SPITFIRE INTERNATIONAL

HELMUT TERBECK,
HARRY VAN DER MEER
and RAY STURTIVANT

An AIR-BRITAIN Publication

Copyright © 2002
Helmut Terbeck, Harry van der Meer
and Ray Sturtivant

Published in the United Kingdom by:

Air-Britain (Historians) Ltd
12 Lonsdale Gardens,
Tunbridge Wells, Kent TN1 1PA

Sales Department:
41 Penshurst Road, Leigh,
Tonbridge, Kent TN11 8HL

Correspondence to:
R.C.Sturtivant, 26 Monks Horton Way,
St.Albans, Herts, AL1 4HA
and not to the Tunbridge Wells address

ISBN 0 85130 250 5

All rights reserved. No part of this publication may be reproduced, stored in a retrieval system or transmitted, in any form or by any means, electronic, mechanical, photocopying, recording or otherwise, without the prior permission of the author and Air-Britain (Historians) Ltd.

Printed in the United Kingdom by:
Ebenezer Baylis & Son Ltd,
The Trinity Press,
London Road,
Worcester WR5 2JH

Origination by Howard Marks, Hastings

Side profile illustrations by Dave Howley

The authors acknowledge the generous and considerable assistance given by Peter Arnold in providing photographs to help illustrate this work.

Front cover: *Spitfire HF.IXe 5518 (TE213) in 1996 with the SAAF Museum Flight at Lanseria, flown as "5553" and marked "AX-K". It was badly damaged in a crash after engine failure on 15th April 2000, but is now under restoration for static display (Herman Potgeiter).*

Back cover: *Swedish Spitfire XIX, 31043/43 (ex PS876) of F 11 Wing, Skavsta, in 1948 (drawing by Dave Howley).*

CONTENTS

	Page
Acknowledgements	5
Introduction	6
Glossary of Terms and Abbreviations	7
Individual Countries:	
Argentina	11
Australia	14
Belgium	57
Brazil	76
Bulgaria	77
Burma	77
Canada	84
China	98
Cuba	98
Czechoslovakia	98
Denmark	108
Egypt	115
Estonia	122
Finland	123
France	123
Germany	157
Greece	161
Hong Kong	169
India	172
Iran	201
Iraq	202
Ireland (Eire)	202
Israel	207
Italy	221
Japan	231
Latvia	231
Lithuania	232
Malta	232
Netherlands	234
New Zealand	247
Norway	250
Poland	263
Portugal	266
Rumania	276
Singapore	277
South Africa	278
Southern Rhodesia	331
Soviet Union	335
Spain	375
Sweden	376
Switzerland	383
Syria	383
Thailand	385
Turkey	390
U.S.A.	409
Yugoslavia	459
Summary of Spitfires and Seafires in foreign services	465
Index of Civil-registered Spitfires	466
Bibliography	467
Index of Names	469

Surviving Spitfire LF.IXc H-15 (ex MK959) displayed on a pole in front of the Officers' Mess at Eindhoven in 1987. This aircraft went to the USA in 1995 for intended restoration to airworthy condition. [MAP]

ACKNOWLEDGEMENTS

The authors wish to thank all those have made contributions to this work to a greater or lesser degree. Without their help it would not have been possible to produce such a comprehensive work. We are particularly grateful for the kind assistance given over the years by the following in response to our many requests:

Argentina
FUERZA AEREA ARGENTINA,
　　Direccion de Estudios Historicos, Buenos Aires
FACULTAD DE INGENIERIA,
　　La Plata, Ricardo Martin LEZON, Buenos Aires
Mrs Jean STOREY, Teignmouth, England

Australia
RAAF & RAN, Dept. of Defence (Air),
　　Historical Section, Canberra, Australia
Frank Olynyk, Aurora, Ohio, USA
Joe BARR, Dunlop, ACT, Australia

Belgium
BELGIAN AIR FORCE (BAF),
　　Centre de Documentation Historique des Forces Armées, Brussels
IPMS BELGIUM, Rudy Binnemans, Deurne/Antwerp
Spitfire Pilots Club, H.A.SAEYS, Schilde
Eric DESSOUROUX, Naninne near Namur
Stefaan VANCAUTEREN, Bruxelles

Brazil
CENTRO TECNICO AEROSPACIAL, S. GIOCONDO,
　　São José dos Campos
MUSEU AEROSPACIAL, A.C. JORDAO, Rio de Janeiro
Roberto Pereira de ANDRADE, São Paulo, Brazil

Burma
Seymour B. FELDMANN, Albuquerque, USA

Canada
CANADIAN WAR MUSEUM, Ottawa, Ontario
NATIONAL ARCHIVES of CANADA, Ottawa
NATIONAL AVIATION MUSEUM, Ottawa
NATIONAL DEFENCE HQ, History Directorate, Ottawa
Leo F PETTIPAS, St.Norbert, Manitoba
Jerry VERNON, Burnaby, British Columbia
Lee W WALSH, Toronto, Ontario

CSSR
Emil F. KNAPP, College Point, USA

Denmark
ROYAL DANISH AIR FORCE, Historical Section at Vedbaek
FLYVEVÅBNETS HISTORISKE SAMLING, Karup
TOJHUSMUSEET, Copenhagen
K.G. Leth FRANDSEN, Vojens
Ole NIKOLAJSEN, Langen, Germany

Egypt
EGYPTIAN AIR FORCE, Air Historical Dept, Cairo
Dr. David NICOLLE, Woodhouse Eaves, UK
Robert van KNORRING, Jarfälla, Sweden
　　(also for India, Ireland and Netherlands, Spitfire T.IX trainer)

France
Archives et Bibliothèques, Service Historique de la Marine Nationale
　　et de l'Armée de l'Air, Château de Vincennes
Michael K. AUSTEN, Lincoln, England
Jean-Pierre DUBOIS, Nice
Serge JOANNE, Bouilland
Phil LISTEMANN, Marseille
Jean-Jacques PETIT, Saint Sever
Claude A. PIERQUET, Quincy-Voisins

Germany
James CROW, Illinois, USA
Peter PETRICK, Berlin

Greece
HELLENIC AIR FORCE, General Staff (Air), History Directorate, Athens

India
INDIAN AIR FORCE MUSEUM at Palam

Ireland
Anthony P. KEARNS, Dublin, Ireland

Israel
ISRAEL DEFENCE FORCE/Air Force,
　　Air Historical Branch and Public Relation Branch, Tel Aviv
Slomo ALONI, Zoran
Paul CRELLIN, Manchester, England
Seymour B. FELDMANN, Albuquerque, USA
Noam HARTOCH, Tel-Aviv
Dr. David NICOLLE, Woodhouse Eaves, England

Italy
STATO MAGGIORE dell' Aeronautica, 5º Reparto, Rome
Gregory ALEGI, Rome

Netherlands
KONINKLIJKE LUCHTMACHT,
　　Sectie Luchtmachthistorie, Ypenburg and Soesterberg, Netherlands

Norway
NORSK FLYHISTORSK FORENING, Oslo, Tom ARHEIM
WARBIRDS OF NORWAY, Mr Øyvind Ellingsen at Sandvika
Bjorn HAFSTEN at Ski and Sverre THUVE at Hosle

Poland
Marian KRZYZAN, Zielona Gora
Wojtek MATUSIAK, Warsaw
James PICKERING, Hinckley, England (also for Portugal)

Portugal
MUSEU DO AR, Alverca, Portugal
Mário Canongia LOPES, Lisbon and Sao Paulo

South Africa
SOUTH AFRICAN AIR FORCE MUSEUM, Pretoria
Ken SMY, Zwartkop
Mike SCHOEMAN, Vlaeberg

Southern Rhodesia
ZIMBABWE Air Force, HQ at Harare (VM ZVOBGO)

Soviet Union
RUSSIAN AVIATION RESEARCH GROUP

Sweden
SWEDEN AIR FORCE, Flygstaben (Info.Dept), Stockholm
KRIGSARKIVET, Stockholm
Ragnar F. BENGTSSON (deceased)
Axel CARLESON, Linköping
Lars R. CRANNING, Karlstad
Sölve FASTH (Flygvapenmuseum Malmen, Linköping)

Thailand
ROYAL THAI AIR FORCE, Directorate of Intelligence, Bangkok

Turkey
GENERALKURMAY BASKANLIGI,
　　Hava Kuvvetleri Komutanligi, Ankara
Ole NIKOLAJSEN, Andorra

U.S.A.
SMITHSONIAN INSTITUTION, National Air Museum, Washington, DC
USAF, Historical Research Agency, Maxwell AFB
USAF, History Support Office, Bolling AFB
George C. COLLINS, Palm Beach, Florida

Yugoslavia
YUGOSLAVIA AIR FORCE MUSEUM, Belgrade

Thanks also for their extremely helpful assistance to:
Peter R. ARNOLD, Newport Pagnell, England
Henry BOOT, Chesterfield, England
Dr. Alfred PRICE, Uppingham, England

Also Air-Britain members Phil Butler, Chris Chatfield, Malcolm Fillmore, Jim Halley, Arno Landewers, Frank McMeiken, Dave Partington, Graham Slack, Barrie Towey and Gerasimos Vevis.

Especial thanks to the Diplomatic Service of the German Government for advice in contacting other countries.

INTRODUCTION

The Vickers-Armstrongs (Supermarine) Spitfire was *the* fighter aircraft of the Royal Air Force and primary equipment of the Royal Australian Air Force, Royal Canadian Air Force and South African Air Force for many years. Its naval adaptation, the Seafire, was also produced in large numbers for carrier operations. Much has been written on the subject, and a considerable number of books have been produced, over the last 60 years.

One aspect that has not received the attention we feel it deserves, however, is the use made by other air forces, of which there were more than thirty in various countries around the world. This book now seeks to remedy that, with concise detailed histories of over 6,000 Spitfires and Seafires which served at some time or other with various overseas and Commonwealth air forces, giving background details of the uses to which they were put and the units which operated them. It also includes details of the many overseas examples in private ownership, both past and present.

The Spitfire first came into service shortly before the outbreak of the Second World War, and its potential was seen immediately. So much so that numerous countries vied with each other to place contracts in order to modernise their air forces, some even seeking licences to produce the type themselves. Events overtook these bids, however, and all such contracts and enquiries were nullified on the outbreak of hostilities. Britain would need all the modern fighters she could produce for the events that lay ahead, and it would be some years before she could consider sparing the precious Spitfires for use by her Allies and friends.

Gradually developed into a robust fighting machine, loved by its pilots and respected by their opponents, the Spitfire saw service everywhere that the British armed forces were in action. By the time production finally ceased, nearly 23,000 Spitfires and Seafires had been produced.

When the war ended there were many thousands in storage at numerous Maintenance Units, and these then became available for sale second-hand at acceptable prices. Not surprisingly, they were sought by various countries seeking to rebuild or re-equip their air forces. The majority of the many Spitfires sold in this way gradually reduced these numbers, but the reputation of this illustrious aircraft was undiminished, and if anything became enhanced. It became sought by collectors around the world and rebuilt examples began to appear increasingly at air shows, where they were one of the star turns. As stock dwindled, prices rose, and a serviceable example can now command a six- or seven-figure price when sold.

Researching the individual histories of aircraft within the scope of the subject of this book has proved to be a mammoth task. Comparatively little official documentation has survived, and consequently the information to be found within the covers of this book has had to be put together piecemeal.

The main starting point was the Aircraft Movement Cards (Air Ministry Form 78), on which are (or should be) recorded the individual movements of RAF aircraft. These are far from complete or accurate, however. Like all handwritten documentation they are subject to copying errors, misinterpretation, illegible writing, abbreviations whose meaning is now lost in the mists of time and numerous other faults. Some have disappeared altogether from the filing system. An added difficulty is that the cards do not record details of the subsequent service of those aircraft which went to the Middle East or Far East.

Searching out the information needed to compile a book of this nature has involved seeking help from numerous individuals, air forces and authorities around the world. The official attitude to security considerations varies from country to country, and from time to time. Some countries proved not to be very forthcoming, other gave help freely. The passage of time during the compilation of the book gradually helped to open doors, particularly after the demise of the Iron Curtain.

Many private researchers and enthusiasts gave us their utmost help and support, often filling gaps with information which official sources could not or would not supply. We are very grateful for all such assistance, both official and private.

Despite all the help we have been given, we are conscious that this record remains incomplete, with much information still missing. Nevertheless, we feel the time is now right to publish what we have achieved so far, and hope that by doing so it will bring to light further information on this unique and timeless topic. We would like very much to hear from anyone who can help in this respect.

Format

The following pages are produced in a concise form for ease of reference. For each country there is a preamble of varying length giving a brief but succinct account of the use, or intended use, of Spitfires (or Seafires) by that county. Where appropriate, this is followed by details of relevant units, giving as far as possible marks flown, codes carried, bases, movement dates, and names of Commanding Officers.

Then follows a list of all known relevant individual aircraft, starting in each case with the basic details from the Aircraft Movement Cards followed, as far as possible, by the serial number allotted by the country concerned and details of its subsequent history including such information as units, dates, codes and ultimate fate where these have been found. There are inevitably some variations in terminology, which we have done our best to respect. For instance a crash resulting in a complete write-off is classified as Category E (Cat.E) by the RAF, the aircraft then being struck off charge (SOC). In Canada it is Struck off Strength (SOS), in the US Navy it would be Stricken, and in Italy it is Fuori Uso (Fu) [Withdrawn from use].

Abbreviations have usually adopted those of the country concerned; for example, Maj or Mjr for Major, Capt or Kapt for Captain. Where known we have included decorations which would have been relevant at the date of the entry, but these are not all shown in source documentation and therefore some may have been omitted inadvertently. In some cases we have anglicised ranks. As far as possible we have used contemporary spelling for the names of countries and places.

GLOSSARY OF TERMS AND ABBREVIATIONS

A/C	Adjudant Chef (F/Sgt, France)
ACB	Air Corps Base, Ireland
ACP	Aircrew Pool
ACSEA	Air Command South East Asia
AD	Aircraft Depot
AD/TU	Aircraft Depot/Test Unit
ADD	Aviatsiya Dal'naya Destviya (Long-Range-Aviation, Soviet Union)
ADEM	Air Defence Eastern Mediterranean
ADGB	Air Defence of Great Britain
ADF	Air Delivery Flight
Adj	Adjutant
ADU	Aircraft Delivery Unit
AFA	Air Force Association, Australia
AFB	Air Force Base (or Air Base)
AFC	Air Force Cross
AFS	Advanced Flying School
AFTS	Advanced Flying Training School
AFU	Advanced Flying Unit
AFW	Army Fighter Wing
AGS	Air Gunnery School
AHQ	Air Headquarters
AM	Aeronáutica Militar (Portuguese Army Air Force)
AMARC	Aircraft Maintenance & Regeneration Centre
AMC	Air Material Command
AMDP	Air Member, Development & Production
AMI	Aeronautica Militare Italiana
AMM	Aviazione per la Marina Militare (Italy)
AMP	Aeronautica Militar Portugal
AMS	Air Material Service (Denmark)
AMTE	Air Mechanical Training Establishment, HMCS *Stadacona*, Canada
ANR	Aeronautica Nazionale Reppublicana (Italy)
ANS	Air Navigation School
AOF	Air Observation Flight
AOpS	Air Operating School
AOS	Air Observation Squadron/School
ARD	Aircraft Repair Depot
ARDU	Aircraft Research and Development Unit
ARF	Aircraft Reception Flight
ARP	ARD-R/P, Replenishment Pool, Australia
AS	Air School (SAAF)
ASC	Air Support Command
Asp	Aspirant (Wt Officer, Oberfähnrich)
ASR	Air-Sea Rescue
ASS	Air Service Squadron
ASSP	Appontage Simulé sur Piste (aerodrome dummy deck landing training, France)
AST	Air Service Training Ltd
ASU	Aircraft Storage Unit
ASWDU	Air Sea Warfare Development Unit
ATC	Air Training Corps
ATG	Air Transport Group
ATU	Air Trials Unit
ATW	Air Transport Wing
Aux	Auxiliary
AVG	American Volunteer Group
AW/CN	Awaiting Collection
A6M	Mitsubishi 'Hamp'
BA	Basi Aeree (Air Base, Italy) or Base Aérea (Air Base, Portugal)
BAF	Belgian Air Force
BAFO	British Air Forces of Occupation
BAN	Base of Aéronautique Navale Française (France)
Banjo	Airfield on Gozo Island
BAOD	Bedek Aircraft Overhaul Depot (Israel)
BAPC	British Aviation Preservation Council
BASTA	Merlin 45 + 66 (boost) modifications
BAT	Blind Approach Training
bboc	brought back on charge
BC	Bomber Command
BCAR	British Classic Aircraft Restorations
BCATP	British Commonwealth Air Training Plan
BCIS	Bomber Command Instructors' School
BE	Base Ecole
BER	Beyond economical repair
Bf	Bayerische Flugzeugwerke (Messerschmitt factories, Germany)
BL	Bezpecnostni Letectvo (Czech border patrol by Air Police)
BO	burnt out
bos	board of survey
bou	breakdown on unit
BRD	Base Repair Depot
BSAA	British South American Airways
BU	broke up (BUA = broke up in air)
c/p	contra-prop (counter-rotating propeller)
CAC	Commonwealth Aircraft Corporation (Fisherman's Bend, Australia) or Central Air Command (Canada)
CAEO	Command Air Extrême-Orient (Indo-China Air Command)
CAF	Confederate Air Force, Texas, USA
CAG	Carrier Air Group
Capt	Captain
Cat	Category
Cat.E	Write-off (E/0 = burnt; E/1= reduced to spares; E/2 = scrap)
Cat.E/FA	Cat.E after flying accident
Cat.E/MI	Cat.E after Major Inspection
Cat.E/stor	Cat.E storage
CATRE	Centre Aérien Technique de Réception et d'Entrainement (Reception and Training Centre, France)
CAV	Centro Addestramento Volo, Flight Training Centre, Italy
CBAF	Castle Bromwich Aircraft Factory
CC	Capitaine de Corvette (French Navy)
Cca	Conversion to components approved, spare parts
CCF	Canadian Car & Foundry Company
CCFATU	Coastal Command (Fighter) Affiliation Training Unit
Cdt	Commandant (S/Ldr, Major)
CEAM	Centre d'Expériences Aériennes Militaire (France)
CEV	Centre d'Essais en Vol (Aircraft Test Centre, France)
CF	Communication Flight, also Capitaine de frégate (France)
CHF	Canadian Heritage Flight
CIC	Centre d'Instruction Chasse (France)
CIG	Cannon instead of Guns
CJATC	Canadian Joint Air Training Centre
CMG	Cannon and Machine Guns
CMU	Civil Maintenance Unit
CN	Constructions Navales (France)
Cne	Capitaine (F/Lt, Hauptmann)
CofR	Certificate of Registration
COGEA	Compagnie Génerale d' Exploitation Aérienne
Col	Colonel
Col.Pil	Colonnello Piloto (Grp Capt equivalent, Italy)
Comm	Commercial contract
Cpt	Captain
CR.3	Civilian Contractor Maintenance (Cat.3)
CRD	Central Recovery Depot
Csa	Conversion in situation approved
CSSR	Czechoslovakia
CSU	Central Servicing Unit
CTA	Centro Técnico de Aeronéutica (Brazil)
CU	Conversion Unit or Communication Unit
CWR	Casualty Wastage Return
CzAF	Czechoslovakian Air Force
d/INV	Deleted from Inventory, USAAF
d/SOX	deleted/SOXO (USAAF)
DA	Deposit Account

DAE	Department or Directorate of Aeronautical Engineering
DanAF	Danish Air Force (Royal Danish AF)
DAP	Department of Aircraft Production
DB	Daimler-Benz
dbp	dive bombing practice
DCAN	Direction des Constructions et Armes Navales (France)
dd	date of delivery
DdAid	Didactic Aid
Del	Delivered
Del Flt	Delivery Flight
Desp	Despatched
dett	Detachment, detached to
DFC	Distinguished Flying Cross
DGMFA	Depósito Geral de Material da Força Aérea (General Deposit of Air Force Equipment, Portugal)
DGRD	Directorate General of Research & Development
div.to	diverted to
DLV	Deutsche Luft und Versuchsanstalt (Test Centre, Germany)
DMAA	Directorate du Matériel de l'Armée de l'Air (France)
DNT	Dutch Naval Transport
DoI	Died of injuries
DoW	Died of wounds
DSD	Department of Supply & Disposal (Australia)
DTD	Directorate of Technical Development
DUKO	US 12th Air Force, Northwest Africa
EAA	Entrepôt de l'Armée de l'Air (France)
EAAF	Egyptian Army Air Force
EAC	Eastern Air Command or East Africa Command
EAE	Ecole de L'Aviation Embarque (France)
EAM	Ecole d'Armement et Méchaniciens Avions
EATS	Empire Air Training Scheme
EC	Escadre de Chasse (Fighter Wing, France)
EcC	Ecole de Chasse, Fighter School (OTU), FAF & BAF
EdM	Ecole de Moniteurs (France)
EPA	Ecole de Pilotage Avece, Belgium
ERC	Escadrille de Réception et de Convoyage (France)
ES	Engineering School
Esk	Escadrille (France, Belgium)
Esk/ESK	Eskadre, Eskadrille (Denmark) or Eskadrila (Yugoslavia)
E.Stelle	Erprobungsstelle (Germany)
Esq	Esquadrilha (Flight, Portugal)
ETO	European Theatre of Operations
EV	Enseigne de Vaisseau (2nd/Lt, French Navy)
(F)	(Fighter)
FAA	Fleet Air Arm or Fuerca Aerea Argentina
FAAMU	Fleet Air Arm Maintenance Unit
FAB	Force Aerienne Belge, Belgian Air Force
FA/E	Flying Accident, Cat.E
FA/E(O)	Flying accident during operations Cat.E
FAF	French Air Force
FALS	French Air Liaison Sector
FAP	Força Aérea Portuguesa (Portuguese Air Force)
FAR	Fighter Aviation Regiment (IAP)
FATU	Fighter Affiliation Training Unit
FB	Fighter-bomber
FB/Ac	Flying Battle damage, Cat.Ac
FB/eac3	damaged by enemy aircraft in flying battle, Cat.3
FC	Flottille de Chasse (France) and Fighter Command
FCCF/FCCS	Fighter Command Communication Flight/Squadron
FCCRS	Fighter Command Control & Reporting School
FEAF	Far East Air Force
FFAF	Free French Air Force
FFP	Fire Fighting Practice
FFS	Fire Fighting School
FFSv	Fire Fighting Service
FG	Fighter Group (USAAF)
FGA	Fighter Ground Attack
Fhr	Fähnrich (Fenrik), Pilot Officer
FIS	Fighter Interception Squadron
Fl/Ch	Flight Charge
FLS	Fighter Leader School
Flt	Flight
F/O	Flying Officer
FR	Fighter Reconnaissance
FRS	Flying Refresher School
FRU	Field Repair Unit or Fleet Requirements Unit
FRV	Foto Rekognoserings Ving (PR unit, Norway)
FS	Fighter Squadron (USAAF) or Fighter Sector
FSTU	Fighter Support Training Unit
FSV	Test & Development Unit
FTG	Fighter Training Group
FTLU	French Technical Liaison Unit
FTR	Failed to return
FTS	Fighter Training Squadron/School
FU	Ferry Unit
FV	Svenska Flygvapnet (Swedish Air Force)
FW	Fighter Wing also Focke-Wulf (Germany)
FWIT	Fighter Weapons Instructor Training
GA	Ground Accident
GAL	General Aircraft Ltd
GAN	Groupement Aéronautique Navale (France)
GATU	Ground Attack Training Unit
GC	Groupe de Chasse (Fighter Sqn, France)
GCC	Group Central Command
GCE	Groupement de Chasse Embarquée (France)
GCF	Group Communication Flight
GCS	Group Communication Squadron
GFAR	Guards Fighter Aviation Regiment (Gv.IAP), Soviet Union
GI	Ground Instructional Airframe
GLUE	Code name for US 9th Air Force
GP	General Purpose
GR	Groupe Reconnaissance (France)
Grp	Group, also Gruppe (Germany)
Grp Capt	Group Captain
GTS	Ground Training (Technical) School
GV	Gvardesjkaya (Guards status, Soviet Union)
Gv.IAP	Gvardejskij Istrebitelnyj Aviatsionnyj Polk (Guards Fighter Aviation Regiment, Soviet Union)
GWP	Group Wastage Pool
G6M	Mitsubishi 'Betty'
Hapmat	Code name for deliveries of aircraft to Soviet Union
HKAAF	Hong Kong Auxiliary Air Force
HMCS	His/Her Majesty's Canadian Ship
HMS	His/Her Majesty's Ship
HQ	Headquarters
HQ8FC	HQ 8th (US)AF, Fighter Command
HT	High Tension
IAC	Irish Air Corps
IAD	Istrebitelnaya Aviatsionnaya Diviziya (Fighter Aviation Division, Soviet Union)
IAF	Indian Air Force
IAI	Israel Aircraft Industries
IAK	Istrebitelnye Aviotsionnye Korpusa (Fighter Aviation Corps, Soviet Union)
IAP	Istrebitelnyj Aviatsionnyj Polk, Fighter Aviation Regiment (Soviet Union) or International Airport
ICAO	International Civil Aviation Organisation
IDF/AF	Israel Defence Force/Air Force
IIT	Indian Institute of Technology
INA	Institute Nautics & Aeronautics
IRAN	Inspection & Repair as necessary
ITA	Instituto Técnologico da Aeronáutica (Brazil)
ItAF	Italian Air Force
ITT	Institute of Technology, Thailand
JAF	Jugoslavian Air Force (see JKRV & JRV)
JG	Jagd-Geschwader (Fighter Wing, Germany)
JKRV	Jugoslovensko Kraljevsko RatnoVazduhoplovstuo (Yugoslav Air Force to 1945)
JNA	Yugoslav National Army of Liberation
JRV	Jugoslovensko Ratno Vazduhoplovstuo (Yugoslav Air Force from 1945)
JVS	Jachtvliegschool (OTU), Netherlands
KAM	Komanda Aerodroma Mostar (Workshop, Yugoslavia)
Kapt	Kaptain / Capt (Flt.Lt)
Ki-46	Mitsubishi 'Dinah'
Ki-48	Kawasaki 'Lily'
Klu	Koninklijke Luchtmacht (Royal Air Force, Netherlands)
Km	Kilometre

Glossary of Terms and Abbreviations

L-09	Liaison aircraft (US 9th AF & French)
Lb	Pound(s) [weight]
LBWG	Langebaanweg Air Station, South Africa
LCL	Lieutenant Colonel (France)
LD	Letecke Divizi (Czech Fighter Wing)
LETS	Luchtmacht Electronische & Technische School, NL
LF	Luft-Flotille, Navy Flight, Denmark
LHS	Letecká Historická Spolecnost, (Aviation Historical Society, Czech)
LLN	Leger Luchtmacht Nederland (Army Air Force, Netherlands)
LPVO	Air Defence Leningrad (Soviet Russia)
LR	Long Range
LSK	Luchtstrijdkrachten (Air Military Forces, Netherlands)
Lt	Lieutenant
LTS	Luftforsvaret Technik Skol (-School), Norway
LV	Lieutenant de Vaisseau (Lt, French Navy)
LVA	Letecke Vojenske Akademie (Czech Military Air Academy)
Lw	Luftwaffe, German Air Force
m	Miles
MAAF	Mediterranean Allied Air Force
MAC	Mediterranean Air Command
MACAF	Mediterranean Allied Coastal Air Forces
MAEE	Marine Aircraft Experimental Establishment
Magg.Pil.	Maggiore Pilota (S/Ldr equivalent, Italy)
Maj	Major
MAP	Ministry of Aircraft Production
MARC	Military Aircraft Restoration Corporation
MASAF	Mediterranean Allied Strategical Air Forces
MATAF	Mediterranean Allied Tactical Air Forces
MCCS	Maintenance Command Communication Sqn
MCS	Metropolitan Communication Squadron
Me	Messerschmitt (Germany)
ME	Middle East
MEAC	Middle East Air Command
MEAF	Middle East Air Force
MI /B	Major inspection /Cat.B
Mjr	Major
Mk	Mark
MM	Matricola Militare (Italian AF serials)
MMI	Marina Militare Italiana
MPFEM	Minnesota's Planes of Fame East Museum
MPVO	Air Defence Moscow (Soviet Russia)
MR/B	Maintenance repair Cat.B
MRAP	Morskoy Razvedyvatel'nyi Aviats.Polk (Maritime Reconnaissance Regiment, Soviet Union)
MSA	Materiale Speciale Aeronautico (Air Depot, Italy)
MTO	Mediterranean Theatre of Operations
MU	Maintenance Unit
MuAid	Mutual Aid
NA	North Africa
NAAF	Northwest African Air Forces
NAASC	Northwest African Air Service Command
NACA	National Advisory Committee for Aeronautics
NACAF	Northwest African Coastal Air Forces
NAFD	Naval Air Fighting Development
NAFS	Naval Air Fighter School
NAP	North Africa Pool
NAPRW	Northwest African Photo Reconnaissance Wing
NASAF	Northwest African Strategical Air Forces
NATAF	Northwest African Tactical Air Forces
NATBF	Northwest African Tactical Bombing Force
NATC	Northwest African Training Command
NAWS	Naval Air Warfare School
NB	New Britain
NEA	Non effective aircraft or Near expired aircraft
NES	Non effective stocks
NethAF	Netherlands Air Force
NFS	Naval Fighter School (NFW = Naval Fighter Wing)
nft	no further trace
NII-VVS	Naoutchno-Ispytatelnyi Institut Voenno-Vozdouchnyi Sil (Research Institute of the Soviet Air Force)
NL	Netherlands
No	Number
NSTT	Netherlands School of Technical Training
NSV	Nucleo Sperimentale Volo (Experimental Flying Unit (later RSV), Italy)
NSW	New South Wales
NT	Northern Territory
NTM	Národni Technické Museum, National Technical Museum Prague, CSSR
ntu	not taken up
NV	Nueleo Volo (Flying Section, Italy)
NVRC	Nucleo Voli del Raggruppamento Caccia (Flying Training Centre (Fighter), Italy)
NWA	North-West Africa
NWAC	North West Air Command
NZ	New Zealand
OADU	Overseas Aircraft Delivery Unit
ObLw	Oberkommando Luftwaffe, HQ German AF
Obs	Observation
OBU	Operation Base Unit, Australia
OCU	Operational Conversion Unit
OE	Officier des Equipages (France)
ofs	output from site
OFTS	Operation Flying Training School
OFU	Overseas Ferry Unit
Ofw	Oberfeldwebel (F/Sgt, Germany)
OGMA	Oficinas Gerais de Material Aeronáutico (Portuguese air material workshop)
OKL	Oberkommando der Luftwaffe (HQ Air Force, Germany)
ORAP	Otdelnyj Razvedyvatelnyj Aviatsionnyj Polk, (Independent Reconnaissance Aviation Regiment, Soviet Union)
ORB	Operations Record Book
OTU	Operational Training Unit
PC	Parc Colonial (France)
PFT	Polish Fighting Team of No.145 Sqn
PG	Pursuit Group
PM	Premier Maitre (Corporal, France)
PMA	Parque de Material de Aeronáutica (Air Equipment Park, Portugal)
PN	Papua-New Guinea
P/O	Pilot Officer
PoW	Prisoner of War
Pp	Lieutenant Colonel (Soviet Union)
PR	Photographic Reconnaissance
Psd SOC	Presumed struck off charge
PSP	Pierced Steel Planking
PSS	Photo Survey Squadron
PTS	Pilots Training School
PVO	Protivovozdushnaya Obornona (Air Defence Force, Soviet Union)
Qld	Queensland
R&R strip	Refuelling and Re-arming airfields
RA	Regia Aeronautica (Italian AF until 6.46)
RAAA	Repaired aircraft awaiting action (later AW/CN)
RAAF	Royal Australian Air Force
RAE	Royal Aircraft Establishment
RAF	Royal Air Force
RAFM	RAF Museum Hendon
RALE	Raggruppamento Aviazione Leggera Esercito, Italy
RAN	Royal Australian Navy
RAP	Reserve Aircraft Pool
RAS	Royal Aeronautical Society / Reserve Aeroplane Sqn
RAuxAF	Royal Auxiliary Air Force
R(B)	beyond repair on site, dismantled to repair in works
RC	Reserve Command
RCAF	Royal Canadian Air Force
RCN	Royal Canadian Navy
RD	Repair Depot
RDanAF	Royal Danish Air Force
RDU	Receipt & Despatch Unit
RE	Regia Esercito (Royal Army, Italy)
REAF	Royal Egyptian Air Force
Re-cat	Recategorised
Reg	Registration
Regd	Registered
Res	Reserve
RHAF	Royal Hellenic Air Force (Greece)

RIAF	Royal Indian Air Force	T/A	Treasury authority
RiW	Repair in works	TAC	Training Air Command
RM	Regia Marine (Italy) and Région Maritime (France)	TAF	Tactical Air Force
RNAS	Royal Naval Air Station	TAG	Trainking Air Group
RNDA	Royal Naval Deposit Account	TAM	Tactical Air Meeting
RNoAF	Royal Norwegian Air Force	TC	Training Command
RNVR	Royal Naval Volunteer Reserve	TCMF	Transport Command Meteorological Flight
RNZAF	Royal New Zealand Air Force	T.Col.Pil	Tenente Colonnello Pilota (Wg Cdr equivalent, Italy)
ROS	Repair on site	TCom	Transport Command
RS	Small repair by squadron (Italy)	TCU	Transport Conversion Unit
RSRA	Riparabile presso Squadra Riparazione Aeroporto (repairable at aerodrome Repair Section, Italy)	TDLMC	Technical Data Laboratory, Material Command (USAAF)
		Temp	Temporary
R&SU	Repair and Salvage Unit	TEU	Tactical Exercise Unit
RSV	Reparto Sperimentale Volo (Experimental Flying Unit, Italy)	TFF	Test & Ferry Flight (No.1 AD), Australia
		TFlt	Towing Flt, Conversion Flight EcC, Belgium
RSwAF	Royal Swedish Air Force (SAF)	TFS	Test & Ferry Sqn or Training (Fighter) Squadron
RTA	Reparto Tecnoccia Aeronautic (Repair & Overhaul Unit, Italy)	TFU	Training (F) Unit
		TG	Training Group or Task Group
rtc	reduced to components	TOC	Taken On Charge
rtp	reduced to produce	TOS	Taken on Strength (RCAF)
rts	reduced to spares	TR/Grp	Tactical Recce Group
RThaiAF	Royal Thai Air Force	TrgD	RAF Training Delegation in France
RTU	Reparto Tecnico Unita Aerea (Technical Unit, Italy)	TrGrp	Transport Group
RVSM	Reparto Volo Stato Maggiore (Air Force Staff Flying Unit, Italy)	trop	tropicalised
		TRU	Tactical (Photo) Reconnaissance Unit
SAAF	South African Air Force	TS	Training Squadron
SABCA	Society Anonyme Belge de Construction Aéronautique, Belgium	TSU	Technical Service Unit
		TT	Target Towing or Target Tug
SA	Squadra Aerea (Air Corps, Italy)	TTC	Technical Training Command
SAF	Sweden Air Force (RSwAF)	TTS	Technical Training Squadron/School
SAMAN	Service d´Approvisionnement en Matériel de l´Aéronautique Navale	TuAF	Turkish Air Force
		TW	Training Wing
SAS	Servicing Aircraft Section	TWDU	Tactical Weapons Development Unit
S/C	Sergent Chef (Sgt, Feldwebel, France)	UBAF	Union of Burma Air Force
ScAdd	Scuola Addestramento Caccia e Bombardieri (Fighter & Bomber Training School, Italy)	UK	United Kingdom
		UMNO	United Malayan National Organization
SCU	Service Commando Unit	u/s	unserviceable
SD	Special Duties	USA	United States of America
SEA	Section Entretien Aéronefs (Maintenance base, France)	USAAF	United States Army Air Force
SEAC	South East Asia Command	USN	U.S. Navy
SEC	Servitudes at Cuers, France	UTI	Uchebno-Trenirovochnyi Istrebitel (Training Fighter, Soviet Union)
SEMA	SEMA, School HQ, Italy		
SF	Severnyj Flot (Northern Fleet, Soviet Union)	VA	Vozdushnaya Armiya (Air Armies, Soviet Union) or Vickers-Armstrongs
SFV	Svenska Flygvapnet, Swedish AF		
SGR	School of General Reconnaissance	VASM	Vickers-Armstrongs, South Marston
SgtM	Sergeant Major	VE-Day	Victory in Europe Day
S&H	Short Brothers & Harland	VF	Volant de fonctionnement (France)
SLA	Section de Liaison Aérienne (France)	Vic	Victoria
S/Ldr	Squadron Leader	VJ-Day	Victory in Japan Day
SLP	Stihaci Letecky Pluk (Czech)	VLU	Vedecky Letecky Ustav, Test Centre, CSSR
S/Lt	Second Lieutenant or Sub-Lt (Navy) or Sous-Lieutenant (Pilot Officer, France)	VMF	Voyenno-Morskoj Flot (Soviet Navy)
		VR	Volunteer Reserve also Volant de réserve (France)
SMER	Section Marine des Ecoles de Rochefort (France)	VVFF	Corpo Nazionale del Vigili del Fuoco, Italy
SNAM	School of Naval Air Maintenance (Canada)	VVS	Voyenno-Vozdushnye Sily, Soviet Air Force
SNCAN	Societe Nationale de Construction Aéronautiques du Nord (France)	VVS VMF	Aviatsiya Voenno-morskogo Flota, Naval Air Force, Soviet Union
SOC	Struck off charge	VVS SF	Voyenno Vozdushniye Sily Severnovo Flota, Northern Fleet Air Force, Soviet Union
SONACA	Societe Nationale de Constructions Aerospatiale		
SOS	Struck off strength (RCAF)	w/o	Written off (Cat."E")
SoTT	School of Technical Training	W/T	Wireless Telegraphy
SOXO	Code name for US 8th Air Force	WA	West Africa or Western Australia
Sqn	Squadron	WAS	Waterkloof Air Station, South Africa
SRA	Squadra Riparazione Aeromobili (Aircraft Repair Scction, Italy)	WASP	Westland aircraft Spitfire production
		WastP	Wastage Pool
SRAM	Squadra Riparazione Aeromobili e Motori (Aircraft repair in special facilities or by manufacturers, Italy)	WDAF	Western Desert Air Force
		WEE	Winter Experimental Establishment
SRAF	Southern Rhodesian Air Force	Wfu	Withdrawn from use (SOC & SOS)
SRC	Section de Réception et de Convoyage (test and delivery, France)	Wg Cdr	Wing Commander
		WU	Western Union
SSEF	Seafire Special Exhibition Flight (Canada)	WW.II	World War II (Second World War)
SSS	Scuola Specialistie e Sottufficiali (Italy)	YAF	Yugoslavian Air Force
St	Staffel (Squadron, Germany)	YPT	Ysterplaat Air Station, South Africa
Stn Flt	Station Flight	YUG	Yugoslavia
Stormo	Wing (Italy)	ZA	Zona Aerea, Italy
SVL	Scuola de Volo de Lecce (Central Flying School, Italy)	ZAS	Zwartkop Air Station, South Africa
Ta	Tank (Professor Tank, Focke-Wulf works, Germany)	ZAT	Zona Aerea Territoriale (Air Traffic Zone, Italy)

ARGENTINA

Spitfire PR.XI LV-NMZ (ex PL972) en route to Argentina, photographed from the accompanying British South American Airways Avro York G-AHFH. For ferrying over such a very long distance it required additional fuel and oil, hence the 170-gallon overload tank under the fuselage.

The Argentine Air Force, the *Fuerca Aerea Argentina* (FAA), asked for Spitfire T.IX trainers, and placed an order for ten of these with Vickers in the fifties. This was later cancelled and Fiat G-55b trainers were purchased instead.

In 1947 a Spitfire F.VIIIc and a Spitfire PR.XI were bought on a private owner basis; also a Spitfire HF.IXe was donated to the Argentine Government, for instructional purposes only. The Argentine Air Force never had Spitfires on unit strength, but one was painted in Air Force colours for some time and another was flown later by the *Fuerca Aerea Argentina* as a test bed.

It has been incorrectly reported that PL194 was flown by "Captain" Storey as LV-NMZ. However, he landed LV-NMZ at Moron airport on 7th May 1947, at which time PL194 was still in storage at No.29 MU High Ercall. LV-NMZ was in fact PL972, a long-range photo-reconnaissance variant of the Spitfire.

"Capt" J E Storey seated in the cockpit of LV-NMZ after arrival at Moron airport on 7th May 1947. At that time he was still hopeful of getting an air mapping contract from the Argentine Government.

The Spitfires were eventually scrapped, and only pieces remained in Argentina. Aviation enthusiasts wished to maintain or restore the aircraft before scrapping, but the official administration refused permission.

Individual Histories

BS116   Spitfire F.IXc; Allocation cancelled; Broken up as scrap by RAF instead

JF275   Spitfire F.VIIIc (Merlin 63); TOC/RAF 24.11.42 - Arrived Buenos Aires 1947; Sold to the firm H Hennequin & Cia, Buenos Aires 13.6.47; The aircraft arrived at the University La Plata (Instituto de Aeronáutica) on 7.4.48 in non-flying condition, with some instruments missing (the exhaust pipes went to Spitfire PL972); Used as ground instructional aid for aeronautical studies; During the early fifties, a group of members of Centro Universitario de Aviacion tried to restore the aircraft, but that was not acceptable to the authorities; Later dismantled, engine sent to a technical school; Fuselage and wings to a Vialidad Nacional depot near Magdalena (Buenos Aires Province) in 1963 or 1968; Sold for scrap some time later
NOTE: Reported also to be painted with FAA insignia, but see PL194

Spitfire JF275, seen here in 1958, was used as a training aid by the University La Plata. In front, Pablo J Ringegni (left), Ing. Alderette (middle) and an unknown.   [Pablo J Ringegni]

Spitfire HF.IXe PL194 in the markings of the Fuerca Aerea Argentina.   [Ricardo M Lezon]

PL194   Spitfire HF.IXe (Merlin 70); TOC/RAF 12.6.44; ex Nos.124 & 287 Sqns - Presented by the British Air Ministry to the Argentine Government for Aeronautical Expositions 20.6.47; Together with a Hurricane IV (KW908) shipped from Liverpool (ex-No.47 MU Sealand) in *SS Durango* 12/13.8.47, arrived Buenos Aires 1.9.47; After Aeronautical expositions in September 1947 (Aeroparque presentation in Buenos Aires from 7.9.47) taken by train to the Escuela de Sub-Oficiales de Aeronautica at Cordoba; Fuselage painted with the insignia of the *Fuerca Aerea Argentina* (but it was never on Argentine Air Force unit strength); In 1950 to the Engineering Faculty of the University of La Plata as a teaching aid; Withdrawn from use in 1966; Scrapped 1968
NOTES: (1) The University of La Plata still owns some aluminium ingots [castings?] of this aircraft; (2) Possibly to aerodrome at Berisso near La Plata, and later to the Vialidad Nacional Depot at Magdalena near Buenos Aires

PL972   Spitfire PR.XI (Merlin 70); Civil reg. *LV-NMZ*; TOC/RAF 9.10.44; Sold back to Vickers via No.6 MU 21.3.47; Equipped with three F.24-8 Williamson cameras; Converted for LR ferry flying, with a 170-gall overload belly tank plus two wing tanks, fuel capacity total 428 gall, estimated endurance 11 hours and a range of 2,300 miles (3,700 km); Weighed 9,700lb (4,400 kg) - Bought by the James & Jack Storey Aerial Photography Company, handed over to James Elwyn Storey (ex F/Lt of the RAF) on 15.4.47; UK Certificate of Airworthiness issued 24.4.47; Ferried out by

A ground shot of LV-NMZ, still fitted with an overload tank.   [Vickers-Armstrongs]

Spitfire PR.XI, LV-NMZ, in delivery scheme, April 1947

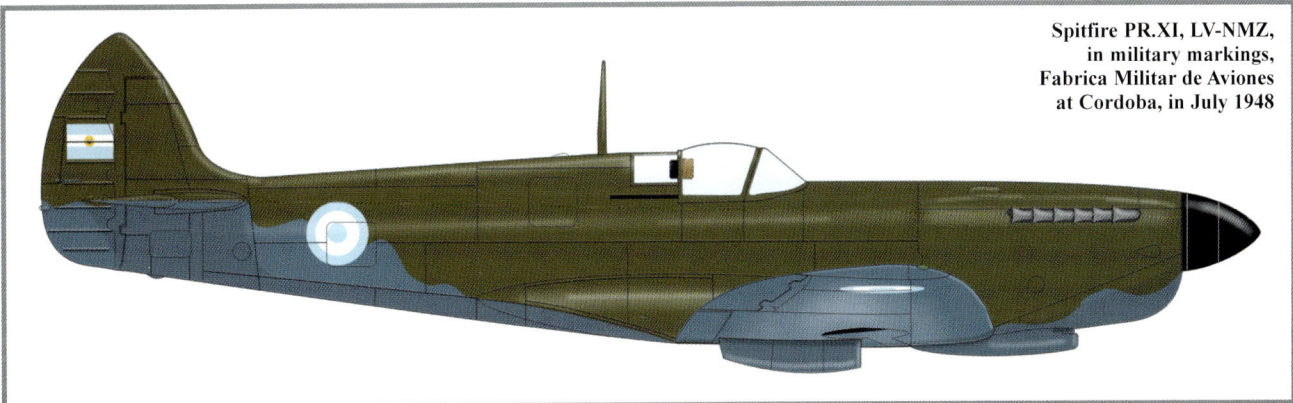

Spitfire PR.XI, LV-NMZ, in military markings, Fabrica Militar de Aviones at Cordoba, in July 1948

Storey to Argentina; The route being London (Hurn airport 29.4.47) - Gibraltar – (Forced landing at Port Etienne, tipped on its nose 1.5.47) - Dakar, then led by an Avro York (*G-AHFH*, 'Star Glitter') of British South American Airways (BSAA) crossing the South Atlantic to Natal in Brazil in 8:40 hours - down to Rio de Janeiro, Montevideo and finally Buenos Aires, where it arrived at Morón Airport 7.5.47; Exhaust stubs had been burned out and replaced by those of JF275; James and Jack Storey wanted to use the Spitfire for their own commercial purposes, but soon after arriving in Argentina they were informed that the Government of Argentina did not recognise his contract for aerial mapping and they then had no use for the aircraft; Finally the *Fuerca Aérea Argentina* (FAA) took it over and Storey, promoted to a Captain of the FAA in the meantime, flew the Spitfire to the Fabrica Militar de Aviones (FMA) at Cordoba on 15.7.48; The FAA used the aircraft for trials by the Instituto Aeronáutico, marked with FAA roundels and having a black spinner, being flown by test pilots Capt JC Doyle, Teniente Luis Valoni and Sub-Oficial Jorge Villegas; On 29.11.51 the Spitfire suffered engine problems and made a wheels-up landing near Alta Gracia (Rosario, Province Córdoba), damaging the propeller, the radiators and the engine (Pilot Teniente L Valoni); The aircraft was not repaired, but remained in storage, and was eventually written off and scrapped.

References:
London to Buenos Aires by Spitfire, The Aeroplane 9 May 1947.
England to Buenos Aires in a Spitfire,
   by Captain James Storey, the Aeroplane 14 November 1947.
Spitfire - The History, Morgan & Shacklady, 1987 (p.379/392).
Spitfire Across the Atlantic, by Ricardo M Lezon & Robert M Stitt,
   Air Enthusiast No.89 (September/October 2000).

A later shot of LV-NMZ about to take off in Argentina, now fitted with the exhaust pipes from JF275. Behind the tail can be seen an Avro York, G-AHFH, and to the right of the picture a Douglas DC-4 is partially visible.

AUSTRALIA

Spitfire F.Vcs of No.452 Sqn, QY-G nearest, dispersed among the palm trees. [MAP]

Eighteen Royal Australian Air Force (RAAF) squadrons served with the Royal Air Force during the Second World War, in the European and Middle East theatres, these being numbered 450 to 467. Of these, Nos.451, 452, 453 and 457 flew Spitfires. On 21st June 1942 Nos.452 and 457 Squadrons and No.54 Sqn RAF left Liverpool in HMT *Stirling Castle*, arriving at No.1 Equipment Depot, Aston Vale, Melbourne on 13th August "minus its aircraft which had been commandeered by the RAF while in transit". In Australia the three squadrons formed No.1 (Fighter) Wing RAAF. From 1944 Nos.548 and 549 Sqns RAF also served in Australia.

For airframe serial numbering purposes, the RAAF allocated the stores prefix "A58-", though not all RAAF Spitfires actually had this painted on.

Between 14th August 1942 and 19th June 1945, 657 Spitfires were received, comprising:

245 Mk.Vc/trop	(RAAF A58- 1 to A58-259)
2 Mk.IIa/Vc	(No RAAF serials)
251 LF.VIIIc	(RAAF A58-300 to A58-550)
159 HF.VIIIc	(RAAF A58-600 to A58-758)

Spitfires thus served in five RAAF units and three RAF Sqns in Australia and the South Pacific, in addition to other types of units. When in October 1948 the RAAF re-equipped with the Mustang, which was superior in range, 13 Spitfire HF.VIIIc and one Mk.Vc were handed over to the Royal Australian Navy.

Additional surviving Spitfires arrived in Australia later.

Australian Spitfire Squadrons of the Royal Air Force

No.**451** Sqn, formed up in Australia February 1941, arrived in the Middle East in May 1941 as an Army Co-operation squadron with Hurricanes; Became a fighter squadron with Spitfires from 2nd February 1943; Then to ADGB 2nd December 1944 and BAFO Germany 13th September 1945 until 21st January 1946.
Spitfire Mks.Vb/c, IXc (ME) - Sqn code: 'BQ'.
Spitfire Mks.IX, XVI, XIV (ETO) - Sqn code: 'NI'.

No.**452** Sqn, in UK from 8th April 1941 until June 1942, then to Australia.
Spitfire Mks.IX, II, Vbs (ETO) - Sqn code: 'DU'.

No.**453** Sqn, in Australia from 13th May 1941 (Singapore July 1941 flying Buffalo); RAF (ETO) from 9th June 1942 with Spitfires, ADGB September 1944 - August 1945, BAFO until 21st January 1946.
Spitfire Mks.Vb, IX, XVI, XIV - Sqn code: 'FU'.

No.**457** Sqn, in UK from 16th June 1941 until June 1942, then to Australia
Spitfire Mks.I, II, Vb (ETO) - Sqn-code: 'BP'.

RAF Spitfire Squadrons in Australia

No.**54** Sqn, re-formed in UK in 1930; Spitfire Mks.I, II & Va/b from March 1939 to June 1942 - Sqn code: 'KL';
To Australia 18th June 1942 - Sqn code (from January 1943): 'DL'
No.1 (F) Wing RAAF from 16th December 1942.
Spitfire Mk.Vc from 29th October 1942; LF.VIIIc from 9th March 1944 and HF.VIIIc from 21 April 1945.
Markings: Sqn code grey with white individual letter; white leading edge [No.1(F)Wing] from December 1943, red spinner in 1944.
Bases:

Left UK for Australia	18.6.42
(in HMT *Stirling Castle*)	
Aston Vale, Melbourne, Vic	13.8.42
Richmond, NSW (NW of Sydney)	24.8.42
[joined No.1 (F) Wing]	

AUSTRALIA

Three Spitfire F.Vc/trop of No.54 Sqn RAAF in formation in late 1942 or early 1943. The nearest machine is BS164 'K' (later A58-63), whose wreckage was recovered in 1991. The other two are BR544 'A' (later A58-50) and BR539 'X' (later A58-45). [Australian War Museum 014383]

Spitfire LF.VIIIc A58-300 (ex JF620) DL-R of No.54 Sqn RAAF being refuelled at Phillip Street, Fannie Bay, Darwin.

Spitfire F.Vc/trop DL-K of No.54 Sqn hidden in trees and disguised by overhead camouflage netting. Depending on the date, it could have been A58-637 (ex BS164), A58-242 (ex MA685) or A58-246 (ex MA863), the last being a survivor.

Winnellie, NT (east of Darwin)	17.1.43
(detts Millingimbi, Drysdale Mission and Learmonth)	
dett Exmouth Gulf	9.5.44
Livingstone, NT (SSE of Darwin)	8.6.44
Darwin Civil, NT	21.10.44
Melbourne, Vic	17.9.45.

Sqn disbanded 31.10.45.
Commanding Officers:
S/Ldr JM Gibbs	10.4.42
S/Ldr RB Newton DFC	11.1.44
S/Ldr S Linnard DFC	27.7.44
S/Ldr JBH Nicholas	1.7.45

No.**548** Sqn, formed at Lawnton, Qld 15th December 1943 [in No.1(F) Wing]; Spitfire LF.VIIIc from 6th April 1944, HF.VIIIc from 23th August 1945 - Sqn code: 'TS'.
Airbases:
Lawnton, Qld (north of Brisbane)	15.12.43
Strathpine, Qld (north of Brisbane)	19.1.44
Amberley, Qld (SW of Brisbane)	28.5.44
Townsville, Qld	6.44
Livingstone, NT (SSE of Darwin)	15.6.44
(dett Truscott)	
Darwin Civil, NT (dett Truscott)	22.10.44.

Sqn disbanded 31.10.45.
Commanding Officers:
S/Ldr WHA Wright	15.12.43
S/Ldr RA Watts	7.44
S/Ldr ED Glaser	2.45.

No.**549** Sqn, formed at Strathpine (north of Brisbane, Qld) 15th December 1943 [in No.1(F) Wing]; Spitfire LF.VIIIc from 7th April 1944 to 26th September 1945 - Sqn code: 'ZF'
Airbases:
Lawnton, Qld (north of Brisbane)	15.12.43
Strathpine, Qld (north of Brisbane)	19.1.44
Amberley, Qld (SW of Brisbane)	25.5.44
Strauss, NT (SSE Darwin)	16.6.44
(dett Truscott)	
Darwin Civil, NT (dett Truscott)	23.10.44.

Sqn disbanded 31.10.45.
Commanding Officer:
S/Ldr EPW Bocock DFC	15.12.43.

Royal Australian Air Force Spitfire units

No.**24** Sqn, with only four Spitfires (A58-1, 2, 6, 93) for pilots training on new aircraft types (awaiting Airacobras), from 26th February 1943 until 25th June 1943 - Unit code: 'GR'.
Airbase: Bankstown, NSW (south of Sydney)	2.43 - 6.43.

Commanding Officer:
S/Ldr B Honey	5.1.43.

No.**79** Sqn, formed 26th April 1943 (No.73 (F) Wing from 16th June 1943, and No.80 (F) Wing from December 1944). Spitfire Mk.Vc from 5th May 1943, LF.VIIIc from 6th December 1944, HF.VIIIc from 14th May 1945 - Sqn code: 'UP'.
Markings: White tail from September 1943, this being a standard Fighter marking in the South-West Pacific area.
Airbases:
Laverton, Vic (west of Melbourne)	26.4.43
Vivigani (Goodenough Island)	16.6.43
(joined No.73 (F) Wing)	
Kiriwina	18.8.43
Los Negros, Momote, Manus Is	16.3.44
Sattler, NT (south of Darwin)	complete 12.1.45
Horn Island	1944
to No.70 (F) Wing	12.44
Morotai, advance party left	6.2.45
Oakey (West of Brisbane)	1945

Sqn disbanded 12.11.45.
Commanding Officers:
S/Ldr AC Rawlinson	26.4.43
S/Ldr MS Bott	8.11.43
S/Ldr SW Galton	16.4.44
S/Ldr KE James	4.5.45

No.**85** Sqn, formed 12th February 1943 for home defence of Western Australia initially equipped with Buffaloes and Boomerangs; Spitfire Mk.Vc from 17th September 1944, 12 on strength by 10th December 1944; Flying ceased 20th September 1944, aircraft departed October 1945 - Code: 'SH'.
Airbases:
Guildford, WA (north of Perth)	27.2.44

Spitfire LF.VIIIcs of No.79 Sqn RAAF in dispersal at Pitoe North airfield, Morotai, in late 1944 or early 1945. In the foreground is Flg Off Norman Smithells' A58-517 UP-F (ex MT594) and behind it is Flg Off Hugh Kennare's A58-492 UP-B (ex MT518), named respectively 'HAVA-GO-JO' and 'MAC III'.

Spitfire HF.VIIIc A58-615 ZP-Y MT834 of No.457 Sqn at Livingstone strip in December 1944, has sharkmouth markings and carries the white "Grey Nurse" inscription forward of the cockpit. [Frank F. Smith]

Pearce, WA (near Perth)	12.5.45
Sqn disbanded 29.11.45.	
Commanding Officers:	
S/Ldr CN Daley	23.2.43
S/Ldr KE James	9.44
S/Ldr MS Lewis	27.3.45

No.**452** Sqn, RAAF unit from September 1942 (No.1 (F) Wing RAAF from 16th December 1942, No.80 (F) Wing RAAF from December 1944).
Spitfire Mk.Vc from 28th September 1942, LF.VIIIc from 6 January 1944,
HF.VIIIc from 26th December 1944 until 6th November 1945 - Code: 'QY'.
Markings: White code and leading edge from December 1943, red spinner from December 1944, "*Ace of Spades*" on rudder.
Airbases:

Richmond, NSW (NW of Sydney)	early 9.42
Mascot, NSW (south of Sydney)	6.9.42
Batchelor, NT (SSE of Darwin)	17.1.43
Strauss, NT (SSE of Darwin)	1.2.43
(joined No.1 (F) Wing)	
detts Wyndham and Millingimbi by	8.43
Guildford, WA (north of Perth)	9.3.44
Strauss, NT (SSE of Darwin	20.3.44
Sattler, NT (SSE of Darwin)	12.5.44
Merauke	16.12.44
Morotai	21.12.44
Tarakan	5.45
Sepinggang	15.7.45
Tarakan	1945
Sqn disbanded 17.10.45.	
Commanding Officers:	
S/Ldr RE Thorold-Smith DFC	18.3.42
S/Ldr RS MacDonald	30.3.43
S/Ldr LT Spence DFC	3.2.44
S/Ldr KM Barclay	4.6.45.

No.**457** Sqn, RAAF unit from September 1942 (No.1 (F) Wing RAAF from 16th December 1942, and No.80 (F) Wing RAAF from December 1944); Spitfire Mk.Vc from 9th November 1942, LF.VIIIc from 2nd July 1944, HF.VIIIc from 15th December 1944 until November 1945.
Sqn code 'XB' from January 1943 until mid 1943, then 'ZP'; Markings: White code, fuselage band and leading edge from December 1943; Red spinner from January 1945, Sharkmouth painted on the cowl and also "*Ace of Spades*" on the rudder, marked "*Grey Nurse Sqn*" on some machines.
Airbases:

Richmond, NSW (NW of Sydney)	6.9.42
(No.1 (F) Wing)	
Camden, NSW (SW of Sydney)	7.11.42
Darwin, NT advance party	31.12.42
Batchelor, NT (SSE of Darwin)	18.1.43
Livingstone, NT (SSE of Darwin)	31.1.43
(to No.78 Wing)	
(detts Millingimbi (6 a/c) 9.5.43 and Drysdale Mission (6 a/c) 4.11.43 to mid-12.43)	
Guildford, WA (north of Perth)	9.3.43
Livingstone, NT (SSE of Darwin)	20.3.43
Sattler, NT (SE of Darwin)	10.1.44
Livingstone, NT (SSE of Darwin)	19.1.44
dett Pearce near Perth	3.44
Guildford, WA (north of Perth)	11.3.44
Livingstone, NT (SSE of Darwin)	25.3.44
Exmouth Gulf, WA	9.5.44
Sattler, NT (SE of Darwin)	24.5.44
(dett Drysdale Mission 1.6.44)	
Morotai	6.2.45
Labuan (to 1st TAF)	17.6.45
Oakey, Qld	31.10.45.
Sqn disbanded 7.11.45.	
Commanding Officers: S/Ldr KE James	18.6.42
S/Ldr TH Trimble	2.2.44
S/Ldr BD Watson	18.12.44
F/Lt DH Maclean	31.8.45.

No.2 OTU (Operational Training Unit) at Mildura, east of Adelaide, Vic.
Commanding Officers:
Wg Cdr P Jeffrey 27.4.42
Grp Capt RW Garrett 20.8.43
Grp Capt WS Arthur 5.7.44
Grp Capt P Jeffrey 27.11.44

No.5 OTU, Williamtown, NSW (near Newcastle, NE of Sydney) - a Beaufighter OTU with only a few Spitfires.

No.8 OTU, Narromine to 25th September 1944, then Parkes (both airfields NW of Sydney, NSW).
Commanding Officer:
Grp Capt WR Garrett 25.6.44

No.1 APU (Aircraft Performance Unit; Later renamed Aircraft Research & Development Unit from September 1947) at Laverton, near Melbourne, Vic.
Commanding Officer:
S/Ldr JH Harper 1.12.42.

No.2 AD/TU (Aircraft Depot, Test Unit of No.2 AP) at Richmond, NSW (NW of Sydney, NSW).

C.G.S. (Central Gunnery School) at Cressy, near Melbourne, Vic.
Commanding Officer:
F/Lt RE Lewis RAF 5.6.42
S/Ldr P Kingsley-Strack (sic) 6.12.43
Wg Cdr RES Polkinghorne 1.10.44

Spitfires used by the Royal Australian Navy (RAN)

In October 1948 the RAAF handed over 13 Spitfire HF.VIIIc and one Mk.Vc to the Royal Australian Navy at Nowra (east of Canberra). They were used for ground handling, instruction and taxying training. The HF.VIIIcs had Merlin 46s in place of the Merlin 70 and were modified by naval artificers using kits made by Clyde Engineering. The last of these were destroyed on the fire dump in 1952.

Remarks:

The Spitfire Vc/trop entered RAAF service on 8th November 1942, being initially referred to as "*Capstans*" with "*Marvel*" engines. From 6th January 1944 the LF.VIIIc came into service, supplemented from 15th December 1944 by HF.VIIIc. Spitfires were phased out generally in November 1945. Then 339 Spitfire Mk.V/VIII were placed in long-term storage in 1946.

Nos.54 (RAF) Sqn, 452 & 457 (RAAF) Squadrons formed No.1 Fighter Wing RAAF (the "*Churchill Wing*") on 16th December 1942. Later Nos.79, 452 & 457 (RAAF) Squadrons formed No.80 Fighter Wing (1st Tactical Air Force) RAAF in December 1944 and Nos.54, 548 & 549 Squadrons then comprised the 1st Fighter Wing.

RAAF Abbreviations:
AD = Aircraft Depot (AD/TFF = ../Test & Ferry Flight)
ARD = Aircraft Repair Depot (-R/P = Replenishment Pool)
Cca = Conversion to components approved
CRD = Central Recovery Depot
DAP = Dept of Aircraft Production, Fishermans Bend, Vic.
DSD = Dept of Supply and Disposal, Melbourne, Vic.
GTS = Ground Training School at Wagga, NSW
OBU = Operational Base Unit
RAN = Royal Australian Navy; Spitfires at Nowra, NSW
R&SU = Repair & Salvage Unit (-R/P = Replenishment Pool).

Individual Histories

P7973 Spitfire F.IIa (Merlin III); TOC/RAF 19.1.41; No.452 Sqn in 4.41 (flown by Wg Cdr Bungey, Sgt Chisholm, F/Lt O'Byrne, S/Ldr Thorold-Smith, S/Ldr "Blue" Truscott, F/Lt Wawn, Air Chief Marshal Sir Andrew Humphrey); Later to CGS with personal code "RH" of Wg Cdr Ray Harris; Shipped 23.2.45 from Liverpool in SS *Fort Adelaide* to Australia as a gift of the British Government - To RAAF, arr Melbourne 17.7.45; Canberra 8.45; AD 8.45; No.2 TMD 5.10.49 (reported in storage RAAF Canberra, cased in open, not on strength); Held for Australian War Memorial, Canberra on 15.11.49; Issued to Australian War Memorial 8.3.50 and displayed marked 'RH', extant - **SURVIVOR**

"R6915" – see LZ844 (prov)

AR510 Spitfire F.Vc/trop (Merlin 46); Became **A58-1**; TOC/RAF 29.6.42 - To RAAF, arr Melbourne 24.12.42; No.1 AD 25.12.42; No.2 OTU 21.1.43; No.24 Sqn 27.2.43; No.2 OTU ('Z') 5.4.43; No.1(F)Wing 9.5.43; No.452 Sqn ('QY-B') 14.5.43; Engine cut out, abandoned 2m E of Point Margaret, S of Tapa Bay, NT 23.6.43; Wreckage to No.7 R&SU 1.7.43; Cca 22.7.43

AR523 Spitfire F.Vc/trop (Merlin 46); Became **A58-2**; TOC/RAF 13.7.42 - To RAAF, arr Melbourne 24.12.42; No.1 AD 25.12.42; No.7 AD 20.1.43; No.2 OTU 23.2.43; No.24 Sqn 27.2.43; No.2 OTU ('T') 5.4.43; No.1(F)Wing 9.5.43; No.452 Sqn ('QY-A') 14.5.43; Engine caught fire during engagement, baled out in rough country 18m SW of Batchelor 30.6.43 (F/Sgt CR Duncan, rescued next day); SOC 4.10.43

AR526 Spitfire F.Vc/trop (Merlin 46); Became **A58-3**; TOC/RAF 11.7.42 - To RAAF, arr Melbourne 24.12.42; No.1 AD 25.12.42; No.7 AD 19.1.43; No.457 Sqn 24.2.43; No.7 R&SU 19.4.43; No.457 Sqn ('ZP-V'), FTR Millingimbi from interception over Arafura Sea 28.5.43 (F/O FB Beale or F/O AH Blake killed - see also BR493); SOC 8.7.43
NOTE: Parts later used for restoration of BL628.

AR532 Spitfire F.Vc/trop (Merlin 46); Became **A58-4**; TOC/RAF 17.7.42 - To RAAF, arr Melbourne 24.12.42; No.1 AD 25.12.42; No.7 AD 9.3.43; No.79 Sqn 16.5.43; No.1 AD 23.5.43; No.79 Sqn ('UP-J') 7.6.43; Taxied into stationary JG796 (A58-175) Vivigani Strip 27.6.43; Take-off collision with BR485 (A58-28), overturned, Momote 16.4.44; No.12 R&SU 17.5.44; Cca 30.5.44

AR558 Spitfire F.Vc/trop (Merlin 46); Became **A58-5**; TOC/RAF 25.7.42 - To RAAF, arr Melbourne 21.11.42; No.1 AD 25.11.42; No.7 AD 28.1.43; No.1 R&SU-R/P 1.5.43; No.457 Sqn 9.5.43; No.7 R&SU 11.5.43; No.457 Sqn 13.5.43; Engine failed, wheels-up landing Darwin 18.8.43; No.7 R&SU 20.8.43; No.452 Sqn 11.10.43; No.14 ARD 25.10.43 (mods); No.452 Sqn 28.10.43; No.14 ARD

NB=New Britain; NSW=New South Wales; NT=Northern Territory; PN=now Papua-New Guinea; Qld =Queensland; SA=South Australia; Vic.=Victoria; WA=Western Australia

AUSTRALIA

14.6.44; No.2 OTU 12.8.44; Oleo leg collapsed in forced landing near Daly Waters, NT 13.8.44; No.14 ARD 18.8.44; Cca 6.6.45; No.8 CRD 16.7.45, SOC

AR563 Spitfire F.Vc/trop (Merlin 46); Became **A58-6**; TOC/RAF 27.7.42 - To RAAF, arr Melbourne 29.11.42; No.2 AD 29.11.42; No.2 OTU 16.12.42; No.24 Sqn 26.2.43; No.2 OTU 5.4.43; No.1(F)Wing 9.5.43; No.452 Sqn ('QY-R') 14.5.43; Air combat 20.6.43 (F/Lt DF Evans); Glycol leak, force-landed, hit anthill W of Middle Arm, Darwin 5.8.43; No.7 R&SU 11.8.43; Cca 28.8.43

AR564 Spitfire F.Vc/trop (Merlin 46); Became **A58-7**; TOC/RAF 4.8.42 - To RAAF, arr Australia 16.4.43; No.1 AD 20.4.43; No.1(F)Wing 13.7.43; No.54 Sqn ('DL-L') 16.7.43; Nosed over in night landing Nightcliffe, Darwin 12.1.44; No.7 R&SU 14.1.44; Cca 17.2.44

AR619 Spitfire F.Vc/trop (Merlin 46); Became **A58-8**; TOC/RAF 3.9.42 - To RAAF, arr Melbourne 28.11.42; No.1 AD 4.12.42; No.7 AD 20.1.43; No.54 Sqn 24.2.43; Shot down by enemy aircraft near Darwin, abandoned Myilly Point 15.3.43 (F/Sgt FL Varney PoW died of wounds 16.3.43); Wreckage to No.7 R&SU 19.3.43; Cca 5.5.43

AR620 Spitfire F.Vc/trop (Merlin 46); Became **A58-9**; TOC/RAF 7.9.42 - To RAAF, arr Melbourne 28.11.42; No.1 AD 6.12.42; No.7 AD 20.1.43; No.452 Sqn, shot down by enemy fighters, abandoned, a/c crashed in Darwin Harbour 15.3.43 (Sgt AE Cooper killed); Cca 6.4.43

AR621 Spitfire F.Vc/trop (Merlin 46); Became **A58-10**; TOC/RAF 7.9.42 - To RAAF, arr Melbourne 28.11.42; No.1 AD 4.12.42; No.2 OTU 19.3.43; Special Duties Flight 16.5.43; No.1 APU 10.1.44; No.1 AD 6.6.44; No.2 OTU 9.6.44; No.8 OTU 1.11.44; Undercarriage leg jammed up, belly-landed Uranquinty, NSW 22.11.44; No.2 CRD 22.5.45; Cca 24.7.45

BL628 Spitfire F.Vb (Merlin 45, hooked Spitfire later); ex No.401 Sqn ('YO-D', flown by GB 'Scottie' Muray, aircraft named "*Marion*"); RNDA 16.1.44; Centre section and cockpit found in farmyard near St.Merryn 1977; Shipped to Australia in 1978 for restoration at Melbourne & Adelaide, but retd UK 1988 for completion; D J T John/Aerofab Restorations, Thruxton, Hants (Civil reg. *G-BTTN* 13.8.91); Shipped to Australia, under restoration as *VH-FVB* (reg 8.6.95) by Mike Aitchison & Peter Croser at Melbourne, Victoria – **SURVIVOR**

BR237 Spitfire F.Vc/trop (Merlin 46); Became **A58-15**; TOC/RAF 22.6.42 - To RAAF, arr Melbourne 23.10.42; No.1 AD 30.10.42; No.452 Sqn 26.11.42; Engine failed during engagement, hit HT wires, crashed Strauss 6.2.43 (Sgt AR Richardson baled out safely); Cca 5.4.43 - NOTE: Sgt Richardson baled out again 6.7.43 (see "Unidentified")

BR238 Spitfire F.Vc/trop (Merlin 46); Became **A58-16**; TOC/RAF 22.6.42 - To RAAF, arr Melbourne 23.10.42; No.1 AD 4.11.42; No.2 OTU 6.12.42; Damaged landing Mildura 15.12.42; Force-landed, wheels-up 4m E of Yatpool 15.2.43; No.2 AD 8.3.43; No.1(F)Wing 11.7.43; No.457 Sqn 14.7.43; Crashed landing Drysdale 12.2.44; No.7 R&SU 15.3.44; No.457 Sqn 27.3.44; No.7 R&SU 21.4.44; No.457 Sqn 7.5.44; No.6 AD 16.7.44; No.85 Sqn ('SH-R') 5.1.45; Wheels-up landing Pearce 29.6.45; No.17 R&SU 3.7.45; No.85 Sqn 23.7.45; No.6 AD 10.10.45; Cat.E storage 22.3.46; SOC 22.5.46; DAP 26.11.47 until 15.11.48

BR239 Spitfire F.Vc/trop (Merlin 46); Became **A58-17**; TOC/RAF 26.6.42 - To RAAF, arr Melbourne 18.10.42; No.1 AD 19.10.42; No.1(F)Wing 10.11.42; No.54 Sqn 11.11.42; Dinah into sea in flames 35m NW of Cape Van Diemen 6.2.43 (F/Lt RW Foster); A6M destroyed, A6M damaged & A6M3 damaged, own aircraft damaged, abandoned over sea 20m SW of Perin Is 2.5.43 (F/O GC Farries, rescued unhurt from dinghy by Walrus after 51 hours); SOC 2.6.43

BR240 Spitfire F.Vc/trop (Merlin 46); Became **A58-18**; TOC/RAF 1.7.42 - To RAAF, arr Melbourne 23.10.42; No.1 AD 4.11.42; No.452 Sqn ('QY-Y') 28.11.42; Air combat 2.5.43 (F/O DF Evans); Selector lever jammed, wheels-up landing Pell Field 23.7.43; No.7 R&SU 25.7.43; No.452 Sqn 9.8.43; No.14 ARD 13.2.44; No.54 Sqn 9.3.44; No.7 R&SU 17.3.44; No.457 Sqn 1.4.44; No.6 AD 16.7.44; No.85 Sqn ('SH-Y') 6.12.44; No.4 AD 8.10.45, No.6 AD 11.2.46; Cat E storage 22.3.46; Cca 30.4.46

BR241 Spitfire F.Vc/trop (Merlin 46); Became **A58-19**; TOC/RAF 4.7.42 - To RAAF, arr Melbourne 23.10.42; Via Commonwealth Aircraft Corp (CAC Australia) to No.1 AD 28.10.42; No.1(F)Wing 9.11.42; No.452 Sqn ('QY-T') 9.11.42; Wheels-up landing Batchelor 23.1.43; No.7 R&SU 14.2.43; No.452 Sqn ('QY-T') 18.2.43; Hit by enemy aircraft, force-landed 2.5.43 (W/O Briggs); Engine cut on interception, overshot landing, Strauss 30.6.43; Cca 21.7.43

BR386 Spitfire F.Vc/trop (Merlin 46); Became **A58-22**; TOC/RAF 10.5.42 - To RAAF, arr Australia 25.8.42; No.1 AD 25.8.42; RAF Training Wing 4.9.42; No.452 Sqn ('QY-K') 28.9.42; Engine failed, force-landed, hit trees on approach, Strauss 21.2.43; No.7 R&SU 24.2.43; Cca 26.3.43

BR462 Spitfire F.Vc/trop (Merlin 46); Became **A58-23**; TOC/RAF 16.5.42 - To RAAF, arr Australia 25.8.42; No.1 AD 25.8.42; RAF Training Wing 4.9.42; Undercarriage collapsed Richmond 21.9.42; No.7 R&SU 25.9.42; No.457 Sqn ('ZP-U') 14.12.42; Wheels-up landing Livingstone 5.3.43; No.7 R&SU 10.3.43; No.457 Sqn ('ZP-U') 23.3.43; Hit by enemy aircraft, force-landed 2.5.43 (W/O Briggs); No.7 R&SU 22.6.43; No.457 Sqn ('ZP-U') 25.6.43; Engine seized during attack on enemy aircraft, force-landed and crashed 20m NW of Tumbling Waters, NT 28.6.43 (pilot safe); No.7 R&SU 1.7.43; Cca 25.8.43

BR468 Spitfire F.Vc/trop (Merlin 46); Became **A58-24**; TOC/RAF 17.5.42 - To RAAF, arr Melbourne 23.10.42; No.1 AD 4.11.42; No.457 Sqn ('ZP-M') 27.11.42; Damaged by enemy action, landed safely Livingstone 15.3.43; No.7 R&SU 12.5.43; No.457 Sqn ('XB-M':'ZP-M') 31.5.43; Air combat 6.7.43 (F/Sgt A E Batcheler); Air combat 7.9.43 (F/Sgt AE Batcheler); Air combat 6.11.43 (F/O AJ Gould); No.7 R&SU 17.12.43; No.14 ARD-R/P 15.2.44; No.15 ARD 13.3.44; No.15 ARD-R/P 18.7.44; No.79 Sqn 7.8.44; No.6 AD 14.11.44; No.8 OTU 7.1.45; No.1 Engineering School 17.1.45; To GI airframe *No. 7 (Engine No.42)* 5.2.45; SOC 24.5.46; DAP 26.1.47 until 8.2.49

BR471 Spitfire F.Vc/trop (Merlin 46); Became **A58-25**; TOC/RAF 21.5.42 - To RAAF, arr Australia 25.8.42; No.1 AD 25.8.42; No.1(F)Wing 4.9.42; No.452 Sqn 5.10.42; Dived into in sea 1m off shore near Wamberal, NSW 9.10.42; SOC 19.1.43

BR480 Spitfire F.Vc/trop (Merlin 46); Became **A58-26**; TOC/RAF 31.5.42 - To RAAF, arr Melbourne 23.10.42; No.1 AD 29.10.42; No.54 Sqn 27.11.42; Engine failed before action, force-landed on beach and submerged by rising tide 4m W of Point Charles, NT 2.5.43 (Sgt Cavanagh OK); Remains to No.7 R&SU 6.5.43; Cca 4.6.43

BR484 Spitfire F.Vc/trop (Merlin 46); Became **A58-27**; TOC/RAF 4.6.42 - To RAAF, arr Melbourne 18.10.42; No.1 AD 21.10.42; No.1(F)Wing 9.11.42; No.54 Sqn 9.11.42; Undershot landing Darwin 16.2.43 (poss. F/Sgt Wellin); No.6 AD 10.2.44; No.2 OTU 11.7.44; No.8 OTU 1.11.44; No.6 AD 28.11.45; Cat.E storage 22.3.46; SOC 22.5.46; DAP 26.11.47 until 15.11.48

BR485 Spitfire F.Vc/trop (Merlin 46); Became **A58-28**; TOC/RAF 4.6.42 - To RAAF, arr Melbourne 18.10.42; No.1 AD 19.10.42; No.79 Sqn ('UP-M') 7.5.43; No.1 AD 24.5.43 (mods); No.79 Sqn 29.5.43; Air combat 21.12.43 (P/O JE Barrie); Hit by AR532 (A58-4) while taxying, Momote 16.4.44; No.12 R&SU 17.5.44; Cca 30.5.44

BR490 Spitfire F.Vc/trop (Merlin 46); Became **A58-29**; TOC/RAF 8.6.42 - To RAAF, arr Melbourne 18.10.42;

No.1 AD 19.10.42; No.1(F)Wing 9.11.42; No.54 Sqn 9.11.42; G6M destroyed, G6M probable & G6M damaged, own aircraft damaged, abandoned 8m NW of Adelaide River, crashed Nightcliffe, Darwin 30.6.43 (F/Sgt AS Laundy wounded), SOC; Cca 17.7.43

BR493 Spitfire F.Vc/trop (Merlin 46); Became **A58-30**; TOC/RAF 13.6.42 - To RAAF, arr Melbourne 18.10.42; No.1 AD 21.10.42; No.1(F)Wing 30.10.42; No.457 Sqn ('ZP-A') 9.11.42; Brakes failed landing, rolled into ditch, Livingstone 12.2.43; FTR Millingimbi from interception over Arafura Sea 28.5.43 (F/O FB Beale or F/O AH Blake killed - see also AR526); SOC 8.7.43

BR495 Spitfire F.Vc/trop (Merlin 46); Became **A58-31**; TOC/RAF 14.6.42 - To RAAF, arr Melbourne 18.10.42; No.1 AD 21.10.42; No.1(F)Wing 9.11.42; No.54 Sqn 9.11.42; G6M destroyed & another probable 30.6.43 (F/Lt RW Foster); Engine ran away, glycol leak, left formation on scramble, force-landed wheels up on beach, Port Patterson, NT 6.7.43; Salvaged from shallow water; No.7 R&SU 29.9.43; No.14 ARD 10.10.43; Cca 4.11.43

BR497 Spitfire F.Vc/trop (Merlin 46); Became **A58-32**; TOC/RAF 14.6.42 - To RAAF, arr Melbourne 18.10.42; No.1 AD 19.10.42; No.1(F)Wing 9.11.42; No.452 Sqn ('QY-C') 9.11.42; Take-off collision with "AR237" 29.5.43; Air combat 30.6.43 (F/O CP Lloyd); Damaged by enemy fighter over Strauss, engine caught fire, abandoned near Murrenja Hill 6.7.43 (F/O Hinds); Cca 14.10.43

BR499 Spitfire F.Vc/trop (Merlin 46); Became **A58-33**; TOC/RAF 15.6.42 - To RAAF, arr Melbourne 18.10.42; No.1 AD 19.10.42; No.1(F)Wing 3.11.42; No.457 Sqn ('ZP-V') 9.11.42; Swung and hit tree landing Livingstone 13.3.43; No.7 R&SU 15.3.43; No.452 Sqn ('QY-A') 13.6.43; Damaged by enemy aircraft during interception 35m E of Anson Bay 6.7.43 (P/O FRJ McDowell killed); Cca 1.9.43

BR526 Spitfire F.Vc/trop (Merlin 46); Became **A58-34**; TOC/RAF 14.6.42 - To RAAF, arr Melbourne 23.10.42; No.1 AD 4.11.42; No.452 Sqn ('QY-J') 30.11.42; Air combat 15.3.43 (F/O AP Goldsmith); Attacked Japanese bombers, then controls shot away by A6M3, pilot thrown out of a/c, a/c crashed in sea 30m NW of Darwin 2.5.43 (F/O Goldsmith parachuted into sea, rescued), SOC

BR527 Spitfire F.Vc/trop (Merlin 46); Became **A58-35**; TOC/RAF 14.6.42 - To RAAF, arr Melbourne 23.10.42; No.1 AD 4.11.42; No.457 Sqn 5.12.42; No.7 R&SU 21.6.43; No.457 Sqn ('ZP-W') 26.6.43; Damaged in combat 28.6.43 (engine change); No.7 R&SU 1.7.43; No.457 Sqn ('ZP-W') 11.7.43; No.7 R&SU 23.12.43; No.14 ARD-R/P 16.2.44; No.15 ARD-R/P 11.3.44; No.15 ARD 7.4.44; No.15 ARD-R/P 14.8.44; No.79 Sqn 9.9.44; No.6 AD 5.12.44; No.3 CRD 20.11.45 (Cca)

BR528 Spitfire F.Vc/trop (Merlin 46); Became **A58-36**; TOC/RAF 14.6.42 - To RAAF, arr Melbourne 23.10.42; No.1 AD 4.11.42; No.54 Sqn 5.12.42; Shot down near Darwin and crashed 30m W of Batchelor on edge of Great Reynolds River swamp 30.6.43 (P/O JC Wellsman killed, aircraft not found until 20.8.43 and remains 29.9.43); Cca 23.9.43

BR530 Spitfire F.Vc/trop (Merlin 46); Became **A58-37**; TOC/RAF 14.6.42 - To RAAF, arr Melbourne 23.10.42; No.1 AD 4.11.42; No.54 Sqn 27.11.42; Ran out of fuel, wheels-up landing Mildura 14.1.43 (Sgt Cooper); Dived into ground after air combat Anson Bay area 30.6.43 (Sgt Holmes OK); No.7 R&SU 6.7.43; Cca 9.8.43

BR531 Spitfire F.Vc/trop (Merlin 46); Became **A58-38**; TOC/RAF 21.6.42 - To RAAF, arr Melbourne 23.10.42; No.1 AD 10.11.42; No.457 Sqn ('ZP-N') 19.11.42; Swung off runway into fallen trees Livingstone 7.9.43; No.7 R&SU 8.9.43; No.14 ARD 1.10.43; No.8 OTU 30.6.45; No.6 AD 28.11.45; Cat.E storage 22.3.46; SOC 22.5.46; DAP 26.11.47 until 15.11.48

BR532 Spitfire F.Vc/trop (Merlin 46); Became **A58-39**; TOC/RAF 20.6.42 - To RAAF, arr Melbourne 18.10.42; No.1 AD 21.10.42; No.1(F)Wing 9.11.42; No.54 Sqn 9.11.42; Low flying Japanese aircraft destroyed 20.6.43 (F/O HO Leonard); A6M damaged 7.9.43 (F/O HO Leonard); No.7 R&SU 7.11.43; No.14 ARD-R/P 15.2.44; No.15 ARD-R/P 13.3.44; No.15 ARD 6.4.44; No.15 ARD-R/P 18.10.44; No.6 AD 23.10.44; No.8 OTU 13.8.45; No.6 AD 14.11.45; SOC 22.5.46; DAP 26.11.47

BR533 Spitfire F.Vc/trop (Merlin 46); Became **A58-40**; TOC/RAF 21.6.42 - To RAAF, arr Melbourne 18.10.42; No.1 AD 21.10.42; No.1(F)Wing 9.11.42; No.457 Sqn 9.11.42; No.6 AD 4.8.44; No.85 Sqn 21.5.45; No.6 AD 10.10.45; Cat.E storage 22.3.46; SOC 22.5.46; DAP 26.11.47 until 15.11.48

BR535 Spitfire F.Vc/trop (Merlin 46); Became **A58-41**; TOC/RAF 25.6.42 - To RAAF, arr Melbourne 23.10.42; No.1 AD 4.11.42; No.54 Sqn 30.11.42; Landing after formation flight, collided on runway with BS158 (A58-11) also landing, Darwin 5.2.43 (Sgt Cooper unhurt); Cca 8.3.43

BR536 Spitfire F.Vc/trop (Merlin 46); Became **A58-42**; TOC/RAF 25.6.42 - To RAAF, arr Melbourne 23.10.42; No.1 AD 30.10.42; No.54 Sqn ('DL-H', named '*Butch II*') 15.11.42; A6M destroyed 15.3.43 (F/Sgt Biggs); Fuel shortage, force-landed off West Point, submerged by rising tide 2.5.43 (Sgt Spencer OK); Salvaged; No.7 R&SU 17.5.43; No.14 ARD 17.5.43; No.14 ARD-R/P 25.10.43; No.54 Sqn 1.11.43; No.7 R&SU 10.1.44; To GI airframe *No.5* 2.3.44; Cca 17.10.45

BR537 Spitfire F.Vc/trop (Merlin 46); Became **A58-43**; TOC/RAF 26.6.42 - To RAAF, arr Melbourne 23.10.42; No.1 AD 29.10.42; No.54 Sqn 27.11.42; Damaged by enemy aircraft, force-landed Darwin 30.6.43; No.7 R&SU 4.7.43; No.452 Sqn ('QY-A') 20.8.43; Ran out of fuel on ferry flight, force-landed and crashed 11m NW of Gin Gin, Qld 11.3.44; No.4 AD 19.3.44; Cca 4.7.44; No.4 CRD 6.7.44

BR538 Spitfire F.Vc/trop (Merlin 46); Became **A58-44**; TOC/RAF 26.6.42 - To RAAF, arr Melbourne 23.10.42; No.1 AD 30.10.42; No.457 Sqn ('U') 27.11.42; Taxying accident Daly Waters 27.11.42; No.7 R&SU 31.1.43; No.457 Sqn ('XB-U':'ZP-U') 11.2.43; Undercarriage failed to lower fully on landing Livingstone 29.4.43; Air combat 7.9.43 (F/O RHW Gregory); Swung landing, lost undercarriage in soft ground, Livingstone 27.1.44; No.7 R&SU 30.1.44; No.14 ARD 1.2.44; Cca 14.2.44

BR539 Spitfire F.Vc/trop (Merlin 46); Became **A58-45**; TOC/RAF 30.6.42 - To RAAF, arr Melbourne 23.10.42; No.1 AD 30.10.42; No.54 Sqn ('X':'DL-X') 15.11.42; Japanese bomber probable & another damaged 15.3.43 (F/Lt RW Foster); Japanese bomber destroyed & A6M damaged 20.6.43 (F/Lt RW Foster); G6M destroyed & another probable 6.7.43 (F/Lt RW Foster); No.452 Sqn 8.6.44; No.14 ARD-R/P 15.6.44; No.2 OTU 17.8.44; No.8 OTU 1.11.44; Force-landed, hit fence, Young 7.12.44; Swung on take-off Parkes 30.3.45; No.2 CRD 22.5.45; Cca 31.7.45

BR540 Spitfire F.Vc/trop (Merlin 46); Became **A58-46**; TOC/RAF 2.7.42 - To RAAF, arr Melbourne 23.10.42; No.1 AD 28.10.42; No.1(F)Wing 9.11.42; No.457 Sqn 9.11.42; Hit truck landing Livingstone 7.3.43; No.7 R&SU 10.3.43; No.457 Sqn ('XB-J':'ZP-J') 7.4.43; Air combat 6.7.43 (F/Lt PH Watson); No.7 R&SU 28.10.43; No.452 Sqn 29.11.43; No.15 ARD-R/P 11.3.44; No.6 AD 23.10.44; No.3 CRD 22.5.45; Cca 15.6.45

BR541 Spitfire F.Vc/trop (Merlin 46); Became **A58-47**; TOC/RAF 4.7.42 - To RAAF, arr Melbourne 23.10.42; No.1 AD 4.11.42; No.457 Sqn ('XB-F':'ZP-F') 15.11.42; Damaged in combat, crashed landing, Livingstone 28.6.43; No.7 R&SU 29.6.43; No.452 Sqn ('QY-Z') 16.7.43; No.14 ARD 24.9.43 (fitted CAAG suiting); No.452 Sqn ('QY-V') 3.10.43; Damaged port leg & undercarriage landing at night, Darwin 16.11.43; No.7 R&SU 18.11.43; No.54 Sqn 12.2.44; No.452 Sqn 29.5.44; No.14 ARD-R/P 1.8.44; No.14 ARD 3.10.44; No.8 OTU 1.3.45; Partial wheels-up landing, Parkes 29.3.45; No.6

AD 14.11.45; Cat.E storage 22.3.46; SOC 22.5.46; DAP 26.11.47 until 15.11.48

BR542 Spitfire F.Vc/trop (Merlin 46); Became **A58-48**; TOC/RAF 7.7.42 - To RAAF, arr Melbourne 23.10.42; No.1 AD 28.10.42; No.1(F)Wing 9.11.42; No.457 Sqn ('XB-Z':'ZP-Z') 9.11.42; Ki-46 destroyed 60m E of Darwin 18.7.43 (S/Ldr KE James); Air combat 7.9.43 (F/O IS Mackenzie); No.7 R&SU 29.3.44; No.457 Sqn 18.4.44; No.6 AD 18.7.44; No.85 Sqn 20.1.45; No.6 AD 10.10.45; Cat.E storage 22.3.46; SOC 22.5.46; DAP 26.11.47 until 15.11.48

BR543 Spitfire F.Vc/trop (Merlin 46); Became **A58-49**; TOC/RAF 8.7.42 - To RAAF, arr Melbourne 23.10.42; No.1 AD 27.10.42; No.1(F)Wing 3.11.42; No.457 Sqn ('ZP-T':'XB-T') 9.11.42; Air combat 20.6.43 (F/Lt JS Newton); Damaged by enemy action over Darwin 28.6.43; No.7 R&SU 1.7.43; No.457 Sqn ('ZP-T') 8.7.43; No.7 R&SU 29.11.43; No.452 Sqn 7.1.44; No.15 ARD-R/P 11.3.44; No.6 AD 26.10.44; Storage 22.11.45; Cat E 22.3.46; SOC 22.5.46; DAP 26.11.47 until 15.11.48

BR544 Spitfire F.Vc/trop (Merlin 46); Became **A58-50**; TOC/RAF 11.7.42 - To RAAF, arr Melbourne 23.10.42; No.1 AD 28.10.42; No.1(F)Wing 9.11.42; No.54 Sqn ('A':'DL-A') 9.11.42; A6M destroyed also 1 probable & 1 damaged 15.3.43 (F/Lt RKC Norwood); Hits on tail of Ki-46 23.5.43 (F/Lt RKC Norwood); Low flying Japanese aircraft destroyed 20.6.43 (P/O WH Appleton); G6M probable 30.6.43 (F/Lt RKC Norwood); No.7 R&SU 25.7.43; No.54 Sqn ('DL-A') 2.8.43; A6M damaged 7.9.43 (F/O Appleton); Caught fire in air, abandoned over Darwin railway station 15.2.44; No.7 R&SU 22.2.44; Cca 14.3.44

BR545 Spitfire F.Vc/trop (Merlin 46); Became **A58-51**; TOC/RAF 13.7.42 - To RAAF, arr Melbourne 23.10.42; No.1 AD 27.10.42; No.54 Sqn ('DL-E', named '*IVY*') 14.11.42; Ran out of fuel on ferry flight between Nightcliffe and Drysdale, force-landed on tidal mud flats on Prince Regent River near Derby, NW Australia 22.12.43 (F/Lt DW Gray) [His log book notes "crashed in swamp, four days and nights in dinghy"; he was recovered 25.12.43]; SOC 22.1.44. - Swamp wreck discovered in 11.87; Hulk stored by the RAAF/RAN Museum, Point Cook, Victoria and currently derelict there - **SURVIVOR**

BR546 Spitfire F.Vc/trop (Merlin 46); Became **A58-52**; TOC/RAF 15.7.42 - To RAAF, arr Melbourne 23.10.42; No.1 AD 4.11.42; No.452 Sqn 27.11.42; Swung and overturned landing Strauss 17.2.43; No.7 R&SU 20.2.43; No.452 Sqn ('QY-S') 23.4.43; Air combat 20.6.43 (F/Sgt KS Cross); Engine cut during interception, force-landed wheels-up on Batchelor-Stapleton road, 15m NW of Batchelor 30.6.43; Cca 17.7.43

BR547 Spitfire F.Vc/trop (Merlin 46); Became **A58-53**; TOC/RAF 20.7.42 - To RAAF, arr Melbourne 23.10.42; No.1 AD 30.10.42; No.1(F)Wing 9.11.42; No.452 Sqn ('QY-S') 9.11.42; FTR from interception 10m W of Fog Bay/near Darwin 2.5.43 (Sgt RS Stagg found alive some days later); SOC 2.6.43

BR548 Spitfire F.Vc/trop (Merlin 46); Became **A58-54**; TOC/RAF 20.7.42 - To RAAF, arr Melbourne 23.10.42; No.1 AD 28.10.42; No.1(F)Wing 9.11.42; No.452 Sqn ('QY-M') 9.11.42; Air combat with A6Ms, controls shot away, crashed landing Strauss 20.6.43 (F/O G A Mawer); No.7 R&SU 21.6.43; No.457 Sqn 4.9.43; No.14 ARD 16.10.43; No.7 R&SU 18.10.43; No.457 Sqn 10.11.43; Swung landing, into drainage ditch, Sattler 19.5.44; Cca 20.6.44

BR549 Spitfire F.Vc/trop (Merlin 46); Became **A58-55**; TOC/RAF 24.7.42 - To RAAF, arr Melbourne 23.10.42; No.1 AD 27.10.42; No.1(F)Wing 9.11.42; No.452 Sqn ('QY-K') 9.11.42; Collided with BS184 (A58-73) 4m SE of Coomalie Creek, NT 27.1.43; Air combat 30.6.43 (G6M destroyed, P/O PD Tully, shared S/Ldr JM Gibbs of No.54 Sqn in BS164); Air combat 6.7.43 (F/O CP Lloyd); Damaged by Japanese fighter and abandoned, dived into ground in Coomalie Creek area, 15m W of Strauss 7.9.43 (P/O PD Tully baled out safely [possibly F/O CP Lloyd, see "Unidentified"); No.7 R&SU 14.9.43; Cca 24.9.43

BR568 Spitfire F.Vc/trop (Merlin 46); Became **A58-56**; TOC/RAF 21.5.42 - To RAAF, arr Australia 25.8.42; No.1 AD 25.8.42; RAF Training Wing 4.9.42; Hit fence landing, Penrith 27.9.42; No.7 R&SU 1.10.42; No.2 AD 8.10.42; No.457 Sqn ('ZP-Y') 28.11.42; Taxying, hit stationary BS171 (A58-66), Livingstone 19.3.43; No.7 R&SU 20.3.43; No.457 Sqn ('ZP-Y') 22.3.43; Glycol leak, abandoned 10m W of Sattler 5.9.43; No.7 R&SU 10.9.43; Cca 1.10.43

BR570 Spitfire F.Vc/trop (Merlin 46); Became **A58-57**; TOC/RAF 20.5.42 - To RAAF, arr Australia 25.8.42; No.1 AD 25.8.42; RAF Training Wing 4.9.42; No.54 Sqn 8.11.42; Possibly take-off crash at Wagga 8.11.42; No.1 AD 8.11.42; No.54 Sqn 12.11.42; Damaged Oodnadatta on ferry flight to Darwin 16.1.43 (F/Lt RKC Norwood); A6M probable 2.5.43 (Sgt Eldred); No.7 R&SU 7.11.43; No.14 ARD-R/P 15.2.44; No.15 ARD 1.3.44; No.79 Sqn 10.8.44; No.6 AD 6.12.44; Cca 24.7.45; No.3 CRD 9.8.45. NOTE: Reported tyre burst on take-off Wagga 8.11.42 (P/O JD Lenagen); Serial-No unknown, see also BR572

BR572 Spitfire F.Vc/trop (Merlin 46); Became **A58-58**; TOC/RAF 20.5.42 - To RAAF, arr Australia 25.8.42; No.1 AD 25.8.42; RAF Training Wing 4.9.42; No.54 Sqn 8.11.42; Possibly take-off crash at Wagga 8.11.42; No.1 AD 8.11.42; No.54 Sqn 14.11.42; Ran out of fuel, ditched 5m W of Point Charles, NT 2.5.43 (F/O Wall rescued by naval launch); SOC 11.6.43
NOTE: For take-off crash Wagga see BR570

BR574 Spitfire F.Vc/trop (Merlin 46); Became **A58-59**; TOC/RAF 26.5.42 - To RAAF, arr Melbourne 2.12.42; No.1 AD 6.12.42; No.7 AD 17.2.43; No.452 Sqn ('QY-D') 30.3.43; Air combat 20.6.43 (S/Ldr RS MacDonald); Hit tree taxying Strauss 1.8.43; No.7 R&SU 9.8.43; No.457 Sqn 14.9.43; No.7 R&SU 29.3.44; No.457 Sqn 28.4.44; Taxying accident after landing Strauss 17.5.44; No.7 R&SU 16.6.44; No.14 ARD-R/P 9.8.44; Crashlanded Alice Springs while ferrying to No.85 Sqn 21.9.44; No.3 AD 29.10.44; No.6 AD 3.11.44; Cca 4.5.45; No.3 CRD 22.5.45

BR584 Spitfire F.Vc/trop (Merlin 46); Became **A58-60**; TOC/RAF 1.6.42 - To RAAF, arr Melbourne 23.10.42; No.1 AD 4.11.42; No.452 Sqn 5.12.42; Undershot landing at night, hit trees, Strauss 17.2.43; No.7 R&SU 18.2.43; Cca 8.3.43

BR589 Spitfire F.Vc/trop (Merlin 46); Became **A58-61**; TOC/RAF 6.6.42 - To RAAF, arr Melbourne 23.10.42; No.1 AD 4.11.42; No.457 Sqn ('XB-P';'ZP-P') 30.11.42; FTR interception 35m E of Anson Bay, NT/Billabong Ridge 6.7.43 (F/O FD Hamilton killed); SOC 11.10.43

BS158 Spitfire F.Vc/trop (Merlin 46); Became **A58-11**; TOC/RAF 18.6.42 - To RAAF, arr Melbourne 18.10.42; No.1 AD 19.10.42; No.1(F)Wing 9.11.42; No.54 Sqn 9.11.42; Landing after formation flight, collided on runway with BR535 (A58-41), Darwin 5.2.43 (F/Sgt PF McCarthy DoI); Cat.FA/E 11.2.43; Cca 8.3.43

BS162 Spitfire F.Vc/trop (Merlin 46); Became **A58-12**; TOC/RAF 22.6.42 - To RAAF, arr Melbourne 18.10.42; No.1 AD 21.10.42; No.1(F)Wing 9.11.42; No.452 Sqn ('QY-F') 9.11.42; Attacked Japanese bomber, then controls shot away by A6M3, baled out 20m W of Perin Is, NT 2.5.43 (F/O AC McNab rescued but died); SOC 2.6.43

BS163 Spitfire F.Vc/trop (Merlin 46); Became **A58-62**; TOC/RAF 22.6.42 - To RAAF, arr Melbourne 23.10.42; No.1 AD 29.10.42; No.452 Sqn ('QY-B') 15.11.42; Hit pipeline landing Strauss 22.3.43; No.7 R&SU; No.14 ARD 5.5.43; Cca 19.6.43

BS164 Spitfire F.Vc/trop (Merlin 46); Became **A58-63**; TOC/RAF 22.6.42 - To RAAF, arr Melbourne 23.10.42; No.1 AD 4.11.42; No.54 Sqn ('K':'DL-K') 30.11.42; A6M destroyed, own aircraft damaged 2.3.43 (S/Ldr JM Gibbs); 2 A6M destroyed & another damaged, also G6M damaged

2.5.43 (S/Ldr JM Gibbs); A6M & G6M destroyed, also another G6M destroyed shared P/O PD Tully of No.452 Sqn, plus 2 G6M damaged 30.6.43 (S/Ldr JM Gibbs); G6M destroyed & another damaged 6.7.43 (S/Ldr JM Gibbs); Mid-air collision with LZ845 (A58-214) during fighter affiliation at 3,000ft, dived into ground 10m ENE of Strauss 13.1.44 (F/Sgt JB Gibbs killed); Cca 16.3.44. - Recovered surface **wreck** by Peter Croser, Melbourne in 1991

BS165 Spitfire F.Vc/trop (Merlin 46); Became **A58-13**; TOC/RAF 26.6.42 - To RAAF, arr Melbourne 23.10.42; No.1 AD 29.10.42; No.54 Sqn 19.11.42; Formation flight, glycol leak, attempted forced landing in field 15m from base, crashed, aircraft burst into flames $^1/_2$m NE of Cattai Public School, NT 25.11.42 (Sgt WK Read killed; too low to bale out safely, parachute opened too late); Cca 22.1.43

BS166 Spitfire F.Vc/trop (Merlin 46); Became **A58-64**; TOC/RAF 26.6.42 - To RAAF, arr Melbourne 23.10.42; No.1 AD 30.10.42; No.54 Sqn 19.11.42; A6M destroyed 20.6.43 (Grp Capt AL Walters); Overshot landing Tennants Creek, NT on ferry flight 31.1.44; No.14 ARD 10.2.44; Cca 14.3.44

BS169 Spitfire F.Vc/trop (Merlin 46); Became **A58-65**; TOC/RAF 28.6.42 - To RAAF, arr Melbourne 23.10.42; No.1 AD 4.11.42; No.452 Sqn 14.11.42; Engine failed, force-landed Palm Beach, Sydney 13.12.42; No.2 AD 29.12.42; No.1 AD 23.4.43; No.79 Sqn 5.5.43; Hit fence landing Wooloomanata 5.5.43; No.1 AD 20.5.43; No.1(F)Wing 11.7.43; No.457 Sqn, air combats 17.8.43 (F/Sgt RW Watson) & 7.9.43 (F/Sgt FC White); R&SU; No.457 Sqn 29.3.44; No.15 R&SU; No.457 Sqn 20.4.44; No.14 ARD-R/P 1.8.44; No.14 ARD 3.10.44; CGS 22.2.45; No.6 AD 22.10.45; Cat.E storage 22.3.46; SOC 22.5.46; DAP 26.11.47 until 15.11.48

BS171 Spitfire F.Vc/trop (Merlin 46); Became **A58-66**; TOC/RAF 3.7.42 - To RAAF, arr Melbourne 23.10.42; No.1 AD 30.10.42; No.457 Sqn ('ZP-B') 27.11.42; Hit stationary BR568 (A58-56) landing Livingstone 19.3.43; No.7 R&SU 20.3.43; No.457 Sqn 4.4.43; Engine failed during interception, abandoned, a/c crashed in sea 60m W of Darwin 2.5.43; SOC 2.6.43

BS173 Spitfire F.Vc/trop (Merlin 46); Became **A58-67**; TOC/RAF 3.7.42 - To RAAF, arr Melbourne 23.10.42; No.1 AD 27.10.42; No.457 Sqn 14.11.42; Swung and hit pipe-line landing Livingstone 19.3.43; No.7 R&SU 20.3.43; No.457 Sqn ('ZP-G') 17.4.43; FTR from interception approx 60m W of Darwin 2.5.43 (F/O GLC Gifford); SOC 26.5.43

BS174 Spitfire F.Vc/trop (Merlin 46); Became **A58-68**; TOC/RAF 3.7.42 - To RAAF, arr Melbourne 23.10.42; No.1 AD 2.11.42; No.1(F)Wing 10.11.42; No.452 Sqn ('QY-W') 11.11.42; No.7 R&SU 24.5.43; No.452 Sqn 9.6.43; Shot down by enemy a/c Koolpinyah Station, N of Adam Bay/10m N of Cape Hotham, NT 20.6.43 (F/Sgt AT Ruskin-Rowe killed); Cca 13.8.43

BS175 Spitfire F.Vc/trop (Merlin 46); Became **A58-69**; TOC/RAF 6.7.42 - To RAAF, arr Melbourne 23.10.42; No.1 AD 5.11.42; No.452 Sqn 15.11.42; Missing on ferry flight, crashed Tabletop Range en route Strauss-Wyndham 27.2.43 (F/O WH Ford killed); Cat.FA/E 4.3.43; Cca 5.4.43

BS178 Spitfire F.Vc/trop (Merlin 46); Became **A58-70**; TOC/RAF 11.7.42 - To RAAF, arr Melbourne 23.10.42; No.1 AD 2.11.42; No.1(F)Wing 10.11.42; No.457 Sqn ('ZP-J':'ZP-D') 11.11.42; Swung on landing, hit trees, Livingstone 31.8.43; No.7 R&SU 2.9.43; No.14 ARD 6.9.43; Cca 22.11.43

BS181 Spitfire F.Vc/trop (Merlin 46); Became **A58-71**; TOC/RAF 13.7.42 - To RAAF, arr Melbourne 23.10.42; No.1 AD 28.10.42; No.54 Sqn 14.11.42; Shot down a Ki-46, the first success of a Spitfire over Australia 6.2.43 (F/Lt RW Foster); No.7 R&SU 5.7.43; No.452 Sqn 11.2.44; No.7 R&SU 27.3.44; No.457 Sqn (ZP-J); Engine failed, force-landed, crashed, Sattler 9.7.44 (F/Sgt G Marks); No.9 R&SU 10.7.44; No.8 CRD 17.7.44; Cca 3.8.44

BS182 Spitfire F.Vc/trop (Merlin 46); Became **A58-72**; TOC/RAF 13.7.42 - To RAAF, arr Melbourne 23.10.42; No.1 AD 28.10.42; No.1(F)Wing 9.11.42; No.54 Sqn 9.11.42; Japanese bomber destroyed 20.6.43 (F/Sgt DM Wheeler); No.452 Sqn 9.3.44; Crashed landing Carnarvon 17.3.44; No.17 R&SU 17.3.44; No.85 Sqn ('SH-N', white fin, red rudder), 17.9.44; No.17 R&SU 31.5.45; Cca 7.8.45

BS184 Spitfire F.Vc/trop (Merlin 46); Became **A58-73**; TOC/RAF 13.7.42 - To RAAF, arr Melbourne 23.10.42; No.1 AD 2.11.42; No.452 Sqn 14.11.42; Mid-air collision with BR549 (A58-55), 4m SE of Coomalie Creek, NT 27.1.43 (Sgt EE Hutchinson killed); Cca 25.2.43

BS186 Spitfire F.Vc/trop (Merlin 46); Became **A58-74**; TOC/RAF 7.7.42 - To RAAF, arr Melbourne 23.10.42; No.1 AD 4.11.42; No.452 Sqn ('QY-L') 27.11.42; Air combat 15.3.43 & 2.5.43 (F/Lt ES Hall); No.7 R&SU 26.6.43; No.452 Sqn 29.6.43; Air combats 30.6.43 & 6.7.43 (F/Lt ES Hall); Air combat 10.8.43 (P/O WM Coombes); No.14 ARD 27.9.43; No.452 Sqn 1.10.43;

The wreckage of Spitfire F.Vc/trop A58-71 ZP-J (ex BS181) of No.457 Sqn at Sattler after the engine failed and it force-landed and crashed on 9th July 1944. [MAP]

AUSTRALIA

The remains of Spitfire F.Vc/trop A58-81 ZP-S (ex BS199) of No.457 Sqn after flying into the ground three miles from Millingimbi airfield during combat with an A6M on 9th May 1943, Plt Off Bruce Little being slightly wounded. Parts of the wreckage were recovered in 1983.

No.7 R&SU 24.10.43; No.452 Sqn 29.11.43; No.7 R&SU 27.3.44; No.14 ARD 4.4.44; No.1 CU 18.6.44; No.1 Engineering School 20.6.44; Converted to GI airframe *No.6* (Engine *No.31*) 21.7.44; SOC 16.5.46; DAP 26.11.47 until 8.2.49

BS187 Spitfire F.Vc/trop (Merlin 46); Became **A58-75**; TOC/RAF 17.7.42 - To RAAF, arr Melbourne 23.10.42; No.1 AD 4.11.42; Crashed on initial test flight, Port Phillip Bay, Vic 1.12.42; Cca 22.1.43

BS188 Spitfire F.Vc/trop (Merlin 46); Became **A58-76**; TOC/RAF 19.7.42 - To RAAF, arr Melbourne 23.10.42; No.1 AD 28.10.42; No.1(F)Wing 10.11.42; No.54 Sqn 11.11.42; Tyre burst on take-off, swung on landing, overturned, Darwin 24.5.43 (F/O RG Ashby); No.7 R&SU 25.5.43; No.14 ARD 6.6.43; Cca 28.10.43

BS190 Spitfire F.Vc/trop (Merlin 46); Became **A58-77**; TOC/RAF 20.7.42 - To RAAF, arr Melbourne 23.10.42; No.1 AD 30.10.42; No.457 Sqn 15.11.42; Damaged by enemy action near Fenton 6.7.43; No.7 R&SU 10.11.43; No.457 Sqn 22.12.43; Damaged by cannon explosion exercising over Shoal Bay 16.6.44; No.9 R&SU 21.6.44; No.14 ARD-R/P 7.8.44; No.14 ARD 30.8.44; CGS 25.6.45; Ferry flight, wheels-up landing Parkes 28.6.45; No.14 ARD; CGS 23.8.45; No.6 AD 22.10.45; Cat.E storage 22.3.46; SOC 22.5.46; DAP 26.11.47 until 15.11.48

BS191 Spitfire F.Vc/trop (Merlin 46); Became **A58-78**; TOC/RAF 20.6.42 - To RAAF, arr Melbourne 23.10.42; No.1 AD 28.10.42; No.1(F)Wing 9.11.42; No.452 Sqn ('QY-X') 9.11.42; Force-landed on beach 12m S of Point Charles 2.5.43; No.7 R&SU 6.5.43; No.14 ARD 17.5.43 (CAAG mod 14.9.43); No.452 Sqn 3.10.43; No.7 R&SU 7.10.43; No.452 Sqn 11.10.43; No.14 ARD 13.2.44; No.54 Sqn 9.3.44; No.7 R&SU 17.3.44; No.457 Sqn 1.4.44; No.7 R&SU 22.4.44; No.457 Sqn 5.5.44; No.6 AD 16.7.44; No.1 AD 4.6.45; SOC 22.5.46; DAP 25.2.49; Sold 20.7.50

BS193 Spitfire F.Vc/trop (Merlin 46); Became **A58-79**; TOC/RAF 27.7.42 - To RAAF, arr Melbourne 14.11.42; No.1(F)Wing 29.11.42; No.452 Sqn 15.12.42; Heavy landing, undercarriage failed Strauss 14.3.43; No.7 R&SU 16.3.43; No.452 Sqn 23.5.43; Air combat 20.6.43 (F/O KL Colyer); Engine failed during engagement 30m N of Fenton 6.7.43 (F/O PStJ Makin baled out safely); No.7 R&SU 15.7.43; No.14 ARD 7.11.43; Cca 12.11.43

BS197 Spitfire F.Vc/trop (Merlin 46); Became **A58-80**; TOC/RAF 28.7.42 - To RAAF, arr Melbourne 23.10.42; No.1 AD 27.10.42; No.457 Sqn 15.11.42; FTR interception c.35m E of Anson Bay 6.7.43 (F/O NF Robinson killed); SOC 11.10.43

BS199 Spitfire F.Vc/trop (Merlin 46); Became **A58-81**; TOC/RAF 29.7.42 - To RAAF, arr Melbourne 14.11.42; No.1(F)Wing 11.42; No.457 Sqn ('ZP-S'), flew into ground in combat with A6M, crashed 3m from Millingimbi airfield 9.5.43 (P/O B Little slightly wounded); Cca 7.6.43 - Parts recovered from surface wreck by Robert L Eastgate, Melbourne, Vic, in 1983 - **SURVIVOR**

BS201 Spitfire F.Vc/trop (Merlin 46); Became **A58-82**; TOC/RAF 1.8.42 - To RAAF, arr Melbourne 29.11.42; No.2 AD 29.11.42; No.457 Sqn ('XB-Q') 15.12.42 (F/O Blake); No.7 R&SU 9.1.44; Landing from ferry flight, ran off runway and hit earth mound, Darwin Civil 16.2.44; No.14 ARD 25.2.44; Cca 16.3.44

BS218 Spitfire F.Vc/trop (Merlin 46); Became **A58-83**; TOC/RAF 12.7.42 - To RAAF, arr Melbourne 23.10.42; No.1 AD 30.10.42; No.1(F)Wing 10.11.42; Engine overheated, force-landed and crashed Norellan, NSW 29.11.42; No.2 AD 7.12.42; No.7 AD 3.2.43; No.54 Sqn 13.5.43; G6M destroyed 6.7.43 (F/O JD Lenagen); Crashed in night landing Darwin 12.10.43 (F/Sgt Finney OK); No.7 R&SU 16.10.43; No.457 Sqn 9.1.44; No.9 R&SU 16.6.44; No.14 ARD-R/P 7.8.44; No.85 Sqn 24.9.44; No.6 AD 10.10.45; Cat.E storage 22.3.46; SOC 22.5.46; DAP 26.11.47 until 15.11.48

BS219 Spitfire F.Vc/trop (Merlin 46); Became **A58-84**; TOC/RAF 19.7.42 - To RAAF, arr Melbourne 23.10.42; No.1 AD 28.10.42; No.1(F)Wing 9.11.42; No.457 Sqn ('XB-X':'ZP-X', named *'JIMINY CRICKET'* figure on the cowling) 9.11.42; Air combat 6.7.43 (F/Sgt RW

Watson) & 17.8.43 (F/Sgt JR Jenkins); Undershot landing Livingstone 12.10.43 (Plt "Butch" Hamilton); No.7 R&SU 13.10.43; No.452 Sqn 14.12.43; No.14 ARD-R/P 16.6.44; No.14 ARD 21.6.44; No.2 OTU 22.9.44; No.8 OTU 1.11.44; Crashed taking off in formation Parkes 19.11.44; No.6 AD 27.3.45; No.3 CRD & Cca 9.8.45

BS220 Spitfire F.Vc/trop (Merlin 46); Became **A58-85**; TOC/RAF 13.8.42 - To RAAF, arr Melbourne 29.11.42; No.2 AD 29.11.42; No.54 Sqn ('DL-Z') 8.12.42; A6M damaged 15.3.43 (F/O IS Taylor); Crashed at end of runway landing, fuel shortage after combat 2.5.43 (F/O IS Taylor OK); No.7 R&SU 3.5.43; No.54 Sqn ('DL-Z') 12.7.43; No.452 Sqn 9.4.44; Crashed landing, brake failure Darwin 29.5.44; No.9 R&SU 31.5.44; No.14 ARD-R/P 13.7.44; No.14 ARD 27.7.44; No.4 ARD-R/P 29.9.44; No.4 AD 3.10.44; No.85 Sqn 18.10.44; No.17 R&SU 10.9.45; Cca 7.11.45

BS221 Spitfire F.Vc/trop (Merlin 46); Became **A58-86**; TOC/RAF 15.8.42 - To RAAF, arr Melbourne 10.11.42; No.1 AD 10.11.42; No.54 Sqn ('DL-N') 27.11.42; B5N damaged smoking 2.3.43 (F/O RG Ashby); Scramble, engine failed before action, CSU failure, glycol leak, abandoned over beach Darwin 2.5.43 (Sgt Fox OK); Cca 2.6.43

BS222 Spitfire F.Vc/trop (Merlin 46); Became **A58-87**; TOC/RAF 26.8.42 - To RAAF, arr Melbourne 21.11.42; No.1 AD 25.11.42; No.2 OTU 17.12.42; Gunnery practice, flew into water, Lake Victoria, NSW (NE of Adelaide) 19.1.43; Cca 17.2.43

BS223 Spitfire F.Vc/trop (Merlin 46); Became **A58-14**; TOC/RAF 1.9.42 - To RAAF, arr Melbourne 21.11.42; No.1 AD 25.11.42; No.2 Fighter Sector 28.2.43; No.2 OTU 26.3.43; No.1(F)Wing 9.5.43; No.452 Sqn 14.5.43; Air combats 20.6.43 (F/O RH Whillans) & 7.9.43 (F/O JDD Bassett); No.14 ARD 20.9.43 (mods); No.452 Sqn 24.9.43; No.7 R&SU 24.4.44; No.452 Sqn 7.5.44; No.14 ARD/R-P 15.6.44; No.2 OTU 17.8.44; Cca 23.8.45

BS224 Spitfire F.Vc/trop (Merlin 46); Became **A58-88**; TOC/RAF 1.9.42 - To RAAF, arr Melbourne 21.11.42; No.1 AD 24.11.42; No.2 OTU 6.12.42; No.24 Sqn 27.2.43; Ground-looped landing Williamtown 25.3.43; No.2 AD 10.4.43; No.2 OTU ('4') 13.6.44; Engine failed, force-landed Mildura 22.6.44; No.8 OTU 1.11.44; No.6 AD 14.11.45; Cat.E storage 22.3.46; SOC 22.5.46; DAP 26.11.47 until 15.11.48

BS225 Spitfire F.Vc/trop (Merlin 46); Became **A58-89**; TOC/RAF 2.9.42 - To RAAF, arr Melbourne 24.12.42; No.1 AD 25.12.42; No.7 AD 17.2.43; No.2 OTU ('5'); No.452 Sqn ('QY-B') 31.3.43; Engine hit in combat with A6M5, dived into Darwin harbour attempting to ditch 2.5.43 (P/O KJ Fox baled out, rescued from dinghy); SOC 11.6.43

BS226 Spitfire F.Vc/trop (Merlin 46); Became **A58-90**; TOC/RAF 7.9.42 - To RAAF, arr Melbourne 21.11.42; No.1 AD 27.11.42; No.7 AD 19.1.43; No.457 Sqn 24.2.43; No.7 R&SU 8.3.43; No.452 Sqn ('QY-A') 13.3.43; Ran out of fuel on interception, crash-landed in shallows off Tumbling Waters, NT 2.5.43; No.7 R&SU 10.5.43; No.14 ARD 23.5.43; Cca 28.10.43

BS230 Spitfire F.Vc/trop (Merlin 46); Became **A58-91**; TOC/RAF 26.7.42 - To RAAF, arr Melbourne 23.10.42; No.1 AD 2.11.42; No.1(F)Wing 10.11.42; No.452 Sqn 11.11.42; Lost wheel on landing, broke up, Bankstown 17.12.42; No.2 AD 22.12.42; Cca 22.1.43

BS231 Spitfire F.Vc/trop (Merlin 46); Became **A58-92**; TOC/RAF 28.7.42 - To RAAF, arr Melbourne 14.11.42; No.2 AD 26.11.42; No.1(F)Wing 29.11.42; No.452 Sqn ('QY-D') 3.12.42; Shot down by fighter near Point Charles, NT 15.3.43 (S/Ldr RE Thorold-Smith killed); Cca 9.4.43. - Partly recovered, displayed at Museum Aviation Society of Northern Territories, Darwin, NT – **SURVIVOR**

BS232 Spitfire F.Vc/trop (Merlin 46); Became **A58-93**; TOC/RAF 11.8.42 - To RAAF, arr Melbourne 29.11.42; No.2 AD 29.11.42; No.2 OTU 16.12.42; No.24 Sqn 27.2.43; Mid-air collision with EE676 (A58-120) over Williamtown 27.4.43; Glycol leak, force-landed wheels-up Mildura, Cat.E 25.6.43; Cca 15.7.43

BS233 Spitfire F.Vc/trop (Merlin 46); Became **A58-94**; TOC/RAF 13.8.42 - To RAAF, arr Melbourne 10.11.42; No.1 AD 10.11.42; No.452 Sqn 19.11.42; No.7 R&SU 23.7.43; No.14 ARD 9.8.43; No.14 ARD-R/P 12.12.43; No.54 Sqn 23.1.44; No.452 Sqn 27.4.44; No.9 R&SU 16.6.44; No.6 AD 4.8.44; No.85 Sqn 17.12.44; Engine failed, force-landed on beach, crashed, 4m N of Stockton, WA, Cat.E 17.12.44; Cca 12.1.45

BS234 Spitfire F.Vc/trop (Merlin 46); Became **A58-95**; TOC/RAF 14.8.42 - To RAAF, arr Melbourne 10.11.42; No.1 AD 10.11.42; No.457 Sqn (Markings "CRC", personal aircraft of Wg Cdr Clive R Caldwell) 26.11.42;

Spitfire F.Vc/trop BS231 (later A58-92) was coded QY-D with No.452 Sqn RAAF when it was shot down by a fighter near Point Charles, NT on 16th March 1943, Sqn Ldr RE Thorold-Smith being killed. Parts of it have been recovered and are now on display at the Museum Aviation Society of Northern Territories, Darwin, NT.

A6M & B5N destroyed 2.3.43 (Wg Cdr Clive R Caldwell); Air combat 2.5.43 (Wg Cdr Clive R Caldwell); No.7 R&SU 3.6.43; No.457 Sqn ("CR-C") 4.6.43; Air combat 6.7.43 (F/O IS Mackenzie); No.7 R&SU 16.4.44; No.457 Sqn ("CRC") 4.5.44; No.14 ARD-R/P 1.8.44; No.2 OTU 21.8.44; No.8 OTU 1.11.44; No.6 AD 22.10.45; Cca 20.11.45

BS235 Spitfire F.Vc/trop (Merlin 46); Became **A58-96**; TOC/RAF 16.8.42 - To RAAF, arr Melbourne 2.12.42; No.1 AD 6.12.42; No.2 OTU 7.1.43; No.24 Sqn 27.2.43; No.2 OTU 25.3.43; No.54 Sqn (DL-Z) 1943; Ran out of fuel on interception, abandoned 60m E of Darwin 23.7.43 (F/Sgt JM Wickman); SOC 4.10.43

BS236 Spitfire F.Vc/trop (Merlin 46); Became **A58-97**; TOC/RAF 17.8.42 - To RAAF, arr Melbourne 2.12.42; No.1 AD 4.12.42; No.7 AD 17.2.43; No.452 Sqn 30.3.43; Air combats 2.5.43 (F/O GA Mawer), 20.6.43 (F/O JHE Bisley) & 6.7.43 (S/Ldr RS MacDonald); No.7 R&SU 2.8.43; No.452 Sqn 9.8.43; Air combat 7.9.43 (F/O GJ Cowell); No.14 ARD 15.9.43 (G-40 mod); No.452 Sqn 18.9.43; No.7 R&SU 6.1.44; No.457 Sqn 2.3.44; No.14 ARD-R/P 1.8.44; CGS 22.9.44; Ground-looped landing, port leg collapsed, Cressy 7.12.44; No.6 AD 15.10.45; Cat.E storage 22.3.46; SOC 22.5.46; DAP 26.11.47 until 15.11.48

BS237 Spitfire F.Vc/trop (Merlin 46); Became **A58-98**; TOC/RAF 20.8.42 - To RAAF, arr Melbourne 2.12.42; No.1 AD 6.12.42; No.7 AD 19.1.43; No.452 Sqn 24.2.43; Damaged by Japanese fighters, glycol leak, abandoned near Fenton, crashed 5-6m S of Strauss 7.3.43 (F/Sgt EM Moore killed); Cca 8.4.43

BS238 Spitfire F.Vc/trop (Merlin 46); Became **A58-99**; TOC/RAF 31.8.42 - To RAAF, arr Melbourne 21.11.42; No.1 AD 27.11.42; No.2 Fighter Sector 28.2.43; No.2 OTU 17.3.43; Force-landed in bad weather, hit fence landing Stroud, near Dungog, NSW 17.3.43; No.2 AD 8.4.43; Cca 10.4.43

BS291 Spitfire F.Vc/trop (Merlin 46); Became **A58-100**; TOC/RAF 11.8.42 - To RAAF, arr Melbourne 29.11.42; No.2 AD 29.11.42; No.2 OTU 16.12.42; Ground-looped landing Mildura 5.1.43; No.2 AD 15.1.43; Converted to GI airframe *No.1* on 17.10.45

BS293 Spitfire F.Vc/trop (Merlin 46); Became **A58-101**; TOC/RAF 11.8.42; Melbourne 29.11.42; No.2 AD 29.11.42; No.452 Sqn ('QY-E') 22.12.42; Damaged by Japanese fighters, abandoned 2.5m W of Picnic Point/10m S of Point Charles, NT 15.3.43; Cca 10.4.43

BS295 Spitfire F.Vc/trop (Merlin 46); Became **A58-20**; TOC/RAF 11.8.42 - To RAAF, arr Melbourne 10.11.42; No.1 AD 10.11.42; No.452 Sqn (marked "CRC", personal code of Wg Cdr Clive R Caldwell) 19.11.42; Air combats 2.3.43, 20.6.43 & 30.6.43 (Wg Cdr Clive R Caldwell); Swung landing, hit water pipe-line Strauss 9.8.43; No.7 R&SU 10.8.43; No.452 Sqn 24.9.43; No.14 ARD 25.10.43 (mods); No.452 Sqn 28.10.43; Hit in rear by EE636 (A58-111) after landing Strauss 1.1.44; No.7 R&SU 3.1.44; No.14 ARD-R/P 16.2.44; No.15 ARD-R/P 11.3.44; Cca 12.2.46
NOTE: Incorrectly as "BR295" in RAAF records, but that operated over Malta and was shot down 7.12.42; BS295 went to Australia

BS298 Spitfire F.Vc/trop (Merlin 46); Became **A58-102**; TOC/RAF 16.8.42 - To RAAF, arr Melbourne 2.12.42; No.1 AD 6.12.42; No.2 Fighter Sector 28.2.43; No.2 OTU 26.3.43; Glycol leak, force-landed, crashed 4m ENE of Williamtown 13.4.43; No.2 AD 23.4.43; Cca 2.6.43

BS300 Spitfire F.Vc/trop (Merlin 46); Became **A58-21**; TOC/RAF 18.8.42 - To RAAF, arr Melbourne 10.11.42; No.1 AD 10.11.42; No.457 Sqn ('ZP-G') 19.11.42; Damaged on take-off Livingstone 23.11.43; No.7 R&SU 25.11.43; No.14 ARD 3.12.43; No.14 ARD-R/P 30.6.44; Hit tender which stalled on taxiway Sattler 16.9.44; No.14 ARD 22.9.44; No.9 R&SU 25.9.44; No.14 ARD-R/P 20.11.44; No.8 OTU 25.2.45; No.2 CRD 21.9.45; Cca 6.10.45
NOTE: Incorrectly as "BR300" in RAAF records, but that was Cat.FB/E (SOC) over Malta in 6.42; BS300 went to Australia

BS305 Spitfire F.Vc/trop (Merlin 46); Became **A58-103**; TOC/RAF 26.8.42 - To RAAF, arr Melbourne 2.12.42; No.1 AD 6.12.42; No.7 AD 20.1.43; No.54 Sqn 24.2.43; A6M destroyed 15.3.43 (F/O GA Mawer); G6M damaged 6.7.43 (F/Sgt Spencer); Caught by sudden gust of wing landing, swung, undercarriage collapsed Darwin 27.10.43 (F/Sgt Kelman); No.7 R&SU 29.10.43; No.452 Sqn 29.11.43; No.7 R&SU 26.3.44; No.457 Sqn 8.4.44; No.14 ARD-R/P 1.8.44; No.85 Sqn 2.10.44; Swung on landing Guildford, WA 20.11.44; Cca 29.12.44; No.4 CRD 5.1.45

EE605 Spitfire F.Vc/trop (Merlin 46); Became **A58-105**; TOC/RAF 14.9.42 - To RAAF, arr Melbourne 21.11.42; No.1 AD 25.11.42; No.54 Sqn ('DL-C') 12.5.43; A6M destroyed 20.6.43 (Sgt AS Laundy); No.7 R&SU 2.9.43; No.54 Sqn ('DL-C') 6.9.43; No.452 Sqn ('QY-P') caught fire, belly-landed Husec airfield 12.11.43 (P/O J King of No.2 Sqn); No.7 R&SU 4.5.44; No.54 Sqn ('DL-C') 18.5.44; No.14 ARD-R/P 2.8.44; CGS ('C') 11.9.44; Crashed landing Mingay 26.7.45; No.6 AD 15.10.45; Cat.E storage 22.3.46; SOC 22.5.46; DAP 26.11.47 until 15.11.48

EE606 Spitfire F.Vc/trop (Merlin 46); Became **A58-106**; TOC/RAF 14.9.42 - To RAAF, arr Melbourne 21.11.42; No.1 AD 25.11.42; No.452 Sqn 12.1.43; Swung into trees landing after Strauss 25.2.43; No.7 R&SU 1.3.43; No.457 Sqn 13.5.43; No.14 ARD 16.9.43 (G-40 mod); No.452 Sqn 21.9.43; No.14 ARD 13.2.44; No.54 Sqn 9.3.44; No.7 R&SU 12.3.44; Test flight, crashed landing Darwin Civil, badly damaged 21.3.44 (F/O Todd unhurt); No.14 ARD 6.4.44; No.8 OTU 30.6.45; No.6 AD 16.11.45; Cat.E storage 22.3.46; SOC 22.5.46; DAP 26.11.47 until 15.11.48; Parts recovered from a farm at Oakey, Queensland; To UK and used as basis for a restoration by Charles Church (Spitfires) Ltd, Winchester/Micheldever (reg *G-MKVC* 18.5.88); ff 20.11.88 as "EE606/DB"; Crashed nr Blackbushe 1.7.89 (Charles Church killed); Wreckage to Warbirds of Great Britain Ltd 1991, then sold Derby 6.92 - **SURVIVOR as wreck only**

EE607 Spitfire F.Vc/trop (Merlin 46); Became **A58-107**; TOC/RAF 14.9.42 - To RAAF, arr Melbourne 28.11.42; No.1 AD 6.12.42; No.7 AD 17.2.43; No.1(F)Wing 28.3.43; No.452 Sqn ('QY-C') 31.3.43; FTR interception, presumed shot down by fighters, NW of Vernon Island 20.6.43 (P/O WE Nichterlein killed); SOC 28.6.43

EE608 Spitfire F.Vc/trop (Merlin 46); Became **A58-108**; TOC/RAF 15.9.42 - To RAAF, arr Melbourne 21.11.42; No.1 AD 25.11.42; No.7 AD 19.1.43; No.452 Sqn ('QY-V') 24.2.43; Glycol trouble, engine cut, belly landed on beach off Lee Point, Shoal Bay, NT 28.6.43 (F/O GJ Cowell OK); No.1 R&SU 8.7.43; No.14 ARD 11.7.43; Cca 28.10.43

EE609 Spitfire F.Vc/trop (Merlin 46); Became **A58-109**; TOC/RAF 15.9.42 - To RAAF, arr Melbourne 21.11.42; No.1 AD 25.11.42; No.7 AD 19.1.43; No.452 Sqn 1943; Overshot and ground-looped Strauss 24.3.43; No.7 R&SU 24.3.43; Hit tree landing Strauss 23.5.43; No.7 R&SU 24.5.43; No.452 Sqn 6.7.43; No.14 ARD 22.9.43; No.452 Sqn 27.9.43; No.7 R&SU 3.11.43; No.452 Sqn 19.11.43; ASI jammed, belly landed, partially burnt, Hughes Field 11.12.43; No.7 R&SU 13.12.43; No.14 ARD 21.12.43; Cca 7.2.44

EE610 Spitfire F.Vc/trop (Merlin 46); Became **A58-110**; TOC/RAF 14.9.42 - To RAAF, arr Melbourne 21.11.42; No.1 AD 25.11.42; Belly-tank fell off, damaged fuselage 5m NNE of Geelong, Vic 15.2.43; No.1 AD 2.43; Special Duties Flight 7.4.43; No.2 AD/TU (No.2 AP) 9.12.43; No.1 APU 7.1.44 (test aircraft, also glider-tug); Fitted special high altitude thermometer 14.11.44; No.8 OTU 4.4.45; No.6 AD 16.11.45; Cat.E storage 22.3.46; SOC 22.5.46; DAP 26.11.47 until 15.11.48

EE636 Spitfire F.Vc/trop (Merlin 46); Became **A58-111**; TOC/RAF 6.10.42 - To RAAF, arr Melbourne 23.1.43;

No.1 AD 24.1.43; No.7 AD 9.3.43; No.54 Sqn 13.5.43; G6M damaged 20.6.43 (F/Sgt G Horkin); G6M damaged 30.6.43 (F/Sgt G Horkin); No.7 R&SU 2.9.43; No.54 Sqn 5.9.43; While stationary, hit by MA389 (A58-239), Darwin 27.10.43; No.7 R&SU 29.10.43; No.452 Sqn 14.12.43; Collided with BS295 (A58-20) after landing Strauss 1.1.44; No.7 R&SU 3.1.44; No.14 ARD 4.1.44; Cca 31.1.44

EE639 Spitfire F.Vc/trop (Merlin 46); Became **A58-112**; TOC/RAF 6.10.42 - To RAAF, arr Melbourne 23.1.43; No.1 AD 24.1.43; No.7 AD 9.3.43; No.2 OTU 25.6.43; No.1 AD 19.8.43; No.2 OTU 2.1.44; Engine failed, force-landed Mildura 16.2.44; Ground-looped, port undercarriage collapsed Mildura 24.10.44; No.8 OTU 2.1.45; Swung and ground looped after landing, Parkes, NSW 1.6.45; No.2 CRD 7.10.45; Cca 31.1.46

EE669 Spitfire F.Vc/trop (Merlin 46); Became **A58-113**; TOC/RAF 20.10.42 - To RAAF, arr Melbourne 11.3.43; No.1 AD 11.3.43; Special Duties Flight 24.5.43; No.1(F)Wing 7.7.43; No.54 Sqn 21.7.43; Flew into ground on night landing, Nightcliffe, Darwin 3.9.43 (F/Sgt Harker OK); No.7 R&SU 6.9.43; No.14 ARD 1.10.43; Cca 30.11.43

EE670 Spitfire F.Vc/trop (Merlin 46); Became **A58-114**; TOC/RAF 20.10.42 - To RAAF, arr Melbourne 23.1.43; No.1 AD 24.1.43; No.7 AD 9.3.43; No.1 FW; No.54 Sqn 15.3.43; Damaged by enemy aircraft, crash-landed Anson Bay, NT 30.6.43 (F/Sgt Harker shaken); No.7 R&SU 6.7.43; Cca 14.8.43

EE671 Spitfire F.Vc/trop (Merlin 46); Became **A58-115**; TOC/RAF 27.10.42 - To RAAF, arr Melbourne 28.2.43; No.1 AD 5.3.43; No.1 APU 17.5.43; No.1 AD 17.6.43; No.452 Sqn 17.7.43; No.14 ARD 16.9.43 (G-40 mod); No.452 Sqn 22.9.43; No.14 ARD 23.2.44; No.2 OTU 2.44; No.14 ARD-R/P; No.54 Sqn 11.3.44; No.7 R&SU 29.5.44 (240 hours inspection); No.452 Sqn 12.6.44; No.14 ARD-R/P 15.6.44; No.85 Sqn 2.10.44; No.17 R&SU 10.7.45; No.6 AD 10.10.45; Cat.E storage 22.3.46; SOC 22.5.46; DAP 26.11.47 until 15.11.48

EE672 Spitfire F.Vc/trop (Merlin 46); Became **A58-116**; TOC/RAF 20.10.42 - To RAAF, arr Melbourne 23.1.43; No.1 AD 24.1.43; No.7 AD 9.3.43; No.1(F)Wing 6.5.43; No.452 Sqn 14.5.43; Air combat 30.6.43 (F/O GJ Cowell); Air combat 10.8.43 (F/O FJ Young); No.7 R&SU 10.9.43; No.14 ARD 7.10.43; No.14 ARD-R/P 14.12.43; No.54 Sqn 23.1.44; Oleo leg collapsed landing Darwin 6.2.44 (F/Sgt Hale); No.7 R&SU 21.2.44; No.457 Sqn 9.3.44; Swung after landing, port oleo leg collapsed, Tennants Creek, NT 10.3.44; No.14 ARD 12.3.44; Cca 13.4.44

EE673 Spitfire F.Vc/trop (Merlin 46); Became **A58-117**; TOC/RAF 27.10.42 - To RAAF, arr Melbourne 28.2.43; No.1 AD 5.3.43; No.1 APU 17.5.43; No.1 AD 3.6.43 (CAAG mod); No.2 AD/TU (No.2 AP) 24.6.43; No.452 Sqn 10.7.43; No.14 ARD 16.12.43; No.54 Sqn 3.1.44; No.452 Sqn 4.4.44; Hit during attack on Ki 46 Dinah, engine failed, abandoned 5m S of Point Blaze, NT 12.6.44 (F/O CH O'Loughlin baled out, rescued); No.9 R&SU 29.8.44; Cca 29.8.44

EE674 Spitfire F.Vc/trop (Merlin 46); Became **A58-118**; TOC/RAF 27.10.42 - To RAAF, arr Melbourne 23.1.43; No.1 AD 24.1.43; No.7 AD 30.3.43; No.457 Sqn 6.5.43; No.7 R&SU 13.5.43; No.457 Sqn 19.5.43; No.7 R&SU 2.6.43; No.457 Sqn ('ZP-S') 4.6.43; Damaged in combat, cannon shell in wing 30.6.43; No.7 R&SU 1.7.43; No.457 Sqn 4.7.43; Air combat 6.11.43 (F/Lt DH Maclean); No.14 ARD-R/P 1.8.44; No.85 Sqn 27.9.44; No.4 AD 2.10.44; No.85 Sqn 1.2.45; No.17 R&SU 17.8.45; No.85 Sqn 4.9.45; No.6 AD 10.10.45; Cat.E storage 22.3.46; SOC 22.5.46; DAP 26.11.47 until 15.11.48

EE675 Spitfire F.Vc/trop (Merlin 46); Became **A58-119**; TOC/RAF 27.10.42 - To RAAF, arr Melbourne 28.2.43; No.1 AD 5.3.43; No.1 APU 17.5.43; No.1 AD 6.6.43 (CAAG mod 8.7.43); No.452 Sqn 10.7.43; No.7 R&SU 5.9.43; No.3 AD 21.4.44; No.6 AD 5.5.44; No.3 CRD 16.6.44; Cca 10.7.44

EE676 Spitfire F.Vc/trop (Merlin 46); Became **A58-120**; TOC/RAF 27.10.42 - To RAAF, arr Melbourne 22.2.43; No.1 AD 24.2.43; No.7 AD; No.2 OTU 4.4.43; Mid-air collision with BS232 (A58-93), crashed 3m SW of Williamtown 27.4.43; Cca 2.6.43

EE677 Spitfire F.Vc/trop (Merlin 46); Became **A58-121**; TOC/RAF 27.10.42 - To RAAF, arr Melbourne 22.2.43; No.1 AD 24.2.43; No.1 APU 17.5.43; No.1 AD 6.6.43 (fitted CAAG suiting 8.7.43); No.452 Sqn 16.7.43; Mid-air collision with JL314 (A58-201) while changing formation, crashed Manton Dam, Strauss 26.9.43 (F/O JP Adam & F/O GA Mawer both killed); No.7 R&SU 27.9.43; No.14 ARD 10.10.43; Cca 12.10.43

EE678 Spitfire F.Vc/trop (Merlin 46); Became **A58-122**; TOC/RAF 27.10.42 - To RAAF, arr Melbourne 22.2.43; No.1 AD 24.2.43; No.7 AD 30.3.43; No.2 OTU 3.4.43; While stationary, taxied into by EE713 (A58-123) on 23.8.43; Bounced, swung and ground-looped landing Mildura 6.1.44; Ground-looped landing Mildura 14.2.44; No.8 OTU 1.11.44; To GI airframe *No.10* 24.8.45; Cca 11.9.45

EE713 Spitfire F.Vc/trop (Merlin 46); Became **A58-123**; TOC/RAF 6.11.42 - To RAAF, arr Melbourne 22.2.43; No.1 AD 24.2.43; No.7 AD 30.3.43; No.2 OTU 25.6.43; Taxied into stationary EE678 (A58-122), Mildura 23.8.43; Mid-air collision with Kittyhawk A29-12, 10m N of Mildura 25.3.44; Cca 1.5.44

EE718 Spitfire F.Vc/trop (Merlin 46); Became **A58-124**; TOC/RAF 17.11.42 - To RAAF, arr Australia 11.4.43; No.2 AD 11.4.43; No.2 OTU 2.5.43; Wheels-up landing 12.10.44; No.8 OTU 9.11.44; Force-landed, crashed Parkes 18.11.44; No.2 CRD 19.2.45; Cca 4.5.45

EE719 Spitfire F.Vc/trop (Merlin 46); Became **A58-125**; TOC/RAF 17.11.42 - To RAAF, arr Australia 11.4.43; No.2 AD 11.4.43; No.2 OTU 2.5.43; Hit by EE737 (A58-132) while taxying Williamtown 7.6.43; Cca 16.2.44

EE728 Spitfire F.Vc/trop (Merlin 46); Became **A58-126**; TOC/RAF 17.11.42 - To RAAF, arr Australia 11.4.43; No.2 AD 11.4.43; No.2 OTU 4.5.43; No.8 OTU 1.11.44; Wheels-up landing Parkes 7.11.44; Hit trees during ground attack practice 8m NE of Parkes (gunnery range), flew back to airfield and crash-landed 30.3.45; No.2 R&SU 13.7.45; No.2 CRD 2.8.45; Cca 29.8.45

EE729 Spitfire F.Vc/trop (Merlin 46); Became **A58-127**; TOC/RAF 17.11.42 - To RAAF, arr Australia 11.4.43; No.2 AD 11.4.43; No.2 OTU 4.5.43; Force-landed Mildura 22.11.43; R&SU; No.8 OTU 1.11.44 (allotted 26.10.44); No.2 OTU; No.8 OTU 9.4.45; No.6 AD 28.11.45; Cat.E storage 22.3.46; SOC 22.5.46; DAP 26.11.47 until 15.11.48

EE731 Spitfire F.Vc/trop (Merlin 46); No RAAF serial allotted; TOC/RAF 17.11.42 - To RAAF, arr Australia 11.4.43; No.2 AD 29.4.43; No.2 OTU 4.5.43; Ran off runway, starboard leg collapsed, Mildura 13.8.43; Authorised to GI *No.2* on 10.9.43, initially on loan without RAAF serial number; Offered to CDC for disposal 9.4.46; SOC 16.5.46; DAP 26.11.47 until 8.2.49

EE733 Spitfire F.Vc/trop (Merlin 46); Became **A58-128**; TOC/RAF 16.11.42 - To RAAF, arr Australia 11.4.43; No.2 AD 11.4.43; No.2 OTU 4.5.43; Force-landed on approach, crashed ½m W of Mildura 25.2.44; Cca 23.3.44

EE734 Spitfire F.Vc/trop (Merlin 46); Became **A58-129**; TOC/RAF 16.11.42 - To RAAF, arr Melbourne 11.3.43; No.1 AD 11.3.43; No.1 APU 17.5.43; No.1 AD 3.6.43; No.2 AD/TU (No.2 AP) 24.6.43 (fitted CAAG suiting 8.7.43); No.452 Sqn 10.7.43; Air combat 7.9.43 (P/O WM Coombes); No.7 R&SU 8.9.43; No.457 Sqn 1.11.43; Prop jammed in course pitch and engine cut, ran off strip on landing, Livingstone 18.2.44; No.7 R&SU 22.2.44; No.14 ARD 7.3.44; Cca 24.3.44

EE735 Spitfire F.Vc/trop (Merlin 46); Became **A58-130**; TOC/RAF 20.11.42 - To RAAF, arr Australia 11.4.43; No.2 AD 11.4.43; No.2 OTU ('130') 4.5.43; Swung off runway, undercarriage collapsed Mildura 22.7.43; No.8

OTU 9.11.44; Stalled on approach, undershot landing, overturned, broke up, Parkes 5.7.45; Cca 24.9.45

EE736 Spitfire F.Vc/trop (Merlin 46); Became **A58-131**; TOC/RAF 23.11.42 - To RAAF, arr Australia 11.4.43; No.2 AD 7.7.43; Damaged in transit, Cat.E 7.7.43; Cca 21.7.43

EE737 Spitfire F.Vc/trop (Merlin 46); Became **A58-132**; TOC/RAF 23.11.42 - To RAAF, arr Australia 11.4.43; No.2 AD 11.4.43; No.2 OTU 4.5.43; Hit EE719 (A58-125) taxying Williamtown 7.6.43; Swung to port landing, undercarriage collapsed Mildura 9.6.43; No.8 OTU 1.4.44; No.6 AD 22.2.45; Cca 30.4.45

EE748 Spitfire F.Vc/trop (Merlin 46); Became **A58-133**; TOC/RAF 2.12.42 - To RAAF, arr Melbourne 11.3.43; No.1 AD 11.3.43; No.1 APU 17.5.43; No.1 AD 6.6.43 (fitted CAAG suiting 8.7.43); No.452 Sqn 10.7.43; Undercarriage collapsed landing Strauss 4.8.43; No.7 R&SU 6.8.43; No.452 Sqn 13.8.43; No.14 ARD 15.8.43; No.452 Sqn 12.12.43; No.14 ARD 14.12.43; No.457 Sqn 17.4.44; No.14 ARD-R/P 1.8.44; No.14 ARD 3.10.44; No.8 OTU ('133') 1.3.45; Force-landed wheels-up, Parkes 27.6.45; Hit tree tops during practice ground attack, force-landed wheels-up, Parkes 23.8.45; Cca 24.9.45

EE751 Spitfire F.Vc/trop (Merlin 46); Became **A58-134**; TOC/RAF 1.12.42 - To RAAF, arr Australia 11.4.43; No.2 AD 11.4.43; No.2 OTU 4.5.43; Force landed, crashed near Mildura 31.3.44; No.8 OTU 30.11.44; Engine failed on take-off, crashed 1m SW of Uranquinty airfield 14.12.44; No.2 CRD 30.1.45; Cca 6.5.45

EE807 Spitfire F.Vc/trop (Merlin 46); Became **A58-135**; TOC/RAF 2.1.43 - To RAAF, arr Australia 16.4.43; No.1 AD 23.4.43 (fitted pressurised tanks); No.13 ARD 16.6.43; No.15 ARD 16.6.43; No.79 Sqn 16.6.43; Crashed on landing Wards Strip 21.6.43; No.15 ARD 24.6.43; Cca 20.10.44

EE834 Spitfire F.Vc/trop (Merlin 46); Became **A58-136**; TOC/RAF 4.1.43 - To RAAF, arr Melbourne 13.4.43; No.1 AD 15.4.43 (fitted pressurised tanks); No.79 Sqn 18.5.43; Crashed, cause unknown, 12m SW of Bacchus Marsh, Vic 26.5.43; No.1 AD 16.6.43; Cca 23.6.43

EE835 Spitfire F.Vc/trop (Merlin 46); Became **A58-137**; TOC/RAF 4.1.43 - To RAAF, arr Melbourne 13.4.43; No.1 AD 15.4.43 (fitted pressurised tanks); No.79 Sqn ('UP-T', marked '*Down With Everything*') 29.5.43; No.6 AD 16.6.44 (240 hours inspection); No.85 Sqn ('SH-W') 22.10.44; Collided with MH644 (A58-257) after landing, Guildford 26.2.45; No.4 CRD 12.3.45; Converted to GI airframe *No.8* and with No.5 Cadet Wing ATC (Australia), Perth 28.3.45

EE836 Spitfire F.Vc/trop (Merlin 46); Became **A58-138**; TOC/RAF 4.1.43 - To RAAF, arr Melbourne 13.4.43; No.1 AD 15.4.43 (fitted pressurised tanks); No.79 Sqn ('UP-F') 28.5.43; No.12 R&SU 21.2.44; No.10 R&SU 13.3.44; No.79 Sqn ('UP-F') 21.3.44; Lost glycol, engine seized, abandoned over southern tip of Los Negros Is 7.6.44; SOC 5.7.44

EE837 Spitfire F.Vc/trop (Merlin 46); Became **A58-139**; TOC/RAF 8.1.43 - To RAAF, arr Australia 16.4.43; No.1

Spitfire F.Vc/trop A58-137 SH-W (ex EE835) of No.85 Sqn RAAF collided with A58-257 SH-U (MH644) after landing at Dunreath airstrip, near Perth, WA, on 26th February 1945. [via M W Prime]

Spitfire F.Vc/trop A58-139 DL-T (ex EE837) of No.54 Sqn after ground looping and going off the runway when a tyre burst on landing at Livingstone on 9th June 1944. [Peter Croser]

Spitfire F.Vc/trop EE851 UP-O (A58-144) of No.79 Sqn RAAF after a wheels-up landing when the engine ran away during an air test from Vivigani Strip, Goodenough Island, on 10th July 1943.

APU 16.6.43; No.1 AD 4.7.43; No.1(F)Wing 7.7.43; No.54 Sqn ('DL-T') 8.7.43; Tyre burst landing, swung off runway Livingstone 9.6.44; No.7 R&SU 10.6.44; No.14 ARD 1.7.44; No.6 AD 26.6.45; Cca 16.10.45

EE842 Spitfire F.Vc/trop; TOC/RAF 23.1.43; Shipped to Australia 4.3.43; Lost when SS *Silver Beech* torpedoed 14.4.43

EE843 Spitfire F.Vc/trop; TOC/RAF 23.1.43; Shipped to Australia 4.3.43; Lost when SS *Silver Beech* torpedoed 14.4.43

EE844 Spitfire F.Vc/trop (Merlin 46); Became **A58-140**; TOC/RAF 23.1.43 - To RAAF, arr Australia 16.4.43; No.1 AD 20.4.43 (fitted pressurised tanks); No.13 ARD-R/P 6.8.43; No.79 Sqn ('UP-E') 3.11.43; Air combat 28.11.44 (F/O AW Moore); Dived into ground on test flight, Vivigani Strip, Goodenough Island 19.2.44; 12.ARD 25.2.44; No.10 R&SU 13.3.44; Cca 14.3.44

EE845 Spitfire F.Vc/trop (Merlin 46); Became **A58-141**; TOC/RAF 27.2.43 - To RAAF, arr Australia 16.4.43; No.1 AD 17.4.43 (fitted pressurised tanks); No.13 ARD 18.6.43; No.12 R&SU 1.7.43; No.79 Sqn ('UP-H' : 'UP-?') 9.7.43; Engine began to smoke after strafing attack Amgen River, abandoned off coast of New Britain 3.2.44; SOC 11.2.44

EE848 Spitfire F.Vc/trop; TOC/RAF 23.1.43; Shipped to Australia 4.3.43; Lost when SS *Silver Beech* torpedoed 14.4.43

EE849 Spitfire F.Vc/trop (Merlin 46); Became **A58-142**; TOC/RAF 23.1.43 - To RAAF, arr Australia 16.4.43; No.1 AD 20.4.43 (fitted pressurised tanks); No.79 Sqn ('UP-E') 6.6.43; Hit truck while taxying for take-off, Vivigani Strip, Goodenough Is 21.9.43; No.12 R&SU 13.2.44; Cca 9.3.44

EE850 Spitfire F.Vc/trop (Merlin 46); Became **A58-143**; TOC/RAF 23.1.43 - To RAAF, arr Australia 16.4.43; No.1 AD 20.4.43 (fitted pressurised tanks); No.79 Sqn 6.6.43 ('UP-Y'); No.6 AD; No.85 Sqn 23.11.44; Cca 18.10.45

EE851 Spitfire F.Vc/trop (Merlin 46); Became **A58-144**; TOC/RAF 23.1.43 - To RAAF, arr Australia 16.4.43; No.1 AD 20.4.43 (fitted pressurised tanks); No.79 Sqn ('UP-O') 28.5.43; Engine ran away on air test, wheels-up landing Vivigani Strip, Goodenough Island 10.7.43; No.26 R&SU 15.7.43; No.15 ARD 15.7.43; Cca 23.8.43

EE852 Spitfire F.Vc/trop (Merlin 46); Became **A58-145**; TOC/RAF 27.1.43 - To RAAF, arr Australia 16.4.43; No.1 AD 17.4.43 (fitted pressurised tanks); No.79 Sqn ('UP-V') 28.5.43; Missing in cloud on sweep over New Britain 31.12.43; SOC 13.1.44

EE853 Spitfire F.Vc/trop (Merlin 46); Became **A58-146**; TOC/RAF 23.1.43 - To RAAF, arr Australia 16.4.43; No.1 AD 20.4.43 (fitted pressurised tanks); No.13 ARD 15.6.43; Badly damaged landing Gurney from Horn Island 21.6.43; No.79 Sqn ('UP-O'); Swung landing and hit embankment, Vivigani Strip 28.8.43; No.26 R&SU 8.9.43; Cca 7.10.43. - Recovered from Goodenough Island, New Guinea by Langdon Badger, Unley Park, Adelaide, South Australia from 5.73, restoration completed 1995; Displayed in private museum as "EE853/UP-O" until moved early 2002 - **SURVIVOR**

EF543 Spitfire F.Vc/trop (Merlin 45); Became **A58-147**; TOC/RAF 13.2.43 - To RAAF, arr Australia 17.5.43; No.1 APU 20.5.43; No.1 AD 23.6.43; No.13 ARD 4.7.43; No.1(F)Wing 4.7.43; No.457 Sqn ('ZP-P') 4.7.43; Air combat 17.8.43 (S/Ldr KE James) & 7.9.43 (F/Lt DH Maclean); Glycol leak, abandoned over Monomah, NT 21.12.43; No.7 R&SU 23.12.43; Cca 23.12.43

EF544 Spitfire F.Vc/trop (Merlin 46); Became **A58-148**; TOC/RAF 24.2.43 - To RAAF, arr Australia 14.6.43; No.1 APU 16.6.43; No.1 AD 2.7.43; No.1(F)Wing 8.7.43; No.54 Sqn 11.7.43; Swung on night landing, hit trees at end of runway Nightcliffe 3.9.43 (F/Sgt Kelman OK); No.7 R&SU 6.9.43; No.457 Sqn ('ZP-J') 28.10.43; Swung on night landing, ran into trees, undercarriage collapsed, Nightcliffe, Livingstone 31.10.43; No.7 R&SU 2.11.43; No.14 ARD 7.11.43; Cca 22.11.43

EF545 Spitfire F.Vc/trop (Merlin 46); Became **A58-149**; TOC/RAF 15.2.43 - To RAAF, arr Australia 17.5.43; No.1 APU 20.5.43; No.1 AD 7.6.43; No.13 ARD 26.6.43; No.79 Sqn ('UP-O') 17.9.43; Tyre failed, overturned 18.9.43; No.15 ARD 18.9.43; No.79 Sqn ('UP-O') 18.9.43; Undercarriage collapsed landing Darwin 12.11.43; Caught fire on ground due to starter trolley fault, Darwin 15.12.43; No.26 R&SU 16.12.43; Cca 4.1.44 - Burnt hulk recovered from Papua-New Guinea (Kiriwina); To New Zealand (*ZK-MKV*), later UK - **SURVIVOR**

EF546 Spitfire F.Vc/trop (Merlin 46); Became **A58-150**; TOC/RAF 15.2.43 - To RAAF, arr Australia 17.5.43; No.1 APU 20.5.43; No.1 AD 30.6.43; No.1(F)Wing 6.7.43; No.452 Sqn 8.7.43; Air combat 17.8.43 (F/Sgt PA Padula);

No.14 ARD 17.9.43 (fitted CAAG suiting); No.452 Sqn 24.9.43; No.14 ARD 2.2.44; No.54 Sqn 9.3.44; No.7 R&SU 12.3.44; No.54 Sqn 17.3.44; No.457 Sqn 30.5.44; No.6 AD 17.7.44; No.85 Sqn ('◇') 4.4.45; Engine failed, force-landed wheels-up 5m S of Rockhampton, WA 10.8.45; Cca 24.9.45

EF556 Spitfire F.Vc/trop (Merlin 46); Became **A58-151**; TOC/RAF 25.2.43 - To RAAF, arr Australia 14.6.43; No.1 APU 16.6.43; No.1 AD 4.7.43; No.1(F)Wing 11.7.43; No.54 Sqn 16.7.43; No.7 R&SU 6.6.44; No.457 Sqn 30.6.44; No.14 ARD-R/P 1.8.44; No.85 Sqn 24.9.44; No.17 R&SU 5.4.45; No.85 Sqn 29.4.45; No.6 AD 5.10.45; No.1 AD 22.3.46; Cat.E 22.5.46; DAP 25.2.49; Sold 20.7.50

EF557 Spitfire F.Vc/trop (Merlin 46); Became **A58-152**; TOC/RAF 24.2.43 - To RAAF, arr Australia 2.8.43; No.1 APU 9.8.43; No.1 AD 24.8.43; No.14 ARD-R/P 7.9.43 (CAAG mod); No.452 Sqn 14.9.43; Stalled from 5ft landing, undercarriage collapsed, Strauss 31.3.44; No.7 R&SU 1.4.44; Cca 3.5.44

EF558 Spitfire F.Vc/trop (Merlin 46); Became **A58-153**; TOC/RAF 24.2.43 - To RAAF, arr Australia 14.6.43; No.1 APU 16.6.43; No.1 AD 11.7.43; No.1(F)Wing 16.7.43; No.54 Sqn 18.7.43; Shot down by enemy aircraft near Pioneer Creek, NT 7.9.43 (F/O WT Hinds killed); No.7 R&SU 14.9.43; Cca 24.9.43

EF559 Spitfire F.Vc/trop (Merlin 46); Became **A58-154**; TOC/RAF 25.2.43 - To RAAF, arr Melbourne 4.7.43; No.1 APU 12.7.43; No.1 AD 20.7.43; No.14 ARD-R/P 27.7.43; No.452 Sqn 13.8.43; Air combat 7.9.43 (F/Sgt JC King); No.7 R&SU 9.9.43; No.452 Sqn 21.9.43; No.14 ARD 29.9.43; No.452 Sqn 30.9.43; No.14 ARD 10.43; No.452 Sqn 20.10.43; No.14 ARD-R/P 13.1.44; No.2 OTU; No.54 Sqn 11.3.44; No.7 R&SU 9.6.44; No.14 ARD-R/P 4.8.44; CGS 11.9.44; Overshot landing, hit soft ground 5.7.45; No.6 AD 29.11.45; Undercarriage leg jammed up on ferry flight and collapsed on landing, Richmond 6.12.45; No.2 AD 2.4.46; Cca 8.5.46

EF560 Spitfire F.Vc/trop (Merlin 46); Became **A58-155**; TOC/RAF 24.2.43 - To RAAF, arr Australia 14.6.43; No.1 APU 16.6.43; No.1 AD 4.7.43; No.1(F)Wing 7.7.43; No.54 Sqn 8.7.43; No.452 Sqn 8.6.44; No.14 ARD-R/P 1.8.44; No.85 Sqn 24.9.44; No.17 R&SU 26.9.44; No.85 Sqn 12.12.44; No.17 R&SU 27.4.45; No.85 Sqn 29.4.45; No.6 AD 10.10.45; SOC 22.5.46; DAP 26.11.47 until 15.11.48

EF562 Spitfire F.Vc/trop (Merlin 46); Became **A58-156**; TOC/RAF 28.2.43 - To RAAF, arr Melbourne 4.7.43; No.1 APU 21.7.43; No.1 AD 2.8.43; No.2 OTU 9.8.43; No.1 AD 15.4.44; Force-landed wheels-up 150m NW of Mildura 8.6.44; No.2 OTU in 1944; No.8 OTU 1.11.44; Engine failed, force-landed and crashed 25.11.44; No.6 AD 21.11.45; Cat.E storage 22.3.46; SOC 22.5.46; DAP 26.11.47 until 15.11.48

EF563 Spitfire F.Vc/trop (Merlin 46); Became **A58-157**; TOC/RAF 28.2.43 - To RAAF, arr Melbourne 4.7.43; No.1 APU 21.7.43; No.1 AD 11.8.43; No.1 APU; No.14 ARD 9.9.43; No.54 Sqn 1.11.43; Hit by landing LZ881 (A58-225) while taxying after landing, Darwin 20.1.44 (F/O Thomas); No.14 ARD 1.2.44; Cca 8.2.44

EF564 Spitfire F.Vc/trop (Merlin 46); Became **A58-104**; TOC/RAF 25.2.43 - To RAAF, arr Australia 16.4.43; No.1 AD 20.4.43; No.79 Sqn ('UP-A') 19.5.43; No.1 AD 29.5.43; Retd No.79 Sqn ('UP-A') .43; Air combat 21.12.43 (F/O JR Richards); No.6 AD 16.6.44; CGS 11.9.44; Taxied into Wirraway A20-640 at Cressy 5.2.45 (Plt WJ Storey); No.6 AD 22.10.45; Cat.E storage 22.3.46; SOC 22.5.46; DAP 26.11.47 until 15.11.48

EF565 Spitfire F.Vc/trop (Merlin 45); Became **A58-158**; TOC/RAF 1.3.43 - To RAAF, arr Melbourne 4.7.43; No.1 APU 22.7.43; No.1(F)Wing 2.8.43; No.1 AD 8.43; No.2 OTU 8.8.43; Engine cut, belly landed 2^{1}/$_{2}$m SE of Mildura 22.11.43; Cca 5.1.44

EF587 Spitfire F.Vc/trop (Merlin 45); Became **A58-159**; TOC/RAF 1.3.43 - To RAAF, arr Melbourne 4.7.43; No.1 APU 13.7.43; No.1 AD 29.7.43; No.2 OTU 1.9.43; Engine cut, belly landed Batchers Swamp, 55m W of Mildura 4.5.44; Cca 30.5.44

Spitfire F.Vc/trop EE853/A58-146 in its original code markings "UP-O". It was with No.79 Sqn RAAF when it swung on landing at Vivigani Strip and hit an embankment on 28th August 1943. It was restored after being recovered in 1973 and is shown here in a private museum at Adelaide around 1980.

EF588   Spitfire F.Vc/trop (Merlin 46); Became **A58-160**; TOC/RAF 8.3.43 - To RAAF, arr Melbourne 4.7.43; No.1 APU 12.7.43; No.1 AD 29.7.43; No.2 OTU 1.8.43; Failed to recover from firing dive, crashed into Lake Victoria, NSW (NE of Adelaide), burst into flames 16.8.43; Cca 6.9.43

EF589   Spitfire F.Vc/trop (Merlin 46); Became **A58-161**; TOC/RAF 8.3.43 - To RAAF, arr Melbourne 4.7.43; No.1 APU 20.7.43; No.1 AD 30.7.43; No.14 ARD-R/P 12.8.43; No.14 ARD 1.11.43; No.54 Sqn 13.1.44; No.452 Sqn 8.6.44; To No.9 R&SU, but tyre burst on landing, swung and hit embankment Sattler, 30.6.44; No.8 CRD 6.7.44; Cca 10.8.44

EF590   Spitfire F.Vc/trop (Merlin 46); Became **A58-162**; TOC/RAF 8.3.43 - To RAAF, arr Australia 10.8.43; No.1 APU 11.8.43; No.1 AD 4.9.43; No.14 ARD-R/P 19.9.43; No.54 Sqn 8.11.43; Caught by sudden gust of wind, u/c collapsed, landed on one wheel Darwin 14.12.43 (F/Lt I Thompson); No.7 R&SU 15.12.43; No.14 ARD 29.12.43; No.54 Sqn 27.3.44; Tyre burst landing, hit petrol tank Port Hedland 10.6.44; No.7 R&SU 11.6.44; No.457 Sqn 20.6.44; No.14 ARD-R/P 1.8.44; No.85 Sqn 24.9.44; Engine failed on take-off, swung on to taxiway, hit ditch, on nose Pearce 14.7.45; No.17 R&SU 17.7.45; No.85 Sqn 25.7.45; No.6 AD 10.10.45; Cat.E storage 22.3.46; SOC 22.5.46; DAP 26.11.47 until 15.11.48

ER735   Spitfire F.Vb (Merlin 46); Became **A58-163**; TOC/RAF 13.10.42 - To RAAF, arr Australia 11.4.43; No.2 AD 11.4.43; No.1 AD 24.4.43 (RAAF mods to Vc/trop); No.79 Sqn ('UP-Q') 6.5.43; No.1 AD 28.5.43; No.79 Sqn ('UP-Q') 1.6.43; Tyre burst, force-landed wheels-up Vivigani Strip 13.9.43; No.6 AD 16.6.44; No.85 Sqn ('SH-E') 14.10.44; No.17 R&SU 6.3.45; No.85 Sqn ('SH-L') 15.3.45; Hit tree low flying 12m SW of Gin Gin, Qld 3.9.45; No.17 R&SU 6.9.45; No.6 AD 10.12.45; Cat.E storage 22.3.46; SOC 22.5.46; For sale, to DAP 26.11.47; Sold & handed over to purchaser same day

ER760   Spitfire F.Vc/trop (Merlin 46); Became **A58-164**; TOC/RAF 12.10.42 - To RAAF, arr Melbourne 23.1.43; No.1 AD 24.1.43; No.1 R&SU-R/P 19.4.43; No.457 Sqn ('XB-B') 9.5.43; No.7 R&SU 11.5.43; No.457 Sqn ('XB-B') 13.5.43; Overturned landing Livingstone 14.6.43; No.7 R&SU 16.6.43; No.457 Sqn ('ZP-B') 11.7.43; Ran off runway on landing, went into soft ground, overturned, Livingstone 16.3.44 (Plt B Hardwik); Cca 26.4.44

ES232   Spitfire F.Vc/trop (Merlin 46); Became **A58-165**; TOC/RAF 28.11.42 - To RAAF, arr Australia 11.4.43; No.2 AD 11.4.43; No.1 AD 23.4.43; No.79 Sqn ('UP-L') 6.5.43; No.1 AD 30.5.43; No.79 Sqn ('UP-L') 1.6.43; No.1 AD 2.6.43; Engine overheated in transit, force-landed Tipton airstrip, Cecil Plains 5.12.44; No.6 AD 6.12.44; Storage 26.11.45; Cat.E storage 22.3.46; SOC 22.5.46; DAP 26.11.47 until 15.11.48

ES238   Spitfire F.Vc/trop (Merlin 46); Became **A58-166**; TOC/RAF 29.11.42 - To RAAF, arr Melbourne 28.2.43; No.1 AD 5.3.43; No.79 Sqn ('UP-R') 14.5.43; No.1 AD 27.5.43; Issued No.6 AD 4.12.44, but left at No.25 OBU with burst tyre 13.12.44; No.79 Sqn; No.6 AD 29.1.45; Cca 16.10.45

ES249   Spitfire F.Vc/trop (Merlin 46); Became **A58-167**; TOC/RAF 28.11.42 - To RAAF, arr Melbourne 28.2.43; No.1 AD 1.3.43; No.79 Sqn ('UP-N') 18.5.43; No.1 AD 27.5.43; No.79 Sqn ('UP-N') 6.6.43; Swung on landing, hit bank, undercarriage collapsed, Momote 25.6.44; No.12 R&SU 13.7.44; Cca 20.11.44

ES259   Spitfire F.Vc/trop (Merlin 46); Became **A58-168**; TOC/RAF 28.11.42 - To RAAF, arr Melbourne 28.2.43; No.1 AD 1.3.43; No.79 Sqn ('UP-B') 28.5.43; No.6 AD 16.6.44; Test & ferry flight 22.1.45; No.1 AD 7.5.45; Test & ferry flight 6.8.45; No.1 AD 17.4.46; SOC 22.5.46; DAP 25.2.49; Sold 20.7.50

ES307   Spitfire F.Vc/trop (Merlin 46); Became **A58-169**; TOC/RAF 29.11.42 - To RAAF, arr Australia 11.4.43; No.2 AD 11.4.43; No.1 AD 23.4.43; No.79 Sqn ('UP-X') 6.5.43; No.1 AD 27.5.43; No.79 Sqn 30.5.43; No.1 AD 2.6.43; No.79 Sqn 6.6.43; Crash landed wheels up, Vivigani Strip 27.6.43; No.26 R&SU 22.8.43; No.79 Sqn ('UP-X') 30.10.43; No.12 R&SU 28.10.44; No.6 AD 26.11.44; No.8 OTU 7.1.45; No.6 AD 27.11.45; SOC 22.5.46; DAP 26.11.47 until 15.11.48

ES367   Spitfire F.Vc/trop (Merlin 46); Became **A58-170**; TOC/RAF 14.12.42 - To RAAF, arr Melbourne 11.3.43; No.1 AD 11.3.43; No.452 Sqn 9.5.43; Air combat 6.7.43 (P/O PD Tully); No.14 ARD-R/P 22.9.43; No.452 Sqn 25.9.43; No.14 ARD-R/P 15.6.44; No.2 OTU 17.8.44; No.8 OTU 1.11.44; No.6 AD 14.7.45; Cca 16.10.45

JF620   Spitfire LF.VIIIc (Merlin 66); Became **A58-300**; TOC/RAF 13.8.43 - To RAAF, arr Melbourne 21.10.43; No.2 AD 14.11.43; No.54 Sqn ('DL-R') 11.3.44; No.2 AD 26.3.44; No.549 Sqn 3.5.44; Mid-air collision with JG429 (A58-364), dived into the ground nr Truscott Strip, WA 16.11.44; Cca 20.12.44 – Wreck recovered c.1972 by John Haslett, Darwin, Northern Territory; To East Point Artillery Museum, Darwin, NT 1973; To Peter Sledge & Garry Cooper, Sydney, New South Wales 1974 ; Parts used to restore RR232 & RM797, also TE294 in South Africa; To Mark de Vries, Bryanston, South Africa and Vancouver, Canada – **SURVIVOR**

JF621   Spitfire LF.VIIIc (Merlin 66); Became **A58-301**; TOC/RAF 14.8.43 - To RAAF, arr Melbourne 21.10.43; No.1 APU 25.10.43; No.1 AD 12.11.43; CAC 15.12.43; No.1 AD 26.12.43; No.452 Sqn 21.3.44; No.54 Sqn 6.4.44; No.7 R&SU 9.6.44; No.54 Sqn 19.6.44; No.7 R&SU 11.12.44; No.54 Sqn 22.2.45; No.549 Sqn 20.7.45; No.6 AD 24.9.45; SOC 22.5.46; Cat.E storage 1.10.46; DAP 7.11.47 until 15.11.48

JF820   Spitfire LF.VIIIc (Merlin 66); Became **A58-302**; TOC/RAF 14.8.43 - To RAAF, arr Melbourne 21.10.43; No.1 APU 2.11.43; No.1 AD 13.12.43; No.54 Sqn 28.3.44; No.452 Sqn 30.3.44; No.7 R&SU 4.4.44; No.54 Sqn 7.5.44; Engine lost power, ditched in deep water 200 yds off Darwin main jetty attempting to land on beach 1.11.44 (W/O SCJ Laundy slightly injured); Cca 14.12.44

JF821   Spitfire LF.VIIIc (Merlin 66); Became **A58-303**; TOC/RAF 14.8.43 - To RAAF, arr Melbourne 21.10.43; No.1 APU 28.10.43 (experimental a/c, oil-cooling test, high-G-trials with CAAG-suit); No.1 AD 19.11.43; No.1 APU 11.1.44; Point Cook 17.4.48; Later DAP until 29.6.51, then sold to R H Grant, Hawthorn, Vic for scrap

JF822   Spitfire LF.VIIIc (Merlin 66); Became **A58-304**; TOC/RAF 14.8.43 - To RAAF, arr Melbourne 21.10.43; No.1 APU 2.11.43; No.1 AD 19.11.43; No.452 Sqn 11.1.44; No.54 Sqn 9.3.44; No.14 ARD-R/P 11.4.44; No.54 Sqn 13.4.44; Tyre burst on landing, crashed, tail damaged RAAF Darwin 8.6.44 (F/Sgt WP Nash); No.7 R&SU 19.6.44; No.549 Sqn ('ZF-K') 5.11.44; No.6 AD 27.3.45; DAP 19.4.45; SOC 22.5.46; Cat.E storage 1.10.46; DAP 7.11.47 until 15.11.48

JF823   Spitfire LF.VIIIc (Merlin 66); Became **A58-305**; TOC/RAF 15.8.43 - To RAAF, arr Melbourne 21.10.43; No.1 APU 28.10.43; No.1 AD 18.11.43; No.452 Sqn 3.7.44; No.9 R&SU 13.12.44; No.6 AD 10.1.45; SOC 22.5.46; Cat.E storage 1.10.46; DAP 7.11.47; DSD 15.11.48

JF824   Spitfire LF.VIIIc (Merlin 66); Became **A58-306**; TOC/RAF 15.8.43 - To RAAF, arr Melbourne 21.10.43; No.2 AD 15.11.43; No.14 ARD-R/P 11.9.44; No.548 Sqn 23.9.44; No.54 Sqn 15.7.45; No.6 AD 13.9.45; SOC 22.5.46; Cat.E storage 1.10.46; DAP 7.11.47; DSD 15.11.48

JF825   Spitfire LF.VIIIc (Merlin 66); Became **A58-307**; TOC/RAF 15.8.43 - To RAAF, arr Melbourne 21.10.43; No.1 APU 25.10.43; No.1 AD 27.3.44; No.452 Sqn ("RHG", personal markings of Wg Cdr RH Gibbes) 3.7.44; Undercarriage collapsed landing Sattler 6.8.44; No.9 R&SU 7.8.44; No.452 Sqn ("RHG") 26.10.44; No.457 Sqn 14.11.44; No.9 R&SU 14.12.44; No.14 ARD 22.1.45; No.54 Sqn 27.2.45; No.548 Sqn 26.7.45; No.6

JF845 Spitfire LF.VIIIc (Merlin 66); Became **A58-308**; TOC/RAF 15.8.43 - To RAAF, arr Melbourne 21.10.43; No.1 APU 3.11.43; No.1 AD 14.12.43; No.452 Sqn 11.1.44; No.7 R&SU 4.4.44; No.549 Sqn 1.7.44; No.7 R&SU 1.8.44; No.8 CRD 24.9.45; Cca 29.10.45

JF846 Spitfire LF.VIIIc (Merlin 66); Became **A58-309**; TOC/RAF 21.8.43 - To RAAF, arr Melbourne 21.10.43; No.1 AD 26.10.43; No.452 Sqn 8.2.44; Crashed in forced landing 4.4.44; No.7 R&SU 5.4.44; No.452 Sqn 6.4.44; No.14 ARD 15.4.44; No.54 Sqn 19.4.44; Engine failed on ferry flight, abandoned c.40m S of Pine Creek, NT 19.4.44; No.7 R&SU; No.14 ARD 8.5.44; Cca 25.5.44
NOTE: Ferry crash reported for "A58-330" on 18.4.44, F/O PGF Brown DoI (see "Unidentified")

JF847 Spitfire LF.VIIIc (Merlin 66); Became **A58-310**; TOC/RAF 16.8.43 - To RAAF, arr Melbourne 21.10.43; No.1 APU 2.11.43; No.1 AD 30.12.43; No.14 ARD 19.1.44; No.452 Sqn 20.1.44; No.54 Sqn 9.3.44; No.452 Sqn 5.4.44; No.14 ARD 13.4.44; Issued No.54 Sqn 12.4.44; No.14 ARD 15.4.44; No.54 Sqn ('DL-Y'), wheels-up landing, badly damaged 7.8.44 (F/Sgt J Blair unhurt); Crashed on air test, Darwin Harbour 5.10.44 (W/O Fox); Cca 3.11.44

JF869 Spitfire LF.VIIIc (Merlin 66); Became **A58-311**; TOC/RAF 23.8.43 - To RAAF, arr Melbourne 21.10.43; No.1 APU 2.11.43; No.1 AD 3.12.43; No.452 Sqn 11.1.44; No.54 Sqn 9.3.44; No.452 Sqn 18.3.44; No.14 ARD 27.3.44; No.54 Sqn 14.4.44; No.7 R&SU 24.10.44; No.6 AD 10.3.45; SOC 22.5.46; Cat.E storage 1.10.46; DAP 26.11.47; DSD 15.11.48

JF870 Spitfire LF.VIIIc (Merlin 66); Became **A58-312**; TOC/RAF 23.8.43 - To RAAF, arr Melbourne 21.10.43; No.1 APU 2.11.43; No.1 AD 25.11.43; No.1 ARD, undercarriage failed, tailwheel collapsed landing Gorrie while ferrying Laverton to Strauss 10.1.44; No.14 ARD 11.1.44; No.452 Sqn 2.3.44; No.54 Sqn 9.4.44; Shot down Ki-46 into sea in flames 5m N of Drysdale Strip, shared JG465 (A58-390) 20.7.44 (F/Lt DM Gossland); No.7 R&SU 8.8.44; No.54 Sqn 17.8.44; No.7 R&SU 6.2.45; Cca 18.4.45

JF871 Spitfire LF.VIIIc (Merlin 66); Became **A58-327**; TOC/RAF 22.8.43 - To RAAF, arr Melbourne 18.1.44; No.1 APU 20.1.44; No.1 AD 3.2.44; No.54 Sqn 4.4.44; Damaged by stone which flew up during touch-and-go, Livingstone 4.8.44; No.7 R&SU 4.8.44; No.54 Sqn 28.8.44; No.7 R&SU 9.3.45; No.54 Sqn ('DL-J') 22.3.45; No.7 R&SU 9.7.45; No.6 AD 10.9.45; SOC 22.5.46; Cat.E storage 1.10.46; DAP 7.11.47 until 15.11.48

JF872 Spitfire LF.VIIIc (Merlin 66); Became **A58-328**; TOC/RAF 22.8.43 - To RAAF, arr Melbourne 18.1.44; No.1 APU 20.1.44; No.1 AD 28.1.44; Tailwheel retracted landing Oodnadatta 18.3.44; No.14 ARD 27.3.44; No.457 Sqn 3.9.44; No.14 ARD 4.12.44; No.54 Sqn 4.5.45; No.549 Sqn 20.7.45; No.6 AD 24.9.45; SOC 22.5.46; Cat.E storage 1.10.46; DAP 7.11.47 until 15.11.48

JF876 Spitfire LF.VIIIc (Merlin 66); Became **A58-313**; TOC/RAF 17.8.43 - To RAAF, arr Melbourne 21.10.43; No.1 APU 25.10.43; No.1 AD 15.11.43; No.452 Sqn 6.1.44; Engine cut, undershot in forced landing, hit trees & telegraph poles 1m N of Narridy, SA 6.1.44; Cca 21.1.44

JF877 Spitfire LF.VIIIc (Merlin 66); Became **A58-314**; TOC/RAF 23.8.43 - To RAAF, arr Melbourne 21.10.43; No.1 APU 2.11.43; No.1 AD 24.11.43; No.452 Sqn 11.1.44; No.54 Sqn 9.3.44; Overshot, landed wheels-up to avoid obstruction at end of runway 16.3.44 (F/Lt I Thompson); No.7 R&SU 17.3.44; No.54 Sqn 10.4.44; No.14 ARD 27.5.44; No.14 ARD-R/P 5.6.44; No.7 R&SU 3.7.44; No.452 Sqn 4.7.44; No.9 R&SU 20.12.44; No.7 R&SU 6.2.45; Cca 30.4.45

JF884 Spitfire LF.VIIIc (Merlin 66); Became **A58-354**; TOC/RAF 18.9.43 - To RAAF, arr Brisbane 30.12.43; No.3 AD 3.1.44; No.54 Sqn 21.5.44; No.6 AD 23.9.45; SOC 22.5.46; Cat.E storage 1.10.46; DAP 7.11.47 until 15.11.48

JF885 Spitfire LF.VIIIc (Merlin 66); Became **A58-356**; TOC/RAF 25.9.43 - To RAAF, arr Brisbane 16.1.44; No.3 AD 23.1.44; No.457 Sqn 29.7.44; No.14 ARD 4.12.44; No.54 Sqn 14.4.45; Undershot landing, hit ditch,

A formation of Spitfire VIIIs, A58-315 (ex JF934) nearest, probably of No.2 Operational Training Unit, Mildura in 1944. [MAP]

overturned, Hughes, NT 2.5.45; No.7 R&SU 4.5.45; Cca 30.5.45

JF933 Spitfire LF.VIIIc (Merlin 66); Became **A58-321**; TOC/RAF 25.8.43 - To RAAF, arr Sydney 28.11.43; No.2 AD 5.12.43; No.54 Sqn 11.3.44; No.2 AD 19.3.44; No.549 Sqn ('ZF-N') 4.5.44; No.6 AD 26.9.45; SOC 22.5.46; Cat.E storage 1.10.46; DAP 7.11.47 until 15.11.48

JF934 Spitfire LF.VIIIc (Merlin 66); Became **A58-315**; TOC/RAF 25.8.43 - To RAAF, arr Melbourne 21.10.43; No.1 APU 25.10.43; No.1 AD 5.11.43; Special Duties Flight 10.11.43; TR5043 VHF tests (with 300-lb bombs) 14.11.44; No.2 OTU Mildura in 1945; No.1 AD 14.3.46; Cca 10.4.46

JF935 Spitfire LF.VIIIc (Merlin 66); Became **A58-316**; TOC/RAF 25.8.43 - To RAAF, arr Melbourne 21.10.43; No.1 APU 25.10.43; No.1 AD 24.11.43; No.452 Sqn 3.7.44; No.9 R&SU 13.12.44; No.7 R&SU 12.2.45; No.54 Sqn 14.7.45; No.6 AD 23.9.45; SOC 22.5.46; Cat.E storage 1.10.46; DAP 7.11.47; DSD 15.11.48

JF936 Spitfire LF.VIIIc (Merlin 66); Became **A58-317**; TOC/RAF 27.8.43 - To RAAF, arr Melbourne 21.10.43; No.1 APU 25.10.43; No.1 AD 18.11.43; No.14 ARD-R/P 22.5.44; No.54 Sqn 2.6.44; Landing from scramble, swung off taxiway, hit tree Livingstone 3.8.44 (F/Sgt J Blair unhurt); No.7 R&SU 4.8.44; No.54 Sqn 21.9.44; No.548 Sqn 19.7.45; No.6 AD 18.9.45; SOC 22.5.46; Cat.E storage 1.10.46; DAP 7.11.47; DSD 15.11.48

JF937 Spitfire LF.VIIIc (Merlin 66); Became **A58-318**; TOC/RAF 27.8.43 - To RAAF, arr Melbourne 21.10.43; No.1 APU 3.11.43; No.1 AD 3.11.43; No.452 Sqn 11.1.44; Wheels-up landing (date unknown); No.7 R&SU 19.1.44; No.452 Sqn 5.2.44; No.54 Sqn 9.3.44; No.452 Sqn 18.3.44; No.14 ARD 27.3.44; No.54 Sqn ('DL-F') 17.4.44; Destroyed beyond repair in heavy night landing, Livingstone 14.6.44; Cca 11.7.44

JF938 Spitfire LF.VIIIc (Merlin 66); Became **A58-329**; TOC/RAF 29.8.43 - To RAAF, arr Melbourne 18.1.44; No.1 APU 20.1.44; No.1 AD 1.2.44; No.54 Sqn 28.3.44; No.7 R&SU 6.2.45; Cca 18.4.45

JF939 Spitfire LF.VIIIc (Merlin 66); Became **A58-330**; TOC/RAF 29.8.43 - To RAAF, arr Melbourne 18.1.44; No.1 APU 18.1.44; No.1 AD 20.1.44; No.452 Sqn 21.3.44; No.54 Sqn 5.4.44; No.14 ARD 17.4.44; No.54 Sqn 19.4.44; Sqn move, overshot landing, gently nosed over, Darwin Civil 8.6.44 (F/O WH Doerr unhurt); No.7 R&SU 7.2.45; Cca 18.4.45
NOTE: Ferry crash reported for "A58-330" on 18.4.44, F/O PGF Brown DoI (see "Unidentified")

JF940 Spitfire LF.VIIIc (Merlin 66); Became **A58-331**; TOC/RAF 30.8.43 - To RAAF, arr Melbourne 18.1.44; No.1 APU 18.1.44; No.1 AD 20.1.44; No.452 Sqn 10.2.44; No.54 Sqn 9.3.44; No.452 Sqn 18.3.44; No.14 ARD 27.3.44; No.54 Sqn ('DL-L') 11.4.44; Tyre burst landing, ran off strip into ditch 18.9.44 (F/O IJ McCrae unhurt); No.7 R&SU 19.9.44; No.6 AD 10.3.45; Cat.E storage 1.10.46; SOC 19.11.46; DAP 26.9.47 until 15.11.48

JF942 Spitfire LF.VIIIc (Merlin 66); Became **A58-322**; TOC/RAF 30.8.43 - To RAAF, arr Sydney 28.11.43; No.2 AD 5.12.43; No.549 Sqn ('ZF-T') 4.5.44; No.6 AD 24.9.45; SOC 22.5.46; Cat.E storage 1.10.46; DAP 7.11.47 until 15.11.48

JF945 Spitfire LF.VIIIc (Merlin 66); Became **A58-323**; TOC/RAF 30.8.43 - To RAAF, arr Sydney 28.11.43; No.2 AD 5.12.43; No.54 Sqn 11.3.44; No.2 AD 19.3.44; No.549 Sqn 3.5.44; No.6 AD 24.9.45; SOC 22.5.46; Cat.E storage 1.10.46; DAP 7.11.47 until 15.11.48

JF965 Spitfire LF.VIIIc (Merlin 66); Became **A58-355**; TOC/RAF 7.9.43 - To RAAF, arr Brisbane 30.12.43; No.3 AD 3.1.44; No.14 ARD-R/P 22.5.44; No.54 Sqn 6.6.44; No.548 Sqn 19.7.45; No.6 AD 21.9.45; SOC 22.5.46; DAP 7.11.47 until 15.11.48

JF966 Spitfire LF.VIIIc (Merlin 66); Became **A58-325**; TOC/RAF 7.9.43 - To RAAF, arr Sydney 7.12.43; No.2 AD 15.12.43; No.548 Sqn 7.5.44; No.6 AD 11.9.45; SOC 22.5.46; DAP 7.11.47; DSD 15.11.48

JF967 Spitfire LF.VIIIc (Merlin 66); Became **A58-324**; TOC/RAF 8.9.43 - To RAAF, arr Sydney 28.11.43; No.2 AD 5.12.43; Storage 19.11.45; SOC 24.5.46; Cat.E storage 1.10.46; DAP 24.6.48; DSD 6.9.49

JG104 Spitfire LF.VIIIc (Merlin 66); Became **A58-326**; TOC/RAF 7.9.43 - To RAAF, arr Sydney 7.12.43; No.2 AD 15.12.43; No.549 Sqn 22.4.44; Undercarriage collapsed while being towed from dispersal bay, Darwin Civil 17.7.44; No.7 R&SU 18.7.44; No.6 AD 24.9.45; SOC 22.5.46; Cat.E storage 1.10.46; DAP 7.11.47 until 15.11.48

JG105 Spitfire LF.VIIIc (Merlin 66); Became **A58-319**; TOC/RAF 9.9.43 - To RAAF, arr Sydney 28.11.43; No.2 AD 6.12.43; No.548 Sqn 7.5.44; No.7 R&SU 17.7.45; Cca 29.10.45

JG106 Spitfire LF.VIIIc (Merlin 66); Became **A58-372**; TOC/RAF 10.9.43 - To RAAF, arr Melbourne 4.2.44; No.2 AD 4.2.44; No.1 AD 9.2.44; No.548 Sqn 6.4.44; Engine failed, dived into sea 16m N of Cape Hotham, NT 31.7.45; SOC 6.12.45

JG107 Spitfire LF.VIIIc (Merlin 66); Became **A58-320**; TOC/RAF 10.9.43 - To RAAF, arr Sydney 28.11.43; No.2 AD 6.12.43; No.548 Sqn ('TS-W') 7.5.44; No.6 AD 11.9.45; SOC 22.5.46; Cat.E storage 1.10.46; DAP 7.11.47; DSD 15.11.48

JG174 Spitfire LF.VIIIc (Merlin 66); Became **A58-332**; TOC/RAF 18.9.43 - To RAAF, arr Brisbane 30.12.43; No.3 AD 3.1.44; No.549 Sqn 27.4.44; Crashed on landing 28.10.44; No.7 R&SU 31.10.44; No.549 Sqn 18.11.44; No.7 R&SU 3.7.45; No.8 CRD 24.9.45; Cca 29.10.45

JG175 Spitfire LF.VIIIc (Merlin 66); Became **A58-333**; TOC/RAF 18.9.43 - To RAAF, arr Brisbane 30.12.43; No.3 AD 3.1.44; No.548 Sqn 4.5.44; No.7 R&SU 23.7.44; No.548 Sqn (date unknown); SOC 22.5.46; No.6 AD 1.10.45; Cat.E storage 1.10.46; DAP 7.11.47 until 15.11.48

JG176 Spitfire LF.VIIIc (Merlin 66); Became **A58-334**; TOC/RAF 16.9.43 - To RAAF, arr Brisbane 30.12.43; No.3 AD 3.1.44; No.548 Sqn 4.5.44; No.6 AD 22.9.45; SOC 22.5.46; Cat.E storage 1.10.46; DAP 7.11.47 until 15.11.48

JG177 Spitfire LF.VIIIc (Merlin 66); Became **A58-335**; TOC/RAF 18.9.43 - To RAAF, arr Brisbane 30.12.43; No.3 AD 3.1.44; No.549 Sqn 21.4.44; Crashed on landing, Darwin Civil 30.10.44; Cca 5.12.44

JG187 Spitfire LF.VIIIc (Merlin 66); Became **A58-336**; TOC/RAF 16.9.43 - To RAAF, arr Brisbane 30.12.43; No.3 AD 3.1.44; No.549 Sqn 7.4.44; No.7 R&SU 22.12.44; No.549 Sqn 19.1.45; No.6 AD 26.9.45; SOC 22.5.46; Cat.E storage 1.10.46; DAP 7.11.47 until 15.11.48

JG188 Spitfire LF.VIIIc (Merlin 66); Became **A58-337**; TOC/RAF 17.9.43 - To RAAF, arr Brisbane 30.12.43; No.3 AD 3.1.44; No.14 ARD-R/P 29.8.44; No.549 Sqn 1.4.45; No.6 AD 24.9.45; SOC 22.5.46; Cat.E storage 1.10.46; DAP 7.11.47 until 15.11.48

JG189 Spitfire LF.VIIIc (Merlin 66); Became **A58-338**; TOC/RAF 17.9.43 - To RAAF, arr Brisbane 30.12.43; No.3 AD 3.1.44; No.548 Sqn ('TS-U') 21.4.44; No.54 Sqn 15.7.45; No.6 AD 23.9.45; SOC 22.5.46; Cat.E storage 1.10.46; DAP 7.11.47 until 15.11.48

JG191 Spitfire LF.VIIIc (Merlin 66); Became **A58-339**; TOC/RAF 18.9.43 - To RAAF, arr Brisbane 30.12.43; No.3 AD 3.1.44; No.14 ARD-R/P 8.8.44; No.452 Sqn 1.9.44; No.9 R&SU 13.12.44; No.7 R&SU 12.2.45; No.54 Sqn 4.8.45; No.6 AD 11.9.45; SOC 22.5.46; Cat.E storage 1.10.46; DAP 7.11.47 until 15.11.48

JG192 Spitfire LF.VIIIc (Merlin 66); Became **A58-340**; TOC/RAF 17.9.43 - To RAAF, arr Brisbane 30.12.43; No.3 AD 3.1.44; No.14 ARD-R/P 6.6.44; No.452 Sqn 15.6.44; No.9 R&SU-R/P 11.12.44; No.6 AD 10.1.45; SOC 22.5.46; Cat.E storage 1.10.46; DAP 7.11.47 until 15.11.48

AUSTRALIA

Spitfire LF.VIIIc A58-377 (ex JG267) of No.452 Sqn RAAF suffered engine failure at 3,000 feet whilst participating in dive bomb attacks near Point Blaize, NT, and ditched 100 yards from the shore on 2nd November 1944. Parts were later recovered and stored in the Darwin Aviation Museum from 1985. [Peter Radtke]

JG239 Spitfire LF.VIIIc (Merlin 66); Became **A58-341**; TOC/RAF 24.9.43 - To RAAF, arr Brisbane 30.12.43; No.3 AD 3.1.44; No.549 Sqn 7.4.44; No.6 AD 23.9.45; SOC 22.5.46; Cat.E storage 1.10.46; DAP 7.11.47 until 15.11.48

JG262 Spitfire LF.VIIIc (Merlin 66); Became **A58-373**; TOC/RAF 7.10.43 - To RAAF, arr Melbourne 4.2.44; No.2 AD 4.2.44; No.549 Sqn 21.4.44; No.7 R&SU 24.7.44; No.549 Sqn 15.8.44; No.6 AD 26.9.45; SOC 22.5.46; Cat.E storage 1.10.46; DAP 7.11.47 until 15.11.48

JG263 Spitfire LF.VIIIc (Merlin 66); Became **A58-374**; TOC/RAF 7.10.43 - To RAAF, arr Sydney 21.1.44; No.2 AD 25.1.44; No.548 Sqn 3.5.44; No.6 AD 11.9.45; SOC 22.5.46; Cat.E storage 1.10.46; DAP 7.11.47 until 15.11.48

JG264 Spitfire LF.VIIIc (Merlin 66); Became **A58-342**; TOC/RAF 8.10.43 - To RAAF, arr Brisbane 30.12.43; No.3 AD 3.1.44; No.452 Sqn 28.6.44; No.9 R&SU-R/P 13.12.44; No.7 R&SU 12.2.45; No.6 AD 10.3.46; SOC 22.5.46; DAP 7.11.47 until 15.11.48

JG265 Spitfire LF.VIIIc (Merlin 66); Became **A58-375**; TOC/RAF 8.10.43 - To RAAF, arr Melbourne 4.2.44; No.2 AD 4.2.44; No.1 AD 9.2.44; No.14 ARD-R/P 30.3.44; No.452 Sqn 31.3.44; No.54 Sqn 6.4.44; No.7 R&SU 1.5.44; No.54 Sqn 24.7.44; No.7 R&SU 26.1.45; No.54 Sqn 12.2.45; No.6 AD 19.11.45; SOC 22.5.46; Cat.E storage 1.10.46; DAP 7.11.47 until 15.11.48

JG266 Spitfire LF.VIIIc (Merlin 66); Became **A58-376**; TOC/RAF 8.10.43 - To RAAF, arr Sydney 21.1.44; No.2 AD 30.1.44; No.548 Sqn 3.5.44; Engine failed after take-off, crashed, destroyed by fire, Livingstone 29.6.44; No.7 R&SU 3.7.44; No.8 CRD 17.7.44; Cca 8.8.44

JG267 Spitfire LF.VIIIc (Merlin 66); Became **A58-377**; TOC/RAF 9.10.43 - To RAAF, arr Sydney 21.1.44; No.2 AD 31.1.44; No.14 ARD-R/P 10.6.44; No.452 Sqn 15.6.44; Participating in dive bomb attacks near Point Blaize, NT, engine failed at 3,000ft, ditched 100yds from shore 2.11.44; SOC 4.12.44 – Recovered shoreline wreck stored in Darwin Aviation Museum from 1985 - **SURVIVOR**

JG269 Spitfire LF.VIIIc (Merlin 66); Became **A58-378**; TOC/RAF 5.10.43 - To RAAF, arr Sydney 21.1.44; No.2 AD 30.1.44; No.548 Sqn 3.5.44; No.6 AD 10.9.45; SOC 22.5.46; Cat.E storage 1.10.46; DAP 7.11.47 until 15.11.48

JG270 Spitfire LF.VIIIc (Merlin 66); Became **A58-379**; TOC/RAF 10.10.43 - To RAAF, arr Sydney 21.1.44; No.2 AD 31.1.44; No.549 Sqn ('ZF-Z') 21.4.44; No.6 AD 24.9.45; SOC 22.5.46; Cat.E storage 1.10.46; DAP 7.11.47 until 15.11.48

JG271 Spitfire LF.VIIIc (Merlin 66); Became **A58-343**; TOC/RAF 10.10.43 - To RAAF, arr Brisbane 30.12.43; No.3 AD 3.1.44; No.549 Sqn 13.4.44; No.7 R&SU 9.11.44; No.549 Sqn 22.1.45; No.6 AD 25.3.45; SOC 22.5.46; Cat.E storage 1.10.46; DAP 7.11.47 until 15.11.48

JG275 Spitfire LF.VIIIc (Merlin 66); Became **A58-384**; TOC/RAF 19.10.43 - To RAAF, arr Sydney 29.1.44; No.2 AD 7.2.44; No.54 Sqn 6.6.44; Undershot, starboard oleo collapsed, Livingstone 17.7.44; No.7 R&SU 17.7.44; No.54 Sqn 24.10.44; No.7 R&SU 27.9.45; SOC 22.5.46; Cat.E storage 1.10.46; DAP 7.11.47 until 15.11.48

JG332 Spitfire LF.VIIIc (Merlin 66); Became **A58-380**; TOC/RAF 1.10.43 - To RAAF, arr Sydney 21.1.44; No.2 AD 31.1.44; No.54 Sqn 11.3.44; No.2 AD 19.3.44; No.2 AD/TU (No.2 AP) 16.11.44; No.2 AD 2.1.45; Storage 19.11.45; Cat.E storage 1.10.46; DAP 24.6.49 until 6.9.49

JG342 Spitfire LF.VIIIc (Merlin 66); Became **A58-392**; TOC/RAF 7.10.43 - To RAAF, arr Melbourne 3.2.44; No.1 AD 7.2.44; No.548 Sqn ('TS-M' or 'TS-N') 7.4.44; Collided with JG350 (A58-393) over Petrie, 5m NW of Strathpine 19.4.44 (Sgt AV Chandler killed); No.3 CRD 24.4.44; Cca 25.5.44

JG343 Spitfire LF.VIIIc (Merlin 66); Became **A58-344**; TOC/RAF 7.10.43 - To RAAF, arr Brisbane 30.12.43;

No.3 AD 3.1.44; No.14 ARD-R/P 6.6.44; No.452 Sqn 15.6.44; No.9 R&SU 20.12.44; No.6 AD 10.9.45; SOC 22.5.46; Cat.E storage 1.10.46; DAP 7.11.47 until 15.11.48

JG345 Spitfire LF.VIIIc (Merlin 66); Became **A58-381**; TOC/RAF 7.10.43 - To RAAF, arr Sydney 21.1.44; No.2 AD 31.1.44; No.549 Sqn 29.4.44; No.7 R&SU 3.7.45; No.6 AD 29.10.45; Cat.E storage; SOC 22.5.46; DAP 7.11.47 until 15.11.48

JG346 Spitfire LF.VIIIc (Merlin 66); Became **A58-345**; TOC/RAF 15.10.43 - To RAAF, arr Brisbane 30.12.43; No.3 AD 3.1.44; No.548 Sqn 3.5.44; Force-landed, crashed 8m N of Proserpine, NT 10.6.44; No.13 ARD 14.6.44; Cca 22.8.44

JG347 Spitfire LF.VIIIc (Merlin 66); Became **A58-382**; TOC/RAF 15.10.43 - To RAAF, arr Sydney 21.1.44; No.2 AD 31.1.44; No.452 Sqn 30.6.44; No.9 R&SU 13.12.44; No.14 ARD 5.1.45; No.54 Sqn 26.3.45; No.7 R&SU 20.4.45; No.548 Sqn 25.6.45; No.6 AD 11.9.45; SOC 22.5.46; Cat.E storage 1.10.46; DAP 7.11.47 until 15.11.48

JG350 Spitfire LF.VIIIc (Merlin 66); Became **A58-393**; TOC/RAF 17.10.43 - To RAAF, arr Melbourne 3.2.44; No.1 AD 7.2.44; No.548 Sqn ('TS-M':'TS-N') 7.4.44; Mid-air collision with JG342 (A58-392) over Petrie, 5m NW of Strathpine 19.4.44 (S/Ldr WHA Wright killed); No.3 CRD 24.4.44; Cca 25.5.44

JG351 Spitfire LF.VIIIc (Merlin 66); Became **A58-346**; TOC/RAF 14.10.43 - To RAAF, arr Brisbane 30.12.43; No.3 AD 3.1.44; No.14 ARD-R/P 15.6.44; No.9 R&SU-R/P 13.12.44; No.7 R&SU 12.2.45; No.6 AD 18.9.45; SOC 22.5.46; Cat.E storage 1.10.46; DAP 7.11.47 until 15.11.48

JG352 Spitfire LF.VIIIc (Merlin 66); Became **A58-347**; TOC/RAF 17.10.43 - To RAAF, arr Brisbane 30.12.43; No.3 AD 3.1.44; No.549 Sqn 13.4.44; Engine lost power, crashed in sea 60m N of Truscott, WA 8.11.44 (pilot killed); SOC 22.11.44

JG353 Spitfire LF.VIIIc (Merlin 66); Became **A58-357**; TOC/RAF 18.10.43 - To RAAF, arr Brisbane 16.1.44; No.3 AD 23.1.44; No.14 ARD-R/P 22.5.44; No.54 Sqn ('DL-M') 6.6.44; No.7 R&SU 18.6.45; No.8 CRD 24.9.45; Cca 19.10.45

JG354 Spitfire LF.VIIIc (Merlin 66); Became **A58-358**; TOC/RAF 17.10.43 - To RAAF, arr Brisbane 16.1.44; No 3 AD 23.1.44; No.457 Sqn 29.7.44; No.9 R&SU 9.12.44; No.14 ARD 23.1.45; No.549 Sqn 3.5.45; No.6 AD 24.9.45; SOC 22.5.46; Cat.E storage 1.10.46; DAP 7.11.47 until 15.11.48

JG355 Spitfire LF.VIIIc (Merlin 66); Became **A58-359**; TOC/RAF 17.10.43 - To RAAF, arr Brisbane 16.1.44; No.3 AD 23.1.44; No.548 Sqn ('TS-V') 20.4.44; Left formation during transit flight, force-landed, crashed 19m ENE of Daly Waters, NT 15.6.44; SOC 3.8.44. – Recovered surface wreck by Langdon Badger, Adelaide, SA; Later to Pearce Dunn/Warbirds Aviation Museum, Mildura, Victoria storage; To Jeff Trappett, Morwell, Vic, storage; In 1988 to Robert L Eastgate, Melbourne, Vic for composite restoration project, RAAF Point Cook, Vic - **SURVIVOR**

JG356 Spitfire LF.VIIIc (Merlin 66); Became **A58-385**; TOC/RAF 19.10.43 - To RAAF, arr Sydney 29.1.44; No.2 AD 7.2.44; No.457 Sqn 2.8.44; No.9 R&SU 13.9.44; No.457 Sqn 12.10.44; No.9 R&SU 9.1.45; No.7 R&SU 29.6.45; No.6 AD 23.9.45; SOC 22.5.46; Cat.E storage 1.10.46; DAP 7.11.47 until 15.11.48

JG371 Spitfire LF.VIIIc (Merlin 66); Became **A58-348**; TOC/RAF 17.10.43 - To RAAF, arr Brisbane 30.12.43; No.3 AD 3.1.44; No.549 Sqn ('ZF-S') 14.4.44; No.7 R&SU 9.10.44; No.549 Sqn ('ZF-S') 15.10.44; No.7 R&SU 3.7.45; No.6 AD 1.10.45; SOC 22.5.46; Cat.E storage 1.10.46; DAP 7.11.47 until 15.11.48

JG372 Spitfire LF.VIIIc (Merlin 66); Became **A58-386**; TOC/RAF 18.10.43 - To RAAF, arr Sydney 29.1.44; No.2 AD 7.2.44; No.14 ARD-R/P 22.5.44; No.54 Sqn 27.5.44; No.7 R&SU 21.6.45; Cca 29.10.45

JG373 Spitfire LF.VIIIc (Merlin 66); Became **A58-394**; TOC/RAF 17.10.43 - To RAAF, arr Melbourne 3.2.44; No.1 AD 7.2.44; No.548 Sqn ('TS-G') 11.4.44 (first Mk.VIIIc of No.548 Sqn); First flight with No.548 Sqn 12.4.44; Engine failed on take-off, crash-landed, Livingstone, NT 31.7.44; No.8 CRD 13.9.44; Cca 26.9.44

JG376 Spitfire LF.VIIIc (Merlin 66); Became **A58-360**; TOC/RAF 24.10.43 - To RAAF, arr Brisbane 16.1.44; No.3 AD 23.1.44; No.14 ARD-R/P 12.8.44; No.452 Sqn 1.9.44; No.9 R&SU-R/P 13.12.44; No.14 ARD 5.1.45; No.54 Sqn ('DL-R') 8.4.45; No.6 AD 22.9.45; SOC 22.5.46; Cat.E storage 1.10.46; DAP 7.11.47 until 15.11.48

JG377 Spitfire LF.VIIIc (Merlin 66); Became **A58-395**; TOC/RAF 23.10.43 - To RAAF, arr Melbourne 3.2.44; No.1 AD 7.2.44; Special Duties Flight; No.2 OTU Mildura (date unknown); No.548 Sqn 16.4.44; No.7 R&SU 31.7.44; No.548 Sqn 10.8.44; No.6 AD 11.9.45; SOC 22.5.46; Cat.E storage 1.10.46; DAP 7.11.47 until 15.11.48

JG382 Spitfire LF.VIIIc (Merlin 66); Became **A58-387**; TOC/RAF 27.10.43 - To RAAF, arr Sydney 29.1.44; No.2 AD 31.1.44; No.452 Sqn 15.7.44; No.9 R&SU 13.12.44; No.7 R&SU 10.2.45; No.6 AD 1.10.45; SOC 22.5.46; Cat.E storage 1.10.46; DAP 7.11.47 until 15.11.48

JG385 Spitfire LF.VIIIc (Merlin 66); Became **A58-448**; TOC/RAF 5.11.43 - To RAAF, arr Sydney 18.4.44; No.2 AD 22.4.44; No.452 Sqn 15.7.44; No.9 R&SU 13.12.44; No.6 AD 4.1.45; SOC 22.5.46; Cat.E storage 1.10.46; DAP 7.11.47 until 15.11.48

JG386 Spitfire LF.VIIIc (Merlin 66); Became **A58-361**; TOC/RAF 5.11.43 - To RAAF, arr Brisbane 16.1.44; No.3 AD 23.1.44; No.14 ARD-R/P 6.6.44; No.452 Sqn 18.6.44; No.9 R&SU 9.10.44; No.452 Sqn 22.10.44; No.9 R&SU 13.12.44; No.14 ARD 22.1.45; No.549 Sqn 28.4.45; No.6 AD 24.9.45; SOC 22.5.46; Cat.E storage 1.10.46; DAP 7.11.47 until 15.11.48

JG387 Spitfire LF.VIIIc (Merlin 66); Became **A58-388**; TOC/RAF 7.11.43 - To RAAF, arr Sydney 29.1.44; No.2 AD 31.1.44; No.548 Sqn ('TS-U') 15.5.45; No.6 AD 11.9.45; SOC 22.5.46; Cat.E storage 1.10.46; DAP 7.11.47 until 15.11.48

JG414 Spitfire LF.VIIIc (Merlin 66); Became **A58-349**; TOC/RAF 15.10.43 - To RAAF, arr Brisbane 30.12.43; No.3 AD 3.1.44; No.14 ARD-R/P 22.5.44; No.54 Sqn ('DL-O') 7.6.44; No.6 AD 10.3.45; DAP Archerfield 17.4.45; No.6 AD 10.6.45; Storage 22.11.45; SOC 22.5.46; Cat.E storage 1.10.46; DAP 7.11.47 until 15.11.48

JG415 Spitfire LF.VIIIc (Merlin 66); Became **A58-383**; TOC/RAF 17.10.43 - To RAAF, arr Sydney 21.1.44; No.2 AD 3.2.44; No.548 Sqn 5.5.44; Force-landed on beach, crashed, near Giru, S of Townsville, Qld 10.6.44; No.13 ARD 14.6.44; Cca 21.8.44

JG416 Spitfire LF.VIIIc (Merlin 66); Became **A58-350**; TOC/RAF 15.10.43 - To RAAF, arr Brisbane 30.12.43; No.3 AD 3.1.44; No.548 Sqn 14.4.44; Taxying crash, hit underground vent, ground-looped, Garbutt 10.6.44; No.13 ARD 29.6.44; No.13 ARD-R/P 19.7.45; Cat.E storage 1.10.46; Cca 29.11.46

JG417 Spitfire LF.VIIIc (Merlin 66); Became **A58-351**; TOC/RAF 15.10.43 - To RAAF, arr Brisbane 30.12.43; No.3 AD 3.1.44; No.549 Sqn 1.5.44; No.6 AD 23.9.45; SOC 22.5.46; Cat.E storage 1.10.46; DAP 7.11.47 until 15.11.48

JG419 Spitfire LF.VIIIc (Merlin 66); Became **A58-362**; TOC/RAF 18.10.43 - To RAAF, arr Brisbane 16.1.44; No.3 AD 23.1.44; No.14 ARD-R/P 22.5.44; No.54 Sqn 6.6.44; Wheel would not lock down, ran off runway landing Darwin Civil, badly damaged 5.11.44 (F/Sgt FR Vanes unhurt); No.7 R&SU 6.11.44; No.6 AD 10.3.45; DAP Archerfield 17.4.45; No.6 AD 10.6.45; SOC 22.5.46; Cat.E storage 1.10.46; DAP 7.11.47 until 15.11.48

JG420 Spitfire LF.VIIIc (Merlin 66); Became **A58-396**; TOC/RAF 19.10.43 - To RAAF, arr Melbourne 3.2.44; No.1 AD 7.2.44; No.548 Sqn 6.4.44; Overshot on night landing during ferry flight, Strathpine 6.4.44; No.6 AD 1.5.44; SOC 22.5.46; Cat.E storage 1.10.46; DAP 7.11.47 until 15.11.48

JG421 Spitfire LF.VIIIc (Merlin 66); Became **A58-352**; TOC/RAF 17.10.43 - To RAAF, arr Brisbane 30.12.43; No.3 AD 3.1.44; No.14 ARD-R/P 22.5.44; No.54 Sqn ('DL-N') 6.6.44; No.548 Sqn 19.7.45; No.6 AD 23.9.45; SOC 22.5.46; Cat.E storage 1.10.46; DAP 7.11.47 until 15.11.48

JG422 Spitfire LF.VIIIc (Merlin 66); Became **A58-353**; TOC/RAF 17.10.43 - To RAAF, arr Brisbane 30.12.43; No.3 AD 3.1.44; No.14 ARD-R/P 31.7.44; No.548 Sqn ('TS-G') 4.8.44; No.7 R&SU 8.9.44; No.548 Sqn 11.10.44; Engine failed, force-landed, crashed, Darwin 16.10.44; No.7 R&SU 18.10.44; No.548 Sqn ('TS-G') 23.10.44; No.54 Sqn 15.7.45; No.6 AD 23.9.45; SOC 22.5.46; Cat.E storage 1.10.46; DAP 7.11.47 until 15.11.48

JG423 Spitfire LF.VIIIc (Merlin 66); Became **A58-397**; TOC/RAF 18.10.43 - To RAAF, arr Melbourne 3.2.44; No.1 AD 7.2.44; No.548 Sqn 11.4.44; No.54 Sqn 15.7.45; No.6 AD 23.9.45; SOC 22.5.46; Cat.E storage 1.10.46; DAP 7.11.47 until 15.11.48

JG424 Spitfire LF.VIIIc (Merlin 66); Became **A58-363**; TOC/RAF 17.10.43 - To RAAF, arr Brisbane 16.1.44; No.3 AD 23.1.44; No.14 ARD-R/P 29.8.44; No.549 Sqn 22.3.45; No.6 AD 24.9.45; SOC 22.5.46; Cat.E storage 1.10.46; DAP 7.11.47 until 15.11.48

JG425 Spitfire LF.VIIIc (Merlin 66); Became **A58-398**; TOC/RAF 19.10.43 - To RAAF, arr Melbourne 3.2.44; No.1 AD 7.2.44; No.548 Sqn 7.4.44; No.7 R&SU 17.7.45; No.6 AD 23.9.45; SOC 22.5.46; Cat.E storage 1.10.46; DAP 7.11.47 until 15.11.48

JG429 Spitfire LF.VIIIc (Merlin 66); Became **A58-364**; TOC/RAF 24.10.43 - To RAAF, arr Brisbane 16.1.44; No.3 AD 23.1.44; No.549 Sqn 4.5.44; Hit in formation by JF620 (A58-300) and abandoned near Truscott, WA 16.11.44; Cca 20.12.44

JG430 Spitfire LF.VIIIc (Merlin 66); Became **A58-389**; TOC/RAF 24.10.43 - To RAAF, arr Sydney 29.1.44; No.2 AD 7.2.44; No.452 Sqn 19.6.44; No.9 R&SU-R/P 11.12.44; No.6 AD 4.1.45; Cat.E storage 1.10.46; SOC 19.11.46; DAP 26.9.47 until 15.11.48

JG431 Spitfire LF.VIIIc (Merlin 66); Became **A58-365**; TOC/RAF 24.10.43 - To RAAF, arr Brisbane 16.1.44; No.3 AD 23.1.44; No.14 ARD-R/P 8.8.44; No.549 Sqn 7.4.45; No.6 AD 24.9.45; SOC 22.5.46; Cat.E storage 1.10.46; DAP 7.11.47 until 15.11.48

JG432 Spitfire LF.VIIIc (Merlin 66); Became **A58-399**; TOC/RAF 22.10.43 - To RAAF, arr Melbourne 3.2.44; No.1 AD 7.2.44; No.548 Sqn 11.4.44; Wheels-up night landing, Darwin 6.10.44; No.7 R&SU 11.10.44; No.548 Sqn 12.3.45; Belly-landed on night approach, burnt out, Truscott 20.5.45; No.8 CRD 27.5.45; Cca 10.7.45

JG465 Spitfire LF.VIIIc (Merlin 66); Became **A58-390**; TOC/RAF 24.10.43 - To RAAF, arr Sydney 29.1.44; No.2 AD 31.1.44; No.54 Sqn 23.5.44; Shot down Ki-46 into sea in flames 5m N of Drysdale Strip, shared JF870 (A58-312) 20.7.44 (F/Lt VF Meakin); Hit treetop and blew up during ground attack exercise, Hughes 28.7.44 (F/Lt VF Meakin killed); SOC 21.8.44

JG466 Spitfire LF.VIIIc (Merlin 66); Became **A58-463**; TOC/RAF 24.10.43 - To RAAF, arr Melbourne 19.5.44; No.1 APU 23.5.44; No.1 AD 23.6.44; No.457 Sqn 17.7.44; No.9 R&SU 9.1.45; No.7 R&SU 13.2.45; No.6 AD 13.2.45; Storage 15.10.45; SOC 22.5.46; Cat.E storage 1.10.46; DAP 7.11.47 until 15.11.48

JG467 Spitfire LF.VIIIc (Merlin 66); Became **A58-405**; TOC/RAF 24.10.43 - To RAAF, arr Sydney 29.2.44; No.1 AD 9.3.44; Special Duties Flight; No.548 Sqn ('TS-D') 15.7.45; No.54 Sqn 15.7.45; No.6 AD 10.9.45; SOC 22.5.46; Cat.E storage 1.10.46; DAP 7.11.47 until 15.11.48

JG468 Spitfire LF.VIIIc (Merlin 66); Became **A58-366**; TOC/RAF 24.10.43 - To RAAF, arr Brisbane 16.1.44; No.3 AD 23.1.44; No.457 Sqn ('ZP-G') 29.7.44; Brakes failed landing, overshot runway into drain, Sattler, WA 28.8.44; No.9 R&SU 29.8.44; No.8 CRD 21.9.44; Cca 26.9.44

JG471 Spitfire LF.VIIIc (Merlin 66); Became **A58-391**; TOC/RAF 27.10.43 - To RAAF, arr Sydney 29.1.44; No.2 AD 31.1.44; No.54 Sqn ('DL-Z') 23.5.44; Undercarriage damaged landing Austin Strip, Snake Bay 17.11.44 (F/Lt MW Grierson-Jackson); No.7 R&SU; No.54 Sqn ('DL-Z') 23.11.44; No.7 R&SU 21.6.45; Cca 29.10.45

JG472 Spitfire LF.VIIIc (Merlin 66); Became **A58-367**; TOC/RAF 27.10.43 - To RAAF, arr Brisbane 16.1.44; No.3 AD 23.1.44; No.6 AD 23.4.44; Belly-landed Amberley 23.11.44; Cca 20.11.45

JG473 Spitfire LF.VIIIc (Merlin 66); Became **A58-368**; TOC/RAF 27.10.43 - To RAAF, arr Brisbane 16.1.44; No.3 AD 23.1.44; No.14 ARD-R/P 8.8.44; No.6 AD 1.10.45; SOC 22.5.46; Cat.E storage 1.10.46; DAP 7.11.47 until 15.11.48

JG474 Spitfire LF.VIIIc (Merlin 66); Became **A58-369**; TOC/RAF 27.10.43 - To RAAF, arr Brisbane 16.1.44; No.3 AD 23.1.44; No.452 Sqn 15.7.44; No.9 R&SU 9.10.44; No.452 Sqn 20.10.44; No.9 R&SU-R/P 11.12.44; No.14 ARD-R/P 26.12.44; No.14 ARD 3.3.45; No.54 Sqn ('DL-F') 10.6.45; No.6 AD 22.9.45; SOC 22.5.46; Cat.E storage 1.10.46; DAP 7.11.47 until 15.11.48

JG481 Spitfire LF.VIIIc (Merlin 66); Became **A58-406**; TOC/RAF 1.12.43 - To RAAF, arr Sydney 29.2.44; No.1 AD 9.3.44; No.549 Sqn 3.5.44; No.6 AD 24.9.45; SOC 22.5.46; Cat.E storage 1.10.46; DAP 7.11.47 until 15.11.48

JG482 Spitfire LF.VIIIc (Merlin 66); Became **A58-407**; TOC/RAF 25.11.43 - To RAAF, arr Sydney 29.2.44; No.1 AD 9.3.44; No.452 Sqn 3.7.44; No.9 R&SU-R/P 13.12.44; No.7 R&SU 13.2.45; No.6 AD 10.9.45; SOC 22.5.46; Cat.E storage 1.10.46; DAP 7.11.47 until 15.11.48

JG484 Spitfire LF.VIIIc (Merlin 66); Became **A58-408**; TOC/RAF 1.12.43 - To RAAF, arr Sydney 29.2.44; No.2 AD 29.2.44; No.54 Sqn ('DL-T') 6.6.44; No.7 R&SU 18.6.45; No.13 ARD 16.10.45; No.6 AD 20.11.45; SOC 22.5.46; Cat.E storage 1.10.46; DAP 7.11.47 until 15.11.48 - Parts recovered in 1993 by Noel Smoothie, Ningi, Qld - **SURVIVOR**

JG485 Spitfire LF.VIIIc (Merlin 66); Became **A58-417**; TOC/RAF 1.12.43 - To RAAF, arr Brisbane 7.4.44; No.3 AD 26.4.44; No.14 ARD-R/P 29.8.44; No.22 R&SU-R/P 26.1.45; No.452 Sqn 10.2.45; No.9 R&SU 6.5.45; 14. R&SU 22.9.45; No.60 OBU 30.10.45; Cca 12.2.46

JG533 Spitfire LF.VIIIc (Merlin 66); Became **A58-418**; TOC/RAF 19.12.43 - To RAAF, arr Brisbane 7.4.44; No.2 AD 13.4.44; No.3 AD 26.4.44; No.14 ARD-R/P 8.8.44; No.457 Sqn ('ZP-Y') 30.9.44; No.9 R&SU 2.1.45; No.7 R&SU 14.2.45; No.549 Sqn 4.8.45; No.7 R&SU 13.9.45; No.6 AD 22.9.45; SOC 22.5.46; Cat.E storage 1.10.46; DAP 7.11.47 until 15.11.48

JG543 Spitfire LF.VIIIc (Merlin 66); Became **A58-484**; TOC/RAF 22.2.44 - To RAAF, arr Melbourne 13.6.44; No.1 APU 20.6.44; No.1 AD 17.7.44; No.457 Sqn (markings "CRC", personal aircraft of Wg Cdr Clive R Caldwell) 19.9.44; No.452 Sqn 8.11.44; No.9 R&SU 14.11.44; No.452 Sqn 10.12.44; Cca 31.1.46

JG549 Spitfire LF.VIIIc (Merlin 66); Became **A58-419**; TOC/RAF 24.12.43 - To RAAF, arr Brisbane 7.4.44; No.3 AD 26.4.44; No.14 ARD-R/P 8.8.44; No.457 Sqn 14.9.44; No.452 Sqn 10.12.44; Engine failure during intruder patrol, ditched off Dyamboela, Ternate Island 13.1.45 (Flt Sgt EMcL Stevenson died as PoW); SOC 16.1.45

JG556 Spitfire LF.VIIIc (Merlin 66); Became **A58-434**; TOC/RAF 12.2.44 - To RAAF, arr Sydney 18.4.44; No.1APU 20.4.44; No.1 AD 31.8.44; No.14 ARD-R/P

Spitfire LF.VIIIc A58-484 (ex JG543) bearing the personal code "CRC" of Wg Cdr Clive R Caldwell, CO of No.80 Fighter Wing RAAF in 1944.
[via R C B Ashworth]

19.9.44; No.79 Sqn 27.1.45; No.9 R&SU 14.2.45; No.79 Sqn .45; FTR sweep over Halmahera Is - Tobela area 27.3.45; SOC 10.4.45

JG557 Spitfire LF.VIIIc (Merlin 66); Became **A58-464**; TOC/RAF 28.1.44 - To RAAF, arr Melbourne 19.5.44; No.1 APU 23.5.44; No.457 Sqn (markings "CRC", personal aircraft of Wg Cdr Clive R Caldwell); No.1 AD 30.8.44; No.8 OTU 2.11.44; No.6 AD 28.11.45; SOC 22.5.46; Cat.E storage 1.10.46; DAP 7.11.47 until 15.11.48

JG558 Spitfire LF.VIIIc (Merlin 66); Became **A58-470**; TOC/RAF 5.2.44 - To RAAF, arr Sydney 9.5.44; No.1 APU 23.5.44; No.1 AD 11.7.44; No.457 Sqn ('ZP-K') 17.7.44; No.9 R&SU 9.1.45; No.7 R&SU 10.2.45; No.54 Sqn 2.7.45; No.6 AD 23.9.45; SOC 22.5.46; Cat.E storage 1.10.46; DAP until 15.11.48

JG566 Spitfire LF.VIIIc (Merlin 66); Became **A58-449**; TOC/RAF 19.12.43 - To RAAF, arr Sydney 18.4.44; No.2 AD 22.4.44; No.14 ARD-R/P 7.8.44; Nosed over in soft ground, prop damaged 12.8.44; No.1 AD 22.8.44; Storage 22.1.46; Cat.E storage 1.10.46; Cca 23.4.51

JG603 Spitfire LF.VIIIc (Merlin 66); Became **A58-370**; TOC/RAF 24.11.43 - To RAAF, arr Brisbane 16.1.44; No.3 AD 23.1.44; No.14 ARD-R/P 8.8.44; No.54 Sqn ('DL-W') 3.4.45; No.6 AD 23.9.45; SOC 22.5.46; Cat.E storage 1.10.46; DAP 7.11.47 until 15.11.48
NOTE: Incorrectly recorded as "JG605"

JG604 Spitfire LF.VIIIc (Merlin 66); Became **A58-409**; TOC/RAF 1.12.43 - To RAAF, arr Sydney 29.2.44; No.1 AD 9.3.44; No.548 Sqn 21.4.44; No.6 AD 11.9.45; SOC 22.5.46; Cat.E storage 1.10.46; DAP 7.11.47 until 15.11.48

JG605 Spitfire LF.VIIIc (Merlin 66); Became **A58-450**; TOC/RAF 2.12.43 - To RAAF, arr Sydney 18.4.44; No.2 AD 22.4.44; No.14 ARD-R/P 2.8.44; No.457 Sqn 8.8.44; No.452 Sqn 16.8.44; While ferrying Sattler to Gorrie, landed in rain, skidded into roller, Katherine, NT 1.12.44; No.14 ARD 8.12.44; No.7 R&SU 9.2.45; Cca 18.4.45

JG607 Spitfire LF.VIIIc (Merlin 66); Became **A58-410**; TOC/RAF 1.12.43 - To RAAF, arr Sydney 29.2.44; No.2 AD 29.2.44; No.14 ARD-R/P 12.6.44; No.452 Sqn 15.6.44; No.457 Sqn 6.12.44; No.9 R&SU 12.12.44; No.7 R&SU 5.2.45; Cca 21.2.45

JG609 Spitfire LF.VIIIc (Merlin 66); Became **A58-451**; TOC/RAF 2.12.43 - To RAAF, arr Sydney 18.4.44; No.2 AD 22.4.44; No.14 ARD-R/P 2.8.44; No.548 Sqn 10.8.44; No.54 Sqn 15.7.45; No.6 AD 23.9.45; SOC 22.5.46; Cat.E storage 1.10.46; DAP 7.11.47 until 15.11.48

JG611 Spitfire LF.VIIIc (Merlin 66); Became **A58-411**; TOC/RAF 2.12.43 - To RAAF, arr Sydney 29.2.44; No.1 AD 9.3.44; No.452 Sqn ('QY-P', named '*Betsy*') 3.7.44; Engine failed, force-landed, wing damaged, Sattler 26.8.44 (Plt Bullock); No.9 R&SU 28.8.44; No.452 Sqn 7.9.44; No.14 ARD 4.12.44; No.6 AD 20.9.45; SOC 22.5.46; Cat.E storage 1.10.46; DAP 7.11.47 until 15.11.48

JG613 Spitfire LF.VIIIc (Merlin 66); Became **A58-452**; TOC/RAF 19.12.43 - To RAAF, arr Sydney 18.4.44; No.2 AD 22.4.44; No.6 AD 8.9.44; SOC 22.5.46; Cat.E storage 1.10.46; DAP 7.11.47 until 15.11.48

JG622 Spitfire LF.VIIIc (Merlin 66); Became **A58-435**; TOC/RAF 24.11.43 - To RAAF, arr Sydney 18.4.44; No.2 AD 20.4.44; No.452 Sqn ('QY-T', "Pegasus" emblem near windscreen) 7.7.44; Flown by F/Lt Ron Cundy some time; Collided with B-24D during fighter affiliation, went into sea, 1m E of Cape Van Diemen, Melville Is, NT 18.9.44; SOC 23.9.44

JG650 Spitfire LF.VIIIc (Merlin 66); Became **A58-485**; TOC/RAF 18.3.44 - To RAAF, arr Brisbane 27.6.44; No.3 AD 4.7.44; No.6 AD 29.9.44; No.1 AD 17.12.44; Test & Ferry Sqn 12.3.46; SOC 22.5.46; Cat.E storage 1.10.46; DAP 19.5.48; DSD 8.8.49

JG652 Spitfire LF.VIIIc (Merlin 66); Became **A58-480**; TOC/RAF 7.3.44 - To RAAF, arr Melbourne 13.6.44; No.1 APU 20.6.44; No.1 AD 17.7.44; No.14 ARD-R/P 5.8.44; No.54 Sqn ('DL-Y') 9.8.44; No.7 R&SU 14.9.44; No.54 Sqn ('DL-Y') 6.10.44; No.6 AD 23.9.45; SOC 22.5.46; Cat.E storage 1.10.46; DAP 7.11.47 until 15.11.48

JG653 Spitfire LF.VIIIc (Merlin 66); Became **A58-481**; TOC/RAF 3.3.44 - To RAAF, arr Melbourne 13.6.44; No.1 APU 27.6.44; No.1 AD 17.7.44; Port leg collapsed landing Gorrie 5.8.44; No.14 ARD-R/P 5.8.44; Cca 1.10.45

JG655 Spitfire LF.VIIIc (Merlin 66); Became **A58-482**; TOC/RAF 11.3.44 - To RAAF, arr Melbourne 13.6.44; No.1 APU 19.6.44; No.1 AD 5.7.44; No.14 ARD-R/P 29.7.44; No.548 Sqn ('TS-M') 2.8.44; No.7 R&SU 9.8.44; No.548 Sqn ('TS-V') 24.8.44; No.6 AD 11.9.44; SOC 22.5.46; Cat.E storage 1.10.46; DAP 7.11.47 until 15.11.48

JG659 Spitfire LF.VIIIc (Merlin 66); Became **A58-483**; TOC/RAF 12.3.44 - To RAAF, arr Melbourne 13.6.44; No.1 APU 19.6.44; No.1 AD 11.7.44; No.14 ARD-R/P 15.8.44; No.549 Sqn 23.4.45; No.6 AD 24.9.45; SOC

- JG664 Spitfire LF.VIIIc (Merlin 66); Became **A58-439**; TOC/RAF 12.3.44 - To RAAF, arr Sydney 19.6.44; No.1 AD 6.7.44; No.14 ARD-R/P 25.9.44; No.54 Sqn 27.7.45; No.6 AD 23.9.45; SOC 22.5.46; Cat.E storage 1.10.46; DAP 7.11.47 until 15.11.48; Head armour with serial and parts currently in Couloundra Air Museum, Queensland - **SURVIVOR**
- JG665 Spitfire LF.VIIIc (Merlin 66); Became **A58-440**; TOC/RAF 12.3.44 - To RAAF, arr Sydney 19.6.44; No.1 AD 6.7.44; No.14 ARD-R/P 6.9.44; No.9 R&SU-R/P 6.12.44; No.452 Sqn 13.12.44; En route to Morotai Is, flown from Sattler to Merauke, Dutch New Guinea 16.12.44; Whilst over Halmaheras hit by ground fire near Cape Gela, Morotai, crashed and burned in heavy timber 3m from Pitoe 7.1.45; No.11 R&SU 16.1.45; Cca 31.1.45
- JG666 Spitfire LF.VIIIc (Merlin 66); Became **A58-486**; TOC/RAF 17.3.44 - To RAAF, arr Brisbane 27.6.44; No.3 AD 4.7.44; No.6 AD 6.10.44; No.8 OTU 24.8.45; No.2 AD 26.2.46; SOC 24.5.46; Cat.E storage 1.10.46; DAP 24.6.48; DSD 6.9.49
- JG668 Spitfire LF.VIIIc (Merlin 66); Became **A58-441**; TOC/RAF 18.3.44 - To RAAF, arr Sydney 19.6.44; No.1 AD 6.7.44; No.14 ARD-R/P 6.9.44; No.9 R&SU 23.10.44; No.14 ARD-R/P 23.11.44; No.6 AD 1.10.45; SOC 22.5.46; DAP 7.11.47 until 15.11.48. – Recovered parts to Ian Mastin, Hoopers Crossing, Vic – **SURVIVOR**
- JG684 Spitfire LF.VIIIc (Merlin 66); Became **A58-511**; TOC/RAF 30.3.44 - To RAAF, arr Sydney 10.7.44; No.2 AD 19.7.44; No.6 AD 19.8.44; No.79 Sqn 12.4.45; No.6 AD 21.5.45; CMU 16.5.46; SOC 19.11.46; Cat.E storage 1.10.46; DAP 26.9.47 until 15.11.48
- JG685 Spitfire LF.VIIIc (Merlin 66); Became **A58-512**; TOC/RAF 28.3.44 - To RAAF, arr Sydney 10.7.44; No.2 AD 21.7.44; No.6 AD 31.8.44; No.79 Sqn 9.3.45; No.9 R&SU 20.8.45; No.79 Sqn 22.9.45; No.60 OBU 23.10.45; Cca 13.12.45
- JG687 Spitfire LF.VIIIc (Merlin 66); Became **A58-513**; Presentation aircraft '*A.V.B. The 1st*' (Australian Victory Bonds); TOC/RAF 4.4.44 - To RAAF, arr Sydney 10.7.44; No.2 AD 21.7.44; No.6 AD 21.8.44; No.79 Sqn ('UP-X') 6.12.44 (some time flown by S/Ldr Ron Susans); No.6 AD 15.1.45; No.79 Sqn ('UP-X') 26.3.45; No.60 OBU 29.10.45; Cca 13.12.45
- JG689 Spitfire LF.VIIIc (Merlin 66); Became **A58-487**; TOC/RAF 4.4.44 - To RAAF, arr Brisbane 27.6.44; No.3 AD 4.7.44; No.6 AD 14.10.44; No.79 Sqn 6.12.44; No.6 AD 15.1.45; No.79 Sqn 9.3.45; Damaged by enemy gunfire Galela 1.5.45; Taxying collision with MT552 (A58-526), Morotai 17.9.45; No.60 OBU 19.10.45; Cca 2.7.46
- JG690 Spitfire LF.VIIIc (Merlin 66); Became **A58-516**; TOC/RAF 6.4.44 - To RAAF, arr Sydney 17.7.44; No.2 AD 24.7.44; No.2 AD/TU (No.2 AP) 13.9.44; No.2 AD 30.9.44; No.14 ARD-R/P 16.10.44; No.9 R&SU-R/P 7.12.44; No.452 Sqn ('QY-T') 10.12.44; No.9 R&SU 12.4.45; No.452 Sqn 15.6.45; Belly-landed, caught fire at Balikpapan 17.7.45 (Plt LS Crompton); No.9 R&SU 19.7.45; Cca 6.9.45
- JG691 Spitfire LF.VIIIc (Merlin 66); Became **A58-501**; TOC/RAF 6.4.44 - To RAAF, arr Melbourne 28.4.44; No.1 AD 12.7.44; No.6 AD 23.8.44; No.79 Sqn 6.12.44; No.6 AD 13.1.45; No.79 Sqn 9.3.45; No.9 R&SU 20.8.45; No.79 Sqn 15.10.45; No.6 AD 5.11.45; SOC 22.5.46; Cat.E storage 1.10.46; DAP 7.11.47 until 15.11.48
- JG728 Spitfire F.Vc/trop (Merlin 46); Became **A58-171**; TOC/RAF 15.12.42 - To RAAF, arr Australia 17.5.43; No.1 APU 20.5.43; No.1 AD 10.6.43; No.13 ARD 4.7.43; To No.1 (F) Wing; No.457 Sqn 12.7.43; No.7 R&SU 25.2.44; No.452 Sqn 9.3.44; Prop went into coarse pitch, lost height, belly landed on beach, Governor Island 23.5.44; No.7 R&SU 20.6.44; No.8 CRD 30.6.44; Cca 1945
- JG731 Spitfire F.Vc/trop (Merlin 46); Became **A58-172**; TOC/RAF 17.12.42 - To RAAF, arr Melbourne 11.3.43; No.1 AD 11.3.43; No.1 R&SU-R/P 4.43; No.54 Sqn 9.5.43; G6M damaged 30.6.43 (F/Sgt JM Wickman); G6M destroyed, then engine failed, pilot baled out at 4,000ft, 35m W of Batchelor/60m E of Darwin 6.7.43 (F/Sgt JM Wickman safe), SOC; Wreckage to No.7 R&SU 2.8.43; Cca 19.8.43
- JG740 Spitfire F.Vc/trop (Merlin 46); Became **A58-173**; TOC/RAF 14.12.42 - To RAAF, arr Melbourne 11.3.43; No.1 AD 11.3.43; No.79 Sqn ('UP-U') 14.5.43; No.1 AD 30.5.43; No.79 Sqn ('UP-U') 6.6.43; No.6 AD 16.6.44; CGS ('E') 11.9.44; Engine failed, force-landed and crashed, 1m SE of Meredith Railway Station, NSW 21.12.44; Cca 6.2.45
- JG795 Spitfire F.Vc/trop (Merlin 46); Became **A58-174**; TOC/RAF 14.12.42 - To RAAF, arr Melbourne 11.3.43; No.1 AD 11.3.43; No.1 R&SU 1.5.43; No.54 Sqn ('DL-H') 13.5.43; Two Japanese bombers destroyed, then engine failed, force-landed wheels-up on beach near Lee Point, seriously damaged 20.6.43 (F/O MC Hughes); No.14 ARD 29.6.43; No.452 Sqn 9.3.44; No.54 Sqn ('DL-V') 11.3.44; Engine failed on take-off, crash-landed, overturned, Wyndham 7.4.44 (P/O Featherstone); No.7 R&SU; Cca 17.5.44
- JG796 Spitfire F.Vc/trop (Merlin 46); Became **A58-175**; TOC/RAF 14.12.42 - To RAAF, arr Melbourne 11.3.43; No.1 AD 11.3.43; No.79 Sqn 10.5.43; No.1 AD 20.5.43; No.79 Sqn 6.6.43; While stationary, taxied into by AR532 (A58-4), Vivigani 27.6.43; To No.6 AD; Partial engine failure on ferry flight, belly landed on beach, overtaken by tide, Debiri Island, Trobriand Is 18.6.44; SOC 8.8.44
- JG807 Spitfire F.Vc/trop (Merlin 46); Became **A58-176**; TOC/RAF 17.12.42 - To RAAF, arr Melbourne 13.4.43; No.1 AD 15.4.43; No.79 Sqn ('UP-P') 18.5.43; No.1 AD 20.5.43; No.79 Sqn 28.5.43; No.1 AD 2.6.43; No.79 Sqn, air combat 31.10.43 (F/Sgt IH Callister); No.6 AD 18.9.44; No.85 Sqn 4.4.45; No.6 AD 10.10.45; No.3 CRD 28.11.45; To CMU Oakley; SOC 22.5.46; DAP 26.11.47; Offered for sale, DAP to purchaser 15.11.48

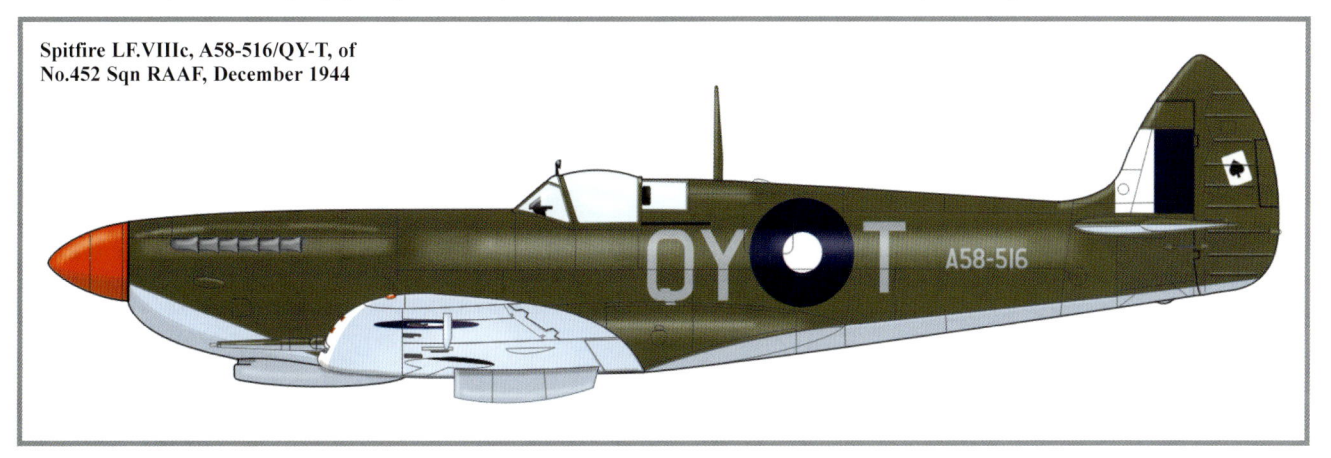

Spitfire LF.VIIIc, A58-516/QY-T, of No.452 Sqn RAAF, December 1944

JG884 Spitfire F.Vc/trop (Merlin 46); Became **A58-177**; TOC/RAF 13.1.43 - To RAAF, arr Australia 17.5.43; No.1 APU 20.5.43; No.1 AD 10.6.43; No.13 ARD 26.6.43; No.12 R&SU 1.7.43; No.79 Sqn 7.7.43; Wheels-up landing 12.8.43; No.26 R&SU 6.9.43; No.79 Sqn 30.9.43; Swung landing, collided with Kittyhawk on runway, damaged beyond repair 6.10.43; Cca 22.11.43

JG891 Spitfire F.Vc/trop (Merlin 46); Became **A58-178**; TOC/RAF 2.1.43 - To RAAF, arr Melbourne 13.4.43; No.1 AD 15.4.43; No.79 Sqn ('UP-G') 7.5.43; No.1 AD to fit tropical air filter 19.5.43; No.79 Sqn ('UP-G') 1.6.43; Returning from scramble, overran wet weather strip landing in gusty weather, swung to avoid another a/c, overturned, badly damaged, Kiriwina 12.1.44 (F/Sgt Dudley Grinlington slightly injured); No.12 R&SU 17.1.44; moved to Momote; No.1 AD 18.1.44; SOC and dumped 26.1.44. - Stripped hulk recovered from Papua-New Guinea (Kiriwina), acquired by N Monty Armstrong and moved to New Zealand 1974; Sold to Don Subritzky, Dairy Flat, Auckland, for restoration to flying condition (reg. *ZK-MKV* 1974); By 1998 moved to Don J Subritzky family workshop/hangar on their North Auckland-Dairy Flat property for restoration to fly with parts from EF545; Sold to Karel Bos (Historic Flying Ltd at Audley End, Essex), arrived in the UK in 7.99 (*G-LFVC*) 28.9.99 – **SURVIVOR**

JG897 Spitfire F.Vc/trop (Merlin 46); Became **A58-179**; TOC/RAF 2.1.43 - To RAAF, arr Australia 16.4.43; No.1 AD 21.4.43; No.79 Sqn 6.6.43; Collided with A58-181 (JG954) on runway after landing, Garbutt airfield near Townsville 13.6.43; No.2 R&SU 12.6.43; No.3 AD 21.6.43; Cca 9.7.43

JG912 Spitfire F.Vc/trop (Merlin 46); Became **A58-180**; TOC/RAF 2.1.43 - To RAAF, arr Melbourne 13.4.43; No.1 AD 15.4.43; No.79 Sqn 7.5.43; No.1 AD 27.5.43; No.79 Sqn 1.6.43; Struck flare path landing from early morning patrol 20.12.43; No.6 AD 16.6.44; Force-landed at end of runway after test flight, Oakey, Qld 17.1.45; No.3 CRD 28.1.45; Cca 14.2.45

JG954 Spitfire F.Vc/trop (Merlin 46); Became **A58-181**; TOC/RAF 2.1.43 - To RAAF, arr Australia 16.4.43; No.1 AD 26.4.43; No.79 Sqn 29.5.43; Collided with A58-179 (JG912) on runway after landing Garbutt airfield near Townsville 13.6.43; No.12 R&SU 12.6.43; Cca 9.7.43

JG957 Spitfire F.Vc/trop (Merlin 46); Became **A58-182**; TOC/RAF 2.1.43 - To RAAF, arr Melbourne 13.4.43; No.1 AD 15.4.43; No.79 Sqn 7.5.43; No.1 AD 27.5.43; No.79 Sqn 1.6.43; No.12 R&SU 18.6.43; No.1 R&SU 22.8.43; No.13 ARD-R/P 21.10.43; Damaged Townsville whilst en route No.79 Sqn 1.1.44, retd No.13 ARD; No.2 OTU Mildura, Vic 20.8.44; No.8 OTU Narromine 1.11.44; Taxied into fence at Parkes 10.11.44; No.6 AD 20.11.45; Cat.E storage 22.3.46; SOC 22.5.46; DAP 26.11.47 until 15.11.48

JK174 Spitfire F.Vc/trop; TOC/RAF 24.1.43; Shipped to Australia 4.3.43; Lost when SS *Silverbeech* torpedoed 28.3.43

JK176 Spitfire F.Vc/trop; TOC/RAF 24.1.43; Shipped to Australia 4.3.43; Lost when SS *Silverbeech* torpedoed 28.3.43

JK181 Spitfire F.Vc/trop; TOC/RAF 28.1.43; Shipped to Australia 4.3.43; Lost when SS *Silverbeech* torpedoed 28.3.43

JK184 Spitfire F.Vc/trop; TOC/RAF 23.1.43; Shipped to Australia 4.3.43; Lost when SS *Silverbeech* torpedoed 28.3.43

JK225 Spitfire F.Vc/trop (Merlin 46); Became **A58-183**; TOC/RAF 3.2.43 - To RAAF, arr Australia 17.5.43; No.1 APU 20.5.43; No.1 AD 6.6.43; No.13 ARD-R/P 29.6.43; No.1(F)Wing 10.7.43; No.457 Sqn 12.7.43; Air combat 11.8.43 (F/Sgt AE Batcheler) & 7.9.43 (F/O JH Smithson); Tyre burst landing, swung off runway, ran into ditch, Livingstone 19.10.43; No.7 R&SU 21.10.43; No.14 ARD 5.2.44; Cca 17.2.44

JK229 Spitfire F.Vc/trop (Merlin 46); Became **A58-184**; TOC/RAF 9.2.43 - To RAAF, arr Australia 16.4.43; No.1 AD 20.4.43; No.79 Sqn 12.5.43; No.1 AD 11.6.43; No.13 ARD 4.7.43; No.79 Sqn 19.8.43; No.13 ARD 21.6.44; No.6 AD 28.9.44; No.4 AD-R/P19.3.45; No.4 AD 21.3.45; No.85 Sqn 30.6.45; No.17 R&SU 27.7.45; Cca 4.10.45

JK231 Spitfire F.Vc/trop (Merlin 46); Became **A58-185**; Presentation aircraft '*SIR HARRY & LADY OAKES III*'; TOC/RAF 9.2.43 - To RAAF, arr Australia 16.4.43; No.1 AD 17.4.43; No.79 Sqn ('UP-D') 12.5.43; No.1 AD 25.5.43; No.79 Sqn 30.5.43; No.6 AD 6.6.44; Central Flying School 20.9.44; Engine failed on take-off, Point Cook 17.5.45; Cat. E storage 22.3.46; No.1 AD 7.5.46; SOC 22.5.46; DAP 25.2.49; Sold 20.7.50

JK257 Spitfire F.Vc/trop; TOC/RAF 29.1.43; Shipped to Australia 4.3.43; Lost when SS *Silverbeech* torpedoed 28.3.43

JK258 Spitfire F.Vc/trop; Presentation aircraft '*SOUTHEND ON SEA*'; TOC/RAF 29.1.43; Shipped to Australia 4.3.43; Lost when SS *Silverbeech* torpedoed 28.3.43

JK273 Spitfire F.Vc/trop; TOC/RAF 29.1.43; Shipped to Australia 4.3.43; Lost when SS *Silverbeech* torpedoed 28.3.43

JK331 Spitfire F.Vc/trop; TOC/RAF 22.1.43; Shipped to Australia 4.3.43; Lost when SS *Silverbeech* torpedoed 28.3.43

JL247 Spitfire F.Vc/trop (Merlin 46); Became **A58-200**; TOC/RAF 19.4.43 - To RAAF, arr Australia 3.7.43; No.1 APU 12.7.43; No.1 AD 16.7.43; No.13 ARD 25.7.43; No.15 ARD-R/P 7.1.44; No.15 ARD 24.2.44; No.79 Sqn ('UP-C') 25.2.44; Hit telephone cables landing Momote 26.7.44; Crash-landed Cecil Strip 5.12.44; No.6 AD 6.12.44; SOC 22.5.46; Cat.E storage 1.10.46; DAP 26.11.47 until 15.11.48

JL314 Spitfire F.Vc/trop (Merlin 50); Became **A58-201**; TOC/RAF 31.5.43 - To RAAF, arr Australia 2.8.43; No.1 APU 8.8.43; No.1 AD 23.8.43; No.14 ARD-R/P 6.9.43; No.452 Sqn 15.9.43; Mid-air collision with EE677 (A58-121), dived into ground Manton Dam, near Strauss 26.9.43 (F/O JP Adam & F/O GA Mawer, both killed); No.7 R&SU 27.9.43; No.14 ARD 4.10.43; Cca 12.10.43

JL348 Spitfire F.Vc/trop (Merlin 46); Became **A58-202**; TOC/RAF 19.4.43 - To RAAF, arr Australia 10.8.43; No.1 APU 16.8.43; No.1 AD 6.9.43; No.13 ARD 13.9.43; No.13 ARD-R/P 2.11.43; Hit by LZ934 (A58-230) while parked Breddan airstrip 24.11.43 (collision also reported at Laverton); No.13 ARD-R/P; No.13 ARD 29.11.43; Cca 7.1.44

JL360 Spitfire F.Vc/trop (Merlin 46); Became **A58-203**; TOC/RAF 19.4.43 - To RAAF, arr Australia 10.8.43; No.1 APU 15.8.43; No.1 AD 24.8.43; No.14 ARD-R/P 9.9.43; No.54 Sqn 8.11.43; No.452 Sqn 9.3.44; Missed runway landing and nosed over in mud, Wyndham 9.3.44; Cca 27.4.44

JL371 Spitfire F.Vc/trop (Merlin 50); Became **A58-204**; TOC/RAF 19.4.43 - To RAAF, arr Australia 3.7.43; No.1 APU 12.7.43; No.2 OTU 6.8.43; Engine lost power, force-landed, crashed 20m NW of Lake Victoria, NSW (NE of Adelaide) 1.12.43; Cca 24.12.43

JL378 Spitfire F.Vc/trop (Merlin 50); Became **A58-205**; TOC/RAF 19.4.43 - To RAAF, arr Australia 3.7.43; No.1 APU 12.7.43; No.1 AD 21.7.43; No.14 ARD-R/P; No.452 Sqn ('QY-Y') 9.8.43; Air combat 7.9.43 (F/Lt AP Goldsmith); Tyre burst landing, swung, port oleo collapsed, Strauss 10.12.43; No.7 R&SU 17.12.43; No.14 ARD 5.2.44; Cca 17.2.44

JL380 Spitfire F.Vc/trop (Merlin 50); Became **A58-206**; TOC/RAF 20.4.43 - To RAAF, arr Australia 10.8.43; No.1 APU 15.8.43; No.1 AD 5.9.43; No.13 ARD 6.10.43; No.15 ARD-R/P 19.11.43; No.79 Sqn 7.1.44; Engine failed, abandoned, a/c crashed in sea 10m SW of Momote 8.5.44; SOC 24.5.44

JL382 Spitfire F.Vc/trop (Merlin 50); Became **A58-207**; TOC/RAF 19.4.43 - To RAAF, arr Australia 3.7.43; No.1

APU 12.7.43; No.1 AD 18.7.43; No.14 ARD-R/P 8.8.43; No.54 Sqn 21.8.43; No.452 Sqn 4.4.44; Hit bank while landing during night flying training, Strauss 5.6.44; No.9 R&SU 7.6.44; Cca 10.7.44

JL386 Spitfire F.Vc/trop (Merlin 46); Became **A58-208**; TOC/RAF 20.4.43 - To RAAF, arr Australia 2.8.43; No.1 APU 9.8.43; No.1 AD 5.9.43; No.14 ARD 19.9.43; No.457 Sqn 30.11.43; No.6 AD 19.7.44; No.85 Sqn 25.11.44; Engine failed, unserviceable, Ceduna 27.12.44; No.6 AD; No.85 Sqn 5.2.45; No.6 AD 10.10.45; SOC 22.5.46; Cat.E storage 1.10.46; DAP 26.11.47 until 15.11.48

JL392 Spitfire F.Vc/trop (Merlin 46); Became **A58-209**; TOC/RAF 19.4.43 - To RAAF, arr Australia 10.8.43; No.1 APU 16.8.43; No.1 AD 5.9.43; No.14 ARD-R/P 9.9.43; No.452 Sqn 30.9.43; No.14 ARD 14.10.43; No.452 Sqn 19.10.43; No.457 Sqn 15.7.44; No.14 ARD-R/P 1.8.44; No.85 Sqn 24.9.44; No.17 R&SU 19.6.45; No.85 Sqn 30.6.45; No.6 AD 10.10.45; SOC 22.5.46; Cat.E storage 1.10.46; DAP 26.11.47 until 15.11.48

JL394 Spitfire F.Vc/trop (Merlin 50); Became **A58-210**; TOC/RAF 20.4.43 - To RAAF, arr Australia 3.7.43; No.1 APU 9.7.43; No.1 AD 15.7.43; No.1 (F) Wing 22.7.43; No.452 Sqn 25.7.43; Air combat 17.8.43 (Wg Cdr Clive R Caldwell); No.54 Sqn; No.7 R&SU 12.3.44; No.54 Sqn 17.3.44; No.7 R&SU 6.6.44; No.457 Sqn 30.6.44; No.14 ARD-R/P 1.8.44; No.85 Sqn 27.9.44; Engine failed, force-landed 70m E of Zanthus, WA 29.9.44; Cca 30.10.44

LV644 Spitfire LF.VIIIc (Merlin 66); Became **A58-453**; TOC/RAF 19.12.43 - To RAAF, arr Sydney 18.4.44; No.2 AD 22.4.44; No.14 ARD-R/P 2.8.44; No.548 Sqn ('TS-A') 7.8.44; No.6 AD 22.9.45; SOC 22.5.46; Cat.E storage 1.10.46; DAP 7.11.47 until 15.11.48

LV647 Spitfire LF.VIIIc (Merlin 66); Became **A58-424**; TOC/RAF 19.12.43 - To RAAF, arr Brisbane 7.4.44; No.3 AD 26.4.44; Eagle Farm (RAAF trials against Ki-61, S/Ldr LV James) 5.8.44; Cca 16.10.45

LV649 Spitfire LF.VIIIc (Merlin 66); Became **A58-425**; TOC/RAF 19.12.43 - To RAAF, arr Brisbane 7.4.44; No.3 AD 26.4.44; Crashed on landing Gorrie airstrip 7.8.44; No.14 ARD-R/P 8.8.44; Cca 24.10.44

LV652 Spitfire LF.VIIIc (Merlin 66); Became **A58-427**; TOC/RAF 19.12.43 - To RAAF, arr Brisbane 7.4.44; No.3 AD 26.4.44; No.14 ARD-R/P 12.8.44; No.22 R&SU 25.1.45; No.452 Sqn ('QY-X') 16.3.45; No.6 AD 6.11.45; SOC 22.5.46; Cat.E storage 1.10.46; DAP 7.11.47 until 15.11.48 (But at Oakes airfield in early fifties)

LV657 Spitfire LF.VIIIc (Merlin 66); Became **A58-454**; TOC/RAF 19.12.43 - To RAAF, arr Sydney 18.4.44; No.2 AD 22.4.44; No.14 ARD-R/P 29.8.44; No.548 Sqn 4.11.44; No.7 R&SU 6.11.44; No.548 Sqn 12.3.45; No.54 Sqn 15.7.45; No.548 Sqn 27.8.45; No.6 AD 10.9.45; SOC 22.5.46; Cat.E storage 1.10.46; DAP 7.11.47 until 15.11.48

LV672 Spitfire LF.VIIIc (Merlin 66); Became **A58-538**; TOC/RAF 28.12.43 - To RAAF, arr Sydney 27.7.44; No.2 AD 29.7.44; No.5 OTU 1.11.44; No.8 OTU 27.11.44; Collided on landing with Wirraway A20-362, Parkes 23.5.45; Cca 15.6.45

LV727 Spitfire LF.VIIIc (Merlin 66); Became **A58-455**; TOC/RAF 21.1.44 - To RAAF, arr Sydney 18.4.44; No.2 AD 22.4.44; No.14 ARD-R/P 11.9.45; No.13 ARD 3.10.45; No.6 AD 26.11.45; SOC 22.5.46; Cat.E storage; DAP 7.11.47 until 15.11.48

LV740 Spitfire LF.VIIIc (Merlin 66); Became **A58-426**; TOC/RAF 27.12.43 - To RAAF, arr Brisbane 7.4.44; No.3 AD 26.4.44; No.6 AD 14.10.44; Storage 22.11.45; No.3 AD; SOC 22.5.46; Cat.E storage 1.10.46; DAP 7.11.47 until 15.11.48

LV750 Spitfire LF.VIIIc (Merlin 66); Became **A58-471**; TOC/RAF 4.2.44 - To RAAF, arr Sydney 9.5.44; No.1 APU 23.5.44; No.1 AD 25.6.44; No.457 Sqn 2.7.44; No.14 ARD 4.12.44; No.8 CRD 3.9.45; Cca 1.10.45 - Buried parts recovered Gorrie airfield, to Alec Wilson, Romsey, Vic; Currently at Yunta, South Australia for restoration of MD338 - **SURVIVOR**

LZ834 Spitfire F.Vc/trop (Merlin 50); Became **A58-211**; TOC/RAF 23.4.43 - To RAAF, arr Australia 30.6.43; No.1 APU 7.7.43; No.1 AD 13.7.43; No.1 (F) Wing 15.7.43; No.452 Sqn 18.7.43; No.14 ARD 24.9.43; No.452 Sqn ('QY-C') 1.10.43; Overshot, lost undercarriage, on nose Strauss 2.10.43; No.7 R&SU 3.10.43; No.457 Sqn 22.12.43; No.6 AD 4.8.44; No.85 Sqn 23.8.45; No.2 AD 26.2.46; Cat.E storage 1.10.46; Allocated for RAN 17.9.48, arr RAN 6.10.48; Ground handling and taxi-training; Destroyed on fire dump later

LZ835 Spitfire F.Vc/trop (Merlin 50); Became **A58-212**; TOC/RAF 25.4.43 - To RAAF, arr Melbourne 18.8.43; No.2 AD 8.43; No.13 ARD-R/P 6.11.43; No.15 ARD-R/P 25.11.43; No.79 Sqn 19.1.44; No.12 R&SU 28.10.44; No.6 AD 5.12.44; No.8 OTU 3.1.45; No.6 AD 28.11.45; SOC 22.5.46; Cat.E storage 1.10.46; DAP 26.11.47 until 15.11.48

LZ842 Spitfire F.IX ex SAAF; Fuselage only via UK to Ross Campbell, Toowoomba, Queensland 12.93; Under restoration for display as "EF-D", one wing from Russia - **SURVIVOR**

LZ844 Spitfire F.Vc/trop (Merlin 50); Became **A58-213**; TOC/RAF 20.4.43 - To RAAF, arr Australia 3.7.43; No.1 APU 13.7.43; No.1 AD 21.7.43; No.13 ARD-R/P 2.8.43; No.79 Sqn (UP-X) 12.9.43; Brakes failed, swung into coral pit, Kiriwina, 11.12.43; No.26 R&SU 16.12.43; No.12 R&SU 30.1.44; SOC 9.3.44

NOTE: LZ844 (prov), rebuilding since 1981: Parts recovered from Kiriwina, Papua-New Guinea in 1974; Owned by Barry Coran, Point Cook Museum; Marked as "R6915"; Rolled out Point Cook, Vic on 12.2.95 - **SURVIVOR**

Spitfire F.Vc/trop LZ844 UP-X (allotted A58-213 but not applied) under repair at No.12 Repair & Salvage Unit, RAAF, Kiriwina Island, Trobriands, Papua, on 31st January 1944. It had been with No.79 Sqn at Kiriwina when the brakes failed and it swung into a coral pit. Parts were later recovered and after restoration it is now in the Point Cook Museum, Vic, marked "R6915". [Australian War Museum OG0628]

LZ845 Spitfire F.Vc/trop (Merlin 50); Became **A58-214**; TOC/RAF 19.4.43 - To RAAF, arr Australia 3.7.43; No.1 APU 9.7.43; No.1 AD 14.7.43; No.452 Sqn 25.7.43; No.7 R&SU 5.8.43; No.452 Sqn 23.8.43; No.7 R&SU 9.9.43; No.54 Sqn ('DL-N') 18.12.43; Mid-air collision at 3,000ft with BS164 (A58-63) during fighter affiliation, crashed 10m ENE of Strauss 13.1.44 (F/Sgt JH Whalley killed); SOC 16.3.44

LZ846 Spitfire F.Vc/trop (Merlin 50); Became **A58-215**; TOC/RAF 23.4.43 - To RAAF, arr Australia 30.6.43; No.1 APU 7.7.43; No.1 AD 14.7.43; No.1 (F) Wing 15.7.43; No.54 Sqn ('DL-N') 17.7.43; Collided with B-24 on landing, Darwin 9.1.44 (Sgt Knapp); Cca 8.2.44

LZ848 Spitfire F.Vc/trop (Merlin 50); Became **A58-216**; TOC/RAF 25.4.43 - To RAAF, arr Australia 30.6.43; No.1

APU 8.7.43; No.1 AD 19.7.43; No.14 ARD-R/P 27.7.43; No.54 Sqn ('DL-U') 1.8.43; Engine failed on take-off from Bathurst Island (emergency landing ground), ground-looped 9.8.43 (F/Lt I Thompson); No.7 R&SU 15.8.43; No.14 ARD-R/P 15.2.44; No.15 ARD-R/P 11.3.44; No.15 ARD 12.3.44; No.15 ARD-R/P 10.5.44; No.79 Sqn 20.5.44; No.12 R&SU 7.12.44; Cca 8.12.45

LZ862 Spitfire F.Vc/trop (Merlin 50); Became **A58-217**; TOC/RAF 23.4.43 - To RAAF, arr Australia 2.8.43; No.1 APU 8.8.43; No.1 AD 15.8.43; No.2 OTU ('862') 13.9.43; Aircraft caught fire, pilot baled out safely, a/c crashed Redcliffs, 13m S of Mildura 23.2.44; Cca 23.3.44

LZ865 Spitfire F.Vc/trop (Merlin 50); Became **A58-218**; TOC/RAF 18.4.43 - To RAAF, arr Australia 10.8.43; No.1 APU 17.8.43; No.1 AD 4.9.43; No.14 ARD-R/P 14.9.43; No.457 Sqn 26.11.43; No.17 R&SU 27.3.44; Damaged while taxying, Laverton 20.6.44; Cca 21.8.44

LZ866 Spitfire F.Vc/trop (Merlin 50); Became **A58-219**; TOC/RAF 23.4.43 - To RAAF, arr Australia 30.6.43; No.1 APU 7.7.43; No.1 AD 15.7.43; No.457 Sqn 25.7.43; Air combat 17.8.43 & 7.9.43 (F/Lt PH Watson); Engine cut after glycol leak, crash-landed in swamp 3m N of Sattler 23.2.44; No.7 R&SU 25.2.44; Cca 14.7.44

LZ867 Spitfire F.Vc/trop (Merlin 50); Became **A58-220**; TOC/RAF 19.4.43 - To RAAF, arr Australia 10.8.43; No.1 APU 17.8.43; No.1 AD 4.9.43; No.14 ARD-R/P 17.9.43; No.452 Sqn ('QY-R') 19.10.43; Swung landing, ran off Strip, Sattler 31.5.44; No.9 R&SU 1.6.44; No.8 CRD 8.6.44; Cca 1.7.44

LZ868 Spitfire F.Vc/trop (Merlin 50); Became **A58-221**; TOC/RAF 23.4.43 - To RAAF, arr Australia 30.6.43; No.1 APU 8.7.43; No.1 AD 19.7.43; No.14 ARD-R/P 13.8.43; No.54 Sqn 9.9.43; No.452 Sqn 9.3.44; No.17 R&SU 9.4.44; No.85 Sqn ('SH-S') 22.9.44; No.17 R&SU 11.4.45; No.85 Sqn 5.6.45; No.6 AD 10.10.45; SOC 22.5.46; Cat.E storage 1.10.46; DAP 26.11.47 until 15.11.48

LZ870 Spitfire F.Vc/trop (Merlin 50); Became **A58-222**; Presentation aircraft '*SIR HARRY & LADY OAKES IV*'; TOC/RAF 24.4.43 - To RAAF, arr Australia 30.6.43; No.1 APU 7.7.43; No.1 AD 15.7.43; No.1 (F) Wing 18.7.43; No.452 Sqn ('QY-N') 21.7.43; No.15 ARD-R/P 11.3.44; No.15 ARD 19.3.44; No.15 ARD-R/P 7.8.44; No.79 Sqn 18.8.44; No.6 AD 5.12.44; No.8 OTU 3.1.45; No.6 AD 20.11.45; SOC 22.5.46; Cat.E storage 1.10.46; DAP 26.11.47 until 15.11.48

LZ873 Spitfire F.Vc/trop (Merlin 50); Became **A58-223**; TOC/RAF 20.4.43 - To RAAF, arr Australia 30.6.43; No.1 APU 4.7.43; No.1 AD 2.8.43; No.13 ARD-R/P 1.9.43; Crashed landing Breddan 2.9.43; No.13 ARD-R/P 1.11.43; No.14 ARD-R/P 16.6.44; No.85 Sqn 2.10.44; Wheels-up landing Guildford 14.10.44; Struck landing beacon, Kalgoorlie 5.10.45; No.4 AD 11.10.45; No.6 AD 3.12.45; SOC 22.5.46; Cat.E storage 1.10.46; DAP 26.11.47 until 15.11.48

LZ874 Spitfire F.Vc/trop (Merlin 50); Became **A58-224**; TOC/RAF 1.5.43 - To RAAF, arr Australia 30.6.43; No.1 APU 7.7.43; No.1 AD 16.7.43; No.14 ARD 27.7.43; No.457 Sqn ('XB-Z':'ZP-Z') 20.8.43; Force-landed wheels-up, Darwin Civil 1.5.44 (P/O TH Trimble); No.7 R&SU 1.5.44; No.457 Sqn ('ZP-Z') 19.5.44; No.14 ARD-R/P 1.8.44; No.14 ARD 7.10.44; No.8 OTU 25.2.45; No.6 AD storage 28.11.45; SOC 22.5.46; Cat.E storage 1.10.46; DAP 26.11.47 until 15.11.48

LZ881 Spitfire F.Vc/trop (Merlin 50); Became **A58-225**; TOC/RAF 23.4.43 - To RAAF, arr Australia 30.6.43; No.1 APU 7.7.43; No.1 AD 16.7.43; No.14 ARD-R/P 2.8.43; Damaged during test flight 9.8.43; No.54 Sqn 9.9.43; Drifted and hit EF563 (A58-157) while landing 20.1.44 (W/O Harker); No.452 Sqn 4.4.44; No.14 ARD-R/P 1.8.44; No.14 ARD 3.10.44; No.6 AD 21.12.44; No.8 OTU; No.6 AD 27.11.45; Storage 28.11.45; SOC 22.5.46; Cat.E storage 1.10.46; DAP 26.11.47 until 15.11.48

LZ883 Spitfire F.Vc/trop (Merlin 50); Became **A58-226**; TOC/RAF 12.5.43 - To RAAF, arr Melbourne 18.8.43; No.2 AD 8.43; No.13 ARD-R/P 1.10.43; No.15 ARD-R/P 19.11.43; No.79 Sqn 26.12.43; Engine cut in cloud after interception, abandoned over sea 70m NE of Los Negros 31.7.44; SOC 11.8.44

LZ884 Spitfire F.Vc/trop (Merlin 50); Became **A58-227**; TOC/RAF 2.5.43 - To RAAF, arr Australia 30.6.43; No.1 APU 9.7.43; No.1 AD 21.7.43; No.14 ARD-R/P 2.8.43; No.452 Sqn ('QY-D') 9.8.43; Abandoned after interception 15m W of Strauss 7.9.43 (S/Ldr RS MacDonald baled out safely); SOC 14.10.43

LZ886 Spitfire F.Vc/trop (Merlin 50); Became **A58-228**; TOC/RAF 2.5.43 - To RAAF, arr Australia 30.6.43; No.1 APU 9.7.43; No.1 AD 29.7.43; Port oleo failed landing Gorrie 14.8.43; No.14 ARD-R/P 15.8.43; No.14 ARD 25.10.43; No.14 ARD-R/P 14.12.43; No.54 Sqn 22.1.44; No.452 Sqn 9.3.44; Air combat 12.6.44 (P/O MJ Beaton); No.457 Sqn 15.7.44; No.14 ARD-R/P 1.8.44; No.14 ARD 3.10.44; No.6 AD 21.12.44; No.8 OTU 19.1.45; Damaged landing Parkes 17.7.45; No.6 AD 20.11.45; SOC 22.5.46; Cat.E storage 1.10.46; DAP 26.11.47 until 15.11.48

LZ926 Spitfire F.Vc/trop (Merlin 50); Became **A58-229**; TOC/RAF 1.5.43 - To RAAF, arr Melbourne 18.8.43; No.1 APU 23.8.43; No.1 AD 22.9.43; No.2 OTU 4.10.43; Crashed in forced landing $^{1}/_{2}$m N of Mildura 31.12.43; To GI airframe *No.4*; Cca 27.4.45

LZ934 Spitfire F.Vc/trop (Merlin 50); Became **A58-230**; TOC/RAF 1.5.43 - To RAAF, arr Australia 2.8.43; No.1 APU 8.8.43; No.1 AD 15.8.43; No.13 ARD-R/P 31.8.43; Hit JL348 (A58-202) after landing Breddan 19.11. or 24.11.43; No.13 ARD 29.11.43; No.13 ARD-R/P 8.1.44; No.15 ARD 11.1.44; Missing on ferry flight, Horn Island to Port Moresby 19.1.44; SOC 11.2.44

MA352 Spitfire F.Vc/trop (Merlin 46); Became **A58-231**; TOC/RAF 29.5.43 - To RAAF, arr Australia 2.8.43; No.1 APU 8.8.43; No.1 AD 24.8.43; No.13 ARD-R/P 3.9.43; No.15 ARD-R/P 31.12.43; No.15 ARD 7.2.44; No.79 Sqn 18.8.44; Engine failed, force-landed wheels-up Los Negros 15.9.44; No.6 AD 26.11.44; No.8 OTU 18.7.45; No.6 AD 14.11.45; SOC 22.5.46; Cat.E storage 1.10.46; DAP 26.11.47 until 15.11.48

MA353 Spitfire F.Vc/trop (Merlin 46); Became **A58-232**; TOC/RAF 30.5.43 - To RAAF, arr Australia 2.8.43; No.1 APU 8.8.43; No.1 AD 4.9.43; No.14 ARD-R/P 9.9.43; No.54 Sqn 18.10.43; No.452 Sqn 9.3.44; Prop hit MA697 (A58-244) on training flight from Strauss, last seen with engine smoking near Port Patterson, NT 24.4.44; SOC 19.5.44 - Fuselage parts salvaged 9.69 by John Haslett, Darwin, NT, from crash site found near Darwin; Engine and wing parts to Darwin Air Museum 1980; Fuselage hulk to Peter Croser, Melbourne 1993 - **SURVIVOR**

MA354 Spitfire F.Vc/trop (Merlin 46); Became **A58-233**; TOC/RAF 29.5.43 - To RAAF, arr Australia 2.8.43; No.1 APU 8.8.43; No.1 AD 15.8.43; No.2 OTU 2.9.43; No.8 OTU 1.11.44; Overturned in forced landing 10m SE of Forbes, NSW 22.1.45; Cca 13.2.45

MA355 Spitfire F.Vc/trop (Merlin 46); Became **A58-234**; TOC/RAF 31.5.43 - To RAAF, arr Australia 2.8.43; No.1 APU 3.8.43; No.1 AD 11.8.43; No.14 ARD-R/P 2.9.43; No.457 Sqn 8.9.43; Air combat 12.11.43 (F/O JH Smithson); Engine failed, force-landed, hit telegraph pole near Guildford 19.3.44; No.17 R&SU 27.3.44; No.457 Sqn 16.5.44; No.14 ARD-R/P 29.7.44; CGS 11.9.44; No.6 AD 15.10.45; SOC 22.5.46; Cat.E storage 1.10.46; DAP 26.11.47 until 15.11.48

MA356 Spitfire F.Vc/trop (Merlin 46); Became **A58-235**; TOC/RAF 2.6.43 - To RAAF, arr Australia 2.8.43; No.1 APU 9.8.43; No.1 AD 24.8.43; No.14 ARD 9.9.43; No.457 Sqn 20.10.43; No.7 R&SU 11.5.44; No.457 Sqn 7.6.44; No.6 AD 16.7.44; No.85 Sqn 4.11.44; Engine overheated on ferry flight, force-landed, crashed 25m E of Balranald, NSW on ferry flight 8.11.44; Cca 14.12.44

MA366 Spitfire F.Vc/trop (Merlin 46); Became **A58-236**; TOC/RAF 9.6.43 - To RAAF, arr Australia 2.8.43; No.1 APU 9.8.43; No.1 AD 17.8.43; No.14 ARD-R/P 11.9.43;

No.54 Sqn (named *'Junior'*) 26.11.43; Engine failed, force-landed 23.12.43 (Plt Beaton Jnr); No.452 Sqn ('QY-G') 6.4.44; No.457 Sqn 15.7.44; No.14 ARD-R/P 1.8.44; No.14 ARD 3.10.44; No.6 AD 18.12.44; No.13 ARD 29.12.44; No.6 AD 25.1.44; SOC 22.5.46; Cat.E storage 1.10.46; DAP 26.11.47 until 15.11.48

MA385 Spitfire F.Vc/trop (Merlin 46); Became **A58-237**; TOC/RAF 6.6.43 - To RAAF, arr Australia 2.8.43; No.1 APU 9.8.43; No.1 AD 17.8.43; No.14 ARD-R/P 19.9.43; No.457 Sqn 13.10.43; No.17 R&SU 27.3.44; No.457 Sqn 18.5.44; No.6 AD 18.7.44; No.8 OTU 8.7.45; No.6 AD 28.11.45; SOC 22.5.46; Cat.E storage 1.10.46; DAP 26.11.47 until 15.11.48

MA387 Spitfire F.Vc/trop (Merlin 46); Became **A58-238**; TOC/RAF 1.6.43 - To RAAF, arr Australia 2.8.43; No.1 APU 3.8.43; No.1 AD 10.8.43; No.14 ARD 2.9.43 (fitted CAAG suiting 8.9.43); No.14 ARD-R/P; No.452 Sqn ('QY-G') 16.9.43; No.7 R&SU 21.11.43; No.14 ARD 24.11.43; Overshot, nosed over in soft ground, Cooktown Civil 2.1.44; Hit concrete tying-down block, undercarriage collapsed, Port Hedland 10.5.44; No.7 R&SU 16.6.44; No.14 ARD-R/P 7.8.44; CGS 11.9.44; No.6 AD 15.10.45; SOC 22.5.46; Cat.E storage 1.10.46; DAP 26.11.47 until 15.11.48

MA389 Spitfire F.Vc/trop (Merlin 46); Became **A58-239**; TOC/RAF 2.6.43 - To RAAF, arr Australia 2.8.43; No.1 APU 3.8.43; No.1 AD 11.8.43; No.14 ARD-R/P 19.8.43; No.54 Sqn 9.9.43; Tyre burst, swung into stationary EE636 (A58-111) 27.10.43 (W/O Ashurst); No.452 Sqn 4.4.44; No.14 ARD-R/P 1.8.44; No.14 ARD 14.8.44; No.8 OTU 19.2.45; No.6 AD 28.11.45; SOC 22.5.46; Cat.E storage 1.10.46; DAP 26.11.47 until 15.11.48

MA394 Spitfire F.Vc/trop (Merlin 46); Became **A58-240**; TOC/RAF 5.6.43 - To RAAF, arr Australia 2.8.43; No.1 APU 8.8.43; No.1 AD 16.8.43; No.14 ARD-R/P 7.9.43; No.452 Sqn 24.9.43; Swung on landing and overturned, Darwin 4.4.44; No.7 R&SU 5.4.44; Cca 12.5.44

MA395 Spitfire F.Vc/trop (Merlin 46); Became **A58-241**; TOC/RAF 30.7.43 - To RAAF, arr Melbourne 18.10.43; No.1 APU 25.10.43; No.1 AD 10.11.43; No.2 OTU 23.11.43; Failed to recover from firing dive and hit bank of Lake Victoria, NSW (NE of Adelaide, c.60m from Mildura) during shadow shooting practice 21.12.43; Cca 6.1.44

MA685 Spitfire F.Vc/trop (Merlin 46); Became **A58-242**; TOC/RAF 12.6.43 - To RAAF, arr Australia 27.9.43; No.1 APU 28.9.43; No.1 AD 27.10.43; No.2 AD/TU (No.2 AP) 15.11.43; No.1 AD 3.12.43; No.14 ARD 9.1.44; No.54 Sqn ('DL K') 22.1.44; No.452 Sqn 6 4 44; No.457 Sqn 18.7.44; No.14 ARD-R/P 1.8.44; CGS 11.9.44; No.6 AD 13.12.45; SOC 22.5.46; Cat.E storage 1.10.46; DAP 26.11.47 until 15.11.48

MA689 Spitfire F.Vc/trop (Merlin 46); Became **A58-243**; TOC/RAF 12.6.43 - To RAAF, arr Australia 2.8.43; No.1 APU 8.8.43; No.1 AD 26.8.43; No.14 ARD-R/P 11.9.43; No.457 Sqn 13.10.43; No.6 AD 17.7.44; No.85 Sqn 2.6.45; No.6 AD 10.10.45; SOC 22.5.46; DAP 26.11.47 until 15.11.48

MA697 Spitfire F.Vc/trop (Merlin 55); Became **A58-244**; TOC/RAF 6.8.43 - To RAAF, arr Australia 16.11.43; No.1 APU 23.11.43; No.1 AD 16.12.43; No.14 ARD-R/P 9.1.44; No.54 Sqn 18.1.44; No.452 Sqn 6.4.44; Mid-air collision with MA353 (A58-232) near Port Patterson, landed safely 24.4.44; No.457 Sqn 15.7.44; No.14 ARD-R/P 1.8.44; CGS ('F':'K') 11.9.44; No.6 AD 22.10.45; SOC 22.5.46; Cat.E storage 1.10.46; DAP 26.11.47 until 15.11.48

MA699 Spitfire F.Vc/trop (Merlin 55); Became **A58-245**; TOC/RAF 7.8.43 - To RAAF, arr Melbourne 21.10.43; No.1 APU 25.10.43; No.1 AD 5.11.43; No.2 AD/TU (No.2 AP) 15.11.43; No.1 AD 15.11.43; No.14 ARD-R/P 27.1.44; No.15 ARD 1.3.44; No.15 ARD-R/P 25.4.44; No.79 Sqn 13.5.44; Crashed in sea 38m NE of Momote 31.7.44; SOC 11.8.44

MA863 Spitfire F.Vc/trop (Merlin 46); Became **A58-246**; TOC/RAF 8.8.43 - To RAAF, arr Melbourne 21.10.43; No.1 APU ('F') 24.10.43; No.1 AD 19.11.43; No.14 ARD-R/P 9.12.43; No.14 ARD 10.12.43; No.54 Sqn ('DL-K') 10.1.44; Overshot landing 21.3.44 (F/Lt Thompson); No.452 Sqn 22.4.44; No.14 ARD-R/P 1.8.44; CGS ('K') 11.9.44; Glycol leak, force-landed near Lake Terang, Vic 26.8.45 (Plt E Gibbs); No.6 AD 22.10.45; SOC 22.5.46; Cat.E storage 1.10.46; DAP 26.11.47 until 15.11.48 - Hulk recovered from a farm by Richard E Hourigan/Moorabin Air Museum; Restoration from 1975 by Ian Whitney, Romsey, Vic., and from 7.98 by Aero Vintage, St.Leonards, Sussex, England (Guy Black); To USAAF Museum in 2000, Wright Patterson in exchange for B-24 Liberator - **SURVIVOR**

Spitfire F.Vc/trop A58-246 K (ex MA863) of the Central Gunnery School at Cressy, near Melbourne, Vic, on 26th August 1945 when it force-landed near Lake Terang, Vic, after suffering a glycol leak. The hulk was later recovered and after restoration in the UK went in 2000 to the USAAF Museum at Wright-Patterson in exchange for a B-24 Liberator.

MB959 Spitfire LF.VIIIc (Merlin 66); Became **A58-494**; TOC/RAF 18.3.44 - To RAAF, arr Brisbane 27.6.44; No.3 AD 4.7.44; No.14 ARD-R/P 25.10.44; No.54 Sqn 1.12.44; No.6 AD 11.9.45; SOC 22.5.46; Cat.E storage 1.10.46; DAP 7.11.47; DSD 15.11.48

MB960 Spitfire LF.VIIIc (Merlin 66); Became **A58-472**; TOC/RAF 28.1.44 - To RAAF, arr Sydney 9.5.44; No.1 APU 23.5.44; No.1 AD 29.7.44; No.14 ARD-R/P 11.8.44; No.6 AD 23.9.44; Cca 16.10.45

MB968 Spitfire LF.VIIIc (Merlin 66); Became **A58-514**; TOC/RAF 31.3.44 - To RAAF, arr Sydney 10.7.44; No.2 AD 19.7.44; No.6 AD 9.9.44; No.79 Sqn 6.12.44; No.6 AD 15.1.45; No.79 Sqn 23.3.45; Undercarriage failed 16.5.45; No.9 R&SU 18.5.45; No.79 Sqn 15.9.45; No.6 AD 6.11.45; SOC 22.5.46; Cat.E storage 1.10.46; DAP 7.11.47 until 15.11.48

MB970 Spitfire LF.VIIIc (Merlin 66); Became **A58-502**; TOC/RAF 6.4.44 - To RAAF, arr Melbourne 7.7.44; No.1 AD 12.7.44; No.14 ARD-R/P 6.9.44; No.9 R&SU 26.10.44; No.452 Sqn 10.12.44; Hit ditch on landing, Croydon Strip, Tarakan 18.7.45; SOC 13.12.45

MB972 Spitfire LF.VIIIc (Merlin 66); Became **A58-503**; TOC/RAF 9.4.44 - To RAAF, arr Melbourne 7.7.44; No.1 AD 16.7.44; No.14 ARD-R/P 19.9.44; No.9 R&SU-R/P 5.12.44; No.452 Sqn 10.12.44; Crash-landed Croydon Strip, Tarakan 10.9.45; No.11 R&SU 13.9.45; Cca 3.12.45

MB974 Spitfire LF.VIIIc (Merlin 66); Became **A58-504**; TOC/RAF 9.4.44 - To RAAF, arr Melbourne 7.7.44; No.1 AD 12.7.44; No.14 ARD-R/P 6.9.44; No.9 R&SU-R/P 5.12.44; No.452 Sqn ('QY-E') 10.12.44; No.9 R&SU 17.4.45; No.452 Sqn ('QY-E') 30.4.45; No.6 AD 6.11.45; SOC 22.5.46; Cat.E storage 1.10.46; DAP 7.11.47 until 15.11.48

MD217 Spitfire LF.VIIIc (Merlin 66); Became **A58-420**; TOC/RAF 27.12.43 - To RAAF, arr Brisbane 7.4.44; No.3 AD 26.4.44; No.14 ARD-R/P 29.8.44; No.22 R&SU 25.1.45; No.452 Sqn 10.2.45; No.6 AD 6.11.45; SOC 22.5.46; DAP 7.11.47 until 15.11.48

MD221 Spitfire LF.VIIIc (Merlin 66); Became **A58-371**; TOC/RAF 24.11.43 - To RAAF, arr Brisbane 16.1.44; No.3 AD 23.1.44; No.14 ARD-R/P 8.8.44; No.54 Sqn 27.7.45; No.6 AD 23.9.45; SOC 22.5.46; Cat.E storage 1.10.46; DAP 7.11.47 until 15.11.48

MD223 Spitfire LF.VIIIc (Merlin 66); Became **A58-400**; TOC/RAF 24.11.43 - To RAAF, arr Sydney 29.2.44; No.2 AD 29.2.44; No.457 Sqn 8.8.44; No.9 R&SU 19.12.44; No.452 Sqn 28.12.44; Brake seized on night take-off, skidded into embankment, Pitoe, Morotai 28.12.44; No.9 R&SU 19.2.45; Cca 15.3.45

MD226 Spitfire LF.VIIIc (Merlin 66); Became **A58-401**; TOC/RAF 2.12.43 - To RAAF, arr Sydney 29.2.44; No.2 AD 29.2.44; No.452 Sqn 15.7.44; Engine lost power, force-landed, overturned on flooded strip, Katherine, NT 2.12.44; Cca 13.3.45

MD228 Spitfire LF.VIIIc (Merlin 66); Became **A58-445**; TOC/RAF 2.12.43 - To RAAF, arr Sydney 18.4.44; No.2 AD 22.4.44; No.14 ARD-R/P 23.9.44; No.6 AD 1.10.45; SOC 22.5.46; Cat.E storage 1.10.46; DAP 7.11.47 until 15.11.48; Scrapped at RAAF Oakey, Qld – Parts recovered from a farm near Oakey by Les Arthur, Toowoomba, Qld; Restoration project from 1993 by Robert L Eastgate, Melbourne, Vic - **SURVIVOR**

MD231 Spitfire LF.VIIIc (Merlin 66); Became **A58-446**; TOC/RAF 2.12.43 - To RAAF, arr Sydney 18.4.44; No.2 AD 1.5.44; No.14 ARD-R/P 2.8.44; No.548 Sqn 10.8.44; No.54 Sqn 15.7.45; No.6 AD 23.10.45; SOC 22.5.46; Cat.E storage 1.10.46; DAP 7.11.47 until 15.11.48

MD232 Spitfire LF.VIIIc (Merlin 66); Became **A58-402**; TOC/RAF 2.12.43 - To RAAF, arr Sydney 29.2.44; No.1 AD 9.3.44; No.549 Sqn 16.4.44; No.2 OTU Mildura (date unknown); No.6 AD 26.9.45; SOC 22.5.46; Cat.E storage 1.10.46; DAP 7.11.47 until 15.11.48

MD234 Spitfire LF.VIIIc (Merlin 66); Became **A58-421**; TOC/RAF 19.12.43 - To RAAF, arr Sydney 7.4.44; No.3 AD 26.4.44; No.14 ARD-R/P 29.8.44; No.9 R&SU 23.10.44; No.14 ARD-R/P 23.11.44; No.549 Sqn 28.4.45; No.6 AD 24.9.45; SOC 22.5.46; Cat.E storage 1.10.46; DAP 7.11.47 until 15.11.48

MD238 Spitfire LF.VIIIc (Merlin 66); Became **A58-403**; TOC/RAF 2.12.43 - To RAAF, arr Sydney 29.2.44; No.2 AD 29.2.44; No.549 Sqn 5.5.44; Engine failed, force-landed, crashed, Darwin Civil 21.11.44; Cca 14.12.44

MD241 Spitfire LF.VIIIc (Merlin 66); Became **A58-404**; TOC/RAF 2.12.43 - To RAAF, arr Sydney 29.2.44; No.2 AD 29.2.44; No.549 Sqn ('ZF-P') 5.5.44; No.6 AD; SOC 22.5.46; Cat.E storage 1.10.46; DAP 7.11.47 until 15.11.48

MD250 Spitfire LF.VIIIc (Merlin 66); Became **A58-412**; TOC/RAF 23.1.44 - To RAAF, arr Sydney 13.3.44; No.2 AD 16.3.44; No.548 Sqn ('TS-S') 10.5.44; No.6 AD 10.9.45; SOC 22.5.46; Cat.E storage 1.10.46; DAP 7.11.47 until 15.11.48

MD251 Spitfire LF.VIIIc (Merlin 66); Became **A58-456**; TOC/RAF 28.1.44 - To RAAF, arr Melbourne 19.5.44; No.1 APU 23.5.44; No.1 AD 23.6.44; No.452 Sqn 3.7.44; No.14 ARD 4.12.44; No.6 AD 1.10.45; SOC 22.5.46; Cat.E storage 1.10.46; DAP 7.11.47 until 15.11.48

MD252 Spitfire LF.VIIIc (Merlin 66); Became **A58-466**; TOC/RAF 4.2.44 - To RAAF, arr Sydney 9.5.44; No.1 APU 23.5.44; No.1 AD 23.6.44; No.457 Sqn ('ZP-H') 17.7.44; No.452 Sqn 10.12.44; Crash-landed Pitoe Strip, Morotai 13.1.45; No.11 R&SU 16.1.45; Cca 5.2.45; No.9 R&SU 7.2.45

MD253 Spitfire LF.VIIIc (Merlin 66); Became **A58-447**; TOC/RAF 23.1.44 - To RAAF, arr Sydney 18.4.44; No.2 AD 22.4.44; No.14 ARD-R/P 19.8.44; No.6 AD 1.10.45; SOC 22.5.46; Cat.E storage 1.10.46; DAP 7.11.47 until 15.11.48

MD281 Spitfire LF.VIIIc (Merlin 66); Became **A58-413**; TOC/RAF 21.1.44 - To RAAF, arr Sydney 13.3.44; No.2 AD 16.3.44; No.548 Sqn ('TS-L') 11.5.44; No.6 AD 24.9.45; SOC 22.5.46; Cat.E storage 1.10.46; DAP 7.11.47 until 15.11.48

MD283 Spitfire LF.VIIIc (Merlin 66); Became **A58-414**; TOC/RAF 21.1.44 - To RAAF, arr Sydney 13.3.44; No.2 AD 16.3.44; No.549 Sqn 7.5.44; No.7 R&SU 3.7.45; No.6 AD 1.10.45; Cat.E storage 22.3.46; Cca 5.7.46

MD286 Spitfire LF.VIIIc (Merlin 66); Became **A58-428**; TOC/RAF 5.2.44 - To RAAF, arr Sydney 18.4.44; No.1 APU 8.6.44; No.1 AD 29.8.44; No.14 ARD-R/P 6.9.44; No.457 Sqn 30.9.44; No.9 R&SU 2.1.45; No.7 R&SU 10.2.45; No.54 Sqn ('DL-B') 11.7.45; No.6 AD 23.9.45; SOC 22.5.46; Cat.E storage 1.10.46; DAP 7.11.47 until 15.11.48

MD296 Spitfire LF.VIIIc (Merlin 66); Became **A58-457**; TOC/RAF 23.1.44 - To RAAF, arr Melbourne 19.5.44; No.1 APU 23.5.44; No.1 AD 23.6.44; No.457 Sqn 2.7.44 ('ZP-Z', named '*SWEET AS A SONG*', flown by S/Ldr Tom Trimble); No.9 R&SU 9.1.45; No.7 R&SU 10.2.45; No.6 AD 10.9.45; SOC 22.5.46; Cat.E storage 1.10.46; DAP 7.11.47 until 15.11.48

MD297 Spitfire LF.VIIIc (Merlin 66); Became **A58-458**; TOC/RAF 28.1.44 - To RAAF, arr Melbourne 19.5.44; No.1 APU 23.5.44; No.1 AD 30.6.44; No.457 Sqn 17.7.44; No.452 Sqn 10.12.44; No.9 R&SU 6.5.45; No.452 Sqn 21.6.45; Bounced on landing, undercarriage leg jammed, hit bank, Pitoe, Morotai 7.7.45; No.9 R&SU 7.7.45; No.14 R&SU 22.9.45; Cca 16.10.45

MD298 Spitfire LF.VIIIc (Merlin 66); Became **A58-459**; TOC/RAF 30.1.44 - To RAAF, arr Melbourne 19.5.44; No.1 APU 23.5.44; No.1 AD 30.6.44; No.457 Sqn 17.7.44; No.14 ARD 4.12.44; No.6 AD 1.10.45; SOC 22.5.46; Cat.E storage 1.10.46; DAP 7.11.47 until 15.11.48

MD299 Spitfire LF.VIIIc (Merlin 66); Became **A58-460**; TOC/RAF 28.1.44 - To RAAF, arr Melbourne 19.5.44; No.1 APU 23.5.44; No.1 AD 21.6.44; No.457 Sqn 2.7.44; No.9 R&SU 9.1.45; No.7 R&SU 12.2.45; No.54 Sqn

1.7.45; No.6 AD 11.9.45; SOC 22.5.46; Cat.E storage 1.10.46; DAP 7.11.47 until 15.11.48

MD300 Spitfire LF.VIIIc (Merlin 66); Became **A58-415**; TOC/RAF 23.1.44 - To RAAF, arr Sydney 13.3.44; No.2 AD 16.3.44; No.549 Sqn 10.5.44; No.6 AD 26.9.45; SOC 22.5.46; Cat.E storage 1.10.46; DAP 7.11.47 until 15.11.48

MD315 Spitfire LF.VIIIc (Merlin 66); Became **A58-461**; TOC/RAF 28.1.44 - To RAAF, arr Melbourne 19.5.44; No.1 APU 23.5.44; No.1 AD 28.6.44; No.457 Sqn 17.7.44; No.14 ARD 4.12.44; No.548 Sqn 20.8.45; No.6 AD 22.9.45; SOC 22.5.46; Cat.E storage 1.10.46; DAP 7.11.47 until 15.11.48

MD317 Spitfire LF.VIIIc (Merlin 66); Became **A58-416**; TOC/RAF 25.1.44 - To RAAF, arr Sydney 13.3.44; No.2 AD 16.3.44; No.549 Sqn 10.5.44; No.6 AD 24.9.45; SOC 22.5.46; Cat.E storage 1.10.46; DAP 7.11.47 until 15.11.48

MD337 Spitfire LF.VIIIc (Merlin 66); Became **A58-462**; TOC/RAF 30.1.44 - To RAAF, arr Melbourne 19.5.44; No.1 APU 23.5.44; No.1 AD 19.7.44; No.14 ARD-R/P 5.8.44; No.54 Sqn ('DL-S') 10.8.44; Caught by gust of wind taxying after landing, weathercocked, into ditch, Darwin 19.7.45 (F/O BR Booker unhurt); Cca 18.10.45

MD338 Spitfire LF.VIIIc (Merlin 66); Became **A58-467**; TOC/RAF 30.1.44 - To RAAF, arr Sydney 9.5.44; No.1 APU 23.5.44; No.1 AD 13.7.44; No.457 Sqn 29.7.44; No.14 ARD 4.12.44; Csa 30.8.45; No.8 CRD 3.9.45; Cca 1.10.45. Buried parts recovered c.1970 from Gorrie strip, NT; Regd 1988 by Alec Wilson, Frome Downs Station, Yunta, South Australia, Vic (Civil reg. *VH-ZPY* ntu) for long term restoration to fly using parts from LV750/A58-471 and MT682/A58-529 - **SURVIVOR**

MD339 Spitfire LF.VIIIc (Merlin 66); Became **A58-429**; TOC/RAF 5.2.44 - To RAAF, arr Sydney 18.4.44; No.2 AD 20.4.44; No.14 ARD 12.7.44; No.452 Sqn 30.7.44; No.9 R&SU-R/P 13.12.44; No.7 R&SU 12.2.45; No.54 Sqn ('DL-H') 11.7.45; No.6 AD 23.9.45; SOC 22.5.46; Cat.E storage 1.10.46; DAP 7.11.47 until 15.11.48

MD341 Spitfire LF.VIIIc (Merlin 66); Became **A58-430**; Presentation aircraft '*RIMA III*'; TOC/RAF 5.2.44 - To RAAF, arr Sydney 18.4.44; No.2 AD 21.4.44; No.452 Sqn ('QY-V', pilot S/Ldr LT Spence); No.2 AD/TU (No.2 AP) 1.9.44; No.2 AD 28.9.44; No.14 ARD-R/P 16.10.44; No.22 R&SU-R/P 26.1.45; Tyre burst landing Croydon Strip, Tarakan 10.7.45; No.452 Sqn ('QY-V') 7.45; Air combat 24.7.45 (F/Lt JC King); Skidded off runway landing in heavy rain, ground-looped. Mokmer, Biak Is 7.11.45; Cca 7.2.46

MD344 Spitfire LF.VIIIc (Merlin 66); Became **A58-473**; TOC/RAF 24.2.44 - To RAAF, arr Melbourne 13.6.44; No.1 APU 19.6.44; No.1 AD 5.7.44; Undercarriage collapsed on landing, Laverton 21.7.44; Cca 22.8.44

MD351 Spitfire LF.VIIIc (Merlin 66); Became **A58-521**; TOC/RAF 25.5.44 - To RAAF, arr Sydney 27.7.44; No.2 AD 29.7.44; No.14 ARD-R/P 23.9.44; No.9 R&SU 23.10.44; No.452 Sqn 10.12.44; No.11 R&SU 1.11.45; Cca 14.12.45

MD355 Spitfire LF.VIIIc (Merlin 66); Became **A58-474**; TOC/RAF 5.2.44 - To RAAF, arr Melbourne 13.6.44; No.1 APU 20.6.44; No.1 AD 17.7.44; No.14 ARD-R/P 5.8.44; No.54 Sqn 6.8.44; Engine cut, bounced on landing and tipped up, Darwin Civil 25.3.45 (F/O F Thomas); No.7 R&SU 26.3.45; No.8 CRD 6.4.45; Cca 24.4.45

MD372 Spitfire LF.VIIIc (Merlin 66); Became **A58-468**; TOC/RAF 8.2.44 - To RAAF, arr Sydney 9.5.44; No.1 APU 23.5.44; No.1 AD 25.6.44; No.14 ARD 31.7.44; No.14 ARD-R/P 21.10.44; No.9 R&SU 23.10.44; No.14 ARD-R/P 23.11.44; No.6 AD 1.10.45; SOC 22.5.46; DAP 7.11.47 until 15.11.48

MD376 Spitfire LF.VIIIc (Merlin 66); Became **A58-469**; TOC/RAF 6.2.44 - To RAAF, arr Sydney 9.5.44; No.1 APU 23.5.44; No.1 AD 23.6.44; No.457 Sqn 29.7.44; No.9 R&SU 9.1.45; No.7 R&SU 13.2.45; No.54 Sqn 4.8.45; No.6 AD 23.9.45; SOC 22.5.46; Cat.E storage 1.10.46; DAP 7.11.47 until 15.11.48

MD380 Spitfire LF.VIIIc (Merlin 66); Became **A58-436**; TOC/RAF 14.3.44 - To RAAF, arr Sydney 19.6.44; No.1 AD 6.7.44; No.14 ARD-R/P 6.9.44; Damaged by light MG fire over Gala Strip, Halmahera Is 18.3.45; No.9 R&SU 12.4.45; No.452 Sqn 24.4.45; No.79 Sqn 28.4.45; Glycol leak on take-off, ground looped, ran off strip over embankment, Pitoe, Morotai 4.5.45; No.9 R&SU 7.5.45; Cca 5.7.45

MD381 Spitfire LF.VIIIc (Merlin 66); Became **A58-437**; TOC/RAF 14.3.44 - To RAAF, arr Sydney 19.6.44; No.1 AD 6.7.44; No.14 ARD-R/P 6.9.44; No.9 R&SU 26.10.44; No.14 ARD-R/P 26.12.44; No.14 ARD 3.3.45; No.54 Sqn 10.4.45; No.6 AD 11.9.45; SOC 22.5.46; Cat.E storage 1.10.46; DAP 7.11.47 until 15.11.48

MD385 Spitfire LF.VIIIc (Merlin 66); Became **A58-475**; TOC/RAF 5.3.44 - To RAAF, arr Melbourne 13.6.44; No.1 APU 19.6.44; No.1 AD 13.7.44; No.457 Sqn 29.7.44; No.9 R&SU 2.1.45; No.7 R&SU 12.2.45; No.6 AD 10.9.45; SOC 22.5.46; Cat.E storage 1.10.46; DAP 7.11.47 until 15.11.48

MD388 Spitfire LF.VIIIc (Merlin 66); Became **A58-438**; TOC/RAF 18.3.44 - To RAAF, arr Sydney 19.6.44; No.1 AD 6.7.44; No.14 ARD-R/P 19.9.44; No.549 Sqn 22.4.45; No.6 AD 24.9.45; SOC 22.5.46; Cat.E storage 1.10.46; DAP 7.11.47 until 15.11.48

MD391 Spitfire LF.VIIIc (Merlin 66); Became **A58-431**; TOC/RAF 12.2.44 - To RAAF, arr Sydney 18.4.44; No.2 AD 20.4.44; No.14 ARD-R/P 12.8.44; No.14 ARD 8.9.44; No.7 R&SU 13.10.44; No.548 Sqn 6.8.45; No.6 AD 11.9.45; SOC 22.5.46; Cat.E storage 1.10.46; DAP 7.11.47 until 15.11.48

MD396 Spitfire LF.VIIIc (Merlin 66); Became **A58-432**; TOC/RAF 12.2.44 - To RAAF, arr Sydney 18.4.44; No.1 APU 20.4.44; No.1 AD 18.7.44; No.14 ARD-R/P 5.8.44; No.54 Sqn 13.8.44; No.548 Sqn 19.7.45; No.6 AD 10.9.45; SOC 22.5.46; Cat.E storage 1.10.46; DAP 7.11.47 until 15.11.48

MD399 Spitfire LF.VIIIc (Merlin 66); Became **A58-433**; TOC/RAF 15.2.44 - To RAAF, arr Sydney 18.4.44; No.2 AD 20.4.44; No.452 Sqn 28.6.44; No.457 Sqn (markings "CRC", personal aircraft of Wg Cdr Clive R Caldwell) 6.12.44; No.9 R&SU-R/P 12.12.44; No.7 R&SU 12.2.45; No.6 AD 27.3.45; SOC 22.5.46; Cat.E storage 1.10.46; DAP 7.11.47 until 15.11.48

MH306 Spitfire F.Vc/trop (Merlin 50); Became **A58-247**; TOC/RAF 31.7.43 - To RAAF, arr Australia 16.11.43; No.1 APU 23.11.43; No.1 AD 27.1.44; No.15 ARD-R/P 24.2.44; No.79 Sqn 3.3.44; No.6 AD 5.12.44; No.8 OTU 27.5.45; Swung on landing on ferry flight, Parkes 27.5.45; No.6 AD 28.11.45; SOC 22.5.46; Cat.E storage 1.10.46; DAP 26.11.47 until 15.11.48

MH566 Spitfire F.Vc/trop (Merlin 55); Became **A58-248**; TOC/RAF 30.7.43 - To RAAF, arr Melbourne 18.10.43; No.1 APU 28.10.43; No.1 AD 18.11.43; No.14 ARD-R/P 16.1.44; No.54 Sqn 7.2.44; No.452 Sqn 4.4.44; Air combat 12.6.44 (F/O KM Gamble); No.14 ARD-R/P 1.8.44; No.85 Sqn ('SH-Z') 24.9.44; No.17 R&SU 27.9.44; No.85 Sqn ('SH-Z') 2.11.44; Engine failed, force-landed, Pearce 16.8.45 (S/Ldr KE James); No.6 AD 11.10.45; SOC 22.5.46; Cat.E storage 1.10.46; DAP 26.11.47 until 15.11.48

MH585 Spitfire F.Vc/trop (Merlin 55); Became **A58-249**; TOC/RAF 31.7.43 - To RAAF, arr Melbourne 18.10.43; No.1 APU 25.10.43; No.1 AD 19.11.43; No.14 ARD-R/P 9.12.43; No.452 Sqn 6.1.44; Wheels-up landed Strauss 5.4.44; No.7 R&SU 5.4.44; No.452 Sqn 24.4.44; No.457 Sqn 15.7.44; No.14 ARD-R/P 1.8.44; CGS 11.9.44; No.6 AD 15.10.45; SOC 22.5.46; Cat.E storage 1.10.46; DAP 26.11.47 until 15.11.48

MH586 Spitfire F.Vc/trop (Merlin 55); Became **A58-250**; TOC/RAF 7.8.43 - To RAAF, arr Australia 16.11.43; No.1 APU 23.11.43; No.1 AD 16.12.43; No.14 ARD-R/P

16.1.44; No.457 Sqn ('SH-K', named '*Marge*') 4.2.44; No.7 R&SU 6.5.44; No.6 AD 16.7.44; No.85 Sqn ('SH-K') 6.11.44; Swung on landing, Pearce 23.5.45; No.17 R&SU 31.5.45; Cca 5.7.45

MH587 Spitfire F.Vc/trop (Merlin 55); Became **A58-251**; TOC/RAF 7.8.43 - To RAAF, arr Melbourne 21.10.43; No.1 APU 25.10.43; No.1 AD 24.11.43; No.14 ARD-R/P 9.12.43; No.452 Sqn 17.12.43; Overshot landing Drysdale 12.2.44; No.6 AD 4.8.44; No.85 Sqn 10.12.44; No.6 AD 12.10.45; SOC 22.5.46; Cat.E storage 1.10.46; DAP 26.11.47 until 15.11.48

MH588 Spitfire F.Vc/trop (Merlin 55); Became **A58-252**; TOC/RAF 5.8.43 - To RAAF, arr Melbourne 21.10.43; No.1 AD 26.10.43; No.15 ARD-R/P 20.6.44; No.79 Sqn 7.8.44; Tyre burst landing, swung off strip, Momote, 4.10.44; Cca 11.12.44

MH589 Spitfire F.Vc/trop (Merlin 55); Became **A58-253**; Presentation aircraft '*RIMA I*'; TOC/RAF 8.8.43 - To RAAF, arr Melbourne 21.10.43; No.1 APU 25.10.43; No.1 AD 10.11.43; No.2 OTU 7.12.43; No.8 OTU 1.11.44; No.6 AD 14.11.45; SOC 22.5.46; Cat.E storage 1.10.46; DAP 26.11.47 until 15.11.48

MH591 Spitfire F.Vc/trop (Merlin 55); Became **A58-254**; Presentation aircraft '*RIMA II*'; TOC/RAF 8.8.43 - To RAAF, arr Melbourne 21.10.43; No.1 APU 25.10.43; No.1 AD 26.11.43; No.14 ARD-R/P 9.12.43; No.452 Sqn ('QY-F') 5.1.44; Undercarriage collapsed taxying Strauss 5.2.44; No.7 R&SU 17.2.44; No.452 Sqn ('QY-V') 9.3.44; No.457 Sqn 15.7.44; No.14 ARD-R/P 1.8.44; CGS 11.9.44; Undercarriage jammed up, belly-landed, Cressy (SW of Melbourne) 18.4.45 (S/Ldr LT Spence of 452 Sqn); No.6 AD 13.12.45; SOC 22.5.46; Cat.E storage 1.10.46; DAP 26.11.47 until 15.11.48

Spitfire F.Vc/trop A58-254 QY-F (ex MH591) of No.452 Sqn RAAF, possibly on 5th February 1944 when the undercarriage collapsed whilst taxying at Strauss.

MH642 Spitfire F.Vc/trop (Merlin 55); Became **A58-255**; TOC/RAF 31.7.43 - To RAAF, arr Melbourne 18.10.43; No.1 APU 25.10.43; No.1 AD 18.11.43; No.2 OTU 28.11.43; Force-landed wheels-up 7m NW of Mildura 9.5.44; No.8 OTU ('255') 1.11.44; Engine failed, force-landed Forbes 16.3.45; Force-landed, crashed, 60m N of Parkes 1.6.45; Cca 5.7.46

MH643 Spitfire F.Vc/trop (Merlin 55); Became **A58-256**; TOC/RAF 31.7.43 - To RAAF, arr Melbourne 18.10.43; No.1 APU 25.10.43; No.1 AD 3.12.43; No.15 ARD-R/P 9.1.44; No.79 Sqn 10.2.44; Tyre burst landing Los Negros 19.4.44; No.6 AD 5.12.44; No.8 OTU 3.1.45; No.6 AD 20.11.45; SOC 22.5.46; Cat.E storage 1.10.46; DAP 26.11.47 until 15.11.48

MH644 Spitfire F.Vc/trop (Merlin 55); Became **A58-257**; TOC/RAF 31.7.43 - To RAAF, arr Melbourne 18.10.43; No.1 APU 3.11.43; No.1 AD 18.11.43; No.14 ARD-R/P 29.11.43; No.452 Sqn 15.12.43; No.457 Sqn 15.7.44; No.14 ARD-R/P 1.8.44; No.85 Sqn 24.9.44; No.17 R&SU 28.9.44; No.85 Sqn ('SH-U') 16.11.44; Hit by EE835 (A58-137) after landing Guildford, port side completely destroyed, Cat E 26.2.45; No.4 CRD 8.3.45; Cca 24.3.45

MH645 Spitfire F.Vc/trop (Merlin 55); Became **A58-258**; TOC/RAF 31.7.43 - To RAAF, arr Australia 16.11.43; No.2 AD 16.11.43; No.15 ARD-R/P 19.2.44; Hit tree during low flying, Chatswood, NSW 2.3.44; No.2 AD/TU (No.2 AP) 2.3.44; No.2 AD 1.4.44; No.2 OTU 7.8.44; No.1 AD 12.8.44; No.2 OTU 29.8.44; No.8 OTU 1.11.44; No.6 AD 14.11.45; SOC 22.5.46; Cat.E storage 1.10.46; DAP 26.11.47 until 15.11.48

MH646 Spitfire F.Vc/trop (Merlin 55); Became **A58-259**; TOC/RAF 31.7.43 - To RAAF, arr Australia 16.11.43; No.1 APU 23.11.43; No.1 AD 30.12.43; No.14 ARD-R/P 16.1.44; No.452 Sqn 30.1.44; No.7 R&SU 22.2.44; No.457 Sqn 15.7.44; No.14 ARD-R/P 1.8.44; No.14 ARD 3.10.44; No.6 AD 21.12.44; Cca 16.10.45

MT502 Spitfire LF.VIIIc (Merlin 66); Became **A58-505**; TOC/RAF 30.3.44 - To RAAF, arr Sydney 10.7.44; No.2 AD 21.7.44; No.6 AD 19.8.44; No.79 Sqn ('UP-S') 20.12.44; No.6 AD 15.1.45; No.79 Sqn 21.4.45; No.6 AD 30.10.45; SOC 22.5.46; Cat.E storage 1.10.46; DAP 7.11.47 until 15.11.48

MT503 Spitfire LF.VIIIc (Merlin 66); Became **A58-506**; TOC/RAF 4.4.44 - To RAAF, arr Sydney 10.7.44; No.2 AD 21.7.44; No.6 AD 9.10.44; No.79 Sqn 6.12.44; No.6 AD 15.1.45; No.79 Sqn 21.4.45; No.6 AD 30.10.45; SOC 22.5.46; Cat.E storage 1.10.46; DAP 7.11.47 until 15.11.48

MT508 Spitfire LF.VIIIc (Merlin 66); Became **A58-507**; TOC/RAF 30.3.44 - To RAAF, arr Sydney 10.7.44; No.2 AD 20.7.44; No.6 AD 25.8.44; No.79 Sqn 10.12.44; No.6 AD 15.1.45; No.79 Sqn 15.3.45; No.6 AD 30.10.45; SOC 22.5.46; Cat.E storage 1.10.46; DAP 7.11.47 until 15.11.48

MT509 Spitfire LF.VIIIc (Merlin 66); Became **A58-489**; TOC/RAF 6.4.44 - To RAAF, arr Brisbane 27.6.44; No.3 AD 4.7.44; No.6 AD 6.10.44; No.79 Sqn ('UP-L') 6.12.44; No.6 AD 15.1.45; No.79 Sqn 23.3.45; Starboard wing hit by flak over Boebale Is 10.5.45; No.9 R&SU 11.5.45; No.79 Sqn 27.5.45; Flew into water and broke up, Galela Lake, Halmaheras 22.9.45; SOC 9.11.45

MT510 Spitfire LF.VIIIc (Merlin 66); Became **A58-495**; TOC/RAF 9.4.44 - To RAAF, arr Melbourne 7.7.44; No.1 AD 12.7.44; No.6 AD 24.8.44; No.79 Sqn 3.1.45; No.6 AD 15.1.45; No.79 Sqn 9.3.45; No.6 AD 5.11.45; SOC 22.5.46; Cat.E storage 1.10.46; DAP 7.11.47; DSD 15.11.48

MT511 Spitfire LF.VIIIc (Merlin 66); Became **A58-490**; TOC/RAF 6.4.44 - To RAAF, arr Brisbane 27.6.44; No.3 AD 4.7.44; No.14 ARD-R/P 16.10.44; No.9 R&SU 6.5.45; No.452 Sqn 6.5.45; No.79 Sqn 15.9.45; No.6 AD 2.11.45; SOC 22.5.46; Cat.E storage 1.10.46; DAP 7.11.47 until 15.11.48

MT512 Spitfire LF.VIIIc (Merlin 66); Became **A58-508**; TOC/RAF 31.3.44 - To RAAF, arr Sydney 10.7.44; No.2 AD 11.7.44; No.6 AD 19.8.44; No.79 Sqn 9.1.45; No.6 AD 15.1.45; No.79 Sqn 23.3.45; No.6 AD 30.10.45; SOC 22.5.46; Cat.E storage 1.10.46; DAP 7.11.47 until 15.11.48

MT513 Spitfire LF.VIIIc (Merlin 66); Became **A58-509**; TOC/RAF 30.3.44 - To RAAF, arr Sydney 10.7.44; No.2 AD 21.7.44; No.6 AD 6.9.44; No.79 Sqn 6.12.44; No.6 AD 15.1.45; No.79 Sqn 26.3.45; No.6 AD 26.10.45; Brakes failed landing, overshot, hit fence, Rockhampton 29.10.45; Cca 31.10.46

MT514 Spitfire LF.VIIIc (Merlin 66); Became **A58-522**; TOC/RAF 27.5.44 - To RAAF, arr Sydney 27.7.44; No.2 AD 29.7.44; No.6 AD 8.9.44; No.79 Sqn ('UP-A') 6.12.44; No.6 AD 15.1.45; No.79 Sqn ('UP-A, named '*Hal Far*') 21.4.45; No.6 AD 5.11.45; SOC 22.5.46; Cat.E storage 1.10.46; DAP 7.11.47 until 15.11.48

MT517 Spitfire LF.VIIIc (Merlin 66); Became **A58-491**; TOC/RAF 6.4.44 - To RAAF, arr Brisbane 27.6.44; No.3

AD 4.7.44; SOC 22.5.46; Cat.E storage 1.10.46; DAP 7.10.44 until 16.9.49

MT518 Spitfire LF.VIIIc (Merlin 66); Became **A58-492**; TOC/RAF 6.4.44 - To RAAF, arr Brisbane 27.6.44; No.3 AD 4.7.44; No.6 AD 14.11.44; No.79 Sqn ('UP-U') 6.12.44; No.6 AD 15.1.45; No.79 Sqn ('UP-B', named '*Mac III*', pilot F/O H Kennare) 9.3.45; No.6 AD 1.10.45; SOC 22.5.46; DAP 7.11.47 until 15.11.48

MT519 Spitfire LF.VIIIc (Merlin 66); Became **A58-515**; TOC/RAF 6.4.44 - To RAAF, arr Sydney 17.7.44; No.2 AD 24.7.44; No.9 R&SU-R/P 23.7.45; Wheels-up landed 2.8.45; No.457 Sqn 3.8.45; No.9 R&SU 11.8.45; No.457 Sqn 17.9.45; No.1 R&SU 1.11.45; Cca 11.1.46

MT524 Spitfire LF.VIIIc (Merlin 66); Became **A58-422**; TOC/RAF 19.12.43 - To RAAF, arr Brisbane 7.4.44; No.3 AD 26.4.44; No.14 ARD-R/P 29.8.44; No.548 Sqn 20.8.45; No.6 AD 11.9.45; SOC 22.5.46; Cat.E storage 1.10.46; DAP until 15.11.48

MT525 Spitfire LF.VIIIc (Merlin 66); Became **A58-423**; TOC/RAF 2.12.43 - To RAAF, arr Brisbane 7.4.44; No.3 AD 26.4.44; SOC 22.5.46; Cat.E storage 1.10.46; DAP 7.10.48 until 10.12.48

MT539 Spitfire LF.VIIIc (Merlin 66); Became **A58-476**; TOC/RAF 29.2.44 - To RAAF, arr Melbourne 13.6.44; No.1 APU 20.6.44; No.1 AD 23.7.44; No.14 ARD-R/P 5.8.44; No.54 Sqn ('DL-W') 9.8.44; No.6 AD 10.3.45; SOC 22.5.46; Cat.E storage 1.10.46; DAP 7.11.47 until 15.11.48

MT540 Spitfire LF.VIIIc (Merlin 66); Became **A58-510**; TOC/RAF 18.3.44 - To RAAF, arr Sydney 10.7.44; No.2 AD 21.7.44; No.14 ARD-R/P 11.9.44; No.22 R&SU 9.1.45; No.452 Sqn 10.2.45; Crash-landed Croydon Strip, Tarakan 18.10.45; No.11 R&SU 22.10.45; Cca 3.12.45

MT541 Spitfire LF.VIIIc (Merlin 66); Became **A58-477**; TOC/RAF 29.2.44 - To RAAF, arr Melbourne 13.6.44; No.1 APU 19.6.44; No.1 AD 19.7.44; No.457 Sqn 15.8.44; No.452 Sqn 14.12.44; No.6 AD 6.11.45; SOC 22.5.46; Cat.E storage 1.10.46; DAP 7.11.47 until 15.11.48

MT542 Spitfire LF.VIIIc (Merlin 66); Became **A58-478**; TOC/RAF 2.3.44 - To RAAF, arr Melbourne 13.6.44; No.1 APU 19.6.44; No.1 AD 11.7.44; No.457 Sqn 29.7.44; No.452 Sqn 10.12.44; Collided with MT550 (A58-525) & MT781 (A58-534) after landing Merauke 17.12.44; SOC 1.2.45

MT543 Spitfire LF.VIIIc (Merlin 66); Became **A58-479**; TOC/RAF 29.2.44 - To RAAF, arr Melbourne 13.6.44; No.1 APU 27.6.44; No.1 AD 24.7.44; No.14 ARD-R/P 5.8.44; No.54 Sqn 13.8.44; Engine failed on approach after air test, dived vertically into ground 1/2m Darwin 17.6.45 (F/O F Thomas killed); Cca 11.7.45

MT545 Spitfire LF.VIIIc (Merlin 66); Became **A58-465**; TOC/RAF 28.1.44 - To RAAF, arr Melbourne 19.5.44; No.1 APU 23.5.44; No.1 AD 28.6.44; No.457 Sqn ('ZP-H') 17.7.44; No.9 R&SU 19.12.44; No.452 Sqn ('QY-K') 4.5.45; Crashed on sweep over Semaloemoeng Is, N of Tarakan Is, off NE Borneo, burnt out 2.7.45; SOC 18.7.45

MT547 Spitfire LF.VIIIc (Merlin 66); Became **A58-523**; TOC/RAF 21.5.44 - To RAAF, arr Sydney 27.7.44; No.2 AD 3.8.44; No.5 OTU 10.10.44; No.8 OTU 27.11.44; Force-landed Parkes 14.8.45; No.6 AD 30.11.45; SOC 22.5.46; Cat.E storage 1.10.46; DAP 7.11.47 until 15.11.48

MT548 Spitfire LF.VIIIc (Merlin 66); Became **A58-539**; TOC/RAF 25.5.44 - To RAAF, arr Brisbane 9.8.44; No.3 AD 21.8.44; No.6 AD 14.11.44; No.79 Sqn 6.12.44; No.9 R&SU-R/P 23.7.45; No.79 Sqn 29.7.45; No.6 AD 30.9.45; SOC 22.5.46; Cat.E storage; DAP 7.11.47 until 15.11.48

MT549 Spitfire LF.VIIIc (Merlin 66); Became **A58-524**; TOC/RAF 22.5.44 - To RAAF, arr Sydney 27.7.44; No.2 AD 31.7.44; No.14 ARD-R/P 16.10.44; No.9 R&SU 7.12.44; No.452 Sqn 10.12.44; Engine cut on night patrol, force-landed, undershot, Pitoe Morotai 19.1.45; No.11 R&SU 25.1.45; Cca 3.3.45

MT550 Spitfire LF.VIIIc (Merlin 66); Became **A58-525**; TOC/RAF 27.5.44 - To RAAF, arr Sydney 27.7.44; No.2 AD 29.7.44; No.14 ARD-R/P 16.10.44; No.9 R&SU-R/P 7.12.44; No.452 Sqn 10.12.44; Collided with MT781 (A58-534) & MT542 (A58-478) after landing, Merauke, NG on 17.12.44; Cca 12.1.45

MT552 Spitfire LF.VIIIc (Merlin 66); Became **A58-526**; TOC/RAF 27.5.44 - To RAAF, arr Sydney 27.7.44; No.2 AD 29.7.44; No.6 AD 9.9.44; No.79 Sqn ('UP-L') 6.12.44; No.6 AD 15.1.45; No.79 Sqn ('UP-L', named '*AVAGROG*') 21.4.45; Ran into stationary JG689 (A58-487) taxying Morotai 17.9.45; Cca 18.12.45

MT593 Spitfire LF.VIIIc (Merlin 66); Became **A58-493**; TOC/RAF 6.4.44 - To RAAF, arr Brisbane 27.6.44; No.3 AD 4.7.44; SOC 22.5.46; Cat.E storage 1.10.46; DAP 7.10.48; DSD 16.9.49

MT594 Spitfire LF.VIIIc (Merlin 66); Became **A58-517**; TOC/RAF 6.4.44 - To RAAF, arr Melbourne 15.7.44; No.1 AD 19.7.44; No.6 AD 24.8.44; No.79 Sqn ('UP-F'; B-Flt, green spinner, named '*HAVA-GO-JO !!*') 10.12.44; No.6 AD 15.1.45; No.79 Sqn 9.3.45; No.9 R&SU 2.8.45; No.79 Sqn 15.9.45; No.6 AD 30.10.45; SOC 22.5.46; Cat.E storage 1.10.46; DAP 7.11.47 until 15.11.48

MT596 Spitfire LF.VIIIc (Merlin 66); Became **A58-496**; TOC/RAF 6.4.44 - To RAAF, arr Melbourne 7.7.44; No.1 AD 16.7.44; No.14 ARD-R/P 15.8.44; No.9 R&SU-R/P 11.12.44; No.452 Sqn 13.12.44; No.6 AD 6.11.45; SOC 22.5.46; Cat.E storage 1.10.46; DAP 7.11.47; DSD 15.11.48

MT607 Spitfire LF.VIIIc (Merlin 66); Became **A58-497**; TOC/RAF 8.4.44 - To RAAF, arr Melbourne 7.7.44; No.1 AD 12.7.44; No.14 ARD-R/P 15.8.44; No.9 R&SU-R/P 12.10.44; No.457 Sqn ('RG-V', marked "*Grey Nurse*") 7.11.44 (Wg Cdr RHM Gibbes aircraft); No.9 R&SU 17.11.44; Engine caught fire in air, crash-landed Sattler 4.12.44; Cca 22.12.44

MT618 Spitfire LF.VIIIc (Merlin 66); Became **A58-518**; TOC/RAF 23.4.44 - To RAAF, arr Melbourne 15.7.44; No.1 AD 19.7.44; No.14 ARD-R/P 6.9.44; No.9 R&SU 20.10.44; No.452 Sqn ('QY-O') 10.12.44; Air combat

Spitfire LF.VIIIc, A58-517/UP-F, of No.79 Sqn RAAF, January 1945

24.12.44 (F/O JA Pretty); FTR raid on Tawao over NE Borneo 10.7.45; SOC 25.7.45

MT620 Spitfire LF.VIIIc (Merlin 66); Became **A58-519**; TOC/RAF 28.4.44 - To RAAF, arr Melbourne 15.7.44; No.1 AD 19.7.44; No.14 ARD-R/P 22.9.44; No.9 R&SU-R/P 6.12.44; No.452 Sqn 14.12.44; Engine failed on patrol over Halmaheras, abandoned over sea off Morotai 24.12.44; SOC 29.12.44

MT621 Spitfire LF.VIIIc (Merlin 66); Became **A58-540**; TOC/RAF 29.4.44 - To RAAF, arr Brisbane 9.8.44; No.3 AD 21.8.44; No.14 ARD 8.11.44; No.22 R&SU-R/P 27.1.45; No.452 Sqn 10.2.45; No.6 AD 6.11.45; SOC 22.5.46; Cat.E storage 1.10.46; DAP 7.11.47 until 15.11.48

MT622 Spitfire LF.VIIIc (Merlin 66); Became **A58-541**; TOC/RAF 28.4.44 - To RAAF, arr Brisbane 9.8.44; No.3 AD 21.8.44; SOC 22.5.46; Cat.E storage 1.10.46; DAP 7.10.48 until 16.9.49

MT624 Spitfire LF.VIIIc (Merlin 66); Became **A58-498**; TOC/RAF 28.4.44 - To RAAF, arr Melbourne 7.7.44; No.1 AD 12.7.44; No.14 ARD-R/P 15.8.44; No.54 Sqn ('DL-D') 7.12.44; No.6 AD 11.9.45; SOC 22.5.46; Cat.E storage 1.10.46; DAP until 15.11.48

MT626 Spitfire LF.VIIIc (Merlin 66); Became **A58-499**; TOC/RAF 30.4.44 - To RAAF, arr Melbourne 7.7.44; No.1 AD 16.7.44; No.1 APU 22.8.44; Crashed in forced landing on test, Laverton 21.5.45; 1 CRD 25.5.45; Cca 5.7.45

MT630 Spitfire LF.VIIIc (Merlin 66); Became **A58-542**; TOC/RAF 7.5.44 - To RAAF, arr Brisbane 9.8.44; No.3 AD 21.8.44; SOC 22.5.46; Cat.E storage 1.10.46; DAP 7.10.48 until 16.9.49

MT632 Spitfire LF.VIIIc (Merlin 66); Became **A58-527**; TOC/RAF 3.4.44 - To RAAF, arr Sydney 27.7.44; No.2 AD 31.7.44; No.9 R&SU-R/P 27.6.45; No.79 Sqn 15.9.45; No.6 AD 2.11.45; SOC 22.5.46; Cat.E storage 1.10.46; DAP 7.11.47 until 15.11.48

MT635 Spitfire LF.VIIIc (Merlin 66); Became **A58-543**; TOC/RAF 7.5.44 - To RAAF, arr Brisbane 9.8.44; No.3 AD 21.8.44; No.6 AD 14.11.44; No.79 Sqn ('UP-M' & 'UP-H') 9.3.45; No.6 AD 30.10.45; SOC 24.5.46; DAP 7.11.47 until 15.11.48

MT649 Spitfire LF.VIIIc (Merlin 66); Became **A58-500**; TOC/RAF 26.4.44 - To RAAF, arr Melbourne 7.7.44; No.1 AD 16.7.44; No.14 ARD-R/P 15.8.44; No.54 Sqn ('DL-R'); No.9 R&SU 26.10.44; No.452 Sqn ('QY-D') 10.12.44; No.9 R&SU 6.5.45; No.60 OBU 30.10.45; Cca 12.2.46

MT650 Spitfire LF.VIIIc (Merlin 66); Became **A58-544**; TOC/RAF 23.4.44 - To RAAF, arr Brisbane 9.8.44; No.3 AD 21.8.44; No.6 AD 15.11.44; No.79 Sqn ('UP-R') 1.1.45; Engine cut of ferry flight, wheels-up landing, Gorrie 10.2.45; No.14 ARD 12.2.45; Cca 8.3.45

MT655 Spitfire LF.VIIIc (Merlin 66); Became **A58-520**; TOC/RAF 23.4.44 - To RAAF, arr Melbourne 15.7.44; No.1 AD 19.7.44; No.14 ARD-R/P 6.9.44; No.9 R&SU 23.10.44; No.452 Sqn 10.12.44; Undercarriage leg collapsed on landing, Merauke, NG 18.12.44; Cca 12.2.45

MT658 Spitfire LF.VIIIc (Merlin 66); Became **A58-545**; TOC/RAF 29.4.44 - To RAAF, arr Brisbane 9.8.44; No.3 AD 21.8.44; No.6 AD 11.12.44; No.79 Sqn 20.12.44; No.6 AD 15.1.45; No.79 Sqn 9.3.45; Hit by ground fire over Miti strip, engine cut, baled out over sea NW of Halmahera Is 12.4.45; SOC 23.4.45

MT672 Spitfire LF.VIIIc (Merlin 66); Became **A58-531**; TOC/RAF 27.5.44 - To RAAF, arr Sydney 27.7.44; No.2 AD 30.7.44; No.6 AD 2.10.44; No.79 Sqn 3.1.45; No.6 AD 15.1.45; No.79 Sqn 9.3.45; Taxied into petrol drum on runway, Morotai 1.9.45; No.60 OBU 19.10.45; Cca 18.12.45

MT673 Spitfire LF.VIIIc (Merlin 66); Became **A58-546**; TOC/RAF 23.5.44 - To RAAF, arr Brisbane 9.8.44; No.3 AD 21.8.44; No.6 AD 29.12.44; No.79 Sqn 9.1.45; No.6 AD 15.1.45; No.79 Sqn 23.3.45; Lost control in cloud during sweep, dived into ground N of Merauke, New Guinea 28.4.45; SOC 31.5.45

MT675 Spitfire LF.VIIIc (Merlin 66); Became **A58-528**; TOC/RAF 18.5.44 - To RAAF, arr Sydney 27.7.44; No.2 AD 29.7.44; No.14 ARD-R/P 11.9.44; No.457 Sqn 26.12.44; No.452 Sqn (markings "CRC", personal aircraft of Wg Cdr Clive R Caldwell) 26.12.44; Crashed Clark Field, East Manila, Philippines 3.5.45; No.9 R&SU 9.5.45; Cca 12.7.45

MT681 Spitfire LF.VIIIc (Merlin 66); Became **A58-547**; TOC/RAF 23.5.44 - To RAAF, despatched 9.6.44, arr Brisbane 9.8.44; No.3 AD 21.8.44; No.6 AD 14.11.44; No.79 Sqn 3.1.45; No.6 AD 15.1.45; No.79 Sqn 9.3.45; No.6 AD 6.11.45; SOC 22.5.46; Cat.E storage 1.10.46; DAP 7.11.47 until 15.11.48
NOTE: As "MT684" in RAAF records, but that was a HF. VIII and arrived later

MT682 Spitfire LF.VIIIc (Merlin 66); Became **A58-529**; TOC/RAF 26.5.44 - To RAAF, arr Sydney 27.7.44; No.2 AD 29.7.44; No.14 ARD-R/P 23.9.44; No.8 CRD 3.9.45; Cca 1.10.45 - Buried parts recovered from Gorrie airfield by Alec Wilson, Romsey, Vic; Currently at Yunta, South Australia for restoration of MD338 - **SURVIVOR**

MT684 Spitfire HF.VIIIc (Merlin 70); Became **A58-603**; TOC/RAF 27.6.44 - To RAAF, arr Brisbane 12.9.44; No.3 AD 19.9.44; No.457 Sqn ('ZP-S') 20.12.44; Engine lost power, force-landed, crashed, Labuan airfield 27.9.45; Cca 18.10.45

MT703 Spitfire LF.VIIIc (Merlin 66); Became **A58-530**; TOC/RAF 27.5.44 - To RAAF, arr Sydney 27.7.44; No.2 AD 29.7.44; No.14 ARD-R/P 11.9.44; No.9 R&SU 12.10.44; No.452 Sqn 10.12.44; Crashed on landing, Pitoe, Morotai 12.3.45; No.9 R&SU 12.3.45; Cca 19.4.45

MT748 Spitfire HF.VIIIc (Merlin 70); Became **A58-678**; TOC/RAF 10.9.44 - To RAAF, arr Sydney 24.11.44; No.2 AD 29.11.44; Storage 7.5.46; SOC 24.5.46; Cat.E storage 1.10.46; DAP 24.6.48; DSD 6.9.49

MT767 Spitfire LF.VIIIc (Merlin 66); Became **A58-548**; TOC/RAF 16.5.44 - To RAAF, arr Brisbane 9.8.44; No.3 AD 21.8.44; SOC 22.5.46; Cat.E storage 1.10.46; DAP 7.10.48 until 16.9.49

MT771 Spitfire LF.VIIIc (Merlin 66); Became **A58-532**; TOC/RAF 18.5.44 - To RAAF, arr Sydney 27.7.44; No.2 AD 29.7.44; No.14 ARD-R/P 23.9.44; No.9 R&SU-R/P 26.12.44; No.452 Sqn ('QY-W') 26.12.44; Fuel system failed, ditched off North Borneo 30.8.45; No.9 R&SU 1.9.45; Cca 12.10.45
NOTE: As "MT770" in RAAF records, but this operated over MTO & cat FB/E (SOC) in 3.45; However, MT771 went to Australia

MT778 Spitfire LF.VIIIc (Merlin 66); Became **A58-533**; TOC/RAF 22.5.44 - To RAAF, arr Sydney 27.7.44; No.2 AD 29.7.44; No.2 AD/TU (No.2 AP) 13.9.44; No.2 AD 2.10.44; No.14 ARD-R/P 16.10.44; No.9 R&SU-R/P 5.12.44; No.452 Sqn 10.12.44; Undershot landing, hit bank of coral and caught fire, Pitoe, Morotai 22.5.45; No.9 R&SU 23.5.45; Cca 25.6.45

MT779 Spitfire LF.VIIIc (Merlin 66); Became **A58-549**; TOC/RAF 22.5.44 - To RAAF, arr Brisbane 9.8.44; No.3 AD 21.8.44; SOC 22.5.46; Cat.E storage 1.10.46; DAP 7.10.48 until 16.9.49

MT781 Spitfire LF.VIIIc (Merlin 66); Became **A58-534**; TOC/RAF 19.5.44 - To RAAF, arr Sydney 27.7.44; No.2 AD 31.7.44; No.14 ARD-R/P 16.10.44; No.9 R&SU-R/P 5.12.44; No.452 Sqn 10.12.44; Collided with MT550 (A58-525) & MT542 (A58-478) landing Merauke 17.12.44; Cca 4.9.46

MT782 Spitfire LF.VIIIc (Merlin 66); Became **A58-535**; TOC/RAF 22.5.44 - To RAAF, arr Sydney 27.7.44; No.2 AD 31.7.44; No.5 OTU 2.10.44; Take-off collision 20.10.44; No.2 R&SU 22.6.45; No.2 AD 27.8.45; SOC 24.5.46; Cat.E storage 1.10.46; DAP 24.6.49; DSD 6.9.49

MT787 Spitfire LF.VIIIc (Merlin 66); Became **A58-550**; TOC/RAF 25.5.44 - To RAAF, arr Brisbane 9.8.44; No.3

Spitfire HF.VIIIc, A58-614/ZP-Q, of No.457 Sqn RAAF, May/June 1945

AD 21.8.44; SOC 22.5.46; Cat.E storage 1.10.46; DAP 7.10.48 until 16.9.49

MT788 Spitfire LF.VIIIc (Merlin 66); Became **A58-536**; TOC/RAF 25.5.44 - To RAAF, arr Sydney 27.7.44; No.2 AD 31.7.44; No.5 OTU 2.10.44; No.8 OTU 27.11.44; No.6 AD 28.11.45; SOC 22.5.46; Cat.E storage 1.10.46; DAP 7.11.47 until 15.11.48

MT794 Spitfire LF.VIIIc (Merlin 66); Became **A58-537**; TOC/RAF 26.5.44 - To RAAF, arr Sydney 27.7.44; No.2 AD 31.7.44; No.14 ARD-R/P 23.9.44; No.9 R&SU 20.10.44; No.452 Sqn 20.10.44; Overshot landing, went into ditch, overturned, Croydon Strip, Tarakan 14.7.45; No.9 R&SU 17.7.45; No.16 ARD 28.7.45; Cca 7.8.45

MT816 Spitfire HF.VIIIc (Merlin 70); Became **A58-604**; TOC/RAF 15.6.44 - To RAAF, arr Brisbane 12.9.44; No.3 AD 16.9.44; No.457 Sqn ('ZP-D', marked "*Grey Nurse*") 15.12.44; Engine failed on take-off 13.8.45; Crashed on landing Pitoe, Morotai 21.10.45; No.60 OBU 30.10.45; Cca 13.12.45

MT817 Spitfire HF.VIIIc (Merlin 70); Became **A58-605**; TOC/RAF 16.6.44 - To RAAF, arr Brisbane 12.9.44; No.3 AD 16.9.44; No.457 Sqn 20.12.44; No.9 R&SU 4.5.45; No.457 Sqn 19.5.45; No.9 R&SU 3.6.45; No.457 Sqn 24.6.45; No.6 AD 30.10.45; SOC 22.5.46; Cat.E storage 1.10.46; DAP 7.11.47 until 15.11.48

MT819 Spitfire HF.VIIIc (Merlin 70); Became **A58-606**; TOC/RAF 30.6.44 - To RAAF, arr Brisbane 12.9.44; No.3 AD 18.9.44; No.457 Sqn ('ZP-W', marked "*Grey Nurse*", named '*MAJIE BULLET*') 20.12.44; Damaged by shrapnel when bomb-laden B-24 blew up on hardstanding 24.2.45; Wheels-up landing from bombing and strafing raid, Labuan 14.7.45 (S/Ldr Bruce Watson); No.9 R&SU 3.8.45; No.6 AD 30.10.45; SOC 22.5.46; Cat.E storage 1.10.46; DAP 7.11.47 until 15.11.48

MT820 Spitfire HF.VIIIc (Merlin 70); Became **A58-607**; TOC/RAF 27.6.44 - To RAAF, arr Brisbane 12.9.44; No.3 AD 16.9.44; No.457 Sqn 20.12.44; No.9 R&SU 7.5.45; No.457 Sqn 1.6.45; No.6 AD 22.10.45; Engine cut on ferry flight, abandoned over sea between Morotai and Biak 23.10.45; SOC 10.12.45

MT821 Spitfire HF.VIIIc (Merlin 70); Became **A58-608**; TOC/RAF 20.6.44 - To RAAF, arr Brisbane 12.9.44; No.3 AD 16.9.44; SOC 22.5.46; Cat.E storage 1.10.46; DAP 7.10.48 until 16.9.49

MT822 Spitfire HF.VIIIc (Merlin 70); Became **A58-609**; TOC/RAF 18.6.44 - To RAAF, arr Brisbane 12.9.44; No.3 AD 16.9.44; No.457 Sqn ('ZP-F') 20.12.44; Wingtip hit MT833 (A58-614) when landing 7.45; No.6 AD 30.10.45; SOC 22.5.46; Cat.E storage 1.10.46; DAP 7.11.47 until 15.11.48

MT825 Spitfire HF.VIIIc (Merlin 70); Became **A58-610**; TOC/RAF 4.7.44 - To RAAF, arr Brisbane 12.9.44; No.3 AD 16.9.44; No.457 Sqn 20.12.44; No.9 R&SU 17.9.45; No.1 R&SU 17.9.45; Cca 11.1.46

MT829 Spitfire HF.VIIIc (Merlin 70); Became **A58-611**; TOC/RAF 7.7.44 - To RAAF, arr Brisbane 12.9.44; No.3 AD 16.9.44; No.457 Sqn ('ZP-B') 15.12.44; No.1 R&SU 1.11.45; No.84 OBU 17.12.45; Cca 11.1.46

MT830 Spitfire HF.VIIIc (Merlin 70); Became **A58-612**; TOC/RAF 6.7.44 - To RAAF, arr Brisbane 12.9.44; No.3 AD 16.9.44; SOC 22.5.46; Cat.E storage 1.10.46; DAP 7.10.48; DSD 16.9.49

MT831 Spitfire HF.VIIIc (Merlin 70); Became **A58-613**; TOC/RAF 14.7.44 - To RAAF, arr Brisbane 12.9.44; No.3 AD 16.9.44; No.457 Sqn 20.12.44; No.9 R&SU 7.5.45; No.60 OBU 30.10.45; Cca 12.2.45

MT833 Spitfire HF.VIIIc (Merlin 70); Became **A58-614**; TOC/RAF 7.7.44 - To RAAF, arr Brisbane 12.9.44; No.3 AD 16.9.44; No.457 Sqn ('ZP-Q', marked "*Grey Nurse*") 15.12.44; Hit by MT822 (A58-609) landing 7.45; No.9 R&SU 7.7.45; No.457 Sqn ('ZP-Q') 17.9.45; No.1 R&SU 1.11.45; Cca 11.1.46

MT834 Spitfire HF.VIIIc (Merlin 70); Became **A58-615**; TOC/RAF 8.7.44 - To RAAF, arr Brisbane 12.9.44; No.3 AD 16.9.44; No.457 Sqn ('ZP-Y', marked "*Grey Nurse*") 15.12.44; No.9 R&SU 7.5.45; No.60 OBU 30.10.45; Cca 12.2.46

MT835 Spitfire HF.VIIIc (Merlin 70); Became **A58-724**; TOC/RAF 15.7.44 - To RAAF, arr Brisbane 5.3.45; No.3 AD 12.3.45; SOC 22.5.46; Cat.E storage 1.10.46; DAP 7.10.48; DSD 16.9.49

MT890 Spitfire HF.VIIIc (Merlin 70); Became **A58-715**; TOC/RAF 9.9.44 - To RAAF, arr Sydney 1.1.45; No.2 AD 22.1.45; Storage 7.5.46; SOC 24.5.46; Cat.E storage 1.10.46; DAP 24.6.48; DSD 9.49

MT891 Spitfire HF.VIIIc (Merlin 70); Became **A58-757**; TOC/RAF 9.9.44 - To RAAF, arr Sydney 14.6.45; No.2 AD 16.6.45; Storage 7.5.46; SOC 24.5.46; Cat.E storage 1.10.46; DAP 24.6.48 until 6.9.49

MT892 Spitfire HF.VIIIc (Merlin 70); Became **A58-669**; TOC/RAF 10.9.44 - To RAAF, arr Brisbane 8.11.44; No.3 AD 13.11.44; Engine failed, force-landed and crashed Amberley 6.4.45; No.3 CRD; Cca 12.6.45

MT893 Spitfire HF.VIIIc (Merlin 70); Became **A58-679**; TOC/RAF 13.9.44 - To RAAF, arr Sydney 24.11.44; No.2 AD 5.12.44; No.6 AD 13.12.45; SOC 22.5.46; Cat.E storage 1.10.46; DAP 7.11.47; DSD 15.11.48

MT894 Spitfire HF.VIIIc (Merlin 70); Became **A58-680**; TOC/RAF 15.9.44 - To RAAF, arr Sydney 24.11.44; No.2 AD 28.11.44; Storage 7.5.46; SOC 24.5.46; Cat.E storage 1.10.46; DAP 24.6.48; DSD 6.9.49

MT895 Spitfire HF.VIIIc (Merlin 70); Became **A58-681**; TOC/RAF 17.9.44 - To RAAF, arr Sydney 24.11.44; No.2 AD 29.11.44; Storage 19.11.45; SOC 24.5.46; Cat.E storage 1.10.46; DAP 24.6.48; DSD 6.9.49

MT896 Spitfire HF.VIIIc (Merlin 70); Became **A58-652**; TOC/RAF 26.9.44 - To RAAF, arr Sydney 30.11.44; No.1 AD 30.11.44; No.9 R&SU-R/P 25.6.45; No.457 Sqn 5.8.45; No.1 R&SU 1.11.45; Cca 11.1.46

MT897 Spitfire HF.VIIIc (Merlin 70); Became **A58-653**; TOC/RAF 25.9.44 - To RAAF, arr Sydney 30.11.44; No.1 AD 30.11.44; No.9 R&SU-R/P 8.5.45; No.452 Sqn 16.5.45; No.18 R&SU 25.10.45; Cca 4.12.45

MT898 Spitfire HF.VIIIc (Merlin 70); Became **A58-749**; TOC/RAF 2.11.44 - To RAAF, arr Sydney 17.4.45; No.2

AD 11.5.45; Storage 7.5.46; SOC 24.5.46; Cat.E storage 1.10.46; DAP 24.6.48; DSD 6.9.49

MT899 Spitfire HF.VIIIc (Merlin 70); Became **A58-712**; TOC/RAF 25.9.44 - To RAAF, arr Brisbane 6.2.45; No.3 AD 12.2.45; SOC 22.5.46; Cat.E storage 1.10.46; DAP 7.10.48; DSD 16.9.49

MT900 Spitfire HF.VIIIc (Merlin 70); Became **A58-654**; TOC/RAF 26.9.44 - To RAAF, arr Sydney 30.11.44; No.1 AD 30.11.44; No.9 R&SU-R/P 22.6.45; No.79 Sqn; Hit tree while strafing on sweep and crashed, Toe Toeli River, Halmahaeras 2.8.45; SOC 29.8.45

MT910 Spitfire HF.VIIIc (Merlin 70); Became **A58-725**; TOC/RAF 23.10.44 - To RAAF, arr Brisbane 5.3.45; No.3 AD 12.3.45; SOC 22.5.46; Cat.E storage 1.10.46; DAP 7.10.48; DSD 16.9.49

MT914 Spitfire HF.VIIIc (Merlin 70); Became **A58-733**; TOC/RAF 23.10.44 - To RAAF, arr Sydney 29.3.45; No.2 AD 10.4.45; Storage 7.5.46; Cat.E storage 1.10.46; Allocated for RAN 11.6.48, arr RAN 25.10.48; Ground handling and taxi training; Destroyed on fire dump later

MV112 Spitfire HF.VIIIc (Merlin 70); Became **A58-616**; TOC/RAF 12.7.44 - To RAAF, arr Brisbane 12.9.44; No.3 AD 16.9.44; No.457 Sqn ('ZP-Y') 15.12.44; Crashed on landing Labuan Strip 18.6.45; No.9 R&SU 7.7.45; Cca 23.8.45

MV113 Spitfire HF.VIIIc (Merlin 70); Became **A58-600**; TOC/RAF 13.7.44 - To RAAF, arr Melbourne 7.9.44; No.1 AD 11.9.44; No.457 Sqn 20.12.44; No.6 AD 30.10.45; SOC 22.5.46; Cat.E storage 1.10.46; DAP 7.11.47 until 15.11.48

MV114 Spitfire HF.VIIIc (Merlin 70); Became **A58-626**; TOC/RAF 15.7.44 - To RAAF, arr Sydney 12.11.44; No.2 AD 22.11.44; No.457 Sqn 26.12.44; No.9 R&SU 2.1.45; No.457 Sqn 8.5.45; No.1 R&SU 1.11.45; Cca 11.1.46

MV115 Spitfire HF.VIIIc (Merlin 70); Became **A58-617**; TOC/RAF 22.7.44 - To RAAF, arr Brisbane 12.9.44; No.3 AD 16.9.44; No.457 Sqn ('ZP-G', marked "*Grey Nurse*") 15.12.44; Engine failed on take-off, force-landed wheels-up Pitoe, Morotai 24.3.45; No.9 R&SU 11.4.45; No.79 Sqn 15.9.45; No.9 R&SU 10.45; No.79 Sqn 2.11.45; No.6 AD 2.11.45; SOC 22.5.46; Cat.E storage 1.10.46; DAP 7.11.47 until 15.11.48

MV116 Spitfire HF.VIIIc (Merlin 70); Became **A58-655**; TOC/RAF 23.7.44 - To RAAF, arr Brisbane 8.11.44; No.3 AD 13.11.44; SOC 22.5.46; Cat.E storage 1.10.46; DAP 7.10.48; DSD 16.9.49

MV117 Spitfire HF.VIIIc (Merlin 70); Became **A58-627**; TOC/RAF 13.8.44 - To RAAF, arr Sydney 12.11.44; No.2 AD 14.11.44; No.457 Sqn ('ZP-Z', marked "*Grey Nurse*") 26.12.44; No.6 AD 30.10.45; SOC 22.5.46; Cat.E storage 1.10.46; DAP 7.11.47 until 15.11.48

MV119 Spitfire HF.VIIIc (Merlin 70); Allotted **A58-601**; TOC/RAF 15.7.44 - To RAAF, arr Melbourne 7.9.44 (the second HF.VIIIc to RAAF); No.1 AD 11.9.44; No.1 APU 31.10.44; No.6 AD 15.10.45; SOC 22.5.46; Cat.E storage 1.10.46; DAP 7.11.47 until 15.11.48

MV120 Spitfire HF.VIIIc (Merlin 70); Became **A58-628**; TOC/RAF 23.7.44 - To RAAF, arr Sydney 12.11.44; No.2 AD 22.11.44; No.6 AD 13.12.45; SOC 22.5.46; Cat.E storage 1.10.46; DAP 7.11.47 until 15.11.48

MV121 Spitfire HF.VIIIc (Merlin 70); Became **A58-629**; TOC/RAF 29.7.44 - To RAAF, arr Sydney 12.11.44; No.2 AD 22.11.44; No.457 Sqn 26.12.44; Crashed landing 17.7.45; No.9 R&SU 26.7.45; No.457 Sqn 17.9.45; No.1 R&SU 1.11.45; Cca 11.1.46

MV123 Spitfire HF.VIIIc (Merlin 70); Became **A58-618**; TOC/RAF 22.7.44 - To RAAF, arr Brisbane 12.9.44; No.3 AD 16.9.44; No.457 Sqn 15.12.44; Hit bomb crater on landing in heavy rain and broke up, Labuan 19.6.45; No.9 R&SU 7.7.45; Cca 23.8.45

MV124 Spitfire HF.VIIIc (Merlin 70); Became **A58-630**; TOC/RAF 23.7.44 - To RAAF, arr Sydney 12.11.44; No.2 AD 14.11.44; No.457 Sqn 26.12.44; Tyre burst landing, swung off runway, Pitoe, Morotai 8.5.45; No.9 R&SU 9.5.45; Cca 25.6.45

MV125 Spitfire HF.VIIIc (Merlin 70); Became **A58-631**; TOC/RAF 28.7.44 - To RAAF, arr Sydney 12.11.44; No.2 AD 14.11.44; No.457 Sqn ('ZP-V', marked "*Grey Nurse*") 26.12.44; No.9 R&SU 9.5.45; No.457 Sqn 13.6.45; Air combat 20.6.45 (F/Lt SG Scrimgeour); No.6 AD 3.10.45; SOC 22.5.46; Cat.E storage 1.10.46; DAP 7.11.47 until 15.11.48

MV128 Spitfire HF.VIIIc (Merlin 70); Became **A58-632**; TOC/RAF 29.7.44 - To RAAF, arr Sydney 12.11.44; No.2 AD 15.11.44; No.6 AD 6.12.45; SOC 22.5.46; Cat.E storage; DAP 7.11.47 until 15.11.48

MV129 Spitfire HF.VIIIc (Merlin 70); Became **A58-633**; TOC/RAF 29.7.44 - To RAAF, arr Sydney 12.11.44; No.2 AD 22.11.44; No.9 R&SU-R/P 13.1.45; No.457 Sqn 22.1.45; Engine cut, abandoned, a/c dived into ground and burnt out, Tenchilian, near Suliman Lake, British North Borneo, 11.7.45; SOC 30.7.45

MV132 Spitfire HF.VIIIc (Merlin 70); Became **A58-634**; TOC/RAF 29.7.44 - To RAAF, arr Sydney 12.11.44; No.2 AD 22.11.44; No.9 R&SU 19.1.45; No.452 Sqn 22.2.45; No.457 Sqn 15.4.45; No.9 R&SU 2.5.45; No.457 Sqn 2.5.45; No.9 R&SU 23.5.45 (Engine changed); No.457 Sqn 24.6.45; No.6 AD 30.10.45; SOC 22.5.46; Cat.E storage 1.10.46; DAP 7.11.47 until 15.11.48

MV133 Spitfire HF.VIIIc (Merlin 70); Became **A58-602**; TOC/RAF 20.8.44 - To RAAF, arr Melbourne 25.10.44; No.1 AD 4.11.44; No.9 R&SU-R/P 20.12.44; No.457 Sqn 9.1.45; No.9 R&SU 11.3.45; Hit by flak over Ternate Is 7.4.45; No.452 Sqn 25.5.45; Damaged landing Croydon Strip, Tarakan 22.7.45; No.6 AD 6.11.45; SOC 22.5.46; Cat.E storage 1.10.46; DAP 7.11.47 until 15.11.48

MV135 Spitfire HF.VIIIc (Merlin 70); Became **A58-619**; TOC/RAF 16.8.44 - To RAAF, arr Melbourne 25.10.44; No.3 AD 28.10.44; No.9 R&SU-R/P 8.5.45; No.452 Sqn 16.5.45; Authorised to abandon remnants of aircraft at Middleburgh Is 3.5.46, SOC

MV136 Spitfire HF.VIIIc (Merlin 70); Became **A58-620**; TOC/RAF 17.8.44 - To RAAF, arr Melbourne 25.10.44; No.1 AD 7.11.44; No.9 R&SU-R/P 27.12.44; No.457 Sqn 5.1.45; Air combat 20.6.45 (F/Lt JGB Campbell); No.6 AD 22.10.45; No.60 OBU 30.10.45; Cca 13.12.45

MV137 Spitfire HF.VIIIc (Merlin 70); Became **A58-656**; TOC/RAF 5.9.44 - To RAAF, arr Brisbane 8.11.44; No.3 AD 13.11.44; SOC 22.5.46; Cat.E storage 1.10.46; DAP 7.10.48; DSD 16.9.49

MV138 Spitfire HF.VIIIc (Merlin 70); Became **A58-621**; TOC/RAF 18.8.44 - To RAAF, arr Melbourne 25.10.44; No.1 AD 4.11.44; No.457 Sqn ('ZP-K') 30.12.44; No.9 R&SU 4.5.45; No.457 Sqn ('ZP-K') 29.5.45; No.9 R&SU 1.11.45; Cca 11.1.46

MV139 Spitfire HF.VIIIc (Merlin 70); Became **A58-622**; TOC/RAF 20.8.44 - To RAAF, arr Melbourne 25.10.44; No.1 AD 3.11.44; No.457 Sqn 18.12.44; Damaged when ran over three flare path lights on ferry flight to Oodnatta 18.12.44; No.1 AD 12.1.45; Failed to recover from dive and crashed on foreshore near Geelong Grammar School, Corio Bay, Vic 4.10.45; No.1 CRD 22.10.45; Cca 11.11.45

MV140 Spitfire HF.VIIIc (Merlin 70); Became **A58-657**; TOC/RAF 31.8.44 - To RAAF, arr Brisbane 8.11.44; No.3 AD 13.11.44 (hack and target aircraft); SOC 22.5.46; Cat.E storage 1.10.46; DAP 7.10.48; DSD 16.9.49

MV141 Spitfire HF.VIIIc (Merlin 70); Became **A58-623**; TOC/RAF 20.8.44 - To RAAF, arr Melbourne 25.10.44; No.1 AD 7.11.44; No.457 Sqn 20.12.44; No.6 AD 2.9.45; SOC 22.5.46; Cat.E storage 1.10.46; DAP 7.11.47 until 15.11.48

MV144 Spitfire HF.VIIIc (Merlin 70); Became **A58-624**; TOC/RAF 27.8.44 - To RAAF, arr Melbourne 25.10.44; No.1 AD 7.11.44; No.9 R&SU-R/P 27.12.44; No.457 Sqn 2.1.45; No.7 R&SU 22.1.45; No.54 Sqn 21.4.45; No.548 Sqn 23.8.45; No.7 R&SU 10.9.45; No.6 AD 29.9.45; SOC 22.5.46; Cat.E storage 1.10.46; DAP 7.11.47 until 15.11.48

MV146 Spitfire HF.VIIIc (Merlin 70); Became **A58-658**; TOC/RAF 7.9.44 - To RAAF, arr Brisbane 8.11.44; No.3

AD 13.11.44; SOC 22.5.46; Cat.E storage 1.10.46; DAP 7.10.48; DSD 16.9.49

MV147 Spitfire HF.VIIIc (Merlin 70); Became **A58-659**; TOC/RAF 5.9.44 - To RAAF, arr Brisbane 8.11.44; No.3 AD 13.11.44; SOC 22.5.46; Cat.E storage 1.10.46; DAP 7.10.48; DSD 16.9.49

MV148 Spitfire HF.VIIIc (Merlin 70); Became **A58-660**; TOC/RAF 31.8.44 - To RAAF, arr Brisbane 8.11.44; No.3 AD 13.11.44; SOC 22.5.46; Cat.E storage 1.10.46; DAP 7.10.48; DSD 16.9.49

MV149 Spitfire HF.VIIIc (Merlin 70); Became **A58-625**; TOC/RAF 28.8.44 - To RAAF, arr Melbourne 25.10.44; No.1 AD 7.11.44; No.9 R&SU-R/P 25.12.44; No.1 AD 1.1.45; No.9 R&SU-R/P 11.7.45; No.49 OBU 17.10.45; Cca 12.2.46

MV150 Spitfire HF.VIIIc (Merlin 70); Became **A58-682**; TOC/RAF 3.10.44 - To RAAF, arr Sydney 17.12.44; No.2 AD 22.12.44; Storage 1.3.46; SOC 24.5.46; Cat.E storage 1.10.46; DAP 24.6.48; DSD 6.9.49

MV151 Spitfire HF.VIIIc (Merlin 70); Became **A58-661**; TOC/RAF 10.9.44 - To RAAF, arr Brisbane 8.11.44; No.3 AD 13.11.44; SOC 22.5.46; Cat.E storage 1.10.46; DAP 7.10.48; DSD 16.9.49

MV152 Spitfire HF.VIIIc (Merlin 70); Became **A58-662**; TOC/RAF 31.8.44 - To RAAF, arr Brisbane 8.11.44; No.3 AD 13.11.44; SOC 22.5.46; Cat.E storage 1.10.46; DAP 7.10.48; DSD 16.9.49

MV153 Spitfire HF.VIIIc (Merlin 70); Became **A58-670**; TOC/RAF 15.9.44 - To RAAF, arr Sydney 24.11.44; No.2 AD 4.12.44; Storage 6.12.45; SOC 22.5.46; Cat.E storage 1.10.46; DAP 7.11.47 until 15.11.48

MV154 Spitfire HF.VIIIc (Merlin 70); Became **A58-671**; TOC/RAF 15.9.44 - To RAAF, arr Sydney 24.11.44; No.2 AD 28.11.44; Storage 7.5.46; MI 22.5.46; Cat.E storage 1.10.46; DAP 24.6.48 until 6.9.48; To the School of Aircraft Production/Sydney Technical Collet, Ultimo, NSW 1.12.49; To A J R Oates, Sydney, NSW 1961; To Sid Marshall, Bankstown Airport, Sydney, NSW 1963, open storage in yard; To Jack P Davidson, NSW 1975; To Brian A Simpson, Sydney, NSW 5.77; Shipped from Sydney to UK 18.9.79 for Robert J Lamplough, Duxford and restored at Filton from 1980; To Fighter Wing Display Team Ltd, Duxford (Civil reg. *G-BKMI* 23.12.82); To Robert J Lamplough, North Weald 1985; ff after restoration 28.5.84 marked "MT928/ZX-M"; To Filton by 2000; Airworthy - **SURVIVOR**

MV155 Spitfire HF.VIIIc (Merlin 70); Became **A58-663**; TOC/RAF 10.9.44 - To RAAF, arr Brisbane 8.11.44; No.3 AD 13.11.44; SOC 22.5.46; Cat.E storage 1.10.46; DAP 7.10.48; DSD 16.9.49

MV156 Spitfire HF.VIIIc (Merlin 70); Became **A58-672**; TOC/RAF 15.9.44 - To RAAF, arr Sydney 24.11.44; No.2 AD 5.12.44; No.9 R&SU-R/P 13.1.45; No.457 Sqn ('ZP-Y', marked "*Grey Nurse*") 22.2.45; No.9 R&SU 18.3.45; No.457 Sqn ('ZP-Y') 7.5.45; 1 R&SU; Cca 11.1.46
Note: Flown with ZP-Y markings, but with light or white spinner, absence of Ace of spades emblem, February/March 1945

MV169 Spitfire HF.VIIIc (Merlin 70); Became **A58-635**; TOC/RAF 20.9.44 - To RAAF, arr Sydney 30.11.44; No.1 AD 30.11.44; No.457 Sqn 27.12.44; No.6 AD 30.10.45; SOC 22.5.46; Cat.E storage 1.10.46; DAP 7.11.47 until 15.11.48

MV170 Spitfire HF.VIIIc (Merlin 70); Became **A58-636**; TOC/RAF 24.9.44 - To RAAF, arr Sydney 30.11.44; No.1 AD 30.11.44; No.1 Engineering School 23.1.45; No.1 AD 12.2.45; No.9 R&SU-R/P 8.5.45; No.452 Sqn 16.5.45; Tyre burst landing, swung off runway, Pitoe, Morotai, Cat.E 1.11.45; Cca 13.11.45

MV171 Spitfire HF.VIIIc (Merlin 70); Became **A58-713**; TOC/RAF 10.9.44 - To RAAF, arr Sydney 1.1.45; No.2 AD 22.1.45; Storage 7.5.46; SOC 24.5.46; Cat.E storage 1.10.46; DAP 24.6.48; DSD 16.9.49

MV172 Spitfire HF.VIIIc (Merlin 70); Became **A58-637**; TOC/RAF 20.9.44 - To RAAF, arr Sydney 30.11.44; No.1 AD 30.11.44; Commonwealth Aircraft Corp (CAC Australia) 27.1.45; No.1 AD 6.11.45; Storage 22.1.46; Cca 12.2.46

MV173 Spitfire HF.VIIIc (Merlin 70); Became **A58-638**; TOC/RAF 25.9.44 - To RAAF, arr Sydney 30.11.44; No.1 AD 30.11.44; Engine fire on ground 16.1.45; No.9 R&SU-R/P 2.7.45; No.79 Sqn 29.7.45; No.60 OBU 29.10.45; Cca 13.12.45

MV174 Spitfire HF.VIIIc (Merlin 70); Became **A58-639**; TOC/RAF 24.9.44 - To RAAF, arr Sydney 30.11.44; No.1 AD 30.11.44; No.9 R&SU-R/P 26.6.45; No.79 Sqn 20.7.45; No.9 R&SU 27.7.45; No.457 Sqn 3.8.45; Engine failed on take-off, ground-looped, Mokmer, Biak Is 26.10.45; Cca 6.2.46

MV175 Spitfire HF.VIIIc (Merlin 70); Became **A58-640**; TOC/RAF 25.9.44 - To RAAF, arr Sydney 30.11.44; No.1

Spitfire HF.VIIIc A58-672 ZP-Y (ex MV156) of No.457 (Grey Nurse) Sqn in flight, flown by F/Lt F J Inger. It was also flown at one time by Wg Cdr G Cooper. It has a large shark mouth, and the absence of a red spinner and Ace of Spades emblem suggests that the photo was taken very early in 1945, before the red spinner was adopted. [RAAF]

MV176 Spitfire HF.VIIIc (Merlin 70); Became **A58-683**; TOC/RAF 12.10.44 - To RAAF, arr Sydney 17.12.44; No.2 AD 22.12.44; Storage 7.5.46; SOC 24.5.46; Cat.E storage 1.10.46; DAP 24.6.48; DSD 6.9.49
MV177 Spitfire HF.VIIIc (Merlin 70); Became **A58-702**; TOC/RAF 1.10.44 - To RAAF, arr Brisbane 6.2.45; No.3 AD 12.2.45; SOC 22.5.46; Cat.E storage 1.10.46; DAP 7.10.48; DSD 16.9.49
MV178 Spitfire HF.VIIIc (Merlin 70); Became **A58-703**; TOC/RAF 1.10.44 - To RAAF, arr Brisbane 6.2.45; No.3 AD 12.2.45; SOC 22.5.46; Cat.E storage 1.10.46; DAP 7.10.48; DSD 16.9.49
MV179 Spitfire HF.VIIIc (Merlin 70); Became **A58-692**; TOC/RAF 13.10.44 - To RAAF, arr Sydney 23.12.44; No.2 AD 26.12.44; Storage 7.5.46; SOC 24.5.46; Cat.E storage 1.10.46; DAP 24.6.48; DSD 6.9.49
MV180 Spitfire HF.VIIIc (Merlin 70); Became **A58-732**; TOC/RAF 24.10.44 - To RAAF, arr Sydney 29.3.45; No.1 AD 29.3.45; No.9 R&SU-R/P 29.6.45; No.79 Sqn 15.9.45; No.6 AD 2.11.45; SOC 22.5.46; Cat.E storage 1.10.46; DAP 7.11.47 until 15.11.48
MV181 Spitfire HF.VIIIc (Merlin 70); Became **A58-734**; TOC/RAF 1.11.44 - To RAAF, arr Sydney 17.4.45; No.2 AD 28.4.45; Cat.E storage 1.10.46; Allocated for RAN 11.6.48, arr RAN 25.10.48; Ground handling and taxi training; Destroyed on fire dump later
MV182 Spitfire HF.VIIIc (Merlin 70); Became **A58-641**; TOC/RAF 25.9.44 - To RAAF, arr Sydney 30.11.44; No.1 AD 30.11.44; No.9 R&SU-R/P 2.7.45; No.452 Sqn 27.7.45; No.6 AD 6.11.45; SOC 22.5.46; Cat.E storage 1.10.46; DAP 7.11.47 until 15.11.48
MV183 Spitfire HF.VIIIc (Merlin 70); Became **A58-704**; TOC/RAF 1.10.44 - To RAAF, arr Brisbane 6.2.45; No.3 AD 12.2.45; SOC 22.5.46; Cat.E storage 1.10.46; DAP 7.10.48; DSD 16.9.49
MV184 Spitfire HF.VIIIc (Merlin 70); Became **A58-717**; TOC/RAF 11.44 - To RAAF, arr Melbourne 6.2.45; No.1 AD 13.2.45; No.1 APU 19.4.45; Cat.E storage 1.10.46; Darwin 22.5.47; Cca 15.9.47
MV185 Spitfire HF.VIIIc (Merlin 70); Became **A58-735**; TOC/RAF 9.11.44 - To RAAF, arr Sydney 17.4.45; No.2 AD 28.4.45; No.13 ARD 17.9.45; No.6 AD 2.10.45; SOC 22.5.46; Cat.E storage 1.10.46; DAP 7.11.47 until 15.11.48
MV186 Spitfire HF.VIIIc (Merlin 70); Became **A58-736**; TOC/RAF 27.10.44 - To RAAF, arr Sydney 17.4.45; No.2 AD 28.4.45; Storage 7.5.46; SOC 24.5.46; Cat.E storage 1.10.46; DAP 24.6.48; RAN 25.10.48 until 6.9.49 (Ground handling & taxi training); Destroyed on fire dump later
MV187 Spitfire HF.VIIIc (Merlin 70); Became **A58-726**; TOC/RAF 24.10.44 - To RAAF, arr Sydney 27.2.45; No.3 AD 16.3.45; SOC 22.5.46; Cat.E storage 1.10.46; DAP 7.10.48; DSD 16.9.49
MV188 Spitfire HF.VIIIc (Merlin 70); Became **A58-750**; TOC/RAF 14.11.44 - To RAAF, arr Sydney 4.5.45; No.2 AD 11.5.45; Storage 7.5.46; Cat.E storage 1.10.46; Allocated for RAN 11.6.48, arr RAN 20.10.48; Ground handling and taxi training; Destroyed on fire dump later
MV189 Spitfire HF.VIIIc (Merlin 70); Became **A58-684**; TOC/RAF 9.10.44 - To RAAF, arr Sydney 17.12.44; No.2 AD 22.12.44; Storage 7.5.46; SOC 24.5.46; Cat.E storage 1.10.46; DAP 24.6.48; DSD 6.9.49
MV190 Spitfire HF.VIIIc (Merlin 70); Became **A58-737**; TOC/RAF 30.10.44 - To RAAF, arr Sydney 17.4.45; No.2 AD 28.4.45; Storage 7.5.46; SOC 24.5.46; Cat.E storage 1.10.46; DAP 24.6.48 until 6.9.49
MV191 Spitfire HF.VIIIc (Merlin 70); Became **A58-738**; TOC/RAF 27.10.44 - To RAAF, arr Sydney 17.4.45; No.2 AD 28.4.45; Storage 7.5.46; SOC 24.5.46; Cat.E storage 1.10.46; DAP 24.6.48 until 6.9.49
MV192 Spitfire HF.VIIIc (Merlin 70); Became **A58-727**; TOC/RAF 23.10.44 - To RAAF, arr Sydney 27.2.45; No.3 AD 16.3.45; SOC 22.5.46; Cat.E storage 1.10.46; DAP 7.10.48; DSD 16.9.49
MV193 Spitfire HF.VIIIc (Merlin 70); Became **A58-739**; TOC/RAF 28.10.44 - To RAAF, arr Sydney 17.4.45; No.2 AD 28.4.45; SOC 24.5.46; Cat.E storage 1.10.46; DAP 24.6.48 until 6.9.49
MV194 Spitfire HF.VIIIc (Merlin 70); Became **A58-740**; TOC/RAF 27.9.44 - To RAAF, arr Sydney 17.4.45; No.2 AD 28.4.45; Storage 7.5.46; SOC 24.5.46; Cat.E storage 1.10.46; DAP 24.6.48 until 6.9.49
MV195 Spitfire HF.VIIIc (Merlin 70); Became **A58-751**; TOC/RAF 23.11.44 - To RAAF, arr Sydney 4.5.45; No.2 AD 11.5.45; Storage 7.5.46; SOC 24.5.46; Cat.E storage 1.10.46; DAP 24.6.48; DSD 6.9.49
MV196 Spitfire HF.VIIIc (Merlin 70); Became **A58-741**; TOC/RAF 17.11.44 - To RAAF, arr Sydney 17.4.45; No.2 AD 20.4.45; No.9 R&SU-R/P 24.7.45; 6.CRD 20.8.45; No.13 ARD 13.2.46; Cca 9.7.46
MV197 Spitfire HF.VIIIc (Merlin 70); Became **A58-742**; TOC/RAF 27.10.44 - To RAAF, arr Sydney 17.4.45; No.2 AD 28.4.45; Undercarriage leg jammed and collapsed landing, Richmond 30.1.46; SOC 24.5.46; Cat.E storage 1.10.46; DAP 24.6.48 until 6.9.49
MV198 Spitfire HF.VIIIc (Merlin 70); Became **A58-743**; TOC/RAF 1.11.44 - To RAAF, arr Sydney 17.4.45; No.2 AD 28.4.45; Storage 7.5.46; SOC 24.5.46; Cat.E storage 1.10.46; DAP 24.6.48; DSD 6.9.49
MV199 Spitfire HF.VIIIc (Merlin 70); Became **A58-728**; TOC/RAF 6.11.44 - To RAAF, arr Sydney 27.2.45; No.3 AD 19.3.45; SOC 22.5.46; Cat.E storage 1.10.46; DAP 7.10.48; DSD 16.9.49
MV200 Spitfire HF.VIIIc (Merlin 70); Became **A58-718**; TOC/RAF 23.10.44 - To RAAF, arr Melbourne 6.2.45; No.1 AD 13.2.45; Wheels-up landed Laverton, Vic 23.3.45; No.1 AD storage 13.5.46; Cat.E storage 1.10.46
MV202 Spitfire HF.VIIIc (Merlin 70); Became **A58-744**; TOC/RAF 29.10.44 - To RAAF, arr Sydney 17.4.45; No.2 AD 28.4.45; Storage 7.5.46; SOC 24.5.46; Cat.E storage 1.10.46; DAP 24.6.48; DSD 6.9.49
MV203 Spitfire HF.VIIIc (Merlin 70); Became **A58-752**; TOC/RAF 18.11.44 - To RAAF, arr Sydney 4.5.45; No.2 AD 14.5.45; Storage 7.5.46; Cat.E storage 1.10.46; Allocated for RAN 11.6.48, arr RAN 27.10.48; Ground handling and taxi training; Destroyed on fire dump later
MV204 Spitfire HF.VIIIc (Merlin 70); Became **A58-753**; TOC/RAF 14.11.44 - To RAAF, arr Sydney 4.5.45; No.2 AD 14.5.45; Storage 7.5.46; Cat.E storage 1.10.46; Allocated for RAN 11.6.48, arr RAN 20.10.48; Ground handling and taxi training; Destroyed on fire dump later
MV206 Spitfire HF.VIIIc (Merlin 70); Became **A58-745**; TOC/RAF 4.11.44 - To RAAF, arr Sydney 17.4.45; No.2 AD 28.4.45; Storage 7.5.46; Cat.E storage 1.10.46; Allocated for RAN 11.6.48, arr RAN 27.10.48; Ground handling and taxi training; Destroyed on fire dump later
MV207 Spitfire HF.VIIIc (Merlin 70); Became **A58-754**; TOC/RAF 18.11.44 - To RAAF, arr Sydney 4.5.45; No.2 AD 11.5.45; Storage 7.5.46; Cat.E storage 1.10.46; Allocated for RAN 11.6.48, arr RAN 25.10.48; Ground handling and taxi training; Destroyed on fire dump later
MV233 Spitfire HF.VIIIc (Merlin 70); Became **A58-755**; TOC/RAF 18.11.44 - To RAAF, arr Sydney 4.5.45; No.2 AD 11.5.45; Storage 7.5.46; SOC 24.5.46; Cat.E storage 1.10.46; DAP 24.6.48 until 6.9.49
MV235 Spitfire HF.VIIIc (Merlin 70); Became **A58-729**; TOC/RAF 6.11.44 - To RAAF, arr Sydney 27.2.45; No.3 AD 19.3.45; SOC 22.5.46; Cat.E storage 1.10.46; DAP 7.10.48; DSD 16.9.49
MV237 Spitfire HF.VIIIc (Merlin 70); Became **A58-746**; TOC/RAF 18.11.44 - To RAAF, arr Sydney 17.4.45; No.2 AD 28.4.45; Storage 1.3.46; SOC 24.5.46; Cat.E storage 1.10.46; DAP 24.6.48; DSD 6.9.49

Spitfire HF.VIIIc A58-758 (ex MV239) had an undistinguished career, remaining in storage until being disposed of to the Sydney Technical College in 1949. It was eventually restored and is seen here in 2001 marked "RG-V" and "Grey Nurse", the markings of RAAF ace Wg Cdr Bobby Gibbes. [Rob Fox]

MV239 Spitfire HF.VIIIc (Merlin 70); Became **A58-758**; TOC/RAF 30.3.45 - To RAAF, arr Sydney 19.6.45; No.2 AD 26.6.45; Crashed landing 7.45; Storage 7.5.46; SOC 24.5.46; Cat.E storage 1.10.46; DAP 24.6.48 until 6.9.49; To Sydney Technical Colle, Ultimo, NSW 9.49; To A J R Oates, Sydney 1961; To Sid Marshall, Bankstown Airport, Sydney 1963, open storage in yard; To Camden Museum of Aviation, NSW on loan 29.7.72, marked "MV239"; To Jack P Davidson, Bankstown & The Oaks, NSW 1975; To Col Pay, Scone, NSW for restoration 6.83 (Civil reg. *VH-HET* 18.12.85); ff 29.12.85 as "A58-758"; Purchased & regd 23.8.00 to David H Lowy, Vaucluse, NSW, (marked "Grey Nurse", flown as "A58-602" and "RG-V") – **SURVIVOR**

MV240 Spitfire HF.VIIIc (Merlin 70); Became **A58-693**; TOC/RAF 15.10.44 - To RAAF, arr Sydney 23.12.44; No.2 AD 26.12.44; Storage 7.5.46; SOC 24.5.46; Cat.E storage 1.10.46; DAP 24.6.48; DSD 6.9.49

MV241 Spitfire HF.VIIIc (Merlin 70); Became **A58-719**; TOC/RAF 22.10.44 - To RAAF, arr Melbourne 6.2.45; No.1 AD 6.2.45; No.9 R&SU-R/P 25.6.45; SOC 22.5.46; DAP 7.11.47; DSD 15.11.48

MV242 Spitfire HF.VIIIc (Merlin 70); Became **A58-747**; TOC/RAF 29.10.44 - To RAAF, arr Sydney 17.4.45; No.2 AD 28.4.45; Storage 7.5.46; SOC 24.5.46; DAP 24.6.48; DSD 6.9.49

MV243 Spitfire HF.VIIIc (Merlin 70); Became **A58-721**; TOC/RAF 22.10.44 - To RAAF, arr Brisbane 10.2.45; No.3 AD 16.2.45; SOC 22.5.46; Cat.E storage 1.10.46; DAP 7.10.48; DSD 16.9.49

MV244 Spitfire HF.VIIIc (Merlin 70); Became **A58-720**; TOC/RAF 22.10.44 - To RAAF, arr Melbourne 6.2.45; No.1 AD 13.2.45; No.9 R&SU-R/P 29.6.45; No.452 Sqn 8.7.45; 16.ARD; No.452 Sqn 15.10.45; No.6 AD 6.11.45; Central Flying School 6.12.45; Ground Training School (TTS) 6.4.49; Cca 14.4.49; DAP 14.4.49

MV321 Spitfire HF.VIIIc (Merlin 70); Became **A58-642**; TOC/RAF 15.9.44 - To RAAF, arr Sydney 30.11.44; No.1 AD 30.11.44; No.9 R&SU-R/P 22.6.45; No.457 Sqn 1.7.45; No.6 AD 30.10.45; SOC 22.5.46; Cat.E storage 1.10.46; DAP 7.11.47 until 15.11.48; Parts recovered from a farm at Oakey, Queensland in 1989, to Bill Martin/Darling Downs Aviation Museum, Oakey, for restoration; To Noel Smoothie, Ningi, Queensland 1996 - **SURVIVOR**

MV322 Spitfire HF.VIIIc (Merlin 70); Became **A58-685**; TOC/RAF 8.10.44 - To RAAF, arr Sydney 17.12.44; No.2 AD 22.12.44; Storage 7.5.46; SOC 24.5.46; Cat.E storage 1.10.46; DAP 24.6.48; DSD 6.9.49

MV323 Spitfire HF.VIIIc (Merlin 70); Became **A58-705**; TOC/RAF 1.10.44 - To RAAF, arr Brisbane 6.2.45; No.2 AD 12.2.45; SOC 22.5.46; Cat.E storage 1.10.46; DAP 7.10.48; DSD 16.9.49

MV324 Spitfire HF.VIIIc (Merlin 70); Became **A58-694**; TOC/RAF 13.10.44 - To RAAF, arr Sydney 23.12.44; No.2 AD 26.12.44; Storage 7.5.46; SOC 24.5.46; Cat.E storage 1.10.46; DAP 24.6.48; DSD 6.9.49

MV325 Spitfire HF.VIIIc (Merlin 70); Became **A58-706**; TOC/RAF 1.10.44 - To RAAF, arr Brisbane 6.2.45; No.3 AD 12.2.45; SOC 22.5.46; Cat.E storage 1.10.46; DAP 7.10.48; DSD 16.9.49

MV342 Spitfire HF.VIIIc (Merlin 70); Became **A58-723**; TOC/RAF 27.10.44 - To RAAF, arr Brisbane 5.3.45; No.3 AD 12.3.45; SOC 22.5.46; Cat.E storage 1.10.46; DAP 7.10.48; DSD 16.9.49

MV344 Spitfire HF.VIIIc (Merlin 70); Became **A58-748**; TOC/RAF 29.10.44 - To RAAF, arr Sydney 17.4.45; No.2 AD 20.4.45; Storage 7.5.46; Cat.E storage 1.10.46; Allocated for RAN 11.6.48, arr RAN 14.10.48; Ground handling and taxi training; Destroyed on fire dump later

MV346 Spitfire HF.VIIIc (Merlin 70); Became **A58-756**; TOC/RAF 10.11.44 - To RAAF, arr Sydney 4.5.45; No.2 AD 14.5.45; Storage 7.5.46; SOC 24.5.46; Cat.E storage 1.10.46; DAP 24.6.48 until 6.9.49

MV460 Spitfire HF.VIIIc (Merlin 70); Became **A58-664**; TOC/RAF 10.9.44 - To RAAF, arr Brisbane 8.11.44; No.3 AD 13.11.44; SOC 22.5.46; Cat.E storage 1.10.46; DAP 7.10.48; DSD 16.9.49

MV461 Spitfire HF.VIIIc (Merlin 70); Became **A58-665**; TOC/RAF 11.9.44 - To RAAF, arr Brisbane 8.11.44; No.3 AD 13.11.44; SOC 22.5.46; Cat.E storage 1.10.46; DAP 7.10.48; DSD 16.9.49

MV463 Spitfire HF.VIIIc (Merlin 70); Became **A58-666**; TOC/RAF 16.9.44 - To RAAF, arr Brisbane 8.11.44; No.3 AD 13.11.44; SOC 22.5.46; Cat.E storage 1.10.46; DAP 7.10.48; DSD 16.9.49

MV464 Spitfire HF.VIIIc (Merlin 70); Became **A58-667**; TOC/RAF 8.9.44 - To RAAF, arr Brisbane 8.11.44; No.3 AD 13.11.44; SOC 22.5.46; Cat.E storage 1.10.46; DAP 7.10.48; DSD 16.9.49

MV465 Spitfire HF.VIIIc (Merlin 70); Became **A58-714**; TOC/RAF 10.9.44 - To RAAF, arr Sydney 1.1.45; No.2 AD 22.1.45; Storage 7.5.46; SOC 24.5.46; Cat.E storage 1.10.46; DAP 24.6.48; DSD 6.9.49

MV466 Spitfire HF.VIIIc (Merlin 70); Became **A58-643**; TOC/RAF 15.9.44 - To RAAF, arr Sydney 30.11.44; No.1 AD 30.11.44; No.9 R&SU-R/P 26.6.45; No.79 Sqn 8.7.45; No.6 AD 5.11.45; SOC 22.5.46; DAP 7.11.47 until 15.11.48

MV467 Spitfire HF.VIIIc (Merlin 70); Became **A58-668**; TOC/RAF 9.9.44 - To RAAF, arr Brisbane 8.11.44; No.3 AD 13.11.44; SOC 22.5.46; Cat.E storage 1.10.46; DAP 7.10.48; DSD 16.9.49

MV468 Spitfire HF.VIIIc (Merlin 70); Became **A58-673**; TOC/RAF 10.9.44 - To RAAF, arr Sydney 24.11.44; No.2 AD 28.11.44; Storage 7.5.46; Cat.E storage 1.10.46; Allocated for RAN 11.6.48, arr RAN 12.10.48; Ground handling and taxi training; Destroyed on fire dump later

MV469 Spitfire HF.VIIIc (Merlin 70); Became **A58-674**; TOC/RAF 15.9.44 - To RAAF, arr Sydney 24.11.44; No.2 AD 28.11.44; Storage 17.5.46; SOC 24.5.46; Cat.E storage 1.10.46; DAP 24.6.48; DSD 6.9.49

MV470 Spitfire HF.VIIIc (Merlin 70); Became **A58-675**; TOC/RAF 15.9.44 - To RAAF, arr Sydney 24.11.44; No.2 AD 5.12.44; No.6 AD 6.12.45; SOC 22.5.46; Cat.E storage 1.10.46; DAP until 15.11.48

MV471 Spitfire HF.VIIIc (Merlin 70); Became **A58-676**; TOC/RAF 16.9.44 - To RAAF, arr Sydney 24.11.44; No.2 AD 29.11.44; Storage 7.5.46; SOC 24.5.46; Cat.E storage 1.10.46; DAP 24.6.48; DSD 6.9.49

MV472 Spitfire HF.VIIIc (Merlin 70); Became **A58-644**; TOC/RAF 18.9.44 - To RAAF, arr Sydney 30.11.44; No.1 AD 30.11.44; SOC 22.5.46; Cat.E storage 11.8.47; DAP 19.5.48 until 8.8.49

MV473 Spitfire HF.VIIIc (Merlin 70); Became **A58-645**; TOC/RAF 17.9.44 - To RAAF, arr Sydney 30.11.44; No.1 AD 30.11.44; No.9 R&SU-R/P 8.5.45; No.79 Sqn 15.5.45; No.9 R&SU 19.5.45; No.79 Sqn 26.5.45; No.6 AD 30.10.45; SOC 22.5.46; Cat.E storage 1.10.46; DAP 7.11.47 until 15.11.48

MV474 Spitfire HF.VIIIc (Merlin 70); Became **A58-646**; TOC/RAF 17.9.44 - To RAAF, arr Sydney 30.11.44; No.1 AD 30.11.44; No.9 R&SU-R/P 22.6.45; No.452 Sqn ('QY-Y') 2.7.45; Prop damaged taxiing Garbutt 6.11.45; Cca 16.7.46

MV475 Spitfire HF.VIIIc (Merlin 70); Became **A58-677**; TOC/RAF 17.9.44 - To RAAF, arr Sydney 24.11.44; No.2 AD 29.11.44; Storage 7.5.46; SOC 24.5.46; Cat.E storage 1.10.46; DAP 24.6.48; DSD 6.9.49

MV476 Spitfire HF.VIIIc (Merlin 70); Became **A58-647**; TOC/RAF 18.9.44 - To RAAF, arr Sydney 30.11.44; No.1 AD 30.11.44; No.9 R&SU-R/P 22.6.45; No.452 Sqn 2.7.45; Hit by ground fire while bombing bridge and crashed in sea off coast, Tawao, NW Borneo 12.7.45 (Flt Lt NJ Cullen killed); SOC 23.7.45

MV477 Spitfire HF.VIIIc (Merlin 70); Became **A58-648**; TOC/RAF 23.9.44 - To RAAF, arr Sydney 30.11.44; No.1 AD 30.11.44; No.9 R&SU 22.6.45; No.457 Sqn 1.7.45; No.6 AD 22.10.45; No.60 OBU 30.10.45; Cca 13.12.45

MV478 Spitfire HF.VIIIc (Merlin 70); Became **A58-649**; TOC/RAF 25.9.44 - To RAAF, arr Sydney 30.11.44; No.1 AD 30.11.44; No.9 R&SU-R/P 22.6.45; No.457 Sqn 1.7.45; No.1 R&SU 1.11.45; Cca 11.1.46

MV479 Spitfire HF.VIIIc (Merlin 70); Became **A58-650**; TOC/RAF 25.9.44 - To RAAF, arr Sydney 30.11.44; No.1 AD 30.11.44; No.9 R&SU-R/P 22.6.45; No.452 Sqn 28.7.45; Brakes seized on take-off, crashed, Croydon Strip, Tarakan 5.8.45; Cca 1.11.45

MV481 Spitfire HF.VIIIc (Merlin 70); Became **A58-708**; TOC/RAF 29.9.44 - To RAAF, arr Brisbane 6.2.45; No.3 AD 12.2.45; SOC 22.5.46; Cat.E storage 1.10.46; DAP 7.10.48; DSD 16.9.49

MV482 Spitfire HF.VIIIc (Merlin 70); Became **A58-730**; TOC/RAF 21.10.44 - To RAAF, arr Sydney 27.2.45; No.3 AD 16.3.45; SOC 22.5.46; Cat.E storage 1.10.46; DAP 7.10.48; DSD 16.9.49

MV484 Spitfire HF.VIIIc (Merlin 70); Became **A58-695**; TOC/RAF 14.10.44 - To RAAF, arr Sydney 23.12.44; No.2 AD 26.12.44; Storage 7.5.46; SOC 24.5.46; Cat.E storage 1.10.46; DAP 24.6.48; DSD 6.9.49

MV485 Spitfire HF.VIIIc (Merlin 70); Became **A58-716**; TOC/RAF 27.9.44 - To RAAF, arr Brisbane 6.2.45; No.3 AD 12.2.45; SOC 22.5.46; Cat.E storage 1.10.46; DAP 7.10.48; DSD 9.49

MV486 Spitfire HF.VIIIc (Merlin 70); Became **A58-651**; TOC/RAF 25.9.44 - To RAAF, arr Sydney 30.11.44; No.1 AD 30.11.44; No.9 R&SU-R/P 8.5.45; No.79 Sqn ('UP-Z', named '*Judy III*') 14.5.45; No.9 R&SU 27.7.45; No.79 Sqn 11.8.45; No.6 AD 5.11.45; SOC 22.5.46; Cat.E storage 1.10.46; DAP 7.11.47 until 15.11.48

MV487 Spitfire HF.VIIIc (Merlin 70); Became **A58-686**; TOC/RAF 1.10.44 - To RAAF, arr Sydney 17.12.44; No.2 AD 26.12.44; Storage 7.5.46; Cat.E storage 1.10.46; Allocated for RAN 11.6.48, arr RAN 19.10.48; Ground handling and taxi training; Destroyed on fire dump later

MV499 Spitfire HF.VIIIc (Merlin 70); Became **A58-707**; TOC/RAF 1.10.44 - To RAAF, arr Brisbane 6.2.45; No.3 AD 12.2.45; SOC 22.5.46; Cat.E storage 1.10.46; DAP 7.10.48; DSD 16.9.49

MV500 Spitfire HF.VIIIc (Merlin 70); Became **A58-709**; TOC/RAF 1.10.44 - To RAAF, arr Brisbane 6.2.45; No.3 AD 12.2.45; SOC 22.5.46; Cat.E storage 1.10.46; DAP 7.10.48; DSD 16.9.49

MV501 Spitfire HF.VIIIc (Merlin 70); Became **A58-710**; TOC/RAF 1.10.44 - To RAAF, arr Brisbane 6.2.45; No.3 AD 12.2.45; SOC 22.5.46; Cat.E storage 1.10.46; DAP 7.10.48; DSD 16.9.49

MV502 Spitfire HF.VIIIc (Merlin 70); Became **A58-696**; TOC/RAF 13.10.44 - To RAAF, arr Sydney 23.12.44; No.2 AD 26.12.44; Storage 7.5.46; SOC 24.5.46; Cat.E storage 1.10.46; DAP 24.6.48; DSD 6.9.49

MV503 Spitfire HF.VIIIc (Merlin 70); Became **A58-687**; TOC/RAF 2.10.44 - To RAAF, arr Sydney 17.12.44; No.2 AD 22.12.44; No.6 AD 13.12.45; SOC 22.5.46; Cat.E storage 1.10.46; DAP 7.11.47; DSD 15.11.48

MV504 Spitfire HF.VIIIc (Merlin 70); Became **A58-688**; TOC/RAF 8.10.44 - To RAAF, arr Sydney 17.12.44; No.2 AD 22.12.44; Storage 7.5.46; SOC 24.5.46; Cat.E storage 1.10.46; DAP 24.6.48; DSD 6.9.49

MV505 Spitfire HF.VIIIc (Merlin 70); Became **A58-689**; TOC/RAF 13.10.44 - To RAAF, arr Sydney 17.12.44; No.2 AD 22.12.44; No.9 R&SU-R/P 15.8.45; No.79 Sqn 15.9.45; No.6 AD 5.11.45; SOC 22.5.46; Cat.E storage 1.10.46; DAP 7.11.47; DSD 15.11.48

MV506 Spitfire HF.VIIIc (Merlin 70); Became **A58-711**; TOC/RAF 6.10.44 - To RAAF, arr Brisbane 6.2.45; No.3 AD 12.2.45; SOC 22.5.46; Cat.E storage 1.10.46; DAP 7.10.48; DSD 16.9.49

MV507 Spitfire HF.VIIIc (Merlin 70); Became **A58-697**; TOC/RAF 15.10.44 - To RAAF, arr Sydney 23.12.44; No.2 AD 26.12.44; Storage 7.5.46; SOC 24.5.46; Cat.E storage 1.10.46; DAP 24.6.48; DSD 6.9.49

MV508 Spitfire HF.VIIIc (Merlin 70); Became **A58-690**; TOC/RAF 8.10.44 - To RAAF, arr Sydney 17.12.44; No.2 AD 22.12.44; Storage 22.11.45; No.1 AD 5.2.46; Storage 5.3.46; SOC 22.5.46; Cat.E storage 1.10.46; DAP 19.5.48; DSD 8.8.49

MV509 Spitfire HF.VIIIc (Merlin 70); Became **A58-698**; TOC/RAF 15.10.44 - To RAAF, arr Sydney 23.12.44; No.2 AD 26.12.44; Storage 7.5.46; Cat.E storage 1.10.46; Allocated for RAN 11.6.48, arr RAN 15.10.48; Ground-handling and taxi-training; Destroyed on fire dump later

MV510 Spitfire HF.VIIIc (Merlin 70); Became **A58-691**; TOC/RAF 8.10.44 - To RAAF, arr Sydney 17.12.44; No.2 AD 26.12.44; Storage 7.5.46; Cat.E storage 1.10.46; Approved for RAN 11.6.48, for ground-handling and taxi-training (issued 20.10.48, but arrival not confirmed); Destroyed on fire dump later

MV511 Spitfire HF.VIIIc (Merlin 70); Became **A58-699**; TOC/RAF 15.10.44 - To RAAF, arr Sydney 23.12.44; No.2 AD 26.12.44; Storage 7.5.46; SOC 24.5.46; Cat.E storage 1.10.46; DAP 24.6.48; DSD 6.9.49

MV512 Spitfire HF.VIIIc (Merlin 70); Became **A58-700**; TOC/RAF 15.10.44 - To RAAF, arr Sydney 23.12.44; No.2 AD 26.12.44; Storage 7.5.46; Cat.E storage 1.10.46; Allocated for RAN 11.6.48, arr RAN 12.10.48; Ground-

AUSTRALIA

handling and taxi-training; Destroyed on fire dump later
MV513 Spitfire HF.VIIIc (Merlin 70); Became **A58-701**; TOC/RAF 15.10.44 - To RAAF, arr Sydney 23.12.44; No.2 AD 26.12.44; Storage 7.5.46; SOC 24.5.46; Cat.E storage 1.10.46; DAP 24.6.48; DSD 6.9.49
MV514 Spitfire HF.VIIIc (Merlin 70); Became **A58-722**; TOC/RAF 22.10.44 - To RAAF, arr Brisbane 10.2.45; No.3 AD 16.2.45; SOC 22.5.46; Cat.E storage 1.10.46; DAP 7.10.48; DSD 16.9.49
NH614 Spitfire HF.VIIIc (Merlin 70); Became **A58-731**; TOC/RAF 9.11.44 - To RAAF, arr Sydney 27.2.45; No.3 AD 19.3.45; SOC 22.5.46; DAP 7.10.48; DSD 16.9.49
PA953 Spitfire LF.VIIIc (Merlin 66); Became **A58-488**; TOC/RAF 17.3.44 - To RAAF, arr Brisbane 27.6.44; No.3 AD 4.7.44; No.6 AD 1.10.44; SOC 22.5.46; Cat.E storage 1.10.46; DAP 7.11.47 until 15.11.48
PA954 Spitfire LF.VIIIc (Merlin 66); Became **A58-442**; TOC/RAF 17.3.44 - To RAAF, arr Sydney 19.6.44; No.1 AD 6.7.44; No.8 OTU 27.11.44; No.6 AD 28.11.45; SOC 22.5.46; DAP 7.11.47 until 15.11.48
PA957 Spitfire LF.VIIIc (Merlin 66); Became **A58-443**; TOC/RAF 18.3.44 - To RAAF, arr Sydney 19.6.44; No.1 AD 6.7.44; No.6 AD 24.8.45; SOC 22.5.46; Cat.E storage 1.10.46; DAP 7.11.47 until 15.11.48
PA958 Spitfire LF.VIIIc (Merlin 66); Became **A58-444** TOC/RAF 12.3.44 - To RAAF, arr Sydney 19.6.44; No.1 AD 6.7.44; No.6 AD 24.8.44; Engine failed on take-off, crashed in attempted forced landing, Oakey 27.7.45; Cca 16.10.45
PK481 Spitfire F 22; Arrived as **SURVIVOR** only- Sold to RAF Association (Brighton & Hove Branch), Shoreham 15.9.55; Transferred to RAAF Association, Perth, Western Australia 5.8.58; Shipped to Australia in SS *Queensland Star*, arrived Fremantle 10.6.59; Exhibited as "AF-A" on pole outside RAAF Association HQ, Adelaide Terrace, Perth from 6.9.59; To Bullcreek, WA, on a pole 13.3.71; To RAAF Association Aviation Museum at Bullcreek, Perth on a pole 11.85 and extant
RM797 Spitfire F.XIVe; Arrived as **SURVIVOR** only; Ex Royal Thai AF *U14-16/93*, collected from Surin airfield in Thailand 24.5.73; Airlifted from Butterworth AFB, Malaysia to Darwin, NT 19.8.73; Stored by Garry Cooper, Alstonville, NSW (Civil reg. *VH-XIV* 1977)
RR232 Spitfire HF.IXe; Arrived as **SURVIVOR** only; Ex SAAF No.*5632*, arr Australia late 1976; Restored by Peter Sledge at AFB Point Cook from 10.12.76, with parts from JF629 (tail) & RM873 (wings); Rolled out Bankstown airport 14.10.84; Loan to the Royal Australian Navy Museum at Nowra, New South Wales late 1985 (exhibited as "DB-N" from 1987); Shipped to UK, arr 13.1.87 for Charles Church, Micheldever; To Sussex Spraying Services Ltd, Shoreham (Civil reg. *G-BRSF* 22.11.89, cancelled 23.6.94); To storage 3.96; to J Pearce, UK; To Martin Phillips, Exeter, January 2000; To Arden Family Trust, Exeter for restoration March 2000 and extant
SW800 Seafire XV; Cockpit section with Peter Croser, Melbourne, Vic since 1991 for restoration project - **SURVIVOR**
TE384 Spitfire LF.XVIe; Arrived as **SURVIVOR** only; RAF GI airframe No.*7207M*, exhibited as "XT-C" at Syerston 1957/58; in Film "*Battle of Britain*"; Storage Henlow 10.68 to 1972; To RAAF Amberley 12.72, storage; On loan to Camden Museum of Aviation, NSW 24.4.75; To Jim F Czerwinski & B Hempel, Toowoomba 9.83; Exhibited in Queensland 1988; Under restoration to flying condition; Civil reg. *VH-XVI* 5.10.88; ff Toowoomba 6.10.88 marked "TE384/XVI"; Later with Hockey Treloar Syndicate, Toowoomba; Flown, but had problems; Regn cancelled 29.9.98; To USA 6.98; US registration candidate 3.8.98
TP298 Spitfire F.XVIII. **SURVIVOR** only. Currently with Garry Cooper / Murray Gilchrist, Alstonville, NSW [see USA for details]

Unidentified Spitfires

19.11.42 No.54 Sqn, engine failed at 3,000ft, force-landed on airfield (F/Lt RKC Norwood)
26.11.42 No.54 Sqn, landing after ferry flight from Melbourne, ran into hole (P/O Wall)
7.3.43 No.457 Sqn, Ki-48 shot down in sea in flames 5m N of Gunn Point
9.5.43 No.457 Sqn, A6M destroyed in Japanese raid on Millingimbi airfield (P/O IS Morse)
9.5.43 No.457 Sqn, A6M destroyed in Japanese raid on Millingimbi airfield (P/O RW Watson)
9.5.43 No.457 Sqn, one A6M probable & two damaged in Japanese raid on Millingimbi airfield
18.5.43 No.54 Sqn, tyre burst landing
28.5.43 No.457 Sqn, three G6M destroyed & others damaged in Japanese raid on Millingimbi airfield [two Spitfires lost, one pilot baled out – see AR526 & BR493. Also one Spitfire damaged on landing]
28.6.43 No.457 Sqn, two A6M destroyed, two A6M & two bombers probable (F/O Brook of No.54 Sqn temp attd No.457 Sqn claimed one of the probables) [two Spits lost, pilots safe; see BR462]
6.7.43 No.452 Sqn, engine failed during engagement (Sgt AR Richardson baled out safely) [NOT BR237 if Cca date correct as 6.7.43 date confirmed in official RAAF war history]
6.7.43 No.452 Sqn, shot down, dived into ground (F/O CP Lloyd baled out safely) [stated by RAAF to be BR549, but this does not fit its known history]
27.10.43 No.54 Sqn, taxying accident (F/Sgt Fox)
18.4.44 "A58-330". No.54 Sqn, ferrying back from Gorrie, pilot baled out too low and fell into blazing wreck of aircraft crashed near Katherine (F/O PGF Brown DoI) [Maybe JF846]
18.12.44 No.54 Sqn, engine failed at 23,000ft, force-landed successfully RAAF Darwin (F/Sgt FR Vanes)
24.7.45 No.54 Sqn, caught by gust, swung, aircraft & flarepath damaged, ROS (F/Sgt AJ Assig unhurt)
8.8.45 No.54 Sqn, engine trouble on Rhubarb, force-landed Coomalie Strip (F/Lt RAS Redd unhurt).

SURVIVORS in Australia

Spitfire Mk II P7973 ("RH")
Spitfire Mk V BL628, BR545 (A58-51), BS164 (A58-63), BS199 (A58-81), BS231 (A58-92), EE853 (A58-146), LZ844 (A58-213/prov "R6915"), MA353 (A58-232)
Spitfire Mk VIII JG267 (A58-377), JG355 (A58-359), JG484 (A58-408), JG668 (A58-441), LV750 (A58-471), MD228 (A58-445), MD338 (A58-467), MT682 (A58-529), MV239 (A58-758)
Spitfire Mk IX LZ842
Spitfire Mk XIV RM797
Spitfire F 22 PK481
Seafire XV SW800

Replicas:
"NH457" - Ed Matthews, Williamtown.
"TB592" - Aviation Heritage Museum, Bull Creek.
"TE283" - Air Force Association, Bull Creek.
"TE351" - Ed Matthews, Williamtown.

[Matthews has made at least two replicas of Spitfires, one marked "CRC" and the other marked "NH457" & "RA-F". Both were on display at the Bicentennial Show at Richmond in 1988]

References:
Aircraft of the RAAF, by Wg Cdr K Isaacs AFC.
RAAF Spitfires, AHSA Journal January 1962 & June 1962.
Spitfires over Darwin, by Fred Morton, Air Classic.
Spitfire Markings of the RAAF, Part 1 & 2, by F Smith, G Pentland & P Malone, Kookaburra Technical Publication., 1970/71.
The Spitfire, Mustang & Kittyhawk in Australian Service, by Stewart Wilson, Aerospace Publication, 1988.
Air War Against Japan 1943 - 1945, by George Odgers, Australian War Memorial, 1957.

Check List of RAAF / RAF Serial Numbers

RAAF Serial No.:	RAF Serial No.:
A58- 1	AR510
A58- 2	AR523
A58- 3	AR526
A58- 4	AR532
A58- 5	AR558
A58- 6	AR563
A58- 7	AR564
A58- 8	AR619
A58- 9	AR620
A58- 10	AR621
A58- 11	BS158
A58- 12	BS162
A58- 13	BS165
A58- 14	BS223
A58- 15	BR237
A58- 16	BR238
A58- 17	BR239
A58- 18	BR240
A58- 19	BR241
A58- 20	BS295
A58- 21	BS300
A58- 22	BR386
A58- 23	BR462
A58- 24	BR468
A58- 25	BR471
A58- 26	BR480
A58- 27	BR484
A58- 28	BR485
A58- 29	BR490
A58- 30	BR493
A58- 31	BR495
A58- 32	BR497
A58- 33	BR499
A58- 34	BR526
A58- 35	BR527
A58- 36	BR528
A58- 37	BR530
A58- 38	BR531
A58- 39	BR532
A58- 40	BR533
A58- 41	BR535
A58- 42	BR536
A58- 43	BR537
A58- 44	BR538
A58- 45	BR539
A58- 46	BR540
A58- 47	BR541
A58- 48	BR542
A58- 49	BR543
A58- 50	BR544
A58- 51	BR545
A58- 52	BR546
A58- 53	BR547
A58- 54	BR548
A58- 55	BR549
A58- 56	BR568
A58- 57	BR570
A58- 58	BR572
A58- 59	BR574
A58- 60	BR584
A58- 61	BR589
A58- 62	BS163
A58- 63	BS164
A58- 64	BS166
A58- 65	BS169
A58- 66	BS171
A58- 67	BS173
A58- 68	BS174
A58- 69	BS175
A58- 70	BS178
A58- 71	BS181
A58- 72	BS182
A58- 73	BS184
A58- 74	BS186
A58- 75	BS187
A58- 76	BS188
A58- 77	BS190
A58- 78	BS191
A58- 79	BS193
A58- 80	BS197
A58- 81	BS199
A58- 82	BS201
A58- 83	BS218
A58- 84	BS219
A58- 85	BS220
A58- 86	BS221
A58- 87	BS222
A58- 88	BS224
A58- 89	BS225
A58- 90	BS226
A58- 91	BS230
A58- 92	BS231
A58- 93	BS232
A58- 94	BS233
A58- 95	BS234
A58- 96	BS235
A58- 97	BS236
A58- 98	BS237
A58- 99	BS238
A58- 100	BS291
A58- 101	BS293
A58- 102	BS298
A58- 103	BS305
A58- 104	EF564
A58- 105	EE605
A58- 106	EE606
A58- 107	EE607
A58- 108	EE608
A58- 109	EE609
A58- 110	EE610
A58- 111	EE636
A58- 112	EE639
A58- 113	EE669
A58- 114	EE670
A58- 115	EE671
A58- 116	EE672
A58- 117	EE673
A58- 118	EE674
A58- 119	EE675
A58- 120	EE676
A58- 121	EE677
A58- 122	EE678
A58- 123	EE713
A58- 124	EE718
A58- 125	EE719
A58- 126	EE728
A58- 127	EE729
A58- 128	EE733
A58- 129	EE734
A58- 130	EE735
A58- 131	EE736
A58- 132	EE737
A58- 133	EE748
A58- 134	EE751
A58- 135	EE807
A58- 136	EE834
A58- 137	EE835
A58- 138	EE836
A58- 139	EE837
A58- 140	EE844
A58- 141	EE845
A58- 142	EE849
A58- 143	EE850
A58- 144	EE851
A58- 145	EE852
A58- 146	EE853
A58- 147	EF543
A58- 148	EF544
A58- 149	EF545
A58- 150	EF546
A58- 151	EF556
A58- 152	EF557
A58- 153	EF558
A58- 154	EF559
A58- 155	EF560
A58- 156	EF562
A58- 157	EF563
A58- 158	EF565
A58- 159	EF587
A58- 160	EF588
A58- 161	EF589
A58- 162	EF590
A58- 163	ER735
A58- 164	ER760
A58- 165	ES232
A58- 166	ES238
A58- 167	ES249
A58- 168	ES259
A58- 169	ES307
A58- 170	ES367
A58- 171	JG728
A58- 172	JG731
A58- 173	JG740
A58- 174	JG795
A58- 175	JG796
A58- 176	JG807
A58- 177	JG884
A58- 178	JG891
A58- 179	JG897
A58- 180	JG912
A58- 181	JG954
A58- 182	JG957
A58- 183	JK225
A58- 184	JK229
A58- 185	JK231
GAP	
A58- 200	JL247
A58- 201	JL314
A58- 202	JL348
A58- 203	JL360
A58- 204	JL371
A58- 205	JL378
A58- 206	JL380
A58- 207	JL382
A58- 208	JL386
A58- 209	JL392
A58- 210	JL394
A58- 211	LZ834
A58- 212	LZ835
A58- 213	LZ844
A58- 214	LZ845
A58- 215	LZ846
A58- 216	LZ848
A58- 217	LZ862
A58- 218	LZ865
A58- 219	LZ866
A58- 220	LZ867
A58- 221	LZ868
A58- 222	LZ870
A58- 223	LZ873
A58- 224	LZ874
A58- 225	LZ881
A58- 226	LZ883
A58- 227	LZ884
A58- 228	LZ886
A58- 229	LZ926
A58- 230	LZ934
A58- 231	MA352
A58- 232	MA353
A58- 233	MA354
A58- 234	MA355
A58- 235	MA356
A58- 236	MA366
A58- 237	MA385
A58- 238	MA387
A58- 239	MA389
A58- 240	MA394
A58- 241	MA395
A58- 242	MA685
A58- 243	MA689
A58- 244	MA697
A58- 245	MA699
A58- 246	MA863
A58- 247	MH306
A58- 248	MH566
A58- 249	MH585
A58- 250	MH586
A58- 251	MH587
A58- 252	MH588
A58- 253	MH589
A58- 254	MH591
A58- 255	MH642
A58- 256	MH643
A58- 257	MH644
A58- 258	MH645
A58- 259	MH646
GAP	
A58- 300	JF620
A58- 301	JF621
A58- 302	JF820

AUSTRALIA

A58- 303	JF821	A58- 368	JG473	A58- 433	MD399	A58- 498	MT624
A58- 304	JF822	A58- 369	JG474	A58- 434	JG556	A58- 499	MT626
A58- 305	JF823	A58- 370	JG603	A58- 435	JG622	A58- 500	MT649
A58- 306	JF824	A58- 371	MD221	A58- 436	MD380	A58- 501	JG691
A58- 307	JF825	A58- 372	JG106	A58- 437	MD381	A58- 502	MB970
A58- 308	JF845	A58- 373	JG262	A58- 438	MD388	A58- 503	MB972
A58- 309	JF846	A58- 374	JG263	A58- 439	JG664	A58- 504	MB974
A58- 310	JF847	A58- 375	JG265	A58- 440	JG665	A58- 505	MT502
A58- 311	JF869	A58- 376	JG266	A58- 441	JG668	A58- 506	MT503
A58- 312	JF870	A58- 377	JG267	A58- 442	PA954	A58- 507	MT508
A58- 313	JF876	A58- 378	JG269	A58- 443	PA957	A58- 508	MT512
A58- 314	JF877	A58- 379	JG270	A58- 444	PA958	A58- 509	MT513
A58- 315	JF934	A58- 380	JG332	A58- 445	MD228	A58- 510	MT540
A58- 316	JF935	A58- 381	JG345	A58- 446	MD231	A58- 511	JG684
A58- 317	JF936	A58- 382	JG347	A58- 447	MD253	A58- 512	JG685
A58- 318	JF937	A58- 383	JG415	A58- 448	JG385	A58- 513	JG687
A58- 319	JG105	A58- 384	JG275	A58- 449	JG566	A58- 514	MB968
A58- 320	JG107	A58- 385	JG356	A58- 450	JG605	A58- 515	MT519
A58- 321	JF933	A58- 386	JG372	A58- 451	JG609	A58- 516	JG690
A58- 322	JF942	A58- 387	JG382	A58- 452	JG613	A58- 517	MT594
A58- 323	JF945	A58- 388	JG387	A58- 453	LV644	A58- 518	MT618
A58- 324	JF967	A58- 389	JG430	A58- 454	LV657	A58- 519	MT620
A58- 325	JF966	A58- 390	JG465	A58- 455	LV727	A58- 520	MT655
A58- 326	JG104	A58- 391	JG471	A58- 456	MD251	A58- 521	MD351
A58- 327	JF871	A58- 392	JG342	A58- 457	MD296	A58- 522	MT514
A58- 328	JF872	A58- 393	JG350	A58- 458	MD297	A58- 523	MT547
A58- 329	JF938	A58- 394	JG373	A58- 459	MD298	A58- 524	MT549
A58- 330	JF939	A58- 395	JG377	A58- 460	MD299	A58- 525	MT550
A58- 331	JF940	A58- 396	JG420	A58- 461	MD315	A58- 526	MT552
A58- 332	JG174	A58- 397	JG423	A58- 462	MD337	A58- 527	MT632
A58- 333	JG175	A58- 398	JG425	A58- 463	JG466	A58- 528	MT675
A58- 334	JG176	A58- 399	JG432	A58- 464	JG557	A58- 529	MT682
A58- 335	JG177	A58- 400	MD223	A58- 465	MT545	A58- 530	MT703
A58- 336	JG187	A58- 401	MD226	A58- 466	MD252	A58- 531	MT672
A58- 337	JG188	A58- 402	MD232	A58- 467	MD338	A58- 532	MT771
A58- 338	JG189	A58- 403	MD238	A58- 468	MD372	A58- 533	MT778
A58- 339	JG191	A58- 404	MD241	A58- 469	MD376	A58- 534	MT781
A58- 340	JG192	A58- 405	JG467	A58- 470	JG558	A58- 535	MT782
A58- 341	JG239	A58- 406	JG481	A58- 471	LV750	A58- 536	MT788
A58- 342	JG264	A58- 407	JG482	A58- 472	MB960	A58- 537	MT794
A58- 343	JG271	A58- 408	JG484	A58- 473	MD344	A58- 538	LV672
A58- 344	JG343	A58- 409	JG604	A58- 474	MD355	A58- 539	MT548
A58- 345	JG346	A58- 410	JG607	A58- 475	MD385	A58- 540	MT621
A58- 346	JG351	A58- 411	JG611	A58- 476	MT539	A58- 541	MT622
A58- 347	JG352	A58- 412	MD250	A58- 477	MT541	A58- 542	MT630
A58- 348	JG371	A58- 413	MD281	A58- 478	MT542	A58- 543	MT635
A58- 349	JG414	A58- 414	MD283	A58- 479	MT543	A58- 544	MT650
A58- 350	JG416	A58- 415	MD300	A58- 480	JG652	A58- 545	MT658
A58- 351	JG417	A58- 416	MD317	A58- 481	JG653	A58- 546	MT673
A58- 352	JG421	A58- 417	JG485	A58- 482	JG655	A58- 547	MT681
A58- 353	JG422	A58- 418	JG533	A58- 483	JG659	A58- 548	MT767
A58- 354	JF884	A58- 419	JG549	A58- 484	JG543	A58- 549	MT779
A58- 355	JF965	A58- 420	MD217	A58- 485	JG650	A58- 550	MT787
A58- 356	JF885	A58- 421	MD234	A58- 486	JG666	GAP	
A58- 357	JG353	A58- 422	MT524	A58- 487	JG689	A58- 600	MV113
A58- 358	JG354	A58- 423	MT525	A58- 488	PA953	A58- 601	MV119
A58- 359	JG355	A58- 424	LV647	A58- 489	MT509	A58- 602	MV133
A58- 360	JG376	A58- 425	LV649	A58- 490	MT511	A58- 603	MT684
A58- 361	JG386	A58- 426	LV740	A58- 491	MT517	A58- 604	MT816
A58- 362	JG419	A58- 427	LV652	A58- 492	MT518	A58- 605	MT817
A58- 363	JG424	A58- 428	MD286	A58- 493	MT593	A58- 606	MT819
A58- 364	JG429	A58- 429	MD339	A58- 494	MB959	A58- 607	MT820
A58- 365	JG431	A58- 430	MD341	A58- 495	MT510	A58- 608	MT821
A58- 366	JG468	A58- 431	MD391	A58- 496	MT596	A58- 609	MT822
A58- 367	JG472	A58- 432	MD396	A58- 497	MT607	A58- 610	MT825

A58-611	MT829	A58-661	MV151	A58-711	MV506	**Without** RAAF SerialNo:	
A58-612	MT830	A58-662	MV152	A58-712	MT899		EE731
A58-613	MT831	A58-663	MV155	A58-713	MV171		
A58-614	MT833	A58-664	MV460	A58-714	MV465	GI airframes:	
A58-615	MT834	A58-665	MV461	A58-715	MT890	No.1	BS291
A58-616	MV112	A58-666	MV463	A58-716	MV485	No.2	EE231
A58-617	MV115	A58-667	MV464	A58-717	MV184	No.3	?
A58-618	MV123	A58-668	MV467	A58-718	MV200	No.4	LZ926
A58-619	MV135	A58-669	MT892	A58-719	MV241	No.5	BR536
A58-620	MV136	A58-670	MV153	A58-720	MV244	No.6	BS186
A58-621	MV138	A58-671	MV154	A58-721	MV243	No.7	BR468
A58-622	MV139	A58-672	MV156	A58-722	MV514	No.8	EE835
A58-623	MV141	A58-673	MV468	A58-723	MV342	No.9	?
A58-624	MV144	A58-674	MV469	A58-724	MT835	No.10	EE678
A58-625	MV149	A58-675	MV470	A58-725	MT910		
A58-626	MV114	A58-676	MV471	A58-726	MV187	**Sunk** in transit to Australia:	
A58-627	MV117	A58-677	MV475	A58-727	MV192		EE842
A58-628	MV120	A58-678	MT748	A58-728	MV199		EE843
A58-629	MV121	A58-679	MT893	A58-729	MV235		EE848
A58-630	MV124	A58-680	MT894	A58-730	MV482		JK174
A58-631	MV125	A58-681	MT895	A58-731	NH614		JK176
A58-632	MV128	A58-682	MV150	A58-732	MV180		JK181
A58-633	MV129	A58-683	MV176	A58-733	MT914		JK184
A58-634	MV132	A58-684	MV189	A58-734	MV181		JK257
A58-635	MV169	A58-685	MV322	A58-735	MV185		JK258
A58-636	MV170	A58-686	MV487	A58-736	MV186		JK273
A58-637	MV172	A58-687	MV503	A58-737	MV190		JK331
A58-638	MV173	A58-688	MV504	A58-738	MV191		
A58-639	MV174	A58-689	MV505	A58-739	MV193	Only temporarily in Australia, returned UK:	
A58-640	MV175	A58-690	MV508	A58-740	MV194		
A58-641	MV182	A58-691	MV510	A58-741	MV196		RR232
A58-642	MV321	A58-692	MV179	A58-742	MV197		
A58-643	MV466	A58-693	MV240	A58-743	MV198	**Survivors** in Australia:	
A58-644	MV472	A58-694	MV324	A58-744	MV202	See after serial number listing	
A58-645	MV473	A58-695	MV484	A58-745	MV206		
A58-646	MV474	A58-696	MV502	A58-746	MV237	**Civil** reg.:	
A58-647	MV476	A58-697	MV507	A58-747	MV242	VH-FVB	BL628
A58-648	MV477	A58-698	MV509	A58-748	MV344	VH-HET	MV239
A58-649	MV478	A58-699	MV511	A58-749	MT898	VH-XIV	RM797
A58-650	MV479	A58-700	MV512	A58-750	MV188	VH-XVI	TE384
A58-651	MV486	A58-701	MV513	A58-751	MV195	VH-ZPY	MD338
A58-652	MT896	A58-702	MV177	A58-752	MV203		
A58-653	MT897	A58-703	MV178	A58-753	MV204		
A58-654	MT900	A58-704	MV183	A58-754	MV207	The following RAAF serial numbers were not allotted:	
A58-655	MV116	A58-705	MV323	A58-755	MV233		
A58-656	MV137	A58-706	MV325	A58-756	MV346		
A58-657	MV140	A58-707	MV499	A58-757	MT891	A58-186 to 199	
A58-658	MV146	A58-708	MV481	A58-758	MV239	A58-260 to 299	
A58-659	MV147	A58-709	MV500			A58-551 to 599	
A58-660	MV148	A58-710	MV501				

Spitfire LF.VIIIc A58-489 UP-L (ex MT509) of No.79 Sqn RAAF formating on a P-38 Lightning in 1945.
[Gene Sommerich/ Howard Levy collection]

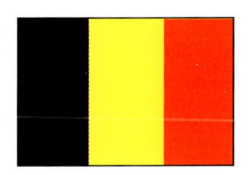

BELGIUM

Belgium's primary interest was in licence-building Spitfires, and at the end of 1937 the Belgian Government asked for one example as a pattern aircraft. After initial discussions, this was increased to ten aircraft, then later to 30 with a licence to build an additional 35 aircraft. On 28th September 1938 a firm quotation was given to Belgium for 15 to 45 Spitfires (Spec.No.456). This was given second place in the priority list, but on the outbreak of the Second World War all were cancelled.

During WWII Belgians flew Spitfires with Nos.349 and 350 Squadrons of the Royal Air Force. From August 1945 they operated under No.160 Wing RAF at Fassberg, Germany (BAFO), moving to Beauvechain, Belgium, on 24th October 1946, to join "A"-Wing of the Belgian Air Force.

Belgian Spitfire units of the Royal Air Force

No.**349** Sqn, formed at Wittering near Stamford on 5th June 1943; Spitfire Mks.V, IX, and LF.XVIe from May 1945; Code "GE".

No.**350** Sqn, formed at Valley in Anglesey on 12th November 1941, from the Belgian flights of Nos.130 & 609 Sqns, successively flying Mks.II, V, IX, XIV, and LF.XVIe from January 1946; Sqn code "MN".

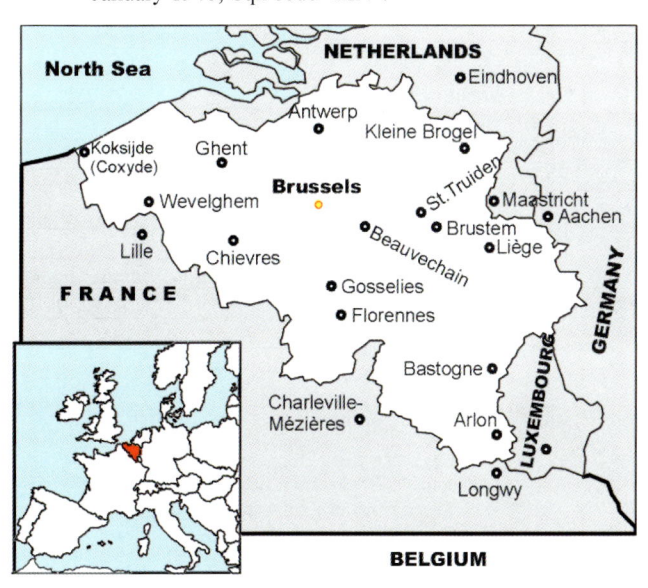

The Belgian Air Force (BAF)

In August 1945 the two squadrons, Nos.349 & 350, which by then formed part of No.123 Wing in No.84 Group, 2nd Tactical Air Force, were grouped as a new No.160 (Belgian) Wing based at Fassberg, Germany. On 15th October 1946 the wing and its squadrons moved to Beauvechain (near Brussels), and on 24th October 1946 this formation was transferred to the re-formed Belgian Air Force (*BAF*), known also as *Aviation Militaire Belge* until January 1949, when it became *Force Aérienne Belge*.

The new built-up Belgian Air Force was eventually to use a total of 203 Spitfires (Mks. IX, XIV & XVI), comprising:

- **26** Spitfire LF.XVIe on loan from the RAF, pending delivery of Mk.XIVs, the last departing in early 1948.
- **43** Spitfire LF.IXc/e, mostly with armament removed, for fighter pilot training by the Ecole de Pilotage Avece (EPA) at Brustem, comprising.
  SM-1 to SM-28 ("SM" = Spitfire/Merlin), delivered August 1947 to November 1948; In service until 1954.
  SM-29 to SM-43 (ex RNethAF range H-50 to H-69), delivered via Fokker (Delivery numbers B-1 to B-15) from June 1952 to March 1954; Remained in service until October 1954.
- **134** Spitfire F/FR.XIVc/e (FRs but without cameras) as replacements for the fighter squadrons and the Ecole de Chasse, remained in service until 1954:
  SG1 to SG-102 ("SG" = Spitfire/Griffon), delivered by air April 1947 to July 1949 (British Comm.No 327)
  SG-103 to SG-132 delivered 1950/51 under Western Union contract. Sold to Belgium, via Vickers-Armstrongs for overhaul.

In addition two Mk.XIVs were delivered for ground instructional use and spares in the autumn of 1947.

Spitfire units of the Belgian Air Force

No.1 Fighter Wing at Beauvechain;
"A" Wing with Spitfire LF.XVIe from 24th October 1946; No.160 Wing with Mk.XIV from 21st April 1947; No.1 (F) Wing from 1 February 1948.
Commanding Officers:

Maj D Le Roy du Vivier, DFC	from 6.46
Maj Léon Prévot, DFC	7.46
Maj Rémy Van Lierde, DFC	6.47
Maj Léopold Collignon, DFC	10.47
Maj A Van de Velde, DFC	7.48
Lt Col Joseph Renier, DFC	1.51

No.1 (F) Wing Flying Group leaders:

Maj Joseph Renier, DFC	10.49
S/Ldr Winskill (RAF)	3.50

No.1 (F) Wing comprised:

No.**349** (F) Sqn [Escadrille]; Spitfire LF.XVIe from October 1946 to November 1947; Mk.XIV from March 1947 to December 1949; Blue spinners; Sqn code 'GE'.
Commanding Officers:

Maj Albert Van De Velde, DFC	from 12.45
Maj LE "Manu" Geerts, DFC	11.46
Maj Paul Deschamps	9.47
Maj Marcel Mullenders	7.48
Capt-Cdt Léon Divoy	8.50.

No.**350** (F) Sqn [Escadrille]; Spitfire LF.XVIe from October 1946 to November 1947; Mk.XIV from October 1947 to December 1949; Red spinners; Sqn code 'MN'.
Commanding Officers:

S/Ldr Rémy Van Lierde, DFC	from 8.45
Capt Roger Duchateau	12.46
Maj Guy de Patoul	8.48

Auxiliary Sqn [Escadrille]; Week-end flyers; Formed 1st December 1949 with Mk.IX, then from 21st January 1950 with Mk.XIV from No.350 Sqn until December 1952, when aircraft transferred to Ecole de Chasse and later to No.10 Fighter Wing; White or silver spinners; Sqn code 'GV'.
Commanding Officers:

Lt Col (Res) Daniel Le Roy du Vivier, DFC & bar	12.49
Maj Léopold Mouzon DFC	in 1952

No.2 Fighter Wing at Florennes;
"B" Wing with Nos.351 & 352 Sqns from December 1946; No.161 Wing from 1 April 1947; No.2 (F) Wing with Nos.1 & 2 Sqns from 1st February 1948, later also No.3 Sqn.

Spitfire FR.XIVe MN-L of No.350 Sqn BAF taxying over grass. It could have been either SG-94 (ex NH984) or SG-31 (ex RN201). [MAP]

Commanding Officers:
Lt Col Raymond Lallemant, DFC & Bar 8.47
Lt Col Albert Custers 6.52

No.2 (F) Wing Flying Group leaders:
Maj Joseph Renier, DFC 9.50
Maj Herman Smets 1.51
Maj Robert Louvigny (interim) 8.52
Maj Roger De Wever 9.52

Spitfire F.XIVe of the Auxiliary Sqn at Beauvechain around 1950-1952. It may have been coded GV-R, which was carried at varous times by NH690, RM726 and RN115.

Spitfire Mk.XIVs of No.2 Escadrille lined up at Florennes. Note the different methods of applying the unit code markings on UR-Z and UR-G.

No.2 (F) Wing comprised:

No.**1** (F) Sqn [Escadrille], ex No.351 Sqn; Spitfire Mk.XIV from October 1947 to April 1952; Emblem: "*Thistle*"; Black spinners; Sqn code '3R'.
Commanding Officers:
Capt Albert Van Eeckhoudt from 11.47
Capt Marcel Mullenders 1.48
Capt Jean Morai 6.48
Capt Albert Van Eeckhoudt (interim) 11.48
Maj Roger De Wever 3.49
Maj Robert Louvigny 9.50

No.**2** Sqn [Escadrille]; ex No.352 Sqn; Mk.XIV from October 1947 to April 1952; Emblem: "*Comet*"; White spinners; Code 'UR'.
Commanding Officers:
Capt Herman Smets 11.47
Capt Guy de Bueger 11.49
Capt Armand Crekillie 9.51

No.**3** Sqn [Escadrille]; Week-end Flyers with Spitfire Mk.XIV from 1st December 1949 to April 1952; Green spinners; "*Holly leaf*" emblem; Sqn code 'YL'.
Commanding Officers:
Maj Léon Vandercruyssen 1.50
Capt Martin Wilmots 9.51
Capt-Cdt Louis Peeters 4.51

No.10 **Fighter Wing** at Kleine-Brogel, later Chievres, became fighter-bomber 1952.
Commanding Officers:
Maj Serge Gheude 12.51
Lt Col Yvan du Monceau de Bergendal 5.52

No.10 (F) Wing Flying Group leaders:
Maj Léon Prevot, DFC 6.52
Maj Roger De Wever 2.53

No.10 Wing comprised:

No.**23** Sqn [Escadrille]; Spitfire Mk.XIV from October 1951 to 1952; Emblem: "*Devil*"; Sqn code 'Z6'.
Commanding Officers:
Capt F Willems 9.51
Capt A Meyvus 10.51
Capt-Cdt E Carpentier 10.52

No.27   Sqn [Escadrille]; Spitfire Mk.XIV from December 1951 to 1952; Emblem: "*Panther*"; Sqn code 'RA'.
Commanding Officers:
Maj S Gheude   from 9.51

No.31   Sqn [Escadrille]; Spitfire Mk.XIV from January 1952 to July 1952; Emblem: "*Tiger*"; Sqn code '8S'.
Commanding Officers:
Capt Louis Lenoble   9.51
Capt Joseph Laloux   12.51
Capt Joseph Van Molkot   2.52
Capt Louis Lenoble   2.52
Maj André Papeians de Morckhoven   5.53

Note: Nos.23 & 27 Sqns were formed in September 1951 and No.31 Sqn in October 1951, joining No.10 Wing on 20th December 1951, with a maximum strength of 26 aircraft each. They used Spitfire Mk.XIVs from No.1 (F) Wing and some from No.2 (F) Wing from December 1951 until December 1952.

Ecole de Pilotage Avece at Brustem (***EPA***) - the Advanced Flying School (AFS) of the BAF; Spitfire LF.IX from July 1947 to October 1954 (22 Spitfires on strength in March 1953, and 17 on 18th May 1954); Yellow fuselage bands and spinners; Digits only (equal to the BAF serial numbers) were carried on the fuselage and wings.
Commanding Officers:
Maj Léon Prevot, DFC   from 5.47
Lt Col Lucien Truyers   9.49
Lt Col Herman De Man   3.52
Maj Joseph Willocq (temp)   5.52
Maj Léopold Collignon   2.53
Maj Joseph Willocq (temp)   8.53

125e Promotion at Brustem, a detachment of the AFS, trained with Harvard T-6 and 15 Spitfire LF.IX from 18th May 1954, after the main body of the EPA (AFS) was transferred to the Kamina airbase in Belgian Congo, making room for the newly-formed No.13 Wing with Meteors at Brustem.
The "125th" Promotion used Spitfires until October 1954.

Spitfire FR.XIVe SG-108 IQ-V (ex NH904) of the Ecole de Chasse in formation with SG-112 IQ-Y (ex MV267) and another machine in 1954. NH604 was later restored and is now with the Planes of Fame East Museum, Flying Cloud, Minnesota, USA, with the civil registration N114BP.

Spitfire LF.IXc MJ783 '15' (later SM-15) of the Ecole de Pilotage Avece, Brustem, around 1948-1951. It is exhibited in the Musée Royal d'Armée et d'Histoire Militaire, Brussels, marked as "MJ360/GE-B".

Ecole de Chasse (*EcC*) at Koksijde (Coxyde), was the OTU of the BAF, also named *Fighter School* or *Jachtvliegschool* ("*JVS*"); Spitfire Mk.XIV from September 1948 until October 1954; Received all the remaining Belgian Spitfire XIVs in July 1952, the maximum strength being 47 Spitfires in 1952/54. Yellow spinners; Unit code 'IQ'.
Commanding Officers:
Maj Giovanni Dieu, DFC from	4.48
Maj Pierre Arend	11.49
Lt Col Edgard Symaes	3.51
Lt Col Léon Vandercruyssen	6.54

Conversion Flight at Koksijde (Coxyde) (also referred to as "*Towing Flight*"), a detachment of the Ecole de Chasse, used Mosquitos and Spitfire Mk.XIV in 1953/54; Unit code 'B2'. Later target towing was done by the COGEA company with Spitfires.

Ecole Technique at Saffraanberg, St.Truiden - a Technical School (SoTT*)* with Spitfire ground instructional airframes for training the technical personnel, from the beginning of 1946; The building burnt down in June 1948 and the school was transferred to Tongeren, returning to Saffraanberg in August 1952; Used Spitfires for ground instructional use until 1954.
Commanding Officers:
Lt Col Auguste Poppe	1.1.50
Lt Col Léon Paulet	3.52

Spitfire F.XIVe NH694/6340M was supplied to Belgium in 1947 as a ground instructional frame for use by the School of Technical Training at Saffraanberg and later at Tongeren, being given the spurious code marking "GD-A".

Air Depot (Aircraft Arsenal) at Wevelghem,
Commanding Officers:
Maj Jean Legrand	12.46
Lt Col Pierre Arend	3.52
Lt Col Guy de Bueger	11.53

Note:
Aircraft repair was undertaken by the Fairey company at Gosselies near Charleroi

Civil user of Spitfires

The COGEA Nouvelle company, *Compagnie Génerale d'Exploitation Aérienne,* used Spitfire LF.IXs for target-towing duties between May 1956 and December 1966, based at Ostende, under Civil registrations:
OO-ARA, Cof R No.1070 - ex MH434 (SM-41)
OO-ARB, Cof R No.1074 - ex MK297 (SM-43)
OO-ARC, Cof R No.1077 - ex NH188 (SM-39)
OO-ARD, Cof R No.1079 - ex MH415 (SM-40)
OO-ARE, Cof R No.1097 - ex NH238 (SM-36)
OO-ARF, Cof R No.1184 - ex MK923 (SM-37)

Personal code letters carried on Belgian Spitfires

"GDA" - With pseudo marking "SR 111", NH694
"MLD" - Wg Cdr Baron MGL Donnet, S/Ldr No.350 Sqn 3.44-10.44, MV381 (SG-34)
"RLD" - Colonel RA Lallemant, S/Ldr (No.349 Sqn) until December 1945, TX995 (SG-49)
"RduV" - Wg Cdr D le Roy du Vivier, No.324 Wing RAF, MJ628
"YVEA" - Spitfire Mk.XIV of No.349 Sqn BAF, RM768 (SG-10)

Individual Histories

EN123 Spitfire LF.IXc (Merlin 66); Became **SM-7**; TOC/RAF 1.11.42 - Del 18.8.47; Ecole de Pilotage Avece (EPA) Brustem ('7') 22.8.47; Force-landed 12.3.48; Accident, Cat.E 18.7.51 (Sgt Dumont killed); R&SU 20.7.51; SOC 8.51

EN568 Spitfire LF.IXc (Merlin 66); Became **SM-6**; TOC/RAF 1.3.43 - Arr Belgium 19.8.47; Ecole de Pilotage Avece (EPA) Brustem ('6') 8.47; 125e Promotion 18.5.54; SOC 10.54

MH366 Spitfire LF.IXc (Merlin 66); Became **SM-12**; TOC/RAF 8.8.43; Despatched to Belgium but crashed on delivery 2.9.47 (Sgt Spiette of No.349 Sqn killed), SOC

MH415 Spitfire LF.IXc (Merlin 66); Became **SM-40**; TOC/RAF 1.8.43; Ex RNethAF (*H-108; H-65*), via Fokker (B-12) to BAF - Del Ecole de Pilotage Avece (EPA) Brustem ('40') 8.4.53; 125e Promotion 18.5.54; SOC 10.54; Sold to COGEA for target towing (Cof R No.1079); Civil reg. *OO-ARD* 15.6.56; Regn cancelled 23.12.66; Sold to T G Mahaddie/Film Aviation Services, Elstree, Hertfordshire, England (reg. *G-AVDJ* 29.12.66); To Spitfire Productions Ltd, Duxford 1.68 *(*used in film *Battle of Britain* as "GW-R"; To Wilson 'Connie' Edwards, Big Springs, Texas, USA 11.68 (*N415MH*; marked "ZD-E"); Offered for sale - **SURVIVOR**

MH424 Spitfire LF.IXc (Merlin 66); Became **SM-32**; TOC/RAF 11.8.43; Ex RNethAF (*H-106; H-53*), via Fokker (B-4) to BAF - Del Ecole de Pilotage Avece (EPA) Brustem 8.8.52; Accident, Cat.A 16.4.54; 125e Promotion 18.5.54; SOC 10.54; w/o 1956

MH434 Spitfire LF.IXc (Merlin 66); Became **SM-41**; TOC/RAF 13.8.43; Ex RNethAF (*H-105; H-68*), via Fokker (B-13) to BAF - Del Ecole de Pilotage Avece (EPA) Brustem ('41') 9.10.53; Accident, 19.3.54; 125e Promotion 18.5.54; SOC 10.54; Sold to COGEA 26.3.56 (CofR No.1070); Reg. *OO-ARA* 23.3.56 for target towing; Regn cancelled 2.7.63; Sold to Tim Davies, Elstree, Hertfordshire, England (reg. *G-ASJV* 29.6.63), used in film as "GW-U"; To T G Mahaddie, Elstree; Sold to Adrian C Swire, Booker 2.69 (marked "AC-S"); Sold to Old Flying Machine Co, Duxford (Ray Hanna) 4.83, extant, airworthy - **SURVIVOR**

MH439 Spitfire LF.IXc (Merlin 66); Became **SM-33**; TOC/RAF 13.8.43; Ex RNethAF (*H-120; H-56*), via Fokker (B-5) to BAF - Del Ecole de Pilotage Avece (EPA) Brustem 3.10.52; Crashed Cat.E 13.1.54 (Sgt Naessens killed); SOC 15.1.54; R&SU 21.1.54 (w/o 1956)

MH485 Spitfire LF.IXc (Merlin 66); Became **SM-30**; TOC/RAF 18.8.43; Ex RNethAF (*H-102; H-51*), via Fokker (B-2) to BAF – Belly-landed on delivery flight 4.6.52; Ecole de Pilotage Avece (EPA) Brustem ('30') 6.52; Broke fuselage, Cat.E 29.4.53; R&SU 2.6.53; SOC 10.4.54

MH725 Spitfire LF.IXc (Merlin 66); Became **SM-38**; TOC/RAF 1.10.43; Ex RNethAF (*H-112; H-63*), via Fokker (B-10) to BAF - Del Ecole de Pilotage Avece (EPA) Brustem ('38') 26.3.53; Accident, Cat.E 6.5.54; R&SU 11.5.54; 125e Promotion 18.5.54; SOC 10.54

MJ244 Spitfire LF.IXc (Merlin 66); Became **SM-11**; TOC/RAF 5.11.43 - Del 2.9.47; Ecole de Pilotage Avece (EPA) Brustem 4.9.47; R&SU 24.6.48; Accident, Cat.3 10.10.52; 125e Promotion 18.5.54; SOC 10.54

MJ332 Spitfire LF.IXc (Merlin 66); Became **SM-14**; TOC/RAF 24.10.43 - Del 18.11.47; Ecole de Pilotage Avece (EPA) Brustem 5.12.47; Belly-landed, Cat.3 9.1.51; R&SU 24.1.51; RiW, Fairey company 5.4.51; SOC 1.4.53; 125e Promotion 18.5.54; SOC 10.54

MJ353 Spitfire LF.IXc (Merlin 66); Became **SM-2**; TOC/RAF 25.11.43 - Del 17.8.47; Ecole de Pilotage Avece (EPA)

Spitfire LF.IXc SM-15 (ex MJ783) shortly after it became a museum aircraft on being struck off charge in 1951.

Brustem 8.9.48; Fairey company, inspection 9.1.49; EPA 2.49; Accident, Cat.E 17.5.50 (Sgt Hernould killed); R&SU 20.5.50; SOC 9.6.50

MJ421 Spitfire LF.IXc (Merlin 66); Became **SM-9**; TOC/RAF 2.11.43 - Del 26.8.47; Ecole de Pilotage Avece (EPA) Brustem 27.8.47; Crashed on landing 8.4.49; R&SU 30.4.49; RiW, Fairey company 30.4.49; EPA in 5.49; Accident, Cat.E 4.8.50 (Sgt Lacroix killed); R&SU 11.8.50; SOC

MJ482 Spitfire LF.IXc (Merlin 66); Became **SM-19**; TOC/RAF 13.11.43 - Del 10.7.48; Ecole de Pilotage Avece (EPA) Brustem 12.7.48; Accident, 20.12.51; Accident, Cat.E 14.1.52 (Corporal Delcon killed); R&SU 18.1.52; SOC

MJ559 Spitfire LF.IXc (Merlin 66); Became **SM-22**; TOC/RAF 24.4.44 - Del Ecole de Pilotage Avece (EPA) Brustem 24.8.48; Accident, Cat.3 13.9.52; SOC 3.11.52; 125e Promotion 18.5.54; w/o 10.54
NOTE: Wings now on MK912 (SM-29)

MJ617 Spitfire LF.IXc (Merlin 66); Became **SM-23**; TOC/RAF 29.11.43 - Del 24.8.48; Ecole de Pilotage Avece (EPA) Brustem 1.9.48; Fairey company, inspection 19.4.51; EPA 20.4.51; Collided with PV189 (SM-26), Cat.E 25.6.52 (Sgt Francotte killed); R&SU 29.6.52; SOC

MJ714 Spitfire LF.IXc (Merlin 66); Became **SM-35**; TOC/RAF 20.12.43; Ex RNethAF (*H-117; H-67*), via Fokker (B-7) to BAF - Del Ecole de Pilotage Avece (EPA) Brustem 29.1.53; Overturned, Cat.E 10.3.54; SOC 9.4.54

MJ783 Spitfire LF.IXc (Merlin 66); Became **SM-15**; TOC/RAF 20.12.43 - Del 3.2.48; Ecole de Pilotage Avece (EPA) Brustem ('15') 4.2.48; Accident, Cat.4 3.7.51; Re-Cat.5; SOC 20.7.51; R&SU 3.8.51; To Musée de l'Armée Militaire/Palais du Cinquantaire, Brussels 1.52; Stored 1978; Exhibited Musée Royal d'Armée et d'Histoire Militaire, Brussels from 1980, marked as "MJ360/GE-B" (with wing from PT643/SM-13) Extant - **SURVIVOR**

MJ893 Spitfire LF.IXc (Merlin 66); Became **SM-42**; TOC/RAF 8.1.44; Ex RNethAF (*H-110; H-69*), via Fokker (B-14) to BAF - Del Ecole de Pilotage Avece (EPA) Brustem 22.4.53; Fuselage broken, Cat.E 6.5.54; R&SU 11.5.54; SOC 6.5.54; w/o 1956

MK153 Spitfire LF.IXc (Merlin 66); Became **SM-28**; TOC/RAF 29.1.44 - Del 20.11.48; Ecole de Pilotage Avece (EPA) Brustem 21.12.48; Crashed on landing, overturned, Cat.4 7.3.51; R&SU 9.3.51; RiW, Fairey company 13.7.51; SOC 2.10.51

MK205 Spitfire LF.IXc (Merlin 66); Became **SM-31**; TOC/RAF 28.1.44; Ex RNethAF (*H-101; H-52*), via Fokker (B-3) to BAF - Del Ecole de Pilotage Avece (EPA) Brustem 26.6.52; Accident, 11.10.52; R&SU 19.11.52; RiW, Fairey company 22.5.53; R&SU 3.5.54; SOC

MK297 Spitfire LF.IXc (Merlin 66); Became **SM-43**; TOC/RAF 30.1.44; Ex RNethAF (*H-116; H-55*), via Fokker (B-15) to BAF - Del Ecole de Pilotage Avece (EPA) Brustem ('43') 16.6.53; Accident, 10.3.54; 125e Promotion 18.5.54; SOC 10.54; Sold to COGEA, Nouvelle, Ostend for target towing (CofR No.1074) Civil reg. *OO-ARB* 5.5.56; Used in film 'The Longest Day' in 1961; Regn cancelled 27.4.64; Sold to J Crewdson / Film Aviation Services Ltd, Biggin Hill, Kent (reg. *G-ASSD* 28.4.64); Sold to R A Wale, London 3.65; To Confederate Air Force, Mercedes, Texas 5.65 (reg. *N11RS* NTU), but remained in UK for filming work, also in France; Retd J Crewdson/Film Aviation Services Ltd, Biggin Hill, Kent 5.66; To H A Rich, Henlow, Bedfordshire 9.66; Used in film *Battle of Britain* as "GW-O"), but damaged at North Weald on 17.5.68; To USA and shipped from Bovingdon to Houston, Texas 11.68 for Aerosmith Corpn, Dallas/Confederate Air Force (reg. *N1882, N11RS, NX9BL*); Destroyed in hangar fire at Hamilton, Canada 2.93; Total loss

MK577 Spitfire LF.IXc (Merlin 66); Became **SM-21**; TOC/RAF 4.4.44 - Del 26.7.48; Ecole de Pilotage Avece (EPA) Brustem 2.8.48; Accident, Cat.4 25.8.49; RiW, Fairey company 19.9.49; EPA in 10.49; Accident, 13.9.52; SoTT Saffraanberg 10.52

MK777 Spitfire LF.IXc (Merlin 66); Became **SM-24**; TOC/RAF

Spitfire LF.IXc SM-29 (ex MK912), minus its engine and wings and marked "MN-P", in storage in the UK in 1989 prior to restoration.

Spitfire LF.IXc SM-29 (ex MK912) after restoration at Audley End, Essex, with the civil registration G-BRRA. It is currently based at Duxford, marked "SH-L" and "FRANCQUI".

2.3.44 - Del Ecole de Pilotage Avece (EPA) Brustem 24.8.48; Melsbroek 11.6.49; R&SU 13.6.49; EPA in 7.49; Crashed 20.7.53; R&SU 25.8.53; SOC 27.8.53

MK912 Spitfire LF.IXc (Merlin 66); Became **SM-29**; TOC/RAF 24.3.44; Ex RNethAF (H-119; H-59), via Fokker (B-1) to BAF - Del Ecole de Pilotage Avece (EPA) Brustem 4.6.52; Accident, Cat.3 17.6.53; SOC 6.53; Extant; Exhibited Belgian Air Force Technical School, Saffraanberg (marked "MN-P") from 8.55 with wing of MJ559/SM-22; To Musée Royal d'Armée et d'Histoire Militaire, Brussels 1988; Sold to Guy Black/Historical Aircraft Collection, Hastings, Sussex, England 22.6.89 (Civil reg. *G-BRRA* 10.10.89*)*; to Historic Aircraft Collection Ltd; Stored at Paddock Wood, Kent from 1993; To Karel Bos/Historic Flying Ltd, Audley End, Essex, for restoration); Airworthy, test flown 8.9.2000 (Plt J Romain); Duxford based, marked "SH-L" and *"Francqui"* - **SURVIVOR**

MK923 Spitfire LF.IXc (Merlin 66); Became **SM-37**; TOC/RAF 24.3.44; Ex RNethAF (*H-104; H-61*), via Fokker (B-9) to

BAF - Del Ecole de Pilotage Avece (EPA) Brustem ('37') 25.2.53; Accident, Cat.3 in 1953; 125e Promotion 18.5.54; SOC 10.54; Sold to COGEA for target towing (CofR No.1184) Civil reg. *OO-ARF* 25.4.58; Used in film *The Longest Day* in France in 1961; Regn cancelled 26.11.63; Sold to Clifford P Robertson, Santa Ana, California USA and airfreighted from Biggin Hill 17.11.63 (Regd *N93081*, then *NX521R*); Kalamazoo Air Zoo Museum Michigan (Cliff Robertson), for display; To Craig McCaw, Washington, DC 1998; To Museum of Flight, Boeing Field, Seattle, May 2001, for display - **SURVIVOR**

ML423 Spitfire LF.IXc (Merlin 66); Became **SM-18**; TOC/RAF 27.4.44 - Del 10.7.48; Ecole de Pilotage Avece (EPA) Brustem ('18') 12.7.48; Force-landed wheels-up in France, Cat.4 13.1.51; R&SU 27.1.51; RiW, Fairey company 3.4.51; EPA; 125e Promotion 18.5.54; SOC 10.54

MV246 Spitfire F.XIVe (Griffon 65); Became **SG-55**; TOC/RAF 29.11.44 - Selected for BAF and flown to Belgium 24.8.48, TOC/BAF 26.8.48; No.349 Sqn ('GE-R'), force-landed Opvelp, Cat.5 11.10.48 (Sgt Saeys safe); SOC 10.8.51; To Musée de l'Armée et d'Histoire Militaire, Brussels, for restoration 25.2.51; Wings from RM860 (SG-37) & RM625 (SG-46), and engine of TZ137 (SG-33); Displayed as "SG-55/GE-R" - **SURVIVOR**

MV248 Spitfire FR.XIVe (Griffon 65); Became **SG-4**; TOC/RAF 30.11.44 - Selected for BAF 24.4.47, flown to Belgium 25.4.47; No.349 Sqn ('GE- ') 8.5.47; Ecole de Chasse ('IQ-O'); Conversion Flight ('B2-H'); SOC 21.9.54; w/o 18.10.54. NOTE: Fitted bubble hood

MV256 Spitfire FR.XIVe (Griffon 65); Became **SG-39**; TOC/RAF 26.12.44 - Selected for BAF and flown to Belgium 22.3.48; SABCA 11.5.48; noted at Evère; SOC 29.10.48 NOTE: Cockpit damaged by accident, arr BAF in unsatisfactory condition, replaced by adding one to Comm.No.327

MV261 Spitfire F.XIVe (Griffon 65); Became **SG-104**; TOC/RAF 18.12.44 - WU-contract: Sold to Belgium, to Vickers-Armstrongs for overhaul 11.1.51; First flight BAF 20.4.51; No.31 Sqn; Ecole de Chasse ('IQ-N'); Accident, Cat.3, Koksijde, 26.2.54; SOC 21.9.54; w/o 18.10.54

MV263 Spitfire F.XIVe (Griffon 65); Became **SG-77**; TOC/RAF 1.45 - Selected for BAF 9.12.48, flown to Belgium 10.12.48; Ecole de Chasse ('IQ-T'); Accident, Cat.3 24.10.49; Engine failed on take-off, force-landed Koksijde, Cat.5 18.7.50 (Sgt G Dubart safe); SOC 21.9.54; w/o 18.10.54

MV265 Spitfire F.XIVe (Griffon 65); Became **SG-103**; TOC/RAF 31.12.44 - WU-contract: Sold to Belgium, to Vickers-Armstrongs for overhaul 15.1.51; First flight BAF 1.5.51; No.2 (F) Wing; No.31 Sqn ('8S-E') 1952; Last public display NATO Meeting at Melsbroek 13.7.52 (1/Lt T de Maere d'Aertrijcke); Ecole de Chasse; Accident, at Chièvres, Cat.4 9.10.52; Re-Cat.5 & SOC 10.52; To No.7 Wing 10.52 for fire fighting practice, still marked "8S-E"

MV267 Spitfire FR.XIVe (Griffon 65); Became **SG-112**; TOC/RAF 4.1.45 - WU-contract: Sold to Belgium, to Vickers-Armstrongs for overhaul 25.8.50; BAF, Conversion Flight ('B2-J'); Ecole de Chasse ('IQ-Y'); Running out of fuel, belly-landed near Mardyck, France, Cat.4 10.5.54 (Sgt Wauters safe); Re-Cat.5 & SOC 24.5.54

MV288 Spitfire FR.XIVe (Griffon 65) Became **SG-30**; TOC/RAF 1.2.45 - Selected for BAF and flown to Belgium 28.1.48; No.350 Sqn ('M'); Ecole de Chasse ('IQ-K'; also reported 'IQ-J') 10.8.51; Engine failed, belly-landed Wevelghem, Cat.4 10.6.50 (Sgt H Stoffels safe); Crashed Koksijde Cat.5 10.8.51 (Sgt Vanderkelen killed) [see also SG-47 crashed previous day by same pilot]; SOC 17.8.51

MV302 Spitfire FR.XIVe (Griffon 65); Became **SG-36**; TOC/RAF 21.2.45 - Selected for BAF and flown to Belgium 22.3.48; No.2 Sqn ('UR-A':'UR-G'), Engine failed, belly-landed Thy-le-Baudouin, Cat.4 2.6.48 (Sgt Kelder safe); Ecole de Chasse ('IQ-K':'IQ-C'); Damaged at Florennes when hangar roof collapsed under weight of snow, Cat.4 10.12.50; Conversion Flight ('B2-R') 1954; SOC 21.9.54; w/o 18.10.54

MV312 Spitfire FR.XIVe (Griffon 65); Became **SG-99**; TOC/RAF 29.3.45 - Selected for BAF and flown to Belgium 22.6.49; No.1 Sqn ('3R-A'); Crashed at Flavion near Florennes after mid-air collision with RM784 (SG-100), Cat.5 23.9.49 (1/Lt Albertus Michiels killed); SOC

MV359 Spitfire FR.XIVe (Griffon 65); Became **SG-131**; TOC/RAF 3.2.45 - WU-contract: Sold to Belgium, to Vickers-Armstrongs for overhaul 15.11.50; Ecole de Chasse ('IQ-S'); Conversion Flight ('B2-O'); SOC 6.4.54

Spitfire F.XIVe SG-55 (ex MV246) 'GE-R' of No.349 Sqn BAF, suffered engine failure after the propeller drive broke in flight, and it force landed wheels-up near Opvelp (Leuven) on 11th October 1948, Sgt Harry A Saeys being fortunately unhurt. This machine is extant in the Military Museum at Brussels.
[Harry A Saeys]

Spitfire LF.IXc SM-39 (ex NH188) with the Ecole de Pilotage Avece (EPA) Brustem around 1953/4. It survives in the Canadian National Aviation Museum at Rockcliffe, Ontario, now marked "AU-H".

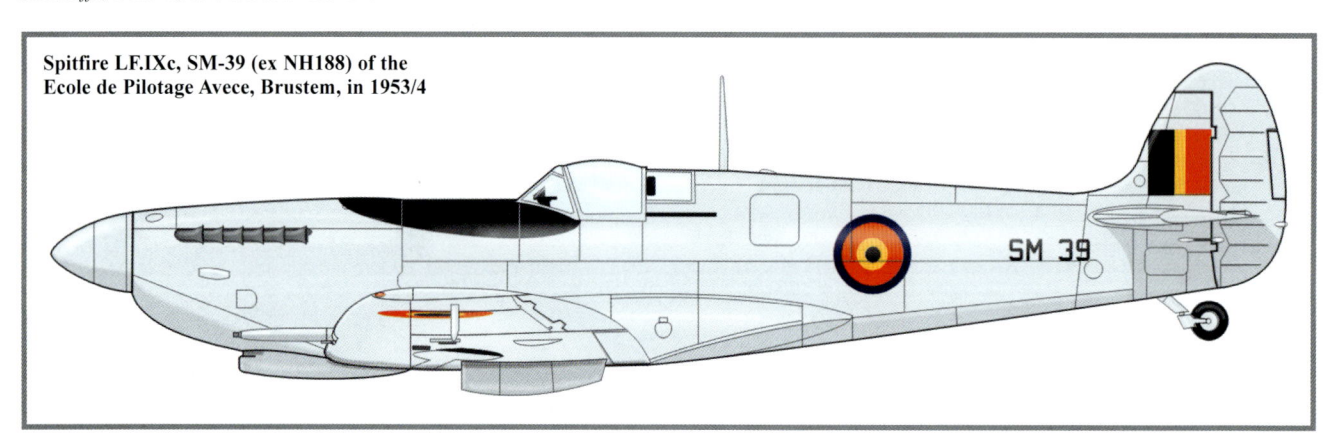

Spitfire LF.IXc, SM-39 (ex NH188) of the Ecole de Pilotage Avece, Brustem, in 1953/4

MV360 Spitfire FR.XIVe; TOC/RAF 17.1.45; Despatched to Belgium, but crashed on ferry flight, Cat.5 9.3.49 (1/Lt T de Maere d'Aertrijcke safe); SOC/RAF 25.3.49

MV369 Spitfire FR.XIVe (Griffon 65); Became **SG-90**; TOC/RAF 3.2.45 - Selected for BAF and flown to Belgium 8.2.49; Ecole de Chasse ('IQ-B'); No.1 Sqn ('3R-D'); Crashed Cat.4 28.3.49 (Capt Louvigny safe); Re-Cat.5 & SOC 7.6.49

MV378 Spitfire FR.XIVe (Griffon 65); Became **SG-50**; TOC/RAF 20.1.45 - Selected for BAF 9.7.48, flown to Belgium 10.7.48; No.1 Sqn ('3R-A'); No.31 Sqn ('8S-R'); No.23 Sqn ('Z6- '); Ecole de Chasse; SOC 21.9.54; w/o 18.10.54

MV381 Spitfire FR.XIVe (Griffon 65); Became **SG-34**; TOC/RAF 21.2.45 - Selected for BAF and flown to Belgium 10.3.48; No.349 Sqn ('GE-B'; Also "MLD" c.6.49, the personal markings of Wg Cdr Baron Michael GL Donnet DFC, Croix de Guerre); No.2 (F) Wing; No.23 Sqn ('Z6- ') 17.10.51; Ecole de Chasse ('IQ- '); SOC 21.9.54; w/o 18.10.54

MV382 Spitfire FR.XIVe (Griffon 65); Became **SG-80**; TOC/RAF 3.2.45 - Selected for BAF 16.12.48, flown to Belgium 17.12.48; No.350 Sqn ('MN-T'); Auxiliary Sqn ('GV-T':'GV-S', also reported 'GV-J'); Crashed on landing Beauvechain, Cat.5 20.7.52 (Lt H Branders safe), SOC

MV383 Spitfire FR.XIVe (Griffon 65); Became **SG-95**; TOC/RAF 14.2.45 - Selected for BAF and flown to Belgium 11.5.49; No.1 Sqn ('3R-D'); Ecole de Chasse ('IQ-N'); Collided with NH863 (SG-93), Cat.5 3.8.53 (Adj E Verschueren killed), SOC

NH188 Spitfire LF.IXc (Merlin 66); Became **SM-39**; TOC/RAF 1.5.44; Ex RNethAF (*H-109; H-64*), via Fokker (B-11) to BAF - Del 22.4.53; Ecole de Pilotage Avece (EPA) Brustem ('39') 4.53; Accident, Cat.3 21.3.54; SOC 12.4.54; Storage. 17.5.54; 125e Promotion 18.5.54; SOC 10.54; Sold to COGEA, Nouvelle, Ostend, for target towing (CofR No.1077) Civil reg. *OO-ARC*, 25.5.56; Regn cancelled 27.12.60; Shipped from UK to John N Paterson, Fort William, Ontario, Canada 8.61 (Civil reg. *CF-NUS*), ff 13.2.62; To the Canadian National Aeronautical Collection/Canadian National Aviation Museum, Rockcliffe, Ontario 6.6.64 (marked "AU-H") - **SURVIVOR**

NH238 Spitfire LF.IXc (Merlin 66); Became **SM-36**; TOC/RAF 6.5.44; Ex RNethAF (*H-103; H-60*), via Fokker (B-8) to BAF - Del Ecole de Pilotage Avece (EPA) Brustem ('36') 29.1.53; 125e Promotion 18.5.54; SOC 10.54; Sold to COGEA, Nouvelles, Ostend for target towing (CofR No.1097) Civil reg. *OO-ARE* 8.9.56. To Beverley Snook/Trans Global Aviation Supply, Southend, Essex, England 27.5.61; Wing damaged by fuel explosion on ground at Elstree 2.6.61; Regn cancelled 24.7.61; Sold to

Beverley Snook, Southend, Essex 1961; Displayed by Taskers of Andover Ltd museum, on an RAF transporter 18.7.61; To Thomas H Pasteur, Eastleigh 22.2.69; To USA 3.7.69, Yesterday AF (*N238V*), flown as "EN398/JE-J"; To UK 1979 (Douglas W Arnold, Blackbushe); Warbirds of Great Britain Ltd, Blackbushe (regd *G-MKIX* 12.12.83); ff 6.5.84; To Biggin Hill 1988; To Flying A Services, stored North Weald - **SURVIVOR**

NH309 Spitfire LF.IXc (Merlin 66); Became **SM-34**; TOC/RAF 5.4.44; Ex RNethAF (*H-113; H-57*), via Fokker (B-6) to BAF - Del Ecole de Pilotage Avece (EPA) Brustem 21.8.52; Overturned, Cat.4 8.4.53; R&SU 18.4.53; RiW, Fairey company 29.5.53; SOC 9.4.54; R&SU 30.4.54; w/o 1956

NH643 Spitfire FR.XIVe (Griffon 65); Became **SG-26**; TOC/RAF 10.3.45 - Selected for BAF and flown to Belgium 14.1.48; No.2 (F) Wing; Ecole de Chasse ('IQ-R'); Ground-collision with RM913 (SG-62) at Koksijde, Cat.3 22.5.50 (Lt Francken); Aux Sqn ('GV-J'); Accident, 23.7.51; Dived into ground near Lamine/Remicourt, Cat.5 10.4.52 (Capt Debie killed); SOC 10.4.52

NH654 Spitfire F.XIVe (Griffon 65); Became **SG-8**; TOC/RAF 11.3.44 - Selected for BAF 24.4.47, flown to Belgium 25.4.47; No.349 Sqn ('GE-P'); No.2 Sqn ('UR-O'); Engine failed, force-landed wheels-up Isnes-les-Temploux, Cat.4 18.11.48 (Capt R Duchateau safe); Engine failed, force-landed Florennes, Cat.5 27.10.50 (Sgt Ossieur injured); SOC 3.2.51

NH655 Spitfire F.XIVc (Griffon 65); Became **SG-1**; TOC/RAF 14.3.44 - Selected for BAF and flown to Belgium 17.4.47; No.349 Sqn ('GE-A') 22.5.47; Belly-landed Beauvechain, Cat.3 1.9.47 (Sgt Claes safe); No.2 Sqn ('UR-2'); Ecole de Chasse ('IQ- '); Undercarriage failed Koksijde, Cat.4 27.8.50 (Adj Renson safe); SOC 21.9.54; w/o 18.10.54

NH658 Spitfire F.XIVc (Griffon 65); Became **SG-113**; TOC/RAF 26.3.44; ex No.350 Sqn RAF - WU-contract: Sold to Belgium, to Vickers-Armstrongs for overhaul 25.8.50; First flight BAF 26.4.51; Ecole de Chasse ('IQ-M'); SOC 6.4.54

NH688 Spitfire FR.XIVe (Griffon 65); Became **SG-16**; TOC/RAF 26.3.44 - Selected for BAF and flown to Belgium 25.7.47; No.349 Sqn ('GE-V'); Belly-landed Beauvechain, Cat.4 12.3.48 (Sgt J Hubert safe); Ecole de Chasse ('IQ-L'); No.2 (F) Wing; No.1 Sqn ('3R-E'); Lost control landing Florennes, Cat.5 3.7.50 (Sgt Deketelaere safe); SOC 18.8.50

NH690 Spitfire F.XIVc (Griffon 65); Became **SG-114**; TOC/RAF 5.4.44 - WU-contract: Sold to Belgium, to Vickers-Armstrongs for overhaul 25.8.50; First flight BAF 14.3.51 (acceptance flight); Aux Sqn ('GV-R'); Ecole de Chasse ('IQ-P'); SOC 6.4.54

NH694 Spitfire F.XIVe (Griffon 65); TOC/RAF 21.4.44; To Ground Instructional No.*6340M*; Allocated BAF 22.5.47; No.47 MU 16.6.47; Liverpool 24.7.47; Despatched to Belgium 24.7.47, arr Antwerp 29.7.47; SoTT Saffraanberg 8.47; SoTT Tongeren 6.48; Exhibited in the Jubelpark "Astridplein" at Antwerp in connection with a film about R J Mitchell; At an airshow at Heizel marked "GD-A" with spurious serial "SR111" in 8.50; Then to the Technical School at Tongeren; SoTT Saffraanberg 8.52; Scrapped 1954

NH702 Spitfire F.XIVc (Griffon 65); Became **SG-115**; TOC/RAF 28.2.44 - WU-contract: Sold to Belgium, to Vickers-Armstrongs for overhaul 25.8.50; BAF, Ecole de Chasse ('IQ-J':'IQ-M'; also reported 'IQ-I'); Accident, Koksijde, Cat.3 24.2.53; Re-Cat.5 & SOC 13.11.53; w/o 21.6.54

NH710 Spitfire F.XIVc (Griffon 65); Became **SG-116**; TOC/RAF 12.3.44 - WU-contract: Sold to Belgium, to Vickers-Armstrongs for overhaul 25.8.50; First flight BAF 21.5.51; Ecole de Chasse; SOC 6.4.54

NH712 Spitfire F.XIVe (Griffon 65); Became **SG-20**; TOC/RAF 6.4.44; Allocated BAF 2.7.47 - Selected for BAF and flown to Belgium 22.9.47; No.350 Sqn ('D'); Ground collision with RM679 (SG-23) at Beauvechain, Cat.3 24.11.47 (1/Lt Labye safe); No.1 Sqn ('3R- '), Engine failed, force-landed Glabbeek/Attenhove-Wever, Cat.5 16.1.48 (Sgt de Maere d'Aertrijcke injured); SOC 17.9.48

NH718 Spitfire F.XIVe (Griffon 65); Became **SG-71**; TOC/RAF 23.4.44 - Selected for BAF 25.11.48, flown to Belgium 26.11.48; Ecole de Chasse ('IQ-A':'IQ-U'); Accident, Landas, France, Cat.4 12.12.49; Accident, Cat.2 on 8.10.52; SOC 20.10.52

Spitfire LF.IX OO-ARE (ex NH238, SM-36), formerly flown by the EPA Brustem, and then in civilian use by the COGEA company, is here seen at Blankensee, Germany, before September 1958 whilst under sub-charter to the Rhein-Flugzeugbau Company. It has a target towing fitment under the rudder.

[K G Genth]

Spitfire F.XIVe SG-105 (ex NH741) was flown for a time with the Ecole de Chasse, later coded 'IQ-R', until being struck of charge in 1954. [G W Harris]

NH720 Spitfire F.XIVe (Griffon 65); Became **SG-73**; TOC/RAF 23.4.44 - Selected for BAF 9.12.48, flown to Belgium 10.12.48; No.1 Sqn ('3R-A'); No.2 Sqn ('UR-A'), Engine failed, force-landed wheels up, fuselage broken, Mellet-Liberchies, Cat.5 14.6.51 (Lt V Absil safe); SOC 5.7.51

NH741 Spitfire F.XIVe (Griffon 65); Became **SG-105**; TOC/RAF 12.44 - WU-contract: Sold to Belgium, to Vickers-Armstrongs for overhaul 10.1.51; First flight BAF 9.4.51 (acceptance flight); BAF, Ecole de Chasse ('IQ-R'); SOC 21.6.54

NH742 Spitfire F.XIVe (Griffon 65); Became **SG-124**; TOC/RAF 29.11.44 - WU-contract: Sold to Belgium, to Vickers-Armstrongs for overhaul 13.11.50; First flight BAF 19.6.51; Ecole de Chasse ('IQ-D'); Accident, Cat.4 23.10.52 (Sgt A Gaye); Re-Cat.5 & SOC 8.11.52

NH743 Spitfire F.XIVe (Griffon 65); Became **SG-123**; TOC/RAF 27.11.44 - WU-contract: Sold to Belgium, to Vickers-Armstrongs for overhaul 10.11.50; First flight BAF 8.6.51; No.3 Sqn ('YL-M'); No.31 Sqn ('8S-A') 4.1.52 (flown by Capt Laloux 4.1.52, the first Spitfire flight of No.31 Sqn); No.23 Sqn ('Z6-A'); Ecole de Chasse ('IQ-W'); Ground collision with NH904 (SG-108), Koksijde, Cat.2 on 5.5.54; Re-Cat.5 & SOC 31.5.54

NH754 Spitfire FR.XIVe (Griffon 65); Became **SG-56**; TOC/RAF 1.3.45 - Selected for BAF and flown to Belgium 24.8.48; No.350 Sqn ('MN-W'); Engine trouble at high speed, force-landed Deurne, Cat.4 10.12.48 (1/Lt F Brosens safe); Ecole de Chasse ('IQ-D'); Stalled on approach Koksijde, Cat.5 5.6.50 (Sgt JF van De Cauter killed); SOC 9.7.50

NH775 Spitfire FR.XIVe (Griffon 65); Became **SG-91**; TOC/RAF 25.2.45 - Selected for BAF and flown to Belgium 8.2.49; No.3 Sqn ('YL-G'); Belly-landed Gütersloh, Germany, Cat.5 13.9.51 (Lt Goemale safe); SOC 19.11.51; To Wevelghem, fire fighting practice, burnt 13.6.52

NH780 Spitfire FR.XIVe (Griffon 65); Became **SG-74**; TOC/RAF 25.2.45 - Selected for BAF 9.12.48, flown to Belgium 10.12.48; No.349 Sqn ('GE-R'); No.3 Sqn ('YL-P'); Mid-air collision with TZ137 (SG-33) & RM759 (SG-32) near Bois du Gros Frene/Lotenne (near Florennes), Cat.3 29.3.50 (Sgt R Delplace safe); Ecole de Chasse ('IQ-U'); Crashed Cat.3 3.5.54; Re-Cat.5 & SOC 21.9.54; w/o 18.10.54

NH789 Spitfire FR.XIVe (Griffon 65); Became **SG-128**; TOC/RAF 1.3.45 - WU-contract: Sold to Belgium, to Vickers-Armstrongs for overhaul 10.11.50; Ecole de Chasse ('IQ-C'); Crashed Avelgem, Cat.5 11.8.52 (Sgt G Lampolle killed); SOC 1952
NOTE: Also reported to be the BAF SG-108 (see NH904)

NH797 Spitfire FR.XIVe (Griffon 65); Became **SG-75**; TOC/RAF 8.3.45 - Selected for BAF 9.12.48, flown to Belgium 10.12.48; No.350 Sqn ('MN-N'); Aux Sqn ('GV-E'); Ecole de Chasse ('IQ- '); SOC 21.9.54; w/o 18.10.54

NH807 Spitfire FR.XIVe (Griffon 65); Became **SG-87**; TOC/RAF 17.3.45 - Selected for BAF 13.1.49, flown to Belgium 15.1.49; Ecole de Chasse ('IQ-N', personal plane of Maj Arend); Mid-air collision Cat.3 22.6.50 (Sgt P Rahir safe); SOC 21.6.54

NH831 Spitfire FR.XIVe (Griffon 65); Became **SG-98**; TOC/RAF 24.3.45 - Selected for BAF and flown to Belgium 11.5.49; No.2 Sqn ('UR-E'); Engine failed, belly-landed Wulpen, Cat.5 17.5.50 (Lt E Cailleau safe); SOC 30.11.50

NH838 Spitfire F.XIVe (Griffon 65); Became **SG-120**; TOC/RAF 3.4.45 - WU-contract: Sold to Belgium, to Vickers-Armstrongs for overhaul 25.8.50; First flight BAF 8.6.51; No.3 Sqn ('YL-P'); No.10 Wing; Ecole de Chasse ('IQ-D'); Emergency wheels-up landing near Nieuwpoort, Cat.4 11.6.54; Re-Cat.5 & SOC 8.7.54

NH857 Spitfire FR.XIVe (Griffon 65); Became **SG-84**; TOC/RAF 10.4.45 - Selected for BAF 13.1.49, flown to Belgium 15.1.49; No.1 Sqn ('3R-O'); Accident, Cat.4 17.5.49; Ecole de Chasse ('IQ-F'); SOC 21.9.54; w/o 18.10.54

NH863 Spitfire FR.XIVe (Griffon 65); Became **SG-93**; TOC/RAF 8.4.45 - Selected for BAF and flown to Belgium 10.3.49; No.350 Sqn ('MN-G'); Aux Sqn ('GV-Q'); No.2 Sqn ('UR-Q'); Ecole de Chasse ('IQ-O'); Collided with MV383 (SG-95), Merkem, Cat.5 3.8.53 (Adj J Peeraer killed), SOC

NH864 Spitfire FR.XIVe (Griffon 65); Became **SG-67**; TOC/RAF 10.4.45 - Selected for BAF and flown to Belgium 29.10.48; No.350 Sqn ('MN-Y'); No.3 Sqn ('YL-D'); Crashed at Pietrebais, Cat.5 28.3.51 (1/Lt V Absil killed); SOC 12.4.51

NH892 Spitfire FR.XIVe (Griffon 65); Became **SG-65**; TOC/RAF 16.3.45 - Selected for BAF and flown to Belgium 5.10.48; No.350 Sqn ('MN-X'); No.1 Sqn ('3R-C'); Aux Sqn ('GV-X'); Conversion Flight; Ecole de Chasse ('IQ-M'); High speed stall, dived into ground near Mannekensvere, Cat.5 14.12.53 (Adj JP Andriaensens killed); SOC 19.12.53

NH894 Spitfire FR.XIVe (Griffon 65); Became **SG-94**; TOC/RAF 31.3.45 - Selected for BAF and flown to Belgium 10.3.49; No.350 Sqn ('MN-L'); Ecole de Chasse ('IQ-L'); Conversion Flight ('B2-M'); Accident, Cat.3 25.2.53; Ecole de Chasse; SOC 21.9.54; w/o 18.10.54

NH904 Spitfire FR.XIVe (Griffon 65); Became **SG-108**; TOC/RAF 24.3.45 - WU-contract: Sold to Belgium, to Vickers-Armstrongs for overhaul 14.11.50; Flown Blackbushe via Coxyde to Brussels-Melsbroek for customs clearance 17.4.51 (Capt-Cdt André Blanco); TOC/BAF 18.4.51; No.31 Sqn ('8S-K'); Collision Cat.2 on 5.5.54; R&SU; Conversion Flight ('B2-K'); Ecole de Chasse ('IQ-V') 1954; SOC 21.9.54; w/o 18.10.54; Stored Wevelghem; Sold to scrap merchant Oscar Dewachter of Stene-Oostende in 1955; Sold to Bunny Brookes of Hoylake/Hooton Park, Cheshire, UK for £250, without wings 12.66 (fitted with RM694 wings for static display at garage); To T G ('Hamish') Mahaddie, stored RAF Henlow, used for film *Battle of Britain*; Restoration commenced by Jeff Hawke at Henlow in 1969; Sold to Sir W J D Roberts 8.71 (Strathallan Collection), then stored Flimwell until to Strathallan 1977; To Spencer R Flack/Classic Air Displays, Elstree, Hertfordshire 1.79 (Civil reg. *G-FIRE* 21.3.79); Restored at Elstree, ff there in the hands of Ray Hanna 14.3.81; To B J Stephen Grey, Duxford 1988; Sold to USA and shipped 12.88; To Planes of Fame East Museum, Flying Cloud, Minnesota (regd *N8118J* 2.89, later *N114BP*) - **SURVIVOR**

NH918 Spitfire FR.XIVe (Griffon 65); Became **SG-129**; TOC/RAF 2.5.45 - WU-contract: Sold to Belgium, to Vickers-Armstrongs for overhaul 13.11.50; First flight BAF 31.8.51; No.31 Sqn until 7.7.52; Conversion Flight ('B2-P'); Ecole de Chasse; Force-landed wheels up Koksijde, Cat.4 17.9.53 (Sgt J Hendricks safe); Re-Cat.5 & SOC 6.4.54

NH922 Spitfire FR.XIVe (Griffon 65); Became **SG-101**; TOC/RAF 1.5.45 - Selected for BAF and flown to Belgium 21.7.49; No.2 (F) Wing; Ecole de Chasse ('IQ-S'); SOC 21.9.54; w/o 18.10.54

PL149 Spitfire LF.IXe (Merlin 66); Became **SM-8**; TOC/RAF 23.6.44 - Del 26.8.47; Ecole de Pilotage Avece (EPA) Brustem ('8') 27.8.47; Overturned on landing, wing broken 16.10.48 (Sgt Bastin); R&SU 18.10.48; SOC 22.3.49

PL190 Spitfire LF.IXe (Merlin 66); Became **SM-4**; TOC/RAF 12.6.44 - Del Ecole de Pilotage Avece (EPA) Brustem 17.8.47; Accident, 24.3.49; R&SU 29.3.49; Accident, 26.6.49 (S/Lt Brosens)

PL224 Spitfire LF.IXe (Merlin 66); Became **SM-20**; TOC/RAF 15.6.44 - Del 10.7.48; Ecole de Pilotage Avece (EPA) Brustem 19.7.48; Fuselage broken, lost wings, Cat.E 1.9.52 (Sgt Frainpont); R&SU 3.9.52; SOC 9.9.52

PL349 Spitfire LF.IXe (Merlin 66); Became **SM-1**; TOC/RAF 21.8.44 - Del 11.8.47; Ecole de Pilotage Avece (EPA) Brustem 17.8.47; Accident, Cat.E 7.52; R&SU 31.7.52; SOC 4.8.52

PT643 Spitfire LF.IXe (Merlin 66); Became **SM-13**; TOC/RAF 27.7.44 - Del Ecole de Pilotage Avece (EPA) Brustem 22.10.47; Accident, Cat.E 20.7.51; R&SU 3.8.51; SOC 7.1.52; Wings now on MJ783 (SM-15) in Military Museum Brussels

PT644 Spitfire LF.IXe (Merlin 66); Became **SM-17**; TOC/RAF 25.7.44 - Del 4.7.48; Ecole de Pilotage Avece (EPA) Brustem 12.7.48; Belly-landed 23.2.51; R&SU 23.2.51; RiW, Fairey company 5.3.51; EPA 1951; Accident, Cat.E 8.9.53; SOC 29.9.53; R&SU 14.10.53

PT853 Spitfire LF.IXe (Merlin 66); Became **SM-16**; TOC/RAF 23.8.44 - Del 25.5.48; Ecole de Pilotage Avece (EPA) Brustem 26.5.48; Accident, Cat.4 21.6.51; R&SU 30.6.51; SOC 7.1.52

PT887 Spitfire LF.IXe (Merlin 66); Became **SM-3**; TOC/RAF 23.8.44 - Del Ecole de Pilotage Avece (EPA) Brustem

Spitfire LF.IXe SM-17 (ex PT644) of the EPA Brustem in the air with weapons removed. As can be seen in this photograph, the Belgian Air Force Spitfires were fitted with both rounded and pointed rudders. [Belgian Air Force]

17.8.47; Accident, 24.1.48; Accident, Cat.E 11.7.49 (Sgt Leclercq); R&SU 3.8.49; SOC

PV189 Spitfire LF.IXe (Merlin 66); Became **SM-26**; TOC/RAF 5.9.44 - Del 25.11.48; Ecole de Pilotage Avece (EPA) Brustem ('26') 26.11.48; Belly-landed 15.4.49; R&SU 22.4.49; RiW, Fairey company 17.8.49; EPA in 9.49; Collided with MJ617 (SM-23) 25.6.52 (Sgt Kleinfeldt killed); Wreckage to R&SU 29.6.52; SOC

RB154 Spitfire F.XIVc (Griffon 65); Became **SG-13**; TOC/RAF 20.12.43 - Selected for BAF 24.7.47, flown to Belgium 26.7.47; No.350 Sqn ('MN-K'); No.349 Sqn ('GE-E'); No.2 Sqn ('UR-Q'); Ecole de Chasse ('IQ-V'); Crashed on landing Koksijde, Cat.3 10.3.50 (1/Lt Boonen safe); Belly-landed Audinghen near Cap Gris-Nez, France, Cat.4 1.4.52 (Sgt P Ros safe); SOC 1952; Fuselage to No.7 Wing for fire-fighting practice (one wing survives in MV246/SG-55, Brussels)

RB156 Spitfire F.XIVc (Griffon 65); Became **SG-68**; TOC/RAF 27.12.43 - Selected for BAF and flown to Belgium 29.10.48; No.349 Sqn ('GE-F'); Ecole de Chasse ('IQ-F'); Crashed Milen-boven-Aalst, Cat.5 14.2.52 (Sgt H Stoffels killed); SOC 1952

RB161 Spitfire F.XIVc (Griffon 65); Became **SG-27**; TOC/RAF 8.1.44 - Selected for BAF and flown to Belgium 14.1.48; No.350 Sqn ('MN-P'); Ecole de Chasse ('IQ-O'); Crashed on landing, Cat.1 on 17.1.52 (Adj P van der Borght); Dived into ground E of St.Pieters Kapelle, Cat.5 31.7.52 (Sgt P Gillis killed); SOC 31.7.52

RB163 Spitfire F.XIVc (Griffon 65); Became **SG-5**; TOC/RAF 20.1.44 - Selected for BAF 25.4.47, flown to Belgium 29.4.47; No.349 Sqn ('GE-Z':'GE-O'); Crashed on landing [date unknown]; Ecole de Chasse ('IQ-E'); Accident, Koksijde, Cat.3 30.7.48 (1/Lt Mathijs safe); To SoTT Saffraanberg as ground instructional airframe 22.8.52; SOC 21.9.54; w/o 18.10.54

RB165 Spitfire F.XIVc (Griffon 65); Became **SG-126**; TOC/RAF 3.2.44 - WU-contract: Sold to Belgium, to Vickers-Armstrongs for overhaul 9.11.50; Ecole de Chasse ('IQ-BB'); SOC 14.8.52

RB166 Spitfire F.XIVc (Griffon 65); Became **SG-2**; TOC/RAF 20.1.44 - Selected for BAF and flown to Belgium 17.4.47; No.349 Sqn (allotted 'GE-B', but not applied); Accident, 21.5.47; Overturned landing Beauvechain, Cat.4 in 9.47 (Adj Lecomte); Re-Cat.5 & SOC 9.47

RB182 Spitfire F.XIVc (Griffon 65); Became **SG-69**; TOC/RAF 15.2.44 - Selected for BAF and flown to Belgium 29.10.48; No.2 (F) Wing; Aux Sqn ('GV-F'); Ecole de Chasse ('IQ-U'); Collided with truck while taxying, Cat.3 31.7.51; SOC 6.4.54

RB186 Spitfire F.XIVc (Griffon 65); Became **SG-40**; TOC/RAF 25.2.44 - Selected for BAF and flown to Belgium 23.4.48; No.349 Sqn ('GE-N'); No.3 Sqn ('YL-S'); Overturned landing Florennes, Cat.5 22.6.51 (Capt Hubert), SOC

RK851 Spitfire LF.IXe (Merlin 66); Became **SM-27**; TOC/RAF 30.9.44 - Del 20.11.48; Ecole de Pilotage Avece (EPA) Brustem 8.12.48; Accident, Cat.5 22.11.51 (Sgt Boulack killed); Remains to R&SU 27.11.51; SOC

RM625 Spitfire FR.XIVe (Griffon 65); Became **SG-46**; TOC/RAF 10.6.44 - Selected for BAF 14.6.48, flown to Belgium 15.6.48; No.2 Sqn ('UR-G'); Ecole de Chasse ('IQ-J'); Ground collision with RM960 (SG-37) at Koksijde, Cat.4 14.1.49 (Adj Champagnac killed); SOC 22.3.49; w/o 21.4.49
NOTE: Wings to MV246 (SG-55), Military Museum Brussels

RM672 Spitfire F.XIVe (Griffon 65); Became **SG-11**; TOC/RAF 28.5.44 - Selected for BAF and flown to Belgium 25.6.47; No.349 Sqn ('GE-T'); Accident, Cat.1 on 6.3.48 (possibly Sgt J Gobert); No.1 Sqn ('3R-T'); Ecole de Chasse ('IQ-C'), Engine failed, belly-landed Koksijde, Cat.3 9.10.53 (Sgt J Janssens safe); Dived into ground at Lammersdorf, Germany, Cat.5 5.8.54; SOC 21.9.54; w/o 18.10.54

RM674 Spitfire F.XIVe (Griffon 65); Became **SG-106**; TOC/RAF 30.7.44 - WU-contract: Sold to Belgium, to Vickers-Armstrongs for overhaul 2.1.51; First flight BAF 14.3.51; Aux Sqn ('GV-G'); Ecole de Chasse ('IQ-Z'); Accident, Brustem, Cat.4 11.7.51; Re-Cat.5 & SOC 20.7.51

RM676 Spitfire F.XIVe (Griffon 65); Became **SG-21**; TOC/RAF 28.5.44; Allocated for Belgium 2.7.47 - Selected for BAF 22.9.47, flown to Belgium 23.9.47; No.350 Sqn ('C') 23.9.47; Engine failed, belly-landed Beauvechain, Cat.5 19.2.48 (Adj C van Hamme safe); SOC 3.4.48

RM679 Spitfire F.XIVe (Griffon 65); Became **SG-23**; TOC/RAF 7.6.44 - Selected for BAF and flown to Belgium 20.10.47; No.1 (F) Wing; No.350 Sqn ('F'); Ground collision with NH712 at Beauvechain, Cat.4 24.11.47 (Sgt Brosens safe); Re-Cat.5 & SOC 3.4.48

RM680 Spitfire F.XIVe (Griffon 65); Became **SG-58**; TOC/RAF 10.6.44 - Selected for BAF and flown to Belgium 20/21.9.48; Aux Sqn ('GV-X'); Ecole de Chasse ('IQ-H':'IQ-DD'); Belly-landed at Haamstede, Netherlands, Cat.3 5.5.50 (Capt G Nossin safe); Stbd undercarriage collapsed landing Koksijde, Cat.3 6.11.53 (Sgt J Janssens safe); Ground collision with SM930 (SG-127), rear fuselage broken, Cat.E 6.3.54; SOC 6.4.54

RM683 Spitfire F.XIVe (Griffon 65); Became **SG-70**; TOC/RAF 18.6.44 - Selected for BAF and flown to Belgium 11.11.48; No.2 Sqn ('UR-C'); Belly-landed, Cat.5 27.4.49; SOC 18.8.50

RM685 Spitfire F.XIVe (Griffon 65); Became **SG-15**; TOC/RAF 27.6.44 - Selected for BAF and flown to Belgium 25.7.47; No.349 Sqn ('GE-Z'); Accident, Cat.1 on 26.1.48; Ground collision with RM770 (SG-35) Beauvechain, Cat.4 25.3.48 (Plt Notte safe); No.2 Sqn ('UR-B'); Ecole de Chasse ('IQ-B'); Touched ground on take-off at Brustem, Cat.3 31.8.50 (Sgt Wodon safe); Crashed on landing, Cat.4 19.1.54; Re-Cat.5 & SOC 6.4.54

RM697 Spitfire FR.XIVe (Griffon 65); Became **SG-42**; TOC/RAF 14.8.44 - Selected for BAF 25.5.48, flown to Belgium 29.5.48; No.349 Sqn ('GE-D'); Ecole de Chasse ('IQ-Z'); Glycol leak, force-landed at Raversijde/Oostende, Cat.5 4.7.50 (Capt Regout injured); SOC 8.7.50

RM700 Spitfire F.XIVe (Griffon 65); Became **SG-107**; TOC/RAF 16.7.44 - WU-contract: Sold to Belgium, to Vickers-

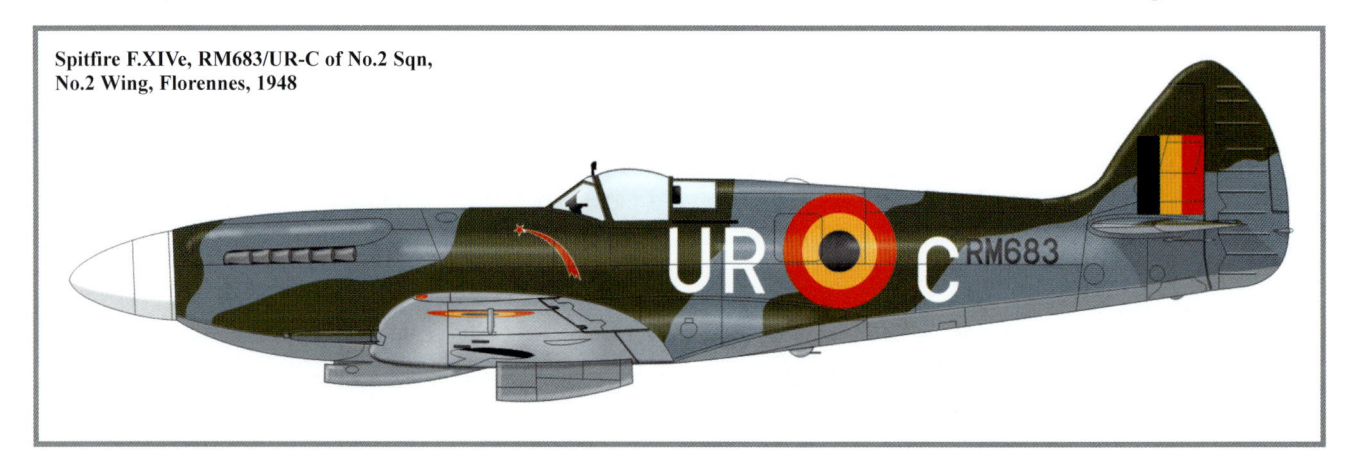

Spitfire F.XIVe, RM683/UR-C of No.2 Sqn, No.2 Wing, Florennes, 1948

Spitfire F.XIVe SG-66 IQ-Q (ex RM705) of the Ecole de Chasse, probably on 24th March 1953 after it crashed on landing at Raversijde, piloted by H Loots.

Armstrongs for overhaul 8.1.51; First flight BAF 9.4.51; No.3 Sqn ('YL-U'); Accident, Cat.1 on 18.9.51 (Plt J Moreau); No.10 Wing; Ecole de Chasse ('IQ- '); SOC 21.9.54; w/o 18.10.54

RM701 Spitfire F.XIVe (Griffon 65); Became **SG-6**; TOC/RAF 1.8.44 - Selected for BAF and flown to Belgium 3.5.47; No.349 Sqn ('GE-E'); No.3 Sqn ('YL- '); No.2 Sqn; Ecole de Chasse ('IQ-C'); Accident, at Florennes, Cat.4 12.5.50 (Sgt de Ketelaere); SOC 8.53 (to spares); w/o 31.5.54

RM703 Spitfire FR.XIVe (Griffon 65); Became **SG-78**; TOC/RAF 16.9.44 - Selected for BAF 16.12.48, flown to Belgium 17.12.48; No.2 Sqn ('UR-E'); Aux Sqn ('GV-E'); Taxying collision with RM726 (SG-14) at Beauvechain, Cat.5 8.9.52; SOC 25.10.52

RM705 Spitfire F.XIVe (Griffon 65); Became **SG-66**; TOC/RAF 26.8.44 - Selected for BAF and flown to Belgium 5.10.48; No.350 Sqn ('MN-V'); Aux Sqn ('GV-V'); Accident, at Beauvechain, Cat.3 13.6.50 (Lt A van Wersch safe); Ecole de Chasse ('IQ-Q'); Accident, at Oostnieuwkerke, Cat.4 24.5.51 (Lt H Branders safe); Ecole de Chasse; Crashed on landing at Raversijde, Cat.5 24.3.53 (Plt H Loots safe); SOC 31.3.53

RM707 Spitfire F.XIVe (Griffon 65); Became **SG-109**; TOC/RAF 21.8.44 - WU-contract: Sold to Belgium, to Vickers-Armstrongs for overhaul 15.1.51; First flight BAF 20.4.51; Ecole de Chasse; Accident, Koksijde, Cat.4 31.7.52; RiW, Fairey company at Gosselies; Re-Cat.5 19.12.52; SOC 1953

RM710 Spitfire F.XIVe (Griffon 65); Became **SG-59**; TOC/RAF 27.8.44 - Selected for BAF and flown to Belgium 20./21.9.48; No.350 Sqn ('MN-V'); No.1 Sqn ('3R-N'); Take-off collision, belly-landed Florennes, Cat.4 6.4.51; Re-Cat.5 & SOC 12.4.51

RM712 Spitfire F.XIVe; TOC/RAF 3.9.44; SOC/RAF 31.12.45 - Arr Belgium 16.1.48; For spare parts

RM726 Spitfire F.XIVe (Griffon 65); Became **SG-14**; TOC/RAF 18.6.44 - Selected for BAF and flown to Belgium 25.7.47; No.349 Sqn ('GE-H'); Accident, Cat.3 5.4.48; No.2 Sqn ('UR-R'); Tipped on nose [date unknown]; Aux Sqn ('GV-R'); Taxying collision with RM703 during NATO exercise "Hold Fast" 20.10.50; Crashed Cat.5 8.9.52, SOC

RM741 Spitfire F.XIVe (Griffon 65); Became **SG-18**; TOC/RAF 7.7.44; Allocated for Belgium 2.7.47 - Selected for BAF and flown to Belgium 22.9.47; No.350 Sqn ('MN-A'); No.2 Sqn ('UR-D'); No.1 Sqn ('3R-E'); No.3 Sqn ('YL-T'); Ecole de Chasse; SOC 1953

RM759 Spitfire F.XIVe (Griffon 65); Became **SG-32**; TOC/RAF 8.44 - Selected for BAF and flown to Belgium 11.2.48; No.349 Sqn ('GE-M'); Tipped on nose (or belly-landed) at Beauvechain, Cat.3 13.8.48 (Lt Mathijs safe); No.3 Sqn ('YL-C'); Mid-air collision with TZ137 (SG-33) and NH780 (SG-74) near Bois du Gros Frene/Lotenne (Florennes), Cat.3 29.3.50 (Lt Wils safe); No.23 Sqn ('Z6- ') 2.1.52; Ecole de Chasse; SOC 6.4.54

RM764 Spitfire F.XIVe (Griffon 65); Became **SG-38**; TOC/RAF 14.8.44 - Selected for BAF and flown to Belgium 22.3.48; No.1 (F) Wing; No.350 Sqn ('M'); No.349 Sqn ('GE-A'); Aux Sqn ('GV-X'); Mechanical problems on test flight, crashed near Bois de Beausart (Beauvechain), Cat.5 24.2.52 (Capt J Rigole killed); SOC 24.2.52

RM768 Spitfire F.XIVc (Griffon 65); Became **SG-10**; TOC/RAF 11.9.44 - Selected for BAF and flown to Belgium 21.6.47; No.349 Sqn ('GE-D':"*YVEA*"); Accident, Cat.1 on 6.1.48 (Plt Lt Remack); No.2 Sqn ('UR-P'); Accident, Cat.3 10.2.48 (Plt L Philippart); No.349 Sqn; Ran off runway at Beauvechain, Cat.4 14.4.48 (Plt Sgt J Gobert safe); Ecole de Chasse ('IQ-G'); SOC 8.53; w/o 8.7.54

RM769 Spitfire F.XIVe; TOC/RAF 18.9.44; Accepted for BAF, but engine seized on approach, crashed at No.33 MU Lyneham before delivery, Cat.E1 on 19.6.47 (Capt J Gueuffen injured); SOC/RAF 25.9.47; Included as part of total for BAF

RM770 Spitfire F.XIVe (Griffon 65); Became **SG-35**; TOC/RAF 26.8.44 - Selected for BAF and flown to Belgium 10.3.48; TOC/BAF 11.3.48; No.350 Sqn ('MN-G'); Ground collision with RM685 (SG-15) at Beauvechain, Cat.3 25.3.48 (Sgt Bayart safe); No.3 Sqn ('YL-F'); Engine failed, dived into ground at Vitrivale, Cat.5 5.6.51 (Adj Roodhans killed); SOC 5.7.51

RM784 Spitfire F.XIVe (Griffon 65); Became **SG-100**; TOC/RAF 27.9.44 - Selected for BAF and flown to Belgium 22.6.49; No.2 (F) Wing; Crashed at Flavion (Florennes) after mid-air collision with MV312 (SG-99), Cat.5 23.9.49 (Plt Meerdaels baled out safely), SOC

Spitfire FR.XIVc SG-10 (ex RM768) 'UR-P' of No.2 Escadrille, Florennes, in 1948.

Spitfire F.XIVe SG-22 IQ-O (ex RM791) of the Ecole de Chasse.

RM787 Spitfire F.XIVe (Griffon 65); Became **SG-28**; TOC/RAF 26.8.44 - Selected for BAF and flown to Belgium 15.1.48; No.350 Sqn ('E'); Crashed on landing, burnt out, Beauvechain, Cat.5 17.3.48 (Sgt Taminiaux safe); SOC 3.4.48

RM790 Spitfire F.XIVe (Griffon 65); Became **SG-117**; TOC/RAF 25.9.44 - WU-contract: Sold to Belgium, to Vickers-Armstrongs for overhaul 25.8.50; First flight BAF 24.5.51; Ecole de Chasse; No.2 Sqn; No.31 Sqn; EcC ('IQ-M'); SOC 21.9.54; w/o 18.10.54

RM791 Spitfire F.XIVe (Griffon 65); Became **SG-22**; TOC/RAF 26.8.44 - Selected for BAF and flown to Belgium 20.10.47; Ecole de Chasse ('IQ-O'); No.2 (F) Wing; No.2 Sqn ('UR- '); Retd EcC; SOC 21.9.54; w/o 18.10.54

RM792 Spitfire F.XIVe (Griffon 65); Became **SG-118**; TOC/RAF 31.8.44 - WU-contract: Sold to Belgium, to Vickers-Armstrongs for overhaul 25.8.50; First flight BAF 28.5.51; Ecole de Chasse ('IQ-J':'IQ-S'); Accident, 26.1.53; SOC 10.3.54

RM795 Spitfire F.XIVe (Griffon 65); Became **SG-125**; TOC/RAF 31.8.44 - WU-contract: Sold to Belgium, to Vickers-Armstrongs for overhaul 10.11.50; Ecole de Chasse ('IQ-T':'IQ-W'); Mid-air collision with RM917 (SG-76), force-landed at Mardyck, France, Cat.5 25.2.53 (Plt J Lambrechts safe); SOC 1953

RM802 Spitfire FR.XIVe (Griffon 65); Became **SG-44**; TOC/RAF 13.9.44 - Selected for BAF and flown to Belgium 10.6.48; No.2 (F) Wing; No.3 Sqn ('YL- '); Crashed near Wulpen,

Cat.4 23.12.49; No.23 Sqn ('Z6- ') 2.1.52; Ecole de Chasse ('IQ-U'); Engine failed on approach, force-landed Koksijde, Cat.5 28.12.53 (Adj Snyers safe); SOC 31.12.53

RM817 Spitfire F.XIVe (Griffon 65); Became **SG-119**; TOC/RAF 1.10.44 - WU-contract: Sold to Belgium, to Vickers-Armstrongs for overhaul 25.8.50; First flight BAF 15.6.51; No.2 Sqn ('YL-E'); No.10 Wing; Ecole de Chasse ('IQ-E'); Taxying collision with RM822 (SG-61) at Koksijde, fuselage broken, Cat.5 17.9.53 (1/Lt R Lecrenier safe); SOC 6.4.54

RM820 Spitfire F.XIVe (Griffon 65); Became **SG-83**; TOC/RAF 22.10.44 - Selected for BAF and flown to Belgium 18.1.49; No.350 Sqn ('MN-E'); Ecole de Chasse ('IQ-C'); Crashed on take-off at Koksijde, Cat.4 6.10.53 (Sgt M Debart safe); Re-Cat.5 & SOC 6.4.54

RM822 Spitfire F.XIVe (Griffon 65); Became **SG-61**; TOC/RAF 29.10.44 - Selected for BAF and flown to Belgium 30.9.48; No.349 Sqn ('GE-P'); Ecole de Chasse ('IQ-Y'); Prop damaged 12.11.51; Taxying collision with RM817 (SG-119) at Koksijde, fuselage broken, Cat.5 17.9.53; SOC in 9.53; w/o 6.4.54

RM841 Spitfire F.XIVe (Griffon 65); Became **SG-72**; TOC/RAF 27.10.44 - Selected for BAF 25.11.48, flown to Belgium 26.11.48; No.1 Sqn ('3R- '); No.2 Sqn ('UR-A'); Mid-air collision with RM857 (SG-53), crashed at Grune/ Nassogne, Cat.5 30.6.49 (1/Lt F Dubois killed), SOC

RM857 Spitfire FR.XIVe (Griffon 65); Became **SG-53**; TOC/RAF 23.10.44 - Selected for BAF and flown to Belgium 27.7.48; No.1 Sqn ('3R-O'); Mid-air-collision with RM841 (SG-72) at Grune/ Nassogne, Cat.5 30.6.49 (1/Lt J Monteyne killed), SOC

RM860 Spitfire F.XIVe (Griffon 65); Became **SG-37**; OC/RAF 11.44 - Selected for BAF and flown to Belgium 23.4.48; No.2 Sqn ('UR-C'); No.3 Sqn ('YL-Q'); Ecole de Chasse ('IQ- '); Ground collision with RM625 (SG-46) at Koksijde, Cat.4 14.1.49 (Adj Campagnac killed); Re-Cat.5 & SOC 22.3.49; Wing & other parts fitted to MV246 (SG-55) in the Military Museum Brussels

RM862 Spitfire FR.XIVe (Griffon 65); TOC/RAF 24.10.44; To Ground Instructional as *6350M* for BAF 5.6.47; Via 47 MU in SS *Electro* to Antwerp - Arr BAF 24.8.47; SoTT Saffraanberg 9.47; SoTT Tongeren 6.48; Scrapped 1952

RM863 Spitfire F.XIVe (Griffon 65); Became **SG-86**; TOC/RAF 29.10.44 - Selected for BAF and flown to Belgium 19.1.49; No.349 Sqn ('GE-K'); No.2 Sqn ('UR-H'); Ecole de Chasse ('IQ-U'); SOC 21.9.54; w/o 18.10.54

RM866 Spitfire F.XIVe (Griffon 65); Became **SG-41**; TOC/RAF 23.9.44 - Selected for BAF and flown to Belgium 22.3.48; No.2 (F) Wing; No.1 Sqn ('3R- '); Engine failed on take-off, crashed Florennes, Cat.5 30.4.48 (Sgt Dechief killed); SOC 7.7.48

RM870 Spitfire F.XIVe (Griffon 65); Became **SG-12**; TOC/RAF 5.10.44 - Selected for BAF and flown to Belgium 3.7.47; No.350 Sqn ('MN-H'); Ecole de Chasse ('IQ-Z'), engine failed, force-landed wheels-up at Koksijde, Cat.5 5.1.50 (Lt Vandenbosch injured); SOC 16.2.50

RM876 Spitfire FR.XIVe (Griffon 65); Became **SG-24**; TOC/RAF 8.10.44 - Selected for BAF and flown to Belgium 14.11.47; No.2 Sqn (ex No.352 Sqn); Accident, Cat.1 on 12.1.48 (Plt E Bouzin); No.1 Sqn ('3R-B') 1.2.48; No.2 Sqn ('UR-B'); Ecole de Chasse ('IQ-B'); Engine failed, force-landed at Wulpen-Booitshoeke, Cat.5 27.12.50 (Sgt Godefroid killed); SOC 3.2.51

RM879 Spitfire F.XIVe (Griffon 65); Became **SG-110**; TOC/RAF 15.10.44 - WU-contract: Sold to Belgium, to Vickers-Armstrongs for overhaul 15.1.51; First flight BAF 8.6.51; No.3 Sqn; No.10 Wing; Ecole de Chasse ('IQ-U'); Engine failed on take-off, crashed Cat.2 on 4.3.54; Re-Cat.5 & SOC 31.5.54

RM882 Spitfire FR.XIVe (Griffon 65); Became **SG-52**; TOC/RAF 27.10.44 - Selected for BAF and flown to Belgium 27.7.48; No.1 Sqn ('3R-V'); Ecole de Chasse ('IQ-S'); Crashed on landing 7.1.49; No.1 Sqn ('3R-V'); Mid-air collision with RN121 (SG-7), force-landed at Evrehailles-Yvoir, fuselage broken, Cat.5 15.3.51 (Plt Leroy safe); SOC 16.3.51; w/o 12.4.51

RM913 Spitfire F.XIVe (Griffon 65); Became **SG-62**; TOC/RAF 9.11.44 - Selected for BAF and flown to Belgium 4.10.48; No.349 Sqn ('GE-P'); No.3 Sqn ('YL- '); Ecole de Chasse ('IQ-P'); Ground collision with NH643 (SG-26) at Koksijde, Cat.3 22.5.50; No.31 Sqn ('8S- '); Tipped on nose [date unknown]; Retd EcC; SOC 21.9.54; w/o 18.10.54

RM916 Spitfire F.XIVe (Griffon 65); Became **SG-3**; TOC/RAF 29.11.44 - Selected for BAF and flown to Belgium 17.4.47; No.349 Sqn ('GE-A'); Fairey company 12.8.47; No.349 Sqn 3.3.48; No.2 Sqn ('UR-M'); Ecole de Chasse ('IQ-J') 4.10.49; Engine failed on take-off, crashed Bray Dunes, France, Cat.4 22.2.50 (1/Lt Corbeel injured); Re-Cat.5 & SOC 26.4.50

RM917 Spitfire F.XIVe (Griffon 65); Became **SG-76**; TOC/RAF 14.1.44 - Selected for BAF 9.12.48, flown to Belgium 10.12.48; No.2 Sqn ('UR-X'); Damaged when hangar roof collapsed, Cat.3 17.12.50; Tipped on nose, Cat.4 12.2.51; Ecole de Chasse ('IQ- '); Mid-air collision with RM795 (SG-125) at Grande-Synthe, France, Cat.5 25.2.53 (Sgt G Govaere killed); SOC 18.10.53

RM918 Spitfire F.XIVe (Griffon 65); Became **SG-111**; TOC/RAF 14.11.44 - WU-contract: Sold to Belgium, to Vickers-Armstrongs for overhaul 8.1.51; First flight BAF 9.4.51; No.3 Sqn; No.10 Wing; Ecole de Chasse ('IQ-E'); Mid-air collision with RN113 (SG-29), crashed at Oudekapelle near Diksmuide, Cat.5 12.9.52 (Sgt G Debras killed); SOC 19.9.52

RM920 Spitfire FR.XIVe (Griffon 65); Became **SG-43**; TOC/RAF 15.11.44 - Selected for BAF 25.5.48, flown to Belgium 29.5.48; No.350 Sqn ('MN-C'); No.1 Sqn ('3R-J'); No.3 Sqn ('YL-A'); Low flying in snowstorm, crashed near Gourdinne/Walcourt, Cat.5 22.2.51 (1/Lt Raick killed), SOC

RM921 Spitfire FR.XIVe (Griffon 65); Became **SG-57**; TOC/RAF 11.44 - Selected for BAF and flown to Belgium 24.8.48; No.2 Sqn ('UR-N') 1.9.48; No.1 (F) Wing 6.1.49; No.2 Sqn 1.3.49; Fairey company 1.12.49; No.3 Sqn ('YL-N'); Accident, Cat.4 12.9.51 (Sgt W Degeyter safe); SOC 19.11.51; Preserved for exhibition 1.2.55; Open display Florennes AFB on pole as "RL-D"; Restoration from 1986; Display in building as "SG57/RL-D" from 24.7.92 - **SURVIVOR**

RM927 Spitfire FR.XIVe (Griffon 65); Became **SG-25**; TOC/RAF 21.11.44 - Selected for BAF and flown to Belgium 14.11.47; No.1 Sqn ('3R-A'); Ecole de Chasse ('IQ-W'); No.1 Sqn 2.10.49; Retd EcC, tyre burst on landing Koksijde, Cat.3 20.6.50 (Maj L Vandercruyssen safe); Accident, Cat.5 (E/2) on 17.6.52; SOC 21.9.54; w/o 18.10.54; Sold as scrap in 1957 to scrap merchant Oscar Dewachter, Ostende; To J Denis Kay/Manchester Tankers Ltd, Charnock Richard, Lancashire, England, arr by road 4.3.67; To A W Francis by road 22.3.69; Sold in USA 1969; Later retd UK, High Wycombe, Bucks (storage) - **SURVIVOR**

RM933 Spitfire F.XIVe (Griffon 65); Became **SG-60**; TOC/RAF 29.11.44 - Selected for BAF and flown to Belgium 20/21.9.48; No.349 Sqn ('GE-S'); No.1 Sqn ('3R-V'); Ecole de Chasse ('IQ-AA'); Undercarriage collapsed on landing Florennes, Cat.4 27.11.50 (Lt J de Bonhomme safe); SOC 21.9.54; w/o 18.10.54

RM935 Spitfire F.XIVe (Griffon 65); Became **SG-17**; TOC/RAF 26.11.44; Allocated for Belgium 2.7.47 - Selected for BAF and flown to Belgium 22.9.47; No.350 Sqn ('V'); Crashed landing Beauvechain, Cat.3 6.1.48 (Capt LV Peeters safe); Accident, Cat.3 12.3.48; Ecole de Chasse ('IQ-E'); Crashed on landing Koksijde, Cat.3 10.7.50 (Sgt Ossieur safe); No.2 Sqn ('UR- '); SOC 2.12.52

RM937 Spitfire F.XIVe (Griffon 65); Became **SG-82**; TOC/RAF 25.11.44 - Selected for BAF and flown to Belgium 19.1.49; Ecole de Chasse ('IQ-W'); No.3 Sqn ('YL-A'); Crashed near La Panne, Cat.5 23.7.51 (Capt P de Ligne safe); SOC 17.8.51

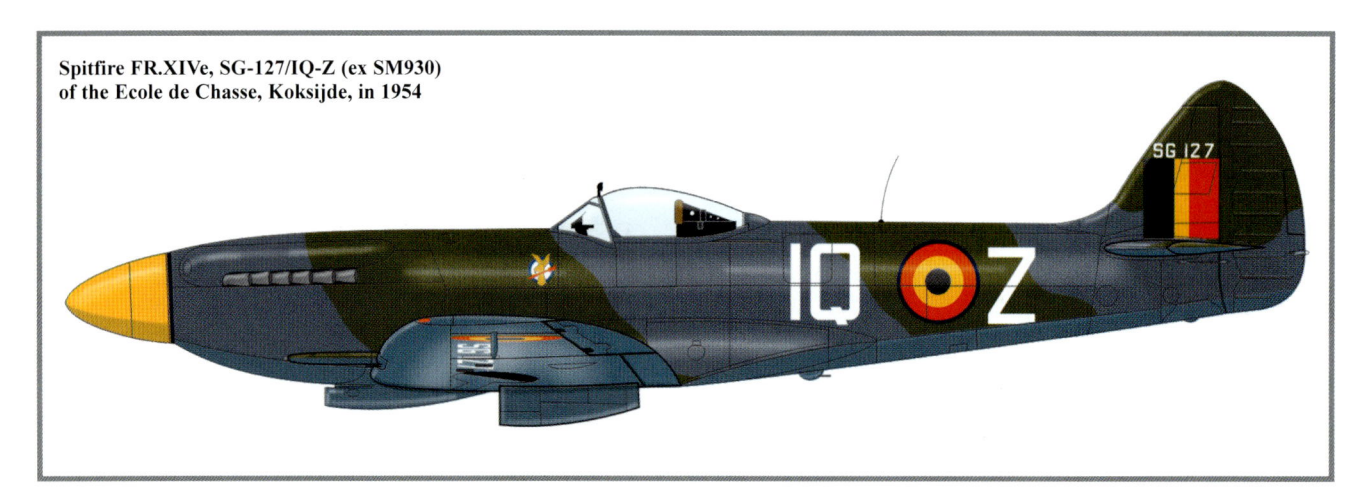

Spitfire FR.XIVe, SG-127/IQ-Z (ex SM930) of the Ecole de Chasse, Koksijde, in 1954

RM938 Spitfire F.XIVe (Griffon 65); Became **SG-92**; TOC/RAF 6.12.44 - Selected for BAF and flown to Belgium 17.2.49; Ecole de Chasse ('IQ- '); Dived into ground on dive bombing practice Lombardsijd, Cat.5 8.4.49 (Sgt J Bastin killed), SOC

RN113 Spitfire F.XIVe (Griffon 65); Became **SG-29**; TOC/RAF 4.11.44 - Selected for BAF 14.1.48, flown to Belgium 15.1.48; No.350 Sqn ('O'); Prop damaged, Cat.3 6.3.48 (Plt A Procureur); No hydraulic pressure, tipped on nose at Beauvechain, Cat.3 25.3.48 (Sgt Guerra safe); No.2 Sqn ('UR-F'); Belly-landed (date unknown); Ecole de Chasse ('IQ-A'); Mid-air collision with RM918 (SG-111), Cat.5 12.9.52; SOC 2.12.52

RN115 Spitfire F.XIVe (Griffon 65); Became **SG-63**; TOC/RAF 6.11.44 - Selected for BAF and flown to Belgium 4.10.48; No.2 (F) Wing; Accident, Cat.4 1.9.49; Aux Sqn ('GV-R'); Ecole de Chasse ('IQ-K'); Tipped on nose while taxying, Cat.5 31.7.51; SOC 17.8.51

RN116 Spitfire F.XIVe (Griffon 65); Became **SG-102**; TOC/RAF 21.11.44 - Selected for BAF and flown to Belgium 21.7.49; No.10 Wing; Ecole de Chasse; Collided with RN124 at Koksijde, Cat.4 1.6.53 (Sgt Fonck safe); Re-Cat.5 & SOC 6.4.54

RN117 Spitfire F.XIVe (Griffon 65); Became **SG-47**; TOC/RAF 9.11.44 - Selected for BAF and flown to Belgium 22.6.48; No.2 Sqn ('UR-E'); Ecole de Chasse ('IQ-J':'IQ-M'); Fuselage broken landing Koksijde, Cat.5 9.8.51 (Sgt Vanderkelen safe, but killed next day in MV288/SG-30); SOC 17.8.51

RN119 Spitfire F.XIVe (Griffon 65); Became **SG-45**; TOC/RAF 8.11.44; Allocated for Belgium 10.6.48 - Selected for BAF and flown to Belgium 19.6.48; No.350 Sqn ('MN-C'); No.2 Sqn ('UR-C'); Tailwheel collapsed landing Koksijde, Cat.3 14.7.48 (Adj B Goosse); Ecole de Chasse ('IQ-W':'IQ-Q'); SOC 21.9.54; w/o 18.10.54

RN121 Spitfire F.XIVe (Griffon 65); Became **SG-7**; TOC/RAF 10.11.44 - Selected for BAF and flown to Belgium 1.5.47; No.349 Sqn; No.351 Sqn; No.1 Sqn ('3R-G'); Collided with RM882 (SG-52) at Evrehailles-Yvoir, Cat.5 15.3.51 (Sgt Colette killed); SOC 12.4.51

RN124 Spitfire F.XIVe (Griffon 65); Became **SG-96**; TOC/RAF 25.11.44 - Selected for BAF and flown to Belgium 11.5.49; No.2 (F) Wing; Ecole de Chasse ('IQ-Z'); Mid-air-collision with RN116 (SG-102) over La Panne, dived into North Sea, Cat.5 1.6.53 (Sgt J Gorris killed), SOC

RN201 Spitfire F.XIVe (Griffon 65); Became **SG-31**; TOC/RAF 22.2.45 - Selected for BAF and flown to Belgium 11.2.48; No.350 Sqn ('MN-L') 3.3.48; No.3 Sqn ('YL-B'); Engine failed, force-landed and crashed Florennes, Cat.5 5.10.50 (Adj Tordeur safe); SOC 10.10.50; w/o 30.11.50; Extant, exhibited on pole near Beauvechain AFB, marked as "SG-3" with code "MN-A" by 1972; Removed and by air to Coltishall, UK 26.4.90; To the Historical Aircraft Collection, Guy Black in Jersey 3.5.90 (Civil reg. *G-BSKP* 27.6.90); 1994 to Duxford for restoration; Stored Paddock Wood, Kent from 1996; To Karel Bos 12.97 (Historic Flying Ltd, Audley End, storage); HFL now based Duxford, first flight pending early 2002 - **SURVIVOR**

RN206 Spitfire F.XIVe (Griffon 65); Became **SG-19**; TOC/RAF 25.2.45; Allocated for Belgium 2.7.47 - Selected for BAF and flown to Belgium 22.9.47; No.3 Sqn ('YL-M':'YL-A'); Aux Sqn; Conversion Flight ('B2-S'); Belly-landed Koksijde Cat.4 5.6.50 (Lt Wils safe); No.31 Sqn ('8S-S'); SOC 8.53; w/o 31.5.54

RN215 Spitfire F.XIVe (Griffon 65); Became **SG-54**; TOC/RAF 7.3.45 - Selected for BAF and flown to Belgium 20.8.48; No.1 Sqn ('3R-M'); Ecole de Chasse ('IQ-K'); Accident, Cat.3 8.10.52; Accident, Cat.5 11.9.53; SOC 6.4.54

RW344 Spitfire LF.XVIe (Merlin 266); No Belgian serial allocated; TOC/RAF 29.6.45; No.350 Sqn from 26.9.46 - Retained by No.350 Sqn BAF ('MN-A') 26.10.46; Accident, Cat.5 1.2.47 (Sgt Limbourg), SOC

SL596 Spitfire LF.XVIe (Merlin 266); No Belgian serial allocated; TOC/RAF 27.8.45; No.349 Sqn from 12.10.46 - Retained by No.349 Sqn BAF ('GE- ') 26.10.46; Force-landed 8.8.47; Retd RAF, No.6 MU 12.8.47; Later Cat E2 on 10.3.48, SOC

SM821 Spitfire F.XIVe (Griffon 65); Became **SG-51**; TOC/RAF 2.3.45 - Selected for BAF and flown to Belgium 27.7.48; No.2 Sqn ('UR-F'); Crashed on landing, fuselage broken, Cat.5 5.5.49 (Lt A Firlefijn safe); SOC 8.6.49

SM829 Spitfire F.XIVe (Griffon 65); Became **SG-122**; TOC/RAF 8.3.45 - WU-contract: Sold to Belgium, to Vickers-Armstrongs for overhaul 10.11.50; First flight BAF 15.6.51 (acceptance flight); No.2 (F) Wing; No.1 Sqn ('3R-A'); No.27 Sqn ('RA-A'); Accident, 25.9.52; Ecole de Chasse; SOC 6.4.54

SM930 Spitfire FR.XIVe (Griffon 65); Became **SG-127**; TOC/RAF 7.7.45 - WU-contract: Sold to Belgium, to Vickers-Armstrongs for overhaul 16.11.50; No.31 Sqn; Accident, Cat.1 on 4.4.52 (Plt Seynhuecq); Last flight with No.31 Sqn 7.7.52; Storage 7.7.52; Conversion Flight ('B2-L'); Ecole de Chasse ('IQ-Z'); Ground collision with RM680 (SG-58) at Koksijde, Cat.3 6.3.54; Re-Cat.5 & SOC 21.9.54; w/o 18.10.54

SM938 Spitfire FR.XIVe (Griffon 65); Became **SG-9**; TOC/RAF 9.8.45 - Selected for BAF and flown to Belgium 3.6.47; No.349 Sqn ('GE-O'); Ecole de Chasse ('IQ-S'); Engine failed, force-landed and crashed Francorchamps, Cat.5 12.5.50 (Lt Marks injured); SOC 9.6.50

TA836 Spitfire LF.IXe (Merlin 66); Became **SM-25**; TOC/RAF 30.9.44 - Del 25.11.48; Ecole de Pilotage Avece (EPA) Brustem 26.11.48; 125e Promotion 18.5.54; SOC 10.54

TA855 Spitfire LF.IXe (Merlin 66); Became **SM-10**; TOC/RAF 2.10.44 - Del 26.8.47; Ecole de Pilotage Avece (EPA) Brustem 27.8.47; Accident, Cat.E 14.12.51 (Sgt Guyot killed); Wreckage to R&SU 18.12.51, SOC

TB348 Spitfire LF.XVIe (Merlin 266); No Belgian serial allocated; TOC/RAF 15.1.45; No.350 Sqn from 17.1.46 - Retained by No.350 Sqn BAF ('MN- ') 26.10.46; Retd to RAF, No.6 MU 6.1.48

TB373 Spitfire LF.XVIe (Merlin 266); No Belgian serial

TB386 Spitfire LF.XVIe (Merlin 266); No Belgian serial allocated; TOC/RAF 17.1.45; No.350 Sqn from 15.1.46 - Retained by No.350 Sqn BAF ('MN-B') 26.10.46; Retd RAF, No.6 MU 6.1.48

TB622 Spitfire LF.XVIe (Merlin 266); No Belgian serial allocated; TOC/RAF 3.2.45; No.349 Sqn from 15.4.46 - Retained by No.349 Sqn BAF 26.10.46; Retd RAF, No.6 MU 27.11.47

TB709 Spitfire LF.XVIe (Merlin 266); No Belgian serial allocated; TOC/RAF 24.2.45; No.350 Sqn from 17.4.46 - Retained by No.350 Sqn BAF ('MN-D') 26.10.46; Not returned to the RAF

TB748 Spitfire LF.XVIe (Merlin 266); No Belgian serial allocated; TOC/RAF 19.2.45; No.350 Sqn from 9.46 - Retained by No.350 Sqn BAF 26.10.46; Crashed Cat E2 on 30.10.46; Retd RAF, No.412 R&SU 30.10.46; No.3 BRU 12.46

TB866 Spitfire LF.XVIe (Merlin 266); No Belgian serial allocated; TOC/RAF 24.2.45; No.349 Sqn from 5.4.46 - Retained by No.349 Sqn BAF ('GE-Q') 26.10.46; Retd RAF, No.6 MU 6.1.48

TB867 Spitfire LF.XVIe (Merlin 266); No Belgian serial allocated; TOC/RAF 10.3.45; No.350 Sqn from 24.1.46 - Retained by No.350 Sqn BAF 26.10.46; Retd RAF, No.6 MU 11.8.47; Later crashed Cat E2 on 16.11.47, SOC

TB868 Spitfire LF.XVIe (Merlin 266); No Belgian serial allocated; TOC/RAF 15.3.45; No.350 Sqn from 18.1.46 - Retained by No.350 Sqn BAF 26.10.46; Retd RAF, No.29 MU 24.7.47; SOC 12.3.48

TB892 Spitfire LF.XVIe (Merlin 266); No Belgian serial allocated; TOC/RAF 25.2.45; No.350 Sqn from 17.1.46 - Retained by No.350 Sqn BAF 26.10.46; Retd RAF, No.9 MU 20.8.47

TB991 Spitfirc LF.XVIe (Merlin 266); No Belgian serial allocated; TOC/RAF 27.2.45; No.349 Sqn from 24.5.45 - Retained by No.349 Sqn BAF ('GE-L', named "*LIEGE*") 26.10.46; Crashed Cat.FA/E 3.2.47 (Adj B Goosse), SOC

TD140 Spitfire LF.XVIe (Merlin 266); No Belgian serial allocated; TOC/RAF 10.3.45; No.349 Sqn from 26.4.45 - Retained by No.349 Sqn BAF 26.10.46; Retd RAF, No.33 MU 22.9.47

TD184 Spitfire LF.XVIe (Merlin 266); No Belgian serial allocated; TOC/RAF 19.3.45; No.349 Sqn from 30.4.45 - Retained by No.349 Sqn BAF ('GE-R') 26.10.46; Retd RAF, No.29 MU 19.8.47

TD188 Spitfire LF.XVIe (Merlin 266); No Belgian serial allocated; TOC/RAF 22.3.45; No.350 Sqn from 16.1.46 - Retained by No.350 Sqn BAF 26.10.46; Retd RAF, No.29 MU 24.7.47

TD231 Spitfire LF.XVIe (Merlin 266); No Belgian serial allocated; TOC/RAF 24.3.45; No.350 Sqn from 15.1.46 - Retained by No.350 Sqn BAF ('MN-J') 26.10.46; Retd RAF, No.29 MU 13.11.47; Became GI No.*6538M* on 6.4.48

TD237 Spitfire LF.XVIe (Merlin 266); No Belgian serial allocated; TOC/RAF 23.3.45; No.349 Sqn from 18.10.45 - Retained by No.349 Sqn BAF 26.10.46; Retd RAF, No.6 MU 6.1.48

TD253 Spitfire LF.XVIe (Merlin 266); No Belgian serial allocated; TOC/RAF 16.3.45; No.350 Sqn from 18.1.46; For BAF, via No.412 R&SU, despatched to Belgium, force-landed and damaged on delivery flight, Cat.E 4.12.46, SOC

TD281 Spitfire LF.XVIe (Merlin 266); No Belgian serial allocated; TOC/RAF 23.3.45; No.350 Sqn from 18.1.46 - Retained by No.350 Sqn BAF ('MN-S') 26.10.46; Retd RAF, No.29 MU 13.11.47; Became GI No.*6540M* on 31.3.48

TD325 Spitfire LF.XVIe (Merlin 266); No Belgian serial allocated; TOC/RAF 4.4.45; No.350 Sqn from 17.1.46 - Retained by No.350 Sqn BAF ('MN-M') 26.10.46; Crashed, Cat.E 20.12.46 (Sgt Bogaerts), SOC

TD348 Spitfire LF.XVIe (Merlin 266); No Belgian serial allocated; TOC/RAF 30.4.45; No.350 Sqn 24.1.-27.9.46; No.349 Sqn from 12.10.46 - Retained by No.349 Sqn BAF 26.10.46; Not returned to the RAF

TD372 Spitfire LF.XVIe (Merlin 266); No Belgian serial allocated; TOC/RAF 12.6.45; No.349 Sqn from 17.5.45 - Retained by No.349 Sqn BAF ('GE-B') 26.10.46; Retd RAF, No.29 MU 24.7.47

TE119 Spitfire LF.XVIe (Merlin 266); No Belgian serial allocated; TOC/RAF 13.4.45; No.349 Sqn from 16.1.46; No.350 Sqn 9.5.46 - Retained by No.350 Sqn BAF 26.10.46; Retd RAF, No.6 MU 24.7.47; Later crashed Cat E2 on 10.3.48, SOC

TE274 Spitfire LF.XVIe (Merlin 266); No Belgian serial allocated; TOC/RAF 18.5.45; No.349 Sqn from 12.10.46 - Retained by No.349 Sqn BAF ('GE-K') 26.10.46; Retd RAF, No.6 MU 9.1.48 (later crashed Cat E2 on 25.5.56, SOC)

TE284 Spitfire LF.XVIe (Merlin 266); No Belgian serial allocated; TOC/RAF 2.6.45; No.349 Sqn from 23.8.46 - Retained by No.349 Sqn BAF 26.10.46; Retd RAF, No.6 MU 1.12.47; Later to Greece 3.49

TE444 Spitfire LF.XVIe (Merlin 266); No Belgian serial allocated; TOC/RAF 25.7.45; No.349 Sqn ('GE-P') from 27.8.46 - Retained by No.349 Sqn BAF 26.10.46; Force-landed at Sylt, Germany 8-15.6.47; Not returned to RAF

TE520 Spitfire LF.IXe (Merlin 66); Became **SM-5**; TOC/RAF 12.6.45 - Del 18.8.47; Ecole de Pilotage Avece (EPA) Brustem 20.8.47; Crashed Cat.E 14.2.52 (Plt Guillaume killed); Wreckage to R&SU 15.2.52, SOC

TX989 Spitfire FR.XIVe (Griffon 65); Became **SG-88**; TOC/RAF 2.5.45 - Selected for BAF and flown to Belgium 8.2.49; No.349 Sqn ('GE-C'); No.1 Sqn ('3R-P'); Burned in hangar when member of ground crew lit cigarette after cleaning aircraft with petrol, Cat.5 14.8.50; SOC 10.10.50 NOTE: Digit '88' on fuselage only

TX992 Spitfire FR.XIVe (Griffon 65); Became **SG-130**; TOC/RAF 30.4.45 - WU-contract: Sold to Belgium, to

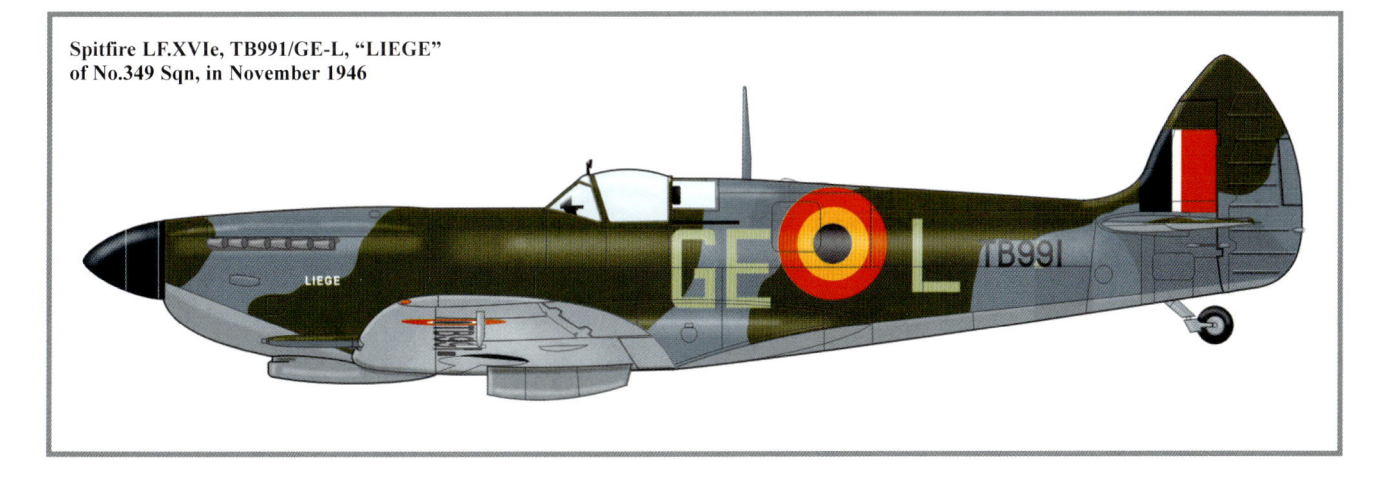

Spitfire LF.XVIe, TB991/GE-L, "LIEGE"
of No.349 Sqn, in November 1946

CHECKLIST OF BELGIAN / RAF SERIAL No's

SM-1 to SM-43: Spitfire LF.IX

BAF Serial No	RAF Serial No	BAF Serial No	RAF Serial No
SM-1	PL349	SM-23	MJ617
SM-2	MJ353	SM-24	MK777
SM-3	PT887	SM-25	TA836
SM-4	PL190	SM-26	PV189
SM-5	TE520	SM-27	RK851
SM-6	EN568	SM-28	MK153
SM-7	EN123	SM-29	MK912 (B1)
SM-8	PL149	SM-30	MH485 (B2)
SM-9	MJ421	SM-31	MK205 (B3)
SM-10	TA855	SM-32	MH424 (B4)
SM-11	MJ244	SM-33	MH439 (B5)
SM-12	MH366	SM-34	NH309 (B6)
SM-13	PT643	SM-35	MJ714 (B7)
SM-14	MJ332	SM-36	NH238 (B8)
SM-15	MJ783	SM-37	MK923 (B9)
SM-16	PT853	SM-38	MH725 (B10)
SM-17	PT644	SM-39	NH188 (B11)
SM-18	ML423	SM-40	MH415 (B12)
SM-19	MJ482	SM-41	MH434 (B13)
SM-20	PL224	SM-42	MJ893 (B14)
SM-21	MK577	SM-43	MK297 (B15)
SM-22	MJ559		

SG-1 to SG-25: Spitfire F/FR.XIVe, deliv. from 17.4.47 to 14.11.47

BAF	RAF	BAF	RAF
SG-1	NH655	SG-14	RM726
SG-2	RB166	SG-15	RM685
SG-3	RM916	SG-16	NH688
SG-4	MV248	SG-17	RM935
SG-5	RB163	SG-18	RM741
SG-6	RM701	SG-19	RN206
SG-7	RN121	SG-20	NH712
SG-8	NH654	SG-21	RM676
SG-9	SM938	SG-22	RM791
SG-10	RM768	SG-23	RM679
SG-11	RM672	SG-24	RM876
SG-12	RM870	SG-25	RM927
SG-13	RB154		

SG-26 to SG-80: Spitfire F/FR.XIVe, deliv. from 14.1.48 to 17.12.48

BAF	RAF	BAF	RAF
SG-26	NH643	SG-54	RN215
SG-27	RB161	SG-55	MV246
SG-28	RM787	SG-56	NH754
SG-29	RN113	SG-57	RM921
SG-30	MV288	SG-58	RM680
SG-31	RN201	SG-59	RM710
SG-32	RM759	SG-60	RM933
SG-33	TZ137	SG-61	RM822
SG-34	MV381	SG-62	RM913
SG-35	RM770	SG-63	RN115
SG-36	MV302	SG-64	TZ192
SG-37	RM860	SG-65	NH892
SG-38	RM764	SG-66	RM705
SG-39	MV256	SG-67	NH864
SG-40	RB186	SG-68	RB156
SG-41	RM866	SG-69	RB182
SG-42	RM697	SG-70	RM683
SG-43	RM920	SG-71	NH718
SG-44	RM802	SG-72	RM841
SG-45	RN119	SG-73	NH720
SG-46	RM625	SG-74	NH780
SG-47	RN117	SG-75	NH797
SG-48	TZ132	SG-76	RM917
SG-49	TX995	SG-77	MV263
SG-50	MV378	SG-78	RM703
SG-51	SM821	SG-79	TZ166
SG-52	RM882	SG-80	MV382
SG-53	RM857		

Vickers-Armstrongs for overhaul 14.11.50; First flight BAF 31.8.51; Ecole de Chasse ('IQ-R'); Running out of fuel, force-landed wheels-up, Longvillers, France 12.3.52; Belly-landed, Cat.4 10.6.52 (Sgt M van der Stockt safe); Re-Cat.5 & SOC 1952

TX995 Spitfire FR.XIVe (Griffon 65); Became **SG-49**; TOC/RAF 12.5.45 - Selected for BAF 9.7.48, flown to Belgium 10.7.48; No.2 (F) Wing ("RLD", personal aircraft of Wg Cdr R Lallemant); No.27 Sqn 5.11.51; No.23 Sqn 7.12.51; No.31 Sqn ('8S-R'); Ecole de Chasse ('IQ- '); SOC 21.9.54; w/o 18.10.54

TZ111 Spitfire FR.XIVe (Griffon 65); Became **SG-89**; TOC/RAF 23.5.45 - Selected for BAF and flown to Belgium 8.2.49; No.350 Sqn ('MN-M'); Ecole de Chasse ('IQ-G'); Engine failed, belly-landed de Mohren, Cat.4 6.3.52 (Adj P van der Borght); Re-Cat.5 & SOC 1952

TZ127 Spitfire FR.XIVe (Griffon 65); Became **SG-81**; TOC/RAF 31.5.45 - Selected for BAF and flown to Belgium 18.1.49; Ecole de Chasse ('IQ-E'); Crashed on take-off Veurne, Cat.5 6.2.50 (1/Lt Emile Dubois killed); SOC 16.2.50

TZ132 Spitfire FR.XIVe (Griffon 65); Became **SG-48**; TOC/RAF 6.6.45 - Selected for BAF 9.7.48, flown to Belgium 10.7.48; No.3 Sqn ('YL-Z'); Ecole de Chasse ('IQ-K'); Accident, 24.11.52; SOC 6.4.54
NOTE: MK.XIV with bubble hood

TZ137 Spitfire FR.XIVe (Griffon 65); Became **SG-33**; TOC/RAF 3.7.45 - Selected for BAF and flown to Belgium 11.2.48; No.350 Sqn ('MN-B'); No.2 (F) Wing; No.3 Sqn ('YL-N'); Mid-air collision with RM759 (SG-32) & NH780 (SG-74) near Bois du Gros Frene/Lotenne, Cat.5 29.3.50 (Capt Lemonne safe); SOC 7.4.50

TZ142 Spitfire FR.XIVe (Griffon 65); Became **SG-121**; TOC/RAF 9.7.45 - WU-contract: Sold to Belgium, to Vickers-Armstrongs for overhaul 25.8.50; First flight BAF 15.6.51; No.3 Sqn; No.27 Sqn; Accident, Cat.1 on 1.4.52

SG-81 to SG-102: Spitfire F/FR.XIVe, deliv. from 18.1.49 to 21.7.49

BAF Serial No	RAF Serial No	BAF Serial No	RAF Serial No
SG-81	TZ127	SG-92	RM938
SG-82	RM937	SG-93	NH863
SG-83	RM937	SG-94	NH894
SG-84	NH857	SG-95	MV383
SG-85	TZ193	SG-96	RN124
SG-86	RM863	SG-97	TZ154
SG-87	NH807	SG-98	NH831
SG-88	TX989	SG-99	MV312
SG-89	TZ111	SG-100	RM784
SG-90	MV369	SG-101	NH922
SG-91	NH775	SG-102	RN116

SG-103 to SG-132: Spitfire F/FR.XIVe, deliv. from 25.8.50 to 15.6.51

BAF	RAF	BAF	RAF
SG-103	MV265	SG-118	RM792
SG-104	MV261	SG-119	RM817
SG-105	NH741	SG-120	NH838
SG-106	RM674	SG-121	TZ142
SG-107	RM700	SG-122	SM829
SG-108	NH904	SG-123	NH743
SG-109	RM707	SG-124	NH742
SG-110	RM879	SG-125	RM795
SG-111	RM918	SG-126	RB165
SG-112	MV267	SG-127	SM930
SG-113	NH658	SG-128	NH789
SG-114	NH690	SG-129	NH918
SG-115	NH702	SG-130	TX992
SG-116	NH710	SG-131	MV359
SG-117	RM790	SG-132	TZ174

Without BAF Serial No: MV360, RM769, RM862

Note:
Spitfire LF.XVIe, on loan pending delivery of Spitfire Mk.XIV, retained RAF serial numbers only, see RW344, SL596, TB348-991, TD140-372, TE119-444. Also TB252.

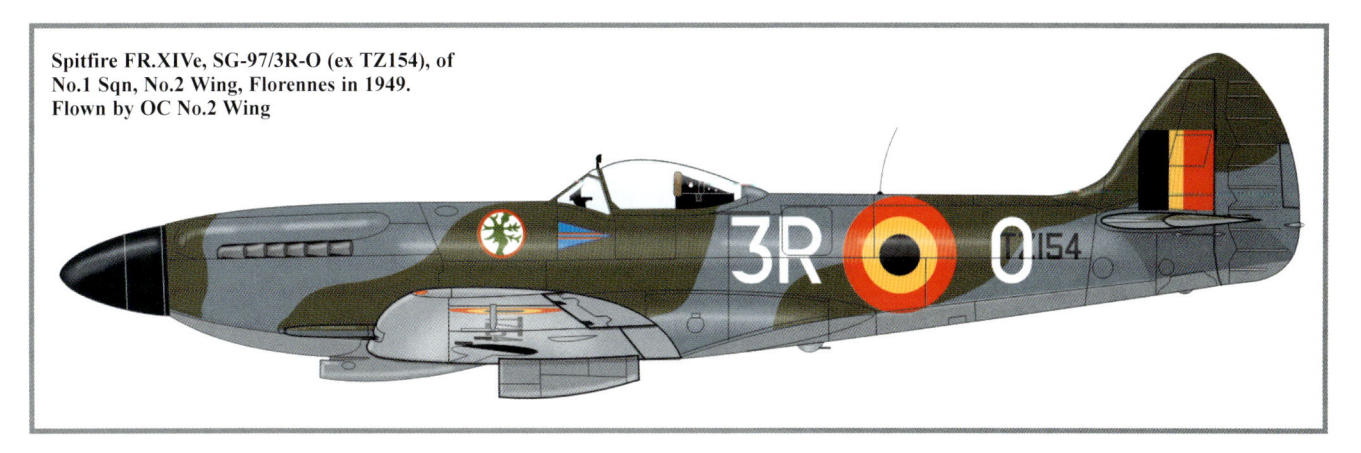

Spitfire FR.XIVe, SG-97/3R-O (ex TZ154), of No.1 Sqn, No.2 Wing, Florennes in 1949. Flown by OC No.2 Wing

(Plt Dome); No.31 Sqn ('8S-A'); Ecole de Chasse ('IQ-S', also reported 'IQ-D'); SOC 18.1.54; w/o 18.10.54

TZ154 Spitfire FR.XIVe (Griffon 65); Became **SG-97**; TOC/RAF 17.7.45 - Selected for BAF and flown to Belgium 11.5.49; No.1 Sqn ('3R-O'); No.3 Sqn ('YL-Q'); Hit tree on take-off Fassberg, Germany Cat.4 20.9.51 (Plt Thierry Woden safe); Re-Cat.5 & SOC 19.11.51

TZ166 Spitfire FR.XIVe (Griffon 65); Became **SG-79**; TOC/RAF 27.8.45 - Selected for BAF 16.12.48, flown to Belgium 17.12.48; No.2 Sqn ('UR-D'); Accident, Cat.3 26.10.49; Crashed Houtain-le-Val, Cat.5 20.9.50 (Capt A Rousseau killed); SOC 29.9.50

TZ174 Spitfire FR.XIVe (Griffon 65); Became **SG-132**; TOC/RAF 12.9.45 - WU-contract: Sold to Belgium, to Vickers-Armstrongs for overhaul 9.11.50; No.31 Sqn ('8S-G'); Connection throttle/engine failed in flight, belly-landed Gottignies (Mons), Cat.5 8.4.52 (Capt J van Molkot, S/Ldr, safe); SOC 1952

TZ192 Spitfire FR.XIVe (Griffon 65); Became **SG-64**; TOC/RAF 1.6.45 - Selected for BAF and flown to Belgium 5.10.48; No.349 Sqn ('GE-P'); No.2 Sqn; Ecole de Chasse ('IQ-F'); Tipped on nose Koksijde, Cat.3 21.3.52 (Sgt J Guerin safe); Stalled in circuit Saffraanberg, Cat.5 23.10.52 (Sgt J Basyn); SOC 5.11.52

TZ193 Spitfire FR.XIVe (Griffon 65); Became **SG-85**; TOC/RAF 14.6.45 - Selected for BAF and flown to Belgium 19.1.49; No.349 Sqn ('GE- '); Accident, Cat.3 11.5.49; Ecole de Chasse ('IQ-X'); SOC 21.9.54; w/o 18.10.54

SURVIVORS in Belgium

MJ783 (SM-15), Armée Museum, Brussels as "MJ360"
MV246 (SG-55), Armée Museum, Brussels
RM921 (SG-57), AFB Florennes
MK912 (SM-29), ex Saffraanberg,
 was sold to Guy Black, Jersey, mid 1989
RN201 (SM-31), ex Beauvechain, via Coltishall, in May 1990,
 to Guy Black in exchange for a Fairey Battle

References:
Vickers Supermarine Spitfire Mk.IX/XVI, Spécial la Dernière Guerre, by J P de Cock, Editions Erasme, Bruxelles-Anvers, 1978.
Belgian Supermarine Spitfire XIV, by Eric Dessouroux, 1985.
IPMS Belgium, Publ.No.57/1985; No.89 & 91/1993; No.95/1994.

Spitfire LF.IXc SM-15 (ex MJ783) photographed in September 1996, by which time it was exhibited in the Musée d'Armée et d'Histoire Militaire, Brussels, marked as "MJ360/GE-B". [PRA]

BRAZIL

Only two Spitfires ever went to Brazil. One Spitfire F.XIVe (RM874) with a Griffon 65 engine arrived in the early fifties, being used initially as teaching aid, then later for test purposes. A Spitfire Mk.IX with a Merlin 70 engine arrived in Brazil recently as a Survivor only.

The Spitfire F.XIVe was bought by the Brazilian Air Attaché for London and Paris, Col H Doytt Fontenelle, as a teaching aid and for test purposes by the Centro Técnico de Aeronáutica (CTA) in Brazil. The idea was to have a modern fighter aircraft for the study by aircraft engineering students of details of high speed aircraft structures.

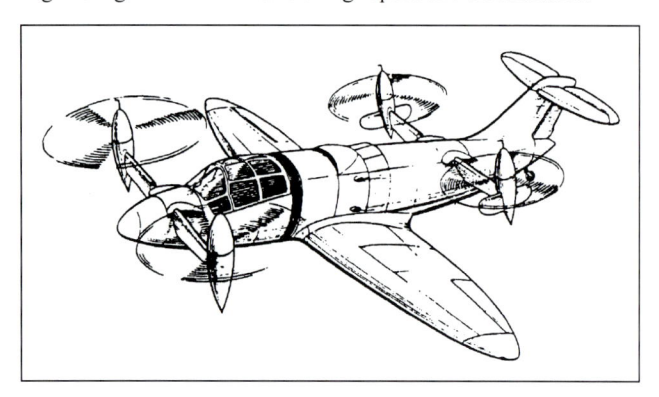

In 1953 the Spitfire F.XIVe went to the Instituto Técnologico da Aeronáutica (ITA) at Sâo José dos Campos, a division of the CTA. The ITA created different programmes for aircraft research. One of these was the helicopter-project *'Heliconair'*, followed by the development of a VTOL-plane - the project *'Convertiplano'*. This VTOL concept was born in 1952/53, and when the need arose for an aeroplane to be modified as a flying test bed, the remains of the Spitfire were available at hand. It was proposed to replace the Griffon 65 engine with an Armstrong-Siddeley Double Mamba turbine, for which the basic Spitfire fuselage would have required very little modification. However, Britain would not allow the sale of that engine, and instead the *'Convertiplano'* engineers acquired an-ex Lockheed Constellation radial engine (2,200hp Wright). This drove the four rotors, which could be moved in the vertical position for take-off and landing or horizontally for normal flying. This required design and construction of a new fuselage, able to accept the big radial engine in the middle for Centre of Gravity reasons. Wings, undercarriage, elevators and modified parts were taken from the Spitfire. A complete test rig was built in the ITA for ground testing of the engine plus its driving systems, while the much modified Spitfire, with reinforced landing gear, waited in a hangar.

Professor H Focke was the leader of the *'Convertiplano'* project, and Messrs Bussmann, Kovacs, Stein and Swoboda were members of the *"Focke-Group"*. The tests continued until 1955, when interest in the project lapsed, and Professor Focke moved to the USA. The engine mount was exhibited in the early sixties, and the airframe was still to be seen in 1967.

The Convertiplano airframe almost complete, with wings, elevator and wheels from Spitfire F.XIVe RM874. [Centro Tecnico Aeroespacial]

The mounting for test of the Wright engine of the Convertiplano, propellers shown in take-off or landing configuration. [Museu Aeroespacial]

F=FRENCH GUYANA, G=GUYANA, S=SURINAME, U=URUGUAY, V=VENEZUELA; SJC=São José dos Campos

Individual Histories

MA793 Spitfire Mk.IX (Merlin 63, now with Merlin 70); ex US 12th AF; Later to South Africa (SAAF); To USA in 1987; Donated by Rolls Royce Derby, England, to the Brazil Flying Museum at Sâo Paulo in March 2000; Arrived in Brazil as **SURVIVOR** only

RM874 Spitfire F.XIVe (Griffon 65); TOC/RAF 8.10.44; Bought by the Brazilian Air Attaché in London 19.12.52 - Arrived Brazil 1953; To the Centro Técnico de Aeronáutica (CTA) as ground instructional airframe for examination by aircraft engineering students; Later components to the Instituto Técnologico da Aeronáutica (ITA) at São José dos Campos for the VTOL-project *'Convertiplano'* 1953/55; Ground tests were undertaken in the early sixties; Airframe ready, storage from 1955; Scrapped after 1967

Reference:
Book *A construção Aeronáutica no Brasil 1910/1976*, by Roberto Pereira de Andrade, p.145.

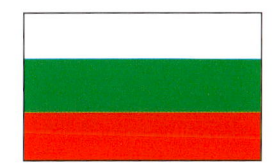

BULGARIA

The Bulgarian Air Force never used the Spitfire, though Bulgaria was interested in having this fighter aircraft when it first became available for overseas sale.

Bulgaria asked for five Spitfire Mk.Ia, known as Spec.No.456, in December 1937. Later the enquiry was increased to twelve aircraft and this was allotted place No.11 in the priority list. A firm quotation was sent to Bulgaria on 30th June 1938 for the Spitfires. The decision of the Air Ministry was deferred until April 1939, then with outbreak of the Second World War the order was automatically cancelled.

Map: see Rumania.

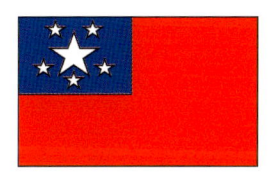

BURMA
(Now MYANMAR)

At the end of the Second World War HQ RAF Burma, which administered Nos.221, 222, 229, 231 and 232 Groups, was established at Rangoon (now Rangun), moving to nearby Mingaladon Airport during January 1947, joining the AHQ Communication Flight which had been based there since November 1945. Both units were disbanded in December 1947. The Communication Flight of No.232 Group, RAF Burma was based at Mingaladon until disbanded in March 1946.

The Union of Burma gained independence on 4th January 1948. However, the country was disrupted following the Chinese Civil War, and a confused situation continued for a long time. All the Burmese Forces fought as a National Army until 1954 when its own Air Force (UBAF) was built up.

The Union of Burma Air Force (UBAF)

Three Spitfire F.XVIIIe from ACSEA (Air Command South East Asia) stocks arrived in Burma during April 1948 for strafing actions against the Communist North. They were incorporated into a training programme for Burmese pilots, supported by the British Services Mission at Mingaladon, near Rangoon. Later a Burmese Conversion Squadron was formed at Llandow in the UK, flying Spitfire F.21s in 1952/53. After the arrival of Spitfire Mk.IXs, the UBAF was assisted by Israel, especially for building up the organisation of an OTU at Hmawbi from 1955 onwards.

In 1951 the Burmese Government ordered 20 de-navalised, reconditioned Seafire F.XVs from Vickers-Armstrongs. These had been re-purchased from Royal Navy stocks and were extensively modified by Airwork General Trading Ltd at Gatwick, Surrey, giving a very similar appearance to the Spitfire Mk.XII. The aircraft lost the arrester hook, catapult and slinging point, and the C-wing was replaced by Seafire Mk.XV-type folding wings with rocket equipment. In the UK they were allocated Class B registrations *G-15-212* to *G-15-231* and delivered to Burma by ship towards the end of 1952.

Given the Burmese serial numbers UB401 to UB420, the Seafire Mk.XVs made their first air tests in Burma between March

Spitfire LF.IXe UB443 (ex IDF/AF 20-87) on delivery from Israel to Burma in December 1954. In the foreground is the ferry pilot, Sqn Ldr Townsend.
[Trevor Williams]

Spitfire ferry flying over 5,000 miles from Israel to Burma

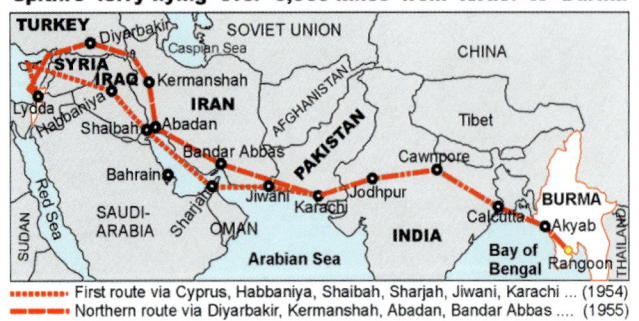

·········· First route via Cyprus, Habbaniya, Shaibah, Sharjah, Jiwani, Karachi ... (1954)
━ ━ ━ Northern route via Diyarbakir, Kermanshah, Abadan, Bandar Abbas .... (1955)

and September 1953. The aircraft moved to the AFB Mingaladon, then to No.1 Sqn at Hmawbi (30 miles north of Rangoon), where they became operational at the end of 1953 for close support operations with the Burmese Army (counter-insurgency and fighter-bomber missions). In 1954/55 they were replaced by Hawker Sea Furies.

Burma also purchased 30 Spitfire LF.IXs (with Merlin 66) from Israel under contracts from 3rd May/17th August 1954: The first twenty with an overhaul-reserve of at least 200 hours, delivery to commence in 1954 (Operation *Orez A*). A further ten were overhauled to zero hours before delivery, which was planned for 1955 (Operation *Orez B*). The price was £5,200 each, plus an extra £1,300 for each of the last ten which had been overhauled.

The Spitfire LF.IXs were equipped with two 20mm cannon and two 0.5-inch guns, plus rocket- and bomb-carriers. For ferry flying to Burma long-range fuel tanks were fitted. Burmese markings and serial numbers UB421 to UB450 were painted on in Israel. The delivery of spare parts, equipment, ammunition and the training of UBAF pilots was also arranged under this deal. Overhaul and refurbishment was undertaken by the Bedek Company at Lydda (Lod) from June 1954 onwards. Due to lack of spares, No.22 Wing IDF/AF (Air/MU) also supported the overhauls.

Burmese pilots arrived in Israel in August 1954 for training, initially on Harvard T-6s at Tel-Nof (ex Ekron/Aqir). Spitfire training was carried out by No 105 Sqn (OTU) at Ramat David until February 1955.

On 10th September 1954 Israel signed a contract with Fieldair Aircraft Services of Croydon, UK, for ferry flying ten Spitfire IXs to Burma. For this transfer, pilots of Israel had to fly the aircraft to Nicosia airport (then in British Cyprus), from where Fieldair pilots would then fly them in batches of four via Habbaniya, Shaibah, Bahrein, Sharjah, Jiwani, Karachi, Jodhpur, Cawnpore, Calcutta and Akyab to Mingaladon. Only eight Spitfires arrived in Burma by this route before the Arab states refused landing and refuelling rights to any aircraft originating in Israel.

The contract with Fieldair ended in December 1954, and the Israeli Ministry of Defence then instigated its own organisation which managed the ferry flying on a northern route direct from Lydda via Diyarbakir (Turkey), Kermanshah, Abadan, Bahrain, Sharjah and Jiwani, then following the known route to Mingaladon near Rangoon.

On the way to Burma several ferry pilots found themselves in difficulties. Three of the Spitfire Mk.IXs turned back to Nicosia, but force-landed in Lebanon due to fuel shortage, and were impounded. Another made a belly landing at Diyarbakir, one was forced to land at Shaibah with engine trouble, one tipped on its nose and a second ground-looped at Bandar Abbas, another made a belly-landing with a seized engine at Dum Dum near Calcutta. Three of the last batch were forced to land in a tropical storm in Burma. Two aircraft were replaced by the IDF/AF. One Spitfire crashed in Israel, still marked as UBAF aircraft.

Only 29 Spitfire LF.IX arrived in Burma, but the UBAF had a high rate of accidents, and therefore the maximum strength was never more than 23 Spitfire Mk.IX. These served with the OTU at Hmawbi, but detachments were sent to Meiktila for action up-country in North-Burma.

Summary - Burma purchased from 1948 to 1954:
        30 Spitfire LF.IXc/e
        20 Seafire F.XVc(e)
        3 Spitfire F.XVIIIe
Total   =   53 aircraft.

Individual Histories

ML119 Spitfire LF.IXc (Merlin 66); Became **UB441**; TOC/RAF 24.3.44; ex Czech AF; Israel *2020*; Selected for UBAF in

Spitfire LF.IXc UB441 (ex ML119) displayed as a gate guardian at Mingaladon air base in May 1987. It was sold in America in 1999 and is now in storage in the UK pending restoration.   *[PRA]*

Another view of Spitfire LF.IXc UB441 (ex ML119) at Mingaladon air base, now camouflaged, in July 1998. [David Gouldsmith]

1954; No.22 Wing IDF/AF 8-10.54; Flown from Lydda (Lod) to Nicosia 30.11.54 - Ferry flight by 'Jacky' Moggridge desp 15.2.55, Sharjah 17.2.55, arr Burma 22.2.55; No.1 Sqn UBAF (personal aircraft of the CO, Col Thura Tin Maung Aye); Crash-landed at Bamtang in 6.55; SOC – Became gate guardian at Mingaladon AFB 1965; Displayed in Aungsan Park, Rangoon 1991-1993; Retd Mingaladon AFB 1994 and restored from 1995; Sold to USA in 1999; Returned to England, Peter Monk & Mike Simpson, Airframe Assemblies, Sandown, Isle of Wight 30.10.2000 – **SURVIVOR**

NH853 Spitfire F.XVIIIe (Griffon 65); TOC/RAF 7.7.45; ACSEA - Arr Burma 22.4.48; Fate unknown

PR355 Seafire F.XV (Griffon VI); Became **UB406**; RNDA 11.6.45; To G-15-217 - Arr Burma 5.52; No.1 Sqn at Hmawbi AFB 1953/54 ; Fate unknown

PR376 Seafire F.XV (Griffon VI); Became **UB409**; RNDA 30.6.45; To G-15-220 - Arr Burma 1952; No.1 Sqn at Hmawbi AFB 1953/54 – Extant, at Shante Air Base near Meiktila 1987, Mingaladon 1995; Now exhibited in the Defence Services Museum at Yangon - **SURVIVOR**

PR400 Seafire F.XV (Griffon VI); Became **UB410**; RNDA

Surviving Spitfire F.XV UB409 (ex PR376) at Mingaladon in January 1995, prior to exhibition at the Defence Museum in Yangon (Rangoon). [PRA]

Seafire F.XV UB415 (ex PR422) of No.1 Sqn at Hmawbi 1953/54. Note the enlarged rudder trim tab and the absence of the arrester hook; also the E-type wing, replacing the original C-type. [UBAF, via Peter Arnold]

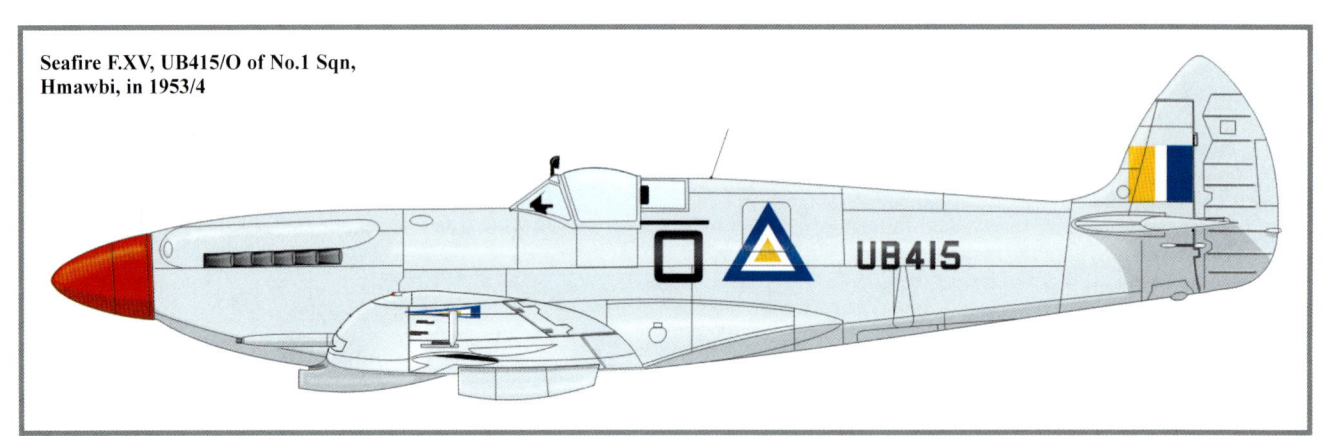

Seafire F.XV, UB415/O of No.1 Sqn, Hmawbi, in 1953/4

28.8.45; To G-15-221 - Arr Burma 1952; No.1 Sqn at Hmawbi AFB 1953/54; Fate unknown
PR407 Seafire F.XV (Griffon VI); Became **UB418**; RNDA 24.7.45; To G-15-229 - Arr Burma 1952; No.1 Sqn at Hmawbi AFB 1953/54 ; Fate unknown
PR422 Seafire F.XV (Griffon VI); Became **UB415**; RNDA 6.9.45; To G-15-226 - Arr Burma 1952; No.1 Sqn at Hmawbi AFB 1953/54. - gate guardian at Hmawbi 1960; Meiktila 1995; Painted as "UB414", for mobile display since 1996 – **SURVIVOR**
PR423 Seafire F.XV (Griffon VI); Became **UB411**; RNDA 5.10.45; To G-15-222 - Arr Burma 6.52; No.1 Sqn at Hmawbi AFB 1953/54; Fate unknown
PR453 Seafire F.XV (Griffon VI); Became **UB413**; RNDA 26.9.45; To G-15-224 - Arr Burma 1952; No.1 Sqn at Hmawbi AFB 1953/54; Fate unknown
PR454 Seafire F.XV (Griffon VI); Became **UB416**; RNDA 29.9.45; To G-15-227 - Arr Burma 1952; No.1 Sqn at Hmawbi AFB 1953/54; Fate unknown
PR455 Seafire F.XV (Griffon VI); Became **UB408**; RNDA 18.1.46; To G-15-219 - Arr Burma 6.52; No.1 Sqn at Hmawbi AFB 1953/54; Fate unknown
PR462 Seafire F.XV (Griffon VI); Became **UB419**; RNDA 19.10.45; To G-15-230 - Arr Burma 1952; No.1 Sqn at Hmawbi AFB 1953/54; Fate unknown
PV270 Spitfire LF.IXe (Merlin 66); Became **UB424**; TOC/RAF 28.9.44; ex Italian AF *MM 4014,* Israel 20*80*; Selected for UBAF 4.54, transfer-order 29.6.54 (to Bedek Company 1.7.54); Flown to Lydda by SB Feldman 1.7.54; Overhaul to zero hours (Operation *Orez B*) - Ferry flight by Leo Gardner desp 29.6.55, arr Burma in 7.55; Service unknown; Extant, Hmawbi AFB on pole as "UB 425"from 1970; Mingaladon AFB in store from 1994; To USA 1999; Purchased by Brendon Deere, New Zealand; Restoration at Dairy Flat, New Zealand, from May 2001 - **SURVIVOR**
SM943 Spitfire F.XVIIIe (Griffon 65); TOC/RAF 23.7.45; ACSEA - Arr Burma 22.4.48; Fate unknown
SR451 Seafire F.XV (Griffon VI); Became **UB401**; RNDA 31.10.44; To G-15-212 - Arr Burma 5.52; Air test in Burma 1953; No.1 Sqn at Hmawbi AFB 1953/54; Fate unknown
SR462 Seafire F.XV (Griffon VI); Became **UB414**; RNDA 10.2.45; To G-15-225 - Arr Burma 1952; No.1 Sqn at Hmawbi AFB 1953/54; gate guardian at Hmawbi as "UB415" from 1970; To storage Mingaladon AFB 1945; sold to USA 1999 – **SURVIVOR**
SR470 Seafire F.XV (Griffon VI); Became **UB417**; RNDA 28.2.45; To G-15-228 - Arr Burma 1952; No.1 Sqn at Hmawbi AFB 1953/54; Fate unknown
SR471 Seafire F.XV (Griffon VI); Became **UB405**; RNDA 13.3.45; To G-15-216 - Arr Burma 1952; No.1 Sqn at Hmawbi AFB 1953/54; Fate unknown
SR534 Seafire F.XV (Griffon VI); Became **UB407**; RNDA 23.4.45; To G-15-218 - Arr Burma 6.52; No.1 Sqn at Hmawbi AFB 1953/54; Fate unknown

SR642 Seafire F.XV (Griffon VI); Became **UB403**; RNDA 18.6.45; To G-15-214 - Arr Burma 6.52; Air test in Burma 3.53; No.1 Sqn at Hmawbi AFB 1953/54; Fate unknown
SW799 Seafire F.XV (Griffon VI); Became **UB402**; RNDA 6.7.45; To G-15-213 - Arr Burma 1952; Air test in Burma 1953; No.1 Sqn at Hmawbi AFB 1953/54; Fate unknown
SW817 Seafire F.XV (Griffon VI); Became **UB412**; RNDA 16.7.45; To G-15-223 - Arr Burma 1952; No.1 Sqn at Hmawbi AFB 1953/54; Fate unknown
SW863 Seafire F.XV (Griffon VI); Became **UB404**; RNDA 1.8.45; To G-15-215 - Arr Burma 5.52; No.1 Sqn at Hmawbi AFB 1953/54; Fate unknown
SW899 Seafire F.XV (Griffon VI); Became **UB420**; RNDA 24.8.45; To G-15-231 - Arr Burma 1952; Air test in Burma 1953; No.1 Sqn at Hmawbi AFB 1953/54; Fate unknown
TE515 Spitfire LF.IXe (Merlin 66); Became **UB439**; TOC/RAF 16.6.45; ex Czech AF; Israel *2058*; Selected for UBAF in 1954, to Bedek Company in 9.54 - Ferry flight by 'Sonny' Banting desp 15.2.55, Sharjah 17.2.55, arr Burma 22.2.55; Fate unknown
TE559 Spitfire LF.IXe (Merlin 66); TOC/RAF 1.6.45; ex Czech AF; Israel *2048*; To Bedek company 1954, as spare parts for overhaul of the UBAF Spitfires
TE564 Spitfire LF.IXe (Merlin 66); Became **UB...** (range 421-450); TOC/RAF 7.6.45; ex Czech AF; Israel *2049* - Arr Burma 1954; Fate unknown
TE578 Spitfire LF.IXc (Merlin 66); ex Israel (IDF/AF) *2028*; (Insurance ID 'SH/CBAF/IX/578'); Selected for UBAF, transfer-order 29.6.54 (to Bedek Company 1.7.54); Test-flown with Burmese marking in Israel 17.8.54; From Lydda to Nicosia by SB Feldman 1.10.54; Vibration, engine replaced at Nicosia; Returned to Israel 4.12.54; Later exhibited Hatzor AFB, marked as "105"; Storage at Hatzerim Museum near Beersheba now - **SURVIVOR**
TP198 Spitfire F.XVIIIe (Griffon 65); TOC/RAF 17.12.45; ACSEA - Arr Burma 22.4.48; Fate unknown

The RAF Serial Nos of the following Spitfire LF.IX are mostly unknown:

UB421 Spitfire LF.IX (Merlin 66); ex Israel (IDF/AF) *2024*; RAF Serial TE5.. (Insurance ID 'SH/CBAF/IX/550'); Selected for UBAF in 4.54, transfer-order 14.6.54 (to Bedek company 15.6.54); Rocket-demonstration in Israel with Burmese markings 11.8.54; Flown 17.8.54; From Lydda to Nicosia by SB Feldman 27.9.54; Test-flying over Cyprus by Philip Gurdon, suffered an oil leak 28/29.9.54 - Ferry flight desp 13.11.54, arr Burma 19.11.54 (Mingaladon 20.11.54); Service unknown; Extant at Meiktila; later Mingaladon 1995; Now exhibited at Defence Services Museum at Yangon (former Rangoon) - **SURVIVOR**
UB422 Spitfire LF.IX (Merlin 66); ex Israel (IDF/AF) *2008*; (Insurance ID '17-676'); Selected for UBAF 4.54, transfer-order 22.6.54 (to Bedek Company in 7.54); Flown in Israel with Burmese markings 3.9-22.9.54; From Lydda to Nicosia 1.10.54 (reported bad belly-tank rubber seals) - Ferry flight by Philip Gurdon desp 3.10.54, Engine rough en route from Habbaniya to Bahrain, belly-landed at Shaibah 4.10.54. Remained there, later taken over by Iraq authority in 5.56; Fate unknown
(2) Replacement - A **second** Spitfire was selected for Burma (IDF/AF Serial No unknown) and became UB422; Overhaul by Bedek Company to zero hours (Operation *Orez B*) - Ferry flight by 'Jacky' Moggridge desp 9.10.55, arr Burma 18.10.55 (force-landed in tropic storm); UBAF, served with the OTU, crashed on landing at Hmawbi, Cat.E 4.11.55, SOC
UB423 Spitfire LF.IX (Merlin 66); ex Israel (IDF/AF) *2009*; (Insurance ID 'SH/CBAF/IX/556'); Selected for UBAF 4.54, transfer-order 14.6.54 (to Bedek Company 15.6.54); Flown in Israel with Burmese markings 23.8.54; From Lydda to Nicosia 27.9.54; Oxygen leak reported 30.9.54 - Ferry flight by CC Lamberton desp 3.10.54, Shaibah 4.10.54, arr Burma (in poor state) 11.10.54; UBAF, crashed on landing at Kain-Ton, Cat.E 18.2.55, SOC
UB424 ex Israel (IDF/AF) *2080*; see PV270 above
UB425 (1) ex Israel (IDF/AF) *2028*; see TE578 above
(2) Replacement - A **second** Spitfire (possibly IDF/AF *2042*) was selected for Burma and became UB425; Overhaul to zero hours (Operation *Orez B*) - Ferry flight by 'Jacky' Moggridge desp 14.8.55, arr Burma 24.8.55; at Hmawbi AFB in 1955 (shown there with Plt Aung Chit Han); Service unknown; Extant with a locally made engine cowling and Harvard tail as "UB424" at Mandalay 1984; Mingaladon 1995; Sold to USA 1999 – **SURVIVOR**
UB426 Spitfire LF.IX (Merlin 66); ex Israel (IDF/AF) *2034*; Selected for UBAF 4.54, transfer-order 22.6/29.6.54 (to Bedek Company 1.7.54); Overhaul to zero hours (Operation *Orez B*) - Ferry flight by Gordon Levett desp 29.6.55, arr Burma 7.55; UBAF, OTU Hmawbi, crash-landed end 1955; Repair, AW/CN 2.56; Fate unknown

Seafire F.XV UB403 (ex SR642) still bearing its Class B registration G-15-214. [via Phillip Jarrett]

UB427 Spitfire LF.IX (Merlin 66); ex Israel (IDF/AF) *2039*; (Insurance ID 'SH/CBAF/IX/566'); Selected for UBAF 4.54, transfer-order 22.6/29.6.54 (to Bedek Company 15.7.54); Flown in Israel with Burmese markings 1.9-22.9.54; From Lydda to Nicosia 6.11.54 - Ferry flight desp 13.11.54, arr Burma in poor condition (oil pipe holed) 19.11.54; UBAF, crashed on landing at Kain-Ton, Cat.E 18.2.55, SOC; Airframe handed over to an Infantry Regiment

UB428 Spitfire LF.IX (Merlin 66); ex Israel (IDF/AF) *2041*; (Insurance ID 'CBAF/IX/2493'); Selected for UBAF 4.54, transfer-order 22.6/29.6.54 (to Bedek Company 15.7.54); Flown in Israel with Burmese markings 17.8.54 - 20.9.54; From Lydda to Nicosia 27.9.54; Oxygen and glycol leak reported 30.9.54 - Ferry flight desp 3.10.54, Shaibah 4.10.54, arr Burma with defect CSU 11.10.54; UBAF, crash-landed at Mingaladon 7.12.54, heavy salvage damage, SOC

UB429 Spitfire LF.IX (Merlin 66); ex Israel (IDF/AF) *2069*; Selected for UBAF 4.54, transfer-order 22.6/29.6.54 (to Bedek Company 15.7.54); Overhaul to zero hours (Operation *Orez B*) - Ferry flight by 'Sonny' Banting desp 14.8.55, arr Burma 24.8.55; UBAF, shown Hmawbi based; Fate unknown

UB430 Spitfire LF.IX (Merlin 66); ex Israel (IDF/AF) *2059*; (Insurance ID 'SH/CBAF/IX/576'); Selected for UBAF 4.54, transfer-order 22.6/29.6.54 (to Bedek Company 1.8.54) - Ferry flight by Gordon Levett desp 2.3.55, stayed at Diyarbekir/Turkey; Crashed on landing at Bandar Abbas: wheels sunk into mud, tipped on nose, propeller damaged c. 6.3.55; Left behind for repair; New propeller fitted, take-off at Bandar Abbas c. 30.3.55, flown via Karachi – Cawnpore – Barrackpore/Calcutta, arr Rangoon 1.4.55; Fate unknown

UB431 Spitfire LF.IXe (Merlin 66); ex Israel (IDF/AF) *2026*; (Insurance ID '17-1337'); Selected for UBAF 4.54, transfer-order 22.6/29.6.54 (to Bedek Company 1.8.54); Flown in Israel with Burmese markings 10.10-13.10.54; From Lydda to Nicosia 26.11.54 - Ferry flight via Bahrain desp 29.11.54 (first leg flown by 'Jacky' Moggridge, final leg by CC Lamberton), arr Burma 7.12.54; UBAF, crashed on landing at Hmawbi, Cat.E 25.2.55 (Plt Than Kyne), SOC; Repaired for instructional purpose and presented by AC Clift (UBAF) 24.4.56, exhibited in the Aung San Park of Royal Lakes at Rangoon; Wrecked in storm 1968; Fuselage remains into a Sea Fury Diorama of UB466 in the Defence Service Museum at Yangon (former Rangoon) - **SURVIVOR**

UB432 Spitfire LF.IXe (Merlin 66); ex Israel (IDF/AF) *2043*; (Insurance ID '17-1357'); Selected for UBAF 4.54, transfer-order 22.6/29.6.54 (to Bedek Company 1.8.54); Flown in Israel with Burmese markings 6.10-13.10.54; From Lydda to Nicosia flown by Lt Akiva Presman 12.11.54 - Ferry flight by Gordon Levett desp 15.2.55, Sharjah 17.2.55, arr Burma 22.2.55; Fate unknown

UB433 Spitfire LF.IXe (Merlin 66); ex Israel (IDF/AF) *2010*; Selected for UBAF 4.54, transfer-order 22.6/29.6.54 (to Bedek Company 1.8.54); Overhaul to zero hours (Operation *Orez B*) - Ferry flight by 'Jacky' Moggridge desp 29.6.55, arr Burma 7.55; Fate unknown

UB434 Spitfire LF.IXe (Merlin 66); ex Israel (IDF/AF) *2077*; Selected for UBAF 4.54, transfer-order 22.6/29.6.54 (to Bedek Company 1.8.54) - Ferry flight by Leo Gardner desp 15.2.55, Sharjah 17.2.55, arr Burma 22.2.55; Fate unknown

UB435 Spitfire LF.IX (Merlin 66); ex Israel (IDF/AF) *2018*; Selected for UBAF in 1954, transfer-order 27.2.55: to Bedek Company, overhaul to zero hours (Operation *Orez B*); No.22 Wing IDF/AF (Air/MU), flown with Burmese markings by Capt AL Ostrof 18.8.55; Test-flight with ferry-tanks, engine failed, crashed near Machane/Lod, Cat.E 22.8.55 (Capt AL Ostrof killed), SOC
NOTE: Report 'OB/CBAF/IX-9-583'; Recorded as UBAF loss, aircraft not replaced by Israel

UB436 Spitfire LF.IXe (Merlin 66); ex Israel (IDF/AF) *2050*; (Insurance ID '17-1342'); Selected for UBAF in 1954, transfer-order 12.8.54 (to Bedek Company until 15.8.54); Test-flown in Israel with Burmese markings 10.10.54; From Lydda to Nicosia 26.11.54 - Ferry flight desp 29.11.54, at Sharjah for maintenance; Engine failed, force-landed wheels-up at Dum Dum/Calcutta; Fuel pump replaced, arr Burma 7.12.54; Fate unknown

UB437 Spitfire LF.IX (Merlin 66); ex Israel (IDF/AF) *2074*; Selected for UBAF in 1954, transfer-order 12.8.54 (to Bedek Company until 15.8.54); Overhaul to zero hours (Operation *Orez B*) - Ferry flight by Gordon Levett desp 14.8.55, arr Burma 24.8.55; Fate unknown

UB438 Spitfire LF.IX (Merlin 66); ex Israel (IDF/AF) *2023*; Selected for UBAF in 1954; 22.Wing IDF/AF, transfer-order 27.8.54 (to Bedek Company 30.8.54); Flown to Lydda by SB Feldman 31.8.54; To Nicosia 30.11.54 - Ferry flight, first leg to Habbaniya flown by Plt Burvill 3.12.54; Then Iraq closed the route; Headed back to Nicosia, force-landed at Beirut/Lebanon 4.12.54 due to fuel shortage; Interned; Later aircraft flown back to Nicosia by Peter Nock 14.3.55; Eventually ferried out to Burma by Gordon Levett, desp 14.4.55, arr Burma 4.55; Fate unknown

UB439 ex Israel (IDF/AF) *2058*; see TE515 above

UB440 Spitfire LF.IX (Merlin 66); ex Israel (IDF/AF) *2070*; Selected for UBAF 4.54, transfer-order 22.6.54 (to Bedek Company 15.8.54); No.22 Wing IDF/AF (Air/MU) 8.54/10.54 - Ferry flight by 'Sonny' Banting desp c. 4.3.55, meet the ferry-group at Diyarbekir/Turkey; Landed at Sharjah instead of Bandar Abbas c. 6.3.55, arr Burma 15.3.55 (Plt Gardner or Moggridge, possibly); Fate unknown

UB441 ex Israel (IDF/AF) *2020*; see ML119 above

UB442 Spitfire LF.IX (Merlin 66); ex Israel (IDF/AF) *20.. ?*; Selected for UBAF 1954/55; Bedek Company for overhaul to zero hours (Operation *Orez B*) - Ferry flight by TJT Maseng desp 9.10.55, arr Burma 18.10.55 (force-landed in tropical storm); Fate unknown

UB443 Spitfire LF.IXe (Merlin 66); ex Israel (IDF/AF) *2087*; No.22 Wing IDF/AF (Air/MU), refurbished for UBAF 10.54/11.54; Test-flown in Israel with Burmese markings 10.11.54; To Lydda 17.11.54, to Nicosia 26.11.54 - Ferry flight by S/Ldr Townsend desp 29.11.54, via Sharjah, arr Burma 7.12.54; UBAF, crashed on landing at Hmawbi 2.1.55 (Plt Saw Pru, CO of the AFB); w/o accepted 31.1.55; Flown after repair 29.1.55; Crashed on landing at Hmawbi, Cat.E 28.2.55 (Plt Than Kyne), SOC

UB444 Spitfire LF.IX (Merlin 66); ex Israel (IDF/AF) *2076*; No.22Wing IDF/AF (Air/MU), refurbished for UBAF 10.54/11.54; Test-flown in Israel with Burmese markings 12.11.54; To Lydda 17.11.54; Bedek Company, returned to No.22 Wing 4.12.54; Test-flown by SB Feldman until 26.1.55 - Ferry flight by 'Jacky' Moggridge desp 2.3.55, stayed at Diyarbekir/Turkey, ground-looped on landing at Bandar Abbas, slight damage only c.6.3.55 (Plt J Moggridge); Take-off with heading to Sharjah c.10.3.55; Continued ferry flight together with UB440 & UB449, arr Burma 15.3.55 (Plt Gardner or Banting, possibly); Fate unknown

UB445 Spitfire LF.IX (Merlin 66); ex Israel (IDF/AF) *2090*; No.22 Wing IDF/AF (Air/MU), refurbished for UBAF 10.54/11.54; Test-flown in Israel with Burmese markings 23.11.54; From Lydda to No.22 Wing 23.11.54 (shown there 12.54 & 2.55); Test-flown by SB Feldman until 9.2.55 - Ferry flight to Burma 2.3.55, damaged at Malatiya/Turkey and returned to Israel; Eventually ferried out by Leo Gardner 14.4.55; On delivery flight, forgot to lower the undercarriage when landing at Diyarbakir/Turkey; Slight damage, repaired by TuAF within four days, arr Burma in 4.55; Fate unknown

UB446 Spitfire LF.IX (Merlin 66); ex Israel (IDF/AF) *2052*; No.22 Wing IDF/AF (Air/MU), refurbished for UBAF 10.54/11.54; Test-flown in Israel with Burmese markings 11.11.54; Bedek Company in 12.54; Flown from Lydda to Nicosia by Capt A Tsivoni 26.11.54 - Ferry flight desp 29.11.54, crashed on landing at Dum Dum/Calcutta: tyre burst, undercarriage leg collapsed 6.12.54; Left behind for repair, arr Burma 11.1.55; Fate unknown

UB447 Spitfire LF.IX (Merlin 66); ex Israel (IDF/AF) *2085*; No.22 Wing IDF/AF (Air/MU), refurbished for UBAF 10.54/11.54; Test-flown in Israel with Burmese markings 11.11-29.11.54; From Lydda to Nicosia 30.11.54 - Ferry flight, first leg to Habbaniya flown by Plt Simmondy 3.12.54; Then Iraq closed the route; Headed back to Nicosia, force-landed at Beirut/Lebanon 4.12.54 due to fuel shortage; Interned; Later flown back to Nicosia by Peter Nock 13.3.55; Eventually ferried out to Burma by 'Sonny' Banting, desp 14.4.55, arr Burma 4.55; Fate unknown

UB448 Spitfire LF.IX (Merlin 66); ex Israel (IDF/AF) *2079*; No.22 Wing IDF/AF (Air/MU), refurbishing for UBAF 10.54/11.54; Test-flown in Israel with Burmese markings from 12/14.11.54; From Lydda to Nicosia 30.11.54 - Ferry flight, first leg to Habbaniya flown by Plt Overburry 3.12.54; Then Iraq closed the route; Headed back to Nicosia, force-landed at Beirut/Lebanon 4.12.54 due to fuel shortage; Interned; Later flown back to Nicosia by Peter Nock 12.3.55; Eventually ferried out to Burma by 'Jacky' Moggridge, desp 14.4.55, arr Burma 4.55; Fate unknown

UB449 Spitfire LF.IX (Merlin 66); ex Israel (IDF/AF) *2013*; No.22 Wing IDF/AF (Air/MU), refurbished for UBAF 10.54/11.54; Test-flown in Israel with Burmese markings 14.11.54 - 10.1.55; From Lydda to No.22 Wing 29.11.54, to Nicosia 2.12.54; Retd to No.22 Wing in 12.54; Aerobatic display in Israel flown by SB Feldman 21.12.54 - Ferry flight by Leo Gardner desp 2.3.55; Stayed at Diyarbekir in Turkey for magneto repair (Plt L Gardner), landed at Sharjah instead of Bandar Abbas, arr Burma 15.3.55 (Plt possibly Banting or Moggridge); Fate unknown

UB450 Spitfire LF.IX (Merlin 66); ex Israel (IDF/AF) *20.. ?*; Bedek Company, overhaul to zero hours (Operation *Orez B*) - Ferry flight by Gordon Levett desp 9.10.55, arr Burma 18.10.55 (force-landed in tropical storm); Fate unknown.

SURVIVORS in Burma
UB409/ PR376 Exhib. Museum Yangon
UB415/ PR422 ("UB414") Hmawbi 1987, Meiktila1995
UB421/ TE5.. Meiktila, Mingaladon; Museum Yangon
UB431/ – Sea-Fury Diorama at Yangon.

Via Mingaladon sold to USA 1999:
UB414 / SR462 ("UB415"); UB424 / PV270 ("UB425"), now in New Zealand; UB425 ("UB424"); UB441 / ML119 ("UB441"), now in UK.

Burmese & British Seafire serial numbers, 1952

Burma Serial	RAF Serial	Delivery No	Burma Serial	RAF Serial	Delivery No
UB401	SR451	G-15-212	UB411	PR423	G-15-222
UB402	SW799	G-15-213	UB412	SW817	G-15-223
UB403	SR642	G-15-214	UB413	PR453	G-15-224
UB404	SW863	G-15-215	UB414	SR462	G-15-225
UB405	SR471	G-15-216	UB415	PR422	G-15-226
UB406	PR355	G-15-217	UB416	PR454	G-15-227
UB407	SR534	G-15-218	UB417	SR470	G-15-228
UB408	PR455	G-15-219	UB418	PR407	G-15-229
UB409	PR376	G-15-220	UB419	PR462	G-15-230
UB410	PR400	G-15-221	UB420	SW899	G-15-231

Spitfire IX Checklist: Israel / Burmese serial numbers

IDF/AF SerialNo	Transfer-order IDF/AF	Gathering in Israel (Bedek+No22Wg)	UBAF SerialNo.
20 .. ?	unknown	unknown	UB442
20 .. ?	unknown	unknown	UB450
2008	22/29.6.54	1.7.54	UB422(1)
20 .. ?	unknown	unknown	UB422(2)
2009	14.6.54	15.6.54	UB423
2010	22/29.6.54	1.8.54	UB433
2013	unknown	? (10.54)	UB449
2018	27.2.55	3-7.55 (8.55)	UB435(*)
2020	unknown	? (8.54)	UB441
2023	27.8.54	30/31.8.54	UB438
2024	14.6.54	15.6.54	UB421
2026	22/29.6.54	1.8.54	UB431
2028	22/29.6.54	1.7.54	UB425(1)
2033	unknown	unknown	UB4..?
2034	22/29.6.54	1.7.54	UB426
2036	unknown	unknown	UB4..?
2039	22/29.6.54	1.8/15.7.54	UB427
2041	22/29.6.54	1.8/15.7.54	UB428
2042	unknown	unknown	UB425(2)
2043	22/29.6.54	15.8/1.8.54	UB432
2048	Spare parts for UBAF		
2050	12.8.54	15.8.54	UB436
2052	unknown	? (10.54)	UB446
2058	unknown	9.54	UB439
2059	22.6/29.7.54	15.8/1.8.54	UB430
2069	22/29.6.54	15.8/15.7.54	UB429
2070	22.6.54	15.8.54 (10.54)	UB440
2072	unknown	unknown	UB4..?
2074	12.8.54	15.8.54	UB437
2076	unknown	? (10.54)	UB444
2077	22./29.6.54	15.8/1.8.54	UB434
2079	unknown	? (10.54)	UB448
2080	29.6.54	1.7.54	UB424
2085	unknown	? (10.54)	UB447
2087	unknown	? (10.54)	UB443
2090	unknown	? (10.54)	UB445

(2) = Replacements   (*) UB435 crashed in Israel 22.8.55

Arrival of Spitfire IX in Burma 1954/55

Arrival date	UBAF Serial No's	Max on Strength	Remarks
11.10.54	UB423, 428	2	1)
19.11.54	UB421, 427	4	
07.12.54	UB431, 436, 443	6	2) 4)
---	(UB438, 447, 448)	6	3)
11.01.55	UB446	7	4)
22.02.55	UB432, 434, 439, 441	9	5)
15.03.55	UB440, 444, 449	10	6) 7)
01.04.55	UB430	11	6)
.... 04.55	UB438, 445, 447, 448	15	3)
.... 07.55	UB424, 426, 433	17	8)
24.08.55	UB425, 429, 437	20	
18.10.55	UB422, 442, 450	**23**	9)

1) The first UB422 left behind at Shaibah, confiscated by Iraq later; replaced by another Spitfire, arrived Burma October 1955.
2) UB428 crashed with UBAF on 7 December 1954, salvage damage, w/o.
3) Turned back for Nicosia, but force-landed in Beirut due to fuel shortage, interned; later to Burma in April 1955.
4) UB446 left behind at Dum Dum, arrived Burma January 1955.
5) UB423 & UB427 crashed on landing with UBAF 18 February 1955.
6) UB430 left behind at Bandar Abbas, arr Burma later.
7) UB431 & UB442 crashed on landing 25 and 28 February 1955, w/o.
8) UB441 crashed on landing with UBAF in June 1955, w/o.
9) Total 29 Spitfire IX arr Burma; maximum strength of UBAF 23 Spitfires; UB435 crashed in Israel, not replaced.

References:
Aviation News 1987, p.666.
FlyPast September 1990, p 52 and November 1996, p.26.
Aeroplane Monthly January 1996, p.24.
Air Enthusiast Sept/Oct 1997, p.48; Nov/Dec.1998, p.34.
Air Enthusiast, Jan/Feb 1999, p.2.

CANADA

A total of 48 Royal Canadian Air Force (RCAF) squadrons fought beside those of the Royal Air Force (RAF) during the Second World War. These included the all-Canadian No.6 Group of Bomber Command, while RCAF fighter units played a major role in the 2nd Tactical Air Force (No.83 Group, 2nd TAF). In the meantime, the RCAF operated the British Commonwealth Air Training Plan (BCATP) in Canada, training a total of more than 130,000 aircrew for the Allied war effort.

Late in 1944 the Canadian Government decided to form carrier air units on two light fleet carriers. The first two fighter squadrons, Nos.803 and 883, flew Seafires, initially under Royal Navy command in the United Kingdom. No.883 Sqn was temporarily disbanded due to manning difficulties, but No.803 Sqn went to Canada with HMCS *Warrior* after becoming a Royal Canadian Navy unit on 24 January 1946.

In all, Canada used 35 Seafire F.XVs and 7 Spitfires. The latter were used in Canada for tests and experiments and as ground instructional airframes; a further three Spitfires arrived for repair work only.

Great numbers of Spitfires served with the RCAF fighter units of the RAF, but these are outside the scope of the present work.

Canadian Spitfire units of the RAF
(Europe, except No.417 Sqn Mediterranean)

No.**400** (*City of Toronto*) Sqn, ex No.110 Sqn RCAF - no code;
Spitfire PR.XI from December 1943 to 7th August 1945.
No.**401** (*Ram*) Sqn, ex No.1 Sqn RCAF - code 'YO';
Spitfire Mks.II/V/IX/XVI/XIV from September 1941 to 23rd June 1945.
No.**402** (*City of Winnipeg*) Sqn, ex No.2 Sqn RCAF - code 'AE';
Spitfire Mks.V/IX/XIV/XVI from March 1942 to 1st July1945.
No.**403** (*Wolf*) Sqn - code 'KH';
Spitfire Mks.I/II/V/IX/XVI from May 1941 to 1st July 1945.
No.**411** (*Grizzly Bear*) Sqn - code 'DB';
Spitfire Mks.I/II/V/IX/XVI/XIV from June 1941 to 15th March 1946.
No.**412** (*Falcon*) Sqn - code 'VZ';
Spitfire Mks.II/V/IX/XVI/XIV from July 1941 to 15th March 1946.
No.**414** (*Sarnia Imperials*) Sqn - code 'RU';
Spitfire Mks.IX/XIV from August 1944 to 7th August 1945.
No.**416** (*City of Oshawa*) Sqn - code 'DN';
Spitfire Mks.II/V/IX/XVI/XIV from November 1941 to 15th March 1946.
No.**417** (*City of Windsor*) Sqn, RAF (ME) - code 'AN';
Spitfire Mks.II/V/VIII/IX from December 1941 to 1st July 1945.
No.**421** (*Red Indian*) Sqn - code 'AU';
Spitfire Mks.V/IX/XVI from April 1942 to 23rd July 1945.
No.**430** (*City of Sudbury*) Sqn - code 'G9';
Spitfire Mk.XIV from November 1944 to 7th August 1945.
No.**441** (*Silver Fox*) Sqn, ex No.125 Sqn RCAF - code '9G';
Spitfire Mks.V/IX from February 1944 to May 1945, then Mustang.
No.**442** (*Caribou*) Sqn, ex No.14 Sqn RCAF - code 'Y2';
Spitfire Mks.V/IX from February 1944 to March 1945, then Mustang.
No.**443** (*Hornet*) Sqn, ex No.127 Sqn RCAF - code '2I';
Spitfire Mks.V/IX/XVI/XIV from February 1944 to 15th March 1946.

No.242 (F) Sqn RAF had many Canadians on strength between 1939 and 1942, but had no Spitfires.

Nos.400, 414 & 430 Sqns were attached to No.39 (Recce) Wing RCAF of the No.83 Group (2nd TAF) from June 1943 to August 1945. Nos.401, 411, 412 Sqn served with No.126 Wing, Nos.403, 416, 421 with No.127 Wing; No.402 Sqn ex No.142 Wing, with No.125 Wing from September 1944, and with No.126 Wing from December 1944; No.441 Sqn with No.144 Wing from May 1944, and with No.125 Wing from July 1944. No.417 Sqn operated over MTO with No.244 Wing (Nos.211 & 205 Groups) from October 1943.

Canadian Seafire Squadrons of the Royal Navy
(Fleet Air Arm)

No.**803** Sqn, formed 15th June 1945 at Arbroath with Seafire Mk.III, then to Nutts Corner August 1945 with Seafire F.XV. Officially became a RCN unit 24th January 1946.

No.**883** Sqn, formed 18th September 1945 at Arbroath with Seafire Mk.III, then to Nutts Corner November 1945 with Seafire F.XV. Disbanded 23rd February 1946. Reformed in Canada 15th May 1947.

SPITFIRES in Canada

The Royal Canadian Air Force (RCAF) used a number of Spitfires for test and trials purposes, especially with the following units:

No.**1**	**Test Centre**	at Edmonton in 1940.
No.**1**	**Training Command**,	HQ at Toronto, Ontario. Spitfires based at Mountain View 1942.
No.**2**	**Training Command**,	HQ at Winnipeg, Manitoba.
No.**3**	**Training Command**,	HQ at Montreal, Quebec.

Note: Card entries for Nos.1, 2 and 3 TC often related to units within those commands, and not to the HQ itself. It is not always possible to establish the actual unit concerned.

No.**2** **Technical Training School** (TTS) at Camp Borden, North of Toronto, Ontario, in 1947.

No.**13** **Photo Survey Squadron** (PSS) of No.7 (PR) Wing, at Rockliffe, East of Ottawa, Ontario, with 3 Spitfires around 1944/45.

WEE **Winter Experimental Establishment** (WEE) at Gimli, Manitoba, a test and development unit in 1944.

One Spitfire Mk.VIII served as a ground instructional airframe in the south of Vancouver Island, at HMCS *Naden*, the Naval base in Victoria, British Columbia, in 1948/49.

SEAFIRES in Canada

In 1946 Canada received 35 Seafire F.XVcs from the United Kingdom, initially on loan. Two returned from the Winter Experimental Establishment (WEE) at Namao to the Royal Navy in 1947. The other 33 were transferred to Canadian charge, most with effect from 1st June 1946. For accounting purposes they were listed in the inventory of the RCAF, being initially on charge with the Eastern Air Command (EAC) until 31st March 1947, and officially from 11th April 1947 with No.10 Group of the Central Air Command (CAC). On 12th July 1947 the Seafires were formally transferred to RCN charge.

Canada also received the carrier HMCS *Warrior* on loan from the Royal Navy. She sailed for Canada on 23rd March 1946 with No.803 Sqn and 32 Seafire F.XVc, arriving at Halifax, Nova Scotia on 31st March 1946, the aircraft being then flown off to the RCN Section Dartmouth, which then became their shore base. HMCS *Warrior* served with the RCN until 23rd March 1948, when she was paid off and returned to the Royal Navy, being replaced by HMCS *Magnificent*.

Canadian airbases with Seafires

RCAF **Dartmouth** near Halifax, Nova Scotia (RCN Section from 31st March 1946, commissioned as RCNAS HMCS *Shearwater* 1 December 1948), home of No.1 TAG and shore base for operational squadrons.

RCAF **Debert** (RCN Air Facility), North of Halifax, Nova Scotia, for short time only.

RCAF **Namao** near Edmonton, Alberta, the Weather Experimental Establishment 1946/47.

RCAF **Rivers**, c.100m NW of Winnipeg, Manitoba (Canadian Joint Air Training Centre) August and September 1948; nearby Camp Shilo bombing range.

Dartmouth near Halifax, NOVA SCOTIA; Edmonton and Calgary, ALBERTA; St.Johns, NEWFOUNDLAND; Vancouver, BRITISH COLUMBIA

HMCS *Tecumseh* near Calgary, Alberta (RCN reserve), ground instructional use.

HMCS *Star* (RCN reserve), Hamilton, Ontario, ground instructional use.

HMCS *Stadacona* (Air Electrical School), Halifax, Nova Scotia, ground instructional use.

Seafire units of the Royal Canadian Navy (RCN)

No.**803** Sqn, an ex Royal Navy unit, became a RCN-unit on 24th January 1946 and sailed with HMCS *Warrior* from UK for Canada on 23rd March 1946, arrived Halifax on 31st March 1946. Based on the Naval Air Section at Dartmouth (HMCS *Shearwater*), this unit trained on ADDLs with Seafire F.XVc from April 1946 to June 1946, and from July 1946 it served on board of HMCS *Warrior*. Together with No.825 (Firefly) Sqn it made up the 19th Carrier Air Group on 15th May 1947. Flying with the Seafire F.XVc was short-lived, however, as most had left the unit by the end of May. In August 1947 No.803 Sqn went to Northern Ireland for re-equipping with Sea Furies.
Markings: Single individual letter on the fuselage only.
Commanding Officers:
L/C AJ Tanner RCNVR   16.11.45
L/C CG Watson RCN   5.46
L/C(A) HJC Bird CD RCN   5.47

No.**883** Sqn was re-formed in Canada on 15th May 1947 and based at HMCS *Shearwater* (RCN Section Dartmouth). The first Seafires arrived on 21st May 1947, the main contingent followed on 29th May 1947. With No.826 (Firefly) Sqn this unit formed the No.18 Carrier Air Group from 2nd June 1947, controlled by No.10 Group of the Central Air Command, and from 12th July 1947 by the RCN HQ. After ADDLs training and dive bombing exercises it served as a carrier unit until 21st November 1947, when the unit returned to the RCN Section Dartmouth. In 1948 No.883 Sqn trained for ground support missions, being based at RCAF Rivers (CJATC) in August and September 1948. During September 1948 the Seafire F.XVcs were used on the Camp Shilo bombing range. Returning to Dartmouth in October 1948, the unit began conversion to Sea Furies. Seafires were phased out in December 1948.
Markings: Call signs in the range 'VG-AAA' to 'VG-AAZ' carried under the wings, being abbreviated to 'AA-A' to 'AA-Z' on the fuselage sides.
Commanding Officers:
L/C RA Monks RCN   15.5.47
L/C JB Fotheringham RCN   1.48 to 12.48

Seafire F.XVs of No.803 Sqn and Fireflies of No.825 Sqn ranged on the flight deck of HMCS Warrior *prior to disembarking for Dartmouth as the vessel returns to Halifax after a training cruise around Bermuda, 14th May 1947.* [R: Ward, James; National Archives of Canada PA-141255]

No.1 **Training Air Group** (No.1 TAG) at Dartmouth, comprising No.743 FRU (Fleet Requirements Unit) and an OTU, which included an Operational Flying Training School (OFTS), began in May 1947 under control of the No.10 Group of the Central Air Command. Seafire F.XVc arrived in July 1947 and flew with No.1 TAG until June 1949 and May 1951 (OFTS & No.743 FRU, respectively). Markings: Call signs in the range 'VG-TGA' to 'VG-TGZ' carried under the wings, being abbreviated to 'TG-A' to 'TG-Z' on the fuselage sides (but in some instances no individual letter was carried).
Commanding Officers:
Lt JN Donaldson RCN   18.9.46
L/C WE Widdows RCN   30.8.47
L/C CG Smith RCN   1.12.48

SSEF **Seafire Special Exhibition Flight** (SSEF), an aerobatic element of No.1 TAG, called *"Watson's Circus"*, was formed at Dartmouth on 1st August 1949. Ten Seafire F.XVc arrived mid August 1949. On 20th August 1949 the SSEF was despatched from HMCS *Shearwater* to Toronto. Returning on 13th September 1949, two pilots and two Seafires being missing after an air-collision over Malton. The last Seafires left the unit on 21st September 1949.
Commanding Officer:
L/C Cliff G Watson RCN (killed in PR502 on 24.8.49).

Repair services

Initially the RCAF helped with overhaul and major repairs, as well as providing logistics for both the RCAF and the RCN at Dartmouth. Minor repairs and inspections were undertaken by the RCN. Technical training was supported by the RCAF and from 1948 onwards by the School of Naval Aircraft Maintenance (SNAM) at HMCS *Shearwater*.

The Canadian Car & Foundry Company (CCF) at Montreal, Quebec, carried out modifications and also overhaul and repair work on the Seafires, with a workshop at Dartmouth. The CCF served as No.11 TSU (Technical Service Unit) and No.11 AID (Aircraft Inspection Directorate) from 1946 to 1948. After that the Fairey Aviation Company of Canada Ltd, Nova Scotia, did repairs and overhaul work from 1949, then also final storage and striking off charge.

Painting of the Seafires in Canada

The Canadian Seafires were at first flown with British-type (RN) markings and painting in Dark Sea (Slate) Grey and Sky, with roundels on wings and fuselage and a red, white and blue fin-flash. Both sides of the rear fuselage were stencilled "ROYAL CANADIAN NAVY" above the serial number.

A new paint scheme was introduced from 1947 when Seafires entered the RCN inventory. Repainting continued until 1948, when the last of the entire fleet of aircraft was shown in a distinctly Canadian Pattern No.2 format, with Dark Grey on the upper fuselage and on the top sides of the wings and tail planes. The fuselage sides and belly, and the under surfaces of the wings and tail planes, were painted Light Grey. Fuselage sides and upper surfaces of the wings carried 18" roundels, outlined yellow and centred by a RCN-style maple leaf. Radio call letters were shown on both sides of the fuselage and under the wings. Stencilled "ROYAL CANADIAN NAVY" and serial number remained on the rear fuselage sides, with a modified flash on the fin.

Canada

End of service

Seafires F.XV served with the first line units of the RCN until autumn 1948. Some Seafires were returned to Nos.803 and 883 Squadrons, but for instruction and display only. For training purposes the Seafires were used until end 1949. Reserve Divisions at Calgary, Hamilton and Toronto flew Seafires still in 1952/53.

Yet in summer 1949 six Seafires were overhauled by Fairey Aviation. In early 1950, c.15 to 18 Seafires were inhibited and stored in hangars Z/1 and Z/2 at Dartmouth. By July 1952 the last Seafires were retired from service and put into storage at Fairey Aviation. The Air Supply Depot at Dartmouth listed 18 Seafires on 30th July 1953.

Officially the last SOC dated from 29th April 1954. Some airframes (without engines) went to the Fire-Fighting Establishment on McNabs Island, being recorded there in March 1955.

Only two Seafires survived in Canada. One of them was transferred to the USA in 1994.

Individual Histories

For easier reading the general known terms "TOC" and "SOC" have been used, though the RCAF & RCN actually used the terms "TOS" & "SOS" (Taken on Strength and Struck off Strength). The term "CR 3" possibly meant "Civil Contractor maintenance (Category 3)".

L1090   Spitfire Mk.Ia (Merlin III); TOC/RAF 29.8.39; Shipped to USAAC Wright Field at Dayton, Ohio for testing 21.9.39; Arr Canada, TOC/RCAF No.1 AD 19.2.40; Comparison and test flying with XP-40 at RCAF Uplands (Ottawa), Ontario, 9.5.40 (S/L EA McNab); Tests at Toronto (date unknown); No.1 Training Air Command 30.5.40; RCAF Stn No.97 on 6.6.40; No.1 AD Ottawa 20.6.40; SOC/RCAF 25.6.40; Departed Ottawa in Canadian National Railway Boxcar No.36531 for England via Montreal 25.6.40; Arr. UK 1.8.40; Converted to GI *3201M*; No.3 SoTT Blackpool 14.4.41; No.14 SoTT Henlow 13.5.44; Cat.E 4.9.44, SOC

P8332   Spitfire Mk.IIb (Merlin XII); Presentation aircraft 'SOEBANG'; First flight 20.3.41; TOC/RAF 29.4.41; Converted to GI *6173M*; To No.82 MU Lichfield for

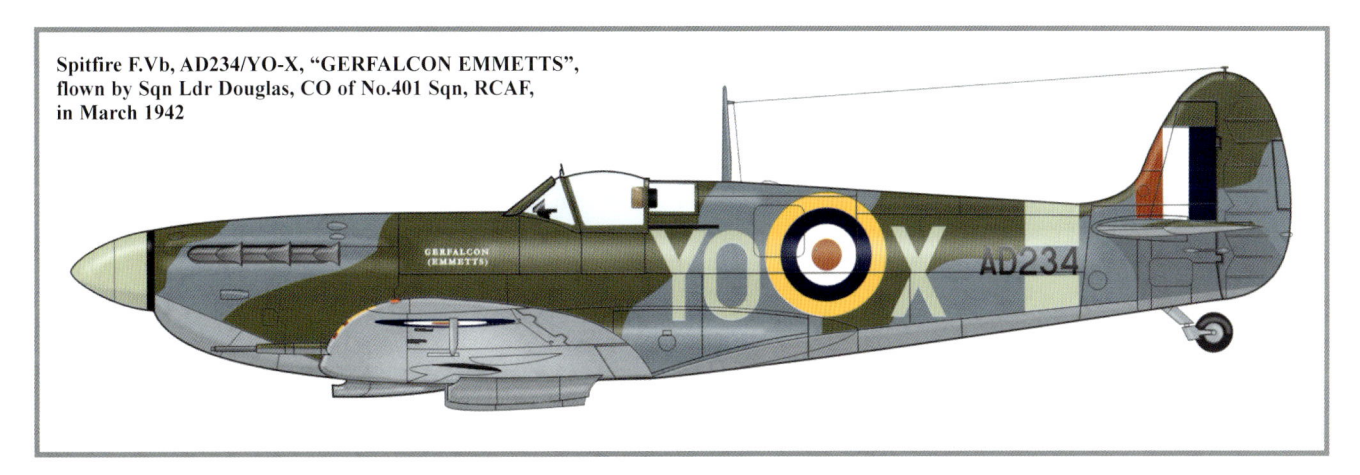

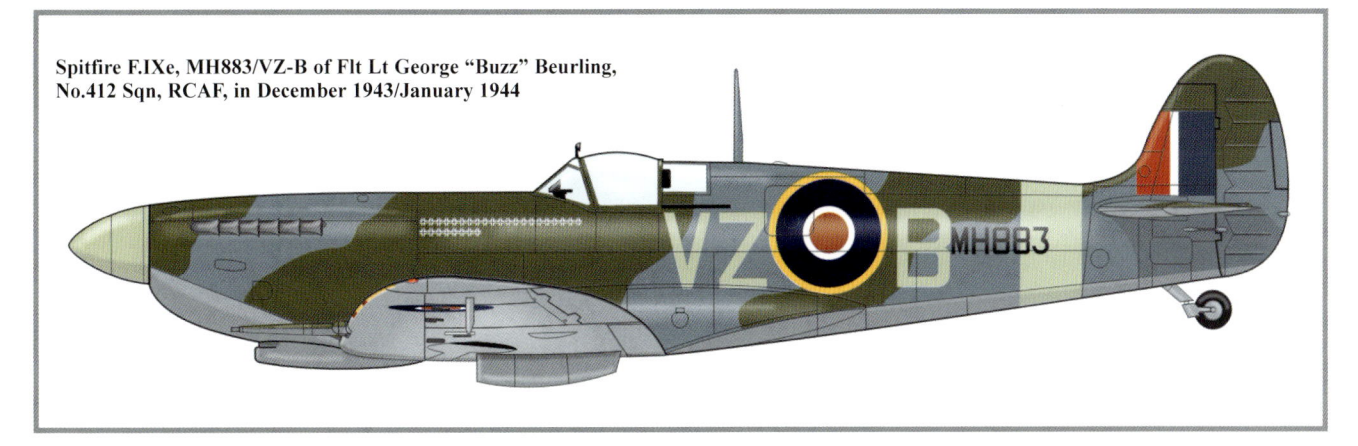

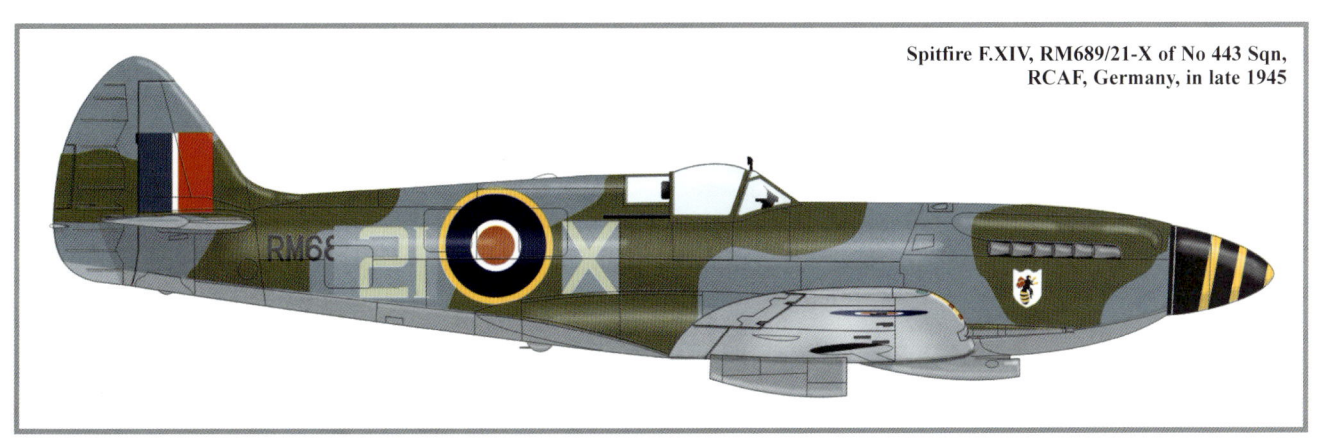

Spitfire F.Vb, AD234/YO-X, "GERFALCON EMMETTS", flown by Sqn Ldr Douglas, CO of No.401 Sqn, RCAF, in March 1942

Spitfire F.IXe, MH883/VZ-B of Flt Lt George "Buzz" Beurling, No.412 Sqn, RCAF, in December 1943/January 1944

Spitfire F.XIV, RM689/21-X of No 443 Sqn, RCAF, Germany, in late 1945 packing, then shipped from Liverpool in SS *Manchester Escort*, arr Montreal 13.4.42; TOC/RCAF No.1 Training Command at Mountain View, Ontario, 7.5.42; GI *A166* at RCAF Rockliffe (Ottawa), Ontario, 7.5.42; Exhibited in front of Toronto City Hall 4.11.43; No.2 Technical Training School at Camp Borden, Ontario, as *166B* from 20.11.47; Canadian National Exhibition at Toronto 8.57 and 9.57; Storage 1960; RCAF Stn Uplands (Ottawa), Ontario, 1962; AW/CN 6.12.64; No.6 RD Trenton, NE Toronto, Ontario, for overhaul from 1.66; Marked "Baron" & "SO-P" in 12.66; On loan to National Museum of Science & Technology, Ottawa 1983; National Aviation Museum Rockliffe, storage 1986; Marked "ZD-L" in 7.88; Canadian War Museum, Ottawa since 9.88 - **SURVIVOR**

R7143 Spitfire Mk.Ia/PR.G (Merlin 46); Presentation aircraft '*WALSALL I*'; TOC/RAF 20.2.41; First flight 2.2.41; No.6 MU, converted to PR.VII (G) 1.6.42; RAF Benson 29.10.42; No.47 MU, armament removed and shipped from Manchester in SS *Manchester Progress* to Canada, arr Montreal 10.2.43; TOC/RCAF No.3 Training Command 26.2.43; On loan from Air Ministry to Home War Establishment at Rockliffe (Ottawa), Ontario, for high altitude testing on behalf of the RAF, telephoto camera installed 7.43; No.13 Photo Survey Sqn (No.7 PR-Wing) at Rockliffe, undercarriage failed, Cat.C accident at Rockliffe 10.9.44; No.1 Air Command 15.1.45; No.9 Transport Group 15.7.46; Awaiting disposal 11.10.46; Air Search and Rescue duties 9.1.47; Transferred to RCN 2.9.47, as surplus to RC.92 (Ottawa) requirements; Flown from Rockliffe to RCNAS Dartmouth; Air Electrical School HMCS *Stadacona* for instructional purposes from 10.47 to 8.50; Fate unknown

X4492 Spitfire Mk.Ia/PR.F (later Merlin 45 & 47); First flight 14.7.40; RAE Farnborough 17.9.40, TOC/RAF 14.11.40; Converted by Heston Aircraft Ltd to PR.IV (D), camera installed; To Rolls-Royce Hucknall for conversion to Mk.Va 18.4.41; No.1 PRU Benson 29.4.41; Later brought up to type PR.F standard with Merlin 47; To No.47 MU Sealand for packing, then shipped from Manchester in SS *Manchester Progress*, arr Montreal (AD) 10.2.43; TOC RCAF No.3 Training Command 26.2.43, on loan from Air Ministry to Home War Establishment, Rockliffe (Ottawa), Ontario, for high altitude testing on behalf of the RAF; No.1 Air Command 15.1.45; No.13 Photo Survey Sqn, Rockliffe 9.7.45, initially to photograph full lunar eclipse (fitted underwing fuel tanks, 36-inch telephoto camera in rear fuselage, later also F-24 oblique camera, flown by Lt T Percival); No.9 Transport Group 15.7.46; Awaiting disposal 11.10.46; Retained for Search and Rescue with No.9 Transport Group 9.1.47; SOC; Transferred to RCN 2.9.47 as surplus to RC.92 (Ottawa) requirements; Fate unknown

X4555 Spitfire Mk.Ia/PR.G (later Merlin 45); Presentation aircraft '*MIMA IV*'; First flight 25.9.40; TOC/RAF 26.9.40; Heston Aircraft Ltd for conversion to PR.IV with Merlin 45 from 29.4.42; No.1 PRU Benson; Converted to PR.VII (G) 15.11.42; To No.47 MU Sealand for packing - Shipped in SS *Tom Couston*, desp to Canada 10.3.43, arr 4.4.43; RCAF No.3 Training Command on loan from Air Ministry to Home War Establishment, Rockliffe (Ottawa), Ontario, 7.4.43 for high altitude testing on behalf of the RAF, 36-inch telephoto camera installed; No.1 Air Command 15.1.45; No.9 Training Group 15.7.46 [possibly No.13 Photo Survey Sqn, Rockliffe]; Awaiting disposal 11.10.46; Retained for Search and Rescue with No.9 Training Group 9.1.47; SOC, transferred by/via X-5 ED to RCN at the Air Electrical School at HMCS *Stadacona* near Halifax, Nova Scotia, on indefinite loan, to train naval personnel on aviation electronics 4.2.47 (it had both wings removed and was lifted up by crane to the third floor of the school, some of the windows being removed in order for it be installed); Officially to Director of Naval Air Services charge 1.8.47; Paint work later entirely removed; No longer there by 8.50; Fate unknown

AR614 Spitfire LF.Vc; ex GI *5378M/6371M/7555M*; Shipped from UK to Air Museum of Calgary, Alberta, in 1964; To Donald Campbell, Kapuskasing, Ontario 1970 (Civil reg. *CF-DUY* 1986); Long term restoration not completed; Shipped to UK for restoration by Old Flying Machine Co, Duxford (reg. *G-BUWA* 19.3.93); Bought by Alpine Fighter Collection, Wanaka, NZ, restored at Audley End, UK, del. to USA 11.99, reg *N614VC* 10.2.00; now with Paul Alan, Seattle, Washington, USA - **SURVIVOR**

ER824 Spitfire LF.Vb/LR/trop; TOC/RAF 18.10.42; Presentation aircraft '*KABIA PROVINCE*'; Shipped to Takoradi 30.11.42; ER824 and two other Spitfires damaged in severe weather in transit to Middle East in SS *Empire Kingsley*, which put into nearest port and arrived St.John's for repair 24.12.42; Put ashore to No.6 Repair Depot RCAF Torbay and ER824 assembled with parts from the other two aircraft 12.2.43; Flown 16.3.43 still in desert camouflage with tropical filter; Shipped to Halifax, NS, then retd UK 6.43; RiW (Phillips & Powis) 2.7.43; Later with No.422 Sqn RAF

ER881 Spitfire F.Vb; TOC/RAF 27.10.42; Shipped to Takoradi ME 30.11.42, damaged in transit (as ER824); No.6 Repair Depot RCAF Torbay, reduced to components and used to rebuild ER824

ES117 Spitfire F.Vc; TOC/RAF 18.11.42; Shipped to Takoradi 30.11.42, but damaged in transit (as ER824); No.6 Repair Depot RCAF Torbay, reduced to components and used to rebuild ER824

JG480 Spitfire LF.VIIIc (Merlin 66); On CRD (Controller of Research & Development) charge at VA Worthy Down 12.12.43; Via No.52 MU shipped to Canada in SS *Indochinois*, arr Montreal 7.3.44; No.8 RD Winnipeg for assembly, test flight 21.3.44; RCAF 23.3.44; No.2 Training Command at Winter Establishment & Test Flt Gimli, Manitoba, 12.4.44; Reserve storage 5.7.44; Displayed in Winnipeg city centre for Victory Bond drive 8.44; No.2 Air Command 1.12.44; storage (serviceable) 25.9.45; North West Air Command 2.1.46; To GI as *A517* 12.7.46; Indefinite loan to RCN Training Establishment (Naval Secretarial & Supply School), HMCS *Naden*, Esquimalt, British Columbia, 12.7.46; Scrapped there around 1950 (RCN personnel cut it up into pieces, keeping some of the parts for themselves; parts to a Museum in British Columbia)

MK923 Spitfire LF.IXc; Arrived as **SURVIVOR** only, Windsor, Ontario, 16.9.72; To USA in 1976

ML196 Spitfire HF.IXe; Arrived as **SURVIVOR** only, ex SAAF Museum, (Serial No. "ML196" provisional only); Shipped to Canada, with Mark de Fries

NH188 Spitfire LF.IXc; Arrived as **SURVIVOR** only, ex *OO-ARC*, John N Paterson, Ontario 8.61; Civil reg. *CF-NUS*; To Canadian National Aeronautical Collection, Rockcliffe, Ontario marked "AU-H" 6.6.64; To National Aviation Museum, Rockcliffe, Ontario 9.82 and extant

PA908 Spitfire PR.XI; Arrived ex India as **SURVIVOR** only, Vancouver, BC, 8.2.85 (bought from IAF by Carl Enzenhofer, John Wilson and Jeet Mehal); To USA 1986

PM627 Spitfire PR.XIX; ex India; Arrived as **SURVIVOR** only, John Weir/Canadian Fighter Pilots Association, Downsview, Ontario dismantled in C-130 3.2.71 (static display as "YO-X" and "DB-X"); To Canadian National Exhibition, Toronto, Ontario 19721; To Ontario Science Centre, Toronto 11.73; To Canadian Warplane Heritage, Toronto 1980; To David C Tallichet/MARC, Chino, California 1983; Now in Sweden

PR375 Seafire F.XVc (Griffon VI); RNDA 2.7.45; No.803 Sqn RCN at Lee-on-Solent 2.46; With HMCS *Warrior* to Canada 23.3.46; Disembarked to Dartmouth 31.3.46; To RCAF charge (EAC) 1.6.46; No.803 Sqn, swung to stbd on take-off, struck runway light 3.2.47 (Lt W Rikeley RCN); Prop touched on take-off at Dartmouth 28.2.47 (S/L AR McBain RCN); No.883 Sqn 29.5.47 (CAC, No.10 Group, No.18 CAG 2.6.47); No.11 TSU (Canadian Car & Foundry Co) 25.6.47; RCN inventory 12.7.47; No.1 TAG

CANADA

Spitfire LF.IXc CF-NUS (ex NH188) with spurious No.421 (RCAF) Sqn code marking "AU-H" and incorrect brown/green camouflage being flown by John Paterson over Thunder Bay, Ontario. This aircraft had, in fact, flown with No.416 (RCAF) Sqn in 1944, being then coded "DN-S". [via John Campbell]

(OFTS) Dartmouth 26.7.47; Tail oleo collapsed & strained stbd undercarriage 11.8.48 (Lt AD Joy RCN); CCF for repair 1.12.48; Reserve storage 15.3.49 (and 1.7.49); Seafire Special Exhibition Flight of No.1 TAG Dartmouth 29.7.49; No.803 Sqn 21.9.49; Reserve storage 9.11.49; Fairey Aviation for final storage 31.1.50; SOC

PR410 Seafire F.XVc (Griffon VI); RNDA, del RDU Culham 14.8.45; No.803 Sqn RCN at Lee-on-Solent 2.46; With HMCS *Warrior* to Canada 23.3.46; Disembarked to Dartmouth 31.3.46; To RCAF charge (EAC) 1.6.46; No.803 Sqn; Canadian Car & Foundry Co 15.4.47; No.11 TSU (CCF), engine change 18.4.47; No.883 Sqn 29.5.47 (CAC, No.10 Group, No.18 CAG 2.6.47); RCN inventory 12.7.47; No.1 TAG (OFTS) Dartmouth 1.10.48; CR.3 on 4.1.49; Fairey Aviation for overhaul 21.5.49; Retd No.1 TAG Dartmouth in 1949; Engine began cutting at 1,000ft, emergency landing 22.7.49 (Lt RA Laidler RCN); HMCS *Star* and Mount Hope (Hamilton), Ontario 8.49; Calgary Technical Training School, HMCS *Tecumseh* (Calgary Flying Club hangar) 1953; SOC 29.4.54; Shown at an air show 1958; Later scrapped at Calgary

PR425 Seafire F.XVc (Griffon VI); RNDA 22.9.45, del RDU Culham 23.9.45; Arr Canada and to RCAF (EAC), stored reserve 7.11.46; RCN inventory 12.7.47; Reserve storage 10.11.47; No.1 TAG (OFTS) Dartmouth ('TG-C') 16.2.48; Throttle linkage detached, emergency landing, tipped on nose 2.3.48 (L/C EB Morris RCN); Reserve storage 15.6.48; No.883 Sqn 1.10.48; Reserve storage 1.12.48; Fairey Aviation for final storage 17.6.49; SOC
Note: Shown with 'TG-C' on the fuselage and 'VG-AA.' markings under the wings, possibly crash 2.3.48.

PR428 Seafire F.XVc (Griffon VI); RNDA, del RDU Culham 15.9.45; Arr Canada and to RCAF (EAC), stored reserve 7.11.46; No.803 Sqn HMCS *Warrior* 1947; RCN inventory 12.7.47; Reported SOC 12.7.47 (rts)

PR434 Seafire F.XVc (Griffon VI); RNDA 26.9.45, del Culham 27.9.45; No.803 Sqn RCN ('N') at Lee-on-Solent 2.46; With HMCS *Warrior* to Canada 23.3.46; Disembarked to Dartmouth 31.3.46; To RCAF charge (EAC) 1.6.46; No.803 Sqn; Free issue RCN 15.7.46; No.803 Sqn 7.11.46; No.883 Sqn 29.5.47 (CAC, No.10 Group, No.18 CAG 2.6.47); RCN inventory 12.7.47; No.11 TSU

Seafire F.XVc PR410 in 1949 at naval reserve shore base HMCS Star, *Mount Hope, Hamilton, Ontario. It was later scrapped at Calgary, Alberta.*
[Jack McNulty]

Seafire F.XV PR425 TG-C of No.1 TAG (OFTS), Dartmouth, tipped on its nose on 14th June 1948. [R. Reid; National Archives of Canada PA-136498]

Seafire F.XVc PR451 became a gate guardian at HMCS Tecumseh *Reserve Station, Calgary, Alberta in 1961. Initially painted with an Ensign as shown here in June 1969, by 1980 it was marked for a period as "PR425/TG-B". It is extant at the Naval Museum of Alberta.*

(Canadian Car & Foundry Co), for engine change 8.8.47; No.883 Sqn ('VG-AAJ') 16.10.47; Reserve storage at Dartmouth 1.2.48; SOC 14.2.49; To Reserve Station Dartmouth (No.6 RD), storage

PR451 Seafire F.XVc (Griffon VI); RNDA 4.10.45, del RDU Culham 5.10.45; No.803 Sqn RCN ('P') at Lee-on-Solent 2.46; Sqn embarking for Canada, struck rounddown & damaged prop HMCS *Warrior* 23.3.46 (S/L HC Rounds RCN); Disembarked to Dartmouth 31.3.46; To RCAF charge (EAC) 1.6.46; 803 Sqn; Accident at HMCS *Warrior* 2.8.46 (Lt HC Rounds); Ground looped landing Dartmouth 14.11.46 (Lt JJ Harvie RCN); Landed with undercarriage retracted Dartmouth 20.11.46 (Lt GH Marlow RCN); No.11 TSU (Canadian Car & Foundry Co) 30.5.47; Engine change 2.6.47; No.883 Sqn ('VG-AAN') 20.6.47 (CAC, No.10 Group, No.18 CAG 23.6.47); RCN inventory 12.7.47; Floated into barrier, Cat.3 on 15.11.47 (Lt RV Bays RCN); Reserve storage 18.11.47; No.1 TAG (OFTS) Dartmouth ('TG-B') summer 1948; CR.3 on 4.1.49; Fairey Aviation 21.5.49; Dartmouth 28.7.49; To the Southern Alberta Institute of Technology, 1953/54; Gate guard, marked as "PR425/TG-B" at HMCS *Tecumseh* Reserve Station, Calgary from 1961; Repainted at some time with the "Red Ensign" fin flag; To Aero Space Museum, Calgary in 1983, restoration until 3.85, marked "VG-AA-N"; To display at CAFB Tecumseh, Calgary 1988 - **SURVIVOR**

PR458 Seafire F.XVc (Griffon VI); RNDA 8.10.45; No.803 Sqn RCN at Lee-on-Solent 2.46; With HMCS *Warrior* to Canada 23.3.46; Disembarked to Dartmouth 31.3.46; To RCAF charge (EAC) 1.6.46; No.803 Sqn, low flying, bird strike near Dartmouth 7.10.46 (Lt JC Sloan RCN); No.11 TSU (Canadian Car & Foundry Co) 15.4.47, Engine change 18.4.47; No.883 Sqn 21.5.47 (CAC, No.10 Group, No.18 CAG); RCN inventory 12.7.47; Reserve storage 1.10.48; Canadian Car & Foundry Co 1.1.49; Reserve storage 14.1.49; Seafire Special Exhibition Flight of No.1 TAG Dartmouth 29.7.49; No.803 Sqn 21.9.49; Reserve storage 9.11.49; Fairey Aviation for storage 14.1.50; HMCS *Tecumseh*, Calgary for exhibition 1961; Fate unknown

PR460 Seafire F.XVc (Griffon VI); RNDA 20.10.45; No.803 Sqn RCN at Lee-on-Solent 2.46; With HMCS *Warrior* to Canada 23.3.46; Disembarked to Dartmouth 31.3.46; To RCAF charge (EAC) 1.6.46; No.803 Sqn; Free issue to RCN 15.7.46; No.803 Sqn, caught No.9 wire, crashed into trucks abaft island HMCS *Warrior* 16.7.46 (Lt JW Logan RCN); Repair; Retd No.803 Sqn 7.11.46; No.11 AID (Canadian Car & Foundry Co) 15.1.47; RCN inventory 12.7.47; Reserve storage 22.12.47; No.1 TAG (OFTS) Dartmouth 24.12.47; Reserve storage 1.10.48; No.883 Sqn ('VG-AAK') 1948/49; Fairey Aviation for final storage 4.6.49; SOC

PR461 Seafire F.XVc (Griffon VI); RNDA 5.10.45; No.803 Sqn RCN ('Z') at Lee-on-Solent 2.46; With HMCS *Warrior* to Canada 23.3.46; Disembarked to Dartmouth 31.3.46; To RCAF charge (EAC) 1.6.46; No.803 Sqn; Free issue RCN 15.7.46; Retd Eastern Air Command (No.803 Sqn) 13.3.47; Canadian Car & Foundry Co 3.5.47; No.11 TSU (CCF) for inspection 5.5.47; No.883 Sqn ('VG-AAC') 21.5.47 (CAC, No.10 Group, No.18 CAG); Engine failure, force-landed wheels up 18.6.47 (Lt BW Mead RCN); CCF for repair 23.6.47; RCN inventory 12.7.47; No.1 TAG (OFTS) Dartmouth 1948; No.883 Sqn ('VG-AAP') 1.11.48; CCF 15.11.48; Reserve storage 3.2.49 (and 1.7.49); Seafire Special Exhibition Flight of No.1 TAG Dartmouth 26.7.49; Collided with PR502 on 24.8.49, during final rehearsal before an air show at Malton Airport (Lt AC Elton killed); Cat.ZZ 24.8.49; SOC 18.10.49

PR470 Seafire F.XVc (Griffon VI); RNDA 11.10.45; No.803 Sqn RCN ('F') at Lee-on-Solent 2.46; With HMCS *Warrior* to Canada 23.3.46; Disembarked to Dartmouth 31.3.46; To RCAF charge (EAC) 1.6.46; No.803 Sqn, undercarriage collapsed on landing Dartmouth 3.2.47 (Lt C Watson); Canadian Car & Foundry Co 30.5.47; No.11 TSU (CCF), Engine change 2.6.47; No.883 Sqn 10.6.47 (CAC, No.10 Group, No.18 CAG); Canadian Car & Foundry Co 11.7.47; RCN inventory and to No.803 Sqn 12.7.47; Probably No.883 Sqn, floated into barrier 11.11.47 (Lt DJ Sheppard RCN); Reserve storage 15.11.47; No.1 TAG (OFTS) Dartmouth 1.12.48; Fairey Aviation for overhaul 17.6.49; Reserve storage 14.12.49; Fairey Aviation for final storage 14.1.50; SOC 15.1.50

PR471 Seafire F.XVc (Griffon VI); RNDA 20.10.45; No.803 Sqn RCN at Lee-on-Solent 2.46; With HMCS *Warrior* to Canada 23.3.46; Disembarked to Dartmouth 31.3.46; To RCAF charge (EAC) 1.6.46; No.803 Sqn, landed with undercarriage retracted 8.7.46 (Lt HP Leidl RCN); No.11 TSU (Canadian Car & Foundry Co) 2.6.47; No.883 Sqn 10.6.47 (CAC, No.10 Group, No.18 CAG); Undercarriage collapsed landing 21.6.47 (Lt DJ Sheppard RCN); RCN

Seafire F.XV PR458 TG served with the Seafire Special Exhibition Flight of No.1 TAG (OFTS), Dartmouth in 1949. [MAP]

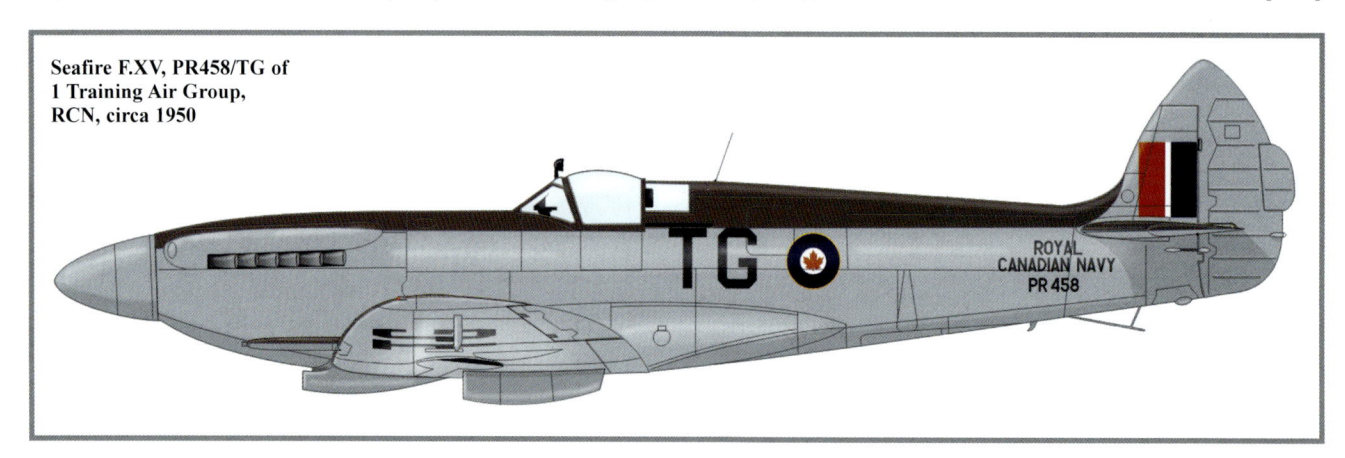

Seafire F.XV, PR458/TG of 1 Training Air Group, RCN, circa 1950

inventory 12.7.47; No.1 TAG (OFTS) Dartmouth, taxied into snow bank, nosed up 19.2.48 (Lt NJ Geary RCN); Engine failure, force-landed wheels-up on hillside 26.11.48 (Lt EJGS Campbell RCN); SOC 12.7.49

PR479 Seafire F.XVc (Griffon VI); RNDA 22.11.45; No.803 Sqn RN ('X') Nutts Corner 11.45; Brake failure, ran onto grass & nosed up Nutts Corner 14.2.46 (S/L HC Rounds RCNR); With HMCS *Warrior* to Canada 23.3.46; Disembarked to Dartmouth 31.3.46; To RCAF charge (EAC) 1.6.46; No.803 Sqn RCN ('L'); Free issue RCN 15.7.46; No.803 Sqn, floated over wires, prop tipped barrier HMCS *Warrior*, unserviceable 15.7.46 (Lt GH Marlow RCN); Tailwheel failed to lower, swerved into ditch, Dartmouth 11.10.46 (Lt JP Whitby RCN); Repair; Retd No.803 Sqn 7.11.46; No.11 AID (Canadian Car & Foundry Co) 11.4.47; No.803 Sqn 11.4.47 (CAC, No.10 Group); Starboard oleo collapsed landing 29.4.47 (Lt JC Sloan RCN); No.883 Sqn ('VG-AAB') 29.5.47 (No.18 CAG 2.6.47); RCN inventory 12.7.47; Canadian Joint Air Training Centre 8.48; over Camp Shilo 9.48; No.883 Sqn 4.11.48; Reserve storage 1.12.48; Fairey Aviation for final storage 4.6.49; SOC

PR494 Seafire F.XVc (Griffon VI); RNDA 30.11.45; No.803 Sqn RCN ('N') at Lee-on-Solent 2.46; With HMCS *Warrior* to Canada 23.3.46; Disembarked to Dartmouth 31.3.46; To RCAF charge (EAC), stored reserve 1.6.46; Allotted to North West Air Command for Winter Experimental Establishment Namao near Edmonton for winterisation trials 4.9.46, together with PR499; Undercarriage damaged during take-off and landing from rough air strips (date unknown); Arrester hook release troublesome during trials; SOC (RCN), returned to UK 16.4.47

PR496 Seafire F.XVc (Griffon VI); RNDA 30.11.45; No.803 Sqn RCN at Lee-on-Solent 2.46; With HMCS *Warrior* to Canada 23.3.46; Disembarked to Dartmouth 31.3.46; To RCAF charge (EAC), stored reserve 1.6.46; No.803 Sqn 5.12.46; CAC, No.10 Group 11.4.47; No.11 AID (Canadian Car & Foundry Co) 11.4.47; No.803 Sqn, hit Seafire SW809, force-landed near Bathurst (New Brunswick) 14.4.47; No.11 TSU (CCF) for repair 11.6.47; RCN inventory 12.7.47; No.1 TAG (OFTS) Dartmouth 13.3.48; Take-off for air-to-air firing, engine failed 13.5.48 (Lt NJ Geary RCN); Reserve storage 19.5.48; CR.3 on 4.1.49; Fairey Aviation for Reserve storage 17.6.49; Fate unknown

PR498 Seafire F.XVc (Griffon VI); RNDA 4.12.45; No.803 Sqn RCN at Lee-on-Solent 2.46; With HMCS *Warrior* to Canada 23.3.46; Disembarked to Dartmouth 31.3.46; To RCAF charge (EAC), stored reserve 1.6.46; RCN inventory 12.7.47; Reserve storage 10.4.48; Fairey, overhaul 17.6.49; Seafire Special Exhibition Flight of No.1 TAG Dartmouth 20.8.49; No.803 Sqn 21.9.49;

Reserve storage 9.11.49; Fairey Aviation for final storage 1.2.50; SOC
PR499 Seafire F.XVc (Griffon VI); RNDA 28.11.45; With HMCS *Warrior* to Canada 23.3.46; Disembarked to Dartmouth 31.3.46; To RCAF charge (EAC), stored reserve 1.6.46; North West Air Command, Winter Experimental Establishment Namao near Edmonton for winterisation trials from 11.9.46, together with PR494; Winter-tests from 12.46 to 1.47; Storage 2.47; SOC (RCN), returned to UK 16.4.47
PR500 Seafire F.XVc (Griffon VI); RNDA (AW/CN) 13.11.45; No.803 Sqn RCN ('R') at Lee-on-Solent 2.46; With HMCS *Warrior* to Canada 23.3.46; Disembarked to Dartmouth 31.3.46; To RCAF charge (EAC) 1.6.46; Free issue RCN 15.7.46; 803 Sqn, caught No.10 wire, stalled on port oleo leg & main plane HMCS *Warrior*, unserviceable 15.7.46 (Lt M Douglas RCN); Repair; Retd No.803 Sqn 7.11.46; No.883 Sqn 29.5.47 (CAC, No.10 Group, No.18 CAG 2.6.47); No.11 TSU (Canadian Car & Foundry Co) 25.6.47; RCN inventory 12.7.47; No.1 TAG (OFTS) Dartmouth ('TG-D') 12.7.47; Swung on take-off, struck light, damaged prop 27.10.47 (Lt JR Sinclair RCN); Mid-air collision with Seafire SW809 on 6.12.48; SOC 12.7.49
PR501 Seafire F.XVc (Griffon VI); RNDA 14.1.46; No.803 Sqn RCN at Lee-on-Solent 2.46; With HMCS *Warrior* to Canada 23.3.46; Disembarked to Dartmouth 31.3.46; To RCAF charge (EAC), stored reserve 1.6.46; CAC, No.10

Seafire F.XV PR479 VG-AAB of No.883 Sqn in 1947. [MAP]

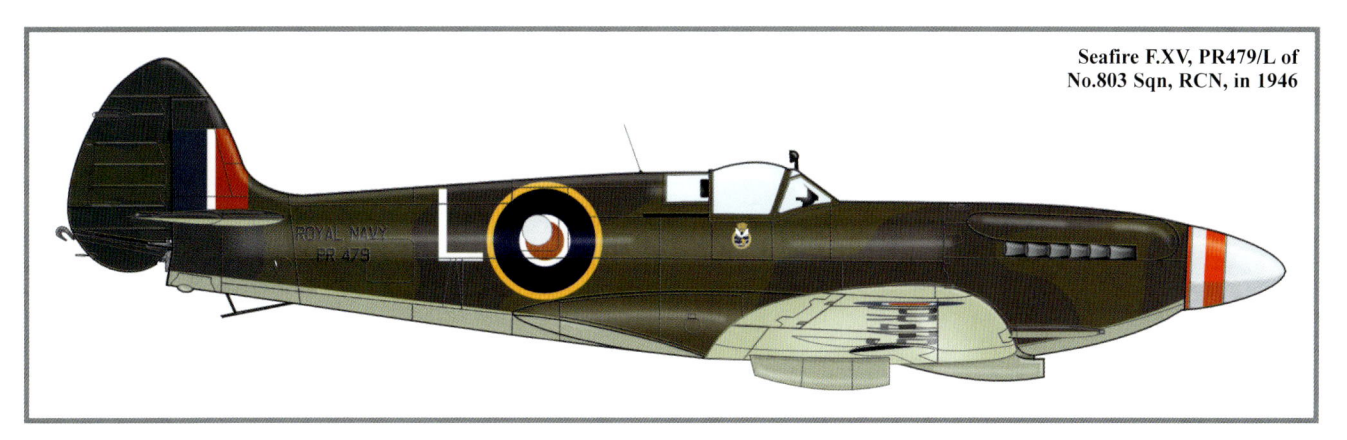

Seafire F.XV, PR479/L of No.803 Sqn, RCN, in 1946

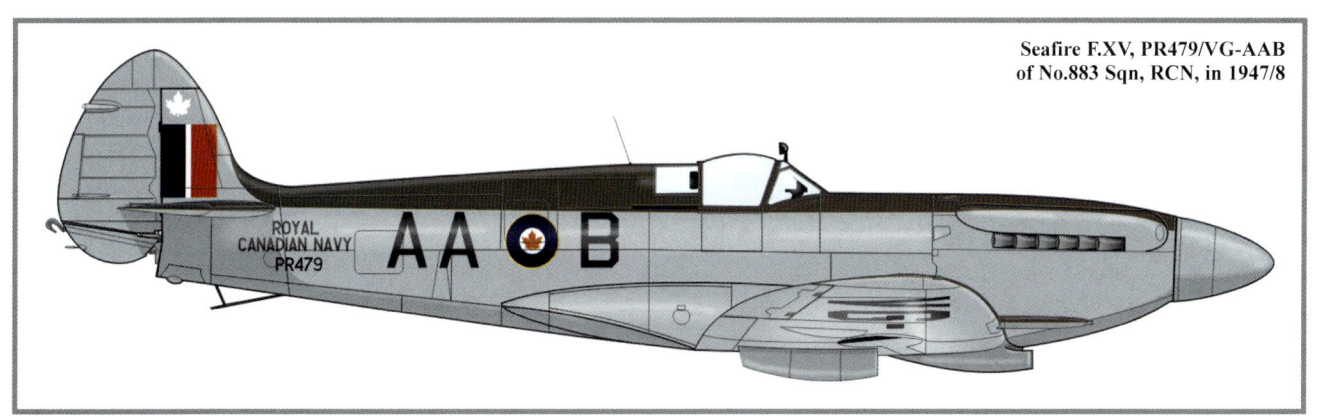

Seafire F.XV, PR479/VG-AAB of No.883 Sqn, RCN, in 1947/8

A parachute bale-out net placed alongside Seafire F.XV PR506 at Dartmouth on 11th April 1950.
[Blakley, Robert W, 1924-1994; National Archives of Canada PA-136514]

Group 7.7.47; RCN inventory 12.7.47; No.1 TAG (OFTS) Dartmouth 12.7.47; Stalled, dropped port wing 16.10.47 (Lt AF Lapres RCN); Spun to stbd, going round again 20 or 23.12.47 (Lt AF Lapres RCN); Workshop reserve for Air Mechanical Training Establishment at HMCS *Stadacona* (AMTE) 11.2.48; Reserve storage 10.4.48; Dartmouth, retired RCN 14.9.48; Ground instructional 23.10.48, to School of Naval Aircraft Maintenance (SNAM) at Dartmouth 1.11.48; Brought back on charge: To Fairey Aviation for overhaul 17.6.49; Seafire Special Exhibition Flight of No.1 TAG Dartmouth 20.8.49; No.803 Sqn 21.9.49; Reserve storage 7.11.49; Fairey Aviation for final storage 1.2.50; SOC

PR502 Seafire F.XVc (Griffon VI); RNDA 18.1.46; No.803 Sqn RCN at Lee-on-Solent 2.46; With HMCS *Warrior* to Canada 23.3.46; Disembarked to Dartmouth 31.3.46; To RCAF charge (EAC) 1.6.46; No.803 Sqn; Storage reserve 11.9.46; CAC, No.10 Group 7.7.47; RCN inventory 12.7.47; Seafire Special Exhibition Flight of No.1 TAG Dartmouth 13.8.49; Collided with PR461 during final rehearsal before an air show at Malton Airport, Cat.ZZ 24.8.49 (L/C Cliff G Watson RCN killed); SOC 18.10.49

PR503 Seafire F.XVc (Griffon VI); RNDA 7.12.45; No.803 Sqn RCN ('K') at Lee-on-Solent 2.46; With HMCS *Warrior* to Canada 23.3.46; Disembarked to Dartmouth 31.3.46; To RCAF charge (EAC) 1.6.46; No.803 Sqn; Reserve storage 11.9.46; No.11 TSU (Canadian Car & Foundry Co) 2.6.47; CAC, No.10 Group 23.6.47; RCN inventory 12.7.47; Reserve storage 30.8.47; No.883 Sqn ('VG-AAA') 1.48; Canadian Joint Air Training Centre at Rivers, Manitoba, 8.48; No.1 TAG (OFTS) Dartmouth, rough running, precautionary landing 30.12.48 (S/L RC Maclean RCN); CR.3 on 14.2.49; Reserve storage 1.7.49; Seafire Special Exhibition Flight of No.1 TAG Dartmouth 13.8.49; Hangar Z/2 Dartmouth 24.8.49; SOC 5.4.50; Salvaged by Peter Myers, Bedford, Nova Scotia 1958 for restoration; To the Experimental Aircraft Association, Dartmouth (Nova Scotia Chapter) 1964 (purchased from Crown Assets 1966); Re-sale to Dennis J Bradley for Canadian Warplane Heritage, Buttonville, Ontario 1970 (at Hamilton, Ontario from 1973, long term restoration); (reserved Civil reg. *C-GCWK* 1985); To Courtesy Aircraft, Rockford, Illinois 1992; Wallace Fisk, Blaine, Minnesota .93; regd *N535R* 12.97; *N503PR* 5.7.00 - **SURVIVOR**

PR504 Seafire F.XVc (Griffon VI); RNDA 7.1.46; No.803 Sqn RCN ('B') at Lee-on-Solent 2.46; With HMCS *Warrior* to Canada 23.3.46; Disembarked to Dartmouth 31.3.46; No.803 Sqn, landed undercarriage retracted Dartmouth 31.5.46 (Lt N J Geary RCN); To RCAF charge (EAC) 1.6.46; Repair; Free issue RCN 15.7.46; No.803 Sqn 7.11.46; Premature undercarriage retraction HMCS *Warrior* 10.4.47 (Lt J C Sloan RCN); No.11 AID (Canadian Car & Foundry Co) 11.4.47; CAC, No.10 Group 11.4.47; No.803 Sqn 15.4.47; Collision 16.4.47 (Lt C Watson); Reserve storage 17.5.47; WSR CAC, No.10 Group 19.5.47; RCN inventory 12.7.47; CCF 22.9.47; No.883 Sqn ('VG-AAD') 17.4.48; Reserve storage 1.12.48; No.1 TAG(OFTS) Dartmouth 5.1.49; Reserve storage 26.1.49; Fairey Aviation for overhaul 17.6.49; Seafire Special Exhibition Flight of No.1 TAG Dartmouth 11.8.49; No.883 Sqn ('VG-AAL') 21.9.49; Reserve storage 9.11.49; Fairey Aviation for final storage 1.2.50; SOC

PR505 Seafire F.XVc (Griffon VI); RNDA 22.1.46; del RDU Culham 28.1.46; With HMCS *Warrior* to Canada 23.3.46; Disembarked to Dartmouth 31.3.46; To RCAF charge

CANADA

(EAC), stored reserve 1.6.46; No.1 TAG (OFTS), for No.883 Sqn ('VG-AAB') 29.5.47; CAC, No.10 Group 7.7.47; RCN inventory 12.7.47 (No.883 Sqn of No.18 CAG); No.11 TSU (Canadian Car & Foundry Co) 8.8.47; No.1 TAG (OFTS) Dartmouth 30.8.47 (TAF); Crashed Dartmouth, Cat.A 22.10.47; WR.CAC 22.10.47; Re-Cat.E1 on 18.11.47; SOC 24.9.48 (rtp)

PR506 Seafire F.XVc (Griffon VI); RNDA 9.1.46; No.803 Sqn RCN at Lee-on-Solent 2.46; With HMCS *Warrior* to Canada 23.3.46; Disembarked to Dartmouth 31.3.46; To RCAF charge (EAC), stored reserve 1.6.46; RCN inventory 12.7.47; Possibly No.883 Sqn 1948? (photographed with 'VG-AA.' markings under wings); Reserve storage 18.6.48; Fairey Aviation for overhaul 17.6.49; Reserve storage 8.12.49; Fairey Aviation for storage 14.1.50; No.1 TAG Dartmouth 21.3.50 (flown by Air Cdre DHP Ryan RCN until 19.7.50); Retained No.1 TAG for ground instructions bale-out procedure; Fairey Aviation for final storage 17.11.50; SOC 27.11.50

SL721 Spitfire LF XVI; Arrived as **SURVIVOR** only (ex Flying Museum Santa Monica; W & C Woods, USA; Civil reg. *N721WK*, cancelled 1.3.02); Acquired by Michael Potter end 2000, to be based at Ottawa, Ontario

SR459 Seafire F.XVc (Griffon VI); RNDA 3.2.45; USNAS Flight Test Centre at Patuxent River 22.6.45; Engine failure, force-landed Fairmont 1.5.46 (Lt BL Hayter RCN); Cat.E1 and to RCAF 10.6.46 (rts); Stored at No.6 RD as workshop reserve 16.7.46 (salvage of airframe, engine removed); No.11 AID (Canadian Car & Foundry Co) for spares 16.10.46; RCN inventory 12.7.47; SOC 11.8.47

SR464 Seafire F.XVc (Griffon VI); RNDA 10.2.45; No.33 MU 21.2.45; With HMCS *Warrior* to Canada 23.3.46; Disembarked to Dartmouth 31.3.46; To RCAF charge (EAC) No.803 Sqn 1.6.46; No.883 Sqn ('VG-AAQ') 29.5.47 (CAC, No.10 Group, No.18 CAG 2.6.47); RCN inventory 12.7.47; Canadian Car & Foundry Co 13.7.47; No.1 TAG (OFTS) Dartmouth 3.8.47; Reserve storage 16.2.48; No.1 TAG (OFTS) Dartmouth 1.12.48; CR.3 (or Storage cat.3) from 26.1.49; Fairey Aviation for overhaul 21.5.49; Flown to Mount Hope (Hamilton), Ontario, via HMCS *Star* 1949; Hamilton Reserve Station, Ontario 1950-1954

SR530 Seafire F.XVc (Griffon VI); RNDA 30.4.45; With HMCS *Warrior* to Canada 23.3.46; Disembarked to Dartmouth 31.3.46; To RCAF charge (EAC) 1.6.46; No.803 Sqn, coolant leak starboard side of engine, Dartmouth 3.4.47 (L/C WD Munro RCN); No.883 Sqn ('VG-AAK') 29.5.47 (CAC, No.10 Group, No.18 CAG 2.6.47); RCN inventory 12.7.47; Fatal crash near Traverse City, Michigan 13.10.48 (Lt Murphy killed); SOC 4.1.49

SR545 Seafire F.XVc (Griffon VI); RNDA 23.11.45; With HMCS *Warrior* to Canada 23.3.46; Disembarked to Dartmouth 31.3.46; To RCAF charge (EAC) 1.6.46; Free issue RCN 15.7.46; No.803 Sqn 7.11.46; Out of fuel, force-landed Dartmouth, Cat.A 15.12.46 (S/L NC Eversfield); No.11 AID (Canadian Car & Foundry Co) 12.2.47; Re-Cat.E1 and SOC 22.4.47 (rts)

SW793 Seafire F.XVc (Griffon VI); RNDA 30.6.45; No.803 Sqn RN ('R') Nutts Corner 9.45; With HMCS *Warrior* to Canada 23.3.46; Disembarked to Dartmouth 31.3.46; To RCAF charge (EAC), stored reserve 1.6.46; No.883 Sqn ('VG-AAL') 29.5.47 (CAC, No.10 Group 7.7.47); RCN inventory 12.7.47; Canadian Car & Foundry Co 26.7.47; No.1 TAG (OFTS) Dartmouth 18.10.47; Reserve storage 13.3.48; Fairey Aviation for overhaul 17.6.49; Reserve storage 27.10.49; Fairey Aviation for final storage 18.1.50; SOC

SW802 Seafire F.XVc (Griffon VI); RNDA 4.7.45; With HMCS *Warrior* to Canada 23.3.46; Disembarked to Dartmouth 31.3.46; To RCAF charge (EAC), stored reserve 1.6.46; No.883 Sqn 29.5.47 (CAC, No.10 Group 7.7.47); RCN inventory 12.7.47; Reserve storage 30.8.47; No.1 TAG (OFTS) Dartmouth 1948; CR.3 on 4.1.49; No.743 FRU of No.1 TAG Dartmouth 18.5.49; Seafire Special Exhibition Flight of No.1 TAG Dartmouth 13.8.49 (flown by Pat Whitby); Exhibition flight, engine failure during inverted flight, power regained 15.8.49 (Lt AT Bice RCN); No.883 Sqn 21.9.49; No.743 FRU of No.1 TAG 27.10.49; Stalled on approach, heavy landing, stbd undercarriage collapsed 25.2.50 (Air Cdre DHP Ryan RCN); Fairey Aviation storage 13.3.50; No.743 FRU of No.1 TAG 12.10.50; Fairey Aviation for final storage 8.5.51; SOC 9.5.51 (121.45 f/hrs: still at Fairey 7.52)

SW809 Seafire F.XVc (Griffon VI); RNDA 14.7.45; No.803 Sqn RCN at Lee-on-Solent 2.46; With HMCS *Warrior* to Canada 23.3.46; Disembarked to Dartmouth 31.3.46; To RCAF charge (EAC) 1.6.46; No.803 Sqn, caught late wire, broke prop on No.1 barrier HMCS *Warrior* 10.7.46 (S/L HP Leidl); Free issue to RCN 15.7.46; No.803 Sqn 7.11.46; CAC, No.10 Group 11.4.47; No.11 AID (Canadian Car & Foundry Co) 11.4.47; No.803 Sqn, hit by PR496, force-landed 14.4.47 (S/L NC Eversfield); No.11 TSU (CCF) for repair 11.6.47; RCN inventory 12.7.47; Reserve storage 27.4.48; No.1 TAG (OFTS) Dartmouth 15.6.48; Mid-air collision with PR500, force-landed on airfield 6.12.48 (Lt EJGS Campbell RCN); Reserve storage 4.5.49; Fairey Aviation for final storage 17.6.49; SOC

SW815 Seafire F.XVc (Griffon VI); RNDA 13.7.45; No.803 Sqn RCN at Lee-on-Solent 2.46; With HMCS *Warrior* to Canada 23.3.46; Disembarked to Dartmouth 31.3.46; To RCAF charge (EAC) 1.6.46; Free issue RCN 15.7.46; No.803 Sqn 7.11.46; No.11 TSU (Canadian Car & Foundry Co) 5.5.47; No.883 Sqn 29.5.47 (CAC, No.10 Group, No.18 CAG); RCN inventory 12.7.47; No.883 Sqn, caught No.10 wire, hit barrier HMCS *Warrior* 19.11.47 (Lt DJ Sheppard RCN); SOC 12.7.49

SW860 Seafire F.XVc (Griffon VI); RNDA 28.7.45; No.803 Sqn RCN at Lee-on-Solent 2.46; With HMCS *Warrior* to Canada 23.3.46; Disembarked to Dartmouth 31.3.46; To RCAF charge (EAC) 1.6.46; Free issue RCN 15.7.46; No.803 Sqn, caught No.5 wire, hook fractured, hit No.1 barrier HMCS *Warrior* 22.7.46 (Lt JW Logan RCN); Repair; No.803 Sqn 7.11.46; No.883 Sqn 29.5.47 (CAC, No.10 Group, No.18 CAG 2.6.47); RCN inventory 12.7.47; Canadian Car & Foundry Co for engine change 11.10.47; No.1 TAG (OFTS) Dartmouth 13.1.48; Premature explosion in stbd Hispano canon 13.5.48 (Lt TEJ Boyle RCN); Reserve storage 19.5.48; No.883 Sqn ('VG-AAH') 1.10.48; No.1 TAG (OFTS) Dartmouth 1.12.48; Reserve storage 28.1.49; Fairey Aviation for final storage 17.6.49; SOC

SW869 Seafire F.XVc (Griffon VI); RNDA 2.8.45; With HMCS *Warrior* to Canada 23.3.46; Disembarked to Dartmouth 31.3.46; To RCAF charge (EAC), stored reserve 1.6.46; No.883 Sqn ('VG-AAH') 29.5.47 (CAC, No.10 Group 7.7.47); RCN inventory 12.7.47; Reserve storage 3.9.47; CR.3 on 4.1.49; Reserve storage 1.7.49; Seafire Special Exhibition Flight of No.1 TAG Dartmouth 13.8.49; No.803 Sqn 21.9.49; Reserve storage 26.10.49; Fairey Aviation for final storage 31.1.50; SOC

SW870 Seafire F.XVc (Griffon VI); RNDA 1.8.45; With HMCS *Warrior* to Canada 23.3.46; Disembarked to Dartmouth 31.3.46; To RCAF charge (EAC), stored reserve 25.5.46; No.11 AID (Canadian Car & Foundry Co) 2.7.46; No.803 Sqn, accident Dartmouth 2.8.46 (Lt JW Logan); No.883 Sqn 21.5.47 (CAC, No.10 Group); RCN inventory 12.7.47; No.883 Sqn, stalled, stbd wing struck runway 6.11.47 (Lt DJ Sheppard RCN); Reserve storage 17.11.47; No.1 TAG (OFTS) Dartmouth 16.4.48; Dartmouth, vapour from coolant leak, precautionary landing 15.12.48 (Lt HD Joy RCN); Reserve storage 30.1.49; Fairey Aviation 7.4.49; Overhaul and reserve storage 27.10.49; Fairey Aviation for final storage 18.1.50; SOC (163.50 f/hrs)

SW909 Seafire F.XVc (Griffon VI); RNDA 31.8.45; No.883 Sqn RN Nutts Corner 12.45; With HMCS *Warrior* to Canada

23.3.46; Disembarked to Dartmouth 31.3.46; To RCAF charge (EAC) 1.6.46; No.803 Sqn; Canadian Car & Foundry Co 17.11.46; No.11 AID (CCF) 23.1.47; RCN inventory, No.883 Sqn 12.7.47; Prop hit runway on landing Presque Isle, Maine 8.8.47 (Lt NJ Geary RCN); No.1 TAG (OFTS) Dartmouth 29.12.47; Ground looped on landing 5.2.48 (Lt KL Gibbs RN); Reserve storage 24.2.48; Workshop Reserve, panel detached, radiator damaged, coolant leak 4.5.48 (L/C EB Morris); No.1 TAG (OFTS) Dartmouth 1.10.48; Reserve storage 26.1.49; Fairey Aviation for overhaul 17.6.49; Seafire Special Exhibition Flight of No.1 TAG Dartmouth 20.8.49; No.883 Sqn 21.9.49; Reserve storage 26.10.49; Fairey Aviation for final storage; SOC 31.1.50 (166.20 f/hrs)

TD314   Spitfire HF.IXe; Cockpit section only, arrived from South Africa as **SURVIVOR** only 11.4.79; To Matt Sattler, Carp, Ontario later Vancouver, BC (to Hull Aero, Ludham, England for restoration 3.95); Extant

TE214   Spitfire LF.XVIe; Arrived on loan to RCAF as **SURVIVOR** only 9.60; RCAF Mountain View, Ontario storage 1960; To RCAF Trenton, Ontario 10.1.63; To Canadian War Museum, Ottawa 1966 marked "DN-T"; National Air Museum, Rockcliffe; To Western Canada Aviation Museum, Winnipeg on loan 12.88; To Canadian Warplane Heritage at Hamilton, Ontario in 4.97

TE294   Spitfire IX; Arrived as **SURVIVOR** (in parts) only; To the Comox Air Museum, British Columbia 28.5.99; Restoration with Merlin 63

TE308   Spitfire T.IX; Arrived ex UK as **SURVIVOR** only, Sold to Don Plumb, Windsor, Ontario 16.7.70 and to Canada, arr Toronto by ship 9.10.70; To Don Plumb, Windsor, Ontario (reg. *CF-RAF* 12.70); Conv single-seater 1975; To USA 1975 (*N92477, N308WK*); Now Bill Greenwood, Aspen, Colorado, airworthy - **SURVIVOR**

TZ138   Spitfire FR.XIVe (Griffon 65); TOC/RAF 7.45; In SS *Alder Province* to Canada for winterisation trials at Winter Experimental Establishment (WEE), Namao near Edmonton, Alberta 11.11.45; RCAF North West Air Command 11.2.46; No.8 RD Winnipeg for assembly, engine changed 6.46; Flown to Lethbridge, Alberta 7.46; Fort Nelson for winter trials 26.11.46; Nosed over in snow (twice) at Le Pas, prop damaged (Plts Badeaux and M Hayward) in 2.47 (41:55 flying hours); Take-off with skis, which were lost in the air, arr Namao 28.2.47; WEE census 8.48; Tested with Tiger Moth skis 12.48; SOC 31.3.49; Awaiting disposal at Edmonton 21.7.49; Sold as surplus by War Assets Corporation 8.49; Civil reg. *CF-GMZ* to Jess Bristow, sponsored by Imperial Oil Co, Edmonton; for racing purposes; Flown for/by F/Lt J H G 'Butch' McArthur in Tinnerman Trophy Race Ohio (Race No.'80') in 1949; To USA 1949 (q.v.); Briefly retd Canada, to Jack Arnold, Brantford, Ontario 1971 (marked 'JR-A'); Then back to USA until sold to Robert Jens, Richmond, British Columbia, Canada (regd *C-GSPT* 18.5.00)– **SURVIVOR**

VN332   Spitfire F.24 (Griffon 61); First flight South Marston 25.2.47; To No.47 MU Sealand for packing 28.5.47; Shipped to Canada in SS *Beaverlake*; Arr Montreal 24.7.47; Winter Experimental Establishment at Namao near Edmonton, for cocooning & winterisation; Test flown 24.8.47; Test-series in 12.47; WEE census 31.7.48; Cocooned for storage 8.48; WEE census 30.12.48; Dismantled 9.49; WEE census 12.49; Sold by War Assets Corp to Lee Fairbrother 1950; (Civil reg. *N7929A* on 21.2.51); To USA 31.3.51; Crashed and destroyed at Teterboro, New Jersey in 1953 (Pilot killed).

SURVIVORS in Canada

P8332, NH188 & TE214 (Hamilton); PR451 (Calgary); SL721 (Ottawa); TZ138 (Richmond); JF620 & TE294 (Comox).

Note: TD314 now in UK; AR614, PA908 & PR503 now in USA.

Bearing the racing number '80', Spitfire FR.XIVe CF-GMZ (ex TZ138) was registered in 1949 to Jess Bristow and sponsored by the Imperial Oil Co., Edmonton, for racing purposes, being flown in the Tinnerman Trophy Race, Ohio. [via Philip Jarrett]

Summary of Royal Canadian Navy Seafire F.XVc (35 aircraft)

Serial No.	TOC / EAC RCAF	No.803 Sqn time (code)	No.883 Sqn time (code)	No.1 TAG time (code)	Fairey storage	Remarks
PR375	1.6.46	1.6.46-29.5.47 21.9.49-9.11.49	29.5.47-25.6.47	26.7.47-1.12.48 (s) 29.7.49-21.9.49	31.1.50	31.5.50 ?
PR410	1.6.46	1.6.46-15.4.47	29.5.47-1.10.48	1.10.48-4.1.49	---	29.4.54 SOC
PR425 *)	7.11.46 (SR)	---	1.10.48-1.12.48 ('VG-...')	16.2.48-15.6.48 ('TG-C')	---	6.49 SOC
PR428 *)	7.11.46 (SR)	1947 ?	---	---	---	12.7.47 rts
PR434	1.6.46	1.6.46-15.7.46 ('N') 7.11.46-29.5.47	29.5.47-1.2.48 ('VG-AAJ')	---	---	14.2.49 SOC No.6 RD
PR451	1.6.46	1.6.46-30.5.47 ('P')	20.6.47-18.11.47 ('VG-AAN')	1948 - 4.1.49 ('TG-B')	21.5.49	25.5.49 SOC
PR458	1.6.46	1.6.46-15.4.47 21.9.49-9.11.49	21.5.47-1.10.48	(s) 29.7.49-21.9.49	14.1.50	Tecumseh
PR460	1.6.46	1.6.46-16.7.46 7.11.46-22.12.47	11.48-5.49 ('VG-AAK')	24.12.47-1.10.48	4.6.49	
PR461	1.6.46	1.6.46-15.7.46 ('Z') 13.3.47-3.5.47	21.5.-18.6.47 ('VG-AAC') 1.11.48-15.11.48 ('VG-AAP')	(s) 26.7.49-24.8.49	---	18.10.49 SOC Coll.PR502
PR470	1.6.46	1.6.46-30.5.47 ('F') 12.7.47-	10.6.47-11.7.47 15.11.47-	1.12.48-17.6.49	14.1.50	15.1.50 SOC
PR471	1.6.46	1.6.46-30.5.47	10.6.47-21.6.47	2.48-26.11.48	---	12.7.49 SOC
PR479	1.6.46	1.6.46-11.10.46 ('L') 7.11.46-29.4.47	29.5.47-1.12.48 ('VG-AAB')	---	4.6.49	
PR494	1.6.46	---	---	---	---	Namao WEE
PR496	1.6.46 (SR)	5.12.46-11.4.47	---	13.3.48-13.5.48	17.6.49	
PR498	1.6.46 (SR)	21.9.49-9.11.49	---	(s) 20.8.49-21.9.49	1.2.50	
PR499	1.6.46 (SR)	---	---	---	---	Namao WEE
PR500	1.6.46	1.6.46-15.7.46 ('R') 7.11.46-29.5.47	29.5.47-25.6.47	12.7.47-6.12.48 ('TG-D')	---	12.7.49 SOC Coll.SW809
PR501	1.6.46 (SR)	21.9.49-7.11.49	---	12.7.47-23.12.47 (s) 20.8.49-21.9.49	1.2.50	
PR502	1.6.46	1.6.46-11.9.46	---	(s) 13.8.49-24.8.49	---	Coll.PR461
PR503	1.6.46	1.6.46-11.9.46 ('K')	1.48-9.48 ('VG-AAA')	12.48-14.2.49 13.8.49-24.8.49		24.8.49 Z2 5.4.50 SOC
PR504	1.6.46	1.6.46-15.7.46 ('B') 7.11.46-11.4.47 15.4.47-17.5.47	17.4.48-1.12.48 ('VG-AAD') 21.9.49-9.11.49 ('VG-AAL')	5.1.49-26.1.49 (s) 11.8.49-21.9.49	1.2.50	
PR505	1.6.46 (SR)	---	29.5.47-8.8.47 ('VG-AAB')	30.8.47-22.10.47	---	24.9.48 SOC
PR506	1.6.46 (SR)	---	- ? -	21.3.50-17.11.50	17.11.50	27.11.50 SOC
SR459 *)	16.7.46 (SR)	---	---	---	---	rts Workshop
SR464	1.6.46	1.6.46-29.5.47	29.5.47-13.7.47 ('VG-AAQ')	3.8.47-16.2.48 1.12.48-26.1.49	---	Hamilton Res
SR530	1.6.46	1.6.46-29.5.47	29.5.47-13.10.48 ('VG-AAK')	---	---	4.1.49 SOC
SR545	1.6.46 (SR?)	7.11.46-15.12.46	---	---	---	22.4.47 rts
SW793	1.6.46 (SR)	---	29.5.47-18.10.47 ('VG-AAL')	18.10.47-13.3.48	18.1.50	
SW802	1.6.46 (SR)	---	29.5.47-30.8.47 21.9.49-27.10.49	1948 + (s) 5.49-9.49 27.10.49-15.2.50 12.10.50-8.5.51	8.5.51	9.5.51 SOC 743 FRU 10.49
SW809	1.6.46	1.6.46-15.7.46 7.11.46-27.4.48	---	15.6.48-4.5.49	17.6.49	Coll PR500
SW815	1.6.46 (SR?)	7.11.46-5.5.47	29.5.47-19.11.47	---	---	12.7.49 SOC
SW860	1.6.46 (SR?)	22.7.46- 7.11.46-29.5.47	29.5.47-13.1.48 2.7.47-29.12.47 21.9.49-26.10.49	13.1.48-19.5.48 29.12.47-4.5.48 1.10.48-26.1.49 (s) 20.8.49-21.9.49	17.6.49 31.1.50	cr. 2.8.46 31.1.50 SOC

*) Seafires arrived in Canada mainly aboard HMCS *Warrior* 31 March 1946, except PR425, PR428 & SR459;
(s) Seafire Special Exhibition Flight (SSEF) of the No.1 TAG in August/September 1949 (10 aircraft).

References:
A History of Canadian Naval Aviation 1918-62, by JDF Kealy and EC Russell, Dept of National Defence, Ottawa, 1965.
RCAF Military Aircraft, by John Griffin, CWM Ottawa, 1969.
The RCN Seafires, by Ingwald Wikene, Willowdale, CAHS Journal December 1970.
History of the Royal Canadian Air Force, by Ch Shores, Bison Books London, 1984.
The Supermarine Seafire in the Royal Canadian Navy, by Leo Pettipas, Winnipeg (Sea Fury) Chapter Canadian Naval Air Group, 1987.
Restoration of a Seafire, Warbirds International February 1989.
Spitfires in Canada (February 1940 – August 1947), by Lee Walsh, 1996.
Canada's Air Force at War and Peace, Vol.1, Spitfires in Canada, by Larry Milberry, Canav Books.

CHINA

China asked to buy the Spitfire in May 1939, but the outbreak of the Second World War circumvented this.

The surrender of Japan in August 1945 did not bring an end to the destruction and misery endured for so long by the Chinese people. The '*Sino*'-Communists refused to acknowledge Chiang Kai-Shek ('*Guomindang*' alliance), and the situation rapidly deteriorated into the Chinese Civil War. This divided China into two parts in January 1949, the mother country with the Communist Chinese Government, and the island of Formosa (Taiwan) with the Nationalist Forces of Chiang Kai-Shek.

The newly formed Communist Chinese Air Force was looking for modern fighter planes, especially P-51 Mustangs and Spitfires. However, the People's Republic of China avoided contact with the West at that time, and therefore the Chinese Government requested Spitfires from the Soviet Union, which had received more than 1,180 Spitfire Mk.IX during the Second World War.

With the beginning of the era of jet fighters the Spitfire lost its primary position in the Soviet Air Force and went to reserve units of the Red Air Force. Some Spitfire Mk.IXs may possibly have then been handed over to the Chinese Air Force, but confirmation is lacking. The Chinese Administration has not commented, and what became of the Spitfires is open to speculation.

However, the Chinese Government contacted the West later. It is known that Vickers-Armstrongs at South Marston received a tentative request from China to build Spitfires under licence, but this was not pursued as new jet fighter aircraft were available from the early fifties.

CUBA

Spitfires never served in Cuba. A private individual purchased a Spitfire Mk.XIV, intending to fly it in Cuba, but it never reached that country.

Individual History

TZ138 Spitfire FR.XIV (Griffon 65); TOC/RAF 7.45; ex RCAF until 31.8.48; To J H G McArthur for the Ohio and Tinnerman race in 1949 (Civil reg *CF-GMZ*); Sold to General Fulgencio Batista, the Cuban dictator, in 1950, flown to the Fort Lauderdale-Hollywood airport, Florida for departure to Cuba and registered as *N20E* to the new owner; But it could not be ferried out as supporters of the Cuban rival Fidel Castro broke off two propeller blades 1.6.51; Remained in USA, Texas 1963 (arr.1965, reg *N5505A*); Made a single flight at Mercedes, Texas on 2 May 1970, piloted by Charlie Liedel. Made a short visit to Windsor, Ontario, Canada; after several owners reg. *N180B* ntu; Reached Bill Destefani at Bakersfield, USA (reg. *N138TZ*) 1992; Restoration to fly by Pete Regina Aviation at van Nuys, California from mid 1998; Santa Monica Flying Museum from autumn 1999 (Civil reg. *N180RB*), based here during air test programme; Offered for sale, sold to Canada, reg. *C-GSPT*, 6.2000 – **SURVIVOR**

Movements of Spitfire TZ138 from 1946 to 2000:

(1) Arr. Canada (St. Johns) 1946
(2) Edmonton, Alberta 1947 B.C. & Manitoba 1948
(3) Ohio Race 1949
(4) Florida 1950, sold to General F. Batista, at Florida damaged 1951, unserviceable
(5) Minnesota 1955, St. Paul 1960
(6) Texas 1963/65, overhaul
(7) Canada & USA 1971-74
(8) In USA from 1974, several owners, offer for sale 1999
(9) Sold to B.C. in 2000

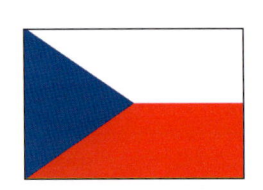

CZECHOSLOVAKIA
(now Czech Republic & Slovak Republic)

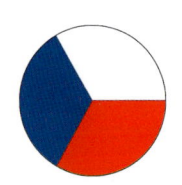

Czechoslovakia was occupied by Germany between 1939 and 1945. During the Second World War, Spitfires were flown by Czechoslovakian pilots of Nos.310, 312 and 313 Sqns RAF, these being grouped as No.134 Airfield Headquarters on 8th November 1943, and renamed No.134 Czech (Fighter) Wing on 12th May 1944.

Spitfire Mk.Vb/trop, captured by the Germans in the Middle East, were tested by the Air Research Institute *Vedecky Letecky Ustav* at Prague-Letnany 1944/45. One of them was exhibited at Melník (near Prague), together with a Russian built La-7 in 1945/46, both in Czechoslovakian colours, and the Spitfire had a Lion Rampant Queue Forchée badge on the cowling. The fate of

Line-up of Spitfire LF.IXes of No.310 Sqn after arriving at Prague-Ruzyne airport on 13th August 1945. The aircraft have the Czech flag on the fin and the unit badge of a lion in front of a sword on the cowling. The third aircraft is coded 'NN-U' and has the RAF serial TE572. [A Vandenameele]

this Spitfire is unknown, possibly it was used as a ground instructional airframe by the new CSSR Air Force, until scrapped in 1948.

After the war, the newly formed Czechoslovakian Air Force received 77 Spitfire LF.IXc/e under a contract signed on 19th February 1945, mainly those with Nos.310, 312 and 313 (Czech) Sqns returning to their home bases. These squadrons came under Czechoslovakian control with effect from 30th August 1945, and officially ceased to be under RAF administration on 15 February 1946. Some fighters were also received from Russia in March 1945.

Czechoslovakian Spitfire Units of the Royal Air Force

No.**310** Sqn - Unit-code: 'NN'
   Formed 10th July 1940, officially disbanded 15th February 1946;
   Spitfire Mks.II, V, VI, IX from October 1941 to February 1946.
No.**312** Sqn - Unit-code: 'DU'
   Formed 29th August 1940, officially disbanded 15th February 1946;
   Spitfire Mks.II, V, IX from October 1941 to February 1946.
No.**313** Sqn - Unit-code: 'RY'
   Formed 10th May 1941, officially disbanded 15th February 1946;
   Spitfire Mks.I, II, V, VI, VI, IX from May 1941 to February 1946.

Czechoslovakian Air Force (CzAF)

To form the new Czechoslovakian Air Force (CzAF), Nos.310, 312 and 313 Squadrons left RAF Manston on 7th August 1945. Led by Wg Cdr Jaroslav Hladó, they flew to Hildesheim in Germany, continuing on 13th August 1945 to Prague-Ruzyne airport, where an official reception was held on 16th August 1945. A second batch, led by Wg Cdr Tomás Vybiral, arrived on 24th August 1945.

Czechoslovakia received a total of 77 Spitfire LF.IXc/e as part of the British Air Ministry Comm.No.322, and designated these as aircraft type No "*S-89*" (S = Stihaci, Fighter). Initially, in 1945, they received 71 aircraft; in 1946 followed five more, and in 1947 one Spitfire Mk.IX. Five of these went to the Security Air Guard (BL), who flew them from 1947 to 1951.

In September 1945 No.310 Sqn moved to Prague-Kbely (LZ-1). No.312 Sqn remained at Prague until 22nd September 1945 when they flew to a new base at Ceské Budejovice (LZ-2) in South Bohemia, and No.313 Sqn flew to their final base at Brno (LZ-3) at the same time.

Three Air-Groups of the CzAF (*Letecká Divize*, short "LD") were equipped with Spitfires: Nos.1, 2 and 3 LD being formed respectively from Nos.310, 312 and 313 Squadrons RAF. Each LD had two Fighter Regiments (*Stihaci Letecky Pluk*, short "SLP"), and each SLP served normally with twelve Spitfires until 1947/48.

The CzAF had 62 Spitfire Mk.IXs still on strength in March 1948, and the Security Air Guard (BL) had two. With the arrival of Russian-built aircraft, the Spitfires were phased out. Fifty-nine airworthy aircraft were sold to Israel in 1948/49, and a further two were supplied for spare parts in November 1949. The first 20 were flown to Israel during Operation s *Velveta I & II* in September 1948 and December 1948 respectively (three losses); a further 39 arrived Israel by ship, mostly in 1949.

After 1949 only three Spitfires remained in the CSSR: The Security Air Guard had two until 1951, and another went in 1950 to the National Technical Museum at Prague for exhibition.

Spitfire Units of Czechoslovakia

No.**1 LD** based at Prague-Kbely (LZ-1) from 14th September 1945, and comprised from 15 February 1946:
   No.**10 SLP**, unit-code: 'KR'
   No.**12 SLP**, unit-code: 'DZ'

A line-up of Spitfire LF.IXes of No.2 Letecká Divize, at České Budejovice, South-Bohemia. [Pavel Kucera]

No.2 LD based at České Budejovice, South-Bohemia (LZ-2) from 22nd September 1945, and comprised from 15 February 1946:
No.4 SLP, unit-code: 'JT'
No.5 SLP, unit-code: 'MP'

No.3 LD based at Brno-Slatina (LZ-3) from 22nd September 1945, and comprised from 15th February 1946:
No.7 SLP, unit-code: 'IV'
No.8 SLP, unit-code: 'LS'

LVA *Letecke Vojenske Akademie* at Hradec Králové, the Military Air Academy (AFS), with its airbase near Pardubice (LZ-5).
From mid 1947 the LVA received Spitfires from the LDs. AFS courses with Spitfires continued from October 1947 to the end 1948, then the aircraft were grounded.
Markings: White letter and three digits on the fuselage, in the range A-701 to A-750.

C.B. = České Budejovice

VLU *Vedecky Letecky Ustav* at Prague-Letnany (an Aviation Research & Test Centre).
Spitfires from March 1946 to 1949; known markings V-7, V-8, V-9, V-12, V-20, IR-1, JP-1, KO-1 & HL M-4.

BL *Bezpecnostni Letectvo,* the National Air Guard (Air-Police), used five Spitfires for border patrol from 1947 until 1951, when only two were left.
Markings: *OK-BXA, OK-BXC, OK-BXD, OK-BXF* and *OK-BXL*.

Markings of Czechoslovakian Spitfires

After the arrival of the Spitfires in Czechoslovakia in August 1945, the RAF fuselage roundels were replaced by white cross-bars between the Squadron codes and the individual letters. The Czech flag was displayed on the fin, and Czech roundels were shown on both sides of the wings, top and bottom; Squadron emblems were painted on both sides of the cowlings.

This paint scheme was used until mid February 1946, when the RAF letters were replaced by the new CzAF markings of the SLPs, and Czech roundels were painted also on the rudder. But instead of a third letter the CzAF normally used digits from "1" to "12" (for reserve "13" & "14") as individual aircraft markings.

Spitfires of the Security Air Guard had completely red noses: Red cowling and red spinner, and also red wing leading edges. The Czechoslovakian 'OK- ' registrations were painted in red (white outlined) on the fuselage sides and on the wings, top and bottom.

Czechoslovakian terminology:

Divize	= Group
Letecky, Letecká	= Aviation, Air, Aero
LD	= Air Group
Pluk	= Regiment
Stihaci	= Fighter
SLP	= Fighter Aviation Regiment

Individual Histories

MH750 Spitfire LF.IXc (Merlin 66); TOC/RAF 19.9.43; RAF Pershore 3.12.46; Ferry flight to Czechoslovakia 6.12.46 – CzAF 12.46; LVA Military Air Academy ('A-717') 10.6.47; Possibly to BL Security Air Guard ('*OK-BX_*') 1947; Later sold to Israel; Operation *Velveta II* ferry flight, arr Israel 12.48

MJ572 Spitfire LF.IXc (Merlin 66); TOC/RAF 22.12.43; ex No.312 Sqn (3.44); No.313 Sqn from 22.7.45; Arr Czechoslovakia 13/24.8.45 – CzAF 30.8.45, to No.3 LD ('RY-.'); No.7 or 8 SLP from 15.2.46; VLU Research & Test Centre 12.3.46

MJ752 Spitfire LF.IXc (Merlin 66); TOC/RAF 20.12.43; No.313 Sqn from 16.7.45; Arr Czechoslovakia 13/24.8.45 – CzAF 30.8.45, to No.3 LD ('RY-N'); No.7 SLP ('IV-7') from 15.2.46; VLU Research & Test Centre (photo equipment trials) 12.3.46; Later sold to Israel, delivered by ship 11.49

MK135 Spitfire LF.IXc (Merlin 66); TOC/RAF 8.1.44; RAF Pershore 2.12.46; Ferry flight to Czechoslovakia 6.12.46 – CzAF 12.46; Possibly to BL Security Air Guard ('*OK-BX_*') 1947; Crashed Zborov near Ceské Budejovice, Cat.E 7.8.47, SOC

MK257 Spitfire LF.IXc (Merlin 66); TOC/RAF 12.2.44; Arr RAF Pershore for Czechoslovakia 5.12.46; Crashed Cat.FA/Ac 12.12.46; ROS - Arr CzAF 10.6.47; To LVA Military Air Academy ('A-7...') 6.47; Shown at Pardubice (LZ-5) still in 6.49; Later sold to Israel, delivered by ship 11.49

ML119 Spitfire LF.IXc (Merlin 66); TOC/RAF 24.3.44; RAF Pershore 3.12.46; Ferry flight to Czechoslovakia 6.12.46 – CzAF 12.46; LVA Military Air Academy ('A-719') in 1947; Later sold to Israel, arr by ship 12.48 (IDF/AF No *2020*); To Burma 1955 (*UB441*); Sold to USA 1999; Returned to UK, P Monk and M Simpson, Kent, 30.10.2000 - **SURVIVOR**

NH174 Spitfire LF.IXe (Merlin 66); TOC/RAF 28.4.44; ex No.310 Sqn 6.44; RAF Pershore 2.12.46; Ferry flight to Czechoslovakia 6.12.46 – CzAF 12.46, to No.2 LD; No.4 SLP ('JT-1'); Later sold to Israel; Operation *Velveta II* ferry flight, arr Israel 12.48

PL250 Spitfire LF.IXe (Merlin 66); TOC/RAF 16.6.44; No.313 Sqn from 22.7.45; Arr Czechoslovakia 13/24.8.45 – CzAF 30.8.45, to No.3 LD ('RY- '); No.7 SLP ('IV-9') from 15.2.46; LVA Military Air Academy ('A-730') in 1947; Tyre burst landing, undercarriage collapsed, Kunovice 30.8.48 (Plt L Dobrovdsky); Repaired; Later sold to Israel, delivered by ship 1948/49

PT621 Spitfire LF.IXe (Merlin 66); TOC/RAF 26.7.44; No.313 Sqn from 19.7.45; Arr Czechoslovakia 13/24.8.45 – CzAF 30.8.45, to No.3 LD ('RY- '); No.7 or 8 SLP from 15.2.46; LVA Military Air Academy ('A-7..'), crashed at Pardubice (LZ-5) 9.10.47; Repaired; Later sold to Israel, delivered by ship 1948/49

PV205 Spitfire LF.IXe (Merlin 66); TOC/RAF 16.9.44; RAF Pershore 5.12.46; Ferry flight to Czechoslovakia 6.12.46 - CzAF 12.46; Possibly to BL Security Air Guard ('*OK-BX_*') 1947; Later sold to Israel, delivered by ship 1948/49

SL594 Spitfire LF.IXe (Merlin 66); TOC/RAF 19.7.45; No.310 Sqn from 7.8.45; Arr Czechoslovakia 13/24.8.45 – CzAF 30.8.45, to No.1 LD ('NN- '); No.10 or 12 SLP from 15.2.46; Later sold to Israel; Operation *Velveta I* ferry flight, arr IDF/AF 27.9.48

SL625 Spitfire LF.IXe (Merlin 66); TOC/RAF 16.6.45; No.312 Sqn from 3.8.45; Arr Czechoslovakia 13/24.8.45 – CzAF 30.8.45, to No.2 LD ('DU-L'); No.4 SLP ('JT-11') from 15.2.46; Ceské Budejovice (LZ-2) in 1948; Later sold to Israel, delivered by ship 1948/49

SL626 Spitfire LF.IXe (Merlin 66); TOC/RAF 19.6.45; No.312 Sqn from 1.8.45; Arr Czechoslovakia 13/24.8.45 – CzAF 30.8.45, to No.2 LD ('DU-R'); No.5 SLP ('MP-5') from 15.2.46; Crashed near Liberec, Cat.E 26.9.46, SOC

SL627 Spitfire LF.IXe (Merlin 66); TOC/RAF 18.6.45; No.312 Sqn from 3.8.45; Arr Czechoslovakia 13/24.8.45 - CzAF 30.8.45, to No.2 LD ('DU-N' ?); No.4 or 5 SLP from

LVA Spitfire LF.IXc MH750 carries the nose emblem of No.2 Letecká Divize, at Ceské Budejovice, South-Bohemia, but the marking 'A-717'. It was one of many Czech aircraft which later went to Israel. [*Jaroslav Voboril*]

15.2.46; Crashed at České Budejovice (LZ-2) 25.7.46; Repaired; Later sold to Israel, delivered by ship 1948/49
NOTE: Reported "SL527" ("DU-X"), possibly 'DU-N' ?

SL628 Spitfire LF.IXe (Merlin 66); TOC/RAF 19.6.45; ex No.312 Sqn; No.310 Sqn from 2.8.45; Arr Czechoslovakia 13/24.8.45 - CzAF 30.8.45, to No.1 LD ('NN- '); No.10 or 12 SLP from 15.2.46; VLU Research & Test Centre ('HL M-4') by 10.6.47; Later sold to Israel; Operation *Velveta II* ferry flight, arr Israel 12.48

SL629 Spitfire LF.IXe (Merlin 66); TOC/RAF 22.6.45; ex No.312 Sqn; No.313 Sqn from 25.7.45; Arr Czechoslovakia 13/24.8.45 - CzAF 30.8.45, to No.3 LD ('RY- '); No.7 SLP ('IV-6') from 15.2.46; Later sold to Israel; Delivery by ship 11.49
NOTE: Reported as "SL625" and "IV-6" at Prostejove air show 29.9.46

SL630 Spitfire LF.IXe (Merlin 66); TOC/RAF 22.6.45; No.313 Sqn from 19.7.45; Arr Czechoslovakia 13/24.8.45 – CzAF 30.8.45, to No.3 LD ('RY- '); No.7 SLP ('IV-10') from 15.2.46; Crashed at Prague-Kbely (LZ-1) 24.10.46; LVA Military Air Academy ('A-7.. '), accident at Pardubice (LZ-5) 14.10.47; Repaired; Later sold to Israel; Operation *Velveta II* ferry flight, arr Israel 12.48

SL631 Spitfire LF.IXe (Merlin 66); TOC/RAF 25.6.45; No.312 Sqn from 1.8.45; Arr Czechoslovakia 13/24.8.45 – CzAF 30.8.45, to No.2 LD ('DU- '); No.5 SLP ('MP-7') from 15.2.46; Crashed at Ceské Budejovice (LZ-2), Cat.E 19.2.48, SOC

SL632 Spitfire LF.IXe (Merlin 66); TOC/RAF 25.6.45; No.312 Sqn from 4.8.45; Arr Czechoslovakia 13/24.8.45 - CzAF 30.8.45, to No.2 LD ('DU- '); No.4 SLP ('JT-4') from 15.2.46; No.5 SLP ('MP- '); Ceské Budejovice (LZ-2) in 1948; Later sold to Israel; Operation *Velveta II* ferry flight, arr 23.12.48 (IDF/AF No *2011*)

SL633 Spitfire LF.IXe (Merlin 66); TOC/RAF 25.6.45; No.312 Sqn from 2.8.45; Arr Czechoslovakia 13/24.8.45 – CzAF 30.8.45, to No.2 LD ('DU-K'); No.4 SLP ('JT-10') from 15.2.46; Shown at Brno (LZ-3) 1946; Possibly LVA Military Air Academy, crashed at Ceské Budejovice (LZ-2) 19.5.48; Repaired; Later sold to Israel, delivered by ship 1948/49

SL634 Spitfire LF.IXe (Merlin 66); TOC/RAF 29.6.45; No.312 Sqn from 17.9.45; Arr Czechoslovakia 13/24.8.45 – CzAF 30.8.45, to No.2 LD ('DU- '); No.4 or 5 SLP from 15.2.46; VLU Research & Test Centre ('JP-1') 10.6.47; Ceské Budejovice (LZ-2) in 1948; Later sold to Israel, delivered by ship 1948/49

SL635 Spitfire LF.IXe (Merlin 66); TOC/RAF 29.6.45; No.313 Sqn from 7.8.45; Arr Czechoslovakia 13/24.8.45 – CzAF 30.8.45, to No.3 LD ('RY- '); No.7 or 8 SLP from 15.2.46

SL648 Spitfire LF.IXe (Merlin 66); TOC/RAF 29.6.45; No.312 Sqn from 4.8.45; Arr Czechoslovakia 13/24.8.45 – CzAF 30.8.45, to No.2 LD ('DU- '); No.4 SLP ('JT-12') from 15.2.46; Ceské Budejovice (LZ-2) in 1948; Later sold to Israel, delivered by ship 1948/49

SL649 Spitfire LF.IXe (Merlin 66); TOC/RAF 29.6.45; No.312 Sqn from 16.8.45; Arr Czechoslovakia 13/24.8.45 – CzAF 30.8.45, to No.2 LD ('DU-Q'); No.5 SLP ('MP-6') from 15.2.46; Ceské Budejovice (LZ-2) in 1948; Later sold to Israel; Operation *Velveta II* ferry flight, arr Israel 12.48

SL650 Spitfire LF.IXe (Merlin 66); TOC/RAF 30.6.45; No.312 Sqn from 23.8.45; Arr Czechoslovakia 13/24.8.45 – CzAF 30.8.45, to No.2 LD ('DU-U'); No.5 SLP ('MP-10') from 15.2.46; Ceské Budejovice (LZ-2) in 1948; Later sold to Israel, delivered by ship 1948/49

SL651 Spitfire LF.IXe (Merlin 66); TOC/RAF 17.7.45; No.310 Sqn from 7.8.45; Arr Czechoslovakia 13/24.8.45 – CzAF 30.8.45, to No.3 LD ('RY- '); No.7 or 8 SLP from 15.2.46; VLU Research & Test Centre ('IR-1') in 1947; Later sold to Israel, delivered by ship 11.49

SL652 Spitfire LF.IXe (Merlin 66); TOC/RAF 23.7.45; No.313 Sqn from 9.8.45; Arr Czechoslovakia 13/24.8.45 – CzAF 30.8.45, to No.3 LD ('RY- '); No.7 or 8 SLP from 15.2.46; Later sold to Israel, delivered by ship 1948/49

SL653 Spitfire LF.IXe (Merlin 66); TOC/RAF 23.7.45; No.312 Sqn from 23.8.45; Arr Czechoslovakia 13/24.8.45 – CzAF 30.8.45, to No.2 LD ('DU- '); No.5 SLP ('MP-9') from 15.2.46; Change to No.3 LD; No.8 SLP ('LS-8'), engine failure, force-landed near Znojmo (Naaceratice) 10.10.47 (P/O V Truhlar killed); Repaired; Ceské Budejovice (LZ-2) in 1948; Later sold to Israel, delivered by ship 1948/49

SL654 Spitfire LF.IXe (Merlin 66); TOC/RAF 19.7.45; No.312 Sqn from 23.8.45; Arr Czechoslovakia 13/24.8.45 – CzAF 30.8.45, to No.2 LD ('DU-G'); No.4 SLP ('JT-8') in 1946; LVA Military Air Academy ('A-7... '), shown at Pardubice (LZ-5) in 6.49; Later sold to Israel, delivered by ship 11.49

SL655 Spitfire LF.IXe (Merlin 66); TOC/RAF 24.7.45; No.310 Sqn from 7.8.45; Arr Czechoslovakia 13/24.8.45 – CzAF

Spitfire LF.IXe SL653 'MP-9' of No.5 Stihaci Letecky Pluk, Ceské Budejovice, South-Bohemia, around 1946. This aircraft was later sold to Israel.
[RAF Museum P13616]

Spitfire LF.IXe TE521 KR-4 and others of No.10 SLP (Fighter Regiment), Prague-Kbely around 1946. [MAP]

30.8.45, to No.1 LD ('NN-T'); No.10 or 12 SLP from 15.2.46; Crashed at Prague-Kbely (LZ-1) 24.9.46; Repaired; Later sold to Israel; Operation *Velveta II* ferry flight, arr Israel 12.48

SL656 Spitfire LF.IXe (Merlin 66); TOC/RAF 24.7.45; No.312 Sqn from 4.8.45; Arr Czechoslovakia 13/24.8.45 – CzAF 30.8.45, to No.2 LD ('DU- '); No.4 or 5 SLP from 15.2.46; Ceské Budejovice (LZ-2) in 1948; Later sold to Israel; Operation *Velveta II* ferry flight, arr Israel 12.48

SL657 Spitfire LF.IXe (Merlin 66); TOC/RAF 24.7.45; No.313 Sqn from 7.8.45; Arr Czechoslovakia 13/24.8.45 – CzAF 30.8.45, to No.3 LD ('RY- '); No.7 SLP ('IV-4') from 15.2.46; Later sold to Israel; Operation *Velveta II* ferry flight, arr Israel 12.48

SL660 Spitfire LF.IXe (Merlin 66); TOC/RAF 25.7.45; No.310 Sqn from 17.8.45; Arr Czechoslovakia 13/24.8.45 – CzAF 30.8.45, to No.1 LD ('NN- '); No.10 or 12 SLP from 15.2.46; LVA Military Air Academy ('A-7..'), dived into ground near Herm, Mestec, Cat E 31.10.47, SOC

SL662 Spitfire LF.IXe (Merlin 66); TOC/RAF 25.7.45; No.310 & 313 Sqns, No.134 (Czech) Wing, Manston from 7.8.45; Arr Czechoslavakia 24.8.45 - CzAF 30.8.45, to No.3 LD ('RY-Z'); No.7 or 8 SLP from 15.2.46; Possibly No.10 SLP ('KR-7') in 1947; LVA Military Air Academy ('A-7..'), crashed near Novy Dvur 14.4.48; Repaired; Shown at Pardubice (LZ-5) in 6.49; Later sold to Israel, delivered by ship 11.49

SL664 Spitfire LF.IXe (Merlin 66); TOC/RAF 23.7.45; No.313 Sqn from 9.8.45; Arr Czechoslovakia 13/24.8.45 – CzAF 30.8.45, to No.3 LD ('RY- '); No.8 SLP ('LS-1') from 15.2.46; LVA Military Air Academy ('A-7..') 1.48; Crashed near Malacky 24.3.48; Repaired; Later sold to Israel; Operation *Velveta II* ferry flight, arr Israel 12.48

TB439 Spitfire LF.IXe (Merlin 66); TOC/RAF 2.1.45; No.312 Sqn from 4.8.45; Arr Czechoslovakia 13/24.8.45 – CzAF 30.8.45, to No.2 LD ('DU- '); No.4 or 5 SLP from 15.2.46; LVA Military Air Academy ('A-7.. '), crashed at Pardubice (LZ-5), Cat E 23.10.47, SOC

TE510 Spitfire LF.IXe (Merlin 66); TOC/RAF 30.5.45; No.310 Sqn from 1.8.45; Arr Czechoslovakia 13/24.8.45 – CzAF 30.8.45, to No.1 LD ('NN- '); No.10 SLP ('KR-2') from 15.2.46 (shown also in 4.46); LVA Military Air Academy ('A-7..'), crashed at Pardubice (LZ-5) 26.9.47; Repaired; LVA 1.48; Crashed near Malacky, Cat.E 15.4.48, SOC

TE512 Spitfire LF.IXe (Merlin 66); TOC/RAF 1.6.45; No.310 Sqn from 2.8.45; Arr Czechoslovakia 13/24.8.45 – CzAF 30.8.45, to No.1 LD ('NN- '); No.10 or 12 SLP from 15.2.46; Later sold to Israel; Operation *Velveta II* ferry flight, crashed in snowstorm over Yugoslavia 18.12.48 (wrecked), SOC

TE513 Spitfire LF.IXe (Merlin 66); TOC/RAF 1.6.45; No.310 Sqn from 2.8.45; Arr Czechoslovakia 9.8.45 - CzAF 30.8.45, to No.1 LD ('NN-G'); No.10 or 12 SLP from 15.2.46; LVA Military Air Academy ('A-731') 1.48; Later sold to Israel, delivered by ship 1948/49

TE515 Spitfire LF.IXe (Merlin 66); TOC/RAF 16.6.45; No.312 Sqn from 3.8.45; Arr Czechoslovakia 13/24.8.45 – CzAF 30.8.45, to No.2 LD ('DU-W'); No.4 or 5 SLP from 15.2.46; VLU Research & Test Centre in 1948; Later sold to Israel, delivered by ship 11.49 (IDF/AF No *2058*)

TE516 Spitfire LF.IXe (Merlin 66); TOC/RAF 1.6.45; No.310 Sqn from 2.8.45; Arr Czechoslovakia 9.8.45 - CzAF 30.8.45, to No.1 LD ('NN-R'); No.10 or 12 SLP from 15.2.46; LVA Military Air Academy ('A-7..') 1.48; Shown at Pardubice (LZ-5) in 6.49; Later sold to Israel, delivered by ship 11.49 (IDF/AF No *2051*)

TE517 Spitfire LF.IXe (Merlin 66); TOC/RAF 2.6.45; No.313 Sqn from 25.7.45; Arr Czechoslovakia 13/24.8.45 – CzAF 30.8.45, to No.3 LD ('RY- '); No.7 SLP ('IV-2') from 15.2.46; Shown in Moravia 2.46; LVA Military Air Academy ('A-702') in 1947; Ceské Budejovice (LZ-2) in 1948; Later sold to Israel, delivered by ship 1948/49 (IDF/AF No *2046*); To UK, Civil reg. *G-BIXP*, regd 3.7.81 to R J Lamplough, cancelled 12.11.84, to *G-CCIX*, regd 9.4.85 to Charles Church (Spitfires) Ltd, Mitcheldever; stored; sold to Kermit Weeks 8.92, regn cancelled 6.1.93 and stored with Personal Plane Services, Booker pending rebuild - **SURVIVOR**

TE518 Spitfire LF.IXe (Merlin 66); TOC/RAF 8.6.45; No.312 Sqn from 3.8.45; Arr Czechoslovakia 13/24.8.45 – CzAF 30.8.45, to No.2 LD ('DU- '); No.5 SLP ('MP-1') from 15.2.46; Ceské Budejovice (LZ-2) in 1948; Later sold to Israel, delivered by ship 1948/49

TE519 Spitfire LF.IXe (Merlin 66); TOC/RAF 9.6.45; No.310 Sqn from 30.7.45; Arr Czechoslovakia 13/24.8.45 – CzAF 30.8.45, to No.1 LD ('NN- '); No.10 or 12 SLP from 15.2.46; Later sold to Israel; Operation *Velveta II* ferry flight, arr Israel 12.48

TE521 Spitfire LF.IXe (Merlin 66); TOC/RAF 15.6.45; No.310 Sqn from 2.8.45; Arr Czechoslovakia 9.8.45 - CzAF 30.8.45, to No.1 LD ('NN- '); No.10 SLP ('KR-4') from 15.2.46; LVA Military Air Academy ('A-7.. '), crashed at Pardubice (LZ-5), Cat.E 17.10.47, SOC

TE522 Spitfire LF.IXe (Merlin 66); TOC/RAF 14.6.45; No.312 Sqn from 3.8.45; Arr Czechoslovakia 13/24.8.45 – CzAF

Spitfire LF.IXe, TE521/KR-4 of No.10 SLP, No.1 LD, Prague-Kbely, 1946/7

30.8.45, to No.2 LD ('DU-C'); No.4 SLP ('JT-2') from 15.2.46; Possibly LVA Military Air Academy, crashed at Ceské Budejovice (LZ-2) 15.10.47; Repaired; Ceské Budejovice in 1948; Later sold to Israel, delivered by ship 1948/49

TE523 Spitfire LF.IXe (Merlin 66); TOC/RAF 14.6.45; ex No.312 Sqn; No.310 Sqn from 2.8.45; Arr Czechoslovakia 13/24.8.45 – CzAF 30.8.45, to No.1 LD ('NN- '); No.10 SLP ('KR-1') from 15.2.46; Ceské Budejovice (LZ-2) in 1948; Later sold to Israel, delivered by ship 1948/49

TE524 Spitfire LF.IXe (Merlin 66); TOC/RAF 16.6.45; No.312 Sqn from 2.8.45; Arr Czechoslovakia 13/24.8.45 – CzAF 30.8.45, to No.2 LD ('DU-F'); No.4 SLP ('JT-5') from 15.2.46; Ceské Budejovice (LZ-2) in 1948; Later sold to Israel, delivered by ship 1948/49

TE527 Spitfire LF.IXe (Merlin 66); TOC/RAF 8.6.45; No.310 & 312 Sqn's from 1.8.45; Arr Czechoslovakia 13/24.8.45 – CzAF 30.8.45, to No.2 LD ('DU-X'); No.4 or 5 SLP from 15.2.46; Later sold to Israel, delivered by ship 1948/49 (IDF/AF No *2027*)

TE531 Spitfire LF.IXe (Merlin 66); TOC/RAF 28.5.45; No.313 Sqn from 20.7.45; Arr Czechoslovakia 13/24.8.45 – CzAF 30.8.45, to No.3 LD ('RY-L'); No.7 or 8 SLP from 15.2.46; Later sold to Israel; Operation *Velveta I* ferry flight, arr IDF/AF 27.9.48

TE532 Spitfire LF.IXe (Merlin 66); TOC/RAF 1.6.45; No.313 Sqn from 30.7.45; Arr Czechoslovakia 13/24.8.45 – CzAF 30.8.45, to No.3 LD ('RY- '); No.7 or 8 SLP from 15.2.46; Later sold to Israel; Operation *Velveta I* ferry flight, arr IDF/AF 27.9.48

TE551 Spitfire LF.IXe (Merlin 66); TOC/RAF 7.6.45; No.310 Sqn from 1.8.45; Arr Czechoslovakia 13/24.8.45 – CzAF 30.8.45, to No.1 LD ('NN-D'); No.10 or 12 SLP from 15.2.46; Later sold to Israel, delivered by ship 1948/49

TE554 Spitfire LF.IXe (Merlin 66); TOC/RAF 26.5.45; No.310 Sqn from 1.8.45; Arr Czechoslovakia 13/24.8.45 – CzAF 30.8.45, to No.1 LD ('NN- '); No.10 SLP ('KR-6') from 15.2.46; Prague-Kbely (LZ-1); LVA Military Air Academy ('A-708') 12.47; Shown Pardubice (LZ-5) in 6.49; Later sold to Israel, delivered by ship 11.49 (IDF/AF No *2057*); Extant, now Hatzerim Museum near Beersheba - **SURVIVOR**

TE555 Spitfire LF.IXe (Merlin 66); TOC/RAF 26.6.45; No.310 Sqn from 3.8.45; Arr Czechoslovakia 13/24.8.45 – CzAF 30.8.45, to No.1 LD ('NN- '); No.10 or 12 SLP from 15.2.46; Crashed at Brno (LZ-3) 24.9.46; Repaired; Later sold to Israel; Operation *Velveta I* ferry flight, belly-landing in Yugoslavia 24.9.48; by air-transport (C-46) to Israel in 11.48

TE556 Spitfire LF.IXe (Merlin 66); TOC/RAF 31.5.45; No.313 Sqn from 19.7.45; Arr Czechoslovakia 13/24.8.45 – CzAF 30.8.45, to No.3 LD ('RY- '); No.7 or 8 SLP from 15.2.46; VLU Research & Test Centre 12.45; Crashed in 1948; To Israel for spare parts 11.49

TE557 Spitfire LF.IXe (Merlin 66); TOC/RAF 26.5.45; No.313 Sqn from 19.7.45; Arr Czechoslovakia 13/24.8.45 – CzAF 30.8.45, to No.3 LD ('RY- '); No.7 or 8 SLP from 15.2.46; Later sold to Israel; Operation *Velveta I* ferry flight, force-landed on Rhodes 27.9.48, interned

TE558 Spitfire LF.IXe (Merlin 66); TOC/RAF 1.6.45; No.313 Sqn from 19.7.45; Arr Czechoslovakia 13/24.8.45 – CzAF 30.8.45, to No.3 LD ('RY-O'); No.7 or 8 SLP from 15.2.46; LVA Military Air Academy ('A-7..') 1.48; Crashed near Malacky 15.3.48; Repaired; Later sold to Israel; Operation *Velveta II* ferry flight, arr Israel 12.48

TE559 Spitfire LF.IXe (Merlin 66); TOC/RAF 1.6.45; No.310 Sqn from 1.8.45; Arr Czechoslovakia 13/24.8.45 – CzAF 30.8.45, to No.1 LD ('NN- '); No.10 or 12 SLP from 15.2.46; Later sold to Israel, delivered by ship 1948/49 (IDF/AF No *2048*)

Spitfire LF.IXe TE524 'JT-5' of No.4 Stihaci Letecky Pluk, Ceské Budejovice, South-Bohemia, around 1946. It was later sold to Israel.

Above: Spitfire LF.IXe TE527 'DU-X' of No.2 Letecká Divize, at Ceské Budejovice, South-Bohemia, having the individual letter painted on in 1945. It later went to Israel as IDF/AF No. 2027.

Right: Spitfire LF.IXe TE561 'LS-6' of No.8 Stihaci Letecky Pluk, Brno-Slatina, on 13th October 1946. It was later sold to Israel.

Below: Spitfire LF.IXe TE563 'NN-O' of No.1 Letecká Divize, Prague-Kbely, after pilot Smira made a wheels-up landing in a field near Lovosice in 1946.

Spitfire LF.IXe TE570 IV-8 of No.7 SLP (Fighter Regiment) photographed shortly before it was lost in a fatal crash at Brno-Slatina in September 1946. [MAP]

Spitfire LF.IXe, TE570/IV-8 of No.7 SLP, No.3 LD, Brno-Slatina in 1946

TE560 Spitfire LF.IXe (Merlin 66); TOC/RAF 31.5.45; No.310 Sqn from 30.7.45; Arr Czechoslovakia 13/24.8.45 – CzAF 30.8.45, to No.1 LD ('NN- '); No.12 SLP ('DZ-7') from 15.2.46; Later sold to Israel, delivered by ship 1948/49

TE561 Spitfire LF.IXe (Merlin 66); TOC/RAF 1.6.45; No.313 Sqn from 25.7.45; Arr Czechoslovakia 13/24.8.45 – CzAF 30.8.45, to No.3 LD ('RY- '); No.8 SLP ('LS-6') from 15.2.46; LVA Military Air Academy ('A-7..') 1.48; Crashed near Malacky 24.3.48; Repaired; Later sold to Israel, delivered by ship 1948/49

TE562 Spitfire LF.IXe (Merlin 66); TOC/RAF 12.6.45; No.310 Sqn from 1.8.45; Arr Czechoslovakia 13/24.8.45 – CzAF 30.8.45, to No.1 LD ('NN- '); No.10 or 12 SLP from 15.2.46

TE563 Spitfire LF.IXe (Merlin 66); TOC/RAF 8.6.45; No.310 Sqn from 1.8.45; Arr Czechoslovakia 13/24.8.45 – CzAF 30.8.45, to No.1 LD ('NN-O'); No.10 or 12 SLP from 15.2.46; Belly-landed near Lovosice, Cat.E in 1946 (Plt Smira), SOC

TE564 Spitfire LF.IXe (Merlin 66); TOC/RAF 7.6.45; No.313 Sqn from 26.7.45; Arr Czechoslovakia 13/24.8.45 – CzAF 30.8.45, to No.3 LD ('RY-X'); No.8 SLP ('LS-7') from 15.2.46; Later sold to Israel; Operation *Velveta I* ferry flight, force-landed on Rhodes 27.9.48, interned; Flown to Israel in 12.50 (IDF/AF No *2049*)

TE565 Spitfire LF.IXe (Merlin 66); TOC/RAF 7.6.45; No.310 Sqn from 30.7.45; Arr Czechoslovakia 13/24.8.45 – CzAF 30.8.45, to No.1 LD ('NN-N'); No.12 SLP ('DZ-6') from 15.2.46; LVA Military Air Academy ('A-712') 12.47; Wheels-up landing at Kunovice in 1948; Salvaged, stored; To Narodni Technicke Museum (National Technical Museum), Prague 22.2.50; Restored by the Aviation Historical Society and the Aero Vodochody aircraft factory 1966/67; To Military Museum, Prague-Kbely airport 1970 and displayed as "NN-N" - **SURVIVOR**

TE566 Spitfire LF.IXe (Merlin 66); TOC/RAF 15.6.45; No.312 Sqn from 3.8.45; Arr Czechoslovakia 13/24.8.45 – CzAF 30.8.45, to No.2 LD ('DU-A'); No.4 or 5 SLP from 15.2.46; LVA Military Air Academy ('A-7..') 12.47; Ceské Budejovice (LZ-2) in 1948; Later sold to Israel, delivered by ship 1948/49 (IDF/AF No *2032*); Extant, via UK to South Africa (Civil reg. *G-BLCK,* regd 22.11.83, to *ZU-SPT* 8.98) – **SURVIVOR**

TE567 Spitfire LF.IXe (Merlin 66); TOC/RAF 25.6.45; No.310 Sqn from 1.8.45; Arr Czechoslovakia 13/24.8.45 – CzAF 30.8.45, to No.1 LD ('NN-X'); No.10 (12) SLP from 15.2.46; Accident at Brno (LZ-3) 31.5.46; Repaired; LVA Military Air Academy ('A-7..') 1.48; VLU Research & Test Centre 1949; Later sold to Israel, delivered by ship 11.49

TE569 Spitfire LF.IXe (Merlin 66); TOC/RAF 18.6.45; No.313 Sqn from 20.7.45; Arr Czechoslovakia 13/24.8.45 – CzAF

30.8.45, to No.3 LD ('RY- '); No.7 or 8 SLP from 15.2.46; LVA Military Air Academy ('A-7.. '), crashed at Pardubice (LZ-5) 2.10.47; Repaired; Later sold to Israel, delivered by ship 1948/49

TE570 Spitfire LF.IXe (Merlin 66); TOC/RAF 12.6.45; No.313 Sqn from 25.7.45; Arr Czechoslovakia 13/24.8.45 – CzAF 30.8.45, to No.3 LD ('RY- '); No.7 SLP ('IV-8') from 15.2.46; Fatal crash at Brno in 9.46, Cat.E (wreck), SOC

TE571 Spitfire LF.IXe (Merlin 66); TOC/RAF 12.6.45; No.310 Sqn from 2.8.45; Arr Czechoslovakia 9.8.45 - CzAF 30.8.45, to No.1 LD ('NN- '); No.10 or 12 SLP from 15.2.46; Force-landed near Hloubetin in Prague district, Cat E in 1946 (Kapt Slouf), SOC

TE572 Spitfire LF.IXe (Merlin 66); TOC/RAF 15.6.45; No.310 Sqn from 2.8.45; Arr Czechoslovakia 9.8.45 - CzAF 30.8.45, to No.1 LD ('NN-U'); No.10 or 12 SLP from

Known markings of Spitfires in Czechoslovakia Air Force Fighter Units

No. 1 LD at Prague-Kbely; Unit code: "NN"

Code	Serial-No
NN-A	
NN-B	
NN-C	
NN-D	TE551
NN-E	
NN-F	
NN-G	TE513
NN-H	
NN-I	
NN-K	
NN-L	
NN-M	

Code	Serial-No
NN-N	TE565
NN-O	TE563
NN-P	
NN-Q	
NN-R	TE516
NN-S	
NN-T	SL655
NN-U	TE572
NN-V	
NN-W	
NN-X	TE567

Served with No. 1 LD, but codes unknown:
SL594; SL628; SL660; TE510; TE512; TE519; TE521; TE523; TE554; TE555; TE559; TE560; TE562; TE571.

Stihacy Letecky Pluk's (1.LD) from 15 February 1946

No. 10 SLP	
KR-1	TE523
KR-2	TE510
KR-3	
KR-4	TE521
KR-5	
KR-6	TE554
KR-7	SL662 ?
KR-8	
KR-9	
KR-10	
KR-11	
KR-12	

No. 12 SLP	
DZ-1	
DZ-2	
DZ-3	
DZ-4	
DZ-5	
DZ-6	TE565
DZ-7	TE560
DZ-8	
DZ-9	
DZ-10	
DZ-11	
DZ-12	

No. 2 LD at České Budějovice; Unit code: "DU"

Code	Serial-No
DU-A	TE566
DU-B	
DU-C	TE522
DU-D	TE575
DU-E	
DU-F	TE524
DU-G	SL654
DU-H	
DU-I	
DU-K	SL633
DU-L	SL625
DU-M	

Code	Serial-No
DU-N	SL627 ?
DU-O	
DU-P	
DU-Q	SL649
DU-R	SL626
DU-S	TE576
DU-T	
DU-U	SL650
DU-V	TE577
DU-W	TE515
DU-X	TE527

Served with No. 2 LD, but codes unknown:
MH758; NH174; SL631; SL632; SL634; SL648; SL653; SL656; TB439; TE518; TE578.

Stihacy Letecky Pluk's (2.LD) from 15 February 1946

No. 4 SLP	
JT-1	NH174
JT-2	TE522
JT-3	TE575
JT-4	SL632
JT-5	TE524
JT-6	
JT-7	
JT-8	SL654
JT-9	
JT-10	SL633
JT-11	SL625
JT-12	SL648

No. 5 SLP	
MP-1	TE518
MP-2	TE577
MP-3	TE578
MP-4	
MP-5	SL626
MP-6	SL649
MP-7	SL631
MP-8	
MP-9	SL653
MP-10	SL650
MP-11	
MP-12	

No. 3 LD at Brno; Unit code: "RY"

Code	Serial-No
RY-A	
RY-B	
RY-C	
RY-D	
RY-E	
RY-F	
RY-G	
RY-H	
RY-I	
RY-K	
RY-L	TE531
RY-M	

Code	Serial-No
RY-N	MJ752
RY-O	TE558
RY-P	
RY-Q	
RY-R	
RY-S	
RY-T	
RY-U	
RY-V	
RY-W	
RY-X	TE564
RY-Z	SL662

Stihacy Letecky Pluk's (3.LD) from 15 February 1946

No. 7 SLP	
IV-1	TE574
IV-2	TE517
IV-3	
IV-4	SL657
IV-5	
IV-6	SL629 ?
IV-7	MJ752
IV-8	TE570 ?
IV-9	PL250
IV-10	SL630
IV-11	
IV-12	

No. 8 SLP	
LS-1	SL664
LS-2	
LS-3	
LS-4	
LS-5	
LS-6	TE561
LS-7	TE564
LS-8	SL653
LS-9	
LS-10	
LS-11	
LS-12	

Served with No. 3 LD, but codes unknown:
MJ572; PL250; PT621; SL629; SL630; SL635; SL651; SL652; SL657; SL664; TE517; TE532; TE556; TE557; TE561; TE569; TE570; TE573; TE574.

15.2.46; Crashed at Prague-Kbely (LZ-1) 17.7.46; Repaired; Later sold to Israel; Operation *Velveta II* ferry flight, crashed in snowstorm over Yugoslavia 18.12.48 (wrecked), SOC

TE573 Spitfire LF.IXe (Merlin 66); TOC/RAF 12.6.45; ex No.310 Sqn; No.313 Sqn from 25.7.45; Arr Czechoslovakia 13/24.8.45 – CzAF 30.8.45, to No.3 LD ('RY- '); No.7 or 8 SLP from 15.2.46; Force-landed near Lomnice/Popelkou 3.12.46 (F/O V Truhlar); Repaired; VLU Research & Test Centre ('KO-1') in 1947; LVA Military Air Academy ('A-7..'), accident at Pardubice (LZ-5) 7.10.47; Repaired; LVA, crashed near Malacky 25.3.48; Repaired; Later sold to Israel, delivered by ship 1948/49

TE574 Spitfire LF.IXe (Merlin 66); TOC/RAF 22.6.45; No.313 Sqn from 19.7.45; Arr Czechoslovakia 13/24.8.45 – CzAF 30.8.45, to No.3 LD ('RY- '); No.7 SLP ('IV-1') from 15.2.46; LVA Military Air Academy ('A-7..') 12.47; Crashed near Novy Dvur 20.4.48; To Israel for spare parts 11.49

TE575 Spitfire LF.IXe (Merlin 66); TOC/RAF 20.6.45; No.312 Sqn from 1.8.45; Arr Czechoslovakia 13/24.8.45 – CzAF 30.8.45, to No.2 LD ('DU-D'); No.4 SLP ('JT-3') from 15.2.46; Later sold to Israel, delivered by ship 1948/49 (IDF/AF No *2035*)

TE576 Spitfire LF.IXe (Merlin 66); TOC/RAF 25.6.45; No.312 Sqn from 2.8.45; Arr Czechoslovakia 13/24.8.45 – CzAF 30.8.45, to No.2 LD ('DU-S'); No.4 or 5 SLP from 15.2.46; Ceské Budejovice (LZ-2) in 1948; LVA Military Air Academy ('A-7..') 1.48; Crashed near Chrudim 7.5.48; Repaired; Later sold to Israel, delivered by ship 1948/49

TE577 Spitfire LF.IXe (Merlin 66); TOC/RAF 25.6.45; No.312 Sqn from 3.8.45; Arr Czechoslovakia 13/24.8.45 – CzAF 30.8.45, to No.2 LD ('DU-V'); No.5 SLP ('MP-2') from 15.2.46; Accident at Ceské Budejovice (LZ-2) 4.9.46; Repaired; No.4 or 5 SLP in 10.46; Possibly LVA, crashed at Ceské Budejovice (LZ-2), Cat.E 2.12.47, SOC

TE578 Spitfire LF.IXe (Merlin 66); TOC/RAF 25.6.45; No.312 Sqn from 2.8.45; Arr Czechoslovakia 13/24.8.45 – CzAF 30.8.45, to No.2 LD ('DU- '); No.5 SLP ('MP-3') from 15.2.46; Crashed Bratislava 22.9.46; Repaired; No.5 SLP 10.46; Crashed Brno (LZ-3) 13.10.46; Repaired; Shown at Ceské Budejovice (LZ-2) in 1948; Later sold to Israel, delivered by ship 1948/49; Extant; now Hatzerim Museum near Beersheba - **SURVIVOR**

SURVIVORS

In the Czech Republic:
One Spitfire LF.IXe survived, this being TE565, which is currently exhibited in the National Technical Museum at Prague-Kbely, marked "NN-N".

Abroad:
ML119, Burma (*UB441*), via USA back to UK.
TE517, flyable in UK (*G-CCIX*).
TE554, Hatzerim Museum near Beersheba, Israel.
TE566, flyable in South-Africa (*ZU-SPT*, ex *G-BLCK*).
TE578, Hatzor, now Hatzerim Museum, Israel.
TE5.., Yangon, Burma (IDF/AF *2024*, *UB421*);
Unknown serial No, IDF/AF *2042*, *UB425*, now USA.

References:
Illustrovaná Historie Letectvi (Edice Triada).
Nase Vojsko, Prague (p.84).
Aeroplane Monthly, April 1995 (p.30).

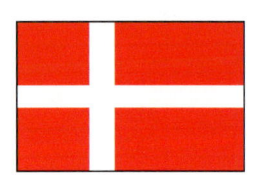

DENMARK

Denmark was invaded by German troops on 9th April 1940, and all Danish airfields were taken over by the German *Luftwaffe*. The situation on 5th May 1945, when the German forces in Denmark capitulated, was that cadres of the Army and Navy Air Forces existed but all training had ceased.

After World War II, Denmark received 48 Spitfires, comprising 38 HF.IXes, three PR.XIs, and a further four Mk.IXs as instructional airframes only, with an additional three Mk.IXs for spare parts. Spitfires served in Denmark from August 1947 to June 1955.

The PR.IXs were delivered under Comm.No 434 from 23rd August 1947 (PL794) and 18th September 1947 and the HF.IXe under Comm.No.320 from 25th October 1947 to 10th February 1949 (MK965 was the last), all ferry-flown to Denmark. The ground instructional airframes arrived by ship from 10th June 1948 to 30th July 1948, under Comm.No.326.

Vickers-Armstrongs test pilot Jeffrey Quill demonstrated the two-seat Mk.VIII (registered *G-ALJM*) in Denmark on 12th October 1949, but the Danish Government was not interested (and eventually this aircraft was sold to Egypt).

The first 25 Danish pilots were trained to fly Spitfires by the RAF during October 1945 to May 1946. Then their own 'Spitfire-Gruppen' (Navy) and the 'Spitfire-Skolen' (Army) in Denmark continued the training.

In February 1948 the Army and the Navy Technical Service (*AMS*) allotted new Danish serial numbers, consisting of a small two-digit aircraft type number and a three-digit individual number for each aircraft. The Spitfire HF.IXe was known as aircraft Type No.41 and the PR.XI as Type No.42.

The HF.IXes were serialled from **41-401** to **41-436** (less two which had crashed before the re-numbering), and the PR.XIs received Nos.**42-451** to **42-453**.

The ground-instructional airframes became **FMSm1** to **FMSm4**.

Spitfire units in Denmark

Marinens Flyvevæsen (Naval Air Service)

Spitfire-Gruppen (Spitfire-Flight) at Kastrup airport, Copenhagen, from 23rd August 1947 to 10th July 1948. The first Spitfire-unit (Reception-unit), founded with PL794, used Spitfire HF.IXe and PR.XI. Later the unit was absorbed into No.2 Luftflotille; Repair and storage then by the Danish Air Material Service (*AMS*) at Værløse.
Commanding Officer:
Lt Cdr KCJ Pedersen, RDN

No.2 Luftflotille ("**2.LF**") at Kastrup airport, Copenhagen, comprised several Flights, also a PR Flight with Spitfire PR.XI from 8th June 1948, and a Fighter Flight with Spitfire HF.IXe from 10th July 1948. The service of this unit continued until 4th January 1950, but from July 1949 the first Spitfires went to No.4 Esk of the Army Air Force.

Commanding Officer:
Capt KCJ Petersen 8.6.48
Unknown 4.1.50
Capt W Lonsdale 1.12.50 until 7.2.51

Hærens Flyvertropper (Army Air Force)

Spitfire-School ("Spitfire-Skolen") at Karup Air Base, used Spitfire HF.IXe from 15th January 1948 to 2nd April 1948. The School was absorbed into the No.5 Esk, although it still retained its separate name until autumn 1948.
Commanding Officer:
First Lt HGP Jensen

No.**1** Esk ("**1 Eskadrille**") at Værløse Air Base, used a few Spitfire HF.IXe for a short period from 1st March 1949 to 30th June 1949, until No.4 Esk was formed.
Commanding Officer:
Capt NVH de Meza von Holstein-Ratlou

No.**4** Esk ("**4 Eskadrille**") at Værløse Air Base, from 1st July 1949 to 19th January 1951 as a Fighter unit, comprised several Flights, including one with Spitfire HF.IXe, and from July 1949 also a PR Flight with Spitfire PR.XI from No.2 Luftflotille.
Commanding Officers:
Capt NVH de Meza von Holstein-Ratlou (until 28.9.49)
Capt G Bouet 1949/50
First Lt POHM Stilling 1950/51

No.**5** Esk ("**5 Eskadrille**") at Karup Air Base, exist from 21st January 1948, became a Fighter unit with Spitfire HF.IXe from 1st April 1948 to 7th February 1951, incorporated the Spitfire-School.
Commanding Officer:
Capt AH Joergensen

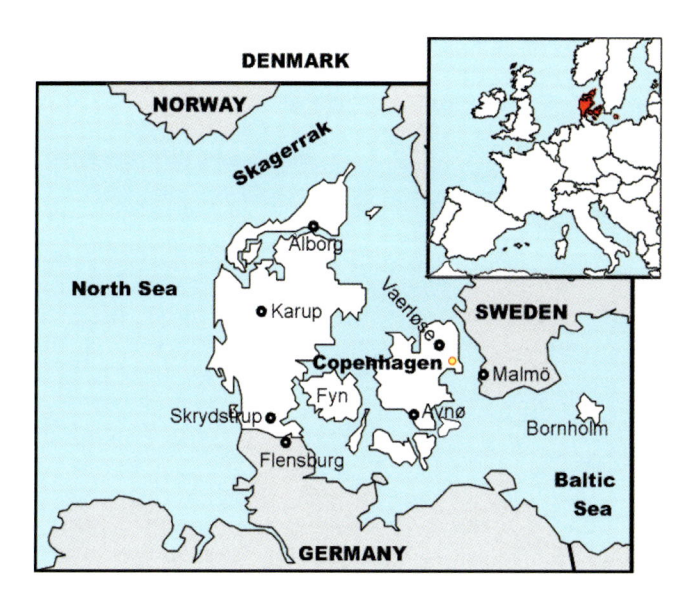

Flyvevåbnet (Royal Danish Air Force)

Law No.242 of 27th May 1950 ordered the formation of the Flyvevåbnet (Royal Danish Air Force) on 1st October 1950 by merging the Army Air Force and the Naval Air Service. The Chief of Defence issued Announcement B.2-1951, dated 8th February 1951, which authorised various unit changes and NATO designations as follows:

● No.2 Luftflotille & No.5 Esk to be disbanded;

● No.4 Esk to be disbanded and material to No.722 ESK;

● No.722 ESK to be formed with material from No.4 Esk;

● No.725 ESK to be formed with Spitfires, until the introduction of F-84G jets.

No.**722** ESK ("**Eskadrille 722**") at Værløse airfield, with Spitfire HF.IXe from 8th February 1951 to 31st May 1955, comprised several flights, also a PR Flight with Spitfire PR.XI of the former No.4 Esk (also an Oxford Flight, a Harvard Flight etc), and later a Training Flight with five Spitfire HF.IX (armament removed) from No.725 ESK from 16th October 1951; Last SOC on 1st June 1955.
Commanding Officers:
First Lt POHM Stilling 8.51
Capt PE Rye-Hansen 1.7.51
Capt GL Reimer 29.12.52
Capt E Moeller 1.2.54
Capt GL Reimer 1.12.54

No.**725** ESK ("**Eskadrille 725**"), initially a fighter OCU at Karup airfield, used Spitfire HF.IXe for a short time as a stop-gap, from 18th May 1951 to 30th September 1951 as the unit was to become the first jet fighter squadron of the RDanAF from 1st October 1951. Then nine of the Spitfires were struck off charge, the remainder being flown on 16th/17th October 1951 to Air Material Service (*AMS*) at Værløse, where they were placed in storage and later scrapped. Only five of the Spitfires went to No.722 ESK, but with weapons removed.
Commanding Officers:
Lt NK Dansing 18.5.51
Capt N Holst-Soerensen 24.6.51

Remarks:
Originally the Danish Air Force named the Spitfire units as "1 Eskadrille" (1 Esk), "4 Eskadrille" (4 Esk) and "5 Eskadrille" (5 Esk). From 1951 the new units were called "Eskadrille 722" (ESK 722) and "Eskadrille 725" (ESK 725).
Navy units were named "Luftflotille" and the Army related units "Eskadrille", both independent flying units below wing level. The term "Eskadre" relates to a Naval fighter squadron.

Flyvemekanikerskolen (School of Technical Training, SoTT)

At Værløse airfield from 30th July 1948. Received four Spitfire Mk.IX airframes, FMSm1 to FMSm4, for training of the ground crews. A further three airframes may have been used for training or spares.
Commanding Officers:
Lt Col PN Brandt-Moeller 5.3.47
Col O Petersen 17.12.51 to 24.3.55

Repair & Storage

This was undertaken by the Danish Air Material Service (*AMS*), later Air Material Command (*AMC*), at Værløse and Karup.
Commanding Officer:
Chief Engineer P Orm Hansen
(later Major General from 1951)

The end of the Spitfire in Denmark

On 31st May 1955 five Spitfires of No.722 ESK (two HF.IX and three PR.XI) made a farewell flight over Værløse. Then the last Danish Spitfires were officially SOC on 1st June 1955 (w/o 17th June 1955) and scrapped. None were sold to other countries. Three went to children playgrounds for some time and were later scrapped. Only one survived.

The Danish Spitfires amassed a total service time of 10,093 flying hours.

Individual Histories

BS248 Spitfire F.IXc (Merlin 61); TOC/RAF 10.42; Converted to GI No. *6516M* - Via No.47 MU shipped from Hull docks to Denmark 16.6.48; Arr Copenhagen 18.6.48; Danish Material Service (AMS) at Værløse 23.6.48; Probably used for spare parts

BS386 Spitfire F.IXc (Merlin 61); TOC/RAF 10.42; Converted to GI No. *6517M* - Via No.47 MU shipped from Hull docks

Surviving Spitfire LF.IXc MA298 during an Open Day at Skrydstrup Air Base on 29th May 1988. It had been sold to Denmark as a ground instructional airframe and numbered FMSm.4, being later retained as a display aircraft with the spurious marking "401".

   to Denmark 8.6.48; Arr Copenhagen 10.6.48; AMS at Værløse 6.48; Probably used for spare parts
LA305 Spitfire F.21; Converted to GI No.*6368M* 10.7.47; Allotted for Denmark 15.7.47, but cancelled 11.8.47; Converted to GI No. *6411M* on 16.8.47 for RAF Melksham, Wiltshire (No 12 SoTT); Scrapped 24.5.54
MA298 Spitfire LF.IXc (Merlin 66); TOC/RAF 27.5.43; Converted to GI No. *6462M*; Became Danish GI No. **FMSm4** - Via No.47 MU shipped from Hull docks to Denmark 20.7.48; Arr Copenhagen 22.7.48; AMS at Værløse 28.7.48; SoTT at Værløse 30.7.48; AMS from 14.4.51; Storage in Tojhuesmuseet Copenhagen (c.1955 with Merlin 70); Loaned Danish Technical Museum, Elsinore for display 1975; To RDAF Historical Section, stored Værløse AFB 1978; Loaned Egeskov Veteranmuseum, Kvaerndrup/Fyn 1982 (painted as "NH417" at one time); Center Mobilium at Billund (Flymuseum Jutland) as "41-401" from 1989; Loaned Danmarks Flyvemuseum, Billund 1993; Storage at Stauning 1998 – **SURVIVOR**
MA803 Spitfire F.IXc (Merlin 63); TOC/RAF 24.7.43; Converted to GI No. *6458M* - Via No.47 MU shipped from Hull docks to Denmark 20.7.48; Arr Copenhagen 22.7.48; AMS at Værløse 28.7.48; Probably used for spare parts
MH450 Spitfire LF.IXc (Merlin 66); TOC/RAF 15.8.43; Converted to GI No. *6461M*; Became Danish GI No. **FMSm3** - Via No.47 MU shipped from Hull docks to Denmark 20.7.48; Arr Copenhagen 22.7.48; AMS at Værløse 28.7.48; SoTT at Værløse 30.7.48; Later SOC, scrapped
MJ329 Spitfire LF.IXc; Converted to GI No. *6370M*; Allotted for Denmark 15.7.47, but cancelled 24.9.47; To No 34 MU in 10.47, scrapped 13.10.47
MK426 Spitfire LF.IXc (Merlin 66); TOC/RAF 25.2.44; Converted to GI No. *6459M*; Became Danish GI No. **FMSm1** - Via No.47 MU shipped from Hull docks to Denmark 20.7.48; Arr Copenhagen 22.7.48; AMS at Værløse 28.7.48; SoTT at Værløse 30.7.48; Later SOC, scrapped
MK681 Spitfire HF.IXe (Merlin 70); Became No.**41-404**; TOC/RAF 28.3.44; Collected and desp. to Denmark 27.10.48, arr Kastrup airport 27.10.48; No.5 Esk in 11.48; AMS storage 5.49; No.4 Esk 1.7.49; AMS Major inspection 11.49 (213 flying hours); Collided with Spitfire 41-412 (PT907) over Arresoe 24.7.50 [Micky Mouse emblem "Pluto" on the cowling] (Lt HJ Corfitzen); AMS for repair 7.50; SOC in 1950 (411 flying hours); Scrapped
MK694 Spitfire HF.IXe (Merlin 70); Became No.**41-405**; TOC/RAF 30.3.44; Collected and desp. to Denmark 12.1.49, arr Kastrup airport 12.1.49; No.5 Esk 12.1.49; No.4 Esk 18.10.50; AMS storage 8.1.51; SOC 13.4.51; Scrapped
MK965 Spitfire HF.IXe (Merlin 70); Became No.**41-406**; TOC/RAF 13.4.44; Collected 8.2.49, desp. to Denmark 10.2.49 (the last delivery batch), arr Kastrup airport 10.2.49; AMS storage 15.2.49; To No.5 Esk in 3.49; Landing accident at Karup 1.4.49 (2/Lt NK Dansing); Engine failure, oil in the cockpit 30.8.49 (2/Lt NK Dansing); AMS at Karup for storage 16.1.51; SOC 13.4.51; AMS at Vaerløse for storage 4.5.51; Scrapped
ML345 Spitfire LF.IXc (Merlin 66); TOC/RAF 28.4.44; Converted to GI No. *6460M*; Became Danish GI No. **FMSm2** - Via No.47 MU shipped from Hull docks to Denmark 27.7.48; Arr Copenhagen 30.7.48; AMS at Værløse 8.48; SoTT at Værløse 8.48; Later SOC, scrapped
NH417 Spitfire HF.IXe (Merlin 70); Became No.**41-401**; TOC/RAF 20.5.44; Collected and desp. to Denmark 12.1.49 – Arr. Kastrup airport, but crashed on landing, undercarriage collapsed 12.1.49 (Lt PB Nissen of No.2 Luftflotille); AMS at Værløse for repair 1.49 (clipped wings replaced by elliptical wings); No.4 Esk 1.7.49; Crashed on landing, collided with ground obstacle at Kastrup 22.4.50 (Lt Aa H Dolleris); Lost exhaust pipe 18.9.50 (Capt G Bouet); To AMS storage 8.1.51; SOC 13.4.51
NOTE: Later reported to be the Survivor - but see MA298
NH478 Spitfire HF.IXe (Merlin 70); Became No.**41-402**; TOC/RAF 23.5.44; Collected and desp. to Denmark 12.1.49 – Arr Kastrup airport 12.1.49; To No.5 Esk 12.1.49; Propeller and engine damaged 28.7.49 (2/Lt HU Darket); AMS at Værløse for repair 2.9.49 (147 flying hours); Belly-landed during test flight 20.4.50 (1/Lt

POHM Stilling); No.4 Esk 26.7.50; AMS storage 8.1.51; No.725 ESK (OCU) 18.5.51; AMS storage 12.10.51; SOC 1.9.52 (314 flying hours); Scrapped

NH582 Spitfire HF.IXe (Merlin 70); Became No.**41-403**; TOC/RAF 6.6.44; Collected 6.7.48, desp to Denmark 8.7.48, arr Værløse 8.7.48 (106 flying hours); AMS storage 13.7.48; To No.5 Esk 2.8.48; Engine failure 22.1.49 (2/Lt F Kofod-Jensen); AMS at Karup for storage 16.1.51; No.725 ESK (OCU) 23.5.51; AMS at Værløse for storage 12.10.51; SOC 1.9.52 (367 flying hours); Scrapped

PL256 Spitfire HF.IXe; Converted to GI No. *6371M* on 10.7.47; Allotted for Denmark 15.7.47, but cancelled 24.9.47; To No.34 MU 8.10.47, scrapped

PL375 Spitfire HF.IXe (Merlin 70); Became No.**41-407**; TOC/RAF 21.6.44; Collected 8.2.49, desp to Denmark 10.2.49 (the last delivery batch), arr Kastrup airport 10.2.49; To No.2 Luftflotille 10.2.49; AMS storage 2.49; No.1 Esk 3.49; No.4 Esk 1.7.49; AMS Major inspection 6.50 (281 flying hours); AMS storage 11.50; No.722 ESK 8.2.51; No.725 ESK (OCU) 18.6.51; AMS storage 16.10.51 (391 flying hours); No.722 ESK from 3.53 (as flying trainer, armament removed); Crashed at Karup, tipped on nose 23.8.53 (Lt R Riisager); Made farewell flight over Værløse 31.5.55; SOC 1.6.55 (482 flying hours); Scrapped

PL392 Spitfire HF.IXe (Merlin 70); Became No.**41-408**; TOC/RAF 24.6.44; Collected 22.3.48, desp to Denmark 23.3.48, arr Kastrup airport 6.4.48 (194 flying hours); To No.5 Esk 7.4.48; AMS at Karup for inspection (260 flying hours); AMS Karup storage 10.50; No.725 ESK (OCU) 18.5.51; Crashed in the skirt of Ringsted, Cat.E 22.9.51 (Lt HJ Brasch); SOC 24.9.51

PL794 Spitfire PR.XI (Merlin 70); Became No.**42-451**; TOC/RAF 18.4.44; Collected 18.8.47, desp. to Denmark 23.8.47, arr Kastrup Airport 23.8.47 (the first Spitfire of Denmark); Spitfire-Gruppen 29.8.47; PR-Flight 8.6.48; No.2 Luftflotille 10.7.48; Landed at Værløse tailwheel retracted, date unknown (Capt PKR Joergensen); No.4 Esk 4.1.50; No.722 ESK (PR-Flight) 8.2.51; AMS Major inspection 10.52 (247 flying hours); No.722 ESK 3.53; Made farewell flight over Værløse 31.5.55; SOC 1.6.55 (w/o 17.6.55; 355 flying hours); Scrapped

PL833 Spitfire PR.XI (Merlin 70); Became No.**42-452**; TOC/RAF 8.5.44; Collected 12.9.47, desp. to Denmark 12.9.47, arr Kastrup airport 18.9.47; To Spitfire-Gruppen 18.9.47; PR-Flight 8.6.48; No.2 Luftflotille 10.7.48; No.4 Esk 4.1.50; No.722 ESK (PR-Flt) 8.2.51; Made farewell flight over Værløse 31.5.55; SOC 1.6.55 (w/o 17.6.55; 292 flying hours); Scrapped

PM134 Spitfire PR.XI (Merlin 70); Became No.**42-453**; TOC/RAF 24.12.44; RAF Pershore, collected 18.8.47, desp. to Denmark 12.9.47, arr Kastrup airport 18.9.47; To Spitfire-Gruppen 18.9.47; Spitfire-School 15.1.48; PR-Flight 8.6.48; No.2 Luftflotille 10.7.48; No.4 Esk 4.1.50; No.722 ESK (PR-Flt) 8.2.51; AMS Major inspection 7.52

Spitfire HF.IXe 41-407 (ex PL375) of Eskadrille 725 at Karup in 1951.
[via R C Jones]

Spitfire PR.XI No.42-453 (RAF Serial No. PM134) of the RDanAF. This aircraft served with the PR-Flight of No.2 Luftflotille (Navy) at Kastrup and later with No.4 Eskadrille. Note the round windows on the belly and provision for two vertical cameras. The window on the top fuselage behind the cockpit was for a third (but oblique) camera. The bulges under the wing leading edges (in front of the wheels and radiators) housed the pumps for the wing tanks (each 66 gallons).
[Royal Danish Air Force]

PT463 Spitfire HF.IXe (Merlin 70); Became No.**41-409**; TOC/RAF 20.7.44; Collected 16.3.48, desp to Denmark 19.3.48, arr Kastrup airport 23.3.48; AMS Værløse for storage 24.3.48; No.5 Esk 2.4.48; AMS inspection 11.48 (286 flying hours); No.5 Esk 9.12.48; AMS Major inspection 19.12.49 (488 flying hours); No.5 Esk 8.5.50; No.4 Esk 19.10.50 (561 flying hours); AMS storage 8.1.51; No.725 ESK (OCU) 18.5.51; AMS at Karup 24.5.51 (for replacement of wings and engine), but SOC 21.6.51 (571 flying hours); AMS Karup storage; Scrapped 16.10.51

PT714 Spitfire HF.IXe (Merlin 70); Became No.**41-410**; TOC/RAF 9.8.44; Collected 21.9.48, desp to Denmark 22.9.48, arr Kastrup airport 22.9.48; AMS Værløse storage 29.9.48 (138 flying hours); No.5 Esk 12.10.48; Undercarriage collapsed at Karup 5.8.49 (2/Lt JA Termoehlen); AMS Karup 24.8.49; AMS Værløse repair 16.9.49 (257 flying hours); No.5 Esk 11.5.50; AMS storage 7.50; No.725 ESK (OCU) 18.5.51; AMS storage 11.10.51 (415 flying hours); No.722 ESK 12.52; SOC 20.8.54 (458 flying hours); Scrapped

PT888 Spitfire HF.IXe (Merlin 70); Became No.**41-411**; TOC/RAF 25.8.44; Collected 8.2.49, desp to Denmark 10.2.49 (the last delivery batch), arr Kastrup airport 10.2.49; To No.5 Esk 10.2.49; AMS storage 7.50 (321 flying hours); No.725 ESK (OCU) 18.6.51; AMS storage 15.10.51; No.722 ESK 4.52; AMS storage 5.52; SOC 2.5.52 (433 flying hours); Scrapped

PT907 Spitfire HF.IXe (Merlin 70); Became No.**41-412**; TOC/RAF 24.8.44; RAF Pershore, collected 23.10.47, desp. to Denmark 24.10.47, arr Kastrup airport 26.10.47 (79 flying hours); Spitfire-Gruppen 26.10.47; Spitfire-School 19.1.48; No.5 Esk 3.4.48; AMS Karup inspection 27.4.48 (124 flying hours); No.5 Esk 4.10.48; No.4 Esk 1.7.49; Collided with Spitfire 41-404 (MK681) over Arresoe 24.7.50 [had a "Micky Mouse" emblem on the cowling; 331 flying hours] (Lt KF Jensen); SOC 31.10.50; Scrapped

PT931 Spitfire HF.IXe (Merlin 70); Became No.**41-413**; TOC/RAF 26.8.44; Collected 6.7.48, desp to Denmark 8.7.48, arr Kastrup airport 8.7.48; AMS storage 13.7.48 (126 flying hours); No.5 Esk 8.48; No.4 Esk 1.7.49; Dived into the water of Oeresund, Cat.E 24.9.49 (Capt NVH de Meza von Holstein-Ratlou); SOC 21.11.49

PV296 Spitfire HF.IXe (Merlin 70); Became No.**41-414**; TOC/RAF 25.9.44; Collected 1.10.48, desp to Denmark 2.10.48, arr AMS at Værløse 2.10.48 (181 flying hours); No.5 Esk 11.48; AMS Karup for storage 16.1.51; SOC 13.4.51; Flown to AMS Værløse for storage 4.5.51; Scrapped

PV303 Spitfire HF.IXe (Merlin 70); Became No.**41-415**; TOC/RAF 3.10.44; Collected 17.11.48, desp to Denmark 20.11.48, arr Kastrup airport 20.11.48; To No.2 Luftflotille 20.11.48; No.5 Esk 12.48; AMS Karup 21.12.48 (engine change); No.5 Esk 11.3.49; AMS storage 11.49; No.5 Esk 24.4.50; No.4 Esk 18.10.50; Crashed, brake failure, tipped on nose 6.12.50 (Lt PS Soerensen); To AMS 7.12.50, storage 8.1.51; No.725 ESK (OCU) 18.5.51; AMS storage 11.10.51; SOC 1.9.52 (489 flying hours); To a playground in Værløse; Removed; Scrapped

PV304 Spitfire HF.IXe (Merlin 70); Became No.**41-416**; TOC/RAF 30.9.44; Collected 12.1.49, desp. to Denmark 12.1.49 – Arr Kastrup airport 12.1.49; No.2 Luftflotille 12.1.49; No.4 Esk 4.1.50; AMS storage 8.1.51; No.725 ESK (OCU) 18.5.51; AMS storage 15.10.51; SOC 2.5.52 (367 flying hours); Scrapped

PV344 Spitfire HF.IXe (Merlin 70); Became No.**41-417**; TOC/RAF 2.10.44; Collected 26.10.48, desp to Denmark 28.10.48, arr Kastrup airport 28.10.48; No.5 Esk 1.11.48; No.4 Esk 18.10.50; AMS storage 8.1.51; SOC 13.4.51; Scrapped

PV354 Spitfire HF.IXe (Merlin 70); Became No.**41-418**; TOC/RAF 29.9.44; Collected 26.10.48, desp to Denmark 28.10.48, arr Kastrup airport 28.10.48; No.5 Esk 1.11.48; AMS Karup for Major inspection 9.50 (390 flying hours); AMS Karup storage; No.725 ESK (OCU) 4.6.51; Belly-landed at Karup 25.6.51 (Lt T Rasmussen); AMS Karup repair 26.6.51; No.725 ESK (OCU) 21.8.51; AMS storage 11.10.51; SOC 1.9.52 (433 flying hours); Scrapped

RK811 Spitfire HF.IXe (Merlin 70); Became No.**41-419**; TOC/RAF 16.9.44; Collected 21.9.48, desp to Denmark 22.9.48, arr Kastrup airport 22.9.48; AMS storage 29.9.48 (160 flying hours); No.5 Esk 11.10.48; Bird strike 2.2.49 (2/Lt F Kofod-Jensen); AMS Karup for replacement of left

Spitfire HF.IXe 41-419 (ex RK811) in formation with 41-422 (ex RR252), probably with No.5 Eskadrille, Karup, around 1949.

Spitfire HF.IXe 41-422 (ex RR252) of No.5 Eskadrille, Karup, on the ground. It has the small aircraft type number "41" above the serial on the rear fuselage. The figure on the cowling indicated service with No.5 Eskadrille. [Royal Danish Air Force]

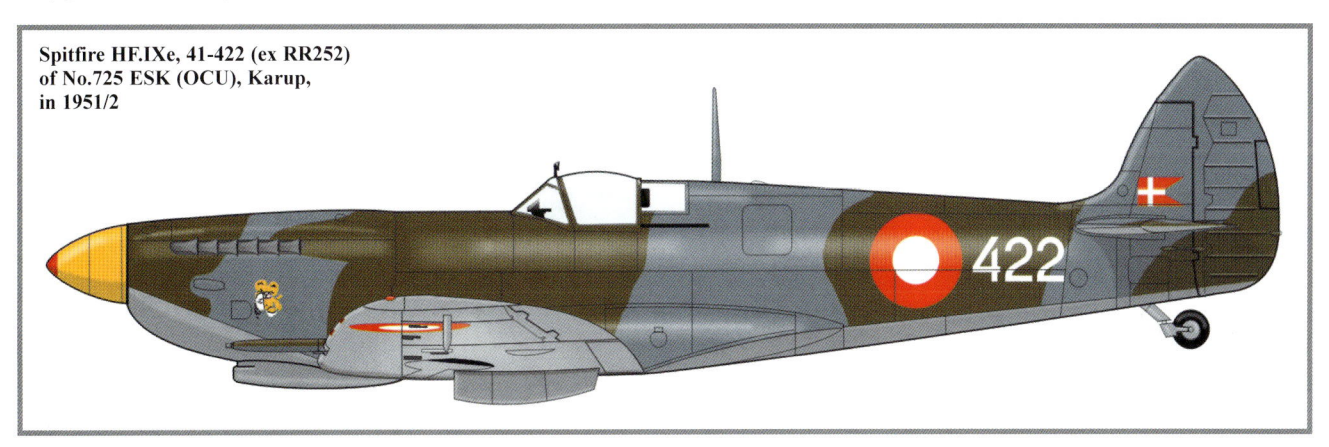

Spitfire HF.IXe, 41-422 (ex RR252) of No.725 ESK (OCU), Karup, in 1951/2

      wing 2.2.49; No.5 Esk 4.3.49; Crashed after take-off from Skrydstrup, force-landed wheels up 2 km from airbase, fuselage broken, Cat.E 27.2.50 (Lt NK Dansing); SOC 18.4.50 (378 flying hours); Scrapped

RK889 Spitfire HF.IXe (Merlin 70); Became No.**41-420**; TOC/RAF 6.10.44; Collected 1.10.48, desp to Denmark 2.10.48, arr AMS at Værløse 2.10.48 (57 flying hours); No.5 Esk 26.10.48; AMS for Major inspection 28.1.50 (199 flying hours); No.5 Esk 16.5.50; AMS for Major inspection 9.50 (299 flying hours); AMS storage 16.1.51; No.725 ESK (OCU) 17.9.51; AMS Værløse storage 12.10.51; No.722 ESK 3.52 (as flying trainer, armament removed); Engine failure, force-landed at Roenne 9.10.54; Crashed at Roenne, Cat.E 20.10.54 (both Capt E Moeller); SOC 5.11.54 (402 flying hours); To a playground in Roenne 5.1.55; Later removed and scrapped

RK911 Spitfire HF.IXe (Merlin 70); None RDanAF Serial No; TOC/RAF 12.10.44; Collected and desp to Denmark 19.3.48, arr Kastrup airport 23.3.48; AMS storage 24.3.48 (174 flying hours); No.5 Esk 2.4.48; AMS Minor inspection 1.8.48 (230 flying hours); No.5 Esk 9.11.48; Crashed near Ikast, Cat E 12.1.49 (2/Lt AL Joergensen); SOC 23.6.49 (264 flying hours)

RR209 Spitfire HF.IXe (Merlin 70); Became No.**41-421**; TOC/RAF 14.10.44; Collected 26.10.48, desp to Denmark 28.10.48, arr Kastrup airport 28.10.48; No.2 Luftflotille 1.11.48; High speed hack aircraft from 2.50; No.4 Esk 10.50; AMS storage 8.2.51; No.725 ESK (OCU) 18.5.51; AMS storage 12.10.51; SOC 1.9.52 (277 flying hours); Scrapped

RR252 Spitfire HF.IXe (Merlin 70); Became No.**41-422**; TOC/RAF 19.10.44; Collected and desp to Denmark 12.3.48, arr Kastrup airport 12.3.48 (161 flying hours); AMS storage 17.3.48; No.5 Esk 1.4.48; SoTT Værløse 24.5.48 (180 flying hours); No.5 Esk 24.2.49; AMS Major inspection 11.50 (382 flying hours); AMS storage 4.51; No.725 ESK (OCU) 30.5.51; AMS storage 12.10.51; SOC 1.9.52 (508 flying hours); Scrapped

SM190 Spitfire LF.XVIe (Merlin 266); TOC/RAF 30.10.44; ex No 403 Sqn; AM (PR.8); No.403 R&SU 6.9.45 (for preparation of a display in Denmark); Ground accident Cat.E 13.10.45; To No.151 RU (fate unknown)

TA812 Spitfire HF.IXe (Merlin 70); Became No.**41-423**; TOC/RAF 11.12.44; Collected 1.10.48, desp to Denmark 2.10.48, arr AMS at Værløse 2.10.48 (60 flying hours); No.5 Esk 26.10.48; Crashed at Holstebro, Cat E 15.11.49 (2/Lt HVB Jensen); SOC 21.11.49 (259 flying hours); Scrapped

TA813 Spitfire HF.IXe (Merlin 70); Became No.**41-424**; TOC/RAF 11.12.44; Collected 17.11.48, desp to Denmark 20.11.48, arr Kastrup airport 20.11.48; No.2 Luftflotille 25.11.48; Crashed at Roenne, into soft ground, tipped on nose 31.8.49 (Lt SG Petersen); Went off runway at Kastrup 4.10.49 (Lt LF Hansen); AMS repair 10.49; No.2

Spitfire HF.IXe TE296 before being reserialled 41-436. [MAP]

Luftflotille 12.49; Crashed at Koege, Cat E 15.2.50 (Lt BE Amled); SOC 18.4.50 (221 flying hours); Used for fire fighting training

TB256 Spitfire LF.XVIe (Merlin 266); TOC/RAF 30.12.44; Allotted for RDanAF 15.7.47, but cancelled 11.8.47; Converted to GI No.*6412M* for RAF on 18.8.47

TB564 Spitfire HF.IXe (Merlin 70); Became No.**41-425**; TOC/RAF 4.2.45; Collected 26.10.48, desp to Denmark 28.10.48, arr Kastrup airport 28.10.48; No.2 Luftflotille 1.11.48; No.4 Esk 29.9.49; AMS storage 8.2.51; No.725 ESK (OCU) 26.5.51; AMS storage 16.10.51; SOC 1.9.52 (386 flying hours); Scrapped

TB570 Spitfire HF.IXe (Merlin 70); Became No.**41-426**; TOC/RAF 4.2.45; Collected 1.10.48, desp to Denmark 2.10.48, arr AMS at Værløse 2.10.48 (159 flying hours); No.5 Esk 26.10.48; AMS Major inspection 9.50 (405 flying hours); AMS storage 5.51; No.722 ESK 4.52 (as flying trainer, armament removed); SOC 20.8.54 (506 flying hours); w/o 22.10.54; Scrapped

TB584 Spitfire HF.IXe (Merlin 70); None RDanAF Serial No; TOC/RAF 10.2.45; Collected and desp to Denmark 28.5.48, arr Kastrup airport 29.5.48, Spitfire Gruppen; AMS storage 31.5.48 (110 flying hours); No.5 Esk 3.6.48; Crashed at Bjerringbro, Cat E on 5.1.49 (2/Lt AS Lygum); SOC 15.1.49; w/o 23.6.49

TB845 Spitfire HF.IXe (Merlin 70); Became No.**41-427**; TOC/RAF 27.2.45; Collected 28.9.48, desp to Denmark 29.9.48, arr Kastrup airport 29.9.48; No.2 Luftflotille 10.48; No.4 Esk 21.9.49; Belly-landed at Værløse 28.12.49 (Capt HOCL Tonnesen); AMS repair 29.12.49; No.4 Esk 15.4.50; AMS Major inspection 8.50; AMS storage 3.51; SOC 1.9.52 (292 flying hours); Scrapped

TD355 Spitfire HF.IXe (Merlin 70); Became No.**41-428**; TOC/RAF 29.3.45; Collected and desp to Denmark 23.10.47, arr Kastrup airport 25.10.47; Spitfire-Gruppen 26.10.47; Spitfire-School 15.1.48; No.2 Luftflotille 10.7.48; Crashed at Roenne, into soft ground, tipped on nose 31.8.49 (Lt CS Boergesen); No.4 Esk 4.1.50; AMS storage 8.2.51; SOC 13.4.51; Scrapped

TD356 Spitfire HF.IXe (Merlin 70); Became No.**41-429**; TOC/RAF 30.3.45; Collected 23.10.47, desp to Denmark 24.10.47, arr Værløse 25.10.47; Spitfire-Gruppen 1.11.47; Spitfire-School 15.1.48; No.5 Esk 8.5.48 (14 flying hours); Crashed during landing at Karup 9.9.49 (2/Lt BE Amled); AMS repair 23.9.49; AMS storage 5.51; No.725 ESK (OCU) 30.6.51; AMS storage 15.10.51; SOC 1.9.52 (229 flying hours); Scrapped

TD362 Spitfire HF.IXe (Merlin 70); Became No.**41-430**; TOC/RAF 5.4.45; Collected 21.9.48; desp to Denmark 22.9.48, arr Kastrup airport 22.9.48; No.2 Luftflotille 10.48; No.4 Esk 4.1.50; AMS Major inspection 2.50 (290 flying hours); No.4 Esk 2.6.50; AMS storage 8.1.51; No.725 ESK (OCU) 22.5.51; Crashed, undercarriage

Check list of Danish / British Serial Nos

Danish Serials	RAF Serials	Arr.DK	Danish Serials	RAF Serials	Arr.DK
Spitfire HF.IXe					
41-401	NH417	12.1.49	41-420	RK889	2.10.48
41-402	NH478	12.1.49	41-421	RR209	28.10.48
41-403	NH582	8.7.48	41-422	RR252	12.3.48
41-404	MK681	27.10.48	41-423	TA812	2.10.48
41-405	MK694	12.1.49	41-424	TA813	20.11.48
41-406	MK965	10.2.49	41-425	TB564	28.10.48
41-407	PL375	10.2.49	41-426	TB570	2.10.48
41-408	PL392	6.4.48	41-427	TB845	29.9.48
41-409	PT463	23.3.48	41-428	TD355	25.10.47
41-410	PT714	22.9.48	41-429	TD356	25.10.47
41-411	PT888	10.2.49	41-430	TD362	22.9.48
41-412	PT907	26.10.47	41-431	TD367	29.9.48
41-413	PT931	8.7.48	41-432	TE197	22.3.48
41-414	PV296	2.10.48	41-433	TE231	23.3.48
41-415	PV303	20.11.48	41-434	TE233	29.5.48
41-416	PV304	12.1.49	41-435	TE236	13.3.48
41-417	PV344	28.10.48	41-436	TE296	29.5.48
41-418	PV354	28.10.48	---	RK911	23.3.48
41-419	RK811	22.9.48	---	TB584	29.5.48
Spitfire PR.XI					
42-451	PL794	23.8.47			
42-452	PL833	18.9.47	for PR-Flight		
42-453	PM134	18.9.47			

Ground-Instructional airframes (SoTT Værløse)			
6459M	MK426	22.7.48	RDanAF No. FMSm1
6460M	ML345	30.7.48	RDanAF No. FMSm2
6461M	MH450	22.7.48	RDanAF No. FMSm3
6462M	MA298	22.7.48	RDanAF No. FMSm4
For spare parts:			
6516M	BS248	18.6.48	AMS Værløse
6517M	BS386	10.6.48	AMS Værløse
6458M	MA803	22.7.48	AMS Værløse

collapsed 6.6.51; AMS Karup repair 7.6.51; No.725 ESK (OCU) 21.9.51; AMS storage 16.10.51 (386 flying hours); No.722 ESK 3.53 (as flying trainer, armament removed); Crashed, tipped on nose 19.4.55 (Lt K Aa Holst); Farewell flight over Værløse 31.5.55; SOC 1.6.55 (485 flying hours); w/o 17.6.55; To a playground in Virum in 1956; To a playground in Værløse in 1961; Removed in 1965; Scrapped ca.1966

TD367 Spitfire HF.IXe (Merlin 70); Became No.**41-431**; TOC/RAF 31.3.45; Collected and desp to Denmark 29.9.48, arr Kastrup airport 29.9.48; No.2 Luftflotille 10.48; Crashed at Avnoe, tipped on nose 23.5.49 (VC K R Ramberg); No.4 Esk 19.1.50; Collided with high-voltage lines 3.4.50 (2/Lt BE Amled); AMS storage 11.50; No.725 ESK (OCU) 18.5.51; AMS storage 16.10.51; SOC 1.9.52 (292 flying hours); Scrapped

TE197 Spitfire HF.IXe (Merlin 70); Became No.**41-432**; TOC/RAF 16.5.45; Collected 16.3.48, desp to Denmark 19.3.48, arr Kastrup airport 22.3.48; Spitfire-Gruppen 23.3.48; No.2 Luftflotille 10.7.48; Bird strike 11.5.49 (Capt CF Soerensen); AMS repair and Major inspection 19.5.49; No.2 Luftflotille 4.10.49; No.4 Esk 4.1.50; AMS storage 8.1.51; SOC 13.4.51; Re-entered inventory (bboc) 8.9.51; No.725 ESK (OCU) 9.51; AMS storage 10.51; SOC 1.9.52 (315 flying hours); Scrapped

TE231 Spitfire HF.IXe (Merlin 70); Became No.**41-433**; TOC/RAF 17.5.45; Collected and desp to Denmark 19.3.48, arr Kastrup airport 23.3.48; Spitfire-Gruppen 23.3.48; No.2 Luftflotille 10.7.48; No.4 Esk 2.50; AMS storage 10.50; SOC 13.4.51; Scrapped

TE233 Spitfire HF.IXe (Merlin 70); Became No.**41-434**; TOC/RAF 16.5.45; Collected and desp to Denmark 28.5.48, arr Kastrup airport 29.5.48; SoTT Værløse 1.6.48 (73 flying hours); No.1 Esk 3.49; No.4 Esk 1.7.49; AMS storage 8.2.51; SOC 13.4.51; Scrapped

TE236 Spitfire HF.IXe (Merlin 70); Became No.**41-435**; TOC/RAF 17.5.45; Collected 12.3.48, desp to Denmark 13.3.48, arr Kastrup airport 13.3.48; Spitfire-Gruppen 13.3.48; No.2 Luftflotille 10.7.48; No.4 Esk 4.1.50; AMS storage 8.2.51; SOC 13.4.51; Scrapped

TE296 Spitfire HF.IXe (Merlin 70); Became No.**41-436**; TOC/RAF 31.5.45; Collected and desp to Denmark 28.5.48, arr Kastrup airport 29.5.48; AMS Værløse 1.6.48 (64 flying hours); No.5 Esk 4.6.48; AMS storage 9.48 (98 flying hours); No.4 Esk 1.7.49; Belly-landed at Værløse 30.6.50 (Lt T Rasmussen); AMS repair 1.7.50; AMS storage 12.50; No.725 ESK (OCU) 18.6.51; AMS storage 15.10.51; SOC 1.9.52 (324 flying hours); Scrapped

References:
British Fighters, procured by Denmark, written by Ole Nikolajsen; Spitfire, Flytyper der har vaeret anvendt i Det danske Flyvervåben, URIAS post June 1968, p.11.
Supermarine Spitfire, Tinbox 4-1978, by Niels H Larsen.
RDAF Spitfires, compiled by Flyvevåbnets Historiske Samling at Karup, January 2001.

EGYPT

Early in 1939 the Royal Egyptian Air Force (REAF) requested the delivery of either 18 Spitfires or Hurricanes. However the RAF had first priority, and the export of Spitfires was restricted.

Shortly before the end of WW.II the first Spitfires were sold to the REAF under treaty arrangements, being delivered via the MUs at Aboukir, Kasfareet, Fayid, Ismailia and later also via RAF Helwan.

In summary, the REAF purchased:
  21 Spitfire Vb/c-trop in 1945
  39 Spitfire F/LF.IX in 1946
  1 Spitfire T.IX in 1950
  19 Spitfire F.22 in 1950

Total = **80** Spitfires.

Egypt also wished to have a further six Spitfire trainers and 20 Mk.XVIIIe, but these were not released by Britain. Similarly an interest was shown by the REAF for six to ten Spitfire PR.IX dissolved.

The Royal Egyptian Air Force (REAF)

The Egyptian Army Air Force (EAAF) was formed under RAF command in 1932. In 1937 command of the then Royal Egyptian Air Force (REAF*)* was taken over by an Egyptian Officer, but the British remained as advisers and as liaison of the British Military mission.

On 1st February 1945 the REAF ceased to be attached to the RAF, and by the end of the Second World War the REAF was organised in five operational and one communication squadrons, with its headquarters at Almaza AFB (Cairo South). Elementary Flying Training (EFTS) was carried out at El Khanka and Intermediate & Advanced Training with the FTS (Initial Training Sqn & Advanced Training Sqn) at Almaza, later moving to Fayid. A Technical Training School, a Signals & Electrical School and an Air Armament School were located at Almaza.

In the first Arabic-Jewish War, 1948/49, Spitfires fought against Spitfires, and Egypt lost more than 20 in this conflict. The first air combat took place on 31st May 1948. Prior to this, on 15th May 1948, a REAF Spitfire LF.IXe had been hit in the glycol tank by Israeli AA fire and force-landed near Tel Aviv. Another was downed near Dalya (Ramat David) on 22nd May 1948. These two provided spare parts for IDF/AF rebuilds D-130 and D-131.

In July 1953 Egypt became a republic, and its Air Force was re-named Egyptian Air Force (EAF).

Spitfire Mk.Vb/c-trop (REAF serial Nos 600 - 620)

Egypt purchased 21 Spitfire Mk.Vb/c (trop) under a contract dated 20th February 1945 at a cost of £10,000 each. The first two Mk.Vs were delivered on 22nd February 1945, and deliveries via Nos.107 and 109 MUs continued during February and March 1945. They served with No.2 Sqn and the FTS (AFS), and later with No.6 Sqn from May 1946. A few were also flown by the Meteorological Flight at Almaza. From October 1948 onwards the surviving Mk.Vs were flown for coastal patrol work.

In 1945 the Spitfires were marked with individual letters (e.g. 'C', 'M', 'B', 'K'), but from 1946 they carried only Arabic serial numbers on the fuselage.

Spitfire Mk.IX (REAF serial Nos 621 - 679)

The first two Spitfire Mk. IX arrived for the REAF via No.132 MU on 25th July 1946. Deliveries continued until July 1947, when the last of the 39 aircraft were handed over via RAF Helwan. Spitfire IXs served mainly with Nos.1 and 2 Sqns, and a few with

Spitfire T.IX was test flown under B-class registration G-15-92, then serialled G-ALJM, for sale to Egypt in April 1950, becoming No.684 of the REAF.
[Egyptian Air Force]

The sole Egyptian Spitfire T.1X, possibly ex MJ113, served with the Advanced Flying School at Almaza as No.684 from 1950. [RAF Museum P11148]

No.6 Sqn, all based at Al Arish from mid-1948. Two Spitfire IXs were in service with the Meteorological Flight in 1947. By 1st January 1950 no Spitfire IXs were in operational units; the Fighter Training Squadron (FTS/AFS) then had 28 Spitfire IX on strength, but ten of these were unserviceable.

Spitfire T.IX (REAF serial No 684)

One Spitfire T.IX (*G-ALJM*, RAF serial number possibly MJ113) was sold to Egypt on 13th April 1950 and received the REAF serial No.684. It served with the FTS (AFS) at Almaza from April 1950, but no details are available.

NOTE: REAF pilots have referred to a second T.IX, but confirmation is lacking

Spitfire F.22 (REAF serial Nos 680 - 683 & 685 - 699)

Sold back from the RAF to Vickers-Armstrongs between 22nd October 1949 and 23rd February 1950, and the Egyptian Government signed an agreement on 1st May 1950 for 20 Spitfire F.22s (Spec.No 480). The aircraft were re-conditioned and sold to the REAF for a sum of £239,000 for nineteen Spitfire F.22 and one T.IX, as replacements for the older Spitfire IX. Allotted Class B registrations *G-15-88* to *G-15-107* for delivery purposes, deliveries began on 14th June 1950, continuing until October 1950 with two Spitfires for each ferry flight. The last one arrived in Egypt on 8th February 1951.

The Spitfire F.22s served with the No.2 (FB) Sqn at Al Arish. Early in 1955 the *EAF* received its first Meteor jet fighters and the

Egypt

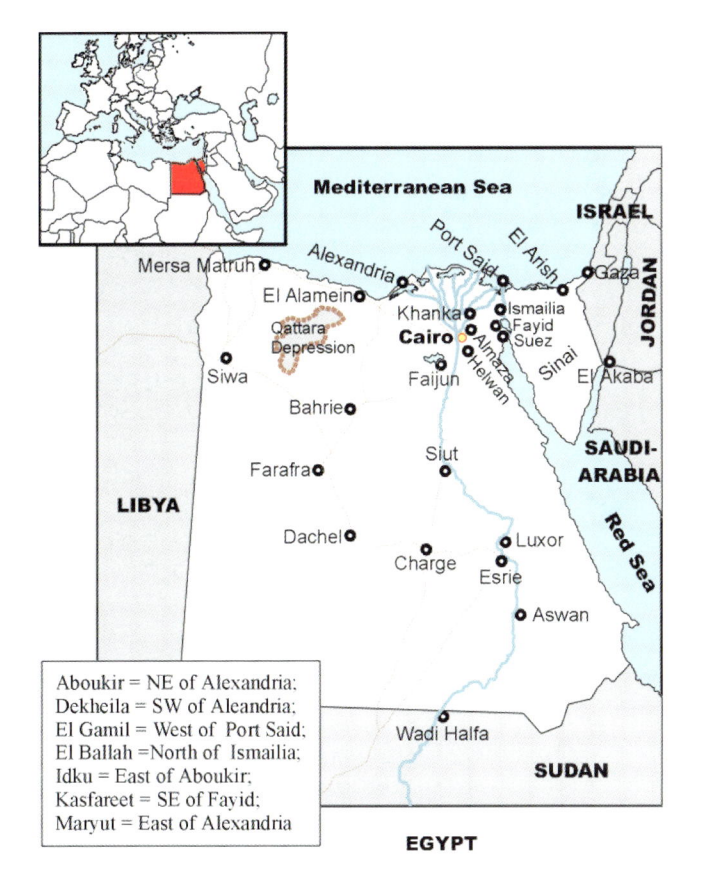

Aboukir = NE of Alexandria;
Dekheila = SW of Aleandria;
El Gamil = West of Port Said;
El Ballah = North of Ismailia;
Idku = East of Aboukir;
Kasfareet = SE of Fayid;
Maryut = East of Alexandria

piston-engined fighters were relegated to the Advanced Training role then. They served with the Fighter Training Sqn (FTS) at Fayid, and some were flown in the Suez campaign in 1956.

Egyptian Spitfire units

No.1 (FR) Sqn, AFB Almaza 1945, FB-training at Helwan July 1946, Al Arish from May 1948 (abandoned 29th December 1948, then to Almaza for short time); Became a TR-Sqn in October 1948.
Spitfire Mk.IX from July 1946 to December 1949.
Commanding Officers: Unknown

No.2 (F) Sqn, AFB Edku & Dakhayla (Dekheila) 1945, Helwan February 1947, Al Arish February 1948, Almaza October 1948, Al Ballah February 1949, FB-Sqn at Al Arish from June 1950.
Spitfire Mk.Vb/c from February 1945 to August 1946; Spitfire LF.IX from July 1946 to October 1948, then Macchi MC.205; Spitfire F.22 from June 1950 to 1956.
Commanding Officers:
S/Ldr M Nasr Al Din
Wg Cdr Said Afifi Al Janzuri
S/Ldr Abd Al Hamid Abu Zaid   from 7.48

No.5 (F) Sqn, awaiting Spitfire IX in 1947; Instead equipped with Italian fighter aircraft Fiat G-55A.

No.6 (F) Sqn, AFB Almaza 1946, Al Arish June 1948 (abandoned 29th December 1948, then to Al Ballah for short time).
Spitfire Mk.Vb/c from May 1946 to December 1948.
Spitfire IX (a few only) from July 1948 to February 1949.
Commanding Officers: Unknown.

Meteorological Flight, known also as the '*Weather Flight*';
Took over from No.1411 (Met) Flight RAF, which disbanded 15th August 1943. Based at Almaza.
Spitfire Mk.V from February 1945, and only a few Spitfire IX in 1946/47.
Commanding Officers: Unknown.

Flying Training School (FTS), Advanced Training Sqn/AFS;
At Almaza, with a Fighter Training Sqn at Fayid from 1955.
Spitfire Mk.Vb/c in 1946; Mk.IX & T.IX from 1947; Spitfire F.22 from 1950 to 1956.
Commanding Officers: Unknown.

Technical Training School (TTS) at Almaza;
Spitfire Mk.V, IX and F.22.
Commanding Officers: Unknown.

Pilots of No.2 Sqn REAF in front of a Spitfire F.22. Third from the left is S/Ldr Zaid, and second from the right is P/O Zaki who later became an Air Marshal.
[T Zaki via Dr. David Nicolle]

Individual Histories

BS339 Spitfire F.IXc; Short loan; TOC/RAF 11.9.42 - Allotted for Egypt 21.6.45; Hand over to REAF not confirmed; possibly to No.2 Sqn; SOC/RAF 26.9.46

EN115 Spitfire F.IXc; Short loan; TOC/RAF 1.12.42; No.107 MU Kasfareet 5.47, to REAF 31.7.47; No.2 Sqn 1947; Retd RAF 28.11.47; SOC 5.2.48

EN193 Spitfire F.IXc (Merlin 61); TOC/RAF 24.11.42, to REAF 26.9.46; No.2 Sqn or No.1 Sqn from 10.46

EN253 Spitfire F.IXc (Merlin 61); TOC/RAF 4.1.43, to REAF 26.9.46; No.2 Sqn or No.1 Sqn from 10.46

EN349 Spitfire F.IXc (Merlin 61); TOC/RAF 6.2.43, to REAF 26.9.46; No.1 Sqn or No.2 Sqn from 10.46; Retd RAF, No.107 MU Kasfareet 5.47
NOTE: Replaced by ML292 in 8.47

EN456 Spitfire F.IXc (Merlin 61); TOC/RAF 21.1.43, to REAF 26.9.46; No.2 Sqn or No.1 Sqn from 10.46

EN482 Spitfire F.IXc (Merlin 61); TOC/RAF 28.2.43, to REAF 31.10.46; No.1 Sqn 11.46

EN521 Spitfire F.IXc allotted for REAF, but cancelled; SOC/RAF 26.9.46

EN925 Spitfire F.Vb/trop (Merlin 45); TOC/RAF 17.5.42, to REAF 29.3.45; No.2 Sqn 4.45; Possibly to No.6 Sqn 5.46

EP652 Spitfire F.Vb/trop (Merlin 46); TOC/RAF 18.7.42, to REAF 29.3.45; No.2 Sqn 4.45; Possibly to No.6 Sqn 5.46

ER207 Spitfire F.Vb/trop (Merlin 46); TOC/RAF 31.8.42, to REAF 29.3.45; No.2 Sqn 4.45; Possibly to No.6 Sqn 5.46

ER625 Spitfire F.Vb/trop (Merlin 46); TOC/RAF 30.9.42, to REAF 29.3.45; No.2 Sqn 4.45; Possibly to No.6 Sqn 5.46

ER640 Spitfire F.Vb/trop (Merlin 46); TOC/RAF 6.10.42, to REAF 29.3.45; No.2 Sqn 4.45; Possibly to No.6 Sqn 5.46

ER713 Spitfire F.IXc (Merlin 63); TOC/RAF 11.6.43, to REAF 26.9.46; No.1 Sqn 10.46

ER973 Spitfire F.Vb/trop (Merlin 46); TOC/RAF 17.11.42, to REAF 29.3.45; No.2 Sqn 4.45; Meteorological Flight in 1946; Minor damage 6.10.46
NOTE: Incorrectly reported as "ES293"

ER991 Spitfire F.Vb/trop (Merlin 46); TOC/RAF 20.11.42, to REAF 22.2.45; No.2 Sqn 2.45; Possibly to No.6 Sqn 5.46

ES284 Spitfire F.Vc/trop (Merlin 46); TOC/RAF 28.11.42, to REAF 29.3.45; No.2 Sqn 4.45; Possibly to No.6 Sqn 5.46

JG925 Spitfire F.Vb/trop (Merlin 46); TOC/RAF 9.12.42, to REAF 22.2.45; No.2 Sqn 2.45; Possibly to No.6 Sqn 5.46

JK195 Spitfire F.Vc/trop (Merlin 46); TOC/RAF 6.2.43, to REAF 22.2.45; No.2 Sqn 2.45; Possibly No.6 Sqn 5.46
NOTE: Shown with REAF markings, coded 'C' in 1945/47; Reported incorrectly "ER602", but could been REAF serial No.602, perhaps

JK371 Spitfire F.Vc/trop (Merlin 46); TOC/RAF 27.2.43, to REAF 22.2.45; No.2 Sqn 2.45; Possibly to 6 Sqn 5.46

JK648 Spitfire F.Vc/trop (Merlin 50A); TOC/RAF 19.2.43, to REAF 22.2.45; No.2 Sqn 2.45; No.6 Sqn 5.46; Minor damage 25.5.46
NOTE: Incorrectly reported as "JK615"

JK722 Spitfire F.Vc/trop (Merlin 46); TOC/RAF 26.2.43, to REAF 29.3.45; No.2 Sqn 4.45; Possibly to No.6 Sqn 5.46

JK728 Spitfire F.Vc/trop (Merlin 46); TOC/RAF 26.2.43, to REAF 22.2.45; No.2 Sqn 2.45; Possibly to No.6 Sqn 5.46

JK739 Spitfire F.Vc/trop (Merlin 46); TOC/RAF 26.2.43, to REAF 22.2.45; No.2 Sqn 2.45; Possibly to No.6 Sqn 5.46

JK834 Spitfire F.Vc/trop (Merlin 50); TOC/RAF 2.4.43, to REAF 29.3.45; No.2 Sqn 4.45; Possibly to No.6 Sqn 5.46

JK835 Spitfire F.Vc/trop (Merlin 50); TOC/RAF 3.4.43 - Arr Egypt 1946; REAF, Meteorological Flight at Almaza 1946 (shown still in RAF markings 1946)

JK968 Spitfire F.Vc/trop (Merlin 46); TOC/RAF 14.3.43, to REAF 22.2.45; No.2 Sqn 2.45; Possibly to No.6 Sqn 5.46

JK984 Spitfire F.Vc/trop (Merlin 45); TOC/RAF 2.4.43, to REAF 22.2.45; No.2 Sqn 2.45; Possibly to No.6 Sqn 5.46

JL177 Spitfire LF.IXc (Merlin 66); TOC/RAF 2.4.43, to REAF 29.8.46; No.2 Sqn 9.46; Minor damage (Cat. unknown) 14.9.46
NOTE: Incorrectly reported as Mk.Vc

JL337 Spitfire F.Vc/trop (Merlin 50); TOC/RAF 1.7.43, to REAF 29.3.45; No.2 Sqn 4.45; Possibly to No.6 Sqn 5.46

JL366 Spitfire LF.IXc (Merlin 66); TOC/RAF 10.9.43, to REAF 31.10.46; No.2 Sqn 11.46

MA248 Spitfire F.IXc (Merlin 61); TOC/RAF 16.5.43, to REAF 26.9.46; No.2 Sqn or No.1 Sqn 10.46
NOTE: Incorrectly reported as "MA428"

MA251 Spitfire F.IXc (Merlin 61); TOC/RAF 13.5.43, to REAF 26.9.46; No.2 Sqn or No.1 Sqn 10.46

MA424 Spitfire F.IXc (Merlin 61); TOC/RAF 20.7.43, to REAF 26.9.46; No.2 or No.1 Sqn 10.46

MA478 Spitfire F.IXc (Merlin 63); TOC/RAF 8.6.43, to REAF 25.7.46; No.2 Sqn 7.46
NOTE: Incorrectly reported as "MA428"

MA514 Spitfire F.IXc allotted for REAF, but cancelled; SOC/RAF 26.9.46

MH547 Spitfire LF.IXc (Merlin 66); TOC/RAF 27.8.43, to REAF 29.8.46; No.2 Sqn 9.46

MH582 Spitfire LF.Vc/trop (Merlin 55M); TOC/RAF 30.7.43, to REAF 29.3.45; No.2 Sqn 4.45; Possibly to No.6 Sqn 5.46

MH653 Spitfire F.IXc (Merlin 63); TOC/RAF 23.8.43, to REAF 29.8.46; No.2 Sqn 9.46

MH656 Spitfire F.IXc (Merlin 63); TOC/RAF 29.8.43, to REAF 26.9.46; No.2 Sqn or No.1 Sqn 10.46

MH677 Spitfire F.IXc (Merlin 63); TOC/RAF 11.9.43, to REAF 26.9.46; No.2 Sqn or No.1 Sqn 10.46

MH697 Spitfire F.IXc (Merlin 63); TOC/RAF 14.9.43, to REAF 26.9.46; No.2 Sqn or No.1 Sqn 10.46

MH715 Spitfire LF.IXc allotted for REAF, but cancelled; SOC/RAF 13.5.48

MH736 Spitfire LF.IXc (Merlin 66); TOC/RAF 16.9.43, to REAF 31.10.46; No.2 Sqn 11.46

MH772 Spitfire LF.IXc allotted for REAF, but cancelled; SOC/RAF 13.5.48

MH795 Spitfire F.IXc (Merlin 63); TOC/RAF 25.9.43, to REAF 26.9.46; No.2 Sqn or No.1 Sqn 10.46

MH931 Spitfire F.IXc (Merlin 63); TOC/RAF 19.9.43, to REAF 29.8.46; No.2 Sqn 9.46

MH932 Spitfire F.IXc (Merlin 63); TOC/RAF 21.9.43, to REAF 26.9.46; No.2 Sqn or No.1 Sqn 10.46

MH993 Spitfire F.IXc allotted for REAF, but cancelled; Later delivered to Greece 3.47

MJ171 Spitfire LF.IXc allotted for REAF, but cancelled; SOC/RAF 27.11.47

MJ191 Spitfire LF.IXc (Merlin 66); TOC/RAF 21.10.43, to REAF 26.9.46; No.2 Sqn or No.1 Sqn 10.46

MJ227 Spitfire F.IXc (Merlin 63); TOC/RAF 18.10.43, to REAF 29.8.46; No.2 Sqn 9.46

MJ462 Spitfire LF.IXc (Merlin 66); TOC/RAF 7.11.43; To REAF 26.9.46; No.2 Sqn or No.1 Sqn 10.46

MJ624 Spitfire LF.IXc (Merlin 66); TOC/RAF 24.11.43, to REAF 26.9.46; No.2 Sqn or No.1 Sqn 10.46

MJ696 Spitfire LF.IXc (Merlin 66); TOC/RAF 12.12.43, to REAF 29.8.46; No.2 Sqn 9.46

MJ847 Spitfire LF.IXc (Merlin 66); TOC/RAF 1.12.43; To REAF 29.8.46; No.2 Sqn 9.46

MK415 Spitfire LF.IXc allotted for REAF, but cancelled; SOC/RAF 5.2.48

MK578 Spitfire LF.IXc (Merlin 66); TOC/RAF 18.3.44, to REAF 31.10.46; No.2 Sqn 11.46

MK841 Spitfire LF.IXc (Merlin 66); TOC/RAF 12.3.44, to REAF 26.9.46; No.2 Sqn or No.1 Sqn 10.46

MK849 Spitfire LF.IXc (Merlin 66); TOC/RAF 19.3.44, to REAF 26.9.46; No.2 Sqn or No.1 Sqn 10.46

ML116 Spitfire LF.IXc (Merlin 66); TOC/RAF 14.4.44, to REAF 26.9.46; No.2 Sqn or No.1 Sqn 10.46

ML292 Spitfire LF.IXc (Merlin 66); TOC/RAF 6.4.44; To REAF 31.7.47; No.2 Sqn 8.47

NH451 Spitfire LF.IXe (Merlin 66); TOC/RAF 26.5.44, to REAF 29.8.46; No.2 Sqn 9.46 (shown in the Arabic/Israeli War 1948)

NH495 Spitfire LF.IXe; Allotted for REAF on loan 27.11.47, via No.109 MU, but hand over not confirmed; Possibly to No.2 Sqn; Retd RAF, storage 11.3.48; SOC/RAF 13.5.48

Egypt

Spitfire F.22 No.681 (ex PK435) of the REAF. In 1950 it served with No.2 Sqn at Al Arish. [via Phillip Jarrett]

PK314 Spitfire F.22 (Griffon 61); Became REAF No.**696**; TOC/RAF 20.4.45; Sold back to Vickers 9.2.50, probably becoming marked G-15-104, to REAF 21.9.50; No.2 Sqn 10.50; Possibly to Fighter Training Sqn 1955

PK319 Spitfire F.22 (Griffon 61); Became REAF No.**695**; TOC/RAF 5.5.45; Sold back to Vickers 22.12.49, probably becoming marked G-15-103, to REAF 12.9.50; No.2 Sqn 9.50; Possibly to Fighter Training Sqn 1955

PK323 Spitfire F.22 (Griffon 61); Became REAF No.**697**; TOC/RAF 11.2.46; Sold to Vickers 9.2.50, probably becoming marked G-15-105, to REAF 21.9.50; 2 Sqn 10.50; Possibly to Fighter Training Sqn 1955

PK327 Spitfire F.22 (Griffon 61); Became REAF No.**693**; TOC/RAF 2.7.45; Sold back to Vickers 22.12.49, probably becoming marked G-15-101, to REAF 10.10.50; No.2 Sqn 10.50; Possibly to Fighter Training Sqn 1955

PK356 Spitfire F.22 (Griffon 61); Became REAF No.**699**; TOC/RAF 3.8.45; Sold back to Vickers 23.2.50, probably becoming marked G-15-107, to REAF 22.8.50; No.2 Sqn 8.50; Possibly to Fighter Training Sqn 1955

PK374 Spitfire F.22 (Griffon 61); Became REAF No.**686**; TOC/RAF 3.9.45; Sold back to Vickers 8.12.49, probably becoming marked G-15-94, to REAF 6.7.50; No.2 Sqn 7.50; Possibly to Fighter Training Sqn 1955

PK390 Spitfire F.22 (Griffon 61); Became REAF No.**691**; TOC/RAF 6.9.45; Sold back to Vickers 21.12.49, probably becoming marked G-15-99, to REAF 22.8.50; No.2 Sqn 8.50; Possibly to Fighter Training Sqn 1955

PK435 Spitfire F.22 (Griffon 61); Became REAF No.**681**; TOC/RAF 3.10.45; Sold back to Vickers 7.12.49, probably becoming marked G-15-89 [or 15-88?] (test flown 2.6.50), to REAF 14.6.50; No.2 Sqn 6.50; Possibly to Fighter Training Sqn 1955

PK484 Spitfire F.22 (Griffon 61); Became REAF No.**682**; TOC/RAF 12.9.45; Sold back to Vickers 7.12.49, probably becoming marked G-15-90 [or 15-89?] (test flown 6.6. & 7.6.50), to REAF 14.6.50; No.2 Sqn 6.50; Possibly to Fighter Training Sqn 1955

PK502 Spitfire F.22 (Griffon 61); Became REAF No.**687**; TOC/RAF 19.9.45; Sold back to Vickers 16.12.49, probably becoming marked G-15-95, to REAF 26.7.50; No.2 Sqn 7.50; Possibly to Fighter Training Sqn 1955

PK509 Spitfire F.22 (Griffon 61); Became REAF No.**692**; TOC/RAF 21.9.45; Sold back to Vickers 21.12.49, probably becoming marked G-15-100, to REAF 12.9.50; No.2 Sqn 9.50; Possibly to Fighter Training Sqn 1955

PK512 Spitfire F.22 (Griffon 61); Became REAF No.**683**; TOC/RAF 25.9.45; Sold back to Vickers 7.12.49, probably becoming marked G-15-91 [or 15-90?] (test flown 7.6.50), to REAF 28.6.50; No.2 Sqn 6.50; Possibly to Fighter Training Sqn 1955

PK516 Spitfire F.22 (Griffon 61); Became REAF No.**698**; TOC/RAF 27.9.45; Sold back to Vickers 9.2.50, probably becoming marked G-15-106, to REAF 10.10.50; No.2 Sqn 10.50; Possibly to Fighter Training Sqn 1955

PK517 Spitfire F.22 (Griffon 61); Became REAF No.**688**; TOC/RAF 27.9.45; Sold back to Vickers 16.12.49, probably becoming marked G-15-96, to REAF 26.10.50; No.2 Sqn 10.50; Possibly to Fighter Training Sqn 1955

PK524 Spitfire F.22 (Griffon 61); Became REAF No.**694**; TOC/RAF 21.9.45; Sold back to Vickers 22.12.49, probably becoming marked G-15-102, to REAF 8.2.51; No.2 Sqn 2.51; Possibly to Fighter Training Sqn 1955

PK541 Spitfire F.22 (Griffon 61); Became REAF No.**680**; TOC/RAF 30.9.45; Sold back to Vickers 22.10.49, probably becoming marked G-15-88 [or 15-91?], to REAF 27.6.50; No.2 Sqn 6.50; Possibly to Fighter Training Sqn 1955

PK562 Spitfire F.22 (Griffon 61); Became REAF No.**689**; TOC/RAF 1.10.45; Sold back to Vickers 20.12.49, probably becoming marked G-15-97, to REAF 26.10.50; No.2 Sqn 10.50; Possibly to Fighter Training Sqn 1955

PK598 Spitfire F.22 (Griffon 61); Became REAF No.**685**; TOC/RAF 22.10.45; Sold back to Vickers 7.12.49, probably becoming marked G-15-93, to REAF 6.7.50; No.2 Sqn 7.50; Possibly to Fighter Training Sqn 1955

PK600 Spitfire F.22 (Griffon 61); Became REAF No.**690**; TOC/RAF 6.12.45; Sold back to Vickers 20.12.49, probably becoming marked G-15-98, to REAF 26.7.50; No.2 Sqn 7.50; Possibly to Fighter Training Sqn 1955

PL168 Spitfire LF.IXe (Merlin 66); TOC/RAF 19.7.44, to REAF 29.8.46; No.2 Sqn 9.46

PL347 Spitfire LF.IXe (Merlin 66); TOC/RAF 26.7.44, to REAF 25.7.46; No.2 Sqn 8.46

PL443 Spitfire LF.IXe (Merlin 66); TOC/RAF 27.6.44, to REAF 29.8.46; No.2 Sqn 9.46

PT705 Spitfire LF.IXe (Merlin 66); TOC/RAF 8.44, to REAF 29.8.46; No.2 Sqn 9.46

PT835 Spitfire HF.IXe allotted for REAF, but cancelled; Later delivered to Greece 1.47

PV259 Spitfire LF.IXe (Merlin 66); TOC/RAF 23.9.44, to REAF 29.8.46; No.2 Sqn 9.46

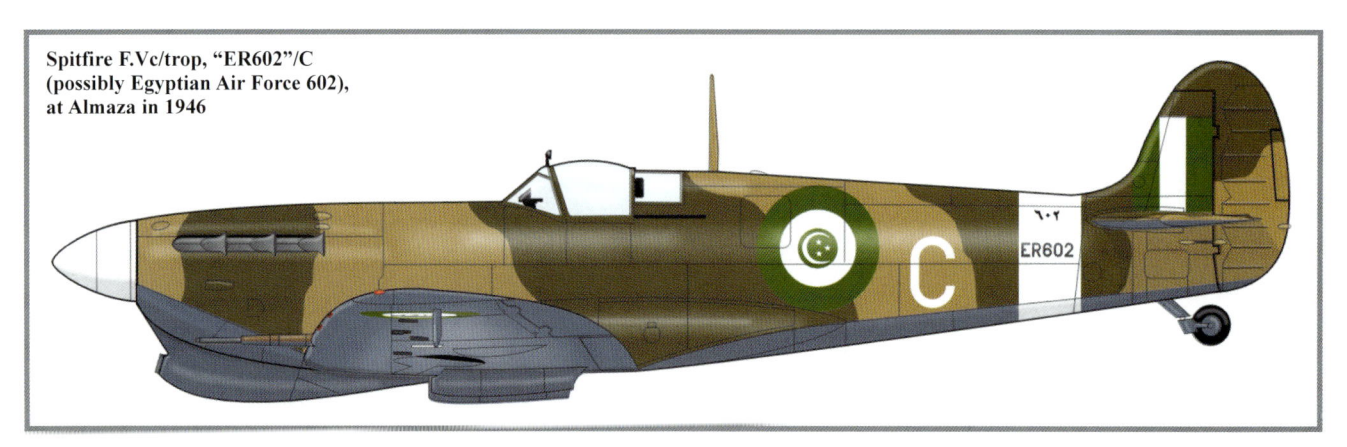

Spitfire F.Vc/trop, "ER602"/C
(possibly Egyptian Air Force 602),
at Almaza in 1946

Spitfire F.22, 681 (ex PK435) of
No.2 Sqn, Egyptian Air Force in 1950

The propeller, engine, front fuselage and wings of Spitfire F.Vc/trop BR491, ex No.92 Sqn RAF, were recovered from the Mediterranean off El Daba in mid-1999 and are now exhibited at the El Alamein Military Museum. It had ditched on 10th October 1942 whilst returning from a ground attack mission in the Daba area, piloted by Wt Off Lloyd George Edwards RCAF who is buried in the Alexandria (Hadra) War Memorial Cemetery.

PV356　Spitfire LF.IXe allotted for REAF, but cancelled; Later delivered to Greece 5.48
RR195　Spitfire LF.IXe (Merlin 66); TOC/RAF 21.9.44, to REAF 31.10.46; No.2 Sqn 11.46

Survivors in Egypt

One Spitfire F.22 survived, and remained in storage at Almaza AFB for some time; fate unknown. [NB. This aircraft had a five-bladed propeller, and might therefore have been a Fury]

Spitfire F.Vc/trop, serial number BR491, ex No 92 Sqn, was partly recovered from the Mediterranean Sea near Al Daba in mid-1999; Prop and engine, front fuselage and wings exhibited in the El Alamein Military Museum from 6th December 2000.

Unidentified aircraft

?　Spitfire LF.IXe (Merlin 66); No.2 Sqn over Israel, force-landed 15.5.48; To IDF/AF for spares.
　NOTE: Unidentified; Attacked Sve Dov, near Tel Aviv, hit by AA, lost coolant, force-landed on beach on the Herzliya seashore (F/Lt Barakat, PoW). REAF deny losing a Spitfire that day, the aircraft did not carry REAF markings. The IDF/AF used parts of this aircraft to build-up its own Spitfire D-130

?　Spitfire LF.IXe (Merlin 66); No.2 Sqn over Israel, force-landed near Majdal 4.6.48 (F/O Jamal Orfan S El-Nasser, POW); To IDF/AF for spares

?　Spitfire F.Vc/trop (Merlin 46); Became REAF No.**610**; No.6 Sqn over Israel, shot down near Majdal by S-199 (Plt Modi Alon) of the IDF/AF 18.7.48 (Wg Cdr Said Afifi Al Janzuri killed)

?　Spitfire LF.IXc (Merlin 66); Became REAF No.**622**; No.2 Sqn over Israel, ran out of fuel, force-landed wheels-up near Majdal 5.11.48 (F/Lt Mustafa Kamal Nasr escaped safe); To IDF/AF for spares

?　Spitfire LF.IXe (Merlin 66); Became REAF No.**624**; Shot down by IDF/AF, force-landed 22.5.48 (F/O Abd Al Rahman Ainan, POW)

?　Spitfire LF.IXe (Merlin 66); Became REAF No.**641**; No.2 Sqn over Israel, force-landed south of Kibbutz Dalya 22.5.48; To IDF/AF for spares

?　Spitfire LF.IXc (Merlin 66); Became REAF No.**664**; No.1 Sqn at Al Arish AFB (marked 'L') 12.48; Captured intact by the IDF/AF 29.12.48; For spare-parts

Spitfire LF.IXc No.664 'L' of No.1 (Fighter Reconnaissance) Sqn, REAF, in its pen at Al Arish, December 1948. On 29th December 1948 it was captured intact by the IDF/AF and used for spare parts.

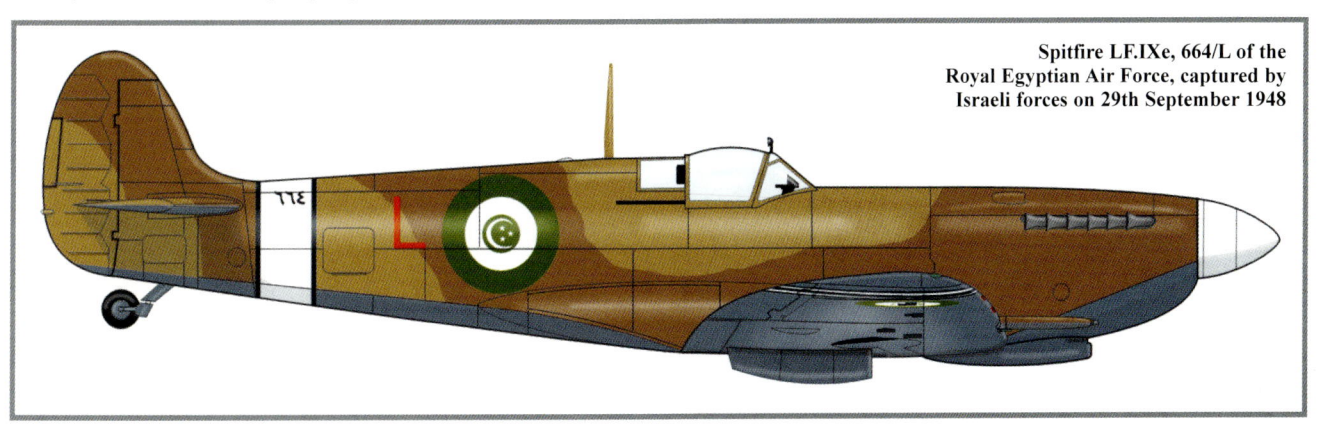

Spitfire LF.IXe, 664/L of the Royal Egyptian Air Force, captured by Israeli forces on 29th September 1948

Spitfire LF.IXc No.622 of No.2 (Fighter) Sqn, REAF Almaza, ran out of fuel and force-landed wheels-up near Majdal on 5th November 1948, the pilot, Flt Lt Mustafa Kamal Nasr, being unhurt. Israeli soldiers are removing the weapons and other parts for use as spares for IDF/AF Spitfires.

?	Spitfire Mk.IX, IDF/AF shot down (probably) four or five Spitfires 16.10.48; REAF confirmed two damaged	
?	Spitfire Mk.IX, IDF/AF claimed one probably	
?	Spitfire Mk.IX, shot down by IDF/AF (Plt Denny Wilson) 31.12.48	
?	Spitfire Mk.IX, shot down and one probably by IDF/AF (Plts SB Feldmann and Boris Senior) 5.1.49	
?	Spitfire LF.IXc (Merlin 66); Became REAF No.**671**; To No.1 Sqn 12.48; Shown at FTS Almaza 1948/49	
?	Spitfire T.IX (Merlin 66); Became REAF No.**684**; ex Vickers-Armstrongs, Civil reg. *G-ALJM*, probably becoming marked G-15-92 - Arr Egypt (Cairo) 17.4.50; Advanced Flying School 4.50	

References:
History of the Egyptian Air Force, by Lon Norden & Dr. David Nicolle, Smithsonian Institute, 1996.
Neutral Allies, The Royal Egyptian Air Force in WW.II, by Dr. David Nicolle, Air Enthusiast No.52.
Spitfire - Star of Israel, by Alex Yofe, Ventura Classic Warbirds No.1 (1996), p.31-35.

ESTONIA

Estonia wished to have Spitfires and asked Supermarine for twelve Mk.Ia in December 1937. Members of the Estonian Air Force visited the Supermarine works for demonstration flights of Spitfires on 5 July 1938.

On 8th July 1938 Supermarine received a provisional order for twelve Spitfire Mk.Ia from Estonia. The next visit followed on 27th July 1938, and the order received a firm quotation on 29th July 1938. The Foreign Office placed the order third on the priority list, dated 17th November 1938, and the Air Ministry approved it on 8th December 1938. Finally a firm contract was made on 2nd March 1939 under No.C.186/39 for twelve Spitfire Mk.Ia, the Type 332 with Frazer-Nash machine guns, delivery to be between July 1939 and June 1940.

The first two Spitfires, L1046 and L1047, were earmarked for Estonia in July 1939, and Estonian pilots and technicians arrived at the factory for acceptance flights. Instead, however, the aircraft went into storage of No.19 MU at St.Athan on 10-11th July 1939. After the outbreak of WW.II, export orders for British military aircraft were cancelled, and both "Estonian" Spitfires went to No.603 Sqn RAF.

Remarks:
Estonia signed a pact of non-aggression with Germany on 7th June 1939, and a mutual assistance pact was concluded with the Soviet Union on 28th September 1939. However, Russia occupied the territory in June 1940, and the Estonian Army became the *22nd Territorial Corps* of the Soviet Army.

Individual Histories

L1046 Spitfire F.Ia; Earmarked for Estonia 7.39, but allotment cancelled; To RAF (later No.603 Sqn, shot down by enemy over Channel, Cat.FB/3 on 28.8.40, SOC)

L1047 Spitfire F.Ia; Earmarked for Estonia 7.39, but allotment cancelled; To RAF (later No.603 Sqn, taxying collision with Spitfire L1059, Cat.E 1.10.39, SOC)

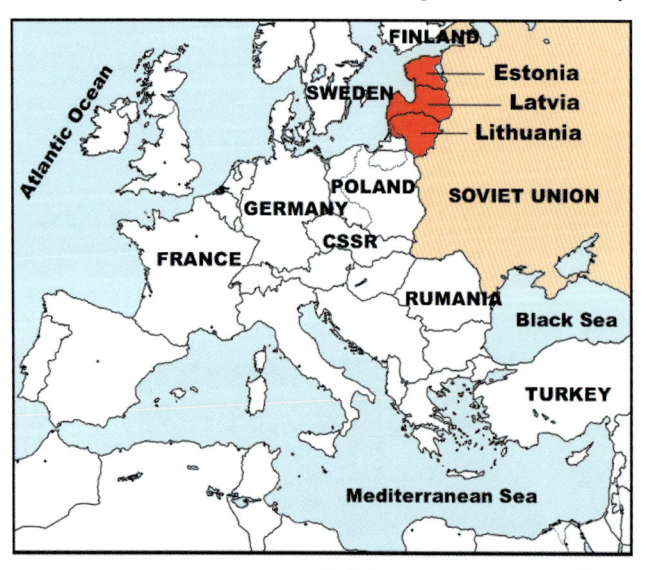

BALTIC interests for Spitfires

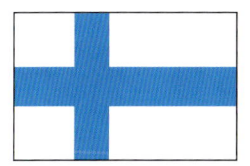

FINLAND

Finland asked to buy Spitfires from Supermarine in 1938 but their inquiry was never followed up and the interest lapsed. Britain accepted an order only for older Gladiator fighters and Blenheim bombers, but not modern fighters.

On 30th November 1939 the Soviet Union attacked Finland. The Finnish Air Force, the *Suomen Ilmvoitmat*, consequently needed more aeroplanes, and eventually bought 35 Fiat G.50s in Italy and 30 M.S.406s in France 1939. In March 1940 ten Hawker Hurricane Mk.Is arrived but by this time the fight was over and Russia and Finland signed a truce on 12th March 1940.

Later, Finland declared the war against the Soviet Union on 26th June 1941. Then, supported by the Axis, the *Suomen Ilmvoitmat* received German aeroplanes (Bf 109 and Ju 88) which were operated until 1944.

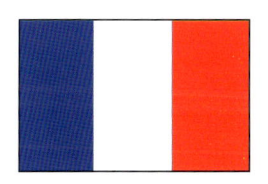

FRANCE

France asked Supermarine for the delivery of Spitfires and received a firm quotation dated 25th April 1938, offering three aircraft. This was placed at the top of the Foreign Office priority list on 17th November 1938. The first French Spitfire, **F.01**, arrived on 18th July 1939, but the other two were never supplied.

After the British evacuation of Dunkirk during June 1940, French pilots joined the RAF and they were formed into Free French units, flying Spitfires with No.340 Squadron from November 1941, followed later by Nos.341, 329 and 345 Sqns. Allied Forces entered North Africa with Operation *'Torch'* in November 1942, and then French units began flying Spitfires during March 1943 under MACAF command. At the end of 1943 these Spitfire units were built up as Nos.326 to 328 Squadrons under RAF command. No.80 (French) OTU of the RAF was especially formed in England in April 1945 for training French personnel.

France received the first Spitfires on loan for GR.II/33 *'Savoie'* and GC.II/18 *'Saintonge'* in mid 1944.

All French Squadrons of the RAF and their equipment were officially handed over to the *Armée de l'Air Française* from 24th - 27th November 1945 (Spitfires via No.81 [French] R&SU, via Nos.340/345 Sqns, or via SNCAN Mureaux after overhaul). Under the terms of the Hartemann-Dickson Agreement, signed in September 1945, deliveries continued and eventually more than 700 Spitfires and Seafires arrived for the French Forces; known:

```
Spitfire Mk.I    =   1 a/c
Spitfire Mk.V    = 150 a/c (incl. 20 instructional a/c)
Spitfire Mk.VIII =  19 a/c (on loan)
Spitfire Mk.IX   = 359 a/c
Spitfire Mk.XVI  =   1 a/c (plus some on loan)
Seafire Mk.III   = 142 a/c
Seafire Mk.XV    =  15 a/c.
```

From 1950 the remaining Spitfires and Seafires in France used radio call-signs, these beginning with the letter 'F- '. Those of GC.I/1 began 'F-UGA_ ' and GC II/1 'F-UGB_ ', plus individual letter; GC I/6 used 'F-UGP_ ' and BE.708 Meknès 'F-TEV_ '. Spitfires and Seafires of the Aéronavale carried 'F-YC_ ', for example those of the 1.Flottille used 'F-YCJ_ ' and those of Esc 1.Serv used 'F-YCA_ '.

The last French Spitfire to be recorded as written off charge was at BE. 708 Meknès in May 1953.

French Spitfire units of the RAF

No.**326** Sqn *'Nice'* (ex GC.II/7) - MTO -
Formed 1st December 1943, disbanded 7th October 1945,
Spitfire Mk. V, VIII, IX;
codes: Mk.V = digits '1' to '25', Mk.VIII & IX = '8J- '.

No.242 Group ORB:
Ground personnel of 2/7 (French) Sqn (Spitfire V) arrived 25th April 1943 at Marylebone from Bou Saada, followed by air party on 28th April 1943 - presumably GC.II/7, which became No.326 Sqn 1st December 1943 at Ajaccio.

No.**327** Sqn *'Corse'* (ex GC.I/3) - MTO -
Formed 1st December 1943, disbanded 6th November 1945,
Spitfire Mk. V, IX, VIIIc;
Sqn codes: Mk.V: Digits '1' to '25',
Mk.IX & VIIIc: Single individual letter 'A' to 'Y'.

No.**328** Sqn *'Provence'* (ex GC.I/7) - MTO -
formed 1st December 1943, disbanded November 1945,
Spitfire Mk. V, VIII, IX;
Sqn code: Mk.V = Digits only,
Mk.IX = Single letter, and Mk.VIII = 'S8'.
[As GC.I/7 it arrived at Oran/Taher 22nd November 1943 with 14 Spitfires to replace GC.II/3 (Hurricanes) in No.332 (Fighter) Wing. After becoming No 328 Sqn on 1st December 1943 it left the Wing 30th April 1944 on moving to Corsica]

No.**329** Sqn *'Cigognes'* (ex GC.I/2) - ETO -
Formed 3rd January 1944, disbanded 17th November 1945,
Spitfire Mk. V, IX, XVI,
Sqn code: Mk.V = Individual letter only,
Mks. IX & XVI = '5A'.

No.**340** Sqn *'Ile de France'* (ex GC.IV/2) - ETO -
formed 7th November 1941, disb. 27th November 1945,
Spitfire Mk. II, V, IX, XVI - Sqn code: 'GW- '.

No.**341** Sqn *'Alsace'* (ex GC.III/2) - ETO -
from 1940 *Free French Flight* of the WDAF, formed as No.341 Sqn on 18th January 1943, disbanded 27th November 1945,
Spitfire Mk. V, IX, XVI - Sqn code: 'NL'.

No.345 Sqn *'Berry'* (ex GC.II/2) - ETO -
Formed 30th January 1944, disbanded 27th November 1945, Spitfire Mk.V, IX, XVI (code: '2Y' until September 1944).

No.80 (French) OTU, formed 23rd April 1945 with Spitfire Mk.IX at Morpeth, moving July 1945 to Ouston where it disbanded 8th March 1946 (Spitfires passed to BE.708 Meknès, NWA).
Unit code: '3H'.

RAF Training Delegation (TRG.DEL.)
Helped to set up the FAF in France soon after WWII. The Delegation formed 8th May 1945 with HQ at Rochefort and EFTS at La Rochelle and Cognac, with A&NBNS at Cazaux, and a Radio School at Pau. The unit disbanded into the RAF Delegation (France) on 10th January 1946.

FRENCH FORCES
L'ARMÉE DE L'AIR FRANÇAISE (FAF)

From 1945 until May 1953 Spitfires served with the FAF in France, North Africa, Germany and Indo-China (Tonkin, Annam, Cochin-China [now Vietnam], Laos and Cambodia).

Combat missions with Spitfires were flown over Indo-China. From January 1946 to December 1950 the Spitfires used mainly the airbases at Hanoi (Bac Mai, Gia-lam & Haiphong) and at Saigon (Bien Hoa & Tan Son Nhut), but also those of Cao Bang and Langson in the north, Dong Hoi, Hué, Seno and Tourane in the middle, Ca Mau, Nha Trang and Phnom Penh in the south.

1. EC (GC I/7 [I/1] *'Provence'* & GC II/7 [II/1] *'Nice'*)
Formed in November 1945, arr Indo-China 25th November 1945 and used Spitfire Mk.IX from 2nd January 1946, and also c.20 Mk.VIIIc (on loan). From 2nd August 1946 most of the Spitfires went to 2.EC, as 1.EC returned to Friedrichshafen, Germany, still flying Spitfire Mk.IX.
On 1st July 1947 the unit was re-formed to become GC I/1 and II/1. Some time later these went to Oran, then to Sidi Ahmed in North Africa, using Spitfire Mk.IX. Re-named as 7Vme EC in November 1950, then with de Havilland Vampire jet-fighters; disbanded September 1951.
Commanding Officers:
LCL M Papin-Labazordière	1.45
Cdt Barbier	2.46
Cdt Maurin	3.46
LCL Louis Delfino	8.46
formerly "Normandie Niémen"	
Cdt Tardy de Montravel	8.47
Cdt Mangin	10.49

COs of GC I/7 (I/1) *'Provence'* :
Cne Madon	3.45
Cne Simard	8.46
Cne Barre de Saint-Venant	1.49
Cne de la Villéon	10.50

COs of GC II/7 (II/1) *'Nice'*:
Cne Jeandet	10.45
Cne Fouchier	12.47
Cne Loubet	11.49

2. EC (GC I/2 *'Cigognes'* & GC III/2 *'Alsace'*)
Formed in November 1945 at Friedrichshafen, Germany, arrived Indo-China on 3rd August 1946, used Spitfire Mk.IX until 16 September 1947 (III/2) and early 1948 (I/2). The Spitfires were then handed over to 4.EC, and 2.EC returned to Friedrichshafen, Germany, and re-equipped with P-47 Thunderbolts.
Commanding Officers:
Cdt Guizard	1946
Cdt Maurin	12.46
Cdt Marchelidon	10.47
Cdt Matras	1.48-5.50

COs of GC I/2 *'Cigognes'*:
Cne de Bordas	3.45
Cne Marchelidon	8.46
Cne Trulla	10.47
Cne Avon	7.48
Cdt Le Groignec	4.50-3.51

COs of GC III/2 *'Alsace'*:
Cne Tanguy	8.45
Cne Peronne	4.46
Cne Guérin	6.46
Cne Tatraux	10.47
Cne Lemaire	2.48
Cne Perseval	10.49.

3. EC (GC I/3 *'Navarre'* & GC II/3 *'Champagne'*)
Formed in November 1945, converted to a Spitfire unit July 1948, arr Indo-China on 26th September 1948 (GC I/3) and 28th December 1948 (GC II/3), received Spitfire Mk.IX from 4.EC for use until 23rd November 1949 (I/3) and 4th April 1950 (II/3). The Spitfire Mk.IX then went to GC I/6.
Commanding Officers:
Cdt d'Anfreville de Jurquet de la Salle	4.48
Cdt Goupy	9.48-10.51

CO of GC I/3 *'Navarre'*:
Cne Segura	1948/49

COs of GC II/3 *'Champagne'*:
Cne Bouton	10.47-11.48
Cne Giraud	1948/49
Cne Chonet	c.1949
Cne Le Dantec	c.1950

4. EC (GC I/4 *'Dauphiné'* & GC II/4 *'La Fayette'*)
Formed January 1947 at Andernach, Germany as a P-47 unit, arr Indo-China on 12th September 1947 and used Spitfire Mk.IX from 2.EC until 28th September 1948 (GC

FRANCE

II/4) & 4th January 1949 (I/4). They then went to the 3.EC, and 4.EC returned to Friedrichshafen, Germany, flew P-47.
Commanding Officers:
Cdt Pape   10.47
Cdt Lansoy   10.48-3.51

COs of GC I/4 *'Dauphiné'*:
Cne Porodo   2.47
Cne Brunet   10.47-12.48

COs of GC II/4 *'La Fayette'*:
Cne Fabry   1947
Cne Charles   1947/50

GC. I/6 *'Corse'* (SPA 69 & 88)
As GC I/3 this unit was part of No.50 (F) Wing, with Mosquitos based at Dijon. In July 1947 the unit was renamed GC I/6.
On 1st April 1950 GC I/6 arr Indo-China receiving the Spitfire Mk.IX of GC I/3 for SPA 69 and those of GC II/3 for SPA 88 in April 1950, both used Spitfires until 14th December 1950.
Call-codes: 'F-UGP_ '.
From 18th November 1950 the GCI/6 converted to a Hellcat unit.
Commanding Officers:
Cne Fuchs   3.50-12.50
Cne de Chavagnac   1950

French Air Force in the Mediterranean Area (AFN)

GR.II/33 *'Savoie'*
A FR-Group North-Africa, used Spitfire Mk.V & IX, but only with the No.2 Esc *'La Mouette'* (B-Flt, *'Sea-Mew'*) from March 1944 until May 1945, and also P-51 from March 1945. Based Laghouat, and Colmar from March 1945.
Commanding Officers:
Cdt Piechon   11.44
Cdt Marcel Martre   1944

GB.II/20 *'Bretagne'*, Free French (Bomber) unit - MTO -
Equipped with B-26 Marauder, reported to have some Spitfires on strength at Kasfareet, Egypt in March 1944.

BE.708 (Base Ecole No 708) at Meknès, Morocco –
Formed as "Centre d' Instruction Chasse" (CIC) on 5th December 1943 [Ecole de Chasse (EcC), a Fighter Pilots School], was renamed AFS *'Christian Martell'* on 31st August 1945, used Spitfire Mk. V & IX from December 1943 to May 1953, but also those of No.80 OTU RAF from 14 March 1946.
Call-codes: 'F-TEV_ ' (Mk.IX only).
Commanding Officers:
Cdt Andrieux   1946/47
LCL Ezanno   1.48-7.48
Col de la Source   1948/50
Col Hugo   7.50-12.53

Forces Aériennes de l'Atlantique

GC.II/18 *'Saintonge'*
Formed on 28th November 1944 at Vannes-Meucon AFB, used Spitfire Mk.V & IX until 20th April 1946. Then disbanded on 22nd June 1946 (pilots were integrated into GC.III/2 *'Alsace'*, Indo-China August 1946).
Commanding Officers GC II/18:
Cdt Thollon   c.1945
Cne Dodet   to 8.46

L'AÉRONAUTIQUE NAVALE FRANÇAISE
– the A.N. - French Naval Air Arm -

The A.N. received 20 Spitfire Mk.IX between March 1946 and July 1946 and 48 Seafire L.IIIc & FR.IIIc from March 1946 to 1947, a further 65 Seafire L.IIIc & FR.IIIc followed in 1947/48.

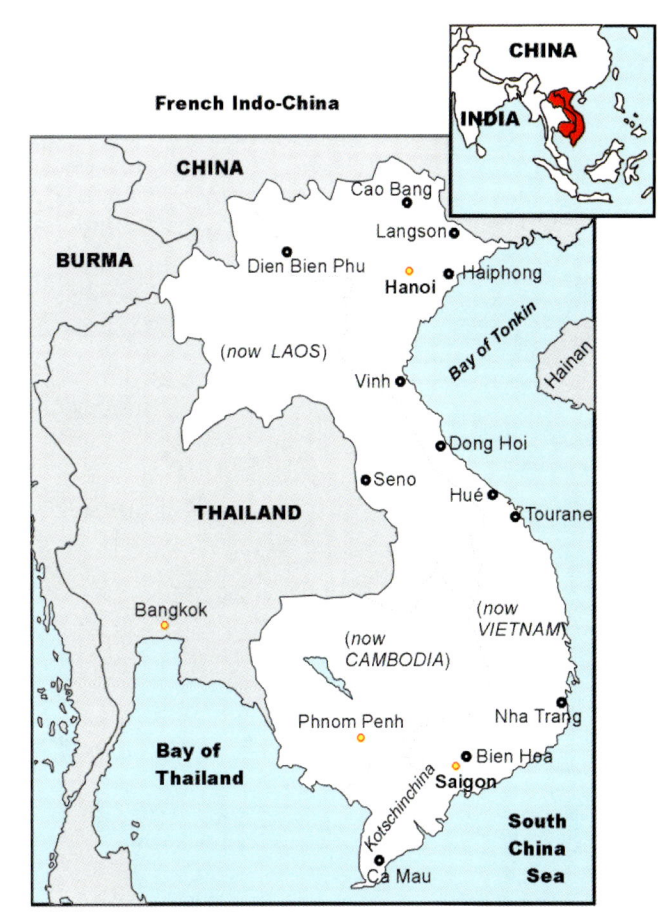

Hanoi = Gialam & Bac Mai AFB; Saigon = Tan Son Nhut AFB

15 Seafire F.XVc arrived for the 1.GCE between 17th June and 28th June 1949.

Total more than 150 Seafires served with the A.N.

The main Naval Air Station was Hyères on the Mediterranean coast, but Cuers (NE of Hyères) and Forcalquier also used Spitfires and Seafires, as did the carriers *Arromanches* and also *Dixmude* (ex HMS *Colossus* and HMS *Biter*, on loan to the A.N. 4th August 1946 and 9th April 1945, respectively; *Arromanches* purchased in 1951).

1. F.C. Flottille de Chasse No.1, became "Flottille 1F" on 1st January 1946;
Formed 6th October 1945 at Cuers and moved to Hyères on 31st December 1945; Red spinner, code '1.F- ', used

Seafire III of L'Aeronautique Navale Francaise marked 'S.2.1' flying over the French coast. [Claude A. Pierquet]

A Corsican guerilla armed with a Sten gun keeps guard over French Spitfires at an aerodrome in Corsica in 1944. [*Official CAN.1834*]

Spitfires 1946-1948, Seafire L(FR).IIIc from April 1946 until 1950, and Seafire F.XVc (also Hellcat) from June 1949 until mid 1950.

With *Arromanches* to North-Africa (Oran) 23rd May - 25th June 1947, to Corsica July - October 1947 and to Indochina desp from Toulon on 30th October 1948, arr Saigon 29th November 1948, returned to France mid-1949.

Commanding Officers:
LV Marius Gleize	from 10.45
LV Roger Pradelles de Latour-Dejean	25.6.47
LV Jean-Michel Lenglet	17.5.49

12. F.C. (Flottille de Chasse No.12)

Formed 1st August 1948 at Hyères, Black spinner, code '12.F- '. Seafire Mk.IIIc from August 1948 until July 1949 and Seafire F.XVc from June 1949 until mid 1950 (*Arromanches* in Sept/Oct 1948 and March 1950).

Commanding Officer:
LV Sanguinetti	(1948-1950)

Note: 1.F with 3.F & 4.F built up "*GAN-2*" by the end of 1945, for development of the ASSP training programme, at first with Spitfires and SBD Dauntless, to be prepared for service with *Arromanches* and *Dixmude* from mid-1946.

Seafire L.IIIc '1.F-22' of Flottille 1F aboard the light fleet carrier Arromanches, *was possibly either PR349 or PX932.*

A Seafire F.XVc of Flottille 1F after running into the barrier on the flight deck of Arromanches. [J J Petit]

Seafire L.IIIc '54.S-17' of Escadrille de Servitude No.54 at Hyères in southern France around 1948/49 for carrier training.

1.F & 12.F formed the 1.GCE (Groupement de Chasse Embarquée) in 1949, with 15 Seafires F.XVc on board *Arromanches*.

Esc 54. Serv. (E.A.E Esc de Servitude No.54) at Hyères
Formed October 1946, Yellow spinner, code '54.S- '. Used SBD Dauntless and also Spitfire Mk.IX from 1946 - 1949, Seafire Mk.IIIc from April 1946 until 1951, and Seafire F.XVc (ex 1.F & 12.F) from February 1950 to 1951 for carrier training (with *Arromanches* April - September 1948).
Commanding Officer:
LV ER Mauban (1946-1950)

Esc 1. Serv. (of 1.RM), based Plessis, from 16th September 1949 at Lanvéoc-Poulmic; Used Spitfire Mk.IX for communication and target towing duties, code '1.S.- '.
Commanding Officers:
LV Louis Carli	from 3.11.45
LV Bernard Thorette	9.46
LV Raoul de Carpentier	1948
LV Marcel Ravet	1949
LV Bernard Maire	1951
LV Jean Delouche	1953

Esc 3. Serv. at Cuers, from 23rd December 1949 at Forcalquier; Used Spitfire Mk.IX for communication, target towing duties and liaison, from 1947 to 1950, code '3.S- '.
Commanding Officers:
LV Paul Ricour	from 13.6.46
LV Pierre Massicot	11.46
LV Georges Martin	1948
LV Albert Lecaque	12.50

Esc 4. Serv. (ex Esc 52.S) AFN; Used Spitfire Mk.IX for training and communication, code '4.S.- '.
Commanding Officers:
LV Pierre Le Mahieu	from 15.4.47
LV Roger Jacquin	1949
LV Michel Palmésani	6.51

Esc 10.Serv, Experimentale du Centre d´Experimentation de Saint-Raphaël (Fréjus), also some Spitfire Mk.IX, code: '10.S.- '.
Commanding Officers:
CC Jean Hervé	from 1.7.45
LV Jean L Lucas	2.47
LV Gilbert Guyon	2.49
LV Jean Mauban	10.50
LV Guy Rivière	9.52

Esc 50. Serv., l'Ecole Navale at Lanvéoc-Poulmic, code '50.S- '; Received some Spitfire Mk.IX as ground instructional airframes in 1950/51.
Commanding Officers:
LV Charles Vaziaga	from 24.5.45
LV Robert Goullet de Rugy	8.46
LV Paul Kerros	5.47
LV François Rondenay	2.49
LV François d'Arcangues	2.51
LV Raymond Vallet	2.53

BE Lartique, l'Ecole Navale at the base d'aéronautique Navale de Lartigue, used some Spitfire Mk.IX for ground instructions in April 1946.
Base commanders:
CC Louis Roussel	from 1.8.44
CC Rémi Duval	11.44
CF Julien Fournier	6.46
CC Guy Lacoste	7.48
CF Jacques Hourdin	9.49

BM 2 (Base Mobile No.2) at Hyères,
A Support-, Depot- and Reserve-Establishment, prepared Seafire Mk.IIIc in 1946 for the use of 1.Flottille (holding unit).
Base commanders:
CF Françis Lainé	from 1.7.45
CF Rémi Duval	7.46
CF René Jalabert	2.47
CV Jean Mouliérac	12.48
CF Raymond Lucas	8.50
CF Michel Ferran	12.52

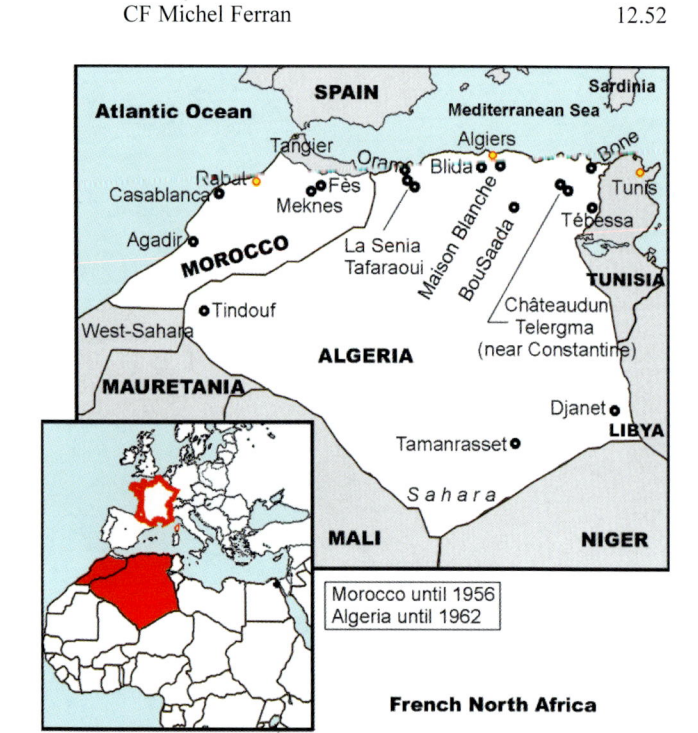

French North Africa

Spitfires & Seafires served also with

CEAM	Centre d'Expériences Aériennes Militaire, Rochefort;
CHAT	Châteaudun, aircraft depot SW of Paris (BA 279);
DMAA	Dir.du Matériel de l'Armée de l'Air (e.g.DMAA 632);
EAA	Entrepôt de l'Armée de l'Air (e.g. Depot No 601);
EAM	Ecole d'Armement et Méchaniciens Avions at Bourget-du-Lac (near Marseille), 1945
EdM	Ecole des Moniteurs (Flight Instructor School) at Tours;
PB 93	Parc Blida No 93 (Depot for GR II/33, too);
PC 257	Parc Colonial No.257 (Depot, R&SU);
PC 482	Parc Colonial No.482 (Depot, R&SU) at Bien Hoa;
SAMAN	Service d´Approvisionnement en Matériel de l´Aéronautique Navale at Toussus-le-Noble;
SEC	Secrétariat of Central Service A.N. at Cuers;
SLA	Section de Liaison Aérienne (e.g. SLA 54);
SMER	Section Marine des Ecoles de Rochefort;
SNCAN	Soc.Nat. de Construction Aéronautiques du Nord at Les Mureaux (aircraft factory, undertook maintenance & overhaul).

French special Abbreviations

AIA	Atelier Industriel de l'Air (assembly, light repair);
ASSP	Appontage Simulé sur Piste, aerodrome dummy deck landing training ;
BAN	Base Aéronautique Navale Française;
CAEO	Cmd Air Extrême-Orient (Indo-China Air Command);
CATRE	Centre Aérien Technique de Réception et d'Entrainement (Reception and Training Centre);
CEV	Centre d'Essais en Vol (Aircraft Test Center);
CIC	Centre d'Instruction Chasse at Meknès, BE708;
CN	Constructions Navale (Ateliers DCAN);
DCAN	Direction des Constructions et Armes Navales;
EAE	Ecole de L'Aviation Embarquée (Carrier Training School), at Hyères;
EC	Escadre de Chasse, a Fighter Wing with 2 GC;

FRANCE

ERC   Esc de Réception et de Convoyage (test- and delivery unit of the A.N.), see also SRC;
FC   Flottille de Chasse
GAN   Groupement Aéronautique Navale, three Flottilles;
GC   Groupe de Chasse, a F-Sqn (contains 2 Esc/Flights);
GCE   Groupement de Chasse Embarquée (1.F & 12.F);
GR   Groupe Reconnaissance;
RM   Région Maritime, Naval areas (1.RM or 3.RM);
SEA   Section Entretien Aéronefs, maintenance base;
SRC   Section de Réception et de Convoyage (test- and delivery unit of the A.N.), see also ERC;
VF   Volant de fonctionnement [operational];
VR   Volant de réserve [reserve].

French damage & crash categories ("degrees"):
cat 2° light damage, repair by FRU within 48 hours;
cat 3° special repair by R&SU within 15 days;
cat 4° repair in works (RiW), SNCAN etc;
cat R   Réformé = SOC

Ranks of FAF and A.N.:
A/C   Adjudant Chef (F/Sgt)
Asp   Aspirant (Warrant Officer)
CC   Capitaine de Corvette (Navy), also "CCV"
Cdt   Commandant (S/Ldr)
CF   Capitaine de frégate
Cne   Capitaine (Flight Lieutenant)
Col   Colonel (Grp Capt)
EV   Enseigne de Vaisseau (2nd/Lt, Navy)
LCL   Lieutenant Colonel (Wg Cdr)
Lt   Lieutenant (Flight Officer)
LV   Lieutenant de Vaisseau (Lt, Navy)
OE   Officier des Equipages
PM   Premier Maitre (Corporal)
S/C   Sergent Chef (Sergeant)
S/Lt   Sous-Lieutenant (Pilot Officer).

Individual Histories

N-21   (F.01) Spitfire F.Ia (Merlin III); The 251st production aircraft, first flown 25.6.39 with Class B Reg. No. *N-21* direct from the Mkrs to France – Arr FAF & TOC as *F.01* on 18.7.39; At Orleans (marked 'FWB'), burnt 6.40; Remains captured by Germans 6.40.
        NOTE: The first French Spitfire (it never had an RAF serial number), fitted with DH two-pitch airscrew: 1938 offer of Vickers-Supermarine also to France for £16,436 for each aircraft; Inquiry of France for three Spitfires on 25.4.38; Confirmation of the Air Ministry for a single aircraft to France on 19.1.39; Contract No. C 590/39 with France for one Spitfire in May 1939
N3200   Spitfire I, recovered wreck from Sangette beach, displayed V3 Museum Fortresse de Mimoyecques
P8718   Spitfire F.Vb (Merlin 45); TOC/RAF 25.7.41 - Arr FAF 19.1.45; GC.II/18 *'Saintonge'* in 1945
P8782   Spitfire F.Vb/trop (Merlin 46); TOC/RAF 5.7.41; via Pershore to Morocco - Arr FAF 10.4.45; BE.708 Meknès 9.9.45; Accident 5.11.45; R&SU; Accident 28.11.45; R&SU; Crashed Cat.E 21.1.47, SOC
P9374   Spitfire I, recovered wreck from Calais beach; parts to Musée de l´Air Paris, storage; Remains acquired by S Marsh and T Kaplan, storage on the Isle of Wight; Civil reg *G-MKIA* on 16.11.2000 - **SURVIVOR**
R7220   Spitfire F.Vb (Merlin 45); Presentation aircraft *'BOURNEMOUTH II'*; TOC/RAF 21.3.41; ex USAAF; Converted to GI No. *5586M* - Shipped to France, arr Bordeaux 3.3.46; FAF, ground instructional airframe only
W3229   Spitfire F.Vb (Merlin 45); TOC/RAF 7.6.41; ex USAAF; Converted to GI No. *5572M* - Shipped to France, arr Bordeaux 3.3.46; FAF, ground instructional airframe only
W3322   Spitfire F.Vb (Merlin 45); TOC/RAF 14.6.41; Converted to GI No. *5584M* - Shipped to France, arr Bordeaux 3.3.46; FAF, ground instructional airframe only
W3328   Spitfire F.Vb (Merlin 50M); Presentation aircraft *'THE FLYING FOX'*; TOC/RAF 19.6.41; ex USAAF; Converted to GI No. *5571M* - Shipped to France, arr Bordeaux 3.3.46; FAF, ground instructional airframe only
W3426   Spitfire F.Vb/trop (Merlin 45); Presentation aircraft *'CHINGLEPUT'*; TOC/RAF 25.6.41; ex No.340 Sqn ('GW-J') - Arr FAF 10.4.45; Possibly GR II/33 *'Savoie'*, service by 20.4.45; BE.708 Meknès 9.10.47
W3619   Spitfire F.Vb (Merlin 45); TOC/RAF 3.8.41 - Arr FAF 19.1.45; GC.II/18 *'Saintonge'* in 1945
W3899   Spitfire LF.Vb (Merlin 50M); Presentation aircraft *'SUN WORKS'* TOC/RAF 19.9.41 - Arr FAF 19.1.45; GC.II/18 *'Saintonge'* in 7.45
W3931   Spitfire F.Vb (Merlin 45); TOC/RAF 1.9.41 - Arr FAF 19.1.45; GC.II/18 *'Saintonge'* in 3.45
W3957   Spitfire F.Vb (Merlin 45); TOC/RAF 1.10.41 - Arr FAF 19.1.45; GC.II/18 *'Saintonge'*, hit by AA, crashed near St.Trelaly, Cat.FB/E 18.4.45 (Sgt Botte), SOC
AA718   Spitfire LF.Vb (Merlin 45M); TOC/RAF 31.8.41 - Arr FAF 19.1.45; GC.II/18 *'Saintonge'* in 3.45 (also 9.45)
AA751   Spitfire LF.Vb (Merlin 50M); TOC/RAF 6.10.41; Converted to GI No. *5583M* - Shipped to France, arr Bordeaux 3.3.46; FAF, ground instructional airframe only
AA875   Spitfire F.Vb (Merlin 45); Presentation aircraft *'MANCHESTER KILLER'*; TOC/RAF 28.10.41 - Arr FAF 19.1.45; GC.II/18 *'Saintonge'*, crashed at Cognac, Cat.E 10.2.45 (S/Ldr Graves), SOC
AA911   Spitfire F.Vb (Merlin 46); TOC/RAF 2.11.41 - Arr FAF 22.1.45; GC.II/18 *'Saintonge'* in 7.45 (also 9.45)
AA969   Spitfire F.Vb (Merlin 45); TOC/RAF 1.11.41; ex USAAF 8th & 9th AF; Converted to GI No. *5596M* - Shipped to France, arr Bordeaux 11.3.46; FAF, ground instructional airframe only
AB139   Spitfire F.Vc (Merlin 46); TOC/RAF 30.11.41; Converted to GI No. *5589M* - Shipped to France, arr Bordeaux 3.3.46; FAF, ground instructional airframe only
AB140   Spitfire F.Vb (Merlin 45); TOC/RAF 25.11.41; ex No.340 Sqn ('GW-E'); Converted to GI No. *5590M* - Shipped to France, arr Bordeaux 3.3.46; FAF, ground instructional airframe only
AB199   Spitfire F.Vb (Merlin 46); Presentation aircraft *'MESOPOTAMIA'*; TOC/RAF 16.12.41; ex USAAF 8th & 9th AF, also No.341 Sqn - Arr FAF 19.1.45; GC.II/18 *'Saintonge'* in 7.45 (also 9.45)
AB202   Spitfire F.Vc (Merlin 46); Presentation aircraft *'PUDUKKOTTAI NAGARATHARS'*; TOC/RAF 24.12.41; Converted to GI No. *5597M* - Shipped to France, arr Bordeaux 3.3.46; FAF, ground instructional airframe only
AB339   Spitfire F.Vb/trop (Merlin 45 with Vokes air filter); TOC/RAF 2.2.42 - Arr FAF 16.3.46
AB501   Spitfire LF.IXc (Merlin 66); TOC/RAF 29.1.42 - Arr FAF 3.6.47; Fate unknown
AB532   Spitfire F.Vc/trop (Merlin 45); TOC/RAF 25.2.42 - Arr FAF 2.5.44; GR.II/33 *'Savoie'* on 2.5.44; Hit by AA 17.6.44; Crashed at Fréjus, Cat.E 26.8. or 27.8.44 (Lt Jean Reder); SOC 31.8.44
AB939   Spitfire LF.Vb (Merlin 50M); TOC/RAF 4.9.41 - Arr FAF 19.1.45; GC.II/18 *'Saintonge'*
AD132   Spitfire F.Vb (Merlin 45); Presentation aircraft *'BIHAR III'*; TOC/RAF 12.9.41 - Arr FAF 1.2.45
AD186   Spitfire F.Vb/trop (Merlin 45); TOC/RAF 8.9.41 - Arr FAF 24.4.45; BE.708 Meknès 7.45; Accident 3.11.45; R&SU; BE.708 by 8.46 (flown by Plt Louis Rat)
AD238   Spitfire LF.Vb (Merlin 50M); Presentation aircraft *'BOROUGH OF BARNES'*; TOC/RAF 16.9.41; ex No.345 Sqn ('M' & 'D') - Arr FAF 19.1.45; GC.II/18 *'Saintonge'* in 3.46
AD248   Spitfire LF.Vb (Merlin 50M); Presentation aircraft *'CHESHIRE COUNTY I'*; TOC/RAF 14.9.41; Converted to GI No. *5591M* - Shipped to France, arr Bordeaux 11.3.46; FAF, ground instructional airframe only

AD288   Spitfire F.Vb (Merlin 45); TOC/RAF 22.9.41; ex USAAF 8 & 9 AF; Converted to GI No. *5599M* - Shipped to France, arr Bordeaux 3.3.46; FAF, ground instructional airframe only

AD324   Spitfire LF.Vb/trop (Merlin 50M); TOC/RAF 13.10.41 - Arr Morocco 10.4.45; FAF, BE.708 Meknès ('T') possibly from 9.10.47

AD508   Spitfire F.Vb (Merlin 45); TOC/RAF 6.11.41; Converted to GI No. *5594M* - Shipped to France, arr Bordeaux 11.3.46; FAF, ground instructional airframe only

AD514   Spitfire LF.Vb (Merlin 50M); TOC/RAF 1.10.41 - Arr FAF 19.1.45; GC.II/18 *'Saintonge'*

AR328   Spitfire LF.Vb/trop LR (Merlin 45M); TOC/RAF 11.2.42 - Arr FAF, Meknès 10.4.47; BE.708 Meknès 9.10.47

AR373   Spitfire F.Vb (Merlin 45); Presentation aircraft *'LULANGURU'*; TOC/RAF 19.3.42; Converted to GI No. *5588M* - Shipped to France, arr Bordeaux 3.3.46; FAF, ground instructional airframe only

AR376   Spitfire F.Vb (Merlin 45); TOC/RAF 17.3.42 - Arr FAF 19.1.45; GC.II/18 *'Saintonge'* in 4.45 (also 4.46)

AR405   Spitfire LF.Vb (Merlin 50M); TOC/RAF 13.4.42 - Arr FAF 19.1.45; GC.II/18 *'Saintonge'* in 3.45

AR451   Spitfire LF.Vb (Merlin 50M); TOC/RAF 16.5.42; ex USAAF; Converted to GI No. *5592M* - Shipped to France, arr Bordeaux 11.3.46; To A.N. as instructional airframe only; SMER/Sect Marine d'Ecoles Rochefort 1946

AR524   Spitfire F.Vc/trop (Merlin 46); TOC/RAF 13.7.42; Gibraltar 6.11.42; NWA 28.2.43 – FFAF (GC.I/7) 1.10.43; No.328 Sqn, crashed at Taher, Cat.FA/3 on 22.3. or 23.3.44 (Lt de Chavaignac), SOC

AR595   Spitfire F.Vc/trop (Merlin 46); TOC/RAF 11.8.42 - ME 28.4.45; possibly FAF, BE.708 Meknès in 1945; Retd RAF (No.1564 Flt, ground collision at Istres, Cat.GA/E 8.6.46); via R&SU to UK on 13.6.46, SOC 27.6.46

AR600   Spitfire F.Vc/trop (Merlin 46); TOC/RAF 17.8.42 - Arr FAF; BE.708 Meknès ('L') 10.9.47 (shown also 5.52)

BL304   Spitfire LF.Vb (Merlin 50M); TOC/RAF 26.2.42 - Arr FAF 19.1.45; GC.II/18 *'Saintonge'* in 5.45 (shown also 7.45)

BL329   Spitfire LF.Vb (Merlin 50M); TOC/RAF 7.2.42; ex No.340 Sqn ('GW-R') - Arr FAF 29.1.45; GC.II/18 *'Saintonge'* in 8.45 (also 11.45)

BL551   Spitfire F.Vb/trop (Merlin 46); TOC/RAF 22.12.41 - Arr FAF, BE.708 Meknès 9.10.47; Ground collision with Spitfire JK105, Cat.GA/E 16.8.48, SOC (Note: Engine cowling to PP972 later)

BL563   Spitfire F.Vb (Merlin 45); TOC/RAF 23.12.41 - Arr FAF 19.1.45; GC.II/18 *'Saintonge'*

BL600   Spitfire LF.Vb (Merlin 50M); Presentation aircraft *'BROMLEY'*; TOC/RAF 25.1.42 - Arr FAF 1.2.45; GC.II/18 *'Saintonge'* in 8.45

BL631   Spitfire F.Vb/trop (Merlin 45); TOC/RAF 27.1.42; ex No.340 Sqn ('GW-U') - Arr FAF, BE.708 Meknès 9.10.47

BL665   Spitfire F.Vb (Merlin 45); Presentation aircraft *'NIGERIA OYO PROVINCE'*; TOC/RAF 10.1.42; Converted to GI No. *5595M* - Shipped to France, arr Bordeaux 3.3.46; FAF, ground instructional airframe only

BL755   Spitfire LF.Vb (Merlin 50M); TOC/RAF 31.1.42; Converted to GI No. *5570M* - Shipped to France, arr Bordeaux 3.3.46; FAF, ground instructional airframe only

BL787   Spitfire LF.Vb/trop (Merlin 50M); TOC/RAF 6.2.42 - Arr FAF, BE.708 Meknès 9.10.47

BL993   Spitfire F.Vb (Merlin 46); TOC/RAF 22.2.42; ex USAAF 8 & 9 AF - Arr FAF 1.2.45; Dijon 3.46; GC.II/18 *'Saintonge'* ('W', named *'PILLY'*) 3.46

BM229   Spitfire F.Vb (Merlin 45); Presentation aircraft *'SILVER BLUE BIRD'*; TOC/RAF 16.3.42; ex USAAF 8th & 9th AF - Arr FAF 1.2.45; GC.II/18 *'Saintonge'* in 3.45 (also noted 2.46)

BM257   Spitfire LF.Vb (Merlin 50M); TOC/RAF 25.3.42 - Arr FAF 19.1.45; GC.II/18 *'Saintonge'* in 3.45

BM262   Spitfire F.Vb (Merlin 45); Presentation aircraft *'THE LINCOLNSHIRE POACHER'*; TOC/RAF 15.3.42 - Arr FAF 19.1.45; GC.II/18 *'Saintonge'*

BM272   Spitfire LF.Vb (Merlin 50M); TOC/RAF 25.3.42 - Arr FAF 19.1.45; GC.II/18 I in 10.45 (also 4.46)

BM295   Spitfire F.Vb/trop (Merlin 45); TOC/RAF 26.3.42 - Arr FAF, BE.708 Meknès 9.10.47 (also noted 6.48)

BM322   Spitfire F.Vb (Merlin 46); Presentation aircraft *'M.A.A.'*; TOC/RAF 27.3.42; Converted to GI No. *5601M* - Shipped to France, arr Bordeaux 3.3.46; FAF, ground instructional airframe only

BM411   Spitfire F.Vb (Merlin 46); TOC/RAF 5.4.42; ex USAAF 8th & 9th AF, and No.340 Sqn ('GW-O'); Converted to GI No. *5600M* - Shipped to France, arr Bordeaux 3.3.46; FAF, ground instructional airframe only

BM412   Spitfire F.Vb (Merlin 45); TOC/RAF 5.4.42; ex No.340 Sqn ('GW-H') - Arr FAF 19.1.45; GC.II/18 *'Saintonge'* in 3.45 (also 4.45)

BM461   Spitfire F.Vb (Merlin 45); TOC/RAF 12.4.42; ex USAAF; Converted to GI No. *5593M* - Shipped to France, arr Bordeaux 3.3.46; FAF, ground instructional airframe only

BM648   Spitfire LF.Vb (Merlin 50M); Presentation aircraft *'TALKA'*; TOC/RAF 5.5.42 - Arr FAF 19.1.45; GC.II/18 *'Saintonge'*

BP906   Spitfire PR IV/D (Merlin 46) TOC/RAF 7.3.42; No.2 PRU, en route to Middle East 1.4.42; Force-landed in French NWA, aircraft & pilot interned 1.4.42, Cat.FA/E 2.4.42; SOC 30.4.42

BR114   Spitfire F.Vc/trop (Merlin 46); Presentation aircraft *'IRENE'*; TOC/RAF 14.3.42 - Arr FAF, GR.II/33 *'Savoie'* on 11.7.44; Hit by AA, Cat.FB/E 1.8.44; SOC/RAF 31.8.44

BR134   Spitfire F.Vc/trop (Merlin 46); TOC/RAF 3.4.42 – Arr FAF, GR.II/33 *'Savoie'* 2.5.44; Crashed 13.5.44; R&SU; Belly-landed, Cat.E 2.10.44, SOC

BR140   Spitfire F.IXc (Merlin 61); TOC/RAF 19.6.42; ex 80 OTU/RAF - Arr FAF, BE.708 Meknès ('E') 14.3.46; Collided on take-off with Spitfire MA591 on 14.2.47; R&SU; BE.708 Meknès 29.7.49 (noted also 11.49)

BR195   Spitfire F.Vc/trop (Merlin 46); TOC/RAF 27.3.42; MAAF (Census 6.45); RAF Training Delegation 27.9.45 - to FAF 27.11.45; Fate unknown

BR202   Spitfire LF.Vc/trop (Merlin 45M); TOC/RAF 1.4.42; Casablanca 2.5.43 – FAF, CIC Meknès, accident 27.9.44 (Sgt Roger Delenatte); SOC/RAF 26.4.45

BR387   Spitfire F.Vc/trop (Merlin 46); TOC/RAF 10.5.42 - Arr FAF, parc Blida in 3.44; GR.II/33 *'Savoie'* 2.5.44 (until 21.10.44 confirmed); SOC/RAF 12.7.45

BS128   Spitfire F.IXc (Merlin 63); TOC/RAF 25.7.42; ex No.340 Sqn ('GW-B'), No.341 Sqn - Arr FAF 10.4.46; BE.708 Meknès 1.4.48

BS131   Spitfire F.IXc (Merlin 61); TOC/RAF 4.8.42 - Arr FAF 16.9.46; 1.EC (F/Wing), ground collision with Spitfire ML422 at Niedermendig, Germany, Cat.E 19.6.47, SOC

BS183   Spitfire F.IXc (Merlin 61); TOC/RAF 23.7.42; ex No.80 OTU ('3H-U') - Arr FAF, BE.708 Meknès 4.4.46; Crashed 20.3.50

BS192   Spitfire F.IXc (Merlin 61); TOC/RAF 26.7.42; ex No.340 Sqn ('GW-A') - Arr FAF 3.6.47; Fate unknown

BS250   Spitfire F.IXc (Merlin 61); TOC/RAF 18.10.42 - Arr FAF 10.4.46; BE.708 Meknès 4.46 (shown also 2.3.49)

BS254   Spitfire F.IXc (Merlin 61); TOC/RAF 8.11.42 - Arr FAF, Châteaudun (ferry flight) 11.8.46; GC.I/4 *'Dauphiné'*, test flight 17.9.48; GC.I/3 *'Navarre'* ('B') 28.9.48; Crashed landing at Gia-lam, Indo-China, Cat.E 18.12.48 (Sgt Baches safe); SOC

BS361   Spitfire PR.IV (D) trop (Merlin 46); TOC/RAF 19.9.42; NAASC 31.10.43 - Arr FAF, GR.II/33 from 31.5.44; Destroyed in ground collision with P-40 at Nettuno, Italy, Cat.FA/3 on 10.6.44, SOC

BS387	Spitfire F.IXc (Merlin 61); Became **F-UGPR**; TOC/RAF 1.10.42 - Arr FAF, Châteaudun (ferry flight) 20.7.46; Shipped to Indo-China; 3.EC ('B'), flown Hanoi to Tourane 29.9.49; GC.I/6 *'Corse'* ('R'; F-UGPR) 4.50, noted also 6.50
BS401	Spitfire F.IXc (Merlin 61); TOC/RAF 25.10.42; ex No.80 OTU - Allotted for FAF 8.3.46, arr BE.708 Meknès 14.3.46; Crashed 14.1.48 (Lt Ronsin); R&SU; Crashed 14.4.49
BS403	Spitfire F.IXc (Merlin 61); TOC/RAF 31.10.42; ex No.80 OTU - Arr FAF, Châteaudun (ferry flight) 20.7.46; GC.I/3 *'Navarre'* 19.4.48; Crashed Bien-Hoa 15.12.48 (Adj Friedrich safe); R&SU; GC.I/3 ('O'), flown Hanoi to Tourane 29.9.49
BS464	Spitfire F.IXc (Merlin 61); Presentation aircraft *'TURF CLUB II'*; TOC/RAF 26.9.42 - Arr FAF 25.6.46; Seen at Villacoublay 1946/47; Musée de l'Air Paris, Le Bourget ("GW-S") 31.12.49; Destoyed in hangar fire, Dugny, 5.90
BS539	Spitfire F.IXc (Merlin 61); TOC/RAF 15.11.42 - Allotted for FAF 5.9.46, arr FAF 12.9.46; Fate unknown NOTE: Spitfire IX full size replica (Hispano-Suiza 12), marked "BS539" (Civil reg *F-WGML*), by Jean-Patrick Dubois, first flown 14.10.94
BS542	Spitfire F.IXc (Merlin 61); TOC/RAF 17.10.42; ex No.340 Sqn ('GW-J'), No.80 OTU - Allotted for FAF 8.3.46, arr BE.708 Meknès 14.3.46; Crashed 29 or 30.11.49 (S/Lt Fequet), BS544 Spitfire F.IXc (Merlin 63); TOC/RAF 21.10.42; - Allotted for FAF 23.9.46, arr FAF 17.10.46; BE.708 Meknès 2.49
BS545	Spitfire F.IXc (Merlin 61); Presentation aircraft *'BRAZIL No.1'*; TOC/RAF 27.10.42 - Arr FAF 24.5.46; BE.708 Meknès ('B'), overshot landing, Cat.E 19.5.49 (Lt Germain), SOC
BS555	Spitfire F.IXc (Merlin 61); TOC/RAF 17.11.42 - Arr FAF 27.7.46; BE.708 Meknès, Taxying collision with Spitfire MA301 on 17.6. or 21.6.49; R&SU; BE.708, crashed 3.10.49 (Sgt Constant)
EE788	Spitfire F.Vc/trop (Merlin 46); TOC/RAF 15.12.42; MAAF Census 6.45; RAF Training Delegation 13.9.45 - to FAF 27.11.45; SMER/Sect. Marine d'Ecoles Rochefort 1949
EE791	Spitfire F.Vc/trop (Merlin 56); TOC/RAF 24.12.42 - Arr FAF 14.2.46; Fate unknown
EF538	Spitfire F.Vc/trop (Merlin 45); TOC/RAF 9.2.43; USAAF until 31.7.43 (NWA) – FFAF (EC.1) 31.10.43; Harbour patrol, starboard undercarriage collapsed after heavy landing airfield Campo del Oro, Ajaccio, Cat.Ac 7.11.43 (Sgt Chef R Paillanay); SOC/RAF 30.6.44
EF548	Spitfire F.Vc/trop (Merlin 46); TOC/RAF 15.2.43; MAAF (Census 6.45); RAF Training Delegation 11.45 - to FAF 27.11.45; Fate unknown
EF568	Spitfire F.Vc/trop (Merlin 45); TOC/RAF 1.3.43; Casablanca 25.4.43; NWA 31.5.43 – FFAF (GC II/7), at Bone, tyre burst on take-off, ground looped, tipped on nose, Cat.B 8.9.43 (Lt R Perrier); R&SU; Later to USAAF 31.12.43
EF602	Spitfire F.Vc/trop (Merlin 50); TOC/RAF 13.3.43; Casablanca 25.4.43; NWA 31.5.43 - FFAF (GC I/7) 14.9.43; Retd RAF 1.10.43; Later to USAAF 30.11.43, then retd to FAF; CIC Meknès, accident 18.7.44 (Cdt Georges Garde)
EF606	Spitfire F.Vc/trop (Merlin 45); TOC/RAF 1.7.43 - Arr FAF 9.10.47, to BE.708 Meknès
EF635	Spitfire F.Vc/trop (Merlin 50); TOC/RAF 2.4.43; MAAF (Census 6.45); RAF Training Delegation 13.9.45 - to FAF 27.11.45; Fate unknown
EF652	Spitfire F.Vc/trop (Merlin 50); TOC/RAF 19.4.43; MAAF (Census 6.45); RAF Training Delegation 13.9.45 - to FAF 27.11.45; Fate unknown
EF686	Spitfire F.Vc/trop (Merlin 46); TOC/RAF 27.5.43 – FFAF (GC.II/7), at Bone, tailwheel damaged by steel strip planking while taxying, Cat.B 15.9.43 (W/O Cazenave); R&SU; Later to Nos.326-328 Sqns - Arr FAF 10.9.47; BE.708 Meknès
EF697	Spitfire F.Vc/trop (Merlin 50); TOC/RAF 17.6.43; Arr FAF, GR.II/33 *'Savoie'* on 25.6.44; SOC/RAF 26.4.45
EF733	Spitfire F.Vc/trop (Merlin 55); TOC/RAF 2.9.43; ex USAAF; MAAF (Census 6.45); RAF Training Delegation 4.10.45 - to FAF 27.11.45; Fate unknown
EF734	Spitfire F.Vc/trop (Merlin 55); TOC/RAF 7.9.43; ex USAAF; MAAF (Census 6.45); RAF Training Delegation 27.9.45 - to FAF 27.11.45; SMER Rochefort
EF736	Spitfire F.Vc/trop (Merlin 55); TOC/RAF 11.9.43; Arr FAF, Parc Blida in 3.44; GR.II/33 *'Savoie'* 2.5.44; Undercarriage failed by cross-wind landing, wheels up at Dijon-Longvic 9.11.44 (Lt Rene Collongues); Fate unknown
EF743	Spitfire F.Vc (Merlin 55); TOC/RAF 5.10.43 - Arr FAF, via parc Blida to GR II/33 ('5-CZ') in 4.44; Ground collision with "JK104" on 9.5.44 (Lt Reder); R&SU;

Spitfire F.Vc/trop EF736, seen here with shark mouth livery, served with GR.II/33 'Savoie' in 1944. [Pierre Gandillet via Charles W Cain]

	Retd to FAF 14.2.46; SMER/Sect. Marine d'Ecoles Rochefort
EF745	Spitfire F.Vc/trop (Merlin 55); TOC/RAF 7.10.43; FALS/NWA from 6.44 - Arr FAF 10.9.47; BE.708 Meknès
EN129	Spitfire F.IXc (Merlin 61); TOC/RAF 20.11.42; ex No.80 OTU - Arr FAF 8.3.46; BE.708 Meknès 14.3.46 (also 12.47 and 1950); Crashed 25.3.50 (Adj Pioch)
EN137	Spitfire F.IXc (Merlin 61); Presentation aircraft *'BAHRAIN III'*; TOC/RAF 22.11.42; ex Nos.326-328 Sqns - Arr FAF 27.11.45; Fate unknown
EN174	Spitfire F.IXc (Merlin 61); TOC/RAF 7.11.42 - Arr FAF 10.4.46; BE.708 Meknès ('S') 1947
EN266	Spitfire F.IXc (Merlin 61); TOC/RAF 21.1.43 - Allotted for FAF 5.9.46, arr FAF 16.9.46; BE.708 Meknès 2.49
EN849	Spitfire LF.Vb (Merlin 50M); TOC/RAF 10.5.42 - Arr FAF 1.2.45; GC.II/18 *'Saintonge'* ('E') 4.45; Belly-landed near Merignac 4.4.45 (Sgt Combrisson); R&SU; GC.II/18 *'Saintonge'* in 9.45
EN893	Spitfire F.Vb/trop (Merlin 45); Presentation aircraft *'BEXLEY'*; TOC/RAF 10.5.42 - Arr FAF, BE.708 Meknès 9.10.47
EN964	Spitfire F.Vb/LR (Merlin 45); TOC/RAF 19.5.42; ex USAAF 9th AF; Converted to GI No. 5585M - Shipped to France, arr Bordeaux 3.3.46; FAF, ground instructional airframe only
EP179	Spitfire F.Vb (Merlin 45); TOC/RAF 14.6.42; ex USAAF 8th & 9th AF - Arr FAF 19.1.45; GC.II/18 *'Saintonge'* in 9.45
EP186	Spitfire F.Vb/trop (Merlin 46); TOC/RAF 1.6.42 - Arr FAF 9.10.47; BE.708 Meknès
EP204	Spitfire F.Vb/trop (Merlin 46); TOC/RAF 20.6.42 - Arr FAF 9.10.47; BE.708 Meknès
EP249	Spitfire F.Vb (Merlin 46); TOC/RAF 5.6.42; ex No.340 Sqn ('GW-P') - Arr FAF 19.1.45; GC.II/18 *'Saintonge'* in 9.45.
EP286	Spitfire F.Vb/trop (Merlin 46); TOC/RAF 7.6.42 - Arr FAF 14.2.46; Fate unknown
EP433	Spitfire F.Vb/trop (Merlin 46); TOC/RAF 25.6.42; FALS/NWA 1943/44 - Arr FAF, BE.708 Meknès 9.10.47 (also noted 1949)
EP597	Spitfire LF.Vb (Merlin 50M); TOC/RAF 22.7.42; ex No.340 Sqn ('GW-K') - Arr FAF 19.1.45; GC.II/18 *'Saintonge'* in 3.45
EP656	Spitfire F.Vb/trop (Merlin 46); TOC/RAF 19.7.42 - Arr FAF, GR.II/33 *'Savoie'* on 3.6.44; Crash-landed 10.7. or 11.7.44 (Lt Guibaud); R&SU; Retd RAF (No.117 MU); SOC/RAF 29.8.46
EP658	Spitfire F.Vb/trop (Merlin 46); TOC/RAF 19.7.42 - Arr FAF 14.3.46; Fate unknown
EP666	Spitfire F.Vb/trop (Merlin 46); TOC/RAF 20.7.42; FALS/NWA 10.43 (Meknès summer 1946) - Arr FAF 9.10.47; BE.708 Meknès
EP689	Spitfire F.Vb/trop (Merlin 46); TOC/RAF 21.7.42; ME 30.10.42; NA 30.11.43 – FAF, CIC Meknès, accident 8.8.44 (Sgt Pierre Klein); Also accident near Ait Raho 28.12.44 (S/Lt Jean Lafargue)
EP720	Spitfire F.Vb/trop (Merlin 46); TOC/RAF 9.8.42 - Arr FAF, GR.II/33 *'Savoie'* on 2.5.44; Ground accident 10.6.44 (Cne A Dupuy); R&SU; SOC/RAF 10.1.46
EP813	Spitfire F.Vb/trop (Merlin 46); TOC/RAF 1.8.42; ex USAAF - Arr FAF, GR.II/33 *'Savoie'* 13.8.44; Engine trouble, crashed in forced-landing at Montoche near Gray 16.11.44 (Cne de Laborderie), SOC
EP903	Spitfire F.Vb/trop (Merlin 46); TOC/RAF 10.8.42; SOC (ME) 1.6.43, bboc (MAAF) - Arr FAF 14.2.46; BE.708 Meknès (possibly marked 'I'), crashed 20.2.47 (Lt Boutan)
EP914	Spitfire F.Vb/trop (Merlin46); TOC/RAF 15.8.42; Gibraltar 1.11.42; NWA 28.2.43 - FFAF (GC.I/7), ran out of fuel near Corsica, which was still held by the enemy, crash-landed in field, struck ditch, overturned, north of Ajaccio 18.9.43 (Adjt J Cazade); Retd RAF 1.10.43; SOC 29.2.44
ER173	Spitfire F.Vb/trop (Merlin 46); TOC/RAF 26.8.42; ex No.326 Sqn (19.5.45-28.6.45) - Arr FAF 27.11.45; Fate unknown
ER228	Spitfire F.Vb/trop (Merlin 46); TOC/RAF 6.9.42; Arr FAF, parc Blida in 3.44; GR.II/33 *'Savoie'* from 2.5.44; Undercarriage not locked, crash-landed at St.Donat 22.5.44 (Lt de Laborderie); R&SU, SOC/RAF 3.8.45
ER249	Spitfire F.Vb/trop (Merlin 46); TOC/RAF 4.9.42; Gibraltar 1.11.42; NWA 28.2.43 – FFAF (GC.II/7) 31.7.43; Group de Chasse at Bone, engine caught fire in circuit after take-off, landed safely, fire put out Salines, Cat.Ac 5.8.43 (Lt Simard); ROS; Later to No.326 Sqn; SOC 26.4.45
ER315	Spitfire F.Vb/trop (Merlin 46); TOC/RAF 4.9.42 - Arr FAF 14.2.46; BE.708 Meknès
ER319	Spitfire F.Vb/trop (Merlin 46); TOC/RAF 10.9.42 - Arr FAF 29.2.44; GR II/33 *'Savoie'*; Retd RAF 1.9.44; Later sold to Turkey 9.44
ER466	Spitfire F.Vb/trop (Merlin 46); TOC/RAF 13.9.42 - Arr FAF 28.2.46; Fate unknown
ER486	Spitfire F.Vb/trop (Merlin 46); TOC/RAF 15.9.42; MAAF; RAF Training Delegation 27.9.45 - to FAF 27.11.45; Fate unknown
ER606	Spitfire F.Vb/trop (Merlin 46); TOC/RAF 25.9.42; Arr FAF, GR.II/33 *'Savoie'* from 13.8.44, lost orientation in bad weather, fuel shortage, force-landed wheels up near Richardmenils (8m south of Nancy), Cat.E 27.11.44 (Lt Guy Daubresse), SOC
ER619	Spitfire F.Vb/trop (Merlin 46); TOC/RAF 1.10.42; NAAF; RAF Training Delegation 13.9.45 - to FAF 27.11.45; Fate unknown
ER647	Spitfire F.Vb/trop (Merlin 46); TOC/RAF 1.10.42; MAAF; RAF Training Delegation 27.9.45 - to FAF 27.11.45; Fate unknown
ER672	Spitfire F.Vb/trop (Merlin 46); TOC/RAF 1.10.42; MAAF; RAF Training Delegation 27.9.45 - to FAF 27.11.45; Fate unknown
ER712	Spitfire F.Vb/trop (Merlin 46); TOC/RAF 25.10.42; Gibraltar 8.1.43; NWA – FFAF (GC.II/7) 7.43; Esc Group de Chasse Armée de l'Air Française, engine failure in flight near Bia Cueniche, force-landed, Cat.B 27.7.43; Retd RAF (RiW)
ER782	Spitfire F.Vc/trop (Merlin 46); Presentation aircraft *'ASSAM X DIGBOI ASSAM'*; TOC/RAF 15.10.42 - Arr FAF 13.3.46; Fate unknown
ER783	Spitfire F.Vb/trop (Merlin 46); Presentation aircraft *'LIMA CHALLENGER II'*; TOC/RAF 16.10.42 - Arr FAF, BE.708 Meknès 3.7.45; Accident 12.12.45 (Cne Brunschwig)
ER809	Spitfire F.Vb/trop (Merlin 46); TOC/RAF 25.10.42 - FFAF 1.10.43; Later Nos.326-328 Sqns; Retd RAF 16.3.45; SOC 29.8.46
ER816	Spitfire F.Vb/trop (Merlin 46); Presentation aircraft *'BHANBA JHANKA III'*; TOC/RAF 24.10.42; Gibraltar 8.12.42; NWA – FFAF (GC II/7), accident near Bone-les-Salines, Cat.FA/E 21.10. or 22.10.43 (Lt Prevost), SOC
ER931	Spitfire F.Vc/trop (Merlin 46); TOC/RAF 6.11.42; ex USAAF and Nos.327 & 328 Sqns from 12.5.45 - Arr FAF 27.11.45; Fate unknown
ER986	Spitfire F.Vb/trop (Merlin 46); TOC/RAF 13.11.42; MAAF; RAF Training Delegation 20.9.45 - to FAF 27.11.45; Fate unknown
ER998	Spitfire F.Vb/trop (Merlin 46); TOC/RAF 4.12.42; French unit (Nos.326-328 Sqns) - Arr FAF 27.11.45; Fate unknown
ES121	Spitfire F.Vb/trop (Merlin 46); TOC/RAF 8.11.42; MAAF; RAF Training Delegation 4.10.45 - to FAF 27.11.45; Fate unknown
ES129	Spitfire F.Vc/trop (Merlin 46); TOC/RAF 17.11.42 - Arr FAF 14.2.46; BE.708 Meknès 1949
ES143	Spitfire F.Vc/trop (Merlin 46); TOC/RAF 8.11.42 - Arr FAF 27.11.45; BE.708 Meknès 30.7.46
ES176	Spitfire F.Vb/trop (Merlin 46); TOC/RAF 6.12.42 - Arr FAF, GR.II/33 *'Savoie'* in 1944; Accident near St.

	Donat 3.4.44 (Lt Collongues); Retd RAF; Later sold to Greece 4.46
ES192	Spitfire F.Vb/trop (Merlin 46); TOC/RAF 6.12.42; French NWA 1943 – FFAF (GC.II/7), Escadrille Group de Chasse, nosed over in soft sand at Bou Saada, Cat.B 23.3.43; R&SU; Ground-collision with Spitfire JK185 at Souk-el-Khemis, Cat.B 2.5.43 (Plt A Deniau); R&SU; Later No.326 Sqn from 1.12.43 - Arr FAF 27.11.45; Arr BE.708 Meknès 28.2.46; Crashed 17.7.46 (Sgt Metayer)
ES195	Spitfire F.Vc/trop (Merlin 46); TOC/RAF 20.12.42; Gibraltar 6.2.43; NWA 28.2.43 - FFAF (EC.1) 31.10.43; Accident airfield Campo del Oro, Ajaccio, Cat.B 7.11.43 (Lt F Brunet); R&SU; Later to USAAF; Retd RAF; No.327 Sqn 1.8.44; SOC 25.7.45
ES229	Spitfire F.Vc/trop (Merlin 46); TOC/RAF 18.11.42 - Arr FAF 14.3.46; Fate unknown
ES231	Spitfire F.Vc/trop (Merlin 46); TOC/RAF 20.11.42; MAAF (Census 6.45); RAF Training Delegation 6.9.45 - to FAF 27.11.45; Fate unknown
ES285	Spitfire F.Vc/trop (Merlin 46); TOC/RAF 24.1.43 - Arr FAF 28.2.46; Fate unknown
ES294	Spitfire F.Vc/trop (Merlin 46); TOC/RAF 29.11.42; FALS/NWA; SOC 8.3.44, bboc (MAAF) - Arr FAF; Arr BE.708 Meknès 10.9.47
JG257	Spitfire LF.VIIIc (Merlin 66); TOC/RAF 3.10.43; ex USAAF & No.328 Sqn - Arr FAF 11.45; 1.EC (F/Wing); SOC/RAF 1.6.47
JG716	Spitfire F.Vc/trop (Merlin 46); TOC/RAF 9.12.42; Gibraltar 9.2.43; NWA 31.3.43; No.326 Sqn – FAF, CIC Meknès, accident at Bou-Kreis 5.10.44 (Aspt Henri Douchet)
JG746	Spitfire F.Vc/trop (Merlin 45); TOC/RAF 15.12.42; NAASC 31.10.43; US 12th AF, div. to French (No.326 Sqn); Possibly later to FAF 11.45; Fate unknown
JG779	Spitfire F Vc/trop (Merlin 46); TOC/RAF 21.12.42; Gibraltar 6.2.43; ex USAAF, retd to RAF in 10.43; RAF Training Delegation 6.9.45 - to FAF 27.11.45; Fate unknown
JG780	Spitfire F.Vc/trop (Merlin 46); TOC/RAF 21.12.42; ex USAAF - Arr FAF 14.2.46; Fate unknown
JG841	Spitfire F.Vc/trop (Merlin 46); TOC/RAF 31.12.42; Gibraltar 16.2.43; NWA 1.10.43 - FFAF (GC.II/7) 1.10.43 (No.326 Sqn RAF from 1.12.43); Retd into RAF inventory 29.3.44; SOC 30.6.44
JG842	Spitfire F.Vc/trop (Merlin 46); TOC/RAF 3.2.43; Casablanca 25.4.43; NWA 31.7.43 - FFAF (GC.II/7) 31.7.43 (No.326 Sqn RAF from 1.12.43); Crash-landed 3.3.44; R&SU; No.318 Sqn from 17.7.44; SOC 30.6.45
JG848	Spitfire F.Vc/trop (Merlin 46); TOC/RAF 17.12.42; Gibraltar 6.2.43; NWA - FFAF (GC.I/7) 31.10.43; Engine caught fire after landing Reghaia, Cat.A 9.11.43; Retd RAF 30.11.43; SOC 14.3.46
JG870	Spitfire F.Vc/trop (Merlin 46); TOC/RAF 22.12.42; Gibraltar 6.2.43; NWA 31.3.43 - FFAF (GC.II/7) , at Bone, swung off runway landing, tipped on nose in soft sand 17.5.43 (S/C A Morizot); GC.II/7 from 1.10.43 (No.326 Sqn RAF from 1.12.43); SOC 26.4.45
JG885	Spitfire F.Vc/trop (Merlin 46); TOC/RAF 22.12.42; ex No.326 Sqn - Arr FAF 27.11.45; Fate unknown
JG896	Spitfire F.Vc/trop (Merlin 46); TOC/RAF 24.12.42 - Arr FAF 14.3.46; Fate unknown
JG899	Spitfire F.Vc/trop (Merlin 46); TOC/RAF 30.12.42; ex No.326 & 328 Sqns - Arr FAF 1944; GR.II/33 'Savoie'; Fate unknown
JG914	Spitfire F.Vc/trop (Merlin 46); TOC/RAF 2.1.43; Gibraltar 6.2.43; NWA – FFAF, accident 15.9.43; USAAF 1.10.43; SOC/RAF 26.4.45
JG925	Spitfire F.Vb/trop (Merlin 46); TOC/RAF 9.12.42 - Arr FAF 29.2.44; GR.II/33 'Savoie'; Retd RAF, later sold to Egypt 2.45
JG944	Spitfire F.Vc/trop (Merlin 46); TOC/RAF 24.12.42; Gibraltar 6.2.43; NWA 31.7.43 - FFAF 1.10.43; Retd RAF 30.11.43; SOC 25.7.46
JK105	Spitfire F.Vc/trop (Merlin 46); TOC/RAF 21.1.43 - Arr FAF 27.11.45; BE.708 Meknès 8.46; Ground-collision with Spitfire BL551 on 16.8.46
JK111	Spitfire F.Vc/trop (Merlin 46); TOC/RAF 31.12.42; Gibraltar 16.2.43; NWA 28.2.43 - FFAF (date unknown); NAASC 31.10.43; Later to SAAF (SOC/RAF 5.1.46)
JK117	Spitfire F Vc/trop (Merlin 46); TOC/RAF 21.1.43; Gibraltar 7.3.43; NWA 31.3.43 – FFAF (GC.II/7), ground collision with P-40 at Sidi Ahmed, Cat.FB/E 29.5.43 (Plt HR Planchard); SOC 31.7.43
JK123	Spitfire F.Vc/trop (Merlin 46); TOC/RAF 22.1.43; Gibraltar 9.3.43; NWA 31.3.43 – FFAF (GC.II/7), crashed on landing at Bou Saada, Cat.FB/E 8.4.43 (Lt de Saint-Marceau), SOC 31.7.43
JK159	Spitfire F.Vc/trop (Merlin 46); TOC/RAF 18.2.43; Casablanca 6.4.43 - FFAF (date unknown); Retd RAF 30.11.43; Later to SAAF (SOC/RAF 26.4.45)
JK143	Spitfire F.Vc/trop (Merlin 46); TOC/RAF 21.1.43 - Arr FAF 28.2.46; Fate unknown
JK178	Spitfire F.Vc/trop (Merlin 46); TOC/RAF 4.2.43; Gibraltar 7.3.43; NWA 31.3.43 - FFAF (GC.I/7) 1.10.43; Convoy protection, undershot landing airfield Campo del Oro, Ajaccio, struck bank, overturned, Cat.FB/E 31.10.43 (Capt R La Maison), SOC
JK179	Spitfire F.Vc/trop (Merlin 46); TOC/RAF 1.2.42; SOC (NWA) 30.6.44; bboc - Arr FAF 14.3.46; BE.708 Meknès 3.48; Crashed 16.3.48 (Sgt Mangin)
JK185	Spitfire F.Vc/trop (Merlin 46); TOC/RAF 29.1.43; Gibraltar 9.3.43; NWA 31.3.43 – FFAF (GC.II/7), ground-collision with Spitfire ES192 Souk-el-Khemis, Cat.B 2.5.43; R&SU; Retd FFAF 31.10.43, later Nos.326 & 327 Sqns; Accident at Ghisonaccia 14.4.44 (Lt Ragot); SOC 5.12.44
JK251	Spitfire F.Vc/trop (Merlin 46); TOC/RAF 6.2.43; Gibraltar 12.4.43 – FFAF (EC.1), search for missing aircraft, Alghero, Cat.FB/B 5.11.43 (Lt J Le Groignec); SOC/RAF 26.4.45
JK266	Spitfire F.Vc/trop (Merlin 45); TOC/RAF 4.2.43; Gibraltar 12.4.43; NWA 30.4.43 - FFAF (date unknown); NAASC 31.10.43; Retd RAF; Later missing (No.249 Sqn), Cat.FB/E 10.6.44, SOC
JK267	Spitfire F.Vc/trop (Merlin 46); TOC/RAF 3.2.43; Gibraltar 12.4.43; NWA 30.4.43 - FFAF 1.10.43; Later to USAAF; Retd RAF 31.5.44; SOC 14.3.46
JK278	Spitfire F Vc/trop (Merlin 46); TOC/RAF 3.2.43; Casablanca 25.4.43; ex USAAF; RAF Training Delegation 1.11.45 - to FAF 27.11.45; Fate unknown
JK315	Spitfire F.Vc/trop (Merlin 46); TOC/RAF 1.2.43; NWA – FFAF (GC.I/7), turned to starboard after landing, port brakes failed, starboard wheel sank in ditch, turned 180° on nose and starboard wheel failed at Reghaia, Cat.FB/Ac 5.11.43 (Sgt R Pizon); Later Nos.326-328 Sqns; ME census 21.6.45; SOC 29.8.46
JK326	Spitfire F.Vc/trop (Merlin 46); TOC/RAF 4.1.43; Gibraltar 6.2.43; ex No.326 Sqn; No.328 Sqn 7.44 & 8.44 (damaged in ground accident at Dijon, S/Lt Rallet); USAAF, div. to French 10.5.45; Possibly later to FAF 11.45
JK342	Spitfire F.Vc/trop (Merlin 46); TOC/RAF 2.2.43; Arr FAF, GR.II/33 'Savoie' 2.5.44; Belly-landed near Gloria 11.6.44 (Lt Reverday); R&SU; SOC/RAF 26.4.45
JK344	Spitfire F Vc/trop (Merlin 46); TOC/RAF 1.2.43; Gibraltar 26.4.43; ex MAAF; RAF Training Delegation 27.9.45 - to FAF 27.11.45; Fate unknown
JK380	Spitfire F.Vc/trop (Merlin 50); TOC/RAF 2.3.43; ex USAAF – Arr FAF; BE.708 Meknès 9.10.47
JK433	Spitfire F Vc/trop (Merlin 46); TOC/RAF 6.2.43; NWA 30.4.43; ex SAAF & MAAF; RAF Training Delegation 13.9.45 - to FAF 27.11.45; Fate unknown
JK437	Spitfire F Vc/trop (Merlin 46); TOC/RAF 11.2.43; NWA 30.4.43; ex USAAF & MAAF; RAF Training Delegation 13.9.45 - to FAF 27.11.45; Fate unknown
JK440	Spitfire F.Vc/trop (Merlin 46); TOC/RAF 7.2.43; Gibraltar 26.4.43; NWA 31.5.43 - FFAF (unit and date unknown); Retd RAF 29.2.44; SOC 31.8.44

JK443   Spitfire F.Vc/trop (Merlin 46); TOC/RAF 6.2.43; Gibraltar 24.3.43; NWA 30.4.43; NAASC 31.10.43 - FFAF (GC I/7); No.327 Sqn, belly-landed 1m E of mouth of Tamar River, Corsica, Cat.FA/E 26.12.43 (Adj D Roncin), SOC

JK449   Spitfire F.Vc/trop (Merlin 46); TOC/RAF 7.2.43; ex Nos.326 & 328 Sqns - Arr FAF 1944, possibly to GR II/33 'Savoie'

JK455   Spitfire F.Vc/trop (Merlin 50A); TOC/RAF 16.2.43; Casablanca 25.4.43; NWA 31.5.43 – FFAF (GC.II/7) Bone, landed at side of runway to avoid hitting leader, overturned in soft sand, Cat.B 11.9.43 (Master Sgt J Sarrail); SOC/RAF 23.10.44

JK465   Spitfire F.Vc/trop (Merlin 50); TOC/RAF 16.2.43; RAF Training Delegation 13.9.45; SMER/Rochefort 10.45 - to FAF 27.11.45, SMER/Sect Marine d'Ecoles Rochefort

JK507   Spitfire F.Vc/trop (Merlin 46); TOC/RAF 27.1.43; Arr FAF, GR.II/33 'Savoie' from 3.6.44; Destroyed in Ground collision with P-40 at Nettuno, Italy, Cat.E 10.6.44, SOC

JK509   Spitfire F.Vc/trop (Merlin 46); Presentation aircraft 'WADI HALFA'; TOC/RAF 6.2.43 - Arr FAF, GR.II/33 'Savoie' 1.10.43; Crashed Cat.E 7.11.44, SOC

JK519   Spitfire F.Vc/trop (Merlin 46); TOC/RAF 13.2.43 – FFAF (GC.II/7), at Bone, tyre burst on take-off, swung off runway landing, overturned in soft ground, Cat.B 10.9.43 (Sgt R Bousqueynard); R&SU; French unit 1.10.43, later Nos.326-328 Sqns RAF - Arr FAF 1944; GR II/33 'Savoie'; SOC/RAF 18.8.44

JK520   Spitfire F.Vc/trop (Merlin 45); Presentation aircraft 'SUNOCO STREAK'; TOC/RAF 15.2.43; Takoradi 20.4.43; M.E. 23.6.43 - FFAF (date unknown); NAAF 1.11.43; SOC 26.4.45

JK524   Spitfire F.Vc/trop (Merlin 46); TOC/RAF 23.2.43; Casablanca 25.4.43 - US 12th AF 31.7.43; Transferred to a French unit 10.43; Fate unknown

JK543   Spitfire F.Vc/trop (Merlin 50); TOC/RAF 20.3.43; ex USAAF; RAF Training Delegation 25.10.45 - to FAF 27.11.45; SMER/Sect Marine d'Ecoles Rochefort 1946/47

JK550   Spitfire F.Vc/trop (Merlin 45); TOC/RAF 26.3.43; ex USAAF - Arr FAF 14.2.46; Fate unknown

JK614   Spitfire F.Vc/trop (Merlin 46); TOC/RAF 16.2.43; FALS/NWA 6.45 - Arr FAF, BE.708 Meknès 1945; SOC/RAF 30.8.45

JK644   Spitfire F.Vc/trop (Merlin 46); Presentation aircraft 'FORWARD IV'; TOC/RAF 21.2.43; RAF Training Delegation 20.9.45 - to FAF 27.11.45; SMER/Sect Marine d'Ecoles Rochefort 1945/46

JK649   Spitfire F.Vc/trop (Merlin 45); TOC/RAF 16.2.43 - Arr FAF 14.2.46; SMER/Sect Marine d'Ecoles Rochefort 1946

JK666   Spitfire F.Vc/trop (Merlin 46); TOC/RAF 24.2.43; Gibraltar 12.4.43; NWA 31.5.43 – FAF, CIC Meknès, accident 1.5.45 (F/Sgt Michel)

JK718   Spitfire F.Vc/trop (Merlin 46); TOC/RAF 28.2.43; Casablanca 25.4.43 – FFAF (GC.II/7), accident at Sidi Ahmed, Cat.FB/E 20.6.43 (S/C Lamblin), SOC

JK727   Spitfire F Vc/trop (Merlin 46); TOC/RAF 26.2.43; NWA 31.5.43; RAF Training Delegation 27.9.45 - to FAF 27.11.45; Fate unknown

JK761   Spitfire F.Vc/trop (Merlin 46); TOC/RAF 1.3.43; Casablanca 25.4.43; NWA 31.5.43 – FFAF (GC.I/7) Ajaccio, overturned in soft ground after tyre burst during take-off, Cat.E 18.10.43 (Sub/Lt RA Martin injured); SOC 29.2.44

JK780   Spitfire F.Vc/trop (Merlin 50); TOC/RAF 6.3.43; NWA 31.5.43; ex USAAF – FFAF until 31.10.43; Retd RAF (later SAAF from 28.2.44)

JK806   Spitfire F.Vc/trop (Merlin 46); TOC/RAF 28.2.43; Casablanca 25.4.43; NWA 31.5.43 – FFAF (GC.II/7), belly landing after convoy escort, Bone, Cat.B 21.8.43 (Sgt J Sarrail); R&SU; Retd FFAF 31.08.43; USAAF; Retd RAF 31.5.44; Later to Turkey 11.44

JK823   Spitfire F.Vc/trop (Merlin 50); TOC/RAF 21.3.43; ex USAAF 12 AF – FFAF (GC.II/7), at Bone, ferrying, undercarriage collapsed landing, Cat.Ac 20.9.43 (Sgt Brown); French Unit NWA [by] 1.10.43; No.328 Sqn from 12.5.45 - Arr FAF 27.11.45; Fate unknown

JK825   Spitfire F.Vc/trop (Merlin 50); TOC/RAF 1.4.43; NWA - FFAF (GC.I/7) 1.10.43; No.328 Sqn, accident at Taher 17.3.44 (Lt Madon) - Arr FAF, GR.II/33 'Savoie' from 15.6.44; Destroyed on take-off at Follonica, Italy, Cat.E 11.7. or 16.7.44 (Cne Amedee Dupuy, also reported: Cne de Laborderie), SOC

JK833   Spitfire F.Vc/trop (Merlin 50); TOC/RAF 31.3.43; Casablanca 17.5.43 - FFAF (GC I/3, date unknown); No.327 Sqn 1.12.43; Escorting C-47, crashed Ghisonaccia, Corsica, Cat.FB/E 16.12.43 (Lt G Pisotte safe), SOC

JK867   Spitfire F.Vc/trop (Merlin 50); TOC/RAF 12.3.43; Casablanca 25.4.43; NWA 31.5.43 – FFAF (GC.I/7), harbour protection, tail struck fence while landing airfield Campo del Oro, Ajaccio, aircraft hit bank, tail broke, overturned, Cat.FB/E 25.10.43 (Capt J Duc injured), SOC

JK886   Spitfire F.Vc/trop (Merlin 46); TOC/RAF 11.3.43; Casablanca 25.4.43, NWA 31.5.43; No.328 Sqn, accident at Taher, Cat.FB/B 7.4.44 (Lt de Beaupuis); R&SU – FAF, CIC Meknès, accident 20.3.45 (F/Sgt de la Flecheres); SOC 5.4.45

JK923   Spitfire F.Vc/trop (Merlin 45); TOC/RAF 26.3.43; NWA - FFAF (GC.II/7) Bone, navigation error, possibly faulty ASI, short of fuel, ditched in sea, Cat.FB/E 17.9.43 (Lt G Amarger rescued unhurt), SOC

JK937   Spitfire F.Vc/trop (Merlin 46); TOC/RAF 17.3.43; Casablanca 25.4.43; NWA 31.5.43 – FFAF (GC.II/7) Bone, engine failure, oil leak, pilot baled out, aircraft crashed in sea 40m NE of Bone/3m E of Fagus, Cat.FB/E 20.9.43 (Lt A Lancois OK), SOC

JK946   Spitfire F.Vc/trop (Merlin 50); TOC/RAF 13.3.43 - Arr FAF 28.2.46; Fate unknown

JK948   Spitfire F.Vc/trop (Merlin 50); TOC/RAF 15.3.43; NWA – FFAF in 8.43; USAAF in 12.43 (lost 27.1.44)

JK972   Spitfire F Vc/trop (Merlin 46); TOC/RAF 20.3.43; N.A. 31.5.43; RAF Training Delegation 27.9.45 - to FAF 27.11.45; Fate unknown

JK980   Spitfire F.IXc (Merlin 63); TOC/RAF 28.3.43, GR.II/33 'Savoie' 1944/45 (loan); Sold to FAF 25.7.46; to A.N.; Esc 4.Serv. ('4.S-10') by 21.3.47 - 6.49; R&SU 11.4.50, for CN Cuers; SOC 2.9.50; confirmed 20.11.50 (3.RM)

JL104   Spitfire F.Vc/trop (Merlin 50); TOC/RAF 9.4.43; Casablanca 17.5.43; NWA 31.5.43 – FFAF (GC.II/7), at Bone, burst tyre on take-off, swung, undercarriage collapsed, Cat.B 15.8.43 (Capt G Prayer); Retd RAF 1.10.43; SOC 27.6.46

JL114   Spitfire F.Vc/trop (Merlin 50); TOC/RAF 25.4.43; Casablanca 14.7.43; NWA – FFAF (GC.II/7), stranger to aerodrome, oil on windscreen, bright sun low in sky, overshot into fence airfield Campo del Oro, Ajaccio, Cat.FA/B 17.9.43; R&SU; Retd RAF 1.10.43 (PSO 1.1.47)

JL121   Spitfire F.Vc/trop (Merlin 50); TOC/RAF 5.5.43; ex USAAF 12th & 8th AF; No.326 Sqn 10.44, No.327 Sqn 12.5.45 - Arr FAF 27.11.45; Fate unknown

JL123   Spitfire F Vc/trop (Merlin 50); TOC/RAF 5.5.43; M.E. 1.10.43; ex MAAF; RAF Training Delegation 1.11.45 - to FAF 27.11.45; Fate unknown

JL160   Spitfire F.Vc/trop (Merlin 45); TOC/RAF 31.3.43; FALS/NWA 1944 - Arr FAF, BE.708 Meknès 9.10.47

JL162   Spitfire F Vc/trop (Merlin 45); TOC/RAF 3.4.43; ex MAAF; RAF Training Delegation 6.9.45 - to FAF 27.11.45; Rochefort, possibly 1949

JL185   Spitfire F.Vc/trop (Merlin 45); TOC/RAF 28.2.43; To French NWA 31.10.43 - FFAF; Later Nos.326 & 328 Sqns, and to FAF 27.11.1945; Fate unknown

JL210   Spitfire F.Vc/trop (Merlin 50); TOC/RAF 2.4.43; Casablanca 17.5.43; NWA – FFAF (GC I/7) 1.10.43; Retd RAF 30.11.43; M.E. 31.8.44; Later to Turkey 9.44

FRANCE

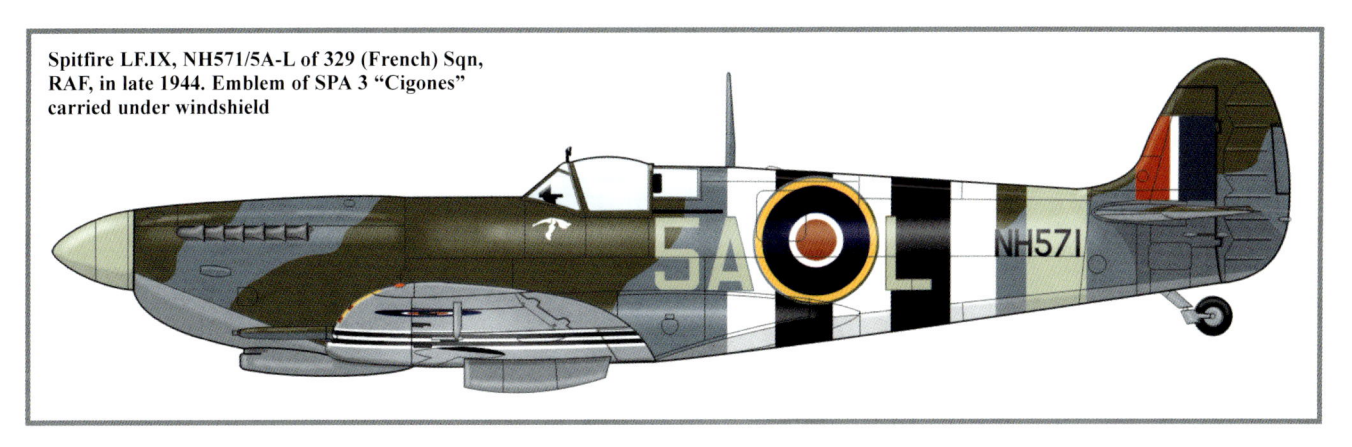

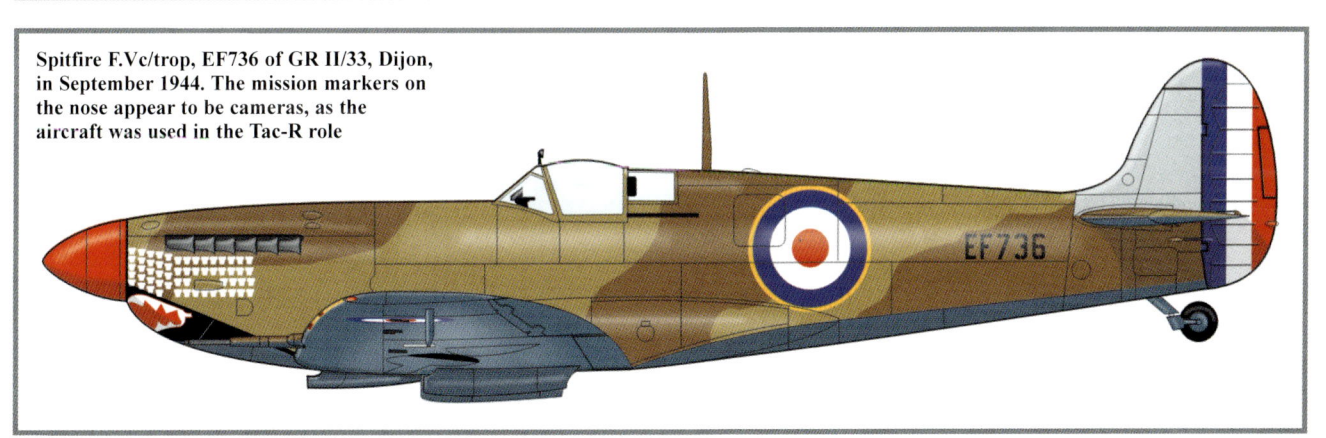

Spitfire LF.IX, NH571/5A-L of 329 (French) Sqn, RAF, in late 1944. Emblem of SPA 3 "Cigones" carried under windshield

Spitfire F.I, F.01/FWB of the French Air Force in 1940

Spitfire F.Vc/trop, EF736 of GR II/33, Dijon, in September 1944. The mission markers on the nose appear to be cameras, as the aircraft was used in the Tac-R role

JL221	Spitfire F.Vc/trop (Merlin 50); TOC/RAF 16.4.43; ex USAAF - Arr FAF 28.2.46; BE.708 Meknès, crashed 6.46
JL234	Spitfire LF.IXc (Merlin 66); TOC/RAF 11.4.43; ex USAAF 12 & 8 AF - Arr FAF, GR.II/33 'Savoie' in 12.44; Ground accident at Luxeuil 2.1. or 2.2.45 (Cdt M Martre); R&SU; No.328 Sqn from 5.4.45 to 25.4.45
JL235	Spitfire F.Vc/trop (Merlin 50); TOC/RAF 4.4.43; NAASC; RAF Training Delegation 25.10.45 - to FAF 27.11.45; to A.N, Esc 5.Serv.; SMER/Sect Marine d'Ecoles Rochefort 1951/52 (still marked '5.S- ')
JL251	Spitfire F.Vc/trop (Merlin 50); TOC/RAF 16.4.43; Casablanca 30.5.43; NWA 30.6.43 - FFAF 31.10.43; Retd RAF; Later to Italy 6.46
JL310	Spitfire F.Vc/trop (Merlin 50); TOC/RAF 14.5.43; Casablanca 15.6.43; NWA 1.7.43 – FFAF (GC.I/7), swung after landing from operation, brake failed, nosed in at Reghaia, Cat.B 9.11.43 (S/Lt G Bouthier); R&SU; Retd RAF; SOC 29.6.44
JL316	Spitfire F.Vc/trop (Merlin 50); TOC/RAF 6.5.43; Casablanca 15.6.43; NWA 1.7.43 - FFAF (GC.II/7) 31.10.43, later No.326 Sqn (marked '2', flown by Lt Claude Mangin 11.43); No.328 Sqn, Ajaccio harbour patrol, accident airfield Campo del Oro, Cat.FB/Ac 6.12.43 (Lt H Jeandet)
JL333	Spitfire F.Vc/trop (Merlin 50); TOC/RAF 30.6.43; Casablanca 19.9.43; N.A. 30.11.43 – FFAF (GC.II/7), then No.326 Sqn 1.12.43; Later to USAAF; Retd RAF 31.5.44 (PSO 1.1.47)
JL374	Spitfire F.Vc/trop (Merlin 50); TOC/RAF 18.4.43; Casablanca 30.5.43; NWA 1.7.43 - FFAF, GC I/3 31.10.43; To USAAF; Retd RAF 31.5.44; Later to Turkey 11.44
JL387	Spitfire F.Vc/trop (Merlin 50); TOC/RAF 19.4.43; Casablanca 30.5.43; NWA 1.7.43 - FFAF (GC.I/7) 1.10.43; Taxied into truck on perimeter at Bone, Cat.B 8.10.43 (Adjt J Monchanin); Retd RAF; SOC 26.4.45
LR793	Seafire L.IIIc (Merlin 55M); RNDA 30.9.43 - Arr A.N. 1948; storage SEC Cuers, tested 9.6.48 and flown to Hyères; SOC 18.6.49
LR815	Seafire L.IIIc (Merlin 55M); RNDA 13.11.43; ex No.894 & 899 Sqn (1944/45) - Arr A.N. 1948; Service unknown; SOC 30.4.49
LV650	Spitfire LF.VIIIc (Merlin 66); TOC/RAF 22.12.43; ex ACSEA - Arr FAF 11.45; 1.EC (F/Wing) 1.1.46 (recorded by 11.1.46); SOC/RAF 9.5.46 NOTE: Serial No also reported "LV659" (TOC/RAF 30.12.43, SOC 14.2.46)
LZ818	Spitfire F.Vc/trop (Merlin 45); TOC/RAF 4.4.43; Casablanca 17.5.43 – FAF, CIC Meknès, crashed 10m from Ras-el-Mah airfield 29.8.44 (Sgt Pierre Maho)

LZ876 Spitfire F.Vc/trop (Merlin 50); TOC/RAF 25.4.43; Casablanca 30.5.43; NWA 1.7.43 – FFAF (EC.1) 31.10.43; Accident Campo del Oro, Ajaccio, Cat.B 7.11.43 (Capt J Duc); Retd RAF; No.327 Sqn 1.12.43, taxy-crash 28.12.43

LZ987 Spitfire F.Vc/trop (Merlin 50); TOC/RAF 21.5.43; NWA 10.43 - FFAF 31.10.43; RAF Training Delegation 4.10.45; To FAF 27.11.45; Fate unknown

MA222 Spitfire LF.IXc (Merlin 66); TOC/RAF 2.5.43; ex No.80 OTU - Allotted for FAF 8.3.46; Arr BE.708 Meknès ('A') 14.3.46 (shown also 1949 & 1950)

MA240 Spitfire F.IXc (Merlin 63); TOC/RAF 13.5.43 - Arr FAF 27.11.45; BE.708 Meknès 1949

MA251 Spitfire F.IXc (Merlin 63); TOC/RAF 13.5.43 - Arr FAF 29.2.44; Retd RAF; Later sold to Egypt 1946

MA254 Spitfire F.IXc (Merlin 63); TOC/RAF 16.5.43 – FFAF (GC.II/7), at Bone, scrambled for operation, undercarriage not locked down, collapsed on landing, Cat.FB/A 27.8.43 (F/Lt H Hoarau de la Source); French unit from 1.10.43 - FAF, GR.II/33 'Savoie' in 3.44; Retd RAF; No.326 Sqn, accident off Iles Sanguinaires 2.8.44 (Lt Roger Laurent missing); SOC 31.8.44

MA301 Spitfire F.IXc (Merlin 63); TOC/RAF 29.5.43 - Arr FAF 25.6.46; BE.708 Meknès 6.49; Ground collision with Spitfire BS555 on 17.6. or 21.6.49

MA307 Spitfire F.IXc (Merlin 63); TOC/RAF 28.5.43; Casablanca 29.6.43; NAAF 1.11.43 – FAF, CIC Meknès, accident 22.2.45 (Aspt Criqui); R&SU; Crashed Cat.FA/E 12.5.45; SOC 23.8.45

MA308 Spitfire F.IXc (Merlin 63); TOC/RAF 29.5.43 - Arr FAF 24.5.46; BE.708 Meknès 10.49; Crashed 5.4.50 (S/M Morant)

MA309 Spitfire F.IXc (Merlin 63); TOC/RAF 30.5.43; ex No.326 Sqn & No.80 OTU - Arr FAF, BE.708 Meknès 14.3.46; Crashed 12.3. or 13.2.47

MA314 Spitfire F.IXc (Merlin 63); TOC/RAF 30.5.43; ex No.80 OTU - Arr FAF, BE.708 Meknès 11.4.46 (noted also 1949)

MA401 Spitfire F.IXc (Merlin 63); TOC/RAF 27.5.43; ex No.328 Sqn; No.326 Sqn, accident at Belfort 10.2.45 (F/Sgt Geremia); R&SU - Arr FAF 27.11.45; GC.I/6 'Corse' Indo-China 1950

MA415 Spitfire F.IXc (Merlin 63); TOC/RAF 25.5.43; ex No.326 Sqn - Arr FAF 7.7.46; GC.I/4 'Dauphiné'; GC.II/4 'La Fayette' 7.47

MA420 Spitfire F.IXc (Merlin 63); TOC/RAF 22.7.43; ex No.80 OTU from 2.6.45 - Arr FAF, BE.708 Meknès 14.3.46; Crashed Cat.E 5.10.49 (Sgt Unuoas); SOC

MA428 Spitfire F.IXc (Merlin 63); TOC/RAF No.9 MU 19.7.43; Casablanca 18.8.43; NWA 1.10.43 - FFAF 30.11.43; Nos.326-328 Sqns from 12.43; No.340 Sqn, dived into sea, Cat.FB/E 29.2.44 (Lt P Borossy), SOC

MA476 Spitfire F.IXc (Merlin 63); TOC/RAF 26.6.43; ex No.80 OTU from 7.6.45 - Allotted for FAF 8.3.46, arr BE.708 Meknès 14.3.46 (shown also 2.49)

MA512 Spitfire F.IXc (Merlin 63); TOC/RAF 13.6.43; ex No.327 & 328 Sqns - Arr FAF 27.11.45; GC.II/7 'Nice' 23.10.46; Tyre burst, Cat.FA/E 25.3.47, SOC

MA528 Spitfire F.IXc (Merlin 63); TOC/RAF 20.6.43; ex No.80 OTU/RAF – Arr FAF, BE.708 Meknès 14.3.46; Crashed 18.6.46 (S/Lt Roncin); R&SU; BE.708, fuel shortage, force-landed wheels-up, Cat.E 11.12.47 (Sgt Binet); SOC

MA534 Spitfire F.IXc (Merlin 63); Presentation aircraft 'LIBERATION'; TOC/RAF 19.6.43; Casablanca 14.7.43; NAASC 31.10.43 – FFAF (GC.II/7) 30.11.43; No.326 Sqn from 1.12.43; Crashed Cat.FB/E 12.2.45, SOC

MA539 Spitfire F.IXc (Merlin 63); TOC/RAF 21.6.43; Casablanca 29.7.43; NWA - FFAF 1.10.43; No.326 Sqn, accident off Calvi 7.8.44 (Adjt Jean Doudies missing); SOC 31.8.44

MA568 Spitfire F.IXc (Merlin 63); TOC/RAF 25.6.43 - Allotted for FAF 17.6.46, arr BE.708 Meknès 25.6.46; Crashed 16.3.47; also crashed 3.4.50 (EV1ère CP Nosneron)

MA571 Spitfire F.IXc (Merlin 63); Became F-UGPW; TOC/RAF 25.6.43 - Allotted for FAF 8.10.46, arr FAF 17.10.46; GC.I/4 'Dauphiné' 1948; Crashlanding, lost undercarriage at PC482 Bien Hoa 21.12.48 (Lt Villien safe); R&SU; GC.I/3 'Navarre' ('D') 26.5.49; Crashed at Lang-Son 1.10.49 (S/Lt Bardou); R&SU 28.10.49; GC.I/6 'Corse' ('W') in 4.50, noted also in 7.50

MA574 Spitfire F.IXc (Merlin 63); TOC/RAF 20.6.43; NWA-FFAF 1.10.43; GC.I/7 ('A') 11.43; No.328 Sqn 1.12.43; Fate unknown

MA591 Spitfire F.IXc (Merlin 63); TOC/RAF 25.6.43 - Arr FAF 25.4.46; BE.708 Meknès ('I'), collided with Spitfire BR140 on take-off 14.2.47 (Plt Noel killed), SOC

MA595 Spitfire F. IXc (Merlin 63); TOC/RAF 30.6.43; Casablanca 29.7.43; USAAF 31.10.43 – FAF; CIC Meknès, accident 16.6.44 (Lt Martinet)

MA600 Spitfire F.IXc (Merlin 63); TOC/RAF 27.6.43; Casablanca 29.7.43; NWA 1.10.43 - FFAF 31.10.43; Retd RAF; SOC 14.3.46

MA622 Spitfire F.IXc (Merlin 63A); TOC/RAF 28.6.43; NWA - FFAF (GC.I/7) 31.10.43; Accident on scramble airfield Campo del Oro, Ajaccio, Cat.FB/Ac 7.11.43 (Lt G Amarger); Later Nos.326-328 Sqns (crash reported for "622": No.327 Sqn off Calvi 13.7.44 (Adjt M Verunes missing)

MA679 Spitfire F.Vc/trop (Merlin 46); TOC/RAF 21.6.43 - Arr FAF, GR II/33 'Savoie' 29.2.44

MA695 Spitfire F.Vc/trop (Merlin 46); TOC/RAF 23.6.43 - Arr FAF, GR.II/33 'Savoie' 29.2.44; Retd RAF; Later to USAAF; Sold to Greece 1946

MA704 Spitfire F.Vc/trop (Merlin 55); TOC/RAF 1.7.43; N.A.; - Arr FAF, GR II/33 'Savoie' 29.2.44; Retd to RAF; Later sold to Greece 25.4.46

MA708 Spitfire F.IXc (Merlin 63); TOC/RAF 1.7.43 - Arr FAF, GR.II/33 'Savoie' 29.2.44; Retd RAF; Later sold to Greece 1946

MA711 Spitfire F.IXc (Merlin 63); TOC/RAF 29.6.43 – FFAF (GC.II/7), Group de Chasse at Bone, scramble, crashed c.20m from Bone, Cat.FB/3 on 27.8.43 (Lt J Lancesseur); bboc; Retd FFAF 1.10.43; Later Nos.326 & 328 Sqns; Possibly to FAF 27.11.45

MA727 Spitfire F.IXc (Merlin 63); TOC/RAF 3.7.43; Casablanca 16.8.43; NWA 1.10.43 - FFAF 30.11.43; Nos.326-328 Sqns from 1.12.43; Crashed Cat.FA/3 on 1.2.44, SOC

MA730 Spitfire F.IXc (Merlin 63); TOC/RAF 30.6.43; Casablanca 16.8.43; No.218 Grp N.A. 30.11.43 - FFAF 30.11.43; Nos.326-328 Sqns; Crashed Cat.FB/3 on 20.2.44 (Adj M Haberkorn); SOC

MA731 Spitfire F.IXc (Merlin 63); TOC/RAF 1.7.43; Casablanca 16.8.43; No.218 Grp N.A. 30.11.43 – FFAF, and Nos.326-328 Sqns from 1.12.43; Crashed Cat.FB/E 12.3.45, SOC

MA735 Spitfire F.IXc (Merlin 63A); TOC/RAF 16.7.43 - Arr FAF 16.4.46; BE.708 Meknès 1949

MA810 Spitfire F.IXc (Merlin 63); TOC/RAF 24.7.43 - Arr FAF 24.5.46; At Oran (unit unknown) 27. or 31.5.46; BE.708 Meknès 1949

MA813 Spitfire F (LF) IXc (Merlin 63, later M.66); TOC/RAF 24.7.43 - Arr FAF, Châteaudun (ferry flight) 15.8.46; GC.I/4 'Dauphiné', test flight 19.9.48; Merlin 66 installed 11.48; GC.I/6 'Corse' 1950

MA818 Spitfire F.IXc (Merlin 63); TOC/RAF 29.7.43; ex No.80 OTU - Allotted for FAF 8.3.46, arr BE.708 Meknès ('P') 14.3.46 (shown also 1949)

MA831 Spitfire F.IXc (Merlin 63); TOC/RAF 21.7.43 - Arr FAF 25.4.46; BE.708 Meknès 1949 (possibly flown by P Lavergne, recorded "MA318"

MA834 Spitfire F.IXc (Merlin 63); TOC/RAF 25.7.43 - Arr FAF 17.6.46; BE.708 Meknès ('P') 1950

MA841 Spitfire F.IXc (Merlin 63); TOC/RAF 24.7.43 - Arr FAF 31.7.46; Unknown unit, engine failure, force-landed, crashed 12.7. or 15.7.47

MA844 Spitfire F.IXc (Merlin 63); TOC/RAF 28.7.43 - Arr FAF 11.7.46; GC.I/3 'Navarre' ('P') 22.3.49; Dived into ground near Bac Hac or Vietri, pilot baled out 26.8.49 (Adj Valentin safe); SOC
NOTE: Reported also as "MA849"

MA882 Spitfire F.Vc/trop (Merlin 55); TOC/RAF 18.7.43 - Arr FAF, GR.II/33 *'Savoie'* 13.8.44; lost orientation, fuel shortage, force-landed near Neufchâteau (Moncourt) 27.11.44 (Cne Sebastien Battle); R&SU

MA893 Spitfire F.Vc/trop (Merlin 55); TOC/RAF 24.7.43; ex USAAF - Arr FAF, BE.708 Meknès 9.10.47

MA898 Spitfire F.Vc/trop (Merlin 46); TOC/RAF 23.6.43 - Arr FAF, GR.II/33 *'Savoie'* 29.2.44; Retd RAF; USAAF; SOC/RAF 11.10.45

MA901 Spitfire F.Vc/trop (Merlin 46); TOC/RAF 26.6.43 - Arr FAF, GR.II/33 *'Savoie'* 29.2.44; Retd RAF; USAAF; SOC/RAF 26.9.46

MB962 Spitfire LF.VIIIc (Merlin 66); TOC/RAF 23.3.44 - Arr FAF 11.45; 1.EC (F/Wing), dived into sea, Cat.E 1.2.46 (Lt Col Papin-Labazordière killed, body not found); SOC 31.10.46

MD215 Spitfire LF.VIIIc (Merlin 66); TOC/RAF 8.1.44; ex ACSEA - Arr FAF 11.45; 1.EC (F/Wing), on ops 27.1.46

MD254 Spitfire LF.VIIIc (Merlin 66); TOC/RAF 8.2.44; ex ACSEA - Arr FAF 11.45; 1.EC (F/Wing), support of ground troops 18.12.45; GC.II/7 *'Nice'*, undershot landing, spun in at Tan Son Nhut, Cat.E/2 (S/Lt de Pradel) 3.2.46, SOC

MD256 Spitfire LF.VIIIc (Merlin 66); TOC/RAF 19.2.44; ex ACSEA - Arr FAF 11.45; 1.EC (F/Wing), noted 6.1.46; SOC/RAF 29.3.46

MD288 Spitfire LF.VIIIc (Merlin 66); TOC/RAF 14.2.44; ex ACSEA - Arr FAF 11.45; 1.EC (F/Wing), system failure, take-off stopped 20.1.46 (Cne du Boucher); SOC/RAF 5.46

MD289 Spitfire LF.VIIIc (Merlin 66); TOC/RAF 8.2.44; ex ACSEA - Arr FAF 11.45; 1.EC (F/Wing), radio call (incorrectly "MD298") 22.12.45; Retd RAF and shipped to India (RIAF), SOC 1.6.47

MH304 Spitfire F.Vc/trop (Merlin 55); TOC/RAF 18.7.43; FALS/NWA 6.45 - Arr FAF 6.45; GR.II/33 *'Savoie'*; SOC/RAF 30.8.45

MH309 Spitfire F.Vc/trop (Merlin 55); TOC/RAF 19.7.43 - Arr FAF, GR.II/33 *'Savoie'* 29.2.44

MH310 Spitfire F.Vc/trop (Merlin 55); TOC/RAF 25.7.43; Casablanca 10.9.43; N.A. 30.11.43 – FFAF, later Nos.326-328 Sqns from 31.12.43; SOC 26.4.45

MH316 Spitfire F.IXc (Merlin 63); TOC/RAF 28.7.43 - Arr FAF 4.7.46; GC.I/4 *'Dauphiné'*, fuel shortage, engine failed, force-landed near Niedermendig, Germany, Cat.FA/E 25.6.47, SOC

MH326 Spitfire F.IXc (Merlin 63); TOC/RAF 31.7.43 - Arr FAF, Châteaudun 31.7.46; GC.I/4 *'Dauphiné'* 9.48; GC.I/3 *'Navarre'* ('E') 1.2.49; Crashed near Tu Ky, Cat.E 23.5.49 (Adj Friedrich safe), SOC

MH331 Spitfire F.IXc (Merlin 61); TOC/RAF 6.8.43; ex No.80 OTU - Arr FAF, BE.708 Meknès 14.3.46; Undercarriage failure, landed wheels-up, Cat.E 25.3.49 (S/Lt Choquet); SOC

MH352 Spitfire F.IXc (Merlin 61); TOC/RAF 31.7.43 - Arr FAF 10.4.46; BE.708 Meknès ('X') 19.2.49; Crashed on landing, Cat.E 4.7.49 (EV1ère Bussiere); SOC

MH353 Spitfire F.IXc (Merlin 63); TOC/RAF 29.7.43; ex No.80 OTU ('3H-J') from 29.5.45 - Allotted for FAF 8.3.46, arr BE.708 Meknès 14.3.46

MH356 Spitfire F.IXc (Merlin 61); TOC/RAF 31.7.43 - Allotted for FAF 6.8.46, arr FAF 11.8.46; Fate unknown

MH368 Spitfire F.IXc (Merlin 63); TOC/RAF 9.8.43 - Arr FAF 26.6.47; Air Depot EAA No.601, engine failure on take-off, crashed at Moutier-Chaume 22.7.47; GC.II/3 *'Champagne' (possibly NH368 ?)*

MH378 Spitfire F.IXc (Merlin 63); TOC/RAF 7.8.43 - Arr FAF, Châteaudun (ferry flight) 7.7.46; GC.I/6 *'Corse'* ('J') 4.50

MH418 Spitfire LF.IXc (Merlin 66); TOC/RAF 11.8.43; ex No.328 Sqn - Arr FAF 27.11.45; GC.I/1 *'Provence'*, undercarriage failed, belly-landed 1.48; R&SU; GC.I/4 *'Dauphiné'*, crashed 11.2.48; R&SU; DMAA 632 (Direct du Materiel de l'Armée de l'Air) 6.51; BE.708 Meknès 9.51

MH482 Spitfire LF.IXc (Merlin 66); TOC/RAF 19.8.43; ex No.329 & 326 Sqns - SNCAN Mureaux 21.6.45, to FAF 27.11.45; BE.708 Meknès 3.47 (also shown 19.10.49)

MH498 Spitfire LF.IXc (Merlin 66); TOC/RAF 20.8.43; ex No.341 Sqn - Arr FAF, Châteaudun (ferry flight) 17.8.46; GC.II/7 *'Nice'*, test flight 13.1.47; 4.EC ('I', or 'T') 8.10.47; GC.II/4 *'La Fayette'* ('T'), noted 8.11.47 (also 4.48); Flat tyre, crashed at Gia-lam 1.12.47 (Asp Bardou); R&SU; GC.II/4 ('I'), undercarriage collapsed, belly-landed at Gia-lam 23.5.48 (Lt Michard safe); R&SU; GC.I/3 *'Navarre'* ('T'), noted 1949

MH545 Spitfire F.IXc (Merlin 63); TOC/RAF 2.9.43; Casablanca 10.10.43; NAASC 31.10.43 – FAF, CIC Meknès, accident 28.12.44 (S/C Julien Ginestet); Retd RAF; Retd FAF 28.3.46, and to A.N.; via Cuers to 1.Flottilla 2.4.46 ('1.F-17', shown in 7.46); Mureaux 25.6.47; RiW SNCAN by 21.11.47, also 13.8.48; SRC to Esc 3.Serv. 8.9.50; General discharge 7.11.50, to Lanvéoc-Poulmic; SOC 13.2.51 (3.RM)

MH594 Spitfire F.Vc/trop (Merlin 55); TOC/RAF 14.8.43; ex USAAF; No.327 Sqn; No.326 Sqn Ajaccio, accident at Campo del Oro 16.7.44 (S/C Rene Bousqueynaud); R&SU; No.326 Sqn, accident at Lyons-Bron 8.9.44 (Lt de Latour-Dejean); FALS/NWA from 6.45 – Arr FAF; BE.708 Meknès 9.10.47

MH596 Spitfire F.Vc/trop (Merlin 55); TOC/RAF 15.8.43 - Arr FAF, GR.II/33 *'Savoie'* from 15.6.44; Engine failure on take-off at Calvi, Cat.E 21.8. or 22.8.44 (Lt Callac); SOC/RAF 31.8.44

MH666 Spitfire F.IXc (Merlin 63); TOC/RAF 4.9.43; ex No.80 OTU - Allotted for FAF 8.3.46, arr BE.708 Meknès 14.3.46 (shown also 29.7.49); Crashed Cat.E 13.5.50 (Lt Berg); SOC

MH671 Spitfire F.IXc (Merlin 63); TOC/RAF 11.9.43 - Arr FAF 25.4.46; Fate unknown

MH717 Spitfire LF.IXc (Merlin 66); TOC/RAF 16.9.43; ex No.326 Sqn - Arr FAF 27.11.45; GC.II/7 *'Nice'* 11.46; GC.I/7 *'Provence'* 1947; GC.I/4 *'Dauphiné'* 1.48; GC.I/1 *'Provence'*, crashed 11.2.48 (Asp Dubarry)

MH732 Spitfire LF.IXc (Merlin 66); TOC/RAF 17.9.43 - Arr FAF 28.3.46; to A.N., 1.Flottille or Esc 54.Serv., crashed at Hyères, aircraft destroyed 19.2.47 (EV1 Pierre Mallez kld), SOC 11.3.47

MH829 Spitfire F.IXc (Merlin 63); TOC/RAF 24.9.43 - Allotted for FAF 25.6.46, arr FAF 9.7.46; BE.708 Meknès 1949

MH840 Spitfire F.IXc (Merlin 63); TOC/RAF 1.10.43; ex No.80 OTU - Arr FAF 14.3.46; SNCAN Mureaux 19.3.46; BE.708 Meknès 4.4.46

MH881 Spitfire F.IXc (Merlin 63); TOC/RAF 2.10.43 - Arr FAF 27.11.45; GC.II/1 *'Nice'* 1949 & 1950

MH894 Spitfire F.IXc (Merlin 63); TOC/RAF 18.9.43; ex No.326 Sqn - Arr FAF 27.11.45; GC.I/1 *'Provence'* 9.48, at Oran 11.48; GC.I/1 *'Provence'* (arr date unknown) until 20.10.49

MH936 Spitfire F.IXc (Merlin 63); TOC/RAF 26.9.43 - Arr FAF, Châteaudun (ferry flight) 20.7.46; GC.I/4 *'Dauphiné'* ('U'), test flight Bien Hoa 9.12.47 (also 13.1. or 19.1.48); Landed crosswind, one leg failed, crashed at Soc Trang 23.3.48 (Sgt Le Goffic safe)

MH988 Spitfire F.IXc (Merlin 63); TOC/RAF 4.9.43; ex USAAF; No.328 Sqn; No.327 Sqn, accident at Borgo 22.6.44 (S/Lt Deniau); R&SU - via Nos.340/345 Sqns to FAF 27.11.45; Fate unknown

MJ114 Spitfire LF.IXc (Merlin 66); TOC/RAF 6.10.43; ex No.327 Sqn - Arr FAF, GC.II/7 *'Nice'* 27.11.45; Undercarriage failed, belly-landed at Oran 16.4.47 (Plt A Jean); Accident Oran 15.6.48 (Sgt Lombard)

MJ133 Spitfire LF.IXc (Merlin 66); TOC/RAF 17.10.43; ex No.327 Sqn - SNCAN Mureaux 21.6.45, to FAF 27.11.45 (shown by 26.7.46); Service unknown; SOC 21.6.47

MJ139 Spitfire LF.IXc (Merlin 66); TOC/RAF 17.10.43 - Arr FAF; GC.I/2 on 15.8.46; GC.III/2, crashed into ground Hoc Mon near Saigon 24.3.47 (S/Lt Meunier killed); SOC

MJ197 Spitfire FR IXc (Merlin 66); TOC/RAF 16.10.43 - Arr FAF, Châteaudun (ferry flight) 15.8.46; GC.I/4 'Dauphiné' ('F'), noted 12.48

MJ198 Spitfire LF.IXc (Merlin 66); Became **F-UGBV**; TOC/RAF 17.10.43; ex No.327 Sqn - Arr FAF 27.11.45; 1.EC, crashed near Freiburg, Germany 26.2.47; R&SU; GC.I/1 'Provence' ('V') in 7.47; GC II/1 'Nice' in 5.50; BE.708 Meknès ('V'), crashed 24.9.51 (Adj Besse)

MJ201 Spitfire LF.IXc (Merlin 66); TOC/RAF 16.10.43 - Arr FAF, Châteaudun (ferry flight) 18.6.46; GC.I/4 'Dauphiné' 10.47, engine failure on take-off, crashed at Tan Son Nhut, Cat.E 11.11.47 (Lt Cazenave safe), SOC

MJ222 Spitfire F.IXc (Merlin 63); TOC/RAF 1.10.43 - Arr FAF 10.4.46; BE.708 Meknès 1949

MJ230 Spitfire LF.IXc (Merlin 66); TOC/RAF 18.10.43; ETO No.6 MU 12.44; No.327 Sqn, accident at Corre 14.3./15 (Sgt Erard); R&SU - SNCAN Mureaux 19.3.46, to FAF; GC.I/1 'Provence' 3.48 until 7.48, also noted 7.49 until 4.11.49

MJ283 Spitfire LF.IXc (Merlin 66); TOC/RAF 24.10.43 - Arr FAF 3.47: Crashed landing at Châteaudun 13.3.47 (Plt safe); R&SU for repair and return to service 5.47; Depot EAA No.601, overshot landing, hit obstacle, crashed at Cuers (Var) 19.8.47; R&SU; GC.I/6 'Corse' 1950; BE.708 Meknès 3.52

MJ285 Spitfire LF.IXc (Merlin 66); TOC/RAF 3.11.43; ex No.327; No.328 Sqn, accident at Entzheim 15.4.45 (Sgt Anina); R&SU - Arr FAF 27.11.45; GC.II/3 'Champagne', belly-landed at Nha Trang 5.2.49 (Cne Chanet safe); R&SU GC.I/6 'Corse' ('J') 1950

MJ298 Spitfire LF.IXc (Merlin 66); TOC/RAF 24.10.43 - Arr A.N. 27.3.46; Cuers to Hyères for 1.Flottille 30.3.46 ('1.F-13'), and as '1.F-15' in 6.46; Belly-landed 13.3.47; Cuers storage autumn 1947; Esc 3.Serv mid 1948 ('3.S-10', shown also in 9.48); Accident 27.6.49; RiW early 1950, selected for overhaul at SNCAN Mureaux 23.9.50; Cuers, SOC 20.11.50

MJ341 Spitfire LF.IXc (Merlin 66); TOC/RAF 11.43 - Allotted for FAF 27.7.46, arr Châteaudun 31.7.46; GC.II/4 'La Fayette' ('Q') 10.47; GC.I/4 'Dauphiné' 1.48; GC II/4 'La Fayette' in 9.48; GC.I/3 'Navarre' ('Q') 10.1.49; Air Depot storage 13.4.49

MJ345 Spitfire LF.IXc (Merlin 66); TOC/RAF 22.11.43; No.326 Sqn ('8J-T'), accident at Colmar 31.3.45 (F/Sgt Geremia); R&SU - Arr FAF 27.11.45; GC.I/7 'Provence' 1947 (also 1948); BE.708 Meknès 3.52

MJ346 Spitfire LF.IXc (Merlin 66); TOC/RAF 14.11.43; ex No.326 Sqn ('8J-E') - Arr FAF 27.11.45; GC.II/1 'Nice' 1949

MJ348 Spitfire LF.IXc (Merlin 66); TOC/RAF 17.11.43; No.327 Sqn, accident at Sersheim 2.5.45 (Sgt Delenatre); R&SU - SNCAN Mureaux, to FAF 27.11.45; GC.I/1 'Provence', dived into ground, Cat.E 3.12.48 (Asp Chauchard killed), SOC

MJ356 Spitfire LF.IXc (Merlin 66); TOC/RAF 23.11.43 - Arr FAF 27.11.45; BE.708 Meknès, take-off crash, Cat.E 1.2.49, SOC

MJ360 Spitfire LF.IXc (Merlin 66); TOC/RAF 29.11.43; ex No.326 Sqn; No.327 Sqn, accident at Le Val d'Ahon 20.11.44 (Cne Felix Brunet); R&SU - Arr FAF 27.11.45; GC.I/1 'Provence', tyre burst landing 14.10.47; R&SU; GC.II/1 'Nice', belly-landed 5.4.48 (Sgt Cave)

MJ395 Spitfire LF.IXc (Merlin 66); TOC/RAF 3.11.43 - Arr FAF 27.11.45; GC.I/3 'Navarre' ('M') 1.10.48, moved to Tourane 29.9.49

MJ408 Spitfire LF.IXc (Merlin 66); TOC/RAF 3.11.43; No.327 Sqn, accident at Strasbourg 9.4.45 (Sgt Aninat); R&SU - Arr FAF 27.11.45; GC.II/7 'Nice' ('A'), collided with Spitfire TA800 on 10.7.47; R&SU; BE.708 Meknès 4.49

MJ415 Spitfire LF.IXc (Merlin 66); TOC/RAF 5.11.43; ex No.328 Sqn - SNCAN Mureaux 7.9.45, to FAF 27.11.45; GC.I/4 'Dauphiné', test flight Bien Hoa 12.1.48; GC.II/4 'La Fayette' ('H'), noted 2.48 and 8.48; GC.I/3 'Navarre' ('H') 2.10.48; Belly-landed at Gia-lam 8.10.48 (Lt Collin); R&SU; GC.I/3 'Navarre', spun landing at Langson 14.2.49 (Lt Binde safe); R&SU; GC.I/3 'Navarre', overshot landing, left runway, struck obstacle at Langson 4.6.49 (S/C Bourreau safe); Cat.E/2 (scrap) 4.9.49

MJ416 Spitfire LF.IXc (Merlin 66); TOC/RAF 5.11.43 - Arr FAF 25.7.46, to A.N.; Esc 1.Serv. at Lanvéoc-Poulmic ('1.S-12') by 31.12.46; Esc 3.Serv. at Cuers ('3.S-11') from 4.47; Take-off accident at Cuers 8.8.47; Force-landed wheels up 12.8.47 (CC Hervé); RiW; Cuers autumn 1947; DCAN, SOC 14.4.48

MJ423 Spitfire LF.IXc (Merlin 66); TOC/RAF 3.11.43; ex Nos.327 & 328 Sqn - Arr FAF 27.11.45; Fate unknown

MJ443 Spitfire LF.IXc (Merlin 66); TOC/RAF 12.11.43 - Arr FAF 27.11.45; BE.708 Meknès, dived into ground, Cat.E 12.10.50 (Sgt Touchard); SOC

MJ456 Spitfire LF.IXc (Merlin 66); TOC/RAF 14.11.43; ex Nos.328 & 327 Sqns - Arr FAF 27.11.45; Indo-China; BE.708 Meknès, tipped on nose landing at Meknès 27.8.51 (Sgt P Rousseau safe)

MJ457 Spitfire LF.IXc (Merlin 66); TOC/RAF 6.11.43; ex No.328 Sqn - Arr FAF 27.11.45; GC.III/2 'Alsace' 1946; GC.I/7 'Provence' 1947 & 1948; BE.708 Meknès, crashed 26.7.51 (S/C Raboxcone)

MJ458 Spitfire LF.IXc (Merlin 66); TOC/RAF 13.11.43; ex No.326 Sqn - Arr FAF 27.11.45; GC.II/18 'Saintonge' in 2.46; GC.III/2 'Alsace' 5.46; GC.II/1 'Nice', crashed 27.10.47 (Sgt E Fleury)

MJ465 Spitfire LF.IXc (Merlin 66); TOC/RAF 6.11.43; ex No.326 Sqn ('8J-S') - Arr FAF 27.11.45; GC.I/1 'Provence', collision with Spitfire MK603 on 30.7. or 31.7.47; BE.708 Meknès, crashed 22.3.51 (Lt Leroy)

MJ475 Spitfire LF.IXc (Merlin 66); TOC/RAF 13.11.43; ex No.326 Sqn - Arr FAF 27.11.45; GC.II/7 'Nice' 1947; BE.708 Meknès 1950

MJ478 Spitfire LF.IXc (Merlin 66); TOC/RAF 13.11.43; ex No.326 Sqn ('GG' – Plts: G Gauthier and Gleyze) 4.45 - Arr FAF 27.11.45; GC.I/4 'Dauphiné' ('J') 11.47 & 10.48

MJ500 Spitfire LF.IXc (Merlin 66); TOC/RAF 12.11.43 - Allotted for FAF 13.8.46, arr FAF 15.8.46; Fate unknown

MJ520 Spitfire LF.IXc (Merlin 66); TOC/RAF 17.11.43 - Arr FAF 12.9.46; GC.I/2 'Cigognes' ('K'), forced landed, overturned in rice field, Cat.E 1.6.47 (S/Lt Schneider injured), SOC

MJ528 Spitfire LF IXc (Merlin 66); TOC/RAF 22.11.43; ex Nos.326 & 340/345 Sqns - Arr FAF 27.11.45, to Indochina; GC II/4 in 1.48 (S/Lt Bardou); 3.EC by 26.9.48 and 17.7.49; Fate unknown

MJ530 Spitfire LF.IXc (Merlin 66); TOC/RAF 24.11.43; ex Nos.327 & 328 Sqns - Arr FAF 27.11.45; GC.I/6 'Corse' 1950

MJ564 Spitfire FR.IXc (Merlin 66); TOC/RAF 2.12.43; ex No.341 Sqn - Arr FAF, GR.II/33 'Savoie' 12.11.44; Taxying accident 1.1.45; R&SU; SNCAN Mureaux 27.11.45; GC.I/1 'Provence' 1947; Taxying collision with Spitfire MK467 in Germany on 30.10.48; R&SU; GC.I/1 'Provence', crashed 3.12.48 (Cne Simard)

MJ605 Spitfire LF.IXc (Merlin 66); TOC/RAF 2.12.43; ex No.327 Sqn - Arr FAF 27.11.45; GC.II/3 'Champagne' 1950 (reported as "MJ803"); GC.I/6 'Corse' ('U') 1950

MJ619 Spitfire LF.IXc (Merlin 66); TOC/RAF 30.11.43 - Arr FAF 27.11.45; GC.I/1 'Provence', crashed 4.8.47; GC.I/7 'Provence' 12.47; 1.EC (F/Wing) 7.48; GC.I/1 'Provence', crashed Cat.E 7.4.49 (Sgt F Richarme); SOC

MJ636 Spitfire LF.IXc (Merlin 66); TOC/RAF 2.3.44 - Arr FAF 25.11.45; GC.II/1 'Nice' ('E'), crashed 15.5.50 (Sgt Lebas)

MJ664 Spitfire F.IXc (Merlin 63); TOC/RAF 2.12.43 - Allotted for FAF 21.5.47, arr FAF 23.5.47; Fate unknown

MJ669 Spitfire LF.IXc (Merlin 66); TOC/RAF 2.12.43 - Arr FAF 28.3.46, to A.N; SNCAN Mureaux; SEA Hyères autumn 1947; R&SU (CN Cuers); Esc 3.Serv 26.7.48, '3.S-11' at Cuers mid 1948; SNCAN Mureaux, SOC 12.6.50

MJ671 Spitfire LF.IXc (Merlin 66); TOC/RAF 2.12.43; ex No.341 Sqn - Allotted for FAF 12.9.46, arr FAF 17.10.46; GC.I/4 *Dauphiné* ('E'), test flight Bien Hoa 12.1.48 (also 21.1.48 and 31.1.49)

MJ686 Spitfire LF IXc (Merlin 66); TOC/RAF 12.12.43, M.E., No.328 Sqn, accident at Selestat/Oberchafolsheim 8.12.44 (Lt Chombard de Lauwe); R&SU – Arr FAF 27.11.45; GC II/4, collision at Langson, Cat.E 17.2.48 (Asp Monthus kld), SOC

MJ712 Spitfire LF.IXc (Merlin 66); TOC/RAF 20.12.43 - Arr FAF, GR.II/33 *'Savoie'* on 12.11.44; Crashed landing at Luxeuil 23.12.44 (Sgt Paul Gerant or Gehant); No.81 R&SU 1.45; No.326 Sqn 24.5.45 until 31.5.45; RiW (SNCAN Mureaux) 28.6.45, to FAF 27.11.45; Fate unknown

MJ723 Spitfire LF.IXc (Merlin 66); TOC/RAF 20.12.43; ex No.341 Sqn - Arr FAF 27.11.45; GC.II/1 *'Nice'* from 28.9.48 until 2.50

MJ737 Spitfire LF.IXc (Merlin 66); TOC/RAF 16.12.43; No.326 Sqn, accident at Luxeuil 1.11.44 (S/C Maurice Gerard) - Arr FAF 27.11.45; GC.II/1 *'Nice'* 12.47 (also in 1950)

MJ742 Spitfire LF.IXc (Merlin 66); TOC/RAF 16.12.43; ex No.326 Sqn; No.328 Sqn, accident at Strasbourg 24.4.45 (Capt Simard); R&SU - Arr FAF 27.11.45; GC.II/1 *'Nice'* from 1948 until 1950; BE.708 Meknès 1952

MJ790 Spitfire LF.IXc (Merlin 66); TOC/RAF 19.12.43 - Arr FAF 27.11.45; 1.EC (F/Wing) 1948; GC.I/1 *'Provence'*; GC.II/1 *'Nice'* (at Oran 10.48)

MJ793 Spitfire LF.IXc (Merlin 66); TOC/RAF 20.12.43; ex No.39 (RCAF Recce) Wing - Arr FAF 12.44; GR.II/33 *'Savoie'*, hydraulic failure, Cat.Ac 1.1.45; R&SU; Crashed Cat.E 22.3.45, SOC

MJ822 Spitfire LF.IXc (Merlin 66); TOC/RAF 20.12.43; ex No.340 Sqn ('GW-U'), and No.326 Sqn from 2.44; No.327 Sqn, accident at Colmar 2.4.45 (S/Lt Genty); R&SU - Arr FAF 27.11.45; GC.I/7 *'Provence'* 11.45; GC.III/2 *'Alsace'* 1946; GC.II/1 *'Nice'* 1947

MJ825 Spitfire LF.IXc (Merlin 66); Became **F-UGPC**; TOC/RAF 4.1.44; ex No.340 Sqn; No.326 Sqn, accident at Entzheim 18.4.45 (Sgt Delime); R&SU - Arr FAF 27.11.45; GC.I/3 *'Navarre'* ('C') 11.7.49; Air Depot 28.10.49; GC.I/6 *'Corse'* ('C'), tipped on nose at Tourane 7.8.50 (Lt de Villepin safe)

MJ848 Spitfire LF.IXc (Merlin 66); TOC/RAF 4.12.43; Nos.327 & 326 Sqns; Accident at Belfort 10.2.45 (Cne Le Borgne); R&SU; No.327 Sqn (marked *"ELIANE"*), accident at Entzheim 8.4.45 (Lt Jacques de Beaucoudray); R&SU - Arr FAF 27.11.45; GC.I/7 *'Provence'* 1947; BE.708 Meknès 1951 (also 1952)

MJ882 Spitfire LF.IXc (Merlin 66); TOC/RAF 24.12.43; ex No.326 Sqn ('8J-K') - Arr FAF 3.46; GC.II/1 *'Nice'* 1948; Wheels-up landing, Cat.E 18.7.50 (Lt Fontvielle); SOC

MJ897 Spitfire LF.IXc (Merlin 66); Presentation name *'CURIEUX'*; TOC/RAF 1.44 - Arr FAF, GR. II/33 *'Savoie'* 17.6.44; Hit by AA (Cdt Martin safe) 5.1.45; No.81 CDR (French) 27.1.45; GR.II/33; No.81 R&SU (RAF) 11.10.45; via Nos.340/345 Sqns to FAF 27.11.45; GC.I/4 *'Dauphiné'* ('H'), test flight Bien Hoa 9.11.48; GC.II/3 *'Champagne'*, accident Tuy Hoa 12.11.49 (Lt Jullien)

MJ908 Spitfire LF.IXc (Merlin 66); Became **F-UGBQ**; TOC/RAF 4.1.44 - Arr FAF 3.6.47; GC.II/1 *'Nice'* ('Q'), missing over Mediterranean (near Zaaf, Algeria), Cat.FB/E 12.9.50 (Cne Marchal); SOC

MJ954 Spitfire LF.IXc (Merlin 66); TOC/RAF 4.1.44; No.328 Sqn, accident at Entzheim 16.4.45 (Sgt Maho); R&SU - Arr FAF 27.11.45; GC.I/4 *'Dauphiné'* ('D'), test flight 12.1.48; Engine failed on take-off at Nha Trang, Cat.E 8.12.48 (Cne Bruyere injured, and three civilians killed), SOC

MJ959 Spitfire LF.IXc (Merlin 66); TOC/RAF 28.1.44; No.328 Sqn, accident at Selz (Bischviller) 11.4. or 12.4.45 (Lt Roesh); No.81 R&SU 12.4.45 - Arr FAF 27.11.45; GC.I/7 *'Provence'* (at Oran 3.48), crashed 7.6.48 (Lt Roche); R&SU; GC.I/7, crashed 9.1.50

MJ960 Spitfire LF.IXc (Merlin 66); TOC/RAF 23.1.44; ex No.340 Sqn ('GW-F') - Arr FAF 27.11.45; Fate unknown

MJ966 Spitfire LF.IXc (Merlin 66); TOC/RAF 25.1.44; ex No.340 Sqn ('GW-B') - Arr FAF, Châteaudun (ferry flight) 27.7.46; GC.II/4 *'La Fayette'* ('R'), tyre burst landing, overturned at Gia-lam, Cat.FA/E 27.10.47 (Adj Raoust safe), SOC

MJ995 Spitfire LF.IXc (Merlin 66); TOC/RAF 8.1.44 - Arr FAF; GR.II/33 *'Savoie'* from 17.6.44; Engine failure, force-landed near Cernay 24.12.44 (Lt Roussel Wilmot); R&SU

MJ998 Spitfire LF.IXc (Merlin 66 TOC/RAF 10.1.44; Cat.FB/Ac 1.4.45 - Arr FAF 27.11.45; 4.EC 3.48 (also noted 4.48); GC.II/3 *'Champagne'* 1949

MK114 Spitfire LF.IXc (Merlin 66); TOC/RAF 30.1.44 - Arr FAF 9.9.46; GC.I/4 *'Dauphiné'* ('M'), test flight Bien Hoa 12.1.48 (noted also 31.1.49); GC.II/3 *'Champagne'* ('M'), dived into ground near Tan Hoi, Cat.E 21.4.49 (Lt Michel killed), SOC

MK127 Spitfire FR IXc (Merlin 66); TOC/RAF 14.1.44; ex Nos.340 ('GW-B':'GW-G') & 328 Sqns - Arr FAF 27.11.45; GC.I/4 *'Dauphiné'* 1947; GC.I/1 *'Provence'* (at Oran 12.47)

MK132 Spitfire LF.IXc (Merlin 66); TOC/RAF 21.1.44; ex Nos.329 ('5A-S') & 326 Sqns - Arr FAF 27.11.45; GC.II/18 *'Saintonge'* in 1946; GC.I/7 *'Provence'* 11.46; GC.II/1 *'Nice'* until 2.48; BE.708 Meknès, undercarriage collapsed landing at Meknès 5.5.51 (S/Lt J Crouzet safe)

MK133 Spitfire LF.IXc (Merlin 66) TOC/RAF 23.1.44 - SNCAN Mureaux 7.45 (SOC/RAF 19.7.45), to FAF 27.11.45; GC.I/4 *'Dauphiné'*, test flight Bien Hoa 3.12.47; Crash-landed at Tan Son Nhut 10.1.48 (S/C Coustie safe)

MK151 Spitfire LF.IXc (Merlin 66); TOC/RAF 25.1.44; ex SAAF - Arr A.N. 27.3.46; Cuers to Hyères for 1.Flottille 30.3.46 ('1.F-14', shown also in 6.46); Cuers, storage mid 1947; Possibly Esc 3.Serv, accident 18.8.47; Esc 3.Serv in 12.47; '3S-11', prep for storage at Cuers, accident 2.2.48; RiW, to VR Cuers 23.3.48; SOC 31.5.50 (confirmed 20.11.50)

MK196 Spitfire LF.IXc (Merlin 66); TOC/RAF 28.1.44; ex No.340 Sqn ('GW-E') - Arr FAF, Châteaudun (ferry flight) 27.7.46; GC.II/4 *'La Fayette'*, crashed landing too fast at night at Gia-lam 26.10.47 (S/C Marillonet safe); R&SU; Mid-air collision with Spitfire MK686, Cat.E 17.2.48 (Cne Wicker killed), SOC

MK234 Spitfire LF.IXc (Merlin 66); TOC/RAF 4.1.44; ex Nos.340 & 326 Sqns - Arr FAF 7.12.45; CEAM (Test Centre Rochefort), belly-landed 18.6 or 19.6.47; R&SU; BE.708 Meknès 1951 (also 1952)

MK259 Spitfire LF.IXc (Merlin 66); TOC/RAF 4.2.44; ex No.345 Sqn; No.327 Sqn, accident at Colmar 4.4.45 (S/Lt Cases); R&SU - Arr FAF 27.11.45; Fate unknown

MK266 Spitfire LF.IXc (Merlin 66); TOC/RAF 12.2.44; ex No.327 Sqn - Arr FAF 27.11.45; GC.II/18 *'Saintonge'* in 3.46; GC.I/7 *'Provence'* 12.46; GC.II/1 *'Nice'* 1.48

MK287 Spitfire LF.IXc (Merlin 66); TOC/RAF 28.1.44; ex No.326 Sqn - Arr FAF 27.11.45; GC.II/18 *'Saintonge'* in 12.45; GC III/2 *'Alsace'*,' crashed 13.3.47 (possibly S/Lt Douchet)

MK292 Spitfire LF.IXc (Merlin 66); TOC/RAF 27.1.44; ex No.326 Sqn ('8J-N') - Arr FAF, GC.II/18 *'Saintonge'* 27.11.45; GC.III/2 *'Alsace'* 6.46; GC.II/7 *'Nice'* 1.47; GC.II/5 in 7.47; BE.708 Meknès 3.52

MK295 Spitfire LF.IXc (Merlin 66); TOC/RAF 23.1.44; ex Nos.327 & 326 Sqns - Arr FAF 27.11.45; GC.I/7 *'Provence'* 1.47; GC.II/1 *'Nice'* 7.47; BE.708 Meknès ('B'), belly-landed 30.1.51 (shown at Meknès 4.52)

MK320 Spitfire LF.IXc (Merlin 66); TOC/RAF 28.1.44; ex No.326 Sqn - Arr FAF 27.11.45; GC.I/1 *'Provence'* from 6.9.48 until 8.11.49

MK365 Spitfire LF.IXc (Merlin 66); TOC/RAF 2.2.44; ex No.341 Sqn - Arr FAF in 7.46; BE.708 Meknès 1951

Spitfire LF.IXc MK295 'B' has the serial painted across the rudder stripes. It was used for flying training by BE.708 Meknès around 1951/52.
[Claude A. Pierquet]

MK378　Spitfire LF.IXc (Merlin 66); TOC/RAF 4.2.44 - Arr FAF 28.3.46; To A.N, via Cuers to 1.Flottille 2.4.46 ('1.F-18' in 7.46); Allotted for Esc 3.Serv. 2.3.50, arr 14.6.50; Cuers, for inspection with engine change 23.9.50; SOC 8.12.50

MK398　Spitfire LF.IXc (Merlin 66); TOC/RAF 11.2.44 - Arr FAF 27.11.45; GC.I/4 *'Dauphiné'* ('B'), noted 9.48; GC.II/3 *'Champagne'*, belly-landed 2.1.49 (Cne Le Dantec safe); Belly-landed at Tourane 3.2.49 (Cne Le Dantec); R&SU; GC.I/6 *'Corse'* ('B'), engine failure, force-landed near Hong Ha 30.6.50 (Lt Mesnard injured) NOTE: Also reported as "TE398"

MK412　Spitfire LF.IXc (Merlin 66); TOC/RAF 11.2.44 - Arr FAF 28.3.46, to A.N. 29.3.46; via Cuers to 1.Flottille 2.4.46 ('1.F-16' in 7.46); SEA Hyères autumn 1947; Esc 54.Serv ('54.S-1'), crashed landing at Luc 19.11.47 (LV Laure safe); RiW; DCAN Cuers 30.9.48; SOC 8.1.49

MK456　Spitfire LF.IXc (Merlin 66); Became **F-UGPQ**; TOC/RAF 15.2.44 – Allotted for FAF 21.6.46, arr Châteaudun 25.6.46; GC.I/6 *'Corse'* ('Q'), noted 8.50 and 11.50

MK464　Spitfire LF.IXc (Merlin 66); TOC/RAF 5.3.44 - Allotted for FAF 9.9.46, arr FAF 16.9.46; GC.I/1 *'Provence'* 1949

MK467　Spitfire LF.IXc (Merlin 66); TOC/RAF 28.2.44; ex No.327 Sqn - Arr FAF 27.11.45; GC.I/1 *'Provence'* (at Oran 5.48); Collided with Spitfire MJ564 on 30.10.48; R&SU; GC.I/1 *'Provence'* 1950

MK473　Spitfire LF.IXc (Merlin 66) TOC/RAF 24.2.44 - Arr FAF 11.45; SNCAN Mureaux, test flight 7.6.48; GC.I/4 *'Dauphiné'* ('T'), test flight 30.10.48; GC.I/6 *'Corse'* ('T'), noted 4.50 and 6.50
NOTE: RAF reported this aircraft missing 27.2.45

MK474　Spitfire LF.IXc (Merlin 66); TOC/RAF 21.2.44; ex No.326 Sqn ('8J-O') - Arr FAF 27.11.45; GC.II/1 *'Nice'* from 2.49 until 6.50

MK484　Spitfire LF.IXc (Merlin 66); TOC/RAF 28.2.44; ex Nos.341 & 328 Sqns; No.327 Sqn, accident at Strasbourg 12.4.45 (Lt Restoux); R&SU - Arr FAF 27.11.45; GC.II/1 *'Nice'* 1948 (also 1950)

MK560　Spitfire LF.IXc (Merlin 66); TOC/RAF 4.3.44 - Allotted for FAF 25.7.46, arr Châteaudun 27.7.46; GC.I/4 *'Dauphiné'* ('K'), undershot, hit obstacle, belly-landed at Nha Trang 25.9.47 (Lt Cazenave safe)

MK590　Spitfire LF.IXc; Allotted for FAF, but cancelled (crashed before delivery)

MK603　Spitfire LF.IXc (Merlin 66); TOC/RAF 23.1.44; No.326 Sqn ('8J-V'), accident at Colmar 24.3.45 (Sgt Habert); R&SU - Arr FAF 27.11.45; GC.I/7 *'Provence'* 1946; Collided with Spitfire MJ465 on 30.7. or 31.7.47; BE.708 Meknès, crashed Cat.E 11.7.51 (Cne Pingoux); SOC

MK619　Spitfire LF.IXc (Merlin 66); TOC/RAF 20.2.44; No.328 Sqn, accident at Entzheim 19.4.45 (Aspt Chaperon); R&SU - Arr FAF 27.11.45; GC.I/1 *'Provence'* 11.47; Crashed landing, Cat.E 16.10.48 (Cne Cuef killed); SOC

MK629　Spitfire LF.IXc (Merlin 66); TOC/RAF 26.2.44; ex No.326 Sqn ('8J-H') - Arr FAF 27.11.45; GC.II/1 *'Nice'* 1950

MK659　Spitfire LF.IXc (Merlin 66); TOC/RAF 17.3.44 - Allotted and arrived FAF 13.8.46; GC.I/2 *'Cigognes'* 1946/47; GC.II/4 *'La Fayette'* ('G'), noted 11.11.47; GC.I/4 *'Dauphiné'*, test flight 20.12.47

MK667　Spitfire LF.IXc (Merlin 66); TOC/RAF 11.3.44 - Arr FAF 27.11.45; GC.II/1 *'Nice'* ('L') from 2.49 until 10.49; BE.708 Meknès 9.51

MK677　Spitfire LF.IXc (Merlin 66); TOC/RAF 22.4.44 - Allotted for FAF 9.9.46, arr 12.9.46; GC.I/7 *'Provence'* (at Oran 1.49, also listed in 10.49); GC.II/1 *'Nice'* 1949 (also shown 1950)

MK680　Spitfire HF.IXe (Merlin 70); TOC/RAF 30.3.44 - Arr FAF 3.12.45; GC.I/2 *'Cigognes'* 1946; GC.I/7 *'Provence'* 1946

MK686　Spitfire LF.IXc (Merlin 66); TOC/RAF 31.3.44 - Arr FAF 31.7.46; 4.EC, mid-air collision with Spitfire MK196 on 17.2.48

MK689　Spitfire LF.IXc (Merlin 66); TOC/RAF 26.3.44 - Arr FAF 27.11.45; GC.I/1 *'Provence'* 26.9.49 until 3.1.50

MK690　Spitfire LF.IXc (Merlin 66); TOC/RAF 22.4.44 - Arr FAF 15.8.46; GC.I/2 *'Cigognes'* 1947; GC.II/7 *'Nice'*, test flight Châteaudun 13.1.47; GC.II/4 *'La Fayette'* ('A') 1947/48; GC.I/3 *'Navarre'* ('A'), collided with Spitfire TE514 on take-off at Seno, Cat.E 27.10.48 (S/C Valiquet safe); SOC 8.11.48

MK713　Spitfire LF.IXc (Merlin 66); TOC/RAF 24.2.44 - Arr FAF, GR.II/33 *'Savoie'* 30.9.44; Crashed on Isle sur le Doubs 25.11.44 (Lt Augustin Rey); Retd RAF; RiW (de Havilland) 18.5.45; SOC 29.7.46

MK716　Spitfire FR.IXc (Merlin 66); TOC/RAF 2.3.44 - SNCAN Mureaux, test flight 26.7.46, to FAF 26.7.46; GC.II/1 *'Nice'*, noted 11.47 and 2.48; GC.I/3 *'Navarre'* ('K')

1949; GC.II/3 *'Champagne'* ('K'), Accident at Kon Tum 6.3.50 (Sgt Crassous)

MK734 Spitfire LF.IXc (Merlin 66); TOC/RAF 15.3.44; ex No.326 Sqn - Arr FAF 27.11.45; GC.II/18 *'Saintonge'* in 12.45

MK743 Spitfire LF.IXc (Merlin 66); TOC/RAF 8.3.44 - Arr FAF 27.11.45; GC.II/3 *'Champagne'*, engine fire, pilot baled out, aircraft dived into ground near Plei Phang, Cat.E 20.2.50 (Lt Laurence safe), SOC

MK756 Spitfire LF.IXc (Merlin 66); Became **F-TEVK**; TOC/RAF 4.3.44; ex Nos.326 & No.327 Sqns - Arr FAF 27.11.45; GC.I/7 *'Provence'* 12.45; GC.II/1 *'Nice'* 1947; BE.708 Meknès ('K'), fatal crash BAN Khouribga 22. or 27.11.50 (EV1 Pilar Bouye of A.N. kld), SOC

MK791 Spitfire LF.IXc (Merlin 66); TOC/RAF 2.3.44 - Allotted for FAF 11.9.46, arr 16.9.46; GC.I/4 *'Dauphiné'* ('K'), noted 12.47 and 11.48; Unknown unit, 1949 (photo)

MK804 Spitfire LF.IXc (Merlin 66); TOC/RAF 11.3.44; ex No.326 Sqn - Arr FAF 27.11.45; GC.II/18 *'Saintonge'* in 1946; GC.II/7 *'Nice'* 1947/48

MK832 Spitfire LF.IXc (Merlin 66); TOC/RAF 11.3.44; ex No.326 Sqn ('8J-C') - Arr FAF 27.11.45; GC.I/4 *'Dauphiné'*, test flight 10.11.48; GC.II/3 *'Champagne'*, crashed at Tourane 30.1.50 (Lt Laurence safe)

MK850 Spitfire LF.IXc (Merlin 66); TOC/RAF 3.7.44 - Allotted for FAF 9.9.46, arr 16.9.46; GC.II/1 *'Nice'* 1949

MK910 Spitfire LF.IXc (Merlin 66); TOC/RAF 19.3.44 - SNCAN Mureaux 28.6.45, to FAF 27.11.45; GC.I/4 *'Dauphiné'*, test flight 9.9.48; GC.I/3 *'Navarre'* ('F'), crashed near Dung Khyet 23.10.48 (Cne Le Corre killed); SOC 24.10.48

MK942 Spitfire LF.IXc (Merlin 66); TOC/RAF 31.3.44 - Arr A.N. 28.3.46; Esc 1.Serv, crashed, undercarriage failed at Toulouse/Francazal 28.3.47 (PM François Borgne safe); R&SU Cuers mid 1947; Esc 1.Serv in 1949; General discharge 7.11.50, Lanvéoc-Poulmic; SOC 1.1.51; As Ground-Instructional airframe for Esc 50.Serv in 1951

MK989 Spitfire LF.IXc (Merlin 66); TOC/RAF 27.3.44 - Arr A.N. 25.7.46; Esc 3.Serv ('3.S-10') Cuers in 1946; reported also Esc 1.Serv ('1.S-11') by 31.12.46; Esc 3.Serv ('3.S-10') Cuers 4.47 – 12.47; VR Cuers, RiW 20.3.48, test flying in 6.49 and 8.49; Esc 3.Serv ('3.S-12'), destroyed by low level flying near Moulin, Forcalqueiret 23.12.49 (EV1 Pierre Louis died in a hospital at Toulon 24.12.49), SOC 12.5.50

MK996 Spitfire LF.IXc – Allotted for FAF, but crashed before delivery

ML137 Spitfire LF.IXc (Merlin 66); TOC/RAF 22.3.44 - Arr FAF 8.8.46; GC.I/2 *'Cigognes'*, crashed landing at Gia-lam 16.5.47 (Lt Ferrando safe); R&SU; GC.II/4 *'La Fayette'* ('P'), flown by Lt Bardou 11.47-1.48, 4.48-6.48 and in 8.48; Went into spin at low altitude, crashed near Lac Tho 11.9.48 (S/C Bigonneau killed), SOC

ML140 Spitfire LF.IXc (Merlin 66); Became **F-UGPG**; TOC/RAF 30.3.44; ex No.327 Sqn - SNCAN Mureaux 9.45 and 10.45; to FAF 27.11.45; GC.I/6 *'Corse'* ('G') 1950

ML214 Spitfire LF.IX (Merlin 66); TOC/RAF 25.4.44 - Arr FAF 14.8.46; 4.EC ('B') Indo-China 13.9.48; GC.I/4 *'Dauphiné'*, crashed at Bien Hoa 25.9. or 27.9.48 (S/C Lacassie safe); PC482 (R&SU); GC.I/4, test flight 30.10.48; GC.I/3 *'Navarre'* ('L') 7.11.48; Hit by AA, force-landed wheels-up near Nam Dinh 26.5.49 (S/C Mesplet safe); R&SU 24.7.49

ML235 Spitfire HF.IXe (Merlin 70); TOC/RAF 13.4.44; ex No.329 Sqn - Arr FAF 24.11.45; Fate unknown

ML270 Spitfire LF.IX (Merlin 66); TOC/RAF 26.4.44; ex Nos.328 & 327 Sqns - Arr FAF 27.11.45; BE.708 Meknès, crashed 20.1.49; R&SU; SNCAN Mureaux, test flight 22.3.49; GC.I/6 *'Corse'* ('S') 11.50

ML271 Spitfire LF.IX (Merlin 66); TOC/RAF 10.5.44 - SNCAN Mureaux 28.6.45, to FAF 27.11.45; GC.I/4 *'Dauphiné'* ('G'), test flight Bien Hoa 11.10.48; GC.I/3 *'Navarre'* ('G'), hit by AA, dived into ground near Bao Ha 8.6.49 (Lt Boursier killed), SOC

ML276 Spitfire LF.IX (Merlin 66); TOC/RAF 18.4.44; ETO; No.326 Sqn 1.12.44; Accident at Luxeuil 16.2.45 (Plt Raymond Bedard); R&SU - Arr FAF 27.11.45; SNCAN Mureaux 1946; GC.II/1 *'Nice'* 1948

ML295 Spitfire IX, recovered wreck (previously reported as "NH341") by Jean-Pierre Benamou, Musée Memorial 1944 Bataille de Normandy at Bayeux - **SURVIVOR**

ML300 Spitfire LF.IX (Merlin 66); TOC/RAF 24.4.44; ex No.326 Sqn ('8J-L') - Arr FAF 27.11.45; GC.I/3 *'Navarre'* ('I') 1948; GC.I/6 *'Corse'* 1950

ML304 Spitfire LF.IX (Merlin 66); TOC/RAF 23.5.44 - Arr FAF 27.11.45; GC.I/1 *'Provence'* ('K'), hit HT wire on 16.8.48 (Asp Villette); R&SU; GC.I/1 *'Provence'* 16.12.49

ML319 Spitfire LF.IX (Merlin 66); TOC/RAF 18.5.44; ex Nos.326 & 340/345 Sqns - Arr FAF 27.11.45; GC.I/3 *'Navarre'* ('E') 10.7.49; Overshot landing, flat tyre, tipped on nose at Gia-lam 30.9.49 (S/Lt Bardou safe); R&SU; GC.I/6 *'Corse'* ('M'), noted at Nha Trang 15.8.50; Engine failed, force-landed, crashed near Tian Vian/Ngoc Tinh Cat.E 5.11.50 (Lt Demanget injured), SOC

ML343 Spitfire LF.IXe (Merlin 66); TOC/RAF 26.4.44 - Arr FAF 3.12.45; GC.II/7 *'Nice'* 1946/47; GC.I/6 *'Corse'* 1950

ML353 Spitfire HF.IXe (Merlin 70); TOC/RAF 19.4.44 - Arr FAF 27.11.45; GC.II/4 *'La Fayette'*, tyre burst landing 21.7. or 22.7.47

ML362 Spitfire LF.IX (Merlin 66); TOC/RAF 21.4.44; Arr FAF, GR.II/33 *'Savoie'* in 1944; Retd RAF 1945; Later sold to Turkey 1947

ML365 Spitfire LF.IX (Merlin 66); Became **F-UGPA**; TOC/RAF 26.4.44; ex No.326 Sqn - Arr FAF 27.11.45; Air Depot EAA 601, undercarriage not locked up, collapsed on landing 29.8.47; GC.I/6 *'Corse'* ('A') 4.50, noted also 7.50

ML381 Spitfire LF.IX (Merlin 66); TOC/RAF 12.5.44; ex Nos.329 & 326 Sqns ('8J-W') - Arr FAF 27.11.45; GC.I/1 *'Provence'* 4.7.49 (also shown 13.2.50)

ML397 Spitfire LF.IX (Merlin 66); TOC/RAF 25.4.44; ex Nos.328 & 327 Sqns - Arr FAF 27.11.45; GC.I/7 *'Provence'* 1946; BE.708 Meknès 1951

ML409 Spitfire LF.IX (Merlin 66); TOC/RAF 25.4.44 - Arr A.N. 28.3.46; Esc 4.Serv 21.3.47 ('4.S-11' from 1947 to 6.49); Cuers (3.RM), general discharge 7.11.50; SOC 8.12.50

ML422 Spitfire LF.IX (Merlin 66); TOC/RAF 5.5.44; ETO, No.125 Wing 9.44; No.326 Sqn, accident at Belfort 10.2.45 (S/Lt Lafargue); R&SU - SNCAN Mureaux 10.45, to FAF 27.11.45; 1.EC, ground collision with Spitfire BS131 at Niedermendig, Germany, Cat.E 19.6.47 (S/C Ruth); SOC

MT521 Spitfire LF.VIIIc (Merlin 66); TOC/RAF 14.4.44; ex ACSEA (No.273 Sqn) - Arr FAF 11.45; 1.EC (F/Wing) 1945 (noted 29.1.46)

MT610 Spitfire LF.VIIIc (Merlin 66); TOC/RAF 24.4.44; ex ACSEA (No.273 Sqn) - Arr FAF 11.45; 1.EC (F/Wing) 1945; GC.I/7 *'Provence'*, noted 12.45 and 1.46; Retd RAF (India), SOC 31.7.47

MT627 Spitfire LF.VIIIc (Merlin 66); TOC/RAF 1.5.44; ex Nos.328 & 327 Sqns - Arr FAF 27.11.45; 1.EC (F/Wing) 1945

MT633 Spitfire LF.VIIIc (Merlin 66); TOC/RAF 7.5.44; ex Nos.326 & 327 Sqns; Accident at Luxeuil 15.10.44 (Lt Gerard); R&SU; No.327 Sqn, accident at Cuers 14.12.44 (Cne Marc Villaceque); R&SU – via SNCAN Mureaux to FAF 11.45; 1.EC (F/Wing) 1945

MT765 Spitfire LF.VIIIc (Merlin 66); TOC/RAF 8.5.44; ex No.327 Sqn - Arr FAF 11.45; 1.EC (F/Wing) 1945

MT791 Spitfire LF.VIIIc (Merlin 66); TOC/RAF 3.6.44; ex ACSEA - Arr FAF 11.45; 1.EC (F/Wing) 25.4.46; SOC/RAF 30.5.46

MT793 Spitfire LF.VIIIc (Merlin 66); TOC/RAF 26.5.44; ex ACSEA - Arr FAF 11.45; 1.EC (F/Wing) 1945; GC.II/4 *'La Fayette'*; Service unknown; SOC/RAF 30.5.46

MT962 Spitfire LF.VIIIc (Merlin 66); TOC/RAF 3.7.44; ex ACSEA - Arr FAF 11.45; 1.EC (F/Wing) 1945; Engine failure, crashed off Phan Ky, Cat.E 14.12.46 (LCL Papin-Labazordière missing); SOC

MV414 Spitfire LF.VIIIc (Merlin 66); TOC/RAF 2.8.44; ex ACSEA (No.273 Sqn) - Arr FAF 11.45; 1.EC (F/Wing) 13.12.45; GC.I/7 *'Provence'*, test flight 14.12.45; Overturned at Tan Son Nhut 28.1.46 (Cne J Bloch safe); SOC/RAF 14.2.46

MV422 Spitfire LF.VIIIc (Merlin 66); TOC/RAF 25.8.44; ex ACSEA (No.273 Sqn) - Arr FAF 11.45; 1.EC (F/Wing) 1945; GC.II/7 *'Nice'*, engine failed on take-off, crashed at Tan Son Nhut 1.1.46 (Cne Brunet injured); SOC/RAF 10.1.46

MV427 Spitfire LF.VIIIc (Merlin 66); TOC/RAF 27.8.44; ex ACSEA (No.273 Sqn) - Arr FAF 27.11.45; 1.EC (F/Wing), ops 20.12.45; SOC/RAF 9.5.46

NF432 Seafire L.IIIc (Merlin 55M); RNDA 19.1.44; ex Nos.885 & 715 Sqns - Arr A.N. 1946/47; VR Cuers, moved to Esc 54.Serv at Hyères 1.8.47; ST Hyères (for discharge), census 7.49; SOC 27.8.49
NOTE: Recorded also as "NN432"

NF454 Seafire L.IIIc (Merlin 55M); RNDA 29.1.44; ex Nos.885, 899 & 879 Sqns - Arr A.N. 1948; Service unknown; SOC 27.8.49

NF482 Seafire L.IIIc (Merlin 55M); RNDA 5.2.44; ex Nos.886, 808, 715, 761 & 772 Sqns - Arr A.N. 1948; Esc 3.Serv ('3.S-11') in spring 1948/mid 1948; SOC 30.4.49

NF507 Seafire L.IIIc (Merlin 55M); RNDA 23.2.44; ex Nos.899 & 794 Sqns (No.52 TAG) - Arr A.N. 9.48, flown from Lee-on Solent to SAMAN at Toussus-le-Noble 16.9.48 (Plt Gicquel, SRC); Unknown unit, Accident 17.2.49; SOC 27.8.49

NF561 Seafire L.IIIc (Merlin 55M); RNDA 24.3.44; ex Nos.899 & 768 Sqns - Arr A.N. 10.4.48; Esc 54.Serv ('54.S-9'), date unknown; SOC 2.11.49

NH176 Spitfire LF.IXe (Merlin 66); TOC/RAF 30.4.44 - Arr FAF 27.11.45; GC.I/3 *'Navarre'* ('J') 1949; Air Depot 28.10.49; GC.I/6 *'Corse'* 1950

NH203 Spitfire LF.IXe (Merlin 66) TOC/RAF 8.5.44 - Arr FAF 11.45; GC.I/4 *'Dauphiné'*, test flight 5.11.48; GC.II/3 *'Champagne'*, explosion in the air, force-landed near Can Tho 9.4.49 (Sgt Chabas safe)
NOTE: RAF reported this serial missing 10.6.44

NH205 Spitfire LF.IXe (Merlin 66); Became **F-UGPV**; TOC/RAF 8.5.44; No.326 Sqn, accident at Belfort 10.2.45 (S/Lt Courteville); R&SU; No.327 Sqn, accident

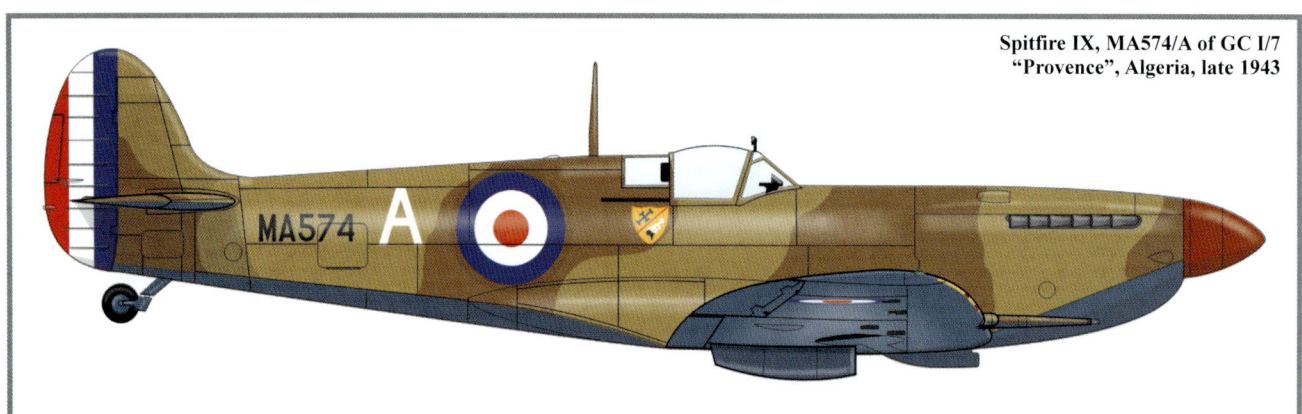

Spitfire IX, MA574/A of GC I/7 "Provence", Algeria, late 1943

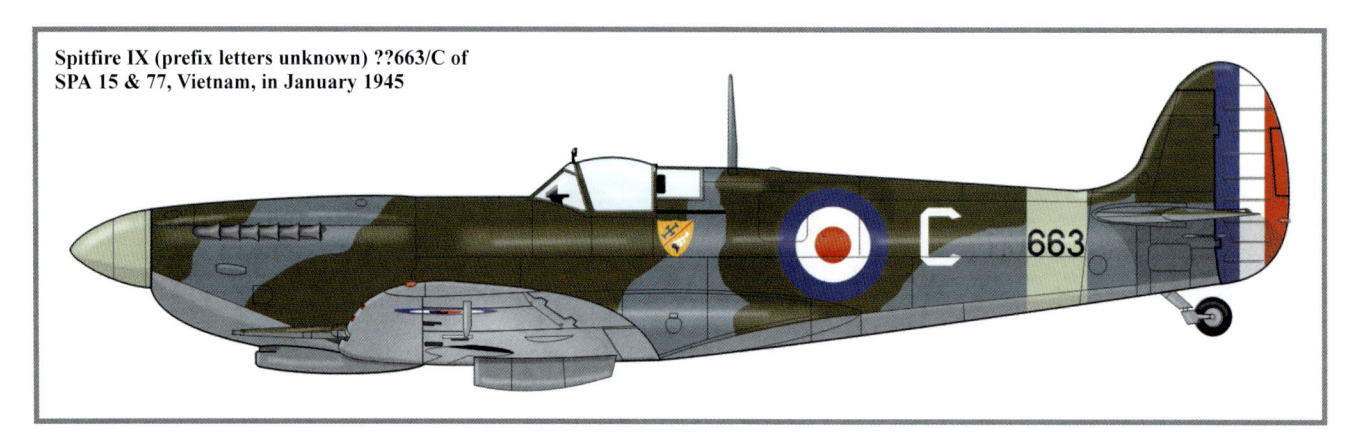

Spitfire IX (prefix letters unknown) ??663/C of SPA 15 & 77, Vietnam, in January 1945

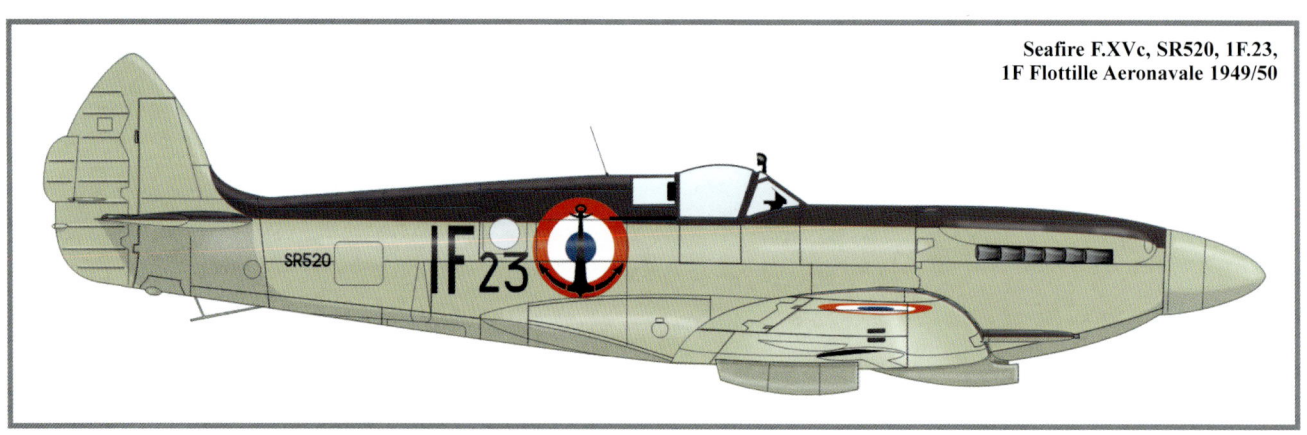

Seafire F.XVc, SR520, 1F.23, 1F Flottille Aeronavale 1949/50

NH240 Spitfire LF.IXe (Merlin 66); TOC/RAF 20.5.44; Allotted 12.9.46 - Arr FAF 16.9.46; Air Depot EAA 601 in 6.49

NH248 Spitfire LF.IXe (Merlin 66); TOC/RAF 11.5.44; ex Nos.327 & 326 Sqns; - FAF, CIC Meknès, accident near base 23.3.45 (Sgt Tranchard); R&SU; Retd to FAF 27.11.45; GC.I/6 *'Corse'* 1950; BE.708 Meknès ('A'), noted 9.51; Tipped on nose landing at Meknès 21.12.51 (Sgt Y Legault)

NH270 Spitfire LF.IXe (Merlin 66); TOC/RAF 15.5.44; ex No.341 Sqn - Arr FAF, GR.II/33 *'Savoie'* in 12.44; Retd RAF (No.414 Sqn, crashed Cat.FB/Ac 24.3.45); ROS; Retd to FAF 27.11.45; BE.708 Meknès, crashed Cat.E 20.1.49 (Lt Nedellec); SOC

NH306 Spitfire LF.IXe (Merlin 66); TOC/RAF 15.5.44; ex Nos.328 & 327 Sqns – Via SNCAN Mureaux to FAF 27.11.45; GC.II/1 *'Nice'* ('O') 1948

NH315 Spitfire LF.IXe (Merlin 66); TOC/RAF 12.5.44; ex No.327 Sqn - Arr FAF 27.11.45; GC.II/1 *'Nice'* 1947; BE.708 Meknès ('F') 1949/50

NH326 Spitfire LF.IXe (Merlin 66); TOC/RAF 23.5.44; ex Nos.326 & 328 Sqns - Arr FAF 27.11.45; GC.II/18 *'Saintonge'* in 1946; GC.I/7 *'Provence'* in 1947; BE.708 Meknès ('I') from 1950; Engine failed, force-landed wheels-up, Cat.E 8.4.52 (Matelot Delord, A.N.), SOC

NH348 Spitfire LF.IXe (Merlin 66); TOC/RAF 26.5.44 - Arr FAF 27.11.45; GC.II/1 *'Nice'* from 1.49 until 5.50

NH351 Spitfire LF.IXe (Merlin 66); TOC/RAF 20.5.44; No.327 Sqn, accident at Strasbourg-Entzheim 9.4.45 (Lt Collomp); R&SU - Arr FAF 27.11.45; SNCAN Mureaux, test flight 2.5.46; GC.I/4 *'Dauphiné'* ('C'), test flight Bien Hoa 3.12.47 (noted also 1.49)

NH368 Spitfire LF.IXe (Merlin 66); TOC/RAF 23.5.44; ex Nos.328 & 327 Sqns - SNCAN Mureaux 18.10.45, to FAF 27.11.45; GC.I/3 *'Navarre'* ('H') 1949; GC.II/3 *'Champagne'* in 10.45; Undercarriage failed, one leg landing at Dong Hoi 29.12.49 (S/C Ruth safe); GC.I/6 *'Corse'* ('U'), ground looped, overturned at Nha Trang 5.7.50 (Cne Seguin safe), SOC

NH400 Spitfire LF.IXe (Merlin 66); TOC/RAF 24.4.44 - Allotted for FAF 14.10.46, arr 18.10.46; GC.I/4 *'Dauphiné'* 12.47; ops 24.1.48 and 28.2.48

NH473 Spitfire LF.IXe (Merlin 66); TOC/RAF 23.5.44 - Arr FAF 27.11.45; GC.I/6 *'Corse'* 1950

NH516 Spitfire LF.IXe (Merlin 66); TOC/RAF 27.5.44 - Allotted for FAF 12.9.46, arr Châteaudun 16.9.46; GC.I/2 *'Cigognes'* 1946/47; Engine fire, force-landed wheels-up near Yam Be, Cat.E 8.6.47 (S/C Mazoyer safe), SOC

NH519 Spitfire LF.IXe (Merlin 66); TOC/RAF 31.5.44; ex Nos.327 & 329 Sqns ('5A-J') - SNCAN Mureaux 28.6.45, to FAF 27.11.45; SNCAN, test flight 22.4.47; GC.I/4 *'Dauphiné'* ('N') 11.47, test flight Bien Hoa 15.12.47 (also 1.2.48 and 31.1.49); GC.II/3 *'Champagne'* 1949; SOC 11.4.49

NH538 Spitfire LF.IXe (Merlin 66); TOC/RAF 8.6.44; ex No.327 Sqn - Arr FAF 27.11.45; BE.708 Meknès, crashed 24.9.51 (pilot of A.N.); R&SU; Crashed Cat.E 4.1.52 (Sgt Y Legault); SOC

NH579 Spitfire LF.IXe (Merlin 66); TOC/RAF 8.6.44; ex Nos.341 & 329 Sqns - Allotted for FAF 25.7.46, arr 27.7.46; GC.I/2 *'Cigognes'*, undercarriage collapsed landing, not locked up, Bien Hoa 27.8.47 (Cne Heliot safe); GC.I/4 *'Dauphiné'* ('B'), noted 12.47 and 1.49; Touched down before runway, crashed at Hué, Cat.E 16.4.48 (S/C Founs safe), SOC

NH585 Spitfire LF.IXe (Merlin 66); TOC/RAF 18.6.44; ex No.326 Sqn - Arr FAF 27.11.45; No.3 AIA (Atelier Industriel de l'Air), crashed 8.1.52 (LCL Rousseau)

NN136 Seafire L.IIIc (Merlin 55M); RNDA 26.5.44; ex Nos.879 & 809 Sqns - Arr A.N. 10.4.48; SEC Cuers 7.48; GCE/Esc 54.Serv, census 7.49; SOC 25.1.50

NN149 Seafire L.IIIc (Merlin 55M); RNDA 3.6.44; ex No.801 Sqn - Arr A.N. 5.48; Esc 54.Serv, air collision with SBD-5 on 29.4.49 (EV1 Albert Esun kld); SOC 18.6.49

NN157 Seafire L.IIIc (Merlin 55M); RNDA 10.6.44; ex Nos.880 & 879 Sqns - Arr A.N. 1948; SEC Cuers, storage; Tested 14.4.48, then flown to Hyères; Possibly with 1.Flottille or Esc 54.Serv; Service unknown; SOC 18.6.49

NN171 Seafire L.IIIc (Merlin 55M); RNDA 10.6.44 - Arr A.N. 7.46, flown from Lee-on-Solent to Mureaux 23.7.46 (LV Lenglet, 1.F); To Lyon 24.7.46, to Cuers 25.7.46; Mentioned in inventory 7.47; Flown to Hyères 1.3.48 (Plt Bomin); SEC Cuers 2.12.48; Esc 54.Serv 8.48 (Plt Conq); SOC 13.7.49
NOTE: Records partly found under "RX171"

NN174 Seafire L.IIIc (Merlin 55M); RNDA 15.6.44; ex Nos.798 & 778 Sqns; Cat.ZZ (E) 12.4.45 - Arr A.N. 1947/48; SEC Cuers, tested 2.2.48; ST Hyères (for discharge), census 7.49; SOC 27.8.49
NOTE: Probably delivered for spare parts

NN178 Seafire L.IIIc (Merlin 55M); RNDA 17.6.44; ex Nos.807 & 757 Sqns - Arr A.N. 7.46; Flown from Lee-on-Solent to Mureaux 31.7.46, to Dijon and Cuers 1.8.46 (LV Marmier); GCE/Esc 54.Serv, census 7.49; Hyères, SOC 10.1.50

NN188 Seafire L.IIIc (Merlin 55M); RNDA 23.6.44; ex No.767 Sqn Milltown ('101 / MV') - Arr A.N. 1948; flown from Cuers to Hyères (Plt Bomin) 2.3.48; Esc 54.Serv ('54.S-28'), crashed into barrier of *Arromanches*, prop damaged, 13.4.48; ST Hyères (for discharge), census 7.49; SOC 27.8.49

NN235 Seafire L.IIIc (Merlin 55M); RNDA 12.7.44; ex Nos.887 & 899 Sqns - Arr A.N. 5.48; GCE/Esc 54.Serv, census 7.49; SOC 25.1.50

NN267 Seafire L.IIIc (Merlin 55M); RNDA 29.7.44 - Arr A.N. 5.48; GCE/Esc 54.Serv, census 7.49; SOC 3.10.50

NN299 Seafire L.IIIc (Merlin 55M); RNDA 4.9.44 - Arr A.N. 1946/47; Mentioned in inventory 7.47, service unknown; SOC 10.3. or 12.3.48 (confirmed by 14.4.48)

NN303 Seafire L.IIIc (Merlin 55M); RNDA 19.8.44; ex Nos.807 & 899 Sqns; AFEE - Arr A.N. 12.1947; Flown from Lee-on-Solent to Mureaux 9.12.47, to Cuers 11.12.47 (LV de Latour-Dejean); Esc 54.Serv by 26.8.48; Accident at Hyères 14.9.48; SOC 30.4.49

NN312 Seafire L.IIIc (Merlin 55M); RNDA 26.8.44; ex Nos.801, 808, 880 & 767 Sqns - Arr A.N. 2.48; Flown from Lee-on-Solent to Mureaux 25.2.48 (Plt Roubaud, SEC); SEC Cuers 9.48; GCE/Esc 54.Serv, census 7.49; Hyères, SOC 26.9.50

NN362 Seafire L.IIIc (Merlin 55M); RNDA 18.6.44; ex No.799 Sqn - Arr A.N. 1948; 54. Serv ('54.S-7'), undercarriage failed, crashed landing, prop damaged (date unknown); SOC 31.3.49

NN391 Seafire L.IIIc (Merlin 55M); RNDA 22.7.44; ex No.899 Sqn - Arr A.N. 1948; SEC Cuers storage, tested 15.4.48, flown to Hyères 16.4.48; 1.Flottille ('1.F-2') 4.49 – 10.49; General discharge 7.11.50; Hyères, SOC 11.12.50

NN396 Seafire L.IIIc (Merlin 55M); RNDA 28.7.44; ex No.879 Sqn - Arr A.N. 1948; Service unknown; SOC 23.2.49

NN402 Seafire L.IIIc (Merlin 55M); RNDA 29.7.44 - Arr A.N. 1946/47; 1.Flottille 8.12.47; SEC Cuers, tested 10.2.48; CAN Cuers (for discharge), census 7.49; SOC approved 28.8.50

NN456 Seafire L.IIIc (Merlin 55M); RNDA 20.9.44; ex No.880 Sqn - Arr A.N. 1948; Esc 54.Serv ('54.S-24'), with *Arromanches* in 1.48; Test flight at Hyères or Cuers 18.3.48 (LV Varela, 54.S); ST Hyères (for discharge), census 7.49; SOC 27.8.49

NN467 Seafire L.IIIc (Merlin 55M); RNDA 28.9.44; ex No.807 Sqn - Arr A.N. 1948; Esc 54.Serv ('54.S-10'), accident at Hyères 25.3.48; RiW; SEC Cuers 10.48; ST Hyères (for discharge), census 7.49; SOC 27.8.49
NOTE: Records partly found under "NN461"

NN546 Seafire L.IIIc (Merlin 55M); RNDA 16.11.44; ex Nos.761 & 794 Sqns - Arr A.N. 1947/48; SEC Cuers,

NN578 Seafire L.IIIc (Merlin 55M); RNDA 8.1.45; ex No.761 Sqn - Arr A.N. 1946/47; Cuers, test flight 13.2.47 (LV Lenglet, 1.F); Mentioned in inventory 7.47; Service unknown; SOC 4.2.49 — accident 7.1.48; Awaiting engine change by 12.2.48; Service unknown; SOC 31.3.49

NN604 Seafire L.IIIc (Merlin 55M); RNDA 12.1.45; ex Nos.802 & 806 Sqns - Arr A.N. 15.1.48; Storage SEC Cuers, tested 14.5.48, flown to Hyères 18.5.48; GCE/Esc 54.Serv, census 7.49; Hyères, SOC 3.10.50

NN609 Seafire L.IIIc (Merlin 55M); RNDA 23.1.45; ex Nos.790 & 805 Sqns - Arr A.N. 1948; CAN Cuers (for discharge), census 7.49; RiW (overhaul): DCAN Toulon by 7.11.50 (general discharge 7.11.50); SOC in 11.50; Flown to SMER Rochefort; Ground instructional airframe
NOTE: Records partly found under "NN600"

NN620 Seafire L.IIIc (Merlin 55M); RNDA 9.2.45 - Arr A.N. 1948; Test flight at Hyères 9.4.48 (LV Sanguinetti, 1.F); Esc 54.Serv 15.4.48; SOC 11.10.48

NN623 Seafire L.IIIc (Merlin 55M); RNDA 13.2.45; R.N. rtp 18.3.48 – Arr A.N. 6.48; Flown from Lee-on-Solent to France 15.6.48; GCE/Esc 54.Serv, census 7.49; Hyères, SOC 19.1.50
NOTE: Probably delivered for spare parts

NN628 Seafire L.IIIc (Merlin 55M); RNDA 15.2.45; ex No.718 Sqn - A.N.1946/47; Mentioned in inventory 7.47; SEC Cuers 10.48 & 11.48; Test flight at Hyères 15.12.48 (PM Moal, 54.S); ST Hyères (for discharge), census 7.49; SOC 27.8.49

NN636 Seafire L.IIIc (Merlin 55M); RNDA 9.2.45 - Arr A.N. 1946; Test flight at Hyères 12.7.46, flown to Cuers 16.7.46 (LV Lenglet, 1.F); Mentioned in inventory 7.47; Storage at Cuers, tested 5.3.48 (Plt Roubaud); SOC 6.7.49

NN641 Seafire L.IIIc (Merlin 55M); RNDA 27.2.45; ex No.748 Sqn; Test flown Lee-on-Solent 8.12.47 (LV Sanguinetti, 1.F) - Arr A.N. 12.47; Service unknown; SOC 23.9.48

PK995 Spitfire LF.IXe (Merlin 66); Presentation aircraft 'FORWARD VII'; TOC/RAF 14.6.44; ex Nos.341, 329 & 327 Sqns - Arr FAF 27.11.45; GC.I/3 'Navarre' ('R'), shot down by AA, crashed near Mai Thong 11.9.49 (Adj Boucherd killed), SOC

PL138 Spitfire LF.IXe (Merlin 66); TOC/RAF 22.6.44; ex Nos.329 & 328 Sqns - Arr FAF 27.11.45; GC.I/7 'Provence' 1946; GC.II/1 'Nice' 1947; BE.708 Meknès 4.52

PL140 Spitfire LF.IXe (Merlin 66); TOC/RAF 12.6.44 - Arr FAF 27.11.45; GC.I/3 'Navarre' ('F') 8.11.48; Hit by AA, force-landed and crashed near Sept Pagodes, Cat.E 18.11.48 (Lt Clem Carrere safe), SOC

PL151 Spitfire LF.IXe (Merlin 66); TOC/RAF 30.6.44; Casablanca 22.8.44 - Arr FAF, GR.II/33 'Savoie'; Collided with a lorry after landing at Lyon-Satolas, Cat.E 11.9.44; R&SU; SOC/RAF 15.3.45
NOTE: Crash date reported also as 26.8.44

PL152 Spitfire LF.IXe (Merlin 66); TOC/RAF 29.6.44; ex Nos.329 & 328 Sqns - Arr FAF 27.11.45; GC.I/7 'Provence', noted 10.46 and 12.46; GC.II/1 'Nice' in 9.47 (also 1948); GC.I/6 'Corse' 1950

PL154 Spitfire LF.IXe (Merlin 66); TOC/RAF 30.6.44 - Arr FAF 27.11.45; GC.II/3 'Champagne', crashed on landing, spun into ground after sharp turn near Nha Trang, Cat.E 20.2.50 (Adj Costes killed), SOC

PL189 Spitfire HF.IXe (Merlin 70); Became F-UGBT; TOC/RAF 12.6.44; ex No.329 Sqn - Arr FAF 27.11.45; GC.I/1 'Provence' ('T'); GC.II/1 'Nice' 1950; BE.708 Meknès, engine failed, force-landed and crashed near Ain Bouda, Cat.E 11.1.51 (A/C P Vivoux), SOC

PL196 Spitfire LF.IXe (Merlin 66); TOC/RAF 12.6.44; ex No.328 Sqn from 3.8.45 - Arr FAF 27.11.45; Fate unknown

PL210 Spitfire LF.IXe (Merlin 66); TOC/RAF 17.6.44; ex Nos.340 ('GW-M'), 345, 326 & 327 Sqns - Arr FAF 27.11.45; GC.I/4 'Dauphiné', test flight 9.9.48; GC.I/3 'Navarre' ('A'), engine failure on take-off, crashed Gia-lam, Cat.E 20.1.49 (S/C Valiquet killed), SOC

PL212 Spitfire LF.IXe (Merlin 66); TOC/RAF 12.6.44; ex No.341 Sqn - Allotted for FAF 9.9.46, arr 16.9.46; GC.I/2 'Cigognes' 1946/47; GC.I/4 'Dauphiné' 1.48

PL265 Spitfire LF.IXe (Merlin 66); TOC/RAF 6.5.44; ex No.327 Sqn - Arr FAF 27.11.45; BE.708 Meknès 1949

PL266 Spitfire LF.IXe (Merlin 66); TOC/RAF 6.5.44 - Arr FAF 4.12.46; GC.I/4 'Dauphiné' by 13.12.47, operational flight 15.1.48 & 14.3.48; With the Wing staff of 4.EC in 9.48; 3.EC ('E') 12.48

PL271 Spitfire LF.IXe (Merlin 66); TOC/RAF 12.5.44; ex No.328 Sqn - Arr FAF 27.11.45; GC.I/7 'Provence' 1946

PL272 Spitfire LF.IXe (Merlin 66); TOC/RAF 8.5.44 - Allotted for FAF 25.7.46, arr Châteaudun 30.8.46; GC.I/4 'Dauphiné' ('R') 10.47, shown also 2.48

PL273 Spitfire LF.IXe (Merlin 66); Became F-YCAA; TOC/RAF 9.5.44; ex No.341 Sqn ('NL-S') - Arr FAF 25.7.46, and immediately to A.N.; 1.S. ('1.S-1') 1947/48; Accident, landed wheels-up, engine broke out at Lanvéoc-Poulmic (date unknown); SOC 9.10.48

PL274 Spitfire LF.IXe – Allotted, but cancelled (hit Dakota at Ciampino, Italy before delivery)

PL286 Spitfire LF.IXe (Merlin 66); TOC/RAF 25.5.44; ex No.326 Sqn - SNCAN Mureaux 28.9.45, to FAF 25.11.45; GC.I/1 'Provence' 10.49 (also shown 3.50)

PL314 Spitfire LF.IXe (Merlin 66); TOC/RAF 2.6.44; ex No.326 Sqn - Arr FAF 27.11.45; GC.II/7 'Nice', crashed at Casablanca 30.5.47 (S/C Broche); R&SU; BE.708 Meknès 1952

PL379 Spitfire HF.IXe (Merlin 70); TOC/RAF 23.6.44; ex No.329 Sqn ('5A-F') - Arr FAF 27.11.45; GC.I/2 'Cigognes' 1946; 1.EC (F/Wing) 1947; BE.708 Meknès 1952

PL390 Spitfire HF.IXe (Merlin 70); TOC/RAF 21.6.44; ex No.329 Sqn - Arr FAF 27.11.45; GC.I/1 'Provence' from 7.47 until 9.47; BE.708 Meknès, crashed Cat.E 23.11.51 (Sgt A Thome); SOC

PL402 Spitfire LF.IXe (Merlin 66); TOC/RAF 27.6.44; ex No.326 Sqn - Arr FAF 27.11.45; Fate unknown

PL438 Spitfire LF.IXe (Merlin 66); TOC/RAF 27.6.44 - Arr FAF 27.11.45; GC.I/4 'Dauphiné' ('W') 10.47; GC.II/4 'La Fayette' ('D') 5.48 and 9.48 - NOTE: 'Amiral' painted

PL452 Spitfire HF.IXe (Merlin 70); TOC/RAF 30.7.44 - Arr FAF 27.11.45; SNCAN Mureaux 2.5.46; 1.EC (F/Wing); GC.I/1 'Provence' 1.7.48; Crashed Cat.E 27.2.50 (Sgt Corcy safe); SOC

PL454 Spitfire LF.IXe (Merlin 66); TOC/RAF 29.6.44; ex No.345 Sqn - Arr FAF 27.11.45; BE.708 Meknès 3.47; GC.I/1 'Provence' 1949

PL495 Spitfire LF.IXe (Merlin 66); TOC/RAF 30.6.44 - Allotted for FAF 9.9.46, arr 12.9.46; GC.II/4 'La Fayette' ('R') 12.47, noted also 4.48

PL983 Spitfire PR.XI arrived as SURVIVOR only 18.11.84; Bought by R Fraisinett 14.4.83 but regd G-PRXI 6.6.83; To Doug Arnold in UK 1987; Fatal crash at Rouen-Boos airport, France 3.6.2001 (Plt Martin Sargeant killed)

PP972 Seafire L.IIIc (Merlin 55M); RNDA 27.9.44; ex Nos.809 & 767 Sqns (Milltown "120 / MV") - Arr A.N. 1948; SEC Cuers 10.48; 1.Flottille ('1.F-9') 1948; 12.Flottille ('12.F-2'); GCE/Esc 54.Serv, census 7.49; Hyères by 7.11.50 (general discharge); SOC 11.12.50 - Wreck at Gâvres 1966; To Jean Fréulaut at Vannes-Meucon 1970; Sold to Doug Arnold, UK and transferred to Biggin Hill 1988/89; Civil reg. G-BUAR (21.1.92); Restoration to fly by Hawker Restorations Ltd at Earls Colne - SURVIVOR

PP990 Seafire L.IIIc (Merlin 55M); RNDA 7.10.44 - Arr A.N. 1948; GCE/Esc 54.Serv, census 7.49; SOC 1.10.49

PR132 Seafire L.IIIc (Merlin 55M); RNDA 9.11.44; ex No.761 Sqn - Arr A.N. 4.48; Flown from Lee-on-Solent to Mureaux 9.4.48 (PM Klein, SRC); Arromanches by 2.7.48, flown to Hyères (PM Moal, 54.S); Test flight at Hyères 13.10.48 (LV Lenglet, 12.F); SOC 30.4.49

Seafire L.IIIcs aboard the light fleet carrier Arromanches *(previously HMS* Colossus*). The nearest machine is PR146 '54.S-14' of Escadrille de Servitude No.54. Also visible are '1.F-1', '1.F-3', '1.F-25' and '1.F-28' of Flottille 1F.*

PR144   Seafire L.IIIc (Merlin 55M); RNDA 28.10.44; ex No.887 Sqn ("129/S") - A.N. by 26.2.46; Esc 54.Serv with *Arromanches* to Algeria 29.4.48; RiW Algiers 5.6.48; ex Maison-Blanche (for discharge), census 7.49; SOC 27.8.49. - NOTE: Records partly found under "PR114"

PR146   Seafire L.IIIc (Merlin 55M); RNDA 28.10.44; ex Nos.899, 894, 794 & 771 Sqns - Arr A.N. 12.47; Flown from Lee-on-Solent to Mureaux 8.12.47, to Hyères 11.12.47 (LV Sanguinetti, 1.F); Esc 54.Serv ('54.S-14'), date unknown; SOC 18.6.49

PR170   Seafire L.IIIc (Merlin 55M); RNDA 31.10.44; ex No.879 Sqn - Arr A.N. 1948; Storage SEC Cuers, tested 21.4.48; To Hyères 28.4.48; 12.Flottille ('12.F-3'); Accident at Hyères 31.8.48; CAN Cuers (for discharge), census 7.49; SOC approved 28.8.50

PR175   Seafire L.IIIc (Merlin 55M); RNDA 29.11.44; ex No.807 Sqn - Arr A.N. 7.46; Flown from Lee-on-Solent to Mureaux 9.7.46, to Hyères 10.7.46 (LV Lenglet, 1.F); SEC Cuers, tested 2.2.48 (Plt Roubaud); Esc 54.Serv ('54.S-18'); Accident at Hyères 26.3.48; SOC 18.6.49

PR176   Seafire L.IIIc (Merlin 55M); RNDA 9.11.44; ex No.801 Sqn - Arr A.N. 1946; Test flight at Mureaux (or Hyères) 30.4.46 (LV de Latour-Dejean); Esc 54.Serv ('54.S-11'); Accident at Cuers 24.2.48; SOC 31.3.49
NOTE: Test flight Mureaux recorded also for "RX176"

PR186   Seafire L.IIIc (Merlin 55M); RNDA 11.11.44 - Arr A.N. 1946; 1.Flottille 30.4.46; Esc 3.Serv by 11.12.46; Engine change 12.2.47; RiW (Mureaux) 21.11.47; SNCAN Mureaux by 13.8.48 and census 7.49; SOC 27.8.49
NOTE: SOC recorded as "PR146"

PR190   Seafire L.IIIc (Merlin 55M); RNDA 25.11.44; ex No.899 Sqn - Arr A.N. 1946/47; SEA Hyères mid 1947; Esc 54.Serv ('54.S-13'), ASSP training at Hyères; Accident 18.9.47 (EV Petit); R&SU; Accident at Hyères 19.3.48 (EV Cremer); SOC 23.4. or 27.4.48
NOTE: Accident 9.47 recorded for "PR140"

PR194   Seafire L.IIIc (Merlin 55M); RNDA 18.11.44; ex No.760 Sqn - Arr A.N. 1946/47; Esc 54.Serv, rtp - approved for spare parts 20.3.47; Mentioned in inventory 7.47; SOC 14.6.48.
NOTE: Spare parts approved (incorrectly) for "PR184"

PR196   Seafire L.IIIc (Merlin 55M); RNDA 18.11.44 - Arr A.N. 1946; Mureaux 5.46; SEC Cuers storage mid 1947, tested 10.9.47; RiW, SNCAN Mureaux 10.3.48; SOC 31.3.49

PR197   Seafire L.IIIc (Merlin 55M); RNDA 25.11.44; ex No.880 Sqn - Arr A.N. 7.46; Flown from Lee-on-Solent to Mureaux, then to Hyères 21.7.46 (LV M Gleize, 1.F); Mentioned in inventory 7.47; SOC 14.6.48

PR204   Seafire L.IIIc (Merlin 55M); RNDA 18.11.44; Test flight at Lee-on-Solent 9.7.46 (LV de Latour-Dejean) - Arr A.N. 7.46; SEC Cuers 7.46; Esc 54.Serv in 3.48; Test flight at Hyères 22.3.48, tested also 17.7. and 21.7.48 (LV Varela); SOC 23.2.49

PR205   Seafire L.IIIc (Merlin 55M); RNDA 25.11.44; ex No.887 Sqn - Arr A.N. 7.46; Lee-on-Solent, tested and flown to Mureaux 9.7.46 (PM Guyot, 1.F); Via Lyon to Hyères 10.7.46 (PM Guyot); Tested at Hyères 12.7.46, to Cuers 13.7.46; 1.Flottille ('1.F-4') 1.48-10.49; GCE/Esc 54.Serv, census 7.49; General discharge 7.11.50; Hyères, SOC 11.12.50

PR249   Seafire L.IIIc (Merlin 55M); RNDA 30.11.44 - Arr A.N. 3.46; Mureaux 17.3.46 (PM Guyot, 1.F), to Hyères 20.3.46 (LV de Latour-Dejean), to BM.2 at Hyères 20.3.46; 1.Flottille by 8.4.46; SEA Hyères autumn 1947; SOC approved 3.10.47, confirmed 28.10.47

PR265   Seafire L.IIIc (Merlin 32); RNDA 16.12.44 - Arr A.N. 3.46; Flown from Mureaux to Hyères 20.3.46, 1.Flottille ('1.F-4') 27.3.46 until 1.48; With *Arromanches* to Oran 5.47; Accident at Sidi Ahmet, tipped on nose 7.6.47; Accident at Hyères 9.9.47; RiW; SOC 17.8.48
NOTE: Records partly found under "PR269"

PR266   Seafire L.IIIc (Merlin 32); RNDA 16.12.44; ex No.880 Sqn; Abbotsinch 2.46 - Arr A.N. 3.46; Flown at Hyères 3.4. and 4.4.46 (LV de Latour-Dejean and LV Sanguinetti, 1.F); 1.Flottille ('1.F-13') 7.47 until 1.48; SOC 18.6.49

PR288   Seafire L.IIIc (Merlin 32); RNDA 16.12.44; Tested at Lee-on-Solent 8.12.47 (LV de Latour-Dejean) - Arr A.N.1947/48; 1.Flottille 1948; SOC 23.9.48

PR293   Seafire L.IIIc (Merlin 55M); RNDA 22.12.44 - Arr A.N. 1948; SEC Cuers 15.9.48; Esc 54.Serv ('54.S-6'), tested at Brétigny 28.10.48 (LV Mauban); Retd to Hyères 17.12.48; Tested at Hyères 12.4.49 (OE Guyot, 1.F); ST Hyères (for discharge), census 7.49; SOC 27.8.49

PR300   Seafire L.IIIc (Merlin 32; M.55M from 3.47); RNDA 31.12.44 - Arr A.N. 7.46; Flown to Mureaux 31.7.46, to Hyères 1.8.46 (LV Lenglet, 1.F), to Cuers 2.8.46 (LV Sanguinetti, 1.F); SEA Hyères, engine changed to Merlin 55M in 3.47; SEA Hyères also mid 1947; Esc 54.Serv ('54.S-12'), with *Arromanches*, crashed landing 11.9.47 (LV Graignic safe); SNCAN Mureaux for overhaul 21.11.47; SOC 9.12.47

PR304   Seafire L.IIIc (Merlin 55M); RNDA 6.1.45; ex No.879 Sqn - Arr A.N. 1948; Service unknown; SOC 18.6.49

PR322   Seafire L.IIIc (Merlin 55M); RNDA 6.1.45 - Arr A.N. 1948; Storage SEC Cuers, tested 14.4.48; Flown to Hyères 15.4.48; Service unknown; ST Hyères (for discharge), census 7.49; SOC 27.8.49

PR329   Seafire L.IIIc (Merlin 32, later M.55M); RNDA 13.1.45; ex No.879 Sqn - Arr A.N. 1946/47; Esc 54.Serv 1946/47 (Engine changed to M.55M on 12.2.47); 1.Flottille ('1.F-3'); Accident at Hyères 24.4.47 (EV1 Thierry d'Argenlieu safe); SOC 29.4.47 (rtp, for spare parts)

PR333   Seafire L.IIIc (Merlin 55M); RNDA 13.1.45; ex No.879 Sqn - Arr A.N. 1948; Service unknown; Hyères, SOC 18.6.49

PR347   Seafire F.XVc (Griffon VI); RNDA 24.5.45; ex Nos.802 & 803 Sqns - Arr A.N. 17.6.49; 12.Flottille ('12.F-15') 6.49

PR349   Seafire F.XVc (Griffon VI); RNDA 29.5.45 - Arr A.N. 17.6.49; Unknown unit ('3') 1949; 1.Flottille ('1.F-25')

PR360   Seafire F.XVc (Griffon VI); RNDA 23.6.45 - Arr A.N. 25.6.49; 1.Flottille ('1.F-22')

PR397   Seafire F.XVc (Griffon VI); RNDA 26.7.45 - Arr A.N. 24.6.49; 54 Esc/Serv ('54.S-22')

PR405   Seafire F.XVc (Griffon VI); RNDA 30.7.45 - Arr A.N. 17.6.49; 1.Flottille '1.F-26'

PR414   Seafire F.XVc (Griffon VI); RNDA 27.8.45; ex No.771 Sqn - Arr A.N. 28.6.49; Unknown unit ('14'); 1.Flottille ('1.F-27')

PR429   Seafire F.XVc (Griffon VI); RNDA 13.9.45; ex No.802 Sqn - Arr A.N. 28.6.49; Fate unknown

PT343   Spitfire LF.IXe (Merlin 66); TOC/RAF 1.6.44; ex No.345 Sqn - Arr FAF 27.11.45; Fate unknown

PT359   Spitfire LF.IXe (Merlin 66); TOC/RAF 30.6.44; ex No.328 Sqn - Arr FAF 2.47; Unknown unit, crashed 30.4.51

PT365   Spitfire LF.IXe (Merlin 66); TOC/RAF 1.7.44 - Arr FAF, GR.II/33 *'Savoie'* from 30.9.44; Hit by AA, force-landed near Dannemarie/Uberstrass, Cat.FB/E 25.11.44 (Cdt Marcel Martre), SOC

PT367   Spitfire LF.IXe (Merlin 66); TOC/RAF 17.7.44; ex Nos.326 & 327 Sqns; No.328 Sqn, accident at Entzheim 25.4.45 (Lt Durand); R&SU - SNCAN Mureaux 11.11.45, to FAF 27.11.45; GC.I/1 *'Provence'* 6.49; GC.I/6 *'Corse'* 4.50

PT376   Spitfire LF.IXe (Merlin 66); TOC/RAF 28.7.44 - Arr FAF 28.3.46, and immediately to A.N.; Cuers, to Esc 10.Serv 10.5.46; Accident at Hyères, tyre burst on take-off 29.6.46; '10.S-23' shown in 9.46 and mid 1947; At Hyères 4.47; Via CN Cuers for Esc 54.Serv 16.12.47; Esc 54.Serv in 4.48; SEC Cuers 1948/49; Esc 3.Serv ('3.S-11') 1949; RiW in early 1950, but lack of spare parts (still marked '3.S-11' in 6.50); SNCAN Mureaux for overhaul 23.9.50; General discharge 7.11.50; Cuers, SOC 20.11.50

PT401   Spitfire LF.IXe (Merlin 66); TOC/RAF 1.7.44; ex Nos.328 & 327 Sqns - Arr FAF 27.11.45; GC.I/2 *'Cigognes'* 1946

PT422   Spitfire LF.IXe (Merlin 66); TOC/RAF 17.7.44 - Arr FAF, GR.II/33 *'Savoie'* from 8.44; Loss of orientation in bad weather, fuel shortage, force-landed wheels up near Dijon-Longvic, Cat.E 9.11.44 (Lt Pierre Sainflou), SOC

PT436   Spitfire LF.IXe (Merlin 66); TOC/RAF 19.7.44; ex Nos.327 & 328 Sqns; Accident at Entzheim 12.4.45 (S/Lt Berthet); R&SU - Arr FAF 27.11.45; Fate unknown

PT454   Spitfire LF.IXe (Merlin 66); TOC/RAF 18.7.44; ex No.326 Sqn - SNCAN Mureaux 1945, to FAF 27.11.45; GC.II/1 *'Nice'* 1949; BE.708 Meknès 1949/50

Seafire F.XVc PR397 '54.S-22' of Escadrille de Servitude No.54, Hyères, around 1950/51.   [Claude A. Pierquet]

PT458 Spitfire LF.IXe (Merlin 66); TOC/RAF 1.8.44 - Arr FAF 28.3.46; A.N. 1946; Cuers, to 10.Serv 10.5.46 ('10.S-24' shown 9.46 to early 1948, but also '10.S-22', reported '10.S-23' end 1947); Possibly '1.S-3' in 1949 (questionable!), still with Esc 10.Serv by 18.3.49 and autumn 1949; Repair approved 15.10.49; BAN St Raphaël from early 1950; SOC 22.7.50

PT467 Spitfire LF.IXe (Merlin 66); TOC/RAF 20.7.44; ex Nos.326 & 328 Sqns - Arr FAF 27.11.45; GC.I/4 *'Dauphiné'*, test flight Bien Hoa 9.9.48; GC.II/3 *'Champagne'* ('C'), belly-landed at Tan Son Nhut 3.2.49 (Lt Mayot safe); R&SU; GC.II/3, force-landed near Sway Rieng, Cat.E 21.7.49 (Lt Mayot safe); SOC

PT494 Spitfire LF.IXe (Merlin 66); TOC/RAF 21.7.44 - Arr A.N. 25.7.46; Esc 3.Serv at Cuers ('3.S-9') in 1946; SOC 16.12.48

PT496 Spitfire LF.IXe (Merlin 66); TOC/RAF 20.7.44; ex Nos.326 & 328 Sqns; Accident at Luxeuil 16.2.45 (Plt Hoot); R&SU - Arr FAF 27.11.45; GC.I/3 *'Navarre'* ('T') 25.7.49 (noted also in 8.49); R&SU 14.10.49; GC.I/6 *'Corse'* 1950; BE.708 Meknès, tipped on nose landing, Cat.E at Meknès, 5.6.52 (Sgt H Gaudin); SOC

PT553 Spitfire LF.IXe (Merlin 66); TOC/RAF 29.8.44; ex No.327 Sqn - Arr FAF 27.11.45; Fate unknown

PT582 Spitfire LF.IXe (Merlin 66); TOC/RAF 20.7.44 – Arr FAF, GR.II/33 *'Savoie'* in 11.44; Retd RAF 2.45 (later Second TAF (No 130 Sqn)

PT612 Spitfire LF.IXe (Merlin 66); TOC/RAF 24.7.44 - Arr FAF at Friedrichshafen, Germany (2.EC) 7.12.45; GC.I/2 *'Cigognes'* 1946; GC.I/7 *'Provence'* 1947

PT623 Spitfire LF.IXe (Merlin 66); TOC/RAF 25.7.44; ex Nos.340 & 345 Sqns - Arr FAF 27.11.45; Fate unknown

PT639 Spitfire LF.IXe (Merlin 66); Became **F-YCAB**; TOC/RAF 4.8.44 - Arr A.N. 28.11.46; SEC Cure storage autumn 1947; Esc 1.Serv ('1.S-2') 1948-1950; Tipped on nose (date unknown); Selected for SOC 2.1.50; Reserve aircraft at Lanvéoc-Poulmic 3.6.50; General discharge 7.11.50; SOC 1.1.51; Possibly via SAMAN at Toussus-le-Noble to Esc 50.Serv

PT671 Spitfire LF.IXe (Merlin 66); TOC/RAF 28.7.44 - Arr FAF 28.3.46, then to A.N.; SEA Hyères autumn 1947; Unknown unit, accident 12.1.48; Storage at Hyères 12.2.48; SOC 17.8.48

PT732 Spitfire LF.IXe (Merlin 66); TOC/RAF 5.8.44; ex Nos.329, 345 & 328 Sqns - Arr FAF 27.11.45; GC.II/1 *'Nice'* 11.47

PT737 Spitfire LF.IXe (Merlin 66); TOC/RAF 9.8.44; ex Nos.340 & 345 Sqns - Arr FAF 14.8.46; GC.I/4 *'Dauphiné'*, FR- mission from Tan Son Nhut 21.12.47; GC.II/4 *'La Fayette'*, lost control in bad visibility and dived into ground near Pat Diem/Tonkin, Cat.E 20.3.48 (Sgt Heroin killed, aircraft wreckage found mid-April 1948), SOC

PT758 Spitfire LF.IXe (Merlin 66); TOC/RAF 5.8.44; ex No.326 Sqn ('8J-X') - Arr FAF 27.11.45; GC.II/18 *'Saintonge'* in 1946

PT783 Spitfire LF.IXe (Merlin 66); TOC/RAF 8.9.44; ex No.326 Sqn - Arr FAF 27.11.45; BE.708 Meknès, tipped on nose 1951

PT819 Spitfire LF.IXe (Merlin 66); TOC/RAF 16.8.44; ex No.341 Sqn - Arr FAF, Châteaudun (ferry flight) 27.2.46; GC.I/2 *'Cigognes'*, engine fire, dived into ground near Cu Linn, SE of Gia-lam, Cat.E 15.9.47 (Lt Serrate), SOC

PT823 Spitfire LF.IXe (Merlin 66); TOC/RAF 16.8.44; ex No.341 & 326 Sqns - SNCAN Mureaux 28.6.45, to FAF 27.11.45; GC.II/4 *'La Fayette'* ('A'), test flight 19.2.48 (noted also in 11.48); GC.II/3 *'Champagne'*, crashed at Nha Trang (Cne Girard) 8.6.49

PT844 Spitfire HF.IXe (Merlin 70); TOC/RAF 24.8.44; ex Nos.345, 340, 341 & 329 Sqns - Arr FAF 27.11.45; GC.I/7 *'Provence'* 1946

PT846 Spitfire LF.IXe (Merlin 66); TOC/RAF 23.8.44 - Arr A.N. 28.3.46; SEA Hyères autumn 1947; Hyères storage 13.2.48; Esc 54.Serv ('54.S-3'); Accident at Hyères 28.8.47 (Plt de Scitivaux); RiW; Hyères, SOC 17.8.48

"PT847" Incorrect report (was lost already 8.11.44)

"PT876" Incorrect report (lost already 30.12.44) - but see PT376

PT894 Spitfire LF.IXe (Merlin 66); TOC/RAF 24.8.44; ex Nos.340 & 345 Sqns - Arr FAF 27.11.45; GC.I/1 *'Provence'* 10.49; BE.708 Meknès ('O') 11.50

PT908 Spitfire LF.IXe (Merlin 66); TOC/RAF 27.8.44; ex Nos.341, 340, 329, 327 & 326 Sqns - Arr FAF 27.11.45; 2.EC (F/Wing) 1946; GC.I/7 *'Provence'* 1947

PT915 Spitfire LF.IXe (Merlin 66); TOC/RAF 26.8.44; ex No.329 Sqn - Arr FAF 27.11.45; Fate unknown

PT959 Spitfire LF.IXe (Merlin 66); TOC/RAF 30.8.44; ex Nos.329, 341 & 328 Sqns - Arr FAF 27.11.45; GC.I/1 *'Provence'* (at Oran in 10.47); 1.EC (F/Wing), crashed 6.3. or 8.3.48

PT991 Spitfire LF.IXe (Merlin 66); TOC/RAF 5.9.44; ex Nos.329 ('5A-R') & 345 Sqns - Arr FAF 27.11.45; GC.II/1 *'Nice'*, crashed 24.10.49 (Lt Hammonton)

PT995 Spitfire LF.IXe (Merlin 66); TOC/RAF 31.8.44; ex No.328 & No.327 Sqns - Arr FAF 27.11.45; GC.I/7 *'Provence'* 1946; GC.II/1 *'Nice'* 1947 (shown also 1948)

PV128 Spitfire LF.IXe (Merlin 66); Became **F-YCJK**; TOC/RAF 14.8.44 – TOC/FAF (officially 28.3.46), arr A.N. 27.3.46; Cuers, for 1.Flottille 27.3.46; Flown to 1.Flottille at Hyères 30.3.46 ('1.F-15'); Marked '1.F-13' in 6.46; For Esc 10.Serv autumn 1946 ('10.S-23'), arrived 31.12.46; Reported as '10.S-20' mid 1947 and '10.S-22' end 1947 to autumn 1948; Moved to Esc 1.Serv at Lanvéoc-Poulmic 7.10.48 ('1.S-1' shown early 1950); Selected for SOC 2.1.50; General discharge 7.11.50; SOC 1.1.51; To Esc 50.Serv., as ground instructional airframe

PV147 Spitfire LF.IXe (Merlin 66); TOC/RAF 5.9.44; ex Nos.327, 329, 340 & 345 Sqns - Arr FAF 27.11.45; Fate unknown

PV155 Spitfire LF.IXe (Merlin 66); TOC/RAF 5.9.44; ex Nos.345 & 326 Sqns - Arr FAF 27.11.45; GC.I/7 *'Provence'* 1946; Collision with **171 on 3.3.47

PV175 Spitfire LF.IXe (Merlin 66); TOC/RAF 5.9.44; ex No.328 Sqn - Arr FAF 27.11.45; GC.III/2 *'Alsace'* 1946

PV180 Spitfire LF.IXe (Merlin 66); TOC/RAF 15.9.44; ex No.328 Sqn - Arr FAF 27.11.45; BE.708 Meknès, crashed 11.1.52 (S/Lt Meunier)

PV187 Spitfire LF.IXe (Merlin 66); TOC/RAF 16.9.44; ex Nos.341 & 340 Sqns - Arr FAF 27.11.45; SNCAN Mureaux, test flight 2.5.46; GC.I/6 *'Corse'* ('F'), test flight 23.7.50 (also noted in 8.50)

PV229 Spitfire LF.IXe (Merlin 66); TOC/RAF 16.9.44; ex Nos.329, 340 ('GW-A') & 345 Sqns - Arr FAF 27.11.45; GC.I/6 *'Corse'* 1950; BE.708 Meknès 4.52

PV232 Spitfire LF.IXe (Merlin 66); Became **F-TEVI**; TOC/RAF 16.9.44; ex No.329 Sqn - Arr FAF 27.11.45; 1.EC, Friedrichshafen 11.46; ELA 55 on 13.6.49; GC.I/6 *'Corse'* ('L') noted 1.4.50 (Plt F Roost); BE.708 Meknès ('I') 1951, also shown in 2.52

PV234 Spitfire LF.IXe (Merlin 66); TOC/RAF 21.9.44; ex No.326 Sqn - Arr FAF 27.11.45; GC.I/4 *'Dauphiné'*, test flight 9.9.48; GC.II/3 *'Champagne'*, belly-landed at Phi Qui, Cat.FB/E 18.5.49 (Lt Mayot safe), SOC

PV235 Spitfire LF.IXe (Merlin 66); TOC/RAF 21.9.44 - Arr FAF 27.11.45; GC.I/6 *'Corse'* ('E') 10.50

PV284 Spitfire LF.IXe (Merlin 66); TOC/RAF 25.9.44; ex No.329 Sqn - Arr FAF 27.11.45; SNCAN Mureaux, test flight 14.2.49; GC.I/6 *'Corse'* ('H'), noted at Nha Trang 23.7.50 (shown also in 12.50); BE.708 Meknès 3.52

PV286 Spitfire LF.IXe (Merlin 66); TOC/RAF 25.9.44; ex Nos.329, 340 & 345 Sqns - Arr FAF 27.11.45; GC.II/7 *'Nice'* 1947/48; BE.708 Meknès ('G') 1949 (also noted 1951)

PV292 Spitfire LF.IXe (Merlin 66); Became **F-TEVF**; TOC/RAF 23.9.44; ex Nos.329, 345 & 326 Sqns - Arr FAF 27.11.45; GC.II/18 *'Saintonge'* in 12.45; GC.I/6

Spitfire LF.IXe PV235 'E' in service with GC.I/6 'Corse' in French Indo-China around 1950. [Annam A502520]

    'Corse' ('M'), noted 7.50 and in 12.50; BE.708 Meknès ('F') 1951

PV343 Spitfire LF.IXe (Merlin 66); TOC/RAF 27.9.44; ex No.329 Sqn - Arr FAF 27.11.45; BE.708 Meknès ('E') 1949 (shown also 1951)

PX916 Seafire L.IIIc (Merlin 55M); RNDA 28.2.45; ex No.767 Sqn - Arr A.N. 1948; Engine failed, force-landed Mureaux 28.2 or 1.3.48 (PM Saout, SRC); RiW; SNCAN Mureaux by 13.8.48, also in 7.49 (census); SOC 1949

PX917 Seafire L.IIIc (Merlin 55M); RNDA 28.2.45 - Arr A.N. 3.46; SNCAN Mureaux 1.8.46; Service unknown; RiW, SNCAN 21.11.47; SRC, test flight 12.3.48 (OE Gicquel); Cuers 19.3.48 (PM Klein, SRC); SEC Cuers storage, tested 22.6.48, flown to Hyères 28.6.48; Test flown 6.8 and 9.8.48 (LV de Latour-Dejean); ST Hyères (for discharge), census 7.49; SOC 27.8.49

PX918 Seafire L.IIIc (Merlin 55M); RNDA 1.3.45 - Arr A.N. 7.46: test flight at Lee-on-Solent and flown to Mureaux 23.7.46 (PM Guyot, 1.F); Via Lyon to Hyères 24.7.46 (PM Guyot), to Cuers 25.7.46; RiW 6.47; SNCAN Mureaux by 21.11.47; Test flight at Hyères 6.8. & 9.8.48 (LV de Latour-Dejean); SNCAN Mureaux by 13.8.48, also census 7.49; SOC 5.4.50

PX919 Seafire L.IIIc (Merlin 55M); RNDA 1.3.45 - Arr A.N. 1947/48; 1.Flottille at Hyères; Deck landing at *Arromanches* 15.4.48; SOC 18.6.49
NOTE: Also reported as "RX219"

PX922 Seafire L.IIIc (Merlin 55M); RNDA 1.3.45 - Arr A.N. 3.46; Flown at Mureaux 28.3.46 (LV Sanguinetti, 1.F); BM.2 Hyères to BAN Cuers 23.4.46; SEC Cuers, tested VHF radio 2.7 & 10.7.47; VR Cuers to 1.Flottille 1.8.47 ('1.F-12' in 12.47 & 1.48); SOC 30.4.49

PX931 Seafire L.IIIc (Merlin 55M); RNDA 5.3.45 - Arr A.N. 1948; GCE/Esc 54.Serv, census 7.49; 1.Flottille ('1.F-10') 4.49 – 10.49; SOC 5.4.50

PX932 Seafire L.IIIc (Merlin 55M); RNDA 3.3.45; ex No.802 Sqn - Arr A.N. 1946; Flown from Cuers to Hyères 23.12.46 (LV de Latour-Dejean); 1.Flottille ('1.F-22') 7.47 – 2.48; SEA Hyères autumn 1947; 1.F, crashed on landing at Algiers/Maison-Blanche 2.2.48 (EV Roy); RiW (Algiers by 5.6.48); GCE/Esc 54.Serv, census 7.49; SOC 27.8.49

PX933 Seafire L.IIIc (Merlin 55M); RNDA 2.3.45 - Arr A.N. 6.46; Flown from Mureaux to Cuers 1.7.46 (LV de Latour-Dejean, 1.F); SNCAN Mureaux for overhaul 29.4.47; 1.Flottille ('1.F-23'), tipped on nose (date unknown); RiW; VR Cuers, allocated for 1.Flottille 24.5.47 (confirmed 5.6.47); RiW, to SNCAN Mureaux 21.11.47, shown there also 13.8.48 and census 7.49; SAMAN Toussus-le-Noble 31.7.49 (OE Gicquel, SRC); General discharge 7.11.50; Hyères, SOC 11.12.50

PX940 Seafire L.IIIc (Merlin 55M); RNDA 12.3.45 - Arr A.N. 1946; SEC Cuers 4.46; 1.Flottille at Hyères 25.9.46; 1.Flottille with *Arromanches*; Accident (engine failure) 20.11.46; Accident 24.12.46; NEA 29.1.47; SOC 27.2.47

PX943 Seafire L.IIIc (Merlin 55M); RNDA 19.3.45 - Arr A.N. 1946/47; 1.Flottille ('1.F-17'), crashed and destroyed near Hyères 25.6.47 (EV2 Guy Moysset killed); SOC approved 7.8.47

PX945 Seafire L.IIIc (Merlin 55M); RNDA 26.3.45 - Arr A.N. 1946/47; Esc 54.Serv 12.6.47; 1.Flottille ('1.F-10') 12.47 & 1.48; ST Hyères (for discharge), census 7.49; SOC 27.8.49

PX946 Seafire L.IIIc (Merlin 55M); RNDA 19.3.45; ex No.794 Sqn - Arr A.N. 1948; SEC Cuers 22.9.48; Service unknown; ST Hyères (for discharge), census 7.49; SOC 27.8.49

PX951 Seafire L.IIIc (Merlin 55M); RNDA 23.3.45 - Arr A.N. 3.46; Mureaux, flown to Hyères 29.3.46 (LV Sanguinetti, 1.F); BM.2 Hyères 3.46; BAN Cuers 23.4.46; Retd to BM.2 on 31.3.47; 1.Flottille ('1.F-14') 7.47 - 1.48; SOC 30.4.49 (confirmed 27.8.49)

PX952 Seafire L.IIIc (Merlin 55M); RNDA 27.3.45 - Arr A.N. 3.46; Cuers, to BM.2 at Hyères 31.3.46; Flown in Mureaux-Beauvais area 17.4.46 (LV M Gleize); Mureaux to Cuers 1.5.46 (LV de Latour-Dejean); Fate unknown

PX953 Seafire L.IIIc (Merlin 55M); RNDA 28.3.45 - Arr A.N. 3.46; Mureaux to Hyères 20.3.46; 1.Flottille ('1.F-5') 27.3.46; SOC 15.10.46

PX954 Seafire L.IIIc (Merlin 55M); RNDA 28.3.45 - Arr A.N. 3.46; Mureaux to Hyères 20.3.46; 1.Flottille ('1.F-6') 27.3.46; VR Cuers (reserve) approved 5.6.47; SOC approved 8.7.47

PX955 Seafire L.IIIc (Merlin 55M); RNDA 30.3.45 - Arr A.N. 3.46; Mureaux, test flown 22.3.46 (LV Sanguinetti and

FRANCE

	LV RP de Latour-Dejean, 1.F); Flown to Hyères 23.3.46; 1.Flottille ('1.F-7') 27.3.46; VR Cuers (discharge approved) 24.5. & 5.6.47; RiW, SNCAN Mureaux 21.11.47, shown there also 13.8.48 and census 7.49; SAMAN Toussus-le Noble, engine tested 24.8.49 (OE Gicquel, SRC); SOC 23.9.50
PX957	Seafire L.IIIc (Merlin 55M); RNDA 30.3.45 - Arr A.N. 1946/47; 1.Flottille ('1.F-14') by 1.7.47; SEC Cuers storage mid 1947; CN Cuers, tested 2.9.47; SOC approved 28.8.50
PX962	Seafire L.IIIc (Merlin 55M); RNDA 31.3.45 - Arr A.N. 1946; Flown Mureaux to Hyères 7.5.46 (LV Sanguinetti, 1.F); SEC Cuers, tested 31.7.47, also VHF tests 9.8.47; VR Cuers, to 1.Flottille 1.8.47 ('1.F-18' shown 12.47 & 1.48); ST Hyères (for discharge), census 7.49; SOC 27.8.49
RK817	Spitfire LF.IXe (Merlin 66); TOC/RAF 18.9.44; ex No.326 Sqn - Arr FAF 24.11.45; GC.II/18 'Saintonge' in 4.46; BE.708 Meknès, crashed 23.10.50
RK853	Spitfire LF.IXe (Merlin 66); TOC/RAF 30.9.44; ex Nos.329, 341 & 326 Sqns - Arr FAF 27.11.45; GC.I/7 'Provence' 1947; GC.II/7 'Nice', crashed 23.4.47
RK900	Spitfire LF.IXe (Merlin 66); TOC/RAF 5.10.44; ex No.327 Sqn - Arr FAF 27.11.45; Fate unknown
RK906	Spitfire LF.IXe (Merlin 66); TOC/RAF 6.10.44; ex Nos.345, 327 & 328 Sqns - Arr FAF 27.11.45; GC.I/7 'Provence', crashed 28.11.46
RR187	Spitfire LF.IXe (Merlin 66); TOC/RAF 30.8.44; ex Nos.341, 340, 345 & 327 Sqns - Arr FAF 27.11.45; GC.II/18 'Saintonge', noted in 2.46; GC.II/3 'Champagne', accident 20.8.49; GC.I/6 'Corse' in 12.50; R&SU; BE.708 Meknès, noted 8.51; Ground collision at Meknès 14.9.51 (Sgt P Rousseau safe)
RR200	Spitfire LF.IXe (Merlin 66); TOC/RAF 15.9.44; ex Nos.345, 327 & 328 Sqns - Arr FAF 27.11.45; GC.I/7 'Provence' 1945; GC.II/1 'Nice' 1947; BE.708 Meknès ('D')
RR263	Spitfire LF.XVIe (Merlin 266); TOC/RAF 19.10.44; ex Nos.66 ('LZ-B') & 416 Sqns, No.4 CAACU; Converted to GI No. *7216M* - Arr France 27.4.67, to Tours 15.5.67; Official hand-over 17.5.67; Storage until 1976; Engine runs 20.5.77; Musée de l'Air at Le Bourget 1984; Display as "TB597" and marked "GW-B" - **SURVIVOR**
RX158	Seafire L.IIIc (Merlin 32); RNDA 3.2.45; ex No.1832 Sqn - Arr A.N. 1948; Esc 54.Serv 3.48; GCE/Esc 54.Serv, census 7.49; General discharge 7.11.50; Hyères, SOC 11.12.50
RX163	Seafire L.IIIc (Merlin 55M); RNDA 27.1.45; ex No.805 Sqn - Arr A.N. 1946; 1.Flottille at Hyères, test flight in 7.46 (PM Conq, 1.F); Esc 54.Serv in 3.47; rtp 20.3.47 (spare parts by Esc 54.Serv) NOTE: Records partly found under "PR163"
RX165	Seafire L.IIIc (Merlin 55M); RNDA 20.1.45 - Arr A.N. 1946/47; Esc 54.Serv ('54.S-12') 15.10.47; SEC Cuers, tested 29.11.47; SOC 31.3.49
RX166	Seafire L.IIIc (Merlin 32); RNDA 10.2.45 - Arr A.N. 1948; SEC Cuers 1.49; 1.Flottille ('1.F-3') 4.49 – 4.50; GCE/Esc 54.Serv, census 7.49; General discharge 7.11.50; Hyères, SOC 11.12.50 NOTE: Left wing later mounted on PP972
RX176	Seafire L.IIIc (Merlin 32); RNDA 10.2.45 - Arr A.N. 3.46; Flown to Mureaux 13.3.36; Test flight at Mureaux or Hyères 30.4.46 (LV RP de Latour-Dejean, 1.F); SEC Cuers, tested 18.7.47; VHF tests 23./24.7.47; VR Cuers, to 1.Flottille 1.8.47, shown as '1.F-2' in 12.47 & 1.48; GCE (with *Arromanches*) 4.49 – 7.49; Aerobatic display 9.8.49; 1.Flottille ('1.F-11') from 10.49 to 4.50; General discharge 7.11.50; Hyères, SOC 11.12.50
RX183	Seafire L.IIIc (Merlin 55M); RNDA 10.2.45; ex No.767 Sqn - Arr A.N.1948; SEC Cuers 9.48; SMER Rochefort by 1.7.49 (for discharge); SOC 3.8.49 (confirmed 27.8.49) NOTE: Delivery-flight 20.1.48 reported for "138"; see also SP183!
RX192	Seafire L.IIIc (Merlin 32); RNDA 24.2.45 - Arr A.N. 3.46; Flown from Mureaux to Hyères 20.3.46; 1.Flottille ('1.F-2') 27.3.46; Crashed on deck landing 4.4.47 (PM Friot); RiW, awaiting 5.6.47; SNCAN Mureaux by 21.11.47, shown there also 13.8.48 and census 7.49; SRC, to SNCAN Mureaux for overhaul 7.11.50 (CC Aragnol); General discharge 7.11.50; to SMER Rochefort (for Instructional purposes); SOC 5.4.51
RX213	Seafire L.IIIc (Merlin 32); RNDA 24.2.45 - Arr A.N. 3.46; Cuers, for 1.Flottille 30.3.46, flown to Hyères for 1.Flottille ('1.F-12') 31.3.46; RiW, awaiting 5.6.47;

Seafire L.IIIc PX955 was flown for a time as '1.F-7' of Flottille 1F at Hyères. [via S P Blandin/Charles W Cain]

Seafire L.IIIc '1.F-12' of Flottille 1F at Hyères in flight. This marking was carried successively by RX213, PX922 and SP190.

	SNCAN Mureaux by 21.11.47, shown there also 13.8.48 and census 7.49; SCR Mureaux 19.10.49 (OE Gicquel); Flown to SAMAN Toussus-le-Noble 21.10.49, engine tested 27.10.49; SOC 5.4.50
RX216	Seafire L.IIIc (Merlin 32); RNDA 24.2.45 - Arr A.N. 3.46; Flown from Belfast to Mureaux 16.3.46 (Lt Cdr PJ Hutton, RN), via Lyon to Hyères 28.3.46; Test flight 29.3.46 (PM Guyot, 1.F); BM.2 at Hyères to BAN Cuers 23.4.46; Retd to BM.2 on 31.3.46; 1.Flottille ('1.F-1') 7.47 – 4.50; GCE/Esc 54.Serv, census 7.49; SOC 25.1.50
RX220	Seafire L.IIIc (Merlin 32); RNDA 24.2.45 - Arr A.N. 1946; SEC Cuers 4.46; CN Cuers, tested 2.9.47, VHF tests 3.9.47; Cuers storage autumn 1947; 1.Flottille ('1.F-28') 12.47 & 1.48, and as '1.F-8' from 7.49 to 4.50; GCE/Esc 54.Serv, census 7.49; General discharge 7.11.50; Hyères, SOC 11.12.50
RX222	Seafire L.IIIc (Merlin 32); RNDA 24.2.45 - Arr A.N. 1946; SEC Cuers 4.46; Tested 8.7.& 16.7.47, VHF tests 23.7.47; VR Cuers, to 1.Flottille 1.8.47, shown as '1.F-7' from 12.47 to 4.50; GCE/Esc 54.Serv, census 7.49; General discharge 7.11.50; Hyères, SOC 11.12.50
RX223	Seafire L.IIIc (Merlin 32); RNDA 24.2.45 - Arr A.N. 3.46; Mureaux to BM.2 at Hyères (VR) 14.4.46; BAN Cuers 23.4.46; Retd to Hyères for 1.Flottille 2.4.47, shown as '1.F-25' from 7.47 to 4.48; Hyères, destroyed in ground collision with Seafire RX227 on 3.4.48; SOC 24.4.48
RX226	Seafire L.IIIc (Merlin 32); RNDA 28.2.45 - Arr A.N. 3.46; Mureaux; Esc 54.Serv 12.6.47; SEC Cuers, tested 1.7.47; 1.Flottille ('1.F-17') 12.47 & 1.48; Hyères, SOC 21.10.48 - NOTE: Reported also as '1.F-6'
RX227	Seafire L.IIIc (Merlin 32); RNDA 24.2.45 - Arr A.N. 4.46; SEC Cuers 4.46; tested 18.4.46 (PM Guyot, 1.F); 1.Flottille 10.12.46 ('1.F-6' from 7.47 to 4.48); Hyères, ground collision with Seafire RX223 on 3.4.48; RiW; CAN Cuers (for discharge), census 7.49; DCAN Toulon, overhaul by 7.11.50 (general discharge); possibly flown to SMER Rochefort (for instructional purposes); SOC 5.4.51
RX228	Seafire L.IIIc (Merlin 32); RNDA 24.2.45; ex No.718 Sqn; Selected for A.N., but crashed 4.4.46, before delivery
RX229	Seafire L.IIIc (Merlin 32); RNDA 24.2.45 - Arr A.N. 1946/47; Allocated for overhaul 21.11.47; SNCAN Mureaux by 13.8.48, also in 7.49 (census) and 7.11.50 (general discharge); SRC, flown to SMER Rochefort for instructional purposes; ERC Mureaux, received 19.1.51 (OE Gicquel); SOC 8.5.51
	NOTE: Records partly found under "RX289"
RX231	Seafire L.IIIc (Merlin 32); RNDA 24.2.45; ex No.802 Sqn - Arr A.N. 15.6.48; GCE/Esc 54.Serv, census 7.49; SOC 19.6.50
RX240	Seafire L.IIIc (Merlin 32); RNDA 28.2.45 - Arr A.N. 3.46; 1.Flottille 9.46 (destined for SOC 2.4.47), but: '1.F-24'; Accident at Quarzazate 6.5.47; for VR Cuers (reserve) 5.6.47; SOC approved 8.7.47
RX241	Seafire FR.IIIc (Merlin 32); RNDA 12.3.45; ex No.794 Sqn - Arr A.N. 1948; Service unknown; ST Hyères (for discharge), census 7.49; SOC 27.8.49
RX242	Seafire FR.IIIc (Merlin 32); RNDA 12.3.45 - Arr A.N. 5.46; Mureaux, tested 6.5.46 (PM Guyot, 1.F); Cuers storage autumn 1947; 1.Flottille in 11.47; SEC, tested by CN Cuers 3/4.9.47; 1.Flottille ('1.F-23'), crashed on deck landing 12.9.47 (LV Schloesing safe); RiW, to SNCAN Mureaux 25.10.47; Overhaul approved 21.11.47; 1.Flottille ('1.F-23') 12.47 & 1.48; SOC 18.6.49
RX244	Seafire FR IIIc (Merlin 32); RNDA 24.3.45; ex No.718 Sqn - Arr A.N. 10.4.48; Flown Mureaux to Cuers 15.4.48 (PM Klein, SRC); Service unknown; GCE/Esc 54.Serv, census 7.49; General discharge 7.11.50; Hyères, SOC 11.12.50
RX247	Seafire L.IIIc (Merlin 32); RNDA 28.3.45 - Arr A.N. 1948; Service unknown; SOC 11.10.48
RX251	Seafire L.IIIc (Merlin 32); RNDA 29.3.45 - Arr A.N. 1946; Allocated for 1.Flottille 28.11.47 (after JATO-mods at Cuers); SEC Cuers storage, tested 11.12.47; Flown to Hyères 16.1.48 (PM Guyot, 1.F); Service unknown; SOC 18.6.49
RX253	Seafire L.IIIc (Merlin 32); RNDA 28.3.45 - Arr A.N. 15.6.48; GCE/Esc 54.Serv, census 7.49; General discharge 7.11.50; Hyères, SOC 11.12.50
RX254	Seafire L.IIIc (Merlin 32); RNDA 28.3.45 - Arr A.N. 3.46; From Mureaux to Hyères for BM.2 (VR) 14.4.46; BM.2 to BAN Cuers 23.4.46; Allocated to 1.Flottille and flown to Hyères 2.4.47; Marked '1.F-26' from 7.47 to 1.48; SOC 4.2.49
	NOTE: Reported also as '1.F-27' on 1.7.47
RX255	Seafire L.IIIc (Merlin 32); RNDA 7.4.45 - Arr A.N. 3.46; Cuers to BM.2 at Hyères 31.3.46; Mureaux, for BM.2 on 14.4.46; To BAN Cuers 23.4.46; Storage SEC Cuers, tested 11.12.47; JATO-mods at Cuers; For 1.Flottille 28.11.47; Service unknown; SOC 31.3.49

RX271　Seafire L.IIIc (Merlin 32); RNDA 7.4.45 - Arr A.N. 5.48; Esc 54.Serv 25.5.48; Deck landing at *Arromanches*, crashed and destroyed 30.9.48 (LV Varela de Casa); SOC 24.11.48

RX279　Seafire L.IIIc (Merlin 32); RNDA 10.4.45 - Arr A.N. 10.4.48; 54 Esc/Serv 2.9.48; SOC 18.6.49

RX281　Seafire FR IIIc (Merlin 32); RNDA 12.4.45 - Arr A.N. 2.48; Flown from Lee-on-Solent to Mureaux 20.2.48 (Plt Roubaud, SEC); SRC, flown 1.3.48 (Plt Gicquel); 12.Flottille ('12.F-3') 1948/49; GCE/Esc 54.Serv, census 7.49; General discharge 7.11.50; Hyères, SOC 11.12.50

RX283　Seafire L.IIIc (Merlin 32); RNDA 13.4.45 - Arr A.N. 5.48; Service unknown; GCE/Esc 54.Serv, census 7.49; Esc 54.Serv ('54.S-3'), flown from Hyéres to Marignane, Bourges, Avord, Brétigny, Blagnac and return 16.4.-22.4.50 (LV Mauban); General discharge 7.11.50; Hyères, SOC 11.12.50

RX286　Seafire L.IIIc (Merlin 32); RNDA 12.4.45; ex No.778 Sqn - Arr A.N. 1948; Esc 3.Serv ('3.S-10') early 1948; GCE/Esc 54.Serv, census 7.49; SOC 1.10.49

RX290　Seafire L.IIIc (Merlin 32); RNDA 20.4.45; ex Nos.760 & 761 Sqns - Arr A.N. 3.46; Flown Mureaux to Hyères 23.3.46; 1.Flottille ('1.F-9') from 27.3.46 to 1.48 (SEA Hyères mid/autumn 1947); CAN Cuers (for discharge), census 7.49; SOC approved 28.8.50

RX293　Seafire L.IIIc (Merlin 32); RNDA 25.4.45 - Arr A.N. 5.46; SNCAN Mureaux, tested 6.5.46, flown via Lyon to Hyères 7.5.46 (PM Guyot, 1.F); 1.Flottille ('1.F-5') 7.47 – 5.48; 1.F. (VR), accident Oran/Arzew 6.5.48 (LV R Vercken, 54.S); SOC 18.6.49

RX296　Seafire L.IIIc (Merlin 32); RNDA 26.4.45 - Arr A.N. 1948; Flown Mureaux to Cuers 28.2.48 (Plt Roubaud, SEC); Service unknown; SOC 6.7.49

RX298　Seafire L.IIIc (Merlin 32); RNDA 26.4.45 - Arr A.N. 1946/47; RiW, awaiting 5.6.47; SNCAN Mureaux repair 21.11.47, shown there also 13.8.48 and 7.49 (census); SRC, flown from Mureaux to SAMAN Toussus-le-Noble 17.2.50 (OE Gicquel); General discharge 7.11.50; Hyères, SOC 11.12.50

RX301　Seafire L.IIIc (Merlin 32); RNDA 30.4.45 - Arr A.N. 1946; SEC Cuers 4.46; Flown to Hyères for 1.Flottille 2.4.47 ('1.F-27' from 7.47 to 6.48); Engine failure, crashed into sea 22.6.48 (EV1 Thierry d'Argenlieu kld); SOC 4.9.48

RX305　Seafire L.IIIc (Merlin 32); RNDA 4.5.45 - Arr A.N. 1946; SEC Cuers 4.46; Flown to Hyères 10.12.46 (PM Guyot, 1.F); 1.Flottille ('1.F-3') 7.47 – 5.48; Accident on *Arromanches* 27.5.48 (LV Sanguinetti); Hyères, SOC 17.8.48

RX307　Seafire L.IIIc (Merlin 32); RNDA 11.5.45 - Arr A.N. 1948; Service unknown; ST Hyères (for discharge), census 7.49; SOC 27.8.49

RX309　Seafire L.IIIc (Merlin 32); RNDA 10.5.45 - Arr A.N. 3.46; Flown from Mureaux to Hyères 23.3.46; 1.Flottille ('1.F-3') 27.3.46; Cuers in 4.46; SOC approved 18.11.46

RX327　Seafire L.IIIc (Merlin 32); RNDA 24.5.45 - Arr A.N. 27.4.48; GCE/Esc 54.Serv, census 7.49; Hyères, SOC 24..8.50

RX333　Seafire L.IIIc (Merlin 32); RNDA 2.6.45; ex No.736 Sqn - Arr A.N. 27.4.48; Unknown unit, cannon failures 20.2.49 (technical report 26.2.49); SOC 18.6.49

RX338　Seafire L.IIIc (Merlin 55M); RNDA 7.6.45; ex A&AEE Boscombe Down (metal elevator tested) - Arr A.N. 3.46; Flown from Mureaux to Hyères 23.3.46; 1.Flottille 27.3.46; Cuers in 4.46; Shown as '1.F-10' by 30.6.46; Destinated for discharge 2.4.47; '1.F-10', crashed on decklanding, into sea Bizerte area 2.6.47 (PM Bozec of Esc 54.Serv missing); SOC approved 7.8.47

RX342　Seafire L.IIIc (Merlin 32); RNDA 16.6.45; ex Nos.761 & 782 Sqns - Arr A.N. 1948; SEC Cuers storage, tested 21.5.48, flown to Hyères 7.6.48; 1.Flottille or Esc 54.Serv., service unknown; SOC 18.6.49

SL658　Spitfire LF.IXe (Merlin 66); TOC/RAF 2.8.45 - For FAF, shipped to Indo-China, desp Birkenhead 29.11.45; Arr Saigon 19.1.46; GC.I/7 *'Provence'*, accident at Gia-lam 22.6.46 (Asp Pechdimaldji); R&SU; GC.I/2 *'Cigognes'* 1946/47; Accident at Gia-lam 25.9.46 (S/C Ginestet safe); R&SU; GC.I/4 *'Dauphiné'* ('R') 1947

SL659　Spitfire LF.IXe (Merlin 66); TOC/RAF 2.8.45 - For FAF desp. Indo-China 29.11.45; Arr Saigon 19.1.46; 1.EC (F/Wing), GC.I/4 *'Dauphiné'* ('T'), engine failure on take-off, crashed at Nha Trang, Cat.E 12.6.48 (Cne Chantier), SOC

SM832　Spitfire F.XIV; ex *G-WWII*; Arr as **SURVIVOR** only 18.1.98 by Chistophe Jacquart, Dijon, France (Civil reg. *F-AZSJ* 20.2.98, operated by Spitfire Warbird Ltd, Eurl, Dijon), flown in SEAC colours, marked "YB-A"

Spitfire F.XIV SM832 in civil guise with the small white registration F-AZSJ *under the tailplane. Registered in February 1998 to Christophe Jacquart of Dijon, it is painted in SEAC colours and carries its original serial number and No.17 Sqn RAF code "YB-A".* [MAP]

Seafire F.IIIc SP136 of the Aéronautique Navale at SEC Cuers in 1947. [J Lebourg via S Joanne]

SP136 Seafire L.IIIc (Merlin 55M); RNDA 31.3.45 - Arr A.N. 1946/47; SEC Cuers, VHF tested 30.7.47 and 5.8.47; VR Cuers, to 1.Flottille ('1.F-16') 1.8.47; Crashed on decklanding 29.9.47; RiW; as '1.F-16' shown in 12.47 & 1.48 (VF/Indisponible); SOC 27.8.49

SP137 Seafire L.IIIc (Merlin 55M); RNDA 11.4.45 - Arr A.N. 5.48; Service unknown; SOC 18.6.49

SP139 Seafire L.IIIc (Merlin 55M); RNDA 6.4.45 - Arr A.N. 1946/47; Storage Cuers mid 1947; SEC Cuers, tests 9.9.& 10.9.47; 1.Flottille in 11.47 ('1.F-20' shown 12.47-3.48); Accident at Hyères 22.3.48 (LV Schloesing, 1.F); CAN Cuers (for discharge), census 7.49; SOC approved 28.8.50

SP143 Seafire L.IIIc (Merlin 55M); RNDA 25.4.45 - Arr A.N. 1946/47; SEA Hyères autumn 1947; 1.Flottille ('1.F-19') 7.47-12.48; Probably accident on *Arromanches* 1.5.48 (EV Robin); Accident at Hyères 17.12.48; SOC 4.2.49

SP144 Seafire L.IIIc (Merlin 55M); RNDA 20.4.45 - Arr A.N. 1946/47; VR Cuers, allocated for 1.Flottille 5.6.47; RiW, SNCAN Mureaux 24.6.47, repair 15.10.47; Overhaul order 21.11.47; SNCAN 13.8.48 and 7.49 (census); Selected for discharge 7.49; SOC 8.49

SP147 Seafire L.IIIc (Merlin 55M); RNDA 28.4.45 - Arr A.N. 1946/47; VR Cuers, allocated for 1.Flottille 5.6.47; RiW, SNCAN Mureaux 24.6.47; Repair 15.10.47; Overhaul order 21.11.47; SNCAN 13.8.48 and 7.49 (census); SRC, received 31.8.49 (OE Gicquel); General discharge 7.11.50; Hyères, SOC 11.12.50

SP148 Seafire L.IIIc (Merlin 55M); RNDA 27.4.45 - Arr A.N. 3.46; Flown from Mureaux to Hyères 23.3.46; 1.Flottille ('1.F-1') 27.3.46; Engine failure, crashed on *Arromanches* 23.1.47 (LV Gleize); Hyères, SOC 19.2.47

SP150 Seafire L.IIIc (Merlin 55M); RNDA 30.4.45 - Arr A.N. 3.46; Mureaux, flown via Lyon to Hyères 23.3.46 (PM Guyot, 1.F); 1.Flottille ('1.F-10') 27.3.46; Shown as '1.F-8' from 7.47 to 1.48; SOC 18.6.49

SP151 Seafire L.IIIc (Merlin 55M); RNDA 30.4.45 - Arr A.N. 3.46; Mureaux, take-off crash 17.3.46; Mureaux, flown via Lyon to Cuers 19.4.46 (PM Guyot, 1.F); 1.Flottille, on *Arromanches* 4.47; Selected for discharge 2.4.47; Crashed on decklanding (Agadir area) 15.4.47; Allotted for VR Cuers 5.6.47; SOC approved 8.7.47

SP156 Seafire L.IIIc (Merlin 55M); RNDA 30.4.45 - Arr A.N. 1946/47; Cuers storage mid 1947; VR Cuers, to 1.Flottille 1.8.47; SEC Cuers, tested 9.9.47; GCE/Esc 54.Serv, census 7.49; SOC 18.11.49

SP163 Seafire L.IIIc (Merlin 55M); RNDA 28.5.45; ex Nos.709 & 741 Sqns - Arr A.N. 1948; 1.Flottille ('1.F-9'), force-landed 16.8.48; R&SU; 1.F in 4.49 and 7.49; GCE/Esc 54.Serv, census 7.49; SOC 19.6.50

SP166 Seafire L.IIIc (Merlin 55M); RNDA 1.6.45; ex Nos.709 & 741 Sqns - Arr A.N. 1948; SEC Cuers 10.48; 1.Flottille ('1.F-5') 4.49-10.49; GCE/Esc 54.Serv, census 7.49; SOC 19.6.50

SP167 Seafire L.IIIc (Merlin 55M); RNDA 2.6.45; ex No.709 Sqn (Lossiemouth "175/LM") - Arr A.N. 1948; SRC, flown Mureaux to Cuers 8.3.48 (OE Gicquel); SEC Cuers by 6.10.48; GCE/Esc 54.Serv, census 7.49; 1.Flottille ('1.F-6') 4.49-3.50; Dived into sea near Toulon 2.3.50 (SM Jean-Pierre Duteil missing); SOC 14.4.50

SP182 Seafire L.IIIc (Merlin 55M); RNDA 6.6.45; ex A&AEE and No.794 Sqn - Arr A.N. 1948; SNCAN Mureaux by 13.8.48, and also census 7.49 (SNCAN for discharge 7.49); SOC 8.49

SP183 Seafire L.IIIc (Merlin 55M); RNDA 5.6.45; ex Nos.771 & 794 Sqns - Arr A.N. 1.48; Flown from Lee-on-Solent to Mureaux 20.1.48 (PM Guyot, 1.F); SEC Cuers 10.48; Service unknown; ST Hyères (for discharge), census 7.49; SOC 27.8.49 - NOTE: Delivery-date recorded for "138" (see also RX183)

SP190 Seafire L.IIIc (Merlin 55M); RNDA 27.6.45; ex Nos.781 & 799 Sqns - Arr A.N. 1948; GCE/Esc 54.Serv, census 7.49; 1.Flottille ('1.F-12') 7.49 - 4.50; General discharge 7.11.50; Hyères, SOC 11.12.50

SP192 Seafire L.IIIc (Merlin 55M); RNDA 3.7.45; ex No.794 Sqn - Arr A.N. 1948; Service unknown; CN Cuers, census 7.49; Hyères, SOC 26.9.50

SR452 Seafire F XVc (Griffon VI); RNDA 31.10.44; ex Nos.778 & 700 Sqns - Arr A.N. 17.6.49; Fate unknown

SR455 Seafire F.XVc (Griffon VI); RNDA 20.1.45; ex No.700 Sqn - Arr A.N. 17.6.49; Fate unknown

SR460 Seafire F.XVc (Griffon VI); RNDA 8.6.45; ex No.761 Sqn - Arr A.N. 24.6.49; 1.Flottille ('1.F-24') 10.49 – 4.50

SR474	Seafire F.XVc (Griffon VI); RNDA 12.3.45; ex No.805 Sqn - Arr A.N. 24.6.49; 1.Flottille ('1.F-21') 8.49 – 4.50 (flown by H Perrin in 8.49)
SR516	Seafire F.XVc (Griffon VI); RNDA 3.4.45; ex Nos.802 & 806 Sqns - Arr A.N. 28.6.49; 1.Flottille with *Arromanches* (date unknown)
SR520	Seafire F.XVc (Griffon VI); RNDA 6.4.45; ex No.802 Sqn - Arr A.N. 28.6.49; 1.Flottille ('1.F-23') 10.49 – 4.50; 12.Flottille; Esc 54.Serv ('54.S-26')
SR522	Seafire F.XVc (Griffon VI); RNDA 6.4.45; ex Nos.802 & 883 Sqns - Arr A.N. 17.6.49; Fate unknown
SR526	Seafire F.XVc (Griffon VI); RNDA 12.4.45 - Arr A.N. 28.6.49; Fate unknown
TA780	Spitfire HF.IXe (Merlin 70); TOC/RAF 12.12.44 - Arr FAF 1.1.46; GC.I/7 *'Provence'* 1947; GC.II/1 *'Nice'* 1948; BE.708 Meknès 1952
TA800	Spitfire HF.IXe (Merlin 70); TOC/RAF 12.12.44 - Arr FAF 24.11.45; GC.II/7 *'Nice'* ('R'), mid-air collision with Spitfire MJ408, Cat.E 10.7.47, SOC
"TB597"	Marked 'GW-B', Musée de l'Air Le Bourget - see RR263
TB844	Spitfire HF.IXe (Merlin 70); TOC/RAF 25.2.45; ex No.329 Sqn - Arr FAF 24.11.45; GC.I/7 *'Provence'* 2.47 (at Oran also in 5.48)
TB981	Spitfire HF.IXe (Merlin 70); TOC/RAF 25.2.45; ex No.329 Sqn - Arr FAF 24.11.45; GC.II/7 *'Nice'* 11.46; BE.708 Meknès, fuel shortage (not refuelled), force-landed near Sebaa-Ayoun, Cat.E 4.12.51 (Sgt P Jaillet); SOC
TB982	Spitfire HF.IXe (Merlin 70); TOC/RAF 27.2.45; ex No.329 Sqn - Arr FAF 24.11.45; GC.II/7 *'Nice'* 11.46
TD202	Spitfire LF.IXe (Merlin 66); TOC/RAF 30.3.45 - For FAF 27.11.45; Shipped to Indo-China, desp. 28.11.45, arr Saigon 3.1.46; GC.III/2 *'Alsace'* ('P') 10.46; GC.I/4 *'Dauphiné'* ('2'), noted 9.47 and 10.47; GC.I/4 ('P'), overturned at Tourane 19.2.48 (Lt Rombi safe); Flown from Nha Trang to Saigon 15.7.48
TD364	Spitfire LF.IXe (Merlin 66); TOC/RAF 16.4.45 - For FAF 27.11.45; Shipped to Indo-China, desp. 28.11.45, arr Saigon 3.1.46; GC.II/7 *'Nice'*, engine failed on take-off at Tan Son Nhut, Cat.E 18.4.46 (S/Lt Maulandy injured), SOC
TD378	Spitfire LF.IXe (Merlin 66); TOC/RAF 23.4.45 - For FAF 27.11.45; Shipped to Indo-China, desp. 28.11.45, arr Saigon 3.1.46; GC.III/2 *'Alsace'* ('C') 8.46
TD396	Spitfire LF.IXe (Merlin 66); TOC/RAF 1.5.45 - For FAF 27.11.45; Shipped to Indo-China, desp. 28.11.45, arr Saigon 3.1.46; GC.III/2 *'Alsace'*, crashed at Nha Trang 20.5.47 (Cne Lemaire safe); R&SU; GC.I/4 *'Dauphiné'* ('H'), engine failed on take-off, crashed at Nha Trang, Cat.E 31.10.47 (Lt Mazo safe), SOC
TD397	Spitfire LF.IXe (Merlin 66); TOC/RAF 2.5.45 - For FAF 27.11.45; Shipped to Indo-China, desp. 28.11.45, arr Saigon 3.1.46; GC.I/2 *'Cigognes'*, oil leak, force-landed near Guynh-Ou, Tonkin 9.8.47 (Cne Carpentier safe); GC.I/6 'Corse' in 12.50; R&SU; BE.708 Meknès, engine failure, force-landed and crashed at Meknès, Cat.E 17.12.51 (S/Lt de Redoul); SOC
TD398	Spitfire LF.IXe (Merlin 66); TOC/RAF 27.4.45 - For FAF 27.11.45; Shipped to Indo-China, desp. 28.11.45, arr Saigon 3.1.46; GC.III/2 *'Alsace'* ('A') 8.46, mid-air collision with Spitfire TE552, dived into ground near Tan Kieu, Cat.E 29.9.46 (Lt de Verneilh killed), SOC
TD399	Spitfire LF.IXe (Merlin 66); TOC/RAF 25.4.45 - For FAF 27.11.45; Shipped to Indo-Cina, desp 28.11.45, arr Saigon 3.1.46; GC.I/4 *'Dauphiné'* ('4') 12.47, operational flight over Go Cong 1.3.48; Test flight 13.6.48 (noted also 31.1.49)
TD954	Spitfire LF.IXe (Merlin 66); TOC/RAF 31.3.45 - For FAF 27.11.45; Shipped to Indo-China, desp. 28.11.45, arr Saigon 3.1.46; 1.EC, mid-air collision with Spitfire TE530 over Tan Son Nhut, dived into ground, pilot baled out, Cat.E 17.5.46 (Cne Bloch injured), SOC
TD981	Spitfire LF.IXe (Merlin 66); TOC/RAF 4.4.45 - For FAF 27.11.45; Shipped to Indo-China, desp. 28.11.45, arr Saigon 3.1.46; GC.I/7 *'Provence'* 3.46 and 5.46; GC.III/2 *'Alsace'*, accident at Tan Son Nhut 7.8.46 (Lt Tatraux safe); R&SU; GC.I/2 *'Cigognes'* ('H') 1946/47; Engine failure, force-landed near Hoa Binh 18.3.47 (Lt Godde)
TD984	Spitfire LF.IXe (Merlin 66); TOC/RAF 2.5.45 - For FAF 8.12.45; Shipped to Indo-China, arr Saigon 19.1.46; GC.I/2 *'Cigognes'*, engine failure, force-landed near Banam/Mekong, Cat.E 12.10.46 (Cne Trulla safe), SOC
TD985	Spitfire LF.IXe (Merlin 66); TOC/RAF 5.4.45 - For FAF 28.11.45; Shipped to Indo-China, desp. 28.11.45, arr Saigon 3.1.46; GC.I/7 *'Provence'* 3.46 and 5.46; GC.III/2 *'Alsace'*, hit by AA, force-landed at Tourane 19.1.47 (S/C Dubreuil safe); R&SU; GC.I/4 *'Dauphiné'* ('G') 11.47, operational flight 13.4.48 (noted also 26.8.48)
TD986	Spitfire LF.IXe (Merlin 66); TOC/RAF 12.4.45 - For FAF 27.11.45; Shipped to Indo-China, desp. 28.11.45, arr Saigon 3.1.46; GC.I/2 *'Cigognes'* ('I') 1946/47; Left the runway whilst taxying at Gia-lam 16.3.47 (C/C Andriot)
TD991	Spitfire LF.IXe (Merlin 66); TOC/RAF 30.4.45 - For FAF 27.11.45; Shipped to Indo-China, desp. 28.11.45, arr Saigon 3.1.46; GC.I/7 *'Provence'*, accident at Gia-lam 3.7.46 (Cne Restoux safe); R&SU; GC.I/2 *'Cigognes'*, crashed at Gia-lam 19.9.46 (S/C Schaferlee safe)
TD994	Spitfire LF.IXe (Merlin 66); TOC/RAF 23.4.45 - For FAF 8.12.45; Shipped to Indo-China, arr Saigon 19.1.46; 2.EC (F/Wing), GC.III/2 *'Alsace'*, engine exploded on ground at Tan Son Nhut, Cat.E/1 on 15.1.47 (Sgt Gastal), SOC
TD996	Spitfire LF.IXe (Merlin 66); TOC/RAF 23.4.45 - For FAF 27.11.45; Shipped to Indo-China, desp. 28.11.45, arr Saigon 3.1.46; GC.I/2 *'Cigognes'*, engine failure, force-landed near Hagia, Cat.E 12.2.47 (Asp Brun killed), SOC
TD997	Spitfire LF.IXe (Merlin 66); TOC/RAF 27.4.45 - For FAF 27.11.45; Shipped to Indo-China, desp. 28.11.45, arr Saigon 3.1.46; GC.I/7 *'Provence'* ('F') 3.46 and 5.46; GC.II/4 *'La Fayette'* ('F'), lost one wheel, crashed on landing at Gia-lam 2.12.47 (S/C Bigonneau safe); R&SU 10.12.47 - NOTE: *'Marcel Farriol'* painted; Shown also numbered "3" in 10.47
TD998	Spitfire LF.IXe (Merlin 66); TOC/RAF 27.4.45 - For FAF 27.11.45; Shipped to Indo-China, desp. 28.11.45, arr Saigon 3.1.46; GC.I/7 *'Provence'*, noted 3.46 and 5.46, belly-landed at Tan Son Nhut 11.6.46 (Cne Simard safe); R&SU; 2.EC ('L'), crashed at Tan Son Nhut 10.12.46 (Cne Helliot); GC.I/2 *'Cigognes'*, crashed landing at Gia-lam 19.3.47 (S/Lt Buffet); GC II/4 *'La Fayette'*, take-off for ground attack near Thai-Nguyen, crashed on landing at Gia-lam, Cat. "R" (FB/E) 26.10.47, SOC
TE121	Spitfire LF.IXe (Merlin 66); TOC/RAF 11.4.45 - For FAF 27.11.45; Shipped to Indo-China, desp. 28.11.45, arr Saigon 3.1.46; GC.I/4 *'Dauphiné'* ('OL'), ground collision with truck at Nha Trang 4.10.47; R&SU; GC.I/4, hit by AA, dived into ground, exploded, 20m south of Tourane, Cat.E 10.11.47 (Lt de Paul killed), SOC
TE123	Spitfire LF.IXe (Merlin 66); TOC/RAF 16.4.45 - For FAF 28.11.45; Shipped to Indo-China, arr Saigon 8.1.46; GC.II/7 *'Nice'*, flew into hill in fog near Ha Nay, Cat.E 8.4.46 (Adj Geremia killed), SOC
TE124	Spitfire LF.IXe (Merlin 66); TOC/RAF 16.4.45 - For FAF 8.12.45; Shipped to Indo-China, arr Saigon 19.1.46; GC.I/7 *'Provence'* 3.46 and 5.46; GC.I/2 *'Cigognes'* 1946/47; Engine failure, force-landed wheels-up at Hanoi, Cat.E 12.2.47 (S/Lt Briffe killed), SOC
TE138	Spitfire LF.IXe (Merlin 66); TOC/RAF 24.4.45 - For FAF 28.11.45; Shipped to Indo-China, arr Saigon 3.1.46; GC.I/7 *'Provence'* 3.46 and 5.46; Mid-air collision with Spitfire TE549 near Gia-lam, landed safely 28.6.46

(Sgt Aue); R&SU; GC.I/2 *'Cigognes'* 1946/47; GC.I/6 in 12.50; BE.708 Meknès, noted 7.51 and 3.52; Mid-air collision with a T-6 over Meknès 28.4.52 (A/C L Belissard or SM Jannic safe)

TE140 Spitfire LF.IXe (Merlin 66); TOC/RAF 27.4.45 - For FAF 28.11.45; Shipped to Indo-China, desp. 28.11.45, arr Saigon 3.1.46; 1.EC (F/Wing) 4.46; GC.III/2 *'Alsace'* ('3') in 9.46; GC.I/4 *'Dauphiné'* 10.48; GC.I/6 in 12.50; BE.708 Meknès ('N') noted 11.50 and 8.51; Crashed landing at Meknès 26.9.51 (Sgt M Garot safe), SOC

TE141 Spitfire LF.IXe (Merlin 66); TOC/RAF 28.4.45 - For FAF 28.11.45; Shipped to Indo-China, desp. 28.11.45, arr Saigon 3.1.46; GC.II/7 *'Nice'* ('J') 6.46

TE143 Spitfire LF.IXe (Merlin 66); TOC/RAF 30.4.45 - For FAF 27.11.45; Shipped to Indo-China, desp. 28.11.45, arr Saigon 3.1.46; GC.I/7 *'Provence'*, operational flight, protection of Spitfire TE149 which force-landed in a rice-field 1m SE of Cholon 26.7.46 (Plt J Sarrail); GC.I/2 *'Cigognes'* ('M') 1946/47; GC.I/4 *'Dauphiné'* 1.48

TE144 Spitfire LF.IXe (Merlin 66); TOC/RAF 30.4.45 - For FAF 27.11.45; Shipped to Indo-China, desp. 28.11.45, arr Saigon 3.1.46; GC.I/7 *'Provence'* 3.46 and 6.46; GC.I/2 *'Cigognes'* 1946/47; GC.I/4 *'Dauphiné'*, flown to Bien Hoa 18.12.47

TE145 Spitfire LF.IXe (Merlin 66); TOC/RAF 1.5.45 - For FAF 28.11.45; Shipped to Indo-China, desp. 28.11.45, arr Saigon 3.1.46; GC.I/7 *'Provence'* 3.46 and 6.46; GC.I/2 *'Cigognes'*; Accident at Moug 19.12.46 (S/C Buge)

TE147 Spitfire LF.IXe (Merlin 66); TOC/RAF 30.4.45 - For FAF 27.11.45; Shipped to Indo-China, desp. 28.11.45, arr Saigon 3.1.46; GC.III/2 *'Alsace'* ('F') 10.46 & 11.46; Tyre burst on take-off at Nha Trang, Cat.E 6.1.47 (Lt Chantier), SOC

TE148 Spitfire LF.IXe (Merlin 66); TOC/RAF 30.4.45 - For FAF 27.11.45; Shipped to Indo-China, desp. 28.11.45, arr Saigon 3.1.46; GC.I/7 *'Provence'* 3.46 and 5.46; GC.I/2 *'Cigognes'* ('A'); Accident at Gia-lam 18.10.48 (Sgt Chanson safe); Hit by AA, lost oil, force-landed at Gia-lam, Cat.FB/E 3.1.47 (Sgt Chanson injured), SOC

TE149 Spitfire LF.IXe (Merlin 66); TOC/RAF 1.5.45 - For FAF 28.11.45; Shipped to Indo-China, desp. 28.11.45, arr Saigon 3.1.46; 1.EC, operational flight 18.4.46; GC.II/7 *'Nice'*, force-landed in a rice field 1m SE of Cholon, Cat.E 26.7.46 (Cne Brunet injured), SOC

TE152 Spitfire LF.IXe (Merlin 66); TOC/RAF 3.5.45 - For FAF 28.11.45; Shipped to Indo-China, desp. 28.11.45, arr Saigon 3.1.46; 1.EC 4.46; GC.III/2 *'Alsace'* ('W'), accident at Nha Trang 7.9.46 (Sgt Tauzy safe); GC.III/2 noted also 10.46 and 1.47; GC.I/4 *'Dauphiné'* ('L'), accident at Nha Trang 8.1.48 (Cne Gerard safe)

TE155 Spitfire LF.IXe (Merlin 66); TOC/RAF 23.5.45 - For FAF 28.11.45; Shipped to Indo-China, desp. 28.11.45, arr Saigon 3.1.46; GC.I/4 *'Dauphiné'* ('F') from 9.47; Belly-landed at Hué 14.3.48 (Lt Mazo)

TE156 Spitfire LF.IXe (Merlin 66); TOC/RAF 3.5.45 - For FAF 28.11.45; Shipped to Indo-China, desp. 28.11.45, arr Saigon 3.1.46; GC.I/2 *'Cigognes'* 1946 (reported as "TE165"); GC.III/2 *'Alsace'*, hit by debris from own bombs, force-landed at Tan Son Nhut, Cat.FB/E 20.8.46 (Lt Tatraux injured), SOC

TE158 Spitfire LF.IXe (Merlin 66); TOC/RAF 23.5.45 - For FAF 27.11.45; Shipped to Indo-China, desp. 28.11.45, arr Saigon 3.1.46; 1.EC, operational flight 2.46; GC.III/2 *'Alsace'* ('D'), noted 10.46 and 12.46; Hit by AA, force-landed at Tourane 25.1.47 (Lt de St.Pulgent safe); Hit obstacle landing at Nha Trang, Cat.E 16.3.47 (Lt Chantier), SOC

TE494 Spitfire LF.IXe (Merlin 66); TOC/RAF 10.5.45 - For FAF 28.11.45; Shipped to Indo-China, desp. 28.11.45, arr Saigon 3.1.46; GC.I/7 *'Provence'*, flown Hanoi to Seno 5.4.46; GC.I/2 *'Cigognes'* ('D') 1946/47; GC.II/4 *'La Fayette'* ('M'), noted 10.47 and 11.47

TE500 Spitfire LF.IXe (Merlin 66); TOC/RAF 30.4.45 - For FAF 27.11.45; Shipped to Indo-China, desp. 28.11.45, arr Saigon 3.1.46; GC.III/2 *'Alsace'*, accident at Tan Son Nhut 20.9.46 (Lt Chantier safe); Belly-landed at Pakse 7.12.46 (Lt de St.Pulgent safe); R&SU; GC.II/4 *'La Fayette'* ('O') 11.47 and 1.48; 3.EC (Bien Hoa) to R&SU 13.4.49

TE501 Spitfire LF.IXe (Merlin 66); TOC/RAF 30.4.45 - For

Spitfire LF.IXe TE494 'D' of GC 1/2 (Spa 103) over French Indo-China around 1946/47. [B Regnier via S Joanne]

Spitfire F.IXc BS464 suspended in the Musée de l'Air, Chalais-Meudon, in the mid-sixties. It later moved to Le Bourget and in May 1990 it was destroyed by fire in a hangar at Dugny. [Phil Butler]

FAF 27.11.45; Shipped to Indo-China, desp. 28.11.45, arr Saigon 3.1.46; GC.III/2 *'Alsace'*, accident at Nha Trang 5.9.46 (Lt Porquet safe)

TE502 Spitfire LF.IXe (Merlin 66); TOC/RAF 30.4.45 - For FAF 27.11.45; Shipped to Indo-China, desp. 28.11.45, arr Saigon 3.1.46; Fate unknown

TE504 Spitfire LF.IXe (Merlin 66); TOC/RAF 30.4.45 - For FAF 27.11.45; Shipped to Indo-China, desp. 28.11.45, arr Saigon 3.1.46; GC.II/7 *'Nice'*, flown from Saigon to Nha Trang 27.5.46; Aerobatic accident, crashed at Nha Trang, Cat.E 22.7.46 (Sgt Combes killed), SOC

TE505 Spitfire LF.IXe (Merlin 66); TOC/RAF 30.4.45 - For FAF 27.11.45; Shipped to Indo-China, desp. 28.11.45, arr Saigon 3.1.46; GC.II/7 *'Nice'*, overshot landing without flaps, crashed at Nha Trang 7.6.46 (S/C Bellissard safe)

TE506 Spitfire LF.IXe (Merlin 66); TOC/RAF 30.4.45 - For FAF 27.11.45; Shipped to Indo-China, desp. 28.11.45, arr Saigon 3.1.46; 2.EC ('F') 1946; GC.I/7 *'Provence'*, noted 3.46 and 5.46; GC.I/2 *'Cigognes'*; Accident at Gia-lam 6.11.46 (Sgt Chanson safe)

TE507 Spitfire LF.IXe (Merlin 66); TOC/RAF 30.4.45 - For FAF 27.11.45; Shipped to Indo-China, desp. 28.11.45, arr Saigon 3.1.46; 1.EC (F/Wing), operational flight 10.2.46; Engine failure, force-landed wheels-up near Long Tanh 15.3.46 (Cdt Barbier murdered by Vietmin), SOC

TE509 Spitfire LF.IXe (Merlin 66); TOC/RAF 25.5.45 - For FAF 27.11.45; Shipped to Indo-China, desp. 28.11.45, arr Saigon 3.1.46; GC.III/2 *'Alsace'*, hit by debris from own bombs, force-landed Tourane 25.1.47 (Sgt Roubaud safe); R&SU; GC.I/4 *'Dauphiné'* ('A'), noted 9.47; Crashed landing at Nha Trang 21.2.48 (Cne Guérin safe); R&SU; Hit by AA or own bombs, dived into ground near Phu Yen/Song Cau, Cat.E 22.3.48 (Cne Gerard killed), SOC

TE514 Spitfire LF.IXe (Merlin 66); TOC/RAF 12.6.45 - For FAF 8.12.45; Shipped to Indo-China, arr Saigon 19.1.46; GC.I/2 *'Cigognes'* 1946/47; GC.II/4 *'La Fayette'* ('N')

5.48 and 6.48; GC.I/3 *'Navarre'*, landing collision with MK690 at Seno, Cat.E 27.10.48 (Adj Valentin), SOC

TE525 Spitfire LF.IXe (Merlin 66); TOC/RAF 23.5.45 - For FAF 27.11.45; Shipped to Indo-China, desp. 28.11.45, arr Saigon 3.1.46; GC.I/2 *'Cigognes'* ('G') 1946/47, take-off at Haiphong for ground-attack, blown up by own bomb, hit ground near Ban Thi, Tonkin (c.20m east-north-east of Bac Kan), Cat "R" (FB/E) 25.8.47 (Lt Combesias Georges missing), SOC
NOTE: Crash 25.8.47 incorrect reported for "TD998", officially corrected to TE525 on 27.8.47

TE526 Spitfire LF.IXe (Merlin 66); TOC/RAF 24.5.45 - For FAF 27.11.45; Shipped to Indo-China, desp. 28.11.45, arr Saigon 3.1.46; GC.I/2 *'Cigognes'* ('L'), engine failure, force-landed in a lake near Hanoi, Cat.E 1.3.47 (S/Lt Astier), SOC

TE528 Spitfire LF.IXe (Merlin 66); TOC/RAF 17.5.45 - For FAF 28.11.45; Shipped to Indo-China, desp. 28.11.45, arr Saigon 3.1.46; GC.III/2 *'Alsace'* ('K') 10.46; Engine failed, force-landed wheels-up near Hué 22.1.47 (Lt Chabot murdered by Vietmin), SOC

TE529 Spitfire LF.IXe (Merlin 66); TOC/RAF 17.5.45 - For FAF 28.11.45; Shipped to Indo-China, desp. 28.11.45, arr Saigon 3.1.46; GC.II/7 *'Nice'*, damaged at Nha Trang 1.6.46 (S/C Bellissard); R&SU; GC.III/2 *'Alsace'* ('K'), noted 10.46; Engine failed on take-off Cam Ranh, Cat.E 1.12.46 (S/C Charollais safe), SOC

TE530 Spitfire LF.IXe (Merlin 66); TOC/RAF 15.5.45 - For FAF 28.11.45; Shipped to Indo-China, desp. 28.11.45, arr Saigon 3.1.46; 1.EC, operational flight 16.2.46; GC.II/7 *'Nice'*, mid-air collision with Spitfire TD954 over Tan Son Nhut 17.5.46 (S/Lt Douchet safe)

TE533 Spitfire LF.IXe (Merlin 66); TOC/RAF 15.5.45 - For FAF 28.11.45; Shipped to Indo-China, desp. 28.11.45, arr Saigon 3.1.46; GC.I/7 *'Provence'* 3.46 and 7.46; GC.I/2 *'Cigognes'* 1946/47; Missing over Phuly Chine 22.3.47 (S/C J Ginestet missing), SOC

TE534 Spitfire LF.IXe (Merlin 66); TOC/RAF 18.5.45 - For FAF 28.11.45; Shipped to Indo-China, desp. 28.11.45,

Although it never served with the Armée de l'Air Française, surviving Spitfire TE184 (alias G-MXVI), seen here at Bournemouth in July 2000, is painted in the authentic colour scheme for those French RAF squadrons operating independently towards the end of the war. [Tony Russo]

arr Saigon 3.1.46; 2.EC ('C') in 1946; GC.I/7 *'Provence'*, noted 3.46 and 7.46; GC.I/2 *'Cigognes'* ('B'), accident at Pochentong 17.8.46 (S/Lt Meunier safe); Engine failed, force-landed wheels-up in rice-field 15m South of Dong Diong, Cat.E 27.2.47 (S/Lt Meunier safe), SOC

TE535　Spitfire LF.IXe (Merlin 66); TOC/RAF 17.5.45 - For FAF 27.11.45; Shipped to Indo-China, desp. 28.11.45, arr Saigon 3.1.46; GC.II/7 *'Nice'*, flown from Hanoi to Nha Trang 27.5.46; GC.I/4 *'Dauphiné'* 11.47, test flight Bien Hoa 15.12.47; Accident at Calbe 27.1.48 (Cne Soula safe)

TE549　Spitfire LF.IXe (Merlin 66); TOC/RAF 18.5.45 - For FAF 28.11.45; Shipped to Indo-China, desp. 28.11.45, arr Saigon 3.1.46; GC.I/7 *'Provence'*, operational flight over Dien Bien Phu 31.5.46; Mid-air collision with Spitfire TE138 near Gia-lam 28.6.46 (S/Lt J Sarrail safe)

TE550　Spitfire LF.IXe (Merlin 66); TOC/RAF 23.5.45 - For FAF 28.11.45; Shipped to Indo-China, desp. 28.11.45, arr Saigon 3.1.46; GC.I/7 *'Provence'* 3.46; Fuel shortage, force-landed wheels-up near Phu Lang Thuong, Cat.E 15.4.46 (Sgt Tron safe), SOC

TE552　Spitfire LF.IXe (Merlin 66); TOC/RAF 23.5.45 - For FAF 28.11.45; Shipped to Indo-China, desp. 28.11.45, arr Saigon 3.1.46; GC.II/7 *'Nice'* ('W') 1946; GC III/2 *'Alsace'* ('W'), mid-air collision with Spitfire TD398 over Tan Kieu/Cholon 29.9.46 (Lt Porquet safe); R&SU; GC.I/4 *'Dauphiné'* ('W'), test flight 19.1.48

TE553　Spitfire LF.IXe (Merlin 66); TOC/RAF 18.5.45 - For FAF 28.11.45; Shipped to Indo-China, desp. 28.11.45, arr Saigon 3.1.46; GC.I/7 *'Provence'* 3.46 and 5.46; GC.II/7 *'Nice'*; Accident at Thereo 24.6.46 (Sgt Combes safe); GC.I/4 *'Dauphiné'* ('V'), noted 1948

TP367　Spitfire FR XVIII, ex Indian AF (*HS-669*); Arr Sandy, Bedfordshire, England as **SURVIVOR** only 17.8.94 en route to storage by JM Limbeuf, Rouen, France.

Unidentified Spitfire

1946　Mk.IX of No.1 EC at Friedrichshafen, Germany, marked with white double circles "⓪", flown by Cdt Louis Delfino (former CO of the "Normandie Niémen" Fighter unit, which fought on side of the Soviets).

"PT847"　LF.IXe - FAF 27.11.45; Unknown unit, crashed 12.3.48 (PT847 was lost already 8.11.44)

SURVIVORS in France

Spitfire Mk XIV: SM832 (*F-AZSJ*), Dijon in 1998.
Spitfire Mk XVI: RR263, marked 'GW-R' ('TB 597'), via Tours to Musée de'l Air at Le Bourget.
Spitfire Mk XVIII: TP367 (ex HS-669), storage at Rouen.
Spitfire BS464 was lost in fire at Le Bourget 1990.
Seafire PP972 of Jean Frélaut moved to D Arnold, England.

Replica

"BS539", Civil reg. *F-WGML* , flyable by J-P Dubois.

References:
Les Francais sur "Spit", by Paul Lambermont.
Ecole de chasse "Christian Martell", by Eric Moreau, Le Fanatique de l'Aviation Nos 111 & 112, February/March 1979.
"Spitfire", Le Trait d'Union, Numero Special 1978, by C.A.Pierquet.
Les "Spitfire" français, by Claude-A.Pierquet, Ouest-France, 1980.
Les "Seafire" dans l'Aeronautique Navale française, by Jean Frélaut and Claude-A. Pierquet, Ouest-France, 1983.
Spitfire français en Indochine, by C.A.Pierquet, 1996.
Supermarine Spitfire Mk.IX, Trait d'Union No.184, by Jean-Pierre Dubois, April 1999.
Supermarine Seafire F.III, Trait d'Union No.185, by Jean-Pierre Dubois, June 1999.
La libération de la Corse, by Christian-Jacques Ehrengardt, Aéro Journal No.10, January 2000.
L'armée de l'Air en Indochine, Fana de l'Aviation, December 2000.

GERMANY

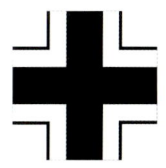

Germany never bought Spitfires, but several captured Spitfires and other Allied types were flown by the German Air Force (*Luftwaffe*, short: Lw) during World War Two. They came into German hands after forced landings or were found by German troops in occupied territories from May 1940.

For example, in October 1943 German troops seized Antimachia airfield on the Greek island of Cos in the Aegean. No.7 (SAAF) Sqn and No.74 Sqn RAF had been unable to fly out their Spitfire Vb/trops, because the runway was cratered. Some were destroyed in the attack, but six were captured intact. Several were tested for the German Air Force by the Czechoslovakian Air Research Institute *Vedecky Letecky Ustav* at Prague-Letnany 1944/45. After the war one of these Spitfires was exhibited at Melník (near Prague), together with a Russian built La-7 in 1945/46, both then in Czechoslovakian colours.

A captured Spitfire V at a flying school at Kolberg on the Baltic coast in north-east Germany. The RAF roundels have been replaced by Luftwaffe *crosses and the marking "G+X". Under the aft fuselage, forward of the tailwheel, is a smoke-making mechanism.*

The same aircraft in flight with RAF roundels repainted for use in a German propaganda film, where it was shown supposedly being attacked by Bf 109 or FW 190 fighters.

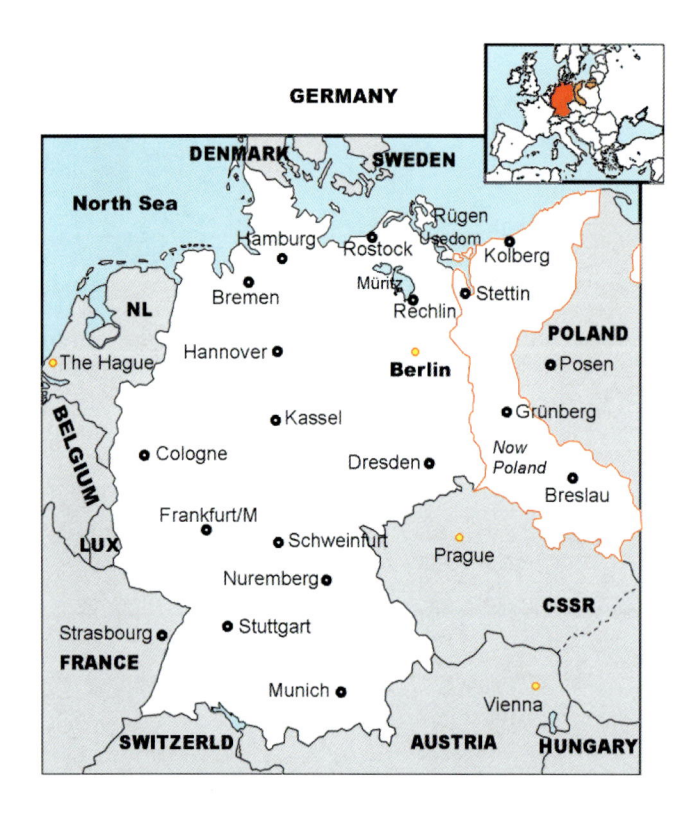

Spitfires were flown by the following German units

DB — Daimler-Benz AG, Testcentre for aero-engines at airfield Echterdingen (near Böblingen, South of Stuttgart).

DLV — Deutsche Luft- und Versuchsanstalt at Oberpfaffenhofen (SW of Munich), a German Aero- and Experimental Establishment; Comparison tests with Spitfires and German aircraft.

E.Stelle — Erprobungsstelle Rechlin, a Military test centre, but also proving centre for new developments of the German Luftwaffe, based near Müritz-See; Comparison tests with Spitfires and German aircraft; The first flying reports for Spitfires dated from January 1941 (test flight Lt.Borris, JG.26).

FW — Focke-Wulf Flugzeugbau GmbH at Bremen, measurements of Spitfire Mk.IX, study 14th April 1944.

Me — Messerschmitt AG, ex Bayerische Flugzeugwerke AG (Bf), at Augsburg (Munich/Stuttgart); Repair of Spitfires; Comparison and measurements on Spitfires.

Kl — Hanns Klemm Flugzeugbau at Böblingen, Stuttgart South; Co-op with Messerschmitt and Daimler-Benz.

2/OKL — "*Zirkus Rosarius*", 2nd Staffel [No.2 Sqn] of the Versuchsverband (Transport) OKL, a test and comparison unit of the HQ German Luftwaffe (Lw), formed at Oranienburg and based at Göttingen, used captured aircraft; Unit-code 'T9+ '. To learn more about Spitfires, especially handling and flying characteristics, the "*Cirkus Rosarius*" visited operational units, where they were flown by unit leaders and experienced pilots from 1943; The inventory listed two Spitfires 20th March 1944, and three Spitfires (Mk.V & IX) in mid 1944; Later two Spitfire PR.XI ('TE+BB' & 'TE+EK') were seen with this unit in 1944, the first being held by the staff and the second by No.2 Sqn of Versuchsverband OKL.
NOTE: No.1426 (Enemy Aircraft Circus) Flight at Duxford, later Collyweston, was a similar RAF establishment.

5/JG.2 — "*Gruppe Bernay*", 5th Staffel [No.5 Sqn] of the 2nd Jagd-Geschwader [No.2 Fighter Wing] in France, also called *Jagdlehrer-Uberprüfungs-Staffel*, a Fighter Leader Training Unit and Flight Instructor Checking Group; Tests and training also with Spitfires and other captured aircraft. Reported Spitfires at Orleans-Bricy and Le Bourget, dett Bernay and Villacoublay in France. For example, a Spitfire Mk.Ia marked '5+2', was used for comparison flying tests against Bf 109 and FW 190s in October 1942. Another Spitfire was here in April 1943, marked '3+9'.

DLV and E-Stelle used the Spitfires for comparison tests with German fighter planes. Spitfires were also tested by German aircraft producers, especially by the Messerschmitt company and by Daimler-Benz Aero engines. The Czechoslovakian VLU Air Research Institute at Prague-Letnany, then controlled by the Germans, also used Spitfires for trials in 1944/45.

Captured Spitfires also featured in Nazi propaganda films. One, which was marked "G-X" and based at Kolberg (Flugzeugführerschule FFS6 (C)), a Flying School in Eastern Germany, on the south coast of the Baltic Sea, now Polish Kolobrzeg), was shown being supposedly attacked by Bf 109 or FW 190 fighters, in October 1940. Despite claims to the contrary, these were not genuine combat films. In a later film, for instance, an obsolete Spitfire Mk.Ia is depicted being supposedly attacked by a much later Ta 152.

A special unit of the German North Africa troops, the "SAS Brandenburger", ferried out a captured Spitfire to Africa. There it gave air cover for troops which were crossing the Tchad, French NW Africa. *See report in FlyPast June 1996 (p.26).*

In July 1942 the Krakow Main Market Square saw the opening of a German exhibition of captured weapons. One of them was a Spitfire with the 'LY'-marking of the No.1 PRU, probably a PR-variant, serial number unknown. In France existed a "Beutepark Luftwaffe No.5" (Booty Collection No.5 of the Lw) at Paris-Nanterre, which had a Spitfire Mk.I at one time.

Most of the force-landed Spitfires were dismantled for spare-parts for the few flyable planes. In early 1944 the Luftwaffe inventory listed four flyable Spitfires: Mks. I, V, IX and XII. By September 1944 only three of these were in use. Additionally two non-flyable Spitfires were held in storage by the 1st Staffel/OKL (No.1 Sqn of the test unit OKL) on 20 March 1944.

After the war another Spitfire arrived in Germany. This was a Spitfire LF.IXc, MK732, ex RNethAF *H-25*, exhibited at the entrance of the former RAF airbase Gütersloh, SW of Bielefeld, from 1956. In 1969 it was returned to the United Kingdom, and later rebuilt for The Netherlands. Since 1994 this aircraft has been flown (Civil reg. *G-HVDM* and *PH-OUQ*), now marked "3W-17".

German Abbreviations:
 Bf = Bayerische Flugzeugwerke (Messerschmitt factories)
 FW = Focke-Wulf aircraft factories (but also Feldwebel/Sgt)
 Grp = Gruppe (I-IV), Group [hierarchy: St-Grp-JG]
 JG = Jagd-Geschwader, Fighter-Wing
 Lw = Luftwaffe, German Air Force
 Ofw = Oberfeldwebel, F/Sgt
 OKL = Oberkommando der Luftwaffe, HQ Air Force
 St = Staffel, Squadron
 Ta = Tank (Professor Tank, Focke-Wulf works)

Individual Histories

F.01 — Spitfire F.Ia (Merlin III); French *F.01* ("FW-B"); Orleans-Bricy, captured by Germans 18.6.40; To the German Test-centre Rechlin (near Müritz-See) in 1940; Fate unknown

K9867 — Spitfire F.Ia (Merlin II); TOC/RAF 18.2.39; No.74 Sqn ('ZP-J'); Force-landed Calais-Marck after air combat

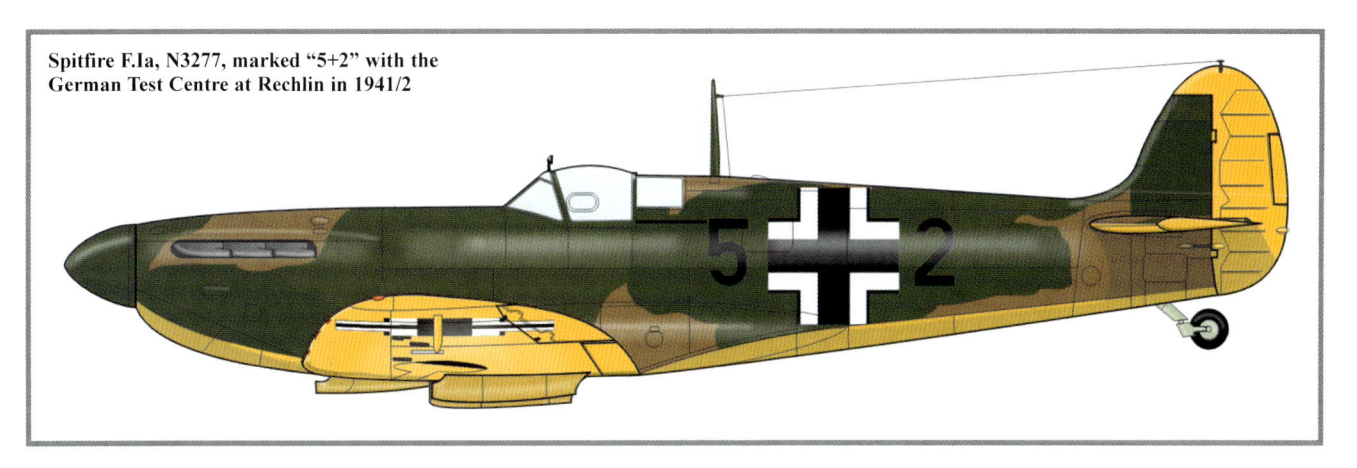

Spitfire F.Ia, N3277, marked "5+2" with the German Test Centre at Rechlin in 1941/2

23.5.40 (S/Ldr FL White safe); Aircraft captured by German troops 26.5.40; To an air depot of the Luftwaffe; Fate unknown

N3277 Spitfire F.Ia (Merlin III); Became (Lw) No.**52**; TOC/RAF 16.1.40; No.234 Sqn ('AZ-H', named "*Dirty Dick*"); Damaged by Bf109 off Swanage, Dorset UK, force-landed near Cherbourg 15.8.40 (P/O R Hardy RCAF, PoW); Repaired, and to the German Testcentre at Rechlin (marked '5+2') from 12.41 to 9.42; Test flown 5.6.42 (Plt HW Lerche); "*Group Bernay*" in France (No.5 Sqn of No.2 (F)Wing [5/JG.2]) in 1942/43; No.26 (F)Wing [JG.26] at Orleans-Bricy, flown 29.3.43 (Ofw Martin); Fate unknown

P7379 Spitfire F.IIa (Merlin XII); TOC/RAF 10.9.40; No.19 Sqn ('QV-U'); Shot down late evening by Bf109 on sweep, force-landed wheels-up near Calais in France 27.6.41 (P/O Andrews, PoW); To an air depot of the Luftwaffe; Fate unknown

P7443 Spitfire F.IIa (Merlin XII); TOC/RAF 1.10.40; No.54.Sqn ('KL-E'); Circus 5, shot down by the first Group of No.2 (F)Wing [I/JG.2], force-landed near Calais 26.2.41 (Sgt H Squire, PoW); SOC/RAF 28.2.41 (98:05 flying hours); To E-Stelle Rechlin; Messerschmitt factory Augsburg from 21.4.41, was to be fitted with a DB601 engine, but this was cancelled; Flown at Echterdingen (near Böblingen, south of Stuttgart,); Retd to Testcentre Rechlin 9.9.42; Fate unknown

P9317 Spitfire F.Ia (Merlin III); TOC/RAF 10.2.40; No.222 Sqn ('ZD-A'); Air combat with Bf 109s and Bf 110s, force-landed at Le Touquet airfield in France, which was held by Germans 1.6.40 (P/O HEL Falkust, PoW); To an air depot of the Luftwaffe; Possibly flown as "G-X" in a propaganda-film, based Kolberg, Eastern Germany; Fate unknown

P9331 Spitfire PR.A (Merlin III); Became Lw.No.**21**; TOC/RAF 29.2.40; No.212 Sqn, glycol leak, force-landed near Reims 7.6.40; Repaired and to German Lw; Testcentre Rechlin ('2+1') in 6.40; Fate unknown

W3824 Spitfire F.Vb (Merlin 45); Presentation aircraft '*HOLT II*'; TOC/RAF 29.8.41; No.129 Sqn ('DV-F') 11.9.41, missing 27.9.41 (Sgt V Ross, PoW); SOC/RAF 28.9.41; Noted in a German air depot (almost intact); Fate unknown

X4260 Spitfire F.Ia (Merlin III); Became Lw.No.**45**; TOC/RAF 23.8.40; No.603 Sqn ('XT-D'); Air combat with first Group of No.54 (F)Wing [I/JG.54] over Pas de Calais, force-landed Guines near Calais 6.9.40 (P/O JR Caister, PoW); SOC/RAF 2.11.40 (9:55 flying hours); To German Lw; With No.2 Sqn of No.54 (F)Wing [2/JG.54] in 11.40; Messerschmitt factory Augsburg ('4+5'), test flown 20.11.40 (Plt Fritz Wendel); Fate unknown

X4385 Spitfire PR.C (Merlin 45); TOC/RAF 14.9.40; No.1 PRU ('LY-B'); Force-landed, undercarriage collapsed at Deelen airfield, Netherlands 22.9.41; Repaired; Testcentre Rechlin 1941/42; Fate unknown

AA835 Spitfire F Vb (Merlin 45); TOC/RAF 10.10.41; No.350 Sqn ('MN-E', marked "*Stella Maris*"); Circus 195 to Hazebrouck marshalling yards, force-landed in German occupied territory 29.6.42 (P/O R de Wever, PoW); To an air depot of the Luftwaffe, Fate unknown

AA837 Spitfire F.Vb (Merlin 45); TOC/RAF 26.9.41; No.501 Sqn (SD-E), force landed on the foreshore near St.Lô after air combat with Bf109s on 4.11.41 (P/O EH Shore PoW); Mostly intact to a Luftwaffe air depot; Fate unknown

AB131 Spitfire PR.IV/D (Merlin 45); TOC/RAF 7.12.41; No.1401 (Met) Flight, force-landed near St.Trond, Belgium 12.4.42 (SOC/RAF 13.4.42; 49.55 flying hours); To an air depot of the Luftwaffe, later to a German Lw Flying School; Fate unknown

AB824 Spitfire F.Vb (Merlin 45); TOC/RAF 30.8.41; No.303 Sqn ('RF-S'), Circus 119, force-landed near St.Omer, France 4.4.42 (F/Lt Z Kurstrzynski, PoW); To an air depot of the Luftwaffe; Fate unknown

AD130 Spitfire F.Vb (Merlin 45); TOC/RAF 31.8.41; No.316 Sqn ('SZ-E'), Circus 122 to Hazebrouck marshalling yards, air combat over St.Omer, shot down by JG.26, force-landed 12.4.42 (F/O BK Buchwald); SOC/RAF 30.4.42; 188:50 flying hours); Almost intact to the Luftwaffe; Fate unknown

AR380 Spitfire F.Vb (Merlin 45); TOC/RAF 17.3.42; No.350 Sqn ('MN-Z'), Dieppe raid, force-landed in France 19.8.42 (P/O HE Marchal rescued); To an air depot of the Luftwaffe; Fate unknown

BL733 Spitfire F.Vb (Merlin 45); TOC/RAF 10.2.42; No.306.Sqn ('UZ-D'), forced landed on French Channel coast 30.7.42 (P/O Roman Pentz PoW); Mostly intact to an air depot of the Luftwaffe; Fate unknown

EN626 Spitfire LF.XIIc (Griffon III); TOC/RAF 19.4.43; No.91 Sqn ('DL-E'), Rhubarb, hit by flak near Gremonville, force-landed near Rouen, France 6.11.43 (W/O RAB Blumer RAAF killed); To an air depot of the Luftwaffe; Fate unknown

EN685 Spitfire PR.XI (Merlin 61); No.542 Sqn; FTR Hannover, force-landed 13.5.44; To the Luftwaffe; Repaired, and to "*Zirkus Rosarius*" (2nd/OKL), marked 'T9+EK'; Flown by Lt KH Messer (First Group of No.53 (F)Wing [I/JG.53]) from Hannover-Wunstorf to Hustedt (NE of Hannover) 31.7.44; Demonstration at Dortmund, Mönchengladbach, Bönninghardt, Bonn, Stadte and Husum from 2.8. to 11.8.44; Flown 21.8.44; Demonstrated by pilots of No.26 (F)Wing [JG.26] at Reinsehlen (near Schneverdingen, c.40m E of Bremen) in 11.44; Fate unknown

EN830 Spitfire F.Vb (Merlin 45); Presentation aircraft '*CHISLEHURST AND SIDCUP*'; TOC/RAF 1.5.42; No.131 Sqn, missing near Ouistreham, force-landed on Jersey after air combat 18.11.42 (P/O BWM Scheidhauer, PoW, murdered); To Messerschmitt factory Augsburg and to Echterdingen (near Böblingen, South of Stuttgart) in 12.42 (test flown by Capt Willy Ellenrieder, Daimler-Benz); Armament & radio removed, 24-volt electrical system and DB605A engine installed; To E-Stelle Rechlin, marked 'CJ+ZY'; Comparison trials with Bf 109G in 1943; Later DB601A engine installed; Technical failure 27.4.44; Destroyed on ground at Echterdingen by an USAAF bombing raid on 14.8.44; Wreck to Klemm company at Böblingen, scrapped there

NOTE: P/O Scheidhauer took part in the Great Escape, but was recaptured at Saarbrucken, and shot dead by the Gestapo on 29 March 1944, along with 50 others who took part

Spitfire F.Vb BL733 'UZ-D' of No.306 (Polish) Sqn RAF is seen after force-landing on the French Channel coast on 30th July 1942, Plt Off Roman Pentz being taken prisoner. It was dismantled and taken to a Luftwaffe air depot.

EP200 Spitfire F.Vb/trop (Merlin 46); TOC/RAF 30.5.42; Arr Malta 8.42; No.185 Sqn ('GL-T'), hit by flak, forced to land, belly-landed near Comiso, Italy 27.8.42 (P/O Woodser PoW); Aircraft almost intact to the German Luftwaffe; Fate unknown

MK698 Spitfire LF.IXc (Merlin 66); TOC/RAF 5.4.44; No.412 Sqn, dive bombing, damaged by Bf 109s south of Wesel, force-landed near Wachtendonk (Krefeld) 5.12.44 (P/O CWH Glithevo, PoW); With "*Zirkus Rosarius*" (2nd/OKL) 12.44; Based Hannover-Wunstorf in 1.45; Fate unknown

MK732 Spitfire LF.IXc; Flown by No.485 Sqn; Arrived as **SURVIVOR** only; Gate-guard at the former AFB Gütersloh (RAF, South of Bielefeld) from 1956; Restored, now flyable in the Netherlands (Civil reg. *G-HVDM* now *PH-OUQ*), marked "3W-17"

MV370 Spitfire FR.XIVe; ex Indian AF, marked 'T44'; via UK (reg. *G-FXIV* 11.4.80, cancelled 5.2.85), arrived as **SURVIVOR** only; Exhibited at Luftfahrtmuseum, Hannover-Laatzen from 11.92, marked "MV370/EB-Q"

PL... ? Spitfire PR.XI (Merlin 70); RAF unit unknown; Force-landed and to Luftwaffe 1944; "*Zirkus Rosarius*" (2nd/OKL), marked 'T9+BB'; Shown Hannover-Wunstorf in 1944; Fate unknown
Possibilities: PL834 (No.16 Sqn), FTR Arnhem 20.9.44; PL904 (No.541 Sqn) FTR Bremen 28.9.44; PL906 (No.542 Sqn) FTR Munich 27.11.44; PL916 (No.683 Sqn) FTR Stuttgart 8.10.44; PL919 (No.541 Sqn) FTR Frankfurt 24.12.44; PL925 (No.400 Sqn) FTR Ruhr 28.10.44.

SURVIVOR
MV370, Spitfire FR.XIVe, ex India, now exhibited at Aviation Museum, Hannover-Laatzen.

References:
Die "Spit" mit dem Balkenkreuz, by Andreas Weise, Model Magazine April 1975 (p.14/15).
Sie flogen mit dem Balkenkreuz, by Paul Hermsen, Modell Fan December 1977 (p.36).
Beuteflugzeuge in Rechlin, by Christoph Regel, Flugzeug January 1985 (p.6) and Alfred Misna, Flugzeug January 1986 (p.5).
E'Stelle Rechlin, by Bruno Lange, German Jägerblatt.
RAF in Luftwaffe colours, by JL Roba and C DeDecker, FlyPast June 1996 (p.24 ff) & July 1996 (p.24).

Spitfire PR.XI, EN685, marked T9+EK with the 2nd OKL at Göttingen in 1944

GREECE

On 21st December 1937 Supermarine reported to the Foreign Orders Committee that an enquiry had been received from Greece about the possibility of a licence for building twelve Spitfire Mk.Ia. Greece signed an order for approximately £66,000 on 14th August 1938, and on 23rd September 1938 received a firm quotation for delivery of twelve Spitfire (Type No.335, price £9,335 each), with an option for a further 12 to 24 to be built under licence. This took place No.10 dated 17th November 1938 in the Foreign Office priority list. Later, with a Greek letter dated 22nd March 1939, the order was increased to 24 Spitfires. The negotiations had reached an advanced stage when the contract No C.315/39 was cancelled.

During the Second World War Greece was occupied by Germany from 1941 until 1944. A number of Greek pilots escaped to the Middle East, to be formed into two RAF squadrons (Nos.335 & 336), both of which were eventually equipped with Spitfires.

After the war the newly-formed Greek Air Force, known as the *Royal Hellenic Air Force* (RHAF), received Spitfires Mks.V, IX & XVI. The Mks.V & IX were delivered from Middle East stocks, but the LF.XVIs were delivered from the UK, being ferry-flown from Manston to Greece (Comm.655). They were used initially for building up the fighter and combat strength, then later the Mk. XVIs, especially, were used within the training and conversion programmes for the new jet fighters. A total of 243 Spitfires was received by the RHAF.

Greek Spitfire units of the RAF

No.335 Sqn; Formed at Gaza 7th October 1941, to Aqir 10th October 1941; To RHAF control at Sedes on 31st July 1946; Sqn code: 'FG ' (possibly denoting "Fighting Greeks").
Spitfire Mk.Vb&c/trop from January 1944.

No.336 Sqn; Formed 25th February 1943 at LG.219 (Almaza, Egypt); To RHAF control at Sedes on 31st July 1946; No squadron code carried on aircraft.
Spitfire Mk.Vc from October 1943 (Mk.IX in May 1944 & June 1944 only).

Both squadrons were handed over from the RAF to Greek Command in December 1944. Official disbandment followed on the 30th June 1946 and 31st July 1946 respectively. The RHAF continued to use Spitfires well after those dates.

Spitfires of the Royal Hellenic Air Force (RHAF)

The initial delivery was of 51 Spitfire F.Vb/c-trop (and five for spares), officially on 25th April 1946, these being mostly those of the two homecoming squadrons, which remained in service until early 1947.

They were replaced by 109 Spitfire Mk.IXc/e received between 30th January 1947 and 10th June 1948 and one PR.XI (EN656) on 29th May 1947, in service until 1953.

Between 9th December 1948 and 21st August 1949, 76 Spitfire LF.XVIe were supplied, these remaining in service until 1954, being largely used in connection with the jet conversion programme. For this the RHAF had engaged a number of pilots between 1949 and 1956, these being trained at Tatoi (EKEX-

Bombing-up a Spitfire LF.XVIe of the RHAF, with the help of a special carrier. [Hellenic Air Force]

School), and also at the Sedes airbase which provided the advanced flying training, both using Spitfires. EKEX stood for Ekpaideytiko Kentro Efedron Heiriston (Reserve Pilots Training Centre), operating a quick training scheme to cover an urgent need for pilots.

Spitfires were phased out from 1953 onwards, the last being written off charge in July 1954.

Spitfire Units of the RHAF

No.**335** (F) Sqn; Based at Hassani/Hellenikon, south of Athens, November 1944; To Sedes airbase in August 1945 (No.113 Combat Wing); Spitfire Mk.Vb/c as front-line aircraft until February 1947, then Spitfire Mks.IX & XVI until October 1953, when re-equipped with F-84 G jets.
Commanding Officers:
F/Lt G Doukas	1.44
F/Lt P Bousios	4.45
S/Ldr I Kartalamakis	7.46
F/Lt A Vlantousis	7.47
S/Ldr E Sinouris	4.49
S/Ldr A Frankias	10.49
F/Lt E Chatzioannou	8.51
F/Lt K Kokkas	9.51
F/Lt E Chatzioannou	1.52
F/Lt P Michelogkonas	2.52
F/Lt E Chatzioannou	12.52
F/Lt D Gounarakis	4.53
P/O D Mitsanas	9.53

No.**336** (F) Sqn; Based at Hassani/Hellenikon November 1944; To Sedes airbase in May 1945; Larisa airbase from February 1949 (No.110 Combat Group); Used Spitfire Mk.Vb/c until February 1947, then Mk.IX until August 1949, when re-equipped with Helldivers.
Commanding Officers:
F/Lt K Chondros	10.44
F/Lt K Koniotakis	4.45
F/Lt L Parisis	11.46
F/Lt A Deligiorgis	11.48
S/Ldr E Athanasoupoulos	5.49

No.**337** (F) Sqn; Formed at airbase Elefsina on 30th March 1948 (No.112 Combat Wing); Used Spitfire Mks.IX & XVI from March 1948 until June 1952, when it re-equipped with F-84G and T-33 jets.

Commanding Officers:
F/Lt Kortronis	3.48
S/Ldr K Loukopoulos	4.49
S/Ldr P Demiris	10.49
S/Ldr E Sinouris	11.49
F/Lt K Kokkas	2.51
F/Lt A Deligeorgis	6.51
F/Lt K Kokkas	8.51
F/Lt A Frankias	9.51
F/Lt E Sinouris	1.52

SA   Air Force Pilots School at Tatoi [Dekelia] airbase (later Sholi Ikaron or '*Icarus*' School from 1954); Spitfire LF.XVIe for jet conversion training (EKEX) from mid-1948 until September 1953.
Commanding Officers:
Grp Cpt P Papapanagiotou	4.47
F/Lt M Kontolefeas	12.49
Wg Cdr A Vlantousis	1.50
Grp Cpt K Margaritis	4.52
Wg Cdr P Mitsakos	5.52

A/FTS   Advanced Flying Training School at Sedes airbase (No.113 Wing); Spitfire LF.XVIe from 1951 until April 1954, also for training of the contract pilots.
Commanding Officers of No.113 CW:
Grp Cpt G Doukas	12.49
Grp Cpt A Nasopoulos	2.51
Grp Cpt K Panagopoulos	6.53

Individual Histories

AB321   Spitfire F.Vb/trop (Merlin 45); TOC/RAF 1.1.42; ex M.E. -To RHAF, No.335 Sqn at Sedes 25.4.46; Fate unknown

AB324   Spitfire F.Vb/trop (Merlin 45); TOC/RAF 1.1.42; ex M.E., No.336 Sqn (crashed 8.9.44) - To RHAF, No.336 Sqn at Sedes 25.4.46; Fate unknown

AR562   Spitfire F.Vc/trop (Merlin 46); TOC/RAF 27.7.42; ex M.E. - To RHAF, No.336 Sqn at Sedes 25.4.46; Fate unknown

BR586   Spitfire F.Vc/trop (Merlin 46); TOC/RAF 1.6.42; ex M.E. - To RHAF, No.336 Sqn at Sedes 25.4.46; No.337 Sqn at Elefsis, crashed 23.12.47

BS129   Spitfire F.IXc (Merlin 61); TOC/RAF 27.7.42 - Arr Greece (via RAF Pershore) 20.4.48; Fate unknown

BS352   Spitfire F.IXc (Merlin 61); TOC/RAF 8.10.42 - Arr Greece 6.5.48; Fate unknown

BS354   Spitfire HF.IXc (Merlin 70); TOC/RAF 28.10.42; ex M.E. - Arr Greece 30.1.47; Fate unknown

BS394   Spitfire F.IXc (Merlin 61); TOC/RAF 8.10.42 - Arr Greece 29.4.48; Fate unknown

BS409   Spitfire F.IXc (Merlin 61); TOC/RAF 31.10.42 - Arr Greece (via RAF Pershore) 29.4.48; Fate unknown

BS508   Spitfire F.IXc (Merlin 61); TOC/RAF 31.10.42 - Arr Greece (via RAF Pershore) 31.3.48; No.336 Sqn at Sedes 31.3.48; Later Larisa airbase from 2.49; Fate unknown

BS558   Spitfire F.IXc (Merlin 61); TOC/RAF 23.11.42; ex NWA - Arr Greece 29.5.47; No.335 Sqn at Sedes 29.5.47; Fate unknown

EE798   Spitfire F.Vc/trop (Merlin 56); TOC/RAF 24.12.42; ex SAAF (M.E.) - To RHAF, No.335 Sqn at Sedes 25.4.46; Fate unknown

EE855   Spitfire F.Vc/trop (Merlin 46); TOC/RAF 23.1.43; ex M.E. – Arr Greece 25.4.46; Fate unknown

EF566   Spitfire F.Vc/trop (Merlin 45); TOC/RAF 1.3.43; ex M.E, No.335 Sqn - to RHAF, No.335 Sqn at Sedes 25.4.46; Dived into ground near Langaja, burnt out, Cat FA/E 2.10.46, SOC

EN143   Spitfire F.IXc (Merlin 61); TOC/RAF 5.12.42; ex USAAF (MAAF) - Arr Greece 29.5.47; Fate unknown

EN254   Spitfire F.IXc (Merlin 61); TOC/RAF 12.1.43; ex SAAF (M.E.) - Arr Greece 30.1.47; Fate unknown

EN286   Spitfire F.IXc (Merlin 61); TOC/RAF 6.12.42; ex M.E. - Arr Greece 27.2.47; Fate unknown

EN656   Spitfire PR XI (Merlin 63); TOC/RAF 6.6.43; ex MAAF - Arr Greece 29.5.47; Fate unknown

GREECE

EP406   Spitfire F.Vb/trop (Merlin 46); TOC/RAF 25.6.42; ex M.E. - To RHAF, No.336 Sqn at Sedes 25.4.46; Fate unknown
EP562   Spitfire F.Vb/trop (Merlin 46); TOC/RAF 5.7.42; SOC 23.10.44 (bboc) - To RHAF 25.4.46, for spares only
EP613   Spitfire F.Vb/trop (Merlin 46); TOC/RAF 19.7.42; ex M.E.; SOC 31.8.44 (bboc); No.1 (M.E.) C&CU, flown from Ismailia to Hassani near Athens 31.8.45/1.9.45 (Plt LW Witham) - To RHAF 25.4.46, for spares only
EP694   Spitfire F.Vb/trop (Merlin 46); TOC/RAF 24.7.42; ex M.E. - To RHAF, No.336 Sqn at Sedes 25.4.46; Fate unknown
EP708   Spitfire F.Vb/trop (Merlin 46); TOC/RAF 25.7.42; ex M.E. - To RHAF, No.336 Sqn at Sedes 25.4.46; Fate unknown
EP772   Spitfire F.Vb/trop (Merlin 46); TOC/RAF 16.8.42; ex USAAF (M.E.) - To RHAF, No.336 Sqn at Sedes 25.4.46; Fate unknown
EP844   Spitfire F.Vb/trop (Merlin 46); TOC/RAF 9.8.42; No.1 (M.E.) C&CU, flown from El Firdan to Kalamaki, Greece 3.5.45 (Plt LW Witham) - To RHAF, Nos.335 or 336 Sqns at Sedes 25.4.46; Fate unknown
EP953   Spitfire F.Vb/trop (Merlin 46); TOC/RAF 13.8.42; ex M.E. - To RHAF, No.336 Sqn at Sedes 25.4.46; Fate unknown
ER128   Spitfire F.Vb/trop (Merlin 46); TOC/RAF 17.9.42; ex NAASC - To RHAF, No.335 Sqn at Sedes 25.4.46; Fate unknown
ER136   Spitfire F.Vb/trop (Merlin 46); TOC/RAF 21.8.42; ex USAAF (MAAF) - To RHAF, No.336 Sqn at Sedes 25.4.46; Fate unknown
ER463   Spitfire F.Vb/trop (Merlin 46); TOC/RAF 13.9.42; ex M.E. - To RHAF, No.336 Sqn at Sedes 25.4.46; Fate unknown
ER717   Spitfire F.Vb/trop (Merlin 46); TOC/RAF 11.10.42; No.1 (M.E.) C&CU, flown from Aboukir to Kalamaki, Greece 28.11.44 (Plt LW Witham) - to RHAF, No.336 Sqn at Sedes 25.4.46; Later Larisa airbase from 2.49; Fate unknown
ER772   Spitfire F.Vb/trop allotted for RHAF, but crashed before delivery
ER773   Spitfire F.Vb/trop (Merlin 46); TOC/RAF 11.10.42; ex M.E., No.336 Sqn RAF, Cat.E 3.3.44 (bboc) - to RHAF 25.4.46, for spares only
ER890   Spitfire F.Vb/trop (Merlin 46); TOC/RAF 6.11.42; ex M.E. - To RHAF, No.335 Sqn at Sedes 25.4.46; Fate unknown
ES144   Spitfire F.Vb/trop (Merlin 46); TOC/RAF 16.11.42; ex M.E., No.335 Sqn RAF - To RHAF, No.335 Sqn at Sedes 25.4.46; Fate unknown
ES176   Spitfire F.Vb/trop (Merlin 46); TOC/RAF 6.12.42; ex M.E. - To RHAF, No.336 Sqn at Sedes 25.4.46; Fate unknown
ES250   Spitfire F.Vc/trop (Merlin 46); TOC/RAF 20.11.42; ex M.E. - To RHAF, No.335 Sqn at Sedes 25.4.46; Fate unknown
JG876   Spitfire F.Vc/trop (Merlin 46); TOC/RAF 23.12.42; ex M.E., No.335 Sqn RAF - To RHAF, No.335 Sqn at Sedes 25.4.46; Fate unknown
JK102   Spitfire F.Vc/trop (Merlin 46); TOC/RAF 2.1.43; ex M.E., USAAF, also No.335 Sqn RAF - To RHAF, No.335 Sqn at Sedes 25.4.46; Fate unknown
JK127   Spitfire F.Vc/trop (Merlin 46); TOC/RAF 22.1.43; ex M.E. - To RHAF, No.336 Sqn at Sedes 25.4.46; Fate unknown
JK170   Spitfire F.Vc/trop (Merlin 46); TOC/RAF 23.1.43; ex SAAF (M.E.), Cat.E 8.3.44 (bboc) -To RHAF 25.4.46, for spares only
JK226   Spitfire F.Vc/trop (Merlin 46); TOC/RAF 3.2.43; ex USAAF (NWA) - to RHAF, No.335 Sqn at Sedes 25.4.46; Fate unknown
JK234   Spitfire F.Vc/trop (Merlin 50); TOC/RAF 15.2.43; ex M.E. - To RHAF, No.335 Sqn at Sedes 25.4.46; Fate unknown

JK256   Spitfire F.Vc/trop (Merlin 46); TOC/RAF 4.2.43; ex M.E. - To RHAF, No.336 Sqn at Sedes 25.4.46; Fate unknown
JK264   Spitfire F.Vc/trop (Merlin 46); TOC/RAF 1.2.43; ex M.E. - To RHAF, No.336 Sqn at Sedes 25.4.46; Fate unknown
JK275   Spitfire F.Vc/trop (Merlin 46); TOC/RAF 1.2.43; ex M.E. - To RHAF, No.336 Sqn at Sedes 25.4.46; Fate unknown
JK306   Spitfire F.Vc/trop (Merlin 50A); TOC/RAF 4.2.43; ex Malta - To RHAF, No.336 Sqn at Larisa 25.4.46, possibly crashed 14.8.49
JK324   Spitfire F.Vc/trop (Merlin 46); TOC/RAF 28.12.42; ex M.E., SOC (bboc) - To RHAF 25.4.46, for spares only
JK327   Spitfire F.Vc/trop (Merlin 46); TOC/RAF 10.1.43; ex M.E. - To RHAF, No.336 Sqn at Sedes 25.4.46; Fate unknown
JK376   Spitfire F.Vc/trop (Merlin 50); TOC/RAF 13.3.43; ex M.E. - To RHAF, No.336 Sqn at Sedes 25.4.46; Fate unknown
JK383   Spitfire F.Vc/trop (Merlin 46); TOC/RAF 2.2.43; ex M.E. - To RHAF, No.336 Sqn at Sedes 25.4.46; Fate unknown
JK408   Spitfire F.Vc/trop (Merlin 46); TOC/RAF 10.2.43; ex SAAF (M.E.) - To RHAF, No.336 Sqn at Sedes 25.4.46; Fate unknown
JK528   Spitfire F.Vc/trop (Merlin 46); TOC/RAF 27.2.43; ex M.E., No.335 Sqn RAF - To RHAF, No.335 Sqn at Sedes 25.4.46; Fate unknown
JK530   Spitfire F.Vc/trop (Merlin 46); TOC/RAF 7.3.43; ex USAAF (M.E.) - To RHAF, Nos.335 or 336 Sqns at Sedes 25.4.46; Take-off crash at Sedes 20.6.46
JK652   Spitfire F.Vc/trop (Merlin 46); TOC/RAF 20.2.43; ex M.E. - To RHAF, No.335 Sqn at Sedes 25.4.46; Fate unknown
JK656   Spitfire F.Vc/trop (Merlin 46); TOC/RAF 23.2.43; ex M.E. - To RHAF, Nos.335 or 336 Sqns at Sedes 25.4.46; Fate unknown
JK782   Spitfire F.Vc/trop (Merlin 46); TOC/RAF 6.3.43; ex M.E. - To RHAF, Nos.335 Sqns at Sedes 25.4.46; Fate unknown
JK809   Spitfire F.Vc/trop (Merlin 46); TOC/RAF 23.2.43; ex USAAF (M.E.) - To RHAF, Nos.335 or 336 Sqns at Sedes 25.4.46; Fate unknown
JK885   Spitfire F.Vc/trop (Merlin 45); TOC/RAF 12.3.43; ex SAAF (M.E.) - To RHAF, Nos.335 or 336 Sqns at Sedes 25.4.46; Force-landed near Tirnavos, Cat.FA/E 27.9.46, SOC
JL139   Spitfire F.Vc/trop (Merlin 46); TOC/RAF 28.3.43; ex SAAF (M.E.) - To RHAF, Nos.335 or 336 Sqns at Sedes 25.4.46; Fate unknown
JL176   Spitfire F.Vc/trop (Merlin 46); TOC/RAF 28.3.43; ex M.E. - To RHAF, Nos.335 or 336 Sqns at Sedes 25.4.46; Fate unknown
JL227   Spitfire F.IXc (Merlin 63); TOC/RAF 3.4.43 - Arr Greece 20.4.48; No.335 Sqn at Sedes 4.48; Fate unknown
LZ828   Spitfire F.Vc/trop (Merlin 45); TOC/RAF 16.8.43; ex SAAF (M.E.) - To RHAF, No.336 Sqn at Sedes 25.4.46; Fate unknown
LZ839   Spitfire F.IXc (Merlin 63); TOC/RAF 24.4.43 - Arr Greece (via RAF Pershore) 31.3.48; No.335 Sqn at Sedes 4.48; Fate unknown
LZ864   Spitfire F.Vc/trop (Merlin 50A); TOC/RAF 23.4.43; ex M.E. - To RHAF, No.335 Sqn at Sedes 25.4.46; Possibly crashed 14.1.49
LZ928   Spitfire F.Vc/trop (Merlin 50); TOC/RAF 30.4.43; ex M.E. - To RHAF, No.336 Sqn at Sedes 25.4.46; Fate unknown
LZ932   Spitfire F.Vc/trop (Merlin 50); TOC/RAF 6.5.43; ex M.E. - To RHAF, No.336 Sqn at Sedes 25.4.46; Fate unknown
MA235   Spitfire F.IXc (Merlin 61); TOC/RAF 15.5.43 - Arr Greece (via RAF Pershore) 31.3.48; No.335 Sqn at Sedes 4.48; Fate unknown
MA257   Spitfire F.IXc (Merlin 63); TOC/RAF 23.5.43; ex SAAF (M.E.) - Arr Greece 30.1.47; No.335 Sqn at Sedes 2.47; Fate unknown
MA422   Spitfire F.IXc (Merlin 61); TOC/RAF 18.7.43 - Arr Greece (via RAF Pershore) 31.3.48; Fate unknown
MA427   Spitfire F.IXc; Allotted for RHAF, but SOC before delivery

Spitfire LF.IXc MH452, seen here being refuelled, served with both No.335 Sqn at Sedes and No.336 Sqn at Larisa.

MA462 Spitfire F.IXc (Merlin 63); TOC/RAF 11.6.43; ex MAAF - Arr Greece 27.2.47; Fate unknown

MA467 Spitfire F.IXc (Merlin 63); TOC/RAF 30.5.43 - Arr Greece 6.5.48; No.337 Sqn at Elefsis 5.48; Fate unknown

MA532 Spitfire F.IXc (Merlin 63); TOC/RAF 13.6.43; ex MAAF - Arr Greece 29.5.47; No.335 Sqn at Sedes 6.47; Fate unknown

MA582 Spitfire F.IXc (Merlin 63); TOC/RAF 25.6.43 - Arr Greece 29.4.48; Fate unknown

MA695 Spitfire F.Vc/trop (Merlin 46); TOC/RAF 23.6.43; ex M.E., No.335 Sqn RAF - To RHAF, No.335 Sqn at Sedes 25.4.46; Fate unknown

MA704 Spitfire F.Vc/trop (Merlin 55); TOC/RAF 1.7.43; ex French (M.E.) - to RHAF, No.335 Sqn at Sedes 25.4.46; Fate unknown

MA791 Spitfire F.IXc (Merlin 63); TOC/RAF 21.7.43; Allotted for RHAF 15.4.48 - Arr Greece 29.4.48; No.337 Sqn at Elefsis 5.48; Fate unknown

MA798 Spitfire F.IXc (Merlin 63); TOC/RAF 18.7.43; ex MAAF - Arr Greece 27.2.47; No.335 Sqn at Sedes 3.47; Fate unknown

MA819 Spitfire F.IXc (Merlin 63); TOC/RAF 28.7.43 - Arr Greece (via RAF Pershore) 20.4.48; Fate unknown

MA904 Spitfire F.Vc/trop (Merlin 50A); TOC/RAF 29.6.43; ex M.E. - To RHAF, No.336 Sqn at Sedes 25.4.46; Fate unknown

MH298 Spitfire F.Vc/trop (Merlin 555); TOC/RAF 1.7.43; ex M.E., No.335 Sqn RAF - To RHAF, No.335 Sqn at Sedes 25.4.46; Flew into mountains, pilot killed 18.12.46, SOC

MH314 Spitfire F.IXc (Merlin 63); TOC/RAF 28.7.43 - Arr Greece 6.5.48; Fate unknown

MH322 Spitfire F.IXc (Merlin 61); TOC/RAF 31.7.43 - Arr Greece 6.5.48; No.335 Sqn at Sedes 5.48; Fate unknown

MH359 Spitfire F.IXc (Merlin 61); TOC/RAF 31.7.43; ex MAAF - Arr Greece 29.5.47; No.336 Sqn at Sedes 6.47, Later Larisa airbase from 2.49; Fate unknown

MH416 Spitfire LF.IXc (Merlin 66); TOC/RAF 11.8.43; ex MAAF - Arr Greece 27.2.47; Fate unknown

MH452 Spitfire LF.IXc (Merlin 66); TOC/RAF 15.8.43; ex MAAF - Arr Greece 27.2.47; No.335 Sqn at Sedes 3.47; No.336 Sqn at Larisa; Fate unknown

MH508 Spitfire LF.IXc (Merlin 66); TOC/RAF 21.8.43; ex MAAF - Arr Greece 27.2.47; No.336 Sqn at Sedes 3.47; Later Larisa airbase 2.49; Possibly crashed at Larisa 14.8.49 - NOTE: Crash reported for "506"

MH558 Spitfire F.IXc (Merlin 63); TOC/RAF 29.8.43; ex NAASC - Arr Greece 31.7.47; No.335 Sqn at Sedes 8.47; Fate unknown

MH590 Spitfire F.Vc/trop (Merlin 55); TOC/RAF 8.8.43; ex M.E. - To RHAF, No.335 Sqn at Sedes 25.4.46; Hit by AA, force-landed near Dendelita in Yugoslavia 6.9.46

MH698 Spitfire F.IXc (Merlin 63); TOC/RAF 10.9.43; ex M.E. - Arr Greece 27.3.47; No.335 Sqn at Sedes 4.47; Fate unknown

MH727 Spitfire LF.IXc (Merlin 66); TOC/RAF 15.9.43; ex MAAF - Arr Greece 30.1.47; Fate unknown

MH774 Spitfire LF.IXc (Merlin 66); TOC/RAF 19.9.43 - Arr Greece (via RAF Pershore) 19.5.48; No.335 Sqn at Sedes 5.48; Fate unknown

MH831 Spitfire F.IXc (Merlin 63); TOC/RAF 1.10.43 - Arr Greece (via RAF Pershore) 20.4.48; Fate unknown

MH853 Spitfire F.IXc (Merlin 63); TOC/RAF 1.10.43 - Arr Greece (via RAF Pershore) 19.5.48; No.335 Sqn at Sedes 5.48; Fate unknown

MH908 Spitfire F.IXc (Merlin 63); TOC/RAF 26.9.43; Allotted for RHAF 22.4.48 - Arr Greece 6.5.48; No.335 Sqn at Sedes 5.48; Fate unknown

MH924 Spitfire F.IXc (Merlin 63); TOC/RAF 14.9.43; ex N.A. - Arr Greece 30.1.47; Fate unknown

MH946 Spitfire LF.IXc (Merlin 66); TOC/RAF 29.8.43; ex M.E. (conv. F.IX to LF.IX 24.7.45) - Arr Greece 30.1.47; No.335 Sqn at Sedes 12.47; Fate unknown

MH993 Spitfire F.IXc (Merlin 63); TOC/RAF 4.9.43; ex NAASC - Arr Greece 27.3.47; No.335 Sqn at Sedes 4.47; Fate unknown

MH996 Spitfire F.IXc (Merlin 61); TOC/RAF 15.9.43; ex MAAF - Arr Greece 27.2.47; No.335 Sqn at Sedes 3.47; Fate unknown

GREECE

MJ292 Spitfire LF.IXc (Merlin 66); TOC/RAF 24.10.43; ex M.E. - Arr Greece 30.1.47; No.335 Sqn at Sedes 2.47; No.336 Sqn at Larisa; Fate unknown
MJ333 Spitfire LF.IXc (Merlin 66); TOC/RAF 24.10.43; ex M.E. - Arr Greece 31.7.47; Fate unknown
MJ391 Spitfire LF.IXc (Merlin 66); TOC/RAF 3.11.43; ex M.E. - Arr Greece 27.2.47; No.335 Sqn at Sedes 3.47; Crashed 29.9.48
MJ446 Spitfire LF.IXc (Merlin 66); TOC/RAF 5.11.43; ex MAAF - Arr Greece 27.2.47; No.335 Sqn at Sedes 3.47; No.336 Sqn at Larisa; Fate unknown
MJ468 Spitfire LF.IXc (Merlin 66); TOC/RAF 16.11.43; ex M.E. - Arr Greece 27.3.47; Fate unknown
MJ474 Spitfire LF.IXc (Merlin 66); TOC/RAF 30.11.43; ex MAAF - Arr Greece 30.1.47; No.335 Sqn at Sedes 2.47; Fate unknown
MJ507 Spitfire LF.IXc (Merlin 66); TOC/RAF 29.11.43; ex MAAF - Arr Greece 27.2.47; Fate unknown
MJ519 Spitfire LF.IXc (Merlin 66); TOC/RAF 22.11.43; ex MAAF - Arr Greece 27.3.47; No.337 Sqn at Elefsis 4.47; Fate unknown
MJ522 Spitfire LF.IXc (Merlin 66); TOC/RAF 2.12.43; ex MAAF - Arr Greece 30.1.47; No.335 Sqn at Sedes 12.47; Fate unknown
MJ556 Spitfire LF.XVIe (Merlin 266); TOC/RAF 4.5.45 - Arr Greece (via RAF Manston) 1.4.49; A/FTS (No.113 Wing) at Sedes; SOC 7.54
MJ577 Spitfire LF.IXc (Merlin 66); TOC/RAF 4.12.43; ex USAAF/MAAF - Arr Greece 29.5.47; No.335 Sqn at Sedes 6.47; Fate unknown
MJ725 Spitfire LF.IXc (Merlin 66); TOC/RAF 12.12.43; ex MAAF - Arr Greece 29.5.47; No.335 Sqn at Sedes 6.47; Crashed 26.2.48
MJ729 Spitfire LF.IXc (Merlin 66); TOC/RAF 16.12.43; ex MAAF - Arr Greece 30.4.47; Fate unknown
MJ755 Spitfire LF.IXc (Merlin 66); TOC/RAF 1.12.43 - Arr Greece 27.2.47; No.335 Sqn at Sedes 4.47; Later to SA (EKEX/Contract pilots training school) at Tatoi airbase, 1949; Overhaul 1950; Last flight 8.9.53; Storage at Hellenikon Airport 1953; To Tatoi airbase Dekelia in 1972 for display; To Hellenic War Museum, Athens, by 1985; To Hellenic Air Force Museum, Tatoi AFB in 1994 (painted "TA854" in 1995) - **SURVIVOR**
MJ839 Spitfire LF.IXc (Merlin 66); TOC/RAF 26.11.43; ex M.E. - Arr Greece 27.3.47; No.335 Sqn at Sedes 4.47; Fate unknown
MJ879 Spitfire LF.IXc (Merlin 66); TOC/RAF 28.12.43; ex MAAF - Arr Greece 30.1.47; Fate unknown
MJ935 Spitfire LF.IXc (Merlin 66); TOC/RAF 27.4.44; ex MAAF - Arr Greece 27.3.47; Fate unknown
MK357 Spitfire LF.IXc (Merlin 66); TOC/RAF 4.2.44; ex MAAF - Arr Greece 30.1.47; No.335 Sqn at Sedes 2.47; Fate unknown
MK361 Spitfire LF.IXc (Merlin 66); TOC/RAF 7.2.44; ex MAAF - Arr Greece 30.1.47; No.335 Sqn at Sedes 2.47; Fate unknown
MK483 Spitfire LF.IXc (Merlin 66); TOC/RAF 23.2.44; ex M.E. - Arr Greece 29.5.47; Fate unknown
MK532 Spitfire LF.IXc (Merlin 66); TOC/RAF 5.3.44; ex MAAF - Arr Greece 27.2.47; No.336 Sqn at Larisa 3.47; Fate unknown
MK571 Spitfire LF.IXc (Merlin 66); TOC/RAF 4.3.44; ex MAAF - Arr Greece 30.4.47; No.336 Sqn at Sedes 5.47; Later Larisa airbase from 2.49; Fate unknown
MK575 Spitfire LF.IXc (Merlin 66); TOC/RAF 12.3.44; ex M.E. (No.137 MU RAF) - Arr Greece 27.5.48; Fate unknown
MK693 Spitfire LF.IXc (Merlin 66); TOC/RAF 31.3.44; ex MAAF - Arr Greece 30.1.47; Fate unknown
MK719 Spitfire LF.IXc (Merlin 66); TOC/RAF 2.3.44; ex MAAF - Arr Greece 30.1.47; Fate unknown
MK746 Spitfire LF.IXc (Merlin 66); TOC/RAF 28.2.44; ex MAAF - Arr Greece 29.5.47; Fate unknown
MK864 Spitfire LF.IXc (Merlin 66); TOC/RAF 5.4.44; ex MAAF - Arr Greece 30.1.47; No.335 Sqn at Sedes 2.47; Fate unknown
MK981 Spitfire LF.IXc (Merlin 66); TOC/RAF 14.4.44; ex M.E. - Arr Greece 30.4.47; No.335 Sqn at Sedes 5.47; Fate unknown
MK991 Spitfire LF.IXc (Merlin 66); TOC/RAF 27.3.44; ex MAAF - Arr Greece 27.2.47; No.335 Sqn at Sedes 3.47; Fate unknown
ML124 Spitfire LF.IXc (Merlin 66); TOC/RAF 27.3.44; ex M.E. (No.137 MU RAF) - Arr Greece 10.6.48; Fate unknown
ML269 Spitfire LF.IXc (Merlin 66); TOC/RAF 19.4.44; ex MAAF - Arr Greece 27.4.47; No.335 Sqn at Sedes 5.47; Fate unknown
NH154 Spitfire LF.IXe (Merlin 66); TOC/RAF 26.4.44 - Arr Greece (via RAF Pershore) 31.3.48; No.335 Sqn at Sedes 4.48; Fate unknown
NH455 Spitfire LF.IXe (Merlin 66); TOC/RAF 20.5.44; ex MAAF - Arr Greece 27.3.47; No.335 Sqn at Sedes 4.47; Crashed 17.3.48
PL135 Spitfire LF.IXe (Merlin 66); TOC/RAF 17.6.44; ex MAAF - Arr Greece 27.2.47; No.335 Sqn at Sedes 3.47; No.337 Sqn at Elefsis 30.3.47; Fate unknown
PL158 Spitfire LF.IXe (Merlin 66); TOC/RAF 30.6.44; ex MAAF - Arr Greece 31.7.47; No.335 Sqn at Sedes 8.47; Fate unknown
PL211 Spitfire LF.IXe (Merlin 66); TOC/RAF 14.6.44; ex MAAF - Arr Greece 30.4.47; No.337 Sqn at Elefsis 5.47; Fate unknown
PL356 Spitfire LF.IXe (Merlin 66); TOC/RAF 29.7.44; ex MAAF - Arr Greece 30.1.47; Fate unknown
PL461 Spitfire LF.IXe (Merlin 66); TOC/RAF 1.7.44; ex MAAF - Arr Greece 27.2.47; Fate unknown
PT369 Spitfire LF.IXe (Merlin 66); TOC/RAF 20.7.44; ex MAAF - Arr Greece 27.3.47; No.335 Sqn at Sedes 4.47; Fate unknown
PT427 Spitfire LF.IXe (Merlin 66); TOC/RAF 17.7.44; ex MAAF - Arr Greece 27.3.47; No.335 Sqn at Sedes 4.47; Crashed 18.8.48; No.337 Sqn at Elefsis; Fate unknown
PT492 Spitfire LF.IXe (Merlin 66); TOC/RAF 22.7.44; ex MAAF - Arr Greece 30.4.47; Fate unknown
PT604 Spitfire LF.IXe (Merlin 66); TOC/RAF 28.7.44; MAAF (SOC/bboc), No.137 MU RAF 29.1.48 - Arr Greece 27.5.48; No.336 Sqn at Larisa 6.48; Fate unknown
PT617 Spitfire LF.IXe (Merlin 66); TOC/RAF 25.7.44; ex M.E. - Arr Greece 30.1.47; No.335 Sqn at Sedes 2.47; Fate unknown
PT660 Spitfire LF.IXe (Merlin 66); TOC/RAF 28.7.44; ex MAAF - Arr Greece 27.2.47; No.335 Sqn at Sedes 3.47; Possibly SOC in 1953 – NOTE: SOC reported for "560".
PT835 Spitfire HF.IXe (Merlin 70); TOC/RAF 17.8.44; ex M.E. - Arr Greece 30.1.47; Fate unknown
PT877 Spitfire LF.IXe, allotted for RHAF, but cancelled & SOC (RAF)
PT898 Spitfire LF.IXe (Merlin 66); TOC/RAF 27.8.44; ex MAAF - Arr Greece 27.2.47; Fate unknown
PT939 Spitfire LF.IXe (Merlin 66); TOC/RAF 27.8.44; ex MAAF - Arr Greece 27.2.47; No.336 Sqn at Larisa 3.47; Fate unknown
PT943 Spitfire LF.IXe (Merlin 66); TOC/RAF 26.8.44; ex MAAF - Arr Greece 30.4.47; No.337 Sqn at Elefsis 5.47; Fate unknown
PV118 Spitfire LF.IXe (Merlin 66); TOC/RAF 28.7.44; ex MAAF - Arr Greece 29.5.47; Fate unknown
PV119 Spitfire LF.IXe (Merlin 66); TOC/RAF 1.8.44; ex MAAF (No.137.MU RAF) - Arr Greece 27.5.48; Fate unknown
PV301 Spitfire LF.IXe (Merlin 66); TOC/RAF 26.9.44; ex MAAF - Arr Greece 31.7.47; No.337 Sqn at Elefsis 8.47; Fate unknown
PV324 Spitfire HF.IXe (Merlin 70); TOC/RAF 28.9.44; ex MAAF - Arr Greece 27.3.47; Fate unknown
PV325 Spitfire LF.IXe (Merlin 66); TOC/RAF 30.9.44; ex MAAF - Arr Greece 27.3.47; Fate unknown
PV349 Spitfire LF.XVIe (Merlin 266); TOC/RAF 3.10.44 - Arr Greece (via RAF Manston) 14.5.49; No.335 Sqn at Sedes 5.49; Fate unknown

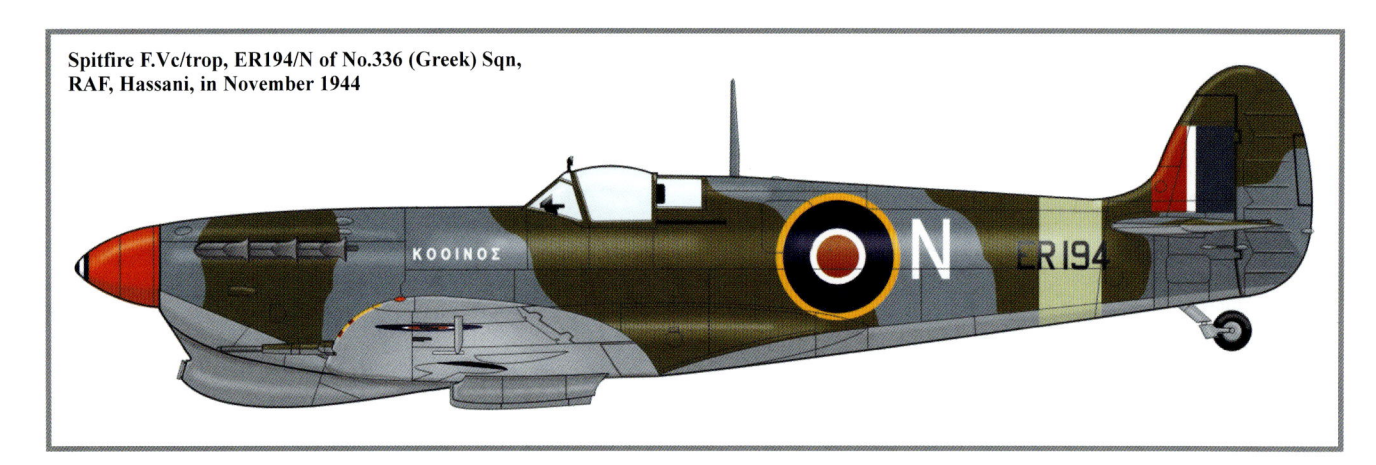

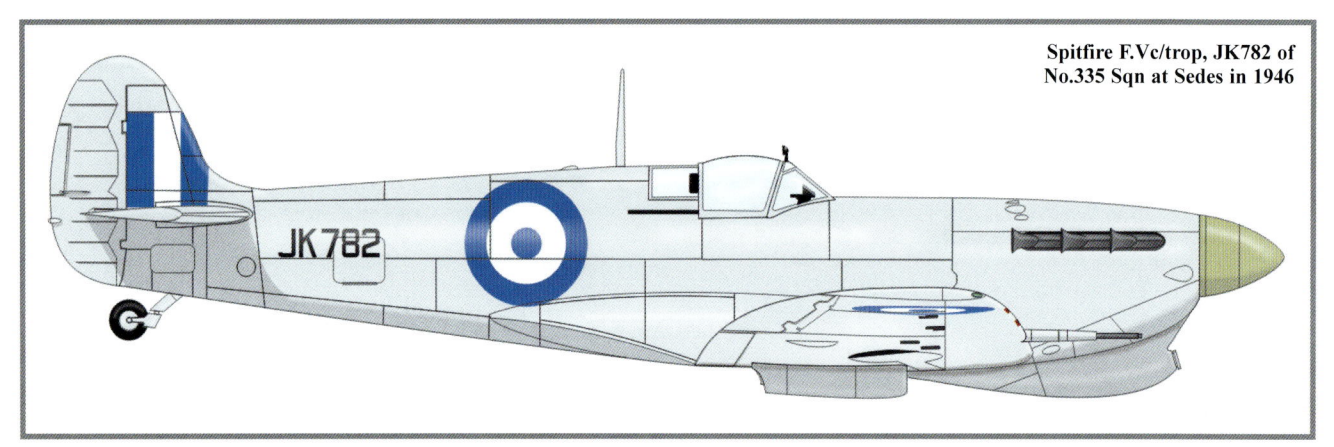

Spitfire F.Vc/trop, ER194/N of No.336 (Greek) Sqn, RAF, Hassani, in November 1944

Spitfire F.Vc/trop, JK782 of No.335 Sqn at Sedes in 1946

PV356 Spitfire LF.IXe (Merlin 66); TOC/RAF 30.9.44; ex MAAF; Allotted for Egypt, but via No.137 MU RAF to RHAF - Arr Greece 27.5.48; Fate unknown

RK856 Spitfire LF.IXe (Merlin 66); TOC/RAF 2.10.44; ex MAAF - Arr Greece 30.1.47; No.335 Sqn at Sedes 2.47; Possibly crashed at Elefsis 23.12.47. NOTE: Crash reported for "586"

RR192 Spitfire LF.IXe (Merlin 66); TOC/RAF 5.9.44; ex M.E. - Arr Greece 30.4.47; No.335 Sqn at Sedes 5.47; Crashed 10.9.48

RR193 Spitfire LF.IXe (Merlin 66); TOC/RAF 11.10.44; ex M.E. - Arr Greece 31.7.47; No.335 Sqn at Sedes 8.47; Fate unknown

RR197 Spitfire LF.IXe (Merlin 66); TOC/RAF 16.9.44; ex M.E. - Arr Greece 27.3.47; Fate unknown

RR203 Spitfire LF.IXe (Merlin 66); TOC/RAF 27.9.44; ex MAAF - Arr Greece 27.2.47; No.335 Sqn at Sedes 3.47; Fate unknown

RR207 Spitfire LF.IXe (Merlin 66); TOC/RAF 12.10.44; ex M.E. - Arr Greece 27.2.47; No.335 Sqn at Sedes 3.47; Fate unknown

RW347 Spitfire LF.XVIe (Merlin 266); TOC/RAF 29.6.45 - Arr Greece (via RAF Manston) 30.4.49; No.335 Sqn at Sedes 5.49; Fate unknown

RW353 Spitfire LF.XVIe (Merlin 266); TOC/RAF 30.6.45 - Arr Greece (via RAF Manston) 14.5.49; Fate unknown

RW354 Spitfire LF.XVIe (Merlin 266); TOC/RAF 24.7.45 - Arr Greece (via RAF Manston) 21.1.49; Fate unknown

RW379 Spitfire LF.XVIe (Merlin 266); TOC/RAF 30.6.45 - Arr Greece (via RAF Manston) 14.4.49; Fate unknown

RW380 Spitfire LF.XVIe (Merlin 266); TOC/RAF 14.8.45 - Arr Greece 21.8.49; A/FTS (No.113 Wing) at Sedes ('2'); SOC 7.54

SL555 Spitfire LF.XVIe (Merlin 266); TOC/RAF 27.7.45 - Arr Greece 2.7.49; Fate unknown

SL573 Spitfire LF.XVIe (Merlin 266); TOC/RAF 15.10.45; Allotted for RHAF 31.1.49 - Arr Greece (via RAF Manston) 9.2.49; Fate unknown

SL608 Spitfire LF.XVIe (Merlin 266); TOC/RAF 31.8.45; Allotted for RHAF 17.3.49 - Arr Greece (via RAF Manston) 30.4.49; Fate unknown

SL623 Spitfire LF.XVIe (Merlin 266); TOC/RAF 8.8.45 - Desp. 8.4.49, ROS; Arr Greece 21.6.49; Fate unknown

SL624 Spitfire LF.XVIe (Merlin 266); TOC/RAF 2.8.45 - Arr Greece 13.7.49; No.337 Sqn; A/FTS (No.113 Wing) at Sedes ('3'); SOC 7.54

SL679 Spitfire LF.XVIe (Merlin 266); TOC/RAF 1.10.45 - Arr Greece 9.2.49; Fate unknown

SL717 Spitfire LF.XVIe (Merlin 266); TOC/RAF 8.8.45; Allotted for RHAF 12.8.49 - Arr Greece (via RAF Manston) 21.8.49; Port oleo collapsed on landing (no date); Fate unknown

SL728 Spitfire LF.XVIe (Merlin 266); TOC/RAF 23.8.45; Allotted for RHAF 28.7.49 - Arr Greece (via RAF Manston) 6.8.49; Fate unknown

SM135 Spitfire LF.IXe (Merlin 66); TOC/RAF 18.9.44; ex M.E. - Arr Greece 30.4.47; No.335 Sqn at Sedes 5.47; No.337 Sqn at Elefsis; Fate unknown

SM172 Spitfire LF.IXe (Merlin 66); TOC/RAF 2.10.44; ex M.E. - Arr Greece 25.9.47; No.335 Sqn at Sedes 10.47; Fate unknown

SM175 Spitfire LF.IXe (Merlin 66); TOC/RAF 9.10.44; ex M.E. - Arr Greece 29.5.47; No.335 Sqn at Sedes 6.47; Fate unknown

SM194 Spitfire LF.XVIe (Merlin 266); TOC/RAF 28.10.44; Allotted for RHAF 30.12.48 - Arr Greece (via RAF Manston) 5.3.49; Fate unknown

SM342 Spitfire LF.XVIe (Merlin 266); TOC/RAF 9.11.44; Allotted for RHAF 18.7.49 - Arr Greece (via RAF Manston) 22.7.49; No.335 Sqn at Sedes 7.49; Fate unknown

SM358 Spitfire LF.XVIe (Merlin 266); TOC/RAF 15.11.44 - Arr Greece (via RAF Manston) 21.6.49; Fate unknown

SM421 Spitfire LF.XVIe (Merlin 266); TOC/RAF 15.11.44; Allotted for RHAF 28.7.49 - Arr Greece (via RAF Manston) 6.8.49; No.337 Sqn at Elefsis 8.49; Fate unknown

SM503 Spitfire LF.XVIe (Merlin 266); TOC/RAF 30.11.44, Allotted for RHAF 22.7.49 - Arr Greece (via RAF Manston) 6.8.49; Fate unknown

TA759 Spitfire LF.XVIe (Merlin 266); TOC/RAF 9.2.45; Allotted for RHAF 3.5.49 - Arr Greece (via RAF Manston)

TA816 Spitfire HF.IXe (Merlin 70); TOC/RAF 11.12.44; ex M.E. - Arr Greece 30.4.47; No.335 Sqn at Sedes 30.4.47; Crashed 2.12.48

TA823 Spitfire LF.IXe (Merlin 66); TOC/RAF 23.9.44; ex MAAF (No.137.MU RAF) - Arr Greece 27.5.48; No.335 Sqn at Sedes 6.48; Fate unknown

TA854 Spitfire LF.IXe (Merlin 66); TOC/RAF 3.10.44; ex MAAF - Arr Greece 27.2.47; No.335 Sqn at Sedes 3.47; Fate unknown NOTE: MJ755, the Survivor at the Hellenic War Museum Athens was painted as "TA854" in 1995

TA859 Spitfire LF.IXe (Merlin 66); TOC/RAF 3.10.44; ex MAAF - Arr Greece 29.5.47; No.335 Sqn at Sedes 6.47; Possibly crashed 14.1.49. NOTE: Crash reported for "869"

TA863 Spitfire LF.IXe (Merlin 66); TOC/RAF 7.10.44; ex M.E. - Arr Greece 29.5.47; No.335 Sqn at Sedes 6.47; Fate unknown

TB130 Spitfire LF.XVIe (Merlin 266); TOC/RAF 30.12.44; Allotted for RHAF 8.4.49 - Arr Greece (via RAF Manston) 30.4.49; A/FTS (No.113 Wing) at Sedes ('4'); SOC 7.54

TB232 Spitfire LF.XVIe (Merlin 266); TOC/RAF 30.12.44; Allotted for RHAF 25.2.49 - Arr Greece (via RAF Manston) 20.3.49; A/FTS (No.113 Wing) at Sedes ('5'); SOC 7.54

TB237 Spitfire LF.XVIe (Merlin 266); TOC/RAF 4.1.45; Allotted for RHAF 30.12.48 - Arr Greece (via RAF Manston) 9.2.49; Fate unknown

TB254 Spitfire LF.XVIe (Merlin 266); TOC/RAF 30.12.44; Allotted for RHAF 26.7.49 - Arr Greece (via RAF Manston) 6.8.49; Fate unknown

TB255 Spitfire LF.XVIe (Merlin 266); TOC/RAF 30.12.44; Allotted for RHAF 20.4.49 - Arr Greece (via RAF Manston) 30.4.49; Fate unknown

TB272 Spitfire LF.XVIe (Merlin 266); TOC/RAF 5.1.45; Allotted for RHAF 15.2.49 - Arr Greece (via RAF Manston) 7.3.49; Fate unknown

TB274 Spitfire LF.XVIe (Merlin 266); TOC/RAF 5.1.45; Allotted for RHAF 4.4.49 - Arr Greece 15.4.49; No.335 Sqn at Sedes 4.49; Crashed 13.8.49

TB340 Spitfire LF.XVIe (Merlin 266); TOC/RAF 7.1.45 - Arr Greece 2.7.49; Fate unknown

TB539 Spitfire LF.IXe (Merlin 66); TOC/RAF 1.2.45; ex MAAF (No.137 MU RAF, conv. HF IX to LF IX 29.1.48) - Arr Greece 27.5.48; No.336 Sqn 6.48; Crashed at Larisa 3.4.49; SOC 1954

TB545 Spitfire LF.IXe (Merlin 66); TOC/RAF 14.2.45; ex MAAF (No.137 MU RAF, conv. HF IX to LF IX 29.1.48) - Arr Greece 27.5.48; No.335 Sqn at Sedes 6.48; Fate unknown

TB577 Spitfire LF.IXe (Merlin 66); TOC/RAF 13.2.45; ex MAAF (No.137 MU RAF, conv. HF IX to LF IX 29.1.48) - Arr Greece 27.5.48; No.335 Sqn at Sedes 6.48; Fate unknown

TB616 Spitfire LF.XVIe (Merlin 266); TOC/RAF 28.1.45; Allotted for RHAF 21.7.49 - Arr Greece 28.7.49; Fate unknown

TB619 Spitfire LF.XVIe (Merlin 266); TOC/RAF 19.2.45; Allotted for RHAF 3.5.49 - Arr Greece (via RAF Manston) 11.5.49; No.335 Sqn at Sedes 5.49; Fate unknown

TB626 Spitfire LF.XVIe (Merlin 266); TOC/RAF 4.2.45; Allotted for RHAF 4.7.49 - Arr Greece 22.7.49; No.335 Sqn at Sedes; Fate unknown

TB859 Spitfire LF.XVIe (Merlin 266); TOC/RAF 24.2.45; Allotted for RHAF 30.12.48 - Arr Greece (via RAF Manston) 21.1.49; No.335 Sqn at Sedes 1.49; Fate unknown

TB886 Spitfire LF.XVIe (Merlin 266); TOC/RAF 15.3.45 - Arr Greece 22.7.49; Fate unknown

TB895 Spitfire LF.XVIe (Merlin 266); TOC/RAF 25.2.45 - Arr Greece 2.7.49; No.335 Sqn at Sedes 2.7.49; Fate unknown

TB901 Spitfire LF.XVIe (Merlin 266); TOC/RAF 17.3.45; Allotted for RHAF 16.2.49 - Arr Greece (via RAF Manston) 7.3.49; Fate unknown

TB908 Spitfire LF.XVIe (Merlin 266); TOC/RAF 28.2.45; Allotted for RHAF 8.4.49 - Arr Greece (via RAF Manston) 15.4.49; Fate unknown

TD114 Spitfire LF.XVIe (Merlin 266); TOC/RAF 1.3.45; Allotted for RHAF 18.7.49 - Arr Greece (via RAF Manston) 22.7.49; Fate unknown

TD126 Spitfire LF.XVIe (Merlin 266); TOC/RAF 10.3.45; Allotted for RHAF 30.12.48 - Arr Greece (via RAF Manston) 30.1.49; Fate unknown

TD133 Spitfire LF.XVIe (Merlin 266); TOC/RAF 20.3.45; Allotted for RHAF 25.2.49 - Arr Greece (via RAF Manston) 26.3.49; A/FTS (No.113 Wing) at Sedes ('7'); SOC 7.54

TD137 Spitfire LF.XVIe (Merlin 266); TOC/RAF 15.3.45 - Arr Greece 13.7.49; Fate unknown

TD141 Spitfire LF.XVIe (Merlin 266); TOC/RAF 9.3.45; Allotted for RHAF 10.2.49 - Arr Greece (via RAF Manston) 20.3.49; Fate unknown

TD145 Spitfire LF.XVIe (Merlin 266); TOC/RAF 8.3.45; Allotted for RHAF 10.2.49 - Arr Greece (via RAF Manston) 8.6.49; Fate unknown

TD147 Spitfire LF.XVIe (Merlin 266); TOC/RAF 10.3.45; Allotted for RHAF 2.5.49 - Arr Greece (via RAF Manston) 8.6.49; Fate unknown

TD176 Spitfire LF.XVIe (Merlin 266); TOC/RAF 10.3.45; Allotted for RHAF 18.2.49 - Arr Greece (via RAF Manston) 5.3.49; A/FTS (No.113 Wing) at Sedes ('8'); SOC 7.54

TD190 Spitfire LF.XVIe (Merlin 266); TOC/RAF 24.3.45 - Arr Greece 2.7.49; Fate unknown

TD191 Spitfire LF.XVIe (Merlin 266); TOC/RAF 23.3.45; Allotted for RHAF 29.10.48 - Arr Greece (via RAF Manston) 11.12.48; Fate unknown

TD229 Spitfire LF.XVIe (Merlin 266); TOC/RAF 23.3.45; Allotted for RHAF 18.1.49 - Arr Greece (via RAF Manston) 30.1.49; Fate unknown

TD235 Spitfire LF.XVIe (Merlin 266); TOC/RAF 26.3.45; Allotted for RHAF 15.3.49 - Arr Greece (via RAF Manston) 14.4.49; No.335 Sqn at Sedes 4.49; Fate unknown

A Spitfire LF.XVIe, probably TD350, with bomb racks and fittings for rocket rails under the wings. This aircraft was serving with No.336 Sqn at Larisa in 1949.
[Hellenic Air Force]

Surviving Spitfire LF.IXc MJ755 of the RHAF at Tatoi air base in 1970. After restoration it was exhibited there in the Hellenic Air Force Museum. [MAP]

Surviving Spitfire LF.IXc MJ755 painted up as "TA854" in the Hellenic Air Force Museum at Tatoi. [D Vogiatzis]

TD239 Spitfire LF.XVIe (Merlin 266); TOC/RAF 27.3.45; Allotted for RHAF 30.12.48 - Arr Greece (via RAF Manston) 21.1.49; Fate unknown

TD241 Spitfire LF.XVIe (Merlin 266); TOC/RAF 30.3.45; Allotted for RHAF 30.12.48 - Arr Greece (via RAF Manston) 21.1.49; Fate unknown

TD243 Spitfire LF.XVIe (Merlin 266); TOC/RAF 21.4.45; Allotted for RHAF 15.2.49 - Arr Greece (via RAF Manston) 7.3.49; Fate unknown

TD246 Spitfire LF.XVIe (Merlin 266); TOC/RAF 4.4.45; Allotted for RHAF 22.2.49 - Arr Greece (via RAF Manston) 11.4.49; Fate unknown

TD285 Spitfire LF.XVIe (Merlin 266); TOC/RAF 23.3.45; Allotted for RHAF 3.3.49 - Arr Greece (via RAF Manston) 15.4.49; No.335 Sqn at Sedes 4.49; A/FTS (No.113 Wing) at Sedes; SOC 7.54

TD320 Spitfire LF.XVIe (Merlin 266); TOC/RAF 20.4.45; Allotted for RHAF 30.12.48 - Arr Greece (via RAF Manston) 21.1.49; No.337 Sqn at Elefsis 1.49; Fate unknown

TD342 Spitfire LF.XVIe (Merlin 266); TOC/RAF 21.4.45; Allotted for RHAF 11.3.49 - Arr Greece (via RAF Manston) 26.3.49; No.335 Sqn at Sedes 4.49; Fate unknown

TD349 Spitfire LF.XVIe (Merlin 266); TOC/RAF 20.4.45; Allotted for RHAF 8.4.49 - Arr Greece (via RAF Manston) 15.4.49; No.335 Sqn at Sedes 4.49; A/FTS (No.113 Wing) at Sedes ('9'); SOC 7.54

TD350 Spitfire LF.XVIe (Merlin 266); TOC/RAF 17.4.45 - Arr Greece (via RAF Manston) 16.6.49; No.336 Sqn at Larisa 6.49; Fate unknown

TD351 Spitfire LF.XVIe (Merlin 266); TOC/RAF 19.4.45; Allotted for RHAF 18.7.49 - Arr Greece (via RAF Manston) 22.7.49; Fate unknown

TD376 Spitfire LF.XVIe (Merlin 266); TOC/RAF 11.4.45; Allotted for RHAF 21.7.49 - Arr Greece (via RAF Manston) 28.7.49; Fate unknown

TD404 Spitfire LF.XVIe (Merlin 266); TOC/RAF 16.5.45;

Allotted for RHAF 6.5.49 - Arr Greece (via RAF Manston) 14.5.49; Fate unknown
TE191 Spitfire LF.XVIe (Merlin 266); TOC/RAF 18.4.45; Allotted for RHAF 16.2.49 - Arr Greece (via RAF Manston) 7.3.49; Fate unknown
TE235 Spitfire LF.XVIe (Merlin 266); TOC/RAF 30.4.45; Allotted for RHAF 31.5.49 - Arr Greece (via RAF Manston) 16.6.49; No.335 Sqn at Sedes 6.49; Fate unknown
TE245 Spitfire LF.XVIe (Merlin 266); TOC/RAF 30.4.45; Allotted for RHAF 31.5.49 - Arr Greece (via RAF Manston) 16.6.49; Fate unknown
TE249 Spitfire LF.XVIe (Merlin 266); TOC/RAF 1.5.45; Allotted for RHAF 8.4.49 - Arr Greece (via RAF Manston) 30.4.49; Fate unknown
TE252 Spitfire LF.XVIe (Merlin 266); TOC/RAF 1.6.45; Allotted for RHAF 31.5.49 - Arr Greece (via RAF Manston) 16.6.49; No.335 Sqn at Sedes 6.49; Fate unknown
TE276 Spitfire LF.XVIe (Merlin 266); TOC/RAF 16.5.45; Allotted for RHAF 17.11.48 - Arr Greece (via RAF Manston) 9.12.48; A/FTS (No.113 Wing) at Sedes ('10'); SOC 7.54
TE284 Spitfire LF.XVIe (Merlin 266); TOC/RAF 2.6.45; Allotted for RHAF 16.2.49 - Arr Greece (via RAF Manston) 5.3.49; Fate unknown
TE346 Spitfire LF.XVIe (Merlin 266); TOC/RAF 20.4.45; Allotted for RHAF 17.11.48 - Arr Greece (via RAF Manston) 9.12.48; Fate unknown
TE350 Spitfire LF.XVIe (Merlin 266); TOC/RAF 12.6.45; Allotted for RHAF 4.11.48 - Arr Greece (via RAF Manston) 11.12.48; No.336 Sqn at Larisa 12.48; Fate unknown
TE381 Spitfire LF.XVIe (Merlin 266); TOC/RAF 15.6.45; Allotted for RHAF 4.11.48 - Arr Greece (via RAF Manston) 11.12.48; No.337 Sqn at Elefsis 12.48; Fate unknown
TE382 Spitfire LF.XVIe (Merlin 266); TOC/RAF 16.6.45; Allotted for RHAF 12.8.49 - Arr Greece (via RAF Manston) 21.8.49; SA (EKEX/Contract pilots training school) at Tatoi airbase; A/FTS (No.113 Wing) at Sedes ('11'); SOC 8.53
TE383 Spitfire LF.XVIe (Merlin 266); TOC/RAF 16.6.45; Allotted for RHAF 17.11.48 - Arr Greece (via RAF Manston) 9.12.48; No.335 Sqn at Sedes; Fate unknown
TE391 Spitfire LF.XVIe (Merlin 266); TOC/RAF 8.8.45; Allotted for RHAF 12.8.49 - Arr Greece (via RAF Manston) 21.8.49; No.335 Sqn at Sedes 8.49; Fate unknown
TE447 Spitfire LF.XVIe (Merlin 266); TOC/RAF 22.6.45; Allotted for RHAF 28.7.49 - Arr Greece (via RAF Manston) 6.8.49; Fate unknown
TE468 Spitfire LF.XVIe (Merlin 266); TOC/RAF 26.6.45; Allotted for RHAF 31.1.49 - Arr Greece (via RAF Manston) 9.2.49; A/FTS (No.113 Wing) at Sedes ('12'); SOC 6.53s

SURVIVOR

Only one Spitfire LF.IXc has survived in Greece, MJ755, exhibited at the Dekelia Air Force Base, Tatoi, Athens.

Remarks:
During Operation *Velveta I*, the delivery of Czech Spitfires to Israel in September 1948, two Spitfires were forced to land in Rhodes, and the Greeks refused to release them until 1950. Only one eventually arrived in Israel, the other having crashed at Rhodes while being test flown in 1950.

HONG KONG

The Hong Kong Auxiliary Air Force (HKAAF) was formed on 1st May 1949. It became the Royal Hong Kong Auxiliary Air Force in 1951, eventually being restyled the Hong Kong Government Flying Service on 1st April 1993.

A Hong Kong Auxiliary Flight was formed at Kai Tak in October 1949. On 1st October 1950 it became the Hong Kong Auxiliary Squadron and four Harvards were added. In April-May 1952 it received eight Spitfire F.24s from FEAF stocks, and two PR.XIXs joined this unit in 1954. The Hong Kong (Auxiliary Air Force) Wing was formed on 24th November 1953 to control the Hong Kong (Fighter) Squadron, the Hong Kong Fighter Control Unit and the Hong Kong Air Traffic Control Centre. The Hong Kong Fighter Squadron flew Spitfires until early 1955 when they were withdrawn.

Commanding Officer:
S/Ldr EJ Gauntlett by December 1953 [killed 12 June 1954]

Individual Histories

PK687 Spitfire F.24 (Griffon 61); TOC/RAF 19.10.46; FEAF 28.3.50; No.80 Sqn 5.9.51 - HKAAF 15.5.52; Service unknown; SOC (Cat.5S) 11.12.53
PK719 Spitfire F.24 (Griffon 61); TOC/RAF 28.9.46; FEAF 28.3.50; No.80 Sqn 20.9.50 - HKAAF 15.5.52; Engine cut during "live" attack on ground target, pulled out sharply from dive and climbed to 1,500ft then stalled and dived vertically into sea off Shelter Island, Cat.5S (dest) 12.6.54 (S/Ldr EJ Gauntlett killed), SOC
PK720 Spitfire F.24 (Griffon 61); TOC/RAF 30.9.46; FEAF 28.3.50; No.80 Sqn 20.7.50 - HKAAF 15.5.52; Engine cut, ditched just short of runway on approach, Kai Tak, Cat.5S (dest) 16.8.53 (F/O HL Mose unhurt), SOC
PS852 Spitfire PR.XIX (Griffon 66); TOC/RAF 9.1.45; FEAF; No.81 Sqn 3.1.51 - HKAAF 25.3.54; In Queen's Birthday Flypast together with PS854, VN318 & VN485 on 21.4.55; Belly-landed Cat.5 on 21.4.55, SOC
PS854 Spitfire PR.XIX (Griffon 66); TOC/RAF 14.1.45; FEAF 23.12.50; No.81 Sqn 3.1.51 - HKAAF 6.8.54; In Queen's Birthday Flypast together with PS852, VN318 & VN485 on 21.4.55; Storage from 1.7.55; SOC 16.9.55

Spitfire PR.XIX PS852 of the Hong Kong Auxiliary Air Force taxying, around 1954/55. [via G Cairns]

Spitfire PR.XIX PS852 of the HKAAF in flight near Hong Kong, around 1954/55. [via G Cairns]

Surviving Spitfire F.24 VN485 of the Hong Kong Auxiliary Air Force in 1954 during the annual camp at Sek Kong. In August 1989 it arrived in the UK on loan to the Imperial War Museum, Duxford, for display. [via G Cairns]

HONG KONG

Spitfire F.24 VN492 'N' of the Hong Kong Auxiliary Air Force, seen on 3rd October 1953 after it swung to port while landing at Sek Kong and went off the runway. The port wheel struck a drainage ditch, the starboard undercarriage was damaged and the aircraft tipped up on its nose; the pilot, Plt Off Rufus 'Red' Heard, fortunately being unhurt. [via G Cairns]

Spitfire F.24 VN318 'E' and others of the Hong Kong Auxiliary Air Force at Kai Tak in 1955. [RAF Museum P7419]

Spitfire F.24, VN318/E of the Hong Kong Auxiliary AF in 1955

SM844   Spitfire FR.XVIIIe (Griffon 66); TOC/RAF 28.5.45; FEAF 19.7.50; No.28 Sqn; SHQ (STG'E) Reinforcement plan 26.2.51 - HKAAF 18.3.51; Cat.5(Comp) 14.11.52, SOC
TP277   Spitfire FR.XVIIIe (Griffon 65); TOC/RAF 18.6.45; FEAF 5.3.50; No.28 Sqn 21.4.50; SHQ (STG'E) Reinforcement plan 26.2.51 - HKAAF 31.3.51; SOC 14.11.52
TP423   Spitfire FR.XVIIIe (Griffon 65); TOC/RAF 11.7.45; FEAF; No.28 Sqn 24.5.50; SHQ (STG'E) Reinforcement plan 16.2.51- HKAAF 16.2.51; SOC 14.11.52
TP431   Spitfire FR.XVIIIe (Griffon 65); TOC/RAF 23.8.45; FEAF; No.28 Sqn 15.8.49; SHQ (STG'E) Reinforcement plan 26.2.51 - HKAAF 16.2.51; SOC 14.11.52
TP434   Spitfire FR.XVIIIe (Griffon 65); TOC/RAF 21.8.45; FEAF; No.28 Sqn; SHQ (STG'E) Reinforcement plan 26.2.51 - HKAAF 26.5.51; SOC 14.11. or 16.11.52
VN308   Spitfire F.24 (Griffon 61); TOC/RAF 26.4.46; No.80 Sqn 15.1.48; FEAF 2.7.49 - HKAAF 15.5.52; Swung after landing cross-wind, undercarriage collapsed, Cat.3R (subs) 15.6.52 (P/O YCD Chen unhurt); FEAF DA/C 16.6.52 - HKAAF 1.2.53; SOC (Cat.5) 11.12.53
VN313   Spitfire F.24 (Griffon 61); TOC/RAF 28.2.46; No.80 Sqn 10.6.49; FEAF 2.7.49 - HKAAF ('M') 15.5.52; Swung to port on landing, port wing hit building, undercarriage collapsed at Sek Kong, Cat.5S (dest) 3.10.53 (P/O G Bain unhurt), SOC
VN318   Spitfire F.24 (Griffon 61); TOC/RAF (Farnborough) 7.46; No.80 Sqn ('W2-F') 23.2.48; FEAF - HKAAF ('E') 1.4.52; Hood disintegrated in flight during dive at 320 knots and struck pilot on forehead, substantial damage to top of fuselage and empennage, normal landing at base, Cat.1 13.12.53 (S/Ldr EJ Gauntlett slightly injured); In Queen's Birthday Flypast together with PS852, PS854 & VN485 on 21.4.55; SOC (WFU) 21.4.55
VN485   Spitfire F.24 (Griffon 61); TOC/RAF 4.9.47 (air tests by No.9 MU before shipment to Hong Kong 23./26.6.49; Wrong type of magneto; Ready for delivery 27.6.49; FEAF 3.10.50; No.80 Sqn ('W2-A', later 'W2-M') 30.9.51 - HKAAF 13.5.52; Engine failed at 35,000ft, force landed downwind, undershot, Cat.2 (subs) 16.1.54 (F/Lt B McConville OK); Farewell flight 15.1.55; In Queen's Birthday Flypast together with PS852, PS854 & VN318 on 21.4.55 (F/Lt Adrian Rowe-Evans); Storage Kai Tak 31.7.55; SOC 30.9.55 (242 flying hours); Converted to GI No. *7326M* on 10.4.56; Retained and preserved by HKAAF (RHKAAF); Issued for exhibition at Science and Space Museum, Kai Tak 30.9.56 ("DW-X"); Arr in UK on loan to Imperial War Museum, Duxford 18.7.89 for display - **SURVIVOR**
VN492   Spitfire F.24 (Griffon 61); TOC/RAF 23.12.47 (air tests by No.9 MU before shipment to Hong Kong 21.6.49; Wrong type of magneto; Ready for delivery 27.6.49; FEAF 3.10.50; No.80 Sqn 1.2.51 - HKAAF ('N') 15.5.52; Swung to port on landing, went off runway, port wheel struck drainage ditch, std undercarriage damaged, tipped up, Sek Kong, Cat.3 (subs) 3.10.53 (P/O R Heard unhurt); FEAF DA/C 3.10.53; DBR; SOC 19.7.54

SURVIVOR

Spitfire F.24 (VN485), Kai Tak Museum, loaned to IWM Duxford, UK for display.

INDIA

India was part of the British Commonwealth. During the Second World War squadrons and units of the Indian Air Force operated under the overall control of RAF India Command. Initially equipped with such types as the Westland Wapiti, Hawker Hart and Westland Lysander, they later progressed to Hawker Hurricanes and Vultee Vengeances. These in turn gave way to Spitfire Mk.VIIIs and later XIVs. The first to receive the former was No.8 Squadron in October 1944, though most squadrons did not re-equip until June 1945 onwards, the aircraft remaining on RAF charge.

In 1945 Indian squadrons equipped with Spitfires were Nos.1 to 4, 6 to 10 and 12, all with LF.VIIIc, but some converted to Mk.XIV in 1945/46.

RAF based in India with Spitfires

No.11   Sqn - No unit code, only individual letter;
         Chettinad, Madura, Spitfire Mk.XIV from June 1945 to September 1945.
No.17   Sqn - unit code: 'YB';
         Sapam & Palel with Mk.VIII from November 1944 to December 1944,
         and Mk.XIV at Madura from June 1945 to September 1945.
No.34   Sqn (ex No.681 Sqn) - No unit code, only individual letter;
         Palam & Kohat with PR.XIX from August 1946 to July 1947.
No.67   Sqn - unit code: 'RD';
         Alipore, Amarda Road, Baigachi, Comilla and Double-Moorings with Mk.VIII from February 1944 to December 1944.
No.81   Sqn - unit code: 'FL';
         Alipore, Imphal, Tulihal, Ramu, Kangla, Kumbhirgram and Amarda Road with Mk.VIII from December 1943 to August 1944 and April 1945 to June 1945.
No.131   Sqn - unit code: 'NX';
         Amarda Road & Dalbumgarh, Mk.VIII from February 1945 to June 1945.
No.132   Sqn - unit code: 'FF';
         Madura with Mk.XIV from June 1945 to August 1945.
No.136   Sqn - unit code: 'HM';
         Sapam, Wangjing and Chittagong with Mk.VIII from March 1944 to June 1944.
No.152   Sqn - unit code: 'UM';
         Baigachi, Double-Moorings, Chittagong, Comilla, Palel, Imphal and Tulihal with Mk.VIII from December 1943 to 1944.
No.155   Sqn - unit code: 'DG';
         Alipore, Baigachi, Kalyanpur, Palel, Sapam and Tulihal with Mk.VIII from January 1944 to January 1945.
No.273   Sqn - unit code: 'MS';
         Chittagong & Coxs Bazaar, Mk.VIII from July 1944 to December 1944.
No.607   Sqn - unit code: 'AF';
         Wangjing, Imphal, Baigachi, Sapam and Tulihal with Mk.VIII from April 1944 to January 1945.
No.615   Sqn - unit code: 'KW';
         Palel, Baigachi, Nidania, Charra, Chakulia and Cuttack with Mk.VIII from June 1944 to June 1945.
No.681   Sqn - No unit code, only individual letter;
         Chandina, Dum Dum and Alipore (dets.) with PR.XI from September 1943 to May 1945, also with PR.XIX at Palam May 1946 to July 1946.

INDIA

From January 1944, RAF units in the Far East were controlled by HQ Air Command South East Asia (ACSEA), this becoming HQ Air Command, Far East on 30th September 1946.

In June 1945 Nos. 81, 131 and 615 Sqns were disbanded and their Spitfire Mk.VIIIs went to the RIAF on loan, as did those of No.17 Sqn which re-equipped with Mk.XIVs at that time. When other squadrons disbanded their aircraft went back into storage at various Maintenance Units, some being subsequently issued to RIAF units and the remainder gradually scrapped. No.681 Sqn was re-numbered on 1st August 1946 to become No.34 Sqn, its PR.XIs being handed over to the RIAF, but its PR.XIXs were retained, these being scrapped when No.34 Sqn disbanded a year later instead of being handed over to the RIAF.

Note: Ceylon now Sri Lanka; East Pakistan now Bangladesh; West Pakistan now Pakistan

Indian Air Force

In March 1945 the designation *Royal Indian Air Force* (RIAF) was approved. On being granted independence on 15th August 1947, the sub-continent was split to create India and Pakistan. India then began to build up its own Air Force, officially taking over Spitfires from the RAF inventory with effect from 29/31 December 1947.

When India became a Republic on 31st December 1949 the name reverted to the *Indian Air Force* (IAF), though by that time the Spitfire had largely given way to the Hawker Tempest.

Spitfire deliveries to the R.I.A.F. from August 1947

29.12.47	14 LF.VIIIc	No RIAF Serial Nos
29/31.12.47	20 F/FR.XIVe	HS351 - HS370 (²)
29/31.12.47	58 F/FR.XVIIIe	HS649 - HS986 range
mid 1949	42 F/FR.XVIIIe	HS649 - HS986 range
31.12.47	1 PR.XI	GI No. *M342*
3.6-15.11.48	10 T.IX	HS534 - HS543
2-6.49	13 PR.XIX	HS693 - HS705
1953	1 PR.XIX	HS964
Total:	159 aircraft	

Notes:
(1) Spitfire T.IX delivered direct from Vickers to India.
(2) Mk.XIV, Serial numbers allotted, but not painted on aircraft. Mk.VIII & XIV retained the RAF serial number.
(3) Mk.XVIIIe were numbered in the range HS649 to HS986, but this included other types of aircraft.
(4) The batch of Mk.XIXs numbered HS693 to HS705 were almost certainly test flown initially with Class B registrations in the range G-15-63 to G-15-75.

Spitfire units of the Indian Air Force

No. **1** (F) Sqn. Formed 1st April 1933 at Drigh Road with Wapiti IIa for army co-op. Later with Hart, Audax and Lysander aircraft. Converted to a fighter unit with Hurricane Mks.I & IIb from September 1942, Hurricane IIc from June 1944. With Spitfire LF.VIIIc from November 1945 at Kohat, moving to Samungli (both now Pakistan) 2nd April 1946, then Yelahanka (near Bangalore) 18th June 1946, with a detachment at Miramshah (now Pakistan) from 27th October 1945 to 7th April 1946 (initially 'A' Flt, but later 'B' Flt), and a further detachment there from 25th February 1947. From March 1947 it also had a few FR.XIVe. Reduced from 16 to 8 Spitfire Mk.VIII 15 May 1947 on moving to Peshawar (Pakistan). Re-equipped with Tempest F.II in July 1947, and transferred to Royal Pakistan Air Force 15th August 1947.
Commanding Officers, before independence:
S/Ldr E Nazirullah 1.8.45
S/Ldr Ranjan Dutt 20.3.46

No. **2** (F) Sqn. Formed 1st April 1941 at Peshawar (now Pakistan) with Wapiti IIa for army co-op. Lysander aircraft from 24th November 1941. Converted to a tactical reconnaissance unit (later also ground attack fighter) with Hurricane IIb from 7th September 1942. With Spitfire LF.VIIIc from January 1946 at Kohat, moving to Samungli 9th November 1946 then Poona 10th February 1947. 'A' Flight was detached to Miramshah from 2nd April 1946, until 6th June 1946 when it was replaced by 'B' Flight, thus being withdrawn August 1946. Reduced from 16 to 8 Spitfire Mk.VIII 31 May 1947. Re-equipped with F/FR.XVIIIe in December 1948 until October 1953, being later based at Peshawar, Palam (near Delhi) and Adampur.
[Indian source says reduced to a number plate basis in December 1947, being reformed at Palam on 15th August 1951 - but this does not fit the above, nor their statement that S/Ldr Singh was appointed CO May 1949]
Commanding Officers:
S/Ldr K Jaswant Singh 1.5.44
S/Ldr M Rabb 23.3.46
S/Ldr A Murat Singh Aulakh 24.3.47
S/Ldr Randhir Singh VrC 5.49
S/Ldr RM Engineer 6.53 to 8.55

No. **3** (F) Sqn. Formed 1st October 1941 as a fighter reconnaissance unit at Peshawar (now Pakistan) with Audax I. Later fighter bomber squadron with Hurricane IIc from November 1943. With 16 Spitfire LF.VIIIc from November 1945 at Risalpur (now Pakistan), moving to Kolar (near Bangalore) 2nd February 1946. Began to re-equip with Tempest F.II in September 1946, and fully equipped from 31st January 1947.
Commanding Officers, before independence:
S/Ldr Shivdev Singh 8.1.45
S/Ldr OP Mehra 22.12.45
F/Lt ML Misra 27.3.46
S/Ldr R Atmaram 6.6.46
S/Ldr MD Suri 30.12.46

No. **4** (F) Sqn. Formed 1st February 1942 as a tactical reconnaissance unit at Peshawar (now in Pakistan) with Lysander II. Received Hurricane IIc for FGA and close support missions from August 1943. With Spitfire LF.VIIIc from June 1945 at Yelahanka (near Bangalore). Some F/FR.XIVe being flown between January 1946 and March 1946. Left for Japan 6th March 1946, and based at Iwakuni from 31st March 1946 with Spitfire F/FR.XIVe, moving to Miho, Hiroshima 6th May 1946. Returned to

Spitfire FR.XIXes of No. 4 (Fighter) Sqn RIAF being hoisted at the end of March 1946 during shipment from Yelahanka (near Bangalore) to Japan as part of the British Commonwealth Occupation Forces. Initially based at Iwakuni, the squadron moved five weeks later to Miho, Hiroshima.

India 19th July 1947, leaving all aircraft in Japan, on decision of Government of India to withdraw its component of British Commonwealth Occupation Forces, Japan. Disembarked Madras 2nd August 1947, then based at Chakeri (Kanpur) and re-equipped with Tempest F.II.

Commanding Officers, before independence:
S/Ldr D Boyd Berry RAF	22.2.45
F/Lt J Chandra (temp)	2.8.45
S/Ldr EW Pinto	12.8.45
S/Ldr J Chandra	2.46
S/Ldr MM Engineer DFC	29.10.46
S/Ldr M Barker	28.5.47

No. 6 (F) Sqn. Formed 1st December 1942 at Trichinopoly (near Madura) with Hurricane IIb (later IIc) for tactical reconnaissance and ground attack missions. With Spitfire LF.VIIIc and F/FR.XIVe from November 1945 at Kohat (now Pakistan), the last Mk.VIII leaving January 1946. Also had a few PR.XI. To Ranchi 10th January 1946, disbanding there on 30th April 1947. Reformed next day at Mauripur (near Karachi, now Pakistan) as a medium range Dakota transport squadron, but ceased to exist as such 15th August 1947 pending re-formation as a Royal Pakistan Air Force squadron. Later reformed as an IAF squadron with B-24s.

Commanding Officers, before independence:
S/Ldr A Lodhie	11.45
S/Ldr JC Varma DFC	1.8.46
S/Ldr H Moolgavkar	11.1.47

No. 7 (F) Sqn. Formed 1st December 1942 at Vizagapatam (eastern India) as a dive-bomber unit with Vengeance I, later also Mk.III. Received Hurricane IIc for ground attack fighter work from November 1944. With Spitfire F/FR.XIVe (also some LF.VIIIc & PR.XI), re-equipping from Hurricane IIc between December 1945 and March 1946 at Maharajpur (Gurgaon) near Delhi. To Kohat (now Pakistan) 4th April 1946, with a detachment at Miramshah until 28th February 1947, then to Risalpur (both now Pakistan) 30th April 1947 reducing to eight Spitfire Mk.XIV. Began to re-equip with Tempest F.II between May 1947 and July 1947, before moving to Agra 15th August 1947, but Spitfires served until early 1948, taking part in Kashmir operations in 1947.

Commanding Officers:
S/Ldr Lal	21.6.44
S/Ldr Masillamani	c.1945
S/Ldr SH Hassan	12.45
S/Ldr ML Misra	5.46
S/Ldr Noronha	12.6.47
Wg Cdr BS Noronha until	16.4.48

No. 8 (F) Sqn. Formed 1st December 1942 at Trichinopoly (near Madura) as a dive-bomber unit with Vengeance I & III. With Spitfire LF.VIIIc for ground attack fighter work from July 1944 at Samungli (now Pakistan), then Amarda Road (near Calcutta) 30th October 1944 (add four Spitfire Mk.V/trop in November 1944), moving to Nidania (now Bangladesh) 29th December 1944, then Baigachi (near Calcutta) 23rd February 1945 using 16 (FB)VIIIs for ground attack work. Embarked for Rangoon 19th July 1945, arriving at Mingaladon 31st July 1945 and taking over 16 Spits from No.607 Sqn RAF. Returned to India by sea 24th January 1946 and at Trichinopoly (near Madura) from 4th February 1946 with Spitfire F/FR.XIVe, then to Kolar (near Bangalore) 4th June 1946. Re-equipped with Tempest F.II from October 1946, the last Spitfires being left behind on moving to Poona 13th May 1947.

Commanding Officers, before independence:
S/Ldr Sutherland, DFC	27.3.44
S/Ldr MW Coombes RAF	10.44
S/Ldr JS Humphreys RAF	5.6.45
S/Ldr MM Engineer DFC	30.11.45
F/Lt KB Joshi	9.10.46
S/Ldr Z Ahmad	12.46
S/Ldr PS Gill	7.47

No. 9 (F) Sqn. Formed 3rd January 1944 at Lahore (now Pakistan) with Hurricane IIc for escort and ground attack fighter missions. With Spitfire LF.VIIIc from May 1945 at Baigachi (near Calcutta). To Ranchi 25th October 1945, then Hmawbi 30th November 1945 with some F/FR.XIVe. Willingdon 22nd January 1946, Maharajpur (Gurgaon) near Delhi 20th February 1946 and Peshawar (now Pakistan) 12th March 1946, now totally re-equipped with F/FR.XIVe. To Bhopal 14th January 1947, then Peshawar (now Pakistan) 8th May 1947, reducing to eight Spitfire Mk.XIV. Re-equipped with Tempest F.II, becoming a Royal Pakistan Air Force unit 15th August 1947. Re-raised as an RIAF unit with Spitfire F/FR.XVIIIe in 1948, and served until October 1953.
Commanding Officers, before independence:
S/Ldr KA Perkin 2.3.44
S/Ldr DA Adams RAF 16.11.44
S/Ldr MA Khan 28.8.45
S/Ldr M Akhtar 24.4.46

No. 10 (F) Sqn. Formed 20th February 1944 at Lahore (now Pakistan) as a fighter-bomber unit with Hurricane IIc. With Spitfire LF.VIIIc from May 1945 at Yelahanka (six LF.VIIIc from No.17 Sqn RAF), moving to Kajamalai/ Trichinopoly 11th May 1945, Ulunderpet (both near Madura) 1st November 1945, Hmawbi (Rangoon) 22nd November 1945, Baigachi 15th February 1946 and Barrackpore (both near Calcutta) 3rd June 1946 with a few FR.XIVe. To Chakeri (Kanpur) 15th May 1947 to re-equip with Tempest F.II.
Commanding Officers:
S/Ldr RFT Deo, DFC & Bar 20.2.44
S/Ldr RW Jones RAF 19.6.45
F/Lt I Adamson 22.10.45
S/Ldr H Raza 5.1.46
S/Ldr MA Rahman 1.8.46
S/Ldr H Moolgavkar 8.5.47

No. 12 (F) Sqn. Formed 1st December 1945 as a fighter unit with Spitfire LF.VIIIc at Kohat. To Risalpur (both now Pakistan) 28th January 1946 and Bairagarh (Bhopal) 23rd June 1946, becoming a Dakota unit August 1946.
Commanding Officer, before independence:
S/Ldr SN Haider 1.12.45
S/Ldr Shiv Dev Singh 1.1.47

No. 14 (F) Sqn. Formed 15th August 1951 with Spitfire F/FR.XVIIIe, based at Ambala, then Barrackpore (near Calcutta) from 1952 until moving to Halwara in 1957.
Note: No.14 Sqn was the last first-line piston-engined IAF fighter unit. Converted to Hawker Hunter in 1957.
Commanding Officers:
S/Ldr LRD Blunt VrC 15.8.51 to 10.6.53
S/Ldr HK Bose 10.10.53 to 30.9.55
S/Ldr JM Fenn 17.10.55 to 12.2.58.

No. 15 (PR) Sqn. Formed 20th August 1951 at Ambala with Spitfire PR.XI. Disbanded in January 1953.
Commanding Officer:
S/Ldr EJ Dhatigara 20.8.51 to 1.53

No. 16 (F) Sqn. Formed in 1951 with Spitfire F/FR.XVIIIe. Ceased to operate Spitfires in 1954.
Commanding Officer:
S/Ldr ASM Bhawnani from 7.1.52.

No. 1 (PR) Squadron. Formed in January 1948 as No.101 (PR) Flight at Jammu, Kashmir, first with Spitfire FR.XVIIIe and from 1949 also with PR.XIX. Became No.1 (Photographic Reconnaissance) Squadron 18th April 1950. Disbanded 1958.
Commanding Officers:
F/Lt JF Shukla 5.49
S/Ldr FVA Scudder 9.51
S/Ldr WVA Lloyd 10.54 to 7.58

AFS (I) Advanced Flying School (India). Formed 1st April 1946 from No.1 (Indian) Advanced Flying Unit, No.1 (Indian) Service Flying Training School and No.151 Operational Training Unit at Ambala, and absorbed into RIAF on 1st June 1947. Flew Spitfire LF.VIIIc, F/FR.XIVe & XVIIIe, later also Spitfire T.IX from 1949 until 1957.

No. 2 Flying Training School (FTS) at Jodhpur, temporarily used Spitfire T.IX between 1949 and 1957.

Spitfires were generally phased out in 1955, only No.1 (PR) Squadron continuing to use Spitfires until 1957/58.

Spitfire FR.XVIIIe HS668 '95' of the Advanced Flying School (India) at Ambala in flight around 1947/48 has the later red-white-green roundels.
[USAAF 39635 AC]

Individual Histories

The following list is far from complete, dates of unit changes, events and crashes being largely unavailable.

JF277 Spitfire F.VIIIc (Merlin 61); TOC/RAF 1.12.42; M.E. 30.11.43; Arr India 1.44; ACSEA - RIAF; No.36 SP, ferrying, force-landed near Bankura, burnt out, Cat.FA/E 5.2.46; SOC 14.3.46

JF289 Spitfire F.VIIIc (Merlin 61); TOC/RAF 13.1.43; M.E. 30.11.43; Arr India 1.12.43; ACSEA (No.152 Sqn) - RIAF, India census 5.46; Service unknown; Retd RAF; SOC 30.1.47

JF292 Spitfire F.VIIIc (Merlin 61); TOC/RAF 21.1.43; M.E. 30.11.43; Arr India 1.44; ACSEA (No.607 Sqn) - RIAF, India census 5.46; Service unknown; Retd RAF; SOC 30.1.47

JF479 Spitfire F.VIIIc (Merlin 63A); TOC/RAF 15.5.43; M.E. 8.43 (No.145 Sqn); NAAF 11.43; Arr India; ACSEA (No.17 Sqn) - RIAF; No.10 Sqn; Fate unknown

JF623 Spitfire F.VIIIc (Merlin 63); TOC/RAF 20.6.43; M.E. 30.11.43; Arr India 1.12.43; ACSEA (Nos.152, 607, 131 Sqns) - RIAF, India census 5.46; Service unknown; Retd RAF; SOC 30.1.47

JF625 Spitfire F.VIIIc (Merlin 63); TOC/RAF 27.6.43; M.E. 30.11.43; Arr India 1.12.43 - RIAF No.8 Sqn, engine failure at 3,000ft, force landing in open country, crashed into 3ft high bank lined with trees, 5m S of Amta, Cat.FA/E 25.3.45 (P/O S Banerje injured); SOC 12.4.45

JF676 Spitfire F.VIIIc (Merlin 63); TOC/RAF 27.7.43; M.E. 30.11.43; Arr India 1.12.43; ACSEA (Nos.152 & 615 Sqns, AFTU) - RIAF, India census 5.46; AFS (I); Retd RAF; SOC 31.10.46

JF694 Spitfire LF.VIIIc (Merlin 66); TOC/RAF 24.7.43; Arr India (Karachi) 9.11.43; ACSEA (No.607 Sqn) - RIAF, India census 5.46; To RIAF inventory 29.12.47; AFS (I); Fate unknown

JF707 Spitfire LF.VIIIc (Merlin 66); TOC/RAF (CRD) 27.6.43; Arr India (Karachi) 17.9.45; ACSEA 27.9.45 - RIAF, India census 5.46; Service unknown; Retd RAF; SOC 30.1.47

JF751 Spitfire LF.VIIIc (Merlin 66); TOC/RAF 6.7.43; N.A. 30.11.43; Arr India 1.44; ACSEA (No.67 Sqn) - RIAF; No.10 Sqn, landed wheels retracted Baigachi, Cat.FA/Ac 14.3.46 (F/O HH Beale OK); SOC 25.4.46

JF755 Spitfire LF.VIIIc (Merlin 66); TOC/RAF 7.7.43; Arr India 29.8.43; ACSEA (No.607 Sqn) - RIAF; No.8 Sqn, engine failed at 15,000ft, lack of fuel after operation, belly landing 11m NW of Cox's Bazaar, Cat.FB/B 9.1.45 (F/Lt AA Narayanan OK); Re-Cat.E, SOC 14.2.45

JF757 Spitfire LF.VIIIc (Merlin 66); TOC/RAF 8.7.43; Arr India 29.8.43; ACSEA (Nos.152, 136,132 Sqns), census 21.6.45 & 30.5.46 - RIAF; Service unknown; Retd RAF; SOC 31.10.46

JF760 Spitfire LF.VIIIc (Merlin 66); TOC/RAF 10.7.43; Arr India 29.8.43; ACSEA (No.136 Sqn) - RIAF, India census 5.46; Service unknown; Retd RAF; SOC 30.1.47

JF764 Spitfire LF.VIIIc (Merlin 66); TOC/RAF 26.7.43; N.A. 30.11.43; Arr India 1.44; ACSEA - RIAF; No.8 Sqn, port tyre burst on take-off, swung off runway, sank in soft ground, nose tipped, Cat.FB/Ac 17.5.45 (F/O AJ Chaves OK); ROS; Crashed 9.7.45; Retd RAF (RiW); No.151 OTU, crashed Cat.FA/E (dbf) 24.1.46; SOC 28.2.46

JF775 Spitfire LF.VIIIc (Merlin 66); TOC/RAF 16.7.43; Arr India (Karachi) 9.11.43; ACSEA - RIAF, India census 5.46; Service unknown; Retd RAF; SOC 30.1.47

JF778 Spitfire LF.VIIIc (Merlin 66); TOC/RAF 18.7.43; Arr India (Karachi) 20.5.44; ACSEA (No.615 Sqn) – To RIAF via No.131 R&SU; No.8 Sqn, engine cut, undershot forced landing, Cat.E 1.3.45; SOC 13.3.45

JF782 Spitfire LF.VIIIc (Merlin 66); TOC/RAF 26.7.43; N.A. 30.11.43; Arr India 1.44; ACSEA (No.81 Sqn) - RIAF; No.2 Sqn ('K') from 21.1.46; Ferrying from Kohat, landed at edge of runway, ran off into rough ground, tyre burst, undercarriage collapsed, Miramshah, Cat.FA/E 23.4.46 (P/O AM Palamkote OK); NWR 25.4.46; SOC 9.5.46

JF785 Spitfire LF.VIIIc (Merlin 66); TOC/RAF 26.7.43; N.A. 30.11.43; Arr India 1.44; ACSEA (Nos.136 & 81 Sqns, 'FL-D') - RIAF; No.2 Sqn, undercarriage collapsed landing after air test, Palam, Cat.FA/Ac 19.3.46 (S/Ldr LW Feltham OK); Retd RAF; SOC 25.4.46

JF789 Spitfire LF.VIIIc (Merlin 66); TOC/RAF 25.7.43; M.E. to India; ACSEA (No.152 Sqn) - RIAF, India census 5.46; AFS (No.151 OTU), engine failed, belly landing at Peshawar, caught fire, extinguished, Cat.FA/E 22.8.46 (P/O AB Patil OK), SOC

JF817 Spitfire LF.VIIIc (Merlin 66); TOC/RAF 12.8.43; Arr India (Karachi) 9.11.43; ACSEA (No.155 Sqn) - RIAF, India census 5.46; Service unknown; Retd RAF; SOC 30.1.47

JF831 Spitfire LF.VIIIc (Merlin 66); TOC/RAF 20.8.43; Arr India 3.11.43; ACSEA - RIAF; No.132 R&SU, engine failure on take-off at Mingaladon, Cat.FA/E 8.1.46; SOC 31.1.46

JF835 Spitfire F.VIIIc (Merlin 63); TOC/RAF 9.8.43; M.E. 30.11.43; Arr India 1.44; ACSEA (No.152 Sqn) - Possibly to RIAF; Fate unknown

JF841 Spitfire LF.VIIIc (Merlin 66); TOC/RAF 13.8.43; Arr India (Karachi) 9.11.43; ACSEA (No.607 Sqn) - RIAF, India census 5.46; Probably with No.8 Sqn; Service unknown; Retd RAF; SOC 30.1.47

JF842 Spitfire LF.VIIIc (Merlin 66); TOC/RAF 13.8.43; Arr India 3.11.43; ACSEA - RIAF, India census 5.46; Service unknown; Retd RAF; SOC 30.1.47

JF843 Spitfire LF.VIIIc (Merlin 66); TOC/RAF 15.8.43; Arr India (Karachi) 11.11.43; ACSEA - RIAF, India census 5.46; Service unknown; Retd RAF; SOC 1.6.47

JF848 Spitfire LF.VIIIc (Merlin 66); TOC/RAF 19.8.43; Arr India (Karachi) 11.11.43; ACSEA (Nos.152 & 136 Sqns) - RIAF, India census 5.46; Service unknown; Retd RAF; SOC 30.1.47

JF883 Spitfire LF.VIIIc (Merlin 66); TOC/RAF 17.9.43; Arr India (Karachi) 26.1.44; ACSEA (No.136 Sqn, No.145 R&SU) – RIAF, No.4 Sqn 6.7.45; Tail chasing exercise, tail hit by pursuing JG620, landed safely Yelahanka, Cat.A(R) 21.7.45 (F/O TN Ghadiok OK); While stationery, run into by MT837 at Yelahanka 28.9.45 (F/O A Qadir OK); India census 5.46; Service unknown; Retd RAF; SOC 31.12.46

JF892 Spitfire LF.VIIIc (Merlin 66); TOC/RAF 3.11.43; Arr India (Karachi) 26.1.44; ACSEA (Nos.607 & 615 Sqns) - RIAF, India census 5.46; Service unknown; Retd RAF; SOC 31.12.46

JF927 Spitfire LF.VIIIc (Merlin 66); TOC/RAF 23.8.43; Arr India (Karachi) 11.11.43; ACSEA - RIAF; No.10 Sqn, rear fuselage found damaged after landing Kajamalai Cat.FA/Ac 26.9.45 (F/O MY Aziz), ROS; Retd RAF; SOC 27.12.45

JF948 Spitfire LF.VIIIc (Merlin 66); TOC/RAF 31.8.43; Arr India (Karachi) 10.1.44; ACSEA (No.152 Sqn) - RIAF, India census 5.46; Service unknown; Retd RAF; SOC 12.9.46

JG113 Spitfire LF.VIIIc (Merlin 66); TOC/RAF 14.9.43; Arr India (Karachi) 10.1.44; ACSEA (No.67 Sqn) - RIAF, India census 5.46; Service unknown; Retd RAF; SOC 30.1.47

JG114 Spitfire LF.VIIIc (Merlin 66); TOC/RAF 14.9.43; Arr India (Bombay) 7.12.43; ACSEA (No.136 Sqn) - RIAF, India census 5.46; Service unknown; Retd RAF; SOC 30.1.47

JG122 Spitfire LF.VIIIc (Merlin 66); TOC/RAF 31.8.43; Arr India (Bombay) 7.12.43; ACSEA (No.67 Sqn) - RIAF, India census 5.46; Service unknown; Retd RAF; SOC 30.1.47

JG171 Spitfire LF.VIIIc (Merlin 66); TOC/RAF 14.9.43; Arr India (Karachi) 16.12.43 - RIAF; No.8 Sqn, overshot landing without flaps, ran into ditch, undercarriage

INDIA

collapsed, Baigachi 10.6.45 (P/O J Bouche); Cat.E 14.6.45 SOC/ACSEA 5.7.45

JG199 Spitfire LF.VIIIc (Merlin 66); TOC/RAF 21.9.43; Arr India (Karachi) 12.1.44; ACSEA (No.67 Sqn) - RIAF, India census 5.46; Service unknown; Retd RAF; SOC 30.1.47

JG200 Spitfire LF.VIIIc (Merlin 66); TOC/RAF 23.9.43; Arr India (Karachi) 12.1.44; ACSEA (Nos.67 & 136 Sqns) - RIAF, India census 5.46; No.10 Sqn ('Z') in 1946; Retd RAF; SOC 24.4.47

JG251 Spitfire LF.VIIIc (Merlin 66); TOC/RAF 1.10.43; Arr India (Karachi) 10.1.44; ACSEA (Nos.67, 155, 273 Sqns) - RIAF, India census 5.46; Service unknown; Retd RAF; SOC 31.10.46

JG257 Spitfire LF.VIIIc (Merlin 66); TOC/RAF 3.10.43; ex USAAF (MTO); Arr India (Karachi) 17.9.45; ACSEA 27.9.45 - RIAF, India census 5.46; Service unknown; Retd RAF; SOC 1.6.47

JG268 Spitfire LF.VIIIc (Merlin 66); TOC/RAF 16.10.43; Arr India (Karachi) 26.1.44; ACSEA (No.152 Sqn) - RIAF, India census 5.46; No.10 Sqn ('G') 1946/47; Retd RAF; SOC 1.6.47

JG314 Spitfire LF.VIIIc (Merlin 66); TOC/RAF 6.11.43; Arr India (Karachi) 6.11.43; ACSEA (Nos.81 & 67 Sqns) - RIAF; No.10 Sqn ('W'), tailwheel failed to lower, DBR on landing, Baigachi, Cat.B 3.4.46 (P/O RL Jebb OK); India census 5.46; Retd RAF; SOC 1.6.47

JG323 Spitfire LF.VIIIc (Merlin 66); TOC/RAF 15.11.43; Arr India (Karachi) 18.2.44; ACSEA (Nos.81 & 132 Sqns) - RIAF; No.4 Sqn 1946; India census 5.46; Retd RAF; SOC 26.6.47

JG325 Spitfire LF.VIIIc (Merlin 66); TOC/RAF 25.11.43; Arr India (Karachi) 18.2.44; ACSEA – RIAF, India census 5.46; No.10 Sqn ('A'); To RIAF inventory 29.12.47; AFS (I); Fate unknown

JG331 Spitfire LF.VIIIc (Merlin 66); TOC/RAF 26.9.43; Arr India (Bombay) 4.7.44; ACSEA (No.3 RFU) - RIAF; Service unknown; Retd RAF; SOC 31.7.47

JG340 Spitfire LF.VIIIc (Merlin 66); TOC/RAF 1.10.43; Arr India (Karachi) 10.1.44; ACSEA (No.81 Sqn); RIAF, India census 5.46; Service unknown; Retd RAF; SOC 30.1.47

JG378 Spitfire LF.VIIIc (Merlin 66); TOC/RAF 24.10.43; Arr India (Karachi) 26.1.44; ACSEA (Nos.136 & 132 Sqns) - RIAF, India census 5.46; AFS(I), undercarriage collapsed landing, Ambala, Cat.E 5.8.47 (P/O RC Malani OK); SOC 28.8.47

JG404 Spitfire LF.VIIIc (Merlin 66); TOC/RAF 25.11.43; Arr India (Karachi) 18.2.44; ACSEA - RIAF, India census 5.46; Service unknown; Retd RAF; SOC 30.1.47

JG405 Spitfire LF.VIIIc (Merlin 66); TOC/RAF 20.12.43; Arr India (Karachi) 20.3.44; ACSEA - RIAF; Nos.8 & 4 Sqns; No.2 Sqn ('C') from 20.1.46 to 4.46; India census 5.46; Retd RAF; SOC 31.7.47

JG406 Spitfire LF.VIIIc (Merlin 66); TOC/RAF 25.11.43; Arr India (Karachi) 12.5.44; ACSEA (No.145 R&SU) – RIAF, No.4 Sqn 6.7.45; Retd RAF; SOC 30.8.45

JG408 Spitfire LF.VIIIc (Merlin 66); TOC/RAF 30.12.43; Arr India (Karachi) 20.3.44; ACSEA (Nos.81, 273, 67 Sqns) - RIAF, India census 5.46; Service unknown; Retd RAF; SOC 31.12.46

JG411 Spitfire LF.VIIIc (Merlin 66); TOC/RAF 16.10.43; Arr India (Karachi) 26.1.44; ACSEA - RIAF, India census 5.46; Service unknown; Retd RAF; SOC 30.1.47

JG413 Spitfire LF.VIIIc (Merlin 66); TOC/RAF 11.10.43; Arr India (Karachi) 26.1.44; ACSEA (No.152 Sqn) - RIAF, India census 5.46; Service unknown; Retd RAF; SOC 30.1.47

JG418 Spitfire LF.VIIIc (Merlin 66); TOC/RAF 18.10.43; Arr India (Karachi) 18.2.44; ACSEA (No.155 Sqn) - RIAF, India census 5.46; Service unknown; Retd RAF; SOC 27.3.47

JG427 Spitfire LF.VIIIc (Merlin 66); TOC/RAF 22.10.43; Arr India (Karachi) 12.1.44; ACSEA (No.152 Sqn) - RIAF, India census 5.46; Service unknown; Retd RAF; SOC 30.1.47

JG477 Spitfire LF.VIIIc (Merlin 66); TOC/RAF 3.11.43; Arr India (Karachi) 26.1.44; ACSEA (No.607 Sqn) - RIAF, India census 5.46; No.1 Sqn, taxied off runway into soft ground, became bogged, Cat.FA/B 3.7.46 (P/O BY Mohona OK); RIW; Retd RAF; SOC 1.6.47

JG478 Spitfire LF.VIIIc (Merlin 66); TOC/RAF 30.11.43; Arr India (Karachi) 7.3.44; ACSEA (Nos.273 & 81 Sqns) - RIAF; No.4 Sqn, night flight, unable to locate airfield, landed on main road, swerved to avoid hillocks, hit ditch, undercarriage collapsed, 12°36'N 77°02'E, Mysore State, Cat.FA/E 27.5.45 (F/Lt DM Finn OK), SOC

JG483 Spitfire LF.VIIIc (Merlin 66); TOC/RAF 2.12.43; Arr India (Karachi) 18.2.44; ACSEA (Nos.681 & 81 Sqns) - RIAF; No.10 Sqn, ran into soft ground taxiing, tipped on nose, Cat.A(R) 6.8.45 (F/O HH Beale); India census 5.46; Retd RAF; SOC 31.1.47

JG489 Spitfire LF.VIIIc (Merlin 66); TOC/RAF 7.11.43; Arr India (Karachi) 18.2.44; ACSEA (Nos.607 & 136 Sqns) - RIAF, India census 5.46; No.1 Sqn, on landing, while leading, run into from behind by MT987, nose tipped, Samungli, Cat.FA/E 6.6.46 (F/O KR Jolly injured); Retd RAF (casualty wastage); SOC 31.10.46

JG497 Spitfire LF.VIIIc (Merlin 66); TOC/RAF 20.12.43; Arr India (Karachi) 20.3.44; ACSEA (Nos.17 & 81 Sqns) - RIAF, India census 5.46; Service unknown; Retd RAF; SOC 30.1.47

JG499 Spitfire LF.VIIIc (Merlin 66); TOC/RAF 15.11.43; Arr India (Karachi) 18.2.44; ACSEA (CCF Mauripur/No.1331 CU) - RIAF, India census 5.46; Service unknown; Retd RAF; SOC 30.1.47

JG500 Spitfire LF.VIIIc (Merlin 66); TOC/RAF 30.11.43; Arr India (Karachi) 7.3.44; ACSEA (No.607 Sqn) - RIAF, India census 5.46; Service unknown; Retd RAF; SOC 31.7.47

JG527 Spitfire LF.VIIIc (Merlin 66); TOC/RAF 4.1.44; Arr India (Karachi) 20.3.44; ACSEA (No.81 Sqn, 'FL-P') - RIAF; No.3 Sqn, engine caught fire on starting up, spread to airframe at Kolar, Cat.FA/E 11.4.46 (F/O S Jamaludin OK); Retd RAF (casualty wastage); SOC 30.5.46

JG529 Spitfire LF.VIIIc (Merlin 66); TOC/RAF 22.12.43; Arr India (Karachi) 20.3.44 - RIAF; No.8 Sqn; Retd RAF; SOC 12.2.45
NOTE: Reported with No.1 Sqn RIAF, but this unit received Spitfires in 11.45

JG544 Spitfire LF.VIIIc (Merlin 66); TOC/RAF 2.1.44; Arr India (Karachi) 20.3.44; ACSEA (Nos.152, 67, 615 Sqns) - RIAF, India census 5.46; Service unknown; Retd RAF; SOC 31.10.46

JG554 Spitfire LF.VIIIc (Merlin 66); TOC/RAF 21.1.44; Arr India (Karachi) 11.5.44; ACSEA (No.17 Sqn) - RIAF, India census 5.46; Service unknown; Retd RAF; SOC 28.8.47

JG560 Spitfire LF.VIIIc (Merlin 66); TOC/RAF 14.11.43; Arr India (Karachi) 18.2.44; ACSEA - RIAF, India census 5.46; Service unknown; Retd RAF; SOC 31.12.46

JG562 Spitfire LF.VIIIc (Merlin 66); TOC/RAF 15.11.43; Arr India (Karachi) 18.2.44; ACSEA (Nos.136 & 81 Sqns, 'FL-O') - RIAF, India census 5.46; Service unknown; Retd RAF; SOC 31.10.46

JG606 Spitfire LF.VIIIc (Merlin 66); TOC/RAF 30.11.43; Arr India (Karachi) 7.3.44; ACSEA (Nos.615 & 67 Sqns) - RIAF, India census 5.46; No.1 Sqn, engine trouble in cross-country, belly-landed, burnt out at Yelahanka, Cat.FA/E 24.11.46 (F/Lt J Marley seriously injured); Retd RAF (casualty wastage); SOC 31.12.46

JG618 Spitfire LF.VIIIc (Merlin 66); TOC/RAF 7.11.43; Arr India (Karachi) 18.2.44; ACSEA (No.607 Sqn) - RIAF, India census 5.46; To RIAF inventory 29.12.47; AFS (I); Fate unknown

JG620 Spitfire LF.VIIIc (Merlin 66); TOC/RAF 14.11.43; Arr India (Karachi) 18.2.44; ACSEA (No.132 Sqn) – RIAF, No.4 Sqn, tail chasing exercise, struck tail of JF883 at 6,000ft, lost prop, belly-landed, undershot, hit tree stump, overturned near Devanhalli, 17m NE of Yelahanka, Mysore State, Cat.FA/E 21.7.45 (F/O YR Agtey seriously injured); To No.39 R&SU 30.7.45; SOC/RAF 16.8.45

JG623 Spitfire LF.VIIIc (Merlin 66); TOC/RAF 20.12.43; Arr India (Karachi) 20.3.44; ACSEA (No.81 Sqn) - RIAF, India census 5.46; No.10 Sqn ('P') in 1946; Retd RAF; SOC 25.9.47

JG624 Spitfire LF.VIIIc (Merlin 66); TOC/RAF 12.3.44; Arr India (Karachi) 18.5.44; ACSEA (No.81 Sqn) - RIAF, India census 5.46; Service unknown; Retd RAF; SOC 27.3.47

JG656 Spitfire LF.VIIIc (Merlin 66); TOC/RAF 11.3.44; Arr India (Karachi) 20.5.44; ACSEA - RIAF, India census 5.46; To RIAF inventory 29.12.47; AFS (I); Fate unknown

JG660 Spitfire LF.VIIIc (Merlin 66); TOC/RAF 17.3.44; Arr India (Karachi) 18.5.44; ACSEA (No.615 Sqn) - RIAF, India census 5.46; Service unknown; Retd RAF; SOC 30.1.47

JG670 Spitfire LF.VIIIc (Merlin 66); TOC/RAF 20.3.44; Arr India (Karachi) 18.5.44; ACSEA (No.615 Sqn) - RIAF; No.1 Sqn in 2.46; Retd RAF; SOC 28.4.46

JG678 Spitfire LF.VIIIc (Merlin 66); TOC/RAF 24.3.44; Arr India (Bombay) 9.6.44; ACSEA- RIAF; No.3 Sqn, hit by MV232 at Nagpur 30.1.46; Engine seized in flight, force landing safely at Kolar, Cat.E 27.4.46 (F/O RS Randhawa OK); Retd RAF; SOC 30.5.46

JG680 Spitfire LF.VIIIc (Merlin 66); TOC/RAF 26.3.44; Arr India (Karachi) 18.5.44; ACSEA - RIAF, India census 5.46; Service unknown; Retd RAF; SOC 27.3.47

JG681 Spitfire LF.VIIIc (Merlin 66); TOC/RAF 26.3.44; Arr India (Bombay) 9.6.44; ACSEA (No.273 Sqn) - RIAF, India census 5.46; Service unknown; Retd RAF; SOC 26.9.46

JG686 Spitfire LF.VIIIc (Merlin 66); TOC/RAF 28.3.44; Arr India (Karachi) 18.5.44; ACSEA - RIAF, India census 5.46; To RIAF inventory 29.12.47; AFS (I); Fate unknown

JG688 Spitfire LF.VIIIc (Merlin 66); TOC/RAF 5.4.44; Arr India (Bombay) 4.7.44; ACSEA (No.67 Sqn) - RIAF, India census 5.46; Service unknown; Retd RAF; SOC 28.8.47

LV643 Spitfire LF.VIIIc (Merlin 66); TOC/RAF 4.11.43; Arr India (Karachi) 18.2.44; ACSEA (Nos.17, 81, 132 Sqns) - RIAF, India census 5.46; Service unknown; Retd RAF; SOC 31.12.46

LV646 Spitfire LF.VIIIc (Merlin 66); TOC/RAF 20.12.43; Arr India (Karachi) 16.3.44; ACSEA - RIAF; No.8 Sqn, inadvertently landed wheels-up, 'George' airstrip, Nidania, Cat.FA/E 11.1.45 (F/Lt DE Colebroke OK), SOC/bboc (ACSEA census 6.45); SOC 4.10.45

LV648 Spitfire LF.VIIIc (Merlin 66); TOC/RAF 20.12.43; Arr India (Karachi) 20.3.44; ACSEA (No.67 Sqn) - RIAF, India census 5.46; Service unknown; Retd RAF; SOC 27.3.47

LV654 Spitfire LF.VIIIc (Merlin 66); TOC/RAF 27.12.43; Arr India (Karachi) 20.3.44; ACSEA (No.607 Sqn) - RIAF, India census 5.46; Service unknown; Retd RAF; SOC 30.1.47

LV656 Spitfire LF.VIIIc (Merlin 66); TOC/RAF 22.12.43; Arr India (Karachi) 20.3.44; ACSEA (No.136 Sqn) - RIAF; No.10 Sqn, accident at Trichinopoly, Cat.A(R) 29.8.45 (F/O H Latimour); India census 5.46; Retd RAF; SOC 11.7.46

LV658 Spitfire LF.VIIIc (Merlin 66); TOC/RAF 31.12.43; Arr India (Karachi) 20.3.44; ACSEA (No.81 Sqn) - RIAF, India census 5.46; No.2 Sqn from 18.1.46 - 9.46; Retd RAF; SOC 31.7.47

LV661 Spitfire LF.VIIIc (Merlin 66); TOC/RAF 1.1.44; Arr India (Karachi) 20.3.44; ACSEA (Nos.136 & 132 Sqns, No.145 R&SU) – RIAF, No.4 Sqn 18.8.45; No.2 Sqn from 21.1.46 to 5.46; India census 5.46; Retd RAF; SOC 31.7.47

LV663 Spitfire LF.VIIIc (Merlin 66); TOC/RAF 18.4.44; Arr India (Bombay) 4.7.44 - RIAF; No.8 Sqn ('V'), while taxying after landing, hit by MD332 at Coxs Bazaar, Cat.E 7.1.45 (F/O KS Thandi OK); Retd RAF; SOC 5.2.45

LV666 Spitfire LF.VIIIc (Merlin 66); TOC/RAF 21.12.43; Arr India (Karachi) 20.3.44; ACSEA - RIAF, India census 5.46; Service unknown; Retd RAF; SOC 27.3.47

LV670 Spitfire LF.VIIIc (Merlin 66); TOC/RAF 22.12.43; Arr India (Karachi) 20.3.44; ACSEA (No.67 Sqn) - RIAF, India census 5.46; Service unknown; Retd RAF; SOC 31.12.47

LV726 Spitfire LF.VIIIc (Merlin 66); TOC/RAF 4.2.44; Arr India (Karachi) 11.5.44; ACSEA (No.615 Sqn) - RIAF, India census 5.46; Service unknown; Retd RAF; SOC 28.8.47

LV732 Spitfire LF.VIIIc (Merlin 66); TOC/RAF 28.12.43; Arr India (Karachi) 20.3.44; ACSEA (No.607 Sqn) - RIAF; No.1 Sqn, tyre burst on take-off, braked hard, swung, tipped up attempting to stop, Samungli, Cat.B 11.4.46 (P/O SR Sowar OK); Recat.E, SOC/RAF 9.5.46

LV735 Spitfire LF.VIIIc (Merlin 66); TOC/RAF 7.1.44; Arr India (Karachi) 30.3.44; ACSEA (No.155 Sqn) - RIAF, India census 5.46; Service unknown; Retd RAF; SOC 30.1.47

LV738 Spitfire LF.VIIIc (Merlin 66); TOC/RAF 2.1.44; Arr India (Karachi) 30.3.44 - RIAF; No.8 Sqn, engine cut, crashed on approach, Samungli, Cat.FA/E 17.10.44; SOC/RAF 15.11.45

LV744 Spitfire LF.VIIIc (Merlin 66); TOC/RAF 10.1.44; Arr India (Karachi) 30.3.44; ACSEA (No.615 & 607 Sqns) - RIAF, India census 5.46; Service unknown; Retd RAF; SOC 27.3.47

LV746 Spitfire LF.VIIIc (Merlin 66); TOC/RAF 14.1.44; Arr India (Karachi) 30.3.44; ACSEA - RIAF, India census 5.46; Service unknown; Retd RAF; SOC 28.8.47

MA364 Spitfire F.Vc/trop (Merlin 55); TOC/RAF 25.7.43; Arr India (Bombay) 27.9.43; ACSEA (No.136 Sqn) – RIAF, No.4 Sqn, engine failed at 30ft on take-off from beach strip, landed wheels down, ran into shallow water, overturned, Murdabahnia, Cat.E 15.1.45 (F/O HS Moolgavkar), SOC

MA368 Spitfire F.Vc/trop (Merlin 55); TOC/RAF 11.6.43; ACSEA 21.6.45; No.607 Sqn; 1 SFTS(I) ("88") in 1946; SOC/RAF 25.4.46

MA672 Spitfire F.Vc/trop (Merlin 50); TOC/RAF 13.6.43; Arr India (Karachi) 18.8.43; ACSEA (No.607 Sqn) - IAF; No.8 Sqn, engine rough at 300ft after take-off, force-landed wheels up, Cat.FA/E 14.11.44 (F/O SA Hussain OK); SOC 27.11.44

MA848 Spitfire T.IX (Merlin 66); Became **HS534**; TOC/RAF 26.7.43; V.A. 22.1.47 (B-class reg. G.15-2) - RIAF 3.6.48; No.2 FTS 1948; AFS Ambala 1949; Fate unknown

MB909 Spitfire PR.XI (Merlin 63); TOC/RAF 19.9.43; Arr India 19.11.43; ACSEA (No.681 Sqn) – RIAF, India census 5.46 (recorded also in 9.46); Service unknown; Retd RAF; SOC 27.2.47

MB910 Spitfire PR.XI (Merlin 63); TOC/RAF 19.9.43; Arr India 30.11.43; ACSEA (No.681 Sqn) – RIAF, India census 5.46 (recorded also in 9.46); Jodhpur, to No.7 Sqn 14.2.47; Retd RAF; SOC 28.8.47

MB961 Spitfire LF.VIIIc (Merlin 66); TOC/RAF 20.3.44; Arr India (Karachi) 18.5.44; ACSEA (Nos.152 & 607 Sqns) - RIAF, India census 5.46; Service unknown; Retd RAF; SOC 27.3.47

MB966 Spitfire LF.VIIIc (Merlin 66); TOC/RAF 24.3.44; Arr India (Karachi) 18.5.44; ACSEA (No.67 Sqn) - RIAF, India census 5.46; Service unknown; Retd RAF; SOC 27.3.47

MB971 Spitfire LF.VIIIc (Merlin 66); TOC/RAF 6.4.44; Arr India (Bombay) 4.7.44; ACSEA - RIAF; No.4 Sqn 11.45 - 12.45; No.2 Sqn ('M') from 21.1.46 (India census 5.46); Ferrying from Kohat, port undercarriage collapsed landing, Miramshah, Cat.FA/E 13.6.46 (F/O WVA Lloyd OK); Retd RAF (casualty wastage); SOC 11.7.46

MD218 Spitfire LF.VIIIc (Merlin 66); TOC/RAF 21.1.44; Arr India (Karachi) 30.3.44; ACSEA (No.136 Sqn) - RIAF, India census 5.46; No.2 Sqn 1946; Retd RAF; SOC 31.10.46

MD219 Spitfire LF.VIIIc (Merlin 66); TOC/RAF 10.1.44; Arr India (Karachi) 30.3.44; ACSEA - RIAF; No.2 Sqn ('G') in 3.45; India census 5.46; Formation flying, engine cut, belly-landed near Mirali, Cat.FA/E 17.5.46 (F/O KL Suri OK); Retd RAF (wastage); SOC 13.6.46

MD222 Spitfire LF.VIIIc (Merlin 66); TOC/RAF 2.12.43; Arr

Spitfire T.IX HS534 (ex MA848), the first of a batch of ten of this variant to be supplied to India, is seen here before despatch.

India (Karachi) 16.3.44; ACSEA - RIAF, India census 5.46; No.10 Sqn, ferrying from Bhopal to Barrackpore, short of fuel, engine cut due to overload tank not operating, turned back to Bamrauli but met monsoon conditions, force-landed Pannganj Robertsgang, 24°77'N 83°24'E, Cat.FA/E 2.8.46 (F/O RL Jebb OK); Retd RAF (casualty wastage); SOC 27.2.47

MD225 Spitfire LF.VIIIc (Merlin 66); TOC/RAF 2.12.43; Arr India (Karachi) 18.2.44; ACSEA (No.293 Wing) - RIAF, India census 5.46; No.10 Sqn ('Y') 1946/47; Retd RAF; SOC 26.6.47

MD236 Spitfire LF.VIIIc (Merlin 66); TOC/RAF 13.12.43; Arr India (Karachi) 16.3.44; ACSEA (No.607 Sqn) - RIAF, India census 5.46; Service unknown; Retd RAF; SOC 30.1.47

MD239 Spitfire LF.VIIIc (Merlin 66); TOC/RAF 19.12.43; Arr India (Karachi) 26.4.44; ACSEA (No.155 Sqn) - RIAF, India census 5.46; Service unknown; Retd RAF; SOC 28.8.47

MD240 Spitfire LF.VIIIc (Merlin 66); TOC/RAF 13.12.43; Arr India (Karachi) 7.3.44; ACSEA (No.273 Sqn, No.315 MU) – RIAF, No.4 Sqn 8.8.45; No.2 Sqn ('W') from 20.1.46 to 6.46; India census 5.46; Retd RAF; SOC 31.10.46

MD243 Spitfire LF.VIIIc (Merlin 66); TOC/RAF 13.12.43; Arr India (Karachi) 7.3.44; ACSEA (No.273 Sqn) - RIAF, India census 5.46; Service unknown; Retd RAF; SOC 1.6.47

MD244 Spitfire LF.VIIIc (Merlin 66); TOC/RAF 13.12.43; Arr India (Karachi) 7.3.44; ACSEA - RIAF, India census 5.46; Service unknown; Retd RAF; SOC 31.7.47

MD255 Spitfire LF.VIIIc (Merlin 66); TOC/RAF 29.1.44; Arr India (Karachi) 30.3.44; ACSEA (No.607 Sqn) - RIAF, India census 5.46; Service unknown; Retd RAF; SOC 30.1.47

MD269 Spitfire LF.VIIIc (Merlin 66); TOC/RAF 21.2.44; Arr India (Karachi) 26.4.44; ACSEA (No.152 Sqn) - RIAF, India census 5.46; No.3 Sqn, bird strike during formation flying, belly-landed 5m from Kolar, Cat.FA/E 17.9.46 (F/O D'Eca OK); Retd RAF (casualty wastage); SOC 31.10.46

MD274 Spitfire LF.VIIIc (Merlin 66); TOC/RAF 23.1.44; Arr India (Karachi) 11.5.44; ACSEA (No.607 Sqn, 'AF-A') - RIAF, India census 5.46; No.10 Sqn ('E') 1946/47; Retd RAF; SOC 27.3.47

MD275 Spitfire LF.VIIIc (Merlin 66); TOC/RAF 20.1.44; Arr India (Karachi) 30.3.44; ACSEA (Nos.67 & 152 Sqns) - RIAF; No.4 Sqn in 12.45; Retd RAF; SOC 10.1.46

MD277 Spitfire LF.VIIIc (Merlin 66); TOC/RAF 20.1.44; Arr India (Karachi) 30.3.44; ACSEA (Nos.607 & 81 Sqns) - RIAF, India census 5.46; No.10 Sqn ('D') 1946/47; Retd RAF; SOC 27.3.47

MD278 Spitfire LF.VIIIc (Merlin 66); TOC/RAF 28.1.44; Arr India (Karachi) 11.5.44; ACSEA (Nos.132 & 136 Sqns) - RIAF; No.1 Sqn ('Q'), engine trouble on air-to-air firing exercise, emergency landing on airfield at Yelahanka, Cat.A(R) 25.6.45 (F/Sgt G Turner); To No.139 R&SU; No.4 Sqn 9.10.45; Formation practice, engine failure at 1,000ft, forced landed safely on airfield, Yelahanka, Cat.A(R) 6.12.45 (F/O L Prince-Foster OK); India census 5.46; SOC/RAF 25.7.46

MD285 Spitfire LF.VIIIc (Merlin 66); TOC/RAF 5.2.44; Arr India (Karachi) 12.5.44; ACSEA – RIAF, No.8 Sqn, engine trouble during formation practice, force-landed at base, Mingaladon, Cat.A(R) 30.10.45 (F/Lt Ranjan Dutt); India census 5.46; SOC/RAF 25.7.46

MD287 Spitfire LF.VIIIc (Merlin 66); TOC/RAF 2.3.44; Arr India (Karachi) 20.5.44; ACSEA – RIAF, No.8 Sqn, scramble for bogey, inadvertently landed wheels-up, 'George' airstrip, Nidania, Cat.Ac 1.2.45 (F/Lt C Foster); India census 5.46; SOC/RAF 27.3.47

MD289 Spitfire LF.VIIIc (Merlin 66); TOC/RAF 8.2.44; Arr India (Karachi) 11.5.44; ACSEA (CCF Mauripur/No.1331.CU); FAF 11.45 - RIAF, India census 5.46; Service unknown; Retd RAF; SOC 1.6.47

MD291 Spitfire LF.VIIIc (Merlin 66); TOC/RAF 20.2.44; Arr India (Karachi) 11.5.44; ACSEA - RIAF; No.10 Sqn, at end of landing run, hit by following MV245 at Hmawbi, Cat.E 20.12.45 (F/O RL Suri seriously injured); SOC 31.1.46

MD303 Spitfire LF.VIIIc (Merlin 66); TOC/RAF 28.1.44; Arr India (Karachi) 11.5.44; ACSEA (No.607 Sqn) - RIAF; No.10 Sqn, propeller blades damaged on take-off, Kajamalai, Cat.A(R) 3.8.45 (F/O OC Shepperd); India census 5.46; SOC/RAF 27.3.47

MD316 Spitfire LF.VIIIc (Merlin 66); TOC/RAF 29.1.44; Arr India (Karachi) 11.5.44; ACSEA (No.615 Sqn) - RIAF,

India census 5.46; No.1 Sqn 2.46; Formation exercise, omitted to lower undercarriage landing, flying control fired Red cartridge too late, Cat.FA/Ac 6.9.46 (P/O RWB Bhardwaj OK); Recat FA/E; SOC 31.10.46

MD318 Spitfire LF.VIIIc (Merlin 66); TOC/RAF 29.1.44; Arr India (Karachi) 11.5.44; ACSEA (No.81 Sqn, 'FL-R') - RIAF, India census 5.46; Service unknown; Retd RAF; SOC 31.10.46

MD323 Spitfire LF.VIIIc (Merlin 66); TOC/RAF 2.3.44; Arr India (Karachi) 20.5.44; ACSEA (No.1331CU & No.151 OTU) - RIAF, India census 5.46; Service unknown; Retd RAF; SOC 31.12.46

MD325 Spitfire LF.VIIIc (Merlin 66); TOC/RAF 21.2.44; Arr India (Karachi) 20.5.44; ACSEA – RIAF, India census 5.46; SOC/RAF 13.6.46

MD328 Spitfire LF.VIIIc (Merlin 66); TOC/RAF 20.2.44; Arr India (Karachi) 26.4.44; ACSEA (No.155 Sqn) - RIAF, India census 5.46; No.8 Sqn, lost on cross-country, short of fuel, force-landed, swung to avoid ditch, tipped up, Chanda, Central Provinces, Cat.E 19.5.46 (F/Lt A Hussain OK); SOC 13.6.46

MD329 Spitfire LF.VIIIc (Merlin 66); TOC/RAF 6.3.44; Arr India (Karachi) 12.5.44; ACSEA – RIAF, India census 5.46; No.1 Sqn 2.46; Squadron move from Nagpur to Hakimpet, engine failed, force-landed wheels-up, undershot selected field, overturned, 20°43'N 79°1'E, 30m S of Nagpur, Cat.E 10.7.46 (P/O LM Katre seriously injured); SOC 31.10.46

MD331 Spitfire LF.VIIIc (Merlin 66); TOC/RAF 8.2.44; Arr India (Karachi) 11.5.44; ACSEA (No.81 Sqn) – RIAF, No.4 Sqn, engine failed at 350ft on take-off, force landing wheels-up in field, 1m S of Yelahanka, Cat.Ac 18.6.45 (F/O YR Agtey OK); SOC/RAF 12.7.45

MD332 Spitfire LF.VIIIc (Merlin 66); TOC/RAF 30.1.44; Arr India (Karachi) 20.5.44 – RIAF, No.8 Sqn ('T' or 'E'), landing from ops, collided with LV663 which had already landed, Coxs Bazaar, Cat.FB/Ac 7.1.45 (F/O SM Zahid OK); Retd RAF; SOC 12.2.45

MD333 Spitfire LF.VIIIc (Merlin 66); TOC/RAF 5.2.44; Arr India (Karachi) 12.5.44; ACSEA – RIAF, No.10 Sqn, undercarriage collapsed on landing Hmawbi, Cat.B 31.1.46 (P/O RD Law OK); SOC/RAF 30.5.46

MD334 Spitfire LF.VIIIc (Merlin 66); TOC/RAF 30.1.44; Arr India (Karachi) 11.5.44; ACSEA (No.81 Sqn) - RIAF, No.4 Sqn to No.139 R&SU 16.7.45; SOC/RAF 30.5.46

MD343 Spitfire LF.VIIIc (Merlin 66); TOC/RAF 11.3.44; Arr India (Karachi) 20.5.44 – RIAF, No.8 Sqn, leeward end of runway obstructed by crashed aircraft, heavy landing downwind, starboard wheel broke off, swung, broken up, 'George' airstrip, Nidania, Cat.E 11.1.45 (P/O E Artus OK), SOC

MD345 Spitfire LF.VIIIc (Merlin 66); TOC/RAF 19.2.44; Arr India (Karachi) 12.5.44; ACSEA - RIAF; No.9 Sqn from 5.45 to 7.45; India census 5.46; No.1 SFTS of AFS (I) in 5.46; To RIAF inventory 29.12.47; Fate unknown

MD347 Spitfire LF.VIIIc (Merlin 66); TOC/RAF 2.3.44; Arr India (Bombay) 4.2.45; ACSEA - RIAF; India census 5.46; No.1 SFTS of AFS (I), heavy landing in low cloud, tyre burst, went round again, belly-landed at Bhopal, Cat.FA/Ac 6.5.46 (P/O WH Walmsley OK); Retd RAF; Re-cat.E, SOC 27.6.46

MD353 Spitfire LF.VIIIc (Merlin 66); TOC/RAF 14.5.44; Arr India (Bombay) 18.7.44; ACSEA - RIAF, India census 5.46; No.2 Sqn ('E') from 20.1.46 to 4.47; Retd RAF; SOC 31.7.47

MD354 Spitfire LF.VIIIc (Merlin 66); TOC/RAF 8.2.44; Arr India (Karachi) 26.4.44 - RIAF; No.8 Sqn, inadvertently landed wheels-up, 'George' airstrip, Nidania, Cat.Ac 6.2.45 (P/O JP Ridgers); Retd RAF; SOC 29.3.45

MD369 Spitfire LF.VIIIc (Merlin 66); TOC/RAF 5.2.44; Arr India (Karachi) 11.5.44; ACSEA - RIAF, India census 5.46; Service unknown; Retd RAF; SOC 31.10.46

MD370 Spitfire LF.VIIIc (Merlin 66); TOC/RAF 5.2.44; Arr India (Karachi) 11.5.44; ACSEA (Nos.67 & 607 Sqns) - RIAF, India census 5.46; Service unknown; Retd RAF; SOC 30.1.47

MD371 Spitfire LF.VIIIc (Merlin 66); TOC/RAF 5.2.44; Arr India (Karachi) 11.5.44; ACSEA (No.228 Gp CF) - RIAF, India census 5.46; No.3 (Indian) Group Comm Flt 1946/47; Retd RAF; SOC 28.8.47

MD379 Spitfire LF.VIIIc (Merlin 66); TOC/RAF 11.3.44; Arr India (Karachi) 18.5.44; ACSEA - RIAF, India census 5.46; Service unknown; Retd RAF; SOC 27.3.47

MD384 Spitfire LF.VIIIc (Merlin 66); TOC/RAF 11.3.44; Arr India (Karachi) 20.5.44; ACSEA (No.81 Sqn) - RIAF, India census 5.46; AFS (I), engine cut on approach, belly-landed at Ambala, Cat.FA/E 10.1.47 (P/O UA Vaz seriously injured); SOC 30.1.47

MD386 Spitfire LF.VIIIc (Merlin 66); TOC/RAF 4.3.44; Arr India (Karachi) 12.5.44; ACSEA (No.615 Sqn); RIAF; No.8 Sqn, engine failed at 300ft during low flight, belly-landed in field, Cat.B 28.9.45 (F/O SM Ahmad); RiW; Retd RAF; SOC 29.11.45

MD387 Spitfire LF.VIIIc (Merlin 66); TOC/RAF 4.3.44; Arr India (Karachi) 12.5.44; ACSEA (No.3 RFU) - RIAF, India census 5.46; No.6 Sqn, tyre burst on take-off, belly-landed alongside runway, Ranchi, Cat.E 18.9.46 (P/O JR Peters OK); SOC 24.4.47

MD390 Spitfire LF.VIIIc (Merlin 66); TOC/RAF 14.2.44; Arr India (Karachi) 12.5.44; ACSEA (Nos.132 & 81 Sqns) - RIAF; No.4 Sqn to No.139 R&SU 4.7.45; SOC/RAF 19.7.45

MD398 Spitfire LF.VIIIc (Merlin 66); TOC/RAF 15.2.44; Arr India (Karachi) 12.5.44; ACSEA - RIAF, India census 5.46; No.2 Sqn ('X') 6.46; Tyre burst on take-off with 4x500-lb bombs, undercarriage collapsed, Miranshah, Cat.FA/E 8.8.46 (F/O DB Rai OK); Retd RAF (casualty wastage); SOC 29.8.46

MD400 Spitfire LF.VIIIc (Merlin 66); TOC/RAF 18.2.44; Arr India (Karachi) 12.5.44; ACSEA (Nos.152 & 273 Sqns) - RIAF; No.1 Sqn, hit slipstream of leading aircraft landing in formation, lost control, heavy landing, tyre burst, undercarriage raised to avoid overturning, Samungli, Cat.B 20.4.46 (F/O BS Dogra OK); Re-cat.E, SOC 9.5.46

MD401 Spitfire LF.VIIIc (Merlin 66); TOC/RAF 21.2.44; Arr India (Karachi) 12.5.44; ACSEA (No.607 Sqn) - RIAF, India census 5.46; No.1 Sqn in 1946; Retd RAF; SOC 1.6.47

MD402 Spitfire LF.VIIIc (Merlin 66); TOC/RAF 12.3.44; Arr India (Karachi) 20.5.44; ACSEA - RIAF; No.10 Sqn, engine trouble, belly-landed in field, 19°18'N 90°17'E, Yedashe, Burma, Cat.E 3.1. or 8.1.46 (F/O RL Sori seriously injured); SOC 14.2.46

MH432 Spitfire T.IX (Merlin 66); Became **HS535**; TOC/RAF 13.8.43; ETO; V.A. 17.10.46; Converted to T.IX 13.5.48 (Class B reg. G.15-3) – RIAF 9.48; AFS (I) Ambala 1949; Fate unknown

MJ177 Spitfire T.IX (Merlin 66); Became **HS536**; TOC/RAF 16.10.43; V.A. 16.4.47; Conv to T.IX 11.5.48 (Class B reg. G.15-4) - RIAF 9.48; AFS (I) Ambala 1949; Fate unknown

MJ276 Spitfire T.IX (Merlin 66); Became **HS537**; TOC/RAF 3.11.43; V.A. 16.4.47; Conv to T.IX 11.5.48 (Class B reg. G.15-5) - RIAF 29.9.48; AFS (I) Ambala 1949; Fate unknown

MJ451 Spitfire T.IX (Merlin 66); Became **HS538**; TOC/RAF 8.11.43; V.A. 30.10.46; Conv to T.IX 26.5.48 (Class B reg. G.15-6) - RIAF 9.48; AFS (I) Ambala 1949; Fate unknown

MJ518 Spitfire T.IX (Merlin 66); Became **HS539**; TOC/RAF 22.11.43; V.A. 30.11.46; Conv to T.IX 11.5.48 (Class B reg. G.15-7) - RIAF 11.48; AFS (I) Ambala 1949; Fate unknown

MK172 Spitfire T.IX (Merlin 66); Became **HS540**; TOC/RAF 20.1.44; V.A. 21.10.46; Conv to T.IX 24.5.48 (Class B reg. G.15-8) - RIAF 11.48; AFS (I) Ambala 1949; Fate unknown

MK176 Spitfire T.IX (Merlin 66); Became **HS541**; TOC/RAF 29.1.44; V.A. 24.10.46; Conv to T.IX 24.5.48 (Class B reg. G.15-9) - RIAF 15.11.48; AFS (I) Ambala 1949; Fate unknown

MK298 Spitfire T.IX (Merlin 66); Became **HS542**; TOC/RAF 4.2.44; V.A. 31.10.46; Conv to T.IX 24.5.48 (Class B reg. G.15-10) - RIAF 15.11.48; AFS (I) Ambala 1949; Fate unknown

ML417 Spitfire T.IX (Merlin 66); Became **HS543**; TOC/RAF 28.4.44; V.A. 31.10.46; Conv to T.IX 25.5.48 (Class B reg. G-15-11) - RIAF 15.11.48; AFS (I) Ambala 1949; Palam until 1967; To Indian Air Force Museum, Palam for storage 1967; Sold to Senator Norman E Gaar, Kansas City, MO 4.71, and shipped to USA 15.3.72; Duxford, UK 7.8.80; First flown after conversion (single seater) 10.2.84; To USA as *N2TF* 2001 - **SURVIVOR**

MT505 Spitfire LF.VIIIc (Merlin 66); TOC/RAF 20.3.44; Arr India (Karachi) 18.5.44; ACSEA - RIAF; No.2 Sqn 5.45; No.4 Sqn, bird strike in formation, starboard mainplane damaged, Yelahanka, Cat.A(R) 27.7.45 (P/O R Khan OK); No.2 Sqn from 21.1.46 to 4.46; India census 5.46; Retd RAF; SOC 30.1.47

MT506 Spitfire LF.VIIIc (Merlin 66); TOC/RAF 21.3.44; Arr India (Karachi) 18.5.44; ACSEA (Nos.155 & 67 Sqns) - RIAF, India census 5.46; Service unknown; Retd RAF; SOC 27.3.47

MT507 Spitfire LF.VIIIc (Merlin 66); TOC/RAF 24.4.44; Arr India (Bombay) 9.7.44; ACSEA (No.136 Sqn) - RIAF, India census 5.46; Service unknown; Retd RAF; SOC 27.2.47

MT516 Spitfire LF.VIIIc (Merlin 66); TOC/RAF 18.4.44; Arr India (Bombay) 4.7.44; ACSEA; No.3 FSTU – RIAF; India census 5.46; AFS (I); Service unknown; SOC/RAF 27.11.47; Became ground instructional airframe

MT520 Spitfire LF.VIIIc (Merlin 66); TOC/RAF 21.4.44; Arr India (Bombay) 4.7.44; ACSEA - RIAF, India census 5.46; No.6 Sqn, transfer ferry flight, fast landing to avoid MV118 turning at end of runway, but hit it, Agra, Cat.FA/E 15.4.47 (F/O JL Payne OK); SOC 26.6.47

MT526 Spitfire LF.VIIIc (Merlin 66); TOC/RAF 15.2.44; Arr India (Karachi) 26.4.44; ACSEA - RIAF, India census 5.46; Service unknown; Retd RAF; SOC 31.12.46

MT554 Spitfire LF.VIIIc (Merlin 66); TOC/RAF 3.6.44; Arr India (Bombay) 4.8.44; ACSEA (No.152 Sqn) - RIAF, India census 5.46; No.10 Sqn ('F') 1946/47; Retd RAF; SOC 26.6.47

MT555 Spitfire LF.VIIIc (Merlin 66); TOC/RAF 4.6.44; Arr India (Bombay) 4.8.44; ACSEA - RIAF, India census 5.46; Service unknown; Retd RAF; SOC 27.11.47; Became ground instructional airframe

MT556 Spitfire LF.VIIIc (Merlin 66); TOC/RAF 3.6.44; Arr India (Bombay) 14.8.44; ACSEA; AFTU (I) – RIAF; India census 5.46; AFS (I); Service unknown; Retd RAF; SOC 13.6.46

MT557 Spitfire LF.VIIIc (Merlin 66); TOC/RAF 4.6.44; Arr India (Bombay) 14.8.44; ACSEA (Nos.152 & 607 Sqns) - RIAF; No.8 Sqn, overshot landing after ops, went into ditch after retracting wheels, Mingaladon, Cat.FB/E 4.8.45 (F/O RS Shipurkar OK); SOC 23.8.45

MT573 Spitfire LF.VIIIc (Merlin 66); TOC/RAF 14.7.44; Arr India (Bombay) 28.9.44; ACSEA - RIAF; No.1 Sqn in 1945; Retd RAF; SOC 30.8.45

MT574 Spitfire LF.VIIIc (Merlin 66); TOC/RAF 18.7.44; Arr India (Bombay) 28.9.44; ACSEA - RIAF, India census 5.46; No.3 FSTU, propeller pecked ground landing at Bhopal, Cat.FA/A 9.5.46 (F/O AR Khan OK); SOC/RAF 25.7.46

MT575 Spitfire LF.VIIIc (Merlin 66); TOC/RAF 20.7.44; Arr India (Bombay) 26.9.44; ACSEA - RIAF, India census 5.46; Service unknown; Retd RAF; SOC 30.1.47

MT576 Spitfire LF.VIIIc (Merlin 66); TOC/RAF 23.7.44; Arr India (Bombay) 26.8.44; ACSEA - RIAF, India census 5.46; Service unknown; Retd RAF; SOC 30.1.47

MT580 Spitfire LF.VIIIc (Merlin 66); TOC/RAF 27.7.44; Arr India (Bombay) 29.10.44; ACSEA - RIAF, India census 5.46; No.10 Sqn in 1946; Retd RAF; SOC 13.6.46

MT581 Spitfire LF.VIIIc (Merlin 66); TOC/RAF 14.8.44; Arr India (Bombay) 4.11.44; ACSEA (Nos.615 & 607 Sqns) - RIAF, India census 5.46; Service unknown; Retd RAF; SOC 28.8.47

MT595 Spitfire LF.VIIIc (Merlin 66); TOC/RAF 5.4.44; Arr India (Bombay) 4.7.44; ACSEA (No.3 RFU) - RIAF, India census 5.46; Service unknown; Retd RAF; SOC 31.12.47

*Dismantled surviving Spitfire T.IX **HS-543** (ex ML417) at Overland Park, Kansas, in November 1972 after being shipped from India. After some 25 years in the UK it is now back in the USA as a single-seater registered N2TF.*

Surviving Spitfire LF.VIIIc T-17 (ex MT719) in a derelict state at Jaipur after being used for some time as a ground instructional airframe. After restoration to flight status in Italy it was sold to the UK and is currently in the USA with the civil registration N719MT.

MT604 Spitfire LF.VIIIc (Merlin 66); TOC/RAF 20.4.44; Arr India (Bombay) 4.7.44; ACSEA (No.81 Sqn, 'FL-N') - RIAF, India census 5.46; Service unknown; Retd RAF; SOC 31.12.46

MT606 Spitfire LF.VIIIc (Merlin 66); TOC/RAF 18.4.44; Arr India (Bombay) 4.7.44; ACSEA (No.152 Sqn) - RIAF; No.1 Sqn in 2.46; India census 5.46; No.2 Sqn in 11.46; Retd RAF; SOC 31.7.47

MT608 Spitfire LF.VIIIc (Merlin 66); TOC/RAF 18.4.44; Arr India (Bombay) 4.7.44; ACSEA (No.17 Sqn) - RIAF, India census 5.46; Service unknown; Retd RAF; SOC 31.10.46

MT610 Spitfire LF.VIIIc (Merlin 66); TOC/RAF 24.4.44; Arr India (Bombay) 4.7.44; ACSEA (Nos.136 & 81 Sqns, 'MT-M') - RIAF, India census 5.46; No.2 Sqn 1.46 (also listed 11.46 - 5.47); Retd RAF; SOC 31.7.47

MT611 Spitfire LF.VIIIc (Merlin 66); TOC/RAF 24.4.44; Arr India (Bombay) 4.7.44; ACSEA - RIAF, India census 5.46; No.2 Sqn ('D') 3.46; Drifted in cross-wind, heavy landing, tyre burst, opened up and belly-landed, Kohat, Cat.FA/E 10.8.46 (P/O AM Palamkote OK); Retd RAF (casualty wastage); SOC 31.10.46

MT615 Spitfire LF.VIIIc (Merlin 66); TOC/RAF 20.4.44; Arr India (Bombay) 4.7.44; ACSEA (No.81 Sqn, 'FL-Y') - RIAF; No.6 Sqn, engine cut after take-off, belly-landed in paddy field 1m NW of Ranchi, Cat.FA/E 9.3.46 (P/O Fernandez seriously injured); SOC 25.4.46

MT623 Spitfire LF.VIIIc (Merlin 66); TOC/RAF 26.4.44; Arr India (Bombay) 4.7.44; ACSEA (No.81 Sqn); RIAF, India census 5.46; No.9 Sqn; Retd RAF; SOC 27.3.47

MT631 Spitfire LF.VIIIc (Merlin 66); TOC/RAF 7.5.44; Arr India (Bombay) 2.7.44; ACSEA - RIAF, India census 5.46; Service unknown; Retd RAF; SOC 1.6.47

MT651 Spitfire LF.VIIIc (Merlin 66); TOC/RAF 22.4.44; Arr India (Bombay) 4.7.44; ACSEA - RIAF, India census 5.46; No.2 Sqn, to Quetta 9.11.46; Retd RAF; SOC 30.1.47
NOTE: Reported for No.2 Sqn as "MT661", which was SOC already on 29.8.46

MT657 Spitfire LF.VIIIc (Merlin 66); TOC/RAF 17.4.44; Arr India (Bombay) 4.7.44; ACSEA - RIAF, India census 5.46; No.1 Sqn, crashed Cat.FA/Ac 12.12.46; Retd RAF; SOC 30.1.47

MT661 Spitfire LF.VIIIc (Merlin 66); TOC/RAF .1944; Arr India (Bombay) 1944; ACSEA - RIAF; No.2 Sqn; SOC 29.8.46

MT662 Spitfire LF.VIIIc (Merlin 66); TOC/RAF 7.5.44; Arr India (Bombay) 4.7.44; ACSEA - RIAF, India census 5.46; No.2 Sqn; No.1 Sqn, tyre burst on heavy night landing, belly-landed at Yelahanka, Cat.FA/E 1.4.47 (F/O W H Walmsley OK); SOC 1.6.47

MT678 Spitfire LF.VIIIc (Merlin 66); TOC/RAF 7.6.44; Arr India (Bombay) 5.9.44; ACSEA – RIAF, India census 5.46; Service unknown; Retd RAF, SOC 13.6.46

MT706 Spitfire LF.VIIIc (Merlin 66); TOC/RAF 3.6.44; Arr India (Bombay) 5.9.44; ACSEA; AFTU (I) - RIAF, India census 5.46; AFS (I) in 1946; SOC/RAF 27.6.46

MT707 Spitfire LF.VIIIc (Merlin 66); TOC/RAF 6.6.44; Arr India (Bombay) 14.8.44; ACSEA; AFTU (I) – RIAF; India census 5.46; AFS (I); Service unknown; Retd RAF; SOC 29.3.47

MT709 Spitfire LF.VIIIc (Merlin 66); TOC/RAF 6.6.44; Arr India (Bombay) 14.8.44; ACSEA (No.151 OTU) - RIAF, India census 5.46; Service unknown; Retd RAF; SOC 31.7.47

MT719 Spitfire LF.VIIIc (Merlin 66); Became **T-17**; TOC/RAF 21.6.44; Arr India (Bombay) 5.9.44; ACSEA (8.45), No.17 Sqn ('YB-J') - RIAF, India census 5.46; To RIAF inventory 29.12.47; Coded '93' at one time; Became ground instructional airframe *T-17* with AFS Cadet Corps at Sanganer-Jaipur until 1977; Hulk recovered Jaipur AFB in 1978 by Ormond and Wensley Haydon-Baillie, Duxford, UK; To Italy 12.79 (Civil reg. *I-SPIT*); To UK 1989 (*G-VIII* 27.4.89); To USA 8.93 (*N719MT*) - **SURVIVOR**

MT725 Spitfire LF.VIIIc (Merlin 66); TOC/RAF 9.12.44; Arr India (Bombay) 19.2.45; ACSEA - RIAF; No.9 Sqn, short of fuel, belly-landed Kodarma, 20m NNE of Hazaribad, Cat.B 18.5.45 (P/O J Selski Can OK); India census 5.46; AFS (I) Ambala, bird strike on radiator during aerobatics, Cat.A 18.6.46 (P/O DC Pears OK); Tyre burst on take-off, landed wheels up, Cat.FA/Ac 19.10.46 (P/O RA Williams OK); Dropped heavily on flapless landing, undercarriage collapsed, Ambala, Cat.FA/E 6.3.47 (P/O AS Bakhshi OK); SOC 27.3.47

MT726 Spitfire LF.VIIIc (Merlin 66); TOC/RAF 11.7.44; Arr India (Bombay) 28.9.44; ACSEA (No.273 Sqn, 'MS-Z') - RIAF; No.1 Sqn ('Z') in 1946; Retd RAF; SOC 9.5.46

INDIA

MT728 Spitfire LF.VIIIc (Merlin 66); TOC/RAF 14.7.44; Arr India (Bombay) 28.9.44; ACSEA (Nos.273 & 67 Sqns) - RIAF; No.1 SFTS of AFS (I), undercarriage jammed, belly-landed, Bhopal, Cat.FA/Ac 18.5.46 (P/O G Haider OK); Retd RAF; Re-cat.E, SOC 30.5.46

MT739 Spitfire LF.VIIIc (Merlin 66); TOC/RAF 24.8.44; Arr India (Bombay) 19.11.44; ACSEA (Nos.155 & 607 Sqns) - RIAF; No.3 Sqn, engine failed at 5,000ft, engine caught fire, belly-landed 15m SSW of Kolar, aircraft caught fire and blew up, Cat.E 2.3.46 (P/O GV Francis seriously injured); SOC 14.3.46

MT740 Spitfire LF.VIIIc (Merlin 66); TOC/RAF 25.8.44; Arr India (Bombay) 4.2.45; ACSEA - RIAF; No.9 Sqn in 1945; Retd RAF (later Cat.E with No.152 Sqn 15.6.45); SOC 12.7.45

MT741 Spitfire LF.VIIIc (Merlin 66); TOC/RAF 29.8.44; Arr India (Bombay) 19.11.44; ACSEA (Nos.155 & 607 Sqns) - RIAF; No.8 Sqn, while taxying collided with petrol bowser crossing taxytrack, Mingaladon, Cat.A(R) 3.10.45 (F/O SM Ahmad); RiW; Retd RAF; SOC 26.9.46

MT742 Spitfire LF.VIIIc (Merlin 66); TOC/RAF 1.9.44; Arr India (Bombay) 19.11.44; ACSEA - RIAF; No.1 Sqn in 2.46; India census 5.46; Retd RAF; SOC 27.11.47; Became ground instructional airframe

MT743 Spitfire LF.VIIIc (Merlin 66); TOC/RAF 6.9.44; Arr India (Bombay) 8.12.44; ACSEA (No.67 Sqn) - RIAF, India census 5.46; Service unknown; Retd RAF; SOC 28.8.47 (bboc, SOC 31.12.47)

MT744 Spitfire LF.VIIIc (Merlin 66); TOC/RAF 6.9.44; Arr India (Bombay) 8.12.44; ACSEA (No.607 Sqn) - RIAF; No.3 Sqn, ferrying, undercarriage not locked down, collapsed on landing, Santa Cruz, Cat.FA/E 12.5.46 (F/O R Singh OK); SOC 30.5.46

MT745 Spitfire LF.VIIIc (Merlin 66); TOC/RAF 4.10.44; Arr India (Bombay) 4.2.45; ACSEA - RIAF, India census 5.46; Service unknown; Retd RAF; SOC 30.1.47

MT746 Spitfire LF.VIIIc (Merlin 66); TOC/RAF 23.10.44; Arr India (Bombay) 4.2.45; ACSEA (No.308 MU) – RIAF; Std mainplane hit stationery MT taxying Bamrauli 23.12.46 (F/O CG Bush OK); To RIAF inventory 29.12.47; AFS (I); Fate unknown

MT747 Spitfire LF.VIIIc (Merlin 66); TOC/RAF 9.10.44; Arr India (Bombay) 8.12.44; ACSEA (No.607 Sqn) - RIAF, India census 5.46; Service unknown; Retd RAF; SOC 30.1.47

MT766 Spitfire LF.VIIIc (Merlin 66); TOC/RAF 9.44; Arr India (Bombay) 8.12.44; ACSEA (No.81 Sqn, 'FL-D') - RIAF, India census 5.46; No.1 SFTS of AFS/I ('70'), flaps failed, overshot landing, undercarriage raised to stop, Peshawar, Cat.FA/Ac 11.10.46 (P/O RA Williams OK); Retd RAF; Re-cat.E, SOC 31.10.46

MT780 Spitfire LF.VIIIc (Merlin 66); TOC/RAF 24.5.44; Arr India (Bombay) 18.7.44; ACSEA - RIAF, India census 5.46; Service unknown; Retd RAF; SOC 30.1.47

MT783 Spitfire LF.VIIIc (Merlin 66); TOC/RAF 22.5.44; Arr India (Bombay) 10.7.44; ACSEA (Nos.3 RFU & 155 Sqn) - RIAF; AFS (I), hit stationery Harvard FT371 taxying, Ambala, Cat.FA/A 13.2.46 (P/O HS Jaggi OK); India census 5.46; Retd RAF; SOC 27.11.47

MT790 Spitfire LF.VIIIc (Merlin 66); TOC/RAF 1.6.44; Arr India (Bombay) 14.8.44; ACSEA; AFTU (I) – RIAF; India census 5.46; AFS (I); Retd RAF; SOC 30.1.47

MT798 Spitfire LF.VIIIc (Merlin 66); TOC/RAF 7.6.44; Arr India (Bombay) 8.12.44; ACSEA (No.81 Sqn, 'FL-Y'); RIAF, India census 5.46; Service unknown; Retd RAF; SOC 30.1.47

MT815 Spitfire LF.VIIIc (Merlin 66); TOC/RAF 18.7.44; Arr India (Bombay) 29.10.44; ACSEA (No.67 Sqn) - RIAF, India census 5.46; No.2 Sqn by 4.46 - 11.46; Retd RAF; SOC 31.7.47

MT828 Spitfire LF.VIIIc (Merlin 66); TOC/RAF 20.7.44; Arr India (Bombay) 19.11.44; ACSEA - RIAF, India census 5.46; No.2 Sqn 11.46; Tyre burst on take-off, belly-landed on airfield Kohat, Cat.E 14.1.47 (P/O MU Ducasse OK); SOC 27.2.47

MT832 Spitfire LF.VIIIc (Merlin 66); TOC/RAF 10.7.44; Arr India (Bombay) 19.11.44; ACSEA (No.17 Sqn) - RIAF, India census 5.46; AFS (I), engine lost power during aerobatics, undershot landing, slipped in on turn, Ambala, Cat.FA/E 15.4.47 (P/O VG Wright injured); SOC 24.4.47

MT836 Spitfire LF.VIIIc (Merlin 66); TOC/RAF 31.12.44; Arr India (Bombay) 28.3.45; ACSEA - RIAF, India census 5.46; Service unknown; Retd RAF; SOC 1.6.47

MT837 Spitfire LF.VIIIc (Merlin 66); TOC/RAF 24.12.44; Arr India (Bombay) 19.2.45 - RIAF; No.9 Sqn, taxied into stationery JF883, propeller damaged, Yelahanka, Cat.A(R) 28.9.45 (F/O AKS Ahmad); Low flying at 50ft, struck by debris thrown up by exploding grenades on ground on range, force-landed wheels up straight ahead, 23°17'N 85°21'E, 75m W of Ranchi, Cat.FA/E 8.10.45 (F/O NG Roy OK); SOC 25.10.45

MT838 Spitfire LF.VIIIc (Merlin 66); TOC/RAF 3.1.45; Arr India (Bombay) 3.4.45; ACSEA (ATP Poona) - RIAF, India census 5.46; No.2 Sqn ('P') in 1946; Retd RAF; SOC 26.9.46

MT839 Spitfire LF.VIIIc (Merlin 66); TOC/RAF 3.1.45; Arr India (Bombay) 20.3.45; ACSEA - RIAF; No.4 Sqn, overshot landing, went into boundary fence and ditch, undercarriage collapsed, Willingdon, Cat.B 8.11.45 (P/O L Prince-Foster OK); Retd RAF; SOC 29.11.45

MT840 Spitfire LF.VIIIc (Merlin 66); TOC/RAF 31.12.44; Arr India (Bombay) 20.3.45 - RIAF; No.9 Sqn, engine failed at 5,000ft, force-landed wheels-up in field near Ranchi, Cat.E 11.6.45 (P/O JM Afridi), SOC

MT841 Spitfire LF.VIIIc (Merlin 66); TOC/RAF 3.1.45; Arr India (Bombay) 12.4.45; ACSEA - RIAF, India census 5.46; No.4 Sqn, engine trouble on cross-country from Arkonam, successful forced landing 13°05'N 79°42'E on 13.7.45 (F/O AIK Suares OK); To No.139 R&SU 16.7.45; No.4 Sqn 18.8.45; No.2 Sqn ('U') from 20.1.46; Engine caught fire after oil leak in circuit, belly-landed on airfield Kohat, Cat.FA/E 29.1.47 (P/O P Callaghan seriously injured); SOC 27.2.47

MT842 Spitfire LF.VIIIc (Merlin 66); TOC/RAF 21.1.45; ACSEA – RIAF, India census 5.46; Service unknown; SOC/RAF 13.6.46

MT843 Spitfire LF.VIIIc (Merlin 66); TOC/RAF 31.12.44; Arr India (Bombay) 19.2.45; ACSEA - RIAF, India census 5.46; No.2 Sqn from 18.1.46 to 11.46; Retd RAF; SOC 31.7.47

MT844 Spitfire LF.VIIIc (Merlin 66); TOC/RAF 30.1.45; ACSEA – RIAF, India census 5.46; Service unknown; SOC/RAF 13.6.46

MT845 Spitfire LF.VIIIc (Merlin 66); TOC/RAF 7.1.45; Arr India (Bombay) 20.3.45; ACSEA - RIAF; No.9 Sqn, undercarriage collapsed landing, Hmawbi, Cat.Ac 9.1.46 (F/O IH Latif OK); Retd RAF; SOC 30.5.46

MT846 Spitfire LF.VIIIc (Merlin 66); TOC/RAF 21.1.45; ACSEA – RIAF, India census 5.46; Service unknown; SOC/RAF 13.6.46

MT848 Spitfire FR.XIVe (Griffon 65); TOC/RAF 8.3.45; Arr India (Karachi) 28.7.45; ACSEA - RIAF, India census 5.46; No.6 Sqn, engine failure while low flying, force-landed wheels up, crashed 4m SW of Ranchi, Cat.FA/E 12.9.46 (F/O TB Chowdhury injured); SOC 31.10.46

MT856 Spitfire FR.XIVe (Griffon 65); TOC/RAF 5.3.45; ACSEA – RIAF, India census 5.46; Service unknown; SOC/RAF 25.7.46

MT872 Spitfire LF.VIIIc (Merlin 66); TOC/RAF 17.8.44; Arr India (Bombay) 19.11.44; ACSEA (No.67 Sqn) - RIAF, India census 5.46; No.2 Sqn ('Y') in 6.46; Engine trouble, then cut, crash-landed avoiding obstruction on approach on approach 1m SE of Kohat, Cat.FA/E 9.9.46 (F/Lt RA Pandit OK); Retd RAF (casualty wastage); SOC 26.9.46

MT873 Spitfire LF.VIIIc (Merlin 66); TOC/RAF 18.8.44; Arr India (Bombay) 4.11.44; ACSEA (No.152 Sqn) - RIAF, India census 5.46; No.1 SFTS (I), oiled windscreen and smoke in cockpit after ground firing practice, cut engine

MT875 Spitfire LF.VIIIc (Merlin 66); TOC/RAF 23.8.44; Arr India (Bombay) 4.11.44; ACSEA - RIAF, India census 5.46; Service unknown; Retd RAF; SOC 30.1.47

MT878 Spitfire LF.VIIIc (Merlin 66); TOC/RAF 25.8.44; Arr India (Bombay) 19.11.44; ACSEA (No.152 Sqn) - RIAF; No.10 Sqn, Accident, DBR Cat.E 20.12.45; SOC 10.1.46

MT880 Spitfire LF.VIIIc (Merlin 66); TOC/RAF 27.8.44; Arr India (Bombay) 4.11.44; ACSEA (No.152 Sqn) - RIAF, India census 5.46; To RIAF inventory 29.12.47; No.2 Sqn or AFS (I); Fate unknown

MT881 Spitfire LF.VIIIc (Merlin 66); TOC/RAF 27.8.44; Arr India (Bombay) 4.11.44; ACSEA (Nos.131 & 615 Sqns) - RIAF, India census 5.46; No.2 Sqn in 11.46; Cyclonic weather over hilly terrain on cross-country, short of fuel, force-landed wheels down, Narayangaon, Cat.E 19.4.47 (F/O DB Pigott OK); Retd RAF; SOC 31.7.47

MT884 Spitfire LF.VIIIc (Merlin 66); TOC/RAF 6.9.44; Arr India (Bombay) 8.12.44; ACSEA; No.3 FSTU - RIAF, India census 5.46; No.9 Sqn; Retd RAF; SOC 13.6.46

MT885 Spitfire LF.VIIIc (Merlin 66); TOC/RAF 5.9.44; Arr India (Bombay) 8.12.44; ACSEA - RIAF, India census 5.46; No.9 Sqn, hit parked bowser taxying Ranchi 16.6.45 (F/O CK Singha OK); Retd RAF; SOC 1.6.47

MT886 Spitfire LF.VIIIc (Merlin 66); TOC/RAF 6.9.44; Arr India (Bombay) 8.12.44; ACSEA - RIAF, India census 5.46; Service unknown; Retd RAF; SOC 30.1.47

MT889 Spitfire LF.VIIIc (Merlin 66); TOC/RAF 17.9.44; Arr India (Bombay) 8.12.44; ACSEA - RIAF, India census 5.46; Service unknown; Retd RAF; SOC 30.1.47

MT901 Spitfire LF.VIIIc (Merlin 66); TOC/RAF 26.9.44; Arr India (Bombay) 8.12.44; ACSEA - RIAF, India census 5.46; No.10 Sqn ('L') 1946; Retd RAF; SOC 31.10.46

MT907 Spitfire LF.VIIIc (Merlin 66); TOC/RAF 29.10.44; Arr India (Bombay) 2.1.45; ACSEA - RIAF, India census 5.46; No.10 Sqn ('T') 1946/47; Retd RAF; SOC 27.3.47

MT908 Spitfire LF.VIIIc (Merlin 66); TOC/RAF 30.10.44; Arr India (Bombay) 4.2.45; ACSEA (No.151 OTU) - RIAF, India census 5.46; Service unknown; Retd RAF; SOC 31.12.46

MT911 Spitfire LF.VIIIc (Merlin 66); TOC/RAF 9.11.44; Arr India (Bombay) 4.2.45; ACSEA - RIAF, India census 5.46; Service unknown; Retd RAF; SOC 26.9.46

MT912 Spitfire LF.VIIIc (Merlin 66); TOC/RAF 7.11.44; Arr India (Bombay) 4.2.45; ACSEA - RIAF; No.9 Sqn, pulled aircraft off ground too soon on take-off, bounced back and damaged starboard undercarriage, Ranchi Cat.Ac 2.6.45 (P/O SC Moulick OK); India census 5.46; No.10 Sqn 1946/47; No.1 SFTS of AFS (I), dived in on low level flight, burnt out, Gara village, 3m S of Ambala, Cat.FA/E 6.7.47 (P/O GS Guron killed); Retd RAF (casualty wastage); SOC 28.8.47

MT913 Spitfire LF.VIIIc (Merlin 66); TOC/RAF 9.11.44; Arr India (Bombay) 2.1.45; ACSEA - RIAF, India census 5.46; Service unknown; Retd RAF; SOC 30.1.47

MT915 Spitfire LF.VIIIc (Merlin 66); TOC/RAF 15.11.44; Arr India (Bombay) 4.2.45; ACSEA - RIAF, India census 5.46; No.2 Sqn from 20.1.46 to 4.47; Retd RAF; SOC 31.7.47

MT933 Spitfire LF.VIIIc (Merlin 66); TOC/RAF 15.6.44; Casablanca 13.7.44 - RIAF; AFS (I), tyre burst on take-off, belly-landed, Cat.E 30.7.47 (P/O KB Majid OK), SOC

MT934 Spitfire LF.VIIIc (Merlin 66); TOC/RAF 18.6.44; Arr India (Bombay) 5.9.44; ACSEA - RIAF, India census 5.46; Service unknown; Retd RAF; SOC 30.1.47

MT940 Spitfire LF.VIIIc (Merlin 66); TOC/RAF 22.6.44; Arr India (Bombay) 5.9.44; ACSEA - RIAF, India census 5.46; AFS (I); To RIAF inventory 29.12.47; Fate unknown

MT941 Spitfire LF.VIIIc (Merlin 66); TOC/RAF 24.6.44; Arr India (Bombay) 5.9.44; ACSEA (Nos.607, 'AF-D') & 152 Sqn) - RIAF; No.2 Sqn from 20.1.46; Retd RAF; SOC 29.8.46

MT946 Spitfire LF.VIIIc (Merlin 66); TOC/RAF 29.6.44; Arr India (Bombay) 5.9.44; ACSEA (No.152 Sqn) - RIAF, India census 5.46; Service unknown; Retd RAF; SOC 30.1.47

MT950 Spitfire LF.VIIIc (Merlin 66); TOC/RAF 16.7.44; Arr India (Bombay) 15.12.44; ACSEA - RIAF, India census 5.46; Service unknown; Retd RAF; SOC 30.1.47

MT959 Spitfire LF.VIIIc (Merlin 66); TOC/RAF 18.7.44; Arr India (Bombay) 29.10.44; ACSEA - RIAF; No.9 Sqn ('N') 6.45; Retd RAF; SOC 11.4.46

MT963 Spitfire LF.VIIIc (Merlin 66); TOC/RAF 3.7.44; Arr India (Bombay) 28.9.44; ACSEA - RIAF, India census 5.46; Service unknown; Retd RAF; SOC 31.12.46

MT964 Spitfire LF.VIIIc (Merlin 66); TOC/RAF 3.7.44; Arr India (Bombay) 28.9.44 - RIAF; No.8 Sqn, engine failed at 500ft on search for crashed aircraft, belly-landing 22°42'N 88°43'E, Cat.Ac 5.4.45 (F/Lt N Dugdale OK); Retd RAF; SOC 31.5.45

MT966 Spitfire LF.VIIIc (Merlin 66); TOC/RAF 7.7.44; ACSEA – RIAF; No.4 Sqn, crashed Cat.FA/E 28.5.45; SOC/RAF 13.6.45

MT967 Spitfire LF.VIIIc (Merlin 66); TOC/RAF 7.7.44; ACSEA – RIAF; Unknown unit, crashed Cat.FA/E 6.3.45; SOC/RAF 17.4.45

MT969 Spitfire LF.VIIIc (Merlin 66); TOC/RAF 7.7.44; Arr India (Bombay) 28.9.44; ACSEA (No.155 Sqn) - RIAF, India census 5.46; Retd RAF (ACSEA) 25.7.46; SOC 30.1.47

MT983 Spitfire LF.VIIIc (Merlin 66); TOC/RAF 14.7.44; Arr India (Bombay) 28.9.44; ACSEA (No.155 Sqn) - RIAF, India census 5.46; AFS (I); To RIAF inventory 29.12.47 (SOC/RAF 28.8.47, bboc 27.11.47); Fate unknown

MT987 Spitfire LF.VIIIc (Merlin 66); TOC/RAF 10.7.44; Arr India (Bombay) 29.9.44; ACSEA (No.615 Sqn) - RIAF, India census 5.46; No.1 Sqn in 2.46; While landing, ran into JG489 leading, undercarriage collapsed, Samungli 6.6.46 (F/Lt AK Gangully seriously injured); Retd RAF; SOC 31.10.46

MT993 Spitfire LF.VIIIc (Merlin 66); TOC/RAF 16.7.44; Arr India (Bombay) 15.10.44; ACSEA (No.131 Sqn) - RIAF, India census 5.46; AFS (I) ['K'], tyre burst on take-off, belly-landed at Ambala, Cat.FA/E 30.7.47; Retd RAF (casualty wastage); SOC 28.8.47

MT994 Spitfire LF.VIIIc (Merlin 66); TOC/RAF 16.7.44; Arr India (Bombay) 28.9.44; ACSEA - RIAF, India census 5.46; Service unknown; Retd RAF; SOC 26.9.46

MT998 Spitfire LF.VIIIc (Merlin 66); TOC/RAF 26.7.44; Arr India (Bombay) 4.11.44; ACSEA - RIAF, India census 5.46; Service unknown; Retd RAF; SOC 27.8.47

MV118 Spitfire LF.VIIIc (Merlin 66); TOC/RAF 27.7.44; Arr India (Bombay) 29.10.44; ACSEA (No.17 Sqn) - RIAF, India census 5.46; No.6 Sqn, while turning at end of runway, run into by MT520 landing, Agra, Cat.FA/E 15.4.47 (F/O NB Menon OK); SOC 26.6.47

MV122 Spitfire LF.VIIIc (Merlin 66); TOC/RAF 12.8.44; Arr India (Bombay) 4.11.44; ACSEA - RIAF, India census 5.46; No.1 Sqn, overshot landing, swung off runway, undercarriage collapsed, Santa Cruz, Cat.Ac 12.12.46 (F/O Powar OK); Retd RAF; SOC 27.2.47

MV143 Spitfire LF.VIIIc (Merlin 66); TOC/RAF 6.10.44; Arr India (Bombay) 8.12.44; ACSEA - RIAF; No.4 Sqn from 11.45 (replaced MT839); Left Sqn 12.45; No.8 Sqn 1.46; Retd RAF; SOC 31.1.46

MV145 Spitfire LF.VIIIc (Merlin 66); TOC/RAF 8.9.44; Arr India (Bombay) 19.11.44; ACSEA - RIAF, India census 5.46; Service unknown; Retd RAF; SOC 1.6.47

MV201 Spitfire LF.VIIIc (Merlin 66); TOC/RAF 14.1.45; ACSEA 5.7.45 – RIAF; India census 5.46; Service unknown; SOC/RAF 13.6.46

MV205 Spitfire LF.VIIIc (Merlin 66); TOC/RAF 2.12.44; Arr India (Bombay) 19.2.45; ACSEA - RIAF, India census 5.46; No.10 Sqn ('X'), engine cut on recce, belly-landed 17m NW of Jessore, Cat.FA/E 25.10.46 (F/O HH Beale seriously injured); Retd RAF (casualty wastage); SOC 31.12.46

MV208 Spitfire LF.VIIIc (Merlin 66); TOC/RAF 24.11.44; Arr India (Bombay) 4.2.45; ACSEA (No.607 Sqn) - RIAF, India census 5.46; No.3 Sqn, hit palm tree on rising

[entry continues] on landing to avoid parked aircraft, overshot into fence, Peshawar, Cat.FA/E 12.10.46 (P/O FD Irani injured); Retd RAF (casualty wastage); SOC 31.10.46

[entry continues] India census 5.46; Service unknown; Retd RAF; SOC 30.1.47

ground while turning on low level cross-country navex, crashed Goridbidnur (near Bangalore), 13°37'N 70°30'E, burnt out 3.7.46 (P/O JM Bose killed); SOC 25.7.46
MV231 Spitfire LF.VIIIc (Merlin 66); TOC/RAF 18.11.44; Arr India (Bombay) 4.2.45; ACSEA (No.131 Sqn) - RIAF; No.9 Sqn, forced landed wheels up, Jhagpani, Bihar, Cat.E 5.10.45 (F/O JS Ingle OK); SOC 29.11.45
MV232 Spitfire LF.VIIIc (Merlin 66); TOC/RAF 2.12.44; Arr India (Bombay) 4.2.45; ACSEA - RIAF; No.3 Sqn, collided with JG678, Nagpur, Cat.Ac 30.1.46; Retd RAF; SOC 9.5.46
MV236 Spitfire LF.VIIIc (Merlin 66); TOC/RAF 18.11.44; Arr India (Bombay) 4.2.45; ACSEA - RIAF, India census 5.46; No.9 Sqn, engine cut on take-off, hit ditch, overturned, Peshawar, Cat.FA/E 4.6.46 (F/O CK Singha injured); SOC 25.7.46
MV245 Spitfire LF.VIIIc (Merlin 66); TOC/RAF 21.11.44; Arr India (Bombay) 4.2.45; ACSEA (No.81 Sqn, 'FL-?') - RIAF; No.10 Sqn ('B'), fast landing, collided with previous MD291 at end of run, Hmawbi, Cat.A 20.12.45 (P/O HR Chitnis); India census 5.46; Retd RAF; SOC 31.10.46
MV250 Spitfire FR.XIVe (Griffon 65); TOC/RAF 13.3.45; Arr India (Karachi) 14.10.45; ACSEA - RIAF; No.4 Sqn 1946; Japan census 9.46; Retd RAF; SOC 24.3.48
MV262 Spitfire FR.XIVe (Griffon 65); TOC/RAF 7.3.45; Arr India (Karachi) 21.5.45; ACSEA (No.202 SP) - RIAF, India census 5.46; To RIAF inventory 29.12.47; Coded '42' and 'G' at different times; To GI at IAF Cadet Corps Calcutta 1977; Hulk recovered by Ormond and Wensley Haydon-Baillie, Duxford, UK in 1978; Arrived crated at Warbirds of Great Britain, Blackbushe 26.5.78; To B J Stephen Grey, Duxford 1985; To Charles Church (Spitfires) Ltd, Winchester 8.86 (Civil reg. *G-CCVV* 18.5.88), but restoration not completed; To The Fighter Collection, Duxford 1992 and stored; Sold to Kermit A Weeks, Tamiami, Florida, USA 10.92 and stored by Personal Plane Services, Booker, since 1996 pending restoration - **SURVIVOR**
MV271 Spitfire FR.XIVe (Griffon 65); TOC/RAF 17.1.45; Arr India (Bombay) 7.6.45; ACSEA - RIAF; No.7 Sqn, bird strike while ferrying Palam to Kohat, landed safely, Cat.A 19.5.46; India census 5.46; Retd RAF; SOC 28.8.47
MV287 Spitfire FR.XIVe (Griffon 65); TOC/RAF 3.2.45; Arr India (Karachi) 28.7.45; ACSEA - RIAF, India census 5.46; Service unknown; Retd RAF; SOC 27.11.47
MV289 Spitfire FR.XIVe (Griffon 65); TOC/RAF 10.2.45; Arr India (Karachi) 30.8.45; ACSEA - RIAF, India census 5.46; Service unknown; Retd RAF; SOC 28.8.47
MV290 Spitfire FR.XIVe (Griffon 65); TOC/RAF 15.4.45; Arr India (Karachi) 18.10.45; ACSEA - RIAF; No.4 Sqn (Japan census 9.46); Retd RAF; SOC 24.3.48
MV292 Spitfire FR.XIVe (Griffon 65); TOC/RAF 10.2.45; Arr India (Karachi) 17.9.45; ACSEA - RIAF; No.6 Sqn, unit move, heavy landing, tailwheel collapsed, Cat.FA/Ac 12.3.46 (F/O NK Mukerjee); Retd RAF; SOC 11.4.46
MV293 Spitfire FR.XIVe (Griffon 65); Became **T20**; TOC/RAF 27.2.45; Arr India (Karachi) 14.10.45 - RIAF; No.8 Sqn, cross-country to Bombay, landed tailwheel retracted, Hakimpet, Cat.Ac 12.5.46 (F/O SM Ahmad OK); To RIAF inventory 29.12.47; No.8 Sqn ('48'); Became ground instructional airframe *T20* at IAF Technical College Jalahalli; Recovered Bangalore 1978; Arr crated. Warbirds of Great Britain Ltd, Blackbushe 26.5.78 (Civil reg. *G-BGHB* 29.12.78 NTU, *G-SPIT* 2.3.79); To The Fighter Collection Duxford for restoration, ff 14.8.92 marked "MV293/OI-C", airworthy - **SURVIVOR**
MV295 Spitfire FR.XIVe (Griffon 65); TOC/RAF 15.3.45; Arr India (Karachi) 14.10.45; ACSEA - RIAF, India census 5.46; No.8 Sqn, propeller tips damaged when aircraft lifted during running up, Kolar, Cat.B 28.7.46; RiW; Retd RAF; SOC 28.8.47
MV297 Spitfire FR.XIVe (Griffon 65); TOC/RAF 28.2.45; Arr India (Bombay) 7.6.45; ACSEA - RIAF, India census 5.46; Service unknown; Retd RAF; SOC 28.8.47
MV298 Spitfire FR.XIVe (Griffon 65); TOC/RAF 15.2.45; Arr India (Karachi) 2.12.45; ACSEA - RIAF, India census 5.46; Service unknown; Retd RAF; SOC 24.3.48
MV301 Spitfire FR.XIVe (Griffon 65); TOC/RAF 24.2.45; Arr India (Karachi) 30.8.45; ACSEA - RIAF, India census 5.46; No.7 Sqn, engine cut on take-off for offensive recce, crash landed, Miranshah, burnt out, Cat.FA/E 8.9.46 (F/O RC Dhawan killed); Retd RAF (casualty wastage); SOC 31.10.46
MV304 Spitfire FR.XIVe (Griffon 65); TOC/RAF 16.3.45; Arr India (Karachi) 16.10.45; ACSEA - RIAF, India census 5.46; No.6 Sqn ('G') 1946/47; Retd RAF; SOC 28.5.47

Surviving Spitfire FR.XIVe MV293 became ground instructional airframe T20 *at the Indian Air Force Technical College at Jalahalli, southern India. It was recovered at nearby Bangalore in 1978 and despatched to the UK. After restoration with civil registration* G-SPIT *it is seen here on the occasion of its first flight at Duxford on 14th August 1992 with its original serial number and the spurious code "OI-C".* [PRA]

Spitfire FR.XIVe MV364 'A' of No. 8 Sqn RIAF in 1946. [Ray Sturtivant]

Spitfire FR.XIVe, MV364/A of No. 8 Sqn, RIAF, Kolar in 1946

MV305 Spitfire FR.XIVe (Griffon 65); TOC/RAF 18.3.45; Arr India (Karachi) 30.8.45; ACSEA - RIAF, India census 5.46; No.6 Sqn ('N'), starboard tyre burst on take-off, belly-landed, Ranchi, Cat.E 7.5.47 (F/O MK Mukherjee seriously injured); SOC 1.6.47

MV306 Spitfire FR.XIVe (Griffon 65); TOC/RAF 26.2.45; Arr India (Karachi) 3.1.46; ACSEA - RIAF, India census 5.46; Service unknown; Retd RAF; SOC 24.3.48

MV308 Spitfire FR.XIVe (Griffon 65); TOC/RAF 3.3.45; Arr India (Karachi) 28.7.45; ACSEA - RIAF, India census 5.46; Service unknown; Retd RAF; SOC 28.8.47

MV317 Spitfire FR.XIVe (Griffon 65); TOC/RAF 31.3.45; Arr India (Karachi) 22.12.45; ACSEA - RIAF, India census 5.46; Service unknown; Retd RAF; SOC 24.3.48

MV318 Spitfire FR.XIVe (Griffon 65); TOC/RAF 2.4.45; Arr India (Karachi) 3.1.46; ACSEA - RIAF, India census 5.46; Service unknown; Retd RAF; SOC 24.3.48

MV328 Spitfire LF.VIIIc (Merlin 66); TOC/RAF 9.11.44; Arr India (Bombay) 4.2.45; ACSEA (No.607 Sqn) - RIAF, India census 5.46; Service unknown; Retd RAF; SOC 30.1.47

MV343 Spitfire LF.VIIIc (Merlin 66); TOC/RAF 6.11.44; Arr India (Bombay) 4.2.45; ACSEA (No.155 Sqn) - RIAF, India census 5.46; Service unknown; Retd RAF; SOC 27.3.47

MV345 Spitfire LF.VIIIc (Merlin 66); TOC/RAF 2.11.44; Arr India (Bombay) 4.2.45; ACSEA - RIAF, India census 5.46; Service unknown; Retd RAF; SOC 30.1.47

MV347 Spitfire FR.XIVe (Griffon 65); TOC/RAF 2.4.45; Arr India (Bombay) 7.6.45; ACSEA - RIAF, India census 5.46; Service unknown; Retd RAF; SOC 28.8.47

MV364 Spitfire FR.XIVe (Griffon 65); TOC/RAF 22.1.45; Arr India (Karachi) 28.7.45; ACSEA - RIAF, India census 5.46; No.8 Sqn ('A') in 1946; Retd RAF; SOC 28.8.47

MV365 Spitfire FR.XIVe (Griffon 65); TOC/RAF 17.1.45; Arr India (Karachi) 28.7.45; ACSEA - RIAF, India census 5.46; Service unknown; Retd RAF; SOC 28.8.47

MV370 Spitfire FR.XIVe (Griffon 65); Became **T44;** TOC/RAF 10.2.45; Arr India (Karachi) 14.10.45; ACSEA 29.11.45 - RIAF, India census 5.46; AFS (I); To RIAF inventory 29.12.47; Became ground instructional airframe T44 at IAF Technical College Jalahalli; At Nagpur c 1970; Hulk recovered there 1977 by Ormond and Wensley Haydon-Baillie, Duxford; To Alan & Keith Wickenden, Hemel Hempstead, Hertfordshire 1978; Regd *G-FXIV* 11.4.80, to Alan & Keith Wickenden and Michael Connor, and stored dismantled at Buckwish Farm, Henfield, Sussex; To Paul Raymond/Whitehall Theatre of War 6.83, displayed as "MV370/AV-L"; Regn cancelled as wfu 5.2.85; Bought at auction by Robert J Lamplough, North Weald 5.6.85; To Old Flying Machine Co, Duxford 1991 for static restoration; To Luftfahrtmuseum, Laatzen, Hanover, Germany 1992 and displayed as "MV370/EB-Q" - **SURVIVOR**

MV371 Spitfire FR.XIVe (Griffon 65); TOC/RAF 5.2.45; Arr India (Karachi) 30.8.45; ACSEA - RIAF, India census 5.46; AFS (I), engine cut, belly-landed, damaged fuselage and mainplanes 8m NW of Ambala, Cat.FA/E 13.2.47 (F/O M Hosain OK); Retd RAF (casualty wastage); SOC 27.3.47

MV372 Spitfire FR.XIVe (Griffon 65); TOC/RAF 16.2.45; Arr India (Bombay) 7.6.45; ACSEA - RIAF, India census 5.46; No.6 Sqn 1947; Retd RAF (No.320 MU); SOC 28.8.47

MV373 Spitfire FR.XIVe (Griffon 65); TOC/RAF 15.2.45; Arr India (Karachi) 28.7.45; ACSEA - RIAF, India census 5.46; No.6 Sqn ('P') 1946/47; Retd RAF (No.320 MU); SOC 28.8.47

MV374 Spitfire FR.XIVe (Griffon 65); Became **M-349**; TOC/RAF 16.2.45; Arr India (Karachi) 14.10.45; ACSEA - RIAF, India census 5.46; No.8 Sqn, tyre burst on take-off, undercarriage swung to std, retracted wheels to avoid collision with dispersed aircraft, Kolar, Cat.B 25.10.46 (P/O PB Bhandarkar OK); Became ground instructional airframe *M-349* ; SOC/RAF 24.4.47;

MV377 Spitfire FR.XIVe (Griffon 65); TOC/RAF 16.2.45; Arr India (Karachi) 14.10.45; ACSEA - RIAF, India census 5.46; No.6 Sqn 1947; Retd RAF (No.320 MU); SOC 28.8.47

MV384 Spitfire FR.XIVe (Griffon 65); TOC/RAF 20.2.45; Arr India (Karachi) 30.8.45; ACSEA - RIAF, India census 5.46; AFS (I); To RIAF inventory 29.12.47; Fate unknown

MV386 Spitfire FR.XIVe (Griffon 65); TOC/RAF 22.2.45; Arr India (Karachi) 17.9.45; ACSEA - RIAF, India census 5.46; No.151 OTU of AFS (I), propeller tipped on take-off at Ambala, Cat.A 27.8.46 (P/O TV Smith OK); Retd RAF; SOC 27.11.47

MV398 Spitfire LF.VIIIc (Merlin 66); TOC/RAF 22.7.44; Arr India (Bombay) 4.11.44; ACSEA (No.607 Sqn) - RIAF; No.8 Sqn, overshot landing after ops, swung off runway to avoid aircraft ahead, ran into bomb crater, Mingaladon, Cat.FB/Ac 3.8.45 (F/O RS Kalayaniwala OK); Retd RAF; SOC 9.5.46

MV399 Spitfire LF.VIIIc (Merlin 66); TOC/RAF 27.7.44; Arr India (Bombay) 29.10.44; ACSEA (No.273 Sqn) - RIAF, India census 5.46; Service unknown; Retd RAF; SOC 24.4.47

MV403 Spitfire LF.VIIIc (Merlin 66); TOC/RAF 1.8.44; Arr India (Bombay) 29.10.44; ACSEA (No.67 Sqn) - RIAF; No.1 Sqn ('K'), unit move, undershot landing, hit soft earth and grass, overturned, Indore, Cat.E 23.6.46 (F/Lt Mehta-Phiroze Shah injured); SOC 11.7.46

MV404 Spitfire LF.VIIIc (Merlin 66); TOC/RAF 29.7.44; Arr India (Bombay) 8.12.44; ACSEA (No.81 Sqn, 'FL-J') - RIAF, India census 5.46; No.10 Sqn ('R') 1946/47; Retd RAF; SOC 1.6.47

MV406 Spitfire LF.VIIIc (Merlin 66); TOC/RAF 13.8.44; Arr India (Bombay) 4.11.44; ACSEA (No.152 Sqn) - RIAF, India census 5.46; AFS (I), ran short of fuel during aerobatics, belly-landed in field, N of Fazilka, Ferozepur, Cat.FA/E 20.6.47 (P/O KB Majid OK); Retd RAF (casualty wastage); SOC 31.7.47

MV409 Spitfire LF.VIIIc (Merlin 66); TOC/RAF 28.7.44; Arr India (Bombay) 29.10.44; ACSEA - RIAF, India census 5.46; Service unknown; Retd RAF; SOC 30.1.47

MV413 Spitfire LF.VIIIc (Merlin 66); TOC/RAF 14.8.44; Arr India (Bombay) 4.11.44; ACSEA (No.67 Sqn) - RIAF, India census 5.46; Service unknown; Retd RAF; SOC 30.1.47

MV418 Spitfire LF.VIIIc (Merlin 66); TOC/RAF 25.8.44; Arr India (Bombay) 19.11.44; ACSEA (No.67 Sqn) - RIAF, India census 5.46; Service unknown; Retd RAF; SOC 28.8.47

MV419 Spitfire LF.VIIIc (Merlin 66); TOC/RAF 23.8.44; Arr India (Bombay) 19.11.44; ACSEA - RIAF, India census 5.46; Service unknown; Retd RAF; SOC 24.4.47

MV420 Spitfire LF.VIIIc (Merlin 66); TOC/RAF 25.8.44; Arr India (Bombay) 19.11.44; ACSEA - RIAF, India census 5.46; Service unknown; Retd RAF; SOC 31.12.46

MV421 Spitfire LF.VIIIc (Merlin 66); TOC/RAF 25.8.44; Arr India (Bombay) 4.11.44; ACSEA (No.131 Sqn) - RIAF; No.4 Sqn, port tyre burst on take-off, swung to port, nosed over, Charbatia (Cuttack), Cat.Ac 9.8.45 (S/Ldr EW Pinto); India census 5.46; Retd RAF; SOC 30.1.47

MV423 Spitfire LF.VIIIc (Merlin 66); TOC/RAF 24.8.44; Arr India (Bombay) 19.11.44; ACSEA (No.131 Sqn) - RIAF, India census 5.46; No.2 Sqn ('J'), tested on 31.3.46 and in 9.46; Service unknown; Retd RAF; SOC 31.12.46

MV427 Spitfire LF.VIIIc (Merlin 66); TOC/RAF 27.8.44; Arr India (Bombay) 8.12.44; ACSEA (No.273 Sqn) - RIAF; No.8 Sqn, bird strike at 1,800ft, Baigachi, Cat.A(R) 6.6.45 (F/O KW Light); Retd RAF; Later on loan to FAF; SOC/RAF 9.5.46

MV430 Spitfire LF.VIIIc (Merlin 66); TOC/RAF 30.8.44; Arr India (Bombay) 8.12.44; ACSEA (No.131 Sqn) - RIAF, India census 5.46; AFS (I), pilot blacked out recovering sharply from dive, looped and crashed, Shahbad bombing range, completely broken up, Cat.FA/E 21.2.47 (P/O HV Smith killed); Retd RAF (casualty wastage); SOC 26.6.47

MV432 Spitfire LF.VIIIc (Merlin 66); TOC/RAF 5.9.44; Arr India (Bombay) 19.11.44; ACSEA (No.67 Sqn) - RIAF, India census 5.46; Service unknown; Retd RAF; SOC 1.6.47

MV434 Spitfire LF.VIIIc (Merlin 66); Became **M-34_** ? TOC/RAF 30.8.44; Arr India (Bombay) 4.11.44; ACSEA (Nos.81, 615, 131 Sqns) - RIAF, India census 5.46; Service unknown; SOC/RAF 27.11.47; Became ground instructional airframe

MV436 Spitfire LF.VIIIc (Merlin 66); TOC/RAF 5.9.44; Arr India (Bombay) 8.12.44; ACSEA - RIAF; No.4 Sqn; No.3 Sqn, belly-landed in error after formation flying, Kolar, Cat.B 28.2.46 (F/O PB Lawar OK); Not repaired; SOC/RAF 11.4.46

MV437 Spitfire LF.VIIIc (Merlin 66); TOC/RAF 5.9.44; Arr India (Bombay) 8.12.44; ACSEA - RIAF, India census 5.46; No.1 Sqn ('F') in 1946; AFS (I); To RIAF inventory 29.12.47; Fate unknown

MV439 Spitfire LF.VIIIc (Merlin 66); TOC/RAF 10.9.44; Arr India (Bombay) 8.12.44; ACSEA; No.1 FSTU - RIAF; No.1 Sqn ('O') in 1946 [bar over letter 'O']; India census 5.46; Retd RAF; SOC 25.7.46

MV459 Spitfire LF.VIIIc (Merlin 66); TOC/RAF 9.9.44; Arr India (Bombay) 8.12.44; ACSEA (No.8 RFU) - RIAF, India census 5.46; AFS (I), engine cut, belly-landed in dry river bed, Mullana village, 10m from Ambala, Cat.FA/E 23.5.47 (P/O A D'Cruz OK); SOC 26.6.47

MV462 Spitfire LF.VIIIc (Merlin 66); TOC/RAF 16.9.44; Arr India (Bombay) 8.12.44; ACSEA - RIAF, India census 5.46; Service unknown; Retd RAF; SOC 31.7.47

MV480 Spitfire LF.VIIIc (Merlin 66); TOC/RAF 23.9.44; Arr India (Bombay) 8.12.44; ACSEA (No.81 Sqn, 'FL-J') - RIAF, India census 5.46; No.10 Sqn ('J', also 'L') 1946/47; Retd RAF; SOC 27.3.47

NH617 Spitfire LF.VIIIc (Merlin 66); TOC/RAF 25.11.44; Arr India (Bombay) 4.2.45; ACSEA - RIAF, India census 5.46; AFS (I); To RIAF inventory 29.12.47; Fate unknown

Spitfire LF.VIIIc, MV480/J of No. 10 Sqn, RIAF, Barrackpore, in 1946

NH618 Spitfire LF.VIIIc (Merlin 66); TOC/RAF 18.11.44; Arr India (Bombay) 4.2.45; ACSEA (No.131 Sqn, No.3 RFU, No.3 FSTU) - RIAF, India census 5.46; Service unknown; Retd RAF; SOC 26.6.47

NH619 Spitfire LF.VIIIc (Merlin 66); TOC/RAF 18.11.44; Arr India (Bombay) 4.2.45; ACSEA - RIAF, India census 5.46; Bhopal to No.2 Sqn 4.7.46; Engine cut on take-off for formation practice, force-landed on rocky surface, 1m N of Miranshah, burnt out, Cat.FA/E 12.9.46 (F/O MU Haq killed); Retd RAF (casualty wastage); SOC 30.1.47

NH620 Spitfire LF.VIIIc (Merlin 66); TOC/RAF 14.11.44; Arr India (Bombay) 4.2.45; ACSEA (GATU) - RIAF; No.9 Sqn from 5.45 to 7.45, heavy landing on starboard wheel in strong cross-wind, tyre burst, Cat.A(R) 24.5.45 (P/O Biwas); RiW; Retd RAF; SOC 11.4.46

NH623 Spitfire LF.VIIIc (Merlin 66); TOC/RAF 29.11.44; Arr India (Bombay) 4.2.45; ACSEA - RIAF; No.9 Sqn, port tyre burst on take-off, landed wheels-up, Ranchi, Cat.Ac 4.6.45 (F/O KG Raman OK); Retd RAF; SOC 11.4.46

NH624 Spitfire LF.VIIIc (Merlin 66); TOC/RAF 9.12.44; Arr India (Bombay) 9.2.45; ACSEA - RIAF, India census 5.46; Service unknown; Retd RAF; SOC 31.12.46

NH625 Spitfire LF.VIIIc (Merlin 66); TOC/RAF 25.11.44; Arr India (Bombay) 4.2.45; SOC/bboc 6.45-8.45 - RIAF, India census 5.46; Retd RAF; SOC 30.1.47 (bboc/SOC 28.8.47)

NH626 Spitfire LF.VIIIc (Merlin 66); TOC/RAF 27.11.44; Arr India (Bombay) 4.2.45; ACSEA (No.3 RFU & No.3 FSTU) - RIAF, India census 5.46; Service unknown; Retd RAF; SOC 26.9.46

NH627 Spitfire LF.VIIIc (Merlin 66); TOC/RAF 2.12.44; Arr

Surviving Spitfire LF.VIIIc NH631 after it went to the Indian Air Force Museum at Palam in 1967. [MAP]

A later photograph of surviving Spitfire LF.VIIIc NH631 in flight in August 1991 with the IAF Historic Flight at Palam after restoration. [Pushpindur Singh]

INDIA

Spitfire FR.XIVe NH786 '48' of No. 1 Service Flying Training School, RIAF Ambala, seen at Peshawar during 1946. It was written off on 2nd August 1946 when the engine cut out during aerobatics, and during the belly landing 12 miles east of Ambala the fuselage broke off just behind the cockpit, Plt Off S M S Haque being injured. [Peter Riley]

India (Bombay) 19.2.45; ACSEA - RIAF, India census 5.46; No.2 Sqn ('A') from 18.1.46 to 9.46; Retd RAF; SOC 31.10.46

NH628 Spitfire LF.VIIIc (Merlin 66); TOC/RAF 29.11.44; Arr India (Bombay) 4.2.45; ACSEA (No.1331 CU & No.151 OTU) - RIAF, India census 5.46; Service unknown; Retd RAF; SOC 31.10.46

NH629 Spitfire LF.VIIIc (Merlin 66); TOC/RAF 24.11.44; Arr India (Bombay) 4.2.45; ACSEA - RIAF, India census 5.46; Service unknown; Retd RAF; SOC 30.1.47 (bboc/SOC 28.8.47)

NH630 Spitfire LF.VIIIc (Merlin 66); TOC/RAF 2.12.44; Arr India (Bombay) 19.2.45; ACSEA - RIAF, India census 5.46; Service unknown; Retd RAF; SOC 31.12.46

NH631 Spitfire LF.VIIIc (Merlin 66); TOC/RAF 16.12.44; Arr India (Bombay) 19.2.45; ACSEA (No.151 OTU) - RIAF, India census 5.46; No.9 Sqn; No.2 Sqn or AFS (I); To RIAF inventory 29.12.47; Bombay No.12 CMU; No.1 Base Repair Depot 22.11.49; HQ Maintenance Command Comm Flt (IAF) 1950; AESS 6.7.64; IAF Museum, Palam, 1967 for exhibition (marked "*Plumber*"); Engine test 7.10.82, first flight after restoration 8.10.82 (Air Cdre P Singh) To IAF Historic Flight, Palam 1988 - **SURVIVOR**

NH633 Spitfire LF.VIIIc (Merlin 66); TOC/RAF 17.12.44; Arr India (Bombay) 19.2.45; ACSEA - RIAF, India census 5.46; No.2 Sqn by 18.2.46 (acceptance test), until 4.47; Retd RAF; SOC 31.7.47

NH634 Spitfire LF.VIIIc (Merlin 66); TOC/RAF 3.1.45; Arr India (Bombay) 20.2.45; ACSEA – RIAF, India census 5.46; Service unknown; Retd RAF, SOC 11.4.46

NH635 Spitfire LF.VIIIc (Merlin 66); TOC/RAF 17.1.45; Arr India (Bombay) 7.6.45; ACSEA - RIAF, India census 5.46; Service unknown; Retd RAF; SOC 12.8.46

NH636 Spitfire LF.VIIIc (Merlin 66); TOC/RAF 11.12.44; Arr India (Bombay) 19.2.45; ACSEA - RIAF; AFS (I), hit by NH901 while stationery with burst tyre, Ambala, Cat.FA/E 9.12.46 (P/O O Brian OK); AHQ (I) 27.12.46; Retd RAF; SOC 31.12.46

NH645 Spitfire FR.XIVe (Griffon 65); TOC/RAF 16.3.45; Arr India (Karachi) 30.8.45; ACSEA 13.9.45 - RIAF, India census 5.46; AFS (I); To RIAF inventory 29.12.47; Fate unknown

NH651 Spitfire FR.XIVe (Griffon 65); TOC/RAF 25.3.45; Arr India (Karachi) 30.8.45; ACSEA - RIAF, India census 5.46; No.7 Sqn, starboard tyre burst on take-off, ran off runway, tipped up, Miranshah, Cat.B 14.2.47 (P/O GE Wilks OK); Retd RAF; SOC 24.4.47

NH656 Spitfire FR.XIVe (Griffon 65); TOC/RAF 23.3.44; Arr India (Bombay) 7.5.45; ACSEA - RIAF, India census 5.46; Service unknown; Retd RAF; SOC 27.3.47

NH749 Spitfire FR.XIVe (Griffon 65); Became **T3_ ?**; TOC/RAF 21.2.45; Arr India (Karachi) 28.7.45; ACSEA - RIAF, India census 5.46; AFS (I); To RIAF inventory 29.12.47; Coded '54' and 'D' at different times; Became ground instructional airframe *T3.(?)* at IAF Technical College Jalahalli; Recovered ex Patna AFB 1977 by Ormond and Wensley Haydon-Baillie, Duxford, England; To Alan & Keith Wickenden, Hemel Hempstead, Hertfordshire 1978 Civil reg. *G-MXIV* 11.4.80); Restored by them at Cranfield, ff 9.4.83 as "NH749/L"; Shipped to USA 4.85 (*NX749DP*) - **SURVIVOR**

NH753 Spitfire FR.XIVe (Griffon 65); TOC/RAF 26.2.45; Arr India (Karachi) 14.10.45; ACSEA - RIAF, India census 5.46; AFS (I); To RIAF inventory 29.12.47; Fate unknown

NH755 Spitfire FR.XIVe (Griffon 65); TOC/RAF 26.2.45; Arr India (Karachi) 14.8.45; ACSEA - RIAF, India census 5.46; Service unknown; Retd RAF; SOC 28.8.47

NH758 Spitfire FR.XIVe (Griffon 65); TOC/RAF 26.2.45; Arr India (Karachi) 14.8.45; ACSEA - RIAF, India census 5.46; AFS(I); Service unknown (see note); Retd RAF; SOC 28.8.47
NOTE: Reported take-off crash and dates as by NH759

NH759 Spitfire FR.XIVe (Griffon 65); TOC/RAF 1.3.45; Arr India (Karachi) 30.10.45; ACSEA - RIAF, India census 5.46; AFS (I), tyre burst on take-off, belly-landed Ambala, Cat.FA/E 30.7.47 (P/O Z Masud OK); Retd RAF (casualty wastage); SOC 28.8.47

NH777 Spitfire FR.XIVe (Griffon 65); TOC/RAF 23.2.45; Arr India (Karachi) 2.12.45; ACSEA - RIAF, India census 5.46; Service unknown; Retd RAF; SOC 25.9.47

NH778 Spitfire FR.XIVe (Griffon 65); TOC/RAF 1.3.45; Arr India (Karachi) 3.1.46; ACSEA (No.11 Sqn) - RIAF, India census 5.46; Service unknown; Retd ACSEA 28.11.46 (in Japan 4.47); SOC 24.3.48

NH781 Spitfire FR.XIVe (Griffon 65); TOC/RAF 1.3.45; Arr India (Karachi) 18.10.45; ACSEA - RIAF, India census 5.46; No.7 Sqn, delivery flight, starboard tyre burst on take-off, selected undercarriage up to stop aircraft, Lahore, Cat.A 21.11.46 (F/O Chaudri); Retd RAF; SOC 28.8.47

NH786 Spitfire FR.XIVe (Griffon 65); TOC/RAF 27.2.45; Arr India (Karachi) 30.10.45; ACSEA - RIAF, India census 5.46; No.1 SFTS of AFS/I ('48'), engine cut during aerobatics, force-landed on belly, fuselage broke off just behind cockpit, 30°25'N 76°54'E, 12m E of Ambala, Cat.FA/E 2.8.46 (P/O SMS Haque injured); Casualty wastage retd RAF; SOC 26.9.46

NH788 Spitfire FR.XIVe (Griffon 65); TOC/RAF 7.3.45; Arr India (Karachi) 17.9.45; ACSEA - RIAF, India census 5.46; No.6 Sqn, lost on navex, overshot into ditch in wheels-up forced landing, Chanbad (near Dhanbad)

NH793 Spitfire FR.XIVe (Griffon 65); TOC/RAF 9.3.45; Arr India (Karachi) 19.10.45; ACSEA - RIAF; No.8 Sqn, engine cut during aerobatic practice, force-landed wheels up near level crossing on Trichinopoly - Puddukkottai road, Rajawil airfield, Cat.E 19.3.46 (P/O CT Muthayah killed); SOC 11.4.46

NH795 Spitfire FR.XIVe (Griffon 65); TOC/RAF 14.3.45; Arr India (Karachi) 28.7.45; ACSEA - RIAF; No.4 Sqn, undershot, struck telegraph wires, undercarriage collapsed on landing, overturned, Cochin, Cat.FA/E 3.4.46 (F/O WRN Dani injured); Retd RAF (casualty wastage); SOC 9.5.46

NH799 Spitfire FR.XIVe (Griffon 65); TOC/RAF 14.3.45; Arr India (Karachi) 28.7.45; ACSEA - RIAF, India census 5.46; No.9 Sqn, cylinder blew when running up on ground, Cat.E 27.2.47 (nobody injured); To RIAF inventory 29.12.47; Sold by IAF to Doug Arnold 1981 and went to his Warbirds of Great Britain Ltd hangar, Blackbushe; On his death bought by Stephen Grey/The Fighter Collection and restored to airworthiness by Historic Flying Ltd, Audley End, Essex (regd *G-BUZU* 1.7.93); To New Zealand 3.94 (*ZK-XIV*) - **SURVIVOR**

NH802 Spitfire FR.XIVe (Griffon 65); TOC/RAF 12.3.45; Arr India (Karachi) 25.6.45; ACSEA - RIAF, India census 5.46; AFS (I); To RIAF inventory 29.12.47; Fate unknown

NH803 Spitfire FR.XIVe (Griffon 65); TOC/RAF 11.3.45; Arr India (Karachi) 30.10.45; ACSEA - RIAF, India census 5.46; No.9 Sqn in 1946; U/c not locked down, collapsed landing at Nagpur, Cat.Ac 20.2.47 (F/O J Zaheer OK); Retd RAF; SOC 26.6.47

NH805 Spitfire FR.XIVe (Griffon 65); TOC/RAF 17.3.45; Arr India (Karachi) 16.10.45; ACSEA - RIAF, India census 5.46; No.1 Sqn in 1946; AFS (I); To RIAF inventory 29.12.47; Fate unknown

NH806 Spitfire FR.XIVe (Griffon 65); TOC/RAF 10.3.45; Arr India (Karachi) 17.9.45; ACSEA - RIAF, India census 5.46; No.7 Sqn, bird strike during cross-country, lost tailplane, crashed Kohat, Cat.FA/E 3.7.46 (F/O RBS Karki killed); SOC 29.8.46

NH810 Spitfire FR.XIVe (Griffon 65); TOC/RAF 17.3.45; Arr India (Karachi) 3.1.46; ACSEA - RIAF, India census 5.46; Service unknown; Retd ACSEA 28.11.46 (in Japan 4.47); SOC 24.3.48

NH837 Spitfire FR.XIVe (Griffon 65); TOC/RAF 31.3.45; Arr India (Karachi) 2.12.45; ACSEA - RIAF, India census 5.46; AFS (I), lost power in circuit, fast approach, raised undercarriage to stop aircraft, Ambala, Cat E 14.5.47 (P/O Ashraf OK); Not repaired; SOC/RAF 26.6.47

NH843 Spitfire FR.XIVe (Griffon 65); TOC/RAF 19.4.45; Arr India (Karachi) 14.10.45; ACSEA - RIAF, India census 5.46; No.6 Sqn; Retd RAF (No.320 MU); SOC 28.8.47

NH845 Spitfire FR.XIVe (Griffon 65); TOC/RAF 23.4.45; Arr India (Karachi) 25.6.45; ACSEA - RIAF, India census 5.46; Service unknown; Retd RAF; SOC 25.9.47
NOTE: Reported with RIAF by 22.6.49

NH846 Spitfire FR.XIVe (Griffon 65); TOC/RAF 25.4.45; Arr India (Karachi) 28.7.45; ACSEA - RIAF; No.9 Sqn ('B'), belly-landed in error, drop tank caught fire on striking metal runway, Gurgaon, Cat.E 19.3.46 (P/O PK Ghosh OK); SOC 28.3.46

NH848 Spitfire F.XVIIIe (Griffon 65); TOC/RAF 23.6.45; Arr India (Karachi) 17.3.46; ACSEA – RIAF, India census 5.46; To RIAF inventory 31.12.47; No.2 or 9 Sqn, AFS (I) or No.101 (PR) Flt; Possibly later to No.14 Sqn; Fate unknown

NH849 Spitfire F.XVIIIe (Griffon 65); TOC/RAF 29.6.45; Arr India 25.2.46; ACSEA 3.46 – RIAF, India census 5.46; Service unknown; Retd RAF 17.10.46 (ACSEA, later No.60 Sqn); SOC 8.3.51
NOTE: Prototype for mods camera mountings

NH850 Spitfire F.XVIIIe (Griffon 65); TOC/RAF 30.6.45; Arr India 17.3.46; ACSEA – RIAF, India census 5.46; Service unknown; Retd RAF (ACSEA, No.60 Sqn); SOC 8.3.51

NH855 Spitfire F.XVIIIe (Griffon 65); TOC/RAF 3.7.45; Arr India (Karachi) 25.2.46; ACSEA - RIAF, India census 5.46; Retd RAF, No.47.MU 1.48; Sold to R J Parkes for RIAF 22.6.49; No.2 or 9 Sqn, AFS (I) or 101 (PR) Flt; Possibly later to No.14 Sqn; Fate unknown

NH858 Spitfire FR.XIVe (Griffon 65); TOC/RAF 12.4.45; Arr India (Karachi) 18.10.45; ACSEA - RIAF, India census 5.46; No.8 Sqn; Retd RAF; SOC 28.8.47

NH861 Spitfire FR.XIVe (Griffon 65); TOC/RAF 7.4.45; Arr India (Karachi) 17.9.45; ACSEA - RIAF, India census 5.46; No.8 Sqn ('Q'), went on nose in 1946; SOC/RAF 27.11.47; Became ground instructional airframe

NH865 Spitfire FR.XIVe (Griffon 65); TOC/RAF 14.4.45; Arr India (Bombay) 7.6.45; ACSEA - RIAF, India census 5.46; No.9 Sqn, engine cut at 200ft, belly-landed 12m W of Hungu, Cat.FA/E 28.5.46 (F/O JR Bearcroft seriously injured); SOC 25.7.46

NH870 Spitfire FR.XIVe (Griffon 65); TOC/RAF 19.4.45; Arr India (Bombay) 7.6.45; ACSEA - RIAF, India census 5.46; Service unknown; Retd RAF; SOC 28.8.47

NH873 Spitfire FR.XIVe (Griffon 65); TOC/RAF 23.4.45; Arr India (Bombay) 7.6.45; ACSEA - RIAF, India census 5.46; AFS (I), tyre burst on take-off, belly-landed on airfield Ambala, Cat.FA/E 16.1.47 (P/O RH Beaupert OK); SOC 30.1.47

NH875 Spitfire FR.XIVe (Griffon 65); TOC/RAF 28.4.45; Arr India (Bombay) 7.6.45; ACSEA (No.11 Sqn) - RIAF; No.1 Sqn ('G') 1946; Retd RAF (Japan census 9.46); SOC 24.3.48

NH893 Spitfire FR.XIVe (Griffon 65); TOC/RAF 14.4.45; Arr India (Karachi) 28.7.45; ACSEA - RIAF, India census 5.46; Service unknown; Retd RAF; SOC 28.8.47

NH901 Spitfire FR.XIVe (Griffon 65); TOC/RAF 3.4.45; Arr India (Karachi) 14.8.45; ACSEA - RIAF, India census 5.46; AFS (I), hit stationery NH636 on taxi track, Ambala, Cat.A 9.12.46 (P/O M Abbas OK); To RIAF inventory 29.12.47; Fate unknown

NH911 Spitfire FR.XIVe (Griffon 65); TOC/RAF 31.3.45; Arr India (Karachi) 3.1.46; ACSEA - RIAF, India census 5.46; Service unknown; Retd ACSEA 28.11.46 (in Japan 4.47); SOC 24.3.48

NH916 Spitfire FR.XIVe (Griffon 65); TOC/RAF 8.4.45; Arr India (Karachi) 18.10.45; ACSEA - RIAF, India census 5.46; No.6 Sqn; Retd RAF (No.320 MU); SOC 28.8.47

NH917 Spitfire FR.XIVe (Griffon 65); TOC/RAF 27.4.45; Arr India (Karachi) 14.10.45; ACSEA - RIAF, India census 5.46; AFS (I); To RIAF inventory 29.12.47; Fate unknown

NH921 Spitfire FR.XIVe (Griffon 65); TOC/RAF 2.5.45; Arr India (Karachi) 30.8.45; ACSEA - RIAF, India census 5.46; Service unknown; Retd RAF; SOC 27.3.47

NH927 Spitfire FR.XIVe (Griffon 65); TOC/RAF 6.5.45; Arr India (Karachi) 14.10.45; ACSEA - RIAF, India census 5.46; No.6 Sqn; Retd RAF (No.320 MU); SOC 28.8.47

NH928 Spitfire FR.XIVe (Griffon 65); TOC/RAF 12.5.45; Arr India (Karachi) 14.10.45; ACSEA - RIAF, India census 5.46; No.6 Sqn; Retd RAF (No.320 MU); SOC 28.8.47

NH929 Spitfire FR.XIVe (Griffon 65); TOC/RAF 17.5.45; Arr India (Karachi) 14.8.45; ACSEA - RIAF, India census 5.46; No.9 Sqn, undercarriage failed to lower after cross-country ferry flight, belly-landed, Cat.Ac 7.1.47 (F/O H Mirza OK); Retd RAF; SOC 28.8.47

PA862 Spitfire PR.XI (Merlin 63); TOC/RAF 4.12.43; ACSEA 25.10.45, ex No.681 Sqn – RIAF, India census 5.46; Service unknown; Retd ACSEA; SOC/RAF 25.7.46

PA896 Spitfire PR.XI (Merlin 63); TOC/RAF 4.1.44; ACSEA 21.2.44, ex No.681 Sqn – RIAF, India census 5.46; Service unknown; Retd ACSEA; SOC/RAF 25.7.46

PA898 Spitfire PR.XI (Merlin 63); TOC/RAF 14.1.44; Arr India 21.2.44; ACSEA (No.681 Sqn) - RIAF, India census 5.46 (also 9.46); Service unknown; Retd RAF; SOC 28.8.47

PA906 Spitfire PR.XI (Merlin 63); TOC/RAF 29.1.44; ACSEA 10.3.44, ex No.681 Sqn – RIAF, India census 5.46; Retd ACSEA; SOC/RAF 31.12.46

PA908 Spitfire PR.XI (Merlin 63); Became No. **M-342**; TOC/RAF 1.44; ACSEA (No.681 Sqn, 'E' & 'I'); Census 8.45; SOC/RAF 9.5.46 (BER) - RIAF 29.12.47; Became ground instructional airframe *M-342* at Allahabad, Indian

Air Training Corps; Later Poona until 1984 then sold by IAF to Carl Enzenhofer, John Wilson and Jeet Mehal, Vancouver, BC, Canada, arr there by ship 8.2.85; To USAAF Museum at Dayton, Ohio, USA in 1986 (painted as "MB950") - **SURVIVOR**

PA934 Spitfire PR.XI (Merlin 63); TOC/RAF 30.1.44; Arr India 23.3.44; ACSEA (No.681 Sqn), India census 5.46 - RIAF 9.46, Service unknown; Retd RAF; SOC 27.2.47

PA952 Spitfire LF.VIIIc (Merlin 66); TOC/RAF 16.3.44; Arr India (Karachi) 18.5.44; ACSEA - RIAF, India census 5.46; Service unknown; Retd RAF; SOC 27.2.47

PL768 Spitfire PR.XI (Merlin 70); TOC/RAF 12.3.44; Arr ACSEA 2.4.44 (No.681 Sqn) - RIAF, India census 5.46; Service unknown; Retd RAF; SOC 27.2.47

PL780 Spitfire PR.XI (Merlin 70); TOC/RAF 2.4.44; Arr ACSEA 8.5.44 (No.681 Sqn) - RIAF, India census 5.46 (also 9.46); Service unknown; Retd RAF; SOC 27.2.47

PL784 Spitfire PR.XI (Merlin 70); TOC/RAF 2.4.44; Arr ACSEA 11.5.44 (No.681 Sqn, 'M') - RIAF, India census 5.46 (also 9.46); Service unknown; Retd RAF; SOC 27.2.47

PL889 Spitfire PR.XI (Merlin 70); TOC/RAF 11.7.44; Arr ACSEA 22.11.44 - RIAF, India census 5.46; Service unknown; Retd RAF; SOC 27.2.47

PL898 Spitfire PR.XI (Merlin 70); TOC/RAF 23.7.44; Arr ACSEA 24.9.44 (No.681 Sqn, 'N') - RIAF, India census 5.46 (also 9.46); Service unknown; Retd RAF; SOC 27.2.47

PL907 Spitfire PR.XI (Merlin 70); TOC/RAF 27.8.44; Arr ACSEA 24.9.44 (No.681 Sqn, 'V') - RIAF, India census 5.46 (also 9.46); Service unknown; Retd RAF; SOC 1.6.47

PL951 Spitfire PR.XI (Merlin 70); TOC/RAF 16.9.44; Arr ACSEA 3.10.44 (No.681 Sqn, 'K') - RIAF, India census 5.46 (also 9.46); No.7 Sqn, nose tipped on running up, Palam, Cat.A (date unknown); Retd RAF; SOC 28.8.47

PL960 Spitfire PR.XI (Merlin 70); TOC/RAF 9.9.44; Arr ACSEA 8.10.44 (No.681 Sqn) - RIAF, India census 5.46 (also 9.46); Service unknown; Retd RAF; SOC 27.2.47

PL988 Spitfire PR.XI (Merlin 70); TOC/RAF 7.11.44; Arr ACSEA 10.12.44 (No.681 Sqn) - RIAF, India census 5.46 (also 9.46); Service unknown; Retd RAF; SOC 27.2.47

PL997 Spitfire PR.XI (Merlin 70); TOC/RAF 25.11.44; Arr ACSEA 10.1.45 (No.681 Sqn, 'S') - RIAF, India census 5.46 (also 9.46); No.6 Sqn; No.7 Sqn, engine cut on take-off, force-landed in field near Kohat, burnt out, Cat.FA/E 14.2.47 (P/O Durney seriously injured); Retd RAF (casualty wastage); SOC 27.3.47

PM516 Spitfire PR.XIX (Griffon 65/66); TOC/RAF 12.6.45; Arr ACSEA 3.9.45 - RIAF, India census 5.46; Service unknown; Retd RAF; SOC 28.8.47

PM536 Spitfire PR.XIX (Griffon 66); TOC/RAF 18.6.45; Arr ACSEA 5.10.45 - RIAF, India census 5.46; Service unknown; Retd RAF; SOC 28.8.47

PM537 Spitfire PR.XIX (Griffon 66); TOC/RAF 18.6.45; Arr ACSEA 10.9.45 - RIAF, India census 5.46; Service unknown; Retd RAF; SOC 27.3.47

PM539 Spitfire PR.XIX (Griffon 66); TOC/RAF 18.6.45; Arr ACSEA 21.10.45 - RIAF, India census 5.46; Service unknown; Retd RAF; SOC 28.8.47

PM542 Spitfire PR.XIX (Griffon 66); TOC/RAF 23.6.45; Arr ACSEA 17.9.45 - RIAF, India census 5.46; Service unknown; Disposed to Army Salvage 28.8.47

PM543 Spitfire PR.XIX (Griffon 66); TOC/RAF 25.6.45; Arr ACSEA 13.2.46 - RIAF, India census 5.46; Service unknown; Retd RAF; SOC 28.8.47

PM545 Spitfire PR.XIX (Griffon 66); TOC/RAF 30.6.45; Arr ACSEA 10.2.46 - RIAF, India census 5.46; Service unknown; Retd RAF; SOC 28.8.47

PM562 Spitfire PR.XIX (Griffon 66); Became HS-..?; TOC/RAF 13.7.45; Sold to V.A. 24.8.48 (G-15-63) - Arr India 22.2.49; No.101 (PR) Flt 22.2.49; No.1 (PR) Sqn in 4.50; Fate unknown

PM563 Spitfire PR.XIX (Griffon 66); Became HS-..?; TOC/RAF 14.7.45; Sold to V.A. 24.8.48 - Arr India 1949; No.101 (PR) Flt 1949; No.1 (PR) Sqn in 4.50; Fate unknown

PM565 Spitfire PR.XIX (Griffon 66); Became HS-..?; TOC/RAF 19.7.45; Sold to V.A. 24.8.48 - Arr India 1949; No.101 (PR) Flt 1949; No.1 (PR) Sqn in 4.50; Fate unknown

PM566 Spitfire PR.XIX (Griffon 66); Became HS-..?; TOC/RAF 19.7.45; Sold to V.A. 24.8.48 - Arr India 1949; No.101 (PR) Flt 1949; No.1 (PR) Sqn in 4.50; Fate unknown

PM569 Spitfire PR.XIX (Griffon 66); Became HS-..?; TOC/RAF 19.7.45; Sold to V.A. 24.8.48 - Arr India 1949; No.101 (PR) Flt 1949; No.1 (PR) Sqn in 4.50; Fate unknown

PM570 Spitfire PR.XIX (Griffon 66); Became **HS-700**; TOC/RAF 19.7.45; Sold to V.A. 24.8.48 (G-15-69) - Arr India 31.3.49; No.101 (PR) Flt 31.3.49; No.1 (PR) Sqn in 4.50; Fate unknown

PM581 Spitfire PR.XIX (Griffon 66); TOC/RAF 31.7.45; Arr ACSEA 30.12.45 - RIAF, India census 5.46; Service unknown; Retd RAF; SOC 28.8.47

PM596 Spitfire PR.XIX (Griffon 66); TOC/RAF 31.7.45; Arr ACSEA 12.11.45 - RIAF, India census 5.46; Service unknown; Retd RAF; SOC 28.8.47

PM602 Spitfire PR.XIX (Griffon 66); Became HS-..?; TOC/RAF 30.8.45; Sold to V.A. 24.8.48 - Arr India 1949; No.101 (PR) Flt 1949; No.1 (PR) Sqn in 4.50; Fate unknown

PM603 Spitfire PR.XIX (Griffon 66); Became HS-..?; TOC/RAF 12.9.45; Sold to V.A. 24.8.48 - Arr India 1949; No.101 (PR) Flt 1949; No.1 (PR) Sqn in 4.50; Fate unknown

PM604 Spitfire PR.XIX (Griffon 66); Became HS-..?; TOC/RAF 31.8.45; Sold to V.A. 24.8.48 - Arr India 1949; No.101 (PR) Flt 1949; No.1 (PR) Sqn in 4.50; Fate unknown

PM605 Spitfire PR.XIX (Griffon 66); Became HS-..?; TOC/RAF 31.8.45; Sold to V.A. 24.8.48 - Arr India 1949; No.101 (PR) Flt 1949; No.1 (PR) Sqn in 4.50; Fate unknown

PM606 Spitfire PR.XIX (Griffon 66); Became **HS-693**; TOC/RAF 6.9.45; Sold to V.A. 24.8.48; Tested with Class B reg. G-15-62 - Arr India 8.2.49; No.101 (PR) Flt 8.2.49; No.1 (PR) Sqn in 4.50; Fate unknown

PM607 Spitfire PR.XIX (Griffon 66); Became HS-..?; TOC/RAF 6.9.45; Sold to V.A. 24.8.48 - Arr India 1949; No.101 (PR) Flt 1949; No.1 (PR) Sqn in 4.50; Fate unknown

PM619 Spitfire PR.XIX (Griffon 66); Became HS-..?; TOC/RAF 3.12.45; Sold to V.A. 11.11.48 - Arr India 1949; No.101 (PR) Flt 1949; No.1 (PR) Sqn in 4.50; Fate unknown

PM627 Spitfire PR.XIX (Griffon 66); Became **HS-694**; TOC/RAF 20.9.45; No.9 MU 4.6.52; Sold V.A. for India 15.2.53 (B class reg. G.15-74) - Arr India 1953; No.1 (PR) Sqn 1953; No.1 Base Repair Depot 1955; No.1 (PR) Sqn in 4.57; Stored Palam until 1970; Recovered, to Canada 3.2.71; To Swedish AF Museum 1982 - **SURVIVOR**

PS916 Spitfire PR.XIX (Griffon 66); TOC/RAF 19.4.45; Arr ACSEA 25.6.45 - RIAF, India census 5.46; Service unknown; Retd RAF; SOC 31.7.47

PS917 Spitfire PR.XIX (Griffon 66); TOC/RAF 21.4.45; Arr ACSEA 16.6.45 - RIAF, India census 5.46; Retd RAF, No.34 Sqn, hit building at Palam, India, Cat.FA/E 26.11.46; SOC 30.1.47

RM742 Spitfire F.XIVe (Griffon 65); TOC/RAF 6.7.44; Arr India (Karachi) 23.5.45; ACSEA - RIAF, India census 5.46; AFS (I); To RIAF inventory 29.12.47; Fate unknown

RM786 Spitfire FR.XIVe (Griffon 65); TOC/RAF 3.2.45; Arr India (Karachi) 17.9.45; ACSEA (No.151 OTU) - RIAF, India census 5.46; No.1 SFTS of AFS (I), lost in bad visibility on Tac/R, ran out of fuel, force-landed wheels-up 1m S of Khaital, Cat.E 13.5.46 (P/O SD Singh OK); SOC 11.7.46 - NOTE: Incorrectly reported as "RM685"

RM816 Spitfire F.XIVe (Griffon 65); TOC/RAF 20.2.45; Arr India (Bombay) 15.5.45; ACSEA - RIAF, India census 5.46; Service unknown; Retd RAF; SOC 31.7.47

RM912 Spitfire F.XIVe (Griffon 65); TOC/RAF 20.11.44; Arr India (Bombay) 4.2.45; ACSEA, TWDU (I) - RIAF, India census 5.46; Service unknown; Retd RAF; SOC 24.4.47

RM926 Spitfire F.XIVe (Griffon 65); TOC/RAF 20.11.44; Arr India (Bombay) 4.2.45; ACSEA - RIAF, India census 5.46; Service unknown; Retd RAF; SOC 31.7.47

RM934 Spitfire F.XIVe (Griffon 65); TOC/RAF 29.11.44; Arr India (Bombay) 4.2.45; ACSEA - RIAF, India census 5.46; Service unknown; Retd RAF; SOC 24.4.47

RM936 Spitfire F.XIVe (Griffon 65); TOC/RAF 5.12.44; Arr India (Bombay) 19.2.45; ACSEA - RIAF, India census 5.46; Service unknown; Retd RAF; SOC 31.7.47

RM940 Spitfire F.XIVe (Griffon 65); TOC/RAF 6.12.44; Arr India (Bombay) 19.2.45; ACSEA - RIAF, India census 5.46; Service unknown; Retd RAF; SOC 25.9.47

RM957 Spitfire F.XIVe (Griffon 65); TOC/RAF 5.12.44; Arr India (Bombay) 19.2.45; ACSEA (TWFU (I) & AFTU (I) - RIAF, India census 5.46; AFS (I); Service unknown; Retd RAF; SOC 11.7.46

RM961 Spitfire F.XIVe (Griffon 65); TOC/RAF 9.12.44; Arr India (Bombay) 19.2.45; ACSEA (No.17 Sqn) - RIAF, India census 5.46; Service unknown; Retd RAF; SOC 25.9.47

RM962 Spitfire F.XIVe (Griffon 65); TOC/RAF 5.12.44; Arr India (Bombay) 19.2.45; ACSEA - RIAF, India census 5.46; Service unknown; Retd RAF; SOC 28.8.47

RM969 Spitfire F.XIVe (Griffon 65); TOC/RAF 7.12.44; Arr India (Bombay) 6.4.45; ACSEA - RIAF, India census 5.46; No.6 Sqn, went out of control during low aerobatics after loop at 3,000ft near Ranchi, Cat.E 30.12.46 (P/O H Rai killed); SOC 24.4.47. NOTE: Incorrectly reported as "SM969"

RM970 Spitfire F.XIVe (Griffon 65); TOC/RAF 7.12.44; Arr India (Bombay) 12.4.45; ACSEA - RIAF, India census 5.46; Service unknown; Retd RAF; SOC 27.3.47

RM973 Spitfire F.XIVe (Griffon 65); TOC/RAF 9.12.44; Arr India (Bombay) 9.2.45; ACSEA (No.136 Sqn) - RIAF, India census 5.46; Service unknown; Retd RAF; SOC 28.8.47

RM977 Spitfire F.XIVe (Griffon 65); TOC/RAF 22.12.44; Arr India (Bombay) 12.4.45; ACSEA - RIAF, India census 5.46; No.9 Sqn ('Q'), bomb carrier dropped off landing, Peshawar, Cat.Ac 2.8.46 (F/O AF Gama); Retd RAF; SOC 31.12.46

RM978 Spitfire F.XIVe (Griffon 65); TOC/RAF 10.12.44; Arr India (Bombay) 19.2.45; ACSEA - RIAF, India census 5.46; Service unknown; Retd RAF; SOC 27.3.47

RM979 Spitfire F.XIVe (Griffon 65); TOC/RAF 16.12.44; Arr India (Bombay) 19.2.45; ACSEA - RIAF, India census 5.46; Service unknown; Retd RAF; SOC 31.7.47

RM980 Spitfire F.XIVe (Griffon 65); TOC/RAF 16.12.44; Arr India (Bombay) 19.2.45; ACSEA - RIAF, India census 5.46; Service unknown; Retd RAF; SOC 25.9.47

RM983 Spitfire F.XIVe (Griffon 65); TOC/RAF 18.12.44; Arr India (Bombay) 20.3.45; ACSEA (No.132 Sqn) - RIAF, India census 5.46; Service unknown; Retd RAF; SOC 31.7.47

RM984 Spitfire F.XIVe (Griffon 65); TOC/RAF 22.12.44; Arr India (Bombay) 20.3.45; ACSEA (No.4 FSTU) - RIAF, India census 5.46; Service unknown; Retd RAF; SOC 31.7.47

RM992 Spitfire F.XIVe (Griffon 65); TOC/RAF 31.12.44; Arr India (Bombay) 12.4.45; ACSEA - RIAF, India census 5.46; No.9 Sqn, nose tipped by airman on starting up, Peshawar, Cat.A 4.11.46; Retd RAF; SOC 31.12.47

RM994 Spitfire F.XIVe (Griffon 65); TOC/RAF 10.1.45; Arr India (Bombay) 12.4.45; ACSEA, No 28 Sqn - RIAF, India census 5.46; Lost en route to India 19.6.46; SOC/RAF 31.10.46

RM995 Spitfire F.XIVe (Griffon 65); TOC/RAF 5.1.45; Arr India (Bombay) 12.4.45; ACSEA - RIAF, India census 5.46; Service unknown; Retd RAF; SOC 31.7.47

RM996 Spitfire F.XIVe (Griffon 65); TOC/RAF 21.1.45; Arr India (Bombay) 6.4.45; ACSEA - RIAF, India census 5.46; Service unknown; Retd RAF; SOC 31.7.47

RN130 Spitfire F.XIVe (Griffon 65); TOC/RAF 5.1.45; Arr India (Bombay) 12.4.45; ACSEA - RIAF, India census 5.46; No.36 SP, ferrying, flew into high ground in sandstorm 38m NE of Agra, Cat.FA/E 23.5.46; CWR 30.5.46; SOC 25.7.46

RN133 Spitfire F.XIVe (Griffon 65); TOC/RAF 5.1.45; Arr India (Bombay) 12.4.45; ACSEA (No.132 Sqn, 'FF-B') - RIAF; Possibly No.4 Sqn, BC Air Station Iwakuni, tyre burst landing after test flight, Cat.FA/Ac 28.7.47 (S/Ldr NUR Khan OK); Retd RAF; SOC 24.7.48

RN134 Spitfire F.XIVe (Griffon 65); TOC/RAF 10.1.45; Arr India (Bombay) 12.4.45; ACSEA (No.3 RFU); Issued to India 30.5.46-25.7.46 - RIAF; No.6 Sqn ('A') 1946/47; Retd RAF (No.320 MU); SOC 28.8.47

RN139 Spitfire F.XIVe (Griffon 65); TOC/RAF 9.1.45; Arr India (Bombay) 6.4.45; ACSEA - RIAF, India census 5.46; Service unknown; Retd RAF; SOC 31.7.47

RN144 Spitfire F.XIVe (Griffon 65); TOC/RAF 20.1.45; Arr India (Bombay) 6.4.45; ACSEA - RIAF, India census 5.46; No.8 Sqn 1946; Retd RAF; SOC 27.11.47; Became ground instructional airframe

RN149 Spitfire F.XIVe (Griffon 65); TOC/RAF 21.1.45; Arr India (Bombay) 15.5.45; ACSEA - RIAF; No.7 Sqn, overshot into rough ground landing, undercarriage collapsed, Maharajpur Cat.E 12.4.46 (F/Lt PK Sarkar OK); India census 5.46; Retd RAF; SOC 25.7.46

RN153 Spitfire F.XIVe (Griffon 65); TOC/RAF 21.1.45; Arr India (Bombay) 6.4.45; ACSEA - RIAF, India census 5.46; Service unknown; Retd RAF; SOC 27.3.47

RN155 Spitfire F.XIVe (Griffon 65); TOC/RAF 3.2.45; Arr India (Bombay) 15.5.45; ACSEA - RIAF, India census 5.46; Service unknown; Retd RAF; SOC 28.8.47

RN157 Spitfire F.XIVe (Griffon 65); TOC/RAF 3.2.45; Arr India (Bombay) 15.5.45; ACSEA - RIAF, India census 5.46; No.8 Sqn, engine cut on air test, belly-landed on airfield, Kolar, Cat.FA/E 14.5.47 (F/O CT Rhenius OK); SOC 1.6.47

RN159 Spitfire F.XIVe (Griffon 65); TOC/RAF 3.2.45; Arr India (Bombay) 15.5.45; ACSEA (No.17 Sqn) - RIAF, India census 5.46; AFS (I); To RIAF inventory 29.12.47; Fate unknown

RN174 Spitfire F.XIVe (Griffon 65); TOC/RAF 3.2.45; Arr India (Bombay) 15.5.45; ACSEA - RIAF, India census 5.46; Service unknown; Retd RAF; SOC 25.9.47

RN178 Spitfire F.XIVe (Griffon 65); TOC/RAF 4.2.45; Arr India (Bombay) 6.4.45; ACSEA - RIAF, India census 5.46; No.6 Sqn ('Q'), engine lost power on cross-country, belly-landed in field 4m E of Lohardanga, Cat.FA/E 26.4.47 (F/Lt DB Naik seriously injured); SOC 28.8.47

RN179 Spitfire F.XIVe (Griffon 65); TOC/RAF 5.2.45; Arr India (Bombay) 6.4.45; ACSEA (No.132 Sqn) - RIAF, India census 5.46; Service unknown; Retd RAF; SOC 28.8.47

RN183 Spitfire F.XIVe (Griffon 65); TOC/RAF 3.2.45; Arr India (Bombay) 6.4.45; ACSEA - RIAF, India census 5.46; Service unknown; Retd RAF; SOC 28.5.47

RN190 Spitfire F.XIVe (Griffon 65); TOC/RAF 5.2.45; Arr India (Bombay) 15.5.45; ACSEA (No.132 Sqn, 'FF-J') - RIAF, India census 5.46; Service unknown; Retd RAF; SOC 31.7.47

RN191 Spitfire F.XIVe (Griffon 65); TOC/RAF 10.2.45; Arr India (Bombay) 15.5.45; ACSEA - RIAF, India census 5.46; Service unknown; Retd RAF; SOC 28.8.47

RN192 Spitfire F.XIVe (Griffon 65); TOC/RAF 7.2.45; Arr India (Bombay) 15.5.45; ACSEA - RIAF, India census 5.46; No.8 Sqn; No.9 Sqn, engine cutting while ferrying, belly-landed in field, Kunkurali (near Raj Samand, Udaipur), Cat.FA/E1 on 27.4.47 (F/O N Zaheer injured); SOC 26.6.47

RN193 Spitfire F.XIVe (Griffon 65); TOC/RAF 10.2.45; Arr India (Bombay) 15.5.45; ACSEA (No.136 Sqn, 'HM-A') - RIAF, India census 5.46; No.2 (India) Grp CF (still 'HM-A') 1947; Disposed of through DGD 25.9.47

RN194 Spitfire F.XIVe (Griffon 65); TOC/RAF 20.2.45; Arr India (Bombay) 11.5.45; ACSEA - RIAF, India census 5.46; Service unknown; Retd RAF; SOC 28.8.47

RN199 Spitfire F.XIVe (Griffon 65); TOC/RAF 20.2.45; Arr India (Karachi) 21.5.45; ACSEA - RIAF, India census 5.46; No.7 Sqn, hit by RN221 whilst formation flying from Miranshah 1.10.46; Hit mud wall at end of runway on low approach Kohat, completely wrecked, Cat.FA/E 21.2.47 (P/O TN Ahmad killed); Retd RAF (casualty wastage); SOC 27.3.47

RN207 Spitfire F.XIVe (Griffon 65); TOC/RAF 21.2.45; Arr India (Bombay) 15.5.45; ACSEA - RIAF, India census 5.46; Service unknown; Retd RAF; SOC 27.3.47

RN209 Spitfire F.XIVe (Griffon 65); TOC/RAF 20.2.45; Arr India (Bombay) 15.5.45; ACSEA - RIAF, India census 5.46; Service unknown; Retd RAF; SOC 28.8.47

RN216 Spitfire FR.XIVe (Griffon 65); TOC/RAF 27.4.45; Arr India (Karachi) 28.7.45; ACSEA - RIAF, India census 5.46; Service unknown; Retd RAF; SOC 25.9.47

RN220 Spitfire FR.XIVe (Griffon 66); TOC/RAF 16.5.45; Arr India (Karachi) 14.8.45, ACSEA - RIAF, India census 5.46; No.7 Sqn, lost way on ferry flight, short of fuel, belly-landed Shikarpur, Cat.E 22.5.47 (F/O HK Patel injured); SOC 26.6.47

RN221 Spitfire FR.XIVe (Griffon 65); TOC/RAF 30.4.45; Arr India (Karachi) 14.10.45; ACSEA - RIAF, India census 5.46; No.7 Sqn, formation flying from Miranshah, hit RN199 and SM819 which had taken up wrong position, Cat.A 1.10.46 (F/O HK Patel OK); Retd RAF; SOC 28.8.47

SM812 Spitfire F.XIVe (Griffon 65); TOC/RAF 25.2.45; Arr India (Bombay) 15.5.45; ACSEA - RIAF, India census 5.46; Service unknown; Retd RAF; SOC 24.4.47

SM815 Spitfire F.XIVe (Griffon 65); TOC/RAF 18.3.45; Arr India (Bombay) 15.5.45; ACSEA - RIAF, India census 5.46; Service unknown; Retd RAF; SOC 31.7.47

SM819 Spitfire F.XIVe (Griffon 65); TOC/RAF 9.3.45; Arr India (Bombay) 15.5.45; ACSEA - RIAF, India census 5.46; No.7 Sqn, took up wrong position while formation flying, hit by RN221, Cat.A 1.10.46; To RIAF inventory 29.12.47; AFS (I); Fate unknown

SM822 Spitfire F.XIVe (Griffon 65); TOC/RAF 9.3.45; Arr India (Bombay) 15.5.45; ACSEA - RIAF, India census 5.46; Service unknown; Retd RAF; SOC 31.7.47

SM832 Spitfire F.XIVe (Griffon 65); TOC/RAF 1.3.45; Arr India 5.45 - To RIAF inventory 29.12.47; AFS (I); To Indian Military Academy, Dehra Dun1972; Recovered by Ormond and Wensley Haydon-Baillie, Duxford, 7.78; To Warbirds of Great Britain, Blackbushe 1979 (Civil reg. *G-WWII* 9.7.79); To The Fighter Collection, Duxford 8.86; To Charles Church (Spitfires) Ltd, Micheldever 11.88; Retd The Fighter Collection, Duxford 11.91; ff 22.5.95 marked "SM832/YB-A"; To France 20.2.98 as *F-AZSJ* and operated by Spitfire Warbird Ltd, Eurl, Dijon - **SURVIVOR**

SM835 Spitfire F.XIVe (Griffon 65); TOC/RAF 13.3.45; Arr India (Bombay) 7.6.45; ACSEA - RIAF, India census 5.46; Service unknown; Retd RAF; SOC 31.7.47

SM836 Spitfire F.XIVe (Griffon 65); TOC/RAF 13.3.45; Arr India (Karachi) 21.5.45; ACSEA - RIAF, India census 5.46; Service unknown; Retd RAF; SOC 31.7.47

SM837 Spitfire F.XIVe (Griffon 65); TOC/RAF 12.3.45; Arr India (Bombay) 7.6.45; ACSEA - RIAF, India census 5.46; Service unknown; Retd RAF; SOC 28.8.47

SM838 Spitfire F.XIVe (Griffon 65); TOC/RAF 15.3.45; Arr India (Karachi) 21.5.45; ACSEA - RIAF, India census 5.46; Service unknown; Retd RAF; SOC 31.7.47

SM840 Spitfire F.XIVe (Griffon 65); TOC/RAF 22.3.45; Arr India (Karachi) 21.5.45; ACSEA - RIAF, India census 5.46; Unknown unit, crashed Cat.FA/E2 on 22.3.47; No.355 MU (RAF); SOC 24.4.47

SM841 Spitfire F.XIVe (Griffon 65); TOC/RAF 22.3.45; Arr India (Karachi) 21.5.45; ACSEA - RIAF, India census 5.46; Service unknown; SOC/RAF 27.3.47; Became ground instructional airframe

SM842 Spitfire F.XIVe (Griffon 65); TOC/RAF 22.3.45; Arr India (Bombay) 7.6.45; ACSEA - RIAF, India census 5.46; Service unknown; Retd RAF; SOC 28.8.47

SM845 Spitfire FR.XVIIIe (Griffon 66); Became **HS-687**; TOC/RAF 28.5.45; Arr India (Karachi) 11.2.46; ACSEA – RIAF, India census 5.46; To RIAF inventory 31.12.47; No.2 or 9 Sqn, AFS (I) or No.101 (PR) Flt; Possibly later to No.14 Sqn; Kalaikunda airfield (west of Calcutta), used as a decoy aircraft; Recovered, via USA to Historic Flying Ltd at Audley End, UK, restoration to airworthy (Civil reg. *G-BUOS* 19.10.92); First flight after restoration 7.7.2000 (F/Lt Charlie Brown) - **SURVIVOR**

SM893 Spitfire FR.XIVe (Griffon 65); TOC/RAF 14.5.45; Arr India (Karachi) 30.8.45; ACSEA - RIAF, India census 5.46; No.8 Sqn, cross-country Bhopal to Nagpur, abandoned when lost in cloud, Lukhander, near Harrai, Madhai Pradesh, 20º42'N 79º5'E, missing Cat.E 4.12.46; SOC 30.1.47

SM894 Spitfire FR.XIVe (Griffon 65); TOC/RAF 17.5.45; Arr India (Karachi) 30.8.45; ACSEA - RIAF, India census 5.46; Service unknown; Retd RAF; SOC 26.6.47

SM895 Spitfire FR.XIVe (Griffon 65); TOC/RAF 18.5.45; Arr India (Karachi) 14.8.45; ACSEA - RIAF, India census 5.46; No.9 Sqn, swung to starboard taxying, hit embankment, nose tipped, Cat.A 9.5.46 (F/O Jaspal Singh OK); Retd RAF; SOC 25.9.47

SM897 Spitfire FR.XIVe (Griffon 65); TOC/RAF 15.5.45; Arr India (Karachi) 14.8.45; ACSEA - RIAF; No.8 Sqn, swung to starboard on take-off, ran off runway, struck a ditch, collided with a steam roller killing two workmen, Mingaladon, Cat.E 21.1.46 (P/O DG Lee injured), SOC

SM898 Spitfire FR.XIVe (Griffon 65); TOC/RAF 16.5.45; Arr India (Karachi) 30.8.45; ACSEA - RIAF, India census 5.46; No.6 Sqn, tyre burst on take-off, swung off runway into soft ground, nose tipped, Ranchi, Cat.A 1.7.46 (P/O TR Peters OK); Retd RAF; SOC 28.8.47

SM915 Spitfire FR.XIVe (Griffon 65); TOC/RAF 2.6.45; Arr India (Karachi) 17.9.45; ACSEA - RIAF; Nos.6 & 1 Sqns in 1946/47; Retd RAF; SOC 28.8.47

SM921 Spitfire FR.XIVe (Griffon 65); TOC/RAF 12.6.45; Arr India (Karachi) 3.1.46; ACSEA - RIAF, India census 5.46; Service unknown; Retd ACSEA 28.11.46; No. 11 Sqn (Japan 4.47); SOC 24.3.48

The derelict remains of Spitfire FR.XVIIIe HS-687 (ex SM845) at Kalaikunda airfield, west of Calcutta, where it had been used as a decoy aircraft. After restoration to airworthy condition in the UK at Audley End it flew again on 7th July 2000 with the civil registration G-BUOS.

SM923 Spitfire FR.XIVe (Griffon 65); TOC/RAF 22.6.45; Arr India (Karachi) 14.10.45; ACSEA - RIAF; No.4 Sqn 1946 (Japan census 9.46); Retd RAF; SOC 24.3.48

SM924 Spitfire FR.XIVe (Griffon 65); TOC/RAF 25.6.45; Arr India (Karachi) 3.1.46; ACSEA - RIAF, India census 5.46; No.4 Sqn in 1946; Retd ACSEA 28.11.46 (in Japan 4.47); SOC 24.3.48

SM925 Spitfire FR.XIVe (Griffon 65); TOC/RAF 29.6.45; Arr India (Karachi) 30.10.45; ACSEA - RIAF; No.4 Sqn, slipstream threw goggles to back of pilot's head on take-off, temporarily lost control, propeller pecked, Miho, Cat.A 16.5.46 (F/O HC Saggal OK); Flying low in mountainous terrain, flew into high ground in cloud while turning in valley while following TX979, Okayama, Japan, Cat.FA/E 11.6.47 (F/O JA Martin killed); SOC 31.7.47

SM933 Spitfire FR.XIVe (Griffon 65); TOC/RAF 17.7.45; Arr India (Karachi) 14.10.45; ACSEA - RIAF, India census 5.46; AFS (I); To RIAF inventory 29.12.47; Fate unknown

SM937 Spitfire FR.XIVe (Griffon 65); TOC/RAF 13.8.45; Arr India (Karachi) 16.10.45; ACSEA - RIAF, India census 5.46; No.1 SFTS of AFS (I), bird strike on canopy and pilot during practice aerobatics, landed safely, Ambala, Cat.A 13.9.46 (P/O S Singh injured); To RIAF inventory 29.12.47; Fate unknown

SM939 Spitfire F.XVIIIe (Griffon 65); TOC/RAF 10.7.45; Arr India (Karachi) 25.2.46; ACSEA 14.3.46 - RIAF, India census 5.46; Retd ACSEA 17.10.46 (later No 60 Sqn); SOC 8.3.51

SM940 Spitfire F.XVIIIe (Griffon 65); TOC/RAF 11.7.45; Arr India (Karachi) 11.2.46; ACSEA - RIAF, India census 5.46; Retd RAF, No.47.MU 21.8.47; Sold to R J Parkes for RIAF 13.7.49; No.2 or 9 Sqn, AFS (I) or No.101 (PR) Flt; Possibly later to No.14 Sqn; Fate unknown

SM941 Spitfire F.XVIIIe (Griffon 65); TOC/RAF 25.7.45; Arr India (Karachi) 25.2.46; ACSEA - RIAF, India census 5.46; Retd RAF, No.47.MU 1.48; Sold to R J Parkes for RIAF 14.6.49; No.2 or 9 Sqn, AFS (I) or No.101 (PR) Flt; Possibly later to No.14 Sqn; Fate unknown

SM942 Spitfire F.XVIIIe (Griffon 65); TOC/RAF 18.7.45; Arr India (Karachi) 25.2.46; ACSEA - RIAF, India census 5.46; Retd RAF, No.47.MU 27.11.47; Sold to R J Parkes for RIAF 9.6.49; No.2 or 9 Sqn, AFS (I) or No.101 (PR) Flt; Possibly later to No.14 Sqn; Fate unknown

SM943 Spitfire F.XVIIIe (Griffon 65); TOC/RAF 23.7.45; Arr India (Karachi) 30.3.46; ACSEA 11.4.46 - RIAF, India census 5.46; Retd ACSEA 17.10.46 (No 60 Sqn, belly-landed 24.12.47); To be issued to Burma 22.4.48

SM944 Spitfire F.XVIIIe (Griffon 65); TOC/RAF 23.7.45; Arr India (Karachi) 14.3.46; ACSEA - RIAF, India census 5.46; Retd RAF, No.47.MU 23.10.47; No.29 MU, to RIAF 14.6.49; No.2 or 9 Sqn, AFS (I) or No.101 (PR) Flt; Possibly later to No.14 Sqn; Fate unknown

SM945 Spitfire F.XVIIIe (Griffon 65); TOC/RAF 31.7.45; Arr India (Karachi) 30.3.46; ACSEA – RIAF, India census 5.46; To RIAF inventory 31.12.47; No.2 or 9 Sqn, AFS (I) or No.101 (PR) Flt; Possibly later to No.14 Sqn; Fate unknown

SM946 Spitfire F.XVIIIe (Griffon 65); TOC/RAF 24.7.45; Arr India (Karachi) 11.2.46; ACSEA - RIAF, India census 5.46; Retd RAF, No.47.MU 21.8.47; Sold to R J Parkes for RIAF 12.7.49; No.2 or 9 Sqn, AFS (I) or No.101 (PR) Flt; Possibly later to No.14 Sqn; Fate unknown

SM947 Spitfire F.XVIIIe (Griffon 65); TOC/RAF 31.7.45; Arr India (Karachi) 17.3.46; ACSEA 28.3.46 - RIAF, India census 5.46; Retd ACSEA 17.10.46 (later No 60 Sqn); SOC 21.12.50

SM950 Spitfire F.XVIIIe (Griffon 65); TOC/RAF 18.8.45; Arr India (Karachi) 25.2.46; ACSEA 14.3.46 - RIAF, India census 5.46; Retd ACSEA 17.10.46; SOC 12.9.50

SM951 Spitfire F.XVIIIe (Griffon 65); TOC/RAF 30.9.45; Arr India (Karachi) 11.2.46; ACSEA - RIAF, India census 5.46; Retd RAF, No.47 MU 24.8.47; Sold to R J Parkes for RIAF 13.7.49; No.2 or 9 Sqn, AFS (I) or No.101 (PR)Flt; Possibly later to No.14 Sqn; Fate unknown

SM952 Spitfire F.XVIIIe (Griffon 65); TOC/RAF 22.8.45; Arr India (Karachi) 30.3.46; ACSEA - RIAF, India census 5.46; To RIAF inventory 31.12.47; No.2 or 9 Sqn, AFS (I) or No.101 (PR)Flt; Possibly later to No.14 Sqn; Fate unknown

SM953 Spitfire F.XVIIIe (Griffon 65); TOC/RAF 23.8.45; Arr India (Karachi) 30.3.46; ACSEA 11.4.46 - RIAF, India census 5.46; Retd ACSEA 17.10.46; SOC 13.8.49

SM954 Spitfire F.XVIIIe (Griffon 65); TOC/RAF 23.8.45; Arr India (Karachi) 30.3.46; ACSEA 11.4.46 - RIAF, India census 5.46; Retd ACSEA 17.10.46; SOC 13.8.49

Surviving Spitfire F.XVIIIe HS-877 (ex SM969) displayed by the Indian Air Force Western Air Command HQ at Delhi Cantonment around 1969. It was later restored in the UK as G-BRAF and is now at North Weald.

Surviving Spitfire F.XVIIIe HS-986 (ex SM986) seen in the Indian Air Force Museum at Palam in June 1991. [PRA]

SM955 Spitfire F.XVIIIe (Griffon 65); TOC/RAF 6.9.45; Arr India (Karachi) 30.3.46; ACSEA 11.4.46 - RIAF, India census 5.46; Retd ACSEA 17.10.46 (later No 60 Sqn 11.48); SOC 8.3.51

SM956 Spitfire F.XVIIIe (Griffon 65); TOC/RAF 6.9.45; Arr India (Karachi) 30.3.46; ACSEA 11.4.46 - RIAF, India census 5.46; Retd ACSEA 17.10.46; SOC 25.8.49

SM968 Spitfire F.XVIIIe (Griffon 65); TOC/RAF 28.8.45; Arr India (Karachi) 17.3.46; ACSEA 28.3.46 - RIAF, India census 5.46; Retd ACSEA 17.10.46 (later No 390 MU in 4.48); SOC 17.6.49

SM969 Spitfire F.XVIIIe (Griffon 65); Became **HS-877**; TOC/RAF 30.8.45; Arr India (Karachi) 11.2.46; ACSEA - RIAF, India census 5.46; No.6 Sqn, crashed on landing, Ranchi 20.12.46; Retd RAF, No.47 MU 24.8.47; Sold to R J Parkes for RIAF 16.7.49; No.2 or 9 Sqn, AFS (I) or No.101 (PR) Flt; Possibly later to No.14 Sqn; To Indian Air Force Western Air Command HQ, Delhi Cantonment 1972, displayed as "HS-877"; Recovered by Ormond and Wensley Haydon-Baillie, Duxford in 1978; To Doug Arnold/ Warbirds of Great Britain Ltd, Blackbushe, arr crated 5.78; *G-BRAF;* 29.12.78 restored, ff 12.10.85 marked "SM969/ D-A"; Storage, later Hurn from 20.11.92; to Wizzard Investments Ltd, North Weald 15.5.98 - **SURVIVOR**

SM971 Spitfire F.XVIIIe (Griffon 65); TOC/RAF 17.9.45; Arr India (Karachi) 11.2.46; ACSEA - RIAF, India census 5.46; Retd RAF, No.47 MU 21.8.47; Sold to R J Parkes for RIAF 27.6.49; No.2 or 9 Sqn, AFS (I) or No.101(PR)Flt; Possibly later to No.14 Sqn; Fate unknown

SM972 Spitfire F.XVIIIe (Griffon 65); TOC/RAF 11.9.45; Arr India (Karachi) 30.3.46; ACSEA 11.4.46 - RIAF, India census 5.46; Retd ACSEA 17.10.46 (later No 60 Sqn); Singapore Auxiliary Air Force 10.5.51; SOC 27.2.53

SM973 Spitfire F.XVIIIe (Griffon 65); TOC/RAF 11.9.45; Arr India (Karachi) 25.2.46; ACSEA 14.3.46 - RIAF, India census 5.46; Retd ACSEA 17.10.46 (later No 60 Sqn); SOC 8.3.51

SM974 Spitfire F.XVIIIe (Griffon 65); TOC/RAF 17.9.45; Arr India (Karachi) 11.2.46; ACSEA - RIAF, India census 5.46; Retd RAF, No.47 MU 25.8.47; Sold to R J Parkes for RIAF 1.7.49; No.2 or 9 Sqn, AFS (I) or No.101(PR)Flt; Possibly later to No.14 Sqn; Fate unknown

SM975 Spitfire F.XVIIIe (Griffon 65); TOC/RAF 5.10.45; Arr India (Karachi) 17.3.46; ACSEA 28.3.46 - RIAF, India census 5.46; Retd ACSEA 17.10.46 (later No 60 Sqn); Seletar, flying accident and SOC 4.5.50

SM976 Spitfire F.XVIIIe (Griffon 65); TOC/RAF 11.10.45; Arr India (Karachi) 12.2.46; ACSEA – RIAF, India census 5.46; To RIAF inventory 31.12.47; No.2 or 9 Sqn, AFS (I) or No.101(PR)Flt; Possibly later to No.14 Sqn; Fate unknown

SM977 Spitfire F.XVIIIe (Griffon 65); TOC/RAF 1.11.45; Arr India (Karachi) 30.3.46; ACSEA 11.4.46 - RIAF, India census 5.46; Retd ACSEA 17.10.46; SOC 13.8.49

SM978 Spitfire F.XVIIIe (Griffon 65); TOC/RAF 11.10.45; Arr India (Karachi) 12.2.46; ACSEA 28.2.46 - RIAF, India census 5.46; Retd ACSEA 17.10.46; MBFE, flying accident Cat.FA/5s and SOC 10.1.50

SM979 Spitfire F.XVIIIe (Griffon 65); TOC/RAF 27.11.45; Arr India (Karachi) 11.2.46; ACSEA - RIAF, India census 5.46; Retd RAF, No.47 MU 25.8.47; Sold to R J Parkes for RIAF 13.7.49; No.2 or 9 Sqn, AFS (I) or No.101(PR)Flt; Possibly later to No.14 Sqn; Fate unknown

SM980 Spitfire F.XVIIIe (Griffon 65); TOC/RAF 17.10.45; Arr India (Karachi) 11.2.46; ACSEA - RIAF, India census 5.46; Retd RAF, No.47 MU 23.10.47; No.29 MU, to RIAF 14.6.49; No.2 or 9 Sqn, AFS (I) or No.101(PR)Flt; Possibly later to No.14 Sqn; Fate unknown

SM981 Spitfire F.XVIIIe (Griffon 65); TOC/RAF 16.11.45; Arr India (Karachi) 11.2.46; ACSEA - RIAF, India census 5.46; Retd RAF, No.47 MU 23.10.47; Sold to R J Parkes for RIAF 22.7.49; No.2 or 9 Sqn, AFS (I) or No.101(PR)Flt; Possibly later to No.14 Sqn; Fate unknown

SM982 Spitfire F.XVIIIe (Griffon 65); TOC/RAF 18.10.45; Arr India (Karachi) 31.1.46; ACSEA - RIAF, India census 5.46; Retd RAF, No.47 MU 23.10.47; Sold to R J Parkes for RIAF 22.7.49; No.2 or 9 Sqn, AFS (I) or No.101(PR)Flt; Possibly later to No.14 Sqn; Fate unknown

SM983 Spitfire F.XVIIIe (Griffon 65); TOC/RAF 18.10.45; Arr India (Karachi) 3.1.46; ACSEA – RIAF, India census 5.46; To RIAF inventory 31.12.47; No.2 or 9 Sqn, AFS (I) or No.101(PR)Flt; Possibly later to No.14 Sqn; Fate unknown

SM984 Spitfire F.XVIIIe (Griffon 65); TOC/RAF 18.10.45; Arr India (Karachi) 31.1.46; ACSEA - RIAF, India census 5.46; Retd RAF, No.47 MU 24.8.47; Sold to R J Parkes for RIAF 16.7.49; No.2 or 9 Sqn, AFS (I) or No.101(PR)Flt; Possibly later to No.14 Sqn; Fate unknown

SM985 Spitfire F.XVIIIe (Griffon 65); TOC/RAF 11.10.45; Arr India (Karachi) 31.1.46; ACSEA - RIAF, India census 5.46; Retd RAF, No.47 MU 25.8.47; Sold to R J Parkes for RIAF 22.7.49; No.2 or 9 Sqn, AFS (I) or No.101(PR)Flt; Possibly later to No.14 Sqn; Fate unknown

SM986 Spitfire F.XVIIIe (Griffon 65); Became **HS-986**; TOC/RAF 11.10.45; ACSEA; No.47 MU in 8.47 - Sold to R J Parkes for RIAF 30.6.49; No.2 or 9 Sqn, AFS (I) or No.101 (PR) Flt; No.1 Base Repair Depot until 5.52; No.14 Sqn in 5.52; No.1 Base Repair Depot in 1.53; No.14 Sqn 15.4.53; No.1 Base Repair Depot in 6.54; Palam 1967; To IAF Museum, Palam, Delhi in 1967 and extant - **SURVIVOR**

SM988 Spitfire F.XVIIIe (Griffon 65); TOC/RAF 27.10.45; Arr India (Karachi) 26.2.46; ACSEA – RIAF, India census 5.46; To RIAF inventory 31.12.47; No.2 or 9 Sqn, AFS (I) or No.101(PR)Flt; Possibly later to No.14 Sqn; Fate unknown

SM989 Spitfire F.XVIIIe (Griffon 65); TOC/RAF 22.10.45; Arr India (Karachi) 11.2.46; ACSEA - RIAF, India census 5.46; Retd RAF, No.47 MU 25.8.47; Sold to R J Parkes for RIAF 16.7.49; No.2 or 9 Sqn, AFS (I) or No.101(PR)Flt; Possibly later to No.14 Sqn; Fate unknown

SM990 Spitfire F.XVIIIe (Griffon 65); TOC/RAF 1.11.45; Arr India (Karachi) 25.2.46; ACSEA – RIAF, India census 5.46; To RIAF inventory 31.12.47; No.2 or 9 Sqn, AFS (I) or No.101(PR)Flt; Possibly later to No.14 Sqn; Fate unknown

SM991 Spitfire F.XVIIIe (Griffon 65); TOC/RAF 1.11.45; Arr India (Karachi) 11.2.46; ACSEA – RIAF, India census 5.46; To RIAF inventory 31.12.47; No.2 or 9 Sqn, AFS (I) or No.101(PR)Flt; Possibly later to No.14 Sqn; Fate unknown

SM992 Spitfire F.XVIIIe (Griffon 65); TOC/RAF 16.11.45; Arr India (Karachi) 11.2.46; ACSEA - RIAF, India census 5.46; Retd RAF, No.47 MU 1.48; Sold to R J Parkes for RIAF 22.6.49; No.2 or 9 Sqn, AFS (I) or No.101(PR)Flt; Possibly later to No.14 Sqn; Fate unknown

TP196 Spitfire F.XVIIIe (Griffon 65); TOC/RAF 27.11.45; Arr India (Karachi) 12.2.46; ACSEA - RIAF, India census 5.46; Retd RAF, No.47 MU 26.11.47; Sold to R J Parkes for RIAF 9.6.49; No.2 or 9 Sqn, AFS (I) or No.101(PR)Flt; Possibly later to No.14 Sqn; Fate unknown

TP203 Spitfire F.XVIIIe (Griffon 65); TOC/RAF 17.12.45; Arr India (Karachi) 25.2.46; ACSEA - RIAF, India census 5.46; Retd RAF, No.47 MU 1.48; Sold to R J Parkes for RIAF 10.6.49; No.2 or 9 Sqn, AFS (I) or No.101(PR)Flt; Possibly later to No.14 Sqn; Fate unknown

TP256 Spitfire FR.XIVe (Griffon 65); TOC/RAF 22.5.45; Arr India (Karachi) 30.8.45; ACSEA - RIAF, India census 5.46; AFS (I), propeller blade came off in flight, engine began smoking, aircraft crashed, Shahbad range area, Cat.E 4.3.47 (P/O H Storey killed); SOC 27.3.47

TP257 Spitfire FR.XVIIIe (Griffon 65); TOC/RAF 29.5.45; Arr India (Karachi) 25.2.46; ACSEA - RIAF, India census 5.46; Retd RAF, No.47 MU 25.8.47; Sold to R J Parkes for RIAF 27.6.49; No.2 or 9 Sqn, AFS (I) or No.101(PR)Flt; Possibly later to No.14 Sqn; Fate unknown

TP258 Spitfire FR.XVIIIe (Griffon 65); TOC/RAF 30.5.45; Arr India (Karachi) 12.2.46; ACSEA – RIAF, India census 5.46; To RIAF inventory 31.12.47; No.2 or 9 Sqn, AFS (I) or No.101(PR)Flt; Possibly later to No.14 Sqn; Fate unknown

TP259 Spitfire FR.XVIIIe (Griffon 65); TOC/RAF 1.6.45; Arr India (Karachi) 31.1.46; ACSEA - RIAF, India census 5.46; To RIAF inventory 31.12.47; No.2 or 9 Sqn, AFS (I) or No.101(PR)Flt; Possibly later to No.14 Sqn; Fate unknown

TP260 Spitfire FR.XVIIIe (Griffon 65); TOC/RAF 1.6.45; Arr India (Karachi) 31.1.46; ACSEA – RIAF, India census 5.46; To RIAF inventory 31.12.47; No.2 or 9 Sqn, AFS (I) or No.101(PR)Flt; Possibly later to No.14 Sqn; Fate unknown

TP262 Spitfire FR.XVIIIe (Griffon 65); TOC/RAF 2.6.45; Arr India (Karachi) 31.1.46; ACSEA - RIAF, India census 5.46; Retd RAF, No.47 MU 1.48; Sold to R J Parkes for RIAF 8.6.49; No.2 or 9 Sqn, AFS (I) or No.101(PR)Flt; Possibly later to No.14 Sqn; Fate unknown

TP263 Spitfire FR.XVIIIe (Griffon 65); Became **HS-649**; TOC/RAF 2.6.45; Arr India (Karachi) 31.1.46; ACSEA – RIAF, India census 5.46; To RIAF inventory 31.12.47; No.2 or 9 Sqn, AFS (I) or No.101(PR)Flt; Possibly later to No.14 Sqn; Coded 'NL' at one time; Fate unknown - **SURVIVOR** NOTE: Part of a Haydon-Baillie recovery of 1977. Fuselage to UK, wings to USA (see RM927). Converted to high back and exchanged with National War & Resistance Museum, Overloon, Netherlands, and marked as "NH649" in lieu of known RAF serial at that time

TP264 Spitfire FR.XVIIIe (Griffon 65); TOC/RAF 9.6.45; Arr India (Karachi) 12.2.46; ACSEA - RIAF, India census 5.46; Retd RAF, No.47 MU 23.10.47; Sold to R J Parkes for RIAF 1.7.49; No.2 or 9 Sqn, AFS (I) or No.101(PR)Flt; Possibly later to No.14 Sqn; Fate unknown

TP265 Spitfire FR.XVIIIe (Griffon 65); TOC/RAF 11.6.45; Arr India (Karachi) 25.2.46; ACSEA - RIAF, India census 5.46; Retd RAF, No.47 MU 1.48; Sold to R J Parkes for RIAF 16.6.49; No.2 or 9 Sqn, AFS (I) or No.101(PR)Flt; Possibly later to No.14 Sqn; Fate unknown

TP266 Spitfire FR.XVIIIe (Griffon 65); TOC/RAF 9.6.45; Arr India (Karachi) 31.1.46; ACSEA – RIAF, India census 5.46; To RIAF inventory 31.12.47; No.2 or 9 Sqn, AFS (I) or No.101(PR)Flt; Possibly later to No.14 Sqn; Fate unknown

TP267 Spitfire FR.XVIIIe (Griffon 65); TOC/RAF 9.6.45; Arr India (Karachi) 25.2.46; ACSEA - RIAF, India census 5.46; To RIAF inventory 31.12.47; No.2 or 9 Sqn, AFS (I) or No.101(PR)Flt; Possibly later to No.14 Sqn; Fate unknown

TP269 Spitfire FR.XVIIIe (Griffon 65); TOC/RAF 13.6.45 arr India (Karachi) 17.3.46; ACSEA - RIAF, India census 5.46; Retd RAF, No.47 MU 28.4.47; Sold to R J Parkes for RIAF 12.7.49; No.2 or 9 Sqn, AFS (I) or No.101 (PR) Flt; Possibly later to No.14 Sqn; Fate unknown

TP274 Spitfire FR.XVIIIe (Griffon 65); TOC/RAF 18.6.45; Arr India (Karachi) 31.1.46; ACSEA - RIAF, India census 5.46; To RIAF inventory 31.12.47; No.2 or 9 Sqn, AFS (I) or No.101(PR)Flt; Possibly later to No.14 Sqn; Fate unknown

TP276 Spitfire FR.XVIIIe (Griffon 65); Became **HS-653**; TOC/RAF 20.6.45; Arr India (Karachi) 12.2.46; ACSEA – RIAF, India census 5.46; To RIAF inventory 31.12.47; No.2 or 9 Sqn, AFS (I) or No.101 (PR) Flt; Possibly later to No 14 Sqn; Coded 'ND' at one time; Barrackpore until 1977 when hulk recovered by Ormond and Wensley Haydon-Baillie, Duxford, UK; To Rudolph A Frasca, Champaign, Illinois, USA, 1978 and after restoration to Frasca Air Museum, Urbana, Illinois - **SURVIVOR**

TP280 Spitfire FR.XVIIIe (Griffon 65); Became **HS-654**; TOC/RAF 19.6.45; Arr India (Karachi) 30.3.46; ACSEA – RIAF, India census 5.46; To RIAF inventory 31.12.47; No.9 Sqn; AFS (I) Kaleikunda until 1977; Coded 'NG' at

INDIA

one time; Hulk recovered at Kalaikunda AFB by Ormond and Wensley Haydon-Baillie, Duxford, UK in 1977; To Rudolph A Frasca/Antiques & Classics Inc, Champaigh, Illinois 1978; Shipped to UK for restoration by Historic Flying Ltd, Audley End, Essex (Civil reg. *G-BTXE* 23.10.91); ff 5.7.92; Shipped back to USA 9.92; To Rudy Frasca/Frasca Air Museum, Urbana, Illinois 2.93 (reg. *N280TP* 2.2.93), flown as "TP280/Z" - **SURVIVOR**

TP282 Spitfire FR.XVIIIe (Griffon 65); TOC/RAF 5.7.45; Arr India (Karachi) 11.2.46; ACSEA – RIAF, India census 5.46; To RIAF inventory 31.12.47; No.2 or 9 Sqn, AFS (I) or No.101(PR)Flt; Possibly later to No.14 Sqn; Fate unknown

TP285 Spitfire FR.XVIIIe (Griffon 65); Became **HS-6..** ?; TOC/RAF 2.7.45; Arr India (Karachi) 12.2.46; ACSEA - RIAF, India census 5.46; To RIAF inventory 31.12.47; No.2 or 9 Sqn, AFS (I) or No.101(PR)Flt; Possibly later to No.14 Sqn; Fate unknown
NOTE: On the tail unit of Spitfire TP263, now exhibited in the War Museum Overloon Netherlands, was found the No. "TP285".

TP287 Spitfire FR.XVIIIe (Griffon 65); TOC/RAF 2.7.45; Arr India (Karachi) 31.1.46; ACSEA – RIAF, India census 5.46; To RIAF inventory 31.12.47; No.2 or 9 Sqn, AFS (I) or No.101(PR)Flt; Possibly later to No.14 Sqn; Fate unknown

TP288 Spitfire FR.XVIIIe (Griffon 65); TOC/RAF 25.6.45; Arr India (Karachi) 30.3.46; ACSEA - RIAF, India census 5.46; Retd RAF, No.47 MU 21.8.47; Sold to R J Parkes for RIAF 27.6.49; No.2 or 9 Sqn, AFS (I) or No.101(PR)Flt; Possibly later to No.14 Sqn; Fate unknown

TP289 Spitfire FR.XVIIIe (Griffon 65); TOC/RAF 2.7.45; Arr India (Karachi) 3.1.46; ACSEA – RIAF, India census 5.46; To RIAF inventory 31.12.47; No.2 or 9 Sqn, AFS (I) or No.101(PR)Flt; Possibly later to No.14 Sqn; Fate unknown

TP290 Spitfire FR.XVIIIe (Griffon 65); TOC/RAF 12.7.45; Arr India (Karachi) 25.2.46; ACSEA – RIAF, India census 5.46; To RIAF inventory 31.12.47; No.2 or 9 Sqn, AFS (I) or No.101(PR)Flt; Possibly later to No.14 Sqn; Fate unknown

TP293 Spitfire FR.XVIIIe (Griffon 65); TOC/RAF 14.7.45; Arr India (Karachi) 12.2.46; ACSEA – RIAF, India census 5.46; To RIAF inventory 31.12.47; No.2 or 9 Sqn, AFS (I) or No.101(PR)Flt; Possibly later to No.14 Sqn; Fate unknown

TP294 Spitfire FR.XVIIIe (Griffon 65); TOC/RAF 25.7.45; Arr India (Karachi) 31.1.46; ACSEA – RIAF, India census 5.46; To RIAF inventory 31.12.47; No.2 or 9 Sqn, AFS (I) or No.101(PR)Flt; Possibly later to No.14 Sqn; Fate unknown

TP296 Spitfire FR.XVIIIe (Griffon 65); TOC/RAF 23.7.45; Arr India (Karachi) 31.1.46; ACSEA – RIAF, India census 5.46; To RIAF inventory 31.12.47; No.2 or 9 Sqn, AFS (I) or No.101(PR)Flt; Possibly later to No.14 Sqn; Fate unknown

TP297 Spitfire FR.XVIIIe (Griffon 65); TOC/RAF 18.7.45; Arr India (Karachi) 31.1.46; ACSEA - RIAF, India census 5.46; Retd RAF, No.47 MU 24.8.47; Sold to R J Parkes for RIAF 16.7.49; No.2 or 9 Sqn, AFS (I) or No.101(PR)Flt; Possibly later to No.14 Sqn; Fate unknown

TP298 Spitfire FR.XVIIIe (Griffon 65); Became **HS-662** ?; TOC/RAF 17.7.45; Arr India (Karachi) 12.2.46; ACSEA – RIAF, India census 5.46; To RIAF inventory 31.12.47; No.2 or 9 Sqn, AFS (I) or No.101 (PR) Flt; Possibly later to No.14 Sqn; Kalaikunda until 1977; Hulk recovered by Ormond and Wensley Haydon-Baillie, Duxford in 1977, to USA 1978 (Civil reg. *N41702, N9323Z*); Fatal crash 19.5.94; Restoration project - **SURVIVOR**

TP319 Spitfire FR.XVIIIe (Griffon 65); TOC/RAF 27.8.45; Arr India (Karachi) 3.1.46; ACSEA – RIAF, India census 5.46; No.2 or 9 Sqn, AFS (I) or No.101(PR)Flt; To RIAF inventory 31.12.47; Possibly later to No.14 Sqn;

TP325 Spitfire FR.XVIIIe (Griffon 65); TOC/RAF 21.8.45; Arr India (Karachi) 31.1.46; ACSEA – RIAF, India census 5.46; To RIAF inventory 31.12.47; No.2 or 9 Sqn, AFS (I) or No.101(PR)Flt; Possibly later to No.14 Sqn; Fate unknown

TP326 Spitfire FR.XVIIIe (Griffon 65); TOC/RAF 28.8.45; Arr India (Karachi) 3.1.46; ACSEA – RIAF, India census 5.46; To RIAF inventory 31.12.47; No.2 or 9 Sqn, AFS (I) or No.101(PR)Flt; Possibly later to No.14 Sqn; Fate unknown

TP333 Spitfire FR.XVIIIe (Griffon 65); TOC/RAF 11.10.45; Arr India (Karachi) 3.1.46; ACSEA – RIAF, India census 5.46; To RIAF inventory 31.12.47; No.2 or 9 Sqn, AFS (I) or No.101(PR)Flt; Possibly later to No.14 Sqn; Fate unknown

TP338 Spitfire FR.XVIIIe (Griffon 65); TOC/RAF 11.10.45; Arr India (Karachi) 31.1.46; ACSEA - RIAF, India census 5.46; Retd RAF, No.47 MU 26.11.47; Sold to R J Parkes for RIAF 10.6.49; No.2 or 9 Sqn, AFS (I) or No.101(PR)Flt; Possibly later to No.14 Sqn; Fate unknown

TP339 Spitfire FR.XVIIIe (Griffon 65); TOC/RAF 11.10.45; Arr India (Karachi) 31.1.46; ACSEA – RIAF, India census 5.46; To RIAF inventory 31.12.47; No.2 or 9 Sqn, AFS (I) or No.101(PR)Flt; Possibly later to No.14 Sqn; Fate unknown

TP342 Spitfire FR.XVIIIe (Griffon 67); TOC/RAF 27.11.45; Arr India (Karachi) 17.3.46; ACSEA - RIAF, India census 5.46; Retd RAF, No.47 MU 28.8.47; Sold to R J Parkes for RIAF 1.7.49; No.2 or 9 Sqn, AFS (I) or No.101 (PR) Flt; Possibly later to No.14 Sqn; Fate unknown

TP344 Spitfire FR.XVIIIe (Griffon 65); TOC/RAF 18.10.45; Arr India (Karachi) 3.1.46; ACSEA – RIAF, India census 5.46; To RIAF inventory 31.12.47; No.2 or 9 Sqn, AFS (I) or No.101(PR)Flt; Possibly later to No.14 Sqn; Fate unknown

TP346 Spitfire FR.XVIIIe (Griffon 67); TOC/RAF 27.12.45; Arr India (Karachi) 25.2.46; ACSEA - RIAF, India census 5.46; To RIAF inventory 31.12.47; No.2 or 9 Sqn, AFS (I) or No.101(PR)Flt; Possibly later to No.14 Sqn; Fate unknown

TP363 Spitfire FR.XVIIIe (Griffon 67); TOC/RAF 18.10.45; Arr India (Karachi) 31.1.46; ACSEA – RIAF, India census 5.46; To RIAF inventory 31.12.47; No.2 or 9 Sqn, AFS (I) or No.101(PR)Flt; Possibly later to No.14 Sqn; Fate unknown

TP366 Spitfire FR.XVIIIe (Griffon 67); TOC/RAF 22.10.45; Arr India (Karachi) 31.1.46; ACSEA – RIAF, India census 5.46; To RIAF inventory 31.12.47; No.2 or 9 Sqn, AFS (I) or No.101 (PR) Flt; Possibly later to No.14 Sqn; Fate unknown

TP367 Spitfire FR.XVIIIe (Griffon 67); Became **HS-669**; TOC/RAF 22.10.45; Arr India (Karachi) 31.1.46; ACSEA – RIAF, India census 5.46; To RIAF inventory 31.12.47; No.2 or 9 Sqn, AFS (I) or No.101(PR)Flt; Possibly later to No.14 Sqn; Coded 'NB' at one time; Indian Institute of Technology, Kharagpur, to Jeet Mahal, Vancouver, BC, Canada 1979, but export not allowed; To Sandy, Bedfordshire, England 17.8.94, en route to J M Limbeuf Rouen, France - **SURVIVOR**

TP370 Spitfire FR.XVIIIe (Griffon 67); Became **HS-674**; TOC/RAF 6.11.45; Arr India (Karachi) 11.2.46; ACSEA -RIAF, India census 5.46; Retd RAF, No.47 MU 27.11.47; Sold to R J Parkes for RIAF 19.6.49; No.2 or 9 Sqn, AFS (I) or No.101(PR)Flt; Possibly later to No.14 Sqn; Fate unknown. NOTE: See also TZ219, there "HS-674" was painted over "HS-683" !

TP379 Spitfire FR.XVIIIe (Griffon 67); TOC/RAF 29.12.45; Arr India (Karachi) 25.2.46; ACSEA – RIAF, India census 5.46; To RIAF inventory 31.12.47; No.2 or 9 Sqn, AFS (I) or No.101(PR)Flt; Possibly later to No.14 Sqn; Fate unknown

TP380 Spitfire FR.XVIIIe (Griffon 67); TOC/RAF 27.10.45; Arr India (Karachi) 11.2.46; ACSEA - RIAF, India census 5.46; To RIAF inventory 31.12.47; No.2 or 9 Sqn, AFS (I) or No.101(PR)Flt; Possibly later to No.14 Sqn; Fate unknown

TP388 Spitfire FR.XVIIIe (Griffon 67); TOC/RAF 6.12.45; Arr India (Karachi) 25.2.46; ACSEA -RIAF, India census 5.46; Retd RAF, No.47 MU 26.11.47; Sold to R J Parkes for RIAF 8.6.49; No.2 or 9 Sqn, AFS (I) or No.101(PR)Flt; Possibly later to No.14 Sqn; Fate unknown

TP392 Spitfire FR.XVIIIe (Griffon 65); TOC/RAF 18.6.45; Arr India (Karachi) 31.1.46; ACSEA - RIAF, India census 5.46; To RIAF inventory 31.12.47; No.2 or 9 Sqn, AFS (I) or No.101(PR)Flt; Possibly later to No.14 Sqn; Fate unknown

TP393 Spitfire FR.XVIIIe (Griffon 65); TOC/RAF 23.6.45; Arr India (Karachi) 31.1.46; ACSEA – RIAF, India census 5.46; To RIAF inventory 31.12.47; No.2 or 9 Sqn, AFS (I) or No.101(PR)Flt; Possibly later to No.14 Sqn; Fate unknown

TP395 Spitfire FR.XVIIIe (Griffon 65); TOC/RAF 22.6.45; Arr India (Karachi) 11.2.46; ACSEA - RIAF, India census 5.46; Retd RAF, No.47 MU 27.11.47; Sold to R J Parkes for RIAF 3.6.49; No.2 or 9 Sqn, AFS (I) or No.101(PR)Flt; Possibly later to No.14 Sqn; Fate unknown

TP396 Spitfire FR.XVIIIe (Griffon 65); TOC/RAF 29.6.45; Arr India (Karachi) 31.1.46; ACSEA - RIAF, India census 5.46; Retd RAF, No.47 MU 27.11.47; Sold to R J Parkes for RIAF 8.6.49; No.2 or 9 Sqn, AFS (I) or No.101(PR)Flt; Possibly later to No.14 Sqn; Fate unknown

TP397 Spitfire FR.XVIIIe (Griffon 65); TOC/RAF 23.6.45; Arr India (Karachi) 31.1.46; ACSEA – RIAF, India census 5.46; To RIAF inventory 31.12.47; No.2 or 9 Sqn, AFS (I) or No.101(PR)Flt; Possibly later to No.14 Sqn; Fate unknown

TP398 Spitfire FR.XVIIIe (Griffon 65); TOC/RAF 25.6.45; Arr India (Karachi) 31.1.46; ACSEA - RIAF, India census 5.46; Retd RAF, No.47 MU 25.8.47; Sold to R J Parkes for RIAF 1.7.49; No.2 or 9 Sqn, AFS (I) or No.101(PR)Flt; Possibly later to No.14 Sqn; Fate unknown

TP401 Spitfire FR.XVIIIe (Griffon 65); TOC/RAF 6.7.45; Arr India (Karachi) 11.2.46; ACSEA - RIAF, India census 5.46; Retd RAF, No.47 MU 26.11.47; Sold to R J Parkes for RIAF 8.6.49; No.2 or 9 Sqn, AFS (I) or No.101 (PR) Flt; Possibly later to No.14 Sqn; Fate unknown

TP403 Spitfire FR.XVIIIe (Griffon 65); TOC/RAF 2.7.45; Arr India (Karachi) 31.1.46; ACSEA – RIAF, India census 5.46; To RIAF inventory 31.12.47; No.2 or 9 Sqn, AFS (I) or No.101(PR)Flt; Possibly later to No.14 Sqn; Fate unknown

TP404 Spitfire FR.XVIIIe (Griffon 65); TOC/RAF 2.7.45; Arr India (Karachi) 31.1.46; ACSEA – RIAF, India census 5.46; To RIAF inventory 31.12.47; No.2 or 9 Sqn, AFS (I) or No.101(PR)Flt; Possibly later to No.14 Sqn; Fate unknown

TP405 Spitfire FR.XVIIIe (Griffon 65); TOC/RAF 24.7.45; Arr India (Karachi) 25.2.46; ACSEA - RIAF, India census 5.46; Retd RAF, No.47 MU 24.8.47; Sold to R J Parkes for RIAF 1.7.49; No.2 or 9 Sqn, AFS (I) or No.101(PR)Flt; Possibly later to No.14 Sqn; Fate unknown

TP425 Spitfire FR.XVIIIe (Griffon 67); TOC/RAF 17.7.45; Arr India (Karachi) 11.2.46; ACSEA RIAF, India census 5.46; Retd RAF, No.47 MU 26.11.47; Sold to R J Parkes for RIAF 3.6.49; No.2 or 9 Sqn, AFS (I) or No.101(PR)Flt; Possibly later to No.14 Sqn; Fate unknown

TP426 Spitfire FR.XVIIIe (Griffon 65); TOC/RAF 17.7.45; Arr India (Karachi) 31.1.46; ACSEA – RIAF, India census 5.46; To RIAF inventory 31.12.47; No.2 or 9 Sqn, AFS (I) or No.101(PR)Flt; Possibly later to No.14 Sqn; Fate unknown

TP435 Spitfire FR.XVIIIe (Griffon 65); TOC/RAF 28.8.45; Arr India (Karachi) 11.2.46; ACSEA - RIAF, India census 5.46; To RIAF inventory 31.12.47; No.2 or 9 Sqn, AFS (I) or No.101(PR)Flt; Possibly later to No.14 Sqn; Fate unknown

TP436 Spitfire FR.XVIIIe (Griffon 65); TOC/RAF 6.9.45; Arr India (Karachi) 31.1.46; ACSEA - RIAF, India census 5.46; Retd RAF, No.47 MU 25.8.47; Sold to R J Parkes for RIAF 28.6.49; No.2 or 9 Sqn, AFS (I) or No.101(PR)Flt; Possibly later to No.14 Sqn; Fate unknown

TP437 Spitfire FR.XVIIIe (Griffon 65); TOC/RAF 11.9.45; Arr India (Karachi) 31.1.46; ACSEA – RIAF, India census 5.46; To RIAF inventory 31.12.47; No.2 or 9 Sqn, AFS (I) or No.101(PR)Flt; Possibly later to No.14 Sqn; Fate unknown

TP439 Spitfire FR.XVIIIe (Griffon 65); TOC/RAF 18.10.45; Arr India (Karachi) 3.1.46; ACSEA – RIAF, India census 5.46; To RIAF inventory 31.12.47; No.2 or 9 Sqn, AFS (I) or No.101(PR)Flt; Possibly later to No.14 Sqn; Fate unknown

TP441 Spitfire FR.XVIIIe (Griffon 67); TOC/RAF 11.10.45; Arr India (Karachi) 3.1.46; ACSEA – RIAF, India census 5.46; To RIAF inventory 31.12.47; No.2 or 9 Sqn, AFS (I) or No.101(PR)Flt; Possibly later to No.14 Sqn; Fate unknown

TP442 Spitfire FR.XVIIIe (Griffon 67); TOC/RAF 18.10.45; Arr India (Karachi) 31.1.46; ACSEA - RIAF, India census 5.46; To RIAF inventory 31.12.47; No.2 or 9 Sqn, AFS (I) or No.101(PR)Flt; Possibly later to No.14 Sqn; Fate unknown

TP444 Spitfire FR.XVIIIe (Griffon 67); TOC/RAF 27.10.45; Arr India (Karachi) 11.2.46; ACSEA – RIAF, India census 5.46; No.47 MU/RAF 23.10.47; Retd RIAF via 29.MU 14.6.49; No.2 or 9 Sqn, AFS (I) or No.101 (PR) Flt; Possibly later to No.14 Sqn; Fate unknown

TX974 Spitfire FR.XIVe (Griffon 65); TOC/RAF 23.8.45; Arr India (Karachi) 2.12.45; ACSEA - RIAF, India census 5.46; No.9 Sqn, engine blew up when started, aircraft broke back, caught fire and burnt out, Peshawar, Cat.E 16.8.46 (F/O R K B Singh injured); Retd RAF (casualty wastage); SOC 31.10.46

TX975 Spitfire FR.XIVe (Griffon 65); TOC/RAF 13.8.45; Arr India (Karachi) 30.10.45; ACSEA - RIAF; No.4 Sqn (Japan census 9.46); Retd RAF; SOC 24.3.48

TX976 Spitfire FR.XIVe (Griffon 65); TOC/RAF 11.8.45; Arr India (Karachi) 14.10.45; ACSEA - RIAF, India census 5.46; No.1 SFTS of AFS (I), stalled on landing, undercarriage collapsed at Ambala, Cat.FA/E 4.5.46 (P/O S Jena seriously injured); SOC 31.10.46

TX977 Spitfire FR.XIVe (Griffon 65); TOC/RAF 30.8.45; Arr India (Karachi) 30.10.45; ACSEA - RIAF; No.4 Sqn (Japan census 9.46); SOC 24.3.48

TX978 Spitfire FR.XIVe (Griffon 65); TOC/RAF 5.9.45; Arr India (Karachi) 18.10.45; ACSEA - RIAF, India census 5.46; No.7 Sqn, engine failed in aerobatics at 3,000ft, emergency landing, landed heavily at Kohat, Cat.FA/B 24.7.46 (F/O GS Dhillon OK); Retd RAF; SOC 29.8.46

TX979 Spitfire FR.XIVe (Griffon 65); TOC/RAF 5.9.45; Arr India (Karachi) 18.10.45; ACSEA - RIAF; No.4 Sqn (Japan census 9.46), flying low in mountainous terrain, flew into high ground in cloud while turning in valley followed by No.2 in SM925, Okayama, Japan, Cat.FA/E 11.6.47 (F/O GS Sekhon killed); SOC 31.7.47

TX986 Spitfire FR.XIVe (Griffon 65); TOC/RAF 27.4.45; Arr India (Karachi) 25.6.45; ACSEA - RIAF; No.4 Sqn (Japan census 9.46); SOC 24.3.48

TX988 Spitfire FR.XIVe (Griffon 65); TOC/RAF 30.4.45; Arr India (Karachi) 14.8.45; ACSEA - RIAF, India census 5.46; No.9 Sqn, engine cut on cross-country, belly-landed Ichawara (near Sehore), 20m SSW of Bhopal, Cat.E 19.2.47 (F/O S Srinivasan minor injuries); SOC 24.4.47

TX990 Spitfire FR.XIVe (Griffon 65); TOC/RAF 30.4.45; Arr India (Karachi) 17.9.45; ACSEA - RIAF, India census 5.46; AFS (I); To RIAF inventory 29.12.47; Fate unknown

TX991 Spitfire FR.XIVe (Griffon 65); TOC/RAF 28.4.45; Arr India (Karachi) 18.10.45; ACSEA - RIAF, India census 5.46; No.8 Sqn, ferrying to join No.9 Sqn, engine cut, force-landed, crashed 30m NW of Secunderabad, Cat.FA/E 15.3.47 (F/O AK Sehgal killed); SOC 24.4.47

Spitfire FR.XIVe TX994 'R' of No. 8 Sqn RIAF in 1946. [via Andy Thomas]

Spitfire FR.XIVe, TX994/R of No. 8 Sqn, RIAF, Kolar in 1946

TX994 Spitfire FR.XIVe (Griffon 65); TOC/RAF 3.5.45; Arr India (Karachi) 30.8.45; ACSEA - RIAF, India census 5.46; No.8 Sqn ('R') in 1946; Retd RAF; SOC 28.8.47

TX996 Spitfire FR.XIVe (Griffon 65); TOC/RAF 29.4.45; Arr India (Karachi) 3.1.46; ACSEA - RIAF, India census 5.46; Service unknown; Retd ACSEA 28.11.46; SOC 13.1.48

TZ104 Spitfire FR.XIVe (Griffon 65); TOC/RAF 4.5.45; Arr India (Karachi) 14.10.45; ACSEA - RIAF, India census 5.46; No.6 Sqn, landed wheels up Ranchi, Cat.Ac 4.1.47 (F/O NB Menon OK); Engine cut on sector recce, pilot struck wing baling out near Palamau, Bihar, Cat.FA/E 18.3.47 (P/O RH Beaupert killed); SOC 26.6.47

TZ107 Spitfire FR.XIVe (Griffon 65); TOC/RAF 11.5.45; Arr India (Karachi) 14.8.45; ACSEA - RIAF; No.8 Sqn, caught fire during servicing, possible petrol vapour in cockpit, Mingaladon, Cat.E 15.1.46; SOC 31.1.46

TZ108 Spitfire FR.XIVe (Griffon 65); TOC/RAF 12.5.45; Arr India (Karachi) 30.8.45; ACSEA - RIAF; No.7 Sqn, swung on landing cross-wind, ran off into bad ground, port wheel bogged, port oleo leg collapsed, Maharajpur, Cat.B 29.3.46 (P/O JR Bankapur); Retd RAF; SOC 25.4.46 (bboc/SOC 30.5.46)

TZ109 Spitfire FR.XIVe (Griffon 65); TOC/RAF 12.5.45; Arr India (Karachi) 14.10.45; ACSEA - RIAF, India census 5.46; No.7 Sqn; No.1 Sqn, took off in cross wind, nose pecked, Nagpur, Cat.Ac 14.4.47 (F/O JI Cohen OK); Retd RAF; SOC 28.8.47

TZ110 Spitfire FR.XIVe (Griffon 65); TOC/RAF 16.5.45; Arr India (Karachi) 20.8.45; ACSEA - RIAF, India census 5.46; No.6 Sqn, engine failed to pick up landing, undershot, Ranchi, Cat.FA/E 3.8.46 (P/O BJG Cazlet OK); Retd RAF (casualty wastage); SOC 25.9.47

TZ113 Spitfire FR.XIVe (Griffon 65); TOC/RAF 23.5.45; Arr India (Karachi) 17.9.45; ACSEA - RIAF, India census 5.46; AFS (I); To RIAF inventory 29.12.47; Fate unknown

TZ114 Spitfire FR.XIVe (Griffon 65); TOC/RAF 23.5.45; Arr India (Karachi) 17.9.45; ACSEA - RIAF, India census 5.46; No.6 Sqn ('L') by 1.47; To RIAF inventory 29.12.47; AFS (I); Fate unknown
NOTE: FR-version, but without camera-installation

TZ118 Spitfire FR.XIVe (Griffon 65); TOC/RAF 23.5.45; Arr India (Karachi) 17.9.45; ACSEA - RIAF, India census 5.46; AFS (I), stalled high while landing, yawed, bounced, nose tipped, undercarriage damaged, Ambala, Cat.FA/E 25.9.46 (P/O SR Bose OK); SOC 31.10.46

TZ119 Spitfire FR.XIVe (Griffon 65); TOC/RAF 23.5.45; Arr India (Karachi) 17.9.45; ACSEA - RIAF, India census 5.46; Service unknown; Retd RAF; SOC 28.8.47

TZ120 Spitfire FR.XIVe (Griffon 65); TOC/RAF 28.5.45; Arr India (Karachi) 17.9.45; ACSEA - RIAF; No.6 Sqn, ferrying from Dum Dum to No.355 MU Salawas, swung landing to avoid obstruction, ran off runway, starboard wheel bogged in soft ground, nose tipped, Jaipur, Cat.FA/Ac 21.7.46 (F/O TR Healey OK); Cross-country

TZ121 Spitfire FR.XIVe (Griffon 65); TOC/RAF 29.5.45; Arr India (Karachi) 30.8.45; ACSEA - RIAF, India census 5.46; Service unknown; Retd RAF; SOC 28.8.47
from Palam to Allahabad, unexpectedly short of fuel in bad weather, force landing wheels-up 2m W of Akrabad 1.8.46 (S/Ldr A Lodhi OK); Retd RAF; SOC 30.1.47

TZ123 Spitfire FR.XIVe (Griffon 65); TOC/RAF 29.5.45; Arr India (Karachi) 30.8.45; ACSEA - RIAF, India census 5.46; No.6 Sqn ('C') 1946/47; Retd RAF (No.320 MU); SOC 28.8.47

TZ124 Spitfire FR.XIVe (Griffon 65); TOC/RAF 29.5.45; Arr India (Karachi) 30.8.45; ACSEA - RIAF, India census 5.46; No.6 Sqn, port tyre burst on formation take-off, swung to port off runway, nose tipped, Ranchi, Cat.A 12.8.46 (F/O Salah-ud-din OK); Retd RAF; SOC 31.12.46

TZ133 Spitfire FR.XIVe (Griffon 65); TOC/RAF 14.6.45; Arr India (Karachi) 2.12.45; ACSEA - RIAF, India census 5.46; Service unknown; Retd RAF; SOC 25.9.47

TZ143 Spitfire FR.XIVe (Griffon 65); TOC/RAF 9.7.45; Arr India (Karachi) 17.9.45; ACSEA - RIAF, India census 5.46; Service unknown; Retd RAF; SOC 26.9.46

TZ145 Spitfire FR.XIVe (Griffon 65); TOC/RAF 12.7.45; Arr India (Karachi) 2.12.45; ACSEA (No.11 Sqn) - RIAF, India census 5.46; Service unknown; Retd ACSEA 28.11.46 (in Japan 4.47); SOC 24.3.48

TZ147 Spitfire FR.XIVe (Griffon 65); TOC/RAF 11.7.45; Arr India (Karachi) 2.12.45; ACSEA (No.11 Sqn) - RIAF, India census 5.46; Service unknown; Retd ACSEA 28.11.46 (in Japan 4.47); SOC 24.3.48

TZ149 Spitfire FR.XIVe (Griffon 65); TOC/RAF 17.7.45; Arr India (Karachi) 2.12.45; ACSEA - RIAF, India census 5.46; Service unknown; Retd RAF; SOC 25.9.47

TZ152 Spitfire FR.XIVe (Griffon 65); TOC/RAF 19.7.45; Arr India (Karachi) 14.10.45; ACSEA - RIAF; No.6 Sqn, unauthorised air combat practice, lost control in half roll, crashed 4m E of Namkum Railway Station, Cat.FA/E 9.4.46 (F/O CA Hall killed); Retd RAF (casualty wastage); SOC 25.4.46 (bboc/SOC 30.5.46)

TZ153 Spitfire FR.XIVe (Griffon 65); TOC/RAF 20.7.45; Arr India (Karachi) 17.9.45; ACSEA - RIAF; No.6 Sqn in 1945; Retd RAF; SOC 27.12.48

TZ155 Spitfire FR.XIVe (Griffon 65); TOC/RAF 21.7.45; Arr India (Karachi) 30.10.45; ACSEA - RIAF, India census 5.46; No.8 Sqn, during ferrying, swung by gust of wind, brakes failed, went into ditch, Barrackpore, Cat.Ac 15.12.45 (F/Lt J Reid OK); No.10 Sqn, undercarriage collapsed landing, Barrackpore, Cat.Ac 14.6.46 (P/O AE Smith OK); Retd RAF; SOC 1.6.47

TZ156 Spitfire FR.XIVe (Griffon 65); TOC/RAF 25.7.45; Arr India (Karachi) 17.9.45; ACSEA - RIAF; No.6 Sqn, became lost during Sqn move from Kohat to Ranchi, force-landed in field, Cat.E 8.1.46 (P/O TO Wynne seriously injured); SOC/RAF 14.2.46

TZ161 Spitfire FR.XIVe (Griffon 65); TOC/RAF 21.8.45; Arr India (Karachi) 18.10.45; ACSEA - RIAF, India census 5.46; No.8 Sqn, bird strike on fin in circuit, Kolar, Cat.A 5.11.46 (F/Lt SA Joseph OK); Retd RAF; SOC 31.7.47

TZ162 Spitfire FR.XIVe (Griffon 65); TOC/RAF 28.7.45; Arr India (Karachi) 14.10.45; ACSEA - RIAF; No.6 Sqn, engine failed, crashed in wheels-up forced landing, Guldhar, Cat.FA/E 5.3.46 (F/O TR Healey seriously injured); SOC 25.4.46 (bboc/SOC 30.5.46); Aircraft later burnt by unidentified natives

TZ163 Spitfire FR.XIVe (Griffon 65); TOC/RAF 13.8.45; Arr India (Karachi) 30.10.45; ACSEA - RIAF, India census 5.46; No.6 Sqn, crashed on take-off at Ranchi, Cat.FA/E 8.11.46; Retd RAF (casualty wastage); SOC 24.4.47

TZ165 Spitfire FR.XIVe (Griffon 65); TOC/RAF 27.8.45; Arr India (Karachi) 18.10.45; ACSEA - RIAF; No.4 Sqn (Japan census 9.46); Retd RAF; SOC 24.3.48

TZ167 Spitfire FR.XIVe (Griffon 65); TOC/RAF 27.8.45; Arr India (Karachi) 30.10.45; ACSEA - RIAF; No.1 SFTS of AFS (I), engine failed at 3,500ft, crashed in wheel-up forced landing in ploughed field, 1m NW of Thanesar, Cat.FA/E 11.4.46 (P/O C Shortlands OK); Retd RAF (casualty wastage); SOC 9.5.46

TZ168 Spitfire FR.XIVe (Griffon 65); TOC/RAF 27.8.45; Arr India (Karachi) 30.10.45; ACSEA - RIAF, India census 5.46; No.8 Sqn; Retd RAF; SOC 28.8.47

TZ169 Spitfire FR.XIVe (Griffon 65); TOC/RAF 27.8.45; Arr India (Karachi) 18.10.45; ACSEA - RIAF, India census 5.46; No.8 Sqn, left peritrack taxying, went into ditch, port mainplane & propeller damaged, Sulur, Cat.FA/E 23.9.46 (F/O S Banerji OK); Retd RAF (casualty wastage); SOC 31.10.46

TZ170 Spitfire FR.XIVe (Griffon 65); TOC/RAF 31.8.45; Arr India (Karachi) 30.10.45; ACSEA - RIAF, India census 5.46; Service unknown; Retd RAF; SOC 28.8.47

TZ171 Spitfire FR.XIVe (Griffon 65); TOC/RAF 31.8.45; Arr India (Karachi) 18.10.45; ACSEA - RIAF, India census 5.46; To RIAF inventory 29.12.47; AFS (I); Fate unknown

TZ172 Spitfire FR.XIVe (Griffon 65); TOC/RAF 5.9.45; Arr India (Karachi) 2.12.45; ACSEA - RIAF, India census 5.46; Service unknown; Retd RAF; SOC 25.9.47

TZ173 Spitfire FR.XIVe (Griffon 65); TOC/RAF 5.9.45; Arr India (Karachi) 18.10.45; ACSEA - RIAF, India census 5.46; Service unknown; Retd RAF; SOC 28.8.47

TZ185 Spitfire FR.XIVe (Griffon 66); Arr India (Karachi) 30.8.45; ACSEA - RIAF, India census 5.46; AFS (I), engine cut on approach after formation flight, belly-landed at Ambala, Cat.FA/E 17.12.46 (P/O PE Harrington OK); SOC 30.1.47

TZ186 Spitfire FR.XIVe (Griffon 65); TOC/RAF 22.5.45; Arr India (Karachi) 28.7.45; ACSEA - RIAF, India census 5.46; No.8 Sqn, engine cut at 800ft in circuit, force-landed wheels-up 4m SSE of Trichinopoly, Cat.FA/E 9.6.46 (F/O VJ Clowsley OK); Retd RAF (casualty wastage); SOC 31.10.46

TZ189 Spitfire FR.XIVe (Griffon 65); TOC/RAF 31.5.45; Arr India (Karachi) 2.12.45; ACSEA (No.11 Sqn) - RIAF, India census 5.46; Service unknown; Retd ACSEA 28.11.46 (in Japan 4.47); SOC 24.3.48

TZ190 Spitfire FR.XIVe (Griffon 65); TOC/RAF 8.6.45; Arr India (Karachi) 14.10.45; ACSEA - RIAF, India census 5.46; Service unknown; Retd RAF; SOC 28.8.47

TZ195 Spitfire FR.XIVe (Griffon 65); TOC/RAF 2.6.45; Arr India (Karachi) 17.9.45; ACSEA - RIAF, India census 5.46; No.7 Sqn, hit ground during dive-bombing practice 6m E of Razmak, burnt out, Cat.E 21.8.46 (F/O PJ Oommen killed); Retd RAF (casualty wastage); SOC 26.9.46

TZ205 Spitfire FR.XVIIIe (Griffon 67); TOC/RAF 14.12.45; Arr India (Karachi) 16.2.46; ACSEA – RIAF, India census 5.46; To RIAF inventory 31.12.47; No.2 or 9 Sqn, AFS (I) or No.101(PR)Flt; Possibly later to No.14 Sqn; Fate unknown

TZ217 Spitfire FR.XVIIIe (Griffon 67); TOC/RAF 6.12.45; Arr India (Karachi) 25.2.46; ACSEA – RIAF, India census 5.46; To RIAF inventory 31.12.47; No.2 or 9 Sqn, AFS (I) or No.101(PR)Flt; Possibly later to No.14 Sqn; Fate unknown

TZ218 Spitfire FR.XVIIIe (Griffon 67); TOC/RAF 14.12.45; Arr India (Karachi) 11.2.46; ACSEA – RIAF, India census 5.46; To RIAF inventory 31.12.47; No.2 or 9 Sqn, AFS (I) or No.101(PR)Flt; Possibly later to No.14 Sqn; Fate unknown

TZ219 Spitfire FR.XVIIIe (Griffon 67); Became **HS-683**; TOC/RAF 8.12.45; Arr India (Karachi) 11.2.46; ACSEA – RIAF, India census 5.46; To RIAF inventory 31.12.47; No.2 or 9 Sqn, AFS (I) or No.101(PR)Flt; Possibly later to No.14 Sqn; Now Punjab Engineering College at Chandigarh, India (Instructional airframe) (painted as "HS-674" – **SURVIVOR**

TZ222 Spitfire FR.XVIIIe (Griffon 67); TOC/RAF 5.12.45; Arr India (Karachi) 11.2.46; ACSEA (India census 5.46); No.47 MU RAF 23.10.47 - Sold to R J Parkes for RIAF 1.7.49; No.2 or 9 Sqn, AFS (I) or No.101(PR)Flt; Possibly later to No.14 Sqn; Fate unknown

INDIA – IRAN

TZ224 Spitfire FR.XVIIIe (Griffon 67); TOC/RAF 21.12.45; Arr India (Karachi) 25.2.46; ACSEA – RIAF, India census 5.46; To RIAF inventory 31.12.47; No.2 or 9 Sqn, AFS (I) or No.101(PR)Flt; Possibly later to No.14 Sqn; Fate unknown

TZ227 Spitfire FR.XVIIIe (Griffon 67); TOC/RAF 17.12.45; Arr India (Karachi) 11.2.46; ACSEA – RIAF, India census 5.46; To RIAF inventory 31.12.47; No.2 or 9 Sqn, AFS (I) or No.101(PR)Flt; Possibly later to No.14 Sqn; Fate unknown

TZ231 Spitfire FR.XVIIIe (Griffon 67); TOC/RAF 27.12.45; Arr India (Karachi) 25.2.46; ACSEA (India census 5.46); No.47 MU RAF 21.8.47 - Sold to R J Parkes for RIAF 28.6.49; No.2 or 9 Sqn, AFS (I) or No.101(PR)Flt; Possibly later to No.14 Sqn; Fate unknown

TZ235 Spitfire FR.XVIIIe (Griffon 67); TOC/RAF 27.12.45; Arr India (Karachi) 25.2.46; ACSEA – RIAF, India census 5.46; To RIAF inventory 31.12.47; No.2 or 9 Sqn, AFS (I) or No.101(PR)Flt; Possibly later to No.14 Sqn; Fate unknown

SURVIVORS

NH631 and SM986 at Palam; TZ219 at Chandigarh.

Unidentified write-offs

28.6.45 No.3 Sqn, crashed at air-to-ground firing range (P/O Buchanan killed), SOC
NOTE: No.3 Sqn officially received Spitfires in 11.45 !

1.8.45 No.8 Sqn, FTR ops, last seen in Kyaukpyu area (F/O SM Zahid), SOC

References:
Indian Air Force, Flying Review November 1968 p. 44.
The Indian Air Force and its aircraft, by W Green, G Swanborough and PS Chopra, Ducimus Books London, 1982.

Checklist – Known previous identities

Indian Serial Nos	RAF Serial Nos
Spitfire T.IX	
HS-534	MA848
HS-535	MH432
HS-536	MJ177
HS-537	MJ276
HS-538	MJ451
HS-539	MJ518
HS-540	MK172
HS-541	MK176
HS-542	MK298
HS-543	ML417

Indian Serial Nos	RAF Serial Nos
Spitfire Mk.XVIII & XIX	
HS-649	TP263
HS-653	TP276
HS-654	TP280
HS-662	TP298
HS-669	TP367
HS-674	TP370
HS-683	TZ219
HS-687	SM845
HS-693	PM606
HS-694	PM627
HS-700	PM570
HS-877	SM969
HS-986	SM986

Spitfire PR.XIX to No.101(PR)Flt - No.1(PR)Sqn (RAF serial numbers mostly unknown)				
	arr. India			arr. India
HS-693	8.2.49		HS-700	31.3.49
HS-694	22.2.49		HS-701	24.5.49
HS-695	22.2.49		HS-702	1.6.49
HS-696	22.3.49		HS-703	8.6.49
HS-697	14.3.49		HS-704	23.6.49
HS-698	14.3.49		HS-705	1953
HS-699	22.3.49			

Ground instructional airframe numbers			
M-341		M-349	MV374
M-342	PA908	M-350	
M-343	MT516		
M-344	MT555	T17	MT719
M-345	MT742	T20	MV293
M-346	MV434		
M-347	NH861	T3. ?	NH749
M-348	RN144		
	SM841	T44	MV370

IRAN

Iran asked for 24 Spitfire Mk.Ia from Supermarine in November 1938. This request was allotted place No.12 on the Foreign Office priority list, dated 17th November 1938, but the inquiry was never followed up, and was eventually cancelled.

Iran was the main delivery route for Spitfires supplied to the Soviet Union. Spitfire F.Vbs and LF.IXs were shipped to the Persian Gulf. The destination was given the code-name "Hapmat", later "Hapmat-South", meaning the ports of Basrah and Abadan on the Shatt-el-Arab. After their assembly by RAF Maintenance Units they were flown by Russian pilots via Teheran to airfields near Baku, Azerbaijan (Caucasian area, near the Caspian Sea).

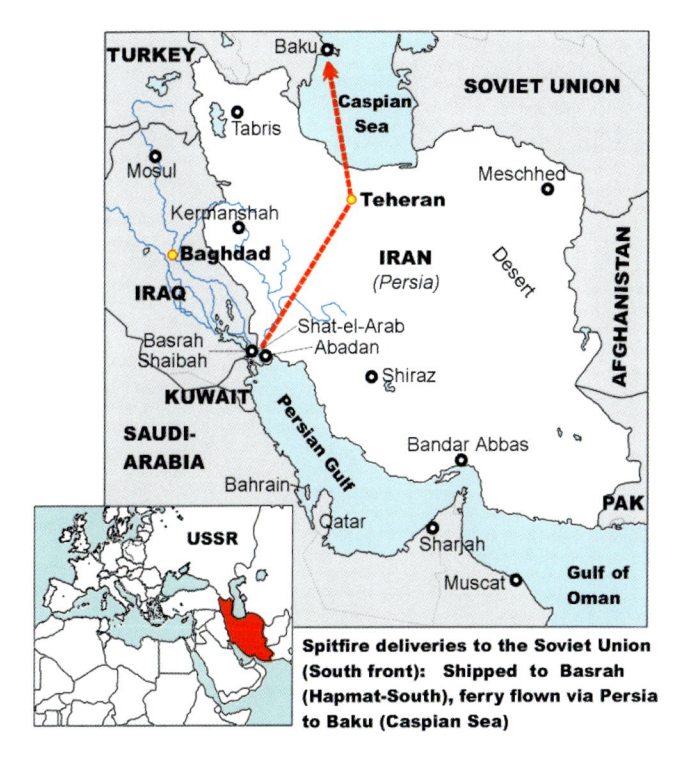

Spitfire deliveries to the Soviet Union (South front): Shipped to Basrah (Hapmat-South), ferry flown via Persia to Baku (Caspian Sea)

IRAQ

On 19th July 1950 Vickers-Armstrongs bought some near-expired Spitfire Mk.IXs from RAF stocks and converted them to Spitfire Trainer T.IX with Merlin 66 engines as Type No.509. Six of these were ordered by the Iraqi Air Force, but later cancelled.

Israel sold 30 Spitfire IXs to Burma in 1953. These were flown over the Persian Gulf and India to Burma. At first they flew also via Iraq. However, on 4th October 1954, whilst en route to Burma, one of them belly-landed at Shaibah (near Basrah), which was then still under RAF control. The aircraft was abandoned, remaining there in storage for a long time. Iraq became a Republic in 1958 and took over the Shaibah station. Subsequently the Spitfire was confiscated by Iraq. Its fate is unknown. It was replaced as *UB422* by another Israeli aircraft.

Note:
In World War Two, No.215 Group (a General Reconnaissance administrative unit) of the RAF served in Iraq from May 1942 until November 1943, controlling various units including Nos.123, 208 and 244 Sqns, a detachment of No.74 Squadron and also No.1438 Flight, but none of these had Spitfires.

IRELAND (EIRE)

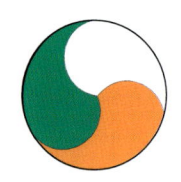

Southern Ireland became independent from Britain as the Irish Free State in January 1922, the six Northern counties remaining part of the UK. Renamed Eire in 1937, the South became the Republic of Ireland in April 1949.

During the Second World War a number of military airfields in Northern Ireland (Ulster) were used by the USAAF and RAF (Eglinton, Aldergrove, Ballyhalbert etc) for training and refresher flying.

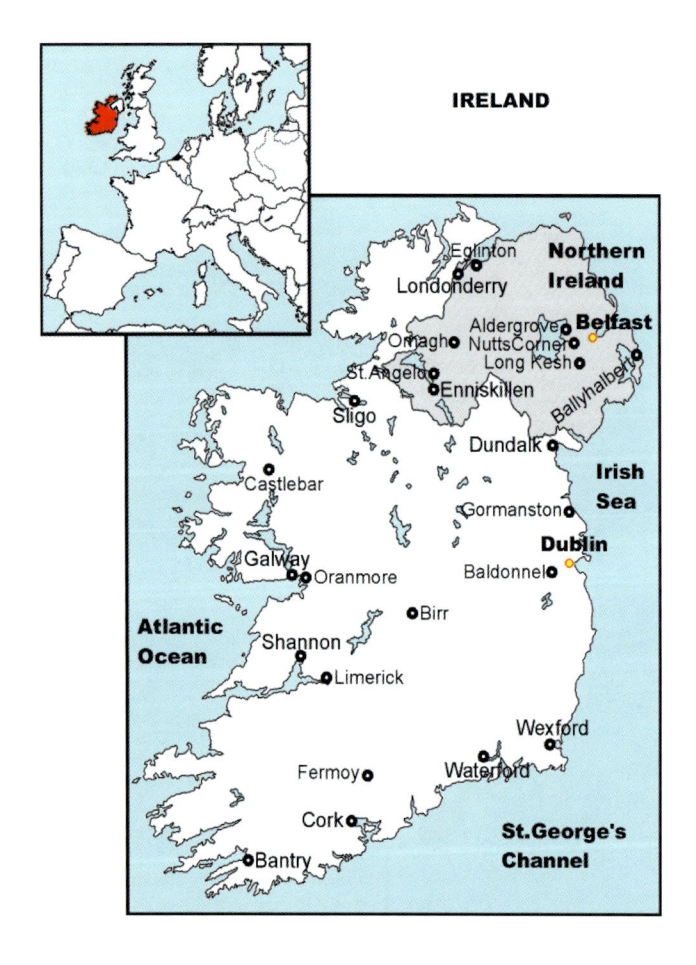

Neutrality was preserved by Southern Ireland throughout the Second World War. Initially, British and German pilots who lost orientation and force-landed were interned in Ireland, and their aircraft confiscated. From mid-1943 the policy changed after some delicate diplomatic negotiations, and aircraft could then be returned. For example the remains of Spitfire P8074 had been retained after a crash at Milladerrach 30th November 1941, but following the relaxation of policy P8267, which force-landed at Clogher Strand while on delivery to Eglinton on 16th December 1941, was returned to the UK in July 1943.

After the Second World War, the military aviation of the Republic of Ireland, the *Irish Air Corps* (IAC), comprised a Headquarters, Depot, Apprentice School, Maintenance Unit (MU), General Purpose Flight (GP Flight), Flying Training School (FTS), and Technical Training Sqn (TTS), all at Baldonnel (known as "Casement Base" from 1965, but since reverted to Baldonnel), and a Fighter Squadron at Gormanston.

In 1947 the IAC received twelve Seafire L.IIIc (converted to Spitfire Mk.Vc standard) these were followed in 1951 by six Spitfire T.IX.

Seafire L.IIIc (de-navalised, Vickers Type No. 506)

The Irish Government asked for twelve Spitfire Mk.IXs for the post-war IAC, but the British Government would not agree to supply them and instead offered twelve Seafire L Mk.IIIc. These were ordered on 31st August 1946 from Vickers-Armstrongs, South Marston Works. The aircraft were delivered from the Royal Navy Aircraft Holding Unit at Abbotsinch, extensively modified and brought up to Spitfire LF Mk.Vc standard. The arrester hooks and all naval attachments were removed and the folding wings were locked in the down position. They were, however, always referred to as Seafires, not Spitfires. A Merlin 55M engine with six exhaust stubs on each side was fitted and a four blade propeller.

The first flight after the modifications was at South Marston on the 2nd September 1946, and the first acceptance flights there were on the 23rd/24th January 1947, the last being on 27th September 1947. The Seafires were flown in batches of four to the MU at Baldonnel on 17th February 1947, 11th July 1947 and 27th September 1947. They were allotted IAC serial numbers 146 to 157.

Seafires served with the No.1 (F) Sqn until 1954. Then they were stored by the MU at Baldonnel, usable spare parts removed, and eventually scrapped 1962/63. Only one survived.

IRELAND

Spitfire T.IX (Vickers-Armstrongs Type No. 502)

The Irish Government ordered six aircraft from Vickers-Armstrongs in September 1950. They were allocated B-class markings *G-15-171* to *G-15-176* and were delivered to Ireland from 5th June 1951 to 30th July 1951 with their IAC serial numbers already painted on, these being respectively 158 to 163.

The Spitfire Trainers served with the School and the Fighter Squadron at various times, and in September 1961 the last Spitfire was transferred to the Technical Training Squadron at Baldonnel.

Five of the Spitfires survived, but not in Ireland.

Spitfire units of the IAC

No. 1 (F) Sqn at Gormanston, North of Dublin;
With twelve Seafire L.IIIc (mod) from February 1947 to June 1954, and three Spitfire T.IX from 1951 to 1961; Five Seafires and one T.IX were lost during the service period.
Camouflage and markings: Mid green overall painted, Serial No on both sides of the rear fuselage and under the starboard wing, Fin-flag; Sqn-emblem (*Black Panthers Head*) on both sides of the cowling.
Commanding Officer:
Cmd Patrick Swan.

(A)FTS at Baldonnel, SW of Dublin;
With five Spitfire T.IX from June 1951 to 1961, and one Seafire L.IIIc (mod) in 1951/53; One Spitfire T.IX was lost 1957;
Markings: Silver overall, Red spinner, serial number on both sides of the rear fuselage and under the starboard wing. None fin-flag. Later anti-dazzle black on the top cowling.
Commanding Officer:
Cmd DJ Healy.

TTS at Baldonnel (training of the ground-crews);
With five Spitfire T.IX from 1960; the last sold 1970.
Commanding Officer:
Unknown.

Individual Histories

MJ627 Spitfire T.IX (Merlin 66); Became IAC No **158**; TOC/RAF 4.12.43 (as LF IX); To Vickers-Armstrongs for conversion to two-seater 19.7.50; Flown as G-15-171; Accepted and flown to Ireland - Arr IAC and to Flying Training School Baldonnel ('158') 5.6.51; Aerobatic display 8.8.51; Technical Training Sqn Baldonnel 4.60; Extant; Offered for sale 1961; Sold 5.11.63 to J Crewdson/Film Aviation Services Ltd, Biggin Hill Kent, England, to UK 13.11.63 and stored dismantled (Civil reg. *G-ASOZ* 19.2.64); Not converted, stored dismantled at Elstree by Tim A Davies from 9.64, and by John Fairey, Stockbridge, Hampshire from 12.67; Restoration begun at Kenilworth by Maurice Bayliss in 1976 and continued at Coventry/Bruntingthorpe by Maurice S Bayliss and Peter K Bayliss from 1978 with wings of IAC No.159 and reg. *G-BMSB* 3.5.78; ff 8.11.93 marked "MJ627/9G-P"), extant, airworthy - **SURVIVOR**

MJ772 Spitfire T.IX (Merlin 66); Became IAC No **159**; TOC/RAF 20.12.43 (as LF IX); To Vickers-Armstrongs for conversion to two-seater 19.7.50; Flown as G-15-172 on 31.5.51; Accepted and flown to Ireland - Arr IAC and to Flying Training School Baldonnel ('159') 5.6.51; Aerobatic display 13.8.51; No.1 Sqn ('A' Flight, mid green camouflage) 1957; Technical Training Sqn 1.60; Offered for sale; Sold 5.11.63 to UK to J Crewdson/Film Aviation Services, Biggin Hill, Kent; To COGEA Nouvelles, Ostend, Belgium, arr by air 1.4.63 and stored dismantled; Retd UK, shipped to N A W Samuelson, Elstree, Hertfordshire 1965, ff 7.67 (Civil reg. *G-AVAV* 8.11.66, cancelled 18.5.75); Flown in film *Battle of Britain* in 1968; Crashed on landing

Maintenance on a Seafire L.IIIc of No. 1 (F) Sqn IAC at Gormanston airfield. [A P Kearns]

Spitfire T.IX No. 158 (MJ627), the first of six which arrived in Ireland in 1951, served with the (A) FTS Baldonnel. [A P Kearns]

Little Staughton 9.7.68;To W J D Roberts 12.69 and in Strathallan Collection, Auchterarder, Scotland from 12.71; Sold to USA 12.74; reg *N8R* Windward Avn Inc, Enid, OK 11.12.75; Now Champlin Fighter Museum, Mesa, Arizona, airworthy - **SURVIVOR**

MK721 Spitfire T.IX (Merlin 66); Became IAC No **160**; TOC/RAF 31.3.44 (as LF IX); To Vickers-Armstrongs for conversion to two-seater 19.7.50; Flown as G-15-173; Accepted and flown to Ireland - Arr IAC and to Flying Training School Baldonnel ('160') 29.6.51; Crashed Cat.E2 15.3.57, SOC; Scrapped

ML407 Spitfire T.IX (Merlin 66); Became IAC No **162**; TOC/RAF 23.4.44 (as LF IX); To Vickers-Armstrongs, as near expired aircraft, for conversion to two-seater 19.7.50; First flight as G-15-175 after conversion at Eastleigh 24.7.51; Accepted and flown via Speke to Ireland – Arr IAC Air Depot Baldonnel 30.7.51; Flying Training School Baldonnel ('B'-Flight) 25.8.51; No.1 Sqn ('A' Flight, mid green camouflage) Gormanston 26.4.57; Flying Training School Baldonnel 28.7.58; No.1 Sqn 28.2.59; FTS from 31.3.59 (last flight 8.7.60); To Technical Training Sqn Baldonnel 8.7.60; SOC 2.64; Offered for sale; Sold to N A W Samuelson, Cricklewood, North London and stored 4.3.68; To Sir William Roberts, Shoreham 23.4.70; To Flimwell 23.4.70; Retd Shoreham 19.3.71; Retd Flimwell 5.10.71; To Strathallan Collection, Auchterarder 2.3.72; To E Nick (& Carolyn) Grace, St.Merryn, Cornwall 9.8.79 for restoration to airworthiness (Civil reg. *G-LFIX* 1.2.80); First flight at St.Merryn after restoration 16.4.85; To Middle Wallop 4.9.85; Southampton Airport (Eastleigh) 16.1.86; Damaged in wheels-up landing at Eastleigh 5.3.86; First flight after repair 25.3.86; Goodwood 25.7.86; To Carolyn S Grace, Winchester; 26.5.89, moved to Duxford 23.9.90, airworthy, marked as "ML407", coded "NL-D" (port) and "OU-V" (starboard) - **SURVIVOR**

PR237 Seafire L.IIIc (Merlin 55M); Became IAC No **155**; RNDA 30.11.44; Vickers-Armstrongs South Marston (conversion to Mk.Vc, probably with wings from NF575 and NF566); Flown to Ireland by Sgt Conway - Arr IAC 27.9.47; No. 1 Sqn Baldonnel ('155') 29.9.47; SOC 19.6.54 (w/o 8.8.54); To MU at Baldonnel; Scrapped 1962

PR302 Seafire L.IIIc (Merlin 55M); Became IAC No **146**; RNDA 6.1.45; Vickers-Armstrongs South Marston (conversion to Mk.Vc); First flight after conversion 4.12.46; Accepted and flown via Speke to Baldonnel - Arr IAC 24.1.47; No.1 Sqn ('146') 17.2.47; SOC 16.6.54; To MU at Baldonnel; Scrapped 1962

PR315 Seafire L.IIIc (Merlin 55M); Became IAC No **147**; RNDA 6.1.45; Vickers-Armstrongs South Marston (conversion to Mk.Vc); First flight after conversion 2.9.46; Accepted and flown via Speke to Baldonnel - IAC 24.1.47; No.1 Sqn ('147') 17.2.47; Force-landed, Cat.E1 5.9.47, SOC; To MU at Baldonnel, for spare parts; Scrapped 1954

PV202 Spitfire T.IX (Merlin 66); Became IAC No **161**; TOC/RAF 18.9.44 (as LF.IX); To Vickers-Armstrongs for conversion to two-seater 19.7.50; Flown as G-15-174; Accepted and flown to Ireland - Arr IAC and to Flying Training School Baldonnel ('161') 29.6.51; Technical Training Sqn Baldonnel 4.12.60; SOC 2.64; Extant; Offered for sale; Sold to N A W Samuelson, Cricklewood, North London, England 4.3.68 and stored dismantled; To Sir William Roberts/Strathallan Collection 4.70 and stored dismantled at Flimwell and Strathallan; To E Nick Grace, St.Merryn 9.8.79; To Steve W Atkins, Battle, Sussex 4.70 (Civil reg. *G-BHGH* allotted 10.10.79 but not taken up); Reg. *G-TRIX* 2.7.80 to Steve W Atkins, Saffron Walden, Essex, ff Dunsfold 23.2.90; To Richard Parker 5.90; To Rick A Roberts, Goodwood 1991; Damaged landing at Goodwood 15.9.96; Repaired at Earls Colne; Sold to Greg McCurragh, South Africa, end March 2000; Fatal crash at Goodwood during conversion training 8.4.00 (pilot Norman Lees and new owner G McCurragh both killed); Currently under rebuild at Historic Flying Ltd, Duxford - **SURVIVOR**

PX915 Seafire L.IIIc (Merlin 55M); Became IAC No **154**; RNDA 22.2.45; Vickers-Armstrongs South Marston (conversion to Mk.Vc); First flight after conversion 8.8.47 (S/Ldr Morgan); Accepted and flown to Baldonnel – Arr IAC and to No.1 Sqn ('154') 27.9.47; Crashed, Cat.E1 28.5.51, SOC; To MU at Baldonnel, for spare parts

PX924 Seafire L.IIIc (Merlin 55M); Became IAC No **153**; RNDA 1.3.45; Vickers-Armstrongs South Marston (conversion to Mk.Vc); First flight after conversion 30.6.47; Accepted and flown to Baldonnel by Lt Creham – Arr IAC and to No.1 Sqn ('153') 11.7.47; SOC 19.6.54; To MU at Baldonnel; Scrapped 1962

Seafire L.IIIc (mod) No. 147 (ex PR315) of No. 1 (Fighter) Sqn at Gormanston, probably after it force-landed on 5th September 1947 and was written off for spares.

Seafire L.IIIc (mod) No. 149 (ex PX948) and others of No. 1 (Fighter) Sqn at Gormanston, north of Dublin.

Seafire L.IIIc, 149 (ex PX948) of No. 1 Sqn, Irish Air Corps, Gormanston 1947-1954

PX929 Seafire L.IIIc (Merlin 55M); Became IAC No **152**; RNDA 3.3.45; Vickers-Armstrongs South Marston (conversion to Mk.Vc); First flight after conversion by John Derry in 6.47; Accepted and flown to Baldonnel by Lt Howard – Arr IAC and to No.1 Sqn ('152') 11.7.47; Crashed, Cat.E1 1.9.49, SOC; To MU at Baldonnel, for spare parts

PX936 Seafire L.IIIc (Merlin 55M); Became IAC No **156**; RNDA 5.3.45; Vickers-Armstrongs South Marston (conversion to Mk.Vc); First flight after conversion by F/Lt Cole 28.4.47; Accepted and flown to Baldonnel by Capt Johnson – Arr IAC and to No.1 Sqn ('156') 27.9.47; SOC 12.6.54; To MU at Baldonnel; Scrapped 1962

PX941 Seafire L.IIIc (Merlin 55M); Became IAC No **151**; RNDA 17.3.45; Vickers-Armstrongs South Marston (conversion to Mk.Vc); First flight after conversion 15.5.47; Accepted and flown to Baldonnel by Lt O'Connell – Arr IAC and to No.1 Sqn ('151') 11.7.47; Crashed, Cat.E1 29.6.51, SOC; To MU at Baldonnel, for spare parts

PX948 Seafire L.IIIc (Merlin 55M); Became IAC No **149**; RNDA 26.3.45; Vickers-Armstrongs South Marston (conversion to Mk.Vc); First flight after conversion 30.12.46; Accepted and flown via Speke to Baldonnel – Arr IAC 24.1.47; No.1 Sqn ('149') 17.2.47; SOC 15.5.54; To MU at Baldonnel; Scrapped 1962

PX950 Seafire L.IIIc (Merlin 55M); Became IAC No **148**; RNDA 26.3.45; Vickers-Armstrongs South Marston (conversion to Mk.Vc); First flight after conversion 3.12.46; Accepted and flown via Speke to Baldonnel - Arr IAC 24.1.47; No.1 Sqn ('148') 17.2.47; Crashed, Cat.E1 22.5.53, SOC; To MU at Baldonnel, for spare parts

RX168 Seafire L.IIIc (Merlin 55M); Became IAC No **157**; RNDA 20.1.45; Vickers-Armstrongs South Marston (conversion to Mk.Vc); First flight after conversion 12.9.47; Accepted and flown to Baldonnel by Sgt Colland – Arr IAC and to No.1 Sqn ('157') 27.9.47; FTS 21.9.51 (oblique photography by Capt H Howard); SOC 27.10.53; To MU

The last of the Spitfire T.IXs (162 and 163) for supply to Ireland awaiting ferrying to Baldonnel in 1951. [Vickers-Armstrongs]

Surviving Spitfire T.IX G-AWGB was formerly No. 163 of the Irish Air Corps, and originally TE308. It is seen here at Baldonnel in May 1968 still with Irish national markings, shortly before being flown to England. It is currently registered N308WK in the USA. [Peter Sargent]

Spitfire T.IX, 163 (ex TE308), of 'A' Flt, No. 1 Sqn, Gormanston 1951-1961

at Baldonnel 1954; Exhibited at Backstreet in Dublin 8.59; To Technical Institute Dublin (probably broken up in parts) 1962; Offered for sale; Sold to UK (Civil reg. *G-BWEM* 28.6.95); Stored by Aerofab Restorations, Andover by 2000; Now Christopher Warrilow (High Wycombe) & Steve Atkins, Exeter (restoration to airworthy) - **SURVIVOR**

RX210 Seafire L.IIIc (Merlin 55M); Became IAC No **150**; RNDA 24.2.45; Vickers-Armstrongs South Marston (conversion to Mk.Vc); First flight after conversion 15.4.47; Accepted and flown to Baldonnel by Capt Ryan – Arr IAC and to No.1 Sqn ('150') 11.7.47; SOC 1953; To MU at Baldonnel

TE308 Spitfire T.IX (Merlin 66); Became IAC No **163**; TOC/RAF 9.6.45 (HF.IX with M.70); To Vickers-Armstrongs for conversion to two-seater 19.7.50; Flown as G-15-176; Accepted and flown to Ireland from Eastleigh via Speke, then north coast of Wales, Rhyl, Great Orme's Head, Holyhead to Flying Training School Baldonnel, undercarriage failed to lock down on arrival, aircraft slid to a less-than-ceremonious halt on its belly, but little damaged on grass airfield 30.7.51 (Capt 'Tim' Healy, IAC) – Arr IAC at Baldonnel 30.7.51; To MU for Repair; No.1 Sqn ('A' Flight, mid green camouflage) 1951; Crashed, Cat.E in 8.61, SOC; To Technical Training Sqn Baldonnel 9.61; Offered for sale 4.3.68; Arr UK 8.5.68 (Civil reg. *G-AWGB* 4.4.68) to N A W Samuelson/ Samuelson Film Services, Elstree (used in film *Battle of Britain* in 1968); To Sir William Roberts, Shoreham 12.69; Sold to Don Plumb, Windsor, Ontario 16.7.70 and to Canada, arr Toronto by ship 9.10.70 (*CF-RAF* 12.70); Conv single-seater 1975; To USA 1975 (*N92477*, then *N308WK* 7.10.79); To Bill Greenwood, Aspen, Colorado, 23.8.83 airworthy - **SURVIVOR**

SURVIVORS

In UK: MJ627; IAC 158 (*G-BMSB*), M&P Bayliss, Coventry.
ML407; IAC 162 (*G-LFIX*), C Grace, Duxford.
PV202; IAC 161 (*G-TRIX*), Historic Flying Ltd, Duxford.
RX168; IAC 157 (*G-BWEM*), Warrillow/ Atkins, Exeter.
In USA: MJ772; IAC 159 (*N8R*), Champlin Fighter Museum Mesa.
TE308; IAC 163 (*N308WK*), B Greenwood, Colorado.

References:
Irish Air Corps Seafires, Readers Write (G Skillen), Air Pictorial 1960.
IAC Spitfires, compiled by AP Kearns, 1984.
Das Irish Air Corps, by AH van der Oever, Flugzeug February 1990, p.28.

Check list of Irish / RAF Serial Numbers

IAC Nos	RAF Serials	Arrival		IAC Nos	RAF Serials	Arrival
Seafire L.IIIc (converted to Spitfire LF Mk.Vc standard):						
146	PR302	24.1.47		152	PX929	11.7.47
147	PR315	24.1.47		153	PX924	11.7.47
148	PX950	24.1.47		154	PX915	27.9.47
149	PX948	24.1.47		155	PR237	27.9.47
150	RX210	11.7.47		156	PX936	27.9.47
151	PX941	11.7.47		157	RX168	27.9.47
Spitfire T.IX:						
158	MJ627	5.6.51		161	PV202	29.6.51
159	MJ772	5.6.51		162	ML407	30.7.51
160	MK721	29.6.51		163	TE308	30.7.51

ISRAEL

Britain's Palestinian Mandate, which had been granted by the League of Nations after the First World War, lapsed on 14th May 1948. Simultaneously the Jews declared the new state of Israel, and the Arabs attacked this from the following day - the first Palestine War continuing until 7th January 1949. On 24th February 1949 an armistice agreement between Israel and Egypt was signed on the island of Rhodes.

The first fighter aircraft to be flown by the new Air Force (Israel Defence Forces/Air Force – IDF/AF, *"HEYL HAVIR"*, and *"CHEL HA' AVIR"*) was the Czech-built Avia S-199 (Bf 109G type with Jumo 211 engine). From May 1948 twenty-five of these were transported by airlift (mostly by Curtiss C-46) from Zatek airfield in Czechoslovakia via Ajaccio to Israel. There the S-199 served with serial numbers D-101 to D-125, and from December 1948 with those of 1900-series.

The second fighter type flown by the new air force was the Spitfire, which began to arrive in August 1948 to become the primary fighter type of the IDF/AF. Together with the S-199 and a few P-51D Mustang they were used to build up No.101 Sqn, then being mostly flown by foreign volunteers, the so-called *"Mahal"* pilots.

The first two Spitfires (*D-130* and *D-131*) were rebuilt aircraft, assembled from downed REAF Spitfires with parts from ex RAF-dumps at Ekron (Aqir) and Ein Shemer. Two further rebuilt (captured) aircraft completed the inventory later.

In March 1948 Czechoslovakia (CSSR) offered its Spitfires for sale. Israel showed provisional interest and on 7th October 1948 final agreement was made and a contract was signed for 50 Spitfire LF.IXs. The price was $23,000 (£5,750) each, including refurbishing and also training of the ferry pilots. Later this order was increased to 59 aircraft plus two for use as spares.

The aircrew flight training began at České Budejovice in June 1948. Refurbishing and conversion for long range were made by the LETOV Aircraft factory at Kunovice (near Uherske Hradiste, later LET Kunovice). This consisted of a belly-tank and two underwing tanks providing a total of an additional 200 gallons of fuel. Eight Spitfires were so equipped.

The first three Czechoslovakian Spitfires arrived in Israel on 27th September 1948 and a further ten followed on 23rd/26th December 1948, after a ferry flight of 1,800 miles (c.2,900 km, Operation *"Velveta I & II"*). The aircraft were given Yugoslav markings with the last three digits of the RAF serial number painted in white on the tail. Take-off was from Kunovice in the CSSR, on the first leg of the 550m journey, landing at Niksic airfield in Yugoslavia (near Podgorica, Albanian border), for re-fuelling. All markings were then changed to the Israel Star of David, and from December 1948 they were given Israeli numbers. In the second leg over 1,250 miles the aircraft had to fly along the coast of the Greek Isles and Crete over the Mediterranean Sea to Ramat David or Tel Nof AFB. A further 39 Spitfires were shipped to Haifa during 1948/49, and three more arrived by air transport (Curtiss C-46) at the end of 1948.

Two Spitfires crashed during the ferry flying. Two others force-landed on Rhodes and were interned, one being allowed to proceed to Israel in 1950.

In 1950 Israel formed a second Spitfire unit, No.105 Sqn (OTU). A further 30 Spitfire Mk IXs were acquired from Italy during 1951/52 (the final contract not being signed until February 1953). These were for use also for the formation of No.107 Sqn. All these aircraft were refurbished by the Ambrosini Company at Foggia in Italy before being ferried out to Israel with delivery numbers from 0600 upwards.

Spitfire LF.IXes No. 2017 '17' and No. 2018 '18', probably of No.101 Sqn, Tel Nof, under the wing of a Boeing B-17 which they were escorting.
[IDF Archive 25964]

Spitfire units of the IDF/AF

No.101 Sqn; Formed at Tel Nof AFB on 3rd June 1948; Initially equipped with S-199, but from August 1948 also with Spitfire LF.IX, and two P-51 added in October 1948. Frontline (F) Sqn with Spitfires until July 1949. Then also OTU and PR Flight. From August 1950 with P-51 Mustang in the fighter role, and Spitfires mainly with the OTU and the PR Flight. Converted to P-51 in February 1953, and the Spitfires went to the new formed No.107 Sqn.
Sqn colours: Red and white striped rudder, red spinner and most white back plate.
Sqn-Emblem: *'Winged Death's Head'*.
Airbases: Tel Nof from 3rd June 1948, Herzliya from 11th June 1948; Hatzor from 9th November 1948; Ramat David from 16th June 1949; later to Beersheba (now Hatzerim).
Commanding Officers:
Mordechai Alon	until 16.10.48
Sydney Cohen	until 4.49
Jack Cohen (temp)	4.49
RT Ezer-Weizman	4.49 - 1950
(later became President of Israel)	
Capt M Ruf	1950 to 1951
Later Mordechai Hod	

No.105 Sqn; Formed as Fighter Sqn & OTU with Spitfire IX in August 1950; Served as an OTU only from February 1953; Spitfires until February 1956; Unit disbanded in October 1956.
Note: This unit received the Spitfires of No.107 Sqn after its disbandment in March 1954.
Sqn colours: Black and yellow striped rudder, yellow spinner with black plate.
Sqn-Emblem: *'Scorpion'*.

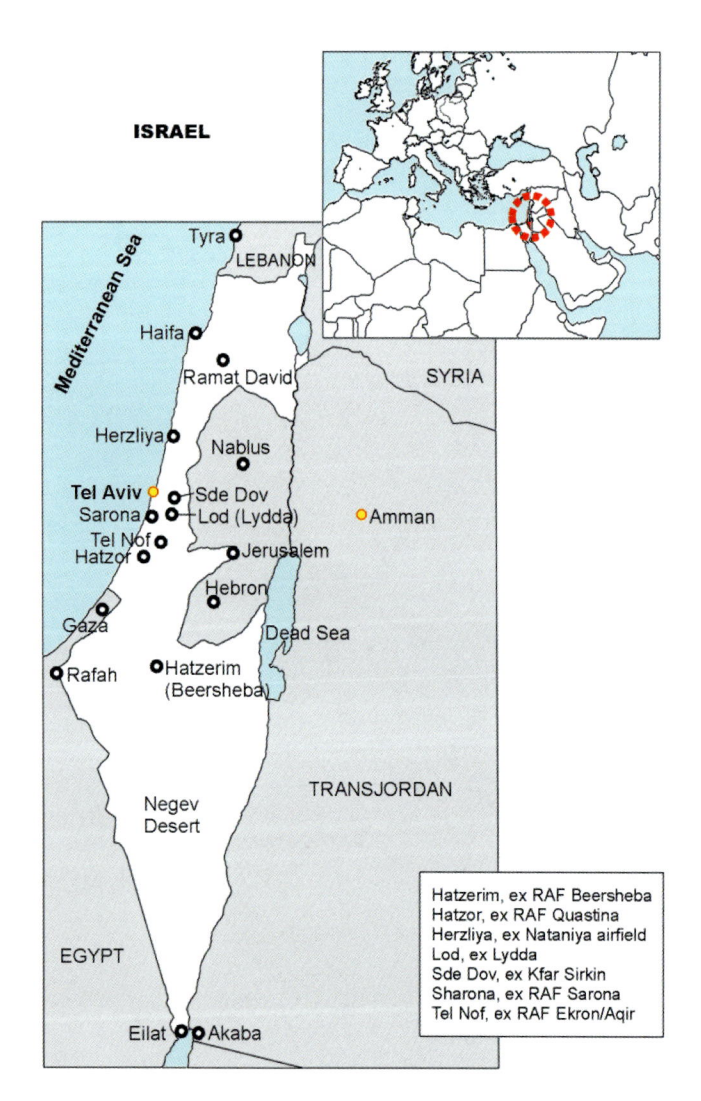

Airbases: Hatzor from August 1950; Ramat David from August 1951 until October 1956.
Commanding Officers:
Maj M Bar	8.50
Capt YS Gazit	8.51
Capt M Peled	4.52
Maj M Bar	6.52
Capt I "Tibbi" Ben-Shahar	4.53
Capt Y Yavneh	4.54
Maj M Tadmor	8.54 until 10.56

No.107 Sqn; Formed as an OTU at Ramat David in January 1953 with Spitfires of No.101 Sqn; Later also Spitfires from the Italian delivery batch. Disbanded in March 1954. The remaining Spitfires then went to No.105 Sqn.
Sqn colours: Blue and silver striped rudder, blue Spinner with silver back plate.
Sqn-Emblem: unknown.
Commanding Officers:
Capt Y Yavneh	1.53
Maj E Eyal	12.53
Capt A Cohen	4.56 until 9.56

Technical Support

Central Maintenance Unit (CMU) at Sharona (Tel Aviv South), with the main airbase at Tel Nof, and from June 1948 at Ma'arabot (near Herzliya).

A Spitfire Brigade was activated at Nataniya (Herzliya) mid August 1948.

In the beginning of the fifties No.22 Wing (Air/MU) was formed. In support of the Bedek Aircraft Overhaul Depot (BAOD) this unit repaired some of the Spitfires which were sold to Burma later.

IDF/AF Serial numbers

Initially mid 1948 the IDF/AF allotted serial numbers from *D-130* upwards for its first Spitfires. D-130 to D-134 saw action with the IDF/AF.

From November 1948 a new serial numbering system was introduced. The Spitfires became aircraft Type No "*20*" with serial numbers in the range from 2001 to 2090, which were marked on the aircraft from 25 December 1948. Spitfires which came to Israel in Operation "*Velveta I*" in September 1948 received the new serials in Israel. The serials and also the two digit radio call sign were painted on the aircraft of Operation "*Velveta II*" during the stay at Niksic (near Podgorica) in Yugoslavia. On later deliveries the serials were painted in Israel.

Serial numbers 2001 & 2002 were rebuilt aircraft; 2003 to 2006 & 2008 to 2059 ex CSSR; 2007 possibly a rebuild; 2060 to 2089 ex Italy; 2090 ex Italy or rebuilt aircraft.

Markings

In the autumn of 1948 the camouflaged Spitfires of No.101 Sqn carried the serial numbers *130 T* to *134 T* (approximately, "T" is the Hebrew letter "D") and a white/blue/white fuselage band. From end December 1948 a two-digit radio callsign, for Spitfires from "*10*" upwards was painted, indicating the sequence of joining No.101 Sqn (Note: The unit used the radio call signs *01* to *09* for the S-199, and those from *40* upwards for the P-51 Mustang). This being different from the serial number. The fuselage band was then abandoned, to be replaced by the red and white striped rudder, and temporary blue and white stripes were painted under the wings until early 1949.

Later, Nos.105 and No.107 Sqns used the last two digits of the serial number as an individual marking (callsign) on the fuselage, the aircraft being then mostly in natural silver and the serial number in black ("*01*", "*03*" etc).

The "*Winged Death's Head*" emblem was used by No.101 Sqn only in 1948, mostly on the cowling. No.105 Sqn used the *Scorpion* emblem on the cowling of their Spitfires.

ISRAEL

The end of Spitfire service

As frontline aircraft the Spitfires were replaced by P-51 Mustangs from August 1950 (No.101 Sqn) and February 1953 (No.105 Sqn), respectively. From 1955 the IDF/AF used Meteors, the Spitfires being phased out in February 1956.

In March 1954 the IDF/AF listed 67 Spitfires on its inventory, but these were surplus.

Thirty Spitfire IXs were sold to Burma in the middle of 1954, some being refurbished by the Bedek Aviation Company (Bedek Aircraft Overhaul Depot [*BAOD*]), a division of Israel Aircraft Industries (*IAI*) at Lod (Lydda), now Ben-Gurion IAP); and also No.22 Wing (Air/MU) of the IDF/AF supported the overhaul. Test-flying was made most by the Chief Test Pilot of the BAOD, Seymour 'Buck' Feldman, an American.

The Spitfires were flown to Burma in batches of two, three or four aircraft, being equipped with special long range fuel tanks. Pilots of the British Fieldair Company at Croydon ferried out the first eight Spitfires via Syria, Iraq and the Persian Gulf in 1954. Later Israel managed the ferry flying with its own contracted pilots. However there was a problem with the delivery as the Arab states refused landing and refuelling facilities to any aircraft originating from Israel. The Spitfires then had to fly a northerly route via Turkey - Iran - Pakistan - India to Burma. Twenty-nine Spitfires arrived in Burma; one Spitfire crashed in Israel, already marked for the UBAF.

The IDF/AF finally phased out the Spitfires from 1955 onwards. The last Spitfires to be struck off charge by the IDF/AF were flown by No.105 Sqn in February 1956. The aircraft then went to Israel Aircraft Industries (IAI) at Lydda, now Lod IAP. A general "write-off" came into effect in April 1956, several aircraft being held in storage during May 1956 for reserve and/or sale, with call signs '4XFOA' to '4XFOX'.

Later some of the aircraft were presented to kibbutzim in Israel, with the suggestion that they were given to playgrounds for children. In the mid-seventies some Spitfires were recovered in Israel, but most were restored in other countries.

Only three Spitfires survive in Israel, and a further nine ex-Israeli Spitfires survive in Burma, South Africa, the UK and the USA.

Individual Histories

(listed in IDF/AF serial number sequence)

xxx ? Spitfire LF(FR) IX (Merlin 66); Became IDF/AF Serial No: **D-130 & 2001**; Rebuilt from wrecked RAF & crashed REAF aircraft, assembled by the CMU at Sharona from 6.48; Arr IDF/AF at Herzliya AFB for engineering tests 7.48; First flight after assembly from Herzliya to the MU at Ma'abarot (Plt Boris Senior) on 23.7.48; Converted to FR version, then to No.101 Sqn ('B' Flt); Test flown by Syd Cohen 5.8.48, PR test and ops by Maurice Mann 8.8.48; Operational flights (as 'D-130') 11.8/17.8.48; Hit by AA 24.8.48; Unserviceable 15.10.48 (Operation Yoav); Operational flights recorded from 17.10.48, with No.101 Sqn this aircraft made a series of recce missions over El Arish, but restricted to 220 mph, only one vertical camera installed, oxygen system not fitted; Long range PR flight over Damascus and El Sacher in Syria 19.11.48, Plt Ezer-Weizman, escorted by P-51; Photo Recce ('D-130') 2.12.48 and 15.12.48; Operational flight (as No '10') 28.12.48; To No.105 Sqn ('01') 1950/51; Engine test at Ramat David, destroyed by electrical fire, Cat.E 12.8.51, w/o 5.52
Remarks: Full wing span, not clipped wings. In 1948 camouflaged, marked with the serial number *'130 T'* *(D-130)* and the white/blue/white fuselage band; Star of David on the fuselage painted too large, went to the top of the fuselage; Initially a figure was sketched in white on the right fuselage behind the cockpit. Four blade prop, mirror not original. No antenna mast, fairings for two 20mm cannon on the wings. Later weapons removed (or reduced, fairings shorter); Camera with 14-inch focal length in the fuselage installed behind the seat; 1948/49 shown in natural silver finish with white-red striped rudder and black '10' on the fuselage. "Winged Death's Head" emblem on the left cowling

xxx ? Spitfire LF.IXc (Merlin 66); Became IDF/AF Serial No: **D-131 & 2002**; Assembled/rebuilt from scrap and crashed aircraft by the CMU Sharona in 6.48, ff 14.10.48 (Plt Maurice Mann); Undercarriage failed 14.10.48; Unserviceable 15.10.48 (Operation *Yoav*); MU at Ma'abarot 16.10.48; No.101 Sqn ('D-131') 21.10.48; Operational flight 22.10.48; Belly landing at Herzliya 1.11.48 (Plt D Wilson safe); To MU at Ma'abarot, test flight 12.11.48, then to No.101 Sqn; Operational flight (as 'D-131') on 24.12.48 and (as No '11') on 27.12.48; Air combat 28.12.48; Operational flight 29/31.12.48; Air collision, propeller broken 6.4.49 (Capt I "Tibbi" Ben-Shahar); MU; No.101 Sqn, accident, Cat.E 11.10.49; SOC 1952, w/o 4.56
Remarks: Rebuilt with parts from wrecked RAF & crashed REAF aircraft. Camouflaged 1948/49, early fuselage band of No.101 Sqn, rudder white only, white No "11" on the fuselage. Later red and white stripes on the rudder shown 6.4.49

Known RAF serial numbers of six aircraft involved in Operation "*Velveta I*" ferry flying 9.48. Only three arrived at that time, and these were initially marked D-132 to 134 (later Nos 2003 to 2005; No 2006 arrived end 1948), but the relationship to the former RAF serial numbers remained mostly unknown.

SL594 Spitfire LF.IXe - TOC/RAF 19.7.45
TE531 Spitfire LF.IXe - TOC/RAF 28.5.45
TE532 Spitfire LF.IXe - TOC/RAF 1.6.45

TE555 Belly-landed in Yugoslavia, to Israel 11.48 (see *2006*)
TE557 Force-landed Rhodes, accident there 1950
TE564 Force-landed Rhodes, to Israel 1950 (see *2049 & 2050*)

xxx ? Spitfire LF.IXe (Merlin 66); Became IDF/AF Serial No: **D-132 & 2003**; ex CSSR - Operation *Velveta I* ferry flight, arr Ramat David AFB in Israel 27.9.48 (Sam Pomerance); TOC/IDF 29.9.48; To Herzliya AFB 2.10.48; To No.101 Sqn ('D-132') 3.10.48; Operational flight 15.10. & 17.10.48; Air combat 21.10.48; Operational flight 13.11., 2.12. & 3.12.48 and (still 'D-132') on 16.12.48; and (as No '12') on 28/31.12.48 & 4.1/5.1/7.1.49; Azion airstrip in the Negev, flown by D Shapira 1949; No.105 Sqn ('03') from 8.50; Crashed on landing 14.1.51; To No.22 Wing/MU; Accident 1.3.51; Crashed, Cat.E 25.12.53, w/o 3.54

xxx ? Spitfire LF.IXe (Merlin 66); Became IDF/AF Serial No: **D-133 & 2004**; ex CSSR - Operation *Velveta I* ferry flight, arr Ramat David AFB 27.9.48 (Syd Cohen); TOC/IDF 29.9.48; To Herzliya AFB 2.10.48; To No.101 Sqn ('D-133') 3.10.48; Operational flight 15.10. & 19.10.48; Still unserviceable 31.10.48; Operational flight (as 'D-133') on 22.12.48 and (as '14') on 22/28.12 & 30.12.48 (Recce); Tyre burst on landing, overturned, Cat.FB/E 4.1.49 (Plt Aaron 'Red' Finkel safe); SOC 21.1.49

xxx ? Spitfire LF.IXe (Merlin 66); Became IDF/AF Serial No: **D-134** (allocated No.**2005**); ex CSSR - Operation *Velveta I* ferry flight, arr Ramat David AFB 27.9.48 (Jack Cohen); to Herzliya AFB 9.10.48; To No.101 Sqn ('D-134') 9.10.48; Operational flight 15.10.48; Crashed on landing at Herzliya, Cat.FB/E 16.10.48 (Plt Maurice Mann safe), SOC

TE557 Spitfire LF.IXe (Merlin 66); Allotment for IDF/AF Serial unknown; TOC/RAF 26.5.45; ex CSSR - Operation *Velveta I* ferry flight, part two from Yugoslavia to Israel

Spitfire ferry flying from Czechoslovakia and Italy to Israel 1948-52

▪▪▪▪▪ from Kunovice via Niksic (nr Podgorica) to Ramat David 1948 (1,800m) ;
▪ ▪ ▪ ▪ from Foggia to Lydda (Lod) in Israel 1951/52 (c.1,200m).

      27.9.48 (Plt Mordechai 'Modi' Alon or Boris Senior): Fuel shortage, forced to land at Maritza airfield on Rhodes, aircraft interned (Plt returned to Israel 12.10.48); Test flown by Greek pilot, crashed in Greece 1950; SOC 1952

TE555 Spitfire LF.IXe (Merlin 66); Became IDF/AF No: **2006**; TOC/RAF 26.6.45; ex CSSR - Operation *Velveta I* ferry flight, part one from CSSR to Yugoslavia: Belly-landed at Niksic airfield 24.9.48 (Plt Naftali 'Tuxi' Blau); Aircraft left behind, with airlift (C-46) to Israel, arr MU at Ma'abarot in 11.48; To No.101 Sqn ('22') in 1.49; reported NTU; SOC 1952

xxx ? Spitfire LF.IX (Merlin 66); Became IDF/AF Serial No: **2007**; Rebuilt from crashed (captured) REAF aircraft at Tel Nof, work completed 1950; To No.101 Sqn in 1950; Damaged 18.6.50; SOC 1952

      Known RAF serial numbers of the 15 aircraft involved in Operation "*Velveta II*" ferry flying 12.48. Numbered 2008 to 2019, but not in RAF serial number order:

MH750 See *2010*
NH174 Spitfire LF.IXe - TOC/RAF 28.4.44
SL628 Spitfire LF.IXe - TOC/RAF 19.6.45
SL629 By ship to Israel in 11.49 (see batch *2050* to *2059*)
SL630 Spitfire LF.IXe - TOC/RAF 22.6.45
SL632 See *2011*
SL649 Spitfire LF.IXe - TOC/RAF 29.6.45
SL655 Spitfire LF.IXe - TOC/RAF 24.7.45
SL656 Spitfire LF.IXe - TOC/RAF 24.7.45
SL657 Spitfire LF.IXe - TOC/RAF 24.7.45
SL664 Spitfire LF.IXe - TOC/RAF 23.7.45
TE512 Crashed in Yugoslavia 18.12.48, wrecked
TE519 Spitfire LF.IXe - TOC/RAF 9.6.45
TE558 See *2012*
TE572 crashed in Yugoslavia 18.12.48, wrecked

xx576 ? Spitfire LF.IXe (Merlin 66); Became IDF/AF Serial No: **2008**; ex CSSR - Operation *Velveta II* ferry flight, arr Hatzor AFB 23.12.48 (Caesar Morton Dangott); To No.101 Sqn 23.12.48; Operational flights (as No '15') 27-31.12.48; Battle damage 27.12.48 (SB Feldman); Operational flight 4.1.49 (D Wilson), 5.1.49 & 7.1.49 (battle damage, J McElroy); Accident at Ramat David, prop damaged in 7.49; to MU; Belly-landed at Ramat David 28.11.50 (Plt Dan Barak); Accident 29.3.51; No.22 Wing 10.52; No.107 Sqn (date unknown); No.105 Sqn ('08') 11.52 & 2-3.53; 5.53 & 8.53; 3.54-5.54 - Selected for Burma 4.54; IDF/AF transfer-order 22./29.6.54; To BAOD (Bedek) 1.7.54; Marked '*UB422*', flown from Lydda to Nicosia/Cyprus 1.10.54; Ferry flight to Burma via Habbaniya by Philip Gurdon, desp 3.10.54, Belly-landed at Shaibah 4.10.54. Aircraft left behind; Later interned and confiscated by Iraq in 5.56, fate unknown
NOTE: Operation *Velveta II* ferry flying from CSSR to Israel with No."576" on the fin; Later this aircraft was destined for Burma ('*UB422*', the first), but then replaced by another Spitfire (IDF/AF serial number unknown), which was ferried out to Burma by 'Jacky' Moggridge 9-18.10.55

xxx ? Spitfire LF.IXe (Merlin 66); Became IDF/AF Serial No: **2009**; ex CSSR - Operation *Velveta II* ferry flight, arr Tel Nof AFB 23.12.48 (G Lichter); To MU at Ma'abarot for engine overhaul 29.12.48; No.101 Sqn 10.1.49; Air collision with 2019 16.2.49; No.22 Wing 1.50 (also 7.52 & 10-11.52); No.107 Sqn ('09') 3.53 (also 10.53 & 1.54); No.105 Sqn ('09') 4&5.54 - Selected for Burma 4.54; IDF/AF transfer-order 14.6.54; To BAOD (Bedek) 15.6.54; Marked '*UB423*', flown from Lydda to Nicosia/Cyprus 27.9.54; Ferry flight to Burma by Charles Lamberton 3-11.10.54

xxx ? Spitfire LF.IXc (Merlin 66); Became IDF/AF Serial No: **2010**; TOC/RAF 19.9.43; ex CSSR - Operation *Velveta II* ferry flight, arr Tel Nof AFB 26.12.48 (Lee Sinclair); Listed unserviceable, for inspection to MU at Ma'abarot with engine and propeller damage 26.12.48; No.101 Sqn ('25') in 2.49; Operational flight 4.49; No.105 Sqn ('10') in 6.51; No.22 Wing 11.51; No.21 TTS as instructional 1.53-2.53; No.107 Sqn ('10') 9.53-11.53 & 1.54-2.54; No.105 Sqn 3.54 & 6.54-7.54 - Selected for Burma 4.54; IDF/AF transfer-order 22/29.6.54; To BAOD 1.8.54 (Bedek, overhaul to zero hours); Marked '*UB433*', ferry flight to Burma by 'Jacky' Moggridge desp 29.6.55, arr Burma 7.55
NOTE: Marked '*VIRGINIA XII*' on the cockpit-door

SL632 Spitfire LF.IXe (Merlin 66); Became IDF/AF Serial No: **2011**; TOC/RAF 25.6.45; ex CSSR - Operation *Velveta II* ferry flight, arr Tel Nof AFB 23.12.48 (Daniel Shapira); Reported cracked engine block, declared unserviceable; To MU at Ma'abarot for engine change in 1.49; No.101 Sqn ('26') in 2.49; Accident, Cat.E 3.11.49; SOC 1952
NOTE: During Operation *Velveta II* an emblem (Eagle with a Spitfire in the talons) under the windscreen, and No."632" on the fin

TE558? Spitfire LF.IXe (Merlin 66); Became IDF/AF Serial No: **2012**; TOC/RAF 1.6.45; ex CSSR - Operation *Velveta II* ferry flight, arr Tel Nof AFB 23.12.48 (Mordechai 'Moti' Hod (former M Fine); To MU at Ma'abarot; No.101 Sqn ('16') 29.12.48; Operational flight 1.1 & 4.1.49; Air combat with Spitfires Mk.XVIIIe of No.26 Sqn RAF, Plts S Goodlin & J McElroy in 2016 & 2012, both claimed TP387 (F Close baled out) 7.1.49; No.105 Sqn ('12'), crashed, Cat.E 4.1.55, SOC 4.4.55
NOTE: Reported also as "TE581"

xxx ? Spitfire LF.IXe (Merlin 66); Became IDF/AF Serial No: **2013**; ex CSSR - Operation *Velveta II* ferry flight, arr Tel Nof AFB 26.12.48 (Arnold Ruch); Listed unserviceable, for inspection to MU at Ma'abarot 26.12.48; To No.101 Sqn ('18') 1.1.49; Operational flight 7.1.49; No.105 Sqn ('13') in 5.51-6.51; 10.52 & 2.53-3.53; No.22 Wing 1.54 & 8.54 - Selected for Burma, No.22 Wing 10.54-11.54; Marked '*UB449*', test flown by SB Feldman (BAOD) 4 & 9.11.54; To Lydda 29.11.54; To Nicosia/Cyprus 2.12.54; Aerobatic display by SB Feldman 21.12.54; Retd No.22 Wing 12.54 (shown there also 1.55); Ferry flight to Burma (Plt Leo Gardner, J Moggridge or S Banting) 2-15.3.55

xxx ? Spitfire LF.IXe (Merlin 66); Became IDF/AF Serial No: **2014**; ex CSSR - Operation *Velveta II* ferry flight, arr Tel Nof AFB 26.12.48 (Jack Cohen); To MU at Ma'abarot with pneumatic leak; No.101 Sqn ('24') in 2.49; Operational flight 14.3.49; Accident, Cat.FA/E 13.12.49, SOC

ISRAEL

Spitfire LF.IXe No. 2011 '26' (ex SL632) of No.101 Sqn at Tel Nof in 1949. It was written off in an accident on 3rd November 1949.

xxx ? Spitfire LF.IXe (Merlin 66); Became IDF/AF Serial No: **2015**; ex CSSR - Operation *Velveta II* ferry flight, part one from CSSR to Yugoslavia, landed at Niksic airfield 19.12.48 (S Jakobs); Aircraft left behind, airlifted by C-46 to Israel 30.12.48; To MU at Ma'abarot; No.101 Sqn ('23') in 2.49; Operational flight 11.4.49; Accident, Cat.FA/E 5.7.49, w/o 1952

xxx ? Spitfire LF.IXe (Merlin 66); Became IDF/AF Serial No: **2016**; ex CSSR - Operation *Velveta II* ferry flight, arr Tel Nof AFB 26.12.48 (Aaron 'Red' Finkel); To MU at Ma'abarot for inspection in 12.48; No.101 Sqn ('21') 5.1.49; Air combat with Spitfires Mk.XVIIIe of 26 Sqn/RAF, Plts S Goodlin & J McElroy in 2016 & 2012, both claimed TP387 (F Close baled out), whilst 2016 claimed TP340 (F/O G Cooper baled out) 7.1.49; Operational flight 23.2.49; Dived into ground with hung-up bomb, Cat.E 28.9.49 (SB Feldman baled out); SOC 4.10.49

xxx ? Spitfire LF.IXe (Merlin 66); Became IDF/AF Serial No: **2017**; ex CSSR - Operation *Velveta II* ferry flight, arr Tel Nof AFB 26.12.48 (Naftali 'Tuxi' Blau); MU at Ma'abarot 12.48; No.101 Sqn ('20') 3.1.49; Operational flight 1.2.49; No.105 Sqn ('17'), crashed with Burmese pilot, Cat.FA/E 9.12.54; SOC 23.5.55

xxx ? Spitfire LF.IXe (Merlin 66); Became IDF/AF Serial No: **2018**; ex CSSR - Operation *Velveta II* ferry flight, arr

Spitfire LF.IXe, 2018/17 of No.101 Sqn, Hatzor, in mid-1949

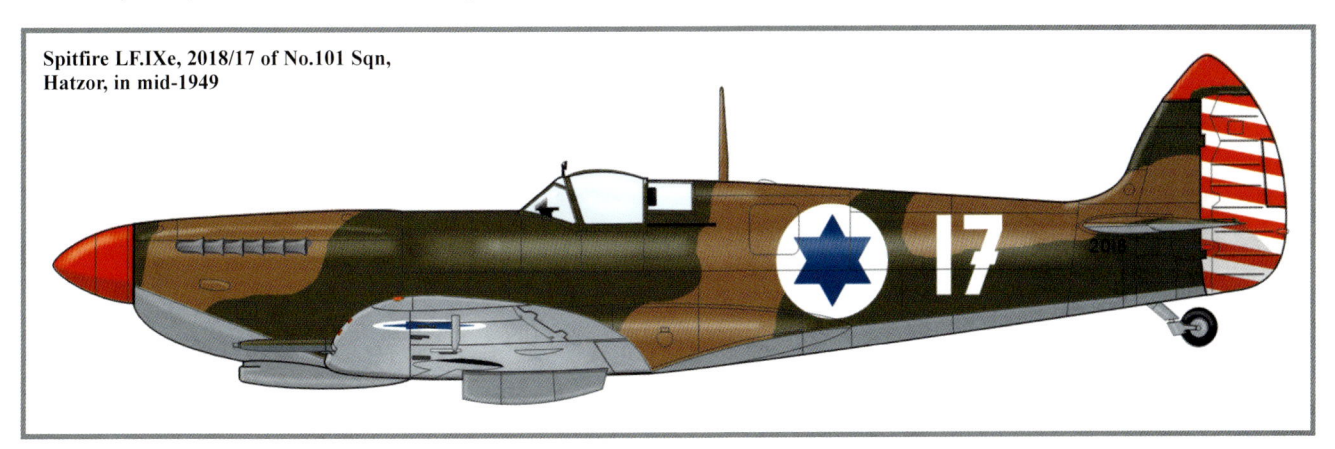

Spitfire LF.IXe, 2021/21 of the Scorpion Sqn (No.105 Sqn) Ramat David, November 1951

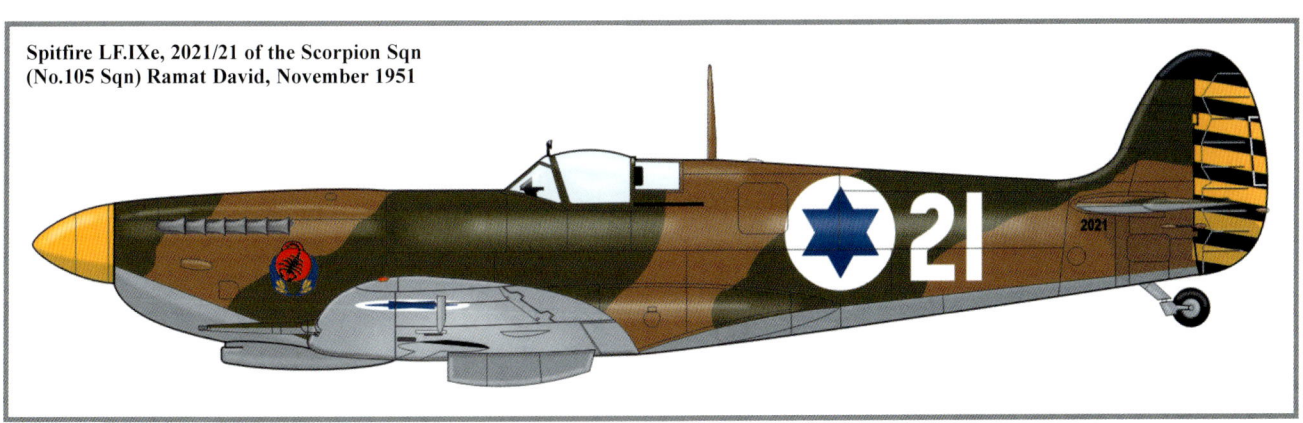

Tel Nof AFB 26.12.48 (W 'Bill' Schroeder, second leg); Listed unserviceable, for inspection to MU at Ma'abarot 26.12.48; No.101 Sqn ('17') 29.12.48; Operational flight 1.2.49; Wing damaged by bomb debris 12.10.49; No.22 Wing 4.51; No.105 Sqn ('18'), force-landed in 7.51; No.22 Wing 2.52 (also 10.52-12.52); No.107 Sqn ('18') 3.53-6.53; Accident (date unknown); No.21 TTS (unserviceable in 2.55) - Selected for Burma, IDF/AF transfer-order 27.2.55; To BAOD (Bedek, overhaul to zero hours); Refurbished and marked *'UB435'*, flown in Israel by Capt AL Ostrof 18.8.55; Crashed in fuel tank test near Machane (Lod/Lydda) 22.8.55 (Capt Ostrof killed), SOC

xxx ? Spitfire LF.IXe (Merlin 66); Became IDF/AF Serial No: **2019**; ex CSSR - Operation *Velveta II* ferry flight, part one from CSSR to Yugoslavia, landed at Niksic 19.12.48 (William 'Bill' Schroeder); Aircraft left behind with fuel leak, airlifted by C-46 to Israel 30.12.48; To MU at Ma'abarot; No.101 Sqn ('19') 2.1.49; Air collision with 2009 16.2.49; to MU for repair; Operational flight 4.4.49; SOC 1952

Shipment from CSSR 1948/49

Known RAF serial numbers of shipment of 29 aircraft from 12.48 and 2.49. Relation to Israeli serial numbers (**2020** to **2048**) mostly unknown:

ML119 See *2020*
PL250 Spitfire LF.IXe - TOC/RAF 16.6.44
PT621 Spitfire LF.IXe - TOC/RAF 26.7.44
PV205 Spitfire LF.IXe - TOC/RAF 16.9.44
SL625 Spitfire LF.IXe - TOC/RAF 16.6.45
SL627 Spitfire LF.IXe - TOC/RAF 18.6.45
SL633 Spitfire LF.IXe - TOC/RAF 25.6.45
SL634 Spitfire LF.IXe - TOC/RAF 29.6.45
SL648 Spitfire LF.IXe - TOC/RAF 29.6.45
SL650 Spitfire LF.IXe - TOC/RAF 30.6.45
SL652 Spitfire LF.IXe - TOC/RAF 23.7.45
SL653 Spitfire LF.IXe - TOC/RAF 23.7.45
TE513 Spitfire LF.IXe - TOC/RAF 1.6.45
TE517 See *2046*
TE518 Spitfire LF.IXe - TOC/RAF 8.6.45
TE522 Spitfire LF.IXe - TOC/RAF 14.6.45
TE523 Spitfire LF.IXe - TOC/RAF 14.6.45
TE524 Spitfire LF.IXe - TOC/RAF 16.6.45
TE527 Spitfire LF.IXe - TOC/RAF 8.6.45 (see *2027*)
TE551 Spitfire LF.IXe - TOC/RAF 7.6.45
TE559 See *2048*
TE560 Spitfire LF.IXe - TOC/RAF 31.5.45
TE561 Spitfire LF.IXe - TOC/RAF 1.6.45
TE566 See *2032*
TE569 Spitfire LF.IXe - TOC/RAF 18.6.45
TE573 Spitfire LF.IXe - TOC/RAF 12.6.45
TE575 See *2035*
TE576 Spitfire LF.IXe - TOC/RAF 25.6.45
TE578 See *2028*

First shipment (10 aircraft)

ML119 Spitfire LF.IXc (Merlin 66); Became IDF/AF Serial No: **2020**; TOC/RAF 24.3.44; ex CSSR - By ship to Israel, arr Haifa in 12.48; MU at Ma'abarot 12.48; No.101 Sqn 5.49; No.22 Wing 12.50-1.51; No.105 Sqn ('20') 5-7.51 & 9.52; No.107 Sqn ('20') 3.53-1.54; No.105 Sqn 3.54 - Selected for Burma, No.22 Wing 8.-10.54; Marked *'UB441'*, flown by SB Feldman (BAOD) 18.8-14.10.54; From Lydda to Nicosia/Cyprus 30.11.54; Ferry flight to Burma by 'Jacky' Moggridge 15-22.2.55
NOTE: Exhibition at Mingaladon and Rangoon; Sold to USA in 1999; Back to UK (P Monk and M Simpson, Kent) 30.10.2000 – **SURVIVOR**

xxx ? Spitfire LF.IXe (Merlin 66); Became IDF/AF Serial No: **2021**; ex CSSR - By ship to Israel, arr Haifa in 12.48; MU at Ma'abarot 12.48; No.101 Sqn ('21') in 5.49; Taxying collision with 2028 3.11.50; No.105 Sqn ('21'), air collision with 2023 27.11.51; SOC 1952

xxx ? Spitfire LF.IXe (Merlin 66); Became IDF/AF Serial No: **2022**; ex CSSR - By ship to Israel, arr Haifa in 12.48; MU at Ma'abarot 12.48; No.101 Sqn 6.49; Accident, Cat.E in 7.50, w/o 1952

xxx ? Spitfire LF.IXe (Merlin 66); Became IDF/AF Serial No: **2023**; ex CSSR - By ship to Israel, arr Haifa in 12.48; MU at Ma'abarot 12.48; No.101 Sqn ('37') in 6.49; No.105 Sqn ('23'), long range flight with slipper tank by Ari Aloef 26.1.51; No.22 Wing 3.51; No.105 Sqn 5.51-6.51 & 11.51; Crash-landed after air collision with 2021 27.11.51; to MU for repair; No.105 Sqn 9.52; No.107 Sqn ('23') 3.53-11.53; No.22 Wing 8.54 - Selected for Burma, IDF/AF transfer-order 27.8.54; Allocated for Bedek Company 30.8.54 (arr. BAOD 31.8.54); Test flown by SB Feldman 23/30.8.54; Marked *'UB438'*, flown from Lydda to Nicosia/Cyprus 30.11.54; Ferry flight by Plt Burvill, first leg Nicosia to Habbaniya 3.12.54; Iraq closed the route; Headed back to Nicosia, forced to land with fuel shortage at Beirut/Lebanon 4.12.54, interned; Retd to Nicosia later, flown by Peter Nock 14.3.55; Eventually ferry flight to Burma by Gordon Levett desp 14.4.55, arr Burma 4.55

TE5.. ? Spitfire LF.IXe (Merlin 66); Became IDF/AF Serial No: **2024**; ex CSSR - By ship to Israel, arr Haifa in 12.48; MU at Ma'abarot 12.48; No.101 Sqn 6.49; Taxying-crash 20.2.50; No.22 Wing 6.52 & 11.52-1.53; No.105 Sqn ('24') in 2.53 & 3.53; No.107 Sqn ('24') 1953; No.105 Sqn 3.54 & 4.54 - Selected for Burma 4.54; IDF/AF transfer-order 14.6.54; To BAOD (Bedek) 15.6.54; Marked *'UB421'*, flown from Lydda to Nicosia/Cyprus by SB Feldman 27.9.54, tested 28/29.9.54; Ferry flight to Burma by Philip Gurdon 13.11-20.11.54
NOTE: Extant Meiktila and Mingaladon, now exhibited in Defence Services Museum at Yangon – **SURVIVOR**

xxx ? Spitfire LF.IXe (Merlin 66); Became IDF/AF Serial No: **2025**; ex CSSR - By ship to Israel, arr Haifa in 12.48; MU at Ma'abarot 12.48; No.101 Sqn ('31') 6.49, shown at Ramat David 10.9.49, but without code number; No.105 Sqn ('25'); Overshot runway at Herzliya, Cat.E 23.9.53, SOC

xxx ? Spitfire LF.IXe (Merlin 66); Became IDF/AF Serial No: **2026**; ex CSSR - By ship to Israel, arr Haifa in 12.48; MU at Ma'abarot 22.12.48; No.101 Sqn 7.49; No.105 Sqn ('26') 9.52 & 10.52; No.22 Wing 11.53; No.107 Sqn ('26') 12.53-1.54; No.105 Sqn 3.54 (also 5.54 & 7.54) - Selected for Burma 4.54; IDF/AF transfer-order 22/29.6.54; To BAOD (Bedek) 1.8.54; Marked *'UB431'*, flown from Lydda to Nicosia/Cyprus 26.11.54; Ferry flight to Burma 29.11.54-7.12.54
NOTE: Extant, presented and exhibited in a park at Rangoon, wrecked 1968; Remains into Sea Fury Diorama of the Defence Service Museum at Yangon - **SURVIVOR**

TE527 Spitfire LF.IXe (Merlin 66); Became IDF/AF Serial No: **2027**; TOC/RAF 8.6.45; ex CSSR - By ship to Israel, arr Haifa in 12.48; MU at Ma'abarot 12.48; No.101 Sqn 25.11.49; No.107 Sqn ('27'); Air collision with Spitfire 2058, spun into ground near Kibbutz Kabri, Cat.FA/E 16.12.53, SOC
NOTE: Reported also as "TE567" (Prod. No. IX-567)

TE578 Spitfire LF.IXe (Merlin 66); Became IDF/AF Serial No: **2028**; TOC/RAF 25.6.45; ex CSSR - By ship to Israel, arr Haifa in 12.48; MU at Ma'abarot 12.48; No.101 Sqn 14.11.49; Taxying collision with 2021 3.11.50; No.22 Wing 6.52-7.52; No.105 Sqn ('28') 10.52 & 2.53-3.53; No.107 Sqn ('28') 8.53; No.22 Wing 5.54; No.105 Sqn 6.54 - Selected for Burma, IDF/AF transfer-order 29.6.54; To BAOD (Bedek) 1.7.54; Marked *'UB425'*, flown from Lydda to Nicosia/Cyprus by SB Feldman 1.10.54; Engine vibration with oil and glycol leaks, engine changed by Cyprus Airways; Returned to Israel 4.12.54; To No.105 Sqn, SOC 2.56; To Israel Aircraft Industries at Lydda (Lod IAP); Call-sign '4XFOA'; IAI storage – Extant, later exhibited at Hatzor AFB, marked "105", temporarily with

Surviving Spitfire LF.IXe No. 2028 (ex TE578) of the IDF/AF exhibited at Hatzor AFB, marked "105". It is now with IDF/AF Museum Hatzerim, near Beersheba, marked as "2011" with code '26'.

racing aerobatic arrow on side; Now IDF/AF Museum Hatzerim near Beersheba, marked as "2011" with '26' code - **SURVIVOR**

xxx ? Spitfire LF.IXe (Merlin 66); Became IDF/AF Serial No: **2029**; ex CSSR - By ship to Israel, arr Haifa in 12.48; MU at Ma'abarot 12.48; No.101 Sqn 12.49; No.105 Sqn; Fate unknown

Second shipment from CSSR

xxx ? Spitfire LF.IXe (Merlin 66); Became IDF/AF Serial No: **2030**; ex CSSR - By ship to Israel, arr Haifa in 2.49; MU at Ma'abarot 3.49; No.101 Sqn 29.12.49; Damaged (date unknown); SOC 1953

xxx ? Spitfire LF.IXe (Merlin 66); Became IDF/AF Serial No: **2031**; ex CSSR - By ship to Israel, arr Haifa in 2.49; MU at Ma'abarot 3.49; No.101 Sqn 22.12.49; Crashed 27.3.50 (repaired); No.105 Sqn (date unknown) - Selected for Burma, to Bedek company in 6.54, but rejected due to excessive flying hours; SOC 1954

TE566 Spitfire LF.IXe (Merlin 66); Became IDF/AF Serial No: **2032**; TOC/RAF 15.6.45; ex CSSR - By ship to Israel, arr Haifa in 2.49; MU at Ma'abarot 3.49; No.101 Sqn 16.2.50; No.107 Sqn; No.105 Sqn ('32'); SOC 2.56; To Israel Aircraft Industries at Lydda (Lod IAP); Call-sign '4XFOB'; IAI storage - hulk recovered from Alonim kibbutz by Robert J Lamplough, arr Duxford 12.76; To Aero Vintage Ltd, St.Leonards, Sussex 1981 (Civil reg. *G-BLCK* 22.11.83); To Historic Aircraft Collections Ltd, Audley End for restoration 5.3.87; ff 2.7.92 in Czech marks as "TE566/DU-A"; Sold to South Africa 12.8.98 (*ZU-SPT*) - **SURVIVOR**

xxx ? Spitfire LF.IXe (Merlin 66); Became IDF/AF Serial No: **2033**; ex CSSR - By ship to Israel, arr Haifa in 2.49; MU at Ma'abarot 3.49; No.101 Sqn 13.2.50; No.105 Sqn ('33'); Belly-landed 22.3.54; To Israel Aircraft Industries at Lydda 1954
Del to Burma (UBAF) 1955, but UBAF Serial-No unknown

xxx ? Spitfire LF.IXc (Merlin 66); Became IDF/AF Serial No: **2034**; ex CSSR - By ship to Israel, arr Haifa in 2.49; MU at Ma'abarot 3.49; No.101 Sqn 22.12.49; No.105 Sqn ('34') 5.51 & 7.51; No.22 Wing 1.53; No.107 ('34') Sqn 3.53-5.53 (also 8.53 & 10.53-2.54); No.105 Sqn 3.54 - Selected for Burma 4.54; IDF/AF transfer-order 22/29.6.54; To BAOD 1.7.54 (Bedek, overhaul to zero hours); Marked *'UB426'*, ferry flight by Gordon Levett desp 29.6.55, arr Burma in 7.55

TE575 Spitfire LF.IXe (Merlin 66); Became IDF/AF Serial No: **2035**; TOC/RAF 20.6.45; ex CSSR - By ship to Israel, arr Haifa in 2.49; MU at Ma'abarot 3.49; No.101 Sqn 3.50; No.107 Sqn; No.105 Sqn ('2035'); Intended for Burma, but NTU; SOC 2.56; To Israel Aircraft Industries at Lydda (Lod IAP); Call-sign '4XFOC'; IAI storage 7.5.56

xxx ? Spitfire LF.IXe (Merlin 66); Became IDF/AF Serial No: **2036**; ex CSSR - By ship to Israel, arr Haifa in 2.49; MU at Ma'abarot 3.49; No.101 Sqn 5.50; No.105 Sqn ('36'); Tipped on nose, date & Cat unknown; To Israel Aircraft Industries at Lydda (Lod IAP) 1954
Del to Burma 1955, but UBAF Serial-No unknown

xxx ? Spitfire LF.IXe (Merlin 66); Became IDF/AF Serial No: **2037**; ex CSSR - By ship to Israel, arr Haifa in 2.49; MU at Ma'abarot 3.49; No.101 Sqn 28.4.50; No.107 Sqn; No.105 Sqn ('37'), engine failure after take-off, crashed, Cat.FA/E 3.1.55 (Burmese pilot Tham Win killed); SOC 1955

xxx ? Spitfire LF.IXe (Merlin 66); Became IDF/AF Serial No: **2038**; ex CSSR - By ship to Israel, arr Haifa in 2.49; MU at Ma'abarot 3.49; No.101 Sqn 16.9.50; No.107 Sqn; No.105 Sqn ('38'); Accident (Cat. and date unknown); SOC 1953
NOTE: Long time reputed to be the '105' of Hatzor, but see 2028

xxx ? Spitfire LF.IXe (Merlin 66); Became IDF/AF Serial No: **2039**; ex CSSR - By ship to Israel, arr Haifa in 2.49; MU at Ma'abarot 3.49; No.101 Sqn 7.50; No.22 Wing 7.50-9.50; No.105 Sqn ('39') in 2.51 (also 7.51); Hit by Syrian AA fire 6.5.51; No.22 Wing 3.53 & 4.53; No.107 Sqn ('39') 5.53-1.54; No.105 Sqn in 5.54 - Selected for Burma 4.54; IDF/AF transfer-order 22/29.6.54; To BAOD (Bedek) 15.7.54; Marked *'UB427'*, flown from Lydda to Nicosia/Cyprus 6.11.54; Ferry flight to Burma 13-19.11.54

Spitfire LF.IXe No. 2036 '36' seen on an unknown date with No.105 Sqn at Ramat David after it had tipped on its nose. Previously in Czechoslovakia, it later went to Burma.

xxx ?	Spitfire LF.IXe (Merlin 66); Became IDF/AF Serial No: **2040**; ex CSSR - By ship to Israel, arr Haifa in 2.49; MU at Ma'abarot 3.49; No.101 Sqn in 10.50; Fate unknown
xxx ?	Spitfire LF.IXe (Merlin 66); Became IDF/AF Serial No: **2041**; ex CSSR - By ship to Israel, arr Haifa in 2.49; MU at Ma'abarot 3.49; No.101 Sqn in 11.50; No.22 Wing 11.50; No.105 Sqn ('41') 5.51-7.51 & 10-11.52; No.22 Wing 8.53 & 9.53; No.107 Sqn ('41') 9.53-1.54; No.105 Sqn 5.54 & 6.54 - Selected for Burma 4.54; IDF/AF transfer-order 22/29.6.54; To BAOD (Bedek) 15.7.54; Marked *'UB428'*, flown from Lydda to Nicosia/Cyprus 27.9.54; Ferry flight to Burma 3-11.10.54
xxx ?	Spitfire LF(FR).IXe (M.66); Became IDF/AF Serial No: **2042**; ex CSSR - By ship to Israel, arr Haifa in 2.49; MU at Ma'abarot 3.49, converted to a FR.IXe; No.101 Sqn in 10.50; No.107 Sqn; No.105 Sqn ('42'); To Israel Aircraft Industries Lydda (Lod IAP) 1954 - Selected for Burma; To BAOD (Bedek, overhaul to zero hours); Became the second *'UB425'*, ferry flight to Burma by 'Jacky' Moggridge 14-24.8.55 Later extant in Burma, exhibited as "UB424" (with Harvard tail unit), at Mandalay; Sold to USA 1999 – **SURVIVOR**
xxx ?	Spitfire LF.IXe (Merlin 66); Became IDF/AF Serial No: **2043**; ex CSSR - By ship to Israel, arr Haifa in 2.49; MU at Ma'abarot 3.49; No.101 Sqn in 10.50; No.22 Wing 10.50-11.50; No.105 Sqn ('43') in 5.51 (also 7.51 & 10.52-11.52); No.22 Wing 8.53-9.53; No.107 Sqn ('43') 1153-12.53; No.105 Sqn 3.54-7.54 - Selected for Burma 4.54; IDF/AF transfer-order 22/29.6.54; To BAOD (Bedek) 1.8.54; Marked *'UB432'*, flown from Lydda to Nicosia/Cyprus by Lt A Presman 12.11.54; Ferry flight to Burma by Gordon Levett 15-22.2.55
xxx ?	Spitfire LF.IXe (Merlin 66); Became IDF/AF Serial No: **2044**; ex CSSR - By ship to Israel, arr Haifa in 2.49; MU at Ma'abarot 3.49; No.101 Sqn in 10.50; Fate unknown
xxx ?	Spitfire LF.IXe (Merlin 66); Became IDF/AF Serial No: **2045**; ex CSSR - By ship to Israel, arr Haifa in 2.49; MU at Ma'abarot in 3.49; No.101 Sqn ('17') in 10.50; No.107 Sqn ('45'), crashed early 1954, SOC
TE517	Spitfire LF.IXe (Merlin 66); Became IDF/AF Serial No: **2046**; TOC/RAF 2.6.45; ex CSSR ('IV-2' & 'A-702') - By ship to Israel, arr Haifa in 2.49; MU at Ma'abarot 3.49; No.101 Sqn in 10.50; No.105 Sqn ('46'); SOC 2.56; To Israel Aircraft Industries at Lydda (Lod IAP) 7.5.56; Call-sign '4XFOD'; IAI storage. - Recovered at Gaaton kibbutz by Robert J Lamplough, arr Duxford for restoration 3.77 (Civil reg. *G-BIXP* 3.7.81); To Charles Church (Spitfires) Ltd to continue restoration 8.84 (reg. *G-CCIX* 9.4.85); To Kermit A Weeks, Florida 10.92, but stored in UK at Booker - **SURVIVOR**
xxx ?	Spitfire LF.IXe (Merlin 66); Became IDF/AF Serial No: **2047**; ex CSSR - By ship to Israel, arr Haifa in 2.49; MU at Ma'abarot 3.49; No.101 Sqn in 20.11.50; Crashed 1952, SOC
TE559	Spitfire LF.IXe (Merlin 66); Became IDF/AF Serial No: **2048**; TOC/RAF 1.6.45; ex CSSR - By ship to Israel, arr Haifa in 2.49; MU at Ma'abarot in 3.49; No.101 Sqn in 24.9.50; No.107 Sqn ('48'); SOC and to Israel Aircraft Industries at Lydda (Lod IAP) 8.54 NOTE: Used as spare parts for Burmese Spitfires - see also 2083 !
TE564	Spitfire LF.IXe (Merlin 66); Became IDF/AF Serial No: **2049**; TOC/RAF 7.6.45; ex CSSR- Operation *Velveta I* ferry flight, part two from Yugoslavia to Israel: fuel shortage, force-landed at Maritza airfield, Rhodes 27.9.48 (Plt B Senior or M Alon), interned (pilot retd Israel 12.10.48); Aircraft ferried out to Israel 10.12.50 (Capt Meir Ruf); No.101 Sqn in 1951; No.107 Sqn and/or No.105 Sqn ('49'); SOC 27.7.54; To Israel Aircraft Industries at Lydda (Lod IAP); Call-sign '4XFOE'; IAI storage NOTE: Possibly del to Burma 1956, UBAF serial No

ISRAEL

Surviving Spitfire LF.IXe No. 2057 '57' (ex TE554). This aircraft was later owned by Ezer Weizman (who became President of Israel), and eventually went to the IDF/AF Museum at Hatzerim, near Beersheba. It is seen here flying near Tel Aviv in 1998 in the paint scheme of an aerobatic team.

unknown. - The IDF/AF listed one of the aircraft which forced to land at Rhodes as "TE574" (but that was still with the LVU of the CSSR in 1949, later delivered to Israel for spares in 11.49); Spitfire TE564 was one of the delivery batch of *Velveta I*, force-landed at Rhodes (see AE No.65 from 10/96 p.64); N Hartoch found a relationship to the IDF/AF No 2049, but also an indication for delivery to Burma (but see also No.2050).

Only ten RAF serial numbers are known from the 11.49 shipment, and only four can be tied to Israeli numbers **2050** to **2059**:

Third shipment from CSSR

MJ752 Spitfire LF.IXe - TOC/RAF 20.12.43
MK257 Spitfire LF.IXc - TOC/RAF 12.2.44
SL629 Spitfire LF.IXe - TOC/RAF 22.6.45 (Operation *Velveta II*)
SL651 Spitfire LF.IXe - TOC/RAF 17.7.45
SL654 Spitfire LF.IXe - TOC/RAF 19.7.45
SL662 Spitfire LF.IXe - TOC/RAF 25.7.45
TE515 see *2058*
TE516 see *2051*
TE554 see *2057*
TE567 see *2055*

xxx ? Spitfire LF.IXe (Merlin 66); Became IDF/AF Serial No: **2050**; ex CSSR - By ship to Israel, arr Haifa in 11.49; To MU 11.49; No.105 Sqn ('50') in 8.50; No.22 Wing, inspection 1.51 (until 3.51); Test flown by SB Feldman 29.1.51; No.105 Sqn, hit by Syrian AA fire 6.5.51; No.22 Wing 6.51-7.51; No.105 Sqn at Ramat David 20.3.52 (105 Sqn also 9.52 & 2.53-3.53); No.107 Sqn ('50') 8.53; Accident 1954 (date unknown); No.22 Wing 5.54-6.54; No.105 Sqn 7.54; No.22 Wing 8.54 - Selected for Burma, IDF/AF transfer-order 12.8.54; To BAOD (Bedek) until 15.8.54; Marked '*UB436*', flown from Lydda to Nicosia/Cyprus 26.11.54; Ferry flight to Burma 29.11.54-7.12.54
NOTE: Insurance No 17-1342 (delivery to Burma) corresponded with the Prod. No. of Spitfire TE564, which force-landed at Rhodes on way from the CSSR to Israel in 1948 (but see also No.2049)

TE516 Spitfire LF.IXe (Merlin 66); Became IDF/AF Serial No: **2051**; TOC/RAF 1.6.45; ex CSSR - By ship to Israel, arr Haifa in 11.49; To MU 11.49; No.105 Sqn ('51'), crashed, Cat.E 7.10.53; SOC 10.6.54; Instructional airframe to TTS Haifa 7.12.54

xxx ? Spitfire LF.IXe (Merlin 66); Became IDF/AF Serial No: **2052**; ex CSSR - By ship to Israel, arr Haifa in 11.49; To MU 11.49; No.105 Sqn ('52') in 8.50, shown at Ramat David 20.3.52; No.105 Sqn also 9.52, 11.52, 1.53-2.53; No.107 Sqn ('52') 10.53 & 1.54; No.105 Sqn 3.54-7.54 - Selected for Burma, No.22 Wing 10.54-11.54; Flown by SB Feldman (BAOD) 4.11.54; IAI 17.11.54; BAOD (Bedek) 12.54; Marked '*UB446*', flown Lydda to Nicosia/Cyprus by Capt A Tsivoni 26.11.54; Ferry flight to Burma desp 29.11.54, crashed on landing at Dum Dum (near Calcutta), flat tyre, undercarriage collapsed 6.12.54; Left behind for repair, arr Burma 11.1.55

xxx ? Spitfire LF.IXe (Merlin 66); Became IDF/AF Serial No: **2053**; ex CSSR - By ship to Israel, arr Haifa in 11.49; To MU 11.49; No.105 Sqn ('53') 27.5.51; damaged 3.52; SOC 1953

xxx ? Spitfire LF.IXe (Merlin 66); Became IDF/AF Serial No: **2054**; ex CSSR - By ship to Israel, arr Haifa in 11.49; To MU 11.49; No.105 Sqn ('54') 30.8.51, shown at Ramat David 20.3.52; Crashed, Cat.E 10.5.53; SOC 29.3.54

TE567 Spitfire LF.IXe (Merlin 66); Became IDF/AF Serial No: **2055**; TOC/RAF 25.6.45; ex CSSR - By ship to Israel, arr Haifa in 11.49; To MU 11.49; No.105 Sqn ('55') 23.7.51; IAI 1954; No.105 Sqn; SOC 2.56; To Israel Aircraft Industries at Lydda (Lod IAP); Call-sign '4XFOF'; IAI storage
NOTE: Reported also as "TE579"

xxx ? Spitfire LF.IXe (Merlin 66); Became IDF/AF Serial No: **2056**; ex CSSR - By ship to Israel, arr Haifa in 11.49; MU 1949/50; No.105 Sqn ('56') 11.9.52; No.107 Sqn, crashed, Cat.E 8.1.54; SOC 4.4.54

TE554 Spitfire LF.IXe (Merlin 66); Became IDF/AF Serial No: **2057**; TOC/RAF 26.5.45; ex CSSR - By ship to Israel, arr Haifa in 11.49; To MU 11.49; No.105 Sqn ('57') in 7.52, flown by Lt A Presman 3.1.55; No.107 Sqn (date unknown); Flown also later by Colonel Oded 'Dedi' Rosentahl, date unknown; SOC 2.56; To Israel Aircraft Industries at Lydda (Lod IAP); Call-sign '4XFOG'. - Flown by the (then) Chief of the Air Force Ezer-Weizman until 1976, and from 1977 flown by Daniel Shapira, then Chief Test Pilot of the IAI, based Ramat David; Now exhibited in IDF/AF Museum at Hatzerim near Beersheba (after more than 500 flying hours); Still airworthy, Rosenthal being the current display pilot – **SURVIVOR**

TE515 Spitfire LF.IXe (Merlin 66); Became IDF/AF Serial No: **2058**; TOC/RAF 16.6.45; ex CSSR - By ship to Israel, arr Haifa in 11.49; To MU 11.49; No.105 Sqn ('58'), personal plane of Maj YS Gazit 5.2.52-20.3.52 (silver finish and black Race-arrow painted); No.107 Sqn ('58') 5.53, force-landed after air collision with 2027 16.12.53 (Cat.3); IAI 1954 - Selected for Burma, to BAOD (Bedek) at Lydda in 9.54; Marked '*UB439*', ferry flight to Burma by 'Sonny' Banting 15.-22.2.55

xxx ? Spitfire LF.IXe (Merlin 66); Became IDF/AF Serial No: **2059**; ex CSSR - By ship to Israel, arr Haifa in 11.49; To MU 11.49; No.105 Sqn ('59') in 8.50; No.22 Wing 5.-6.52 (also 12.52 & 2.53); No.107 Sqn ('59') 4.53-5.53 (also 11.53 & 1.54); No.105 Sqn 3.54, crashed, Cat.E 27.7.54; IAI 1954 - Selected for Burma 4.54; IDF/AF transfer-order 22/29.6.54 & 29.7.54; To BAOD (Bedek) 1.8.54; Marked '*UB430*', ferry flight to Burma by Gordon Levett 2.3.55; prop damaged at Bandar Abbas; Left behind for repair, arr Burma 1.4.55

Deliveries from Italy

RAF serial numbers of Italian Spitfires, which arrived by ferry flying 1952. Relationship to IDF/AF serials **2060** to **2089** mostly unknown:

EN145 See *2078*
EN632 See *2083*
MA453 See *2086*
MA617 See *2081*
MA618 See *2084*
MH785 Spitfire LF.IXc - TOC/RAF 22.9.43; Italy *MM 4066*
MH985 Spitfire LF.IXe - TOC/RAF 5.9.43; Italy *MM 4128*
MJ571 See *2068*
MJ673 See *2065*
MJ730 See *2066*
MJ830 See *2063*
MK207 Spitfire LF.IXc - TOC/RAF 26.1.44; Italy *MM 4120*
MK679 Spitfire LF.IXc - TOC/RAF 14.4.44; Italy *MM 4135*
ML410 See *2060*
ML416 See *2062*
NH242 Spitfire LF.IXe - TOC/RAF 18.5.44; Italy *MM 4095*
NH431 Spitfire LF.IXe - TOC/RAF 23.5.44; Italy *MM 4027*
PL127 Spitfire LF.IXe - TOC/RAF 19.6.44; Italy *MM 4099*
PT462 See *2067*
PT481 See *2082*
PT625 Spitfire LF.IXe - TOC/RAF 26.7.44; Italy *MM 4048*
PV270 See *2080*
RR191 Spitfire FR IXe - TOC/RAF 5.9.44; ex Italy *MM 4119*
RR251 Spitfire HF.IXe - TOC/RAF 14.10.44; Italy *MM4113*
(Also a further six, RAF serials unknown)

ML410 Spitfire LF.IXc (Merlin 66); Became IDF/AF Serial No: **2060**; TOC/RAF 25.4.44; ex Italy (*MM 4123*); Delivery No. 0600 - Flown to Israel, arr IAI at Lydda (Lod IAP) 24.4.51; No.105 Sqn ('60'), dived into ground and exploded 28.9.55 (Lt Amir Shapira killed), SOC xxx ? Spitfire LF.IXe (Merlin 66); Became IDF/AF Serial No: **2061**; ex Italy (*MM...* ? "*SM-92*"); Delivery No. uncertain - Flown to Israel, arr IAI at Lydda (Lod IAP) 25.3.52; No.107 Sqn and/or No.105 Sqn ('61'); IAI in 1.55; Test flown by SB Feldman 23/26.1.55 & 2.2.55; No.105 Sqn, SOC 2.56; Take-off crash 17.4.56; To Israel Aircraft Industries at Lydda (Lod IAP); Call-sign '4XFOI'; IAI storage

ML416 Spitfire LF.IXc (Merlin 66); Became IDF/AF Serial No: **2062**; TOC/RAF 1.5.44; ex Italy (*MM 4125*); Delivery No. 0602 - Flown to Israel, arr IAI at Lydda (Lod IAP) 19.4.52; No.107 Sqn and/or No.105 Sqn ('62'); To Israel Aircraft Industries at Lydda in 10.54, flown by SB Feldman 14.10.54; No.105 Sqn, crashed, Cat.E 9.12.54; SOC 12.5.55

MJ830 Spitfire LF.IXc (Merlin 66); Became IDF/AF Serial No: **2063**; TOC/RAF 22.12.43; ex Italy (*MM 4070*); Delivery No. 0604 - Flown to Israel, arr IAI at Lydda (Lod IAP) 16.4.52; No.107 Sqn and/or No.105 Sqn ('63'); Aerobatic display by SB Feldman 20.1.55; To Israel Aircraft Industries at Lydda in 2.55, test flown by S B Feldman 6-10.2.55; No.105 Sqn, crashed on landing at Ramat David, Cat.E 1.6.55; SOC 24.8.55

xxx ? Spitfire LF.IXe (Merlin 66); Became IDF/AF Serial No: **2064**; ex Italy (*MM...* ?); Delivery No. 0601 - Flown to Israel, arr IAI at Lydda (Lod IAP) 22.4.52; No.105 Sqn ('64'); IAI in 2.55, test flown by S B Feldman 3-10.2.55; No.105 Sqn; SOC 2.56, w/o 17.4.56; To Israel Aircraft Industries at Lydda (Lod IAP); Call-sign '4XFOJ'; IAI storage from 7.5.56

MJ673 Spitfire LF.IXc (Merlin 66); Became IDF/AF Serial No: **2065**; TOC/RAF 2.12.43; ex Italy (*MM 4059*); Delivery No. 0605 - Flown to Israel, arr IAI at Lydda (Lod IAP) 20.4.52; No.105 Sqn ('65'); IAI in 2.55, test flown by S B Feldman 10.2.55; SOC 2.56; To Israel Aircraft Industries at Lydda (Lod IAP); Call-sign '4XFOK'; IAI storage
NOTE: UB425 shows "2065" hand painted under the fuel tank

MJ730 Spitfire LF.IXc (Merlin 66); Became IDF/AF Serial No: **2066**; TOC/RAF 12.12.43; ex Italy (*MM 4094*); Delivery No. 0606 - Flown to Israel, arr IAI at Lydda (Lod IAP) 25.4.52; No.107 Sqn and/or No.105 Sqn ('66'); IAI in 1.55, test flying by S B Feldman from 14.1 to 3.2.55; No.105 Sqn; SOC 2.56; Intended for Burma 4.56, but NTU; To Israel Aircraft Industries at Lydda (Lod IAP); Call-sign '4XFOL'; IAI storage from 7.5.56
NOTE: Hulk recovered from a kibbutz at Kabri by Robert J Lamplough in 1976, to Nailsworth, Gloucestershire, England 6.78; To Aero Vintage Ltd, Hastings, Sussex for restoration 10.80; Intended 4.82 for Fred Smith/Federal Express, Memphis, Tennessee, USA but NTU; (Civil reg. *G-BLAS* 22.11.83) To David W Pennell, ff at East Midlands Airport 12.11.88; To David W Pennell at Gloucester marked as "MJ730/GZ-?" (Reg. *G-HFIX* 22.8.89); To Training Services Inc, Virginia Beach, USA 23.3.00 as *N730MJ* – **SURVIVOR**

PT462 Spitfire HF.IXe (Merlin 70); Became IDF/AF Serial No: **2067**; TOC/RAF 21.7.44; ex 253 Sqn and Italian Air Force (*MM 4100*); Delivery No. 0607 - Flown to Israel, arr IAI at Lydda (Lod IAP) 25.4.52; No.105 Sqn ('67'); SOC 2.56; To Israel Aircraft Industries at Lydda; Call-sign '4XFOM'; IAI storage from 7.5.56 – **SURVIVOR**
NOTE: Forward fuselage hulk recovered from town dump in Gaza Strip 5.83, to Fowlmere, UK by Robert J Lamplough, Duxford, England; To Charles Church (Spitfires) Ltd, Winchester, Hampshire 7.74 and converted to two-seater (Civil reg. *G-CTIX* 9.4.85); ff 25.7.87, operated by Dick Melton Aviation, Winchester from 1991; To USA as *N462JC* 25.7.94; Retd UK 28.4.98, *G-CTIX*

MJ571 Spitfire FR IXc (Merlin 66); Became IDF/AF Serial No: **2068**; TOC/RAF 22.12.43; ex Italy (*MM 4102*); Delivery No. 0608 - Flown to Israel, arr IAI at Lydda (Lod IAP) 11.6.52; No.107 Sqn and/or No.105 Sqn ('68'); IAI in 12.54, test flown by S B Feldman 22.12.54 & 5.1.55; No.105 Sqn; SOC 2.56; To Israel Aircraft Industries at Lydda (Lod IAP) 30.4.56

xxx ? Spitfire LF.IXe (Merlin 66); Became IDF/AF Serial No: **2069**; ex Italy (*MM...* ?); Delivery No. 0609 - Flown to Israel, arr IAI at Lydda (Lod IAP) 25.5.52; No.22 Wing in 2.53-3.53 & 8.53-9.53; No.107 Sqn ('69') 8.53-10.53 & 12.53-1.54; No.105 Sqn ('69') 7.54 - Selected for Burma 4.54; IDF/AF transfer-order 22/29.6.54; To BAOD 15.7.54 (Bedek, overhaul to zero hours); Marked *'UB429'*, ferry flight to Burma by 'Sonny' Banting 14.-24.8.55

xxx ? Spitfire LF.IXe (Merlin 66); Became IDF/AF Serial No: **2070**; ex Italy (*MM...* ?); Delivery No. 0700 - Flown to

Surviving Spitfire LF.IXc No. 2066 '66' (ex MJ730) and others at Ramat David around 1955/56. After restoration in the UK it went to the USA in February 2000 as N730MJ.

Spitfire LF.IXe No. 2069 '69' served during 1953/54 with Nos.107 and 105 Sqns, both at Ramat David. In 1955 it was despatched to Burma as 'UB429'.

	Israel, arr IAI at Lydda (Lod IAP) 8.51; No.105 Sqn ('70') 1952; No.22 Wing 1.54; No.105 Sqn 5.54-8.54 - Selected for Burma 4.54; IDF/AF transfer-order 22.6.54; To BAOD (Bedek) 15.8.54; No.22 Wing 854.-10.54; Marked *'UB440'*, six test-flights by S B Feldman from 20.8.54 to 5.10.54; IAI 5.10.54; Ferry flight to Burma (by 'Sonny' Banting, J Moggridge or L Gardner) in 3.55, arr Burma 15.3.55
xxx ?	Spitfire LF.IXe (Merlin 66); Became IDF/AF Serial No: **2071**; ex Italy (*MM...* ?); Delivery No. 0701 - Flown to Israel, arr IAI at Lydda (Lod IAP) 17.7.52; No.105 Sqn ('71'); Belly-landed 15.6.53; No.22 Wing/MU; Crashed on landing, left wing torn off, Cat.E 1.8.54; SOC 1.2.55
xxx ?	Spitfire LF.IXe (Merlin 66); Became IDF/AF Serial No: **2072**; ex Italy (*MM...* ?); Delivery No. 0702 - Flown to Israel, arr IAI at Lydda (Lod IAP) 8.51; No.105 Sqn ('72') in 1952; training of Burmese pilots at Ramat David 1954/55; IAI in 10.54, test flown by S B Feldman 11.10.54; Sold to Burma (SOC IDF/AF 6.12.54, w/o 5.4.55), but UBAF Serial No unknown
xxx ?	Spitfire LF.IXe (Merlin 66); Became IDF/AF Serial No: **2073**; ex Italy (*MM...* ?); Delivery No. 0703 - Flown to Israel, arr IAI at Lydda (Lod IAP) 1951/52; No.105 Sqn ('73') in 1952; SOC 2.56; To Israel Aircraft Industries at Lydda; Call-sign '4XFOO'; IAI storage NOTE: Intended for Burma, possibly delivered as replacement or spare parts 1956
xxx ?	Spitfire LF.IXe (Merlin 66); Became IDF/AF Serial No: **2074**; ex Italy (*MM...* ?); Delivery No. 0704 - Flown to Israel, arr IAI at Lydda (Lod IAP) 5.52; No.107 Sqn ('74') 4.53; No.22 Wing 3.54 & 5.54-7.54; to Ramat David, No.105 Sqn ('74') 9.7.54; with No.105 Sqn also in 8.54 and 11.54 - Selected for Burma, IDF/AF transfer-order 12.8.54; Allocated for BAOD 15.8.54, arr 16.8.54; (Bedek, overhaul to zero hours); Marked *'UB437'*, ferry flight to Burma by Gordon Levett 14-24.8.55
xxx ?	Spitfire LF.IXe (Merlin 66); Became IDF/AF Serial No: **2075**; ex Italy (*MM...*?); Delivery No. 0705 - Flown to Israel, arr IAI at Lydda (Lod IAP) 7.10.51; No.105 Sqn ('75'); w/o 14.2.56; To Israel Aircraft Industries at Lydda (Lod IAP)
xxx ?	Spitfire LF.IXe (Merlin 66); Became IDF/AF Serial No: **2076**; ex Italy (*MM...* ?); Delivery No. 0706 - Flown to Israel, arr IAI at Lydda (Lod IAP) 1951/52; No.105 Sqn ('76') in 1952 - Selected for Burma, No.22 Wing 10.-11.54; Marked *'UB444'*, IAI 17.11.54, flown by S B Feldman to Lydda (BAOD, Bedek) 17.11.54; Retd No.22 Wing 4.12.54 (shown there also 1.55); Ferry flight to Burma (by 'Jacky' Moggridge, L Gardner or S Banting) 2-15.3.55
xxx ?	Spitfire LF.IXe (Merlin 66); Became IDF/AF Serial No: **2077**; ex Italy (*MM...* ?); Delivery No. 0707 - Flown to Israel, arr IAI at Lydda (Lod IAP) 1951/52; No.105 Sqn ('77') in 1952; No.22 Wing 3.53-5.53 & 10.53; No.105 Sqn 3.54 (also 5.54-6.54) - Selected for Burma 4.54; IDF/AF transfer-order 22/29.6.54; To BAOD (Bedek) 1.8.54; Marked 'UB434', ferry flight to Burma by Leo Gardner 15.-22.2.55
EN145	Spitfire F.IXc (Merlin 63); Became IDF/AF Serial No: **2078**; TOC/RAF 6.12.42; ex 12(US)AF NWA; ex Italy (*MM 4116*); Delivery No. 0708 - Flown to Israel, arr IAI at Lydda (Lod IAP) 1951/52; No.105 Sqn ('78') in 1952; IAI in 1.55, test flown by S B Feldman 31.1.55.-10.2.55; 105 Sqn; SOC 2.56; To Israel Aircraft Industries at Lydda (Lod IAP); Call-sign '4XFOQ'; IAI storage from 11.5.56 – Extant, displayed Ramat David AFB from 1960; To Carmiel 29.5.89 for restoration, then to IDFAF Museum at Hatzerim, near Beersheba 1990 and extant – **SURVIVOR**
xxx ?	Spitfire LF.IXe (Merlin 66); Became IDF/AF Serial No: **2079**; ex Italy (*MM...* ?); Delivery No. 0709 - Flown to Israel, arr IAI at Lydda (Lod IAP) 10.7.52; No.22 Wing 3.53; No.107 Sqn ('79') 4.53-5.53 (also 9.53 & 12.53-1.54); No.105 Sqn (date unknown) - Selected for Burma;

ISRAEL

No.22 Wing 10.54-11.54; Marked *'UB448'*, flown by S B Feldman to Lydda (BAOD) 30.11.54, to Nicosia/Cyprus 30.11.54; Ferry flight by Plt Overburry, first leg Nicosia to Habbaniya 3.12.54; Iraq closed the route; Headed back to Nicosia, forced to land with fuel shortage at Beirut/Lebanon 4.12.54, interned; Retd to Nicosia later, flown by Peter Nock 12.3.55; Eventually ferry flight to Burma by 'Jacky' Moggridge desp 14.4.55, arr Burma 4.55

PV270 Spitfire LF.IXe (Merlin 66); Became IDF/AF Serial No: **2080**; ex Italy (*MM4014*); Delivery No. 0809 - Flown to Israel, arr IAI at Lydda (Lod IAP) 14.5.52; No.22 Wing in 2.53; No.107 Sqn ('80') 4.53-5.53 & 12.53 - Selected for Burma 4.54; IDF/AF transfer-order 29.6.54; Flown to BAOD (Bedek) by S B Feldman 1.7.54; Overhaul by Bedek to zero hours; Marked *'UB424'*, ferry flight to Burma by Leo Gardner from 29.6.55, arr Burma in 7.55

NOTE: Extant Hmwabi and Mingaladon as "UB425"; Sold to USA 1999; To Brendon Deere (restoration at Dairy Flat), New Zealand, May 2001 - **SURVIVOR**

MA617 Spitfire F.IXc (Merlin 63A); Became IDF/AF Serial No: **2081**; TOC/RAF 29.6.43; ex Italy (*MM 4044*); Delivery No. 0801 - Flown to Israel, arr IAI at Lydda (Lod IAP) 6.12.51; No.105 Sqn ('81') in 1952; Hit ground by low level flying, Cat.E 4.4.54 (1/Lt David Ratner killed); SOC 25.9.54

PT481 Spitfire HF.IXe (Merlin 70); Became IDF/AF Serial No: **2082**; TOC/RAF 17.7.44; ex Italy (*MM 4126*); Delivery No. 0802 - Flown to Israel, arr IAI at Lydda (Lod IAP) 1951/52; No.105 Sqn ('82'); SOC 2.56; To Israel Aircraft Industries at Lydda (Lod IAP); Call-sign '4XFOR'; IAI storage

NOTE: Intended for Burma, possibly delivered as replacement in 1956

Surviving Spitfire F.IXc No. 2078 (ex EN145) at Carmiel around January 1990 after restoration, still bearing code '78' with the black and yellow striped rudder and yellow spinner of No.105 Sqn. It is now in the IDF/AF Museum at Hatzerim, near Beersheba. [Cyclone Aviation]

Spitfire LF.IXe No. 2079 on take-off, serving with No.107 Sqn at Ramat David around 1953. Code '79' is identical with the last two digits of the serial number which is carried under the tailplane. This aircraft was later sold to Burma and flew as UB448. [IDF]

EN632 Spitfire LF.IXc (Merlin 66); Became IDF/AF Serial No: **2083**; TOC/RAF 30.5.43; ex Italy (*MM 4051*); Delivery No. 0803 - Flown to Israel, arr IAI at Lydda (Lod IAP) 29.5.52; No.107 Sqn; No.105 Sqn ('83'), belly-landed 2.5.55; No.22 Wing/MU; No.105 Sqn, belly-landed, Cat.E 20.9.55; SOC 28.9.55 (Broken up for spare parts - see also No.2048)

xxx ? Spitfire LF.IXe (Merlin 66); Became IDF/AF Serial No: **2084**; TOC/RAF 28.6.43; ex Italy (*MM...* ?); Delivery No. 0804 - Flown to Israel, arr IAI at Lydda (Lod IAP) 1951/52; No.105 Sqn ('84') in 1952; SOC 2.56; To Israel Aircraft Industries at Lydda (Lod IAP)
NOTE: Reported as "TE518", but that was not from Italy

xxx ? Spitfire LF.IXe (Merlin 66); Became IDF/AF Serial No: **2085**; ex Italy (*MM...* ?); Delivery No. 0805 - Flown to Israel, arr IAI at Lydda (Lod IAP) 1951/52; No.105 Sqn ('85') in 1952 - Selected for Burma; No.22 Wing 10.-11.54; To BAOD (Bedek company); Marked '*UB447*', test flown by S B Feldman 9./10.11.54; From Lydda to Nicosia/Cyprus 30.11.54; Ferry flight by Plt Simmondy, first leg Nicosia to Habbaniya 3.12.54; Iraq closed the route; Headed back to Nicosia, forced to land with fuel shortage at Beirut/Lebanon 4.12.54, interned; Retd to Nicosia later, flown by Peter Nock 13.3.55; Eventually ferry flight to Burma by 'Sonny' Banting desp 14.4.55, arr Burma 4.55

MA453 Spitfire F.IXc (Merlin 63); Became IDF/AF Serial No: **2086**; TOC/RAF 8.6.43; ex Italy (*MM 4031*); Delivery No. 0806 - Flown to Israel, arr IAI at Lydda (Lod IAP) 1951/52; No.105 Sqn ('86') in 1952; Accident (date and Cat unknown); IAI in 9.54; Test flown by S B Feldman 8.9.54; SOC in 1954, w/o 1955

xxx ? Spitfire LF.IXe (Merlin 66); Became IDF/AF Serial No: **2087**; ex Italy (*MM...* ?); Delivery No. 0807 - Flown to

Spitfires of Israel (IDF/AF)

No 101 Sqn IDF/AF, development of strength 1948/49

Month	Avia S-199	Spitfire	P-51
6.48	11	0	0
8.48	9	1	0
9.48	9 (13)	1 (2)	0 (2)
10.48	8	4 (5)	2
1.49	6	14	2
6.49	?	21 (47)	2

(13) S-199 listed, but 4 were u/s; (2) repair, one or two; (5) D-134 crashed October 1948; (47) 26 Spitfires unassembled

Known Spitfire callsigns of No.101 Sqn IDF/AF:

call	Serial	to 101 Sqn	call	Serial	to 101 Sqn
10	2001	8.48	20	2017	1.49
11	2002	9.48	21	2016	1.49
12	2003	10.48	21	2021	5.49
13	?		22	2006	1.49
14	2004	10.48	23	2015	2.49
15	2008	12.48	24	2014	2.49
			25	2010	2.49
16	2012	12.48	26	2011	2.49
17	2018	12.48	27	?	
17	2045	10.50	31	2025	6.49
18	2013	1.49	37	2023	6.49
19	2019	1.49	39	?	

ICAO codes for Spitfires (IAI storage 1956):

Code	Serial No		Code	Serial No	
4XFOA	2028	Surv.	4XFOL	2066	Surv.
4XFOB	2032	Surv.	4XFOM	2067	Surv.
4XFOC	2035		4XFON	?	
4XFOD	2046	Surv.	4XFOO	2073	
4XFOE	2049		4XFOP	?	
4XFOF	2055		4XFOQ	2078	Surv.
4XFOG	2057	Surv.	4XFOR	2082	
4XFOH	?		4XFO ?	?	
4XFOI	2061				
4XFOJ	2064		4XFOW	2088	
4XFOK	2065		4XFOX	2089	

Surv. = Survivor

Check list of Burmese & IDF/AF Serial Nos

UBAF Serial No	Transfer-order (IDF)	Gathering Bedek (&22.Wg)	IDF/AF Serial No
UB4.. ?	unknown	unknown	2033
UB4.. ?	unknown	unknown	2036
UB4.. ?	unknown	unknown	2072
UB421	14.6.54	15.6.54	2024
UB422(1)	22/29.6.54	1.7.54	2008
UB422(²)	unknown	unknown	20.. ? **)
UB423	14.6.54	15.6.54	2009
UB424	29.6.54	1.7.54	2080
UB425(1)	22/29.6.54	1.7.54	2028
UB425(²)	unknown	unknown	2042
UB426	22/29.6.54	1.7.54	2034
UB427	22/29.6.54	1.8/15.7.54	2039
UB428	22/29.6.54	1.8/15.7.54	2041
UB429	22/29.6.54	15.8/15.7.54	2069
UB430	226./29.7.54	15.8/1.8.54	2059
UB431	22/29.6.54	1.8.54	2026
UB432	22/29.6.54	15.8./1.8.54	2043
UB433	22/29.6.54	1.8.54	2010
UB434	22/29.6.54	15.8/1.8.54	2077
UB435 *)	27.2.55	3-7.55 (8.55)	2018
UB436	12.8.54	15.8.54	2050
UB437	12.8.54	15.8.54	2074
UB438	27.8.54	30/31.8.54	2023
UB439	unknown	9.54	2058
UB440	22.6.54	15.8.54 (10.54)	2070
UB441	unknown	? (8.54)	2020
UB442	unknown	unknown	20.. ? **)
UB443	unknown	? (10.54)	2087
UB444	unknown	? (10.54)	2076
UB445	unknown	? (10.54)	2090
UB446	unknown	? (10.54)	2052
UB447	unknown	? (10.54)	2085
UB448	unknown	? (10.54)	2079
UB449	unknown	? (10.54)	2013
UB450	unknown	?	20.. ? **)
--	Spare parts for UBAF		2048

(1) for Burma, but replaced; (²) = Replacements
*) crashed in Israel August 1955
**) poss. IDF/AF 2033, 2036, 2072; Bedek Company (BAOD), (Bedek Aircraft Overhaul Depot)

New airfield names
The IDF/AF renamed her airfields and gave new (Hebrew) names:
Hatzerim   – ex RAF Beersheba
Hatzor   – ex RAF Qastina
Herzliya   – ex Nataniya airfield
Lod airport – ex Lydda airfield (Ben Gurion airport, Tel Aviv)
Sde Dov   – ex Kfar Sirkin (East Tel Aviv)
Sharona   – ex RAF Sarona (Petah Tiqva)
Tel Nof   – ex Ekron (Aqir/Akir).

Israel, arr IAI at Lydda (Lod IAP) 7.7.52; No.107 Sqn and/or No.105 Sqn ('87') - Selected for Burma, No.22 Wing 10.-11.54; To BAOD (Bedek Company); Marked *'UB443'*, test flown by S B Feldman 2.11.54; IAI 17.11.54; From Lydda to Nicosia 26.11.54; Ferry flight to Burma 29.11.54-7.12.54

xxx ? Spitfire LF.IXe (Merlin 66); Became IDF/AF Serial No: **2088**; ex Italy (*MM...* ?); Delivery No. 0808 - Flown to Israel, arr IAI at Lydda (Lod IAP) 1951/52; No.105 Sqn ('88'); SOC 2.56; To Israel Aircraft Industries at Lydda (Lod IAP); Call-sign '4XFOW'; IAI storage from 7.5.56

xxx ? Spitfire LF.IXe (Merlin 66); Became IDF/AF Serial No: **2089**; ex Italy (*MM...* ?); Delivery No. 0800 - Flown to Israel, arr IAI at Lydda (Lod IAP) 5.51; No.105 Sqn ('89') in 1952; SOC 2.56; To Israel Aircraft Industries at Lydda (Lod IAP); Call-sign '4XFOX'; IAI storage from 7.5.56

xxx ? Spitfire LF.IXe (Merlin 66); Became IDF/AF Serial No: **2090**; Assembled from captured or crashed aircraft (or an additional supply from Italy ?); CMU at Sharona 1948; MU at Ma'abarot 1949; No.101 Sqn 1949; No.107 Sqn; No.105 Sqn ('90'); No.22 Wing 7.53 (also 3.54, 5.54, 7.54-8.54) - Selected for Burma; test flown by S B Feldman (BAOD) 22.8.54; No.22 Wing 10.-11.54; To BAOD (Bedek company) 17.11.54; Marked *'UB445'*, test flown by S B Feldman 7.11.54; IAI 17.11.54; From Lydda to Nicosia/Cyprus 23.11.54; Retd No.22 Wing 12.54 (shown there also in 2.55); Ferry flight to Burma, desp 2.3.55, damaged at Malatiya Turkey and retd to Israel; Second departure by Leo Gardner 14.4.55, arr Burma in 4.55
NOTE: Herein lies a mystery: The ItAF contracted for the delivery of 30 aircraft with the IDF/AF Nos 2060 to 2089, but numbers 2060 to 2090 were issued. There was however, the REAF Spit at Al Arish (REAF No 664), and another downed aircraft rebuilt with parts from REAF. But see also No.2007.

Crashed on delivery flight to Israel

TE512 Spitfire LF.IXe (Merlin 66); TOC/RAF 1.6.45; ex CSSR; Operation *Velveta II* ferry flight, part one from Kunovice/CSSR to Niksic airfield in Yugoslavia: Force-landed in snowstorm over Yugoslavia, aircraft destroyed by fire 18.12.48 (Plt William 'Bill' Pomerantz safe), SOC

TE572 Spitfire LF.IXe (Merlin 66); TOC/RAF 15.6.45; ex CSSR; Operation *Velveta II* ferry flight, part one from Kunovice/CSSR to Niksic airfield in Yugoslavia: Crashed in snowstorm over Yugoslavia, Cat.E 18.12.48 (Plt Samuel Pomerance killed), SOC

Delivered from the CSSR for spare-parts

TE556 Spitfire LF.IXe; TOC/RAF 31.5.45; ex CSSR unserviceable; To Israel by sea 11.49

TE574 Spitfire LF.IXe; TOC/RAF 22.6.45; ex CSSR unserviceable; To Israel by sea 11.49

SURVIVORS

In Israel

EN145	2078	IDF/AF Museum Hatzerim [static display]
TE554	2057	AF Museum Hatzerim (near Beersheba) [airworthy]
TE578	2028	Hatzor; now Hatzerim as "2011" ('26') [static display]

In Burma

ML119	2020	UB441	Mingaladon, sold to USA 1999, to UK 30.10.00
xx ?	2026	UB431	Remains in Diorama at Yangon
xx ?	2042	UB425	Mandalay, sold to USA 1999
PV270	2080	UB424	Hmwabi, sold to USA 1999, to New Zealand 12.5.01
TE5...	2024	UB421	Yangon (formerly Rangoon)

Elsewhere

MJ730	2066	UK G-BLAS, G-HFIX, USA N730MJ
PT462	2067	UK G-CTIX, USA N462JC, G-CTIX
TE517	2046	UK G-CCIX (has never flown)
TE566	2032	UK G-BLCK, South-Africa ZU-SPT

References:
Aeroplane Monthly May 1990, p.264 & April 1995, p.30.
Air Enthusiast May/June 1996 p.17; Sept/Oct 1996 p.64, Nov/Dec.1998, p.34 & Jan/Feb.1999, p.2.
FlyPast Sept 1990, p 45.
'Spitfires over Israel', by B Cull/S Aloni/D Nicolle, Grub Street Publication, London, 1994.
Yorek, the Supermarine Spitfire IX in Israel, Research by Noam Hartoch and Shlomo Aloni, 1999.

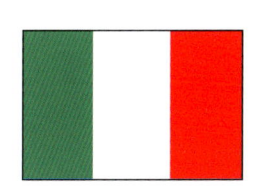

ITALY

Italy became one of the Axis Powers when it declared war on Britain and her Allies on 10th June 1940, after the fall of France. Three years later Allied Forces occupied Southern Italy in the autumn of 1943; Nos.254 & 281 Wings of the RAF and their Repair & Salvage Units, also Nos.110 & 159 MUs being based at Brindisi (NW Lecce), Canne (NW Foggia) and satellite stations. After the armistice from 8th September 1943 the Italian Air Force switched to the Allied side and became attached to the Balkan Air Force from the summer of 1944.

The first Spitfire Mks.Vb and Vc went to the Italian Air Force on loan in September 1944. The 51° Stormo had 33 Spitfire Mk.Vs on strength in autumn 1944, and a total of 53 Mk.V served with this unit during the Second World War. The 51° Stormo became operational on 23rd October 1944 and flew Spitfire Mk.Vs with its 20° Gruppo and their Squadriglie from Italian bases. The Spitfires carried Italian roundels, though the unit the came under RAF command 1944/45.

The RAF handled the loan of Spitfire Mk.Vb/cs as an internal matter, and therefore surviving records are sparse. Few surviving Italian records refer to the borrowed aircraft.

Post-war, the Italian Air Force received 14 Spitfire Mk.Vb/cs. In RAF documents the official hand-over was dated 27th June 1946. Some of the Spitfires were relegated to training duties with the Flying School at Lecce by 1948.

After WWII the RAF possessed many surplus aircraft which were left behind in Italy. For example, a large batch of Spitfire IXs was stored near Treviso. Italy bought 141 Spitfire IXs from RAF (Middle East) stocks in three stages: on 30th May 1946 (40 aircraft), on 27th June 1946 (18 aircraft) and on 26th June 1947 (83 aircraft). A further two Spitfire IXs arrived from Turkey (TuAF) in May 1949.

Deliveries totalled 143 Spitfire Mk.IXs.

The Italian Air Force (ItAF)

Italy was a Monarchy during WWII, and the Italian Air Force (ItAF) was then named *Regia Aeronautica* (RA). In 1946 Italy became a Republic, and consequently the ItAF was re-named *Aeronautica Militare Italiano* (AMI) from 3rd June 1946.

Operational units of the ItAF were designated 'Stormo', 'Gruppo' and 'Squadriglia'. A Stormo was equal to a RAF Wing, comprising two or more Gruppi. A Gruppo consisted of two or three Squadriglie.

Italian Spitfires served operationally with the 5° and the 51° Stormo. Later the Air Force Staff at Centocelle, the Test and Trial Establishment at Guidonia, the Flying School at Lecce, the OTU at Frosinone and several Flying Training Centres also used Spitfires.

The 20° Gruppo of the 51° Stormo was the first Italian user of Spitfires (September 1944), being the only Italian Air Force unit to fly Spitfire Mk.Vs operationally. The 5° Stormo served only with Spitfire Mk.IXs.

Initially all Italian Spitfires were flown with RAF serial numbers. They were changed on 16th December 1947, when all serviceable Spitfire Mks.V & IX were given Italian serial numbers in the ranges **MM4000** to **MM4143**, plus **MM4284** and **MM4285.**

A Spitfire F.IXC of the Aeronautica Militare Italiano being prepared at Foggia in 1953 for despatch to Israel. [via Gregory Alegi]

A Spitfire Mk.IX, marked 'S3-10' used as a ground instructional airframe by the Technical Trailing School at Caserta 1952/53. [Gregory Alegi]

Spitfire F.IXes of No.51° Stormo lined up at Treviso on 12th February 1948. The aircraft in the foreground was named "Altair", the second "Oldtra". It has the No.51° insignia painted on the fin. [Gregory Alegi]

Italy joined NATO on 4th April 1949. The purchase of English aircraft then ended, and American weapons were used instead. However, two Spitfire IXs arrived from Turkey around this time and were numbered **MM4286** and **MM4287**.

Problems with the wing attachments grounded all Spitfires for a short period after 12th June 1948. Spitfire Mk.IXs served as front-line aircraft of the Italian Air Force until 1951, when P-47D replaced them. Some time later the general phase-out began, the aircraft being mostly scrapped or burnt on fire-fighting exercises, apart from a few which remained for flying training until 1952. The last flight of a Spitfire was recorded by the SVL at Lecce in 1952.

Israel bought 30 Spitfire Mk.IXs from the Italian Air Force. These were selected 1951/52 and went to the Ambrosini works at Foggia for overhaul, before being flown to their new country under the Delivery numbers 0600 to 0900. For this deal the final contract was signed on 2nd February 1953.

Only one Spitfire survives in Italy, being now on display in the ItAF Museum at Vigna di Valle.

Spitfire units of the Italian Air Force

5°   **Stormo** – No.5 (FB) Wing -
at B.A. Galatina (c.15m South of Lecce) from October 1944, Orio al Serio (Bergamo, c.20m East of Milan) from May 1947, Vicenza from July 1949;
Spitfire Mk.IX from 1946 to October 1949.
Commanding Officers:

Magg.Pil. (S/Ldr) Mario Bacich	6.44
T.Col.Pil. (Wg Cdr) Gustavo Garretto	3.46
T.Col.Pil. (Wg Cdr) Domenico La Tarda	5.47
T.Col.Pil. (Wg Cdr) Guiseppe Mauriello	5.48
T.Col.Pil. (Wg Cdr) Ercolano Ercolani	8.48
T.Col.Pil. (Wg Cdr) Giuliano Giacomelli	9.49

51°   **Stormo** – No.51 (FB) Wing -
at B.A. Leverano (NW Lecce) from August 1944, Lecce from October 1944, Treviso from August 1947;
Spitfire Mk.V from September 1944, Mk.IX from 1946 to 1950.
Commanding Officers:

T.Col.Pil. (Wg Cdr) Duilio Fanali	9.43
Magg.Pil. (S/Ldr) Gino Callieri	10.44
T.Col.Pil. (Wg Cdr) Francesco Beccaria	4.47
T.Col.Pil. (Wg Cdr) Francesco Sforza	4.48
T.Col.Pil. (Wg Cdr) Roberto Fassi	9.48
Col.Pil. (Grp Capt) Delio Guizzon	5.50
Col.Pil. (Grp Capt) Gino Callieri	6.52

R.V.S.M. (**Reparto Volo Stato Maggiore**) - Staff Flying Unit - from 1946 at Urbe, from 1948 at Centocelle (both Rome);
Spitfire IX from 1946 to 1952.
Commanding Officers:

T.Col.Pil. (Wg Cdr) G Battista Vassallo	4.46
Magg.Pil. (S/Ldr) Oscar Pegna (temp)	1.47
T.Col.Pil. (Wg Cdr) Gastone Valentini	5.47
Magg.Pil. (S/Ldr) Flavio Danieli (temp)	7.48
T.Col.Pil. (Wg Cdr) Giulio Cesare Villa	11.48
T.Col.Pil. (Wg Cdr) Massimo Giovannozzi	1.50
T.Col.Pil. (Wg Cdr) Venanzio Bresciani	1.51
T.Col.Pil. (Wg Cdr) Tanrico Chiantia	1.52
Col.Pil. (Grp Capt) Felice Santini	10.52

R.S.V. (**Reparto Sperimentale de Volo**) –
Experimental Flying Unit at B.A. Guidonia (near Rome);
Spitfire IX from 1948 to 1952.
Commanding Officers:

T.Col.Pil. (Wg Cdr) Paolo Moci	from 3.48
Col.Pil. (Grp Capt) Giovanni Zappetta	10.50

S.V.L (**Scuola Volo Lecce**) – Flying School at Lecce, part of the 3° GrSc (School Group) with Spitfire Mks.V & IX from 1946 to 1952.
Commanding Officers:

Magg.Pil. (S/Ldr) Mario Frulla from	7.44
T.Col.Pil. (Wg Cdr) Edoardo Travaglini	4.45
Col.Pil. (Grp Capt) Roberto Fassi	2.46
Col.Pil. (Grp Capt) Antonio Lippi	5.47
Col.Pil. (Grp Capt) Luigi Bianchi	8.48
Col.Pil. (Grp Capt) Bruno Ricco	10.51

Aircraft of the Scuola Volo Lecce (flying school) at Lecce. As well as Spitfire Mks.V and IX, P-38s and MC-202s were also in use.

ScAdd (Scuola Addestramento Caccia e Bombardieri) at **Frosinone** - a Fighter & Bomber Training School (approx. similar as an OTU), Spitfire Mk.Vb/c in 1945, later also Mk.IX.
Commanding Officers:
Unknown

Individual Histories

BS168 Spitfire F.Vc/trop (Merlin 46); TOC/RAF 26.6.42; Malta 1.10.43 - To ItAF, on loan to 51° Stormo; 20° Gruppo 9.44; SRA (Repair Section/51° St) 16.12.44; Retd RAF; SOC 30.6.45

EE841 Spitfire F.Vc/trop (Merlin 46); TOC/RAF 23.1.43; M.E. 27.5.43 – To ItAF, on loan to 51° Stormo 9.44; 20° Gruppo; To SRA (Repair Section/51° St) 16.12.44; Retd RAF Canne 22.3.45; SOC 20.6.45

EF553 Spitfire F.Vc/trop (Merlin 46); TOC/RAF 16.2.43; NWAAF 31.5.43 – To ItAF, on loan to 51° Stormo, 20° Gruppo from 13.11.44; 360ª Squadriglia end 1944; Retd RAF, to No.110 MU Lissa (Vis Is.) 12.3.45; SOC 26.4.45

EF640 Spitfire F.Vc/trop (Merlin 50); TOC/RAF 5.4.43; N.A. 30.11.43; ex No.352 Sqn – To ItAF, on loan to 51° Stormo, 20° Gruppo from 15.9.44; Hit by AA on 4.11.44; Retd RAF 9.11.44; SOC 26.4.45

EF649 Spitfire F.Vc/trop (Merlin 50); Became **MM4053**; TOC/RAF 13.4.43; NWAAF by 1.7.43; ex No.352 Sqn – To ItAF, on loan to 51° Stormo, 20° Gruppo from 15.9.44; SRA (Repair Section/51° St) 16.12.44; MAAF census (RAF) 21.6.45; ItAF census 8.8.45; Italy to own from 27.6.46

EN144 Spitfire F.IXc (Merlin 61); Became **MM4115**; TOC/RAF 5.12.42 – To Italy (ItAF) 26.6.47; Fate unknown

EN145 Spitfire F.IXc (Merlin 63); Became **MM4116**; TOC/RAF 6.12.42 - To Italy (ItAF) 26.6.47; RVSM at Centocelle ('31') 15.12.47; Crashed (undercarriage failed, date unknown); Test flown by unit in 6.48; RTU; Later sold to Israel (*2078*) in 1951/52; Delivery No 0708; Now IDF/AF Museum Hatzerim – **SURVIVOR**

EN445 Spitfire F.IXc (Merlin 61); Became **MM4029**; TOC/RAF 13.1.43 - To Italy (ItAF) 26.6.47; Fate unknown

EN510 Spitfire F.IXc (Merlin 63A); Became **MM4036**; TOC/RAF 11.5.43 – To Italy (ItAF) 30.5.46; 20° Gruppo at Lecce in 3.47; SVL Flying School at Lecce later

EN583 Spitfire LF.IXc (Merlin 66); Became **MM4038**; TOC/RAF 21.5.43; ex SAAF (No.3 Sqn) - Arr ItAF 30.5.46; Fate unknown

EN630 Spitfire LF.IXc (Merlin 66); Became **MM4103**; TOC/RAF 30.5.43 - Arr ItAF 26.6.47; Fate unknown

EN632 Spitfire LF.IXc (Merlin 66); Became **MM4051**; TOC/RAF 30.5.43 - To Italy (ItAF) 30.5.46; 51° Stormo from 27.5.46 to 15.12.47 (Accident 21.3.47); Reserve storage ('59') in 12.48; RVSM at Centocelle ('SM-32'); Later sold to Israel (*2083*) in 5.52; Delivery No. 0803

EN635 Spitfire LF.IXc (Merlin 66); Became **MM4106**; TOC/RAF 7.6.43 - To Italy (ItAF) 26.6.47; Fate unknown

EN843 Spitfire F.IXc (Merlin 63); Became **MM4138**; TOC/RAF 10.6.43; ex SAAF (No.41 Sqn) - To Italy (ItAF) 26.6.47; Fate unknown

EP617 Spitfire F.Vc/trop (Merlin 46); TOC/RAF 19.7.42; NWAAF 28.2.43 – To ItAF, on loan to 51° Stormo, 20° Gruppo 9.44; 360ª Squadriglia end 1944; Retd RAF, No.110 MU Lissa (Vis Is.) 12.3.45; SOC 30.8.45

EP669 Spitfire F.Vb/trop (Merlin 46); TOC/RAF 27.7.42; Malta (SOC) 27.4.43; bboc – To ItAF, on loan to 51° Stormo, 20° Gruppo from 13.11.44; 360ª Squadriglia end 1944; Retd RAF; MAAF census 21.6.45; SOC (NWAAF) 30.8.45

EP758 Spitfire F.Vb/trop (Merlin 46); TOC/RAF 14.8.42; M.E. 9.11.42 – To ItAF, on loan to 51° Stormo, 20° Gruppo 23.3.45; MAAF census 21.6.45; Italy to own from 27.6.46; 51° Stormo

EP829 Spitfire F.Vb/trop (Merlin 46); Became **MM4069**; TOC/RAF 2.8.42; dis. ME 1.7.43 – To ItAF, on loan to 51° Stormo, 20° Gruppo 9.44; 360ª Squadriglia end 1944; MAAF census 21.6.45; ItAF census 8.8.45; storage ComSc/SEMA (School HQ); Italy to own from 27.6.46; At Lecce 31.12.47

EP886 Spitfire F.Vb/trop (Merlin 46); Became **MM4071**; TOC/RAF 11.8.42; dis. NA 1.7.43; ex No.352 Sqn; No.110 MU - To ItAF, on loan to 51° Stormo, 20° Gruppo from 16.5.45; MAAF census 21.6.45; ItAF census 8.8.45; storage ComSc/SEMA (School HQ); Italy to own from 27.6.46; At Lecce 31.12.47

ER200 Spitfire F.Vb/trop (Merlin 46); TOC/RAF 28.8.42; Gibraltar 1.11.42; ex SAAF 3.43; No.281 Wing Canne – To ItAF, on loan to 51° Stormo, 20° Gruppo 1944/45; 51° Stormo by 10.4.45; Fate unknown
NOTE: Reported as "BR200"

ER655 Spitfire F.Vc/trop (Merlin 46); Became **MM4055**; TOC/RAF 9.10.42; ex USAAF – To ItAF, on loan to 51° Stormo, 20° Gruppo 9.44; 360ª Squadriglia end 1944; MAAF census 21.6.45; ItAF census 8.8.45; storage ComSc/SEMA (School HQ); Italy to own from 27.6.46; ItAF, At Lecce 31.12.47

ER821 Spitfire F.Vb/trop (Merlin 46); Became **MM4068**; TOC/RAF 24.10.42; NAASC 1.11.43 – To ItAF, on loan to 51° Stormo, 20° Gruppo from 23.3.45; MAAF census 21.6.45; ItAF census 8.8.45; storage ComSc/SEMA (School HQ); Italy to own from 27.6.46; At Lecce 31.12.47

ER880 Spitfire F.Vc/trop (Merlin 46); TOC/RAF 7.11.42; ex USAAF; NWAAF 31.5.44 - To ItAF, on loan to 51° Stormo, 20° Gruppo from 13.11.44; 356ª Squadriglia end 1944; Retd RAF Canne 22.3.45; SOC 30.6.45
NOTE: Reported as "EF880"

ER886 Spitfire F.Vb/trop (Merlin 46); TOC/RAF 4.12.42; M.E. 30.11.44 – To ItAF, on loan to 51° Stormo, 20° Gruppo from 16.3.45; MAAF census 21.6.45; Italy to own from 14.3.46

ER893 Spitfire F.Vb/trop (Merlin 46); TOC/RAF 7.11.42; NAAF 11.43; No.2 FTLU – To ItAF (on loan); ScAdd Frosinone (Scuola Addestramento, OTU) from 19.5.45; MAAF census 21.6.45; Italy to own from 27.6.46

ES142 Spitfire F.Vc/trop (Merlin 46); TOC/RAF 8.11.42; NAAF 30.11.43; ex No.352 Sqn – To ItAF, on loan to 51° Stormo, 20° Gruppo from 15.9.44; In between to RAF, retd to 20° Gruppo 7.11.44; Crashed on take-off at Balasso, collision with Spitfire JL363 28.11.44 (Lt Casabeltrame); To RTU 30.11.44; SRA (Rgp Caccia/2° Rep Ric e Rip) end 1944; 356ª Squadriglia from 15.12.44; Unserviceable, retd RAF, to No.110 MU Lissa (Vis Is.) 30.4.45; SOC 30.6.45

ES148 Spitfire F.Vc/trop (Merlin 46); TOC/RAF 9.12.42; NAAF 1.11.43 – To ItAF, on loan to 51° Stormo, 20° Gruppo 9.44; 360ª Squadriglia end 1944; Retd RAF, to No.110 MU Lissa (Vis Is.) 29.4.45; MAAF census 21.6.45; SOC 30.8.45

ES257 Spitfire F.Vc/trop (Merlin 46); Became **MM4013**; TOC/RAF 21.11.42; dis. ME 1.7.43 – To ItAF, on loan to 51° Stormo, 20° Gruppo 9.44; 356ª Squadriglia end 1944; MAAF census 21.6.45; ItAF census 8.8.45; Italy to own from 27.6.46; SVL (Flying School Lecce) 25.3.47; 3° School Group ('38') by 31.12.47

JG878 Spitfire F.Vc/trop (Merlin 46); TOC/RAF 21.1.43; ex USAAF; NWAAF 31.3.43 – To ItAF, on loan to 51° Stormo, 20° Gruppo 9.44; Taxied into Macchi C-205 (MM92173) 23.10.44; To No.110 MU Canne 28.10.44; SRA (Rgp Caccia/2° Rep Ric e Rip) end 1944; Retd RAF 28.4.45; M.E. census 21.6.45; SOC 25.7.46

JG950 Spitfire F.Vc/trop (Merlin 46); TOC/RAF 22.1.43; NAASC 31.10.43; ex Nos.111 & 352 Sqns – To ItAF, on loan to 51° Stormo, 20° Gruppo by 23.3.45; Crashed 28.4.45; Retd RAF, to No.110 MU Lissa (Vis Is.) 4.5.45; Census 21.6.45; SOC 30.8.45
NOTE: Reported as "JK950"

JK130 Spitfire F.Vc/trop (Merlin 46); Became **MM4001**; TOC/RAF 20.1.43; M.E. 30.3.43; No.254 Wing; R&SU at Canne – To ItAF, on loan to 51° Stormo, 20° Gruppo from 5.5.45; MAAF census 21.6.45; ItAF census 8.8.45; storage ComSc/SEMA (School HQ); Italy to own from 27.6.46; At Lecce 31.12.47

JK161 Spitfire F.Vc/trop (Merlin 46); TOC/RAF 29.1.43; NWAAF 31.3.43 – To ItAF, on loan to 51° Stormo, 20° Gruppo 9.44; 360ª Squadriglia end 11.44; Retd RAF Canne 29.12.44; MAAF census 21.6.45; Crashed, Cat.E 18.10.45; SOC 28.10.45

JK165 Spitfire F.Vc/trop (Merlin 46); Became **MM4005**; TOC/RAF 27.1.43; NAASC 31.10.43; ex No.352 Sqn – To ItAF, on loan to 51° Stormo, 20° Gruppo from 15.9.44; 356ª Squadriglia end 1944; MAAF census 21.6.45; ItAF census 8.8.45; storage ComSc/SEMA (School HQ); Italy to own from 27.6.46; At Lecce by 31.12.47

JK177 Spitfire F.Vc/trop (Merlin 46); TOC/RAF 24.1.43; NAAF 1.11.43 – To ItAF, on loan to 51° Stormo, 20° Gruppo 9.44; 356ª Squadriglia end 1944; Ground accident, Cat.E 8.3.45; SOC/RAF 26.4.45 (bboc, MAAF census 21.6.45; SOC 30.8.45)

JK385 Spitfire F.Vc/trop (Merlin 46); TOC/RAF 4.2.43; ex USAAF; NWAAF 31.8.43 – To ItAF, on loan to 51° Stormo, 20° Gruppo from 16.3.45; Unserviceable, retd RAF 25.3.45; MAAF census 21.6.45; SOC 19.7.45

JK392 Spitfire F.Vc/trop (Merlin 46); Became **MM4067**; TOC/RAF 6.2.43; NWAAF 31.5.43 – To ItAF, on loan to 51° Stormo, 20° Gruppo from 5.5.45; MAAF census 21.6.45; ItAF census 8.8.45; storage ComSc/SEMA (School HQ); Italy to own from 27.6.46; At Lecce 31.12.47

JK509 Spitfire F.Vc/trop (Merlin 46); Presentation aircraft '*WADI HALFA*'; TOC/RAF 6.2.43; ex French; NWAAF 1.10.43; MAAF; ex No.352 Sqn – To ItAF, on loan to 51° Stormo, 20° Gruppo from 15.9.44; 360ª Squadriglia, force-landed in a field near San Cesareo, Cat.FB/E 7.11.44; Retd RAF & SOC 9.11.44

JK675 Spitfire F.Vc/trop (Merlin 50); TOC/RAF 21.2.43; NWAAF 30.4.43 – To ItAF (on loan); ScAdd Frosinone (Scuola Addestramento, OTU) in 1945; Unserviceable, retd RAF No.159 MU 18.6.45; SOC 20.9.45

JK720 Spitfire F.Vc/trop (Merlin 46); Became **MM 4061**; TOC/RAF 26.2.43; NAAF 30.11.43 – To ItAF, on loan to 51° Stormo, 20° Gruppo 9.44; MAAF census 21.6.45; ItAF census 8.8.45; storage ComSc/SEMA (School HQ); Italy to own from 27.6.46; At Lecce 31.12.47

JK784 Spitfire F.Vc/trop (Merlin 50); Became **MM4065**; TOC/RAF 6.3.43; NWAAF 1.10.43 – To ItAF, on loan to 51° Stormo, 20° Gruppo from 18.10.44; Hit by AA 4.11.44; In between to RAF on 9.11.44; MAAF census 21.6.45; Retd ItAF (census 8.8.45); Italy to own from 27.6.46

JK803 Spitfire F.Vc/trop (Merlin 46); TOC/RAF 12.2.43; dis. Italy 1.11.43 – To ItAF, on loan to 51° Stormo, 20° Gruppo 9.44; 356ª Squadriglia, failed to return from ops, Cat.FB/E 4.11.44 (Lt A Veronese killed); SOC/RAF in 11.44

JK805 Spitfire F.Vc/trop (Merlin 46); TOC/RAF 27.2.43; NWAAF 31.5.43; ex No.352 Sqn – To ItAF, on loan to 51° Stormo, 20° Gruppo from 15.9.44; 356ª Squadriglia, ground-looped on take-off 16.11.44 (Lt Fio Jannicelli); SRA (Rgp Caccia/2° Rep Ric e Rip) end 1944; Retd to 20° Gruppo 9.12.44; MAAF census 21.6.45; SOC/RAF 30.8.45

JK875 Spitfire F.Vc/trop (Merlin 50); TOC/RAF 7.3.43; ex USAAF; NWAAF 31.5.44; ex No.352 Sqn – To ItAF, on loan to 51° Stormo, 20° Gruppo from 15.9.44; 360ª Squadriglia end 1944; Crashed, Cat.FA/E 8.3.45; Retd RAF in 4.45; MAAF census 21.6.45; SOC 30.8.45

JK878 Spitfire F.Vc/trop (Merlin 46); TOC/RAF 10.3.43; M.E. 31.8.44; ex No.352 Sqn – To ItAF, on loan to 51° Stormo, 20°Grp from 15.9.44; SOC/RAF 31.5.45

JL251 Spitfire F.Vc/trop (Merlin 50); Became **MM4012**; TOC/RAF 16.4.43; ex French unit – To ItAF, on loan to 51° Stormo, 20° Gruppo from 15.9.44; 356ª Squadriglia end 1944; Crashed, Cat.FA/Ac 24.5.45 (Sgt M Fattoreti); MAAF census 21.6.45; ItAF census 8.8.45; Italy to own from 27.6.46; SVL (Flying School Lecce) from 18.3.47; 3° School Group ('36') by 31.12.47

JL363 Spitfire F.Vc/trop (Merlin 46); TOC/RAF 27.4.43; ex SAAF; NWAAF 1.7.43 – To ItAF, on loan to 51° Stormo, 20° Gruppo from 13.11.44; Take-off crash at Belasso, collision with Spitfire ES142 28.11.44; To RTU 30.11.44; SRA (Rgp Caccio/2° Rep Ric e Rip) end 1944; SOC/RAF 30.6.45

LZ949 Spitfire F.IXc (Merlin 63); Became **MM4074**; TOC/RAF 30.4.43 – To Italy (ItAF) 30.5.46; Fate unknown

LZ952 Spitfire F.IXc (Merlin 63); Became **MM4075**; TOC/RAF 28.4.43 - To Italy (ItAF) 26.6.47; Fate unknown

LZ991 Spitfire F.IXc (Merlin 63); Became **MM4142**; TOC/RAF 16.5.43 - To Italy (ItAF) 26.6.47; Fate unknown

MA256 Spitfire F.IXc (Merlin 63); TOC/RAF 21.5.43; ex SAAF (No.41 Sqn) - To Italy (ItAF) 26.6.47; Crashed in 1947

MA315 Spitfire LF.IXc (Merlin 66); Became **MM4081**; TOC/RAF 31.5.43 - To Italy (ItAF) 27.6.46; Fate unknown

MA369 Spitfire F.IXc (Merlin 63); Became **MM4023**; TOC/RAF 15.8.43 - To Italy (ItAF) 30.5.46; Fate unknown

MA426 Spitfire F.IXc (Merlin 63); Became **MM4086**; TOC/RAF 18.7.43 - To Italy (ItAF) 30.5.46; Fate unknown

MA447 Spitfire F.IXc (Merlin 63); Became **MM4030**; TOC/RAF 6.6.43 - To Italy (ItAF) 30.5.46; Fate unknown

MA453 Spitfire F.IXc (Merlin 63); Became **MM4031**; TOC/RAF 8.6.43; MAAF census 6.45 – To Italy (ItAF) 30.5.46; 51° Stormo at Lecce from 21.5.46 to 15.12.47; 1° RTA; 3° School Group (SVL) from 25.11.49; Later sold to Israel (*2086*) in 1951/52; Delivery No 0806

MA471 Spitfire F.IXc (Merlin 63); Became **MM4035**; TOC/RAF 3.6.43 - To Italy (ItAF) 26.6.47; Fate unknown

MA559 Spitfire F.IXc (Merlin 63); Became **MM4040**; TOC/RAF 19.6.43; Arr NWAAF 31.7.43 - Possibly sold to ItAF 30.5.46; Fate unknown
NOTE: Not confirmed, but RAF movement card shows presumed SOC in 1947

MA617 Spitfire F.IXc (Merlin 63A); Became **MM4044**; TOC/RAF 29.6.43 - To Italy (ItAF) 30.5.46; 51° Stormo at Lecce ('31') from 5.7.46 to 15.12.47; For overhaul to Aero Macchi 30.6.49; Test flown 15.1.51; AW/CN 27.1.51; To RVSM at Centocelle 31.3.51; Later sold to Israel (*2081*) in 12.51; Delivery No 0801

MA618 Spitfire F.IXc (Merlin 63A); Became **MM4045**; TOC/RAF 28.6.43 - To Italy (ItAF) 30.5.46; Later sold to Israel (*2084*) 1951/52; Delivery No 0804

MA630 Spitfire F.IXc (Merlin 63); Became **MM4049**; TOC/RAF 30.6.43 - To Italy (ItAF) 26.6.47; Fate unknown

MA632 Spitfire F.IXc (Merlin 63); Became **MM4050**; TOC/RAF 29.6.43 - To Italy (ItAF) 30.5.46; Fate unknown

MA751 Spitfire F.IXc (Merlin 61); TOC/RAF 18.7.43 - To Italy (ItAF) 26.6.47; Crashed in 1947

MH526 Spitfire LF.IXc (Merlin 66); Became **MM4037**; TOC/RAF 21.8.43 - To Italy (ItAF) 26.6.47; 51° Stormo

MH599 Spitfire LF.IXc (Merlin 66); Became **MM4284**; TOC/RAF 23.8.43 - To Italy (ItAF) 26.6.47; Fate unknown

MH602 Spitfire F.IXc (Merlin 63); Became **MM4041**; TOC/RAF 2.9.43 - To Italy (ItAF) 30.5.46; Fate unknown

MH604 Spitfire F.IXc (Merlin 63); Became **MM4042**; TOC/RAF 9.9.43; ex USAAF - To Italy (ItAF) 30.5.46; Fate unknown

MH615 Spitfire LF.IXc (Merlin 66); Became **MM4043**; TOC/RAF 23.8.43; ex USAAF - To Italy (ItAF) 26.6.47; Fate unknown

MH619 Spitfire F.IXc (Merlin 63); Became **MM4046**; TOC/RAF 14.9.43 - To Italy (ItAF) 26.6.47; Fate unknown

MH621 Spitfire LF.IXc (Merlin 66); Became MM4047; TOC/RAF 31.8.43 - To Italy (ItAF) 30.5.46; Fate unknown

MH635 Spitfire F.IXc (Merlin 63); Became **MM4052**; TOC/RAF 11.9.43 - To Italy (ItAF) 26.6.47; Fate unknown

MH648 Spitfire F.IXc (Merlin 63); Became **MM4134**; TOC/RAF 22.8.43 - To Italy (ItAF) 26.6.47; Fate unknown

MH691 Spitfire F.IXc (Merlin 63); Became **MM4136**; TOC/RAF 10.9.43; ex USAAF - To Italy (ItAF) 26.6.47; Fate unknown

MH720 Spitfire LF.IXc (Merlin 66); Became **MM4062**; TOC/RAF 16.9.43 - To Italy (ItAF) 26.6.47; Fate unknown

MH779 Spitfire LF.IXc (Merlin 66); Became **MM4107**; TOC/RAF 1.10.43 - To Italy (ItAF) 26.6.47; Fate unknown

MH785 Spitfire LF.IXc (Merlin 66); Became **MM4066**; TOC/RAF 22.9.43 - To Italy (ItAF) 30.5.46; ItAF on own 26.6.47; 5° Stormo by 15.12.47; Later sold to Israel in 1951/52

MH896 Spitfire F.IXc (Merlin 63); Became **MM4072**; TOC/RAF 14.9.43; ex USAAF - To Italy (ItAF) 26.6.47; Fate unknown

MH945 Spitfire F.IXc (Merlin 63); Became **MM4285**; TOC/RAF 29.8.43 - To Italy (ItAF) 26.6.47; Fate unknown

MH947 Spitfire F.IXc (Merlin 63); Became **MM4073**; TOC/RAF 26.8.43 - To Italy (ItAF) 30.5.46; Fate unknown

MH954 Spitfire LF.IXc (Merlin 66); Became **MM4141**; TOC/RAF 30.8.43 - To Italy (ItAF) 26.6.47; Fate unknown

MH985 Spitfire LF.IXc (Merlin 66); Became **MM4128**; TOC/RAF 5.9.43 - To Italy (ItAF) 29.8.46; ItAF on own 26.6.47; 5° Stormo by 15.12.47; Later sold to Israel in 1951/52

MH997 Spitfire F.IXc (Merlin 63); Became **MM4092**; TOC/RAF 4.9.43; ex USAAF - To Italy (ItAF) 30.5.46; Fate unknown

MJ297 Spitfire LF.IXc (Merlin 66); Became **MM4015**; TOC/RAF 27.10.43 - To Italy (ItAF) 30.5.46; 51° Stormo by 17.6.46

MJ358 Spitfire LF.IXc (Merlin 66); Became **MM4021**; TOC/RAF 23.11.43 - To Italy (ItAF) 30.5.46; 51° Stormo

MJ404 Spitfire LF.IXc (Merlin 66); Became **MM4098**; TOC/RAF 3.11.43 - To Italy (ItAF) 26.6.47; Fate unknown

MJ525 Spitfire LF.IXc (Merlin 66); Became **MM4087**; TOC/RAF 30.11.43; ex USAAF - To Italy (ItAF) 27.6.46; Fate unknown

MJ527 Spitfire LF.IXc (Merlin 66); Became **MM4127**; TOC/RAF 24.11.43 - To Italy (ItAF) 26.6.47; Fate unknown

MJ561 Spitfire LF.IXc (Merlin 66); Became **MM4131**; TOC/RAF 22.12.43 - To Italy (ItAF) 26.6.47; Fate unknown

MJ571 Spitfire LF(FR).IXc (Merlin 66); Became **MM4102**; TOC/RAF 22.12.43 - To Italy (ItAF) 26.6.47; 5° Stormo

ITALY

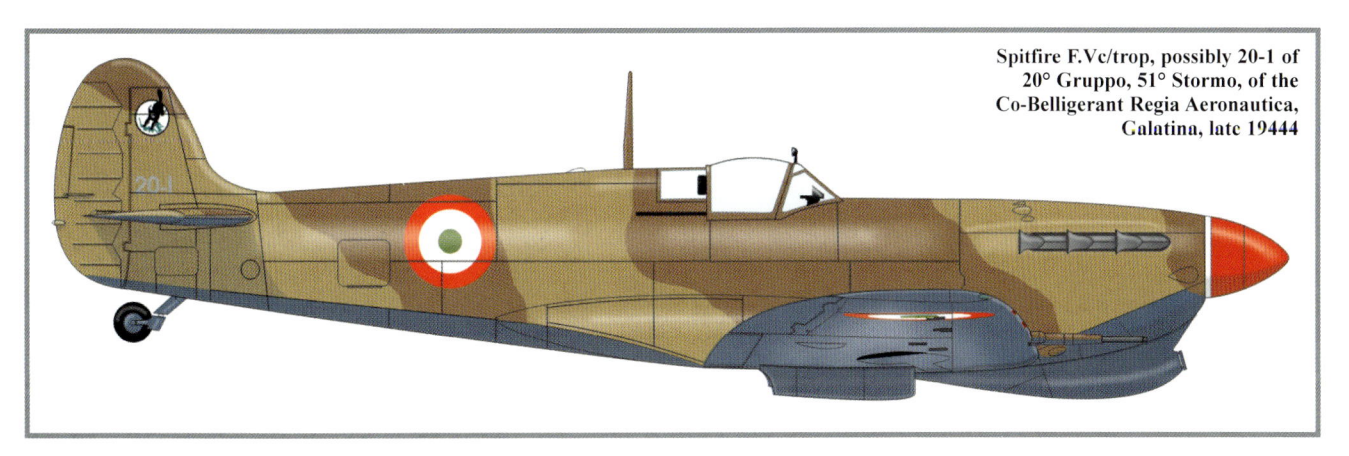

Spitfire F.Vc/trop, possibly 20-1 of 20° Gruppo, 51° Stormo, of the Co-Belligerant Regia Aeronautica, Galatina, late 1944

Spitfire LF(FR).IXc, MM4102, 51-31, of 21° Gruppo, 51° Stormo, AMI, Treviso, circa 1950. Note camera ports under wing root

by 15.12.47; To 51° Stormo; 155ª Gruppo ('51-31'); Later sold to Israel (*2068*) in 6.52; Delivery No 0608
MJ587 Spitfire LF.IXc (Merlin 66); Became **MM4039**; TOC/RAF 25.11.43 - To Italy (ItAF) 26.6.47; Fate unknown
MJ630 Spitfire LF.IXc (Merlin 66); Became **MM4133**; TOC/RAF 30.11.43 - To Italy (ItAF) 26.6.47; Fate unknown
MJ668 Spitfire LF.IXc (Merlin 66); Became **MM4058**; TOC/RAF 30.11.43 - To Italy (ItAF) 26.6.47; Fate unknown
MJ673 Spitfire LF.IXc (Merlin 66); Became **MM4059**; TOC/RAF 2.12.43 - To Italy (ItAF) 30.5.46; 51° Stormo in 3.47; SVL (Flying School Lecce); Later sold to Israel (*2065*) in 4.52; Delivery No 0605
MJ730 Spitfire LF.IXc (Merlin 66); Became **MM4094**; TOC/RAF 12.12.43 - To Italy (ItAF) 27.6.46; 1° RTA, stored at Linate (for spares) 15.12.47; For overhaul to Aero Macchi 11.5.48; At Varese, test flown 29.11.50; RVSM at Centocelle 2.2.51; Later sold to Israel (*2066*) in 4.52; Delivery No 0606 – **SURVIVOR**
NOTE: To *G-BLAS* reg. 22.11.83 and later *G-HFIX* reg. 9.11.87. Now in USA as *N730J*

MJ731 Spitfire LF.IXc (Merlin 66); Became **MM4063**; TOC/RAF 16.12.43 - To Italy (ItAF) 27.6.46; Fate unknown
MJ778 Spitfire LF.IXc (Merlin 66); Became **MM4137**; TOC/RAF 1.1.44 - To Italy (ItAF) 26.6.47; Fate unknown
MJ829 Spitfire LF.IXc (Merlin 66); Became **MM4108**; TOC/RAF 24.12.43 - To Italy (ItAF) 26.6.47; Fate unknown
MJ830 Spitfire LF.IXc (Merlin 66); Became **MM4070**; TOC/RAF 22.12.43 - To Italy (ItAF) 26.6.47; 1° RTU/NV, Accident 5.12.47 (RSRA); SRA (Repair Section) at Bresso 15.12.47; Later sold to Israel (*2063*) in 4.52; Delivery No 0604
MJ841 Spitfire LF.IXc (Merlin 66); Became **MM4109**; TOC/RAF 28.11.43 - To Italy (ItAF) 26.6.47; Fate unknown
MJ849 Spitfire LF.IXc (Merlin 66); Became **MM4139**; TOC/RAF 4.12.43 - To Italy (ItAF) 26.6.47; Fate unknown
MJ955 Spitfire LF.IXc (Merlin 66); TOC/RAF 20.1.44 - To Italy (ItAF) 26.6.47; Unknown unit, crashed, Cat.E2 on 25.11.47, SOC

Spitfire LF.XIc (ex MJ996), marked 'A-32', serving with the Reparto Volo Stato Maggiore (Staff Flying Unit) at Centocelle, near Rome in 1949.
[Stato Maggiore dell'Aeronautica]

MJ996 Spitfire LF.IXc (Merlin 66); Became **MM4079**; TOC/RAF 10.1.44 - To Italy (ItAF) 27.6.46; RVSM at Centocelle ('A-32') in 1949
MK154 Spitfire LF.IXc (Merlin 66); Became **MM4083**; TOC/RAF 20.1.44 - To Italy (ItAF) 27.6.46; 51° Stormo
MK155 Spitfire LF.IXc (Merlin 66); Became **MM4117**; TOC/RAF 4.2.44 - To Italy (ItAF) 26.6.47; 51° Stormo
MK156 Spitfire LF.IXc (Merlin 66); Became **MM4004**; TOC/RAF 12.2.44 - To Italy (ItAF) 30.5.46; 51° Stormo from 25.5.46
MK193 Spitfire LF.IXc (Merlin 66); Became **MM4008**; TOC/RAF 20.1.44 - To Italy (ItAF) 30.5.46; 51° Stormo, destroyed in crash landing, Cat.E 12.8.47, SOC
MK194 Spitfire LF.IXc (Merlin 66); Became **MM4010**; TOC/RAF 23.1.44 - To Italy (ItAF) 30.5.46; SVL (Flying School Lecce), crashed, Cat.E 20.12.47; SOC
MK207 Spitfire LF.IXc (Merlin 66); Became **MM4120**; TOC/RAF 26.1.44; Italy to own from 26.6.47; 5° Stormo by 15.12.47; To 1° RTA 30.6.49; Later sold to Israel in 1951/52
MK227 Spitfire LF.IXc (Merlin 66); Became **MM4082**; TOC/RAF 24.12.43 - To Italy (ItAF) 27.6.46; 5° Stormo
MK302 Spitfire LF.IXc (Merlin 66); Became **MM4017**; TOC/RAF 28.1.44 - To Italy (ItAF) 26.6.47; Fate unknown
MK375 Spitfire LF.IXc (Merlin 66); Became **MM4077**; TOC/RAF 9.2.44 - To Italy (ItAF) 27.6.46; 51° Stormo at Lecce ('46') in 3.47
MK413 Spitfire LF.IXc (Merlin 66); Became **MM4124**; TOC/RAF 10.2.44 - To Italy (ItAF) 26.6.47; Fate unknown
MK419 Spitfire LF.IXc (Merlin 66); Became **MM4085**; TOC/RAF 21.2.44 - To Italy (ItAF) 27.6.46; SVL (Flying School Lecce) 27.6.46 until 18.10.50; Fire Fighting Practice (near Rome) in 10.50
MK555 Spitfire LF.IXc (Merlin 66); Became **MM4114**; TOC/RAF 24.2.44 - To Italy (ItAF) 26.6.47; Unknown unit, crashed, Cat.E 6.10.47, SOC
MK557 Spitfire LF.IXc (Merlin 66); Became **MM4101**; TOC/RAF 1.3.44 - To Italy (ItAF) 27.6.46; Fate unknown
MK569 Spitfire LF.IXc (Merlin 66); Became **MM4132**; TOC/RAF 12.3.44 - To Italy (ItAF) 26.6.47; Fate unknown
MK586 Spitfire LF.IXc (Merlin 66); TOC/RAF 24.3.44 - To Italy (ItAF) 26.6.47; Unknown unit, crashed 1947
MK636 Spitfire LF.IXc (Merlin 66); Became **MM4080**; TOC/RAF 9.3.44 - To Italy (ItAF) 30.5.46; Fate unknown
MK679 Spitfire LF.IXc (Merlin 66); Became **MM4135**; TOC/RAF 14.4.44 - To Italy (ItAF) 26.6.47; 5° Stormo 15.12.47; Later sold to Israel in 1951/52
MK770 Spitfire LF.IXc (Merlin 66); Became **MM4064**; TOC/RAF 2.3.44 - To Italy (ItAF) 26.6.47; Fate unknown
MK805 Spitfire LF.IXc (Merlin 66); Became **MM4084**; TOC/RAF 11.3.44 – To Italy (ItAF) 29.6.46; SVL (Flying School Lecce) by 25.8.47; Nettuno 19.12.47; On pole at Foce Verde Artillery School, Nettuno 1948; Salvaged, and to Museu Storico Dell'Aeronautica Militare Italiana, Vigna di Valle AFB 1976; Restored by the 3° RTA at Lecce; Delivered to GAVS at Rome for finishing in 2.89; Painted as "MM4079" and marked "A-32"; On display in IAF Museum Vigna di Valle from 14.7.89 – **SURVIVOR**
MK906 Spitfire LF.IXc (Merlin 66); Became **MM4110**; TOC/RAF 17.3.44 - To Italy (ItAF) 26.6.47; Fate unknown
MK916 Spitfire LF.IXc (Merlin 66); TOC/RAF 23.3.44 - To Italy (ItAF) 30.5.46; Unknown unit, crashed, Cat.E2 23.9.47, SOC
ML129 Spitfire LF.IXc (Merlin 66); Became **MM4000**; TOC/RAF 18.3.44 - To Italy (ItAF) 30.5.46; Fate unknown
ML134 Spitfire LF.IXc (Merlin 66); Became **MM4002**; TOC/RAF 20.3.44 - To Italy (ItAF) 30.5.46; 51° Stormo (before 1948) until 8.48; 5° Stormo in summer 1948
ML139 Spitfire LF.IXc (Merlin 66); Became **MM4003**; TOC/RAF 27.3.44 - To Italy (ItAF) 26.6.47; Fate unknown
ML180 Spitfire LF.IXc (Merlin 66); Became **MM4090**; TOC/RAF 5.4.44 - To Italy (ItAF) 30.5.46; Fate unknown
ML193 Spitfire LF.IXe (Merlin 66); Became **MM4009**; TOC/RAF 18.4.44 - To Italy (ItAF) 26.6.47; 51° Stormo (before 1948); RVSM at Centocelle in 1951
ML371 Spitfire LF.IXc (Merlin 66); Became MM4024; TOC/RAF 25.4.44 - To Italy (ItAF) 30.5.46; Fate unknown
ML410 Spitfire LF.IXc (Merlin 66); Became **MM4123**; TOC/RAF 25.4.44 - To Italy (ItAF) 26.6.47; Later sold to Israel (*2060*) in 5.51; Delivery No 0600
ML416 Spitfire LF.IXc (Merlin 66); Became **MM4125**; TOC/RAF 1.5.44 - To Italy (ItAF) 26.6.47; 5° Stormo by 15.12.47; Storage at Bresso in 1951 (marked '4125-R'); CAV Iª ZAT (Flying Training Centre); Later sold to Israel (*2062*) in 4.52; Delivery No 0602
MT719 Spitfire LF.VIIIc; ex Indian A.F.; Arrived as **SURVIVOR** only; Hulk recovered Jaipur AFB in 1978 by Ormond and

Surviving Spitfire LF.VIIIc MT719 seen at Middle Wallop on 11th July 1986 with the small Italian civil registration **I-SPIT** *on the rudder and painted up in SEAC markings with No.17 Sqn RAF code "YB-J". It was previously an RIAF aircraft, and is now extant in the USA as N719MT.* [*Ray Sturtivant*]

ITALY

Wensley Haydon-Baillie, Duxford, UK; Sold to Franco Actis, Turin, Italy (Civil reg. *I-SPI T*12.79); Restored Vergiate and ff 27.10.82 marked "MT719/YB-J"; To Reynard Racing Cars Ltd, Bicester 5.11.88 (reg. *G-VIII* 27.4.89); To Aircraft Investments Ltd 1993, Sold to USA (*N719MT*), crated ex Micheldever 25.6.93

NH182 Spitfire LF.IXe (Merlin 66); Became **MM4104**; TOC/RAF 29.4.44 - To Italy (ItAF) 26.6.47; Fate unknown

NH184 Spitfire LF.IXe (Merlin 66); Became **MM4118**; TOC/RAF 6.5.44 - To Italy (ItAF) 26.6.47; Fate unknown

NH242 Spitfire LF.IXe (Merlin 66); Became **MM4095**; TOC/RAF 18.5.44 - To Italy (ItAF) 27.6.46; 1° RTA, storage at Linate (for spares) 15.12.47; For overhaul to Aero Macchi 29.4.48; Test flown 9.1.50; AW/CN 20.1.50; 51° Stormo from 11.2.50; 5° Stormo ('5-19'); Later sold to Israel in 1951/52

NH247 Spitfire LF.IXe (Merlin 66); Became **MM4096**; TOC/RAF 9.5.44 - To Italy (ItAF) 26.6.47; Fate unknown

NH297 Spitfire HF.IXe (Merlin 70); Became **MM4016**; TOC/RAF 15.5.44 - To Italy (ItAF) 30.5.46; Fate unknown

NH307 Spitfire LF.IXe (Merlin 66); Became **MM4018**; TOC/RAF 12.5.44 - To Italy (ItAF) 30.5.46; Fate unknown

NH319 Spitfire LF.IXe (Merlin 66); Became **MM4019**; TOC/RAF 20.5.44 - To Italy (ItAF) 27.6.46; Fate unknown

NH426 Spitfire LF.IXe (Merlin 66); Became **MM4105**; TOC/RAF 19.5.44 - To Italy (ItAF) 26.6.47; Fate unknown

NH431 Spitfire LF.IXe (Merlin 66); Became **MM4027**; TOC/RAF 23.5.44 - To Italy (ItAF) 26.6.47; 5° Stormo 15.12.47; For overhaul to 1° RTA 18.7.49; Later sold to Israel 1951/52

NH468 Spitfire LF.IXe (Merlin 66); Became **MM4034**; TOC/RAF 26.5.44 - To Italy (ItAF) 30.5.46; Fate unknown

NH599 Spitfire LF.IXe (Merlin 66); Became **MM4130**; TOC/RAF 10.6.44 - To Italy (ItAF) 30.5.46; Fate unknown

PL127 Spitfire LF.IXe (Merlin 66); Became **MM4099**; TOC/RAF 19.6.44 - To Italy (ItAF) 26.6.47; 5° Stormo 15.12.47; Accident, propeller broken 12.5.48; To 1° RTA 11.2.49; Later sold to Israel in 1951/52

PL164 Spitfire LF.IXe (Merlin 66); TOC/RAF 17.7.44 - To Italy (ItAF) 26.6.47; Crashed 1947

PL328 Spitfire LF.IXe (Merlin 66); Became **MM4121**; TOC/RAF 21.6.44 - To Italy (ItAF) 26.6.47; Fate unknown

PL330 Spitfire LF.IXe (Merlin 66); Became **MM4020**; TOC/RAF 19.6.44 - To Italy (ItAF) 26.6.47; Fate unknown

PL388 Spitfire HF.IXe (Merlin 70); Became **MM4122**; TOC/RAF 21.6.44 - To Italy (ItAF) 26.6.47; Fate unknown

PL458 Spitfire HF.IXe (Merlin 70); Became **MM4032**; TOC/RAF 30.6.44 - To Italy (ItAF) 26.6.47; Fate unknown

PT396 Spitfire LF.IXe (Merlin 66); Became **MM4025**; TOC/RAF 1.7.44 - To Italy (ItAF) 26.6.47; Fate unknown

PT414 Spitfire LF.IXe (Merlin 66); Became **MM4026**; TOC/RAF 18.7.44 - To Italy (ItAF) 27.6.46; Fate unknown

PT460 Spitfire HF.IXe (Merlin 70); Became **MM4033**; TOC/RAF 14.10.44 - To Italy (ItAF) 30.5.46; Fate unknown

PT462 Spitfire HF.IXe (Merlin 70); Became **MM4100**; TOC/RAF 21.7.44 - To Italy (ItAF) 26.6.47; 5° Stormo 15.12.47; Accident, tyre burst 4.3.48; RSRA 13.4.48; Later sold to Israel (*2067*) in 4.52; Delivery No 0607; Now in UK
NOTE: Civil reg. *G-CTIX* 9.4.85; To USA 8.94 as *N462JC*; Retd to UK *G-CTIX* 28.4.98 and now with Anthony Hodgson, North Wales; Converted to a two-seater, airworthy (marked "SW-A") - **SURVIVOR**

PT481 Spitfire LF.IXe (Merlin 70); Became **MM4126**; TOC/RAF 17.7.44 - To Italy (ItAF) 26.6.47; 21° Grp (of 51° Stormo) from 20.10.47 until 15.12.47; For overhaul to 1° RTA 7.6.49; Later sold to Israel (*2082*) in 1951/52; Delivery No 0802

PT590 Spitfire LF.IXe (Merlin 66); TOC/RAF 22.7.44 - To Italy (ItAF) 30.5.46; unknown unit, crashed, Cat.E2 7.3.47, SOC

PT625 Spitfire LF.IXe (Merlin 66); Became **MM4048**; TOC/RAF 26.7.44 - To Italy (ItAF) 30.5.46; 51° Stormo from 4.7.46 to 15.12.47 (Accident 16.7.46); Unknown unit, crashed, left wing and undercarriage broken 5.5.48; For overhaul to Aero Macchi 31.5.48; Test flown 15.11.48; AW/CN 3.2.49; 51° Stormo from 18.2.50 (shown with underwing bomb racks); Later sold to Israel in 1951/52

PT653 Spitfire LF.IXe (Merlin 66); Became **MM4093**; TOC/RAF 27.7.44 - To Italy (ItAF) 27.6.46; 51° Stormo (marked '*Antares*')

PT654 Spitfire LF.IXe (Merlin 66); Became **MM4054**; TOC/RAF 28.7.44 - To Italy (ItAF) 26.6.47; 5° Stormo until 19.7.48; To Aero Macchi for destruction tests 20.7.48

PT656 Spitfire LF.IXe (Merlin 66); Became **MM4129**; TOC/RAF 27.7.44 - To Italy (ItAF) 26.6.47; Fate unknown

PT666 Spitfire LF.IXe (Merlin 66); Became **MM4056**; TOC/RAF 30.7.44 - To Italy (ItAF) 26.6.47; Fate unknown

PT667 Spitfire LF.IXe (Merlin 66); Became **MM4057**; TOC/RAF 29.7.44 - To Italy (ItAF) 30.5.46; Fate unknown

PT677 Spitfire LF.IXe (Merlin 66); Became **MM4060**; TOC/RAF 29.7.44 - To Italy (ItAF) 26.6.47; Fate unknown

PT957 Spitfire LF.IXe (Merlin 66); Became **MM4076**; TOC/RAF 30.8.44 - To Italy (ItAF) 30.5.46; Fate unknown

PT994 Spitfire LF.IXe (Merlin 66); Became **MM4143**; TOC/RAF 30.8.44 - To Italy (ItAF) 26.6.47; Fate unknown

PV115 Spitfire LF.IXe (Merlin 66); Became **MM4097**; TOC/RAF 2.8.44 - To Italy (ItAF) 26.6.47; Fate unknown

PV122 Spitfire LF.IXe (Merlin 66); Became **MM4088**; TOC/RAF 2.8.44 - To Italy (ItAF) 27.6.46; Fate unknown

PV140 Spitfire LF.IXe (Merlin 66); Became **MM4286**; TOC/RAF 5.9.44; ex TuAF – To Italy (ItAF), arr Brindisi in 1949; MSA air depot; SVL (Flying School Lecce) 19.5.49; SOC short time later

PV270 Spitfire LF.IXe (Merlin 66); Became **MM4014**; TOC/RAF 28.9.44 - To Italy (ItAF) 26.6.47; 5° Stormo by 15.12.47; Vickers-Armstrongs 5.12.49; Later sold to Israel (*2080*) 1952; Delivery No 0809; Re-sold to Burma (*UB424*) later - **SURVIVOR**
NOTE: Painted in Burma as "UB425"; Sold to USA 1999; Now in New Zealand for restoration

PV359 Spitfire LF.IXe (Merlin 66); Became **MM4022**; TOC/RAF 12.10.44 - To Italy (ItAF) 26.6.47; Fate unknown

RK803 Spitfire LF.IXe (Merlin 66); Became **MM4287**; TOC/RAF 21.9.44; ex TuAF – To Italy (ItAF), arr Brindisi in 1949; MSA air depot; SVL (Flying School Lecce) 19.5.49; SOC short time later

RR191 Spitfire LF (FR) IXe (Merlin 66) Became **MM4119**; TOC/RAF 5.9.44 - To Italy (ItAF) 26.6.47; 5° Stormo by 15.12.47; SRA at Guidonia (for camera installation); To NSV (Experimental Flying Unit) in 1948; To 1° RTA 16.11.48; Later sold to Israel in 1951/52

RR204 Spitfire LF.IXe (Merlin 66); Became **MM4011**; TOC/RAF 18.9.44 - To Italy (ItAF) 26.6.47; Fate unknown

RR235 Spitfire HF.IXe (Merlin 70); Became **MM4112**; TOC/RAF 14.10.44 - To Italy (ItAF) 26.6.47; Fate unknown

RR239 Spitfire HF.IXe (Merlin 70); Became **MM4091**; TOC/RAF 18.10.44 - To Italy (ItAF) 30.5.46; Fate unknown

RR251 Spitfire HF.IXe (Merlin 70); Became **MM4113**; TOC/RAF 14.10.44 - To Italy (ItAF) 26.6.47; 5° Stormo 15.12.47; To 1° RTA 13.7.49; Later sold to Israel in 1951/52
NOTE: Survived partly (wings to TE517 later)

SM171 Spitfire LF.IXe (Merlin 66); Became **MM4006**; TOC/RAF 2.10.44 - To Italy (ItAF) 30.5.46; 51° Stormo; Engine failure, force-landed, Cat.E 15.9.47, SOC

SM173 Spitfire LF.IXe (Merlin 66); Became **MM4007**; TOC/RAF 5.10.44 - To Italy (ItAF) 26.6.47; Fate unknown

SM174 Spitfire LF.IXe (Merlin 66); Became **MM4089**; TOC/RAF 2.10.44 - To Italy (ItAF) 27.6.46; Fate unknown

SM441 Spitfire LF.IXe (Merlin 66); TOC/RAF 12.10.44 - To Italy (ItAF) 26.6.47; Unknown unit, crashed, Cat.E2 in 9.47, SOC

SM445 Spitfire LF.IXe (Merlin 66); Became **MM4028**; TOC/RAF 17.10.44 - To Italy (ItAF) 30.5.46; Fate unknown

TB909 Spitfire HF.IXe (Merlin 70); Became **MM4111** (also allotted MM4140 in error); TOC/RAF 3.3.45 - To Italy (ItAF) 26.6.47; Fate unknown

TB983 Spitfire HF.IXe (Merlin 70); Became **MM4078**; TOC/RAF 3.3.45 - To Italy (ItAF) 26.6.47; RVSM at Centocelle ('SM33'); Fire Fighting Practice at Guidonia, burnt 12.12.51, SOC

Check list of Italian & RAF Serial Nos

Italian Serial MM	RAF Serial No.	Italian Serial MM	RAF Serial No.	Italian Serial MM	RAF Serial No.
4000	ML129	4054	PT654	4108	MJ829
4001	JK130	4055	ER655	4109	MJ841
4002	ML134	4056	PT666	4110	MK906
4003	ML139	4057	PT667	4111 *)	TB909
4004	MK156	4058	MJ668	4112	RR235
4005	JK165	4059	MJ673	4113	RR251
4006	SM171	4060	PT677	4114	MK555
4007	SM173	4061	JK720	4115	EN144
4008	MK193	4062	MH720	4116	EN145
4009	ML193	4063	MJ731	4117	MK155
4010	MK194	4064	MK770	4118	NH184
4011	RR204	4065	JK784	4119	RR191
4012	JL251	4066	MH785	4120	MK207
4013	ES257	4067	JK392	4121	PL328
4014	PV270	4068	ER821	4122	PL388
4015	MJ297	4069	EP829	4123	ML410
4016	NH297	4070	MJ830	4124	MK413
4017	MK302	4071	EP886	4125	ML416
4018	NH307	4072	MH896	4126	PT481
4019	NH319	4073	MH947	4127	MJ527
4020	PL330	4074	LZ949	4128	MH985
4021	MJ358	4075	LZ952	4129	PT656
4022	PV359	4076	PT957	4130 **)	NH599
4023	MA369	4077	MK375	4131	MJ561
4024	ML371	4078	TB983	4132	MK569
4025	PT396	4079	MJ996	4133	MJ630
4026	PT414	4080	MK636	4134	MH648
4027	NH431	4081	MA315	4135	MK679
4028	SM445	4082	MK227	4136	MH691
4029	EN445	4083	MK154	4137	MJ778
4030	MA447	4084	MK805	4138	EN843
4031	MA453	4085	MK419	4139	MJ849
4032	PL458	4086	MA426	4140 *)	(TB909)
4033	PT460	4087	MJ525	4141	MH954
4034	NH468	4088	PV122	4142	LZ991
4035	MA471	4089	SM174	4143	PT994
4036	EN510	4090	ML180	4284	MH599
4037	MH526	4091	RR239	4285	MH945
4038	EN583	4092	MH997	4286	PV140
4039	MJ587	4093	PT653	4287	RK803
4040 **)	MA559?	4094	MJ730		
4041	MH602	4095	NH242	Without Italian MM-No's (crashed before 16 December 1947):	
4042	MH604	4096	NH247		
4043	MH615	4097	PV115		
4044	MA617	4098	MJ404	----	EP758
4045	MA618	4099	PL127	----	ER893
4046	MH619	4100	PT462	----	MA256
4047	MH621	4101	MK557	----	MA751
4048	PT625	4102	MJ571	----	MJ955
4049	MA630	4103	EN630	----	MK586
4050	MA632	4104	NH182	----	MK916
4051	EN632	4105	NH426	----	PL164
4052	MH635	4106	EN635	----	PT590
4053	EF649	4107	MH779	----	SM441

*) MM4140 also allotted to TB909, which was already MM4111
**) NH599 to MM4130 & MM4040; one could been MA559, perhaps

SURVIVORS

In Italy
MK805 (MM4084), ItAF Museum Vigna di Valle, on display.

Abroad
EN145 (*2078*), IDF/AF Museum Hatzerim, Israel, display;
MJ730 (*2066*), airworthy, now US (N730MJ);
PT462 (*2067*), airworthy, now UK (G-CTIX);
PV270 (*2080, UB424*), ex Hmawbi, Burma, sold to USA, resold to New Zealand.
(The ex Indian Spitfire MT719, which was flown with Italian civil Reg. *I-SPIT*, was sold to the USA in 1995)

ITALIAN abbreviations

AMI	Aeronautica Militare Italiano, the name of the Italian Air Force from 3 June 1946
ANR	Aeronautica Nazionale Repubblicana, Northern Italy, fought with the Axis after the armistice from 8 September 1943
BA	Basi Aeree (Airbase, AFB)
CAV	Centro Addestramento Volo (Flight Training Centre), for each ZAT; Spitfires served in Nos.1, 3 & 4 ZAT
FU	Fuori Uso (date of a fatal crash, cat.E or written off)
GrSc	Gruppo Scuola (School Group of SVL)
ItAF	Italian Air Force - see "AMI" and "RA"
MM	Matricola Militare (ItAF serial numbers)
MSA	Materiale Speciale Aeronautico (a depot for aircraft stores/parts/equipment on every Italian base)
NSV	Nucleo Sperimentale Volo (previous name of RSV)
NV	Flying Section
NVRC	Nucleo Voli del Raggruppamento Caccia (Flying Training Centre)
RA	Regia Aeronautica, the name of the Royal Italian Air Force from 28 March 1923 until 2 June 1946
RS	Small repair by the Squadrons
RSRA	Riparabile presso Squadra Riparazione Aeroporto (repairable at aerodrome Repair Section, see SRA)
RSV	Reparto Sperimentale Volo (Experimental Flying Unit), ex NSV
RTA	Reparto Tecnoccia Aeronautic (repair & overhaul); e.g. 3rd RTA at Lecce
RTU	Reparto Tecnico Unita Aerea (Technical Unit) at Lecce. It later developed to several RTAs in various locations (e.g. 3rd RTA at Lecce)
RVSM	Reparto Volo Stato Maggiore (Air Force Staff Flying Unit) at Centocelle near Rome
SA	Squadra Aerea (Air Corps)
ScAdd	Scuola Addestramento Caccia e Bombardieri (Fighter and Bomber Training School, similar to an OTU) at Frosinone
SRA	Aircraft Repair Section (Squadron maintenance & depot)
SRAM	Aircraft repair in special facilities or by manufacturers

ITALY – JAPAN – LATVIA

Surviving Spitfire LF.IXc MM4084 (ex MK805) seen outside the Rome Aero Club hangar at Urbe in July 1989 bearing its original RAF serial number. Prior to this it had been painted as "MM4079" and marked "A-32". It is now in the Italian Air Force Museum at Vigna di Valle.

	(approx. similar to RiW of the RAF); Later work done by RTU
Sqn	Squadriglia (Sqns/Squadriglie)
SSS	Scuola Specialisti e Sottufficiali, at Caserta
Stormo	Wing (CO: Lt Col), with two or three Gruppi (CO: Major), each with two or three Squadriglie (CO: Capt)
SVL	Scuola di Volo di Lecce (Central Flying School), at Lecce); Part of the 3rd School Group
ZAT	Zona Aerea Territoriale (Air Traffic Zone); each ZAT had its own CAV.

References:
Italian Air Force, Flying Review 1962, Vol.XVII No.12, p.20.
GLI Spitfires dell' AMI, by Gregory Alegi,
   Aerofan February 1982, p. 22.
Italian Spitfire Saga, Fly Past July 1983, p. 49.

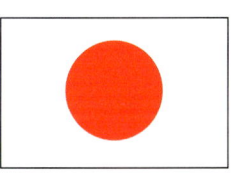

JAPAN

In April 1937 Japan asked for delivery of one Spitfire F.Ia, but this was not acceptable to the British authorities.

Major differences existed between Japan and America, culminating in the surprise attack by the Japanese on Pearl Harbor on 7th December 1941, resulting in the USA joining the Allied powers and Japan becoming one of the Axis powers. After the surrender of Japan in 1945, units of the Allied Forces occupied the country, including RAF Spitfires of Nos.11 & 27 Sqns, ACSEA. However, Spitfires were never bought by that country, nor have they ever been purchased by private collectors.

LATVIA

In January 1938 Latvia enquired about a delivery of Spitfires. This request was confirmed with an order for twelve Spitfire Mk.Ia on 24th May 1939, but the contract was cancelled when the Soviet Union occupied the territory of Latvia in June 1940.

The Soviet Air Force then served in Latvia from June 1940, except from 1941 until 1944 when Germany controlled this country.

Remarks:
The Latvian Army was re-named the 24th Territorial Corps of the Soviet Army in 1940.

Map: see Lithuania.

LITHUANIA

Lithuania asked for delivery of 14 Spitfire Mk.Ia on 12th March 1937, and in October 1937 a further enquiry arrived for a licence to build Spitfires. However, this inquiry never had a priority in the list of the Foreign Office orders, dated 17th November 1938. In the absence of Air Ministry approval, it eventually lapsed.

The Red Air Force of occupation then served in Lithuania from June 1940, except from 1941 until 1944 when Germans controlled this country.

Remarks:
The Lithuanian Army was re-named the 23rd Territorial Corps of the Soviet Army in 1940.

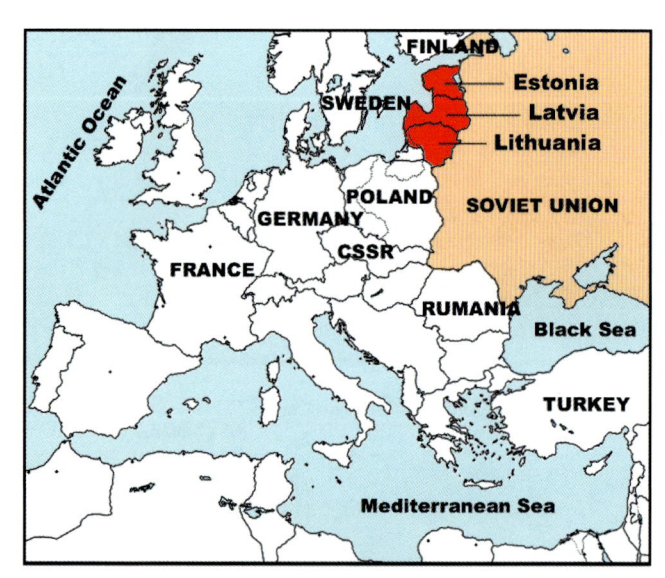

BALTIC interests for Spitfires

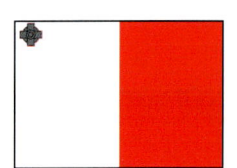

MALTA

During the Second World War Malta was held by British and Allied troops despite continuous German and Italian attacks. The RAF operated from airfields at Hal Far, Krendi, Luqa, Safi, Ta Kali (Ta' Qali) and also Kalafrana seaplane base. The Spitfire units Nos.69 (PR only), 126, 185, 229, 249, 683 Sqns, No.1435 Flight and No.40 (SAAF) Sqn operated from Malta bases.

One incomplete Spitfire (EN199) survived, and a group of enthusiasts has completed reconstructing this into a whole aircraft for the National War Museum at Valletta, Malta. In addition, two salvaged remains were exhibited in the Malta National Museum at Valletta, one a Spitfire Mk.Vc and the other a Seafire Mk.IIc, both having been recovered from the sea around Malta. One of these is now in the UK.

Individual Histories of Survivors in Malta

BR108　Spitfire F.Vc/trop (Merlin 46). TOC/RAF 8.3.42; With No.249 Sqn when shot down into sea 8.7.42; Remains salvaged from Marsalforn Bay, Gozo, in 1968; To National War Museum, Fort St.Elmo, Valletta 5.75 for exhibition (**wreckage of fuselage and wings only**)

EN199　Spitfire F.IXc (Merlin 60). TOC/RAF 1.12.42; With No.73 Sqn when blown over at Luqa in a gale on 23.12.46 (Cat.E & w/o). - Presented by Air Vice-Marshal KBB Lloyd 27.5.47; Displayed in Civil Defence area at Targa Gap; Air Scouts HQ at Floriana, Malta in 1947; Later wings to UK, but fuselage and tail section remained in Civil Defence yard, Malta; To National War Museum, Fort St.Elmo, Valletta in 1990; Total restoration at Ta' Qali with Merlin 500 engine, roll-out 10.7.93; Restoration completed with wings, marked '*Mary Rose*', displayed in Palace Square, Valletta 5.95; Then exhibited in the National War Museum, Valletta; now in the Malta Aviation Museum at Ta' Qali – **SURVIVOR**

MB293　Seafire LF.IIc (Merlin 46). To RNDA 12.42: With No.879 Sqn and HMS '*Attacker*' c.9.44 - 10.44. Wreck recovered near Gozo island 25.4.94; To the National War Museum, Fort St.Elmo, Valletta for exhibition (**wreck only**); Later stored in the museum's restoration facility at Ta Kali; Sold, exchanged to the UK 3.01 - **SURVIVOR**

MALTA

Right: Derelict Spitfire F.IXc EN199 outside the Air Scouts Headquarters at Floriana, Malta. It had been written off with No.73 Sqn when it was blown backwards into a quarry at Luqa during a gale on 23rd December 1946.

Below: Spitfire F.IXc EN199 was totally restored at Ta'Qali with a Merlin 500 engine, being rolled out on 10th July 1993. It is seen here displayed in Palace Square, Valletta on VE-Day 1995 marked 'Mary Rose'.

Bottom: Surviving Spitfire F.IXc EN199 in the Malta Aviation Museum at Ta'Qali. [MAP]

NETHERLANDS

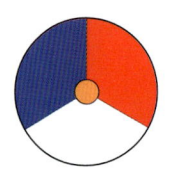

A row of Dutch Air Force Spitfires in a large hangar at Leeuwarden in 1948.

The Netherlands made an enquiry in August 1937 to buy a single Spitfire Mk.Ia, then requested on 29th July 1938 to build 40 more under licence. Supermarine offered delivery for £9,335 each. In the priority list of the Foreign Office dated 17th November 1938 the inquiry reached place No.9, for 18 to 36 Spitfires. Test flying by Dutch pilots was carried out in September 1939, but with the outbreak of the Second World War the order was cancelled.

Netherlands pilots flew Spitfires during the war in No.167 Sqn RAF, this being re-numbered No.322 (Dutch) Sqn on 12th June 1943.

After WWII the Netherlands rebuilt its Air Force and used Spitfires out of surplus RAF stocks from mid-1946 for pilot flying and technical training. The Netherlands Air Force allotted the serial numbers **H-1 to H-35** for the first batch of Spitfire LF.IXs, and numbers **H-97 to H-99** for the trainer aircraft Spitfire T.IXs respectively. These being carried from August 1947.

The Netherlands Government had controlled the Netherlands East Indies ("*Dutch Indië*") - Java, Sumatra, Celebes, Moluccas, and partly Borneo and New Guinea - since 1596. Japan occupied these islands in 1942 and established the Indonesian Republic, which sought independence after the war. The Netherlands, however, attempted to retake control with military power. For this task they bought a second batch of 20 Spitfire LF.IXs in 1946, these remaining in storage in the UK until May 1947, when they were despatched by road to Tilbury Docks and shipped to Java in June 1947. On arrival No.322 Sqn temporarily numbered the aircraft as *H-101 to H-120*, but at the end of 1948 the Dutch Air Force serial numbers **H-50 to H-69** were allotted.

The three Spitfire T.IX conversions H-97 (ex MK715), H-98 (ex BS274) and H-99 (ex BS147) at Eastleigh awaiting delivery to Valkenburg on 26th March 1948.
[Vickers-Armstrongs]

NETHERLANDS

With the arrival of the Gloster Meteor at JVS Twenthe in June 1948, Spitfires became second-line aircraft. They were later used for weekend flying by reserve pilots. After its return from Java No.322 Sqn used these Spitfires from February 1950.

Fifteen of the eighteen Java Spitfires, which remained in crates after their arrival in Holland, were sold to Belgium on 30th April 1952 and reached the Belgian Air Force (BAF) after overhaul by Fokker at Schiphol.

The surviving Dutch Spitfires was all ordered to be struck off charge in September 1953.

Dutch Spitfire units of the RAF

No.167 Sqn - code: 'VL'.
Formed as (Fighter) Sqn at Scorton 6th April 1942, with a Dutch flight, used Spitfire Mk.Vb/c; Disbanded (and re-numbered as No.322 Sqn) at Woodvale 12th June 1943.

No.322 Sqn - code: 'VL', changed in 1944 to '3W '.
Formed at Woodvale 12th June 1943 from Dutch personnel of No.167 Sqn; Based at Woensdrecht NL from 3rd January 1945; Disbanded at Wunstorf in Germany 7th October 1945.
Spitfire Mk.Vb/c, XIV, IX & XVI.

Netherlands Air Force

The Netherlands Air Force (NethAF, *Dutch Air Force*) was named "*Leger Luchtmacht Nederland*" (LLN) from 1945 to 1948. Then this changed to "*Luchtstrijdkrachten*" (LSK), until being re-named to "*Koninklijke Luchtmacht*" (KLu) in March 1953 – today internationally known as the "Royal Netherlands Air Force" (RNethAF).

The Netherlands Air Force received
(under Comm.Nos.291, 348, 426 & 559) =
    35 LF.IXc/e for the JVS (Nos. H-1 to H-35)
    20 LF.IXc/e for No.322 Sqn Java (Nos. H-50 to H-69)
    3 T.IX for the JVS (Nos. H-97 to H-99)
    11 Mks.V, IX, XVI, XIX, F.22 (on loan)
        for technical training at NSTT Langham, UK
    8 Mks.XI, XIV, XVI
        for technical training of LETS Deelen, Netherlands

Total = 77 Spitfires.

A further two Spitfires were privately owned in Holland.

Spitfire Units of the Netherlands Air Force

Netherlands Air Force Technical Training School (NSTT) Langham, Norfolk, England

The School of Technical Training (NSTT) opened at Langham in June 1946 to provide ground instruction for Dutch Air Force personnel. Eleven Spitfires arrived on loan from the RAF on 3rd October 1946 for this purpose, remaining in use until July 1947, when the Netherlands personnel went to LETS Deelen.
Commanding Officer:
Lt Kol G van der Tak   15.7.46 to 24.9.47

LETS at Deelen in Holland

Technical training commenced at the Luchtmacht Electronische and Technische School at Deelen (near Arnhem) in Holland in July 1947. Eight Spitfires were received for ground instructional purposes, the first arrived at AFB Twenthe on 10th July 1947 and another on 31st July 1947. They were all flown from Twenthe to Deelen on 6th August 1947, remaining in use until l951/52.
Commanding Officer:
Lt Kol G van der Tak   25.9.47 to 1.7.51

Jachtvliegschool (JVS) at Twenthe in Holland

This Fighter Pilots School (OTU) was formed on 1st March 1946 and opened at Twenthe 19th July 1946, at first with Oxfords. Spitfires arrived some time later, in all 35 aircraft (serial numbers **H-1 to H-35**). By the end of November 1946, 21 Spitfire LF.IX were in use, being followed until October 1948 by a further 14 Mk.IX. They carried the serials in big letters on the fuselage.

No.322 Sqn was re-formed at Twenthe on 17th February 1947, being despatched to the Netherlands East Indies on 10 September 1947.

In March 1948 three Spitfire trainer (T.IX) arrived the JVS at Twenthe (Serial Numbers **H-97 to H-99**).

The JVS used Spitfires until 1st June 1950, then only Gloster Meteor for the regular flying. Members of No.322 Sqn, which arrived from Java in December 1949, then flew the Spitfires of the JVS.

Commanding Officers of the JVS:
Maj W M van den Bosch	1946
Maj J L Flinterman	7.47
Maj A J "Rooie" de Vries	
Maj W M van den Bosch	1950
Kapt Johnny W Dekker	1951
Maj A J W Wijting	1951/52

No.322 Sqn in Java, Dutch India

Ordered on 27th September 1946, the re-formation of No.322 Sqn officially began at Twenthe on 17th February 1947. After re-commencement of flying in March 1947 the training for this unit continued until 10th September 1947, when No.322 Sqn was despatched to the Netherlands East Indies. Pilots of No.322 Sqn, who had trained at the JVS Twenthe, and the technical personnel arrived at Tandjong Priok (Batavia) harbour in Java on 7th October 1947.Twenty Spitfire LF.IXc/e were bought from RAF stocks and despatched to Java from Tilbury docks in SS *Rotti* (Comm.No.559) 13th June 1947, arriving at Tandjong Priok on 13 July 1947. The Spitfires were transported to Kalidjati airfield for assembly and test flying. In February 1948, No.322 Sqn was at full strength with twelve Spitfires. Reserve aircraft were stored in an aircraft depot at Andir near Bandoeng.

At first the Spitfires were provisionally numbered *H-101 to H-120*, these being later changed to **H-50 to H-69**. The aircraft carried large fuselage serials. In December 1948 both the provisional and the later numbers were in use (e.g. MK205 had 'H-101', MH485 carried 'H-51'), but from April 1949 only the newer numbers were used.

Netherlands East Indies (Dutch Indies), now Indonesia

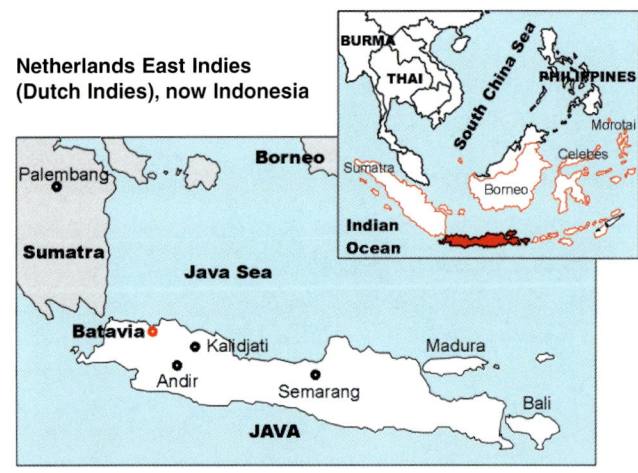

Batavia [harbour Tandjong Priok] now Djakarta

The first flight of a Spitfire over Java was recorded on 24th October 1947 (NH238); the twentieth aircraft had its first flight over Java on 16th March 1948 (MH439). The operational base was Semarang, with Kalidjati being used as a base for overhaul and inspection. No.322 Sqn used the Spitfires for ground attack missions until 15th September 1949. Then, after a heavy protest by the United Nations, the Netherlands eventually accepted the sovereignty of Indonesia with agreement from 2nd November 1949. The Squadron returned home on 30th November 1949, arrived Holland in December 1949. The surviving 18 Spitfires followed in crates in July 1950. Fifteen of these were sold to the Belgian Air Force (BAF Serial Numbers *SM-29* to *SM-43*) on 30th April 1952. The other three were used for spares.

Commanding Officer:
Maj WM van den Bosch (from 9.47 to 1950)

No.322 Sqn back in Holland

Squadron personnel arrived in Holland at AFB Twenthe in December 1949, but the unit was non-active. The JVS was operating Spitfires and Meteors at that time.

Pilots of No.322 Sqn used the Spitfires of the JVS for monthly flying training ("weekend-warriors") from 1st February 1950. The unit re-formed and build up its strength as an LSK unit flying Spitfires regularly from February 1951. The Squadron became operational in summer of that year. Then the Spitfires were painted silver and carried the squadron code '3W', but with arabic numbers instead of individual letters. On 31st August 1951 the unit moved to AFB Soesterberg, where in July 1952 it split into two sections, one with Meteors and one with Spitfires until September 1953.

Commanding Officers:
Maj HC 'Bas' Asjes 1.6.50
Maj Jhr B Sandberg 15.2.51
Maj W de Wolf 1.11.52
Maj AJW Wijting 17.3.53

Schreiner Aero Ypenburg, Holland

Four Spitfires of No.322 Sqn (formerly JVS aircraft) went to the Schreiner Company on loan for target towing duties. The first two (BS147 & MK475) were flown in September 1953 to Aero Ypenburg, where they received modifications for the new owner and were Civil reg. as *PH-NFO* (ex MK475) on 22nd September 1954, *PH-NFN* (ex BS147) on 6th October 1954.. On 13th July 1955 *PH-NFP* (ex PT986) followed, then *PH-NFR* (ex MJ828) on 3rd January 1956.

For target towing duties the Spitfires were modified at Ypenburg and became orange colour overall. They were based at the Texel airfield. Withdrawal from the register was recorded on 7th August 1957.

Other users

One Spitfire Mk.IX was in use by the Technical College at Delft, and one PR.XI was held by a museum at Rotterdam, dismantled and used for ground instruction only.

Individual Histories

W3250 Spitfire LF.Vb (Merlin 50M); TOC/RAF 18.5.41; Became GI No. *5938M*; ex No.12 SoTT – Arr NethAF (on loan), NSTT Langham 25.11.46

BS147 Spitfire T.IX (Merlin 66); Became **H-99**; TOC/RAF 1943; ex No.122 Sqn; To V.A. (G-15-1), test flight as T.IX 22.3.48 - Del to Holland 23.3.48; JVS ('H-99') 26.3.48; To Fokker (MI) 24.2.49; Painted silver, Retd to JVS Twenthe 13.10.49; Used by reserve pilots from 2.50; No.322 Sqn ('3W-22') in 2.51; Engine replaced (No.178859 from BS274) 24.4.52; Belly-landed Soesterberg 13.5.53; Repaired; Service until 9.53; Open storage; On sale 5.54; SOC 4.6.54; CofR No.360 to Schreiner & Co; To Aero Ypenburg 6.10.54 (Civil reg. *PH-NFN* 22.9.54); Test flown 18.8.55; Based at Texel (*Donald Duck* insignia on the cowling); Test flight, overshot landing 22.11.55 (Plt B de Geus); New wing mounted; Crashed on belly-landing 4.5.57 at Texel, reg cancelled 7.8.57; Scrapped

BS274 Spitfire T.IX (Merlin 66); Became **H-98**; TOC/RAF 20.12.42; ex A&AEE; To V.A. 1.47; Converted to T.IX; First flight (N-42) 17.3.48 - Arr Holland 23.3.48; JVS 26.3.48; Belly-landed Twenthe 16.5.49; To Fokker 28.6.49 (MI); Painted silver, retd Twenthe 14.8.50; No.322 Sqn ('H-98'), crashed at Volkel, undercarriage failed, belly-landed, Cat.E 7.2.51; SOC 7.5.51; w/o 13.6.51 (for spare parts)

NOTE: Mispainted as "BF274"; Code "3W-20" allotted, but not applied; Engine to BS147 in 4.52

BS4..? Spitfire F.IXc (Merlin 61); TOC/RAF 1942 - To the Technical College at Delft in 4.46; Broken up 1958; Wings there 1960/70; Remains collected for Spitfire restoration in UK early 1980

NOTE: Probably BS461

EN560 Spitfire LF.IXc (Merlin 66); Became H-118, later **H-54**; TOC/RAF in 3.43; ex No.485 Sqn; Selected for Netherlands 1946; Storage until 16.5.47; - Shipped to Java, arr Tandjong Priok 13.7.47; First flight NethAF 19.2.48 (Plt T Bruggink); Storage at air depot Andir 4.48, also by 26.11.48; Shipped to Holland 1950, storage; Cat.E1 & SOC 12.3.53 (used for spare parts)

NOTE: Only storage in Java, not flown with No 322 Sqn; Serial Nos. H-118 & H-54 allotted, but not painted on aircraft

MH415 Spitfire LF.IXc (Merlin 66); Became H-108, later **H-65** from 8.48; TOC/RAF 8.43; ex No.222 Sqn; Selected for Netherlands 16.8.46; Tilbury 15.5.47 – Shipped to Java, arr Tandjong Priok 13.7.47; First flight NethAF 22.12.47; No.322 Sqn 30.1.48; Air depot Andir 9.49; Shipped to Holland 1950; At Rotterdam from 1950 until 1953; Sold to Belgium 30.4.52; Fokker (B-12), test flown 14.2.53; To BAF (*SM-40*) 8.4.53; Later to COGEA (*OO-ARD*); Extant; Via UK (Civil reg. *G-AVDJ* 29.12.66) to 'Connie' Edwards, Big Springs, USA (*N415MH*) 11.68; In storage, offered for sale 2002 - **SURVIVOR**

MH424 Spitfire LF.IXc (Merlin 66); Became H-106, later **H-53** from 8.48; TOC/RAF 11.8.43; ex No.222 Sqn; Sold the Netherlands 5.9.46; Tilbury 15.5.47 - Shipped to Java, arr Tandjong Priok 13.7.47; First flight NethAF 13.12.47; No.322 Sqn 22.12.47; Kalidjati 2.48; Test flown 25.2.48; No.322 Sqn by 19.12.48; Air depot Andir 9.50; Shipped to Holland; Rotterdam 1950 until 1952; Sold to Belgium 30.4.52; Fokker (B-4), test flown 23.6.52; To BAF (*SM-32*) 8.8.52

NOTE: *Donald Duck* emblem on the cowling, bright orange spinner

MH434 Spitfire LF.IXc (Merlin 66); Became H-105, later **H-68** from 7.48; TOC/RAF 13.8.43; ex No.222 Sqn; Selected for Netherlands 7.46; Tilbury 6.47 – Shipped to Java, arr Tandjong Priok 13.7.47; First flights NethAF 31.10.47; Test flight 10.11.47, test of drop tank 17.11.47; No.322 Sqn 22.12.47, also by 19.12.48; Short of fuel, belly-landed Semarang 15.4.49 (Lt G Nijwening); Repaired and flown

Spitfire T.IX H-99 (ex BS147) in flight with the Jachtvliegschool at Twenthe around 1948/49. It later became civilianised as PH-NFN.

Spitfire T.IX PH-NFN (ex H-99) was originally F.IX BS147, serving for a time with No.322 Sqn at Twenthe and later Soesterberg as '3W-22'. It was civilianised in 1954, but was scrapped after a wheels-up landing on 4th May 1957. [R C B Ashworth]

Surviving Spitfire LF.IXc H-68 (ex MH434) was originally H-105 until July 1948. Shipped to Java, it is seen here probably on 15th April 1949 when it ran short of fuel and Lt G Nijwening of No.322 Sqn belly-landed at Semarang. It was sold in the UK in 1963, becoming G-ASJV, and is now at Duxford.

from 20.5.49; Air depot Andir 9.49; Shipped to Holland 1950; Sold to Belgium 30.4.52; Fokker (B-13), test flown 10.3.53 & 29.4.53 (Plt More); To BAF (*SM-41*) 9.10.53; Later to COGEA (*OO-ARA*) 26.3.56; To UK, delivered to Tim A Davies, Elstree, Hertfordshire (Civil reg. *G-ASJV* 2.7.63); To T G Mahaddie/Film Aviation Services, Elstree 11.67 (flown in Battle of Britain film in 1968); To Adrian C Swire, Booker & Duxford 2.69; To Ray Hanna/Nalfire Aviation Ltd, Duxford 14.4.83; To Old Flying Machine Co, Duxford 1987; Rebuild completed 1995 and flown as "MH434/ZD-B"; Stored without engine 7.99 - **SURVIVOR**

MH439 Spitfire LF.IXc (Merlin 66); Became H-120, later **H-56**; TOC/RAF 13.8.43; ex Nos.222 & 350 Sqns; Selected for Netherlands autumn 1946; Tilbury 6.47 – Shipped to Java, arr Tandjong Priok 13.7.47; First flight NethAF 16.3.48; Test flown 19.3.48; Storage at air depot Andir 25.3.48, also by 26.11.48; No.322 Sqn by 19.12.48; Engine failed on take-off, landed wheels up, propeller damaged 27.1.49 (Lt G Nijwening); AD Andir 9.49; Shipped to Holland in 1950; Sold to Belgium 30.4.52; Fokker (B-5), test flights 28.8.52 to 3.10.52; To BAF (*SM-33*) 3.10.52

MH473 Spitfire LF.IXc (Merlin 66); TOC/RAF 20.8.43; ex No.485 Sqn & CFE; Became GI No. *6142M* - Arr NethAF (on loan), NSTT Langham 10.10.46; Retd to RAF 7.47

MH477 Spitfire LF.IXc (Merlin 66); Became **H-6**; TOC/RAF 16.8.43; ex Nos.341, 411, 33 Sqns and USAAF; Selected for Netherlands 23.7.46 - Arr Twenthe (JVS) 31.7.46; Fokker (MI) 14.5.49; Painted silver, storage; Retd Twenthe 10.5.50, for monthly flyers; No.322 Sqn 2.51, marked '3W-6' in mid-1951; Engine changed (No.179731) 7.5.52; Engine exploded in flight, belly-landed Soesterberg, burnt, Cat.E 11.9.52; SOC 9.10.52 (w/o 4.6.54); Scrapped

MH485 Spitfire LF.IXc (Merlin 66); Became H-102, later **H-51** from 4.48; TOC/RAF 18.8.43; ex Nos.129 & 66 Sqns; Selected for Netherlands 16.10.46; Tilbury 19.5.47 – Shipped to Java, arr Tandjong Priok 13.7.47; Kalidjati 11.47; First flight NethAF 5.12.47 (Plt Tub Bruggink); Test flown 13.12.47; No.322 Sqn 22.12.47; Undercarriage failed, belly-landed 30.1.48 (Kapt F de Grave); Retd No. 322 Sqn (reported by 19.12.48); Air depot Andir 9.49; Shipped to Holland in 1950; Sold to Belgium 30.4.52; Fokker (B-2), test flown 24.4.52 (Plt J Mol), also 4.6.52; To BAF (*SM-30*), but landed wheels-up on arrival 4.6.52

MH723 Spitfire LF.IXc (Merlin 66); Became **H-7**; TOC/RAF 14.9.43; ex Nos.317, 66, 485 Sqns; Test flown (Lt F Vijzelaar) 16.9.46, selected for Netherlands - Arr Twenthe 1.10.46; To Valkenburg 1.10.46; JVS 3.10.46; 'H-7' marked in 9.47; Engine changed (date unknown); Fokker (MI) 20.6.49; Painted silver, storage; Retd Twenthe 22.6.50, for monthly flyers; No.322 Sqn 2.51; marked '3W-7' in mid-1951; Based Soesterberg from 31.8.51; Engine changed (No.181069) 15.4.53; Crashed landing 9.53; SOC 4.6.54; Gate guardian at Leeuwarden 7.54; Burnt in 1956

MH725 Spitfire LF.IXc (Merlin 66); Became H-112, later **H-63** from 1.49; TOC/RAF 1.10.43; ex Nos 317 & 401 Sqns; Selected for the Netherlands 1946; Tilbury 15.5.47 – Shipped to Java, arr Tandjong Priok 13.7.47; First flight NethAF 20.1.48; Test flown 22.1.48; No.322 Sqn, belly-landed 23.1.48 (Plt G Nijwening); Storage air depot Andir from 2.48 to 12.48; No.322 Sqn by 19.12.48; AD Andir 9.49; Shipped to Holland 1950; Sold to Belgium 30.4.52; Fokker (B-10), test flights 22.1 to 26.3.53; To BAF (*SM-38*) 26.3.53

MH940 Spitfire F.IXc (Merlin 63); TOC/RAF 26.9.43; ex Nos.331, 611, 312 Sqns and CFE; Became GI No. *6146M* - Arr NethAF (on loan), NSTT Langham 3.10.46; Retd RAF 7.47

MJ143 Spitfire LF.IXc (Merlin 66); Became **H-1**; TOC/RAF 16.10.43; ex Nos.485 & 66 Sqns; Selected for Netherlands 1946 - Arr Valkenburg 17.7.46, then to JVS ('H-1'); Public presentation Twenthe in July 1946; Engine changed 5.4.49; Fokker (MI) 20.8.49; Painted silver, storage; Retd Twenthe 16.9.50; Valkenburg 10.50 & 11.50; Monthly flyers at Twenthe from 2.50; No.322 Sqn from 2.51; Marked '3W-1' in 7.51; grounded 9.53; SOC 5.54; Transferred for storage to Gilze-Rijen 20.7.54; To Aeroplanorama Museum, Schiphol, for display 28.3.60; Militaire Luchtvaart Museum, Soesterberg 18.6.68; Displayed as 'H-1' from 26.4.73; Loaned to Deelen for 60th Anniversary of RNethAF from 30.6.73 to 4.7.73; Placed in storage 9.76; Back on display as 'H-1' in 4.77 (temporary Rotterdam in 1985) - **SURVIVOR**

MJ152 Spitfire LF.IXc (Merlin 66); Became **H-31**; TOC/RAF 16.10.43; ex Nos 317 & 401 Sqns; Selected for the Netherlands 1946; Dagenham docks 6.47, shipped to Netherlands - Arr Amsterdam 13.6.47; To Leeuwarden AFB; JVS Twenthe ('H-31') 10.10.48, storage; Erected until 3.12.49, used by monthly flyers; Taxying collision with MJ957 ('H-24') at Twenthe, Cat.E 6.4.50 (Plt van Gastel); w/o 5.7.50; Scrapped

MJ271 Spitfire LF.IXc (Merlin 66); Became **H-8**; TOC/RAF 24.10.43; ex Nos.118, 132, 401 Sqns; Test flown 11.11.46 (Plt F Vijzelaar), selected for Netherlands - Arr JVS

Spitfire LF.IXc H-1 (ex MJ143) of the JVS, flown on Public Display at Twenthe in July 1946. [*RNethAF*]

Surviving Spitfire LF.IXc MJ271 in the Aviodome Museum, Schiphol in 1982. It was ex H-8, but was painted up as "H-53" and "MH424" with a Donald Duck motif on the cowling.

Twenthe ('H-8') 25.11.46; Engine changed (No.162999) in 9.48; Fokker Schiphol (MI) 14.6.49; Painted silver; Test flown 26.10.50, 6.11.50 & 13.2.51; Acceptance flight 19.2.51 (Lt Jaap Eden); No.322 Sqn Twenthe in 2.51 (marked '3W-8') in summer 1951; Based Soesterberg from 31.8.51; Last flight by Lt Jan Breman 29.9.53; SOC in 5.54 (w/o 4.6.54); Open storage at Volkel AFB 7.7.54; With No.313 Sqn at Volkel in 1956; "TA-26" painted on the cowling; To War Museum, Delfzijl (incomplete) 6.1.59, exhibited on top of a building; To Anthony Fokker Technical School, Den Haag, for restoration 4.4.73 (Engine No 162999 in 1974); Work continued in the Aviodome Museum, Schiphol from 22.3.78 until 1982; Exhibited at Aviodome as "H-53" & "MH424", with engine No.159933 from 12.1.82 - **SURVIVOR**

MJ361 Spitfire LF.IXc (Merlin 66); Became **H-20**; TOC/RAF 30.11.43; Test flown 11.11.46, selected for Netherlands - Arr JVS Twenthe 25.11.46; Engine failed, force-landed and crashed 25.7.47 (Plt Gys Noyons injured), SOC (w/o 15.3.48)

MJ469 Spitfire LF.IXc (Merlin 66); Became **H-9**; TOC/RAF 8.11.43 - Arr JVS Twenthe 30.7.46; Marked 'H-9' in 1947; Engine changed (No.180589); Fokker (MI) 14.6.49; Retd Twenthe 20.7.50 (flown by Maj HC 'Bas' Asjes); Used by monthly flyers; No.322 Sqn from 2.51 (marked '3W-9' from 20.7.50); Based at Soesterberg from 31.8.51; Communications aircraft of Transport Command Valkenburg from 5.11.51; Crashed on landing, overturned, Soesterberg 22.2.52; SOC 9.53 (w/o 4.6.54); Gate guardian at Twente AFB since 7.54; Display Twenthe-Overmaat 1956; Scrapped 1960

MJ479 Spitfire LF.IXc (Merlin 66); Became **H-10**; TOC/RAF 29.11.43; Test flown Langham 25.6.46 - Arr Twenthe (JVS) 12.7.46; Engine changed (No.186543) 2.4.48; Fokker (MI) 24.2.49; Painted silver; Retd JVS 5.1.50; Used by monthly flyers; No.322 Sqn in 2.51 (marked '3W-10' in 7.51); Engine failed, force-landed wheels-up near Hilversum 10.7.53 (Plt M Determeyer safe); Storage; SOC 4.6.54; Fire Fighting School at Deelen 30.6.54; Burnt out 1955

Spitfire LF.IXc, H-9 (ex MJ469) of the JVS, Twenthe, 1946-50

Spitfire LF.IXc H-11 (ex MJ642) was used by JVS Twenthe between 1946 and 1951, later joining No.322 Sqn.

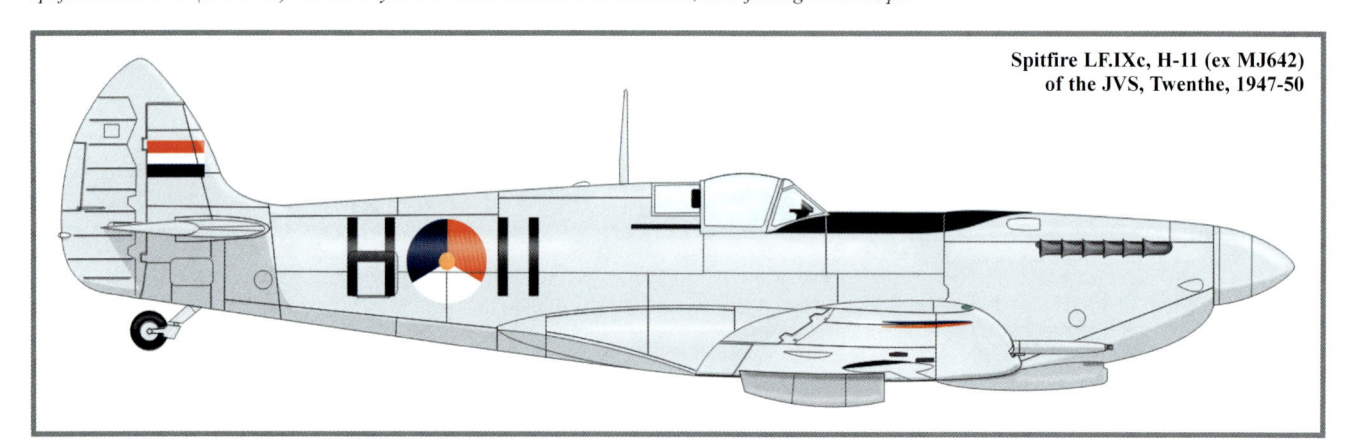

Spitfire LF.IXc, H-11 (ex MJ642) of the JVS, Twenthe, 1947-50

Spitfire LF.IXc H-11 now marked '3W-11' (ex MJ642) with No.322 Sqn, Soesterberg, around 1952/53. It became a gate guardian at Twenthe in 1954, but was scrapped in 1958.
[via R C B Asworth]

NETHERLANDS

MJ536 Spitfire LF.IXc (Merlin 66); Became H-107, later **H-66** from 8.48; TOC/RAF 24.12.43; ex No.411 Sqn; Selected for Netherlands 8.7.46; Tilbury 19.5.47 – Shipped to Java, arr Tandjong Priok 13.7.47; First flight NethAF 21.12.47; No.322 Sqn from 6.1.48; Crashed on landing, brake failure, Cat.E 16.10.48 (Kapt Thijssen), SOC; Abandoned, wreck left behind at Semarang

MJ580 Spitfire LF.IXc (Merlin 66); Became **H-35**; TOC/RAF 29.11.43; Selected for Netherlands 1946; Acceptance flight in UK 13.10.48 - Arr Twenthe (JVS) 27.10.48; Later used by monthly flyers 1950; No.322 Sqn in 2.51 (Painted silver and '3W-5' marked in summer 1951); Engine failure, force-landed wheels-up Hilversum, Cat.E 17.5.52 (Lt Jan Breman safe), SOC (w/o 10.7.52)

MJ614 Spitfire LF.IXc (Merlin 66); Became **H-2**; TOC/RAF 30.11.43; Selected for Netherlands 1946 - Arr Twenthe (JVS) 1.10.46; Fokker (MI) 1948; Painted silver, marked 'H-2'; Retd to JVS 3.5.49; Engine changed (No.181057) 12.9.49; Used by monthly flyers 1950; Exercise "*Cupola*" 8.50; Dived into ground near Etten/Leur, Cat.E 27.8.50 (Lt Jan Welte killed), SOC (w/o 6.11.50)

MJ642 Spitfire LF.IXc (Merlin 66); Became **H-11**; TOC/RAF 4.12.43; Selected for Netherlands 1946; Test flown 12.9.46 - Arr Twenthe (JVS) 31.10.46; Marked 'H-11' in 7.47; Engine changed in 9.48; Prop hit ground low flying, force-landed on belly at Vlieland 3.12.48 (Plt Bill Jansen); To Fokker for repair; Retd JVS Twenthe 21.7.49; Used by monthly flyers 1950; No.322 Sqn in 2.51; Engine changed 25.4.51 (marked '3W-11' in 7.51); Engine changed 28.1.53, changed once more to engine No.178531 on 25.2.53; Last flown in 9.53; SOC 4.6.54; Gate guardian at Twenthe 7.7.54; Scrapped 1958

MJ714 Spitfire LF.IXc (Merlin 66); Became H-117, later **H-67** from 8.48; TOC/RAF 20.12.43; ex Nos 310 & 421 Sqns; Selected for Netherlands 26.7.46; Tilbury 6.47 – Shipped to Java, arr Tandjong Priok 13.7.47; First flight NethAF 4.3.48; Storage air depot Andir 16.3.48, reported there also by 26.11.48; Shipped to Holland 1950; Sold to Belgium 30.4.52; Fokker (B-7), test flown 31.10.52 (Plt Jas Mol); To BAF (*SM-35*) 29.1.53

MJ828 Spitfire LF.IXc (Merlin 66); Became **H-30**; TOC/RAF 20.12.43; Selected for Netherlands 1946 - Arr Amsterdam by ship 13.6.47; To Depot Materiel at Leeuwarden for storage 6.47; To Twenthe 10.10.48; Erected until 20.7.49, to JVS Twenthe; Engine changed (No.161599) 30.11.49; Used by monthly flyers from 2.50; No.322 Sqn in 2.51 ('3W-2' marked 7.51); Based at Soesterberg from 31.8.51; Communications aircraft for Transport Command Valkenburg; SOC 4.6.54; By road to Soesterberg 10.5.55; CofR No.391 to Schreiner & Co; Collected for Aero Ypenburg (Civil reg. *PH-NFR* 3.1.56), test flown 3.1.56 (Plt Ben de Geus), then flown to Texel; Taxying accident, undercarriage collapsed, propeller and wing damaged 21.12.56; Regn cancelled 25.5.57; Sold for scrap 8.57

MJ874 Spitfire LF IXc (Merlin 66); TOC/RAF 28.12.43; No.416 Sqn, dived into ground, Kekerdam near Nijmegen, Cat.FB/E 29.9.44 (W/O RE Chambers killed); Recovered 1997; Remains to DAEG Museum Deelen, storage

MJ893 Spitfire LF.IXc (Merlin 66); Became H-110, later **H-69** from 1.49; TOC/RAF 8.1.44; ex Nos 312 & 302 Sqns; Selected for Netherlands 26.7.46; Tilbury 19.5.47 – Shipped to Java, arr Tandjong Priok 13.7.47; Kalidjati 1.48; First flight NethAF 9.1.48; No.322 Sqn 30.1.48, reported also by 19.12.48; Storage air depot Andir 9.49; Shipped to Holland 1950; Sold to Belgium 30.4.52; Fokker (B-14), test flown 10.3.53; To BAF (*SM-42*) 22.4.53

MJ953 Spitfire LF.IXc (Merlin 66); Became **H-12**; TOC/RAF 20.1.44; Selected for Netherlands 1946 - Arr Holland 29.7.46; JVS Twenthe 30.7.46; 'H-12' marked 8.47; Crashed on landing, ran into trench 29.10.47 (Plt Theo Verhey); Repaired; Engine failed, force-landed wheels-up near Zwolle, Cat.E 26.7.48, SOC (w/o 18.8.48); Scrapped

MJ957 Spitfire LF.IXc (Merlin 66); Became **H-24**; TOC/RAF 20.1.44; ex No.443 Sqn; Selected for Netherlands 1946 - Arr Amsterdam 13.6.47; To Depot Materiel at Leeuwarden 6.47; Twenthe 10.10.48; Fokker 1950; To JVS Twenthe 11.3.50; Taxying collision with MJ152 ('H-31') on 6.4.50 (Plt Baanstra); To Fokker Schiphol for repair; Retd JVS; Used by monthly flyers in 1950; No.322 Sqn 2.51; '3W-12' marked 7.51; Soesterberg based 31.8.51; Engine changed (to No.157983) 10.11.52; Engine changed to No.181367 on 4.12.52; Last flown 9.53; SOC 4.6.54; Gate guardian at Leeuwarden from 7.54 with spurious marking "4R"; Broken up, burnt 1956

MK121 Spitfire LF.IXc (Merlin 66); Became **H-18**; TOC/RAF 30.1.44; ex Nos 331 & 421 Sqns; Selected for Netherlands 1946; Pershore 25.9.46 – Flown to Valkenburg 26.9.46; Ferry flight to JVS Twenthe but crashed on landing, tipped on nose, Twenthe AFB 27.9.46 (Lt Hendrikx); Repaired and retd to JVS (marked 'H-18' summer 1947); Landed wheels-up Twenthe 7.47 (Plt Jas Mol), SOC (w/o 15.3.48)

MK128 Spitfire LF.IXc (Merlin 66); Became **H-3**; TOC/RAF 14.1.44; Selected for Netherlands 1946; Test flown 11.11.46 – Flown from Pershore, arr JVS Twenthe 25.11.46; Force-landed in Germany 3.3.49; To Fokker for repair and MI 7.3.49; Engine changed 27.4.49; Painted silver, marked 'H-3'; Retd JVS 30.3.50; Used for monthly flyers from 2.50; No.322 Sqn 2.51; Exercise "*Archilles*", based Valkenburg, crashed Cat.E 25.4.51, SOC (w/o 10.7.51); Scrapped

MK188 Spitfire LF.IXc (Merlin 66); Became **H-23**; TOC/RAF 2.2.44; ex No.64 Sqn; Selected for Netherlands 1946; Test flown 15.7.48 (Lt F Vijzelaar) – Ferry flight from Pershore to Twenthe, arr JVS 4.8.48; Communications aircraft of Transport Command Valkenburg 5.7.50 (Lt Kol van der Giessen); No.322 Sqn ('3W-13') at Soesterberg from 19.7.52; Engine changed (to No.156467) 14.11.51; Engine fire, force-landed and crashed near Breda, Cat.E 25.3.53 (Plt H van der Roer); w/o 17.4.53

MK202 Spitfire LF.IXc (Merlin 66); Became **H-32**; TOC/RAF 28.1.44; Selected for Netherlands 16.5.47 - Arr by ship Amsterdam 13.6.47; To Depot Materiel at Leeuwarden; To Twenthe 10.10.48; JVS early 1949; Engine failure over Germany, crashed in forced landing, Cat.E 9.6.49, SOC; Engine removed 13.10.49 (w/o 27.6.50)

MK205 Spitfire LF.IXc (Merlin 66); Became H-101, later **H-52** from 4.49; TOC/RAF 28.1.44; ex Nos 313, 205, 332, 453 Sqns; Selected for Netherlands 8.7.46; Dagenham 25.5.47 – Shipped to Java, arr Tandjong Priok 13.7.47; Kalidjati 11.47; First flight NethAF 5.12.47 (Plt Tub Bruggink); Test flown 10.12. and 12.12.47; No.322 Sqn ('H-101') 22.12.47, also by 19.12.48; Marked 'H-52' in 4.49; Crashed on landing, brake failure, ground-looped at Kalidjati 23.6.49; Repaired; Stored air depot Andir 9.49; Shipped to Holland 1950; Sold to Belgium 30.4.52; Fokker (B-3), test flown 10.5.52 (Plt Burgerhout); To BAF (*SM-31*) 26.6.52

MK230 Spitfire LF.IXc (Merlin 66); Became H-114, later **H-58** from 6.48; TOC/RAF 24.12.43; ex No.442 Sqn; Selected for Netherlands 13..8.46 – Shipped to Java, arr Tandjong Priok 13.7.47; Kalidjati 1.48; First flight NethAF 29.1.48; Test flown 2.2.48; No.322 Sqn in 2.48 (marked "MK230" and later 'H-58'); Engine failure, force-landed on belly 20.12.48 (Plt Henk Rauwerdink); Repaired, retd No.322 Sqn; Storage air depot Andir 9.49; Shipped to Holland c. 1950; To Fokker for spares for the Belgium Spitfires; SOC (Cat.E1), w/o 12.3.53

MK249 Spitfire FR.IXc (Merlin 66); Became **H-21**; TOC/RAF 20.1.44; ex No.485 Sqn; Selected for Netherlands 1946 - Arr JVS Twenthe 30.7.46; Marked 'H-21' from 1947; Engine failure, force-landed early 1948; Repaired, engine changed (to No.179081); Engine failed, force-landed and crashed Cat.E 29.8.49 (Lt A de Jong injured), SOC; Engine removed 7.9.49 (w/o 27.6.50)

MK297 Spitfire LF.IXc (Merlin 66); Became H-116, later **H-55** from 8.48; TOC/RAF 30.1.44; ex Nos.66, 485, 132 Sqns; Selected for Netherlands 26.7.46 – Shipped to Java, arr Tandjong Priok 13.7.47; Kalidjati 2.48; First flight

**Spitfire T.IX, H-97 (ex MK715)
of the JVS Twenthe, 1948-50**

NethAF 16.2.48 (Plt Tub Bruggink); Test flown 16.3.48, then stored air depot Andir (AD also by 26.11.48); Not flown with No.322 Sqn; Shipped to Holland 1950; Sold to Belgium 30.4.52; Fokker (B-15), test flown 16.4. and 16.6.53; To BAF (*SM-43*) 16.6.53, flown by Kapt Dien; Later to COGEA (*OO-ARB*); Via UK (Civil reg. *G-ASSD* 28.4.64), to USA 5.69 (*N1882, N11RS, NX9BL)*; Hangar fire at Hamilton, Canada, destroyed 15.2.93

MK403 Spitfire LF.IXc (Merlin 66); Became **H-29**; TOC/RAF 12.2.44; ex Nos.302 & 303 Sqns; Selected for Netherlands; Test flown 3.5.48 - Arr JVS Twenthe 21.5.48; Engine changed (No.178777) 12.5.49, also engine change (No.194333) 19.10.50; Fokker (MI) 29.4.51; Declared Cat.E1 in 5.51 (w/o 12.3.53); Spent spares for the overhaul of the Belgian Spitfires

MK475 Spitfire LF.IXc (Merlin 66); Became **H-28**; TOC/RAF 2.3.44; ex No.56 Sqn; Selected for Netherlands; Test flown 12.4.48 (Lt F Vijzelaar) - Arr JVS Twenthe 4.5.48; Engine changed (No.180725) 23.6.49, also engine change (No.159571) 27.9.49; Fokker (MI) 12.2.51; Engine changed (No.159403) 5.11.51; No.322 Sqn at Soesterberg (Painted silver, '3W-14' marked) 6.11.51; Transport Command Valkenburg 8.12.52; Engine failed on take-off, crashed 14.4.53; Repaired, retd to Valkenburg; SOC in 9.53; On sale 4.6.54; CofR No.359 to Schreiner & Co; To Aero Ypenburg 6.10.54 (Civil reg. *PH-NFO* 22.9.54); Based at Texel for towing duties; Engine failure, crashed 4.6.57 (Plt Ben de Geus injured); Wreck scrapped 8.57; Regn cancelled 7.8.57

MK606 Spitfire LF.IXc (Merlin 66); Became H-111, later **H-50** from 12.48; TOC/RAF 29.1.44; ex No.322 Sqn; Selected for Netherlands 1946 – Shipped to Java, arr Tandjong Priok 13.7.47; Kalidjati 1.48; First flight NethAF 20.1.48; No.322 Sqn 6.2.48 (rudder white painted); Landed without brake pressure, date unknown, S/Ldr W van den Bosch; Stored air depot Andir 9.49; Shipped to Holland 1950; Fokker factory, declared Cat.E1 & SOC (w/o 12.3.53); Spare parts for the Belgium Spitfires

MK630 Spitfire LF.IXc (Merlin 66); Became **H-19**; TOC/RAF 26.2.44; ex Nos.411, 442, 412, 602, 453 Sqns; Test flown Langham 25.6.46 (Plt F Vijzelaar); Selected for Netherlands 4.7.46; - Arr JVS Twenthe 12.7.46; Marked 'H-19' in 8.47; Engine changed (No.180355) 3.11.48; Farewell flight for No.322 Sqn 20.9.47 (Kapt HC 'Bas' Asjes); Fokker (MI) 4.3.49; Painted silver, retd JVS 11.11.49; Used for monthly flyers from 2.50; No.322 Sqn 2.51; Engine changed (No.180767) 21.5.51; Marked '3W-19' in 7.51; Based Soesterberg from 31..8.51; w/o 4.6.54; To Volkel AFB as gate guardian 7.7.54; Bomb demonstration, destroyed with napalm, burnt out 29.5.57

MK632 Spitfire LF.IXc (Merlin 66); Became **H-13**; TOC/RAF 1.3.44; Selected for Netherlands 1946; Test flown Langham 25.6.46 - Arr Twenthe (JVS) 30.7.46; Overshot landing, tipped on nose at Twenthe 9.10.47; Repaired, Painted silver; Crashed Twenthe, Cat.E2 on 30.3.49, SOC; To Fokker 5.7.49; Engine removed 11.11.49 (w/o 17.2.50); Scrapped

MK715 Spitfire T.IX (Merlin 66); Became **H-97**; TOC/RAF 28.2.44; Sold to V.A. 2.1.47; Converted to T.IX; Test flown (N-41) by Lt F Vijzelaar 9.3.48 – Delivered to Twenthe 23.3.48; JVS 26.3.48; Used for monthly flyers from 2.50; Undercarriage failed, belly-landed Twenthe 1.6.50 (Sqn Cdr Maj HC 'Bas' Asjes, with Kol van der Giessen); Repaired, retd 20.6.50; No.322 Sqn 2.51; Marked '3W-21' in 6.51; Based Soesterberg from 31.8.51; Crashed Soesterberg, Cat.E 20.9.51 (Kapt JD Sandberg injured, Lt A van Tienhoven died of injuries); w/o 22.10.51; Scrapped

MK732 Spitfire LF.IXc (Merlin 66); Became **H-25**; TOC/RAF 8.3.44; ex No.485 Sqn; For Netherlands 22.4.47; Test flown 3.6. and 9.6.48 (Lt F Vijzelaar) - Arr Twente via Valkenburg 27.6.48; Depot Materiel Leeuwarden, storage 13.7.48; JVS 31.3.49; Hit HT cable, force-landed, prop damaged near Lichtenvoorde 10.11.49 (Sgt PPA van Eijsden); Fokker Schiphol for repair 14.11.49; Engine changed 18.1.50; Painted silver and marked 'H-25' to No.322 Sqn at Twenthe 27.4.51; Marked '3W-17' in 6.51; Based Soesterberg from 31.8.51; Last flight 9.53; SOC 4.6.54; Transported to Eindhoven AFB as gate guardian 30.6.54; Displayed by No.14 Sqn RAF, Oldenburg, Germany 1956 (later Ahlhorn from 9.57); Superficial restoration commenced; Gate guardian outside Officers Mess RAF Gütersloh 1960; Dismantled and flown to RAF Brize Norton, England for storage 27.6.69; By road to RAF St.Athan10.7.69 and given GI No *8633M*; Restored planned, but NTU; To No.71 MU Bicester and stored dismantled 3.12.70; To RAF Coltishall for use as spares for Battle of Britain Memorial Flight 23.10.74; To RAF Coningsby 1978; To RAF St.Athan 8.79; To RAF Abingdon 9.80; Entire tail assembly removed and sent to Peter Croser & Michael Aitchison, Sydney, Australia (Spitfire Mk.Vb BL628); Airframe returned to RAF St.Athan for storage 12.11.80; Agreement signed for return to No.332 Sqn RNethAF 30.8.83; Left St.Athan 11.3.84; Arrived Schiphol 13.4.84; Displayed at Hilversum Air Show 20.5.84, then returned to Schiphol; To Gilze-Rijen AFB 29.11.85; Restoration commenced with Packard-built Merlin in 1990; First flight after restoration by DSF (Guernsey) Ltd as *G-HVDM* (reg. 18.1.91) with "H-25" marking and named 'Baby Bea V' from Lydd Airport 10.6.93 (pilot Peter Kynsey); First flying debut in Holland 12.6.93 (AFB Leeuwarden, Plt Dan Griffith, RAF); Repainted as "OU-U" for D-Day 50th Anniversary, flew in formation with ML407; Owner RNethAF (from 1999 operated by the Netherlands Air Force Historic Flight, based at Gilze-Rijen); Heavy landing at Rochester Airport, took off again and diverted to RAF Manston where it ground looped due to earlier damage 26.8.95; Belly-landed at Volkel 19.5.96; Flown again as "OU-U" on 11.11.97; Reserved as *PH-OUQ* 24.2.99, regd 11.10.00; Painted silver and marked "3W-17" from March 2000 - **SURVIVOR**

MK901 Spitfire LF.IXc (Merlin 66); Became **H-14**; TOC/RAF 15.3.44; Selected for Netherlands 1946 - Arr Twenthe

NETHERLANDS
243

Surviving Spitfire LF.IXc H-25 (ex MK732), gate guard at RAF Gütersloh in Germany in August 1966.

Parts of LF.IXc H-25 (ex MK732) displayed at an air show at Hilversum in The Netherlands on 20th May 1984. It had been returned to Holland after being used as spares for the Battle of Britain Memorial Flight.

Spitfire LF.IXc H-25 (ex MK732), extant in No.322 Sqn RNethAF colours, silver overall and "3W-17" marked, at Gilze-Rijen airbase early in 2000. After rebuilding it was initially camouflaged and marked "H-25" with name "Baby Bea V", being first flown on 10th June 1993. [Harry van der Meer]

(JVS) 12.7.46; Dived into ground near Epe, Germany (Lt H Fabius killed) 9.4.48, SOC

MK912 Spitfire LF.IXc (Merlin 66); Became H-119, later **H-59** from 8.48; TOC/RAF 24.3.44; ex No.312 Sqn; Selected for Netherlands 26.7.46; Tilbury 19.5.47 – Shipped to Java, arr Tandjong Priok 13.7.47; Kalidjati 3.48; First flight NethAF 10.3.48; Storage air depot Andir 23.3.48, also by 26.11.48, spent spare parts; Shipped to Holland 1950; Sold to Belgium 30.4.52; Fokker (B-1), test flown 21.4.52 (Plt Jas Mol); To BAF (*SM-29*) 4.6.53; On pole at Saffraenberg St.Truiden, Belgium; Via Guy Black, UK to Karel Bos (restoration Historic Flying Ltd, Audley End), Civil reg *G-BRRA* 10.10.89; Rebuilding 1997; Airworthy, test flown 8.9.2000 - **SURVIVOR**

MK913 Spitfire LF.IXc (Merlin 66); Became **H-34**; TOC/RAF 22.3.44; Selected for Netherlands 1947 – Via Dagenham shipped to Holland by Dutch Naval Transport 13.6.47; Depot Materiel at Leeuwarden, storage from 6.47; To Twente AFB 10.10.48; JVS 20.7.49; Painted silver 1950; Used by monthly flyers from 2.50; No.322 Sqn in 2.51; Marked '3W-18' in 7.51; Based Soesterberg from 31.8.51; SOC 9.53 (w/o 4.6.54); Gate guardian at Leeuwarden AFB ("4R") from 7.7.54; To Fire Fighting Group, burnt 1956

MK923 Spitfire LF.IXc (Merlin 66); Became H-104, later **H-61** from 8.48; TOC/RAF 24.3.44; ex No.126 Sqn; Selected for Netherlands 1946 – Shipped to Java, arr Tandjong Priok 13.7.47; Kalidjati, first flight NethAF 17.11.47 (Plt Tub Bruggink); Test flights 5.12.47; No.322 Sqn, first to the Training Flight, ops 19.12.48 (probably as 'H-61'); Hit water while low flying, propeller damaged 11.7.49 (Plt H van Gorkom); Storage air depot Andir 9.49; Shipped to Holland in 1950; Sold to Belgium 30.4.52; Fokker (B-9), test flown 26.11.52 (Plt Jas Mol); To BAF (*SM-37*) 25.2.53; Later to COGEA (*OO-ARF*); Extant; To USA, Cliff Robertson, regd *N93081* 1963, various owners and re-regd *NX521R* 2.66; Extant, owner Apex Foundation, Belleview, WA, on display at Museum of Flight, Seattle, Washington, USA, airworthy - **SURVIVOR**

MK959 Spitfire LF.IXc (Merlin 66); Became **H-15**; TOC/RAF 15.4.44; ex Nos.302, 329, 165 Sqns; Selected for Netherlands 25.9.46 – Flown from Pershore to Twenthe (JVS) 26.9.46 (F/Sgt SK Aertsen); Accident at Twenthe 16.3.49; To Fokker Schiphol for overhaul; Painted silver, retd JVS Twenthe 16.3.50; No.322 Sqn in 2.51; Marked '3W-15' in 6.51; Engine changed 25.8.52; Based Soesterberg 31.8.51; Last flight 9.53; SOC 4.6.54; Gate guardian at Eindhoven AFB 7.7.54; Temporary on loan to No.14 Sqn RAF; Retd RNethAF 4.10.61; Engine removed for use in glider winch at AFB Eindhoven in 1962; Later displayed on pole in front of the officers mess Eindhoven as "VL-V" & "MJ289" from early 1964; Restoration from 5.81; Sold to Raybourne Thomson jnr, Houston, USA 1995 for restoration to airworthy - **SURVIVOR**

MK962 Spitfire LF.IXc (Merlin 66); Became **H-4**; TOC/RAF 1.4.44; Selected for Netherlands 1946 – Flown from Pershore to Twenthe (JVS) 30.7.46; Marked 'H-4' from 7.47; Fokker (MI) in 1949; Painted silver; Used by monthly flyers from 2.50; No.322 Sqn in 2.51; Marked '3W-4' in 7.51; Based Soesterberg 31.8.51; Engine changed (No.157983) 3.4.50; Poor condition, grounded in summer 1952; Cat.E1 on 16.9.52, SOC (w/o 9.10.52)

MK993 Spitfire LF.IXc (Merlin 66); Became H-115, later **H-62** from 8.48; TOC/RAF 30.3.44; Selected for Netherlands 16.8.46; Tilbury – Shipped to Java, arr Tandjong Priok 13.7.47; Kalidjati for assembly 1.48; First flight NethAF 10.2.48; Storage air depot Andir 19.2.48; No.322 Sqn in 4.48, also by 19.12.48; Overshot landing, tipped on nose, fuselage broken, Cat.E1 on 27.1.49, SOC (Plt Gijs Noyons unhurt); Abandoned, wreck left behind at Semarang

MK998 Spitfire LF.IXc (Merlin 66); Became **H-16**; TOC/RAF 6.4.44; ex Nos.1 & 91 Sqns; Selected for Netherlands 1946 - Flown from Pershore to Twenthe (JVS) 12.7.46;

Surviving Spitfire H-60 (ex NH238) was initially serialled H-103 but this was changed to H-60 in 1948, three leaping white mice being painted on the cowling. Since 1979 it has been in the UK, registered G-MKIX.

Crashed on landing, undercarriage collapsed, ground-looped 14.7.47 (Sgt van Spaendonk); Cat.E2 & SOC 6.10.47 (w/o 18.8.48)

ML262 Spitfire LF.IXc (Merlin 66); Became **H-17**; TOC/RAF 18.4.44; Test flown 11.11.46 (Lt F Vijzelaar); Selected for Netherlands 1946 - Arr Twenthe (JVS) 25.11.46; 'H-17' marked summer 1947; Grounded early 1948; SOC 6.8.48 (w/o 9.11.48)

MT853 Spitfire FR.XIVe (Griffon 65); TOC/RAF 1.3.45; ex Nos 36 & 26 Sqns; Selected for Netherlands 10.7.47 – Flown to Twenthe AFB 10.7.47; Flown to LETS Deelen 6.8.47; Exhibited at Rotterdam ('XC- ') in 10.47; Propeller damaged; Retd LETS Deelen for display; To Army shooting range Harskamp in 1952; Scrapyard Gilze-Rijen 7.4.59

NH188 Spitfire LF.IXc (Merlin 66); Became H-109, later **H-64** from 7.48; TOC/RAF 1.5.44; ex Nos.308 & 416 Sqns; Selected for Netherlands 1946; - Shipped to Java, arr Tandjong Priok 13.7.47; Kalidjati 12.47; First flight NethAF 12.1.48 (Plt Tub Bruggink); Test flown ('H-109') on 23.1.48; No.322 Sqn in 2.48; Storage air depot Andir 3.48, also by 26.11.48; Flown to Tjililitan for Dutch Air Force celebration, ground-display (light blue overall, 'H-64' marked) in 7.48; Andir storage later; Shipped to Holland 1950; Sold to Belgium 30.4.52; Fokker (B-11), test flown 2.3.53 (Plt Jas Mol); To BAF, EPA Brustem (*SM-39*) 22.4.53; Later COGEA (*OO-ARC*); Extant; To the Canadian National Air Museum Rockliffe (Civil reg *CF-NUS*), on display - **SURVIVOR**

NH197 Spitfire LF.IXe (Merlin 66); Became **H-33**; TOC/RAF 8.5.44; ex Nos.302, 313, 308 Sqns; Selected for Netherlands 1946 - Shipped to Amsterdam 13.6.47; Depot Materiel at Leeuwarden, storage 6.47; To Twente AFB 10.10.48; JVS 28.6.49; Dived into buildings at Twenthe, Cat.E 18.11.49 (Eerste Lt Joep Huistee and three civilians killed), SOC (w/o 27.6.50)

NH212 Spitfire LF.IXe (Merlin 66); Became **H-22**; TOC/RAF 5.5.44; ex Nos.132, 412, 453 Sqns; Test flown 14.4.48 (Lt F Vijzelaar); Selected for Netherlands - Flown to the JVS Twenthe 3.5.48; Marked 'H-22'; Engine changed (No.162489, date unknown); Force-landed wheels-up near Markelo 2.6.49; To Fokker for repair; Painted silver; Retd JVS 18.4.50; No.322 Sqn 2.51; Marked '3W-3' in 7.51; Based Soesterberg 31.8.51; Engine changed (No.179717) 31.3.52; Last flown 9.53; SOC 4.6.54; To Eindhoven AFB as gate guardian 10.9.54; Burnt 1956

NH238 Spitfire LF.IXe (Merlin 66); Became H-103, later **H-60**; TOC/RAF 6.5.44; Selected for Netherlands 1946 – Shipped to Java, arr Tandjong Priok 13.7.47; Kalidjati 10.47; First flight NethAF 24.10.47 (Plt Tub Bruggink); Test flown 4.11.47; No.322 Sqn ('H-103') 22.12.47; Marked 'H-60' in 7.48 (three mice painted on the cowling); No.322 Sqn by 19.12.48; Storage air depot Andir 9.49; Shipped to Holland 1950; Sold to Belgium 30.4.52; Fokker (B-8), test flown 5.11.52; To BAF (*SM-36*) 29.1.53; Later to COGEA (*OO-ARE*); Extant; Sold to USA (reg. *N238V* 3.7.69); To Douglas Arnold, UK 1979 (reg. *G-MKIX* 12.12.83), stored with Flying A Services, North Weald - **SURVIVOR**

NH309 Spitfire LF.IXe (Merlin 66); Became H-113, later **H-57** from 1.49; TOC/RAF 1.5.44; Selected for Netherlands 1946 – Shipped to Java, arr Tandjong Priok 13.7.47; Kalidjati 1.48; 2.2.48; First flight NethAF 28.1.48; Test flown 2.2.48; Storage air depot Andir from 2.48; No.322 Sqn ('H-57') 26.11.48; Storage AD Andir 9.49; Shipped to Holland 1950; Sold to Belgium 30.4.52; Fokker (B-6), test flown 24.7.52 (Plt Jas Mol); To BAF (*SM-34*) 21.8.52

PK318 Spitfire F.22 (Griffon 61); TOC/RAF 26.5.45; Became GI No. *6255M* – Arr NethAF (on loan), NSTT Langham 31.1.47; Retd RAF; SOC 11.11.47

PL854 Spitfire PR.XI (Merlin 70); TOC/RAF 17.6.44; ex No 16 Sqn, SOC/RAF 14.8.45 – Presented by the Military Attaché UK to the Institute for Nautics & Aeronautics at Rotterdam 10.1.46 (without wings and engine); Used until 1968; To the HTS Haarlem 1974; Scrapped
NOTE: Flying panel to MJ143, Military Aviation Museum, Soesterberg

PL912 Spitfire PR.XI (Merlin 70); TOC/RAF 21.8.44; ex No 16 Sqn - Arr Twente AFB 10.7.47; To LETS Deelen 6.8.47; Remains dumped 1952

PL965 Spitfire PR.XI (Merlin 70); TOC/RAF 2.10.44; ex No.16 Sqn; Selected for Netherlands 7.47 - Arr Twente AFB 10.7.47; To LETS Deelen 6.8.47; Marked '03'; SOC 1952; Rescued from scrapyard 1955, re-assembled with parts from PM156, PL998 & TD402; Selected for Schiphol Museum in 1956, but went to the National War & Resistance Museum, Overloon 9.12.60; Exhibited there as "3W- " with an orange triangle; 1973 restoration, re-painted in blue, only "PL965" marked; Exhibited until 16.3.87; Then dismantled to E Nick Grace, Chichester, Sussex, in England (exchanged for TP263) in 1986; To Christopher P B Horsley/Medway Aircraft Preservation Society for rebuild at Rochester 2.87 (Civil reg *G-MKXI* 13.11.89); ff 23.12.92; Flown with Old Flying Machine Co, Duxford; Damaged nr Ashford, Kent 2.8.98; To Real Aeroplane Company, Breighton, East Yorkshire; Painted pink and marked "R" with USAAF markings, rollout 13.3.2000, airworthy in USA 9.01 - **SURVIVOR**

PL998 Spitfire PR XI (Merlin 70); TOC/RAF 18.11.44; ex No.400 Sqn; Selected for Netherlands 8.7.47 - Arr Twente AFB 10.7.47; LETS Deelen from 6.8.47 to 1952

PM133 Spitfire PR XI (Merlin 70); TOC/RAF 6.12.44; ex No.400 Sqn; Selected for Netherlands 1947 – Flown to Twente AFB 10.7.47; LETS Deelen 6.8.47, broken up for instructional parts, in use until 1952

PM633 Spitfire PR XIX (Griffon 66); TOC/RAF 6.11.45; Became GI No. *6453M* – Arr NethAF (on loan), NSTT Langham 6.11.46; Retd RAF & SOC 17.12.47

PT669 Spitfire LF.IXe (Merlin 66); Became **H-5**; TOC/RAF 1.8.44; Selected for Netherlands 1946 – Flown from Pershore to Twenthe (JVS) 17.7.46; Marked 'H-5' from 8.47; Engine failed, force-landed wheels-up near Usselo, Cat.E 9.6.49 (Lt Jaap Eden) 9.6.49, SOC (w/o 27.6.50)

PT873 Spitfire LF.IXe (Merlin 66); Became **H-26**; TOC/RAF 23.8.44; ex Nos.222 & 485 Sqns; Test flown 3.6. and 9.6.48 (Lt F Vijzelaar); Selected for Netherlands – Flown from Pershore to Twenthe 26.6.48; Depot Materiel at Leeuwarden, storage from 6.48; JVS Twenthe ('H-26') 30.3.49; Used by monthly flyers from 2.50; Engine failure, force-landed wheel-up, Cat.E 14.7.50, SOC (w/o 6.11.50); Kept for spare parts, later scrapped

PT986 Spitfire LF.IXe (Merlin 66); ; Became **H-27**; TOC/RAF 1.9.44; Test flown 16.9.48 (Lt F Vijzelaar); Selected for Netherlands – Flown to Twenthe (JVS) 1.10.48; Marked 'H-27'; Engine changed (No.178439, date unknown); Engine failed, force-landed wheels-up near Markelo 6.9.49 (Plt DA Uytenboogaart); To Fokker for repair 12.10.49; Engine changed (No.194119) 30.3.51; Painted silver; No.322 Sqn 26.4.51; Marked '3W-16' in 7.51; Based Soesterberg from 31.8.51 (used for weekend flying); To Transport Group at Valkenburg AFB 14.4.53; No.322 Sqn Soesterberg 29.12.53; Offered for sale 4.6.54; CofR No.375 to Schreiner & Co; To Aero Ypenburg on loan (Civil reg. *PH-NFP* 13.7.54); Test flown 12.7.55 (Jaap Zwaan); Based at Texel, belly-landed 6.8.55 (Lody Huizinga); Test flown 17.9.55; Grounded 4.6.57; Regn cancelled 7.8.57; Sold for scrap 8.57

RB155 Spitfire F.XIVc (Griffon 65); TOC/RAF 24.12.43; ex No.350 Sqn; Selected for Netherlands 31.7.47 – Arr Twente AFB 31.7.47; Flown to LETS Deelen 6.8.47 (Kapt F de Grave); Engine removed; Fire Fighting Group 1950; Burnt

SL595 Spitfire LF.IXe (Merlin 66); TOC/RAF 25.7.45 – Arr NethAF (on loan), NSTT Langham 11.12.46; Retd RAF 19.12.47; Allocated for Norway 11.12.47, but cancelled; Sold for scrap 3.2.50

Check list Netherlands AF / RAF Serial Numbers

Neth Nos.	RAF Nos.	Arrival Date
H-1	MJ143	17.7.46
H-2	MJ614	3.10.46
H-3	MK128	25.11.46
H-4	MK962	30.7.46
H-5	PT669	17.7.46
H-6	MH477	31.7.46
H-7	MH723	3.10.46
H-8	MJ271	25.11.46
H-9	MJ469	30.7.46
H-10	MJ479	12.7.46
H-11	MJ642	31.10.46
H-12	MJ953	30.7.46
H-13	MK632	30.7.46
H-14	MK901	12.7.46
H-15	MK959	26.9.46
H-16	MK998	12.7.46
H-17	ML262	25.11.46
H-18	MK121	26.9.46
H-19	MK630	12.7.46
H-20	MJ361	25.11.46
H-21	MK249	30.7.46
H-22	NH212	3.5.48
H-23	MK188	14.8.48
H-24	MJ957	13.6.47
H-25	MK732	28.6.48
H-26	PT873	27.6.48
H-27	PT986	1.10.48
H-28	MK475	4.5.48
H-29	MK403	21.5.48
H-30	MJ828	13.6.47

Neth. Nos.	Prov. Nos.	RAF Nos.	Arrival Date
H-31		MJ152	13.6.47
H-32		MK202	13.6.47
H-33		NH197	13.6.47
H-34		MK913	13.6.47
H-35		MJ580	27.10.48
Spitfire LF.IX in Java			
H-50	-111	MK606	13.7.47
H-51	-102	MH485	13.7.47
H-52	-101	MK205	13.7.47
H-53	-106	MH424	13.7.47
H-54	-118	EN560	13.7.47
H-55	-116	MK297	13.7.47
H-56	-120	MH439	13.7.47
H-57	-113	NH309	13.7.47
H-58	-114	MK230	13.7.47
H-59	-119	MK912	13.7.47
H-60	-103	NH238	13.7.47
H-61	-104	MK923	13.7.47
H-62	-115	MK993	13.7.47
H-63	-112	MH725	13.7.47
H-64	-109	NH188	13.7.47
H-65	-108	MH415	13.7.47
H-66	-107	MJ536	13.7.47
H-67	-117	MJ714	13.7.47
H-68	-105	MH434	13.7.47
H-69	-110	MJ893	13.7.47
Spitfire T.IX			
H-97		MK715	26.3.48
H-98		BS274	26.3.48
H-99		BS147	26.3.48

Ground Instructional Airframes (GI)

NTTS Langham, UK

GI Nos.	RAF Serial Nos.	Arrival Date
5938M	W3250	25.11.46
6142M	MH473	10.10.46
6144M	TB920	3.10.46
6145M	TD358	3.10.46
6146M	MH940	3.10.46
6224M	TD187	13.12.46
6255M	PK318	31.01.47
6323M	SM247	22.04.47
6453M	PM633	6.11.46
	TZ197	3.10.46
	SL595	11.12.46

LETS Deelen, Holland

RAF Serial Nos.	Arrival Date
RB155	31.7.47
MT853	10.7.47
PL912	10.7.47
PL965	10.7.47
PL998	10.7.47
PM133	10.7.47
TD264	10.7.47
TD402	10.7.47

Technical College at Delft

RAF Serial	Date
BS4..?	..4.46
Broken up in parts	

Institute for Nautics and Aeronautics, Rotterdam

RAF Serial	Date
PL854	10.1.46
Fuselage only	

Civil registrations for Schreiner Aero, Ypenburg:

Code	Reg. Date	NethAF Nos.	RAF Serial Nos.
PH-NFN	6.10.54	H-99	BS147
PH-NFP	13.7.55	H-27	PT986
PH-NFO	22.9.54	H-28	MK475
PH-NFR	3.1.56	H-30	MJ828

SM247 Spitfire LF.XVIe (Merlin 266); TOC/RAF 23.10.44; Became GI No. *6323M* – Arr RNethAF (on loan), NSTT Langham 22.4.47; Retd RAF in 7.47

TB920 Spitfire HF.IXe (Merlin 70); TOC/RAF 28.2.45; ex No.164 Sqn; Became GI No. *6144M* – Arr NethAF (on loan), NSTT Langham 3.10.46; Retd RAF in 7.47

TD187 Spitfire LF.XVIe (Merlin 266); TOC/RAF 17.3.45; ex Nos.416 & 164 Sqns, No.1687 Flt; Became GI No. *6224M* – Arr NethAF (on loan), NSTT Langham 13.12.46; Retd RAF in 7.47

TD264 Spitfire LF.XVIe (Merlin 266); TOC/RAF 19.3.45; ex Nos.421, 416. 164, 63 Sqns; Selected for Netherlands 8.7.47 – Flown to Twenthe AFB 10.7.47; LETS Deelen 6.8.47 until 1952; scrapped

TD358 Spitfire HF.IXe (Merlin 70); TOC/RAF 29.3.45; ex No.164 Sqn; Became GI No. *6145M* – Arr NethAF (on loan), NSTT Langham 3.10.46; Retd RAF in 7.47

TD402 Spitfire LF.XVIe (Merlin 266); TOC/RAF 18.5.45; Selected for Netherlands 8.7.47 - Arr Twente AFB 10.7.47; Test flown 26.7.47 (Kapt HC 'Bas' Asjes); LETS Deelen 6.8.47 until 1952; Scrapped

TP263 Spitfire FR.XVIIIe (Griffon 65); ex India (*HS-649*); arrived as **SURVIVOR** only 1987, (from Nick Grace, England) to the War & Resistance Museum Overloon (in exchange for PL965); Exhibition as "*NH649*" and marked "3W-F"
NOTE: Number "TP285" found on the tail-unit

TZ197 Spitfire FR.XIVe (Griffon 65); TOC/RAF 29.6.45; ex No.61 OTU – Arr RNethAF (on loan), NSTT Langham 3.10.46; Retd RAF 7.47; SOC (Cat.E2) 17.12.47

SURVIVORS
In the Netherlands

MJ143 (H-1) Military Aviation Museum, Soesterberg
MJ271 (H-8) Aviodome, Schiphol Airport, Amsterdam as "H-53"
MK732 (H-25) Airworthy, "3W-17", based Gilze-Rijen
TP263 National War & Resistance Museum, Overloon, as "3W-F" & "NH649".

SURVIVORS
Elsewhere

MH415 In USA, 'Connie' Edwards, Big Springs, USA (*N415MH*); In storage, offered for sale
MH434 In UK, now OFMC Duxford, airworthy (*G-ASJV*)
MK912 In UK, to Karel Bos (restoration Historic Flying Ltd, Audley End), *G-BRRA*, airworthy
MK923 (H-61) In USA, *NX521R*, on display Museum of Flight, Seattle, Washington
MK959 (H-15) ex Eindhoven, sold to USA in October 1994
NH188 In Canada, on display in Canadian National Air Museum, Rockliffe (*CF-NUS*)
NH238 In UK, stored at North Weald, UK (*G-MKIX*)
PL965 ex Overloon, was exchanged with Nick Grace, UK in 1987, now *G-MKXI*.

Replicas in Holland

"P7981" at Veghel
"MJ881" at Soesterberg (as "3W-B")
"MJ964" at Leeuwarden (as "3W-V")
"MK732" "H-25" (retd to UK)
"MK959" at Eindhoven (as "H-15")
– Alu-Replica Mk.IX "*WILLEM SIEBEN*" displayed Flying Museum at Seppe

References:
De Nederlandse Spitfires van 1945 tot 1976; Nederlandse Vliegtuig Encyclopedie January 1976;
   by Harry van der Meer en Hugo Hooftman.
Nederlandse Spitfires, by Fred Bachofner
   & Harry van der Meer, Modellbouw in Plastic, 1986.
Dutch Spitfires, by Harry van der Meer, part 1 & 2,
   Airnieuws Nederland, Rotterdam, 1986.

NEW ZEALAND

The remains of surviving Spitfire F.Vc/trop A58-178 (ex JG891) were recovered at Kiriwina, Papua New Guinea, and assembly was then commenced with a collection of parts at the Don J Subritzky Facility at Auckland, New Zealand, with the civil registration ZK-MKV from 1990. It later went to the UK and is seen here in August 1999 under restoration to airworthy at Audley End, being allocated the British registration G-LFVC. [PRA]

New Zealand became a British colony in 1840, and achieved Dominion status in 1907. Under a statute of Westminster of 1931 it became a fully independent nation within the British Commonwealth of Nations.

The New Zealand Permament Air Force was formed in June 1923, being re-named the Royal New Zealand Air Force (RNZAF) on 27th February 1934. Under the terms of the Empire Air Training Scheme (EATS) deliveries of military material expanded from 1940, and it was given the task of training around 900 RNZAF pilots per annum. A further 500 were sent from elementary flying training schools to Canada for advanced training under the British Commonwealth Air Training Plan (BCATP).

Spitfires were never operated by the Royal New Zealand Air Force, but many New Zealand pilots flew Spitfires in the RAF.

After the Second World War a few Spitfires went to private owners in New Zealand either for exhibition purposes or for flying – they arrived in New Zealand as Survivors only. They were mostly flown by the Alpine Fighter Collection (AFC) of Sir Tim Wallis at Wanaka.

New Zealand Spitfire unit of the RAF

No.**485** (New Zealand) Sqn was formed at Driffield, UK, on 1st March 1941 and disbanded at Drope, Germany on 26th August 1945.
  Sqn-code - 'OU '.
  Flew Spitfire Mks.I, II, V and IX in the European theatre (ETO) at that time.

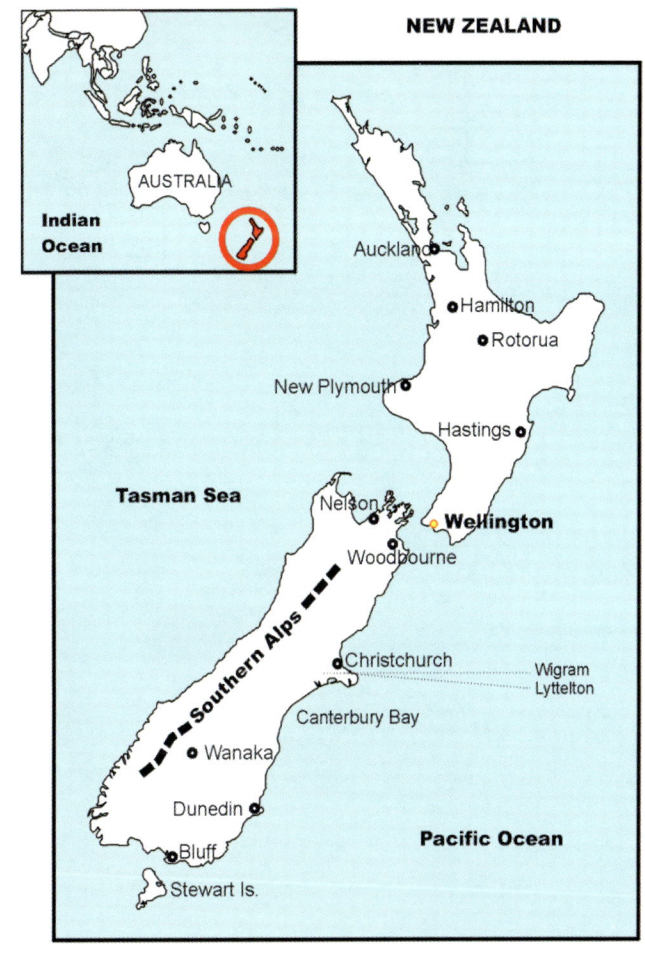

Surviving Spitfire LF.XVIe TE288 seen at the RNZAF Museum at Wigram, near Christchurch, in late 1986, with the spurious code marking "DU-V" and the name "Rongotea".

[RNZAF photo]

NEW ZEALAND

Spitfire LF.XVIe TE288 mounted on a plinth at Christchurch in 1978. It is now displayed in the RNZAF Museum at Wigram, near Christchurch. [MAP]

Individual Histories

AR614 Spitfire Vc; Became GI No. *5378M*, *6371M*, *7555M*; Civil reg. *CF-DUY* & *G-BUWA* (reg. 19.3.93); Restored by Hawker Restorations Ltd, Earls Colne and Historic Flying Ltd, Audley End, UK; Purchased by the Alpine Fighter Collection (AFC); First flown UK after restoration 5.10.96; Sold to Vintage Wings, Seattle, USA; Departed from the UK to USA in 11.99 (reg. *N614VC*) 10.2.00 Flying Heritage Inc, Seatle 25.4.01 - **SURVIVOR**

EF545 Spitfire F.Vc/trop; ex RAAF *A58-149*; Burnt hulk recovered in 1974 from Papua-New Guinea (Kiriwina) by N Monty Armstrong, Auckland; Regd *ZK-MKV* reserved to G S Smith, Auckland 7.11.83; To J Shivas, Ashburton, New Zealand 1984; To Don J Subritzky, Auckland - Dairy Flat 1986 (parts used to restore *JG891 - see below*); Parts traded in 1992 to Chris Warrilow, High Wycombe, Bucks, UK; Sold on in 2001; As at 2.02 with Peter Arnold in transit to Guy Black at Northiam, where it arrived 23.3.02 - **SURVIVOR**

JG891 Spitfire F.Vc/trop; ex RAAF *A58-178*; Civil reg. *ZK-MKV*; Recovered at Kiriwina, Papua New Guinea - Assembled from a collection of parts by Don J Subritzky Facility at Auckland 1990; Restoration to airworthy; Sold to Karel Bos, Audley End, UK (Historic Flying Ltd) and arrived in UK 7.99 (reg. *G-LFVC* 28.9.99) - **SURVIVOR**

NH799 Spitfire FR.XIVe; Civil reg. *ZK-XIV* 28.3.94 (ex *G-BUZU*, regd 1.7.93); Bought by the Alpine Fighter Collection of Sir Tim Wallis; First flight after restoration at Historic Flying Ltd, Audley End, UK 21.1.94; Later marked "AP-V" - Dismantled for shipment 14.2.94, arrived Auckland 29.3.94; Crashed and badly damaged on take-off at Wanaka 2.1.96 (pilot Tim Wallis injured); Aircraft salvage for sale 3.96; Sold to Brian Hare & Paul E Page; Storage by Pacific Aerospace Corp. Ltd, Hamilton, NZ; Under restoration at Avspecs, Rotorua, NZ by 1998 - **SURVIVOR**

PV270 Spitfire LF IX; ex Italy *MM4014*; Israel *2080*; Burma *UB424*; Arr as **SURVIVOR** only; Cassville, Missouri, USA 1999; Sold to Brendon Deere in New Zealand, restoration at Dairy Flat from May 2001

TB863 Spitfire LF.XVIe; Civil reg. *ZK-XVI*; Metro-Goldwyn-Meyer, Pinewood Studios, England in 1955 for use in film Reach for the Sky; To A William Francis, Southend, Essex, for restoration project 12.68 (displayed Historic Aircraft Museum, Southend from 1972); To J Parkes and A W Francis, Booker (Civil reg. *G-CDAN* 30.11.82); To The Fighter Collection, Duxford 1984; Sold to Sir Tim Wallis/Alpine Fighter Collection, Ardmore, NZ - crated for delivery in 1.88 and arrived New Zealand in 2.88 (reg. 17.1.89); Re-assembled at Wanaka (AFC), first flight in New Zealand 25.1.89; Engine failure, force landed at Waipukurau, severe damage 29.1.89 (pilot Tim Wallis unhurt); Damaged landing Woodbourne 18.11.92; Repaired; Currently airworthy with Alpine Fighter Collection, Wanaka - **SURVIVOR**

TE288 Spitfire LF.XVIe; ex No.501 Sqn ('RAB-D'); Became GI No. *7287M*; Film "Reach for the Sky" in U.K. (temporarily marked as "AR251") in 8.55; Displayed Battle of Britain weeks 1959/61; Presented to the Brevet Club, Canterbury, NZ in 1962 - Shipped SS *Hinapura* from Liverpool 19.4.63, arrived Lyttelton, NZ 28.6.63; Assembled at RNZAF Wigram 11.63; Exhibited in Agricultural Show at Addington; To the Brevet Club Canterbury in 3.64, mounted on a plinth in front of the club's memorial hall near Christchurch airport, then still marked as "AR251". Moved to Woodbourne for restoration and making a replica (for Bull Creek, Australia); Now displayed in the RNZAF Museum at Wigram AFB near Christchurch as TE288 – **SURVIVOR**

TE330 Spitfire LF.XVIe; Became GI No. *7449M*; ex Dayton, Ohio, USA; Imported by James Slade (Hong Kong) for restoration 4.97; Sold to Don and Mike Subritzky at Auckland, NZ for restoration - **SURVIVOR**

TE456 Spitfire LF.XVIe; ex No.501 Sqn ('RAB-J') & No.3 CAACU ('43') - Arrived in New Zealand in 10.56, to Domain War Memorial at Auckland; Original code "RAB-J" marked 1997 - **SURVIVOR**

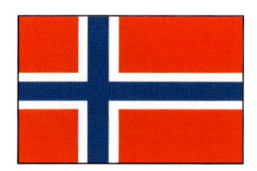

NORWAY

As with others countries, Norway expressed an interest in receiving Spitfire Mk.Is, and in 1939 asked for a quotation, but with the outbreak of the Second World War nothing came of this.

Germany invaded Norway in April 1940, but numbers of Norwegian pilots escaped to serve with RAF units including Nos.331 and 332 (Norwegian) Spitfire Squadrons. With the return home of these units after the war 36 almost brand-new Spitfire IXs arrived in Norway on 19th May 1945, remaining there at first with the RAF, but becoming wholly RNoAF from 22nd November 1945.

The initial post-war requirement of the RNoAF was for a total of 78 Spitfire Mk.IXs for three fighter units. Beside the two Spitfire units, which returned from the RAF, a third squadron was planned at Bardufoss. However, lack of personnel caused their requirement to be cut back to 68 Spitfires in two squadrons only. Eventually Norway signed an agreement dated 27th September 1946 for a

A line-up of No.331 (Norwegian) Sqn Spitfires shortly after arrival at Gardermoen on 22nd May 1945. The nearest aircraft, MJ931 'FN-L' had the typical No.331 Sqn markings of flag-stripes on the spinner as well as on a band around the rear fuselage. The colours were red-white-blue-white-red. [Bjørn Hafsten]

Spitfires (ex No.331 skv) and Harvards of the operational training unit at Feltflyvingen, in front of B hangar at Gardermoen in January 1946. Note RNoAF roundel applied directly over the old RAF roundel. The Spitfires appear to be devoid of serial numbers. [Bjørn Hafsten]

further 32 Spitfire LF.IXc/es. Norway also wished to buy eight Spitfire Mk.Vs for training purposes, but this was cancelled, and three Spitfire PR.XIs were purchased. With that, the interest of Norway for a conversion of some Spitfires to type PR.IX lapsed.

Norway later took an interest in training aircraft, and on 18th October 1949 Spitfire T.VIII (Civil reg. *G-ALJM*) arrived at Oslo for demonstrations, later going to Gardermoen Air Station, north of Oslo. Norway asked for conversion of some LF.IXs to T.IX standard at a quoted price of £5,200 to £5,700 each, but agreement could not be reached.

Spitfire deliveries to Norway:

```
36 LF.IXc/e in 1945, by returning of Nos.331 & 332 Sqns
 1 LF.IXc in November 1945, left by No.165 Sqn
31 LF.IXe in 1947/48 (Comm.No.321)
 3 PR.XI in 8.47 (Comm.No.326)
 3 LF.IX left behind for the LTS in 1945
```

Total = 74 Spitfires, plus some for spares.

Norwegian Spitfire units of the RAF

No.**331** Sqn, unit code 'FN'.
Formed Catterick 21st July 1941, Gardermoen near Oslo from 22nd May 1945, disbanded and to RNoAF 21st November 1945;
Spitfire Mks.IIa, Vb & LF.IXc/e from November 1941 until November 1945.

No.**332** Sqn, unit code 'AH'.
Formed Catterick 16th January 1942, Gardermoen from 22nd May 1945, Værnes 16th July 1945, disbanded and to RNoAF 21st November 1945;
Spitfire Mks.Va/b & LF.IXc/e from January 1942 until November 1945.

Both squadrons served with No.132 (Norwegian) Wing, No.84 Group, of the 2nd TAF. Nos.331 & 332 Sqns were withdrawn from operations on 22nd April 1945 and came under control of No.128 (Recce) Wing on 7th May 1945. They flew on 12th May 1945 to RAF Dyce near Aberdeen, Scotland, en route for Norway - landed in Stavanger/Sola on 19th May 1945 and arrived at Gardermoen airbase near Oslo on 22nd May 1945. Officially disbanded from RAF strength and incorporated into the RNoAF on 21st November 1945.

Both units used red/white/blue/white/red stripes on the propellers. Additionally No.331 Sqn used a white/blue/white fuselage-band, whilst No.332 Sqn painted an equals sign on the fin.

The Royal Norwegian Air Force (RNoAF)

In 1915 Norway formed small air services for the Army (*Hærens Flyvevaesen*) and for the Navy (*Marinens Flyvevaesen*), re-named in 1925 to become *Hærens Flyvevåben* and *Marinens Flyvevåben* respectively.

The RNoAF re-formed on 10th November 1944 with British concepts and equipment, nationally known as "*Kongelige Norske Luftforsvaret*" [except from 1954 to 1957 as "*...Flyvåpen*" (Flyvåpnet)], with four Air Commands. The RNoAF then consisted of three Fighter Squadrons (*Jagervinger*, each 12 aircraft), two Bomber & Recce Sqns (each 9 aircraft), one Maritime Patrol Sqn and one Transport Sqn. On joining NATO in 1951 the strength was increased; for example, eight Fighter Squadrons were built up with 25 jet aircraft for each unit. Two Air Commands have existed since 1957, one for the South and one for the North (*Sør-Norge* and *Nord-Norge*).

Spitfire units of the Royal Norwegian Air Force

No.**331** Sqn (skvadron, skv) with Spitfire LF.IXc/e from 21st November 1945 to 20th November 1951; Unit code: 'FN- ' (except August 1946 - January 1951, then RNoAF serial codes only).
Incorporated into an OTU ("*Feltflyvingen*") from 22nd November 1945 to 26th March 1947, used Spitfires together with North American Harvards and Fairchild Cornells; Reformed as fighter unit No.331 Sqn (skv) on 20th October 1948; Disbanded 1st December 1951 (re-formed with F-84G on 15th July 1952).
[From 10th May 1948 to 15th July 1949 No.331 Sqn (skv) comprised also a special Vampire-"ving" (12 aircraft); later this Vampire unit formed the No.336 skv];
Airbases: Gardermoen near Oslo from 22nd May 1945 (RNoAF from 21st November 1945); dett to Kjevik (B-Flight) October 1948; Værnes near Trondheim from 20th October 1949.
Commanding Officers:
Maj Nils A Ringdal   3.3.45
Maj Reidar Isachsen   1.8.45
Maj John Ryg (OTU, "*Feltflyvingen*")   1.1.46
Maj Olav Ullestad   20.10.48 - 1.12.51

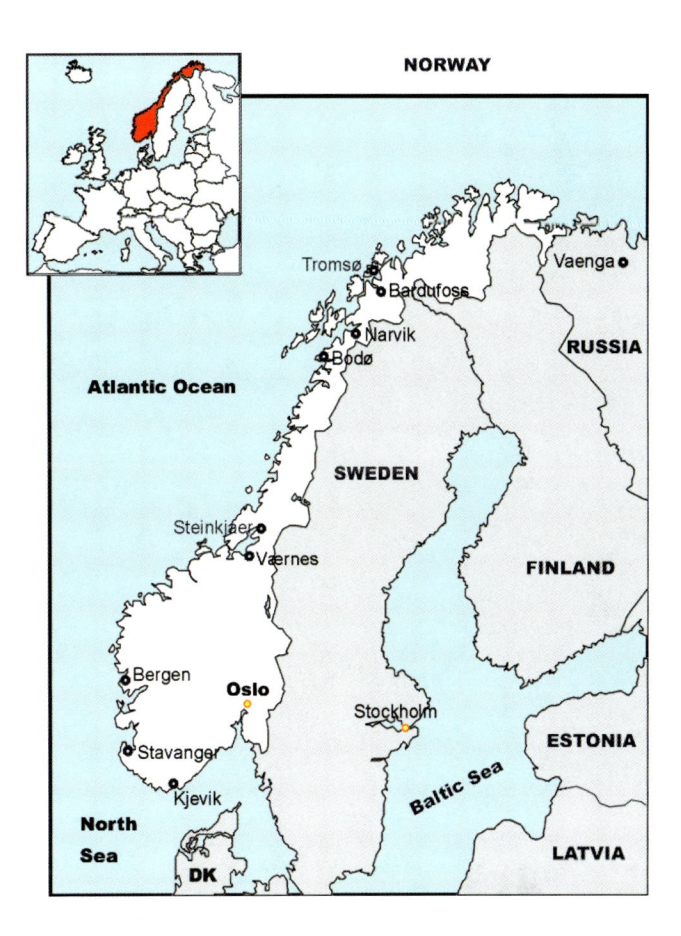

Remarks:
The OTU "*Feltflyvingen*" was formed at Gardermoen airfield with aircraft from No.331 Sqn (skv) and elements from the Flying School (Harvards and Cornells) on 22nd November 1945. Disbanded 20th October 1948, then the Spitfire element re-formed the same day as No.331 Sqn (skv).

No.**332** Sqn (skvadron, skv) with Spitfire LF.IXc/e from 21st November 1945 to 1st July 1952; Unit code: 'AH' (except August 1946 - January 1951, then RNoAF serial codes only).
Temporarily inactivated, reduced to a maintenance basis only from 1st January 1946; Re-activated to No.332 Sqn (skv) on 12th April 1948; Disbanded 1st July 1952 (re-formed with F-84G on 23rd February 1953).
Airbases: Værnes near Trondheim from 16th July 1945 (RNoAF from 22nd November 1945) (dett Bardufoss June 1948 to October 1949); Bardufoss from October 1949.
Commanding Officers:
Maj Ola G Aanjesen   3.4.45 - 6.10.45
Maj B Eivind Tjensvoll   12.4.48
Maj Martin Gran   1.11.49
Maj B Eivind Tjensvoll   10.1.51 - 1.7.52

Spitfire LF.IXes of No.332 Sqn lined up at Værnes around 1945/46. The nearest aircraft is PT529 AH-G. [via Nils Mathisrud]

No.1 PRU - the *"First Fotorekognoseringsving"* - formed with three Spitfire PR.XI on 9th August 1949 (no unit code, only RNoAF serial codes painted); Temporarily disbanded 26th March 1954 (re-formed with F-84E on 5th May 1954, eventually became No.717 skv).
Airbases: Gardermoen near Oslo from 9th August 1949; Bardufoss 11th September 1949; Værnes near Trondheim 7th October 1949; Gardermoen 4th November 1949; Bardufoss 15th June 1950; Værnes 16th October 1950; Kjeller near Oslo 16th November 1950; Værnes 14th May 1951; Kjevik near Kristiansand 23th December 1951; Værnes 13th May 1952; Kjevik (dett Bardufoss) 10th February 1953 - March 1954.
Commanding Officers:
Kapt Kristian Nyerrød 8.8.49
Kapt Harald Meland 24.11.52
 (killed 19.8.53 in PL994)
Lt Jens Chr Width 20.8.53

LTS The Luftforsvarets Tekniske Skolesenter (Air Force Technical School), formed at Kjevik near Kristiansand 1st February 1946, from a temporary base at Kjeller near Oslo, used Spitfires for ground instructions from spring 1946 onwards.
Commanding Officer:
Lt Col Asbjørn Hassel 1.2.46
Lt Col Olav Unhammer 19.9.48

AD Aircraft Depots
ARD Kjeller (main supply, maintenance and repair depot, incl. Flyfordelingskontore [a distribution office])
ASU Gardermoen ("Lagringssveiten")
ASU Værnes ("Lagringsavdelingen")
LTS Kjevik, held also Spitfires on storage.

End of Spitfire flying in Norway

At the end of 1948 twelve of the Spitfires were withdrawn from use. The inventory list on 30th June 1950 showed 47 Spitfires in service with the RNoAF (23 aircraft on strength of the three Spitfire units, a further 20 in storage and four in repair or overhaul). In December 1951 the number was reduced to 30 Spitfires.

Jet fighters in the shape of de Havilland Vampires had arrived in Norway in May 1948, but general re-equipment with F-84E & G and T-33 continued until 1951, the Spitfires then being phased out. The last LF.IXe as withdrawn from use in August 1952, and the last PR.XI in May 1954. Only two Spitfires survived, all the other being scrapped.

Markings of the Norwegian Spitfires

The two Spitfire squadrons initially used the RAF coding system, retaining RAF roundels and fin flashes. Following a competition within the RNoAF, a new Norwegian roundel was introduced on all aircraft with effect from 1st December 1945, and all previous RAF nationality markings were to be removed. However, at first the RNoAF roundels were just painted over the former RAF fuselage and wing roundels, the RAF serial number being retained but now painted on the fin.

Then on 15th August 1946, the RNoAF Technical Division ordered the Eastern and Trøndelag Air Commands to be marked in accordance with a new system. This was based on an individual letter for each type of aircraft in the RNoAF inventory; the Spitfire being given the type-letter "A". This letter was followed by two letters identifying each individual aircraft. The first aircraft would have the letters -AB, then -AC, -AD to -AZ, then -BA to -BZ and -CA to -CZ; gaps could be made for practical reasons. The markings were to be read from left to right irrespective of the position of the fuselage roundel, so might appear, for instance, as A-CD on one side of the fuselage but AC-D on the opposite side. Following the delivery of new aircraft from the UK during 1947/48, the RNoAF Technical Division issued a new standard for the size of roundels and identification letters in the spring of 1948.

This system continued for the operational units until January 1951, when pressure from leading personnel led to the Technical Division reinstating the wartime coding system, the two Spitfire Squadrons then reverting to their war-time codes, 'FN' for No.331 Sqn (skv) and 'AH' for No.332 Sqn (skv). At the same time, the RAF serials were again painted on the aft fuselage sides, in at least some cases. No.1 PRU (*"Fotorekognoseringsving"*), not being regarded as a first line unit, continued to use the old coding system, however, with aircraft marked A-ZA to A-ZC until disbandment.

Individual Histories

JL361 Spitfire LF.IXc (Merlin 66); Became **A-CD**; TOC/RAF 18.4.43; Tests and trials at Boscombe Down and Farnborough 1943/44 - Selected for Norway 15.7.47; Arr Norway 31.7.47; RNoAF (TOC) 7.8.47; Storage, coded 'A-CD' after 8.46 (ASU Gardermoen, still on storage 6.3.48); No.331 Sqn from 7.48; Marked 'FN-D' after 1.51; Storage 1.52; No.332 Sqn ('AH-D') from 5.52; SOC in 7.52; ASU Værnes, storage (554:40 flying hours)

MH350 Spitfire LF.IXc (Merlin 66); Became **A-BM**; TOC/RAF 7.8.43; No.332 Sqn - Arr Norway 19.5.45; RNoAF,

No.332 Sqn ('AH-V') 22.11.45; To ASU Værnes, airworthy, in 1.46; Coded 'A-BM' after 8.46; No.331 Sqn, first flown with this unit 13.12.50; Marked 'FN-M' after 1.51; Taxying accident 5.2.51; ROS; Storage, due to lack of engine spares 15.2.51; Last flown 15.11.51 (Lt Lien, No.331 Sqn); SOC 12.51, storage (168:20 flying hours); Exhibited Norwegian Armed Forces Museum, Akershus Castle, Oslo, for 50th Anniversary of Norwegian Air Force 7-23.5.59; Retd to storage at Værnes; Moved to Bodø for restoration 5.61; Displayed as 'FN-T' for 30th Anniversary of No.331 Sqn 21.7.71; Displayed in Norwegian Armed Forces Museum (Forrsvarsmuseet), Akershus Castle, Oslo from 9.82; Moved to Bodø for display at the Air Force Museum, which opened in 1994 (now with E-type wing) - **SURVIVOR**

MJ217 Spitfire LF.IXc (Merlin 66); Became **A-AT**; TOC/RAF 20.1.44; ex Nos.331 ('FN-X') & 66 Sqns; No.165 Sqn 10.6.45; No.88 GSU to No.128 Wing & No.331 Sqn 19.7.45 – RNoAF, OTU "*Feltflyvingen*" at Gardermoen ('FN-B') 22.11.45; Coded 'A-AT' after 8.46; No.331 Sqn, engine failure, force-landed at Gardermoen 1.7.48 (Lt Harby safe); Engine trouble, force-landed at Fornebu airfield (near Oslo) 3.7.48; Take-off crash, lost power, overshot the runway, overturned, Gardermoen, Cat.E 30.9.49 (Sgt Per Holter-Sørensen safe), SOC (458:30 flying hours)

MJ409 Spitfire LF.IXc (Merlin 66); Became **A-CW**; TOC/RAF 6.11.43 – Selected for Norway 5.7.48; Engine changed; Arr RNoAF 10.9.48; Storage, coded 'A-CW'; No.332 Sqn from 5.49; Crashed on landing at Bardufoss, hydraulic system failed, no flaps and brakes, undercarriage collapsed, Cat.E1 5.12.49; w/o 9.2.50; Used for spares (187:35 flying hours)

MJ418 Spitfire LF.IXe (Merlin 66); Became **A-BY**; TOC/RAF 3.11.43 – Selected for Norway 16.6.47; Desp. 18.6.47, arr Norway 19.6.47; RNoAF (TOC) 26.6.47; Storage, coded

Spitfire IX A-CD with RAF serial JL361 in black on the fin. It was delivered to Norway in August 1947 and remained in service to the bitter end in 1952.
[Bjørn Hafsten]

Surviving Spitfire LF.IXc MH350 (ex A-BM) displayed in RAF colours with the spurious code "FN-T" in the Norwegian Air Force Museum at Bodø in August 1997.
[S Vancanteren]

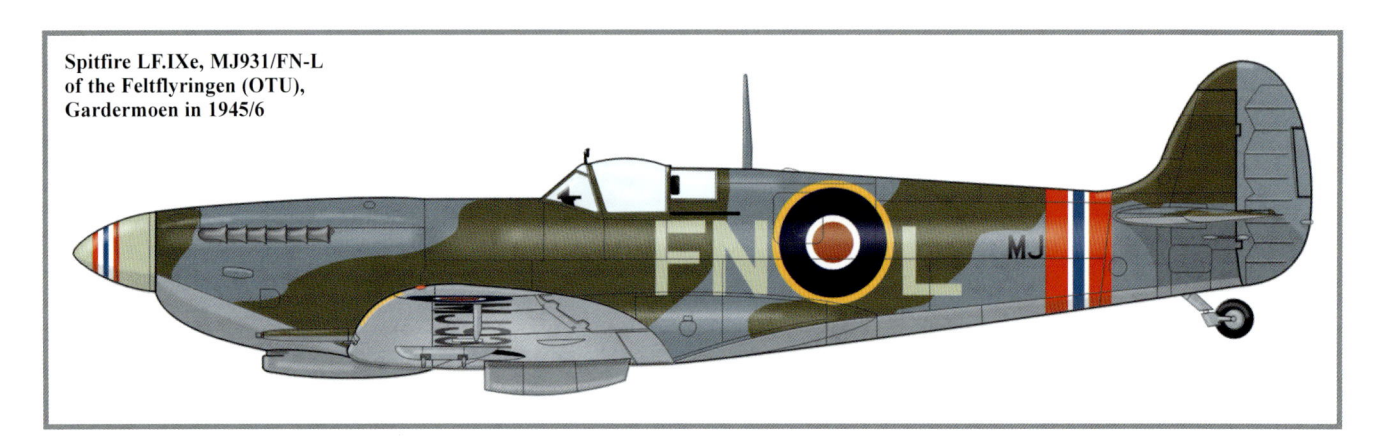

Spitfire LF.IXe, MJ931/FN-L of the Feltflyringen (OTU), Gardermoen in 1945/6

'A-BY' after 8.46; No.332 Sqn from 3.49; Taxying after landing at Værnes, hit truck, undercarriage broken, Cat.E 30.8.50 (Lt Frithjof Torkehagen safe); w/o 29.8.51 (202:00 flying hours)

MJ471 Spitfire LF.IXc (Merlin 66); Became **A-AP**; TOC/RAF 14.11.43; No.331 Sqn 30.4.45 - Arr Norway 19.5.45 (Accident Gardermoen 14.8.45, Plt C Christensen); RNoAF, OTU "*Feltflyvingen*" at Gardermoen ('FN-V') 22.11.45; Coded 'A-AP' after 8.46; No.331 Sqn, crashed on landing at Værnes, nosed over 17.8.47 (Kapt E Tjensvoll safe); Prop damaged on landing Værnes 5.5.48 (Fenrik [P/O] K Aagaard safe); Storage; No.332 Sqn from 3.49; Storage 9.49; No.331 Sqn ('FN-B') from 4.51; SOC in 1.52, storage
NOTE: 434:30 flying hours on 17.8.47; Total 576:10 f/hr

MJ633 Spitfire LF.IXc (Merlin 66); Became **A-BR**; TOC/RAF 29.11.43; ex No.331 Sqn ('FN-J') – Selected for Norway 7.5.47; Desp. 8.5.47, arr RNoAF 9.5.47; Storage, coded 'A-BR' after 8.46; Not in Sqn service; SOC and used for spares; w/o 30.9.49 (315:55 flying hours)

MJ792 Spitfire LF.IXc (Merlin 66); Became **A-BS**; TOC/RAF 8.1.44; ex Nos.312 & 308 Sqns - Selected for Norway 7.5.47; Desp. 8.5.47, arr RNoAF 9.5.47; Storage, coded 'A-BS' after 8.46; No.331 Sqn (B Flight at Kjevik), issued before 6.48; LTS Kjevik 8.48; Kjeller air depot 3.51; No.331 Sqn ('FN-E') from 6.51; Last flown with No.331 Sqn 20.11.51; Storage 1.52; No.332 Sqn ('AH-F') from 3.52; SOC in 7.52; ASU Værnes, storage (385:20 flying hours)

MJ855 Spitfire LF.IXc (Merlin 66); Became **A-BL**; TOC/RAF 22.12.43; ex Nos.416, 421 & 165 Sqns ('SK-Z') - No.332 Sqn RAF in Norway ('AH- ') 15.11.45; RNoAF 22.11.45; Storage, coded 'A-BL' after 8.46; Service unknown; SOC in 9.49; Used for spares (321:30 flying hours)

MJ931 Spitfire LF.IXc (Merlin 66); Became **A-AI**; TOC/RAF 4.1.44; ex Nos.312 & 302 Sqns; No.331 Sqn from 10.5.45 - Arr Norway 19.5.45; RNoAF, OTU "*Feltflyvingen*" at Gardermoen ('FN-L') 22.11.45; Overshot landing Gardermoen, nosed over 3.5.46 (Sgt E Magnussøn safe); Coded 'A-AI' after 8.46; No.331 Sqn, collision with Spitfire PL448 during take-off at Gardermoen, caught fire, burnt out, Cat.E 16.12.47 (Sgt Gotaas), SOC
NOTE: 219:30 flying hours on 3.5.46

MJ951 Spitfire LF.IXc (Merlin 66); Became **A-AO**; TOC/RAF 24.12.43; ex Nos.421, 401 & 442 Sqns; No.331 Sqn from 17.5.45 - Arr Norway 19.5.45; RNoAF, OTU

Spitfire LF.IXc MK671 AH-H as a ground instructional airframe at Kjevik after ending its operational career with No.332 Sqn. [via Nils Mathisrud]

"*Feltflyvingen*" at Gardermoen ('FN-S') 22.11.45; Coded 'A-AO' after 8.46; SOC (date unknown, for use as spare parts); w/o 31.7.49 (563:20 flying hours on 30.6.48; Total 681:05 f/hrs)

MK304 Spitfire LF.IXc; TOC/RAF 23.1.44; ex Nos.310, 442 & 412 Sqns; No.331 Sqn, arr Norway 19.5.45; Engine failure, force-landed on belly near Gjøvik, Cat.FA/E 21.9.45, SOC; Remains to LTS Kjevik

MK631 Spitfire LF.IXc (Merlin 66); Became **A-AD**; TOC/RAF 1.3.44; ex No.132 Sqn; No.331 Sqn from 5.45 - Arr Norway 19.5.45; RNoAF, OTU "*Feltflyvingen*" at Gardermoen ('FN-E') 22.11.45; Coded 'A-AD' after 8.46; No.331 Sqn, engine failure, force-landed and crashed Værnes, Cat.E 11.8.47 (Lt Egil Stokstad safe), SOC (299:15 flying hours)

MK671 Spitfire LF.IXc (Merlin 66); Became **A-AK**; TOC/RAF 28.3.44; ex No.317 Sqn; No.331 Sqn from 5.45 - Arr Norway 19.5.45; RNoAF, OTU "*Feltflyvingen*" at Gardermoen ('FN-M') 22.11.45; Coded 'A-AK' after 8.46; No.331 Sqn, engine failure, force-landed Gardermoen 16.4.48 (Maj Tharald Weisteen safe); Repaired, back to No.331 Sqn; Storage 5.50; Kjeller air depot 1951 (marked 'AH-H'); No.332 Sqn ('AH-H') from 4.51; SOC 6.52, storage
NOTE: 293:05 flying hours on 16.4.48; Total 568:50 f/hrs

MK799 Spitfire LF.IXc (Merlin 66); Became **A-CK**; TOC/RAF 19.3.44; ex Nos.222, 485 & 349 Sqns; No.332 Sqn ('AH-W') 22.2.45 – Selected for Norway 3.11.47; Desp. 13.11.47, arr RNoAF 14.12.47; Storage, coded 'A-CK' after 8.46 (ASU Gardermoen, still on storage 6.3.48); No.331 Sqn (issued) before 6.48; Taxying Gardermoen, tipped on nose, propeller damaged 4.8.49 (Lt K Bjørge-Hansen safe); Storage 9.50; No.332 Sqn ('AH-N') from 4.51; SOC in 7.52; ASU Værnes, storage (617:05 flying hours)

MK839 Spitfire LF.IXc (Merlin 66); Became **A-AR**; TOC/RAF 11.3.44; ex Nos.302, 310, 329 & 165 Sqns; No.331 Sqn 30.4.45 - Arr Norway 19.5.45; RNoAF, OTU "*Feltflyvingen*" at Gardermoen ('FN-X') 22.11.45; Coded 'A-AR' after 8.46; No.331 Sqn, propeller damaged on take-off at Gardermoen 17.12.48 (Lt T Ludvigsen safe); Storage 6.50; No.331 Sqn from 7.51; To ARD Kjeller for major overhaul in 11.51; No.332 Sqn at Bardufoss from 3.52; SOC in 7.52, storage (570:50 flying hours)

MK866 Spitfire LF.IXc (Merlin 66); Became **A-CR**; TOC/RAF 9.5.44; ex Nos.222, 485 & 411 Sqns – Selected for Norway 26.11.47; No.5 MU, ready 8.4.48; Arr RNoAF in 5.48; Storage, coded 'A-CR'; No.332 Sqn from 3.49; Marked 'AH-B' after 1.51; SOC in 7.52; To air depot Kjeller, storage (654:40 flying hours)

MK886 Spitfire LF.IXc (Merlin 66); Became **A-AG**; TOC/RAF 24.3.44; ex No.485 Sqn; No.331 Sqn from 10.5.45 - Arr Norway 19.5.45 (Accident, propeller tip broken 3.9.45; Sgt B Ringstad); RNoAF, OTU "*Feltflyvingen*" at Gardermoen ('FN-J') 22.11.45; Coded 'A-AG' after 8.46; SOC in 5.50; Used for spares; w/o 29.8.51 (675:50 flying hours)

MK897 Spitfire LF.IXc (Merlin 66); Became **A-AX**; TOC/RAF 19.3.44; ex No.485 Sqn; No.332 Sqn 1.5.45 - Arr Norway 19.5.45; RNoAF, No.332 Sqn ('AH- ') 22.11.45; Storage, coded 'A-AX' after 8.46; No.331 Sqn from 9.50; Marked 'FN-X' after 1.51; Crashed on take-off at Værnes, Cat.FA/E 12.4.51; w/o 9.5.51 (427:35 flying hours); Scrapped

MK904 Spitfire LF.IXc (Merlin 66); Became **A-BX**; TOC/RAF 19.3.44; ex Nos.485, 222, 331 & 349 Sqns – Selected for Norway 26.8.47; Desp. 28.8.47, arr RNoAF 29.8.47; Storage, coded 'A-BX'; No.332 Sqn from 3.49; Oil on windscreen, hit snowdrift by landing, overturned on Andsvann field airstrip, Cat.E 9.3.50 (Sgt Hosel safe), SOC (421:15 flying hours)

MK983 Spitfire LF.IXc (Merlin 66); Became **A-BG**; TOC/RAF 20.3.44; ex No.302 Sqn; No.332 Sqn 10.5.45 - Arr Norway 19.5.45; RNoAF, No.332 Sqn ('AH- ') 22.11.45; Coded 'A-BG' after 8.46; Crashed on landing at Værnes, minor damage on prop and left wingtip 6.12.48 (Sgt Frithjof Torkehagen safe); Overshot landing at Værnes, overturned, Cat.FA/E 19.2.49 (Sgt F Torkehagen safe); w/o 8.9.49 (319:55 flying hours); Used for spare parts

Spitfire LF.IXc MK904 A-BX, possibly with No.332 Sqn after it crashed at Andsvann airstrip on 9th March 1950 and overturned. [via Nils Mathisrud]

Spitfire LF.IXe, NH193/A-CI, RNoAF in 1946/7

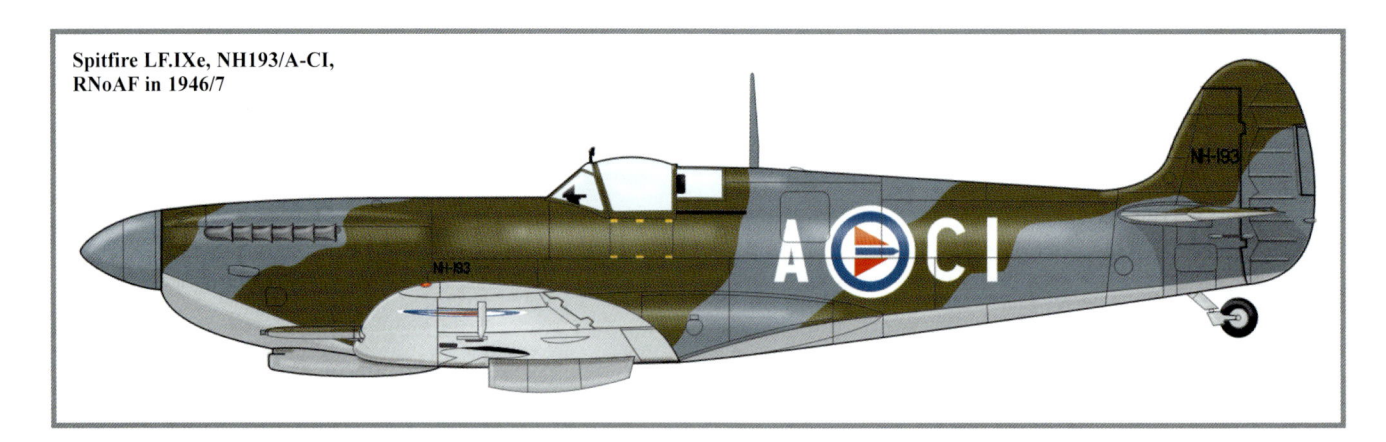

Spitfire LF.IXe A-CI (ex NH193) in flight around 1949.

Spitfire LF.IXe NH193 FN-I at either Kjevik or Vaernes in 1951. [via Nils Mathisrud]

MK997 Spitfire LF.IXc (Merlin 66); Became **A-CP**; TOC/RAF 3.4.44; ex No.1 Sqn – Selected for Norway 18.11.47; No.5 MU, ready 14.4.48; Arr. RNoAF 1.5.48; Storage, coded 'A-CP'; No.331 Sqn from 2.50; Low-level flying south of the Lake Selbusjøen, hit surface of lake Samsjøen near Værnes, exploded, Cat.FA/E 4.8.50 (Fenrik [P/O] Finn Thorstensen), SOC (263:50 flying hours)

ML132 Spitfire LF.IXc (Merlin 66); Became **A-AV**; TOC/RAF 28.3.44; ex No.317 Sqn; No.332 Sqn 30.4.45 - Arr Norway 19.5.45; RNoAF, No.332 Sqn 22.11.45; Storage; Coded 'A-AV' after 8.46; No.322 Sqn at Bardufoss from 7.48; Storage 12.49; w/o 2.12.51; To LTS Kjevik as ground instructional airframe

ML178 Spitfire LF.IXc (Merlin 66); Became **A-BB**; TOC/RAF 14.4.44; ex Nos.317 & 403 Sqns; No.332 Sqn 12.5.45 - Arr Norway 19.5.45 (Flying accident, hit HT cables North of Grue near Kongsvinger 13.7.45, Lt Egil Stigset); RNoAF, No.332 Sqn ('AH-K') 22.11.45; Storage, coded 'A-BB' after 8.46; No.332 Sqn ('AH-E') from 1.51; SOC in 5.52, storage (343:55 flying hours)

ML363 Spitfire LF.IXc (Merlin 66); Became **A-BC**; TOC/RAF 25.4.44; ex No.66 Sqn; No.332 Sqn 12.5.45 - Arr Norway 19.5.45; RNoAF, No.332 Sqn ('AH-L') 22.11.45; Storage, coded 'A-BC' after 8.46; No.331 Sqn ('FN-C') from 2.51; SOC in 1.52, storage (306:00 flying hours)

NH171 Spitfire LF.IXe (Merlin 66); Became **A-BK**; TOC/RAF 30.4.44; ex Nos.332, 602, 412, 604, 453 & 165 Sqns - No.332 Sqn (in Norway) 15.11.45; RNoAF, No.332 Sqn ('AH-Z') 22.11.45; Storage, coded 'A-BK' after 8.46; No.331 Sqn ('FN-K') from 6.51; SOC in 11.51; To air depot at Kjeller, possibly used for spares; w/o 26.6.52 (396:30 flying hours)

NH193 Spitfire LF.IXe (Merlin 66); Became **A-CI**; TOC/RAF 1.5.44; ex No.308 Sqn – Selected for Norway 13.11.47; Desp. 13.11.47, arr RNoAF 14.12.47; Storage, coded 'A-CI' (ASU Gardermoen, still on storage 6.3.48); Shown over Oslo 6.49; No.331 Sqn; Marked 'FN-I' after 1.51; SOC in 1.52; ASU Værnes, storage

NH208 Spitfire LF.IXe (Merlin 66); Became **A-BT**; TOC/RAF 8.5.44; ex Nos.453 & 443 Sqns – Selected for Norway 7.5.47; Desp. 8.5.47, arr RNoAF 9.5.47; Storage, coded 'A-BT'; No.331 Sqn (B Flight at Kjevik), issued before 6.48; LTS Kjevik 8.48; Kjeller air depot 3.51; No.332 Sqn ('AH-W') from 4.51; SOC in 6.52 (417:20 flying hours)

NH213 Spitfire LF.IXe (Merlin 66); Became **A-BZ**; TOC/RAF 5.5.44; ex Nos.453 & 412 Sqns – Selected for Norway 7.5.47; Desp. 8.5.47, arr RNoAF 9.5.47; Storage; Wrongly coded 'A-BO' up to 6.3.48; Re-coded 'A-BZ'; No.332 Sqn from 6.50; Marked 'AH-V' after 1.51; SOC in 7.52; ASU Værnes, storage (272:40 flying hours)

NH253 Spitfire LF.IXe (Merlin 66); Became **A-CU**; TOC/RAF 8.5.44; ex No.1 Sqn – Selected for Norway 26.11.47; No.5 MU, ready 23.4.48; Arr RNoAF 1.5.48; Storage, coded 'A-CU'; No.332 Sqn from 3.49; Collided with another aircraft landing Værnes 2.6.49 (Sgt Oddvar Lien); Marked 'AH-C' after 1.51; SOC in 5.52; Communication Ving LKN Bardufoss, for storage at ASU Værnes in 7.52 (639:40 flying hours)

NH261 Spitfire LF.IXe (Merlin 66); Became **A-CB**; TOC/RAF 9.5.44; ex Nos.349, 485, 74 & 332 Sqns - Selected for Norway 3.9.47; Arr RNoAF 5.9.47; Storage, coded 'A-CB' (ASU Gardermoen, still in storage 6.3.48); Cocooning trials at Kjeller from 8.6.48 to 6.3.50; Storage; No.332 Sqn ('AH-K') from 1.51; SOC in 7.52; ASU Værnes, storage (495:35 flying hours)

NH316 Spitfire LF.IXe (Merlin 66); Allotted **A-BD**; TOC/RAF 19.5.44; ex Nos.313 & 127 Sqns; No.332 Sqn 1.5.45 - Arr Norway 19.5.45; RNoAF, No.332 Sqn ('AH-O') 22.11.45; Propeller damage by low level flying, crashed in forced landing, overturned, Værnes airfield, Cat.FA/E 20.2.46 (Lt HW Rohde safe); w/o 23.3.46 (169:00 flying hours)

NH357 Spitfire LF.IXe (Merlin 66); Became **A-BV**; TOC/RAF 30.5.44; ex Nos.453, 412 & 411 Sqns - Selected for Norway 31.7.47; Arr RNoAF 31.7.47; Storage, coded 'A-BV'; No.331 Sqn from 5.50; No.332 Sqn from 6.50; Marked 'AH-X' after 1.51; SOC in 7.52; ASU Værnes, storage (428:55 flying hours)

NH372 Spitfire LF.IXe (Merlin 66); Became **A-BN**; TOC/RAF 15.6.44; ex No.341 Sqn; No.332 Sqn 29.4.45 - Arr Norway 19.5.45 (bird strike by low level flying 23.8.45, Plt E Anosen); RNoAF, No.332 Sqn ('AH-D') 22.11.45; Hit snow drift taxying at Værnes, propeller damage, engine vibrated in flight, but safe landing 31.1.46 (Lt Thor Werner); Coded 'A-BN' after 8.46; Crashed on landing, Værnes, Cat. FA/E on 30.6.49, SOC; Used for spares
NOTE: 135:15 flying hours on 31.1.46

NH401 Spitfire LF.IXe (Merlin 66); Allotted **A-CN**; TOC/RAF 2.6.44; ex Nos.165, 91 & 1 Sqns – Selected for Norway 9.10.47; Arr RNoAF 15.11.47; Storage at ASU Gardermoen (reported still on storage by 6.3.48); Flown to Kjeller, swung off runway and into snowdrift, Cat.FA/E 9.3.48 (Major John Ryg), SOC (291:10 flying hours)

NH423 Spitfire LF.IXe (Merlin 66); Became **A-CE**; TOC/RAF 23.5.44; ex Nos.310, 33, 331, 349, 412 Sqns – Selected, and desp. to Norway 28.8.47; Arr. Norway 29.8.47; RNoAF (TOC) 4.9.47; Storage, coded 'A-CE' (ASU Gardermoen, still on storage 6.3.48); No.332 Sqn at Værnes 29.4.49; SOC in 5.49; Used for spares (269:30 flying hours)

NH460 Spitfire LF.IXe (Merlin 66); Became **A-BH**; TOC/RAF 23.5.44; ex Nos.310, 33, 39 Sqns; No.332 Sqn 10.5.45 - Arr Norway 19.5.45; RNoAF, No.332 Sqn ('AH- ') 22.11.45; Storage, coded 'A-BH' after 8.46; Crashed on landing, Værnes 18.11.48 (Sgt Frithjof Torkehagen safe); Storage 9.49; No.331 Sqn ('FN-T') from 5.51; Storage 12.51; No.332 Sqn (allocated) 28.4.52; SOC in 7.52, storage (425:50 flying hours)

NH475 Spitfire LF.IXe (Merlin 66); Became **A-AY**; TOC/RAF 23.5.44; ex Nos.310, 33, 222 Sqns; No.332 Sqn 30.4.45 - Arr Norway 19.5.45; RNoAF, No.332 Sqn ('AH-F') 22.11.45; Storage, coded 'A-AY' after 8.46; No.332 Sqn from 7.48; Bardufoss based from 3.49 (B Flight); Crashed on landing at Bardufoss, brake failure, undercarriage collapsed, Cat.FA/E 5.7.49 (Fenrik [P/O] N Rødberg-Nilsen safe); w/o 29.7.49, scrapped (258:15 flying hours)

NH485 Spitfire LF.IXe (Merlin 66); TOC/RAF 26.5.44; ex No.349 Sqn; No.128 Wing (Norway) 19.7.45; No.332 Sqn ('AH-R') 6.45; Overshot landing at Fornebu airfield (near Oslo), overturned, Cat.FA/E 11.8.45 (Sgt B Djupvik safe), SOC

NH520 Spitfire LF.IXe (Merlin 66); Became **A-CV**; TOC/RAF 26.5.44; ex Nos.313 & 329 Sqns – Selected for Norway 26.11.47; No.5 MU, ready 23.4.48; Arr. RNoAF 13.5.48; Storage, coded 'A-CV'; LTS Kjevik, storage 6.48; Kjeller air depot 9.48; No.331 Sqn from 1.49; Caught in slipstream of another a/c when landing, hit snowdrift, nosed over, Værnes 14.12.50 (Fenrik [P/O] Jan Sandvik safe); Repaired, marked 'FN-V' after 1.51; SOC in 12.51, storage (420:10 flying hours)

NH540 Spitfire LF.IXe (Merlin 66); Became **A-CT**; TOC/RAF 30.5.44; ex Nos.329, 345, 331 Sqns ('FN-A') – Selected for Norway 22.12.47; No.5 MU, ready 7.4.48; Arr RNoAF 1.5.48; Storage, coded 'A-CT'; No Sqn service; w/o 23.8.49; To LTS Kjevik as ground instructional
NOTE: 239:15 flying hours by 23.8.49; Aircraft later used in a film, marked then "FN-C"

NH550 Spitfire LF.IXe (Merlin 66); Became **A-BO**; TOC/RAF 31.5.44; ex Nos.312, 74 & 442 Sqns; No.332 Sqn 10.5.45 - Arr Norway 19.5.45; RNoAF, No.332 Sqn ('AH-S') 22.11.45; Storage, coded 'A-BO' after 8.46; No.332 Sqn at Bardufoss from 7.48; Marked 'AH-Z' after 1.51; SOC 29.5.52, storage (465:25 flying hours)

NH576 Spitfire LF.IXe (Merlin 66); Became **A-BW**; TOC/RAF 10.6.44; ex Nos.74, 341 & 329 Sqns - Selected for Norway 9.6.47; No.29 MU, ready 2.9.47; Desp. 5.9.47; Arr. RNoAF 5/6.9.47; Storage, coded 'A-BW'; No.331 Sqn (B Flight Kjevik), issued before 6.48; LTS Kjevik, storage 8.48; No.331 Sqn ('FN-F') from 6.51; Storage 1.52;

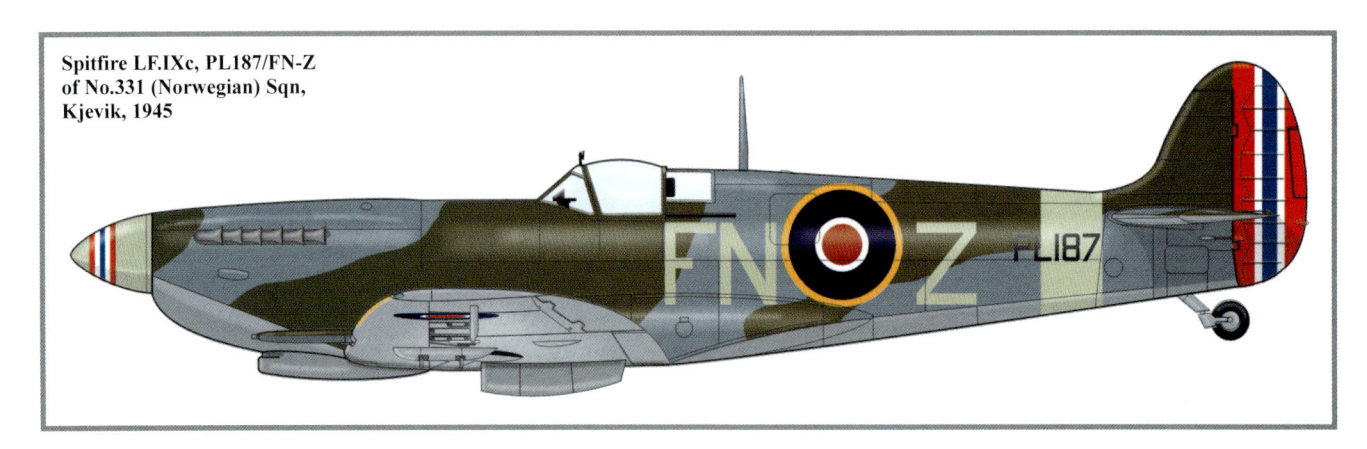

Spitfire LF.IXc, PL187/FN-Z of No.331 (Norwegian) Sqn, Kjevik, 1945

No.332 Sqn ('AH-R') from 3.52; SOC in 7.52; To Kjeller air depot (243:10 flying hours)

NH584 Spitfire LF.IXe (Merlin 66); Became **A-BE**; TOC/RAF 6.6.44; ex Nos.312 & 74 Sqns; No.332 Sqn 29.4.45 - Arr Norway 19.5.45; RNoAF, No.332 Sqn ('AH-X') 22.11.45; Storage, coded 'A-BE' after 8.46; No.332 Sqn, engine failed on test flight, burnt, approached for forced landing but dived into ground near Ydstines in Stjørdal, 1-2m E of Værnes airfield, Cat.FA/E 15.6.48 (Lt Kristian Aagaard killed), SOC (249:13 flying hours)

PL185 Spitfire LF.IXe (Merlin 66); Became **A-CA**; TOC/RAF 12.6.44; ex Nos.329, 345, 332, 485 & 74 Sqns - Selected for Norway 9.6.47; Desp. 18.6.47, arr Norway 19.6.47; RNoAF (TOC) 26.6.47; ASU Gardermoen ("*Flylagringssveiten*") for storage, coded 'A-CA' (reported still on storage 6.3.48); No.331 Sqn, engine trouble near Kragerø (Killefjorden), vibrated and smoked, pilot baled out, aircraft crashed in an old farm building near Sandnes in Søndeled, c.10m SW Risør, Cat.E 4.5.48 (Major John Ryg safe), SOC (280:20 flying hours)

PL187 Spitfire LF.IXe (Merlin 66); Became **A-AS**; TOC/RAF 13.6.44; Nos.332 ('AH-O') & 331 Sqns from 3.8.44; Accident, Cat.FA/B 31.12.44, RiW (PSO); No.331 Sqn 5.45 - Arr Norway 19.5.45; RNoAF, OTU "*Feltflyvingen*" at Gardermoen ('FN-Z') 22.11.45; Coded 'A-AS' after 8.46; No.331 Sqn, engine failure by low level training flight, pilot baled out, into Lake Soneren, Sigdal, Cat.E 22.6.49 (Sgt Jostein Hoset safe), SOC (349:30 flying hours)

PL221 Spitfire LF.IXe (Merlin 66); Became **A-AL**; TOC/RAF 17.6.44; ex No.340 Sqn; No.331 Sqn 10.5.45 - Arr Norway 19.5.45; RNoAF, OTU "*Feltflyvingen*" at Gardermoen ('FN-N') 22.11.45; Crashed on landing at Gardermoen, tipped on nose 30.4.46 (Sgt M Sandvik safe); Coded 'A-AL' after 8.46; No.331 Sqn, accident Cat.E (total loss) in 9.48, SOC (138:15 flying hours)

PL226 Spitfire LF.IXe (Merlin 66); Became **A-BA**; TOC/RAF 17.6.44; ex No.132 Sqn; No.332 Sqn 12.5.45 - Arr Norway 19.5.45; RNoAF, No.332 Sqn ('AH-A') 22.11.45; Storage; Coded 'A-BA' after 8.46; No.332 Sqn from 1948; Marked 'AH-S' after 1.51; SOC in 8.52; ASU Værnes, storage

PL255 Spitfire LF.IXe (Merlin 66); Became **A-CS**; TOC/RAF 17.6.44; ex Nos.341 & 33 Sqns – Selected for Norway 26.11.47; No.5 MU, ready 23.4.48; Arr. RNoAF 1.5.48; Storage, coded 'A-CS'; No.331 Sqn ('FN- ') from 5.51; No.332 Sqn ('AH-L') from 11.51; Storage 1.52; No.332 Sqn from 3.52; SOC in 7.52; ASU Værnes, storage (131:40 flying hours)

PL327 Spitfire LF.IXe (Merlin 66); Became **A-CC**; TOC/RAF 19.6.44; ex No.33 Sqn – Selected for Norway 19.8.47;

Spitfire LF.IXe PL221 FN-N of the RNoAF, OTU "Feltflyvingen" at Gardermoen in early 1946. [via Nils Mathisrud]

Desp. & arr. RNoAF 28.8.47; ASU Gardermoen storage, coded 'A-CC' (still on storage 6.3.48); Crashed on landing at Kjeller (AD), hit snowdrift, tipped on nose (date unknown, Lt O Harby safe); No.331 Sqn, engine failed, pilot baled out too low, aircraft dived into ground near Domkirkeodden at Hamar, Cat.E 6.7.48 (Fenrik [P/O] Per Marum killed); w/o 22.7.48

PL408 Spitfire LF.IXe (Merlin 66); Became **A-BF**; TOC/RAF 23.6.44; No.331 Sqn 3.8.44; No.332 Sqn 5.5.45 - Arr Norway 19.5.45; RNoAF, No.332 Sqn ('AH-P') 22.11.45; Storage, coded 'A-BF' after 8.46; No.332 Sqn from 3.49; Storage 9.49; No.331 Sqn ('FN-F', named 'Donald') from 1.51; Engine failure, pilot baled out, aircraft dived into Trondheim Fjord, NW of Ekne, between Vestrumholmen and Ytterøy, Cat.FA/E 9.8.51 (Sgt Leif Lyngby safe); w/o 24.8.51 (285:50 flying hours)
NOTE: *Donald Duck* (head) emblem and "*Donald*" painted on the fuselage

PL448 Spitfire LF.IXe (Merlin 66); Became **A-AU**; TOC/RAF 29.6.44; ex Nos.132, 411, 412 & 130 Sqns - No.331 Sqn (in Norway) c.6.45; RNoAF, OTU "*Feltflyvingen*" at Gardermoen ('FN-T') 22.11.45; Coded 'A-AU' after 8.46; No.331 Sqn, taxying collision at Gardermoen with MJ931, Cat.E 16.12.47 (Fenrik [P/O] Knut Urdahl killed), SOC

PL463 Spitfire LF.IXe (Merlin 66); Became **A-CF**; TOC/RAF 29.6.44; ex Nos.66, 331 & 349 Sqns – Selected and desp. to Norway 28.8.47, arr Norway 29.8.47; RNoAF (TOC) 4.9.47; Storage, coded 'A-CF' (ASU Gardermoen, still in storage 6.3.48); No.332 Sqn from 3.49; Take-off at Værnes, Seagull hit radiator, safe landing, Cat.E1 8.8.49 (Sgt Frithjof Torkehagen safe); w/o 30.11.49; Used for spares (191:10 flying hours)

PL861 Spitfire PR.XI (Merlin 70); Became **A-ZA**; TOC/RAF 6.44 - Arr Norway 31.7.47; RNoAF (TOC) 7.8.47; ASU Gardermoen, storage (still in storage 6.3.48); No.1 PRU "*Fotorekognoseringsving*" ('A-ZA') 9.8.49; Hit snowdrift landing Kjevik, lost a wheel, belly-landed, Cat.E 24.3.54 (Lt Jens Chr Width safe); SOC 18.5.54; w/o 20.5.54 (447:45 flying hours); Parts to LTS Kjevik later

PL979 Spitfire PR.XI (Merlin 70); Became **A-ZB**; TOC/RAF 17.10.44 - Arr Norway 31.7.47; RNoAF (TOC) 7.8.47; ASU Gardermoen, storage (still in storage 6.3.48); To No.331 Sqn temporary; No.1 PRU "*Fotorekognoseringsving*"('A-ZB') from 11.49; Engine trouble on take-off, retracted undercarriage, force-landed on belly, Værnes 4.8.51 (Kapt Kristian Nyerrød safe); Repaired and back to No.1 PRU (some time flown by Fenrik [P/O] Reidar Ludt 1952/53); Last flown 25.3.54 (Fenrik Amund Klepp); w/o 18.5.54; Storage at Kjevik; Film as "FN-Z" 1957; Exhibited as "AH-O" in Oslo 1962; Coded "A-ZB" in 5.69 (Oslo); Storage at Rygge AFB in 6.75 (Offered to the Kingsford Smith Memorial Committee in Australia 10.5.61, but deal not completed); Sold for NOK 1,00 to a private owner; To RNoAF Defence Museum/ Forvarsmuseet Flysamlingn, Gardermoen, Oslo 16.6.84, exhibition - **SURVIVOR**
NOTE: 266:15 flying hours on 4.8.51; Total 460:10 f/hrs

PL994 Spitfire PR.XI (Merlin 70); Became **A-ZC**; TOC/RAF 14.11.44 - Arr Norway 31.7.47; RNoAF (TOC) 7.8.47; ASU Gardermoen, storage (still in storage 6.3.48); To No.331 Sqn 28.3.49; No.1 PRU "*Fotorekognoseringsving*" ('A-ZC') 10.49; ARD Kjeller, overhaul from 1.51 to 6.51; Retd to No.1 PRU in 6.51; Engine failed on ferry flight from Sola airfield (Stavanger) to Kjevik, pilot baled out too low, aircraft dived into ground at Lille Djupedal, E of Egersund, Cat.E 19.8.53 (Kapt Harald Meland killed); w/o 21.10.53 (398:35 flying hours)

PT396 see PT726

PT399 Spitfire LF.IXe (Merlin 66); Became **A-BU**; TOC/RAF 1.7.44; ex Nos.329, 74 & 345 Sqns - Selected for Norway 9.6.47; Desp. 18.6.47, arr Norway 19.6.47; RNoAF (TOC) 26.6.47; Storage, coded 'A-BU'; To No.331 Sqn, B-Flight at Kjevik from 31.5.48; Engine trouble, force-landed at Kjevik 1.6.48 (Lt Herfjord); Grounded; LTS Kjevik 8.48; Kjeller air depot in 2.51; No.331 Sqn ('FN-J') from 6.51; Storage 12.51; No.332 Sqn ('AH-A') from 3.51; SOC in 7.52; ASU Værnes, storage (193:15 flying hours)

PT529 Spitfire LF.IXe (Merlin 66); Became **A-AZ**; TOC/RAF 11.8.44; ex No.66 Sqn; No.332 Sqn 10.5.45 - Arr Norway 19.5 45; RNoAF, No.332 Sqn ('AH-G') 22.11.45; Storage, coded 'A-AZ' after 8.46; No.331 Sqn from 9.50; No.332 Sqn from 12.50; Marked 'AH-Y' after 1.51; SOC in 6.52; ASU Værnes, storage (314:55 flying hours)

PT536 Spitfire LF.IXe (Merlin 66); Became **A-AC**; TOC/RAF 14.8.44; ex No.341 Sqn; No.331 Sqn 10.5.45 (marked 'JR', Wg Cdr John Ryg) - Arr Norway 19.5.45; RNoAF, OTU "*Feltflyvingen*" at Gardermoen ('FN-D') 22.11.45; Coded 'A-AC' after 8.46; No.331 Sqn, crashed after wing failure, Cat.E 2.10.48 (Maj Jon Ryg), SOC (117:35 flying hours)

PT658 Spitfire LF.IXe (Merlin 66); Became **A-AW**; TOC/RAF 27.7.44; ex Nos.39 & 33 Sqns; No.332 Sqn 10.5.45 - Arr Norway 19.5.45; RNoAF, No.332 Sqn ('AH- ') 22.11.45; Storage, coded 'A-AW' after 8.46; No.332 Sqn at Bardufoss from 7.48; Crashed on landing, fuselage and wing broken, total loss, Bardufoss, Cat.FA/E 30.10.48 (Fenrik [P/O] Odd Haabet safe), SOC (201:55 flying hours)

PT726 Spitfire LF.IXe (Merlin 66); TOC/RAF 9.8.44; No.331 Sqn from 31.8.44 (No.420 RSU 19.-26.10.44) - Arr Norway in 5.45; RNoAF 22.11.45; LTS Kjevik (marked 'L-TS') by 3.5.47
NOTE: Aircraft marked '*Asbjørn*'; Reported as "PT396"

PT727 Spitfire LF.IXe (Merlin 66); Became **A-AE**; TOC/RAF 9.8.44; ex No.74 Sqn; No.331 Sqn 9./10.5.45 - Arr Norway 19.5.45; RNoAF, OTU "*Feltflyvingen*" at Gardermoen ('FN-F') 22.11.45; Coded 'A-AE' after 8.46; No.331 Sqn, exercise "*Svenor*", engine failure, dived into Skagerak (NW of Väderöerna), Cat.E 10.5.49 (Sgt Olav Tradin killed); w/o 27.6.49 (285:35 flying hours)

PT754 Spitfire LF.IXe (Merlin 66); TOC/RAF 9.8.44; No.332 Sqn ('AH-J') from 9.44; No.132 Wing 19.4.45 - Arr Norway 19.5.45; RNoAF 22.11.45; To LTS Kjevik 1946

PT775 Spitfire LF.IXe; TOC/RAF 16.8.44; ex No.74 Sqn; No.332 Sqn ('AH-R') 12.5.45; Arr Norway 19.5.45; Take-off crash, Gardermoen, Cat.E 17.6.45; SOC 2.7.45 (No.88 Group RAF Oslo)

PT827 Spitfire LF.IXe; TOC/RAF 23.8.44; ex Nos.340 & 341 Sqns; No.332 Sqn ('AH-M') 29.4.45; Arr Norway 19.5.45; Aerobatics, dived into ground near Askim, Cat.FA/E 14.6.45 (Sgt Wilmar Wik killed), SOC

PT833 Spitfire LF.IXe (Merlin 66); Became **A-AB**; TOC/RAF 15.8.44; ex Nos.341 & 222 Sqns; No.331 Sqn from 9.5.45 - Arr Norway 19.5.45; RNoAF, OTU "*Feltflyvingen*" at Gardermoen ('FN-A') 22.11.45; Coded 'A-AB' after 8.46; Storage; No.331 Sqn from 8.50; No.332 Sqn from 12.50; Marked 'AH-D' after 1.51; SOC 29.3.52; To Kjeller air depot, storage; w/o 26.6.52

PT858 Spitfire LF.IXe (Merlin 66); Became **A-BP**; TOC/RAF 24.8.44; ex Nos.74 & 329 Sqns - Selected for Norway 7.5.47; Desp. 8.5.47, arr RNoAF 9.5.47; Storage; No.332 Sqn ('A-BP') from 10.50; Marked 'AH-T' after 1.51; SOC in 7.52; ASU Værnes, storage (266:45 flying hours)

PT882 Spitfire LF.IXe (Merlin 66); Became **A-AH**; TOC/RAF 23.8.44; ex No.329 Sqn; No.331 Sqn 10.5.45 - Arr Norway 19.5.45; RNoAF, OTU "*Feltflyvingen*" at Gardermoen ('FN-K') 22.11.45; Fuel shortage, belly-landed at Gardermoen 8.1.46 (Fenrik [P/O] Egil Stigseth); One wheel landing, skidded on the belly at Gardermoen 30.4.46 (Sgt Per Jansen); Coded 'A-AH' after 8.46; No.331 Sqn, crash-landed Kjevik, Cat.E 23.9.49 (Sgt Jens Lie-Slathein); w/o 22.11.49; Wreckage to LTS Kjevik 21.2.50
NOTE: Marked '*UNNi*'; Total 202:00 flying hours

PT884 Spitfire LF.IXe (Merlin 66); Became **A-CG**; TOC/RAF 24.8.44; ex Nos.331 & 332 Sqns 14.9.44-24.3.45 – Selected for Norway 7.5.47; Desp. 8.5.47, arr RNoAF 9.5.47; Storage, coded 'A-CG' (ASU Gardermoen, still in storage 6.3.48); No.331 Sqn from 3.50; Marked 'FN-G'

Surviving Spitfire PR.XI A-ZB (ex PL979) displayed in the RNoAF Defence Museum/Forvarsmuseet Flysamlingn, Gardermoen, Oslo, in May 1992. [PRA]

Spitfire PR.XI, A-ZC (PL994), receiving engine maintenance and camera installation. The long focus of the camera indicated that it was a Type F-52.
[Øyvind Ellingsen]

PT912 Spitfire LF.IXe (Merlin 66); Became **A-CL**; TOC/RAF 29.8.44; ex Nos.127, 74, 341, 340, 345, 331 & 349 Sqns – Selected for Norway 13.11.47; Desp. 13.11.47, arr RNoAF 14.12.47; Storage, coded 'A-CL' (ASU Gardermoen, still in storage 6.3.48); No.331 Sqn (issued before 6.48); Storage 6.50; No.331 Sqn ('FN-L') from 3.51; SOC in 12.51; ASU Værnes, storage (437:55 flying hours)

PT934 Spitfire LF.IXe; TOC/RAF 30.8.44; ex Nos.127 Sqn; No.331 Sqn ('FN-C') 30.4.45; Arr Norway 19.5.45; Taxying, hit parked truck, Gardermoen, Cat.FA/E 15.7.45 (Plt O Roald); SOC 20.7.45; Remains left behind, to LTS Kjevik spring 1946

PT937 Spitfire LF.IXe (Merlin 66); Became **A-CH**; TOC/RAF 30.8.44; ex Nos.341, 74 & 345 Sqns – Selected for Norway 18.11.47; Desp. 18.11.47, arr Norway 19.11.47; RNoAF (TOC) 22.11.47; Storage, coded 'A-CH'; ASU Gardermoen (still in storage by 6.3.48), test flight from Kjeller, belly-landed at Gardermoen, propeller damaged 11.6.48 (Kapt Eirik Sandberg safe); Repaired, then storage; No.331 Sqn from 7.48; Overshot landing, ground-looped at Værnes 15.11.50 (Sgt John A Larsen); No.332 Sqn ('AH-J') from 11.51; Storage 1.52; No.332 Sqn from 3.52; SOC in 7.52; ASU Værnes, storage
NOTE: 172:15 flying hours 15.11.50; Total 216:25 f/hrs

PT940 Spitfire LF.IXe (Merlin 66); Became **A-AM**; TOC/RAF 5.9.44; ex No.66 Sqn; No.331 Sqn 30.4.45 - Arr Norway 19.5.45; RNoAF, OTU "*Feltflyvingen*" at Gardermoen ('FN-P') 22.11.45; Coded 'A-AM' after 8.46; Storage; No.332 Sqn from 3.49; Storage 9.49; No.331 Sqn ('FN-A') from 4.51; Last flown with No.331 Sqn 20.11.51; SOC in 1.52, storage (361:10 flying hours)

PT942 Spitfire LF.IXe (Merlin 66); Became **A-CM**; TOC/RAF 5.9.44; ex Nos.66 & 345 Sqns – Selected for Norway 18.11.47; Desp. 18.11.47, arr RNoAF 22.11.47; Storage, coded 'A-CM' (ASU Gardermoen, still in storage 6.3.48); None Sqn service; w/o 30.11.49; Used for spares (116:45 flying hours)

PT949 Spitfire LF.IXe (Merlin 66); Became **A-CO**; TOC/RAF 30.8.44; ex No.66 Sqn – Selected for Norway 14.11.47; Desp. 15.11.47, arr Norway 16.11.47; RNoAF (TOC) 22.11.47; Storage, coded 'A-CO' (ASU Gardermoen, still

after 1.51; Exercise "*Stiklestad*", take-off Værnes 26.5.51 (22:45 flying hours), just after midnight the engine failed, aircraft dived into ground c.5m NE of Steinkjaer, Cat.E 27.5.51 (Sgt Ivar Strøm killed); w/o 3.10.51 (337:35 flying hours)

Check list of RNoAF / RAF Serial numbers

RNoAF Code	TOC	RAF SerialNo	RNoAF Code	TOC	RAF SerialNo
Spitfire LF.IXc/e					
A-AB	21.9.45	PT833	A-BP	9.5.47	PT858
A-AC	21.9.45	PT536	A-BR	9.5.47	MJ633
A-AD	21.9.45	MK631	A-BS	9.5.47	MJ792
A-AE	21.9.45	PT727	A-BT	9.5.47	NH208
A-AF	21.9.45	SM668	A-BU	19.6.47	PT399
A-AG	21.9.45	MK886	A-BV	31.7.47	NH357
A-AH	21.9.45	PT882	A-BW	5.9.47	NH576
A-AI	21.9.45	MJ931	A-BX	28.8.47	MK904
A-AK	21.9.45	MK671	A-BY	18.6.47	MJ418
A-AL	21.9.45	PL221	A-BZ	9.5.47	NH213
A-AM	21.9.45	PT940			
A-AN	21.9.45	PV190	A-CA	19.6.47	PL185
A-AO	21.9.45	MJ951	A-CB	5.9.47	NH261
A-AP	21.9.45	MJ471	A-CC	28.8.47	PL327
A-AR	21.9.45	MK839	A-CD	31.7.47	JL361
A-AS	21.9.45	PL187	A-CE	28.8.47	NH423
A-AT	21.9.45	MJ217	A-CF	28.8.47	PL463
A-AU	21.9.45	PL448	A-CG	9.5.47	PT884
A-AV	21.9.45	ML132	A-CH	19.11.47	PT937
A-AW	21.9.45	PT658	A-CI	14.11.47	NH193
A-AX	21.9.45	MK897	A-CK	14.11.47	MK799
A-AY	21.9.45	NH475	A-CL	14.11.47	PT912
A-AZ	21.9.45	PT529	A-CM	19.11.47	PT942
			A-CN	15.11.47	NH401
A-BA	21.9.45	PL226	A-CO	16.11.47	PT949
A-BB	21.9.45	ML178	A-CP	1.5.48	MK997
A-BC	21.9.45	ML363	A-CR	1.5.48	MK866
A-BD	21.9.45	NH316	A-CS	1.5.48	PL255
A-BE	21.9.45	NH584	A-CT	1.5.48	NH540
A-BF	21.9.45	PL408	A-CU	1.5.48	NH253
A-BG	21.9.45	MK983	A-CV	13.5.48	NH520
A-BH	21.9.45	NH460	A-CW	10.9.48	MJ409
A-BI	21.9.45	PV215			
A-BK	15.11.45	NH171	**Spitfire PR.XI**		
A-BL	15.11.45	MJ855	A-ZA	31.7.47	PL861
A-BM	21.9.45	MH350	A-ZB	31.7.47	PL979
A-BN	21.9.45	NH372	A-ZC	31.7.47	PL994
A-BO	21.9.45	NH550			

To LTS Kjevik: PT726, PT754, PV153, and spare parts from MK304, PT775/ 827/ 934

Spitfire LF.IXe PV190 FN-R of the RNoAF, OTU "Feltflyvingen" at Gardermoen around 1945/46. It was written off there when it hit a snowblower on take-off on 6th February 1946.
[via Nils Mathisrud]

Typical post-January 1951 markings of RNoAF Spitfire IXs. No.332 Sqn's 'AH-F' with serial number SM668 in black on the rear fuselage. This minor accident at Bardufoss on 4th February 1952 caused the aircraft to be written off. No repairs were undertaken at this late stage in its service career.
[Bjørn Hafsten]

in storage 6.3.48); No.332 Sqn 29.4.49; Accident at Værnes airfield, prop and wingtip damaged on landing 2.6.49 (Sgt Einar Weisteen safe); With No.332 Sqn to Bardufoss from 10.49; Marked 'AH-A' after 1.51; Crashed on landing at Bardufoss (shows marking 'A-AH'), stalled and turned over, Cat.E2 11.7.51 (Sgt Jan Steen Härum of No.331 Sqn safe); w/o 1.8.51 (315:20 flying hours)

PV153 Spitfire LF.IXe (Merlin 66); TOC/RAF 15.9.44; No.331 Sqn ('FN-D') 19.10.44 - Arr Norway in 5.45; RNoAF 22.11.45; To LTS Kjevik 1946

PV190 Spitfire LF.IXe (Merlin 66); Allotted **A-AN**; TOC/RAF 15.9.44; ex No.442 Sqn; No.331 Sqn 14.5.45 - Arr Norway 19.5.45; RNoAF, OTU "*Feltflyvingen*" at Gardermoen ('FN-R') 22.11.45; Hit snowblower on take-off, Gardermoen, Cat.E 6.2.46 (Sgt B Ringstad safe), SOC

PV215 Spitfire LF.IXe (Merlin 66); Became **A-BI**; TOC/RAF 18.9.44; ex Nos.222 & 485 Sqns; FSU Dyce 19.6.45; No.128 Wing 19.7.45 - No.332 Sqn (in Norway) 19.6.45; RNoAF, No.332 Sqn ('AH-M') 22.11.45; Coded 'A-BI' after 8.46; ASU Værnes, storage from 25.10.47 to 8.3.50; No.331 Sqn (issued 8.3.50); Engine failure over Steinkjaer, crashed in forced landing at Bardalgård in Beistad, c.40m NW of Værnes, Cat.FA/E 26.9.50 (Sgt Asbjørn Andreas Thunes killed), SOC

SL595 Spitfire LF.IXe; On loan to Netherlands Air Force (NSTT Langham 12.46-12.47); Allocated for Norway 11.12.47, but cancelled and scrapped 2.50

SM668 Spitfire LF.IXe (Merlin 66); Became **A-AF**; TOC/RAF 5.12.44; No.331 Sqn 12.5.45 - Arr Norway 19.5.45; RNoAF, OTU "*Feltflyvingen*" at Gardermoen ('FN-H') 22.11.45; Coded 'A-AF' after 8.46; Storage 8.50; No.332 Sqn ('AH-F') from 4.51; Undercarriage failed, belly-landed, Bardufoss, Cat.E 4.2.52; w/o 28.3.52 (466:25 flying hours)
NOTE: Aircraft carried the name "*Bente*"

Unidentified

18.10.48 No.331 Sqn, crashed on approach, Gardermoen (Sgt Jan Christian Amundsen)
18.10.48 No.331 Sqn, crashed on approach, Gardermoen (Sgt Kjell Lindboe).

SURVIVORS in Norway

MH350 RNoAF Museum Bodø
BP929? RNoAF Museum Bodø, recovered Russian PR.IV wreck. Since acquired by Swedish enthusiast Sven Kindblom of Stockholm. [Previous identity BP929 provisional, but this went to the USAAF. From the Soviet Union listing BP923 would seem more likely]
PL979 RNoAF Museum Gardermoen.

References:
Norwegian Air Force, RAF Flying Review 1962 (p.20 & 48).
Sentinel of the Fjords, by William Green, Flying Review International April 1969 (p.50 ff) and May 1969 (p.54f).
From Spitfire to Fighting Falcon, No.332 Sqn RNoAF, by S Stenersen and B Olsen, Air Pictorial June 1983 (p.212).
History of the Nos.331 & 332 Sqns, RNoAF 1991/92.
Nr.1 Fotorekognoseringsving by Bjørn Hafsten and Tom Arheim.
Supermarine Spitfire in the Royal Norwegian Air Force 1945-54, by Bjørn Hafsten (Norsk Flyhistorisk Forening).
Warbirds of Norway, Vol.11, No.1 (1996).

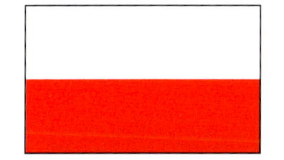

POLAND

Two Spitfire LF.XVIes, TB292 marked 'QH-Z' (No.302 Sqn) and TB581 marked 'JH-Q' (No.317 Sqn) after their arrival at Okecie airport, Warsaw, on 25th October 1945. [Andrzej Glass via Wojtek Matusiak]

In August 1939 a single example of a Spitfire Mk.Ia (L1066) was despatched for Poland. However, Polish resistance to the occupying German forces collapsed whilst it was en route, and it was diverted instead to Turkey.

During the Second World War Polish pilots flew Spitfires with the RAF, seven Polish Air Force fighter squadrons being formed under RAF control.

Shortly after the war ended Poland received three Spitfire LF.XVIes for display. One was returned to the RAF in Germany (BAFO) in 1945. The other two were exhibited in Warsaw from 1945 until both were scrapped at the end of 1950.

In July 1977, the Aviation Museum at Krakow received a further Spitfire LF.XVIe in exchange for the fuselage of a DH.9a for the Royal Air Force Museum at Hendon

Polish Spitfire units of the RAF

No.**145** Sqn, *Polish Fighting Team* - Unit code 'ZX';
While based in North Africa, this unit received a third flight with Polish pilots, the '*Polish Fighting Team*' (PFT), which used Spitfire Mk.IX from 12th March 1943 until 30th June 1943. PFT aircraft wore individual numbers instead of the individual letters of other aircraft of No.145 Sqn.

No.**302** '*Poznanski*' Sqn - Unit code 'WX'; from August 1945 'QH';
Formed Leconfield 13th July 1940, disbanded Hethel 18th December 1946; Spitfire Mks.II (few for training only), V, IX and XVI between October 1941 and December 1946.

No.**303** '*Warszawski*' – '*T Kosciuszko*' Sqn - Unit code 'RF';
Formed Northolt 22th July 1940, disbanded Hethel 11th December 1946; Spitfire Mks. I, II, V and IX (and one LF.XVIe) from January 1941 to April 1945; then Mustang I & IV.

No.**306** '*Torunski*' Sqn - Unit code 'UZ';
Formed Church Fenton 29th August 1940, disbanded Coltishall 6th January 1947; Spitfire Mks.II, V and IX between June 1941 and April 1944; then Mustang III.

No.**308** '*Krakowski*' Sqn - Unit code 'ZF';
Formed Squires Gate 5th September 1940, disbanded Hethel 18th December 1946; Spitfire Mks.I, II, V, IX and XVI between March 1941 and December 1946.

No.**315** '*Deblinski*' Sqn - Unit code 'PK';
Formed Acklington 8th January 1941, disbanded

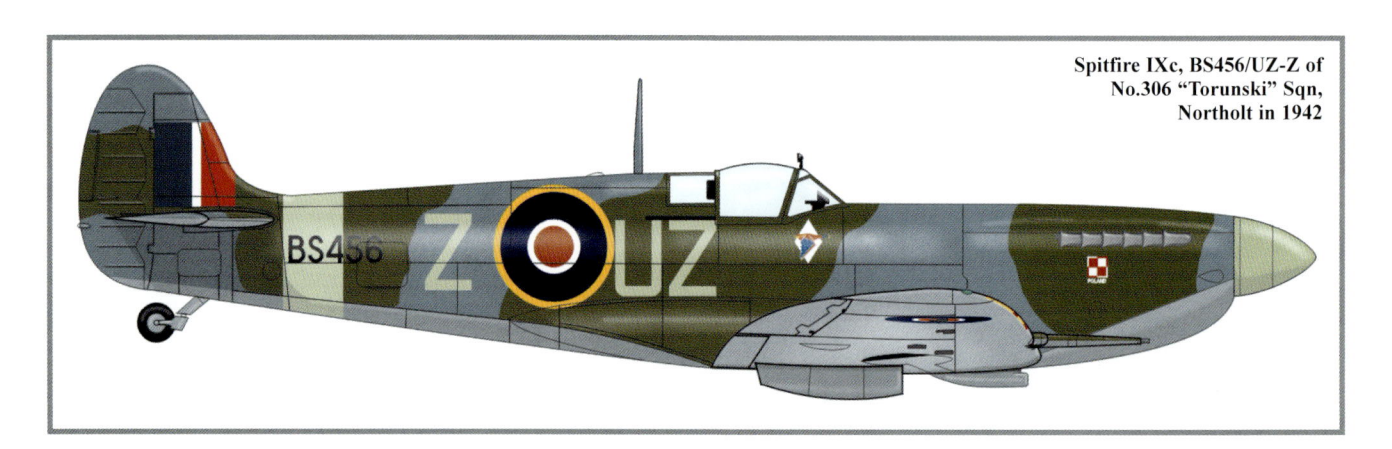

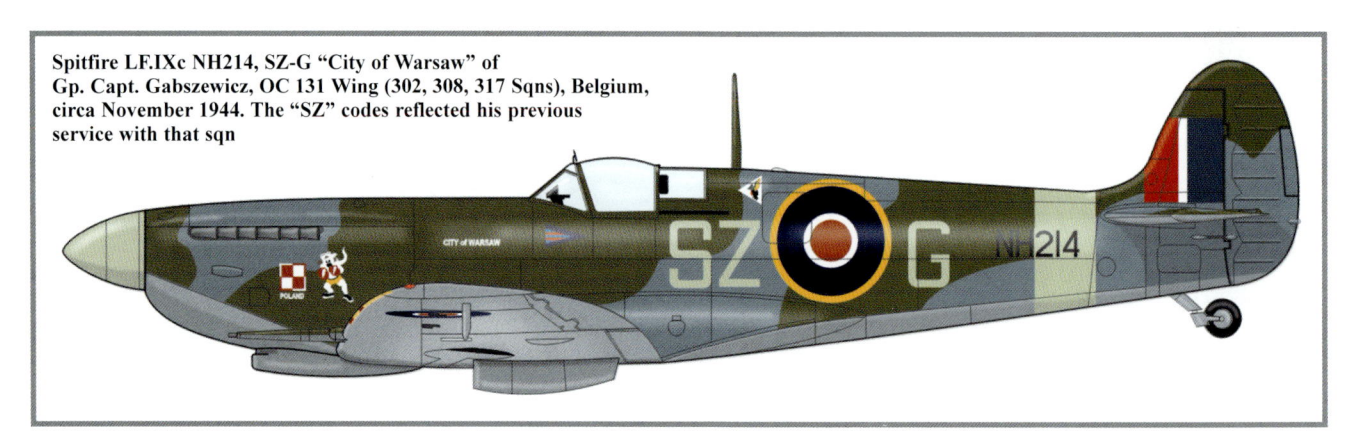

Spitfire IXc, BS456/UZ-Z of
No.306 "Torunski" Sqn,
Northolt in 1942

Spitfire LF.IXc NH214, SZ-G "City of Warsaw" of
Gp. Capt. Gabszewicz, OC 131 Wing (302, 308, 317 Sqns), Belgium,
circa November 1944. The "SZ" codes reflected his previous
service with that sqn

Surviving Spitfire LF.XVIe SM411 was exhibited in the Muzeum Lotnictwa Polskiego (Polish Aviation Museum) at Krakow and marked "SM411/AU-Y", but by June 2000 was repainted as "TB995" and coded "ZF-O" as seen here at Goraska. [Wojtek Matusiak]

POLAND

Spitfire LF.XVIe TB581 'JH-Q' served with No.317 (Polish) Sqn RAF and was flown to Warsaw for exhibition in front of the National Museum in October 1945, being later shown at Katowice. This aeroplane remained in Poland until 1950, when it was scrapped. Note the Polish insignia on the cowling.
[Marian Krzyzan (above) and Ryszard Witkowski (below)]

Coltishall 14th January 1947; Spitfire Mks.II, V and IX between July 1941 and April 1944; then Mustang III.

No.316 *'Warszawski'* Sqn - Unit code 'SZ';
Formed Pembrey 12th February 1941, disbanded at Hethel 11th December 1946; Spitfire Mks.II (few for training only), V and IX between October 1941 and April 1944; then Mustang III.

No.317 *'Wilenski'* Sqn - Unit code 'JH';
Formed Acklington 19th February 1941, disbanded Hethel 18th December 1946; Spitfire Mks.V, IX and XVI from October 1941 to December 1946.

No.318 *'Gdanski'* Sqn - Unit code 'LW';
Formed Detling 20th March 1943, Middle East from August 1943 to August 1946, disbanded Coltishall 12th December 1946; Spitfire Mks.V and IX between March 1944 and July 1946.

Individual Histories

SM411 Spitfire LF.XVIe; ex GI No. *7242M*; Arr Poland 1977; Currently exhibited in the Muzeum Lotnictwa Polskiego (Polish Aviation Museum), Krakow and marked "SM411/AU-Y"; Temporary exhibition in Warsaw 13-15.2.98; Recently painted as 'TB995' and coded 'ZF-O' – **SURVIVOR**

TB292 Spitfire LF.XVIe (Merlin 266); TOC/RAF 3.1.45; ex No.302 Sqn RAF ('QH-Z'); Prepared by No.411 R&SU for a flight to Poland 20.10.45 (No.412 R&SU 25.10.45);

Handed over to British pilots for flying to Warsaw 22.10.45; Arr Warsaw-Okecie airport 25.10.45; Exhibited in the Polish Army Museum at Warsaw from 1946; Scrapped in 12.50

TB581 Spitfire LF.XVIe (Merlin 266); TOC/RAF 4.2.45; ex No.317 Sqn RAF ('JH-Q'); Prepared by No.411 R&SU 20.10.45 (No.412 R&SU 25.10.45); To British pilots for flying to Warsaw 22.10.45; Arr Warsaw-Okecie airport 25.10.45; Dismantled and by truck to Warsaw City, assembled in front of the Polish Army Museum, exhibition 29.10.45; Later the British Government gifted the aircraft to Poland; Scrapped in 11.50

TB890 Spitfire LF.XVIe (short stay in Poland only); TOC/RAF 25.2.45; ex No.308 Sqn RAF ('ZF-V'); Destined for an exhibition in Poland (on loan); No 411 R&SU 20.10.45 (No.412 R&SU 25.10.45); To the British pilot P/O AR Cox 22.10.45; During the ferry flight the pilot lost his bearing, force-landed at Poznan (Posen) on Lawica airfield 25.10.45; Soviets would not allow to continue the flight to Warsaw, but only gave permission to return to the BAFO at Ahlhorn, Germany; Later the aircraft served with No.302 Sqn from 6.3.46 to 19.8.46.

Unidentified

On 26 July 1942 the Krakow Main Market Square saw the opening of a German exhibition of captured weapons, also one Spitfire of No.1 PRU (code 'LY'), probably a PR-variant; Serial number unknown.

SURVIVOR in Poland

SM411 Muzeum Lotnictwa Polskiego, Krakow.

Reference:
Spitfires in Poland, by Wojtek Matusiak, FlyPast 5.98, p.49.

PORTUGAL

The Portuguese Air Force originally came under the control of the Portuguese Army, being then the Army Air Force and known as *Arma de Aeronáutica Militar* (*AM*). Alongside this existed an Air Arm of the Navy (*Aviação Naval*). Both were merged into the *Força Aérea Portuguesa* (*FAP*) from 1st July 1952.

In the late thirties the Portuguese Air Force wished to modernise it equipment, and the Foreign Orders Committee (British Air Ministry) first considered an enquiry from Portugal for ten or fifteen Spitfire Mk.Ia on 3rd February 1938. On 16th February 1938 Supermarine sent a quotation to Portugal for 15 aircraft. In the priority list of the Foreign Office, dated 17th November 1938, Portugal was allocated sixth place. In April 1939 the Portuguese Government ordered 15 Spitfire Mk.Ia (Type 336, with Merlin III), and under No C.972/39 a contract was signed in the autumn 1939. With the outbreak of the Second World War delivery dates were revised, and eventually interest lapsed.

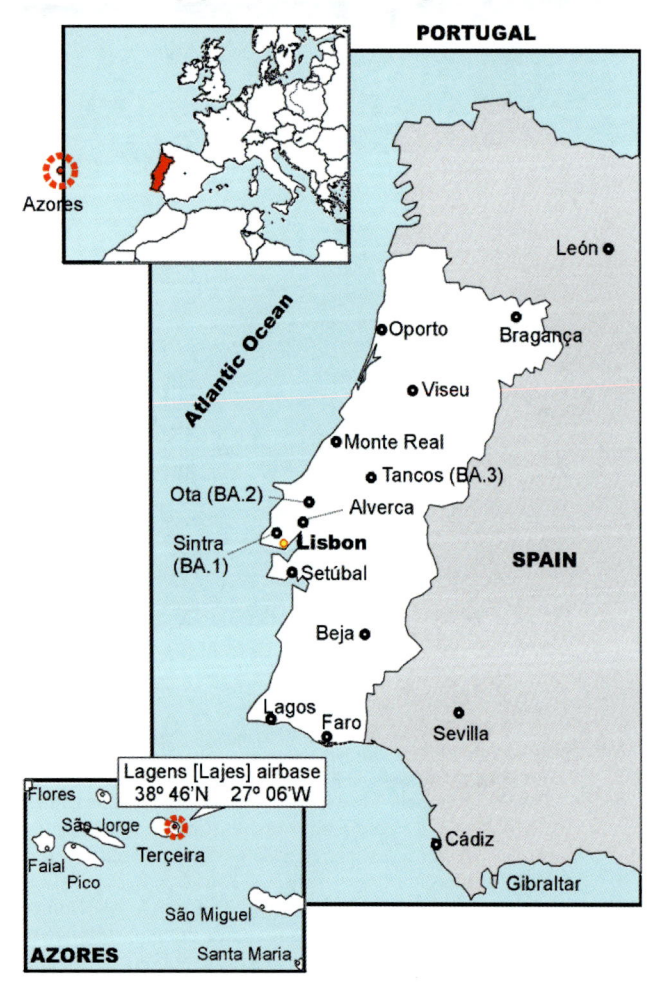

The Portuguese Air Force then used equipment from various countries, including Britain, Germany and the USA, and the training of the pilots was also carried out abroad. Portugal remained neutral throughout the war, but as Britain's oldest ally it received favourable consideration, and in the autumn of 1941 fifteen Curtiss Mohawk IVs were sent from RAF reserve stocks. The Portuguese Air Force asked for more of these, but as no more were available they were offered Spitfires instead.

British interests and activities

Portugal recognised the vital interest of Britain in the strategic position of the Azores and its need for free passage to Gibraltar. On the other hand it wished to avoid confrontation with Germany or Spain. Protection of the Azores was therefore initially undertaken by Portuguese troops. However, Britain requested the use of an airfield there, and from 1941 gave help for the enlargement of the airfield at Lagens (Lajes) on Terçeira Island.

By 1943 Portugal was becoming concerned that they might be attacked by Axis forces. Britain looked into the possibility of providing some form of defence, and on 3rd July 1943 "*Task Force 130*" was formed at Air Ministry headquarters in Whitehall, London. On 6th July 1943 the Air Component of this Force became No.246 (Special Operations) Group, to control Nos. 96, 130 & 234 Sqns for Operation *Kaolin* (later Operation *Lemonade*), for the planned defence of Portuguese airfields and the ports of Lisbon and Oporto. No.96 Sqn used Beaufighter VIF at that time. Nos.130 & 234 Sqns assembled at Honiley with Spitfire Mk.Vs to be fitted with long-range tanks and were to have proceeded overseas in company with No.98 Sqn Mitchells acting as guides, a detachment of this unit being based at Honiley from 15th July 1943 to 1st August 1943. A month later the plan was cancelled, and the Spitfire squadrons left Honiley for West Malling on 4th August 1943. No.246 Group was disbanded on 9th August 1943.

PORTUGAL

A line-up of Spitfire F.Ias of the XZ-Esq and Spitfire F.Vbs of the RL- and MR Esqs at BA.2 Ota in August 1944. In the left foreground is No.370 (ex X4339), marked 'XZ+A'.
[Mário Canonglia Lopes]

The same place, but three or four years later, with newly-delivered Spitfire LF.Vbs on the ground. Nearest are EP785 and W3248, which became AM Nos. 75 and 76 respectively, arriving at Ota in January 1948. In the background are older F.Vbs with RL- and MR- markings. The six-stub exhaust pipes of the later LF.Vbs are interesting.
[Mário Canonglia Lopes]

Under the terms of an agreement signed on 17th August 1943 between the two countries, British forces were based on the Azores from 8 October 1943 until 2nd June 1946. Among them was No.247 Group RAF, which included Nos.206 & 220 Sqns with Fortress II & No.269 Sqn with Spitfire Mk.V at Lagens (Lajes), and the Royal Navy at Port Horta, Faial Is). In return Britain supplied additional military equipment, including aircraft. From 1944 the USAAF also held bases on the Azores, using airfields on Santa Maria.

The Portuguese Air Force

At the beginning of the forties the Portuguese Army Air Force (AM) consisted of a small bombing element of four Esquadrilhas (each with 5 aircraft) at Ota (BA.2), and a Recce Esquadrilha (9 aircraft) at Tancos (BA.3). Liaison and training was carried out with Tiger Moths, Dragon IIs etc, based at Sintra (BA.1), where a Practice School was established with the firing range of Espino. Two Fighter units existed with British Gladiator II biplanes, serving as Nos.1 & 2 Expeditionary Fighter Esquadrilhas for the

Azores from 1941, when Portugal received 15 Mohawk IV for a further fighter unit, the XY-Esquadrilha. Nineteen USAAF P-39 Airacobras with a lone Lightning (P-38), all force-landed and were interned by Portugal, forming the OK-Esquadrilha in 1943. During that period Spitfire Mk.Ias flew with the XZ-Esquadrilha, and Hawker Hurricanes arrived for building up five new fighter units, the VX-, SU-, TY-, RV- and GL-Esquadrilhas at Sintra, Ota and Tancos.

Portuguese *Spitfire* inventory:

Nos. 370 to 387,	del. 11.42 - 10.43	=	18 Mk.Ia
Nos. 1 to 34,	del. 10.43 - 2.44	=	34 Mk.Vb/c
Nos. 35 to 93,	del. 4.47 - 1.48	=	59 LF.Vb
	Total	=	111

By the end of 1943 Portugal had a sizeable Air Force, and on 6th May 1944 over 200 aircraft were assembled at Ota for flight demonstrations and mock attacks, with President Carmona and Prime Minister Salazar in attendance. The flying display included Spitfire Mk.Ia of the XZ-Esquadrilha, whilst Spitfire Mk.Vs were in the static display.

Under order No.10711 of the 18th July 1944 the Portuguese Air Force was re-organised. At Ota (BA.2) a Fighting Aviation Group (*Grupo de Esquadrilhas de Aviação de Caça*) was formed comprising Esquadrilhas (Nos.1 & 2 Esq [MR-/RL-Esq] with Spitfire Mk.Vb/cs, No.3 Esquadrilha [XZ-Esq] with Spitfire Mk.Ias and No.4 Esquadrilha [OK-Esq] with Airacobras).

A further re-organisation of the Portuguese Air Force was made under Decree No.12194 dated 19th December 1947. Then a Spitfire Fighter Aviation Group was formed at Ota, comprising three Esquadrilhas: Nos.1 & 2 Esq [MR- & RL-Esq] with Spitfire Mk.Vb/cs and a third unit the ZE-Esquadrilha (formerly a Blenheim unit, then an OTU with Spitfire LF.Vbs, AT-6s, Magisters & Gladiatorss). Simultaneously the XZ-Esquadrilha was disbanded, and all Spitfire Mk.Ias were struck off charge, the last being scrapped in 1948/50. Later the Group moved from Ota to Tancos (BA.3) in April 1952 with 50 Spitfires.

Meanwhile, on 1st July 1952, the Portuguese Air Force became an independent service, no longer under Army control, and combined with the *Aviação Naval* to form the *Força Aérea Portuguesa* (*FAP*). As part of NATO, the primary (Fighter) operational unit was now to be a 25-aircraft *Esquadra* (Squadron) to conform with USAF practice. At the same time the FAP announced a new four-digit aircraft numbering system in which the first digit indicated the military class (role), the second digit the aircraft type and the last two the individual number. The block *4300* onwards was allocated for the Spitfires, which were used for jet transition training at that time. However, by then they were nearing the end of their service time, and consequently never took up the new allocation, retaining the old serials until the end.

Spitfire Mk.Ia

Portugal requested additional Mohawks, but the UK supplied ten Spitfire Mk.Ias instead between November 1942 and January 1943 (Price **£8,400** each). These arrived by sea at Lisbon, and after assembly in the *Oficinas Gerais de Material Aeronáutico* (OGMA workshop) at Alverca they went to the BA.3 at Tancos to build up the XZ-Esquadrilha.

A further eight Spitfire Mk.Ias were sent to Portugal in August to October 1943. The 18 aircraft now supplied were given the Portuguese serial numbers **370 to 387**. However, the hot Iberian climate proved unsuitable for the Spitfire Mk.Ia. Consideration was given to basing the aircraft in the cooler climate of the Azores, as a No.4 Expeditionary Fighter Flight, but this was never put into effect. Instead they became part of the *Fighting Aviation Group* (No.3 Esq) at Ota from 1st August 1944.

A general SOC for the last serviceable Spitfire Mk.Ia was given with order from 19th December 1947. All were scrapped.

Spitfire Mk.Vb/c

The Azores agreement led to an expansion of the military deliveries from Great Britain.

The first 13 Spitfire F.Vbs and two F.Vcs arrived for BA.2, Ota, in March 1944 to build up the new RL-Esquadrilha, these aircraft being given serial numbers **1 to 15**. In March/April 1943, a further 15 Mk.Vbs (including one LF.Vb) were supplied for the new formed MR-Esquadrilha, these being numbered **16 to 30** plus **33** (except No.27). An additional one Spitfire LF.Vb and three F.Vbs reached the airbase in June 1944, carried the numbers **27** and **31, 32 & 34**; two of these going to RL-Esquadrilha and the other two to the MR-Esquadrilha.

After World War Two, 59 Spitfire LF.Vbs arrived in Portugal, being serialled **35 to 93**. These had been refurbished by Reid & Sigrist Ltd at Desford, near Leicester, before being ferried out by air via Dunsfold to the OGMA at Alverca 1947/48. The pilot of a further Spitfire LF.Vb (AA753) lost his bearing on delivery to Portugal, and landed in Spain, where his aircraft was interned and eventually struck off charge.

From August 1944 the *Fighting Aviation Group* at Ota served with Spitfire Mk.Vb/cs in two Esquadrilhas. After being re-formed in early 1948 the *Spitfire Fighter Aviation Group* used Spitfire F.Vb/c and LF.Vb in three Esquadrilhas.

In April 1952, under NATO control, the Spitfire Group moved with 50 Spitfire Mk.Vs from Ota to Tancos (BA.3). In the meantime 20 Spitfires has been written off before February 1952; a further 24 were struck off charge between February 1952 and April 1952. Shortly afterwards the Group became a second-line unit.

With the arrival of the F-84G *Thunderjet* in 1953 the Spitfires were phased out. By September 1954 only about a dozen Spitfire Mk.Vs were flying, and these moved to Sintra (BA.1) to be used for ground instructional purposes, but by now they were in a poor state and not worth repair. The last known flight was recorded on 1 March 1955. All Spitfires were scrapped by the DGMFA at Alverca.

Camouflage

The Portuguese Spitfires used dark green/ocean grey (RAF day fighter) camouflage. The unit code and an individual letter were painted on the fuselage sides, centred by the Portuguese cross; on the rear fuselage the Portuguese serial number was applied in white; on both wings, top and bottom, the Portuguese cross was painted in a white circle. The Mk.Vs carried a fuselage band in unit-colours.

In 1952 the camouflage of fighter aircraft was changed to olive green overall with grey under-surface. The national insignia was painted on one wing only, in a white circle, then also on the fuselage; the serial number was applied in white on the fin (trainer aircraft in natural metal shows black numbers). From April 1952 the Spitfires became reserve aircraft, and fuselage bands were no longer carried. Some time later the FAP ceased using unit code-letters. Instead the serial number was painted in big digits on the fuselage, together with the Portuguese cross and an individual letter.

Spitfire units of the Portuguese Air Force

XZ - Esquadrilha; Formed early 1943 at Tancos (BA.3) with Spitfire Mk.Ia; To Ota (BA.2) on 18th July 1944 and No.**3** Esq of the *Fighting Aviation Group* from 1st August 1944; End 1947 disbanded; All Spitfire Mk.Ia scrapped.
Markings: Spinner Sky-coloured, no fuselage bands.
Commanding Officer:
Capt Sarmento

MR- Esquadrilha; Formed in March 1944 at Ota (BA.2) with

Spitfire F.Vb/c; No.**1** Esq of the *Fighting Aviation Group* at Ota from 1st August 1944; No.**1** Esq of the *Spitfire Fighter Aviation Group* at Ota from January 1948, partly re-equipped with Spitfire LF.Vb; Second-line unit with Spitfires at Tancos (BA.3) from April 1952 to August 1954.
Markings: Yellow spinner and yellow fuselage bands.
Commanding Officers:
Capt Fernando de Oliveira e Sousa
Capt Artur Tamagnini Barbosa in 2.52

RL - Esquadrilha; Formed in March 1944 at Ota (BA.2) with Spitfire F.Vb and two LF.Vb; No.**2** Esq of the *Fighting Aviation Group* at Ota from 1st August 1944; No.**2** Esq of the Spitfire Fighter Aviation Group at Ota from January 1948, partly re-equipped with Spitfire LF.Vb; Second-line unit with Spitfires at Tancos (BA.3) from April 1952 to August 1954.
Markings: Blue spinner and blue fuselage bands.
Commanding Officers:
Lt Rogerio de Oliveira Seixas
Capt Rui Braz de Oliveira in 2.52

ZE - Esquadrilha; Ex day bombing unit (Blenheim & Ju 86); Re-formed as No.**3** Esq (OTU) of the Spitfire Fighter Aviation Group at Ota (BA.2) in January 1948, with Spitfire LF.Vb plus AT-6s, Magisters and Gladiators; Second-line unit at Tancos (BA.3) from April 1952 to August 1954.
Unit inactive from 1945 to 1947, after the fatal crash of its CO, Capt Ferreira. With the arrival of the Spitfire LF.Vb in 1947/48 and the disbandment of the XZ-Esquadrilha, this unit was resurrected.
Commanding officers:
Capt Joao Jose Ribeiro Ferreira (killed in accident 12.8.44)
Unknown (1948)
Capt Fernando Pereira Caldas in 2.52

Portuguese Abbreviations:
AM = Aeronáutica Militar (Portuguese Army Air Force) until June 1952.
BA = Base Aérea (Air Base).
DGMFA = Depósito Geral de Material da Força Aérea (General Depot of Air Force Equipment), a storage unit at Alverca.
Esq = Esquadrilha ("Flight"); Fighter Esq 10-15 aircraft).
FAP = Força Aérea Portuguesa (Portuguese Air Force) from July 1952.
IRAN = Inspection & Repair as necessary.
OGMA = Oficinas Gerais de Material Aeronáutico (Aeronautical Equipment General Plants), a production, reception and maintenance unit at Alverca.
PMA = Parque de Material de Aeronáutica (Equipment Park) at Alverca, became OGMA in 1928.

Individual Histories

[Individual information is regrettably sparse. General fates are given with the Notes, but individual aircraft may have had a shorter service time, as it is known, for instance, that by 1952 more than forty Spitfire Vs were no longer on charge]

K9828 Spitfire F.Ia (Merlin III); Became A.M. No. **3**xx (range 380-383); TOC/RAF 18.12.38 - Arr Lisbon by ship 29.8.43; OGMA workshop Alverca for assembly; XZ-Esquadrilha at BA.3 Tancos in 10.43; Fighting Aviation Group at BA.2 Ota (No.3 Esq) from 1.8.44; Latest SOC end 1947; Scrapped 1948/50

K9991 Spitfire F.Ia (Merlin III); Became A.M. No. **384**; TOC/RAF 31.5.39 - Arr Lisbon by ship 18.9.43; OGMA workshop Alverca for assembly; XZ-Esquadrilha ('XZ+P') at BA.3 Tancos in 10.43; Fighting Aviation Group at BA.2 Ota (No.3 Esq) from 1.8.44; Latest SOC end 1947; Scrapped 1948/50

P8788 Spitfire LF.Vb (Merlin 45M); Became A.M. No. **73**; TOC/RAF 7.7.41; Reid & Sigrist, Desford 12.11.46 - Dunsfold, en route for Portugal 22.8.47, arr. OGMA Alverca; BA.2 Ota 12.12.47; Spitfire Fighter Aviation Group (Nos.1, 2 or 3 Esq) from 1.48; To BA.3 Tancos (No.3 Esq) in 4.52; FAP 7.52 [see Note 3)]
NOTE: FB-version, with underwing bomb racks.

P8791 Spitfire LF.Vb (Merlin 55M); Became A.M. No. **79**; TOC/RAF 24.7.41; ex USAAF; Reid & Sigrist, Desford 9.12.46 - Dunsfold, en route for Portugal 12.11.47, arr. OGMA Alverca; BA.2 Ota 12.1.48; Spitfire Fighter Aviation Group (Nos.1, 2 or 3 Esq) from 1.48; To BA.3 Tancos (No.3 Esq) in 4.52; FAP 7.52 [see Note 3)]

P9544 Spitfire F.Ia (Merlin III); Became A.M. No. **387**; TOC/RAF 6.5.44 - Arr Lisbon by ship 7.10.43; OGMA workshop Alverca for assembly; XZ-Esquadrilha ('XZ+S') at BA.3 Tancos in 11.43; Fighting Aviation Group at BA.2 Ota (No.3 Esq) from 1.8.44; Latest SOC end 1947; Scrapped 1948/50

R6626 Spitfire F.Ia (Merlin III); Became A.M. No. **3**xx (range 380-383); TOC/RAF 25.5.44 - Arr Lisbon by ship 29.8.43; OGMA workshop Alverca for assembly; XZ-Esquadrilha at BA.3 Tancos in 10.43; Fighting Aviation Group at BA.2 Ota (No.3 Esq) from 1.8.44; Latest SOC end 1947; Scrapped 1948/50

R6920 Spitfire F.Ia (Merlin III); Became A.M. No. **3**xx (range 372-374); TOC/RAF 12.7.40 - Arr Lisbon by ship 12.12.42; OGMA workshop Alverca for assembly; XZ-Esquadrilha at BA.3 Tancos in 1.43; Fighting Aviation Group at BA.2 Ota (No.3 Esq) from 1.8.44; Latest SOC end 1947; Scrapped 1948/50
NOTE: A.M. No. **372**, Mk.Ia ('XZ+C'), collided in the air with No. **375** (X4716), safe belly landing, light tail damage (Sgt Ismael Canavilhas), date unknown.

R6987 Spitfire F.Ia (Merlin III); Became A.M. No. **3**xx (range 376-379); TOC/RAF 23.7.40 - Arr Lisbon by ship 20.1.43; OGMA workshop Alverca for assembly; XZ-Esquadrilha at BA.3 Tancos in 3.43; Fighting Aviation Group at BA.2 Ota (No.3 Esq) from 1.8.44; Latest SOC end 1947; Scrapped 1948/50

R7027 Spitfire F.Ia (Merlin III); Became A.M. No. **3**xx (range 376-379); TOC/RAF 15.2.41 - Arr Lisbon by ship 20.1.43; OGMA workshop Alverca for assembly; XZ-Esquadrilha at BA.3 Tancos in 3.43; Fighting Aviation Group at BA.2 Ota (No.3 Esq) from 1.8.44; Latest SOC end 1947; Scrapped 1948/50

R7071 Spitfire F.Ia (Merlin III); Became A.M. No. **385**; Presentation aircraft '*PERSEUS*'; TOC/RAF 15.2.41 - Arr Lisbon by ship 26.9.43; OGMA workshop Alverca for assembly; XZ-Esquadrilha ('XZ-Q') at BA.3 Tancos in 11.43; Fighting Aviation Group at BA.2 Ota (No.3 Esq) from 1.8.44; Latest SOC end 1947; Scrapped 1948/50

R7123 Spitfire F.Ia (Merlin III); Became A.M. No. **3**xx (range 376-379); Presentation aircraft '*CAPUT INTER NIBILA*'; TOC/RAF 14.2.41 - Arr Lisbon by ship 20.1.43; OGMA workshop Alverca for assembly; XZ-Esquadrilha at BA.3 Tancos in 3.43; Fighting Aviation Group at BA.2 Ota (No.3 Esq) from 1.8.44; Latest SOC end 1947; Scrapped 1948/50

R7146 Spitfire PR.C (Merlin III); Became A.M. No. **3**xx (range 380-383); TOC/RAF 23.2.41 - Arr Lisbon by ship 29.8.43; OGMA workshop Alverca for assembly; XZ-Esquadrilha at BA.3 Tancos in 10.43; Fighting Aviation Group at BA.2 Ota (No.3 Esq) from 1.8.44; Latest SOC end 1947; Scrapped 1948/50

R7159 Spitfire F.Ia (Merlin III); Became A.M. No. **3**xx (range 372-374); Presentation aircraft '*KAMBU MERU*'; TOC/RAF 3.3.41 - Arr Lisbon by ship 12.12.42; OGMA workshop Alverca for assembly; XZ-Esquadrilha at BA.3 Tancos in 1.43; Fighting Aviation Group at BA.2 Ota (No.3 Esq) from 1.8.44; Latest SOC end 1947; Scrapped 1948/50

W3128 Spitfire LF.Vb (Merlin 45M); Became A.M. No. **68**; TOC/RAF 24.4.41; Reid & Sigrist, Desford 20.11.46 - Dunsfold, en route for Portugal 17.9.47, arr. OGMA Alverca; BA.2 Ota 12.12.47; Spitfire Fighter Aviation

Group (Nos.1,2 or 3 Esq) from 1.48; To BA.3 Tancos (No.1 Esq) in 4.52; FAP 7.52 [see Note 3)]

W3180 Spitfire LF.Vb (Merlin 50M); Became A.M. No. **59**; Presentation aircraft '*FIJI VII*'; TOC/RAF 16.5.41; Reid & Sigrist, Desford in 12.46 - Dunsfold, en route for Portugal 17.4.47, arr. OGMA Alverca; BA.2 Ota 14.10.47; Fighting Aviation Group; Spitfire Fighter Aviation Group (Nos.1, 2 or 3 Esq) from 1.48; Still at Ota in 2.52, not to Tancos, SOC between 2.52 and 4.52

W3248 Spitfire LF.Vb (Merlin 50M); Became A.M. No. **76**; Presentation aircraft '*LETCHWORTH*'; TOC/RAF 18.5.41; Reid & Sigrist, Desford 4.12.46 - Dunsfold, en route for Portugal 15.10.47, arr. OGMA Alverca; BA.2 Ota 12.1.48; Spitfire Fighter Aviation Group (No.1, 2 or 3 Esq) from 1.48; Still at Ota in 2.52, not to Tancos, SOC between 2.52 and 4.52

W3430 Spitfire F.Vb (Merlin 45); Became A.M. No. **1**; TOC/RAF 26.6.41 - Arr Lisbon by ship 19.10.43; OGMA workshop Alverca for assembly; BA.2 Ota 2.3.44; To RL-Esquadrilha ('RL+A'); Fighting Aviation Group (No.2 Esq) from 1.8.44; Spitfire Fighter Aviation Group from 1.48; To BA.3 Tancos (No.1 Esq) 4.52; F.A.P. 7.52; Flown by Brig. JO Mourao 17.8.53 [see Note 3)]

W3431 Spitfire LF.Vb (Merlin 50M); Became A.M. No. **70**; Presentation aircraft '*KAAPSTAD III*'; TOC/RAF 1.7.41; ex USAAF; Reid & Sigrist, Desford 25.11.46 - Dunsfold, en route for Portugal 22.9.47, arr. OGMA Alverca; BA.2 Ota 12.12.47; Spitfire Fighter Aviation Group (Nos.1, 2 or 3 Esq) from 1.48; To BA.3 Tancos (No.1 Esq) in 4.52; FAP 7.52 [see Note 3)]
NOTE: FB-version, with underwing bomb racks

W3518 Spitfire LF.Vb (Merlin 55M); Became A.M. No. **58**; TOC/RAF 22.6.41; ex USAAF; Reid & Sigrist, Desford 5.11.46 - Dunsfold, en route for Portugal 14.7.47, arr. OGMA Alverca; BA.2 Ota 14.10.47; Fighting Aviation Group; Spitfire Fighter Aviation Group (Nos.1, 2 or 3 Esq) from 1.48; To BA.3 Tancos (No.1 Esq) in 4.52; FAP 7.52 [see Note 3)]

W3519 Spitfire LF.Vb (Merlin 55M); Became A.M. No. **74**; Presentation aircraft '*ASANSOL II*'; TOC/RAF 22.6.41; Reid & Sigrist, Desford 20.11.46 - Dunsfold, en route for Portugal 22.8.47, arr. OGMA Alverca; BA.2 Ota 12.12.47; Spitfire Fighter Aviation Group (Nos.1, 2 or 3 Esq) from 1.48; Still at Ota in 2.52, not to Tancos, SOC between 2.52 and 4.52

W3641 Spitfire LF.Vb (Merlin 45M); Became A.M. No. **67**; TOC/RAF 20.7.41; Reid & Sigrist, Desford 25.11.46 - Dunsfold, en route for Portugal 25.8.47, arr. OGMA Alverca; BA.2 Ota 12.12.47; Spitfire Fighter Aviation Group (Nos.1, 2 or 3 Esq) from 1.48; Still at Ota in 2.52, not to Tancos, SOC between 2.52 and 4.52

W3648 Spitfire LF.Vb (Merlin 45M); Became A.M. No. **27**; Presentation aircraft '*WISBECH*'; TOC/RAF 3.8.41 - Arr Lisbon by ship 17.2.44; OGMA workshop Alverca for assembly; BA.2 Ota 29.6.44; To MR-Esquadrilha ('MR+L'); Fighting Aviation Group (No.1 Esq) from 1.8.44; Spitfire Fighter Aviation Group from 1.48; To BA.3 Tancos (No.3 Esq) 4.52; F.A.P. 7.52 [see Note 3)]
NOTE: Shown with clipped wings

W3803 Spitfire LF.Vb (Merlin 45M); Became A.M. No. **20**; Presentation aircraft '*POPOCATAPETL I*'; TOC/RAF 29.8.41 - Arr Lisbon by ship 28.1.44; OGMA workshop Alverca for assembly; BA.2 Ota 25.4.44; To MR-Esquadrilha ('MR+E'); Fighting Aviation Group (No.1 Esq) 1.8.44; Spitfire Fighter Aviation Group from 1.48; To BA.3 Tancos (No.3 Esq) in 4.52; FAP 7.52 [see Note 3)]
NOTE: Shown with clipped wings

W3902 Spitfire LF.Vb (Merlin 50M); Became A.M. No. **87**; Presentation aircraft '*GILBERT & ELLICE II*'; TOC/RAF 26.9.41; ex USAAF; Reid & Sigrist,, Desford 9.12.46 - Dunsfold, en route for Portugal 8.1.48, arr. OGMA Alverca; BA.2 Ota 11.2.48; Spitfire Fighter Aviation Group (No.1, 2 or 3 Esq) from 2.48; To BA.3 Tancos (No.3 Esq) in 4.52; FAP 7.52 [see Note 3)]

W3950 Spitfire LF.Vb (Merlin 45M); TOC/RAF 26.9.41; To Reid & Sigrist,, Desford for refurbishing 26.11.46 – Dunsfold, en route for Portugal 29.10.47; Crashed Cat.E (date unknown); w/o 30.1.48, SOC
NOTE: Replaced by EP766

W3951 Spitfire F.Vb (Merlin 45); Became A.M. No. .. ? (range 21-26); TOC/RAF 26.9.41 - Arr Lisbon by ship 9.11.43; OGMA workshop Alverca for assembly; BA.2 Ota 25.4.44; To MR-Esquadrilha; Fighting Aviation Group (No.1 Esq) from 1.8.44 [see Notes 1) - 3)]

X4339 Spitfire F.Ia (Merlin III); Became A.M. No. **370**; TOC/RAF 4.9.40 - Arr Lisbon by ship 21.11.42; OGMA workshop Alverca for assembly; XZ-Esquadrilha ('XZ+A') at BA.3 Tancos in 1.43; Shown at Ota in 7.44; Fighting Aviation Group at BA.2 Ota (No.3 Esq) from 1.8.44; Latest SOC end 1947; Scrapped 1948/50
NOTE: AM Serial No.370 allotted also for a Valparaiso III, which became SOC in 12.42

X4589 Spitfire F.Ia (Merlin III); Became A.M. No. **371**; TOC/RAF 29.9.40 - Arr Lisbon by ship 21.11.42; OGMA workshop Alverca for assembly; XZ-Esquadrilha ('XZ+B') at BA.3 Tancos in 1.43; Fighting Aviation Group at BA.2 Ota (No.3 Esq) from 1.8.44; Latest SOC end 1947; Scrapped 1948/50

X4617 Spitfire F.Ia (Merlin III); Became A.M. No. **386**; Presentation aircraft '*FALKLAND ISLANDS III*'; TOC/RAF 16.10.40 - Arr Lisbon by ship 28.9.43; OGMA workshop Alverca for assembly; XZ-Esquadrilha ('XZ+R') at BA.3 Tancos in 11.43; Fighting Aviation Group at BA.2 Ota (No.3 Esq) from 1.8.44; Latest SOC end 1947; Scrapped 1948/50

X4716 Spitfire F.Ia (Merlin III); Became A.M. No. **375**; TOC/RAF 10.11.40 - Arr Lisbon by ship 12.12.42; OGMA workshop Alverca for assembly; XZ-Esquadrilha ('XZ+F') at BA.3 Tancos in 1.43; Propeller hit tail of No.372, both aircraft landed safely [date unknown]; Fighting Aviation Group at BA.2 Ota (No.3 Esq) from 1.8.44; Latest SOC end 1947; Scrapped 1948/50

X4855 Spitfire F.Ia (Merlin III); Became A.M. No. **3xx** (range 372-374); TOC/RAF 16.12.40 - Arr Lisbon by ship 12.12.42; OGMA workshop Alverca for assembly; XZ-Esquadrilha at BA.3 Tancos in 1.43; Fighting Aviation Group at BA.2 Ota (No.3 Esq) from 1.8.44; Latest SOC end 1947; Scrapped 1948/50

X4857 Spitfire F.Ia (Merlin III); Became A.M. No. **382**; TOC/RAF 21.12.40 - Arr Lisbon by ship 29.8.43; OGMA workshop Alverca for assembly; XZ-Esquadrilha ('XZ+N') at BA.3 Tancos in 10.43; Fighting Aviation Group at BA.2 Ota (No.3 Esq) from 1.8.44; Latest SOC end 1947; Scrapped 1948/50

X4920 Spitfire F.Ia (Merlin III); Became A.M. No. **3xx** (range 376-379); Presentation aircraft '*VICTOR*'; TOC/RAF 9.1.41 - Arr Lisbon by ship 20.1.43; OGMA workshop Alverca for assembly; XZ-Esquadrilha at BA.3 Tancos in 3.43; Fighting Aviation Group at BA.2 Ota (No.3 Esq) from 1.8.44; Latest SOC end 1947; Scrapped 1948/50

AA728 Spitfire LF.Vb (Merlin 45M); Became A.M. No. **37**; TOC/RAF 11.9.41; ex USAAF; Reid & Sigrist,, Desford 2.10.46 - Dunsfold, en route for Portugal 6.5.47, arr. OGMA Alverca; BA.2 Ota 16.6.47; Fighting Aviation Group; Spitfire Fighter Aviation Group (Nos.1, 2 or 3 Esq) 1.48; Still at Ota in 2.52, not to Tancos, SOC between 2.52 and 4.52

AA729 Spitfire LF.Vb (Merlin 45M); Became A.M. No. **47**; TOC/RAF 11.9.41; ex USAAF; Reid & Sigrist,, Desford 27.9.46 - Dunsfold, en route for Portugal 6.5.47, arr. OGMA Alverca; BA.2 Ota 16.6.47; Fighting Aviation Group; Spitfire Fighter Aviation Group (Nos.1, 2 or 3 Esq) 1.48; To BA.3 Tancos (No.2 Esq) in 4.52; FAP 7.52 [see Note 3)]

AA753 Spitfire LF.Vb (Merlin 55); TOC/RAF 6.10.41; ex USAAF; Reid & Sigrist,, Desford in 12.46; Dunsfold, en route for Portugal 18.4.47, lost orientation and landed in León, Spain; Interned, SOC

AA756 Spitfire LF.Vb (Merlin 55M); Became A.M. No. **91** (?); TOC/RAF 1.10.41; ex USAAF; Reid & Sigrist, Desford 16.6.47 - Dunsfold, en route for Portugal 19.1.48, arr. OGMA Alverca; BA.2 Ota 11.5.48; Spitfire Fighter Aviation Group (No.1, 2 or 3 Esq) from 5.48; Possibly to BA.3 Tancos (No.3 Esq) in 4.52; FAP 7.52 [see Note 3)]

AA862 Spitfire LF.Vb (Merlin 50M); Became A.M. No. **43**; Presentation aircraft '*BLACKBURN II*'; TOC/RAF 22.10.41; Reid & Sigrist, Desford 23.9.46 - Dunsfold, en route for Portugal 28.4.47, arr. OGMA Alverca; BA.2 Ota 16.6.47; Fighting Aviation Group; Spitfire Fighter Aviation Group (Nos.1, 2 or 3 Esq) from 1.48; To BA.3 Tancos (No.3 Esq) in 4.52; FAP 7.52 [see Note 3)]

AA881 Spitfire LF.Vb (Merlin 45M); Became A.M. No. **88**; Presentation aircraft '*MANCHESTER CORPORATION TRANSPORTER*'; TOC/RAF 29.10.41; Reid & Sigrist, Desford 3.6.47 - Dunsfold, en route for Portugal 8.1.48, arr. OGMA Alverca; BA.2 Ota 11.2.48; Spitfire Fighter Aviation Group (No.1, 2 or 3 Esq) from 2.48; To BA.3 Tancos (No.2 Esq) in 4.52; FAP 7.52 [see Note 3)]

AA946 Spitfire F.Vb (Merlin 45); Became A.M. No. **16**; TOC/RAF 22.11.41 - Arr Lisbon by ship 9.11.43; OGMA workshop Alverca for assembly; BA.2 Ota 3.3.44; To MR-Esquadrilha ('MR+A'); Fighting Aviation Group (No.1 Esq) from 1.8.44; Spitfire Fighter Aviation Group from 1.48; Still at Ota in 2.52, not to Tancos, SOC between 2.52 and 4.52 - Note: Clipped wings

AA967 Spitfire LF.Vb (Merlin 45M); Became A.M. No. **77**; Presentation aircraft '*INDIAN TELEPHONES*'; TOC/RAF 1.11.41; Reid & Sigrist, Desford 9.12.46 - Dunsfold, en route for Portugal 4.11.47, arr. OGMA Alverca; BA.2 Ota 12.1.48; Spitfire Fighter Aviation Group (No.1, 2 or 3 Esq) from 1.48; Still at Ota in 2.52, not to Tancos, SOC between 2.52 and 4.52

AA979 Spitfire LF.Vb (Merlin 55M); Became A.M. No. **56**; Presentation aircraft '*YAOUNDE*'; TOC/RAF 12.11.41; Reid & Sigrist, Desford 25.9.46 - Dunsfold, en route for Portugal 17.7.47, arr. OGMA Alverca; BA.2 Ota 14.10.47; Fighting Aviation Group; Spitfire Fighter Aviation Group (No.2 Esq - marked 'RL+U') from 1.48; To BA.3 Tancos (No.1 Esq) in 4.52; FAP 7.52 [see Note 3)]

AB133 Spitfire F.Vb (Merlin 45); Became A.M. No. .. ? (range 28-34); TOC/RAF 20.11.41 - Arr Lisbon by ship 28.1.44; OGMA workshop Alverca for assembly; BA.2 Ota 25.4.44; MR- or RL-Esquadrilha; Fighting Aviation Group (No.1 or 2 Esq) from 1.8.44 [see Notes 1) - 3)]

AB191 Spitfire F.V<u>c</u> (Merlin 46); Became A.M. No. .. ? (range 2-15); TOC/RAF 5.12.41 - Arr Lisbon by ship 19.10.43; OGMA workshop Alverca for assembly; BA.2 Ota 2.3.44; To RL-Esquadrilha; Fighting Aviation Group (No.2 Esq) from 1.8.44 [see Notes 1) - 3)]

AB203 Spitfire LF.Vb (Merlin 50M); Became A.M. No. **48**; TOC/RAF 15.12.41; Reid & Sigrist, Desford 30.9.46 - Dunsfold, en route for Portugal 8.5.47, arr. OGMA Alverca; BA.2 Ota 16.6.47; Fighting Aviation Group; Spitfire Fighter Aviation Group (Nos.1, 2 or 3 Esq) 1.48

AB487 Spitfire LF.Vb (Merlin 55M); Became A.M. No. **36**; TOC/RAF 31.1.42; Reid & Sigrist, Desford 1.11.46 - Dunsfold, en route for Portugal 22.4.47, arr. OGMA Alverca; BA.2 Ota 16.6.47; Fighting Aviation Group; Spitfire Fighter Aviation Group (No.1 Esq - marked 'MR+S') from 1.48; Crashed, tipped on nose (location and date unknown); To BA.3 Tancos (No.2 Esq) in 4.52; FAP 7.52 [see Note 3)]

AB862 Spitfire LF.Vb (Merlin 45M); Became A.M. No. **41**; TOC/RAF 24.7.41; ex USAAF; Reid & Sigrist, Desford 25.9.46 - Dunsfold, en route for Portugal 28.4.47, arr. OGMA Alverca; BA.2 Ota 16.6.47; Fighting Aviation Group; Spitfire Fighter Aviation Group (Nos.1, 2 or 3 Esq) from 1.48; Still at Ota in 2.52, not to Tancos, SOC between 2.52 and 4.52

AB895 Spitfire F.Vb (Merlin 45); Became A.M. No. .. ? (range 21-26); TOC/RAF 15.8.41 - Arr Lisbon by ship 8.12.43; OGMA workshop Alverca for assembly; BA.2 Ota 25.4.44; To MR-Esquadrilha; Fighting Aviation Group (No.1 Esq) from 1.8.44 [see Notes 1) - 3)]

AB935 Spitfire F.Vb (Merlin 45); Became A.M. No. .. ? (range 2-15); Presentation aircraft '*GINGERBREAD*'; TOC/RAF 27.8.41 - Arr Lisbon by ship 19.10.43; OGMA workshop Alverca for assembly; BA.2 Ota 2.3.44; To RL-Esquadrilha; Fighting Aviation Group (No.2 Esq) from 1.8.44 [see Notes 1) -3)]

AB988 Spitfire LF.Vb (Merlin 45MA); Became A.M. No. **84**; TOC/RAF 7.10.41; ex USAAF; Reid & Sigrist, Desford 25.11.46 - Dunsfold, en route for Portugal 21.10.47, arr. OGMA Alverca; BA.2 Ota 11.2.48; Spitfire Fighter Aviation Group (No.1, 2 or 3 Esq) from 2.48; Still at Ota in 2.52, not to Tancos, SOC between 2.52 and 4.52

AD191 Spitfire LF.Vb (Merlin 45M); Became A.M. No. **66**; TOC/RAF 12.10.41; ex USAAF 8.AF; Reid & Sigrist, Desford 26.9.46 - Dunsfold, en route for Portugal 18.4.47, arr. OGMA Alverca; BA.2 Ota 12.12.47; Spitfire Fighter Aviation Group (Nos.1, 2 or 3 Esq) from 1.48; To BA.3 Tancos (No.1 Esq) in 4.52; FAP 7.52 [see Note 3)]

AD294 Spitfire LF.Vb (Merlin 45M); Became A.M. No. **38**; Presentation aircraft '*Miss A.B.C. III*'; TOC/RAF 26.9.41; ex USAAF; Reid & Sigrist, Desford 12.9.46 - Dunsfold, en route for Portugal 28.4.47, arr. OGMA Alverca; BA.2 Ota 16.6.47; Fighting Aviation Group; Spitfire Fighter Aviation Group (Nos.1, 2 or 3 Esq) from 1.48; Still at Ota in 2.52, not to Tancos, SOC between 2.52 and 4.52

AD383 Spitfire LF.Vb (Merlin 50M); Became A.M. No. **49** (?); TOC/RAF 23.10.41; Reid & Sigrist, Desford 19.9.46 - Dunsfold, en route for Portugal 17.4.47, arr. OGMA Alverca; BA.2 Ota 21.7.47; Fighting Aviation Group; Spitfire Fighter Aviation Group (possibly No.1 Esq - marked 'MR+GG') from 1.48; To BA.3 Tancos (No.2 Esq) in 4.52; FAP 7.52 [see Note 3)]

AD464 Spitfire LF.Vb (Merlin 55M); Became A.M. No. **57**; TOC/RAF 16.10.41; ex USAAF; Reid & Sigrist, Desford 26.9.46 - Dunsfold, en route for Portugal 14.7.47, arr. OGMA Alverca; BA.2 Ota 14.10.47; Fighting Aviation Group; Spitfire Fighter Aviation Group (Nos.1, 2 or 3 Esq) from 1.48; Still at Ota in 2.52, not to Tancos, SOC between 2.52 and 4.52

AD499 Spitfire LF.Vb (Merlin 50M); Became A.M. No. **42**; TOC/RAF 22.10.41; Reid & Sigrist, Desford 8.10.46 - Dunsfold, en route for Portugal 6.5.47, arr. OGMA Alverca; BA.2 Ota 16.6.47; Fighting Aviation Group; Spitfire Fighter Aviation Group (Nos.1, 2 or 3 Esq) from 1.48; To BA.3 Tancos (No.2 Esq) in 4.52; FAP 7.52 [see Note 3)]

AD511 Spitfire F.Vb (Merlin 45); Became A.M. No. .. ? (range 2-15); TOC/RAF 8.11.41; ex USAAF - Arr Lisbon by ship 19.10.43; OGMA workshop Alverca for assembly; BA.2 Ota 2.3.44; To RL-Esquadrilha; Fighting Aviation Group (No.2 Esq) from 1.8.44 [see Notes 1) - 3)]

AR366 Spitfire LF.Vb (Merlin 50M); Became A.M. No. **40**; TOC/RAF 7.3.42; Reid & Sigrist, Desford 30.9.46 - Dunsfold, en route for Portugal 17.4.47, arr. OGMA Alverca; BA.2 Ota 16.6.47; Fighting Aviation Group; Spitfire Fighter Aviation Group (Nos.1, 2 or 3 Esq) from 1.48; To BA.3 Tancos (No.2 Esq) in 4.52; FAP 7.52 [see Note 3)]

AR367 Spitfire F.Vb (Merlin 46); Became A.M. No. .. ? (range 21-26); Presentation aircraft '*SCOTIA*'; TOC/RAF 7.3.42 - Arr Lisbon by ship 8.12.43; OGMA workshop Alverca for assembly; BA.2 Ota 25.4.44; To MR-Esquadrilha; Fighting Aviation Group (No.1 Esq) 1.8.44 [see Notes 1) -3)]

AR404 Spitfire LF.Vb (Merlin 45M); Became A.M. No. **52**; TOC/RAF 11.4.42; ex USAAF; Reid & Sigrist, Desford 2.10.46 - Dunsfold, en route for Portugal 12.6.47, arr. OGMA Alverca; BA.2 Ota 21.7.47; Fighting Aviation Group; Spitfire Fighter Aviation Group (Nos.1, 2 or 3 Esq) 1.48; To BA.3 Tancos (No.1 Esq) in 4.52; FAP 7.52 [see Note 3)]

AR438 Spitfire LF.Vb (Merlin 45M); Became A.M. No. **69**; TOC/RAF 27.4.42; ex USAAF; Reid & Sigrist, Desford

Spitfire F.Vb, 19/ZE-D (ex BL690) of ZE-Esquadrilha, Ota, circa 1946

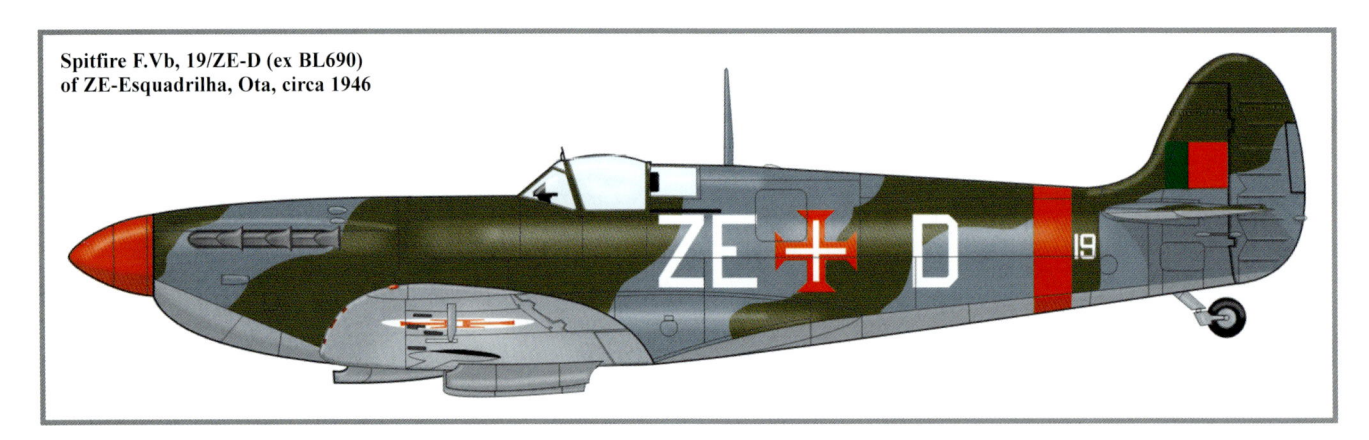

2.12.46 - Dunsfold, en route for Portugal 22.9.47, arr. OGMA Alverca; BA.2 Ota 12.12.47; Spitfire Fighter Aviation Group (Nos.1, 2 or 3 Esq) from 1.48; Still at Ota in 2.52, not to Tancos, SOC between 2.52 and 4.52

BL355 Spitfire F.Vb (Merlin 45); Became A.M. No. .. ? (range 28-34); Presentation aircraft '*PUNJAB POLICE V*'; TOC/RAF 23.11.41 - Arr Lisbon by ship 28.1.44; OGMA workshop Alverca for assembly; BA.2 Ota 25.4.44; To MR- or RL-Esquadrilha; Fighting Aviation Group (No.1 or 2 Esq) from 1.8.44 [see Notes 1) -3)]

BL368 Spitfire LF.Vb (Merlin 50M); Became A.M. No. **86**; TOC/RAF 21.11.41; ex USAAF; Reid & Sigrist, Desford 20.3.47 - Dunsfold, en route for Portugal 23.12.47, arr. OGMA Alverca; BA.2 Ota 11.2.48; Spitfire Fighter Aviation Group (No.1, 2 or 3 Esq) in 2.48

BL374 Spitfire LF.Vb (Merlin 50M); Became A.M. No. **62**; TOC/RAF 1.12.41; Reid & Sigrist, Desford 1.11.46 - Dunsfold, en route for Portugal 24.6.47, arr. OGMA Alverca; BA.2 Ota 14.10.47; Fighting Aviation Group; Spitfire Fighter Aviation Group (Nos.1, 2 or 3 Esq) 1.48

BL437 Spitfire LF.Vb (Merlin 45M); Became A.M. No. **65**; TOC/RAF 10.12.41; ex USAAF; Reid & Sigrist, Desford 9.11.46 - Dunsfold, en route for Portugal 1.8.47, arr. OGMA Alverca; BA.2 Ota 14.10.47; Fighting Aviation Group; Spitfire Fighter Aviation Group (Nos.1, 2 or 3 Esq) from 1.48; To BA.3 Tancos (No.1 Esq) in 4.52; FAP 7.52 [see Note 3)]

BL449 Spitfire F.Vb (Merlin 45); Became A.M. No. .. ? (range 21-26); TOC/RAF 5.12.41; ex USAAF - Arr Lisbon by ship 8.12.43; OGMA workshop Alverca for assembly; BA.2 Ota 25.4.44; To MR-Esquadrilha; Fighting Aviation Group (No.1 Esq) from 1.8.44 [see Notes 1) -3)]

BL496 Spitfire LF.Vb (Merlin 50M); Became A.M. No. **50**; TOC/RAF 8.1.42; Reid & Sigrist, Desford 28.10.46 - Dunsfold, en route for Portugal 20.5.47, arr. OGMA Alverca; BA.2 Ota 21.7.47; Fighting Aviation Group; Spitfire Fighter Aviation Group (Nos.1, 2 or 3 Esq) from 1.48; To BA.3 Tancos (No.3 Esq) in 4.52; FAP 7.52 [see Note 3)]

BL572 Spitfire F.Vb (Merlin 45); Became A.M. No. .. ? (range 2-15); TOC/RAF 20.2.42 - Arr Lisbon by ship 19.10.43; OGMA workshop Alverca for assembly; BA.2 Ota 2.3.44; To RL-Esquadrilha; Fighting Aviation Group (No.2 Esq) from 1.8.44 [see Notes 1) -3)]

BL636 Spitfire F.Vb (Merlin 45); Became A.M. No. .. ? (range 28-34); Presentation aircraft '*BOROUGH OF ACTON*'; TOC/RAF 10.3.42 - Arr Lisbon by ship 17.2.44; OGMA workshop Alverca for assembly; BA.2 Ota 29.6.44; To RL- or MR-Esquadrilha; Fighting Aviation Group (No.1 or 2 Esq) from 1.8.44 [see Notes 1) -3)]

BL646 Spitfire LF.Vb (Merlin 45M); Became A.M. No. **44**; TOC/RAF 28.1.42; Reid & Sigrist, Desford 17.9.46 - Dunsfold, en route for Portugal 14.4.47, arr. OGMA Alverca; BA.2 Ota 16.6.47; Fighting Aviation Group; Spitfire Fighter Aviation Group (Nos.1, 2 or 3 Esq) 1.48

BL664 Spitfire F.Vb (Merlin 45); Became A.M. No. .. ? (range 2-15); Presentation aircraft '*MUNTOK*'; TOC/RAF 22.1.42 - Arr Lisbon by ship 19.10.43; OGMA workshop Alverca for assembly; BA.2 Ota 2.3.44; To RL-Esquadrilha; Fighting Aviation Group (No.2 Esq) from 1.8.44 [see Notes 1) -3)] - Note: Shown with clipped wings

BL671 Spitfire LF.Vb (Merlin 50M); Became A.M. No. **81**; TOC/RAF 28.1.42; Reid & Sigrist, Desford 14.1.47 - Dunsfold, en route for Portugal 8.12.47, arr. OGMA Alverca; BA.2 Ota 12.1.48; Spitfire Fighter Aviation Group (No.3 Esq - marked 'ZE+K') from 1.48; To BA.3 Tancos (No.3 Esq) in 4.52; FAP 7.52 [see Note 3)]

BL684 Spitfire F.Vb (Merlin 45); Became A.M. No. **17**; TOC/RAF 26.1.42 - Arr Lisbon by ship 9.11.43; OGMA workshop Alverca for assembly; BA.2 Ota 3.3.44; To MR-Esquadrilha ('MR+B'); Fighting Aviation Group (No.1 Esq) from 1.8.44

BL690 Spitfire F.Vb (Merlin 46); Became A.M. No. **19**; TOC/RAF 24.1.42 - Arr Lisbon by ship 8.12.43; OGMA workshop Alverca for assembly; BA.2 Ota 25.4.44; To MR-Esquadrilha ('MR+D'); Fighting Aviation Group (No.1 Esq) from 1.8.44; ZE-Esquadrilha ('ZE+D') @ 1946

BL821 Spitfire LF.Vb (Merlin 45M); Became A.M. No. **90** (?); TOC/RAF 6.2.42; Reid & Sigrist, Desford 17.4.47 - Dunsfold, en route for Portugal 14.1.48, arr. OGMA Alverca; BA.2 Ota 11.5.48; Spitfire Fighter Aviation Group (No.1, 2 or 3 Esq) from 5.48; Still at Ota in 2.52, not to Tancos, SOC between 2.52 and 4.52

BL850 Spitfire LF.Vb (Merlin 50M); Became A.M. No. **45**; TOC/RAF 14.2.42; Reid & Sigrist, Desford 12.9.46 - Dunsfold, en route for Portugal 9.4.47, arr. OGMA Alverca; BA.2 Ota 16.6.47; Fighting Aviation Group; Spitfire Fighter Aviation Group (Nos.1, 2 or 3 Esq) from 1.48; To BA.3 Tancos (No.2 Esq) in 4.52; FAP 7.52 [see Note 3)]

BL890 Spitfire F.Vb (Merlin 45); Became A.M. No. **18** (?); TOC/RAF 12.2.42 - Arr Lisbon by ship 9.11.43; OGMA workshop Alverca for assembly; BA.2 Ota 25.4.44; To MR-Esquadrilha (possibly 'MR+C'); Fighting Aviation Group (No.1 Esq) from 1.8.44 [see Notes 1) -3)]

BL898 Spitfire LF.Vb (Merlin 55MA); Became A.M. No. **92** (?); TOC/RAF 14.2.42; ex USAAF; Reid & Sigrist, Desford 8.10.47 - Dunsfold, en route for Portugal 28.1.48, arr. OGMA Alverca; BA.2 Ota 11.5.48; Spitfire Fighter Aviation Group (No.1, 2 or 3 Esq) in 5.48; Possibly to BA.3 Tancos (No.2 Esq) in 4.52; FAP 7.52 [see Note 3)]

BL970 Spitfire LF.Vb (Merlin 55M); Became A.M. No. **72**; TOC/RAF 24.2.42; Reid & Sigrist, Desford 9.10.46 - Dunsfold, en route for Portugal 8.8.47, arr. OGMA Alverca; BA.2 Ota 12.12.47; Spitfire Fighter Aviation Group (Nos.1, 2 or 3 Esq) from 1.48; To BA.3 Tancos (No.3 Esq) in 4.52; FAP 7.52 [see Note 3)]

BL976 Spitfire LF.Vb (Merlin 50M); Became A.M. No. **89** (?); TOC/RAF 27.2.42; Reid & Sigrist, Desford 28.10.46 - Dunsfold, en route for Portugal 3.6.47, arr. OGMA Alverca; BA.2 Ota 11.5.48; Spitfire Fighter Aviation Group (No.1, 2 or 3 Esq) from 1.48; Still at Ota in 2.52, not to Tancos, SOC between 2.52 and 4.52

BL978 Spitfire F.Vb (Merlin 45); Became A.M. No. **30**; TOC/RAF 19.2.42; ex USAAF - Arr Lisbon by ship

Portugal

28.1.44; OGMA workshop Alverca for assembly; BA.2 Ota 29.4.44; To MR-Esquadrilha ('MR+O'); Fighting Aviation Group (No.1 Esq) from 1.8.44; Repair & Storage 1947 (in unit replaced by EP411); To BA.3 Tancos (No.1 Esq) in 4.52; FAP 7.52 [see Note 3)]

BL981 Spitfire LF.Vb (Merlin 50M); Became A.M. No. **63**; TOC/RAF 22.2.42; Reid & Sigrist, Desford 31.10.46 - Dunsfold, en route for Portugal 23.7.47, arr. OGMA Alverca; BA.2 Ota 14.10.47; Fighting Aviation Group; Spitfire Fighter Aviation Group (Nos.1, 2 or 3 Esq) from 1.48; To BA.3 Tancos (No.1 Esq) in 4.52; FAP 7.52 [see Note 3)]

BM131 Spitfire LF.Vb (Merlin 45M); Became A.M. No. **78**; TOC/RAF 19.4.42; Reid & Sigrist, Desford 4.12.46 - Dunsfold, en route for Portugal 22.10.47, arr. OGMA Alverca 23.10.47; BA.2 Ota 12.1.48; Spitfire Fighter Aviation Group (No.1, 2 or 3 Esq) from 1.48; Still at Ota in 2.52, not to Tancos, SOC between 2.52 and 4.52

BM176 Spitfire F.Vb (Merlin 45); Became A.M. No. **34**; TOC/RAF 21.3.42 - Arr Lisbon by ship 17.2.44; OGMA workshop Alverca for assembly; BA.2 Ota 29.6.44; To MR-Esquadrilha ('MR+Q'); Fighting Aviation Group (No.1 Esq) from 1.8.44; Spitfire Fighter Aviation Group from 1.48; To BA.3 Tancos (No.2 Esq) in 4.52; FAP 7.52 [see Note 3)]

BM177 Spitfire F.Vb (Merlin 45); Became A.M. No. .. ? (range 2-15); TOC/RAF 4.3.42 - Arr Lisbon by ship 19.10.43; OGMA workshop Alverca for assembly; BA.2 Ota 2.3.44; To RL-Esquadrilha; Fighting Aviation Group (No.2 Esq) from 1.8.44 [see Notes 1) -3)] - Note: Clipped wings

BM298 Spitfire LF.Vb (Merlin 50M); Became A.M. No. **46**; TOC/RAF 25.3.42; Reid & Sigrist, Desford 8.10.46 - Dunsfold, en route for Portugal 22.4.47, arr. OGMA Alverca; BA.2 Ota 16.6.47; Fighting Aviation Group; Spitfire Fighter Aviation Group (Nos.1, 2 or 3 Esq) from 1.48; To BA.3 Tancos (No.2 Esq) in 4.52; FAP 7.52 [see Note 3)]

BM300 Spitfire F.Vb (Merlin 46); Became A.M. No. .. ? (range 21-26); TOC/RAF 27.3.42 - Arr Lisbon by ship 8.12.43; OGMA workshop Alverca for assembly; BA.2 Ota 25.4.44; To MR-Esquadrilha; Fighting Aviation Group (No.1 Esq) from 1.8.44 [see Notes 1) -3)]

BM311 Spitfire F.Vb (Merlin 46); Became A.M. No. .. ? (range 21-26); TOC/RAF 28.3.42 - Arr Lisbon by ship 9.11.43; OGMA workshop Alverca for assembly; BA.2 Ota 25.4.44; To MR-Esquadrilha; Fighting Aviation Group (No.1 Esq) from 1.8.44 [see Notes 1) -3)]

BM313 Spitfire F.Vb (Merlin 45); Became A.M. No. .. ? (range 28-34); TOC/RAF 28.3.42 - Arr Lisbon by ship 28.1.44; OGMA workshop Alverca for assembly; BA.2 Ota 29.6.44; To RL- or MR-Esquadrilha; Fighting Aviation Group (No.1 or 2 Esq) from 1.8.44 [see Notes 1) -3)]

BM343 Spitfire LF.Vb (Merlin 50M); Became A.M. No. **54**; TOC/RAF 28.3.42; Reid & Sigrist, Desford 1.11.46 - Dunsfold, en route for Portugal 9.6.47, arr. OGMA Alverca; BA.2 Ota 21.7.47; Fighting Aviation Group; Spitfire Fighter Aviation Group (Nos.1, 2 or 3 Esq) from 1.48; Still at Ota in 2.52, not to Tancos, SOC between 2.52 and 4.52

BM364 Spitfire F.Vb (Merlin 45); Became A.M. No. .. ? (range 2-15); TOC/RAF 1.4.42 - Arr Lisbon by ship 19.10.43; OGMA workshop Alverca for assembly; BA.2 Ota 2.3.44; To RL-Esquadrilha; Fighting Aviation Group (No.2 Esq) from 1.8.44 [see Notes 1) -3)] - Note: Clipped wings

BM479 Spitfire F.Vb (Merlin 45); Became A.M. No. .. ? (range 21-26); TOC/RAF 13.4.42; ex USAAF - Arr Lisbon by ship 8.12.43; OGMA workshop Alverca for assembly; BA.2 Ota 25.4.44; To MR-Esquadrilha; Fighting Aviation Group (No.1 Esq) from 1.8.44 [see Notes 1) -3)]

BM514 Spitfire LF.Vb (Merlin 50M); Became A.M. No. **64**; TOC/RAF 26.4.42; Reid & Sigrist, Desford 24.10.46 - Dunsfold, en route for Portugal 25.7.47, arr. OGMA Alverca; BA.2 Ota 14.10.47; Fighting Aviation Group; Spitfire Fighter Aviation Group (Nos.1, 2 or 3 Esq) from 1.48; To BA.3 Tancos (No.3 Esq) in 4.52; FAP 7.52 [see Note 3)]

BM594 Spitfire LF.Vb (Merlin 50M); Became A.M. No. **35**; TOC/RAF 24.4.42; Reid & Sigrist, Desford 30.9.46 - Dunsfold, en route for Portugal 29.4.47, arr. OGMA Alverca; BA.2 Ota 16.6.47; Fighting Aviation Group; Spitfire Fighter Aviation Group (No.1 Esq - marked 'MR+R') 1.48; To BA.3 Tancos (No.2 Esq) in 4.52; FAP 7.52 [see Note 3)]

BM624 Spitfire F.Vb (Merlin 45); Became A.M. No. .. ? (range 2-15); Presentation aircraft '*GO TO IT*'; TOC/RAF 26.4.42 - Arr Lisbon by ship 19.10.43; OGMA workshop Alverca for assembly; BA.2 Ota 2.3.44; To RL-Esquadrilha; Fighting Aviation Group (No.2 Esq) 1.8.44 [see Notes 1) -3)]

EE620 Spitfire F.Vc (Merlin 46); Became A.M. No. .. ? (range 2-15); TOC/RAF 26.9.42 - Arr Lisbon by ship 19.10.43; OGMA workshop Alverca for assembly; BA.2 Ota 2.3.44; To RL-Esquadrilha; Fighting Aviation Group (No.2 Esq) from 1.8.44 [see Notes 1) -3)]

EN419 Spitfire PR.XI TOC/RAF 24.3.43; No.1 OADU, delivery flight from Portreath, flown over Portugal, force-landed at Furadouro beach, aircraft interned 5.5.43 (pilot safe); Cat.FA/E 7.5.43, SOC (RAF)

EN775 Spitfire LF.Vb (Merlin 50M); Became A.M. No. **83**; TOC/RAF 29.4.42; Reid & Sigrist, Desford 15.1.47 - Dunsfold, en route for Portugal 16.12.47, arr. OGMA Alverca; BA.2 Ota 11.2.48; Spitfire Fighter Aviation Group (No.1, 2 or 3 Esq) from 2.48; To BA.3 Tancos (No.3 Esq) in 4.52; FAP 7.52 [see Note 3)]

EN800 Spitfire LF.Vb (Merlin 50M); Became A.M. No. **60**; TOC/RAF 1.5.42; Reid & Sigrist, Desford 24.10.46 - Dunsfold, en route for Portugal 3.7.47, arr. OGMA Alverca; BA.2 Ota 14.10.47; Fighting Aviation Group; Spitfire Fighter Aviation Group (Nos.1, 2 or 3 Esq) from 1.48; Still at Ota in 2.52, not to Tancos, SOC between 2.52 and 4.52

EN903 Spitfire LF.Vb (Merlin 50M); Became A.M. No. **53**; TOC/RAF 10.5.42; ex USAAF; Reid & Sigrist, Desford 24.10.46 - Dunsfold, en route for Portugal 9.6.47, arr. OGMA Alverca; BA.2 Ota 21.7.47; Fighting Aviation Group; Spitfire Fighter Aviation Group (Nos.1, 2 or 3 Esq) from 1.48
NOTE: FB-version, with underwing bomb racks

EN928 Spitfire LF.Vb (Merlin 50M); Became A.M. No. **55**; TOC/RAF 16.5.42; ex USAAF; Reid & Sigrist, Desford 24.10.46 - Dunsfold, en route for Portugal 24.6.47, arr. OGMA Alverca; BA.2 Ota 21.7.47; Fighting Aviation Group; Spitfire Fighter Aviation Group (Nos.1, 2 or 3 Esq) from 1.48

EP242 Spitfire LF.Vb (Merlin 45M); Became A.M. No. **82**; TOC/RAF 6.6.42; Reid & Sigrist, Desford 3.1.47 - Dunsfold, en route for Portugal 17.12.47, arr. OGMA Alverca; BA.2 Ota 11.2.48; Spitfire Fighter Aviation Group (No.1, 2 or 3 Esq) from 2.48; To BA.3 Tancos (No.3 Esq) in 4.52; FAP 7.52 [see Note 3)]

EP244 Spitfire LF.Vb (Merlin 45M); Became A.M. No. **61**; TOC/RAF 5.6.42; Reid & Sigrist, Desford 31.10.46 - Dunsfold, en route for Portugal 3.7.47, arr. OGMA Alverca; BA.2 Ota 14.10.47; Fighting Aviation Group; Spitfire Fighter Group (Nos.1, 2 or 3 Esq) from 1.48; Still at Ota in 2.52, not to Tancos, SOC between 2.52 and 4.52

EP335 Spitfire F.Vb (Merlin 46); Became A.M. No. .. ? (range 2-15); TOC/RAF 17.6.42 - Arr Lisbon by ship 19.10.43; OGMA workshop Alverca for assembly; BA.2 Ota 2.3.44; To RL-Esquadrilha; Fighting Aviation Group (No.2 Esq) from 1.8.44 [see Notes 1) -3)]

EP350 Spitfire F.Vb (Merlin 46); Became A.M. No. .. ? (range 2-15); TOC/RAF 18.6.42 - Arr Lisbon by ship 19.10.43; OGMA workshop Alverca for assembly; BA.2 Ota 2.3.44; To RL-Esquadrilha; Fighting Aviation Group (No.2 Esq) from 1.8.44 [see Notes 1) -3)]

EP411 Spitfire LF.Vb (Merlin 45M); Became A.M. No. **85**; TOC/RAF 26.6.42; Reid & Sigrist, Desford 14.1.47 - Dunsfold, en route for Portugal 23.12.47, arr. OGMA

Alverca; BA.2 Ota 11.2.48; Spitfire Fighter Group (No.1 Esq - marked 'MR+O') from 2.48; To BA.3 Tancos (No.2 Esq) in 4.52; FAP 7.52 [see Note 3)]

EP452 Spitfire LF.Vb (Merlin 45M); Became A.M. No. **39**; TOC/RAF 26.6.42; Reid & Sigrist, Desford 31.10.46 - Dunsfold, en route for Portugal 6.5.47, arr. OGMA Alverca; BA.2 Ota 16.6.47; Fighting Aviation Group; Spitfire Fighter Aviation Group (Nos.1, 2 or 3 Esq) 1.48

EP492 Spitfire F.Vb (Merlin 46); Became A.M. No. .. ? (range 2-15); TOC/RAF 19.7.42; ex USAAF - Arr Lisbon by ship 19.10.43; OGMA workshop Alverca for assembly; BA.2 Ota 2.3.44; To RL-Esquadrilha; Fighting Aviation Group (No.2 Esq) from 1.8.44 [see Notes 1) -3)]

EP538 Spitfire F.Vb (Merlin 46); Became A.M. No. .. ? (range 2-15); TOC/RAF 3.7.42 - Arr Lisbon by ship 19.10.43; OGMA workshop Alverca for assembly; BA.2 Ota 2.3.44; To RL-Esquadrilha; Fighting Aviation Group (No.2 Esq) from 1.8.44 [see Notes 1) -3)]

EP560 Spitfire LF.Vb (Merlin 45M); Became A.M. No. **71**; TOC/RAF 3.7.42; Reid & Sigrist, Desford 12.11.46 - Dunsfold, en route for Portugal 1.8.47, arr. OGMA Alverca; BA.2 Ota 12.12.47; Spitfire Fighter Aviation Group (No.1, 2 or 3 Esq) from 1.48; To BA.3 Tancos (No.3 Esq) in 4.52; FAP 7.52 [see Note 3)]

EP605 Spitfire LF.Vb (Merlin 55M); Became A.M. No. **80**; TOC/RAF 1.8.42; ex USAAF; Reid & Sigrist, Desford 12.11.46 - Dunsfold, en route for Portugal 26.11.47, arr. OGMA Alverca; BA.2 Ota 12.1.48; Spitfire Fighter Aviation Group (No.1, 2 or 3 Esq) from 1.48; Still at Ota in 2.52, not to Tancos, SOC between 2.52 and 4.52

EP699 Spitfire F.Vb (Merlin 46); Became A.M. No. .. ? (range 2-15); TOC/RAF 28.7.42 - Arr Lisbon by ship 19.10.43; OGMA workshop Alverca for assembly; BA.2 Ota 2.3.44; To RL-Esquadrilha; Fighting Aviation Group (No.2 Esq) from 1.8.44 [see Notes 1) -3)]

EP766 Spitfire LF.Vb (Merlin 55M); Became A.M. No. **94** (?); TOC/RAF 10.8.42; Reid & Sigrist, Desford 16.12.47 (as Replacement for W3950) - Dunsfold, en route for Portugal 30.1.48 (ferried out by Skyway Ltd), arr. OGMA Alverca; BA.2 Ota 13.10.48; Spitfire Fighter Aviation Group (No.1, 2 or 3 Esq) in 10.48; Possibly to BA.3 Tancos (No.3 Esq) in 4.52; FAP 7.52 [see Note 3)]

EP767 Spitfire LF.Vb (Merlin 45M); Became A.M. No. **51**; TOC/RAF 10.8.42; Reid & Sigrist, Desford 31.10.46 - Dunsfold, en route for Portugal 3.6.47, arr. OGMA Alverca; BA.2 Ota 21.7.47; Fighting Aviation Group; Spitfire Fighter Aviation Group (Nos.1, 2 or 3 Esq) from 1.48; To BA.3 Tancos (No.1 Esq) in 4.52; FAP 7.52 [see Note 3)]

EP785 Spitfire LF.Vb (Merlin 45M); Became A.M. No. **75**; TOC/RAF 26.7.42; Reid & Sigrist, Desford 2.12.46 - Dunsfold, en route for Portugal 24.9.47, arr. OGMA Alverca; BA.2 Ota 12.1.48; Spitfire Fighter Aviation Group (No.1, 2 or 3 Esq) from 1.48; To BA.3 Tancos (No.2 Esq) in 4.52; FAP 7.52 [see Note 3)]

ML255 Spitfire HF.IXe; Ex SAAF, rebuild with parts from various aircraft (SAAF Nos.5503, 5563 & 5632); arrived as **SURVIVOR** only; To Museu do Ar, Alverca do Ribatejo, in 1989; Exhibition as "MR+Z".

Notes:
1) Possibly later to the Spitfire Fighter Aviation Group in January 1948;
2) Possibly later to BA.3, Tancos in April 1952; FAP in July 1952;

Ex-SAAF Spitfire HF.IXe ML255 was rebuilt with parts from various aircraft, then sent in 1989 to Portugal to be exhibited at the Museu do Ar, Alverca do Ribatejo in Portuguese markings as "MR+Z".
[Dave Becker]

Portugal

3) Possibly later to BA.1, Sintra for instructional purposes in September 1954; Some time later scrapped.

SURVIVORS in Portugal

None of the original Portuguese Spitfires survive, all having been scrapped.

However, ex-SAAF Spitfire IX ML255 arrived later in exchange for a Beaufighter, and is now exhibited in the Museu do Ar at Alverca do Ribatejo.

References:
Spitfires and Hurricanes in Portugal,
by Mário Canongia Lopes, Dinalivro Publication, Lisbon, 1992.
The Airplanes of the Cross of Christ,
by Mário Canongia Lopes, Dinalivro Publication, Lisbon, 2001.

Check list of Portuguese AF Serials and Deliveries

18 Spitfire Mk.Ia, Portuguese A.F. Serial Nos.: **370 – 387**

Deliv. by ship	Desp.	Arrival	RAF Serial Nos.
Baron Forbes	7.11.42	21.11.42	X4339, X4589
Castillan	27.11.42	12.12.42	R6920/7159, X4716/4855
City/Lancaster	7. 1.43	20. 1.43	R6987/7027/7123, X4920
Empire Rhodeo	14. 8.43	29. 8.43	K9828, R6626/7146, X4857
Rugeley	4. 9.43	18. 9.43	K9991
OceanVolunteer	14. 9.43	26. 9.43	R7071
Fort Ellice	12. 9.43	28. 9.43	X4617
Tellesfora de Laminaga	25. 9.43	7.10.43	P9544

A.M. Serial Nos. **370-387**

A.M. No.	Code	RAF Serial
370	XZ+A	**X4339**
371	XZ+B	**X4589**
372	XZ+C	R6920
373	XZ+D	R7159
374	XZ+E	X4855
375	XZ+F	**X4716**
376	XZ+G	R6987
377	XZ+H	R7027
378	XZ+I	R7123
379	XZ+J	X4920

A.M. No.	Code	RAF Serial
380	XZ+L	*)
381	XZ+M	*)
382	XZ+N	**X4857**
383	XZ+O	*)
384	XZ+P	**K9991**
385	XZ+Q	**R7071**
386	XZ+R	**X4617**
387	XZ+S	**P9544**
Indiv.letter "K" not employed; Last SOC 1948, all scrapped

*) Nos. 380+381+383: K9828, R6626, R7146

60 Spitfire LF Vb, Portuguese Air Force Serial Nos.: **35 – 93**
Dunsfold, en route for Portugal (ferry flown):

Desp.	RAF Serial Nos.	Desp.	RAF Serial Nos.
9.4.47	BL850	17.9.47	W3128
14.4.47	BL646	22.9.47	W3431, AR438
17.4.47	W3180,AD383, AR366	24.9.47	EP785
18.4.47	AD191, AA753 **)	15.10.47	W3248
22.4.47	AB487, BM298	21.10.47	AB988
28.4.47	AA862,AB862,AD294	22.10.47	BM131
29.4.47	BM594	(29.10.47)	W3950 *
6.5.47	AA728/729,AD499, EP452	4.11.47	AA967
8.5.47	AB203	12.11.47	P8791
20.5.47	BL496	26.11.47	EP605
3.6.47	BL976, EP767	8.12.47	BL671
9.6.47	BM343, EN903	16.12.47	EN775
12.6.47	AR404	17.12.47	EP242
24.6.47	BL374, EN928	23.12.47	BL368, EP411
3.7.47	EN800, EP244		
14.7.47	W3518, AD464		
17.7.47	AA979	8.1.48	W3902, AA881
23.7.47	BL981	14.1.48	BL821
25.7.47	BM514	19.1.48	AA756
1.8.47	BL437, EP560	28.1.48	BL898
8.8.47	BL970	30.1.48	EP766
22.8.47	P8788, W3519	* W3950 crashed by test flying;
25.8.47	W3641	** AA753 lost on delivery route

34 Spitfire Mk.Vb/c, Portuguese A.F. Serial Nos.: **1 – 34**

Deliv. by ship	Desp.	Arrival	RAF Serial Nos.
Empire Ortolan	6.10.43	19.10.43	W3430, AB191/935, AD511, BL572/664, BM177/364/624, EE620, EP335/350/492/538/699
Baron Forbes	16.10.43	9.11.43	AA946, BL684/890, BM311
City/Lancaster	27.10.43	9.11.43	W3951
Pandorian	25.11.43	8.12.43	AB895, AR367, BL449/690, BM300/479
Dromore	9. 1.44	28. 1.44	W3803, AB133, BL355/978, BM313
Empire Cormorant	3. 1.44	17. 2.44	W3648, BL636, BM176

A.M. Serial Nos. **1 - 34**

A.M No.	(¤)	Code	RAF Serial
1	(1)	RL+A	**W3430**
2	(1)	RL+B	
3	(1)	RL+C	AB191
4	(1)	RL+D	AB935
5	(1)	RL+E	AD511
6	(<)	RL+F	BL572
7	(1)	RL+G	BL664
8	(3)	RL+H	BM177
9	(~)	RL+I	BM364
10	(~)	RL+J	BM624
11	(3)	RL+K	EE620 EP335
12	(<)	RL+L	EP350
13	(<)	RL+M	EP492
14	(<)	RL+N	EP538
15	(<)	RL+O	EP699

A.M No.	(¤)	Code	RAF Serial
16	(~)	MR+A	**AA946**
17	(<)	MR+B	**BL684**
18	(2)	MR+C	BL890 ?
19	(<)	MR+D	**BL690**
20	(3)	MR+E	**W3803**
21	(2)	MR+F	BM311
22	(~)	MR+G	W3951
23	(2)	MR+H	AB895
24	(~)	MR+I	AR367
25	(<)	MR+J	BL449
26	(2)	MR+K	BM300 BM479
27	(3)	MR+L	**W3648**
28	(<)	MR+M	?
29	(<)	MR+N	?
30	(1)	MR+O	**BL978**

| 31 | (<) | RL+P | ? |
| 32 | (<) | RL+Q | ? |

| 33 | (~) | MR+P | ? |
| 34 | (2) | MR+Q | **BM176** |

A.M. Serial Nos. **35 – 93**

A.M No.	(¤)	Code	RAF Serial	A.M No.	(¤)	Code	RAF Serial
35	(2)	MR+R	BM594	65	(1)		BL437
36	(2)	MR+S	AB487	66	(1)		AD191
37	(~)		AA728	67	(~)		W3641
38	(~)		AD294	68	(1)		W3128
39	(~)		EP452	69	(~)		AR438
40	(2)		AR366	70	(1)		W3431
41	(~)		AB862	71	(3)		EP560
42	(2)		AD499	72	(3)		BL970
43	(3)		AA862	73	(3)		P8788
44	(<)		BL646	74	(~)		W3519
45	(2)		BL850	75	(2)		EP785
46	(2)		BM298	76	(~)		W3248
47	(2)		AA729	77	(~)		AA967
48	(<)		AB203	78	(~)		BM131
49	(2)	MR+GG:	AD383 ?	79	(3)		P8791
50	(3)		BL496	80	(~)		EP605
51	(1)		EP767	81	(3)	ZE+K	BL671
52	(1)		AR404	82	(3)		EP242
53	(<)		EN903	83	(3)		EN775
54	(~)		BM343	84	(~)		AB988
55	(<)		EN928	85	(2)	MR+O	EP411
56	(1)	RL+U	AA979	86	(<)		BL368
57	(~)		AD464	87	(3)		W3902
58	(1)		W3518	88	(2)		AA881
59	(~)		W3180	89	(~)		BL976
60	(~)		EN800	90	(~)		BL821
61	(~)		EP244	91	(3)		AA756
62	(<)		BL374	92	(2)		BL898
63	(1)		BL981	93	(3)		EP766
64	(3)		BM514	1 a/c lost on delivery (AA753)

(¤) To Tancos (BA.3) in April 1952 = No (1), (2) or (3) Esquadrilha;
(<) SOC before February 1952;
(~) SOC from February 1952 to April 1952, still at Ota;
Code: Known markings until February 1952

RUMANIA

Rumania was one of several foreign Air Forces interested in the Spitfire, and in 1937 an order was placed for ten Mk.Is. A firm quotation was given on 29 March 1938, and place number five was allotted in the Foreign Office priority list dated 17th November 1938.

In the autumn of 1939 Supermarine prepared Spitfire K9791 for test flying by foreign pilots. This commenced on 12th September with the Belgians, and next day Yugoslav pilots flew this aircraft. Rumanians should have flown it in the second half of September 1939, but it was not to be. With the outbreak of the Second World War, all foreign orders were cancelled.

Russia occupied North-Bucovina and Moldavia in June 1940, bringing Rumania onto the side of Germany against Russia. The Air Force of Rumania, the *Fortele Aeriene Regale Romane*, then received German fighter aircraft types He 112, Bf 109E and Bf 110C, also Bf 109G later. Following very heavy air attacks against the Ploesti oilfield and the arrival of the Soviet Army on the frontier, Rumania changed sides, and on 25th August 1944 declared war on Germany.

After the Second World War, Rumania became part of the Soviet bloc, and never ordered further Spitfires.

Rumania was interested in buying Spitfires, but never received them. The picture shows Prince Michael of Rumania inspecting a Spitfire F.Ia in the UK, 1938. [Wojtek Matusiak]

SINGAPORE

Spitfire F.24 PK683, gate guardian at RAF Changi in August 1965. It subsequently returned to the UK.

Singapore was British-controlled from 1824. In the Second World War Japan occupied this territory from 1942 until 1945. After the war Singapore became a British Colony in 1946 and took part in the United Malayan National Organization (UMNO) in the same year. It was part of the Malayan Federation from 1948, but became independent in 1959, as a member of the British Commonwealth. With Malaya, Sarawak and Sabah it formed the Federation of Malaysia in 1963, but in 1965 Singapore separated to become a republic.

An Auxiliary Fighter Squadron (Singapore) was formed at Tengah on 1st March 1950 with four Tiger Moths, later receiving one Spitfire F.XVIIIe, some Spitfire F.24s and two Harvards from FEAF stocks, and becoming the Singapore Fighter Squadron, Malayan Auxiliary Air Force in October 1951. From July 1952 the Squadron came under the control of the newly-formed Singapore Wing, Malayan Auxiliary Air Force. On 20th June 1955 the title of the unit changed to Singapore Squadron, Malayan Auxiliary Air Force, and on 1st April 1958 it moved to Seletar, where it was disbanded on 30th September 1960, but Spitfires had been phased out in April 1954.

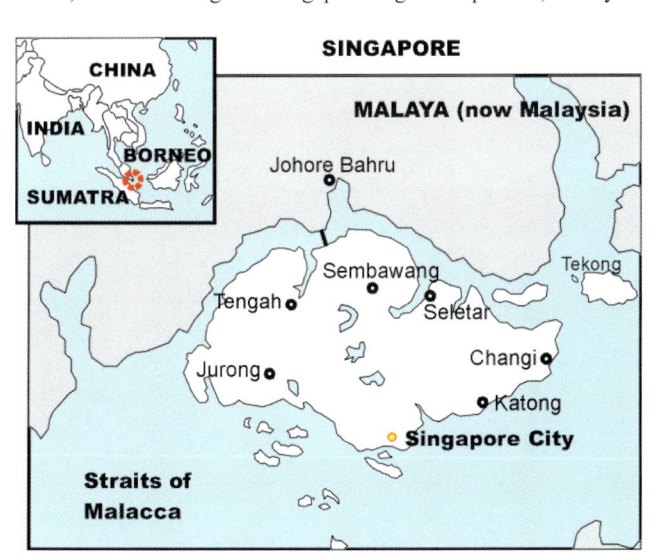

Individual Histories

PK681 Spitfire F.24 (Griffon 61); TOC/RAF 28.11.46; Seletar, Singapore.12.8.49 - Singapore Aux.A.F. 20.7.51; Malayan Aux.A.F. 10.51; Hit PK683 while taxiing at Tengah 29.9.52; SOC 15.4.54

PK683 Spitfire F.24 (Griffon 61); TOC/RAF 13.8.46; FEAF 7.9.50 - Singapore Aux.A.F. 24.7.51; Malayan Aux.A.F. 10.51; Hit by PK681 while taxiing at Tengah 29.9.52; Retd RAF, to No.390 MU 10.2.53; Not repaired; SOC, converted to ground instructional No.*7150M* 15.4.54; To the Singapore Air Training Corps 5.54; To gate guardian at RAF Changi 1954; Displayed RAF Seletar 1968; Flown to UK in an RAF Belfast; Arr No.71 MU at Bicester 16.4.70; Restoration; RAF Kemble 30.6.72; To RAF Museum, RAF Colerne 11.72; To RAF Shawbury 21.8.75; ; To R J Mitchell Museum, Southampton 7.2.76; To Hall of Aviation, Southampton 5.84; Still on exhibition – **SURVIVOR**

SM972 Spitfire F.XVIIIe (Griffon 65); TOC/RAF 11.9.45; ACSEA 11.4.46; No.60 Sqn (Seletar) 2.8.49 – Singapore Aux.A.F. 10.5.51; Retd RAF, SOC 27.2.53

TP205 Spitfire F.XVIIIe (Griffon 65); TOC/RAF 5.1.46; ex No 60 Sqn ACFE; MBFE Repair Cat.4R 2.2.50; Re-Cat.5 (GI), issued to Malayan Aux.(F) Sqn Penang 26.6.50

VN494 Spitfire F.24 (Griffon 61); TOC/RAF 14.1.48; FEAF 22.10.50 - Singapore Aux.A.F. 23.7.51; Malayan Aux.A.F. 10.51; Service unknown; SOC 18.2.54.

SOUTH AFRICA

A line-up of rocket-equipped post-war Spitfire HF.IXes, stated to include 5583, 5517, 5599, 5518 and 5537 at the Air Operational School, Langebaanweg.
[SAAF Museum]

South Africa was British controlled from 1795 (Cape Colony) and 1877 (Transvaal) respectively. In 1910 these formed the Union of South Africa, with a mandate for South-West Africa (now Namibia) from 1920 to 1966. The Union attained independence in 1931, and became the Republic of South Africa in 1961.

The South African Air Force (SAAF) - or *Sudafrikaanse Lugmag* (SALM) in Afrikaans - was formed with the support of the U.K. after World War One on 1st February 1920. It was re-organised in 1936, and within a short time after the outbreak of World War two the SAAF intensified coastal patrols. Construction of new airfields enabled training of both SAAF and RAF pilots from June 1940 under a Joint Training Scheme, part of the British Commonwealth Air Training Plan. The SAAF fought very closely with the RAF in the Mediterranean area (MTO). It was an integral arm of the Allied Forces, but with its own organisation, largely under the overall control of the RAF in the field.

SAAF in World War Two (MTO)

A number of units of the South African Air Force (SAAF), including several Spitfire squadrons, served in cooperation with the RAF in North Africa and later Italy (MTO). More than 900 Spitfires (mostly Mks.V & IX) served with the following SAAF units from late 1942:

No. 1 (F) Squadron - Sqn code: "AX".
Spitfire Vb/c from 4th November 1942 to August 1943, Mk.VIIIc from August 1943 to June 1944, Mk.IX from June 1943 to October 1943 and from April 1944 to June 1945 (No.1 Sqn handed over ten Mk.IX to No.7 Sqn in exchange for ten Mk.Vc/trop, keeping only five Mk.IX, on 2nd March 1944).
Operated over Egypt, Libya, Tunisia, Malta, Sicily, Italy and the Balkans. With the Western Desert Air Force (No.212 Group, No.243 Wing) in October 1942; NAAF (DAF), No.211 Group, No.244 Wing [from 7th November 1942] in July 1943; To No.7 (SAAF) Wing 18th September 1943.
Bases: LG.172 from 23.10.42; LG.05 from 17.11.42; Martuba 20.11.42; Msus 25.11.42; El Hasseiat 3.12.42; Agedabia 9.12.42; Merduma 21.12.42; El Chel 31.12.42; Hamraiet Main 6.1.43; Wadi Sirru 19.1.43; Castel Benito 7.2.43; Hazbub 24.2.43; Ben Gardane 2.3.43; Bu Gara 10.3.43; La Fauconnerie 11.4.43; Goubrine 15.4.43; Hergla 6.5.43; Ben Gardane 20.5.43; Luqa, Malta 14.6.43; Pachino, Sicily 13.7.43; Cassibile 17.7.43; Lentini West 26.7.43; Isola/Crotone, Italy 18.9.43; Cassano 19.9.43; Scanzano 22.9.43; Gioia del Colle 2.10.43; Palata 15.10.43; Trigno 17.12.43; Sinello 5.5.44; Marcigliano 14.6.44; Orvieto 23.6.44; Foiano 16.7.44; Rimini 11.10.44; Bellaria 7.11.44; Forli 8.12.44; Ravenna 3.3.45; Lavariano 18.5.45; Sqn disbanded 12.7.45.
Commanding Officers:
Mjr G J Le Mesurier	4.42
Mjr P C R Metelerkamp	13.11.42
S/Ldr P Olver, RAF (temp)	29.12.42
Mjr D D Moodie	26.1.43
Mjr J M Faure	24.7.43
Mjr J T Seccombe	14.2.44
Mjr G B Lipawsky	24.10.44

No. 2 (FB) Squadron - Sqn code: "DB".
Spitfire Vb & Vc from 7th July 1943 to March 1944. A few Mk.IX flown from 10th August 1943 but these were

withdrawn October 1943. Re-equipped fully with Mk.IX from February 1944 to July 1945, also one F.VIIIc in October 1944.

Operated over Tunisia, Sicily, Italy and the Balkans. With Western Desert Air Force (No.211 Group, No.233 Wing) in October 1942; NAAF (DAF), No.211 Group; To No.7 (SAAF) Wing by July 1943.

Bases: Ben Gardane North 24.6.43; El Houaria 14.7.43; Pachino, Sicily 18.8.43; Faro 28.8.43; Isolo/Crotone, Italy 18.9.43; Cassano 19.9.43; Scanzano 23.9.43; Gioia del Colle 2.10.43; Palata 18.10.43; Trigno 22.12.43; Sinello 5.5.44; Marigliana 14.6.44; Cisterna 23.6.44; Foiano 16.7.44; Rimini 25.10.44; Bellaria 6.11.44; Forli 8.12.44; Ravenna 3.3.45; Tissano 18.5.45; Sqn disbanded 12.7.45.

Commanding Officers:
Mjr T P L Murray	4.43
Mjr J H Gaynor	3.1.44
Capt D A Ruiter (temp)	5.3.44
Mjr S A Finney	3.44
Mjr L Dawson-Smith	5.44
Mjr S A Finney	10.44

No. 3 (F) Squadron - Sqn code: "CA";
Spitfire IX from February 1944 to October 1945, Mk.Vb/c from March 1944 to August 1944.

Operated over Italy, the Balkans and Egypt. Air Defence Middle East (No.210 Group) July 1943; Joined No.8 (SAAF) Wing 24th September 1944.

Bases: Italy from 27.7.43; Bari 1.8.44; Foiano 22.8.44; Borghetto 25.9.44; Fano 2.10.44; Peretola 12.11.44; Pontedera 2.1.45; Villafranca 31.4.45; Udine/Campoformido 16.5.45; Fayid, Egypt 30.9.45; Sqn disbanded 7.10.45.

Commanding Officers:
Mjr B A A Wiggett	2.44
Mjr E K Dunning	22.5.44
Capt C A Golding	20.12.44

No. 4 (FB) Squadron - Sqn code: "KJ".
Spitfire Vb/c from July 1943 to May 1944 and Mk.IX from May 1944 to July 1945 (few Mk.VIIIc in October 1944).

Operated over Tunisia, Sicily, Italy and the Balkans. With Western Desert Air Force (No.211 Group, No.233 Wing) in October 1942; NAAF (DAF, No.211 Group); To No.7 (SAAF) Wing by April 1943.

Bases: Ben Gardane 25.6.43; El Haouaria 14.7.43; Pachino, Sicily 2.8.43; Cassibile 31.8.43; Faro 6.9.43; Scanzano, Italy 24.9.43; Gioia del Colle 1.10.43; Palata 15.10.43; Trigno 21.10.43; Sinello 5.5.44; Marcigliano 14.6.44; Cisterna 23.6.44; Foiano 16.7.44; Rimini 12.10.44; Bellaria 6.11.44; Forli 8.12.44; Ravenna 1.3.45; Tissano 18.5.45; Sqn disbanded 12.7.45.

Commanding Officers:
Mjr D W Golding	5.43
Mjr C A van Vliet	10.11.43

Spitfire IXs of No. 1 Sqn SAAF including 5516 'AX-M' lined up at Waterkloof.

Spitfire F.Vc/trop KJ-T of No. 4 Sqn SAAF has an EF600-series serial number and a leaping springbok badge on the rudder. [SAAF Museum]

A line-up of Spitfire F.Vb/trops of No. 40 Sqn SAAF in mid-1943, the nearest four being EP826 WR-B, EP192 WR-O, EP894 WR/J and ER549 WR-L.
[SAAF Museum]

Snow-covered Spitfire WR-K of No. 40 Sqn SAAF, possibly LF(FR).IXc MH550 in 1945.

Mjr W J Wheeler	2.1.44
Mjr P D Bryant	24.1.44
Mjr B J L Boyle	17.2.44
[arrived then, but did not take over Sqn until 4.44]	
Capt R D B Morton (temp)	27.7.44
Mjr J M Faure	3.8.44
Mjr C J O Swales	18.11.44
Mjr D Hilton-Barber	20..2.45 [killed 25.2.45]
Capt W V Brunton	26.2.45
Mjr W V Brunton [promoted]	4.45

No. 7 (F) Squadron - Sqn code: "TJ".
Spitfire Vb/c from July 1943 to March 1944 and Mk.IX from 9th October 1943 to July 1945; No.1 Sqn handed over ten Mk.IX to No.7 Sqn in exchange for ten Mk.Vc/trop on 2nd March 1944; Mid July 1944 exchanged Merlin 66 engined aircraft for Merlin 63 engined ones.
[Note: Uncertain whether 'TJ' code actually applied before moving to Italy.]

Operated over Libya, Palestine, Egypt, Cyprus, Italy and the Balkans. With Western Desert Air Force (No.211 Group) in October 1942; HQ Air Defence Middle East (No.212 Group) in July 1943 [by April 1943]; Later No.7 (SAAF) Wing.

Bases: Derna 30.5.43; St.Jean 17.8.43; El Gamil 1.9.43; Cos/Antimachia (dett) 9.43 to 2.10.43; Savoia 2.11.43; El Gamil 9.11.43; Nicosia, Cyprus (dett) 14-30.11.43; Cairo West (dett) 18.11.43 to 12.12.43; Savoia 24.2.44; Trigno, Italy 10.4.44; Sinello 6.5.44; Marcigliano 14.6.44; Orvieto 23.6.44; Foiano 16.7.44; Rimini 7.10.44 (dett. from 25.9.44); Bellaria 6.11.44; Forli 8.12.44; Ravenna 1.3.45; Lavariano 18.5.45; Sqn disbanded 12.7.45.

Commanding Officers:
Mjr C A van Vliet	4.43
Mjr W P Stanford	6.11.43
Mjr R H C Kershaw	21.10.44
Capt K A Young (temp)	16.3.45
Mjr D M Brebner	8.4.45

This Spitfire IX of No. 40 Sqn SAAF carried the squadron code letters 'WR', the name 'Imp VI' and the squadron's "cat-and-magnifying glass" motif.
[SAAF Museum]

No. 9 (F) Squadron – (Sqn code unknown).
Spitfire Vb/c from June 1944 to February 1945 and Mk.IX from July 1944 to February 1945.
Operated over Egypt, Palestine, Cyprus and Libya. In No.219 Group September 1944. Lakatamia detachment with No.259 Wing.
Bases: El Gamil 28.6.44; St.Jean (dett) 12.7.44 to 12.8.44; Lakatamia (dett) 12.7.44 to 10.9.44; Edku (dett) 11.9.44 to 16.11.44; Savoia 14.9.44; dett from Tocra to Gamil 23.1.45; Sqn disbanded 1.2.45.
Commanding Officer:
Mjr H E N Wildsmith   5.44
Mjr H C W Liebenberg   11.44

No. 10 (F) Squadron – (no Sqn code);
Spitfire Vb/c from June 1944 to October 1944 and Mk.IX from July 1944 to October 1944.
Operated over Egypt, Palestine and Libya. In No.209 Group. To No.219 Group by August 1944.
Bases: Almaza 25.5.44; Minnick 3.6.44; Edku 28.6.44; Mersa Matruh (dett) 28.6.44 to 8.9.44; Savoia 12.9.44; Sqn disbanded 31.10.44:
Commanding Officer:
Mjr C J O Swales   25.5.44

No.11 (F) Squadron - Sqn code: "ND";
Spitfire Vb/c in July and August 1944; Kittyhawk from September 1944 to August 1945; Spitfire Mk.IX from August 1945 to October 1945.
Operated with Mk.V over Egypt, Italy, with Mk.IX over Egypt. In No.8 (SAAF) Wing.
Bases: Almaza 29.6.44; Edku 19.7.44; Re-equipped Kittyhawk 8.44; Villafrancha, Italy (Spitfire) 8.45; Fayid, Egypt 29.9.45; Sqn disbanded 30.10.45.
Commanding Officer:
Mjr C J Laubscher   6.44
Mjr D C Dove   24.4.45

No. 40 (TR) Squadron - Sqn code: "WR";
Spitfire Mk.Vb/c from February 1943 to September 1944 (several FR.Vb for recce missions), Mk.IX from August 1944 to October 1945 and PR.XI in September and October 1945.
Operated over Tunisia, Malta, Sicily, Italy, Greece and Austria. With Western Desert Air Force (No.285 Wing) in October 1942; To AHQ Malta July 1943; dett. NAAF (DAF, No.285 Wing) in July 1943; Detachment with No.337 Wing 10th December 1944 to 14th January 1945; To No.324 Wing 10th August 1945.
Bases: Castel Benito 24.1.43; El Assa 14.2.43; Nefatia 25.2.43; Nefatia South 8.3.43; Bu Grara 10.3.43; Gabes Town 4.4.43; La Fauconnerie 11.4.43; Goubrine 15.4.43; Ben Gardane North 18.5.43; Luqa, Malta 23.6.43; Pachino 15.7.43; Cassibile 18.7.43; Lentini West 27.7.43; San Francesco 14.9.43; Bari (dett) 16-29.9.43; Grottaglie, Italy 16.9.43; Palazzo 29.9.43; Foggia Main 5.10.43; Foggia No.1 from 18.10.43; Trigno 17.12.43; Lago 16.3.44; Marcianise 2.4.44; San Angelo 25.4.44; Venafro 22.5.44; Aquino 5.6.44; Osa 11.6.44; Orvieto 23.6.44; Castiglione del Lago 6.7.44; Malignano 1.8.44; Chiaravalle 25.8.44; Piagiolino 31.8.44; Cassandro 18.9.44; Rimini 27.9.44; Bellaria 7.11.44; Forli 4.12.44; Araxos (dett) 10.12.44 to 14.1.45; La Russia 3.5.45; Treviso 6.5.45; Rissano 14.5.45; Moderndorf 27.5.45; Klagenfurt, Austria 12.9.45; Sqn disbanded 20.10.45.
Commanding Officers:
Col C M S Gardner   2.43
Mjr (later Lt Col) J P Blaauw   17.4.43
Lt Col W A Nel   23.8.43
Mjr (later Lt Col) R H Rogers   8.8.44

No. 41 (F) Squadron – (no Sqn code).
Spitfire Mk.IX from 24th February 1944 to July 1944 and Mk.Vb/c from March 1944 to November 1944.
Operated over Egypt and Palestine. AHQ Malta (No.207

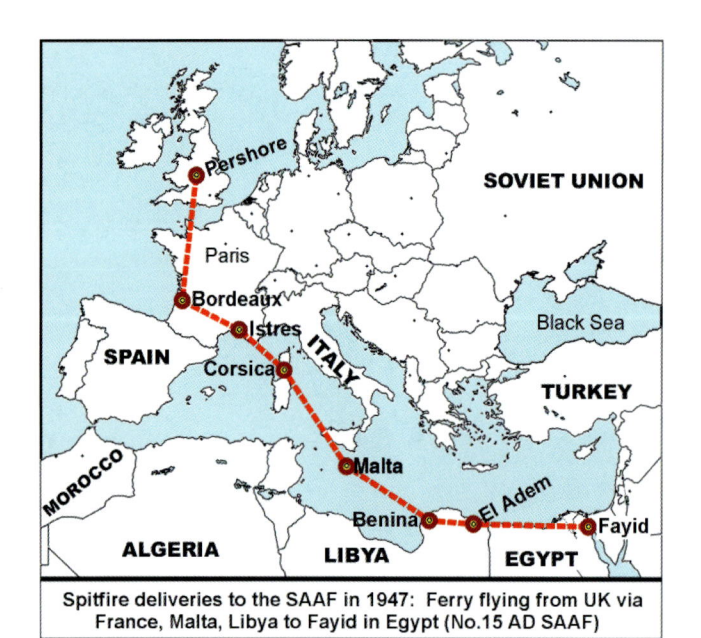

Spitfire deliveries to the SAAF in 1947: Ferry flying from UK via France, Malta, Libya to Fayid in Egypt (No.15 AD SAAF)

Group, No.246 Wing) in October 1942; HQ Air Defence Middle East (No.212 Group) in July 1943.
Bases: Savoia 31.1.44; LG.07 from 25.2.44; St.Jean d'Acre (dett) 3.5.44 to 13.7.44; El Gamil 9.5.44; Almaza 28.7.44; St.Jean d'Acre 8.8.44; Sqn disbanded 8.11.44.
Commanding Officer:
Mjr G C Krummeck 2.44
Mjr T Murray 9.44

No. 7   **Wing** Training Flight
used Spitfire Mk.V (see JK159 & JK433).

Nos.1, 2, 4 and 7 Squadrons operated with No.7 (SAAF) Wing, and Nos.3 and 11 Squadrons with No.8 (SAAF) Wing.
No.40 Squadron was attached to No.285 Wing RAF.
[The High Altitude Flight of No.244 Wing was attached to No.1 Sqn for local defence 5th September 1943 to 6th November 1943, equipped with Spitfire IX.]
One Spitfire F.VIIIc served with No.4 Sqn in October 1944. Another F.VIIIc was used by No.11 OTU at Waterkloof AFB from 1944 until November 1948.

No. 7 (SAAF) Wing

Formed 12th August 1942 at LG.93 Amiriya (Egypt) in No.212 Group with Nos. 80, 127, 247 & 335 Sqns RAF; 17th December 1942 took over Nos.2 & 4 Sqns SAAF from No.233 Wing; 11th January 1943 Belandah (Libya); 16th January 1943 Hamraiet; 31st January 1943 Darragh Main; 31st January 1943 Zuara; 23rd February 1943 Neffatia (Tunisia); 21st March 1943 Hazbub Main; 12th April 1943 Sfax; 17th April 1943 El Adem (Libya); by April 1943 in No.211 Group; 18th May 1943 Sorman; by September 1943 Isola (Italy); 19th September 1943 Cassano; 22nd September 1943 Scanzano; 18th September 1943 No.1 Sqn SAAF joined ex No.244 Wing; 1st October 1943 Gioia; 14th October 1943 Palata; 14th December 1943 Trigno; April 1944 No.7 Sqn SAAF to No.7 Wing; 5th May 1944 at Sinello; 14th June 1944 Marcigliana (now in Desert Air Force); 22nd June 1944 Orvieto; 18th July 1944 Foiano; 1st October 1944 Rimini; 7th November 1944 Bellaria; 8th December 1944 Forli; 1st March 1945 Ravenna; 16th May 1945 Tissano No.2; 13th August 1945 left Desert Air Force; 11th September 1945 arr South Africa; 17th October 1945 re-established at Waterkloof (where disbanded).

No. 8 (SAAF) Wing

Formed 24th June 1944 at Bari (Italy); Took over Nos.3 (Spitfire) & 11 (Kittyhawk) Sqns by 31st August 1944 Chiaravalle; By July 1945 Campoformido; 25th September 1945 to Fayid; Disbanded 24th October 1945.

SAAF at home - New order from 1947

After the war South Africa ordered 136 Spitfire Mk.IX, mainly HF.IXe (Comm.No.362). These were delivered between April 1947 and October 1949, being given the SAAF designation Spitfire "IXA, IXB, IXC" (equivalent to F/LF/HF, respectively).

Negotiations were completed in September 1946 for the supply of 136 Spitfires. It was planned at that time to equip five fighter squadrons with 16 aircraft each. 80 aircraft were to be supplied on free transfer and 56 on repayment terms. These were to comprise 50 F.IXe (Merlin 63) and 86 HF.IXe (Merlin 70). The aircraft were to fly out to Egypt (originally to have been Heliopolis but later changed to No.109 MU Fayid, to which was attached to No.15 Air Depot SAAF) by RAF pilots of No.46 Group (Transport Command), staging through Bordeaux and Istres (France), Elmas (Corsica), Luqa (Malta), Benina and El Adem (Libya). SAAF crews would then take over for the remainder of the trip to Zwartkop AFB in South Africa. The rate of delivery was planned to be ten each month from February to April 1947, then 15 per month from May to October, and finally 16 in November 1947.

In the event, only 53 aircraft were flown by RAF pilots from RAF Pershore near Birmingham to Fayid in Egypt from 23rd April 1947, then by SAAF pilots to South Africa, these being given SAAF serial numbers **5502 to 5554** (the first six arrived at Zwartkop on 9th June 1947). The remaining 83 were shipped to South Africa (82 to Cape Town and one to Durban), seventy-nine from Birkenhead and four from Liverpool, between 9th April 1948 and 6th October 1949, these being given SAAF serials **5555 to 5637**.

Spitfire Mk.IX served post-war with the following units of the SAAF:

No. 1   **Squadron** - Sqn code: "AX".
Spitfires from June 1947 to 1950, at Waterkloof AFB (WKF, c.6-8m SE of Pretoria).
Commanding Officer:
Mjr A C Bosman

No. 1   **(Aux) Sqn,** a Citizen force element of No.1 Sqn; Reserve unit for "Weekend-flyers" at Waterkloof AFB, established 16th August 1947; Became No.4 Sqn on 1st January 1951.
Commanding Officer:
Capt M.MacRobert

No. 2   **Squadron** - Sqn code: "DB".
Spitfires from June 1947, at Waterkloof AFB (WKF).
Commanding Officer:
Capt K Kuhlmann 1.12.48
Cdt S van Breda Theron 9.50 [in Korea with F-51s]

No. 35 **Squadron** - Sqn codes: "RB" & "AX".
Spitfires from March 1948 to May 1949, based at Stamford Hill (near Durban).
Note: No.35 Sqn used officially the code-letters "RB", but all the Spitfires wore the letters "AX", so were probably on loan from No.1 Sqn.
Commanding Officer:
Unknown

No. 60 **Squadron** - Sqn code: "JS";
Spitfires from January 1949 to July 1950, at Zwartkop (Swartkop) AFB (SKP), c.5-7m south of Pretoria.
Remarks: One aircraft was painted "J-SD" due to the position of the roundels on the starboard side
Commanding Officer:
Unknown

No. 68 **Air School** (for Technical Training) - No code letters
Spitfires from February 1948 to June 1954, at Lyttelton AFB (LYT, c. 6-8m SE of Pretoria, between Zwartkop and Waterkloof).
Commanding Officer:
Unknown

SOUTH AFRICA

AOS Air Operational School - No code letter; Spitfires from August 1948 to August 1953, Langebaanweg AFB (LBWG, on the west coast, some 60m north of Cape Town, near Saldahna Bay).
Commanding Officer:
Unknown

CFS **Central Flying School** - No code letter; Spitfires from December 1947 to March 1950, at Dunnottar AFB (near Nigel), c.30m SE of Johannesburg; CFS temporary also used for some courses.
Commanding Officer:
Unknown.

The last Spitfire was withdrawn from SAAF service on 7 April 1954.

SAAF abbreviations

10 AD	=	No 10 Air Depot at Voortrekkerhoogte
15 AD	=	No 15 Air Depot at Fayid, later to Valhalla (Pretoria)
AOS	=	Air Operational School at Langebaanweg (LBWG)
68 AS	=	No 68 Air School (Technical Training) at Lyttelton
BMSpT	=	Bloemspruit AFB (near Bloemfontein)
bos	=	board of survey (held on every aircraft to determine disposal)
FCS	=	"Flying Cheetah" Sqn (No.2 Sqn SAAF)
LBWG	=	Langebaanweg AFB (c.60m N of Cape Town, coast)
LYT	=	Lyttelton AFB (SE of Pretoria)
11 OTU	=	Operational Training Unit at Waterkloof
SKP	=	Swartkop (Zwartkop) AFB (South of Pretoria)
T/A	=	Treasury authority (disposal)
WAS	=	Waterkloof Air Station
WKF	=	Waterkloof AFB (c.10m SE Pretoria)
YPT	=	Ysterplaat AFB (north of Cape Town)
ZAS	=	Zwartkop (Swartkop) AFB, Air Station.

Individual Histories

AB320   Spitfire F.Vb/trop (Merlin 45); TOC/RAF 25.2.42; M.E. 12.42 – SAAF (MTO), No.1 Sqn ('AX-L') by 3.43; Me 210 shot down 30m WNW of Gabes 27.3.43 (Lt DS Rogan DSO); Engine failed at 21,000ft on swccp, suggested coolant leak, glided to 500ft then abandoned over Gulf of Hammamet, Cat.FB/E 27.4.43 (Lt CA Halliday rescued unhurt by Walrus), SOC

AB345   Spitfire F.Vb/trop (Merlin 45); TOC/RAF 4.2.42; M.E. 16.5.42 - SAAF (MTO), No.40 Sqn, seat broke loose, unable to get wheels down, belly-landed on airfield, Carabully Gasr, Castel Verde, Cat.A 25.2.43 (Lt RD Steinbach); Retd RAF; Later to Turkey 28.9.44

AB536   Spitfire F.Vc/trop (Merlin 46); TOC/RAF 26.2.42; Malta 8.42; dis. NA 7.43 - SAAF (MTO), No.4 Sqn ('KJ-R'), hit by flak, crash-landed, Cat.FB/3 8.11.43 (Lt DJ Campbell killed), SOC

AR469   Spitfire F.Vc/trop (Merlin 45); TOC/RAF 28.5.42; M.E. 14.10.42 – SAAF (MTO), No.1 Sqn, glycol leak in formation operational flight, broke formation, forced landed at Advanced New Zealand HQ on hillside near battle front, "did well to get to our lines", Cat.B 14.4.43 (Lt GW Hillary OK); Retd RAF; SOC 8.3.44

AR593   Spitfire F.Vc/trop (Merlin 46); TOC/RAF 9.8.42; NWA 28.2.43 - SAAF (MTO), No.4 Sqn, to No.117 MU 25.4.44; No.4 Sqn from 26.4.44 until 21.5.44 (used by Wing Leader, No.7 Wing Training Flight from 5.5.44); Retd RAF; SOC 29.2.45

AR598   Spitfire F.Vb/trop (Merlin 46); TOC/RAF 12.8.42; M.E. 7.12.42 - SAAF (MTO), No.1 Sqn ('AX-Y'), MC 202 damaged 12m NW of Medenine 7.3.43 (Lt DL Quin); To R&SU; Ferrying back to No.1 Sqn in poor visibility, ran out of fuel, force-landed 10m SSW of Burg el Arab, Cat.A 16.4.43 (Lt GT van der Veen OK); Retd RAF (converted to Vc/trop 10.45)

AR618   Spitfire F.Vc/trop (Merlin 46); TOC/RAF 13.10.42; NWA 31.8.43; M.E. 1.9.43 - SAAF (MTO), No.40 Sqn,

Rocket-equipped Spitfire HF.IXe 5582 of the SAAF.

	hit wing of B-24 taxying, propeller damaged Cat.2 17.10.43 (Lt GC Dent); Retd RAF; SOC 26.4.45		Araldi/Jet Cap Aviation, Lakeland, Florida 1994; Now in USA at Barton, Florida - **SURVIVOR**
BP978	Spitfire F.Vc/trop (Merlin 46); TOC/RAF 2.4.42; M.E. - SAAF (MTO), No.1 Sqn, while stationary in dark, hit by JG939, Luqa, Cat.B 8.7.43 (Lt RC Cherrington); Retd RAF (later missing 19.11.43)	BS125	Spitfire F.IXc (Merlin 61); Became SAAF No. **5...** (range 5555-5637); TOC/RAF 24.7.42; Arr South Africa, Cape Town (via Birkenhead) 28.4.48 – SAAF; Fate unknown
BP985	Spitfire F.Vc/trop (Merlin 46); TOC/RAF 12.4.42; M.E. 1.8.42 - SAAF (MTO), No.9 Sqn by 6.44; Glycol leak, engine cut, blower rear bearing broke up, force-landed wheels-up on beach, hit soft patch, overturned 10m W of El Gamil, Cat.E1 7.10.44 (Lt W J Bartman OK); SOC 27.10.44	BS200	Spitfire F.IXc (Merlin 61); Became SAAF No. **5...** (range 5555-5637); TOC/RAF 9.8.42; Arr South Africa, Cape Town (via Birkenhead) 24.12.48 – SAAF; Fate unknown
BR166	Spitfire F.Vc/trop (Merlin 46); TOC/RAF 15.3.43; N.A. 30.11.43; Malta - SAAF (MTO), No.40 Sqn, fuel shortage, forced landing Tracchi area, Cat.FB/A 1.6.44 (Lt N G Boys) [listed as "666"]; Engine cut, forced landing 5m SE of Rimini LG, Cat.FB/E 18.9.44 (Lt D H Robinson slightly injured), SOC	BS309	Spitfire F.IXc (Merlin 61); TOC/RAF 31.8.42; Casablanca 17.5.43 - SAAF (MTO), No.1 Sqn, hit by AA, Cat.FB/Ac 11.11.44 (Lt WA Dowden); ROS; Bomb dropped off and exploded on take-off, damaging MA687 & PT591, Cat. FB/E2 14.12.44 (Lt BD Mair killed); SOC 31.1.45
BR175	Spitfire F.Vc/trop (Merlin 46); TOC/RAF 15.3.42; M.E. 1.7.42 - SAAF (MTO), No.7 Sqn by 16.1.44; No.41 Sqn 8.3.44; No.132 MU, to No.10 Sqn 21.9.44; No.136 MU 26.9.44; SAAF Conv Flt, crashed Cat.FA/E 14.12.44; Retd RAF; SOC 29.8.46	BS344	Spitfire F.IXc (Merlin 63); Became SAAF No. **55..** (range 5502-5554); TOC/RAF 24.9.42; Flown to ME, arr No.15 AD Fayid 31.7.47 – SAAF, Zwartkop Air Station in 9.47; Fate unknown
BR299	Spitfire F.Vc/trop (Merlin 46); TOC/RAF 26.4.42; N.A. 1.44 - SAAF (MTO), No.9 Sqn by 6.44; No.10 Sqn 10.8.44; Brake failure, ran off runway landing, undercarriage collapsed 24.9.44 (Lt JG Segalla); Retd RAF (No.136 MU) 25.9.44; SOC 30.4.47	BS408	Spitfire F.IXc (Merlin 63); Became SAAF No. **5564**; TOC/RAF 31.10.42; Arr South Africa, Cape Town (via Birkenhead) 21.6.48 – SAAF, Lyttelton AFB; Service unknown; Later ground instructional airframe; No.15 AD 10.12.53; For sale 9.5.55
BR363	Spitfire F.Vc/trop (Merlin 46); TOC/RAF 5.5.42; M.E. 7.42 - SAAF (MTO), No.7 Sqn, to No.3 Sqn 5.3.44; Retd RAF; SOC 31.5.45	BS431	Spitfire F.IXc (Merlin 61); TOC/RAF 30.8.42; NWA 10.43 - SAAF (MTO), No.4 Sqn ('KJ-L') 14.9.44; Took off with bombs, port tyre burst, swung and overturned at Bellaria, Cat.FB/2 4.12.44 (Lt KJA de Graaf seriously injured); Retd RAF; SOC 2.8.45
BR375	Spitfire F.Vc/trop (Merlin 46); TOC/RAF 23.4.42; Malta 8.42 - SAAF (MTO), No.2 Sqn ('DB-K') by 12.43; Tyre came off on take-off, belly-landed, Cat.FB/2 13.1.44 (Lt W J Geering); Retd RAF (RiW); SOC 9.8.45	BS451	Spitfire F.IXc (Merlin 61); Became SAAF No. **55..** (range 5502-5554); TOC/RAF 16.9.42; Flown to ME, arr No.15 AD Fayid 20.9.47 – SAAF, Zwartkop Air Station 1947; Fate unknown
BR390	Spitfire F.Vc/trop (Merlin 46); TOC/RAF 15.5.42; via Takoradi to M.E. 18.7.42; No.92 Sqn, Cat.FA/2 29.9.42; SOC 30.9.42 (bboc) - SAAF (MTO), No.1 Sqn ('AX-B') by 2.43; Ju 87 destroyed & another probable 10m NW of Medenine 6.3.43 (Lt AF Tyrrell); Collided with MC 202, both broke up Gabes-El Hamma, crashed 8m S of Gabes, Cat.FB/E 25.3.43 (Lt H F Smith killed), SOC	BS512	Spitfire F.IXc (Merlin 61); Became SAAF No. **5507**; TOC/RAF 27.3.43; Flown to ME, arr No.15 AD Fayid 17.5.47 – SAAF, Zwartkop Air Station in 7.47; No.1 Sqn, taxying accident (Mjr GC Krummeck) 6.11.48; R&SU; SOC 14.10.49
BR494	Spitfire F.Vc/trop (Merlin 46); TOC/RAF 13.6.42; M.E. 8.42 (also 11.44) - SAAF (MTO), No.9 Sqn, glycol leak, landed undercarriage up at El Gamil, Cat.Ac 28.6.44 (Lt K E F George); Retd RAF; SOC 26.9.46	BS538	Spitfire F.IXc (Merlin 61); Became SAAF No. **5...** (range 5555-5637); TOC/RAF 11.10.42; Arr South Africa, Cape Town (via Liverpool) 4.12.48 – SAAF; Fate unknown
BR520	Spitfire F.Vc/trop (Merlin 46); TOC/RAF 6.42; Malta 7.43 - SAAF (MTO), No.1 Sqn by 6.43; Hit by ground fire while strafing gharris 1m NE of Randazzo 6.8.43 (Lt RB Peel slightly wounded); Retd RAF (RiW); No.2 Sqn, lost power 23.1.44; Retd RAF (Census 6.45); SOC 29.8.46	BS553	Spitfire F.IXc (Merlin 61); TOC/RAF 17.11.42; NWA 28.2.43 - SAAF (MTO), No.4 Sqn ('KJ-D':'KJ-E'), squadron move, crowded in formation take-off by leader swinging towards him, attempted to lift off in 300yds to clear crashed aircraft near boundary, struck wall, Gioia del Colle, Cat.3 18.10.43 (Lt K F Huskisson OK), SOC
BR521	Spitfire F.Vc/trop (Merlin 46); TOC/RAF 6.42; M.E. 27.9.42 - SAAF (MTO), No.41 Sqn, undercarriage damaged landing but pulled up and ordered to crash land at No.104 MU, Cat.FB/2 29.8.44 (Lt DG Nunan); Retd RAF (R&SU); SOC 16.9.46	EE741	Spitfire F.Vc/trop (Merlin 46); TOC/RAF 12.42; M.E. 20.4.43; N.A. 30.11.43 - SAAF (MTO), No.2 Sqn ('DB-R') by 12.43; Retd RAF; Later No.229 Sqn, Cat.FB/3 24.4.44, SOC
BR580	Spitfire F.Vc/trop (Merlin 46); TOC/RAF 29.5.42; M.E. 30.7.42; No.92 Sqn - SAAF (MTO), No.7 Sqn, tipped on nose landing Antimachia, Cos from scramble, Cat.FB/1 24.9.43; Retd RAF; SOC 28.4.45	EE749	Spitfire F.Vc/trop (Merlin 46); TOC/RAF 12.42; NWA 28.2.43 - SAAF (MTO), No.2 Sqn, damaged 10.12.43; Retd RAF (No.114 MU) 10.12.43
BR601	Spitfire F.IXc (Merlin 61 & 63); Became SAAF No. **5631**; TOC/RAF 17.6.42 - Arr South Africa, Cape Town 13.3.49; SAAF, Ysterplaat AFB; AOS, swung on landing, Cat.1a 5.4.51 (2/Lt RV Sherwood); Swung on landing, Cat.1 11.5.51 (2/Lt de Jongh); Overshot landing Ysterplaat, Cat.2 6.5.52 (Lt DR Leathers); SOC 1952; To Ysterplaat AFB (syn) in 6.54; Sold to Harold Barnett /South African Metal & Machinery Co, Salt River, Cape Town 10.3.55; Displayed there on pole as "PV260/DB-P"; Shipped to UK and auctioned in London 31.10.87; To Thruxton 6.7.89 for restoration to fly; Stored dismantled at Biggin Hill 1992; To Mike	EE779	Spitfire F.Vc/trop (Merlin 46); TOC/RAF 7.12.42; Gibraltar 13.1.43 - SAAF (MTO), No.4 Sqn ('KJ-D'), hit by AA 5m W of Pescara, retd to base, Cat.FB/2 18.11.43 (Lt G P Rabie); Retd RAF (RiW)
		EE785	Spitfire F.Vc/trop (Merlin 46); TOC/RAF 14.12.42; M.E. 23.4.43 - SAAF (MTO), No.1 Sqn ('AX-H'), crashed on landing 16.4.43; No.136 MU 13.5.43; No.1 Sqn, formation attacked in poor visibility by Bf 109Gs and a FW 190 at 7,000ft over Randazzo, Sicily, shot down by Hptm Franz Beyer of IV/JG3, broke up in air, crashed, burnt out, Cat.FB/E 19.7.43 (Lt C A Halliday killed), SOC
		EE786	Spitfire F.Vc/trop (Merlin 46); TOC/RAF 15.12.42; M.E. 25.5.43 - SAAF (MTO), No.7 Sqn, attack on island by Bf 109s and Ju 88s, shot down by Bf 109s over Cos, Cat. FB/E 28.9.43 (Capt E A Rorvik killed), SOC

Spitfire F.Vs of No. 4 Sqn SAAF lined up at Trigno, Italy, in the winter of 1943/44. The two nearest machines are EF682 KJ-E and EE779 KJ-D, and at the far end of the line can be seen Mk.VIII AX-T of No. 1 Sqn SAAF, which was also based there at that time. [via Ron Backhouse]

EE798   Spitfire F.Vc/trop (Merlin 56); TOC/RAF 24.12.42; M.E. 5.43 - SAAF (MTO); Lydda to No.7 Sqn 18.12.43; Tyre burst on take-off for Gamil, landed Aboukir en route, ran off tarmac runway, nosed up in sand, propeller damaged 16.2.44 (Lt JA Gilbert); ROS; Retd RAF; Later to Greece 25.4.46

EE808   Spitfire F.Vc/trop (Merlin 46); TOC/RAF 2.1.43; M.E. 9.8.43 - SAAF (MTO), No.40 Sqn, hit by AA in Atino area, engine fire, crash-landed, burnt out, Cat.FB/E 23.4.44 (Lt CR Dent slightly injured), SOC

EE847   Spitfire F.Vc/trop (Merlin 46); TOC/RAF 23.1.43; M.E. 26.5.43 - SAAF (MTO), No.3 Sqn ('CA-P'), tyre burst on take-off, overturned landing, Savoia, Cat.FB/3 12.5.44 (Lt DJF Huyser slightly injured); SOC (RAF) 25.6.44

EE856   Spitfire F.Vc/trop (Merlin 45); TOC/RAF 23.1.43; NWA 31.3.43; ex No.326 (French) Sqn 31.3.43; NAASC 31.10.43 - SAAF (MTO), No.4 Sqn from 8.4.44; Engine failed, caught fire, pilot baled out 20m N of S of Andria, aircraft crashed in sea, Cat.3 17.4.44 (Lt FC Hamilton killed, last seen next day, dinghy found empty), SOC

EF535   Spitfire F.Vc/trop (Merlin 45); TOC/RAF 8.2.43; NWA 31.5.43 - SAAF (MTO), No.7 Sqn, crashed El Gamil; Retd RAF (No.58 R&SU) 18.10.43

EF537   Spitfire F.Vc/trop (Merlin 45); TOC/RAF 8.2.43; M.E. 9.4.43 - SAAF (MTO), No.7 Sqn, hit tractor taxying, tipped on nose, Cat.B 15.10.43 (Lt ACG Binedell); Retd RAF (No.58 R&SU); No.10 Sqn by 6.44; Retd RAF; No.94 Sqn RAF to No.10 Sqn SAAF 1.8.44; Retd No.94 Sqn RAF 28.8.44

EF552   Spitfire F.Vc/trop (Merlin 46); TOC/RAF 18.2.43; NWA 31.5.43; M.E. from 30.11.43 - SAAF (MTO), No.7 Sqn 12.43; Propeller damaged low flying 10.12.43 (Lt LF Morrison); Still No.7 Sqn to at least 16.2.44; Retd RAF; No.130 MU, to No.7 Sqn 28.2.44; No.41 Sqn 8.3.44 to at least 10.44; Retd RAF (Cat.E 13.9.45, SOC)

EF566   Spitfire F.Vc/trop (Merlin 46); TOC/RAF 1.3.43; NWA 31.5.43 - SAAF (MTO), No.40 Sqn; No.117 MU; No.4 Sqn from 9.4.44; Retd RAF (No.117 MU) 25.4.44

EF591   Spitfire F.Vc/trop (Merlin 46); TOC/RAF 8.3.43; NWA 31.5.43; M.E. 7.43 - SAAF (MTO), No.2 Sqn, damaged, Cat.FB/2 3.9.43; Retd RAF (RiW); SOC 26.4.45

EF601   Spitfire F.Vc/trop (Merlin 50A); TOC/RAF 15.3.43; NWA 31.5.43; dis. ME 7.43 - SAAF (MTO), No.2 Sqn by 7.43; Retd RAF; SOC 13.9.45

EF604   Spitfire F.Vc/trop (Merlin 50); TOC/RAF 15.3.43; NAASC 31.10.43; M.E. 30.11.43 - SAAF (MTO), No.9 Sqn by 6.44; Hydraulic failure, ground looped landing Idku, Cat.Ac 10.7.44 (Lt N Bremner); Retd RAF; SOC 31.5.45

EF607   Spitfire F.Vc/trop (Merlin 45); TOC/RAF 15.3.43; M.E. 7.43 - SAAF (MTO), No.2 Sqn, engine failure returning from op, broken con-rod, landed Catania, Cat.FB/2 2.9.43 (Mjr T P L Murray); RiW; Retd RAF (FB/E 6.4.44, SOC)

EF611   Spitfire F.Vc/trop (Merlin 45); TOC/RAF 22.3.43; Malta 8.43 - SAAF (MTO), No.4 Sqn, hit by flak over Chieti area, glycol leak, pilot baled out over sea, Cat.FB/3 22.12.43 (Lt R K Hall picked OK up by ASR Walrus), SOC

EF629   Spitfire F.Vc/trop (Merlin 45); TOC/RAF 26.3.43 - SAAF (MTO) 30.11.43; No.3 Sqn, abandoned after glycol leak on convoy escort, Cat.FB/E2 23.6.44 (Lt Kinsey picked up by destroyer, retd 30.6.44), SOC

EF631   Spitfire F.Vc/trop (Merlin 46); TOC/RAF 29.3.43; M.E. 16.4.43 - SAAF (MTO), No.7 Sqn by 17.1.44; No.3 Sqn 5.3.44; Engine cut, crash-landed 20m E of Savoia, Cat.FB/3 7.4.44; SOC 12.4.44

EF637   Spitfire F.Vc/trop (Merlin 50); TOC/RAF 29.3.43; M.E. 7.43 - SAAF (MTO), No.2 Sqn, hit by P-40 of FFAF, Cat. GA/2 16.8.43; Retd RAF (RiW); SOC 31.10.43

EF638   Spitfire F.Vc/trop (Merlin 50); TOC/RAF 2.4.43; Malta - SAAF (MTO), No.2 Sqn, hit by P-40 of FFAF, force-landed El Haouaria LG, Cat.A 16.8.43; SOC (RAF) 17.11.43

EF639   Spitfire F.Vc/trop (Merlin 50); TOC/RAF 5.4.43; M.E. 9.43 - SAAF (MTO), No.2 Sqn ('DB-U') by 18.10.43; Hit while parked by ER893 of No.4 Sqn, Palata, burnt out, Cat. E 24.10.43, SOC

EF642   Spitfire F.Vc/trop (Merlin 50); TOC/RAF 6.4.43; M.E. 16.7.43 - SAAF (MTO), No.10 Sqn until retd RAF (No.94 Sqn) 28.8.44; No.136 MU retd to No.10 Sqn 29.10.44; Sqn disbanded and aircraft to No.9 Sqn 31.10.44; Retd RAF (SOC 29.8.46)

EF643 Spitfire F.Vc/trop (Merlin 50); TOC/RAF 5.4.43; M.E. 13.7.43 - SAAF (MTO), No.40 Sqn [no date]; Retd RAF; Later with No.225 Sqn, destroyed in air raid, Cat.E 18.9.43, SOC

EF649 Spitfire F.Vc/trop (Merlin 50); TOC/RAF 13.4.43; NWA 7.43 - SAAF (MTO), No.3 Sqn, due for major inspection 25.8.44; Retd RAF; Later to Italy (*MM4053*) 27.6.46
NOTE: Reported also as "EF647"

EF651 Spitfire F.Vc/trop (Merlin 50); TOC/RAF 17.4.43; M.E. 9.43; NAAF 1.11.43 - SAAF (MTO), No.4 Sqn, hit retd to base, by flak, Cat.FB/2 7.11.43 (F/O WP Pistorius); Swung landing in strong cross-wind, tipped up, Cat.FB/2 8.2.44 (Lt RK Hall unhurt); Retd RAF (M.E. 31.1.45); Later to Turkey 22.2.45

EF673 Spitfire F.Vc/trop (Merlin 50); TOC/RAF 27.4.43; M.E. 9.43 - SAAF (MTO), No.4 Sqn, tyre burst landing, swung, went off runway into sand and overturned Trigno, Cat.E 31.12.43 (Capt DF de Wet injured), SOC

EF682 Spitfire F.Vc/trop (Merlin 50); TOC/RAF 17.5.43; NWA in 10.43 - SAAF (MTO), No.40 Sqn; No.4 Sqn ('KJ-E'), hit by AA over Korcula, force-landed Cat.FB/2 8.3.44 (F/O WP Pistorius); R&SU; No.4 Sqn ('KJ-S') by 17.3.44; Hit by AA, retd to base, Cat.FB/2 30.3.44 (Lt DJ de Villiers); Retd RAF (No.59 R&SU) 30.3.44

EF692 Spitfire F.Vc/trop (Merlin 50); TOC/RAF 9.6.43; NWA 10.43; FFAF to RAF 30.11.43 - SAAF (MTO), No.2 Sqn ('DB-R') by 12.43; Retd RAF (FB/E 29.10.44, SOC)

EF694 Spitfire F.Vc/trop (Merlin 50); TOC/RAF 9.6.43; M.E. 9.43 - SAAF (MTO), No.9 Sqn, crashed in sea 3m off Alexandria, Cat.FB/E 25.10.44 (Lt WD Bell killed), SOC

EF702 Spitfire F.Vc/trop (Merlin 55); TOC/RAF 28.6.43; N.A. 30.11.43 - SAAF (MTO), No.117 MU to No.4 Sqn 30.3.44; Retd RAF (No.208 Sqn) 25.4.44

EF705 Spitfire F.Vc/trop (Merlin 55); TOC/RAF 30.6.43; N.A. 30.11.43 - SAAF (MTO), No.1 Sqn; To No.3 Sqn 3.9.44; No.40 Sqn, landing from operation in poor visibility, collided with MA736 landing from opposite direction, Forli, Cat.FB/E 13.2.45 (F/Lt AP Buxton OK), SOC

EF722 Spitfire LF.Vc/trop (Merlin 55M); TOC/RAF 21.8.43; NAASC 31.10.43 - SAAF (MTO), No.40 Sqn, hit by AA in Cassino/San Giorgo area, force-landed undercarriage up, Cat.FB/2 3.5.44 (Lt NG Boys); Repair; Hit by flak and abandoned NW of Florence, Cat.FB/3 5.8.44 (Lt WB Sobey PoW), SOC

EF726 Spitfire LF.Vc/trop (Merlin 55M); TOC/RAF 21.8.43; NAASC 31.10.43; ex USAAF 29.2.44 - SAAF (MTO), No.40 Sqn, heavy landing, undercarriage collapsed in soft patch, Cat.FB/2 17.7.44 (Lt FE Vincent); Retd RAF (RiW); SOC 26.4.45

EF728 Spitfire F.Vc/trop (Merlin 55); TOC/RAF 2.9.43; NAASC 31.10.43 - SAAF (MTO), No.40 Sqn, hit by AA over Anzio, Cat.FB/E 6.3.44 (Lt JC Aronson killed), SOC

EF732 Spitfire F.Vc/trop (Merlin 55); TOC/RAF 2.9.43; NAASC 31.10.43 - SAAF (MTO), No.40 Sqn ('WR-B' & 'WR-M'), hit by AA over Impruneta, force-landed and crashed, Cat.FB/E 28.7.44 (Lt JH du Plessis killed), SOC

EF735 Spitfire F.Vc/trop (Merlin 55); TOC/RAF 8.9.43; NAASC 31.10.43, ex USAAF 29.2.44 - SAAF (MTO), No.40 Sqn, wing dropped landing, undercarriage collapsed, Cat.FB/2 23.4.44 (Lt RC Theunissen); Retd RAF (RiW); SOC 26.4.45

EF737 Spitfire F.Vc/trop (Merlin 55); TOC/RAF 17.9.43; N.A. 31.11.43; M.E. - SAAF (MTO), No.7 Sqn, failed to return, Cat.FA/3 23.11.43, SOC

EF738 Spitfire F.Vc/trop (Merlin 55); TOC/RAF 17.9.43; N.A. 30.11.43 - SAAF (MTO), No.40 Sqn, engaged by Four FW 190, damaged one of them 26.3.44 (Capt FE Welgemoed); Hit by AA near Orvieto, too low to bale out, dived in at 45°, and exploded, Cat.FB/3 13.6.44 (Capt INL Taylor killed), SOC

EN138 Spitfire F.IXc (Merlin 61); TOC/RAF 22.11.42; NWA 28.2.43 - SAAF (MTO), No.10 Sqn by 8.44 and 10.44; Retd RAF; SOC 31.1.45

EN140 Spitfire F.IXc (Merlin 61); TOC/RAF 28.11.42; NWA 31.5.43 - SAAF (MTO), No.1 Sqn, lost control on take-off, dived in from 40ft on turn, hit tree Rimini, burnt out, presumed glycol leak, Cat.FA/E2 16.10.44 (Lt WJ Antony injured), SOC

EN156 Spitfire F.IXc (Merlin 61); TOC/RAF 22.12.42; NAAF 1.11.43 - SAAF (MTO), No.1 Sqn, hit by debris on strafing 8.11.44 (Lt TE Wallace); Swung after landing, hit PT451 of No.4 Sqn in standby position, Bellaria, Cat.E1 4.12.44 (Lt BD Mair OK); SOC 2.8.45

EN182 Spitfire F.IXc (Merlin 61); Became SAAF No. **55..** (range 5502-5554); TOC/RAF 17.11.42; MED 3.8.47; No.15 AD Fayid 5.8.47 – SAAF, Zwartkop Air Station 1947; Fate unknown

EN186 Spitfire F.IXc (Merlin 61); TOC/RAF 24.11.42; N.A. - SAAF (MTO), No.2 Sqn, damaged, Cat.2 5.9.43; Retd RAF (RiW); No.40 Sqn, overshot landing on new runway, nosed up, port oleo collapsed, went into soft sand at Bellaria, Cat.B 7.11.44 (Lt SM Cornelius OK); Retd RAF; SOC 2.8.45

EN195 Spitfire F.IXc (Merlin 61); TOC/RAF 24.11.42; NWA 28.2.43 - SAAF (MTO), No.4 Sqn, lost power on sweep, emergency landing, overshot, crashed when opened up to go round again, hit small house 1m NW of Bari Main, Cat.E 24.9.43 (Lt AC Paterson seriously injured); SOC 25.9.43

EN202 Spitfire F.IXc (Merlin 61); TOC/RAF 1.12.42; NWA 28.2.43 - SAAF (MTO), No.1 Sqn, fuselage wrinkled, possible sharp turn on ground or lorry backed into it, Cat.FB/2 18.3.45 (Lt JS de Villiers OK); Retd RAF; SOC 14.3.46

EN242 Spitfire F.IXc (Merlin 61); TOC/RAF 24.12.42; NWA 28.2.43 - SAAF (MTO), No.1 Sqn, unable to land after sortie due to collision between JK884 & ES185, had to land at dusk, hit airfield boundary barrel at Palata, Cat.FB/2 4.11.43 (Lt HP Freeman); Retd RAF; SOC 11.4.46

EN254 Spitfire F.IXc (Merlin 61); TOC/RAF 12.1.43; M.E. 7.43 - SAAF (MTO), No.10 Sqn from 15.7.44; To No.94 Sqn RAF 31.7.44; No.10 Sqn SAAF 28.8.44; Landed undercarriage retracted Idku, Cat.FB/2 28.8.44 (2/Lt L de Klerk OK); Retd RAF (No.109 MU) 30.8.44; Later to Greece 30.1.47

EN257 Spitfire F.IXc (Merlin 61); TOC/RAF 26.1.43; NWA 30.4.43 - SAAF (MTO), No.1 Sqn, disappeared from formation at dusk, failed to pull out of dive, crashed in sea 15m SSW of Pozzallo after chasing Bf 109s towards Sicily, Cat.FB/E 25.6.43 (Lt AdeL Rossouw killed), SOC [Possibly the Spitfire claimed as shot down by Uffz Hans Jürgens of 5/JG27]

EN265 Spitfire F.IXc (Merlin 61); TOC/RAF 2.1.43; NAASC 10.43 - SAAF (MTO), No.4 Sqn ('KJ-E') by 25.8.44; While attd No.3 Sqn, hit by AA and exploded in bombing dive on sheds 5m E of Dicomano, Cat.FB/E 30.8.44 (Lt PO Dawber killed), SOC
NOTE: Crash reported also for EN268

EN267 Spitfire F IXc (Merlin 63); TOC/RAF 23.1.43; Gibraltar 7.3.43; NWA 31.3.43 - SAAF (MTO), No.1 Sqn ('AX-5') by 19.7.43; NAASC 31.10.43; Fate unknown (PSO 1.1.47)

EN268 Spitfire F.IXc (Merlin 61); TOC/RAF 13.1.43; NAASC 31.10.43 - SAAF (MTO), No.117 MU to No.1 Sqn ('AX-H') 4.44; No.4 Sqn?; Retd RAF (MAAF census 6.45); SOC 14.3.46

EN269 Spitfire F.IXc (Merlin 61); TOC/RAF 13.1.43; NAASC 31.10.43 - SAAF (MTO), No.2 Sqn, hit by AA, retd to base 29.7.44 (Lt WR Powell); Armed recce carrying bomb, landed heavily, tailwheel damaged, went round again, tailwheel collapsed on landing, Cat.FB/Ac 2.9.44

SOUTH AFRICA

Spitfire F.IXc EN286 AX-8 of No. 1 Sqn SAAF around July-August 1943. Beneath the front of the cockpit is the name "Cire Cooks VIII" [SAAF Museum]

Spitfire F.IXc 5502 AX-A (ex EN314) of No. 1 Sqn SAAF taxying at Waterkloof around 1948. [via Ken Smy]

      (Lt JS Aberdien); ROS; Retd RAF (No.357 MU) 12.11.44; Later accident Cat.FA/E 9.2.45 (No.5 RFU), SOC

EN286 Spitfire F.IXc (Merlin 61); TOC/RAF 6.12.42; NWA 31.3.43 - SAAF (MTO), No.1 Sqn ('AX-8', named 'Cire Cooks VIII', flown by Lt MES Robinson) by 19.7.43; Bf 109G destroyed nr Randazzo (Obgfr Reinhard Hagedorn of 11 Staffel killed) 19.7.43 (Lt WD Wikner); Out of fuel on operation, force-landed well down runway, swung to avoid another aircraft, round into mound of earth, Lentini West, Cat.FB/B 13.8.43 (Lt HN Taylor); RiW; No.357 MU, to No.2 Sqn 12.5.45-6.45; Retd RAF; Later to Greece 27.2.47

EN291 Spitfire F.IXc (Merlin 61); TOC/RAF 14.12.42; NWA 28.2.43 - SAAF (MTO), No.1 Sqn, shot down by P-38 of USAAF (306th FW), crashed on landing, overturned, Cat.3 20.4.44 (Lt HP Freeman wounded); Retd RAF (No.59 R&SU), SOC

EN296 Spitfire F.IXc (Merlin 61); TOC/RAF 21.12.42; N.A. 30.11.43 - SAAF (MTO), No.1 Sqn ('AX-W') by 15.4.44; Hit by AA, Cat.FB/Ac 7.6.44 (Lt CWL Boyd); ROS; Retd RAF (No.43 Sqn, Cat.FB/E 21.2.45, SOC)

EN300 Spitfire F.IXc (Merlin 61); TOC/RAF 23.12.42; NWA 28.2.43; M.E. - SAAF (MTO), No.1 Sqn ('AX-9'); Abandoned at 5,000ft after shot down (by "friendly" P-38) 5m off Catania, Cat.FB/E 14.7.43 (Lt MES Robinson baled out and rescued unhurt by Greek destroyer), SOC

EN314 Spitfire F.IXc (Merlin 63); Became SAAF No. **5502**; TOC/RAF 1.5.43; Flown to ME, arr No.15 AD Fayid 23.4.47 – SAAF, Zwartkop Air Station 5.47; No.107

	MU Kasfareet 5.47; No.60 ('JS-D') Sqn for PR duties; No.1 Sqn ('AX-A'), mid-air collision with 5520 5.8.48 (2/Lt MH Rorke); AOS, propeller hit ground on run-up, Cat.1 29.9.52 (2/Lt H Ludick); No.15 AD in 6.54; For sale 9.5.55; To S&D Metal NOTE: "EN314" was reported with REAF-markings, but in fact this aircraft went to SAAF. Possibly an error for EN349, which went to the REAF
EN315	Spitfire F.IXc (Merlin 61); TOC/RAF 11.1.43; Malta 7.43 - SAAF (MTO), No.40 Sqn; No.1 Sqn, landed downwind from operation out of fuel, overshot, swung into pile of rocks at Luqa, Cat.FB/A 10.7.43 (Lt WH Greeff); Re-Cat.E, SOC 16.7.43
EN333	Spitfire F.IXc (Merlin 61); TOC/RAF 21.1.43; NWA 31.3.43; N.A. 30.11.43 - SAAF (MTO), No.1 Sqn, hit by AA in dive-bombing attack, caught fire, baled out near River Po, Cat.FB/E2 14.9.44 (Lt CWL Boyd safe); SOC 23.10.44
EN339	Spitfire F.IXc (Merlin 61); TOC/RAF 26.1.43; NWA 31.3.43 - SAAF (MTO), No.2 Sqn ('DB-G') by 11.44; Hit by AA over target, Cat.FB/Ac 1.12.44 (Lt M Flynn); Hood came off in dive, hit tailplane, Cat.Ac 18.1.45 (Lt TJMcD Breakey); Retd RAF (No.110 MU) 11.4.45; MAAF census 6.45
EN345	Spitfire F.IXc (Merlin 61); Became SAAF No. **5...** (range 5555-5637); TOC/RAF 2.2.43; Arr South Africa, Cape Town (del via Liverpool) 14.5.49 – SAAF; Fate unknown
EN350	Spitfire F.IXc (Merlin 61); TOC/RAF 10.2.43; Malta 6.43 - SAAF (MTO), No.7 Sqn ('TJ-E'), while stationery awaiting take-off, hit by MJ506 of No.40 Sqn landing, Rimini, Cat.FB/2 12.10.44 (Lt NGN Atmore OK); R&SU; Retd RAF; SOC 5.6.45
EN352	Spitfire F.IXc (Merlin 61); TOC/RAF 21.1.43; NWA 31.3.43; ex FFAF - SAAF (MTO), No.1 Sqn ('AX-I') by 9.44; Me 410 crashed in flames 8m NE of Modena, shared with MH901 & MA532 10.9.44 (Lt JBS Ross); Stbd mainplane hit by AA while strafing, Cat.FB/2 17.9.44 (Lt FW Whittaker); Retd RAF (No.5 RFU) 6.12.44
EN357	Spitfire F.IXc (Merlin 61 & 63); TOC/RAF 1.2.43; NAASC 31.10.43 - SAAF (MTO), No.7 Sqn from 18.7.44 (Merlin 63); Hit by flak but retd safely 12.9.44 (Lt P Maxwell); To No.7 Wing Servicing Flight; Retd No.7 Sqn; Loss of hydraulic pressure after mission, flapless landing, no brakes, swung, retracted undercarriage to stop, hit tractor, nosed up, Cat.FB/Ac 13.10.44 (Lt DC Bosch OK); R&SU; No.7 Sqn, hit by flak, crash landed Forli LG, Cat.FB/2 9.12.44 (Lt P Maxwell); Retd RAF; SOC 9.8.45
EN365	Spitfire F.IXc (Merlin 61); TOC/RAF 3.3.43; NWA 30.4.43; NAASC 1.11.43 - SAAF (MTO), No.117 MU to No.4 Sqn from 26.4.44; No.110 MU 5.6.44; No.2 Sqn ('DB-H'), tyre burst landing, ran off runway, Cat.A 7.10.44 (Lt P Marshall); Engine trouble, retd to base 15.12.44 (Lt MH Rorke); No.7 Wing SAAF 19.12.44 (engine change); No.4 Sqn, crashed Cat.FA/E 1.5.45 (pilot OK); SOC 30.8.45
EN390	Spitfire F.IXc (Merlin 61 & 63); TOC/RAF 7.2.43; M.E. 8.43 - SAAF (MTO), No.7 Sqn from 19.7.44 (Merlin 63); Hit by AA, force-landed, hit bump at end of landing run, port wheel and oleo broke off, crack in pintle pin, Cat.FB/B 1.9.44 (Lt L Symons); Retd RAF (RiW); MAAF in 6.45; SOC 14.3.46
EN392	Spitfire F.IXc (Merlin 63); TOC/RAF 7.2.43; Italy 1.11.43; SOC 31.8.44 (bboc) - SAAF (MTO), No.357 MU to No.2 Sqn ('DB-Y') 2.3.45; Hit by AA 3m SSE of Argenta, Cat.FB/Ac 19.3.45 (Lt JE Harley); No.7 Wing SAAF for repair 21.3.45; Retd to No.2 Sqn; Hit by AA 13m NE of Ferrara, Cat.FB/Ac 1.4.45 (Capt GLH Tatham); Retd RAF (No.256 Sqn) 29.4.45; SOC 30.4.47
EN399	Spitfire F.IXc (Merlin 63); TOC/RAF 25.2.43; M.E. 7.43 - SAAF (MTO), No.41 Sqn, lost power, landed safely 21.4.44; Retd RAF (census 6.45); SOC 26.8.45
EN402	Spitfire F.IXc (Merlin 63); TOC/RAF 7.3.43; Malta 6.43 - SAAF (MTO), No.7 Sqn ('TJ-F') 8.44; Hit by flak attacking locomotives, pilot failed to bale out, dived into ground in flames near Polesella (E of Copparo), burnt out, Cat.FB/E 24.10.44 (F/O GS Richardson of No.93 Sqn RAF attd No.7 Sqn killed), SOC
EN405	Spitfire F.IXc (Merlin 63); TOC/RAF 18.3.43; Casablanca 25.4.43 - SAAF (MTO), No.3 Sqn ('CA-M'); Retd RAF (MAAF census 6.45); SOC 31.7.47
EN430	Spitfire PR.XI (Merlin 61); TOC/RAF 13.4.43; MAC 5.5.43 - SAAF (MTO), No.40 Sqn from 21.9.45; Retd RAF; SOC 27.3.47
EN446	Spitfire F.IXc (Merlin 61); TOC/RAF 15.1.43; M.E. 30.9.43; N.A. 30.11.43 - SAAF (MTO), No.2 Sqn ('DB-T') c.11.44; No.357 MU 12.11.44 (for repair); Retd No.2 Sqn by 2.45; SOC (RAF) 2.8.45
EN451	Spitfire F.IXc (Merlin 61); TOC/RAF 21.1.43; Gibraltar 9.3.43; M.E - SAAF (MTO), No.1 Sqn, hit by small arms fire Cat.FB/1 1.12.44 (Lt HJ Kritzinger); Retd RAF (RiW); SOC 14.3.46
EN453	Spitfire F.IXc (Merlin 61); TOC/RAF 21.1.43; NWA 30.4.43; USAAF 31.10.43 - SAAF (MTO), No.2 Sqn, tail oleo broke landing Foiano, Cat.B 21.8.44 (Lt JB Miller); Hit by AA, baled out, Cat.FB/E 11.9.44 (Capt HCW Liebenberg), SOC
EN476	Spitfire F.IXc (Merlin 61); TOC/RAF 16.2.43; M.E; USAAF 31.1.44 - SAAF (MTO), No.4 Sqn ('KJ-X'), engine cut when hit by light AA in dive bombing attack, forced landing wheels-up at Mapref, Cat.FB/E1 20.11.44 (Lt CWL Boyd of No.1 Sqn OK), SOC
EN500	Spitfire F.IXc (Merlin 63); TOC/RAF 20.4.43; NAAF 1.11.43 - SAAF (MTO), No.4 Sqn ('KJ-X') from 13.10.44; Armed Recce, hit by AA, Cat.FB/2 20.11.44 (Lt HW Tatham); Retd RAF (MAAF census in 6.45)
EN516	Spitfire F.IXc (Merlin 63); TOC/RAF 6.2.43; NWA 31.5.43 - SAAF (MTO), No.162 MU to No.2 Sqn 11.8.43; Ferrying, engine failed shortly after take-off, belly-landed short of airfield, Scanzana LG, Cat.FA/2 2.10.43 (Capt PD Bryant seriously injured); Retd RAF (RiW); Fate unknown
EN517	Spitfire F.IXc (Merlin 63); TOC/RAF 10.2.43; NWA, ex No.111 Sqn - SAAF, No.2 Sqn ('DB-S') 1943/44 (service unknown); retd RAF, SOC 2.8.45
EN521	Spitfire F.IXc (Merlin 63); TOC/RAF 13.2.43; NWA 30.4.43 - SAAF (MTO), No.1 Sqn, over-ran forming up, fin and rudder hit stbd mainplane of MH949, Cat.Ac 24.11.44 (Capt HT Snyman OK); ROS; Hit by small arms fire, Cat.FB/Ac 28.12.44 (Lt EA Shores); ROS; Hit by AA 3m NW of Lugo, Cat.FB/Ac 20.1.45 (Lt JS de Villiers); Retd RAF; SOC 26.9.45
EN524	Spitfire F.IXc (Merlin 61); Became SAAF No. **55..** (range 5502-5554); TOC/RAF 21.2.43; Flown to ME, arr No.15 AD Fayid 20.9.47 – SAAF, Zwartkop Air Station 1947; Fate unknown
EN528	Spitfire F.IXc (Merlin 63); TOC/RAF 21.2.43; NAASC 31.10.43 - SAAF (MTO), No.7 Sqn from 9.44 (arrived in bad weather); Hit by flak and spun in while dive bombing artillery positions, Cat.FB/E 6.11.44 (Lt PJ du Toit killed), SOC
EN531	Spitfire F.IXc (Merlin 63); TOC/RAF 5.3.43; Malta 1.6.43 - SAAF (MTO), No.3 Sqn ('CA-L'), hit by flak while strafing barges on long range reconnaissance mission, abandoned over enemy territory, crashed in river Po 15m S of Pealeta, Cat.FB/E 25.4.45 (Lt NPG Fischer retd Sqn 27.4.45), SOC
EN583	Spitfire LF.IXc (Merlin 66); TOC/RAF 21.5.43; Casablanca 29.6.43; No.72 Sqn - SAAF (MTO), No.4 Sqn from 2.5.44 (fighter-bomber); Unable to jettison LR tank, it came off in dive and struck fuselage, retd to base, Cat.FB/3 19.5.44 (Capt PB Lee OK); No.3 Sqn until retd RAF 20.9.45; Later to Italy (*MM4038*) 30.5.46
EN673	Spitfire PR.XI (Merlin 63); TOC/RAF 18.7.43; MAC 13.8.43 - SAAF (MTO), No.40 Sqn from 4.9.45; Retd RAF; SOC 27.2.47

EN843　Spitfire F.IXc (Merlin 63); TOC/RAF 10.6.43; M.E. 1.9.43; No.74 Sqn - SAAF (MTO), No.41 Sqn ('C') by 16.4.44; No.4 Sqn 2.5.44; No.9 Sqn by 7.44; Retd RAF; Later to Italy (*MM 4138*) 26.6.47

EN968　Spitfire F.Vb/trop (Merlin 46); TOC/RAF 23.5.42; Malta 8.42; dis. NA 6.43 - SAAF (MTO), No.4 Sqn, hit by flak, retd to base, Cat.FB/2 11.11.43 (Lt HF Marshall unhurt); Retd RAF; SOC 26.4.45

EP187　Spitfire F.Vb/trop (Merlin 46); TOC/RAF in 6.42; Malta 8.42; dis. NA 7.43 - SAAF (MTO), No.4 Sqn 12.43; Retd RAF; SOC 28.4.45

EP192　Spitfire F.Vb/trop (Merlin 46); TOC/RAF 31.5.42; RAFME, ex No.94 Sqn, No.238 Sqn - SAAF, 40 Sqn ('WR-O'); retd RAF; No.225 Sqn, swung on landing and hit ER181 and JL358, burnt out, Palazzo 1.10.43

EP201　Spitfire F.Vb/trop (Merlin 46); TOC/RAF 31.5.42; dis. NA 6.43 - SAAF (MTO), No.10 Sqn by 8.7.44 (inspection); Retd RAF (No.336 Sqn) 16.7.44

EP204　Spitfire F.Vb/trop (Merlin 46); TOC/RAF 20.6.42; M.E. 22.10.42; NAASC 31.10.43; NAAF 1.11.43 - SAAF (MTO), No.1 Sqn ('AX-F':'AX-E') by 11.42 & 1.43; Bf 109G shot down in flames nr Mersa El Brega 27.11.42 (Capt JM Faure); Retd RAF (Census 6.45); Later to France 9.10.47

EP205　Spitfire F.Vb/trop (Merlin 45); TOC/RAF 31.5.42; dis. N.A. 6.43 - SAAF (MTO), No.40 Sqn, failed to return artillery reconnaissance W of Arezzo, Cat.FB/3 12.7.44 (Lt P Naylor killed), SOC

EP303　Spitfire F.Vb/trop (Merlin 46); TOC/RAF 14.6.42; M.E. 28.9.42 - SAAF (MTO), No.1 Sqn ('AX-S'); Shot down El Hamma during attack on large formation of Me 210s and Bf 109s, crashed 35m W of Gabes, Cat.FB/E 25.3.43 (Lt AF Tyrrell killed); SOC 10.4.43
NOTE: Serial reported also as "xx903" for 14.1.43

EP305　Spitfire F.Vb/trop (Merlin 46); TOC/RAF 12.6.42; dis. NA 6.43; M.E. - SAAF (MTO), No.2 Sqn, smoke from engine after take-off for air test, landed straight ahead in marshy ground, overturned, pilot thrown out, aircraft burnt out, Lentini LG, Cat.FA/E3 26.8.43 (Lt JM Sweeney minor facial injuries); SOC 30.9.43

EP537　Spitfire F.Vb/trop (Merlin 46); TOC/RAF 2.7.42; NWA 28.2.43 - SAAF (MTO), No.10 Sqn 25.6.44; Retd RAF; SOC 31.3.45

EP573　Spitfire F.Vb/trop (Merlin 46); TOC/RAF 5.7.42; N.A. 1.44 - SAAF (MTO), No.10 Sqn 26.5.44; Retd RAF (No.336 Sqn) 16.7.44

EP617　Spitfire F.Vb/trop (Merlin 46); TOC/RAF 19.7.42; NWA 28.2.43 - SAAF (MTO), No.40 Sqn (date unknown); Retd RAF (MAAF census 6.45); Later to Italy on loan in 11.44; To Yugoslavia 18.5.45 (crashed 30.8.45)

EP638　Spitfire F.Vb/trop (Merlin 46); TOC/RAF 16.7.42; M.E. 29.9.42 - SAAF (MTO), No.136 MU to No.3 Sqn 24.6.44; Retd RAF; SOC 28.7.46

EP649　Spitfire F.Vb/trop (Merlin 46); TOC/RAF 20.7.42; M.E. 30.10.42 - SAAF (MTO), No.1 Sqn ('AX-B') by 27.11.42; Damaged by Bf 109, Cat.FB/2 13.12.42 (Lt HF Smith); Bf 109 probable 14.1.43 (Lt HF Smith); Retd RAF (MAAF census 6.45); SOC 19.7.45

EP655　Spitfire F.Vb/trop (Merlin 46); TOC/RAF 19.7.42; M.E. 1.11.42 - SAAF (MTO), No.1 Sqn ('AX-U':'AX-E' or 'AX-Q') by 27.11.42; Badly damaged by light AA at Marble Arch 13.12.42 (Lt GG Paterson); Attack on Bf 109 over Tamet, glycol leak, pilot passed out from fumes in cockpit at 13,000ft, force-landed 6m SSE of Sirte, Cat.FB/2 12.1.43 (Lt GG Paterson minor injuries, retd Sqn next day); Salvaged 30.9.43; SOC (RAF) 8.3.44

EP656　Spitfire F.Vb/trop (Merlin 46); TOC/RAF 19.7.42; M.E. 14.10.42; NAASC - SAAF (MTO), No.40 Sqn, tyre burst taxying for take-off on Tac/R, swung, undercarriage collapsed at Foggia No.1, Cat.FB/B 16.11.43 (Lt G Orchard); Retd RAF; SOC 29.8.46

EP666　Spitfire F.Vb/trop (Merlin 46); TOC/RAF 20.7.42; M.E. 5.11.42 - SAAF (MTO), No.1 Sqn ('AX-M') by 27.11.42 - @13.12.42; Retd RAF (MAAF census 6.45); Later to France 9.10.47

EP682　Spitfire F.Vb/trop (Merlin 46); TOC/RAF 23.7.42; M.E. 26.9.42 - SAAF (MTO), No.1 Sqn ('AX-F') by 13.12.42; MC 202 destroyed near Castelverde 21.1.43 (Capt JH Gaynor); Struck a bump and drifted off runway landing in cross-wind, hit Kittyhawk FR359 of No.250 Sqn dispersed clear of runway, overturned Castel Benito, Cat.FA/3 11.2.43 (Lt GB Lipawsky badly injured), SOC

EP688　Spitfire FR Vb/trop (Merlin 46); TOC/RAF 27.7.42; Malta 7.43; Sicily (dis) 1.8.43 - SAAF (MTO), No.40 Sqn ('WR-R'), failed to become airborne, swung to avoid stationary aircraft, undercarriage collapsed, Grottaglie, Cat.B 21.9.43 (Lt JC Aronson); Retd RAF; SOC 26.4.45

EP689　Spitfire F.Vb/trop (Merlin 46); TOC/RAF 21.7.42; M.E. 30.10.42; N.A. 30.11.43 - SAAF (MTO), No.40 Sqn, hit

Spitfire F.Vb/trop EP649 'B' of No. 1 Sqn SAAF taxying on a desert airfield around 1942/43. [via SAAF Museum]

EP690 Spitfire F.Vb/trop (Merlin 46); TOC/RAF 22.7.42; M.E. 30.10.42 - SAAF (MTO), No.1 Sqn ('AX-A') 11.42; 07.30 patrol, Bf 109G damaged nr Mersa el Brega 27.11.42; 15.30 patrol, Bf 109 destroyed 27.11.42 (both Mjr PCR Metelerkamp); Landing in dust cloud at El Hassiet, came down on top of ER245, Cat.B 4.12.42 (Lt DS Rogan unhurt); No.40 Sqn, shot down by (RAF or USAAF) Spitfire 2m E of Syracuse, Cat.FB/E 10.7.43 (Capt CG Le Roux DFC killed), SOC [More likely shot down by a MC 202 of 4°Stormo]

EP692 Spitfire F.Vb/trop (Merlin 46); TOC/RAF 23.7.42; M.E. 23.9.42 - SAAF (MTO), No.1 Sqn ('AX-E') by 11.42; Retd RAF (M.E. census 6.45); SOC 26.9.46

EP694 Spitfire F.Vb/trop (Merlin 46); TOC/RAF 24.7.42; M.E. 11.42 - SAAF (MTO), No.9 Sqn, crashed in river 3m N of Alexandria, Cat.E 25.10.44 (Lt RD Bar), SOC/bboc (M.E. census 6.45); Later to Greece 4.46

EP777 Spitfire F.Vb/trop (Merlin 46); TOC/RAF 24.8.42; M.E. 5.11.42 - SAAF (MTO), No.40 Sqn, short of fuel on ferry flight in bad weather, belly-landed on disused airstrip on island of Zante, Cat.FA/E 10.12.44 (Lt NK McCullum OK); SOC 24.12.44

EP792 Spitfire F.Vb/trop (Merlin 46); TOC/RAF 8.42; M.E. 30.10.42 - SAAF (MTO), No.1 Sqn ('AX-C') by 27.11.42; Retd RAF; No.40 Sqn SAAF by c.11.43 and 12.43; No.11 Sqn, forced landing 35m NE of Alexandria 28.8.44 (Lt JQ de Kema); Retd RAF; SOC 13.9.45

EP793 Spitfire F.Vb/trop (Merlin 46); TOC/RAF 1.8.42; M.E. 30.10.42 - SAAF (MTO), No.1 Sqn ('AX-E'), shot down in engagement with Bf 109G, hit ground, exploded 27m NE of Mersa El Brega, Cat.FB/E 27.11.42 (Capt WR Thomson killed); SOC (RAF) 2.12.42

EP826 Spitfire F.Vb/trop (Merlin 46); TOC/RAF 12.8.42; NAAF - SAAF, No.40 Sqn ('WR-B') 6.43; retd RAF; 73 OTU ('28') in 1945; SOC 29.8.46

EP827 Spitfire F.Vb/trop (Merlin 46); TOC/RAF 9.8.42; M.E. 11.42 - SAAF (MTO), No.1 Sqn ('AX-C') by 21.1.43; Ju 88 destroyed 12m NW of Medenine, shared with ER882/'AX-F' 7.3.43 (Lt SW van der Merwe); MC 202 destroyed Gabes-El Hamma 25.3.43 (Lt S W van der Merwe); Damaged in combat 30m NW of Gabes (hit either by flak or by rear gunner of Me 210), cockpit filled with smoke, forced landing, overturned, crashed in New Zealand lines 27.3.43 (Lt D L Quin seriously injured); Salvaged, retd RAF (NAASC 10.43)

EP876 Spitfire F.Vb/trop (Merlin 46); TOC/RAF 28.8.42; M.E. 28.2.43 - SAAF (MTO), No.40 Sqn, hit by AA, Cat.FB/Ac 18.11.44 (Lt DW Swart); Fate unknown

EP878 Spitfire FR Vb/trop (Merlin 46); TOC/RAF 24.9.42; NWA 10.42 - SAAF (MTO), No.40 Sqn in 11.42; Retd RAF (ME); No.40 Sqn SAAF from 28.2.43; Crashed 15m S of Gabes, Cat.FB/3 22.3.43 (Lt G Lloyd DFC killed), SOC

EP888 Spitfire F.Vb/trop (Merlin 46); TOC/RAF 16.8.42; Gibraltar in 11.42 - SAAF (MTO), No.1 Sqn ('AX-S':'AX-E') by 27.11.42 and 2.43; Fate unknown
NOTE: Reported also as "xx688"

EP891 Spitfire F.IXc (Merlin 63); TOC/RAF 9.6.43; M.E. in 9.43; NAAF 1.11.43 - SAAF (MTO), No.2 Sqn, hit by flak, glycol leak, abandoned 3m NNE of Porto Gruaro, Cat.FB/E 5.3.45 (Lt WR Lawrie evaded capture, retd 4.5.45), SOC
NOTE: Originally built as F.Vb/trop, but crashed on delivery flight, repaired and converted to F IXc in 6.43

EP894 Spitfire F.Vb/trop (Merlin 46); TOC/RAF 10.8.42; M.E. 5.11.42 - SAAF (MTO), No.40 Sqn, stream landing, oil and dust on windscreen, slowed up on runway, hit from behind by ER227 at Luqa, Cat.E 23.6.43 (Capt BAA Wiggett unhurt), SOC

EP896 Spitfire F.Vb/trop (Merlin 46); TOC/RAF 10.8.42; M.E. 5.11.42 - SAAF (MTO), No.1 Sqn ('AX-O'), accident Cat.FB/2 13.12.42; Still No.1 Sqn 10-20.3.43 (reported as "xx693"); Retd RAF (MAAF in 10.44)

EP897 Spitfire F.Vb/trop (Merlin 46); TOC/RAF 14.8.42; via Takoradi to M.E. 5.11.42 - SAAF (MTO), No.1 Sqn ('AX-L'), failed to return engagement with Bf 109G, crashed, burnt out, 10m S of Agedabia, Cat.FB/E 27.11.43 (2/Lt JM Bredenkamp killed); SOC 8.3.44

EP953 Spitfire F.Vb/trop (Merlin 46); TOC/RAF 13.8.42; M.E. 5.11.42 - SAAF (MTO), No.10 Sqn from/by 19.7.44; Retd RAF 27.8.44; Later to Greece 25.4.46

EP960 Spitfire F.Vb/trop (Merlin 46); TOC/RAF 14.8.42; M.E. 11.11.42; N.A. 30.11.43 - SAAF (MTO), No.40 Sqn, port undercarriage leg failed to lower, Cat.2 27.3.44 (Lt Col WA Nel); Re-Cat.E, SOC 31.3.44

EP977 Spitfire F.Vb/trop (Merlin 46); TOC/RAF 18.8.42; Gibraltar 11.42 - SAAF (MTO), No.10 Sqn by 22.6.44; Crashed in upward roll at low altitude, Cat.E 23.6.44 (Capt SW Rabie DFC killed), SOC

EP979 Spitfire F.Vb/trop (Merlin 46); TOC/RAF 21.8.42; Gibraltar 1.11.42 - SAAF (MTO), No.40 Sqn by 6.44; Hit by light AA in dive in Radda area, glycol leak, force-landed in field 1m SW of Rapplano 13.7.44 (Capt PH Donnelly retd Sqn); Retd RAF; SOC 26.4.45

ER116 Spitfire F.Vb/trop (Merlin 46); TOC/RAF 4.9.42; M.E. 9.11.42 - SAAF (MTO), No.1 Sqn ('AX-N'), MC 202 probable 21.1.43 (Lt DS Rogan); Me 210 crashed and burnt out destroyed & Bf 109F damaged 25m SW of Gabes 25.3.43 (Lt MES Robinson); Shot down by Bf 109 at 20,000ft off Cap Bon, Cat.FB/E 16.4.43 (Lt V Mundell PoW), SOC

ER117 Spitfire F.Vb/trop (Merlin 46); TOC/RAF 3.9.42; via Takoradi to M.E. 30.10.42 - SAAF (MTO), No.1 Sqn ('AX-W'), spun in, pilot possibly blacked out, 13m E of bay of Mersa El Brega 27.11.42 (Lt LM Marshall killed); SOC 3.1.43

ER126 Spitfire F.IXb (Merlin 63); TOC/RAF 7.6.43; M.E. - SAAF (MTO), No.2 Sqn, hit by AA, crashed spinning in flames 15m SW of Termoli, Cat.FB/E 3.10.43 (Lt D Driver PoW DoW 3.10.43); SOC 29.2.44

ER143 Spitfire F.Vb/trop (Merlin 46); TOC/RAF 24.8.42; M.E. 17.4.43 - SAAF (MTO), No.11 Sqn, hit boundary fence on turn after take-off Idku, Cat.B 24.8.44 (2/Lt AJ Hoffe OK); Retd RAF (SOC 26.4.45/bboc/M.E. census 21.6.45); SOC 1.46

ER168 Spitfire F.Vb/trop (Merlin 46); TOC/RAF 26.8.42; via Takoradi arr M.E.29.10.42 - SAAF (MTO), No.1 Sqn ('AX-R'), failed to return, glycol tank hit in attack on Ju 88, crashed 16m N of Benghazi, Cat.FB/E 13.12.42 (Mjr PCR Metelerkamp killed), SOC

ER171 Spitfire F.Vb/trop (Merlin 46); TOC/RAF 24.8.42; M.E. 5.11.42 - SAAF (MTO), No.1 Sqn ('AX-V':'AX-D') by 9.11.42; Two Bf 109 damaged nr Mersa el Brega 27.11.42 (Lt JH Gaynor); Bf 109G destroyed NE of Sfax 2.4.43 (Lt MES Robinson); Retd RAF; SOC 26.4.45

ER178 Spitfire F.Vb/trop (Merlin 46); TOC/RAF 28.8.42; M.E. 11.42 - SAAF (MTO), No.1 Sqn ('AX-P'), Bf 109F damaged, then crashed Cat.FB/2 13.12.42 (Lt D S Rogan); R&SU; Retd No.1 Sqn ('AX-P') by 1.43; Retd RAF (Malta) 1.7.43

ER181 Spitfire F.Vb/trop (Merlin 46); TOC/RAF 29.8.42; M.E. 6.1.43 - SAAF (MTO), No.40 Sqn, while parked, run into by EP192 (No.225 Sqn) which swung on take-off Palazzo, Cat.E 1.10.43; SOC 8.3.44
NOTE: Reported No.40 Sqn, hit by AA in Gioia area, force-landed 4.6.44 (Lt P McClure)

ER200 Spitfire F.Vb/trop (Merlin 46); TOC/RAF 28.8.42; Gibraltar in 11.42; M.E. - SAAF (MTO), No.1 Sqn ('AX-B'), Me 210 damaged 30m NW of Gabes 27.3.43 (Lt GW Hillary); Fate unknown
NOTE: Serial prefix not confirmed, perhaps ES200

ER208 Spitfire F.Vb/trop (Merlin 46); TOC/RAF 9.9.42; M.E. 12.42 - SAAF (MTO), No.1 Sqn ('AX-V'), Bf 109G

Spitfire F.Vb/trop ER171 AX-D of No. 1 Sqn SAAF parked at Castel Benito in Libya around February 1943. It carries the name 'Maureen'. Lt J H Gaynor damaged two Bf 109s near Mersa el Brega in this aircraft on 27th November 1942, and on 2nd April 1943 Lt M E S Robinson destroyed a Bf 109G northeast of Sfax. *[via SAAF Museum]*

	damaged nr Zembra island 21.4.43 (Lt A Higgo); One Me 323Me 323 destroyed off Zembra island and another shared with JG945/'AX-Z' 22.4.43 (Lt A Higgo); Retd RAF; No.10 Sqn SAAF, retd RAF (No.94 Sqn) 17.7.44; SOC 23.10.44 NOTE: Reported as "ES208" and also "xx208"
ER214	Spitfire F.Vb/trop (Merlin 46); TOC/RAF 2.9.42; M.E. 5.11.42 - SAAF (MTO), No.1 Sqn ('AX-N') by 27.11.42; No.40 Sqn, engine failed, glycol leak, force-landed on beach 3m W of Sabratha LG, Cat.FA/3 3.8.43 (Lt DL Robinson), SOC
ER222	Spitfire F.Vb/trop (Merlin 46); TOC/RAF 31.8.42; M.E. 10.11.42 - SAAF (MTO), No.40 Sqn, landed from operation, undercarriage would not lower, landed wheels-up Luqa, Cat.FB/A 27.6.43 (Lt ECT Webb unhurt); Retd RAF; SOC 23.8.45
ER226	Spitfire F.Vb/trop (Merlin 46); TOC/RAF 3.9.42; NAASC 31.10.43 - SAAF (MTO), No.41 Sqn, engine failed, force-landed Ramat David 23.8.44 (Lt Basson); Retd RAF (census 6.45)
ER227	Spitfire F.Vb/trop (Merlin 46); TOC/RAF 3.9.42; M.E. 20.12.42 - SAAF (MTO), No.40 Sqn, streamed landing, collided with EP894 which slowed down in front, Luqa, Cat.FB/A 23.6.43 (Lt PH Donnelly unhurt); Retd RAF; SOC 8.3.44
ER229	Spitfire F.Vb/trop (Merlin 46); TOC/RAF 31.8.42; M.E. 11.11.42 - SAAF (MTO), No.1 Sqn ('AX-W') by 1.43; Hit obstruction landing cross-wind on bad surface with an oiled-up windscreen at Castel Benito, Cat.FB/A 10.2.43 (Lt DRH McLoughlin unhurt); No.40 Sqn, force-landed in Sangro River area 8.12.43 (Lt Col WA Nel); Retd RAF; SOC 29.12.44
ER245	Spitfire F.Vb/trop (Merlin 46); TOC/RAF 2.9.42; M.E. 1.11.42 - SAAF (MTO), No.1 Sqn ('AX-D') by 11.42; Became stuck in sand after landing El Hassiet, landed on by EP690, Cat.B 4.12.42 (2/Lt DT Gilson unhurt); SOC 8.3.44
ER246	Spitfire F.Vb/trop (Merlin 46); TOC/RAF 31.8.42; N.A. 30.11.43 - SAAF (MTO), No.10 Sqn 25.6.44 (off strength); Engine change 12.7.44; Retd No.10 Sqn 17.7.44; No.10 Sqn dett Mersa Matruh 27.8.44; SOC 15.3.45
ER247	Spitfire F.Vb/trop (Merlin 46); TOC/RAF 3.9.42; M.E.; NWA 28.2.43 - SAAF (MTO), No.1 Sqn, crashed Cat. FA/3 4.3.43, SOC
ER274	Spitfire F.Vb/trop (Merlin 46); TOC/RAF 9.9.42; M.E. 9.2.43 - SAAF (MTO), No.40 Sqn, landing in strong cross-wind, swung off runway, struck bad ground, overturned Castelverde, Cat.B 3.3.43 (Lt Col CMS Gardner slightly injured); SOC 1.11.43
ER278	Spitfire F.Vb/trop (Merlin 46); TOC/RAF 9.9.42; M.E. 12.11.42 - SAAF (MTO), No.1 Sqn ('AX-Y'), damaged by Bf 109, Cat.FB/2 13.12.42 (Capt JH Slater); No.40 Sqn by 7.43; Retd RAF
ER280	Spitfire F.Vc/trop (Merlin 46); TOC/RAF 10.9.42; M.E. 5.11.42 - SAAF (MTO), No.1 Sqn, crashed 25m S of Gabes, possible flak damage, Cat.FB/E 25.3.43 (Lt DRH McLoughlin seriously injured), SOC
ER299	Spitfire F.Vb/trop (Merlin 46); TOC/RAF 18.9.42; Gibraltar in 11.42; M.E - SAAF (MTO), No.103 MU to No.10 Sqn by 28.9.44; Retd RAF (No.94 Sqn); Cat.E 25.12.44, SOC
ER301	Spitfire F.Vb/trop (Merlin 46); TOC/RAF 22.9.42; M.E. 16.12.42 - SAAF (MTO), No.10 Sqn 25.6.44 to at least 9.44; Retd RAF (Census 6.45); SOC 26.9.46
ER303	Spitfire F.Vb/trop (Merlin 46); TOC/RAF 23.9.42; M.E. 31.1.43 - SAAF (MTO), No.40 Sqn, hit by AA over Gasta Point, baled out, aircraft crashed in sea, Cat.FB/E 19.3.44 (Capt RH van der Poel rescued slightly injured), SOC
ER305	Spitfire F.Vb/trop (Merlin 46); TOC/RAF 24.9.42; M.E. 1.43 - SAAF (MTO), No.7 Sqn, in use at Daba by 16.1.44; To No.58 R&SU, engine change 18.1.44; To RAF charge (No.58 R&SU) 1.2.44; SOC 3.3.44
ER313	Spitfire F.Vb/trop (Merlin 46); TOC/RAF 3.9.42; M.E. 16.12.42 - SAAF (MTO), No.40 Sqn, shot down by Re 2005 (Ten Giulio Torresi of 362^a Squadriglia) over Catania, Sicily, Cat.FB/E 12.7.43 (Lt K Robinson killed); SOC 8.3.44
ER318	Spitfire F.Vb/trop (Merlin 46); TOC/RAF 10.9.42; N.A. (dis) 1.7.43 - SAAF (MTO), No.1 Sqn ('AX-A'), MC 202 destroyed 21.1.43 (S/Ldr P Olver DFC); MC 202 dest, shared with ER666/'AX-O', and Bf 109F damaged 17.4.43 (S/Ldr P Olver DFC); Retd RAF; No.10 Sqn SAAF from 16.6.44; Landed undercarriage retracted Savoia 5.9.44 (Lt JG Segalla); Unserviceable 5-26.9.44; Retd RAF (Census 6.45)
ER319	Spitfire F.Vb/trop (Merlin 46); TOC/RAF 10.9.42; M.E. 23.12.42 - SAAF (MTO), No.1 Sqn, while landing Castel Benito, hit lorry track with ridge of hard mud,

undercarriage collapsed, Cat.B 23.2.43 (Lt BW Haynes unhurt); Retd RAF (R&SU); No.1 Sqn ('AX-V') by 20-29.3.43; FW 190 probably destroyed 28m SW of Medenine 20.3.43 (Lt WD Wikner); Bf 109F dest, shared with 'AX-O' (xx607 ?) & Bf 109F damaged 20m NW of Gabes 29.3.43 (Capt JH Gaynor); Retd RAF; To France (GR 2/33) on loan; Later to Turkey 28.9.44
NOTE: Also reported as "xx193"

ER321 Spitfire F Vb/trop (Merlin 46); TOC/RAF 13.9.42; Gibraltar 6.11.42; NWA 28.2.43 - SAAF (MTO), No.1 Sqn ('AX-E'), Ju 87 damaged 10m NW of Medenin 6.3.43 (Lt DL Quin); Fate unknown (PSO 1.1.47)

ER323 Spitfire F.Vb/trop (Merlin 46); TOC/RAF 17.9.42; M.E. 10.2.43 - SAAF (MTO), No.40 Sqn (date unknown); SOC 8.3.44; but bboc (ME census 6.45)

ER335 Spitfire F.Vb/trop (Merlin 46); TOC/RAF 13.9.42; M.E. 13.1.43 - SAAF (MTO), No.7 Sqn, failed to return scramble 55m off Port Said, Cat.FB/E 4.9.43 (Lt HFP Boyer killed), SOC

ER342 Spitfire F.Vb/trop (Merlin 46); TOC/RAF 8.9.42; M.E. 5.11.42; Sicily 8.43 - SAAF (MTO), No.40 Sqn by 7.43; Hit by flak, crashed in sea in Margherita area, Cat.FB/E 20.9.43 (Lt RW Passmore killed); SOC 29.2.44

ER344 Spitfire F.Vb/trop (Merlin 46); TOC/RAF 9.9.42; M.E. 4.11.42 - SAAF (MTO), No.1 Sqn ('AX-K'), failed to return combat with Bf 109s near Marble Arch, Cat.FB/E 13.12.42 (2/Lt RR Scott killed), SOC

ER386 Spitfire F.Vc/trop (Merlin 46); TOC/RAF 2.2.43; M.E. - SAAF (MTO), No.40 Sqn, glycol leak, force-landed on beach nr Giarre, Sicily, Cat.E 25.8.43 (Lt JC Kruger slightly injured)

ER465 Spitfire F.Vb/trop (Merlin 46); TOC/RAF 10.9.42; NAAF 1.11.43 - SAAF (MTO), No.40 Sqn, shot down by flak over Mainella Mountains, near Sulmona, Cat.FB/3 8.2.44 (Capt AC Warner PoW), SOC

ER468 Spitfire F.Vb/trop (Merlin 46); TOC/RAF 11.9.42; M.E. 17.11.42 - SAAF (MTO), No.1 Sqn ('AX-L'), Bf 109G probable 12.1.43 (Lt DS Rogan); Taxied into an obstruction at Castel Benito, Cat.A 26.2.43 (Lt SW van der Merwe unhurt); Retd RAF; SOC 19.8.46

ER473 Spitfire F.Vb/trop (Merlin 46); TOC/RAF 11.9.42; M.E. 9.11.42 - SAAF (MTO), No.1 Sqn ('AX-M') by 6-20.3.43; MC 202 probable W of Medenine 7.3.43 (Lt DM Brebner); No.7 Sqn; No.1 Sqn ('AX-M') 3.5.44; No.10 Sqn by 19.7.44 (retd from Matruh dett); Back to Matruh dett 28.8.44; No.103 MU at Aboukir for mods 30.8.44; Retd No.10 Sqn by 14.9.44; Retd RAF (No.94 Sqn); Crashed Cat.E 13.9.45
NOTE: For Nos.1 & 7 Sqns reported only as "xx473", serial prefix not confirmed

ER476 Spitfire F.Vb/trop (Merlin 46); TOC/RAF 16.9.42; M.E. 31.12.42 - SAAF (MTO), No.1 Sqn ('AX-W') by 10.3.43 - 26.4.43; FW 190 probably destroyed 28m SW of Medenine 20.3.43 (Lt B Rose-Christie) [serial prefix xx476/'AX-W' unconfirmed]; No.9 Sqn by 6.44; Engine change 11.8.44; Still No.9 Sqn 30.1.45; Retd RAF; Later to Turkey 26.4.45

ER481 Spitfire F.Vb/trop (Merlin 46); TOC/RAF 11.9.42; M.E. 12.11.42 - SAAF (MTO), No.7 Sqn ('TJ-C') by 16.1.44; Retd RAF (No.55 R&SU) 21.2.44; Later to Turkey 22.2.45

ER482 Spitfire F.Vb/trop (Merlin 46); TOC/RAF 12.9.42; M.E. 6.12.42 - SAAF (MTO), No.40 Sqn, ran out of fuel and force-landed in field, overshot into bank, overturned nr Taormina, Sicily, Cat.E 24.8.43 (Lt NP Prinsloo slightly injured), SOC

ER487 Spitfire F.Vb/trop (Merlin 46); TOC/RAF 16.9.42; M.E. 1.12.42 - SAAF (MTO), No.10 Sqn by 6.44; Taxying accident, propeller damaged Idku 29.6.44 (Lt RG Whitehorn); Propeller u/s 4.7.44; Belly-landed Cat.2 30.7.44 (2/Lt JG Doveton-Helps); Retd RAF (No.103 MU) 1.8.44; Later No.74 OTU, crashed 7.4.45

ER493 Spitfire F.Vb/trop (Merlin 46); TOC/RAF 13.9.42; M.E. 31.12.42 - SAAF (MTO), No.11 Sqn, became lost, looked at map and hit pole low flying, crashed in field Ahmadia, Egypt, Cat.E 4.8.44 (2/Lt BJ Kirby injured), SOC

ER508 Spitfire F.Vb/trop (Merlin 46); TOC/RAF 17.9.42; Gibraltar 1.11.42 - SAAF (MTO), No.40 Sqn, ran short of fuel on ferry flight in bad weather, belly-landed on disused airstrip on Zante Island, Cat.B 10.12.44 (Capt HH Davidson OK); SOC
NOTE: Reported also with No.81 Sqn, Cat.FB/3 (EAC) 1.1.43

ER510 Spitfire F.Vb/trop (Merlin 46); TOC/RAF 17.9.42; NWA; USAAF 31.7.43 - SAAF (MTO), No.1 Sqn ('AX-G'), Bf 109G destroyed on ground, shared 27.5.44 (Lt TE Wallace); Fate unknown

ER525 Spitfire F.Vb/trop (Merlin 46); TOC/RAF 21.9.42; NWA 28.2.43 - SAAF (MTO), No.1 Sqn ('AX-X') by 27.3.43; Overshot, opened up, engine cut at 150ft, crash-landed 1m S of Ben Gardane, Cat.A 20.5.43 (Lt DT Gilson); Retd RAF; No.10 Sqn SAAF by 15.6.44; Belly-landed, Cat.A 21.6.44 (Capt CJ Laubscher injured); Retd RAF (No.94 Sqn) 28.8.44; SOC 22.8.46

ER546 Spitfire F.Vb/trop (Merlin 46); TOC/RAF 10.42; M.E. 23.12.42; N.A. 30.11.43 - SAAF (MTO), No.40 Sqn, swung on take-off, ran off runway, tipped up, Cat.2 16.3.44 (Capt PC Campbell); Retd RAF (RiW); SOC 31.8.44

ER549 Spitfire F.Vb/trop (Merlin 46); TOC/RAF 21.9.42; NAAF - SAAF, No.1 Sqn ('WR-L'); retd RAF; No.145 Sqn, No.244 Wing Training Flight; No.249 Sqn; SOC 25.4.45

ER565 Spitfire F.Vb/trop (Merlin 46); TOC/RAF 27.9.42; via Basrah (16.1.43) to NWA - SAAF (MTO), No.40 Sqn, crashed on landing during delivery flight, premature take-off at Marble Arch on bad surface under repair, undercarriage damaged on bouncing back on airfield, Cat.FA/B 10.3.43 (Lt E Hodgson unhurt); Retd RAF (RiW); Later to USAAF 31.1.44

ER566 Spitfire F.Vb/trop (Merlin 46); TOC/RAF 25.9.42; M.E. 28.1.43 - SAAF (MTO), No.40 Sqn, leader swerved on take-off, lost height, belly-landed trying to avoid parked aircraft at Bu Grara, Cat.FB/B 29.3.43 (Capt CP Geere unhurt); Retd RAF (RiW); M.E. census 6.45

ER583 Spitfire F.Vb/trop (Merlin 46); TOC/RAF 30.9.42; M.E. 18.1.43 - SAAF (MTO), No.1 Sqn ('AX-E') by 21-27.4.43; Bf 109G damaged nr Zembra island 21.4.43 (Lt DM Brebner); Damaged Bf 109G while returning from escorting an ASR Walrus 25.4.43 (Lt DM Brebner); Retd RAF (Cat.FA/E 18.7.44)

ER584 Spitfire F.Vb/trop (Merlin 46); TOC/RAF 8.10.42; M.E. 28.1.43 - SAAF (MTO), No.40 Sqn, tyre burst on take-off, went on nose at El Adem, Cat.B 3.3.43 (Lt AF Whilby unhurt); No.40 Sqn by 7.43; Retd RAF; SOC 30.9.43

ER587 Spitfire F.Vb/trop (Merlin 46); TOC/RAF 9.10.42; M.E. 18.1.43 - SAAF (MTO), No.40 Sqn, flap stuck landing from ferry flight, overshot, went on nose at Neffatia, Cat.FA/B 7.3.43 (Lt JHP Miles seriously injured); Retd RAF; SOC 30.5.46

ER588 Spitfire F.Vb/trop (Merlin 46); TOC/RAF 30.9.42; NWA 28.2.43 - SAAF (MTO), No.40 Sqn failed to return tactical reconnaissance, dived inverted into ground at Avezzano, 2m NE of Cerchio, Cat.FB/E 1.2.44 (Lt JR Harmer missing, but returned later), SOC

ER604 Spitfire F.Vb/trop (Merlin 46); TOC/RAF 1.10.42; M.E. 20.12.42 - SAAF (MTO), No.40 Sqn, overshot landing from tactical reconnaissance, hit parked Bombay L5827 of No.216 Sqn, Francavilla di Sicilia, Cat.2 9.8.43 (2/Lt JP du Plessis); Accident Cat.FA/2 3.11.43; Retd RAF (RiW); SOC 8.3.44

ER622 Spitfire LF.Vb/trop (Merlin 50M); TOC/RAF 30.9.42; NWA 30.4.43; SOC (bboc); NAASC 31.10.43; Conv to LF.Vb - SAAF (MTO) No.40 Sqn ('WR-D') 12.43; Hit by AA S of Villemarna, Cat.FB/2 5.1.44 (Capt AC Warner); Retd RAF; Later to Turkey 22.2.45

ER639 Spitfire F.Vb/trop (Merlin 46); TOC/RAF 3.10.42; NWA 28.2.43 - SAAF (MTO), via Perugia to No.3 Sqn 24.8.44; Retd RAF; SOC 26.2.45

ER648 Spitfire F.Vb/trop (Merlin 46); TOC/RAF 7.10.42; M.E. 9.3.43; NAASC 31.10.43; NAAF 1.11.43 - SAAF (MTO), No.40 Sqn, brakes failed landing, undercarriage collapsed on turning, Cat.2 24.5.44 (Lt WE Bayford); Retd RAF (RiW); SOC 26.4.45

ER666 Spitfire F.Vc/trop (Merlin 46); TOC/RAF 17.11.42; M.E. 8.3.43 - SAAF (MTO), No.1 Sqn ('AX-O'), MC 202 destroyed, shared with ER318, and Bf 109F damaged 17.4.43 (Lt DT Gilson); Bf 109G probable in Cap Bone area and also damaged another which was then shot down by a USAAF P-40 21.4.43 (Lt ME Robinson); Bf 109G damaged in attack on Soliman LGs 26.4.43 (Lt JLRH Brent); No.4 Sqn 2.4.44; Retd RAF (No.117 MU) 25.4.44; Later to Turkey in 2.45

ER703 Spitfire F.Vb/trop (Merlin 46); TOC/RAF 18.10.42; M.E. 17.1.43 - SAAF (MTO), No.7 Sqn until retd RAF (No.103 MU) 29.12.43; SOC 26.4.45

ER706 Spitfire F.Vb/trop (Merlin 46); TOC/RAF 18.10.42; M.E. 28.1.43 - SAAF (MTO), No.40 Sqn, on wrong course returning from ops, out of fuel, baled out, aircraft ditched 8m N of Malta, Cat.FB/E 10.7.43 (Lt ECT Webb picked up unhurt from dinghy by British destroyer), SOC

ER742 Spitfire F.Vb/trop (Merlin 46); TOC/RAF 12.10.42; Gibraltar 9.11.42 - SAAF (MTO), No.4 Sqn, hit by AA nr San Benedetto, retd to base, Cat.FB/2 26.12.43 (Lt RW Rowan OK); Retd RAF (later No.243 Sqn, Cat.FB/E 15.7.44, SOC)

ER744 Spitfire F.Vb/trop (Merlin 46); TOC/RAF 11.10.42; NWA 28.3.43 - SAAF (MTO), No.132 MU to No.3 Sqn 12.5.44; No.11 Sqn, oil leak, high coolant temperature, overshot, went off runway, overturned at Idku, Cat.B 5.8.44 (2/Lt JF Steinhobel OK); Retd RAF; SOC 17.3.46

ER788 Spitfire F.Vb/trop (Merlin 46); TOC/RAF 12.10.42; NWA 28.2.43 - SAAF (MTO), No.40 Sqn; Later No.225 Sqn RAF and No.40 Sqn SAAF; Retd RAF; SOC 26.4.45

ER808 Spitfire F.Vb/trop (Merlin 46); TOC/RAF 15.10.42; NWA 28.2.43 - SAAF (MTO), No.3 Sqn for training from 3.9.44; Fate unknown
NOTE: Reported shot down with No.229 Sqn RAF 19.7.43, but that was LZ808 !

ER812 Spitfire F.Vb/trop (Merlin 46); TOC/RAF 18.10.42; NWA 28.2.43, NAASC 31.10.43 - SAAF (MTO), No.40 Sqn, hit by AA over Miglianico area, Cat.FB/2 13.3.44 (Lt PAJ K'Anval-Aimee); Retd RAF; SOC 26.4.45

ER819 Spitfire F.Vb/trop (Merlin 46); TOC/RAF 18.10.42; NWA 28.2.43 - SAAF (MTO), No.9 Sqn ('T'), tyre burst taxying Abu Sueir 8.12.44 (Lt RO Petit); Retd RAF (M.E. census 6.45); SOC 13.9.45

ER828 Spitfire F.Vb/trop (Merlin 46); TOC/RAF 24.10.42; M.E. 8.3.43 - SAAF (MTO), No.132 MU to No.1 Sqn ('AX-B') 3.43; Squadron scrambled at same time as No.601 Sqn came in to land short of fuel, dust on runway, landed on by EE796 of No.601 Sqn, Goubrine, Cat.FB/E 29.4.43 (Lt JLRH Brent); Retd RAF; SOC 8.3.44

ER829 Spitfire F.Vb/trop (Merlin 46); TOC/RAF 20.11.42; NWA 28.2.43 - SAAF (MTO), No.40 Sqn, forced landing 4.5.44; Hit by AA in Frosinone area, crashed Cat.FB/E 29.5.44 (Capt EIH Sturgeon, PoW injured, escaped from hospital, retd Sqn 30.6.44), SOC

ER867 Spitfire F.Vb/trop (Merlin 46); TOC/RAF 26.10.42; M.E. 13.3.43 - SAAF (MTO), No.7 Sqn (date unknown); Retd RAF 9.9.43 (No.58 R&SU for engine change, then to No.103 MU 24.9.43)

ER872 Spitfire F.Vc/trop (Merlin 46); TOC/RAF 31.10.42; M.E. 9.3.43; NAAF 1.44 - SAAF (MTO), No.40 Sqn, attacked by three Bf 109, force-landed on coast in Anzio area N of Gaeta, Cat.FB/E 26.3.44 (Lt EA Brande PoW), SOC

ER874 Spitfire F.Vb/trop (Merlin 46); TOC/RAF 25.10.42; M.E. 5.3.43 - SAAF (MTO), No.1 Sqn ('AX-N'), engine cut on take-off for sweep, belly-landed 11m E of Goubrine, Cat.FB/B 17.4.43 (Lt SW van der Merwe); Retd RAF (NAAF 1.11.43)

ER882 Spitfire F.Vb/trop (Merlin 46); TOC/RAF 25.10.42; M.E. 9.3.43 - SAAF (MTO), No.132 MU to No.1 Sqn ('AX-F') by 6.3.43 & 17.4.43; Ju 88 destroyed 12m NW of Medenine, shared with EP827 ('AX-C') 7.3.43 (Lt J

Spitfire F.Vb/trops of No. 1 Sqn SAAF, ER882 AX-F nearest, being refuelled in North Africa. [IWM via Ken Smy]

Spitfire F.Vb/trop ES127 KJ-I of No. 4 Sqn is seen fitted out as an unofficial two-seat field conversion by No. 118 MU at Catania, Sicily, where this photograph was taken in the shadow of Mount Etna, which can just be seen in the distance. It has been suggested that the modification was made in order to carry a very small batman, though it would have been a tight fit, and he would certainly have been able to keep his feet warm sitting so close to the engine!

[via Ron Backhouse]

R Lanham); FW 190 destroyed 28m SW of Medenine 20.3.43 (Lt JR Lanham); Pilot baled out at 3,000ft NW of the Kerkenna Islands, 35m SE of Sfax, Cat.FB/E 22.5.43 (Capt J R Lanham killed, body never found), SOC

NOTE: Reported also as "xx188"

ER887   Spitfire F.Vc/trop (Merlin 46); TOC/RAF 18.11.42; M.E. 11.3.43 - SAAF (MTO), No.1 Sqn ('AX-K') by 22.4.43 - @5.43; Retd RAF (No.113 MU) Castel Benito, hit hump landing, tipped on nose on arrival, Cat.Ac 2.6.43 (Lt G T van der Veen); ROS; No.10 Sqn SAAF by 7.44; Compressor unserviceable 5.7.44; Camshaft u/s 13.7.44; Retd RAF (No.336 Sqn) 16.7.44; SOC 31.5.45

ER891   Spitfire F.Vb/trop (Merlin 46); TOC/RAF 6.11.42; M.E. 9.2.43; NAAF 1.11.43 - SAAF (MTO), No.1 Sqn, stbd tyre burst taxying, tipped on nose Azizia, Cat.A 26.6.43 (Lt D S Hastie); No.40 Sqn, hit truck on take-off for operations, Foggia No.1, Cat.E 4.12.43 (Lt W R Sobey); SOC (RAF) 31.8.44

ER893   Spitfire F.Vb/trop (Merlin 46); TOC/RAF 7.11.42; NWA 28.2.43; M.E. 1.9.43 - SAAF (MTO), No.4 Sqn, overshot landing from sweep, swung, collided with JG713 then both hit parked No.2 Sqn aircraft LZ930, EF639 & ES141 at Palata, Cat.FB/2 24.10.43 (Lt J G Strydom); Retd RAF (RiW); Later to Italy 27.6.46

ER941   Spitfire F.Vb/trop (Merlin 46); TOC/RAF 8.11.42; M.E. 25.2.43 - SAAF (MTO), No.132 MU to No.1 Sqn ('AX-B':'AX-U' or 'AX-E') by 3.43; MC 202 destroyed Gabes-El Hamma 25.3.43 (Lt D M Brebner); Me 210 damaged 30m NW of Gabes 27.3.43 (Lt B Rose-Christie); Bf 109F damaged 6.4.43 (Lt D M Brebner); Still No.1 Sqn 22.4.43; Retd RAF (NAAF 11.43); Later to USAAF 31.1.44

ER983   Spitfire F.Vb/trop (Merlin 46); TOC/RAF 13.11.42; M.E. 28.2.43 - SAAF (MTO), No.1 Sqn ('AX-Y') by 25.3.43 - @22.4.43; Retd RAF (bboc, NAAF 1.11.43); SOC 29.2.44

ER987   Spitfire F.Vb/trop (Merlin 46); TOC/RAF 15.11.42; M.E. 28.2.43 - SAAF (MTO), No.40 Sqn, tactical reconnaissance, glare from salt lake, deceived as to actual height, flew into ground, Cat.FA/3 15.4.43 (Lt R T Nicholson injured), SOC

ES107   Spitfire F.IXc (Merlin 61); TOC/RAF 10.2.43; N.A. 30.11.43 - SAAF (MTO), No.1 Sqn ('AX-D'), FW 190 destroyed 27.5.44 (Capt DR Judd); Taxying collision with JG739, Cat.2 24.6.44 (Lt SC Langton); No.4 Sqn ('KJ-E') from 2.9.44; Hit by AA, retd to base, Cat.FB/1 2.9.44 (Capt R D B Morton); Retd RAF (R&SU) 3.9.44; SOC 13.9.45

ES120   Spitfire F.Vc/trop (Merlin 46); TOC/RAF 8.11.42; M.E. 25.2.43 - SAAF (MTO), No.2 Sqn ('DB-B':'DB-L') by 18.10.43; Accident Cat.2 29.11.43; RiW & engine change (No.59 R&SU); Accident, retd RAF (No.110 MU) in 2.44; SOC 18.8.44

ES127   Spitfire F.Vb/trop (Merlin 46); TOC/RAF 10.11.42; N.A. 30.11.43 - SAAF (MTO), No.4 Sqn ('KJ-I'), coolant leak 4.9.43; Retd RAF, became unofficial two-seat field conversion by No.118 MU, still marked 'KJ-I'; SOC 8.3.44; bboc (census 6.45); Later used as ground instructional airframe from 10.47

ES129   Spitfire F.Vc/trop (Merlin 46); TOC/RAF 17. 11.42; NWA 28.2.43 - SAAF (MTO), No.2 Sqn ('DB-F'), damaged Cat.2 10.12.43; Retd RAF (No.114 MU); Later to France 14.2.46

ES133   Spitfire F.Vb/trop (Merlin 46); TOC/RAF 13.11.42; M.E. 20.2.43 - SAAF (MTO), No.7 Sqn, to No.58 R&SU 9.9.43 (engine change, then to No.103 MU 24.9.43); Retd SAAF, at No.10 Sqn by 15.7.44; Retd RAF (No.94 Sqn) 28.8.44

ES141   Spitfire F.Vc/trop (Merlin 46); TOC/RAF 15.11.42; M.E. 31.3.43 - SAAF (MTO), No.1 Sqn ('AX-T') by 28.4.43; No.2 Sqn ('DB-E') by 18.10.43; Hit by ER893 of No.4 Sqn while parked at Palata, Cat.E 24.10.43; SOC 29.2.44

NOTE: Serial (prefix) for No.1 Sqn not confirmed

ES144   Spitfire F.Vb/trop (Merlin 46); TOC/RAF 16.11.42; M.E. 22.2.43 - SAAF (MTO), No.40 Sqn, undercarriage failed to lower properly, force-landed on beach nr San Salvo LG, Cat.FB/2 29.1.44 (Lt M A Parker unhurt); Retd RAF; Later to Greece 25.4.46

ES150   Spitfire F.Vc/trop (Merlin 46); TOC/RAF 20.11.42; M.E. 21.2.43 - SAAF (MTO), No.1 Sqn ('AX-S':'AX-L') by 3.43; Me 210 damaged 30m NW of Gabes 27.3.43 (Capt S de K Viljoen); Re 2001 damaged while escorting Kittyhawks on anti-shipping patrol 8.5.43 (Lt

	D S Rogan DSO); FW 190 shot down into sea, shared JK393, nr Augusta (Oblt Fritz Holzapfel of 13/SKG10 baled out but killed) 19.7.43 (Lt SW van der Merwe); Retd RAF (crashed 17.1.45); SOC 22.2.45
ES154	Spitfire F.Vc/trop (Merlin 46); TOC/RAF 13.11.42; M.E. 31.1.43 - SAAF (MTO), No.1 Sqn ('AX-G') by 21-26.4.43; Retd RAF (lost 20.8.44); SOC 31.8.44
ES172	Spitfire F.Vb/trop (Merlin 46); TOC/RAF 10.11.42; M.E. 31.3.43 - SAAF (MTO), No.40 Sqn by 7.43; Retd RAF; SOC 26.4.45
ES178	Spitfire F.Vc/trop (Merlin 46); TOC/RAF 10.1.43; Casablanca 17.5.43; M.E. - SAAF (MTO), No.40 Sqn, badly shot up when attacked by six FW 190, landed safely, Cat.FB/2 29.4.44 (Lt ECT Webb unhurt); Retd RAF; SOC 28.4.45
ES185	Spitfire F.IXc (Merlin 63); TOC/RAF 9.6.43; M.E. 1.9.43 - SAAF (MTO), No.2 Sqn ('DB-Z') by 18.10.43; No.1 Sqn ('AX-P') by 11.43; Bf 109G probable 3.11.43 (Lt SA Finney); Hit by JK884 on ground, Palata, Cat.3 4.11.43 (Lt GT van der Veen); SOC 29.2.44
ES191	Spitfire F.Vb/trop (Merlin 46); TOC/RAF 4.12.42; NWA 28.2.43 - SAAF (MTO), No.10 Sqn 15.6.44; Retd RAF 27.8.44; SOC 30.11.44
ES200	Spitfire F.Vc/trop (Merlin 46); TOC/RAF 17.11.42; M.E. 16.2.43 - SAAF (MTO), No.1 Sqn ('AX-C': 'AX-U') by 17.4. & 21.4.43; Long-range fuel test, stalled landing at dusk, belly-landed Hergla South, Cat.FA/B 14.5.43 (Capt WM Langerman); Retd RAF; SOC 26.3.45 NOTE: Serial prefix for 4.43 doubtful, perhaps ER200; Reported as 'AX-U', but also as 'AX-C'
ES202	Spitfire F.Vc/trop (Merlin 46); TOC/RAF 15.11.42; Casablanca 29.9.43 - SAAF (MTO), No.1 Sqn 10.43; No.2 Sqn ('DB-A'), hit by AA nr Pescara, crashed 50yds offshore, 5m NNW of Pescara, Cat.FB/E 13.12.43 (Lt BH Stewart PoW), SOC
ES209	Spitfire F.Vb/trop (Merlin 46); TOC/RAF 20.11.42; M.E. 18.2.43 - SAAF (MTO), No.132 MU to No.1 Sqn 3.43; Retd RAF (census 6.45)
ES211	Spitfire F.Vc/trop (Merlin 46); TOC/RAF 16.11.42; M.E. 26.2.43 - SAAF (MTO), No.132 MU to No.1 Sqn ('AX-Z') by 20.3.43; Bf 109F destroyed Gabes-El Hamma 25.3.43 (Lt GH O'Farrell); Engine failed, glycol loss on ops, force landing, crashed NE of Sfax, Cat.B 15.4.43 (Lt DR Davies OK); Retd RAF (Cat.E 13.9.45)
ES227	Spitfire F.Vb/trop (Merlin 46); TOC/RAF 16.11.42; NWA 28.2.43 - SAAF (MTO), No.2 Sqn, retd RAF (No.59 R&SU) 31.1.44; SOC 13.9.45
ES231	Spitfire F.Vc/trop (Merlin 46); TOC/RAF 20.11.42; M.E. 9.3.43; ex No.80 Sqn - SAAF (MTO), No.4 Sqn ('KJ-V') from 3.4.44; Destroyed Ju 88 crashed into hillside, shared with JL169 6.4.44 (Lt DM Scott); Retd RAF (No.114 MU) 18.4.44
ES242	Spitfire F.Vc/trop (Merlin 46); TOC/RAF 28.11.42; M.E. 10.5.43; NAAF 11.43 - SAAF (MTO), No.2 Sqn, damaged Cat.2 29.11.43; Fate unknown
ES244	Spitfire F Vb/trop (Merlin 46); TOC/RAF 29.11.42; Gibraltar 18.1.43; NWA - SAAF (MTO), No.40 Sqn, damaged by Re 2001, Cat.FB/2 12.7.43 (Lt BV Clarence OK); Retd RAF (RiW); Later to USAAF 31.7.43; SOC (RAF) 14.3.46
ES254	Spitfire F.Vc/trop (Merlin 46); TOC/RAF 28.11.42; Gibraltar 13.1.43 - SAAF (MTO), No.9 Sqn, hit wall on take-off El Gamil for scramble, crashed in lake, Cat.FB/E1 11.9.44 (Lt LW Gillman injured), SOC
ES281	Spitfire F.Vc/trop (Merlin 46); TOC/RAF 9.12.42; NWAAF 31.3.43; NAAF 1.11.43 - SAAF (MTO), No.4 Sqn until retd RAF (No.59 R&SU) 30.3.44; Later crashed Cat.FA/E 24.8.44, SOC (DBR)
ES289	Spitfire F.Vc/trop (Merlin 46); TOC/RAF 4.12.42; N.A. 30.11.43 - SAAF (MTO), No.2 Sqn ('DB-A') in 12.43; Damaged by debris from target, glycol failure, baled out 10m SW of Aquila, Cat.FB/E 22.1.44 (Lt BJG Keyter PoW), SOC
ES292	Spitfire F.Vc/trop (Merlin 46); TOC/RAF 10.12.42; M.E. (dis) 10.43 - SAAF (MTO), No.4 Sqn ('KJ-M'), hit by 88mm flak, abandoned near Pescara Valley, Cat.FB/E 23.1.44 (Mjr WJ Wheeler killed), SOC
ES308	Spitfire F.Vc/trop (Merlin 46); TOC/RAF 20.12.42; NAASC 1.11.43 - SAAF (MTO), No.132 MU to No.7 Sqn 15.2.44; No.3 Sqn 5.3.44; No.10 Sqn 17.7.44; Retd RAF (No.94 Sqn) 28.8.44
ES335	Spitfire F.Vc/trop (Merlin 46); TOC/RAF 9.12.42; M.E. 21.4.43 - SAAF (MTO), No.9 Sqn by 6.44; Damaged on ferry flight, undercarriage failed to lock down, Cat.FA/Ac 10.7.44 (Lt KEF George); Retd RAF (RiW); SOC 30.6.45
ES342	Spitfire F.Vc/trop (Merlin 46); TOC/RAF 9.12.42; NWA 10.43 - SAAF (MTO), No.4 Sqn (fighter-bomber) until 15.3.44; Repair; No.4 Sqn; Retd RAF (No.117 MU) 25.4.44
ES343	Spitfire F.Vc/trop (Merlin 46); TOC/RAF 9.12.42; Gibraltar 18.1.43 - SAAF (MTO), No.4 Sqn ('KJ-B'), tyre burst on take-off, overturned, wings torn off, Cat.FB/3 8.1.44 (Lt R Mark injured), SOC
ES359	Spitfire F.Vc/trop (Merlin 46); TOC/RAF 20.12.42; M.E. 30.3.43 - SAAF (MTO), No.9 Sqn by 6.44 - @30.1.45; Retd RAF; Later to Turkey 29.3.45
ES369	Spitfire F.Vc/trop (Merlin 46); TOC/RAF 10.12.42; To Casablanca 25.4.43; M.E. - SAAF (MTO), No.40 Sqn (date unknown); Retd RAF (No.118 MU, Malta) 31.1.44; Later to Yugoslavia (No.9483) 18.5.45
JF294	Spitfire F.VIIIc (Merlin 61A); Became SAAF No. **5501**; TOC/RAF 1.43 - Arr South Africa 3.44 (Ferry flight, high speed dash Cairo-Cape Town 3.3.44 (F/O GE Camplin); From March to September 1944 demonstrations flying by F/O Camplin and exhibition during the Liberty Cavalcades of the Union of South Africa (at Cape Town, Bloemfontein, Kimberly, East London, Port Elizabeth, Durban and Johannesburg); To SAAF 10.44; No.11 OTU until November 1948 (personal aircraft of Lt Col D H Loftus); SOC at Lyttelton AFB 17.11.48; To the South African National Military Museum, Saxonwold, Johannesburg 12.11.48;

A composite photograph assembled digitally from ten frames of 8mm cinefilm taken in 1944 at Wonderboom. JF294, in high altitude day fighter finish, was flown to the Cape for the 'Liberty Cavalcades' and subsequently became the first post-war SAAF Spitfire – 5501. [Fred Mills]

Exhibited as "5501" in high gloss polished natural finish; Officially bought 9.8.55 (sale No. 153), extant - **SURVIVOR**
NOTE: F.VIIIc, delivered and flown with extended wing tips

JF322 Spitfire F.VIIIc (Merlin 61); TOC/RAF 9.2.43; Casablanca 29.7.43; M.E. - SAAF (MTO), No.1 Sqn ('AX-B', named *'BILLY BOY II'*) by 1.44; Hit by AA over Aquila, Cat.FB/2 25.1.44 (2/Lt JA Kayser); Me 410 destroyed 4m off Penna Point 14.3.44 (Lt SJ Richards); FW 190 destroyed over Ortona 19.3.44 (Lt DS Hastie); Two Bf 109G destroyed 8.4.44 (Lt SJ Richards); Retd RAF; SOC 15.3.45

JF346 Spitfire F.VIIIc (Merlin 63A); TOC/RAF 7.3.43; M.E. 8.43 - SAAF (MTO), No.1 Sqn, shot down by FW 190s over Sangro, crashed 12m NNW of fork of Sangro River, 6m S of Castel Frentano/35m W of Termoli, Cat.FB/E 28.11.43 (Lt LJ Oates killed), SOC

JF353 Spitfire F.VIIIc (Merlin 63A); TOC/RAF 14.3.43; M.E. 9.43; NAAF 11.43 - SAAF (MTO), No.2 Sqn ('DB-1'), weather recce and top cover; Damaged Cat.2 16.12.43; Retd RAF (No.244 Wing); SOC 28.11.46

JF405 Spitfire F.VIIIc (Merlin 63); TOC/RAF 2.4.43; Casablanca 17.5.43 - SAAF (MTO), No.1 Sqn, LR tanks ran dry on ops, unable to turn on to main tanks, baled out Messina, Cat.E 2.9.43 (Wg Cdr WGG Duncan-Smith DSO DFC, No.244 Wing Sweep-Leader, unhurt), SOC

JF406 Spitfire F.VIIIc (Merlin 63); TOC/RAF 3.4.43; M.E. 30.9.43 - SAAF (MTO), No.1 Sqn ('AX-A', named *'DIL-EMMA'* by Lt LH Brown), date unknown; Retd RAF; SOC 30.6.45

JF417 Spitfire F.VIIIc (Merlin 63); TOC/RAF 11.4.43; NWA 7.43 - SAAF (MTO), No.1 Sqn ('AX-5') by 8.43; FW 190 damaged 10.8.43 (Lt SJ Richards); Shot down Bf 109G which exploded on hitting ground 2.9.43 (Lt H Taylor); ASR sortie, engine cutting 10m SW of Capo Vaticano, Sicily, turned back, crashed in sea, assumed allowed LR tanks to run dry, Cat.FB/E 5.9.43 (Capt CE Martin killed), SOC

JF421 Spitfire F.VIIIc (Merlin 63); TOC/RAF 10.4.43; Casablanca 17.5.43; M.E. - SAAF (MTO), No.1 Sqn ('AX-4') by 19.7.43; Retd RAF (lost No.185 Sqn 12.9.44)

JF445 Spitfire F.VIIIc (Merlin 63); TOC/RAF 17.4.43; NWA 7.43; M.E. - SAAF (MTO), No.1 Sqn ('AX-9') by 19.7.43; Damaged MC 202, own aircraft damaged, coolant leak, caught fire, baled out, aircraft crashed in sea 2m SE of Reggio, Cat.FB/E 3.9.43 (Lt DS Hastie rescued), SOC

JF446 Spitfire F.VIIIc (Merlin 63); TOC/RAF 18.4.43; M.E. 1.8.43 - SAAF (MTO), No.1 Sqn ('AX-K') by 2.9.43; Failed to return, squadron formation entered dense black thundercloud at 12,000ft en route to Kuna, Yugoslavia, believed hit by lightning over sea nr Delgara, Cat.FB/E 29.10.43 (Lt HN Taylor killed), SOC

JF448 Spitfire F.VIIIc (Merlin 63); TOC/RAF 18.4.43; NWA 7.43; M.E. 8.43 - SAAF (MTO), No.1 Sqn, hit cement block on river bank during forced landing in Trigno River, about 9m W of Termoli, Cat.FB/3 7.12.43 (Lt AF Staples killed), SOC

JF460 Spitfire F.VIIIc (Merlin 63); TOC/RAF 25.4.43; NWA 7.43; M.E. 8.43 - SAAF (MTO), No.1 Sqn ('AX-E') by 11.43; Bf 109G damaged 3.11.43 (Capt JT Seccombe); Engine trouble approaching coast after sweep, had encountered heavy AA but reported not hit, attempted to bale out at 50ft, aircraft crashed in sea near mouth of Sangro River/off Foccacesia, 70m W of Termoli, Cat.FB/E 18.12.43 (Lt B Trotter drowned); SOC 29.2.44

JF467 Spitfire F.VIIIc (Merlin 63); TOC/RAF 30.4.43; M.E. 8.43; NAAF 11.43 - SAAF (MTO), No.1 Sqn, overshot landing Trigno, Cat.FB/2 28.1.44 (Lt CC Shaw); Retd RAF; SOC 25.4.46

JF475 Spitfire LF.VIIIc (Merlin 66); TOC/RAF 13.5.43; NWA 7.43; M.E. 1.8.43 - SAAF (MTO), No.1 Sqn ('AX-7') by 8.43; FW 190 (Uffz August Woletering) destroyed, crashed in sea nr Augusta, Sicily 10.8.43 (Capt JT Seccombe); Still No.1 Sqn 2.9.43; Retd RAF; Later to USAAF 29.2.44

JF485 Spitfire F.VIIIc (Merlin 63); TOC/RAF 20.5.43; M.E. 1.8.43; NAAF 1.11.43 - SAAF (MTO), No.117 MU to No.1 Sqn 4.44; Retd RAF (later No.253 Sqn, missing Cat FB/E 6.12.44); SOC 31.1.45

JF505 Spitfire F.VIIIc (Merlin 63A); TOC/RAF 22.5.43; M.E. 8.43 - SAAF (MTO), No.1 Sqn ('AX-3') by 19.7.43; RiW; Me 210 destroyed 15.10.43 (Capt J van Nus); Me 210 destroyed, shared with JF559 15.10.43 (Capt J van Nus); Fighter sortie, undercarriage defect, belly-landed Palata LG, Cat.FB/A 2.11.43 (Lt GT van der Veen); Still No.1 Sqn ('AX-V') 2.12.43; Retd RAF; SOC 23.10.44

JF519 Spitfire F.VIIIc (Merlin 63); TOC/RAF 30.5.43; Casablanca 14.7.43 - SAAF (MTO), No.1 Sqn ('AX-D'), Service unknown; Retd RAF; SOC 30.6.45

JF521 Spitfire F.VIIIc (Merlin 63); TOC/RAF 30.5.43; M.E. 8.43; NAAF 11.43 - SAAF (MTO), No.2 Sqn ('DB-2'), damaged 16.12.43; Retd RAF (No.244 Wing); SOC 28.4.45

JF523 Spitfire F.VIIIc (Merlin 63); TOC/RAF 1.6.43; N.A. 30.11.43 - SAAF (MTO), No.1 Sqn ('AX-A') by 2.4.44; Retd RAF; SOC 28.4.45

JF528 Spitfire F.VIIIc (Merlin 63); TOC/RAF 6.6.43; M.E. 9.43; NAAF 11.43 - SAAF (MTO), No.1 Sqn, hit by light AA 3m SE of Sora, Cat.FB/2 25.1.44 (Lt RE de Jongh); Retd RAF; SOC 30.6.44

JF559 Spitfire F.VIIIc (Merlin 63); TOC/RAF 6.6.43; M.E. 9.43 - SAAF (MTO), No.1 Sqn ('AX-G'), Me 210 destroyed, shared with JF505 15.10.43 (Lt B Trotter); Retd RAF (later No.92 Sqn, crashed 30.1.45)

JF562 Spitfire F.VIIIc (Merlin 63); TOC/RAF 9.6.43; M.E. 9.43; NAAF 1.11.43 - SAAF (MTO), No.1 Sqn ('AX-H') by 12.43; FW 190 damaged 3.12.43 (Lt RE de Jongh); Engine cut on weather recce towards Rome, abandoned at 8,000ft near Casoli, Cat.FB/E 23.2.44 (Capt JW Ross, buried Civitella Pescorocchiano cemetery), SOC

JF578 Spitfire F.VIIIc (Merlin 63); TOC/RAF 31.5.43; M.E. 1.9.43 (sic) - SAAF (MTO), No.1 Sqn ('AX-L', named *'OLD FAITHFUL'*) 28.8.43; FW 190 destroyed 2.12.43 (Lt RE de Jongh); Retd RAF 20.3.44; SOC 31.8.44

JF581 Spitfire F.VIIIc (Merlin 63); TOC/RAF 8.6.43; M.E. 9.43; NAAF 1.11.43 - SAAF (MTO), No.1 Sqn, hit by flak in attack on train near Antrodocu, caught fire, pilot unsuccessfully attempted to bale out in Chieti area, aircraft dived into ground 10m SE of Avezza, Cat.FB/E 27.2.44 (Lt EE Sisson killed), SOC

JF582 Spitfire F.VIIIc (Merlin 63); TOC/RAF 8.6.43; M.E. 9.43 - SAAF (MTO), No.1 Sqn, struck by lightning on ops, aircraft became uncontrollable, pilot blacked out, recovered at 1,000-2,000ft, force-landed under control, Cat.FB/A 29.10.43 (Lt DJ Lindsay injured); Retd RAF (NAAF 1.11.43); SOC 30.6.45

JF620 Spitfire LF.VIIIc; ex RAAF (*A58-300*); Recovered surface wreck; Arrived as **SURVIVOR** only; Project by Mark de Vries, Bryanston, SA

JF626 Spitfire F.VIIIc (Merlin 63); TOC/RAF 29.6.43; M.E. 9.43; NAAF 1.11.43 - SAAF (MTO), No.1 Sqn ('AX-W') by 12.43; FW 190 destroyed 2.12.43 (Capt JH Gaynor); On sweep, glycol leak, engine cut at 4,000ft, baled out over sea at 900ft near mouth of Sangro River, 6m N of Ortona, Cat.E 25.12.43 (Lt JR Spencer seriously injured), SOC

JF659 Spitfire F.VIIIc (Merlin 63); TOC/RAF 29.6.43; Casablanca 29.7.43 - SAAF (MTO), No.1 Sqn, heavy landing, undercarriage collapsed Trigno LG, Cat.FB/2 22.1.44 (Lt J Landman); Retd RAF (RiW); SOC 30.6.44

JF704 Spitfire F.VIIIc (Merlin 63); TOC/RAF 22.6.43; M.E. 9.43; NAAF 11.43 - SAAF (MTO), No.1 Sqn, hit sand

	bank landing Trigno LG, Cat.2 9.1.44 (Lt SJ Richards); Retd RAF (RiW); SOC 23.10.44	JG778	Spitfire F.Vc/trop (Merlin 46); TOC/RAF 2.1.43; N.A. 30.11.43 - SAAF (MTO), No.3 Sqn 25.8.44; Retd RAF; SOC in 10.44
JG316	Spitfire F.VIIIc (Merlin 63); TOC/RAF 13.11.43; Casablanca 22.12.43 - SAAF (MTO), No.1 Sqn, lost leader in dense cloud then control at 10,000ft, baled out, Cat.FB/E 25.3.44 (Lt AW Homer rescued from dinghy by Walrus), SOC	JG839	Spitfire F.Vc/trop (Merlin 46); TOC/RAF 21.1.43; M.E. 31.3.43 - SAAF (MTO), No.10 Sqn by 8.8.44; Retd RAF 27.8.44 (Psd SOC in 1.47)
JG318	Spitfire F.VIIIc (Merlin 63); TOC/RAF 13.11.43; Casablanca 22.12.43 - SAAF (MTO), No.1 Sqn ('AX-D') by 4.44; Bf 109G damaged 4.4.44 (Lt RE de Jongh); Bf 109G destroyed and another damaged 12.4.44 (Lt RJ Barnwell); Retd RAF (later No.241 Sqn, missing FB/E 7.6.44, SOC)	JG844	Spitfire F.Vc/trop (Merlin 46); TOC/RAF 21.1.43; M.E. 6.5.43 - SAAF (MTO), No.7 Sqn, shot down in engagement with five Bf 109s over Cos, Cat.FB/3 27.9.43 (Lt JH Hynd killed); SOC 1.11.43
		JG864	Spitfire F.Vc/trop (Merlin 46); TOC/RAF 21.12.42; M.E. 20.4.43; Malta 7.43 - SAAF (MTO), No.1 Sqn late 7.43; Retd RAF (lost 6.2.44)
JG338	Spitfire LF.VIIIc (Merlin 66); TOC/RAF 3.10.43; NA 30.11.43 - SAAF (MTO), Service unknown; Retd RAF (later No.145 Sqn, shot down attacking MT 31.8.44, Cat.FB/E 2.9.44, SOC)	JG867	Spitfire F.Vc/trop (Merlin 45); TOC/RAF 21.12.42; NAASC 10.43 - SAAF (MTO), No.4 Sqn by 1.44; Hit by AA in Florence area, retd to base, Cat.FB/2 11.1.44 (Lt GW Pitout); Engine caught fire returning from patrol, abandoned over Sangro, burnt out Cat.FB/E 19.1.44 (Lt RK Atkinson unhurt), SOC
JG616	Spitfire F.VIIIc (Merlin 63); TOC/RAF 9.11.43; Casablanca 22.12.43 - SAAF (MTO), No.4 Sqn ('KJ-F') 26.4.44; To RAF, retd SAAF; No.1 Sqn ('AX-F'), FW 190 destroyed 27.5.44 (Lt DM Brebner); Flown by Lt Col AC Bosman (No.7 Wing), two Bf 109G destroyed mid 1944; No.4 Sqn ('KJ-F'), flown by Lt Col GC Krummeck 21.7.44 and 23.5.45; Weather recce, due to fly out 12.10.44; Retd RAF (MAAF); SOC 31.12.46	JG869	Spitfire F.Vc/trop (Merlin 46); TOC/RAF 22.12.42; NAAF 1.11.43 - SAAF (MTO), No.117 MU to No.4 Sqn 18.4.44; To No.241 Sqn RAF 5.5.44; No.7 (SAAF) Wing 6.5.44; Retd RAF; SOC 23.10.44
		JG874	Spitfire F.Vc/trop (Merlin 46); TOC/RAF 21.1.43; M.E. 1.11.43 - SAAF (MTO), No.10 Sqn (illegible name under cockpit) by 5.7.44 - @8.10.44; Undergoing mods at Aboukir 29.8.44; Retd RAF; SOC 29.8.46
JG617	Spitfire F.VIIIc (Merlin 63); TOC/RAF 13.11.43; Casablanca 22.12.43 - SAAF (MTO), No.1 Sqn (possibly 'AX-S'), glycol leak, caught fire, baled out, Cat.E 24.5.44 (Lt DT Gilson picked up from sea by Walrus), SOC	JG880	Spitfire F.Vb/trop (Merlin 46); TOC/RAF 21.12.42; NAASC 31.10.43 - SAAF (MTO), No.7 Sqn ('TJ-C') by 11.43; No.10 Sqn 15.6.44; Retd RAF 17.6.44; SOC 31.1.46
JG713	Spitfire F.Vc/trop (Merlin 46); TOC/RAF 10.12.42; NWA 28.2.43 - SAAF (MTO), No.4 Sqn, returning from sweep, fast landing too far to port, collided with ER893 then both hit parked aircraft LZ930, EF639 & ES141 at Palata, Cat.E 24.10.43 (Lt H McLeod injured); SOC 29.2.44	JG881	Spitfire F.Vc/trop (Merlin 46); TOC/RAF 29.12.42; M.E. 8.5.43 - SAAF (MTO), No.7 Sqn, ('R') by 9.43; 07.04h mission, Ju 88 destroyed, shared with JK140 18.9.43 (Lt DR Fisher); Shot down while taking off on 15.10 scramble, Cat.FB/3 18.9.43 (Lt AEF Cheesman killed), SOC
JG720	Spitfire F.Vc/trop (Merlin 46); TOC/RAF 17.12.42; M.E. 17.4.43 - SAAF (MTO), No.1 Sqn ('AX-N' : 'AX-C') by 6.43; Landed on one wheel Luqa, Cat.B 14.6.43 (Lt MES Robinson); Damaged Do 217E which was attacking JK834 16.7.43 (Lt SW van der Merwe); Still No.1 Sqn 19.7.43; Retd RAF; SOC 28.4.45	JG886	Spitfire F.Vc/trop (Merlin 46); TOC/RAF 31.12.42; M.E. 8.5.43; N.A. 30.11.43 - SAAF (MTO), No.4 Sqn, swung on landing, tipped up at Trigno LG, Cat.FB/2 14.2.44 (2/Lt HG Chapman unhurt); Re-Cat.E, SOC
		JG893	Spitfire F.Vc/trop (Merlin 46); TOC/RAF 24.12.42; M.E. 22.3.43; NA 30.11.43 - SAAF (MTO), No.117 MU to No.4 Sqn 12.4.44; Hit obstruction take-off, force-landed on LG, Cat.2 12.4.44 (Lt GT van Rooyen); Retd RAF (No.59 R&SU) 13.4.44; Later Cat.FB/3 11.5.44, SOC
JG721	Spitfire F.Vc/trop (Merlin 45); TOC/RAF 15.12.42; M.E. 9.5.43 - SAAF (MTO), No.2 Sqn ('DB-T'), took off with air mechanic on tail, crash-landed in field near Palata, air mechanic thrown off on touchdown, Cat.B 17.12.43 (Lt J Lenards OK; A/M BL Watson DoI); SOC 25.12.43	JG899	Spitfire F.Vc/trop (Merlin 46); TOC/RAF 30.12.42; NWA 28.2.43; French 31.7.43 - SAAF (MTO), No.40 Sqn, ran short of fuel on ferry flight in bad weather, belly-landed on disused airstrip on island of Zante, Cat.FA/B 10.12.44 (Lt AC De Villers OK); Fate unknown
JG732	Spitfire F.Vc/trop (Merlin 46); TOC/RAF 21.1.43; M.E. 10.6.43 - SAAF (MTO), No.1 Sqn, on take-off for harbour patrol, stbd wingtip struck civilian horse-drawn cart crossing runway Lentini West, carried out patrol and landed safely, Cat.FB/E (bboc) 31.7.43 (Lt GW Hillary); Retd RAF (ME 31.8.44, Psd SOC 1.47)	JG915	Spitfire F.Vc/trop (Merlin 46); TOC/RAF 31.12.42; M.E. 9.5.43 - SAAF (MTO), No.2 Sqn, engine failed, suspect bearing failure, El Haouaria LG, Cat.B 22.7.43; Retd RAF; Later USAAF 3.44; SOC 26.4.45
JG736	Spitfire F.Vc/trop (Merlin 46); TOC/RAF 15.12.42; NWA 28.2.43 - SAAF (MTO), No.2 Sqn ('DB-D') by 18.10.43; Landing accident, Cat.1 5.1.44; To No.114 MU 5.1.44; SOC (RAF) 29.8.46 NOTE: Reported for No.1 Sqn, taxying collision with ES107, Cat.Ac 24.6.44 (Lt JR Spencer) - but see JG739	JG916	Spitfire F.Vc/trop (Merlin 46); TOC/RAF 22.1.43; M.E. 22.4.43 - SAAF (MTO), No.7 Sqn, test flown 5.1.44; Still with No.7 Sqn 18.1.44; No.41 Sqn 8.3.44 to at least 5.44; No.9 Sqn, landed undercarriage retracted during night flying training, St.Jean 27.7.44 (Capt HCW Liebenberg); SOC 31.8.44
JG737	Spitfire F.Vc/trop (Merlin 46); TOC/RAF 15.12.42; NWA 28.2.43 - SAAF (MTO), No.4 Sqn ('KJ-V'), hit by flak, retd to base, Cat.FB/2 8.11.43 (Lt DF Hanafey); Lost in Chieta area, believed hit by AA, Cat.FB/E 20.12.43 (Lt GP Rabie PoW), SOC	JG928	Spitfire F.Vc/trop (Merlin 46); TOC/RAF 13.12.42; M.E. 9.43; NAAF - SAAF (MTO), No.2 Sqn ('DB-P') by 12.43; Loss power, Cat.1 (date unknown); Retd RAF (No.117 MU, W/E 20.1.44); Later No.185 Sqn, FB/E 1.9.44, SOC
JG739	Spitfire F.IXc (Merlin 63); TOC/RAF 13.6.43; M.E. 9.43; NAAF 11.43 - SAAF (MTO), No.1 Sqn, taxying collision with ES107, Cat.Ac 24.6.44 (Lt JR Spencer); Retd RAF; SOC 18.10.45	JG931	Spitfire F.Vc/trop (Merlin 46); TOC/RAF 22.1.43; M.E. 9.5.43 - SAAF (MTO), No.40 Sqn (date unknown); SOC 8.3.44 (but bboc)
JG752	Spitfire F.Vc/trop (Merlin 46); TOC/RAF 14.12.42; NWA 28.2.43; ex No.80 Sqn - SAAF (MTO), No.4 Sqn from 3.4.44; Believed shot down a Bf 109G or C205V, then himself shot down in flames by a Bf 109 near Termi, Cat.FB/3 7.4.44 (Lt RRW Sutton killed), SOC	JG937	Spitfire F.Vc/trop (Merlin 45); TOC/RAF 7.2.43; NWA 30.4.43; N.A. 30.11.43; No.94 Sqn - SAAF (MTO), No.10 Sqn from 1.8.44; Retd RAF; SOC 26.4.45 NOTE: Reported also as "JG397"

Spitfire F.Vc/trop JG959 AX-N Sqn SAAF around April-May 1943, with the name 'Cire Cooks VI' beneath the cockpit. [SAAF Museum]

JG939 Spitfire F.Vc/trop (Merlin 46); TOC/RAF 21.12.42; M.E. 2.4.43 - SAAF (MTO), No.1 Sqn ('AX-N') by 4.43; Convoy escort, collided in dark with stationary BP978, Luqa, Cat.FB/B 8.7.43 (Capt WM Langerman); Retd RAF; SOC 26.4.45

JG942 Spitfire F.Vc/trop (Merlin 46); TOC/RAF 22.1.43; M.E. 10.6.43; NAAF 11.43 - SAAF (MTO), No.40 Sqn, hit by AA nr Monte Cairo, Cat.FB/2 8.5.44 (Lt NG Boys OK); Retd RAF (RiW); SOC 26.4.45

JG945 Spitfire F.Vc/trop (Merlin 45); TOC/RAF 21.1.43; M.E. 22.3.43 - SAAF (MTO), No.1 Sqn, ('AX-Z') by 21.4.43; Two Me 323 destroyed off Zembra island and another shared with ER208/'AX-V', then forced landing near an advanced New Zealand MDS, fuel shortage, Cat.FB/B 22.4.43 (Lt GT van der Veen unhurt); Retd RAF (failed to return 10.7.43, SOC)

JG949 Spitfire F.Vc/trop (Merlin 46); TOC/RAF 2.1.43; Gibraltar 6.2.43; ex USAAF 31.10.43 - SAAF (MTO), No.2 Sqn ('DB-E') by 12.43; Short of fuel, force-landed 10m from Trigno LG, Cat.2 31.1.44 (Lt IT Gowar); Retd RAF (No.59 R&SU); Fate unknown

JG959 Spitfire F.Vc/trop (Merlin 46); TOC/RAF 10.1.43; M.E. 24.3.43 - SAAF (MTO), No.1 Sqn ('AX-N') by 4.43 - 5.43; Two Bf 109f destroyed in Cap Bon area 22.4.43 (Lt MES Robinson); Retd RAF; SOC 10.1.46

JK104 Spitfire F.Vc/trop (Merlin 46); TOC/RAF 21.1.43; NWA 31.3.43; M.E. 1.11.43 - SAAF (MTO), No.40 Sqn (date unknown); Retd RAF; SOC 26.4.45

JK108 Spitfire F.Vc/trop (Merlin 46); TOC/RAF 10.1.43; M.E. 29.5.43 - SAAF (MTO), No.7 Sqn by 16.1.44; No.3 Sqn 5.3.44; Accident Cat.FB/3 18.3.44, SOC

JK111 Spitfire F.Vc/trop (Merlin 46); TOC/RAF 31.12.42; NWA 28.2.43; ex French; NAASC 31.10.43 - SAAF (MTO), No.7 Sqn (service unknown); Retd RAF; SOC 5.1.46

JK112 Spitfire F.Vc/trop (Merlin 46); TOC/RAF 21.1.43; NWA 30.4.43 - SAAF (MTO), No.4 Sqn, hit by flak, retd to base, Cat.FB/2 6.11.43 (Lt KF Huskisson OK); Retd RAF; SOC 14.3.46

JK115 Spitfire F.Vc/trop (Merlin 46); TOC/RAF 21.1.43; M.E. 27.5.43 - SAAF (MTO), No.9 Sqn, undercarriage collapsed landing El Gamil, Cat.B 14.6.44 (Capt RC Lever); On ferry flight 10.7.44; No.136 MU, to No.10 Sqn 30.9.44; Retd RAF; SOC 13.9.45

JK122 Spitfire F.Vc/trop (Merlin 46); TOC/RAF 22.1.43; Gibraltar 25.2.43; N.A; Malta 1.5.43; Crashed Cat.FA/2 24.10.43; No.229 Sqn, Cat.FA/2 2.7.44 - SAAF (MTO), No.4 Sqn (date unknown); Retd RAF 6.11.44; Later No.352 Sqn, and to Yugoslavia (*No.9477*) 18.5.45

JK132 Spitfire F.Vc/trop (Merlin 46). Presentation aircraft *'EL FASER/DARFUR PROVINCE'*; TOC/RAF 22.1.43; NAAF 1.11.43 - SAAF (MTO), No.3 Sqn, glycol leak, force-landed wheels-up, hit stone wall in undergrowth, ground looped, overturned, burnt out, 5m NNW of Beda Littoria, Cat.FB/2 23.6.44 (Lt FD Wilson minor injuries); SOC 29.6.44

JK140 Spitfire F.Vc/trop (Merlin 46); TOC/RAF 21.1.43; M.E. 27.5.43 - SAAF (MTO), No.7 Sqn ('O'), 07.04 mission, Ju 88 destroyed, shared with JK140 18.9.43 (Lt RP Burl); 15.10 scramble, shot down by Bf 109s 4m N of Cos, Cat.FB/3 18.9.43 (Lt AG Turner killed), SOC

JK142 Spitfire F.Vc/trop (Merlin 46); TOC/RAF 21.1.43; M.E. 30.3.43 - SAAF (MTO), No.11 Sqn, hit by 3-ton truck while jacked up in dispersal Idku, Cat.Ac 19.8.44; ROS (further fate unknown)

JK159 Spitfire F.Vc/trop (Merlin 46); TOC/RAF 18.2.43; N.A. 30.11.43 - SAAF (MTO), No.7 Wing Training Flight, crashed Madna LG, Italy 25.4.44 (Lt JP Hogan slightly injured); Retd RAF; SOC 26.4.45

JK165 Spitfire F.Vc/trop (Merlin 46); TOC/RAF 27.1.43; NWA 30.4.43; M.E - SAAF (MTO), No.114 MU to No.4 Sqn 3.4.44; Oil leak in propeller 23.3.45; Retd RAF; Later to Italy (*MM4005*) 27.6.46

JK170 Spitfire F.Vc/trop (Merlin 46); TOC/RAF 23.1.43; M.E. 26.3.43 - SAAF (MTO), No.1 Sqn ('AX-D') by 21-22.4.43; No.130 MU, to No.7 Sqn SAAF 28.3.44; No.3 Sqn 5.3.44; Retd RAF 8.3.44; Later to Greece 25.4.46

JK182 Spitfire F.Vc/trop (Merlin 46); TOC/RAF 30.1.43; M.E, dis. NAAF - SAAF (MTO), No.4 Sqn, hit by AA 4.11.43 (Lt H Crosley OK); Hit by AA over Metkovic, Yugoslavia, retd to base, Cat.FB/2 14.11.43 (Lt KF Huskisson); Retd RAF (No.118.MU) 31.1.44

JK186 Spitfire F.Vc/trop (Merlin 46); TOC/RAF 6.2.43; M.E. 30.11.43; ex SHQ Idku - SAAF (MTO), No.10 Sqn 7.9.44 - 10.44; Retd RAF (Census 6.45)

JK187 Spitfire F Vc/trop (Merlin 46); TOC/RAF 1.2.43; Takoradi 2.4.43; M.E. 8.5.43 - SAAF (MTO), No.40 Sqn, hit by AA at 1,500ft nr Randazzo, abandoned near Gerbini airfield, Cat.FB/E 8.8.43 (Lt DS Waugh OK), SOC
NOTE: Serial No unconfirmed, but JK187 lost with unidentified unit that day

JK221 Spitfire F.Vc/trop (Merlin 46); TOC/RAF 2.2.43; NWA 30.4.43; M.E. 30.9.43 - SAAF (MTO), No.4 Sqn

South Africa

JK232 Spitfire F.Vc/trop (Merlin 50A); TOC/RAF 15.2.43; M.E. 30.11.43 - SAAF (MTO), No.7 Sqn ('TJ-N') by 16.1.44; Swung off runway landing, nosed up at Mersa Matruh, Cat.2 16.2.44 (Lt WL Strong); Retd RAF (fighter-bomber) from 6.1.44; Left Sqn 17.3.44; To USAAF; Retd RAF, SOC 14.3.46

JK233 Spitfire F.Vc/trop (Merlin 46); TOC/RAF 9.2.43; Casablanca 6.4.43; NWA 31.5.43; Malta 6.43 – SAAF (MTO), No.1 Sqn ('AX-H'), two Me 323 destroyed off Zembra island 22.4.43 (Lt DT Gilson); Retd RAF (No.229 Sqn, missing 12.7.43, SOC)
NOTE: Reported also No.1 Sqn by 20.3.43 or 20.4.43

JK236 Spitfire F.Vc/trop (Merlin 50); TOC/RAF 1.4.43; Casablanca 20.9.43; NAASC 31.10.43 - SAAF (MTO), No.9 Sqn by 30.1.45; Retd RAF; Later to Turkey 26.4.45

JK254 Spitfire F.Vc/trop (Merlin 46); TOC/RAF 29.1.43; M.E. 16.6.43 - SAAF (MTO), No.40 Sqn, hit by AA during recce over Francoville, spun in from 2,000ft, baled out too low and parachute failed to open properly, Bronte, Sicily, Cat.FB/E 13.8.43 (Lt OL Dugmore killed), SOC

JK281 Spitfire F.Vc/trop (Merlin 50A); TOC/RAF 2.2.43; NWA 31.3.43 - SAAF (MTO), No.2 Sqn, hit by debris while strafing 2m E of Munik airfield, retd to base, Cat.FB/2 24.2.44 (Lt IT Gowar); Retd RAF (RiW); SOC 26.4.45

JK282 Spitfire F.Vc/trop (Merlin 46); TOC/RAF 3.2.43; NAASC 31.10.43 - SAAF (MTO), No.130 MU to No.7 Sqn 28.2.44 to at least 9.3.44; Retd RAF; No.9 Sqn SAAF by 6.44; R/T failure 29.7.44; Retd RAF (Census 6.45)

JK306 Spitfire F.Vc/trop (Merlin 50A); TOC/RAF 4.2.43; NWA 30.4.43; SOC 8.3.44 (bboc) - SAAF (MTO), No.136 MU to No.3 Sqn 30.6.44; No.136 MU, to No.10 Sqn 30.9.44 - 10.44; Retd RAF; Later to Greece 25.4.46

JK307 Spitfire F.Vc/trop (Merlin 46); TOC/RAF 3.2.43; NAASC 31.10.43 - SAAF (MTO), No.3 Sqn 30.6.44; Retd RAF; SOC 26.4.45 - NOTE: Reported also as "JK302"

JK328 Spitfire F.Vc/trop (Merlin 46); TOC/RAF 22.1.43; M.E. 27.3.43 - SAAF (MTO), No.9 Sqn by 30.1.45; Retd RAF; SOC 25.7.46

JK340 Spitfire F.Vc/trop (Merlin 46); TOC/RAF 1.2.43; Gibraltar 26.4.43; NWA - SAAF (MTO), No.2 Sqn, damaged Cat.FB/2 7.9.43; Retd RAF (RiW); Later to Turkey 26.4.45

JK383 Spitfire F.Vc/trop (Merlin 46); TOC/RAF 2.2.43; M.E. 9.5.43; No.59 R&SU - SAAF (MTO), No.4 Sqn 19.4.44; Retd RAF (No.117 MU) 25.4.44; Later to Greece 25.4.46

JK386 Spitfire F.Vc/trop (Merlin 46); TOC/RAF 2.2.43; M.E. - SAAF (MTO), No.40 Sqn, glycol leak, force-landed on beach near Giarre, Sicily, Cat.E 25.8.43 (Lt JC Kruger slightly injured), SOC

JK387 Spitfire F.Vc/trop (Merlin 46); TOC/RAF 7.4.43; Malta 7.43 - SAAF (MTO), No.2 Sqn ('DB-F'), hit by AA, baled out Peljesaur Peninsula, aircraft crashed in sea 3m S of Kalogee Island, nr Dubrovnik, Cat.FB/E 29.11.43 (Lt NM MacDonald PoW), SOC

JK388 Spitfire F.Vc/trop (Merlin 46); TOC/RAF 6.2.43; Gibraltar 24.3.43 - SAAF (MTO), No.2 Sqn ('DB-N') by 12.43; Reported engine trouble [shot down 8m S of Pescara?], last seen off Ortona, crashed in sea, Cat.FB/E 9.1.44 (Lt LA Legoff killed), SOC

JK393 Spitfire F.Vc/trop (Merlin 46); TOC/RAF 7.2.43; M.E. 23.4.43 - SAAF (MTO), No.1 Sqn ('AX-A': 'AX-X') by 7.43; FW 190 shot down into sea, shared with ES150, Augusta (Oblt Fritz Holzapfel of 13/SKG10 baled out but killed) 19.7.43 (Capt JM Faure); Taxied into parked aircraft, Lentini West, Cat.B 31.8.43 (Lt AJ Biden); Retd RAF; Later to Turkey 30.11.44

JK396 Spitfire F.Vc/trop (Merlin 46); TOC/RAF 7.2.43; NWA 31.5.43 - SAAF (MTO), No.1 Sqn ('AX-M') by 19.7.43; Retd RAF, and to USAAF 31.7.43

JK397 Spitfire F.Vc/trop (Merlin 46); TOC/RAF 4.2.43; M.E. 7.43 - SAAF (MTO), No.4 Sqn, shipping patrol, very bad weather, ran out of fuel, force landing Terlizzi, crashed Cat.FB/2 6.10.43 (F/O BR Dodd RAF seriously injured); Re-Cat.E; SOC 1.11.43

JK398 Spitfire F.Vc/trop (Merlin 46); TOC/RAF 4.2.43; NWA 30.4.43 - SAAF (MTO), No.40 Sqn, hit by light AA over Atina, crash-landed in flames, overturned, Cat.FB/3 3.4.44 (Lt PTC O'Keeffe), SOC

JK401 Spitfire F.Vc/trop (Merlin 46); TOC/RAF 2.2.43; NWA 30.4.43 - SAAF (MTO), No.4 Sqn, hit by flak during attack on camp at Metkovic, Yugoslavia, lost glycol, engine failure, crashed in sea in Chieti area, Cat.FB/E 14.11.43 (Lt PGF Bailey killed); SOC 17.11.43

JK405 Spitfire F.Vc/trop (Merlin 46); TOC/RAF 6.2.43; NWA 30.3.43 - SAAF (MTO), No.2 Sqn, hit by AA nr Guiliano, N of Chieti, spun down in flames, Cat.FB/E 2.12.43 (Lt EC Jordan killed), SOC

JK407 Spitfire F.Vc/trop (Merlin 46); TOC/RAF 7.2.43; N.A. 30.11.43 - SAAF (MTO), No.2 Sqn ('DB-T') by 18.10.43; No.9 Sqn by 6.44-7.44; Undercarriage collapsed landing Minnick, Cat. AR 24.6.44 (Lt DR Collins); Retd RAF (later No.73 OTU, crashed 6.9.44)

JK408 Spitfire F.Vc/trop (Merlin 46); TOC/RAF 10.2.43; M.E. 26.5.43 - SAAF (MTO), No.7 Sqn ('C') from 23.2.44; No.3 Sqn 2.3.44; No.10 Sqn 15.6.44; Retd RAF (No.94 Sqn) 28.8.44; Later to Greece 25.4.46

JK425 Spitfire F.Vc/trop (Merlin 46); TOC/RAF 11.2.43; M.E. 27.5.43; N.A. 30.11.43 - SAAF (MTO), No.9 Sqn ('H') by 8.44-2.45; Retd RAF; Later to Turkey 31.5.45

JK430 Spitfire F.Vc/trop (Merlin 46); TOC/RAF 6.2.43; NWA 30.4.43; M.E. 30.9.43 - SAAF (MTO), No.3 Sqn (Service unknown); Retd RAF, SOC 26.4.45

JK431 Spitfire F.Vc/trop (Merlin 46); TOC/RAF 7.2.43; NWA 31.5.43 - SAAF (MTO), No.3 Sqn until 30.8.44; Retd RAF (MU); SOC 29.8.46

JK433 Spitfire F.Vc/trop (Merlin 46); TOC/RAF 6.2.43; NWA 30.4.43 - SAAF (MTO), No.4 Sqn, to No.59 R&SU 8.4.44; No.4 Sqn 26.4.44; No.7 Wing Training Flight (Wing Leader) 5.5.44; Retd RAF (MAAF census 6.45)

JK435 Spitfire F.Vc/trop (Merlin 50A); TOC/RAF 13.2.43; M.E. 13.12.43 - SAAF (MTO), No.4 Sqn from 2.4.44; RiW; No.10 Sqn from 5.8.44; Tyre burst on take-off 11.8.44 (2/Lt DJ Taylor); Retd RAF; SOC 13.9.45

JK453 Spitfire F.Vc/trop (Merlin 46); TOC/RAF 11.2.43; M.E. 6.5.43 - SAAF (MTO), No.10 Sqn until 28.8.44; Retd RAF (No.94 Sqn) 28.8.44; No.9 Sqn SAAF (service unknown)

JK456 Spitfire F.Vc/trop (Merlin 46); TOC/RAF 7.2.43; NAAF 1.11.43 - SAAF (MTO), No.4 Sqn ('KJ-Z') by 22.2.44; Damaged by AA and abandoned near Carsoli, Cat.FB/E2 11.3.44 (2/Lt GW Pitout PoW), SOC

JK461 Spitfire F.Vc/trop (Merlin 50A); TOC/RAF 13.2.43; M.E. 12.4.43 - SAAF (MTO), No.1 Sqn by 5.43; Retd RAF (No.154 Sqn, lost 25.7.43, SOC)

JK466 Spitfire F.Vc/trop (Merlin 50); TOC/RAF 13.2.43; M.E. 25.5.43 - SAAF (MTO), No.7 Sqn by 9.43; Damaged Ju 88, then own aircraft damaged by Bf 109, force-landed near Cos town 19.9.43 (Lt RP Burl); Fate unknown
NOTE: Reported SOC 25.5.43; RAF Movement Card: Psd SOC 1.47

JK517 Spitfire F.Vc/trop (Merlin 46); TOC/RAF 12.2.43; M.E. 26.5.43 - SAAF (MTO), No.2 Sqn, ferry flight, engine failed, force-landed and crashed near Taranto, Cat.FA/3 2.10.43 (Lt JM Sweeney seriously injured); SOC 1.11.43

JK540 Spitfire F.Vc/trop (Merlin 46); TOC/RAF 29.4.43; NWA 7.43; M.E. 14.7.43 - SAAF (MTO), No.7 Sqn, swung on heavy landing, cannon dug in at Gamil, Cat.FB/3 15.9.43 (2/Lt JWS Fisher); Retd RAF (No.58 R&SU) 16.9.43

JK545 Spitfire F.Vc/trop (Merlin 50); TOC/RAF 29.4.43; NWA 7.43 - SAAF (MTO), No.2 Sqn ('DB-U':'DB-S') by 28.11.43-12.43; No.4 Sqn, retd RAF 8.4.44; SOC 28.4.45

JK608 Spitfire F.Vc/trop (Merlin 50); TOC/RAF 14.2.43; M.E. 7.5.42 - SAAF (MTO), No.10 Sqn, heavy landing, swung off runway 14.6.44 (2/Lt PB During); Retd RAF; SOC 26.4.45

JK613 Spitfire F.Vc/trop (Merlin 50); TOC/RAF 15.2.43; M.E. 30.11.43 - SAAF (MTO), No.7 Sqn by 15.2.44; Retd to RAF (No.103 MU) 22.2.44; No.40 Sqn SAAF, overshot in flapless landing, into ditch, Cat.2 8.2.44 (Lt JR Harmer); Retd RAF; SOC 25.7.46

JK654 Spitfire F.Vc/trop (Merlin 46); TOC/RAF 18.2.43; Casablanca 6.4.43 - SAAF (MTO), No.7 Sqn ('TJ-H') 9-13.2.44; Retd RAF (ME Census 6.45); SOC 29.8.46

JK658 Spitfire F.Vc/trop (Merlin 46); TOC/RAF 18.2.43; Casablanca 6.4.43 - SAAF (MTO), No.40 Sqn, failed to return artillery recce 6m N of Gridolfo, crashed SE of Morgiano, Cat.FB/E 1.9.44 (Lt G Morgan killed); SOC 23.10.44

JK667 Spitfire F.Vc/trop (Merlin 50); TOC/RAF 21.2.43; NWA 30.4.43; M.E. 1.8.43 - SAAF (MTO), No.7 Sqn, shot down in engagement with five Bf 109s 10m S of Cos, Cat.FB/E 27.9.43 (Lt KW Prescott killed), SOC

JK671 Spitfire F.Vc/trop (Merlin 50); TOC/RAF 21.2.43; M.E. 7.5.43 - SAAF (MTO), No.1 Sqn, formation attacked by three Bf 109s over Gulf of Santa Eufemia, crashed in sea in flames NE of Capo Vatinico, Cat.FB/E 2.9.43 (Lt RL Cherrington killed), SOC

JK674 Spitfire F.Vc/trop (Merlin 46); TOC/RAF 25.2.43; Malta 7.43 - SAAF (MTO), No.2 Sqn ('DB-S'), believed hit by AA, last seen spinning down NE of Chieti-Cinliano, failed to return, Cat.FB/E 2.12.43 (Lt RE Laing killed), SOC

JK677 Spitfire F.Vc/trop (Merlin 50); TOC/RAF 21.2.43; M.E. 7.5.43 - SAAF (MTO), No.7 Sqn, shot down a Bf 109 then spun into sea off Cos while chasing another, Cat.FB/E 19.9.43 (Lt IM Seel killed); SOC 1.11.43

JK740 Spitfire F.Vc/trop (Merlin 50); TOC/RAF 27.2.43; M.E.; NAASC 31.10.43 - SAAF (MTO), No.40 Sqn (date unknown); Retd RAF; SOC 22.2.45

JK742 Spitfire F.Vc/trop (Merlin 50); TOC/RAF 2.3.43; M.E. 1.11.43 - SAAF (MTO), No.7 Sqn ('H'), gun test 8.12.43; No.103 MU 6.2.44; No.11 Sqn SAAF, engine failed, glycol leak, forced crash landed near Buseili, 35m NE of Alexandria, Egypt, Cat.FB/2 25.8.44 (2/Lt JR Derema injured); Retd RAF (RiW); SOC 27.10.44

JK760 Spitfire F.Vc/trop (Merlin 50); TOC/RAF 28.2.43; M.E. 31.8.44 - SAAF (MTO), No.4 Sqn by 3.44; Retd RAF (No.144 MU) 3.4.44; SOC 28.12.44

JK778 Spitfire F.Vc/trop (Merlin 46); TOC/RAF 10.3.43; M.E. 7.43 - SAAF (MTO), No.130 MU to No.7 Sqn ('N') 19.2.44; No.3 Sqn 5.3.44; Retd RAF (No.136 MU for 280 hr inspection) early 7.44; No.3 Sqn SAAF by 25.8.44; Retd RAF; SOC 10.11.44

JK780 Spitfire F.Vc/trop (Merlin 50); TOC/RAF 6.3.43; ex USAAF 31.7.43 (FFAF); NAASC 31.10.43 - SAAF (MTO), No.130 MU to No.7 Sqn 28.2.44; SOC 29.2.44

JK815 Spitfire F.Vc/trop (Merlin 46); TOC/RAF 8.3.43; NWA 31.5.43; Malta 8.43 - SAAF (MTO), No.2 Sqn ('DB-R') by 18.10.43; Damaged Cat.2 18.11.43; Retd RAF (RiW); SOC 26.4.45

JK822 Spitfire F.Vc/trop (Merlin 46); TOC/RAF 21.3.43; Casablanca 25.4.43; NAAF - SAAF (MTO), No.4 Sqn, hit by AA over Pescara River, abandoned 4m N of Casoli, Cat.FB/E 7.11.43 (Lt BA Bird killed), SOC

JK830 Spitfire F.Vc/trop (Merlin 45); TOC/RAF 28.3.43; NAASC 31.10.43; N.A. - SAAF (MTO), No.40 Sqn, crashed in enemy territory in Ortona area, Cat.FB/E 30.12.43 (Lt DS Waugh killed, buried Morro River Military Cemetery), SOC

JK834 Spitfire F.Vc/trop (Merlin 50); TOC/RAF 2.4.43; Malta 1.8.43 - SAAF (MTO), No.1 Sqn ('AX-O') by 16.7.43, hit by ground fire nr Gerbini, engine failed, overheating, forced landed successfully 1m W of Priolo, Cat.B 17.7.43 (Lt GT van der Veen OK); Retd RAF; Later to Egypt 29.3.45

JK837 Spitfire F.Vc/trop (Merlin 50); TOC/RAF 2.4.43; M.E. - SAAF (MTO), No.4 Sqn, ran into JK866 also taxying, Faro LG, Cat.B 30.8.43 (Lt HF Marshall); Retd RAF; SOC (FB/E2) 28.4.44

JK865 Spitfire F.Vc/trop (Merlin 50); TOC/RAF 7.3.43; NWA 31.5.43 - SAAF (MTO), No.4 Sqn (date unknown); No.2 Sqn, heavy landing, bounced, undercarriage collapsed, overturned Ben Gardane, Cat.B 10.7.43 (Lt JFJ Stone); Reported No.7 Wing, Cat.3 22.7.43; Retd RAF; SOC 1.9.45

JK866 Spitfire F.Vc/trop (Merlin 50); TOC/RAF 6.3.43; NWA 31.5.43 - SAAF (MTO), No.4 Sqn, while taxying, run into by JK837, Faro LG, Cat.Ac 30.8.43 (Lt H Crosley); Retd RAF; No.103 MU, to No.10 Sqn SAAF 10.10.44; Retd RAF; SOC 26.4.45

JK872 Spitfire F.Vc/trop (Merlin 50); TOC/RAF 12.3.43; NAAF 1.11.43 - SAAF (MTO), No.4 Sqn ('KJ-A'), hit by AA, retd to base, Cat.FB/2 11.11.43 (Lt GT van Rooyen unhurt); Repair; Damaged by flak Frosinone area, abandoned near Valmontone, burnt out, Cat.FB/E2 24.2.44 (Lt KF Huskinsson evaded capture), SOC

JK873 Spitfire F.Vc/trop (Merlin 50); TOC/RAF 6.3.43; NWA - SAAF (MTO), No.40 Sqn, tailwheel damaged in PSP, Cat.FB/Ac 13.3.44 (Capt WG Andrew); Retd RAF (later No.32 Sqn, missing Cat.FB/E 23.10.44, SOC)

JK878 Spitfire F.Vc/trop (Merlin 46); TOC/RAF 10.3.43; M.E. 31.8.44 - SAAF (MTO), No.2 Sqn, swung landing, overturned, Cat.2 10.1.44 (Lt VH Martin); Retd RAF (RiW); SOC 31.5.45

JK884 Spitfire F.IXc (Merlin 63); TOC/RAF 27.3.43; M.E. 7.43; NAASC 31.10.43 - SAAF (MTO), No.2 Sqn ('DB-Y') by 18.10.43; No.1 Sqn, flaps not working, landed downhill and slightly downwind at dusk using flarepath, tyre burst, collided with ES185 landing Palata, Cat.B 4.11.43 (Lt DS Hastie); SOC 29.2.44 (bboc); Lost 26.1.45

JK885 Spitfire F.Vc/trop (Merlin 45); TOC/RAF 12.3.43; NAAF 1.11.43 - SAAF (MTO), No.3 Sqn from 25.8.44 until 30.11.44; Retd RAF; Later to Greece 25.4.46

JK922 Spitfire F.Vc/trop (Merlin 50); TOC/RAF 12.3.43; NWA 31.5.43 - SAAF (MTO), No.4 Sqn ('KJ-N'), hit by flak and blew up in air attacking MT near Bariscaino, Cat.FB/E2 8.2.44 (Capt JW Meiring killed), SOC

JK936 Spitfire F.Vc/trop (Merlin 45); TOC/RAF 23.3.43; Casablanca 17.5.43 - SAAF (MTO), No.1 Sqn ('AX-M'), air combat Bf 109G damaged in Syracuse area 13.7.43 (Lt CA Halliday); Bf 109G damaged 19.7.43 (Lt GW Hillary); Malta-Sicily 1.8.43; N.A. 30.11.43; Unknown unit, crashed Cat.FB/3 22.3.44, SOC

JK967 Spitfire F.Vc/trop (Merlin 45); TOC/RAF 20.3.43; NWA 31.5.43; M.E. 8.43 - SAAF (MTO), No.4 Sqn ('KJ-P') by 7.4.44; Retd RAF (No.117 MU) 16.4.44; No.352 Sqn, failed to return, Cat.FB/E 16.9.44, SOC

JK973 Spitfire F.Vc/trop (Merlin 45); TOC/RAF 20.3.43; M.E. 30.9.43; NAAF 1.11.43 - SAAF (MTO), No.4 Sqn ('KJ-Q'), hit by AA, engine seen pouring out glycol and smoke in dive on target 10m W of Chieti, crashed Tollo, Cat.FB/E 31.12.43 (Capt HJ Buch killed), SOC

JK977 Spitfire F.Vc/trop (Merlin 46); TOC/RAF 20.3.43; N.A. 30.11.43; No.94 Sqn - SAAF (MTO), No.10 Sqn 1.8.44; Retd RAF 27.8.44 (Cat FB/E 19.10.44, SOC)

JK985 Spitfire F.Vc/trop (Merlin 45); TOC/RAF 7.4.43; NAASC 31.10.43 - SAAF (MTO), No.10 Sqn 15.6.44, but due for engine change; Retd RAF 16.6.44; Retd No.10 Sqn SAAF; Retd RAF 27.8.44

JL111 Spitfire LF.IXc (Merlin 66); TOC/RAF 16.8.43; N.A. 30.11.43 - SAAF (MTO), No.7 Sqn, to No.41 Sqn 7.3.44; No.7 Sqn ('TJ-E') by 11.3.44; Hit by Seafire MB245 of No.879 Sqn (FAA) while taxying Orvieto 13.7.44 (Lt MGM Atmore OK); Retd RAF (RiW); SOC in 2.45

JL113 Spitfire F.Vc/trop (Merlin 50); TOC/RAF 21.4.43; NWA 7.43 - SAAF (MTO), No.1 Sqn ('AX-W') by 10.43, damaged Cat.1 and retd RAF (No.114 MU) 5.1.44; SOC 26.4.45

JL115　Spitfire F.Vc/trop (Merlin 50); TOC/RAF 27.4.43; NWA 7.43 - SAAF (MTO), No.2 Sqn ('DB-V') by 28.11.43; Bf 109F damaged leaving long white trail 29.11.43 (Lt DV Ducasse); Glycol leak, Cat.1; Retd RAF (No.117 MU, W/E) 20.1.44; Later No.253 Sqn, missing, presumed shot down by flak near Khalkados, Cat.FB/E 21.9.44, SOC

JL126　Spitfire F.Vc/trop (Merlin 45); TOC/RAF 30.3.43; N.A. 30.11.43; No.2 R&SU - SAAF (MTO), No.7 Wing Training Flight, crashed nr Madna LG, Cat.E 4.5.44 (Lt AB Barter killed), SOC
NOTE: Incorrectly shown in RAF records as "JG126", which is a blackout serial

JL132　Spitfire LF.IXc (Merlin 66); TOC/RAF 27.3.43; N.A. 30.11.43 - SAAF (MTO), No.4 Sqn (date unknown); No.41 Sqn, to No.7 Sqn 8.3.44; Retd RAF (No.225 Sqn), SOC 27.8.44

JL134　Spitfire F.IXc (Merlin 63); TOC/RAF 28.3.43; Casablanca 17.5.43; NWA; ex USAAF 31.7.43 - SAAF (MTO), No.1 Sqn ('AX-W'), Me 410 into sea on fire, own engine hit, landed safely Bifeno LG, Cat.FB/2 2.4.44 (Lt RJ Barnwell); Engine failed at 1,000ft, baled out into sea, Cat.E2 1.5.44 (Lt JO Newton-Thompson rescued by ASR Walrus), SOC

JL139　Spitfire F.Vc/trop (Merlin 46); TOC/RAF 28.3.43; M.E. 1.11.43 - SAAF (MTO), No.7 Sqn by 16.1.44; No.3 Sqn 5.3.44; Retd RAF (No.136 MU for 180hr inspection) 8.5.44; Later to Greece 25.4.46

JL162　Spitfire F.Vc/trop (Merlin 45); TOC/RAF 3.4.43; MAAF 31.1.44 - SAAF (MTO), No.4 Sqn, hit by cannon shell, Cat.FB/2 7.4.44; Retd RAF (census 21.6.45); RAF Training Delegation 6.9.45; To France 29.11.45

JL163　Spitfire LF.IXc (Merlin 66); TOC/RAF 26.3.43; N.A. 30.11.43 - SAAF (MTO), No.357 MU to No.4 Sqn ('KJ-U') 31.7.44; Hit by flak in dive bombing attack on bridge, glycol leak, caught fire, baled out but parachute not fully opened, crashed Cat.FB/E 28.8.44 (Lt PJ Welmann killed), SOC

JL168　Spitfire F.Vc/trop (Merlin 45); TOC/RAF 31.3.43; M.E. 7.43 - SAAF (MTO), No.2 Sqn, damaged Cat.2 9.9.43; Retd RAF (RiW); Later to Yugoslavia (*No.9480*) 18.5.45

JL169　Spitfire F.Vc/trop (Merlin 50); TOC/RAF 2.4.43; M.E. 8.43; NAAF 1.11.43 - SAAF (MTO), No.2 Sqn, damaged by AA while strafing S of Pinan-Jane, Yugoslavia 3.3.44 (Lt GT Fowles); No.4 Sqn (KJ-W), Ju 88 crashed into hillside, shared with ES231 6.4.44 (Lt MWV Odendaal); Air combat over Termi, hit by cannon shell, crashed on landing Biferno, Cat.FB/3 7.4.44 (Lt FC Hamilton), SOC

JL172　Spitfire LF.IXc (Merlin 66); TOC/RAF 27.3.43; Casablanca 16.8.43 - SAAF (MTO), No.7 Sqn from 11.7.44; Hit by flak, crashed 1m E of target, Cat.FB/E 17.11.44 (Lt DC Bosch killed), SOC

JL174　Spitfire F.Vc/trop (Merlin 46); TOC/RAF 28.3.43; M.E. 7.43 - SAAF (MTO), No.4 Sqn, lost power 3.9.43; Retd RAF; Accident Cat.FA/3 10.9.43 (No.40 PTC), SOC

JL176　Spitfire F.Vc/trop (Merlin 46); TOC/RAF 28.3.43; NWA 10.43 - SAAF (MTO), No.4 Sqn until retd RAF (No.117 MU) 16.4.44; Later to Greece

JL184　Spitfire F.Vc/trop (Merlin 45); TOC/RAF 2.4.43; M.E. 19.6.43 - SAAF (MTO), No.40 Sqn (date unknown); Retd RAF, (No.225 Sqn), destroyed in air raid, Cat.E 18.9.43, SOC)

JL211　Spitfire F.Vc/trop (Merlin 50); TOC/RAF 4.4.43; M.E.; NAAF 11.43 - SAAF (MTO), No.4 Sqn, hit by AA, retd to base, Cat.FB/2 4.11.43 (Mjr SF du Toit OK); Retd RAF (RiW); SOC 26.4.45

JL216　Spitfire F.Vc/trop (Merlin 46); TOC/RAF 10.4.43; M.E. 23.6.43 - SAAF (MTO), No.41 Sqn (date unknown); No.3 Sqn for conversion training 29.2.44; Retd RAF (No.237 Sqn) 3.44; No.3 Sqn SAAF for ops, but found to be in poor condition 7.4.44; Engine failed on take-off for shipping patrol, crashed Savoia airfield, Cat.FB/3 17.4.44 (Lt AP du Preez slightly injured); SOC 24.4.44

JL226　Spitfire F.IXc (Merlin 63); TOC/RAF 11.4.43; NAAF 8.43 - SAAF (MTO), No.4 Sqn ('KJ-O') from 2.9.44; Engine cut on return from army support mission, abandoned inside lines S of Lucia, Cat.FB/E2 4.9.44 (Lt WM Thompson OK), SOC

JL236　Spitfire F.Vc/trop (Merlin 50); TOC/RAF 8.4.43; NWA - SAAF (MTO), No.4 Sqn, lost speed on take-off, struck ground but landed safely Ben Gardane, Cat.A 9.7.43 (Lt GT van Rooyen); Retd RAF; SOC 10.1.46

JL238　Spitfire F.Vc/trop (Merlin 45); TOC/RAF 19.4.43; NWA 7.43; M.E. 7.43 - SAAF (MTO), No.2 Sqn, shipping patrol, tyre burst landing, swung, undercarriage collapsed, Gioia LG, Cat.FB/2 11.10.43 (Lt JA Gilbert); Retd RAF (later No.352 Sqn, missing Cat.FA/E 3.5.45, SOC)

JL250　Spitfire F.Vc/trop (Merlin 45); TOC/RAF 11.4.43; M.E. 7.43 - SAAF (MTO), No.4 Sqn (fighter-bomber), retd RAF 5.11.43; SOC 14.3.46

JL254　Spitfire F.IXc (Merlin 63); TOC/RAF 9.4.43; Casablanca (NWA) 17.5.43 - SAAF (MTO), No.7 Sqn (possibly 'TJ-A') from 11.9.44; Hit by flak, crash-landed in enemy territory, on beach, Lake Commachio, Cat.FB/E 13.11.44 (Lt JC Buddell PoW), SOC

JL255　Spitfire F.IXc (Merlin 63); TOC/RAF 10.4.43; M.E. 8.43; NAASC 31.10.43 - SAAF (MTO), No.1 Sqn, port mainplane hit by AA over Castiglione, Cat.FB/Ac 14.9.44 (Lt DP Farrell); Retd RAF; SOC 26.9.46

JL308　Spitfire F.Vc/trop (Merlin 50); TOC/RAF 11.5.43; M.E. 28.8.43 - SAAF (MTO), No.41 Sqn by 8.44; Engine failed, attempted to return to base but crashed in forced landing 1m W of Nicosia, Cat.FA/E 15.9.44 (Lt IS de Klerk DoI), SOC

JL313　Spitfire F.Vc/trop (Merlin 50); TOC/RAF 22.5.43; M.E. 13.8.43 - SAAF (MTO), No.7 Sqn, landed downwind, stbd wheel went into ditch taxying, went on nose, Savoia, Cat.B 5.11.43 (Lt JWS van Heerden); Retd RAF; SOC 25.7.46

JL337　Spitfire F.Vc/trop (Merlin 50); TOC/RAF 1.7.43; N.A. 30.11.43 - SAAF (MTO), No.2 Sqn, braked to avoid jeep while taxying, tipped on nose, wingtip hit jeep, Cat.E 30.12.43 (Mjr TPL Murray OK); SOC 29.2.44 (bboc, MAAF); Later to Egypt 29.3.45

JL338　Spitfire F.Vc/trop (Merlin 50); TOC/RAF 26.5.43; M.E. 23.8.43 - SAAF (MTO), No.4 Sqn, heavy landing, swung, overturned, Cat.FB/3 14.2.44 (Lt DF de Wet unhurt), SOC

JL357　Spitfire F.Vc/trop (Merlin 50); TOC/RAF 18.4.43; M.E. 16.7.43 - SAAF (MTO), No.9 Sqn, tyre burst taxying Abu Sueir, Cat.Ac 8.12.44 (Lt WR Lawrie); Hit starter trolley taxying, undercarriage collapsed El Gamil, Cat. R 10.1.45 (Lt FM Carrington OK); Still No.9 Sqn 30.1.45; Retd RAF; SOC 29.8.46

JL358　Spitfire F.Vc/trop (Merlin 50); TOC/RAF 18.4.43; M.E. 13.7.43 - SAAF (MTO), No.40 Sqn, while parked, run into by EP192 (No.225 Sqn) which swung on take-off Palazzo, Cat.FA/3 1.10.43 (bboc); M.E. to NAAF 11.43; N.A. 30.11.43; SOC 26.4.45

JL363　Spitfire F.Vc/trop (Merlin 46); TOC/RAF 27.4.43; NWA 7.43 - SAAF (MTO), No.117 MU to No.4 Sqn 8.4.44; Retd RAF (No.117 MU) 25.4.44; No.4 Sqn SAAF 26.4.44; To No.7 Wing Training Flight at Madna 4.5.44; Retd RAF; SOC 30.6.45

JL365　Spitfire F.Vc/trop (Merlin 45); TOC/RAF 10.4.43; M.E. 5.8.43 - SAAF (MTO), No.136 MU to No.3 Sqn ('CA-P') 16.5.44; Retd RAF (No.94 Sqn); Lost 23.10.44

JL366　Spitfire LF.IXc (Merlin 66); TOC/RAF 10.9.43; N.A. 30.11.43 - SAAF (MTO), No.357 MU to No.2 Sqn ('DB-A', *diving girl* on nose) 5.1.45 to at least 16.4.45; Still No.2 Sqn 30.1.45; Retd RAF; Later to Egypt 31.10.46

JL369　Spitfire LF.IXc (Merlin 66); TOC/RAF 11.4.43; Casablanca 29.9.43 - SAAF (MTO), No.2 Sqn, port tyre

JL370　Spitfire LF.IXc (Merlin 66); TOC/RAF 21.8.43; Casablanca 29.9.43 - SAAF (MTO), No.2 Sqn, hit by AA, baled out, Cat.FB/E2 22.8.44 (Lt JB Miller came down in front lines, got through and retd same evening); SOC 31.8.44

JL372　Spitfire LF.IXc (Merlin 66); TOC/RAF 11.4.43; NAASC 31.10.43 - SAAF (MTO), No.41 Sqn, to No.7 Sqn 8.3.44; Failed to return, crashed on escort Serravelle, Cat.FB/3 13 or 18.4.44 (Lt JE Brand killed), SOC

JL377　Spitfire F.IXc (Merlin 63); TOC/RAF 9.4.43; N.A. 31.10.43 - SAAF (MTO), No.7 Sqn, hit by flak in Po Valley, landed Forli LG, Cat.FB/Ac 18.3.45 (Lt MH Steyn); Failed to return strafing attack on MT 3m N of Cavarzere, belly-landed 19m SSE of Padua, Cat.FB/E2 26.4.45 (Lt Peter B During PoW but escaped), SOC

JL385　Spitfire LF.IXc (Merlin 66); TOC/RAF 23.10.43; Casablanca 17.2.44 - SAAF (MTO), No.2 Sqn ('DB-B'), hit by AA, Cat.FB/Ac 18.7.44 (Lt NC Harrison); Tailwheel strut broke on landing Foiano 26.8.44 (Lt H Nash-Webber); Retd RAF (No.110 MU) 21.12.44, time expired; SOC 30.4.47

LR651　Seafire FR.IIc (Merlin 50); RNDA 27.4.43; No.787 Sqn - Attd to No.4 Sqn SAAF 28.6.44 -17.7.44

LR665　Seafire F.IIc (Merlin 50); RNDA 18.5.43; No.879 Sqn - Attd to No.7 Sqn SAAF 7.7.44 (Sqn Ldr JM Howden)

LR692　Seafire F.IIc (Merlin 50); RNDA 3.6.43; Nos 842 & 880 Sqns – Attd to No.4 Sqn SAAF 10.7-15.7.44

LR783　Seafire F.IIIc (Merlin 55); RNDA 28.8.43 - Attd to No.7 Sqn SAAF in 6.44 - 7.44

LZ823　Spitfire F.Vc/trop (Merlin 50); TOC/RAF 11.4.43; M.E. 2.7.43; N.A. 30.11.43 - SAAF (MTO), No.2 Sqn, damaged Cat.2 6.12.43; Retd RAF (RiW); SOC 29.2.44

LZ827　Spitfire F.Vc/trop (Merlin 50); TOC/RAF 14.4.43; M.E. 28.4.45 - SAAF (MTO), No.40 Sqn (date unknown); Retd RAF; SOC 27.6.46

LZ828　Spitfire F.Vc/trop (Merlin 45); TOC/RAF 16.8.43; NAASC 10.43 - SAAF (MTO), No.41 Sqn, swung off runway landing, ground looped, St.Jean d'Acre, Cat.FB/2 28.9.44 (Lt CL Stevenson); Retd RAF; Later to Greece 25.4.46

LZ832　Spitfire F.IXc (Merlin 63); Became SAAF No. **5...** (range 5555-5637); TOC/RAF 16.4.43; Arr South Africa, Cape Town (via Birkenhead) 11.5.48 - SAAF (Fate unknown)

LZ833　Spitfire F.IXc (Merlin 61); TOC/RAF 14.4.43; NAAF 1.11.43 - SAAF (MTO), unit and date unknown; Retd RAF; SOC 18.4.45

LZ842　Spitfire F.IXc (Merlin 63); Became SAAF No. **5...** (range 5555-5637); TOC/RAF 17.4.43; Arr South Africa, Cape Town (via Birkenhead) 28.4.48 – SAAF, AD 25.11.48; service unknown; SOC 1952; To South African Metal & Machinery Co, Salt River, scrapyard at Cape Town; Front fuselage recovered from scrapyard by Larry Barnett, Johannesburg in late 1960's; To SAAF Museum 1978 and stored Lanseria AFB; To Steve W Atkins & Chris Warrilow, Oxford, England 1989; to Ross Campbell, Toowoomba, Qld, Australia in 1991 for static restoration (with Australian wings) - **SURVIVOR**

LZ861　Spitfire F.IXc (Merlin 63); TOC/RAF 17.4.43; M.E. 8.43; NAASC 31.10.43 - SAAF (MTO), No.1 Sqn ('AX-A', named *DIL-EMMA II*'), hit by flak on sweep, last seen gliding under control 7m SW of Sarsina (Mercatino), baled out, Cat.FB/3 3.7.44 (Lt LH Brown later retd Sqn), SOC

LZ877　Spitfire F.Vc/trop (Merlin 50); TOC/RAF 27.4.43; NAAF 1.11.43 - SAAF (MTO), No.4 Sqn, hit by flak, retd to base, Cat.FB/2 7.11.43 (Lt RW Rowan); Retd RAF (later No.71 OTU, Cat.FA/E 26.3.45); SOC 13.9.45

LZ880　Spitfire F.Vc/trop (Merlin 50); TOC/RAF 30.4.43; NWA 7.43; M.E. 9.43 - SAAF (MTO), No.2 Sqn ('DB-H'), hit bump on runway while landing, bounced, port wheel dug into soft ground and undercarriage leg collapsed at Palata, Cat.FB/3 16.12.43 (Capt PD Bryant OK); Remains to RAF (No.59 R&SU), SOC

LZ885　Spitfire F.Vc/trop (Merlin 50); TOC/RAF 27.4.43; M.E. 8.43 - SAAF (MTO), No.10 Sqn by 30.7.44; No.103 MU at Aboukir for mods 30.8.44; Retd No.10 Sqn by 10.9.44-21.10.44; Retd RAF; No.11 Sqn SAAF, Fate unknown (Psd SOC 1.47)

LZ889　Spitfire F.IXc (Merlin 63); TOC/RAF 18.4.43; M.E. 8.43 - SAAF (MTO), No.1 Sqn ('AX-6') by 19.7.43; Retd RAF; SOC 26.9.46

LZ894　Spitfire F.IXc (Merlin 63); TOC/RAF 17.4.43; M.E. 8.43 - SAAF (MTO), No.41 Sqn ('V') by 16.4.44; Ju 88 shot down in sea, shared with MA257 25.4.44 (Lt JC Silberbauer); Ju 88 destroyed 24.6.44; Ju 88 damaged, shared MA257 11.7.44 (both Capt RP Burl); No.9 Sqn ('V'), destroyed Ju 88, three bullet holes in own tail, 40m W of Limassol, Cat.A 29.7.44 (Lt Joubert); Retd RAF (Census 6.45); SOC 29.8.46

LZ896　Spitfire F.IXc (Merlin 63); TOC/RAF 21.4.43; M.E. 8.43; NAAF 11.43 - SAAF (MTO), No.1 Sqn, swung on landing, hit two dispersed aircraft, Trigno, Cat.FB/3 4.4.44 (Capt E Odendaal), SOC

LZ918　Spitfire F.IXc (Merlin 63); TOC/RAF 25.4.43; N.A. (FFAF) 2.44 - SAAF (MTO), unknown unit in 2.44; No.7 Sqn from 18.7.44; 20mm round went off in breach of one of cannons, Cat.1 21.8.44 (Capt AW Meikle); Hit by light flak, abandoned near Figlioni, burnt out, Cat.FB/E 14.9.44 (Capt AW Meikle retd unit 4 hrs later); SOC 23.10.44

LZ930　Spitfire F.Vc/trop (Merlin 50); TOC/RAF 2.5.43; NWA 7.43 - SAAF (MTO), No.2 Sqn ('DB-S') by 18.10.43; Hit while parked by ER893 of No.4 Sqn at Palata, Cat.E 24.10.43; Re-Cat B, RiW; No.4 Sqn by 2.44; SOC 16.3.44

LZ947　Spitfire F.IXc (Merlin 63); TOC/RAF 28.4.43; Casablanca 29.11.43 - SAAF (MTO), No.1 Sqn ('AX-F') by 25.4.44; Bf 109G damaged 27.5.44 (Lt JA Kayser); Retd RAF; SOC 30.8.45

LZ949　Spitfire F.IXc (Merlin 63); TOC/RAF 30.4.43; NAAF 1.11.43 - SAAF (MTO), No.1 Sqn ('AX-Z'), Ju 88 destroyed and Bf 109G damaged 12.4.44 (Lt EF Harriss); Heavy landing, tailwheel strut broke, Cat.FB/2 14.6.44 (Lt T Schorn); Retd RAF; Later to Italy (*MM4074*) 30.5.46

LZ956　Spitfire F.IXc (Merlin 63); TOC/RAF 30.4.43; NAAF 1.11.43 - SAAF (MTO), No.117 MU to No.4 Sqn ('KJ-O'), as fighter-bomber from 5.9.44 until 4.3.45; Retd RAF; SOC 6.9.45

LZ976　Spitfire F.Vc/trop (Merlin 50); TOC/RAF 15.5.43; Casablanca 15.6.43; NWA 7.43; ex No.253 Sqn – SAAF (MTO), No.4 Sqn ('KJ-B') by 16.10.44 & 4.3.45 (Lt Cuff); But reported No.352 Sqn 27.11.44 ! Retd RAF, MAAF census 6.45; SOC 19.7.45
NOTE: Serial number correlated with LZ956

LZ979　Spitfire F.Vc/trop (Merlin 50); TOC/RAF 21.5.43; To M.E. 10.8.43 - SAAF (MTO), No.10 Sqn from 15.6.44; Retd RAF 16.6.44; Later to Turkey 26.4.45

LZ980　Spitfire F.Vc/trop (Merlin 50); TOC/RAF 15.5.43; NWA 7.43 - SAAF (MTO), No.4 Sqn, tailwheel torn off taxying on PSP, Cat.FB/E1 14.2.44 (Lt GV Hardingham), SOC

LZ998　Spitfire F.IXc (Merlin 63); TOC/RAF 13.5.43; NWA 31.7.43 - SAAF (MTO), No.2 Sqn ('DB-C'), damaged Cat.2 27.9.43; Ferry flight, bad visibility, became lost, force-landed in dark near convoy, crashed 15m from Taranto, Cat.FA/E 2.10.43 (Lt A F Allen-White OK), SOC

MA229　Spitfire F.IXc (Merlin 63); Became SAAF No. **5...** (range 5555-5637); TOC/RAF 11.5.43; Arr South Africa, Cape Town (via Birkenhead) 23.2.49 – SAAF; Fate unknown

MA232　Spitfire F.IXc (Merlin 63); Became SAAF No. **55..**

MA237 Spitfire F.IXc (Merlin 63); TOC/RAF 14.5.43; M.E. 8.43 - SAAF (MTO), No.2 Sqn, damaged Cat.2 5.9.43; Retd RAF (RiW); N.A. 11.43; Fate unknown
(range 5502-5554); TOC/RAF 11.5.43; Flown to ME, arr No.15 AD Fayid 11.7.47 – SAAF, Zwartkop Air Station in 9.47; Fate unknown
MA245 Spitfire F.IXc (Merlin 63); TOC/RAF 16.5.43; M.E. 8.43; NAAF 1.11.43 - SAAF (MTO), No.1 Sqn, stbd tyre burst on take-off for weather recce, belly-landed on return, Cat.FB/2 17.3.45 (Lt LN Bulley OK); Accident Cat.E 20.9.45, SOC
MA247 Spitfire F.IXc (Merlin 63); TOC/RAF 16.5.43; NAAF 1.11.43 - SAAF (MTO), No.7 Sqn (date unknown); No.10 Sqn 1943/44; No.1 Sqn ('AX-P') by 8.4.44; FW 190 destroyed April/May 1944 (Lt DM Brebner); Undercarriage leg failed to lower, climbed to 5,000ft and baled out, Cat.E 28.5.44 (Lt CWL Boyd), SOC
MA251 Spitfire F.IXc (Merlin 63); TOC/RAF 16.5.43; M.E. 8.43; NAAF 11.43; French 2.44 - SAAF (MTO), No.1 Sqn, damaged on landing 10.44; Hit by shrapnel, Cat.FB/2 4.12.44 (Lt WA Dowden); Retd RAF; Later to Egypt 26.9.46
MA256 Spitfire F.IXc (Merlin 63); TOC/RAF 21.5.43; M.E. 8.43; No.145 MU, undercarriage collapsed landing on delivery to Sorman West, Cat.B 20.7.43 (Lt JA Kayser) - SAAF (MTO), No.41 Sqn ('E') by 16.4.44; Rev counter unserviceable 22.6.44; No.9 Sqn by 7.44; Retd RAF; Later to Italy 26.6.47
MA257 Spitfire F.IXc (Merlin 63); TOC/RAF 23.5.43; M.E. 8.43 - SAAF (MTO), No.41 Sqn ('X') by 3.44; Ju 88 shot down in sea, shared with LZ894 25.4.44 (Lt AH Hartogh); With Lakatamia dett; Inadvertently hit by fire from Baltimore, Cat.A 15.6.44 (Lt MH Hartogh slightly wounded); Ju 88 damaged, shared with LZ894 11.7.44 (Lt AE Brokensha); Retd RAF; Later to Greece 30.1.47
MA258 Spitfire F.Vc/trop (Merlin 46); TOC/RAF 22.5.43; NWA 10.43 - SAAF (MTO), No.1 Sqn ('AX-Z'), Bf 109G probable 3.11.43 (Lt SJ Richards); Retd RAF; SOC 26.6.47
MA260 Spitfire F.IXc (Merlin 63); TOC/RAF 23.5.43; M.E. 8.43; NAAF 1.11.43 - SAAF (MTO), No.1 Sqn, hit by AA, Cat.FB/Ac 27.6.44 (Lt CWL Boyd); Three direct hits by AA while pulling out of dive, pilot baled out on return journey, Cat.FB/E 8.8.44 (Lt CWL Boyd slightly injured baling out); SOC 31.8.44
MA261 Spitfire F.Vc/trop (Merlin 50); TOC/RAF 15.5.43; M.E. 8.43; NAAF 1.11.43 - SAAF (MTO), No.40 Sqn, landed on by P-47 at Nettuno LG 6.6.44 (Capt RK Dunkerley DoI 11.6.44); Retd RAF for repair; SOC 31.8.44
MA264 Spitfire F.Vc/trop (Merlin 46); TOC/RAF 1.6.43 - SAAF (MTO), No.7 Sqn (engine change 11.12.43); From No.7 Sqn to No.41 Sqn 8.3.44; No.7 Sqn, crashed 40m SE of LG.121, Cat.E 15.3.44 (Lt HD Ratcliff killed), SOC
MA287 Spitfire F.Vc/trop (Merlin 50); TOC/RAF 22.5.43; M.E. 31.8.43 - SAAF (MTO), No.41 Sqn by 8.44 - 10.44; Retd RAF (conv to Mk.Vb 11.45); SOC 29.8.46
MA291 Spitfire F.Vc/trop (Merlin 50); TOC/RAF 20.5.43; NWA 7.43 - SAAF (MTO), No.2 Sqn, ferried Sorman to El Haouaria 19.7.43; No.3 Sqn (date unknown); Retd RAF (later No.32 Sqn, missing 25.8.44, SOC)
MA293 Spitfire F.Vc/trop (Merlin 46); TOC/RAF 25.5.43; M.E. 13.9.43 - SAAF (MTO), No.7 Sqn ('D') by 5.2.44; No.3 Sqn 5.3.44; No.11 Sqn, crashed in Lake Idku, Cat.FB/E2 29.7.44 (2/Lt IA MacKenzie killed), SOC
MA294 Spitfire F.Vc/trop (Merlin 46); TOC/RAF 25.5.43; M.E. 23.8.43; No.1 ADU - SAAF (MTO), fuel shortage on delivery ferry flight to No.7 Sqn, overload tank had fallen off, precautionary landing airfield Zaria, Cat.FA/A 4.9.43 (Lt JE Brand); No.7 Sqn, hit ground at end of runway during attempted slow roll at 250ft over airfield, exploded, burnt out, El Gamil, Cat.FB/E (Cat.3) 3.1.44 (Lt SA Hartley killed); SOC 1.2.44
MA310 Spitfire F.IXc (Merlin 63); TOC/RAF 1.6.43; Casablanca 29.6.43 - SAAF (MTO), No.40 Sqn, landed heavily in cross-wind, wing dropped, undercarriage collapsed, Malignano, Cat.B 17.9.44 (2/Lt JMcL Basson OK); Retd RAF; SOC 31.5.45
MA313 Spitfire F.IXc (Merlin 63); TOC/RAF 6.6.43; M.E. 8.43 - SAAF (MTO), No.1 Sqn ('AX-X'), hit by AA in attack on MT 5m E of Loiano, baled out at 3,500ft 7m NE of Firenzuola, aircraft crashed 15m S of Bologna, Cat.FB/E 23.9.44 (Capt E Wayburne PoW), SOC

Spitfire F.IXc MA313 AX-X of No. 1 Sqn SAAF in mid-1944. [SAAF Museum]

Spitfire F.Vc/trop MA350 served with No. 7 Sqn at Savoia, Libya, around February 1944. Code 'Z', which appears to have been roughly altered to '2', may relate to that period, though by then this aircraft was probably in Sicily or Italy. [J M Bruce/G S Leslie collection]

MA315	Spitfire F.IXc (Merlin 63); TOC/RAF 31.5.43; M.E. 8.43; NAAF 1.11.43 - SAAF (MTO), No.3 Sqn, engine failed, force-landed Rimini, Cat.2 7.11.44 (Lt JH Holton); Retd RAF; Later to Italy (*MM4081*) 27.6.46
MA328	Spitfire F.Vc/trop (Merlin 50); TOC/RAF 24.8.43; NWA 7.43; M.E. 7.43 - SAAF (MTO), No.2 Sqn ('DB-A') by 18.10.43; Hit by AA over Mostar LG, Yugoslavia, Cat.FB/E 29.11.43 (Lt CMD Reitz PoW), SOC
MA337	Spitfire F.Vc/trop (Merlin 50); TOC/RAF in 5.43; NAAF 1.11.43 - SAAF (MTO), No.9 Sqn ('Y'), glycol leak, ditched in lake just short of airfield, nr El Gamil, Cat.FA/E1 21.9.44 (2/Lt MH Pitcher), SOC
MA340	Spitfire F.Vc/trop (Merlin 46); TOC/RAF 6.5.43; NAAF 1.11.43 - SAAF (MTO), No.3 Sqn 25.8.44; Retd RAF (No.4 ADU) 4.9.44; SOC 11.4.46
MA350	Spitfire F.Vc/trop (Merlin 45); TOC/RAF 16.5.43; M.E. 13.12.43 - SAAF (MTO), No.7 Sqn by 4-5.2.44; Retd RAF; SOC 20.8.46
MA351	Spitfire F.Vc/trop (Merlin 46); TOC/RAF 16.5.43; M.E. 28.8.43 - SAAF (MTO), No.7 Sqn by 11.43; No.3 Sqn 5.3.44; Tyre burst on take-off, belly-landed, Cat.FB/2 16.6.44 (Lt AP du Preez); Retd RAF; SOC 4.9.45
MA360	Spitfire F.Vc/trop (Merlin 50); TOC/RAF 6.6.43; M.E. 10.9.43 - SAAF (MTO), No.10 Sqn (date unknown); Retd RAF; SOC 27.6.46
MA403	Spitfire F.IXc (Merlin 63); TOC/RAF 24.5.43; M.E. 9.43 - SAAF (MTO), No.41 Sqn ('L') 1943; Ops 16-20.4.44; Retd RAF (later lost 19.1.45)
MA407	Spitfire F.IXc (Merlin 63); TOC/RAF 26.5.43; M.E. 9.43 - SAAF (MTO), No.41 Sqn ('T') by 16.4.44; Shared Ju 88 damaged with MH786 24.4.44 (Lt JJ de Klerk); Retd RAF (crashed Cat.FA/E 14.3.45); SOC 29.3.45
MA414	Spitfire F.IXc (Merlin 63); TOC/RAF 23.5.43; N.A. 30.11.43; No.4 ADU - SAAF (MTO), No.7 Sqn 19.8.44; Hit petrol bowser taxying Rimini, Cat.FB/2 17.10.44 (Lt EE Stott OK); Retd RAF; SOC 5.6.45
MA424	Spitfire F.IXc (Merlin 63); TOC/RAF 20.7.43; NAASC 31.10.43 - SAAF (MTO), No.2 Sqn, crash landing Rimini, swung off runway, retracted undercarriage on soft ground, Cat.FB/B 7.10.44 (Lt RN du Play OK); Retd RAF; Later to Egypt 26.9.46
MA425	Spitfire F.IXc (Merlin 63); TOC/RAF 21.7.43; N.A. (No. 218 Grp) 30.11.43 - SAAF (MTO), No.1 Sqn ('AX-Y'), failed to return attack on village of Livergnano, near Loiano, seen to burst into flakes just after commencing dive-bombing attack from 8,000ft, probably hit by flak, Cat.FB/E 4.10.44 (Lt TJC Hopkins killed), SOC
MA427	Spitfire F.IXc (Merlin 63); TOC/RAF 21.7.43; M.E. 11.43 - SAAF (MTO), No.10 Sqn from 15.7.44; No.94 Sqn RAF 31.7.44; No.10 Sqn SAAF 27.8.44; Hit by enemy aircraft over Crete, Cat.FB/Ac 7.10.44 (Lt JH du Toit); No.9 Sqn 31.10.44; No.7 Sqn; Retd RAF; Later to Greece 27.3.47
MA451	Spitfire F.IXc (Merlin 63); TOC/RAF 3.6.43; M.E. 8.43; NAAF 1.11.43 - SAAF (MTO), No.7 Sqn, collided with fuel bowser taxying 27.4.44 (Lt JL Spencer); No.59 R&SU; No.4 Sqn (KJ-N') from 16.10.44 until 7.11.44 (Bombing 6.11.44, Lt TF Vollmer); Retd RAF; SOC 6.9.45
MA454	Spitfire F.IXc (Merlin 63); TOC/RAF 8.6.43; M.E. 9.43; NAAF - SAAF (MTO), No.1 Sqn, hit by flak 5m SE of Udine, baled out in Italy, Cat.FB/E 20.2.45 (Capt HT Snyman PoW), SOC
MA469	Spitfire F.IXc (Merlin 63); TOC/RAF 4.6.43; Casablanca 14.7.43; ME 1.9.43 - SAAF (MTO), No.2 Sqn ('DB-Q') by 18.10.43 (NAAF 1.11.43); Retd RAF; Later No.1435 Sqn, Cat.FB/3 17.1.44, SOC
MA474	Spitfire F.IXc (Merlin 63); TOC/RAF 7.6.43; Casablanca 14.7.43 - SAAF (MTO), No.1 Sqn ('AX-A') by 10.43; Forced down Ca311bis with Yugoslavian crew NW of Palata, shared MA475 on 31.10.43 (Lt GT van der Veen); Retd RAF (lost 8.3.44)
MA475	Spitfire F.IXc (Merlin 63); TOC/RAF 1.6.43; M.E. 8.43; NAAF 1.11.43 - SAAF (MTO), No.2 Sqn, damaged Cat.2 4.10.43; No.1 Sqn ('AX-G'), forced down Ca311bis with Yugoslavian crew NW of Palata, shared MA474 31.10.43 (Lt D Tribelhorn); Became lost, ran out of fuel on dive-bombing mission, crash landed 8m S of Ancona 1.9.44, Cat.FB/2 2.9.44 (Lt RD Marshall of No.3 Sqn seriously injured), SOC
MA477	Spitfire F.IXc (Merlin 63); Became SAAF No. **5...** (range 5555-5637); TOC/RAF 31.5.43; Arr South Africa, Cape Town (via Birkenhead) 21.6.48 – SAAF; Fate unknown
MA501	Spitfire F.IXc (Merlin 63); TOC/RAF 11.6.43; M.E. 8.43; NAAF 1.11.43 - SAAF (MTO), No.3 Sqn ('CA-H'), hit tree on approach, went round again, belly-landed, Peretola, Cat.FB/2 7.12.44 (Lt DH Lucas OK); Retd RAF; SOC 30.5.46
MA504	Spitfire F.IXc (Merlin 63); TOC/RAF 13.6.43; M.E. 9.43 - SAAF (MTO), No.10 Sqn from 19.7.44; No.9 Sqn 11.9.44; Retd RAF (No.94 Sqn); SOC 28.2.46

MA506 Spitfire F.IXc (Merlin 63); TOC/RAF 18.8.43; Casablanca 19.10.43; N.A (No.218 Grp) 30.11.43 - SAAF (MTO), No.40 Sqn, hit by AA in Pastorella area, retd to base, Cat.FB/2 11.4.45 (Lt PH Taylor); Retd RAF (RiW); SOC 20.9.45

MA508 Spitfire F.IXc (Merlin 63); TOC/RAF 13.6.43; N.A. 30.11.43 - SAAF (MTO), No.41 Sqn ('Z') by 16-25.4.44; No.94 Sqn RAF; No.10 Sqn SAAF 28.8.44; No.9 Sqn 31.10.44; Stbd tyre burst landing, swung off runway, tipped on nose at Tocra, Cat.A 21.1.45 (Lt KO Embling); Retd RAF; SOC 17.10.45

MA510 Spitfire F.IXc (Merlin 63); TOC/RAF 13.6.43; Casablanca 14.7.43; N.A (No.218 Grp) 30.11.43; USAAF until 29.2.44 - SAAF (MTO), No.1 Sqn, swung landing, hit marker, Cat.Ac 29.6.44 (Lt TJC Hopkins); ROS; Hit by AA, abandoned 30m NNE of Arezzo, Cat.FB/E 3.7.44 (Lt DR Judd killed, grave found 8 months later at Monte Petra, 22m SE of Forli), SOC

MA519 Spitfire F.IXc (Merlin 63); TOC/RAF 17.6.43; Casablanca 14.7.43; M.E. 9.43 - SAAF (MTO), No.2 Sqn, damaged Cat.2 9.9.43; Retd RAF; SOC 8.3.44

MA526 Spitfire F.IXc (Merlin 63); TOC/RAF 12.6.43; NAAF 1.11.43 - SAAF (MTO), No.1 Sqn ('AX-V') 1944; No.10 Sqn from 15.7.44; No.94 Sqn RAF 31.7.44; No.10 Sqn SAAF 27.8.44; Engine cut on reconnaissance mission, force-landed in Crete, Cat.FB/E 16.10.44 (Lt JO Brown picked up unhurt by a Commando unit and retd Sqn 3.11.44), SOC

MA527 Spitfire F.IXc (Merlin 63); TOC/RAF 13.6.43; M.E. 9.43 - SAAF (MTO), No.1 Sqn by 9.9.43; Retd RAF (crashed 19.11.43); SOC 8.3.44

MA529 Spitfire F.IXc (Merlin 63); TOC/RAF 19.6.43; M.E. 9.43; NAAF 1.11.43 - SAAF (MTO), No.1 Sqn ('AX-O') by 9.44; Bf 109 attacked nr Faenza 11.9.44 (Lt JO Newton-Thompson); Dive bombing attack on Barco village, hit by AA, crashed 15m NE of Florence, Cat.FB/E 17.9.44 (Lt GA Roy killed), SOC

MA530 Spitfire F.IXc (Merlin 63); TOC/RAF 19.6.43; M.E. 9.43; NAAF 1.11.43 - SAAF (MTO), No.1 Sqn ('AX-Z'), damaged by debris and ground contact while strafing, then evaded at low level, Cat.FB/Ac 16.10.44 (Lt JBS Ross); Retd RAF; SOC 31.10.46

MA531 Spitfire F.IXc (Merlin 63); TOC/RAF 17.6.43; Casablanca 14.7.43 - SAAF (MTO), No.162 MU to No.2 Sqn 11.8.43; Damaged Cat.2 25.9.43; Retd RAF (No.94 Sqn, lost 28.2.44)

MA532 Spitfire F.IXc (Merlin 63); TOC/RAF 13.6.43; M.E. 8.43; NAAF 1.11.43 - SAAF (MTO), No.1 Sqn ('AX-H':'AX-Z'), Me 410 crashed in flames 8m NE of Modena, shared with EN352 & MH901 10.9.44 (Lt TE Wallace); Accident Cat.1 16.10.44; Retd RAF; Later to Greece 29.5.47

MA541 Spitfire F.IXc (Merlin 63); TOC/RAF 20.6.43; M.E. 9.43; NAAF 1.11.43 - SAAF (MTO), No.1 Sqn, hit by AA, Cat.FB/1 1.12.44 (Lt T Schorn); Repair; No.4 Sqn ('KJ-V') from 19.3.45; Test flown 28.6.45 (Lt Styger); Retd RAF; SOC 6.9.45
NOTE: "MH541" and "ML541" reported for No 4 Sqn.

MA544 Spitfire F.IXc (Merlin 63); TOC/RAF 19.6.43; Casablanca 29.7.43 - SAAF (MTO), No.4 Sqn ('KJ-V') from 20.10.44; Bombing 7.11.44 (Lt McChesney); Retd RAF; SOC 6.9.45

MA545 Spitfire F.IXc (Merlin 63); TOC/RAF 20.6.43; NWA 31.7.43 - SAAF (MTO), No.162 MU to No.2 Sqn 11.8.43; Engine failed on ops, forced landing on airfield, undershot, stalled, heavy landing, undercarriage collapsed at Bari LG, Cat.B 24.9.43 (Mjr TPL Murray DFC); Retd RAF; SOC 15.10.45

MA563 Spitfire F.IXc (Merlin 63); Became SAAF No. 5... (range 5555-5637); TOC/RAF 25.6.43; Arr South Africa, Cape Town (via Birkenhead) 28.9.48 – SAAF; Fate unknown

MA565 Spitfire F.IXc (Merlin 63); TOC/RAF 20.6.43; M.E. 9.43; NAAF 1.11.43 - SAAF (MTO), No.1 Sqn ('AX-6'), Ju 88 damaged (W/O R Fry of High Altitude Flight attd No.1 Sqn); No.40 Sqn, hit by AA in Argenta area, abandoned, Cat.FB/E 5.3.45 (Lt W S Parker PoW), SOC

Spitfire F.IXc MA506 of No. 40 Sqn returned safely to its base at Forli after being hit by AA in the Pastorella area on 11th April 1945, piloted by Lt P H Taylor.

MA587 Spitfire F.IXc (Merlin 63); Became SAAF No. **55..** (range 5502-5554); TOC/RAF 24.6.43; Flown to ME, arr No.15 AD Fayid 20.11.47 – SAAF, Zwartkop Air Station 1947; Fate unknown

MA588 Spitfire F.IXc (Merlin 63); TOC/RAF 27.6.43; Casablanca 29.7.43 - SAAF (MTO), No.10 Sqn from 15.7.44; No.94 Sqn RAF 31.7.44; No.10 Sqn SAAF 28.8.44; Failed to lock down undercarriage, Idku 2.9.44 (2/Lt L de Klerk); No.103 MU 2.9.44; No.109 MU, to No.10 Sqn SAAF 9.44; No.9 Sqn 31.10.44; Retd RAF (No.94 Sqn); SOC 31.7.47

MA589 Spitfire F.IXc (Merlin 63); TOC/RAF 24.6.43; Casablanca 29.7.43 - ME 1.9.43 - SAAF (MTO), No.2 Sqn ('DB-H') by 18.10.43; Retd RAF (NAAF) 1.11.43; Later No.43 Sqn, failed to return ops, Cat.FB/E 22.1.44, SOC

MA592 Spitfire F.IXc (Merlin 63); Became SAAF No. **5...** (range 5555-5637); TOC/RAF 26.6.43; Arr South Africa, Cape Town (via Birkenhead) 20.7.48 – SAAF; Fate unknown

MA593 Spitfire F.IXc (Merlin 63); Became SAAF No. **5...** (range 5555-5637); TOC/RAF 26.6.43; Arr South Africa, Cape Town (via Birkenhead) 26.9.48 – SAAF; Fate unknown

MA619 Spitfire F.IXc (Merlin 63); TOC/RAF 27.6.43; M.E. 9.43; NAAF 1.11.43 - SAAF (MTO), No.1 Sqn, hit by AA in Mont Selice area, Cat.FB/Ac 19.3.45 (Lt WA Dowden); Retd RAF; SOC 11.4.46

MA628 Spitfire F.IXc (Merlin 63); Became SAAF No. **5...** (range 5555-5637); TOC/RAF 6.8.43; Arr South Africa, Cape Town (via Birkenhead despatched. Durban) 15.9.48 – SAAF; Fate unknown

MA638 Spitfire F.IXc (Merlin 63); TOC/RAF 30.6.43; N.A. (No.218 Grp) 30.11.43 - SAAF (MTO), No.1 Sqn ('AX-C'), attacked gun positions 7m W of Cesana, light and heavy AA, flicked into spin pulling out of dive, crashed Cat.FB/E 20.10.44 (Lt HM Fisher killed), SOC

MA640 Spitfire F.IXc (Merlin 63); TOC/RAF 30.6.43; NWA 10.43 - SAAF (MTO), No.7 Sqn, shot down by enemy, failed to return ground attack mission, Cat.FB/E 2.12.44 (Capt HG Nisbet PoW); SOC 31.1.45

MA643 Spitfire F.Vc/trop (Merlin 50); TOC/RAF 21.5.43; NWA 7.43 - SAAF (MTO), No.1 Sqn, ground collision, unable to taxi out of way of landing aircraft, brake failure, Lentini East, Cat.Ac 26.7.43 (Mjr JM Faure); ROS; No.4 Sqn, hit by flak, force-landed wheels down in field SE of Termoli, Cat.FB/2 8.11.43 (Lt GW Pitout unhurt); Retd RAF (RiW); SOC 29.8.46

MA682 Spitfire F.Vc/trop (Merlin 50); TOC/RAF 22.6.43; M.E. 9.43; NAASC 31.10.43 - SAAF (MTO), No.4 Sqn (fighter-bomber) until retd RAF (No.59 R&SU) 30.3.44; Back to No.4 Sqn until retd RAF (No.59 R&SU) 25.4.44; SOC 29.8.46

MA687 Spitfire F.IXc (Merlin 63); TOC/RAF 23.8.43; ex No.93 Sqn - SAAF (MTO), No.7 Sqn from 18.7.44 (silver overall); Damaged at dispersal when bomb fell from BS309 (No.1 Sqn) on take-off at Forli, Cat.FB/2 14.12.44; Retd RAF; SOC 2.8.45

MA706 Spitfire F.IXc (Merlin 63); TOC/RAF 30.6.43; Casablanca 29.7.43 - SAAF (MTO), No.40 Sqn, lost in bad weather, fuel shortage, precautionary landing, overturned, Reggio, Cat.FB/2 26.4.45 (Lt PJE Luyt OK); Retd RAF; SOC 30.8.45

MA708 Spitfire F.IXc (Merlin 63); TOC/RAF 30.6.43; NWA 10.43; No.4 ADU - SAAF (MTO), No.117 MU to No.4 Sqn ('KJ-C') 5.9.44; Run into from behind by MH556 while taxying out for take-off, Forli, Cat.Ac 3.3.45 (Lt J Pollock OK); Offensive Patrol 6.3.45 (Lt HA Carter); Retd RAF 6.3.45; SOC 12.7.45

MA728 Spitfire F.IXc (Merlin 63A); TOC/RAF 3.7.43; M.E. 31.12.43 - SAAF (MTO), No.7 Sqn, hit by small arms fire, retd to base, Cat.FB/A 3.1.45 (Lt HB Potter); Hit by flak, force-landed, crashed 3m NW of Monselice, Cat.FB/E2 28.1.45 (Lt CC Schoombie PoW), SOC

MA729 Spitfire F.IXc (Merlin 63); TOC/RAF 1.7.43; N.A. 30.11.43 - SAAF (MTO), No.4 Sqn ('KJ-W'), engine caught fire on starting up, Bellaria, Cat.Ac 14.11.44 (Lt RG Bosch OK); Retd RAF (R&SU); SOC 9.8.45

MA732 Spitfire F.IXc (Merlin 63A); TOC/RAF 3.7.43; N.A. 30.11.43 - SAAF (MTO), No.41 Sqn ('T') by 16.4.44; Engine cutting out, landed OK 22.6.44; Retd RAF; No.9 Sqn SAAF, test flight, tyre burst on take-off, overturned in soft sand at El Gamil, Cat.FB/2 13.7.44 (Capt CR Sinclair); Retd RAF; SOC 30.11.44

MA736 Spitfire F.IXc (Merlin 63); TOC/RAF 3.7.43; Casablanca 29.7.43 - SAAF (MTO), No.40 Sqn, collided with EF705 landing from opposite direction at Forli, Cat.FB/E 13.2.45 (Capt DP Young OK); SOC (MAAF) 2.8.45

MA745 Spitfire F.IXc (Merlin 63); TOC/RAF 3.7.43; NWA 10.43 - SAAF (MTO), No.40 Sqn, undercarriage trouble landing, port oleo collapsed, hit bank at edge of runway at Forli, Cat.FB/B 17.1.45 (Lt EG Dowell OK); Retd RAF; SOC 9.8.45

MA746 Spitfire F.IXc (Merlin 61); TOC/RAF 4.7.43; Casablanca 16.8.43; N.A (No.218 Grp) 30.11.43 - SAAF (MTO), No.1 Sqn, hit by AA while strafing E of Bologna, belly-landed Basu, Cat.FB/2 16.8.44 (Lt HP Freeman severely wounded); Retd RAF (RiW); SOC 2.8.45

MA752 Spitfire LF.IXc (Merlin 66); TOC/RAF 14.1.44 - SAAF (MTO), No.4 Sqn ('KJ-R') from 24.5.44; Lost height, engine caught fire, propeller ran away, abandoned safely, Cat.FB/3 26.5.44 (Lt HC Chandler minor injuries), SOC

MA756 Spitfire F.IXc (Merlin 63); Became SAAF No. **5509**; TOC/RAF 17.7.43; Flown to ME, arr No.15 AD Fayid 18.6.47 – SAAF, Zwartkop Air Station in 8.47; No.35 Sqn, undercarriage collapsed landing, Cat.2 3.3.49 (Lt Morrison); R&SU; b.o.s. 16.4.52; FC 7.1.53; SOC 24.5.53; No.15 AD in 6.54

MA761 Spitfire F.IXc (Merlin 63); TOC/RAF 18.7.43; N.A. 11.43 - SAAF (MTO), No.117 MU to No.4 Sqn ('KJ-A') 28.5.44; Hit by AA, propeller & mainplane damaged, Cat.FB/A 13.7.44 (Lt TF Vollmer); No.2 (SA) R&SU 15.7.44 (repair mainplane damage); Retd No.4 Sqn 21.7.44; Hit tree after strafing, climbed to safe height, baled out 1m S of Bibbienna, aircraft crashed in flames, Cat.FB/E2 17.8.44 (Lt JJ Booyens landed safely in vineyard, PoW), SOC

MA765 Spitfire F.IXc (Merlin 63); TOC/RAF 18.7.43; Casablanca 18.8.43; NWA; ex USAAF 1.10.43 - SAAF (MTO), No.3 Sqn, engine cut on armed recce, forced landing wheels-up on unused strip due to burst tyre on take-off, Piagiolino, Cat.FB/2 15.10.44 (Lt OEG Bezuindenhout OK); Retd RAF; No.357 Sqn, to No.2 Sqn SAAF ('DB-S') 21.3.45; Port tyre burst on take-off, stbd tyre burst landing, tipped on nose, Ravenna, Cat.FB/2 12.5.45 (Lt DR Phelan OK); To No.7 Wing SAAF 12.5.45; Retd RAF; SOC 6.9.45

MA793 Spitfire F.IXc (Merlin 63); Became SAAF No. **5601**; TOC/RAF 19.7.43; Arr South Africa, Cape Town 26.9.48 - SAAF (no details of service); SOC 14.10.49; Meerhof School, Johannesburg (plaything) 1954 until 1967; To Larry Barnett & Alan Lurie, Johannesburg in 8.69 and restored; ff 29.9.75 at Johannesburg - Jan Smuts marked as "PT672", with code "WR-RR" and name "*Evelyn*"; Waterkloof AFB 10.6.76; Zwartkop AFB 6.3.79; Loaned to the museum facility at Lanseria airport, nr Johannesburg (parts to PT672); To USA 4.87; Now in Brazil - **SURVIVOR**

MA797 Spitfire F.IXc (Merlin 63); TOC/RAF 18.7.43; N.A. (No.218 Grp) 30.11.43 - SAAF (MTO), No.41 Sqn; Fate unknown
NOTE: Reported as "MA791", but that served over ETO

MA801 Spitfire F.IXc (Merlin 63); TOC/RAF 20.7.43; N.A. 30.11.43 - SAAF (MTO), No.1 Sqn ('AX-M', named

Surviving Spitfire F.IX 5601 (ex MA793) marked as "PT672", with code "WR-RR" and named "Evelyn" is here seen at Lanseria airport, nr Johannesburg in July 1981. It is now in Brazil. [PRA]

'*MAUD*'), hit by AA 5m NE of Godiloro, Cat.FB/Ac 10.3.45 (Lt GD Doveton); Shot down by flak in attack on MT near Polesella (10m NE of Ferrara), baled out at 500ft, Cat.FB/E 22.3.45 (Lt WA Dowden PoW unhurt), SOC

MA805   Spitfire F.IXc (Merlin 63); TOC/RAF 21.7.43; N.A. 30.11.43 - SAAF (MTO), No.1 Sqn ('AX-L'), hit by flak, crash-landed 10m W of Bologna, Cat.FB/E 22 or 27.8.44 (Lt S Schneider slightly injured, evaded capture and joined partisans, later killed in action in Bologna using the name *John Klem* - his aircraft was destroyed by a No.7 Sqn strafing mission), SOC

MA815   Spitfire F.IXc (Merlin 63); Became SAAF No. **55..** (range 5502-5554); TOC/RAF 25.7.43; Flown to ME, arr No.15 AD Fayid 25.9.47 – SAAF, Zwartkop Air Station 1947; Fate unknown

MA849   Spitfire F.IXc (Merlin 63); Became SAAF No. **5...** (range 5555-5637); TOC/RAF 28.7.43; Arr South Africa, Cape Town (via Birkenhead) 11.5.48 – SAAF; Fate unknown

MA853   Spitfire F.Vc/trop (Merlin 50); TOC/RAF 27.6.43 - SAAF (MTO), No.4 Sqn, as fighter-bomber (date unknown); No.7 Wing, Sweep Leader (personal code '*DUT*', personal aircraft of CO, Lt Col SF du Toit by 12.43); No.4 Sqn, retd RAF (No.208 Sqn) 25.4.44; SOC 26.4.45

MA856   Spitfire LF.Vc/trop (Merlin 55M); TOC/RAF 7.43; NWA 10.43 - SAAF (MTO), No.2 Sqn ('DB-Y') by 12.43; Retd RAF; No.4 Sqn SAAF by 3.44; To 80hrs inspection 15.4.44; Retd RAF (No.208 Sqn) 25.4.44; SOC 27.6.46

MA877   Spitfire F.Vc (Merlin 55); TOC/RAF 17.7.43; NWA 10.43 - SAAF (MTO), No.4 Sqn, damaged Cat.2 11.11.43; Hit by flak at Tollo, belly-landed, overturned near Sangro, Cat.FB/3 30.12.43 (Capt WJ Wheeler injured), SOC

MA894   Spitfire F.Vc/trop (Merlin 55); TOC/RAF 24.7.43; Casablanca 8.43; N.A. 30.11.43 - SAAF (MTO), No.40 Sqn, ran short of fuel on ferry flight in bad weather, belly-landed on disused airstrip on island of Zante, Cat.FA/B 10.12.44 (Lt RT Joyner OK); Fate unknown

MA896   Spitfire F.Vc/trop (Merlin 50); TOC/RAF 15.8.43; Casablanca 20.9.43; N.A. 30.11.43 - SAAF (MTO), No.2 Sqn ('DB-Q') by 12.43; Retd RAF; SOC 26.4.45

MA904   Spitfire F.Vc/trop (Merlin 50A); TOC/RAF 29.6.43; N.A. 30.11.43 - SAAF (MTO), No.1 Sqn by 10.44 (major inspection); Retd RAF; Later to Greece 25.4.46

MB888   Spitfire PR.XI (Merlin 63); TOC/RAF 20.8.43; N.W.A. 1.10.43 - SAAF (MTO), No.40 Sqn from 5.9.45; To No.8 ARD 21.9.45 (mainplane and engine change); Retd RAF; SOC 28.2.46

MB938   Spitfire PR.XI (Merlin 63); TOC/RAF 26.9.43; M.A.C. 10.43; No.8 ARD - SAAF (MTO), No.40 Sqn from 1.10.45; Retd RAF; SOC 29 5.47

MH332   Spitfire F.IXc (Merlin 61); Became SAAF No. **55..** (range 5502-5554); TOC/RAF 9.8.43; Flown to ME, arr No.15 AD Fayid 22.8.47 – SAAF, Zwartkop Air Station 1947; Fate unknown

MH355   Spitfire F.IXc (Merlin 61); Became SAAF No. **5...** (range 5555-5637); TOC/RAF 31.7.43; Arr South Africa, Cape Town (via Birkenhead) 17.3.49 – SAAF; Fate unknown

MH373   Spitfire F.IXc (Merlin 63); Became SAAF No. **55..** (range 5502-5554); TOC/RAF 5.8.43; Flown to ME, arr No.15 AD Fayid 18.6.47 – SAAF, Zwartkop Air Station in 8.47; Fate unknown

MH380   Spitfire F.IXc (Merlin 63); Became SAAF No. **55..** (range 5502-5554); TOC/RAF 9.8.43; Flown to ME, arr No.15 AD Fayid 20.9.47 – SAAF, Zwartkop Air Station 1947; Fate unknown

MH444   Spitfire LF.IXc (Merlin 66); TOC/RAF 15.8.43; NAASC 31.10.43, ex USAAF 31.1.44 - SAAF (MTO), No.3 Sqn ('CA-H') by 12.44; Shot down by flak attacking MT, Cat.FB/E 20.2.45 (Lt MFW Austin killed), SOC

MH499   Spitfire LF IXc (Merlin 66); TOC/RAF 19.8.43; MAAF 26.2.45 - SAAF (MTO), No.3 Sqn, hit by AA, Cat. FB/Ac 17.4.45 (Lt RO Petit); Retd RAF; SOC 26.9.46

MH511   Spitfire LF.IXc (Merlin 66); TOC/RAF 22.8.43; NAASC 31.10.43 - SAAF (MTO), No.4 Sqn as fighter-bomber ('KJ-A') by 7.5.44; Hit by flak, glycol leak, Cat.FB/2 26.5.44 (Lt JJ Booyens); Retd RAF (No.59

MH530 Spitfire LF.IXc (Merlin 66); TOC/RAF 22.8.43; NAASC 31.10.43; No.4 FU - SAAF (MTO), No.1 Sqn ('AX-X') by 15.12.44; Hit by AA nr Rovigo 11.1.45 (Lt LH Brown); Retd RAF; SOC 13.9.45

R&SU) 27.5.44; No.4 Sqn ('KJ-M') 3.6.44; Lost wheel on take-off, landed undercarriage up on return from op, Cat.FB/2 18.7.44 (Lt HC Chandler); Retd RAF (No.59 R&SU) 20.7.44; SOC 5.6.45

MH536 Spitfire LF.IXc (Merlin 66); TOC/RAF 23.8.43; NAASC 31.10.43 - SAAF (MTO), No.117 MU to No.4 Sqn 25.4.44; Undercarriage failed to lock down, collapsed taxying after landing, Cat.2 14.6.44 (Lt MWV Odendaal OK); Re-Cat.E 16.6.44 (bboc); No.40 Sqn, army co-op recce, hit by AA, forced landing nr Forli, Cat.FB/E 24.10.44 (Lt ARS Dorning PoW); Salvaged by No.59 R&SU; SOC 19.7.45

MH537 Spitfire LF.IXc (Merlin 66); TOC/RAF 22.8.43; NAASC 31.10.43 - SAAF (MTO), No.3 Sqn, to No.7 Sqn 5.3.44; No.136 MU for long range mods 16.3.44; No.4 Sqn ('KJ-Q') 19.7.44; Failed to return attack on shipping weather reconnaissance on River Po, believed fuel shortage after hit by AA, Cat.FB/E2 5.8.44 (Lt BD Jenkins killed), SOC

MH540 Spitfire LF.IXc (Merlin 66); TOC/RAF 26.8.43; NAASC 31.10.43 - SAAF (MTO), No.7 Sqn, failed to return, hit by flak in San Lorenzo de Vallo area/4m S of Zagreb, Cat.FB/E 2.5.45 (Lt JCG Logan PoW); SOC 31.5.45

MH544 Spitfire F.IXc (Merlin 63); TOC/RAF 27.8.43; NAASC 31.10.43 - SAAF (MTO), No.357 MU to No.2 Sqn ('DB-Z') 5.1.45; No.7 Wing for overhaul 14.4.45; No.1 Sqn, unable to lower undercarriage landing at dusk, engine cut on second circuit, short of fuel, belly-landed, Cat.B, Ravenna 24.4.45 (Capt PCW England); To No.7 Wing for repair 24.4.45; Retd RAF; SOC 30.8.45

MH548 Spitfire LF.IXc (Merlin 66); TOC/RAF 24.8.43; NAASC 10.43 - SAAF (MTO), No.3 Sqn, to No.7 Sqn ('TJ-D') 5.3.44 to at least 25.4.44; No.4 Sqn ('KJ-O') from or by 31.7.44; Damaged by flak attacking MT, glycol leak, abandoned, aircraft crashed in flames, Cat.FB/E 25.8.44 (Lt EDK Franck landed safely, retd Sqn after 14 days), SOC

MH549 Spitfire LF.IXc (Merlin 66); TOC/RAF 23.8.43; NAASC 31.10.43 - SAAF (MTO), No.41 Sqn, to No.7 Sqn 8.3.44; No.136 MU for long range mods 11.3.44; Hit by AA 27.5.44 (Capt GR Connell); Retd RAF (No.59 R&SU); SOC 15.3.45

MH550 Spitfire LF(FR).IXc (Merlin 66); TOC/RAF 27.8.43; NAASC 31.10.43 - SAAF (MTO), No.40 Sqn ('WR-K') by 5.9.45; SOC 6.9.45

MH551 Spitfire F.IXc (Merlin 63); TOC/RAF 27.8.43; NAASC 31.10.43 - SAAF (MTO), No.9 Sqn, while ferrying, swung off runway into soft ground, pecked, Mariut, Cat.FA/Ac 25.1.45 (Lt B Doyle OK); Retd RAF; SOC 31.1.46

MH552 Spitfire F.IXc (Merlin 63); TOC/RAF 29.8.43; Casablanca 6.4.44 - SAAF (MTO), No.1 Sqn ('AX-H'), damaged Cat.1 12.10.44; Retd RAF; SOC 24.6.48

MH554 Spitfire LF.IXc (Merlin 66); TOC/RAF 24.8.43; NAASC 31.10.43 - SAAF (MTO), No.3 Sqn, to No.7 Sqn 5.3.44; No.136 MU for long range mods 11.3.44; Hit by vehicle during night, Cat.FA/E (DBR) 5.6.45, SOC

MH556 Spitfire F.IXc (Merlin 63); TOC/RAF 29.8.43; Casablanca 12.43 - SAAF (MTO), No.4 Sqn ('KJ-A') by 11.1.45; Ran into MA708 in front while taxying out, Forli, Cat.B 3.3.45 (Lt JG Segalla OK); Bombing, hit by MG fire, engine failed, abandoned safely near Lake Commachio, Cat.FB/E2 20.3.45 (Lt DJ Taylor evaded capture), SOC

MH557 Spitfire F.IXc (Merlin 66); TOC/RAF 24.8.43; NAASC 31.10.43 - SAAF (MTO), No.357 MU to No.2 Sqn ('DB-E') 13.12.44; Glycol system hit by AA, pilot believed baled out too low, aircraft crashed in River Montone, E of San Michele, Cat.FB/E 28.12.44 (Lt M Flynn killed), SOC

MH558 Spitfire F.IXc (Merlin 63); TOC/RAF 29.8.43; NAASC 31.10.43; No.94 Sqn - SAAF (MTO), No.10 Sqn 28.8.44; Damaged by enemy aircraft, Cat.FB/Ac 7.10.44 (Lt TR Fryer); No.136 MU for repair 7.10.44;

Spitfire F.IXc MH558 A of either No. 9 or No. 10 Sqn SAAF on its nose around 1945. [SAAF Museum]

MH563	Retd No.10 Sqn; No.9 Sqn 31.10.44; Swung landing, port oleo collapsed, El Gamil, Cat.A 18.1.45 (Lt FM Carrington OK); No.1 Sqn (date unknown); Retd RAF; Later to Greece 31.7.47
MH563	Spitfire F.IXc (Merlin 63); TOC/RAF 27.8.43; NAASC 10.43 - SAAF (MTO), No.7 Sqn from 19.7.44; Hit by flak, Cat.A 15.8.44; Armed reconnaissance, shot down by flak nr Pontepetri/E of San Marcello, Cat.FB/E 2.9.44 (Lt SP Griessel baled out but killed), SOC
MH582	Spitfire LF Vc/trop (Merlin 55M); TOC/RAF 30.7.43; N.A. 30.11.43 - SAAF (MTO), No.10 Sqn, swung landing, ran off runway 12.6.44 (Lt JJ Roelofse); Retd RAF; Later to Egypt 29.3.45
MH584	Spitfire F.Vc/trop (Merlin 55M); TOC/RAF 20.7.43; NAASC 31.10.43 - SAAF (MTO), No.3 Sqn ('CA-J') by 3.45 - 5.45; SOC 26.4.45 NOTE: Reported "MH444" for No.3 Sqn
MH592	Spitfire F.Vc/trop (Merlin 55); TOC/RAF 14.8.43; Casablanca 10.10.43; NAASC 31.10.43 - SAAF (MTO), No.41 Sqn by 4.44 - 5.44, R/T failure 21.4.44; Retd RAF; Later to Yugoslavia (No.9486) 18.5.45
MH600	Spitfire F.Vc/trop (Merlin 55); TOC/RAF 22.8.43; NAASC 31.10.43 - SAAF (MTO), No.2 Sqn ('DB-B'), flak damage, Cat.1 10.12.43 (Capt WAT Johl); Retd RAF; No.4 Sqn SAAF as fighter-bomber (date unknown); Retd RAF (No.208 Sqn) 25.4.44; SOC 26.4.45
MH603	Spitfire F.IXc (Merlin 63); Became SAAF No. 5... (range 5555-5637); TOC/RAF 15.10.43; Arr South Africa, Cape Town (via Birkenhead) 10.3.49 – SAAF; Service unknown; Ysterplaat AFB; Scrapyard Cape Town; SAAF Museum storage Snake Valley; Major parts to John Sykes, Oxford, England in 1989; To USA (Joe Scogna, Fort Collins, Colorado) in 1993; Restoration to fly - **SURVIVOR**
MH605	Spitfire F.IXc (Merlin 63); TOC/RAF 29.8.43; NAASC 31.10.43; ex USAAF 31.12.43 - SAAF (MTO), No.1 Sqn, swung into soft sand on landing, overturned Ravenna, Cat.E 22.4.45 (Lt I Rowden OK); SOC 19.7.45
MH606	Spitfire F.IXc (Merlin 63); Became SAAF No. 5... (range 5555-5637); TOC/RAF 7.10.43; Arr South Africa, Cape Town (via Birkenhead) 26.9.48 – SAAF; Fate unknown
MH609	Spitfire F.IXc (Merlin 63); TOC/RAF 3.9.43; Casablanca 10.10.43; NAASC 31.10.43 - SAAF (MTO), No.1 Sqn, hit by AA, belly landing 3m N of Pierantonio, nr Perugia, FB/E 27.6.44 (Lt JR Spencer); SOC 30.6.44
MH612	Spitfire LF.IXc (Merlin 66); TOC/RAF 22.8.43; NAASC 31.10.43 - SAAF (MTO), No.3 Sqn ('CA-F'), Ju 88 crashed and burst into flames 12m SE of Derna, shared with MH971, own aircraft hit by 13mm bullet, Cat.FB/1 29.2.44 (Lt HTR du Preez); No.7 Sqn ('TJ-F') 5.3.44; Crash-landed near Callefagato, Cat.FB/3 13.5.44 (2/Lt WL Strong PoW), SOC
MH613	Spitfire LF.IXc (Merlin 66); TOC/RAF 22.8.43; Casablanca 29.9.43; NAASC 31.10.43 - SAAF (MTO), No.2 Sqn ('DB-Q') c.11.44; To No.110 MU 31.12.44; Retd No.2 Sqn by 2.45; Retd RAF; SOC 30.8.45
MH614	Spitfire LF.IXc (Merlin 63); TOC/RAF 23.8.43; NAASC 31.10.43 - SAAF (MTO), No.7 Sqn from 19.7.44; Damaged when hit runway indicator landing from op, Foiano LG, Cat.FB/Ac 29.8.44 (Lt BN Ackerman); ROS; Hit by flak, new stbd wing fitted 5.9.44 (Lt AW Allen); While stationery, hit by MJ506 of No.40 Sqn at Rimini 12.10.44; ROS; Retd RAF (No.5 RFU); SOC 19.11.44
MH619	Spitfire F.IXc (Merlin 63); TOC/RAF 14.9.43; N.A. 30.11.43 - SAAF (MTO), No.1 Sqn, port oleo collapsed in heavy landing, Foiano, Cat.Ac 1.9.44 (Lt GA Roy OK); Retd RAF; Later to Italy (*MM4046*) 26.6.47
MH621	Spitfire LF.IXc (Merlin 66); TOC/RAF 31.8.43; Casablanca 10.10.43; NAASC 31.10.43 - SAAF (MTO), No.2 Sqn ('DB-P') 11.44; Retd RAF (No.110 MU for engine change) 23.2.45; Later to Italy (*MM4047*) 30.5.46
MH635	Spitfire F.IXc (Merlin 63); TOC/RAF 11.9.43; Casablanca 19.10.43; N.A. 30.11.43 - SAAF (MTO), No.2 Sqn ('DB-E') c.11.44; No.5 RFU 11.12.44; Retd No.2 Sqn by 2.45; Retd RAF; Later to Italy (*MM4052*) 26.6.47
MH657	Spitfire F.IXc (Merlin 63); TOC/RAF 2.9.43; NAASC 31.10.43 - SAAF (MTO), No.7 Sqn, crashed Cat.FB/3 27.1.44; R&SU; No.7 Sqn, hit by flak, abandoned near Ravenna/Forli Cat.FB/E 3.1.45 (Lt AL Basson retd OK), SOC
MH658	Spitfire F.IXc (Merlin 63); TOC/RAF 2.9.43; NAASC 31.10.43 - SAAF (MTO), No.7 Sqn 13.12.44; Hit by flak Castel Bolognese, crash-landed Forli, Cat.FB/2 21.2.45 (Lt N Bremner OK); Retd RAF, not repaired, SOC 30.8.45
MH663	Spitfire F.IXc (Merlin 63); Became SAAF No. **5**... (range 5555-5637); TOC/RAF 5.9.43; Arr South Africa, Cape Town (via Birkenhead) 13.3.49 – SAAF; Fate unknown
MH664	Spitfire LF.IXc (Merlin 66); TOC/RAF 5.9.43; Casablanca 17.2.44 - SAAF (MTO), No.1 Sqn, bombing attack on gun positions 4m NW of Traversa, radioed petrol in cockpit, climbed to 6,000ft, apparently overcome by fumes, seen to peel off to port and dive in 20m NNE of Florence, burnt out, Cat.FB/E 17.9.44 (Lt DP Farrell killed), SOC
MH674	Spitfire F.IXc (Merlin 63); Became SAAF No. **55**.. (range 5502-5554); TOC/RAF 9.9.43; Flown to ME, arr No.15 AD Fayid 18.6.47 - SAAF, Zwartkop Air Station in 8.47; Fate unknown
MH692	Spitfire F.IXc (Merlin 63); Became SAAF No. **5**... (range 5555-5637); TOC/RAF 10.9.43; Arr South Africa, Cape Town (via Birkenhead) 26.11.48 – SAAF; Fate unknown
MH694	Spitfire F.IXc (Merlin 63A); Became SAAF No. **5**... (range 5555-5637); TOC/RAF 10.9.43; Arr South Africa, Cape Town (via Birkenhead) 16.11.48 – SAAF; Fate unknown
MH698	Spitfire F.IXc (Merlin 63); TOC/RAF 10.9.43; N.A. 30.11.43 - SAAF (MTO), No.10 Sqn 27.8.44; No.9 Sqn, Engine lost power on take-off, sank back, belly-landed El Gamil, Cat.Ac 10.9.44 (Mjr CJO Swales of No.10 Sqn injured); Retd RAF (No.103 MU) 11.9.44; Later to Greece 27.3.45
MH703	Spitfire F.IXc (Merlin 63); TOC/RAF 14.9.43; N.A. 30.11.43 - SAAF (MTO), No.10 Sqn (date unknown); Retd RAF (crashed 5.5.44); SOC 29.6.44
MH705	Spitfire F.IXc (Merlin 63); TOC/RAF 14.9.43; N.A. 30.11.43 - SAAF (MTO), No.10 Sqn 27.8.44; No.9 Sqn 31.10.44; Engine failed on return from strafing op to Crete, baled out at 4,000ft 100m N of Derna, Cat.E 4.12.44 (Lt KEF George seen in dinghy but never picked up despite search), SOC
MH711	Spitfire F.IXc (Merlin 63); TOC/RAF 14.9.43; NAASC 31.10.43; ex USAAF 31.1.44 - SAAF (MTO), No.1 Sqn, reported smoke in cockpit after attack on lorries, failed to bale out, dived in vertically and broke up 9m NE of Bologna, Cat.FB/E 23.1.45 (Lt CWL Boyd killed, buried Bentivolglio cemetery); SOC 25.2.45
MH715	Spitfire LF.IXc (Merlin 66); TOC/RAF 15.9.43; MAAF 24.4.45 - SAAF (MTO); No.357 MU to No.2 Sqn 26.4.45; SOC 13.5.48 NOTE: Allocated for Egypt 4.47, but remained in storage
MH736	Spitfire LF.IXc (Merlin 66); TOC/RAF 16.9.43; Casablanca 1.45 - SAAF (MTO), No.3 Sqn ('CA-R') by 4.45-5.45; Damaged on armed recce, Cat.FB/1 12.4.45; Retd RAF; Later to Egypt 31.10.46
MH751	Spitfire LF.IXc (Merlin 66); TOC/RAF 19.9.43 - SAAF (MTO), No.117 MU to No.4 Sqn 28.5.44; Retd RAF (later missing 25.9.44, SOC) NOTE: Reported also "MH761"

MH752	Spitfire LF.IXc (Merlin 66); TOC/RAF 18.9.43; N.A. 30.11.43 - SAAF (MTO), No.41 Sqn, to No.7 Sqn 8.3.44; Bomb failed to release, aircraft overstressed 25.5.44 (Lt JC Beddell); No.3 Sqn, damaged in attack on buildings, Cat.FB/1 16.4.45; Retd RAF; SOC 23.12.45
MH755	Spitfire LF.IXc (Merlin 66); TOC/RAF 18.9.43; N.A. 30.11.43 - SAAF (MTO), No.4 Sqn ('KJ-A'); No.2 Sqn ('DB-E') 5.44; Hit by AA, landed at base undercarriage up, Cat.FB/2 29.7.44 (Lt JH Meintjies); No.10 Sqn (date unknown); Retd RAF; SOC 13.9.45
MH764	Spitfire LF.IXc (Merlin 66); TOC/RAF 19.9.43; N.A. 30.11.43 - SAAF (MTO), No.3 Sqn, to No.7 Sqn 5.3.44; Hit bump landing, swung, oleo torn off, Cat/B2 8.7.44 (Lt DC Bosch); Retd RAF (R&SU); No.7 Sqn, holed by flak while strafing, Cat.1 4.4.45 (pilot unhurt); Hit by AA, retd to Forli LG, Cat.FB/2 29.4.45 (Lt AT Tennant); Collided with RR190 in formation, baled out, crashed 7m S of Udine, burnt out, Cat.FA/E 15.6.45 (Lt JJ van der Watt OK), SOC
MH765	Spitfire LF.IXc (Merlin 66); TOC/RAF 19.9.43; N.A. 30.11.43 - SAAF (MTO), No.3 Sqn, to No.7 Sqn 5.3.44; Holed in attack on road junction 13.7.44 (Lt DB Tribelhorn); ROS; Grounded after 300hrs 9.9.44 (unfit for further tour, last of No.7 Squadron's original complement with which it arrived in Italy); Retd RAF; SOC 14.3.46
MH771	Spitfire LF.IXc (Merlin 66); TOC/RAF 24.9.43; N.A. 30.11.43 - SAAF (MTO), No.7 Sqn 11.9.44; Damaged by AA, Cat.FB/2 1.4.45 (Lt HG Gericke); Retd RAF; SOC 20.9.45
MH772	Spitfire LF.IXc (Merlin 66); TOC/RAF 19.9.43; Casablanca 17.11.43; N.A. (No.218 Grp) 30.11.43 - SAAF (MTO), No.4 Sqn ('KJ-Z') from 19.1.45; Training flight 28.6.45 (Lt Tatham); Retd RAF; Allotted for Egypt (REAF), but SOC 13.5.45
MH776	Spitfire LF.IXc (Merlin 66); TOC/RAF 22.9.43; N.A. 30.11.43 - SAAF (MTO), No.41 Sqn (possibly 'P'), engine failed, ditched on anti-submarine sweep off Egyptian coast, Cat.FB/E 23.3.44 (Lt A Thomson killed), SOC
MH777	Spitfire LF.IXc (Merlin 66); Became SAAF No. **5...** (range 5555-5637); TOC/RAF 28.9.43; Arr South Africa, Cape Town (via Birkenhead) 26.11.48 – SAAF; Fate unknown
MH780	Spitfire LF.IXc (Merlin 66); TOC/RAF 23.9.43; N.A. 30.11.43 - SAAF (MTO) as fighter-bomber; No.3 Sqn, to No.7 Sqn 5.3.44; No.136 MU for long range mods 15.3.44; No.41 Sqn by 16.4.44; No.7 Sqn, to No.4 Sqn ('KJ-L') 19.7.44; No.59 R&SU 14.9.44; No.4 Sqn, Bombing 3.10.44 (Lt Messo); No.2 Sqn SAAF ('DB-Q') from 24.3.45; To No.7 Wing for engine change 21.5.45; Retd No.2 Sqn 30.5.45-6.45; Retd RAF; SOC 23.8.45
MH784	Spitfire LF.IXc (Merlin 66); TOC/RAF 24.9.43; N.A. 30.11.43 - SAAF (MTO), No.3 Sqn ('CA-D'), overshot landing, tipped on nose, Peretola/Florence, Cat.FB/2 1.12.44 (Lt DIG Gibson OK); Hit by AA, retd to base Cat.FB/Ac 20.1.45 (Lt JS Aberdien); Damaged by AA in attack on bridge, Cat.FB/2 27.2.45 (Lt G Kinsey); No.11 Sqn ('ND-R'); Retd RAF (No.107 MU); SOC 28.8.47 (still coded 'ND-R')
MH786	Spitfire LF.IXc (Merlin 66); TOC/RAF 21.9.43; N.A. 30.11.43 – SAAF (MTO), No.41 Sqn ('K' : 'E') 1943 [possibly from 30.11.43], ops 16-24.4.44; Shared Ju 88 damaged with MA407 24.4.44 (Lt JC Silberbauer); No.4 Sqn (date unknown); No.1 Sqn, hit by AA N of Bologna, Cat.FB/Ac 18.1.45 (Lt GD Doveton); Retd RAF; SOC 18.8.44
MH789	Spitfire LF.IXc (Merlin 66); TOC/RAF 24.9.43; N.A. 30.11.43 - SAAF (MTO), No.40 Sqn by 5.9.45; Forced off peritrack by B-17 taxying in opposite direction, stbd wheel bogged in soft ground, pecked, Ciampino, Cat.Ac 30.9.45 (Lt I Angus Leppan OK); Fate unknown
MH813	Spitfire F.IXc (Merlin 63); TOC/RAF 25.9.43; N.A. 30.11.43 - SAAF (MTO), No.7 Sqn ('TJ-C'), hit by flak W of Florence, engine cut, abandoned aircraft nr Rignano, dived into British lines, Cat.FB/E 12.8.44 (Lt JA Gilbert retd Sqn same day); SOC 31.8.44
MH830	Spitfire F.IXc (Merlin 63); Became SAAF No. **5...** (range 5555-5637); TOC/RAF 28.9.43; Arr South Africa, Cape Town (via Birkenhead) 22.10.48 – SAAF; Fate unknown
MH832	Spitfire F.IXc (Merlin 63); Became SAAF No. **55..** (range 5502-5554); TOC/RAF 1.10.43; Flown to ME, arr No.15 AD Fayid 22.8.47 - SAAF, Zwartkop Air Station 1947; Fate unknown
MH834	Spitfire F.IXc (Merlin 63); TOC/RAF 24.9.43; N.A. (No. 218 Grp) 30.11.43 - SAAF (MTO), No.9 Sqn ('S'), damaged on ground when IFF detonator exploded on test 23.9.44; Fate unknown
MH838	Spitfire F.IXc (Merlin 63A); TOC/RAF 27.9.43; N.A. 30.11.43 - SAAF (MTO), No.10 Sqn 27.8.44; Engine run, tipped on nose then fell back, fuselage buckled at Savoia 6.10.44 (Capt D Herboldt); No.136 MU 6.10.44; No.9 Sqn 31.10.44; Retd RAF (M.E. census 6.45); Later converted to LF.IX 3.8.45
MH851	Spitfire F.IXc (Merlin 63); Became SAAF No. **5...** (range 5555-5637); TOC/RAF 1.10.43; Arr South Africa, Cape Town (via Birkenhead) 11.5.48 – SAAF; Fate unknown
MH855	Spitfire F.IXc (Merlin 63); Became SAAF No. **5...** (range 5555-5637); TOC/RAF 13.10.43; Arr South Africa, Cape Town (via Birkenhead) 3.11.48 – SAAF; Fate unknown
MH869	RegNo: 5555-5637;Spitfire F.IXc (Merlin 63); TOC/RAF 2.10.43; Arr South Africa, Cape Town (via Birkenhead) 21.5.49 - SAAF; Fate unknown
MH871	RegNo: 5555-5637;Spitfire F.IXc (Merlin 63); TOC/RAF 1.10.43; Arr South Africa, Cape Town (via Birkenhead) 11.5.48 - SAAF; Fate unknown
MH875	Spitfire F.IXc (Merlin 63); Became SAAF No. **5...** (range 5555-5637); TOC/RAF 2.10.43; Arr South Africa, Cape Town (via Birkenhead) 21.6.48 - SAAF; Fate unknown
MH876	Spitfire LF.IXc (Merlin 66); Became SAAF No. **55..** (range 5502-5554); TOC/RAF 2.10.43; Flown to ME, arr No.15 AD Fayid 22.8.47 - SAAF, Zwartkop Air Station 1947; Fate unknown
MH889	Spitfire LF.IXc (Merlin 66); TOC/RAF 4.9.43; N.A. 30.11.43; ex USAAF 31.1.44 - SAAF (MTO), No.7 Sqn from 18.7.44; Retd RAF (MAAF, Cat.FA/E 14.2.45)
MH891	Spitfire F.IXc (Merlin 63); TOC/RAF 11.9.43; N.A. 30.11.43 - SAAF (MTO), No.7 Sqn ('H') by 10.44; Damaged by 20mm ball ammo in supercharger while attacking train, landed safely, Cat.FB/Ac 24.10.44 (Lt WF Anderson unhurt); Failed to return close support mission 2m SW of Imola, Cat.FB/E 4.1.45 (Lt RG Whitehorn buried Bologna Empire Cemetery), SOC
MH895	Spitfire F.IXc (Merlin 63); TOC/RAF 11.9.43; N.A. (No.218 Grp) 30.11.43; ex USAAF 31.1.44 - SAAF (MTO), No.1 Sqn ('AX-X') by 12.4.44; Retd RAF (lost 8.2.45)
MH901	Spitfire F.IXc (Merlin 63); TOC/RAF 24.10.43; Casablanca 22.12.43 - SAAF (MTO), No.1 Sqn ('AX-G'), Me 410 crashed in flames 8m NE of Modena, shared with EN352 & MA532 10.9.44 (Capt DM Brebner); Hit by AA, Cat.FB/Ac 22.11.44 (Lt T Mitchell); Engine caught fire starting up Forli, burnt out, Cat.E2 4.1.45 (Lt MHL Tweedie OK), SOC
MH904	Spitfire F.IXc (Merlin 63); TOC/RAF 24.9.43; N.A. (No. 218 Grp) 30.11.43 - SAAF (MTO), No.1 Sqn ('AX-E') by 7.44; Retd RAF (No.93 Sqn, failed to return, Cat.FB/E 18.4.45, SOC)
MH925	Spitfire F.IXc (Merlin 63); TOC/RAF 17.9.43; N.A. (No.218 Grp) 30.11.43 - SAAF (MTO), No.117 MU to No.4 Sqn ('KJ-Y') 26.8.44; Ran off end of runway, tipped up on nose at Forli, Cat.Ac 8.12.44 (Lt MF

Reim); Training flight 13.2.45 (Lt TF Vollmer); No.4 Sqn ('KJ-M') from 20.2.45; Port gun exploded while strafing 15m W of Padua, Cat.FB/Ac 24.3.45 (Lt DJ Murray); Bombing 6.4.45 (Lt Thomson); Retd RAF 6.4.45; SOC 6.9.45

MH930 Spitfire F.IXc (Merlin 63); TOC/RAF 19.9.43 - SAAF (MTO), No.40 Sqn, hit by flak on artillery spotting sortie, crashed NW of Cesenatico, Cat.FB/E 17.10.44 (Lt DGC Cheesman PoW wounded), SOC

MH931 Spitfire F.IXc (Merlin 63); TOC/RAF 19.9.43; N.A. (No. 218 Grp) 30.11.43 - SAAF (MTO), No.41 Sqn by 8.44 (natural metal finish); No.9 Sqn by 7.44 - 9.44; Retd RAF; Later to Egypt 19.8.46
NOTE: Reported also as "MH936", but that served in ETO, later FAF

MH939 Spitfire F.IXc (Merlin 63); Became SAAF No. **55..** (range 5502-5554); TOC/RAF 3.10.43; Flown to ME, arr No.15 AD Fayid 18.6.47 - SAAF, Zwartkop Air Station in 8.47; Fate unknown

MH941 Spitfire LF.IXc (Merlin 66); TOC/RAF 14.1.44 (ETO); Arr MAAF 25.2.45 - SAAF (MTO), No.1 Sqn; No.357 MU, to No.2 Sqn 12.4.45; Hit by 20mm AA 30m NE of Padua, Cat.FB/Ac 29.4.45 (Lt RD Pritchard); No.7 Wing for repair 29.4.45; No.2 Sqn 4.5.45; Retd RAF; SOC 10.5.46

MH944 Spitfire LF.IXc (Merlin 66); TOC/RAF 29.8.44; NAASC 10.43 - SAAF (MTO), No.3 Sqn, to No.7 Sqn ('W') 5.3.44; Stbd wing damaged on runway 25.4.44; Still No.7 Sqn 22.5.44; No.7 Sqn ('TJ-W'), hit by flak and exploded in dive while attacking MT NW of Massa Lombarda, 5m NW of Lugo, Cat.FB/E2 13.4.45 (Lt N Bremner killed), SOC

MH946 Spitfire F.IXc (Merlin 63); TOC/RAF 29.8.43; NAASC 31.10.43; No.94 Sqn - SAAF (MTO), No.9 Sqn 11.8.44; No.10 Sqn 11.9.44 - @13.9.44; Retd RAF; Later as LF IXc (M.66) to Greece 30.1.47
NOTE: Reported also as "MA946"

MH948 Spitfire LF.IXc (Merlin 66); TOC/RAF 30.8.43; NAASC 31.10.43 - SAAF (MTO), No.7 Sqn, accident Cat.FA/3 29.2.44, SOC

MH949 Spitfire F.IXc (Merlin 63); TOC/RAF 27.8.43; NAASC 31.10.43 - SAAF (MTO), No.1 Sqn ('AX-A'), hit by AA and debris while strafing, Cat.2 16.10.44 (Capt RJ Barnwell); While forming up, stbd mainplane hit by EN521, Cat.Ac 24.11.44 (Lt FW Whittaker OK); Retd RAF; SOC 14.3.46

MH951 Spitfire LF.IXc (Merlin 66); TOC/RAF 29.8.43; NAASC 31.10.43 - SAAF (MTO), No.41 Sqn, to No.7 Sqn ('TJ-I') 8.3.44; No.136 MU for long range mods 11-15.3.44; Investigation 4.9.44 (following crash of EN390 revealed crack in pintle pin of undercarriage 1.9.44); Due for MI 19.9.44; No.1 Sqn (date unknown); Retd RAF; SOC 18.10.45

MH952 Spitfire LF.IXc (Merlin 66); TOC/RAF 30.8.43; NAASC 31.10.43 - SAAF (MTO), No.3 Sqn ('CA-B') by 12.44; Hit by AA, Cat.FB/Ac 27.1.45 (Lt G Kinscy); Damaged in attack on gun, Cat.FB/A 18.3.45 (Lt DH Lucas); Retd RAF; SOC 11.4.46

MH953 Spitfire LF.IXc (Merlin 66); TOC/RAF 30.8.43; NAASC 31.10.43 - SAAF (MTO), No.41 Sqn ('P') by 16-22.4.44; Retd RAF; SOC 30.4.47

MH955 Spitfire LF.IXc (Merlin 66); TOC/RAF 29.8.43; NAASC 31.10.43 - SAAF (MTO), No.41 Sqn (date unknown); No.3 Sqn, to No.7 Sqn ('TJ-C') 5.3.44; Bf 109 possibly damaged 25.4.44 (Mjr WP Stanford); No.4 Sqn ('KJ-O') 19.7.44; Bombing, hit by AA, flew into hillside while attacking MT, burst into flames, Cat.FB/E 25.7.44 (Lt E Williams killed), SOC

MH957 Spitfire LF.IXc (Merlin 66); TOC/RAF 30.8.43; NAASC 31.10.43 - SAAF (MTO), No.2 Sqn, hit by flak 8m SE of Amendola, abandoned 5m S of Farindol, Cat.FB/3 12.6. or 14.6.44 (Lt RD McKechnie evaded capture and retd next day), SOC

MH970 Spitfire LF.IXc (Merlin 66); TOC/RAF 30.8.43; NAASC 31.10.43 - SAAF (MTO), No.357 MU to No.2 Sqn ('DB-V') 4.4.45; Hit by AA 10m NE of Bologna, Cat.FB/Ac 17.4.45 (Lt JE Harley); To No.7 Wing SAAF for repair 18.4.45; Retd No.2 Sqn 1.5.45; No.7 Wing for repair 8.6.45; Retd No.2 Sqn 18.6.45; Retd RAF; SOC (No.107 MU) 28.8.47, but still coded 'DB-V'

MH971 Spitfire LF.IXc (Merlin 66); TOC/RAF 2.9.43; NAASC 31.10.43 - SAAF (MTO), No.3 Sqn ('CA-H'), Ju 88 crashed and burst into flames 12m SE of Derna, shared with MH612 29.2.44 (Lt HA Geater); No.7 Sqn 5.3.44; No.136 MU, long range mods 16.3.44; Hit by flak attacking MT, abandoned 3m NE of Umbertide, Cat.FB/E 3.7.44 (Lt H Matthews retd 8.7.44), SOC

MH975 Spitfire LF.IXc (Merlin 66); TOC/RAF 2.9.43; Casablanca 10.10.43; NAASC 31.10.43 - SAAF (MTO), No.40 Sqn, hit by AA nr Signa, force-landed nr Artimino, crashed in flames, Cat.FB/E 3.8.44 (Lt NG Boys killed), SOC

MH976 Spitfire LF.IXc (Merlin 66); TOC/RAF 29.8.43; N.A. 10.43; ex USAAF 1.44 - SAAF (MTO), No.117 MU to No.4 Sqn 23.8.44 ('KJ-F', to 'KJ-E' by 17.9.44), flown by CO Mjr JM Faure; Hit by light AA and caught fire in bombing dive, abandoned at 5,000ft S of Ravenna, landed nr target, Cat.FB/E 13.11.44 (Lt WM Thompson killed), SOC

MH985 Spitfire F.IXc (Merlin 63); TOC/RAF 5.9.43; NAASC 31.10.43 - SAAF (MTO), No.2 Sqn ('DB-H') from 20.3.45; Hit by AA 14m E of Bologna, Cat.FB/Ac 15.4.45 (Lt AR Cowsge-Crosse); No.7 Wing SAAF for repair 15.4.45; Retd to No.2 Sqn 17.4.45; Retd RAF (No.2 FTLU) 28.4.45; Later conv to LF IXc (M.66) and to Italy (*MM4128*) 26.6.47

MH990 Spitfire F.IXc (Merlin 63); TOC/RAF 10.9.43; N.A. (No.218 Grp) 30.11.43 - SAAF (MTO), No.1 Sqn ('AX-B': 'AX-G'), Me 410 destroyed 15.4.44 (Capt AJ Biden) 15.4.44; Attacked by P-38s while covering a RAAF pilot in his dinghy, but undamaged 20.4.44 (Capt AJ Biden); Destroyed Bf 109G on ground which exploded as he passed over it, hit by debris and also by a single 20mm AA round, Cat.FB/Ac 11.5.44 (Lt RJ Barnwell); Engine fire on starting 23.7.44; Retd RAF; SOC 13.9.45

MH993 Spitfire F.IXc (Merlin 63); TOC/RAF 4.9.43; NAASC 31.10.43 - SAAF (MTO), No.41 Sqn (silver overall, date unknown); Retd RAF; Later to Greece 27.3.47

MH995 Spitfire F.IXc (Merlin 63); TOC/RAF 5.9.43; NAASC 31.10.43 - SAAF (MTO), No.357 MU to No.4 Sqn ('KJ-Q', then 'KJ-G') 9.8.44; Hit by flak attacking MT and abandoned successfully, aircraft in flames, Cat.FB/E2 20.10.44 (Capt EW Sturgess PoW), SOC

MJ118 Spitfire LF.IXc (Merlin 66); TOC/RAF 8.10.43; MAAF 10.2.45 - SAAF (MTO), No.4 Sqn ('KJ-C') from or by 19.3.45; Practice flight 9.6.45 (Lt Goldsworthy); Retd RAF (M.E. 8.45); SOC 31.10.46

MJ121 Spitfire LF.IXc (Merlin 66); TOC/RAF 21.10.43; Casablanca 22.12.43 - SAAF (MTO), No.7 Sqn, to No.4 Sqn ('KJ-Y') 19.7.44; Hit tree attacking MT near Forli and crash-landed in river bed, Cat.FB/E 24.8.44 (Lt MWV Odendaal evaded capture and returned), SOC

MJ123 Spitfire LF.IXc (Merlin 66); TOC/RAF 8.10.43; Casablanca 29.11.43 - SAAF (MTO), No.7 Sqn, hit by flak, caught fire and abandoned 3m NW of Pescina, Cat.FB/3 16.5.44 (Lt JW Swanepoel seen being assisted by civilians, PoW), SOC

MJ129 Spitfire F.IXc (Merlin 63); Became SAAF No. **55..** (range 5502-5554); TOC/RAF 13.10.43; Flown to ME, arr No.15 AD Fayid 20.11.47 - SAAF, Zwartkop Air Station 1947; Fate unknown

MJ156 Spitfire LF.IXc (Merlin 66); TOC/RAF 21.10.43; Casablanca 22.12.43 - SAAF (MTO), No.40 Sqn, hit by AA, engine fire, forced landing, hit tree, Cat.FB/E 4.1.45 (Lt BK Ross injured); SOC 4.1.45

MJ185 Spitfire LF.IXc (Merlin 66); TOC/RAF 19.10.43; Casablanca 29.11.43 - SAAF (MTO), No.2 Sqn, engine

MJ191 Spitfire LF.IXc (Merlin 66); TOC/RAF 21.10.43; Casablanca 22.12.43 - SAAF (MTO), No.2 Sqn ('DB-Z') by 10.44; Tyre burst on take-off, belly-landed, Cat.Ac 11.10.44 (Lt H Nash-Webber OK); Engine failure on bombing attack, forced landed out of petrol, Cat.FB/B 5.1.45 (Lt CC Hitchins OK); Retd RAF; Later to Egypt 26.9.46 cut, abandoned 20m E of Penna Point, Cat.FB/3 20.3.44 (Lt WJ Geering picked up OK by Walrus), SOC

MJ195 Spitfire LF.IXc (Merlin 66); TOC/RAF 5.11.43; Casablanca 22.12.43; MAAF - SAAF (MTO), No.117 MU to No.4 Sqn 25.4.44; No.2 Sqn, tailwheel damaged in PSP taxying, Cat.A 7.4.44 (Lt GE Conning); Tyre burst landing, swung, tipped up, Cat.A 2.5.44 (Lt IT Gowar); Hit by AA in Imola/Faenza area, belly-landed at base, Cat.FB/2 7.7.44 (Capt CN Shone); Retd RAF; SOC 29.4.45

MJ196 Spitfire LF.IXc (Merlin 66); TOC/RAF 5.11.43; Casablanca 8.1.44 - SAAF (MTO), No.2 Sqn, hit by flak, abandoned 7m SE of Lagosta Island, Cat.FB/E 19.3.44 (Capt G Ogilvie-Watson rescued by Jugoslavian partisans and retd Sqn 30.3.44), SOC

MJ220 Spitfire F.IXc (Merlin 63); Became SAAF No. 5... (range 5555-5637); TOC/RAF 1.10.43; Arr South Africa, Cape Town (via Birkenhead) 28.4.48 - SAAF; Fate unknown

MJ224 Spitfire F.IXc (Merlin 63); Became SAAF No. 5... (range 5555-5637); TOC/RAF 11.10.43; Arr South Africa, Cape Town (via Birkenhead) 28.4.48 - SAAF; Fate unknown

MJ225 Spitfire LF.IXc (Merlin 66); Became SAAF No. 5... (range 5555-5637); TOC/RAF 11.10.43; Arr South Africa, Cape Town (via Birkenhead) 2.1.49 - SAAF; Fate unknown

MJ227 Spitfire F.IXc (Merlin 63); TOC/RAF 18.10.43; Casablanca 22.12.43; MAAF, ex "HA Special Flt" - SAAF (MTO), No.10 Sqn 11.7.44; No.103 MU 13.8.44; No.4 Sqn by 4.9.44; Retd RAF; Later to Egypt 29.8.46 Note: Reported for No.4 Sqn as "JL277"

MJ247 Spitfire LF.IXc (Merlin 66); TOC/RAF 19.10.43; Casablanca 22.12.43 - SAAF (MTO), No.2 Sqn ('DB-F'), Trigno early 1944; No.7 Sqn ('TJ-M'), holed by flak, Cat.1 3.1.45; Hit by flak in dive, retd to base, Cat.FB/Ac 27.1.45 (Lt PA Leslie); Escorting Kittyhawks, tyre burst on take-off, belly-landed Ravenna, Cat.B 12.3.45 (Lt JCG Logan OK); Retd RAF (No.59 R&SU); Later crashed 15.8.47, SOC

MJ251 Spitfire LF.IXc (Merlin 66); TOC/RAF 22.10.43; ex USAAF; N.A. 31.1.44 - SAAF (MTO), No.3 Sqn ('CA-X') 7.9.45; Retd RAF; SOC 26.9.46

MJ254 Spitfire LF.IXc (Merlin 66); TOC/RAF 22.10.43; Casablanca 22.12.43 - SAAF (MTO), No.2 Sqn, ran off side of runway, undercarriage leg collapsed, Cat.Ac 3.4.44 (Lt ER Powell); Stalled high on landing, undercarriage collapsed, Cat.FB/2 31.5.44 (Lt P Marshall); No.4 Sqn ('KJ-M') from or by 7.4.45; Testflight 27.6.45 (Lt J Pollock); Retd RAF; SOC 11.4.46

MJ256 Spitfire LF.IXc (Merlin 66); TOC/RAF 20.10.43; Casablanca 29.11.43 - SAAF (MTO), No.4 Sqn ('KJ-S') from or by 22.3.45; Training flight 26.6.45 (Lt Styger); Retd RAF 6.45 (M.E, crashed 1.6.46); SOC 25.7.46

MJ258 Spitfire LF.IXc (Merlin 66); TOC/RAF 20.10.43; Casablanca 29.11.43 - SAAF (MTO), No.117 MU to No.4 Sqn ('KJ-X') 27.5.44; Bombing 7.10.44 (Lt Martin); Retd RAF 13.10.44; SOC 14.3.46

MJ272 Spitfire LF.IXc (Merlin 66); TOC/RAF 20.10.43; Casablanca 29.11.43 - SAAF (MTO), No.2 Sqn ('DB-S') from 1.45; Damaged by flak, glycol leak, crash-landed nr Villanova/2m SE of Fusignano, Cat.FB/E2 19.3.45 (Lt DR Phelan retd same day); Recovered; Retd RAF; SOC 14.3.46

MJ273 Spitfire LF.IXc (Merlin 66); TOC/RAF 18.10.43; Casablanca 22.12.43 - SAAF (MTO), No.2 Sqn, hit by AA in Arezzo area, retd to base, Cat.FB/1 1.7.44 (Lt RB McKenzie); Retd RAF; SOC 28.4.45

MJ280 Spitfire LF.IXc (Merlin 66); TOC/RAF 23.10.43; Casablanca 22.12.43 - SAAF (MTO), No.2 Sqn, hit by AA, San Guistina, Cat.FB/Ac 30.6.44 (Lt P Marshall); Retd RAF; SOC 23.10.44

MJ282 Spitfire LF.IXc (Merlin 66); TOC/RAF 20.10.43 - SAAF (MTO), No.3 Sqn 20.9.45; Retd RAF; SOC 26.9.46

MJ290 Spitfire LF.IXc (Merlin 66); TOC/RAF 22.10.43; Casablanca 29.11.43 - SAAF (MTO), No.2 Sqn, hit HT cables during ground attack mission, crashed SE of Carsoli, Cat.FB/E 3.3.44 (Mjr JH Gaynor killed), SOC

MJ294 Spitfire LF.IXc (Merlin 66); TOC/RAF 23.1.44; MAAF 17.5.45 - SAAF (MTO), No.357 MU to No.2 Sqn 15.5.45 - 6.45; Retd RAF; SOC 6.12.45

MJ308 Spitfire LF.IXc (Merlin 66); TOC/RAF 24.10.43; Casablanca 29.11.43 - SAAF (MTO), No.357 MU to No.2 Sqn ('DB-Q') 21.12.44; Possibly hit by flak, lost glycol, engine temperature went off clock, seen to dive vertically, crashed 11m SE of Montelice, Cat.FB/E 24.3.45 (Lt L de Klerk killed), SOC

MJ328 Spitfire F.IXc (Merlin 63); TOC/RAF 20.10.43; Casablanca 29.11.43; MAAF; No.94 Sqn - SAAF (MTO), No.10 Sqn 28.8.44; No.9 Sqn 31.10.44; Retd RAF; SOC 20.8.46

MJ333 Spitfire LF.IXc (Merlin 66); TOC/RAF 24.10.43 - SAAF (MTO), No.7 Sqn, hit by AA in Padua/Mestre area, retd to base, Cat.FB/A 6.4.45 (Lt BR Oldridge); Retd RAF; Later to Greece 31.7.47

MJ339 Spitfire LF.IXc (Merlin 66); TOC/RAF 3.11.43 - SAAF (MTO), No.2 Sqn ('DB-P') in 4.45; No.40 Sqn, hit by AA in Portomaggiore area, retd to base, Cat.FB/Ac 17.4.45 (Lt P McClure); Retd RAF; SOC 30.8.45

MJ367 Spitfire LF.IXc (Merlin 66); TOC/RAF 2.12.43; Casablanca 17.2.44; No.4 ADU - SAAF (MTO), No.4 Sqn 10.6.44; No.2 Sqn ('DB-V'), possibly by 7.44; Hit by AA in Po estuary area, abandoned, Cat.FB/E 6.9.44 (Capt GH Wates PoW), SOC

MJ368 Spitfire LF.IXc (Merlin 66); TOC/RAF 2.12.43; MAAF 31.1.44 - SAAF (MTO), No.117 MU to No.4 Sqn ('KJ-T') 27.5.44; Hit by 40mm flak, force-landed undercarriage up 15m SSW of Florence, crashed in Allied lines, FB/E 13.7.44 (Capt RDB Morton minor injuries); SOC 18.8.44

MJ383 Spitfire LF.IXc (Merlin 66); TOC/RAF 5.11.43; Casablanca 22.12.43 - SAAF (MTO), No.2 Sqn, hit by AA, engine failed, crashed SW of Bologna, Cat.FB/E 27.9.44 (Lt SP Healey PoW), SOC

MJ410 Spitfire LF.IXc (Merlin 66); TOC/RAF 5.11.43; Casablanca 22.12.43 - SAAF (MTO), No.2 Sqn, hit by AA nr Pescina, retd to base, Cat.FB/2 2.5.44 (Lt CFG Greenham); Retd RAF; SOC 23.10.44

MJ416 Spitfire LF.IXc (Merlin 66); TOC/RAF 5.11.43; Casablanca 8.1.44 - SAAF (MTO), No.357 MU to No.2 Sqn ('DB-E', named 'SCAT') 29.12.44; Hit by AA 10m SSE of Ferrara, Cat.FB/Ac 14.4.45 (Lt TJ McBreakey); No.7 Wing SAAF for repair 14.4.45; No.357 MU, to No.2 Sqn 20.4.45; To No.7 Wing 6.6.45; Retd No.2 Sqn 18.6.45; Retd RAF; Later to France 25.7.46

MJ472 Spitfire LF.IXc (Merlin 66); TOC/RAF 22.11.43; Casablanca 17.2.44 - SAAF (MTO), No.4 Sqn from 17.4.44; No.7 Sqn 3.5.44; Heavy landing, swung, oleo collapsed, Cat.B 14.7.44 (Lt DC Bosch); Retd RAF; SOC 31.5.45

MJ506 Spitfire LF.IXc (Merlin 66); TOC/RAF 22.11.43; MAAF 31.1.44; ex USAAF 29.2.44 - SAAF (MTO), No.40 Sqn, engine rough at 9,000ft, glycol loss, undershot approach and hit EN350 and MH614 in standby area, Rimini, Cat.E 12.10.44 (Lt SSM Gray OK), SOC

MJ521 Spitfire LF.IXc (Merlin 66); TOC/RAF 29.11.43; MAAF 12.4.45 - SAAF (MTO), No.7 Sqn, hit by AA 15m S of Oguvin, Cat.FB/E 2.5.45 (Lt EE Stott retd to Sqn on 6.5.44); SOC 31.5.45

South Africa

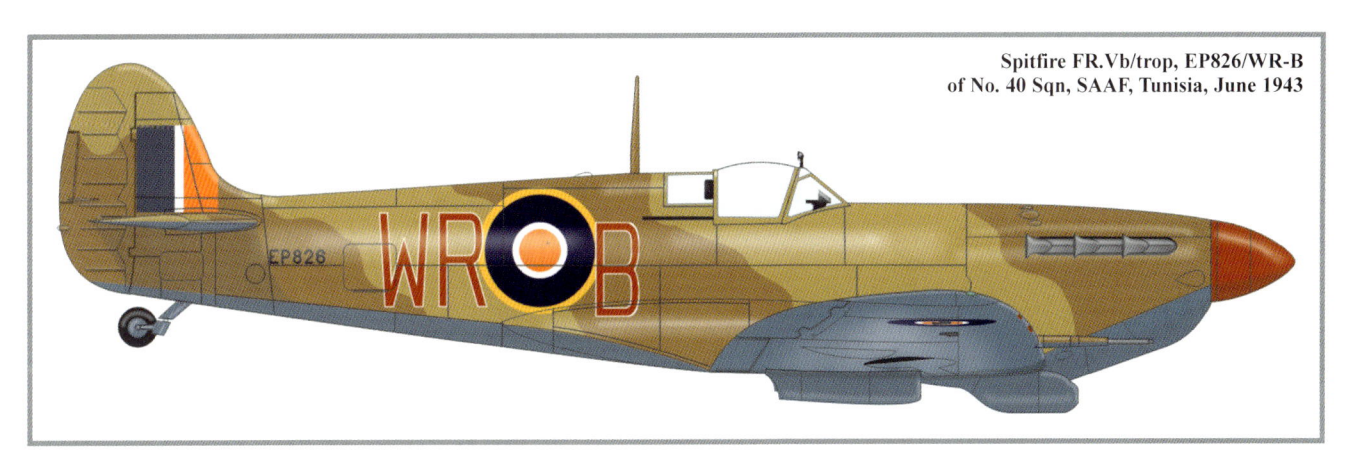

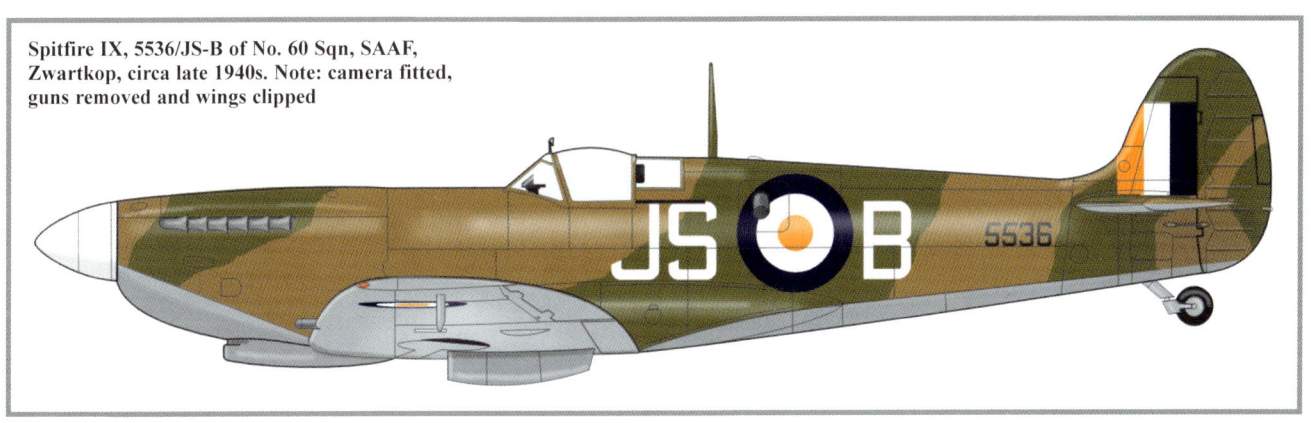

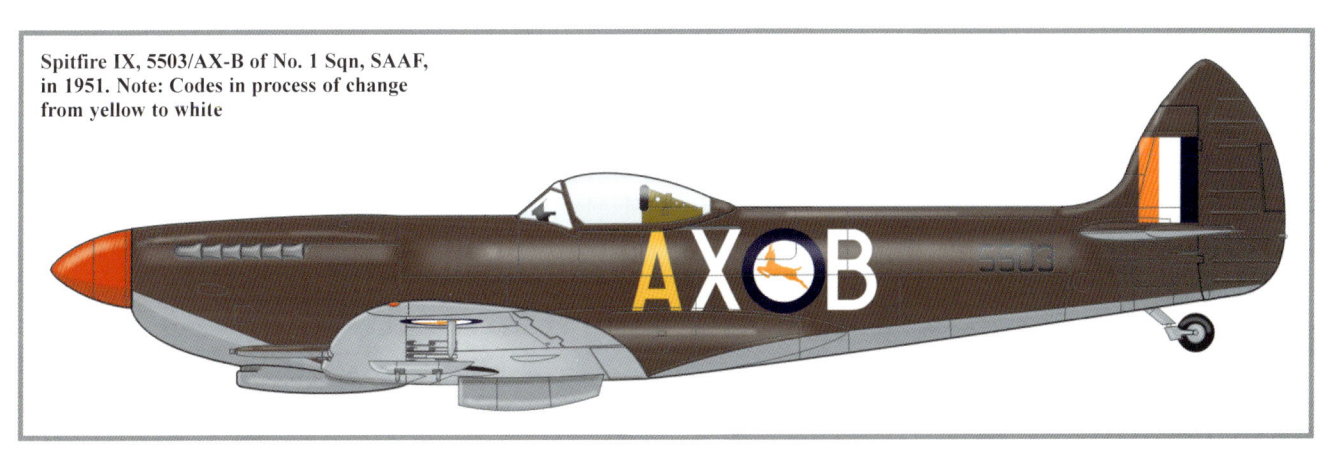

Spitfire FR.Vb/trop, EP826/WR-B of No. 40 Sqn, SAAF, Tunisia, June 1943

Spitfire IX, 5536/JS-B of No. 60 Sqn, SAAF, Zwartkop, circa late 1940s. Note: camera fitted, guns removed and wings clipped

Spitfire IX, 5503/AX-B of No. 1 Sqn, SAAF, in 1951. Note: Codes in process of change from yellow to white

MJ526 Spitfire LF.IXc (Merlin 66); TOC/RAF 22.11.43; Casablanca 8.1.44; MAAF 31.1.44 - SAAF (MTO), No.2 Sqn, engine failure, force-landed on airfield, Cat.E 2.5.44 (Capt EK Dunning); Retd RAF; Later GI *6079M* from 15.8.46

MJ527 Spitfire LF.IXc (Merlin 66); TOC/RAF 24.11.43; Casablanca 17.2.44; MAAF - SAAF (MTO), No.2 Sqn, hit by AA, Cat.FB/1 22.6.44 (Lt CFG Greenham); ROS; Retd RAF; Later to Italy (*MM4127*) 26.8.47

MJ533 Spitfire LF.IXc (Merlin 66); TOC/RAF 23.11.43; Casablanca 22.12.43 - SAAF (MTO), No.2 Sqn ('DB-F'), ran into soft ground taxying 7.10.44 (Lt HPS Broome); Hit by AA, engine fire, force-landed 12m S of Ferrara, Cat.FB/E 15.4.45 (Lt HPS Broome retd to Sqn), SOC

MJ535 Spitfire LF.IXc (Merlin 66); TOC/RAF 2.12.43; MAAF 31.1.44 - SAAF (MTO), No.40 Sqn, port undercarriage would not retract after take-off and could not be locked down, collapsed on landing, Bellaria, Cat.FB/Ac 19.11.44 (Capt LR Hartley OK); Retd RAF; SOC 14.3.46

MJ573 Spitfire LF.IXc (Merlin 66); TOC/RAF 24.12.43 - SAAF (MTO), No.357 MU to No.2 Sqn ('DB-B') 14.12.44; Hit by AA 12m NE of Venice, Cat.FB/Ac 14.3.45 (Lt NC Harrison); No.110 MU for complete overhaul 28.3.45; No.3 Sqn 6.9.45; Retd RAF; SOC 23.9.46

MJ574 Spitfire LF.IXc (Merlin 66); TOC/RAF 24.12.43; Casablanca 17.2.44 - SAAF (MTO), No.2 Sqn, collided on landing, Cat.2 8.4.44 (Lt RB Peel wounded); Retd RAF; SOC 22.11.45

MJ578 Spitfire LF.IXc (Merlin 66); TOC/RAF 24.11.43; Casablanca 8.1.44; MAAF 31.1.44 - SAAF (MTO), No.2 Sqn, hit barrel marker landing into sun, Sinello, Cat.FB/1 27.5.44 (Lt SB Healey); Retd RAF; SOC 11.4.46

MJ588 Spitfire LF.IXc (Merlin 66); TOC/RAF 25.11.43; Casablanca 8.1.44; MAAF 31.1.44 - SAAF (MTO), No.2 Sqn, bad swing on landing, retracted undercarriage, Cat.A 14.4.44 (Lt ER Powell); No.4 Sqn ('KJ-X') from or by 3.3.45; Escort, engine failed, baled out 5m NE of Cervia, Cat.FB/E2 18.3.45 (Lt HA Carter retd same day), SOC

MJ603 Spitfire LF.IXc (Merlin 66); TOC/RAF 10.1.44; Casablanca 17.3.44 - SAAF (MTO), No.40 Sqn, landed undercarriage retracted, Cat.A 28.8.44 (Lt P McClure); Hit by AA in Rimini area, Cat.FB/Ac 18.9.44 (Lt SM Cornelius); Heavy landing after op, port oleo collapsed,

	Cat.FB/Ac 13.10.44 (Lt BK Ross OK); Hit tree in Argenta area, retd to base, Cat.2 27.1.45 (Lt BK Ross); Retd RAF; SOC 30.8.45
MJ609	Spitfire LF.IXc (Merlin 66); TOC/RAF 30.11.43; MAAF 31.1.44 - SAAF (MTO), No.1 Sqn, hit by AA 4m NW of Lugo, Cat.FB/Ac 20.2.45 (Lt H Foster); No.7 Sqn, holed by MG while strafing, Cat.FB/1 6.4.45 (pilot unhurt); Hit by flak, abandoned 5m NW of Ostalleto, burnt out, Cat.FB/E2 20.4.45 (Capt B Guest PoW but released, evaded capture and retd Sqn 29.4.45), SOC
MJ613	Spitfire LF.IXc (Merlin 66); TOC/RAF 26.11.43; Casablanca 12.2.44 - SAAF (MTO), No.117 MU to No.4 Sqn 19.4.44; Retd RAF (No.59 R&SU) 4.6.44; No.117 MU, to No.4 Sqn SAAF from 20.4.44; Retd RAF (No.59 R&SU, engine change) 29.7.44; Back to No.4 Sqn SAAF 1.8.44; Engine failed on landing, bounced, ran off runway, undercarriage collapsed, damaged prop, belly & engine mounting, Cat.FA/2 13.8.44 (Lt GV Hardingham); To R&SU 14.8.44; Retd No.4 Sqn ('KJ-K') 25.8.44; Hit by flak, force-landed Florence, Cat.FB/2 1.10.44 (Lt NP Victor slightly wounded); No.59 R&SU 1.10.44; Back to No.4 Sqn SAAF ('KJ-K') 5.10.44; Test flight, undershot landing on PSP, undercarriage collapsed Rimini, Cat.E1 29.10.44 (Lt RG Dyason injured); Retd RAF; SOC 2.8.45
MJ620	Spitfire LF.IXc (Merlin 66); TOC/RAF 30.11.43; MAAF 31.1.44 - SAAF (MTO), No.144 MU, possibly to No.4 Sqn 3.4.44; No.2 Sqn, damaged by bomb splinters, crash landed nr Capestrand [?], Cat.FB/3 2.6.44 (Lt JG de Wet PoW), SOC NOTE: Reported as "JK620" for No.4 Sqn
MJ621	Spitfire LF.IXc (Merlin 66); TOC/RAF 4.12.43; Casablanca 8.1.44 - SAAF (MTO), No.40 Sqn (date unknown); Retd RAF; SOC 14.3.46
MJ632	Spitfire LF.IXc (Merlin 66); TOC/RAF 2.12.43, MAAF - SAAF, No.2 Sqn ('DB-T') 1944; retd RAF; 72 Sqn, caught fire in bombing dive and crashed 5m N of Portomaggiore, 10.4.45
MJ665	Spitfire LF.IXc (Merlin 66); TOC/RAF 2.12.43; Casablanca 8.1.44; MAAF 31.1.44 - SAAF (MTO), No.40 Sqn, hit by AA over Rolesella, retd to base, Cat.FB/1 24.4.45 (2/Lt EH Pike); Retd RAF; SOC 20.9.45
MJ666	Spitfire LF.IXc (Merlin 66); TOC/RAF 12.12.43; Casablanca 17.2.44 - SAAF (MTO), No.7 Sqn, hit by flak, Cat.FB/2 2.3.44; RiW; Retd No.7 Sqn; Hit by flak while strafing S of Citta di Castello, abandoned nr Celleno, 5m W of Marscian, aircraft dived into ground, Cat.FB/3 16.6.44 (Lt DJ Lindsay retd sqn), SOC
MJ669	Spitfire LF.IXc (Merlin 66); TOC/RAF 2.12.43; Casablanca 8.1.44; MAAF 31.1.44 - SAAF (MTO), No.2 Sqn, hit mound at end of runway while landing, Cat.A 31.3.44 (Lt JP Irving); Retd RAF; Later to France 28.3.46
MJ670	Spitfire LF.IXc (Merlin 66); TOC/RAF 4.12.43; MAAF 31.1.44 - SAAF (MTO), No.7 Sqn, stbd tyre burst on take-off for ops, completed mission, landed on one wheel, undercarriage collapsed at end of run, Cat.FB/2 14.3.45 (Lt KO Embling OK); Retd RAF; SOC 20.9.45
MJ672	Spitfire LF.IXc (Merlin 66); TOC/RAF 2.12.43; Casablanca 17.2.44 - SAAF (MTO), No.117 MU to No.4 Sqn ('KJ-J') 19.4.44; Bombing mission 17.10.44 (Lt Barrell); Retd RAF; No.357 MU, to No.2 Sqn SAAF 2.3.45; Retd RAF (No.357 MU) 7.5.45; SOC 14.3.46
MJ673	Spitfire LF.IXc (Merlin 66); TOC/RAF 2.12.43; Casablanca 17.2.44; MAAF - SAAF (MTO), No.4 Sqn ('KJ-Z') by 18.11.44; Retd RAF; Later to Italy (*MM4059*) 30.5.46
MJ675	Spitfire LF.IXc (Merlin 66); TOC/RAF 13.12.43; Casablanca 17.2.44 - SAAF (MTO), No.117 MU to No.4 Sqn ('KJ-U') 21.5.44; Bumpy landing, wing hit runway, Citerno LG, Cat.Ac 23.6.44 (2/Lt HG Chapman); No.2 (SA) R&SU 24.6.44; Retd No.4 Sqn 25.6.44; Hit by AA NW of Arezzo, abandoned, aircraft burnt, Cat.FB/E 14.7.44 (2/Lt HG Chapman PoW); SOC 18.8.44
MJ680	Spitfire LF.IXc (Merlin 66); TOC/RAF 11.12.43; Casablanca 17.2.44 - SAAF (MTO), No.3 Sqn ('CA-E'), Hit by AA on armed recce, blew up in bombing dive, NW of Forli, Cat.FB/E 5.11.44 (Lt HD Wheeler killed), SOC
MJ688	Spitfire LF.IXc (Merlin 66); TOC/RAF 2.12.43; Casablanca 17.2.44 - SAAF (MTO), No.2 Sqn ('DB-B'), caught fire and exploded in bombing dive, crashed near Popoli/Pratola, Cat.FB/3 25.5.44 (Capt JO de Waal killed), SOC
MJ692	Spitfire LF.IXc (Merlin 66); TOC/RAF 11.12.43; Casablanca 17.2.44; No.208 Sqn - SAAF (MTO), No.4 Sqn from 3.5.44; Bombing mission, direct hit by AA San Benedetto/Porto Reconati, caught fire in dive at 5-4,000ft, exploded, crashed Cupra Maritima, Cat.FB/3 17.5.44 (Lt DJ de Villiers killed), SOC
MJ713	Spitfire LF.IXc (Merlin 66); TOC/RAF 12.12.43; Casablanca 17.2.44 - SAAF (MTO), No.117 MU to No.4 Sqn 19.4.44; Hit oil drum on take-off Cisterna, Cat.FB/E 1.7.44 (Lt PJ Welman), SOC
MJ715	Spitfire LF.IXc (Merlin 66); TOC/RAF 11.12.43; Casablanca 17.2.44 - SAAF (MTO), No.7 Sqn by 16.5.44; Wingtip hit barrel taxying after op 1.7.44 (Lt FB Richter); To RAF (No.59 R&SU) 1.7.44; No.4 Sqn ('KJ-W') 30.7.44; Bombing 12.11.44 (Lt MF Reim); No.2 Sqn in 6.45; Retd RAF; SOC 26.4.47
MJ718	Spitfire LF.IXc (Merlin 66); TOC/RAF 12.12.43; Casablanca 17.2.44 - SAAF (MTO), No.3 Sqn, hit by AA, retd to base, Cat.FB/1 15.1.45 (Capt FE Potgieter); Port tyre burst on take-off Pontedera for bombing raid, swung landing, nosed over on soft ground, Cat.FB/2 6.2.45 (Capt FE Potgieter OK); Retd RAF; SOC 2.8.45
MJ727	Spitfire LF.IXc (Merlin 66); TOC/RAF 11.12.43; Casablanca 17.2.44 - SAAF (MTO), No.117 MU to No.4 Sqn 25.4.44; Hit by gunfire over Yugoslavia, crashed in flames, Cat.FB/E 14.5.44 (Lt RW Rowan killed), SOC
MJ729	Spitfire LF.IXc (Merlin 66); TOC/RAF 16.12.43; MAAF 11.2.45; No.185 Sqn - SAAF (MTO), No.11 Sqn 7.8.45; Landed in strong cross-wind, stalled onto runway, port tyre burst, swung off runway, Cat.B 13.8.45 (Lt AC Wilson OK); Retd RAF; Later to Greece 30.4.47
MJ738	Spitfire LF.IXe (Merlin 66); TOC/RAF 13.12.43; Casablanca 2.44 - SAAF (MTO), No.4 Sqn, engine failed on take-off, stalled on approach, undershot, bomb exploded Sinello, Cat.FB/E 21.5.44 (Capt PLR Burger injured), SOC
MJ739	Spitfire LF.IXe (Merlin 66); TOC/RAF 13.12.43; Casablanca 17.2.44; No.72 Sqn - SAAF (MTO), No.4 Sqn ('KJ-Z') 3.5.44; No.59 R&SU 4.9.44; No.4 Sqn 6.9.44; Bombing, hit by AA, pilot baled out, aircraft crashed in Forli town, Cat.FB/3 18.11.44 (Lt HA Carter); SOC 23.12.44
MJ754	Spitfire LF.IXe (Merlin 66); TOC/RAF 10.1.44; Casablanca 17.3.44 - SAAF (MTO), No.2 Sqn ('DB-R'), hit by flak, abandoned near Veghereto, Cat.FB/E 27.7.44 (Lt DJS Jansen van Rensburg PoW), SOC
MJ755	Spitfire LF.IXe (Merlin 66); TOC/RAF 10.1.44; Casablanca - SAAF (MTO), No.2 Sqn, engine failed in circuit, force-landed wheels up 2m N Foiana, Cat.2 19.8.44 (Lt CFG Greenham); Retd RAF; Later to Greece in 1947
MJ769	Spitfire LF.IXe (Merlin 66); TOC/RAF 13.12.43; Casablanca 2.44 - SAAF (MTO), No.7 Sqn, hit by AA, Cat.FB/2 8.8.44 (Lt L Symons); Retd RAF (No.59 R&SU; Census 6.45); SOC 6.12.45
MJ775	Spitfire LF.IXe (Merlin 66); TOC/RAF 22.12.43; Casablanca 17.2.44 - SAAF (MTO), No.2 Sqn, hit by flak, abandoned near Spoleto, aircraft crashed 1m S of Spoleto, Cat.FB/3 13.6.44 (Lt BD Shelver PoW), SOC

MJ788 Spitfire LF.IXc (Merlin 66); TOC/RAF 22.12.43; Casablanca 17.2.44 - SAAF (MTO), No.117 MU to No.4 Sqn 19.4.44; Retd RAF (R&SU) 17.8.44; No.4 Sqn SAAF ('KJ-V') 8.44; Bombing, hit by flak and abandoned, Cat.FB/E2 3.10.44 (Capt IG Will), SOC

MJ830 Spitfire LF.IXe (Merlin 66); TOC/RAF 22.12.43; Casablanca 17.2.44 - SAAF (MTO), No.117 MU to No.4 Sqn ('KJ-P') 19.4.44; No.117 MU, retd to No.4 Sqn 16.7.44; Hit by AA, retd to base, Cat.FB/Ac 19.7.44 (Lt JC Booysens); Retd RAF 17.10.44; Later to Italy (*MM4070*) 26.6.47

MJ837 Spitfire LF.IXe (Merlin 66); TOC/RAF 24.11.43, MAAF 31.1.44 - SAAF (MTO), No.2 Sqn ('DB-Y'), Bf 109G destroyed 16.4.44 (Lt HJC Dyason); Hit by AA NW of Chieti, belly-landed Ginella LG, Cat.FB/Ac 10.6.44 (Capt RE Gray); Retd RAF; SOC 21.8.45

MJ838 Spitfire LF.IXe (Merlin 66); TOC/RAF 24.11.43; MAAF 31.1.44; ex USAAF 29.2.44 - SAAF (MTO) No.40 Sqn (date unknown); Retd RAF; SOC 20.9.45

MJ839 Spitfire LF.IXe (Merlin 66); TOC/RAF 26.11.43; Casablanca 17.2.44 - SAAF (MTO), No.117 MU to No.4 Sqn ('KJ-E') 27.5.44; R&SU 8.8.44; No.4 Sqn SAAF by 8.8.44, ops 22.8.44 (Lt EDK Franck); Later to Greece 27.3.47

MJ875 Spitfire LF.IXc (Merlin 66); TOC/RAF 24.12.43; Casablanca 17.2.44; No.4 FU - SAAF (MTO), No.7 Sqn ('R') 25.2.45; Hit by flak attacking barges on River Po, abandoned Pilastro, Cat.FB/E 1.4.45 (Lt KO Embling killed), SOC

MJ885 Spitfire LF.IXc (Merlin 66); TOC/RAF 22.12.43; Casablanca 17.2.44; No.72 Sqn - SAAF (MTO), No.4 Sqn ('KJ-T') 2.5.44; Hit by AA, abandoned after glycol leak, Cat.FB/E 26.5.44 (Capt RDB Morton), SOC

MJ886 Spitfire LF.IXc (Merlin 66); TOC/RAF 29.12.43; MAAF 3.3.45 - SAAF (MTO), No.1 Sqn, hit by AA 10m E of Bologna, Cat.FB/Ac 17.4.45 (Lt LC Clarke); Retd RAF; SOC 18.10.45

MJ894 Spitfire LF.IXc (Merlin 66); TOC/RAF in 1.44; Casablanca 17.3.44 - SAAF (MTO), No.2 Sqn ('DB-K') by 11.44; Hit by AA over target, Cat.FB/Ac 1.12.44 (Lt JP Hogan); Retd RAF (No.110 MU) 2.3.45; SOC 30.4.47

MJ895 Spitfire LF.IXe (Merlin 66); TOC/RAF 4.1.44; Casablanca 17.3.44 - SAAF (MTO), No.2 Sqn ('DB-S') by 10.44; Accident Cat.Ac 10.10.44; Hit by AA in Argenta area, Cat.FB/Ac 11.10.44 (Lt NC Harrison); Sweep N of Porto Maggiore, shot down W of Lake Commachio, Cat.FB/E 31.12.44 (Lt RF Bell evaded capture), SOC

MJ901 Spitfire LF.IXe (Merlin 66); TOC/RAF 4.1.44; Casablanca 3.44 - SAAF (MTO), No.7 Sqn, hit by flak nr Castel Bolognese, retd to base, Cat.FB/Ac 21.2.45 (Lt LH Deary); Bomb hung up, abandoned near Ravenna, aircraft dived into ground, Cat.FB/E2 14.3.45 (Lt JCG Logan), SOC

MJ904 Spitfire LF.IXc (Merlin 66); TOC/RAF 29.12.43; Casablanca 17.2.44 - SAAF (MTO), No.2 Sqn, bombs came off landing, ground looped, tipped up, Liverna LG, Cat.FB/Ac 24.6.44 (Lt JP Irving); Hit by AA, abandoned over Lake Trasimena, FB/E 13.7.44 (Lt KB Borcherds survived); SOC 18.8.44

MJ913 Spitfire LF.IXc (Merlin 66); TOC/RAF 1.1.44; Casablanca 17.3.44 - SAAF (MTO), No.117 MU to No.4 Sqn 25.4.44; Engine cut while changing tanks, abandoned 12m N of Pescara, Cat.FA/3 26.5.44 (Lt RG Bosch), SOC

MJ926 Spitfire LF.IXc (Merlin 66); TOC/RAF 24.12.43; Casablanca 2.44 - SAAF (MTO), No.4 Sqn ('KJ-D') 23.4.44; Failed to return attack on tank near Corletto, dived into ground, Cat.FB/E 24.10.44 (Capt JV Rochford killed), SOC

MJ933 Spitfire LF.IXc (Merlin 66); TOC/RAF 10.1.44; Casablanca 17.3.44 - SAAF (MTO), No.40 Sqn, damaged by FW 190, abandoned W of Cattaligo/near Rimini, Cat.FB/E 4.9.44 (Lt FP Lee retd Sqn 6.9.44), SOC

MJ943 Spitfire LF.IXc (Merlin 66); TOC/RAF 4.1.44; Casablanca 6.4.44 - SAAF (MTO), No.4 Sqn 15.5.44; Retd RAF (No.237 Sqn), SOC 9.6.44

MJ948 Spitfire LF.IXc (Merlin 66); TOC/RAF 4.1.44, Casablanca 17.3.44 - SAAF (MTO), No.117 MU to No.4 Sqn 15.5.44; Direct hit by flak from MV in Ancona harbour, Cat.FB/3 17.5.44 (Lt RE Chaplin killed), SOC

MJ956 Spitfire LF.IXc (Merlin 66); TOC/RAF 20.1.44; Casablanca 17.3.44 - SAAF (MTO), No.40 Sqn, hit by AA nr Rimini, Cat.FB/Ac 4.9.44 (Mjr FE Welgemoed); Hit by AA over Forli LG, Cat.FB/Ac 2.12.44 (Lt Col RHD Rogers); Hit by AA, engine cut, pilot baled out S of Milano, Cat.FB/E 23.1.45 (Capt DL Robinson safe), SOC

MJ993 Spitfire LF.IXc (Merlin 66); TOC/RAF 10.1.44; Casablanca 17.3.44 - SAAF (MTO), No.40 Sqn, hit by AA in Forli area, Cat.FB/E 6.11.44 (Lt SSM Gray PoW), SOC

MJ994 Spitfire LF.IXc (Merlin 66); TOC/RAF 14.1.44; MAAF 8.5.45 - SAAF (MTO), No.357 MU to No.2 Sqn 15.5.45 - 6.45; Retd RAF

MK125 Spitfire LF.IXc (Merlin 66); TOC/RAF 14.1.44; Casablanca 17.3.44; MAAF - SAAF (MTO), No.4 Sqn ('KJ-Y') from 7.3.45; Bombing 4.4.45 (Lt Carter); Retd RAF; SOC 26.9.46

MK133 Spitfire LF.IXc (Merlin 66); TOC/RAF 23.1.44; Casablanca 17.3.44 - SAAF (MTO), No.7 Sqn, swung off PSP on landing, overturned Ravenna, Cat.FB/2 7.4.45 (Lt AT Tennant); Retd RAF by 6.45; SOC

MK134 Spitfire LF IXc (Merlin 66); TOC/RAF 14.1.44; Casablanca 17.3.44 - SAAF (MTO), No.3 Sqn, hit during bombing attack on Villa Aisne in bad weather, engine failed, pilot baled out, Cat.FB/E 25.11.44 (Capt FE Potgieter); SOC 23.12.44

MK143 Spitfire LF.IXc (Merlin 66); TOC/RAF 14.1.44; Casablanca 17.3.44 - SAAF (MTO), No.3 Sqn ('CA-T'), hit by AA, Cat.FB/1 26.2.45 (Capt FE Potgieter); Retd RAF; No.3 Sqn SAAF 7.9.45; Smoke in cockpit, baled out, aircraft crashed 2m S of Campo Larghetto, Cat.3 27.9.45 (Lt GG Robbs OK), SOC

MK151 Spitfire LF.IXc (Merlin 66); TOC/RAF 25.1.44; Casablanca 17.3.44 - SAAF (MTO), No.40 Sqn ('WR-F'), by 5.9.45; Retd RAF; Later to France (Aeronavale) 28.3.46

MK158 Spitfire LF.IXc (Merlin 66); TOC/RAF 30.1.44; Casablanca 17.3.44; MAAF - SAAF (MTO), No.2 Sqn ('DB-Y') by 11.44; No.110 MU 2.3.45; No.357 MU, to No.2 Sqn 28.4.45 - 6.45; Retd RAF; SOC 30.10.47

MK174 Spitfire LF.IXc (Merlin 66); TOC/RAF 26.1.44; Casablanca 17.3.44 - SAAF (MTO), No.117 MU to No.4 Sqn ('KJ-L') 3.6.44; Bombing, hit by AA, abandoned after glycol leak, crashed 11m SE of Florence, Cat.FB/3 18.7.44 (Capt PCR Burger killed), SOC

MK189 Spitfire LF.IXc (Merlin 66); TOC/RAF 28.1.44; MAAF 2.4.45 - SAAF (MTO), No.7 Sqn, hit by AA, Cat.2 22.4.45; Retd RAF (R&SU); Later Cat.E 20.9.45

MK197 Spitfire LF.IXc (Merlin 66); TOC/RAF 11.2.44; MAAF 10.5.45 - SAAF (MTO), No.3 Sqn ('CA-M') 7.9.45; Retd RAF; SOC 31.7.47

MK231 Spitfire LF.IXc (Merlin 66); TOC/RAF 24.12.43; Casablanca 17.2.44 - SAAF (MTO), No.2 Sqn ('DB-I'); Bf 109G destroyed NW of Termi 12.4.44 (Capt DA Ruiter); Engine cut after bombing, abandoned 6m E of Fano, Cat.FB/3 26.6.44 (Capt NM Phillips PoW), SOC

MK243 Spitfire LF.IXc (Merlin 66); TOC/RAF 10.1.44; Casablanca 17.3.44 - SAAF (MTO), No.117 MU to No.4 Sqn ('KJ-N') 18.5.44; Bombing, hit by AA, retd to base, Cat.FB/2 13.10.44 (Lt HC Chandler); Retd RAF; SOC 30.8.45

MK313 Spitfire LF.IXc (Merlin 66); TOC/RAF 28.1.44; Casablanca 17.3.44 - SAAF (MTO), No.7 Sqn 18.9.44; Glycol leak after strafing MT, force-landed, Ravenna, Cat.AR 20.2.45 (Lt NJ Hamilton OK); Retd RAF; SOC 20.9.45

MK314 Spitfire LF.IXc (Merlin 66); TOC/RAF 2.2.44; Casablanca 5.4.44 - SAAF (MTO), No.3 Sqn ('CA-W') by 4.45; Retd RAF (No.410 R&SU) 8.7.45; MAAF census 21.6.45; MED/ME census 26.6.47; SOC (BER) 31.7.47

MK348 Spitfire LF.IXc (Merlin 66); TOC/RAF 9.2.44; Casablanca 3.44 - SAAF (MTO), No.117 MU to No.4 Sqn ('KJ-Q') 20.5.44; Hit by flak, caught fire, abandoned, Cat.FB/3 13.7.44 (Lt FA O'Connor killed), SOC

MK361 Spitfire LF.IXc (Merlin 66); TOC/RAF 7.2.44; Casablanca 25.1.45; MAAF - SAAF (MTO), No.357 MU to No.2 Sqn 19.4.45 to 6.45; Retd RAF; Later to Greece 30.1.47

MK372 Spitfire LF.IXc (Merlin 66); TOC/RAF 8.2.44; Casablanca 6.4.44 - SAAF (MTO), No.40 Sqn, wing damaged by AA, Cat.FB/Ac 13.10.44 (Lt DH Robinson); Retd RAF (FB/E 18.4.45); SOC 14.6.45

MK402 Spitfire LF.IXc (Merlin 66); TOC/RAF 15.2.44; Casablanca 6.4.44 - SAAF (MTO), No.1 Sqn ('AX-K'), crashed on landing at Forli, hit barrel, Cat.Ac 24.2.45 (Lt SC Langton OK); Retd RAF 18.10.45

MK408 Spitfire LF.IXc (Merlin 66); TOC/RAF 21.2.44; Casablanca 6.4.44 - SAAF (MTO), No.7 Sqn, hit by AA 15.6.44 (Lt AW Allen); Hit by flak, flew into mountain in cloud 6m SE of Firenzuola, Cat.FB/E 21.7.44 (Capt GR Connell evaded capture), SOC

MK410 Spitfire LF.IXc (Merlin 66); TOC/RAF 15.2.44; Casablanca 6.4.44 - SAAF (MTO), No.40 Sqn, ran out of fuel, abandoned 5m N of Cesenatico, Cat.E 22.12.44 (Lt C Rose OK); SOC 31.1.45

MK440 Spitfire LF.IXc (Merlin 66); TOC/RAF 25.2.44; Casablanca 6.4.44 - SAAF (MTO), No.1 Sqn, stbd wing hit truck taxying after op at Forli, Cat.FB/Ac 19.2.45 (Lt CS Bender OK); Retd RAF (MAAF census 6.45); SOC 20.9.45

MK447 Spitfire LF.IXc (Merlin 66); TOC/RAF 22.2.44; Casablanca 6.4.44 - SAAF (MTO), No.1 Sqn, failed to return, engine failed, possibly hit by 40mm AA, abandoned aircraft 12m N of Padua, Cat.FB/E 6.3.45 (Lt FW Whittaker PoW), SOC

MK467 Spitfire LF.IXc (Merlin 66); TOC/RAF 28.2.44; Casablanca 12.5.44 - SAAF (MTO), No.1 Sqn, accident 24.4.45; Retd RAF; Later SNCAN 6.45, possibly to France

MK485 Spitfire LF.IXc (Merlin 66); TOC/RAF 25.2.44; Casablanca 6.4.44 - SAAF (MTO), No.2 Sqn ('DB-H'), hit by flak, abandoned 20m N of Florence, Cat.FB/E 1.8.44 (Lt JH Meintjies PoW), SOC

MK501 Spitfire LF.IXc (Merlin 66); TOC/RAF 25.2.44; Casablanca 4.44 - SAAF (MTO), No.4 Sqn, hit by AA, retd to base, Cat.FB/2 26.5.44 (Lt JG Booysens); RiW; No.7 Sqn, hit bump landing, Cat.Ac 9.8.44 (Lt JC Buddell); Unable to land at base due to Marauder crash, fuel shortage prevented diversion to more suitable airfield, landed on unoccupied airfield, hit soft patch on runway, tipped on nose, Creta LG, Cat.FB/2 9.9.44 (Lt LF Morrison OK); Retd RAF; SOC 2.8.45

MK555 Spitfire LF.IXc (Merlin 66); TOC/RAF 24.2.44; Casablanca 6.4.44 - SAAF (MTO), No.2 Sqn ('DB-A'), canopy jammed, hit fin when released, Cat.Ac 8.8.44 (Mjr L Dawson-Smith); No.110 MU 7.1.45 (engine change); Retd No.2 Sqn by 2.45; Later to Italy (*MM4114*) 26.6.47

MK627 Spitfire LF.IXc (Merlin 66); TOC/RAF 26.2.44; Casablanca 6.4.44 - SAAF (MTO), No.40 Sqn, hit tree, crashed on tactical reconnaissance near Forli, Cat.FB/E 12.11.44 (Capt PH Donnelly seriously injured), SOC

MK634 Spitfire LF.IXc (Merlin 66); TOC/RAF 29.2.44; Casablanca 6.4.44 - SAAF (MTO), No.117 MU to No.4 Sqn ('KJ-W') 7.5.44; No.4 ADU, to No.4 Sqn 6.6.44; Bombing, hit by flak over Bibbiana, abandoned, Cat.FB/E 18.7.44 (Lt AI Bristol evaded capture and retd sqn), SOC

MK662 Spitfire LF.IXc (Merlin 66); TOC/RAF 28.2.44; Casablanca 6.4.44; No.4 ADU - SAAF (MTO), No.2 Sqn ('DB-C') 16.6.44; Tyre came off on take-off, undercarriage collapsed, Citerno, Cat.Ac 30.6.44 (Capt CN Shone); Hit by debris from MT explosion, retd to base, Cat.FB/Ac 16.7.44 (Lt RB McKechnie); Cannon shell exploded in gun, damaged wing radiator 22.8.44 (Lt RB McKechnie); Hit by flak near Castiglione, crash landed, Cat.FB/E 14.9.44 (Lt RB McKechnie evaded capture, retd Sqn 30.9.44), SOC

MK675 Spitfire HF.IXc (Merlin 70); Became SAAF No. **5...** (range 5555-5637); TOC/RAF 30.3.44; Arr South Africa, Cape Town (via Birkenhead) 5.8.48 – SAAF; Service unknown; No.15 AD in 6.54; For sale 9.5.55

MK728 Spitfire LF.IXc (Merlin 66); TOC/RAF 8.3.44, Casablanca 12.5.44 - SAAF (MTO), No.7 Sqn 4.1.45 (sic); Hit by flak but retd to base safely 3.1.45 (Lt HB Potter wounded); Retd RAF; SOC 27.11.47

MK783 Spitfire LF.IXc (Merlin 66); TOC/RAF 7.3.44; Casablanca 12.5.44 - SAAF (MTO), No.7 Sqn, swung on landing in cross-wind after op when propeller struck PSP, port tyre burst, ran off runway, port oleo collapsed, Ravenna, Cat.FB/2 19.3.45 (Lt AL Basson OK); Retd RAF (MAAF census 6.45); SOC 30.8.45

MK784 Spitfire LF.IXc (Merlin 66); TOC/RAF 8.3.44; MAAF 12.5.45 - SAAF (MTO), No.7 Sqn mid 1945; Retd RAF; SOC 10.6.48

MK842 Spitfire HF.IXe (Merlin 70); Became SAAF No. **55..** (range 5502-5554); TOC/RAF 15.5.44; Flown to ME, arr No.15 AD Fayid 11.7.47 - SAAF, Zwartkop Air Station in 9.47; Fate unknown

MK989 Spitfire LF.IXc (Merlin 66); TOC/RAF 27.3.44; MAAF 25.2.45 - SAAF (MTO), No.357 MU to No.2 Sqn 28.4.45 to 6.45; Retd RAF; Later to France 25.7.46

ML116 Spitfire LF.IXc (Merlin 66); TOC/RAF 14.4.44; MAAF 21.2.45 - SAAF (MTO), No.2 Sqn ('DB-K') from 18.3.45 - 6.45; Retd RAF; Later to Egypt 26.9.46

ML131 Spitfire LF.IXc (Merlin 66); TOC/RAF 24.3.44; Casablanca 25.1.45; MAAF - SAAF (MTO), No.4 Sqn ('KJ-Y') from 10.4.45; Comm flight 25.6.45 (Lt Barrell); Retd RAF; SOC 26.6.47

ML145 Spitfire HF.IXe (Merlin 70); Became SAAF No. **5557**; TOC/RAF 27.3.44; Arr South Africa, Cape Town 28.4.48 – SAAF; No.7 Wing, stalled into ground during battle formation flight, crashed Vaaldam, Cat.3 13.7.50 (Lt GE Conning killed); SOC 14.10.50; FC 23.10.53

ML146 Spitfire LF.IXc (Merlin 66); TOC/RAF 28.3.44; MAAF 3.3.45 – SAAF, unknown unit, crashed Cat.FB/E 26.4.45; SOC (RAF) 23.8.45

ML148 Spitfire HF.IXe (Merlin 70); Became SAAF No. **5...** (range 5555-5637); TOC/RAF 26.3.44; Arr South Africa, Cape Town (via Birkenhead) 20.7.48 - SAAF; Fate unknown

ML151 Spitfire LF.IXc (Merlin 66); TOC/RAF 24.3.44; MAAF 4.2.45 - SAAF (MTO), No.4 Sqn ('KJ-K') from 19.3.45; Comm flight 24.6.45 (Lt Goldsworthy); Retd RAF 6.45; SOC 31.12.46

ML189 Spitfire LF.IXc (Merlin 66); TOC/RAF 5.4.44; Casablanca 15.1.45 - SAAF (MTO), No.7 Sqn, hit while strafing, retd to base, Cat.FB/1 23.4.45 (Lt PA Leslie); Retd RAF; SOC 20.9.45

ML196 Spitfire HF.IXe (Merlin 70); Became SAAF No. **5...** (range 5555-5637); TOC/RAF 28.4.44; Arr South Africa, Cape Town (via Birkenhead) 10.8.48 – SAAF; Service unknown; Ysterplaat AFB; To South African Metal & Machinery Co, Salt River, Cape Town, scrapyard 1954; To SAAF Museum 1981, storage at Snake Valley; To Graham McDonald, Durban for restoration 1995; Now project by Mark de Vries,

	Bryanston, South Africa (Serial No. "ML196" provisional only); Shipped to Canada, with Mark de Vries - **SURVIVOR**
ML197	Spitfire HF.IXe (Merlin 70); Became SAAF No. **5...** (range 5555-5637); TOC/RAF 13.4.44; Arr South Africa, Cape Town (via Birkenhead) 13.2 49 - SAAF; Fate unknown
ML243	Spitfire HF.IXe (Merlin 70); Became SAAF No. **55..** (range 5502-5554); TOC/RAF 15.4.44; Flown to ME, arr No.15 AD Fayid 2.6.47 - SAAF, Zwartkop Air Station in 8.47; Fate unknown
ML246	Spitfire HF.IXe (Merlin 70); Became SAAF No. **5...** (range 5555-5637); TOC/RAF 18.5.44; Arr South Africa, Cape Town (via Birkenhead) 16.11.48 - SAAF; Fate unknown
ML255	Spitfire HF.IXe (Merlin 70); Became SAAF No. **5563**; TOC/RAF 19.4.44; Arr South Africa, Cape Town 16.11.48 - SAAF Ysterplaat AFB, propeller hit ground on take-off, Cat.1 6.9.51 (Lt AB Retief); AOS, mid-air collision with Harvard No.7284, Cat.1 23.10.51 (2/Lt BC Barnard); Ysterplaat AFB; SOC 22.1.54; To South African Metal & Machinery Co, Salt River, Cape Town, scrapyard 1954; To SAAF Museum 1981, storage at Snake Valley; Static restoration by Atlas Aircraft Ltd; To Museo do Ar, Alverca-Ribalejo, Lisbon, Portugal 1989, displayed as "ML255/MR-2" - **SURVIVOR**
ML259	Spitfire HF.IXe (Merlin 70); Became SAAF No. **5...** (range 5555-5637); TOC/RAF 13.4.44; Arr South Africa, Cape Town (via Birkenhead) 19.12.48 - SAAF; Fate unknown
ML292	Spitfire LF.IXc (Merlin 66); TOC/RAF 6.4.44; MAAF 2.2.45 - SAAF (MTO), No.1 Sqn, damaged tailwheel landing, Ravenna, Cat.Ac 2.4.45 (Lt LC Bartel OK); Hit by AA 9m NE of Bologna, Cat.FB/Ac 18.4.45 (Capt TR Fryer); Retd RAF; Later to Egypt 31.7.47
ML306	Spitfire LF.IXe (Merlin 66); TOC/RAF 29.5.44; MAAF 2.2.45 - SAAF (MTO), No.7 Sqn, hit by flak while strafing barges N of Ferrola on armed recce, Cat.FB/Ac 21.4.45 (Lt ER Phelan wounded); Retd RAF; SOC 11.6.46
ML356	Spitfire HF.IXe (Merlin 70); Became SAAF No. **5...** (range 5555-5637); TOC/RAF 21.4.44; Arr South Africa, Cape Town (via Birkenhead) 10.8.48 - SAAF; Fate unknown
ML409	Spitfire LF.IXe (Merlin 66); TOC/RAF 25.4.44; MAAF 26.2.45 - SAAF (MTO), No.3 Sqn, hit by AA, Cat.FB/A 16.4.45 (Lt SM Brown); Damaged in attack on river barge, Cat.FB/2 22.4.45 (Lt WC Price); Retd RAF; Later to France (Aeronavale) 28.3.46
NH190	Spitfire HF.IXe (Merlin 70); Became SAAF No. **5...** (range 5555-5637); TOC/RAF 8.5.44; Arr South Africa, Cape Town (via Birkenhead) 10.8.48 - SAAF; Fate unknown
NH235	Spitfire LF. IXe (Merlin 66); TOC/RAF 5.5.44; MAAF 10.2.45 - SAAF (MTO), No.1 Sqn ('AX-P'), flak damage, Cat.2 22.4.45 (Lt AG Frisby); Retd RAF; SOC 20.9.45
NH275	Spitfire HF.IXe (Merlin 70); Became SAAF No. **5...** (range 5555-5637); TOC/RAF 10.5.44; Arr South Africa, Cape Town (via Birkenhead) 5.8.48 - SAAF; Fate unknown
NH295	Spitfire LF.IXe (Merlin 66); TOC/RAF 16.5.44; MAAF 14.5.45 - SAAF (MTO), No.4 Sqn ('KJ-D') from 9.6.45; Training flight 27.6.45 (Lt Goldsworthy); No.11 Sqn ('ND-K'); Retd RAF; SOC (No.107 MU) 28.8.47, but still coded 'ND-K'
NH307	Spitfire LF.IXe (Merlin 66); TOC/RAF 12.5.44 - SAAF (MTO), No.3 Sqn 3.4.44; No.1 Sqn, hit by AA 4m NE of Imola, Cat.FB/Ac 17.4.45 (Lt JBS Ross); Retd RAF (MAAF census 6.45); To Italy (*MM4018*) 30.5.46
NH345	Spitfire LF.IXe (Merlin 66); TOC/RAF 19.5.44; Casablanca 25.1.45; MAAF - SAAF (MTO), No.4 Sqn ('KJ-E') from 10.4.45; Comm flight 29.6.45 (Lt Montgomery); Retd RAF 6.45; SOC 28.11.46
NH355	Spitfire LF.IXe (Merlin 66); TOC/RAF 26.5.44; MAAF 16.2.45; No.185 Sqn - SAAF (MTO), No.11 Sqn 7.8.45; Failed to pull out of dive in aerobatics, crashed into sea 10m SW of Grado, Cat.FA/E 30.8.45 (Lt GV Marks killed), SOC
NH358	Spitfire LF.IXe (Merlin 66); TOC/RAF 30.5.44 - SAAF (MTO), No.3 Sqn 7.9.45; Off Sqn for major inspection 8.9.45; Retd RAF; SOC 14.3.46
NH451	Spitfire LF.IXe (Merlin 66); TOC/RAF 26.5.44 Casablanca 25.1.45; MAAF - SAAF (MTO), No.4 Sqn ('KJ-V') from or by 19.3.45; Retd RAF 5.45; Later to Egypt 29.8.46
NH467	Spitfire LF.IXe (Merlin 66); TOC/RAF 26.5.44; Casablanca 15.1.45; MAAF - SAAF (MTO), No.1 Sqn, hit by AA 12m SE of Ferrara, Cat.FB/Ac 11.4.45 (Lt JS de Villiers); Retd RAF; SOC 5.2.48
NH513	Spitfire HF.IXe (Merlin 70); Became SAAF No. **55..** (range 5502-5554); TOC/RAF 28.5.44; Flown to ME, arr No.15 AD Fayid 20.9.47 - SAAF, Zwartkop Air Station 1947; Fate unknown
NH532	Spitfire LF.IXe (Merlin 66); TOC/RAF 2.6.44; Casablanca 15.1.45 - SAAF (MTO), No.7 Sqn, hit by AA S of San Alberto, abandoned, Cat.FB/E 19.4.45 (Mjr DM Brebner retd Sqn by lunchtime), SOC
NH534	Spitfire HF.IXe (Merlin 70); Became SAAF No. **5503**; TOC/RAF 31.5.44; Flown to ME, arr No.15 AD Fayid 2.6.47 - SAAF, Zwartkop Air Station in 8.47; No.1 Sqn ('AX-B'), heavy landing 28.1.48 (Lt HJ Hanreek); R&SU; Engine cut in circuit 14.10.50 (Lt PJ Strydom); R&SU; Engine overheated on ground, Waterkloof, Cat.2 20.2.51 (Cpl PC Frisby); R&SU; AOS, engine failed on take-off, crashed Langebaanweg, Cat.1a 16.3.51 (Lt MJR Kempster); R&SU; Engine failed, force-landed, crashed 1m SW of Tulbach, Cat.3 25.1.52 (Lt WRO Doyle killed); SOC 16.2.54
NH535	Spitfire LF.IXe (Merlin 66); TOC/RAF 28.5.44; MAAF 15.3.45 - SAAF (MTO), No.40 Sqn (date unknown); Retd RAF; SOC 29.8.46
NH539	Spitfire HF.IXe (Merlin 70); Became SAAF No. **5...** (range 5555-5637); TOC/RAF 5.6.44; Arr South Africa, Cape Town (via Birkenhead) 5.8.48 - SAAF; Fate unknown
NH573	Spitfire LF.IXc (Merlin 66); TOC/RAF 8.6.44; MAAF 7.3.45 - SAAF (MTO), No.3 Sqn, propeller blade damaged in bomb attack on Salsomaggiore oilfield, Cat.FB/E1 29.3.45 (Lt MG Royston); Retd RAF (bboc); SOC 18.10.45
NH606	Spitfire LF.IXe (Merlin 66); TOC/RAF 12.6.44; Casablanca 22.9.44; MAAF - SAAF (MTO), No.4 Sqn ('KJ-W') from 17.2.45; Bombing 9.3.45 (Capt Schoeman); Retd RAF 9.3.45; SOC 31.7.47
NH611	Spitfire HF.IXe (Merlin 70); Became SAAF No. **5...** (range 5555-5637); TOC/RAF 14.6.44; Arr South Africa, Cape Town (via Birkenhead) 21.6.48 - SAAF; Fate unknown
NN573	Seafire L.IIIc (Merlin 55M); RNDA 9.1.45; Attached to No.3 Sqn SAAF, damaged Cat.3 29.3.45, SOC
PA910	Spitfire PR.XI (Merlin 63); TOC/RAF 2.2.44; MAC 1.3.44 - SAAF (MTO), No.40 Sqn by 5.9.45; Retd RAF (MAAF); SOC 27.2.47
PL134	Spitfire LF.IXe (Merlin 66); TOC/RAF 14.6.44; Casablanca 22.8.44; MAAF - SAAF (MTO), No.4 Sqn ('KJ-P') from 23.11.44; Cover, flown by Capt Heugh 12.3.45; Retd RAF 12.3.45; SOC 31.5.45
PL158	Spitfire LF.IXe (Merlin 66); TOC/RAF 30.6.44; MAAF 6.45 - SAAF (MTO), No.3 Sqn 7.9.45; Retd RAF; Later to Greece 31.7.47
PL164	Spitfire LF.IXe (Merlin 66); TOC/RAF 17.7.44; MAAF 23.2.45 - SAAF (MT), No.1 Sqn, two flak hits, one in engine which was cutting intermittently all the way back, retd base 20.4.45 (Lt LN Bulley); Retd RAF; Later to Italy 26.6.47
PL166	Spitfire LF.IXe (Merlin 66); TOC/RAF 21.7.44; Casablanca 3.9.44 - SAAF (MTO), No.40 Sqn, unit

PL192 Spitfire HF.IXe (Merlin 70); Became SAAF No. **5508**; TOC/RAF 16.6.44; Flown to ME, arr No.15 AD Fayid 23.4.47 - SAAF, Zwartkop Air Station 9.6.47; CFS in 1948/50; Heavy landing, Cat.1a 21.3.50 (Lt J H Haskins); R&SU; AOS, propeller hit ground on take-off, Cat.1 on 18.9.52 (2/Lt J P Visser); Zwartkop AFB 25.2.54; No.15 AD 12.4.54; For sale 9.5.55

PL201 Spitfire LF.IXe (Merlin 66); TOC/RAF 12.6.44; MAAF - SAAF (MTO), No.357 MU to No.2 Sqn from 15.5.45 to 6.45; Retd RAF; SOC 26.9.46

PL203 Spitfire HF.IXe (Merlin 70); Became SAAF No. **5...** (range 5555-5637); TOC/RAF 14.6.44; Arr South Africa, Cape Town (via Liverpool) 19.6.49 - SAAF; Fate unknown

PL209 Spitfire HF.IXe (Merlin 70); Became SAAF No. **55..** (range 5502-5554); TOC/RAF 15.6.44; Flown to ME, arr No.15 AD Fayid in 12.47 - SAAF, Zwartkop Air Station in 12.47; Fate unknown

PL215 Spitfire HF.IXe (Merlin 70); Became SAAF No. **5...** (range 5555-5637); TOC/RAF 16.6.44; Arr South Africa, Cape Town (via Birkenhead) 21.6.48 - SAAF; Fate unknown

PL253 Spitfire HF.IXe (Merlin 70); Became SAAF No. **5558**; TOC/RAF 29.6.44; Arr South Africa, Cape Town (via Birkenhead) 11.5.48 – SAAF; No.60 Sqn ('JS-C'), service unknown; No.15 AD in 6.54; For sale 9.5.55 (sold without engine)

PL261 Spitfire HF.IXe (Merlin 70); Became SAAF No. **5...** (range 5555-5637); TOC/RAF 22.6.44; Arr South Africa, Cape Town (via Birkenhead) 13.2.49 - SAAF; Fate unknown

PL268 Spitfire LF.IXe (Merlin 66); TOC/RAF 6.5.44; MAAF 20.4.45 - SAAF (MTO), No.3 Sqn ('CA-S'), service unknown; Retd RAF; SOC (No.107 MU) 28.8.47, but still coded 'CA-S'

PL273 Spitfire LF.IXe (Merlin 66); TOC/RAF 9.5.44; MAAF 20.4.45 - SAAF (MTO), No.357 MU to No.2 Sqn 28.4.45 - 6.45; Retd RAF; Later to France 25.7.46

PL274 Spitfire LF.IXe (Merlin 66); TOC/RAF 15.5.44; MAAF - SAAF (MTO), No.1 Sqn, hit by AA 6m NE of Ferrara, Cat.FB/Ac 1.4.45 (Lt J Mitchell); Retd RAF (crashed 13.9.46)

PL338 Spitfire LF.IXe (Merlin 66); TOC/RAF 22.6.44; Casablanca 23.8.44 - SAAF (MTO), No.40 Sqn, undercarriage failed to lock down, collapsed on landing, Bellaria, Cat.Ac 20.11.44 (Lt DW Swart OK); Hit by AA N of Fusignano, forced landed NE of Lugo, Cat.FB/2 22.3.45 (Lt S Cooper unhurt); Retd RAF (ME) SOC 26.9.46

PL342 Spitfire LF.IXe (Merlin 66); TOC/RAF 15.7.44; Casablanca 22.8.44 - SAAF (MTO), No.7 Sqn, hit by ground fire while strafing, Cat.1 6.4.45 (pilot unhurt); Retd RAF; SOC 14.3.46

PL345 Spitfire LF.IXe (Merlin 66); TOC/RAF 17.7.44; Casablanca 23.9.44 - SAAF (MTO), unknown unit, missing (FB/E) 7.10.44, SOC

PL348 Spitfire LF.IXe (Merlin 66); TOC/RAF 17.7.44; MAAF 6.45 - SAAF (MTO), No.3 Sqn ('CA-M'), hit by AA, retd to base, Cat.FB/Ac 18.1.45 (Lt AR Blair); Damaged in attack on bridge, Cat.FB/1 27.2.45; Stbd radiator fairing attachment failed while bombing oil fields, Cat.FB/Ac 1.4.45 (Lt G Kinsey OK); Undershot landing on bad ground, undercarriage torn off Iesi, Cat.FB/2 6.9.45 (Lt JO Allen OK); Retd RAF (R&SU) 7.9.45; SOC 13.12.45

PL351 Spitfire LF.IXe (Merlin 66); TOC/RAF 27.7.44; Casablanca 3.9.44 - SAAF (MTO), No.3 Sqn, wings wrinkled in dive bombing attack on road bridge, Cat.FB/1 6.1.45 (Capt GC Southey OK); Retd RAF (FB/E 19.3.45); SOC 14.6.45

move, engine cut, crash landed 2m S of Lavariano airfield, Cat.B 14.5.45 (2/Lt DP Bolitho OK); Not repaired; SOC 23.8.45

PL356 Spitfire LF.IXe (Merlin 66); TOC/RAF 29.7.44; MAAF 12.3.45 - SAAF (MTO), No.1 Sqn ('AX-Z'), date unknown; No.357 MU, to No.2 Sqn 28.4.45-6.45; Retd RAF; Later to Greece 30.1.47

PL376 Spitfire HF.IXe (Merlin 70); TOC/RAF 20.6.44; Casablanca 22.8.44 - SAAF (MTO), No.4 Sqn ('KJ-A') from or by 29.11.44; Tyre burst on take-off, swung off runway while landing, overturned, Forli, Cat.B 9.12.44 (Lt DN de Jongh OK); Retd RAF; SOC 2.8.45

PL377 Spitfire HF.IXe (Merlin 70); TOC/RAF 21.6.44; Casablanca 22.8.44 - SAAF (MTO), No.4 Sqn ('KJ-W') from 18.11.44; Stbd mainplane leading edge damaged on ops, Cat.FB/Ac 26.12.44 (Capt GW Summers OK); Training flight 10.2.45 (Capt WV Brunton); No.4 Sqn ('KJ-T') by 19.2.45; Hit by AA while strafing, Cat.FB/2 14.3. or 17.3.45 (Capt WV Brunton); Retd RAF; SOC 30.8.45

PL384 Spitfire HF.IXe (Merlin 70); TOC/RAF 22.6.44; Casablanca 22.8.44 - SAAF (MTO), No.4 Sqn ('KJ-E') 14.11. - 16.12.44 and from 5.1.45 to 4.45; Bombing 6.4.45 (Lt Cohen); Retd RAF, SOC 31.5.45

PL400 Spitfire HF.IXe (Merlin 70); TOC/RAF 24.6.44; Casablanca 22.8.44 - SAAF (MTO), No.2 Sqn ('DB-D') by 11.44; Wheels ran over end of runway after landing, nosed up, Cat.Ac 4.3.45 (Lt WG Gordon OK); Hit by flak over Legnano, force-landed NE of Dignano/11m NE of Pola, Cat.FB/E 6.4.45 (Lt JP Hogan PoW), SOC

PT369 Spitfire LF.IXe (Merlin 66); TOC/RAF 20.7.44; Casablanca 23.8.44 - SAAF (MTO), No.7 Wing Training Flight (Wing Leader); No.7 Sqn, tailwheel hit railway line taxying across airfield at Bari, Cat.Ac 2.6.45 (Col DD Moodie OK); Retd RAF; Later to Greece 27.3.47

PT375 Spitfire LF.IXe (Merlin 66); TOC/RAF 24.7.44; Casablanca 23.8.44 - SAAF (MTO), No.7 Sqn from 19.8.44 (recorded as being IXb); Hit while strafing, probably own ricochet, abandoned over Adriatic, aircraft dived into sea 15m off coast, Cat.FB/E 21.10.44 (Capt AW Meikle picked up from dinghy by ASR Catalina), SOC

PT426 Spitfire LF.IXe (Merlin 66); TOC/RAF 17.7.44; Casablanca 23.8.44 - SAAF (MTO), No.3 Sqn (date unknown); No.2 Sqn ('DB-T'), hit by flak in dive attack, exploded and burst into flames, 1m W of Capparo, Cat.FB/E 20.2.45 (Lt JB Miller killed), SOC

PT427 Spitfire LF.IXe (Merlin 66); TOC/RAF 17.7.44; Casablanca 22.8.44; MAAF - SAAF (MTO), No.4 Sqn ('KJ-L') from 15.12.44; Bombing 3.4.45 (Lt Hawky); Retd RAF 5.4.45; Later to Greece 27.3.47

PT434 Spitfire HF.IXe (Merlin 70); Became SAAF No. **5...** (range 5555-5637); TOC/RAF 1.7.44; Arr South Africa, Cape Town (via Birkenhead) 23.2.49 - SAAF; Fate unknown

PT451 Spitfire LF.IXe (Merlin 66); TOC/RAF 17.7.44; Casablanca 22.8.44 - SAAF (MTO), No.4 Sqn ('KJ-X') from 26.11.44; Bombing 2.12.44 (Lt Martin); While in standby position, hit by EN156 of No.1 Sqn at Bellaria, Cat.FB/2 4.12.44; Retd RAF; SOC 23.11.45

PT453 Spitfire LF.IXe (Merlin 66); TOC/RAF 19.7.44; Casablanca 23.8.44 - SAAF (MTO), No.1 Sqn, engine cut at 400ft after take-off, crash-landed in field 3m SE of Forli, Cat.E1 27.12.44 (Lt JBS Ross OK); SOC 29.12.44

PT455 Spitfire HF.IXe (Merlin 70); TOC/RAF 19.7.44; Casablanca 8.44 - SAAF (MTO), No.3 Sqn ('CA-P') by 1.45; Hit by flak, Cat.FB/A 7.3.45 (Lt AR Blair); Engine cut while escorting C-47s on supply drop mission, abandoned 5m SW of Frassinoro, Cat.FB/E1 29.3.45 (Lt DG Nunan baled out, retd Sqn 4.4.45), SOC

PT458 Spitfire LF.IXe (Merlin 66); TOC/RAF 1.8.44; Casablanca 9.44 - SAAF (MTO), No.3 Sqn, engine failed on take-off for op, ran off runway onto soft ground, tipped on nose, Pontedera, Cat.FB/A 11.2.45 (Lt DC Stewart seriously injured); Damaged in attack

PT462   on bridge, Cat.FB/1 27.2.45; Damaged in attack on gun, Cat.FB/2 20.3.45 (Lt MG Royston); Retd RAF (RiW); Later to France (Aeronavale) 28.3.46

PT462 Spitfire HF.IXe (Merlin 70); TOC/RAF 21.7.44; Casablanca 23.8.44; MAAF - SAAF (MTO), No.4 Sqn ('KJ-Z') from 19.11.44; Bombing 4.1.45 (Lt Barrell); Retd RAF 5.1.45; Later to Italy (*MM4100*) 26.6.47, and then to Israel (*20-67*); Via UK (*G-CTIX* 9.4.85) to USA (*N462JC* 25.7.94); Retd UK (*G-CTIX* 28.4.98), airworthy, marked "SW-A" - **SURVIVOR**

PT466 Spitfire HF.IXe (Merlin 70); TOC/RAF 20.7.44; Casablanca 3.9.44 - SAAF (MTO), No.7 Sqn, swung landing, went off runway, nosed up at Ravenna, Cat.FB/2 31.3.45 (Lt HJ Myhill OK); Retd RAF (RiW); SOC 13.12.45

PT472 Spitfire LF.IXe (Merlin 66); Became SAAF No. **5...** (range 5555-5637); TOC/RAF 26.8.44; Arr South Africa, Cape Town (via Birkenhead) 16.11.48 - SAAF; Fate unknown

PT477 Spitfire LF.IXe (Merlin 66); TOC/RAF 31.7.44; Casablanca 23.9.44 - SAAF (MTO), No.3 Sqn ('CA-R'), hit by AA, retd to base, Cat.FB/2 15.12.44 (Lt WC Price); Port tyre burst on take-off, swung off runway, hit ditch, tipped on nose, Pontedera, Cat.E1 12.3.45 (Lt JJ Lawrence OK); Retd RAF (bboc/MAAF); SOC 25.9.47

PT482 Spitfire LF.IXe (Merlin 66); TOC/RAF 19.7.44; Casablanca 23.8.44; MAAF - SAAF (MTO), No.4 Sqn ('KJ-W') from 22.3.45; Training flight 23.6.45 (Lt Walters); Retd RAF 6.45; SOC 26.9.46

PT484 Spitfire LF.IXe (Merlin 66); TOC/RAF 18.7.44; Casablanca 23.8.44 - SAAF (MTO), No.7 Sqn, hit by AA, Cat.FB/Ac 21.11.44 (Lt ITM Angus); ROS; Hit by flak while attacking strong points 5m N of Imola, believed baled out, crashed NE of Imola, Cat.FB/E 22.12.44 (Lt CHL Paull PoW), SOC

PT491 Spitfire LF.IXe (Merlin 66); TOC/RAF 22.7.44; Casablanca 23.8.44 - SAAF (MTO), No.117 MU to No.4 Sqn ('KJ-A') 19.9.44; Presumed shot down by flak, broke up in air E of Faenza, Cat.FB/E 21.11.44 (Capt IG Will killed), SOC

PT494 Spitfire LF.IXe (Merlin 66); TOC/RAF 21.7.44; Casablanca 23.8.44; MAAF - SAAF (MTO), No.4 Sqn ('KJ-J') from 19.10.44; Bombing 4.4.45 (Lt Carter); Training flight 7.4.45 & 25.6.45 (Lt Montgomery); Retd RAF 6.45; Later to France 25.7.46

PT495 Spitfire LF.IXe (Merlin 66); TOC/RAF 20.7.44; Casablanca 8.44 - SAAF (MTO), No.117 MU to No.4 Sqn 18.9.44 (initially used by Mjr Faure as 'KJ-F', then by Mjr Swales as 'KJ-S' from 26.11.44, and to 'KJ-Y' by 20.2.45); Flew into a house while strafing MT 6m N of Bondeno, disintegrated, Cat.FB/E 25.2.45 (Mjr G Hilton-Barber killed), SOC

PT498 Spitfire LF.IXe (Merlin 66); TOC/RAF 22.7.44; Casablanca 3.9.44 - SAAF (MTO), No.3 Sqn ('CA-F') by 1.45; Retd RAF (No.73 Sqn, missing Cat.FB/E 16.4.45); SOC 14.6.45

PT539 Spitfire LF.IXe (Merlin 66); TOC/RAF 15.8.44; Casablanca 23.8.44 - SAAF (MTO), No.3 Sqn ('CA-E'), collided with parked P-38 while taxying in strong wind, Peretola, Cat.Ac 27.12.44 (Lt DH Lucas OK); Damaged in attack on gun, Cat.FB/1 4.3.45; Retd RAF 6.9.45; SOC 14.3.46

PT541 Spitfire LF.IXe (Merlin 66); TOC/RAF 17.8.44; Casablanca 23.9.44 - SAAF (MTO), No.1 Sqn, hit by AA, Cat.FB/Ac 29.10.44; Hit by AA, Cat.FB/Ac 12.11.44 (both Capt RB McKechnie); Hit by AA, Cat.FB/Ac 3.12.44 (Lt AG Frisby); Damaged propeller on tree while strafing N of Bologna, belly-landed, Cat.FB/E 23.1.45 (Lt HJ Kritzinger evaded capture, retd Sqn 7.4.45), SOC

PT545 Spitfire LF.IXe (Merlin 66); TOC/RAF 23.8.44; Casablanca 23.9.44 - SAAF (MTO), No.7 Sqn, hit by flak, crashed 1m SW of airfield in emergency approach, Bellaria, Cat.FB/E 26.12.44 (Lt PW Nourse killed), SOC

PT566 Spitfire LF.IXe (Merlin 66); TOC/RAF 29.8.44; Casablanca 23.9.44 - SAAF (MTO), No.40 Sqn, hit by AA, crashed E of Cotignola, burnt out, Cat.FB/E 30.3.45 (Lt RF Krynauw killed), SOC

PT591 Spitfire LF.IXe (Merlin 66); TOC/RAF 22.7.44; Casablanca 23.9.44 - SAAF (MTO, No.2 Sqn ('DB-V'), damaged by flak 11.10.44; Damaged at dispersal when bomb fell from BS309 on take-off at Forli 14.12.44 (Lt G van der Spuy); Tailwheel came off on take-off 10.1.45 (Lt HD Carolin); Hit by AA 20m NE of Venice, Cat.FB/Ac 31.3.45 (Lt HPS Broome); No.7 Wing SAAF for repair 1.4.45; Retd RAF; SOC 19.7.45

PT594 Spitfire LF.IXe (Merlin 66); TOC/RAF 25.7.44; Casablanca 23.9.44; MAAF - SAAF (MTO), No.4 Sqn ('KJ-P') from 21.3.45; Training flight 28.6.45 (Lt Goldsworthy); Retd RAF 6.45; SOC 31.10.46

PT601 Spitfire HF.IXe (Merlin 70); Became SAAF No. **5573**; TOC/RAF 22.7.44; Arr South Africa, Cape Town 5.8.48 – SAAF; AOS, swung off runway landing Langebaanweg, Cat.1a 21.11.50 (Lt I J Strydom); R&SU; Flew into hillside, Cat.3 14.3.51 (Lt F B Coetzee killed); b.o.s. 9.8.51; SOC 14.8.51
NOTE: Wreck to SAAF Museum, now at Lanseria AFB

PT614 Spitfire HF.IXe (Merlin 70); Became SAAF No. **5555**; TOC/RAF 24.7.44; Arr South Africa, Cape Town 28.4.48 – SAAF; CFS, undercarriage collapsed landing, not fully down, Cat.1a 9.1.50 (2/Lt Kruger); R&SU; AOS, belly-landed, Cat.1 7.8.51 (Lt LW Parsonson); R&SU; Engine change in 1954; Zwartkop AFB 20.3.54; No.15 AD 12.4.54; For sale 9.5.55

PT615 Spitfire LF.IXe (Merlin 66); TOC/RAF 28.7.44; Casablanca 3.9.44 - SAAF (MTO), No.3 Sqn ('CA-V':'CA-U') by 12.44 to 5.45; Holed by flak in attack on gun, Cat.FB/1 25.3.45 (Lt PB Broken); Retd RAF; SOC 28.2.46

PT618 Spitfire LF.IXe (Merlin 66); TOC/RAF 26.7.44; M.E. 28.12.44 - SAAF (MTO), No.11 Sqn ('ND-L'), date unknown; Retd RAF; SOC (No.107 MU) 28.8.47, but still coded 'ND-L'

PT619 Spitfire HF.IXe (Merlin 70); Became SAAF No. **5...** (range 5555-5637); TOC/RAF 22.7.44; Arr South Africa, Cape Town (via Birkenhead) 13.2.49 - SAAF; Fate unknown

PT625 Spitfire LF.IXe (Merlin 66); TOC/RAF 26.7.44; Casablanca 2.9.44 - SAAF (MTO), No.3 Sqn ('CA-T') by 1.45; Hit by flak, Cat.FB/Ac 21.2.45 (Lt DG Nunan); Retd RAF 6.9.45; Later to Italy (*MM4048*) 30.5.46

PT647 Spitfire LF.IXe (Merlin 66); TOC/RAF 1.8.44 - SAAF (MTO), No.7 Sqn, hit by flak, engine rough and streaming glycol on close support bombing, force-landed wheels up SW of Ravenna, Cat.FB/2 3.1.45 (Lt DH Theron OK); Fate unknown

PT654 Spitfire LF.IXe (Merlin 66); TOC/RAF 28.7.44; Casablanca 8.9.44 - SAAF (MTO), No.3 Sqn, wings wrinkled pulling sharply out of dive bombing dive, Cat.FB/1 5.11.44 (Lt MFW Austin OK); Retd RAF; Later to Italy (*MM4054*) 26.6.47

PT655 Spitfire LF.IXe (Merlin 66); TOC/RAF 29.7.44; Casablanca 11.9.44 - SAAF (MTO), No.3 Sqn (date unknown); Retd RAF (ME); SOC 10.6.48

PT660 Spitfire LF.IXe (Merlin 66); TOC/RAF 28.7.44; Casablanca 3.9.44 - SAAF (MTO), No.3 Sqn ('CA-D') by 3.45; Later to Greece 27.2.47

PT664 Spitfire LF.IXe (Merlin 66); TOC/RAF 28.7.44; Casablanca 3.9.44 - SAAF (MTO), No.3 Sqn, dive bombing attack, wings wrinkled pulling out, hit air pocket and aircraft thrown on back, Cat.FB/B 8.11.44 (Lt DJF Huyser OK); Retd RAF (M.E. 31.5.45); Fate unknown

PT667 Spitfire LF.IXe (Merlin 66); TOC/RAF 29.7.44 – SAAF (MTO), attd to No.2 Sqn from 28.1.45; No.318 Sqn RAF 1.3.45; MAAF 6.45; No.3 Sqn SAAF 7.9.45; Retd RAF (Desert Air Force HQ) 10.9.45; Later to Italy (*MM4037*) 30.5.46

Above: A line-up of CA-coded Spitfire LF.IXs of No. 3 Sqn SAAF around 1944/45, the nearest machine having serial in the PT660-range.
[via Ken Smy]

Left: Spitfire LF.IXe PT672 of No. 40 Sqn SAAF bearing the personal code 'WR-RR' of Lt Col R H D Rogers in 1945 (see page 329).

PT672   Spitfire LF.IXe (Merlin 66); TOC/RAF 28.7.44 - SAAF (MTO), No.40 Sqn ('WR-F':'WR-RR') by 9.44; Concrete surface of runway collapsed while taxying, nosed up, Russi LG, Cat.Ac 6.5.45 (Lt Col RHD Rogers OK); Retd RAF; SOC 30.4.47

PT679   Spitfire LF.IXe (Merlin 66); TOC/RAF 30.7.44; Casablanca 23.9.44 - SAAF (MTO), No.4 Sqn ('KJ-V') 9.11.44; Hit on ground by enemy aircraft in raid, Cat.Ac 11.12.44; Wing skin wrinkled, overstressed in dive nr Forli, Cat.FB/1 2.1.45 (Lt FA Hawley OK); Recce mission 30.1.45 (Lt McChesney); Retd RAF (MAAF) 30.1.45; SOC 13.9.45

PT709   Spitfire LF.IXe (Merlin 66); TOC/RAF 1.8.44; Casablanca 11.9.44 - SAAF (MTO), No.3 Sqn, failed to return, last seen in strafing dive, Cat.FB/E 17.2.45 (Lt JS Aberdien killed), SOC

PT728   Spitfire LF.IXe (Merlin 66); TOC/RAF 4.8.44; Casablanca 11.9.44 - SAAF (MTO), No.1 Sqn, strafing attack after bombing strong point 8m SW of Faenza, engine hit by flak, crashed near Forli, Cat.FB/E 18.11.44 (Capt RB McKechnie seriously injured), SOC

PT760   Spitfire HF.IXe (Merlin 70); TOC/RAF 11.8.44; Casablanca 23.9.44 - SAAF (MTO), No.40 Sqn, hit by AA W of Rovigo, retd to base, Cat.FB/Ac 26.4.45 (Capt PAJ K'Anval-Aimee); Retd RAF; SOC 30.8.45

PT765   Spitfire HF.IXe (Merlin 70); TOC/RAF 11.8.44; Casablanca 23.9.44; MAAF - SAAF (MTO), No.4 Sqn ('KJ-K') from 13.11.44; Training flight 10.3.45 (Lt TF Vollmer); Retd RAF 10.3.45; SOC 6.9.45

PT773   Spitfire LF.IXe (Merlin 66); TOC/RAF 12.8.44; Casablanca 23.9.44 - SAAF (MTO), No.3 Sqn ('CA-D') by 2.45; SOC 4.45

PT781   Spitfire HF.IXe (Merlin 70); Became SAAF No. 5... (range 5555-5637); TOC/RAF 15.8.44; Arr South Africa, Cape Town (via Birkenhead) 2.1.49 - SAAF; Fate unknown

PT787   Spitfire HF.IXe (Merlin 70); Became SAAF No. 5... (range 5555-5637); TOC/RAF 15.8.44; Arr South Africa, Cape Town (via Birkenhead) 13.2.49 - SAAF; Fate unknown

PT788   Spitfire LF.IXe (Merlin 66); TOC/RAF 14.8.44; MAAF 17.2.45 - SAAF (MTO), No.1 Sqn, hit by AA 5m SE of Rovigo, Cat.FB/1 29.3.45 (Lt WJ Bartman); Retd RAF; SOC 14.3.46

PT791   Spitfire LF.IXe (Merlin 66); TOC/RAF 14.8.44; Casablanca 23.9.44 - SAAF (MTO), No.1 Sqn, hit by flak on weather recce, climbed to 3,000ft and baled out, into sea nr Porto Garibaldi, Cat.FB/E 10.1.45 (Lt MHL Tweedie killed), SOC

PT792   Spitfire LF.IXe (Merlin 66); TOC/RAF 14.8.44; Casablanca 23.9.44; MAAF - SAAF (MTO), No.357 MU to No.2 Sqn ('DB-R') 7.11.44; No.7 Wing 3.5.45 (engine change); Retd No.2 Sqn 8.5.45; Retd RAF (No.2ftLU) 13.5.45; SOC 20.9.45

PT793   Spitfire LF.IXe (Merlin 66); TOC/RAF 12.8.44; Casablanca 23.9.44 - SAAF (MTO), No.7 Sqn, holed by flak while strafing, Cat.1 4.4.45 (pilot unhurt); Shot down by flak near Budrio, 10m NE of Bologna, burnt out, Cat.FB/E2 13.4.45 (Lt G F McCormick killed), SOC

PT820   Spitfire LF.IXe (Merlin 66); TOC/RAF 16.8.44; Casablanca 23.8.44 - SAAF (MTO), No.7 Sqn, hit by flak while strafing 5m N of Imola, baled out, Cat.FB/E 22.12.44 (Capt RN Day killed), SOC

PT821   Spitfire LF.IXe (Merlin 66); TOC/RAF 16.8.44; Casablanca 15.1.45; MAAF - SAAF (MTO), No.1 Sqn, hit by AA 10m NE of Vicenza, Cat.FB/Ac 5.4.45 (Lt GD Doveton); Retd RAF; SOC 27.2.47

PT822   Spitfire LF.IXe (Merlin 66); TOC/RAF 17.8.44; Casablanca 23.9.44 - SAAF (MTO), No.1 Sqn, hit by AA, Cat.FB/Ac 14.12.44 (Lt CMT Pare); Hit by AA 16m SW of Udine, Cat.FB/Ac 23.3.45 (Lt EJ Strick); Both mainplanes wrinkled during dive-bombing attack from 9,000ft to 3,000ft, Cat.FB/1 2.4.45 (Lt JS de Villiers OK); Re-Cat.E, SOC

PT831   Spitfire LF.IXe (Merlin 66); TOC/RAF 14.8.44; Casablanca 23.9.44 - SAAF (MTO), No.4 Sqn ('KJ-Q'); Armed recce, hit by flak while strafing HDVs on road near Cento, abandoned and landed safely, aircraft burst into flames and crashed, Cat.FB/E 17.11.44 (Capt MWV Odendaal PoW), SOC

PT845   Spitfire LF.IXe (Merlin 66); TOC/RAF 23.8.44; Casablanca 23.9.44 - SAAF (MTO), No.1 Sqn, overstressed, both mainplanes wrinkled during dive-bombing Cat.FB/1 11.4.45 (Lt TR Fryer OK); Retd RAF, SOC 14.6.45

PT850   Spitfire LF.IXe (Merlin 66); TOC/RAF 24.8.44; Casablanca 23.9.44; MAAF - SAAF (MTO), No.4 Sqn ('KJ-D') from 6.11.44, also by 25.2.45; Practice flight 5.6.45 (Lt J Pollock); Retd RAF 5.6.45; SOC 20.9.45 NOTE: Reported as "PT650", but that operated in ETO

PT886   Spitfire LF.IXe (Merlin 66); TOC/RAF 25.8.44; MAAF 6.45 - SAAF (MTO), No.3 Sqn ('CA-L'), damaged in attack on ammunition dump, Cat.FB/1 16.3.45; Hit by AA, Cat.FB/A 22.4.45 (Lt AR Blair); Retd RAF 6.9.45; SOC 14.3.46

PT897   Spitfire LF.IXe (Merlin 66); TOC/RAF 24.8.44; Casablanca 2.10.44 - SAAF (MTO), No.7 Sqn, hit by flak, retd to base, Cat.FB/Ac 2.1.45 (Mjr RHC Kershaw); Hit by debris while strafing, abandoned 5m E of Adria, burnt out, Cat.FB/E2 10.3.45 (Mjr RHC Kershaw PoW), SOC

PT898   Spitfire LF.IXe (Merlin 66); TOC/RAF 27.8.44; MAAF - SAAF (MTO), No.4 Sqn ('KJ-B') from 3.5.45, Comm Flt 20.6.45 (Lt Tatham); Retd RAF 6.45; Later to Greece 27.2.47

PT900   Spitfire LF.IXe (Merlin 66); TOC/RAF 30.8.44; Casablanca 2.10.44 - SAAF (MTO), No.7 Sqn, hit by flak, crashed on landing Forli, Cat.FB/2 4.1.45 (Capt KA Young); Retd RAF (MAAF 6.45); SOC 2.8.45

PT905 Spitfire HF.IXe (Merlin 70); Became SAAF No. **5...** (range 5555-5637); TOC/RAF 26.8.44; Arr South Africa, Cape Town (via Birkenhead) 16.4.49 - SAAF; Fate unknown

PT910 Spitfire HF.IXe (Merlin 70); Became SAAF No. **5522**; TOC/RAF 29.8.44; Flown to ME, arr No.15 AD Fayid 23.4.47 - SAAF, Zwartkop Air Station 9.6.47; Service unknown; No.15 AD in 6.54; For sale 9.5.55

PT941 Spitfire HF.IXe (Merlin 70); Became SAAF No. **5...** (range 5555-5637); TOC/RAF 29.8.44; Arr South Africa, Cape Town (via Birkenhead) 13.2.49 - SAAF from 15.2.49; Fate unknown

PT954 Spitfire LF.IXe (Merlin 66); TOC/RAF 29.8.44; Casablanca 2.10.45 - SAAF (MTO), No.4 Sqn ('KJ-X') from 11.12.44; Weather recce, engine cut, abandoned over Adriatic, Cat.FB/E 20.2.45 (Capt TA Harris PoW), SOC

PT955 Spitfire LF.IXe (Merlin 66); TOC/RAF 30.8.44; MAAF 12.5.45 - SAAF (MTO), No.11 Sqn ('ND-S'), date unknown; Retd RAF; SOC (No.107 MU) 28.8.47, but still coded 'ND-S'

PT962 Spitfire LF.IXe (Merlin 66); TOC/RAF 30.8.44; Casablanca 2.10.44 - SAAF (MTO), No.3 Sqn ('CA-F') by 4.45; Hit by flak, Cat.FB/A 1.4.45 (Lt AR Blair); Failed to return, hit by flak in Sassuola area, Cat.FB/E 17.4.45 (Capt RC Egner PoW but retd Sqn 1.5.45), SOC

PT994 Spitfire LF.IXe (Merlin 66); TOC/RAF 30.8.44; Casablanca 24.9.44; MAAF - SAAF (MTO), No.1 Sqn, hit by AA 9m W of Luco, Cat.FB/2 3.3.45 (Lt WA Dowden); Retd RAF; Later to Italy (*MM4143*) 26.6.47

PV115 Spitfire LF.IXe (Merlin 66); TOC/RAF 2.8.44; Casablanca 11.9.44; MAAF - SAAF (MTO), No.1 Sqn, hit by AA, Cat.FB/Ac 4.12.44 (Lt HJ Kritzinger); Retd RAF; Later to Italy (*MM4097*) 26.6.47

PV122 Spitfire LF.IXe (Merlin 66); TOC/RAF 2.8.44; Casablanca 23.9.44; MAAF - SAAF (MTO), No.1 Sqn, hit by AA 10m SE Ragno, Cat.FB/Ac 21.1.45 (Capt RJ Barnwell); ROS; Hit by AA nr Porto Garibardi, Cat.FB/Ac 20.2.45 (Capt RJ Barnwell); Retd RAF; Later to Italy (*MM4088*) 27.6.46

PV136 Spitfire LF.IXe (Merlin 66); TOC/RAF 31.8.44; Casablanca 23.9.44; MAAF - SAAF (MTO), No.4 Sqn ('KJ-N') from 8.11.44; Training flight 25.6.45 (Lt Wakers); Retd RAF 6.45; SOC 28.2.46

PV191 Spitfire LF.IXe (Merlin 66); TOC/RAF 16.9.44; Casablanca 3.11.44 - SAAF (MTO), No.40 Sqn (date unknown); Retd RAF; SOC 13.9.45

PV202 See note at end

PV260 Spitfire LF.IXe (Merlin 66); TOC/RAF 23.9.44; Casablanca 23.11.44 - SAAF (MTO), No.357 MU to No.2 Sqn ('DB-V') 23.2.45; Hit by AA in attack of enemy transport, dived into ground 17m NE of Ferrara, Cat.FB/E 25.4.45 (Lt TJ McD Breakey killed), SOC

PV269 Spitfire HF.IXe (Merlin 70); Became SAAF No. **5...** (range 5555-5637); TOC/RAF 25.9.44; Arr South Africa, Cape Town (via Birkenhead) 13.2.49 - SAAF; Fate unknown

PV315 Spitfire LF.IXe (Merlin 66); TOC/RAF 2.10.44; Casablanca 3.11.44 - SAAF (MTO), No.40 Sqn, bad weather, short of fuel, force-landed Wiener Neustadt in Russian Zone 21.8.45 (Lt DP Bolitho); Retd Sqn 24.8.45; No.8 ARD 5.9.45; Retd No.40 Sqn 7.9.45; Retd RAF (No.225 Sqn in 7.46); SOC 31.10.46

PV320 Spitfire LF.IXe (Merlin 66); TOC/RAF 28.9.44; Casablanca 3.11.44 - SAAF (MTO), No.40 Sqn, hit by AA W of Valacu, crash landed Rivolto LG, Cat.FB/2 8.5.45 (2/Lt EH Pike); Retd RAF; SOC 26.9.45

PV325 Spitfire LF.IXe (Merlin 66); TOC/RAF 30.9.44; Casablanca 11.44; No.4 FU - SAAF (MTO), No.3 Sqn ('CA-A') 25.2.45; Damaged when 20mm wing gun exploded, Cat.2 3.3.45 (Lt CE Hedgecock); Damaged by AA in attack on methane gas field, Cat.FB/A 3.4.45 (Lt AR Blair); Retd RAF; Later to Greece 27.3.47

RK856 Spitfire LF.IXe (Merlin 66); TOC/RAF 2.10.44; Casablanca 3.11.44 - SAAF (MTO), No.3 Sqn ('CA-G') 19.4.45; Retd RAF; Later to Greece 30.1.47

RK862 Spitfire LF.IXe (Merlin 66); TOC/RAF 3.10.44; Casablanca 3.11.44; MAAF - SAAF (MTO), No.40 Sqn ('WR-A') by 5.9.45; VIP escort, heavy landing, tail oleo collapsed, swung onto stony ground, stbd tyre burst, nosed up at Peretola, Cat.FB/2 1.10.45 (Lt G Cuyler OK); Retd RAF (No.159 MU) 8.10.45; SOC 28.2.46

RK890 Spitfire LF.IXe (Merlin 66); TOC/RAF 12.10.44; Casablanca 23.11.44 - SAAF (MTO), No.2 Sqn ('DB-W') from 23.2.45; Hit by AA 11m E of Bologna, force-landed Cat.FB/Ac 16.4.45 (Lt DW Haines); No.7 Wing SAAF for repair 6.4.45; Retd No.2 Sqn 11.4.45; Hit by AA 18m NE of Ferrara, Cat.FB/Ac 18.4.45 (Lt JE Harley); No.7 Wing for repair 18.4.45; Retd RAF; SOC 20.9.45

RK907 Spitfire LF.IXe (Merlin 66); TOC/RAF 9.10.44; Casablanca 23.11.44 - SAAF (MTO), No.357 MU to No.2 Sqn ('DB-B') 26.3.45; Hit by AA, abandoned 4m E of Ferrara, Cat.FB/E 25.4.45 (Lt PD Leppen retd Sqn same day), SOC

RK917 Spitfire HF.IXe (Merlin 70); Became SAAF No. **5...** (range 5555-5637); TOC/RAF 10.10.44; Arr South Africa, Cape Town (via Birkenhead) 9.3.49 - SAAF; Fate unknown

RK924 Spitfire HF.IXe (Merlin 70); Became SAAF No. **5...** (range 5555-5637); TOC/RAF 12.10.44; Arr South Africa, Cape Town (via Birkenhead) 13.10.48 - SAAF; Fate unknown

RR184 Spitfire LF.IXe (Merlin 66); TOC/RAF 30.8.44; Casablanca 23.9.44 - SAAF (MTO), No.4 Sqn ('KJ-A') by 26.12.44; Escort duty, spun into marsh while gliding back with dead engine, NE of Cesenatico, Cat.FB/E2 4.1.45 (Lt JJ Roelofse killed), SOC

RR189 Spitfire LF.IXe (Merlin 66); TOC/RAF 5.9.44; Casablanca 2.10.44 - SAAF (MTO), No.357 MU to No.2 Sqn ('DB-H') 21.12.44; Hit by AA, glycol leak, abandoned during ground attack mission N of Lake Commachio/2m S of Migharino, Cat.FB/E 3.1.45 (Lt A Assad PoW), SOC

RR190 Spitfire LF.IXe (Merlin 66); TOC/RAF 5.9.44; Casablanca 2.10.44 – SAAF (MTO), No.7 Sqn, collided with MH764 in formation, crashed 7m S of Udine, burnt out, Cat.E 15.6.45 (Lt JWS van Heerden OK), SOC

RR197 Spitfire LF.IXe (Merlin 66); TOC/RAF 16.9.44; Casablanca 3.11.44 - SAAF (MTO), No.4 Sqn ('KJ-B') from 7.3.45; Strafing mission, brake closed in vertical dive, pulled out sharply, stbd mainplane wrinkled, Cat.FB/A 29.4.45 (Lt F Mendelsohn OK); Retd RAF; Later to Greece 27.3.47

RR203 Spitfire LF.IXe (Merlin 66); TOC/RAF 27.9.44; Casablanca 23.11.44 - SAAF (MTO), No.3 Sqn ('CA-J') by 2.45; Damaged in attack on gun, Cat.FB/A 3.3.45 (Capt DC Theron); Retd RAF; Later to Greece 27.2.47

RR207 Spitfire LF.IXe (Merlin 66); TOC/RAF 12.10.44; Casablanca 23.11.44 - SAAF (MTO), No.7 Sqn, strafing attack, faulty bullet burst cannon barrel and damaged aircraft, mainplane wrinkled, Cat.FB/A 25.3.45 (Capt KA Young OK); Retd RAF (MAAF); Later to Greece 27.2.47

RR210 Spitfire LF.IXe (Merlin 66); TOC/RAF 12.10.44; Casablanca 3.11.44 - SAAF (MTO), No.40 Sqn ('WR-W'), cross-country flight, short of fuel, force-landed in haze in field near Puntigram, Cat.FA/E 10.7.45 (Lt GFR Paxton seriously injured, retd Sqn 14.7.45); Retd RAF (bboc); SOC in 11.45

RR232 Spitfire HF.IXe (Merlin 70); Became SAAF No. **5632**; TOC/RAF 14.10.44; Arr South Africa 21.5.49 – SAAF; No.2 Sqn ('DB-N'), crashed landing, Cat.2 14.2.50 (Lt WF Maritz); R&SU; No.2 Sqn, brake failure on landing, Cat.1 27.4.50 (Lt AM Cooke); R&SU; AOS, crashed on landing, Cat.2 21.6.51 (Lt AR Beamish); SOC, Ysterplaat AFB 16.1.54; Remains South African Metal & Machinery Co, Salt River, Cape Town by 1954;

Spitfire FR.IXe SM143 KJ-T of No. 4 Sqn SAAF has the squadron's "bat" motif on the engine cowling. [SAAF Museum]

Recovered by Larry Barnett and Alan Lurie, Johannesburg (tail section to MA793 rebuild); To Australia 1976, RAN Museum Australia 1985; To Jim Pearce, Sussex, England 13.1.87 (Civil reg. *G-BRSF* 22.11.89) - composite using parts from Mk.VIII JF629 from Western Australia and wings of Thai AF Mk.XVI U14-5/93 (RM873); Stored 3.96; Now Martin Phillips, Exeter, UK - **SURVIVOR**

RR264   Spitfire HF.IXe (Merlin 70); TOC/RAF 18.10.44; Casablanca 15.1.45; MAAF - SAAF (MTO); No. 7 Wing, to No.2 Sqn ('DB-D') 10.4.45; Retd RAF (No.2ftLU) 13.5.45; SOC 6.9.45

SM141   Spitfire LF.IXe (Merlin 66); TOC/RAF 28.9.44; Casablanca 3.11.44 - SAAF (MTO), No.40 Sqn; Retd RAF (MAAF); SOC 30.4.47

SM143   Spitfire LF.IXe (Merlin 66); TOC/RAF 25.9.44; MAAF 7.2.45 - SAAF (MTO), No.4 Sqn ('KJ-T') from 25.3.45; Comm Flt 6.7.45 (Lt Metcalf); Retd RAF 6.7.45; SOC 14.3.46

SM149   Spitfire LF.IXe (Merlin 66); TOC/RAF 2.10.44; Casablanca 23.11.44 - SAAF (MTO), No.4 Sqn ('KJ-V') from 17.2.45; Shot down FW 190, but hit by enemy aircraft over Oderzo, baled out nr Conegliano, burnt out, Cat.FB/E 3.3.45 (Lt MF Reim murdered while trying to evade capture); SOC

SM441   Spitfire LF.IXe (Merlin 66); TOC/RAF 12.10.44; Casablanca 3.11.44; No.324 (Wing) R&SU - SAAF (MTO), No.40 Sqn 13.10.45; Retd RAF; Later to Italy 26.6.47

SM444   Spitfire LF.IXe (Merlin 66); TOC/RAF 16.10.44; Casablanca 23.11.44 - SAAF (MTO), No.3 Sqn, damaged in attack on flak, Cat.FB/A 3.3.45 (Capt FE Potgieter); Hit by AA, crashed on landing, Cat.FB/2 20.4.45 (Lt MH Hartogh); Retd RAF; SOC 13.12.45

SM505   Spitfire HF.IXe (Merlin 70); Became SAAF No. **5...** (range 5555-5637); TOC/RAF 23.11.44; Arr South Africa, Cape Town (via Birkenhead) 13.2.49 - SAAF; Fate unknown

SM506   Spitfire HF.IXe (Merlin 70); Became SAAF No. **5556**; TOC/RAF 23.11.44; Arr South Africa, Cape Town 28.4.48 – SAAF; AOS, dived into sea after drogue attack 3.10.52 (2/Lt van der Heever killed); b.o.s. 5.8.53; SOC 11.8.53; FC 15.10.53

SM520   Spitfire HF.IXe (Merlin 70); Became SAAF No. **5...** (range 5555-5637); TOC/RAF 23.11.44; Arr South Africa, Cape Town (via Birkenhead) 21.6.48 – SAAF; Service unknown; In scrapyard South African Metal & Machinery Co, Salt River, Cape Town 1954; Hulk to SAAF Museum, Snake Valley 1981; To Steve W Atkins, Oxford, England; Restoration to fly in UK (Civil reg. *G-BXHZ* 9.6.97), To Alan G Dunkerley, Edenfield, Lancashire and last known in Oxfordshire (restoration by C W Engineering) - **SURVIVOR**

SM523   Spitfire HF.IXe (Merlin 70); Became SAAF No. **5504**; TOC/RAF 2.12.44; Flown to ME, arr No.15 A D Fayid 17.5.47 - SAAF, Zwartkop Air Station in 7.47; Service unknown; SOC 14.10.49; FC 23.10.53

TA802   Spitfire HF.IXe (Merlin 70); Became SAAF No. **5505**; TOC/RAF 9.12.44; Flown to ME, arr No.15 A D Fayid 16.5.47 - SAAF, Zwartkop Air Station 7.47; No.35 Sqn, landed undercarriage not locked down 2.11.48 (Lt SI Botes); R&SU; b.o.s. 11.6.53; SOC 3.7.53

TA805   Spitfire HF.IXe (Merlin 70); Became SAAF No. **5...** (range 5555-5637); TOC/RAF 3.1.45; Arr South Africa, Cape Town (via Birkenhead) 16.4.49 - SAAF; Service unknown; To scrapyard South African Metal & Machinery Co, Salt River, Cape Town 1954; To SAAF Museum, Snake Valley AFB 1981; To Steve W Atkins, Oxford, England 1989 for restoration project (Civil reg. *G-PMNF* 29.4.96), Peter Monk & Mike Simpson, Airframe Assemblies, Sandown, Isle of Wight - **SURVIVOR**

TA816   Spitfire HF.IXe (Merlin 70); TOC/RAF 13.12.44; MAAF 8.3.45 - SAAF (MTO), No.4 Sqn from 9.4.45 ('KJ-L'); Cover, flown by Capt Cohen 25.4.45; Marked 'KJ-Q', Training flight by Lt Walters 25.4.45 & 25.6.45; Retd RAF 6.45; Later to Greece 30.4.47

TA854   Spitfire LF.IXe (Merlin 66); TOC/RAF 3.10.44; Casablanca 2.11.44; MAAF - SAAF (MTO), No.9 Sqn, to No.2 Sqn ('DB-G') 6.4.45; Retd RAF (No.2 FTLU) 27.4.45; Later to Greece 27.2.47

TB568   RegNo: 5511;Spitfire HF.IXe (Merlin 70); TOC/RAF 5.2.45; Flown to ME, arr No.15 AD Fayid 2.6.47 - SAAF, Zwartkop Air Station in 8.47; Fate unknown

TB569   Spitfire HF.IXe (Merlin 70); Became SAAF No. **5...** (range 5555-5637); TOC/RAF 5.2.45; Arr South Africa, Cape Town (delivered via Liverpool) 4.12.48 - SAAF; Fate unknown

TB576   Spitfire HF.IXe (Merlin 70); Became SAAF No. **5506**; TOC/RAF 14.2.45; Flown to ME, arr No.15 AD Fayid

	23.4.47 - SAAF, Zwartkop Air Station 9.6.47; No.68 Air School (TTS) 25.5.54; No.15 AD 20.6.54; For sale 16.5.57
TB985	Spitfire HF.IXe (Merlin 70); Became SAAF No. **55..** (range 5502-5554); TOC/RAF 28.2.45; Flown to ME, arr No.15 AD Fayid 4.8.47 - SAAF, Zwartkop Air Station 1947; Fate unknown
TB986	Spitfire HF.IXe (Merlin 70); Became SAAF No. **5510**; TOC/RAF 28.2.45; Flown to ME, arr No.15 AD Fayid 2.6.47 - SAAF, Zwartkop Air Station in 8.47; CFS, engine failed on approach, crashed, Cat.FA/3 29.1.51 (2/Lt F Muller), SOC
TB987	Spitfire HF.IXe (Merlin 70); Became SAAF No. **55..** (range 5502-5554); TOC/RAF 28.2.45; Flown to ME, arr No.15 AD Fayid 4.8.47 - SAAF, Zwartkop Air Station 1947; Fate unknown
TB988	Spitfire HF.IXe (Merlin 70); Became SAAF No. **55..** (range 5502-5554); TOC/RAF 1.3.45; Flown to ME, arr No.15 AD Fayid 17.5.47 - SAAF, Zwartkop Air Station in 7.47; Fate unknown
TD310	Spitfire HF.IXe (Merlin 70); Became SAAF No. **5...** (range 5555-5637); TOC/RAF 27.3.45; Arr South Africa, Cape Town (via Birkenhead) 23.2.49 - SAAF; Fate unknown
TD314	Spitfire HF.IXe (Merlin 70); Became SAAF No. **5...** (range 5555-5637); TOC/RAF 30.3.45; Arr South Africa 11.5.48, Cape Town 12.5.48 – SAAF; Service unknown; Ysterplaat AFB; Scrapyard Cape Town; Recovered by Larry Barnett; Cockpit section only, arrived in UK from South Africa 11.4.79; To Matt Sattler, Ontario; Now in UK, restoration - **SURVIVOR**
TD315	Spitfire HF.IXe (Merlin 70); Became SAAF No. **5...** (range 5555-5637); TOC/RAF 29.3.45; Arr South Africa, Cape Town (via Birkenhead) 10.8.48 - SAAF; Fate unknown
TD352	Spitfire HF.IXe (Merlin 70); Became SAAF No. **5...** (range 5555-5637); TOC/RAF 29.3.45; Arr South Africa, Cape Town (via Birkenhead) 10.3.49 - SAAF; Fate unknown
TD353	Spitfire HF.IXe (Merlin 70); Became SAAF No. **55..** (range 5502-5554); TOC/RAF 29.3.45; Flown to ME, arr No.15 AD Fayid 2.6.47 - SAAF, Zwartkop Air Station in 8.47; Fate unknown
TE205	Spitfire HF.IXe (Merlin 70); Became SAAF No. **55..** (range 5502-5554); TOC/RAF 15.5.45; Flown to ME, arr No.15 AD Fayid 20.9.47 - SAAF, Zwartkop Air Station 1947; Fate unknown
TE211	Spitfire HF.IXe (Merlin 70); Became SAAF No. **55..** (range 5502-5554); TOC/RAF 23.5.45; Flown to ME, arr No.15 AD Fayid 18.6.47 - SAAF, Zwartkop Air Station in 8.47; Fate unknown
TE212	Spitfire HF.IXe (Merlin 70); Became SAAF No. **55..** (range 5502-5554); TOC/RAF 23.5.45; Flown to ME, arr No.15 AD Fayid 11.7.47, left Fayid for South Africa 14.8.47 - SAAF, Zwartkop Air Station 1947; Fate unknown
TE213	Spitfire HF.IXe (Merlin 70); Became SAAF No. **5518**; TOC/RAF 15.5.45; Flown to ME, arr No.15 AD Fayid 31.7.47, left Fayid for South Africa 14.8.47 - SAAF, Zwartkop Air Station in 8.47; To Waterkloof AFS 4.12.48; No.7 Wing in 12.48; Mid-air collision with 5516, Cat.1 25.6.49 (Lt Gow); R&SU; AOS Langebaanweg 4.51; Struck drogue cable, Cat.1 12.9.51 (2/Lt CJ Pappas); R&SU; No.1 Sqn, Zwartkop in 6.53; SOC 7.4.54; No.15 AD in 6.54; Waterkloof from 14.3.55; Exhibited outside on a pole as "W5581" (also "W5851"); To the South African Museum at Waterkloof in 11.78; To the museum's facility at Lanseria airport nr Johannesburg 29.3.79 (with parts of MA793); Restoration by No.1 Air Depot at Zwartkop AFB; Airworthy, first flight after restoration 7.10.95 (Test pilot Rick Cullpan); SAAF Museum Flight Lanseria, flown as "*5553*" and marked 'AX-K' in 1996; Engine failed, badly damaged in crash at Zwartkop AFB 15.4.2000 (Col Neil Thomas safe); Restorable to static display only - **SURVIVOR**
TE215	Spitfire HF.IXe (Merlin 70); Became SAAF No. **55..** (range 5502-5554); TOC/RAF 18.5.45; Flown to ME, arr No.15 AD Fayid 22.8.47 - SAAF, Zwartkop Air Station 1947; Fate unknown
TE230	Spitfire HF.IXe (Merlin 70); Became SAAF No. **5...** (range 5555-5637); TOC/RAF 23.5.45; Arr South Africa, Cape Town (via Birkenhead) 13.3.49 - SAAF; Fate unknown
TE232	Spitfire HF.IXe (Merlin 70); Became SAAF No. **55..** (range 5502-5554); TOC/RAF 16.5.45; Flown to ME, arr No.15 AD Fayid 4.8.47 - SAAF, Zwartkop Air Station 1947; Fate unknown
TE234	Spitfire HF.IXe (Merlin 70); Became SAAF No. **55..** (range 5502-5554); TOC/RAF 17.5.45; Flown to ME, arr No.15 AD Fayid 17.5.47 - SAAF, Zwartkop Air Station in 7.47; Fate unknown
TE238	Spitfire HF.IXe (Merlin 70); Became SAAF No. **55..** (range 5502-5554); TOC/RAF 18.5.45; Flown to ME, arr No.15 AD Fayid 20.9.47 - SAAF, Zwartkop Air Station 1947; Fate unknown
TE289	Spitfire HF.IXe (Merlin 70); Became SAAF No. **55..** (range 5502-5554); TOC/RAF 29.5.45; Flown to ME, arr No.15 AD Fayid 5.8.47 - SAAF, Zwartkop Air Station 1947; Fate unknown
TE290	Spitfire HF.IXe (Merlin 70); Became SAAF No. **55..** (range 5502-5554); TOC/RAF 8.6.45; Flown to ME, arr No.15 AD Fayid 22.8.47 - SAAF, Zwartkop Air Station 1947; Fate unknown
TE292	Spitfire HF.IXe (Merlin 70); Became SAAF No. **5...** (range 5555-5637); TOC/RAF 6.45; Arr South Africa, Cape Town (via Birkenhead) 17.3.49 - SAAF; Fate unknown
TE293	Spitfire HF.IXe (Merlin 70); Became SAAF No. **55..** (range 5502-5554); TOC/RAF 4.6.45; Flown to ME, arr No.15 AD Fayid 5.8.47 - SAAF, Zwartkop Air Station 1947; Fate unknown
TE294	Spitfire HF.IXe (Merlin 70); Became SAAF No. **5519**; TOC/RAF 7.6.45; Flown to ME, arr No.15 AD Fayid 31.7.47, left Fayid for South Africa 14.8.47 – SAAF; Zwartkop Air Station 1947; No.1 Sqn, taxying accident 24.7.48 (Capt Duigan); AOS, undercarriage collapsed on landing, Cat.2 4.1.52 (2/Lt JN Lellyet); Ysterplaat AFB, SOC 22.1.54; Cape Town, scrapyard; SAAF Museum, storage Snake Valley; Front fuselage to Mark de Vries, Bryanston, SA; To the Air Museum at Comox, British Columbia in Canada (with Merlin 63) for restoration 5.99 - **SURVIVOR**
TE297	Spitfire HF.IXe (Merlin 70); Became SAAF No. **5...** (range 5555-5637); TOC/RAF 6.45; Arr South Africa, Cape Town (via Birkenhead) 16.4.49 - SAAF; Fate unknown
TE298	Spitfire HF.IXe (Merlin 70); Became SAAF No. **55..** (range 5502-5554); TOC/RAF 28.5.45; Flown to ME, arr No.15 AD Fayid 31.7.47 - SAAF, Zwartkop Air Station 1947; Fate unknown
TE301	Spitfire HF.IXe (Merlin 70); Became SAAF No. **55..** (range 5502-5554); TOC/RAF 4.6.45; Flown to ME, arr No.15 AD Fayid 4.10.47 - SAAF, Zwartkop Air Station 1947; Fate unknown
TE303	Spitfire HF.IXe (Merlin 70); Became SAAF No. **5...** (range 5555-5637); TOC/RAF 6.45; Arr South Africa, Cape Town (via Birkenhead) 22.5.49 - SAAF; Fate unknown
TE305	Spitfire HF.IXe (Merlin 70); Became SAAF No. **55..** (range 5502-5554); TOC/RAF 31.5.45; Flown to ME, arr No.15 AD Fayid 11.7.47, left Fayid for South Africa 14.8.47 - SAAF, Zwartkop Air Station 1947; Fate unknown
TE306	Spitfire HF.IXe (Merlin 70); Became SAAF No. **55..** (range 5502-5554); TOC/RAF 12.6.45; Flown to ME, arr No.15 AD Fayid 18.6.47 - SAAF, Zwartkop Air Station in 8.47; Fate unknown

TE307 Spitfire HF.IXe (Merlin 70); Became SAAF No. **5...** (range 5555-5637); TOC/RAF 31.5.45; Arr South Africa, Cape Town (via Birkenhead) 21.6.48 - SAAF; Fate unknown

TE309 Spitfire HF.IXe (Merlin 70); Became SAAF No. **5637**; TOC/RAF 6.45; Arr South Africa 6.10.49; Cape Town (via Birkenhead) 6.10.49 – SAAF; AOS, swung landing, tyre burst, Cat.1 21.6.51 (Lt MS Pretorius); No.1 Sqn, propeller hit ground on take-off, Cat.1 14.8.53 (Cdt Verster); Zwartkop Air Station, ground accident 20.11.53 (Sgt Pohl); No.1 Sqn, crashed on landing, Cat.3 15.12.53 (Cdt WR Spies killed); No.15 AD, Zwartkop AFB 17.12.53 (engine removed); SOC 17.8.54

TE312 Spitfire HF.IXe (Merlin 70); Became SAAF No. **5...** (range 5555-5637); TOC/RAF 6.45; Arr South Africa, Cape Town (via Birkenhead) 22.10.48 - SAAF; Fate unknown

TE313 Spitfire HF.IXe (Merlin 70); Became SAAF No. **5...** (range 5555-5637); TOC/RAF 6.45; Arr South Africa, Cape Town (via Birkenhead) 22.11.48 - SAAF; Fate unknown

TE315 Spitfire HF.IXe (Merlin 70); Became SAAF No. **55..** (range 5502-5554); TOC/RAF 2.6.45; Flown to ME, arr No.15 AD Fayid in 12.47 - SAAF, Zwartkop Air Station in 12.47; Fate unknown

TE329 Spitfire HF.IXe (Merlin 70); Became SAAF No. **5...** (range 5555-5637); TOC/RAF 4.6.45; Arr South Africa, Cape Town (via Birkenhead) 21.6.48 - SAAF; Fate unknown

TE331 Spitfire HF.IXe (Merlin 70); Became SAAF No. **5...** (range 5555-5637); TOC/RAF 7.6.45; Arr South Africa, Cape Town (via Birkenhead) 3.11.48 - SAAF; Fate unknown

TE333 Spitfire HF.IXe (Merlin 70); Became SAAF No. **5...** (range 5555-5637); TOC/RAF 4.6.45; Arr South Africa, Cape Town (via Birkenhead) 21.6.48 - SAAF; Fate unknown

TE336 Spitfire HF.IXe (Merlin 70); Became SAAF No. **55..** (range 5502-5554); TOC/RAF 6.45; Flown to ME, arr No.15 AD Fayid 11.7.47 - SAAF, Zwartkop Air Station 1947; Fate unknown

TE337 Spitfire HF.IXe (Merlin 70); Became SAAF No. **55..** (range 5502-5554); TOC/RAF 2.6.45; Flown to ME, arr No.15 AD Fayid 5.8.47 - SAAF, Zwartkop Air Station 1947; Fate unknown

TE343 Spitfire HF.IXe (Merlin 70); Became SAAF No. **5636**; TOC/RAF 6.45; Arr South Africa, Cape Town (via Birkenhead) 6.10.49 – SAAF; Langebaanweg AFB; No.15 AD; Service unknown; Zwartkop AFB 25.2.54; No.15 AD from 12.4.54; For sale 9.5.55

TE566 Spitfire LF.IXe (Merlin 66); ex CSSR & Israel (*2032*); Recovered and to UK 12.76 (*G-BLCK* 22.11.83) - Arrived in South Africa as **SURVIVOR** only: To Andrew J Torr, Zwartkop AFB 8.98 (reg. *ZU-SPT* 12.8.98)

SAAF at home (new order)

Regrettably, the records giving dates of service with units, and those listing the relationship to RAF serial numbers have not survived. The original RAF serial numbers of these aircraft are therefore mostly unknown:

5501	see	JF294
5502	see	EN314
5503	see	NH534
5504	see	SM523
5505	see	TA802
5506	see	TB576
5507	see	BS512
5508	see	PL192
5509	see	MA756
5510	see	TB986
5511	see	TB568

5512 Spitfire HF.IXe (Merlin 70); Flown to No.15 AD Fayid 1947 - SAAF, Zwartkop Air Station 1947; No.1 Sqn, undercarriage failure, belly-landed 9.9.48 (Lt KB McDonald)

5513 Spitfire HF.IXe (Merlin 70); Flown to No.15 AD Fayid 1947 - SAAF, Zwartkop Air Station 1947; Fate unknown

5514 Spitfire HF.IXe (Merlin 70); Flown to No.15 AD Fayid 1947 - SAAF, Zwartkop Air Station 1947; No.7 Wing, engine failure, force-landed, Cat.3 17.6.49 (Lt JB Rossiter); SOC 14.10.49

5515 Spitfire HF.IXe (Merlin 70); Flown to No.15 AD Fayid 1947 - SAAF, Zwartkop Air Station 1947; No.1 Sqn, propeller damage 13.3.48 (Lt AB Bridgers); No.2 Sqn, crashed on landing, brake failure, Cat.2 6.7.50 (Lt DD Grace); AOS, hit fence landing, Bloemspruit, Cat.1 18.9.52 (Lt AS Rae); No.1 Sqn, failed to recover from spin, dived into ground, Cat.3 8.9.53 (Cdt AC Cillie killed); No.15 AD; b.o.s. 5.11.53; SOC 13.11.53

5516 Spitfire IX (Merlin 70 ?); Flown to No.15 AD Fayid 1947 - SAAF, Zwartkop Air Station 1947; No.7 Wing; No.1 Sqn ('AX-M'), mid-air collision with 5518, Cat.1 25.6.49 (Capt JFO Davis); Engine failure on take-off 16.9.49 (Capt JFO Davis); Radiator cowling came off, Cat.1 21.3.50 (Capt JFO Davis); No.2 Sqn, engine failed on take-off Waterkloof, Cat.3 3.8.50 (Lt JA Joubert); b.o.s. 5.1.51; FC 30.10.52

5517 Spitfire HF.IXe (Merlin 70); Flown to No.15 AD Fayid 1947 – SAAF; Unknown unit, engine failed, force-landed Zwartkop, Cat.1b 24.12.49 (Lt FB Richter); AOS, crashed on landing, brake failure, Cat.1 6.7.51 (Lt B Wilson); No.15 AD in 6.54; For sale 9.5.55

5518 see TE213

5519 see TE294

5520 Spitfire IX (Merlin 70 ?); Flown to No.15 AD Fayid 1947 - SAAF, Zwartkop Air Station 1947; No.1 Sqn, mid-air collision with 5502 5.8.48 (Capt K Kuhlmann); Ground looped landing 31.8.48 (2/Lt MH Rorke); Engine failure, force-landed, Cat.3 23.3.50 (Lt Lello); b.o.s. 28.7.50; SOC 10.8.50

5521 Spitfire IX (Merlin 70 ?); Flown to No.15 AD Fayid 1947 - SAAF, Zwartkop Air Station 1947; No.1 Sqn, engine failure, force-landed, Cat.3 10.1.50 (Lt CP Starck); b.o.s. 28.7.50; SOC 10.8.50

5522 see PT910

5523 Spitfire IX (Merlin 70 ?); Flown to No.15 AD Fayid 1947 - SAAF, Zwartkop Air Station 1947; No.15 AD in 6.54; For sale without engine 9.5.55

5524 Spitfire HF.IXe (Merlin 70); Flown to No.15 AD Fayid 1947 - SAAF, Zwartkop Air Station 1947; AOS, belly landing, Cat.1a 23.12.52 (2/Lt DC Louw); Zwartkop AFB 18.11.53; No.15 AD 12.4.54 (engine changed, then No.185031); For sale 9.5.55

5525 Spitfire HF.IXe (Merlin 70); Flown to No.15 AD Fayid 1947 - SAAF, Zwartkop Air Station 1947; AOS, engine failure, pilot baled out, dived into ground, Cat.3 21.4.52 (Lt GG Paterson); b.o.s. 3.2.53; SOC 10.2.53

5526 Spitfire IX (Merlin 70 ?); Flown from RAF Pershore to No.15 AD Fayid 1947 - SAAF, Zwartkop Air Station 1947; Service unknown; SOC 14.10.49

5527 Spitfire HF.IXe (Merlin 70); Flown to No.15 AD Fayid 1947 - SAAF, Zwartkop Air Station 1947; No.60 Sqn, propeller struck ground on take-off, Zwartkop, Cat.1a 18.7.50 (Lt RB Wheeldon); No.15 AD in 6.54; For sale 9.5.55

5528 Spitfire IX (Merlin 70 ?); Flown to No.15 AD Fayid 1947 - SAAF, Zwartkop Air Station 1947; CFS, tyre flat, overturned on landing, Cat.FA/3 25.3.49 (Lt HH or KB MacDonald); SOC 14.10.49

5529 Spitfire IX (Merlin 70 ?); Flown to No.15 AD Fayid 1947 - SAAF, Zwartkop Air Station 1947; Unknown unit, ground looped landing 21.8.48 (2/Lt WE Wilson); Fate unknown

5530 Spitfire IX (Merlin 70 ?); Flown to No.15 AD Fayid 1947 - SAAF, Zwartkop Air Station 1947; Fate unknown

5531 Spitfire HF.IXe (Merlin 70); Flown to No.15 AD Fayid 1947 - SAAF, Zwartkop Air Station 1947; No.1 Sqn ('AX-X'), crashed on landing, held off to high, Cat.2 20.1.50 (Lt NC Maritz); No.15 AD in 6.54; For sale 9.5.55 (S&D); SOC 28.10.55

5532 Spitfire IX (Merlin 70 ?); Flown to No.15 AD Fayid 1947 - SAAF, Zwartkop Air Station 1947; No.1 Sqn, engine cut out, force-landed, Cat.1a 30.1.51 (Lt JH Haskins); AOS, engine failure, pilot baled out, a/c dived into ground, Cat.3 4.7.51 (Lt AJ Meiring); b.o.s. 1.2.52; SOC 5.2.52

5533 Spitfire IX (Merlin 70 ?); Flown to No.15 AD Fayid 1947 - SAAF, Zwartkop Air Station 1947; Service unknown; No.15 AD in 6.54; For sale 9.5.55 (without engine)

5534 Spitfire IX (Merlin 70 ?); Flown to No.15 AD Fayid 1947 - SAAF, Zwartkop Air Station 1947; No.1 Sqn 1947; AOS, dived into sea after launching rocket-projectile, Toothrock, Cat.3 12.5.51 (2/Lt CH Venter killed); b.o.s. 9.8.51; SOC 14.8.51

5535 Spitfire HF.IXe (Merlin 70); Flown to No.15 AD Fayid 1947 - SAAF, Zwartkop Air Station 1947; AOS, tyre burst on landing, Cat.1 11.5.51 (2/Lt ER Keevy); No.15 AD in 6.54; For sale 9.5.55

5536 Spitfire FR.IXe (Merlin 70); Flown to No.15 AD Fayid 1947 - SAAF, Zwartkop Air Station 1947; No.60 Sqn ('JS-B'), mods for PR duties (field-conversion to FR.IXe); No.15 AD in 6.54; For sale 9.5.55

5537 Spitfire IX (Merlin 70 ?); Flown to No.15 AD Fayid 1947 - SAAF, Zwartkop Air Station 1947; Service unknown; b.o.s. 14.6.48; SOC 23.6.48

5538 Spitfire HF.IXe (Merlin 70); Flown to No.15 AD Fayid 1947 - SAAF, Zwartkop Air Station 1947; No.15 AD in 6.54; For sale 9.5.55

5539 Spitfire F.IX (Merlin 63); Flown to No.15 AD Fayid 1947 - SAAF, Zwartkop Air Station 1947; No.1 Sqn ('AX-G'); Lyttelton AFB; b.o.s. 31.7.52; SOC 12.8.52; No.15 AD 17.5.54; For sale 9.5.55; S&D 28.10.55

5540 Spitfire HF.IXe (Merlin 70); Flown from RAF Pershore to No.15 AD Fayid 1947 - SAAF, Zwartkop Air Station 1947; AOS, flew into drogue cable, Cat.1 17.11.51 (Lt A Gardiner-Atkinson); No.1 Sqn, canopy blew off on take-off, Cat.2 9.10.53 (Cdt Crafford); Crashed on landing, held off too high 21.10.53 (2/Lt HJ Yates); No.15 AD 9.1.54; For sale 9.5.55

5541 Spitfire IX (Merlin 70 ?); Flown to No.15 AD Fayid 1947 - SAAF, Zwartkop Air Station 1947; SOC 14.10.49

5542 Spitfire IX (Merlin 70 ?); Flown to No.15 AD Fayid 1947 - SAAF, Zwartkop Air Station 1947; AOS, engine failure after bird-strike, crashed at Langebaanweg, Cat.3 8.12.50 (Lt IJ Strydom); b.o.s. 7.10.51; SOC 13.11.51

5543 Spitfire HF.IXe (Merlin 70); Flown from RAF Pershore to No.15 AD Fayid 1947 - SAAF, Zwartkop Air Station 1947; No.1 Sqn, damaged by bomb fragments 28.9.48 (Capt JFO Davis); No.2 Sqn ('DB-A'), swung on landing, Cat.2 7.1.50 (Lt RM Savage); No.1 Sqn, crashed on landing, undercarriage not locked down, Cat.1 26.10.50 (2/Lt RL Staats); AOS, hit drogue, forced landed Toothrock, Cat.1a 24.6.52 (Capt JF Nortje); Zwartkop AFB 21.11.53; No.15 AD 12.4.54; For sale 9.5.55

5544 Spitfire IX (Merlin 70 ?); Flown to No.15 AD Fayid 1947 - SAAF, Zwartkop Air Station 1947; AOS, engine failure, force-landed, Langebaanweg, Cat.3 30.10.50 (Lt DR Leathers); b.o.s. 5.1.51; SOC 9.2.51

5545 Spitfire F.IX (Merlin 63); Flown to No.15 AD Fayid 1947 - SAAF, Zwartkop Air Station 1947; No.15 AD in 6.54; For sale 9.5.55

5546 Spitfire IX (Merlin 70 ?); Flown to No.15 AD Fayid 1947 - SAAF, Zwartkop Air Station 1947; No.2 Sqn, undercarriage retracted too soon on take-off, crashed, Cat.2 4.2.49 (Lt BJ Geldenhuys); b.o.s. 4.12.50; SOC 12.1.51

5547 Spitfire IX (Merlin 70 ?); Flown to No.15 AD Fayid 1947 - SAAF, Zwartkop Air Station 1947; No.15 AD in 6.54; For sale without engine 9.5.55

5548 Spitfire F.IX (Merlin 63); Flown to No.15 AD Fayid 1947 - SAAF, Zwartkop Air Station 1947; No.1 Sqn, engine failure landing, crashed, Cat.2 16.8.49 (Lt DD Grace); b.o.s. 28.7.50; SOC 10.8.50

5549 Spitfire HF IXe (Merlin 70); Flown to No.15 AD Fayid 1947 - SAAF, Zwartkop Air Station 1947; Fate unknown

5550 Spitfire IX (Merlin 70 ?); Flown to No.15 AD Fayid 1947 - SAAF, Zwartkop Air Station 1947; No.15 AD in 6.54; For sale 9.5.55 (S&D Metal); SOC 28.10.55 (sold without engine)

5551 Spitfire IX (Merlin 70 ?); Flown to No.15 AD Fayid 1947 - SAAF, Zwartkop Air Station 1947; No.15 AD in 6.54; For sale 9.5.55 (without engine)

5552 Spitfire IX (Merlin 70 ?); Flown to No.15 AD Fayid 1947 - SAAF, Zwartkop Air Station 1947; b.o.s. 14.10.49; FC 23.10.53

5553 Spitfire HF.IXe (Merlin 70); Flown to No.15 AD Fayid 1947 - SAAF, Zwartkop Air Station 1947; No.1 Sqn ('AX-K'), propeller hit ground landing, Cat.1 7.10.50 (Lt GD Wiehahn); Propeller hit ground landing, Cat.1 9.10.50 (Lt GD Wiehahn); Fuel shortage, forced landed, crashed, Vereeniging, Cat.2 8.12.50 (2/Lt E Downie); Zwartkop AFB 15.3.54; No.15 AD 12.4.54; For sale 9.5.55

5554 Spitfire HF.IXe (Merlin 70); Flown to No.15 AD Fayid 1947 - SAAF, Zwartkop Air Station 1947; No.1 AD, damaged during hailstorm, Cat.1 25.11.49 (Lt AM Cooke); No.1 Aux Sqn, swung on landing, Cat.1a 15.2.50 (2/Lt FG Coetzee); Undercarriage collapsed landing, Cat.2 23.9.50 (Capt GC Dent); No.15 AD 12.4.54; For sale 9.5.55

5555 see PT614

5556 see SM506

5557 see ML145

5558 see PL253

5559 Spitfire IX (Merlin 70 ?); Shipped to Cape Town 1948 – SAAF; Service unknown; SOC 14.10.49

5560 Spitfire IX (Merlin 70 ?); Shipped to Cape Town 1948 – SAAF; Service unknown; SOC 14.10.49

5561 Spitfire IX (Merlin 70 ?); Shipped to Cape Town 1948 – SAAF; AOS, collided with 5616 on landing Ysterplaat AFB, Cat.3 31.3.52 (2/Lt EAC Pienaar); b.o.s. 3.2.53; SOC 10.2.53

5562 Spitfire IX (Merlin 70 ?); Shipped to Cape Town 1948 – SAAF; Service unknown; SOC 14.10.49

5563 see ML255

5564 see BS408

5565 Spitfire F.IX (Merlin 63); Shipped to Cape Town 1948 – SAAF; Service unknown; No.15 AD in 6.54; For sale 9.5.55

5566 Spitfire F.IX (Merlin 63); Shipped to Cape Town 1948 – SAAF; No.68 Air School (TTS), ground accident, Cat.1 24.4.51 (Sgt Stopberg); No.15 AD in 6.54; For sale 9.5.55

5567 Spitfire IX (Merlin 63, later Merlin 70); Shipped to Cape Town 1948 – SAAF; AOS, engine failure, force-landed wheels-up, Cat.1 2.11.51 (Lt RW Clark); Merlin 70 installed 5.52; Ysterplaat AFB; SOC 16.2.54

5568 Spitfire IX (Merlin 70 ?); Shipped to Cape Town 1948 – SAAF; No.15 AD; Ysterplaat AFB; AOS, engine failure, dived into ground, pilot baled out, Cat.3 30.1.51 (Lt JH Haskins); b.o.s. 7.10.51; SOC 13.11.51;

5569 Spitfire IX (Merlin 70 ?); Shipped to Cape Town 1948 – SAAF; Service unknown; No.15 AD in 6.54; For sale 9.5.55 (without engine)

5570 Spitfire HF.IXe (Merlin 70); Shipped to Cape Town 1948 – SAAF; No.2 Sqn, ground looped after landing,

	Cat.2 30.7.49 (2/Lt IJ Gow); Zwartkop AFB 9.1.54; No.15 AD 12.4.54; For sale 9.5.55
5571	Spitfire IX (Merlin 70 ?); Shipped to Cape Town 1948 – SAAF; No.2 Sqn, pilot blacked out in dive, crashed, Cat. 3 18.8.49 (Capt RE Gray killed); b.o.s. 28.7.50; SOC 10.8.50
5572	Spitfire IX (Merlin 70 ?); Shipped to Cape Town 1948 – SAAF; No.15 AD, undercarriage failed to lower on landing, Cat.2 13.7.49 (Lt FB Richter); AOS, undercarriage collapsed on landing, Cat.1a 27.3.50 (Lt OJ van Niekerk); Engine failure, crashed, Cat.3 19.7.50 (Lt JR Morris); b.o.s. 4.12.50; SOC 12.1.51
5573	see PT601
5574	Spitfire HF.IXe (Merlin 70); Shipped to Cape Town 1948 – SAAF; AOS, engine failure. Cat.1a 28.4.50 (Lt GA Page); No.2 Sqn, landing collision with 5596, Cat.3 22.2.54 (Mjr RH Rogers); Bloemspruit AFB 25.2.54; FC 28.7.55; To Zwartkop AFB
5575	Spitfire IX (Merlin 70 ?); Shipped to Cape Town 1948 – SAAF; Service unknown; SOC 14.10.49
5576	Spitfire IX (Merlin 70 ?); Shipped to Cape Town 1948 - SAAF; Service unknown; SOC 14.10.49
5577	Spitfire HF.IXe (Merlin 70); Shipped to Cape Town 1948 - SAAF; Service unknown; No.15 AD in 6.54; For sale 9.5.55
5578	Spitfire HF.IXe (Merlin 70); Shipped to Cape Town 1948 - SAAF; Service unknown; No.15 AD in 6.54; For sale 9.5.55
5579	Spitfire IX (Merlin 70?); Shipped to Cape Town 1948 - SAAF; Service unknown; No.15 AD in 6.54; For sale 9.5.55
5580	Spitfire HF.IXe (Merlin 70); Shipped to Cape Town 1948 – SAAF; AOS, ran off runway landing, Cat.1 9.10.51 (2/Lt MB Clur); No.1 Sqn, ground accident 1.2.54; Zwartkop AFB 1.2.54; Engine changed (to No.184901) from 16.2.54; No.15 AD 12.4.54; For sale 9.5.55
5581	Spitfire HF.IXe (Merlin 70); Shipped to Cape Town 1948 – SAAF; No.1 Sqn ('AX-M') by 1950; Nosed over during run-up, Cat.1 26.10.53 (2/Lt G Nettleton); Zwartkop Air Station; Engine changed (to No.189951) 23.1.54; No.15 AD 12.4.54; Zwartkop AFB 12.4.54; For sale 9.5.55
5582	Spitfire HF.IXe (Merlin 70); Shipped to Cape Town 1948 – SAAF; CFS, landed with undercarriage not fully locked down, Cat.FA/1a 1.2.51 (2/Lt MO Grunder); No.1 Sqn, swung on landing Zwartkop, Cat.1 16.7.53 (Cdt Vermeulen); Zwartkop Air Station 16.7.53; No.15 AD in 6.54; For sale 9.5.55
5583	Spitfire HF.IXe (Merlin 70); Shipped to Cape Town 1948 – SAAF; No.1 Sqn, engine failure, forced landed, Cat.3 20.11.53 (2/Lt NP Friedricks); No.15 AD 23.11.53; SOC 17.8.54
5584	Spitfire HF.IXe (Merlin 70); Shipped to Cape Town 1948 – SAAF; AOS, ran into 5622, Cat.2 19.9.52 (2/Lt H Ludick); Zwartkop AFB 17.12.53; No.15 AD 22.12.53; For sale 9.5.55
5585	Spitfire HF.IXe (Merlin 70); Shipped to Cape Town 1948 – SAAF; No.1 AD, undercarriage failed to lower landing, Cat.1 27.1.50 (Lt AD Lawrenson); No.15 AD in 6.54; For sale 9.5.55
5586	Spitfire F.IX (Merlin 63); Shipped to Cape Town 1948 - SAAF; Service unknown; Bloemspruit AFB in 6.54; For sale 10.3.55
5587	Spitfire IX (Merlin 70 ?); Shipped to Cape Town 1948 - SAAF; Service unknown; SOC 14.10.49
5588	Spitfire IX (Merlin 70 ?); Shipped to Cape Town 1948 - SAAF; Service unknown; SOC 14.10.49
5589	Spitfire HF.IXe (Merlin 70 ?); Shipped to Cape Town 1948 - SAAF; Service unknown; SOC 14.10.49
5590	Spitfire HF.IXe (Merlin 70); Shipped to Cape Town 1948 – SAAF; No.1 Sqn, heavy landing, Cat.2 20.3.51 (2/Lt PJT Retief); b.o.s. 29.9.52; SOC 17.10.52
5591	Spitfire HF.IXe (Merlin 70); Shipped to Cape Town 1948 – SAAF; No.2 Sqn, engine failure on take-off, Cat.2 18.9.50 (Lt DW Featherstone); No.15 AD in 6.54; For sale 9.5.55
5592	Spitfire HF IXe (Merlin 70); Shipped to Cape Town 1948 – SAAF; Service unknown; SOC 14.10.49
5593	Spitfire HF.IXe (Merlin 70); Shipped to Cape Town 1948 – SAAF; No.1 Sqn, fuel shortage, force-landed and crashed, Baragwanath 8.12.50 (2/Lt RL Staats); No.6 Sqn (date unknown); Ground instructional at Ysterplaat AFB in 6.54; For sale 30.5.55
5594	Spitfire IX (Merlin 70 ?); Shipped to Cape Town 1948 - SAAF; Service unknown; SOC 14.10.49

Post-war Spitfire HF.IXe 5593 seen in a hangar. [SAAF Museum]

Spitfire HF.IXes of No. 1 Sqn SAAF in loose formation around 1951. They have varied roundels and cockpit hood designs. The only identifiable serial number is that of the second from the front, which appears to be 5596. [SAAF]

5595	Spitfire IX (Merlin 70 ?); Shipped to Cape Town 1948 - SAAF; Service unknown; SOC 14.10.49
5596	Spitfire HF.IXe (Merlin 70); Shipped to Cape Town 1948 – SAAF; No.1 Sqn, propeller hit ground on take-off, Cat.1 5.1.51 (Lt FK Grobler); No.2 Sqn, collided with 5574 on landing, Cat.3 22.2.54 (2/Lt PC Franz); Bloemspruit AFB 25.2.54; For sale 10.3.55
5597	Spitfire HF.IXe (Merlin 70); Shipped to Cape Town 1948 – SAAF; No.60 Sqn, stalled on approach, crashed Zwartkop, Cat.2 27.6.50 (Lt J W Hill); Zwartkop Air Station 27.6.50; Swung on take-off, Cat.1 27.10.50 (Capt JC Collins); No.15 AD in 6.54; For sale 9.5.55
5598	Spitfire IX (Merlin 70 ?); Shipped to Cape Town 1948 - SAAF; Service unknown; SOC 14.10.49
5599	Spitfire HF.IXe (Merlin 70); Shipped to Cape Town 1948 – SAAF; No.1 AD, heavy landing 10.5.51 (Lt BJ Grove); AOS, struck by stone during low level flying, Cat.FA/1a 18.10.51 (Capt JG Villiers); Propeller hit ground landing, Cat.FA/1 27.3.52 (Lt R Richards); No.15 AD in 6.54; For sale 9.5.55
5600	Spitfire IX (Merlin 70 ?); Shipped to Cape Town 1948 - SAAF; Service unknown; SOC 14.10.49
5601	see MA793
5602	Spitfire IX (Merlin 70 ?); Shipped to Cape Town 1948 - SAAF; Service unknown; SOC 14.10.49
5603	Spitfire F.IX (Merlin 63); Shipped to Cape Town 1948 - SAAF; Service unknown; Bloemspruit AFB in 6.54; For sale 10.3.55
5604	Spitfire HF.IXe (Merlin 70); Shipped to Cape Town 1948 – SAAF; No.15 AD, belly-landed, pilot forget to lower undercarriage, Cat.2 23.6.50 (Lt G G Paterson); Zwartkop AFB 15.3.54; No.15 AD from 2.4.54; For sale 9.5.55
5605	Spitfire HF.IXe (Merlin 70); Shipped to Cape Town 1948 – SAAF; Service unknown; Zwartkop AFB 22.12.53; No.15 AD 12.4.54; For sale 9.5.55
5606	Spitfire IX (Merlin 70 ?); Shipped to Cape Town 1948 – SAAF; AOS, engine failure, force-landed and crashed Cat.FA/3 30.1.51 (Lt WDB Boyes killed); b.o.s. 1.2.52; SOC 5.2.52

5607 Spitfire IX (Merlin 70 ?); Shipped to Cape Town 1948 - SAAF; Service unknown; No.15 AD in 6.54; For sale 9.5.55 (without engine)

5608 Spitfire F.IX (Merlin 63); Shipped to Cape Town 1949 – SAAF; AOS, engine failure, pilot baled out, aircraft dived into ground Kliphuvel, Cat.FA/3 3.4.52 (Lt R Richards); Ysterplaat AFB in 4.52; SOC 16.2.54

5609 Spitfire IX (Merlin 70 ?); Shipped to Cape Town 1949 – SAAF; No.2 Sqn, dived into sea during low level bombing, Cat.3 26.1.51 (2/Lt SV van Reenen killed); b.o.s. 21.6.51; SOC 28.6.51

5610 Spitfire IX (Merlin 70 ?); Shipped to Cape Town 1949 – SAAF; No.1 Sqn, engine failure, force-landed 12.1.51 (Lt SJ Richards); No.15 AD in 6.54; SOC 28.10.55; For sale 9.5.55 (without engine)

5611 Spitfire IX (Merlin 70 ?); Shipped to Cape Town 1949 – SAAF; No.2 Sqn, partial engine failure, force-landed 11.9.50 (Lt FB Richter); Engine failed, force-landed, crashed, Cat.3 12.1.51 (Lt SJ Richards); b.o.s. 4.10.51; SOC 9.10.51

5612 Spitfire IX (Merlin 70 ?); Shipped to Cape Town 1949 - SAAF; Service unknown; No.15 AD in 6.54; For sale 9.5.55 (without engine)

5613 Spitfire IX (Merlin 70 ?); Shipped to Cape Town 1949 - SAAF; Service unknown; No.15 AD in 6.54; For sale 9.5.55 (without engine)

5614 Spitfire IX (Merlin 70 ?); Shipped to Cape Town 1949 - SAAF; Service unknown; No.15 AD in 6.54; For sale 9.5.55 (without engine)

5615 Spitfire IX (Merlin 70 ?); Shipped to Cape Town 1949 – SAAF; No.1 AD, ground accident, Cat.1 11.2.50; AOS, engine failure, dived into ground, Cat.FA/3 17.7.51 (Lt AJ McLeod baled out); b.o.s. 1.2.52; SOC 5.2.52

5616 Spitfire IX (Merlin 70 ?); Shipped to Cape Town 1949 – SAAF; AOS, collided with 5561 while landing Ysterplaat, Cat.FA/3 31.3.52 (2/Lt R Turner); Ysterplaat AFB until 16.2.54, SOC

5617 Spitfire F.IX (Merlin 63); Shipped to Cape Town 1949 - SAAF; Service unknown; No.15 AD in 6.54; For sale 9.5.55

5618 Spitfire IX (Merlin 63); Shipped to Cape Town 1949 – SAAF; AOS, tipped on nose, Cat.FA/1 9.8.51 (Lt F Gouws); Merlin 70 installed 5.52; Ysterplaat AFB until 16.2.54; SOC 16.2.54

5619 Spitfire IX (Merlin 63); Shipped to Cape Town 1949 – SAAF; AOS, propeller hit ground during engine run-up, Cat.1 9.11.51 (Lt A Gardiner-Atkinson); Merlin 70 installed 5.52; Ysterplaat AFB until 16.2.54; SOC 16.2.54

5620 Spitfire IX (Merlin 70 ?); Shipped to Cape Town 1949 – SAAF; No.2 Sqn, tailwheel collapsed landing, Cat.1a 19.8.50 (Lt DG van der Byl); Waterkloof Air Station 19.8.50; AOS, taxying-accident, brake failure, Cat.2 10.6.52 (Lt HG Holthauzen); Ysterplaat AFB until 22.1.54; SOC 22.1.54

5621 Spitfire HF.IXe (Merlin 70); Shipped to Cape Town 1949 – SAAF; No.1 Sqn ('AX-N'); No.15 AD from 12.4.54; Zwartkop AFB 12.4.54; Engine changed (to No.185233); For sale 9.5.55

5622 Spitfire HF.IXe (Merlin 70); Shipped to Cape Town 1949 – SAAF; No.2 Sqn, swung on landing, Cat.2 22.12.49 (Lt WDB Boyes); Swung on landing, Cat.2 25.1.50 (Lt WDB Boyes); AOS, Hit on ground collision by 5584 while stationary, Cat.FA/2 19.9.52; No.1 Sqn, propeller hit ground on take-off, Cat.1 22.10.53 (Lt L Weeks); No.10 AD 15.12.53; Engine failure, force-landed, overshot Zwartkop, Cat.3 3.4.54 (Lt HF Pretorius killed); No.15 AD 5.4.54; For sale 9.5.55

5623 Spitfire IX (Merlin 70 ?); Shipped to Cape Town 1949 – SAAF; Service unknown; No.15 AD in 6.54; For sale 9.5.55 (without engine)

5624 Spitfire IX (Merlin 70 ?); Shipped to Cape Town 1949 - SAAF; Service unknown; No.15 AD in 6.54; For sale 9.5.55 (without engine)

5625 Spitfire IX (Merlin 70 ?); Shipped to Cape Town 1949 – SAAF; AOS, engine failure, pilot baled out, aircraft dived into ground, Cat.FA/3 3.5.51 (2/Lt JFG Howe); b.o.s. 9.8.51; SOC 14.8.51

5626 Spitfire IX (Merlin 70 ?); Shipped to Cape Town 1949 – SAAF; No.1 Aux Sqn, swung taxying, Cat.1 15.2.50 (2/Lt AJ Hoogland); AOS, engine failed, force-landed and crashed Cat.FA/3 26.1.51 (Lt E Downie); b.o.s. 2.10.51; SOC 13.11.51

5627 Spitfire HF.IXe (Merlin 70); Shipped to Cape Town 1949 - SAAF; Service unknown; No.15 AD 12.4.54; Zwartkop AFB 12.4.54; For sale 16.5.55

5628 Spitfire F.IX (Merlin 63); Shipped to Cape Town 1949 - SAAF; Service unknown; Bloemspruit AFB in 6.54; For sale 10.3.55

5629 Spitfire IX (Merlin 70 ?); Shipped to Cape Town 1949 - SAAF; Service unknown; No.15 AD in 6.54; For sale 9.5.55 (without engine)

5630 Spitfire HF.IXe (Merlin 70); Shipped to Cape Town 1949 – SAAF; AOS, propeller hit ground on take-off, Cat.FA/1 18.6.51 (2/Lt C Lombard); No.15 AD in 6.54; For sale 9.5.55

5631 see BR601

5632 see RR232

5633 Spitfire IX (Merlin 70 ?); Shipped to Cape Town 1949 - SAAF; Service unknown; No.15 AD in 6.54; For sale 9.5.55 (without engine)

5634 Spitfire HF.IXe (Merlin 70); Shipped to Cape Town 1949 - SAAF; Service unknown; Zwartkop AFB; No.15 AD in 6.54; For sale 9.5.55 (S&D Metal); SOC 28.10.55

5635 Spitfire IX (Merlin 70 ?); Shipped to Cape Town 1949 - SAAF; Service unknown; No.15 AD in 6.54; For sale 9.5.55 (without engine)

5636 see TE343

5637 see TE309

Unidentified Spitfires, SAAF in WWII (MTO)

xx112 (Mk.V) No.41 Sqn by 9.44
xx167 (Mk.V) No.1 Sqn ('AX-H') by 6.3.43
xx174 (Mk.V) No.5 Sqn, ferried Sorman to Ben Gardane (too early for MK174) [JL174?], date missed
xx242 (Mk.Vb) No.40 Sqn 7.43 [EN242 or ES242?]
xx256 (Mk.V) No.40 Sqn 6.44
xx267 (Mk.V) No.41 Sqn by 9.44
xx281 (Mk.V) No.1 Sqn ('AX-G') by 7-20.3.43; MC 202 damaged 12m NW of Medenine 7.3.43 (Lt H van N Fouché)
xx286 (Mk.V) No.1 Sqn ('AX-W') by 11.42
xx310 (Mk.V) No.41 Sqn by 5.44
xx312 (Mk.Vc) No.9 Sqn by 6.44 - 7.44
xx330 (Mk.V) No.41 Sqn by 9.44
xx397 (Mk.V) No.5 Sqn ferry to No.7 Wing Gardane-El Djem-El Haouaria [date missed]
xx408 (Mk.V) No.41 Sqn by 3.44
xx455 (Mk.IX) No.41 Sqn by 5.44 - 6.44
xx458 (Mk.V) No.1 Sqn ('AX-L') by 10.3.43 [middle digit unclear on microfilm]
xx470 (Mk.V) No.9 Sqn by 6.44
xx474 (Mk.V or IX) No.9 Sqn by 11.44
xx475 (Mk.V) No.40 Sqn, swung landing, tipped on nose 5.1.44 (Lt PAJ K'Anval-Aimee) [but see xx975]
xx501 (Mk.V) No.41 Sqn by 4.44
xx549 (Mk.Vb) No.40 Sqn by 7.43 [ER549 might fit - see accident 3.12.43]
xx590 (Mk.V) No.1 Sqn ('AX-M') by 25.3.43; Bf 109F destroyed Gabes-El Hamma 25.3.43 (Lt J van Nus); Me 210 destroyed 30m NW of Gabes 27.3.43 (Lt W M Langerman); Bf 109F destroyed 20m NW of Gabes 29.3.43 (Lt DM Brebner); Me 210 damaged 28.4.43 (Lt D T Gilson)
xx593 (Mk.Vc) No.1 Sqn ('AX-V') by 4.43
xx598 (Mk.V) No.41 Sqn by 6.44

xx607	(Mk.V) No.1 Sqn ('AX-O') by 27.3.43; Bf 109F destroyed, shared with xx193/'V' 20m NW of Gabes 29.3.43 (Lt W D Wikner)	xx943	(Mk.V) No.5 Sqn by 13.7.43
xx618	(Mk.V) No.41 Sqn by 8.44	xx960	(Mk.V) No.1 Sqn ('AX-H'), Bf 109F destroyed SW of Tamet 14.1.43 (Lt M E S Robinson)
xx649	(Mk.V) No.41 Sqn by 4.44; No.9 Sqn by 7.44	xx972	(Mk.Vb) No.40 Sqn by 7.43
xx653	(Mk.Vc) No.1 Sqn ('AX-X') by 11.42	xx973	(Mk.IX) No.9 Sqn by 8.44
xx660	(Mk.Vc) No.1 Sqn ('AX-O') by 4.43	xx975	(Mk.V) No.40 Sqn, crashed on landing, tipped on nose 5.1.44 (Lt PAJ K'Anval-Aimee) [but see xx475]
xx680	(Mk.V) No.41 Sqn by 4.44 - 6.44; No.9 Sqn by 8.44	xx981	(Mk.Vb) No.1 Sqn (AX-T), air combat 27.11.42 (Lt J H Gaynor)
xx694	(Mk.V) No.41 Sqn by 4.44 - 6.44		
xx704	(Mk.V) No.41 Sqn by 8.44	xx982	(Mk.V) No.1 Sqn ('AX-Z') by 11.42 - 14.1.43
xx729	(Mk.IX) No.9 Sqn by 8.44	xx991	(Mk.IX) No.9 Sqn by 8.44
xx731	(Mk.Vb) No.9 Sqn by 6.44 - 8.44	xx993	(Mk.IX) No.9 Sqn by 8.44
xx740	(Mk.V) No.41 Sqn by 9.44 - 10.44	"MJ73x"	(Mk.IX) No.1 Sqn ('AX-Y')
xx758	(Mk.Vc) No.1 Sqn ('AX-U'), Ju 88 probably destroyed 13.12.42 (Lt G H O'Farrell); FW 190 probably destroyed 28m SW of Medenine 20.3.43 (Lt W M Langerman)	"JG397"	(Mk.Vc/trop) No.10 Sqn 1.9.44
		"MA330"	(F.Vc/trop) SAAF in 11.43, and No.7 Sqn 16.1.44
		"MH413"	No.3 Sqn ('CA-S') by 2.45
		"MH936"	No.3 Sqn ('CA-R') by 3.45
xx776	(Mk.V) No.9 Sqn by 6.44	"MJ392"	No.40 Sqn, crashed on landing at Castiglione, Cat.Ac 11.7.44 (Lt BM de Plooy); Take-off crash, force-landed in football field, hit fence, Cat.2 18.1.45 (Lt N D Broom)
xx777	(Mk.Vc) No.1 Sqn by 6.43		
xx792	(SHF) No.9 Sqn by 8.44		
xx793	(Mk.V) No.1 Sqn ('AX-E') by 27.11.42		
xx818	(Mk.V) No.41 Sqn by 5.44	"MJ608"	No.2 Sqn ('DB-A') by 3.44
xx841	(Mk.V) No.41 Sqn by 4.44	"PL272"	(Mk.IX) No.1 Sqn, hit by 40mm AA in attack on tank 11m E of Bacara, Cat.FB/Ac 15.4.45 (Lt J L J Slaven unhurt)
xx843	(Mk.IX) No.9 Sqn by 7.44		
xx867	(Mk.Vc) No.9 Sqn by 6.44		
xx877	(Mk.V) No.41 Sqn by 5.44	5.3.43	(Mk.V) No.40 Sqn, ferrying from Delta, burst tyre and crashed on take-off El Adem (Lt Wilsby unhurt)
xx888	(Mk.V) No.41 Sqn by 8.44 - 10.44		
xx895	(Mk.Vc) No.1 Sqn by 1.43 - 2.43	6.4.43	(Mk.V) No.40 Sqn, shot down by AA fire, force-landed safely behind lines (Lt T W Iles unhurt) [ES339 was lost that date, no details or Sqn]
xx897	(Mk.V) No.1 Sqn ('AX-L') by 27.11.42		
xx903	(Mk.V) No.1 Sqn ('AX-S'), Bf 109F probably destroyed 14.1.43 (Lt D T Gilson)		
		31.8.43	No.40 Sqn, took off with A/M Carter on tail, landed safely Gerbini Main (Lt T W Iles and airman unhurt)
xx904	(Mk.IX) No.9 Sqn by 6.44		
xx913	(Mk.V) No.41 Sqn by 8.44 - 10.44		
xx920	(Mk.V) No.41 Sqn by 3.44	27.9.43	(Mk.V) No.7 Sqn, Bf 109 destroyed Cos, believed Bf 109G of III/JG27 from which Uffz Jakob Herweg baled
xx941	(Mk.V) No.41 Sqn by 10.44		

General R H D Rogers standing in front of surviving Spitfire F.IX 5601 (ex MA793) painted up as his wartime aircraft with serial number "PT672", and code "WR-RR". Left is Alan Lurie and right is Larry Barnett, owners and restorers of the aircraft.

27.9.43	out and was rescued (Mjr C A van Vliet)
27.9.43	(Mk.V) No.7 Sqn, in company with Mjr van Vliet, Bf 109 destroyed Cos, then shot down, baled out (Lt A L Basson rescued) [JK667?]
3.9.43	"EN300" No.1 Sqn, MC 202 damaged 3.9.43 (Lt D S Hastie)
28.9.43	No.7 Sqn, attack on island by Bf 109s and Ju 88s, shot down by Bf 109s over Cos, baled out (Lt E M Taylor rescued) [ES204 was lost that date, squadron unknown]
18.10.43	No.2 Sqn, Me 210 last seen streaming glycol (Mjr T P L Murray & others)

Spitfire Deliveries to South Africa

SAAF Serial Nos: **5502 - 5554**

53 Spitfire Mk. IX, delivered 1947.
Ferried from RAF Pershore to No.15 AD at Fayid, Egypt:

Desp.	Arrival	RAF Serial No's	Qty.
16.4.47	23.4.47	EN314, PL192, PT910, TB576	4
16.4.47	25.9.47	MA815	1
8.5.47	16.5.47	TA802	1
8.5.47	17.5.47	BS512, SM523, TB988, TE234	4
8.5.47	22.8.47	TE215	1
28.5.47	2.6.47	ML243, NH534, TB568/986, TD353	5
11.6.47	18.6.47	MA756, MH373/674/939, TE211/306	6
11.6.47	4.8.47	TB987	1
4.7.47	11.7.47	MA232, MK842, TE212/305/336	5
18.7.47	31.7.47	BS344, TE294/298/213	4
31.7.47	4.8.47	TB985, TE232	2
31.7.47	5.8.47	EN182, TE289/293/337	4
15.8.47	22.8.47	MH332/832/876, TE290	4
26.8.47	20.9.47	NH513, TE205	2
26.8.47	4.10.47	TE301	1
10.9.47	20.9.47	BS451, EN524, MH380, TE238	4
14.11.47	20.11.47	MA587, MJ129	2
7.12.47	12.47	PL209, TE315	2

Spitfire F VIIIc JF 294 (No. 5501 SAAF), arrived in March 1944!

A collection of Spitfire HF.IXes in storage at No. 15 Air Depot, Zwartkop, awaiting sale around 1954/55. The only serial number visible is "P5585" on an aircraft in the centre of the aircraft. The reason for the "P" prefix to its serial number is unknown. [SAAF]

SAAF Serial Nos: **5555 - 5637**

83 Spitfire IX, shipped to Cape Town (except one to Durban) 1948/49, despatched. Birkenhead (79 a/c) and Liverpool (4 a/c)

Desp.	Arrival	Ship	RAF Serial Nos	Qty.
9.4.48	28.4.48	Clan Forbes	BS125, LZ842, MJ220/224, ML145, PT614, SM506	7
23.4.48	11.5.48	Clan Chattan	LZ832, MA849, MH851/871, PL253, TD314	6
26.5.48	21.6.48	Halesius	NH611	1
27.5.48	21.6.48	City of Cape Town	BS408, MA477, MH875, PL215, SM520, TE307/329/333	8
4.6.48	20.7.48	Clan McKay	MA592, ML148	2
17.6.48	5.8.48	Clan McFaydon	MK675, NH275, NH539, PT601	4
6.7.48	10.8.48	Clan McDonald	ML196/356, NH190, TD315	4
11.8.48	15.9.48	Clan Cumming	MA628	1 *)
13.8.48	26.9.48	Clan Campbell	MA593/793, MH606	3
24.8.48	28.9.48	Clan McBride	MA563	1
31.8.48	22.10.48	Clan Kenneth	MH830, TE312	2
10.9.48	13.10.48	Lanarkshire	RK924	1
1.10.48	3.11.48	Clan McKenzie	MH855, TE331	2
1.10.48	22.11.48	Clan Mc Kendrick	TE313	1
6.10.48	16.11.48	City of Kimberley	MH694, ML246, ML255, PT472	4
16.10.48	26.11.48	Merchant	MH692/777	2
1.11.48	19.12.48	Clan McFarlane	ML259	1
6.11.48	24.12.48	Caledon Monarch	BS200	1
10.11.48	4.12.48	Brisbane Star	BS538, TB569	2 (L)
4.12.48	2.1.49	Clan McLeod	MJ225, PT781	2
30.12.48	13.2.49	Coulgoem	ML197, PL261, PT619/787, PT941, PV269, SM505	7
17.1.49	23.2.49	Clan McKinley	MA229, PT434, TD310	3
27.1.49	13.3.49	Clan McKellar	BR601, MH663, TE230	3
1.2.49	10.3.49	Clan Campbell	MH603, TD352	2
3.2.49	9.3.49	Clan Brodie	RK917	1
3.2.49	17.3.49	Geologist	MH355, TE292	2
11.3.49	10.4.49	Clan McLeod	PT905, TA805, TE297	3
9.4.49/L	14.5.49	Clan McKenzie	EN345	1 (L)
21.4.49	21.5.49	City of Cape Town	MH869, RR232	2
7.5.49/L	19.6.49	Riodene	PL203	1 (L)
14.5.49	22.5.49	City of London	TE303	1
8.9.49	6.10.49	Student	TE309/343	2

*) = deliv. to Durban (MA628)
(L) = desp. Liverpool (BS538, EN345, PL203 & TB569)

6.12.43	No.7 Sqn, formation practice, force-landed (Lt VC Inggs)
4.1.44	No.7 Sqn, slight mid-air collision during camera gunning (Lt DS de Jager & Lt JE Brand both landed safely)
11.1.44	No.4 Sqn, lost tailwheel on take-off, landed safely at Palata LG
19.1.44	No.2 Sqn ('DB-Y'?), shot up by AA in Francavilla-Tollo area, Cat.1 (Lt RJ Greaves) [MA856?]
6.3.44	(Mk.V) No.40 Sqn, landed too close to aircraft in front, swung, tipped up, Cat.2 (Lt TW Lyle)
15.3.44	(Mk.Vc) No.3 Sqn, unable to lower undercarriage, belly-landed, Cat.2 (Lt Cochrane-Murray)
17.3.44	No.3 Sqn, engine failed over coast at 3,000ft, force-landed and crashed 7m NW of Cyrene, Cat.3 (Lt DE Hough OK)
29.4.44	(Mk.IX) No.2 Sqn, wingtip hit airman working on taxiway (Lt KB Borcherds)
27.5.44	No.7 Wing, two Bf 109 destroyed in Foligno area, at least one of which was a Bf 109G of I.Gruppo CT, RSI and another shared on the ground (Col AC Bosman)
27.5.44	No.1 Sqn, Bf 109G damaged (squadron)
29.7.44	No.9 Sqn ('X'), attacked Ju 88 (Lt AB Retief)
9.8.44	No.7 Wing, Fi 156 destroyed on ground Borolone airfield (Col AC Bosman)
2.9.44	No.7 Wing, Me 210 destroyed on ground Ferrara (Col AC Bosman)
8.45	(Mk.IX) No.11 Sqn: 17 Spitfire Mk.IX (ex No.185 Sqn), all to Fayid, Egypt 9.45
15.8.45	(Mk.IX) No.3 Sqn, two aircraft collided during formation flight, both Cat.A.

SURVIVORS

In South Africa

JF294 (5501)
TE213 (5518 & "5553")
TE566

Elsewhere

BR601 (5631)	To USA
LZ842	Via UK to Australia
MA793 (5601)	To USA
MH603	Via UK to USA
ML196	To Canada
ML255 (5589)	To Portugal
PT462	To UK
RR232 (5632)	Via Australia to UK
SM520	To UK
TA805	To UK
TD314	Via Canada to UK
TE294 (5519)	To Canada

Note
PV202, a T.IX (Merlin 66) (reg. *G-BHGH* 1979 & *G-TRIX* 2.7.80) was sold to Greg McCurragh, a South African, in March 2000. It never reached South Africa, however, as it crashed when it hit a tree during flying training at Goodwood aerodrome, West Sussex on 8 April 2000. Pilot Norman Lees and the new owner were both killed. Aircraft for rebuild at Historic Flying Ltd, Duxford.

Reference:
The Liberty Calvalcades, Spitfire JF294 (5501),
 by GE Camplin AFC, Spitfire Society DCO spring 1999 (p.6).

SOUTHERN RHODESIA
(now ZIMBABWE)

Southern Rhodesia and Northern Rhodesia were British from 1891 initially as protectorates. Both became British colonies in 1923/24, and as such part of the British Empire. In 1953 they united with Nyasaland to become a Federation, but the union was dissolved in 1963. One year later Northern Rhodesia was re-named *Zambia,* and Nyasaland became *Malawi.* Southern Rhodesia became the Republic of Rhodesia in 1970, but in 1980 the name was changed to *Zimbabwe.*

The first Air Section was formed in Southern Rhodesia in 1936. After the Second World War the Southern Rhodesian Air Force (SRAF) was re-formed with one operational auxiliary squadron, mainly for training and communication purposes. It was the air arm of the Southern Rhodesia Army. From 15th October 1954, during Federation with Nyasaland, the name changed to Rhodesian Air Force, then the Royal Rhodesian Air Force (RRAF) from 1955. At that time the RRAF flew also from satellite bases between N'dola and Blantyre and Bulawayo.

Rhodesian units of the RAF in WWII

The Rhodesian Air Training Group was the first to open an Elementary Flying Training School under the British Commonwealth Air Training Plan, in May 1940.

In the Middle East No.1 (Rhodesian) Squadron became No.237 Sqn RAF. This unit was manned mainly by colonials. It served with the Desert Air Force throughout the Italian campaign and helped cover the Allied landings in Southern France in August 1944.

No. 237 ("*Rhodesia*"), ex No.1 Sqn SRAF, code 'DV'.
 Middle East – Based in Kenya (Nairobi) from April 1940; At Sudan (Wadi Halfa) June 1941; To Egypt July 1941; Idku 9th September 1943, Savoia 7th December 1943, Sidi Barrani 31st January 1944, Idku 25th February 1944; Corsica (Poretta) 19th April 1944; Serregia 23rd May 1944; St.Catharines 9th July 1944; France (Cuers) 25th August 1944; Italy (Falconara) 4th October 1944, Rossignano 9th February 1945, Lavariano 8th October 1945; Re-numbered No.93 Sqn 1st January 1946.
 Spitfire Mk.Vc/trop from December 1943 and Mk. IX from March 1944.

Note:
Nos.44 (Bomber) and 266 (Fighter) Squadrons of the RAF had "Rhodesia" included in their titles, as their equipment had been subscribed by that country, but they did not have Rhodesian personnel.

Spitfires of the Southern Rhodesian Air Force (SRAF)

Post-war, the SRAF ordered twenty-two Spitfire F.22s from surplus RAF stocks to form a Fighter squadron. The first two of these were selected under Comm.No.742 on 22nd February 1951, four more on 23rd February 1951, five on 12th March 1951 and the last eleven on 4th December 1951.

An advance party sailed to the UK on 16th December 1950 under the command of Lt Col E Jacklin to prepare for Spitfire

Spitfire ferry flying from U.K. to Southern Rhodesia in 1951

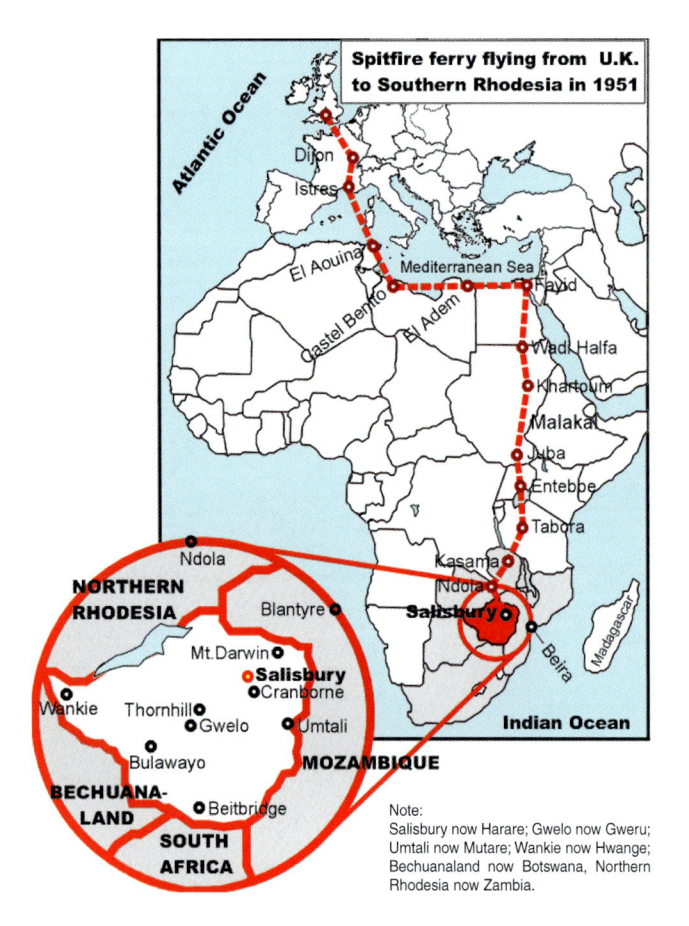

delivery. The ferry pilots left Salisbury (now Harare) on 22nd January 1951 in a Dakota (*SR25*) to ferry out the first batch of Spitfires. The aircraft were flown to the Overseas Ferry Unit at Chivenor where the pilots familiarised themselves with the Spitfires, converting at No.6 MU Brize Norton on a 20-hours flying course. In two batches each of eleven aircraft the Spitfires were flown to Southern Rhodesia.

The first ferry flight began on 14th March 1951 and staged via Dijon, Istres (France), El Aouina (Tunisia), Castel Benito, El Adem (both Libya), Fayid (Egypt), Wadi Halfa, Khartoum (both Sudan - partly the old Egypt ferry route), Malakal, Juba (Sudan), Entebbe (Uganda), Tabora (Tanganyika), Kasama, N'dola (both Zambia), arriving at Salisbury on 22nd March 1951. One aircraft (PK576) had to be left at Juba due to coolant pipe failure on take-off, being later shipped to Beira, Mozambique. By the following month most SRAF pilots, who normally flew transport aircraft, had converted to the Spitfire.

The second batch of Spitfires left Abingdon, where the Overseas Ferry Unit was now based, at 2 p.m. on 7th December 1951 in three sections, but one aircraft (PK344) crashed and was written off in France the same day, the pilot being killed. On 16th December 1951 another (PK482) was also lost when it crashed on landing at Entebbe, but the remaining aircraft arrived at Salisbury on 19th.

The 20 Spitfires which reached the Southern Rhodesian Air Force (*SRAF*) received the serial Nos. **SR58 to SR68** and **SR80 to SR88**.

With the creation of the Rhodesian Air Force (soon to become the Royal Rhodesian Air Force) aircraft serial number prefixes were changed from "SR" to "RRAF", but this did not affect the Spitfires, which were no longer in use, having been withdrawn from service in June 1954. However, two museum aircraft were given RRAF (later "R") serial prefixes.

Spitfire unit of the SRAF

No. 1 (Auxiliary) Sqn at Cranborne; New Sarum Air Station (Salisbury Airport) from 1952.
Spitfire F.22 from March 1951 until June 1954, when re-equipped with Vampires.
Sqn-markings: Red spinner, fuselage roundels with green/yellow flanking bars next to type D roundels RAF. [These were later changed to three assegais on a type D roundel c.1954, possibly when the RRAF formed, therefore after the Spitfire went out of service]
Commanding Officer:
Mjr Hardwick Holderness

Four Spitfire F.22 were lost during service with the SRAF. The remainder were finally SOC in 1954.

The first eleven, SR58, SR59, SR61 – SR63, SR66 - SR68 and SR81 – SR83 were ordered to be scrapped, authority being given on 17 September 1954 (Authority Ref 1088/1) for them to be towed to No.1 Salvage Dump and broken up after stripping, the wings being broken off. On 8th November 1954 authority was given for five more to suffer a similar fate, these being SR60, SR80, SR85, SR87 and SR88 (Ref 1088/2), and on 18th January 1955 Spitfire airframes were offered for scrap (Ref Box 38885). But on 16th March 1955 seven Spitfire airframes and spares were to have been sold to the Syrian Air Force for £1,200 each plus £2,000 for the spares. (Authority ref 2249/10 dated 10th March 1955), these being SR60, SR65, SR67, SR80, SR85, SR87 and SR88, but the sale appears to have been cancelled and the aircraft mainly scrapped.

Only two Spitfires remained in Southern Rhodesia (now Zimbabwe), SR64 and SR65 being officially placed on RRAF charge on 30 June 1955 to be retained as Museum exhibits.

Individual Histories

PK326 Spitfire F.22 (Griffon 61); Became **SR80**; TOC/RAF 26.6.45; Ferry flight to Southern Rhodesia (Lt OD Penton) - Arr SRAF 19.12.51; No.1 Sqn 12.51
PK330 Spitfire F.22 (Griffon 61); Became **SR63**; TOC/RAF 29.6.45; Ferry flight to Southern Rhodesia (WO1 M Schuman, Red Section) - Arr SRAF 25.3.51; No.1 Sqn 28.3.51

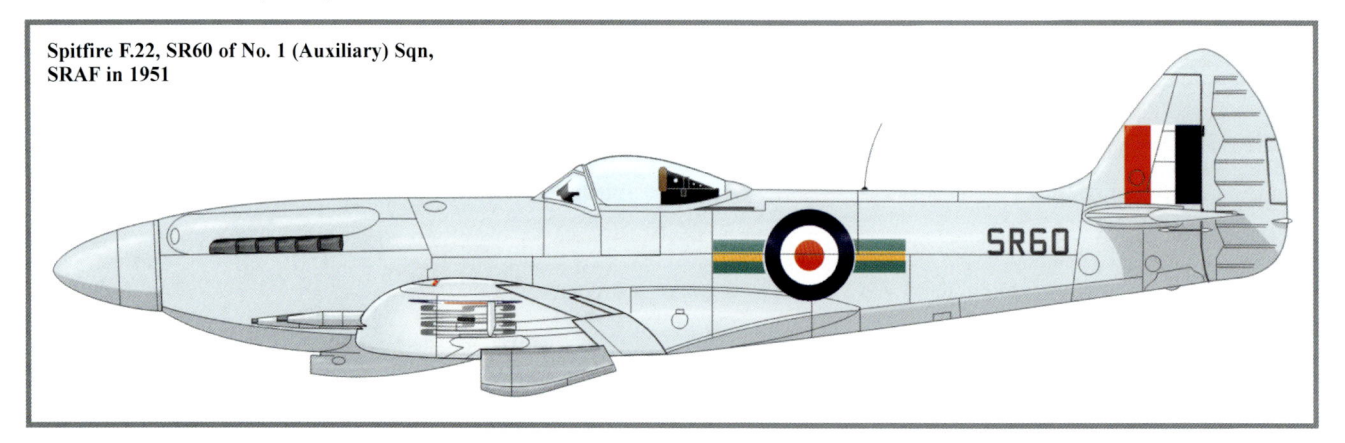

Spitfire F.22, SR60 of No. 1 (Auxiliary) Sqn, SRAF in 1951

Spitfire F.22 SR60 of No. 1 (Auxiliary) Sqn SRAF, Cranborne, in 1951. [Brian Sharman via Roger Lindsay]

PK344 Spitfire F.22 (Griffon 61); TOC/RAF 31.7.45; Despatched to SRAF, in company with PK328, PK494 & PK548 on ferry flight from Abingdon, lost contact with the others while climbing through low cloud from 700ft to 2,000ft, crashed Hameau d'Auvilliers, 5m SW of Clermont in France, Cat.FA/E 7.12.51 (Lt O Love RAF killed), SOC (RAF)

PK350 Spitfire F.22 (Griffon 61); Became **SR64** (RRAF64 & R64); TOC/RAF 31.7.45; Ferry flight to Southern Rhodesia (Lt DA Bradshaw); Arr SRAF 25.3.51; No.1 Sqn 28.3.51; Landed wheels-up at Cranborne 1.6.51 (Capt D McGibbon); Repaired (estimated at £1,226.5s.6d); Last flight 18.12.54; SOC 1954; Retained on RRAF charge as exhibit at Bulawayo Museum 30.6.55; Displayed on a pole at New Sarum AFB from 1955; To Capt Jack Malloch/Air Trans Africa, Salisbury/Harare, Zimbabwe 1978; Restored and flown as "*JM-M*" from 29.3.80; Dived into ground, Goromiorzi, near Harare 26.3.82 (Jack Malloch killed); **Wreck** to W H Owens at Gweru in 1983

PK355 Spitfire F.22 (Griffon 61); Became **SR-65** (RRAF65 & R65); TOC/RAF 1.8.45; Ferry flight to Southern Rhodesia (Lt J Malloch); Arr SRAF 25.3.51; No.1 Sqn 28.3.51; Propeller damaged 30.4.51; SOC 1954; Retained on RRAF charge as exhibit at Bulawayo Museum 30.6.55; Loaned to Bulawayo RAF Association 8.10.57; Later gate guardian on pole at Thornhill AFB (near Gwelo) 1978; To Zimbabwe Air Force Museum, New Sarum AFB (near Salisbury) 1981; Exhibited in National Museum, Gweru, Zimbabwe from 1993; Advertised for sale 9.95 - **SURVIVOR**

PK370 Spitfire F.22 (Griffon 61); Became SR..? (80-88 range); TOC/RAF 10.8.45; Ferry flight to Southern Rhodesia; Arr SRAF 19.12.51; No.1 Sqn

PK401 Spitfire F.22 (Griffon 61); Became **SR86**; TOC/RAF 2.8.45; Ferry flight to Southern Rhodesia; Arr SRAF 19.12.51; No.1 Sqn

PK408 Spitfire F.22 (Griffon 61); Became SR..? (58-68 range); TOC/RAF 31.8.45; Ferry flight to Southern Rhodesia (Capt RH Barber, Yellow Section); Arr SRAF 25.3.51; No.1 Sqn 28.3.51

PK432 Spitfire F.22 (Griffon 61); Became SR..? (80-88 range); TOC/RAF 25.9.45; Ferry flight to Southern Rhodesia; Arr SRAF 19.12.51; No.1 Sqn

Spitfire F.22 RRAF 64 (ex PK350) displayed on a pole at New Sarum AFB around April 1969. It was later restored and flown as "JM-M" from March 1980, but on 26th March 1982 it dived into the ground at Goromiorzi, near Harare, and the pilot, Jack Malloch, was killed. [via A Thomas]

A line-up of Spitfires of No. 1 (Auxiliary Sqn) SRAF at Cranborne, SR65 nearest. In the background is Anson C.19 srs 2 SR30. [via Ken Smy]

PK482 Spitfire F.22 (Griffon 61); TOC/RAF 31.8.45; Despatched to SRAF 7.12.51; During delivery flight, landed in rain, misjudged height of runway and stalled, aircraft cartwheeled at Entebbe, Cat.FA/E 16.12.51 (Lt Richards SAAF slightly injured), SOC.

PK494 Spitfire F.22 (Griffon 61); Became SR..? (80-88 range); TOC/RAF 6.9.45; Ferry flight to Southern Rhodesia (Lt O'Hara); Arr. SRAF 19.12.51; No.1 Sqn

PK506 Spitfire F.22 (Griffon 61); Became SR..? (58-68 range); TOC/RAF 12.9.45; Ferry flight to Southern Rhodesia (WO1 CH Paxton, Yellow Section); Arr SRAF 25.3.51; No.1 Sqn 28.3.51

PK514 Spitfire F.22 (Griffon 61); Became **SR59**; TOC/RAF 17.9.45; Ferry flight to Southern Rhodesia (Lt D Bellingan, Yellow Section); Arr SRAF 25.3.51; No.1 Sqn 28.3.51; Engine failed, landed safely N.S.A. 4.9.51 (Lt J H Deale)

PK548 Spitfire F.22 (Griffon 61); Became SR..? (80-88 range); TOC/RAF 27.9.45; Ferry flight to Southern Rhodesia (Lt Pascoe); Arr SRAF 19.12.51; No.1 Sqn

PK572 Spitfire F.22 (Griffon 61); Became SR..? (80-88 range); TOC/RAF 10.10.45; Ferry flight to Southern Rhodesia; Arr SRAF 19.12.51; No.1 Sqn

PK575 Spitfire F.22 (Griffon 61); Became **SR62**; TOC/RAF 10.10.45; Ferry flight to Southern Rhodesia (WO1 R Blair & Lt BTA Bone, Blue Section); Arr SRAF 25.3.51; No.1 Sqn 28.3.51

PK576 Spitfire F.22 (Griffon 61); Became SR..? (58-68 range); TOC/RAF 18.10.45; Desp. to SRAF 14.3.51; Engine seized on ferry flight; Engine coolant pipe failure on take-off, force-landed and left at Juba in Sudan 19.3.51 (Lt OD Penton, Red Section); Aircraft shipped to harbour of Beira, Mozambique; Engine changed; Flown to Southern Rhodesia, arr SRAF 5.4.51; To No.1 Sqn

PK594 Spitfire F.22 (Griffon 61); Became SR..? (80-88 range); TOC/RAF 15.10.45; Ferry flight to Southern Rhodesia; Arr SRAF 19.12.51; No.1 Sqn

PK625 Spitfire F.22 (Griffon 61); Became SR..? (58-68 range); TOC/RAF 19.12.45; Ferry flight to Southern Rhodesia (WO1 JH Deall, Blue Section); Arr SRAF 25.3.51; No.1 Sqn 28.3.51

PK649 Spitfire F.22 (Griffon 61); Became **SR84**; TOC/RAF 20.12.45; Ferry flight to Southern Rhodesia; Arr SRAF 19.12.51; Possibly No.1 Sqn, crashed in high speed turn during formation flight at low level, on a farm named "Birrteg", c.25m SE of Salisbury (now Harare) 11.12.53 (Lt Ray Maritz killed), SOC.

PK663 Spitfire F.22 (Griffon 61); Became SR..? (58-68 range); TOC/RAF 1.1.46; Ferry flight to Southern Rhodesia (Lt BTA Bone & Lt DM Barbour, Yellow Section); Arr SRAF 25.3.51; No.1 Sqn 28.3.51

PK672 Spitfire F.22 (Griffon 61); Became **SR68**; TOC/RAF 27.12.45; Ferry flight to Southern Rhodesia (Lt Col E Jacklin, Red Section); Arr SRAF 25.3.51; No.1 Sqn 28.3.51.

Unidentified

SR88, crashed after take-off 14.6.54 (F/O CV Dams).

SURVIVORS

PK 350/SR64 (RRAF64), crashed with J Malloch in 1982, wreck to WH Owens at Gweru.

PK 355/SR65 (RRAF65 & R65), gate guardian at Thornhill (near Gweru) and New Sarum (near Harare); Now exhibited in Military Museum at Gweru.

References:
SRAF Spitfire F.22, Delivery report 12 March - 22 March 1951.
Rhodesian Air Force, Air Pictorial, December 1965, p.417.
Airfix Magazine April 1971, p.418.

Check list of SRAF / RAF Serial Numbers

SRAF Serial-Nos.	RAF Serial-Nos.	Arr. SRAF	Remarks
SR58	*)		
SR59	PK514	25.3.51	
SR60	*)		
SR61	*)		
SR62	PK575	25.3.51	
SR63	PK330	25.3.51	
SR64	PK350	25.3.51	Survivor, crashed 26.3.82
SR65	PK355	25.3.51	Survivor, Gweru Museum
SR66	*)		
SR67	*)		
SR68	PK672	25.3.51	
Second delivery batch:			
SR80	PK326	19.12.51	
SR81	**)	19.12.51	
SR82	**)	19.12.51	
SR83	**)	19.12.51	
SR84	PK649	19.12.51	crashed 11.12.53
SR85	**)	19.12.51	
SR86	PK401	19.12.51	
SR87	**)	19.12.51	
SR88	**)	19.12.51	
Lost during ferry flying:			
	PK344		crashed 7.12.51
	PK482		crashed 16.12.51

*) PK408/PK506/PK576/PK625/PK663;
**) PK370/PK432/PK494/PK548/PK572/PK594.

SOVIET UNION
[U.S.S.R. – Russia]

German forces invaded Russia on 22nd June 1941. Russia then sought military supplies from Britain and the USA, and on 20th August 1941 a Russian test pilot flew a Spitfire at Duxford. Two days later the Naval and Air Attachés of the Soviet Union visited this airfield. Shortly before this the Hurricanes of Nos.81 and 134 Sqns, No.151 Wing RAF, were sent to Russia, arriving 30th August 1941 at Archangel, to be based at Vaenga from 7th September 1941 until 16th November 1941. In the meantime, on 1st October 1941 representatives of the American, British and Soviet Governments signed the first Lend-Lease contract for the supply of Allied aeroplanes to Russia, but Spitfires were not included at this time.

In September 1942 the first four Spitfire PR.IV (D) arrived in the north of the Soviet Union for PQ-convoy protection and reconnaissance missions, flown by RAF pilots (Operation "*Orator*"). A further six Spitfire PR.IVs arrived in 1943/44. Six, plus one for spares, were handed to the Soviets.

On 4th October 1942 the Soviet Ambassador in London asked for Spitfire fighter aircraft. Deliveries commenced on 10th January 1943 and continued until 24th March 1943 when the last of 143 Spitfire F.Vbs arrived at Basrah in the Persian Gulf. They were newly-marked locally as Soviet aircraft with the Red Star by Nos.118 and 119 MUs, assembly units at Basrah and Shaibah respectively, and handed over to the Soviet Mission, where they were collected by Russian pilots and flown home to USSR bases in the South.

A Spitfire F.Vb with the Russian No."65" had a fixed loop-aerial for the RPK-10M radio compass, but in general they had the TR-9D radio set installed.

Deliveries of Spitfire Mk.IXs began in February 1944, arriving Basrah on 5th April 1944. The first were despatched from RAF storage units, but later aircraft went direct from the Castle Bromwich production line to Russia. By 12th June 1945 a total of 1,183 Spitfire LF.IXc/es and two HF.IXes had arrived (Comm.No.507).

Russia also showed an interest in the Spitfire T.IX trainer, though the Red Air Force had converted some from her own Spitfire LF.IXes. A photograph of a two-seater Spitfire LF.IXe (UTI) shows a normal blister canopy for a second cockpit in the fuselage immediately behind the regular seat with an additional transparent fairing between both.

Altogether the Soviet Union received 1,335 Spitfires - comprising 7 Spitfire PR.IV/D, 143 F.Vb and 1,185 Mk.IX.

Note:
Russia, the Ukraine and White-Russia formed the Soviet Union (USSR) in 1922. This Federation expanded with Armenia, Azerbaijan, Georgia, Kazakhstan, Kirgizia, Tadzhikistan, Turkmenistan, Uzbekistan in 1926/36, and with Estonia, Latvia, Lithuania and Moldavia in 1940. The USSR was dissolved in 1991.

Spitfire delivery routes to the Soviet Union

The first four Spitfire PR.IVs (long range PR-type D) arrived in Russia by ferry-flying direct from the Shetlands to Vaenga near Murmansk in Northern Russia in September 1942 (Operation "*Orator*"). Further PR.IVs followed in this way 1943/44.

Spitfire Mks.V and IX were shipped to the Soviet Air Force from 1943 onwards. All the Spitfire Mk.Vbs went to the Middle East and were delivered to Basrah (Iraq) on the Persian Gulf from January to March 1943. There the erected Spitfires were handed over to pilots of the Soviet Air Force, which flew the Spitfires to a Depot and Replacement Centre near Baku (Caspian Sea).

The Persian Gulf - Caspian Sea overland route became a supply line for Allied materials to reach the Russian armies on their Southern front. The arrival of Spitfire Mk.IXs in the Soviet Union

This Spitfire PR.IV (D) served with the RAF in Operation Orator *from Vaenga airbase in 1942. The aircraft later went to the Soviet Air Force, marked '01', and was tested by the NII VVS Research Institute at Zhukovskyi near Moscow in 1943.* [Wojtek Matusiak]

Spitfire F.Vbs at Abadan airfield mid-1943. Delivered via Basrah harbour, the aircraft were then moved to either Shaibah or Abadan for assembly by RAF MUs, being finally flown by Russian pilots to the Southern front (Caucasus). [Victor Kulikov]

continued from April 1944 to June 1945. The first were delivered via Middle East. But some later Mk.IXs came to Russia by a Northern route, arriving direct at Murmansk and nearby harbours.

RAF documentation often referred only to destinations "*Hapmat*", "Hapmat-South" or "Hapmat-North", these being code names for the delivery routes to Russia. Hapmat and Hapmat-South referred to delivery through the Shatt-el-Arab ports of Basrah (Iraq) and Abadan (Iran). Hapmat-North indicated delivery by the northern route, to Murmansk or Bakaritsa (otherwise Molotowsk, now Severomorsk, near Archangel).

Services of the Soviet Air Force

The Air Forces of the Soviet Union formed integral parts of the Army and Navy, and were divided as follows in that time:
- Air Armies (Nos. 1-17 VAs);
- Air Defence Force;
- Long-Range Bomber Force (No. 18 VA);
- Air Forces of the Fleets (VVS VMF).

By then the Soviet Air Force consisted of 18 Air Armies ("*Vozdushnaya Armiya*"), with subordination to the respective ground forces for Nos.1 to 17 VAs. Only No.18 VA, the re-formed Long-Range Bomber Force, became an independent arm in December 1944, controlled directly by the supreme HQ of the Soviet Air Force.

Strategic targets in Russia became protected by the Air Defence Force ("PVO"). Several Air Defence Fighter Regiments ("IAP.PVO") fought with Spitfires in the Murmansk area, in the Leningrad and Moscow Air Defence Sectors ("IAP.LPVO" & "IAP.MPVO"), over Stalingrad (now Volgograd) and in the Caucasian area.

The Naval air arm ("*Aviatsiya Voenno-morskogo flota*") was divided into the Baltic Fleet (KBF), the Northern Fleet (SF), the Black Sea Fleet (ChF) and the Pacific Fleet (TOF). The Northern Fleet and the Black Sea Fleet used also Spitfire PR.IV/D and F.Vb, respectively.

Fighter units of the Air Armies and the Air Defence Force were controlled by Fighter Aviation Corps ("IAK"). The largest flying formation was the Fighter Air Division ("IAD", c.120-125 aircraft), which comprised most three Fighter Air Regiments ("IAP", c.40 aircraft each). A Regiment being normally made up of three Squadrons (Eskadrilyas).

Guard Air Regiments and Divisions ("GvIAP" & "GvIAD") were so designated as a mark of distinguished service in combat.

The Spitfire F.Vb served as a pure fighter aircraft, without bomb racks and rocket equipment. Spitfire F.Vbs saw operational service in the Black Sea coast area, and also in the middle sectors and over Moscow. Late in 1943 the German JG.52 (No.52 Fighter Wing), was engaged in a fight against 25 Russian Spitfire F.Vbs in the Orel area, c.170 miles south of Moscow. In 1943 the Red Air

E = Estonia; Hu = Hungary; La = Latvia; Li = Lithuania; NS = Nowaja Semlja; Ru = Rumania - Note: Molotowsk (Bakaritsa) now Severodvinsk

Force lost 28 Spitfire F.Vbs in air combat. Fighter units listed 12 serviceable Spitfire F.Vbs in November 1945.

The Air Defence Force received the first 20 Spitfire F.Vbs in 1943. Later inventory lists show 297 Spitfire LF.IXs on strength of the "PVOs" in 1944. In April 1945 the Air Defence shows 26 of the 81 Regiments equipped with Spitfire LF.IXs.

In total, the inventories of all Fighter and Air Defence units listed 843 serviceable Spitfires in May 1945. Generally the Spitfire LF.IXs remained in service until 1948, but the last were phased out in 1951.

The RAF in the Soviet Union

No.151 Wing RAF sailed to the Soviet Union in August 1941 ("*Force Benedict*"). Led by Wg Cdr Ramsbottom-Isherwood, the two fighter units, Nos.81 and 134 Sqns, arrived at Vaenga in Northern Russia on 7th September 1941, both with Hurricanes. The task ended in mid November 1941, and all serviceable Hurricanes then went to the Soviet Navy.

To protect convoy PQ.18, which sailed for Russia on 3rd September 1942, a detachment of three Spitfire PR.IV/Ds of No.1 PRU RAF went to the Soviet Union on 1st September 1942 (Operation "*Orator*"). Led by F/Lt EA Fairhurst, they were flown in a first step from the Shetlands to the Afrikanda airfield near the White Sea, north Russia. In a second leg the unit flew to its operational airbase Vaenga near Murmansk on 2nd September 1942. A fourth Spitfire PR.IV (D) followed on 19th September 1942 as replacement for one which was heavily damaged by an enemy bombing raid ten days before. Another Spitfire was lost over Altenfjord, Norway on 27th September 1942. On completion of the task, the surviving two Spitfires (plus one damaged for spares) were handed over to the Soviet Northern Fleet with date of 18th October 1942.

Later, with Operation "*Source*" (3rd September - 31st October 1943) and Operation "*Tungsten*" (7th March -31st May 1944) a further six Spitfire PR IV (D)s arrived in the Soviet Union. Only five arrived at the Vaenga airfield, however, one having been shot down by flak on the ferry route to Vaenga c.10th March 1944. Another PR.IV crashed in a forced landing on 19th April 1944. Eventually four of these Spitfires remained with the Northern Fleet after return of the RAF personnel, mainly for use by No.3 Eskadrilya of No.118 ORAP. Later one PR.IV was flown by a Russian test centre in March 1943, and was displayed in the Murmansk Fleet Museum in 1946.

Known Spitfire units of the Soviet Union

No.7   IAP.ChF, a Fighter Aviation Regiment of the Black Sea Fleet, used Spitfires by No.3 Eskadrilya over the Crimea (Sevastopol, Taman area) 1943/45. Spitfire Mk.Vbs in 1943. The service list shows ten Spitfire F.Vbs in November 1944.
Commanding Officers:
Lt Col AZ Dushin; Lt Col KD Denisov; Lt Col VM Yankovskij (by October 1943)

No.11   GvIAP.PVO, a Guards Fighter Aviation Regiment of the Leningrad Air Defence (No.2 GvIAK) 1943/45; ex No.44 IAP.PVO; Spitfire F.Vbs in July 1943, Spitfire LF.IX in March 1945.
Commanding Officers:
Kapt SP Danilov; Lt Col VG Blagoveshchenskiy; Lt Col IP Neustroyev

No.16   IAP.PVO, a Fighter Aviation Regiment of the Moscow Air Defence (No.6 IAK), based at Ljuberzij, with Spitfire F.Vbs in 1943 (operation reported 22nd August 1943), and LF.IX in August 1944.
Commanding Officer:
Lt Col FM Prutskov (1941)

No.24   Carrier Aviation Sqn at Alma-Tomat airfield, received ten Spitfire F.Vb in autumn 1944. Experimental unit, carrier launch trials.
Commanding Officers:
Unknown

No.25   ZAP, a Reserve Aviation Regiment, based at Adzikabul near Baku, Caspian Sea (Azerbaijan), served as an OCU with Spitfire Mk.Vbs from early 1943; e.g. Pilots conversion training of No.57 GvIAP. Later some Spitfire F.Vbs handed over to No.821 IAP in August 1943.
Commanding Officers:
Unknown

No.26   GvIAP.PVO, a Guards Fighter Aviation Regiment of the Leningrad Air Defence (No.2 GvIAK) 1943/45; ex No. 26 IAP.PVO; Spitfire F.Vbs in July 1943, LF.IXs in August 1944 (twelve LF.IXs on strength in December 1945). Trials with RD-1 television navigation system on two Spitfires in 1945.
Commanding Officer:
Lt Col BN Romanov; Maj GG Petrov

No.27   GvIAP.PVO, a Guards Fighter Aviation Regiment of the Leningrad Air Defence (No.2 GvIAK) 1943/45; ex No.123 IAP.PVO; Spitfire F.Vbs in July 1943; LF.IX in August 1944.
Commanding Officers:
Maj BN Surin; Lt Col FM Mishchenko; Lt Col NP Mazhayev

No.57   GvIAP, a Guards Fighter Aviation Regiment (No.9 GvIAD, No.4 Air Army, South front), the first Soviet Fighter unit with Spitfires:
As No.36 IAP pulled back from the Caucasian front to the Adzikabul airfield near Baku, Caspian area (Azerbaijan) in December 1942, to be brought up to strength and to train with Spitfire F.Vbs by No.25 ZAP (OCU). Then each pilot had to make six ferry flights from Shaibah and Basrah via Teheran for delivery of Spitfires for other Regiments.
On 8th February 1943 No.36 IAP was re-designated as No.57 GvIAP. This Guards Regiment departed from Baku to arrive on the Krasnodar airfield in the North of the Black Sea 23rd April 1943. There the Spitfires operated over the Kuban river, being used for bomber escorts and interception missions. Reports show the Spitfires F.Vbs engaged in air combats over Krymskaya, Neberdjeevskaya, Abinskaya from 28th April 1943. Moved to the Slavyanskaya airfield 15th May 1943. But the unit suffered a high rate of failures and losses, and in July 1943 it re-equipped with P-39s and Russian-built aircraft.
Commanding Officer:
Lt Col AA Osipov

No.67   IAP.PVO, a Fighter Aviation Regiment of the Moscow Air Defence, with Spitfire F.Vbs in 1943 (operation reported 6th September 1943).
Commanding Officer:
Maj BA Rudakov

No.67   GvIAP, a Guards Fighter Aviation Regiment, ex No.436 IAP, served with Spitfire LF.IXs over Leningrad, Moscow and Stalingrad (No.273 IAD).
Commanding Officers
Lt Col AB Panov (until 12th September 1944)

No.100 GvIAP, a Guards Fighter Aviation Regiment, ex No.45 IAP.PVO, with Spitfires based at Krasnodar, operated over the Crimea and Kuban river, reported over Sevastopol (No.9 GvIAD).
Commanding Officers:
Lt Col IM Dzusov; Lt Col SI Lukyanov

No.102 **GvIAP.PVO**, a Guards Fighter Aviation Regiment of the Leningrad Air Defence (No.2 GvIAK) 1943/45; ex-No.124 IAP, Moscow Defence; Spitfire F.Vbs in July 1943, LF.IXs in March 1945.
Commanding Officers:
Lt Col MG Trunov; Maj AG Pronin

No.117 **GvIAP**, a Guards Fighter Aviation Regiment (No.236 IAD); ex No.975 IAP; Spitfire F.Vbs at Krasnodar May 1943, operated over the Caucasus (Kuban river) and over the Ukraine;
Commanding Officer:
Lt Col GI Grozhovetskiy

No.177 **IAP.PVO**, a Fighter Aviation Regiment of the Moscow Air Defence (No.6 IAK), based Ljuberzij with Spitfire LF.IXs in 1944/45; served with Spitfire LF.IXs until 1948, then Yak-17.
Commanding Officer:
Maj MI Korolev (1941)

No.768 **IAP.PVO**, a Fighter Aviation Regiment of the Murmansk Air Defence (No.122 IAD), with Spitfire LF.IXs in 1944/45.
Commanding Officers:
Unknown

No.769 **IAP.PVO**, a Fighter Aviation Regiment of the Murmansk Air Defence (No.122 IAD), with Spitfire LF.IXs in 1944/45.
Commanding Officers:
Unknown

No.802 **IAP.PVO**, a Fighter Aviation Regiment, Air Defence with Spitfire LF.IXs at Poltava, Ukraine in September 1944.
Commanding Officers:
Unknown

No.821 **IAP.PVO**, a Fighter Aviation Regiment for Air Defence in the Caucasian area (No.236 IAD); Spitfire

A fighter training course of the Soviet Air Force in 1945. Instructor, pilots and pupils stand in front of a Spitfire Mk.IX UTI two-seater, converted by the Red Air Force from an LF.IXe. [Victor Kulikov]

No.178 **IAP.PVO**, a Fighter Aviation Regiment of the Moscow Air Defence (No.6 IAK); with Spitfire LF.IXs in 1944/45. Reported also over Kaluga and Podolsk.
Commanding Officer:
Maj RI Rakov (1941)

No.480 **IAP.PVO**, a Fighter Aviation Regiment for Air Defence, with Spitfire LF.IXs in 1944/45.
Commanding Officers:
Unknown

No.767 **IAP.PVO**, a Fighter Aviation Regiment of the Murmansk Air Defence (No.122 IAD), with Spitfire LF.IXs in August 1944.
Commanding Officers:
Unknown

F.Vbs from July 1943, based Shakhty & Chapayevka (north of the Azov Sea, Donez/Don estuary), with 29 Spitfire F.Vbs on strength 4 August 1943; Operations over Molochnaya and Miyus rivers from 26th August 1943. Some accidents with Spitfires, spare parts lacking. The unit was soon sent to the rear for re-equipment in September 1943.
Commanding Officer:
Maj V Chalov

No.118 **ORAP/SF**, a Reconnaissance Aviation Regiment of the Navy (North-Fleet), formed in March 1943, flew reconnaissance duties with four Eskadrilyas. The first three Spitfire PR.IV/D were handed over to No.28 ORAE [Eskadrilya] in October 1942, which merged into No.118 ORAP later. From March 1943 the

SOVIET UNION

Two views of a Spitfire F.Vb of the NII VVS/RKKA (Research and Test Institute) during catapult trials from the cruiser Molotov *in 1946.*

A further view of a Spitfire F.Vb of the NII VVS/RKKA (Research and Test Institute) during catapult trials from the cruiser Molotov *in 1946.*

Spitfires mainly served with No.3 Eskadrilya of No.118 ORAP at Vaenga for short-range reconnaissance missions. One of the Spitfires went to a Russian test centre in May 1943. A further three Spitfire PR.IV were received from No.543 Sqn in 1943 and another one from No.542 Sqn RAF in 1944. But the Soviets suffered many losses, and No.118 ORAP never listed more than four Spitfires in use at the same time: By 1st January 1943 only three, on 1st June 1944 four, and by 1st February 1945 only two Spitfire PR.IV (D) were serviceable with No.3 Esk of No.118 ORAP. Later one of them with the white marking '*02*' went to the Fleet Museum at Murmansk.
Commanding Officers:
Unknown

NII VVS / RKKA, a Research and Test Institute of the Soviet Air Force, based at Zhukovskyi near Moscow, used Spitfires for tests and trials. For example, a Spitfire PR.IV/D with the code '*01*' was there from March 1943 to *May* 1943, and a F.Vb was tested in May-June 1943; a LF.IXe (Merlin 66) was there in September 1944, a second in April 1945, and a HF.IXe (Merlin 70) in May to August 1945. Trials with a Mk.IX UTI were reported in October 1945. Also cockpit hood jettison tests were made in 1945/46. A Spitfire F.Vb undertook catapult trials from the cruiser "*Molotov*" in 1946.
Commanding Officers:
Unknown

Remarks
Little is known about the Red Air Force Spitfires. They may have been served with many other units. For example, 26 of the 81 Air Defence Regiments used Spitfire LF.IXs in 1945, but only a few of them are known. Russian archives are restricted, or remain unknown. Official support was not forthcoming, and information came from private sources only.

Abbreviations of the Soviet Union

Gv	Gvardejskaya (Guards status)
IAD	Istrebitelnaya Aviotsionnaya Diviziya (Fighter Aviation Division)
IAK	Istrebitelnye Aviotsionnye Korpusa (Fighter Aviation Corps)
IAP	Istrebitelnyj Aviatsionnyj Polk (Fighter Aviation Regiment)
LPVO	Air Defence Force Leningrad
MPVO	Air Defence Force Moscow
NII-VVS	Naoutchno-Ispytatelnyi Institut Voenno Vozdouchnyi Sil (Research Institute of the Soviet Air Force)
ORAP	Otdelnyj Razvedyvatelnyj Aviatsionnyj Polk (Independent Recce Aviation Regiment)
Pp	Podpolk (rank of Lt Col)
PVO	Protivovozdushnaya Obornona (Air Defence Force)
SF	Severnyj Flot (Northern Fleet)
UTI	Uchebno-Trenirovochnyi Istrebitel (Training Fighter)
VA	Vozdushnaya Armiya (Air Armies)
VMF	Voyenno-Morskoj Flot (Soviet Navy)
VVS	Voyenno-Vozdushnye Sily (Soviet Air Force).

Individual Histories

P8755   Spitfire F.Vb (Merlin 45); TOC/RAF 29.6.41; via No.222 MU and Birkenhead to Russia; Arr Basrah 17.3.43; Fate unknown

P8783   Spitfire F.Vb (Merlin 45); TOC/RAF 6.7.41; via No.82 MU and Glasgow to Russia; Arr Basrah 24.3.43; No.57 GvIAP; Fate unknown

W3818   Spitfire F.Vb (Merlin 45); TOC/RAF 25.8.41; via No.222 MU and Manchester to Russia; Arr Basrah 17.3.43; No.57 GvIAP; Fate unknown

AA908   Spitfire F.Vb (Merlin 45); TOC/RAF 1.11.41; via No.76 MU and Swansea to Russia; Arr Basrah 16.2.43; No.821 IAP, Caucasian front; Fate unknown

SOVIET UNION

AB132 Spitfire PR.IV/D (Merlin 45); TOC/RAF 30.11.41; No.1 PRU 27.1.42 (officially No.542 Sqn 30.9.42); Operation "O*rator*", *a*rr Vaenga, Russia in 9.42; To No.118 ORAP (No.3 Esk) 18.10.42; Fate unknown
NOTE: Possibly No. "01", shown at the NII VVS Test-/Reserach Institute at Zhukovskyi 3.43-5.43

AB423 Spitfire PR.IV (Merlin 46); TOC/RAF 12.1.42; No.543 Sqn; Possibly Operation "*Source*", arr. Vaenga, Russia in 9.43; To No.118 ORAP (No.3 Esk) 1.11.43; Fate unknown

AB427 Spitfire PR.IV (Merlin 46); TOC/RAF 28.1.42; No.543 Sqn; Possibly Operation "*Source*", arr. Vaenga, Russia in 9.43; To No.118 ORAP (No.3 Esk) 1.11.43; Fate unknown

AB781 Spitfire F.Vb (Merlin 45); TOC/RAF 31.7.41; via No.222 MU and Manchester to Russia; Arr Basrah 17.3.43; Fate unknown

AB896 Spitfire F.Vb (Merlin 45); TOC/RAF 10.8.41; ex USAAF (5th Sqn, 52nd FG); via No.3 PATP to Russia; Arr Basrah 24.3.43; No.821 IAP; Fate unknown

AB901 Spitfire F.Vb (Merlin 45); TOC/RAF 9.8.41; ex USAAF (308th Sqn, 31st FG); via No.76 MU and Swansea to Russia; Arr Basrah 16.2.43; Fate unknown

AD176 Spitfire F.Vb (Merlin 45); TOC/RAF 19.9.41; via No.82 MU and Glasgow to Russia; Arr Basrah 24.3.43; Fate unknown

AD190 Spitfire F.Vb (Merlin 45); TOC/RAF 15.10.41; ex USAAF (2nd Sqn, 52nd FG); via No.215 MU and Cardiff to Russia; Arr Basrah 6.2.43; Fate unknown

AD194 Spitfire F.Vb (Merlin 45); TOC/RAF 15.9.41; via No.82 MU and Glasgow to Russia; Arr Basrah 24.3.43; Fate unknown

AD225 Spitfire F.Vb (Merlin 45); TOC/RAF 13.9.41; via No.76 MU and Swansea to Russia; Arr Basrah 16.2.43; Fate unknown

AD236 Spitfire F.Vb (Merlin 45); TOC/RAF 14.9.41; via No.222 MU and Cardiff to Russia; Arr Basrah 6.2.43; Fate unknown

AD319 Spitfire F.Vb (Merlin 45); TOC/RAF 17.10.41; via No.222 MU and Birkenhead to Russia; Arr Basrah 17.3.43; Fate unknown

AD418 Spitfire F.Vb (Merlin 45); TOC/RAF 15.10.41; via No.82 MU and Glasgow to Russia; Arr Basrah 24.3.43; Fate unknown

AD461 Spitfire F.Vb (Merlin 45); TOC/RAF 23.10.41; via No.76 MU and Swansea to Russia; Arr Basrah 16.2.43; No.821 IAP; Lost in action 9.8.43, SOC

AD473 Spitfire F.Vb (Merlin 45); TOC/RAF 9.11.41; via No.222 MU and Swansea to Russia; Arr Basrah 16.2.43; No.821 IAP; Fate unknown

AD505 Spitfire F.Vb (Merlin 45); TOC/RAF 23.10.41; via No.215 MU & No.3 PATP, Glasgow to Russia; Arr Basrah 24.3.43; No.821 IAP; Lost in accident 3.8.43, SOC

BL257 Spitfire F.Vb (Merlin 45); TOC/RAF 7.11.41; via No.215 MU & No.3 PATP, Glasgow to Russia; Arr Basrah 24.3.43; No.821 IAP; Repair 19.8.43; Fate unknown

A Spitfire F.Vb coded '65' seen at an airfield near Moscow. In the background can be seen a line-up of La-5FNs. [Russian Aviation Research Group]

Spitfire F.Vb, '65' was based at an airfield near Moscow circa 1943

Spitfire F.Vbs, BM185 nearest, at Abadan in March 1943, being prepared for delivery to the Soviet Union. [G Petrov]

BL289 Spitfire F.Vb (Merlin 45); TOC/RAF 23.11.41; via No.215 MU & No.3 PATP, Glasgow to Russia; Arr Basrah 24.3.43; No.57 GvIAP; Fate unknown

BL327 Spitfire F.Vb (Merlin 45); TOC/RAF 18.11.41; via No.82 MU and Glasgow to Russia; Arr Basrah 24.3.43; No.821 IAP; Fate unknown

BL352 Spitfire F.Vb (Merlin 45); TOC/RAF 23.11.41; via No.76 MU and Swansea to Russia; Arr Basrah 16.2.43; No.821 IAP; Fate unknown

BL353 Spitfire F.Vb (Merlin 45); TOC/RAF 23.11.41; via No.222 MU and Southport to Russia; Arr Basrah 17.3.43; No.821 IAP; Fate unknown

BL431 Spitfire F.Vb (Merlin 45); TOC/RAF 30.11.41; via No.215 MU and Cardiff to Russia; Arr Basrah 6.2.43; No.821 IAP; Shot down by enemy 7.8.43, SOC

BL467 Spitfire F.Vb (Merlin 45); TOC/RAF 1.12.41; via No.82 MU and Glasgow to Russia; Arr Basrah 24.3.43; Fate unknown

BL485 Spitfire F.Vb (Merlin 45); TOC/RAF 23.12.41; via No.215 MU and Cardiff to Russia; Arr Basrah 6.2.43; Fate unknown

BL513 Spitfire F.Vb (Merlin 45); TOC/RAF 13.12.41; via No.82 MU and Liverpool to Russia; Arr Basrah 30.1.43; Fate unknown

BL618 Spitfire F.Vb (Merlin 45); TOC/RAF 6.1.42; via No.215 MU & No.3 PATP to Russia; Arr Basrah 24.3.43; Fate unknown

BL625 Spitfire F.Vb (Merlin 45); TOC/RAF 4.1.42; via No.82 MU and Glasgow to Russia; Arr Basrah 24.3.43; No.821 IAP; Fate unknown

BL645 Spitfire F.Vb (Merlin 45); TOC/RAF 17.1.42; via No.76 MU and Birkenhead to Russia; Arr Basrah 30.1.43; Fate unknown

BL685 Spitfire F.Vb (Merlin 45); TOC/RAF 28.1.42; via No.82 MU and Glasgow to Russia; Arr Basrah 24.3.43; Fate unknown

BL764 Spitfire F.Vb (Merlin 45); TOC/RAF 25.1.42; via No.222 MU and Manchester to Russia; Arr Basrah 17.3.43; Fate unknown

BL771 Spitfire F.Vb (Merlin 45); TOC/RAF 8.2.42; via No.22 MU and Birkenhead to Russia; Arr Basrah 17.3.43; Fate unknown

BL801 Spitfire F.Vb (Merlin 45); TOC/RAF 10.2.42; via No.76 MU and Birkenhead to Russia; Arr Basrah 30.1.43; No.821 IAP; Fate unknown

BL808 Spitfire F.Vb (Merlin 45); TOC/RAF 14.2.42; via No.215 MU & No.3 PATP to Russia; Arr Basrah 24.3.43; Fate unknown

BL823 Spitfire F.Vb (Merlin 45); TOC/RAF 11.2.42; via No.222 MU and Swansea to Russia; Arr Basrah 16.2.43; Fate unknown

BM154 Spitfire F.Vb (Merlin 45); TOC/RAF 8.3.42; via No.82 MU and Glasgow to Russia; Arr Basrah 24.3.43; Fate unknown

BM184 Spitfire F.Vb (Merlin 45); TOC/RAF 10.3.42; via No.82 MU and Glasgow to Russia; Arr Basrah 24.3.43; Fate unknown

BM185 Spitfire F.Vb (Merlin 46); TOC/RAF 9.3.42; via No.82 MU and Glasgow to Russia; Arr Basrah 24.3.43; No.57 GvIAP; Fate unknown

BM189 Spitfire F.Vb (Merlin 45); TOC/RAF 13.3.42; via No.215 MU & No.3 PATP to Russia; Arr Basrah 24.3.43; No.821 IAP; Fate unknown

BM270 Spitfire F.Vb (Merlin 45); TOC/RAF 18.3.42; via No.222 MU and Swansea to Russia; Arr Basrah 16.2.43; Fate unknown

BM359 Spitfire F.Vb (Merlin 46); TOC/RAF 27.3.42; via No.82 MU and Glasgow to Russia; Arr Basrah 24.3.43; Fate unknown

BM365 Spitfire F.Vb (Merlin 45); TOC/RAF 1.4.42; via No.222 MU and Swansea to Russia; Arr Basrah 16.2.43; Fate unknown

BM372 Spitfire F.Vb (Merlin 45); TOC/RAF 12.4.42; via No.76 MU and Swansea to Russia; Arr Basrah 16.2.43; Fate unknown

BM460 Spitfire F.Vb (Merlin 45); TOC/RAF 12.4.42; via No.82 MU and Glasgow to Russia; Arr Basrah 24.3.43; No.821 IAP; Fate unknown

BM462 Spitfire F.Vb (Merlin 45); TOC/RAF 11.4.42; via No.222 MU and Swansea to Russia; Arr Basrah 16.2.43; Fate unknown

BM520 Spitfire F.Vb (Merlin 45); TOC/RAF 18.4.42; via No.82 MU and Glasgow to Russia; Arr Basrah 24.3.43; Fate unknown

BM595 Spitfire F.Vb (Merlin 45); TOC/RAF 25.4.42; via No.76 MU and Swansea to Russia; Arr Basrah 16.2.43; No.821 IAP; Lost in action 9.8.43, SOC

BP884 Spitfire PR.IV (Merlin 46); TOC/RAF 15.2.42; No.542 Sqn; Operation "*Tungsten*", arr Vaenga, Russia in 3.42; To Soviet Air Force and possibly still on charge 1.6.44

BP889 Spitfire PR IV/D (Merlin 46); TOC/RAF 15.2.42; 542 Sqn; Operation "*Orator*", arr Vaenga, Russia in 9.42; Recce over Altenfjord, Norway, shot down north of Banak airfield by an enemy aircraft (possibly an FW 190A of II/JG5 based at Alta 27.9.42 (F/O GW Walker killed, buried Tromsø cemetery post-war); Cat.FB/E 14.12.42, SOC

BP891 Spitfire PR IV/D (Merlin 46); TOC/RAF 15.2.42; No.1 PRU 7.5.42 (officially No.541 Sqn 30.9.42); Operation "*Orator*", arr Vaenga, Russia in 9.42; To No.118 ORAP (No.3 Esk) 18.10.42; Fate unknown

BP917 Spitfire PR IV/D (Merlin 46); TOC/RAF 26.3.42; No.542 Sqn; Operation "*Tungsten*", arr Vaenga, Russia in 3.42; To Soviet Air Force and still on charge 1.6.44

BP923 Spitfire PR IV/D (Merlin 46); TOC/RAF 30.3.42; No.1 PRU 5.5.42 (officially No.542 Sqn 30.9.42); Operation "*Orator*", arr Vaenga, Russia in 9.42; To No.118 ORAP (No.3 Esk) 18.10.42; Fate unknown

BP926 Spitfire PR IV/D (Merlin 46); TOC/RAF 3.4.42; No.542 Sqn; Operation "*Tungsten*", arr Vaenga, Russia in 3.42; To Soviet Air Force and still on charge 1.6.44

BP929 Spitfire PR IV/D (Merlin 46); TOC/RAF 13.4.42; No.542 Sqn; Operation "*Tungsten*", arr Vaenga, Russia in 3.42; To Soviet Air Force and still on charge 1.6.44

BR658 Spitfire PR.IV/D (Merlin 46); TOC/RAF 21.7.42; No.543 Sqn; Possibly Operation "*Source*", arr. Vaenga, Russia in 9.43; To No.118 ORAP (No.3 Esk) 1.11.43; Lost in action 29.2.44; SOC 9.12.44

EN785 Spitfire F.Vb (Merlin 45); TOC/RAF 1.5.42; via No.76 MU and Birkenhead to Russia; Arr Basrah 30.1.43; Fate unknown

EN797 Spitfire F.Vb (Merlin 45); TOC/RAF 2.5.42; via No.222 MU and Manchester to Russia; Arr Basrah 17.3.43; Fate unknown

EN859 Spitfire F.Vb (Merlin 45); TOC/RAF 10.5.42; via No.3 PATP to Russia; Arr Basrah 10.1.43; No.821 IAP; Fate unknown

EN911 Spitfire F.Vb (Merlin 46); TOC/RAF 3.6.42; via No.76 MU & No.3 PATP, Glasgow to Russia; Arr Basrah 10.1.43; Fate unknown

EN923 Spitfire F.Vb (Merlin 45); TOC/RAF 16.5.42; ex USAAF (309th, 31st FG); via No.76 MU and Birkenhead to Russia; Arr Basrah 30.1.43; Fate unknown

EN930 Spitfire F.Vb (Merlin 45); TOC/RAF 16.5.42; via No.215 MU and Cardiff to Russia; Arr Basrah 6.2.43; Fate unknown

EN967 Spitfire F.Vb (Merlin 45); TOC/RAF 30.5.42; via No.76 MU and Manchester to Russia; Arr Basrah 10.1.43; Fate unknown

EN970 Spitfire F.Vb (Merlin 45); TOC/RAF 23.5.42; via No.82 MU & No.3 PATP to Russia; Arr Basrah 16.2.43; Fate unknown

EN977 Spitfire F.Vb (Merlin 45); TOC/RAF 29.5.42; via No.76 MU and Manchester to Russia; Arr Basrah 10.1.43; Fate unknown

EP120 Spitfire F.Vb (Merlin 46); TOC/RAF 23.5.42; via No.82 MU & No.3 PATP to Russia; Arr Basrah 11.1.43; Fate unknown

EP145 Spitfire F.Vb (Merlin 46); TOC/RAF 18.6.42; via No.76 MU & No.3 PATP to Russia; Arr Basrah 11.1.43; Fate unknown

EP149 Spitfire F.Vb (Merlin 46); TOC/RAF 30.5.42; via No.76 MU & No.3 PATP to Russia; Arr Basrah 10.1.43; No.821 IAP; Fate unknown

EP150 Spitfire F.Vb (Merlin 46); TOC/RAF 14.6.42; via No.76 MU & No.3 PATP to Russia; Arr Basrah 1.3.43; Fate unknown

EP151 Spitfire F.Vb (Merlin 46); TOC/RAF 30.5.42; via No.76 MU & No.3 PATP to Russia; Arr Basrah 10.1.43; No.821 IAP; Fate unknown

EP165 Spitfire F.Vb (Merlin 45); TOC/RAF 21.5.42; via No.222 MU and Birkenhead to Russia; Arr Basrah 17.3.43; No.821 IAP; Fate unknown

EP184 Spitfire F.Vb (Merlin 46); TOC/RAF 1.6.42; via No.76 MU & No.3 PATP to Russia; Arr Basrah 1.3.43; Fate unknown

EP185 Spitfire F.Vb (Merlin 46); TOC/RAF 30.5.42; via Nos.47 MU & 1 PATP, Hull to Russia; Arr Basrah 10.1.43; Fate unknown

EP210 Spitfire F.Vb (Merlin 46); TOC/RAF 2.6.42; via Nos.76 & 82 MUs & No.3 PATP, Glasgow desp.to Basrah 23.10.42; Arr Basrah for Russia 11.1.43; Guards unit, with Soviet Red Star and numbered "538" c.1943; Fate unknown

Spitfire F.Vb EP210 coded '538' with an unidentified Guards unit around 1943. [Russian Aviation Research Group]

Spitfire F.Vb EP356 arrived at Basrah on 1st March 1943, then flew to join the Soviet Air Force. It is here shown with fin marking '20'.

EP212 Spitfire F.Vb (Merlin 46); TOC/RAF 4.6.42; via No.82 MU & No.3 PATP to Russia; Arr Basrah 16.2.43; Fate unknown

EP213 Spitfire F.Vb (Merlin 46); TOC/RAF 1.6.42; via No.82 MU & No.3 PATP to Russia; Arr Basrah 10.1.43; Fate unknown

EP230 Spitfire F.Vb (Merlin 46); TOC/RAF 4.6.42; via No.76 MU & No.3 PATP to Russia; Arr Basrah 10.1.43; No.821 IAP; Fate unknown

EP231 Spitfire F.Vb (Merlin 46); TOC/RAF 5.6.42; via No.82 MU & No.3 PATP to Russia; Arr Basrah 10.1.43; Fate unknown

EP232 Spitfire F.Vb (Merlin 46); TOC/RAF 5.6.42; via No.82 MU & No.3 PATP to Russia; Arr Basrah 11.1.43; Fate unknown

EP239 Spitfire F.Vb (Merlin 46); TOC/RAF 5.6.42; via No.82 MU & No.3 PATP to Russia; Arr Basrah 11.1.43; Fate unknown

EP241 Spitfire F.Vb (Merlin 46); TOC/RAF 7.6.42; via No.82 MU & No.3 PATP to Russia; Arr Basrah 10.1.43; No.821 IAP; Fate unknown

EP243 Spitfire F.Vb (Merlin 46); TOC/RAF 6.6.42; via No.76 MU & No.3 PATP to Russia; Arr Basrah 10.1.43; Fate unknown

EP246 Spitfire F.Vb (Merlin 46); TOC/RAF 6.6.42; via No.76 MU & No.3 PATP to Russia; Arr Basrah 10.1.43; Fate unknown

EP247 Spitfire F.Vb (Merlin 46); TOC/RAF 6.6.42; via No.76 MU & No.3 PATP to Russia; Arr Basrah 10.1.43; No.57 GvIAP; Fate unknown

EP248 Spitfire F.Vb (Merlin 46); TOC/RAF 6.6.42; via No.76 MU & No.3 PATP to Russia; Arr Basrah 10.1.43; Fate unknown

EP256 Spitfire F.Vb (Merlin 46); TOC/RAF 9.6.42; via No.76 MU & No.3 PATP to Russia; Arr Basrah 11.1.43; Fate unknown

EP282 Spitfire F.Vb (Merlin 46); TOC/RAF 25.6.42; via No.82 MU and Glasgow to Russia; Arr Basrah 24.3.43; No.821 IAP; Fate unknown

EP292 Spitfire F.Vb (Merlin 46); TOC/RAF 9.6.42; via No.76 MU and Manchester to Russia; Arr Basrah 10.1.43; Fate unknown

EP307 Spitfire F.Vb (Merlin 46); TOC/RAF 21.6.42; via Nos.47 MU & 1 PATP, Hull to Russia; Arr Basrah 10.1.43; Fate unknown

EP311 Spitfire F.Vb (Merlin 46); TOC/RAF 20.6.42; via No.82 MU & No.3 PATP to Russia; Arr Basrah 1.3.43; Fate unknown

EP314 Spitfire F.Vb (Merlin 46); TOC/RAF 16.6.42; via No.82 MU & No.3 PATP to Russia; Arr Basrah 11.1.43; Fate unknown

EP333 Spitfire F.Vb (Merlin 46); TOC/RAF 18.6.42; via No.76 MU and Hull to Russia; Arr Basrah 10.1.43; Fate unknown

EP337 Spitfire F.Vb (Merlin 46); TOC/RAF 20.6.42; via No.76 MU and Hull to Russia; Arr Basrah 10.1.43; No.821 IAP; Fate unknown

EP348 Spitfire F.Vb (Merlin 46); TOC/RAF 16.6.42; via No.76 MU and Glasgow to Russia; Arr Basrah 16.2.43; Fate unknown

EP351 Spitfire F.Vb (Merlin 46); TOC/RAF 17.6.42; via No.82 MU & No.3 PATP to Russia; Arr Basrah 10.1.43; Fate unknown

EP353 Spitfire F.Vb (Merlin 46); TOC/RAF 21.6.42; via No.76 MU & No.3 PATP to Russia; Arr Basrah 11.1.43; Fate unknown

EP356 Spitfire F.Vb (Merlin 46); TOC/RAF 20.6.42; via No.76 MU & No.3 PATP to Russia; Arr Basrah 1.3.43; Soviet Air Force, shown with Red Star and fin marked '*20*'; further fate unknown

EP357 Spitfire F.Vb (Merlin 46); TOC/RAF 20.6.42; via No.82 MU & No.3 PATP to Russia; Arr Basrah 11.1.43; Fate unknown

EP358 Spitfire F.Vb (Merlin 46); TOC/RAF 21.6.42; via No.76 MU & No.3 PATP, Glasgow & Hull to Russia; Arr Basrah 10.1.43; Fate unknown

EP359 Spitfire F.Vb (Merlin 46); TOC/RAF 21.6.42; via No.76 MU & No.3 PATP, Glasgow to Russia; Arr Basrah 11.1.43; Fate unknown

EP363 Spitfire F.Vb (Merlin 46); TOC/RAF 20.6.42; via No.76 MU & No.3 PATP, Glasgow to Russia; Arr Basrah 1.3.43; Fate unknown

EP366 Spitfire F.Vb (Merlin 46); TOC/RAF 21.6.42; via No.76 MU & No.3 PATP to Russia; Arr Basrah 11.1.43; No.821 IAP; Fate unknown

EP382 Spitfire F.Vb (Merlin 46); TOC/RAF 5.7.42; via No.82 MU and Glasgow to Russia; Arr Basrah 24.3.43; Fate unknown

EP383 Spitfire F.Vb (Merlin 46); TOC/RAF 27.6.42; via No.222 MU and Cardiff to Russia; Arr Basrah 6.2.43; Fate unknown

EP386 Spitfire F.Vb (Merlin 46); TOC/RAF 5.7.42; via No.82 MU and Glasgow to Russia; Arr Basrah 24.3.43; Fate unknown

EP389 Spitfire F.Vb (Merlin 46); TOC/RAF 20.6.42; via No.82 MU & No.3 PATP to Russia; Arr Basrah 11.1.43; No.821 IAP; Fate unknown

EP391 Spitfire F.Vb (Merlin 46); TOC/RAF 20.6.42; via No.215 MU & No.3 PATP to Russia; Arr Basrah 24.3.43; No.821 IAP; Fate unknown

EP392 Spitfire F.Vb (Merlin 46); TOC/RAF 21.6.42; via No.76 MU and Hull to Russia; Arr Basrah 10.1.43; Fate unknown

EP396 Spitfire F.Vb (Merlin 46); TOC/RAF 22.6.42; via Nos.47 MU & 1 PATP, Hull to Russia; Arr Basrah 10.1.43; Fate unknown

EP400 Spitfire F.Vb (Merlin 46); TOC/RAF 22.6.42; via No.76 MU and Hull to Russia; Arr Basrah 10.1.43; Fate unknown

EP402 Spitfire F.Vb (Merlin 46); TOC/RAF 21.6.42; via No.82 MU & No.3 PATP to Russia; Arr Basrah 10.1.43; No.821 IAP; Fate unknown

EP403 Spitfire F.Vb (Merlin 46); TOC/RAF 21.6.42; via No.76 MU & No.3 PATP, Glasgow to Russia; Arr Basrah 11.1.43; Fate unknown

EP408 Spitfire F.Vb (Merlin 46); TOC/RAF 28.6.42; via Nos.47 MU & 1 PATP, Hull to Russia; Arr Basrah 10.1.43; Fate unknown

EP414 Spitfire F.Vb (Merlin 46); TOC/RAF 23.6.42; via No.82 MU & No.3 PATP to Russia; Arr Basrah 11.1.43; Fate unknown

EP415 Spitfire F.Vb (Merlin 46); TOC/RAF 25.6.42; via No.82 MU & No.3 PATP to Russia; Arr Basrah 10.1.43; Fate unknown

EP416 Spitfire F.Vb (Merlin 46); TOC/RAF 25.6.42; via No.82 MU & No.3 PATP to Russia; Arr Basrah 10.1.43; No.821 IAP; Lost in action 9.8.43, SOC

EP417 Spitfire F.Vb (Merlin 46); TOC/RAF 25.6.42; via Nos.47 MU & 1 PATP to Russia; Arr Basrah 10.1.43; Fate unknown

EP431 Spitfire F.Vb (Merlin 46); TOC/RAF 24.6.42; via No.76 MU & No.3 PATP, Glasgow to Russia; Arr Basrah 1.3.43; Fate unknown

EP434 Spitfire F.Vb (Merlin 46); TOC/RAF 24.6.42; via No.47 MU and Hull to Russia; Arr Basrah 10.1.43; No.821 IAP; Lost in action 9.8.43, SOC

EP446 Spitfire F.Vb (Merlin 46); TOC/RAF 28.6.42; via Nos.47 MU & 1 PATP, Hull to Russia; Arr Basrah 10.1.43; Fate unknown

EP450 Spitfire F.Vb (Merlin 46); TOC/RAF 28.6.42; via No.215 MU & No.3 PATP, Avonmouth to Russia; Arr Basrah 1.3.43; Fate unknown

EP454 Spitfire F.Vb (Merlin 46); TOC/RAF 27.6.42; via No.222 MU and Cardiff to Russia; Arr Basrah 6.2.43; Fate unknown

EP462 Spitfire F.Vb (Merlin 46); TOC/RAF 27.6.42; via No.82 MU & No.3 PATP to Russia; Arr Basrah 1.3.43; Fate unknown

EP466 Spitfire F.Vb (Merlin 46); TOC/RAF 28.6.42; via Nos.47 MU & 1 PATP to Russia; Arr Basrah 10.1.43; Fate unknown

EP468 Spitfire F.Vb (Merlin 46); TOC/RAF 28.6.42; via No.76 MU & No.3 PATP, Glasgow to Russia; Arr Basrah 1.3.43; No.821 IAP; Fate unknown

EP469 Spitfire F.Vb (Merlin 46); TOC/RAF 28.6.42; via No.47 MU and Liverpool to Russia; Arr Basrah 10.1.43; Fate unknown

EP486 Spitfire F.Vb (Merlin 46); TOC/RAF 3.7.42; via No.82 MU and Glasgow to Russia; Arr Basrah 24.3.43; No.821 IAP; Fate unknown

EP488 Spitfire F.Vb (Merlin 46); TOC/RAF 16.7.42; via No.82 MU and Glasgow to Russia; Arr Basrah 24.3.43; No.821 IAP; Fate unknown

EP490 Spitfire F.Vb (Merlin 46); TOC/RAF 5.7.42; via No.82 MU and Glasgow to Russia; Arr Basrah 24.3.43; Fate unknown

EP494 Spitfire F.Vb (Merlin 46); TOC/RAF 21.6.42; via No.222 MU and Birkenhead to Russia; Arr Basrah 30.1.43; Fate unknown

EP495 Spitfire F.Vb (Merlin 46); TOC/RAF 21.6.42; via No.222 MU and Swansea to Russia; Arr Basrah 16.2.43; No.821 IAP; Lost in action 9.8.43, SOC

EP497 Spitfire F.Vb (Merlin 46); TOC/RAF 28.6.42; via No.82 MU and Glasgow to Russia; Arr Basrah 24.3.43; No.821 IAP; Fate unknown

Spitfire F.Vbs including EP386 or EP486 at Abadan in March 1943 before flying to join the Soviet Air Force.

Spitfire F.Vbs at Abadan around March-April 1943 awaiting delivery to the Soviet Union. The nearest aircraft is EP495. [Russian Aviation Research Group]

EP498 Spitfire F.Vb (Merlin 46); TOC/RAF 2.7.42; via No.82 MU and Glasgow to Russia; Arr Basrah 24.3.43; Fate unknown

EP501 Spitfire F.Vb (Merlin 46); TOC/RAF 1.7.42; via No.222 MU and Birkenhead to Russia; Arr Basrah 17.3.43; Fate unknown

EP502 Spitfire F.Vb (Merlin 46); TOC/RAF 2.7.42; via No.222 MU and Cardiff to Russia; Arr Basrah 6.2.43; Fate unknown

EP505 Spitfire F.Vb (Merlin 46); TOC/RAF 8.7.42; via No.222 MU and Swansea to Russia; Arr Basrah 16.2.43; No.821 IAP; Fate unknown

EP510 Spitfire F.Vb (Merlin 46); TOC/RAF 22.7.42; via No.76 MU and Birkenhead to Russia; Arr Basrah 30.1.43; Fate unknown

EP512 Spitfire F.Vb (Merlin 46); TOC/RAF 1.8.42; via No.76 MU and Birkenhead to Russia; Arr Basrah 30.1.43; No.821 IAP; Fate unknown

EP513 Spitfire F.Vb (Merlin 46); TOC/RAF 29.7.42; via No.76 MU and Birkenhead to Russia; Arr Basrah 30.1.43; No.821 IAP; Fate unknown

EP514 Spitfire F.Vb (Merlin 46); TOC/RAF 1.8.42; via No.76 MU and Birkenhead to Russia; Arr Basrah 30.1.43; No.821 IAP; Fate unknown

EP540 Spitfire F.Vb (Merlin 46); TOC/RAF 1.7.42; via No.82 MU & No.3 PATP, Avonmouth to Russia; Arr Basrah 1.3.43; No.821 IAP; Fate unknown

EP565 Spitfire F.Vb (Merlin 46); TOC/RAF 5.7.42; via Nos.47 MU & 1 PATP, Hull to Russia; Arr Basrah 10.1.43; Fate unknown

EP566 Spitfire F.Vb (Merlin 46); TOC/RAF 5.7.42; via No.47 MU and Hull to Russia; Arr Basrah 10.1.43; Fate unknown

EP596 Spitfire F.Vb (Merlin 46); TOC/RAF 20.7.42; via No.222 MU and Cardiff to Russia; Arr Basrah 6.2.43; No.821 IAP; Lost in action 9.8.43, SOC

EP598 Spitfire F.Vb (Merlin 46); TOC/RAF 23.7.42; via No.222 MU and Cardiff to Russia; Arr Basrah 6.2.43; No.821 IAP; Fate unknown

EP599 Spitfire F.Vb (Merlin 46); TOC/RAF 24.7.42; via No.82 MU and Glasgow to Russia; Arr Basrah 24.3.43; Fate unknown

EP602 Spitfire F.Vb (Merlin 46); TOC/RAF 29.7.42; via No.76 MU and Birkenhead to Russia; Arr Basrah 30.1.43; Fate unknown

EP623 Spitfire D Vb (Merlin 46); TOC/RAF 26.7.42; via No.82 MU and Glasgow to Russia; Arr Basrah 24.3.43; No.821 IAP; Lost in action 9.8.43, SOC

EP760 Spitfire F.Vb (Merlin 46); TOC/RAF 1.8.42; via No.222 MU and Swansea to Russia; Arr Basrah 16.2.43; No.821 IAP; Fate unknown

EP761 Spitfire F.Vb (Merlin 46); TOC/RAF 1.8.42; via No.222 MU and Birkenhead to Russia; Arr Basrah 17.3.43; No.821 IAP; Fate unknown

EP764 Spitfire F.Vb (Merlin 46); TOC/RAF 1.8.42; via No.76 MU and Manchester to Russia; Arr Basrah 30.1.43; Fate unknown

EP765 Spitfire F.Vb (Merlin 46); TOC/RAF 1.8.42; via No.76 MU and Birkenhead to Russia; Arr Basrah 30.1.43; Fate unknown

EP788 Spitfire F.Vb (Merlin 46); TOC/RAF 31.7.42; ME 11.42; Shaibah 31.3.43; disposed for Russia since 31.3.43; Fate unknown

MJ188 Spitfire LF.IXc (Merlin 66); TOC/RAF 5.11.43; via No.82 MU and Glasgow to Russia; Arr Hapmat 9.1.45; Fate unknown

SOVIET UNION

MJ242 Spitfire LF.IXc (Merlin 66); TOC/RAF 5.11.43; via No.52 MU and Salford to Russia; Arr Hapmat 9.1.45; Fate unknown
MJ249 Spitfire LF.IXc (Merlin 66); TOC/RAF 5.11.43; via No.82 MU and Birkenhead to Russia; Arr Hapmat-South 12.8.44; Fate unknown
MJ335 Spitfire LF.IXc (Merlin 66); TOC/RAF 31.10.43; via No.52 MU and Manchester to Russia; Arr Hapmat 9.1.45; Fate unknown
MJ336 Spitfire LF.IXc (Merlin 66); TOC/RAF 31.10.43; via No.82 MU and Glasgow to Russia; Arr Hapmat 9.1.45; Fate unknown
MJ337 Spitfire LF.IXc (Merlin 66); TOC/RAF 2.11.43; via No.82 MU and Glasgow to Russia; Arr Hapmat 9.1.45; Fate unknown
MJ354 Spitfire LF.IXc (Merlin 66); TOC/RAF 27.6.44; via No.47 MU and Manchester to Hapmat-North for Russia; Arr Hapmat 27.8.44; Fate unknown
MJ357 Spitfire LF.IXc (Merlin 66); TOC/RAF 25.11.43; via No.222 MU to Hapmat-South for Russia; Arr Basrah 23.4.44; NII VVS/RKKA (Research institute) in 9.44; Fate unknown
MJ362 Spitfire LF.IXc (Merlin 66); TOC/RAF 30.11.43; via No.222 MU to Hapmat-South for Russia; Arr Basrah 23.4.44; Fate unknown
MJ400 Spitfire LF.IXc (Merlin 66); TOC/RAF 5.11.43; via No.82 MU and Glasgow to Russia; Arr Hapmat 9.1.45; Fate unknown
MJ459 Spitfire LF.IXc (Merlin 66); TOC/RAF 7.11.43; via No.82 MU to Russia; Arr Hapmat 8.12.44; Fate unknown
MJ508 Spitfire LF.IXc (Merlin 66); TOC/RAF 22.11.43; via No.222 MU to Russia; Arr Hapmat-South 23.4.44; Fate unknown
MJ510 Spitfire LF.IXc (Merlin 66); TOC/RAF 23.11.43; via No.222 MU to Hapmat-South for Russia; Arr Basrah 23.4.44; Fate unknown
MJ531 Spitfire LF.IXc (Merlin 66); TOC/RAF 19.12.43; via No.82 MU to Hapmat-South for Russia; Arr Basrah 23.4.44; Fate unknown
MJ550 Spitfire LF.IXc (Merlin 66); TOC/RAF 18.3.44; via No.52 MU and Birkenhead to Russia; Arr Hapmat 5.7.44; Fate unknown
MJ555 Spitfire LF.IXc (Merlin 66); TOC/RAF 19.12.43; via No.52 MU and Middlesbrough to Russia; Arr Hapmat 8.12.44; Fate unknown
MJ560 Spitfire LF.IXc (Merlin 66); TOC/RAF 19.12.43; via No.52 MU and Birkenhead to Russia; Arr Hapmat 6.7.44; Fate unknown
MJ568 Spitfire LF.IXc (Merlin 66); TOC/RAF 1.5.44; via No.52 MU and Birkenhead to Russia; Arr Hapmat-South 12.8.44; Fate unknown
MJ576 Spitfire LF.IXc (Merlin 66); TOC/RAF 30.11.43; via No.222 MU to Hapmat-South for Russia; Arr Basrah 23.4.44; Fate unknown
MJ606 Spitfire LF.IXc (Merlin 66); TOC/RAF 29.11.43; via No.82 MU to Hapmat-South for Russia; Arr Basrah 23.4.44; Fate unknown
MJ607 Spitfire LF.IXc (Merlin 66); TOC/RAF 13.12.43; via No.82 MU to Hapmat-South for Russia; Arr Basrah 23.4.44; Fate unknown
MJ610 Spitfire LF.IXc (Merlin 66); TOC/RAF 30.11.43; via No.82 MU and Birkenhead to Russia; Arr Hapmat-South 12.8.44; Fate unknown
MJ622 Spitfire LF.IXc (Merlin 66); TOC/RAF 16.12.43; via No.52 MU and Salford to Russia; Arr Hapmat 9.1.45; Fate unknown
MJ635 Spitfire LF.IXc (Merlin 66); TOC/RAF 13.12.43; via No.82 MU to Hapmat-South for Russia; Arr Basrah 23.4.44; Fate unknown
MJ638 Spitfire LF.IXc (Merlin 66); TOC/RAF 19.12.43; via No.222 MU to Hapmat-South for Russia; Arr Basrah 23.4.44; Fate unknown
MJ640 Spitfire LF.IXc (Merlin 66); TOC/RAF 13.12.43; via No.82 MU to Hapmat-South for Russia; Arr Basrah 23.4.44; Fate unknown
MJ667 Spitfire LF.IXc (Merlin 66); TOC/RAF 13.12.43; via No.82 MU to Hapmat-South for Russia; Arr Basrah 23.4.44; Fate unknown
MJ683 Spitfire LF.IXc (Merlin 66); TOC/RAF 13.12.43; via No.222 MU to Hapmat-South for Russia; Arr Basrah 23.4.44; Fate unknown
MJ687 Spitfire LF.IXc (Merlin 66); TOC/RAF 13.12.43; via No.222 MU to Hapmat-South for Russia; Arr Basrah 23.4.44; Fate unknown
MJ690 Spitfire LF.IXc (Merlin 66); TOC/RAF 19.12.43; via No.82 MU to Hapmat-South for Russia; Arr Basrah 5.4.44; Fate unknown
MJ693 Spitfire LF.IXc (Merlin 66); TOC/RAF 20.12.43; via No.222 MU to Hapmat-South for Russia; Arr Basrah 23.4.44; Fate unknown
MJ695 Spitfire LF.IXc (Merlin 66); TOC/RAF 12.12.43; via No.222 MU to Hapmat-South for Russia; Arr Basrah 23.4.44; Fate unknown
MJ697 Spitfire LF.IXc (Merlin 66); TOC/RAF 13.12.43; via No.82 MU to Hapmat-South for Russia; Arr Basrah 5.4.44; Fate unknown
MJ698 Spitfire LF.IXc (Merlin 66); TOC/RAF 13.12.43; via No.82 MU to Hapmat-South for Russia; Arr Basrah 23.4.44; Fate unknown
MJ716 Spitfire LF.IXc (Merlin 66); TOC/RAF 12.12.43; via No.52 MU and Glasgow to Russia; Arr Hapmat-South 9.7.44; Fate unknown
MJ717 Spitfire LF.IXc (Merlin 66); TOC/RAF 13.12.43; via No.222 MU to Hapmat-South for Russia; Arr Basrah 23.4.44; Fate unknown
MJ721 Spitfire LF.IXc (Merlin 66); TOC/RAF 13.12.43; via No.222 MU to Hapmat-South for Russia; Arr Basrah 23.4.44; Fate unknown
MJ740 Spitfire LF.IXc (Merlin 66); TOC/RAF 19.12.43; via No.222 MU to Hapmat-South for Russia; Arr Basrah 28.4.44; Fate unknown
MJ747 Spitfire LF.IXc (Merlin 66); TOC/RAF 13.12.43; via No.82 MU to Hapmat-South for Russia; Arr Basrah 23.4.44; Fate unknown
MJ749 Spitfire LF.IXc (Merlin 66); TOC/RAF 19.12.43; via No.82 MU to Hapmat-South for Russia; Arr Basrah 28.4.44; Fate unknown
MJ750 Spitfire LF.IXc (Merlin 66); TOC/RAF 13.12.43; via No.222 MU to Hapmat-South for Russia; Arr Basrah 23.4.44; Fate unknown
MJ753 Spitfire LF.IXc (Merlin 66); TOC/RAF 20.12.43; via No.222 MU to Hapmat-South for Russia; Arr Basrah 23.4.44; Fate unknown
MJ756 Spitfire LF.IXc (Merlin 66); TOC/RAF 19.12.43; via No.222 MU to Hapmat-South for Russia; Arr Basrah 23.4.44; Fate unknown
MJ771 Spitfire LF.IXc (Merlin 66); TOC/RAF 20.12.43; via No.82 MU to Russia; Arr Hapmat-South 28.4.44; Fate unknown
MJ773 Spitfire LF.IXc (Merlin 66); TOC/RAF 16.12.43; via No.82 MU to Hapmat-South for Russia; Arr Basrah 23.4.44; Fate unknown
MJ776 Spitfire LF.IXc (Merlin 66); TOC/RAF 20.12.43; via No.82 MU to Hapmat-South for Russia; Arr Basrah 23.4.44; Fate unknown
MJ777 Spitfire LF.IXc (Merlin 66); TOC/RAF 19.12.43; via No.82 MU to Hapmat-South for Russia; Arr Basrah 5.4.44; Fate unknown
MJ781 Spitfire LF.IXc (Merlin 66); TOC/RAF 13.12.43; via No.82 MU to Hapmat-South for Russia; Arr Basrah 23.4.44; Fate unknown
MJ782 Spitfire LF.IXc (Merlin 66); TOC/RAF 20.12.43; via No.222 MU to Hapmat-South for Russia; Arr Basrah 23.4.44; Fate unknown
MJ791 Spitfire LF.IXc (Merlin 66); TOC/RAF 19.12.43; via No.82 MU to Hapmat-South for Russia; Arr Basrah 5.4.44; Fate unknown
MJ800 Spitfire LF.IXc (Merlin 66); TOC/RAF 19.12.43; via No.82 MU to Hapmat-South for Russia; Arr Basrah 23.4.44; Fate unknown

MJ819 Spitfire LF.IXc (Merlin 66); TOC/RAF 20.12.43; via No.82 MU to Hapmat-South for Russia; Arr Basrah 5.4.44; Fate unknown
MJ821 Spitfire LF.IXc (Merlin 66); TOC/RAF 20.12.43; via No.222 MU to Hapmat-South for Russia; Arr Basrah 23.4.44; Fate unknown
MJ842 Spitfire LF.IXc (Merlin 66); TOC/RAF 28.11.43; via No.82 MU and Birkenhead to Russia; Arr Hapmat-South 12.8.44; Fate unknown
MJ846 Spitfire LF.IXc (Merlin 66); TOC/RAF 1.12.43; via No.82 MU and Birkenhead to Russia; Arr Hapmat-South 12.8.44; Fate unknown
MJ850 Spitfire LF.IXc (Merlin 66); TOC/RAF 18.12.43; via No.52 MU and Salford to Russia; Arr Hapmat 9.1.45; Fate unknown
MJ856 Spitfire LF.IXc (Merlin 66); TOC/RAF 19.12.43; via No.222 MU to Hapmat-South for Russia; Arr Basrah 23.4.44; Fate unknown
MJ858 Spitfire LF.IXc (Merlin 66); TOC/RAF 19.12.43; via No.222 MU to Hapmat-South for Russia; Arr Basrah 23.4.44; NII VVS/RKKA (Research institute); Test flying 9.44; Fate unknown
MJ902 Spitfire LF.IXc (Merlin 66); TOC/RAF 4.1.44; via No.82 MU to Hapmat-South for Russia; Arr Basrah 5.4.44; Fate unknown
MJ936 Spitfire LF.IXc (Merlin 66); TOC/RAF 1.5.44; via No.52 MU and Glasgow to Russia; Arr Hapmat-South 9.7.44; Fate unknown
MJ937 Spitfire LF.IXc (Merlin 66); TOC/RAF 1.5.44; via No.52 MU and Birkenhead to Russia; Arr Hapmat-South 12.8.44; Fate unknown
MJ946 Spitfire LF.IXc (Merlin 66); TOC/RAF 29.4.44; via No.52 MU and Birkenhead to Russia; Arr Hapmat-South 12.8.44; Fate unknown
MJ949 Spitfire LF.IXc (Merlin 66); TOC/RAF 21.1.44; via No.52 MU to Hapmat-South for Russia; Arr Basrah 29.5.44; Fate unknown
MJ961 Spitfire LF.IXc (Merlin 66); TOC/RAF 21.1.44; via No.52 MU to Russia; Arr Hapmat-South 15.5.44; Fate unknown
MK146 Spitfire LF.IXc (Merlin 66); TOC/RAF 2.2.44; via No.52 MU to Russia; Arr Hapmat-South 15.5.44; Fate unknown
MK209 Spitfire LF.IXc (Merlin 66); TOC/RAF 23.1.44; via No.52 MU to Hapmat-South for Russia; Arr Basrah 29.5.44; Fate unknown
MK262 Spitfire LF.IXc (Merlin 66); TOC/RAF 10.2.44; via No.52 MU to Russia; Arr Hapmat-South 15.5.44; Fate unknown
MK268 Spitfire LF.IXc (Merlin 66); TOC/RAF 20.2.44; via No.52 MU to Russia; Arr Hapmat-South 15.5.44; Fate unknown
MK282 Spitfire LF.IXc (Merlin 66); TOC/RAF 23.1.44; via No.52 MU to Russia; Arr Hapmat-South 15.5.44; Fate unknown
MK307 Spitfire LF.IXc (Merlin 66); TOC/RAF 10.2.44; via No.52 MU to Russia; Arr Hapmat-South 15.5.44; Fate unknown
MK310 Spitfire LF.IXc (Merlin 66); TOC/RAF 21.2.44; via No.52 MU to Russia; Arr Hapmat-South 15.5.44; Fate unknown
MK345 Spitfire LF.IXc (Merlin 66); TOC/RAF 10.2.44; via No.52 MU to Russia; Arr Hapmat-South 15.5.44; Fate unknown
MK349 Spitfire LF.IXc (Merlin 66); TOC/RAF 8.2.44; via No.52 MU to Russia; Arr Hapmat-South 15.5.44; Fate unknown
MK351 Spitfire LF.IXc (Merlin 66); TOC/RAF 5.2.44; via No.52 MU to Russia; Arr Hapmat-South 15.5.44; Fate unknown
MK352 Spitfire LF.IXc (Merlin 66); TOC/RAF 20.2.44; via No.52 MU to Russia; Arr Hapmat-South 15.5.44; Fate unknown
MK368 Spitfire LF.IXc (Merlin 66); TOC/RAF 8.2.44; via No.52 MU to Russia; Arr Hapmat-South 15.5.44; Fate unknown
MK371 Spitfire LF.IXc (Merlin 66); TOC/RAF 9.2.44; via No.52 MU to Hapmat-South for Russia; Arr Basrah 29.5.44; Fate unknown
MK377 Spitfire LF.IXc (Merlin 66); TOC/RAF 21.2.44; via No.52 MU to Russia; Arr Hapmat-South 15.5.44; Fate unknown
MK395 Spitfire LF.IXc (Merlin 66); TOC/RAF 20.2.44; via No.52 MU to Russia; Arr Hapmat-South 15.5.44; Fate unknown
MK401 Spitfire LF.IXc (Merlin 66); TOC/RAF 15.2.44; via No.52 MU to Hapmat-South for Russia; Arr Basrah 29.5.44; Fate unknown
MK409 Spitfire LF.IXc (Merlin 66); TOC/RAF 15.2.44; via No.52 MU to Russia; Arr Hapmat-South 15.5.44; Fate unknown
MK427 Spitfire LF.IXc (Merlin 66); TOC/RAF 25.2.44; via No.52 MU to Russia; Arr Hapmat-South 15.5.44; Fate unknown
MK428 Spitfire LF.IXc (Merlin 66); TOC/RAF 25.2.44; via No.52 MU to Hapmat-South for Russia; Arr Basrah 29.5.44; Fate unknown
MK442 Spitfire LF.IXc (Merlin 66); TOC/RAF 24.2.44; via No.52 MU and Birkenhead to Russia; Arr Hapmat 5.7.44; Fate unknown
MK446 Spitfire LF.IXc (Merlin 66); TOC/RAF 28.2.44; via No.52 MU to Russia; Arr Hapmat-South 15.5.44; Fate unknown
MK450 Spitfire LF.IXc (Merlin 66); TOC/RAF 20.2.44; via No.52 MU to Russia; Arr Hapmat-South 15.5.44; Fate unknown
MK451 Spitfire LF.IXc (Merlin 66); TOC/RAF 21.2.44; via No.52 MU to Russia; Arr Hapmat-South 15.5.44; Fate unknown
MK452 Spitfire LF.IXc (Merlin 66); TOC/RAF 21.2.44; via No.52 MU to Russia; Arr Hapmat-South 15.5.44; Fate unknown
MK455 Spitfire LF.IXc (Merlin 66); TOC/RAF 21.2.44; via No.52 MU to Hapmat-South for Russia; Arr Basrah 29.5.44; Fate unknown
MK457 Spitfire LF.IXc (Merlin 66); TOC/RAF 1.3.44; via No.52 MU to Hapmat-South for Russia; Arr Basrah 29.5.44; Fate unknown
MK461 Spitfire LF.IXc (Merlin 66); TOC/RAF 21.2.44; via No.52 MU to Russia; Arr Hapmat-South 15.5.44; Fate unknown
MK470 Spitfire LF.IXc (Merlin 66); TOC/RAF 20.2.44; via No.52 MU to Russia; Arr Hapmat-South 15.5.44; Fate unknown
MK477 Spitfire LF.IXc (Merlin 66); TOC/RAF 21.2.44; via No.52 MU to Russia; Arr Hapmat-South 15.5.44; Fate unknown
MK499 Spitfire LF.IXc (Merlin 66); TOC/RAF 24.2.44; via No.52 MU to Hapmat-South for Russia; Arr Basrah 29.5.44; Fate unknown
MK502 Spitfire LF.IXc (Merlin 66); TOC/RAF 25.2.44; via No.52 MU to Russia; Arr Hapmat-South 15.5.44; Fate unknown
MK505 Spitfire LF.IXc (Merlin 66); TOC/RAF 21.2.44; via No.52 MU to Hapmat-South for Russia; Arr Basrah 29.5.44; Fate unknown
MK506 Spitfire LF.IXc (Merlin 66); TOC/RAF 1.3.44; via No.52 MU and Birkenhead to Russia; Arr Hapmat 6.7.44; Fate unknown
MK509 Spitfire LF.IXc (Merlin 66); TOC/RAF 25.2.44; via No.52 MU to Russia; Arr Hapmat-South 15.5.44; Fate unknown
MK518 Spitfire LF.IXc (Merlin 66); TOC/RAF 25.2.44; via No.222 MU to Hapmat-South for Russia; Arr Basrah 29.5.44; Fate unknown
MK522 Spitfire LF.IXc (Merlin 66); TOC/RAF 24.2.44; via No.52 MU to Russia; Arr Hapmat-South 15.5.44; Fate unknown
MK523 Spitfire LF.IXc (Merlin 66); TOC/RAF 8.3.44; via No.52 MU to Hapmat-South for Russia; Arr Basrah 29.5.44; Fate unknown
MK525 Spitfire LF.IXc (Merlin 66); TOC/RAF 22.2.44; via No.52 MU to Hapmat-South for Russia; Arr Basrah 29.5.44; Fate unknown
MK526 Spitfire LF.IXc (Merlin 66); TOC/RAF 24.2.44; via No.52 MU to Hapmat-South for Russia; Arr Basrah 29.5.44; Fate unknown
MK527 Spitfire LF.IXc (Merlin 66); TOC/RAF 2.3.44; via No.52 MU and Birkenhead to Russia; Arr Hapmat 5.7.44; Fate unknown
MK533 Spitfire LF.IXc (Merlin 66); TOC/RAF 28.2.44; via No.52 MU to Russia; Arr Hapmat-South 15.5.44; Fate unknown
MK548 Spitfire LF.IXc (Merlin 66); TOC/RAF 20.2.44; via No.52 MU to Russia; Arr Hapmat-South 15.5.44; Fate unknown
MK550 Spitfire LF.IXc (Merlin 66); TOC/RAF 20.2.44; via No.52 MU to Russia; Arr Hapmat-South 15.5.44; Fate unknown
MK554 Spitfire LF.IXc (Merlin 66); TOC/RAF 1.3.44; via No.52 MU and Birkenhead to Russia; Arr Hapmat 6.7.44; Fate unknown
MK556 Spitfire LF.IXc (Merlin 66); TOC/RAF 21.2.44; via No.52 MU to Hapmat-South for Russia; Arr Basrah 29.5.44; Fate unknown
MK584 Spitfire LF.IXc (Merlin 66); TOC/RAF 21.3.44; via No.52 MU to Hapmat-South for Russia; Arr Basrah 29.5.44; Fate unknown

SOVIET UNION

MK613 Spitfire LF.IXc (Merlin 66); TOC/RAF 8.2.44; via No.52 MU to Russia; Arr Hapmat-South 15.5.44; Fate unknown

MK615 Spitfire LF.IXc (Merlin 66); TOC/RAF 8.2.44; via No.52 MU to Russia; Arr Hapmat-South 15.5.44; Fate unknown

MK617 Spitfire LF.IXc (Merlin 66); TOC/RAF 24.5.44; via No.52 MU and Birkenhead to Hapmat-South for Russia; Arr Basrah 12.8.44; Fate unknown
NOTE: This was the second aircraft to bear the serial MK617, the first having crashed on delivery and been written off

MK626 Spitfire LF.IXc (Merlin 66); TOC/RAF 26.2.44; via No.52 MU to Russia; Arr Hapmat-South 15.5.44; Fate unknown

MK641 Spitfire LF.IXc (Merlin 66); TOC/RAF 11.3.44; via No.52 MU and Glasgow to Russia; Arr Hapmat-South 9.7.44; Fate unknown

MK642 Spitfire LF.IXc (Merlin 66); TOC/RAF 11.3.44; via No.52 MU to Hapmat-South for Russia; Arr Basrah 29.5.44; Fate unknown

MK643 Spitfire LF.IXc (Merlin 66); TOC/RAF 11.3.44; via No.52 MU and Birkenhead to Russia; Arr Hapmat 5.7.44; Fate unknown

MK645 Spitfire LF.IXc (Merlin 66); TOC/RAF 17.3.44; via No.52 MU and Birkenhead to Russia; Arr Hapmat 6.7.44; Fate unknown

MK646 Spitfire LF.IXc (Merlin 66); TOC/RAF 18.3.44; via No.52 MU and Birkenhead to Russia; Arr Hapmat 5.7.44; Fate unknown

MK660 Spitfire LF.IXc (Merlin 66); TOC/RAF 12.4.44; via No.52 MU and Birkenhead to Russia; Arr Hapmat 6.7.44; Fate unknown

MK665 Spitfire LF.IXc (Merlin 66); TOC/RAF 25.2.44; via No.52 MU to Russia; Arr Hapmat-South 15.5.44; Fate unknown

MK685 Spitfire LF.IXc (Merlin 66); TOC/RAF 4.4.44; via No.52 MU and Birkenhead to Russia; Arr Hapmat 6.7.44; Fate unknown

MK699 Spitfire LF.IXc (Merlin 66); TOC/RAF 15.4.44; via No.52 MU and Birkenhead to Russia; Arr Hapmat 6.7.44; Fate unknown

MK718 Spitfire LF.IXc (Merlin 66); TOC/RAF 24.2.44; via No.52 MU and Birkenhead to Russia; Arr Hapmat 5.7.44; Fate unknown

MK735 Spitfire LF.IXc (Merlin 66); TOC/RAF 15.3.44; via No.52 MU to Hapmat-South for Russia; Arr Basrah 29.5.44; Fate unknown

MK740 Spitfire LF.IXc (Merlin 66); TOC/RAF 7.3.44; via No.52 MU and Birkenhead to Russia; Arr Hapmat 5.7.44; Fate unknown

MK741 Spitfire LF.IXc (Merlin 66); TOC/RAF 28.2.44; via No.52 MU to Russia; Arr Hapmat-South 15.5.44; Fate unknown

MK748 Spitfire LF.IXc (Merlin 66); TOC/RAF 28.2.44; via No.52 MU to Russia; Arr Hapmat-South 15.5.44; Fate unknown

MK779 Spitfire LF.IXc (Merlin 66); TOC/RAF 15.3.44; via No.52 MU and Birkenhead to Russia; Arr Hapmat 5.7.44; Fate unknown

MK781 Spitfire LF.IXc (Merlin 66); TOC/RAF 1.3.44; via No.52 MU to Hapmat-South for Russia; Arr Basrah 29.5.44; Fate unknown

MK785 Spitfire LF.IXc (Merlin 66); TOC/RAF 4.3.44; via No.52 MU and Birkenhead to Russia; Arr Hapmat 5.7.44; Fate unknown

MK789 Spitfire LF.IXc (Merlin 66); TOC/RAF 8.3.44; via No.52 MU to Russia; Arr Hapmat-South 29.5.44; Fate unknown

MK792 Spitfire LF.IXc (Merlin 66); TOC/RAF 8.3.44; via No.52 MU to Russia; Arr Hapmat-South 29.5.44; Fate unknown

MK802 Spitfire LF.IXc (Merlin 66); TOC/RAF 6.3.44; via No.52 MU to Hapmat-South for Russia; Arr Basrah 29.5.44; Fate unknown

MK828 Spitfire LF.IXc (Merlin 66); TOC/RAF 17.3.44; via No.52 MU and Birkenhead to Russia; Arr Hapmat 6.7.44; Fate unknown

MK847 Spitfire LF.IXc (Merlin 66); TOC/RAF 21.3.44; via No.52 MU and Birkenhead to Russia; Arr Hapmat 5.7.44; Fate unknown

MK848 Spitfire LF.IXc (Merlin 66); TOC/RAF 12.3.44; via No.52 MU and Birkenhead to Russia; Arr Hapmat 5.7.44; Fate unknown

MK851 Spitfire LF.IXc (Merlin 66); TOC/RAF 15.3.44; via No.52 MU and Birkenhead to Russia; Arr Hapmat 5.7.44; Fate unknown

MK856 Spitfire LF.IXc (Merlin 66); TOC/RAF 12.3.44; via No.52 MU and Birkenhead to Russia; Arr Hapmat 5.7.44; Fate unknown

MK857 Spitfire LF.IXc (Merlin 66); TOC/RAF 17.3.44; via No.52 MU and Birkenhead to Russia; Arr Hapmat 5.7.44; Fate unknown

MK858 Spitfire LF.IXc (Merlin 66); TOC/RAF 15.3.44; via No.52 MU and Birkenhead to Russia; Arr Hapmat 6.7.44; Fate unknown

MK860 Spitfire LF.IXc (Merlin 66); TOC/RAF 20.3.44; via No.52 MU and Birkenhead to Russia; Arr Hapmat 6.7.44; Fate unknown

MK861 Spitfire LF.IXc (Merlin 66); TOC/RAF 12.3.44; via No.52 MU and Birkenhead to Russia; Arr Hapmat 5.7.44; Fate unknown

MK865 Spitfire LF.IXc (Merlin 66); TOC/RAF 17.3.44; via No.52 MU and Birkenhead to Russia; Arr Hapmat 5.7.44; Fate unknown

MK884 Spitfire LF.IXc (Merlin 66); TOC/RAF 15.3.44; via No.52 MU and Birkenhead to Russia; Arr Hapmat 5.7.44; Fate unknown

MK887 Spitfire LF.IXc (Merlin 66); TOC/RAF 15.3.44; via No.52 MU and Birkenhead to Russia; Arr Hapmat 5.7.44; Fate unknown

MK891 Spitfire LF.IXc (Merlin 66); TOC/RAF 30.4.44; via No.52 MU and Birkenhead to Hapmat-South for Russia; Arr Basrah 12.8.44; Fate unknown

MK894 Spitfire LF.IXc (Merlin 66); TOC/RAF 17.3.44; via No.52 MU and Birkenhead to Russia; Arr Hapmat 5.7.44; Fate unknown

MK900 Spitfire LF.IXc (Merlin 66); TOC/RAF 18.3.44; via No.52 MU and Birkenhead to Russia; Arr Hapmat 5.7.44; Fate unknown

MK903 Spitfire LF.IXc (Merlin 66); TOC/RAF 17.3.44; via No.52 MU and Birkenhead to Russia; Arr Hapmat 5.7.44; Fate unknown

MK908 Spitfire LF.IXc (Merlin 66); TOC/RAF 17.3.44; via No.52 MU and Birkenhead to Russia; Arr Hapmat 5.7.44; Fate unknown

MK911 Spitfire LF.IXc (Merlin 66); TOC/RAF 18.3.44; via No.52 MU and Birkenhead to Russia; Arr Hapmat 5.7.44; Fate unknown

MK925 Spitfire LF.IXc (Merlin 66); TOC/RAF 17.3.44; via No.52 MU and Birkenhead to Russia; Arr Hapmat 5.7.44; Fate unknown

MK945 Spitfire LF.IXc (Merlin 66); TOC/RAF 12.4.44; via No.52 MU and Birkenhead to Russia; Arr Hapmat 6.7.44; Fate unknown

MK949 Spitfire LF.IXc (Merlin 66); TOC/RAF 12.4.44; via No.52 MU and Birkenhead to Russia; Arr Hapmat 6.7.44; Fate unknown

MK952 Spitfire LF.IXc (Merlin 66); TOC/RAF 19.3.44; via No.52 MU and Birkenhead to Russia; Arr Hapmat 5.7.44; Fate unknown

MK954 Spitfire LF.IXc (Merlin 66); TOC/RAF 15.4.44; via No.52 MU and Birkenhead to Russia; Arr Hapmat 6.7.44; Fate unknown

MK956 Spitfire LF.IXc (Merlin 66); TOC/RAF 15.4.44; via No.52 MU and Birkenhead to Hapmat-South for Russia; Arr Basrah 12.8.44; Fate unknown

MK957 Spitfire LF.IXc (Merlin 66); TOC/RAF 18.4.44; via No.52 MU and Birkenhead to Russia; Arr Hapmat 6.7.44; Fate unknown

MK960 Spitfire LF.IXc (Merlin 66); TOC/RAF 18.4.44; via No.52 MU and Birkenhead to Russia; Arr Hapmat 6.7.44; Fate unknown

MK961 Spitfire LF.IXc (Merlin 66); TOC/RAF 18.4.44; via No.52 MU and Glasgow to Russia; Arr Hapmat-South 9.7.44; Fate unknown

MK985 Spitfire LF.IXc (Merlin 66); TOC/RAF 20.3.44; via No.52 MU and Birkenhead to Russia; Arr Hapmat 6.7.44; Fate unknown

ML114 Spitfire LF.IXc (Merlin 66); TOC/RAF 12.4.44; via No.52 MU and Birkenhead to Russia; Arr Hapmat 6.7.44; Fate unknown

ML121 Spitfire LF.IXc (Merlin 66); TOC/RAF 19.3.44; via No.52 MU and Birkenhead to Russia; Arr Hapmat 5.7.44; Fate unknown

ML127 Spitfire LF.IXc (Merlin 66); TOC/RAF 19.3.44; via No.52 MU and Birkenhead to Russia; Arr Hapmat 5.7.44; Fate unknown

ML155 Spitfire LF.IXc (Merlin 66); TOC/RAF 5.4.44; via No.52 MU and Birkenhead to Russia; Arr Hapmat 6.7.44; Fate unknown

ML188 Spitfire LF.IXc (Merlin 66); TOC/RAF 4.4.44; via No.52 MU and Birkenhead to Russia; Arr Hapmat 6.7.44; Fate unknown

ML190 Spitfire LF.IXc (Merlin 66); TOC/RAF 15.4.44; via No.52 MU and Birkenhead to Russia; Arr Hapmat 6.7.44; Fate unknown

ML203 Spitfire LF.IXc (Merlin 66); TOC/RAF 4.4.44; via No.52 MU and Birkenhead to Russia; Arr Hapmat 6.7.44; Fate unknown

ML229 Spitfire **HF**.IXe (Merlin 70); TOC/RAF 13.4.44; via No.52 MU and Birkenhead to Russia; Arr Hapmat 6.7.44; To NII VVS/RKKA (Research Institute); Trials in 5.45-8.45; Fate unknown

ML237 Spitfire LF.IXc (Merlin 66); TOC/RAF 13.4.44; via No.52 MU and Birkenhead to Russia; Arr Hapmat 6.7.44; Fate unknown

ML256 Spitfire LF.IXc (Merlin 66); TOC/RAF 26.4.44; via No.52 MU and Birkenhead to Russia; Arr Hapmat 6.7.44; Fate unknown

ML291 Spitfire LF.IXc (Merlin 66); TOC/RAF 15.4.44; via No.52 MU and Birkenhead to Russia; Arr Hapmat 6.7.44; Fate unknown

ML297 Spitfire LF.IXc (Merlin 66); TOC/RAF 21.4.44; via No.52 MU and Birkenhead to Russia; Arr Hapmat 6.7.44; Fate unknown

ML298 Spitfire LF.IXc (Merlin 66); TOC/RAF 20.4.44; via No.52 MU and Birkenhead to Russia; Arr Hapmat 6.7.44; Fate unknown

ML299 Spitfire LF.IXc (Merlin 66); TOC/RAF 26.4.44; via No.52 MU and Glasgow to Russia; Arr Hapmat-South 9.7.44; Fate unknown

ML302 Spitfire LF.IXc (Merlin 66); TOC/RAF 29.4.44; via No.52 MU and Glasgow to Russia; Arr Hapmat-South 9.7.44; Fate unknown

ML340 Spitfire LF.IXc (Merlin 66); TOC/RAF 18.4.44; via No.52 MU and Birkenhead to Russia; Arr Hapmat 6.7.44; Fate unknown

ML344 Spitfire LF.IXc (Merlin 66); TOC/RAF 20.4.44; via No.52 MU and Birkenhead to Russia; Arr Hapmat 6.7.44; Fate unknown

ML352 Spitfire LF.IXc (Merlin 66); TOC/RAF 20.4.44; via No.52 MU and Birkenhead to Russia; Arr Hapmat 6.7.44; Fate unknown

ML359 Spitfire LF.IXc (Merlin 66); TOC/RAF 29.4.44; via No.52 MU and Birkenhead to Hapmat-South for Russia; Arr Basrah 12.8.44; Fate unknown

ML369 Spitfire LF.IXc (Merlin 66); TOC/RAF 26.4.44; No.222 MU and Birkenhead to Hapmat-South for Russia; Arr Basrah 12.8.44; Fate unknown

ML375 Spitfire LF.IXc (Merlin 66); TOC/RAF 6.5.44; via No.82 MU and Birkenhead to Hapmat-South for Russia; Arr Basrah 12.8.44; Fate unknown

ML402 Spitfire LF.IXc (Merlin 66); TOC/RAF 29.4.44; via No.52 MU and Glasgow to Russia; Arr Hapmat-South 9.7.44; Fate unknown

ML408 Spitfire LF.IXc (Merlin 66); TOC/RAF 26.4.44; via No.52 MU and Birkenhead to Russia; Arr Hapmat-South 9.7.44; Fate unknown

ML426 Spitfire LF.IXc (Merlin 66); TOC/RAF 26.4.44; via No.52 MU and Glasgow to Russia; Arr Hapmat-South 9.7.44; Fate unknown

NH149 Spitfire LF.IXe (Merlin 66); TOC/RAF 30.4.44; via No.52 MU and Glasgow to Russia; Arr Hapmat-South 9.7.44; Fate unknown

NH156 Spitfire LF.IXe (Merlin 66); TOC/RAF 29.4.44; via No.52 MU and Glasgow to Russia; Arr Hapmat-South 9.7.44; Fate unknown

NH177 Spitfire LF.IXe (Merlin 66); TOC/RAF 1.5.44; via No.52 MU and Birkenhead to Hapmat-South for Russia; Arr Basrah 12.8.44; Fate unknown

NH180 Spitfire LF.IXe (Merlin 66); TOC/RAF 30.4.44; via No.52 MU and Glasgow to Russia; Arr Hapmat-South 9.7.44; Fate unknown

NH185 Spitfire LF.IXe (Merlin 66); TOC/RAF 1.5.44; via No.52 MU and Birkenhead to Hapmat-South for Russia; Arr Basrah 12.8.44; Fate unknown

NH187 Spitfire LF.IXe (Merlin 66); TOC/RAF 2.5.44; via No.52 MU and Glasgow to Russia; Arr Hapmat-South 9.7.44; Fate unknown

NH192 Spitfire LF.IXe (Merlin 66); TOC/RAF 2.5.44; via No.52 MU and Glasgow to Russia; Arr Hapmat-South 9.7.44; Fate unknown

NH202 Spitfire LF.IXe (Merlin 66); TOC/RAF 8.5.44; via No.82 MU and Birkenhead to Hapmat-South for Russia; Arr Basrah 12.8.44; Fate unknown

NH216 Spitfire LF.IXe (Merlin 66); TOC/RAF 6.5.44; via No.52 MU and Birkenhead to Hapmat-South for Russia; Arr Basrah 12.8.44; Fate unknown

NH234 Spitfire LF.IXe (Merlin 66); TOC/RAF 8.5.44; via No.222 MU and Birkenhead to Hapmat-South for Russia; Arr Basrah 12.8.44; Fate unknown

NH237 Spitfire LF.IXe (Merlin 66); TOC/RAF 6.5.44; via No.52 MU and Birkenhead to Hapmat-South for Russia; Arr Basrah 12.8.44; Fate unknown

NH264 Spitfire LF.IXe (Merlin 66); TOC/RAF 11.5.44; via No.222 MU and Birkenhead to Hapmat-South for Russia; Arr Basrah 12.8.44; Fate unknown

NH291 Spitfire LF.IXe (Merlin 66); TOC/RAF 16.5.44; via No.215 MU and Birkenhead to Hapmat-South for Russia; Arr Basrah 12.8.44; Fate unknown

NH292 Spitfire LF.IXe (Merlin 66); TOC/RAF 16.5.44; via No.215 MU and Birkenhead to Hapmat-South for Russia; Arr Basrah 12.8.44; Fate unknown

NH301 Spitfire LF.IXe (Merlin 66); TOC/RAF 11.5.44; via No.222 MU and Liverpool to Russia; Arr Hapmat-South 9.7.44; Fate unknown

NH303 Spitfire LF.IXe (Merlin 66); TOC/RAF 18.5.44; via No.52 MU and Birkenhead to Hapmat-South for Russia; Arr Basrah 12.8.44; Fate unknown

NH308 Spitfire LF.IXe (Merlin 66); TOC/RAF 18.5.44; via No.52 MU and Birkenhead to Hapmat-South for Russia; Arr Basrah 12.8.44; Fate unknown

NH324 Spitfire LF.IXe (Merlin 66); TOC/RAF 17.5.44; via No.215 MU and Birkenhead to Hapmat-South for Russia; Arr Basrah 12.8.44; Fate unknown

NH393 Spitfire LF.IXe (Merlin 66); TOC/RAF 20.4.44; via No.52 MU and Birkenhead to Russia; Arr Hapmat 6.7.44; Fate unknown

NH394 Spitfire LF.IXe (Merlin 66); TOC/RAF 21.4.44; via No.52 MU and Birkenhead to Russia; Arr Hapmat 6.7.44; Fate unknown

NH395 Spitfire LF.IXe (Merlin 66); TOC/RAF 20.4.44; via No.52 MU and Birkenhead to Russia; Arr Hapmat 6.7.44; Fate unknown

NH396 Spitfire LF.IXe (Merlin 66); TOC/RAF 21.4.44; via No.52 MU and Birkenhead to Russia; Arr Hapmat 6.7.44; Fate unknown

NH399 Spitfire LF.IXe (Merlin 66); TOC/RAF 20.4.44; via No.52 MU and Birkenhead to Russia; Arr Hapmat 6.7.44; Fate unknown

NH416 Spitfire LF.IXe (Merlin 66); TOC/RAF 1.5.44; via No.52 MU and Glasgow to Russia; Arr Hapmat-South 9.7.44; Fate unknown

Soviet Union

NH558 Spitfire LF.IXe (Merlin 66); TOC/RAF 8.6.44; via Nos.52 MU & 1 PATP to Russia; Arr Hapmat 27.8.44; Fate unknown

PL144 Spitfire LF.IXe (Merlin 66); TOC/RAF 27.6.44; via No.52 MU and South Shields to Hapmat-North for Russia; Arr Hapmat 27.8.44; Fate unknown

PL147 Spitfire LF.IXe (Merlin 66); TOC/RAF 27.6.44; via No.52 MU and South Shields to Hapmat-North for Russia; Arr Hapmat 27.8.44; Fate unknown

PL148 Spitfire LF.IXe (Merlin 66); TOC/RAF 27.6.44; via No.47 MU and Manchester to Hapmat-North for Russia; Arr Hapmat 27.8.44; Fate unknown

PL150 Spitfire LF.IXe (Merlin 66); TOC/RAF 27.6.44; via No.52 MU and Salford to Russia; Arr Hapmat 27.8.44; Fate unknown

PL195 Spitfire LF.IXe (Merlin 66); TOC/RAF 10.6.44; via No.52 MU and Salford to Hapmat-North for Russia; Arr Hapmat 27.8.44; Fate unknown

PL197 Spitfire LF.IXe (Merlin 66); TOC/RAF 13.6.44; via No.52 MU and Salford to Hapmat-North for Russia; Arr Hapmat 27.8.44; Fate unknown

PL199 Spitfire LF.IXe (Merlin 66); TOC/RAF 16.6.44; via No.52 MU and Salford to Hapmat-North for Russia; Arr Hapmat 27.8.44; Fate unknown

PL200 Spitfire LF.IXe (Merlin 66); TOC/RAF 14.6.44; via No.82 MU and South Shields to Hapmat-North for Russia; Arr Hapmat 27.8.44; Fate unknown

PL205 Spitfire LF.IXe (Merlin 66); TOC/RAF 13.6.44; via No.52 MU and Salford to Hapmat-North for Russia; Arr Hapmat 27.8.44; Fate unknown

PL208 Spitfire LF.IXe (Merlin 66); TOC/RAF 13.6.44; via No.52 MU and Salford to Hapmat-North for Russia; Arr Hapmat 27.8.44; Fate unknown

PL270 Spitfire LF.IXe (Merlin 66); TOC/RAF 18.5.44; via No.52 MU and Birkenhead to Hapmat-South for Russia; Arr Basrah 12.8.44; Fate unknown

PL285 Spitfire LF.IXe (Merlin 66); TOC/RAF 24.5.44; via No.52 MU and Birkenhead to Hapmat-South for Russia; Arr Basrah 12.8.44; Fate unknown

PL329 Spitfire LF.IXe (Merlin 66); TOC/RAF 21.6.44; via No.82 MU and Middlesbrough to Russia; Arr Hapmat 27.8.44; Fate unknown

PL331 Spitfire LF.IXe (Merlin 66); TOC/RAF 27.6.44; via No.52 MU and South Shields to Hapmat-North for Russia; Arr Hapmat 27.8.44; Fate unknown

PL335 Spitfire LF.IXe (Merlin 66); TOC/RAF 24.6.44; via No.52 MU to Russia; Arr Hapmat 27.8.44; Fate unknown

PL336 Spitfire LF.IXe (Merlin 66); TOC/RAF 30.6.44; via No.52 MU to Russia; Arr Hapmat 27.8.44; Fate unknown

PL339 Spitfire LF.IXe (Merlin 66); TOC/RAF 24.7.44; via No.82 MU and Salford to Russia; Arr Hapmat 23.9.44; Fate unknown

PL341 Spitfire LF.IXe (Merlin 66); TOC/RAF 15.7.44; via No.82 MU and Middlesbrough to Russia; Arr Hapmat 27.8.44; Fate unknown

PL343 Spitfire LF.IXe (Merlin 66); TOC/RAF 24.7.44; via No.82 MU and Middlesbrough to Russia; Arr Hapmat 27.8.44; Fate unknown

PL346 Spitfire LF.IXe (Merlin 66); TOC/RAF 24.7.44; via No.82 MU and Middlesbrough to Russia; Arr Hapmat 27.8.44; Fate unknown

PL350 Spitfire LF.IXe (Merlin 66); TOC/RAF 24.7.44; via No.82 MU and Middlesbrough to Russia; Arr Hapmat 27.8.44; Fate unknown

PL354 Spitfire LF.IXe (Merlin 66); TOC/RAF 29.7.44; via No.52 MU to Russia; Arr Hapmat 23.9.44; Fate unknown

PL381 Spitfire LF.IXe (Merlin 66); TOC/RAF 21.6.44; via No.82 MU and Middlesbrough to Russia; Arr Hapmat 27.8.44; Fate unknown

PL382 Spitfire LF.IXe (Merlin 66); TOC/RAF 25.6.44; via No.52 MU and Salford to Hapmat-North for Russia; Arr Hapmat 27.8.44; Fate unknown

PL383 Spitfire LF.IXe (Merlin 66); TOC/RAF 24.6.44; via No.52 MU to Russia; Arr Hapmat 27.8.44; Fate unknown

PL389 Spitfire LF.IXe (Merlin 66); TOC/RAF 25.6.44; via No.52 MU and South Shields to Hapmat-North for Russia; Arr Hapmat 27.8.44; Fate unknown

PL391 Spitfire LF.IXe (Merlin 66); TOC/RAF 23.6.44; via No.82 MU and Middlesbrough to Russia; Arr Hapmat 27.8.44; Fate unknown

PL397 Spitfire LF.IXe (Merlin 66); TOC/RAF 25.6.44; via No.52 MU and Salford to Russia; Arr Hapmat 27.8.44; Fate unknown

PL399 Spitfire LF.IXe (Merlin 66); TOC/RAF 27.6.44; via No.82 MU and Middlesbrough to Russia; Arr Hapmat 27.8.44; Fate unknown

PL404 Spitfire LF.IXe (Merlin 66); TOC/RAF 24.6.44; via No.52 MU to Russia; Arr Hapmat 27.8.44; Fate unknown

PL406 Spitfire LF.IXe (Merlin 66); TOC/RAF 25.6.44; via No.52 MU and Salford to Russia; Arr Hapmat 27.8.44; Fate unknown

PL407 Spitfire LF.IXe (Merlin 66); TOC/RAF 24.6.44; via No.82 MU and Middlesbrough to Russia; Arr Hapmat 27.8.44; Fate unknown

PL425 Spitfire LF.IXe (Merlin 66); TOC/RAF 25.6.44; via No.82 MU and South Shields to Hapmat-North for Russia; Arr Hapmat 27.8.44; Fate unknown

PL428 Spitfire LF.IXe (Merlin 66); TOC/RAF 23.6.44; via No.52 MU to Russia; Arr Hapmat 27.8.44; Fate unknown

PL429 Spitfire LF.IXe (Merlin 66); TOC/RAF 25.6.44; via No.82 MU and South Shields to Hapmat-North for Russia; Arr Hapmat 27.8.44; Fate unknown

PL435 Spitfire LF.IXe (Merlin 66); TOC/RAF 25.6.44; via No.52 MU and South Shields to Hapmat-North for Russia; Arr Hapmat 27.8.44; Fate unknown

PL442 Spitfire LF.IXe (Merlin 66); TOC/RAF 30.6.44; via No.52 MU to Russia; Arr Hapmat 27.8.44; Fate unknown

PL445 Spitfire LF.IXe (Merlin 66); TOC/RAF 27.6.44; via No.52 MU and South Shields to Hapmat-North for Russia; Arr Hapmat 27.8.44; Fate unknown

PL446 Spitfire LF.IXe (Merlin 66); TOC/RAF 25.6.44; via No.52 MU and South Shields to Hapmat-North for Russia; Arr Hapmat 27.8.44; Fate unknown

PL447 Spitfire LF.IXe (Merlin 66); TOC/RAF 27.6.44; via No.52 MU and Salford to Hapmat-North for Russia; Arr Hapmat 27.8.44; Fate unknown

PL449 Spitfire LF.IXe (Merlin 66); TOC/RAF 27.6.44; via No.52 MU and South Shields to Hapmat-North for Russia; Arr Hapmat 27.8.44; Fate unknown

PL456 Spitfire LF.IXe (Merlin 66); TOC/RAF 29.6.44; via No.82 MU and Middlesbrough to Russia; Arr Hapmat 27.8.44; Fate unknown

PL460 Spitfire LF.IXe (Merlin 66); TOC/RAF 29.6.44; via No.82 MU and Middlesbrough to Russia; Arr Hapmat 27.8.44; Fate unknown

PL494 Spitfire LF.IXe (Merlin 66); TOC/RAF 30.6.44; via No.52 MU to Russia; Arr Hapmat 27.8.44; Fate unknown

PL496 Spitfire LF.IXe (Merlin 66); TOC/RAF 30.6.44; via No.82 MU and Middlesbrough to Russia; Arr Hapmat 27.8.44; Fate unknown

PL499 Spitfire LF.IXe (Merlin 66); TOC/RAF 30.6.44; via No.52 MU to Russia; Arr Hapmat 27.8.44; Fate unknown

PT355 Spitfire LF.IXe (Merlin 66); TOC/RAF 29.6.44; via No.82 MU and South Shields to Hapmat-North for Russia; Arr Hapmat 27.8.44; Fate unknown

PT356 Spitfire LF.IXe (Merlin 66); TOC/RAF 29.6.44; via No.82 MU and South Shields to Hapmat-North for Russia; Arr Hapmat 27.8.44; Fate unknown

PT358 Spitfire LF.IXe (Merlin 66); TOC/RAF 29.6.44; via No.82 MU and South Shields to Hapmat-North for Russia; Arr Hapmat 27.8.44; Fate unknown

PT363 Spitfire LF.IXe (Merlin 66); TOC/RAF 30.6.44; via No.82 MU and Middlesbrough to Russia; Arr Hapmat 27.8.44; Fate unknown

PT373 Spitfire LF.IXe (Merlin 66); TOC/RAF 22.6.44; via No.82 MU and Middlesbrough to Russia; Arr Hapmat 27.8.44; Fate unknown

PT374 Spitfire LF.IXe (Merlin 66); TOC/RAF 22.6.44; via No.82 MU to Russia; Arr Hapmat 23.9.44; Fate unknown

PT380 Spitfire LF.IXe (Merlin 66); TOC/RAF 29.6.44; via No.47 MU and Manchester to Hapmat-North for Russia; Arr Hapmat 27.7.44; Fate unknown

PT400 Spitfire LF.IXe (Merlin 66); TOC/RAF 8.7.44; via No.82 MU and Middlesbrough to Russia; Arr Hapmat 27.8.44; Fate unknown

PT404 Spitfire LF.IXe (Merlin 66); TOC/RAF 1.7.44; via No.52 MU and Salford to Russia; Arr Hapmat 27.8.44; Fate unknown

PT406 Spitfire LF.IXe (Merlin 66); TOC/RAF 15.7.44; via No.52 MU to Russia; Arr Hapmat 27.8.44; Fate unknown

PT408 Spitfire LF.IXe (Merlin 66); TOC/RAF 15.7.44; via No.82 MU and Middlesbrough to Russia; Arr Hapmat 27.8.44; Fate unknown

PT418 Spitfire LF.IXe (Merlin 66); TOC/RAF 17.7.44; via No.52 MU to Russia; Arr Hapmat 27.8.44; Fate unknown

PT425 Spitfire LF.IXe (Merlin 66); TOC/RAF 15.7.44; via No.82 MU and Middlesbrough to Russia; Arr Hapmat 27.8.44; Fate unknown

PT428 Spitfire LF.IXe (Merlin 66); TOC/RAF 15.7.44; via No.52 MU to Russia; Arr Hapmat 27.8.44; Fate unknown

PT429 Spitfire LF.IXe (Merlin 66); TOC/RAF 17.7.44; via No.82 MU and Middlesbrough to Russia; Arr Hapmat 27.8.44; Fate unknown

PT430 Spitfire LF.IXe (Merlin 66); TOC/RAF 15.7.44; via No.82 MU and Middlesbrough to Russia; Arr Hapmat 27.8.44; Fate unknown

PT431 Spitfire LF.IXe (Merlin 66); TOC/RAF 17.7.44; via No.82 MU and Middlesbrough to Russia; Arr Hapmat 27.8.44; Fate unknown

PT435 Spitfire LF.IXe (Merlin 66); TOC/RAF 17.7.44; via No.82 MU and Middlesbrough to Russia; Arr Hapmat 27.8.44; Fate unknown

PT459 Spitfire LF.IXe (Merlin 66); TOC/RAF 17.7.44; via No.82 MU and Middlesbrough to Russia; Arr Hapmat 27.8.44; Fate unknown

PT469 Spitfire LF.IXe (Merlin 66); TOC/RAF 14.8.44; via No.52 MU to Russia; Arr Hapmat 23.9.44; Fate unknown

PT471 Spitfire LF.IXe (Merlin 66); TOC/RAF 17.7.44; via No.82 MU and Middlesbrough to Russia; Arr Hapmat 27.8.44; Fate unknown

PT528 Spitfire LF.IXe (Merlin 66); TOC/RAF 3.8.44; via No.52 MU and Salford to Russia; Arr Hapmat 23.9.44; Fate unknown

PT533 Spitfire LF.IXe (Merlin 66); TOC/RAF 12.8.44; via No.52 MU and Middlesbrough to Russia; Arr Hapmat 23.9.44; Fate unknown

PT544 Spitfire LF.IXe (Merlin 66); TOC/RAF 18.8.44; via No.52 MU and Middlesbrough to Russia; Arr Hapmat 23.9.44; Fate unknown

PT558 Spitfire LF.IXe (Merlin 66); TOC/RAF 29.8.44; via No.52 MU and Salford to Murmansk; Arr Russia 30.10.44; Fate unknown

PT561 Spitfire LF.IXe (Merlin 66); TOC/RAF 5.9.44; via No.52 MU and Salford to Russia; Arr Hapmat 9.1.45; Fate unknown

PT563 Spitfire LF.IXe (Merlin 66); TOC/RAF 31.8.44; via No.52 MU and Salford to Murmansk; Arr Russia 30.10.44; Fate unknown

PT564 Spitfire LF.IXe (Merlin 66); TOC/RAF 18.9.44; via No.52 MU and Middlesbrough to Murmansk; Arr Russia 30.10.44; Fate unknown

PT567 Spitfire LF.IXe (Merlin 66); TOC/RAF 29.8.44; via No.52 MU and Salford to Murmansk; Arr Russia 30.10.44; Fate unknown

PT586 Spitfire LF.IXe (Merlin 66); TOC/RAF 24.7.44; via No.82 MU and Salford to Russia; Arr Hapmat 23.9.44; Fate unknown

PT589 Spitfire LF.IXe (Merlin 66); TOC/RAF 25.7.44; via No.52 MU to Russia; Arr Hapmat 23.9.44; Fate unknown

PT599 Spitfire LF.IXe (Merlin 66); TOC/RAF 30.7.44; via No.52 MU to Russia; Arr Hapmat 23.9.44; Fate unknown

PT602 Spitfire LF.IXe (Merlin 66); TOC/RAF 22.7.44; via No.82 MU to Russia; Arr Hapmat 23.9.44; Fate unknown

PT607 Spitfire LF.IXe (Merlin 66); TOC/RAF 27.7.44; via No.52 MU to Russia; Arr Hapmat 23.9.44; Fate unknown

PT611 Spitfire LF.IXe (Merlin 66); TOC/RAF 3.8.44; via No.52 MU to Russia; Arr Hapmat 23.9.44; Fate unknown

PT616 Spitfire LF.IXe (Merlin 66); TOC/RAF 24.7.44; via No.82 MU and Salford to Russia; Arr Hapmat 23.9.44; Fate unknown

PT626 Spitfire LF.IXe (Merlin 66); TOC/RAF 25.7.44; via No.39 MU and Middlesbrough to Russia; Arr Hapmat 27.8.44; Fate unknown

PT645 Spitfire LF.IXe (Merlin 66); TOC/RAF 26.7.44; via No.82 MU to Russia; Arr Hapmat 23.9.44; Fate unknown

PT651 Spitfire LF.IXe (Merlin 66); TOC/RAF 26.7.44; via No.82 MU and Salford to Russia; Arr Hapmat 23.9.44; Fate unknown
NOTE: Mov.Card (RAF) shows the arrival at Hapmat, but then also at home census 3.46; the latter possibly in error

PT663 Spitfire LF.IXe (Merlin 66); TOC/RAF 30.7.44; via No.52 MU to Russia; Arr Hapmat 23.9.44; Fate unknown

PT670 Spitfire LF.IXe (Merlin 66); TOC/RAF 5.8.44; via No.82 MU and Manchester to Russia; Arr Hapmat 23.9.44; Fate unknown

PT674 Spitfire LF.IXe (Merlin 66); TOC/RAF 30.7.44; via No.52 MU to Russia; Arr Hapmat 23.9.44; Fate unknown

PT675 Spitfire LF.IXe (Merlin 66); TOC/RAF 30.7.44; via No.52 MU to Russia; Arr Hapmat 23.9.44; Fate unknown

PT678 Spitfire LF.IXe (Merlin 66); TOC/RAF 30.7.44; via No.52 MU to Russia; Arr Hapmat 23.9.44; Fate unknown

PT682 Spitfire LF.IXe (Merlin 66); TOC/RAF 30.7.44; via No.52 MU to Russia; Arr Hapmat 23.9.44; Fate unknown

PT683 Spitfire LF.IXe (Merlin 66); TOC/RAF 3.8.44; via No.52 MU to Russia; Arr Hapmat 23.9.44; Fate unknown

PT697 Spitfire LF.IXe (Merlin 66); TOC/RAF 3.8.44; via No.52 MU and Salford to Russia; Arr Hapmat 23.9.44; Fate unknown

PT703 Spitfire LF.IXe (Merlin 66); TOC/RAF 23.8.44; via No.52 MU and Middlesbrough to Russia; Arr Hapmat 23.9.44; Fate unknown

PT710 Spitfire LF.IXe (Merlin 66); TOC/RAF 30.7.44; via No.52 MU to Russia; Arr Hapmat 23.9.44; Fate unknown

PT711 Spitfire LF.IXe (Merlin 66); TOC/RAF 1.8.44; via No.52 MU and Salford to Russia; Arr Hapmat 23.9.44; Fate unknown

PT713 Spitfire LF.IXe (Merlin 66); TOC/RAF 4.8.44; via No.82 MU and Manchester to Russia; Arr Hapmat 23.9.44; Fate unknown

PT719 Spitfire LF.IXe (Merlin 66); TOC/RAF 3.8.44; via No.52 MU and Salford to Russia; Arr Hapmat 23.9.44; Fate unknown

PT722 Spitfire LF.IXe (Merlin 66); TOC/RAF 3.8.44; via No.52 MU and Salford to Russia; Arr Hapmat 23.9.44; Fate unknown

PT731 Spitfire LF.IXe (Merlin 66); TOC/RAF 3.8.44; via No.52 MU and Salford to Russia; Arr Hapmat 23.9.44; Fate unknown

PT759 Spitfire LF.IXe (Merlin 66); TOC/RAF 14.8.44; via No.52 MU to Russia; Arr Hapmat 23.9.44; Fate unknown

PT771 Spitfire LF.IXe (Merlin 66); TOC/RAF 12.8.44; via No.52 MU to Russia; Arr Hapmat 23.9.44; Fate unknown

PT780 Spitfire LF.IXe (Merlin 66); TOC/RAF 14.8.44; via No.52 MU to Russia; Arr Hapmat 23.9.44; Fate unknown

PT782 Spitfire LF.IXe (Merlin 66); TOC/RAF 18.10.44; via No.52 MU to Russia; Arr Hapmat 8.12.44; Fate unknown

PT785 Spitfire LF.IXe (Merlin 66); TOC/RAF 14.8.44; via No.52 MU to Russia; Arr Hapmat 23.9.44; Fate unknown

PT786 Spitfire LF.IXe (Merlin 66); TOC/RAF 14.8.44; via No.52 MU to Russia; Arr Hapmat 23.9.44; Fate unknown

PT794 Spitfire LF.IXe (Merlin 66); TOC/RAF 14.8.44; via No.52 MU and Middlesbrough to Russia; Arr Hapmat 23.9.44; Fate unknown

PT795 Spitfire LF.IXe (Merlin 66); TOC/RAF 17.8.44; via No.52 MU and Middlesbrough to Russia; Arr Hapmat 23.9.44; Fate unknown

Spitfire LF.IXe PT879 served with No. 767 IAP PVO, Air Defence Murmansk, until being lost in an accident on 18th May 1945. Half a century later it was recovered from the barren Kola Peninsula area, and the wreckage sent to the UK. It is seen here on the Isle of Wight in March 1998, and is now in storage, civil registration G-BYDE having been allotted. [PRA]

PT824 Spitfire LF.IXe (Merlin 66); TOC/RAF 24.8.44; via No.52 MU and Middlesbrough to Russia; Arr Hapmat 23.9.44; Fate unknown

PT825 Spitfire LF.IXe (Merlin 66); TOC/RAF 30.8.44; via No.52 MU and Salford to Murmansk; Arr Russia 30.10.44; Fate unknown

PT829 Spitfire LF.IXe (Merlin 66); TOC/RAF 17.8.44; via No.52 MU and Salford to Murmansk; Arr Russia 30.10.44; Fate unknown

PT832 Spitfire LF.IXe (Merlin 66); TOC/RAF 17.8.44; via No.52 MU to Russia; Arr Hapmat 23.9.44; Fate unknown

PT837 Spitfire LF.IXe (Merlin 66); TOC/RAF 24.8.44; via No.52 MU and Middlesbrough to Russia; Arr Hapmat 23.9.44; Fate unknown

PT859 Spitfire LF.IXe (Merlin 66); TOC/RAF 24.8.44; via No.52 MU and Salford to Murmansk; Arr Russia 30.10.44; Fate unknown

PT874 Spitfire LF.IXe (Merlin 66); TOC/RAF 17.8.44; via No.52 MU to Russia; Arr Hapmat 23.9.44; Fate unknown

PT875 Spitfire LF.IXe (Merlin 66); TOC/RAF 24.8.44; via No.52 MU and Middlesbrough to Russia; Arr Hapmat 23.9.44; Fate unknown

PT878 Spitfire LF.IXe (Merlin 66); TOC/RAF 24.8.44; via No.52 MU and Middlesbrough to Russia; Arr Hapmat 23.9.44; Fate unknown

PT879 Spitfire LF.IXe (Merlin 66); TOC/RAF 24.8.44; via No.52 MU and Salford to Murmansk; Arr Russia 30.10.44; No.767 IAP.PVO, Air Defence Murmansk; Lost in accident 18.5.45, SOC – Recovered from the barren Kola Peninsula area in NW Russia; Owner Angela Soper; to Airframe Assemblies Ltd, Isle of Wight for restoration 16.3.98; Civil reg. *G-BYDE* 11.11.98 - **SURVIVOR**

PT880 Spitfire LF.IXe (Merlin 66); TOC/RAF 24.8.44; via No.52 MU and Salford to Murmansk; Arr Russia 30.10.44; Fate unknown

PT893 Spitfire LF.IXe (Merlin 66); TOC/RAF 29.8.44; via No.52 MU and Salford to Murmansk; Arr Russia 30.10.44; Fate unknown

PT895 Spitfire LF.IXe (Merlin 66); TOC/RAF 25.8.44; via No.52 MU and Salford to Murmansk; Arr Russia 30.10.44; Fate unknown

PT899 Spitfire LF.IXe (Merlin 66); TOC/RAF 27.8.44; via No.52 MU and Salford to Murmansk; Arr Russia 30.10.44; No.768 IAP.PVO, Air Defence Murmansk; Fate unknown

PT901 Spitfire LF.IXe (Merlin 66); TOC/RAF 24.8.44; via No.52 MU and Middlesbrough to Russia; Arr Hapmat 23.9.44; Fate unknown

PT933 Spitfire LF.IXe (Merlin 66); TOC/RAF 31.8.44; via No.52 MU and Salford to Murmansk; Arr Russia 30.10.44; Fate unknown

PT952 Spitfire LF.IXe (Merlin 66); TOC/RAF 29.8.44; via No.52 MU to Murmansk; Arr Russia 30.10.44; Fate unknown

PT958 Spitfire LF.IXe (Merlin 66); TOC/RAF 29.8.44; via No.52 MU and Salford to Murmansk; Arr Russia 30.10.44; Fate unknown

PT967 Spitfire LF.IXe (Merlin 66); TOC/RAF 30.8.44; via No.52 MU and Salford to Murmansk; Arr Russia 30.10.44; Fate unknown

PT969 Spitfire LF.IXe (Merlin 66); TOC/RAF 30.8.44; via No.52 MU and Salford to Murmansk; Arr Russia 30.10.44; Fate unknown

PT970 Spitfire LF.IXe (Merlin 66); TOC/RAF 30.8.44; via No.52 MU and Salford to Murmansk; Arr Russia 30.10.44; Fate unknown

PT987 Spitfire LF.IXe (Merlin 66); TOC/RAF 30.8.44; via No.52 MU and Salford to Murmansk; Arr Russia 30.10.44; Fate unknown

PT989 Spitfire LF.IXe (Merlin 66); TOC/RAF 31.8.44; via No.52 MU and Salford to Murmansk; Arr Russia 30.10.44; No.767 IAP.PVO, Air Defence Murmansk; Lost in accident 18.5.45, SOC

PT990 Spitfire LF.IXe (Merlin 66); TOC/RAF 5.9.44; via No.52 MU and Salford to Murmansk; Arr Russia 30.10.44; Fate unknown

PV125 Spitfire LF.IXe (Merlin 66); TOC/RAF 2.8.44; via No.52 MU to Russia; Arr Hapmat 23.9.44; Fate unknown

PV129 Spitfire LF.IXe (Merlin 66); TOC/RAF 14.8.44; via No.52 MU and Middlesbrough to Russia; Arr Hapmat 23.9.44; Fate unknown

PV130 Spitfire LF.IXe (Merlin 66); TOC/RAF 30.8.44; via No.52 MU and Salford to Murmansk; Arr Russia 30.10.44; Fate unknown

PV131 Spitfire LF.IXe (Merlin 66); TOC/RAF 14.8.44; via No.52 MU and Middlesbrough to Russia; Arr Hapmat 23.9.44; Fate unknown

PV132 Spitfire LF.IXe (Merlin 66); TOC/RAF 30.8.44; via No.52 MU and Salford to Murmansk; Arr Russia 30.10.44; Fate unknown

PV133 Spitfire LF.IXe (Merlin 66); TOC/RAF 15.8.44; via No.52 MU and Middlesbrough to Russia; Arr Hapmat 23.9.44; Fate unknown

A photograph of a two-seater Spitfire LF.IXe (UTI) modified as a trainer with a normal blister canopy for a second cockpit in the fuselage immediately behind the regular seat with an additional transparent fairing between both. [Russian Aviation Research Group]

PV135 Spitfire LF.IXe (Merlin 66); TOC/RAF 3.10.44; via No.52 MU and Middlesbrough to Russia; Arr Hapmat 8.12.44; Fate unknown

PV150 Spitfire LF.IXe (Merlin 66); TOC/RAF 5.9.44; via No.52 MU and Salford to Murmansk; Arr Russia 30.10.44; Fate unknown

PV158 Spitfire LF.IXe (Merlin 66); TOC/RAF 13.9.44; via No.52 MU and Salford to Murmansk; Arr Russia 30.10.44; Fate unknown

PV174 Spitfire LF.IXe (Merlin 66); TOC/RAF 16.9.44; via No.52 MU and Middlesbrough to Murmansk; Arr Russia 30.10.44; Fate unknown

PV178 Spitfire LF.IXe (Merlin 66); TOC/RAF 13.9.44; via No.52 MU and Salford to Murmansk; Arr Russia 30.10.44; Fate unknown

PV179 Spitfire LF.IXe (Merlin 66); TOC/RAF 5.9.44; via No.52 MU and Salford to Murmansk; Arr Russia 30.10.44; Fate unknown

PV182 Spitfire LF.IXe (Merlin 66); TOC/RAF 25.9.44; via No.52 MU and Middlesbrough to Murmansk; Arr Russia 30.10.44; Fate unknown

PV183 Spitfire LF.IXe (Merlin 66); TOC/RAF 16.9.44; via No.52 MU and Salford to Murmansk; Arr Russia 30.10.44; Fate unknown

PV184 Spitfire LF.IXe (Merlin 66); TOC/RAF 15.9.44; via No.52 MU and Salford to Murmansk; Arr Russia 30.10.44; Fate unknown

PV188 Spitfire LF.IXe (Merlin 66); TOC/RAF 13.9.44; via No.52 MU and Salford to Murmansk; Arr Russia 30.10.44; Fate unknown

PV194 Spitfire LF.IXe (Merlin 66); TOC/RAF 13.9.44; via No.52 MU and Salford to Murmansk; Arr Russia 30.10.44; Fate unknown

PV195 Spitfire LF.IXe (Merlin 66); TOC/RAF 21.9.44; via No.82 MU and Middlesbrough to Murmansk; Arr Russia 30.10.44; Fate unknown

PV196 Spitfire LF.IXe (Merlin 66); TOC/RAF 16.9.44; via No.52 MU and Middlesbrough to Murmansk; Arr Russia 30.10.44; Fate unknown

PV198 Spitfire LF.IXe (Merlin 66); TOC/RAF 15.9.44; via No.52 MU and Middlesbrough to Murmansk; Arr Russia 30.10.44; Fate unknown

PV200 Spitfire LF.IXe (Merlin 66); TOC/RAF 8.9.44; via No.52 MU and Salford to Murmansk; Arr Russia 30.10.44; Fate unknown

PV201 Spitfire LF.IXe (Merlin 66); TOC/RAF 16.9.44; via No.52 MU and Middlesbrough to Murmansk; Arr Russia 30.10.44; Fate unknown

PV204 Spitfire LF.IXe (Merlin 66); TOC/RAF 15.9.44; via No.52 MU and Salford to Murmansk; Arr Russia 30.10.44; Fate unknown

PV206 Spitfire LF.IXe (Merlin 66); TOC/RAF 21.11.44; via No.52 MU and Birkenhead to Russia; Arr Hapmat 9.1.45; Fate unknown

PV207 Spitfire LF.IXe (Merlin 66); TOC/RAF 30.9.44; via No.52 MU and Middlesbrough to Russia; Arr Hapmat 8.12.44; Fate unknown

PV214 Spitfire LF.IXe (Merlin 66); TOC/RAF 15.9.44; via No.52 MU and Middlesbrough to Murmansk; Arr Russia 30.10.44; Fate unknown

PV236 Spitfire LF.IXe (Merlin 66); TOC/RAF 23.9.44; via No.82 MU to Murmansk; Arr Russia 30.10.44; Fate unknown

PV242 Spitfire LF.IXe (Merlin 66); TOC/RAF 23.9.44; via No.82 MU and Manchester to Murmansk; Arr Russia 30.10.44; Fate unknown

PV244 Spitfire LF.IXe (Merlin 66); TOC/RAF 16.9.44; via No.52 MU and Middlesbrough to Murmansk; Arr Russia 30.10.44; Fate unknown

PV247 Spitfire LF.IXe (Merlin 66); TOC/RAF 23.9.44; via No.52 MU and Middlesbrough to Murmansk; Arr Russia 30.10.44; Fate unknown

PV248 Spitfire LF.IXe (Merlin 66); TOC/RAF 23.9.44; via No.82 MU and Middlesbrough to Murmansk; Arr Russia 30.10.44; Fate unknown

PV249 Spitfire LF.IXe (Merlin 66); TOC/RAF 23.9.44; via No.52 MU and Middlesbrough to Murmansk; Arr Russia 30.10.44; Fate unknown

PV250 Spitfire LF.IXe (Merlin 66); TOC/RAF 21.9.44; via No.52 MU and Middlesbrough to Murmansk; Arr Russia 30.10.44; Fate unknown

PV251 Spitfire LF.IXe (Merlin 66); TOC/RAF 21.9.44; via No.82 MU and Middlesbrough to Murmansk; Arr Russia 30.10.44; Fate unknown

PV252 Spitfire LF.IXe (Merlin 66); TOC/RAF 23.9.44; via No.82 MU and Middlesbrough to Murmansk; Arr Russia 30.10.44; Fate unknown

PV254 Spitfire LF.IXe (Merlin 66); TOC/RAF 23.9.44; via No.82 MU and Manchester to Murmansk; Arr Russia 30.10.44; Fate unknown

PV255 Spitfire LF.IXe (Merlin 66); TOC/RAF 21.9.44; via No.52 MU and Middlesbrough to Murmansk; Arr Russia 30.10.44; Fate unknown

PV256 Spitfire LF.IXe (Merlin 66); TOC/RAF 23.9.44; via No.52 MU and Middlesbrough to Murmansk; Arr Russia 30.10.44; Fate unknown

PV257 Spitfire LF.IXe (Merlin 66); TOC/RAF 21.9.44; via No.52 MU and Middlesbrough to Murmansk; Arr Russia 30.10.44; Fate unknown

PV258 Spitfire LF.IXe (Merlin 66); TOC/RAF 23.9.44; via No.82 MU and Middlesbrough to Murmansk; Arr Russia 30.10.44; Fate unknown

PV262 Spitfire LF.IXe (Merlin 66); TOC/RAF 25.9.44; via No.82 MU and Liverpool to Murmansk; Arr Russia 30.10.44; Fate unknown

PV265 Spitfire LF.IXe (Merlin 66); TOC/RAF 23.9.44; via No.82 MU and Manchester to Murmansk; Arr Russia 30.10.44; Fate unknown

PV266 Spitfire LF.IXe (Merlin 66); TOC/RAF 23.9.44; via No.52 MU and Salford to Murmansk; Arr Russia 30.10.44; Fate unknown

PV267 Spitfire LF.IXe (Merlin 66); TOC/RAF 23.9.44; via No.52 MU and Salford to Murmansk; Arr Russia 30.10.44; Fate unknown

PV268 Spitfire LF.IXe (Merlin 66); TOC/RAF 23.9.44; via No.82 MU and Middlesbrough to Murmansk; Arr Russia 30.10.44; Fate unknown

PV285 Spitfire LF.IXe (Merlin 66); TOC/RAF 25.9.44; via No.82 MU and Middlesbrough to Murmansk; Arr Russia 30.10.44; Fate unknown

PV287 Spitfire LF.IXe (Merlin 66); TOC/RAF 23.9.44; via No.82 MU and Manchester to Murmansk; Arr Russia 30.10.44; Fate unknown

PV297 Spitfire LF.IXe (Merlin 66); TOC/RAF 27.9.44; via No.82 MU to Murmansk; Arr Russia 30.10.44; Fate unknown

PV298 Spitfire LF.IXe (Merlin 66); TOC/RAF 28.9.44; via No.82 MU to Murmansk; Arr Russia 30.10.44; Fate unknown

PV309 Spitfire LF.IXe (Merlin 66); TOC/RAF 25.9.44; via No.82 MU to Murmansk; Arr Russia 30.10.44; Fate unknown

PV317 Spitfire LF.IXe (Merlin 66); TOC/RAF 27.9.44; via No.52 MU and Salford to Russia; Arr Hapmat 9.1.45; Fate unknown

PV319 Spitfire LF.IXe (Merlin 66); TOC/RAF 2.10.44; via No.82 MU and Liverpool to Murmansk; Arr Russia 30.10.44; Fate unknown

PV322 Spitfire LF.IXe (Merlin 66); TOC/RAF 30.9.44; via No.82 MU and Liverpool to Murmansk; Arr Russia 30.10.44; No.177 IAP.PVO, Air Defence Moscow; Fate unknown
NOTE: Incorrectly reported as "TE322"

PV326 Spitfire LF.IXe (Merlin 66); TOC/RAF 28.9.44; via No.82 MU and Liverpool to Murmansk; Arr Russia 30.10.44; Fate unknown

PV341 Spitfire LF.IXe (Merlin 66); TOC/RAF 28.9.44; via No.82 MU and Manchester to Murmansk; Arr Russia 30.10.44; No.769 IAP.PVO, Air Defence Murmansk; Fate unknown

PV345 Spitfire LF.IXe (Merlin 66); TOC/RAF 30.9.44; via No.82 MU and Manchester to Russia; Arr Hapmat 8.12.44; Fate unknown

Nothing is known of the service history of Spitfire LF.IXe RK858, but its wreckage is seen here around 1990/91 after its recovery in Russia. It is now at Duxford.

PV348 Spitfire LF.IXe (Merlin 66); TOC/RAF 28.9.44; via No.82 MU and Manchester to Murmansk; Arr Russia 30.10.44; Fate unknown

PV350 Spitfire LF.IXe (Merlin 66); TOC/RAF 28.9.44; via No.82 MU to Murmansk; Arr Russia 30.10.44; Fate unknown

PV351 Spitfire LF.IXe (Merlin 66); TOC/RAF 30.9.44; via No.82 MU and Liverpool to Murmansk; Arr Russia 30.10.44; Fate unknown

PV355 Spitfire LF.IXe (Merlin 66); TOC/RAF 27.9.44; via No.82 MU and Glasgow to Russia; Arr Hapmat 9.1.45; Fate unknown

PV357 Spitfire LF.IXe (Merlin 66); TOC/RAF 2.10.44; via No.52 MU and Middlesbrough to Russia; Arr Hapmat 8.12.44; Fate unknown

PV358 Spitfire LF.IXe (Merlin 66); TOC/RAF 2.10.44; via No.82 MU and Liverpool to Murmansk; Arr Russia 30.10.44; Fate unknown

RK798 Spitfire LF.IXe (Merlin 66); TOC/RAF 18.9.44; via No.52 MU and Middlesbrough to Murmansk; Arr Russia 30.10.44; Fate unknown

RK799 Spitfire LF.IXe (Merlin 66); TOC/RAF 30.8.44; via No.52 MU and Salford to Murmansk; Arr Russia 30.10.44; Fate unknown

RK801 Spitfire LF.IXe (Merlin 66); TOC/RAF 18.9.44; via No.52 MU and Middlesbrough to Murmansk; Arr Russia 30.10.44; Fate unknown

RK805 Spitfire LF.IXe (Merlin 66); TOC/RAF 18.9.44; via No.52 MU and Middlesbrough to Murmansk; Arr Russia 30.10.44; Fate unknown

RK807 Spitfire LF.IXe (Merlin 66); TOC/RAF 15.9.44; via No.52 MU and Middlesbrough to Murmansk; Arr Russia 30.10.44; Fate unknown

RK808 Spitfire LF.IXe (Merlin 66); TOC/RAF 13.9.44; via No.52 MU and Salford to Murmansk; Arr Russia 30.10.44; Fate unknown

RK813 Spitfire LF.IXe (Merlin 66); TOC/RAF 18.9.44; via No.82 MU and Manchester to Murmansk; Arr Russia 30.10.44; Fate unknown

RK814 Spitfire LF.IXe (Merlin 66); TOC/RAF 18.9.44; via No.52 MU and Middlesbrough to Murmansk; Arr Russia 30.10.44; Fate unknown

RK815 Spitfire LF.IXe (Merlin 66); TOC/RAF 23.9.44; via No.52 MU and Middlesbrough to Murmansk; Arr Russia 30.10.44; Fate unknown

RK816 Spitfire LF.IXe (Merlin 66); TOC/RAF 18.9.44; via No.52 MU and Salford to Murmansk; Arr Russia 30.10.44; Fate unknown

RK818 Spitfire LF.IXe (Merlin 66); TOC/RAF 23.9.44; via No.52 MU and Middlesbrough to Murmansk; Arr Russia 30.10.44; Fate unknown

RK819 Spitfire LF.IXe (Merlin 66); TOC/RAF 23.9.44; via No.52 MU and Middlesbrough to Murmansk; Arr Russia 30.10.44; Fate unknown

RK836 Spitfire LF.IXe (Merlin 66); TOC/RAF 30.9.44; via No.82 MU and Manchester to Murmansk; Arr Russia 30.10.44; Fate unknown

RK839 Spitfire LF.IXe (Merlin 66); TOC/RAF 30.9.44; via No.82 MU to Murmansk; Arr Russia 30.10.44; Fate unknown

RK841 Spitfire LF.IXe (Merlin 66); TOC/RAF 30.9.44; via No.82 MU and Middlesbrough to Russia; Arr Hapmat 9.1.45; Fate unknown

RK843 Spitfire LF.IXe (Merlin 66); TOC/RAF 2.10.44; via No.52 MU and Middlesbrough to Russia; Arr Hapmat 8.12.44; Fate unknown

RK844 Spitfire LF.IXe (Merlin 66); TOC/RAF 3.10.44; via No.52 MU and Middlesbrough to Russia; Arr Hapmat 8.12.44; Fate unknown

RK845 Spitfire LF.IXe (Merlin 66); TOC/RAF 3.10.44; via No.52 MU and Salford to Russia; Arr Hapmat 8.12.44; Fate unknown

RK847 Spitfire LF.IXe (Merlin 66); TOC/RAF 30.9.44; via No.52 MU and Salford to Russia; Arr Hapmat 8.12.44; Fate unknown

RK852 Spitfire LF.IXe (Merlin 66); TOC/RAF 2.10.44; via No.52 MU and Salford to Russia; Arr Hapmat 8.12.44; Fate unknown

RK854 Spitfire LF.IXe (Merlin 66); TOC/RAF 3.10.44; via No.52 MU and Salford to Russia; Arr Hapmat 9.1.45; Fate unknown

RK858 Spitfire LF.IXe (Merlin 66); TOC/RAF 2.10.44; via No.52 MU and Middlesbrough to Russia; Arr Hapmat 8.12.44; Service unknown - Wreck recovered, to The Fighter

Collection, Duxford, England (St.Grey) in 1992 - **SURVIVOR**

RK863 Spitfire LF.IXe (Merlin 66); TOC/RAF 3.10.44; via No.82 MU and Manchester to Russia; Arr Hapmat 8.12.44; Fate unknown

RK864 Spitfire LF.IXe (Merlin 66); TOC/RAF 30.9.44; via No.82 MU and Manchester to Murmansk; Arr Russia 30.10.44 Fate unknown

RK867 Spitfire LF.IXe (Merlin 66); TOC/RAF 3.10.44; via No.52 MU and Middlesbrough to Russia; Arr Hapmat 8.12.44; Fate unknown

RK885 Spitfire LF.IXe (Merlin 66); TOC/RAF 27.10.44; via No.82 MU and Manchester to Russia; Arr Hapmat 8.12.44; Fate unknown

RK887 Spitfire LF.IXe (Merlin 66); TOC/RAF 5.10.44; via No.52 MU and Manchester to Russia; Arr Hapmat 9.1.45; Fate unknown

RK894 Spitfire LF.IXe (Merlin 66); TOC/RAF 6.10.44; via No.52 MU and Middlesbrough to Russia; Arr Hapmat 8.12.44; Fate unknown

RK898 Spitfire LF.IXe (Merlin 66); TOC/RAF 10.10.44; via No.52 MU and Salford to Russia; Arr Hapmat 8.12.44; Fate unknown

RK899 Spitfire LF.IXe (Merlin 66); TOC/RAF 12.10.44; via No.52 MU and Middlesbrough to Russia; Arr Hapmat 8.12.44; Fate unknown

RK909 Spitfire LF.IXe (Merlin 66); TOC/RAF 12.10.44; via No.52 MU and Salford to Russia; Arr Hapmat 8.12.44; Fate unknown

RK914 Spitfire LF.IXe (Merlin 66); TOC/RAF 19.10.44; via No.82 MU and Manchester to Russia; Arr Hapmat 8.12.44; Fate unknown

RK915 Spitfire LF.IXe (Merlin 66); TOC/RAF 10.10.44; via No.52 MU and Salford to Russia; Arr Hapmat 8.12.44; Fate unknown

RK919 Spitfire LF.IXe (Merlin 66); TOC/RAF 12.10.44; via No.52 MU and Salford to Russia; Arr Hapmat 8.12.44; Fate unknown

RK923 Spitfire LF.IXe (Merlin 66); TOC/RAF 12.10.44; via No.52 MU and Salford to Russia; Arr Hapmat 8.12.44; Fate unknown

RR181 Spitfire LF.IXe (Merlin 66); TOC/RAF 17.8.44; via No.52 MU and Middlesbrough to Russia; Arr Hapmat 23.9.44; Fate unknown

RR202 Spitfire LF.IXe (Merlin 66); TOC/RAF 18.9.44; via No.52 MU and Salford to Russia; Arr Hapmat 8.12.44; Fate unknown

RR208 Spitfire LF.IXe (Merlin 66); TOC/RAF 19.10.44; via No.52 MU and Salford to Russia; Arr Hapmat 8.12.44; Fate unknown

RR237 Spitfire LF.IXe (Merlin 66); TOC/RAF 19.12.44; via No.82 MU and Manchester to Russia; Arr Hapmat 20.3.45; Fate unknown

RR253 Spitfire LF.IXe (Merlin 66); TOC/RAF 18.10.44; via No.52 MU and Middlesbrough to Russia; Arr Hapmat 8.12.44; Fate unknown

SM140 Spitfire LF.IXe (Merlin 66); TOC/RAF 23.9.44; via No.52 MU and Middlesbrough to Murmansk; Arr Russia 30.10.44 Fate unknown

SM142 Spitfire LF.IXe (Merlin 66); TOC/RAF 23.9.44; via No.82 MU and Middlesbrough to Murmansk; Arr Russia 30.10.44 Fate unknown

SM144 Spitfire LF.IXe (Merlin 66); TOC/RAF 25.9.44; via No.82 MU and Middlesbrough to Murmansk; Arr Russia 30.10.44 Fate unknown

SM145 Spitfire LF.IXe (Merlin 66); TOC/RAF 28.9.44; via No.82 MU and Salford to Russia; Arr Hapmat 8.12.44; Fate unknown

SM146 Spitfire LF.IXe (Merlin 66); TOC/RAF 30.9.44; via No.52 MU and Salford to Russia; Arr Hapmat 8.12.44; Fate unknown

SM148 Spitfire LF.IXe (Merlin 66); TOC/RAF 30.9.44; via No.52 MU and Salford to Russia; Arr Hapmat 8.12.44; Fate unknown

SM240 Spitfire LF.IXe (Merlin 66); TOC/RAF 24.11.44; via No.82 MU and Manchester to Russia; Arr Hapmat 9.1.45; Fate unknown

SM425 Spitfire LF.IXe (Merlin 66); TOC/RAF 25.11.44; via No.82 MU and Manchester to Russia; Arr Hapmat 9.1.45; Fate unknown

SM442 Spitfire LF.IXe (Merlin 66); TOC/RAF 17.10.44; via No.52 MU and Middlesbrough to Russia; Arr Hapmat 8.12.44; Fate unknown

SM447 Spitfire LF.IXe (Merlin 66); TOC/RAF 23.10.44; via No.52 MU to Russia; Arr Hapmat 8.12.44; Fate unknown

SM448 Spitfire LF.IXe (Merlin 66); TOC/RAF 20.10.44; via No.52 MU and Manchester to Russia; Arr Hapmat 8.12.44; Fate unknown

SM449 Spitfire LF.IXe (Merlin 66); TOC/RAF 23.10.44; via No.52 MU and Salford to Russia; Arr Hapmat 8.12.44; Fate unknown

SM450 Spitfire LF.IXe (Merlin 66); TOC/RAF 2.11.44; via No.82 MU and Manchester to Russia; Arr Hapmat 8.12.44; Fate unknown

SM451 Spitfire LF.IXe (Merlin 66); TOC/RAF 27.10.44; via No.82 MU and Manchester to Russia; Arr Hapmat 8.12.44; Fate unknown

SM452 Spitfire LF.IXe (Merlin 66); TOC/RAF 2.11.44; via No.82 MU and Middlesbrough to Russia; Arr Hapmat 8.12.44; Fate unknown

SM453 Spitfire LF.IXe (Merlin 66); TOC/RAF 29.10.44; via No.82 MU and Manchester to Russia; Arr Hapmat 8.12.44; Fate unknown

SM454 Spitfire LF.IXe (Merlin 66); TOC/RAF 4.11.44; via No.82 MU and Salford to Russia; Arr Hapmat 8.12.44; Fate unknown

SM455 Spitfire LF.IXe (Merlin 66); TOC/RAF 27.10.44; via No.82 MU and Manchester to Russia; Arr Hapmat 8.12.44; Fate unknown

SM456 Spitfire LF.IXe (Merlin 66); TOC/RAF 30.10.44; via No.82 MU and Manchester to Russia; Arr Hapmat 8.12.44; Fate unknown

SM457 Spitfire LF.IXe (Merlin 66); TOC/RAF 2.11.44; via No.82 MU and Manchester to Russia; Arr Hapmat 8.12.44; Fate unknown

SM458 Spitfire LF.IXe (Merlin 66); TOC/RAF 4.11.44; via No.52 MU and Salford to Russia; Arr Hapmat 8.12.44; Fate unknown

SM459 Spitfire LF.IXe (Merlin 66); TOC/RAF 2.11.44; via No.52 MU and Middlesbrough to Russia; Arr Hapmat 8.12.44; Fate unknown

SM460 Spitfire LF.IXe (Merlin 66); TOC/RAF 1.11.44; via No.82 MU and Middlesbrough to Russia; Arr Hapmat 8.12.44; Fate unknown

SM461 Spitfire LF.IXe (Merlin 66); TOC/RAF 1.11.44; via No.82 MU and Middlesbrough to Russia; Arr Hapmat 9.1.45; Fate unknown

SM462 Spitfire LF.IXe (Merlin 66); TOC/RAF 1.11.44; via No.82 MU and Manchester to Russia; Arr Hapmat 8.12.44; No.767 IAP.PVO, Air Defence Murmansk; Lost in accident 13.6.45, SOC

SM463 Spitfire LF.IXe (Merlin 66); TOC/RAF 8.11.44; via No.52 MU and Salford to Russia; Arr Hapmat 9.1.45; Fate unknown

SM508 Spitfire LF.IXe (Merlin 66); TOC/RAF 24.11.44; via No.82 MU and Birkenhead to Russia; Arr Hapmat 13.2.45; Fate unknown

SM509 Spitfire LF.IXe (Merlin 66); TOC/RAF 23.11.44; via No.52 MU and Birkenhead to Russia; Arr Hapmat 9.1.45; Fate unknown

SM510 Spitfire LF.IXe (Merlin 66); TOC/RAF 25.11.44; via No.52 MU and Birkenhead to Russia; Arr Hapmat 9.1.45; Fate unknown

SM514 Spitfire LF.IXe (Merlin 66); TOC/RAF 23.11.44; via No.82 MU and Birkenhead to Russia; Arr Hapmat 9.1.45; Fate unknown

SM517 Spitfire LF.IXe (Merlin 66); TOC/RAF 21.11.44; via No.82 MU and Middlesbrough to Russia; Arr Hapmat 9.1.45; Fate unknown

SM519 Spitfire LF.IXe (Merlin 66); TOC/RAF 23.11.44; via No.82 MU and Middlesbrough to Russia; Arr Hapmat 9.1.45; Fate unknown
SM521 Spitfire LF.IXe (Merlin 66); TOC/RAF 24.11.44; via No.82 MU and Manchester to Russia; Arr Hapmat 9.1.45; Fate unknown
SM522 Spitfire LF.IXe (Merlin 66); TOC/RAF 24.11.44; via No.82 MU and Manchester to Russia; Arr Hapmat 9.1.45; Fate unknown
SM524 Spitfire LF.IXe (Merlin 66); TOC/RAF 20.11.44; via No.82 MU and Birkenhead to Russia; Arr Hapmat 9.1.45; Fate unknown
SM525 Spitfire LF.IXe (Merlin 66); TOC/RAF 20.11.44; via No.82 MU and Middlesbrough to Russia; Arr Hapmat 9.1.45; Fate unknown
SM526 Spitfire LF.IXe (Merlin 66); TOC/RAF 28.11.44; via No.82 MU and Manchester to Russia; Arr Hapmat 9.1.45; Fate unknown
SM527 Spitfire LF.IXe (Merlin 66); TOC/RAF 24.11.44; via No.82 MU and Middlesbrough to Russia; Arr Hapmat 9.1.45; Fate unknown
SM528 Spitfire LF.IXe (Merlin 66); TOC/RAF 21.11.44; via No.82 MU and Middlesbrough to Russia; Arr Hapmat 9.1.45; Fate unknown
SM529 Spitfire LF.IXe (Merlin 66); TOC/RAF 20.11.44; via No.82 MU and Middlesbrough to Russia; Arr Hapmat 9.1.45; Fate unknown
SM530 Spitfire LF.IXe (Merlin 66); TOC/RAF 23.11.44; via No.82 MU and Middlesbrough to Russia; Arr Hapmat 9.1.45; Fate unknown
SM531 Spitfire LF.IXe (Merlin 66); TOC/RAF 24.11.44; via No.82 MU and Manchester to Russia; Arr Hapmat 9.1.45; Fate unknown
SM532 Spitfire LF.IXe (Merlin 66); TOC/RAF 24.11.44; via No.52 MU and Birkenhead to Russia; Arr Hapmat 9.1.45; Fate unknown
SM533 Spitfire LF.IXe (Merlin 66); TOC/RAF 24.11.44; via No.82 MU and Middlesbrough to Russia; Arr Hapmat 9.1.45; Fate unknown
SM534 Spitfire LF.IXe (Merlin 66); TOC/RAF 24.11.44; via No.82 MU and Manchester to Russia; Arr Hapmat 9.1.45; Fate unknown
SM535 Spitfire LF.IXe (Merlin 66); TOC/RAF 20.11.44; via No.82 MU and Middlesbrough to Russia; Arr Hapmat 9.1.45; Fate unknown
SM536 Spitfire LF.IXe (Merlin 66); TOC/RAF 7.12.44; via No.82 MU and Salford to Russia; Arr Hapmat 13.2.45; Fate unknown
SM537 Spitfire LF.IXe (Merlin 66); TOC/RAF 24.11.44; via No.52 MU and Newport to Russia; Arr Hapmat 9.1.45; Fate unknown
SM539 Spitfire LF.IXe (Merlin 66); TOC/RAF 21.11.44; via No.52 MU and Birkenhead to Russia; Arr Hapmat 9.1.45; Fate unknown
SM540 Spitfire LF.IXe (Merlin 66); TOC/RAF 21.11.44; via No.82 MU and Middlesbrough to Russia; Arr Hapmat 9.1.45; Fate unknown
SM541 Spitfire LF.IXe (Merlin 66); TOC/RAF 24.11.44; via No.82 MU and Manchester to Russia; Arr Hapmat 9.1.45; Fate unknown
SM542 Spitfire LF.IXe (Merlin 66); TOC/RAF 29.11.44; via No.82 MU and Glasgow to Russia; Arr Hapmat 9.1.45; Fate unknown
SM543 Spitfire LF.IXe (Merlin 66); TOC/RAF 25.11.44; via No.52 MU and Newport to Russia; Arr Hapmat 9.1.45; Fate unknown
SM544 Spitfire LF.IXe (Merlin 66); TOC/RAF 25.11.44; via No.82 MU and Manchester to Russia; Arr Hapmat 9.1.45; Fate unknown
SM545 Spitfire LF.IXe (Merlin 66); TOC/RAF 24.11.44; via No.52 MU and Birkenhead to Russia; Arr Hapmat 9.1.45; Fate unknown
SM546 Spitfire LF.IXe (Merlin 66); TOC/RAF 24.11.44; via No.82 MU and Manchester to Russia; Arr Hapmat 9.1.45; Fate unknown
SM547 Spitfire LF.IXe (Merlin 66); TOC/RAF 23.11.44; via No.52 MU and Birkenhead to Russia; Arr Hapmat 9.1.45; Fate unknown
SM548 Spitfire LF.IXe (Merlin 66); TOC/RAF 25.11.44; via No.82 MU and Middlesbrough to Russia; Arr Hapmat 9.1.45; Fate unknown
SM563 Spitfire LF.IXe (Merlin 66); TOC/RAF 24.11.44; via No.82 MU and Manchester to Russia; Arr Hapmat 9.1.45; Fate unknown
SM564 Spitfire LF.IXe (Merlin 66); TOC/RAF 24.11.44; via No.82 MU and Middlesbrough to Russia; Arr Hapmat 9.1.45; Fate unknown
SM565 Spitfire LF.IXe (Merlin 66); TOC/RAF 9.12.44; via No.52 MU and Newport to Russia; Arr Hapmat 9.1.45; Fate unknown
SM566 Spitfire LF.IXe (Merlin 66); TOC/RAF 24.11.44; via No.52 MU and Birkenhead to Russia; Arr Hapmat 9.1.45; Fate unknown
SM567 Spitfire LF.IXe (Merlin 66); TOC/RAF 25.11.44; via No.52 MU and Newport to Russia; Arr Hapmat 9.1.45; Fate unknown
SM568 Spitfire LF.IXe (Merlin 66); TOC/RAF 29.11.44; via No.82 MU and Newport to Russia; Arr Hapmat 9.1.45; Fate unknown
SM569 Spitfire LF.IXe (Merlin 66); TOC/RAF 25.11.44; via No.52 MU and Birkenhead to Russia; Arr Hapmat 9.1.45; Fate unknown
SM570 Spitfire LF.IXe (Merlin 66); TOC/RAF 28.11.44; via No.52 MU and Newport to Russia; Arr Hapmat 9.1.45; Fate unknown
SM571 Spitfire LF.IXe (Merlin 66); TOC/RAF 25.11.44; via No.52 MU and Newport to Russia; Arr Hapmat 9.1.45; Fate unknown
SM572 Spitfire LF.IXe (Merlin 66); TOC/RAF 29.11.44; via No.82 MU and Glasgow to Russia; Arr Hapmat 9.1.45; Fate unknown
SM573 Spitfire LF.IXe (Merlin 66); TOC/RAF 25.11.44; via No.52 MU and Birkenhead to Russia; Arr Hapmat 9.1.45; Fate unknown
SM574 Spitfire LF.IXe (Merlin 66); TOC/RAF 7.12.44; via No.82 MU and Birkenhead to Russia; Arr Hapmat 13.2.45; Fate unknown
SM575 Spitfire LF.IXe (Merlin 66); TOC/RAF 20.11.44; via No.82 MU and Middlesbrough to Russia; Arr Hapmat 9.1.45; Fate unknown
SM576 Spitfire LF.IXe (Merlin 66); TOC/RAF 24.11.44; via No.52 MU and Birkenhead to Russia; Arr Hapmat 9.1.45; Fate unknown
SM577 Spitfire LF.IXe (Merlin 66); TOC/RAF 24.11.44; via No.82 MU and Manchester to Russia; Arr Hapmat 9.1.45; Fate unknown
SM578 Spitfire LF.IXe (Merlin 66); TOC/RAF 24.11.44; via No.82 MU and Manchester to Russia; Arr Hapmat 9.1.45; Fate unknown
SM579 Spitfire LF.IXe (Merlin 66); TOC/RAF 25.11.44; via No.52 MU and Newport to Russia; Arr Hapmat 9.1.45; Fate unknown
SM580 Spitfire LF.IXe (Merlin 66); TOC/RAF 29.11.44; via No.82 MU and Manchester to Russia; Arr Hapmat 9.1.45; Fate unknown
SM581 Spitfire LF.IXe (Merlin 66); TOC/RAF 24.11.44; via No.82 MU and Middlesbrough to Russia; Arr Hapmat 9.1.45; Fate unknown
SM582 Spitfire LF.IXe (Merlin 66); TOC/RAF 24.11.44; via No.82 MU and Manchester to Russia; Arr Hapmat 9.1.45; Fate unknown
SM583 Spitfire LF.IXe (Merlin 66); TOC/RAF 25.11.44; via No.52 MU and Birkenhead to Russia; Arr Hapmat 9.1.45; Fate unknown
SM584 Spitfire LF.IXe (Merlin 66); TOC/RAF 6.12.44; via No.82 MU and Birkenhead to Russia; Arr Hapmat 13.2.45; Fate unknown
SM585 Spitfire LF.IXe (Merlin 66); TOC/RAF 28.11.44; via No.82 MU and Middlesbrough to Russia; Arr Hapmat 9.1.45; Fate unknown

SM586 Spitfire LF.IXe (Merlin 66); TOC/RAF 24.11.44; via No.52 MU and Birkenhead to Russia; Arr Hapmat 9.1.45; Fate unknown
SM587 Spitfire LF.IXe (Merlin 66); TOC/RAF 25.11.44; via No.52 MU and Newport to Russia; Arr Hapmat 9.1.45; Fate unknown
SM588 Spitfire LF.IXe (Merlin 66); TOC/RAF 29.11.44; via No.82 MU and Glasgow to Russia; Arr Hapmat 9.1.45; Fate unknown
SM589 Spitfire LF.IXe (Merlin 66); TOC/RAF 28.11.44; via No.52 MU and Newport to Russia; Arr Hapmat 9.1.45; Fate unknown
SM590 Spitfire LF.IXe (Merlin 66); TOC/RAF 29.11.44; via No.52 MU and Newport to Russia; Arr Hapmat 9.1.45; Fate unknown
SM591 Spitfire LF.IXe (Merlin 66); TOC/RAF 24.11.44; via No.82 MU and Manchester to Russia; Arr Hapmat 9.1.45; Fate unknown
SM592 Spitfire LF.IXe (Merlin 66); TOC/RAF 29.11.44; via No.82 MU and Middlesbrough to Russia; Arr Hapmat 9.1.45; Fate unknown
SM593 Spitfire LF.IXe (Merlin 66); TOC/RAF 24.11.44; via No.82 MU and Middlesbrough to Russia; Arr Hapmat 9.1.45; Fate unknown
SM594 Spitfire LF.IXe (Merlin 66); TOC/RAF 28.11.44; via No.52 MU and Birkenhead to Russia; Arr Hapmat 9.1.45; Fate unknown
SM595 Spitfire LF.IXe (Merlin 66); TOC/RAF 29.11.44; via No.82 MU and Glasgow to Russia; Arr Hapmat 9.1.45; Fate unknown
SM596 Spitfire LF.IXe (Merlin 66); TOC/RAF 29.11.44; via No.82 MU and Birkenhead to Russia; Arr Hapmat 9.1.45; Fate unknown
SM597 Spitfire LF.IXe (Merlin 66); TOC/RAF 28.11.44; via No.82 MU and Manchester to Russia; Arr Hapmat 9.1.45; Fate unknown
SM610 Spitfire LF.IXe (Merlin 66); TOC/RAF 6.12.44; via No.82 MU and Salford to Russia; Arr Hapmat 13.2.45; Fate unknown
SM611 Spitfire LF.IXe (Merlin 66); TOC/RAF 28.11.44; via No.52 MU and Newport to Russia; Arr Hapmat 9.1.45; Fate unknown
SM612 Spitfire LF.IXe (Merlin 66); TOC/RAF 29.11.44; via No.52 MU and Newport to Russia; Arr Hapmat 9.1.45; Fate unknown
SM613 Spitfire LF.IXe (Merlin 66); TOC/RAF 28.11.44; via No.82 MU and Middlesbrough to Russia; Arr Hapmat 9.1.45; Fate unknown
SM614 Spitfire LF.IXe (Merlin 66); TOC/RAF 28.11.44; via No.52 MU and Newport to Russia; Arr Hapmat 9.1.45; Fate unknown
SM615 Spitfire LF.IXe (Merlin 66); TOC/RAF 29.11.44; via No.82 MU and Manchester to Russia; Arr Hapmat 9.1.45; Fate unknown
SM616 Spitfire LF.IXe (Merlin 66); TOC/RAF 28.11.44; via No.52 MU and Newport to Russia; Arr Hapmat 9.1.45; Fate unknown
SM617 Spitfire LF.IXe (Merlin 66); TOC/RAF 29.11.44; via No.82 MU and Middlesbrough to Russia; Arr Hapmat 9.1.45; Fate unknown
SM618 Spitfire LF.IXe (Merlin 66); TOC/RAF 29.11.44; via No.82 MU and Salford to Russia; Arr Hapmat 13.2.45; Fate unknown
SM619 Spitfire LF.IXe (Merlin 66); TOC/RAF 29.11.44; via No.82 MU and Glasgow to Russia; Arr Hapmat 9.1.45; Fate unknown
SM620 Spitfire LF.IXe (Merlin 66); TOC/RAF 29.11.44; via No.82 MU and Birkenhead to Russia; Arr Hapmat 9.1.45; Fate unknown
SM621 Spitfire LF.IXe (Merlin 66); TOC/RAF 28.11.44; via No.52 MU and Newport to Russia; Arr Hapmat 9.1.45; Fate unknown
SM622 Spitfire LF.IXe (Merlin 66); TOC/RAF 29.11.44; via No.82 MU and Manchester to Russia; Arr Hapmat 9.1.45; NII VVS/RKKA, Research and Test Institute, used for trials; Fate unknown
SM623 Spitfire LF.IXe (Merlin 66); TOC/RAF 6.12.44; via No.82 MU and Birkenhead to Russia; Arr Hapmat 13.2.45; Fate unknown
SM624 Spitfire LF.IXe (Merlin 66); TOC/RAF 6.12.44; via No.52 MU and Manchester to Russia; Arr Hapmat 13.2.45; Fate unknown
SM625 Spitfire LF.IXe (Merlin 66); TOC/RAF 30.11.44; via No.52 MU and Newport to Russia; Arr Hapmat 9.1.45; Fate unknown

Spitfire LF.IXe SM622 was used for trials in early 1945 by the NII VVS/RKKA, Research and Test Institute at Zhukovsky, near Moscow.

SM626 Spitfire LF.IXe (Merlin 66); TOC/RAF 28.11.44; via No.52 MU and Newport to Russia; Arr Hapmat 9.1.45; Fate unknown

SM627 Spitfire LF.IXe (Merlin 66); TOC/RAF 29.11.44; via No.52 MU and Newport to Russia; Arr Hapmat 9.1.45; Fate unknown

SM628 Spitfire LF.IXe (Merlin 66); TOC/RAF 6.12.44; via No.82 MU and Middlesbrough to Russia; Arr Hapmat 20.3.45; Fate unknown

SM629 Spitfire LF.IXe (Merlin 66); TOC/RAF 6.12.44; via No.82 MU and Salford to Russia; Arr Hapmat 13.2.45; Fate unknown

SM630 Spitfire LF.IXe (Merlin 66); TOC/RAF 28.11.44; via No.82 MU and Salford to Russia; Arr Hapmat 9.1.45; Fate unknown

SM631 Spitfire LF.IXe (Merlin 66); TOC/RAF 6.12.44; via No.82 MU and Manchester to Russia; Arr Hapmat 20.3.45; Fate unknown

SM632 Spitfire LF.IXe (Merlin 66); TOC/RAF 28.11.44; via No.52 MU and Newport to Russia; Arr Hapmat 9.1.45; Fate unknown

SM633 Spitfire LF.IXe (Merlin 66); TOC/RAF 6.12.44; via No.52 MU and Manchester to Russia; Arr Hapmat 13.2.45; Fate unknown

SM634 Spitfire LF.IXe (Merlin 66); TOC/RAF 6.12.44; via No.82 MU and Salford to Russia; Arr Hapmat 13.2.45; Fate unknown

SM635 Spitfire LF.IXe (Merlin 66); TOC/RAF 29.11.44; via No.52 MU and Newport to Russia; Arr Hapmat 9.1.45; Fate unknown

SM636 Spitfire LF.IXe (Merlin 66); TOC/RAF 6.12.44; via No.82 MU and Salford to Russia; Arr Hapmat 13.2.45; Fate unknown

SM637 Spitfire LF.IXe (Merlin 66); TOC/RAF 6.12.44; via No.82 MU and Glasgow to Russia; Arr Hapmat 9.1.45; Fate unknown

SM638 Spitfire LF.IXe (Merlin 66); TOC/RAF 7.12.44; via No.82 MU and Salford to Russia; Arr Hapmat 13.2.45; Fate unknown

SM639 Spitfire LF.IXe (Merlin 66); TOC/RAF 6.12.44; via No.82 MU and Birkenhead to Russia; Arr Hapmat 13.2.45; Service unknown - Recovered wreck to AJD Engineering, Mildenhall, Suffolk, England 1995; To Chris Lawrence, Norwich, 3.96 (storage awaiting restoration) - **SURVIVOR**

SM640 Spitfire LF.IXe (Merlin 66); TOC/RAF 8.12.44; via No.82 MU and Middlesbrough to Russia; Arr Hapmat 20.3.45; Fate unknown

SM641 Spitfire LF.IXe (Merlin 66); TOC/RAF 30.11.44; via No.52 MU and Newport to Russia; Arr Hapmat 9.1.45; Fate unknown

SM642 Spitfire LF.IXe (Merlin 66); TOC/RAF 6.12.44; via No.52 MU and Manchester to Russia; Arr Hapmat 13.2.45; Fate unknown

SM643 Spitfire LF.IXe (Merlin 66); TOC/RAF 29.11.44; via No.52 MU and Newport to Russia; Arr Hapmat 9.1.45; Fate unknown

SM644 Spitfire LF.IXe (Merlin 66); TOC/RAF 29.11.44; via No.82 MU and Middlesbrough to Russia; Arr Hapmat 9.1.45; Fate unknown

SM645 Spitfire LF.IXe (Merlin 66); TOC/RAF 6.12.44; via No.52 MU and Manchester to Russia; Arr Hapmat 13.2.45; Fate unknown

SM647 Spitfire LF.IXe (Merlin 66); TOC/RAF 29.11.44; via No.82 MU and Birkenhead to Russia; Arr Hapmat 9.1.45; Fate unknown

SM663 Spitfire LF.IXe (Merlin 66); TOC/RAF 6.12.44; via No.82 MU and Glasgow to Russia; Arr Hapmat 9.1.45; Fate unknown

SM666 Spitfire LF.IXe (Merlin 66); TOC/RAF 6.12.44; via No.82 MU and Southport to Russia; Arr Hapmat 25.4.45; Fate unknown

SM669 Spitfire LF.IXe (Merlin 66); TOC/RAF 12.12.44; via No.82 MU and Birkenhead to Russia; Arr Hapmat 13.2.45; Fate unknown

TA738 Spitfire LF.IXe (Merlin 66); TOC/RAF 2.12.44; via No.82 MU and Salford to Russia; Arr Hapmat 13.2.45; Fate unknown

TA740 Spitfire LF.IXe (Merlin 66); TOC/RAF 2.12.44; via No.52 MU and Manchester to Russia; Arr Hapmat 13.2.45; Fate unknown

TA742 Spitfire LF.IXe (Merlin 66); TOC/RAF 2.12.44; via No.52 MU and Manchester to Russia; Arr Hapmat 20.3.45; Fate unknown

TA743 Spitfire LF.IXe (Merlin 66); TOC/RAF 7.12.44; via No.52 MU and Newport to Russia; Arr Hapmat 9.1.45; Fate unknown

TA744 Spitfire LF.IXe (Merlin 66); TOC/RAF 2.12.44; via No.52 MU and Manchester to Russia; Arr Hapmat 20.3.45; Fate unknown

TA745 Spitfire LF.IXe (Merlin 66); TOC/RAF 13.12.44; via No.82 MU and Salford to Russia; Arr Hapmat 13.2.45; Fate unknown

TA747 Spitfire LF.IXe (Merlin 66); TOC/RAF 5.12.44; via No.82 MU and Salford to Russia; Arr Hapmat 13.2.45; Fate unknown

TA748 Spitfire LF.IXe (Merlin 66); TOC/RAF 5.12.44; via No.82 MU and Salford to Russia; Arr Hapmat 13.2.45; Fate unknown

TA749 Spitfire LF.IXe (Merlin 66); TOC/RAF 5.12.44; via No.52 MU and Newport to Russia; Arr Hapmat 9.1.45; Fate unknown

TA750 Spitfire LF.IXe (Merlin 66); TOC/RAF 4.12.44; via No.82 MU and Glasgow to Russia; Arr Hapmat 9.1.45; Fate unknown

TA751 Spitfire LF.IXe (Merlin 66); TOC/RAF 6.12.44; via No.82 MU and Birkenhead to Russia; Arr Hapmat 13.2.45; Fate unknown

TA752 Spitfire LF.IXe (Merlin 66); TOC/RAF 2.12.44; via No.82 MU and Salford to Russia; Arr Hapmat 13.2.45; Fate unknown

TA753 Spitfire LF.IXe (Merlin 66); TOC/RAF 4.12.44; via No.82 MU and Salford to Russia; Arr Hapmat 13.2.45; Fate unknown

TA754 Spitfire LF.IXe (Merlin 66); TOC/RAF 2.12.44; via No.82 MU and Southport to Russia; Arr Hapmat 20.3.45; Fate unknown

TA755 Spitfire LF.IXe (Merlin 66); TOC/RAF 6.12.44; via No.82 MU and Salford to Russia; Arr Hapmat 13.2.45; Fate unknown

TA756 Spitfire LF.IXe (Merlin 66); TOC/RAF 5.12.44; via No.52 MU and Manchester to Russia; Arr Hapmat 13.2.45; Fate unknown

TA757 Spitfire LF.IXe (Merlin 66); TOC/RAF 5.12.44; via No.82 MU and Birkenhead to Russia; Arr Hapmat 13.2.45; Fate unknown

TA758 Spitfire LF.IXe (Merlin 66); TOC/RAF 2.12.44; via No.82 MU and Glasgow to Russia; Arr Hapmat 9.1.45; Fate unknown

TA760 Spitfire LF.IXe (Merlin 66); TOC/RAF 12.1.45; via No.52 MU and Manchester to Russia; Arr Hapmat 20.3.45; Fate unknown

TA761 Spitfire LF.IXe (Merlin 66); TOC/RAF 7.12.44; via No.82 MU and Salford to Russia; Arr Hapmat 13.2.45; Fate unknown

TA762 Spitfire LF.IXe (Merlin 66); TOC/RAF 21.1.45; via No.82 MU and Manchester to Russia; Arr Hapmat 20.3.45; Fate unknown

TA763 Spitfire LF.IXe (Merlin 66); TOC/RAF 6.12.44; via No.82 MU and Salford to Russia; Arr Hapmat 13.2.45; Fate unknown

TA764 Spitfire LF.IXe (Merlin 66); TOC/RAF 5.12.44; via No.52 MU and Newport to Russia; Arr Hapmat 9.1.45; Fate unknown

TA765 Spitfire LF.IXe (Merlin 66); TOC/RAF 5.12.44; via No.52 MU and Manchester to Russia; Arr Hapmat 13.2.45; Fate unknown

TA766 Spitfire LF.IXe (Merlin 66); TOC/RAF 6.12.44; via No.82 MU and Birkenhead to Russia; Arr Hapmat 13.2.45; Fate unknown

Spitfire HF.IXe TA810 with the NII VVS/RKKA (Research Institute) for trials and test flying around May-August 1945. [Russian Aviation Research Group]

TA767 Spitfire LF.IXe (Merlin 66); TOC/RAF 5.12.44; via No.52 MU and Newport to Russia; Arr Hapmat 9.1.45; Fate unknown

TA768 Spitfire LF.IXe (Merlin 66); TOC/RAF 6.12.44; via No.82 MU and Birkenhead to Russia; Arr Hapmat 13.2.45; Fate unknown

TA769 Spitfire LF.IXe (Merlin 66); TOC/RAF 5.12.44; via No.82 MU and Manchester to Russia; Arr Hapmat 20.3.45; Fate unknown

TA770 Spitfire LF.IXe (Merlin 66); TOC/RAF 6.12.44; via No.82 MU and Birkenhead to Russia; Arr Hapmat 13.2.45; Fate unknown

TA771 Spitfire LF.IXe (Merlin 66); TOC/RAF 11.12.44; via No.82 MU and Salford to Russia; Arr Hapmat 13.2.45; Fate unknown

TA773 Spitfire LF.IXe (Merlin 66); TOC/RAF 5.12.44; via No.82 MU and Newport to Russia; Arr Hapmat 9.1.45; Fate unknown

TA774 Spitfire LF.IXe (Merlin 66); TOC/RAF 9.12.44; via No.82 MU and Birkenhead to Russia; Arr Hapmat 13.2.45; Fate unknown

TA775 Spitfire LF.IXe (Merlin 66); TOC/RAF 9.2.45; via No.82 MU and Manchester to Murmansk; Arr Russia 25.4.45; Fate unknown

TA776 Spitfire LF.IXe (Merlin 66); TOC/RAF 9.12.44; via No.82 MU and Birkenhead to Russia; Arr Hapmat 13.2.45; Fate unknown

TA777 Spitfire LF.IXe (Merlin 66); TOC/RAF 7.12.44; via No.82 MU and Manchester to Russia; Arr Hapmat 20.3.45; Fate unknown

TA778 Spitfire LF.IXe (Merlin 66); TOC/RAF 9.12.44; via No.82 MU and Southport to Russia; Arr Hapmat 20.3.45; Fate unknown

TA779 Spitfire LF.IXe (Merlin 66); TOC/RAF 9.12.44; via No.52 MU and Manchester to Russia; Arr Hapmat 13.2.45; Fate unknown

TA793 Spitfire LF.IXe (Merlin 66); TOC/RAF 7.12.44; via No.82 MU and Salford to Russia; Arr Hapmat 13.2.45; Fate unknown

TA797 Spitfire LF.IXe (Merlin 66); TOC/RAF 7.12.44; via No.52 MU and Manchester to Russia; Arr Hapmat 13.2.45; Fate unknown

TA799 Spitfire LF.IXe (Merlin 66); TOC/RAF 18.12.44; via No.82 MU and Southport to Russia; Arr Hapmat 20.3.45; Fate unknown

TA801 Spitfire LF.IXe (Merlin 66); TOC/RAF 17.12.44; via No.82 MU and Birkenhead to Russia; Arr Hapmat 13.2.45; Fate unknown

TA803 Spitfire LF.IXe (Merlin 66); TOC/RAF 6.12.44; via No.82 MU and Salford to Russia; Arr Hapmat 13.2.45; Fate unknown

TA810 Spitfire HF.IXe (Merlin 70); TOC/RAF 9.12.44; via No.82 MU and Manchester to Russia; Arr Hapmat 20.3.45; Soviet Air Force; To NII VVS/RKKA (Research and Test Institute), trials and test flying 5.45-8.45; Fate unknown

TA814 Spitfire LF.IXe (Merlin 66); TOC/RAF 17.12.44; via No.82 MU and Manchester to Russia; Arr Hapmat 20.3.45; Fate unknown

TA815 Spitfire LF.IXe (Merlin 66); TOC/RAF 17.12.44; via No.52 MU and Manchester to Russia; Arr Hapmat 13.2.45; Fate unknown

TA818 Spitfire LF.IXe (Merlin 66); TOC/RAF 17.12.44; via No.82 MU and Middlesbrough to Russia; Arr Hapmat 20.3.45; Fate unknown

TA819 Spitfire LF.IXe (Merlin 66); TOC/RAF 17.12.44; via No.82 MU and Manchester to Russia; Arr Hapmat 20.3.45; Fate unknown

TA820 Spitfire LF.IXe (Merlin 66); TOC/RAF 17.12.44; via No.82 MU and Salford to Russia; Arr Hapmat 13.2.45; Fate unknown

TA821 Spitfire LF.IXe (Merlin 66); TOC/RAF 23.9.44; via No.82 MU and Middlesbrough to Murmansk; Arr Russia 30.10.44; Fate unknown

TA824 Spitfire LF.IXe (Merlin 66); TOC/RAF 23.9.44; via No.82 MU and Middlesbrough to Murmansk; Arr Russia 30.10.44; Fate unknown

TA826 Spitfire LF.IXe (Merlin 66); TOC/RAF 25.9.44; via No.82 MU and Middlesbrough to Murmansk; Arr Russia 30.10.44; Fate unknown

TA827 Spitfire LF.IXe (Merlin 66); TOC/RAF 20.9.44; via No.52 MU and Salford to Russia; Arr Hapmat 8.12.44; Fate unknown

TA828 Spitfire LF.IXe (Merlin 66); TOC/RAF 25.9.44; via No.82 MU and Middlesbrough to Murmansk; Arr Russia 30.10.44; Fate unknown

TA830 Spitfire LF.IXe (Merlin 66); TOC/RAF 25.9.44; via No.52 MU and Middlesbrough to Murmansk; Arr Russia 30.10.44; Fate unknown

TA832 Spitfire LF.IXe (Merlin 66); TOC/RAF 25.9.44; via No.82 MU and Manchester to Murmansk; Arr Russia 30.10.44; Fate unknown

TA833 Spitfire LF.IXe (Merlin 66); TOC/RAF 2.10.44; via No.52 MU and Salford to Russia; Arr Hapmat 9.1.45; Fate unknown
TA834 Spitfire LF.IXe (Merlin 66); TOC/RAF 28.9.44; via No.82 MU and Middlesbrough to Russia; Arr Hapmat 30.10.44; Fate unknown
TA835 Spitfire LF.IXe (Merlin 66); TOC/RAF 28.9.44; via No.82 MU and Manchester to Murmansk; Arr Russia 30.10.44; Fate unknown
TA840 Spitfire LF.IXe (Merlin 66); TOC/RAF 2.10.44; via No.52 MU and Salford to Russia; Arr Hapmat 8.12.44; Fate unknown
TA856 Spitfire LF.IXe (Merlin 66); TOC/RAF 2.10.44; via No.52 MU and Salford to Russia; Arr Hapmat 9.1.45; Fate unknown
TA860 Spitfire LF.IXe (Merlin 66); TOC/RAF 2.10.44; via No.82 MU and Manchester to Russia; Arr Hapmat 8.12.44; Fate unknown
TA865 Spitfire LF.IXe (Merlin 66); TOC/RAF 7.10.44; via No.82 MU and Manchester to Russia; Arr Hapmat 8.12.44; Fate unknown
TA867 Spitfire LF.IXe (Merlin 66); TOC/RAF 12.10.44; via No.52 MU and Salford to Russia; Arr Hapmat 8.12.44; Fate unknown
TA868 Spitfire LF.IXe (Merlin 66); TOC/RAF 16.10.44; via No.52 MU and Middlesbrough to Russia; Arr Hapmat 8.12.44; Fate unknown
TA869 Spitfire LF.IXe (Merlin 66); TOC/RAF 16.10.44; via No.52 MU and Middlesbrough to Russia; Arr Hapmat 8.12.44; Fate unknown
TA870 Spitfire LF.IXe (Merlin 66); TOC/RAF 17.10.44; via No.52 MU and Salford to Russia; Arr Hapmat 8.12.44; Fate unknown
TA871 Spitfire LF.IXe (Merlin 66); TOC/RAF 27.10.44; via No.82 MU and Manchester to Russia; Arr Hapmat 8.12.44; Fate unknown
TA872 Spitfire LF.IXe (Merlin 66); TOC/RAF 19.10.44; via No.52 MU and Salford to Russia; Arr Hapmat 8.12.44; Fate unknown
TA873 Spitfire LF.IXe (Merlin 66); TOC/RAF 23.10.44; via No.52 MU and Salford to Russia; Arr Hapmat 8.12.44; Fate unknown
TA874 Spitfire LF.IXe (Merlin 66); TOC/RAF 19.10.44; via No.52 MU and Salford to Russia; Arr Hapmat 8.12.44; Fate unknown
TA875 Spitfire LF.IXe (Merlin 66); TOC/RAF 23.10.44; via No.82 MU and Manchester to Russia; Arr Hapmat 8.12.44; Fate unknown
TA876 Spitfire LF.IXe (Merlin 66); TOC/RAF 23.10.44; via No.82 MU and Manchester to Russia; Arr Hapmat 8.12.44; Fate unknown
TA877 Spitfire LF.IXe (Merlin 66); TOC/RAF 23.10.44; via No.52 MU and Salford to Russia; Arr Hapmat 8.12.44; Fate unknown
TA878 Spitfire LF.IXe (Merlin 66); TOC/RAF 24.10.44; via No.52 MU and Middlesbrough to Russia; Arr Hapmat 8.12.44; Fate unknown
TA879 Spitfire LF.IXe (Merlin 66); TOC/RAF 24.10.44; via No.52 MU and Salford to Russia; Arr Hapmat 8.12.44; Fate unknown
TA880 Spitfire LF.IXe (Merlin 66); TOC/RAF 30.10.44; via No.82 MU and Manchester to Russia; Arr Hapmat 8.12.44; Fate unknown
TA881 Spitfire LF.IXe (Merlin 66); TOC/RAF 27.10.44; via No.82 MU and Manchester to Russia; Arr Hapmat 8.12.44; Fate unknown
TA882 Spitfire LF.IXe (Merlin 66); TOC/RAF 2.11.44; via No.82 MU and Middlesbrough to Russia; Arr Hapmat 8.12.44; Fate unknown
TA883 Spitfire LF.IXe (Merlin 66); TOC/RAF 28.10.44; via No.82 MU and Manchester to Russia; Arr Hapmat 8.12.44; Fate unknown
TA884 Spitfire LF.IXe (Merlin 66); TOC/RAF 27.10.44; via No.82 MU and Manchester to Russia; Arr Hapmat 8.12.44; Fate unknown
TA885 Spitfire LF.IXe (Merlin 66); TOC/RAF 27.10.44; via No.82 MU and Manchester to Russia; Arr Hapmat 8.12.44; Fate unknown
TA886 Spitfire LF.IXe (Merlin 66); TOC/RAF 30.10.44; via No.82 MU and Middlesbrough to Russia; Arr Hapmat 8.12.44; Fate unknown
TA887 Spitfire LF.IXe (Merlin 66); TOC/RAF 30.10.44; via No.52 MU and Salford to Russia; Arr Hapmat 8.12.44; Fate unknown
TA888 Spitfire LF.IXe (Merlin 66); TOC/RAF 2.11.44; via No.82 MU and Middlesbrough to Russia; Arr Hapmat 8.12.44; Fate unknown
TA905 Spitfire LF.IXe (Merlin 66); TOC/RAF 28.10.44; via No.52 MU and Salford to Russia; Arr Hapmat 8.12.44; Fate unknown
TA906 Spitfire LF.IXe (Merlin 66); TOC/RAF 30.10.44; via No.52 MU and Salford to Russia; Arr Hapmat 8.12.44; Fate unknown
TA907 Spitfire LF.IXe (Merlin 66); TOC/RAF 30.10.44; via No.52 MU and Salford to Russia; Arr Hapmat 8.12.44; Fate unknown
TA908 Spitfire LF.IXe (Merlin 66); TOC/RAF 30.10.44; via No.82 MU and Middlesbrough to Russia; Arr Hapmat 8.12.44; Fate unknown
TA909 Spitfire LF.IXe (Merlin 66); TOC/RAF 30.10.44; via No.82 MU and Manchester to Russia; Arr Hapmat 8.12.44; Fate unknown
TA910 Spitfire LF.IXe (Merlin 66); TOC/RAF 4.11.44; via No.52 MU and Salford to Russia; Arr Hapmat 8.12.44; Fate unknown
TA911 Spitfire LF.IXe (Merlin 66); TOC/RAF 9.11.44; via No.52 MU and Manchester to Russia; Arr Hapmat 9.1.45; Fate unknown
TA912 Spitfire LF.IXe (Merlin 66); TOC/RAF 4.11.44; via No.82 MU and Glasgow to Russia; Arr Hapmat 9.1.45; Fate unknown
TA913 Spitfire LF.IXe (Merlin 66); TOC/RAF 1.11.44; via No.82 MU and Middlesbrough to Russia; Arr Hapmat 8.12.44; Fate unknown
TA914 Spitfire LF.IXe (Merlin 66); TOC/RAF 1.11.44; via No.82 MU and Manchester to Russia; Arr Hapmat 8.12.44; Fate unknown
TA915 Spitfire LF.IXe (Merlin 66); TOC/RAF 4.11.44; via No.52 MU and Salford to Russia; Arr Hapmat 8.12.44; Fate unknown
TA916 Spitfire LF.IXe (Merlin 66); TOC/RAF 1.11.44; via No.82 MU and Middlesbrough to Russia; Arr Hapmat 8.12.44; Fate unknown
TA917 Spitfire LF.IXe (Merlin 66); TOC/RAF 7.11.44; via No.82 MU and Birkenhead to Russia; Arr Hapmat 9.1.45; Fate unknown
TA918 Spitfire LF.IXe (Merlin 66); TOC/RAF 4.11.44; via No.52 MU and Salford to Russia; Arr Hapmat 8.12.44; Fate unknown
TA919 Spitfire LF.IXe (Merlin 66); TOC/RAF 4.11.44; via No.52 MU and Salford to Russia; Arr Hapmat 8.12.44; Fate unknown
TA920 Spitfire LF.IXe (Merlin 66); TOC/RAF 19.11.44; via No.82 MU and Middlesbrough to Russia; Arr Hapmat 9.1.45; Fate unknown
TA921 Spitfire LF.IXe (Merlin 66); TOC/RAF 15.11.44; via No.52 MU and Manchester to Russia; Arr Hapmat 9.1.45; Fate unknown
TA922 Spitfire LF.IXe (Merlin 66); TOC/RAF 21.11.44; via No.82 MU and Glasgow to Russia; Arr Hapmat 9.1.45; Fate unknown
TA923 Spitfire LF.IXe (Merlin 66); TOC/RAF 21.11.44; via No.52 MU and Birkenhead to Russia; Arr Hapmat 9.1.45; Fate unknown
TA924 Spitfire LF.IXe (Merlin 66); TOC/RAF 21.11.44; via No.82 MU and Middlesbrough to Russia; Arr Hapmat 9.1.45; Fate unknown
TA925 Spitfire LF.IXe (Merlin 66); TOC/RAF 21.11.44; via No.52 MU and Birkenhead to Russia; Arr Hapmat 9.1.45; Fate unknown

TA926 Spitfire LF.IXe (Merlin 66); TOC/RAF 21.11.44; via No.52 MU and Birkenhead to Russia; Arr Hapmat 9.1.45; Fate unknown

TA927 Spitfire LF.IXe (Merlin 66); TOC/RAF 21.11.44; via No.82 MU and Manchester to Russia; Arr Hapmat 9.1.45; Fate unknown

TA928 Spitfire LF.IXe (Merlin 66); TOC/RAF 21.11.44; via No.82 MU and Glasgow to Russia; Arr Hapmat 9.1.45; Fate unknown

TA929 Spitfire LF.IXe (Merlin 66); TOC/RAF 21.11.44; via No.52 MU and Birkenhead to Russia; Arr Hapmat 9.1.45; Fate unknown

TA930 Spitfire LF.IXe (Merlin 66); TOC/RAF 28.11.44; via No.82 MU and Middlesbrough to Russia; Arr Hapmat 9.1.45; Fate unknown

TA931 Spitfire LF.IXe (Merlin 66); TOC/RAF 28.11.44; via No.82 MU and Middlesbrough to Russia; Arr Hapmat 9.1.45; Fate unknown

TA932 Spitfire LF.IXe (Merlin 66); TOC/RAF 21.11.44; via No.82 MU and Manchester to Russia; Arr Hapmat 9.1.45; Fate unknown

TA933 Spitfire LF.IXe (Merlin 66); TOC/RAF 21.11.44; via No.82 MU and Glasgow to Russia; Arr Hapmat 9.1.45; Fate unknown

TA934 Spitfire LF.IXe (Merlin 66); TOC/RAF 23.11.44; via No.52 MU and Birkenhead to Russia; Arr Hapmat 9.1.45; Fate unknown

TA935 Spitfire LF.IXe (Merlin 66); TOC/RAF 28.11.44; via No.82 MU and Manchester to Russia; Arr Hapmat 9.1.45; Fate unknown

TA936 Spitfire LF.IXe (Merlin 66); TOC/RAF 6.12.44; via No.52 MU and Manchester to Russia; Arr Hapmat 13.2.45; Fate unknown

TA937 Spitfire LF.IXe (Merlin 66); TOC/RAF 30.11.44; via No.82 MU and Manchester to Russia; Arr Hapmat 9.1.45; Fate unknown

TA938 Spitfire LF.IXe (Merlin 66); TOC/RAF 6.12.44; via No.52 MU and Manchester to Russia; Arr Hapmat 13.2.45; Fate unknown

TA939 Spitfire LF.IXe (Merlin 66); TOC/RAF 7.12.44; via No.82 MU and Salford to Russia; Arr Hapmat 13.2.45; Fate unknown

TA940 Spitfire LF.IXe (Merlin 66); TOC/RAF 30.11.44; via No.52 MU and Newport to Russia; Arr Hapmat 9.1.45; Fate unknown

TA941 Spitfire LF.IXe (Merlin 66); TOC/RAF 30.11.44; via No.82 MU and Glasgow to Russia; Arr Hapmat 9.1.45; Fate unknown

TA943 Spitfire LF.IXe (Merlin 66); TOC/RAF 7.12.44; via No.82 MU and Salford to Russia; Arr Hapmat 13.2.45; Fate unknown

TA944 Spitfire LF.IXe (Merlin 66); TOC/RAF 2.12.44; via No.82 MU and Manchester to Russia; Arr Hapmat 20.3.45; Fate unknown

TA945 Spitfire LF.IXe (Merlin 66); TOC/RAF 2.12.44; via No.82 MU and Salford to Russia; Arr Hapmat 13.2.45; Fate unknown

TA946 Spitfire LF.IXe (Merlin 66); TOC/RAF 2.12.44; via No.82 MU and Salford to Russia; Arr Hapmat 13.2.45; Fate unknown

TA947 Spitfire LF.IXe (Merlin 66); TOC/RAF 4.12.44; via No.52 MU and Manchester to Russia; Arr Hapmat 13.2.45; Fate unknown

TA948 Spitfire LF.IXe (Merlin 66); TOC/RAF 11.12.44; via No.82 MU and Salford to Russia; Arr Hapmat 13.2.45; Fate unknown

TA960 Spitfire LF.IXe (Merlin 66); TOC/RAF 7.12.44; via No.82 MU and Birkenhead to Russia; Arr Hapmat 13.2.45; Fate unknown

TA961 Spitfire LF.IXe (Merlin 66); TOC/RAF 18.12.44; via No.82 MU and Manchester to Russia; Arr Hapmat 13.2.45; Fate unknown

TA962 Spitfire LF.IXe (Merlin 66); TOC/RAF 18.12.44; via No.82 MU and Salford to Russia; Arr Hapmat 13.2.45; Fate unknown

TA963 Spitfire LF.IXe (Merlin 66); TOC/RAF 9.12.44; via No.82 MU and Salford to Russia; Arr Hapmat 13.2.45; Fate unknown

TA964 Spitfire LF.IXe (Merlin 66); TOC/RAF 11.12.44; via No.82 MU and Salford to Russia; Arr Hapmat 13.2.45; Fate unknown

TA965 Spitfire LF.IXe (Merlin 66); TOC/RAF 18.12.44; via No.82 MU and Birkenhead to Russia; Arr Hapmat 13.2.45; Fate unknown

TA966 Spitfire LF.IXe (Merlin 66); TOC/RAF 7.2.45; via No.82 MU and Middlesbrough to Murmansk; Arr Russia 25.4.45; Fate unknown

TA967 Spitfire LF.IXe (Merlin 66); TOC/RAF 11.12.44; via No.82 MU and Salford to Russia; Arr Hapmat 13.2.45; Fate unknown

TA968 Spitfire LF.IXe (Merlin 66); TOC/RAF 7.12.44; via No.82 MU and Manchester to Russia; Arr Hapmat 20.3.45; Fate unknown

TA969 Spitfire LF.IXe (Merlin 66); TOC/RAF 31.12.44; via No.82 MU and Manchester to Russia; Arr Hapmat 20.3.45; Fate unknown

TA970 Spitfire LF.IXe (Merlin 66); TOC/RAF 11.12.44; via No.52 MU and Manchester to Russia; Arr Hapmat 13.2.45; Fate unknown

TA971 Spitfire LF.IXe (Merlin 66); TOC/RAF 2.11.44; via No.82 MU and Manchester to Russia; Arr Hapmat 8.12.44; Fate unknown

TA972 Spitfire LF.IXe (Merlin 66); TOC/RAF 6.11.44; via No.52 MU and Salford to Russia; Arr Hapmat 9.1.45; Fate unknown

TA973 Spitfire LF.IXe (Merlin 66); TOC/RAF 6.11.44; via No.82 MU and Glasgow to Russia; Arr Hapmat 9.1.45; Fate unknown

TA974 Spitfire LF.IXe (Merlin 66); TOC/RAF 16.11.44; via No.52 MU and Manchester to Russia; Arr Hapmat 9.1.45; Fate unknown

TA975 Spitfire LF.IXe (Merlin 66); TOC/RAF 9.12.44; via No.82 MU and Manchester to Murmansk; Arr Russia 25.4.45; Fate unknown

TA976 Spitfire LF.IXe (Merlin 66); TOC/RAF 16.11.44; via No.52 MU and Manchester to Russia; Arr Hapmat 9.1.45; Fate unknown

TA977 Spitfire LF.IXe (Merlin 66); TOC/RAF 25.11.44; via No.82 MU and Middlesbrough to Russia; Arr Hapmat 9.1.45; Fate unknown

TA978 Spitfire LF.IXe (Merlin 66); TOC/RAF 23.11.44; via No.52 MU and Birkenhead to Russia; Arr Hapmat 9.1.45; Fate unknown

TA979 Spitfire LF.IXe (Merlin 66); TOC/RAF 24.11.44; via No.82 MU and Manchester to Russia; Arr Hapmat 9.1.45; Fate unknown

TA980 Spitfire LF.IXe (Merlin 66); TOC/RAF 20.11.44; via No.52 MU and Birkenhead to Russia; Arr Hapmat 9.1.45; Fate unknown

TA981 Spitfire LF.IXe (Merlin 66); TOC/RAF 23.11.44; via No.52 MU and Birkenhead to Russia; Arr Hapmat 9.1.45; Fate unknown

TA982 Spitfire LF.IXe (Merlin 66); TOC/RAF 23.11.44; via No.52 MU and Birkenhead to Russia; Arr Hapmat 9.1.45; Fate unknown

TA983 Spitfire LF.IXe (Merlin 66); TOC/RAF 23.11.44; via No.52 MU and Birkenhead to Russia; Arr Hapmat 9.1.45; Fate unknown

TA984 Spitfire LF.IXe (Merlin 66); TOC/RAF 23.11.44; via No.52 MU and Newport to Russia; Arr Hapmat 9.1.45; Fate unknown

TA985 Spitfire LF.IXe (Merlin 66); TOC/RAF 1.12.44; via No.82 MU and Salford to Russia; Arr Hapmat 13.2.45; Fate unknown

TA986 Spitfire LF.IXe (Merlin 66); TOC/RAF 24.11.44; via No.82 MU and Manchester to Russia; Arr Hapmat 9.1.45; Fate unknown

TA987 Spitfire LF.IXe (Merlin 66); TOC/RAF 29.11.44; via No.52 MU and Newport to Russia; Arr Hapmat 9.1.45; Fate unknown

TA988 Spitfire LF.IXe (Merlin 66); TOC/RAF 1.12.44; via No.82 MU and Manchester to Russia; Arr Hapmat 9.1.45; Fate unknown

TA989 Spitfire LF.IXe (Merlin 66); TOC/RAF 2.12.44; via No.82 MU and Manchester to Russia; Arr Hapmat 20.3.45; Fate unknown

TA990 Spitfire LF.IXe (Merlin 66); TOC/RAF 29.11.44; via No.82 MU and Manchester to Russia; Arr Hapmat 9.1.45; Fate unknown

TA991 Spitfire LF.IXe (Merlin 66); TOC/RAF 29.11.44; via No.82 MU and Glasgow to Russia; Arr Hapmat 9.1.45; Fate unknown

TA992 Spitfire LF.IXe (Merlin 66); TOC/RAF 2.12.44; via No.82 MU and Manchester to Russia; Arr Hapmat 20.3.45; Fate unknown

TA993 Spitfire LF.IXe (Merlin 66); TOC/RAF 1.12.44; via No.52 MU and Southport to Russia; Arr Hapmat 9.1.45; Fate unknown

TA994 Spitfire LF.IXe (Merlin 66); TOC/RAF 2.12.44; via No.82 MU and Southport to Murmansk; Arr Russia 25.4.45; Fate unknown

TA995 Spitfire LF.IXe (Merlin 66); TOC/RAF 18.12.44; via No.82 MU and Birkenhead to Russia; Arr Hapmat 13.2.45; Fate unknown

TA996 Spitfire LF.IXe (Merlin 66); TOC/RAF 3.1.45; via No.82 MU and Manchester to Russia; Arr Hapmat 20.3.45; Fate unknown

TA997 Spitfire LF.IXe (Merlin 66); TOC/RAF 4.1.45; via No.82 MU and Manchester to Russia; Arr Hapmat 20.3.45; Fate unknown

TA998 Spitfire LF.IXe (Merlin 66); TOC/RAF 18.12.44; via No.82 MU and Birkenhead to Russia; Arr Hapmat 13.2.45; Fate unknown

TA999 Spitfire LF.IXe (Merlin 66); TOC/RAF 3.1.45; via No.82 MU and Middlesbrough to Russia; Arr Hapmat 20.3.45; Fate unknown

TB115 Spitfire LF.IXe (Merlin 66); TOC/RAF 4.1.45; via No.82 MU and Manchester to Russia; Arr Hapmat 20.3.45; Fate unknown

TB116 Spitfire LF.IXe (Merlin 66); TOC/RAF 31.12.44; via No.82 MU and Manchester to Russia; Arr Hapmat 13.2.45; Fate unknown

TB117 Spitfire LF.IXe (Merlin 66); TOC/RAF 31.12.44; via No.82 MU and Birkenhead to Russia; Arr Hapmat 13.2.45; Fate unknown

TB118 Spitfire LF.IXe (Merlin 66); TOC/RAF 31.12.44; via No.82 MU and Birkenhead to Russia; Arr Hapmat 13.2.45; Fate unknown

TB119 Spitfire LF.IXe (Merlin 66); TOC/RAF 17.12.44; via No.82 MU and Middlesbrough to Russia; Arr Hapmat 20.3.45; Fate unknown

TB120 Spitfire LF.IXe (Merlin 66); TOC/RAF 31.12.44; via No.82 MU and Middlesbrough to Russia; Arr Hapmat 20.3.45; Fate unknown

TB121 Spitfire LF.IXe (Merlin 66); TOC/RAF 17.12.44; via No.52 MU and Manchester to Russia; Arr Hapmat 13.2.45; Fate unknown

TB122 Spitfire LF.IXe (Merlin 66); TOC/RAF 4.1.45; via No.82 MU and Middlesbrough to Russia; Arr Hapmat 20.3.45; Fate unknown

TB123 Spitfire LF.IXe (Merlin 66); TOC/RAF 4.1.45; via No.82 MU and Manchester to Russia; Arr Hapmat 20.3.45; Fate unknown

TB124 Spitfire LF.IXe (Merlin 66); TOC/RAF 31.12.44; via No.82 MU and Birkenhead to Russia; Arr Hapmat 13.2.45; Fate unknown

TB125 Spitfire LF.IXe (Merlin 66); TOC/RAF 12.1.45; via No.82 MU and Manchester to Russia; Arr Hapmat 20.3.45; Fate unknown

TB126 Spitfire LF.IXe (Merlin 66); TOC/RAF 5.1.45; via No.82 MU and Southport to Russia; Arr Hapmat 20.3.45; Fate unknown

TB127 Spitfire LF.IXe (Merlin 66); TOC/RAF 6.1.45; via No.82 MU and Manchester to Russia; Arr Hapmat 20.3.45; Fate unknown

TB128 Spitfire LF.IXe (Merlin 66); TOC/RAF 6.1.45; via No.82 MU and Manchester to Russia; Arr Hapmat 20.3.45; Fate unknown

TB129 Spitfire LF.IXe (Merlin 66); TOC/RAF 4.1.45; via No.82 MU and Middlesbrough to Russia; Arr Hapmat 20.3.45; Fate unknown

TB133 Spitfire LF.IXe (Merlin 66); TOC/RAF 22.1.45; via No.82 MU and Manchester to Murmansk; Arr Russia 25.4.45; Fate unknown

TB134 Spitfire LF.IXe (Merlin 66); TOC/RAF 17.1.45; via No.82 MU and Manchester to Russia; Arr Hapmat 20.3.45; Fate unknown

TB135 Spitfire LF.IXe (Merlin 66); TOC/RAF 17.1.45; via No.82 MU and Middlesbrough to Russia; Arr Hapmat 20.3.45; Fate unknown

TB142 Spitfire LF.IXe (Merlin 66); TOC/RAF 17.1.45; via No.82 MU and Manchester to Russia; Arr Hapmat 20.3.45; Fate unknown

TB143 Spitfire LF.IXe (Merlin 66); TOC/RAF 17.1.45; via No.82 MU and Middlesbrough to Russia; Arr Hapmat 20.3.45; Fate unknown

TB144 Spitfire LF.IXe (Merlin 66); TOC/RAF 22.1.45; via No.82 MU and Manchester to Russia; Arr Hapmat 20.3.45; Fate unknown

TB145 Spitfire LF.IXe (Merlin 66); TOC/RAF 7.2.45; via No.82 MU and Southport to Murmansk; Arr Russia 25.4.45; Fate unknown

TB146 Spitfire LF.IXe (Merlin 66); TOC/RAF 7.2.45; via No.82 MU and Manchester to Murmansk; Arr Russia 25.4.45; Fate unknown

TB147 Spitfire LF.IXe (Merlin 66); TOC/RAF 7.2.45; via No.82 MU and Middlesbrough to Murmansk; Arr Russia 25.4.45; Fate unknown

TB148 Spitfire LF.IXe (Merlin 66); TOC/RAF 7.2.45; via No.82 MU and Middlesbrough to Murmansk; Arr Russia 25.4.45; Fate unknown

TB149 Spitfire LF.IXe (Merlin 66); TOC/RAF 22.1.45; via No.82 MU and Manchester to Russia; Arr Hapmat 20.3.45; Fate unknown

TB150 Spitfire LF.IXe (Merlin 66); TOC/RAF 7.2.45; via No.82 MU and Manchester to Murmansk; Arr Russia 22.5.45; Fate unknown

TB168 Spitfire LF.IXe (Merlin 66); TOC/RAF 17.12.44; via No.82 MU and Southport to Russia; Arr Hapmat 20.3.45; Fate unknown

TB169 Spitfire LF.IXe (Merlin 66); TOC/RAF 17.12.44; via No.82 MU and Manchester to Russia; Arr Hapmat 20.3.45; Fate unknown

TB170 Spitfire LF.IXe (Merlin 66); TOC/RAF 17.12.44; via No.82 MU and Manchester to Russia; Arr Hapmat 20.3.45; Fate unknown

TB171 Spitfire LF.IXe (Merlin 66); TOC/RAF 17.12.44; via No.82 MU and Salford to Russia; Arr Hapmat 13.2.45; Fate unknown

TB172 Spitfire LF.IXe (Merlin 66); TOC/RAF 17.12.44; via No.82 MU and Southport to Russia; Arr Hapmat 20.3.45; Fate unknown

TB173 Spitfire LF.IXe (Merlin 66); TOC/RAF 17.12.44; via No.82 MU and Southport to Russia; Arr Hapmat 20.3.45; Fate unknown

TB174 Spitfire LF.IXe (Merlin 66); TOC/RAF 17.12.44; via No.82 MU and Birkenhead to Russia; Arr Hapmat 13.2.45; Fate unknown

TB175 Spitfire LF.IXe (Merlin 66); TOC/RAF 4.1.45; via No.82 MU and Middlesbrough to Russia; Arr Hapmat 20.3.45; Fate unknown

TB176 Spitfire LF.IXe (Merlin 66); TOC/RAF 17.12.44; via No.82 MU and Southport to Russia; Arr Hapmat 20.3.45; Fate unknown

TB177 Spitfire LF.IXe (Merlin 66); TOC/RAF 17.12.44; via No.82 MU and Middlesbrough to Russia; Arr Hapmat 20.3.45; Fate unknown

TB178 Spitfire LF.IXe (Merlin 66); TOC/RAF 17.12.44; via No.82 MU and Manchester to Russia; Arr Hapmat 20.3.45; Fate unknown

TB179 Spitfire LF.IXe (Merlin 66); TOC/RAF 18.12.44; via No.52 MU and Manchester to Russia; Arr Hapmat 13.2.45; Fate unknown
TB180 Spitfire LF.IXe (Merlin 66); TOC/RAF 31.12.44; via No.82 MU and Southport to Russia; Arr Hapmat 20.3.45; Fate unknown
TB181 Spitfire LF.IXe (Merlin 66); TOC/RAF 17.12.44; via No.82 MU and Manchester to Russia; Arr Hapmat 20.3.45; Fate unknown
TB182 Spitfire LF.IXe (Merlin 66); TOC/RAF 17.12.44; via No.82 MU and Southport to Russia; Arr Hapmat 20.3.45; Fate unknown
TB183 Spitfire LF.IXe (Merlin 66); TOC/RAF 17.12.44; via No.82 MU and Manchester to Russia; Arr Hapmat 20.3.45; Fate unknown
TB184 Spitfire LF.IXe (Merlin 66); TOC/RAF 18.12.44; via No.82 MU and Salford to Russia; Arr Hapmat 13.2.45; Fate unknown
TB185 Spitfire LF.IXe (Merlin 66); TOC/RAF 3.1.45; via No.82 MU and Manchester to Russia; Arr Hapmat 20.3.45; Fate unknown
TB186 Spitfire LF.IXe (Merlin 66); TOC/RAF 18.12.44; via No.52 MU and Manchester to Russia; Arr Hapmat 13.2.45; Fate unknown
TB187 Spitfire LF.IXe (Merlin 66); TOC/RAF 31.12.44; via No.82 MU and Salford to Russia; Arr Hapmat 13.2.45; Fate unknown
TB189 Spitfire LF.IXe (Merlin 66); TOC/RAF 3.1.45; via No.82 MU and Middlesbrough to Russia; Arr Hapmat 20.3.45; Fate unknown
TB190 Spitfire LF.IXe (Merlin 66); TOC/RAF 4.1.45; via No.82 MU and Manchester to Russia; Arr Hapmat 20.3.45; Fate unknown
TB191 Spitfire LF.IXe (Merlin 66); TOC/RAF 21.1.45; via No.82 MU and Southport to Murmansk; Arr Russia 25.4.45; Fate unknown
TB192 Spitfire LF.IXe (Merlin 66); TOC/RAF 3.1.45; via No.82 MU and Middlesbrough to Russia; Arr Hapmat 20.3.45; Fate unknown
TB193 Spitfire LF.IXe (Merlin 66); TOC/RAF 17.12.44; via No.82 MU and Salford to Russia; Arr Hapmat 13.2.45; Fate unknown
TB195 Spitfire LF.IXe (Merlin 66); TOC/RAF 31.12.44; via No.82 MU and Salford to Russia; Arr Hapmat 13.2.45; Fate unknown
TB196 Spitfire LF.IXe (Merlin 66); TOC/RAF 31.12.44; via No.82 MU and Middlesbrough to Russia; Arr Hapmat 20.3.45; Fate unknown
TB213 Spitfire LF.IXe (Merlin 66); TOC/RAF 4.1.45; via No.82 MU and Middlesbrough to Russia; Arr Hapmat 20.3.45; Fate unknown
TB214 Spitfire LF.IXe (Merlin 66); TOC/RAF 18.12.44; via No.82 MU and Salford to Russia; Arr Hapmat 13.2.45; Fate unknown
TB215 Spitfire LF.IXe (Merlin 66); TOC/RAF 3.1.45; via No.82 MU and Middlesbrough to Russia; Arr Hapmat 20.3.45; Fate unknown
TB216 Spitfire LF.IXe (Merlin 66); TOC/RAF 17.12.44; via No.82 MU and Salford to Russia; Arr Hapmat 13.2.45; Fate unknown
TB217 Spitfire LF.IXe (Merlin 66); TOC/RAF 3.1.45; via No.82 MU and Manchester to Russia; Arr Hapmat 20.3.45; Fate unknown
TB218 Spitfire LF.IXe (Merlin 66); TOC/RAF 18.12.44; via No.82 MU and Salford to Russia; Arr Hapmat 13.2.45; Fate unknown
TB219 Spitfire LF.IXe (Merlin 66); TOC/RAF 18.12.44; via No.82 MU and Manchester to Russia; Arr Hapmat 13.2.45; Fate unknown
TB220 Spitfire LF.IXe (Merlin 66); TOC/RAF 17.12.44; via No.82 MU and Birkenhead to Russia; Arr Hapmat 13.2.45; Fate unknown
TB221 Spitfire LF.IXe (Merlin 66); TOC/RAF 18.12.44; via No.82 MU and Birkenhead to Russia; Arr Hapmat 13.2.45; Fate unknown
TB222 Spitfire LF.IXe (Merlin 66); TOC/RAF 31.12.44; via No.82 MU and Middlesbrough to Russia; Arr Hapmat 20.3.45; Fate unknown
TB223 Spitfire LF.IXe (Merlin 66); TOC/RAF 18.12.44; via No.82 MU and Salford to Russia; Arr Hapmat 13.2.45; Fate unknown
TB224 Spitfire LF.IXe (Merlin 66); TOC/RAF 3.1.45; via No.82 MU and Manchester to Russia; Arr Hapmat 20.3.45; Fate unknown
TB225 Spitfire LF.IXe (Merlin 66); TOC/RAF 18.12.44; via No.82 MU and Middlesbrough to Russia; Arr Hapmat 20.3.45; Fate unknown
TB226 Spitfire LF.IXe (Merlin 66); TOC/RAF 3.1.45; via No.82 MU and Manchester to Russia; Arr Hapmat 20.3.45; Fate unknown
TB227 Spitfire LF.IXe (Merlin 66); TOC/RAF 8.1.45; via No.82 MU and Southport to Russia; Arr Hapmat 20.3.45; Fate unknown
TB228 Spitfire LF.IXe (Merlin 66); TOC/RAF 3.1.45; via No.82 MU and Manchester to Russia; Arr Hapmat 20.3.45; Fate unknown
TB229 Spitfire LF.IXe (Merlin 66); TOC/RAF 3.1.45; via No.82 MU and Manchester to Russia; Arr Hapmat 20.3.45; Fate unknown
TB230 Spitfire LF.IXe (Merlin 66); TOC/RAF 31.12.44; via No.82 MU and Southport to Russia; Arr Hapmat 20.3.45; Fate unknown
TB231 Spitfire LF.IXe (Merlin 66); TOC/RAF 4.1.45; via No.82 MU and Manchester to Russia; Arr Hapmat 20.3.45; Fate unknown
TB233 Spitfire LF.IXe (Merlin 66); TOC/RAF 4.1.45; via No.82 MU to Murmansk; Arr Russia 20.3.45; Fate unknown
TB234 Spitfire LF.IXe (Merlin 66); TOC/RAF 3.1.45; via No.82 MU and Manchester to Russia; Arr Hapmat 20.3.45; Fate unknown
TB235 Spitfire LF.IXe (Merlin 66); TOC/RAF 31.12.44; via No.82 MU and Middlesbrough to Russia; Arr Hapmat 20.3.45; Fate unknown
TB236 Spitfire LF.IXe (Merlin 66); TOC/RAF 8.1.45; via No.82 MU and Salford to Russia; Arr Hapmat 13.2.45; Fate unknown
TB238 Spitfire LF.IXe (Merlin 66); TOC/RAF 4.1.45; via No.82 MU and Manchester to Russia; Arr Hapmat 20.3.45; No.178 IAP.PVO, Air Defence Moscow; Fate unknown
TB239 Spitfire LF.IXe (Merlin 66); TOC/RAF 31.12.44; via No.82 MU and Middlesbrough to Russia; Arr Hapmat 20.3.45; Fate unknown
TB240 Spitfire LF.IXe (Merlin 66); TOC/RAF 17.1.45; via No.82 MU and Manchester to Russia; Arr Hapmat 20.3.45; Fate unknown
TB242 Spitfire LF.IXe (Merlin 66); TOC/RAF 31.12.44; via No.82 MU and Manchester to Russia; Arr Hapmat 20.3.45; Fate unknown
TB243 Spitfire LF.IXe (Merlin 66); TOC/RAF 18.12.44; via No.82 MU and Birkenhead to Russia; Arr Hapmat 13.2.45; Fate unknown
TB249 Spitfire LF.IXe (Merlin 66); TOC/RAF 31.12.44; via No.82 MU and Salford to Russia; Arr Hapmat 13.2.45; Fate unknown
TB251 Spitfire LF.IXe (Merlin 66); TOC/RAF 3.1.45; via No.82 MU and Manchester to Russia; Arr Hapmat 20.3.45; Fate unknown
TB253 Spitfire LF.IXe (Merlin 66); TOC/RAF 4.1.45; via No.82 MU and Middlesbrough to Russia; Arr Hapmat 20.3.45; Fate unknown
TB393 Spitfire LF.IXe (Merlin 66); TOC/RAF 28.1.45; via No.82 MU and Middlesbrough to Murmansk; Arr Russia 25.4.45; Fate unknown
TB413 Spitfire LF.IXe (Merlin 66); TOC/RAF 20.12.44; via No.82 MU and Salford to Russia; Arr Hapmat 13.2.45; Fate unknown
TB414 Spitfire LF.IXe (Merlin 66); TOC/RAF 5.12.44; via No.82 MU and Manchester to Russia; Arr Hapmat 13.2.45; Fate unknown

TB415 Spitfire LF.IXe (Merlin 66); TOC/RAF 1.12.44; via No.82 MU and Birkenhead to Russia; Arr Hapmat 13.2.45; Fate unknown

TB416 Spitfire LF.IXe (Merlin 66); TOC/RAF 2.12.44; via No.82 MU and Salford to Russia; Arr Hapmat 13.2.45; Fate unknown

TB417 Spitfire LF.IXe (Merlin 66); TOC/RAF 6.12.44; via No.82 MU and Manchester to Russia; Arr Hapmat 20.3.45; Fate unknown

TB418 Spitfire LF.IXe (Merlin 66); TOC/RAF 8.12.44; via No.82 MU and Birkenhead to Russia; Arr Hapmat 13.2.45; Fate unknown

TB419 Spitfire LF.IXe (Merlin 66); TOC/RAF 8.12.44; via No.82 MU and Birkenhead to Russia; Arr Hapmat 13.2.45; Fate unknown

TB420 Spitfire LF.IXe (Merlin 66); TOC/RAF 4.1.45; via No.82 MU and Manchester to Russia; Arr Hapmat 20.3.45; No.480 IAP.PVO; Fate unknown
NOTE: Incorrectly reported as "TB402"

TB421 Spitfire LF.IXe (Merlin 66); TOC/RAF 11.12.44; via No.52 MU and Manchester to Russia; Arr Hapmat 13.2.45; Fate unknown

TB422 Spitfire LF.IXe (Merlin 66); TOC/RAF 9.12.44; via No.82 MU and Birkenhead to Russia; Arr Hapmat 13.2.45; Fate unknown

TB423 Spitfire LF.IXe (Merlin 66); TOC/RAF 8.1.45; via No.82 MU and Manchester to Russia; Arr Hapmat 20.3.45; Fate unknown

TB424 Spitfire LF.IXe (Merlin 66); TOC/RAF 11.12.44; via No.52 MU and Manchester to Russia; Arr Hapmat 13.2.45; Fate unknown

TB425 Spitfire LF.IXe (Merlin 66); TOC/RAF 12.12.44; via No.82 MU and Salford to Russia; Arr Hapmat 13.2.45; Fate unknown

TB426 Spitfire LF.IXe (Merlin 66); TOC/RAF 18.12.44; via No.52 MU and Manchester to Russia; Arr Hapmat 13.2.45; Fate unknown

TB427 Spitfire LF.IXe (Merlin 66); TOC/RAF 31.12.44; via No.82 MU and Southport to Russia; Arr Hapmat 20.3.45; Fate unknown

TB428 Spitfire LF.IXe (Merlin 66); TOC/RAF 30.12.44; via No.82 MU and Southport to Russia; Arr Hapmat 20.3.45; Fate unknown

TB429 Spitfire LF.IXe (Merlin 66); TOC/RAF 30.12.44; via No.82 MU and Southport to Russia; Arr Hapmat 20.3.45; Fate unknown

TB430 Spitfire LF.IXe (Merlin 66); TOC/RAF 30.12.44; via No.82 MU and Salford to Russia; Arr Hapmat 13.2.45; Fate unknown

TB431 Spitfire LF.IXe (Merlin 66); TOC/RAF 30.12.44; via No.82 MU and Middlesbrough to Russia; Arr Hapmat 20.3.45; Fate unknown

TB432 Spitfire LF.IXe (Merlin 66); TOC/RAF 4.1.45; via No.82 MU and Southport to Russia; Arr Hapmat 20.3.45; Fate unknown

TB433 Spitfire LF.IXe (Merlin 66); TOC/RAF 31.12.44; via No.82 MU and Manchester to Russia; Arr Hapmat 20.3.45; Fate unknown

TB434 Spitfire LF.IXe (Merlin 66); TOC/RAF 1.1.45; via No.82 MU and Southport to Russia; Arr Hapmat 20.3.45; Fate unknown

TB435 Spitfire LF.IXe (Merlin 66); TOC/RAF 4.1.45; via No.82 MU and Manchester to Russia; Arr Hapmat 20.3.45; Fate unknown

TB436 Spitfire LF.IXe (Merlin 66); TOC/RAF 4.1.45; via No.82 MU and Southport to Russia; Arr Hapmat 20.3.45; Fate unknown

TB437 Spitfire LF.IXe (Merlin 66); TOC/RAF 5.1.45; via No.82 MU and Middlesbrough to Russia; Arr Hapmat 20.3.45; Fate unknown

TB438 Spitfire LF.IXe (Merlin 66); TOC/RAF 2.1.45; via No.82 MU and Middlesbrough to Russia; Arr Hapmat 20.3.45; Fate unknown

TB440 Spitfire LF.IXe (Merlin 66); TOC/RAF 20.1.45; via No.82 MU and Manchester to Russia; Arr Hapmat 20.3.45; Fate unknown

TB441 Spitfire LF.IXe (Merlin 66); TOC/RAF 20.1.45; via No.82 MU and Manchester to Russia; Arr Hapmat 20.3.45; Fate unknown

TB442 Spitfire LF.IXe (Merlin 66); TOC/RAF 5.1.45; via No.82 MU and Manchester to Russia; Arr Hapmat 20.3.45; Fate unknown

TB443 Spitfire LF.IXe (Merlin 66); TOC/RAF 7.2.45; via No.82 MU and Middlesbrough to Murmansk; Arr Russia 25.4.45; Fate unknown

TB444 Spitfire LF.IXe (Merlin 66); TOC/RAF 7.2.45; via No.82 MU and Middlesbrough to Murmansk; Arr Russia 25.4.45; Fate unknown

TB445 Spitfire LF.IXe (Merlin 66); TOC/RAF 10.2.45; via No.52 MU and Southport to Murmansk; Arr Russia 22.5.45; Fate unknown

TB446 Spitfire LF.IXe (Merlin 66); TOC/RAF 9.2.45; via No.82 MU and Middlesbrough to Murmansk; Arr Russia 25.4.45; Fate unknown

TB447 Spitfire LF.IXe (Merlin 66); TOC/RAF 7.2.45; via No.52 MU and Southport to Murmansk; Arr Russia 25.4.45; Fate unknown

TB448 Spitfire LF.IXe (Merlin 66); TOC/RAF 19.2.45; via No.52 MU and Middlesbrough to Murmansk; Arr Russia 22.5.45; Fate unknown

TB449 Spitfire LF.IXe (Merlin 66); TOC/RAF 9.2.45; via No.82 MU and Manchester to Murmansk; Arr Russia 25.4.45; Fate unknown

TB450 Spitfire LF.IXe (Merlin 66); TOC/RAF 9.2.45; via No.82 MU and Middlesbrough to Murmansk; Arr Russia 25.4.45; Fate unknown

TB464 Spitfire LF.IXe (Merlin 66); TOC/RAF 7.2.45; via No.52 MU and Southport to Murmansk; Arr Russia 25.4.45; Fate unknown

TB465 Spitfire LF.IXe (Merlin 66); TOC/RAF 20.2.45; via No.82 MU and Manchester to Murmansk; Arr Russia 25.4.45; Fate unknown

TB466 Spitfire LF.IXe (Merlin 66); TOC/RAF 19.2.45; via No.52 MU and Middlesbrough to Murmansk; Arr Russia 22.5.45; Fate unknown

TB467 Spitfire LF.IXe (Merlin 66); TOC/RAF 20.2.45; via No.82 MU and Middlesbrough to Murmansk; Arr Russia 25.4.45; Fate unknown

TB468 Spitfire LF.IXe (Merlin 66); TOC/RAF 9.2.45; via No.82 MU and Middlesbrough to Murmansk; Arr Russia 25.4.45; Fate unknown

TB469 Spitfire LF.IXe (Merlin 66); TOC/RAF 9.2.45; via No.82 MU and Manchester to Murmansk; Arr Russia 25.4.45; Fate unknown

TB470 Spitfire LF.IXe (Merlin 66); TOC/RAF 9.2.45; via No.82 MU and Manchester to Murmansk; Arr Russia 25.4.45; Fate unknown

TB471 Spitfire LF.IXe (Merlin 66); TOC/RAF 10.2.45; via No.52 MU and Middlesbrough to Murmansk; Arr Russia 22.5.45; Fate unknown

TB472 Spitfire LF.IXe (Merlin 66); TOC/RAF 10.2.45; via No.82 MU and Manchester to Murmansk; Arr Russia 22.5.45; Fate unknown

TB473 Spitfire LF.IXe (Merlin 66); TOC/RAF 9.2.45; via No.82 MU and Middlesbrough to Murmansk; Arr Russia 25.4.45; Fate unknown

TB474 Spitfire LF.IXe (Merlin 66); TOC/RAF 20.2.45; via No.82 MU and Middlesbrough to Murmansk; Arr Russia 25.4.45; Fate unknown

TB477 Spitfire LF.IXe (Merlin 66); TOC/RAF 19.2.45; via No.82 MU and Manchester to Murmansk; Arr Russia 25.4.45; Fate unknown

TB479 Spitfire LF.IXe (Merlin 66); TOC/RAF 19.2.45; via No.82 MU and Middlesbrough to Murmansk; Arr Russia 25.4.45; Fate unknown

TB482 Spitfire LF.IXe (Merlin 66); TOC/RAF 20.2.45; via No.82 MU and Manchester to Murmansk; Arr Russia 25.4.45; Fate unknown

The wreckage of a Spitfire coded '18' crashed among trees. [Russian Aviation Research Group]

TB483 Spitfire LF.IXe (Merlin 66); TOC/RAF 20.2.45; via No.52 MU and Southport to Murmansk; Arr Russia 25.4.45; Fate unknown

TB484 Spitfire LF.IXe (Merlin 66); TOC/RAF 9.2.45; via No.82 MU and Middlesbrough to Murmansk; Arr Russia 25.4.45; Fate unknown

TB485 Spitfire LF.IXe (Merlin 66); TOC/RAF 19.2.45; via No.82 MU and Manchester to Murmansk; Arr Russia 25.4.45; Fate unknown

TB486 Spitfire LF.IXe (Merlin 66); TOC/RAF 13.2.45; via No.82 MU and Middlesbrough to Murmansk; Arr Russia 22.5.45; Fate unknown

TB487 Spitfire LF.IXe (Merlin 66); TOC/RAF 20.2.45; via No.82 MU and Middlesbrough to Murmansk; Arr Russia 22.5.45; Fate unknown

TB488 Spitfire LF.IXe (Merlin 66); TOC/RAF 21.2.45; via No.82 MU and Manchester to Murmansk; Arr Russia 22.5.45; Fate unknown

TB489 Spitfire LF.IXe (Merlin 66); TOC/RAF 13.2.45; via No.82 MU and Manchester to Murmansk; Arr Russia 22.5.45; Fate unknown

TB490 Spitfire LF.IXe (Merlin 66); TOC/RAF 25.2.45; via No.52 MU and Southport to Murmansk; Arr Russia 25.4.45; Fate unknown

TB491 Spitfire LF.IXe (Merlin 66); TOC/RAF 21.2.45; via No.82 MU and Middlesbrough to Murmansk; Arr Russia 22.5.45; Fate unknown

TB499 Spitfire LF.IXe (Merlin 66); TOC/RAF 28.1.45; via No.82 MU and Manchester to Russia; Arr Hapmat 20.3.45; Fate unknown

TB500 Spitfire LF.IXe (Merlin 66); TOC/RAF 4.2.45; via No.82 MU and Middlesbrough to Murmansk; Arr Russia 25.4.45; Fate unknown

TB503 Spitfire LF.IXe (Merlin 66); TOC/RAF 21.1.45; via No.82 MU and Manchester to Russia; Arr Hapmat 20.3.45; Fate unknown

TB516 Spitfire LF.IXe (Merlin 66); TOC/RAF 22.1.45; via No.82 MU and Manchester to Russia; Arr Hapmat 20.3.45; Fate unknown

TB518 Spitfire LF.IXe (Merlin 66); TOC/RAF 7.3.45; via No.52 MU and Manchester to Molotowsk; Arr Russia 12.6.45; Fate unknown

TB523 Spitfire LF.IXe (Merlin 66); TOC/RAF 28.1.45; via No.82 MU and Manchester to Murmansk; Arr Russia 25.4.45; Fate unknown

TB524 Spitfire LF.IXe (Merlin 66); TOC/RAF 4.2.45; via No.82 MU and Middlesbrough to Russia; Arr Hapmat 20.3.45; Fate unknown

TB527 Spitfire LF.IXe (Merlin 66); TOC/RAF 28.1.45; via No.82 MU and Manchester to Russia; Arr Hapmat 20.3.45; Fate unknown

TB529 Spitfire LF.IXe (Merlin 66); TOC/RAF 28.1.45; via No.82 MU and Manchester to Russia; Arr Hapmat 20.3.45; Fate unknown

TB530 Spitfire LF.IXe (Merlin 66); TOC/RAF 4.2.45; via No.82 MU and Manchester to Murmansk; Arr Russia 25.4.45; Fate unknown

TB531 Spitfire LF.IXe (Merlin 66); TOC/RAF 13.2.45; via No.82 MU and Manchester to Murmansk; Arr Russia 25.4.45; Fate unknown

TB533 Spitfire LF.IXe (Merlin 66); TOC/RAF 10.2.45; via No.82 MU and Manchester to Murmansk; Arr Russia 25.4.45; Fate unknown

TB534 Spitfire LF.IXe (Merlin 66); TOC/RAF 28.1.45; via No.82 MU and Manchester to Murmansk; Arr Russia 25.4.45; Fate unknown

TB535 Spitfire LF.IXe (Merlin 66); TOC/RAF 4.2.45; via No.82 MU and Manchester to Murmansk; Arr Russia 25.4.45; Fate unknown

TB536 Spitfire LF.IXe (Merlin 66); TOC/RAF 28.1.45; via No.82 MU and Manchester to Russia; Arr Hapmat 20.3.45; Fate unknown

TB538 Spitfire LF.IXe (Merlin 66); TOC/RAF 21.1.45; via No.82 MU and Manchester to Russia; Arr Hapmat 20.3.45; Fate unknown

TB541 Spitfire LF.IXe (Merlin 66); TOC/RAF 28.1.45; via No.82 MU and Manchester to Murmansk; Arr Russia 25.4.45; Fate unknown

TB543 Spitfire LF.IXe (Merlin 66); TOC/RAF 9.2.45; via No.82 MU and Middlesbrough to Murmansk; Arr Russia 25.4.45; Fate unknown

TB547 Spitfire LF.IXe (Merlin 66); TOC/RAF 28.1.45; via No.82 MU and Manchester to Murmansk; Arr Russia 25.4.45; Fate unknown

TB563 Spitfire LF.IXe (Merlin 66); TOC/RAF 22.1.45; via No.82 MU and Manchester to Murmansk; Arr Russia 25.4.45; Fate unknown

TB566 Spitfire LF.IXe (Merlin 66); TOC/RAF 22.1.45; via No.82 MU and Manchester to Russia; Arr Hapmat 20.3.45; Fate unknown

TB571 Spitfire LF.IXe (Merlin 66); TOC/RAF 10.2.45; via No.82 MU and Middlesbrough to Murmansk; Arr Russia 25.4.45; Fate unknown

TB573 Spitfire LF.IXe (Merlin 66); TOC/RAF 13.2.45; via No.82 MU and Manchester to Murmansk; Arr Russia 22.5.45; Fate unknown

TB575 Spitfire LF.IXe (Merlin 66); TOC/RAF 10.2.45; via No.52 MU and Southport to Murmansk; Arr Russia 25.4.45; Fate unknown

TB579 Spitfire LF.IXe (Merlin 66); TOC/RAF 28.1.45; via No.82 MU and Manchester to Murmansk; Arr Russia 22.5.45; Fate unknown

TB638 Spitfire LF.IXe (Merlin 66); TOC/RAF 10.2.45; via No.82 MU and Manchester to Murmansk; Arr Russia 25.4.45; Fate unknown

TB640 Spitfire LF.IXe (Merlin 66); TOC/RAF 10.2.45; via No.82 MU and Middlesbrough to Murmansk; Arr Russia 22.5.45; Fate unknown

TB641 Spitfire LF.IXe (Merlin 66); TOC/RAF 9.2.45; via No.82 MU and Middlesbrough to Murmansk; Arr Russia 25.4.45; Fate unknown

TB642 Spitfire LF.IXe (Merlin 66); TOC/RAF 10.2.45; via No.82 MU and Middlesbrough to Murmansk; Arr Russia 25.4.45; Fate unknown

TB643 Spitfire LF.IXe (Merlin 66); TOC/RAF 10.2.45; via No.52 MU and Southport to Murmansk; Arr Russia 22.5.45; Fate unknown

TB644 Spitfire LF.IXe (Merlin 66); TOC/RAF 9.2.45; via No.82 MU and Manchester to Murmansk; Arr Russia 22.5.45; Fate unknown

TB645 Spitfire LF.IXe (Merlin 66); TOC/RAF 10.2.45; via Nos.33 MU & 1 PATP to Murmansk; Arr Russia 22.5.45; Fate unknown

TB646 Spitfire LF.IXe (Merlin 66); TOC/RAF 10.2.45; via No.82 MU and Manchester to Murmansk; Arr Russia 25.4.45; Fate unknown

TB647 Spitfire LF.IXe (Merlin 66); TOC/RAF 14.2.45; via No.52 MU and Southport to Murmansk; Arr Russia 22.5.45; Fate unknown

TB648 Spitfire LF.IXe (Merlin 66); TOC/RAF 9.2.45; via No.82 MU and Manchester to Murmansk; Arr Russia 25.4.45; Fate unknown

TB649 Spitfire LF.IXe (Merlin 66); TOC/RAF 9.2.45; via No.82 MU and Manchester to Murmansk; Arr Russia 25.4.45; Fate unknown

TB650 Spitfire LF.IXe (Merlin 66); TOC/RAF 9.2.45; via No.82 MU and Middlesbrough to Murmansk; Arr Russia 25.4.45; Fate unknown

TB651 Spitfire LF.IXe (Merlin 66); TOC/RAF 10.2.45; via No.82 MU and Manchester to Murmansk; Arr Russia 25.4.45; Fate unknown

TB652 Spitfire LF.IXe (Merlin 66); TOC/RAF 10.2.45; via No.52 MU and Southport to Murmansk; Arr Russia 25.4.45; Fate unknown

TB653 Spitfire LF.IXe (Merlin 66); TOC/RAF 10.2.45; via No.82 MU and Middlesbrough to Murmansk; Arr Russia 25.4.45; Fate unknown

TB654 Spitfire LF.IXe (Merlin 66); TOC/RAF 13.2.45; via No.82 MU and Manchester to Murmansk; Arr Russia 25.4.45; Fate unknown

TB655 Spitfire LF.IXe (Merlin 66); TOC/RAF 10.2.45; via No.82 MU and Manchester to Murmansk; Arr Russia 25.4.45; Fate unknown

TB656 Spitfire LF.IXe (Merlin 66); TOC/RAF 9.2.45; via No.82 MU and Middlesbrough to Murmansk; Arr Russia 22.5.45; Fate unknown

TB657 Spitfire LF.IXe (Merlin 66); TOC/RAF 9.2.45; via No.82 MU and Middlesbrough to Murmansk; Arr Russia 25.4.45; Fate unknown

TB658 Spitfire LF.IXe (Merlin 66); TOC/RAF 25.2.45; via Nos.39 MU & 1 PATP to Murmansk; Arr Russia 22.5.45; Fate unknown

TB659 Spitfire LF.IXe (Merlin 66); TOC/RAF 10.2.45; via No.82 MU and Manchester to Murmansk; Arr Russia 25.4.45; Fate unknown

TB674 Spitfire LF.IXe (Merlin 66); TOC/RAF 13.2.45; via No.52 MU and Southport to Murmansk; Arr Russia 25.4.45; Fate unknown

TB676 Spitfire LF.IXe (Merlin 66); TOC/RAF 9.2.45; via No.82 MU and Manchester to Murmansk; Arr Russia 25.4.45; Fate unknown

TB677 Spitfire LF.IXe (Merlin 66); TOC/RAF 13.2.45; via No.82 MU and Middlesbrough to Murmansk; Arr Russia 25.4.45; Fate unknown

TB678 Spitfire LF.IXe (Merlin 66); TOC/RAF 10.2.45; via No.82 MU and Manchester to Murmansk; Arr Russia 22.5.45; Fate unknown

TB679 Spitfire LF.IXe (Merlin 66); TOC/RAF 10.2.45; via No.82 MU and Middlesbrough to Murmansk; Arr Russia 22.5.45; Fate unknown

TB680 Spitfire LF.IXe (Merlin 66); TOC/RAF 13.2.45; via No.82 MU and Middlesbrough to Murmansk; Arr Russia 25.4.45; Fate unknown

TB681 Spitfire LF.IXe (Merlin 66); TOC/RAF 21.2.45; via No.82 MU and Manchester to Murmansk; Arr Russia 25.4.45; Fate unknown

TB682 Spitfire LF.IXe (Merlin 66); TOC/RAF 10.2.45; via No.82 MU and Manchester to Murmansk; Arr Russia 22.5.45; Fate unknown

TB683 Spitfire LF.IXe (Merlin 66); TOC/RAF 14.2.45; via No.82 MU and Southport to Murmansk; Arr Russia 25.4.45; Fate unknown

TB684 Spitfire LF.IXe (Merlin 66); TOC/RAF 27.2.45; via No.82 MU and Manchester to Murmansk; Arr Russia 22.5.45; Fate unknown

TB685 Spitfire LF.IXe (Merlin 66); TOC/RAF 28.2.45; via No.52 MU and Southport to Murmansk; Arr Russia 22.5.45; Fate unknown

TB686 Spitfire LF.IXe (Merlin 66); TOC/RAF 27.2.45; via No.52 MU and Middlesbrough to Murmansk; Arr Russia 22.5.45; Fate unknown

TB687 Spitfire LF.IXe (Merlin 66); TOC/RAF 13.2.45; via No.82 MU and Manchester to Murmansk; Arr Russia 25.4.45; Fate unknown

TB688 Spitfire LF.IXe (Merlin 66); TOC/RAF 21.2.45; via No.52 MU and Southport to Murmansk; Arr Russia 22.5.45; Fate unknown

TB689 Spitfire LF.IXe (Merlin 66); TOC/RAF 14.2.45; via No.82 MU and Manchester to Murmansk; Arr Russia 25.4.45; Fate unknown

TB690 Spitfire LF.IXe (Merlin 66); TOC/RAF 13.2.45; via Nos.52 MU & 1 PATP to Murmansk; Arr Russia 22.5.45; Fate unknown

TB691 Spitfire LF.IXe (Merlin 66); TOC/RAF 25.2.45; via No.82 MU and Middlesbrough to Murmansk; Arr Russia 22.5.45; Fate unknown

TB692 Spitfire LF.IXe (Merlin 66); TOC/RAF 14.2.45; via No.52 MU and Manchester to Murmansk; Arr Russia 25.4.45; Fate unknown

TB693 Spitfire LF.IXe (Merlin 66); TOC/RAF 25.2.45; via Nos.52 MU & 1 PATP to Murmansk; Arr Russia 22.5.45; Fate unknown

TB694 Spitfire LF.IXe (Merlin 66); TOC/RAF 20.2.45; via No.82 MU and Manchester to Murmansk; Arr Russia 25.4.45; Fate unknown

TB695 Spitfire LF.IXe (Merlin 66); TOC/RAF 20.2.45; via No.82 MU and Manchester to Murmansk; Arr Russia 25.4.45; Fate unknown

SOVIET UNION

TB696 Spitfire LF.IXe (Merlin 66); TOC/RAF 21.2.45; via Nos.52 MU & 1 PATP to Murmansk; Arr Russia 22.5.45; Fate unknown
TB697 Spitfire LF.IXe (Merlin 66); TOC/RAF 13.2.45; via No.52 MU and Southport to Murmansk; Arr Russia 22.5.45; Fate unknown
TB698 Spitfire LF.IXe (Merlin 66); TOC/RAF 8.3.45; via No.52 MU and Manchester to Molotowsk; Arr Russia 12.6.45; Fate unknown
TB699 Spitfire LF.IXe (Merlin 66); TOC/RAF 4.2.45; via No.82 MU and Manchester to Murmansk; Arr Russia 22.5.45; Fate unknown
TB700 Spitfire LF.IXe (Merlin 66); TOC/RAF 14.2.45; via No.82 MU and Manchester to Murmansk; Arr Russia 22.5.45; Fate unknown
TB701 Spitfire LF.IXe (Merlin 66); TOC/RAF 27.2.45; via No.52 MU and Southport to Murmansk; Arr Russia 22.5.45; Fate unknown
TB703 Spitfire LF.IXe (Merlin 66); TOC/RAF 25.2.45; via No.82 MU and Middlesbrough to Murmansk; Arr Russia 22.5.45; Fate unknown
TB704 Spitfire LF.IXe (Merlin 66); TOC/RAF 27.2.45; via No.82 MU and Manchester to Murmansk; Arr Russia 22.5.45; Fate unknown
TB705 Spitfire LF.IXe (Merlin 66); TOC/RAF 14.2.45; via No.52 MU and Manchester to Murmansk; Arr Russia 25.4.45; Fate unknown
TB706 Spitfire LF.IXe (Merlin 66); TOC/RAF 27.2.45; via No.52 MU and Southport to Murmansk; Arr Russia 22.5.45; Fate unknown
TB707 Spitfire LF.IXe (Merlin 66); TOC/RAF 25.2.45; via No.82 MU and Manchester to Murmansk; Arr Russia 22.5.45; Fate unknown
TB708 Spitfire LF.IXe (Merlin 66); TOC/RAF 27.2.45; via No.52 MU and Middlesbrough to Murmansk; Arr Russia 22.5.45; Fate unknown
TB710 Spitfire LF.IXe (Merlin 66); TOC/RAF 20.2.45; via No.82 MU and Middlesbrough to Murmansk; Arr Russia 22.5.45; Fate unknown
TB711 Spitfire LF.IXe (Merlin 66); TOC/RAF 27.2.45; via No.82 MU and Middlesbrough to Murmansk; Arr Russia 22.5.45; Fate unknown
TB712 Spitfire LF.IXe (Merlin 66); TOC/RAF 25.2.45; via No.82 MU and Manchester to Murmansk; Arr Russia 22.5.45; Fate unknown
TB717 Spitfire LF.IXe (Merlin 66); TOC/RAF 27.2.45; via No.82 MU and Manchester to Murmansk; Arr Russia 22.5.45; Fate unknown
TB718 Spitfire LF.IXe (Merlin 66); TOC/RAF 25.2.45; via No.82 MU and Manchester to Murmansk; Arr Russia 22.5.45; Fate unknown
TB736 Spitfire LF.IXe (Merlin 66); TOC/RAF 27.2.45; via No.82 MU and Middlesbrough to Murmansk; Arr Russia 22.5.45; Fate unknown
TB740 Spitfire LF.IXe (Merlin 66); TOC/RAF 21.2.45; via No.82 MU and Middlesbrough to Murmansk; Arr Russia 25.4.45; Fate unknown
TB771 Spitfire LF.IXe (Merlin 66); TOC/RAF 1.2.45; via No.82 MU and Manchester to Murmansk; Arr Russia 25.4.45; Fate unknown
TB772 Spitfire LF.IXe (Merlin 66); TOC/RAF 8.1.45; via No.82 MU and Manchester to Russia; Arr Hapmat 20.3.45; Fate unknown
TB773 Spitfire LF.IXe (Merlin 66); TOC/RAF 17.1.45; via No.82 MU and Manchester to Murmansk; Arr Russia 25.4.45; Fate unknown
TB774 Spitfire LF.IXe (Merlin 66); TOC/RAF 17.1.45; via No.82 MU and Manchester to Russia; Arr Hapmat 20.3.45; Fate unknown
TB775 Spitfire LF.IXe (Merlin 66); TOC/RAF 17.1.45; via No.82 MU to Russia; Arr Hapmat 20.3.45; Fate unknown
TB776 Spitfire LF.IXe (Merlin 66); TOC/RAF 9.1.45; via No.82 MU and Southport to Russia; Arr Hapmat 20.3.45; Fate unknown
TB777 Spitfire LF.IXe (Merlin 66); TOC/RAF 17.1.45; via No.82 MU and Manchester to Murmansk; Arr Russia 25.4.45; Fate unknown
TB778 Spitfire LF.IXe (Merlin 66); TOC/RAF 9.1.45; via No.82 MU and Salford to Russia; Arr Hapmat 13.2.45; Fate unknown
TB779 Spitfire LF.IXe (Merlin 66); TOC/RAF 17.1.45; via No.82 MU and Manchester to Murmansk; Arr Russia 25.4.45; Fate unknown
TB780 Spitfire LF.IXe (Merlin 66); TOC/RAF 10.2.45; via No.52 MU and Southport to Murmansk; Arr Russia 25.4.45; Fate unknown
TB781 Spitfire LF.IXe (Merlin 66); TOC/RAF 20.1.45; via No.82 MU and Manchester to Murmansk; Arr Russia 25.4.45; Fate unknown
TB782 Spitfire LF.IXe (Merlin 66); TOC/RAF 19.1.45; via No.82 MU and Manchester to Murmansk; Arr Russia 25.4.45; Fate unknown
TB783 Spitfire LF.IXe (Merlin 66); TOC/RAF 28.2.45; via No.52 MU and Manchester to Molotowsk; Arr Russia 12.6.45; Fate unknown
TB784 Spitfire LF.IXe (Merlin 66); TOC/RAF 19.1.45; via No.82 MU and Manchester to Murmansk; Arr Russia 25.4.45; Fate unknown
TB785 Spitfire LF.IXe (Merlin 66); TOC/RAF 19.1.45; via No.82 MU and Middlesbrough to Murmansk; Arr Russia 25.4.45; Fate unknown
TB786 Spitfire LF.IXe (Merlin 66); TOC/RAF 1.2.45; via No.82 MU and Manchester to Murmansk; Arr Russia 25.4.45; Fate unknown
TB787 Spitfire LF.IXe (Merlin 66); TOC/RAF 20.1.45; via No.82 MU and Manchester to Murmansk; Arr Russia 25.4.45; Fate unknown
TB788 Spitfire LF.IXe (Merlin 66); TOC/RAF 3.2.45; via No.82 MU and Manchester to Russia; Arr Hapmat 20.3.45; Fate unknown
TB789 Spitfire LF.IXe (Merlin 66); TOC/RAF 3.2.45; via No.82 MU and Manchester to Russia; Arr Hapmat 20.3.45; Fate unknown
TB790 Spitfire LF.IXe (Merlin 66); TOC/RAF 7.2.45; via No.82 MU and Manchester to Murmansk; Arr Russia 25.4.45; Fate unknown
TB791 Spitfire LF.IXe (Merlin 66); TOC/RAF 1.2.45; via No.82 MU and Manchester to Murmansk; Arr Russia 25.4.45; Fate unknown
TB792 Spitfire LF.IXe (Merlin 66); TOC/RAF 5.2.45; via No.52 MU and Southport to Murmansk; Arr Russia 25.4.45; Fate unknown
TB793 Spitfire LF.IXe (Merlin 66); TOC/RAF 9.2.45; via No.82 MU and Middlesbrough to Murmansk; Arr Russia 25.4.45; Fate unknown
TB794 Spitfire LF.IXe (Merlin 66); TOC/RAF 7.2.45; via No.82 MU and Manchester to Murmansk; Arr Russia 25.4.45; Fate unknown
TB795 Spitfire LF.IXe (Merlin 66); TOC/RAF 24.2.45; via No.82 MU and Manchester to Murmansk; Arr Russia 22.5.45; Fate unknown
TB796 Spitfire LF.IXe (Merlin 66); TOC/RAF 7.2.45; via No.82 MU and Manchester to Murmansk; Arr Russia 25.4.45; Fate unknown
TB797 Spitfire LF.IXe (Merlin 66); TOC/RAF 13.2.45; via No.82 MU and Manchester to Murmansk; Arr Russia 22.5.45; Fate unknown
TB798 Spitfire LF.IXe (Merlin 66); TOC/RAF 9.2.45; via No.52 MU and Manchester to Murmansk; Arr Russia 25.4.45; Fate unknown
TB799 Spitfire LF.IXe (Merlin 66); TOC/RAF 7.2.45; via No.52 MU and Manchester to Murmansk; Arr Russia 25.4.45; Fate unknown
TB800 Spitfire LF.IXe (Merlin 66); TOC/RAF 13.2.45; via No.52 MU and Manchester to Murmansk; Arr Russia 25.4.45; Fate unknown
TB801 Spitfire LF.IXe (Merlin 66); TOC/RAF 10.2.45; via No.82 MU and Manchester to Murmansk; Arr Russia 22.5.45; Fate unknown

TB802 Spitfire LF.IXe (Merlin 66); TOC/RAF 13.2.45; via No.52 MU and Southport to Murmansk; Arr Russia 25.4.45; Fate unknown
TB803 Spitfire LF.IXe (Merlin 66); TOC/RAF 21.2.45; via No.82 MU and Manchester to Murmansk; Arr Russia 22.5.45; Fate unknown
TB804 Spitfire LF.IXe (Merlin 66); TOC/RAF 21.2.45; via No.82 MU and Middlesbrough to Murmansk; Arr Russia 22.5.45; Fate unknown
TB805 Spitfire LF.IXe (Merlin 66); TOC/RAF 25.2.45; via No.82 MU and Middlesbrough to Murmansk; Arr Russia 22.5.45; Fate unknown
TB806 Spitfire LF.IXe (Merlin 66); TOC/RAF 28.2.45; via No.82 MU and Middlesbrough to Murmansk; Arr Russia 22.5.45; Fate unknown
TB807 Spitfire LF.IXe (Merlin 66); TOC/RAF 21.2.45; via No.52 MU and Middlesbrough to Murmansk; Arr Russia 22.5.45; Fate unknown
TB808 Spitfire LF.IXe (Merlin 66); TOC/RAF 21.2.45; via No.52 MU and Manchester to Molotowsk; Arr Russia 12.6.45; Fate unknown
TB824 Spitfire LF.IXe (Merlin 66); TOC/RAF 25.2.45; via Nos.39 MU & 1 PATP to Murmansk; Arr Russia 22.5.45; Fate unknown
TB825 Spitfire LF.IXe (Merlin 66); TOC/RAF 25.2.45; via Nos.39 MU & 1 PATP to Murmansk; Arr Russia 22.5.45; Fate unknown
TB826 Spitfire LF.IXe (Merlin 66); TOC/RAF 25.2.45; via Nos.39 MU & 1 PATP to Murmansk; Arr Russia 22.5.45; Fate unknown
TB827 Spitfire LF.IXe (Merlin 66); TOC/RAF 28.2.45; via No.82 MU and Manchester to Murmansk; Arr Russia 25.4.45; Fate unknown
TB830 Spitfire LF.IXe (Merlin 66); TOC/RAF 28.2.45; via No.82 MU and Middlesbrough to Murmansk; Arr Russia 11.6.45; Fate unknown
TB837 Spitfire LF.IXe (Merlin 66); TOC/RAF 28.2.45; via No.52 MU and Manchester to Molotowsk; Arr Russia 12.6.45; Fate unknown
TB838 Spitfire LF.IXe (Merlin 66); TOC/RAF 28.2.45; via No.82 MU and Middlesbrough to Murmansk; Arr Russia 22.5.45; Fate unknown
TB839 Spitfire LF.IXe (Merlin 66); TOC/RAF 1.3.45; via No.82 MU and Manchester to Murmansk; Arr Russia 22.5.45; Fate unknown
TB840 Spitfire LF.IXe (Merlin 66); TOC/RAF 1.3.45; via No.52 MU and Manchester to Molotowsk; Arr Russia 12.6.45; Fate unknown
TB841 Spitfire LF.IXe (Merlin 66); TOC/RAF 6.3.45; via No.82 MU and Manchester to Murmansk; Arr Russia 22.5.45; Fate unknown
TB842 Spitfire LF.IXe (Merlin 66); TOC/RAF 1.3.45; via No.82 MU and Manchester to Murmansk; Arr Russia 22.5.45; Fate unknown
TB843 Spitfire LF.IXe (Merlin 66); TOC/RAF 5.3.45; via No.82 MU to Murmansk; Arr Soviet Union 22.5.45; Fate unknown
TB848 Spitfire LF.IXe (Merlin 66); TOC/RAF 7.3.45; via No.82 MU and Manchester to Murmansk; Arr Russia 22.5.45; No.480 IAP.PVO; Fate unknown
NOTE: Incorrectly reported "TA848"
TB849 Spitfire LF.IXe (Merlin 66); TOC/RAF 7.3.45; via No.82 MU and Manchester to Bakaritsa; Arr Russia 11.6.45; Fate unknown
TB850 Spitfire LF.IXe (Merlin 66); TOC/RAF 5.3.45; via No.52 MU and Manchester to Murmansk; Arr Russia 25.4.45; Fate unknown
TB851 Spitfire LF.IXe (Merlin 66); TOC/RAF 8.3.45; via No.52 MU and Manchester to Molotowsk; Arr Russia 12.6.45; Fate unknown
TB852 Spitfire LF.IXe (Merlin 66); TOC/RAF 12.3.45; via No.82 MU and Manchester to Murmansk; Arr Russia 22.5.45; Fate unknown
TB853 Spitfire LF.IXe (Merlin 66); TOC/RAF 15.3.45; via No.82 MU and Manchester to Murmansk; Arr Russia 22.5.45; Fate unknown
TB854 Spitfire LF.IXe (Merlin 66); TOC/RAF 13.3.45; via No.82 MU and Middlesbrough to Murmansk; Arr Russia 22.5.45; Fate unknown
TB855 Spitfire LF.IXe (Merlin 66); TOC/RAF 17.3.45; via No.82 MU and Middlesbrough to Murmansk; Arr Russia 22.5.45; Fate unknown
TB856 Spitfire LF.IXe (Merlin 66); TOC/RAF 16.3.45; via No.82 MU and Manchester to Murmansk; Arr Russia 22.5.45; Fate unknown
TB857 Spitfire LF.IXe (Merlin 66); TOC/RAF 16.3.45; via No.82 MU and Middlesbrough to Murmansk; Arr Russia 11.6.45; Fate unknown
TB938 Spitfire LF.IXe (Merlin 66); TOC/RAF 2.3.45; via No.82 MU and Manchester to Murmansk; Arr Russia 22.5.45; Fate unknown
TB939 Spitfire LF.IXe (Merlin 66); TOC/RAF 24.2.45; via No.82 MU and Manchester to Murmansk; Arr Russia 22.5.45; Fate unknown
TB940 Spitfire LF.IXe (Merlin 66); TOC/RAF 24.2.45; via No.82 MU and Manchester to Murmansk; Arr Russia 22.5.45; Fate unknown
TB941 Spitfire LF.IXe (Merlin 66); TOC/RAF 13.2.45; via No.52 MU and Manchester to Murmansk; Arr Russia 25.4.45; Fate unknown
TB942 Spitfire LF.IXe (Merlin 66); TOC/RAF 24.2.45; via No.82 MU and Manchester to Murmansk; Arr Russia 22.5.45; Fate unknown
TB943 Spitfire LF.IXe (Merlin 66); TOC/RAF 20.3.45; via No.82 MU and Manchester to Bakaritsa; Arr Russia 11.6.45; Fate unknown
TB944 Spitfire LF.IXe (Merlin 66); TOC/RAF 27.2.45; via No.82 MU and Manchester to Murmansk; Arr Russia 22.5.45; Fate unknown
TB945 Spitfire LF.IXe (Merlin 66); TOC/RAF 24.2.45; via No.52 MU and Southport to Murmansk; Arr Russia 22.5.45; Fate unknown
TB946 Spitfire LF.IXe (Merlin 66); TOC/RAF 28.2.45; via No.82 MU and Middlesbrough to Murmansk; Arr Russia 11.6.45; Fate unknown
TB947 Spitfire LF.IXe (Merlin 66); TOC/RAF 24.2.45; via No.52 MU and Southport to Murmansk; Arr Russia 22.5.45; Fate unknown
TB948 Spitfire LF.IXe (Merlin 66); TOC/RAF 28.2.45; via No.82 MU and Middlesbrough to Murmansk; Arr Russia 22.5.45; Fate unknown
TB949 Spitfire LF.IXe (Merlin 66); TOC/RAF 2.3.45; via No.52 MU and Manchester to Murmansk; Arr Russia 25.4.45; Fate unknown
TB950 Spitfire LF.IXe (Merlin 66); TOC/RAF 28.2.45; via No.82 MU and Middlesbrough to Murmansk; Arr Russia 11.6.45; Fate unknown
TB951 Spitfire LF.IXe (Merlin 66); TOC/RAF 2.3.45; via No.52 MU and Manchester to Molotowsk; Arr Russia 12.6.45; Fate unknown
TB952 Spitfire LF.IXe (Merlin 66); TOC/RAF 2.3.45; via No.52 MU and Manchester to Murmansk; Arr Russia 25.4.45; Fate unknown
TB953 Spitfire LF.IXe (Merlin 66); TOC/RAF 1.3.45; via No.82 MU and Manchester to Murmansk; Arr Russia 22.5.45; Fate unknown
TB954 Spitfire LF.IXe (Merlin 66); TOC/RAF 5.3.45; via No.39 MU & PATP to Murmansk; Arr Russia 22.5.45; Fate unknown
TB955 Spitfire LF.IXe (Merlin 66); TOC/RAF 2.3.45; via No.52 MU and Manchester to Murmansk; Arr Russia 25.4.45; Fate unknown
TB956 Spitfire LF.IXe (Merlin 66); TOC/RAF 15.3.45; via No.52 MU and Manchester to Molotowsk; Arr Russia 12.6.45; Fate unknown
TB957 Spitfire LF.IXe (Merlin 66); TOC/RAF 5.3.45; via No.82 MU and Middlesbrough to Murmansk; Arr Russia 22.5.45; Fate unknown

TB958 Spitfire LF.IXe (Merlin 66); TOC/RAF 10.3.45; via No.82 MU and Manchester to Murmansk; Arr Russia 22.5.45; Fate unknown

TB959 Spitfire LF.IXe (Merlin 66); TOC/RAF 5.3.45; via No.52 MU and Manchester to Molotowsk; Arr Russia 12.6.45; Fate unknown

TB971 Spitfire LF.IXe (Merlin 66); TOC/RAF 5.3.45; via No.82 MU and Manchester to Murmansk; Arr Russia 22.5.45; Fate unknown

TB972 Spitfire LF.IXe (Merlin 66); TOC/RAF 8.3.45; via No.52 MU and Manchester to Molotowsk; Arr Russia 12.6.45; Fate unknown

TB973 Spitfire LF.IXe (Merlin 66); TOC/RAF 5.3.45; via No.82 MU and Manchester to Murmansk; Arr Russia 22.5.45; Fate unknown

TB974 Spitfire LF.IXe (Merlin 66); TOC/RAF 16.4.45; via No.82 MU and Manchester to Molotowsk; Arr Russia 12.6.45; Fate unknown

TB975 Spitfire LF.IXe (Merlin 66); TOC/RAF 29.3.45; via No.82 MU and Southport to Bakaritsa; Arr Russia 11.6.45; Fate unknown

TB976 Spitfire LF.IXe (Merlin 66); TOC/RAF 12.3.45; via No.82 MU and Manchester to Murmansk; Arr Russia 22.5.45; Fate unknown

TB977 Spitfire LF.IXe (Merlin 66); TOC/RAF 22.3.45; via No.52 MU and Manchester to Bakaritsa; Arr Russia 11.6.45; Fate unknown

TB978 Spitfire LF.IXe (Merlin 66); TOC/RAF 15.3.45; via No.82 MU and Manchester to Bakaritsa; Arr Russia 11.6.45; Fate unknown

TB979 Spitfire LF.IXe (Merlin 66); TOC/RAF 22.3.45; via No.52 MU and Manchester to Bakaritsa; Arr Russia 11.6.45; Fate unknown

TB980 Spitfire LF.IXe (Merlin 66); TOC/RAF 20.3.45; via No.52 MU and Manchester to Molotowsk; Arr Russia 12.6.45; Fate unknown

TD155 Spitfire LF.IXe (Merlin 66); TOC/RAF 7.5.45; via No.82 MU and Manchester to Molotowsk; Arr Russia 12.6.45; Fate unknown

TD175 Spitfire LF.IXe (Merlin 66); TOC/RAF 17.3.45; via No.82 MU and Middlesbrough to Murmansk; Arr Russia 22.5.45; Fate unknown

TD178 Spitfire LF.IXe (Merlin 66); TOC/RAF 16.3.45; via No.82 MU and Middlesbrough to Murmansk; Arr Russia 22.5.45; Fate unknown

TD179 Spitfire LF.IXe (Merlin 66); TOC/RAF 21.3.45; via No.82 MU and Manchester to Bakaritsa; Arr Russia 11.6.45; Fate unknown

TD180 Spitfire LF.IXe (Merlin 66); TOC/RAF 20.3.45; via No.52 MU and Manchester to Molotowsk; Arr Russia 12.6.45; Fate unknown

TD181 Spitfire LF.IXe (Merlin 66); TOC/RAF 20.3.45; via No.82 MU and Manchester to Bakaritsa; Arr Russia 11.6.45; Fate unknown

TD182 Spitfire LF.IXe (Merlin 66); TOC/RAF 20.3.45; via No.82 MU and Middlesbrough to Murmansk; Arr Russia 11.6.45; Fate unknown

TD183 Spitfire LF.IXe (Merlin 66); TOC/RAF 22.3.45; via No.82 MU and Manchester to Bakaritsa; Arr Russia 11.6.45; Fate unknown

TD192 Spitfire LF.IXe (Merlin 66); TOC/RAF 24.3.45; via No.82 MU and Middlesbrough to Murmansk; Arr Russia 22.5.45; Fate unknown

TD193 Spitfire LF.IXe (Merlin 66); TOC/RAF 23.3.45; via No.82 MU and Middlesbrough to Murmansk; Arr Russia 22.5.45; Fate unknown

TD194 Spitfire LF.IXe (Merlin 66); TOC/RAF 22.3.45; via No.82 MU and Manchester to Molotowsk; Arr Russia 12.6.45; Fate unknown

TD195 Spitfire LF.IXe (Merlin 66); TOC/RAF 26.3.45; via No.82 MU and Middlesbrough to Murmansk; Arr Russia 11.6.45; Fate unknown

TD196 Spitfire LF.IXe (Merlin 66); TOC/RAF 24.3.45; via No.82 MU and Middlesbrough to Murmansk; Arr Russia 22.5.45; Fate unknown

TD197 Spitfire LF.IXe (Merlin 66); TOC/RAF 24.3.45; via No.82 MU and Manchester to Murmansk; Arr Russia 22.5.45; Fate unknown

TD198 Spitfire LF.IXe (Merlin 66); TOC/RAF 29.3.45; via No.52 MU and Manchester to Molotowsk; Arr Russia 12.6.45; Fate unknown

TD199 Spitfire LF.IXe (Merlin 66); TOC/RAF 26.3.45; via No.82 MU and Manchester to Bakaritsa; Arr Russia 11.6.45; Fate unknown

TD200 Spitfire LF.IXe (Merlin 66); TOC/RAF 29.3.45; via No.52 MU and Manchester to Molotowsk; Arr Russia 12.6.45; Fate unknown

TD201 Spitfire LF.IXe (Merlin 66); TOC/RAF 30.3.45; via No.82 MU and Middlesbrough to Murmansk; Arr Russia 11.6.45; Fate unknown

TD203 Spitfire LF.IXe (Merlin 66); TOC/RAF 31.3.45; via No.82 MU and Middlesbrough to Murmansk; Arr Russia 11.6.45; Fate unknown

TD204 Spitfire LF.IXe (Merlin 66); TOC/RAF 30.3.45; via No.82 MU and Manchester to Molotowsk; Arr Russia 12.6.45; Fate unknown

Two Spitfire LF.IXs in April 1945 with personnel of 26 Gv.IAP of the Leningrad Air Defence. Visible aft of the cockpit is the Guards emblem.
[Russian Aviation Research Group]

TD207 Spitfire LF.IXe (Merlin 66); TOC/RAF 4.4.45; via No.82 MU and Middlesbrough to Murmansk; Arr Russia 11.6.45; Fate unknown

TD208 Spitfire LF.IXe (Merlin 66); TOC/RAF 4.4.45; via No.52 MU and Manchester to Molotowsk; Arr Russia 12.6.45; Fate unknown

TD209 Spitfire LF.IXe (Merlin 66); TOC/RAF 4.4.45; via No.52 MU and Manchester to Molotowsk; Arr Russia 12.6.45; Fate unknown

TD210 Spitfire LF.IXe (Merlin 66); TOC/RAF 4.4.45; via No.52 MU and Manchester to Molotowsk; Arr Russia 12.6.45; Fate unknown

TD211 Spitfire LF.IXe (Merlin 66); TOC/RAF 4.4.45; via No.52 MU and Manchester to Bakaritsa; Arr Russia 11.6.45; Fate unknown

TD212 Spitfire LF.IXe (Merlin 66); TOC/RAF 11.4.45; via No.82 MU and Middlesbrough to Murmansk; Arr Russia 11.6.45; Fate unknown

TD213 Spitfire LF.IXe (Merlin 66); TOC/RAF 11.4.45; via No.82 MU and Middlesbrough to Murmansk; Arr Russia 22.5.45; Fate unknown

TD287 Spitfire LF.IXe (Merlin 66); TOC/RAF 22.3.45; via No.82 MU and Manchester to Bakaritsa; Arr Russia 11.6.45; Fate unknown

TD290 Spitfire LF.IXe (Merlin 66); TOC/RAF 23.3.45; via No.82 MU and Middlesbrough to Murmansk; Arr Russia 11.6.45; Fate unknown

TD291 Spitfire LF.IXe (Merlin 66); TOC/RAF 24.3.45; via No.82 MU and Middlesbrough to Murmansk; Arr Russia 11.6.45; Fate unknown

TD292 Spitfire LF.IXe (Merlin 66); TOC/RAF 21.3.45; via No.52 MU and Manchester to Molotowsk; Arr Russia 12.6.45; Fate unknown

TD294 Spitfire LF.IXe (Merlin 66); TOC/RAF 23.3.45; via No.52 MU and Manchester to Molotowsk; Arr Russia 12.6.45; Fate unknown

TD295 Spitfire LF.IXe (Merlin 66); TOC/RAF 21.3.45; via No.52 MU and Manchester to Molotowsk; Arr Russia 12.6.45; Fate unknown

TD296 Spitfire LF.IXe (Merlin 66); TOC/RAF 26.3.45; via No.82 MU and Manchester to Murmansk; Arr Russia 22.5.45; Fate unknown

TD297 Spitfire LF.IXe (Merlin 66); TOC/RAF 26.3.45; via No.82 MU and Manchester to Murmansk; Arr Russia 22.5.45; Fate unknown

TD298 Spitfire LF.IXe (Merlin 66); TOC/RAF 20.3.45; via No.82 MU and Manchester to Bakaritsa; Arr Russia 11.6.45; Fate unknown

TD299 Spitfire LF.IXe (Merlin 66); TOC/RAF 23.3.45; via No.82 MU and Manchester to Murmansk; Arr Russia 22.5.45; Fate unknown

TD300 Spitfire LF.IXe (Merlin 66); TOC/RAF 23.3.45; via No.82 MU and Manchester to Murmansk; Arr Russia 22.5.45; Fate unknown

TD301 Spitfire LF.IXe (Merlin 66); TOC/RAF 23.3.45; via No.82 MU and Middlesbrough to Murmansk; Arr Russia 11.6.45; Fate unknown

TD302 Spitfire LF.IXe (Merlin 66); TOC/RAF 23.3.45; via No.82 MU and Middlesbrough to Murmansk; Arr Russia 11.6.45; Fate unknown

TD303 Spitfire LF.IXe (Merlin 66); TOC/RAF 22.3.45; via No.82 MU and Middlesbrough to Murmansk; Arr Russia 11.6.45; Fate unknown

TD304 Spitfire LF.IXe (Merlin 66); TOC/RAF 22.3.45; via No.82 MU and Middlesbrough to Murmansk; Arr Russia 11.6.45; Fate unknown

TD306 Spitfire LF.IXe (Merlin 66); TOC/RAF 26.3.45; via No.82 MU and Manchester to Murmansk; Arr Russia 22.5.45; Fate unknown

TD307 Spitfire LF.IXe (Merlin 66); TOC/RAF 24.3.45; via No.82 MU and Middlesbrough to Murmansk; Arr Russia 11.6.45; Fate unknown

TD308 Spitfire LF.IXe (Merlin 66); TOC/RAF 26.3.45; via No.82 MU and Middlesbrough to Murmansk; Arr Russia 11.6.45; Fate unknown

TD309 Spitfire LF.IXe (Merlin 66); TOC/RAF 26.3.45; via No.82 MU and Manchester to Murmansk; Arr Russia 22.5.45; Fate unknown

TD311 Spitfire LF.IXe (Merlin 66); TOC/RAF 27.3.45; via No.82 MU and Middlesbrough to Murmansk; Arr Russia 22.5.45; Fate unknown

TD312 Spitfire LF.IXe (Merlin 66); TOC/RAF 29.3.45; via No.52 MU and Manchester to Bakaritsa; Arr Russia 11.6.45; Fate unknown

TD354 Spitfire LF.IXe (Merlin 66); TOC/RAF 9.4.45; via No.82 MU and Middlesbrough to Murmansk; Arr Russia 11.6.45; Fate unknown

TD357 Spitfire LF.IXe (Merlin 66); TOC/RAF 13.4.45; via No.52 MU and Manchester to Molotowsk; Arr Russia 12.6.45; Fate unknown

TD360 Spitfire LF.IXe (Merlin 66); TOC/RAF 30.3.45; via No.82 MU and Manchester to Bakaritsa; Arr Russia 11.6.45; Fate unknown

TD365 Spitfire LF.IXe (Merlin 66); TOC/RAF 10.4.45; via No.82 MU and Manchester to Molotowsk; Arr Russia 12.6.45; Fate unknown

TD368 Spitfire LF.IXe (Merlin 66); TOC/RAF 9.4.45; via No.82 MU and Middlesbrough to Murmansk; Arr Russia 11.6.45; Fate unknown

TD371 Spitfire LF.IXe (Merlin 66); TOC/RAF 10.4.45; via No.82 MU and Manchester to Molotowsk; Arr Russia 12.6.45; Fate unknown

TD373 Spitfire LF.IXe (Merlin 66); TOC/RAF 14.4.45; via No.82 MU and Manchester to Molotowsk; Arr Russia 12.6.45; Fate unknown

TD374 Spitfire LF.IXe (Merlin 66); TOC/RAF 11.4.45; via No.52 MU and Manchester to Bakaritsa; Arr Russia 11.6.45; Fate unknown

TD379 Spitfire LF.IXe (Merlin 66); TOC/RAF 21.4.45; via No.82 MU and Manchester to Molotowsk; Arr Russia 12.6.45; Fate unknown

TD395 Spitfire LF.IXe (Merlin 66); TOC/RAF 24.4.45; via No.82 MU and Manchester to Molotowsk; Arr Russia 12.6.45; Fate unknown

TD952 Spitfire LF.IXe (Merlin 66); TOC/RAF 22.3.45; via No.52 MU and Manchester to Molotowsk; Arr Russia 12.6.45; Fate unknown

TD953 Spitfire LF.IXe (Merlin 66); TOC/RAF 20.3.45; via No.52 MU and Manchester to Molotowsk; Arr Russia 12.6.45; Fate unknown

TD955 Spitfire LF.IXe (Merlin 66); TOC/RAF 20.3.45; via No.82 MU and Middlesbrough to Murmansk; Arr Russia 11.6.45; Fate unknown

TD956 Spitfire LF.IXe (Merlin 66); TOC/RAF 21.3.45; via Nos.52 MU & 1 PATP to Murmansk; Arr Russia 22.5.45; Fate unknown

TD957 Spitfire LF.IXe (Merlin 66); TOC/RAF 23.3.45; via No.82 MU and Middlesbrough to Murmansk; Arr Russia 22.5.45; Fate unknown

TD958 Spitfire LF.IXe (Merlin 66); TOC/RAF 26.3.45; via No.82 MU and Manchester to Bakaritsa; Arr Russia 11.6.45; Fate unknown

TD970 Spitfire LF.IXe (Merlin 66); TOC/RAF 4.4.45; via No.82 MU and Manchester to Bakaritsa; Arr Russia 11.6.45; Fate unknown

TD971 Spitfire LF.IXe (Merlin 66); TOC/RAF 4.4.45; via No.82 MU and Manchester to Bakaritsa; Arr Russia 11.6.45; Fate unknown

TD972 Spitfire LF.IXe (Merlin 66); TOC/RAF 26.3.45; via No.52 MU and Manchester to Molotowsk; Arr Russia 12.6.45; Fate unknown

TD973 Spitfire LF.IXe (Merlin 66); TOC/RAF 27.3.45; via No.52 MU and Manchester to Molotowsk; Arr Russia 12.6.45; Fate unknown

TD974 Spitfire LF.IXe (Merlin 66); TOC/RAF 29.3.45; via No.52 MU and Manchester to Molotowsk; Arr Russia 12.6.45; Fate unknown

TD975 Spitfire LF.IXe (Merlin 66); TOC/RAF 4.4.45; via No.82 MU and Middlesbrough to Murmansk; Arr Russia 11.6.45; Fate unknown

TD976 Spitfire LF.IXe (Merlin 66); TOC/RAF 4.4.45; via No.82 MU and Middlesbrough to Murmansk; Arr Russia 11.6.45; Fate unknown

TD977 Spitfire LF.IXe (Merlin 66); TOC/RAF 4.4.45; via No.82 MU and Manchester to Molotowsk; Arr Russia 12.6.45; Fate unknown

TD978 Spitfire LF.IXe (Merlin 66); TOC/RAF 4.4.45; via No.82 MU and Middlesbrough to Murmansk; Arr Russia 11.6.45; Fate unknown

TD979 Spitfire LF.IXe (Merlin 66); TOC/RAF 4.4.45; via No.52 MU and Manchester to Molotowsk; Arr Russia 12.6.45; Fate unknown

TD980 Spitfire LF.IXe (Merlin 66); TOC/RAF 21.4.45; via No.82 MU and Manchester to Molotowsk; Arr Russia 12.6.45; Fate unknown

TD982 Spitfire LF.IXe (Merlin 66); TOC/RAF 16.4.45; via No.52 MU and Manchester to Molotowsk; Arr Russia 12.6.45; Fate unknown

TD983 Spitfire LF.IXe (Merlin 66); TOC/RAF 4.4.45; via No.52 MU and Manchester to Molotowsk; Arr Russia 12.6.45; Fate unknown

TD987 Spitfire LF.IXe (Merlin 66); TOC/RAF 12.4.45; via No.82 MU and Manchester to Molotowsk; Arr Russia 12.6.45; Fate unknown

TD988 Spitfire LF.IXe (Merlin 66); TOC/RAF 13.4.45; via No.82 MU and Middlesbrough to Murmansk; Arr Russia 11.6.45; Fate unknown

TD989 Spitfire LF.IXe (Merlin 66); TOC/RAF 16.4.45; via No.52 MU and Manchester to Molotowsk; Arr Russia 12.6.45; Fate unknown

TD990 Spitfire LF.IXe (Merlin 66); TOC/RAF 19.4.45; via No.82 MU and Manchester to Bakaritsa; Arr Russia 11.6.45; Fate unknown

TD992 Spitfire LF.IXe (Merlin 66); TOC/RAF 7.5.45; via No.52 MU and Manchester to Bakaritsa; Arr Russia 11.6.45; Fate unknown

TD993 Spitfire LF.IXe (Merlin 66); TOC/RAF 1.5.45; via No.82 MU and Manchester to Molotowsk; Arr Russia 12.6.45; Fate unknown

TD995 Spitfire LF.IXe (Merlin 66); TOC/RAF 23.4.45; via No.82 MU and Manchester to Bakaritsa; Arr Russia 11.6.45; Fate unknown

TD999 Spitfire LF.IXe (Merlin 66); TOC/RAF 25.4.45; via No.52 MU and Manchester to Bakaritsa; Arr Russia 11.6.45; Fate unknown

TE115 Spitfire LF.IXe (Merlin 66); TOC/RAF 9.4.45; via No.82 MU and Manchester to Murmansk; Arr Russia 22.5.45; Fate unknown

TE118 Spitfire LF.IXe (Merlin 66); TOC/RAF 12.4.45; via No.82 MU and Manchester to Bakaritsa; Arr Russia 11.6.45; Fate unknown

TE122 Spitfire LF.IXe (Merlin 66); TOC/RAF 14.4.45; via No.82 MU and Manchester to Bakaritsa; Arr Russia 11.6.45; Fate unknown

TE125 Spitfire LF.IXe (Merlin 66); TOC/RAF 17.4.45; via No.82 MU and Manchester to Bakaritsa; Arr Russia 11.6.45; Fate unknown

TE126 Spitfire LF.IXe (Merlin 66); TOC/RAF 19.4.45; via No.52 MU and Manchester to Bakaritsa; Arr Russia 11.6.45; Fate unknown

TE127 Spitfire LF.IXe (Merlin 66); TOC/RAF 19.4.45; via No.52 MU and Manchester to Bakaritsa; Arr Russia 11.6.45; Fate unknown

TE128 Spitfire LF.IXe (Merlin 66); TOC/RAF 21.4.45; via No.82 MU and Manchester to Bakaritsa; Arr Russia 11.6.45; Fate unknown

TE129 Spitfire LF.IXe (Merlin 66); TOC/RAF 29.4.45; via No.82 MU and Manchester to Molotowsk; Arr Russia 12.6.45; Fate unknown

TE130 Spitfire LF.IXe (Merlin 66); TOC/RAF 28.4.45; via No.82 MU and Manchester to Bakaritsa; Arr Russia 11.6.45; Fate unknown

TE131 Spitfire LF.IXe (Merlin 66); TOC/RAF 21.4.45; via No.52 MU and Manchester to Bakaritsa; Arr Russia 11.6.45; Fate unknown

TE132 Spitfire LF.IXe (Merlin 66); TOC/RAF 23.4.45; via No.52 MU and Manchester to Bakaritsa; Arr Russia 11.6.45; Fate unknown

TE133 Spitfire LF.IXe (Merlin 66); TOC/RAF 21.4.45; via No.82 MU and Manchester to Molotowsk; Arr Russia 12.6.45; Fate unknown

TE134 Spitfire LF.IXe (Merlin 66); TOC/RAF 23.4.45; via No.82 MU and Manchester to Molotowsk; Arr Russia 12.6.45; Fate unknown

TE135 Spitfire LF.IXe (Merlin 66); TOC/RAF 21.4.45; via No.52 MU and Manchester to Bakaritsa; Arr Russia 11.6.45; Fate unknown

TE136 Spitfire LF.IXe (Merlin 66); TOC/RAF 23.4.45; via No.82 MU and Manchester to Bakaritsa; Arr Russia 11.6.45; Fate unknown

TE137 Spitfire LF.IXe (Merlin 66); TOC/RAF 27.4.45; via No.82 MU and Middlesbrough to Murmansk; Arr Russia 11.6.45; Fate unknown

TE139 Spitfire LF.IXe (Merlin 66); TOC/RAF 25.4.45; via No.82 MU and Manchester to Molotowsk; Arr Russia 12.6.45; Fate unknown

TE142 Spitfire LF.IXe (Merlin 66); TOC/RAF 30.4.45; via No.82 MU and Manchester to Molotowsk; Arr Russia 12.6.45; Fate unknown

TE146 Spitfire LF.IXe (Merlin 66); TOC/RAF 1.5.45; via No.82 MU and Manchester to Bakaritsa; Arr Russia 11.6.45; Fate unknown

TE150 Spitfire LF.IXe (Merlin 66); TOC/RAF 1.5.45; via No.82 MU and Manchester to Bakaritsa; Arr Russia 11.6.45; Fate unknown

TE151 Spitfire LF.IXe (Merlin 66); TOC/RAF 7.5.45; via No.52 MU and Manchester to Bakaritsa; Arr Russia 11.6.45; Fate unknown

TE154 Spitfire LF.IXe (Merlin 66); TOC/RAF 1.5.45; via No.82 MU and Manchester to Molotowsk; Arr Russia 12.6.45; No.177 IAP.PVO, Moscow Air Defence; Fate unknown

TE157 Spitfire LF.IXe (Merlin 66); TOC/RAF 7.5.45; via No.82 MU and Manchester to Molotowsk; Arr Russia 12.6.45; Fate unknown

TE493 Spitfire LF.IXe (Merlin 66); TOC/RAF 27.4.45; via No.82 MU and Manchester to Bakaritsa; Arr Russia 11.6.45; Fate unknown

TE495 Spitfire LF.IXe (Merlin 66); TOC/RAF 30.4.45; via No.82 MU and Manchester to Bakaritsa; Arr Russia 11.6.45; Fate unknown

TE496 Spitfire LF.IXe (Merlin 66); TOC/RAF 2.5.45; via No.82 MU and Manchester to Molotowsk; Arr Russia 12.6.45; Fate unknown

TE497 Spitfire LF.IXe (Merlin 66); TOC/RAF 4.5.45; via No.82 MU and Manchester to Molotowsk; Arr Russia 12.6.45; Fate unknown

TE498 Spitfire LF.IXe (Merlin 66); TOC/RAF 4.5.45; via No.52 MU and Manchester to Bakaritsa; Arr Russia 11.6.45; Fate unknown

TE499 Spitfire LF.IXe (Merlin 66); TOC/RAF 10.5.45; via No.82 MU and Manchester to Bakaritsa; Arr Russia 11.6.45; Fate unknown

Unidentified

xx.5.43 Spitfire PR.IV (D), marked '**01**'; ex No.1 PRU, arr Vaenga in 9.42 (Operation "Orator"); To No.118 ORAP (No.3 Esk) Soviet Air Force (North Fleet) 18.10.42; With NII VVS/RKKA (Research Institute) from 3.43 to 5.43
NOTE: X-equipment (three F-24 cameras); Red Stars painted on both sides of the fin, rear fuselage and cowling

xx. 43 Spitfire PR IV (D), marked '**02**'; Possibly No.118 ORAP (No.3 Esk); Crashed at Pumanki airport (date unknown); Later transferred to the Northern Fleet Museum at Murmansk 1946
NOTE: Digit '2' painted on the fin and "*Meibl*" on the cowling; Flown by Iosif A Platonov 1944

4.9.43 Spitfire PR IV (D) of No.118 ORAP (No.3 Esk), Recce mission over Kaafjord, shot down by German fighters, crashed into the mountainside of Vad'dasgaissa near lake Levnasjavvre 4.9.43 or 29.2.44 (pilot killed, probably Lt Solovkin)

NOTE: Wreck recovered, exhibited in the Air Force Museum Bodø (a part with found No "139"; mirror marked AR257 - which only few in the UK)

16.5.44 Spitfire PR.IV of No.118 ORAP (No.3 Esk), shot down during recce to Kirkenes by Ltn Werener Gayko of IX/JG5 (No.9 Sqn of No.5 Fighter Wing) near Midthaugen, Norway 16.5.44 (Kapt VV Aleksandrov killed)

17.6.44 Spitfire PR.IV shot down during recce over Kirkenes by Oberfeldwebel W Schuck of III/JG5 (Senr Ltr Popovich baled out safely and landed in Soviet-held territory)

29.6.44 Spitfire PR.IV damaged by German fighters during recce to Varanger Peninsula, force landed Pummanki airfield in Rubachi Peninsula (Kapt IA Platonov)

It has been suggested that a number of Soviet Spitfires were transferred to Communist China in the 1950s, but confirmation of this is lacking.

Spitfire F Mk. Vb
shipped to Basrah for Russia

Ship	Departure Ports	Despatch Date	Arrival Date	Quantity
City of Derby	Glas, Hul, Liv, Man	1.11.42	10.1.43	35
Bandor Shahpour	Glas	23.10.42	11.1.43	14
Palma	Bir, Liv, Man	5.12.42	30.1.43	13
Nanking	Car	28.11.42	6.2.43	10
City of Lille	Glas,Swan	8.12.42	16.2.43	18
Canada	Avo, Glas	3.12.42	1.3.43	10
Kartago & Nargahus	Bir,Man,SP	19.12.42	17.3.43	11
Baron Inchcape	Glas	18.12.42	24.3.43	32
dis./ME account for Russia	to Shaibah	(EP 788)	31.3.43	(?)
Spitfire F.Vb for Russia, total				**143**

Remarks:
AB 868, AD 301, BL 441, BL 621, EN 901, EP 511 (F VB): allotted for Russia, but damaged in transit (SS "City of Lille"), reduced to produce 5th March 1943;
EN 913 (LF Vb), issued for SS "Palma", but to No.39 MU 31st Dec 1942;
EP 242 (F Vb), arr. Basrah, but via No.35 MU to No.129 Sqn RAF, later to Portugal;
EP 704 (F Vb), disposed for Russia, but SOC before delivery;
EP 970 (F Vb), allotted for Russia, but cancelled;
ER 565 (F Vb/trop), arr. Basrah 10th January 1043, to USAAF in NWA.

Abbreviations for Delivery Ports, etc:
Departure: Avo - Avonmouth   Arrival: Bak - Bakaritsa
          Bir - Birkenhead   Bas - Basrah
          Car - Cardiff   HAP - Hapmat
          Glas - Glasgow   HaN - Hapmat-North
          Hul - Hull   HaS - Hapmat-South
          Liv - Liverpool   Mol - Molotowsk
          Man - Manchester   Murm - Murmansk
          Mid - Middlesbrough
          Newp - Newport
          Sal - Salford
          SP - Southport
          SS - South Shields
          Swan - Swansea

Spitfire LF.IX (incl. two HF.IX)
shipped to Russia (mostly via Nos.52 & 82 MUs):

Ship	Departure Ports	Arrival Port	Despatch Date	Arrival Date	Quantity
City of Eastbourne		HaS	10.2.44	5.4.44	6
Eurybates		HaS	2..3.44	23.4.44	31
Samana		HaS	12.3.44	28.4.44	3
Avristan		HaS	30.3.44	15.5.44	15
St. Claas		HaS	3.4.44	15.5.44	20
Marsdale		HaS	22.4.44	29.5.44	21
Afghanistan	Bir	HAP	12.5.44	5.7.44	27
Inverbank	Bir	HAP	21.5.44	6.7.44	35
Empire Glade	Glas,Liv	HAP	1.6.44	9.7.44	16
Arabistan	Bir	HaS	29.6.44	12.8.44	27
Samconstantan	Man,Sal	HaN	17.7.44	27.8.44	10
Sansuva	SS	HaN	21.7.44	27.8.44	14
Samgara (SS 243)	Mid	HAP	1.8.44	27.8.44	12
Samannon (SS 244)	Mid	HAP	5.8.44	27.8.44	12
Samsaedy	Sal	HaN	11.8.44	27.8.44	16
Empire Celia	Mid	HAP	4.9.44	23.9.44	14
Ad.S.Ottis	Man,Sal	HAP	8.9.44	23.9.44	18
Samaritan		HAP	8..9.44	23.9.44	18
SS 255	Mid,Sal	Murm	12.10.44	30.10.44	42
SS 256	Sal	Murm	13.10.44	30.10.44	18
SS 257	Mid,Sal	Murm	13.10.44	30.10.44	29
SS 258		Murm	15.10.44	30.10.44	9
Fort Boise	Mid	HAP	4.11.44	8.12.44	12
Empire Stalwart	Mid	HAP	4.11.44	8.12.44	14
Fort Island		HAP	11.11.44	8.12.44	18
Fort Massac (262)	Mid	HAP	11.11.44	8.12.44	11
Fort Highfield (263)	Man	HAP	18.11.44	8.12.44	30
Henry Villard (269)	Bir	HAP	15.12.44	9.1.45	31
Thomas Scott (267)	Sal	HAP	18.12.44	9.1.45	10
EmpireArcher (270)	Glas	HAP	20.12.44	9.1.45	23
J.D. Yeager (268)	Man	HAP	20.12.44	9.1.45	33
Empire Celia (265)		HAP	23.12.44	9.1.45	16
Ed Fanning (271)	Newp	HAP	23.12.44	9.1.45	32
Samaritan (264)	Mid	HAP	25.12.44	9.1.45	9
Joyce Kilmer (274)	Man,Sal	HAP	19.1.45	13.2.45	17
SS 275	Man,Sal	HAP	19.1.45	13.2.45	36
SS 276	Bir	HAP	25.1.45	13.2.45	29
SS 273	Sal	HAP	26.1.45	13.2.45	17
Fort Masrac (277)	Mid	HAP	16.2.45	20.3.45	7
W.R. Grace (280)	Man,SP	HAP	26.2.45	20.3.45	43
Emp.Stalwart (272)	ManMid	HAP	26.2.45	20.3.45	24
Fort Yukon (SS279)	Man,SP	HAP	27.2.45	20.3.45	25
Fort Boise (SS 278)	Man,SP	HAP	28.2.45	20.3.45	13
Benj.H.Hill (SS282)	Man,SP	Murm	27.3.45	25.4.45	33
ParkBenjamin(281)	ManMid	Murm	30.3.45	25.4.45	30
Samaritan (SS 283)	Man,SP	Murm	30.3.45	25.4.45	37
EmpirePowess (286)	Man	Murm	29.4.45	22.5.45	36
Ad.S.Gehs (SS 284)	Mid	Murm	30.4.45	22.5.45	34
Fort Highfield (285)	Man,SP	Murm	5.5.45	22.5.45	30
Fort Graham (287)	Mid	Murm	31.5.45	11.6.45	26
Samsturdy (SS 288)	Man	Bak	1.6.45	11.6.45	41
Sannythian (SS 289)	Man	Mol	1.6.45	12.6.45	53
other					2
Spitfire Mk.IX for Russia, total					**1,185**

Remarks:
LV677/743/744 (Mk.VIIIc) arr. Basrah, but to India;
MK942 (Mk.IXc) arr. Hapmat (Basrah), but to FAF!

Note:
The SS numbers were not coded ship's names but berthing numbers at the loading port. In some cases the actual ship has not been identified.

SURVIVORS

Spitfire PR.IV, code No.'*02*', carrying the name '*Mable*' exhibited in the Murmansk Fleet Museum in 1946; Fate unknown.
PT879, recovered wreck, now Isle of Wight, UK.
RK858, recovered wreck, now at Duxford, UK.
SM639, recovered wreck, now Norfolk, UK.
A crashed Russian Spitfire PR.IV was recovered in Norway. This wreckage is now stored in the Museum at Bodø, a part bears the number "139", and on the mirror is marked "AR257".

References:
Red Stars - Soviet Air Force in World War Two, by Geust, Keskinen & Stenman, Kustantaja Ar-Kustannus oy, Kangasala, Finland, 1993.
Stalin's Eagles, by Hans D Seidl,
   Schiffer Military History, Atglen, USA, 1998.
Les Spitfires dans le ciel soviétique, by Victor Kulikov, 1999.
Spitfires in USSR, by Vladimir Kotelnikov & G Sloutski, 1999.
Unarmed, Unafraid and Unaccompanied, article
   by Wojtek Matusiak, Air Enthusiast November/December 2000.

SPAIN

Spain remained neutral during the Second World War, though it gave support to the Axis countries. Spanish troops were sent to the Eastern front against Russia (Soviet Union). They included a small air contingent, using Bf 109Es and FW 190A-3s.

For example, the German No.VIII Air-Corps included the 1ª Escuadrilla de Caza from September 1941. This unit was replaced by the 2ª Esc in June 1942; other replacements (3ª to 5ª Esc) followed later.

After the disasters of El Alamein and Stalingrad in 1942/43 the policy of Spain changed. Pressed by the Allies, General Franco ordered the return of all Spanish troops in early 1944.

The country always took a neutral position against Allied airmen who force-landed in Spanish territory. Their aircraft were retained and the crews interned.

Spain did not see Spitfires until 1943, when an occasional RAF Spitfire en route to Gibraltar or flying with Gibraltar air defence, force-landed in Spain or Spanish Morocco. These were interned until the end of the war, when they were offered to the British Embassy at Madrid, but by then the aircraft were unserviceable and so were written off instead.

Individual Histories

ER248 Spitfire F.Vb/trop (Merlin 46); TOC/RAF 4.9.42; Shipped to Gibraltar, arrived 27.10.42; Possibly lost in action, force-landed in Spanish territory; Disposed of by Air Attache at Madrid; SOC/RAF 30.4.48

JG864 Spitfire F.Vc/trop (Merlin 46); TOC/RAF 21.12.42; M.E. 20.4.43; Defence Flight Gibraltar ('G') 23.10.43; Damaged on operations, forced to land on the beach of Spanish Morocco (Playa de Geremias near Tangier) 7.2.44; Interned; SOC/RAF (Cat.FB/3) on 7.2.44

PA847 Spitfire PR.XI (Merlin 63); TOC/RAF 9.11.43; No.1 OADU, failed to reach Gibraltar, force-landed in Spain 14.12.43; Interned; Disposed of by the British Air Attache at Madrid; SOC/RAF 30.4.48

PL777 Spitfire PR.XI (Merlin 70); TOC/RAF: 27.3.44; OADU, desp to MAAF 18.4.44; On ferry flight to Gibraltar on 18.4.44 when it force-landed short of fuel 8 miles north of Larache, Spanish Morocco; Cat.FB/E (missing) 18.4.44; Disposed of by Air Attaché at Madrid; SOC/RAF 30.4.48

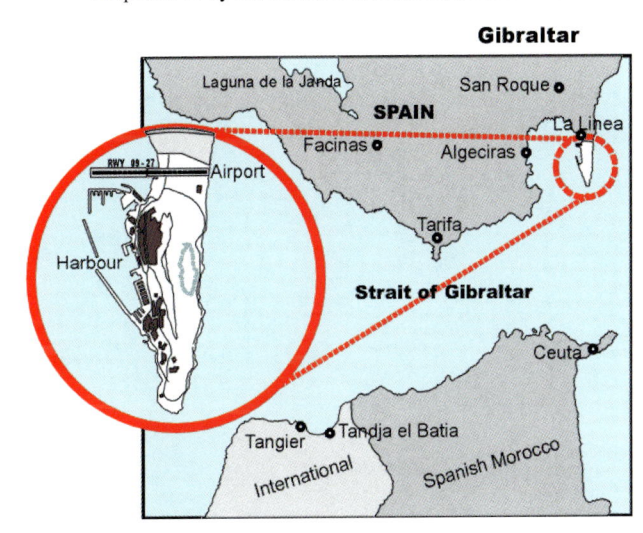

Note:

Gibraltar, at the South of the Iberian peninsula, has been British since 1713. North Front airfield at Gibraltar saw many Allied aircraft movements in World War Two. With Takoradi (West Africa), Gibraltar was one of the main doors for deliveries to the Middle East. Especially later, after Operation "*Torch*", it became of increased importance, because it was within ferry range from England.

SWEDEN

The Kingdom of Sweden held strict neutrality in the Second World War, and also afterwards. Spitfires arrived there only after the war, except for one RAF aircraft which experienced fuel shortage and force-landed in that country, where it was interned in 1942.

Before the Second World War the Swedish Air Force was interested in the Spitfire Mk.Ia. On 12th May 1939 Sweden placed an order for an immediate delivery of 15 aircraft, but with the outbreak of war that was cancelled.

On 25th April 1944 an offer was made to equip some of its fighter units with Spitfires in order to persuade Sweden to reduce ball-bearing supplies to Germany. Sweden wanted 25 Spitfire Mk.IXs to be delivered by 10th December 1944, but instead received P-51D Mustangs.

Sweden ordered 50 Spitfire PR.XIXs for reconnaissance duties in 1948. These remained in use until 1955.

Later, a 51st Spitfire PR.XIX was bought especially for museum purposes.

The Swedish Air Force

The Air Force of the Kingdom of Sweden was formed in July 1926. Together with the Field-Telegraph Corps Flying Company and the Marine Flying Service they built up the *Flyvapnet* (FV), the Royal Swedish Air Force (RSwAF) or *"Kunliga Svenska Flygvapnet"*. After 1975 the word "Royal" was dropped from the title.

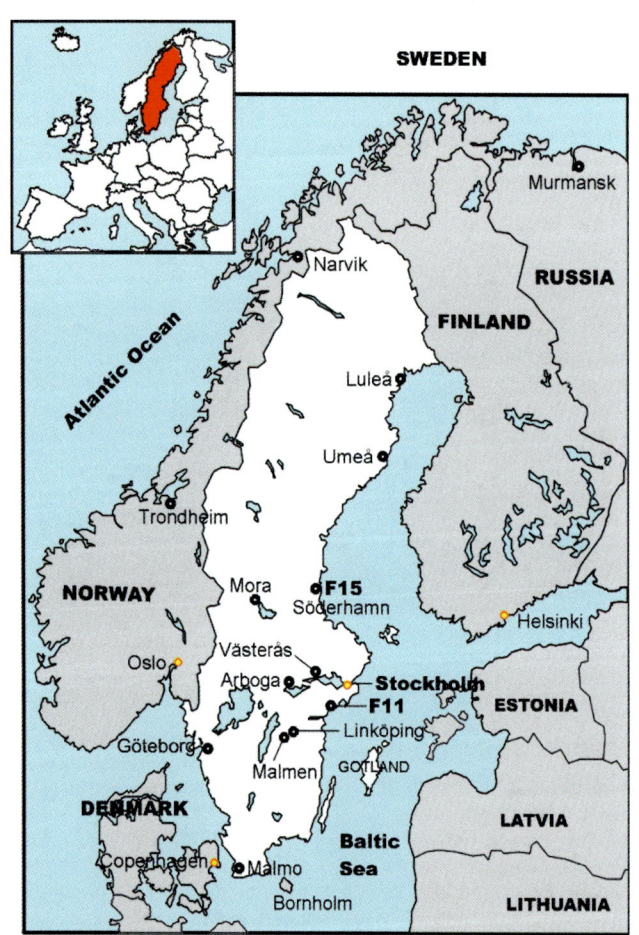

During the period Spitfires were flown, the Royal Swedish Air Force consisted of four Air Groups, Nos. 1, 3 & 4 with HQ at Stockholm and No.2 with HQ at Göteborg. Each comprised three or four Wings, and each Wing comprised four Squadrons, of which two were fully operational, one was devoted to flying training and the other undertook technical training of ground personnel.

A Flying Training Centre was established at Luleå. Three aircraft depots (*Centrala Flygverkstäder*) were in use, all also with repair workshops, based at Malmslätt (airbase Malmen), Västerås and Arboga, respectively.

The aircraft of the RSwAF were officially identified by the following class letters:

A = Attacker, B = Bomber, G = Glider, J = Fighter, P = Experimental, Prototype, S = Recce (e.g.: S31/Spitfire), Se = Sailplane, Sk = Trainer, T = Torpedo bomber, Tp = Transport.

Spitfires of the Royal Swedish Air Force

The RSwAF ordered 70 unused surplus Spitfire PR.XIXs from the UK. in 1948 at £5,380 each, the order being reduced to 50 aircraft before delivery. The total price was £269,004. For this deal the Spitfires were sold back by the RAF to Vickers-Armstrongs and test flown with Class B Registrations *G-15-12* to *G-15-61*. After refurbishing and overhaul the Spitfires went to South Marston (except the first four to Chilbolton) for customer clearance. There they were handed over to RSwAF pilots, who ferried out the aircraft in batches of four or six via Netherlands and Germany to Sweden. The first ferry flight started at Chilbolton on 6th October 1948, landed at Hamburg-Fuhlsbüttel, Germany, for refuelling, and arrived in Sweden the following day. Later delivery batches flew with 90-gallon slipper tanks non-stop to Sweden in about four hours. The last delivery flight was recorded on 11th May 1949.

In Sweden the Spitfire PR.XIXs were designated "**S 31**" and serialled from **31001** to **31050**. Approval tests for the FV-serviceable certificates continued from January to June 1949.

The Spitfires served with Nos.1, 2, 3 & 5 Sqns of the F 11 Wing (Flottilj No.11 Wing of No.4 Air Group [Fjärde Flygeskadern], a long-range PR-unit), based at Skavsta airbase near Nyköping, SW of Stockholm. One Spitfire (No.31004) was never flown after its first touch-down in Sweden, being stored for spare parts until December 1951.

Commanding Officers:
F11 Wing: Grp Capt Greger Falk
(Adjutant: F/O [Löjtnant] Axel Carleson)
Grp Capt Nordström

No.1 Sqn	F/Lt Folke Ringborg	(Adj: F/O D Holmström)
No.2 Sqn	F/Lt Gösta Lundström	(Adj: F/O I Wängström)
No.3 Sqn	F/Lt B Sundberg	(Adj: F/O Jan Sjökvist)
No.5 Sqn	F/Lt Evert Tibell	(Adj: F/O Gösta Aulin)

No.2 Sqn was the school and training unit, with F/O [Löjtnant] Ingemar Wängström ("*Mr. Spitfire*") as a Flight Instructor for S 31; No.4 Sqn was only a technical ground echelon, none flying.

Delivery of the Saab S.29C "Tunnan" towards 1953/54 indicated that time was beginning to run out for the Spitfires. In fact, their service ended in 1955, when they were superseded by more modern jet aircraft. The last were written off charge on 20th August 1955.

All Spitfires were subsequently scrapped, the last (31039, ex PS929) in 1962.

F11 airbase Skavsta nr Nyköping; Malmen airbase at Malmslätt nr Linköping

Identification markings

In England, for the delivery-flight to Sweden the black "11" Wing number was painted on the aft fuselage sides of each aircraft, the yellow-blue Swedish Air Force emblem being carried on wings and fuselage.

For identification purposes in Sweden, large two-digit numbers were painted in white on the fins, these being originally connected with the last two figures of the Swedish serial number: Initially, each fin number was 20 higher than the last two serial digits, for example 31003 had the white fin marking "23", and 31040 had "60". That changed later. From 1949 the fin identity numbers were painted in yellow and reverted to being the last two digits of the serial number, 31003, for instance, now carrying "3" on the fin, and 31040 having "40" in the same position.

Unit colours

Wing Staff = white spinners;
No.1 Sqn = red,
No.2 Sqn = blue,
No.3 Sqn = yellow,
No.5 Sqn = black spinners
(No.4 Sqn none)
A white line around the spinner was used later.

Aircraft of the F 11 Wing carried the "SÖRMLANDSGRIPEN" emblem on the fuselage, immediately under the front screen; near the end of the Spitfire flying a crown was painted on the top of the emblem.

Emblem of F 11 Wing RSwAF the "Sörmlandsgripen"

Individual Histories

BP929? Ex RNoAF Museum Bodø, recovered Russian PR.IV wreck; Since acquired by Swedish enthusiast Sven Kindblom of Stockholm. [Previous identity BP929 provisional, but this went to the USAAF. From the Soviet Union listing BP923 would seem more likely - q.v.] - **SURVIVOR**

PM497 Spitfire PR.XIX (Griffon 66, unpressurised cockpit); Became FV No. **31025**; TOC/RAF 23.5.45; Sold back to Vickers-Armstrongs 8.48; B-class G-15-36 – South Marston, handing over to RSwAF delegation 19.1.49; Flown to Sweden 19.1.49 (Sgt Sven Elmegård); Arr F11 Wing 22.1.49; FV certificated 14.2.49; Service unknown [Markings: '45' (white), later '25' (yellow) from 9.49]; w/o 20.8.55 (472 flying hours)
NOTE: Spitfires PM497 to PM503 were built with Griffon 65 engines, but converted to Griffon 66 before delivery to Sweden

PM498 Spitfire PR.XIX (Griffon 66, unpressurised cockpit); Became FV No. **31004**; TOC/RAF 5.45; Sold back to Vickers-Armstrongs 7.48; B-class G-15-15 - Chilbolton, handing over to RSwAF delegation 5.10.48; Flown to Sweden 6/7.10.48 (F/O [Löjtnant] Ingemar Wängström); Arr F11 Wing 7.10.48; FV certificated 5.1.49; Never flown by the RSwAF after delivery, used for spare parts only; w/o 18.12.51 (11 flying hours)

PM499 Spitfire PR.XIX (Griffon 66, unpressurised cockpit); Became FV No. **31030**; TOC/RAF 26.5.45; Sold back to Vickers-Armstrongs 10.48; B-class G-15-41 – South Marston, handing over to RSwAF delegation 11.2.49; Flown to Sweden 12.2.49 (F/O [Löjtnant] Bernt GR Fyhrlund); Arr F11 Wing 2.3.49; FV certificated 23.3.49; [Markings: '50' (white), later '30' (yellow) from 9.49]; Engine failure during low level flying, force-landed wheels-up near Grisslehamn 14.5.52; Not repaired; w/o 16.2.53 (180 flying hours)

PM502 Spitfire PR.XIX (Griffon 66, unpressurised cockpit); Became FV No. **31026**; TOC/RAF 29.5.45; Sold back to Vickers-Armstrongs 10.48; B-class G-15-37 - South Marston, handing over to RSwAF delegation 11.2.49; Flown to Sweden 12.2.49 (F/O [Löjtnant] Gösta Ström); Arr F11 Wing 20.2.49; FV certificated 10.3.49; Service unknown [Markings: '46' (white), later '26' (yellow) from 9.49]; w/o 20.8.55 (360 flying hours)

PM503 Spitfire PR.XIX (Griffon 66, unpressurised cockpit); Became FV No. **31003**; TOC/RAF 5.45; Sold back to Vickers-Armstrongs 7.48; B-class G-15-14 – Chilbolton, handing over to RSwAF delegation 5.10.48; Flown to Sweden 6/7.10.48 (F/O [Löjtnant] Erik Goliath); Arr F11 Wing 7.10.48; FV certificated 5.1.49; Service unknown [Markings: '23' (white), later '03' (yellow) from 9.49]; w/o 20.8.55 (541 flying hours)

PM554 Spitfire PR.XIX (Griffon 66); Became FV No. **31027**; TOC/RAF 3.7.45; Sold back to Vickers-Armstrongs 10.48; B-class G-15-38 – South Marston, handing over to RSwAF delegation 11.2.49; Flown to Sweden 12.2.49 (F/O [Löjtnant] Roy H Muchow); Arr F11 Wing 20.2.49; FV certificated 10.3.49; [Markings: '47' (white), later '27' (yellow) from 9.49]; Engine failure, oil on windscreen, force-landed at Bromma airfield (near Stockholm), destroyed by fire, Cat.E 3.6.51; w/o 7.7.51 (129 flying hours)

PM556 Spitfire PR.XIX (Griffon 66); Became FV No. **31031**; TOC/RAF 7.7.45; Sold back to Vickers-Armstrongs 10.48; B-class G-15-42 - South Marston, handing over to RSwAF delegation 24.2.49; Flown to Sweden 24.2.49 (F/O [Löjtnant] Roy H Muchow); Arr F11 Wing 25.2.49; FV certificated 10.3.49; [Markings: '51' (white), later '31' (yellow) from 9.49]; Engine failure, baled out, aircraft dived into ground c.3m NW of Mora, Cat.E 15.6.53 (P/O Bengt Palmqvist safe); w/o 13.11.53 (287 flying hours)

PM559 Spitfire PR.XIX (Griffon 66); Became FV No. **31032**; TOC/RAF 14.7.45; Sold back to Vickers-Armstrongs 10.48; B-class G-15-43 – South Marston, handing over to RSwAF delegation 24.2.49; Flown to Sweden 24.2.49 (F/O [Löjtnant] Rune Hallander); Arr F11 Wing 25.2.49; FV certificated 10.3.49; Service unknown [Markings: '52' (white), later '32' (yellow) from 9.49]; w/o 20.8.55 (386 flying hours)

PM560 Spitfire PR.XIX (Griffon 66); Became FV No. **31033**; TOC/RAF 11.7.45; Sold back to Vickers-Armstrongs 10.48; B-class G-15-44 – South Marston, handing over to RSwAF delegation 24.2.49; Flown to Sweden 24.2.49 (F/O [Löjtnant] Arne Carlsson); Arr F11 Wing 25.2.49; FV certificated 10.3.49; Service unknown [Markings: '53' (white), later '33' (yellow) from 9.49]; w/o 20.8.55 (266 flying hours)

PM561 Spitfire PR.XIX (Griffon 66); Became FV No. **31034**; TOC/RAF 11.7.45; Sold back to Vickers-Armstrongs 11.48; B-class G-15-45 – South Marston, handing over to RSwAF delegation 16.3.49; Flown to Sweden 16.3.49 (F/O [Löjtnant] Gösta Lundström); Arr F11 Wing 23.3.49; FV certificated 19.4.49; Service unknown [Markings: '54' (white), later '34' (yellow) from 9.49]; w/o 20.8.55 (323 flying hours)

Spitfire PR.XIX 31034 (ex PM561) on the ground, marked with a white "54" on the fin, some time before September 1949. [Lars Cranning]

Spitfire PM627, an ex-Indian Air Force PR.XIX. It arrived in Sweden via Canada in October 1982 and after restoration was painted up as 31061 '51' of F11 Wing for static display. It is seen here photographed at a difficult angle in Flygvapenmuseum at Malmen airbase, Malmslätt, southwest of Linköping, in February 1997. [Wojtek Matusiak]

Spitfire PR.XIX 31050 (ex PS850) and others of F11 Wing lined up at Skavsta airbase, near Nyköping, southwest of Stockholm, in the early fifties.

PM627 Spitfire PR.XIX, ex Indian AF *HS964* - arrived as **SURVIVOR** only 22.10.82; Marked "**31.051**"; Now exhibited in the Flygvapenmuseum at airbase Malmen, Malmslätt, c.3m SW of Linköping.
NOTE: In 1980 an offer was received from Canada suggesting that PM627 could be exchanged for a Skyraider, Hunter or Vampire. Price reduced to $125,000 (of which $12,500 was kept back to cover to cost of replacing missing parts); Arrived in Sweden in a C-130 Hercules 22.10.82; A few days later it was transported to the Flygvapenmuseum, Linkping for restoration; Front screen, canopy and upper fuselage fuel tank had been preserved from Spitfire 31039 (PS929); A box of Spitfire parts was found at the Flygvapenmuseum, also some 5-bladed propellers were preserved in Sweden, one at Skavsta airfield near Nyköping; Displayed as "Fv31051"

PS850 Spitfire PR.XIX (Griffon 66); Became FV No. **31050**; TOC/RAF 3.1.45; Sold back to Vickers-Armstrongs 10.48; B-class G-15-61 – South Marston, handing over to RSwAF delegation 11.5.49; Flown to Sweden 11.5.49 (F/O [Löjtnant] Gösta Aulin); Arr F11 Wing 13.5.49; FV certificated 3.6.49; Service unknown [Markings: '50' in yellow]; w/o 20.8.55 (277 flying hours)

PS859 Spitfire PR.XIX (Griffon 66); Became FV No. **31049**; TOC/RAF 7.2.45; Sold back to Vickers-Armstrongs 10.48; B-class G-15-60 - South Marston, handing over to RSwAF delegation 11.5.49; Flown to Sweden 11.5.49 (F/Sgt [Fanjunkare] Harry Molander); Arr F11 Wing 13.5.49; FV certificated 3.6.49; Service unknown [Markings: '49' in yellow]; w/o 20.8.55 (442 flying hours)

PS860 Spitfire PR.XIX (Griffon 66); Became FV No. **31009**; TOC/RAF 10.2.45; Sold back to Vickers-Armstrongs 5.8.48; B-class G-15-20 - South Marston, handing over to RSwAF delegation 3.12.48; Flown to Sweden 4.12.48 (F/O [Löjtnant] Folke Ringborg); Arr F11 Wing 5.12.48; FV certificated 5.1.49; Service unknown [Markings: '29' (white), later '09' (yellow) from 9.49]; w/o 20.8.55 (498 flying hours)

PS861 Spitfire PR.XIX (Griffon 66); Became FV No. **31013**; TOC/RAF 10.2.45; Sold back to Vickers-Armstrongs 16.8.48; B-class G-15-24 – South Marston, handing over to RSwAF delegation 19.1.49; Flown to Sweden 19.1.49 (F/O [Löjtnant] Folke Ringborg); Arr F11 Wing 22.1.49; FV certificated 14.2.49; Service unknown [Markings: '33' (white), later '13' (yellow) from 9.49]; w/o 20.8.55 (360 flying hours)

PS862 Spitfire PR.XIX (Griffon 66); Became FV No. **31015**; TOC/RAF 13.2.45; Sold back to Vickers-Armstrongs 20.8.48; B-class G-15-26 – South Marston, handing over to RSwAF delegation 19.1.49; Flown to Sweden 19.1.49 (Sgt Kjell-Göran Aulin); Arr F11 Wing 22.1.49; FV certificated 14.2.49; Service unknown [Markings: '35' (white), later '15' (yellow) from 9.49]; w/o 20.8.55 (356 flying hours)

PS863 Spitfire PR.XIX (Griffon 66); Became FV No. **31010**; TOC/RAF 14.2.45; Sold back to Vickers-Armstrongs 9.8.48; B-class G-15-21 – South Marston, handing over to RSwAF delegation 3.12.48; Flown to Sweden 4.12.48 (Sgt Holger Sundell); Arr F11 Wing 8.12.48; FV certificated 5.1.49; Service unknown [Markings: '30' (white), later '10' (yellow) from 9.49] w/o 20.8.55 (503 flying hours)

PS864 Spitfire PR.XIX (Griffon 66); Became FV No. **31017**; TOC/RAF 14.2.45; Sold back to Vickers-Armstrongs 20.7.48; B-class G-15-28 – South Marston, handing over to RSwAF delegation 11.2.49; Flown to Sweden 11.2.49 (F/O [Löjtnant] Per Axel Persson); Arr F11 Wing 20.2.49; FV certificated 10.3.49; Service unknown [Markings: '37' (white), later '17' (yellow) from 9.49]; w/o 20.8.55 (444 flying hours)

PS865 Spitfire PR.XIX (Griffon 66); Became FV No. **31045**; TOC/RAF 25.2.45; Sold back to Vickers-Armstrongs 10.48; B-class G-15-56 – South Marston, handing over to RSwAF delegation 11.5.49; Flown to Sweden 11.5.49 (Plt Gregor Falk); Arr F11 Wing 13.5.49; FV certificated 3.6.49; Service unknown [Markings: '45' in yellow]; w/o 20.8.55 (368 flying hours)

PS866 Spitfire PR.XIX (Griffon 66); Became FV No. **31006**; TOC/RAF 22.2.45; Sold back to Vickers-Armstrongs 26.7.48, B-class G-15-19 – South Marston, handing over to RSwAF delegation 26.10.48; Flown to Sweden 26.10.48 (S/Ldr DW Morgan, Vickers-Armstrongs); Arr F11 Wing 26.10.48; FV certificated 5.1.49; Service unknown [Markings: '26' (white), later '06' (yellow) from 9.49]; w/o 20.8.55 (430 flying hours)

PS867 Spitfire PR.XIX (Griffon 66); Became FV No. **31046**; TOC/RAF 1.3.45; Sold back to Vickers-Armstrongs 22.10.48; B-class G-15-57 – South Marston, handing over to RSwAF delegation 11.5.49; Flown to Sweden 11.5.49 (Plt Nils Ehrning); Arr F11 Wing 13.5.49; FV certificated 3.6.49; [Markings: '46' in yellow]; Crashed on landing at Barkarby (F8 airbase), undercarriage broken, Cat.E 1.8.50; w/o 5.9.50 (120 flying hours)

PS868 Spitfire PR.XIX (Griffon 66); Became FV No. **31018**; TOC/RAF 26.2.45; Sold back to Vickers-Armstrongs 13.8.48; B-class G-15-29 – South Marston, handing over to RSwAF delegation 11.2.49; Flown to Sweden 11.2.49 (F/O [Löjtnant] Ingemar Wängström); Arr F11 Wing 3.3.49; FV certificated 23.3.49; Service unknown [Markings: '38' (white), later '18' (yellow) from 9.49]; w/o 20.8.55 (424 flying hours)

PS869 Spitfire PR.XIX (Griffon 66); Became FV No. **31021**; TOC/RAF 4.2.45; Sold back to Vickers-Armstrongs 12.8.48; B-class G-15-32 – South Marston, handing over to RSwAF delegation 3.12.48; Flown to Sweden 4.12.48 (F/O [Löjtnant] Sven Forsberg); Arr F11 Wing 5.12.48; FV certificated 5.1.49; [Markings: '41' (white), later '21' (yellow) from 9.49]; Take-off collision with Spitfire 31007 at Skavsta F11 airbase (Nyköping), Cat.E 12.8.53; w/o 23.6.54 (208 flying hours)

PS870 Spitfire PR.XIX (Griffon 66); Became FV No. **31023**; TOC/RAF 1.3.45; Sold back to Vickers-Armstrongs 13.8.48; B-class G-15-34 – South Marston, handing over to RSwAF delegation 19.1.49; Flown to Sweden 19.1.49 (F/O [Löjtnant] Erik Goliath); Arr F11 Wing 22.1.49; FV certificated 14.2.49; Service unknown [Markings: '43' (white), later '23' (yellow) from 9.49]; w/o 20.8.55 (347 flying hours)

PS871 Spitfire PR.XIX (Griffon 66); Became FV No. **31016**; TOC/RAF 27.2.45; Sold back to Vickers-Armstrongs 20.8.48; B-class G-15-27 – South Marston, handing over to RSwAF delegation 19.1.49; Flown to Sweden 19.1.49 (Sgt Holger Sundell); Arr F11 Wing 22.1.49; FV certificated 14.2.49; Service unknown [Markings: '36' (white), later '16' (yellow) from 9.49]; w/o 20.8.55 (374 flying hours)

PS872 Spitfire PR.XIX (Griffon 66); Became FV No. **31029**; TOC/RAF 3.45; Sold back to Vickers-Armstrongs 29.10.48; B-class G-15-40 – South Marston, handing over to RSwAF delegation 11.2.49; Flown to Sweden 12.2.49 (F/O [Löjtnant] Edward Jacobi); Arr F11 Wing 18.2.49; FV certificated 10.3.49; Service unknown [Markings: '49' (white), later '29' (yellow) from 9.49]; w/o 20.8.55 (359 flying hours)

PS873 Spitfire PR.XIX (Griffon 66); Became FV No. **31028**; TOC/RAF 3.3.45; Sold back to Vickers-Armstrongs 27.10.48; B-class G-15-39 – South Marston, handing over to RSwAF delegation 11.2.49; Flown to Sweden 12.2.49 (F/O [Löjtnant] Nils Olof Norin); Arr F11 Wing 18.2.49; FV certificated 10.3.49; Service unknown [Markings: '48' (white), later '28' (yellow) from 9.49]; w/o 20.8.55 (394 flying hours)

PS874 Spitfire PR.XIX (Griffon 66); Became FV No. **31008**; TOC/RAF 7.3.45; Sold back to Vickers-Armstrongs 29.7.48; B-class G-15-17 – South Marston, handing over to RSwAF delegation 5.11.48; Flown to Sweden 5.11.48 (P/O [Fähnrik] Axel Carleson, call sign SM5QR); Arr F11 Wing 9.11.48; FV certificated 5.1.49; Service unknown

Spitfire PR.XIX 31043 (ex PS876), marked "43" in yellow, seen some time after September 1949, when the last two digits of the serial became used as the code. [Axel Carleson]

The first Swedish Spitfire PR.XIX, 31001 (ex PS935), awaiting delivery around October 1948. [Vickers-Armstrongs]

PS875 Spitfire PR.XIX (Griffon 66); Became FV No. **31040**; TOC/RAF 9.3.45; Sold back to Vickers-Armstrongs 4.11.48; B-class G-15-51 – South Marston, handing over to RSwAF delegation 11.4.49; Flown to Sweden 13.4.49 (F/O [Löjtnant] Jan Sjökvist); Arr F11 Wing 14.4.49; FV certificated 27.4.49; Service unknown [Markings: '60' (white), later '40' (yellow) from 9.49]; w/o 20.8.55 (440 flying hours)

[Markings: '28' (white), later '08' (yellow) from 9.49]; w/o 20.8.55 (489 flying hours)

PS876 Spitfire PR.XIX (Griffon 66); Became FV No. **31043**; TOC/RAF 9.3.45; Sold back to Vickers-Armstrongs 4.11.48; B-class G-15-54 – South Marston, handing over to RSwAF delegation 20.4.49; Flown to Sweden 20.4.49 (S/Ldr WJG Morgan, Vickers-Armstrongs); Arr F11 Wing 21.4.49; FV certificated 2.5.49; [Markings: '43' in yellow]; Recce training flight 15.6.53 (flown by Lars R Cranning, call sign SM4RKS); Probably crashed Cat.E in 1954 (date unknown); w/o 20.8.55 (332 flying hours)

PS877 Spitfire PR.XIX (Griffon 66); Became FV No. **31044**; TOC/RAF 11.3.45; Sold back to Vickers-Armstrongs 11.11.48; B-class G-15-55 – South Marston, handing over to RSwAF delegation 20.4.49; Flown to Sweden 20.4.49 (Plt PG Robarts, Vickers-Armstrongs); Arr F11 Wing 21.4.49; FV certificated 2.5.49; Service unknown [Markings: '44' in yellow]; w/o 20.8.55 (259 flying hours)

PS878 Spitfire PR.XIX (Griffon 66); Became FV No. **31007**; TOC/RAF 13.3.45; Sold back to Vickers-Armstrongs 6.8.48; B-class G-15-16 – South Marston, handing over to RSwAF delegation 5.11.48; Flown to Sweden 5.11.48 (P/O [Fähnrik] Karl Evert Tyrling); Arr F11 Wing 9.11.48; FV certificated 5.1.49; Service unknown [Markings: '27' (white), later '07' (yellow) from 9.49]; Parked on runway at Skavsta F11 airbase (Nyköping), hit by Spitfire 31021 on take-off 12.8.53; Repaired; w/o 20.8.55 (361 flying hours)

PS879 Spitfire PR.XIX (Griffon 66); Became FV No. **31024**; TOC/RAF 14.3.45; Sold back to Vickers-Armstrongs 8.48; B-class G-15-35 – South Marston, handing over to RSwAF delegation 19.1.49; Flown to Sweden 19.1.49 (P/O [Fähnrik] Karl Evert Tyrling); Arr F11 Wing 22.1.49; FV certificated 14.2.49; Service unknown [Markings: '44' (white), later '24' (yellow) from 9.49]; Crashed, ground-looped 28.9.49; Repaired; w/o 20.8.55 (445 flying hours)

PS880 Spitfire PR.XIX (Griffon 66); Became FV No. **31041**; TOC/RAF 10.3.45; Sold back to Vickers-Armstrongs 2.11.48; B-class G-15-52 – South Marston, handing over to RSwAF delegation 11.4.49; Flown to Sweden 13.4.49 (F/O [Löjtnant] Folke Ringborg); Arr F11 Wing 14.4.49; FV certificated 27.4.49; [Markings: '41' in yellow]; Crashed on landing at Skavsta F11 airbase (Nyköping), ground-looped, undercarriage and prop. broken, Cat.E 12.5.49; w/o 4.3.52 (9 flying hours)

PS881 Spitfire PR.XIX (Griffon 66); Became FV No. **31020**; TOC/RAF 18.3.45; Sold back to Vickers-Armstrongs 12.8.48; B-class G-15-31 – South Marston, handing over to RSwAF delegation 3.12.48; Test flown by Sgt Kjell-Göran Aulin RSwAF, touched the top of a tree by approach, propeller blades splintered, undercarriage damaged; Repair Vickers-Armstrongs (£105); Flown to Sweden 15.12.48 (Sgt KG Aulin); Arr F11 Wing 19.12.48; FV certificated 5.1.49; Service unknown [Markings: '40' (white), later '20' (yellow) from 9.49]; w/o 20.8.55 (318 flying hours)

PS882 Spitfire PR.XIX (Griffon 66); Became FV No. **31048**; TOC/RAF 21.3.45; Sold back to Vickers-Armstrongs 17.11.48; B-class G-15-59 – South Marston, handing over to RSwAF delegation 11.5.49; Ferry flight en route for Sweden 11.5.49, suffered engine troubles, forced to land on Beldringe airfield near Odensee, Denmark (Plt Sture Hägg); Arr F11 Wing 15.5.49; FV certificated 3.6.49; Service unknown [Markings: '48' in yellow]; w/o 20.8.55 (397 flying hours)

PS883 Spitfire PR.XIX (Griffon 66); Became FV No. **31011**; TOC/RAF 22.3.45; Sold back to Vickers-Armstrongs 6.8.48; B-class G-15-22 – South Marston, handing over to RSwAF delegation 3.12.48; Flown to Sweden 4.12.48 (P/O [Fähnrik] Karl Evert Tyrling); Arr F11 Wing 5.12.48; FV certificated 5.1.49; Service unknown [Markings: '31' (white), later '11' (yellow) from 9.49]; Crashed on landing at Söderhamn (F15 base), burnt, Cat.E 26.9.52 (Plt killed); w/o 16.2.53 (305 flying hours)

PS884 Spitfire PR.XIX (Griffon 66); Became FV No. **31047**; TOC/RAF 24.3.45; Sold back to Vickers-Armstrongs 17.11.48; B-class G-15-58 – South Marston, handing over to RSwAF delegation 11.5.49; Flown to Sweden 11.5.49 (Plt Ulf Hjelm); Arr F11 Wing 13.5.49; FV certificated 3.6.49; Service unknown [Markings: '47' in yellow]; w/o 20.8.55 (384 flying hours)

PS886 Spitfire PR.XIX (Griffon 66); Became FV No. **31035**; TOC/RAF 23.6.45; Sold back to Vickers-Armstrongs 25.11.48; B-class G-15-46 – South Marston, handing over to RSwAF delegation 16.3.49; Flown to Sweden 16.3.49 (P/O [Fähnrik] Axel Carleson, call sign SM5QR); Arr F11 Wing 23.3.49; FV certificated 19.4.49; Service unknown [Markings: '55' (white), later '35' (yellow) from 9.49]; w/o 20.8.55 (396 flying hours)

PS891 Spitfire PR.XIX (Griffon 66); Became FV No. **31022**; TOC/RAF 9.4.45; Sold back to Vickers-Armstrongs 17.8.48; B-class G-15-33 – South Marston, handing over to RSwAF delegation 15.12.48; Flown to Sweden 15.12.48 (F/O [Löjtnant] Sven Forsberg); Arr F11 Wing 19.12.48; FV certificated 5.1.49; Service unknown [Markings: '42' (white), later '22' (yellow) from 9.49]; w/o 20.8.55 (344 flying hours)

PS893 Spitfire PR.XIX (Griffon 66); Became FV No. **31019**; TOC/RAF 24.4.45; Sold back to Vickers-Armstrongs 11.8.48; B-class G-15-30 – South Marston, handing over to RSwAF delegation 5.11.48; Flown to Sweden 5.11.48 (Sgt Sven Elmegård); Arr F11 Wing 9.11.48; FV certificated 5.1.49; Service unknown [Markings: '39' (white), later '19' (yellow) from 9.49]; w/o 20.8.55 (525 flying hours)

PS909 Spitfire PR.XIX (Griffon 66); Became FV No. **31036**; TOC/RAF 28.4.45; Sold back to Vickers-Armstrongs

Spitfire XIX, 31036/36 (ex PS909) of F 11 Wing, Skavsta in 1948

PS923 Spitfire PR.XIX (Griffon 66); Became FV No. **31005**; TOC/RAF 7.5.45; Sold back to Vickers-Armstrongs 27.7.48; B-class G-15-18 – South Marston, handing over to RSwAF delegation 5.11.48; Flown to Sweden 5.11.48 (F/O [Löjtnant] Erik Goliath); Arr F11 Wing 9.11.48; FV certificated 5.1.49; Service unknown [Markings: '25' (white), later '05' (yellow) from 9.49]; Crashed on landing at Skavsta F11 airbase (Nyköping), overturned, Cat.E 24.1.51; w/o 15.2.51 (131 flying hours)

7.12.48; B-class G-15-47 – South Marston, handing over to RSwAF delegation 16.3.49; Flown to Sweden 17.3.49 (F/O [Löjtnant] Bo Sundberg); Arr F11 Wing 23.3.49; FV certificated 19.4.49; Service unknown [Markings: '56' (white), later '36' (yellow) from 9.49]; w/o 20.8.55 (349 flying hours)

PS924 Spitfire PR.XIX (Griffon 66); Became FV No. **31037**; TOC/RAF 12.5.45; Sold back to Vickers-Armstrongs 7.12.48; B-class G-15-48 – South Marston, handing over to RSwAF delegation 16.3.49; Flown to Sweden 16.3.49 (F/O [Löjtnant] Birger Nilsson); Arr F11 Wing 23.3.49; FV certificated 19.4.49; Service unknown [Markings: '57' (white), later '37' (yellow) from 9.49]; w/o 20.8.55 (366 flying hours)

PS926 Spitfire PR.XIX (Griffon 66); Became FV No. **31038**; TOC/RAF 11.5.45; Sold back to Vickers-Armstrongs 13.12.48; B-class G-15-49 – South Marston, handing over to RSwAF delegation 16.3.49; Flown to Sweden 17.3.49 (P/O [Fähnrik] Owe Frösell); Arr F11 Wing 23.3.49; FV certificated 19.4.49; [Markings: '58' (white), later '38' (yellow) from 9.49]; Crashed on landing at Nyköping (F11 base), rudder failed, overshot into field and overturned, Cat.E 18.3.54; w/o 22.4.54 (487 flying hours)

PS927 Spitfire PR.XIX (Griffon 66); Became FV No. **31042**; TOC/RAF 12.5.45; Sold back to Vickers-Armstrongs 16.12.48; B-class G-15-53 – South Marston, handing over to RSwAF delegation 11.4.49; Flown to Sweden 13.4.49 (F/O [Löjtnant] Arne Carlsson); Arr F11 Wing 14.4.49; FV certificated 27.4.49; Service unknown [Markings: '42' in yellow]; w/o 20.8.55 (389 flying hours)

PS928 Spitfire PR.XIX (Griffon 66); Became FV No. **31014**; TOC/RAF 18.5.45; Sold back to Vickers-Armstrongs 10.8.48; B-class G-15-25 – South Marston, handing over to RSwAF delegation 19.1.49; Flown to Sweden 19.1.49 (P/O [Fähnrik] Bengt Palmqvist); Arr F11 Wing 22.1.49; FV certificated 14.2.49; Service unknown [Markings: '34' (white), later '14' (yellow) from 9.49]; w/o 20.8.55 (465 flying hours)

PS929 Spitfire PR.XIX (Griffon 66); Became FV No. **31039**; TOC/RAF 5.5.45; Sold back to Vickers-Armstrongs in 11.48; B-class G-15-50 – South Marston, handing over to RSwAF delegation 16.3.49; Flown to Sweden 17.3.49 (F/O [Löjtnant] Holger Hansson); Arr F11 Wing 23.3.49; FV certificated 19.4.49; Service unknown [Markings: '59' (white), later '39' (yellow) from 9.49]; w/o 20.8.55 (364 flying hours); Instructional airframe for technical training; Scrapped in 1962

PS931 Spitfire PR.XIX (Griffon 66); Became FV No. **31002**; TOC/RAF 16.5.45; Sold back to Vickers-Armstrongs 27.7.48; B-class G-15-13 – Chilbolton, handing over to RSwAF delegation 5.10.48; Flown to Sweden 6/7.10.48 (Plt Sten Brycker); Arr F11 Wing 7.10.48; FV certificated 5.1.49; [Markings: '22' in white]; Crashed on landing at Skavsta F11 airbase (Nyköping), landed downwind, undercarriage collapsed, Cat.E 15.6.49; SOC 20.7.49; w/o 20.8.55 (291 flying hours)

PS933 Spitfire PR.XIX (Griffon 66); Became FV No. **31012**; TOC/RAF 18.5.45; Sold back to Vickers-Armstrongs 10.8.48; B-class G-15-23 – South Marston, handing over to RSwAF delegation 3.12.48; Flown to Sweden 4.12.48 (P/O [Fähnrik] Bengt Palmqvist); Arr F11 Wing 5.12.48; FV certificated 5.1.49; Service unknown [Markings: '32' (white), later '12' (yellow) from 9.49]; w/o 20.8.55 (301 flying hours)

PS935 Spitfire PR.XIX (Griffon 66); Became FV No. **31001**; TOC/RAF 22.5.45; Sold back to Vickers-Armstrongs 26.7.48; B-class G-15-12 - Chilbolton, handing over to RSwAF delegation 5.10.48; Flown to Sweden 6./7.10.48 (Plt Nils Ehrning); Arr F11 Wing 7.10.48; FV certificated 5.1.49; Service unknown [Markings: '21' (white), later '01' (yellow) from 9.49]; w/o 20.8.55 (352 flying hours)

Check list of Royal Swedish Air Force / RAF serial numbers

RSwAF (FV) Nos.	RAF Serial Nos.	C/Nos: 6S -	arrived F11 Wing	RSwAF w/o
31001	PS935	-585141	7.10.48	20.8.55
31002	PS931	-585134	7.10.48	20.8.55 1)
31003	PM503	-683430	7.10.48	20.8.55
31004	PM498	-585144	7.10.48	18.12.51 2)
31005	PS923	-585129	9.11.48	15.2.51 1)
31006	PS866	-594690	26.10.48	20.8.55
31007	PS878	-585098	9.11.48	20.8.55 1)
31008	PS874	-594697	9.11.48	20.8.55
31009	PS860	-594684	5.12.48	20.8.55
31010	PS863	-594687	8.12.48	20.8.55
31011	PS883	-585103	5.12.48	16.2.53 1)
31012	PS933	-585139	5.12.48	20.8.55
31013	PS861	-594685	22.1.49	20.8.55
31014	PS928	-585137	22.1.49	20.8.55
31015	PS862	-594686	22.1.49	20.8.55
31016	PS871	-594694	22.1.49	20.8.55
31017	PS864	-594688	20.2.49	20.8.55
31018	PS868	-594673	3.3.49	20.8.55
31019	PS893	-585113	9.11.48	20.8.55
31020	PS881	-585101	19.12.48	20.8.55
31021	PS869	-594692	5.12.48	23.6.54 1)
31022	PS891	-585111	19.12.48	20.8.55
31023	PS870	-594693	22.1.49	20.8.55
31024	PS879	-585099	22.1.49	20.8.55 1)
31025	PM497	-585143	22.1.49	20.8.55
31026	PM502	-683429	20.2.49	20.8.55
31027	PM554	-683465	20.2.49	7.7..51 1)
31028	PS873	-594696	18.2.49	20.8.55
31029	PS872	-594695	18.2.49	20.8.55
31030	PM499	-585145	2.3.49	16.2.53 1)
31031	PM556	-683467	25.2.49	13.11.53 1)
31032	PM559	-683470	25.2.49	20.8.55
31033	PM560	-683471	25.2.49	20.8.55
31034	PM561	-683472	23.3.49	20.8.55
31035	PS886	-585106	23.3.49	20.8.55
31036	PS909	-585115	23.3.49	20.8.55
31037	PS924	-585130	23.3.49	20.8.55
31038	PS926	-585132	23.3.49	22.4.54 1)
31039	PS929	-585135	23.3.49	20.8.55
31040	PS875	-594698	14.4.49	20.8.55
31041	PS880	-585100	14.4.49	4.3.52 1)
31042	PS927	-585133	14.4.49	20.8.55
31043	PS876	-594699	21.4.49	20.8.55
31044	PS877	-594700	21.4.49	20.8.55
31045	PS865	-594689	13.5.49	20.8.55
31046	PS867	-594691	13.5.49	5.9..50 1)
31047	PS884	-585104	13.5.49	20.8.55
31048	PS882	-585102	13.5.49	20.8.55
31049	PS859	-594683	13.5.49	20.8.55
31050	PS850	-594674	13.5.49	20.8.55
"31051"	PM627	-699626	1981	3)

Notes: 1) Crashed; 2) For spares only; 3) For Museum only (SURVIVOR)

SURVIVORS in Sweden

BP929? Ex RNoAF Museum Bodø, recovered Russian PR.IV, substantial wreck. Acquired December 2000 by Sven Kindblom, Stockholm. [Previous identity provisionally BP929, but this went to the USAAF. From the Soviet Union listing BP923 would seem more likely]

PM627 Ex Indian A.F. (*HS964*); Flygvapenmuseum at airbase Malmen (Malmslätt near Linköping), numbered "31051" and marked "51", exhibition.

References:
S31 Spitfire Mk.XIX i den Svenska Flygspaningen, by Axel Carleson, 1996;
Flyghistoriskt Månadsblad, November 1974; "S-31", by S Sandberg & SH Anderson.

SWITZERLAND – SYRIA

SWITZERLAND

In the late 1930s, Supermarine sent specific quotations for the supply of Spitfires to several foreign governments. Switzerland asked for delivery of between ten and twenty Mk.Ias in 1937/38, with a licence to build a further 100 to 120 aircraft. In August 1938 this country was awaiting permission to licence build the Spitfire Mk.Ia. It placed a general order for 15 Spitfire Mk.Ia, which reached place No.7 in the priority list of the Foreign Office, dated 17th November 1938. Later the order was increased to 30 or 40 aircraft with delivery scheduled for 1939/40.

Test-flying with Spitfire K9791 took place in September 1939, and Swiss pilots had the opportunity to check the Spitfire in the air on 29th September 1939. They claimed the handling was good, but gliding and landing were inferior to the German Bf 109. Switzerland amended its order to "three plus fifteen Spitfire Mk.Ia, plus the opportunity to licence-build Spitfires later". That became contract No C.638B, but with the outbreak of the Second World War earlier that month the order could not be fulfilled and was consequently cancelled.

Spitfires never served in Switzerland, but this country received ten Bf 109D from Germany in 1938/39, and later thirty Bf 109E.

After the war a Spitfire LF.XVIe (TE191 of No 349 Sqn, marked 'GE-G') was exhibited at Zurich in the spring of 1946.

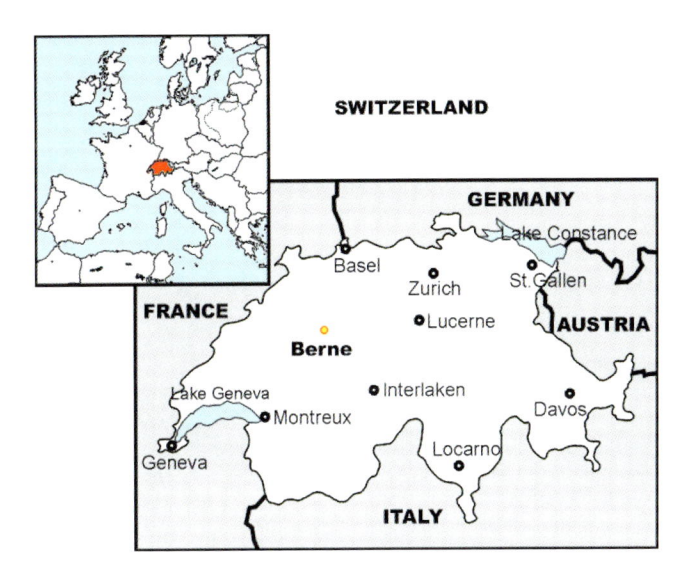

SYRIA

On 26th January 1953 the Syrian Government signed a contract No. C 148/53 with Vickers-Armstrongs for the supply of 20 Spitfire F.22. The aircraft were overhauled and refurbished by Airwork General Trading Ltd at Gatwick, probably under sub-contract.

Six aircraft, selected by agency of D Squire on 24 February 1953, were to be ready for shipment on 31st May 1954 and the balance in two batches on 30th June 1954 and 31st July 1954.

The Syrian Spitfires were test flown in England under Class B registrations *G-15-232* to *G-15-251*, before being given Syrian serial numbers **501** to **520** in sequence.

Later the Royal Rhodesian Air Force (RRAF) offered Spitfire F.22s to Syria. On 16th March 1955 seven airframes (SR60, SR65, SR67, SR80, SR85, SR87 and SR88) were sold for £1,200 each plus £2,000 for spares, but the order was not completed.

Little is known about the service of the Syrian Spitfires; individual dates are lacking. Some went to a scrapyard at an airfield near Damascus around 1960, but 14 still existed by about 1967. Four were then near Damascus and a further ten in the desert, north of the city.

Eventually only one Spitfire survived, but its fate and location remain unknown.

Individual Histories

PK337 Spitfire F.22 (Griffon 61); Became No **5..** (in range 514-520); TOC/RAF: 2.7.45; Sold back to V.A. 5.5.53; Shipped to Syria; Arr Syrian Air Force 8.54

PK348 Spitfire F.22 (Griffon 61); Became No **5..** (in range 507-513); TOC/RAF: 28.7.45; Sold back to V.A. 27.4.53; Shipped to Syria; Arr Syrian Air Force 7.54

PK383 Spitfire F.22 (Griffon 61); Became No **5..** (in range 501-506); TOC/RAF: 27.8.45; Sold back to V.A. via agency D Squire 24.2.53; Shipped to Syria; Arr Syrian Air Force 6.54

PK386 Spitfire F.22 (Griffon 61); Became No **5..** (in range 507-513); TOC/RAF: 31.8.45; Sold back to V.A. 27.4.53; Shipped to Syria; Arr Syrian Air Force 7.54

Spitfire F.22 PK658 with the Class B registration G-15-235 outside an Airwork hangar prior to delivery to Syria as No. 504. [MAP]

A derelict Spitfire F.22 of the Syrian Air Force, one of a number at an airfield scrapyard near Damascus around 1967. Efforts to purchase them were unsuccessful. [Bob Diemart]

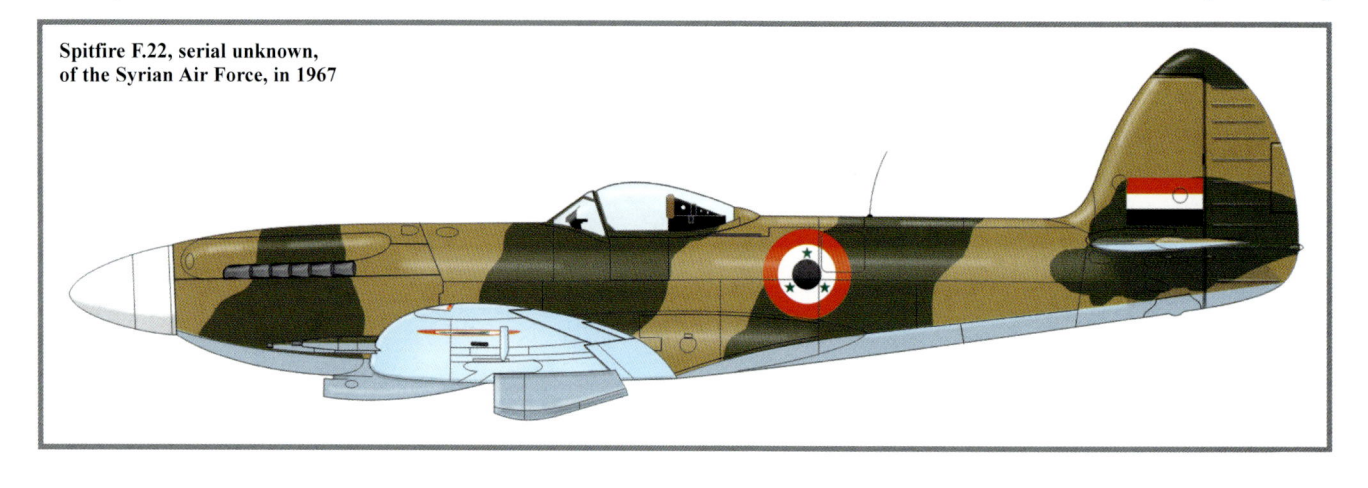

Spitfire F.22, serial unknown, of the Syrian Air Force, in 1967

PK389 Spitfire F.22 (Griffon 61); Became No **5..** (in range 514-520); TOC/RAF: 5.9.45; Sold back to V.A. 5.5.53; Shipped to Syria; Arr Syrian Air Force 8.54
PK504 Spitfire F.22 (Griffon 61); Became No **5..** (in range 507-513); TOC/RAF: 7.9.45; Sold back to V.A. 20.4.53; Shipped to Syria; Arr Syrian Air Force 7.54
PK549 Spitfire F.22 (Griffon 61); Became No **5..** (in range 507-513); TOC/RAF: 28.9.45; Sold back to V.A. 20.4.53; Shipped to Syria; Arr Syrian Air Force 7.54
PK558 Spitfire F.22 (Griffon 61); Became No **5..** (in range 501-506); TOC/RAF: 1.10.45; Sold back to V.A. via agency D Squire 24.2.53; Shipped to Syria; Arr Syrian Air Force 6.54
PK578 Spitfire F.22 (Griffon 61); Became No **5..** (in range 514-520); TOC/RAF: 15.10.45; Sold back to V.A. 5.5.53; Shipped to Syria; Arr Syrian Air Force 8.54
PK604 Spitfire F.22 (Griffon 61); Became No **5..** (in range 514-520); TOC/RAF: 13.12.45; Sold back to V.A. 5.5.53; Shipped to Syria; Arr Syrian Air Force 8.54
PK610 Spitfire F.22 (Griffon 61); Became No **5..** (in range 501-506); TOC/RAF: 27.10.45; Sold back to V.A. via agency D Squire 24.2.53; Shipped to Syria; Arr Syrian Air Force 6.54
PK616 Spitfire F.22 (Griffon 61); Became No **5..** (in range 501-506); TOC/RAF: 17.12.45; Sold back to V.A. via agency D Squire 24.2.53; Shipped to Syria; Arr Syrian Air Force 6.54
PK619 Spitfire F.22 (Griffon 61); Became No **5..** (in range 514-520); TOC/RAF: 5.12.45; Sold back to V.A. 5.5.53; Shipped to Syria; Arr Syrian Air Force 8.54
PK650 Spitfire F.22 (Griffon 61); Became No **5..** (in range 514-520); TOC/RAF: 3.1.46; Sold back to V.A. 5.5.53; Shipped to Syria; Arr Syrian Air Force 8.54
PK652 Spitfire F.22 (Griffon 61); Became No **5..** (in range 507-513); TOC/RAF: 20.12.45; Sold back to V.A. 24.4.53; Shipped to Syria; Arr Syrian Air Force 7.54
PK655 Spitfire F.22 (Griffon 61); Became No **5..** (in range 501-506); TOC/RAF: 13.12.45; Sold back to V.A. 22.2.53; Sold to Syria via agency D Squire; Shipped to Syria; Arr Syrian Air Force 6.54
PK658 Spitfire F.22 (Griffon 61); Became No **504**; TOC/RAF: 3.12.45; Sold back to V.A. via agency D Squire 24.2.53; Shipped to Syria; Arr Syrian Air Force 6.54; Later shown near Damascus, but fate unknown – **SURVIVOR**
PK660 Spitfire F.22 (Griffon 61); Became No **5..** (in range 507-513); TOC/RAF: 20.12.45; Sold back to V.A. 24.4.53; Shipped to Syria; Arr Syrian Air Force 7.54
PK668 Spitfire F.22 (Griffon 61); Became No **5..** (in range 514-520); TOC/RAF: 6.12.45; Sold back to V.A. 5.5.53; Shipped to Syria; Arr Syrian Air Force 8.54
PK671 Spitfire F.22 (Griffon 61); Became No **5..** (in range 507-513); TOC/RAF: 3.12.45; Sold back to V.A. 24.4.53; Shipped to Syria; Arr Syrian Air Force 7.54.

SURVIVOR

PK658 (Syrian No.**504**) reported near Damascus, probably in the eighties.

THAILAND
(formerly SIAM)

A Spitfire FR.XIVe of the RThaiAF, serial unknown. National markings above and below both wings, and on both fuselage sides. Note the under-wing fitment for rocket projectiles, indicating the use of the aircraft for ground attack. [RThaiAF]

One of the last users of Spitfires was the Royal Thai Air Force (RThaiAF). This country was a main customer in the Far East for Spitfire Mks.XIV and XIX, together with India.

Thailand was formerly known as Siam. In 1939 the name was changed to the Kingdom of Thailand. Japan occupied the country between 1942 and 1945.

Thailand received 30 reconditioned Spitfire F/FR.XIVc/es from Vickers-Armstrongs under a contract signed on 18th April 1950.

These were purchased by the company from RAF stocks on 10th-12th May 1950, and after reconditioning were test flown in the UK with B-class Registrations *G-15-111 to G-15-140*. They were delivered to Thailand between 13th December 1950 and 4th July 1951, being given the RThaiAF serial numbers **U14-1/93** to **U14-30/93**.

At first the Spitfire Mk.XIV served with the No.1 Wing, then with No.4 Wing from February/March 1951.

The RThaiAF changed the numbering system for its units in

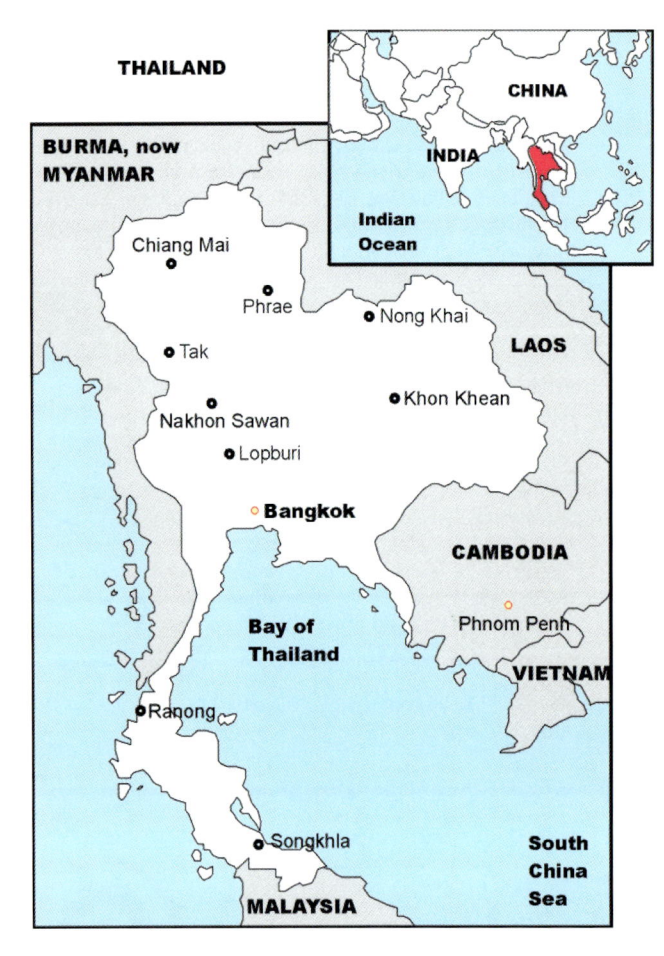

1953/54. No.1 Sqn of No.1 Wing was renamed No.11 Sqn, No.2 Sqn became No.12 Sqn, No.3 Sqn became No.13 Sqn. Similarly No.1 Sqn of No.4 Wing became No.41 Sqn and No.2 Sqn became No.42 Sqn, etc.

Finally all Spitfire Mk.XIVs were re-assigned to No.12 (F) Sqn from April 1954, for a short time only. The last Spitfire Mk.XIV being recorded as struck off charge on 26th April 1955. They were replaced by Bearcats.

Thailand also bought three Spitfire PR.XIXs for ground instructional use from the RAF (Comm.No.311). These were delivered from Far East Air Force stocks to the Directorate of Aeronautical Engineering (DAE) on 21st June 1954 and serialled **U14-25/97** to **U-14-27/97**. However, they were in poor condition, and served for only a short time, being struck off charge in April 1955.

Spitfire units of the Royal Thai Air Force

No. **1** Wing at Don Muang (near Bangkok),
No. 1 Sqn with Spitfire Mk.XIV from 16th-20th February 1951, built up its strength with 14 Spitfires from March to July 1951. Served with Spitfires until April 1954.
No. 12 (F) Sqn took over the Spitfire Mk.XIV of the No.1 Sqn and also those of the No.4 Wing in April 1954. Service with Spitfires until April 1955.
Commanding Officer:
Wg Cdr Thep Ketmoot

No. **2** Wing at Lopburi,
Spitfire Mk.XIV from 1951 to 1954.
Commanding Officer:
Wg Cdr Saun Sukserm

No. **4** Wing at Takli,
No.1 (Spec) Sqn received the first Spitfire Mk.XIV on 27th March 1951, built up its strength with nine Spitfires until August 1951; a tenth Spitfire arrived in January 1952. Service with Spitfires continued until April 1954, when they went to No.12 (F) Sqn of No.1 Wing.
Commanding Officers:
S/Ldr Watchara Jutairat 1951/52
S/Ldr Prakong Bintaboot 1952
Grp Capt Wong Poompoolpol 1952/54
Grp Capt Korn Kanittanon 1954/55

DAE Directorate of Aeronautical Engineering at Chiang Mai, received three Spitfire PR.XIX for ground instructional purposes from 21st June 1954 to April 1955.
Leader: Unknown.

Remarks for the Serial Nos of the RThaiAF:
"U" - is a letter of the Thai alphabet, which signifies a Fighter aircraft. Digit "14" indicates Spitfire Mk.XIV/XIX, and the following two digits (Mk.XIV=01 to 30; PR XIX=25 to 27) signify the sequence in which the aircraft was obtained; the last two figures ("93" or "97") signify the year in the Buddhist era in which the aircraft was commissioned.

For example: **U14- 1/93** (SM 914) means =
Fighter "SPITFIRE XIV", serial number 1 in 1951;
and: **U14-25/97** (PS 888) means =
Fighter "SPITFIRE XIX", serial number 25 in 1955.

Civil user

On 7th August 1954 a fourth Spitfire PR.XIX came to Thailand, for use in the Institute of Technology (ITT) at Trat. To Bangsue district of Bangkok by 1986

Individual Histories

MV350 Spitfire FR.XIVe (Griffon 65); Became **U14-..?/93**; TOC/RAF 31.3.45; Sold to V.A. 10.5.50; Arr RThaiAF 1951; No.1 Wing (No.1 Sqn) in 1951; No.4 Wing (No.1 Sqn); Service unknown; SOC 1955; scrapped

MV352 Spitfire FR.XIVe (Griffon 65); Became **U14-..?/93**; TOC/RAF 8.4 45; Sold to V.A. 12.5.50; Arr RThaiAF 1951; No.1 Wing (No.1 Sqn) in 1951; No.4 Wing (No.1 Sqn); Service unknown; SOC 1955; scrapped

NH639 Spitfire FR.XIVe (Griffon 65); Became **U14-..?/93**; TOC/RAF 4.3.45; Sold to V.A. 10.5.50; Arr RThaiAF 1951; No.1 Wing (No.1 Sqn) in 1951; No.4 Wing (No.1 Sqn); Service unknown; SOC 1955; scrapped

NH646 Spitfire FR.XIVe (Griffon 65); Became **U14-..?/93**; TOC/RAF 22.3.45; Sold to V.A. 10.5.50; Arr RThaiAF 1951; No.1 Wing (No.1 Sqn) in 1951; No.4 Wing (No.1 Sqn); Service unknown; SOC 1955; scrapped

NH657 Spitfire F.XIVe (Griffon 65); Became **U14-..?/93**; TOC/RAF 26.8.44; Sold to V.A. 10.5.50; Arr RThaiAF 1951; No.1 Wing (No.1 Sqn) in 1951; No.4 Wing (No.1 Sqn); Service unknown; SOC 1955; scrapped

NH698 Spitfire F.XIVe (Griffon 65); Became **U14-10/93**; TOC/RAF 21.2.44; Sold to V.A. 10.5.50; B-class reg. G-15-120; Test flown 17.11.50; Arr RThaiAF 1951; No.4 Wing (No.1 Sqn) 16.5.51; Service unknown; SOC 26.4 55; scrapped

NH714 Spitfire F.XIVe (Griffon 65); Became **U14-9/93**; TOC/RAF 18.3.44; Sold to V.A. 10.5.50; B-class reg. G-15-119; Test flown in 11.50; Arr RThaiAF 1951; No.4 Wing (No.1 Sqn) 27.3.51; Service unknown; SOC 26.4 55; scrapped

NH794 Spitfire FR.XIVe (Griffon 65); Became **U14-12/93**; TOC/RAF 9.3.44; Sold to V.A. 10.5.50; B-class reg. G-15-122; Test flown in 11.50; Arr RThaiAF 1951; No.1 Wing (No.1 Sqn) 12.7.51; Cat.E/1 on 20.10.51, SOC; Spare parts

NH800 Spitfire FR.XIVe (Griffon 65); Became **U14-25/93**; TOC/RAF 13.3.45; Sold to V.A. 10.5.50; B-class reg. G-15-135; Test flown in 4.51; Arr RThaiAF 1951; Air depot, storage from 1951; For spare parts

NH833 Spitfire FR.XIVe (Griffon 65); Became **U14-..?/93**; TOC/RAF 25.3.45; Sold to V.A. 10.5.50; Arr RThaiAF

THAILAND

1951; No.1 Wing (No.1 Sqn) in 1951; No.4 Wing (No.1 Sqn); Service unknown; SOC 1955; scrapped
NH834 Spitfire FR.XIVe (Griffon 65); Became **U14-..?/93**; TOC/RAF 30.3.45; Sold to V.A. 10.5.50; Arr RThaiAF 1951; No.1 Wing (No.1 Sqn) in 1951; No..4 Wing (No.1 Sqn); Service unknown; SOC 1955; scrapped
PM630 Spitfire PR.XIX (Griffon 66); TOC/RAF 26.11.45; Ex FEAF; Via No.390 MU transferred to the RThaiAF, arr 7.8.54; But only for exhibition, never on strength of the RThaiAF; Instructional airframe at the Institute of Technology at TRAT 7.8.54 (ITT); Exhibited in poor condition at a school playground at Trat some time (seen there in 3.80); Stored at Bangkok 1994/95; Now AFB Bangsue, Bangkok, static display - **SURVIVOR**
PS836 Spitfire PR.XIX (Griffon 66); Became **U14-27/97**; TOC/RAF 31.12.44; Ex FEAF; Arr Thailand 21.6.54; Instructional airframe by the Directorate of Aeronautical Engineering (DAE) from 21.6.54; SOC 26.4.55; Located

Surviving Spitfire PR.XIX PM630, seen here on display at Bangsue air base, Bangkok in March 1996, was taken over by the Royal Thai Air Force in August 1954 for ground instructional use only, never having received a RThaiAF serial number. [PRA]

Spitfire PR.XIX PS836, seen here dismantled at Don Muang airport, near Bangkok, around 1954, was previously U14-27/97, though only used as a ground instructional airframe. It was under restoration there from 1994, and is extant. [Merle Olmstad]

A Thai Spitfire PR.XIX with RAF serial PS888 later to become U14-25/97. The RAF fuselage roundel has been painted over but is still visible. The aircraft was used as a ground instructional airframe by the Directorate of Aeronautical Engineering (DAE) from June 1954. [via Phillip Jarrett]

at Technical school, Chiang Mei in 2.60; Derelict, bought by a British collector c.1979; To the Thai Airways Engineering Facility at Don Muang airport (near Bangkok), for restoration (with parts of RM873 & PM630) from 1994 - **SURVIVOR**

PS888 Spitfire PR.XIX (Griffon 66); Became **U14-25/97**; TOC/RAF 30.3.45; Ex FEAF; Arr Thailand 21.6.54; Instructional airframe by the Directorate of Aeronautical Engineering (DAE) from 21 6.54; SOC 26.4.55; scrapped

PS890 Spitfire PR.XIX (Griffon 66); Became **U14-26/97**; TOC/RAF 9.4.45; Ex FEAF; Arr Thailand 21.6.54; Instructional airframe by the Directorate of Aeronautical Engineering (DAE) from 21 6.54; SOC 26.4.55; Exhibited Bangkok Museum until 1962, then to USA; Restoration to airworthy; Reg. *N219AM* 7.1.99 to Air Museum, Chino, CA; and expected to fly in 2002 - **SURVIVOR**

RB164 Spitfire F.XIVc (Griffon 65); Became **U14-..?/93**; TOC/RAF 30.1.44; Sold to V.A. 10.5.50; Arr RThaiAF 1951; No.1 Wing (No.1 Sqn) in 1951; No.4 Wing (No.1 Sqn); Service unknown; SOC 1955; scrapped

RB174 Spitfire F.XIVc (Griffon 65); Became **U14-..?/93**; TOC/RAF 3.2.44; Sold to V.A. 10.5.50; Arr RThaiAF 1951; No.1 Wing (No.1 Sqn) in 1951; No.4 Wing (No.1 Sqn); Service unknown; SOC 1955; scrapped

RB181 Spitfire F.XIVc (Griffon 65); Became **U14-..?/93**; TOC/RAF 14.2.44; Sold to V.A. 10.5.50; Arr RThaiAF

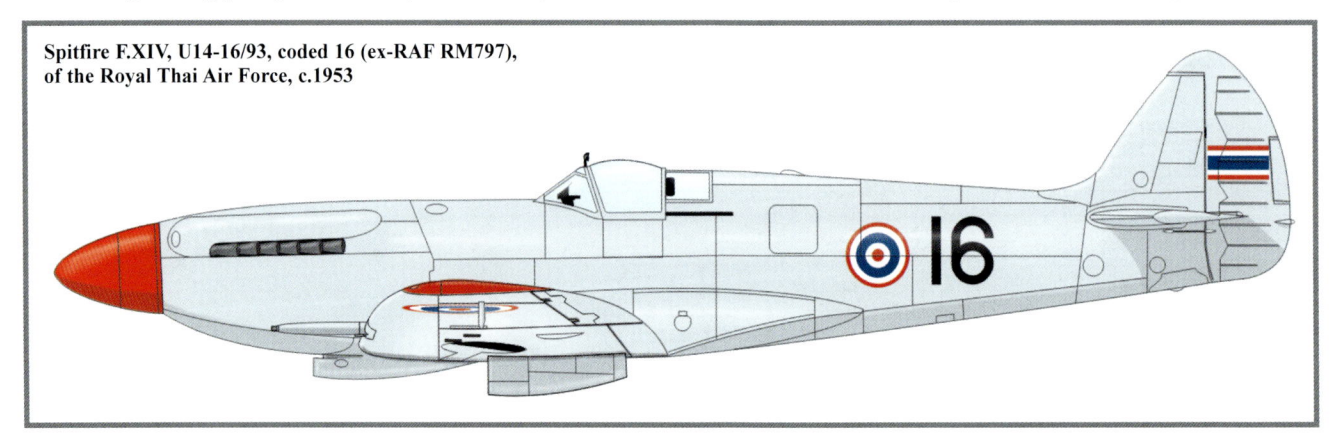

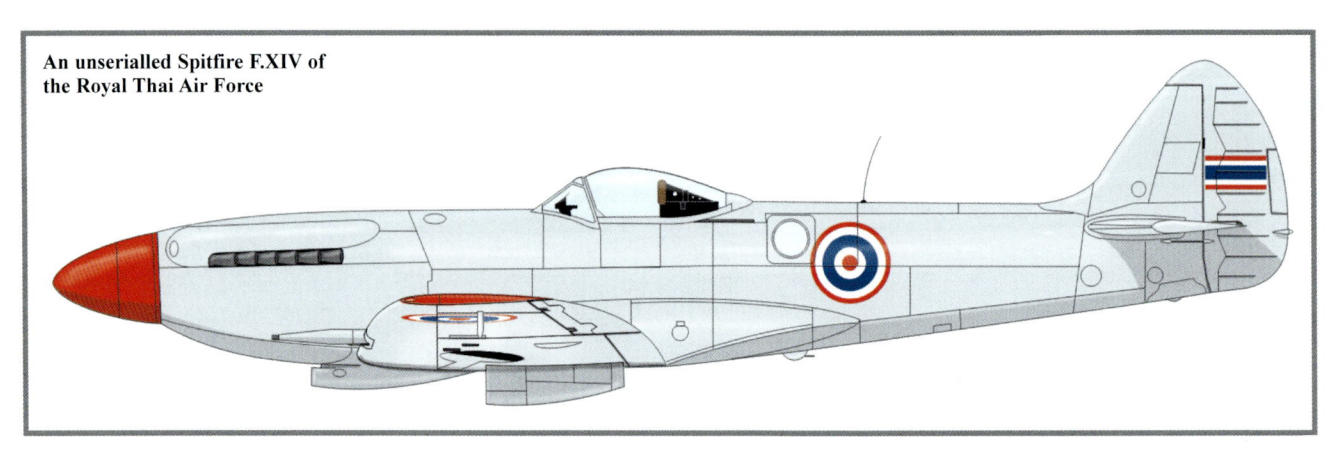

Spitfire F.XIV, U14-16/93, coded 16 (ex-RAF RM797), of the Royal Thai Air Force, c.1953

An unserialled Spitfire F.XIV of the Royal Thai Air Force

RB184 Spitfire F.XIVc (Griffon 65); Became **U14- 3/93**; TOC/RAF 21.3.44; Sold to V.A. 10.5.50; B-class reg. G-15-113; Test flown 16.10.50; Arr RThaiAF 1951; No.1 Wing (No.1 Sqn) 5.6.51; Dived into ground, Cat.FA/E 8.6.51; SOC in 7.51

RB188 Spitfire F.XIVc (Griffon 65); Became **U14-18/93**; TOC/RAF 20.2.44; Sold to V.A. 10.5.50; B-class reg. G-15-128; Test flown in 12.50; Arr RThaiAF 1951; No.4 Wing (No.1 Sqn) in 8.51; Dived into ground, Cat.FA/E on 26.1 53; SOC in 2.53

RB189 Spitfire F.XIVc (Griffon 65); Became **U14-..?/93**; TOC/RAF 4.3.44; Sold to V.A. 10.5.50; Arr RThaiAF 1951; No.1 Wing (No.1 Sqn) in 1951; No.4 Wing (No.1 Sqn); Service unknown; SOC 1955; scrapped

RM621 Spitfire F.XIVe (Griffon 65); Became **U14-30/93**; TOC/RAF 7.5.44; Sold to V.A. 10.5.50; B-class reg. G-15-140; Test flown 27.4.51; Arr RThaiAF 1951; To air depot (MU, storage) 1951; Spare parts

RM682 Spitfire F.XIVe (Griffon 65); Became **U14-..?/93**; TOC/RAF 14.6.44; Sold to V.A. 10.5.50; Arr RThaiAF 1951; No.1 Wing (No.1 Sqn) in 1951; No.4 Wing (No.1 Sqn); Service unknown; SOC 1955; scrapped

RM692 Spitfire F.XIVe (Griffon 65); Became **U14-24/93**; TOC/RAF 4.9.44; Sold to V.A. 10.5.50; B-class reg. G-15-134; Test flown 16.4.51; Arr RThaiAF 1951; No.4 Wing (No.1 Sqn) 25.1 52; Cat.E/1 on 25.8.53, SOC; Spare parts

RM728 Spitfire F.XIVe (Griffon 65); Became **U14-..?/93**; TOC/RAF 19.6.44; Sold to V.A. 10.5.50; Arr RThaiAF 1951; No.1 Wing (No.1 Sqn) in 1951; No.4 Wing (No.1 Sqn); Service unknown; SOC 1955; scrapped

RM747 Spitfire F.XIVe (Griffon 65); Became **U14-..?/93**; TOC/RAF 17.7.44; Sold to V.A. 10.5.50; Arr RThaiAF 1951; No.1 Wing (No.1 Sqn) in 1951; No.4 Wing (No.1 Sqn); Service unknown; SOC 1955; scrapped

RM757 Spitfire F.XIVe (Griffon 65); Became **U14-..?/93**; TOC/RAF 1.7.44; Sold to V.A. 10.5.50; Arr RThaiAF 1951; No.1 Wing (No.1 Sqn) in 1951; No.4 Wing (No.1 Sqn); Service unknown; SOC 1955; scrapped

RM797 Spitfire F.XIVe (Griffon 65); Became **U14-16/93**; TOC/RAF 1.9.44; Sold to V.A. 10.5.50; B-class reg. G-15-126; Test flown in 12.50; Arr RThaiAF 1951; No.1 Wing (No.1 Sqn) 27.6.51; Service unknown; SOC 27.1.54; Located at Surin AFB in Thailand early 1973 by Capt G Cooper, collected 24.5.73, to Darwin, Australia on 19.8.73, later to Sydney (engine replaced, restoration to fly as "*VH-XIV*"); Now at Alstonville, NSW - **SURVIVOR**

RM873 Spitfire F.XIVe (Griffon 65); Became **U14-5/93**; TOC/RAF 8.10.44; Sold to V.A. 10.5.50; B-class reg. G-15-115; Test flown 15.10.50; Arr RThaiAF 20.3.51; No.1 Wing (No.1 Sqn) 3.51; Service unknown; SOC 25.8.53; Fuselage only survived: Displayed at Sawankalok, Central Thailand; The fuselage has been stored at Bangkok since 1994/95, and parts were used for restoration of PS836 (wings to Peter Sledge, Australia, for RR232) - **SURVIVOR**

RN198 Spitfire F.XIVe (Griffon 65); Became **U14-..?/93**; TOC/RAF 14.2.45; Sold to V.A. 10.5.50; Arr RThaiAF 1951; No.1 Wing (No.1 Sqn) in 1951; No.4 Wing (No.1 Sqn); Service unknown; SOC 1955; scrapped

Checklist of RThaiAF / RAF serial numbers

RThaiAF No. U14–	RAF Serial No.	Construct. No. 6S -	B-class Reg.No. G.15 -	Test-flown (V.A.)	R.Thai.A.F. TOC	R.Thai.A.F. Unit	R.Thai.A.F. SOC	Remarks
Spitfire Mk.XIV								
1/93	SM914	585092	111	15.1.51	20.2.51	1/1	26.4.55	Survivor
2/93	?	585074	112	3.10.50	16.2.51	1/1	22.7.52	
3/93	RB184	364205	113	16.10.50	5.6.51	1/1	6.51	crashed 8.6.51
4/93	?	507148	114	18./20.10.50	16.3.51	1/1	27.1.54	
5/93	RM873	432296	115	15./24.10.50	20.3.51	1/1	27.1.54	
6/93	?	507129	116	4.11.50	20.3.51	1/1	25.8.53	
7/93	?	501102	117	4.11.50	16.5.51	1/1	27.1.54	
8/93	?	585007	118	13.11.50	22.8.51	4/1	27.1.54	
9/93	NH714	687154	119	11.50	27.3.51	4/1	26.4.55	
10/93	NH698	648264	120	17.11.50	16.5.51	4/1	26.4.55	
11/93	?	501127	121	?	23.3.51	1/1	7.52	crashed 22.7.52
12/93	NH794	507158	122	11.50	12.7.51	1/1	20.10.51	
13/93	?	432256	123	7.12.50	14.6.51	1/1	22.7.52	
14/93	?	364209	124	?	28.5.51	1/1	27.1.54	
15/93	?	364202	125	?	27.6.51	1/1	27.1.54	
16/93	RM797	507183	126	12.50	27.6.51	1/1	27.1.54	Survivor
17/93	?	687152	127	?	27.6.51	1/1	26.4.55	
18/93	RB188	585072	128	12.50	8.51	4/1	1.53	crashed 26.1.53
19/93	?	432266	129	26.1./16.4.51	11.8.51	4/1	27.1.54	
20/93	?	643807	130	?	8.51	4/1	22.7.52	
21/93	?	643790	131	?	22.8.51	4/1	7.52	crashed 22.7.52
22/93	?	364195	132	?	22.8.51	4/1	7.52	crashed 22.7.52
23/93	?	642797	133	27.2.51	22.8.51	4/1	1.54	crashed 27.1.54
24/93	RM692	643806	134	16.4.51	25.1.52	4/1	25.8.53	
25/93	NH800	501086	135	4.51	1951	MU		for spares only
26/93	?	432239	136	27.2.51	1951	MU		for spares only
27/93	?	676463	137	?	1951	MU		for spares only
28/93	?	364185	138	?	1951	MU		for spares only
29/93	?	663414	139	16.4.51	1951	MU		for spares only
30/93	RM621	648270	140	27.4.51	1951	MU		for spares only
Spitfire PR.XIX								
25/97	PS888	?	None		21.6.54	DAE	26.4.55	Instructional airframe
26/97	PS890	?	None		21.6.54	DAE	26.4.55	Instructional airframe; Survivor
27/97	PS836	?	None		21.6.54	DAE	26.4.55	Instructional airframe; Survivor
Private Owner:								
None	PM630	?	None		7.8.54	ITT		Instructional at Trat; Survivor

DAE = Directorate of Aeronautical Engineering; ITT = Institute of Technology at Trat

Surviving Spitfire FR.XIVe SM914, seen here on display devoid of identification markings in March 1996 at the Royal Thai Air Force Museum at Don Muang Airport, near Bangkok, was flown as U14-1/93 between 1951 and 1955, when it was relegated to display purposes.

SM914 Spitfire FR.XIVe (Griffon 65); Became **U14-1/93**; TOC/RAF 29.5.45; Sold to V.A. 12.5.50; B-class reg. G-15-111; Test flown 15.1.51; Arr RThaiAF 1951; No.1 Wing (No.1 Sqn) 20.2.51; Service unknown; SOC 26.4.55; To the RThaiAF Museum at Don Muang Airport (near Bangkok), display since 1955 - **SURVIVOR**

TP236 Spitfire FR.XIVe (Griffon 65); Became **U14-..?/93**; TOC/RAF 1 10.45; Sold to V.A. 10.5.50; Arr RThaiAF 1951; No.1 Wing (No.1 Sqn) in 1951; No.4 Wing (No.1 Sqn); Service unknown; SOC 1955; scrapped

TX993 Spitfire FR.XIVe (Griffon 65); Became **U14-..?/93**; TOC/RAF 2.5.45; Sold to V.A. 10.5.50; Arr RThaiAF 1951; No.1 Wing (No.1 Sqn) in 1951; No.4 Wing (No.1 Sqn); Service unknown; SOC 1955; scrapped

TZ183 Spitfire FR.XIVe (Griffon 65); Became **U14-..?/93**; TOC/RAF 17.10.45; Sold to V.A. 10.5.50; Arr RThaiAF 1951; No.1 Wing (No.1 Sqn) in 1951; No.4 Wing (No.1 Sqn); Service unknown; SOC 1955; scrapped

SURVIVORS in Thailand

PM630 Bangsue AFB, Bangkok.
PS836 Under restoration at Don Muang, Bangkok.
RM873 Museum at Don Muang, Bangkok.
SM9l4 Museum at Don Muang.

TURKEY

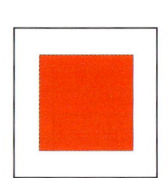

Turkey lay between the Allied and Axis powers during the Second World War. It was ready to defend it territory, but wished to remain neutral, having a pact with Britain as well as a non-aggression pact with Germany. Consequently the Turkish Air Force used aircraft from both sides. For example, the 5th Air Regiment had both British Spitfires and the German FW 190 on its strength. The Central Flying School trained with American, British, French and German aircraft, and flying training was supported by the RAF in the UK and in Egypt. Towards the end of the Second World War, on 23 February 1945, Turkey declared war against Germany.

The Turkish Air Force (TuAF)

Until 1944 the Turkish Air Force ["*Türk Hava Kuvvetleri*"] was part of the Turkish Army. It then became an independent arm and was organised in two Air Divisions, the first with HQ at Eskisehir (100m SW of Ankara), the second at Gaziemir (near Izmir). In 1947 a third was formed with HQ at Erzincan. The HQ of the TuAF was at Ankara.

Each Division controlled a number of Air Regiments ["*Hava Alay(lar)*", formerly named "*Tayyare Alay(lar)*"]. Each Fighter Regiment comprised two Battalions ["*Tabur(lar)*"], each Battalion with two Companies ["*Bölük(ler)*"]. In general the Companies of each Air Regiment were numbered 1 to 4 (1st & 2nd Companies for the first Battalion, 3rd & 4th for the second; but before 1943 another system with individual numbered Tabur(*lar*) and Bölük(*ler*) was in use - see 42nd Company of the 4th Air Regiment.

Under an order dated 31st March 1951 the TuAF was re-organised into Airbases and Squadrons with effect from 1st June 1951. At that time the last Spitfire Mk.Vs were phased out and the remaining Spitfire Mk.IXs went to the 4th Air Base ["*4.Hava Üssü*"] at Merzifon for the 141st & 142nd Sqns ["*Filo(lar)*"]; but the PR & FR-variants of Spitfires were sent to the First Air Base ["*1.H.Ü.*"] at Eskisehir for using by 113th Sqn ["*Filo*"].

Flying Training of the TuAF

The TuAF trained their pilots at a large Flying School (CFS) at Eskisehir ("*Hava Okulu*"), which included a Fighter Conversion Unit (FCU). This establishment used American Curtiss Hawk IIs and CW-22s, British Ansons, Magisters and others; French MS.406s; German FW 58s and GO 145As; Polish PLZ P.24s and from 1948 also Harvard T-6s. Spitfire Mk.Vc/trops arrived in 1947, later also some Mk.IXs.

Some pilots of the TuAF trained with the RAF during the war. Initial conversion training to the Spitfire Mk.V took place on airfields in Egypt, mainly at Abu Sueir and El Ballah (two ex-Turkish Spitfire Mk.Is were based there in 1942).

Spitfire deliveries

Originally Turkey asked on 8th January 1937 for a supply of 30 Spitfire Mk.Ia. Subsequently it requested a licence to build a further 30 aircraft, and on 3rd February 1938 the Air Ministry's Foreign Orders Committee (FOC) discussed a changed order for 50 Spitfires. On 17th November 1938 the request was allotted priority No.4, by the Foreign Office, for 30+30 Spitfires.

The first Spitfire F.Ia (L1066) arrived in Turkey with SS *Lassell* on 18th September 1939 and was serialled **2901**. It had been intended for Poland, but with the collapse of that country it was offered instead to Turkey. After test flying by Turkish pilots on 26th and 27th September 1939 the Turkish Air Force wanted to order a further 45 sets of components for licence-building with a letter of 15th May 1940. Eventually a contract was made under No. C1060/40 for 15 Spitfire Mk.Ias, the Type 341. The actual invoice price was £12,000. However, only two further Spitfire (Nos.**2902 & 2903**) were received at this time, after having been test flown in the UK under B-class registrations *N22* & *N23*. Thirteen others were retained for RAF use (eight of them are known to have been test flown in the UK under B-class registrations *N24* to *N31*). Spitfire Mk.Ias served with the 4th Air Regiment ["*4th Hava Alayi*"], which also used 15 Hurricane Mk.Is at that time.

Deliveries of Allied aircraft were later virtually ceased in an attempt to pressure the country into cutting off trade and diplomatic relations with Germany. Turkey had initially requested 132 Spitfire Mk.Vb/c-trop, this number being reduced to 105 aircraft. TuAF serial numbers were allotted in the range **5501** to **5536** (Spitfire Mk.Vb/trop) & **5701** to **5769** (supposed to be Spitfire Mk.Vc/trop).

In 1943 the TuAF was awaiting the first Spitfire Mk.Vb/trop, which were offered as Lend-Lease aid by the British Government following the military agreement from 30th/31st January 1943 (Adana conference). However, it was not until September 1944 that the first Mk.Vb arrived. Later a further 69 Mk.Vb/c-trops and a single F.IXc followed between November 1944 and May 1945. All the Mk.Vs came from RAF Middle East stocks, mostly in poor condition. Some were withdrawn from use within a year. None returned to the RAF. Spitfire Mk.Vb/c-trops were used primarily for training purposes by the 5th and 6th Air Regiments until 1948 (Mk.Vb) and 1949 (Mk.Vc), when they were replaced by the American P-47 and Spitfire Mk.IX, respectively. Only a few Spitfire Mk.Vcs survived within the Flying School until 1951.

Three reconnaissance Spitfire Mk.V of the TuAF served with the HQ Liaison and PR-detachment "*Yüksek Irtifa Foto Kesif Kitasi*" [High Altitude Photo Recce Unit] from 1945 to 1948, these being Spitfire Mk.Vb/c-trops with special equipment; they became TuAF Serial Nos.**5801-5803**.

A Spitfire PR.XIX of the Yüksek Irtifa Foto Kesif Kitasi. [Ole Nikolajsen]

Spitfire LF.IXs lined up at Nicosia whilst en route to Turkey around 1946/7. [L Le Moignan]

Pilots of the 4th Regiment TuAF standing in front of a Spitfire F.Ia, serial unknown. [Ole Nikolajsen]

Additionally, Turkey received from the RAF a total of 197 Spitfire F. & LF.IXc/es (Comm.No.361), the first 169 of these being given Serial Nos.**6201** to **6369**. Supplies began in January 1947 and continued until autumn 1948. Nine crashed before or during delivery flight, and of these only two were given a TuAF serial number.

The Spitfire Mk.IXs were flown from England to Turkey via Bordeaux, Istres/Marseilles and Corsica (France), Italy, Malta and over Mediterranean Sea to Turkey. To increase the range, slipper-tanks were installed. The aircraft had underwing bomb release-gear and clipped wings for fighter-bomber purposes, as well as in the fighter role. In England the Spitfires were marked with the TuAF national emblems on wings and fuselage and the national flag of Turkey on both sides of the fin, but they retained their RAF serials. On arriving in Turkey each aircraft was given a TuAF Serial No painted on the fuselage in black or white digits.

Spitfire Mk.IXs served in five Air Regiments (Nos.4 to 8 *Hava Alay(lar)* from 1947 to 1951, each company within these regiments initially receiving nine aircraft, but these were gradually replaced by Republic P-47D Thunderbolts. When the Turkish Air Force a reorganised on 31 March 1951 the 4th Air Regiment at Merzifon became the 4th Air Base, and the remaining Spitfire IXs were

Summary of Spitfire deliveries

TuAF Serial Nos	Mk.-Type	Order Vol.	Deliv. Vol.	Deliv. dates	Notes (user / unit)
2901-2903	Mk.Ia	3	3	8.39 - - 5.40	(1.A/12.Bl)
4501-4515	Mk.Ia	15	0	---	1939/42; cancelled
5501-5536	Mk.Vb	36	36	28.9.44	selected 5.9.44 (6.A & 5.A)
5701-5769	Mk.Vc	69	69	11.44 - - 5.45	selected 10.-12.44 (6.A)
5801-5803	Mk.V - Recce	3	3	9.44 - - 1.45	(Yük.Irt.Kş.Foto. Kt. & 10.A)
5804-5827	Mk.V	24	0	---	cancelled
5851	PR.XI	1	0	---	no trace
6201-6369 6347 6370	Mk.IX FR.IXc F IXc	168 1 1	168 1 1	1.47 - - 2.48; 3.45	(4.-8.A & 4.HÜ) (as Nos 6551-54)
unknown	Mk.IX	?	28	1948/49	also replacements
6551-6554	PR.XIX	4	4	3.-4.47	(Yük.Irt.Kş.Foto. Kt,10.A& 113.Filo)
Total		325	313		

regrouped into the newly formed 141st & 142nd Squadrons ["*Filo(lar)*"], each with 25 aircraft. They were the country's only air defence fighters until November 1954 when they were replaced by the North American F-86E Sabre.

Also reported was a Spitfire PR.XI with the TuAF Serial No.5851, which served in co-operation with the Spitfire PR.XIXs and the Mk.V recce variants with the Yüksek Irtifa Foto Kesif Kitasi in 1947/48, and later with the 10th Recce Regiment ["*10.Kesif Alayi*"]. However, the 113th Squadron ["*Filo*"] reported a Mk.IX in use until 1953. RAF records shows no trace of a PR.XI being delivered to Turkey, but a Spitfire FR.IXc (formerly MK915) is mentioned, this becoming No **6347**.

The TuAF received four Spitfire PR.XIX in 1947 after overhaul by Vickers-Armstrongs, which had bought the Spitfires from the RAF on 12th November 1946. They were test flown under Class B registrations *N-131* to *N-134*, being later given TuAF Serial Nos.**6551** to **6554**. Spitfire PR.XIXs served first with the Yüksek Irtibat Kesif Foto Kitaati in 1947 and 1948. Later they went to the 10th Recce Regiment ["*10.Kesif Alayi*"] which flew communication and reconnaissance missions, being based at Afyon until 1951. One had been struck off charge by 1951, but the other three flew with the 113th Squadron ["*Filo*"] at Eskisehir from 1951 to 1953.

Abbreviations of the TuAF

A.   Alayi (Regiment)
Bl.   Bölük (Company)
F.   Filo (Squadron)
Hv.   Hava (Air)
HÜ   Hava Üssü (Air Base)
Ks.   Kesif (Reconnaissance)
Tb.   Taburu (Battalions)

For example "4.A/II.Tb/3.Bl" means the No.3 Company of the Second Battalion within the 4th Air Regiment, but sometimes also written without the Battalion (e.g.: "4.A/3.Bl").

Spitfire units of the Turkish Air Force (TuAF)

4th   Air Regiment ["*4 ncü Hava Alayi*"]; Based at Kütahya from 4th February 1937, at Çorlu 1939/40 and at Merzifon from 26th July 1942 to 31st May 1951 (airbase became 4th Hava Üssü, see by 141st & 142nd Filo); Comprised the 42nd, 43rd, 57th & 58th Companies ["*Bölük(ler)*"] with Hurricane Mk.I and MS.406C in 1939/40, the 42nd Company ["*Bölük*"] also with three Spitfire Mk.Ia at that time; Later the 4th Air Regiment (1st - 4th Companies) served with Spitfire Mk.IX from March 1947 to May 1951. - Unit code: 'YV'.

Commanding Officers:
Lt Col Ferruh Sahinbas   2.37
Col Muzaffer Göksenin   1.38
Col I Hakki Akkus   1.40
Col Seyfi Turagay   8.44
Col Ziya Zeyrek   8.45
Col H Suphi Göker   8.46

Spitfire LF.IXe TE511 (TuAF 6281) at Bordeaux in France on the way from the UK to Turkey in June 1947. The aircraft served with the 3rd Company, 7th Air Regiment at Kütahya from July 1947.   *[J Delmas via Claude A Pierquet]*

Col M Ali Pekman	8.48
Col Hidayet Göksel	8.49
Lt Col Suat Eraybar	8.50
Col Necmi Akyildiz	9.51
Col Semi Karacehennem	9.52

5th Air Regiment ["*5 nci Hava Alayi*"]; Based at Bursa from 1944 to 1952 (airbase became 5th Hava Üssü mid 1951); With FW 190A-3 from 1943 to 1947, but the 1st & 2nd Companies ["*Bölük(ler)*"] with Spitfire F.Vb/c-trop from 1945-48; The 3rd & 4th Companies with Spitfire Mk.IX from October 1947. In May 1948 this Air Regiment converted to the American P-47D Thunderbolt. - Unit code: 'YL'.

Commanding Officers:
Lt Col Enver Akoglu	3.45
Col Rahmi Uçari	9.47
Col Seyfi Turagay	12.48
Col Talat Biringen	8.50
Col Hidayet Göksel	8.51

6th Air Regiment ["*6 nci Hava Alayi*"]; Formed at Gaziemir (near Izmir) with Curtiss P-40 on 12th February 1943, based at Bandirma from 20th May 1949; Disbanded 15th February 1950. 1st & 3rd Companies ["*Bölük(ler)*"] with Spitfire Mk.Vb/trop from September 1944; 1st - 4th Companies with Spitfire Mk.Vb/c-trop from 1945 to 1949;

Spitfire IXs of the 4th Air Regiment at Kütahya around 1948/50, the nearest aircraft being coded 'YV.85'. [via Phillip Jarrett]

Spitfire IXs of the 4th Air Regiment lined up at Merzifon around 1948/50, the nearest aircraft being coded 'YV.17'. [via Phillip Jarrett]

Spitfire Mk.IX from May 1949 to February 1950. Unit code: 'FT'.
Commanding Officers:
Maj Enver Akoglu 4.43
Col Hidayet Göksel 4.44
Col Sabri Göknart 8.47
Lt Col M Ali Pekman 7.49

7th Air Regiment ["*7 nci Hava Alayi*"]; Formed at Kütahya 11th March 1947; disbanded 1st March 1950; The 1st - 4th Companies ["*Bölük(ler)*"] with Spitfire Mk.IX from May 1947 to February 1950.
Commanding Officers:
Col Gavsi Uçagök 4.47
Col Seyfi Turagay 8.48
Col Rahmi Uçari 12.48

8th Air Regiment ["*8 nci Hava Alayi*"]; Formed at Erzincan 4th April 1947, based there until 23rd June 1952 (the airbase became 8 Hava Üssü mid 1951); The 1st - 4th Companies ["*Bölük(ler)*"] with Spitfire Mk.IX from August 1947 to January 1949. Unit code: 'DE'.
Commanding Officers:
Lt Col Rahmi Uçari 5.47
Col Enver Akoglu 8.47
Col Tekin Ariburun 2.48
Col Nevzat Gökeri 8.50

Yüksek Irtifa Foto Kesif Kitasi (*Yük.Irt. Foto Ks.Kt.*); Formed as a Liaison and high level Photo-Recce detachment of the TuAF HQ 1946, attached to the "*Irtibat Nakliye*" Battalion (II.Nk.Tab Ks, ve irt.böl) at Eskisehir in 1946/47; Also with Spitfire Mk.V/Recce and PR.XIX and a PR.XI (possibly a FR.IXc); Spitfires to the 10th Recce Regiment in August 1948.
Commanding Officers:
Unknown

10th (Recce) Regiment ["*10 ncu Kesif Alayi*"]
Formed at Afyon 23rd August 1948, disbanded there 31st May 1951; 3rd Company ["*Bölük*"] with Spitfire PR.XIX, Mk.V/Recce and a PR.XI (possibly FR.IXc) from August 1948 to 1951. Then the remaining Spitfires went to the First Air Base (113th Squadron). - Unit Code: 'SK'.
Commanding Officers:
Unknown

113th (Recce) Squadron ["*113.Filo*"]
Formed 1st June 1951 on the First Air Base ["*1 Hava Üssü*"] at Eskisehir, used three Spitfire PR.XIX and a FR.IXc until 1953, when the unit was reformed with F-84G.
Commanding Officer:
Unknown

141st (F) Squadron ["*141.Filo*"]
Formed on the Fourth Air Base ("*4.Hava Üssü*") at Merzifon on 1st June 1951 and served with Spitfire Mk.IX until 1953. Received F-86E Sabre in 1954.

Commanding Officers:
Mjr Mustafa Azakli 8.51 to 10.53
Mjr Selçuk Okyay 8.54 to 12.54

142nd (F) Squadron ["*142.Filo*"]
Formed on the Fourth Air Base ("*4.Hava Üssü*") at Merzifon on 1st June 1951 and served with Spitfire Mk.IX until 1953. Received F-86E Sabre in 1954.
Commanding Officers:
Mjr Ihsan Aras 8.51 to 8.52
Mjr Bülent Sakarya 1952/53

CFS Central Flying School ["*Hava Okulu*"] at Eskisehir, included also a Fighter Conversion Unit (FCU); Spitfire Mk.Vc/trop from 1948 to 1950; possibly also Spitfire Mk.IX from 1949 to 1953 - Unit code: 'OK'.
Commanding Officers:
Unknown

Technical Training

A Technical School at Yesilkoy (near Istanbul) provided technical training.

Storage

Air depots exist at Afyon, Ankara, Eskisehir, Kasseri, and Malatya; Eskisehir and Kayseri also have repair depots (ARD).

The end of Spitfire flying by the TuAF

TuAF census showed 93+3 Spitfire Mk.V on strength in June 1946. It listed 72+2 Spitfire Mk.V, 170 Mk.IX and 4 PR.XIX to October 1949. In 1951 63 Mk.IX and 3 PR.XIX were counted.

The Spitfire Mk.Is were grounded because lack of spares in 1940, but two later went to Egypt (El Ballah) in 1942. They were not officially listed as withdrawn from use by the TuAF until 1950. Spitfire Mk.Vs were phased out mostly in 1948 (Vb) and 1949 (Vc), the last became SOC in 1951. Spitfire Mk.IXs & XIXs remained in service until 1953/54; one of the last crashed on 5th August 1954, see TuAF No 6251 (PT680). Two Mk.IXs were sold to Italy after they had emergency landed there and joined the Italian Air Force in 1949. All the other Spitfires were scrapped, none survived.

Individual Histories

(Only general information on TuAF service is available. Individual histories are known only for a few aircraft; see Notes at the end of this section.)

TuAF Serial Nos. 2901 - 2903: Spitfire Mk.Ia, served with 42nd Company ["42 *Bölük*"] of the 4th Air Regiment ["4 *Hava Alayi*"], detached to Çorlu 1939/40

L1066 Spitfire F.Ia (Merlin III); Became TuAF No. **2901**; TOC/RAF 31.7.39 - Arr TuAF 19.8.39; 42nd Company of 4th Air Regiment in 8.40, detached to Çorlu; Grounded due to lack of spares 12.40; Fate unknown

Spitfire F.Ia, 2902/2 of 42nd Bölük (Company) of 4 Hava Alayi (Air Regiment), Turkish Air Force, Çorlu, August 1940

Spitfire F.Vb/trop 5512 was flown by the 2nd Company of the 6th Air Regiment at Gaziemir. It is seen here flying in company with a FW 190A-5 marked '36'.
[via Phillip Jarrett]

Spitfire F.Vb/trop 5514 TuAF being manhandled. It served with the 1st Company, 5th Air Regiment at Bursa.
[IWM CMA3687]

P9566 Spitfire F.Ia (Merlin III); Became TuAF No. **2902**; Class B reg. N-22 - Arr TuAF in 5.40; 42nd Company of 4th Air Regiment in 8.40; Detached to Çorlu; Grounded due to lack of spares 12.40; Abu Sueir, Egypt, flown to No.1 (ME) Training School at El Ballah c. 4.42 (F/O NF Duke); Re-serialled HK954 by 25.4.42; Fate unknown

P9567 Spitfire F.Ia (Merlin III); Became TuAF No. **2903**; Class B reg. N-23 - Arr TuAF in 5.40; 42nd Company of 4th Air Regiment in 8.40; Detached to Çorlu; Grounded due to lack of spares 12.40; Abu Sueir, Egypt, flown to No.1 (ME) Training School at El Ballah c. 4.42 (F/O NF Duke); Re-serialled HK956 by 25.4.42; Fate unknown

TuAF Serial Nos. 5501 - 5539: Spitfire Mk.Vb/trop,
delivered 28 September 1944; 6th & 5th Air Regiments, 1944-48

Nos.5501 to 5531 went direct to the Regiments. But three of them were in such a poor condition that they could not be used, another four went into storage 1944/45.
Nos.5532 to 5539 stored as reserve; some perhaps used for ground instructional use later.

5501 Spitfire F.Vb/trop (Merlin 46); Arr 28.9.44; To 6th Air Regiment (1st Company) at Gaziemir; SOC by 1951
5502 Spitfire F.Vb/trop (Merlin 46); Arr 28.9.44; To 6th Air Regiment (1st Company) at Gaziemir; SOC by 1951
5503 Spitfire F.Vb/trop (Merlin 46); Arr 28.9.44; To Afyon Depot; SOC by 1951
5504 Spitfire F.Vb/trop (Merlin 46); Arr 28.9.44; To 6th Air Regiment (4th Company) at Gaziemir; SOC by 1951
5505 Spitfire F.Vb/trop (Merlin 46); Arr 28.9.44; To 5th Air Regiment (2ns Company) at Bursa; SOC by 1951
5506 Spitfire F.Vb/trop (Merlin 46); Arr 28.9.44; To 6th Air Regiment (1st Company) at Gaziemir; SOC by 1951
5507 Spitfire F.Vb/trop (Merlin 46); Arr 28.9.44; To 6th Air Regiment (1st Company) at Gaziemir; SOC by 1951
5508 Spitfire F.Vb/trop (Merlin 46); Arr 28.9.44; To 6th Air Regiment (1st Company) at Gaziemir; SOC by 1951
5509 Spitfire F.Vb/trop (Merlin 46); Arr 28.9.44; To 6th Air Regiment (1st Company) at Bursa; SOC by 1951
5510 Spitfire F.Vb/trop (Merlin 46); Arr 28.9.44; No details; SOC by 1951
5511 Spitfire F.Vb/trop (Merlin 46); Arr 28.9.44; To 6th Air Regiment (1st Company) at Gaziemir; SOC by 1951
5512 Spitfire F.Vb/trop (Merlin 46); Arr 28.9.44; To 6th Air Regiment (2nd Company) at Gaziemir; SOC by 1951
5513 Spitfire F.Vb/trop (Merlin 46); Arr 28.9.44; To Ankara Depot; SOC by 1951
5514 Spitfire F.Vb/trop (Merlin 46); Arr 28.9.44; To 5th Air Regiment (1st Company) at Bursa; SOC by 1951
5515 Spitfire F.Vb/trop (Merlin 46); Arr 28.9.44; To 6th Air Regiment (2nd Company) at Gaziemir; SOC by 1951
5516 Spitfire F.Vb/trop (Merlin 46); Arr 28.9.44; To 6th Air Regiment (2nd Company) at Gaziemir; SOC by 1951
5517 Spitfire F.Vb/trop (Merlin 46); Arr 28.9.44; To 6th Air Regiment (2nd Company) at Gaziemir; SOC by 1951
5518 Spitfire F.Vb/trop (Merlin 46); Arr 28.9.44; To 5th Air Regiment (2nd Company) at Bursa; SOC by 1951
5519 Spitfire F.Vb/trop (Merlin 46); Arr 28.9.44; To Afyon Depot; SOC by 1951
5520 Spitfire F.Vb/trop (Merlin 46); Arr 28.9.44; To 6th Air Regiment (4th Company) at Gaziemir; SOC by 1951
5521 Spitfire F.Vb/trop (Merlin 46); Arr 28.9.44; To 6th Air Regiment (3rd Company) at Gaziemir; SOC by 1951
5522 Spitfire F.Vb/trop (Merlin 46); Arr 28.9.44; To 6th Air Regiment (1st Company) at Gaziemir; SOC by 1951
5523 Spitfire F.Vb/trop (Merlin 46); Arr 28.9.44; To 6th Air Regiment (1st Company) at Gaziemir; SOC by 1951
5524 Spitfire F.Vb/trop (Merlin 46); Arr 28.9.44; To 6th Air Regiment (4th Company) at Gaziemir; SOC by 1951
5525 Spitfire F.Vb/trop (Merlin 46); Arr 28.9.44; Not accepted
5526 Spitfire F.Vb/trop (Merlin 46); Arr 28.9.44; Not accepted; Placed in reserve, wfu
5527 Spitfire F.Vb/trop (Merlin 46); Arr 28.9.44; Not accepted; Placed in reserve, wfu
5528 Spitfire F.Vb/trop (Merlin 46); Arr 28.9.44; To 6th Air Regiment (2nd Company) at Gaziemir; SOC by 1951
5529 Spitfire F.Vb/trop (Merlin 46); Arr 28.9.44; To 6th Air Regiment (2nd Company) at Gaziemir; SOC by 1951
5530 Spitfire F.Vb/trop (Merlin 46); Arr 28.9.44; To 6th Air Regiment (3rd Company) at Gaziemir; SOC by 1951
5531 Spitfire F.Vb/trop (Merlin 46); Arr 28.9.44; To 6th Air Regiment (3rd Company) at Gaziemir; SOC by 1951
5532 Spitfire F.Vb/trop (Merlin 46); Arr 28.9.44; To reserve storage
5533 Spitfire F.Vb/trop (Merlin 46); Arr 28.9.44; To reserve storage
5534 Spitfire F.Vb/trop (Merlin 46); Arr 28.9.44; To reserve storage
5535 Spitfire F.Vb/trop (Merlin 46); Arr 28.9.44; To reserve storage
5536 Spitfire F.Vb/trop (Merlin 46); Arr 28.9.44; To reserve storage
5537 Spitfire F.Vb/trop (Merlin 46); Arr 28.9.44; To reserve storage
5538 Spitfire F.Vb/trop (Merlin 46); Arr 28.9.44; To reserve storage
5532 Spitfire F.Vb/trop (Merlin 46); Arr 28.9.44; To reserve storage

EP195 Spitfire F.Vb/trop (Merlin 46); Became TuAF No. **55..** ? TOC/RAF 31.5.42; Selected for Turkey 5.9.44 - Arr TuAF 28.9.44; 6th Air Regiment at Gaziemir 10.44 [see Note 1)]; SOC by 1948
ER277 Spitfire F.Vb/trop (Merlin 46); Became TuAF No. **55..** ? TOC/RAF 8.9.42; ex USAAF; Selected for Turkey 5.9.44 - Arr TuAF 28.9.44; 6th Air Regiment at Gaziemir [see Note 1)]; SOC by 1948
ER319 Spitfire F.Vb/trop (Merlin 46); Became TuAF No. **55..** ? TOC/RAF 10.9.42; ex FFAF; Selected for Turkey 5.9.44 - Arr TuAF 28.9.44; 6th Air Regiment at Gaziemir [see Note 1)]; SOC by 1948
JL210 Spitfire F.Vc/trop (Merlin 50); Became TuAF No. **55..** ? TOC/RAF 2.4.43; ex FFAF; Selected for Turkey 5.9.44 - Arr TuAF 28.9.44; 6th Air Regiment at Gaziemir [see Note 1)]; SOC by 1951
? Spitfire F.Vb/trop (M. 45/46); Became TuAF No. **55..** ? further 32 aircraft selected 5.9.44, arrived TuAF as lend lease aid 28.9.44 (RAF Serial Nos unknown); To 6th Air Regiment at Gaziemir 10.44; To 5th Air Regiment at Bursa in 1945; SOC latest 1948 (None returned to the RAF)

TuAF Serial Nos 5701 - 5769: Spitfire Mk.Vb/c-trop
selected October-December 1944, delivered November 1944 - May 1945; To 6th & 5th Air Regiments 1945 - 1949; CFS from 1948 - 1950

5701 Arr 18.10.44; To Afyon Depot; SPOC by 1951
5702 Arr 18.10.44; To 6th Air Regiment (4th Company) at Gaziemir; SOC by 1951
5703 Arr 18.10.44; To 6th Air Regiment (3rd Company) at Gaziemir; SOC by 1951
5704 Arr 18.10.44; To 6th Air Regiment (1st Company) at Gaziemir; SOC by 1951
5705 Arr 18.10.44; To 6th Air Regiment (3rd Company) at Gaziemir; SOC by 1951
5706 Arr 18.10.44; No information
5707 Arr 18.10.44; To 6th Air Regiment (3rd Company) at Gaziemir; SOC by 1951
5708 Arr 18.10.44; To 6th Air Regiment (3rd Company) at Gaziemir; SOC by 1951
5709 Arr 20.10.44; To 6th Air Regiment (3rd Company) at Gaziemir; SOC by 1951
5710 Arr 18.10.44; To Ankara Depot
5711 Arr 20.10.44; No information
5712 Arr 22.10.44; To 6th Air Regiment (3rd Company) at Gaziemir; SOC by 1951
5713 Arr 22.10.44; To 6th Air Regiment (3rd Company) at Gaziemir; SOC by 1951

5714	Arr 22.10.44; To 6th Air Regiment (2nd Company) at Gaziemir; SOC by 1951
5715	Arr 22.10.44; To 6th Air Regiment (3rd Company) at Gaziemir; SOC by 1951
5716	Arr 22.10.44; To 6th Air Regiment (2nd Company) at Gaziemir; SOC by 1951
5717	Arr 22.10.44; To 6th Air Regiment (4th Company) at Gaziemir; SOC by 1951
5718	Arr 22.10.44; To 5th Air Regiment (2nd Company) at Bursa; SOC by 1951
5719	Arr 22.10.44; To 6th Air Regiment (4th Company) at Gaziemir; SOC by 1951
5720	Arr 22.10.44; To 6th Air Regiment (4th Company) at Gaziemir; SOC by 1951
5721	Arr 7.11.44; To 6th Air Regiment (4th Company) at Gaziemir; SOC by 1951
5722	Arr 7.11.44; To 6th Air Regiment (4th Company) at Gaziemir; SOC by 1951
5723	Arr 7.11.44; To 6th Air Regiment (3rd Company) at Gaziemir; SOC by 1951
5724	Arr 7.11.44; To 6th Air Regiment (4th Company) at Gaziemir; SOC by 1951
5725	Arr 7.11.44; To 6th Air Regiment (4th Company) at Gaziemir; SOC by 1951
5726	Arr 7.11.44; To 6th Air Regiment (4th Company) at Gaziemir; SOC by 1951
5727	Arr 7.11.44; To 6th Air Regiment (2nd Company) at Gaziemir; SOC by 1951
5728	Arr 7.11.44; To 6th Air Regiment at Gaziemir; SOC by 1951
5729	Arr 7.11.44; Placed in reserve, wfu
5730	Arr 7.11.44; To 6th Air Regiment at Gaziemir; SOC by 1951
5731	Arr 7.11.44; U/s in 1945
5732	Arr 7.11.44; To 5th Air Regiment (1st Company) Bursa at Gaziemir; SOC by 1951
5733	Arr 7.11.44; U/s in 1945
5734	Arr 7.11.44; To 5th Air Regiment (1st Company) at Bursa; SOC by 1951
5735	Arr 15.11.44; To 5th Air Regiment (1st Company) at Bursa; SOC by 1951
5736	Arr 15.11.44; No information
5737	Arr 15.11.44; To 5th Air Regiment (1st Company) at Bursa; SOC by 1951
5738	Arr 15.11.44; To 5th Air Regiment (1st Company) at Bursa; SOC by 1951
5739	Arr 15.11.44; To 5th Air Regiment (2nd Company) at Bursa; SOC by 1951
5740	Arr 15.11.44; To 5th Air Regiment (2nd Company) at Bursa; SOC by 1951
5741	Arr 15.11.44; To 5th Air Regiment (2nd Company) at Bursa; SOC by 1951
5742	Arr 15.11.44; To 5th Air Regiment (2nd Company) at Bursa; SOC by 1951
5743	Arr 15.11.44; U/s in 1945
5744	Arr 15.11.44; No information
5745	Arr 16.12.44; No information
5746	Arr 16.12.44; To 5th Air Regiment (2nd Company) at Bursa; SOC by 1951
5747	Arr 16.12.44; To 6th Air Regiment (2nd Company) at Gaziemir; SOC by 1951
5748	Arr 16.12.44; To 5th Air Regiment (2nd Company) at Bursa; SOC by 1951
5749	Arr 16.12.44; To 6th Air Regiment (2nd Company) at Gaziemir; SOC by 1951
5750	Arr 16.12.44; To 6th Air Regiment (2nd Company) at Gaziemir; SOC by 1951
5751	Arr 16.12.44; To 5th Air Regiment (1st Company) at Bursa; SOC by 1951
5752	Arr 16.12.44; To 5th Air Regiment (1st Company) at Bursa; SOC by 1951
5753	Arr 16.12.44; To 5th Air Regiment (1st Company) at Bursa; SOC by 1951
5754	Arr 16.12.44; To 5th Air Regiment (1st Company) at Bursa; SOC by 1951
5755	Arr 16.12.44; U/s in 1945
5756	Arr 25.12.44; To 5th Air Regiment (2nd Company) at Bursa; SOC by 1951
5757	Arr 25.12.44; To 5th Air Regiment (2nd Company) at Bursa; SOC by 1951
5758	Arr 25.12.44; To 5th Air Regiment (2nd Company) at Bursa; SOC by 1951
5759	Arr 25.12.44; To 5th Air Regiment (2nd Company) at Bursa; SOC by 1951
5760	Arr 25.12.44; To 6th Air Regiment (4th Company) at Gaziemir; SOC by 1951
5761	Arr 25.12.44; To 6th Air Regiment (4th Company) at Gaziemir; SOC by 1951
5762	Arr 25.12.44; To 6th Air Regiment (4th Company) at Gaziemir; SOC by 1951
5763	Arr 25.12.44; To 6th Air Regiment (4th Company) at Gaziemir; SOC by 1951
5764	Arr 25.12.44; To 6th Air Regiment (1st Company) at Gaziemir; SOC by 1951
5765	Arr 25.12.44; To 5th Air Regiment (2nd Company) at Bursa; SOC by 1951
5766	Arr 25.12.44; To 6th Air Regiment (1st Company) at Gaziemir; SOC by 1951
5767	Arr 25.12.44; To 5th Air Regiment (2nd Company) at Bursa; SOC by 1951
5768	Arr 25.12.44; To 5th Air Regiment (2nd Company) at Bursa; SOC by 1951
5769	Arr 25.12.44; To 6th Air Regiment (1st Company) at Gaziemir; SOC by 1951
BR113	Spitfire F.Vc/trop (Merlin 46); Became TuAF No. **57..** ? TOC/RAF 16.3.42 - Arr TuAF 29.3.45; 5th or 6th Air Regiment at Bursa or Gaziemir; SOC by 1951
EE774	Spitfire F.Vc/trop (Merlin 46); Became TuAF No. **57..** ? TOC/RAF 10.12.42 - Arr TuAF 29.3.45; 5th or 6th Air Regiment at Bursa or Gaziemir; SOC by 1951
EE865	Spitfire F.Vc/trop (Merlin 45); Became TuAF No. **57..** ? TOC/RAF 4.2.43; ex USAAF - Arr TuAF 30.11.44; 6th Air Regiment at Gaziemir; SOC by 1951
EF539	Spitfire F.Vc/trop (Merlin 45); Became TuAF No. **57..** ? TOC/RAF 8.2.43 - Arr TuAF 28.12.44; 6th Air Regiment at Gaziemir; SOC by 1951
EF542	Spitfire F.Vc/trop (Merlin 45); Became TuAF No. **57..** ? TOC/RAF 13.2.43 - Arr TuAF 22.2.45; 5th or 6th Air Regiment at Bursa or Gaziemir; SOC by 1951
EF651	Spitfire F.Vc/trop (Merlin 50); Became TuAF No. **57..** ? TOC/RAF 17.4.43 - Arr TuAF 22.2.45; 5th or 6th Air Regiment at Bursa or Gaziemir; SOC by 1951
EF690	Spitfire F.Vc/trop (Merlin 50); Became TuAF No. **57..** ? TOC/RAF 1.6.43 - Arr TuAF 30.11.44; 6th Air Regiment at Gaziemir; SOC by 1951
EP258	Spitfire F.Vb/trop (Merlin 46); Became TuAF No. **57..** ? TOC/RAF 7.6.42; - Arr TuAF 29.3.45; 5th or 6th Air Regiment at Bursa or Gaziemir; SOC by 1951
ER476	Spitfire F.Vb/trop (Merlin 46); Became TuAF No. **57..** ? TOC/RAF 16.9.42; Selected for Turkey 5.9.44; No.1 (ME) C&CU, flown from Aboukir via Lydda to Adana, Turkey 30.3.45 (Plt LW Witham) - Arr TuAF 26.4.45; 5th or 6th Air Regiment at Bursa or Gaziemir; SOC by 1951
ER481	Spitfire F.Vb/trop (Merlin 46); Became TuAF No. **57..** ? TOC/RAF 11.9.42; ex No.7 Sqn SAAF - Arr TuAF 22.2.45; 5th or 6th Air Regiment at Bursa or Gaziemir; SOC by 1951
ER590	Spitfire F.Vb/trop (Merlin 46); Became TuAF No. **57..** ? TOC/RAF 18.10.42 - Arr TuAF 30.11.44; 6th Air Regiment at Gaziemir; SOC by 1951
ER622	Spitfire LF.Vb/trop (Merlin 50M); Became TuAF No **57..**? TOC/RAF 30.9.42; ex No.40 Sqn SAAF - Arr TuAF 22.2.45; 5th or 6th Air Regiment at Bursa or Gaziemir; SOC by 1951
ER643	Spitfire F.Vb/trop (Merlin 46); Became TuAF No. **57..** ? TOC/RAF 6.10.42 - Arr TuAF 26.4.45; 5th or 6th Air Regiment at Bursa or Gaziemir; SOC by 1951

ER661   Spitfire F.Vb/trop (Merlin 46); Became TuAF No. **57..** ? TOC/RAF 6.10.42 - Arr TuAF 29.3.45; 5th or 6th Air Regiment at Bursa or Gaziemir; SOC by 1951

ER666   Spitfire F.Vc/trop (Merlin 46); Became TuAF No. **57..** ? TOC/RAF 17.11.42 - Arr TuAF 22.2.45; 5th or 6th Air Regiment at Bursa or Gaziemir; SOC by 1951

ER810   Spitfire F.Vb/trop (Merlin 46); Became TuAF No. **57..** ? Presentation aircraft '*INCA*'; TOC/RAF 16.10.42 - Arr TuAF 28.12.44; 6th Air Regiment at Gaziemir; SOC by 1951

ER938   Spitfire F.Vb/trop (Merlin 46); Became TuAF No. **57..** ? TOC/RAF 17.11.42 - Arr TuAF 22.2.45; 5th or 6th Air Regiment at Bursa or Gaziemir; SOC by 1951

ER985   Spitfire F.Vb/trop (Merlin 46); Became TuAF No. **57..** ? TOC/RAF 13.11.42 - Arr TuAF 30.11.44; 6th Air Regiment at Gaziemir; SOC by 1951

ES243   Spitfire F.Vc/trop (Merlin 46); Became TuAF No. **57..** ? TOC/RAF 6.12.42 - Arr TuAF 29.3.45; 5th or 6th Air Regiment at Bursa or Gaziemir; SOC by 1951

ES251   Spitfire F.Vc/trop (Merlin 46); Became TuAF No. **57..** ? TOC/RAF 18.11.42 - Arr TuAF 22.2.45; 5th or 6th Air Regiment at Bursa or Gaziemir; SOC by 1951

ES295   Spitfire F.Vc/trop (Merlin 46); Became TuAF No. **57..** ? TOC/RAF 9.12.42 - Arr TuAF 29.3.45; 5th or 6th Air Regiment at Bursa or Gaziemir; SOC by 1951

ES300   Spitfire F.Vc/trop (Merlin 46); Became TuAF No. **57..** ? TOC/RAF 9.12.42 - Arr TuAF 28.12.44; 6th Air Regiment at Gaziemir; SOC by 1951

ES305   Spitfire F.Vc/trop (Merlin 46); Became TuAF No. **57..** ? TOC/RAF 28.11.42 - Arr TuAF 28.12.44; 6th Air Regiment at Gaziemir; SOC by 1951

ES348   Spitfire F.Vc/trop (Merlin 46); Became TuAF No. **57..** ? TOC/RAF 4.12.42 - Arr TuAF 22.2.45; 5th or 6th Air Regiment at Bursa or Gaziemir; SOC by 1951

ES359   Spitfire F.Vb/trop (Merlin 46); Became TuAF No. **57..** ? Presentation aircraft '*H.C.R. (G.P.O.)*'; TOC/RAF 20.12.42 - Arr TuAF 29.3.45; 5th or 6th Air Regiment at Bursa or Gaziemir; SOC by 1951

JG733   Spitfire F.Vc/trop (Merlin 46); Became TuAF No. **57..** ? TOC/RAF 15.12.42 - Arr TuAF 29.3.45; 5th or 6th Air Regiment at Bursa or Gaziemir; SOC by 1951

JG744   Spitfire F.Vc/trop (Merlin 46); Became TuAF No. **57..** ? TOC/RAF 14.12.42 - Arr TuAF 28.12.44; 6th Air Regiment at Gaziemir; SOC by 1951

JG788   Spitfire F.Vc/trop (Merlin 46); Became TuAF No. **57..** ? TOC/RAF 29.1.43 - Arr TuAF 30.11.44; 6th Air Regiment at Gaziemir; SOC by 1951

JG851   Spitfire F.Vc/trop (Merlin 46); Became TuAF No. **57..** ? TOC/RAF 21.1.43 - Arr TuAF 28.12.44; 6th Air Regiment at Gaziemir; SOC by 1951

JG938   Spitfire F.Vc/trop (Merlin 46); Became TuAF No. **57..** ? TOC/RAF 1.1.43 - Arr TuAF 29.3.45; 5th or 6th Air Regiment at Bursa or Gaziemir; SOC by 1951

JG955   Spitfire F.Vc/trop (Merlin 46); Became TuAF No. **57..** ? TOC/RAF 10.1.43 - Arr TuAF 28.12.44; 6th Air Regiment at Gaziemir; SOC by 1951

JK139   Spitfire F.Vc/trop (Merlin 46); Became TuAF No. **57..** ? TOC/RAF 20.1.43 - Arr TuAF 29.3.45; 5th or 6th Air Regiment at Bursa or Gaziemir; SOC by 1951

JK164   Spitfire F.Vc/trop (Merlin 46); Became TuAF No. **57..** ? TOC/RAF 28.1.43 - Arr TuAF 28.12.44; 6th Air Regiment at Gaziemir; SOC by 1951

JK236   Spitfire F.Vc/trop (Merlin 50); Became TuAF No. **57..** ? TOC/RAF 1.4.43 - Arr TuAF 26.4.45; 5th or 6th Air Regiment at Bursa or Gaziemir; SOC by 1951

JK340   Spitfire F.Vc/trop (Merlin 46); Became TuAF No. **57..** ? TOC/RAF 1.2.43 - Arr TuAF 26.4.45; 5th or 6th Air Regiment at Bursa or Gaziemir; SOC by 1951

JK362   Spitfire F.Vc/trop (Merlin 46); Became TuAF No. **57..** ? TOC/RAF 28.2.43 - Arr TuAF 30.11.44; 6th Air Regiment at Gaziemir; SOC by 1951

JK381   Spitfire F.Vc/trop (Merlin 46); Became TuAF No. **57..** ? TOC/RAF 7.3.43 - Arr TuAF 30.11.44; 6th Air Regiment at Gaziemir; SOC by 1951

JK393   Spitfire F.Vc/trop (Merlin 46); Became TuAF No. **57..** ? TOC/RAF 7.2.43 - Arr TuAF 30.11.44; 6th Air Regiment at Gaziemir; SOC by 1951

JK425   Spitfire F.Vc/trop (Merlin 46); Became TuAF No. **57..** ? TOC/RAF 11.2.43 - Arr TuAF 31.5.45; 5th or 6th Air Regiment at Bursa or Gaziemir; SOC by 1951

JK458   Spitfire F.Vc/trop (Merlin 46); Became TuAF No. **57..** ? TOC/RAF 11.2.43 - Arr TuAF 28.12.44; 6th Air Regiment at Gaziemir; SOC by 1951

JK526   Spitfire F.Vc/trop (Merlin 46); Became TuAF No. **57..** ? TOC/RAF 19.2.43; ex USAAF - Arr TuAF 29.3.45; 5th or 6th Air Regiment at Bursa or Gaziemir; SOC by 1951

JK664   Spitfire F.Vc/trop (Merlin 46); Became TuAF No. **57..** ? TOC/RAF 21.2.43 - Arr TuAF 29.3.45; 5th or 6th Air Regiment at Bursa or Gaziemir; SOC by 1951

JK665   Spitfire F.Vc/trop (Merlin 46); Became TuAF No. **57..** ? TOC/RAF 21.2.43 - Arr TuAF 28.12.44; 6th Air Regiment at Gaziemir; SOC by 1951

JK676   Spitfire F.Vc/trop (Merlin 46); Became TuAF No. **57..** ? TOC/RAF 1.3.43 - Arr TuAF 30.11.44; 6th Air Regiment at Gaziemir; SOC by 1951

JK710   Spitfire F.Vc/trop (Merlin 46); Became TuAF No. **57..** ? TOC/RAF 23.2.43 - Arr TuAF 28.12.44; 6th Air Regiment at Gaziemir; SOC by 1951

JK806   Spitfire F.Vc/trop (Merlin 46); Became TuAF No. **57..** ? TOC/RAF 28.2.43; ex FAF, USAAF - Arr TuAF 30.11.44; 6th Air Regiment; SOC by 1951

JK931   Spitfire F.Vc/trop (Merlin 50); Became TuAF No. **57..** ? TOC/RAF 14.3.43 - Arr TuAF 28.12.44; 6th Air Regiment at Gaziemir; SOC by 1951

JL374   Spitfire F.Vc/trop (Merlin 46); Became TuAF No. **57..** ? TOC/RAF 18.4.43; ex FFAF & USAAF - Arr TuAF 30.11.44; 6th Air Regiment at Gaziemir; SOC by 1951

LZ829   Spitfire F.Vc/trop (Merlin 50); Became TuAF No. **57..** ? TOC/RAF 16.4.43 - Arr TuAF 30.11.44; 6th Air Regiment at Gaziemir; SOC by 1951

LZ927   Spitfire F.Vc/trop (Merlin 50); Became TuAF No. **57..** ? TOC/RAF 1.5.43; No.1(ME)C&CU, air test Helwan 3.11.44, flown via Ramat David to Adana, Turkey 3.11.44 (Plt LW Witham) - Arr TuAF 30.11.44; 6th Air Regiment at Gaziemir; SOC by 1951

LZ979   Spitfire F.Vc/trop (Merlin 50); Became TuAF No. **57..** ? TOC/RAF 21.5.43; ex No.10 Sqn SAAF - Arr TuAF 26.4.45; 5th or 6th Air Regiment at Bursa or Gaziemir; SOC by 1951

MA700   Spitfire F.Vc/trop (Merlin 46); Became TuAF No. **57..** ? TOC/RAF 25.6.43 - Arr TuAF 28.12.44; 6th Air Regiment at Gaziemir; SOC by 1951

MA703   Spitfire F.Vc/trop (Merlin 46); Became TuAF No. **57..** ? TOC/RAF 27.6.43 - Arr TuAF 30.11.44; 6th Air Regiment at Gaziemir; SOC by 1951

?   Spitfire F.Vc/trop (M. 46/50); Became TuAF No. **57..** ? further **16** aircraft to Turkey in 1945; Serial Nos and fates unknown. SOC by 1951

TuAF Serial Nos.5801 - 5803: Spitfire Mk.V "Recce" variants, with the Yüksek Irtifa Foto Kesif Kitası at Eskisehir 1945-48 and with the 10th Recce Regiment 1948/49

AB345   Spitfire F.Vb/trop (Merlin 45); Became TuAF No. **5801**; TOC/RAF 4.2.42; NWA, ex 12th(US)AF; Selected for Turkey 5.9.44 - Arr TuAF 28.9.44; Yük.Irt. Foto Ks.Kt. at Eskisehir from 1945 to 1948; SOC by 1948/49

BP882   Spitfire PR.G (Merlin 46) TOC/RAF 31.1.42; No.680 Sqn RAF, ran out of fuel, force-landed in Turkey, date unknown, interned (fate unknown)

BR644   Spitfire PR.G (Merlin 46) TOC/RAF 26.6.42; No.680 Sqn RAF, ran out of fuel, force-landed in Turkey, Cat.FB/E on 26.9.43, interned (fate unknown)

JK190   Spitfire F.Vc/trop (Merlin 46); Became TuAF No. **5802**; TOC/RAF 3.2.43 - Arr TuAF 22.2.45; Yük.Irt.Foto Ks.Kt. at Eskisehir from 1945 to 1948; SOC by 1948/49

JL240　Spitfire F.Vc/trop (Merlin 50); Became TuAF No. **5803**; TOC/RAF 16.4.43 - Arr TuAF 22.2.45; Yük.Ks.Irt.Foto Kt. at Eskisehir from 1945 to 1948; SOC by 1948/49

TuAF Serial Nos. 5804 - 5827: Spitfire Mk.V "Recce" variants, 24 aircraft, order 15 January 1945 - Cancelled

?　　Note: Serial No 5808 not mentioned in the TuAF list.
　　Spitfire PR.XI (Merlin 63 or 70); Reported TuAF No.**5851** at Eskisehir in 1947; No trace in RAF records, Serial No unknown.
　　NOTE: Spitfire MK915 (FR.IXc) became No.6347

TuAF Serial Nos. 6201 - 6369: Spitfire Mk.IXc/e;
4th Air Regiment 1947-51; 5th Air Regiment 1947/48; 6th Air Regiment 1949/50; 7th Air Regiment 1947-50; 8th Air Regiment 1947-49; 141st & 142nd Sqns 1951-54; CFS 1949-53

EN579　Spitfire LF.IXc (Merlin 66); Became TuAF No. **6346**; TOC/RAF 13.5.43; Selected for Turkey 21.8.47 - Arr TuAF 29.8.47; 8th Air Regiment (3rd Company) at Erzincan from 9.47 [see Notes 2) & 4)]; SOC by 1954

EN633　Spitfire LF.IXc (Merlin 66); Became TuAF No. **6314**; TOC/RAF 2.6.43; Selected for Turkey 30.7.47 - Arr TuAF 2.8.47; 8th Air Regiment (2nd Company) at Erzincan from 8.47 [see Notes 2) & 4)]; SOC by 1954

EN636　Spitfire LF.IXc (Merlin 66); Became TuAF No. **6271**; TOC/RAF 4.6.43; Selected for Turkey 15.10.47 - Arr TuAF 22.1.48; 7th Air Regiment (2nd Company) at Kütahya from 2.48 [see Notes 3) & 4)]; SOC by 1954

JL106　Spitfire LF.IXc (Merlin 66); Became TuAF No. **6268**; TOC/RAF 10.4.43; Selected for Turkey 11.7.47 - Arr TuAF 17.7.47; 7th Air Regiment (2nd Company) at Kütahya from 7.47 [see Notes 3) & 4)]; SOC by 1954

JL229　Spitfire F.IXc (Merlin 63); None TuAF No known [see Note 6)]; TOC/RAF 2.4.43; ex USAAF NWA 10.43 - Arr TuAF 29.3.45; Air depot, storage; Fate unknown (together with the Mk.Vcs delivered in 1945, but no trace of usage); SOC by 1954

JL359　Spitfire LF.IXc (Merlin 66); Became TuAF No. **6284**; TOC/RAF 21.4.43; Selected for Turkey 24.1.48 - Arr TuAF 1.2.48; 7th Air Regiment (3rd Company) at Kütahya from 2.48 [see Notes 3) & 4)]; SOC by 1954

LZ843　Spitfire F.IXc (Merlin 63); Became TuAF No. **6280**; TOC/RAF 17.4.43; Selected for Turkey 11.7.47 - Arr TuAF 16.7.47; 7th Air Regiment (3rd Company) at Kütahya from 7.47 [see Notes 3) & 4)]; SOC by 1954

MA255　Spitfire F.IXc (Merlin 63); Became TuAF No. **6205**; Presentation aircraft '*URUGUAY X*'; TOC/RAF 18.6.43; Selected for Turkey 18.12.46 - Arr TuAF 20.1.47; 4th Air Regiment (1st Company) at Merzifon from 3.47; Staff of 4.Alayi, fatal crash near Merzifon 21.12.48 (Plt Sulhi Altinok killed); SOC

MH374　Spitfire LF.IXc (Merlin 66); Became TuAF No. **6258**; TOC/RAF 6.8.43; Selected for Turkey 15.10.47 - Arr TuAF 30.12.47; 7th Air Regiment (1st Company) at Kütahya from 1.48 [see Notes 3) & 4)]; SOC by 1954

MH414　Spitfire LF.IXc (Merlin 66); Became TuAF No. **6361**; TOC/RAF 11.8.43; Selected for Turkey 3.9.47 - Arr TuAF 4.9.47; 8th Air Regiment (4th Company) at Erzincan from 9.47 [see Notes 2) & 4)]; SOC by 1954

MH883　Spitfire LF.IXc (Merlin 66); Became TuAF No. **6220**; TOC/RAF 7.10.43; Selected for Turkey 16.1.47 - Arr TuAF 4.6.47; Written off on delivery

MJ147　Spitfire LF.IXc (Merlin 66); Became TuAF No. **6213**; TOC/RAF 16.10.43; Selected for Turkey 18.12.46 - Arr TuAF 11.3.47; 4th Air Regiment (2nd Company) at Merzifon from 4.47 [see Note 4)]; SOC by 1954

MJ180　Spitfire LF.IXc (Merlin 66); Became TuAF No. **6255**; TOC/RAF 16.10.43; Selected for Turkey 11.7.47 - Arr TuAF 15.7.47; 7th Air Regiment (1st Company) at Kütahya from 7.47 [see Notes 3) & 4)]; SOC by 1954

MJ313　Spitfire LF.IXc (Merlin 66); Became TuAF No. **6254**; TOC/RAF 16.10.43; Selected for Turkey 26.6.47 - Arr TuAF 4.7.47; 7th Air Regiment (1st Company) at Kütahya from 7.47 [see Notes 3) & 4)]; SOC by 1954

MJ344　Spitfire LF.IXc (Merlin 66); Became TuAF No. **6230**; TOC/RAF 29.11.43; Selected for Turkey 17.1.47 - Arr TuAF 14.4.47; 4th Air Regiment (3rd Company) at Merzifon from 5.47 [see Note 4)]; SOC by 1954

MJ369　Spitfire LF.IXc (Merlin 66); Became TuAF No. **6293**; TOC/RAF 19.12.43; Selected for Turkey 22.7.47 - Arr TuAF 23.7.47; 7th Air Regiment (4th Company) at Kütahya from 7.47 [see Notes 3) & 4)]; SOC by 1954

MJ387　Spitfire LF.IXc (Merlin 66); Became TuAF No. **6305**; TOC/RAF 2.11.43; Selected for Turkey 7.8.47 - Arr TuAF 9.8.47; 8th Air Regiment (1st Company) at Erzincan from 9.47 [see Notes 2) & 4)]; SOC by 1954

MJ388　Spitfire LF.IXc (Merlin 66); Became TuAF No. **6278**; TOC/RAF 3.11.43; Selected for Turkey 10.4.47 - Arr TuAF 9.7.47; 7th Air Regiment (3rd Company) at Kütahya from 7.47 [see Notes 3) & 4)]; SOC by 1954

MJ396　Spitfire LF.IXc (Merlin 66); Became TuAF No. **6216**; TOC/RAF 6.11.43; Selected for Turkey 20.3.47 - Arr TuAF 4.4.47; 4th Air Regiment (2nd Company) at Merzifon from 4.47 [see Note 4)]; SOC by 1954

MJ448　Spitfire LF.IXc (Merlin 66); Became TuAF No. **6287**; TOC/RAF 7.11.43; Selected for Turkey 2.5.47 - Arr TuAF 12.6.47; 7th Air Regiment (4th Company) at Kütahya from 6.47 [see Notes 3) & 4)]; SOC by 1954

MJ566　Spitfire LF.IXc (Merlin 66); Became TuAF No. **6244**; TOC/RAF 21.12.43; Selected for Turkey 15.4.47 - Arr TuAF 7.5.47; 4th Air Regiment (4th Company) at Merzifon from 5.47 [see Note 4)]; SOC by 1954

MJ567　Spitfire LF.IXc (Merlin 66); Became TuAF No. **6340**; TOC/RAF 22.12.43; Selected for Turkey 9.10.47 - Arr TuAF 16.10.47; 5th Air Regiment (4th Company) at Bursa from 10.47 [see Notes 2) & 4)]; SOC by 1954

MJ575　Spitfire LF.IXc (Merlin 66); Became TuAF No. **6362**; TOC/RAF 24.11.43; Selected for Turkey 2.9.47 - Arr TuAF 4.9.47; 8th Air Regiment (4th Company) at Erzincan from 9.47 [see Notes 2) & 4)]; SOC by 1954

MJ780　Spitfire LF.IXc (Merlin 66); Became TuAF No. **6320**; TOC/RAF 20.12.43; Selected for Turkey 24.10.47 - Arr TuAF 8.11.47; 8th Air Regiment (2nd Company) at Erzincan from 12.47 [see Notes 2) & 4)]; SOC by 1954

Spitfire IX YV-17 of the Turkish Air Force, late 1940s

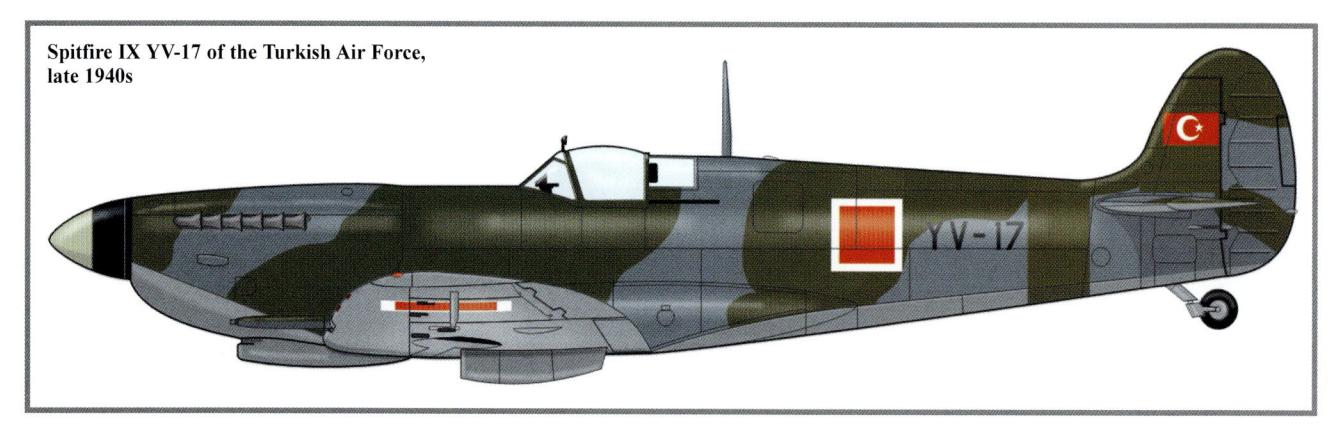

MJ799 Spitfire LF.IXc (Merlin 66); Became TuAF No. **6229**; TOC/RAF 28.12.43; Selected for Turkey 23.1.47 - Arr TuAF 7.4.47; 4th Air Regiment (3rd Company) at Merzifon from 4.47 [see Note 4)]; SOC by 1954

MJ872 Spitfire LF.IXc (Merlin 66); Became TuAF No. **6327**; TOC/RAF 24.12.43; Selected for Turkey 25.9.47 - Arr TuAF 2.10.47; 5th Air Regiment (3rd Company) at Bursa from 10.47 [see Notes 2) & 4)]; SOC by 1954

MJ883 Spitfire LF.IXc (Merlin 66); Became TuAF No. **6231**; TOC/RAF 24.12.43; Selected for Turkey 18.12.46 - Arr TuAF 14.4.47; 4th Air Regiment (3rd Company) at Merzifon from 4.47 [see Note 4)]; SOC by 1954

MJ888 Spitfire LF.IXc (Merlin 66); Became TuAF No. **6297**; TOC/RAF 28.12.43; Selected for Turkey 22.7.47 - Arr TuAF 24.7.47; 8th Air Regiment (1st Company) at Erzincan from 8.47 [see Notes 2) & 4)]; SOC by 1954

MJ963 Spitfire LF.IXc (Merlin 66); Became TuAF No. **6201**; TOC/RAF 2.2.44; Selected for Turkey 18.12.46 - Arr TuAF 10.1.47; 4th Air Regiment (1st Company) at Merzifon from 3.47 [see Note 4)]; SOC by 1954

MK147 Spitfire LF.IXc (Merlin 66); Became TuAF No. **6355**; TOC/RAF 14.1.44; Selected for Turkey 1.10.47 - Arr TuAF 30.10.47; 8th Air Regiment (3rd Company) at Erzincan from 12.47 [see Notes 2) & 4)]; SOC by 1954

MK178 Spitfire LF.IXc (Merlin 66); Became TuAF No. **6341**; TOC/RAF 30.1.44; Selected for Turkey 9.10.47 - Arr TuAF 17.10.47; 5th Air Regiment (4th Company) at Bursa from 10.47 [see Notes 2) & 4)]; SOC by 1954

MK183 Spitfire LF.IXc (Merlin 66); Became TuAF No. **6292**; TOC/RAF 23.1.44; Selected for Turkey 11.7.47 - Arr TuAF 20.7.47; 7th Air Regiment (4th Company) at Kütahya from 7.47 [see Notes 3) & 4)]; SOC by 1954

MK195 Spitfire LF.IXc (Merlin 66); Became TuAF No. **6264**; TOC/RAF 23.1.44; Selected for Turkey 17.1.47 - Arr TuAF 14.6.47; 7th Air Regiment (2nd Company) at Kütahya from 6.47 [see Notes 3) & 4)]; SOC by 1954

MK201 Spitfire LF.IXc (Merlin 66); Became TuAF No. **6317**; TOC/RAF 23.1.44; Selected for Turkey 13.8.47 - Arr TuAF 15.8.47; 8th Air Regiment at Erzincan from 9.47 [see Notes 2) & 4)]; SOC by 1954

MK228 Spitfire LF.IXc (Merlin 66); Became TuAF No. **6257**; TOC/RAF 24.12.43; Selected for Turkey 18.7.47 - Arr TuAF 22.7.47; 7th Air Regiment (1st Company) at Kütahya from 7.47 [see Notes 3) & 4)]; SOC by 1954

MK246 Spitfire LF.IXc (Merlin 66); Became TuAF No. **6286**; TOC/RAF 20.1.44; Selected for Turkey 17.1.47 - Arr TuAF 28.5.47; 7th Air Regiment (4th Company) at Kütahya from 5.47 [see Notes 3) & 4)]; SOC by 1954

MK288 Spitfire LF.IXc (Merlin 66); Became TuAF No. **6249**; TOC/RAF 4.2.44; Selected for Turkey 1.5.47 - Arr TuAF 9.5.47; 7th Air Regiment (1st Company) at Kütahya from 5.47 [see Notes 3) & 4)]; SOC by 1954

MK294 Spitfire LF.IXc (Merlin 66); Became TuAF No. **6356**; TOC/RAF 30.1.44; Selected for Turkey 24.10.47 - Arr TuAF 8.11.47; 8th Air Regiment (3rd Company) at Erzincan from 12.47 [see Notes 2) & 4)]; SOC by 1954

MK308 Spitfire LF.IXc (Merlin 66); Became TuAF No. **6316**; TOC/RAF 4.2.44; Selected for Turkey 6.8.47 - Arr TuAF 8.8.47; 8th Air Regiment (2nd Company) at Erzincan from 9.47 [see Notes 2) & 4)]; SOC by 1954

MK309 Spitfire LF.IXc (Merlin 66); Became TuAF No. **6348**; TOC/RAF 29.1.44; Selected for Turkey 23.8.47 - Arr TuAF 2.9.47; 8th Air Regiment(3rd Company) at Erzincan from 9.47 [see Notes 2) & 4)]; SOC by 1954

MK317 Spitfire LF.IXc (Merlin 66); Became TuAF No. **6358**; TOC/RAF 30.1.44; Long range test aircraft, crossed the North Atlantic from USA to UK early 7.44; Selected for Turkey 22.8.47 - Arr TuAF 29.8.47; 8th Air Regiment (4th Company) at Erzincan from 9.47 [see Notes 2) & 4)]; SOC by 1954

MK517 Spitfire LF.IXc (Merlin 66); Became TuAF No. **6308**; TOC/RAF 2.3.44; Selected for Turkey 23.10.47 - Arr TuAF 8.11.47; 8th Air Regiment (1st Company) at Erzincan from 12.47 [see Notes 2) & 4)]; SOC by 1954

MK534 Spitfire LF.IXc (Merlin 66); Became TuAF No. **6324**; TOC/RAF 12.3.44; Selected for Turkey 25.9.47 - Arr TuAF 27.9.47; 5th Air Regiment (3rd Company) at Bursa from 10.47 [see Notes 2) & 4)]; SOC by 1954

MK559 Spitfire LF.IXc - TOC/RAF 1.3.44; Selected for TuAF 17.1.47, but crashed on or before delivery flight

MK564 Spitfire LF.IXc (Merlin 66); Became TuAF No. **6283**; TOC/RAF 5.3.44; Selected for Turkey 14.10.47 - Arr TuAF 20.1.48; 7th Air Regiment (3rd Company) at Kütahya from 2.48 [see Notes 3) & 4)]; SOC by 1954

MK565 Spitfire LF.IXc (Merlin 66); Became TuAF No. **6225**; TOC/RAF 1.3.44; Selected for Turkey 20.1.47 - Arr TuAF 11.3.47; 4th Air Regiment (3rd Company) at Merzifon from 4.47 [see Note 4)]; SOC by 1954

MK583 Spitfire LF.IXc (Merlin 66); Became TuAF No. **6238**; TOC/RAF 19.3.44; Selected for Turkey 23.1.47 - Arr TuAF 28.3.47; 4th Air Regiment (4th Company) at Merzifon from 4.47 [see Note 4)]; SOC by 1954

MK628 Spitfire LF.IXc (Merlin 66); Became TuAF No. **6243**; TOC/RAF 20.2.44; Selected for Turkey 15.4.47 - Arr TuAF 26.4.47; 4th Air Regiment (4th Company) at Merzifon from 5.47 [see Note 4)]; SOC by 1954

MK663 Spitfire LF.IXc (Merlin 66); Became TuAF No. **6363**; TOC/RAF 7.3.44; Selected for Turkey 5.9.47 - Arr TuAF 9.9.47; 8th Air Regiment (4th Company) at Erzincan from 9.47 [see Notes 2) & 4)]; SOC by 1954

MK678 Spitfire LF.IXc (Merlin 66); Became TuAF No. **6282**; TOC/RAF 5.4.44; Selected for Turkey 1.10.47 - Arr TuAF 13.1.48; 7th Air Regiment (3rd Company) at Kütahya from 1.48 [see Notes 3) & 4)]; SOC by 1954

MK688 Spitfire LF.IXc (Merlin 66); Became TuAF No. **6299**; TOC/RAF 15.4.44; Selected for Turkey 22.7.47 - Arr TuAF 27.7.47; 8th Air Regiment (1st Company) at Erzincan from 8.47 [see Notes 2) & 4)]; SOC by 1954

MK726 Spitfire LF.IXc (Merlin 66); Became TuAF No. **6279**; TOC/RAF 15.3.44; Selected for Turkey 11.7.47 - Arr TuAF 15.7.47; 7th Air Regiment (3rd Company) at Kütahya from 7.47 [see Notes 3) & 4)]; SOC by 1954

MK733 Spitfire LF.IXc (Merlin 66); Became TuAF No. **6276**; TOC/RAF 11.3.44; Selected for Turkey 2.5.47 - Arr TuAF 12.6.47; 7th Air Regiment (3rd Company) at Kütahya from 6.47 [see Notes 3) & 4)]; SOC by 1954

MK747 Spitfire LF.IXc (Merlin 66); Became TuAF No. **6306**; TOC/RAF 2.3.44; Selected for Turkey 10.10.47 - Arr TuAF 17.10.47; 8th Air Regiment (1st Company) at Erzincan from 10.47 [see Notes 2) & 4)]; SOC by 1954

MK754 Spitfire LF.IXc (Merlin 66); Became TuAF No. **6275**; TOC/RAF 5.3.44; Selected for Turkey 30.4.47 - Arr TuAF 4.6.47; 7th Air Regiment (3rd Company) at Kütahya from 6.47 [see Notes 3) & 4)]; SOC by 1954

MK786 Spitfire LF.IXc (Merlin 66); Became TuAF No. **6207**; TOC/RAF 11.3.44; Selected for Turkey 16.1.47 - Arr TuAF 20.1.47; 4th Air Regiment (1st Company) at Merzifon from 3.47 [see Note 4)]; SOC by 1954

MK787 Spitfire LF.IXc (Merlin 66); Became TuAF No. **6295**; TOC/RAF 11.3.44; Selected for Turkey 15.10.47 - Arr TuAF 25.1.48; 7th Air Regiment (4th Company) at Kütahya from 2.48 [see Notes 3) & 4)]; SOC by 1954

MK852 Spitfire LF.IXc (Merlin 66); Became TuAF No. **6366**; TOC/RAF 19.3.44; Selected for Turkey 9.10.47 - Arr TuAF 21.10.47; Air depot, reserve storage [see Note 4)]; SOC by 1954

MK863 Spitfire LF.IX (Merlin 66); Became TuAF No. **6319**; TOC/RAF 18.4.44; Selected for Turkey 20.10.47 - Arr TuAF 8.11.47; 8th Air Regiment (2nd Company) at Erzincan from 12.47 [see Notes 2) & 4)]; SOC by 1954

MK868 Spitfire LF.IXc (Merlin 66); Became TuAF No. **6291**; TOC/RAF 15.3.44; Selected for Turkey 11.7.47 - Arr TuAF 15.7.47; 7th Air Regiment (4th Company) at Kütahya from 7.47 [see Notes 3) & 4)]; SOC by 1954

MK889 Spitfire LF.IXc (Merlin 66); Became TuAF No. **6332**; TOC/RAF 15.3.44; Selected for Turkey 15.10.47 - Arr TuAF 13.1.48; Air depot, unserviceable [see Note 4)]; Not accepted

MK893 Spitfire LF.IXc (Merlin 66); Became TuAF No. **6312**; TOC/RAF 24.3.44; Selected for Turkey 22.7.47 - Arr TuAF 29.7.47; 8th Air Regiment (2nd Company) at Erzincan from 8.47 [see Notes 2) & 4)]; SOC by 1954

MK907 Spitfire LF.IXc (Merlin 66); Became TuAF No. **6289**; TOC/RAF 19.3.44; Selected for Turkey 26.6.47 - Arr TuAF 1.7.47; 7th Air Regiment (4th Company) at Kütahya from 7.47 [see Notes 3) & 4)]; SOC by 1954

MK915 Spitfire **FR.IXc** (Merlin 66); Became TuAF No. **6347**; TOC/RAF 19.3.44; Blackbushe, selected for Turkey 7.7.47 - Arr TuAF 30.8.47; 8th Air Regiment (3rd Company) at Erzincan from 9.47 (Possibly to Yüksek Irtibat Kesif Foto Kitaati at Eskisehir 1948 and to 10th Recce Regiment [3rd Company] at Afyon 1948-51; 113th Sqn at Eskisehir 1951-53); SOC by 1954
NOTE: Yüksek Irtibat Kesif Foto Kitaati and 10th Regiment reported a Spitfire PR.XI (TuAF No 5851), but 113th Sqn a Mk.IX

MK947 Spitfire LF.IXc (Merlin 66); Became TuAF No. **6219**; TOC/RAF 6.4.44; Selected for Turkey 25.3.47 - Arr TuAF 14.4.47; 4th Air Regiment (2nd Company) at Merzifon from 5.47 [see Note 4)]; SOC by 1954

MK948 Spitfire LF.IXc (Merlin 66); Became TuAF No. **6349**; TOC/RAF 22.3.44; Selected for Turkey 28.8.47 - Arr TuAF 4.9.47; 8th Air Regiment (3rd Company) at Erzincan from 9.47 [see Notes 2) & 4)]; SOC by 1954

MK986 Spitfire LF.IXc (Merlin 66); Became TuAF No. **6237**; TOC/RAF 25.3.44; Selected for Turkey 24.1.47 - Arr TuAF 11.3.47; 4th Air Regiment (4th Company) at Merzifon from 4.47 [see Note 4)]; SOC by 1954

MK988 Spitfire LF.IXc (Merlin 66); Became TuAF No. **6345**; TOC/RAF 25.3.44; Selected for Turkey 12.8.47 - Arr TuAF 15.8.47; 8th Air Regiment (3rd Company) at Erzincan from 9.47 [see Notes 2) & 4)]; SOC by 1954

MK995 Spitfire LF.IXc (Merlin 66); Became TuAF No. **6274**; TOC/RAF 30.3.44; Selected for Turkey 20.3.47 - Arr TuAF 19.5.47; 7th Air Regiment (3rd Company) at Kütahya from 5.47 [see Notes 3) & 4)]; SOC by 1954

ML115 Spitfire LF.IXc (Merlin 66); Became TuAF No. **6342**; TOC/RAF 12.4.44; Selected for Turkey 29.4.47 - Arr TuAF 12.6.47; Unserviceable after delivery; Air depot [see Note 4)]; Not accepted

ML126 Spitfire LF.IXc (Merlin 66); Became TuAF No. **6335**; TOC/RAF 23.3.44; Selected for Turkey 25.9.47 - Arr TuAF 26./27.9.47; 5th Air Regiment (4th Company) at Bursa from 10.47 [see Notes 2) & 4)]; SOC by 1954

ML143 Spitfire LF.IXc (Merlin 66); Became TuAF No. **6248**; TOC/RAF 27.3.44; Selected for Turkey 1.10.47 - Arr TuAF 30.12.47; 4th Air Regiment (4th Company) at Merzifon from 1.48 [see Note 4)]; SOC by 1954

ML147 Spitfire LF.IXc (Merlin 66); Became TuAF No. **6247**; TOC/RAF 31.3.44; Selected for Turkey 10.4.47 - Arr TuAF 23.12.47; 4th Air Regiment (4th Company) at Merzifon from 1.48 [see Note 4)]; SOC by 1954

ML156 Spitfire LF.IXc (Merlin 66); Became TuAF No. **6259**; TOC/RAF 6.4.44; Selected for Turkey 14.10.47 - Arr TuAF 20.1.48; 7th Air Regiment (1st Company) at Kütahya from 1.48 [see Notes 3) & 4)]; SOC by 1954

ML173 Spitfire LF.IXc (Merlin 66); Became TuAF No. **6202**; TOC/RAF 4.4.44; Selected for Turkey 18.12.46 - Arr TuAF 18.1.47; 4th Air Regiment (1st Company) at Merzifon from 3.47 [see Note 4)]; SOC by 1954

ML175 Spitfire LF.IXc (Merlin 66); Became TuAF No. **6224**; TOC/RAF 5.4.44; Selected for Turkey 3.11.47 - Arr TuAF 30.12.47; 4th Air Regiment (2nd Company) at Merzifon from 1.48 [see Note 4)]; SOC by 1954

ML191 Spitfire LF.IXc (Merlin 66); Became TuAF No. **6329**; TOC/RAF 14.4.44; Selected for Turkey 13.10.47 - Arr TuAF 16.10.47; 5th Air Regiment (3rd Company) at Bursa from 10.47 [see Notes 2) & 4)]; SOC by 1954

ML202 Spitfire LF.IXc (Merlin 66); Became TuAF No. **6367**; TOC/RAF 31.3.44; Selected for Turkey 24.10.47 - Arr TuAF 8.11.47; 8th Air Regiment (4th Company) at Erzincan from 12.47 [see Notes 2) & 4)]; SOC by 1954

ML208 Spitfire LF.IXc (Merlin 66); Became TuAF No. **6261**; TOC/RAF 6.4.44; Selected for Turkey 16.4.47 - Arr TuAF 14.5.47; 7th Air Regiment (2nd Company) at Kütahya from 5.47 [see Notes 3) & 4)]; SOC by 1954

ML265 Spitfire LF.IXc (Merlin 66); Became TuAF No. **6338**; TOC/RAF 28.4.44; Selected for Turkey 25.9.47 - Arr TuAF 30.9.47; 5th Air Regiment (4th Company) at Bursa from 10.47 [see Notes 2) & 4)]; SOC by 1954

ML266 Spitfire LF.IXc (Merlin 66); Became TuAF No. **6315**; TOC/RAF 14.4.44; Selected for Turkey 30.7.47 - Arr TuAF 2.8.47; 8th Air Regiment (2nd Company) at Erzincan from 9.47 [see Notes 2) & 4)]; SOC by 1954

ML268 Spitfire LF.IXc (Merlin 66); Became TuAF No. **6313**; TOC/RAF 21.4.44; Selected for Turkey 30.7.47 - Arr TuAF 1.8.47; 8th Air Regiment (2nd Company) at Erzincan from 8.47 [see Notes 2) & 4)]; SOC by 1954

ML273 Spitfire LF.IXc (Merlin 66); Became TuAF No. **6321**; TOC/RAF 27.4.44; Selected for Turkey 15.9.47 - Arr TuAF 18.9.47; 5th Air Regiment (3rd Company) at Bursa from 10.47 [see Notes 2) & 4)]; SOC by 1954

ML274 Spitfire LF.IXc (Merlin 66); TOC/RAF 18.4.44; For TuAF, but crashed before delivery; Cancelled

ML293 Spitfire LF.IXc (Merlin 66); Became TuAF No. **6273**; TOC/RAF 22.4.44; Selected for Turkey 16.4.47 - Arr TuAF 13.5.47; 7th Air Regiment (3rd Company) at Kütahya from 5.47 [see Notes 3) & 4)]; SOC by 1954

ML313 Spitfire LF.IXc (Merlin 66); Became TuAF No. **6353**; TOC/RAF 11.5.44; Selected for Turkey 15.9.47 - Arr TuAF 18.9.47; 8th Air Regiment (3rd Company) at Erzincan from 9.47 [see Notes 2) & 4)]; SOC by 1954

ML320 Spitfire LF.IXc (Merlin 66); Became TuAF No. **6357**; TOC/RAF 19.5.44; Selected for Turkey 21.8.47 - Arr TuAF 29.8.47; 8th Air Regiment (4th Company) at Erzincan from 9.47 [see Notes 2) & 4)]; SOC by 1954

ML321 Spitfire LF.IXc (Merlin 66); Became TuAF No. **6307**; TOC/RAF 15.5.44; Selected for Turkey 15.10.47 - Arr TuAF 29.10.47; To 5th Air Regiment at Bursa, Reserve aircraft [see Notes 2) & 4)]; SOC by 1954

ML362 Spitfire LF.IXc (Merlin 66); Became TuAF No. **6326**; TOC/RAF 21.4.44; Selected for Turkey 25.9.47 - Arr TuAF 30.9.47; 5th Air Regiment (3rd Company) at Bursa from 10.47 [see Notes 2) & 4)]; SOC by 1954

ML368 Spitfire LF.IXc (Merlin 66); Became TuAF No. **6233**; TOC/RAF 18.4.44; Selected for Turkey 10.4.47 - Arr TuAF 7.5.47; 4th Air Regiment (3rd Company) at Merzifon from 5.47 [see Note 4)]; SOC by 1954

ML376 Spitfire LF.IXc (Merlin 66); Became TuAF No. **6337**; TOC/RAF 23.4.44; Selected for Turkey 25.9.47 - Arr TuAF 28.9./30.9.47; 5th Air Regiment (4th Company) at Bursa from 10.47 [see Notes 2) & 4)]; SOC by 1954

ML414 Spitfire LF.IXc (Merlin 66); Became TuAF No. **6245**; TOC/RAF 25.4.44; Selected for Turkey 10.4.47 - Arr TuAF 9.5.47; 4th Air Regiment (4th Company) at Merzifon from 5.47 [see Note 4)]; SOC by 1954

ML424 Spitfire LF.IXc (Merlin 66); Became TuAF No. **6300**; TOC/RAF 23.4.44; Selected for Turkey 22.7.47 - Arr TuAF 29.7.47; 8th Air Regiment (1st Company) at Erzincan from 8.47 [see Notes 2) & 4)]; SOC by 1954

NH155 Spitfire LF.IXe (Merlin 66); Became TuAF No. **6339**; TOC/RAF 28.4.44; Selected for Turkey 25.9.47 - Arr TuAF 2.10.47; 5th Air Regiment (4th Company) at Bursa from 10.47 [see Notes 2) & 4)]; SOC by 1954

NH158 Spitfire LF.IXe (Merlin 66); Became TuAF No. **6298**; TOC/RAF 30.4.44; Selected for Turkey 22.7.47 - Arr TuAF 24.7.47; 8th Air Regiment (1st Company) at Erzincan from 8.47 [see Notes 2 & 4)]; SOC by 1954

NH179 Spitfire LF.IXe (Merlin 66); Became TuAF No. **6322**; TOC/RAF 30.4.44; Selected for Turkey 18.9.47 - Arr TuAF 20.9.47; 5th Air Regiment (3rd Company) at Bursa from 10.47 [see Notes 2) & 4)]; SOC by 1954

NH200 Spitfire LF.IXe (Merlin 66); Became TuAF No. **6354**; TOC/RAF 10.5.44; Selected for Turkey 6.10.47 - Arr TuAF 18.10.47; Air depot, reserve storage [see Note 4)]; SOC by 1954

NH206 Spitfire LF.IXe (Merlin 66); Became TuAF No. **6208**; TOC/RAF 25.5.44; Selected for Turkey 17.1.47 - Arr TuAF 24.1.47; 4th Air Regiment (1st Company) at Merzifon from 3.47 [see Note 4)]; SOC by 1954

NH244 Spitfire LF.IXe (Merlin 66); Became TuAF No. **6209**; TOC/RAF 10.5.44; Selected for Turkey 17.1.47 - Arr TuAF 28.1.47; 4th Air Regiment (1st Company) at Merzifon from 3.47 [see Note 4)]; SOC by 1954

NH246 Spitfire LF.IXe (Merlin 66); Became TuAF No. **6330**; TOC/RAF 17.5.44; Selected for Turkey 10.10.47 - Arr TuAF 17.10.47; Unserviceable after delivery ("w/o"); Air depot, repair [see Note 4)]; SOC by 1954

NH250 Spitfire LF.IXe (Merlin 66); Became TuAF No. **6223**; TOC/RAF 13.5.44; Selected for Turkey 15.10.47 - Arr TuAF 23.12.47; 4th Air Regiment (2nd Company) at Merzifon from 1.48 [see Note 4)]; SOC by 1954

NH257 Spitfire LF.IXe (Merlin 66); Became TuAF No. **6221**; TOC/RAF 20.5.44; Selected for Turkey 15.4.47 - Arr TuAF 7.5.47; 4th Air Regiment (2nd Company) at Merzifon from 5.47 [see Note 4)]; SOC by 1954

NH268 Spitfire LF.IXe (Merlin 66); Became TuAF No. **6236**; TOC/RAF 11.5.44; Selected for Turkey 3.11.47 - Arr TuAF 27.12.47; 4th Air Regiment (3rd Company) at Merzifon from 1.48 [see Note 4)]; SOC by 1954

NH361 Spitfire LF.IXe (Merlin 66); Became TuAF No. **6228**; TOC/RAF 31.5.44; Selected for Turkey 24.3.47 - Arr TuAF 4.4.47; 4th Air Regiment (3rd Company) at Merzifon from 5.47 [see Note 4)]; SOC by 1954

NH414 Spitfire LF.IXe (Merlin 66); Became TuAF No. **6239**; TOC/RAF 1.5.44; Selected for Turkey 23.1.47 - Arr TuAF 3.4.47; 4th Air Regiment (4th Company) at Merzifon from 4.47 [see Note 4)]; SOC by 1954

NH419 Spitfire LF.IXe (Merlin 66); Became TuAF No. **6328**; TOC/RAF 23.5.44; Selected for Turkey 13.10.47 - Arr TuAF 16.10.47; 5th Air Regiment (3rd Company) at Bursa from 10.47 [see Notes 2) & 4)]; SOC by 1954

NH427 Spitfire LF.IXe (Merlin 66); Became TuAF No. **6232**; TOC/RAF 8.6.44; Selected for Turkey 25.3.47 - Arr TuAF 26.4.47; 4th Air Regiment (3rd Company) at Merzifon from 5.47 [see Note 4)]; SOC by 1954

NH434 Spitfire LF.IXe (Merlin 66); Became TuAF No. **6203**; TOC/RAF 24.5.44; Selected for Turkey 18.12.46 - Arr TuAF 18.1.47; 4th Air Regiment (1st Company) at Merzifon from 3.47 [see Note 4)]; SOC by 1954

NH456 Spitfire LF.IXe (Merlin 66); Became TuAF No. **6368**; TOC/RAF 23.5.44; Selected for Turkey 14.10.47 - Arr TuAF 27.11.47; 8th Air Regiment (4th Company) at Erzincan from 12.47 [see Notes 2) & 4)]; SOC by 1954

NH457 Spitfire LF.IXe (Merlin 66); Became TuAF No. **6212**; TOC/RAF 23.5.44; Selected for Turkey 23.10.47 - Arr TuAF 5.12.47; 5th Air Regiment at Bursa, Reserve aircraft [see Notes 2) & 4)]; SOC by 1954

NH462 Spitfire LF.IXe (Merlin 66); Became TuAF No. **6272**; TOC/RAF 23.5.44; Selected for Turkey 13.11.47 - Arr TuAF 1.2.48; 7th Air Regiment (2nd Company) at Kütahya from 2.48; Staff of 7th Alayi, crashed Yesilköy 23.7.49 (Plt Fethi Serim killed); SOC

NH469 Spitfire LF.IXe (Merlin 66); Became TuAF No. **6250**; TOC/RAF 24.5.44; Selected for Turkey 16.4.47 - Arr TuAF 18.5.47; 7th Air Regiment (1st Company) at Kütahya from 5.47 [see Notes 3) & 4)]; SOC by 1954

NH472 Spitfire LF.IXe (Merlin 66); Became TuAF No. **6343**; TOC/RAF 20.5.44; Selected for Turkey 23.10.47 - Arr TuAF 15.1.48; Unserviceable after delivery; Air depot, repair [see Note 4)]; Not accepted

NH487 Spitfire LF.IXe (Merlin 66); Became TuAF No. **6369**; TOC/RAF 27.5.44; Selected for Turkey 26.6.47 - Arr TuAF 7.7.47; Burnt during delivery; Air depot, repair; To 4th Air Regiment at Merzifon [see Note 4)]; SOC by 1954

NH490 Spitfire LF.IXe (Merlin 66); Became TuAF No. **6234**; TOC/RAF 2.6.44; Selected for Turkey 9.10.47 - Arr TuAF 5.12.47; 4th Air Regiment (3rd Company) at Merzifon from 1.48 [see Note 4)]; SOC by 1954

NH524 Spitfire LF.IXe (Merlin 66); Became TuAF No. **6331**; TOC/RAF 26.5.44; Selected for Turkey 12.11.47 - Arr TuAF 6.12.47; For 4th Air Regiment at Merzifon, but unserviceable on acceptance [see Note 4)]; SOC by 1954

NH551 Spitfire LF.IXe (Merlin 66); Became TuAF No. **6260**; TOC/RAF 5.6.44; Selected for Turkey 15.10.47 - Arr TuAF 1.2.48; 7th Air Regiment (1st Company) at Kütahya from 2.48; 4th Air Base at Merzifon; Air Collision 27.1.53 (Plt Mahmut Nedim Sengü killed); SOC

NH554 Spitfire LF.IXe (Merlin 66); Became TuAF No. **6269**; TOC/RAF 31.5.44; Selected for Turkey 22.7.47 - Arr TuAF 23.7.47; 7th Air Regiment (2nd Company) at Kütahya from 7.47 [see Notes 3) & 4)]; SOC by 1954

NH589 Spitfire LF.IXe (Merlin 66); Became TuAF No. **6227**; TOC/RAF 17.6.44; Selected for Turkey 23.1.47 - Arr TuAF 28.3.47; 4th Air Regiment (3rd Company) at Merzifon from 4.47 [see Note 4)]; SOC by 1954

NH601 Spitfire LF.IXe (Merlin 66); Selected for Turkey 18.12.46; SOC before delivery; Cancelled

NH604 Spitfire LF.IXe (Merlin 66); Became TuAF No. **6267**; TOC/RAF 7.6.44; Selected for Turkey 11.7.47 - Arr TuAF 15.7.47; 7th Air Regiment (2nd Company) at Kütahya from 7.47 [see Notes 3) & 4)]; SOC by 1954

NH607 Spitfire LF.IXe (Merlin 66); Became TuAF No. **6296**; TOC/RAF 10.6.44; Selected for Turkey 14.10.47 - Arr TuAF 7.2.48; 7th Air Regiment (4th Company) at Kütahya from 2.48 [see Notes 3) & 4)]; SOC by 1954

NH609 Spitfire LF.IXe (Merlin 66); Became TuAF No. **6256**; TOC/RAF 8.6.44; Selected for Turkey 11.7.47 - Arr TuAF 16.7.47; 7th Air Regiment (1st Company) at Kütahya from 7.47 [see Notes 3) & 4)]; SOC by 1954

PK994 Spitfire LF.IXe (Merlin 66); TOC/RAF 10.6.44; Selected for TuAF 17.1.47, but crashed on or before delivery

PL124 Spitfire LF.IXe (Merlin 66); Became TuAF No. **6301**; TOC/RAF 30.5.44; Selected for Turkey 22.7.47 - Arr TuAF 29.7.47; 8th Air Regiment (1st Company) at Erzincan from 8.47 [see Notes 2) & 4)]; SOC by 1954

PL125 Spitfire LF.IXe (Merlin 66); Became TuAF No. **6235**; TOC/RAF 16.6.44; Selected for Turkey 15.10.47 - Arr TuAF 6.12.47; 4th Air Regiment (3rd Company) at Merzifon from 1.48 [see Note 4)]; SOC by 1954

PL129 Spitfire LF.IXe (Merlin 66); Became TuAF No. **6310**; TOC/RAF 17.6.44; Selected for Turkey 22.7.47 - Arr TuAF 24.7.47; 8th Air Regiment (2nd Company) at Erzincan from 8.47 [see Notes 2) & 4)]; SOC by 1954

PL136 Spitfire LF.IXe (Merlin 66); Became TuAF No. **6325**; TOC/RAF 10.6.44; Selected for Turkey 25.9.47 - Arr TuAF 28.9.47; 5th Air Regiment (3rd Company) at Bursa from 10.47 [see Notes 2) & 4)]; SOC by 1954

PL161 Spitfire LF.IXe (Merlin 66); Became TuAF No. **6359**; TOC/RAF 17.7.44; Selected for Turkey 28.8.47 - Arr TuAF 2.9.47; Written off on delivery; Air depot, repair [see Note 4)]; SOC by 1954

PL163 Spitfire LF.IXe (Merlin 66); Became TuAF No. **6336**; TOC/RAF 17.7.44; Selected for Turkey 25.9.47 - Arr TuAF 28.9.47; Unserviceable after delivery, but repaired; 5th Air Regiment (4th Company) at Bursa from 10.47 [see Notes 2) & 4)]; SOC by 1954

PL165 Spitfire LF.IXe (Merlin 66); Became TuAF No. **6290**; TOC/RAF 17.7.44; Selected for Turkey 11.7.47 - Arr TuAF 14.7.47; 7th Air Regiment (4th Company) at Kütahya from 7.47; Fatal crash 7.8.50 (Plt Fuat Çerençe killed, 8th Air Base Staff); SOC

PL213 Spitfire LF.IXe (Merlin 66); Became TuAF No. **6302**; TOC/RAF 15.6.44; Selected for Turkey 30.7.47 - Arr TuAF 2.8.47; 8th Air Regiment (1st Company) at Erzincan from 9.47 [see Notes 2) & 4)]; SOC by 1954

PL260 Spitfire LF.IXe (Merlin 66); Became TuAF No. **6252**; TOC/RAF 19.6.44; Selected for Turkey 2.5.47 - Arr TuAF 12.6.47; 7th Air Regiment (1st Company) at Kütahya from 6.47 [see Notes 3) & 4)]; SOC by 1954

PL320 Spitfire LF.IXe (Merlin 66); Became TuAF No. **6277**; TOC/RAF 7.6.44; Selected for Turkey 26.6.47 - Arr TuAF 1.7.47; 7th Air Regiment (3rd Company) at Kütahya from 7.47 [see Notes 3) & 4)]; SOC by 1954

PL332　Spitfire LF.IXe (Merlin 66); Became TuAF No. **6214**; TOC/RAF 22.6.44; Selected for Turkey 3.3.47 - Arr TuAF 22.3.47; 4th Air Regiment (2nd Company) at Merzifon from 4.47 [see Note 4)]; SOC by 1954

PL398　Spitfire LF.IXe (Merlin 66); Became TuAF No. **6246**; TOC/RAF 22.6.44; Selected for Turkey 24.1.47 - Arr TuAF 5.12.47; 4th Air Regiment at Merzifon from 1.48 [see Note 4)]; SOC by 1954

PL423　Spitfire LF.IXe (Merlin 66); TOC/RAF 24.6.44; Selected for TuAF 17.1.47, but crashed on delivery-flight

PL462　Spitfire LF.IXe (Merlin 66); Became TuAF No. **6344**; TOC/RAF 30.6.44; Selected for Turkey 15.10.47 - Arr TuAF 1.2.48; Air depot, storage; 8th Air Regiment (Staff), fatal crash at Erzincan 10.5.49 (Plt Turan Karatekin killed); SOC

PL493　Spitfire LF.IXe (Merlin 66); Became TuAF No. **6215**; TOC/RAF 1.7.44; Selected for Turkey 20.1.47 - Arr TuAF 28.3.47; 4th Air Regiment (2nd Company) at Merzifon from 4.47 [see Note 4)]; SOC by 1954

PT402　Spitfire LF.IXe (Merlin 66); Became TuAF No. **6285**; TOC/RAF 1.7.44; Selected for Turkey 30.4.47 - Arr TuAF 18.5.47; 7th Air Regiment (4th Company) at Kütahya from 5.47; Later with 4th Air Regiment at Merzifon, marked 'YV.85' [see Note 4)]; SOC by 1954

PT405　Spitfire LF.IXe (Merlin 66); Became TuAF No. **6365**; TOC/RAF 1.7.44; Selected for Turkey 15.9.47 - Arr TuAF 18.9.47; 8th Air Regiment (4th Company) at Erzincan from 9.47 [see Notes 2) & 4)]; SOC by 1954

PT413　Spitfire LF.IXe (Merlin 66); Became TuAF No. **6204**; TOC/RAF 18.7.44; Selected for Turkey 18.12.46 - Arr TuAF 19.1.47; 4th Air Regiment (1st Company) at Merzifon from 3.47 [see Note 4)]; SOC by 1954

PT525　Spitfire LF.IXe (Merlin 66); Became TuAF No. **6323**; TOC/RAF 8.8.44; Selected for Turkey 25.9.47 - Arr TuAF 27.9.47; 5th Air Regiment (3rd Company) at Bursa from 10.47 [see Notes 2) & 4)]; SOC by 1954

PT537　Spitfire LF.IXe (Merlin 66); Became TuAF No. **6222**; TOC/RAF 14.8.44; Selected for Turkey 23.10.47 - Arr TuAF 5.12.47; 4th Air Regiment (2nd Company) at Merzifon from 1.48 [see Note 4)]; SOC by 1954

PT592　Spitfire LF.IXe (Merlin 66); Became TuAF No. **6309**; TOC/RAF 22.7.44; Selected for Turkey 22.7.47 - Arr TuAF 24.7.47; 8th Air Regiment (2nd Company) at Erzincan from 8.47 [see Notes 2) & 4)]; SOC by 1954

PT680　Spitfire LF.IXe (Merlin 66); Became TuAF No. **6251**; TOC/RAF 15.8.44; Selected for Turkey 6.5.47 - Arr TuAF 28.5.47; 7th Air Regiment (1st Company) at Kütahya from 6.47; 4th Air Base at Merzifon; Fatal crash 5.8.54 (Plt Lütfü Elgin killed); SOC

PT734　Spitfire LF.IXe (Merlin 66); Became TuAF No. **6263**; TOC/RAF 9.8.44; Selected for Turkey 16.4.47 - Arr TuAF 4.6.47; 7th Air Regiment (2nd Company) at Kütahya from 6.47 [see Notes 3) & 4)]; SOC by 1954

PT763　Spitfire LF.IXe (Merlin 66); Became TuAF No. **6206**; TOC/RAF 14.8.44; Selected for Turkey 16.1.47 - Arr TuAF 20.1.47; 4th Air Regiment (1st Company) at Merzifon from 3.47; Staff of 4th Alayi, fatal crash 13.9.50 (Plt Fikret Vural killed); SOC

PT842　Spitfire LF.IXe (Merlin 66); Became TuAF No. **6311**; TOC/RAF 17.8.44; Selected for Turkey 17.4.47 - Arr TuAF 2.5.47; 8th Air Regiment (2nd Company) at Erzincan from 8.47 [see Notes 2) & 4)]; SOC by 1954

PT843　Spitfire LF.IXe (Merlin 66); TOC/RAF 17.8.44; Selected for TuAF 25.3.47; Despatched 5.47, but crashed on delivery-flight

PT851　Spitfire LF.IXe (Merlin 66); Became TuAF No. **6253**; TOC/RAF 24.8.44; Selected for Turkey 1.4.47 - Arr TuAF 1.7.47; 7th Air Regiment (1st Company) at Kütahya from 7.47; Staff of 7th Alayi, crashed en route from Kütahya to Balikesir 6.9.49 (Plt Muzaffer Gürler and another killed); SOC
NOTE: Perhaps air collision, or a second person on board?

PT852　Spitfire LF.IXe (Merlin 66); Became TuAF No. **6318**; TOC/RAF 23.8.44; Selected for Turkey 6.10.47 - Arr TuAF 21.10.47; Air depot, storage [see Notes 2) & 4)]; SOC by 1954

PT883　Spitfire LF.IXe (Merlin 66); TOC/RAF 24.8.44; Selected for TuAF 22.8.47; Desp 11.47, but crashed on delivery-flight

PT938　Spitfire LF.IXe (Merlin 66); Became TuAF No. **6266**; TOC/RAF 26.8.44; Selected for Turkey 7.7.47 - Arr TuAF 14.7.47; 7th Air Regiment (2nd Company) at Kütahya from 7.47 [see Notes 3) & 4)]; SOC by 1954

PT947　Spitfire LF.IXe (Merlin 66); Became TuAF No. **6226**; TOC/RAF 27.8.44; Selected for Turkey 20.1.47 - Arr TuAF 21.3.47; 4th Air Regiment (3rd Company) at Merzifon from 4.47 [see Note 4)]; SOC by 1954

PT968　Spitfire LF.IXe (Merlin 66); Became TuAF No. **6288**; TOC/RAF 30.8.44; Selected for Turkey 23.1.47 - Arr TuAF 24.6.47; 7th Air Regiment (4th Company) at Kütahya from 7.47 [see Notes 3) & 4)]; SOC by 1954

PV126　Spitfire LF.IXe (Merlin 66); Became TuAF No. **6262**; TOC/RAF 3.8.44; Selected for Turkey 9.5.47 - Arr TuAF 28.5.47; 7th Air Regiment (2nd Company) at Kütahya from 5.47 [see Notes 3) & 4)]; SOC by 1954

PV146　Spitfire LF.IXe (Merlin 66); Became TuAF No. **6240**; TOC/RAF 31.8.44; Selected for Turkey 17.1.47 - Arr TuAF 5.4.47; 4th Air Regiment (4th Company) at Merzifon from 4.47 [see Note 4)]; SOC by 1954

PV149　Spitfire LF.IXe (Merlin 66); Became TuAF No. **6265**; TOC/RAF 5.9.44; Selected for Turkey 27.6.47 - Arr TuAF 1.7.47; 7th Air Regiment (2nd Company) at Kütahya from 7.47 [see Notes 3) & 4)]; SOC by 1954

PV159　Spitfire LF.IXe (Merlin 66); Became TuAF No. **6294**; TOC/RAF 5.9.44; Selected for Turkey 4.11.47 - Arr TuAF 16.1.48; 7th Air Regiment (4th Company) at Kütahya from 1.48 [see Notes 3) & 4)]; SOC by 1954

PV176　Spitfire LF.IXe (Merlin 66); Became TuAF No. **6333**; TOC/RAF 8.9.44; Selected for Turkey 18.9.47 - Arr TuAF 19.9.47; 5th Air Regiment (4th Company) at Bursa from 10.47 [see Notes 2) & 4)]; SOC by 1954

PV199　Spitfire LF.IXe (Merlin 66); Became TuAF No. **6352**; TOC/RAF 16.9.44; Selected for Turkey 5.9.47 - Arr TuAF 9.9.47; 8th Air Regiment (3rd Company) at Erzincan from 9.47 [see Notes 2) & 4)]; SOC by 1954

PV231　Spitfire LF.IXe (Merlin 66); Became TuAF No. **6350**; TOC/RAF 21.9.44; Selected for Turkey 2.9.47 - Arr TuAF 4.9.47; 8th Air Regiment (3rd Company) at Erzincan from 9.47 [see Notes 2) & 4)]; SOC by 1954

PV263　Spitfire LF.IXe (Merlin 66); Became TuAF No. **6217**; TOC/RAF 25.9.44; Selected for Turkey 24.3.47 - Arr TuAF 14.4.47; 4th Air Regiment (2nd Company) at Merzifon from 5.47 [see Note 4)]; SOC by 1954

PV305　Spitfire LF.IXe (Merlin 66); Became TuAF No. **6351**; TOC/RAF 26.9.44; Selected for Turkey 5.9.47 - Arr TuAF 9.9.47; 8th Air Regiment (3rd Company) at Erzincan from 9.47 [see Notes 2) & 4)]; SOC by 1954

PV342　Spitfire LF.IXe (Merlin 66); Became TuAF No. **6218**; TOC/RAF 30.9.44; Selected for Turkey 24.3.47 - Arr TuAF 14.4.47; 4th Air Regiment (2nd Company) at Merzifon from 5.47 [see Note 4)]; SOC by 1954

RK848　Spitfire LF.IXe (Merlin 66); Became TuAF No. **6304**; TOC/RAF 30.9.44; Selected for Turkey 6.8.47 - Arr TuAF 8.8.47; 8th Air Regiment (1st Company) at Erzincan from 9.47 [see Notes 2) & 4)]; SOC by 1954

RR182　Spitfire LF.IXe (Merlin 66); Became TuAF No. **6334**; TOC/RAF 25.8.44; Selected for Turkey 18.9.47 - Arr TuAF 20.9.47; 5th Air Regiment (4th Company) at Bursa from 10.47 [see Notes 2) & 4)]; SOC by 1954

SL661　Spitfire LF.IXe (Merlin 66); Became TuAF No. **6360**; TOC/RAF 14.8.45; Selected for Turkey 28.8.47 - Arr TuAF 2.9.47; 8th Air Regiment (4th Company) at Erzincan from 9.47 [see Notes 2) & 4)]; SOC by 1954

SL665　Spitfire LF.IXe (Merlin 66); Became TuAF No. **6303**; TOC/RAF 31.7.45; Selected for Turkey 30.7.47 - Arr TuAF 2.8.47; 8th Air Regiment (1st Company) at Erzincan from 9.47 [see Notes 2) & 4)]; SOC by 1954

SM139　Spitfire LF.IXe (Merlin 66); Became TuAF No. **6210**; TOC/RAF 22.9.44; Selected for Turkey 16.10.47 - Arr

TA858 Spitfire LF.IXe (Merlin 66); Became TuAF No. **6270**; TOC/RAF 2.10.44; Selected for Turkey 3.11.47 - Arr TuAF 15.1.48; 7th Air Regiment (2nd Company) at Kütahya from 1.48 [see Notes 3) & 4)]; SOC by 1954

TE153 Spitfire LF.IXe (Merlin 66); Became TuAF No. **6242**; TOC/RAF 28.5.45; Selected for Turkey 24.3.47 - Arr TuAF 14.4.47; 4th Air Regiment (4th Company) at Merzifon from 4.47 [see Note 4)]; SOC by 1954

TE503 Spitfire LF.IXe (Merlin 66); Became TuAF No. **6211**; TOC/RAF 30.4.45; Selected for Turkey 1.10.47 - Arr TuAF 5.12.47; Reserve, then 4th Air Regiment at Merzifon from 1.48 [see Note 4)]; SOC by 1954

TE508 Spitfire LF.IXe (Merlin 66); Became TuAF No. **6241**; TOC/RAF 30.5.45; Selected for Turkey 24.3.47 - Arr TuAF 14.4.47; 4th Air Regiment (4th Company) at Merzifon from 5.47 [see Note 4)]; SOC by 1954

TE511 Spitfire LF.IXe (Merlin 66); Became TuAF No. **6281**; TOC/RAF 31.5.45; Selected for Turkey 10.4.47 - Arr TuAF 12.6.47; 7th Air Regiment (3rd Company) at Kütahya from 7.47 [see Notes 3) & 4)]; SOC by 1954

TE568 Spitfire LF.IXe (Merlin 66); Became TuAF No. **6364**; TOC/RAF 12.6.45; Selected for Turkey 10.9.47 - Arr TuAF 13.9.47; 8th Air Regiment (4th Company) at Erzincan from 9.47 [see Notes 2) & 4)]; SOC by 1954

Unknown TuAF Serial Nos: **Spitfire Mk. IXc/e;**
Allocation for Turkey in RAF documents (28 aircraft), but no trace in TuAF records [see Note 6)] =

MJ386 Spitfire LF.IXc (Merlin 66); Became TuAF No. .... ? TOC/RAF 5.11.43; Selected for Turkey 3.11.47 - Arr TuAF 1948/49; Air depot, storage; Fate unknown [see Note 4)]; SOC by 1954

MJ801 Spitfire LF.IXc (Merlin 66); Became TuAF No. .... ? TOC/RAF 21.12.43; Selected for Turkey 14.10.47 - Arr TuAF 1948/49; Fate unknown [as MJ386, above]

MJ871 Spitfire LF.IXc (Merlin 66); Became TuAF No. .... ? TOC/RAF 28.12.43; Selected for Turkey 1.10.47 - Arr TuAF 1948/49; Fate unknown [as MJ386, above]

MJ589 Spitfire LF.IXc (Merlin 66); Became TuAF No. .... ? TOC/RAF 4.12.43; Selected for Turkey 16.10.47 - Arr TuAF 1948/49; Fate unknown [as MJ386, above]

MK347 Spitfire LF.IXc (Merlin 66); Became TuAF No. .... ? TOC/RAF 30.1.44; Selected for Turkey 1.10.47 - Arr TuAF 1948/49; Fate unknown [as MJ386, above]

MK838 Spitfire LF.IXc (Merlin 66); Became TuAF No. .... ? TOC/RAF 30.3.44; Selected for Turkey 3.11.47 - Arr TuAF 1948/49; Fate unknown [as MJ386, above]

MK896 Spitfire LF.IXc (Merlin 66); Became TuAF No. .... ? TOC/RAF 17.3.44; Selected for Turkey 4.11.47 - Arr TuAF 1948/49; Fate unknown [as MJ386, above]

MK899 Spitfire LF.IXc (Merlin 66); Became TuAF No. .... ? TOC/RAF 4.4.44; Selected for Turkey 3.11.47 - Arr TuAF 1948/49; Fate unknown [as MJ386, above]

MK926 Spitfire LF.IXc (Merlin 66); Became TuAF No. .... ? TOC/RAF 24.3.44; Selected for Turkey 23.10.47 - Arr TuAF 1948/49; Fate unknown [as MJ386, above]

ML125 Spitfire LF.IXc (Merlin 66); Became TuAF No. .... ? TOC/RAF 19.3.44; Selected for Turkey 3.11.47 - Arr TuAF 1948/49; Fate unknown [as MJ386, above]

ML181 Spitfire LF.IXc (Merlin 66); Became TuAF No. .... ? TOC/RAF 20.4.44; Selected for Turkey 5.9.47 - Arr TuAF 1948/49; Fate unknown [as MJ386, above]

ML184 Spitfire LF.IXc (Merlin 66); Became TuAF No. .... ? TOC/RAF 13.4.44; Selected for Turkey 4.11.47 - Arr TuAF 1948/49; Fate unknown [as MJ386, above]

ML186 Spitfire LF.IXc (Merlin 66); Became TuAF No. .... ? TOC/RAF 14.4.44; Selected for Turkey 15.10.47 - Arr TuAF 1948/49; Fate unknown [as MJ386, above]

ML205 Spitfire LF.IXc (Merlin 66); Became TuAF No. .... ? TOC/RAF 6.4.44; Selected for Turkey 21.10.47 - Arr TuAF 1948/49; Fate unknown [as MJ386, above]

ML264 Spitfire LF.IXc (Merlin 66); Became TuAF No. .... ? TOC/RAF 27.4.44; Selected for Turkey 6.4.48 - Arr TuAF 1948/49; Fate unknown [as MJ386, above]

ML411 Spitfire LF.IXc (Merlin 66); Became TuAF No. .... ? TOC/RAF 26.4.44; Selected for Turkey 14.10.47 - Arr TuAF 1948/49; Fate unknown [as MJ386, above]

NH214 Spitfire LF.IXe (Merlin 66); Became TuAF No. .... ? TOC/RAF 6.5.44; Selected for Turkey 16.10.47 - Arr TuAF 1948/49; Fate unknown [as MJ386, above]

NH255 Spitfire LF.IXe (Merlin 66); Became TuAF No. .... ? TOC/RAF 18.5.44; Selected for Turkey 15.10.47 - Arr TuAF 1948/49; Fate unknown [as MJ386, above]

NH313 Spitfire LF.IXe (Merlin 66); Became TuAF No. .... ? TOC/RAF 17.5.44; Selected for Turkey 15.10.47 - Arr TuAF 1948/49; Fate unknown [as MJ386, above]

NH349 Spitfire LF.IXe (Merlin 66); Became TuAF No. .... ? TOC/RAF 25.5.44; Selected for Turkey 26.7.48 (Replacement) - Arr TuAF 1948/49; Fate unknown [as MJ386, above]

PL143 Spitfire LF.IXe (Merlin 66); Became TuAF No. .... ? TOC/RAF 20.6.44; Selected for Turkey 14.10.47 - Arr TuAF 1948/49; Fate unknown [as MJ386, above]

PL223 Spitfire LF.IXe (Merlin 66); Became TuAF No. .... ? TOC/RAF 15.6.44; Selected for Turkey 16.10.47 - Arr TuAF 1948/49; Fate unknown [as MJ386, above]

PT415 Spitfire LF.IXe (Merlin 66); Became TuAF No. .... ? TOC/RAF 1.7.44; Selected for Turkey 23.8.48 (Replacement) - Arr TuAF 1948/49; Fate unknown [as MJ386, above]

PT538 Spitfire LF.IXe (Merlin 66); Became TuAF No. .... ? TOC/RAF 15.8.44; Selected for Turkey 16.10.47 - Arr TuAF 1948/49; Fate unknown [as MJ386, above]

PT565 Spitfire LF.IXe (Merlin 66); Became TuAF No. .... ? TOC/RAF 5.9.44; Selected for Turkey 5.4.48 - Arr TuAF 1948/49; Fate unknown [as MJ386, above]

PT826 Spitfire LF.IXe (Merlin 66); Became TuAF No. .... ? TOC/RAF 17.8.44; Selected for Turkey 15.10.47 - Arr TuAF 1948/49; Fate unknown [as MJ386, above]

PV140 Spitfire LF.IXe (Merlin 66); No TuAF No; TOC/RAF 5.9.44; ex No.332 Sqn; Selected for Turkey 15.10.47 - On delivery route from England to Turkey force-landed in Italy; Later sold to Italy (*MM4286*) in 5.49
NOTE: Picture shows the aircraft in TuAF markings, equipped with long range ferry tank *(see page 406)*

RK803 Spitfire LF.IXe (Merlin 66); No TuAF No; TOC/RAF 21.9.44; ex Nos.331, 349, 401, 130 Sqns; Selected for Turkey 12.7.48 - On delivery route force-landed in Italy; Later sold to Italy (*MM4287*) in 5.49

TuAF Serial Nos. 6551 - 6554: Spitfire PR.XIX,
with Yüksek Irtibat Kesif Foto Kitaati 1946-48; 10th Recce Regiment 1948-51; 113th Sqn 1951-53

PM548 Spitfire PR.XIX (Griffon 66); Became TuAF No. **6551**; TOC/RAF 30.6.45; Sold to V.A. 12.11.46 (B-class reg. N-133) - Arr TuAF 11.3.47; Yük.Irt.Ks.Foto Kt. (Photo Recce) at Eskisehir 1947/48; 10th Recce Regiment (3rd Company) at Afyon 1948-51; 113th Sqn at Eskisehir 1951-53; SOC by 1953 [see Note 5)]

PM654 Spitfire PR.XIX (Griffon 66); Became TuAF No. **6552**; TOC/RAF 26.11.45; Sold to V.A. 12.11.46 (B-class reg. N-131) - Arr TuAF 26.4.47; Yük.Irt.Ks.Foto Kt. (Photo Recce) at Eskisehir 1947/48; 10th Recce Regiment (3rd Company) at Afyon 1948-51; 113th Sqn at Eskisehir 1951-53; SOC by 1953 [see Note 5)]

PM656 Spitfire PR.XIX (Griffon 66); Became TuAF No. **6553**; TOC/RAF 21.3.46; Sold to V.A. 12.11.46 (B-class reg. N-134) - Arr TuAF 10.3.47; Yük.Irt.Ks.Foto Kt. (Photo Recce) at Eskisehir 1947/48; 10th Recce Regiment (3rd Company) at Afyon 1948-51; 113th Sqn at Eskisehir 1951-53; SOC by 1953 [see Note 5)]

Spitfire LF.IXe PV140, seen here with a long-range ferry tank, force landed in Italy whilst en route to Turkey. It was later sold to Turkey. [MAP]

Spitfire LF.IXe, PV140 of the Turkish AF, circa 1948/9

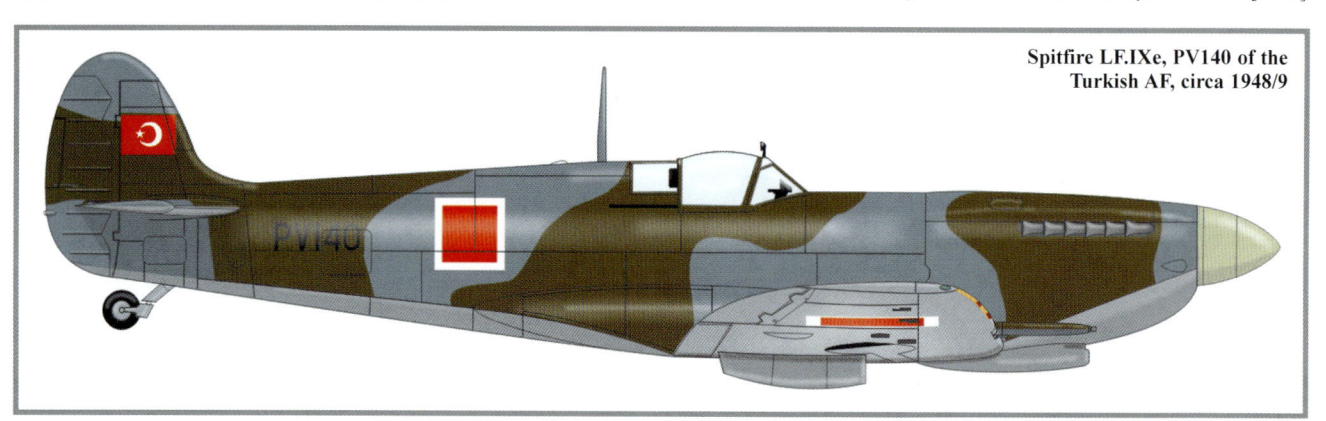

PM657 Spitfire PR.XIX (Griffon 66); Became TuAF No. **6554**; TOC/RAF 27.11.45; Sold to V.A. 12.11.46 (B-class reg. N-132) - Arr TuAF 10.3.47; Yük.Irt.Ks.Foto Kt. (Photo Recce) at Eskisehir 1947/48; 10th Recce Regiment (3rd Company) at Afyon 1948-51; 113th Sqn at Eskisehir 1951-53; SOC by 1953 [see Note 5)].

Notes
Only general fates are known.
The aircraft could have served also as follows:
1) possibly with the 5th Air Regiment at Bursa from 1945.
2) possibly with the 6th Air Regiment at Bandirma in May 1949.
3) possibly with the 4th Air Regiment at Merzifon in March 1950.
4) possibly with the 141st Sqn & 142nd Sqn at Merzifon in April 1951.
5) one PR.XIX became SOC between November 1949 and 1951.
6) TuAF inventory list told 170 Spitfire Mk.IX by 31 October 1949.

Regarding notes 1) - 4): Some aircraft were involved in crashes and phased out earlier.

Unidentified fatal crashes

25.10.44 Spitfire; Crashed in UK; Plt Emin Dönmez of Hava Okulu
10.11.44 Spitfire; Crashed in UK; Plt M Hüdai Toros of Hava Okulu
25.12.44 Two Spitfire F.Vb/c trop; Flown from Egypt to Adana by RAF; Taken over by TuAF, mid-air collision during ferry flight from Adana to Izmir; Pilots Suat Çantay (6.A/1.Bl) and Ismail Erkan (6.A/3.Bl)
25. 3.46 Spitfire F.Vb/c trop, TuAF No.5760; Crashed en route Izmir-Gaziemir; Plt H Nafiz Hazneci (6.A/3.Bl)
27. 7.46 Spitfire F.Vb/c trop, TuAF No.5737; Crashed Bursa; Plt Seyfi Baybora (5.A/1.Bl)
2.10.46 Spitfire F.Vb/c trop, TuAF No.5759; Crashed Kizilcullu
28.12.46 Spitfire F.Vb/c trop, TuAF No.5767; Crashed Bursa; Plt Osman Kaya (5.A/2.Bl, School Grp)
25. 2.47 Spitfire F.Vb/c trop; Crashed Istinye Köyü; Plt Muhtar Özgören (5.A, Staff)
7. 5.47 Spitfire F.Vb/c trop; Crashed Inegöl; Plt Mustafa Atalay (5.A, Staff)
2.10.47 Spitfire LF.IX; Crashed Kütahya; Plt Hüsnü Kurban (7.A/1.Bl)
3. 1.48 Two Spitfire LF.IX; Mid-air collision 12m from Merzifon; pilots Elibollu and Serafettin Gürsoy (both 4.A/1.Bl)
9. 2.48 Spitfire LF.IX of 5.Alay; Lost bearing, penetrated into Bulgarian air space, shot down by Bulgarian AA
27. 3.48 Spitfire LF.IX; Plt Ismail Casin (8.A, Staff)

Check list of TuAF / RAF Serial Nos

TuAF Serial	RAF No.	Arr. TuAF
2901	L1066	8.39
2902	P9566	5.40
2903	P9567	5.40
Spitfire Mk. V		
5501-5539	Relation unknown	
5701-5769	Relation unknown	
5801	AB345	9.44
5802	JK190	2.45
5803	JL240	2.45
Spitfire Mk. IX		
6201	MJ963	1.47
6202	ML173	1.47
6203	NH434	1.47
6204	PT413	1.47
6205	MA255	1.47
6206	PT763	1.47
6207	MK786	1.47
6208	NH206	1.47
6209	NH244	1.47
6210	SM139	12.47
6211	TE503	12.47
6212	NH457	12.47
6213	MJ147	3.47
6214	PL332	3.47
6215	PL493	3.47
6216	MJ396	4.47
6217	PV263	4.47
6218	PV342	4.47
6219	MK947	4.47
6220	MH883	6.47
6221	NH257	5.47
6222	PT537	12.47
6223	NH250	12.47
6224	ML175	12.47
6225	MK565	3.47
6226	PT947	3.47
6227	NH589	3.47
6228	NH361	4.47
6229	MJ799	4.47
6230	MJ344	4.47
6231	MJ883	4.47
6232	NH427	4.47
6233	ML368	5.47
6234	NH490	12.47
6235	PL125	12.47
6236	NH268	12.47
6237	MK986	3.47
6238	MK583	3.47
6239	NH414	4.47
6240	PV146	4.47
6241	TE508	4.47
6242	TE153	4.47
6243	MK628	4.47
6244	MJ566	5.47
6245	ML414	5.47
6246	PL398	12.47
6247	ML147	12.47
6248	ML143	12.47
6249	MK288	5.47
6250	NH469	5.47
6251	PT680	5.47
6252	PL260	6.47
6253	PT851	7.47
6254	MJ313	7.47
6255	MJ180	7.47

TuAF Serial	RAF No.	Arr. TuAF
6256	NH609	7.47
6257	MK228	7.47
6258	MH374	12.47
6259	ML156	1.48
6260	NH551	2.48
6261	ML208	5.47
6262	PV126	5.47
6263	PT734	6.47
6264	MK195	6.47
6265	PV149	7.47
6266	PT938	7.47
6267	NH604	7.47
6268	JL106	7.47
6269	NH554	7.47
6270	TA858	1.48
6271	EN636	1.48
6272	NH462	2.48
6273	ML293	5.47
6274	MK995	5.47
6275	MK754	6.47
6276	MK733	6.47
6277	PL320	7.47
6278	MJ388	7.47
6279	MK726	7.47
6280	LZ843	7.47
6281	TE511	6.47
6282	MK678	1.48
6283	MK564	1.48
6284	JL359	2.48
6285	PT402	5.47
6286	MK246	5.47
6287	MJ448	6.47
6288	PT968	6.47
6289	MK907	7.47
6290	PL165	7.47
6291	MK868	7.47
6292	MK183	7.47
6293	MJ369	7.47
6294	PV159	1.48
6295	MK787	1.48
6296	NH607	2.48
6297	MJ888	7.47
6298	NH158	7.47
6299	MK688	7.47
6300	ML424	7.47
6301	PL124	7.47
6302	PL213	8.47
6303	SL665	8.47
6304	RK848	8.47
6305	MJ387	8.47
6306	MK747	10.47
6307	ML321	10.47
6308	MK517	11.47
6309	PT592	7.47
6310	PL129	7.47
6311	PT842	5.47
6312	MK893	7.47
6313	ML268	8.47
6314	EN633	8.47
6315	ML266	8.47
6316	MK308	8.47
6317	MK201	8.47
6318	PT852	10.47
6319	MK863	11.47
6320	MJ780	11.47
6321	ML273	9.47
6322	NH179	9.47
6323	PT525	9.47
6324	MK534	9.47

TuAF Serial	RAF No.	Arr. TuAF
6325	PL136	9.47
6326	ML362	9.47
6327	MJ872	10.47
6328	NH419	10.47
6329	ML191	10.47
6330	NH246	10.47
6331	NH524	12.47
6332	MK889	1.48
6333	PV176	9.47
6334	RR182	9.47
6335	ML126	9.47
6336	PL163	9.47
6337	ML376	9.47
6338	ML265	9.47
6339	NH155	10.47
6340	MJ567	10.47
6341	MK178	10.47
6342	ML115	6.47
6343	NH472	1.48
6344	PL462	2.48
6345	MK988	8.47
6346	EN579	8.47
6347	MK915	8.47
6348	MK309	9.47
6349	MK948	9.47
6350	PV231	9.47

TuAF Serial	RAF No.	Arr. TuAF
6351	PV305	9.47
6352	PV199	9.47
6353	ML313	9.47
6354	NH200	10.47
6355	MK147	10.47
6356	MK294	11.47
6357	ML320	8.47
6358	MK317	8.47
6359	PL161	9.47
6360	SL661	9.47
6361	MH414	9.47
6362	MJ575	9.47
6363	MK663	9.47
6364	TE568	9.47
6365	PT405	9.47
6366	MK852	10.47
6367	ML202	11.47
6368	NH456	11.47
6369	NH487	7.47
Spitfire PR.XIX		
6551	PM548	3.47
6552	PM654	4.47
6553	PM656	3.47
6554	PM657	3.47

20.04.48 Spitfire LF.IX of 5.Alay; Crashed Yesilköy
11. 5.48 Spitfire LF.IX; Crashed Bozüyük; Plt Selahattin Yentürk (5.A/4.Bl)
2. 9.48   Spitfire LF.IX; Crashed Yesilköy; Plt Bahattin Seylan (7.A/1.Bl)
5.10.48   Spitfire LF.IX; Crashed Erzincan; Plt H Bahattin Erkmenalp (3rd Div., Staff)
25.10.48 Spitfire F.Vb/c trop & Spitfire LF.IX; Mid-air collision near K Maras; Plt's Mustafa Küçükel of CFS (OTU) and Esref Pitrak (5.A, Staff)
9. 4.49   Spitfire LF.IX; Crashed Yesilköy; Plt Dündar Alp (7.A, Staff)
6. 9.49   Spitfire LF.IX; Crashed en route Kütahya-Balikesir, possibly air collision; Plt Muhtesem Esiner (7.A, Staff) - see also PT851, TuAF No 6253
25. 4.50 Spitfire LF.IX; Plt Nejat Gençer (8th Air Base, Staff)
21. 8.51 Spitfire LF.IX; Plt Ismet Uysal (4th Air Base, Staff)
27. 1.53 Spitfire LF.IX; Mid-air collision with No.6260 (ex NH551); Plt Gani Yazici (4th Air Base, Staff)
14. 7.53 Spitfire LF.IX; Dived into ground during flying display for AA training; Plt Nizamettin Benli (AA Co-op unit at Polati)
9.10.53   Spitfire LF.IX; Plt Orhan Tunçöz (4th Air Base, Staff)
3.12.53   Three Spitfire LF.IX; Night flying exercise of 141st Sqn, fuel shortage, three pilots tried to emergency land, but crashed; Pilots Sezai Aydin, Servet Ilksümer and Salim Pamukçu killed (Note: In this event a further 5 or 6 Spitfires of 141st Sqn crashed, but their pilots baled out and survived).

SURVIVORS

None survived, only a replica of a Spitfire being exhibited in the Military Museum at Ankara.

References:
Turkish Spitfires, Air International September 1985 (p.151/152), letters to the editor, by Ole Nikolajsen and ASC Lumsden.
Spitfire sales, Air International December 1985 (p.310), letter to the editor, by Ken J Rutterford.
Turkish Military Aircraft 1912-1999, by Ole Nikolajsen, Air-Britain Publication in preparation.

Two restored Spitfires in formation. "HL-K" in USAAF colours is actually LF.XVIe G-MXVI (ex TE184), whilst PT642 "SW-A" is a T.IX registered G-CTIX. The latter, which is ex Italy and Israel, was previously with the Harry Stenger Facility at Bartow, Florida (Jet-Cap Aviation Corpn, Lakeland, Florida), registered N462JC. [Cliff Knox]

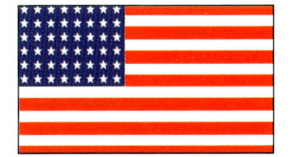

UNITED STATES OF AMERICA

Spitfire F.Vc/trop XR-K of the 334th Fighter Sqn, 4th Fighter Group has its serial number painted over but is possibly EN783 which was with that squadron at Debden in late 1941. [MAP]

A number of American pilots joined the RAF as individuals early in the Second World War, and this was formalised on 19th September 1940 when No.71 Sqn was formed at Church Fenton as the first of three 'Eagle' squadrons manned by American volunteers. It was followed by No.121 Sqn at Kirton-in-Lindsey on 14 May 1941 and No.133 Sqn at Coltishall on 1st August 1941. All were initially equipped with Hurricanes, but No.71 Sqn converted to Spitfire Mk.IIs at North Weald in August 1941, followed by No.121 Sqn at Kirton-in-Lindsey in October 1941 and No.133 Sqn at Eglinton the same month.

The United States officially entered the war against all the Axis powers following the Japanese Navy's surprise attack on the Pearl Harbor naval base on 7th December 1941, and American forces began to arrive in Britain, the US 8th Air Force being established on 18th June 1942. In the autumn of 1942 the three 'Eagle' squadrons were absorbed into the US 8th Air Force; Nos.71, 121 and 133 Sqns then forming the 4th Fighter Group, based at Debden.

Meanwhile other British-based American units were receiving Spitfires. In June 1942 the 31st Fighter Group arrived at Atcham and one month later the 52nd Fighter Group at Eglinton. In November 1942, Operation *'Torch'* saw British and American forces landing in Northwest Africa (NWA), including the US 12th Air Force with the 31st and 52nd Fighter Groups using Spitfires.

Spitfires were transferred to the USAAF under Lend-Lease exchange arrangements between the USA and Great Britain, a total of more than a thousand Spitfires & Seafires being eventually used by the Americans.

In addition to Lend-Lease arrangements in the UK and Mediterranean area, a small number of Spitfires and Seafires were used for test flying and comparison purposes at home bases in the USA.

Post-war, the USA has more surviving restored Spitfires in flying condition than any other country.

EAGLE SQUADRONS - the American Spitfire units of the RAF

No. 71   Sqn, formed at Church Fenton 19th September 1940. Sqn code 'XR'; Spitfire Mks.IIa & Vb from 20th August 1941 to 29th September 1942.

No.121   Sqn, formed at Kirton-in-Lindsey 5th May 1941. Sqn code 'AV'; Spitfire Mks.IIa & Vb from 17th October 1941 to 29th September 1942.

No.133   Sqn, formed at Coltishall 31st July 1941. Sqn code 'MD'; Spitfire Mks.IIa, Va/b & IX from October 1941 to 29th September 1942.

The 'Eagle' *Squadrons* were officially transferred to the 4th Fighter Group of the USAAF on 29th September 1942 and given squadron numbers 334, 335 and 336.

Spitfire units of the USAAF

The USAAF operated over the European Theatre of Operations (ETO) with the 8th (Strategic) Air Force from mid-1942, this being joined later by the 9th Air Force which operated as a tactical element from early 1944.

In the Mediterranean Theatre of Operations (MTO), the US 12th AF operated within the Mediterranean Air Command (MAC) from the end of 1942 onwards, and additionally the US 15th AF built up strategic power from Italian bases after the 9th AF went to ETO at the end of 1943.

The Far East (FE) was mostly the operating area of the US Navy, together with the 5th, 10th, 13th, 14th and 20th (US) Air Forces, based at Okinawa, China (SEAC), Philippines and Marianas. After VE-Day the 8th AF was partly incorporated, based at Okinawa.

Spitfire units of the 8th & 9th US Air Forces in Europe ("*SOXO*" & "*GLUE*")

The 4th Fighter Group

Formed on 22nd August 1942 and activated at Bushey Hall, England on 12th September 1942. Moved to Debden and officially took over the former RAF 'Eagle' Squadrons on 29th September 1942, these retaining their RAF squadron codes. It was part of the 65th Fighter Wing in the 2nd Air Division within the US 8th Air Force.

Spitfire Mk.Vb (336th Sqn also Mk.IXc) from October 1942 to March 1943 (then P-47, converting to P-51 from April 1944).
Commanding Officers:
Col Edward W Anderson 9.42
Col Chesley G Peterson 8.43
Col Donald JM Blakeslee 1.44

334th Sqn (ex No.71 Sqn RAF), at Debden - code 'XR'; became an OTU in January 1943, with P-47 Thunderbolt.
Commanding Officer:
Mjr A "Gus" Daymond DFC 29.9.42

335th Sqn (ex No.121 Sqn RAF), at Debden - code 'AV'.
Commanding Officers:
[S/Ldr WA Williams DFC on 29.9.42]
Mjr R Daley by 10.42
Mjr R Evans by 11.42

336th Sqn (ex No.133 Sqn RAF), Great Sampford, code 'MD- '.
Commanding Officer:
[S/Ldr CW McColpin DFC on 29.9.42]
Mjr OH Coen by 1.43

The 31st Fighter Group (ETO)

Formed as a Pursuit Group in February 1940 with the Nos.39, 40 & 41 Pursuit Sqns (later re-named Fighter Sqns), commanded then by Col HH George.

At Atcham (19th Air Base, Atcham Field) from 15th June 1942 as part of the US 8th Air Force, equipped with Spitfire Mk.Vbs from June 1942 to October 1942. It comprised the 307th and 308th Fighter Squadrons at Atcham and the 309th Fighter Squadron at High Ercall. First operational flight 26th July 1942; Dieppe raid 19th August 1942 (Lt SF Junkin jr shot down a FW 190, reported to be the first kill by a US pilot over ETO). From 23rd August 1942 based at Westhampnett with all three squadrons.

On 9th October 1942 the 31st FG was withdrawn from action to prepare for a move to North Africa. Some of its Spitfires were distributed to other USAAF units in the UK, the remainder returned to the RAF. The unit went initially to Gibraltar, being re-assigned to the US 12th AF in order to participate in Operation '*Torch*', the Allied landings on 8th November 1942 (see MTO, below).
Commanding Officer:
Col John R Hawkins 7.41

307th Sqn, Atcham from 11th June 1942. To Biggin Hill 1st August 1942, Westhampnett 23rd August 1942, then to Merston 24th August 1942. Sqn code: 'MX'.
Commanding Officers:
Mjr Marvin L McNickle 1.42
Mjr George J La Breche 9.42

308th Sqn, Atcham from 11th June 1942, to Kenley 1st August 1942, then to Westhampnett 24th August 1942 until 21st October 1942. Sqn code: 'HL'.
Commanding Officers:
Mjr Fred M Dean 1.42
Mjr Delwin B Avery 9.42

309th Sqn, High Ercall from 11.6.42. To Westhampnett 4.8.42 until 21.10.42. Sqn code: 'WZ- '.
Commanding Officer:
Mjr Harrison R Thyng 1.42

The 52nd Fighter Group (ETO)

Constituted as 52nd Pursuit Group on 20th November 1940. Activated 15th January 1941, re-designed 52th Fighter Group in May 1942. Training with P-39 and P-40. Moved to the UK, arrived Liverpool on 12th July 1942.

At Eglinton, Northern Ireland from 13th July 1942. Later dett Maydown satellite and to Biggin Hill and Kenley; only the 5th FS remaining at Eglinton, except for a flight which went to Ballyhalbert on 24th August 1942. 52nd FG to Goxhill on 13th September 1942 with all three squadrons reunited.

Spitfire Mk.Vb/c until the beginning of October 1942. Then re-assigned to the US 12th AF for Operation '*Torch*' in NWA 8th November 1942 (see MTO, below).
Commanding Officer:
Col Dixon M Allison from 27.2.42.

2nd Sqn at Eglinton 13th July 1942, dett Maydown satellite 7th August 1942; To Biggin Hill 26th August 1942, to Goxhill 13th September 1942; Sqn code: 'QP'.
Commanding Officers:
1/Lt Robert C Richardson 1.42
1/Lt Ralph E Keyes 1942
Capt Graham W West 10.42

4th Sqn, at Eglinton 13th July 1942; To Kenley 27th August 1942, to Goxhill 13th September 1942; Sqn code: 'WD'.
Commanding Officers:
Mjr Robert Levine 5.42

5th Sqn, at Eglinton 13th July 1942; Goxhill 13th September 1942; Code: 'VF- '.
Commanding Officers:
1/Lt James F Whisenand 1942
Capt Thomas A Holdiman 1942
Mjr George C Deaten 5.42

The 82nd Fighter Group (ETO)

In the UK from October 1942, comprising the 95th, 96th and 97th Fighter Squadrons, flying training with P-38s and few Spitfire Mk.Vbs at Eglinton from 5th October 1942. The 97th FS moved to Maydown 6th October 1942. 82nd FG via St.Eval to the US 12th AF in North Africa in December 1942 (MAC/NASAF, 47th Wing with P-38 in July 1943).
Commanding Officer:
Lt Col William E Covington

The 7th Photographic Reconnaissance & Mapping Group

Activated and based at Mount Farm, Oxfordshire, from 7th July 1943; moving 22nd March 1945 to Chalgrove; at Hitcham from 25th October 1945 until disbanded 21st November 1945. Re-designated the 7th Photographic Group (Reconnaissance) November 1943, and 7th Reconnaissance Group June 1945.

UNITED STATES OF AMERICA

The 7th (PR) Grp formed part of the 325th Photographic Wing, which came under the US 8th Air Force. It comprised the 13th, 14th, 22nd and 27th Photographic Reconnaissance Squadrons, all equipped with F-5 (PR Lightning). Technical and Maintenance support was given by the 381st Air Service Sqn (No.381 ASS) at Mount Farm.

On 3rd June 1943 the 7th (PR) Group received five Spitfire Mk.Vs (clipped wings, weapons removed), first for maintenance training, but from mid-June 1943 these also for flying training. Spitfire PR.XIs arrived in November 1943 and were used for long range or high ceiling reconnaissance missions. At first Nos.13, 14 and 22 Sqns also flew Spitfire PR.XIs, but after an order from 7th January 1944 the Spitfires served only with the Third Flight of No.14 Sqn (*Spitfire Flight*), until end of March 1945.

PR escort was supported by nearby US Fighter Squadrons. Later the 7th (PR) Group received own P-51 Mustang, and conversion was given by the 181st Mobile Training Unit (No.181 MTU) in January 1945. The first P-51 fighters of the 7th (PR) Group were assigned to the 22nd Sqn; they flew her first escort on 13th January 1945.

Markings: Aircraft of the 7th (PR) Group had dark blue spinners. No unit code was used (only large size tail serial numbers). Sqn-colours on the rudder, see below.

Commanding Officers:
Col James G Hall	7.43
Col Homer L Sanders	9.43
Col Paul T Cullen	1.44
Lt Col George A Lawson	2.44
Lt Col Norris E Hartwell	5.44
Lt Col Clarence A Shoop	8.44
Col George W Humbrecht	10.44
Mjr Hubert M Childress	6.45

13th (PR) Sqn, activated in USA 20th June 1942; To Mount Farm in March 1943 (order 16th February 1943), operational 27th March 1943, first sortie 28th March 1943; Served with F-5; Few Spitfire PR.XI in December 1943 and January 1944. Unit colours: Red rudder.
Commanding Officers:
Lt Shipway	6.42
Mjr Eidson	6.42
1/Lt LH Richardson	8.42
Mjr J Hall	9.42
Capt H Parsons	7.43
Capt R Mitchell	11.43
Mjr RR Smith	5.44

14th (PR) Sqn, activated in USA 20th June 1942; To Mount Farm 12th May 1943, operational from 7th August 1943 Served with F-5, but the third Flight with Spitfire PR.XI from November 1943; The only unit with Spitfires of the 7th (PR) Grp from January 1944 until early April 1945. Unit colours: Green rudder.
Commanding Officers:
2/Lt RW Willis	3.43
Capt M Wayne	3.43
Mjr WL Weitner	1.44
Mjr CT Haugen	5.44
Mjr KE Bliss	6.44
Capt RJ Dixon	7.44
Capt GM Adams	2.45

22nd (PR) Sqn, activated in USA 2nd September 1942; To Mount Farm 8th June 1943; First sortie (over French coast) 26th June 1943; Served with F-5, and some Spitfire PR.XI from November 1943 to early January 1944; Received later also P-51 Mustang for PR-escort early 1945, first escort mission flown on 13th January 1945. Unit colours: White rudder.
Commanding Officers:
1/Lt Tracy	9.42
Capt GA Lawson	12.42
Mjr RR Smith	2.44
Mjr WL Weitner	5.44

27th (PR) Sqn, activated in USA 9th February 1943; To Mount Farm 4th November 1943; A70 airfield (Laon/Couvron, France) in October 1944; A83 airfield (Denain/Prouvy) January 1945; First sortie 20th December 1943; Assigned to 7th (PR) Grp 21st December 1943; Served with F-5 (PR-Lightning).
Commanding Officers:
2/Lts Kappes & Willis from	2.43
2/Lt Cameron, Lt Baird	3.43
Lt Hardee	3.43
1/Lt CT Haugen, Mjr Smith	5.43
Mjr Mitchell	5.43
Capt HM Childress	8.44

The **67th Observation Group**

Constituted as 67th Observation Group 21st August 1941, activated 1st September 1941, moved to the UK in August 1942 with 12th, 107th, 109th and 153rd (Observation) Squadrons; also with 113th Sqn, which had no Spitfires. Assigned to US 8th AF, based at Membury from September 1942, moved to Middle Wallop in December 1943 and to Le Molay, France in July 1944.

Spitfire Mk.Vb (12th Sqn also Mk.II, from January 1943 together with A-20) from September 1942 to 1945; from April 1944 also F-6 (PR-*Mustang*), and P-51 for escort.

The 67th (TR) Group changed to the US 9th AF (within AEAF, alongside 2nd TAF) in November 1943; Spitfires were handed over from the 8th AF to the inventory of the 9th AF mostly with effect from 1st February 1944.

NOTE: Became 67th Reconnaissance Group from May 1943, then 67th Tactical Reconnaissance Group from November 1943, reverting to 67th Reconnaissance Group from June 1945.
Commanding Officers:
Col Frederick R Anderson	5.42
Col George W Peck	12.43
Lt Col Richard S Leghorn	5.45

12th (Obs) Sqn, based at Membury September 1942; Greenham Common December 1943; Aldermaston January 1944; Chilbolton March 1944; Middle Wallop March 1944; To Le Molay July 1944; Rennes August 1944; Châteaudun August 1944; Sqn code: 'ZM'.
Commanding Officers:
Capt James R Haun from	7.42
Mjr Russell E Berg	10.43
Capt Dickman R French	12.43
Capt Gordon H Woodrow	2.44

107th (Recce) Sqn, based at Membury September 1942; Middle Wallop December 1943 (first sortie 20th December 1943); TR-Sqn from 28th December 1943; To Le Molay July 1944; Sqn code: 'AX- '.
Commanding Officer:
Unknown

109th (Recce) Sqn at Membury September 1942; Atcham November 1942 to May 1943, then to Membury; TR-Sqn from 13th November 1943; To Middle Wallop December 1943; To Le Molay, France July 1944; Sqn code: 'VX'.
Commanding Officer:
Unknown

153rd (Obs) Sqn, based at Keevil August 1942; Membury September 1942; Liaison Sqn from 5th July 1943; Middle Wallop December 1943; Erlestoke,Wilts 13th March 1944; To Le Molay, France July 1944; Sqn code: 'ZS'.
Commanding Officer:
Unknown

Spitfire F.Vb W3364 of the 153 Sqn, 67th (Observer) Group, bearing the personal code 'EPA' of Captain Emmette P Allen, probably at Keevil in 1943.

Other USAAF units with Spitfires on strength (ETO)

6th   **Fighter Wing**, Combat Training Replacement Centre (CTRC), re-activated 7th June 1942; Arrived Swansea 18th August 1942; Bushey c.24 August 1942; Atcham from 9th September 1942 until disbanded 13th September 1943.
Commanding Officers:
Lt Col Paul M Jacobs from   13.7.42
Lt Col John W Ranson   18.9.42
Lt Col Jack W Hickman   13.3.43
Col Ross G Hoyt   18.3.43

66th   **Fighter Wing** from July 1943 (55th, 78th, 353rd, 358th, 359th & 361st FG) at Duxford, Swanston from 20th August 1943, some Spitfire Vb in September 1943.
Commanding Officer:
Brig Gen Murray C Woodbury

14th   **Fighter Group** (with 48th, 49th & 50th FS), training at Atcham from 18th August 1942 with P-38 and few Spitfires; assigned to US 12th AF (MAC/NASAF, 5th Wing, with P-38 in July 1943).
Commanding Officers:
Col Thayer S Olds

31st   **Air Transport Group** (31st ATG) of the 302nd ATW, US 9th AF, Service Command at Grove 1944 (C-47).
Commanding Officers:
Unknown

81st   **Fighter Group** (with 91st, 92nd and 93rd FS), training at Atcham with P-39 and few Spitfires from November 1942; Later to US 12th AF early 1943 (MAC/NACAF, 242nd Grp, Oran Sector with P-39 in July 1943).
Commanding Officers:
Lt Col Kenneth S Wade   7.42
Col Philip B Klein   5.43

350th   **Fighter Group**, activated at Bushey Hall 2nd October 1942, training at Duxford with P-39D and few Spitfire Vb from October 1942, before deployment to US 12th AF in January 1943 (MAC/NACAF with P-39 in July 1943).
Commanding Officer:
Lt Col Richard P Klocko

495th   **Fighter Training Group** (Observation Training) at Atcham, formed 26th October 1943, used few Spitfire Mk.V from October 1943 to January 1945.

6th   **Fighter Training Squadron** (6th TFS), ex ADV Flt, at Defford 1943.

555th   **Fighter Training Squadron** of the 496th Fighter Training Group, operated as an OTU at Goxhill in US 9th AF from 25th December 1943 and Halesworth from February 1944; Flew P-51 Mustang by February 1944; Only few Spitfire Mk.V in 1944. Sqn code: ' C7 '.

The **(F & B) Comm Flt/Sqn.** at Bovingdon also used Spitfires.

Spitfire units of the 12th US Air Force in Northwest Africa ("*DUKO*")

In November 1942 the 12th US Air Force operated with Spitfires over Northwest Africa. The RAF flew with this command and also with the Eastern Air Command over the Middle East. Mediterranean Air Command (MAC) formed at Algiers on 17th February 1943, comprising both USAAF and RAF elements, the latter including SAAF units.

This command comprised (**a**) Northwest African Air Forces (NAAF), Northwest African Tactical Air Forces (NATAF), Northwest African Strategical Air Forces (NASAF), Northwest African Coastal Air Forces (NACAF), Northwest African Training Command (NATC), Northwest African Air Service Command (NAASC) and Northwest African Photo Reconnaissance Wing, also (**b**) Malta Air Command and (**c**) Middle East Air Command. On 10th December 1943 it became Rear HQ Mediterranean Allied Air Forces.

By February 1944, administrative units were based in both northern Africa and Italy, most having been either replaced or renamed. They now included Mediterranean Air Command (MAC), Mediterranean Allied Tactical Air Forces (MATAF), Mediterranean Allied Strategical Air Forces (MASAF) and Mediterranean Allied Coastal Air Forces (MACAF).

The **31st Fighter Group (64th FW /XII.ASC) - MTO**

31st FG fought over ETO from July 1942 to end 9.42, then this Group moved to NWA, arrived Tafaraoui, Algeria (south of Oran)

UNITED STATES OF AMERICA

8th November 1942; to La Senia, Algeria (south of Oran) c.12th November 1942; Thelepte, Tunisia (south of Bone) c.7th February 1943; Tebessa, Algeria (SE of Bone) 17th February 1943; Youks-les-Bains, Algeria 21st February 1943; Kalaa Djerda, Tunisia c.25th February 1943; Thelepte, Tunisia 11th March 1943; Djilmas, Tunisia 7th April 1943; Le Sers, Tunisia 12th April 1943; Korba, Tunisia 15th May 1943; Gozo, Malta c.30th June 1943; Ponte Olivo, Sicily c.12th July 1943; Agrigento, Sicily 21st July 1943; Termini, Sicily 2nd August 1943; Milazzo, Sicily 2nd September 1943; Montecorvino, Italy 20th September 1943; Pomigliano, Italy 14th October 1943; Castel Volturno, Italy 19th January 1944; San Severo, Italy 2nd April 1944.

Spitfire Mks.V/trop & IX from November 1942 to April 1944 (Mk.IX most from March 1943), except 308th FS with Mk. V & VIII.

To the US 15th AF with P-51 Mustang on 1st April 1944. The last formation flight with Spitfires over Rome was on 29th March 1944.

Commanding Officers:
Col John R Hawkins   1.7.41
Col Fred M Dean   5.12.42
  (personal code 'F-MD'; 'FM-D')
Lt Col Frank A Hill   7.43
  (personal code 'FA-H')
Col Charles M McCorkle   9.43
  ('CM-M'; aircraft marked '*BETTY JANE*')

307th   Sqn, Unit code: 'MX- '.
Arr Tafaraoui, Algeria 9th November 1942; La Senia, Algeria 12th November 1942; Maison Blanche, Algeria 21st December 1942; Thelepte, Tunisia 7th February 1943; Tebessa, Algeria 17th February 1943; Du Kouif 21st February 1943; Youks-les-Bains, Algeria 22nd February 1943; Kalaa Djerda, Tunisia 25th February 1943; Thelepte, Tunisia 11th March 1943; Djilmas, Tunisia 7th April 1943; Le Sers, Tunisia 12th April 1943; Korba, Tunisia c.15th May 1943; Gozo, Malta c.30th June 1943; Ponte Olivo, Sicily c.14th July 1943; Agrigento, Sicily 21st July 1943; Palermo, Sicily 27th July 1943; Termini, Sicily 1st August 1943; Milazzo, Sicily 3rd September 1943; Montecorvino, Italy 21st September 1943; Pomigliano, Italy 13th October 1943; Castel Volturno, Italy 18th January 1944; San Severo, Italy 2nd April 1944.
To the US 15th AF with P-51 Mustang in April 1944.
Commanding Officers:
Unknown   11.42 onwards
Mjr V Fields (killed 6.2.44)
Mjr AC Gillem

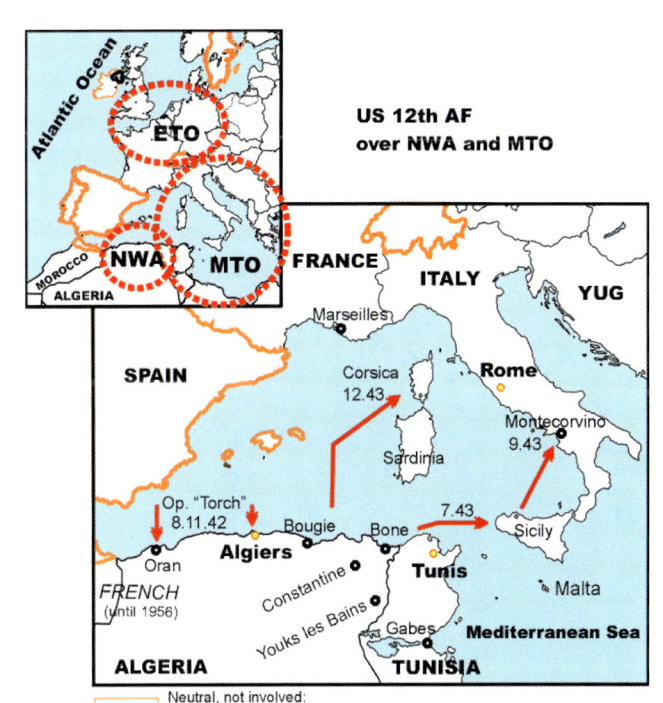

308th   Sqn, Unit code: 'HL- '.
Arr Tafaraoui, Algeria 8th November 1942; Maison Blanche 21th December 1942 (Morocco 10th-31st January 1943, protection of the Casablanca conference); Thelepte, Tunisia 6th February 1943; Tebessa, Algeria 17th February 1943; Canrobert (Du Kouif), Algeria 21st

Spitfire F.Vc/trop HL-U of the 308th Fighter Sqn, 31st Fighter Group, in a pen at Gozo in mid-1943.

Spitfire F.Vc/trop HL-J of the 308th Fighter Sqn, 31st Fighter Group, in mid-1943. [R C Jones]

Spitfire F.VIII, HL-MM, "Lonesome Polecat", flown by 2/Lt William Skinner of the 308 FS, 31 FG, Castel Volturno, Italy in 1944

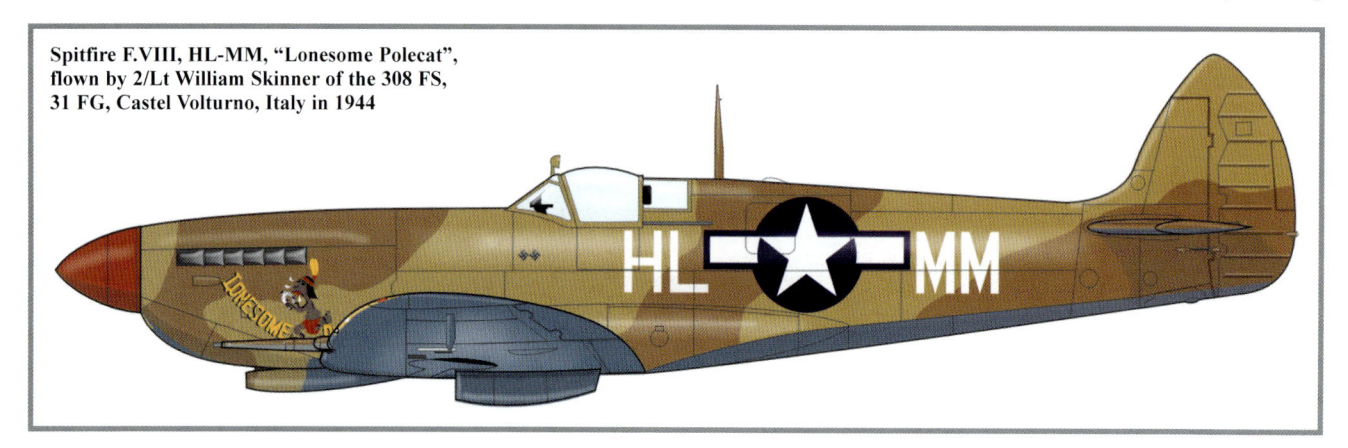

February 1943; Kalaa Djerda, Tunisia 25th February 1943; Thelepte, Tunisia 11th March 1943; Djilmas, Tunisia 7th April 1943; Le Sers, Tunisia 12th April 1943; Korba, Tunisia 20th May 1943; Gozo, Malta c.30th June 1943; Ponte Olivo, Sicily c.14th July 1943; Agrigento, Sicily 19th July 1943; Termini, Sicily c.2nd August 1943; Milazzo, Sicily 2nd September 1943; Montecorvino, Italy 20th September 1943; Pomigliano, Italy 14th October 1943; Castel Volturno, Italy 14th January 1944; San Severo, Italy 2nd April 1944.
Spitfire Mk.VIIIc in August 1943, marked with yellow band on the wingtips.
To the US 15th AF with P-51 Mustang in April 1944.
Commanding Officer:
Mjr Frank A Hill by 4.43

309th Sqn, Unit code: 'WZ'.
Arr Tafaraoui, Algeria 8th November 1942; La Senia, Algeria 14th November 1942; Thelepte, Tunisia 6th February 1943; Tebessa, Algeria 17th February 1943; Du Kouif 21st February 1943; Youks-les-Bains, Algeria 22nd February 1943; Kalaa Djerda, Tunisia 26th February 1943; Thelepte, Tunisia 11th March 1943; Djilmas, Tunisia 7th April 1943; Le Sers, Tunisia 12th April 1943; Korba, Tunisia 17th May 1943; Gozo, Malta 3rd July 1943; Ponte Olivo, Sicily 13th July 1943; Agrigento, Sicily 21st July 1943; Termini, Sicily 5th August 1943; Milazzo, Sicily 5th September 1943; Montecorvino, Italy 21st September 1943; Pomigliano, Italy 14th October 1943; Castel Volturno, Italy c.19th January 1944; San Severo, Italy 4th April 1944.
Spitfire Mk.IX, with red band on the wingtips.

Spitfires flown out to Pomigliano 30th March 1944; To the US 15th AF with P-51 Mustang in April 1944.
Commanding Officers:
Mjr HR Thyng by 3.43
Mjr JS Thorsen by 2.44

The 52nd Fighter Group (63rd FW/XII.FC) - MTO

Built up its strength and learned tactics over ETO from July 1942 to end September 1942, the 52nd FG moved to NWA and arrived Tafaraoui, Algeria (south of Oran) 9th November 1942; La Senia, Algeria (south of Oran) 14th November 1942; Orleansville, Algeria (100m SW of Algiers) c.12th January 1943; Telergma, Algeria c.17th January 1943; Youks-les-Bains, Algeria c.9th March 1943; Le Sers, Tunisia 14th April 1943; La Sebala, Tunisia 14th April 1943; Unknown; Retd La Sebala, Tunisia 21st May 1943; Boccadifalco, Sicily 20th July 1943; Corsica 1st December 1943.

Spitfire Mks.V/trop & IX from November 1942 to March 1944 (mainly Mk.IX from June 1943).

52nd FG was attached to No.335 Wing RAF 15th October 1943 until it left for Corsica 1st December 1943. To the US 15th AF in April 1944 and re-equipped with P-51 Mustang; first operational flight with P-51 on 10 May 1944, then moved to Italy.
Commanding Officers:
Col Dixon M Allison 27.2.42
Lt Col Graham W West 1.3.43
Lt Col James S Coward 24.7.43
Lt Col Richard A Ames 1.9.43
Col Marvin L McNickle 6.9.43
Lt Col Robert Levine 25.2.44

UNITED STATES OF AMERICA

2nd **Sqn**, Unit code: 'QP- '.
Arr Tafaraoui, Algeria 8th November 1942 (air echelon); La Senia, Algeria 12th November 1942 (The 2nd FS joined the 322nd Wing at Bone on 27th November 1942); Orleansville, Algeria 1st January 1943; from Bone to Biskra 4th January 1943; Telergma, Algeria 19th January 1943; Youks-les-Bains, Algeria 8th March 1943; Le Sers, Tunisia 12th April 1943; La Sebala, Tunisia 20th May 1943; Boccadifalco, Sicily 1st August 1943 (Palermo Sector 5th August 1943); Corsica c.3th December 1943.
Commanding Officers:
Capt Ralph E Keyes	11.42
Capt James S Coward	12.42
Capt Arnold E Vinson	3.43
Capt George V Williams	4.43
Capt Bert S Sandborn	8.43

4th **Sqn**, Unit code: 'WD- '.
Arr Tafaraoui, Algeria 8th November 1942 (air echelon); La Senia, Algeria 12th November 1942; Orleansville, Algeria 1st January 1943; Bone 5th January 1943; Thelepte 17th January 1943; Telergma, Algeria 19th January 1943; Youks-les-Bains, Algeria 8th March 1943; Le Sers, Tunisia 12th April 1943; La Sebala, Tunisia 20th May 1943; Boccadifalco, Sicily 1st August 1943 (Palermo Sector 5th August 1943); Corsica 4th December 1943.
Commanding Officers:
Mjr Robert Levine	5.42
Capt William Houston	6.43
Capt Lee M Trowbridge	2.44

5th **Sqn**, Unit code: 'VF'.
Arr Tafaraoui, Algeria 8th November 1942 (air echelon);

Spitfires of the 309th FS, 31st Fighter Group, US 12th Air Force, 'WZ-VV' nearest, lined up at Castel Volturno on 30th March 1944, the day they were flown back to Naples to be returned to the RAF. [Lt J E Fawcett via Henry Boot]

Tribesmen examining the wreckage of Spitfire Vb/trop QP-L of the 2nd Fighter Squadron, 52nd Fighter Group, possibly at La Sebala in mid-1943. The serial number appears to have an EP-prefix.

La Senia, Algeria 12th November 1942; Orleansville, Algeria 1st January 1943; Telergma, Algeria 19th January 1943; Youks-les-Bains, Algeria 8th March 1943; Le Sers, Tunisia 12th April 1943; La Sebala, Tunisia 20th May 1943; Boccadifalco, Sicily 1st August 1943 (Palermo Sector 5th August 1943); Corsica 1st December 1943.
Commanding Officers:
Mjr George C Deaten 5.42
Mjr William J Payne 5.43
Mjr Everett K Jenkins 11.43

The **Fighter Training Center (FTC) in Morocco**

The FTC was assigned to the XIIth Training & Replacement Command NWA, activated 18th February 1943, based at Berrachid, French Morocco; HQ temporary Villa Maas, later to Constantine, Algeria 28th July 1943; Primary P-38 and P-40 were used for training purposes, but also twelve Spitfire Mk.V/trop entered the service there in early 1943; Disbanded 20th July 1944.
Commanding Officers:
Brig Gen John K Cannon 2.43
Col John W Monahan 5.43

The U.S. Navy

Spitfires

VCS-7 was a part of the Air Spotting Pool of the 2nd TAF, together with Nos.808, 885, 886 & 897 Sqns of the 3rd Naval (Fighter) Wing and Nos.26 & 63 Sqns of the RAF. US Navy pilots trained with Spitfires of the 67th (TR) Group at Middle Wallop from February 1944. To RNAS Lee-on-Solent on 8th May 1944, used Spitfire Mk.Vb for air spotting during Operation *'Neptune'*, Cherbourg until 26th June 1944. These Spitfires were noted in records as *"L-09"* aircraft (Liaison aircraft), diverted from the US 8th AF to the Navy. Known markings: '4Q', '4R', '4X', '4Z'.
Commanding Officers:
Lt RW Calland 2.44
Lt Cdr W Denton Jnr 5.44

Seafires

FAW-7: In August 1944 a number of Seafire L.IIc were transferred to the US Navy Liberator Wing "FAW-7" (Fleet Air Wing No.7) at Dunkeswell in Devon. Six Seafires L.IIc were used for air combat training for the patrol squadron crews, to acquaint them with tactics to be expected from European-style fighter aircraft.
Commanding Officers:
Unknown

Seafires flown in the USA

One Seafire Mk.IIc went to the USA in April 1943. Registered as '**F.S.-1**' by the US Navy.

A Seafire F.XVc arrived at the US Naval Test Centre in June 1945.

Remarks

At the beginning of World War Two the Air Force was named "US Army Air Corps" (USAAC). Officially this was changed to "US Army Air Force" (USAAF) on 20th June 1940, but in RAF records the term "USAAC" remained in use until 1943. It was not until 18th September 1947 that the "Army" prefix was dropped and it became an independent air arm, named "United States Air Force" (USAF), operating alongside the US Army and the US Navy.

The USAAF at first constituted the fighter units as "Pursuit Groups" (PG) and "Pursuit Squadrons" (PS). In May 1942 these were redesignated as "Fighter Groups" and "Fighter Squadrons" (FG & FS). Similarly the Observer Sqns were abbreviated to "OS".

USAAF aircraft records used the term *"SOXO"* to denote the US 8th Air Force, *"GLUE"* for the US 9th Air Force, and *"DUKO"* for the US 12th Air Force in Northwest Africa. For example, the term *"SOXO, del/inv"* meant deleted from the inventory of the US 8th AF, though this did not necessarily mean the aircraft was struck off charge, as it could simply mean that it was transferred to some other command. The 9th Air Force equivalent was *"GLUE* (condemned) HQ".

Middle Wallop housed the headquarters of the US 9th Air Force from 30th November 1943, and a number of aircraft are referred to as being allocated to *"SOXO, 8916"* from December 1943, often also from 1st February 1944. This term is connected with the change-over of the 67th (TR) Group to the US 9th AF. However, the reason for this is not readily apparent, since that the base was officially known by the USAAF as Station No.449. Also it may be just coincidence that the headquarters of the 19th Air Support Command was based at Middle Wallop from 4th January 1944 until moving to Aldermaston Court on 1 February 1944.

Individual Histories

K9871   Spitfire F.Va [ex Mk.Ia] (Merlin 45); TOC/RAF 21.2.39 - US 8th AF; 52nd FG Eglinton, 5th FS in 8.42; Retd RAF; SOC 15.10.45

L1090   Spitfire F.Ia (Merlin III); TOC/RAF 29.8.39; To USA, arr USAAC Dayton in 9.39; To Canada, RCAF 19.2.40; Retd to UK later. Became GI No. *3201M* in 5.44

N3098   Spitfire F.Va/trop [ex F.Ia] (Merlin 45); TOC/RAF 19.10.39; US 8th AF – 82nd FG Eglinton 8.11.42; 96th FS Eglinton, taxying accident, Cat.A 21.11.42 (2/Lt Zubarik OK); Flying accident Cat.A 9.2.43, Re-Cat.B (RiW); USAAF Atcham, accident at base 4.5.43 (Lt SO Buck); Retd RAF, to No.61 OTU 23.10.43

P7287   Spitfire F.Va (Merlin 45); TOC/RAF 13.7.40 - US 8th AF; 52nd FG Eglinton, 2nd FS 6.8.42; Later 5th FS (also reported with 'HW-A' markings, a personal code); Fate unknown

P7297   Spitfire F.Va (Merlin 45); TOC/RAF 27.7.40; ex No.71 Sqn RAF - US 8th AF; 52nd FG Eglinton, 2nd FS in 8.42; Later 5th FS; Retd RAF; SOC 21.11.44

P7447   Spitfire F.Va (Merlin 45); TOC/RAF 29.9.40 - US 8th AF; 52nd FG Eglinton, 2nd FS 1.8.42; 5th FS 22.8.42; Retd RAF 8.11.42

P7629   Spitfire F.Va (Merlin 45); TOC/RAF 13.11.40 - US 8th AF; 52nd FG Eglinton 12.7.42; 4th FS, heavy landing, Cat.Ac 26.7.42 (2/Lt DH Williams OK); ROS 31.7.42; Re-Cat.B, Retd RAF (RiW, Short & Harland) 7.8.42

P7672   Spitfire F.Va (Merlin 45); TOC/RAF 20.11.40 - US 8th AF; 52nd FG Eglinton, 2nd FS 1.8.42; 5th FS from 22.8.42 to 7.9.42; To 67th (Obs) Grp; 12th Sqn, taxied into hole after landing Membury, Cat.A 8.4.43 (2/Lt RG Ogilvie); Overshot landing Aberporth 27.6.43 (Lt AM Rusten); Retd RAF; Later No.61 OTU

P7686   Spitfire F.Va (Merlin 45); TOC/RAF 24.11.40 - US 8th AF; 52nd FG Eglinton, 2nd FS 7.8.42; 5th FS 22.8.42; Retd RAF 8.11.42

P7692   Spitfire F.Va (Merlin 45); TOC/RAF 27.11.40 - US 8th AF; 82nd FG Eglinton 12.11.42; Retd RAF 6.12.42 (crashed 26.7.43, SOC)

P7789   Spitfire F.Va (Merlin 45); TOC/RAF 16.12.40 - US 8th AF; 52nd FG Eglinton 12.7.42; Undershot landing, Cat.B 23.7.42 (2/Lt RB Gabriel OK); Retd RAF (RiW); SOC 27.9.45

P7849   Spitfire F.Va (Merlin 45); Presentation aircraft *'ARMAGH'*; TOC/RAF 9.1.41; US 8th AF from 18.11.42 - 67th (Obs) Grp, 109th Sqn Atcham, collided with BL660 over Shropshire 29.3.43 (Lt DR Scott), SOC

P7906   Spitfire F.Va [ex Mk.IIa] (Merlin 45); TOC/RAF 4.2.41 - US 8th AF; 6th FW Atcham 24.11.42; Accident at Atcham 5.12.42 (Lt DW Koon); Retd RAF (RiW) 13.3.43

P7965   Spitfire F.Va (Merlin 45); TOC/RAF 5.2.41 - US 8th AF; 52nd FG Eglinton, 2nd FS 6.8.42; 5th FS 22.8.42; Retd RAF 8.11.42; Retd USAAF; 67th (Obs) Grp, 109th Sqn, accident at Atcham 12.3.43 (Lt WO Brite); US 8th AF, condemned 21.12.43, SOC

P8038   Spitfire F.Vb (Merlin 45); TOC/RAF 23.2.41 - US 8th AF; 52nd FG Eglinton, 2nd FS 26.8.42; USAAF Bovingdon, tipped on nose landing Pershore, Cat.A 28.11.42; Retd RAF 2.4.43

UNITED STATES OF AMERICA

P8086 Spitfire F.Va (Merlin 45); Presentation aircraft *'GARFIELD WESTON VIII'*; TOC/RAF 1.3.41 - US 8th AF; 52nd FG Eglinton, 2nd FS 21.8.42; 5th FS 22.8.42; Retd RAF 13.9.42

P8095 Spitfire F.Va (Merlin 45); Presentation aircraft *'HALIFAX III'*; TOC/RAF 11.3.41 - US 8th AF; 52nd FG Eglinton 12.7.42; 5th FS 22.8.42; Retd RAF 8.11.42; Retd USAAF; 67th (Obs) Grp, 109th Sqn Atcham, accident at base 23.1.43 (Lt PW McKennon); Fate unknown

P8099 Spitfire F.Va (Merlin 45); Presentation aircraft *"THE BLUE PENCIL"*; TOC/RAF 31.3.41; - US 8th AF; 52nd FG Eglinton, 2nd FS 4.8.42; 5th FS 22.8.42; 82nd FG 18.11.42; Accident at Atcham 11.12.42 (Lt LE Tourville); Retd RAF 11.3.43

P8436 Spitfire F.Va (Merlin 45); Presentation aircraft *'MORVI II'*; TOC/RAF 8.5.41; US 8th AF – 67th (Recce) Grp Membury 30.8.43; 12th Sqn 2.9.43; BC Bovingdon; To US 9th AF 2.4.44; Retd RAF 1.7.44; SOC 12.10.45

P8585 Spitfire F.Vb (Merlin 45); Presentation aircraft *'TELING TINGGI'*; TOC/RAF 10.6.41 - US 8th AF; 52nd FG Eglinton, 5th FS 7.8.42; While ferrying, undershot in gusty weather, heavy landing, knocked off port undercarriage, belly-landed, Cat.Ac 20.8.42 (2/Lt EG Steinbrenner OK); ROS 28.8.42; Re-Cat.B 4.9.42; Retd RAF (RiW) 4.9.42

P8708 Spitfire F.Vb (Merlin 45); TOC/RAF 5.7.41 - US 8th AF; 31st FG Atcham 21.6.42; Retd RAF (No.111 Sqn) 24.6.42; Later to Royal Navy (as hooked Spitfire)

P8741 Spitfire F.Vb (Merlin 45); Presentation aircraft *'BHAVNAGAR'*; TOC/RAF 15.6.41 - US 8th AF; 52nd FG, 5th FS Eglinton 5.9.42; While ferrying, stopped with overheated engine, taxied into by AB897, Cat.B 10.9.42 (2/Lt GE Montour OK); Retd RAF (RiW) 13.9.42

P8791 Spitfire F.Vb (Merlin 45); TOC/RAF 24.7.41; ex No.133 Sqn - US 8th AF; 4th FG, 336th FS Great Sampford 1.10.42; RiW, AST 12.11.42; AW/CN 23.12.42; 67th (TR) Grp Membury 6.12.43; Condemned 12th Sqn 15.4.44; Retd RAF (RiW) 17.4.44; Later to Portugal as LF.Vb (Merlin 45M) in 11.47

P8798 Spitfire F.Vb (Merlin 45); TOC/RAF 6.7.41 - US 8th AF; 52nd FG Eglinton 11.7.42; 2nd FS 22.8.42; Accident, Bovingdon 26.9.42 (Lt MJ Gordon); Retd RAF 21.10.42

P9306 Spitfire F.Ia (Merlin III); TOC/RAF 22.1.40; To USA, arr New York 19.9.44; Museum of Science & Industry, Chicago, Illinois, from 10.11.44, for exhibition and extant - **SURVIVOR** NOTE: See also AA963

P9326 Spitfire F.Ia (Merlin III); TOC/RAF 13.2.40 - US 8th AF; 31st FG Atcham 14.6.42; Retd RAF (No.53 OTU) 9.8.42

P9329 Spitfire F.Ia (Merlin III); TOC/RAF 14.2.40 - US 8th AF; 31st FG Atcham 13.6.42; Retd RAF (No.61 OTU) 11.8.42

R6602 Spitfire F.Va (Merlin 45); TOC/RAF 13.5.40 - US 8th AF; 52nd FG Eglinton, 2nd FS 4.8.42; Undershot landing, Cat.Ac 9.8.42 (1/Lt H Peabody OK); ROS; Retd RAF 15.8.42

R6623 Spitfire F.Va (Merlin 45); TOC/RAF 26.5.40 - US 8th AF; 52nd FG Eglinton, 4th FS 15.7.42; Landing collision with EN848, Cat.B 28.7.42 (2/Lt FD Camp OK); Retd RAF (RiW) 3.8.42

R6835 Spitfire F.Vb (Merlin 45); TOC/RAF 1.7.40 - US 8th AF; 31st FG Atcham 13.6.42; Accident 17.6.42 (Lt LP Wells Jnr); 307th FS 25.6.42; 308th FS; Retd RAF 14.8.42

R6888 Spitfire F.Vb [ex F.Ia (Ib)] (Merlin 45); TOC/RAF 5.7.40 - US 8th AF; 31st FG, 309th FS High Ercall 21.6.42; Retd RAF (No.302 Sqn) 12.9.42

R6895 Spitfire F.Ia (Merlin III); TOC/RAF 5.7.40 - US 8th AF; 31st FG Atcham 13.6.42 (for training only); Accident 19.6.42 (Lt KR Dziesinski); 307th FS & 308th FS; Retd RAF in 7.42; SOC 6.3.45

R6963 Spitfire F.Ia (Merlin III); TOC/RAF 16.7.40 - US 8th AF; 31st FG Atcham (for training only), 307th FS 25.6.42; 308th FS; Retd RAF 12.8.42

R6993 Spitfire F.Ia (Merlin III); TOC/RAF 22.7.40 - US 8th AF; 31st FG (for training only), 309th FS High Ercall 15.6.42; Retd RAF in 8.42; Later No.61 OTU and FAA

R7147 Spitfire PR.III/C (Merlin III); TOC/RAF 23.2.41; RAF Benson 3.7.42 - US 8th AF, Bomber Command Bovingdon 14.8.42; Accident at *"Station No.634"* 10.11.42 (Lt L Beirne); Accident Cat.FA/Ac 5.1.43; ROS 5.1.43; BC Bovingdon 26.1.43; Accident 11.2.44 (Lt O Norris); Accident, Cat.B in 7.44; RiW, de Havilland 26.7.44; Re-Cat.E 16.8.44, SOC

R7196 Spitfire F.Va (Merlin 45); Presentation aircraft *'HOLMEWOOD II'*; TOC/RAF 5.3.41 - US 8th AF; 52nd FG Eglinton, 2nd FS 5.8.42, Sqn moved to Maydown, ran off peritrack landing, Cat.Ac 7.8.42 (2/Lt WA Beard OK); Retd RAF 30.12.42

R7220 Spitfire F.Va (Merlin 45); Presentation aircraft *'BOURNEMOUTH II'*; TOC/RAF 21.3.41 - US 8th AF; 82nd FG Eglinton 8.11.42; Retd RAF (RiW, de Havilland.) 14.2.43; Later as GI No. *5586M* to France in 3.46

R7256 Spitfire F.Va (Merlin 45); Presentation aircraft *'ZIRA'*; TOC/RAF 8.4.41 - US 8th AF; 52nd FG Eglinton, 2nd FS 3.8.42; 5th FS 22.8.42; HQ 8th FC USAAC, taxying in strong wind, swung into soft ground, went on nose Bradwell Bay, Cat.Ac 29.12.42 (Lt A Lukas OK); ROS 4.1.43; To USAAF Eglinton 10.2.43; Retd RAF 24.9.43

R7261 Spitfire F.Vb (Merlin 45); Presentation aircraft *'BOLSOVER I'*; TOC/RAF 30.3.41 - US 8th AF; 52nd FG Eglinton, 2nd FS 12.7.42; 5th FS 22.8.42; Struck HT cables, Cat.B 2.9.42 (Lt FE Campbell OK); Retd RAF (RiW) 14.9.42

R7292 Spitfire F.Vb (Merlin 45); Presentation aircraft *'NEWBURY I'*; TOC/RAF 4.4.41; ex No.71 Sqn - US 8th AF; 31st FG Atcham, 308th FS 20.8.42; Crashed Cat.FB/Ac 14.10.42; ROS; Re-Cat.B; Retd RAF (RiW) 19.10.42

R7297 Spitfire F.Va (Merlin 45); Presentation aircraft *'IDEAL'*; TOC/RAF 11.4.41 - US 8th AF; 52nd FG Eglinton, 5th FS 9.7.42; 12th FC Bovingdon from 16.9.42; Retd RAF 2.6.44

R7298 Spitfire F.Vb (Merlin 45); Presentation aircraft *'ROTHERHAM & DISTRICT'*; TOC/RAF 5.4.41 - US 8th AF; 31st FG Westhampnett, 309th FS 22.8.42; 67th (Obs) Grp Membury, 153rd Sqn, tyre burst landing, swung off runway, overturned, Cat.A 11.11.42 (2/Lt FJ Dillon OK); Retd RAF (later No.61 OTU); SOC 9.11.44

R7343 Spitfire F.Va (Merlin 45); Presentation aircraft *'HEXHAM & DISTRICT'*; TOC/RAF 18.5.42 - US 8th AF; 52nd FG Eglinton 11.7.42; Landed wheels-up 7.8.42 (2/Lt EP Gardner OK); ROS; Re-Cat.B; Retd RAF (RiW) 14.8.42

R7344 Spitfire F.Vb (Merlin 45); Presentation aircraft *'BOROUGH OF HALESOWEN'*; TOC/RAF 12.4.41 - US 8th AF; 31st FG Atcham, 308th FS 14.7.42; Took off 10.02, missing near Dieppe, Cat.FB/E 19.8.42 (1/Lt WAM Dabney killed), SOC

R7347 Spitfire F.Va (Merlin 45); TOC/RAF 1.4.41; To USA, arr Dayton, Ohio in 5.41; To NACA test centre Langley Field, Virginia; NACA report 15.1.43 (stalling characteristics of Mk.Va, also measurements of flying qualities; Conclusions - satisfactory); Fate unknown

W3110 Spitfire F.Va (Merlin 45); Presentation aircraft *'HOLYROOD'*; TOC/RAF 10.5.41; - US 8th AF; 52nd FG Eglinton, 2nd FS 3.8.42; 5th FS 22.8.42; 67th (Obs) Grp, 109th Sqn, accident at Atcham 2.4.43 (Lt AV Degenaro); Accident at Atcham 3.5.43 (Lt WM Kelley); 6th FW, taxying accident Atcham, Cat.A 1.8.43 (S/Sgt TH/JH Schmoker); 496th FTG Goxhill; Retd RAF 10.8.43; Condemned 496th FTG 10.10.44

W3114 Spitfire F.Va (Merlin 45); TOC/RAF 16.5.41 - US 8th AF; 82nd Grp Eglinton 8.11.42; Retd RAF 6.12.42

W3119 Spitfire F.Va (Merlin 45); TOC/RAF 25.4.41; To USA, arr Dayton, Ohio in 5.41; To NACA test centre Langley Fields in 12.41 (tests with special engine and manifold fitments); Fate unknown

W3129 Spitfire F.Vb (Merlin 45); Presentation aircraft *'ABEOKUTO PROVINCE'*; TOC/RAF 26.4.41 - US 8th AF; 52nd FG Eglinton, 5th FS 8.9.42; Station Flight Eglinton from 13.9.42 to 23.10.42; Retd RAF; SOC 8.8.43

W3133 Spitfire F.Vb (Merlin 45); TOC/RAF 28.4.41 - US 8th AF; 52nd FG Eglinton 12.7.42, 2nd FS ('QP-N') 22.8.42; Accident at Goxhill 21.9.42 (Lt JA Carey); Retd RAF (No.332 Sqn) 8.11.42; Retd USAAF; 67th (Obs) Grp Atcham, crashed 3m from Frampton, Cat.E 18.2.43 (Lt EW Wallace); SOC 19.2.43

W3138 Spitfire F.Va (Merlin 45); Presentation aircraft *'CAWNPORE I'*; TOC/RAF 4.5.41 - US 8th AF; 82nd FG Eglinton 11.11.42; ROS (RAF) 17.11.42; Retd to US 8th AF 13.7.43; HQ 8th Air Force 29.8.43; Landing accident Maghaberry, Cat.Ac 18.10.43 (1/Lt AAG Talbot); ROS; Re-Cat.B; Retd RAF (RiW) 22.10.43

W3209 Spitfire F.Vb (Merlin 45); Presentation aircraft *'EDMONTON - (LONDON - ALBERTA)'*; TOC/RAF 13.5.41; ex No.133 Sqn - US 8th AF; 4th FG, 336th FS Great Sampford 1.10.42; Retd RAF (RiW, AST) 25.3.43

W3213 Spitfire F.Va (Merlin 45); Presentation aircraft *'CECIL McKAY'*; TOC/RAF 16.5.41 - US 8th AF; 52nd FG Eglinton, 2nd FS 7.8.42; 5th FS 22.8.42; 82nd FG Eglinton, 97th FS 18.11.42; Ran off runway, nosed up in soft ground, Cat.A 22.11.42 (2/Lt HR Decker OK); 67th (Obs) Grp, accident at Membury 3.6.43 (Lt J Thompson Jnr); Detached service 27.10.43; Retd RAF (No.9 MU) 21.3.44

W3229 Spitfire F.Vb (Merlin 45); TOC/RAF 7.6.41 - US 8th AF; 52nd FG Eglinton, 4th FS 12.8.42; 67th (Obs) Grp Membury, 12th Sqn, starboard wheel left runway after landing, tipped on nose in soft ground, Cat.A 13.2.43 (1/Lt DR Sherwood OK); Struck obstacle low flying Middle Wallop, Cat.Ac 19.5.43 (Lt AM Rusten); ROS 29.5.43; 12th Sqn 14.7.43; Retd RAF 4.10.43; Later as GI No. *5572M* to France on SS *'Hickory Isle'* in 3.46

W3236 Spitfire F.Vb (Merlin 45); Presentation aircraft *'LLANELLY'*; TOC/RAF 17.5.41 - US 8th AF; 31st FG, 307th FS Biggin Hill 22.8.42; Retd RAF 12.9.42

W3245 Spitfire F.Vb (Merlin 45); Presentation aircraft *'LINCOLN IMP'*; TOC/RAF 18.5.41 - US 8th AF; 52nd FG Eglinton, 4th FS 4.8.42; Retd RAF 8.11.42 - US 9th AF; 67th (TR) Grp 9.5.44; Diverted to US Navy VCS-7 at Lee-on-Solent 29.5.44; Retd RAF 17.7.44

W3262 Spitfire F.Vb (Merlin 45); TOC/RAF 2.6.41 - US 8th AF; 31st FG Atcham, 307th FS 14.7.42; Retd RAF (No.350 Sqn) 12.9.42

W3264 Spitfire F.Vb (Merlin 45); TOC/RAF 2.6.41 - US 8th AF; 52nd FG Eglinton, 5th FS 6.8.42; 2nd FS 22.8.42; Taxied into tractor, Goxhill, Cat.A 21.10.42 (Lt MR Lynn Jnr); ROS 2.11.42; 82nd FG Eglinton 27.11.42; Retd RAF (No.332 Sqn) 3.12.42; Retd USAAF; 6th FW Atcham, port brake seized, yawed to starboard at night, Cat.Ac 8.9.43 (Lt WG Kis); ROS; SOXO (8th AF), delete inventory 29.11.43

W3309 Spitfire F.Vb (Merlin 45); Presentation aircraft *'THE WILTSHIRE I'*; TOC/RAF 7.6.41 - US 8th AF; 31st FG Atcham, 307th FS 20.6.42; Port undercarriage collapsed landing, Cat.Ac 28.8.42 (2/Lt JM Winkler); ROS; 307th FS 16.9.42; Retd RAF 24.10.42

W3328 Spitfire F.Vb (Merlin 45); Presentation aircraft *'THE FLYING FOX'*; TOC/RAF 19.6.41 - US 8th AF; 52nd FG Eglinton, 4th FS 12.8.42; Retd RAF 8.11.42; Retd US 8th AF; Atcham, overturned on take-off, Cat.Ac 29.5.43; ROS; 82nd FG 18.7.43; Retd RAF 25.9.43; Later as GI No. *5571M* to France in 3.46

W3364 Spitfire F.Vb (Merlin 45); TOC/RAF 18.5.41 - US 8th AF; 52nd FG Eglinton, 2nd FS 5.8.42; 5th FS 22.8.42; 82nd FG Eglinton 18.11.42; Retd RAF 6.12.42; Retd USAAF; 67th (Obs) Grp, 153rd Sqn ('EP-A'), Keevil-based; Landed too fast, encountered soft surface, nosed over, South Marston 21.2.43 (Capt Emmette P Allen); Retd RAF (Hurn) 2.3.43; SOC

W3370 Spitfire F.Vb (Merlin 45); TOC/RAF 1.6.41 - US 8th AF; 31st FG, 307th FS Biggin Hill 20.8.42; Retd RAF 12.9.42

W3405 Spitfire F.Vb (Merlin 45); Presentation aircraft *'MONMOUTH, CHEPSTOW & FOREST OF DEAN SPITFIRE'*; TOC/RAF 11.6.41 - US 8th AF; 52nd FG Eglinton 11.7.42; 4th FS 6.8.42; No.3501 SU 8.11.42 - US 9th AF; 67th (TR) Grp Membury 20.12.43; Accident at Aldermaston 3.2.44 (Lt RT Simpson); To No.5 Air Depot; Retd RAF 20.6.44

W3407 Spitfire F.Vb (Merlin 45); TOC/RAF 18.6.41 - US 9th AF; 67th (TR) Grp Membury 6.12.43; Accident at Middle Wallop 2.1.44 (Lt FM Robinson); Retd RAF 16.6.44

W3423 Spitfire F.Vb (Merlin 45); TOC/RAF 23.6.41 - US 8th AF; 52nd FG Eglinton, 2nd FS 31.7.42; 4th FS 13.9.42; 67th (Obs) Grp Membury, 107th Sqn 22.11.42; Accident Membury 22.1.43 (Lt WP Chattaway); Accident at Membury 3.5.43 (Lt JW McAllister); Retd RAF 4.11.43; Later converted to GI No. *5383M*

W3425 Spitfire F.Vb (Merlin 45); TOC/RAF 23.6.41 - US 8th AF; 52nd FG Eglinton, 4th FS 5.8.42; Retd RAF 24.9.42

W3427 Spitfire F.Vb (Merlin 45); Presentation aircraft *'SPIT FIGHTER'*; TOC/RAF 25.6.41 - US 8th AF; 31st FG Atcham, 307th FS 13.7.42; Taxied into battery cart landing at Biggin Hill, Cat.A 18.8.42 (2/Lt J Ford OK); Re-Cat.B, Retd RAF (RiW) 18.8.42

W3431 Spitfire F.Vb (Merlin 45); Presentation aircraft *'KAAPSTAD III'*; TOC/RAF 1.7.41 - US 8th AF; 52nd FG Eglinton, 5th FS 6.8.42; 2nd FS 22.8.42; Retd RAF 11.11.43; Later to Portugal as LF.Vb (Merlin 45M) in 10.47

W3439 Spitfire LF.Vb (Merlin 45M); Presentation aircraft *'KAAPSTAD IV'*; TOC/RAF 27.6.41 - US 9th AF; 67th (TR) Grp Middle Wallop 7.5.44; Diverted to US Navy VCS-7 at Lee-on-Solent 29.5.44; Retd RAF (No.6 MU) 17.7.44

W3456 Spitfire F.Vb (Merlin 45); Presentation aircraft *'WATFORD'*; TOC/RAF 14.7.41; Westhampnett 22.7.41 - US 8th AF; 31st FG, 309th FS High Ercall 21.6.42; Retd RAF (No.302 Sqn) 12.9.42

W3505 Spitfire F.Vb (Merlin 45); Presentation aircraft *'HENDON ENDEAVOUR'*; TOC/RAF 22.6.41 - US 8th AF; 52nd FG Eglinton 11.7.42; 5th FS 22.8.42; 67th (Obs) Grp Membury, 109th Sqn Atcham, mid-air collision with W3797, crashed near Chetwynd, Cat.E 14.2.43 (2/Lt DE Lambert injured), SOC

W3518 Spitfire F.Vb (Merlin 45); TOC/RAF 22.6.41 - US 8th AF; 52nd FG Eglinton, 2nd FS 12.7.42; Mid-air collision with AR429, Cat.A 30.7.42 (2/Lt NL McDonald OK); ROS; 2nd FS 22.8.42; Retd RAF 28.1.43; Later to Portugal as LF.Vb in 7.47

W3619 Spitfire F.Vb (Merlin 45); TOC/RAF 3.8.41 - US 8th AF; 31st FG Atcham, 307th FS 20.6.42; Retd RAF 12.9.42; Later to France in 1.45

W3632 Spitfire F.Vb (Merlin 45); Presentation aircraft *'BAHRAIN'*; TOC/RAF 21.7.41 - US 8th AF; 52nd FG Eglinton, 5th FS 6.8.42; 2nd FS ('QP-Z') 22.8.42; Retd RAF (No.332 Sqn) 8.11.42; US 8th AF, 67th (Obs) Grp Membury, 109th Sqn, MI Cat.B 28.2.43; Retd RAF (RiW) 12.3.43

W3636 Spitfire F.Vb (Merlin 45); TOC/RAF 19.7.41; ex No.71 Sqn - US 8th AF; 4th FG Debden, 334th FS ('XR-C') 26.10.42; Collided with EN915 over Debden, crashed Cat.FB/E 26.11.42 (Capt RS Sprague killed, buried Cambridge), SOC

W3657 Spitfire F.Vb (Merlin 45); Presentation aircraft *'PENDLE'*; TOC/RAF 10.8.41 - US 8th AF; 31st FG, 309th FS High Ercall 20.6.42; Retd RAF (No.308 [Polish] Sqn from 12.9.42)

W3702 Spitfire F.Vb (Merlin 45); TOC/RAF 25.8.41 - US 8th AF; 31st FG, 309th FS High Ercall 20.6.42; Retd RAF (No.308 [Polish] Sqn from 12.9.42)

W3713 Spitfire F.Vb (Merlin 45); TOC/RAF 6.8.41 - US 8th AF; 52nd FG Eglinton, 5th FS 5.9.42; Station Flight Eglinton 13.9.42; Retd RAF 16.10.42

W3718 Spitfire F.Vb (Merlin 45); TOC/RAF 11.8.41 - US 8th AF; 52nd FG Eglinton, 4th FS 6.8.42; 67th (Obs) Grp Membury, 12th Sqn, engine failed at 6,000ft, water and dirt in fuel line, forced landing wheels up, Cat.B 28.3.43 (2/Lt CE Louden injured); Retd RAF (RiW) 9.4.43

UNITED STATES OF AMERICA

W3721　Spitfire F.Vb (Merlin 45); TOC/RAF 14.8.41 - US 8th AF; 67th (Obs) Grp 8.12.42; Retd RAF 31.12.44

W3766　Spitfire F.Vb (Merlin 45); Presentation aircraft *'WANDSWORTH, PUTNEY, ROEHAMPTON & SOUTHFIELDS'*; TOC/RAF 18.8.41 - US 8th AF; 52nd FG Eglinton, 5th FS 7.9.42; Station Flight Eglinton 13.9.42; Retd RAF 16.10.42

W3797　Spitfire F.Vb (Merlin 45); TOC/RAF 21.8.41 - US 8th AF; 52nd FG Eglinton, 5th FS 6.8.42; 4th FS 9.8.42; 67th (Obs) Grp Membury, 109th Sqn Atcham, mid-air collision with W3505, crashed near Chetwynd, Cat.E2 14.2.43 (Lt JR Warburton killed), SOC

W3815　Spitfire F.Vb (Merlin 45); Presentation aircraft *'SIERRA LEONE'*; TOC/RAF 24.8.41 - US 8th AF; 52nd FG Eglinton, 4th FS 5.8.42; 67th (Obs) Grp Membury, 109th Sqn 8.11.42; Undercarriage collapsed landing cross-wind Atcham, Cat.Ac 12.2.43 (Lt WA Watkins); ROS; US 9th AF - 496th FTG, 555th FS (OTU) Goxhill ('C7-M') 1944; Salvaged 31.1.44; Retd RAF; To GI No. *5388M* 17.7.45

W3825　Spitfire F.Vb (Merlin 45); Presentation aircraft *'HOLT III'*; TOC/RAF 29.8.41 - US 8th AF; 52nd FG Eglinton, 2nd FS 7.8.42; 4th FS 14.8.42; Retd RAF 2.3.43; US 9th AF, 67th (TR) Grp Middle Wallop 8.5.44; Diverted to US Navy VCS-7 at Lee-on-Solent 29.5.44; Retd RAF 28.9.44

W3828　Spitfire F.Vb (Merlin 45); Presentation aircraft *'HOLT VI'*; TOC/RAF 30.8.41 - US 8th AF; 31st FG, 309th FS High Ercall 30.7.42; Retd RAF 12.9.42

W3834　Spitfire F.Vb (Merlin 45); Presentation aircraft *'HOLT XII'* (later *'CORPS OF IMPERIAL FRONTIERSMEN'*); TOC/RAF 5.9.41 - US 8th AF; 52nd FG Eglinton, 5th FS 6.8.42; 2nd FS 22.8.42; Retd RAF 10.3.43; Later converted to LF.Vb (Merlin 55M)

W3837　Spitfire F.Vb (Merlin 45); Presentation aircraft *'KETTERING BOROUGH'*; TOC/RAF 7.9.41 - US 9th AF; 67th (TR) Grp Middle Wallop 6.1.44; Accident at Hawarden 8.1.44 (Lt FM Robinson); Retd RAF 10.3.44

W3848　Spitfire F.Vb (Merlin 45); Presentation aircraft *'TRAVANCORE II'*; TOC/RAF 11.9.41 - US 9th AF; 67th (TR) Grp 2.11.43, 12th Sqn in 1944; Accident at Chilbolton 13.3.44 (Lt LF Skenyon); Detached service 14.3.44; Condemned 369th (AS) Sqn 2.4.44; Retd RAF 16.6.44; Later converted to LF.Vb (Merlin 45M)

W3899　Spitfire F.Vb (Merlin 45); Presentation aircraft *'SUN WORKS'*; TOC/RAF 19.9.41 - US 8th AF; 4th FG Debden, 335th FS ('AV-M') 1.10.42; Retd RAF 27.3.43; Later to France as LF.Vb (Merlin 45M) in 1.45

W3902　Spitfire LF.Vb (Merlin 45M); Presentation aircraft *'GILBERT & ELLICE II'*; TOC/RAF 26.9.41 - US 9th AF; 67th (TR) Grp 7.5.44; Diverted to US Navy VCS-7 at Lee-on-Solent 29.5.44; Retd RAF 18.7.44; Later to Portugal in 1.48

W3931　Spitfire F.Vb (Merlin 45); TOC/RAF 1.9.41 - US 8th AF; 52nd FG Eglinton, 4th FS 5.8.42; 67th (Obs) Grp Membury, 153rd Sqn, swung landing, tipped on nose in soft ground, Cat.A 9.2.43 (2/Lt HP Cole OK); Accident Keevil 20.3.43 (Lt LF Huston); Retd RAF 30.3.43 - US 9th AF; 67th (TR) Grp, 153rd Sqn in 1944; Retd RAF; Later to France in 1.45

W3939　Spitfire F.Vb (Merlin 45); TOC/RAF 7.9.41 - US 8th AF; 52nd FG Eglinton, 5th FS 12.8.42; 2nd FS ('QP-M') 22.8.42; Retd RAF 5.3.43

W3942　Spitfire F.Vb (Merlin 45); TOC/RAF 13.9.41 - US 8th AF; 52nd FG, Eglinton 9.7.42; 4th FS 13.9.42; 67th (Obs) Grp Membury, flying accident at Keevil, Cat.E2 30.5.43 (Lt OF Harlan), SOC

W3960　Spitfire F.Vb (Merlin 45); TOC/RAF 3.10.41 - US 8th AF; 67th (Obs) Grp 25.2.43; Accident Membury 2.9.43 (Lt JS Vestal); Retd RAF 15.9.43; SOXO (8th AF), delete inventory 21.12.43

W3965　Spitfire F.Vb (Merlin 45); TOC/RAF 14.10.41 - US 9th AF; No.1 FLD/62 on 17.1.44, Damage Cat.B; RiW, Scottish Aviation (date unknown); Retd RAF (No.6 MU) 29.2.44

X4174　Spitfire F.Ia (Merlin III); TOC/RAF 13.8.40 - US 8th AF; 31st FG Atcham (for training only) 13.6.42; Accident 28.6.42 (Lt HJ Robb); Retd RAF 30.6.42

X4180　Spitfire F.Va (Merlin 45); TOC/RAF 13.8.40; ex No.121 & 133 Sqns - US 8th AF; 52nd FG Eglinton, 2nd FS 6.8.42; 5th FS 22.8.42; 67th (Obs) Grp Membury, 109th Sqn 14.12.42; Forced landed in bad visibility, ran of runway, tipped up in soft ground High Ercall, Cat.Ac 10.1.43 (2/Lt JD Dye OK); ROS; 6th FG 23.2.43; 67th (Obs) Grp Membury, 109th Sqn, collided with obstruction taxying Atcham, Cat.Ac 18.4.43 (Lt DC Fleming); ROS; 6th FG Atcham 22.5.43; Flying accident, Cat.Ac 21.9.43; ROS; 6th FG Atcham 13.10.43; Flying accident, Cat.Ac 10.1.44; ROS; 495th FTG Atcham 28.1.44; Retd RAF 28.2.44

X4234　Spitfire F.Ia (Merlin III); TOC/RAF 16.8.40 - US 8th AF; 31st FG Atcham (for training only), 307th FS 12.6.42; Accident 27.6.42 (Lt JH Cooper); 308th FS; Retd RAF 18.8.42

X4280　Spitfire F.Va (Merlin 45); TOC/RAF 29.8.40 - US 8th AF; 67th (Obs) Grp 25.3.43; Retd RAF 29.9.43

X4486　Spitfire F.Ia (Merlin III); TOC/RAF 20.4.40 - US 8th AF; 31st FG (for training only), 309th FS High Ercall 12.6.42; Retd RAF 15.8.42

X4606　Spitfire F.Ia (Merlin III); Presentation aircraft *'CEYLON V'*; TOC/RAF 7.10.40 - US 8th AF; 52nd FG Eglinton, 2nd FS 1.9.42; 5th FS 3.9.42; Retd RAF 27.7.43

X4669　Spitfire F.Va (Merlin 45); Presentation aircraft *'KAFFRARIA II'*; TOC/RAF 11.5.41 - US 8th AF; 52nd FG Eglinton 6.42; 4th FS until 4.7.42; Station Flight Eglinton 15.7.42; 52nd FG, 5th FS 22.8.42; 6th FW, crashed near Kings Nordley, Shropshire, Cat.E 27.3.43 (Lt JL Beck survived), SOC

X4709　Spitfire F.Va (Merlin 45); TOC/RAF 7.11.40 - US 8th AF; 82nd FG, 95th F Sqn, accident Eglinton 26.11.42 (Lt AK Hamrik) - US 8th AF; 82nd FG 15.7.43; Retd RAF 22.6.44

X4721　Spitfire F.Va (Merlin 45); TOC/RAF 13.11.40 - US 8th AF; 52nd FG Eglinton 11.7.42; 5th FS 22.8.42; 82nd FG 18.11.42; 6th FW, went off runway taxying High Ercall, Cat.A 7.12.42 (Lt FO Trafton); Retd RAF 25.9.43

X4821　Spitfire F.Va (Merlin 45); TOC/RAF 27.11.40 - US 8th AF; 52nd FG Eglinton 11.7.42; 5th FS 22.8.42; 67th (Obs) Grp; Retd RAF 11.3.43

X4828　Spitfire F.Ia (Merlin III); TOC/RAF 29.11.40 - US 8th AF; 31st FG (for training only), 309th FS High Ercall 12.6.42; Retd RAF 1.9.42

X4845　Spitfire F.Ia (Merlin III); TOC/RAF 12.12.40 - US 8th AF; 31st FG Atcham (for training only) 13.6.42; 307th FS in 6.42; 308th FS; Retd RAF 9.8.42

X4908　Spitfire F.Va (Merlin 45); Presentation aircraft *'SOUTHERN RAILWAY – INVICTA'*; TOC/RAF 4.1.41 - US 8th AF; 52nd FG Eglinton 11.7.42; 5th FS 22.8.42; Station Flight Eglinton 13.9.42 - US 12th AF; BC Bovingdon (HQ) 16.9.42; Retd RAF 6.1.43

AA720　Spitfire F.Vb (Merlin 45); TOC/RAF 31.8.41; ex No.121 Sqn - US 8th AF; 4th FG Debden, 335th FS ('AV-G') 1.10.42; Retd RAF 2.2.43

AA728　Spitfire LF.Vb (Merlin 45M); TOC/RAF 11.9.41 - US 9th AF; 67th (TR) Grp Middle Wallop 8.5.44; SOXO, diverted to US Navy ("L-09") for VCS-7 29.5.44; Retd RAF (No.33 MU) 18.7.44; Later via Reid & Sigrist to Portugal in 5.47

AA729　Spitfire F.Vb (Merlin 45); TOC/RAF 11.9.41 - US 8th AF; 67th (Recce) Grp Membury 20.12.43; SOXO (8th AF), census 31.12.43; "8916" 5.1.44; GLUE (9th AF) 3.4.44; Retd RAF 16.6.44; Later as LF.Vb via Reid & Sigrist to Portugal in 5.47

AA750　Spitfire F.Vb (Merlin 45); TOC/RAF 1.10.41; ex No.71 Sqn - US 8th AF; 52nd FG Eglinton, 5th FS 10.9.42; Flying accident, Cat.A 15.9.42; Station Flight Eglinton from 16.9.42; Retd RAF 25.10.42; Later converted to Seafire Mk.Ib (NX946)

AA752　Spitfire F.Vb (Merlin 45); TOC/RAF 1.10.41; ex No.121 Sqn - US 8th AF; 4th FG Debden, 335th FS 1.10.42; Dived into sea on Rhubarb, Cat.FB/E 21.11.42 (pilot picked up by Walrus), SOC

AA753 Spitfire F.Vb (Merlin 45); TOC/RAF 6.10.41 - US 8th AF; 52nd FG Eglinton 11.7.42; 2nd FS 22.8.42; Retd RAF 23.10.42; Later to Portugal as LF.Vb in 4.47
AA754 Spitfire F.Vb (Merlin 45); TOC/RAF in 7.41 - US 8th AF; 52nd FG Eglinton 7.42; 2nd Sqn Kenley, accident at Biggin Hill, Cat.Ac 29.8.42 (Lt HL Williamson); ROS; Retd RAF (No.411 Sqn, dived into sea after air collision 21.1.43, SOC)
AA756 Spitfire F.Vb (Merlin 45); TOC/RAF in 10.41 - US 8th AF; 52nd FG Eglinton, 5th FS 7.9.42; Station Flight Eglinton 13.9.42; Retd RAF; To Portugal as LF.Vb in 1.48
AA764 Spitfire F.Vb (Merlin 45); TOC/RAF in 10.41 - US 8th AF; USAAC Bovingdon 22.12.42; 7th (PR) Grp Mount Farm, 13th Sqn 19.7.43; Accident Mount Farm 27.8.43 (Lt RM Hairston); Crashed Cat.E2 5.9.43; SOXO (8th AF), deleted inventory 1.2.44; SOC
AA841 Spitfire F.Vb (Merlin 45); TOC/RAF 28.9.41; ex No.121 Sqn - US 8th AF; 4th FG Debden, 335th FS ('AV-D') 1.10.42; Op flt, FW 190 destroyed 5m E of Calais 2.10.42 (Mjr J Daley); Engine failure on take-off, Cat.B 20.1.43 (2/Lt SN Pissanos minor injuries); RiW; Re-Cat.E; SOC 20.1.43
AA858 Spitfire F.Vb (Merlin 46); TOC/RAF 11.10.41 - US 8th AF; 31st FG Atcham, 309th FS 31.7.42; Retd RAF 12.9.42
AA860 Spitfire F.Vb (Merlin 45); TOC/RAF 11.10.41 - US 8th AF; 67th (Obs) Grp 18.2.43; 12th Sqn 8.6.43; Retd RAF (RiW) 9.10.43; SOXO (8th AF), deleted inventory 1.2.44; Converted to LF.Vb; Later to GI No. *5028M*
AA877 Spitfire F.Vb (Merlin 46); Presentation aircraft '*MANCHESTER CHAIRMAN*'; TOC/RAF 26.10.41; ex No.71 Sqn - US 8th AF; 4th FG Debden, 334th FS ('XR-F') 22.11.42; Retd RAF 25.3.43
AA882 Spitfire F.Vb (Merlin 45); Presentation aircraft '*BOROUGH OF WANSTEAD & WOODFORD*'; TOC/RAF 29.10.41 - US 8th AF; 67th (Recce) Grp Membury 2.7.43; 107th Sqn 10.7.43; "8916" 31.1.44; SOXO (8th AF), deleted inventory 1.2.44; US 9th AF 1.2.44 - GLUE (9th AF), delivered to RAF 16.6.44; Retd RAF (RiW, de Havilland) 17.6.44
AA903 Spitfire F.Vb (Merlin 45); TOC/RAF 25.10.41 - US 8th AF; 52nd FG Eglinton, 2nd FS 3.8.42; Practice flight, crashed a few miles NW of Coleraine, Cat.E 11.8.42 (2/Lt EL Sharpe of 4th FS killed); SOC 19.8.42
AA912 Spitfire F.Vb (Merlin 45); TOC/RAF 2.11.41 - US 8th AF; 31st FG, 309th FS High Ercall 20.6.42; Overshot landing, Cat.B 28.7.42 (1/Lt WC Bryson); Retd RAF (RiW) 31.7.42
AA918 Spitfire F.Vb (Merlin 45); TOC/RAF 18.11.41 - US 8th AF; 52nd FG Eglinton 12.7.42; 2nd FS ('QP-O') 22.8.42; Retd RAF 11.2.43
AA920 Spitfire F.Vb (Merlin 45); TOC/RAF 18.11.41; ex No.71 Sqn - US 8th AF; 4th FG Debden, 334th FS 1.10.42; 335th FS ('AV-G'); 334th FS, hit tree on take-off, landed wheels-up to keep speed up 16.11.42 (Lt JA Clark OK); Retd RAF (RiW, AST) 25.11.42
AA924 Spitfire F.Vb (Merlin 45); Presentation aircraft '*TREGGANU II*'; TOC/RAF 11.41; ex No.133 Sqn; - US 8th AF; 4th FG, 336th FS Great Sampford 1.10.42; Flying accident Cat.E2 9.3.43; bboc; 6th FW, 342nd Sqn, hit Mosquito II HJ643 (Cat.E2, pilot killed) 1m south of Atcham, Cat.E 28.7.43 (Mjr HO Asselin injured), SOC
AA963 Spitfire F.Vc (Merlin 45); Presentation aircraft '*BOROUGH OF SOUTHGATE*'; TOC/RAF 12.11.41; with SS '*Evanger*' to USA 21.2.42; Special commitment tests in USA in 3.42; For exhibition to Chicago 5.42; Fate unknown - NOTE: See also P9306
AA964 Spitfire F.Vb (Merlin 45); Presentation aircraft '*DIRTY GERTIE, VANCOUVER*'; TOC/RAF 1.11.41 - US 8th AF; 67th (Recce) Grp Membury 17.5.43; 109th Sqn 16.6.43; Retd RAF 21.11.43; RiW, No.1 CRU 22.11.43; To US 9th AF 31.1.44; SOXO (8th AF), delete inventory 1.2.44; GLUE (9th AF), retd RAF 1.2.44; Later RNDA 21.4.44
AA966 Spitfire F.Vb (Merlin 45); TOC/RAF 1.11.41 - US 8th AF; 52nd FG Eglinton, 4th FS 12.8.42; Retd RAF 8.11.42

AA969 Spitfire F.Vb (Merlin 45); TOC/RAF 1.11.41 - US 8th AF; 67th (TR) Grp Membury 22.11.43; SOXO (8th AF), "8916" 5.1.44; US 9th AF 1.2.44; RiW, Scottish Aviation 12.4.44; GLUE (9th AF), deleted inventory 31.10.44; Later as GI No. *5596M* to France in 4.46
AA982 Spitfire F.Vb (Merlin 45); Presentation aircraft '*CITY OF LIVERPOOL V*'; TOC/RAF 22.11.41; US 8th AF 31.12.43 - SOXO (8th AF) 5.1.44; 67th (TR) Grp 6.1.44; 12th Sqn; SOXO (8th AF), delete inventory 6.4.44; Retd RAF (RiW) 12.4.44
AB168 Spitfire F.Vb/trop (Merlin 45); TOC/RAF 7.12.41; ME 1.11.43; NAASC 31.10.43 - US 12th AF 31.10.43; Retd RAF (ME) 28.4.45
AB192 Spitfire F.Vb (Merlin 45); Presentation aircraft '*ORGANILIL*'; TOC/RAF 5.12.41; ex No.133 Sqn - US 8th AF; 4th FG, 336th FS Great Sampford 1.10.42; SOXO (8th AF) 8.10.43; SOXO, delete inventory 23.1.44; Retd RAF 1.3.44 (No.7 SoTT as *4462M* from 2.3.44)
AB199 Spitfire F.Vb (Merlin 46); Presentation aircraft '*MESOPOTAMIA*'; TOC/RAF 16.12.41 - US 8th AF; 67th (TR) Grp Middle Wallop 9.5.44; Crashed Cat.Ac 22.6.44; ROS; 302nd (Transport) Wing, to US 9th AF 1.7.44; GLUE (9thAF), delete inventory 2.7.44; 31st ATG 9.7.44; Retd RAF (RiW) 22.7.44; Later to France in 1.45
AB252 Spitfire F.Vb/trop (Merlin 45); TOC/RAF 26.2.42; ME, NAASC 31.10.43 - US 12th AF 31.10.43; Unknown unit, crashed near Aboukir/Helwan 5.5.44; R&SU; Retd RAF (ME) 21.6.45
AB256 Spitfire F.Vb (Merlin 46); TOC/RAF 8.12.41 - US 8th AF; 67th (Obs) Grp 9.2.43; 12th Sqn 17.6.43; Crashed Cat.B 9.10.43; Retd RAF (RiW) 9.10.43; SOXO (8th AF), delete inventory 1.2.44
AB257 Spitfire F.Vb (Merlin 45); TOC/RAF 8.12.41 - US 8th AF; 52nd FG Eglinton, 4th FS 9.8.42; Engine failure, forced landing, overshot, hit wall, overturned & caught fire at Kenley, Cat.E 10.9.42 (Lt EM Scott survived), SOC
AB264 Spitfire F.Vb/trop (Merlin 45); TOC/RAF 30.1.42; NWA 1.10.43 - US 12th AF 1.10.43; Retd RAF (ME) 31.8.44
AB271 Spitfire F.Vb (Merlin 45); TOC/RAF 13.12.41; ex No.133 Sqn - US 8th AF; 4th FG, 336th FS Great Sampford ('MD-E', marked '*DOREEN I*') 1.10.42; Taxied into stationery beacon on peritrack Debden, Cat.B 16.11.42 (2/Lt KD Peterson OK); Retd RAF (RiW) 25.11.42
AB345 Spitfire F.Vb/trop (Merlin 45); TOC/RAF 4.2.42; NAASC - US 12th AF 31.10.43; Retd RAF (ME) 31.8.44; Later to Turkey in 9.44
AB532 Spitfire F.Vc/trop (Merlin 45); TOC/RAF 25.2.42; Malta 1.8.42 - US 12th AF 31.10.43; Retd RAF (MAAF) 31.1.44; Later to FAF in 5.44
AB789 Spitfire F.Vb (Merlin 45); TOC/RAF 1.8.41 - US 8th AF; 67th (TR) Grp Membury 22.11.43; SOXO (8th AF), "8916" 5.1.44; From Middle Wallop, accident at Bury St.Edmunds 31.1.44 (Lt EW Murphy); GLUE (9th AF), delete inventory 31.5.44; Retd RAF (crashed Cat.B 19.9.44; RiW, AST 27.9.44)
AB792 Spitfire F.Vb (Merlin 45); TOC/RAF 27.7.41 - US 8th AF; 52nd FG Eglinton, 5th FS 5.9.42; Station Flight Eglinton 13.9.42; Retd RAF; SOC 11.10.42
AB803 Spitfire F.Vb (Merlin 45); TOC/RAF 13.8.41 - US 8th AF; 31st FG Atcham, 308th FS 5.8.42; Retd RAF 12.8.42
AB809 Spitfire F.Vb (Merlin 45); TOC/RAF 24.8.41; ex No.71 Sqn - US 8th AF; 4th FG Debden, 334th FS 1.10.42; Taxied into petrol tanker at Debden, Cat.Ac 12.12.42 (Lt DW Beeson OK); ROS; Retd RAF; Later converted to Seafire Mk.Ib NX963
AB811 Spitfire F.Vb (Merlin 45); TOC/RAF 16.8.41 - US 8th AF; 31st FG, 309th FS High Ercall 21.6.42; Missing off Dieppe, Cat.FB/E 19.8.42 (Lt S Junkin Jnr wounded, baled out and returned), SOC
AB862 Spitfire F.Vb (Merlin 45); TOC/RAF 24.7.41 - US 8th AF; 52nd FG Eglinton, 4th FS 6.8.42; 67th (Obs) Grp Membury, 153rd Sqn, canopy slid forward and hit pilot's head, right wheel went off peritrack into soft ground, braked and tipped nose, Cat.A 24.11.42 (1/Lt JH Corbin

UNITED STATES OF AMERICA

OK); ROS 30.11.42; Swung off runway landing, nosed up in soft ground at Keevil, Cat.A 24.1.43 (1/Lt JR Cooper OK); Accident 3m S of Keevil 13.2.43 (Lt LF Houston); 82nd FG Eglinton; RiW 22.2.43; AW/CN 3.7.43; No.340 Sqn RAF 23.8.43; USAAF, 67th (TR) Grp, 153rd Sqn Membury 22.11.43; SOXO (8th AF), "8916" 5.1.44; US 9th AF 1.2.44; GLUE, delete inventory 20.4.44; Retd RAF 16.6.44; RiW, de Havilland 17.6.44; Later to Portugal as LF.Vb in 5.47

AB870 Spitfire F.Vb (Merlin 45); Presentation aircraft 'HAWKES BAY I'; TOC/RAF 2.8.41 - US 8th AF; 31st FG Atcham 20.6.42; 308th FS Kenley 1.8.42; Westhampnett 24.8.42; Retd RAF 26.10.42

AB871 Spitfire F.Vb (Merlin 45); TOC/RAF 24.8.41 - US 8th AF; 52nd FG Eglinton, 5th FS 8.9.42; Station Flight Eglinton from 13.9.42; Retd RAF 30.5.43; Later converted to GI No. *4353M*

AB896 Spitfire F.Vb (Merlin 45); TOC/RAF 10.8.41; ex No.71 Sqn - US 8th AF; 52nd FG Eglinton, 5th FS 5.9.42; Station Flight Eglinton 13.9.42; Retd RAF 16.10.42; Later to Soviet Union (Russia) in 3.43

AB897 Spitfire F.Vb (Merlin 45); TOC/RAF 20.8.41 - US 8th AF; 52nd FG Eglinton, 5th FS 5.9.42; While ferrying, taxied into P8741, Cat.A 10.9.42 (1/Lt GA Zientowski OK); Station Flight Eglinton 13.9.42; Retd RAF (No.45 MU) 1.11.42

AB898 Spitfire F.Vb (Merlin 45); TOC/RAF 15.8.41 - US 8th AF; 52nd FG Eglinton 13.7.42; Retd RAF 21.10.42 - US 9th AF; 67th (TR) Grp Middle Wallop 9.5.44; 369th (AS) Sqn; GLUE (9th AF), delete inventory 13.5.44; Retd RAF (No.39 MU) 18.7.44

AB899 Spitfire F.Vb (Merlin 45); TOC/RAF 17.8.41 - US 8th AF; 4th FG Debden, 334th FS ('XR-J') 1.12.42; Crashed at Debden, Cat.Ac 12.12.42 (Lt DW Beeson); ROS; Re-Cat.B 24.12.42; Retd RAF (RiW, AST) 31.12.42

AB901 Spitfire F.Vb (Merlin 45); TOC/RAF 9.8.41 - US 8th AF; 31st FG Atcham, 308th FS 20.6.42; Crashed Cat.Ac 25.6.42 (Lt E Dalrymple); ROS; Re-Cat.B; Retd RAF (RiW) 15.7.42; Later to Soviet Union (Russia) in 2.43

AB904 Spitfire F.Vb (Merlin 45); TOC/RAF 22.8.41 - US 8th AF; 52nd FG Eglinton, 2nd FS ('QP-I') in 9.42; Retd RAF in 9.43; Later converted to GI No. *5349M* from 7.45

AB907 Spitfire F.Vb (Merlin 45); TOC/RAF 20.8.41; ex No.71 Sqn - US 8th AF; 52nd FG Eglinton, 5th FS 6.8.42; 2nd FS 22.8.42; 82nd FG Eglinton; USAAF Aldermaston, accident at base 3.1.43 (Lt WW Story); ROS 8.1.43; 82nd FG 6.2.43; 67th (Obs) Grp Membury, accident at base 24.2.43 (Lt SC Arnold); Retd RAF (MR/Cat.E) 28.6.43, SOC (scrapped)

AB918 Spitfire F.Vb (Merlin 45); Presentation aircraft 'WELLINGTON I'; TOC/RAF 6.7.41 - US 8th AF; 52nd FG Eglinton, 5th FS 9.8.42; 2nd FS 22.8.42; 67th (Obs) Grp Membury, 12th Sqn, poor visibility, landed wheels-up, Cat.B 16.11.42 (1/Lt AE Hauert OK); RiW 24.11.42; AW/CN 14.1.43; 67th (TR) Grp Membury 20.12.43; SOXO (8th AF), census 31.12.43; "8916" 5.1.44; US 9th AF 1.2.44; Retd RAF; GLUE, delete inventory 31.10.44

AB920 Spitfire F.Vb (Merlin 45); TOC/RAF 24.8.41; US 8th AF – 6th AFW, as GI No. *2656M* from 9.4.43; Fate unknown

AB929 Spitfire F.Vb (Merlin 45); TOC/RAF 28.8.41; ex No.71 Sqn - US 8th AF; 4th FG Debden, 334th FS 1.10.42; Retd RAF 2.4.43

AB936 Spitfire F.Vb (Merlin 45); TOC/RAF 30.8.41 - US 8th AF; 52nd FG Eglinton 11.7.42; Retd RAF (No.45 MU) 24.10.42

AB941 Spitfire F.Vb (Merlin 45); TOC/RAF 3.9.41; ex No.71 Sqn - US 8th AF; 4th FG Debden, 334th FS 1.10.42; Hit by AA, dived into English Channel, Cat.FB/E 26.1.43 (2/Lt RA Boock rescued), SOC

AB970 Spitfire F.Vb (Merlin 46); TOC/RAF 31.8.41 - US 8th AF; 52nd FG Eglinton, 5th FS 6.7.42; 2nd FS 22.8.42; 67th (Obs) Grp Membury, 12th Sqn 22.11.42; Wheels-up landing, Cat.A 2.1.43 (Capt RA Berg OK); Accident Membury 13.2.43 (Lt FD Burt); ROS 18.2.43; 67th (Obs) Grp 4.4.43, 12th Sqn 17.6.43; RiW, No.1 CRU 6.1.44; AW/CN 17.3.44; No.345 Sqn RAF 6.6.44; Crashed Cat.FB/E 8.6.44; SOXO (8th AF), delete inventory 31.10.44; SOC

AB974 Spitfire F.Vb (Merlin 45); Presentation aircraft 'B B & C I RAILWAY No.III'; TOC/RAF 12.9.41; ex No.121 Sqn - US 8th AF; 4th FG Debden, 335th FS ('AV-J') 1.10.42; Retd RAF 23.3.43

AB975 Spitfire F.Vb (Merlin 45); TOC/RAF 31.8.41; ex No.121 Sqn - US 8th AF; 4th FG Debden, 335th FS ('AV-A') 1.10.42; Retd RAF 2.4.43

AB976 Spitfire F.Vb (Merlin 46); TOC/RAF 30.8.41 - US 8th AF; 31st FG Atcham 20.6.42; 67th (Obs) Grp 16.10.42; Based Membury, accident Keevil 7.3.43 (Lt DR Smith); Accident Membury 17.3.43 (Lt JW Braucht); 107th Sqn 9.6.43; Crashed Cat.B 28.9.43; RiW 29.9.43; SOXO (8th AF), delete inventory 1.2.44; AW/CN 11.2.44 (No.39 MU 25.3.44); US 9th AF, 31st ATG 26.5.44; GLUE (9th AF), retd RAF 1.7.44 (RiW 7.7.44)

AB982 Spitfire F.Vb (Merlin 45); Presentation aircraft 'WEST BORNEO IV'; TOC/RAF 7.9.41 - US 8th AF; 31st FG, 309th FS High Ercall 11.8.42; 308th FS 15.8.42; Retd RAF 1.10.42

AB988 Spitfire F.Vb (Merlin 45); TOC/RAF 7.10.41 - US 8th AF; 4th FG Debden, 336th FS, claimed a Bf 109F 22.1.43 (2/Lt Joseph A Matthews); Crashed (Cat. & date unknown); Retd 336th FS 3.2.43; SOXO (HQ US 8th AF) 5.6.43; No.3501 SU 19.9.43; 67th (TR) Grp Membury 22.11.43; SOXO (8th AF), condemned 14.3.44; MR 17.4.44; Retd RAF (RiW) 21.4.44; Later to Portugal as LF.Vb in 11.47

AB989 Spitfire F.Vb (Merlin 45); TOC/RAF 26.8.41 - US 8th AF; 52nd FG 12.7.42; Retd RAF; SOC 12.4.45

AD113 Spitfire F.Vb (Merlin 45); TOC/RAF 16.8.41 - US 8th AF; 31st FG Atcham, 307th FS 20.6.42; Landed cross-wind, undercarriage collapsed, Cat.Ac 4.8.42 (Lt JH Cooper OK); ROS 7.8.42; 307th FS 9.8.42; Retd RAF 12.9.42

AD116 Spitfire F.Vb (Merlin 45); Presentation aircraft 'TWICKENHAM I'; TOC/RAF 19.9.41 - US 8th AF; 52nd FG Eglinton, 5th FS 8.9.42; Station Flight Eglinton from 13.9.42; Retd RAF 30.9.42

AD118 Spitfire F.Vb (Merlin 45); TOC/RAF 4.9.41; US 8th AF 8.10.43; SOXO (HQ US 8th AF), condemned 16.10.43; 67th (Recce) Grp 17.10.43; SOXO, delete ("8916") 31.1.44; US 9th AF 1.2.44; GLUE, retd RAF 31.5.44 (AFDU 14.6.44)

AD127 Spitfire F.Vb (Merlin 45); TOC/RAF 6.9.41; ex No.71 Sqn - US 8th AF; 4th FG Debden, 334th FS ('XR-F') 27.10.42; Landed downwind, overshot, swung to avoid obstruction at Southend, Cat.B 17.11.42; Retd RAF (RiW); Later converted to LF.Vb; To FAA (R.N.)

AD181 Spitfire F.Vb (Merlin 45); TOC/RAF 14.9.41 - US 8th AF; 67th (Obs) Grp Membury 24.3.43; 12th Sqn 17.6.43; Crashed Ellington, Cat.E2 6.12.43 (Lt FP Viviano); SOXO (8th AF), delete inventory 1.2.44, SOC

AD187 Spitfire F.Vb (Merlin 45); TOC/RAF 10.9.41 - US 8th AF; 31st FG Atcham 14.7.42; 309th FS High Ercall 16.7.42; 67th (Obs) Grp Membury, 107th Sqn, turned at excessive speed after landing, left runway, tipped on nose at Farnborough, Cat.A 2.12.42 (1/Lt HC Conner); Accident Membury 11.1.43 (Lt RW Booze); Delivery to ATA White Waltham, landing accident on arrival, Cat.FA/Ac 23.1.43 (Lt LK Martin); ROS 24.1.43; Re-Cat.B; Retd RAF (RiW) 3.2.43

AD190 Spitfire F.Vb (Merlin 45); TOC/RAF 15.10.41 - US 8th AF; 52nd FG Eglinton, 2nd FS 8.8.42; Station Flight Eglinton from 13.9.42; Retd RAF (No.8 MU) 16.10.42; Later to Soviet Union (Russia) in 2.43

AD191 Spitfire F.Vb (Merlin 45); TOC/RAF 12.10.41 - US 8th AF; 67th (TR) Grp Membury 6.12.43; SOXO, census 31.12.43; "8916" 5.1.44; US 9th AF 1.2.44; GLUE, retd RAF 16.6.44; Later to Portugal in 4.47

AD199 Spitfire F.Vb (Merlin 45); TOC/RAF 7.9.41; ex No.71 & 121 Sqns - US 8th AF; 4th FG Debden, 335th FS 1.10.42;

Accident at Bodney 15.1.43 (Col JC Harrington); Retd RAF 26.1.43

AD231 Spitfire F.Vb (Merlin 45); Presentation aircraft *'WEST BORNEO II'*; TOC/RAF 13.9.41 - US 8th AF; 31st FG Atcham, 307th FS ('MX-K') 26.8.42; Retd RAF 12.9.42. - NOTE: Also reported as "AD237"

AD247 Spitfire F.Vb (Merlin 45); Presentation aircraft *'RAJNAGAR'*; TOC/RAF 14.9.41 - US 8th AF; 67th (Obs) Grp Membury 12.4.43; Accident Keevil 15.4.43 (Lt JS Conner); 12th Sqn 8.6.43; Accident Membury 1.12.43 (Lt JB Perry); Condemned HQ US 8th AF 9.12.43; RiW, No.1 CRU 9.12.43; SOXO (8th AF), delete inventory 1.2.44; Retd RAF (AW/CN 12.2.44); SOC 26.7.44

AD253 Spitfire F.Vb (Merlin 45); TOC/RAF 19.9.41 - US 8th AF; 31st FG, 309th FS High Ercall 20.6.42; Retd RAF (No.39 MU) 26.10.42

AD260 Spitfire F.Vb (Merlin 45); Presentation aircraft *'MISS A.B.C. 1'*; TOC/RAF 27.9.41 - US 8th AF; 31st FG Atcham 20.6.42; 308th FS 1.8.42; Westhampnett 24.8.42; Retd RAF 4.11.42

AD274 Spitfire F.Vb (Merlin 45); Presentation aircraft *'MOKHOTLONG'*; TOC/RAF 26.9.41 - US 8th AF; 31st FG, 309th FS High Ercall 31.7.42; Collided with EN823 while taxying, Cat.Ac 6.8.42 (Capt CE Wilson OK); ROS 12.8.42; 309th FS 15.8.42; 8th AF, Comm.- Sqn 27.10.42; 67th (Obs) Grp 31.1.43; Retd RAF 15.2.43; Later converted to Seafire Mk.Ib (NX926)

AD288 Spitfire F.Vb (Merlin 45); TOC/RAF 22.9.41; ex No.71 Sqn - US 8th AF; 67th (TR) Grp Membury 20.11.43; SOXO (US 8th AF), census 31.12.43; "8916" 5.1.44; SOXO (8th AF), delete inventory 1.2.44; GLUE (9th AF) 15.2.44; Retd RAF (RiW, de Havilland) 16.6.44; Later as GI No. *5599M* to France in 3.46

AD294 Spitfire F.Vb (Merlin 45); Presentation aircraft *'MISS A.B.C. III'*; TOC/RAF 26.9.41 - US 8th AF; 31st FG Atcham 20.6.42; 307th FS in 7.42; Retd RAF 12.9.42; Later to Portugal as LF.Vb in 5.47

AD299 Spitfire F.Vb (Merlin 45); TOC/RAF 27.9.41; ex No.133 Sqn - US 8th AF; 4th FG, 336th FS Great Sampford 1.10.42; 335th FS 15.2.43; Retd RAF 23.3.43; Later converted to LF.Vb; Became GI No. *5717M* in 10.45

AD321 Spitfire F.Vb (Merlin 45); Presentation aircraft *'FIREFLY'*; TOC/RAF 6.10.41 - US 8th AF; 67th (Recce) Grp 4.6.43; 107th Sqn 17.6.43; SOXO "8916" (delete) 31.1.44; Retd RAF (RiW, AST) 1.3.44

AD324 Spitfire F.Vb (Merlin 45); TOC/RAF 13.10.41; ex No.121 Sqn - US 8th AF; 4th FG Debden, 335th FS 1.10.42; Retd RAF 23.3.43; Later to France as LF.Vb in 10.47

AD353 Spitfire F.Vb (Merlin 45); TOC/RAF 12.10.41 - US 8th AF; 52nd FG Eglinton, 4th FS 6.8.42; RiW; 4th FS 27.8.42; 82nd FG 13.11.42; 67th (Recce) Grp Membury, 107th Sqn 24.10.43; US 9th AF 1.2.44; 67th (TR) Grp, 12th Sqn; Storage 1.3.44; GLUE (9th AF), retd RAF 6.4.44

AD357 Spitfire F.Vb (Merlin 45); Presentation aircraft *'NATIONAL FEDERATION OF HOSIERY MANUFACTURERS ASSOCIATION LEICESTER SECTION'*; TOC/RAF 2.10.41 - US 8th AF; 31st FG, 309th FS High Ercall 30.7.42; Retd RAF 29.10.42; Later converted to Seafire Mk.Ib (PA112)

AD359 Spitfire F.Vb (Merlin 45); TOC/RAF 19.10.41 - US 8th AF; 52nd FG Eglinton, 2nd FS 11.7.42; Landing collision with AB270 of No.152 Sqn RAF which had run off runway landing, overshot into ditch, Cat.Ac 27.7.42 (2/Lt WL Yorke OK); ROS; Re-Cat.B; Retd RAF (RiW) 3.8.42

AD378 Spitfire F.Vb (Merlin 45); TOC/RAF 28.10.41 - US 8th AF; 52nd FG Eglinton, 5th FS 6.9.42; Station Flight Eglinton from 13.9.42; Retd RAF 30.9.42

AD385 Spitfire F.Vb (Merlin 45); TOC/RAF 15.10.41 - US 8th AF; 4th FG, 336th FS Great Sampford 23.11.42; SOXO (8th AF USAAF HQ), condemned 3.11.43; RiW 4.11.43; 67th (TR) Grp. 23.11.43; Retd RAF (RiW); No.39 MU 13.2.44

AD388 Spitfire F.Vb (Merlin 45); Presentation aircraft *'AMBALA II'*; TOC/RAF 17.10.41; ex No.121 Sqn - US 8th AF; 4th FG Debden, 335th FS ('AV-Z') 1.10.42; Retd RAF 23.3.43

AD416 Spitfire F.Vb (Merlin 45); TOC/RAF 15.10.41 - US 8th AF; 31st FG Atcham, 307th FS 31.7.42; Retd RAF (No.93 Sqn) 13.9.42

AD417 Spitfire LF.Vb (Merlin 45M); Presentation aircraft *'YR HEN BONT'*; TOC/RAF 13.10.41 - US 9th AF; 67th (TR) Grp Middle Wallop 9.5.44; GLUE (9th AF), retd RAF 25.5.44 (RW/AST 30.5.44)

AD422 Spitfire F.Vb (Merlin 45); TOC/RAF 16.10.41 - US 8th AF; 52nd FG Eglinton, 5th FS 6.8.42; 2nd FS 22.8.42; 67th (Recce) Grp Membury, 109th Sqn 8.7.43; RiW 9.10.43; AW/CN 31.12.43; SOXO (8th AF), delete inventory 1.2.44; Retd RAF; SOC 28.3.46

AD451 Spitfire F.Vb (Merlin 45); TOC/RAF 28.11.41 - US 8th AF; 4th FG Debden, 336th FS 23.11.42; Taxying in high wind, tipped on nose Bradwell Bay, Cat.A 14.1.43; Heavy landing Atcham, Cat.Ac 30.4.43 (Lt RE Belliveau); ROS 5.5.43; 336th FS Debden 20.6.43; No.3501 SU 19.9.43; 67th (TR) Grp Membury 20.12.43; SOXO (8th AF), census 31.12.43; Accident at Middle Wallop 2.1.44 (Lt HJ Skinner); US 9th AF 1.2.44; GLUE (9th AF), delete inventory 2.4.44; Detached service 10.5.44; Retd RAF 18.5.44 (RiW, de Havilland 16.6.44)

AD464 Spitfire F.Vb (Merlin 45); TOC/RAF 16.10.41 - US 8th AF; 31st FG Atcham, 308th FS 20.6.42; Flying accident, Cat.Ac 28.6.42; ROS 3.7.42; 308th FS 28.7.42; Retd RAF, No.71 Sqn ('XR-L') 12.8.42; US 8th AF, 308th FS 24.8.42; 4th FG Debden, 334th FS 1.10.42; SOXO, delivered to RAF 6.7.44; Retd RAF 12.7.44; Later to Portugal as LF.Vb (Merlin 55M)

AD506 Spitfire F.Vb (Merlin 45); Presentation aircraft *'MISS HERRIN'*; TOC/RAF 28.10.41 - US 8th AF; 67th (Obs) Grp Membury 19.4.43; 12th Sqn 17.6.43; SOXO (8th AF), retd RAF 6.4.44 (RiW 12.4.44)

AD511 Spitfire F.Vb (Merlin 45); TOC/RAF 8.11.41; ex No.121 Sqn - US 8th AF; 4th FG Debden, 335th FS ('AV-E') 1.10.42; Retd RAF 9.10.42 (No.1 Air Delivery Flight); USAAF, 6th AFW Atcham, heavy landing, Cat.Ac 20.5.43 (Lt MC Wood); ROS; Retd RAF; Later to Portugal in 10.43

AD564 Spitfire F.Vb (Merlin 45); TOC/RAF 1.12.41; ex No.71 Sqn - US 8th AF; 4th FG Debden, 334th FS 1.10.42; USAAF Atcham, accident at base 7.5.43 (Lt JW Icard); Crashed 2m NE of Newport, Shropshire, Cat.E 26.5.43 (Lt J Woods killed), SOC

AD566 Spitfire F.Vb (Merlin 45); TOC/RAF 1.12.41 - US 8th AF; 31st FG Atcham, 308th FS 1.8.42; Brakes failed taxying, raised undercarriage to avoid hitting building at Kenley, Cat.Ac 11.8.42 (T/Sgt EJ Howell OK); ROS; Re-Cat.B; Retd RAF (RiW); Later converted to Seafire Mk.Ib NX922

AD573 Spitfire F.Vb (Merlin 45); TOC/RAF 29.10.41 - US 8th AF; 4th FG Debden, 335th FS ('AV-H') 23.11.42; Accident at Atcham 29.4.43 (Lt JJ Klein); RiW; US 8th AF HQ 11.8.43; 4th FG, 336th FS 19.9.43; Vickers-Armstrongs 25.12.43; No.3501 SU 27.1.44; RiW, de Havilland 6.6.44; AW/CN 1.9.44; No.8 MU 16.9.44; 1695.Flt 3.10.44; USAAF, 495th FTG Atcham; SOXO (8th AF), retd RAF 10.10.44; Later converted to GI No. *5555M*

AD574 Spitfire F.Vb (Merlin 45); TOC/RAF 20.10.41 - US 8th AF; 31st FG Atcham 20.6.42; 308th FS 4.8.42; Westhampnett 24.8.42; Retd RAF 12.9.42

AD580 Spitfire F.Vb (Merlin 45); TOC/RAF 23.11.41 - US 8th AF; 31st FG Atcham 20.6.42; 308th FS 1.8.42; Westhampnett 24.8.42; Retd RAF 12.9.42; Later converted to Seafire Mk.Ib (NX914)

AR232 Spitfire F.Ia (Merlin III); TOC/RAF 13.10.41 - US 8th AF; 31st FG Atcham, 308th FS 5.7.42; Retd RAF 7.8.42

AR275 Spitfire F.Vb (Merlin 45); TOC/RAF 16.12.41 - US 8th AF; 31st FG, 308th FS 18.9.42; Retd RAF 11.10.42

AR278 Spitfire F.Vb (Merlin 46); TOC/RAF 5.2.42 - US 9th AF; 31st ATG Grove 31.5.44; GLUE (9th AF), retd RAF 1.7.44 (RiW 25.7.44)

UNITED STATES OF AMERICA

AR283　Spitfire F.Vb (Merlin 45); TOC/RAF 12.1.42 - US 8th AF; 31st FG Atcham, 307th FS 14.7.42; 67th (Obs) Grp Membury, 153rd Sqn, starboard brake failed, ran off runway, tipped nose in muddy ground, Cat.A 14.11.42 (1/Lt WL Boone OK); Crashed Cat.Ac 20.11.42; ROS 20.11.42; SOXO 23.1.43; Retd RAF (RiW, Heston) 7.4.43

AR295　Spitfire F.Vb (Merlin 46); TOC/RAF 26.1.42 - US 9th AF; 31st ATG Grove 2.6.44; GLUE (9th AF), retd RAF 1.7.44 (RiW, Scottish Aviation 5.7.44)

AR323　Spitfire F.Vb (Merlin 45); TOC/RAF 12.2.42; US 8th AF 6.1.44, SOXO (8th AF), census 31.12.43; "8916" 5.1.44; 67th (TR) Grp 6.1.44; 12th Sqn, accident at Aldermaston (Lt FS Aldridge); SOXO (8th AF), delete inventory 1.2.44; GLUE, retd RAF 2.4.44; RiW, No.1 CRU 22.2.44; Later converted to LF.Vb (Merlin 45M)

AR335　Spitfire F.Vb (Merlin 45); TOC/RAF 16.2.42 - US 8th AF; 52nd FG Eglinton, 5th FS 5.9.42; Station Flight Eglinton from 13.9.42; Retd RAF 24.10.42

AR336　Spitfire F.Vb (Merlin 45); TOC/RAF 16.2.42; ex No.133 Sqn - US 8th AF; 4th FG, 336th FS Great Sampford 1.10.42; *Circus 253*, Escorting four Bostons to bomb St.Omer airfield, Bf 109f destroyed between Mardyk and Dunkirk, then taxying accident (or overshot landing) Penshurst, Cat.A 22.1.43 (2/Lt JG Matthews); Re-Cat.B; Retd RAF (RiW) 28.1.43

AR341　Spitfire F.Vb (Merlin 45); TOC/RAF 24.2.42; ex No.133 Sqn - US 8th AF; 4th FG, 336th FS Great Sampford 1.10.42; Convoy patrol, engine failed, ditched off Harwich, Cat.E 13.2.43 (2/Lt JA Powell killed, buried Cambridge), SOC

AR372　Spitfire F.Vb (Merlin 45); TOC/RAF 14.3.42; ex No.133 Sqn - US 8th AF; 4th FG, 336th FS Great Sampford 1.10.42; SOXO, 7th (PR) Grp Mount Farm (aircraft named '*The Sad Sack*'), 13th Sqn 23.6.43; 14th Sqn; Detached service 21.9.44; Retd RAF (RiW, AST) 18.12.44

AR390　Spitfire LF.Vb (Merlin 45M); TOC/RAF 27.3.42 - US 9th AF; 67th (TR) Grp Middle Wallop 8.5.44; SOXO (8th AF), diverted to US Navy VCS-7 at Lee-on-Solent ("L-09") 29.5.44; Retd RAF (MR/RiW), No.39 MU 17.7.44

AR393　Spitfire F.Vb (Merlin 46); TOC/RAF 1.4.42; US 8th AF 12.43; SOXO (8th AF), census 31.12.43; "8916" 5.1.44; 67th (TR) Grp 6.1.44; From Middle Wallop, accident at Rhua Farm 28.1.44 (Lt FM Robinson); US 9th AF 1.2.44; GLUE, retd RAF 16.6.44 (RiW, Heston Aircraft 17.6.44)

AR395　Spitfire LF.Vb (Merlin 45M); TOC/RAF 1.4.42 - US 9th AF; 67th (TR) Grp Middle Wallop 10.5.44; SOXO (8th AF), diverted to US Navy VCS-7 at Lee-on-Solent ("L-09") 29.5.44; Retd RAF (No.33 MU) 15.7.44

AR404　Spitfire F.Vb (Merlin 45); TOC/RAF 11.4.42 - US 8th AF; 52nd FG Eglinton 12.7.42; 2nd FS 22.8.42; Force-landed or crashed Thornton Abbey while low flying 2m miles from Goxhill, Cat.E 21.10.42 (Lt EM Boughton); Re-Cat.B; RiW, AST 4.11.42; Converted to LF.Vb, Merlin 45M installed, AW/CN 11.3.43; SOXO (8th AF), 67th (TR) Grp Mount Farm 9.11.43; Accident Mount Farm 25.11.43 (Lt AW Clark); US 9th AF 1.2.44; Retd to RAF 3.4.44; Retd to US 8th AF, 7th (PR) Grp; Accident 21.8.44 (Lt CJ Goffin); Retd RAF 5.9.44; Later to Portugal as LF.Vb (Merlin 45M) in 6.47

AR427　Spitfire F.Vb (Merlin 45); TOC/RAF 17.4.42; US 8th AF in 5.43 - 67th (Recce) Grp Membury, 107th Sqn, accident at base 23.5.43 (Lt RW Booze); Crashed Cat.B 9.10.43; Retd RAF (RiW) 9.10.43; SOXO (8th AF), delete inventory 1.2.44

AR429　Spitfire F.Vb (Merlin 46); TOC/RAF 20.4.42 - US 8th AF; 52nd FG Eglinton 12.7.42; Mid-air collision with W3518, Cat.A 30.7.42 (Capt WJ Payne OK); ROS; 2nd FS 22.8.42; Station Flight Eglinton 31.12.42; Retd RAF 3.43

AR435　Spitfire F.Vb (Merlin 45); TOC/RAF 25.4.42 - US 8th AF; 52nd FG Eglinton, 2nd FS 12.7.42; Ground collision with EN766, Cat.A 28.7.42 (2/Lt MA Dodd OK); ROS; 2nd FS 22.8.42; Retd RAF 30.11.42

AR438　Spitfire LF.Vb (Merlin 45M); TOC/RAF 27.4.42; US 8th AF 11.43; No.3501 SU 18.11.43; No.411 ARF 2.12.43; SOXO (8th AF), 495th FTG Atcham in 12.43; Flying accident, Cat.Ac 15.4.44; ROS 23.4.44; No.411 ARF 4.5.44; Retd RAF (No.39 MU) 9.5.44; GLUE (9th AF), delete inventory 1.7.44; Later to Portugal as LF.Vb in 10.47

AR451　Spitfire F.Vb (Merlin 45); TOC/RAF 16.5.42 - US 8th AF; 67th (TR) Grp Middle Wallop 26.1.44; US 9th AF 1.2.44; 67th (TR) Grp Aldermaston, accident at base 17.2.44 (Lt CB East); Retd RAF 6.6.44; Later as GI No. *5592M* to France in 3.46

AR464　Spitfire F.Vc/trop (Merlin 46); TOC/RAF 16.5.42; Malta 1.8.42; NWA 1.5.43 - SOXO (US 8th AF); N.A. - US 12th AF (DUKO), received 6.7.43; Fate unknown

AR524　Spitfire F.Vc/trop (Merlin 46); TOC/RAF 13.7.42; NWA 28.2.43 - US 12th AF; 52nd FG, 2nd FS, force-landed Affreville 7.2.43; No.107 R&SU Blida 8.2.43; Retd 2nd FS 27.2.43; Later to FFAF (GC I/7) 10.43, then No.328 Sqn 12.43

AR600　Spitfire F.Vc/trop (Merlin 46); TOC/RAF 17.8.42; NWA 31.5.43 - US 12th AF; 31st FG, 309th FS ('WZ-N'), hit pothole, overturned, landing Termini 29.8.43 (Lt Boardman); Retd RAF 29.2.44; Later to France in 9.47

AR602　Spitfire F.Vc/trop (Merlin 46); TOC/RAF 20.8.42; NWA 31.7.43 - US 12th AF 31.7.43; Retd RAF 1.10.43; French unit

AR614　Spitfire F.Vc; Became GI No. *5378M, 6371M, 7555M*; Civil reg. *CF-DUY* 1986 & *G-BUWA* 19.3.93; Arrived as **SURVIVOR** only: Restored by Hawker Restorations at Earls Colne and Historic Flying Ltd, at Audley End, UK from 1994; Purchased by the Alpine Fighter Collection at Wanaka, New Zealand; First flown after restoration in UK 5.10.96; Sold to the Paul Alan, Seattle/Vintage Wings, Seattle, Washington, USA; Departed from the UK to USA in 11.99; Regd *N614VC* 10.2.00 to Flying Heritage Collection, Bellevue, Washington; Regd 25.4.01 to Flying Heritage Inc, Seattle, Washington and extant

AR615　Spitfire F.Vc/trop (Merlin 46); TOC/RAF 28.8.42; NWA 28.2.43 - US 12th AF in 9.43; Retd RAF 29.2.44

BL239　Spitfire F.Vb (Merlin 45); TOC/RAF 2.11.41; ex No.121 Sqn - US 8th AF; 31st FG Atcham, 308th FS 15.6.42; RAF 28.8.42; US 8th AF, 308th FS 7.9.42; Retd RAF 8.1.43; Later converted to Seafire Mk.Ib (NX981)

BL240　Spitfire F.Vb (Merlin 45); TOC/RAF 1.11.41; ex No.133 Sqn - US 8th AF; 4th FG, 336th FS Great Sampford 1.10.42; Engine failure, force-landed Manston, Cat.Ac 13.1.43 (Lt Bishop OK); ROS 22.1.43; 336th FS 29.1.43; Shot down by enemy aircraft 10m off St.Omer, Cat.FB/E 12.3.43 (2/Lt HS Anderson, PoW), SOC

BL243　Spitfire F.Vb (Merlin 45); TOC/RAF 22.12.41 - US 8th AF (HQ) 16.10.43; 67th (Recce) Grp Membury 17.10.43; No.3501 SU on 2.11.43; No."8916" 5.1.44; 67th (TR) Grp 17.1.44; Accident at Aldermaston 12.1.44 (Lt SA Mecca); US 9th AF 1.2.44; GLUE (9th AF), delete inventory 6.6.44; Retd RAF 20.7.44 (Westland Ltd 18.8.44; RiW 26.8.44)

BL247　Spitfire LF.Vb (Merlin 45M); TOC/RAF 1.12.41 - US 9th AF; 67th (TR) Grp Middle Wallop 9.5.44; SOXO, diverted to US Navy VCS-7 at Lee-on-Solent ("L-09") 29.5.44; Retd RAF (No.39 MU) 18.7.44

BL255　Spitfire F.Vb (Merlin 45); TOC/RAF 5.12.41; ex No.133 Sqn - US 8th AF; 4th FG, 336th FS Great Sampford ('MD-T', marked '*Buckeye Don*', Lt D Gentile) 1.10.42; Heavy landing, tyre burst, swung, undercarriage collapsed, Cat.Ac 26.11.42 (2/Lt J Mitchellweis OK); ROS 3.12.42; 336th FS 23.1.43; Crashed on forced landing Cat.Ac 10.2.43 (Lt A Warren OK); Retd RAF 14.3.43

BL267　Spitfire F.Vb (Merlin 45); TOC/RAF 6.11.41 - US 8th AF; 67th (TR) Grp Middle Wallop, 12th Sqn 31.12.43; "8916" 5.1.44; US 9th AF 1.2.44; GLUE (9th AF), retd RAF 13.5.44 (RiW, AST 24.5.44)

BL291　Spitfire F.Vb (Merlin 45); TOC/RAF 9.11.41 - US 8th AF; 31st FG Atcham in 6.42; 308th FS Atcham 3.7.42; 308th FS to Kenley 4.8.42; 308th FS to Westhampnett 24.8.42; Retd RAF 27.10.42; Later to GI No. *5389M* in 7.45

BL338 Spitfire F.Vb (Merlin 45); TOC/RAF 15.11.41 - US 8th AF; 31st FG, 309th FS High Ercall 20.6.42; Temp. missing 19.8.42; 308th FS Westhampnett, crashed landing, Cat.A 26.8.42 (2/Lt WR Waltner OK); Re-Cat.B; Retd RAF (RiW, date unknown)

BL347 Spitfire F.Vb (Merlin 45); TOC/RAF 26.2.42 - US 8th AF; 31st FG, 309th FS High Ercall 6.42; Retd RAF in 11.42

BL365 Spitfire F.Vb (Merlin 45); Presentation aircraft '*SHREWSBURY*'; TOC/RAF 18.11.41 - US 8th AF; 67th (TR) Grp Middle Wallop 26.1.44; SOXO (8th AF), "8916" 31.1.44; Accident at Chilbolton 3.3.44 (Lt J Robertson); RiW, AST 21.3.44; SOXO (8th AF), retd RAF 2.4.44; Later to GI No. *5381M* in 7.45

BL368 Spitfire LF.Vb (Merlin 45M); TOC/RAF 21.11.41 - US 9th AF; 67th (TR) Grp Middle Wallop 9.5.44; SOXO, diverted to US Navy VCS-7 at Lee-on-Solent ("L-09") 29.5.44; Retd RAF (No.39 MU) 18.7.44; Later to Portugal as LF.Vb in 1.48

BL370 Spitfire F.Vb (Merlin 45); Presentation aircraft '*GURGAON II PUNJAB*'; Rebuilding in UK; Arrived as **SURVIVOR** only; Restored from wreck by Star Aircraft, California for Patrick Taylor and donated to the New Orleans D-Day Museum (exhibited as "SH-J", marked "Gurgaon II Punjab") from 6.6.00 and extant

BL376 Spitfire F.Vb (Merlin 45); TOC/RAF 12.12.41; ex No.71 Sqn - US 8th AF; 4th FG Debden, 334th FS ('XR-B') 1.10.42; Crashed Cat.Ac 15.12.42; ROS 21.12.42; 334th FS 25.1.43; 335th FS ('AV-T') 28.1.43; Engine failure on take-off, forced landing, crashed Debden, Cat.Ac 1.3.43 (2/Lt SN Pissanos unhurt); ROS 5.3.43; 335th FS 23.3.43; Retd RAF 28.3.43.
NOTE: 4th FG, 334th FS, Ju 52 probable, seen with port engine on fire in flat spin at 1,000ft 1m S of Flushing (Shared by 1/Lt SM Anderson & Sgt RA Boock); Andersons aircraft was damaged by shrapnel 15.12.42, possibly BL376

BL379 Spitfire F.Vb (Merlin 46); TOC/RAF 21.11.41 - US 8th AF; 31st FG Atcham 20.6.42; 308th FS Kenley 1.8.42; 308th FS to Westhampnett 24.8.42; Retd RAF 12.9.42

BL383 Spitfire F.Vb (Merlin 45); TOC/RAF 20.11.41 - US 8th AF; 4th FG Debden, 336th FS ('MD-J') 13.2.43; ROS 6.9.43; 336th FS 9.9.43; Crashed Membury 22.10.43 (Lt HJ Skinner); Condemned HQ US 8th AF 27.10.43; SOXO (8th AF), retd RAF in 12.43 (RiW; AW/CN 8.1.44)

BL409 Spitfire F.Vb (Merlin 46); TOC/RAF 5.12.41 - US 8th AF; 31st FG Atcham 20.6.42; 308th FS Kenley 1.8.42; 308th FS to Westhampnett 24.8.42; SOXO (8th AF), 67th (Recce) Grp, 109th Sqn 15.6.43; Condemned HQ US 8th AF 7.11.43; Retd RAF (RiW) 8.11.43

BL422 Spitfire F.Vb (Merlin 45); TOC/RAF 29.3.42; ex No.71 Sqn - US 8th AF; 4th FG Debden, 334th FS ('XR-J') 1.10.42; Run into by BL449 after landing, Cat.B 25.10.42 (Lt DW Beeson OK); Retd RAF (RiW, No.1 CRU) 3.11.42

BL425 Spitfire F.Vb (Merlin 45); TOC/RAF 25.11.41 - US 8th AF; 52nd FG Eglinton 12.7.42; Taxied into soft ground, Cat.B 23.7.42 (2/Lt PW Tedford OK); Re-Cat.A; Later to No.61 OTU

BL426 Spitfire F.Vb (Merlin 45); TOC/RAF 24.12.41 - US 8th AF; 52nd FG Eglinton, 5th FS in 7.42; Crashed Cat.B 9.8.42; Retd RAF (RiW) in 8.42

BL437 Spitfire F.Vb (Merlin 45); TOC/RAF 10.12.41; ex No.71 Sqn - US 8th AF; 4th FG Debden, 334th FS ('XR-M') 1.10.42; Taxied into BL449 Debden, Cat.A 30.12.42 (Lt VJ France); 335th FS ('AV-N'); Retd RAF 23.3.43; US 9th AF; 67th (TR) Grp Middle Wallop 9.5.44; SOXO, diverted to US Navy VCS-7 at Lee-on-Solent ("L-09") 29.5.44; Retd RAF (No.6 MU) 17.7.44; Later to Portugal in 8.47

BL449 Spitfire F.Vb (Merlin 45); TOC/RAF 5.12.41; ex No.71 Sqn - US 8th AF; 4th FG Debden, 334th FS 1.10.42; Tyre burst on touchdown, swung off runway into BL422 at Debden, Cat.A 25.10.42 (1/Lt GH Whitlow OK); Taxied into by BL437 Debden, Cat.B 30.12.42 (Lt GG Ross); Retd RAF 12.1.43; Later to Portugal in 12.43

BL477 Spitfire F.Vb (Merlin 45); TOC/RAF 8.12.41; ex No.121 Sqn - US 8th AF; 4th FG Debden, 335th FS ('AV-S') 1.10.42; Retd RAF 23.3.43 (later converted LF.Vb)

BL481 Spitfire F.Vb (Merlin 46); TOC/RAF 15.3.42; US 8th AF, census 31.12.43; "8916" 5.1.44; 67th (TR) Grp 6.1.44; US 9th AF 1.2.44; 67th (TR) Grp, 12th Sqn; Accident at Chilbolton 2.3.44 (Lt TH Milner); GLUE (9th AF), retd RAF 14.5.44 (RiW, AST 25.5.44)

BL488 Spitfire F.Vb (Merlin 45); TOC/RAF 5.12.41; ex No.71 Sqn - US 8th AF; 4th FG Debden, 334th FS ('XR-E') 1.10.42; 336th FS 23.8.43; Retd RAF (No.6 MU) 11.11.43; SOXO (8th AF), delete inventory 1.2.44

BL512 Spitfire F.Vb (Merlin 45); TOC/RAF 14.12.41 - US 8th AF; 67th (Obs) Grp 9.2.43; 109th Sqn 16.6.43; Crashed Cat.C; Re-Cat.B 4.10.43; Retd RAF (RiW) 4.10.43; SOXO (8th AF), delete inventory 1.2.44

BL516 Spitfire F.Vb (Merlin 45); TOC/RAF 14.12.41 - US 8th AF; 52nd FG Eglinton, 5th FS 6.9.42; Station Flight Eglinton 13.9.42; Retd RAF (No.453 Sqn) 19.9.42; Later converted to LF.Vb

BL523 Spitfire F.Vb (Merlin 45); TOC/RAF 4.1.42; ex No.133 Sqn - US 8th AF; 4th FG, 336th FS Great Sampford 1.10.42; Retd RAF 23.3.43; Later converted to GI No. *4368M*

BL530 Spitfire F.Vb (Merlin 45); Presentation aircraft '*TASLUS II*'; TOC/RAF 17.12.41 - US 8th AF in 9.42; 4th FG, 336th FS Great Sampford 1.10.42; No.436 ARF 25.10.42 (RiW); No.6 MU 28.11.42; 334th FS Debden ('XR-B') 17.12.42; Escorting 4 Bostons to bomb St. Omer airfield, destroyed FW190, own aircraft shot-up 22.1.43 (1/Lt Stanley M Anderson); 336th FS 15.2.43; Swung landing, undercarriage collapsed at Llanbedr, Cat.Ac 4.6.43 (2/Lt DM Funchean); ROS; Re-Cat.B, RiW 18.6.43; US 9th AF, 67th (TR) Grp Middle Wallop 9.5.44; SOXO, diverted to US Navy VCS-7 at Lee-on-Solent ("L-09") 29.5.44; Retd RAF 17.7.44

BL545 Spitfire F.Vb (Merlin 46); TOC/RAF 27.12.41 - US 8th AF; 4th FG, 336th FS ('MD-L') Great Sampford 27.10.42; Escorting 4 Bostons to bomb St. Omer airfield, FW190 destroyed W of Dunkirk 22.1.43 (Mjr OH Coen); HQ US 8th AF 30.7.43; ROS 6.9.43; 4th FG Debden, 336th FS 16.9.43; 6th FW Atcham in 10.43; No.3501 SU 9.10.43; Retd RAF (RiW) 10.11.43; SOXO (8th AF), delete inventory 1.2.44

BL550 Spitfire F.Vb (Merlin 45); TOC/RAF 5.1.42; ex No.71 Sqn - US 8th AF; 4th FG Debden, 334th FS ('XR-Q') 1.10.42; 335th FS ('AV-U'); SOXO (8th AF) 6.7.43; Retd RAF; No.3501 SU 19.9.43; No.52 OTU 5.10.43; Fighter Leader School (FLS) 2.2.44; USAAF, 495th FTG Atcham; SOXO (8th AF), delete inventory 10.10.44; Retd RAF; No.41 OTU 21.9.44

BL564 Spitfire F.Vb (Merlin 45); TOC/RAF 22.12.41 - US 8th AF; 4th FG Debden, 335th FS 10.3.43; Retd RAF 23.3.43

BL565 Spitfire F.Vb (Merlin 45); Presentation aircraft '*SOUTHERN CROSS*'; TOC/RAF 21.2.42 - US 8th AF; 52nd FG Eglinton, 5th FS 5.9.42; Station Flight Eglinton from 13.9.42; Retd RAF 30.9.42

BL571 Spitfire F.Vb (Merlin 45); Presentation aircraft '*WYVERN II*'; TOC/RAF 15.3.42 - US 8th AF; 67th (TR) Grp Membury 22.11.43; SOXO (8th AF), "8916" 5.1.44; US 9th AF 1.2.44; 67th (TR) Grp, 12th Sqn; RiW, Scottish Aviation Ltd 12.4.44; GLUE (9th AF), retd RAF 5.5.44

BL582 Spitfire F.Vb (Merlin 45); TOC/RAF 24.12.41; ex No.71 Sqn - US 8th AF; 4th FG Debden, 334th FS 1.10.42, claimed a FW 190 2.10.42 (Wg Cdr R Duke-Woolley RAF); 336th FS; HQ US 8th AF 4.6.43, crashed Cat.B 20.12.43; Condemned 20.12.43; Retd RAF (RiW) 21.12.43; SOXO (8th AF), delete inventory 1.2.44

BL617 Spitfire F.Vb (Merlin 45); TOC/RAF 28.12.41 - US 8th AF; 67th (Obs) Grp 9.2.43; 109th Sqn 16.7.43; Crashed Cat.B 4.10.43; Retd RAF (RiW) 4.10.43; SOXO (8th AF), delete inventory 1.2.44

BL628 Spitfire F.Vb (Merlin 45); TOC/RAF 25.1.42 - US 8th AF; 31st FG Atcham, 308th FS 5.8.42; Retd RAF 12.8.42; Later converted to hooked Spitfire. - Remains now with P Croser, Australia – **SURVIVOR**

BL629 Spitfire F.Vb (Merlin 45); Presentation aircraft '*GARONTALO*' (later '*MEDWAY METEOR*'); TOC/ RAF

Spitfire F.Vb BL680 of the 7th (PR) Group, US 8th Air Force, at Mount Farm, where it was used in 1944 as a hack aircraft, with fin code 'A'. [MAP]

25.1.42 - US 8th AF; ADV Flight Defford 15.10.43; MI Cat.B, Retd RAF (RiW) 23.3.44

BL639　Spitfire F.Vb (Merlin 45); TOC/RAF 9.1.42 - US 8th AF; 52nd FG Eglinton, 5th FS 31.7.42; 2nd FS 22.8.42; Retd RAF 23.10.42; Later converted to Seafire Mk.Ib (NX959)

BL641　Spitfire F.Vb (Merlin 45); TOC/RAF 6.1.42 - US 8th AF; 52nd FG Eglinton, 4th FS 5.8.42; 67th (Obs) Grp Membury 22.11.42; 153rd Sqn, brakes failed, weathercocked into soft earth and nosed over at Keevil, Cat.A 31.3.43 (2/Lt RP Humphrey OK); 109th Sqn 12.7.43; Retd RAF (RiW) 9.10.43; SOXO (8th AF), delete inventory 1.2.44

BL660　Spitfire F.Vb (Merlin 45); TOC/RAF 16.5.42 - US 8th AF; 31st FG Atcham, 307th FS 21.6.42; Bounced landing rough ground, tyre burst Merston, Cat.Ac 16.9.42 (1/Lt ET White injured); ROS 2.10.42; 307th FS Merston 3.10.42; HQ US 8th AF (FC) 21.10.42; 67th (Obs) Grp, 109th Sqn Atcham, accident at Perton 18.2.43 (Lt W Hopkins); Air collision with P7849 over Shropshire, Cat.E 29.3.43 (Lt ED Smith); SOC

BL663　Spitfire F.Vb (Merlin 45); TOC/RAF 18.1.42; US 8th AF 31.12.43; 67 (TR) Grp 6.1.44; Accident at Aldermaston 8.2.44 (Lt MF Johnson); ROS 16.2.44; Retd RAF; No.3501 SU 26.4.44; RiW 15.6.44; SOXO (8th AF), delete inventory 31.10.44

BL670　Spitfire F.Vb (Merlin 45); Presentation aircraft '*EVER READY II*'; TOC/RAF 31.1.42; US 8th AF 31.12.43; 1.FLD/62 17.1.44; US 9th AF 15.2.44; Fate unknown

BL673　Spitfire F.Vb (Merlin 45); TOC/RAF 25.1.42 - US 8th AF; 4th FG Debden, 336th FS 23.1.43, claimed a FW 190 over Audruieq 12.3.43 (1/Lt Don Gentile); SOXO (HQ 8th AF) 9.8.43; Condemned HQ US 8th AF 4.11.43; Retd RAF (RiW, AST) 17.11.43 (later converted LF.Vb)

BL680　Spitfire F.Vb (Merlin 45); TOC/RAF 31.1.42 - US 8th AF 15.11.43; 7th (PR) Grp Mount Farm ('A') as hack aircraft in 1944; Accident at Mount Farm 27.1.44 (Lt CF Parker); Accident at Kings Cliffe 31.3.44 (Lt RC Garrett); SOXO (HQ US 8th AF), condemned 31.3.44

BL688　Spitfire F.Vb (Merlin 45); TOC/RAF 25.1.42 - US 8th AF; 4th FG Debden, 335th FS 11.3.43; Retd RAF 23.3.43

BL692　Spitfire F.Vb (Merlin 45); TOC/RAF 22.1.42 - US 8th AF; 4th FG Debden, 334th FS 22.11.42; Retd RAF 1.4.43

BL722　Spitfire F.Vb (Merlin 45); TOC/RAF 22.1.42; ex No.133 Sqn - US 8th AF; 4th FG, 336th FS Great Sampford ('MD-B') 1.10.42; USAAF Atcham, accident at base 6.5.43 (Lt FJ Christensen Jnr); Accident Chivenor 28.10.43 (Lt DE Colton); SOXO (HQ US 8th AF), condemned 4.11.43; Diverted to US Navy ("L-09") 4.11.43; SOXO ("8916") 5.1.44; Retd RAF (RiW, No.1 CRU) 15.1.44; SOXO (8th AF), delete inventory 1.2.44

BL727　Spitfire F.Vb (Merlin 45); TOC/RAF 6.2.42 - US 8th AF; 67th (TR) Grp Membury in 11.43; 12th Sqn Membury 16.11.43; Retd RAF (No.602 Sqn) 25.1.44; SOXO (8th AF), delete inventory 1.2.44

BL729　Spitfire LF.Vb (Merlin 45M); TOC/RAF 5.2.42 - US 9th AF; 67th (TR) Grp Middle Wallop 9.5.44; SOXO (8th AF), diverted to US Navy VCS-7 at Lee-on-Solent ("L-09") 29.5.44; Retd RAF 17.6.44

BL770　Spitfire F.Vb (Merlin 45); TOC/RAF 7.2.42 - US 8th AF; 52nd FG Eglinton 11.7.42; 2nd FS 22.8.42; Taxying accident Goxhill, Cat.B 21.10.42 [or 21.9.42] (Lt WL Morgan); RiW; Crashed Cat.Ac 3.11.42; Re-Cat.B; Retd RAF (RiW) 3.11.42; Later converted to Seafire Mk.Ib PA113

BL773　Spitfire F.Vb (Merlin 45); TOC/RAF 6.2.42; ex No.133 Sqn - US 8th AF; 4th FG, 336th FS Great Sampford 1.10.42; Retd RAF 31.12.42; Later converted to LF.Vb (Merlin 45M)

BL776　Spitfire F.Vb (Merlin 45); TOC/RAF 14.2.42; ex No.133 Sqn - US 8th AF; 4th FG, 336th FS Great Sampford ('MD-C') 1.10.42; SOXO (8th AF), 7th (PR) Grp Mount Farm, 13th Sqn 10.8.43; Retd RAF (RiW, de Havilland.) 18.8.43; SOXO (8th AF), delete inventory 1.2.44

BL778　Spitfire F.Vb (Merlin 45); TOC/RAF 11.2.42 - US 8th AF; 52nd FG Eglinton, 4th FS 1.8.42; Ran off runway, went on nose, Cat.A 9.8.42 (2/Lt EL Sharpe OK); RAF 2.12.42; 6th FW Atcham 20.4.43; Retd RAF in 5.43

BL832　Spitfire F.Vb (Merlin 45); Presentation aircraft '*ELEANOR*'; TOC/RAF 22.2.42 - US 8th AF; 31st FG, 309th FS High Ercall 12.8.42; Retd RAF 26.10.42

BL848　Spitfire F.Vb (Merlin 46); TOC/RAF 8.2.42 - US 9th AF; 31st ATG Grove 9.6.44; GLUE (9th AF), retd RAF 1.7.44

BL862　Spitfire F.Vb (Merlin 46); TOC/RAF 6.2.42 - US 8th AF; 4th FG Debden, 334th FS 2.11.42; ROS 21.11.42; 334th FS 24.12.42; Retd RAF in 1.43

BL888　Spitfire F.Vb (Merlin 46); TOC/RAF 10.2.42; US 8th AF 17.1.44; "8916" 31.1.44; US 9th AF 1.2.44; 67th (TR) Grp; GLUE (9th AF), retd RAF 29.5.44 (AFDU 14.6.44)

BL898 Spitfire F.Vb (Merlin 45); TOC/RAF 14.2.42 - US 8th AF; 52nd FG Eglinton, 5th FS 3.8.42; 2nd FS 22.8.42; 67th (Obs) Grp Membury, 109th Sqn, accident at Atcham, Cat.A 13.2.43 (Lt WF Kaiser); Taxied into parked van at Atcham, Cat.Ac 11.3.43 (Lt GS Dietz); ROS 18.3.43; 82nd FG 12.5.43; 67th (Recce) Grp Membury, 109th Sqn 23.10.43; SOXO (8th AF), "8916" 5.1.44; SOXO, delete inventory 31.1.44; US 9th AF 1.2.44; GLUE, retd RAF (RiW) 16.6.44; Later to Portugal as LF.Vb in 2.48

BL918 Spitfire F.Vb (Merlin 45); TOC/RAF 11.2.42 - US 8th AF in 1943; US 9th AF 1.2.44; 67th (TR) Grp; GLUE (9th AF), retd RAF 16.6.44 (RiW)
NOTE: Reported (temp.) missing No 124 Sqn 27.4.42.

BL920 Spitfire F.Vb (Merlin 45); TOC/RAF 11.2.42 - US 8th AF; 6th AFW 11.6.43; SOXO, HQ US 8th AF 3.9.43; 67th (Recce) Gp Membury, crashed 1m E of Bishops Caundle, Dorset, Cat.E2 9.9.43 (Lt IR Henry); Condemned HQ US 8th AF 10.9.43; SOC (scrapped)

BL958 Spitfire F.Vb (Merlin 45); TOC/RAF 17.2.42 - US 8th AF; 52nd FG Eglinton in 7.42, engine failure, force landed on beach near Portrush, Cat.FA/Ac 10.8.42 (2/Lt RW Raup safe); Re-Cat.B; Retd RAF (RiW, Short & Harland) 15.8.42; Later converted to Seafire Mk.Ib (NX898)

BL962 Spitfire LF.Vb (Merlin 45M); TOC/RAF 22.2.42; ex No.133 Sqn - US 9th AF; 67th (TR) Grp Middle Wallop 9.5.44; GLUE (9th AF), retd RAF 26.7.44

BL964 Spitfire F.Vb (Merlin 45); TOC/RAF 24.2.42 - US 8th AF; 31st FG, 309th FS High Ercall 20.6.42; Flying with No.412 Sqn in sweep to St.Omer, shot down over Abbeville-Domart, Cat.FB/E 25.7.42 (Lt Col AP Clark PoW), SOC

BL975 Spitfire F.Vb (Merlin 45); TOC/RAF 14.2.42; ex No.133 & 71 Sqns - US 8th AF; 4th FG Debden, 334th FS ('XR-H') 1.10.42; Caught by strong wind while taxying, swung off runway into mud hole, tipped on nose at Ford, Cat.A 6.11.42 (Lt JF Lutz OK); 335th FS ('AV-I'); Retd RAF 23.3.43 (later converted LF.Vb LR)

BL978 Spitfire F.Vb (Merlin 45); TOC/RAF 19.2.42 - US 8th AF; 31st FG, 309th FS High Ercall 11.8.42; Retd RAF 12.9.42; Later to Portugal in 1.44

BL986 Spitfire F.Vb (Merlin 45); TOC/RAF 28.2.42; ex No.121 Sqn - US 8th AF; 4th FG Debden, 335th FS 1.10.42; Retd RAF 7.12.42; Later converted to Seafire Mk.Ib (NX908)

BL991 Spitfire F.Vb (Merlin 45); TOC/RAF 25.2.42; ex No.133 Sqn - US 8th AF; 31st FG, 309th FS High Ercall 20.6.42; Westhampnett 23.8.42; Retd RAF 12.9.42

BL993 Spitfire F.Vb (Merlin 46); TOC/RAF 22.2.42 - US 9th AF; 31st ATG Grove 31.5.44; 369th (AS) Sqn; RiW, London Midland & Scottish Railway workshops 23.7.44; GLUE (9th AF), retd RAF 24.7.44; Later to France in 2.45

BL994 Spitfire F.Vb (Merlin 45); Presentation aircraft 'MANCHESTER GRANDOTEL' (later 'NIGERIA .. PROVINCE'); TOC/RAF 3.42; ex No.133 Sqn - US 8th AF; 4th FG, 336th FS Great Sampford 1.10.42; Retd RAF (RiW, Heston) 21.1.43; Later converted to Seafire Mk.Ib (NX989)

BM117 Spitfire F.Vb (Merlin 45); TOC/RAF 28.2.42; ex No.71 Sqn - US 8th AF; 4th FG Debden, 334th FS 1.10.42; Retd RAF 29.10.42; Later converted to LF.Vb (Merlin 50M)

BM143 Spitfire F.Vb (Merlin 45); TOC/RAF 27.2.42; ex No.71 Sqn - US 8th AF; 4th FG Debden, 334th FS 1.10.42; Retd RAF 29.10.42

BM147 Spitfire F.Vb (Merlin 46); TOC/RAF 8.3.42 - US 8th AF; 67th (Recce) Grp Membury 17.10.43; No.3501 SU 2.11.43; Retd RAF (scrapped 9.47)

BM181 Spitfire F.Vb (Merlin 45); TOC/RAF 22.3.42 - US 8th AF; 67th (Recce) Grp Membury 23.6.43; 107th Sqn ('AX-D') 18.7.43; Retd RAF (RiW, Morris) 21.1.44; SOXO (8th AF), delete inventory 1.2.44

BM190 Spitfire LF.Vb (Merlin 45M); TOC/RAF 9.3.42 - US 9th AF; 67th (TR) Grp Middle Wallop 9.5.44; SOXO, diverted to US Navy VCS-7 at Lee-on-Solent ("L-09") 29.5.44; Retd RAF (CGS via No.9 MU) 30.9.44.

BM193 Spitfire F.Vb (Merlin 45); TOC/RAF 10.3.42; ex No.71 Sqn - US 8th AF; 4th FG Debden, 334th FS 1.10.42; On convoy patrol, engine failed, exploded 10m E of Harwich, dived into sea, Cat.FB/E 20.10.42 (1/Lt AJ Seaman killed), SOC

BM229 Spitfire F.Vb (Merlin 45); Presentation aircraft 'SILVER BLUE'; TOC/RAF 16.3.42 - US 8th AF, census 31.12.43; "8916" 5.1.44; 67th (TR) Grp 6.1.44; GLUE (9th AF) 20.4.44; RiW, de Havilland 12.6.44; GLUE (9th AF), retd RAF 13.6.44; Later to France in 2.45

BM293 Spitfire F.Vb (Merlin 45); TOC/RAF 25.3.42; ex No.71 Sqn - US 8th AF; 4th FG Debden, 334th FS ('XR-W') 1.10.42; 335th FS ('AV-L'); Retd RAF 2.4.43

BM309 Spitfire F.Vb (Merlin 45); Presentation aircraft 'BOMBAY CITY 3'; TOC/RAF 28.3.42 - US 8th AF; 4th FG Debden, 334th FS ('XR-S'), claimed a FW 190 10m NW of Dunkirk 22.1.43 (2/Lt Robert A Boock); 335th FS ('AV-V') 29.1.43; Retd RAF 6.6.43

BM316 Spitfire LF.Vb (Merlin 45M); TOC/RAF 27.3.42 - US 9th AF; 67th (TR) Grp Middle Wallop 10.5.44; SOXO, diverted to US Navy VCS-7 at Lee-on-Solent ("L-09") 29.5.44; Retd RAF (No.33 MU) 15.7.44

BM318 Spitfire F.Vb (Merlin 46); TOC/RAF 27.3.42 - US 8th AF; 67th (TR) Grp Middle Wallop 26.1.44; Accident at Aldermaston 22.1.44 (Lt WJ Boyle); SOXO ("8916"), 31.1.44; US 9th AF 1.2.44; GLUE, retd RAF 11.6.44 (RiW 20.6.44); Later converted to LF.Vb (Merlin 45M)

BM371 Spitfire F.Vb (Merlin 45); TOC/RAF 1.4.42 - US 8th AF; 31st FG Atcham 24.6.42; 309th FS High Ercall ('WZ-R') 30.6.42; Hit pillbox on approach, lost starboard undercarriage, took off again, landed with port wheel retracted High Ercall, Cat.Ac 30.6.42 (2/Lt B Chandler unhurt); ROS 4.7.42; 309th FS Westhampnett 11.9.42; 67th (Obs) Grp Membury, 107th Sqn, raised tail too soon take-off, nose pecked ground, Cat.A 9.11.42 (2/Lt EL Cook OK); ROS 25.11.42; 109th Sqn 12.7.43; Crashed Cat.B 6.10.43; Retd RAF (RiW) 6.10.43; SOXO (8th AF), delete inventory 1.2.44

BM380 Spitfire F.Vb (Merlin 45); Presentation aircraft 'FAVERSHAM'; TOC/RAF 5.4.42 - US 8th AF; 52nd FG Eglinton 12.7.42; 2nd FS 22.8.42; Accident Goxhill 11.10.42 (Lt RC Newberry); Retd RAF 9.3.43

BM408 Spitfire F.Vb (Merlin 45); TOC/RAF 9.4.42 - US 8th AF; 4th FG Debden, 335th FS 3.2.43; Retd RAF 23.3.43

BM411 Spitfire F.Vb (Merlin 46); TOC/RAF 5.4.42 - US 9th AF; 67th (TR) Grp Middle Wallop 9.5.44; GLUE (9th AF), retd RAF (RiW, de Havilland) 16.6.44; Later as GI No. 5600M to France in 2.46

BM417 Spitfire F.Vb (Merlin 45); TOC/RAF 7.4.42 - US 8th AF; 31st FG Atcham 24.6.42; 308th FS Kenley 1.8.42; 308th FS Westhampnett 24.8.42; SOXO, 67th (Recce) Grp Membury, 12th Sqn ('ZM-H') 12.7.43; Crashed Peasemore, near East Ilsley, Berks, Cat.E 29.7.43 (Capt DR Sherwood killed); Condemned HQ US 8th AF 4.2.44, SOC (scrapped)

BM430 Spitfire F.Vb (Merlin 45); TOC/RAF 6.4.42 - US 9th AF; 67th (TR) Grp Middle Wallop 7.5.44; SOXO, diverted to US Navy VCS-7 at Lee-on-Solent ("L-09") 29.5.44; Retd RAF (No.6 MU) 17.7.44

BM454 Spitfire F.Vb (Merlin 45); TOC/RAF 12.4.42 - US 8th AF; 31st FG Atcham 20.6.42; 309th FS, flying accident Cat.B 28.6.42 (Lt ER Cobb); Retd RAF (RiW) 28.6.42

BM461 Spitfire F.Vb (Merlin 45); TOC/RAF 12.4.42 - US 8th AF; 4th FG Debden, 335th FS ('AV-F') 29.1.43; USAAF Bovingdon, landed downwind and turned violently to avoid hedge Hockley Heath RLG 1.6.43; ROS 8.6.43; 335th FS 1.7.43; 7th (PR) Grp Mount Farm 10.7.43; MI Cat.B 30.9.43; RiW 3.10.43; SOXO (8th AF), delete inventory 1.2.44; GLUE (9th AF) 1.2.44; 31st ATG Grove 9.6.44; Retd RAF 1.7.44; Later to France as GI No. 5593M in 3.46

BM472 Spitfire F.Vb (Merlin 45); TOC/RAF 12.4.42 - US 8th AF; 31st FG Atcham 21.6.42; 308th FS Kenley 4.8.42; Crashed Kenley, Cat.FB/Ac 19.8.42; ROS; 52nd FG from 29.8.42; 31st FG, 308th FS 5.9.42; Retd RAF 12.9.42

BM479 Spitfire F.Vb (Merlin 45); TOC/RAF 13.4.42 - US 8th AF; 52nd FG Eglinton 9.7.42; 2nd FS ('QP-J') 22.8.42;

UNITED STATES OF AMERICA

Accident at Goxhill 3.10.42 (Lt GA Newman Jnr); ROS 13.10.42; 82nd FG Eglinton 21.10.42; Retd RAF 2.3.43; Later to Portugal in 12.43

BM510 Spitfire F.Vb (Merlin 45); TOC/RAF 12.4.42; ex No.71 Sqn - US 8th AF; 4th FG Debden, 334th FS ('XR-A') 1.10.42; Crashed on landing 25.10.42 (Mjr A "Gus" Daymond OK); 335th FS ('AV-F'); Retd RAF 25.3.43

BM511 Spitfire F.Vb (Merlin 45); TOC/RAF 18.4.42 - US 8th AF; 31st FG, 309th FS High Ercall 20.6.42; Dived into ground on night flight, suspected oxygen-failure, Cat.FA/E 16.7.42 (1/Lt HR Kerr killed, buried Cambridge); SOC 25.7.42

BM512 Spitfire F.Vb (Merlin 45); TOC/RAF 13.4.42; SOXO (US 8th AF), census 31.12.43; "8916" 5.1.44; US 9th AF 1.2.44; 67th (TR) Grp, 12th Sqn; Damaged, failed rudder; Retd RAF (RiW); AEAF 13.8.44

BM523 Spitfire F.Vb (Merlin 45); TOC/RAF 16.4.42; ex No.71 Sqn - US 8th AF; 52nd FG Eglinton 9.7.42; 4th FS 28.8.42; 2nd FS, altitude formation combat, engine failed, force landed wheels-up Kenley, Cat.Ac 2.9.42 (2/Lt S Feld OK); ROS 7.9.42; 4th FS Kenley 12.9.42; Retd RAF 8.11.42; Retd USAAF; Accident at Atcham 26.5.43 (Lt GS Wright); SOXO (HQ US 8th AF) 30.8.43; 66th FW 6.9.43; 495th FTG Atcham; Retd RAF 10.10.43; RiW 29.10.43; SOXO, delete inventory 31.10.43

BM526 Spitfire F.Vb (Merlin 46); TOC/RAF 19.4.42 - US 9th AF; 31st ATG Grove 5.6.44; SOXO, diverted to US Navy VCS-7 at Lee-on-Solent ("L-09") 7.6.44; GLUE (9th AF), retd RAF 5.7.44

BM530 Spitfire F.Vb (Merlin 45); TOC/RAF 18.4.42; ex No.133 Sqn - US 8th AF; 4th FG, 336th FS Great Sampford 1.10.42; Heavy landing, undercarriage collapsed Great Sampford, Cat.Ac 24.10.42 (2/Lt DK Cameron OK); ROS 4.11.42; 336th FS 21.11.42; RAF 13.4.43; US 8th AF in 5.43; Retd RAF in 11.43

BM532 Spitfire F.Vb (Merlin 45); TOC/RAF 24.4.42 - US 8th AF; 31st FG Atcham, 307th FS 21.6.42; Crashed at Atcham, Cat.FA/E (Re-Cat.B) 12.7.42 (2/Lt WA Thomas Jnr OK); Retd RAF (RiW, AST) 17.7.42

BM537 Spitfire F.Vb (Merlin 46); TOC/RAF 18.4.42; ex No.133 Sqn - US 8th AF; 4th FG, 336th FS Great Sampford 1.10.42; Crashed Cat.Ac (Re-Cat.B) 31.12.42; Retd RAF (RiW) 14.1.43

BM538 Spitfire F.Vb (Merlin 45); TOC/RAF 18.4.42; ex No.71 Sqn - US 8th AF; 4th FG Debden, 334th FS 1.10.42; Retd RAF (No.401 Sqn) 5.12.42

BM540 Spitfire F.Vb (Merlin 45); TOC/RAF 18.4.42 - US 8th AF; 67th (Recce) Grp Membury 28.6.43; 12th Sqn 1.7.43; MI 3.10.43; Crashed Codford, Wilts, Cat.E 6.11.43 (Lt RP Humphrey); Condemned HQ US 8th AF 12.11.43; SOC (scrapped)

BM559 Spitfire F.Vb (Merlin 45); TOC/RAF 19.4.42 - US 8th AF; 52nd FG Eglinton, 5th FS 6.9.42; Station Flight Eglinton from 13.9.42; Retd RAF 23.10.42; Later converted to Seafire Mk.Ib (NX945)

BM560 Spitfire F.Vb (Merlin 45); TOC/RAF 10.4.42 - US 8th AF; 52nd FG Eglinton 8.7.42; 4th FS 27.8.42; Retd RAF 8.11.42

BM563 Spitfire F.Vb (Merlin 45); TOC/RAF 1.5.42 - US 8th AF; 31st FG Atcham 20.6.42; 307th FS Atcham, hit EN832 from above on approach, Cat.FA/E 10.7.42 (Lt CK Gray RAF injured); SOC 18.7.42

BM564 Spitfire F.Vb (Merlin 45); Presentation aircraft 'LEOPOLDVILLE'; TOC/RAF 19.4.42 - US 8th AF; 4th FG Debden, 335th FS in 3.43; Retd RAF (No.501 Sqn) 4.4.43

BM567 Spitfire F.Vb (Merlin 45); TOC/RAF 19.4.42 - US 8th AF; 52nd FG Eglinton 8.7.42; 4th FS 29.8.42; Retd RAF (332 Sqn) 8.11.42; USAAF Atcham, accident at base 26.12.42 (Lt DE Wilkes); Retd RAF (No.341 & 340 Sqns in 3.43)

BM578 Spitfire F.Vb (Merlin 45); TOC/RAF 19.4.42 - US 8th AF; ex No.121 Sqn - US 8th AF; 4th FG Debden, 335th FS ('AV-Q') 1.10.42; Hit truck on runway on take-off Debden, Cat.Ac 3.1.43 (Lt PM Elington OK); ROS 13.1.43; 335th FS 14.1.43; Retd RAF 23.3.43 (later converted to LF.Vb LR)

BM581 Spitfire F.Vb (Merlin 50); TOC/RAF 26.4.42; ex No.121 Sqn - US 8th AF; 4th FG Debden, 335th FS ('AV-K') 1.10.42; Retd RAF 2.4.43

BM582 Spitfire F.Vb (Merlin 45); TOC/RAF 26.4.42 - US 8th AF; 52nd FG, 5th FS Eglinton 14.7.42; Hit object in flight, Cat.E 27.9.42 (1/Lt GT Keough killed, buried Cambridge), SOC (RAF Mov.card: Cat.E 24.10.42)

BM585 Spitfire F.Vb (Merlin 45); TOC/RAF 1.5.42 - US 8th AF; 31st FG, 309th FS High Ercall 20.6.42; Retd RAF 31.10.42

BM586 Spitfire F.Vb (Merlin 45); TOC/RAF 1.5.42 - US 8th AF; 31st FG, 309th FS High Ercall 20.6.42; Flying accident, Cat.A 11.8.42; Retd RAF 27.10.42

BM587 Spitfire F.Vb (Merlin 45); TOC/RAF 7.5.42 - US 8th AF; 31st FG, 309th FS High Ercall ('WZ-W') 20.6.42; Retd RAF 12.9.42

BM588 Spitfire F.Vb (Merlin 45); Presentation aircraft 'WILLIAM E ROOTES'; TOC/RAF 24.4.42 - US 8th AF; 52nd FG Eglinton 13.7.42; 4th FS Goxhill 27.8.42; RAF 8.11.42; USAAF; 67th (Obs) Grp, accident at Atcham 31.3.43 (Lt WA Marangello); Retd RAF; Later converted to GI No. 5524M

BM590 Spitfire F.Vb (Merlin 45); TOC/RAF 25.4.42; ex No.121 Sqn - US 8th AF; 4th FG Debden, 335th FS ('AV-R', also 'Olga') 1.10.42; 7th (PR) Grp Mount Farm, 13th Sqn 16.8.43; Engine failed on take-off, crashed, burnt out Mount Farm, Cat.E 7.10.43 (Lt VN Luber); SOXO (HQ US 8th AF), condemned 7.10.43, SOC

BM593 Spitfire F.Vb (Merlin 45); TOC/RAF 24.4.42 - US 8th AF; 52nd FG Eglinton 14.7.42; Flying accident, Cat.Ac 25.7.42; ROS; 2nd FS 26.7.42; ROS 18.8.42; RAF 15.10.42; USAAF; 67th (TR) Grp Membury 20.12.43; US 8th AF, census 31.12.43; "8916" 5.1.44; Retd RAF (RiW) 7.2.44; SOXO (8th AF), delete inventory 31.10.44

BM630 Spitfire F.Vb (Merlin 45); TOC/RAF 25.4.42; ex No.121 Sqn - US 8th AF; 4th FG Debden, 335th FS ('AV-B') 1.10.42; 67th (Obs) Grp Membury, 109th Sqn, main bearing failed, wheels-up landing, Cat.Ac 20.4.43 (Lt RV Hearn); ROS 23.4.43; 109th Sqn in 7.43; No.906 Grp (2909) 21.8.43; SOXO (8th AF), delete inventory 1.2.44; GLUE (9th AF) received 25.2.44; USAAF Bottisham, accident at Tuddenham 25.2.44 (Lt JM Todd); Retd RAF 26.7.44

BM635 Spitfire F.Vb (Merlin 46); TOC/RAF 7.5.42 - US 8th AF; 31st FG, 309th FS High Ercall ('WZ-Y') 21.6.42; Flying accident, Cat.B 29.6.42 (Lt DE Shafer Jnr); RAF (RiW) 7.42; 67th (Obs) Grp Membury, 12th Sqn, ran off runway into soft ground, tipped on nose, Cat.A 2.11.42 (1/Lt GH Woodrow OK); SOXO, 67th (Recce) Grp Membury, 109th Sqn 8.7.43; Retd RAF (RiW) 1.11.43; SOXO (8th AF), delete inventory 1.2.44

BM636 Spitfire F.Vb (Merlin 45); TOC/RAF 9.5.42 - US 8th AF; 31st FG Atcham 21.6.42; HQ US 8th AF (FC) 21.10.42; USAAF Kings Cliffe, flying accident at base, Cat.Ac 14.12.42 (Lt GE Sanford); ROS 17.12.42; US 8th AF 17.3.43; Retd RAF 27.3.43

BM637 Spitfire F.Vb (Merlin 45); TOC/RAF 10.5.42 - US 8th AF; 52nd FG Eglinton 11.7.42; 2nd FS 22.8.42; 67th (Obs) Grp Membury, 153rd Sqn, undercarriage collapsed taxying Keevil, Cat.B 17.3.43 (2/Lt OF Harlan OK); Retd RAF 23.3.43; Later converted to GI No. 3688M in 4.43

BP860 Spitfire F.Vc/trop (Merlin 46); TOC/RAF 24.2.42; NWA 1.5.43 - US 12th AF 31.10.43; Retd RAF 15.3.45

BP959 Spitfire F.Vc/trop (Merlin 46); TOC/RAF 23.3.42; NAASC 1.11.43 - US 12th AF; SOXO (8th AF) diverted to French ("L-09") 10.5.45; possibly to France later

BP975 Spitfire F.Vc/trop (Merlin 46); TOC/RAF 3.4.42; NWA 31.8.43 - US 12th AF 31.8.43; Retd RAF 26.4.45, SOC

BR130 Spitfire F.Vc/trop (Merlin 46); TOC/RAF 29.3.42; NWA 1.10.43 - US 12th AF in 10.43; Diverted to French unit 1.10.43; Retd RAF 31.10.43; Later via No.352 Sqn to Yugoslavia (No 9478) in 5.45

BR387 Spitfire F.Vc/trop (Merlin 46); TOC/RAF 10.5.42; Malta 1.6.42; FAF, GR II/33 from 2.5.44 to 31.12.44 - US 8th

Spitfire F.Vb BM635 WZ-Y of the 309th Sqn, 31st FG, High Ercall, in 1942. [P H T. Green]

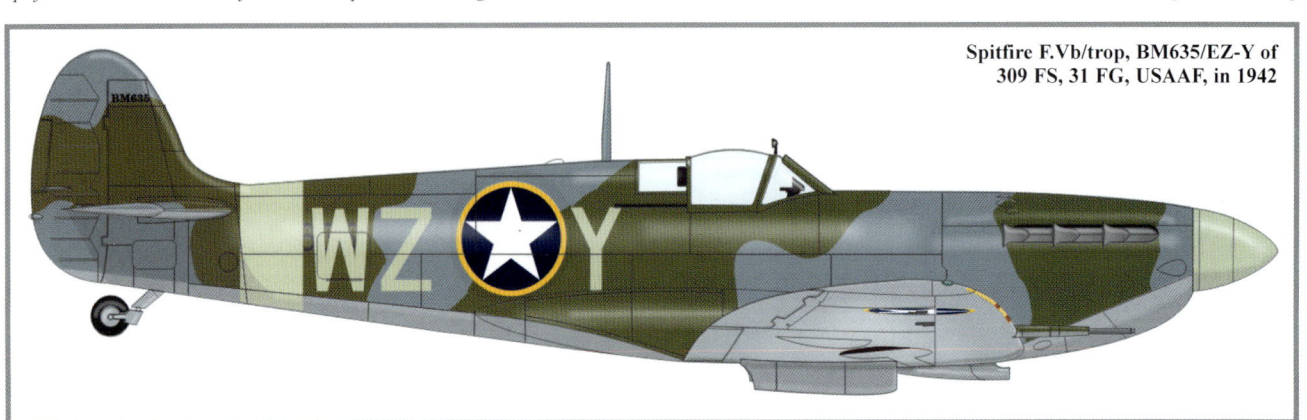

Spitfire F.Vb/trop, BM635/EZ-Y of 309 FS, 31 FG, USAAF, in 1942

       AF; SOXO (8th AF), diverted to French ("L-09") 10.5.45; Retd RAF, SOC 12.7.45

BR565 Spitfire F.Vc/trop (Merlin 46); TOC/RAF 16.5.42; NWA 1.10.43 - US 12th AF 1.10.43; RAF 31.10.43 - US 12th AF 30.11.43; Retd RAF 15.3.44

BR601 Spitfire F.IX; ex SAAF; Ex Thruxton, England 9.90; Arrived as **SURVIVOR** only, to Harry Stenger Facility, Bartow, Florida (Jet Cap Aviation) for restoration; Extant

BS161 Spitfire F.Vc/trop (Merlin 46); TOC/RAF 20.6.42; Malta 3.8.42 - US 12th AF 31.8.43; Fate unknown

BS344 Spitfire F.IXc (Merlin 61); TOC/RAF 24.9.42; NWA 28.2.43; French (No.326 Sqn) 1.8.44, arr. U.K. 28.1.45 - US 8th AF; SOXO, diverted to French ("L-09") 10.5.45; Retd RAF (RiW), AW/CN 6.6.45; Later with Merlin 63 to South Africa in 1947

EE664 Spitfire F.Vc/trop (Merlin 46); TOC/RAF 19.10.42; NWA 31.5.43 - US 12th AF 31.7.43; Retd RAF 15.3.45

EE784 Spitfire F.Vc/trop (Merlin 46); TOC/RAF 14.12.42; M.E. 18.4.43 - US 12th AF 31.1.44; Retd RAF 31.1.45

EE793 Spitfire F.Vc/trop (Merlin 46); TOC/RAF 24.12.42; Arr Takoradi 10.3.43, to M.E. - US 12th AF; 52nd FG; La Sebala, accident at base, Cat.FA/E 26.5.43 (Lt WR Joy), SOC
NOTE: Reported "JK795", but this operated over ETO

EE794 Spitfire F.Vc/trop (Merlin 56); TOC/RAF 24.12.42; NWA 31.5.43 - US 12th AF 31.7.43; Fate unknown

EE858 Spitfire F.Vc/trop (Merlin 45); TOC/RAF 23.1.43; NWA 31.3.43 - US 12th AF 31.10.43; Retd RAF 29.2.44

EE865 Spitfire F.Vc/trop (Merlin 45); TOC/RAF 4.2.43; NAASC 1.11.43 - US 12th AF 29.2.44; Retd RAF 31.5.44; Later to Turkey in 11.44

EF526 Spitfire F.Vc/trop (Merlin 45); TOC/RAF 2.2.43; NWA 30.4.43 - US 12th AF 29.2.44; Retd RAF 25.2.45

EF529 Spitfire F.Vc/trop (Merlin 45); TOC/RAF 5.2.43; NWA 31.5.43 - US 12th AF 31.8.43; N.A. in 2.44; Fate unknown

EF538 Spitfire F.Vc/trop (Merlin 45); TOC/RAF 9.2.43; NWA 31.7.43 - US 12th AF 31.7.43; Retd RAF 31.10.43; Later to FFAF

EF540 Spitfire F.Vc/trop (Merlin 45); TOC/RAF 8.2.43; NWA 31.5.43 - US 12th AF 31.1.44; Crashed Cat.FA/3 26.1.45, SOC

EF568 Spitfire F.Vc/trop (Merlin 45); TOC/RAF 1.3.43; NWA 31.5.43 - US 12th AF 31.12.43; Fate unknown

EF585 Spitfire F.Vc/trop (Merlin 45); TOC/RAF 1.3.43; To Malta, disembarked Gozo for US 12th AF 1.8.43; Retd RAF 31.10.43

EF586 Spitfire F.Vc/trop (Merlin 46); TOC/RAF 1.3.43; Casablanca 25.4.43 – US 12th AF (DUKO) 8.7.44; MAAF to ME 15.3.45; Crashed, Cat.E 27.9.45, SOC

EF592 Spitfire F.Vc/trop (Merlin 46); TOC/RAF 8.3.43; NWA 31.7.43 - US 12th AF 31.7.43; Fate unknown

EF600 Spitfire F.Vc/trop (Merlin 50); TOC/RAF 15.3.43; NWA 31.5.43 - US 12th AF 31.7.43; Fate unknown

EF602 Spitfire F.Vc/trop (Merlin 50); TOC/RAF 13.3.43; NWA 31.5.43; FFAF from 6.43 to 9.43 - US 12th AF 30.11.43;

UNITED STATES OF AMERICA

EF614   to FAF (CIC Meknes), Accident 18.7.44
EF614   Spitfire F.Vc/trop (Merlin 45); TOC/RAF 22.3.43; NWA 31.5.43 - US 12th AF ("USAAC") 31.7.43; Retd RAF 1.10.43, SOC
EF632   Spitfire F.Vc/trop (Merlin 46); TOC/RAF 29.3.43; Arr Casablanca 17.5.43 - US 12th AF; 31st FG, 309th FS ('WZ-W'), while stationery hit by ER165 of 308th FS, killing 2 fitters, aerodrome '*Banjo*' (Gozo), wrecked Cat.E 30.6.43 (Lt GB Stevens Jnr), SOC
EF647   Spitfire F.Vc/trop (Merlin 50); TOC/RAF 14.4.43; NAASC 31.10.43 - US 12th AF; 52nd FG Corsica 30.11.43; Missing over Italy, Cat.FB/E 9.2.44, SOC
EF679   Spitfire F.Vc/trop (Merlin 50); TOC/RAF 29.5.43; NWA 1.10.43 - US 12th AF; 52nd FG Sicily 1.10.43; Missing, Cat.FB/E 24.1.44 (1/Lt HO Schellhase of 2nd FS or 2/Lt TE Watts of 4th FS killed), SOC
EF691   Spitfire F.Vc/trop (Merlin 50); TOC/RAF 7.6.43; Casablanca 14.7.43 - US 12th AF; 52nd FG 12.43; Missing over Italy, Cat.FB/E 19.12.43; SOC 29.2.44
EF693   Spitfire F.Vc/trop (Merlin 50); TOC/RAF 9.6.43; NWA 1.10.43 - US 12th AF; 52nd FG 1.10.43; Missing over Italy, Cat.FB/E 7.2.44 (Lt WB Canning), SOC
EF698   Spitfire F.Vc/trop (Merlin 55); TOC/RAF 22.6.43; N.A. 30.11.43 - US 12th AF 31.1.44; SOC 31.8.44
EF699   Spitfire F.Vc/trop (Merlin 55); TOC/RAF 22.6.43; N.A. 31.1.44 - US 12th AF 31.1.44; SOC 30.6.44
EF700   Spitfire F.Vc/trop (Merlin 55); TOC/RAF 22.6.43; NAASC 31.10.43 - US 12th AF; 52nd FG Corsica 31.1.44; Missing, Cat.FB/E 19.2.44, SOC
EF701   Spitfire F.Vc/trop (Merlin 55); TOC/RAF 22.6.43; N.A. 30.11.43 - US 12th AF 31.1.44; Retd RAF 31.5.44
EF703   Spitfire F.Vc/trop (Merlin 55); TOC/RAF 28.6.43; NAASC 31.10.43 - US 12th AF; 52nd FG Corsica 31.1.44; 5th FS, leading flight over Italian coast, bounced by FW 190, shot down into sea, Cat.FB/E 19.3.44 (Capt EG Steinbrenner DFC killed), SOC
EF704   Spitfire F.Vc/trop (Merlin 55); TOC/RAF 28.6.43; NAASC 31.10.43 - US 12th AF; 52nd FG Corsica 29.2.44; Retd RAF (MAAF) 25.2.45
EF706   Spitfire F.Vc/trop (Merlin 55); TOC/RAF 9.7.43; N.A. 30.11.43 - US 12th AF 31.1.44; 63rd FW; 52nd FG; Retd RAF 31.5.44
EF707   Spitfire F.Vc/trop (Merlin 55); TOC/RAF 13.7.43; N.A. 30.11.43 - US 12th AF; 52nd FG 5th FS Corsica 31.1.44; Brought down by AA, Cat.FB/E 19.2.44 (2/Lt SH Cooper), SOC
EF708   Spitfire F.Vc/trop (Merlin 55); TOC/RAF 13.7.43; NWA 1.10.43 - US 12th AF 31.12.43; Retd RAF 31.5.44
EF709   Spitfire F.Vc/trop (Merlin 55); TOC/RAF 16.7.43; N.A. 30.11.43 - US 12th AF 31.1.44; Retd RAF 28.4.45, SOC
EF710   Spitfire F.Vc/trop (Merlin 55); TOC/RAF 16.7.43; N.A. 30.11.43 - US 12th AF; 52nd FG Corsica 31.1.44; Missing, Cat.FB/E 19.2.44, SOC
EF716   Spitfire F.Vc/trop (Merlin 55); TOC/RAF 29.7.43; NAASC 31.10.43 - US 12th AF 29.2.44; Retd RAF in 1944 (No.326.Sqn, ditched 11.6.44)
EF717   Spitfire F.Vc/trop (Merlin 55); TOC/RAF 4.8.43; N.A. 30.11.43 - US 12th AF 31.1.44; Retd RAF 31.5.44
EF724   Spitfire F.Vc/trop (Merlin 55); TOC/RAF 17.8.43; NAASC 31.10.43 - US 12th AF 29.2.44; Retd RAF; SOC 26.4.45
EF726   Spitfire LF.Vc/trop (Merlin 55M); TOC/RAF 21.8.43; NAASC 31.10.43 - US 12th AF 29.2.44; Retd RAF; SOC 26.4.45
EF727   Spitfire F.Vc/trop (Merlin 55); TOC/RAF 24.8.43; NAASC 31.10.43 - US 12th AF 29.2.44; Retd RAF; Later via No.352 Sqn to Yugoslavia (No.*9488*) 18.5.45
EF728   Spitfire F.Vc/trop (Merlin 55); TOC/RAF 2.9.43; NAASC 31.10.43 - US 12th AF 29.2.44; Later to SAAF, No.40 Sqn, crashed Cat.FB/3 6.3.44, SOC
EF729   Spitfire F.Vc/trop (Merlin 55); TOC/RAF 31.8.43; NAASC 31.10.43 - US 12th AF 29.2.44; Retd RAF; SOC 30.6.44
EF730   Spitfire F.Vc/trop (Merlin 55); TOC/RAF 2.9.43; NAASC 31.10.43 - US 12th AF 29.2.44; Retd RAF; SOC 30.6.45
EF732   Spitfire F.Vc/trop (Merlin 55); TOC/RAF 2.9.43; NAASC 31.10.43 - US 12th AF 29.2.44; Later to SAAF, No.40 Sqn, crashed Cat. FB/3 28.7.44, SOC
EF733   Spitfire F.Vc/trop (Merlin 55); TOC/RAF 2.9.43; NAASC 31.10.43 - US 12th AF 29.2.44; Retd RAF (MAAF Census in 6.45); Training Delegation 4.10.45; To France 11.45
EF734   Spitfire F.Vc/trop (Merlin 55); TOC/RAF 7.9.43; Casablanca 19.10.43 - US 12th AF 29.2.44; Retd RAF 21.6.45
EF735   Spitfire F.Vc/trop (Merlin 55); TOC/RAF 8.9.43; NAASC 31.10.43 - US 12th AF 29.2.44; Retd RAF; SOC 26.4.45
EF736   Spitfire F.Vc/trop (Merlin 55); TOC/RAF 11.9.43; N.A. 30.11.43 - US 12th AF 29.2.44; To FAF (GR 2/33) in 5.44 (belly-landed 9.11.44); Then to R&SU
EF738   Spitfire F.Vc/trop (Merlin 55); TOC/RAF 17.9.43; N.A. 30.11.43 - US 12th AF 29.2.44; Later to SAAF, No.40 Sqn, crashed Cat.FB/3 13.6.44, SOC
EF739   Spitfire F.Vc/trop (Merlin 55); TOC/RAF 28.9.43; N.A. 30.11.43 - US 12th AF 29.2.44; Fate unknown
EF740   Spitfire F.Vc/trop (Merlin 55); TOC/RAF 1.10.43; Casablanca 29.11.43 - US 12th AF 29.2.44; Retd RAF in 1944 (No.253 Sqn missing 11.5.44)
EF741   Spitfire F.Vc/trop (Merlin 55); TOC/RAF 5.10.43; Casablanca 29.11.43 - US 12th AF; 52nd FG 29.2.44; Hit by AA over Italy, Cat.FB/E 15.3.44 (1/Lt AB Tower PoW), SOC
EF742   Spitfire F.Vc/trop (Merlin 55); TOC/RAF 5.10.43; Casablanca 29.11.43 - US 12th AF 29.2.44; Retd RAF 28.12.44
EF743   Spitfire F.Vc/trop (Merlin 55); TOC/RAF 5.10.43; Casablanca 29.11.43 - US 12th AF 29.2.44; Retd RAF (MAAF); Later to France 14.2.46
EF744   Spitfire F.Vc/trop (Merlin 55); TOC/RAF 7.10.43; N.A. 30.11.43 - US 12th AF 29.2.44; Retd RAF 31.1.45
EF745   Spitfire F.Vc/trop (Merlin 55); TOC/RAF 7.10.43; Casablanca 29.11.43 - US 12th AF 29.2.44; Retd RAF 31.5.44; Later to France in 9.47
EF746   Spitfire F.Vc/trop (Merlin 55); TOC/RAF 12.10.43; Casablanca 29.11.43 - US 12th AF; 52nd FG Corsica 29.2.44; Missing, Cat.FB/E 29.2.44, SOC
EF747   Spitfire F.Vc/trop (Merlin 55); TOC/RAF 13.10.43; Casablanca 29.11.43 - US 12th AF 29.2.44; Retd RAF 31.5.44
EF748   Spitfire F.Vc/trop (Merlin 55); TOC/RAF 19.10.43; Casablanca 29.11.43 - US 12th AF 29.2.44; Retd RAF; SOC 30.6.45
EF749   Spitfire LF.Vc/trop (Merlin 55M); TOC/RAF 19.10.43; Casablanca 22.12.43 - US 12th AF 29.2.44; 52nd FG, 5th FS ('VF-R'), air combat, hit by 20 mm shell from a Bf 109 (date unknown); Retd RAF 31.5.44
EF750   Spitfire LF.Vc/trop (Merlin 55M); TOC/RAF 22.10.43; Casablanca 22.12.43 - US 12th AF 29.2.44; Retd RAF (M.E.); SOC 22.3.45
EF751   Spitfire LF.Vc/trop (Merlin 55M); TOC/RAF 26.10.43; Casablanca 22.12.43 - US 12th AF; 52nd FG 5th FS Corsica 29.2.44; Shot down in sea, Cat.FB/E 17.3.44, SOC
EF753   Spitfire LF.Vc/trop (Merlin 55M); TOC/RAF 5.11.43; Casablanca 22.12.43 - US 12th AF 29.2.44; Fate unknown
EN125   Spitfire F.IXc (Merlin 61); TOC/RAF 8.11.42 - US 8th AF; 4th FG Debden, 336th FS 8.11.42; Retd RAF 22.11.42
EN126   Spitfire F.IXc (Merlin 61); TOC/RAF 8.11.42 - US 8th AF; 4th FG Debden, 336th FS 8.11.42; Retd RAF 22.11.42
EN127   Spitfire F.IXc (Merlin 61); TOC/RAF 8.11.42 - US 8th AF; 4th FG Debden, 336th FS 8.11.42; Retd RAF 26.11.42
EN143   Spitfire F.IXc (Merlin 61); TOC/RAF 5.12.42; M.E. 30.10.43; NAAF 1.11.43 - US 12th AF; 31st FG, 308th FS 1944; Retd RAF in 1944; Later to Greece in 5.47
EN145   Spitfire F.IXc (Merlin 61); TOC/RAF 6.12.42; Arr Gibraltar 13.1.43, NWA - US 12th AF; 52nd FG Gedim, accident at base 23.4.43 (Lt LM Trowbridge); Retd RAF;

Later to Italy (*MM4116*), then to Israel (No *20-78*); Displayed at Hatzerim AF Museum; Recently to Peter Arnold, Newport Pagnell, Buckinghamshire, England – **SURVIVOR**

EN180 Spitfire F.IXc (Merlin 61); Presentation aircraft '*ALDABRA*'; TOC/RAF 17.11.42 - US 8th AF; 4th FG Debden, 336th FS 17.11.42; Retd RAF 22.11.42

EN181 Spitfire F.IXc (Merlin 61); TOC/RAF 17.11.42 - US 8th AF; 4th FG Debden, 336th FS 17.11.42; Retd RAF 22.11.42

EN182 Spitfire F.IXc (Merlin 61); TOC/RAF 17.11.42 - US 8th AF; 4th FG Debden, 336th FS 17.11.42; Retd RAF 22.11.42

EN183 Spitfire F.IXc (Merlin 61); TOC/RAF 17.11.42 - US 8th AF; 4th FG Debden, 336th FS 17.11.42; Retd RAF 26.11.42

EN184 Spitfire F.IXc (Merlin 61); TOC/RAF 17.11.42 - US 8th AF; 4th FG Debden, 336th FS 17.11.42; Retd RAF 23.11.42

EN185 Spitfire F.IXc (Merlin 61); TOC/RAF 17.11.42 - US 8th AF; 4th FG Debden, 336th FS 17.11.42; Retd RAF 23.11.42

EN201 Spitfire F.IXc (Merlin 61); TOC/RAF 1.12.42; NWA 28.2.43 - US 12th AF 31.10.43; Retd RAF (MAAF); Census 6.45; SOC 13.9.45

EN202 Spitfire F IXc (Merlin 61); TOC/RAF 1.12.42; NWA 28.2.43 - US 12th AF 1943; Later to SAAF 1944; Retd RAF (MAAF Census 6.45); SOC 14.3.46

EN207 Spitfire F.IXc (Merlin 61); TOC/RAF 6.12.42; NWA 28.2.43 - US 12th AF; 31st FG, 309th FS Westhampnett ('WZ-GG') 31.8.43, also with 309th FS 1.12.43 - 13.1.44; Fate unknown

EN249 Spitfire F.IXc (Merlin 61); TOC/RAF 21.12.42; NWA 31.3.43 - US 12th AF; 31st FG, 309th FS Westhampnett ('WZ-XX') in 10.43 (and by 13.12.43); Retd RAF; SOC 10.44

EN255 Spitfire F.IXc (Merlin 61); TOC/RAF 12.1.43; NWA 31.3.43 - US 12th AF; 31st FG Italy 9.43; Shot down into sea near Nettuno by AA, Cat.FB/E 19.11.43 (Lt Van Natta PoW); HQ 12AF, condemned 19.11.43, SOC

EN302 Spitfire F.IXc (Merlin 61); TOC/RAF 23.12.42; NWA 31.3.43 - US 12th AF in 10.43; Retd RAF 31.12.43

EN307 Spitfire F.IXc (Merlin 61); TOC/RAF 29.12.42; NWA 31.3.43 - US 12th AF; 31st FG, 307th FS ('MX-D') 10.43; Radioed he was flying on the deck and doubted he would make it back, force-landed, Italy, Cat.FB/E 15.12.43 (Lt Walker), SOC

EN345 Spitfire F.IXc (Merlin 61); TOC/RAF 2.2.43; NWA 31.5.43 - US 12th AF 31.7.43; Retd RAF 28.2.45; Later to South Africa 1949

EN354 Spitfire F.IXc (Merlin 61); TOC/RAF 29.1.43; NWA 31.3.43 - US 12th AF; 52nd FG, 4th FS ('WD-W') in 9.43; Retd RAF; SOC 15.3.45

EN369 Spitfire F.IXc (Merlin 63); TOC/RAF 1.2.43; NWA 31.3.43 - US 12th AF; 31st FG, 309th FS ('WZ-KK') 31.1.44; Retd RAF 29.2.44
NOTE: Incorrectly "EN639" ('WZ-KK') recorded by 309th (US) Sqn 12.11. and 2.12.43

EN430 Spitfire PR.XI (Merlin 61); TOC/RAF 13.4.43; dis. MAC, ferry flight 5.5.43 - US 12th AF; 31st FG in 6.43; Retd RAF 1944; Later MAAF in 1945; SOC 27.3.47

EN453 Spitfire F.IXc (Merlin 61); TOC/RAF 21.1.43; NWA 30.4.43 - US 12th AF; 31st FG, 309th FS ('WZ-BB') 31.10.43 (also by 11.1.44); Retd RAF in 1944; Later to the SAAF

EN460 Spitfire F.IXc (Merlin 61); TOC/RAF 3.2.43; NWA 31.5.43 - US 12th AF; 31st FG, 309th FS ('WZ-YY') in 10.43, also by 5.2.44; Retd RAF (MAAF census 6.45); SOC 26.8.45

EN463 Spitfire F.IXc (Merlin 61); TOC/RAF 2.2.43; NWA 31.3.43 - US 12th AF in 9.43; Retd RAF 1.10.43

EN474 Spitfire F.VIIc (Merlin 64); Became: **FE.400**; TOC/RAF 13.3.43; No.47 MU RAF Sealand, Cheshire, for packing 13.3.43; Shipped to USA with SS G*lena* 10.4.43; Arr New York 2.5.43; Allocated US Serial No."FE.400" (Foreign Equipment inventory); To Technical Data Laboratory of Material Command (TDLMC) at Dayton in 5.43; Tested at Wright Field, Dayton, Ohio; Issued to HQ transfer 6.1.45; To Freeman Field, Indiana 1946; To the National Air Museum in 1947, storage at Park Ridge, Illinois (O'Hare airport) until early 1950's, then to Silver Hill, Maryland (near Washington) 1952; From 1969 displayed in its 1943 camouflage, later repainted and restored with its original Merlin 64 for the National Air & Space Museum, Washington DC (Smithsonian Institution), on display and extant – **SURVIVOR**
NOTE: Delivered and flown with extended wingtips; Reported also US Serial No."161.522"

Replacement for the 4th Sqn, 52nd FG, Spitfire F.IXc EN354 'WD-W' at Le Sebala airfield in Tunisia, June 1943. Note the marking "Doris fume it" on the nose.
[James Crow]

Surviving Spitfire F.VIIc EN474 was shipped to the USA in 1943 for evaluation. It was retained after World War II for museum purposes and is seen here, still in RAF colours but somewhat weathered, at Silver Hill, Washington, in June 1972. It is extant in the National Air & Space Museum, Washington, DC.
[PRA]

EN476 Spitfire F.IXc (Merlin 63); TOC/RAF 16.2.43; Arr Gibraltar 12.4.43 - US 12th AF 31.1.44; Retd RAF; SOC 23.12.44

EN492 Spitfire F.IXc (Merlin 63A); TOC/RAF 1.3.43; N.A. 30.11.43 - US 12th AF 31.1.44; Fate unknown

EN564 Spitfire LF.IXc (Merlin 66); TOC/RAF 1.3.43 - US 8th AF; 67th (Recce) Grp, 12th Sqn 7.43; Shot down in air combat with FW 190 of JG2 over Bernay, France, Cat.FB/E 14.7.43 (Capt JR Walker killed, named on Wall of Missing at Cambridge), SOC

EN766 Spitfire F.Vb (Merlin 46); TOC/RAF 28.4.42 - US 8th AF; 52nd FG Eglinton, 2nd FS 11.7.42; Ground collision with AR435, Cat.A 28.7.42; ROS; 2nd FS 22.8.42; ROS 2.11.42; 82nd FG Eglinton 7.11.42; 67th (Obs) Grp Membury, 153rd Sqn, hit lorry which was parked on runway, swung, undercarriage collapsed at Keevil, Cat.A 1.12.42 (1/Lt EW Hansen OK); ROS 7.12.42; 82nd FG 27.2.43; 67th (Recce) Grp 6.7.43; 153rd Sqn, crashed Cat.B (date unknown); Retd RAF (RiW 11.1.44); AW/CN 13.3.44

EN768 Spitfire F.Vb (Merlin 45); TOC/RAF 26.4.42; ex No.121 Sqn - US 8th AF; 4th FG Debden, 335th FS ('AV-W') 15.10.42; Retd RAF 27.3.43

EN772 Spitfire F.Vb (Merlin 45); TOC/RAF 26.4.42 - US 8th AF; 52nd FG Eglinton 9.7.42; 2nd FS 22.8.42; Accident at Atcham 15.1.43 (Lt RV Douglas); Crashed, Cat.E, Shrewsbury, 16.1.43 (Lt GT Parker); SOC 17.1.43

EN776 Spitfire F.Vb (Merlin 45); TOC/RAF 28.4.42 - US 8th AF; 31st FG Atcham, 307th FS 20.6.42; Crashed Cat.FB/B 19.8.42; Retd RAF (RiW) 10.5.43

EN778 Spitfire F.Vb (Merlin 45); TOC/RAF 28.4.42 - US 8th AF; 31st FG, 309th FS High Ercall 21.6.42; Shot down on Dieppe raid, Cat.FB/E 19.8.42 (Lt Collins PoW), SOC

EN783 Spitfire F.Vb (Merlin 46); TOC/RAF 30.4.42; ex No.71 Sqn - US 8th AF; 31st FG Atcham, 308th FS 15.7.42; 309th FS Westhampnett 24.8.42; No.71 Sqn RAF 12.9.42; US 4th FG Debden, 334th FS ('XR-K') 1.10.42; 335th FS ('AV-D'); Retd RAF 30.3.43

EN784 Spitfire F.Vb (Merlin 45); TOC/RAF 7.5.42 - US 8th AF; 31st FG Atcham, 308th FS (poss. 'HL-U') 21.6.42; Taxying too fast, ran into parked aircraft at Atcham, Cat.A 9.7.42 (2/Lt HE Daniels OK); Collided with parked aircraft while taxying Atcham, Cat.A 12.7.42 (2/Lt DK Smith OK); Retd RAF 18.8.42

EN792 Spitfire F.Vb (Merlin 45); TOC/RAF 30.4.42 - US 8th AF; 31st FG Atcham 20.6.42; 308th FS Kenley 1.8.42; Shot down during Dieppe raid, Cat.FB/E 19.8.42 (1/Lt RD Ingram PoW, picked up by German boat), SOC

EN793 Spitfire F.Vb (Merlin 46); TOC/RAF 1.5.42; ex No.121 & 133 Sqn - US 8th AF; 4th FG, 336th FS Great Sampford ('MD-L') 1.10.42; *Circus 253*, escorting four Bostons to bomb St.Omer airfield, undercarriage collapsed on landing Debden, Cat.Ac 22.1.43 (Lt BB Leicester OK); ROS 25.1.43; 336th FS Debden 22.2.43; Retd RAF 13.4.43

EN799 Spitfire F.Vb (Merlin 45); TOC/RAF 2.5.42 - US 8th AF; 31st FG Atcham, 307th FS (MX-R) 20.6.42; HQ 8th AF (FC) 21.10.42; 6th TFS 21.10.42; On delivery-flight, crashed Enson Moor, 6m N of Stafford, Cat.B 14.12.42 (Sgt FE Hope injured); Re-Cat.E 15.12.42, SOC 24.12.42

EN823 Spitfire F.Vb (Merlin 45); TOC/RAF 15.5.42 - US 8th AF; 31st FG, 309th FS High Ercall 21.6.42; While stationery, hit by AD274, Cat.B 6.8.42; Retd RAF (RiW) 13.8.42

EN826 Spitfire F.Vb (Merlin 45); TOC/RAF 29.5.42 - US 8th AF; 52nd FG Eglinton, 4th FS in 7.42; Retd RAF 30.7.42

EN832 Spitfire F.Vb (Merlin 45); TOC/RAF 4.5.42 - US 8th AF; 31st FG Atcham 24.6.42; 308th FS, hit from above by BM563 on approach, Cat.FA/E1 10.7.42 (Lt FA Hill OK); SOC 18.7.42

EN833 Spitfire F.Vb (Merlin 45); TOC/RAF 8.5.42 - US 8th AF; 31st FG Atcham 20.6.42; 307th FS; 308th FS, flying accident Cat.FA/B 18.10.42; Retd RAF (RiW) 18.10.42; Later converted to GI No. No.*3414M*

EN834 Spitfire F.Vb (Merlin 45); TOC/RAF 4.5.42 - US 8th AF; 4th FG Debden, 336th FS 4.3.43; USAAF Atcham, accident at base 14.5.43 (Lt BC Wyman); SOXO (8th AF) 23.10.43; To RAF, via No.6 MU to Vickers-Armstrongs 24.12.43; No.9 MU 23.2.44; USAAF, 67th (TR) Grp; SOXO (8th AF), delete inventory 2.4.44; US 9th AF; 31st ATG Grove 9.6.44; Retd RAF (RiW) 19.6.44

EN837 Spitfire F.Vb (Merlin 45); TOC/RAF 7.5.42 - US 8th AF; 31st FG Atcham 20.6.42; US 8th AF HQ (FC) 21.10.42; Retd RAF 4.3.43

EN838 Spitfire F.Vb (Merlin 45); TOC/RAF 8.5.42 - US 8th AF; 31st FG Atcham, 308th FS 20.6.42; Flying accident, Cat.Ac 24.6.42 (Lt SM Lymberis); ROS; 308th FS 10.7.42; ROS 14.7.42; 308th FS 15.7.42; ROS 4.8.42; 308th FS 5.8.42; Undercarriage collapsed landing, Cat.Ac 11.8.42 (1/Lt JB Fleming OK); ROS 15.8.42; 308th FS in 8.42; Structural failure, crashed Arundel Park, Arundel Castle, Cat.E 9.10.42 (Lt WC Ward killed), SOC

EN839 Spitfire F.Vb (Merlin 45); TOC/RAF 14.5.42 - US 8th AF; 31st FG Atcham 20.6.42; 308th FS Kenley 1.8.42; 308th FS Westhampnett 24.8.42; 67th (Obs) Grp Membury, 12th Sqn, engine failure, force-landed wheels-up in field near Mildenhall, Cat.B 2.12.42 (Capt WW Berg OK); Retd RAF (RiW) 16.12.42; Later converted to Seafire Mk.Ib NX925

EN842 Spitfire F.Vb (Merlin 45); TOC/RAF 10.5.42 - US 8th AF; 31st FG Atcham 20.6.42; 308th FS Kenley 1.8.42; 308th FS Westhampnett 24.8.42; Retd RAF 24.10.42

EN847 Spitfire F.Vb (Merlin 45); TOC/RAF 3.5.42 - US 8th AF; 31st FG Atcham 20.6.42; 308th FS, stalled on approach, spun in Atcham, Cat.FA/E 29.6.42 (Lt AW Giacomini died on way to hospital), SOC
NOTE: Reported to be the first US 8th AF casualty in UK

EN848 Spitfire F.Vb (Merlin 45); TOC/RAF 7.5.42 - US 8th AF; 52nd FG Eglinton, 4th FS 12.7.42; Landing collision with R6623, Cat.E 28.7.42 (2/Lt RB Gabriel injured), SOC

EN851 Spitfire F.Vb (Merlin 45); Presentation aircraft '*LIMA CHALLENGER*'; TOC/RAF 7.5.42 - US 8th AF; 31st FG Atcham 20.6.42; 307th FS ('MX-D'); 67th (Obs) Grp Membury, 107th Sqn, overshot landing due to tractor pulling out onto runway, went into pile of sand, nosed over, Cat.A 10.11.42 (2/Lt SE Marsh OK); Retd RAF 16.11.42; Later converted to Seafire Mk.Ib NX952

EN853 Spitfire F.Vb (Merlin 45); TOC/RAF 10.5.42; ex No.121 Sqn - US 8th AF; 4th FG Debden, 335th FS ('AV-D') 1.10.42; *Circus 253*, escorting four Bostons to bomb St.Omer airfield, hit by FW 190, pilot baled out off French coast 22.1.43, Cat.FB/E 23.1.43 (2/Lt CP Grimm kld, buried Cambridge), SOC

EN854 Spitfire F.Vb (Merlin 46); TOC/RAF 7.5.42 - US 8th AF; 31st FG Atcham 20.6.42; HQ US 8th AF (FC) 21.10.42; Retd RAF 9.3.43; Later converted to LF.Vb (LR)

EN855 Spitfire F.Vb (Merlin 45); TOC/RAF 8.5.42 - US 8th AF; 31st FG Atcham 20.6.42; 307th FS, took off 09.55, crashed on Dieppe raid, Cat.FB/E 19.8.42 (2/Lt RG Wright killed, buried Ardennes), SOC

EN860 Spitfire F.Vb (Merlin 45); TOC/RAF 9.5.42 - US 8th AF; 52nd FG Eglinton 9.7.42; Heavy landing, Cat.Ac, Re-Cat.B 29.7.42 (2/Lt EC Smithers OK); Retd RAF (RiW) 29.7.42

EN862 Spitfire F.Vb (Merlin 45); TOC/RAF 8.5.42 - US 8th AF; 52nd FG Eglinton 12.7.42; 2nd FS 22.8.42; SOXO, 67th (Recce) Grp 6.7.43; Crashed Cat.B 6.10.43; Retd RAF (RiW) 6.10.43; SOXO, delete inventory 1.2.44; Later converted to GI No. *5397M* from 17.7.45

EN863 Spitfire F.Vb (Merlin 45); TOC/RAF 10.5.42 - US 8th AF; 31st FG Atcham 21.6.42; 308th FS Kenley 1.8.42; Crashed Cat.FB/Ac 19.8.42; ROS; Westhampnett 24.8.42; Retd RAF (No.38 MU) 27.10.42

EN864 Spitfire F.Vb (Merlin 45); TOC/RAF 9.5.42 - US 8th AF; 31st FG Atcham 20.6.42; 309th FS High Ercall 21.6.42; ROS 24.10.42; 4th FG Debden, 335th FS 8.11.42; 336th FS, Flying accident, Cat.FA/E 23.11.42, Re-Cat.B 15.12.42; RiW; 67th (Obs) Grp, 107th Sqn Membury, crashed, burnt, Great Shefford, Cat.FA/E2 23.5.43 (1/Lt HC Conner), SOC 23.5.43

EN867 Spitfire F.Vb (Merlin 45); TOC/RAF in 5.42 - US 8th AF; 4th FG Debden; Atcham 20.6.42; 336th Sqn, landing collision with Beaufighter X7924 at Coltishall, Cat.FA/E 23.11.42 (Lt CM Kirschner); bboc, later converted to Seafire Mk.Ib (NX962). NOTE: Also reported crashed Hendon 4.12.42 (Lt WC Wren)

EN890 Spitfire F.Vb (Merlin 45); TOC/RAF 14.5.42 - US 8th AF; 31st FG Atcham, 307th FS in 7.42; Retd RAF 16.3.43; Later converted to Seafire (NX909)

EN894 Spitfire F.Vb (Merlin 45); TOC/RAF 13.5.42 - US 8th AF; 52nd FG Eglinton 9.7.42; 4th FS 27.8.42; Crashed Membury 22.1.43 (Lt T Martin); Re-Cat.Ac 6.2.43; ROS 18.2.43; USAAF Eglinton 15.3.43; 67th (Obs) Grp, accident at Membury 15.5.43 (Lt JT Riggins); Retd RAF 19.5.43

EN897 Spitfire F.Vb (Merlin 45); TOC/RAF 16.5.42 - US 8th AF; 31st FG Atcham 22.6.42; HQ US 8th (FC) 21.10.42; ROS 25.10.42; HQ 8th AF (FC) in 11.42; ROS 19.2.43; HQ 8th (FC) 24.3.43; SOXO No."8672" on 6.7.43; MI 29.9.43; Retd RAF (RiW) 10.10.43

EN899 Spitfire F.Vb (Merlin 45); TOC/RAF 9.5.42; No.71 Sqn 2.6.42 - US 8th AF; 52nd FG Eglinton 11.7.42; Retd RAF (No.501 Sqn) 4.4.43

EN900 Spitfire F.Vb (Merlin 45); TOC/RAF 10.5.42 - US 8th AF; 4th FG Debden, 334th FS ('XR-J') 7.12.42; 336th FS in 4.43; ROS 6.9.43; 334th FS Debden 6.9.43; USAAF Atcham, accident at base 1.3.44 (Lt RF Hilse); SOXO (8th AF), retd RAF 10.7.44

EN902 Spitfire F.Vb (Merlin 45); TOC/RAF 14.5.42 - US 8th AF; 31st FG Atcham, 307th FS 21.6.42; Undershot, wheels hit edge of runway, tyre burst, Cat.B 28.7.42 (2/Lt Robinson OK); Retd RAF (RiW) 5.8.42

EN903 Spitfire F.Vb (Merlin 45); TOC/RAF 10.5.42 - US 8th AF; 31st FG Atcham 20.6.42; 308th FS Kenley 1.8.42; Westhampnett 24.8.42; Retd RAF 27.10.42; Later to Portugal as LF.Vb in 6.47

EN904 Spitfire F.Vb (Merlin 45); TOC/RAF 21.5.42 - US 8th AF (SOXO), allotted 7.11.43, arr 15.11.43; 7th (PR) Grp Mount Farm 15.11.43; Accident Mount Farm 20.12.43 (Lt JA McGlynn Jnr); Accident 2.8.44 (Lt PA Balogh); Crashed Cat.E 26.3.45, SOC

EN909 Spitfire F.Vb (Merlin 45); TOC/RAF 14.5.42 - US 8th AF; 31st FG, 309th FS High Ercall 21.6.42; Spun in, Westhampnett, Cat.E 1.10.42 (Capt W L Chambers killed), SOC

Spitfire F.Vb EN851 'MX-D' of the 307th FS, 31st FG was a presentation aircraft named 'LIMA CHALLENGER', being one of three donated by a Mr. H L Woodhouse of Lima, Peru. It is seen here at Merston around July-August 1942, the pilot being Lt R Hooten. [via R C B Ashworth]

UNITED STATES OF AMERICA

EN913 Spitfire F.Vb (Merlin 45); TOC/RAF 14.5.42 - US 8th AF; 31st FG, 309th FS High Ercall 21.6.42; Retd RAF (No.39 MU) 26.10.42; Later converted to GI No. *5380M*

EN915 Spitfire F.Vb (Merlin 45); Presentation aircraft '*S.M.M.T.*'; TOC/RAF 17.5.42, ex No.71 Sqn - US 8th AF; 4th FG Debden, 334th FS ('XR-I') 1.10.42; Mid-air collision with W3636 over Debden on operational flight, crashed on landing, Cat.FB/Ac 26.11.42 (Col JC Harrington OK); ROS 1.12.42; 336th FS, crashed on landing at Bradwell Bay 14.1.43 (2/Lt J Mitchellweis); RiW; 336th FS (sic), possibly 335th FS Debden 26.1.43; RiW 13.4.43; TFU Defford 1.10.43; Dived into ground, pilot baled out, Cat.FA/E 1.2.45, SOC

EN918 Spitfire F.Vb (Merlin 45); TOC/RAF 15.5.42; ex No.121 Sqn - US 8th AF; 4th FG Debden, 335th FS ('AV-X') 1.10.42; Crashed, overturned 14.1.43; Hit by AA from a ship, crashed in sea off Walcheren, Netherlands, Cat.FB/E 5.2.43 (Capt WP Kelly killed, buried Netherlands), SOC

EN920 Spitfire F.Vb (Merlin 45); TOC/RAF 15.5.42 - US 8th AF; 31st FG Atcham 21.6.42; Attd No.131 Sqn RAF, collided with lorry on take-off Merston, Cat.B 28.7.42; Retd RAF 31.7.42; Re-Cat.E and SOC 8.8.42

EN921 Spitfire F.Vb (Merlin 45); TOC/RAF 14.5.42 - US 8th AF; 31st FG, 309th FS High Ercall 21.6.42; Good landing, tailwheel caught in steel mesh of runway, Merston, Cat.B 21.7.42 (Lt Col AP Clark OK); ROS 24.7.42; Retd 309th FS 7.8.42; Retd RAF (No.412 Sqn) 3.9.42

EN923 Spitfire F.Vb (Merlin 45); TOC/RAF 16.5.42 - US 8th AF; 31st FG Atcham 22.6.42; Flying accident, Cat.FA/B 29.6.42; 309th FS 30.6.42; Retd RAF 8.7.42; Later to Soviet Union (Russia) in 1.43

EN928 Spitfire F.Vb (Merlin 45); TOC/RAF 16.5.42 - US 8th AF; 31st FG Atcham 21.6.42; 308th FS Kenley 1.8.42; Westhampnett 24.8.42; 67th (Obs) Grp Membury, 153rd Sqn, accident Keevil 30.12.42 (2/Lt RP Humphrey); SOXO, 67th (Recce) Grp Membury, 12th Sqn 19.7.43 (sic); Accident 12.7.43 (Lt DE Frye); Accident 26.8.43 (Lt SE Marsh); Crashed Cat.B 6.10.43; Retd RAF (RiW) 6.10.43; SOXO (8th AF), delete inventory 1.2.44; Later to Portugal as LF.Vb in 7.47

EN929 Spitfire F.Vb (Merlin 45); TOC/RAF 16.5.42 - US 8th AF; 31st FG Atcham 20.6.42; 307th FS, took off 12.25, FTR Dieppe raid, in sea 2m off Camber, Sussex, Cat.FB/E 19.8.42 (2/Lt LP Wells Jnr killed, body picked up by ASR, buried Cambridge), SOC

EN944 Spitfire F.Vb (Merlin 45); Presentation aircraft '*BROMLEY*'; TOC/RAF 21.5.42 - US 8th AF; 31st FG Atcham 20.6.42; 308th FS Kenley 1.8.42; Westhampnett 24.8.42; Retd RAF 12.9.42

EN945 Spitfire F.Vb (Merlin 45); TOC/RAF 21.5.42 - US 8th AF; 31st FG Atcham 22.6.42; 67th (Obs) Grp Membury, 153rd Sqn, overshot landing, tipped on nose, Membury, Cat.A 28.12.42 (2/Lt RP Humphrey); Accident Keevil 26.1.43 (Lt JS Evans); 67th (Recce) Grp Membury, crashed 3m from Wantage, Cat.E2 14.6.43 (Lt CF Stone), SOC
NOTE: Also reported as "DR945" USAAF Bovingdon, accident 14.6.43 (Lt JB Foster)

EN947 Spitfire F.Vb (Merlin 45); TOC/RAF 28.5.42 - US 9th AF; 31st ATG Grove 7.6.44; GLUE (9th AF), retd RAF 1.7.44 (RiW 7.7.44)

EN952 Spitfire F.Vb (Merlin 45); TOC/RAF 16.5.42 - US 8th AF; 31st FG Atcham 23.6.42; HQ US 8th AF (FC) 21.10.42; Spun in Walthamstow, Cat.E 22.11.42 (Lt HD Johnson killed), SOC

EN957 Spitfire F.Vb (Merlin 46); Presentation aircraft '*LONDON TRANSPORT*'; TOC/RAF 22.5.42 - US 8th AF; 31st FG Atcham 20.6.42; 308th FS Kenley 4.8.42; Westhampnett 24.8.42; 67th (Obs) Grp Membury, 109th Sqn, tyre burst landing, swung, starboard wheel went into hole, tipped on nose, Cat.A 6.11.42 (1/Lt PH Morris OK); ROS 23.11.42; 67th (Obs) Grp Membury, 107th Sqn, undercarriage collapsed on landing Membury, Cat.Ac 6.12.42 (1/Lt RE Phillips OK); Accident Aldermaston 21.12.42 (1/Lt RE Phillips); ROS 30.12.42; 67th (Recce) Grp Membury, 107th Sqn 16.7.43; SOXO, delete inventory 1.2.44; Retd RAF (RiW, AST Hamble 14.3.44)

EN964 Spitfire F.Vb/LR (Merlin 45); TOC/RAF 19.5.42; US 9th AF in 2.44; RNDA 14.2.44; US 369th (AS) Sqn; GLUE (9th AF), delete inventory 12.8.44; RNDA 12.8.44; Retd RAF 12.5.45; Later as GI No. *5585M* to France in 2.46

EN981 Spitfire F.Vb/trop (Merlin 45); TOC/RAF 23.5.42; Arr Gibraltar 27.9.42 - US 12th AF; 52nd FG, 5th FS, landing accident Maison Blanche, Cat.E 26.11.42 (Lt OR Duff); Possibly 950th Sqn, destroyed in air raid in North Africa 31.1.43; SOC

EP110 Spitfire F.Vb (Merlin 46); TOC/RAF 6.6.42; US 8th AF 31.12.43 - 67th (TR) Grp 6.1.44; US 9th AF 1.2.44; GLUE (9th AF), retd RAF 14.4.44; SOXO (8th AF), delete inventory 15.4.44

EP111 Spitfire F.Vb (Merlin 46); TOC/RAF 6.6.42 - US 8th AF; 31st FG Atcham 21.6.42; 307th FS, took off 09.55, FTR Dieppe raid, Cat.FB/E 19.8.42 (1/Lt EA Tovrea PoW), SOC

EP112 Spitfire F.Vb (Merlin 45); TOC/RAF 7.6.42 - US 8th AF; 52nd FG Eglinton 9.7.42; 2nd FS 22.8.42; RAF (No.332 Sqn) 8.11.42; HQ US 8th AF 8.8.43; Retd RAF (RiW) 5.1.44; SOXO (8th AF), delete inventory 1.2.44

EP143 Spitfire F.Vb (Merlin 45); TOC/RAF 14.6.42 - US 8th AF; 31st FG Atcham 20.6.42; 308th FS in 7.42; Flying accident, Cat.FA/A 9.7.42; HQ US 8th AF (FC) 21.10.42; SOXO (8th AF) 6.7.43; No.3501 SU 24.9.43; Crashed Cat.B 5.10.43; Retd to RAF (RiW) 5.10.43; To US 9th AF (FC); Retd RAF 10.10.44

EP167 Spitfire F.Vb – Allotment to US cancelled – No.133 Sqn (RAF), Cat.FA/E 19.9.42, SOC 25.9.42

EP169 Spitfire F.Vb (Merlin 45); TOC/RAF 31.5.42; 121 Sqn 7.7.42 - US 8th AF; 52nd FG Eglinton 11.7.42, crashed Cat.FA/B 21.7.42; Retd RAF (RiW, Short & Harland) 29.7.42; Later RNDA (to be *NX898*, but NTU and return to RAF); Became GI No. *5396M* for 5 SoTT Locking 17.7.45

EP172 Spitfire F.Vb (Merlin 45); TOC/RAF 2.6.42 - US 8th AF; 31st FG Atcham 20.6.42; 309th FS High Ercall ('WZ-A'); Retd RAF 26.10.42

EP173 Spitfire F.Vb (Merlin 45); TOC/RAF 4.6.42 - US 8th AF; 31st FG Atcham 21.6.42; 308th FS Kenley 1.8.42; Westhampnett 24.8.42; Retd RAF (No.33 MU) 24.10.42

EP174 Spitfire F.Vb (Merlin 46); TOC/RAF 6.6.42 - US 8th AF; 31st FG Atcham 23.6.42; 308th FS 1.8.42; Crashed Kenley, Cat.FB/Ac 19.8.42; ROS; Westhampnett 24.8.42; SOXO, 67th (Obs) Grp 16.2.43; 107th Sqn 7.6.43; Crashed Cat.B 5.10.43; Retd RAF (RiW) 5.10.43; SOXO (8th AF), delete inventory 1.2.44

EP175 Spitfire F.Vb (Merlin 45); TOC/RAF 7.6.42 - US 8th AF; 31st FG Atcham 24.6.42; 308th FS Kenley 1.8.42; Westhampnett 24.8.42; Retd RAF 24.10.42

EP176 Spitfire F.Vb (Merlin 45); TOC/RAF 10.6.42 - US 8th AF; 31st FG, 309th FS High Ercall ('WZ-A') 21.6.42; HQ US 8th AF (FC) 27.10.42; 4th FG Debden, 335th FS, landed wheels-up Duxford, Cat.Ac 30.11.42 (2/Lt FW Campbell OK); ROS 8.12.42; HQ US 8th AF (FC) 30.12.42; 4th FG, 334th FS Debden 15.1.43; 67th (Obs) Grp Membury, 109th Sqn 21.1.43; Accident at Atcham 11.3.43 (Lt JF Casey); Hit truck while taxying Atcham, Cat.Ac 18.5.43 (Lt EG Stiff); ROS 22.5.43; USAAC 11.7.43; SOXO (8th AF), 906th Grp (2909) 11.8.43; HQ US 8th AF, Condemned 16.10.43; Rep (DR) 28.3.44; Retd RAF 9.7.44

EP179 Spitfire F.Vb (Merlin 45); TOC/RAF 14.6.42; ex No.71 Sqn - US 8th AF; 4th FG Debden, 334th FS 1.10.42; Taxied into by EE742 of No.350 Sqn RAF at Debden 5.3.43 (Lt Col CG Peterson); SOXO (8th AF), 67th (Recce) Grp Membury, 109th Sqn 23.10.43; Accident at Chilbolton 5.3.44 (Lt JF McCormick); Crashed Cat.B 31.3.44; RiW (AST) 31.3.44; US 9th AF, Retd RAF 2.4.44; Later to France in 1.45

EP183 Spitfire F.Vb (Merlin 46); TOC/RAF 21.6.42 - US 9th AF; 67th (TR) Grp Middle Wallop 9.5.44; GLUE (9th AF), retd RAF 25.5.44

EP249 Spitfire F.Vb (Merlin 46); TOC/RAF 5.6.42 - US 8th AF; 67th (TR) Grp Membury 15.11.43; 7th (PR) Grp Mount Farm, accident at Wendling 15.3.44 (Lt JJ Mann); Detached service 21.9.44; Retd RAF 13.12.44; Later to France in 1.45

EP285 Spitfire F.Vb (Merlin 45); TOC/RAF 25.6.42 - US 8th AF 31.12.43; 67th (TR) Grp 6.1.44; Middle Wallop, flying accident [forced landed?], Tangley, Wilts, Cat.FA/B 12.2.44 (Lt RH Cassady); Retd RAF (RiW, via No.3501 SU) 18.4.44; SOC 29.11.45

EP309 Spitfire F.Vb/trop (Merlin 46); TOC/RAF 14.6.42; M.E. 14.10.42 - US 12th AF; 31st FG, 309th FS ('WZ-K') in 11.42; FTR, Cat.FB/E 17.3.43 (Lt Col FA Hill not seen again); SOC 20.3.43

EP315 Spitfire F.Vb/trop (Merlin 46); TOC/RAF 14.6.42; NAASC 31.10.43 - US 12th AF 31.1.44; poss. 52nd FG, accident at Telergma 19.1.44 (Lt RN Evans)

EP332 Spitfire F.Vb/trop (Merlin 46); TOC/RAF 14.6.42; NWA 31.8.43 - US 12th AF 31.8.43; Fate unknown

EP380 Spitfire F.Vb (Merlin 45); TOC/RAF 21.6.42 - US 9th AF; 67th (TR) Grp Middle Wallop 9.5.44; Detached service 12.5.44; Retd RAF 25.5.44; Later converted to GI No. *5931M*

EP385 Spitfire F.Vb (Merlin 46); TOC/RAF 23.6.42 - US 9th AF; 67th (TR) Grp 15.2.44; SOXO (8th AF), "8916" 15.2.44; RiW 18.4.44; US 369th (AS) Sqn; GLUE (9th AF), retd RAF (FLS) 26.7.44

EP401 Spitfire F.Vb/trop (Merlin 46); TOC/RAF 22.6.42; NAAF 1.11.43 - US 12th AF 31.1.44; Accident at Telergma 3.3.44 (Lt WC Zelinski); Retd RAF; SOC 28.4.45

EP404 Spitfire F.Vb/trop (Merlin 46); TOC/RAF 24.6.42; NWA 1.10.43 - US 12th AF 1.10.43; Retd RAF; SOC 28.4.45

EP492 Spitfire F.Vb (Merlin 46); TOC/RAF 19.7.42 - US 8th AF; 52nd FG Eglinton, 5th FS 13.9.42; Retd RAF (No.169 Sqn) 20.9.42; Later to Portugal in 10.43

EP496 Spitfire F.Vb (Merlin 46); TOC/RAF 27.6.42 - US 8th AF; 67th (TR) Grp 2.11.43; SOXO (8th AF) No."8916" 21.2.44; GLUE (9th AF), retd RAF 17.6.44 (RiW 20.6.44)

EP520 Spitfire F.Vb/trop (Merlin 46); TOC/RAF 28.6.42; Malta 1.11.42; dis. NA 1.6.43 - US 12th AF 30.11.43; Fate unknown

EP605 Spitfire LF.Vb (Merlin 55MA); TOC/RAF 1.8.42 - US 9th AF; 31st ATG Grove 30.5.44; GLUE (9th AF), retd RAF 1.7.44 (RiW 7.7.44); Later to Portugal as LF.Vb in 12.47

EP615 Spitfire F.IXb (Merlin 63); TOC/RAF 11.6.42; N.A. 30.11.43 - US 12th AF; 31st FG, 309th FS ('WZ-GG') 31.1.44, named '*THURLA MAE III*', flown by Lt R Belmont in 2.44; Shot down over Anzio beachhead, crashed Falgagnano, Cat.FB/E 5.2.44 (Lt BW Collins killed); SOC 7.2.44

EP668 Spitfire F.Vb/trop (Merlin 46); TOC/RAF 1.8.42; NWA 28.2.43 - US 12th AF; 31st FG, collided with lorry at Es-Souda, Cat.E 16.5.43 (W/O Otto wounded, died later in hospital), SOC

EP698 Spitfire F.Vb/trop (Merlin 46); TOC/RAF 24.7.42; NWA 1.10.43 - US 12th AF in 9.43; RAF 1.10.43; Retd US 12th AF 30.11.43; Retd RAF (NWA); SOC 1.4.44

EP712 Spitfire F.Vb/trop (Merlin 46); TOC/RAF 25.7.42; Malta 6.9.42; dis. NA 1.7.43 - US 12th AF; 31st FG, 309th FS ('WZ-C'), overturned 17.9.43 (Lt Stone); Served with 309th FS also 31.10.43 and 12.1.44; Fate unknown
NOTE: A Spitfire Vb coded 'WZ-C' had '*MILLIE*' on filter and '*SNATCHES SNAFU*' on nose 12.43

EP728 Spitfire F.Vb/trop (Merlin 46); TOC/RAF 31.7.42; NWA 31.8.43 - US 12th AF; 31st FG, 309th FS ('WZ-A') 31.8.43; Operational flight, Anzio fighter cover 25.1.44; Retd RAF 29.2.44

EP768 Spitfire F.Vb (Merlin 46); Presentation aircraft '*LORD AUSTIN*'; TOC/RAF 10.8.42 - US 8th AF; 67th (TR) Grp Middle Wallop 20.12.43; SOXO (8th AF), census 31.12.43; 7th (PR) Grp, Mount Farm; Retd RAF 14.5.44 (RiW, AST 11.8.44)

EP769 Spitfire F.Vb (Merlin 46); TOC/RAF 17.8.42; US 8th AF, census 31.12.43; "8916" 5.1.44; 67th (TR) Grp 6.1.44; 12th Sqn, accident at Aldermaston 21.1.44 (Lt WD Lacy Jnr); Retd RAF 10.4.44; Later converted to LF.Vb (Merlin 45M)

EP772 Spitfire F.Vb/trop (Merlin 46); TOC/RAF 16.8.42; Arr Gibraltar 14.9.42; NWA - US 12th AF in 1943; Retd RAF 1.10.43; Later to Greece in 4.46

EP774 Spitfire F.Vb/trop (Merlin 46); TOC/RAF 21.8.42; NWA 28.2.43 - US 12th AF; 52nd FG 31.11.43; Missing Italy, Cat.FB/E 29.12.43 (1/Lt RW Hine killed, buried Florence), SOC

EP783 Spitfire F.Vb/trop (Merlin 46); TOC/RAF 8.42; Arr Gibraltar 27.9.42 - US 12th AF; 52nd FG, 4th FS, crashed Gedim, Cat.E 8.5.43, (Lt AA Alenius killed), SOC

EP791 Spitfire F.Vb/trop (Merlin 46); TOC/RAF 31.7.42; Malta 1.11.42; NWA 31.3.43 - US 12th AF 1.10.43; Retd RAF (ME census 6.45); SOC 14.3.46

EP795 Spitfire F.Vb/trop (Merlin 46); TOC/RAF 1.8.42; Arr Gibraltar 1.11.42; NWA 31.7.43 - US 12th AF 31.7.43; Retd RAF (ME); SOC 26.4.45

EP813 Spitfire F.Vb/trop (Merlin 46); TOC/RAF 1.8.42; Arr Gibraltar 27.9.42; NWA 31.7.43 - US 12th AF 31.7.43; Retd RAF in 1944; Later to FAF 13.8.44 (scrapped 23.11.44)

EP824 Spitfire F.Vb/trop (Merlin 46); TOC/RAF 2.8.42; Arr Gibraltar 27.9.42; NWA 1.10.43 - US 12th AF 1.10.43; Retd RAF 31.5.44

EP835 Spitfire F.Vb/trop (Merlin 46); TOC/RAF 10.8.42; Malta 1.11.42; dis. NA 2.6.43 - US 12th AF 31.10.43; Retd RAF 31.5.44

EP837 Spitfire F.Vb/trop (Merlin 46); TOC/RAF 9.8.42; Arr Gibraltar 27.9.42 - US 12th AF; 31st FG, 308th FS ('HL-L') in 10.43; Over Tunisia in 1943; Fate unknown

EP841 Spitfire F.Vb/trop (Merlin 46); TOC/RAF 9.8.42; Arr Gibraltar 27.9.42 - US 12th AF; 52nd FG, 5th FS, accident Telergma 19.1.43 (Lt EJ Odom); Retd RAF (lost No.328 Sqn 2.6.44)

EP843 Spitfire F.Vb/trop (Merlin 46); TOC/RAF 9.8.42; Malta 1.11.42; M.E. 1.9.43 - US 12th AF 1.9.43; Retd RAF; SOC 31.5.45

EP901 Spitfire F.Vb/trop (Merlin 46); TOC/RAF 12.8.42; Arr Gibraltar 27.9.42; NWA - US 12th AF; 52nd FG, 5th FS ('VF-N') in 11.42; Shot down by enemy, forced landed, Cat.FB/E in 12.42, SOC

EP907 Spitfire F.Vb/trop (Merlin 46); TOC/RAF 12.8.42; Arr Gibraltar 18.1.43 - US 12th AF 31.1.44; Retd RAF; SOC 30.6.44

EP912 Spitfire F.Vb/trop (Merlin 46); TOC/RAF 13.8.42; Arr Gibraltar 1.11.42 - US 12th AF in 9.43; Retd RAF 1.10.43; SOC 29.2.44

EP971 Spitfire F.Vb/trop (Merlin 46); TOC/RAF 18.8.42; Arr Gibraltar 1.11.42; NWA 31.7.43 - US 12th AF 31.7.43; Retd RAF; SOC 28.4.45

EP978 Spitfire F.Vb/trop (Merlin 46); TOC/RAF 17.8.42; NAASC 31.10.43 - US 12th AF 31.1.44; Retd RAF (ME census 21.6.45); SOC 29.8.46

EP989 Spitfire F.Vb/trop (Merlin 46); TOC/RAF 23.8.42; Arr Gibraltar 1.11.42 - US 12th AF; 31st FG, 309th FS ('WZ-G') in 9.43, also by 4.1.44; Retd RAF (Census 6.45); SOC 29.8.46

EP990 Spitfire F.Vb/trop (Merlin 46); TOC/RAF 20.8.42; Arr Gibraltar 11.42 - US 12th AF; Afreville, accident at base 4.1.43 (Lt JT Kemp jr); Fate unknown

ER120 Spitfire F.Vb/trop (Merlin 46); TOC/RAF 4.9.42; Arr Gibraltar 1.11.42 - US 12th AF; 52nd FG, 5th FS ('VF-D') in 1943; Crashed on landing, Cat.E 7.43; SOC 31.7.43

ER130 Spitfire F.Vb/trop (Merlin 46); TOC/RAF 18.10.42; Arr Gibraltar 23.11.42; NWA 28.2.43 - US 12th AF; 31st FG, 307th FS, fighter cover over Anzio beachhead, shot down by Bf 109 near lakes, Cat.FB/E 6.2.44 (Mjr V Fields, CO killed); SOC 29.2.44.
NOTE: Mis-reported as "ER730"

ER136 Spitfire F.Vb/trop (Merlin 46); TOC/RAF 21.8.42; M.E. 1.8.43; dis. NAAF 30.9.43 - US 12th AF 31.10.43; Retd RAF in 1944; Later to Greece in 4.46

ER161 Spitfire F.Vb/trop (Merlin 46); TOC/RAF 24.8.42; Arr Gibraltar 1.11.42; NWA 31.7.43 - US 12th AF 31.7.43; Retd RAF; SOC 26.6.45

ER165 Spitfire F.Vb/trop (Merlin 46); TOC/RAF 22.8.42; Arr Gibraltar 1.11.42 - US 12th AF; 31st FG mid 1943; 308th FS ('HL-W'), bounced landing on slope, carried by wind on top of wrecked EF632 ('WZ-W') of 31st FG (309th FS) being serviced by four RAF fitters, killing two of them and injuring the other two, "Banjo" airstrip, Gozo, Cat.E 30.6.43 (1/Lt EL Fardella seriously injured), SOC

ER180 Spitfire F.Vb/trop (Merlin 46); TOC/RAF 27.8.42; Arr Gibraltar 11.42 - US 12th AF – 31st FG, 307th FS (MX-P) in 1943; Fate unknown

ER187 Spitfire F.Vb/trop (Merlin 46); TOC/RAF 27.8.42; Arr Gibraltar 11.42; NWA 28.2.43 - US 12th AF; 31st FG, 309th FS ('WZ-C') by 6.5.43 (marked '*LINDY AND FRANK*', flown by Mjr FA Hill); Fate unknown

ER219 Spitfire F.Vb/trop (Merlin 46); TOC/RAF 31.8.42; Arr Gibraltar 1.11.42; NWA - US 12th AF; unknown unit ('K') in 11.42; Retd RAF in 1943; SOC 30.4.43

ER277 Spitfire F.Vb/trop (Merlin 46); TOC/RAF 8.9.42; Arr Gibraltar 1.11.42 - US 12th AF in 1943; NAASC 31.10.43; US 12th AF 31.1.44; Accident at Telergma 10.3.44 (Lt AJ Carey); Retd RAF 31.8.44; Later to Turkey in 9.44

ER306 Spitfire F.Vb/trop (Merlin 46); TOC/RAF 25.9.42; NAASC 31.10.43 - US 12th AF 31.1.44; Fate unknown

ER314 Spitfire F.Vb/trop (Merlin 46); TOC/RAF 4.9.42; Arr Gibraltar 6.11.42 - US 12th AF 31.7.43; NAASC 31.10.43; Fate unknown

ER320 Spitfire F.Vb/trop (Merlin 46); TOC/RAF 13.9.42; Arr Gibraltar 6.11.42 - US 12th AF; 52nd FG Orleansville, accident at base 4.10.43 (Lt GC Deaton); Fate unknown

ER324 Spitfire F.Vb/trop (Merlin 46); TOC/RAF 16.9.42; Arr Gibraltar 23.11.42; No.111 Sqn RAF - US 12th AF; 52nd FG, 2nd FS, accident at Telergma 2.2.43 (Lt WL Morgan); Retd RAF; SOC 31.7.43

ER325 Spitfire F.Vb/trop (Merlin 46); TOC/RAF 18.9.42; Arr Gibraltar 6.11.42 - US 12th AF; 52nd FG, La Senia, accident at base 27.12.42 (Lt WR Williams); Retd RAF 1.10.43

ER477 Spitfire F.Vb/trop (Merlin 46); TOC/RAF 13.9.42; Arr Gibraltar 6.11.42 - US 12th AF 31.7.43; Retd RAF 1.10.43

ER503 Spitfire F.Vb/trop (Merlin 46); TOC/RAF 18.9.42; Arr Gibraltar 1.11.42; US 12th AF - 31st FG, 308th FS 8.11.42; 307th FS ('MX-P', sharkmouth on nose) by 11.42 (flown by Capt Holloway); Fate unknown

ER510 Spitfire F.Vb/trop (Merlin 46); TOC/RAF 17.9.42; Arr Gibraltar 1.11.42; SAAF; NWA 31.7.43 - US 12th AF 31.7.43; Fate unknown

ER538 Spitfire F.Vb/trop (Merlin 46); TOC/RAF 23.9.42; Arr Gibraltar 6.11.42 - US 12th AF; 52nd FG Orleansville, accident at Maison Blanche 3.1.43 (Lt W MacGregor); Fate unknown

ER557 Spitfire F.Vb/trop (Merlin 46); TOC/RAF 6.10.42; NWA 28.2.43 - US 12th AF 29.2.44; Retd RAF 25.2.45

ER559 Spitfire F.Vb/trop (Merlin 46); TOC/RAF 27.9.42; Arr Gibraltar 6.11.42; NWA - US 12th AF; 52nd FG, accident at Telergma 1.2.43 (Lt JD Templeton); Retd RAF; SOC 31.7.43

ER565 Spitfire F.Vb/trop (Merlin 46); TOC/RAF 27.9.42; NAAF 1.11.43 - US 12th AF 31.1.44; Fate unknown

ER569 Spitfire F.Vb/trop (Merlin 46); TOC/RAF 23.9.42; NWA 28.2.43 - US 12th AF 1.10.43; Retd RAF 31.8.44

ER570 Spitfire F.Vb/trop (Merlin 46); TOC/RAF 25.9.42; Arr Gibraltar 9.11.42; NWA 31.7.43 - US 12th AF; 52nd FG, 4th FS ('WD-Q') 31.7.43; Retd RAF (MAAF); Cat.E 14.1.45, SOC

ER614 Spitfire F.Vc/trop (Merlin 46); Presentation aircraft '*WAD MEDANI / BLUE NILE*'; TOC/RAF 22.1.43; NWA 31.3.43 - US 12th AF 31.10.43; Retd RAF; SOC 29.2.44

ER647 Spitfire F.Vb/trop (Merlin 46); TOC/RAF 1.10.42; Malta 1.12.42; dis. NA 1.6.43 - US 12th AF 29.2.44; Retd RAF (MAAF census 6.45); Later Training Delegation 27.9.45; To France 11.45

ER653 Spitfire F.Vb/trop (Merlin 46); TOC/RAF 6.10.42; NWA 28.2.43 - US 12th AF; 52nd FG 12.43; Dived into Mediterranean, Cat.FB/E 10.1.44; SOC 27.1.44

ER655 Spitfire F.Vc/trop (Merlin 46); TOC/RAF 9.10.42; Arr Gibraltar 9.11.42; NWA 31.7.43 - US 12th AF 31.7.43; Retd RAF in 1944; Later sold to Italy 27.6.46

ER705 Spitfire F.Vb/trop (Merlin 46); TOC/RAF 18.10.42; M.E. 31.1.43 - US 12th AF 31.1.44; Flying accident, Cat.FA/E 15.2.45, SOC

ER710 Spitfire F.Vb/trop (Merlin 46); USAAF Telergma, accident at base 29.3.44 (Lt EF Jones)

ER730 Spitfire F.Vb/trop (Merlin 46); TOC/RAF 27.10.42; NWA 28.2.43 - US 12th AF 1.10.43; Crashed in lake, Cat.E 17.10.44, SOC

The remains of Spitfire F.Vb/trop ER120 VF-D of the 5th Fighter Sqn, 52nd Fighter Group, which crashed on landing at La Sebala in July 1943.

Spitfire F.Vb/trop ER570 'WD-Q', serving with the 4th F Sqn, 52nd FG, 12th (US)AF in Tunisia around June 1943, flown by Major Levine. [James Crow]

Another view of Spitfire F.Vb/trop ER570, which joined the 4th Sqn, 52nd FG, 12th (US)AF on 31st July 1943. Next day the squadron moved from La Sebala in Tunisia to Boccadifalco in Sicily, where this photo was taken. [via Henry Boot]

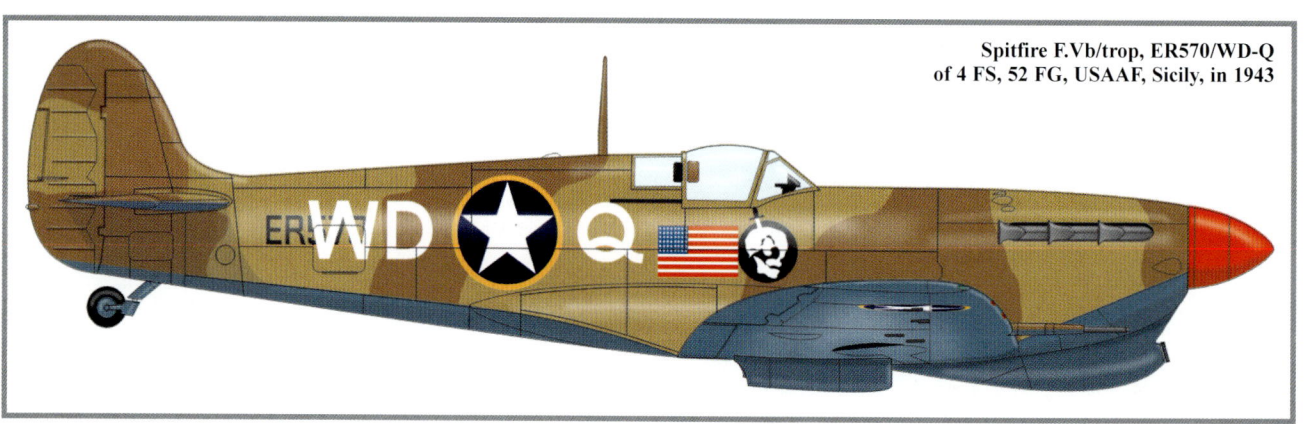

Spitfire F.Vb/trop, ER570/WD-Q of 4 FS, 52 FG, USAAF, Sicily, in 1943

ER759 Spitfire F.Vb/trop (Merlin 46); TOC/RAF 10.10.42; Arr Gibraltar 9.11.42; NWA 28.2.43 - US 12th AF; 52nd FG, La Sebala, accident at base 9.6.43 (1/Lt DW Markley killed)

ER780 Spitfire F.Vb/trop (Merlin 46); TOC/RAF 11.10.42 – US 12th AF; 52nd FG La Sebala, accident at base 29.5.43 (Lt CR Brown); NWA 31.5.43 (12th AF reported also 31.7.43); Retd RAF 31.1.44

ER815 Spitfire F.Vb/trop (Merlin 46); Presentation aircraft '*NORTH WESTERN RAILWAY III PUNJAB*'; TOC/RAF 18.10.42; Arr Gibraltar 4.11.42; Cat.FB/2 22.12.42; Cat.FB/3 25.2.43 (No.93 Sqn) - US 12th AF mid 1943; Retd RAF (NWA) 31.7.43

ER826 Spitfire F.Vb/trop (Merlin 46); TOC/RAF 21.10.42; Arr Gibraltar 23.11.42 - US 12th AF; 52nd FG, accident at Bone 7.9.43 (Lt RP Hagen); Fate unknown

ER880 Spitfire F.Vc/trop (Merlin 46); TOC/RAF 7.11.42; NWA 25.2.43 - US 12th AF 31.1.44; Retd RAF 31.5.44

ER886 Spitfire F.Vb/trop (Merlin 46); TOC/RAF 4.12.42; NWA 28.2.43 - US 12th AF 31.1.44; Retd RAF 30.11.44

ER926 Spitfire F.Vb/trop (Merlin 46); TOC/RAF 20.11.42; Arr Gibraltar 13.1.43; NWA 31.7.43 - US 12th AF 31.7.43; Fate unknown

ER931 Spitfire F.Vc/trop (Merlin 46); TOC/RAF 6.11.42; Arr Gibraltar 8.1.43; NWA 31.7.43 - US 12th AF 31.7.43; Retd RAF 30.11.44; Later to France in 11.45

ER941 Spitfire F.Vb/trop (Merlin 46); TOC/RAF 8.11.42; NAASC 31.10.43; NAAF 1.11.43 - US 12th AF 31.1.44; Retd RAF; SOC 26.4.45

ER970 Spitfire F.Vb/trop (Merlin 46); TOC/RAF 6.12.42; Arr Gibraltar 13.1.43 - US 12th AF; 52nd FG, 5th FS, accident Telergma 28.1.43 (1/Lt GA Zientowski); Fate unknown

ER976 Spitfire F.Vc/trop (Merlin 46); TOC/RAF 19.12.42; NWA 28.2.43 - US 12th AF 31.10.43; Retd RAF 31.5.44

ES118 Spitfire F.Vc/trop (Merlin 46); TOC/RAF 8.11.42; Arr Gibraltar 13.1.43 - US 12th AF; 52nd FG Telergma, accident at base 21.2.43 (Lt EJ Gebhart); Retd RAF, NWA 31.7.43 (SOC 26.4.45)

ES123 Spitfire F.Vb/trop (Merlin 46); TOC/RAF 10.11.42; Arr Gibraltar 8.1.43 - US 12th AF 31.10.43; Diverted to French unit (No.326 Sqn); Retd RAF 31.5.44

ES138 Spitfire F.Vc/trop (Merlin 46); TOC/RAF 10.11.42; NWA 28.2.43 - US 12th AF; 52nd FG 31.8.43; 4th FS ('WD-N') in 1943; Fate unknown

ES177 Spitfire F.Vb/trop (Merlin 46); TOC/RAF 19.11.42; NWA 28.2.43 - US 12th AF mid 1943; Retd RAF 31.7.43

ES182 Spitfire F.Vc/trop (Merlin 46); TOC/RAF 22.12.42; Arr Gibraltar 6.2.43 - US 12th AF; 31st FG, 308th FS in 3.43; Shot down over Malta, engine failure, overshot landing Gozo, crashed into sea 500yds off northern shore in 36ft of water, no attempt made at rescue, Cat.FB/E 30.6.43 (2/Lt JB Stephens Jnr killed), SOC

ES186 Spitfire F.Vb/trop (Merlin 46); TOC/RAF 4.12.42; N.A. 29.9.43 - US 12th AF; 52nd FG 31.10.43, 4th FS ('WD-N') in 11.43; Retd RAF in 1944

ES195 Spitfire F.Vc/trop (Merlin 46); TOC/RAF 20.12.42; NWA 28.2.43 - US 12th AF in 1943/44 (French unit end 1943); Retd RAF 31.5.44

ES244 Spitfire F.Vb/trop (Merlin 46); TOC/RAF 29.11.42; Arr Gibraltar 18.1.43; NWA 31.7.43 - US 12th AF 31.7.43; Retd RAF; SOC 3.46

ES261 Spitfire F.Vb/trop (Merlin 46); TOC/RAF 28.11.42; Arr Gibraltar 13.1.43; NWA - US 12th AF; 52nd FG, accident Gedim 18.4.43 (Lt VN Cabas); Retd RAF, SOC 31.7.43

ES264 Spitfire F.Vb/trop (Merlin 46); TOC/RAF 6.12.42; Arr Gibraltar 13.1.43; US 12th AF, NWA - 52nd FG in 3.43; 2nd FS ('QP-V'); Retd RAF 1.10.43

ES276 Spitfire F.Vb/trop (Merlin 46); TOC/RAF 25.11.42; Arr Gibraltar 13.1.43 - US 12th AF; 31st FG, 309th FS ('WZ-Y') 31.10.43, also by 2.1.44; Retd RAF 31.1.45

ES277 Spitfire F.Vc/trop (Merlin 46); TOC/RAF 4.12.42; Arr Gibraltar 13.1.43; NWA - US 12th AF; 52nd FG, 4th FS, La Senia, accident at base 27.2.43 (Lt NNV Bolle); SOC/RAF 30.4.43

ES284 Spitfire F.Vc/trop (Merlin 46); TOC/RAF 28.11.42; NWA 28.2.43 - US 12th AF in 4.43; Retd RAF 1.10.43; Later to Egypt in 3.45

ES296 Spitfire F.Vc/trop (Merlin 46); TOC/RAF 29.11.42; Arr Gibraltar 18.1.43 - US 12th AF 31.12.43; SOC/RAF 29.2.44

ES297 Spitfire F.Vc/trop (Merlin 46); TOC/RAF 10.12.42; NWA 28.2.43 - US 12th AF 31.10.43; Fate unknown

ES306 Spitfire F.Vc/trop (Merlin 46); TOC/RAF 9.12.42; arr Gibraltar 18.1.43 - US 12th AF; 31st FG, 308th FS Sqn ('HL-D') in 3.43 (flown by Capt FA Hill); Retd RAF (No.249 Sqn)

ES317 Spitfire F.Vc/trop (Merlin 46); TOC/RAF 9.12.42; Arr Gibraltar 18.1.43; NWA - US 12th AF; 31st FG, 307th FS ('MX-F') in 3.43; Fate unknown

ES340 Spitfire F.Vc/trop (Merlin 46); TOC/RAF 6.12.42; Arr Gibraltar 18.1.43 - US 12th AF; 31st FG, 307th FS, hit by US Navy flak near shore, engine problems, attempted to force land on beach, crashed in sea near shore, Pantellaria 11.7.43 (2/Lt AL Goldenberg killed), SOC

ES360 Spitfire F.Vc/trop (Merlin 46); TOC/RAF 15.12.42; Arr Gibraltar 18.1.43 - US 12th AF; 52nd FG Youks-les-Bains, accident at base 24.3.43 (1/Lt EC Smithers); Fate unknown

ES362 Spitfire F.Vc/trop (Merlin 46); TOC/RAF 11.12.42; Arr Gibraltar 6.2.43; NWA US 12th AF in 4.43; Retd RAF 30.11.43

ES363 Spitfire F.Vc/trop (Merlin 46); TOC/RAF 9.12.42; Arr Gibraltar 18.1.43; NWA 31.7.43 - US 12th AF 31.7.43; Retd RAF 31.1.45

ES364 Spitfire F.Vc/trop (Merlin 46); TOC/RAF 10.12.42; NWA 28.2.43; US 12th AF, NWA - 52nd FG, 4th FS ('WD-F') in 3.43; Belly-landed, date unknown; Retd RAF (RiW); SOC 28.4.45

JF296 Spitfire F.VIIIc (Merlin 61); TOC/RAF 27.1.43; Casablanca 6.4.44; No.328 Sqn 3.9.44 (crashed Epinal 1.10.44, Plt de Montrachu) - US 12th AF; 31st FG, 308th FS; SOXO, diverted to French ("L-09") 10.9.45; Retd RAF (RiW) 14.9.45; Later converted to GI No. *5835M*

JF331 Spitfire F.VIIIc (Merlin 63); TOC/RAF 27.2.43; Arr Gibraltar 12.4.43; NWA 31.7.43 - US 12th AF; 31st FG, 308th FS 31.7.43; 52nd FG, 2nd FS, over Sicily in 8.43; Fate unknown

JF333 Spitfire F.VIIIc (Merlin 63); TOC/RAF 25.2.43; NWA 31.5.43 - US 12th AF; 31st FG, 308th FS 31.7.43; Retd RAF 31.5.44

JF340 Spitfire F.VIIIc (Merlin 63); TOC/RAF 6.3.43; Casablanca 30.7.43 - US 12th AF; 31st FG, 308th FS in 8.43; Shot down by FW 190 over Gaeta, Cat.FB/E 11.11.43 (1/Lt EL Fardella killed), SOC

JF345 Spitfire F.VIIIc (Merlin 63A); TOC/RAF 12.3.43; Casablanca 24.4.43; NWA 31.5.43 - US 12th AF; 31st FG, 308th FS 31.7.43; Fate unknown

JF347 Spitfire F.VIIIc (Merlin 63); TOC/RAF 7.3.43 - US 12th AF; 31st FG, 308th FS 1.10.43; SOC/RAF 30.6.45

JF351 Spitfire F.VIIIc (Merlin 63); TOC/RAF 14.3.43 - US 12th AF; 31st FG, 308th FS 31.7.43; Retd RAF 29.2.44

JF359 Spitfire F.VIIIc (Merlin 63); TOC/RAF 22.3.43 - US 12th AF; 31st FG, 308th FS 31.7.43; Fate unknown

JF360 Spitfire F.VIIIc (Merlin 63); TOC/RAF 22.3.43 - US 12th AF; 31st FG, 308th FS 31.10.43; Fate unknown

JF363 Spitfire F.VIIIc (Merlin 63); TOC/RAF 27.3.43; Casablanca 17.5.43; NAASC 1.11.43 - US 12th AF in 11.43; DUKO, retd RAF 6.7.44

JF400 Spitfire F.VIIIc (Merlin 63); TOC/RAF 28.3.43; NAASC 31.10.43 - US 12th AF; 31st FG, 308th FS 31.10.43; M.E. dis. NAAF 1.11.43; SOC/RAF 30.6.45

JF416 Spitfire F.VIIIc (Merlin 63); TOC/RAF 8.4.43; NWA 1.7.43 - US 12th AF; 31st FG, 308th FS 30.11.43; Retd RAF 31.5.44

JF444 Spitfire F.VIIIc (Merlin 63); TOC/RAF 15.4.43; NWA 1.7.43 - US 12th AF; 31st FG, 308th FS 30.11.43; Retd RAF 31.5.44

JF455 Spitfire F.VIIIc (Merlin 63A); TOC/RAF 24.4.43; NWA 7.43 - US 12th AF 30.11.43; Retd RAF; SOC 28.4.45

Spitfire F.VIIIc JF331 of the 2nd FS, 52nd FG at Palermo, Sicily, in August 1943. In the foreground is 'Mullegan John' wearing his Brazilian flying boots.
[Lt J E Fawcett via Henry Boot]

JF456   Spitfire F.VIIIc (Merlin 63); TOC/RAF 21.4.43; NWA 1.7.43 - US 12th AF; 31st FG, 308th FS 30.11.43; Retd RAF 28.2.44

JF470   Spitfire F.VIIIc (Merlin 63); TOC/RAF 5.5.43; Arr Casablanca 15.6.43; NWA 7.43; ME 8.43; NAASC 11.43 - US 12th AF; 31st FG, 308th FS ('HL-R') as hack aircraft in 1944; unknown unit, crashed, Cat FB/E 1.10.44, SOC

JF475   Spitfire LF.VIIIc (Merlin 66); TOC/RAF 13.5.43; M.E. 1.8.43; NAAF 1.11.43 - US 12th AF; 31st FG, 308th FS 29.2.44; Fate unknown

JF511   Spitfire F.VIIIc (Merlin 63); TOC/RAF 25.5.43; NWA 1.10.43 - US 12th AF; 31st FG, 308th FS 30.11.43; Fate unknown

JF569   Spitfire LF.VIIIc (Merlin 66); TOC/RAF 12.6.43; M.E. 1.9.43; NAAF 1.11.43 - US 12th AF; 31st FG, 308th FS 31.1.44; Fate unknown

JF576   Spitfire F.VIIIc (Merlin 63); TOC/RAF 22.6.43; Casablanca 29.7.43 - US 12th AF; 31st FG, 308th FS 31.10.43; Retd RAF 31.5.44

JF577   Spitfire F.VIIIc (Merlin 63); TOC/RAF 25.6.43; Casablanca 29.7.43 - US 12th AF; 31st FG, 308th FS 30.11.43; Flying accident, Cat.FA/3 11.4.44, SOC

JF628   Spitfire F.VIIIc (Merlin 63); TOC/RAF 29.6.43; Casablanca 29.7.43 - US 12th AF; 31st FG, 308th FS 30.11.43; Retd RAF 31.5.44

JF658   Spitfire F.VIIIc (Merlin 63); TOC/RAF 1.7.43; NWA 1.10.43 - US 12th AF; 31st FG, 308th FS 30.11.43; Fate unknown

JF660   Spitfire F.VIIIc (Merlin 63); TOC/RAF 2.7.43; Casablanca 29.7.43 - US 12th AF; 31st FG, 308th FS 30.11.43; Shot down over Italy, pilot baled out near Valmontone, Cat.FB/E 22.2.44 (Lt R Hackbarth killed), SOC

JF661   Spitfire F.VIIIc (Merlin 63); TOC/RAF 2.7.43; Casablanca 29.7.43 - US 12th AF; 31st FG, 308th FS 31.10.43; Retd RAF 31.5.44; Later converted to GI No. *5832M*

JF699   Spitfire F.VIIIc (Merlin 63); TOC/RAF 27.7.43; Casablanca 22.12.43 - US 12th AF; 31st FG, 308th FS 31.1.44; Fate unknown

JF706   Spitfire F.VIIIc (Merlin 63); TOC/RAF 25.6.43; Casablanca 29.7.43 - US 12th AF; 31st FG, 308th FS 30.11.43; Fate unknown

JF708   Spitfire F.VIIIc (Merlin 63); TOC/RAF 25.6.43; Casablanca 29.7.43 - US 12th AF; 31st FG, 308th FS 31.10.43; Retd RAF; SOC 30.6.44

JF749   Spitfire LF.VIIIc (Merlin 66); TOC/RAF 3.7.43; N.A. 30.11.43; No.326 (French) Sqn in 8.44 - SOXO (US 8th AF), diverted to French ("L-09") 10.5.45; No.327 (French) Sqn 12.5.45 & 24.5.45; No.339 (French) Wing 9.8.45; SNCAN (for repair) 11.10.45; Possibly to France 11.45

JF873   Spitfire LF.VIIIc (Merlin 66); TOC/RAF 27.8.43; NAASC 31.10.43 - US 12th AF; 31st FG, 308th FS 31.1.44; Retd RAF; SOC 30.6.44

JF874   Spitfire LF.VIIIc (Merlin 66); TOC/RAF 27.8.43; NAASC 31.10.43 - US 12th AF; 31st FG, 308th FS 31.1.44; Retd RAF 31.5.44

JF880   Spitfire LF.VIIIc (Merlin 66); TOC/RAF 3.9.43; NAASC 31.10.43 - US 12th AF; 31st FG, 308th FS 31.1.44; Retd RAF 31.5.44

JF894   Spitfire F.VIIIc (Merlin 63); TOC/RAF 7.11.43; MAAF 31.1.44 - US 12th AF; 31st FG, 308th FS 29.2.44; Crashed Cat.FB/E 12.11.44, SOC

JF899   Spitfire F.VIIIc (Merlin 63); TOC/RAF 13.11.43; MAAF 31.1.44 - US 12th AF; 31st FG, 308th FS 29.2.44; Retd RAF 31.5.44

JF930   Spitfire LF.VIIIc (Merlin 66); TOC/RAF 24.8.43; NAASC 31.10.43 - US 12th AF; 31st FG, 308th FS 31.1.44; Retd RAF 31.5.44

JF932   Spitfire LF.VIIIc (Merlin 66); TOC/RAF 24.8.43; NAASC 31.10.43 - US 12th AF; 31st FG, 308th FS 31.1.44; SOC/RAF 31.1.45

JF949   Spitfire LF.VIIIc (Merlin 66); TOC/RAF 31.8.43; NAASC 31.10.43 - US 12th AF; 31st FG, 308th FS 31.1.44; SOC/RAF 31.8.44

JF951   Spitfire LF.VIIIc (Merlin 66); TOC/RAF 2.9.43; NAASC 31.10.43 - US 12th AF; 31st FG, 308th FS 31.1.44; SOC/RAF 10.44

JF954   Spitfire LF.VIIIc (Merlin 66); TOC/RAF 2.9.43; NAASC 31.10.43 - US 12th AF; 31st FG, 308th FS 31.1.44; Retd RAF; SOC (dbf) 15.4.45

UNITED STATES OF AMERICA

JG108 Spitfire LF.VIIIc (Merlin 66); TOC/RAF 11.9.43; NAASC 31.10.43 - US 12th AF; 31st FG, 308th FS 31.1.44; Fate unknown
JG120 Spitfire LF.VIIIc (Merlin 66); TOC/RAF 29.8.43; Casablanca 22.12.43; MAAF 31.1.44 - US 12th AF; 31st FG, 308th FS 31.1.44; Fate unknown
JG123 Spitfire LF.VIIIc (Merlin 66); TOC/RAF 31.8.43; NAASC 31.10.43 - US 12th AF; 31st FG, 308th FS 31.1.44; Crashed Cat.E 25.4.45, SOC
JG124 Spitfire LF.VIIIc (Merlin 66); TOC/RAF 31.8.43; Casablanca 10.10.43; NAASC 31.10.43 - US 12th AF; 31st FG, 308th FS 31.1.44; DUKO (12th AF), retd RAF 9.7.44
JG157 Spitfire LF.VIIIc (Merlin 66); TOC/RAF 2.9.43; NAASC 31.10.43 - US 12th AF; 31st FG, 308th FS 31.1.44; Fate unknown
JG163 Spitfire LF.VIIIc (Merlin 66); TOC/RAF 4.9.43; Casablanca 10.10.43; NAASC 31.10.43 - US 12th AF; 31st FG, 308th FS 31.1.44; Flying accident, Cat.FA/E 12.6.44; DUKO (12th AF), retd RAF; SOC 9.7.44
JG165 Spitfire LF.VIIIc (Merlin 66); TOC/RAF 6.9.43; NAASC 31.10.43 - US 12th AF; 31st FG, 308th FS 29.2.44; SOC/RAF 31.8.44
JG186 Spitfire LF.VIIIc (Merlin 66); TOC/RAF 25.9.43; Casablanca 17.11.43; N.A. 30.11.43 - US 12th AF; 31st FG, 308th FS 31.1.44; SOC/RAF 30.6.44
JG197 Spitfire LF.VIIIc (Merlin 66); TOC/RAF 19.9.43; NAASC 31.10.43 - US 12th AF; 31st FG, 308th FS 31.1.44; Retd RAF in 1944 (MAAF census 6.45); SOC 27.3.47
JG242 Spitfire LF.VIIIc (Merlin 66); TOC/RAF 26.9.43; Casablanca 17.11.43; N.A. 30.11.43 - US 12th AF; 31st FG, 308th FS 31.1.44; Retd RAF 31.5.44
JG245 Spitfire LF.VIIIc (Merlin 66); TOC/RAF 26.9.43; Casablanca 17.11.43; N.A. 30.11.43 - US 12th AF; 31st FG, 308th FS 31.1.44; Retd RAF and to No.327.Sqn, Accident 1.1.45
JG248 Spitfire LF.VIIIc (Merlin 66); TOC/RAF 30.9.43; Casablanca 17.11.43; N.A. 30.11.43 - US 12th AF; 31st FG, 308th FS 31.1.44; Retd RAF 31.5.44
JG257 Spitfire LF.VIIIc (Merlin 66); TOC/RAF 3.10.43; Casablanca 17.11.43; N.A. 30.11.43 - US 12th AF; 31st FG, 308th FS 31.1.44; No.328 (French) Sqn in 10.44, crashed 7.10.44; SOXO (8th AF), diverted to French ("L-09") 10.5.45; SOC/RAF 1.6.47
JG317 Spitfire F.VIIIc (Merlin 63); TOC/RAF 16.11.43; Casablanca 8.1.44; MAAF 31.1.44 - US 12th AF; 31st FG, 308th FS 29.2.44; Retd RAF in 1944 (MAAF census 6.45); SOC 31.12.46
JG337 Spitfire LF.VIIIc (Merlin 66); TOC/RAF 2.10.43; Casablanca 17.11.43; N.A. 30.11.43 - US 12th AF; 31st FG, 308th FS 29.2.44; Retd RAF in 1944 (MAAF census 6.45); SOC 23.11.45
JG384 Spitfire LF.VIIIc (Merlin 66); TOC/RAF 5.11.43; Casablanca 22.12.43 - US 12th AF; 31st FG, 308th FS 29.2.44; Crashed Cat.FB/E 4.7.44, SOC
JG490 Spitfire LF.VIIIc (Merlin 66); TOC/RAF 5.11.43; Casablanca 22.12.43 - US 12th AF; 31st FG, 308th FS 31.1.44; Fate unknown
JG492 Spitfire F.VIIIc (Merlin 63); TOC/RAF 13.11.43; Casablanca 22.12.43 - US 12th AF; 31st FG, 308th FS 29.2.44; Retd RAF in 4.44 (No.241 Sqn, missing 20.4.44)
JG538 Spitfire LF.VIIIc (Merlin 66); TOC/RAF 3.11.43; Casablanca 22.12.43 - US 12th AF; 31st FG, 308th FS 31.1.44; Retd RAF 31.5.44
JG541 Spitfire F.VIIIc (Merlin 63); TOC/RAF 7.11.43; Casablanca 22.12.43 - US 12th AF; 31st FG, 308th FS 29.2.44; Retd RAF 31.5.44
JG542 Spitfire LF.VIIIc (Merlin 66); TOC/RAF 30.10.43; Casablanca 22.12.43 - US 12th AF; 31st FG, 308th FS 29.2.44; SOC/RAF 31.8.44
JG729 Spitfire F.Vc/trop (Merlin 46); TOC/RAF 15.12.42; NWA 28.2.43 - US 12th AF in 1943; Retd RAF 29.2.44
JG744 Spitfire F.Vc/trop (Merlin 46); TOC/RAF 14.12.42; Arr Gibraltar 18.1.43 - US 12th AF; 52nd FG Telergma, accident at base 21.2.43 (Lt DC Wolfe); Retd RAF; Later to Turkey in 12.44
JG746 Spitfire F.Vc/trop (Merlin 45); TOC/RAF 15.12.42; NWA 28.2.43; NAASC 31.10.43 - US 12th AF end 1943; SOXO (8th AF), diverted to French ("L-09") 10.5.45; No.326 (French) Sqn; Possibly to France 11.45
JG748 Spitfire F.Vc/trop (Merlin 46); TOC/RAF 14.12.42; Arr Gibraltar 18.1.43 - US 12th AF; 52nd FG Telergma, crashed 6m SSW of Benimansour, Cat.FB/E (Lt JC Roberts, date unknown), SOC
JG750 Spitfire F.Vc/trop (Merlin 46); TOC/RAF 15.12.42; Arr Gibraltar 6.2.43; NWA 28.2.43 - US 12th AF; 52nd FG, accident La Senia 17.3.43 (Lt JK Blythe); Based Youks-les-Bains, accident Gedim 16.4.43 (Lt PJ Fox); Retd RAF, SOC 28.4.45
JG779 Spitfire F.Vc/trop (Merlin 46); TOC/RAF 21.12.42; Arr Gibraltar 6.2.43 - US 12th AF mid 1943; Retd RAF 1.10.43
JG780 Spitfire F.Vc/trop (Merlin 46); TOC/RAF 21.12.42; Arr Gibraltar 18.1.43; NWA 31.7.43 - US 12th AF 31.7.43; Retd RAF in 1944 (MAAF census 6.45); Later to France in 2.46
JG800 Spitfire F.Vc/trop (Merlin 46); TOC/RAF 22.1.43; NWA 31.3.43 - US 12th AF 31.10.43; Retd RAF in 1944 (No.73 Sqn, missing 26.5.44)
JG873 Spitfire F.Vc/trop (Merlin 46); TOC/RAF 21.12.42; Arr Gibraltar 18.1.43; NWA 28.2.43 - US 12th AF; 52nd FG Telergma, accident at base 28.2.43 (Lt OR McDuff); SOC/RAF 31.7.43
JG878 Spitfire F.Vc/trop (Merlin 46); TOC/RAF 21.1.43; NWA 31.3.43 - US 12th AF; 52nd FG, 4th FS ('WD-V') in 10.43; Retd RAF in 1944 (ME in 4.45); SOC 25.7.46
JG883 Spitfire F.Vc/trop (Merlin 46); TOC/RAF 24.12.42; Arr Gibraltar 16.2.43; NWA 31.3.43 - US 12th AF; 31st FG, 309th FS ('WZ-W') 31.8.43; Retd RAF 29.2.44
NOTE: Misreported as "JG685" in 10.43. Also reported Mk.Vb of 31st FG, 309th FS ('WZ-W'), pilot baled out when engine seized 27.7.43 (Lt Mehroff). ["JG883 had been with 309th FS since Tafaraoui [= 11.42], mechanics cheered when they heard"]. But this must have been another aircraft
JG885 Spitfire F.Vc/trop (Merlin 46); TOC/RAF 22.12.42; ME 19.5.43; NA 30.11.43 - US 12th AF end 1944 (No.326 (French) Sqn in 4.45); SOXO (8th AF), diverted to French ("L-09") 10.5.45; No.326 Sqn RAF 19.5.45; No.81 R&SU 25.7.45; Possibly to France in 11.45
JG914 Spitfire F.Vc/trop (Merlin 46); TOC/RAF 2.1.43; Arr Gibraltar 6.2.43; NWA 1.10.43 - US 12th AF 1.10.43; Retd RAF; SOC 26.4.45
JG915 Spitfire F.Vc/trop (Merlin 46); TOC/RAF 31.12.42; Arr Takoradi 20.4.43; ME 9.5.43; SAAF 7.43; NAAF 11.43 - US 12th AF; 52nd FG (possibly), accident at Telergma 29.3.44 (Lt JAC Andrews); Retd RAF, SOC 26.4.45
JG926 Spitfire F.Vc/trop (Merlin 46); TOC/RAF 11.12.42; Arr Gibraltar 18.1.43; NWA 31.7.43 - US 12th AF 31.7.43; Retd RAF in 1944 (MAAF census 6.45); SOC 19.7.45
JG930 Spitfire F.Vc/trop (Merlin 46); TOC/RAF 21.12.42; Arr Gibraltar 6.2.43; NWA 28.2.43 - US 12th AF; 52nd FG La Sebala, accident at base 31.5.43 (Lt TD Litchfield); Fate unknown
JG949 Spitfire F.Vc/trop (Merlin 46); TOC/RAF 2.1.43; Arr Gibraltar 6.2.43 - US 12th AF 31.10.43; Fate unknown
JG952 Spitfire F.Vc/trop (Merlin 46); TOC/RAF 4.1.43; Arr Gibraltar 16.2.43; NWA 31.3.43 - US 12th AF; 52nd FG La Sebala, accident at base 4.43 or 5.43 (Lt SA Rollag), date unknown; SOC/RAF 28.4.45
JK102 Spitfire F.Vc/trop (Merlin 46); TOC/RAF 2.1.43; Arr Gibraltar 6.2.43 - US 12th AF 1943; Retd RAF 1.10.43; Later to Greece in 4.46
JK160 Spitfire F.Vc/trop (Merlin 46); TOC/RAF 29.1.43; NWA 31.3.43 - US 12th AF; 52nd FG, 2nd FS Corsica 31.12.43; Shot down over France, Cat.FB/E 9.2.44, SOC
JK162 Spitfire F.Vc/trop (Merlin 46); TOC/RAF 22.1.43; NWA 31.3.43 - US 12th AF 31.8.43; Retd RAF 1.10.43

Spitfire F.Vc/trop JG878 'WD-V' of the 4th Sqn, 52nd FG, 12th (UA)AF in October 1943.

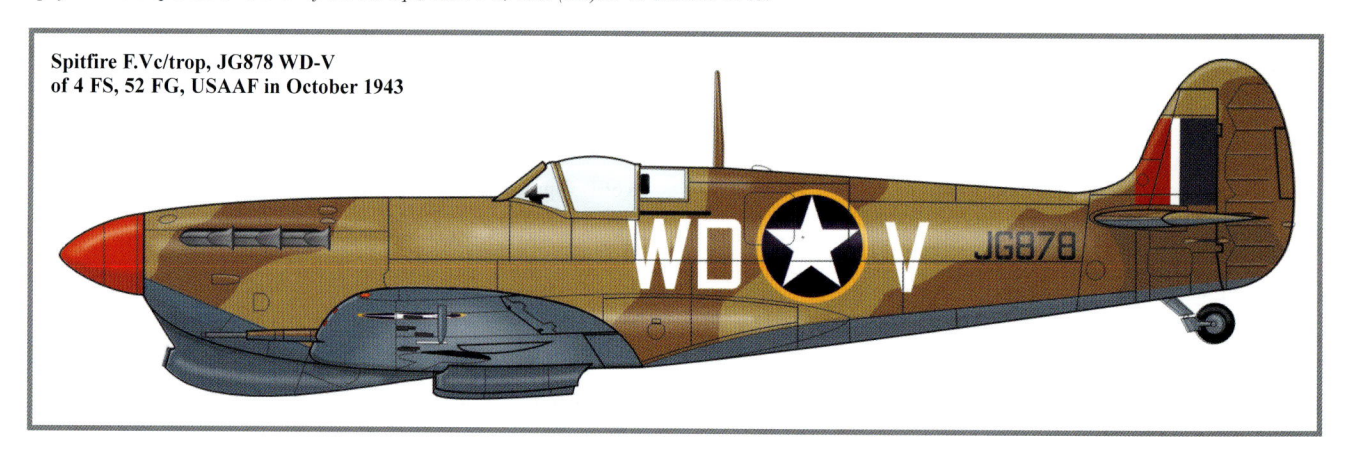

**Spitfire F.Vc/trop, JG878 WD-V
of 4 FS, 52 FG, USAAF in October 1943**

JK167   Spitfire F.Vc/trop (Merlin 46); TOC/RAF 1.2.43; NWA 31.3.43 - US 12th AF 1.10.43; Fate unknown
JK171   Spitfire F.Vc/trop (Merlin 46); TOC/RAF 24.1.43; NWA 31.3.43 - US 12th AF; 52nd FG in 1943; Dived into Mediterranean, Cat.FB/E 3.4.44, SOC
JK183   Spitfire F.Vc/trop (Merlin 46); TOC/RAF 24.1.43; Arr Gibraltar 9.3.43; NWA 25.4.43 (missing Cat.FB/E) - US 12th AF 1.10.43; Fate unknown
JK188   Spitfire F.Vc/trop (Merlin 46); Presentation aircraft *'KHARTOUM CITY AND PROVINCE'*; TOC/RAF 1.2.43; N.A. 30.11.43 - US 12th AF 31.1.44; Retd RAF 31.5.44
JK192   Spitfire F.Vc/trop (Merlin 46); TOC/RAF 2.43; Arr Gibraltar 7.3.43; NWA 31.3.43 - US 12th AF; 52nd FG Youks-el-Bains, accident La Sebala 11.4.43 (Lt W Goldstein); SOC/RAF 31.7.43
JK218   Spitfire F.Vc/trop (Merlin 46); TOC/RAF 3.2.43; NWA 30.4.43 - US 12th AF in 5.43; Retd RAF 30.11.43
JK221   Spitfire F.Vc/trop (Merlin 46); TOC/RAF 2.2.43; Arr Gibraltar 24.3.43; NWA 30.4.43; M.E. 9.43; NAAF 11.43; SAAF 1.3.44 - US 12th AF; 52nd FG (poss.), accident at Telergma 27.3.44 (Lt RJ Goebel); SOC/RAF 14.3.46
JK222   Spitfire F.Vc/trop (Merlin 46); TOC/RAF 13.2.43; NWA 31.5.43 - US 12th AF 1.10.43; Retd RAF 29.2.44
JK226   Spitfire F.Vc/trop (Merlin 46); TOC/RAF 3.2.43; NWA 30.4.43 - US 12th AF; 31st FG, 308th FS ('HL-AA') in 1943; Retd RAF 31.8.44; Later to Greece in 4.46
JK235   Spitfire F.Vc/trop (Merlin 46); TOC/RAF 2.3.43; NWA 31.5.43 - US 12th AF 31.7.43; Fate unknown
JK252   Spitfire F.Vc/trop (Merlin 46); TOC/RAF 6.2.43; Casablanca 6.4.43; NWA 30.4.43 - US 12th AF 31.7.43; DUKO (12th AF), retd RAF 24.6.44
JK255   Spitfire F.Vc/trop (Merlin 46); Presentation aircraft *'BARAKAT/BLUE NILE'*; TOC/RAF 27.1.43; NWA 31.5.43 - US 12th AF; 52nd FG 31.8.43; Dived into Mediterranean, pilot baled out, Cat.FB/E 13.1.44 (1/Lt JT Nangle DoI), SOC
JK261   Spitfire F.Vc/trop (Merlin 46); TOC/RAF 3.2.43; Arr Gibraltar 26.4.43; NWA 31.7.43 - US 12th AF 31.7.43; Retd RAF 31.5.44
JK267   Spitfire F.Vc/trop (Merlin 46); TOC/RAF 3.2.43; Arr Gibraltar 12.4.43; NWA 30.4.43 - US 12th AF 1943/44 (French-unit 1.10.43); Retd RAF 31.5.44
JK278   Spitfire F.Vc/trop (Merlin 46); TOC/RAF 3.2.43; Casablanca 25.4.43; NWA 31.7.43 - US 12th AF 31.7.43; Retd RAF; Training Delegation 1.11.45; To France 11.45

United States of America

JK284   Spitfire F.Vc/trop (Merlin 46); TOC/RAF 2.2.43; NWA 31.5.43 - US 12th AF 31.7.43; Retd RAF 31.5.44; Via No.352 Sqn to Yugoslavia (No 9481) in 5.45
JK309   Spitfire F.Vc/trop (Merlin 46); TOC/RAF 2.2.43; NWA 30.4.43; US 12th AF, Sicily in 1943; Retd RAF 30.11.43
JK322   Spitfire F.Vc/trop (Merlin 46); Presentation aircraft '*JOY*'; TOC/RAF 6.2.43; NAAF 1.11.43 - US 12th AF 31.1.44; Fate unknown
JK326   Spitfire F.Vc/trop (Merlin 46); TOC/RAF 4.1.43; Arr Gibraltar 6.2.43 - US 12th AF 1944; No.326 & 328 (French) Sqns in 7.44 & 8.44; Damaged 21.9.44; SOXO (8th AF), diverted to French ("L-09") 10.5.45; Possibly to France 11.45
JK360   Spitfire F.Vc/trop (Merlin 50); TOC/RAF 15.2.43; NWA 31.5.43 - US 12th AF 31.7.43; Retd RAF in 1944
JK363   Spitfire F.Vc/trop (Merlin 46); TOC/RAF 18.2.43; NWA 31.5.43 - US 12th AF 31.7.43; Retd RAF (MAAF) 22.2.45; SOC 29.3.45
JK367   Spitfire F.Vc/trop (Merlin 46); TOC/RAF 23.2.43; NWA 31.5.43 - US 12th AF 31.7.43; SOC/RAF 26.4.45
JK369   Spitfire F.Vc/trop (Merlin 46); TOC/RAF 11.4.43; M.E. 1.7.43 - US 12th AF in 1943 (also listed 6.44); Fate unknown
JK378   Spitfire F.Vc/trop (Merlin 50); TOC/RAF 6.3.43; Arr Casablanca 25.4.43; NAASC 31.10.43; US 12th AF – 52nd FG (possibly), accident at Telergma 23.2.44 (Lt CR Denham); SOC/RAF 26.4.45
JK380   Spitfire F.Vc/trop (Merlin 50); TOC/RAF 2.3.43; NWA 30.4.43 - US 12th AF 29.2.44; Retd RAF 31.5.44; Later to France in 10.47
JK381   Spitfire F.Vc/trop (Merlin 46); TOC/RAF 7.3.43; Arr Casablanca 24.4.43; NWA - US 12th AF; 52nd FG, 4th FS, Accident at Calvi, Corsica 12.1.44 (Lt TE Watts); Retd RAF; Later to Turkey in 11.44
JK382   Spitfire F.Vc/trop (Merlin 50); TOC/RAF 2.3.43; NWA 31.5.43 - US 12th AF; 52nd FG, 4th FS ('WD-D') 31.5.43 (also seen over Corsica 4.44); Retd RAF (ME census 6.45); SOC 29.3.46
JK385   Spitfire F.Vc/trop (Merlin 46); TOC/RAF 4.2.43; NWA 30.4.43 - US 12th AF 31.7.43; Retd RAF 31.5.44
JK390   Spitfire F.Vc/trop (Merlin 46); TOC/RAF 3.2.43; NWA 30.4.43 - US 12th AF; 52nd FG, 2nd FS in 7.43; RAF 1.10.43; To US 12th AF 30.11.43; Retd RAF 31.5.44
JK396   Spitfire F.Vc/trop (Merlin 46); TOC/RAF 7.2.43; NWA 31.5.43 - US 12th AF 31.7.43; Fate unknown
JK402   Spitfire F.Vc/trop (Merlin 46); TOC/RAF 9.2.43; NWA 30.4.43 - US 12th AF 31.7.43; Retd RAF 31.5.44
JK403   Spitfire F.Vc/trop (Merlin 46); TOC/RAF 6.2.43; NWA 31.5.43; Malta 1.8.43 - US 12th AF 1.8.43; dis. Gozo; Fate unknown
JK437   Spitfire F.Vc/trop (Merlin 46); TOC/RAF 11.2.43; NWA 30.4.43 - US 12th AF 31.7.43; Retd RAF (MAAF census 6.45); Training Delegation 13.9.45; Later to France
JK464   Spitfire F.Vc/trop (Merlin 46); TOC/RAF 11.2.43; NWA 30.4.43 - US 12th AF in 7.43; Retd RAF 1.10.43
JK521   Spitfire F.Vc/trop (Merlin 46); TOC/RAF 15.2.43; Arr Casablanca 25.4.43; NWA 31.5.43; NAASC 10.43 - US 12th AF; 52nd FG La Sebala, accident at base (Lt SA Rollag, date unknown); Retd RAF, SOC 28.4.45
JK523   Spitfire F.Vc/trop (Merlin 46); TOC/RAF 15.2.43; NWA 31.5.43 - US 12th AF 31.7.43; Fate unknown
JK524   Spitfire F.Vc/trop (Merlin 46); TOC/RAF 23.2.43; Casablanca 25.4.43 - US 12th AF 31.7.43; Transferred to a French unit 10.43
JK526   Spitfire F.Vc/trop (Merlin 46); TOC/RAF 19.2.43; NWA 31.5.43 - US 12th AF 31.7.43; Retd RAF 31.5.44; Later to Turkey in 3.45
JK528   Spitfire F.Vc/trop (Merlin 46); TOC/RAF 27.2.43; NWA 30.4.43 - US 12th AF in 7.43; Retd RAF 31.10.43; Later to Greece in 4.46
JK530   Spitfire F.Vc/trop (Merlin 46); TOC/RAF 7.3.43; NWA 31.5.43 - US 12th AF 31.7.43; Retd RAF 31.1.44; Later to Greece in 5.45
JK531   Spitfire F.Vc/trop (Merlin 46); Named '*MISS MAUD*'; TOC/RAF 13.3.43; NAAF 1.11.43 - US 12th AF; 52nd FG, 2nd FS ('QP-XX') in 11.43 (later seen marked 'M218' in 1944); Retd RAF (ME census 6.45); SOC 4.10.45
JK537   Spitfire F.Vc/trop (Merlin 45); TOC/RAF 18.3.43; NWA 31.5.43 - US 12th AF 31.7.43; Fate unknown
JK541   Spitfire F.Vc/trop (Merlin 46); TOC/RAF 14.3.43; NWA 31.5.43; M.E. 8.43 - US 12th AF; 31st FG (Malta) 31.1.44; Fate unknown
JK542   Spitfire F.Vc/trop (Merlin 50); TOC/RAF 20.3.43; NWA 31.5.43 - US 12th AF in 7.43; Retd RAF 31.10.43
JK543   Spitfire F.Vc/trop (Merlin 50); TOC/RAF 20.3.43; NWA 31.5.43 - US 12th AF in 7.43; Retd RAF 31.7.43; Later to France in 10.43
JK550   Spitfire F.Vc/trop (Merlin 45); TOC/RAF 26.3.43; Casablanca 17.5.43 - US 12th AF 31.7.43; Retd RAF in 1944; Later to France in 2.46
JK551   Spitfire F.Vc/trop (Merlin 45); TOC/RAF 27.3.43; NWA 31.5.43 - US 12th AF 31.7.43; Fate unknown
JK602   Spitfire F.Vc/trop (Merlin 50); TOC/RAF 14.2.43; NWA 31.5.43 - US 12th AF; 52nd FG 31.8.43; Lost over France, Rhone area, Cat.FB/E 27.1.44 (2/Lt LR Kater killed), SOC
JK604   Spitfire F.Vc/trop (Merlin 50); TOC/RAF 16.2.43; NWA 30.4.43; M.E. 1.8.43 - US 12th AF 31.10.43; DUKO (12th AF), retd RAF 6.7.44
JK607   Spitfire F.Vc/trop (Merlin 46); TOC/RAF 18.2.43; NWA 30.4.43 - US 12th AF 30.11.43; Retd RAF in 1944; SOC 26.4.45
JK609   Spitfire F.Vc/trop (Merlin 46); TOC/RAF 18.2.43; Casablanca 6.4.43; NWA 31.5.43 - US 12th AF; 31st FG in 7.43; Shot down by flak whilst on patrol 20m N of Venafro, Cat.FB/E 5.11.43 (Lt E Frost PoW), SOC
JK612   Spitfire F.Vc/trop (Merlin 46); TOC/RAF 16.2.43; Casablanca 25.4.43; Malta 1.7.43; NAAF 1.11.43 - US 12th AF 31.1.44; Fate unknown
JK648   Spitfire F.Vc/trop (Merlin 50A); TOC/RAF 19.2.43; NWA 31.5.43 - US 12th AF 31.7.43; Retd RAF 31.1.44; Later to Egypt 2.45
JK653   Spitfire F.Vc/trop (Merlin 46); TOC/RAF 24.2.43; M.E. 30.9.43 - US 12th AF 1.10.43; SOC/RAF 8.3.44
JK661   Spitfire F.Vc/trop (Merlin 46); TOC/RAF 19.2.43; Arr Gibraltar 12.4.43; NWA 30.4.43 - US 12th AF 31.7.43; Retd RAF 31.5.44
JK668   Spitfire F.IXc (Merlin 63); TOC/RAF 4.4.43; Casablanca 17.5.43; NWA - US 12th AF 31.7.43; Fate unknown
JK673   Spitfire F.Vc/trop (Merlin 46); TOC/RAF 24.2.43; Arr Gibraltar 12.4.43; NWA 31.5.43 - US 12th AF in 7.43; Retd RAF 31.7.43
JK705   Spitfire F.Vc/trop (Merlin 46); TOC/RAF 27.2.43; Casablanca 6.4.43 - US 12th AF; 52nd FG 29.2.44; 4th FS, lost over France, shot down by aircraft, FTR ops, Cat.FB/E 27.1.44 [Mov.card 27.4.44], (2/Lt Harold Beedle Jnr missing), SOC
JK707   Spitfire F.Vc/trop (Merlin 50); TOC/RAF 24.2.43; NWA 30.4.43 - US 12th AF; 31st FG, 307th FS ('MX-P') in 7.43; Force-landed on beach near Salerno in 9.43, Cat.FB/E (1/Lt CA Pryblo), SOC
JK711   Spitfire F.Vc/trop (Merlin 46); TOC/RAF 23.2.43; NWA 31.5.43 - US 12th AF in 7.43; Retd RAF 29.2.44
JK716   Spitfire F.Vc/trop (Merlin 50); TOC/RAF 26.2.43; NWA 31.5.43 - US 12th AF in 7.43; Retd RAF 31.7.43
JK717   Spitfire F.Vc/trop (Merlin 50); TOC/RAF 25.2.43; Arr Gibraltar 12.4.43; NWA 31.5.43 - US 12th AF 31.8.43; Fate unknown
JK719   Spitfire F.Vc/trop (Merlin 46); TOC/RAF 25.2.43; NWA 31.5.43 - US 12th AF 31.7.43; Fate unknown
JK724   Spitfire F.Vc/trop (Merlin 46); TOC/RAF 26.2.43; NWA 31.5.43 - US 12th AF 31.7.43; Retd RAF; SOC 28.4.45
JK729   Spitfire F.Vc/trop (Merlin 46); TOC/RAF 27.2.43; Arr Gibraltar 12.4.43; NWA 30.4.43 - US 12th AF; 52nd FG Bone, accident at Borgo 11.1.44 (Lt A G Johnson Jnr); Fate unknown
JK732   Spitfire F.Vc/trop (Merlin 46); TOC/RAF 27.2.43; Casablanca 6.4.43 - US 12th AF in 7.43; Retd RAF 1.10.43

JK734 Spitfire F.Vc/trop (Merlin 46); TOC/RAF 6.3.43; Arr Gibraltar 12.4.43 - US 12th AF in 7.43; 52nd FG, 2nd FS ('QP-E', marked 'KAY II'); NAASC 31.10.43 - US 12th AF 29.2.44; Flying accident, Cat.FB/3 31.3.44, SOC

JK735 Spitfire F.Vc/trop (Merlin 46); TOC/RAF 28.2.43; Arr Gibraltar 6.4.43; NWA 31.5.43 - US 12th AF 1.10.43; Accident Naples 30.11.43 (Lt AC Gillem); Accident Telergma 12.1.44 (Lt HC Lane Jnr); Fate unknown

JK736 Spitfire F.Vc/trop (Merlin 46); TOC/RAF 26.2.43; NWA 31.5.43 - US 12th AF 31.8.43; Fate unknown

JK763 Spitfire F.Vc/trop (Merlin 46); TOC/RAF 28.2.43; NWA 30.4.43 - US 12th AF in 7.43; Retd RAF 31.10.43 (Cat.FB/3 2.2.44, SOC)

JK765 Spitfire F.Vc/trop (Merlin 45); TOC/RAF 1.3.43; NWA 31.5.43 - US 12th AF 31.10.43; SOC/RAF 26.4.45

JK768 Spitfire F.Vc/trop (Merlin 50); TOC/RAF 6.3.43; NWA 31.5.43 - US 12th AF 31.7.43; Retd RAF 31.1.44 (NAAF)

JK772 Spitfire F.Vc/trop (Merlin 50A); TOC/RAF 6.3.43; NWA 31.5.43 - US 12th AF 31.8.43; Fate unknown

JK774 Spitfire F.Vc/trop (Merlin 46); TOC/RAF 28.2.43; NWA 31.5.43 - US 12th AF 31.7.43; Fate unknown

JK775 Spitfire F.Vc/trop (Merlin 46); TOC/RAF 28.2.43; Casablanca 25.4.43; NWA - US 12th AF 31.7.43; RAF 1.10.43; To 12th AF 29.2.44; Fate unknown

JK776 Spitfire F.Vc/trop (Merlin 50); TOC/RAF 6.3.43; Casablanca 25.4.43; NWA - US 12th AF 31.7.43; Fate unknown

JK777 Spitfire F.Vc/trop (Merlin 46); Presentation aircraft 'PUNJAB POLICE V'; TOC/RAF 6.3.43; Casablanca 25.4.43; NWA 31.5.43 - US 12th AF 31.7.43; 52nd FG, 2nd FS ('QP-Z') 7.43; Retd RAF (MAAF census 6.45); SOC 22.11.45

JK780 Spitfire F.Vc/trop (Merlin 50); TOC/RAF 6.3.43; NWA 31.5.43 - US 12th AF 31.7.43; Retd RAF in 10.43 (French unit until 31.10.43); SAAF from 28.2.44

JK788 Spitfire F.Vc/trop (Merlin 46); TOC/RAF 6.3.43; NWA 31.5.43 - US 12th AF 31.7.43; Retd RAF 31.8.44

JK791 Spitfire F.Vc/trop (Merlin 46); TOC/RAF 7.3.43; NWA 31.5.43 - US 12th AF 31.7.43; Fate unknown

JK804 Spitfire F.Vc/trop (Merlin 46); TOC/RAF 26.2.43; Casablanca 25.4.43; NWA 31.8.43 - US 12th AF 31.8.43; DUKO (12th AF), retd RAF 19.8.44

JK806 Spitfire F.Vc/trop (Merlin 46); TOC/RAF 28.2.43 (French unit 31.8.43) - US 12th AF 1943/44; Retd RAF 31.5.44; Later to Turkey in 11.44

JK809 Spitfire F.Vc/trop (Merlin 46); TOC/RAF 23.2.43; NWA 30.4.43 - US 12th AF 31.1.44; Retd RAF 30.11.44; Later to Greece in 4.46

JK810 Spitfire F.Vc/trop (Merlin 46); TOC/RAF 25.2.43; NWA 31.5.43; Malta 1.7.43; N.A. 30.11.43 - US 12th AF 31.1.44; Fate unknown

JK811 Spitfire F.Vc/trop (Merlin 46); TOC/RAF 1.3.43; NWA 31.5.43 - US 12th AF; 52nd FG, 2nd FS 31.8.43; Retd RAF 31.5.44

JK813 Spitfire F.Vc/trop (Merlin 46); TOC/RAF 1.3.43; NWA 30.4.43 - US 12th AF 31.7.43; Fate unknown

JK818 Spitfire F.Vc/trop (Merlin 46); TOC/RAF 15.3.43; NWA 31.5.43 - US 12th AF 31.7.43; Retd RAF 29.2.44

JK823 Spitfire F.Vc/trop (Merlin 50); TOC/RAF 21.3.43; Casablanca 25.4.43; French unit NWA 1.10.43; NAASC 31.10.43 - US 12th AF in 1943; DUKO (12th AF), diverted to French ("L-09") 10.5.45; No.328 (French) Sqn 12.5.45; No.81 R&SU 25.7.45; Later to France in 11.45

JK827 Spitfire F.Vc/trop (Merlin 45); TOC/RAF 28.3.43; Casablanca 17.5.43 - US 12th AF 31.10.43; Retd RAF 31.5.44

JK828 Spitfire F.Vc/trop (Merlin 45); TOC/RAF 26.3.43; NWA, Malta 31.5.43 - US 12th AF 31.7.43; Fate unknown

JK839 Spitfire F.Vc/trop (Merlin 50); TOC/RAF 3.4.43; NWA 31.5.43 - US 12th AF 31.7.43; Crashed Cat.FB/E 19.10.44, SOC

JK861 Spitfire F.Vc/trop (Merlin 46); TOC/RAF 7.3.43; NWA 31.5.43 - US 12th AF 31.7.43; Retd RAF 31.10.43

JK862 Spitfire F.Vc/trop (Merlin 50); TOC/RAF 6.3.43; NWA 31.5.43 - US 12th AF 31.8.43; Fate unknown

JK864 Spitfire F.Vc/trop (Merlin 50); TOC/RAF 7.3.43; M.E. 30.9.43; NWA 1.10.43 - US 12th AF 31.10.43; Fate unknown

JK870 Spitfire F.Vc/trop (Merlin 46); TOC/RAF 11.3.43; Casablanca 25.4.43; NWA 31.5.43 - US 12th AF; 31st FG, 309th FS ('WZ-P') 31.7.43; Shot down on patrol by Bf 109 north of Terracina [N of Gaeta], Cat.FB/E 2.12.43 (Lt H Arrelson PoW), SOC

JK875 Spitfire F.Vc/trop (Merlin 50); TOC/RAF 7.3.43; NWA 31.5.43 - US 12th AF in 7.43; RAF 31.7.43; To 12th USAF 1.10.43; Retd RAF 31.5.44

JK881 Spitfire F.IXc (Merlin 63); TOC/RAF 28.3.43; Casablanca 17.5.43 - US 12th AF in 1943; SOXO (8th AF), diverted to French ("L-09") 10.5.44; Retd RAF; SOC 26.3.45

JK883 Spitfire F.IXc (Merlin 63); TOC/RAF 26.3.43; Casablanca 17.5.43; NWA - US 12th AF 31.7.43; Fate unknown

JK941 Spitfire F.Vc/trop (Merlin 50); TOC/RAF 14.3.43; NWA 31.5.43; US 12th AF 1.10.43; Crashed Cat.FB/3 27.5.44, SOC

JK948 Spitfire F.Vc/trop (Merlin 50); TOC/RAF 15.3.43; French unit 8.43 - US 12th AF; 52nd FG in 12.43; 4th FS, lost over France, shot down by enemy aircraft, Cat.FB/E 27.1.44 (1/Lt Ottaway B Cornwell missing), SOC

JK976 Spitfire F.Vc/trop (Merlin 46); TOC/RAF 17.3.43; NWA 31.5.43 - US 12th AF in 7.43; Retd RAF 31.7.43

JL121 Spitfire F.Vc/trop (Merlin 50); TOC/RAF 5.5.43; Casablanca 15.6.43; NWA 1.7.43 - US 12th AF 1943/44; No.326 (French) Sqn in 10.44; SOXO (8th AF), diverted to French ("L-09") 10.5.45; No.327 Sqn RAF 12.5.45 (also shown in 10.45); Later to France in 11.45

JL129 Spitfire F.Vc/trop (Merlin 46); TOC/RAF 28.3.43; NWA 31.5.43 - US 12th AF 31.8.43; Fate unknown

JL131 Spitfire F.Vc/trop (Merlin 45); TOC/RAF 22.3.43; NWA 31.5.43; M.E. 1.9.43 - US 12th AF 1.10.43; Retd RAF 31.5.44

JL133 Spitfire F.Vc/trop (Merlin 45); TOC/RAF 22.3.43; Casablanca 17.5.43; NWA 31.5.43; N.A. 30.11.43 - US 12th AF 31.1.44; Fate unknown

JL134 Spitfire F.IXc (Merlin 63); TOC/RAF 28.3.43; Casablanca 17.5.43; NWA - US 12th AF 31.7.43; Fate unknown

JL135 Spitfire F.IXc (Merlin 63); TOC/RAF 28.3.43; Casablanca 17.5.43; NAASC 31.10.43 - US 12th AF end 1943; RiW, AST Hamble 23.3.45; SOXO (8th AF), diverted to French ("L-09") 10.5.45; Retd RAF in 7.45

JL140 Spitfire F.Vc/trop (Merlin 50); TOC/RAF 22.3.43; Arr Casablanca 25.4.43; NWA - US 12th AF; Accident Ain Seymour 16.10.43 (Lt R Savoy); SOC/RAF 26.4.45

JL182 Spitfire F.Vc/trop (Merlin 45); TOC/RAF 30.3.43; Casablanca 17.5.43; NAAF 1.11.43 - US 12th AF 31.1.44; Fate unknown

JL183 Spitfire F.Vc/trop (Merlin 46); TOC/RAF 31.3.43; Casablanca 17.5.43; NWA - US 12th AF 31.7.43; Fate unknown

JL221 Spitfire F.Vc/trop (Merlin 50); TOC/RAF 16.4.43; NAASC 31.10.43 - US 12th AF 31.1.44; Retd RAF 28.12.44; Later to France in 2.46

JL229 Spitfire F.IXc (Merlin 63); TOC/RAF 2.4.43; NWA 1.10.43 - US 12th AF 31.10.43; Retd RAF in 1944; Later to Turkey in 3.45

JL234 Spitfire LF.IXc (Merlin 66); TOC/RAF 11.4.43; Casablanca 29.9.43 - US 12th AF end 1943; Luxeuil 12.44; FAF GR.2/33 in 1.45; Damaged 2.1.45; No.328 Sqn 5.4.45; SOXO (8th AF), diverted to French ("L-09") 10.5.45; Possibly to France in 11.45

JL237 Spitfire F.Vc/trop (Merlin 45); TOC/RAF 4.4.43; Casablanca 17.5.43 - US 12th AF; 31st FG, 309th FS ('WZ-J') in 7.43; Landed wheels up, Milazzo, Cat.E 2.9.43 (Lt RC Stone); bboc; 31st FG, 309th FS, Gulf patrol of Gaeta 27.10.43 (Lt RJ Connor); Fate unknown

JL244 Spitfire F.Vc/trop (Merlin 50); TOC/RAF 11.4.43; M.E. 2.7.43; NAASC 31.10.43 - US 12th AF 31.1.44; Coded '7' with an all-French unit of the USAAF 10.44; Retd RAF (M.E. census 6.45); SOC 14.3.46

UNITED STATES OF AMERICA

JL253　Spitfire F.IXc (Merlin 63); TOC/RAF 2.4.43; M.E. 1.9.43; NAAF 1.11.43 - US 12th AF; 31st FG, 309th FS ('WZ-FF') in 11.43; Lost over Anzio beachhead, crashed Falgagnano, Cat.FB/E 5.2.44 (Lt Yocum PoW?); SOC 7.2.44 - But note: Reported Anzio patrol (JL253) by Lt RJ Connor 6.2.44.

JL301　Spitfire F.Vc/trop (Merlin 50); TOC/RAF 20.5.43; M.E. 1.8.43; NAAF 1.11.43; No.118 MU - US 12th AF 31.1.44; Fate unknown

JL309　Spitfire F.Vc/trop (Merlin 50); TOC/RAF 15.5.43; NWA 1.7.43 - US 12th AF 1.10.43; Retd RAF 30.11.43

JL318　Spitfire F.Vc/trop (Merlin 50); TOC/RAF 15.5.43; NWA 1.7.43 - US 12th AF 31.12.43; Fate unknown

JL323　Spitfire F.Vc/trop (Merlin 50); TOC/RAF 17.6.43; Casablanca 18.8.43 - US 12th AF 1.10.43; Retd RAF (MAAF census 6.45); SOC 30.6.45

JL333　Spitfire F.Vc/trop (Merlin 50); TOC/RAF 30.6.43; N.A. 30.11.43; (French unit 31.12.43) - US 12th AF in 1944; Retd RAF 31.5.44

JL374　Spitfire F.Vc/trop (Merlin 46); TOC/RAF 18.4.43; NWA 1.10.43; French unit end 1943 - US 12th AF in 1944; Retd RAF 31.5.44; Later to Turkey in 11.44

JL381　Spitfire F.Vc/trop (Merlin 46); TOC/RAF 13.4.43; Casablanca 30.5.43; Gozo - US 12th AF 1.8.43; NAAF 1.11.43; Retd 12th AF 31.1.44; Retd RAF 29.2.44

JL384　Spitfire F.IXc (Merlin 63); TOC/RAF 11.4.43; Casablanca 30.5.43; NWA 1.7.43 - US 12th AF end 1943; SOXO (8th AF), diverted to French ("L-09") 10.5.45; Retd RAF (No.29 MU) 2.8.45

JL389　Spitfire F.Vc/trop (Merlin 50); TOC/RAF 25.4.43; Casablanca 30.5.43; Malta 7.43; Gozo 1.8.43 - US 12th AF 1.8.43; DUKO (12th AF), crashed Cat.A 8.7.44; Retd RAF 22.7.44

JL391　Spitfire F.Vc/trop (Merlin 50); TOC/RAF 27.4.43; Casablanca 30.5.43; NWA 1.7.43 - US 12th AF 31.8.43; Fate unknown

LZ809　Spitfire F.Vc/trop (Merlin 45); TOC/RAF 1.4.43; Casablanca 17.5.43; Malta 1.8.43; dis. NA 1.10.43 - US 12th AF 31.12.43; Fate unknown

LZ820　Spitfire F.Vc/trop (Merlin 50); TOC/RAF 5.4.43; Casablanca 7.5.43 - US 12th AF; 52nd FG, 4th FS ('WD-E') in 9.43; Missing, forced landed near Borgataro, Italy, Cat.E 19.12.43, SOC

LZ863　Spitfire F.Vc/trop (Merlin 50); TOC/RAF 27.4.43; NWA 1.7.43 - US 12th AF; 52nd FG; Missing over Corsica, Cat.FB/E 29.1.44, SOC
NOTE: Reported also with 52nd FG, 2nd FS, hit by small arms fire crossing Italian coast on recce trip to Rome/ Florence area, turn back but forced to bale out 500yds from SE tip of Elba 29.1.44 (Lt Haskins PoW) [probably LZ863]

LZ869　Spitfire F.Vc/trop (Merlin 50); TOC/RAF 27.4.43; N.A. 30.11.43 - US 12th AF 31.1.44; Retd RAF 31.5.44

LZ888　Spitfire F.IXc (Merlin 63); TOC/RAF 18.4.43; NWA 1.7.43; NAASC 31.10.43 - US 12th AF 29.2.44; Retd RAF (No.93 Sqn, Cat.FB/E 4.2.45)

LZ931　Spitfire F.Vc/trop (Merlin 50); TOC/RAF 3.5.43; NWA 1.7.43 - US 12th AF; 31st FG in 1944; Crashed Cat.FB/3 27.2.44, SOC

MA242　Spitfire F.IXc (Merlin 63); TOC/RAF 12.5.43; NWA 1.7.43 - US 12th AF 31.8.43; Fate unknown

MA248　Spitfire F.IXc (Merlin 63); TOC/RAF 16.5.43; NWA 1.7.43 - US 12th AF 31.7.43; Retd RAF 31.12.43; Later to Egypt 9.46

MA279　Spitfire F.Vc/trop (Merlin 46); TOC/RAF 15.5.43; NWA 1.7.43; NAASC 1.11.43 - US 12th AF 31.12.43; Fate unknown

MA335　Spitfire F.Vc/trop (Merlin 46); TOC/RAF 27.4.43; NWA 30.6.43 - US 12th AF; 52nd FG in 7.43; 5th FS, dived into Mediterranean, Cat.FB/E 29.12.43 (1/Lt I Gottlieb killed); SOC 29.2.44
NOTE: Also reported sugar in tank 28.12.43 (Lt D P Anderson killed)

MA336　Spitfire F.Vc/trop (Merlin 46); TOC/RAF 27.4.43; NAASC 31.10.43 - US 12th AF 30.11.43; Retd RAF (M.E. census 6.45); SOC 10.1.46

MA344　Spitfire F.Vc/trop (Merlin 46); TOC/RAF 9.5.43; NWA 1.7.43 - US 12th AF 31.8.43; Retd RAF 31.5.44

MA421　Spitfire F.IXc (Merlin 63); TOC/RAF 18.7.43; No.218 Grp N.A. 30.11.43 - US 12th AF 30.11.43; Fate unknown

MA483　Spitfire F.IXc (Merlin 63); TOC/RAF 31.5.43; NWA 31.7.43 - US 12th AF; 31st FG, 309th FS ('WZ-OO', 'FREDI III') in 10.43 - 3.44 (Lt RJ Connor in 2.44, Lt RC Stone in 3.44); Retd RAF (MAAF census 6.45); SOC 18.10.45

MA506　Spitfire F.IXc (Merlin 63); TOC/RAF 18.8.43; No.218 Grp N.A. 30.11.44 - US 12th AF; 31st FG, 309th FS ('WZ-KK') flown 12.1.44, tested 15.2.44 (Lt RJ Connor); Retd RAF; SOC 20.9.45

MA507　Spitfire F.IXc (Merlin 63); Presentation aircraft 'URUGUAY XII'; TOC/RAF 13.6.43; M.E. 1.9.43 - US 12th AF; 31st FG, 309th FS ('WZ-II') in 9.43 (shown also 11.43); Veered off runway in cross-wind 2.9.43 (Lt Souch); Overshot runway, crashed, engine torn out, Cat.E 7.9.43 (Lt Souch); dis. NAAF 30.11.43; bboc; still with 309th FS, Anzio fighter cover 28.1.44 (Lt RJ Connor); Fate unknown

MA510　Spitfire F.IXc (Merlin 63); Presentation aircraft 'URUGUAY XV'; TOC/RAF 13.6.43; No.218 Grp N.A. 30.11.43 - US 12th AF in 12.43; Retd RAF 29.2.44

MA522　Spitfire F.IXc (Merlin 63); TOC/RAF 17.6.43; Casablanca 14.7.43 - US 12th AF 31.1.44; Retd RAF 31.5.44

MA533　Spitfire F.IXc (Merlin 63); TOC/RAF 17.6.43; NWA 31.7.43 - US 12th AF in 9.43; Unknown unit (code 'V') in 9.43; Retd RAF (MAAF census 6.45); SOC 30.5.46

MA559　Spitfire F.IXc (Merlin 63); TOC/RAF 19.6.43; NWA 31.7.43 - US 12th AF; 31st FG, 309th FS ('WZ-PP') in 9.43; Fighter cover over Anzio beachhead, engine failed, force landed on beach, just made it to shore just N of Isola di Ischia 29.1.44 (Lt RJ Connor OK); SOC

MA580　Spitfire F.IXc (Merlin 63); TOC/RAF 21.6.43; M.E. 1.9.43; NAAF 30.9.43 - US 12th AF 31.10.43; Retd RAF (MAAF); SOC 28.4.45

MA595　Spitfire F.IXc (Merlin 63); TOC/RAF 30.6.43; Casablanca 29.7.43 - US 12th AF 31.10.43; Fate unknown

MA616　Spitfire F.IXc (Merlin 63); TOC/RAF 27.6.43; No.218 Grp. N.A. 30.11.43 - US 12th AF; 31st FG 30.11.43; 307th FS, bounced by Bf 109s over Liri Valley, radioed turning back with rough engine, FTR, Cat.FB/E 15.12.43 (Lt W Archer killed), SOC

MA625　Spitfire F.IXc (Merlin 63); TOC/RAF 28.6.43; Casablanca 20.7.43 - US 12th AF; 31st FG, 309th FS ('WZ-NN'), hit by flak on patrol over Anzio, Italy, baled out, Cat.FB/E 29.2.44 (Lt WG Nisbet killed), SOC

MA695　Spitfire F.Vc/trop (Merlin 46); TOC/RAF 23.6.43; Casablanca 20.9.43; NAASC 31.10.43; French unit 29.2.44 - US 12th AF in 5.44; Retd RAF 31.5.44; Later to Greece in 4.46

MA698　Spitfire F.Vc/trop (Merlin 46); TOC/RAF 8.8.43; Casablanca 29.9.43; NAASC 31.10.43 - US 12th AF 21.12.43; Retd RAF 31.5.44

MA702　Spitfire LF.Vc/trop (Merlin 55M); TOC/RAF 4.7.43; N.A. 30.11.43 - US 12th AF 31.1.44; Retd RAF 31.5.44

MA705　Spitfire F.IXc (Merlin 63); TOC/RAF 1.7.43; NWA 1.10.43 - US 12th AF 31.10.43; SOC/RAF 28.12.44

MA734　Spitfire F.IXc (Merlin 63); TOC/RAF 4.7.43; NWA 1.10.43 - US 12th AF 31.10.43; Retd RAF 30.11.43

MA765　Spitfire F.IXc (Merlin 63); TOC/RAF 18.7.43; Casablanca 18.8.43; NWA - US 12th AF 1.10.43; Retd RAF in 1944; SOC 6.9.45

MA793　Spitfire F.IXc (Merlin 63); TOC/RAF 19.7.43; NWA 1.10.43 - US 12th AF; 31st FG, 309th FS 31.10.43; Retd RAF, later to SAAF as 5601 31.5.44
NOTE: Airworthy (Merlin 70); Ex South Africa to Larry Barnett International California Inc, Los Angeles, California (reg. N930LB 29.9.86); ff 1.1.87; Operated by David Price/Donald Douglas Museum of Flying, Santa Monica California in 1987 (flown in RAF colours as

Surviving Spitfire F.IXc N930LB (ex MA793) in 1995, being operated by David Price/Donald Douglas Museum of Flying, Santa Monica, California, and flown in RAF colours as "EN398/JE-J". It is now in the Brazil Flying Museum at Sao Paulo.

"EN398/JE-J"); Sold to Rolls-Royce 21.1.00; Donated to the Brazil Flying Museum at Sao Paulo 3.00 - **SURVIVOR**

MA800 Spitfire F.IXc (Merlin 63); TOC/RAF 20.7.43; Casablanca 10.9.43; NAASC 31.10.43 - US 12th AF 31.1.44; Retd RAF in 1944 (No.241 Sqn, missing 21.3.44)

MA804 Spitfire F.IXc (Merlin 63); TOC/RAF 25.7.43; Casablanca 19.10.43; No.218 Grp. N.A. 30.11.43 - US 12th AF 31.12.43; Retd RAF 31.5.44

MA850 Spitfire LF.Vc/trop (Merlin 55M); TOC/RAF 1.7.43; Casablanca 10.9.43; N.A. 30.11.43 - US 12th AF 29.2.44; Retd RAF (M.E. census 6.45); SOC 29.8.46

MA861 Spitfire F.Vc/trop (Merlin 55); TOC/RAF 17.7.43; NWA 1.10.43 - US 12th AF 31.12.43; Fate unknown

MA862 Spitfire LF.Vc/trop (Merlin 55M); TOC/RAF 1.7.43; Casablanca 10.9.43; N.A. 30.11.43 - US 12th AF 31.1.44; Retd RAF in 1944 (No.253 Sqn, crashed Cat.FB/3 19.5.44); SOC

MA863 Spitfire F.Vc/trop; Arrived as **SURVIVOR** only; Restoration Imperial War Museum Duxford and Airframe Assemblies UK, rollout 16.2.00; On the way to USA by 15.3.00; Arr. USAF Museum at Dayton, Ohio; Exhibited in colours of No.71 [Eagle] Sqn as "XR-T" and extant

MA883 Spitfire F.Vc/trop (Merlin 55); TOC/RAF 8.8.43; Casablanca 20.9.43; NAASC 31.10.43 - US 12th AF; 52nd FG 31.12.43; Lost over France, Cat.FB/E 9.2.44, SOC

MA884 Spitfire F.IXc (Merlin 63); TOC/RAF 18.9.43; Casablanca 19.10.43; No.218 Grp N.A. 30.11.43 - US 12th AF 31.1.44; Retd RAF (MAAF census 6.45); SOC 30.8.45

MA886 Spitfire F.Vc/trop (Merlin 55); TOC/RAF 22.7.43; N.A. 30.11.43 - US 12th AF 29.2.44; Retd RAF 31.5.44.

MA887 Spitfire F.Vc/trop (Merlin 55); TOC/RAF 22.7.43; N.A.

Surviving ex-RAAF Spitfire F.Vc/trop MA863 was restored at Duxford before going to the USAF Museum at Dayton, Ohio, where it is seen here in mid-2000, exhibited in the colours of No. 71 (Eagle) Sqn as "XR-T".

30.11.43 - US 12th AF 29.2.44; Retd RAF; SOC 26.4.45
MA889 Spitfire F.Vc/trop (Merlin 55); TOC/RAF 18.7.43; N.A. 30.11.43 - US 12th AF 29.2.44; Retd RAF in 1944; Later to No.326 (French) Sqn, lost over sea 6.6.44, SOC
MA890 Spitfire F.Vc/trop (Merlin 55); TOC/RAF 26.7.43; NAASC 31.10.43 - US 12th AF; 52nd FG 31.1.44; Lost over Italy, Cat.FB/E 19.2.44, SOC
MA893 Spitfire F.Vc/trop (Merlin 55); TOC/RAF 24.7.43; Casablanca 18.8.43 - US 12th AF 29.2.44; Retd RAF (MAAF census 6.45); Later to France in 10.47
MA898 Spitfire F.Vc/trop (Merlin 46); TOC/RAF 23.6.43; N.A. 30.11.43; French unit 29.2.44 - US 12th AF in 5.44; Retd RAF 31.5.44
MA901 Spitfire F.Vc/trop (Merlin 46); TOC/RAF 26.6.43; N.A. 30.11.43; French unit 29.2.44 - US 12th AF in 5.44; Retd RAF 31.5.44
MA912 Spitfire F.IXc (Merlin 63); TOC/RAF 1.7.43 - US 12th AF in 1944; Fate unknown
MA996 Seafire L.IIc (Merlin 45); RNDA 5.9.42; On loan to US Navy at FAW-7 Dunkeswell 8.44; Retd R.N., later to No.768 Sqn in 11.44
MB113 Seafire F IIc (Merlin 46); RNDA 29.8.42; 885 Sqn 10.42; Op *'Torch'* 11.42: marked 'US Navy' and '6H-B', but with US star and Royal Navy fin flag; RN No.897 Sqn 10.43
MB190 Seafire F IIc (Merlin 46); RNDA 24.10.42; Shipped to USA 3.4.43; Became No. **FS-1**; Arr Floyd Bennet Field in 4.43; New York 10.11.43 (flown there by the pilots Clarkson and D B Law); sent to the US Navy at Patuxent River for comparison test with current carrier aircraft 3.44; Belly-landed 3.5.44 (Lt Flint); At Patuxent until 5.45; Fate unknown
MB263 Seafire L.IIc (Merlin 45); RNDA 6.12.42; On loan to US Navy at FAW-7 Dunkeswell 8.44; Ground-looped landing 16.9.44 (Lt Cdr RD Garland USNR); Retd R.N., major overhaul required
MB... ? Seafire L.IIc (Merlin 45); On loan to US Navy at FAW-7 Dunkeswell 8.44; Serial & Fate unknown (perhaps NM... serial number)
MB... ? Seafire L.IIc (Merlin 45); On loan to US Navy at FAW-7 Dunkeswell 8.44; Serial & Fate unknown (perhaps NM... serial No)
MB... ? Seafire L.IIc (Merlin 45); On loan to US Navy at FAW-7 Dunkeswell 8.44; Serial & Fate unknown (perhaps NM... serial No)
MB... ? Seafire L.IIc (Merlin 45); On loan to US Navy at FAW-7 Dunkeswell 8.44; Serial & Fate unknown (perhaps NM... serial No)
MB945 Spitfire PR.XI (Merlin 63); TOC/RAF 7.10.43 - US 8th AF; 7th (PR) Grp Mount Farm 30.10.43; 14th Sqn by 3.11.43; 22nd Sqn by 30.12.43; 14th Sqn 5.1.44 until 3.44; Recce over Aschersleben and Brunswick in Germany, abandoned, aircraft dived into English Channel, Cat.FB/E 1.3.44 (Lt Franklyn Van Wart, POW), SOC
MB946 Spitfire PR.XI (Merlin 63); TOC/RAF 9.10.43 - US 8th AF; 7th (PR) Grp Mount Farm 12.11.43; Camera trials in 12.43; 13th Sqn in 12.43; 14th Sqn from 29.1.44 (except 25.2.44, flown by Capt Chapman of 22nd Sqn); Recce over Romilly-sur-Seine and Dieppe, accident 24.6.44 (Lt JR Richards); Repair; 14th Sqn from 4.7.44 to 7.10.44; Retd RAF (MI/RiW) 30.3.45
MB948 Spitfire PR.XI (Merlin 63); TOC/RAF 10.43 – US 8th AF; 7th (PR) Grp Mount Farm; 22nd Sqn by 18.-28.11.43; 14th Sqn by 23.11.43 and from 14.1.44 to 6.10.44; further fate unknown
MB949 Spitfire PR.XI (Merlin 63); TOC/RAF 16.10.43 - US 8th AF; 7th (PR) Grp Mount Farm, 14th Sqn 12.11.43; Accident Mount Farm 18.11.43 (Lt RR Smith); Retd RAF 23.11.43; 7th (PR) Grp, condemned 10.10.44
MB950 Spitfire PR.XI (Merlin 63); TOC/RAF 18.10.43 - US 8th AF; 7th (PR) Grp Mount Farm 13.11.43; 22nd Sqn 25.11.43 to 7.1.44; 14th Sqn from 14.1.44 to 7.10.44: Accident at Mount Farm 29.2.44 (Capt RN Sheble); Accident at Bradwell Bay 6.3.44 (Lt VK Davidson); Retd RAF (MI/RiW) 29.3.45
NOTE: Incorrect reported as "PA950"
MB952 Spitfire PR.XI (Merlin 63); TOC/RAF 5.11.43 - US 8th AF; 7th (PR) Grp Mount Farm 23.11.43; 22nd Sqn 26.11.-24.12.43; 14th Sqn from 30.12.43: Mapping Siegfried Line, lost over Mersch Belgium, Cat.FB/E 8.9.44 (Lt Charles JJ Goffin kld), SOC
MB955 Spitfire PR.XI (Merlin 63); TOC/RAF 5.11.43 - US 8th AF; 7th (PR) Grp Mount Farm 5.12.43; 22nd Sqn 20.12.-30.12.43; 14th Sqn from 6.1.44: Recce over Bitche, Zweibrücken, St.Wendoz, lost over Langkamp Germany, Cat.FB/E 19.9.44 (Lt Paul A Balogh killed, buried Epinal); SOC 20.9.44
MB956 Spitfire PR.XI (Merlin 63); TOC/RAF 5.11.43 - US 8th AF; 7th (PR) Grp, Mount Farm 13.12.43; 14th Sqn 23.12.43; Recce over Germany (Barmen-Sterkrade-Wanne-Eickel-Kamen area), short of fuel, force-landed 2m N of Loddiswell, Kingsbridge, South Devon, Cat.FB/B 23.12.43 (Capt WJ Simon); Recce over St.Florentin, Pacy-sur-Armancon, Montdidier, accident 11.8.44 (Lt IL Rawlings); Repair; 14th Sqn until 7.10.44; Retd RAF (MI/RiW) 29.3.45
MH367 Spitfire F.IX. Firewall with provenance incorporated into R Melton airframe by Harry Stenger Facility, Bartow,

Spitfire PR.XI MB955 was flown by the 14th (PR) Sqn, 7th (PR) Group, Mount Farm, from January 1944 until being lost over Germany on 19th September 1944.

Florida, manufactured to airworthy condition and then adopted this serial as a legitimate identity, owned by Mr Hunter; Sold to Peter Godrey, Aerofab, Bartow, Florida 12.99 and extant- **SURVIVOR**

MH415 Spitfire LF.IX; Ex RNethAF, BAF and UK; Arrived ex Bovingdon, Hertfordshire, as **SURVIVOR** only in 1.69. Regd 11.68 Wilson "Connie" Edwards, Edwards Ranch, Big Springs, Texas for restoration; ff 1973; Civil reg. *N415MH*; To storage 1996; Offered for sale 8.98; Sold in North or South Dakota and extant

MH444 Spitfire LF.IXc (Merlin 66); TOC/RAF 15.8.43; Casablanca 10.10.43; NAASC 31.1.44 - US 12th AF 31.1.44; Retd RAF in 1944; Later No.3 Sqn SAAF missing, Cat.FB/E 20.2.45, SOC

MH477 Spitfire LF.IXc (Merlin 66); TOC/RAF 16.8.43; US 9th AF 25.11.44; Retd RAF in 2.45; Later to Netherlands 7.46

MH562 Spitfire F.IXc (Merlin 63); TOC/RAF 29.8.43; Casablanca 10.10.43; NAASC 31.10.43 - US 12th AF 31.1.44; Retd RAF (No.73 Sqn, crashed Cat.FB/E 23.9.44); SOC

MH564 Spitfire LF.Vc/trop (Merlin 55M); TOC/RAF 29.7.43; Casablanca 1.9.43; N.A. 30.11.43 - US 12th AF; 52nd FG 31.1.44; Lost over Italy, Cat.FB/E 19.2.44, SOC

MH565 Spitfire F.Vc/trop (Merlin 55); TOC/RAF 26.7.43; Casablanca 10.9.43; N.A. 30.11.43 - US 12th AF 31.1.44; Fate unknown

MH581 Spitfire LF.Vc/trop (Merlin 55M); TOC/RAF 28.7.43; Casablanca 1.9.43; N.A. 30.11.43 - US 12th AF 31.1.44; Retd RAF (M.E. census 6.45); SOC 29.8.45

MH593 Spitfire F.Vc/trop (Merlin 55); TOC/RAF 14.8.43; Casablanca 20.9.43 - US 12th AF 29.2.44; Retd RAF (No.253 Sqn, missing 22.5.44); SOC

MH594 Spitfire F.Vc/trop (Merlin 55); TOC/RAF 14.8.43; Casablanca 20.9.43; N.A. 30.11.43 - US 12th AF 27.2.44; Retd RAF in 1944; Later to France in 10.47

MH597 Spitfire F.IXc (Merlin 63); TOC/RAF 30.8.43; Casablanca 10.10.43; NAASC 31.10.43 - US 12th AF 31.1.44; Flying accident Cat.FA/3 29.2.44, SOC

MH603 Spitfire F.IXc (Merlin 63); ex SAAF; Arrived as **SURVIVOR** only; To Joe Scognia, QG Aviation, Fort Collins, Colorado 1993 for restoration, operated by Ray Middleton and extant [US registration candidate 13.8.98]

MH604 Spitfire F.IXc (Merlin 63); TOC/RAF 9.9.43; N.A. 30.11.43 - US 12th AF 31.1.44; Retd RAF in 1944; Later to Italy 5.46

MH605 Spitfire F.IXc (Merlin 63); TOC/RAF 29.8.43; Casablanca 10.10.43; NAASC 31.10.43 - US 12th AF; 52nd FG, 4th FS ('WD-D') 31.12.43; Crashed in Italy, Cat.FB/E 29.2.44; bboc; 4th FS, damaged over Italy Cat.FB/Ac 5.8.44; Retd RAF; No. 1 Sqn SAAF, crashed landing, Cat.FA/E 22.4.45; SOC 19.7.45. - NOTE: Reported as "NH605", but that served in ETO at that time

MH611 Spitfire F.IXc (Merlin 63); TOC/RAF 5.9.43; NAASC 31.10.43 - US 12th AF 31.1.44; Retd RAF (MAAF census 6.45); SOC 22.11.45

MH615 Spitfire LF.IXc (Merlin 66); TOC/RAF 23.8.43; Casablanca 29.9.43; NAASC 31.10.43 - US 12th AF 29.2.44; Retd RAF in 1944; Later to Italy 6.47

MH618 Spitfire F.IXc (Merlin 63); TOC/RAF 8.9.43; Casablanca 19.10.43; N.A. 30.11.43 - US 12th AF; 31st FG, 309th FS ('WZ-ZZ') 31.1.44; Anzio fighter cover and patrol 3.2.-13.2.44 (Lt RJ Connor); Retd RAF 31.5.44

MH651 Spitfire F.IXc (Merlin 63); TOC/RAF 23.8.43; Casablanca 10.10.43; NAASC 31.10.43; MAAF 31.1.44 - US 12th AF 31.1.44; Retd RAF (MAAF census 6.45); SOC 22.11.45

MH654 Spitfire F.IXc (Merlin 63); TOC/RAF 25.8.43; Casablanca 29.9.43; NAASC 31.10.43 - US 12th AF; 31st FG, 309th FS ('WZ-XX') 31.1.44; Retd RAF in 1944 (MAAF); Crashed Cat.FB/E 21.10.44, SOC

MH655 Spitfire F.IXc (Merlin 63); TOC/RAF 29.8.43; Casablanca 10.10.43; NAASC 31.10.43 - US 12th AF 31.1.44; Retd RAF 31.5.44

MH656 Spitfire F.IXc (Merlin 63); TOC/RAF 29.8.43; Casablanca 10.10.43; NAASC 31.10.43 - US 12th AF; 31st FG, 309th FS ('WZ-RR', painted *THATS ALL FOLKS – PORKY II*') in 1944; Retd RAF (RiW, AST) 29.5.44; MAAF census 6.45; Later to Egypt in 9.46

MH672 Spitfire F.IXc (Merlin 63); TOC/RAF 9.9.43; Casablanca 19.10.43; N.A. 30.11.43 - US 12th AF; 31st FG, 309th FS ('WZ-HH'); painted '*AUDREY*' under nose and '*ITS A LULU*' under cowling, shown in 1.44 (Lt Hank Hughes); Anzio, bomber escort 6.2.44 (Lt RJ Connor); Retd RAF (Later crashed Cat.FA/E 11.2.45); SOC - NOTE: A Spitfire IXc marked 'WZ-HH' was named '*Skipper*'

MH675 Spitfire F.IXc (Merlin 63); TOC/RAF 11.9.43; Casablanca 19.10.43; N.A. 30.11.43 - US 12th AF 31.1.44; Fate unknown

MH677 Spitfire F.IXc (Merlin 63); TOC/RAF 11.9.43; Casablanca 19.10.43; N.A. 30.11.43 - US 12th AF 31.1.44; Retd RAF (MAAF census 6.45); Later to Egypt 9.46

MH691 Spitfire F.IXc (Merlin 63); TOC/RAF 10.9.43; Casablanca 19.10.43; N.A. 30.11.43 - US 12th AF 31.1.44; Retd RAF (MAAF census 6.45); Later to Italy 6.47

MH701 Spitfire F.IXc (Merlin 63); TOC/RAF 15.9.43; Casablanca 19.10.43; N.A. 30.11.43 - US 12th AF; 31st FG, 309th FS ('WZ-SS'), on patrol 9.1.44 and 10.1.44 (Lt RJ Connor); Engine failed, pilot baled out over Allied-held territory, Cat.FB/E 14.3.44 (Lt Faxon picked up safely by British and retd Sqn), SOC

MH704 Spitfire F.IXc (Merlin 63); TOC/RAF 14.9.43; N.A. 30.11.43 - US 12th AF 31.1.44; Retd RAF in 1944; MAAF, crashed FB/E 26.2.45, SOC

MH710 Spitfire F.IXc (Merlin 63); TOC/RAF 15.9.43; N.A. 30.11.43 - US 12th AF 31.1.44; Fate unknown

MH711 Spitfire F.IXc (Merlin 63); TOC/RAF 14.9.43; Casablanca 19.10.43; NAASC 31.10.43 - US 12th AF 31.1.44; Retd RAF in 1944; SOC 25.2.45

MH750? Spitfire LF IX; ex Myanmar (Burma) UB425; Arr as **SURVIVOR** only, at Cassville, Missouri 1999; Extant Lee Maples, Brad Eppel & Wes Strickler Sy, Columbia, Missouri

MH762 Spitfire LF.IXc (Merlin 66); TOC/RAF 19.9.43; No.218 Grp N.A. 30.11.43 - US 12th AF 31.1.44; Fate unknown

MH778 Spitfire LF.IXc (Merlin 66); TOC/RAF 21.9.43; No.218 Grp N.A. 30.11.43 - US 12th AF 31.1.44; Retd RAF 31.5.45

MH794 Spitfire LF.IXc (Merlin 66); TOC/RAF 23.9.43; No.218 Grp N.A. 30.11.43 - US 12th AF 31.1.44; Retd RAF 31.3.44

MH795 Spitfire F.IXc (Merlin 63); TOC/RAF 25.9.43; No.218 Grp N.A. 30.11.43 - US 12th AF 31.1.44; Retd RAF in 1944 (MAAF 12.44); Later to Egypt 9.46

MH814 Spitfire LF.IXc (Merlin 66); TOC/RAF 25.9.43; No.218 Grp N.A. 30.11.43 - US 12th AF 31.1.44; Retd RAF 31.5.44

MH816 Spitfire F.IXc (Merlin 63); TOC/RAF 27.9.43; No.218 Grp N.A. 30.11.43 - US 12th AF 29.2.44; Retd RAF; SOC 30.6.44

MH884 Spitfire LF.IXc (Merlin 66); TOC/RAF 22.10.43; Casablanca 29.11.43 - US 12th AF; 31st FG, 309th FS ('WZ-CC') in 1.44; Anzio patrol 9.2.44 (Lt RJ Connor); Retd RAF (MAAF census 6.45); SOC (dbf) 15.4.48

MH889 Spitfire LF.IXc (Merlin 66); TOC/RAF 4.9.43; Casablanca 19.10.43; No.218 Grp N.A. 30.11.43 - US 12th AF 31.1.44; Retd RAF 1944; Later to SAAF in 1944

MH894 Spitfire F.IXc (Merlin 63); TOC/RAF 18.9.43; Casablanca 17.11.43; No.218 Grp N.A. 30.11.43 - US 12th AF; 31st FG, 309th FS ('WZ-JJ', painted '*Lady Ellen III*') in 1.44; No.326 (French) Sqn 19.4.45; Later to France in 11.45

MH895 Spitfire F.IXc (Merlin 63); TOC/RAF 11.9.43; Casablanca 19.10.43; No.218 Grp N.A. 30.11.43 - US 12th AF 31.1.44; Retd RAF; MAAF, missing 8.2.45, SOC

MH896 Spitfire F.IXc (Merlin 63); TOC/RAF 14.9.43; Casablanca 19.10.43; No.218 Grp N.A. 30.11.43 - US 12th AF 31.1.44; Retd RAF (MAAF census 6.45); Later to Italy 6.47

MH897 Spitfire F.IXc (Merlin 63); TOC/RAF 17.9.43; No.218 Grp N.A. 30.11.43 - US 12th AF 31.1.44; Fate unknown

MH898 Spitfire F.IXc (Merlin 63); TOC/RAF 18.9.43; No.218 Grp N.A. 30.11.43 - US 12th AF 31.1.44; Fate unknown

MH902 Spitfire F.IXc (Merlin 63); TOC/RAF 22.9.43; No.218 Grp

Spitfire F.IXc MH894 'WZ-JJ', named 'Lady Ellen III' of the 309th FS, 31st Fighter Group, US 12th Air Force, in January 1944.
[R Mackay via John Hamlin]

       N.A. 30.11.43 - US 12th AF 29.2.44; Retd RAF 31.5.44

MH912 Spitfire F.IXc (Merlin 63); TOC/RAF 14.9.43; No.218 Grp N.A. 30.11.43 - US 12th AF 31.12.43; Fate unknown

MH930 Spitfire F.IXc (Merlin 63); TOC/RAF 19.9.43; No.218 Grp N.A. 30.11.43 - US 12th AF 31.1.44; Retd RAF; No.40 Sqn SAAF, crashed Cat.FB/E 17.10.44, SOC

MH976 Spitfire LF.IXc (Merlin 66); TOC/RAF 29.8.43; Casablanca 10.10.43; NAASC 31.10.43 - US 12th AF 31.1.44; Retd RAF; No. 4 Sqn SAAF, crashed Cat.FB/E 13.11.44, SOC

MH988 Spitfire F.IXc (Merlin 63); TOC/RAF 4.9.43; No.218 Grp N.A. 30.11.43 - US 12th AF 29.2.44; Retd RAF 31.5.44; Later to France in 11.45

MH997 Spitfire F.IXc (Merlin 63); TOC/RAF 4.9.43; Casablanca 10.10.43; NAASC 31.10.43 - US 12th AF 31.1.44; Retd RAF (MAAF census 6.45); Later to Italy 5.46

MH999 Spitfire F.IXc (Merlin 63A); TOC/RAF 5.9.43; Casablanca 19.10.43; No.218 Grp N.A. 30.11.43 - US 12th AF; 31st FG 31.12.43; 307th FS, shot down near Cassino, Cat.FB/E 18.3.44 (2/Lt JL O'Brien killed), SOC

MJ194 Spitfire LF.IXc (Merlin 66); TOC/RAF 30.10.43; Casablanca 22.12.43 - US 12th AF 31.1.44; Retd RAF; SOC 31.8.44

MJ234 Spitfire LF.IXc (Merlin 66); TOC/RAF 21.10.43; Casablanca 29.11.43 - US 12th AF 31.1.44; Retd RAF (MAAF census 6.45); SOC 26.9.46

MJ251 Spitfire LF.IXc (Merlin 66); TOC/RAF 22.10.43; Casablanca 29.11.43 - US 12th AF 31.1.44; Retd RAF (MAAF census 6.45); Later No. 3 Sqn SAAF in 9.45

MJ257 Spitfire LF.IXc (Merlin 66); TOC/RAF 21.10.43; Casablanca 22.12.43 - US 12th AF 29.2.44; Retd RAF 31.5.44

MJ349 Spitfire LF.IXc (Merlin 66); TOC/RAF 23.11.43; Casablanca 8.1.44; MAAF 31.1.44 - US 12th AF 29.2.44; Retd RAF 31.5.44

MJ389 Spitfire LF.IXc (Merlin 66); TOC/RAF 27.10.43; Casablanca 22.12.43 - US 12th AF 29.2.44; Retd RAF 31.5.44

MJ447 Spitfire LF.IXc (Merlin 66); TOC/RAF 5.11.43; Casablanca 22.12.43; ROS 27.2.44 - US 12th AF in 3.44; Retd RAF 31.5.44

MJ505 Spitfire LF.IXc (Merlin 66); TOC/RAF 23.11.43; Casablanca 8.1.44; MAAF 31.1.44 - US 12th AF 29.2.44; Flying accident Cat.FA/E 3.6.44, SOC

MJ506 Spitfire LF.IXc (Merlin 66); TOC/RAF 22.11.43; Casablanca 8.1.44; MAAF 31.1.44 - US 12th AF; 31st FG, 309th FS ('WZ-PP') 29.2.44; Retd RAF 31.5.44; Later No.40 Sqn SAAF, crashed on landing, Cat.E 12.10.44, SOC

MJ525 Spitfire LF.IXc (Merlin 66); TOC/RAF 30.11.43; Casablanca 8.1.44; MAAF 31.1.44 - US 12th AF 29.2.44; Retd RAF (MAAF census 6.45); Later to Italy 6.46

MJ552 Spitfire LF.IXc (Merlin 66); TOC/RAF 2.12.43; Casablanca 8.1.44; MAAF 31.1.44 - US 12th AF 29.2.44; Retd RAF 31.5.44

MJ561 Spitfire LF.IXc (Merlin 66); TOC/RAF 22.12.43 - US 8th AF 9.1.44; Retd RAF (RiW) 25.1.44; Later sold to Italy 1947
NOTE: Reported US 12th AF missing 18.11.44, but at that time MJ561 was being prepared for shipment to Casablanca [Also quoted as "NJ561"]

MJ577 Spitfire LF.IXc (Merlin 66); TOC/RAF 4.12.43; Casablanca 8.1.44; MAAF 31.1.44 - US 12th AF 29.2.44; Retd RAF (MAAF census 6.45); Later to Greece in 5.47

MJ579 Spitfire LF.IXc (Merlin 66); TOC/RAF 22.11.43; Casablanca 8.1.44; MAAF 31.1.44 - US 12th AF 29.2.44; Retd RAF (MAAF census 6.45); SOC 14.3.46

MJ582 Spitfire LF.IXc (Merlin 66); TOC/RAF 25.11.43; Casablanca 8.1.44; MAAF 31.1.44 - US 12th AF 29.2.44; Fate unknown

MJ646 Spitfire LF.IXc (Merlin 66); TOC/RAF 30.11.43; Casablanca 8.1.44; MAAF 30.1.44 - For US 12th AF, N.A., but crashed on ferry flight Cat.FA/3 30.1.44, SOC

MJ685 Spitfire LF.IXc (Merlin 66); TOC/RAF 4.12.43; Casablanca 8.1.44; MAAF 31.1.44 - US 12th AF 29.2.44; Retd RAF 31.5.44

MJ730 Spitfire LF.IX; Arr as **SURVIVOR** only; Sold to Fred Smith/Federal Express, Memphis, Tennessee 4.82 but NTU; To Aero Vintage Ltd, St.Leonards, Sussex 11.83 (Civil reg. *G-BLAS* 22.11.83); Restored in UK, first flight East Midlands after restoration 12.11.88; To David W Pennell, Staverton, Gloucestershire (Civil reg. *G-HFIX* 22.8.89); Last flight in UK on 11.1.00, then crated and shipped to USA for Jerry Yagen, Tidewater Tech, Suffolk, Virginia; Regd *N730MJ* 23.3.00 to Training Services Inc, Virginia Beach, Virginia, marked "GZ-?" and extant

MJ772 Spitfire LF.IX; (ex *G-AVAV* reg.8.11.66); Arrived as **SURVIVOR** only in 11.74; Douglas Champlin/Windward Aviation, Enid, Oklahoma 12.74 (Civil reg. *N8R* 11.12.75 - see also SL721*)*; To Champlin Fighter Museum, Mesa, Arizona 1980; Damaged landing Amarillo, Texas whilst ferrying to Mesa 22.7.80; Rebuilt as single-seater at Mesa, ff 10.85; Marked "NL-R" by 3.93; Sold to Seattle Museum of Flight, Seattle end 2000 (move planned for 2003)

MJ838 Spitfire LF.IXc (Merlin 66); TOC/RAF 24.11.43; Casablanca 8.1.44; MAAF 31.1.44 - US 12th AF 29.2.44; Retd RAF 31.5.44

MK210 Spitfire LF.IXc (Merlin 66); TOC/RAF 30.1.44; With SS *'Carnarvon Castle'* to USA 25.2.44; Arr New York 10.3.44; Wright Field at Dayton, Ohio in 5.44; Tankage modified: Additional two (P-51 Mustang) under wing drop-tanks (each 62 gall), flexible fuel tanks in the leading edges of each wing (each 16.5 gall) and a 43 gall fuel tank in the rear fuselage installed; Total 285 gall of fuel, military equipment removed; Arr Grenier Field 5.6.44, painted *'Tolly'* and *'hello'*; Escorted by a B-25, the aircraft was flown across the Atlantic via Labrador, Greenland and Iceland to the U.K. by Maj G E Lundquist (test pilot of Wright Field); Engine failure after take-off at Bluie West Eight in Greenland, force-landed on its belly, repaired in three weeks; Arr UK together with MK317 early 7.44; Handling trials and tank dropping tests at A&AEE Boscombe Down (report 6.7.44, picture 20.9.44); To CRD Rolls-Royce 28.9.44 with Merlin 66 for carburetion tests; Later converted to GI No. *4988M* and to No.1 SoTT at Halton in 1.45

NOTE: For the Atlantic flight the aircraft was equipped with an ADF radio compass, bearing a loop aerial on the top of the rear fuselage

MK297 Spitfire LF.IX; Arrived as **SURVIVOR** only in 11.68 (ex *G-ASSD*), shipped from Bovingdon to Houston, Texas for Aerosmith Corpn, Dallas (reg. *N1882 5.69*) (operated by Confederate Air Force); To Confederate Air Force, Harlingen, Texas 20.6.73 (reg. *N11RS, NX9BL*); Damaged landing 5.81 (repaired); Regd 27.8.91 to American Airpower Heritage Flying Museum, Midland, Texas; Marked "MH434/SM-43"; Destroyed in hangar fire, Hamilton Airport, Ontario, Canada 15.2.93; Total loss; Regn cancelled 1.98

MK317 Spitfire LF.IXc (Merlin 66); TOC/RAF 30.1.44; With SS *'Carnarvon Castle'* to USA 25.2.44; Arr New York 10.3.44; Dayton Wright Field in 5.44; For comparison additional tankage fitted (as MK210); Total 285 gall of fuel; Arr Dow Field 1.7.44; Escorted by a B-25, the aircraft was flown across the Atlantic via Labrador, Greenland and Iceland to the UK by GR Ayle; Met MK210 at Bluie West Eight, Greenland, both arrived UK 6.7.44; Test flying and comparison by Supermarine; AST Hamble for repair (RiW) 24.9.45; Later sold to Turkey in 8.47

NOTE: Test report 28.7.44 confirmed the superiority of the British 90 gall slipper-tanks to the two 62 gall (P-51) drop-tanks with a speed of up to 12 mph at 10.000 ft

MK923 Spitfire LF.IX; Arrived as **SURVIVOR** only 17.11.63 (ex *OO-ARF*); Airfreighted from Biggin Hill, Kent, England to USA for Clifford P Robertson, Santa Ana, California (later Oxnard) (Civil reg. *N93081* 1963); Displayed Tallmantz/Movieland of Air Museum 1964; Clifford P Robertson and Jerry Billing, Los Angeles, California, from 2.66 (reg. *NX521R*), marked as "MJ923/5J-Z"; Based Windsor, Ontario Canada, 1972; Retd USA 1976; Regd to Fleet National Bank, Hartford, Connecticut 6.1.86; Kalamazoo Air Zoo Museum, Michigan 8.87; Sold 27.7.98 and regd to Security Aviation Inc [escrow agent]; Sold 4.8.98 and regd 15.9.98 to GV Leasing Llc, Water Mill. New York; Sold 14.5.99 and regd 15.6.99 to Flight Management Llc, Kirkland, Washington; Regd 28.9.99 to State Street Bank, Hartford, Connecticut; Regd 6.1.00 to First Security Bank; Regd 1.3.01 to Aircraft Holdings Llc, Kirkland, Washington; Regd 12.7.01 to Wells Fargo Bank, Salt Lake City, Utah; Regd 12.12.01 to Apex Foundation, Bellevue, Washington

[Passed to Craig McCaw, The Museum of Flight, Seattle, Washington 1999 painted as '5J-Z'; To Boeing Field, Seattle in 2000, to the Museum Flight for display in the Great Gallery 15.5.01 and extant]

MK959 Spitfire LF.IX (Merlin 66); ex RNethAF H-15; Arr 1995 as **SURVIVOR** only to Raybourne Thomson jnr, Houston, Texas and extant; Regd *N959RT* 22.4.01

ML119 Spitfire LF.IX; ex Myanmar (Burma) UB441; Arr ex Burma as **SURVIVOR** only, to a syndicate at Cassville Missouri 1999; To Peter Monk & Mike Simpson, Airframe Assemblies, Sandown, Isle of Wight 30.12.00 for eventual restoration

ML417 Spitfire LF.IX; Arrived as **SURVIVOR** only in 1971, ex Indian Air Force Museum, Palam; Sold to Senator Norman E Gaar, Kansas City, MO 4.71, and shipped to USA 15.3.72; Restoration begun at Fort Collins, Colorado; Sold to B J Stephen Grey, Duxford 11.6.80, and shipped to UK, arr 7.8.80; To The Fighter Collection, Duxford 28.1.91 to complete restoration, completed at Booker as a Mk.IXc single-seater and ff 10.2.84 marked "ML416/2I-T"; Chino Spitfires Llc, Houston, Texas sold to Friedkin, Chino, California 2.01 (Civil reg. *N2TF* 12.12.01) - **SURVIVOR**

MT719 Spitfire LF.VIII; Arrived as **SURVIVOR** only in 1989 ex *I-SPIT, G-VIII*); Jim Cavanaugh/Cavanaugh Collection Inc, trading as Cavanaugh Flight Museum, Addison, Dallas, Texas 10.8.93; Marked 'YB-J'; Civil reg. *N719MT* 29.9.93; and extant

MT818 Spitfire T.VIII; Arrived as **SURVIVOR** only in 1985 (ex *G-AIDN*); Sold by Vickers-Armstrongs to Vivian H Bellamy, Eastleigh 8.56; To John S Fairey, Eastleigh 8.63 (later Andover, with Tim Davies from 1967) To M S Bayliss, Baginton 1976; To George F.Miller, Baginton 9.77; Undercarriage collapsed landing Baginton 6.2.78; Rebuilt by 1982 as "MT818/G-M"; Sold in USA, shipped in 1983 to George F.Miller, Houston, Texas; Jim Cavanaugh, Cavanaugh Flight Museum, Dallas, Texas 10.8.93; Jack Erickson, Erickson Aircrane Inc, Medford, Oregon 7.86 (based Tillamook); Civil reg. *N58JE 13.8.*86 and extant

MV262 Spitfire FR.XIV; Sold as **SURVIVOR** only in 1992 (ex Indian AF and *G-CCVV*) to Kermit A Weeks, Tamiami, Florida, USA 10.92 and stored by Personal Plane Services, Booker, since 1996 pending restoration (never delivered to the USA) - **SURVIVOR**

MV358 Spitfire FR.XIVe (Griffon 65); TOC/RAF 17.1.45; Glasgow, with LS2707 *'Empire Severn'* shipped to New York for comparison tests; Retd UK 22.1.47; sold as scrap 6.1.50

MV361 Spitfire FR.XIVe (Griffon 65); TOC/RAF 17.1.45; To USA, arr New York 15.6.45; 3-weather tests on RAF charge in 1945; Retd 22.1.47; Arr UK in 2.47

NH238 Spitfire LF.IX; ex RNethAF (H-60), BAF (SM36), COGEA (OO-ARE 8.9.56); Shipped from UK, arr as **SURVIVOR** only Galveston, Texas 14.6.70; To Ed Jurist & Bruce Farkas, Sugarland, Texas (Civil reg. *N238V* 3.7.69) (operated by Confederate Air Force); Regd to David C Tallichet/MARC, Chino, California 4.75; Sold to Douglas Arnold 1979; To UK, Hull Aviation Inc for restoration, Warbirds of Great Britain Ltd (reg. *G-MKIX* 12.12.83); Flown in film *A Piece of Cake* 10.7.88; Retd to Florida, USA 1994, marked "EN398/JE-J"; To Flying 'A' Services North Weald, Essex, England 1998 and extant

NH749 Spitfire FR.XIV; Arrived ex UK as **SURVIVOR** only in 5.85 (ex RIAF, then *G-MXIV*); Bought by David G Price, Portland, Oregon 4.3.85; Shipped UK to Chino, California 4.85; Regd *NX749DP* 17.5.85 to David Glyn Price, Portland, Oregon (based with Museum of Flying, Santa Monica, California; ff Chino 24.7.85 marked "H749/L"; Crashed on landing at Oshkosh, Wisconsin 1985; Sold 2.4.96 and regd 17.5.96 to Museum of Flying Support Fund, Santa Monica, California and extant

NH904 Spitfire FR.XIV (ex BAF *SG-108;* Civil reg. *G-FIRE*); Arrived as **SURVIVOR** only ex UK in 12.88; Registration candidate 27.12.88; Regd to Robert J Pond, Plymouth, operated by Planes of Fame East, Minneapolis-Flying Cloud, Minnesota (reg. *N8118J* 2.89); Regd. to Robert J Pond, Eden Prairie, Minnesota 27.2.89; Re-regd *N114BP* 4.91; Palm Springs Air Museum, California from 1994; Regd 26.3.01 to Pond Warbirds Llc, Palm Springs,

UNITED STATES OF AMERICA

Surviving Spitfire LF.VIII N719M (ex MT719) in 1994 with a gauntlet motif on the nose. It is currently operated by Cavanaugh Flight Museum, Addison, Dallas, Texas, in SEAC camouflage with its original serial number and has the spurious code marking "YB-J".

California; Marked 'W2-P' and extant

PA841 Spitfire PR.XI (Merlin 63); TOC/RAF 6.11.43 - US 8th AF; 7th (PR) Grp Mount Farm 5.12.43; 13th Sqn in 12.43; 14th Sqn from 6.2.44; Recce in Ostend-Ghent-Brussels area, accident at Bradwell Bay 5.3.44 (Lt GM Adams); Take-off crash 26.8.44 (Lt IL Rawlings); Repair; 14th Sqn until 7.10.44; Detached service 3.4.45; Retd RAF 5.4.45

PA842 Spitfire PR.XI (Merlin 63); TOC/RAF 5.11.43 - US 8th AF; 7th (PR) Grp Mount Farm 23.11.43; 13th Sqn in 12.43; 22nd Sqn 4.1.44; 14th Sqn from 5.2.44 (except 8.4.44, Capt Carl Chapman of 22nd Sqn over Quackenbrück, Oldenburg, Wilhelmshaven); Accident 4.12.44 (Lt DW Werner); Retd RAF 29.3.45

PA851 Spitfire PR.XI (Merlin 63); TOC/RAF 5.11.43 - US 8th AF; 7th (PR) Grp Mount Farm 28.11.43; 22nd Sqn from 12.12.43; Recce over Osnabrück and Münster, Germany, engine failed, dived into North Sea, Cat.FB/E 23.12.43 (Capt Steven Scott killed), SOC

PA892 Spitfire PR.XI (Merlin 63); TOC/RAF 6.11.43 - US 8th AF; 7th (PR) Grp Mount Farm 17.1.44; 22nd Sqn 31.12.43-5.1.44; 14th Sqn from 14.1.44; Recce over Berlin and Hannover 6.3.44 (Mjr WL Weitner); Recce in Nancy-Le Touquet area, accident at Mount Farm 24.3.44 (Mjr WL Weitner); Repair; 14th Sqn from 30.5.44 to 7.10.44; Retd RAF 3.4.45

PA908 Spitfire PR.XI; Ex Indian Air Force; Arrived ex Canada as **SURVIVOR** only in 1986; USAF Museum Wright-Patterson AFB, Dayton, Ohio; Restoration by Pete Regina, Van Nuys, California 1992; Marked "MB950" in US 8th Air Force colours; Extant

Surviving Spitfire FR.XIV NX749DP (ex NH749) in 1995, spuriously coded "L" and painted in SEAC colours. It was then owned by David Glyn Price of Portland, Oregon, and based with the Museum of Flying, Santa Monica, California. [MAP]

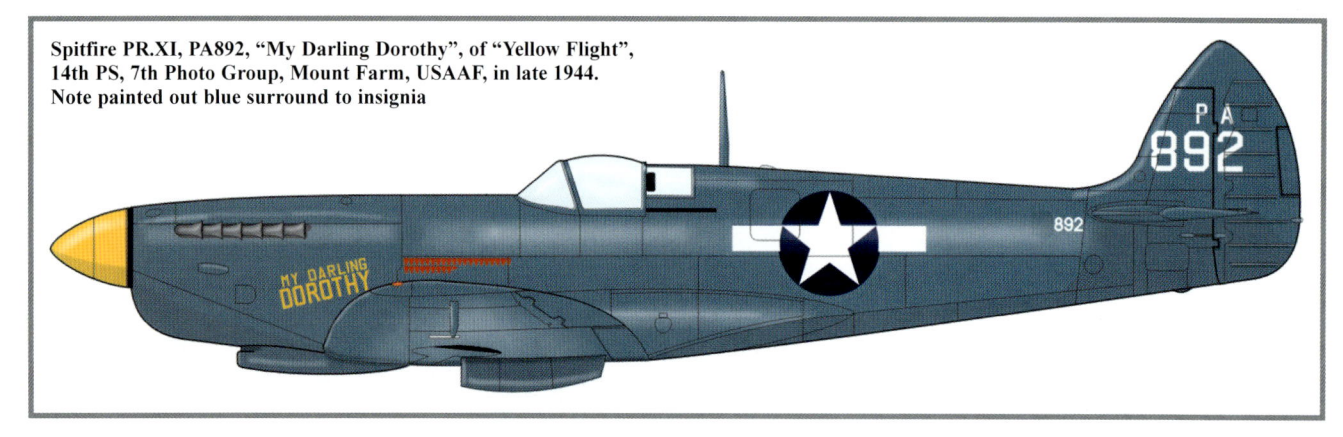

Spitfire PR.XI, PA892, "My Darling Dorothy", of "Yellow Flight", 14th PS, 7th Photo Group, Mount Farm, USAAF, in late 1944. Note painted out blue surround to insignia

PA944   Spitfire PR.XI (Merlin 63); TOC/RAF 14.2.44 - US 8th AF; 7th (PR) Grp Mount Farm 20.4.44; 14th Sqn from 29.4.44; Recce over Hanau-Eisenach Germany, accident 12.9.44 (Lt JS Blyth); Repair; Detached service 3.4.45; Retd RAF 5.4.45

PL344   Spitfire LF.IXc; For USA as **SURVIVOR** only: Sold to Kermit A Weeks, Florida, USA in 11.92 (Civil reg. *G-IXCC*; Restoration by Personal Plane Services, Wycombe Air Park, England, also Hull Aero, Norwich); After rebuilding flown at Booker, Bucks 7.2.2001 (marked as "Y2-P"); Regd 13.12.01 as *N644TB* to Southern Aircraft Leasing Inc (Tom Blair), Gaitherburg, MD for Kermit A Weeks, at Harry Stenger Facility, Bartow, Florida and extant

PL767   Spitfire PR.XI (Merlin 70); TOC/RAF 23.3.44 - US 8th AF; 7th (PR) Grp Mount Farm 20.4.44; 14th Sqn from 28.5.44; Recce in Paris area, crashed N of Mount Farm (near Combe, Oxfordshire), Cat.FB/E 28.6.44 (Mjr CT Haugen kld); Salvaged by 4th (MRR) Sqn 28.6.44, SOC

PL782   Spitfire PR.XI (Merlin 70); TOC/RAF 2.4.44 - US 8th AF; 7th (PR) Grp Mount Farm 20.4.44; 14th Sqn from 1.6.44; Recce over Stuttgart-Karlsruhe-Ludwigshaven Germany, shot down by enemy aircraft near Feuerbach (or: dived into North Sea), abandoned, Cat.FB/E 5.9.44 (Lt RB Hilborn, POW), SOC

PL790   Spitfire PR.XI (Merlin 70); TOC/RAF 6.4.44 - US 8th AF; 7th (PR) Grp Mount Farm 20.4.44; 14th Sqn from 29.5.44; Recce in Paris area, lost over England, Cat.FB/E 15.6.44 (Lt R Diderickson kld), SOC

PL866   Spitfire PR.XI (Merlin 70); TOC/RAF 8.7.44 - US 8th AF; 7th (PR) Grp Mount Farm 7.44; 14th Sqn from 31.7.44; Accident 15.1.45 (Lt IL Rawlings); Recce over Halle and Leuna Leipzig, Germany, hit by AA, dived into ground, abandoned, Cat.FB/E 14.2.45 (Capt RJ Dixon, POW), SOC

PL914   Spitfire PR.XI (Merlin 70); TOC/RAF 2.9.44 - US 8th AF; 7th (PR) Grp Mount Farm, 14th Sqn 2.10.44; Retd RAF 3.4.45

PL959   Spitfire PR.XI (Merlin 70); TOC/RAF 15.9.44 - US 8th AF; 7th (PR) Grp Mount Farm 27.9.44; 14th Sqn from 6.10.44 to 15.10.44; Retd RAF 3.4.45

PL962   Spitfire PR.XI (Merlin 70); TOC/RAF 24.9.44 - US 8th AF; 7th (PR) Grp Mount Farm 3.10.44; 14th Sqn, recce in Lille area, dived into ground, Cat.FB/E 14.1.45 (Lt James F Tostevin killed); Salvaged 20.1.45, SOC

PL965   Spitfire PR XI (Merlin 70); TOC/RAF 2.10.44; ex RNethAF, LETS Deelen 1947; National War & Resistance Museum at Overloon from 1960; To UK, Civil reg. *G-MKXI*; First flight after restoration 23.12.92; Painted pink and marked "R" in 3.00; Arrived USA as **SURVIVOR** only in 9.01; On loan for air display by Tony 'Taff' Smith and Robert Fleming, Real Aeroplane Company Breighton, Florida. Temporary import operated Leeward Air Ranch, Florida and extant

PL972   Spitfire PR.XI (Merlin 70); TOC/RAF 9.10.44 - US 8th AF; 7th (PR) Grp Mount Farm, 14th Sqn 9.3.45; Retd RAF (IP&IP Benson) 3.4.45; Later to Argentina in 5.47

PL983   Spitfire PR.XI (Merlin 70); TOC/RAF 24.11.44; Race aircraft in 1947 (flown by Miss L Curtiss); To Air Attache, US Embassy London and based Hendon (courier aircraft, Civil reg. *N74138* 27.1.48); Sold back to Vickers-Armstrongs 1949 (G-15-109); Sold to Shuttleworth Trust, Old Warden for static display 1950; By road to Duxford 30.8.75 and restored to fly by 1983; Sold to Roland Fraissinet, Marseilles, France 14.4.83, but based in UK (Civil reg. *G-PRXI* 6.6.83) and ff East Midlands Airport 17.7.84; To Douglas Arnold/Warbirds of Great Britain Ltd 1.10.87 (restored with a fighter windscreen); To Flying 'A' Services, North Weald 1998; Bought by Justin Fleming and moved to a strip in Kent 3.12.99; Fatal crash at Rouen-Boos, France 3.6.01 – **SURVIVOR**

PM153   Spitfire PR.XI (Merlin 70); TOC/RAF 22.1.45; US 8th AF, 7th (PR) Grp Mount Farm, 14th Sqn 4.2.45; Retd RAF 3.4.45

PM157   Spitfire PR.XI (Merlin 70); TOC/RAF 3.2.45 - US 8th AF; 7th (PR) Grp Mount Farm, 14th Sqn 22.2.45; Retd RAF 3.4.45

PR503   Seafire F.XV; ex Canada (RCN); Arrived as **SURVIVOR** only (ex *C-GCWK*); To Courtesy Aircraft, Rockford, Illinois 1992; To Wallace Fisk, Amjet Facility/Polar Aviation Museum, Anoka County Airport, Blaine, Minnesota 1993, under restoration to fly from 1994; Reserved as *N535R* 12.97 and regd 14.1.98 to Amjet Aircraft Corp; Re-regd *N503PR* 5.7.00 and extant

PS890   Spitfire PR.XIX; Ex Thai Air Force *U14-26/97*; Arrived as **SURVIVOR** only in 1962, donated by King Bhumiphol of Siam and airfreighted to Burbank, California in an L-1049 for Edward Maloney, The Air Museum, Claremont, California; To Planes of Fame Museum, Chino, California, in 1971, for restoration; Reg candidate 4.9.98 for C Schall; Civil reg. *N219AM* 7.1.99 to Air Museum, Chino, California and expected to fly in 2002

PT462   Spitfire T.IX; Arrived (ex Italy, Israel and UK) as **SURVIVOR** only in 1994; Harry Stenger Facility at Bartow, Florida (Jet-Cap Aviation Corpn, Lakeland, Florida), marked "SW-A" (Civil reg. *N462JC* 25.7.94); Regn cancelled and retd to UK 4.98 (Anthony Hodgson/Aircraft Restoration Co, Duxford) *G-CTIX* 28.4.98

PV270   Spitfire LF IX; ex Italy *MM4014*, Israel *2080*, Burma *UB424*; Arr as **SURVIVOR** only, at Cassville, Missouri 1999; Sold to Brendon Deere in New Zealand; Restoration at Dairy Flat, New Zealand, from May 2001

RM694   Spitfire F.XIV; Arrived ex UK as **SURVIVOR** (Fuselage only, wings to NH904) in 1972; RAF Dishforth as scrap, to A H 'Bunny' Brooks, Hoylake, Cheshire 1966; Fuselage only to J Denis Kay/Manchester Tankers Ltd, Charnock Richard, Lancashire, 1966 (fuselage used at Henlow *for Battle of Britain* film in 1967); To A W Francis, Southend, Essex 1.68; Sold to John Lowe and Larry Matt, Riverside, Illinois c.1972 for restoration with various wings (stored at Victory Air Museum, Mundelein, Illinois); Retd to UK 1985, to Warbirds of Great Britain Ltd, Bitteswell, Warwickshire; Back to USA in 1989, Don L Knapp/DK Precision, Fort Lauderdale, Florida; To storage with Vern Schuppan, Florida 1995; Now storage at High Wycombe, Buckinghamshire, England

UNITED STATES OF AMERICA

Spitfire PR.XI N74138 (ex PL983) was allocated to the US Air Attaché in London in early 1948, being flown for a time from Hendon as a courier aircraft. It later became G-PRXI *but suffered a fatal crash at Rouen-Boos, France, on 3rd June 2001.* [Vickers-Armstrongs]

RM927 Spitfire FR.XIV; Ex BAF; Arrived ex Belgium & UK as **SURVIVOR** only in 1969; Sold to John Lowe and Larry Matt, Riverside, Illinois 1969 (stored at Victory Air Museum, Mundelein, Illinois); To Larry Matt, Chicago, Illinois 1982 for restoration with wings of IAF HS649 (ex TP263); To Don L Knapp/DK Precision, Fort Lauderdale, Florida in 1987; To storage with Vern Schuppan, Florida 1995; To England, restoration with HS649 wings at High Wycombe, Buckinghamshire

RW382 Spitfire LF.XVI; Arrived as **SURVIVOR** only in 1994; Ex RAF Uxbridge to Tim Routis/Historic Flying Ltd, Cambridge 26.8.88; To David C Tallichet/MARC, Chino, California, USA 1989; To Historic Flying Ltd, Audley End, Essex, England (Civil reg. *G-XVIA* 2.7.91); ff Audley End 3.7.91 as "RW382/NG-C"; Retd David C Tallichet/MARC, Chino, California, USA 1991 (but based UK to 1995); To Barrie Jackson, Manitoba, Canada 1994; Del Audley End 13.2.95 for export to USA and British reg. Cancelled 17.3.95; US registration candidate 22.3.95; Regd 21.8.95 to Bernie F.Jackson [Trustee], San Jose, California & Barrie Jackson, Manitoba 8.95 (Civil reg. *NX382RW*); Crashed and written off, Blue Canyon, Nevada 3.6.98 (Thomas Jackson killed); Regd 30.10.01 to Stephen H Vizard; Reg. cancelled 11.2.02, to UK

SL542 Spitfire LF.XVI (Merlin 266); Arrived ex UK as **SURVIVOR** only (via Jeet Mahal, Vancouver, BC 1992); To Pegasus Investments Inc, West Palm Beach, Florida 1994/6 (Civil reg. *N2289J* 11.5.94); To Harry Stenger

Surviving Spitfire T.IX N462JC (ex PT462) was registered as such to the Jet-Cap Aviation Corporation, Lakeland, Florida, and marked "SW-A". It is now at Duxford, re-registered G-CTIX. [MAP]

Facility, Bartow, Florida for restoration for Anthony Jurak; Possibly now in Canada with Anthony Jurak, Quebec [Cancelled to UK 11.2.02]

SL574 Spitfire LF.XVI; Arrived as **SURVIVOR** only in 1988; San Diego Aerospace Museum, Balboa Park, California (presentation to the American 'Eagle' Squadrons), marked "MD-T"; Extant

SL721 Spitfire LF.XVI; Arrived as **SURVIVOR** only in 12.65; ex RAF to Beaulieu Motor Museum on loan 6.10.58; To Monty Thackray/M D Thackray Ltd 9.7.65; To USA 12.65, William D Ross, Du Page, Illinois; Restored at Atlanta, Georgia, ff 11.5.67 marked "SL721/JM-R" (it was the former personal aircraft of AVM Sir James Robb); Retd William D Ross at Du Page, Illinois 1967 (Civil reg. *N8R*); Shipped UK for Douglas W Arnold/Fairoaks Aviation Services, arr Leavesden, Hertfordshire 28.3.73 (reg *G-BAUP* 4.4.73); Assembled at Blackbushe and flew as "SL721/DA"; Retd USA, shipped 8.77 to Woodson K Woods, Scottsdale, Arizona (Reg. *N8WK* 21.7.77); ff Deer Valley 18.9.77; Became *N721WK* 2.82 - Woodson K Woods/Aero Meridian Corpn, Scottsdale, Arizona (operated by Carefree Flying Museum); On loan to San Diego Aerospace Museum, California 21.2.83; To Fort Collins, California for restoration 1990; Retd Scottsdale 23.2.92 marked "SL721/WK-W"; Damaged landing Albuquerque, New Mexico 7.10.95; Sold 20.9.99 and regd 18.1.00 to Woods Aviation Llc, Carefree, Arizona; Regd 6.10.00 to MTW Aviation Inc Trustee, Washington Delaware; Acquired by Michael Potter end 2000 (to be based Ottawa); Reg. cancelled 1.3.02, to Canada; Extant

SM845 Spitfire FR.XVIII (Griffon 66); ex Indian AF (*HS-687*); Arrived 1978 as a **SURVIVOR** only, purchased by Marshall Moss and Richard A Boolootian, Lancaster, California; To David C Tallichett/MARC, Chino, California 1982; To UK, Adrian Reynard & R Synge, Kidlington, Oxfordshire 1.88; To Park Avenue Investments Ltd, Witney, Oxfordshire 1992, for restoration by Historic Flying Ltd, Audley End, Essex, (Civil reg. *G-BUOS* 19.10.92); First flight after restoration 7.7.00 (F/Lt Charlie Brown)

SR459 Seafire F.XVc (Griffon VI); RNDA 3.2.45; Arr USNAS Patuxent River (armour plates stripped) in 6.45; Demonstration flying; To Canada 10.6.46

SR462 Seafire F.XV; ex Myanmar (Burma) *UB414*; Arr as **SURVIVOR** only; At Cassville, Missouri 1999; 3.02 owned by Lee Maples, Brad Eppel & Wes Strickler Sy, Columbia, Missouri

TD135 Spitfire LF.XVI; Arrived ex UK as **SURVIVOR** only in 1975; Bought by Percy Sheppard, The Spitfire Inn, Leominster 1964; To Worral Granger/Connie Motors 1975; To USA 1975 for Larry Higgins/Thunderbird Aviation, Deer Valley, Arizona; To David Boyd and Hurley Bowler, Tulsa, Oklahoma 1967; To Ray Stutsman, Elkhart, Indiana 1985; to William C Anderson. Genesio, New York State (1941 Historical Aircraft Group) 20.1.86 for long term rebuild at Palmyra and Genesco; Extant

TE308 Spitfire T.IX; Arrived as single-seater ex Canada (*CF-RAF*) as **SURVIVOR** only in 1975; To USA (Civil reg. *N92477* 1975), to Thomas J Watson, Owls Head Transport, Owls Head, ME; To Woodson K Woods, Scottsdale, Arizona (reg. *N308WK* 7.10.79); Conv back to two-seater; Operated by Carefree Aviation Museum, Scottsdale, Arizona; Regd to Aero Meridian Corpn, Scottsdale, Arizona 11.1.82; Regd 23.8.83 to William S Greenwood, Aspen, Colorado, airworthy, marked "TE308/RJ-M" in 1991 and extant - **SURVIVOR**

TE330 Spitfire LF.XVI; Arrived as **SURVIVOR** only; Presented to the USAF Academy, Colorado Springs (South of Denver) 2.7.58 (del ex RAF Odiham in a C-124 Globemaster); Owned from 1961 by USAF Museum, Wright-Patterson AFB, Dayton, Ohio for display (Civil reg. *N75460)*; Sold 9.5.96 and regd 4.6.96 to World Wide Aeronautical Industries Inc, Moorpark, California; Regn cancelled 3.97; Imported by James Slade (of Hong Kong) for restoration in 4.97; Now owned by Don and Mike Subritzky at Auckland, New Zealand

TE356 Spitfire LF XVI; Arrived as **SURVIVOR** only in 1.90; Sold ex RAF (*6709M*, *7001M*) to Warbirds of Great Britain Ltd, Bitteswell & Biggin Hill (Civil reg. *G-SXVI* 25.2.87); Restored at East Midlands airport and ff 16.12.87; Regd 18.1.90 to Delford M Smith/Evergreen Ventures Inc, McMinnville, Oregon (reg. *N356EV*); Regd 4.90 to Evergreen Heritage Collection, Marana, Arizona and marked "TE356/DE-D" named *Carolyn*; Re-regd *N356TE* 15.3.91 to 747 Inc, McMinnville, Oregon (marked *NX356TE*); Regd 8.7.97 to Evergreen Ventures Inc, McMinnville, Oregon; Sold 30.3.99 and regd 23.4.99 to Evergreen Vintage Aircraft Inc, McMinnville, Oregon; Extant

TE384 Spitfire LF.XVIe; Arrived 6.98 as **SURVIVOR** from UK and Australia; To Ken McBride, Hollister, Los Angeles, CA and extant, under restoration at St.Jose, CA

TE392 Spitfire LF.XVI; Arrived ex UK as **SURVIVOR** only in 1995; Jet Cap Aviation, Lakeland, Florida; To Harry

Surviving Spitfire T.IX N308WK (ex TE308) in 1994. It is registered to William S Greenwood of Aspen, Colorado, and carries its genuine serial number with the spurious code "RJ-M". [MAP]

Surviving Spitfire LF.XVI NX356TE (ex TE356) in 1995, marked "D-DE" on the port side and "DD-E" on the starboard side, with the name 'Carolyn' on the nose. Since 23rd April 1999 it has been registered to Evergreen Vintage Aircraft Inc, McMinnville, Oregon. [MAP]

Stenger Facility, Bartow, Florida, for Lone Star Flight Museum/Texas Aviation Hall of Fame, Galveston, Texas (Civil reg. *N97RW* 6.10.99); First flight after restoration in Florida 24.12.99, flown back to Houston 27.4.01, marked "ZX-Z"; Extant

TE476 Spitfire LF.XVI; Arrived ex UK as **SURVIVOR** only in 8.95; Ex RAF to Historic Flying Ltd, Rayne and Cambridge (Civil reg. *G-XVIB* 3.7.89); Sold to Kermit A Weeks, Weeks Air Museum, Polk City, Miami, Florida 2.2.90 (reg. *N476TE* 13.3.91); Regn cancelled 29.4.95; Shipped to UK; Regd *G-XVIB* to Personal Plane Services Ltd, Booker for restoration 3.5.94; ff 20.6.95 marked "TE476/GE-D"; Sold 5.12.95 and retd to Kermit A Weeks, Polk City, Florida, regn restored as *N476E* 11.1.96; Extant

TE517 Spitfire LF.IXe; Sold ex UK as **SURVIVOR** only in 1994; To Kermit A Weeks, Polk City, Florida 10.92, but stored at Personal Plane Services, Booker, UK (Civil reg. *G-CCIX*); For sale 1999 [Never to USA]

TP276 Spitfire FR.XVIII; Ex Indian Air Force; Arrived as **SURVIVOR** only in 1978 - to Rudolph A Frasca/Antiques & Classics Inc, Champaign, Illinois for restoration; To Rudy Frasca/Frasca Air Museum, Urbana, Illinois 1986 (restoration); Extant

TP280 Spitfire FR.XVIII; Ex Indian Air Force; Arrived ex UK as **SURVIVOR** only in 1978 - to Rudolph A Frasca/Antiques & Classics Inc, Champaigh, Illinois 1978; Shipped to UK for restoration by Historic Flying Ltd, Audley End, Essex (Civil reg. *G-BTXE* 23.10.91); ff 5.7.92; Shipped back to USA 9.92; To Rudy Frasca/Frasca Air Museum/Frasca International Inc, Urbana, Illinois 2.93 (reg. *N280TP* 3.2.93), flown as "TP280/Z"; Extant

TP298 Spitfire FR.XVIII; Ex Indian Air Force; Arrived as **SURVIVOR** only in 1978, to Marshall Moss and Richard A Boolootian, Lancaster, California; To David C Tallichet/MARC, China, California c.1981; To UK for rebuild at Colchester, Essex 1988; Retd Military Aircraft Restoration Corp, Anaheim, California (Civil reg. *N41702*, 2.7.91); ff Chino 6.7.92 as "TP298/UM-T"; Regd to John Breit, Denver, Colorado 19.1.94 (*N9323Z*); Flown into mountainside, Geyser, MT 20.5.94 (Plt Larry Diehl killed), aircraft destroyed
NOTE: Restoration project by P Goichelaar, Orford, New Hampshire, USA

TZ138 Spitfire FR.XIV (Griffon 65); TOC/RAF 7.45; ex RCAF until 31.8.48; To JHG 'Butch' McArthur, third in the Tinnermann Trophy Race Ohio 1949, 360 mph (Civil reg. *CF-GMZ*, race No *'80'*); Sold to Cuban, Fulgencio Batista, in 1950, flown to the Hollywood airport at Florida for departure to Cuba and registered as *N20E* to the new owner, but remained in the USA at Miami from 28.9.49; To Opa Locka, Florida, USA 1950, later North Perry, Florida, USA; It could not be ferried out as supporters of the Cuban rival, Fidel Castro, broke off two propeller blades 1.6.51; To US Customs Service, Miami, Florida; Sold to Lloyd B Milner, Minneapolis, Minnesota, USA 12.59; Sold to John L Russell 1960; Sold to M W Fairbrother, Rosemont, Minnesota 1960; Regd to Harvey J Ferguson, McAllen, Texas, 1963 (regd *N5505A* 7.7.65) (operated by Confederate Air Force); To Charles H Liedel, Mercedes, Texas (and Fergus Falls, Minnesota) 1969; Engine failure, force landed, crashed on test flight 2.5.70; Sold to Jack Arnold, Brantford, Ontario, Canada 1971 (marked 'JR-A'); To Max R Hoffman, Fort Collins, Colorado, USA 6.10.71; Sold to Don Plumb, Windsor, Ontario, Canada 28.6.74; Sold to Ray Jones, Pontiac, Michigan, USA 9.74; To Leonard A Tanner, New Braintree, Connecticut, USA 7.75 (reg. *N138TZ* reserved); Loaned to Bradley Air Museum, Windsor Locks, Connecticut 1979; To Don L Knapp/DK Precision, Fort Lauderdale, Florida 1988 (regd *N5505A*, also allocated *N180B* 11.88 but NTU); To Lone Star Flight Museum, Galveston, Texas 1990; To Bill Destefani, Bakersfield, California 1991; To David Price (Santa Monica Museum), California, USA (now regd *N180RB?*); Under restoration to fly by Pete Regina Aviation, Van Nuys, California from mid-1998; Regd 28.10.98 to Liberty Aero Corpn, Santa Monica, California (based Santa Monica Flying Museum from autumn 1999 (reg. *N180RB*), for air test programme); Sold to Robert Jens, Vancouver, British Columbia, Canada, spring 2000 (regd *C-GSPT*) – **SURVIVOR**

VN332 Spitfire F.24; Arrived as survivor only in 1951; Practicing for New Zealand Race; Destroyed in a fatal crash nr Teterboro Airport, New Jersey (oxygen failed at 20,000 ft) 1953; reg. *N7929A*

VP441 Seafire FR.47; Arrived ex UK as **SURVIVOR** only in or by 11.75 - to John J Stokes/Rebel Aviation, San Antonio, Texas; Confederate Air Force, Harlingen/Midland, Texas (Civil reg. *N47SF* 4.12.80); Later renamed American Airpower Heritage Flying Museum, Midland, Texas 5.9.91; Sold 14.9.95 to James E Smith, Montana; Regd 22.9.95 to Nelson E Ezell, Breckenridge, Texas; Rewgd 10.9.97 to James E Smith, Kalispell, Montana; Extant

Spitfire F.24 N7929A (VN332) was destroyed in a fatal crash near Teterboro Airport, New Jersey, in 1953 after oxygen failure at 20,000 feet.

Unidentified

?.7.42	31st FG, 309th FS, no details but possibly mid-air collision (Lt Sidney Simms killed)
19.8.42	31st FG, 307th FS, FW 190 probable 15m NW of Dieppe (shared by Capt J C Robertson & Lt J H White)
19.8.42	31st FG, 307th FS, FW 190 destroyed 15m NW of Dieppe (shared by Lt WB Whisonant & Lt R Wooten)
19.8.42	31st FG, 308th FS, FW 190 probably destroyed over Dieppe (2/Lt F A Hill).
19.8.42	31st FG, 309th FS, FW 190 probable Dieppe (Mjr H R Thyng)
19.8.42	31st FG, 309th FS, Do 217 damaged on convoy patrol (Shared by Capt J S Thorsen, Lt C W Payne & Lt H R L Bisgard)
22.9.42	31st FG, 309th FS, Ju 88 probably destroyed 60m S of Selsey Bill (shared by Mjr H R Thyng & Lt B Chandler)
2.10.42	4th FG, 334th FS, FW 190 destroyed SW of Dunkirk (shared by Lt J A Clark and "W.C.")
2.10.42	4th FG, 334th FS, FW 190 destroyed 10m SW of Dunkirk (Capt O H Coen)
2.10.42	4th FG, 334th FS, FW 190 damaged S of Nieuport (Lt W B Morgan)
2.10.42	4th FG, 334th FS, FW 190 destroyed SW of Dunkirk (1/Lt S M Anderson)
2.10.42	4th FG, 335th FS, FW 190 destroyed S of Dunkirk (Lt G B [Tilson?])
2.10.42	4th FG, 335th FS, Fi 156 Storch destroyed SE of Furnes (Shared by 2/Lt R W Evans & 2/Lt F J Smolinksi); Evans aircraft then hit by flak, baled out safely near Foulness Point
8.11.42	31st FG, 309th FS, Algeria, shot down by Dewoitine D-520 whilst landing Tafaraoui (2/Lt J C Byrd killed)
8.11.42	31st FG, shot down by US fire, Tafaraoui (Capt La Breche returned to Sqn)
8.11.42	31st FG, 307th FS, shot down by US fire (1/Lt W A Thomas Jnr returned to sqn)
8.11.42	31st FG, 307th FS, shot down by ground fire, force-landed 8m from Tafaraoui (Lt R Wooten walked back)
10.11.42	31st FG, shot down by flak over Les Trembles, forced landed (Lt Colney PoW, taken to Sidi-bel-Abbes hospital where he was released after French surrendered)
19.11.42	4th FG, 335th FS, FW 190 destroyed 10m SW of Flushing (2/Lt F J Smolinski)
20.11.42	4th FG, 335th FS, Debden, mechanical failure, ditched in Channel (Mjr R Evans)
4.12.42	52nd FG, 2nd FS, Sqn bounced by Bf 109s, formed Lufbury circle, shot down near Tebourba (Lt W A Kari killed)
4.12.42	52nd FG, 2nd FS, sqn bounced by Bf 109s, formed Lufbury circle, baled out (Lt F B Short picked up by British recce unit)
4.12.42	52nd FG, 2nd FS, sqn bounced by Bf 109s, formed Lufbury circle, tried to land Bone but only one flap came down, crashed (Lt S Freel killed)
4.12.42	52nd FG, 2nd FS, sqn bounced by Bf 109s, formed Lufbury circle, baled out (Lt J M Shuck, PoW)
20.12.42	52nd FG, shot down a RAF Spitfire during engagement with enemy aircraft over Bone (Lt J R Ludlow)
21.12.42	31st FG, 307th FS, force-landed at Samda, 75m S of Maison Blanche after escort to Telergma (Lt W B Whisonant uninjured, returned to sqn 28.12.42)
21.12.42	31st FG, force-landed at Samda, 75m S of Maison Blanche after escort to Telergma (Lt Colney uninjured, returned to sqn 28.12.42)
?.1.43	31st FG, 307th FS, hit tractor on take-off from Telergma, aircraft destroyed by fire (Lt Roche injured)
3.1.43	52nd FG, 4th FS, lost on move from Orleansville to Bone (Capt J E Garvey, PoW)
3.1.43	52nd FG, 4th FS, lost on move from Orleansville to Bone (Lt R W Rivers, PoW)
3.1.43	52nd FG, 4th FS, lost on move from Orleansville to Bone (Lt A W Vogtle, PoW)
6.1.43	52nd FG, 4th FS, harbour patrol from Bone, attacked 3 FW 190 and shot one down, then himself shot down by II/JG.2 and seen to dive into sea 5m N of La Calle (Capt DH Williams killed)
6.1.43	31st FG, 307th FS, two aircraft belly-landed at Youks-les-Bains, undercarriage would not lower, aircraft repaired (2/Lt J Klaas OK and Lt Langberg)
9.1.43	31st FG, blew tyre landing, tipped over, probably repaired (Capt Zimlich)
9.1.43	4th FG, 336th FS, came in too high, crashed, wrecked (Lt R Mirsch, who was flying Lt L Gover's 'Sondra Lee')
14.1.43	4th FG, 334th FS, two FW 190 destroyed 3m W of Ostend (one shared by 1/Lt S M Anderson & Sgt R A Boock, and one by Boock alone)
14.1.43	4th FG, 335th FS, FW 190 down in sea W of Dunkirk (1/Lt S M Anderson)
14.1.43	4th FG, 336th FS, Rhubarb, shot up by ground fire exiting Dunkirk, crash-landed Bradwell Bay (Lt K D Peterson)
14.1.43	4th FG, 336th FS, Rhubarb, shot up by ground fire exiting Dunkirk, crashed on landing [at base] (Lt R Mirsch)

UNITED STATES OF AMERICA

14.1.43	4th FG, 336th FS, Rhubarb, shot up by ground fire exiting Dunkirk, landed North Weald; Retd to base same day (Lt L Gover)
20.1.43	31st FG, two aircraft collided just after take off, both destroyed by fire (Mjr HR Thyng and Capt R Mitchell OK)
22.1.43	4th FG, 335th FS, FW 190 damaged 10m NW of Dunkirk (1/Lt G B Fetrow)
22.1.43	4th FG, 336th FS, Circus 253 escorting four Bostons to bomb St.Omer airfield, shot up (Lt R Mirsch)
22.1.43	4th FG, 336th FS, Circus 253 escorting four Bostons to bomb St.Omer airfield, shot up (Lt Boehle)
24.1.43	52nd FG 4th FS, hit by flak, belly-landed in enemy territory (Lt N Boyce, PoW)
30.1.43	4th FG, 336th FS, on landing, braked hard to avoid a truck which drove onto runway, nosed over and damaged prop, then dropped back and broke tail section, aircraft scrapped (Lt L Gover)
4.2.43	52nd FG, 5th or 6th FS, escorting P-39s on recce, met FW 190s of II/JG.2, shot down over Fondouk, crashed in flames SW of Kel el Abur (Lt HL Pederson)
4.2.43	52nd FG, 5th or 6th FS, escorting P-39s on recce, met FW 190s of II/JG.2, shot down over Fondouk, baled out, landed in Allied lines (Lt Rudorffer leg wound)
4.2.43	52nd FG, 5th or 6th FS, escorting P-39s on recce, met FW 190s of II/JG.2, shot down [could this third pilot be Roberts, listed below as 14.2.43?]
4.2.43	USAAF Bovingdon, accident at base 4.2.43 (Lt J R Westwood)
10.2.43	31st FG, shot down, details missing (Capt Bissgard)
14.2.43	52nd FG, 5th FS, circumstances unknown (2/Lt J C Roberts killed)
15.2.43	31st FG, 308th FS, one of four aircraft airfield patrol when airfield attacked by four Bf 109 & four FW 190, shot down by enemy aircraft over Thelepte airfield, Tunisia (1/Lt J C Reed killed)
15.2.43	31st FG, 307th FS, six Spitfires shot up on ground at Thelepte by attacking Bf 109s and FW 190s (all six aircraft destroyed when airfield evacuated 17.2.43)
16.2.43	52nd FG, aircraft lost over Tebassa, Algeria
17.2.43	52nd FG, 2nd FS, escort to six A-20 and four P-39 to south of Feriana, just south of Thelepte, shot down by ground fire (1/Lt R C Newberry killed)
17.2.43	52nd FG, 2nd FS, escort to six A-20 and four P-39 to south of Feriana, just south of Thelepte, forced down (Mjr J S Coward)
17.2.43	52nd FG, 2nd FS, escort to six A-20 and four P-39 to south of Feriana, just south of Thelepte, landed in desert in dark, pilot spent night in aircraft (Lt Petot)
18.2.43	52nd FG, 4th FS, circumstances unknown (Lt T H Evans Jnr killed)
24.2.43	52nd FG, shot down over El Agunire, Tunisia
4.3.43	52nd FG, performed roll at low altitude over airfield, failed to pullout when inverted, hit ground and exploded (Lt J A Baldwin killed)
4.3.43	52nd FG, hit flock of sheep landing (Capt G V Williams)
8.3.43	31st FG, 307th FS, shot down by FW 190s of II/JG.2, spun down inverted, exploded on hitting ground, S of Pichon, Tunisia (1/Lt W A Thomas Jnr killed)
8.3.43	31st FG, 307th FS, shot down by FW 190s of II/JG.2, S of Pichon, Tunisia (1/Lt M P Mitchell, PoW)
12.3.43	31st FG, 307th FS, two aircraft damaged by bombs
15.3.43	31st FG, 308th FS, B-25 escort, shot up by ten to fifteen Bf 109, forced landed in desert, St.de Mezzou, Tunisia (Lt Mosby retd Sqn)
17.3.43	31st FG, 307th FS, lost (Lt R Mandeville killed)
20.3.43	31st FG, chased by six Bf 109s of II/JG.51, shot down, forced landed in desert, Tunisia (Lt Barber injured)
20.3.43	31st FG, 307th FS, forgot to lower undercarriage, belly-landed, Thelepte (2/Lt J Klaas)
20.3.43	31st FG, 307th FS, shot down, baled out near Maknassy (Lt Langberg walked back three days later)
21.3.43	31st FG, 309th FS, shot down a Ju 87, then badly shot up by a Bf 109, pilot baled out near Maknassy, Tunisia (Lt Langberg)
21.3.43	52nd FG, 4th FS, bomber escort, shot down 6m SW of Sened (Lt G St.Germain killed)
22.3.43	31st FG, shot down by Bf 109, belly-landed in friendly territory, aircraft repaired (Lt Carver)
23.3.43	31st FG, 309th FS, FTR sweep, shot down by Bf 109, Tunisia (Lt N G Earley PoW)
23.3.43	31st FG, 309th FS, sweep, Bf 109 damaged, then shot down by another Bf 109, force-landed Tunisia (1/Lt J A Juhnke retd Sqn on foot)
23.3.43	52nd FG, 2nd FS, collided with Bf 109 piloted by Mjr Joachim Muenchenberg (134 victories) south of Es Sened (Capt T R Sweetland and Mjr Muenchenberg killed)
23.3.43	52nd FG, 2nd FS, collided with Lt Strasen [Mjr Joachim Muencheber's number Two] (Capt H L Williamson)
23.3.43	31st FG, 309th FS, hit by flak, forced landing, overturned (Lt Wolfe rescued and taken to No.77 Evacuation Hospital at Youks-les-Bains)
1.4.43	31st FG, 308th FS, shot down spinning in flames by Bf 109 over Guettar, Tunisia (2/Lt W C O'Brien killed)
1.4.43	31st FG, 309th FS, hit by flak, forced landing in desert but crashed into American tank, Tunisia (2/Lt F M Strole killed)
1.4.43	31st FG, 309th FS, shot down by enemy aircraft, burnt out, Tunisia (1/Lt J A Juhnke killed)
1.4.43	52nd FG, 2nd FS, shot down by Bf 109 at Bou Hamrain (1/Lt E M Boughton killed)
1.4.43	31st FG, 308th FS, crash-landed at Gafsa (2/Lt R L Peebles retd to sqn)
1.4.43	31st FG, hit parked Spitfire on take-off, both aircraft destroyed by fire (Lt Colney uninjured)
3.4.43	52nd FG, 2nd FS, engaged Ju 87s over Guetter, shot down S of Djebel Hamadt (Capt A E Vinson DFC killed)
3.4.43	31st FG, 307th FS, shot down by flak in Djebel Chemas area, crash-landed in flames NE of Gafsa (Lt Baltezor minor injuries, picked up by Americans and retd to Sqn)
4.4.43	31st FG, 309th FS, escort A-20s to La Fauconnerie, shot down by FW 190 (Lt B J Roche retd to sqn later)
5.4.43	31st FG, 308th FS, undercarriage failed to lower fully, ground-looped, Thelepte (1/Lt C R Ramsey)
5.4.43	52nd FG, 4th FS, top squadron escort to A-20s bombing La Fauconnerie, bounced by Bf 109s & FW 190s, shot down 4m SW of target (1/Lt RI East killed)
5.4.43	31st FG, 307th FS, escort to A-20s bombing La Fauconnerie, bounced by Bf 109s & FW 190s, shot down (2/Lt B J Roche killed) - NOTE: Lt Henry Roche flew Mk.IX 'FLYING COCKROCHE'
6.4.43	31st FG, 307th FS, escorting A-20s to La Fauconnerie, shot down by Bf 109s, Tunisia (2/Lt J Klaas, PoW)
6.4.43	52nd FG, 2nd FS, shot down by flak, forced landing, crashed 10m N of Maknassy (Lt J A Carey)
6.4.43	52nd FG, shot down by flak, forced landing, crashed 10m N of Maknassy (Lt J T Nangle)
6.4.43	52nd FG, shot down by fighters 10m NW of Maknassy (Lt JG Doigherty)
6.4.43	52nd FG, 4th FS, shot down by fighters 10m NW of Maknassy (1/Lt D W Markley DFC found by Arabs and taken to hospital
6.4.43	52nd FG, shot down by flak during strafing, crashed 8m N of Maknassy (Lt G E Montour)
6.4.43	52nd FG, 5th FS ('VF-S'), shot down by flak during strafing, crashed 8m N of Maknassy (Lt J S White)
7.4.43	31st FG, 308th FS, escort to A-20s to Mezzouna/Fatnassa area, bounced by Bf 109s & FW 190s, shot down by enemy aircraft Tunisia (1/Lt D Miller baled out safely, PoW)
9.4.43	52nd FG, 2FS, sqn bounced by Ju 88s in Kairouan area, shot down by return fire from Ju 88, crash-landed in enemy territory (Lt M K Langberg evaded capture and retd to sqn)

9.4.43	52nd FG, 5th FS ('VF-D'), hit by flak, crash-landed on a ridge (Lt E G Steinbrenner)
16.4.43	("xx721") 52nd FG, 4th FS, crashed on take-off Gedim (1/Lt MR Blais killed)
17.4.43	31st FG, 309th FS (Mk.IX), sweep to Tunis area, shot down by flak at 23,000ft (Lt Strawn baled out, picked up by Germans and taken PoW, to Tunis hospital, released when Tunis fell)
19.4.43	52nd FG, 4th FS, damaged, crash-landed 8m E of Mateur (1/Lt EC Smithers killed)
19.4.43	52nd FG, 2nd FS, shot down on sweep to La Sebala, seen to force-land (Lt MK Langberg)
20.4.43	52nd FG, 4th FS, shot down in Tunis area (1/Lt JD Harvey killed)
20.4.43	52nd FG, 4th FS, last seen chasing Bf 109 north of Tunis (Capt FB Camp killed)
20.4.43	52nd FG, 2nd FS, shot down in Tunis area (Lt WF Higgins, PoW)
20.4.43	52nd FG, 2nd FS, shot down in Tunis area (Lt LS Williamson, PoW)
20.4.43	52nd FG, 2nd FS, shot down over La Marsa LG (S/Sgt JE Butler killed)
21.4.43	31st FG, 308th FS, shot down by enemy aircraft on sweep to La Sebala, pilot baled out (1/Lt R C Corrigan, PoW)
21.4.43	31st FG, 308th FS ('HL-Q'), shot down by enemy aircraft, crash-landed Tunisia (2/Lt RL Peebles, PoW injured)
25.4.43	31st FG, 308th FS, shot down by aircraft in Allied territory, Tunisia (Lt AD Callander retd sqn same day)
25.4.43	31st FG, shot down by enemy aircraft in Allied territory, Tunisia (Lt Ramer retd sqn same day)
18.5.43	4th FG, 334th FS, circumstances unknown (1/Lt RA Boock killed, buried Henri St.Chapelle)
21.5.43	4th FG, 334th FS, circumstances unknown (2/Lt L L MacFarlane killed, buried Cambridge) [unconfirmed that there was anyone of this name with the FG at this time]
23.5.43	(Mk.Vb) 31st FG ('WZ-R'), engine blew up on ferry trip to Korba (Lt O'Brien safe)
7.6.43	31st FG, one aircraft lost on Korbe raid
7.6.43	31st FG, 309th Sqn, FW 190 damaged over Pantellaria (1/Lt RM Lupton Jnr)
9.6.43	31st FG, 308th FS, shot down off Pantellaria by Ten Ugo Drago in Bf 109G 363-7 of 363^Squadriglia, crashed in sea on return due to falling oil pressure (1/Lt SE McCann [McMann?] rescued after 6 hours in water)
9.6.43	31st FG, attacked by aircraft Pantellaria, pilot baled out 8m off Pantellaria (Lt Rich picked up by ASR Walrus)
10.6.43	31st FG, 307th FS, shot down in error by P-40 of 99th FS off Pantellaria, crashed in sea (1/Lt GV Gooding killed)
11.6.43	31st FG, 308th FS, shot down Pantellaria, radioed wing shot off then nothing further heard (1/Lt M P Smith Jnr killed)
11.6.43	31st FG, shot down by enemy aircraft Pantellaria (Lt Rich, PoW)
14.6.43	4th FG, 336th FS, lost escorting bombers to Abbeville (1/Lt GC King killed, buried Cambridge)
20.6.43	52nd FG, HQ Sqn, circumstances unknown (1/Lt HH Brians killed)
26.6.43	31st FG, one aircraft lost en route Gozo
6.7.43	31st FG, 308th FS, shot in flames by a Bf 109 over Comiso, Sicily (Capt TB Fleming killed)
6.7.43	31st FG, 308th FS, shot down by a Bf 109 Sicily (1/Lt Babcock, PoW)
7.7.43	31st FG, 308th FS, baled out over friendly territory (Lt Miller - ex RAF)
8.7.43	31st FG, 308th FS, crashed on take-off, destroyed by fire, Gozo (Lt Van Ausdell uninjured)
10.7.43	31st FG, 307th FS, hit by gunfire from a US Navy LST, engine failure, force-landed 2m from Gela Bay, Sicily (Lt JE Johnston rescued unhurt by US troops)
10.7.43	31st FG, 307th FS, hit by US Navy gunfire off Sicily (Lt JE Conley baled out into sea, rescued by USN destroyer)
11.7.43	31st FG, 307th FS, FW 190 shot down nr Gela (Capt JD Collinsworth)
11.7.43	31st FG, 307th FS, Bf 109 probable [claimed as Do 217] Gela (1/Lt Wright)
11.7.43	31st FG, 307th FS, Fw 190 shot down Gela (Capt J M Winkler)
11.7.43	31st FG, 309th FS, Ju 88 shot down 15m NE of Gela (shared Mjr FA Hill & Capt B Chandler)
11.7.43	31st FG, 309th FS, Bf 109 shot down (Capt C W Payne)
11.7.43	31st FG, 308th FS, Bf 110 of II/ZG1 shot down [claimed as Do 217] (Capt JH Paulk)
11.7.43	31st FG, 308th FS, Bf 110 of II/ZG1 shot down [claimed as Do 217] (1/Lt AD Callander)
11.7.43	31st FG, 308th FS, Bf 110 of II/ZG1 shot down [claimed as Do 217] (1/Lt WW Waltner)
12.7.43	31st FG, 307th FS, FW 190 of Stab/SKG10 (Fw Hermann Heiss) shot down (Capt HL Barr)
14.7.43	4th FG, 335th FS, circumstances unknown (2/Lt W K Wortman killed, buried Normandy) [not listed with 4th FG?]
16.7.43	31st FG, 307th FS, no details (Lt C Hoffman killed)
16.7.43	31st FG, shot down by American flak while flying over convoy (Lt Colney picked up safe)
19.7.43	52nd FG, 2nd FS, gun practice, crashed in sea while shadow shooting, neither aircraft nor body found (2/Lt GL Bailey killed)
28.7.43	31st FG, 309th FS, hit by AA near San Fratello, destroyed by fire, Sicily (2/Lt RF Heil killed)
30.7.43	4th FG, 335th FS, circumstances unknown (1/Lt FD Merritt killed, buried Cambridge) [not listed with 4 FG?]
30.7.43	31st FG, 309th FS, Bf 109 probable off Randazzo (2/Lt FO Trafton)
30.7.43	31st FG, 309th FS, Bf 109 probable off Randazzo (2/Lt Mutchler)
1.8.43	52nd FG, 2nd FS, Do 217 shot down 60m N of Salina Island (2/Lt NE English)
1.8.43	52nd FG, 2nd FS, Do 217 shot down 15m NE of Stromboli Island (Capt NL McDonald)
6.8.43	52nd FG, 4th FS, Bf 109 shot down 40m NE of Palermo (1/Lt LV Helton)
8.8.43	31st FG, 308th FS, FW 190 shot down off Cape Orlando (Capt JH Paulk)
8.8.43	31st FG, 308th FS, FW 190 shot down off Cape Orlando (1/Lt CR Ramsey)
8.8.43	31st FG, 308th FS, FW 190 shot down off Cape Orlando (2/Lt RF Hurd)
11.8.43	31st FG, 308th FS, involved in fight with FW 190s, crash-landed due to glycol leak, aircraft destroyed by fire, San Stefano (2/Lt RF Hurd)
11.8.43	31st FG, crashed on landing Gozo (pilot unhurt) [lost Cayve Orlando?]
11.8.43	31st FG, 307th FS, MC 202 shot down off Cape Orlando (2/Lt RB Chaddock)
11.8.43	31st FG, 307th FS, FW 190 shot down off Cape Orlando (shared by 1/Lt CA Pryblo & 2/Lt DG Graham)
11.8.43	31st FG, 308th FS, FW 190 shot down off Cape Orlando (Capt RN Baker)
12.8.43	31st FG, crashed on landing Gozo (pilot unhurt) [was one of these JK403?]
28.8.43	52nd FG, 2nd FS, engine failed over Sicily, force-landed, hit two stone walls (Lt WL Bryan Jnr injured but retd Sqn)
28.8.43	52nd FG, 5th FS, Bf 109G shot down S of Naples (2/Lt RW Hine)
29.8.43	52nd FG, 5th FS, Me 410, probably of 2(F)/122, shot down off Ustica island (1/Lt EJ Odom)
29.8.43	(Mk.VIII) 31st FG, 309th FS ('WZ-G'), taxied into pothole, tipped on nose (Lt McCarthy); see also AR600
2.9.43	4th FG, 334th FS, shot down Provins, 50m SE of Paris (1/Lt DB Leaf killed, buried Ardennes) [poss. P-47]
9.9.43	31st FG, 307th FS, hit by return fire from Do 217, crash-landed on beach, Italy (Lt V Fields)
10.9.43	31st FG, 309th FS, undershot overturned, Milazzo, Cat.E (Lt Webster injured)
10.9.43	31st FG, 307th FS, glycol leak, force-landed at Preia te Mare (2/Lt DG Graham returned to sqn by Italians)

11.9.43 31st FG, 309th Sqn, oil pressure failed, force-landed Paestum (1/Lt RM Lupton Jnr)
11.9.43 31st FG, 309th Sqn, taxied into parked Spitfire (Lt Jamison)
13.9.43 31st FG, crash-landed in southern Italy after fuel tank tap came off in pilots hand (Mjr JH Paulk)
13.9.43 31st FG, 308th FS, baled out 25m W of Cape Bonifati due to main tank being unserviceable (Lt Overend floated in water all night and was picked up next morning)
13.9.43 (Mk.Vb) 31st FG, 309th FS ('WZ-B'), ground-looped (Lt Nelson)
17.9.43 (Mk.IX) 31st FG, 309th FS ('WZ-BB'), pilot baled out after engine failure (Lt Weismueller) [RAF flew in replacement aircraft but pranged it on landing; Later repaired]
21.9.43 31st FG, 309th FS, FTR ops (Lt W Imwall killed)
22.9.43 52nd FG, 2nd FS, Sgt Varnell ran into rear of Fuller's aircraft breaking off entire tail section
22.9.43 52nd FG, 2nd FS, hit rock taxying, lost tail wheel (Lt CS Cleveland)
26.9.43 31st FG, 309th FS, damaged on take off (Lt H Hughes)
2.10.43 52nd FG, 2nd FS, very strong wind damaged many aircraft parked in field, including Mk.VIII 'QP-R' which was SOC after being blown from dispersal area to engineering area
13.10.43 52nd FG, 5th FS, circumstances unknown (2/Lt FW Holmberg killed)
17.10.43 52nd FG, force-landed Vis with oil leak due to mice chewing flexi-pipe for nesting material (Lt Toombs flew it back next day)
18.10.43 "..533", accident Duxford (Lt EL Bryan)
20.10.43 52nd FG, 4th FS, forced landing, crashed (Capt EN Scott killed)
25.10.43 52nd FG, 5th FS, circumstances unknown (Sgt LE Aubertin killed)
1.11.43 31st FG, one aircraft lost at Cassino
3.11.43 4th FG, 334th FS, escorting 400 B-17s to Wilhelmshaven, bounced at coast by Bf 109s, shot down (Lt FD Gallion killed, buried Netherlands)
3.11.43 4th FG, 334th FS, escorting 400 B-17s to Wilhelmshaven, bounced at coast by Bf 109s, shot down (1/Lt IR Moon killed, buried Netherlands)
7.11.43 31st FG, engine failed, force-landed, crashed Pomigliano (pilot unhurt)
12.11.43 31st FG, 308th FS, pilot forgot to lower undercarriage, burnt out (2/Lt RF Hurd)
18.11.43 31st FG, 307th FS, Gaeta, engine failed on take-off, force-landed, crashed in poor visibility (1/Lt EF Mann killed)
18.11.43 31st FG, 309th FS, nosed over taxying, repaired (Lt Hurter)
18.11.43 31st FG, nosed over, repaired (Lt Midgett)
19.11.43 52nd FG, 2nd FS, shot down by flak over Cape Limaro
19.11.43 31st FG, one aircraft shot down by flak into water
24.11.43 31st FG, 309th FS ('WT-Z'), spun in Pomigliano (2/Lt Shenberger killed)
24.11.43 52nd FG, 2nd FS, landing from cross-country flight, caught by strong wind, ground-looped, flipped on to one wing (Lt Williams)
27.11.43 31st FG, 307th FS ('MX-EE'), written off (Lt Amyx)
1.12.43 31st FG, three aircraft FTR (all pilots PoW)
3.12.43 52nd FG, 2nd FS, move to Borgo, tipped on nose landing at Olbia, Sardinia
14.12.43 31st FG, 309th FS, shot down by three British aircraft (Lt Walker FTR) [EN307?]
15.12.43 31st FG, 309th FS, escorting A-20s to Frosinone, damaged by Bf 109, glided back over Allied lines (Lt Lyman baled out safely, retd to sqn by L-4 spotter aircraft)
19.12.43 31st FG, hit while parked Pomigliano
19.12.43 52nd FG, 4th FS, circumstances unknown (Lt H W Dorland killed)
19.12.43 52nd FG, 4th FS, circumstances unknown (1/Lt L V Helton, PoW)
19.12.43 52nd FG, 4th FS, circumstances unknown (Lt J Ennis PoW)
19.12.43 52nd FG, 4th FS, force-landed, sugar in tank (Lt JW Massey, PoW) [above presumably included EF691 & LZ820]
21.12.43 31st FG, 307th FS, mid-air collision near Capua with Lt Amyx, pilot baled out safely (Lt Place unhurt)
21.12.43 31st FG, 307th FS, mid-air collision near Capua with Lt Place, pilot baled out safely (Lt Amyx unhurt)
21.12.43 31st FG, 307th FS, hit by AA (Capt Clark seriously injured)
21.12.43 52nd FG, 2nd FS, shipping recce with Lt B Kellam, hit water, skipped about 50yds, pulled up to 400ft, then dived into water, disappeared (1/Lt N E English killed)
27.12.43 31st FG, crash-landed near Capua, suspect fuel, it was later discovered that fuel was being drawn off at supply depot by GIs and replaced with water (Lt Gompf)
28.12.43 31st FG, 307th FS, engine failed, belly-landed near Venafro (Lt W Schanning killed)
6.1.44   52nd FG, pilot killed strafing E-Boats
13.1.44 52nd FG, 2nd Sqn, recce, coolant leak, force-landed OK on Pianosa (unable to rescue Lt J D Myers as Germans still holding island)
15.1.44 52nd FG, 5th FS, baled out (2/Lt C T J O'Connor dead by time A S R Walrus arrived)
22.1.44 52nd FG, 2nd FS ('QP-A'), hit by flak, no flaps, ran off end of runway landing and onto road, aircraft SOC (Lt Alexander)
23.1.44 52nd FG, 2nd FS, shot down by return fire from Do 217 near Viareggio, baled out off coast near Leghorn, pilot appeared unhurt (Lt CS Cleveland)
23.1.44 31st FG, 309th FS, tipped over onto back landing after patrol (Lt Lyman safe)
23.1.44 31st FG, 309th FS, blew tyre on take off, Cat.E, SOC (Lt Mann)
25.1.44 31st FG, lost three aircraft (one shot down by a P-40)
28.1.44 31st FG, 307th FS, collided with Bf 109 over Anzio (Lt Frank Haberle buried Nettuno cemetery)
28.1.44 31st FG, hit by debris of FW 190, pilot baled out N of Ponziane Island (Lt Terry picked up by personal launch of General Donovan of the OSS after 6 hours in water)
3.2.44   31st FG, one Spitfire destroyed and one damaged by shelling during night, Nettuno
5.2.44   31st FG, 307th FS, airfield shelled, two Spitfire Cat.E, two damaged, Nettuno
5.2.44   31st FG, 309th FS, force-landed Nettuno, engine problems (Lt Nelson)
5.2.44   31st FG, 307th FS, Nettuno shelled, two Spitfire destroyed, sqn flew out 14 aircraft to Castel Volturno
9.2.44   31st FG, crashed short of runway in soft dirt (Lt Sturm head & face injuries)
9.2.44   52nd FG, 4th FS, FTR (Lt RA Hoover PoW)
9.2.44   52nd FG, 4th FS, FTR (Lt JH Montgomery Jnr killed) [above were EF647 & MA883]
15.2.44 31st FG, hit by flak (Lt A Tower killed)
19.2.44 52nd FG, 2nd FS, strafing fighter airfield at Viterbo, near Lake Bolsena, sqn bounced by 30+ Bf 109s, shot down, baled out (Lt M Encinias, PoW)
19.2.44 52nd FG, 2nd FS, strafing fighter airfield at Viterbo, near Lake Bolsena, sqn bounced by 30+ Bf 109s, hit, crash-landed in olive grove, wings and engine broke off, fuselage came to rest upside down, pilot rescued by monks (Lt Liebl taken PoW by German ski troops)
19.2.44 52nd FG, 5th FS, FTR (1/Lt WD Gahagen killed) [EF700, EF710, MA890 or MH564 would all fit]
19.2.44 31st FG, tyre blew on take-off, continued patrol force-landed at Capodichino (Lt Ainley)
21.2.44 31st FG, 309th FS, aircraft hit, crash-landed inside Allied territory (Mjr JS Thorsen retd to sqn)
24.2.44 Accident Great Ashfield (Lt B Raeder)
24.2.44 31st FG, 307th FS, shot down by flak, crashed near Lanuvio (Lt Horace Comstock killed)
28.2.44 4th FG, 334th FS, circumstances unknown (1/Lt RB Fraser killed, buried Cambridge)

1.3.44	31st FG, hit by flak strafing Cisterna road, crash-landed near front line (Capt Clark picked up by ground patrol)
2.3.44	4th FG, 336th FS, circumstances unknown (1/Lt GK Villinger DFC killed, buried Netherlands)
3.3.44	4th FG, 336th FS, circumstances unknown (1/Lt GW Barnes killed, buried Netherlands)
3.3.44	52nd FG, 2nd FS, escorting B-26s to Rome, engine failed, pilot baled out at 4,000ft, landed in water 25m W of Civitavecchia, dinghy exploded during inflation so relied on half inflated Mae West (Lt Adam picked up OK after one hour by ASR Walrus)
4.3.44	4th FG, 336th FS, circumstances unknown (1/Lt RH Roberts killed, buried Cambridge)
6.3.44	4th FG, 334th FS, circumstances unknown (1/Lt ED Whalen killed)
6.3.44	31st FG, 309th FS ('WZ-V'), engine failed, pilot baled out near airfield into Gulf of Yalta (Lt Harmeyer picked up by Walrus)
7.3.44	31st FG, 309th FS, engine failure, pilot baled out Gulf of Yalta (pilot picked by ASR Walrus)
8.3.44	52nd FG, 4th FS, FTR (2/Lt BW Jones killed)
15.3.44	52nd FG, 4th FS, shot down strafing (2/Lt RM Moore killed)
16.3.44	4th FG, 336th FS, circumstances unknown (1/Lt ER Skilton killed, buried Lorraine)
18.3.44	31st FG, belly-landed out of fuel at base, Cat.B (Lt Hardage)
19.3.44	52nd FG, 5th FS, shot down by enemy aircraft off Italian coast, near Port Ecole, rescue flight could not find dinghy (2/Lt RC Boyd, PoW)
19.3.44	52nd FG, 5th FS, flight bounced by FW 190s over Italian coast, shot up, tipped on nose landing at base (Lt DeVoe wounded)
21.3.44	4th FG, 335th FS, circumstances unknown (Lt J Goetz killed, buried Brittany)
21.3.44	31st FG, 309th FS, nosed over on landing (Lt Fawcett)
22.3.44	52nd FG, 4th FS, circumstances unknown (2/Lt G St Germain killed)
22.3.44	52nd FG, 4th FS, circumstances unknown (Capt NNV Bolle, PoW)
31.3.44	4th FG, 336th FS, circumstances unknown (1/Lt PG Lehman DFC killed, buried Cambridge)
31.3.44	31st FG, FTR from strafing
11.4.44	52nd FG, 2nd FS, recce/strike, hit by flak, pilot baled out NW of San Vicenzo, (Mjr BS Sandborn, CO, picked up by ASR Walrus)
12.4.44	52nd FG, 2nd FS, two Spitfires made wheel-ups landings
12.4.44	Accident at Eshott (no unit or pilot given)
12.6.44	Crashed in France (no unit or pilot given).

SURVIVORS in USA

Spitfire Mk.I	P9306
Spitfire Mk.V	BL370, MA863
Spitfire Mk.VIIc	EN474
Spitfire Mk.VIII	MT719
Spitfire T.VIII	MT818
Spitfire Mk.IX	BR601, MH367, MH415, MH603, MH750(?), MJ730, MK923, MK959, ML417, PL344
Spitfire T.IX	MJ772, TE308
Spitfire PR.XI	PA908
Spitfire Mk.XIV	NH749, NH904
Spitfire Mk.XVI	SL542, SL574, TD135, TE356, TE384, TE392, TE476
Spitfire Mk.XVIII	TP276, TP280
Spitfire PR.XIX	PS890
Seafire Mk.XV	PR503, SR462
Seafire Mk.47	VP441

Note

MA793 (Mk.IX)	To Brazil
MK297 (Mk.IX)	Destroyed by fire
ML119 (Mk.IX)	Back to UK
PV270 (Mk.IX)	To New Zealand
RW382 (Mk.XVI)	Back to UK
SL721 (Mk.XVI)	To Canada
TE330 (Mk.XVI)	To Australia/New Zealand
TP298 (Mk.XVIII)	To Australia
TZ138 (Mk.XIV)	To Canada

References:

Air Force Combat Units of World War II, by Maurer Maurer, US Armament Printing Office Washington DC, 1961.
The Mighty Eighth, by Roger A Freeman, Macdonald & Company London, 1970.
The Army Air Forces in World War II (Vol.Two), University Chicago Press, p.55.
Yankee Spitfires, by Chris F Shores, Air Classics, p.51.
America's Spitfires, by Ch. Shores, Air Enthusiast sixteen, p.13.
Naval Aviators in Spitfires (VCS-7), by Cmd P Mersky, Proceedings December 1986, p.105.
American Spitfire, Camouflage & Markings, by P Ludwig and M Laird, Ventura Publication, 1998.
Spitfires over Sicily, by Brian Cull with Nicola Malizia and Frederick Galea, Grub Street, 2000.

Synopsis of American Spitfires & Seafires

Mk Type	ETO 8 & 9th (US) AF	MTO 12th (US)AF	Sum ETO & MTO	in USA only*	USA total
F.Ia	10	-	10	2	12
PR.C & D	1	1	2	-	2
F/LF.V b/c	382	279	661	7	668
F.VIIc	-	-	-	1	1
F/LF.VIIIc	2	56	58	2	60
F/LF.IXc/e	13	104	117	14	131
PR.XI	23	1	24	2	26
F.XIVc/e	-	-	-	7	7
LF.XVIe	-	-	-	8	8
F/FR.XVIIIe	-	-	-	7	7
PR. XIX	-	2	2	1	3
F.24	-	-	-	1	1
SF F.Ib	-	12	12	-	12
SF F.IIc	6	42	48	1	49
SF F.XVc	-	-	-	2	2
SF FR.47	-	-	-	1	1
Total	**437**	**497**	**934**	**56**	**990**

ETO = European Territory (UK, France, Belgium, NL, Germany)
MTO = Mediterranean Territory (NA, NWA, Italy)
SF = Seafire

* in USA: incl USAAC at home, but also those for civil purposes and those which arrived as Survivors later !

Remarks

Over **1,000** Spitfires and Seafires served with the US forces.
This survey lists only those aircraft, which were shown, photographed or listed in surviving British and American records as having served with American forces.
There were probably others as yet unidentified, especially in North Africa where, for instance, some Spitfires served with both French and American units.

YUGOSLAVIA
[now the Republics of Bosnia-Herzegovina, Croatia, Macedonia, Slovenia and Yugoslavia (Serbia & Montenegro)]

In a letter dated 28th January 1937 the *Kraljevina Jugoslavija* (Kingdom of Yugoslavia) inquired about Spitfires generally, then in November 1937, following the visit of a Col Rabchitch, requested a firm delivery date for an order of twelve Spitfires and permission to build 30 under licence. A quotation for twelve aircraft was sent on 25th February 1938, and on 17th November 1938 the Foreign Office gave the Yugoslavian order place No. 8 on its priority list.

In 1939 Yugoslavian pilots arrived in England to test-fly Spitfire K9791. The first such flight was to have taken place on 13th September 1939, but with the outbreak of the Second World War all foreign orders were cancelled.

[Note: Yugoslavia also asked in January 1938 for the German Bf 109E. A contract for a delivery of 50 Bf 109Es was made in April 1939, later increased to 100 aircraft in June 1939, but only 73 arrived.]

After the occupation of Yugoslavia by Germany and Italy in 1941, some pilots of the *JKRV* (Yugoslav Royal Air Force) escaped to the Middle East. They gained Spitfire experience with No.2 ADU (M.E.), and in 1943 they flew with No.71 OTU, then with No.94 Sqn RAF from September 1943 to August 1944.

On 22nd March 1944 an agreement was signed between the

A Spitfire F.Vb/trop coded 'L' of No. 352 Sqn RAF, serving with the Balkan Air Force. [IWM CNA3102]

Spitfire F.Vb/trop of No. 352 Sqn RAF on the ground, serving with the Balkan Air Force. Shortly before the unit switched to the Yugoslavian Air Force their Spitfires were replaced. These older aircraft, JK544 'M', JG948 'J' and JK608 'C', were returned to the RAF. [IWM CMA3097]

Spitfire F.Vb/trop JK544 'M' of No. 352 (Jugoslav) Sqn, RAF, being armed up in 1944/45.

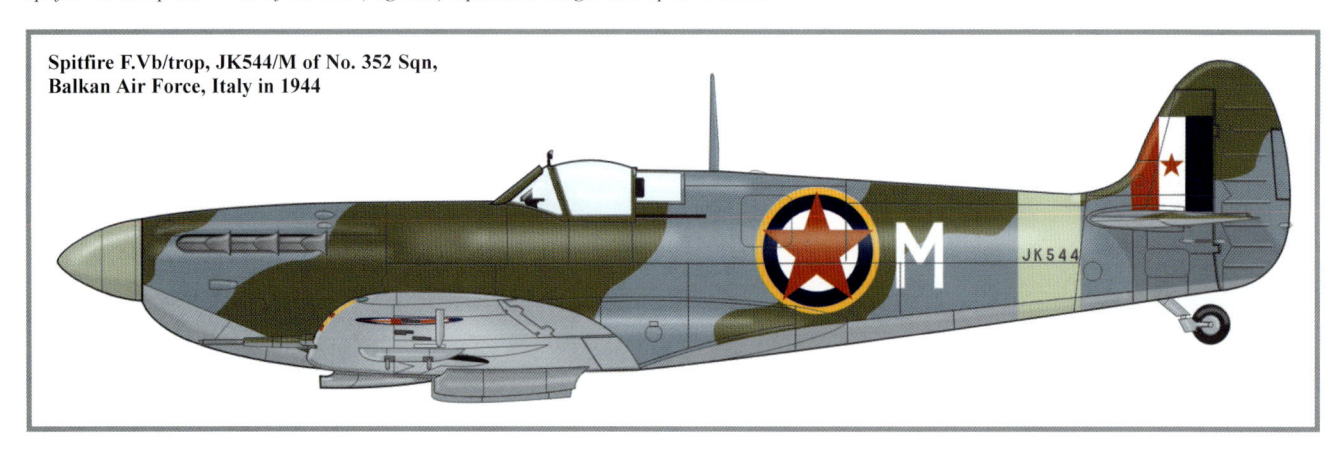

Spitfire F.Vb/trop, JK544/M of No. 352 Sqn, Balkan Air Force, Italy in 1944

British Government and Marshal Tito, commanding the *Yugoslav National Army of Liberation* (JNA), whereby a special Yugoslav air contingent was formed within the framework of the RAF. In the Summer of 1944 a Yugoslav fighter squadron (No.352 Sqn), completely manned by Yugoslav personnel and equipped with Spitfires, went into action as a unit of the No.281 Tactical Wing of the Balkan Air Force in support of Yugoslav operations. The numbers of Yugoslav airmen becoming available were such that a second fighter unit (No.351 Sqn) was operational in October 1944, but equipped with Hurricanes.

After World War Two Yugoslavia received 19 Spitfire Mk.V/trops and three Mk.IXs from RAF (M.E.) stocks.

Nine Spitfires were lost during service with the Yugoslavian Air Force. The remaining aircraft were phased out from early 1952 onwards, and with effect from 18th August 1952 the last became SOC and were scrapped.

Only one Spitfire survived. It is now on exhibition in the Aeronautical Museum at Surcin airport, Belgrade.

Yugoslavian Spitfire unit of the RAF

No.**352** Sqn, formed at Benina in Libya on 22nd April 1944; Lete 6th May 1944; Canne 9th August 1944; Vis 25th January 1945 (dett 18th October 1944); Prkos (near Zadar on the Adriatic coast) from 12th April 1945; disbanded 15th June 1945.

First equipped with Hurricanes, No.352 Sqn began conversion to Spitfire Mk.Vb/c (trop) on 25th June 1944. Complete with 16 Spitfires this unit joined No.281 Wing in August 1944 and was part of the Balkan Air Force.

No squadron insignia were painted on the Spitfires, which bore only individual letters. The Spitfires carried a red star superimposed on the centre of the RAF roundels, on fuselage and wings, and also in the central white portion of the fin flag stripes.

No.352 Sqn RAF was formally transferred to Yugoslavia on 18th May 1945, though not officially disbanded as an RAF unit until 15th June 1945. Under Yugoslav Command this unit became No.1 Eskadrila, and then No.351 Sqn RAF switched to No.2 Eskadrila. Both built up the No.1 Fighter Regiment (Wing) of the *JRV*.

Spitfire F.Vb/trop JK808 'B' of No. 352 Sqn (Jugoslav) Sqn, RAF, around 1944/45.

The Yugoslavian Air Force (JRV)

Until 1945 Yugoslavia was officially a Kingdom, although in fact occupied by Germany and Italy from 1941 to 1944. Partisans were the main combatants against the Axis, later supported by the Soviet and Allied Forces, being provided with aircraft mainly by the British.

Before WWII the Air Force of Yugoslavia was named "*Jugoslovensko Kraljevsko Ratno Vazduhoplovstuo*" (Yugoslav Royal Air Force) - short 'JKRV'. During World War Two Tito's troops were called "*Yugoslav National Army of Liberation*", the 'JNA'. Yugoslavia became a Republic in 1945, and the Air Force was then named "*Jugoslovensko Ratno Vazduhoplovstuo*" ('JRV').

Spitfires were flown by a Fighter Regiment in 1945 and 1946. Then the unit was disbanded, and the Spitfires went into storage with a Workshop at Mostar airfield (III.District), "*Komanda Aerodroma Mostar*" ('KAM'). There they were converted to FR-variants, using Russian-built cameras, and from May 1947 to 1952 they served with a Recce Aviation Regiment.

The Yugoslavian Air Force allotted own Serial-Nos in 1947/48. The Spitfire Mk.V/trops became Nos **9476 – 9493**, and the Spitfire Mk.IXs the Nos **9501 – 9503**.

Spitfires were replaced by Mosquito NF38 in 1952.

Spitfire units of the Yugoslavian Air Force

No. **1** (F) Aviation Regiment, formed 18th May 1945 at Prkos, to Mostar in August 1945. This unit comprised:
No. 1 Eskadrila with Spitfire Mk.Vb/c trop;
No. 2 Eskadrila with Hurricane Mk.IV.
Disbanded in 1946 (date unknown). Spitfires went into storage at *KAM* Mostar.

No.**112** (F) Regiment at Mostar, equipped with Yak-3, received three Spitfire Mk.V in 1947 for comparison and test flying.

No.**103** (Recce) Aviation Regiment;
Formed as Recce Aviation Regiment at Mostar on 10th May 1947; re-named No.103 (Recce) Aviation Regiment mid 1948; To Pancevo near Belgrade in February 1949. This unit comprised:
No.**1 (Recce)** Eskadrila with Spitfire (FR) Vb/c trop;
No.**2 (Recco)** Eskadrila with Hurricane Mk.IV.
Served with Spitfires from May 1947 to August 1952.

Individual Histories

BR130 Spitfire F.Vc/trop (Merlin 46); Became JRV No **9478**; TOC/RAF 29.3.42; ex USAAF; No.352 Sqn RAF ('D') - To JRV 18.5.45; No.1 (F) Av.Regiment & No.1 Esk ('D') at Mostar in 8.45; 'KAM' storage 1946; Engine change, Merlin 46 (ex EP782) installed; No.103 (Recce) Av.Regiment 10.5.47; SOC in 1952

EF727 Spitfire F.Vc/trop (Merlin 45); Became JRV No **9488**; TOC/RAF 24.8.43; ex No.352 Sqn RAF - To JRV 18.5.45; No.1 (F) Av.Regiment & No.1 Esk at Mostar in 8.45; 'KAM' storage 1946; Engine change at Mostar; No.103 (Recce) Av.Regiment 10.5.47; Tactical exercise in Sumadija area autumn 1949; Crashed on landing, tyre burst, tipped nose, prop and wing damaged 28.9.49 (Plt Srecko Gozivoda); Repaired; Flown by Ivan Katic mid 1952; SOC 18.8.52; Later to Technical School at Sombor as ground instructional airframe
NOTE: Reported to be "EP727", but that crashed Cat.FA/3 on 12.10.42; ORB No.352 Sqn mentioned "EF727" in 4.45

EN513 Spitfire F IXc (Merlin 63); Became JRV No **9503**; TOC/RAF 17.5.43; Arr Casablanca 15.6.43; M.E.1.8.43; NAAF & MAAF – To JRV (non-operational) 18.5.45; No.1 (F) Av.Regiment & No.1 Esk 8.45; 'KAM' storage 1946; (Perhaps with No.103 (Recce) Av.Regiment from 5.47, but confirmation lacking); No.163 Repair Unit 1951/52; SOC 18.8.52; Engine removed and to the central depot at Bukovaci, went later to the Air Force Museum

EP579 Spitfire F.Vb/trop (Merlin 45); Became JRV No **9484**; TOC/RAF 5.7.42; ex No.352 Sqn RAF - To JRV 18.5.45; No.1 (F) Av.Regiment & No.1 Esk at Mostar in 8.45; 'KAM' storage 1946; Engine changed (removed Merlin 45 in JK360 by 5.47); No.254 (F) Regiment 1946; No.103 (Recce) Av.Regiment 10.5.47; For Liaison duties to No. III Air Division at Borongaj (near Zagreb); SOC 18.8.52; Remained with the Air Division for display and as ground instructional airframe; Engine later to the Air Force Museum Surcin - see JK808

EP617 Spitfire F.Vc/trop (Merlin 46); Became JRV No **9487**; TOC/RAF 19.7.42; ex No.352 Sqn RAF - To JRV 18.5.45; No.1 (F) Av.Regiment & No.1 Esk; Crashed, Cat.E in 8.45; SOC/RAF 30.8.45; To No.163 Repair Unit; Engine removed, went to a Depot at Mostar (later to JL168)

EP782 Spitfire F.Vb/trop (Merlin 46); Became JRV No **9492**; TOC/RAF 30.8.42; ex No.352 Sqn RAF ('K') - To JRV 18.5.45; No.1 (F) Av.Regiment & No.1 Esk ('K') at Mostar in 8.45; 'KAM' storage 1946; To No.112 (F) Wing for comparison and trials with Yak-3 in 1946/47; No.103 (Recce) Av.Regiment 10.5.47; SOC 29.9.48; Engine removed, went to No.103 Regiment Depot (later to BR130)
NOTE: Reported to be "EP872", but that was SOC 8.3.44, not in ORB No.352 Sqn 4.45

ER585 Spitfire F.Vb/trop (Merlin 45); Became JRV No **9485**; TOC/RAF 30.9.42; ex No.352 Sqn RAF ('J')- To JRV 18.5.45; No.1 (F) Av.Regiment & No.1 Esk ('J') at Mostar in 8.45; 'KAM' storage 1946; Airshow Zemun (near Belgrade) 1946; No.103 (Recce) Av.Regiment 10.5.47; Aerobatic flight, engine failed, normal landing in 1949; Tipped on nose, engine damaged and propeller broken 8.5.50; SOC 18.8.52

ES146 Spitfire F.Vc/trop (Merlin 46); Became JRV No **9479**; TOC/RAF 17.11.42; ex No.352 Sqn RAF ('O') - To JRV 18.5.45; No.1 (F) Av.Regiment & No.1 Esk ('O') at Mostar in 8.45; 'KAM' storage 1946; Engine changed; No.103 (Recce)Av.Regiment 10.5.47; SOC 18.8.52

ES369 Spitfire F.Vc/trop (Merlin 55); Became JRV No **9483**; TOC/RAF 10.12.42; ex No.352 Sqn RAF - To JRV18.5.45; No.1 (F) Av.Regiment & No.1 Esk at Mostar in 8.45; 'KAM' storage 1946; No.103 (Recce) Av.Regiment 10.5.47; Tactical exercise and air combat training with Yak-3 in Sumadija area, stalled and dived into ground, burnt out 23.9.49 (Plt Dragurin Mirosa), SOC
NOTE: Reported to be "ES368" (Merlin 55), but that was Cat.FB/3 on 5.2.43; ORB No.352 Sqn shows "ES368" on 5.4.45 only, otherwise ES369 was mentioned, before and later

JG871 Spitfire F.Vc/trop (Merlin 46); Became JRV No **9491**; TOC/RAF 24.12.42; ex No.352 Sqn RAF ('N') - To JRV 18.5.45; No.1 (F) Av.Regiment & No.1 Esk ('N') at Mostar in 8.45; 'KAM' storage 1946; Possibly to No.103

Flown with the Balkan Air Force, Spitfire F.Vc/trop ES146 'O' of No. 352 Sqn went to the Yugoslavian Air Force, becoming JRV No. 9479.

Spitfire F.Vb/trop, JK808/B of No. 352 Sqn, Balkan Air Force, Italy in 1944

(Recce) Av.Regiment 10.5.47; Fatal crash Cat.E 6.10.47, SOC; Engine removed and to No.103 Regiment Depot for spares

JK103　Spitfire F.Vc/trop (Merlin 46); Became JRV No **9476**; TOC/RAF 2.1.43; ex No.352 Sqn RAF ('S') - To JRV 18.5.45; No.1 (F) Av.Regiment & No.1 Esk ('S') at Mostar in 8.45; 'KAM' storage 1946; No.103 (Recce) Av.Regiment 10.5.47; Overshot landing, tipped on nose in soft ground 8.3.50 (Plt Erdeljan Svetolik); Repaired, engine change, Merlin 46 (ex ES146) installed; Engine failure, destroyed in forced landing 14.8.51 (Plt Stewan Krnjaic); SOC 19.11.51

JK122　Spitfire F.Vc/trop (Merlin 46); Became JRV No **9477**; TOC/RAF 22.1.43; ex No.352 Sqn RAF ('M') - To JRV 18.5.45; No.1 (F) Av.Regiment & No.1 Esk ('M') at Mostar in 8.45; 'KAM' storage 1946; No.103 (Recce) Av.Regiment 10.5.47; Forgot to lower the undercarriage landing, prop damage 9.2.49 (Plt Zivadin Bokovic); SOC 18.8.52

JK284　Spitfire F.Vc/trop (Merlin 46); Became JRV No **9481**; TOC/RAF 2.2.43; ex USAAF; No.352 Sqn RAF ('R') - To JRV 18.5.45; No.1 (F) Av.Regiment & No.1 Esk ('R') at Mostar in 8.45; 'KAM' storage 1946; No.254 (F) Regiment in 1946; No.103 (Recce) Av.Regiment 10.5.47; Tyre burst landing, tipped on wing, Cat.E 24.2.49 (Plt Radetom Kojicem), SOC

JK360　Spitfire F.Vc/trop (Merlin 45); Became JRV No **9493**; TOC/RAF 15.2.43; Arr Casablanca 6.4.43; NWA 31.5.43; ex No.352 RAF ('A'); Crashed in Middle Bosnia Cat.FB/E 26.2.45, bboc - To JRV possibly 1945/46; Merlin 45 (ex EP579) installed; No.103 (Recce) Av.Regiment 10.5.47; Engine failure, crashed in forced landing 31.5.51 (Plt Ivan Katic); No.170 Repair Unit until SOC 18.8.52; Engine removed, to JK808 later

JK361　Spitfire F.Vc/trop (Merlin 55); Became JRV No **9482**; TOC/RAF 15.2.43; ex No.352 Sqn RAF - To JRV 18.5.45; No.1 (F) Av.Regiment & No.1 Esk at Mostar in 8.45; 'KAM' storage 1946; No.254 (F) Regiment in 1946; Engine changed in 1947; Possibly to No.103 (Recce) Av.Regiment 5.47, but confirmation lacking; No.163 Repair Unit until SOC 18.8.52

JK448　Spitfire F.Vc/trop (Merlin 46); JRV No unknown; TOC/RAF 7.2.43; ex No.352 Sqn RAF ('W'); SOC 30.11.44 – Yugoslavia 1945, non-active. Perhaps storage for spares from 1946 to 1952; Reported to have been in the Museum

JK808　Spitfire F.Vc/trop (Merlin 45); Became JRV No **9489**; TOC/RAF 4.3.43; ex No.352 Sqn RAF ('B') - To JRV 18.5.45; No.1 (F) Av.Regiment & No.1 Esk ('B') at Mostar in 8.45; Engine change 1946; 'KAM' storage 1946; To No.112 (F) Regiment for comparison trials with Yak-3 in 1946/47; No.103 (Recce) Av.Regiment 10.5.47; Belly-landed at Mostar 18.2.49 (Plt Milan Bernatic); Repaired; Engine failure, force-landed on belly 24.2.50 (Plt Marko Bukija); Engine changed; SOC 18.8.52
NOTE: Crash report "Boraie, Algerie Cat.E 22.4.43" refers to JG808)

JK830　Spitfire F.Vc/trop (Merlin 45); Became JRV No **9490**; TOC/RAF 28.3.43; ex No.352 Sqn RAF ('K') - To JRV 18.5.45; No.1 (F) Av.Regiment & No.1 Esk ('K') at Mostar in 8.45; 'KAM' storage 1946; No.103 (Recce) Av.Regiment 10.5.47; Throttle lever blocked, landed cross-wind, went into ditch 24.3.50 (Plt Gojko Berovic injured), SOC
NOTE: Reported to be "LZ830", but that was not listed in the No.352 Sqn ORB in 4.45; "JK830" was mentioned in several times (but reported crash Cat.FB/E 30.12.43)

JL168　Spitfire F.Vc/trop (Merlin 46); Became JRV No **9480**; TOC/RAF 31.3.43; ex No.352 Sqn RAF ('P') - To JRV 18.5.45; No.1 (F) Av.Regiment & No.1 Esk ('P') at Mostar

Spitfire F.Vc/trop 9486 (ex MH592) parked under trees at Kalemagdon Park with a tarpaulin over the engine and cockpit. Previously aircraft 'G' of No. 352 (Jugoslav) Sqn, RAF, it was handed over in May 1945 to the Jugoslovensko Ratno Vazduhoplovstuo, serving until August 1952 when it was struck off charge.
[Ken Smy]

Exhibited in the Yugoslav Aeronautical Museum, Belgrade as "JK808/B", as seen here in March 1990, the provenance of this Spitfire F.Vc/trop survivor is disputed. Although it carried the livery of JK448 'W' in the 1980s, it is, in fact, the former 'Kalemagden' Spitfire 9486 (ex MH592). [PRA]

in 8.45; 'KAM' storage 1946; Engine change, Merlin 46 (ex EP617) installed; To No.112 (F) Wing for comparison trials with Yak-3 in 1946/47; No.103 (Recce) Av.Regiment 10.5.47; Engine failed after take-off, normal landing 19.7.50 (Plt Georg Petrovic); SOC 18.8.52
NOTE: Reported to be "JK168", but that was SOC 31.8.44; No.352 Sqn ORB mentioned "JL168" in 4.45

MH592 Spitfire F.Vc/trop (Merlin 46); Became JRV No **9486**; TOC/RAF 14.8.43; ex No.352 Sqn RAF ('G') - To JRV 18.5.45; No.1 (F) Av.Regiment & No.1 Esk ('G') at Mostar in 8.45; 'KAM' storage 1946; No.103 (Recce) Av.Regiment 10.5.47; Engine change in 5.47; Crashed on landing, jumped, damaged left wing and undercarriage 28.3.50 (Plt Marko Bucija); Repaired; Airshow Pancevo 1951; SOC 18.8.52; Later to the Flying School at Rajlouvac as ground instructional airframe

Extant - Handed over to the Military Museum, Kalamagden Park, Belgrade for display 26.1.53; Display in 1950's; Marked "JRV 9486" by 4.61 (Document from 24.7.61 has JRV No 9489); Open storage at Zemun airbase 7.65 and Surcin airport 1968, marked 'H'; Restoration 1973 by the Technical Service of the Jugoslavian Aerotransport (JAT); Exhibited in the Surcin Aviation Museum as "JK448" (code 'W', inscription "*CRVENA ARMIJA*"); Second restoration in the 80's, marked "JK808" (code 'B'); Static display in the Yugoslav Aeronautical Museum, Belgrade from 1984 with Merlin 45 (Engine No.91217, ex JK360) – **SURVIVOR**

MK444 Spitfire LF IXc (Merlin 66); Became JRV No **9502**; TOC/RAF 15.2.44; Arr Casablanca 6.4.44; M.E. (MAAF) 28.12.44; ex No.73 Sqn – To JRV (non-operational) 18.5.45; No.1 (F) Av.Regiment & No.1 Esk at Mostar in 8.45; 'KAM' storage 1946; No.103 (Recce) Av.Regiment 10.5.47; Engine failure, stalled and dived into ground at Mostar aerodrome 28.6.51 (Plt Peter Knezevic killed), SOC

NH271 Spitfire HF IXe (Merlin 70); Became JRV No **9501**; TOC/RAF 16.5.44; Arr Casablanca 13.6.44; M.E. (MAAF); ex No.73 Sqn (Cat.FA/E 7.2.45) – To JRV (non-operational) 18.5.45; No.1 (F) Av.Regiment & No.1 Esk at Mostar in 8.45; 'KAM' storage 1946; No.103 (Recce) Av.Regiment 10.5.47; No.163 Repair Unit, engine tested, run over brake-block, tipped on nose, light damage (3 Mechanics injured) 26.10.49; Ferry flight after repair to Pancevo, engine failed, aircraft stalled and dived into ground 25.4.50 (Plt Janes Habijan killed), SOC.

Check list of JRV / RAF Serial Nos

JRV Serial Nos.	RAF Serial Nos.	Mk.-Type (Eng.-Type)	Markings No.1 Esk
9476	JK103	F.Vc/trop (M46)	'S'
9477	JK122	F.Vc/trop (M46)	'M'
9478	BR130	F.Vc/trop (M46)	'D'
9479	ES146	F.Vc/trop (M46)	'O'
9480	JL168	F.Vc/trop (M46)	'P'
9481	JK284	F.Vc/trop (M46)	'R'
9482	JK361	F.Vc/trop (M55)	-
9483	ES369	F.Vc/trop (M55)	-
9484	EP579	F.Vb/trop (M45)	-
9485	ER585	F.Vb/trop (M45)	'J'
9486	MH592	F.Vc/trop (M46)	'G'
9487	EP617	F.Vc/trop (M46)	-
9488	EF727	F.Vc/trop (M45)	-
9489	JK808	F.Vc/trop (M45)	'B'
9490	JK830	F.Vc/trop (M45)	'K'
9491	JG871	F.Vc/trop (M46)	'N'
9492	EP782	F.Vb/trop (M46)	'K'
9493	JK360	F.Vc/trop (M45)	'A'
9501	NH271	HF.IXe (M70)	-
9502	MK444	LF.IXc (M66)	-
9503	EN513	F.IXc (M63)	
JRV 9486	(JK448/808)	F.Vc/trop (M45)	**Museum**

SURVIVOR

"JK808" (MH592), Aviation Museum, Surcin Airport, Belgrade.

References:
Aeroplan BPOJ 1 "*Yugoslav Spitfires*", p.40.
Spitfires of the JNA, Air Force Museum Belgrade, C Janic, February 1984.
Spitfire Yugoslav Mystery, FlyPast April 1992, p.70/71.

Summary of Spitfires and Seafires in foreign services

Country	Spitfire Merlin	Spitfire Griffon	Seafire Merlin	Seafire Griffon	Sum	Sub-deliv.	Survivors	Remarks
Argentina	3	0	0	0	3	0	0	Mks. VIII, IX, XI
Australia	657	0	0	0	657	0	8	Mks. II, V, VIII
Belgium	69	134	0	0	203	15	3	Mks. IX, XIV, XVI
Brazil	0	1	0	0	1	0	1	Mk. XIV
Bulgaria	0	0	0	0	0	0	0	Request only
Burma	30	3	0	20	53	30	3	Mks. IX, XVIII & SF.XV
Canada	6	1	0	35	42	0	5	Mks. I/II, VIII, XIV & SF.XV
China	0	0	0	0	0	0	0	Request only
Cuba	0	1	0	0	1	1	0	bought, but not arrived in Cuba
Czechoslovakia	77	0	0	0	77	0	1	Mk. IX
Denmark	48	0	0	0	48	0	1	Mks. IX & XI, incl. 4 Instructionals
Egypt	61	19	0	0	80	0	0	Mks. V, IX, T.IX, F.22
Estonia	0	0	0	0	0	0	0	Ordered (12 a/c), but not delivered
Finland	0	0	0	0	0	0	0	Request only
France	c.531	0	142	15	c.688	0	3	Mks. I, V, VIII, IX, XVI & SF.III, XV
Germany	3	1	0	0	4	0	1	Mks. V, IX, XI, XII
Greece	243	0	0	0	243	0	1	Mks. V, IX, XI, XVI
Hong Kong	0	15	0	0	15	0	1	Mks. XVIII, XIX, F.24
India	24	135	0	0	159	0	3	Mks. VIII, T.IX, XIV, XVIII, XIX
Iran	0	0	0	0	0	0	0	Request only
Iraq	1	0	0	0	1	1	0	T.IX order (6 a/c) not realised
Ireland	18	0	0	0	18	0	0	T.IX & SF.III
Israel	90	0	0	0	90	90	3	Mk. IX
Italy	157	0	0	0	157	2	1	Mks. Vb/c & IX
Japan	0	0	0	0	0	0	0	Request only
Latvia	0	0	0	0	0	0	0	Request only
Lithuania	0	0	0	0	0	0	0	Request only
Malta	0	0	0	0	0	0	1	remained as scrap, now Survivor
Netherlands	73	5	0	0	78	0	4	Mks. IX/T.IX &V,XIV,XVI,XIX,F.22
New Zealand	0	0	0	0	0	0	5	arrived as Survivors only
Norway	74	0	0	0	74	0	2	Mks. IX, XI
Poland	3	0	0	0	3	0	1	Mk. XVI
Portugal	112	0	0	0	112	0	1	Mks. I & V, Survivor Mk.IX
Rumania	0	0	0	0	0	0	0	Order (10 a/c) not realised
Singapore	0	4	0	0	4	0	0	Mk. XVIII & F.24
South Africa	c.1036	0	0	0	c.1036	17	5	c.900 (Mks.V&IX)MTO, 136 (IX)home
South. Rhodesia	0	22	0	0	22	0	1	F.22
Soviet Union	1335	0	0	0	1335	0	0	PR.IV, Mk. V & IX
Spain	3	0	0	0	3	0	0	interned aircraft only, Mks. V & XI
Sweden	0	51	0	0	51	1	1	PR. XIX
Switzerland	0	0	0	0	0	0	0	Order (c.18 a/c) not realised
Syria	0	20	0	0	20	0	1	F. 22
Thailand	0	34	0	0	34	0	4	Mk. XIV & 4 Instructionals (PR.XIX)
Turkey	309	4	0	0	313	0	0	Mks. I, V, IX, XIX
U.S.A.	c.990	0	10	0	c.1000	0	33	MksV,VIII,IX&SF.II,most ETO&MTO
Yugoslavia	22	0	0	0	22	0	1	Mk. V
Total =	**c.5975**	**450**	**152**	**70**	**c.6647**	**157**	**95**	

Notes:
Sub-deliveries: Handover from Country to Country, but not from U.K.; c.= circa, exact delivery numbers unknown;
Survivors and Extants, but only complete aircraft, flyable or for exhibition, in each country, including those which only arrived as Survivors later.

INDEX OF CIVIL REGISTRATIONS

Entries in italics indicate illustrations

Regn.	Serial	Page
CF-DUY	AR614	88, 249, 423
CF-GMZ	TZ138	96, *96,* 98, 453
CF-NUS	NH188	64, *64,* 88, *89,* 245, 246
CF-RAF	TE308	96, 206, 452
C-GCWK	PR503	94, 450
C-GSPT	TZ138	96, 98, 453
F-AZSJ	SM832	151, *151,* 156, 193
F-WGML	'BS539'	131
G-AIDN	MT818	449
G-ALJM	MJ113?	108, 116, *116,* 122, 251
G-ASJV	MH434	60, *237,* 238, 246
G-ASOZ	MJ627	203
G-ASSD	MK297	61, 242, 448
G-AVAV	MJ772	203, 447
G-AVDJ	MH415	60, 236
G-AWGB	TE308	206, *206*
G-BAUP	SL721	452
G-BGHB	MV293	185
G-BHGH	PV202	204, 331
G-BIXP	TE517	103, 214
G-BKMI	MV154	49
G-BLAS	MJ730	217, 227, 447
G-BLCK	TE566	106, 213, 221, 324
G-BMSB	MJ627	203, 206
G-BRAF	SM969	*194,* 195
G-BRRA	MK912	62, *62,* 244, 246
G-BRSF	RR232	53, 322
G-BSKP	RN201	72
G-BTTN	BL628	19
G-BTXE	TP280	197, 453
G-BUAR	PP972	144
G-BUOS	SM845	193, 452
G-BUWA	AR614	88, 249, 423
G-BUZU	NH799	190, 249
G-BWEM	RX168	206
G-BXHZ	SM520	322
G-BYDE	PT879	*353,* 354
G-CCIX	TE517	103, 214, 221, 453
G-CCVV	MV262	185, 449
G-CDAN	TB863	249
G-CTIX	PT462	217, 221, 229, 319, *408,* 450
G-FIRE	NH904	67, 450
G-FXIV	MV370	160, 186
G-HFIX	MJ730	217, 221, 227, 447
G-HVDM	MK732	158, 160, 242
G-IXCC	PL344	450
G-LFIX	ML407	204, 206
G-LFVC	JG891	38, 247, 249
G-MKIA	P9374	129
G-MKIX	NH238	65, *244,* 245, 246, 449
G-MKVC	EE606	25
G-MKXI	PL965	245, 246, 450
G-MXIV	NH749	189, 449
G-MXVI	TE184	*156,* 408
G-PMNF	TA805	322
G-PRXI	PL983	144, 450
G-SPIT	MV293	185, *185*
G-SXVI	TE356	452
G-TRIX	PV202	204, 206, 331
G-VIII	MT719	182, 229, 449
G-WWII	SM832	151, 193
G-XVIA	RW382	451
G-XVIB	TE476	453
I-SPIT	MT719	182, *228,* 229, 449
LV-NMZ	PL972	11, *11,* 12, *12,* 13, *13*
N11RS	MK297	61, 242, 448
N114BP	NH904	67, 448
N138TZ	TZ138	98, 453
N180B	TZ138	98, 453
N180RB	TZ138	98, 453
N1882	MK297	242, 448
N2TF	ML417	181, 449
N20E	TZ138	98, 453
N219AM	PS890	388, 450
N2289J	SL542	451
N238V	NH238	65, 245, 449
N280TP	TP280	197, 453
N308WK	TE308	96, 206, *206,* 452, *452*
N356EV	TE356	452
N356TE	TE356	452, *453*
N415MH	MH415	60, 236, 246, 446
N41702	TP298	197, 453
N462JC	PT462	217, 221, 229, 319, 408, 450, *451*
N47SF	VP441	453
N476E	TE476	453
N476TE	TE476	453
N503PR	PR503	94, 450
N535R	PR503	94, 451
N5505A	TZ138	98, 453
N58JE	MT818	449
N614VC	AR614	88, 249, 423
N644TB	PL344	450
N719MT	MT719	182, *182,* 229, 449, *449*
N721WK	SL721	95, 452
N730MJ	MJ730	217, *217,* 221, 447
N74138	PL983	451, *450*
N75460	TE330	452
N7929A	VN332	453, *454*
N8118J	NH904	67, 448
N8R	MJ772	204, 206, 447
	SL721	452
N8WK	SL721	452
N92477	TE308	96, 206, 452
N930LB	MA793	444, *444*
N93081	MK923	63, 244, 448
N9323Z	TP298	197, 453
N959RT	MK959	449
N97RW	TE392	453
NX382RW	RW382	451
NX521R	MK923	63, 244, 246, 449
NX749DP	NH749	189, 449, *449*
NX9BL	MK297	61, 242, 448
OK-BXA	-	100
OK-BXC	-	100
OK-BXD	-	100
OK-BXF	-	100
OK-BXL	-	100
OO-ARA	MH434	60, 238
OO-ARB	MK297	60, 61, 242
OO-ARC	NH188	60, 64, *64,* 88, 245
OO-ARD	MH415	60, 236
OO-ARE	NH238	60, 64, *65,* 245, 449
OO-ARF	MK923	60, 63, 244, 448
PH-NFN	BS147	236, *237*
PH-NFO	MK475	242
PH-NFP	PT986	245
PH-NFR	MJ828	241
PH-OUQ	MK732	158, 160, 242
VH-FVB	BL628	19, 56
VH-HET	MV239	51, *51,* 56
VH-XIV	RM797	53, 56, 389
VH-XVI	TE384	53, 56
VH-ZPY	MD338	43, 56
ZK-MKV	EF545	28, 249
	JG891	38, 249
ZK-XIV	NH799	190, 249
ZK-XVI	TB863	249
ZU-SPT	TE566	106, 213, 221, 324

BIBLIOGRAPHY

AIRCRAFT CAMOUFLAGE and MARKINGS 1907 - 1954,
   by Robertson & Hepworth, Harleyford Publication, 1966
AIRCRAFT MARKINGS of the WORLD 1912-1967,
   by Bruce Robertson, Harleyford Publication, 1967
AIRCRAFT of the R.A.F since 1918,
   by Owen Thetford, Putnam, London, 1962
AIRCRAFT of the ROYAL NAVY since 1945,
   by David Hobbs, Maritime Books, Liskeard, Cornw., 1970
AIRCRAFT of WORLD WAR II,
   by Kenneth Munson, Ian Allan Ltd. London, 1962
BIRTH of a SPITFIRE, by Gordon Beckles, 1941
BRITISH CIVIL AIRCRAFT 1919 - 1959,
   by A J Jackson, Putnam London, 1960
BRITISH CIVIL AVIATION REGISTERS 1919 to 1999,
   by Michael Austin with Kevin Evans and
   Malcolm P Fillmore, Air-Britain (Historians) Ltd, 1999
BRITISH FIGHTERS of WORLD WAR TWO,
   by Mason & Goulding, Hylton Lacy Publishing Ltd., 1970
BRITISH MILITARY AIRCRAFT SERIALS 1912 - 1966,
   by Bruce Robertson, Ian Allan Ltd., London, 1966
COMBAT AIRCRAFT of the WORLD 1909 to the present,
   by J W Taylor, Putnam New York, 1969
DESERT AIR FORCE at WAR,
   by Chaz Bowyer & Chris Shores, 1981
In ENEMY HANDS, by Bryan Philpott, 1981
FALLEN EAGLES, by Edward Doylerush,
   Midland Counties Publ., 1990/93
FAMOUS FIGHTERS of the SECOND WORLD WAR,
   by W Green, Mac Donald, London, 1962
FAMOUS PILOTS and THEIR PLANES,
   by Francis K Mason, 1981
FIGHTER SQUADRONS of the RAF and their Aircraft,
   John D R Rawlings, Macdonald & Janes, London, 1976
FLEET AIR ARM AIRCRAFT 1939 to 1945, by Ray Sturtivant
   with Mick Burrow, Air-Britain (Historians) Ltd, 1995
JANE'S ALL THE WORLD'S AIRCRAFT,
   Janes Publ., London, 1947
LUFTKAMPF - JAGDFLUGZEUGE im II.WELTKRIEG,
   by Alfred Price, Stalling Hamburg, 1976
LUFTKÄMPFE über FELS und WÜSTE - Tunesien 1942/43
   by Shores/Ring/Hess, Motorbuchverlag, Stuttgart, 1981
MALTA - the SPITFIRE YEAR 1942,
   by Shores, Cull & Malizia, Grubb Street Press, 1991
MISSION SANS RETOUR, by MN Cuich, 1975
OUTSTANDING MILITARY AIRCRAFT of WW II,
   by E R Atkins, Superscale Arlington, USA, 1961
PRESENTATION AIRCRAFT of TWO WORLD WARS,
   by G R Duval, Bradford Barton Ltd., 1976
RAF FIGHTER COMMAND LOSSES
of the Second World War (Vol.1-3), by Norman L R Franks,
   Midland Publishing Ltd, 1997 to 2000
RAF FIGHTERS (Part 3), by W Green and G Swanborough,
   Jane's London & Sydney, 1981
RAF FLYING TRAINING & SUPPORT UNITS,
   by Ray Sturtivant, John Hamlin & J J Halley,
   Air-Britain (Historians) Ltd, 1997
RAF SQUADRONS, by C G Jefford, Airlife Publ.Ltd, 1988
SAMOLOT MYSLIWSKI SPITFIRE Mk.I - V,
   by Choloniewski & Jonca, W.M.O.N. Warszawa, 1979
SAMOLOT MYSLIWSKI SPITFIRE IX/XVI,
   by Choloniewski & Iwanski, W.M.O.N. Warszawa, 1987
The SEAFIRE, by D Brown, Ian Allan Ltd., Shepperton, 1973
SEVENTY FIGHTERS of the WORLD WAR II,
   Aireview, Kantosha Co., Tokyo, 1963
SPITFIRE, by Sweetman & Watanabe, Janes Publ. London, 1980
SPITFIRE, by Taylor & Allward, Harborough, 1946
SPITFIRE, by John Vader, Pan/Ballantine Ltd. London, 1972
SPITFIRE & SEAFIRE, PILOT'S NOTES,
   Air Ministry/Air Publications, 1940 ff
The SPITFIRE - 50 YEARS on,
   by Michael J F Bowyer, P Stephens Ltd., 1986
SPITFIRE - 50TH ANNIVERSARY,
   Portmouth & Sunderland News, 1986
SPITFIRE - CLASSIC AIRCRAFT No.1,
   by Cross & Scarborough, Airfix, 1971
SPITFIRE - a DOCUMENTARY HISTORY,
   by Alfred Price, Macdonald & Janes, London, 1977
SPITFIRE en ACTION, by A Price, EPA, 1979
SPITFIRE in ACTION, by Jerry Scutts,
   Squadron/Signal Publ. (Aircraft No.39), 1980
SPITFIRE - the COMBAT History,
   by Robert Jackson, Airlife, Shrewsbury, 1995
SPITFIRE - the story of a FAMOUS FIGHTER,
   by Bruce Robertson, Harleyford, Letchworth, 1973
SPITFIRE - GEGNER der Me 109,
   by H J Nowarra, Podzun-Pallas, Friedberg, 1977
SPITFIRE - the HISTORY,
   by Morgan & Shacklady, Key Publications, Stamford, 1987
SPITFIRES OVER SICILY, by Brian Cull with
   Nicola Malizia & Frederick Galea, Grub Street, 2000
SPITFIRE SPECIAL,
   by T Hooton, Ian Allan Ltd., Shepperton, 1972
SPITFIRE! SPITFIRE! by Michael Burns, Blandford Press, 1986
The SPITFIRE STORY, by Alfred Price, Janes, London, 1982
SPITFIRE SURVIVORS - round the WORLD,
   by Riley & Trant, Aston, 1986
SPITFIRE at WAR (Vols. I & II),
   by Alfred Price, Ian Allan Ltd., Shepperton, 1974-85
SPITFIRE Z DRUTEM CZY BEZ,
   by Wojtek Matusiak, Skrzydlata Polska 1994
SPITFIRE I-XVI, FAMOUS AIRPLANES of the WORLD,
   No.3 Bunrin-Do, Tokyo, Koku-Fan 1975
SPITFIRE XII-24 & SEAFIRES, FAMOUS AIRPLANES,
   No.9 Bunrin-Do, Tokyo, Koku-Fan 1975
The SQUADRONS of the ROYAL AIR FORCE &
COMMONWEALTH 1918-1988,
   by James J Halley, Air-Britain (Historians) Ltd, 1988
SUPERMARINE AIRCRAFT since 1914,
   by Andrews & Morgan, Putnam, London, 1981
SUPERMARINE SEAFIRES (MERLINS),
   by L Bachelor, Profile Publication No.221, 1971
SUPERMARINE SPITFIRE, Model Art Ltd., Japan, 1996
SUPERMARINE SPITFIRE - 40 YEARS on,
   by G N M Gingell, R.A.E. Southampton, 1976
SUPERMARINE SPITFIRE,
   by E T Maloney & U Feist, Aero Series No.10, 1966
SUPERMARINE SPITFIRE - Remembered,
   by Ph. J R Moyes, Wingspan No.2, 1975
SUPERMARINE SPITFIRE (CZ.1),
   by Alfred Price, Monografie Lotnicze No.38, 1997
SUPERMARINE SPITFIRE (CZ.2 to 4) by Wojtek Matusiak,
   Monografie Lotnicze Nos.39, 40 & 71, 1998 to 2000
SUPERMARINE SPITFIRE - WARPLANES in COLOUR,
   by Chaz Bowyer, Arms & Armour Press, London, 1980
SUPERMARINE SPITFIRE I & II,
   by Ph. J R Moyes, Aerodata International No.2, 1977
The SUPERMARINE SPITFIRE I & II,
   by Ph. J R Moyes, Profile Publications No.41, 1965
SUPERMARINE SPITFIRE I - Archive,
   by Peter Moss, Container Publications, London, 1978
The SUPERMARINE SPITFIRE V Series,
   by E N Hooton, Profile Publications No.166, 1967
SUPERMARINE SPITFIRE V,
   by Wojtek Matusiak, Aero Technika Lotnicza 1992

SUPERMARINE SPITFIRE I - XVI,
    by R Ward & T Hooton, Aircam Series No.4, 1970
SUPERMARINE SPITFIRE I - XVI,
    by P Moss, Ducimus Books, 1970
SUPERMARINE SPITFIRE Mk.IX,
    by Moss & Bachelor, Profile Publication No.206, 1970
SUPERMARINE SPITFIRE Mk.XII-24 & SEAFIRE I-47,
    by R Ward & T Hooton, Aircam No.8, 1970
SUPERMARINE SPITFIRE Mk.XIV & XVIII (GRIFFON),
    by L J Bachelor, Aircraft Profile No.246, 1972
SZPIEGOWSKIE SPITFIRE'F, Spy Spits,
    by Wojtek Matusiak, Aeroplan, 1994
VETERAN and VINTAGE AIRCRAFT,
    by Leslie Hunt, Garnstone Press Ltd., London, 1974
VICKERS SUPERMARINE SPITFIRE IX & XVI,
    Spécial la Dernière Guerre, 1979
WARBIRDS DIRECTORY, 3rd Edition, by John Chapman
    & Geoff Goodall, Warbirds Media Co Ltd, 1999
WAR PLANES of the SECOND WORLD WAR - FIGHTERS
    (Vol.II), by W Green, MacDonald & Co., London, 1966
WINGS of the NAVY,
    by Brown & Green, Janes Publishing, London, 1980
WRECKS & RELICS, 17th Edition,
    by Ken Ellis, Midland Publishing, Earl Shilton, 2000

Country specific literature

Australia
SPITFIRE MARKINGS of the RAAF (Part 1 & 2), by Smith,
Pentland & Malone, Kookaburra Techn. Publication, 1970/71

Belgium
BELGIAN Spitfires, by R Binnemans & J Govaerts,
    IPMS Belgium Nos.57 (1985), 89 & 91 (1993) & 95 (1994)

Canada
History of the ROYAL CANADIAN AIR FORCE,
    by Christopher Shores, Bison Books Ltd, 1984
SPITFIRE - the CANADIANS (I & II),
    by Robert BRACKEN, Boston Mills Press, 1995/97
SUPERMARINE SEAFIRE in the CANADIAN NAVY,
    by Leo Pettipas, Winnipeg (Sea Fury) Chapter,
    Canadian Naval Air Group, 1987

Egypt
History of the EGYPTIAN AIR FORCE,
    by L Norden & Dr. D Nicolle, Smithsonian Institute, 1996

France
Les COMMANDEMENTS DE L'AERONAUTIQUE
    NAVALE (1912-1994), by Norbert Desgouttes, 1994
Les PILOTES de CHASSE FRANÇAIS 1939-45,
    by P Listemann & Tilley (Aero Edition Fleurance), 1999
Les SEAFIRE dans L'AERONAUTIQUE NAVALE
    FRANÇAIS, by Frelaut & Pierquet, Ouest France, 1983
Les SEAFIRE FRANÇAIS,
    by Claude A Pierquet, Le Trait d'Union, 1975
SPITFIRE FRANÇAIS, by Claude A Pierquet,
    Le Trait d'Union Numero Special, 1978
Les SPITFIRE FRANÇAIS,
    by Claude A Pierquet, Ouest France, 1980

Israel
SPITFIRES over ISRAEL, by B Cull, S Aloni and D Nicolle,
    Grub Street, London, 1994;
SPITFIRE - Star of ISRAEL,
    by Alex Yofe, Ventura Publication, 1996

Italy
La GUERRA in ITALIA,
    by Emiliani & Ghergo, Aviazione Italiana, 1982
ITALIAN MILITARY AVIATION,
    by Frank M C Meiken, 1984
SPITFIRE - Le MONOGRAFIE,
    Aeronautiche Italiane No.52, 1985

Netherlands
DUTCH SPITFIRES,
    by Harry van der Meer, Airnieuwe Nederland, 1986
DUTCH SPITFIRES - a TECHNICAL STUDY,
    by H v.d. Meer & T Melchers, Repro Holland, Alphen, 1988
De NEDERLANDSE SPITFIRE van 1945 - 1976,
    by H v.d. Meer & H Hooftman, Cockpit Bennekom, 1976
NEDERLANDSE SPITFIRES, by Fred Bachofner
    & Harry van der Meer, Modellbouw in Plastic, 1986
SQUADRONS van de KONINKLIJKE LUCHTMACHT,
    by Willem Helfferich, Uniboek, Bussum, Netherlands, 1983

Norway
LUFTFORSVARETT - 332 SKVADRON 50 AR,
    RNoAF, 1992
NORWEGIAN SPITFIRES, by Øyvind Ellingsen, R Meum
    & L Lyngby, Warbirds of Norway (WON), 1996

Poland
History of the POLISH AIR FORCE 1918 - 1968,
    by J B Cynk, Osprey Publ. London, 1972
POLISH WINGS on the WEST, by Bohdan Arct, 1971
POLSKIE SAMOLOTY WOJSKOWE 1939 - 1945,
    by A Morgala, M.O.N. Warszawa, 1976
SPITFIRE in POLAND,
    by Wojtek Matusiak, Aeroplan, 1996

Portugal
The AIRPLANES of the CROSS OF CHRIST, Portugal,
    by Mário Canongia Lopes, Dinalivro Publ., Lisbon, 2000
SPITFIRES and HURRICANES in PORTUGAL,
    by Mário Canongia Lopes (Dinalivro at Lisboa), 1994

Soviet Union
PR-Spitfires over Russia,
    by V Kotelnikov, Aviation World Magazine, 1993
RED STARS, Soviet Air Force in WW.II, by C F Geust,
    K Keskinen & K Stenman, Ar-Kustannus Oy, 1993

Sweden
S 31 SPITFIRE Mk.XIX i den SVENSKA FLYGSPANINGEN,
    by Axel Carleson, Östergötlands Flyghistoriska Sällskap, 1996

Turkey
TURKISH MILITARY AIRCRAFT, since 1912,
    by Ole Nikolajsen, Air-Britain (Historians) Ltd, due 2003

USA
AMERICAN SPITFIRE - CAMOUFLAGE & MARKINGS,
    by P Ludwig & M Laird, Ventura Publ.,Wellington, NZ, 1998
BRITISH AIRCRAFT in USAAF SERVICE 1942-45,
    by R A Freeman, Ducimus Books, London
    (Camouflage No.21), 1980
The EAGLE SQUADRONS,
    by Vern Haugland, David & Charles Ltd., 1980
EYES of the EIGHTH, The 7th (US) PR.Grp 1942/45,
    by Patricia Fussel Keen, Cava Publishers, Sun City, AZ, 1996
OVER-SEXED, OVER-PAID and OVER HERE,
    by J Goodson & N Franks, Wingham Press Ltd, 1991.

INDEX OF NAMES

ARGENTINA
Doyle Capt Jack, 13
Storey Jack, 12, 13
Storey James Elwyn, 11, 12, 13
Villega Sub-Oficial Jorge, 13
Valoni Teniente Luis, 13

AUSTRALIA
Adam F/O JP, 26, 38
Aitchison Mike, 19
Appleton F/O, 21
Armstrong NM, 38
Arthur Les, 42
Ashby F/O RG, 23, 24
Assig F/Sgt AJ, 53
Badger Langdon, 28, 34
Barclay S/Ldr KM, 17, 18
Barrie P/O JE, 19
Bassett F/O JDD, 24
Batcheler F/Sgt AE, 19, 38
Beale F/O FB, 18, 20
Beaton P/O MJ, 40
Beaton Jnr, 41
Biggs F/Sgt, 20
Black Guy, 41
Blair F/Sgt J, 31, 32
Blake F/O AH, 18, 20
Bocock S/Ldr EPW, 16
Booker F/O BR, 43
Bos Karel, 38
Bott S/Ldr MS, 16
Briggs W/O, 19
Brook F/O, 53
Brown F/O PGF, 31, 53
Bullock, 36
Bungey Wg Cdr, 18
Caldwell Wg Cdr CR, 24, 25, 35, 36, *36*, 43, 46
Callister F/Sgt IH, 37
Cavanagh Sgt, 19
Chandler Sgt AV, 33
Chisholm, 18
Church Charles, 25, 53
Colyer, F/O KL, 23
Coombes P/O WM, 22
Cooper Sgt AE, 19
Cooper Gary, 30, 53
Cooper Wg Cdr G, *49*
Cooper Sgt, 20
Coran Barry, 39
Cowell F/O GJ, 25, 26
Crompton LS, 37
Croser Peter, 19, 22, 40, 53
Cross F/Sgt KS, 21
Cullen Lt NJ, 52
Cundy F/Lt R, 36
Czerwinski, 53
Daley S/Ldr CN, 17, 18
Davidson Jack P, 49, 51
De Vries Mark, 30
Doerr F/O WH, 31
Duncan F/Sgt CR, 18
Dunn Pearce, 34
Eastgate RL, 23, 34, 42
Eldred Sgt, 21
Evans F/Lt DF, 19

Farrier F/O GC, 19
Featherstone P/O, 37
Ford F/O WH, 22
Foster F/Lt RW, 19, 20, 22
Fox Sgt, 24
Fox P/O KJ, 24
Fox F/Sgt, 53
Fox W/O, 31
Galton S/Ldr SW, 16
Gibbes Wg Cdr RH, 30, 45
Gibbs E, 41
Gibbs F/Sgt JB, 22
Gibbs S/Ldr JM, 16 , 21, 22
Gifford F/O GLC, 22
Gilchrist Murray, 53
Glaser S/Ldr ED, 16
Goldsmith F/Lt AP, 20, 38
Gossland F/Lt DM, 31
Grant RH, 30
Gray F/Lt DW, 21
Gregory F/O RHW, 20
Grierson-Jackson F/Lt MW, 35
Grinlington F/Sgt D, 38
Hale F/Sgt 26
Hall F/Lt ES, 22
Hamilton F/O FD, 21
Hamilton 'Butch', 24
Hardwik B, 30
Harker W/O, 26, 40
Harris Wg Cdr R, 18
Haslett John, 30
Hempel B, 53
Hinds F/O, 20
Hinds F/O WT, 29
Holmes Sgt, 20
Honey S/Ldr B, 16
Horkin F/Sgt G, 26
Hourigan Richard E, 41
Hughes F/O MC, 37
Humphrey Air Chief Marshal Sir Andrew, 18
Hutchinson Sgt EE, 22
James S/Ldr KE, 16, 17, 18, 21, 28, 43
James S/Ldr LV, 39
Jenkins F/Sgt JR, 24
John DJT, 19
Kelman F/Sgt, 25, 28
Kennare F/O H, 45
King P/O J, 25
King F/Lt JC, 43
Knapp Sgt, 39
Lamplough Robert J, 49
Laundy F/Sgt AS, 20, 25
Laundy W/O SCJ, 30
Lenagen P/O JD, 21, 23
Leonard F/O HO, 20
Lewis S/Ldr MS, 17, 18
Linnard S/Ldr S, 16
Little P/O B, 23, *23*
Lloyd F/O CP, 20, 21, 53
Lowy David, 51
MacDonald S/Ldr RS, 17, 18, 21, 25, 40
Mackenzie F/O IS, 21
Maclean F/Lt DH, 17, 18, 26

Makin F/O PStJ, 23
Marks F/Sgt G, 22
Marshall Sid, 49, 51
Martin Bill, 51
Matthjews Ed, 53
Mawer F/O GA, 21, 25, 26, 38
McCarthy F/Sgt PF, 21
McDowell P/O FRJ, 20
McNab F/O AC, 21
McRae F/O IJ, 31
Meakin F/Lt VF, 35
Moore F/Sgt EM, 25
Morse P/O IS, 53
Muray GB, 19
Nash F/Sgt WP, 30
Newton F/Lt JS, 21
Newton S/Ldr RB, 16
Nicholas S/Ldr JBH, 16
Nichterlein P/O WE, 25
Norwood F/Lt RKC, 21, 53
Oates A.J.R, 49
O'Byrne F/Lt, 18
O'Loughlin F/P CH, 26
Padula F/Sgt PA, 28
Pay Col, 51
Pearce, 53
Phillips J, 53
Pretty F/O JA, 46
Rawlinson S/Ldr AC, 16
Read Sgt WK, 22
Redd F/.Sgt RAS, 53
Richardson Sgt AR, 19, 53
Robertson F/O NF, 23
Ruskin-Rowe F/Sgt AT, 22
Scrimgeour F/L SG, 48
Sledge Peter, 30
Smoothie Noel, 51
Spence S/Ldr LT, 17, 18, 43, 44
Spencer Sgt, 20
Spencer F/Sgt, 25
Stagg Sgt RS, 21
Stevenson F/Sgt EMcL, 35
Storey WJ, 29
Subritzky Don, 38
Susans S/Ldr R, 37
Taylor F/O IS, 24
Thomas F/O F, 43, 45
Thompson F/Lt I, 30, 31, 40
Thorold-Smith S/Ldr RE, 17, 18, 24, *24*
Todd F/O, 25
Trappett Jeff, 34
Trimble S/Ldr TH, 17, 18, 40
Truscott, S/Ldr 'Blue', 18
Tully P/O PD, 21, 22
Vanes F/Sgt FR, 34, 53
Varney F/Sgt FL, 19
Wall F/O, 21, 53
Walters Gp Capt AL, 22
Watson F/Lt PH, 20
Watson S/Ldr BD, 17, 18, 47
Watson F/Lt PH, 40
Watson F/Sgt RW, 22, 23/4
Watts S/Ldr RA, 16
Wawn F/Ly, 18
Wellsman P/O JC

Wheeler F/Sgt DM, 22
Whalley F/Sgt JH, 39
Whillans F/O RH, 24
White F/Sgt FC, 22
Whitney Ian, 41
Wickman F/Sgt JM, 25, 37
Wilson Alec, 39, 43, 46
Wright S/Ldr WHA , 16, 34
Young F/O FJ, 26

BELGIUM
Absil 1/Lt V, 66
Andriaensens Adj JP, 66
Arend Lt Col Pierre, 60
Arnold Douglas W, 65
Bastin Sgt J, 72
Bastin Sgt, 67
Basyn Sgt J, 75
Bayart Sgt, 69
Black Guy, 72
Black Guy, 75
Bogaerts Sgt, 73
Boonen 1/Lt, 68
Born S/Lt, 73
Bos Karel, 62
Bos Karel, 72
Boulack Sgt, 68
Branders Lt H, 64, 69
Brookes Bunny, 67
Brosens 1/Lt F, 66, 67
Brosens Sgt, 68
Cailleau Lt E, 66
Carpentier Capt-Cdt E, 58
Champagnac Adj, 68
Claes Sgt, 65
Colette Sgt, 72
Collignon Maj Léopold, 57, 59
Corbeel 1/Lt, 71
Crekillie Capt Armand, 58
Crewdson J, 61
Custers Lt Col Albert, 58
d'Aertrijcke 1/Lt T de Maere, 64, 65
Davies Tim, 60
de Bergendal Lt Col Yvan du Monceau, 58
de Bonhomme Lt J, 71
de Bueger Capt Guy, 58
De Cauter Sgt JF van, 66
de Ketelaere Sgt, 69
de Ligne Capt P, 71
De Man Lt Col Herman, 59
de Morckhoven Maj André Papeians, 59
de Patoul Maj Guy, 57
de Velde Maj A Van, 57
De Wever Maj Roger, 58
Debart Sgt M, 71
Debie Capt, 65
Debras Sgt G, 71
Dechief Sgt, 71
Degeyter Sgt W, 71
Deketelaere Sgt, 65
Delcon Corporal, 61
Delplace Sgt R, 66
Deschamps Maj Paul, 57

Dewachter Oscar, 67
Dieu Maj Giovanni, 60
Divoy Capt-Cdt Léon, 57
Dome Plt, 75
Donnet Wg Cdr Baron MGL, 60, 64
du Vivier Lt Col Daniel Le Roy, 57, 60
Dubart Sgt G, 63
Dubois 1/Lt Emile, 74
Dubois 1/Lt F, 71
Duchateau Capt R, 57, 65
Dumont Sgt, 60
Edwards Wilson 'Connie', 60
Firlefijn Lt A, 72
Flack Spencer R, 67
Fonck Sgt, 72
Francis AW, 71
Francken Lt, 65
Francotte Sgt, 61
Gaye Sgt A, 66
Geerts Maj LE "Manu", 57
Gheude Maj S, 58, 59
Gillis Sgt P, 68
Gobert Sgt J, 68, 69
Godefroid Sgt, 71
Goemale Lt, 66
Goosse Adj B, 72, 73
Gorris Sgt J, 72
Govaere Sgt G, 71
Guerin Sgt J, 75
Guerra Sgt, 72
Gueuffen Capt J, 69
Guillaume, 73
Guyot Sgt, 72
Hanna Ray, 67
Hendricks Sgt J, 67
Hernould Sgt, 61
Hubert Capt, 68
Hubert Sgt J, 65
Janssens Sgt J, 68
Kay J Denis, 71
Kelder Sgt, 63
Kleinfeldt Sgt, 68
Lacroix Sgt, 61
Lallemant Lt Col RA, 58, 60, 74
Laloux Capt Joseph, 59
Lambrechts J, 70
Lampolle Sgt G, 66
Leclercq Sgt, 68
Lecomte Adj, 68
Lecrenier 1/Lt R, 71`
Legrand Maj Jean, 60
Lemonne Capt, 74
Lenoble Capt Louis, 59
Leroy, 71
Limbourg Sgt, 72
Loots H, 69
Louvigny Capt, 64
Louvigny Maj Robert, 58
Mahaddie TG, 60, 67
Marks Lt, 72
Mathijs 1/Lt, 68t, 69
McCaw Craig, 63
Meerdaels, 69
Meyvus Capt A, 58
Michiels 1/Lt Albertus, 63
Mitchell RJ, 65
Monteyne 1/Lt J, 71

Morai Capt Jean, 58
Moreau Plt J, 69
Mouzon Maj Léopold, 57
Mullenders Maj Marcel, 57, 58
Naessens Sgt, 60
Nossin Capt G, 68
Notte Plt, 68
Ossieur Sgt, 65, 71
Pasteur Thomas H, 65
Paterson John N, 64
Paulet Lt Col Léon, 60
Peeters Capt LV, 71
Peeters Capt-Cdt Louis, 58
Philippart L, 69
Poppe Lt Col Auguste, 60
Prévot Maj Léon, 57, 58, 59
Procureur A, 72
Rahir Sgt P, 66
Raick 1/Lt, 71
Regout Capt, 68
Remack Lt, 69
Renier Lt Col Joseph, 57, 58
Renson Adj, 65
Rich HA, 61
Rigole Capt J, 69
Roberts Sir WJD, 67
Robertson Clifford P, 63
Roodhans Adj, 69
Ros Sgt P, 68
Rousseau Capt A, 75
Seynhuecq, 72
Smets Maj Herman, 58
Snook Beverley, 64, 65
Snyers Adj, 71
Spiette Sgt, 60
Stoffels Sgt H, 63, 68
Swire Adrian C, 60
Symaes Lt Col Edgard, 60
Taminiaux Sgt, 70
Tordeur Adj, 72
Truyers Lt Col Lucien, 59
van der Borght Adj P, 68, 74
van der Stockt Sgt M, 74
Van Eeckhoudt Capt Albert, 58
van Hamme Adj C, 68
Van Lierde Maj Rémy, 57
van Molkot Capt J, 59, 75
van Wersch Lt A, 69
Vandenbosch Lt, 71
Vandercruyssen Lt Col Léon, 58, 60, 71
Vanderkelen Sgt, 63, 72
Verschueren Adj E, 64
Wauters Sgt, 63
Willems Capt F, 58
Willocq Maj Joseph, 59
Wilmots Capt Martin, 58
Wils Lt, 69, 72
Winskill S/Ldr, 57
Wodon Sgt, 68
Wodon Thierry, 75

BRAZIL
Bussman, 76
Focke Professor H, 76
Kovacs, 76
Stein, 76
Swoboda, 76

BURMA
Banting 'Sonny', 81, 82, 83
Burvill, 82
Deere Brendon, 80
Feldman SB, 80, 82, 83
Gardner Leo, 80, 82, 83
Gurdon Philip, 81
Han Aung Chit, 81
Lamberton CC, 81, 82
Levett Gordon, 81, 82, 83
Maseng TJT, 83
Moggridge 'Jacky', 81, 82, 83
Nock Peter, 82, 83
Ostraf Capt AL, 82
Presman Lt Akiva, 82
Pru Saw, 83
Townsend Sqn Ldr, 77, 83
Tsivoni Capt A, 83

CANADA
Arnold Jack, 96
Badeaux, 96
Bays Lt RV, 91
Beurling Flt Lt George, *87*
Bice Lt AT, 95
Bird L/C HJC, 85
Boyle Lt TEJ, 95
Bradley Denni J, 94
Bristow Jess, 96, *96*
Campbell Lt EJGS, 92, 95
Donaldson Lt JN, 86
Douglas Sqn Ldr AG, 87
Douglas Lt M, 93
Elton Lt AC, 91
Enzenhofer Carl, 88
Eversfield S/L NC, 95
Fairbrother Lee, 96
Fotheringham L/C JB, 85
Geary Lt NJ, 92, 94, 96
Gibbs Lt KL, 96
Greenwood Bill, 96,
Harvie Lt JJ, 91
Hater Lt BL, 95
Hayward M, 96
Jens Robert, 96
Joy Lt AD, 88
Laidler Lt RA, 88
Lapres Lt AF, 94
Leidl S/L HP, 95
Logan Lt JW, 95
Maclean S/L RC, 94
Marlow Lt GH, 91, 92
McArthur JHG 'Butch', 96
McBain S/L AR, 88
Mead Lt BW, 91
Mehal Jeet, 88
Monks L/C RA
Morris L/C EB, 88, 96
Munro L/C WD, 95
Murphy Lt, 95
Plumb Don, 96
Potter Michael, 95
Rikely Lt W, 88
Rounds S/L HC, 91
Ryan Air Cdre DHP, 95
Sattler Matt, 96
Sheppard, Lt DJ, 91, 95
Sloan Lt JC, 92
Smith L/C CG, 86

Tallichet David C, 88
Tanner L/C AJ, 85
Watson Lt C, 91, 94
Watson L/C CG, 85, 86, 94
Whitby Lt JP, 92, 95
Widdows L/C WE, 86
Wilson John, 88

CHINA
Kai-Shek Chiang, 98

CUBA
Batista General Fulgencio, 98
Castro Fidel, 98
Destefani Bill, 98
Liedel Charles, 98
McArthur JHG, 96

CZECHOSLOVAKIA
Lamplough Robert J, 103
Truhlar P/O V, 102
Vybiral Wg Cdr T, 99
Weeks Kermit A, 103

DENMARK
Amled Lt BE, 114
Boergesen Lt CS, 114
Bouet Capt G, 109, 110
Brandt-Moeller Lt Col PN, 109
Brasch Lt HJ, 111
Corfitzen Lt HJ, 110
Dansing Lt NK, 109, 110
Darket 2/Lt HU, 110
Dolleris Lt AaH, 110
Hansen Chief Eng P Orm, 109
Holst Lt KAa, 115
Holst-Soerensen Capt N, 109
Jensen 1/Lt HGP, 109
Jensen 2/Lt HVB, 113
Jensen Lt KF, 112
Joergensen Capt AH, 109
Joergensen 2/Lt AL, 113
Joergensen Capt PKR, 111
Kofod-Jensen 2/Lt F, 111, 112
Lonsdale, Capt W, 109
Lygum 2/Lt AS, 114
Moeller Capt E, 109, 113
Nissen Lt PB, 110
Pedersen Capt KCJ, 108, 109
Petersen Col O, 109
Petersen Lt SG, 113
Ramberg VC KR, 115
Rasmussen Lt T, 112, 114
Reimer Capt GL, 109
Riisager Lt R, 111
Rye-Hansen Capt PE, 109
Soerensen Capt CF, 115
Soerensen Lt PS, 112
Stilling 1/Lt POHM, 109, 110/1
Termoehlen 2/Lt JA, 112
Tonnesen Capt HOCL, 114
Quill Jeffrey, 108
von Holstein-Ratlou Capt NVH de Meza, 109, 112

EGYPT
Ainan F/O Abd Al Rahman, 121
Barakat F/Lt, 121
Din S/Ldr M Nasr Al, 117

INDEX

Edwards W/O LG, 120
El-Nasser F/O Jamal Orfan S, 121
Feldmann SB, 122
Janzuri Wg Cdr Said Afifi Al, 117, 121
Nasr F/Lt Mustafa Kamal, 121, *122*
Senior Boris, 122
Wilson Denny, 122
Zaid S/Ldr Al Hamid Abu, 117, *117*
Zaki Air Marshal, *117*

FRANCE
Amarger Lt G, 134
Andrieux Cdt, 125
Andriot C/C, 153
Aninat Sgt, 138
Aragnol CC, 149
Arnold Doug, 144, 156
Astier S/Lt, 155
Aue Sgt, 153/4
Avon Cne, 124
Baches Sgt, 129
Barbier Cdt, 124, 155
Bardou Aspt, 137
Bardou Lt, 141
Bardou Sgt 136
Bardou S/Lt, 138, 141
Barre de Saint-Venant Cne, 124
Battle Cne Sebastien, 137
Bedard Raymond, 141
Belissard A/C L, 154
Bellissard S/C, 155
Berg Lt, 137
Berthet S/Lt, 146
Besse Adj, 138
Bigonneau Lt, 141
Biginneau S/C, 153
Binde Lt, 138
Binet Sgt, 136
Bloch Cne J, 142
Bloch Cne, 153
Bomin, 143
Borgne PM François, 141
Borgne Cne Le, 139
Borossy Lt P, 136
Botte Sgt, 129
Boucherd Adj, 144
Bourreau S/C, 138
Boursier Lt, 141
Bousqueynard Sgt R, 134, 137
Boutan Lt, 132
Bouthier S/Lt G, 135
Bouton Cne, 124
Bouye EV1 Pilar, 141
Bozec PM, 151
Briffe S/Lt, 153
Brown Sgt, 134
Brun Asp, 153
Brunet Cne Felix, 125, 133, 138, 142, 154
Brunschwig Cne, 132
Bruyere Cne, 139
Buge S/C, 154
Callac Lt, 137
Carli LV Louis, 128
Carpentier Cne, 153

Carrere Lt Clem, 144
Cases S/Lt, 139
Cave Sgt, 138
Cazade Adj J, 132
Cazenave Lt, 138, 140
Cazenave W/O, 131
Chabas Sgt, 142
Chabot Lt, 155
Chanet Cne, 138
Chanson Sgt, 154, 155
Chantier Cne, 151
Chantier Lt, 154
Chapeon Aspt, 140
Charles Cne, 125
Charollais S/C, 155
Chauchard Asp, 138
Chonet Cne, 124
Choquet S/Lt, 137
Collomp Lt, 143
Collongues Lt, 131, 133
Combes Sgt, 155, 156
Combrisson Sgt, 132
Conq PM, 143, 149
Constant Sgt, 131
Corcy Sgt, 144
Costes Adj, 144
Courteville S/Lt, 142
Coustie S/C, 139
Crassous Sgt, 141
Cremer EV, 145
Criqui Aspt, 136
Crouzet S/Lt J, 139
Cuef Cne, 140
d'Arcangues LV François, 128
d'Argenlieu EV1 Thierry, 146, 151
Daubresse Lr Guy, 132
de Beaucoudray Lt Jacques, 139
de Beaupuis Lt, 134
de Bordas Cne, 124
de Carpentier LV Raoul, 128
de Casa LV Varela, 151
de Chavaignac Lt, 130
de Chavagnac Cne, 125
de la Salle Cdt d'Anfreville de Jurquet, 124
de Laborderie Cne, 132
de la Flecheres Sgt, 134
de la Source F/Lt HH, 136
de la Source Col, 125
de Latour-Dejean LV RP, 126, 137, 143, 145, 146, 148, 149
de Lauwe Lt Chombard, 139
de la Villéon Cne, 124
Delenatre Sgt, 138
Delenatte Sgt Roger, 130
Delfino LCL, 124, 156
Delime Sgt, 139
Delord Matelot, 143
Delouche LV Jean, 128
Demanget Lt, 141
Deniau S/Lt, 137
Deny A, 133
de Paul Lt, 153
de Pradel S/Lt, 137
de Redoul S/Lt, 153
de Rugy LV Robert Goullet, 128
de Saint-Marceau Lt, 133
de Scitivaux, 147

de St.Pulgent Lt, 154
de Vereilh Lt, 153
de Villepin Lt, 139
Dodet Cne, 125
Douchet S/Lt, 139, 155
Douchet Aspt Henri, 133
Doudis Adj Jean, 136
Dubarry Asp, 137
Dubois Jean-Patrick, 131, 156
Du Boucher Cne, 137
Dubreuil S/C, 153
Duc Capt J, 134, 136
Dupuy Cne Amadee, 132
Durand Lt, 146
Duteil SM Jean-Pierre, 152
Duval CC/CF Rémi, 128
Esun EV1 Albert, 143
Ezanno LCL, 125
Fabry Cne, 125, 134
Fequet S/Lt, 131
Ferran CF Michel, 128
Ferrando Lt, 141
Fleury Sgt E, 138
Fontvielle Lt, 139
Fouchier Cne, 124
Founs S/C, 143
Fournier CF Julien, 128
Fraisinett R, 144
Frélaut Jean, 144, 156
Friedrich Adj, 131, 137
Friot PM, 149
Fuchs Cne, 125
Garde Cdt Georges, 131
Garot Sgt M, 154
Gastal Sgt, 153
Gaudin Sgt H, 147
Gauthier G, 138
Genty S/Lt, 139
Georges Lt Combesias, 155
Geramia Adj, 153
Gerant/Gehant Sgt Paul, 139
Gerard Cne, 154, 155
Gerard Lt, 141
Gerard S/C Maurice, 139
Geremia F/Sgt, 136
Germain Lt, 131
Gicquel OE, 138, 148, 149, 150, 151, 152
Ginestet S/C Julien, 137, 151, 155
Giraud/Girard Cne, 124, 147
Gleize LV Marius, 126, 145, 148, 152
Gleyze, 138
Godde Lt, 153
Goupy Cdt, 124
Graignic LV, 146
Guérin Cne, 124, 155
Guibard Lt, 131
Guizard Cdt, 124
Guyon LV Gilbert, 128
Guyot PM, 145, 146, 148, 150, 151, 152
Haberkorn Adj M, 136
Habert Sgt, 140
Hammonton Lt, 147
Heliot/Helliot Cne, 143, 153
Heroin Sgt, 147
Hervé CC Jean, 128, 138

Hoot, 147
Hourdin CF Jacques, 128
Hugo Col, 125
Hutton Lt Cdr PJ, 150
Jacquart Christophe, 151, *151*
Jacquin LV Roger, 128
Jaillet Sgt P, 153
Jalabert CF René, 128
Jannic SM, 153
Jean A, 137
Jeandet Lt H, 135
Jeandet Cne, 124
Jullien Lt, 139
Kaplan T, 129
Kerros LV Paul, 128
Klein Sgt Piere, 131
Klein PM, 144, 148, 150
Lacassie S/C, 141
Lacoste CC Guy, 128
Lafargue S/Lt, 141
Lafargue S/Lt Jean, 131
Lainé CF Françis, 128
Lamblin S/C, 134
La Maison Capt R, 133
Lancesseur Lt J, 136
Lancois Lt A, 134
Lansoy Cdt, 125
Laure LV, 140
Laurence Lt, 140, 141
Laurent Lt Roger, 136
Lebas Sgt, 138
Lecaque LV Albert, 128
Le Corre Cne, 141
Legault Sgt Y, 143
Leglet LV Jean-Michel, 126
Le Goffic Sgt, 137
Le Groignec Cdt, 124, 133
Le Mahieu LV Pierre, 128
Lemaire Cne, 124, 153
Lenglet LV, 143, 144, 145, 146
Leroy Sgt, 138
Limbard Sgt, 137
Limbeuf JM, 156
Loubet Cne, 124
Louis EV1 Pierre, 141
Lucas LV Jean L, 128
Madon Cne, 124
Madon Lt, 134
Maho Sgt, 139
Maho Sgt Piere, 135
Maire LV Bernard, 128
Mallez EV1 Pierre, 137
Mangin Lt Claude, 135
Mangin Cdt, 124
Mangin Sgt, 133
Marchelidon Cdt, 124
Marchelidon Cne, 124
Marmier LV, 143
Marrillonet S/C, 139
Marsh S, 129
Martin Cdt, 139
Martin LV Georges, 128
Martin Sub-Lt RA, 134
Martinet Lt, 134
Martre Cdt Marcel, 125, 135, 146
Massicot LV Pierre, 128
Matras Cdt, 124
Mauban LV ER, 128

Mauban LV Jean, 128
Maubin LV, 146, 151
Maulandy S/Lt, 153
Maurin Cdt, 124
Mayot Lt, 147
Mazo Lt, 153, 154
Mazoyer S/C, 143
Mesnard Lt, 140
Mesplet S/C, 141
Metayer Sgt, 133
Meunier Sgt, 137
Meunier S/Lt, 147, 156
Michel F/Sgt, 134
Michel Lt, 139
Moal PM, 144
Monchanin Adj J, 135
Monthus Asp, 139
Morant S/M, 136
Morizot S/C A, 133
Mouliérac CV Jean, 128
Moysset EV2, 148
Nedellec Lt, 143
Noel, 136
Nosneron EV 1ere CP, 136
Paillanay Sgt Chef R, 131
Palmésani LV Michel, 128
Pape Cdt, 125
Papin-Labazordière LCL M, 124, 137, 142
Pechdimaldjii Asp, 151
Peronne Cne, 124
Perrier Lt R
Perrin H, 153
Petit EV, 145
Piechon Cdt, 125
Pingoux Cne, 140
Pioch Adj, 131
Pisotte Lt G, 134
Pizon Sgt R, 133
Planchard HR, 133
Porodo Cne, 125
Porquet Lt, 155, 156
Prayer Capt G, 134
Prevost Lt, 132
Raboxcone S/C, 138
Ragot Lt, 133
Rallet S/Lt, 133
Raoust Adj, 139
Rat Louis, 129
Ravet LV Marcel, 128
Reder Lt Jean, 129
Restoux Lt, 140
Restoux, 153
Reverday Lt, 133
Rey Lt Augustin, 140
Richarme Sgt F, 138
Ricour LV Paul, 128
Rivière LV Guy, 128
Robin EV, 152
Roche Lt, 139
Roesh Lt, 139
Rombi Lt, 147
Roncin Adj D, 134
Roncin S/Lt, 136
Rondenay LV François, 128
Ronsin Lt, 131
Roost F, 147
Roubaud, 143, 144, 145, 151
Rousseau LCL, 143

Rousseau Sgt P, 138, 149
Roussel CC Louis, 128
Roy EV, 148
Ruth S/C, 141, 143
Sainflou Lt Pierre, 146
Sanguinetti LV, 144, 145, 146, 148, 149, 151
Saout PM, 148
Sargeant Martin, 144
Sarrail S/Lt J, 134, 154, 156
Schloesing LV, 152
Schmidt Sgt, 143
Schneider S/Lt, 138
Seguin Cne, 143
Segura Cne, 124
Serrate Lt, 147
Simard Capt, 139
Simard Cne, 124, 132, 138, 153
Soula Cne, 156
Tanguy Cne, 124
Tardy de Montravel Cdt, 124
Tatraux Cne, 124, 156
Tauzy Sgt, 154
Thollon Cdt, 125
Thome Sgt A, 144
Thorette LV Bernard, 128
Touchard Sgt, 138
Trachard Sgt, 143
Tron Sgt, 156
Trulla Cne, 124, 153
Unuoas Sgt, 136
Valentin Adj, 136, 155
Valiquet S/C, 140, 144
Vallet LV Raymond, 128
Varela LV, 143
Vaziaga LV Charles, 128
Vercken LV R, 151
Veunes Adj M, 136
Villaceque Cne Marc, 141
Villette Asp, 141
Villien Lt, 136
Vivoux A/C P, 144
Wicker Cne, 139
Wilmot Lt Roussel, 139

GERMANY
Andrews P/O, 159
Blumer W/O RAB, 159
Buchwald F/O BK, 159
Caister P/O JR, 159
de Wever P/O R, 159
Ellenrieder Capt Willy, 159
Falkust P/O HEL, 159
Glithevo P/O CWH, 160
Hardy P/O R, 159
Kurstrzynski F/Lt Z, 159
Lerche HW, 159
Marchal P/O HE, 159
Martin Ofw, 159
Messer Lt KH, 159
Pentz P/O Roman, 159, *160*
Ross Sgt V, 159
Scheidhauer P/O BWM, 159
Shore P/O EH, 159
Squire Sgt H, 159
Wendel Fritz, 159
Woodser P/O, 160

GREECE
Athanasoupoulos S/Ldr E, 162
Bousios F/Lt P, 162
Chatzioannou F/Lt E, 162
Chondros F/Lt K, 162
Deligeorgis F/Lt A, 162
Demiris S/Ldr P, 162
Doukas Grp Cpt G, 162
Frankias S/Ldr A, 162
Gounarakis F/Lt D, 162
Kartalamakis S /Ldr I, 162
Kokkas F/Lt K, 162
Koniotakis F/Lt K, 162
Kontolefeas F/Lt M, 162
Kortronis F/Lt, 162
Loukopoulos S/Ldr K, 162
Margaritis Grp Cpt K, 162
Michelogkonas F/Lt P, 162
Mitsakos Wg Cdr P, 162
Mitsanas P/O D, 162
Nasopoulos Grp Cpt A, 162
Panagopoulos Grp Cpt K, 162
Papapanagiotou Grp Cpt P, 162
Parisis F/Lt L, 162
Sinouris F/Lt E, 162
Sinouris S/Ldr E, 162
Vlantousis Wg Cdr A, 162
Witham LW, 163

HONG KONG
Bain P/O G, 172
Chen P/O YCD, 172
Gauntlett S/Ldr EJ, 169, 172
Heard P/O R, *171*, 172
McConville F/Lt B, 172
Mose F/O HL, 169
Rowe-Evans F/Lt Adrian, 172

INDIA
Abbas P/O M, 190
Adams S/Ldr DA, 175
Adamson F/Lt I, 175
Afridi P/O JM, 183
Agtey F/O YR, 177, 180
Ahmad, F/O AKS, 183
Ahmad F/O SM, 180, 183, 185
Ahmad P/O TN, 192
Ahmad S/Ldr Z, 174
Akhtar S/Ldr M, 175
Arnold Doug, 190, 195
Artus P/O E, 180
Ashraf P/O, 190
Atmaram S/Ldr R, 173
Aulakh S/Ldr A Murat Singh, 173
Aziz F/O MY, 176
Bakhshi P/O AS, 182
Banerje F/O S, 176, 200
Bankapur P/O JR, 199
Barker S/Ldr M, 174
Beale F/O HH, 176, 177, 184
Bearcroft F/O JR, 190
Beaupert P/O RH, 190, 199
Berry S/Ldr D Boyd, 174
Bhandarkar P/O PB, 187
Bhardwaj P/O RWB, 180
Bhawnani S/Ldr ASM, 175
Biwas P/O, 187
Blunt S/Ldr LRD, 175

Bose S/Ldr HK, 175
Bose P/O JM, 185
Bose P/O SR, 199
Bouche P/O J, 177
Brian P/O O, 189
Brown F/Lt Charlie, 193
Buchanan P/O, 201
Bush F/O CG, 183
Callaghan P/O P, 183
Cazlet P/O BJG, 199
Chandra S/Ldr J, 174
Chaudri F/O, 189
Chaves F/O AJ, 176
Chitnis P/O HR, 185
Chowdhury F/O TB, 183
Church Charles, 185, 193
Clowsley F/O VJ, 200
Cohen F/O JI, 199
Colebroke F/Lt DE, 178
Connor Michael, 186
Coombes S/Ldr MW, 174
Dani F/O WRN, 190
D'Cruz P/O A, 187
D'Eca F/O, 179
Deo S/Ldr RFT, 175
Dhatigara S/Ldr EJ, 175
Dhawan F/O RC, 185
Dhillon F/O GS, 198
Dogra F/O BS, 180
Ducasse, P/O MU, 183
Dugdale F/Lt N, 184
Durney P/O, 191
Dutt S/Ldr Ranjan, 173, 179
Engineer S/Ldr MM, 174
Engineer S/Ldr RM, 173
Enzenhofer Carl, 191
Feltham S/Ldr LW, 176
Fenn S/Ldr JM, 175
Fernandez P/O, 182
Finn F/Lt DM, 177
Foster F/Lt C, 179
Francis P/O GV, 183
Frasca Rudolph A, 197
Gaar Norman E, 181
Gama F/O AF, 192
Gangully F/Lt AK, 184
Ghadiok F/O TN, 176
Ghosh P/O PK, 190
Gill S/Ldr PS, 174
Grey BJ Stephen, 185, 190
Guron P/O GS, 184
Haider P/O G, 183
Haider S/Ldr SN, 175
Hall F/O CA, 200
Haq F/O MU, 188
Haque P/O SMS, 189
Harrington P/O PE, 200
Hassan S/Ldr SH, 174
Haydon-Baillie Ormond, 182, 185, 186, 189, 193, 195, 196, 197
Haydon-Baillie Wensley, 182, 185, 186, 189, 193, 195, 196, 197
Healey F/O TR, 199
Hosain F/O M, 186
Humphreys S/Ldr JS, 174
Hussain F/Lt A, 180
Hussain F/O SA, 178

INDEX

Ingle F/O JS, 185
Irani P/O FD, 183
Jaggi, P/O HS, 183
Jamaludin F/O S, 177
Jebb P/O RL, 177, 179
Jena P/O S, 198
Jolly F/O KR, 177
Jones S/Ldr RW, 175
Joseph F/Lt SA, 200
Joshi F/Lt KB, 174
Kalayaniwala F/O RS, 187
Karki F/O RBS, 190
Katre P/O LM, 180
Khan F/O AR, 181
Khan S/Ldr MA, 175
Khan S/Ldr NUR, 192
Khan P/O R, 181
Lal S/Ldr, 174
Lamplough Robert J, 186
Latif F/O IH, 183
Law P/O RD, 180
Lawar F/O PB, 187
Lee P/O DG, 193
Light F/O KW, 187
Limbeuf JM, 197
Lloyd S/Ldr WVA, 175, 178
Lodhie S/Ldr A, 174, 200
Majid P/O KB, 184, 187
Malani P/O RC, 177
Marley F/Lt J, 177
Martin F/O JA, 194
Masillamani S/Ldr, 174
Masud P/O Z, 189
Mehal Jeet, 191, 197
Mehra S/Ldr OP, 173
Menon F/O NB, 184, 199
Mirza F/O H, 190
Misra S/Ldr ML, 173, 174
Mohona P/O BY, 177
Moolgavkar S/Ldr HS,
    174, 175, 178
Moulick P/O SC, 184
Mukerjee F/O NK, 185
Mukherjee F/O MK, 186
Muthayah P/O CT, 190
Naik F/Lt DB, 192
Narayanan F/Lt AA, 176
Nazirullah S/Ldr E, 173
Noronha S/Ldr, 174
Noronha Wg Cdr BS
Palamkote P/O AM, 176, 182
Pandit F/Lt RA, 183
Parkes RJ,
    194, 195, 196, 197, 201
Patel F/O HK, 193
Patil P/O AB, 176, 190
Payne F/O JL, 181
Pears P/O DC, 182
Perkin S/Ldr KA, 175
Peters P/O JR, 180
Peters P/O TR, 193
Piggott F/O DB, 184
Pinto S/Ldr EW, 174, 187
Powar F/O, 184
Prince-Foster F/O L, 179, 183
Qadir F/O A, 176
Oommen F/O PJ, 200
Rabb S/Ldr M, 173
Rahman S/Ldr MA, 175

Rai, F/O DB, 180
Rai P/O H, 192
Raman F/O KG, 187
Randhawa F/O RS, 178
Raymond Paul, 186
Raza S/Ldr H, 175
Reid F/Lt J, 200
Rhenius F/O CT, 192
Ridgers P/O JP, 180
Roy F/O NG, 183
Saggal F/O HC, 194
Salah-ud-din F/O, 200
Sarkar F/Lt PK, 192
Scudder S/Ldr FVA, 175
Sehgal F/O AK, 198
Sekhon F/O GS, 198
Selski P/O J, 182
Shah F/Lt Mehta-Phiroze, 187
Shepperd F/O OC, 179
Shipurkar F/O RS, 181
Shortlands P/O C, 200
Shukla F/Lt JF, 175
Singh F/O Jaspal, 193
Singh S/Ldr K Jaswant, 173
Singh Air Cdre P, 189
Singh F/O R, 183
Singh S/Ldr Randhir, 173
Singh F/O RKB, 198
Singh P/O S, 194
Singh P/O SD, 191
Singh S/Ldr Shiv Dev, 173, 175
Singha F/O CK, 184, 185
Smith P/O AE, 200
Smith P/O HV, 187
Smith P/O TV, 187
Soear P/O SR, 178
Sori F/O RL, 180
Srinivasan F/O S, 198
Storey P/O H, 196
Suares F/O AIK, 183
Suri F/O KL, 178
Suri S/Ldr MD, 173
Suri F/O RL, 179
Sutherland S/Ldr, 174
Thandi F/O KS, 178
Turner F/Sgt G, 179
Varma S/Ldr JC, 174
Vaz P/O UA, 180
Walmsley P/O WH, 180, 182
Weeks Kermit A, 185
Wickenden Alan, 186, 189
Wickenden Keith, 186, 189
Wilks P/O GE, 189
Williams P/O RA, 182, 183
Wilson John, 191
Wright P/O VG, 183
Wynne P/O TO, 200
Zaheer F/O J, 190
Zaheer F/O N, 192
Zahid F/O SM, 180, 201

IRELAND
Atkins Steve W, 204
Bayliss Maurice S, 203, 206
Bayliss Peter K, 203, 206
Cole F/Lt, 204
Colland Sgt, 205
Creham Lt, 204
Crewdson J, 203

Davies Tim A, 203
Derry John, 204
Fairey John, 203
Grace Carolyn S, 204, 206
Grace E Nick, 204
Grrenwood Bill, 206
Healy Cmd HR, 203
Healy Capt Tim, 206
Howard Capt H, 205
Howard Lt, 205
Johnson Capt, 205
Lees Norman, 204
McCurragh Greg, 204
Morgan S/Ldr, 204
O'Connell Lt, 205
Parker Richard, 204
Plumb Don, 206
Roberts WJD, 204
Roberts Sir William, 206
Rayn Capt, 206
Samuelson NAW, 203, 204, 206
Swan Cmd Patrick, 203
Warrilow Christopher, 206

ISRAEL
Alon Mordechai,
    208, 210, 214
Banting S,
    210, 216, 217, 218, 220
Bar Maj M, 208
Barak, 210
Ben-Shahar Capt I, 208, 209
Blau Naftali, 210, 211
Burvill, 212
Close F, 211
Cohen Capt A, 208
Cohen Jack, 209, 210
Cohen Sydney, 208, 209
Cooper F/O G, 211
Dangott Caesar Morton, 210
Deere Brendon, 219
Eyal Maj E, 208
Feldman Seymour, 209, 210,
    211, 212, 216, 216, 217, 218,
    220, 221
Finkel Aaron, 209
Ezer-Weizman RT, 208, 209, 216
Gardner Leo, 218, 219, 221
Goodlin S, 210, 211
Gurdon Philip, 210
Hartoch N, 216
Hod Mordechai, 208, 210.
Jack Cohen, 208
Jakobs S, 211
Lamberton Charles, 210
Lamplough Robert J, 213, 217
Levett Gordon,
    212, 213, 216, 218
Lichter, 210
Mann Maurice, 209
McElroy J, 210, 211
Melton Dic, 217
Moggridge Jacky,
    210, 212, 214, 218, 219
Monk P, 212
Nock Peter, 219, 220
Ostroj Capt AL, 212
Overburry, 219
Peled Capt M, 208

Pennell David W, 217
Pomerance Sam, 209, 221
Pomerantz William, 221
Presman Lt A, 214
Ratner 1/Lt David, 219
Rosentahl Col Oded, 216
Ruf Capt M, 208, 214
Schroeder W, 212
Senior Boris, 209, 210, 214
Shapira Lt Amir, 216
Shapira Daniel, 209, 210, 216
Simmondy, 220
Simpson M, 212
Sinclair, 210
Smith Fred, 217
Tadmor Maj M, 208
Tsivoni Capt A, 216
Weeks Kermit A, 214
Wilson D, 209, 210
Win Tham, 213
Yavneh Capt Y, 208

ITALY
Bacich Magg.Pil. Mario, 223
Beccaria T Col.Pil. Francesco,
    223
Bianchi Col.Pil. Luigi, 223
Bresciani T Col.Pil. Venanzio,
    223
Callieri Col.Pil. Gino, 223
Callieri Magg.Pil. Gino, 223
Casabeltrame Lt, 225
Chiantia T Col.Pil. Tanrico, 223
Danieli Magg.Pil. Flavio, 223
Ercolani T Col.Pil. Ercolano, 223
Fanali T Col.Pil. Duilio, 223
Fassi Col.Pil. Roberto, 223
Fattoreti Sgt N, 226
Frulla Magg.Pil. Mario, 223
Garretto T Col.Pil. Gustavo, 223
Giacomelli T Col.Pil. Giuliano,
    223
Giovannozzi T Col.Pil. Massimo,
    223
Guizzon Col.Pil. Delio, 223
Haydon-Baillie Ormond, 228
Haydon-Baillie Wensley, 229
Jannicelli Lt Fio, 226
La Tarda T Col.Pil. Domenico
Lippi Col.Pil. Antonio, 223
Mauriello T Col.Pil. Guiseppe,
    223
Moci T Col.Pil. Paolo, 223
Pegna Magg.Pil. Oscar, 223
Ricco Col.Pil. Bruno, 223
Santini Col.Pil. Felice, 223
Sforza T Col.Pil. Francesco, 223
Travaglini T Col.Pil. Edoardo,
    223
Valentini T Col.Pil. Gastone,
    223
Vassallo T Col.Pil. G. Battista,
    223
Veronese Lt A, 226
Villa T Col.Pil. Giulio Cesare,
    223
Zappetta Col.Pil. Giovanni, 223

MALTA
Lloyd AVM KBB, 232

NETHERLANDS
Aertson F/Sgt SK, 244
Aitchison Michael, 242
Asjes Maj HC,
    236, 239, 242, 246
Baanstra, 241
Bos Karel, 244, 246
Breman Lt Jan, 239, 241
Bruggink Tub, 236, 238, 241,
    242, 244, 245
Burgerhout, 241
Chambers W/O RE, 241
Croser Peter, 242
Davies Tim A, 238
De Geus Ben, 236, 241, 242
De Grave Kapt F, 238, 245
De Jong Lt A, 241
Dekker Kapt Johhny W, 235
Determeyer M, 239
De Vries Maj AJ, 235
De Wolf Maj W, 236
Eden Jaap, 239, 245
Edwards 'Connie', 236, 246
Fabius Lt H, 244
Flinterman Maj JL, 235
Grace E Nick, 245, 246
Griffith Dan, 242
Hanna Ray, 238
Hendrikx Lt, 241
Horeley Christopher PB, 245
Huistee Eerste Lt Joep, 245
Jansen Bill, 241
Kynsey Oeter, 242
Mahaddie TG, 238
McCaw Craig, 244, 246
Mol Jas, 238, 241, 244, 245
Nijwening Lt G, 236, 238
Noyons Gys, 239, 244
Rauwerdink Henk, 241
Robertson Cliff, 244
Sandberg Maj Jhr B/JD, 235, 242
Swire Adrian C, 238
Thijsen Kapt, 241
Thomson Raybourne, 244
Uytenboogaart DA, 245
van den Bosch Maj WM,
    235, 234, 242
van der Giessen Lt Kol, 241, 242
van der Roer J, 241
van der Tak Lt Kol, 235
van Eijsden Sgt PPA, 242
van Gorkom H, 244
van Spaendonk Sgt, 245
Verhey Theo, 241
Vijzelaar Lt F, 238, 241, 242, 245
Welte Lt Jan, 241
Wijting Maj AJW, 235, 236
Zwaan Jaap, 245

NEW ZEALAND
Arnold Peter, 249
Bos Karek, 249
Deere Brendon, 249
Francis A.William, 249
Hare Brian, 249
Page Paul E, 249

Parkes J, 249
Shivas J, 249
Slade James, 249
Smith GS, 249
Subritsky Don J, 249
Subritsky Mike, 249
Wallis Sir Tim, 249
Warrilow Chris, 249

NORWAY
Aagaard Lt K, 254, 258
Aanjesen Maj Ola G, 251
Amundsen Sgt Jan Christian,
    262
Anosen E, 257
Bjørge-Hansen Lt K, 255
Djupvik Sgt B, 257
Gotaas Sgt, 254
Gran Maj Martin, 251
Haabet Fenrik Odd, 259
Harby Lt, 254
Härum Sgt Jan Steen, 262
Hassel Lt Col Asbjørn, 251
Herfjord Lt, 259
Holter-Sørensen Sgt Per, 254
Hosel Sgt, 255
Hoset Sgt Jostein, 258
Isachsen Maj Reidar, 251
Jansen Sgt Per, 259
Klepp Fenrik Amund, 259
Larsen Sgt John A, 261
Lien Sgt Oddvar, 257
Lie-Slathein Sgt Jens, 259
Lindboe Sgt Kjell, 262
Ludt Fenrik Reidar, 259
Ludvigsen Lt T, 255
Lyngby Sgt Leif, 259
Magnussøn, 254
Marum Fenrik Per, 259
Meland Kapt Harald, 251, 259
Nyerrød Kapt Kristian, 251, 259
Rohde Lt HW, 257
Ringstad Sgt B, 255, 262
Ringdal Maj Nils A, 251
Roald O, 261
Rødberg-Nilsen Fenrik N, 257
Ryg Wg Cdr John,
    251, 257, 258, 259
Sandberg Kapt Eirik, 261
Sandvik Fenrik Jan, 257
Sandvik Sgt M, 258
Stigset/Stigseth Lt Egil, 257, 259
Stokstad Lt Egil, 255
Strøm Sgt Ivar, 261
Thorstensen Fenrik Finn, 257
Thunes Sgt Asbjørn Andreas, 262
Tjensvoll Maj B Eivind, 251, 254
Torkehagen Lt Frithjof,
    254, 255, 257, 259
Tradin Sgt Olav, 259
Ullestad Mah Olav, 251
Unhammer Lt Col Olav, 251
Urdahl Fenrik Knut, 259
Weisteen Sgt Einar, 262
Weisteen Maj Tharald, 255
Werner Lt Thor, 257
Width Lt Jens Chr, 251, 259
Wik Sgt Wilmar, 259

PORTUGAL
Barbosa Capt Artur Tamagnani,
    269
Caldas Capt Fernando Pereira,
    269
Canavilhas Sgt Ismael, 269
De Oliveira Capt Rus Braz, 269
Ferreira Capt Joao Jose, 269
Sarmento Capt, 268
Seixas Lt Rogeria de Oliveira,
    269
Sousa Capt Fernando de Oliveira,
    269

SOUTH AFRICA
Aberdien Lt JS, 287, 310, 320
Ackerman Lt BN, 309
Allen Lt AW, 309
Allen Lt JO, 318
Allen-White Lt AF, 302
Anderson Lt WF, 310
Andrew Capt WG, 300
Angu Lt ITM, 319
Antony Lt WJ, 286
Araldi Mike, 284
Aronson Lt JC, 286, 289
Assad Lt A, 321
Atkins Steve W, 302, 322
Atkinson Lt RK, 297
Atmore Lt NGN/MGM, 288, 300
Austin Lt MFW, 307, 319
Bailey Lt PGF, 299
Bar Lt RD, 290
Barnard 2/Lt FC, 317
Barnett Larry, 306, 322, 323, 329
Barnwell Capt RJ,
    297, 301, 311, 321
Barrell Lt, 314, 316, 317
Bartel Lt LC, 317
Barter Lt AB, 301
Bartman Lt WJ, 284, 320
Basson Lt AL, 309, 316, 330
Basson Lt L, 291
Basson Lt JMcL, 303
Bayford Lt WE, 293
Beamish Lt AR, 321
Beddell Lt JC, 310
Bell Lt RF, 315
Bell Lt WD, 286
Bender Lt C, 316
Beyer Hptm Franz, 284
Bezuindenhout Lt OEG, 306
Biden Capt AJ, 299, 311
Binedell Lt ACG, 285
Bird Lt DA, 300
Blaauw Lt Col JP, 281
Blair Lt AR, 318, 320, 321
Bolitho Lt DP, 318, 321
Booyens Lt JJ, 306, 307
Booysens Lt JC/JG, 315, 316
Borcherds Lt KB, 315, 331
Bosch Lt DC, 288, 301, 310, 312
Bosch Lt RG, 306, 315
Bosman Lt Col AC,
    282, 297, 331
Botes Lt SI, 322
Boyd Lt CWL,
    287, 288, 303, 309
Boyer Lt HFP, 292

Boyes Lt WDB, 327, 328
Boyle Mjr BJL, 280
Boys Lt NG, 284, 286, 298, 311
Brand Lt JE, 302, 303, 331
Brande Lt EA, 293
Breakey Lt TJMcD, 288, 321
Brebner Mjr DM, 280, 292, 294,
    297, 303, 310, 317, 328
Bredenkamp 2/Lt JM, 290
Bremner Lt N, 285, 309, 311
Brent Lt JLRH, 293
Bridgers Lt AB, 324
Bristol Lt AI, 316
Brokensha Lt AE, 303
Broken Lt PB, 319
Broom Lt ND, 329
Broome Lt HPS, 313, 319
Brown Lt JO, 305
Brown Lt LH, 296, 302, 308
Brown Lt SM, 317
Brunton Mjr WV, 280, 318
Bryant Mjr PD, 280, 288, 302
Buch Capt HJ, 300
Buddell Lt JC, 301, 316
Bulley Lt LN, 303, 317
Burger Capt PLR/PCR,
    314, 315
Burl Capt RP, 298, 299, 302
Buxton F/Lt AP, 286
Campbell Lt DJ, 283
Campbell Capt PC, 292
Camplin F/O, 295
Carolin Lt HD, 319
Carrington Lt FM, 301, 309
Carter A/M, 329
Carter Lt, 315, 319
Carter Lt HA, 306, 313, 314
Chandler Lt HG/HC,
    306, 308, 315
Chaplin Lt RE, 315
Chapman 2/Lt HG, 297, 313
Cheesman Lt AEF, 297
Cheesman Lt DGF, 311
Cherrington Lt RC, 284, 300
Cillie Cdt AC, 324
Clarence Lt BV, 295
Clarke Lt RW, 325
Clarke Lt LC, 315
Clur 2/Lt MB, 326
Cochrane-Murray Lt, 331
Coetzee Lt FB, 319
Coetzee 2/Lt FG, 325
Cohen Capt, 322
Cohen Lt, 318
Collins Lt DR, 299
Collins Capt JC, 327
Connell Capt GR, 308, 316
Conning Lt GE, 312, 316
Cooke Lt AM, 319, 325
Cooper Lt S, 318
Cornelius Lt SM, 286, 313
Cowsge-Crosse Lt AR, 311
Crafford Cdt, 325
Crosley Lt H, 300
Cullpan Rick, 323
Cuyler Lt G, 321
Davidson Capt HH, 292
Davies Lt DR, 295
Davis Capt JFO, 324, 325

INDEX

Dawber Lt PO, 286
Dawson-Smith Mjr L, 279, 316
Day Capt RN, 320
Deary Lt LH, 315
de Graaf Lt KJA, 284
de Jager Lt DS, 331
de Jongh 2/Lt, 284
de Jongh Lt DN, 318
de Jongh Lt RE, 296, 297
de Klerk Lt IS, 301
de Klerk Lt JJ, 304
de Klerk 2/Lt L, 286, 306, 312
Dent Lt CR, 285
Dent Capt GC, 325
de Plooy Lt BM, 329
Dertema 2/Lt JR
De Villers Lt AC, 297
de Villiers Lt DJ, 286, 314
de Villiers Lt JS,
   286, 288, 317, 320
de Vries Mark,
   296, 316, 317, 323
de Waal Capt JO, 314
de Wet Capt DF 286, 301
de Wet Lt JG, 313
Dodd F/O BR, 299
Donnelly Capt PH, 290, 291, 316
Dorning Lt ARS, 308
Dove Mjr DC, 281
Doveton Lt GD, 310, 320
Doveton-Helps 2/Lt JG, 292
Dowden Lt WA,
   284, 303, 306, 307, 321
Downie Lt E, 325, 328
Dowell Lt EG, 306
Doyle Lt B, 308
Doyle Lt WRO, 317
Driver Lt D, 290
Ducasse Lt DV, 301
Dugmore Lt OL, 299
Duigan Capt, 323
Duncan-Smith Wg Cdr WGG,
   296
Dunkeley Alan, 322
Dunkerley Capt REK, 303
Dunning Mjr EK, 279, 313
During 2/Lt PB, 300, 302
du Play Lt R, 303
du Plessis Lt JH, 286
du Plessis 2/Lt JP, 292
du Preez Lt AP, 301, 304
du Preez Lt HTR, 309
du Toit Lt JH, 304
du Toit Lt PJ, 288
du Toit Lt Col SF, 301, 307
Dyason Lt HJC, 315
Dyason Lt RG, 314
Egner Capt RC, 321
Embling Lt KO, 305, 313, 315
England Capt PCW, 308
Farrell Lt DP, 301, 309
Faure Mjr JM,
   278, 280, 289, 306, 311
Featherstone Lt DW, 326
Finney Mjr SA, 279, 295
Fischer Lt NPG, 288
Fisher Lt DR, 297
Fisher Lt HM, 306
Fisher 2/Lt JWS, 299

Flynn Lt M, 288, 308
Foster Lt H, 314
Fowles Lt GT, 301
Franck Lt EDK, 308, 315
Franz 2/Lt PC, 327
Freeman Lt HP, 286, 287, 306
Friedricks 2/Lt NP, 326
Frisby Lt AG, 317, 319
Frisby Cpl PC, 317
Fry W/O R, 305
Fryer Capt TR, 308, 317, 320
Gardiner-Atkinson Lt A, 325, 328
Gardner Lt Col CMS, 281, 291
Gaynor Mjr JH, 279, 289, 290,
   291, 292, 296, 312, 329
Geater Lt HA, 311
Geere Capt CP, 293
Geering Lt WJ, 284, 312
Geldenhuys Lt BJ, 325
George Lt KEF, 284, 295, 309
Gericke Lt HG, 310
Gibson Lt DIG, 310
Gilbert Lt JA, 285, 301, 310
Gillman Lt LW, 295
Gilson Lt DT,
   291, 292, 293, 297, 299, 328
Golding Capt CA, 279
Golding Mjr DW, 279
Goldsworthy Lt,
   311, 316, 317, 319
Gordon Lt WG, 302, 318
Gouws Lt F, 328
Gow 2/Lt IJ, 326G, 302, 318
Gow Lt, 323
Gowar Lt IT, 298, 298, 312
Grace Lt DD, 324, 325
Gray Capt RE, 315, 326
Gray Lt SSM, 312, 315
Greaves Lt RJ, 331
Greeff Lt WH, 288
Greenham Lt CFG, 312, 313, 314
Griesse Lt SP, 309
Grobler Lt FK, 327
Grove Lt BJ, 327
Grunder 2/Lt MO, 326
Guest Capt B, 314
Hagedorn Obgfr Reinhard, 287
Haines Lt DW, 321
Hall Lt RK, 285 286
Halliday Lt CA, 283, 284, 300
Hamilton Lt FC, 285, 301
Hamilton Lt NJ, 316
Hanreek Lt HJ, 317
Hardingham Lt GV, 302, 314
Harley Lt JE, 288, 311, 321
Harmer Lt JR, 292, 300
Harris Capt TA, 321
Harrison Lt NC, 302, 313, 315
Hartley Capt LR, 313
Hartley Lt SA, 303
Hartogh Lt MH, 303, 322
Haskins Lt JH, 325
Hastie Lt DS, 294, 296, 300, 330
Hawley Lt FA, 319
Haynes Lt BW, 291
Healey Lt SB, 313
Healey Lt SP, 312
Hedgecock Lt CE, 321
Herboldt Capt D, 310

Heugh Capt, 317
Higgo Lt A, 291
Hill Lt JW, 327
Hillary Lt GW, 283, 290, 297, 300
Hilton-Barber Mjr D, 280, 319
Hitchins Lt CC, 312
Hodgson Lt, 292
Hoffe 2/Lt AJ, 290
Hogan Lt JP, 298, 315, 318
Holthausen Lt HG, 328
Holton Lt JH, 304
Holzapfel Oblt Fritz, 299
Hoogland 2/Lt AJ, 328
Hopkins Lt TJC, 304, 305
Homer Lt AW, 297
Hough Lt DE, 331
Howe 2/Lt JFG, 328
Huskisson Lt KF, 284, 297
Huyser Lt DJF, 285, 319
Hynd Lt JH, 297
Iles Lt TW, 329
Inggs Lt VC, 331
Irving Lt JP, 313, 315
Jenkins Lt BD, 308
Johl Capt WAT, 309
Jordan Lt EC, 299
Joubert Lt, 302
Joyner Lt RT, 307
Judd Capt DR, 294, 305
K'Anval-Aimee Lt PAJ,
   293, 320, 328
Kayser 2/Lt JA, 296, 303
Keevy 2/Lt ER, 325
Kempster Lt MJR, 317
Kershaw Mjr RHC, 280, 320
Keyter Lt BJG, 295
Kinsey Lt G, 310, 311, 318
Kirby 2/Lt BJ, 292
Kritzinger Lt HJ, 288, 319, 321
Kruger 2/Lt, 319
Kruger Lt JC, 292, 299
Krummeck Lt Col GC,
   282, 284, 297
Kuhlmann, Capt K, 324
Joubert Lt JA, 324
Jrynauw Lt RF, 319
Laing Lt RE, 300
Landman Lt J, 296
Langerman Capt WM,
   295, 298, 328
Langton Lt SC, 294, 316
Lanham Capt JR, 294
Laubscher Mjr CJ, 281, 292
Lawrence Lt JJ, 319
Lawrenson Lt AD, 326
Lawrie Lt WR, 290, 301
Leathers Lt DR, 284, 325
Lee Lt FP, 315
Lee Capt PB, 288
Lees Norman, 331
Legoff Lt LA, 299
Lello Lt, 324
Lellyat 2/Lt JN, 323
Le Mesurier Mjr GJ, 278
Lenards Lt J, 297
Leppan Lt I Angus, 310
Leppen Lt PD, 321
Le Roux Capt CG, 290
Leslie Lt PA, 312, 316

Lever Capt RC, 298
Liebenberg Mjr HCW,
   281, 288, 297
Lindsay Lt DJ, 296, 314
Lipawsky Lt GB, 289
Lloyd Lt G, 290
Loftus Lt Col DH, 295
Logan Lt JCG, 308, 312, 315
Lombard 2/Lt C, 328
Louw 2.Lt DC, 324
Lucas Lt DH, 304, 31, 3191
Ludick 2/Lt H, 288, 326
Lurie Alan, 306, 322, *329*
Luyt Lt PJE, 306
Lyle Lt TW, 331
MacDonald Lt HH, 324
MacDonald Lt KB, 324
MacDonald Lt NM, 299
MacKenzie 2/Lt IA, 303
MacRobert Capt M, 282
Mair Lt BD, 284, 286
Maritz Lt NC, 325
Maritz Lt WF, 321
Mark Lt R, 295
Marks Lt GV, 317
Marshall Lt HF, 289, 300
Marshall Lt LM, 290
Marshall Lt P, 288, 312
Marshall Lt RD, 304
Martin Lt, 312, 318
Martin Capt CE, 296
Martin Lt VH, 300
Matthews Lt H, 311
Maxwell Lt P, 288
McBreakey Lt TJ, 312
McChesney Lt, 305, 320
McClure Lt P, 290, 312, 313
McCormick Lt GF, 320
McCullum, Lt NK, 290
McCurragh Greg, 331
McDonald Graham, 316
McDonald Lt KB, 324
McKechnie Capt RB, 319, 320
McKechnie Lt RD, 311, 316
McKenzie Lt RB, 312
McLeod Lt AJ, 328
McLeod Lt H, 297
McLoughlin Lt DRH, 291
Meikle Capt AW, 302, 318
Meintjies Lt JH, 310, 316
Meiring Lt AJ, 325
Meiring Capt JW, 300
Mendelsohn Lt F, 321
Metcalf Lt, 322
Meterlekamp Mjr PCR, 278, 290
Miles Lt JHP, 292
Miller Lt JB, 288, 302, 318
Mitchell Lt J, 318
Mitchell Lt T, 310
Monk Peter, 322
Montgomery Lt, 317, 319
Moodie Mjr DD, 278, 318
Morgan Lt G, 300
Morris Lt JR, 326
Morrison Lt, 306
Morrison Lt LF, 316
Morton Capt RDB,
   280, 294, 312, 315
Muller 2/Lt F, 323

Mundell Lt V, 290
Murray Lt DJ, 311
Murray Mjr T, 282
Murray Mjr TPL,
    279, 285, 301, 305, 330
Myhill Lt HJ, 318
Nash-Webber Lt H, 302, 312
Naylor Lt P, 289
Nel Lt Col WA, 281, 290, 291
Nettleton 2/Lt G, 326
Newton Thompson Lt JO,
    301, 305
Nicholson Lt RT, 294
Nisbet Capt HG, 306
Nortje Capt JF, 325
Nourse Lt PW, 319
Nunan Lt DG, 284, 318, 319
Oates Lt LJ, 296
O'Connor Lt FA, 316
Odendaal, Capt E, 302
Odendaal, Capt MWV,
    301, 308, 311, 320
O'Farrell Lt GH, 295, 328
Ogilvie-Watson Capt G, 312
O'Keeffe Lt PTC, 290, 299
Oldridge Lt BR, 312
Olver S/Ldr P, 278, 291
Orchard Lt G, 289
Pappas 2/Lt CJ, 323
Page Lt GA, 326
Pare Lt CMT, 320
Parker Lt MA, 294
Parker Lt WS, 305
Parsonson Lt LW, 319
Passmore Lt RW, 292
Paterson Lt AC, 286
Paterson Lt GG, 289, 324, 327
Paxton Lt GFR, 319
Paull Lt CHL, 319
Pearce Jim, 322
Peel Lt RB, 284, 313
Petit Lt RO, 293
Phelan Lt DR, 306, 312
Phelan Lt EL, 317
Phillips Martin, 322
Phillips Capt NM, 315
Pienaar 2/Lt EAC, 325
Pike 2/Lt EH, 313, 321
Pistorius F/O WP, 286
Pitcher 2/Lt MH, 304
Pitout Lt GW, 297, 299, 306
Pohl Sgt, 324
Pollock Lt J, 306, 312, 320
Potgieter Capt FE, 314, 315
Potter Lt HB, 306, 316
Powell Lt ER, 312, 313
Powell Lt WR, 286
Prescott Lt KW, 300
Ptetorius Lt HG, 328
Pretorius Lt MS, 324
Price Lt WC, 317, 319
Prinsloo Lt NP, 292
Pritchard Lt RD, 311
Quin Lt DL, 283, 290, 292
Rabie Lt GP, 284, 297
Rabie Capt SW, 290
Rae Lt AS, 324
Ratcliff Lt HD, 303
Reaim Lt MF, 309/310

Reim Lt MF, 314
Retief Lt AB, 316, 331
Retief 2/Lt PJT, 326
Richards Lt R, 327, 328
Richards Lt SJ,
    296, 297, 303, 328
Richardson F/O GS, 288
Richter Lt FB, 314, 324, 326, 328
Robbs Lt GG, 315
Robinson Lt DH, 284, 316
Robinson Lt DL, 291, 315
Robinson Lt K, 291
Robinson Lt ME, 293
Robinson Lt MES,
    287, 290, 297, 298, 328
Rochford Capt JV, 315
Roelofse Lt JJ, 309, 321
Rogan Lt DS, 283, 290, 292, 295
Rogers General RHD,
    281, 315, *320*, 326, *329*
Rorke Lt MH, 288, 324
Rorvik Capt EA, 284
Rose Lt C, 316
Rose-Christie Lt B, 292, 294
Ross Lt BK, 314
Ross Lt JBS, 288, 305, 317, 318
Rossiter Lt JB, 324
Rossouw Lt AdeL, 286
Rowan Lt RW, 293, 302, 314
Rowden Lt I, 309
Roy Lt GA, 305, 309
Royston Lt MG, 317, 319
Ruiter Capt DA, 279, 315
Sattler Matt, 323
Schneider Lt S, 307
Schoeman Capt, 317
Schoombie Lt CC, 306
Schorn Lt T, 302, 305
Scogna Joe, 309
Scott Lt DM, 295
Scott 2/Lt RR, 292
Seccombe Mjr GB, 278
Seccombe Capt JT, 296
Seel Lt IM, 300
Segalla Lt JG, 284, 291, 308
Shelver Lt BD, 314
Sherwood 2/Lt RV, 284
Shone Capt CN, 312, 316
Shore Lt CC, 296
Shores Lt EA, 288
Silberbauer Lt JC, 310
Simpson Mike, 322
Sinclair Capt CR, 306
Sisson Lt RE, 296
Slater Capt JH, 291
Slaven Lt JLJ, 329
Smith Lt HF, 284, 289
Snyman Capt HT, 288, 304
Sobey Lt WR, 294
Southey Capt GC, 318
Spencer Lt JL, 304
Spencer Lt JR, 296, 297, 309
Spies Cdt WR, 324
Staats 2/Lt RL, 325
Stanford Mjr WP, 280, 311
Staples Lt AF, 296
Starck Lt CP, 324
Steinbach Lt RD, 283
Steinhobel 2/Lt JF, 293

Stevenson Lt CL, 302
Stewart Lt DC, 318
Stewart Lt BH, 295
Steyn Lt MH, 302
Stone Lt JFJ, 300
Stopberg, 325
Stott Lt EE, 303, 312
Strick Lt EJ, 320
Strong Lt WL, 299, 309
Strydom Lt IJ, 317, 325
Strydom Lt JG, 294
Strydom Lt PJ, 317
Sturgeon Capt EIH, 293
Sturgess Capt EW, 311
Styger Lt, 305, 312
Summers Capt GW, 318
Sutton Lt RRW, 297
Swales Mjr CJO,
    280, 281, 309, 319
Swanepoel Lt JW, 311
Swart Lt DW, 290, 318
Sweeney Lt JM, 289, 299
Sykes John, 309
Symons Lt L, 288, 314
Tatham Lt, 310, 320
Tatham Capt GLH, 288
Tatham Lt HW, 288
Taylor Lt DJ, 299, 308
Taylor Lt EM, 330
Taylor Lt H, 296
Taylor Lt HN, 287, 296
Taylor Capt INL, 286
Taylor Lt PH, 305
Tennant Lt AT, 310, 315
Theron Capt DC, 321
Theron Lt DH, 319
Theunissen Lt RC, 286
Thomas Col Neil, 323
Thompson Lt WM, 301, 311
Thomson Lt A, 310
Thomson Capt WR, 290
Torr Andrew J, 324
Torresi Ten Giulio, 291
Tribelhorn Lt D, 304
Tribelhorn Lt DB, 310
Trotter Lt B, 296
Turner Lt AG, 298
Turner Lt R, 328
Tweedie Lt MHL, 310, 320
Tyrrell Lt AF, 284, 289
van der Byl Lt DG, 328
van der Heever Lt, 322
van der Merwe Lt SW,
    290, 292, 293, 295, 297
van der Poel Capt RH, 291
van der Spuy Lt G, 319
van der Veen Lt GT, 283, 294,
    295, 296, 297, 300, 304
van der Watt Lt JJ, 310
van Heerden Lt JWS, 301, 321
van N Fouché Lt H, 328
van Niekerk Lt OJ, 326
van Nus Capt J, 296, 328
van Reenan 2/Lt SV, 328
van Rensburg Lt DJS Jansen, 314
van Rooyen Lt GT, 297, 300, 301
van Vliet Mjr CA, 279, 280
Venter 2/Lt CH, 325
Vermeulen Cdt, 326

Verster Cdt, 323
Victor Lt NP
Villers Capt JG, 327
Viljoen Capt SdeK, 294
Vincent Lt FE, 286
Visser 2/Lt JP, 318
Vollmer Lt TF, 304, 306, 311, 319
Wakers Lt, 321
Wallace Lt TE, 286, 292, 305
Walters Lt, 319, 322
Warner Capt AC, 292
Warrilow Chris, 302
Wates Capt GH, 312
Watson A/M BL, 297
Waugh Lt DS, 298, 300
Wayburne Capt E, 303
Webb Lt ECT, 291, 293, 295
Weeks Lt L, 328
Welgemoed Mjr FE, 286, 315
Welmann Lt PJ, 301, 314
Wheeldon Lt RB, 324
Wheeler Lt HD, 314
Wheeler Mjr WJ, 280, 295, 307
Whilby Lt AF, 292
Whitehorn Lt RG, 292, 310
Whittaker Lt FW, 288, 311, 316
Wiehahn Lt GD, 325
Wiggett Mjr BAA, 279, 290
Wikner Lt WD, 287, 292, 329
Will Capt IG, 315, 319
Williams Lt E, 311
Wilsby Lt, 329
Wilson Lt AC, 314
Wilson Lt B, 324
Wilson Lt FD, 298
Wilson Lt WE, 324
Wildsmith Mjr HEB, 281
Woletering Uffz August, 296
Yates 2/Lt HJ
Young Capt DP, 306
Young Capt KA, 280, 320, 321

SOUTHERN RHODESIA
Barber Capt RH, 333
Barbour Lt DM, 334
Bellingan Lt D, 334
Blair WO1 R, 334
Bone Lt BTA, 334
Bradshaw Lt DA, 333
Deale Lt JH, 334
Deall WO1 JH, 334
Jacklin Lt Col E, 334
Love Lt O, 333
Malloch Lt J, 333, 334
Maritz Lt Ray, 334
McGibbon Capt D, 333
Owens WH, 333, 334
Pascoe Lt, 334
Paxton WO1 CH, 334
Penton Lt OD, 334
Richards Lt, 334

SOVIET UNION
Aleksandrov Kapt VV, 375
Blagoveshchenskjy Lt Col VG,
    227
Chalov Maj V, 338
Danilov Kapt SP, 337
Denisov Lt Col KD, 337

INDEX

Dushin Lt Col AZ, 337
Dzusov Lt Col IM, 337
Fairhurst F/Lt EA, 337
Gayko Ltn Werener, 375
Grozhovetsklj Lt Col GI, 338
Korolev Maj MI, 338
Lukyanov Lt Col SI, 337
Mazhayev Lt Col NP, 337
Mischchenko Lt Col FM, 337
Neustroyev Lt Col IP, 337
Osipov Lt Col AA, 337
Panov Lt Col AB, 337
Petrov Maj GG, 337
Platonov Kapt IA, 375
Popovich Senr Lt, 375
Pronin Maj AG, 338
Prutskov Lt Col FM, 337
Rakob Mah RI, 338
Romanov Lt Col BN, 337
Rudakov Maj BA, 337
Schuck Oberfeldwebel, 375
Solovkin Lt, 375
Soper Angela, 338
Surin Maj BN, 337
Trunov Lt Col MG, 338
Walker F/O GW, 338
Yankovkij Lt Col VM, 337

SWEDEN
Aulin F/O Gösta, 377, 379
Aulin Sgt Kjell-Göran, 379
Brycker Sten, 382
Carleson P/O Axel, 379, 381
Carlsson F/O Arne, 377, 382
Ehrning Nils, 379, 382
Elmegård Sgt Sven, 381
Falk Grp Capt Greger, 376, 379
Forsberg F/O Sven, 379, 381
Frösell P/O Owe, 382
Fyhrlund F/O Bernt GR, 377
Goliath F/O Erik, 377, 379, 382
Hägg Sture, 381
Hallander F/O Rune, 377
Hansson F/O Holger, 382
Hjelm Ulf, 381
Holmström F/O D, 376
Jacobi F/O Edward, 379
Kindblom Sven, 377
Lundström F/Lt Göste, 376, 377
Molander F/Sgt Harry, 379
Morgan S/Ldr DW, 379
Morgan S/Ldr WJG, 381
Muchow F/O Roy H, 377
Nilsson F/O Birger, 382
Nordström Grp Capt, 376
Norn F/O Nils Olof, 379
Palmqvist P/O Bengt, 377, 382
Persson F/O Per Axel, 370
Ringborg F/Lt Folke, 376, 379, 381
Robarts PG, 381
Sjökvist F/O Jan, 376, 381
Ström F/O Gösta, 377
Sundberg F/Lt B, 376, 382
Sundell Sgt Holger, 379
Tibell F/Lt Evert, 376
Tyrling P/O Karl Evert, 381
Wangström F/O I, 376, 377, 379

SYRIA
Squire D, 383

THAILAND
Bintaboot S/Ldr Prakong, 386
Jutairat S/Ldr Watchara, 386
Ketmoot Wg Cdr Thep, 386
Poompoolpol Grp Capt Wong, 386
Sukserm Wg Cdr, 386

TURKEY
Akku Col I Jakki, 393
Akoglu Lt Col Enver, 394, 395
Akyildiz Col Necmi, 394
Alp Dündar, 407
Aras Mjr Ihsan, 395
Ariburun Col Tekin, 395
Atalay Mustafa, 406
Aydin Sezai, 407
Azakli Mjr Mustafa, 395
Baybora Seyfi, 406
Benli Nizamettin, 407
Biringen Col Tata, 394
Çantay Suat, 406
Casin Ismail, 406
Dönmez Emin, 406
Duke F/O NF, 397
Elgin Lütfü, 404
Elibollu, 406
Eraybar Lt Col Suat, 394
Erkan Ismail, 406
Erkmenalp H Bahattin, 407
Esiner Muhtesem, 407
Gençer Nejat, 407
Göker Col H Suphi, 393
Gökeri Col Nevzat, 395
Goknart Col Sabri, 395
Göksel Col Hidayet, 394, 395
Göksenin Col Muzaffer, 393
Gürler Musaffer, 404
Gürsoy Serafettin, 406
Hazneci J Nafiz, 406
Ilksümer Servet, 407
Karacehennem Col Semi, 394
Kaya Osman, 406
Küçükel Mustafa, 407
Kurban Hüsnü, 406
Okyay Mjr Selçuk, 395
Özgören Muhtar, 406
Pamukç Salim 407
Pekman Col M Ali, 394, 395
Pitrak Esref, 407
Sahinbas Lt Col Ferruh, 393
Sakarya Mjr Bülent, 395
Sengü Mahmut Nedim, 403
Serim Fethi, 403
Seylan Bahattin, 407
Toros M Hüdai, 406
Tunçöz Orhan, 407
Turagay Col Seyfi, 393, 394, 395
Uçagök Col Gavsi, 395
Uçari Lt Col Rahmi, 394, 395
Uysal Ismet, 407
Vural Fikret, 404
Yazici Gani, 407
Yentürk Selahattin, 407
Zeyrek Col Ziya, 393

UNITED STATES
Adam Lt, 458
Adams Capt GM, 411, 449
Ainley Lt, 457
Alan Paul, 423
Aldridge Lt FS, 423
Alenius Lt AA, 434
Alexander Lt, 457
Allen Capt Emmette P, 418
Allison Col Dixon M, 410, 414
Ames Lt Col Richard A, 414
Amyx Lt, 457
Anderson Lt DP, 443
Anderson Col Edward W, 410
Anderson Col Frederick R, 411
Anderson 2/Lt HS, 423
Anderson 1/Lt SM, 424, 454
Anderson William C, 452
Andrews Lt JAC, 439
Archer Lt W, 443
Arnold Douglas W, 448, 450, 452
Arnold Jack, 453
Arnold Peter, 430
Arrelson Lt H, 442
Asselin Mjr HO, 420
Aubertin Sgt LE, 457
Avery Mjr Delwin B, 410
Ayle GR, 447
Babcock 1/Lt, 456
Bailey 2.Lt GL, 456
Baird 2/Lt, 411
Baker Capt RN, 456
Baldwin Lt JA, 455
Balogh Lt PA, 432, 445
Baltezer Lt, 455
Barnes 1/Lt GW, 458
Barber Lt, 455
Barr Capt HL, 456
Batista Fulgencio, 453
Bayliss MS, 448
Beard 2/Lt WA, 417
Beck Lt JL, 419
Beedle 2/Lt H, 441
Beirne Lt K, 417
Bellamy Vivian H, 448
Belliveau Lt RE, 422
Berg Capt RA, 421
Berg Mjr Russell E, 411
Berg Capt WW, 432
Bhumiphol King of Siam, 450
Billing Jerry, 448
Bisgard Lt HRL, 454
Bishop Lt, 423
Bissgard Capt, 455
Blair Tom, 450
Blais 1/Lt MR, 456
Blakeslee Col Donald JM, 410
Bliss Mjr KE, 411
Blyth JS, 450
Blythe Lt JK, 437
Boardman Lt, 423
Boehle Lt, 455
Bolle Capt NNV, 437, 458
Boock 1/Lt RA, 421, 424, 426, 454, 456
Boolootian Richard A, 452, 453
Boone 1/Lt WL, 423
Booze Lt RW, 421, 423

Boughton Lt EM, 423, 455
Bowler Hurley, 452
Boyce Lt N, 455
Boyd David, 452
Boyd 2/Lt RC, 458
Boyle Lt WJ, 426
Braucht Lt JW, 421
Breit John, 453
Brians 1/Lt HH, 456
Brite Lt WO, 416
Brooks AH, 450
Brown F/Lt Charlie, 452
Brown Lt CR, 437
Bryan Lt EL, 457
Bryan Lt WL, 456
Bryson 1/Lt WC, 420
Buck Lt SO, 416
Burt Lt FD, 421
Butler S/Sgt JE, 456
Byrd 2/Lt JC, 454
Cabas Lt VN, 437
Calland Lt RW, 416
Callander 1/Lt AD, 456
Cameron 2/Lt, 411
Cameron 2/Lt DK, 427
Camp Capt FB, 456
Camp 2/Lt FD, 417
Campbell Lt FE, 417
Campbell 2/Lt FW, 433
Cannon Brig Gen John K, 416
Carey Lt AJ, 435
Carey Lt JA, 418, 455
Carver Lt, 455
Casey Lt JF, 433
Cassady Lt RH, 434
Castro Fidel, 453
Cavanaugh Jim, 448
Chaddock 2/Lt RB, 456
Chambers Capt WL, 432
Champlin, 447
Chandler 2/Lt B, 426, 454, 456
Chapman Capt Carl, 449
Chattaway Lt WP, 418
Chennault Claire, 449, *449*
Childress Mjr Hubert M, 411
Christensen Lt FJ, 425
Clark Capt, 457, 458
Clark Lt Col AP, 426, 433
Clark Lt AW, 423
Clark Lt JA, 420, 454
Clarkson, 445
Cleveland Lt CS, 457
Cobb Lt ER, 426
Coen Mjr OH, 410, 424, 454
Cole 2/Lt HP, 419
Collins Lt, 431
Collins Lt BW, 434
Collinsworth Capt JD, 456
Colney Lt, 454, 455, 456
Colton Lt DE, 425
Comstock Lt Horace, 457
Conley Lt JE, 456
Conner 1/Lt HC, 421, 432
Conner Lt JS, 422
Connor Lt RJ, 442, 443, 446
Cook 2/Lt EL, 426
Cooper Lt JH, 419, 421
Cooper 1/Lt JR, 421
Corbin 1/Lt JH, 420

Cornwell 1/Lt Ottaway B, 442
Corrigan 1/Lt RC, 456
Covington Lt Col William E, 410
Coward Lt Col James S, 414, 415, 455
Cullen Col Paul T, 411
Curtiss Miss L, 450
Dabney 2/Lt WAM, 417
Daley Mjr J, 420
Daley Mjr R, 410
Dalrymple Lt E, 421
Daniels 2/Lt HE, 431
Davidson Lt VK, 445
Davies Tim, 448
Daymond Mjr A, 410, 427
Dean Mjr Fred M, 410, 413
Deaten Mjr George C, 410, 416, 435
Decker 2/Lt HR, 418
Deere Brendan, 450
Degenaro Lt AV, 417
de Montrachu, 437
Denham Lt CR, 441
Denton Lt Cdr W, 416
Destefani Bill, 453
De Voe Lt, 458
Diderickson Lt R, 450
Diehl Larry, 453
Dietz Lt GS, 426
Dillon 2/Lt FJ, 417
Dixon Capt RJ, 411, 450
Dodd 2/Lt MA, 423
Doigherty Lt JG, 455
Dorland Lt HW, 457
Douglas Lt RV, 431
Duff Lt OR, 433
Duke-Woolley Wd Cdr R, 424
Dye 2/Lt JD, 419
Dziesinski Lt KR, 417
Earley Lt NG, 455
East Lt CB, 423
East 1/Lt RI, 455
Edwards Wilson, 446
Eidson Mjr, 411
Elington Lt PM, 427
Encinias Lt M, 457
English 1/Lt NE, 456, 457
Ennis Lt J, 457
Eppel Brad, 446, 452
Erickson Jack, 448
Evans Lt JS, 433
Evans Mjr R, 410, 454
Evans 2/Lt RW, 454
Evans Lt RN, 434
Evans Lt TH, 455
Ezell Nelson E, 453
Fairbrother MW, 455
Fairey John S, 448
Fardella 1/Lt EL, 435, 437
Farkas Bruce, 448
Fawcett Lt, 458
Faxon Lt, 446
Feld 2/Lt S, 427
Ferguson Harvey J, 453
Fetrow 1/Lt GB, 455
Fields Mjr V, 413, 434, 456
Fisk Wallace, 450
Fleming Lt DC, 419
Fleming 1/Lt JB, 431

Fleming Justin, 450
Fleming Robert, 450
Fleming Capt TB, 456
Flint Lt, 445
Ford 2/Lt J, 418
Foster Lt JB, 433
Fox Lt PJ, 437
Fraissinet Roland, 450
France Lt VJ, 424
Francis AW, 450
Frasca Rudolph A, 453, 454
Fraser 1/Lt RB, 457
Freel Lt S, 454
French Capt Dickman R, 411
Frost Lt E, 441
Frye Lt DE, 433
Funchean 2/Lt DM, 424
Gaar Norman E, 448
Gabriel 2/Lt RB, 416, 432
Gahegan 1/Lt WD
Gallion Lt FD, 457
Gardner 2/Lt EP, 417
Garland Lt Cdr RD, 445
Garrett Lt RC, 425
Garvey Capt JE, 454
Gebhart Lt EJ, 437
Gentile 1/Lt D, 423, 425
Giacomini Lt AW, 432
Gillem Mjr AC, 413, 442
Godrey Peter 446
Goebel Lt RJ, 440
Goetz Lt J, 458
Goffin Lt CJ, 423, 445
Goichelaar P, 453
Goldenberg 2/Lt AL, 437
Goldstein Lt W, 440
Gompf Lt, 457
Gooding 1/Lt GV, 456
Gordon Lt MJ, 417
Gottlieb 1/Lt I, 443
Gover Lt L, 454
Graham 2/Lt DG, 456
Granger Worral, 452
Greenwood William S, 452, *452*
Gray Lt CK, 427
Grey BJ Stephen, 448
Grimm 2/Lt CP, 432
Haberle Lt F, 457
Hackbarth Lt R, 438
Hagen Lt RP, 437
Hairston Lt RM, 420
Hall Mjr J, 411
Hall Col James G, 411
Hamrik Lt AK, 419
Hansen 1/Lt EW, 431
Hardage Lt, 458
Hardee Lt, 411
Harlan Lt OF, 419, 424
Harmeyer Lt, 458
Harrimgton Col JC, 422, 432
Hartwell Lt Col Norris E, 411
Harvey 1/Lt JD, 456
Haskins Lt, 443
Hauert 1/Lt AE, 421
Haugen Mjr CT, 411, 450
Haun Capt James R, 411
Hawkins Col John R, 410, 413
Hearn Lt RV, 427
Heil 2/Lt RF, 456

Heiss Fw Hermann, 456
Helton 1/Lt LV, 456, 457
Henry Lt IR, 426
Hickman Lt Col Jack W, 412
Higgins Larry, 452
Higgins Lt WF, 456
Hilborn Lt RB, 450
Hill Lt Col Frank A, 413, 414, 431, 434, 435, 437, 454, 456
Hilse Lt RF, 432
Hine 1/Lt RW, 434, 456
Hodgson Anthony, 450
Hoffman Lt C, 456
Hoffman Max R, 453
Holdiman Capt Thomas A, 410
Holloway Capt, 435
Holmberg 2/Lt FW, 457
Hooten Lt R, *432*
Hoover Lt RA, 457
Hope Sgt FE, 431
Hopkins Lt W, 425
Houston Lt LF, 421
Houston Capt William, 415
Howell T/Sgt EJ Howell, 422
Hoyt Col Ross G, 412
Hughes Lt Hank, 446, 458
Humbrecht Col George W, 411
Humphrey 2/Lt RP, 425, 427, 433
Hunter Mr, 446
Hurd 2/Lt RF, 456, 457
Hurter Lt, 457
Huston Lt LF, 419
Icard Lt JW, 422
Imwall Lt W, 457
Ingram 1/Lt RD, 431
Jacobs Lt Col Paul M, 412
Jackson Barrie, 451
Jackson Bernie F, 451
Jackson Thomas, 451
Jamison Lt, 457
Jenkins Mjr Everett K, 416
Jens Robert 455
Johnson Lt AG, 441
Johnson Lt HD, 433
Johnson Lt MF, 425
Johnston Lt JE, 456
Jones 2/Lt BW, 458
Jones Lt EF, 437
Jones Ray, 453
Juhnke 1/Lt JA, 455
Junkin Lt S, 420
Jurak Anthony, 452
Jurist Ed, 448
Kaiser Lt WF, 426
Kappes 2/Lt, 411
Kari Lt WA, 454
Kater 2/Lt LR, 441
Kay J Denis, 450
Kellam Lt B, 457
Kelley Lt WM, 417
Kelly Capt WP, 432
Kemp Lt JT, 434
Keough 1/Lt GT, 427
Kerr 1/Lt HR, 427
Keyes Capt Ralph E, 410, 415
King 1/Lt GC, 456
Kirschner Lt CM, 432
Kis Lt WG, 418
Klaas 2/Lt J, 454, 455

Klein Lt JJ, 422
Klein Col Philip B, 412
Knapp Don L, 450, 451, 453
Koon Lt DW, 416
La Breche Capt, 455
La Breche Mjr George J, 410, 454
Lacy Lt WD, 434
Lambert 2/Lt DE, 418
Lane Lt HC, 442
Langberg Lt, 455
Langberg Lt MK, 455
Law Lt DB, 445
Lawson Lt Col George A, 410, 411
Leaf 1/Lt DB, 456
Leghorn Lt Col Richard S, 411
Lehman 1/Lt PG, 458
Leicester Lt BB, 431
Levine Lt Col Robert, 410, 414, 415, *436*
Liebl Lt, 457
Liedel Charles H, 453
Litchfield Lt TD, 439
Louden 2/Lt CE, 418
Lowe John, 450, 451
Luber Lt VN, 427
Ludlow Lt, 454
Lukas Lt A, 417
Lunquist Maj GE, 447
Lupton 1/Lt RM, 457
Lutz Lt JF, 426
Lyman Lt, 457
Lymberis Lt SM, 431
Lynn Lt MR, 418
MacFarlane 2/Lt LL, 456
MacGregor Lt W, 435
Mahal Jeet, 451
Maloney Edward, 450
Mandeville Lt R, 455
Mann Lt, 457
Mann 1/Lt EF, 457
Mann Lt JJ, 434
Maples Lee, 446, 452
Marangello Lt WA, 427
Markley 1/Lt DW, 437, 455
Marsh 2/Lt SE, 432, 433
Martin Lt LK, 421
Martin Lt T, 432
Massey, Lt JW, 457
Matt Larry, 450, 451
Matthews 2/Lt Joseph A, 421
Matthews 2/Lt JG, 423
McAllister Lt JW, 418
McArthur JHG, 453
McBride Ken, 452
McCann/McMann 1/Lt DE, 456
McCarthy Lt, 456
McCaw Craig, 448
McColpin S/Ldr CW, 410
McCorkle Col Charles M, 413
McCormick Lt JF, 433
McDonald 2/Lt NL, 418, 456
McDuff Lt OR, 439
McGlynn Lt JA, 432
McKennon Lt PW, 417
McNickle Mjr Marvin L, 410, 414
Mehroff Lt, 439
Merritt 1/Lt FD, 456
Middleton Ray, 446

INDEX

Midgett Lt, 457
Miller Lt, 456
Miller 1/Lt D, 455
Miller George F, 448
Milner Lloyd B, 453
Milner Lt TH, 424
Mirsch Lt R, 454, 455
Mitchell Mjr, 411
Mitchell 1/Lt MP, 455
Mitchell Capt R, 411, 455
Mitchellweis 2/Lt J, 423, 432
Monahan Col John W, 416
Monk Peter, 448
Montgomery Lt JH, 4577
Montour Lt GE, 417, 455
Moon 1/Lt IR, 457
Moore 2/Lt RM, 458
Morgan Lt WB, 454
Morgan Lt WL, 425, 435
Morris 1/Lt PH, 433
Mosby Lt, 455
Moss Marshall, 452, 453
Muenchenberg Mjr Joachim, 455
Murphy Lt EW, 420
Mutchler 2/Lt, 456
Myers Lt JD, 457
Nangle 1/Lt JT, 440, 455
Nelson Lt, 457
Newberry Lt RC, 426, 455
Newman Lt GA, 427
Nisbet Lt WG, 443
Norris Lt O, 417
O'Brien Lt, 456
O'Brien 2/Lt JL, 447
O'Brien 2/Lt WC, 455
O'Connor 2/Lt CTJ, 457
Odom Lt EJ, 434, 456
Ogilvie 2/Lt RG, 416
Olds Col Thayer S, 412
Otto W/O, 434
Overend Lt, 457
Parker Lt GT, 431
Parsons Capt H, 411
Paulk Capt JH, 456, 457
Payne Capt CW, 454, 456
Payne Mjr William J, 416, 423
Peabody 1/Lt H, 417
Peck Col George W, 411
Pederson Lt HL, 455
Peebles 2/Lt RL, 455, 456
Pennell David W, 447
Perry Lt JB, 422
Peterson Lt Col Chesley G, 410, 433
Peterson 2/Lt KD, 420, 454
Petot Lt, 455
Phillips 1/Lt RE, 433
Pissanos 2/Lt SN, 420, 424
Place Lt, 457
Plumb Don, 453
Pond Robert J, 448
Potter Michael, 452
Powell 2/Lt JA, 423
Price David G, 443, *444*, 448, 450, 453
Pryblo 1/Lt CA, 441, 456
Raeder Lt B, 457
Ramer Lt, 456
Ramsey 1/Lt CR, 455, 456

Ranson Lo Col John W, 412
Raup 2/Lt RW, 425
Rawlings Lt IL, 445, 449, 450
Reed 1/Lt JC, 455
Regina Pete, 449, 453
Reynard Adrian, 452
Rich Lt, 456
Richards Lt JR, 445
Richardson 1/Lt LH, 411
Richardson 2/Lt Robert R, 410
Riggins Lt JT, 432
Rivers Lt RW, 454
Robb Lt HJ, 419
Robb AVM Sir James, 452
Roberts Lt JC, 439, 455
Roberts 1/Lt RH, 458
Robertson Clifford P, 448, 449
Robertson Lt J, 424
Robertson Capt JC, 454
Robinson 2/Lt, 432
Robinson Lt FM, 418, 419, 423
Roche Lt, 454
Roche Lt BJ, 455
Rollag Lt SA, 439
Ross William D, 452
Rudorffer Lt, 455
Russell John J, 453
Rusten Lt AM, 416, 418
Sandborn Capt Bert S, 415, 458
Sanders Col Homer L, 411
Sanford Lt GE, 427
Savoy Lt R, 442
Schall C, 450
Schanning Lt W, 457
Schellhase 1/Lt HO, 429
Schmoker S/Sgt TH/JT, 417
Schuppen Vern, 450, 451
Scognia Joe, 446
Scott Lt DR, 416
Scott Lt EM, 420
Scott Capt EN, 457
Scott Capt Steven, 449
Seaman 1/Lt AJ, 426
Shafer Lt DE, 427
Sharpe 2/Lt EL, 420, 425
Sheble Capt RN, 445
Shenburger 2/Lt, 457
Sheppard Percy, 452
Sherwood Capt DR, 418, 426
Shipway Lt, 411
Shoop Lt Col Clarence A, 411
Short Lt FB, 454
Shuck Lt JM, 454
Simms Lt Sidney, 454
Simon Capt WJ, 445
Simpson Mike, 448
Simpson Lt RT, 418
Skenyon Lt LF, 419
Skilton 1/Lt ER, 458
Skinner Lt HJ, 424
Skinner 2/Lt William, *414*
Slade James, 452
Smith Mjr, 411
Smith 2/Lt DK, 431
Smith Delford M, 452
Smith Lt DR, 421
Smith Lt ED, 425
Smith Fred, 447
Smith James E, 453

Smith 1/Lt M, 456
Smith Mjr RR, 411, 445
Smith Tony, 450
Smithers 1/Lt EC, 432, 437, 456
Smolinski 2/Lt FJ, 454
Souch Lt, 443
Sprague Capt RS, 418
Steinbrenner Capt EG, 417, 429, 455
Stenger Harry, 428, 446, 450, 451, 453
Stephens 2/Lt JB, 437
Stevens Lt GB, 428
St.Germain Lt G, 455, 458
Stiff Lt EG, 433
Stokes John J, 453
Stone Lt, 434
Stone Lt CF, 433
Stone Lt RC, 442
Story Lt WW, 421
Strasen Lt, 455
Strawn Lt, 456
Strole 2/Lt FM, 455
Stutsman Ray, 452
Subritzky Don, 452
Subritzky Mike, 452
Sweetland Capt TR, 455
Sy Wes Strickler, 446, 452
Synge R, 452
Talbot 1/Lt AAG, 418
Tallichet David C, 448, 451, 452, 453
Tanner Leonard A, 453
Taylor Patrick, 424
Tedford 2/Lt PW, 424
Templeton Lt JD, 435
Terry Lt, 457
Thackray Monty, 452
Thomas 2/Lt WA, 427, 454, 455
Thompson Lt J, 418
Thomson Raybourne, 448
Thorsen Mjr JS, 414, 454, 457
Thyng Mjr Harrison R, 410, 414, 454
Tilson Lt GB, 454
Todd Lt JM, 427
Toombs Lt, 457
Tostevin Lt James F, 450
Tourville Lt LE, 417
Tovrea 1/Lt EA, 433
Tower Lt A, 457
Tower 1/Lt EB, 429
Tracy 1/Lt, 411
Trafton Lt FO, 419, 456
Trowbridge Capt Lee M, 415, 429
Van Ausdell Lt, 456
Van Natta Lt, 430
Van Wart Lt Franklyn, 445
Vestal Lt JS, 419
Villinger 1/Lt GK, 458
Vinson Capt Arnold E, 415, 455
Viviano Lt FP, 421
Vizard Stephen H, 451
Vogtle Lt AW, 454
Wade Lt Col Kenneth S, 412
Walker Lt, 430, 457
Walker Capt JR, 431
Wallace Lt EW, 418
Waltner 2/Lt WR, 424

Waltner 1/Lt WW, 456
Warburton Lt JR, 419
Ward Lt WC, 431
Warren Lt A, 423
Watkins Lt WA, 419
Watson Thomas J, 452
Watts Lt TE, 441
Wayne Capt M, 411
Webster Lt, 456
Weeks Kermit A, 448, 450, 453
Weismueller Lt, 457
Weitner Mjr WL, 411, 449
Wells 2/Lt LP, 433
Werner Lt DW, 449
West Lt Col Graham W, 410, 414
Westwood Lt JR, 455
Whalen 1/Lt ED, 458
Whisenand 1/Lt James F, 410
Whisonant Lt WB, 454
White 1/Lt ET, 425
White Lt JH, 454
White Lt JS, 455
Whitlow 1/Lt GH, 424
Wilkes Lt DE, 427
Williams Lt, 457
Williams 2/Lt DH, 416, 454
Williams Capt George V, 415, 455
Williams S/Ldr WA, 410
Williams Lt WR, 435
Williamson Capt HL, 420, 455
Williamson Lt LS, 456
Willis 2/Lt RW, 411
Wilson Capt CE, 422
Winkler Capt JM, 418, 456
Wolfe Lt, 455
Wolfe Lt DC, 439
Wood Lt MC, 422
Woodbury Brig Gen Murray C, 412
Woodhouse HL, *432*
Woodrow Capt Gordon H, 411, 427
Woods Lt J, 422
Woods Woodson K, 452
Wooten Lt R, 454
Wortman 2/Lt WK, 456
Wren Lt WC, 432
Wright 1/Lt, 456
Wright 2/Lt RG, 432
Wyman Lt BC, 431
Yagen Jerry, 447
Yocum Lt, 443
Yorke 2/Lt WL, 422
Zelinski Lt WC, 434
Zientowski 1/Lt GA, 421, 437
Zimlich Capt, 454

YUGOSLAVIA

Bernatic Milan, 463
Berovic Gojko, 464
Bokovic Zivadin, 463
Bucija Marko, 464
Bukija Marko, 463
Gozivoda Srecko, 462
Habijan Janes, 464
Katic Ivan, 463
Knezevic Peter, 464
Kojicem Radetom, 463
Krnjaic Stewan, 463
Mirosa Dragurin, 462
Petrovic Georg, 464
Svetolik Erdeljan, 463

AIR-BRITAIN - THE INTERNATIONAL ASSOCIATION OF AVIATION HISTORIANS - FOUNDED 1948

Since 1948, Air-Britain has recorded aviation events as they have happened, because today's events are tomorrow's history. In addition, considerable research into the past has been undertaken to provide historians with the background to aviation history. Over 18,000 members have contributed to our aims and efforts in that time and many have become accepted authorities in their own fields.

Every month, *AIR-BRITAIN NEWS* covers the current civil and military scene. Quarterly, each member receives *AIR-BRITAIN DIGEST* which is a fully-illustrated journal containing articles on various subjects, both past and present.

For those interested in military aviation history, there is the quarterly *AEROMILITARIA* which is designed to delve more deeply into the background of, mainly, British and Commonwealth military aviation than is possible in commercial publications and whose format permits it to be used as components of a filing system which suits the readers' requirements. This publication is responsible for the production of the present volume and other monographs on military subjects. Also published quarterly is *ARCHIVE*, produced in a similar format but covering civil aviation history in depth on a world-wide basis. Both magazines are well-illustrated by photographs and drawings.

In addition to these regular publications, there are monographs covering type histories, both military and civil, airline fleets, Royal Air Force registers, squadron histories and the civil registers of a large number of countries. Although our publications are available to non-members, prices are considerably lower for Air-Britain members, who have priority over non-members when availability is limited. The accumulated price discounts for which members qualify when buying Air-Britain books can far exceed the annual subscription rates.

A large team of aviation experts is available to answer members' queries on most aspects of aviation. If you have made a study of any particular subject, you may be able to expand your knowledge by joining those with similar interests. Also available to members are libraries of colour slides and photographs which supply slides and prints at prices considerably lower than those charged by commercial firms.

There are local branches of the Association in Blackpool, Bournemouth, Chiltern, Heston, London, Luton, Manchester, Merseyside, North-East England, Rugby, Scotland, Severnside, Solent, South-West Essex, Stansted, West Cornwall and West Midlands. Overseas in France and the Netherlands.

If you would like to receive samples of Air-Britain magazines, please write to the following address enclosing 50p and stating your particular interests. If you would like only a brochure, please send a stamped self-addressed envelope to the same address (preferably 230mm by 160mm or over) - Air-Britain Membership Enquiries (Mil), 1 Rose Cottages, 179 Penn Road, Hazlemere, High Wycombe, Bucks., HP15 7NE.

Our website may be found at www.air-britain.com.

MILITARY AVIATION PUBLICATIONS IN PRINT
(prices are for members/non-members and are post-free)

Royal Air Force Aircraft series

J1-J9999	(£8.00/£10.00)	K1000-K9999	(see The K-File)	L1000-N9999	(£12.00/£15.00)
P1000-R9999	(£11.00/£14.00)	T1000-V9999	(£12.00/£15.00)	W1000-Z9999	(£13.00/£16.50)
AA100-AZ999	(£13.00/£16.50)	BA100-BZ999	(New edition in preparation)	DA100-DZ999	(£5.00/£6.00)
EA100-EZ999	(£5.00/£6.00)	FA100-FZ999	(£5.00/£6.00)	HA100-HZ999	(£6.00/£7.50)
JA100-JZ999	(£6.00/£7.50)	KA100-KZ999	(£6.00/£7.50)	LA100-LZ999	(£7.00/£8.50)
MA100-MZ999	(£8.00/£10.00)	NA100-NZ999	(£8.00/£10.00)	PA100-RZ999	(£10.00/£12.50)
WA100-WZ999	(New edition in preparation)	XA100-XZ999	(£9.00/£11.00)		

Type Histories

The Battle File	(£20.00/£25.00)	The Beaufort File	(£11.00/£13.50)	The Camel File	(£13.00/£16.00)
The Defiant File	(£12.50/£16.00)	The DH4/DH9 File	(£24.00/£30.00)	The S.E.5 File	(£16.00/£20.00)
The Harvard File	(£8.00/£9.50)	The Hoverfly File	(£16.50/£19.50)	The Martinsyde File	(£24.00/£30.00)
The Norman Thompson File	(£13.50/£17.00)	The Oxford, Consul & Envoy File	(£25.00/£32.00)	The Scimitar File	(£26.00/£32.00)
		The Sopwith Pup File	(in preparation)		

Individual R.A.F. Squadron Histories

Hawks Rising - The History of No.25 Squadron (£25.00/£32.00)
United in Effort - The Story of No.53 Squadron (£15.00/£19.00)
Always Prepared – the History of No.207 Squadron (£22.00/£27.50)
Flat Out – The History of No.30 Squadron (£27.00/£34.00)
Scorpions Sting - The Story of No.84 Squadron (£12.00/£16.50)
The Hornet Strikes - The Story of No.213 Squadron (£20.00/£25.00)
Rise from the East - The History of No.247 Squadron (£13.00/£16.50)

Naval Aviation titles

The Squadrons of the Fleet Air Arm (£24.00/£30.00)
Royal Navy Aircraft Serials and Units 1911 - 1919 (£12.00)
Fleet Air Arm Fixed Wing Aircraft since 1946 (in preparation)
Royal Navy Shipboard Aircraft Developments 1912 - 1931 (£12.00)
Fleet Air Arm Aircraft, Units and Ships 1920 - 1939 (£26.00/£32.50)
Fleet Air Arm Aircraft 1939 - 1945 (new edition in preparation)
Royal Navy Instructional Airframes (£14.00/£17.50)

Other titles

The K-File (the RAF of the 1930s) (£23.00/£30.00)
Aviation in Cornwall (£14.00/£17.50)
Aerial Refuelling at Farnborough 1924 – 1937 (£11.00/£14.00)
World Military Transport Fleets 2002 (£15.00/£19.00)
The British Aircraft Specifications File (£20.00/£25.00)
British Air Commission and Lend-Lease (£23.00/£29.00)
Broken Wings – Post-War RAF accidents (£21.00/£26.00)
U.K. Military Flight Testing Accidents 1940 - 1971 (in preparation)

The above are available from Air-Britain (Historians) Ltd, 41 Penshurst Rd, Leigh, Tonbridge, Kent TN11 8HL
or by e-mail to mike@sales.demon.co.uk. Payment in Sterling only. Overseas carriage 15% of book price, minimum £1.50.
Visa, Mastercard, Delta/Visa accepted with card number and expiry date, also Switch (with Issue number).